ISBN 978-1-333-06511-9
PIBN 10461792

ALUMNI CANTABRIGIENSES

Five hundred copies of this book have been printed and the type has been distributed.

This copy is No. 488

CAMBRIDGE UNIVERSITY PRESS
C. F. CLAY, MANAGER
LONDON : FETTER LANE, E.C. 4

NEW YORK : THE MACMILLAN CO.
BOMBAY
CALCUTTA } MACMILLAN AND CO., LTD.
MADRAS
TORONTO : THE MACMILLAN CO. OF CANADA, LTD.
TOKYO : MARUZEN-KABUSHIKI-KAISHA

ALUMNI CANTABRIGIENSES

A BIOGRAPHICAL LIST OF ALL KNOWN STUDENTS, GRADUATES AND HOLDERS OF OFFICE AT THE UNIVERSITY OF CAMBRIDGE, FROM THE EARLIEST TIMES TO 1900

COMPILED BY

JOHN VENN, Sc.D., F.R.S., F.S.A.,
PRESIDENT OF GONVILLE AND CAIUS COLLEGE

AND

J. A. VENN, M.A.,
GILBEY LECTURER IN THE HISTORY AND ECONOMICS OF AGRICULTURE

PART I

FROM THE EARLIEST TIMES TO 1751

VOLUME II

DABBS—JUXTON

CAMBRIDGE
AT THE UNIVERSITY PRESS
1922

PRINTED IN GREAT BRITAIN

PREFACE

THIS Volume is of course continued on exactly the same lines as Volume I. But readers will find that it is appreciably fuller, both in respect of the proportion of names which we have succeeded in identifying, and of the amount of information furnished as to careers. This is due partly to the even more generous help accorded us by those to whom we have already expressed our indebtedness in the preface to Volume I and partly to the considerable access of new helpers which the publication of that volume has brought us. Amongst the latter we must particularly mention the following: Mr E. Axon of Buxton, well known for his extensive investigations into the history of Lancashire and Cheshire families; the Rev. A. G. Kealy, late chaplain R.N., of Maltby, Yorkshire, who has opened up for us an entirely new source of information, viz. that of former chaplains in the Royal Navy; the Very Rev. B. Zimmerman, Prior of the Carmelites, who has given us much that is new about early members of his Order; the Rev. E. A. Irons, Rector of North Luffenham, has added many facts to our Northamptonshire names; the Rev. G. Montagu Benton, Vicar of Fingringhoe, has supplied much help in the task of identifying incumbents in Essex; to the Rev. Harold Smith, D.D., Principal of St John's Hall, Highbury, we are indebted for assistance in assigning Institutions and Ordinations during the Interregnum period. We much regret that by an unaccountable oversight the name of our principal Lincolnshire helper was omitted in Volume I, viz. the Rev. Canon E. Foster, Rector of Timberland. It was to him that we owe most of the Lincoln ordinations, as well as a mass of information regarding early institutions in that county.

Readers are reminded that Volume IV of this work will contain an extensive Appendix recording additions and corrections received as the first three Volumes go through the press. We shall therefore be glad if they will let us have all that they can supply in time for insertion in that Volume, which it is hoped will be published at the end of next year.

J. VENN
J. A. VENN

CAMBRIDGE,
September, 1922

ALUMNI CANTABRIGIENSES

FROM THE EARLIEST TIMES TO 1751

DABBS, JOHN. Adm. pens. (age 17) at EMMANUEL, Nov. 25, 1717. Of Warwickshire. Matric. 1717; B.A. 1721-2; M.A. 1725. Fellow, 1724. Ord. deacon (Ely) Sept. 20, 1724; priest (Lincoln) Dec. 19, 1725. R. of Gayhurst, Bucks., 1725-50. R. of Stoke Goldington, 1736-50. Died 1750. Will, P.C.C. (*Lipscomb*, IV. 162.)

DABELL, ——. M.A. 1478.

DABRIDGECOURT, JOHN. Matric. pens. from ST JOHN'S, Easter, 1584. Probably of Ossington, Notts., and of Staple Inn; when adm. at Gray's Inn, Apr. 27, 1586.

DABRIDGCOURT, ROBERT. Clerk; of Lichfield diocese. Studied arts at Cambridge. (*Cal. of Papal Letters*, 1408.)

DACIE or DACY, JOHN. Adm. pens. (age 20) at PEMBROKE, Apr. 28, 1658. S. of Robert, of Buckland Brewer, Devon. Matric. 1659, as 'Ducy'; B.A. 1661-2, as Dacie; M.A. 1665. Will of one of these names (Exeter) 1716; of Upton Helions, Devon, clerk.

DACIE, JOHN. Adm. sizar at CHRIST'S, June 23, 1689. Matric. 1689; Scholar, 1690. Will of one of these names (Exeter) 1723; of Crediton, Devon, clerk.

DACK, ROBERT. Adm. pens. at EMMANUEL, Mar. 1, 1731-2. Of Norfolk. Matric. 1732; M.B. 1737. Admitted student at Leyden, Sept. 17, 1737. Practised physic at Norwich. Of Kerdiston, Norfolk, M.D. Died Aug. 8, 1792, aged 78. M.I. at Reepham. Will, P.C.C. (G. *Mag.*)

DAK, WILLIAM. B.Can.L. 1454-5. V. of Meldreth, Cambs., till 1475. Will (P.C.C.) 1495; 'clerk, of Sudborne, Suffolk.' Perhaps the Mr Dacke excused from processions, etc., 1476-7. (*Gr. Bk*, A, 118.)

DACKOMBE, JOHN. Adm. Fell.-Com. (age 17) at CAIUS, Dec. 4, 1624. S. of Sir John, Knt., of Temple Combe, Somerset. B. in London. School, Isleworth, Middlesex (Mr Willis). Matric. 1624. Of Edmonton in 1649. (*Venn*, I. 269; *Vis. of Dorset*, 1623.)

DACKWOOD, SAMUEL. Adm. sizar at ST CATHARINE'S, Sept. 13, 1678.

DACRES, ARTHUR. Matric. pens. from MAGDALENE, Michs. 1642. S. of Sir Thomas (1603), of Cheshunt, Herts., Knt. B. there. Bapt. Apr. 18, 1624. B.A. 1645-6; M.A. 1649; M.D. 1654. Fellow, 1646. Assistant physician at St Bartholomew's, 1653-78. Professor of Geometry at Gresham College, 1664-5. F.R.C.P. 1665. Censor, 1672. Died Sept. 1678. Buried at St Bartholomew-the-Less, London. Will, P.C.C. Brother of Richard (1647), John (1634) and Thomas (1632). (*Munk*, I. 354; *D.N.B.*; *Vis. of Herts.*, 1634.)

DACRES, CHRISTOPHER. Matric. Fell.-Com. from PETERHOUSE, Easter, 1555.

DACRES, EDWARD. Adm. at KING'S, a scholar from Eton, Michs. 1611. S. of Sir Thomas, of Cheshunt, Herts., Knt. B.A. 1615. Fellow, till 1617. Adm. at Lincoln's Inn, Aug. 9, 1617. Of Bedwell Park. Buried at Cheshunt, July 7, 1659, aged 66. M.I. (*Vis. of Herts.*, 1634; *Clutterbuck*, II. 101.)

DAKER, HENRY. Matric. sizar from CHRIST'S, Nov. 1554. Of Carlisle diocese. Received tonsure (London) Apr. 1556. Probably migrated to Oxford. B.A. from Queen's College, 1560. R. of Skelton, Cumberland, 1562-97; when he resigned. (*Peile*, I. 59; *Al. Oxon.*)

DACRES, HUGH. Incorp. 1493, from a foreign University. Archdeacon of Carlisle, -1490-1503-. Will (P.C.C.) 1509: 'of Dacre, Cumberland, Netherbury, Dorset, and Wem, Salop.'

DACRES, HUMPHREY. Adm. pens. (age 18) at TRINITY, June 18, 1685. S. of George. B. at Old Warden, Beds., Oct. 13, 1665. School, Westminster. Matric. 1685; Scholar, 1686; B.A. 1688-9; M.A. 1692. Fellow, 1691.

DACRES, JOHN. Matric. pens. from MAGDALENE, Michs. 1634; B.A. 1637-8; M.A. 1641. Probably s. of Sir Thomas, of Cheshunt, Herts., Knt. Bapt. May 7, 1617. Brother of Arthur (1642) and Richard (1647). (*Vis. of Herts.*, 1634.)

DACRES, JOHN. Adm. pens. (age 18) at MAGDALENE, Nov. 6, 1690. 3rd s. of Sir Robert, of Cheshunt, Herts., Knt. B. at Clerkenwell, Middlesex. School, Charterhouse. Matric. 1690. Adm. at Lincoln's Inn, Dec. 10, 1694. Married and had issue. Buried May 21, 1705. Brother of Thomas (1687), father of Richard (1714). (Le Neve, *Knights*.)

DACRES or DAKERS, PERCIVAL. Matric. sizar from QUEENS', Michs. 1572. Of Yorkshire. B.A. 1577-8. C. of Boynton, near Bridlington, 1582.

DACRES, RICHARD. Adm. pens. (age 18) at MAGDALENE, July 5, 1647. S. of Sir Thomas (1603), Knt., of Cheshunt, Herts. Bapt. July 5, 1627. School, Hertford. Matric. 1647; B.A. 1650-1. Adm. at the Inner Temple, Nov. 1652. Barrister, 1660. Brother of Arthur (1642), John (1634) and Thomas (1632). (*Vis. of Herts.*, 1634.)

DACRES, RICHARD. Adm. Fell.-Com. (age 17) at MAGDALENE, July 8, 1714. S. of John (1690), Esq., deceased. B. at Cottenham, Cambs. School, Bishop's Stortford, Herts. Matric. 1714. Migrated to Pembroke, Sept. 18, 1718.

DACRES, ROBERT. Adm. pens. at EMMANUEL, 1585. Matric. Michs. 1585. Doubtless s. of George, of Cheshunt, Herts. Brother of Walter (1585) and Thomas (1571).

DACRES, THOMAS (*alias* LEMORE). Probably of CLARE, as he was V. of Gt Gransden, Hunts. (Clare living), 1478-82.

DACRES, THOMAS. Matric. Fell.-Com. from TRINITY, Easter, 1571. Probably s. of George, of Cheshunt, Herts. (The same, or another, adm. at King's, as Fell.-Com. 1573.) Adm. at Lincoln's Inn, from Furnival's Inn, June 10, 1576. Of Hertfordshire. Knighted, 1604. Sheriff of Herts., 1614. Buried at Cheshunt, July 31, 1615.

DACRES, THOMAS. Matric. Fell.-Com. from ST JOHN'S, Easter, 1603. Probably s. of Sir Thomas, Knt., of Cheshunt. Knighted, Feb. 22, 1616-7. M.P. for Higham Ferrers, 1626; for Herts., 1626, 1628, and 1641-8. Buried Dec. 26, 1668. Brother of Edward (1611), father of Arthur, of John (1634), Richard (1647), and the next.

DACRES, THOMAS. M.A. 1632 (incorp. from Oxford). S. of Sir Thomas (1603), of Cheshunt, Herts., Knt. Matric. from Exeter College, Oct. 16, 1629, age 20. M.A. (Oxford) Nov. 12, 1629. Adm. at Lincoln's Inn, 1631. M.P. for Callington, Cornwall, 1646. Knight of the Royal Oak, 1660. Died 1668. Will, P.C.C. (*Al. Oxon.*; *Cussans*, II. 101; *Vis. of Herts.*, 1634.)

DACRES, THOMAS. Adm. Fell.-Com. (age 16) at MAGDALENE, May 13, 1687. S. of Sir Robert, of Cheshunt, Knt. B. at Clerkenwell, Middlesex. School, Berkhampstead, Herts. Matric. 1688. Adm. at Lincoln's Inn, Jan. 22, 1691-2. S. and h. of Sir Robert, of Clerkenwell, Knt. Married Elizabeth, dau. of Major Bull, of Marwell, Hants. Buried at Owselsbury, Hants. Brother of John (1690). (*Cussans*, II. 101.)

DACRES, WALTER. Adm. pens. at EMMANUEL, 1585. Matric. 1585. Doubtless 5th s. of George, of Cheshunt, Herts. Buried May 22, 1632. Brother of Robert (1585) and perhaps of Thomas (1571).

DAKERS or DAKER, WILLIAM. Adm. pens. (age 17) at TRINITY, June 27, 1685. S. of William, of Condover, Salop. B. at Wheathill, Salop. School, Newport, Salop (Mr Samuel Edwards). Matric. 1685; Scholar, 1687; B.A. 1688-9; M.A. 1692. C. of Aston, Salop. Perhaps R. of Selattyn, 1713-9.

DACRES, WILLOUGHBY. Adm. at KING'S, a scholar from Eton, 1625. Matric. Michs. 1625. Fellow till his death, of small-pox, Sept. 28, 1628. Admon. in King's College.

DACRES, ——. Of ST NICHOLAS HOSTEL, 1529-30. 'Parson Dakers of St Nich. Hostel' is complained of by the Vice-Chancellor (Dr Wm Buckmaster) for his violent behaviour, *c.* 1530. (J. Lamb, *Documents*, 24.)

DADDOW, JONATHAN. Adm. sizar (age 24) at PEMBROKE, J 17, 1715. S. of Joseph. B. at St Blazey, Cornwall, 1687. Matric. 1715; B.A. 1718-9; M.A. 1739. Ord. deacon (Ely) Feb. 22, 1718-9. Admon. (Exeter) 1743; of St Wenn, Cornwall, clerk.

DADE, FRANCIS. Matric. pens. from TRINITY HALL, Easter, 1637; LL.B. 1643. Fellow, 1647.

DADE, FRANCIS. Adm. pens. (age 15) at CAIUS, Jan. 26, 1673-4. S. of Thomas (1631), Esq., of Tannington, Suffolk. B. there, Feb. 2, 1658-9. School, Bury. Matric. 1674; Scholar, 1674-81; B.A. 1677-8; M.A. 1681. Ord. deacon (Norwich) Sept. 1683; priest, May, 1684. V. of Bramford, Suffolk and of Baylham, 1692-1722. Married Sarah, dau. of William Lodge, of Nettlestead, Nov. 19, 1689. Died June 8, 1722. Buried at Bramford. Brother of John (1665-6) and Nathaniel (1667). (*Venn*, I. 450.)

DADE, HENRY. Matric. pens. from TRINITY HALL, Lent, 1597–8; Scholar, 1600; LL.B. 1603–4. Perhaps 2nd s. of Thomas (1631), of Tannington, Suffolk. Commissary for Suffolk Archdeaconry, 1640. His proceedings in the Ecclesiastical Court mentioned in *Newes from Ipswich*. Died Sept. 15, 1653, aged 71. M.I. at Dallinghoe, Suffolk. Will (P.C.C.) 1654. (*Misc. Gen. et Her.*, 2nd S., I. 186, 327; Le Neve, *Mon.*, IV. 24; V. B. Redstone.)

DADE, JOHN. Perhaps B.A. 1500–1. Author on Heraldry. (Bodleian MS.) (*Cooper*, I. 44.)

DADE, JOHN. Adm. at CORPUS CHRISTI, 1636. Of Suffolk. B.A. 1639–40.

DADE, JOHN. Adm. pens. (age 14) at CAIUS, Mar. 12, 1665–6. S. of Thomas (1631), gent., of Tannington, Suffolk. B. there, Sept. 4, 1651. Schools, Mr Crachnall and Bury St Edmunds. Scholar, 1666–73; Matric. 1667; B.A. 1669–70; M.A. 1673; M.D. 1683. Fellow, 1674–94. Practised in Ipswich. Died May 2, 1732. M.I. at Tannington. Brother of Francis (1673–4). Apparently father of John (1743), and William (1744). (*Venn*, I. 426.)

DADE, JOHN. Adm. sizar at TRINITY, June 22, 1674. Matric. 1676; B.A. 1677–8. Ord. deacon (York) June, 1680; priest, May, 1681.

DADE, JOHN. Adm. pens. (age 17) at ST JOHN'S, July 13, 1743. S. of John (1665–6), M.D., of Suffolk. B. at Ipswich. School, Monk-Soham, Suffolk (Mr Ray). Matric. 1743–4. Of Debenham and Ipswich. Major, East Suffolk Militia. Free burgess of Ipswich, 1753. Died Jan. 8, 1811. Brother of William (1744). (V. B. Redstone; Cole, *Suffolk MSS.*)

DADE, JONATHAN. Adm. sizar at TRINITY, May 22, 1668. Matric. 1668; Scholar, 1671; B.A. 1671–2. Ord. deacon (York) Feb. 1674–5; priest, Mar. 1674–5. V. of Whitkirk, Leeds, Yorks., 1675–88.

DADE, NATHANIEL. Adm. pens. (age 14) at CAIUS, Aug. 2, 1667. 4th s. of Thomas (1631), Esq., of Tannington. B. there, Dec. 30, 1652. School, Bury. Matric. 1667–8; Scholar, 1668–70. Died 1670. Brother of Francis (1673) and John (1665–6). (*Venn*, I. 432; *Misc. Gen. et Her.*, 2nd S., I. 201.)

DADE, RICHARD. B.A. 1500–1. A Richard Dade, V. of Henham, Essex, 1514–31. R. of Cotton, Suffolk, 1515. Died 1531. Will (P.C.C.) 1532; 'of Henham, Essex; and R. of Cotton, Suffolk. To be buried at Cotton.' (*Cott. MS.* II. 13; V. B. Redstone.)

DADE, ROBERT. Adm. at CORPUS CHRISTI, 1591. Of Norfolk. B.A. 1594–5; M.A. 1598. Ord. priest (Norwich) Jan. 1, 1600–1, age 25. C. of Buckenham St Martin, Norfolk. R. of Thelnetham, Suffolk, 1612–38. Buried Aug. 27, 1638. Father of the next.

DADE, ROBERT. Adm. pens. (age 16) at CAIUS, June 30, 1643. Of Suffolk. S. of Robert (above), R. of Thelnetham. School, Norwich. Matric. 1644; Scholar, 1644–50; B.A. 1646–7; M.A. 1650. Fellow of Peterhouse, 1651. Died 1652–3. Will, P.C.C. (*T. A. Walker*, 97; *Venn*, I. 350.)

DADE, THOMAS (*jun.*). Adm. pens. (age 16) at CAIUS, Apr. 27, 1631. S. of Thomas, gent., of Tannington, Suffolk. B. there. School, Bury. Matric. 1631. Perhaps scholar of Trinity Hall, 1632–7. Of Pettistree, Suffolk, gent. Adm. at Gray's Inn, Feb. 6, 1636–7. Called to the Bar, 1645. Succeeded his father at Tannington. Died July 20, 1688. Buried at Bramford. Half-brother of William (1598). (*Venn*, I. 298; *Vis. of Suffolk*, 1664.)

DADE, THOMAS (*sen.*). Adm. pens. (age 17) at CAIUS, Apr. 27, 1631. S. of William, gent. (1598). B. at Tannington. School, Bury. Matric. 1631. Adm. at Gray's Inn, Apr. 14, 1632. Called to the Bar, 1638. Ancient, 1658. Of Tannington, Esq. Died Sept. 15, 1685. Buried at Tannington. Will (Archd. Suff.) 1685. Father of Francis (1673–4), John (1665–6), Nathaniel (1667) and Thomas (1661). (*Venn*, I. 298.)

DADE, THOMAS. Adm. pens. (age 16) at CAIUS, May 28, 1661. S. of Thomas (1631), Esq., of Tannington, Suffolk. B. there, Aug. 27, 1644. Schools, Ipswich (Mr Woodside) and Bury. Matric. 1661; Scholar, 1661–4; M.A. 1669–70 (*Lit. Reg.*—He was of royal descent, through his grandmother, Mary Winkfield). Adm. at Gray's Inn, Apr. 1, 1664. Called to the Bar 1671. Ancient, 1687. Of Tannington, Esq. Died Dec. 14, 1697. Will (P.C.C.) 1698. (*Venn*, I. 413; *Vis. of Suffolk*, 1664.)

DADE, THOMAS. Adm. sizar at CHRIST'S, Mar. 31, 1687. Matric. 1687; B.A. 1690–1; M.A. 1694. Ord. deacon (Ely) Feb. 1691–2; priest (York) June, 1698. R. of Sneaton in Cleveland, Yorks., 1699–1708. V. of Otley, 1701–8. Died Dec. 25, 1708. (*Peile*, II. 104.)

DADE, THOMAS. Adm. sizar at QUEENS', Oct. 7, 1718. Of Yorkshire. Matric. 1718–9; B.A. 1722–3; M.A. 1735. Ord. deacon (York) June, 1723; priest, Sept. 1726. V. of Ergham, Yorks., 1731–59. R. of Barmston and Burton Agnes, 1735–59. Died Sept. 28, 1759. (*G. Mag.*)

DADE, WILLIAM. Adm. pens. (age 18) at CAIUS, May 1, 1598. S. of Thomas, gent. B. at Witton, Norfolk. Schools, Brandiston (Mr Rason) and Worlingworth (Mr Grundy). Adm. at Gray's Inn, Apr. 21, 1600. Of Ipswich, Esq. Died Feb. 22, 1659–60. M.I. at Tannington. Father of Thomas (1631). (*Venn*, I. 164; *Vis. of Suffolk*, 1664; Le Neve, *Mon.*, IV. 71.)

DADE, WILLIAM. Adm. pens. (age 17) at PEMBROKE, June 26, 1744. S. of [John] (1665–6), of Tannington, Suffolk, M.D. B. at Ipswich. Matric. 1744; B.A. 1747–8; M.A. 1751. Fellow, 1749. Free burgess of Ipswich, 1753. Died May 28, 1755. M.I. at Tannington. Brother of John (1743).

DADE, ——. Adm. at CORPUS CHRISTI, 1577.

DADE, ——. Adm. at CORPUS CHRISTI, 1584.

DADLEY, RICHARD. Matric. pens. from CHRIST'S, July, 1618, as 'Dudley'; B.A. 1621–2; M.A. 1625. Ord. deacon (Peterb.) Oct. 23; priest, Oct. 24, 1625. (*Peile*, I. 323.)

DAFFERNE, RICHARD. Matric. sizar from ST JOHN'S, Michs. 1576.

DAFFORNE, ROBERT. Matric. sizar from JESUS, Easter, 1568; B.A. 1571–2.

DAFFY, ELIAS. Adm. Fell.-Com. at CAIUS, Aug. 4, 1681. S. of Anthony, citizen of London. B. there. Schools, London, Hertford (Mr Howard) and Saumur. Matric. 1681; M.B. 1687. Probably practised in London. One of the makers of the 'Elixir.' (*Venn*, I. 468.)

DAFFY, THOMAS. Adm. pens. (age 18) at ST JOHN'S, June 16, 1666. S. of Thomas, clerk, R. of Harby and Redmile, Leics. B. at Leicester. School, Melton (Mr Stokes). Matric. 1667; B.A. 1669–70; M.A. 1674. Head Master of Melton Mowbray School, 1673. His father was the inventor of the well-known 'Elixir.' (See *D.N.B.*)

DAGGE, JOHN. M.A. from PEMBROKE, 1734. S. of Jonathan, of Fowey, Cornwall, clerk. Matric. from Queen's College, Oxford, July 11, 1722, age 18; B.A. (Oxford) 1726. Died Feb. 1753–4. Will (Exeter) 1754; of Fowey, clerk. (*Al. Oxon.*)

DAGGET, ARTHUR. Adm. pens. (age 18) at SIDNEY, May 6, 1714. S. of William, R. of Birmingham. B. there. School, Coxwold, Yorks. Matric. 1714; B.A. 1717–8; M.A. 1721. V. of Theddingworth, Leics., 1723–38. Buried there 1738. Admon., Leicester. (*Nichols*, II. 828.)

DAGGET, JOHN. Adm. sizar (age 17) at SIDNEY, Apr. 14, 1623. S. of Robert, gent. B. at Howe, near Thirsk, Yorks. School, Topcliffe (Mr Ri. Crowe). Matric. 1623; B.A. 1626–7; M.A. 1630.

DAGGET, ROBERT. Adm. pens. at SIDNEY, June 3, 1605. Matric. 1605; B.A. 1608–9; M.A. 1612; B.D. 1619. Fellow. Incorp. at Oxford, 1614. Ord. deacon (Peterb.) Sept. 19; priest, Sept. 20, 1613. R. of Kirklington, Yorks., 1640. Died Aug. 19, 1644. Buried at Kirklington. (McCall, *Churches of Richmondshire.*)

DAGGOTT, THOMAS. B.Can.L. 1503–4. R. of Knapwell, Cambs. (*See also* Thomas Docket, 1509–10.)

DAGGET, WILLIAM. Adm. sizar (age 18) at SIDNEY, June 21, 1628. S. of William, draper. B. at Ripon, Yorks. School, Ripon (Mr Palmes). B.A. 1631–2; M.A. 1635; B.D. 1642. Fellow. Ord. deacon (Peterb.) May 20, 1638; priest, June 9, 1639. Will proved (V.C.C.) 1642.

DAGGET, WILLIAM. Adm. sizar (age 16) at SIDNEY, Apr. 1, 1682. 1st s. of William, yeoman, deceased. B. at Boroughbridge, Yorks. Schools, Leeds and Coxwold. Matric. 1682; B.A. 1685–6. Of Boroughbridge, in 1694. (M. H. Peacock.)

DAGGETT, ——. Adm. sizar at EMMANUEL, Sept. 27, 1610.

DAGNALL, THOMAS. Matric. sizar from KING'S, Easter, 1622; B.A. 1625–6; M.A. 1630.

DAGNALL, WILLIAM. Adm. pens. (age 19) at CAIUS, May 7, 1645. S. of Samuel, gent. B. at Berkhampstead St Peter, Herts. Schools, Berkhampstead (Mr Sayer) and Tring (Mr Holmes). Matric. 1645; Scholar, 1645–9; B.A. 1648–9.

DAILLONIUS or DALLION, DANIEL. Incorp. M.A. at PEMBROKE, 1682. Of Rochefoucalt (Rupifucaldiensis).

DAINTREE or DAYNTIE, ARTHUR. Matric. pens. from CHRIST'S, Feb. 1563–4; Scholar.

DAINTREE, BENJAMIN. Adm. pens. at PETERHOUSE, Apr. 16, 1658. Of Leicestershire. Matric. 1658; Scholar, 1658; B.A. 1661–2; M.A. 1665. Ord. priest (Peterb.) May 21, 1665. R. of Aldwinkle St Peter, Northants., 1684–1707. Died June 9, 1707, aged 66. M.I. (H. I. Longden.)

DANTREY or DAUTREY, JOHN. Matric. sizar from CHRIST'S, c. 1601.

DAINTREY, JOHN. Adm. sizar (age 22) at TRINITY, June 7, 1720. S. of Brian, of Stafford. School, Birmingham (Mr Perkinson). Matric. 1724–5; LL.B. 1726.

DAINTRY, WILLIAM. Adm. pens. (age 16) at PETERHOUSE, Apr. 23, 1650. Of Leicestershire. School, Coventry. Scholar, 1651; Matric. 1652; B.A. 1653-4; M.A. 1657. Fellow, 1656.

DAKER, see DACRES.

DAKEYNE, HENRY. Adm. pens. (age 16) at SIDNEY, May 17, 1632. S. of Arthur, Esq., of Ashover, Derbs. B. at Nottingham. Schools, Dronfield (Mr Sim. Peck) and Mansfield (Mr Ri. Poynton). Matric. 1632. Of Stubbing Edge, Derbs. Died 1671. (*F.M.G.*, 1018; *Vis. of Derbs.*, 1662.)

DAKEYNE, HENRY. Adm. pens. at QUEENS', Apr. 2, 1719. S. of Digby, of Dalbury, Derbs. Migrated to Emmanuel, June 15. Matric. 1719; B.A. 1722-3; M.A. 1726. Clerk, of Staffordshire. Died aged about 27. (*F.M.G.*, 1018.)

DAKYN, JOHN. B.Civ.L. 1524-5; D.Civ.L. 1528-9. Of ST NICHOLAS HOSTEL. Probably a monk of St Mary's, York. Adm. advocate, Nov. 25, 1529. Chancellor of Wells, 1543, and treasurer, 1554. R. of Kirkby Ravensworth, Yorks., 1548-54. Preb. of York, 1550-8. Archdeacon, East Riding, 1551-8. Commissary for the Bishop of Chester. Founded a hospital and Grammar School at Kirkby Ravensworth. Died Nov. 9, 1558. (*Cooper*, I. 181; M. H. Peacock.)

DAKEINE, SAMUEL. Adm. sizar (age 16) at ST JOHN'S, Nov. 3, 1676. S. of John, deceased, of Parwich, Derbs. B. there. School, Hartington. Matric. 1676; B.A. 1680-1; M.A. 1684. Fellow, 1683. Taxor, 1690. Ord. deacon (Peterb.) Dec. 18, 1681. V. of Holme-on-Spalding-Moor, Yorks., 1690-1703. Died 1703.

DAKIN, SAMUEL. Adm. sizar (age 16) at CHRIST'S, April 6, 1688. S. of Edward. B. at Fairfield, Derbs. School, Macclesfield (Mr Ashworth). Matric. 1688; Scholar, 1689; B.A. 1691-2. Ord. deacon (Lichfield) Mar. 1693-4; priest, July, 1691; as 'praelector' at Ashbourne. Perhaps assistant Master at Derby School, 1705-14. (*Peile*, II. 108.)

DAKIN, THOMAS. Matric. sizar from PEMBROKE, Easter, 1660.

DAKIN, THOMAS. Adm. sizar (age 23) at ST JOHN'S, May 18, 1730. S. of Edward, husbandman, of Derbyshire. B. at Bakewell. School, Stockport, Cheshire. Matric. 1734.

DAKIN, ——. Adm. at PEMBROKE, June 16, 1659.

DAKYNS, ARTHUR. Matric. pens. from TRINITY, Michs. 1567; B.A. 1570-1. Perhaps s. of George, of Linton, Yorks. Knighted, 1604. Will (P.C.C.) 1632; of St Andrew's, Holborn. One of these names adm. at Gray's Inn, 1575, from Staple Inn; Ancient, 1598. An Oxford contemporary was B.C.L. 1557. (*Vis. of Yorks.*, 1612; J. Ch. Smith.)

DAYKYNS, EDWARD. Matric. pens. from ST JOHN'S, Easter, 1550.

DAKYNS, EDWARD. Matric. pens. from PETERHOUSE, Easter, 1571. S. of John, gent., of Brandesburton, Yorks. School, Pocklington. B.A. 1574-5; M.A. from Trinity Hall, 1578. Adm. Fell.-Com. at Caius, Dec. 7, 1578, age 24. Joined the Church of Rome. Ord. sub-deacon (Laon) Mar. 8, 1581-2; deacon (Chalons) 1582; priest, 1582. Sent to England, 1584; banished and returned to Douay, 1585; again sent to England, 1586. (*Venn*, I. 99.)

DAKYNS, GEORGE. Matric. pens. from TRINITY, Michs. 1567.

DAKYNS, HILARY. Matric. pens. from PETERHOUSE, Easter, 1571. Of Brandesburton, Esq. Probably brother of Edward (1571). A Romanist. (*T. A. Walker*.)

DAKYNS, JOHN. Matric. sizar from ST JOHN'S, Michs. 1556. Of Derbyshire. B.A. 1559-60; M.A. 1563. Fellow, 1560. Will proved (V.C.C.) 1566.

DAKINS, PHILIP. Adm. pens. (age 17) at ST JOHN'S, Apr. 16, 1670. S. of Edward, mercer, of Woodbridge, Suffolk. B. there. School, Ipswich. Matric. 1670; B.A. 1673-4.

DAKENS, ROBERT. Matric. sizar from JESUS, Michs. 1546. Of Derbyshire. B.A. 1551-2; M.A. from St John's, 1555. Fellow of St John's, 1553. Fellow of Trinity, 1560.

DAKYNS, WILLIAM. Matric. pens. from CHRIST'S, May, 1544; B.A. 1548-9; M.A. 1552. Fellow, 1549-54. Ord. priest (London) May, 1552. V. of Ashwell, Herts., 1559-99. Died Feb. 18, 1598-9, aged 75. M.I. at Ashwell. Perhaps father of the next. (*Peile*, I. 35; *Clutterbuck*, III. 487.)

DAKYNS, WILLIAM. Matric. pens. from TRINITY, Michs. 1586. Scholar from Westminster. Perhaps s. of William, V. of Ashwell (above). B.A. 1590-1; M.A. 1594; B.D. 1601. Fellow, 1593. V. of Trumpington, Cambs., 1603-5. Professor of Divinity at Gresham College, 1604-7. One of the translators of the Bible. Died Feb. 1606-7. (*Cooper*, II. 444; *D.N.B.*)

DALBY, EDWARD. Matric. sizar from TRINITY, Easter, 1620; Scholar, 1624; B.A. 1624-5; M.A. 1628. Ord. deacon (Peterb.) May 29; priest, May 30, 1627. V. of Exton, Rutland, 1647.

DALBY, EDWARD. B.A. 1635 (incorp. from Oxford). S. of Thomas, of London. Matric. from New College, Aug. 19, 1634, age 19; B.A. from Wadham College, 1635. Adm. at the Inner Temple, 1632. Barrister, 1641. Steward of Reading. (*Al. Oxon.*; *Vis. of Berks.*, 1665.)

DALBIE, FERDINAND. Scholar of TRINITY, 1602; B.A. 1603-4.

DALBY, FRANCIS. Adm. at CORPUS CHRISTI, 1673. Of Lincolnshire. Matric. Easter, 1674; B.A. 1676-7; M.A. 1680. Ord. deacon (Peterb.) Sept. 23, 1677; priest, Sept. 19, 1680.

DALBY, HENRY. Adm. pens. at CLARE, Easter, 1647.

DALBY, HUMPHREY. Adm. sizar (age 18) at MAGDALENE, June 13, 1674. S. of Humphrey, of Stamford, Lincs. School, Stamford. Matric. 1674; B.A. 1677-8. Ord. deacon (Peterb.) Sept. 22, 1678.

DALBY, JOHN. Adm. sizar at EMMANUEL, Dec. 9, 1734. B. at Castle Donington, Leics. Matric. 1735; B.A. 1738-9; M.A. 1758. Ord. deacon (Lincoln) Mar. 18, 1738-9; priest, June 1, 1740. R. of Lambley, Notts. V. of Castle Donington, Leics., 1758-80. Died Dec. 20, 1780. M.I. at Castle Donington. Will, P.C.C. (*Nichols*, III. 782.)

DALBY, SAMUEL. Adm. at CORPUS CHRISTI, 1661. Of Lincolnshire. Matric. 1661; B.A. 1664-5.

DALBY, TOBIAS. Matric. pens. from JESUS, Michs. 1580. Ord. priest (Peterb.) June 17, 1586, as 'B.A.' R. of Quinton, Northants., 1586-1606.

DALBY, W. Matric. sizar from QUEENS', Michs. 1565.

DALBY, W. Matric. pens. from QUEENS', Michs. 1568 (perhaps same as the above).

DALBY, WILLIAM. Adm. pens. (age 13) at CAIUS, May 24, 1589. S. of James, V. of Howden. B. at Hemingbrough, Yorks. School, Adlingfleet. B.A. from St John's, 1592-3; M.A. 1596. Ord. priest (Durham) Sept. 30, 1599. R. of St Peter-at-Arches, Lincoln, 1604-12. V. of Haxey, Lincs., 1606. Official of Howden, Yorks., in 1636. (*Venn*, I. 137; Robinson, *Snaith*.)

DALBY, WILLIAM. Matric. sizar from JESUS, c. 1596; B.A. (? 1602-3); M.A. 1606. Ord. deacon and priest (Lincoln) Mar. 12, 1608-9. V. of Kirmond, Lincs., 1610-23. Perhaps R. of Broughton, 1623. Preb. of Lincoln, 1624.

DALBY, WILLIAM. Adm. sizar at JESUS, May 19, 1619. Matric. 1619. Ord. deacon (Peterb.) Mar. 12; priest, Mar. 13, 1624-5, as 'B.A.' Perhaps V. of Anstey, Leics., c. 1627.

DOLBY, ——. Scholar of CHRIST'S, 1531-2.

DALE, CHRISTOPHER. Matric. pens. from CHRIST'S, Nov. 1544.

DALE, CUTHBERT. Matric. sizar from TRINITY, Michs. 1570; Scholar, 1575; B.A. 1576-7; M.A. 1580; B.D. 1587. Fellow, 1579. Ord. deacon (Peterb.) Apr. 3; priest, Apr. 11, 1584. V. of St Andrew's, Histon, Cambs., 1589-92. R. of Branston, Lincs., 1591. Will (Cons. C. Lincoln) 1638; of Branston, Lincs., clerk.

DALE, CUTHBERT. Matric. sizar from TRINITY, Easter, 1611; Scholar, 1614; B.A. 1614-5; M.A. 1618. Ord. deacon (Peterb.) Apr. 26; priest, Apr. 27, 1618. V. of Gt Wymondley, Herts., 1618-30. Perhaps father of the next.

DALE, CUTHBERT. Adm. sizar at JESUS, Feb. 21, 1637-8. Of Hertfordshire. Perhaps s. of Cuthbert (above), V. of Gt Wymondley. Matric. 1638; B.A. 1641.

DALE, DAMASCENE. M.A. 1545. (No B.A.) C. of St Giles', Cambridge, in 1543.

DALE, DANIEL. Matric. pens. from TRINITY, Easter, 1617; Scholar, 1619; B.A. 1620-1; M.A. 1624. Ord. deacon (Peterb.) Sept. 25; priest, Sept. 26, 1625. R. of Snelland, Lincs., 1633.

DALE, FRANCIS. Adm. sizar at TRINITY, June 1, 1653. Of Lincolnshire. Scholar, 1655; B.A. 1656-7; M.A. 1660. R. of Addlethorpe, Lincs., 1662-70. R. of Hagworthingham, 1671-1708. Will (P.C.C.) 1708. Doubtless father of the next.

DALE, FRANCIS. Adm. pens. (age 17) at TRINITY, Apr. 13, 1687. S. of Francis, of Hagworthingham, Lincs. School, Lincoln (Mr Sam. Garnstone). Matric. 1687.

DALE or DALLE, GEOFFREY. Adm. pens. at PETERHOUSE, June 19, 1632. Of Lincolnshire. Matric. 1632; Scholar, 1633; B.A. 1635-6. Ord. deacon (Peterb.) Sept. 24, 1637.

DALE, HENRY. Matric. sizar from TRINITY, Michs. 1627; B.A. 1630-1; M.A. 1634. V. of Dunholme, Lincs., 1633-42. V. of Upton with Kexby, 1642.

DALE, HENRY. Adm. sizar at TRINITY, Mar. 17, 1654-5. Of Lincolnshire. Matric. 1656; B.A. 1658-9.

DALE, JOHN. Scholar of CHRIST'S, 1540-1; B.A. 1542-3; M.A. 1546; B.D. 1556. Fellow of Queens', 1542-8. Chaplain and Cross-bearer of the University, 1554. 'Severely reprimanded by Ormaneto (whom *see*), Cardinal Pole's delegate to visit the University, for bringing a chalice with the Hoste in his bosom, instead of a Pyx with a Relick which he had purposed to present to the University' (Cole, *Suff. MSS.*). R. of Little Shelford, Cambs., 1557. Perhaps R. of St Margaret, New Fish St, London, 1556. R. of Wetheringsett, Suffolk, 1557; did not subscribe to the oath of allegiance, 1558. A recusant after 1558; 'not altogether unlearned, but very perverse.' (Stokes, *Chaplains*, 86; *Peile*, I. 27; *Cooper*, I. 212.)

DALE, JOHN. Adm. sizar at QUEENS', Oct. 16, 1672. Of Warwickshire. Matric. 1672; B.A. 1676-7. Will of one of these names, of Stillington, Yorks., clerk, proved (York) 1717.

DALE, JOHN. Adm. at KING'S, a scholar from Eton, 1722. S. of John. B. at Christchurch, Hants. Bapt. there Aug. 11, 1709. Matric. 1723. Fellow, 1726. Adm. at the Middle Temple, Mar. 11, 1725, as s. and h. of John, gent., of Chewton, Mitton, Hants. Secretary in Lord Townshend's Office. Afterwards became insane. (For his dispute with the College, *see Hist. of King's College*, 181.)

DALE, JOHN. Adm. sizar (age 19) at TRINITY, June 29, 1726. S. of Christopher, of Pickhill, Yorks. School, Pickhill. Matric. 1726; B.A. 1729-30. Perhaps C. of Masham, Yorks., 1736; and V. of Kirby-Hill. Buried at Watlass, Apr. 28, 1778. (J. Fisher, *Masham*, 335.)

DALE, JOHN. Adm. sizar (age 17) at ST JOHN'S, Mar. 25, 1728. S. of Thomas, of Cheshire. B. at Stockport. School, Stockport (Mr Dale). Matric. 1728; M.B. 1734.

DALE, NATHANIEL. Adm. sizar at JESUS, July 1, 1645. Of Suffolk.

DALE, RICHARD. B.Can.L. V. of Barton, Cambs., 1457.

DALE, RICHARD. B.Can.L. 1520-1. V. of Swaffham St Cyriac, Cambs., 1526.

DALE, RICHARD. Adm. sizar at MAGDALENE, June 1, 1700. S. of Edward, gent. B. at Lusby, Lincs. School, Ashby, Lincs. (private). Matric. 1700; B.A. 1703-4. Ord. deacon (Lincoln) June 8, 1707; priest, Sept. 19, 1708. R. of Dalderby, Lincs., 1709. C. of Lusby. V. of Gt Stourton, 1720. V. of Mareham-on-the-Hill.

DALE, RICHARD. Adm. sizar (age 19) at ST JOHN'S, Mar. 21, 1737-8. S. of John, saddler, of Yorks. B. at Beverley. School, Beverley (Mr Clarke). Matric. 1738; B.A. 1742-3. Ord. deacon (Norwich) 1742; priest (York) Sept. 22, 1745; C. of Beeford, Yorks.

DALE, ROBERT. B.A. 1511-2; M.A. (Oxford) 1531-2.

DALE, ROBERT. Adm. scholar at TRINITY HALL, Jan. 5, 1729-30. Of Whippingham, Isle of Wight. Matric. 1729-30; LL.B. 1734; LL.D. 1739. Fellow, 1734-86. Admon. (P.C.C.) of one of these names, 1789; of W. Cowes, Isle of Wight.

DALE, ROGER. Adm. at EMMANUEL, Apr. 29, 1613. Perhaps s. of Roger, Bencher and Treasurer of the Inner Temple; adm. there, 1610. (*Vis. of Chesh.*, 1613; *Vis. of London*, 1568.)

DALE, ROGER. Adm. pens. (age 18) at MAGDALENE, Apr. 15, 1680. S. of William. B. at Sandbach, Cheshire. School, Sandbach.

DALE, SAMUEL. Matric. sizar from MAGDALENE, Easter, 1616; B.A. from Trinity Hall, 1619-20.

DALE, VALENTINE. LL.D. 1562 (incorp. from Orleans). B.A. (Oxford) 1541; B.C.L. 1545. Incorp. D.C.L. 1562 (from Orleans). Fellow of All Souls', 1542. V. of Winterbourne Earls, Wilts., 1550. R. of Llandyssul, Cardigan, 1554. Adm. advocate, Jan. 14, 1553-4. M.P. for Taunton, 1555, 1558, 1559; for Chichester, 1572, 1584, 1586, 1588; for Hindon, 1584. Master of the Court of Requests. Ambassador in Flanders, 1563. Dean of Wells, 1575-89. Master of Sherburn Hospital, Durham, 1585. Judge of the Court of Admiralty, 1585-9. Died Nov. 17, 1589. Buried in St Gregory by St Paul, London. Will, P.C.C. (*Cooper*, II. 62; *D.N.B.*)

DALE, WILLIAM. Matric. from ST JOHN'S, Michs. 1579. Bapt. at St Michael's, Cornhill, Sept. 29, 1563. William Dale was adm. at the Middle Temple, Jan. 13, 1582, as s. and h. of George, merchant, of London. Buried at St Michael's, Cornhill, Dec. 31, 1594. Will (P.C.C.), 'of the Middle Temple, and Staynes, Middlesex.'

DALE, WILLIAM. Matric. sizar from TRINITY, c. 1591. B. c. 1573. S. of Jeffrey, V. of Boughton, Northants. (will, 1593). Scholar, 1593; B.A. 1593-4. Ord. deacon and priest (Peterb.) June 16, 1595. V. of Moulton, Northants., 1598-1607. R. of South Stoke, Lincs., 1608-19. R. of Hagworthingham, 1619. Will proved (Lincoln) 1638.

DALE, WILLIAM. Adm. sizar at EMMANUEL, Easter, 1627. Of Lincolnshire. Matric. 1627; B.A. 1630-1; M.A. 1634. Ord. deacon (Peterb.) June 5, 1631. Probably R. of Hagworthingham, Lincs. Will (Lincoln) 1668.

DALE, WILLIAM. Adm. sizar (age 16) at CHRIST'S, June 19, 1635. S. of Ralph. B. at Dalby, Lincs. Matric. 1635.

DALE, ——. *Com.* for M.A. or higher degree, 1468-9. Perhaps William, V. of Barrington, Cambs.; resigned, 1476.

DALECHAMP, CALEB. B.A. 1624; M.A. from TRINITY, 1624; B.D. 1633. Had studied 10 years at Cambridge and then at Sedan, before B.A. Incorp. at Oxford, 1627. V. of Ingham, Lincs., 1632. R. of South Ferriby, 1634. Father of the next.

DALECHAMP or DE LA CHAMP, ROBERT. Adm. pens. (age 20) at ST JOHN'S, June 4, 1662. S. of Caleb, above, clerk, deceased, of Ingham, Lincs. B. there. School, St Paul's, London. Matric. 1662; B.A. 1665-6; M.A. 1669. Signs for deacon's orders (London) June 9, 1666. C. of Little Sampford, Essex. Signs for priest's orders, Mar. 1, 1666-7. C. to Dr Peter Du Moulin. Buried in Canterbury Cathedral Cloisters, Jan. 11, 1678-9.

DALENDAR, HENRY. Adm. pens. (age 16) at CAIUS, June 27, 1617. S. of Sir William, Knt., of Buckland, Surrey. Schools, Croydon, 'Kent' (Mr Davie) and Charlwood, Surrey (Mr Bristow). Matric. 1617; B.A. 1620-1; M.A. (Oxford) 1627. R. of Headley, Surrey, till sequestered, 1645. Will of Henry Dallender (Chichester) 1661; of Wisborough Green, Sussex, minister. Brother of the next. (*Venn*, I. 236; *Vis. of Surrey*.)

DALENDER, RODOLPH. Adm. Fell.-Com. (age 14) at CAIUS, July 5, 1613. S. of William, Esq., of Buckland, Surrey. Matric. 1614. Lord of the manor of Buckland. Brother of Henry (above). (*Venn*, I. 222; *Vis. of Surrey*.)

DALGARNO, THOMAS. Adm. pens. (age 17) at ST JOHN'S, Apr. 1, 1698. S. of Arthur, clerk (preb. of York). B. at Etton, near Beverley, Yorks. School, Beverley (Mr Lambert). Matric. 1698; B.A. 1701-2. Ord. priest (York) Sept. 1706. V. of Lund, Yorks., 1706-17. Died 1717.

D'ALGRE, Sir GASPARD, Count of Beauvoir, Baron of Vivroux. Incorp. at Oxford, Aug. 24, 1624, as 'M.A. of Cambridge,' Captain of 50 chevaliers in attendance on the King of France. (*Al. Oxon.*; *Fasti*, I. 418.)

DALIELL, ROBERT. Incorp. M.A. 1663, from Edinburgh (M.A. there, 1640). Master of Dedham School, Essex, in 1663. R. of Stratford St Mary, Suffolk, 1663-77.

DALKEITH, Earl of. LL.D. 1749; *see* Scott, Francis.

DALL, ——. B.Civ.L. 1473.

DALLAND, SIMON. Matric. pens. from CLARE, Easter, 1584; B.A. from Jesus, 1587-8, as Dollond.

DALLAWAY, GEORGE. Adm. pens. at CLARE, Oct. 17, 1747. B. at Birmingham. Matric. 1748; B.A. 1752.

DALLING, SIMON. Fellow of TRINITY HALL. Ord. sub-deacon (Norwich) Dec. 21, 1419; priest, Dec. 19, 1422. R. of All Saints', Warham, Norfolk. Master of Trinity Hall, 1443-53; under whom the college greatly increased. (*Coll. Hist.*, 63.)

DALLING, WILLIAM. B.Can.L. 1460-1; D.Can.L. 1472. Master of TRINITY HALL, 1471-1500. Benefactor to the College. R. of Holywell, Hunts., 1461-1500. R. of St Andrew's, Huntingdon, 1474. R. of Over, Cambs., 1500. Will (P.C.C.) 1500; described as of Over, Cambs. (*Coll. Hist. of Trinity Hall*; *Warren*.)

DALLINGTON, ROBERT. Scholar at CORPUS CHRISTI, c. 1575-80. B. at Geddington, Northants., 1561. Schoolmaster in Norfolk. Afterwards travelled in France and Italy. There is no record of his graduation as M.A. at Cambridge, but he was incorporated at Oxford as such, Apr. 6, 1601. Gentleman of the Privy chamber to Prince Charles. Master of the Charter House, 1624-37. Knighted, Dec. 30, 1624. Author, *Aphorisms Civil and Military*. Died 1637. Buried in the Charter House. Benefactor to Geddington. Will (P.C.C.) 1638. (*Masters*; *D.N.B.*)

DALLION, ——, *see* DAILLONIUS.

DALLISON, EDWARD. Matric. pens. from JESUS, Michs. 1559.

DALISON, JAMES. Adm. sizar at KING'S, Lent, 1544-5.

DALLISON, JOHN. Matric. pens. from TRINITY, Easter, 1637.

DALLISON, ROGER. B.A. 1519-20; M.A. from ST JOHN'S, 1523; B.D. 1531-2; D.D. 1535. Fellow of St John's, 1523. Ord. priest (Lincoln) Mar. 7, 1529-30. V. of Ravensthorpe, Northants., 1531-4. V. of Standon, Herts., 1537. Dean of Thornton, Lincs. Preb. and Precentor of Lincoln, 1554-66. Died, July 24, 1566. Will (P.C.C.) 1566. (*Cooper*, I. 243.)

DALISON, ROGER. Adm. at KING'S, a scholar from Eton, 1533; B.A. 1537-8; M.A. 1541.

DALYSON, THOMAS. Adm. Fell.-Com. (age 19) at TRINITY, May 18, 1704. S. of Thomas, of Hampton, Kent. School, Enfield, Middlesex (Mr Uvedale). Probably M.A. 1705 (*Com. Reg.*). Adm. at the Middle Temple, Feb. 12, 1701-2. Of Manton, Lincs., and Hampton, Kent, Esq. Died at Plaxtol, Kent, Aug. 4, 1741. Father of the next, and of William (1748). (Burke, *Ext. Bart.*; *Vis. of Sussex*; G. *Mag.*)

DALYSON, THOMAS. Adm. pens. (age 17) at ST JOHN'S, Oct. 18, 1750. S. of Thomas, Esq. (above), of Middlesex. B. in London. School, Tonbridge. Matric. 1750; B.A. 1755. Ord. deacon (Lincoln) Sept. 25; priest, Dec. 18, 1757. R. of Manton, Lincs., 1757–92. P.C. of Plaxtol, Kent, 1768–91. Died 1792. Will, P.C.C. Brother of William (1748). (*Scott-Mayor*, III. 603.)

DALLISON, WILLIAM. Studied in Cambridge. S. of William, of Laughton, Lincs. Perhaps of KING'S HALL, 1532–43. Afterwards of Gray's Inn, 1535. Barrister, 1537. Reader, 1548. Serjeant-at-law, 1552. M.P. for Co. Lincoln, 1553. Justice K.B., 1556. Knighted. Died Jan. 18, 1558–9. Buried in Lincoln Cathedral. Will, P.C.C. (*Cooper*, I. 191; *D.N.B.*; Burke, *Ext. Bart.*)

DALYSON, WILLIAM. Adm. Fell.-Com. at ST JOHN'S, Jan. 23, 1748–9. S. of Thomas (1704). B. in London. School, Tonbridge. Matric. 1748–9. Adm. at the Inner Temple, Feb. 5, 1750–1, as s. and h. of Thomas, late of West Peckham, Kent, Esq. Colonel of the West Kent Militia. Died Jan. 11, 1809. Brother of Thomas (1750). (*Scott-Mayor*, III. 584.)

DALYSON, ——. B.Civ.L. or B.Can.L. 1500–1.

DALLOCK, THOMAS. Matric. pens. from CLARE, Easter, 1579; B.A. 1582–3; M.A. 1586. Ord. deacon and priest (Peterb.) Sept. 3, 1587.

DALLY or DALLAY, HENRY. Adm. pens. at CLARE, Aug. 12, 1647. Matric. 1647–8; B.A. 1651–2; M.A. 1655.

DALLYS, HENRY. Matric. pens. from PETERHOUSE, Easter, 1565.

DALRYMPLE, JOHN. Adm. Fell.-Com. at TRINITY HALL, Oct. 20, 1746. John, 4th Bart., of Consland and Cranstoun. Eldest s. of Sir William. B. 1726. Advocate at the Scottish Bar, 1748. Solicitor to the Board of Excise. Succeeded as Bart., 1771. Baron of the Court of Exchequer, 1776–1807. Took the name Dalrymple-Hamilton-Macgill. Author, Historical, etc. Died Feb. 26, 1810. (*D.N.B.*; *G.E.C.*)

DALSTON, FRANCIS. Matric. pens. from CHRIST'S, Easter, 1603.

DALSTON, GEORGE. Matric. Fell.-Com. from QUEENS', *c.* 1596, as Dolston. Of Cumberland. S. of Sir John, of Dalston, Knt. Knighted, June 26, 1607. M.P. for Cumberland, 1620, 1624, 1628, 1640–3. Royalist. During the siege of Carlisle forced to retire before General Lesley. Died Sept. 1657. His funeral sermon was preached at Dalston, by Jeremy Taylor. Will (P.C.C.) 1657. Father of William (1631). (*Vis. of Cumberland*; *G.E.C.*; G. B. Routledge; A. B. Beaven.)

DALSTONE, JOHN. Matric. pens. from ST JOHN'S, Michs. 1580.

DALSTONE, JOHN. Matric. pens. from CHRIST'S, Easter, 1603; B.A. 1606–7.

DALSTON, THOMAS. Matric. pens. from JESUS, Michs. 1570.

DALSTON, WILLIAM. Adm. Fell.-Com. (age 17) at ST JOHN'S, July 6, 1631. S. of Sir George (1596), Knt., of Dalston Hall, Cumberland. B. at Smardale in Kirkby Stephen, Westmorland. Adm. at Gray's Inn, Dec. 7, 1631. Of Dalston, Cumberland, Knt. M.P. for Carlisle, Apr. to May, 1640; and Nov. 1640. Created Bart., Feb. 15, 1640–1. Knighted, 1641. Colonel of Horse in the King's Army. Royalist. Died Jan. 13, 1683. (G.E.C.)

DALTON, CHARLES. Adm. pens. (age 16) at CHRIST'S, Mar. 6, 1730–1. S. of Darcy (next), R. of Aston, near Rotherham, Yorks. B. there. School, Westminster. Matric. 1731; Scholar, 1733; B.A. 1734–5; M.A. 1739. R. of Hauxwell, Yorks., 1737–88. Succeeded to the Hauxwell estate, 1747. Died, at the Hall, Dec. 22, 1788. Buried at Hauxwell. M.I. Brother of D'arcy (1720). (*Peile*, II. 223.)

DALTON, DARCY. Adm. pens. (age 17) at CHRIST'S, Apr. 20, 1688. S. of Sir William, of Hauxwell, Yorks., Knt. B. there. School, Bury St Edmunds. Matric. 1688; B.A. 1691–2; M.A. 1695. Ord. deacon (Ely) Sept. 1693; priest (Peterb.) June 3, 1694. V. of Lissington, Lincs., 1697. R. of Binbrooke St Mary, 1699–1704. R. of Hauxwell, Yorks., 1703–11. Preb. of Ripon, 1705–13. R. of Aston, Yorks., 1712–34. Preb. of York, 1713–34. Died Mar. 27, 1734. Buried at Aston. M.I. Father of the above and next. (*Peile*, II. 108; *F.M.G.*)

DALTON, D'ARCY. Adm. pens. at CHRIST'S, June 7, 1720. Eldest s. of Darcy (above), R. of Cold Aston, Yorks. School, Beighton, Derbs. (Mr Drake). Matric. 1720; Scholar, 1721; B.A. 1724–5. Died unmarried. Buried at Hauxwell, 1746. Brother of Charles (1730). (*Whitaker*, I. 328; *Peile*, II. 198.)

DALTON, EDWARD. B.A. from ST JOHN'S, 1606–7. Ord. deacon (York) Nov. 1608; priest, Sept. 1609. V. of Foston, Yorks., 1609. *Cooper* (III. 15) makes him a younger half-brother of Oliver (1607); but the latter was bapt. at Wratting, July 5, 1609.

DALTON, FRANCIS. Matric. pens. from TRINITY, Easter, 1570. S. of Roger, of Kirby Misperton, Yorks., Esq. B. there, *c.* 1550. Scholar, 1573; B.A. 1573–4; M.A. 1577; B.D. 1586. Fellow, 1576. University preacher. Incorp. at Oxford, 1586. Ord. deacon and priest (Lincoln) Dec. 30, 1583. V. of Trumpington, Cambs., 1584–6. R. of Houghton, Hunts., 1586–8. R. of Slaidburn, Yorks., 1588–91. R. of St Dionis Backchurch, London, 1591–6. V. of Tilmanstone, Kent, 1597–9. R. of Calverton, Bucks., 1600–4. R. of Hope All Saints, Kent, 1606–8. Died 1608. (*Vis. of Yorks.*, 1564.)

DALTON, GEORGE. Matric. sizar from TRINITY, Easter, 1584; B.A. 1588–9.

DALTON, ISAAC. Adm. sizar at TRINITY, Apr. 24, 1674. Matric. 1674; Scholar, 1676; B.A. 1677–8.

DALTON, JEREMY. Matric. sizar from ST CATHARINE'S, Easter, 1627. Of Hertfordshire. B.A. 1632–3.

DALTON, J. Fee for B.A. 1468–9; M.A. Of Ely diocese. Ord. deacon (Lincoln) Feb. 29, 1479–80; title, St Radegund's, Cambridge.

DALTON, JOHN. Matric. sizar from TRINITY, Easter, 1586; B.A. 1571–2, as Dawlton. Perhaps R. of Pudding-Norton, Norfolk, 1576. C. at Roydon, 1582.

DALTON, JOHN. Adm. pens. (age 16) at CAIUS, Mar. 12, 1622–3. S. of Edmund, yeoman, of Ipswich. School, Ipswich. Matric. 1623; Scholar, 1626–30; B.A. 1626–7; M.A. 1630. Ord. deacon (Peterb.) June 5; priest, Dec. 18, 1631. Probably R. of Depden, Suffolk. V. of Gt Abington, Cambs., 1633–43. Minister at Walthamstow, 1647–8. Perhaps V. of Aylesbury, 1665–88. Father of Nathaniel (1660). (*Venn*, I. 261; *East Anglian*, I. 414; *Al. Oxon.*)

DALTON, JOHN. Adm. pens. at EMMANUEL, Feb. 14, 1626–7. Matric. sizar, Lent, 1626–7; B.A. 1630–1; M.A. 1634.

DALTON, JOHN. Matric. pens. from KING'S, Michs. 1642. S. of Corleby (?), of Richmond, gent. Migrated to Magdalene, Dec. 22, 1648, age 20. B.A. 1648–9; M.A. from St John's, 1652. Fellow of Magdalene. Intruded fellow of St John's, Dec. 19, 1650. One of these names V. of Aylesbury, Bucks., 1665–88, but *see* above.

DALTON, JOHN. Adm. sizar (age 18) at ST JOHN'S, Mar. 4, 1672–3. S. of John, yeoman, of Eastham, Cheshire. B. there. School, Chester. Matric. 1672, as 'Dutton.'

DALTON, JOHN. Adm. pens. (age 16) at ST JOHN'S, May 23, 1681. S. of Thomas (1625), D.D., preb. of Durham. B. there. School, Durham. Matric. 1681. Adm. at Lincoln's Inn, May 6, 1684.

DALTON, JOHN. Adm. sizar (age 20) at ST JOHN'S, July 1, 1724. S. of John, husbandman, of Nottinghamshire. B. at South Scarle. School, Newark (Mr Warburton). Matric. 1724; B.A. 1727–8. Ord. deacon (Lincoln) Mar. 17, 1727–8; priest, Sept. 21, 1729. V. of South Scarle, Notts., 1730–69. R. of North Scarle, 1742–69. (*Scott-Mayor*, III. 374.)

DALTON, MARMADUKE. Adm. pens. (age 17) at CHRIST'S, May 24, 1654. S. of John, of Hauxwell, Yorks. B. there. School, Bedale (Mr Rawlin). Matric. 1654, as 'Bolton.' Died without issue. Will proved, 1695. Brother of Thomas (1650) and William (1647). (*Peile*, I. 563; *F.M.G.*, 913; *Vis. of Yorks.*, 1665.)

DALTON, MARMADUKE. Adm. Fell.-Com. at CHRIST'S, Apr. 16, 1672. S. of Sir William (1647), of Hauxwell, Yorks., Knt. B. there. School, Bury St Edmunds. Matric. 1672. Succeeded his father, 1675. Knighted, Nov. 2, 1676. Drowned at Dalton Bridge, Feb. 19, 1680; buried at Hauxwell. M.I. (*Vis. of Yorks.*, 1665; *Peile*, II. 42; *F.M.G.*)

DALTON, MICHAEL. Matric. pens. from TRINITY, Lent, 1579–80. Doubtless s. of Thomas, of Hildersham, Cambs. Adm. at Lincoln's Inn, from Furnival's Inn, Nov. 25, 1581. Of West Wratting, Cambs. J.P. for Cambs., and commissioner for sequestrations, 1648. Author, *The Country Justice*, 1618, etc. Died *c.* 1650. Father of Thomas (1610) and Oliver. (*D.N.B.*)

DALTON, NATHANIEL. Scholar at TRINITY HALL, 1660. S. of John (1622–3), clerk. B. at Abington, Cambs., Aug. 16, 1641. School, Merchant Taylors'. Matric. pens. Michs. 1660; LL.B. 1665. Signs for deacon's orders (London) Dec. 16, 1664; but cancelled. R. of Cucklington, Somerset, 1674–1706. R. of Holton, Lincs., 1681–1706. Died 1708. (*East Anglian*, I. 414.)

DALTON, OLIVER. Matric. Fell.-Com. from PETERHOUSE, Easter, 1607. S. of Michael (above), of West Wratting, Cambs., Esq. Adm. at Lincoln's Inn, Jan. 24, 1609–10. Died Jan. 19, 1618–9. M.I. at Little Abington. Brother of Thomas (1610). (*Vis. of Cambs.*, 1619.)

DALTON, RICHARD. B.A. 1520–1.

DALTON, RICHARD. Adm. Fell.-Com. at QUEENS', Sept. 9, 1595. Of Lancashire.

DALTON, RICHARD. M.A. 1682 (*Com. Reg.*). One of these names, s. and h. of Thomas, of Abington, Cambs., deceased; adm. at Lincoln's Inn, May 5, 1656.

DAWLTON, RO. Matric. pens. from ST JOHN'S, Michs. 1545.

DALTON, ROBERT. Incorp. M.A. 1661, from Queen's College, Oxford. Matric. there, Mar. 17, 1653-4; B.A. (Oxford) 1657-8; M.A. 1660. Fellow of Queen's College, 1660. R. of Oaksey, Wilts., 1670. (*Al. Oxon.*)

DALTON, ROGER. Matric. pens. from TRINITY, Easter, 1570. Perhaps adm. at Lincoln's Inn, Feb. 8, 1573-4. Of Yorkshire. One of these names M.P. for Lancaster, 1588; for Scarborough, 1593.

DALTON, SAMUEL. Adm. pens. (age 17) at CHRIST'S, May 1, 1672. S. of John. B. at Nottingham. School, Mackworth, Derbs. (private; Mr Ogden). Probably adm. at the Inner Temple, 1674. Of Derby, gent.

DALTON, THOMAS. Adm. at KING'S, a scholar from Eton, 1448. Ord. priest (Ely) Mar. 24, 1458-9; M.A.; M.D. 'A celebrated physician.' (*Harwood.*)

DALTON, THOMAS. Adm. pens. at SIDNEY, Jan. 1601-2. B. at Wratting, Cambs. Matric. 1601. Probably LL.B. 1611-2.

DALTON, THOMAS. Fell.-Com. at PETERHOUSE, 1610-9. S. of Michael (1579-80). Adm. at Lincoln's Inn, Apr. 27, 1616. Of Little Abington, Cambs. Brother of Oliver (1607). (*T. A. Walker.*)

DALTON, THOMAS. Matric. sizar from TRINITY, Easter, 1625; Scholar, 1627; B.A. 1628-9; M.A. 1632; B.D. 1639; D.D. 1661 (*Lit. Reg.*). R. of Dalham, Suffolk, 1633. R. of Redgrave, 1661. Perhaps R. of Barwick-in-Elmet, Yorks., 1661-72. Preb. of Durham, 1660-72. Died 1672. Father of John (1681).

DALTON, THOMAS. Adm. pens. (age 16) at CHRIST'S, May 11, 1650. S. of John, of Hauxwell, Yorks. B. at Caley Hall, near Otley, Yorks. School, York. Matric. 1650. Adm. at Gray's Inn, May 17, 1650; and at Lincoln's Inn, May 23, 1650. Married Anne, dau. of Sir Marm. Wyvill, of Burton Constable, Knt. Of York, and afterwards of Bedale, Esq. Will (York) 1710. Brother of William (1647) and Marmaduke (1654). (*Peile*, I. 534; *Vis. of Yorks.*, 1665; *Whitaker*, I. 328.)

DALTON, THOMAS. Adm. at CORPUS CHRISTI, 1706. Of Norfolk. Matric. 1707; B.A. 1710-1. Ord. deacon (Ely) Sept. 20, 1713; priest (Norwich) Oct. 28, 1715. R. of Crostwight, Norfolk, 1715-24. R. of Whinburgh. R. of Thuxton, 1728-42. R. of Reymerston, 1728-42.

DALTON, THOMAS. Adm. Fell.-Com. (age 17) at TRINITY, July 29, 1717. S. of ——, of Bury, Suffolk. School, Bishop's Stortford, Herts. (Dr Tooke).

DALTON, TIMOTHY. Matric. sizar from ST JOHN'S, Michs. 1610, as 'Dolson.' B. *c.* 1588. B.A. 1613-4. Ord. priest, June 19, 1614. V. of Woolverstone, Suffolk, 1615-36: suspended by Bishop Wren. R. of Flowton, 1616-24. Went to New England, 1636. At first resided at Watertown and Dedham, Mass. One of the founders of Hampton, N.H. Minister there, 1639, until his death. Died there, Dec. 28, 1661. (*Felt*, 397; J. G. Bartlett.)

DALTON, TIRRELL. Adm. pens. (age 16) at CAIUS, Feb. 9, 1684-5. S. of Tirrell, of Fulbourn, Cambs., Esq. B. there. School, Norwich. Of Fulbourn, Esq. Lord of the manor of Shalford, Essex. (*Venn*, I. 477.)

DALTON, WILLIAM. University Bedell, *c.* 1460. (Stokes, *Bedells*, 67.)

DALTON, WILLIAM. A priest. B.Can.L. 1519-20.

DALTON, WILLIAM. Adm. pens. (age 17) at CAIUS, Feb. 11, 1584-5. S. of Thomas, gent., Mayor of Hull. B. there. School, Hull (Mr Margetts). Adm. at Lincoln's Inn, Oct. 11, 1588. Recorder of Hull. Attorney-general to the Northern court at York. Knighted, Apr. 28, 1629. Buried in York Minster, Jan. 25, 1649-50. Will, York. (*Venn*, I. 123; *Vis. of Yorks.*, 1665.)

DALTON, WILLIAM. Matric. pens. from CHRIST'S, Easter, 1609; B.A. 1615-6. ('Balton,' in *Grace*.) Probably ord. deacon (Peterb.) Dec. 22, 1616, as 'B.A. of Pembroke'; priest, Mar. 9, 1616-7.

DALTON, WILLIAM. Adm. Fell.-Com. (age 17) at CHRIST'S, May 7, 1647. S. of John, of Hauxwell, near Richmond, Yorks. B. at Caley Hall, near Otley, Yorks. School, York. Adm. at Gray's Inn, May 17, 1650. Knighted, June 5, 1660. Of Hauxwell. Married Elizabeth, dau. of Sir Marmaduke Wyvill, of Burton Constable. Died Mar. 23, 1675. Buried at Hauxwell. M.I. Father of Marmaduke (1672). Brother of Thomas (1650) and Marmaduke (1654). (*Peile*, I. 513; *F.M.G.*, 913; *Vis. of Yorks.*, 1665.)

DALTON, WILLIAM. Adm. pens. (age 18) at ST JOHN'S, June 29, 1652. S. of William, gent., of Sotton-in-Holderness, Yorks. B. there. School, Pocklington (Mr Llewellyn). Matric. 1652. Adm. at Lincoln's Inn, June 28, 1652.

DALTON, WILLIAM. Adm. at CORPUS CHRISTI, 1678. Of Lincolnshire. Matric. 1679; B.A. 1682-3; M.A. 1687. Ord. deacon (Norwich) Mar. 1682-3; priest, June, 1683. R. of Spixworth, Norfolk, 1688-1704. R. of St Edward and St Julian, Norwich, 1691-1704. R. of All Saints', 1691-1704.

DALTON, WILLIAM. Adm. sizar at ST CATHARINE'S, Jan. 15, 1736-7. Of Over Penn, Staffs. Matric. 1737; B.A. 1740-1; M.A. 1744. Fellow, 1742. Proctor, 1767. V. of Coton, Cambs., 1748. Died 1780. (G. *Mag.*)

DALTON, ——. B.Can.L. 1476-7.

DALTON, ——. B.Civ.L. 1503-4.

DALTON, ——. Scholar of TRINITY, 1548.

DALTON, ——. Adm. sizar at SIDNEY, July, 1603.

DALTON, ——. Adm. Fell.-Com. at TRINITY, 1656.

DAMASON or DAMERON, ROBERT. B.A. 1525-6.

DAMAT, ——. Matric. sizar from CHRIST'S, Dec. 1608.

DAME, ——. B.Can.L. 1485-6.

DAMIAN, HENRY. Adm. at KING'S, a scholar from Eton, 1459; B.A. 1463-4; M.A. 1467. Died at Canterbury, 'much esteemed for his piety and worth.' (*Harwood.*)

DAMLET, HUGH. Fellow of PEMBROKE, as B.A. 1426. Proctor, 1431-2. Master of Pembroke, 1447-50. R. of St Peter's, Cornhill, London, 1447-76. Referred to as 'Master Hugh Damelet, D.D.' in will of John Dun, mercer, of London (P.C.C., 1478). One of the framers of the statutes of Queens' College. Died May 17, 1476. Will (Commis. C. London) 1476. Bequests to Queens' and Pembroke. (J. Ch. Smith.)

DAMMANT, WILLIAM. Adm. sizar (age 17) at ST JOHN'S, Apr. 29, 1738. S. of William, surgeon. B. at Colchester. Schools, Colchester (Mr Smythies) and Bury, Suffolk. Matric. 1738; B.A. 1741-2. Ord. deacon (Lincoln) June 9, 1745; C. of Kempston, Beds.; priest (Norwich) Sept. 1753.

DAMME, ——. B.A. 1474-5.

DAMMER or DAMER, EDWARD. Adm. sizar (age 18) at CHRIST'S, July 1, 1650. S. of John (Damony or Damer). B. at Godmanstone, Dorset. School, Bridport (Mr Hallet). Matric. 1650; B.A. 1653. R. of Wyke Regis, Dorset, 1658-62. Chaplain to Jersey Garrison; ejected, 1660. Afterwards at Dorchester, preaching occasionally. Steward to Denzil, Lord Holles. (*Peile*, I. 538; Hutchins, *Dorset*, II. 856, and IV. 387.)

DAMORY, NICHOLAS. One of the earliest 'King's scholars' at Cambridge, Apr. 14, 1318. (He and his brothers seem also called 'Pour'; *Trin. Coll. Admissions*, I. 83.)

DAMORY, RICHARD. 'King's scholar,' Apr. 14, 1318. Perhaps the nephew of Baron Roger D'Amorie, Knt. Summoned to Parliament in 1326. Died 1330. (Nicolas, *Peerage of England*.)

DAMORY, WILLIAM. 'King's scholar,' Apr. 14, 1318.

DAMPIER, THOMAS. Adm. at KING'S, a scholar from Eton, 1731. S. of William. B. at Blackford, Somerset. Matric. 1732; B.A. 1735-6; M.A. 1741; D.D. 1755. Fellow, 1735. Under-Master at Eton, 1745. Preb. of Canterbury, 1765-9. Fellow of Eton College, 1767. Canon of Windsor, 1769-74. Preb. of Durham, 1771-3. Master of Sherburn Hospital, 1773-4; resigned in favour of his son Thomas. Dean of Durham, 1774. Died at Bath, July 31, 1777. Buried there. Will, P.C.C. (*Harwood*, 95; H. M. Wood.)

DAMPORT, *see* also **DAVENPORT.**

DAMPORT, CHRISTOPHER. B.A. 1511-2.

DAMPORT or DAVENPORT, EDMUND. Adm. pens. (age 16) at CAIUS, May 15, 1612. S. of Robert, Esq., of Manby, Lincs. School, Roxby (Mr Welby). Matric. as Fell.-Com. 1612. Adm. at Gray's Inn, 1615.

DAMPORT, RICHARD, *see* **DANFORD.**

DAMPORT, SAMPSON Matric. sizar from ST JOHN'S, Easter, 1625; B.A. 1628-9; M.A. 1632. Ord. deacon (Peterb.) Dec. 18, 1631; priest, Feb. 26, 1631-2. V. of Thurcaston, Leics., 1633.

DAMPORT, W. Matric. pens. from ST JOHN'S, Michs. 1561.

DAN, EDWARD. Matric. sizar from ST JOHN'S, Easter, 1582.

DAN, JOHN. Matric. pens. from ST JOHN'S, Lent, 1563-4.

DAN or DANN, JOHN. Adm. sizar (age 17) at ST JOHN'S, June 17, 1668. S. of John, of Wigston, Leics. B. there. School, Oakham. Matric. 1668; B.A. 1672-3; M.A. 1677.

DANN, OLYMPAS. Matric. sizar from TRINITY, Easter, 1604; B.A. from Sidney, 1606-7.

DAN, THOMAS. Matric. pens. from CHRIST'S, July 5, 1627; B.A. 1629-30.

DAN or DANN, WILLIAM. Adm. pens. at EMMANUEL, Sept. 9, 1710. Of Cambridgeshire. Matric. 1710-1; B.A. 1714-5.

DANBY, CHARLES. Adm. pens. (age 16) at Caius, July 2, 1661. 4th s. of Sir Thomas (1626), Knt., of Farnley, Yorks. B. there. School, Farnley (Mr Lovell). Matric. 1661. Adm. at Gray's Inn, Jan. 29, 1663-4. Died 1672. Will (York) 1672. (*Venn*, I. 414.)

DANBY, FRANCIS. Adm. Fell.-Com. at Jesus, May 6, 1632. Of Yorkshire. Matric. 1632. Perhaps s. of Thomas, of Kirkby Knowle, Thirsk, Yorks. Of South Cave. Major in the Royal army; surrendered to Lord Fairfax at the taking of York, 1644. Died 1672. (A. Gray.)

DANBYE, JAMES. Matric. sizar from Michael House, Easter, 1545.

DANBY, JOHN. Matric. pens. from St John's, Michs. 1608. One of these names ord. priest (Peterb.) 1621. C. of Westacre, Norfolk, in 1635.

DANBY, JOHN. Adm. sizar (age 17) at Christ's, Sept. 23, 1674. S. of Thomas, V. of Keighley, Yorks. B. there. School, Bingley (Mr Rawson). Matric. 1674; B.A. 1678-9. Ord. deacon (York) Dec. 1679. Brother of Thomas (1674).

DANBY, NATHANIEL. Adm. sizar at Emmanuel, Easter, 1623. Of Northamptonshire. S. of John, alderman, of Northampton. Matric. 1623. Migrated to Queens', July, 1626. B.A. 1626-7. Of Northamptonshire. Married Mary, dau. of W. Ward, of Breafield, Northants. Buried, at All Saints', Northampton, May 7, 1644. Will (Archd. Northants.) 1645. (H. I. Longden.)

DANBY, ROGER. Matric. pens. from St John's, Michs. 1601; B.A. 1605-6. Will of one of these names (Dublin) 1626; of Dublin, clerk.

DANBIE, THOMAS. Matric. pens. from St John's, Easter, 1619. Will (York) 1621; 'of Sleningford, Yorks.,' late student of St John's; to be buried at Burneston. (J. Ch. Smith.)

DANBY, THOMAS. Matric. Fell.-Com. from St John's, Lent, 1626-7. Doubtless s. and h. of Christopher, of Thorpe Perrow and Farnley, Yorks., age 2 in 1612. Succeeded to his father's estates in 1624. Married Catherine Wandesford, of Kirklington, Yorks., 1630. Commissioner of the Peace for the North Riding of Yorkshire. High Sheriff of Yorkshire, 1637-8. Colonel in the army. M.P. for Richmond, 1640-5. Knighted, 1640. A staunch Royalist and supporter of his cousin and patron the Earl of Stafford. Imprisoned and heavily fined. Created a Knight of the Royal Oak, 1660. Died Aug. 5, 1660. Buried in York Minster. Father of Charles (1661). (*Vis. of Yorks.*, 1612; John Fisher, *History of Masham*.)

DANBY, THOMAS. Adm. sizar (age 14) at Christ's, Sept. 23, 1674. S. of Thomas, V. of Keighley, Yorks. B. there. School, Bingley (Mr Rawson). Matric. 1674; B.A. 1678-9. Ord. deacon (York) Mar. 1681-2; priest, Feb. 1683-4. V. of Fawsley, Northants., 1699-1720. Perhaps R. of Shawell, Leics., 1692. V. of Preston-Capes, Northants., 1720-3. Buried there, 1723-4. Brother of John (1674). (*Peile*, II. 56; *Baker*, I. 388.)

DANBY, WILLIAM. Matric. pens. from St Catharine's, Lent, 1653-4. One of these names, s. and h. of James, of City of York, gent., adm. at Gray's Inn, Oct. 24, 1653. Called to the Bar, 1661.

DANBY, WILLIAM. Adm. Fell.-Com. at St Catharine's, Aug. 11, 1730. Matric. 1730. Adm. at the Middle Temple, Aug. 6, 1730. S. of Abstrupus, of Farnley, Yorks., Esq. Of Swinton. Married Mary, dau. of Gilbert Affleck, Esq., of Dalham Hall, Sussex. Died Apr. 8, 1781, aged 69. M.I. at Masham. (J. Fisher, *Masham*, 384.)

DANCE or DANNCE, GEORGE. Matric. sizar from St John's, Easter, 1617; B.A. 1619-20. Ord. deacon (Peterb.) May 11; priest, Sept. 24, 1620.

DANCE, THOMAS. B.A. from St John's, 1611-2.

DAND, EMERY. Matric. sizar from Pembroke, Michs. 1558, as 'Ed.' Of Durham diocese. Ord. deacon (London) Feb. 17, 1558-9. R. of Oakington, Cambs., 1559-64 (deprived).

DAND, FRANCIS. Matric. pens. from St John's, May, 1576. S. of Rowland, of Mansfield-Woodhouse, Notts. Migrated to Christ's. B.A. 1579-80; M.A. 1583. Died Oct. 28, 1627, aged 67. Father of Oliver (1619). (*Peile*, I. 140; *F.M.G.*, 1003.)

DAND, JOHN. Adm. Fell.-Com. (age 18) at Christ's, June 26, 1651. Eldest s. of Sir Roland, of Mansfield-Woodhouse, Notts., Knt. B. Dec. 3, 1632. School, Nottingham (Mr Leake). Matric. 1651. Adm. at Gray's Inn, Nov. 25, 1654. Of Mansfield-Woodhouse, Esq. (*Peile*, I. 544; *F.M.G.*)

DANDE, OLIVER. Matric. pens. from St John's, Michs. 1619. Of Nottinghamshire. S. of Francis (1576), of Mansfield. B.A. 1623-4; M.A. 1627; B.D. 1634. Fellow, 1626; senior fellow, 1645. Incorp. at Oxford, 1628. R. of Warsop, Notts., 1647. Died May 4, 1661. Buried at Warsop. (*F.M.G.*, 1004; *Al. Oxon.*)

DANDE, THOMAS. Matric. sizar from Trinity, Michs. 1614; B.A. 1618; M.A. 1622. Doubtless s. of Thomas, of Mansfield, Notts., clerk. Died at Dronfield, Mar. 31, 1669, aged 71.

DAND, THOMAS. Adm. sizar at Emmanuel, Mar. 23, 1704-5. Of Leicestershire. Matric. 1705; B.A. 1708-9. Ord. deacon (Peterb.) June 19, 1709; priest (Lincoln) May 27, 1711, as Thos. Raye Dand. C. of Ason (? Ayston, Rutland). Will (Leicester) 1732; of Sheepy Magna, Leics.

DANDE, WILLIAM. Matric. sizar from St John's, c. 1596.

DAND, WILLIAM. Matric. from Pembroke, Easter, 1681; B.A. 1684-5. Ord. priest (Lincoln) Dec. 22, 1695. V. of Sproxton, Leics., 1695-1704. V. of Saltby, 1704-16. V. of Granby, Notts., 1716-20. V. of Howes, 1718. Died 1720. Buried at Granby. (*Nichols*, II. 306, 330.)

DAND, WILLIAM JOHN. Adm. sizar (age 17) at St John's, May 8, 1703. S. of John, clerk. B. in London. School, Kilworth (under his father), Leics. Matric. 1703; B.A. 1707-8. Ord. deacon (Lincoln) June 19, 1709; priest, Mar. 5, 1709-10. C. of Kibworth Beauchamp, 1709. School-master there.

DANDY, EDMUND. Matric. pens. from St John's, Easter, 1604. Probably s. of Thomas, of Combes, Suffolk; adm. at Gray's Inn, Apr. 30, 1605. (Pedigree in *Vis. of Suff.*, 1664.)

DANDY, FRANCIS. Adm. sizar at Emmanuel, May 12, 1669. Of Northamptonshire. Matric. 1669.

DANDY, HENRY. Adm. pens. at Jesus, Feb. 18, 1644-5. Of Suffolk. Matric. 1645.

DANDY, JAMES. Adm. pens. at Clare, Apr. 19, 1683. Matric. 1683; B.A. 1686-7.

DANDYE, THOMAS. Matric. pens. from Clare, Easter, 1576.

DANDY or DENDY, THOMAS. Adm. pens. at Emmanuel, Mar. 21, 1653-4. Of Suffolk.

DANDY, ——. Adm. pens. at Emmanuel, Easter, 1626. Possibly Edmund, s. and h. of Edmund, of Finningley, Suffolk; adm. at Gray's Inn, Aug. 9, 1626.

DANE, FRANCIS. Matric. sizar from King's, Easter, 1633. S. of John and Frances Dane. Bapt. at Bishop's Stortford, Nov. 20, 1615. Went to New England, with his parents, c. 1636. Minister at Andover, Mass., 1648-97. Died there Feb. 17, 1696-7. (J. G. Bartlett.)

DANES, *see* **DAYNES.**

DANFIELD, ROBERT. D.D. 1488.

DANFORD or DAMPORT, RICHARD. Adm. sizar at Sidney, June 23, 1603. Matric. 1604; B.A. 1606-7; M.A. 1610; B.D. 1617. Fellow. Ord. deacon (Peterb.) Sept. 19; priest, Sept. 20, 1613. R. of Stowlangtoft, Suffolk, 1625-31, as Damport. R. of Feltwell, Norfolk, 1630; ejected, but reinstated, 1660. Will proved Oct. 11, 1666. (*E. Anglian*, I. 75, 82.)

DANIEL, BRIAN. Fellow of Queens', 1484-6.

DANIEL, CHARLES. Adm. pens. at Caius, Aug. 4, 1655. S. of Edward, of Yorkshire, of the Merchant Adventurers' Company. B. at Dantzig. School, Thorne. Matric. 1655. Readm. as Fell.-Com. Oct. 24, 1655; LL.B. 1660. Perhaps adm. at Leyden, Dec. 13, 1660. (*Venn*, I. 392.)

DANIEL, EDWARD. B.A. 1516-7; M.A. 1520.

DANIEL, EDWARD. Adm. at Corpus Christi, 1704. Of London. Matric. 1704. Migrated to Christ's, 1706. B.A. 1707-8.

DANIELL, FRANCIS. Matric. sizar from St John's, c. 1601; B.A. 1605-6; M.A. 1609. Ord. deacon (York) Dec. 1609; schoolmaster and curate at Saxton, Yorks. Ord. priest, Mar. 1611-2. Licensed to preach, 1612.

DANIELL, GEORGE. Adm. sizar at Sidney, June, 1599. Of Sussex. B.A. 1599-1600; M.A. 1603. Ord. deacon (Colchester) June 21; priest, June 28, 1601. V. of Bromham. Beds., 1605-8. V. of Stevington, 1608. Perhaps R. of Irthlingborough, Northants., 1601-61.

DANIEL, HENRY. Matric. sizar from St John's, Easter, 1576; B.A. from Corpus Christi, 1578-9; M.A. 1582. Probably V. of Blockley, Worcs., 1586-1627.

DANYELL, HENRY. Matric. pens. from Peterhouse, Easter, 1584.

DANIELL, INGLEBY. Adm. pens. (age 15) at Caius, Oct. 11, 1588. S. and h. of William, Esq. B. at Beswick, Yorks. School, Beswick. Matric. 1588. Knighted, July 23, 1603. Of Beswick, Yorks. Died c. Jan. 1645-6. (*Venn*, I. 134; *Vis. of Yorks.*, 1584.)

DANYELL, JAMES. Adm. pens. (age 14) at Caius, Sept. 17, 1622. S. of John, brewer, of Norwich. School, Norwich. Matric. 1623; Scholar, 1624-31; B.A. 1626-7; M.A. 1630. Fellow, 1631-6. Ord. deacon (Norwich) Sept. 23, 1632. Died in College, of the plague. Buried at St Michael's, Cambridge, Oct. 27, 1636. (*Venn*, I. 259.)

DANIEL, JAMES. Adm. sizar at ST CATHARINE'S, 1710. Matric. 1711.

DANIELL, JOHN. Matric. pens. from QUEENS', Michs. 1569. Perhaps adm. at the Middle Temple, Mar. 21, 1570-1; as s. and h. of Edmund, Esq., of Mining Beynerds, Essex (? in Messing parish: *see Morant*, II. 176. If so, he inherited the estate, and died Dec. 15, 1596).

DANIELL, JOHN. Matric. sizar from CAIUS, Easter, 1583.

DANIEL, JOHN. Matric. pens. from TRINITY, *c.* 1592. One of these names, of Kilnwick, Yorks., adm. at Gray's Inn, Feb. 11, 1594-5.

DANIEL, JOHN. Adm. sizar (age 19) at CHRIST'S, Apr. 4, 1677. S. of John. B. at Hartshorne, Derbs. School, Repton. Matric. 1678; B.A. 1680-1. V. of Croxall, Derbs., 1690-1728. Father of Thomas (1717) and brother of Samuel (1674). (*Peile*, II. 63.)

DANIEL or DONELLAN, NEHEMIAH. Matric. sizar from KING'S, Lent, 1579-80. B. in Galway. B.A. from St Catharine's, 1581-2. Returned to Ireland, and acted as Coadjutor to the Archbishop of Tuam; whom he succeeded as Archbishop, Aug. 17, 1595; resigned, 1609; died soon after. A skilled Irish scholar. (*Cooper*, III. 15; *D.N.B.*; under Donellan.)

DANIELL, PETER. Adm. Fell.-Com. at EMMANUEL, Apr. 8, 1626. Perhaps s. and h. of Peter, of Tabley, Cheshire, Esq.; adm. at Gray's Inn, Aug. 9, 1626. Age 3 in 1613. (*Vis. of Chesh.*, 1613.)

DANIELL, RICHARD. Matric. pens. from ST JOHN'S, Michs. 1568; B.A. 1572-3.

DANIELL, RICHARD. Matric. pens. from QUEENS', Michs. 1587. Of Cheshire. Perhaps 2nd s. of Thomas, of Tabley. Died 1605. (*Genealogist*, N.S., XXXII.)

DANIELL, RICHARD. B.A. from TRINITY, 1596-7; M.A. 1600. Perhaps R. of Radclive with Chackmore, Bucks., 1603. But *see* a contemporary in *Al. Oxon.*

DANIEL, RICHARD. Adm. pens. (age 18) at ST JOHN'S, July 1, 1717. S. of John, grocer (apothecary), of Colchester. B. at Colchester. Schools, Felsted and Charterhouse. Matric. 1717; M.B. 1723. Practised physic at Colchester. Died 1772. Will, P.C.C. (*Scott-Mayor*, III. 314.)

DANIELL, ROBERT. Adm. pens. at TRINITY, Apr. 25, 1649. Of London. One of these names, s. of Robert, merchant, of London. B. 1631.

DANIEL, ROBERT. Matric. pens. from CORPUS CHRISTI, Easter, 1654. Of Norwich. B.A. 1657-8; M.A. 1661. Ord. deacon (Norwich) May 18; priest, May 23, 1696. One of these names R. of Hawkinge, Kent, 1696-1713. Died 1713. (*Vis. of London*, 1634.)

DANIEL, ROBERT. Adm. pens. at CHRIST'S, Oct. 1, 1706, from Corpus Christi (according to *Peile*, II. 165; probably a mistake for Edward).

DANIELL, SAMUEL. Matric. pens. from ST JOHN'S, Michs. 1566. B. at Colchester. Ord. deacon (London) Jan. 6, 1573-4, age 25; of Thorpe, Essex (? Curate).

DANIELL, SAMUEL. Adm. pens. at TRINITY, June 22, 1666. Matric. 1667; B.A. 1672-3. Ord. deacon (York) Dec. 1674; priest, Sept. 1675.

DANIELL, SAMUEL. Adm. pens. at TRINITY, Feb. 23, 1673-4. B. 1656. Matric. 1674. Adm. at the Middle Temple, Nov. 26, 1674; as s. and h. of Thomas, of Over Tabley, Cheshire. Of Over Tabley. Knighted, Feb. 21, 1708-9. Died Dec. 24, 1726. M.I. at Over Tabley. (*Ormerod*, I. 341.)

DANIEL, SAMUEL. Adm. sizar (age 20) at CHRIST'S, July 1, 1674. S. of John. B. at Hartshorne, Derbs. School, Repton. Matric. 1674; B.A. 1677-8; M.A. 1683. Ord. deacon (Lichfield) Sept. 1678; priest (Lincoln) June, 1680. V. of Rothley, Leics., 1691-1734. Chaplain to the Earl of Burlington. R. of Cossington, 1704. Died Oct. 30, 1735. Buried at Rothley. M.I. Brother of John (1677). (*Peile*, II. 54.)

DANIELL, THOMAS. M.A. from JESUS, 1625.

DANIEL, THOMAS. Adm. pens. at TRINITY, July 1, 1646. Of London. Matric. 1646; Scholar, 1649; B.A. 1650-1. Perhaps s. and h. of Roger, of London, gent.; adm. at Gray's Inn, Dec. 31, 1650.

DANIELL, THOMAS. Adm. pens. (age 17) at ST JOHN'S, July 21, 1654. S. of Richard, druggist, of Colchester. B. there. School, St Paul's, London. Matric. 1658; B.A. 1658-9; M.A. 1662. Signs for deacon's and priest's orders (London) June 4, 1664. V. of St Pancras, Kentish Town, London, 1664. V. of Bengeo, Herts., 1668. R. of St Andrew's, Hertford, 1675.

DANIEL, THOMAS. Adm. sizar (age 18) at CHRIST'S, Apr. 25, 1717. S. of John (1677), V. of Croxall, Derbs. School, Loughborough (Mr Martin). Scholar, 1719; B.A. 1720-1; M.A. 1724. Ord. priest (Lichfield) June, 1723. Master of Abbot's Bromley School, Staffs., 1734. P.C. of Stowe, Staffs., 1724. (*Peile*, II. 192.)

DANIEL, WILLIAM. Adm. at KING'S, a scholar from Eton, 1545. Left in 1548.

DANIELL, WILLIAM. Matric. pens. from PEMBROKE, Easter, 1572; B.A. 1575-6; M.A. 1579. Fellow, 1578. R. of Springfield Richards, Essex, 1582-1604. R. of Runwell, 1587-1604. Will (Cons. C. London) 1604; of Springfield.

DANIEL, WILLIAM. Matric. sizar from EMMANUEL, Easter, 1586; Scholar, on founder's nomination; B.A. 1589-90; M.A. 1593.

DANIELL, WILLIAM. Adm. pens. (age 16) at CAIUS, Oct. 11, 1588. S. of William, Esq. B. at Beswick, Yorks. School, Beswick (Mr Todd). Matric. 1588; B.A. (? 1594-5); M.A. 1598. Perhaps adm. at Gray's Inn, June 5, 1594, from Staple Inn; s. of William, of Kilnwick, Yorks. Died without issue. (*Vis. of Yorks.*, 1584; *Venn*, I. 134.)

DANIELL, WILLIAM. Matric. pens. from JESUS, *c.* 1595; B.A. 1598-9; M.A. 1603. Ord. deacon (London) Sept. 7; priest, Sept. 14, 1600. R. of Beaumont, Essex, 1603. R. of Markshall till 1642. Died 1642.

DANIELL, WILLIAM. Adm. pens. at SIDNEY, June 29, 1653. S. of Thomas, Esq., of Flitton, Beds. Bapt. there, Mar. 26, 1635. Schools, Hitchin (Mr Jos. Kempe) and Cambridge (Mr Moore). Adm. at Gray's Inn, May 12, 1652; as s. of Thomas, of Silsoe, Beds.

DANIEL, ——. Of ST MARY HOSTEL. Fee for B.A. 1456-7.

DANYALL, ——. Resident graduate at CORPUS CHRISTI, 1480.

DANIEL, ——. B.Civ.L. 1497-8.

DANIEL, ——. B.A. 1498-9.

DANIELL, ——. Adm. sizar at CHRIST'S, Easter, 1564.

DANIELL, ——. Matric. Fell.-Com. from QUEENS', *c.* 1591.

DANKES, CHARLES. Adm. sizar (age 14) at PETERHOUSE, July 4, 1656. Of Cambridge. Doubtless s. of John, cook of Peterhouse. Matric. 1657; Scholar; B.A. 1660-1; M.A. from Jesus, 1664. Fellow of Jesus, 1663-70. Ord. deacon (Ely) Mar. 1663-4; priest, Mar. 1665-6. P.C. of St Giles', Cambridge, 1666-70. V. of Elm and Emneth, Cambs., 1676-98. Buried at Emneth, Sept. 17, 1698. Brother of the next.

DANKES, THEOPHILUS. Adm. sizar at JESUS, Feb. 6, 1662-3. Of Cambridge. S. of John, cook of Peterhouse. Matric. 1663; B.A. 1666-7. Buried at Little St Mary's, Cambridge, Dec. 26, 1666. Brother of Charles (above).

DANN, *see* DAN.

DANNACKE, NICHOLAS. Matric. pens. from TRINITY, Easter, 1575.

DANNET, GER. Matric. sizar from MAGDALENE, Easter, 1548. Probably Gerard Dannett, s. of John, of Leicestershire. Adm. at Gray's Inn, 1556. (*Vis. of Leics.*, 1619.)

DANNETT or DONAT, MATTHEW. Adm. at KING'S, a scholar from Eton, 1605. Matric. 1606; B.A. 1609-10; M.A. 1613. Fellow, till 1614. V. of Newington, Kent, 1613-? 26.

DANNET, THOMAS. Incorp. D.D. 1479-80. Chaplain of the King. Principal of Alban Hall, Oxford, 1468-83. Canon of Windsor, 1472. Dean, 1481. Died Sept. 18, 1483. Buried at Windsor.

DANNET, THOMAS. Matric. sizar from MAGDALENE, Easter, 1548.

DANNET, THOMAS. Matric. sizar from ST JOHN'S, Easter, 1548. Doubtless s. of John, of Leicestershire, and brother of Gerard. Perhaps the translator of *Comines*, and other historical works. (See *D.N.B.*)

DANNET, THOMAS. Adm. Fell.-Com. at KING'S, Easter, 1574.

DANNETT, THOMAS. Adm. pe . (age 14) at PEMBROKE, Oct. 10, 1633. Eldest s. of John, of Peterborough, Northants., Esq. (and Margaret, dau. of Thomas Dove, Bishop of Peterborough). Bapt. at St John's, Peterborough, Aug. 5, 1619. Matric. 1633. (H. I. Longden.)

DANNOTT, SAMUEL. Matric. sizar from CHRIST'S, Dec. 1609.

DANNY, ROBERT. Adm. at CORPUS CHRISTI, 1695. Of Norwich. S. of Robert, of Barrow by Mattishall, Norfolk. Matric. 1696; B.A. 1699-1700; M.A. 1703; B.D. 1711; D.D. 1717. Fellow, 1702-13. Junior Proctor, 1708-9. Chaplain to the Duke of Somerset, Chancellor of the University. Ord. priest (Ely) June 19, 1709. R. of Spofforth, Yorks., 1709. Preb. of Southwell, 1724. Died 1729. (*Masters*.)

DANSER, THOMAS. Adm. sizar at QUEENS', July 4, 1699. Of Northamptonshire. Matric. 1701; B.A. 1702-3. Ord. deacon (Peterb.) 1704; priest, May 19, 1706. V. of Duston, Northants., 1706-38. V. of Dallington, 1720-38. Died Oct. 27, 1738, aged 58. Buried at Duston. M.I. Will (Archd. Northants.) 1738. (H. I. Longden.)

DANSON, PETER. B.A. from CHRIST'S, 1603-4. B. at Cartmell, Lancs. M.A. 1607. Incorp. at Oxford, 1607. V. of Carshalton, Surrey, 1613-24 (as Dawson). R. of Camberwell, 1618; sequestered, 1643. Will (P.C.C.) 1653; as of Camberwell. (*Peile*, I. 235.)

DANSON, THOMAS. Adm. pens. (age 17) at ST JOHN'S, July 6, 1637. S. of Thomas, of Roosecote in Dalton, Lancs., gent. Matric. 1637.

DANSON, THOMAS. M.A. 1654 (Incorp. from Oxford). Adm. at New Inn Hall, Oxford, 1648. Chaplain of Corpus, 1648. B.A. (Oxford) 1649-50; M.A. 1652. Fellow of Magdalen College, Oxford, 1652. Macray says that he was born at St Mary-le-Bow; otherwise it would be possible that he was the same as the last. R. of Sandwich St Peter, till 1660 (ejected). Minister at Sibton, Suffolk, 1661; ejected, 1662. Minister at Abingdon, Berks. Author, theological. Died 1694. (*Calamy*, III. 286; *D.N.B.*; *Al. Oxon.*)

DANSON, THOMAS. Adm. sizar (age 20) at ST JOHN'S, June 13, 1715. S. of Thomas, husbandman. B. at Cross, in Millom, Cumberland. School, Cross (Mr Steele). Matric. 1715; B.A. 1718-9. Ord. priest (Norwich) Sept. 1720. R. of Maltby, Lincs., 1721. Brother of William (1718).

DANSON or DAUSON, WILLIAM. Adm. Fell.-Com. (age 16) at CHRIST'S, Apr. 29, 1659. S. of George. B. at Azerley, near Ripon. Schools, York and Blewhouse, Barnet (Mr Lovell). Matric. 1659.

DANSON, WILLIAM. Adm. sizar (age 21) at ST JOHN'S, May 24, 1718. S. of Thomas, husbandman, of Cumberland. B. at Cross, near Bootle. School, Millom (Mr Steele). Matric. 1718; B.A. 1722-3; M.A. 1728. Ord. deacon (Lincoln) May 20, 1722; priest (York) Dec. 22, 1723. V. of Bilsby, Lincs., 1727-47. Brother of Thomas (1715).

DANSOR, ——. Resident student at JESUS, 1539-40.

DANSY, WILLIAM. Fined 5*s*. for disturbance of the peace, 1466-7. (*Gr. Bk*, A, 61.)

DANTON, ——. Resident graduate at CORPUS CHRISTI in the fifteenth century.

DANVERS, DANIEL. M.A. 1655 (Incorp. from Oxford). Of Byfield, Northants. S. of William, of London. Intruded fellow of New College, 1648. B.A. from Trinity College, Oxford, 1651; M.A. 1654; M.B. and M.D. 1666. Fellow of Trinity College, Oxford, 1654. Died May 12, 1699. Buried at All Saints', Northampton. M.I. there. (*Memorials of the Danvers family*, by Macnamara, 405-6; Le Neve, *Mon.*, III. 179; *Al. Oxon.*)

DANVERS or DAVERS, HENRY. Adm. Fell.-Com. at EMMANUEL, July 21, 1648. Of Middlesex. S. and h. of Sir John, of Dauntsey, Wilts., Knt. B. Dec. 5, 1633. M.A. 1650 (*fil. nob.*). Adm. at Lincoln's Inn, Nov. 14, 1648. Died Dec. 12, 1654, of small-pox, aged 21. M.I. at West Lavington, Wilts. (*Memorials of the Danvers family*, by F. N. Macnamara.)

DANVERS, HENRY. Adm. pens. at CLARE, June 16, 1705. B. at Newington, Middlesex. Matric. 1705. Perhaps adm. at Lincoln's Inn, Oct. 4, 1707; as 2nd s. of Samuel, late of Swithland, Leics., Esq., deceased. Buried Oct. 2, 1708. (*Nichols*, IV. 189.)

DANVERS, WILLIAM. Matric. pens. from CHRIST'S, Feb. 1579-80. Perhaps s. of Mark, of Clare, Suffolk. B.A. 1583-4; M.A. 1587. One of these names, of 'Wennington,' Essex, ord. deacon (London) 1587, ag 25; priest, Nov. 1589. R. of Wennington, 1589-1616; deprived. (*Peile*, I. 158.)

DANWELL, RICHARD. Adm. sizar at EMMANUEL, Oct. 30, 1611. Matric. 1611.

DANYE, JONATHAN. Matric. pens. from ST JOHN'S, Michs. 1619.

DANYTH, ——. Rector of a parish. Fee for M.A. or higher degree, 1468-9.

D'ARANDA, PETER. M.A. from ST CATHARINE'S, 1705. S. of Philip, of Canterbury, clerk. Matric. from University College, Oxford, Oct. 27, 1694, age 20; B.A. (Oxford) 1697. Ord. priest (Lincoln) Dec. 24, 1699. P.C. of Upper Gravenhurst and of Lower Gravenhurst, Beds., 1699-1731. (*Al. Oxon.*)

DARANT, LEONARD. Adm. sizar (age 17) at TRINITY, Apr. 12, 1699. S. of Simon, deceased, of London. School, St Paul's. Matric. 1699; B.A. 1702-3. Ord. deacon (London) May 23, 1703. Lecturer at Berwick-on-Tweed. V. of Alnwick, Northumberland, 1722-37. V. of Tynemouth, 1723-36. Married, at Berwick, Apr. 5, 1712, Mary Horne, widow. (H. M. Wood.)

DARBY, *see also* DERBY.

DARBY, CHARLES. Adm. pens. at JESUS, Apr. 21, 1652. Of Suffolk. Probably s. of John (brother of Luke, 1612). B. at Bramford. Matric. 1652; Scholar, 1653; B.A. 1655-6; M.A. 1659. Fellow, 1657-66. Ord. deacon (Lincoln) Sept. 27, 1662; priest (Ely) Se . 19, 1663. R. of Kedington, Suffolk, 1664-1709. Author of *Psalms in English Metre*, 1704. Buried at Kedington, Sept. 19, 1709. Father of Edward (1692) and the next. (V. B. Redstone; *Surtees Soc. Pub.*, 17; *Camden Soc.*, Woodcock Papers.)

DARBY, CHARLES. Adm. pens. at JESUS, Mar. 4, 1683-4. S. of Charles (above), R. of Kedington, Suffolk. B. at Kedington, 1666. Bapt. there, Oct. 12, 1667. Matric. 1684; Scholar, 1685; B.A. 1687-8; M.A. 1691. Fellow, 1692-1702. Died of small-pox, Oct. 14, 1702. Buried in the College Chapel. Brother of Edward (1692). (A. Gray.)

DARBY, EDWARD. Matric. sizar from JESUS, Michs. 1578; B.A. 1581-2.

DARBY, EDWARD. Adm. pens. at JESUS, June 29, 1692. S. of Charles (1652), R. of Kedington, Suffolk. Bapt. at Kedington, Jan. 6, 1678-9. Died in College. Buried in the Chapel, May 5, 1693. Brother of Charles (1683-4). (A. Gray.)

DARBY, HENRY. Adm. pens. at JESUS, Nov. 30, 1699. Of Suffolk. Doubtless s. of Charles (1652). Bapt. at Kedington, Nov. 5, 1685. Matric. 1700; Scholar, 1700; B.A. 1703-4; M.A. 1707. Ord. deacon (London) May 19, 1706; priest, Sept. 25, 1709. V. of Stowmarket, Suffolk, 1710. V. of Bramford and R. of Baylham, 1722. R. of Combs, 1723-35. Died Dec. 10, 1735. Father of the next, and Samuel (1739).

DARBY, HENRY HARWARD. Adm. sizar (age 19) at ST JOHN'S, Apr. 17, 1735. S. of Henry (above), of Suffolk. B. at Stowmarket. School, Suffolk (private; Mr Ray). Matric. 1735; B.A. 1738-9; M.A. 1742. Fellow, 1739-51. Ord. deacon (Norwich) Sept. 23, 1739; priest, Sept. 20, 1741. V. of Fordham, Cambs., 1754-68. Died at Boxford, Suffolk, Apr. 1, 1800. Brother of Samuel (1739). (*Scott-Mayor*, III. 465.)

DARBY, JOHN. Adm. at CORPUS CHRISTI, 1639. Of Norwich. Matric. 1640; B.A. 1643-4; M.A. 1647.

DARBY, JOSEPH. Adm. sizar at EMMANUEL, Oct. 28, 1676. Of Derbyshire. School, Ashby-de-la-Zouch. B.A. 1680-1; M.A. 1684. Perhaps V. of Waltham Abbey, 1693.

DARBY, LUKE. Adm. at EMMANUEL, June 4, 1612. Matric. pens. from St John's, Easter, 1612. Probably 1st s. of John, of Bramford, Suffolk. Of Ipswich, merchant. (V. B. Redstone.)

DARBY, SAMUEL. Adm. sizar at JESUS, Sept. 7, 1739. Of Suffolk. S. of Henry (1699), clerk, deceased. Rustat scholar. Matric. 1740; B.A. 1743-4; M.A. 1749. Fellow, 1749-73. Ord. deacon (Rochester) Dec. 25, 1744; priest (Norwich) Sept. 1748. V. of Fordham, Cambs., 1768-73. R. of Whatfield, Suffolk, 1773. V. of St Mary, Stowmarket, and Stow Upland 1785-8. V. of Bradfield, Suffolk. Married Martha, dau. of Dr Jortin. Died at Ipswich, Mar. 31, 1794, aged 72. (A. Gray.)

DARBY, THOMAS. Matric. pens. from EMMANUEL, Easter, 1623.

DARBY, —— Doctor in some faculty, in 1444.

DARBYSHIRE, JOHN. Matric. sizar from CHRIST'S, 1590-1, as Darbisher; B.A. 1593-4.

DARBISHIRE, JOHN. Adm. sizar at TRINITY, Aug. 2, 1654. Of Lancashire. Matric. 1654; Scholar, 1657; B.A. 1658-9. R. of Piddletrenthide, Dorset, 1680-2. R. of Portland, 1682-1712.

DARBISHIRE, THOMAS. Matric. pens. from TRINITY, Michs. 1619.

DARBYSHIRE or DERBISHIRE, THOMAS. Adm. sizar (age 18) at ST JOHN'S, Oct. 25, 1707. S. of John, husbandman. B. at Dalton, Lancs. School, Sedbergh. Matric. 1707; B.A. 1711-2. R. of Davenham, Cheshire, 1725-45. Buried Jan. 23, 1744-5.

DARCET, JAMES. Matric. sizar from QUEENS', Easter, 1610, as 'Tasset.' Of Warwickshire.

DARCH, ROBERT. Adm. pens. (age 18) at PETERHOUSE, June 19, 1736. Of Somerset. School, Tiverton. Matric. 1736; Scholar, 1736; B.A. 1740-1; M.A. 1744. Perhaps R. of Tillingham, Lincs. Died Nov. 17, 1768. (*G. Mag.*)

DARCIE or DARSEY, ARTHUR. Matric. Fell.-Com. from TRINITY, Michs. 1561. Of London. Adm. at the Inner Temple, Nov. 1564. Perhaps s. of Thomas, of Tolleshunt, Essex. (*Vis. of Essex*, 1558.)

DARCIE, BRIAN. Adm. pens. (a 15) at CAIUS, Oct. 10, 1604. S. of John, Esq., of Berechurch, near Colchester. School, Brentwood (Mr Greenwood). Probably adm. at Lincoln's Inn, 1606. (*Vis. of Essex*, 1558.)

DARCIE, CONYERS. Adm. Fell.-Com. (age 17) at CAIUS, Dec. 10, 1588. Of Hornby Castle, Yorks. S. of Thomas. Bapt. at St Michael-le-Belfry, York, Aug. 27, 1570. School, York. Adm. at the Inner Temple, May 22, 1593. Knighted, July 23, 1603. Succeeded his father, 1605. Title restored to him, in 1641, of Baron Darcy and Conyers. Died Mar. 3, 1653-4. Buried at Hornby. Father of Marmaduke (1631). (*Venn*, I. 135; M. H. Peacock.)

DARCEY, CONYERS. Matric. Fell.-Com. from KING'S, Easter, 1703. Doubtless s. of John, of Aske, Yorks. Comptroller of the King's Household. Lord Lieutenant of the North Riding, 1722-40. M.P. for Yorks., 1707-8, 1747-58; for Newark, 1715-22; for Richmond, 1722-7, 1728-47. Died Dec. 1, 1758, aged 73. M.I. at Hornby. Brother of Robert (1698). (Whitaker, *Richmondshire*, II. 46; M. H. Peacock; A. B. Beaven.)

DARSEY, EDWARD. Matric. Fell.-Com. from TRINITY, Michs. 1561. Of Stamford, Yorks. Adm. at the Inner Temple, Nov. 1561. Perhaps created M.A. at Oxford, 1588 (*Al. Oxon.*; where the date given is 1592). If so, probably s. of Sir Arthur. M.P. for Truro, 1584. Knighted, Apr. 23, 1603. Died Oct. 28, 1612, aged 69.

DARCIE, FRANCIS. Matric. Fell.-Com. from ST JOHN'S, Easter, 1571. Perhaps knighted, 1591.

DARCY, GEORGE. Adm. Fell.-Com. (age 16) at CHRIST'S, Oct. 24, 1649. S. of Sir William, Knt. B. at Hornby Castle, Yorks. Matric. 1650. Adm. at Gray's Inn, Mar. 20, 1649-50. (*Peile*, I. 530.)

DARCY, JAMES. Adm. pens. ('age 15') at SIDNEY, Apr. 11, 1668. S. of James, of Sedbury Park, Yorks. B. at Richmond, Yorks., Aug. 25, 1650. Matric. 1668, as 'Jenner.' M.P. for Richmond, 1698, 1702. Created Lord Darcy of Navan, 1721. Died July 19, 1731. Buried at Gilling. Brother of Marmaduke (1668). (*Vis. of Yorks.*, 1665; J. Ch. Smith; *G.E.C.*)

DARCY, JAMES. Adm. Fell.-Com. at CLARE, Apr. 21, 1722. Probably s. of James, of Bromehall, Yorks. (and grandson of James, above). B. in London. Matric. 1723. Succeeded as Baron, 1731. Died June 15, 1733, aged 26. Buried at Gilling. (*G.E.C.*)

DARCIE, JOHN. Matric. Fell.-Com. from ST JOHN'S, Easter, 1571.

DARCY, JOHN. Matric. Fell.-Com. from QUEENS', Easter, 1577. Of Essex.

DARCYE, JOHN. Adm. Fell.-Com. (age 15) at CAIUS, Oct. 22, 1585. S. of Brian, gent., of St Osyth, Essex. Schools, Walden and Dedham. Adm. at Lincoln's Inn, Feb. 11, 1592-3. Barrister. Died 1638. Brother of Robert (1595-6). (*Vis. of Essex*, 1558; *Venn*, I. 126.)

DARCY, JOHN. Matric. Fell.-Com. from ST JOHN'S, c. 1594. Adm. at the Middle Temple, Oct. 1595, as s. and h. of Michael, Esq., of Aston, Yorks. Succeeded his grandfather as Lord Darcy, 1602. Died July, 1635. (Hunter, *S. Yorks.*, II. 165.)

DARCY, JOHN. Adm. pens. at TRINITY, June 10, 1636. Matric. 1635; Scholar, 1638.

DARCY, MARMADUKE. Matric. pens. from TRINITY, Easter, 1631. S. of Sir Conyers Darcy (1588), of Hornby Castle, Yorks. Bapt. at Hornby, June 4, 1615. Adm. at Lincoln's Inn, Nov. 2, 1633. Created M.A. at Oxford, 1663. Gentleman Usher of the Privy Chamber to Charles II. M.P. for Richmond, 1665-79. Died, unmarried, July 3, 1687. Buried at Windsor. (*Al. Oxon.*)

DARCY, MARMADUKE. Adm. pens. (age 16) at SIDNEY, Apr. 11, 1668. S. of James, of Sedbury Park, Richmond, Yorks. B. at Richmond. Matric. 1668. Adm. at Lincoln's Inn, May 19, 1670. Died s.p. Will (York) 1713. Brother of James (1668). (*Vis. of Yorks.*, 1665.)

DARCY, ROBERT. Adm. pens. (age 17) at CAIUS, Feb. 25, 1595-6. S. of Brian, gent., of Tiptree Priory, Essex. School, Chelmsford (Mr Bradway). Matric. 1596. Of Tiptree, Esq. (*Vis. of Essex*, 1634.)

DARCY, ROBERT. Matric. Fell.-Com. from KING'S, Easter, 1698. S. of John, M.P. for Yorks. B. in London, Nov. 24, 1681. Succeeded his grandfather in 1692, as 3rd Earl of Holderness. Lord Lieutenant of the North Riding, 1714-22. First Commissioner of Trade, 1718. P.C. Died at Bath, Jan. 20, 1721-2. Buried at Hornby. Brother of Conyers (1703), father of Robert, Earl of Holderness. (*G.E.C.*)

DARCY, ROBERT (1732), *see* HOLDERNESS, Earl of.

DARCEY, THOMAS. Adm. Fell.-Com. (age 15) at CAIUS, Apr. 22, 1601. S. of Thomas, Baron Darcy. B. at St Osyth, Essex. Matric. 1601. Adm. at Gray's Inn, Mar. 10, 1600-1. Died 1614. Buried at Hengrave. M.I. there. (*Venn*, I. 175.)

DARCEY, THOMAS. Matric. pens. from QUEENS', Lent, 1618-9. Of Suffolk. B.A. 1621-2; M.A. 1625.

DARCIE or DARSEY, THOMAS. Matric. pens. from TRINITY, Easter, 1631.

DARCY, THOMAS. Adm. Fell.-Com. at JESUS, May 28, 1650. Of Essex. B. 1632. Matric. 1650. Adm. at Gray's Inn, Feb. 12, 1651-2, as s. and h. of Thomas, late of Pattiswick, Essex. Created Bart., June 19, 1660. M.P. for Maldon, 1679, 1681, 1685, 1689, 1690. Died 1693. Father of Thomas (1683). (*G.E.C.*)

DARCY, THOMAS. Adm. pens. at JESUS, May 14, 1652. Of Yorkshire. Matric. 1652; Scholar, 1653; B.A. 1655-6.

DARCY, THOMAS. Adm. pens. at CHRIST'S, Jan. 12, 1653-4. S. of Sir William, of Wilton Castle, Knt. Matric. 1653-4; B.A. 1657. Obtained a mandate for a fellowship at Christ's, and at Trinity, 1660. Brother of George (1649) and William (1651).

DARCY, THOMAS. Adm. Fell.-Com. at JESUS, Apr. 10, 1683. S. of Sir Thomas, Bart. (1650), of St Osyth and Tiptree, Essex. Died in College of small-pox, July 7, 1683. M.I. in the Chapel, erected by his father. (A. Gray.)

DARCY, WILLIAM. Adm. Fell.-Com. at CHRIST'S, Dec. 2, 1651. S. of Sir William, of Wilton Hall, Yorks., Knt. Brother of Thomas (1653-4) and George (1649).

DARCEY, ——. Matric. Fell.-Com. from TRINITY, Easter, 1615.

DARDIS, JOHN. Matric. pens. from TRINITY, Michs. 1585.

DAREY, ROBERT. Matric. sizar from PETERHOUSE, Lent, 1597-8.

DARGENT, JAMES. Adm. Fell.-Com. (age 25) at SIDNEY, Jan. 31, 1749-50. S. of John, deceased. B. in London. School, St Paul's. Matric. 1750. F.R.S. 1768. Surgeon, of London.

DARICK, JOHN (1688), *see* DERRICK.

DARINGTON, *see* also DORINGTON.

DARINGTON, NICHOLAS. B.A. 1510-1; M.A. 1514; B.D. 1524-5. Fellow of ST JOHN'S, 1516. Preb. of Lichfield, 1524. Died c. 1542. Will (P.C.C.) 1543; of Wybunbury, Cheshire; s. of Nicholas. (J. Ch. Smith.)

DARKER, EDWARD. Matric. from MAGDALENE, Michs. 1689; B.A. 1692-3. (Perhaps adm. in College as 'Henry.')

DARKER, GEORGE. Adm. pens. (age 16) at CAIUS, May 14, 1625. Of Scalford, Lincs. S. of Edward, gent. Matric. 1625; Scholar. Living, 1651. (*Venn*, I. 271.)

DARKER, HENRY (perhaps a mistake for Edward). Adm. sizar (age 17) at MAGDALENE, July 4, 1689. S. of Henry. B. at Wisbech, Isle of Ely. School, Wisbech.

DARKNOLL, PHINEAS. B.A. 1609 (Incorp. from Oxford). Of Kent. B.A. (Oxford) 1608-9; M.A. 1612. R. of Titscy, Surrey, 1619. Buried there Oct. 12, 1662. (*Al. Oxon.*; which dates his matriculation in 1577; 'aged 15.')

DARLEY, BENJAMIN. Adm. pens. at TRINITY, June 9, 1656. Of Yorkshire. S. and h. of Richard, of Bishop Wilton, Yorks., Esq. Bapt there, Nov. 12, 1639. Matric. 1656. Adm. at Gray's Inn, June 21, 1658. Died 1659. Brother of Joshua (1660) and William (1652). (*F.M.G.*, 994.)

DARLEY, BRIAN. B.A. 1489-90; M.A. 1493-4. Described as D.D. from c. 1512. Fellow of PETERHOUSE, 1494-1512. Bursar, 1502-3. R. of St Mary, Calais, 1509. Custos of the Collegiate Church of Ulcombe, 1512. R. of St Botolph, Bishopsgate till 1512. R. of Gt Linford, Bucks., 1518. Preb. of the Free Chapel of Tamworth, till 1527. Died 1526-7. Will (P.C.C.) 1527; to be buried at Elsing Spital. (*Lipscomb*, IV. 224; *T. A. Walker*; *Hennessy*.)

DARLEY, GEORGE. Matric. pens. from ST JOHN'S, Easter, 1571; B.A. 1574-5, as Darlowe. Perhaps V. of Ugley, Essex, 1580-96.

DARLY, HENRY. Matric. pens. from TRINITY, Michs. 1611. Henry Darley, s. and h. of Richard (1586), Esq., adm. at Gray's Inn, May 18, 1610. M.P. for Aldborough, 1628; for Malton, 1641-53; for East Riding, 1656. Parliamentarian. Taken prisoner to Scarborough, June, 1644. Of Buttercrambe, Yorks., Esq. Age 16, in 1612. (*F.M.G.*, 995; *Vis. of Yorks.*, 1612; *Vis. of London*, 1634.)

DARLEY, HENRY. Adm. Fell.-Com. at TRINITY, May 9, 1681. One of these names, s. and h. of Richard, of Aldby, Yorks., Esq., adm. at Gray's Inn, Nov. 27, 1680. Of Buttercrambe, Esq. Died June 24, 1720, aged 58. (*F.M.G.*, 994.)

DARLEY, JOHN. Matric. sizar from CHRIST'S, Michs. 1544. One of these names R. of Henstead, Suffolk, 1558. R. of North Cove, 1567-80.

DARLEY, JOHN. Matric. sizar from TRINITY, Easter, 1578.

DARLEY, JOHN. B.A. from MAGDALENE, 1615–6. S. of Nathan, of Beccles, Suffolk. Matric. (Oxford) Apr. 23, 1613. Incorp. B.A. at Oxford from Cambridge, 1618; M.A. (Oxford) 1618; B.D. 1627. R. of Northill, Cornwall, 1619–64. Buried there Nov. 9, 1664. Admon. (Exeter) 1665. (*Al. Oxon.*)

DARLEY, JOSEPH. Adm. sizar at TRINITY, Apr. 8, 1657. Of Yorkshire. S. of Thomas, gent. School, Pocklington. Matric. 1660; B.A. 1660–1.

DARLEY, JOSHUA. Adm. pens. (age 18) at SIDNEY, June 1, 1660. S. of Richard, Esq., of Yorks. B. at Bishop Wilton. Schools, Pocklington (Mr Greenwood) and Coxwold (Mr Littelton). Matric. 1660; B.A. 1663–4; M.A. 1667. Fellow, 1664. Chaplain, East India Co., 1673. Drowned in the Hughli, 1676 or 1678. Brother of Benjamin (1656) and William (1652). (*F.M.G.*, 994; *F. Penny.*)

DARLEY, RICHARD. Matric. Fell.-Com. from JESUS, Michs. 1586. S. of Richard, of Buttercrambe. Age 16 in 1584. Doubtless of Buttercrambe, Yorks., adm. at Gray's Inn, Nov. 21, 1588. J.P. Knighted, Apr. 11, 1617. Married and had issue. Father of Henry (1611). (*F.M.G.*, 994; *Vis. of Yorks.*, 1584.)

DARLEY, ROBERT. Adm. sizar at TRINITY, Apr. 16, 1651. Of Suffolk. Matric. 1651; B.A. 1654–5; M.A. 1658. Ord. deacon (Norwich) Sept. 1661. V. of Ludham, Norfolk, 1662. V. of Swaffham St Mary, Cambs., 1664–7.

DARLEY, THOMAS. Adm. at CORPUS CHRISTI, 1577. Matric. 1577; B.A. 1580–1; M.A. 1584. R. of Benacre, Suffolk, 1595–1613. Will proved, 1613 (Norwich). Father of the next.

DARLIE, THOMAS. Adm. pens. (age 17) at CAIUS, Apr. 26, 1608. S. of Thomas (above), R. of Benacre, Suffolk. B. at Beccles. Matric. 1608; Scholar, 1608–12; B.A. 1611–2; M.A. 1615.

DARLEY, WILLIAM. B.A. 1493; M.A. 1497–8. Of York diocese. Ord. sub-deacon (Ely) Apr. 4, 1495.

DARLEY, WILLIAM. Adm. pens. at TRINITY, Oct. 25, 1652. Of Yorkshire. S. and h. of Richard, of Bishop Wilton, Yorks., Esq. Adm. at Gray's Inn, June 6, 1655. Buried Sept. 3, 1656, aged 21. Brother of Benjamin (1656) and Joshua (1660). (*F.M.G.*, 994.)

DARLING or **DARLYN, JOHN.** Matric. sizar from TRINITY HALL, Easter, 1580. S. of John. B. at Stevenage, Herts. Schools, Letchworth, Stevenage and Hitchin. Migrated to Caius, Nov. 3, 1580, age 16. Scholar of Caius; B.A. 1583–4. V. of Codicote, Herts., 1593–1609. Died 1609. Admon. (Archd. St Albans). (*Venn*, I. 108.)

DARLING, JOHN (1588), *see* **DERLINGE.**

DARLING, WILLIAM. Adm. pens. at EMMANUEL, as Dearlinge, Sept. 13, 1595. B. at Clifton, Staffs., 1580. Matric. 1595; B.A. 1598–9; M.A. 1602. Ord. deacon (Lichfield), Sept. 29, 1606. V. of Ashby-de-la-Zouch, Leics., 1606. V. of Packington-on-the-Heath, 1610. Buried at Clifton, Mar. 12, 1612.

DARNALD or **DARNOLD, THOMAS.** Adm. Fell.-Com. at ST CATHARINE'S, May 1, 1661.

DARNALL, HENRY. Matric. pens. from TRINITY, Michs. 1580. Of Middlesex, late of Barnard's Inn, gent., when adm. at Gray's Inn, June 27, 1582. Utter-barrister, 1590. Ancient, 1598. Died Feb. 1607–8, aged 42. M.I. at Essendon, Herts.

DARNELL, JEREMY. Matric. pens. from CLARE, 1569; B.A. 1573–4, as Henry; M.A. 1578. Ord. priest (Lincoln) Oct. 21, 1580. V. of Dunton, Beds., 1580.

DARNELL, JOHN. Matric. pens. from ST JOHN'S, Easter, 1551; *impubes.*

DARNALL or **DARNELL, JOHN.** Matric. Fell.-Com. from KING'S, Easter, 1662. S. and h. of Ralph, of Gray's Inn and Loughton's Hope, Pembridge, Heref. Adm. at Gray's Inn, Dec. 2, 1662. Serjeant-at-law, 1692. King's Serjeant, 1698. Knighted, June 1, 1699. Died Dec. 14, 1706. Buried in St Clement Danes, London. (*D.N.B.*)

DARNELL, RALPH. Adm. sizar at CHRIST'S, May 1, 1624. Of Hertfordshire. Matric. 1624. Attorney in the Court of Wards. Subscribed to the New Building of Christ's. (*Peile*, I. 358.)

DARNELL, ROBERT. Matric. sizar from TRINITY, Easter, 1570. Ord. deacon (Lincoln) June 22, 1582; priest Jan. 16, 1582–3. V. of Eyeworth, Beds. Perhaps V. of Bentley Magna, Essex, 1585–1602. Will (Consist. C. London) 1602.

DARNELL, THOMAS. Matric. sizar from TRINITY, Michs. 1606; Scholar, 1608; B.A. 1609–10; M.A. 1613. V. of Thorpe-le-Soken, Essex; ejected, 1642.

DARNILL, THOMAS. Matric. Fell.-Com. from ST JOHN'S, Easter, 1610.

DARNELLY, DANIEL. M.A. 1634–5 (Incorp. from Oxford). S. of Daniel, of London, clerk. Bapt. at St Mary Woolchurch, Dec. 2, 1604. Matric. from New College, Oxford, Nov. 14, 1623, age 19; B.A. 1627; M.A. 1629–30. R. of Currey Mallett, Somerset, 1632. V. of Walden St Paul, Herts., 1634. R. of Teversham, Cambs., 1635–46 (sequestered). Father of the next. (*Al. Oxon.*)

DARNELLY, DANIEL. Matric. pens. from TRINITY HALL, Easter, 1652, as 'Davine.' S. of Daniel (above). Bapt. at Teversham, Cambs., Aug. 18, 1636. B.A. 1655–6; M.A. 1659. Fellow, 1656–9. Died Sept. 23, 1659. M.I. in the College Chapel. (Le Neve, *Mon.*, IV. 70.)

DARNLEY, RICHARD. Adm. Fell.-Com. at TRINITY, Nov. 15, 1649. Of Yorkshire.

DARNELLY, RICHARD. Adm. pens. (age 15) at ST JOHN'S, Oct. 24, 1668. S. of Richard, of Thames Street, London (who was probably a brother of Daniel, of 1634–5). B. there. School, Tottenham. Matric. 1668; M.B. 1674; M.D. 1681. Candidate, R.C.P. 1682. Fellow, 1685. Censor. Died Jan. 11, 1732–3. (*Munk*, I. 434.)

DARNTON, HENRY. Matric. sizar from TRINITY, Lent, 1579–80; Scholar, 1584; B.A. 1584–5; M.A. 1588.

DARNTON, HENRY. Matric. sizar from PETERHOUSE, Michs. 1584; B.A. 1588–9, as Darton. Incorp. at Oxford, 1588–9; M.A. (Oxford) 1596. R. of Goldsborough, Yorks., 1592; and of West Tanfield, 1601. (*Al. Oxon.*)

DARNTON, JOHN. Adm. pens. (age 17) at ST JOHN'S, May 29, 1647. S. of Richard (next), R. of Tanfield, Yorks. School, Sedbergh. Matric. 1647; B.A. 1650–1; M.A. 1654. Incorp. at Oxford, 1654. Adm. at Gray's Inn, 1647. V. of Bedlington, Northumberland, till 1662 (ejected). Died at Tanfield, Yorks., July 9, 1680. (*Calamy*, III. 55.)

DARNTON, RICHARD. Matric. pens. from ST JOHN'S, Easter, 1615; B.A. 1618–9; M.A. 1622. Ord. deacon (York) Sept. 1620; priest, May, 1624. R. of Tanfield, Yorks., 1657–64. Buried Feb. 16, 1664. Father of John (above).

DAROURY (? **DICONRY**), **RICHARD.** Matric. pens. from TRINITY, Easter, 1620.

DARRELL, *see also* **DORRELL.**

DARRELL or **DORRELL, CHARLES.** Adm. pens. at CHRIST'S, July 3, 1648. S. of Sampson. B. at Fulmer, Bucks. School, Hertford (Mr Minors). Matric. 1649; B.A. 1651.

DARRELL, CHARLES. Adm. at CORPUS CHRISTI, 1676. Of London. Matric. 1677; B.A. 1679–80; M.A. 1683; B.D. 1691. Fellow, 1682–1700. Died 1700. (*Masters.*)

DARRELL, EDWARD. Matric. pens. from PETERHOUSE, Lent, 1582–3.

DARELL, GEORGE. Matric. sizar from TRINITY, Easter, 1554.

DARRELL, GEORGE. Adm. pens. at EMMANUEL, June 27, 1588. Matric. Michs. 1587, from Magdalene, as Dorrell. George Darrell, s. and h. of John, of Little Chart, Kent, Esq., was adm. at Gray's Inn, Feb. 3, 1590–1. Died before 1619. Brother of Robert (1588). (Darrell pedigree in *Kent Vis.*)

DARRELL, GEORGE. M.A. 1601 (Incorp. from Oxford). S. of Edward, of Pagham, Sussex, gent. Matric. from New College, Oct. 25, 1589, age 14; B.A. from All Souls, 1594; M.A. 1597–8; B.D. 1605; D.D. 1607–8. Proctor, 1604. R. of Digswell, Herts., 1606–12. Preb. of Westminster, 1607–31. R. of Wormley, 1610–30; of West Hanningfield, Essex, 1611–30. Preb. of Lincoln, 1618–31. R. of Beaconsfield, Bucks., 1630–1. Died Oct. 31, 1631. Buried in Westminster Abbey. Will, P.C.C. (*Al. Oxon.*; A. B. Beaven; J. Ch. Smith.)

DARELL, HENRY. Matric. sizar from TRINITY, Easter, 1554 (*impubes*).

DARRELL, HUMPHREY. Adm. at KING'S, a scholar from Eton, 1523; B.A. 1527–8; M.A. 1531. R. of Cogenhoe, Northants., 1538. R. of Drayton Beauchamp, Bucks., till 1547. 'Eminently learned in Latin and Greek.' (*Harwood.*)

DARRELL, JOHN. B.Can.L. 1523–4. V. of Cressing, Essex, 1526–8. Perhaps R. of Holy Trinity-the-Less, London, 1534–55. (Called B.D.) Died 1555.

DARRELL, JOHN. Matric. sizar from QUEENS', June, 1575. Probably B. at Mansfield, Notts., *c.* 1562. B.A. 1578–9. Studied law in London. Returned to Mansfield where he became a preacher and exorcist. Resided at Bulwell, Notts., and at Ashby-de-la-Zouch. amined at Lambeth, 1599; pronounced an impostor, degraded from the Ministry and committed to the Gatehouse. Author of works on the detection of witchcraft, etc. (*Cooper*, II. 380; *D.N.B.*)

DARRELL or **DORRELL, JOHN.** Adm. Fell.-Com. at EMMANUEL, Feb. 12, 1632–3. Of Kent. Doubtless s. of Sir Robert (1588), of Little Chart. Bapt. there, Jan. 28, 1615–6. Aged 5 in 1621. Matric. 1633. Adm. at Gray's Inn, Oct. 10, 1634. Knighted, 1670. Died 1675. (*Vis. of Kent*, 1619; *Le Neve*, 240.)

DARELL, NICHOLAS. Incorp. M.A. from Oxford, 1677; M.D. from CAIUS, 1678 (*Lit. Reg.*). S. of Marmaduke, of Horkstow, Lincs., gent. Matric. from Lincoln College, Oxford, May 21, 1669, age 17; B.A. (Oxford) 1672–3; M.A. 1675. Adm. candidate R.C.P. Sept. 30, 1678. Buried at St Stephen's, Walbrook, London, Mar. 18, 1678–9. Admon. (P.C.C.) 1679. (*Al. Oxon.*; *Venn*, I. 457.)

DARRELL, ROBERT. Matric. from MAGDALENE, Michs. 1587, as Dorrell. Adm. pens. at Emmanuel, June 27, 1588; B.A. from Corpus Christi, Oxford, 1590–1; M.A. 1594. S. and h. of John, of Little Chart, Kent, Esq.; adm. at Gray's Inn, June 5, 1594. Knighted, Apr. 1, 1614. Died 1645, aged 76. Brother of George (1588), father of John (1632–3). (*Vis. of Kent*, 1663; *Al. Oxon.*; *Hasted*, III. 224.)

DARRELL or DORRELL, THOMAS. Matric. pens. from CHRIST'S, Oct. 1564. Perhaps s. and h. of Nicholas, gent., of Leman, Kent. Adm. at the Middle Temple, from Staple Inn, Oct. 1572.

DARELL, WILLIAM. Resident M.A. at CORPUS CHRISTI, in Aug. 1564. Preb. of Canterbury, 1554–70. Sub-dean, 1560. Chaplain to the Queen. Chancellor of Bangor, 1565–70. Author of a treatise on the Kentish Castles. Died 1570. (*Cooper*, I. 430; *D.N.B.* No such M.A. degree found at Cambridge. Jos. Foster gives one at Oxford, B.A. and M.A. 1554; with a list of benefices in Kent. Probably the same.)

DARRYS, ——. Adm. at CORPUS CHRISTI, 1563.

DARTE, CHARLES. Matric. pens. from QUEENS', Michs. 1608. Of Cornwall. Adm. at the Inner Temple, 1609. Of Plymouth.

D'ARTIGUES, JOHN. Adm. sizar at CLARE, Jan. 25, 1730–1. B. at Bury, Suffolk. Matric. 1731; B.A. 1734–5. Ord. deacon (Norwich) June, 1735. V. of Gooderston, Norfolk, 1740–4. C. of Wereham, till 1744. Died 1744. M.I. at Wereham.

DARTNOLL, WILLIAM. Adm. sizar at EMMANUEL, Mar. 12, 1592–3. Matric. c. 1593; Scholar; B.A. 1596–7; M.A. 1600.

DARWENT, ROBERT. Adm. pens. (age 16) at ST JOHN'S, Apr. 23, 1685. S. of Charles, gent. B. at Rotherham, Yorks. School, Rotherham (Mr Ferrer). Matric. 1685.

DARWENT, THOMAS. Adm. sizar (age 18) at ST JOHN'S, Apr. 6, 1726. S. of Robert, clerk, of Yorkshire. B. at Rotherham. School, Rotherham (Mr Withers). Matric. 1726. R. of West Itchenor, Sussex, in 1735. Died soon after. (*Scott-Mayor*, III. 394.)

DARWIN, ERASMUS. Adm. pens. (age 18) at ST JOHN'S, June 30, 1750. 4th s. of Robert, barrister. B. at Elston, Notts. School, Chesterfield. Scholar; M.B. 1755. Studied medicine at Edinburgh. Established a practice at Lichfield. F.R.S. 1761. Author on evolution, and poet. Died at the Priory, near Derby, Apr. 18, 1802. Grandfather of Charles. Brother of the next two. (*D.N.B.*; *Scott-Mayor*, III. 601.)

DARWIN, JOHN. Adm. pens. (age 19) at ST JOHN'S, June 30, 1750. S. of Robert, barrister, of Elston, Notts. B. at Elston. School, Chesterfield, Derbs. Matric. 1750; B.A. 1754; M.A. 1757. Ord. deacon (Lincoln) Mar. 4, 1754; priest, May 25, 1755. R. of Carlton Scroop, Lincs, 1762–1805. R. of Elston, Notts., 1766–1805. Died 1805. Brother of the above and next. (*Scott-Mayor*, III. 601.)

DARWIN, ROBERT (WARING). Adm. pens. (age 19) at ST JOHN'S, July 1, 1743. S. of Robert, barrister, of Elston, Notts. B. at Elston. School, Chesterfield (Mr Burrow). Matric. 1743–4. Adm. at Lincoln's Inn, June 18, 1743. Barrister, 1751. Probably Solicitor to Gray's Inn Society. Succeeded his father at Elston, 1754. Author, botanical. Died, unmarried, Nov. 3, 1816. Brother of Erasmus and John (above). (*Scott-Mayor*, III. 538.)

DARWIN, THOMAS. Adm. at CORPUS CHRISTI, 1598. Of Lincolnshire. Perhaps s. of Richard, of Marton. B.A. 1600–1; M.A. 1604. Of Fenton. Died c. 1632. Buried in Kettlethorpe Church. One of these names, M.A., V. of Shenstone, Staffs., 1631–? 1635. (*Misc. Gen. et Her.*, 2nd S., III. 13.)

DARWIN, WILLIAM. Matric. Fell.-Com. from MAGDALENE, Easter, 1640. S. and h. of William, late of Cletham, Lincs., gent., deceased. Adm. at Lincoln's Inn, Oct. 24, 1645. Recorder of the City of Lincoln. Will proved, Nov. 23, 1675. Doubtless father of the next. (*Misc. Gen. et Her.*, 2nd S., III. 14.)

DARWYN, WILLIAM. Adm. pens. (age 17) at MAGDALENE, Apr 3, 1672. S. of William, Esq., of Lincoln. School, Lincoln. Matric. 1672. Adm. at Lincoln's Inn, Apr. 17, 1673. Died Aug. 28, 1682, at Elston. M.I. (*Misc. Gen. et Her.*, 2nd S., III. 15.)

DARWIN, WILLIAM MORGAN. Adm. pens. at JESUS, May 27, 1730. Of Nottingham. S. of William, of Cleatham, Lincs. B. at Newark, 1710. Matric. 1730; M.B. 1736. Practised medicine at Gainsborough. Died there July 20, 1762. (*Misc. Gen. et Her.*, 2nd S., III. 16.)

DASH, THOMAS. Matric. sizar from TRINITY, Easter, 1604. Probably s. of John Dasche and Alice (Coleman). B. at Long Melford, Suffolk. B.A. 1607–8; M.A. 1611. Ord. deacon (London) Sept. 25, 1609, age 24; C. of High Ongar, Essex; priest, Sept. 22, 1611. V. of West Mersea, Essex, 1628. Admon. (Cons. C. London) Aug. 14, 1630. (V. B. Redstone; J. Ch. Smith.)

DASHFIELD, JOHN. B.A. from ST CATHARINE'S, 1621. Probably the student, adm. at Magdalen Hall, Oxford, Mar. 12, 1618–9, age 16. Of Surrey. V. of Littleport, Cambs., 1627–38. Perhaps R. of All Saints', Colchester, 1639–40. One of these names R. of Sutton Bonnington, Notts., 1662–5. Preb. of Bristol. Died Apr. 1665. (*Al. Oxon.*)

DASHWOOD, GEORGE. Adm. sizar (age 18) at CAIUS, Mar. 27, 1697. S. of Samuel, citizen of London (? afterwards Lord Mayor). B. at Salisbury. Schools, Broome, Norfolk (Mr Robbins) and Norwich. Matric. 1697. (Apparently adm. at Magdalen College, Oxford, Oct. 25, 1698.) Scholar of Caius, 1697–1701; B.A. 1700–1. Probably adm. at the Inner Temple, May 11, 1697; at Lincoln's Inn, Apr. 3, 1702; and at Gray's Inn, Nov. 16, 1709 and called to the Bar, 1709. If so, M.P. for Sudbury, 1703–5; for Stockbridge, 1710–3. Died 1762. (*Venn*, I. 499; *Al. Oxon.*)

DASHWOOD, LEONARD. Matric. pens. from ST CATHARINE'S, Easter, 1631. Of Dorset. B.A. 1634–5.

DASHWOOD, WILLIAM. M.A. from KING'S, 1710. S. of Robert, of Stogumber, Somerset. Matric. from Balliol College, Oxford, Mar. 18, 1688–9, age 15; B.A. (Oxford) 1694. R. of Little Thurrock, Essex, 1697. V. of West Thurrock, 1710. R. of Enborne, Berks., 1718. Died July 10, 1734. M.I. at Enborne. Will (Archd. Berks.) 1734. (*Al. Oxon.*)

DASSET, JOHN. Adm. sizar at TRINITY, May 19, 1669; B.A. 1672–3.

D'ASSIGNY, MARIUS. B.D. 1668 (*Lit. Reg.*). 'After long and painful study in foreign universities.' S. of Peter, French Protestant Minister at Norwich. B. 1643. Chaplain at Tangier, to the forces. V. of Penrith, Cumberland, 1667–8. V. of Cutcombe, Somerset, 1672–99. R. of Tidmarsh, Berks., 1702. V. of Aveley, Essex, 1706–12. V. of Blackmore, 1712. Author, classical, etc. Died Nov. 14, 1717. Buried at Woodham Walter, Essex. M.I. Will (Commis. C. Essex), 1718. (*D.N.B.*; J. Ch. Smith.)

DASTON, RICHARD. Adm. pens. (age 18) at ST JOHN'S, July 2, 1745. S. of Richard, gent., of Isleham, Cambs. B. at Isleham. School, Bury. Matric. 1746. Migrated to Emmanuel, Dec. 9, 1747; B.A. 1749–50. Adm. at the Middle Temple, Aug. 12, 1747. Died at Isleham, Feb. 28, 1758. (G. *Mag.*)

DAUBNEY, *see* DAWBNEY.

DAUBURNE or DAWBURNE, ROBERT. Matric. sizar from KING'S, 1598. Donor to the Library.

DAUBUZ or DAWBUZ, CHARLES. Adm. sizar at QUEENS', Jan. 10, 1689–90. S. of Isaie d'Aubus, protestant pastor at Nérac, Guienne. B. there, 1673. Refugee family of Hugenots. School, Merchant Taylors'. Matric. 1690; B.A. 1693–4; M.A. 1697. Master of Sheffield Grammar School, 1696–9. Ord. deacon (York) Sept. 1698; priest, 1698. V. of Brotherton, Yorks., 1699–1717. Author, theological. Died June 14, 1717. Father of the next. (*D.N.B.*)

DAUBUZ, CLAUDE. Adm. sizar at ST CATHARINE'S, Oct. 20, 1722. Of Brotherton, Yorks. S. of Charles (above). Matric. 1722; B.A. 1726–7; M.A. 1749. Incorp. at Oxford, 1749. Preb. of Southwell, 1750–60. V. of Huddersfield, c. 1750. Died at Pontefract, Sept. 11, 1760. (G. *Mag.*)

DAUDESON (? DANDESON), JOHN. B.Can.L. 1488–9.

DAULING, *see* DAWLING.

DAULY (? DANBY), ALFRED. Matric. pens. from ST JOHN'S, Easter, 1609.

DAUNCIE, GERVASE. Matric. sizar from TRINITY, Michs. 1609.

DAUS, *see* DAWES.

DAUTRE or DAUNTRE, LIONEL. Scholar at KING'S HALL, 1359. Left 1362.

DAVELL, RICHARD. Matric. pens. from TRINITY, Easter, 1570.

DAVELL, ROBERT. B.A. 1504–5. Perhaps V. of Gt Bursted, Essex, 1512. One of these names (Davell or Dovell) Archdeacon of Northumberland, 1518–57. Died 1557.

DAVENANT, CHARLES. Incorp. LL.D. 1675, from Oxford. S. of Sir William, the poet. B. in London, 1656. School, 'Gbedin' (? Cheam), Surrey. Matric. Fell.-Com. from Balliol College, Oxford, July 21, 1671, age 15. Practised at Doctors' Commons. Commissioner of Excise, 1678–89. M.P. for St Ives, Cornwall, 1685; for Gt Bedwyn, 1698, 1701. Inspector-General of the Customs, 1703–14. Died Nov. 6, 1714. (*D.N.B.*; *Al. Oxon.*; A. B. Beaven.)

DAVENANT, EDWARD. Matric. pens. from QUEENS', Lent, 1584-5. S. of John. B. in London. Bapt. at All Hallows, Bread St, Jan. 29, 1568-9. Of Whiddy Island, Cork. Died at Salisbury. Will, P.C.C. Brother of John (1587), William (1590) and George (1602), father of the next. (J. Ch. Smith.)

DAVENANT, EDWARD. Matric. pens. from QUEENS', Easter, 1610. S. of Edward (above). Bapt. at All Hallows, Bread St, Apr. 25, 1596. B.A. 1613; M.A. 1617; B.D. 1624; D.D. 1629. Incorp. at Oxford, 1619. Fellow, 1615-25. Ord. deacon (Peterb.) Sept. 23; priest, Sept. 24, 1621. R. of Poulshot, Wilts., 1623. V. of Gillingham, Dorset, 1626-80. Archdeacon of Berks., 1630. R. of North Morton, Bucks., 1631. Treasurer of Salisbury, 1634. Died Mar. 12, 1679-80, aged 84. M.I. at Gillingham. Will (P.C.C.) 1680. Father of George (1657), Ralph (1663) and William (1659). (*Al. Oxon.*)

DAVENANT, GEORGE. Adm. pens. at QUEENS', 1602. Of London. S. of John. Bapt. at All Hallows, Bread St, Oct. 1, 1587. Matric. 1604; B.A. 1605-6; M.A. 1609. Fellow, 1608-14. Buried at St Botolph's, Cambridge, Apr. 2, 1614. Brother of Edward (1584-5), John (1587) and William (1590).

DAVENANT, GEORGE. M.A. 1657 (Incorp. from Oxford). S. of Edward (1610), D.D., V. of Gillingham, Dorset. Matric. from Queen's College, Oxford, Nov. 18, 1650; B.A. 1651-2; M.A. 1655. Fellow of Oriel College, 1653. Died at Gillingham, Dorset, Sept. 11, 1661. Will, P.C.C. Brother of Ralph (1663) and William (1659). (*Al. Oxon.*)

DAVENANT, JOHN. Matric. pens. from QUEENS', Michs. 1587. 2nd s. of John, citizen and merchant taylor, of London. B. in Watling Street, London. Bapt. at All Hallows, Bread St, May 25, 1572. B.A. 1590-1; M.A. 1594; B.D. 1601; D.D. 1609. Fellow, 1597-1614. President, 1614-21. Lady Margaret Professor of Divinity, 1609-21. R. of Fleet, Lincs., 1609. R. of Leake, Notts., 1612. R. of Cottenham, Cambs., 1620. Bishop of Salisbury, 1621-41. One of the delegates at the Synod of Dort. Author, theological. Died Apr. 20, 1641. Will, P.C.C. Uncle of Thomas Fuller, the divine. Brother of Edward (1584-5), William (1590) and George (1602). (*D.N.B.*)

DAVENANT, JOHN. Matric. pens. from QUEENS', Easter, 1636. Of Nottinghamshire. B.A. 1639-40; M.A. 1643; M.D. 1661 (*Lit. Reg.*)

DAVENANT, RALPH. M.A. from TRINITY HALL, 1663. S. of Edward (1610), D.D., V. of Gillingham, Dorset. Fellow, July, 1664-9 (by royal recommendation). Matric. from Oriel College, Oxford, July 25, 1655; (? B.A. Oxford). R. of St Mary Matfellon, Whitechapel, 1668-81. R. of Stepney, 1669-81. Canon of Exeter, 1677. Died Mar. 1680-1. Will (P.C.C.) 1681. Brother of George (1657) and William (1659). (*Al. Oxon.*)

DAVENANT, WILLIAM. Matric. pens. from JESUS, Michs. 1552.

DAVENANT, WILLIAM. Adm. pens. at QUEENS', Apr. 9, 1590. Of London. 3rd s. of John. Bapt. at All Hallows, Bread St, Mar. 13, 1574-5. Brother of Edward (1584-5), John (1587) and George (1602).

DAVENANT, WILLIAM. M.A. from QUEENS', 1659 (Incorp. from Oxford). S. of Edward (1610). Matric. from Queen's, Oxford, July 15, 1652; B.A. 1654; M.A. from Magdalen Hall, 1657. Fellow of Trinity Hall, Cambridge, 1659-61. V. of Watford, Herts., 1661-2. Buried May 15, 1662, at Gillingham, Dorset. Will, P.C.C. Brother of George (1657), Ralph (1663) and William (1659). (Hutchins, *Dorset*, III. 643.)

DAVENPORT, *see also* DAMPORT.

DAVENPORT, ADAM. Scholar at KING'S HALL, 1372. Beneficed, 1376.

DAVENPORT, BOSVILE. Adm. pens. at JESUS, May 30, 1692. Of Lancashire. School, Charterhouse. Matric. 1693; Scholar, 1693; B.A. 1695-6; M.A. 1699. Died in College. Buried at All Saints', Cambridge, Sept. 27, 1701. (A. Gray.)

DAVENPORT, CHRISTOPHER. Matric. sizar from TRINITY, Easter, 1602. Perhaps s. of Henry, of Coventry. B.A. 1606-7; M.A. 1610. (*Vis. of Warws.*, 1619.)

DAVENPORT, CHRISTOPHER. Adm. pens. at TRINITY, Sept. 11, 1673.

DAVENPORT, EDWARD. Adm. pens. at SIDNEY, July 15, 1604; B.A. 1606-7; M.A. 1611. Incorp. at Oxford, 1611. R. of Edgmond, Salop, 1620.

DAVENPORT, EDWARD. Adm. sizar (age 24) at ST JOHN'S, Apr. 2, 1650. S. of John (1605), of Didsbury, Lancs. School, Didsbury (private). M.B. (Oxford) 1657. Afterwards practised in London. Married Ellen, dau. of William Newton, of Wilmslow, Cheshire. Father of the next. (*Al. Oxon.*; Mumford, *Manch. Gr. Sch.*; *Vis. of Lancs.*, 1664.)

DAVENPORT, FRANCIS. Adm. pens. (age 17) at ST JOHN'S, July 4, 1668. S. of Edward, M.B. (above). School, Manchester. (*Vis. of Lancs.*, 1664.)

DAVENPORT, GEORGE. Adm. pens. at EMMANUEL, May 1, 1646. Of Leicestershire. B. at Wigston. Matric. 1647; B.A. 1649-50; M.A. 1653. R. of Houghton-le-Spring, Durham, 1664-77. Perhaps R. of St Peter, Cheapside, London, 1661-5. Died July 6, 1677. Buried at Houghton-le-Spring. Brother of John (1642). (Le Neve, *Mon.*, IV. 176; *Nichols*, IV. 38.)

DAVENPORT, GEORGE. Adm. pens. (age 15) at PETERHOUSE, Oct. 15, 1668. Of Leicester. Probably s. of Stephen. School, Leicester. Matric. 1669; Scholar, 1669; B.A. 1672-3; M.A. 1676. R. of Steeple, Essex, 1678. V. of Althorne.

DAVENPORT, GEORGE. Adm. pens. at EMMANUEL, May 1, 1695. Of Lincolnshire. Matric. 1695; B.A. 1698-9; M.A. 1712. Ord. priest (Peterb.) Sept. 20, 1712; C. of Wardley, Rutland.

DAVENPORT, HENRY. Matric. pens. from QUEENS', Easter, 1634. S. and h. of John, Esq., of Burley Park, Leicester. Adm. at the Middle Temple, Oct. 26, 1635.

DAVENPORT, HENRY. Adm. pens. (age 17) at PETERHOUSE, Feb. 26, 1637-8. Of Coventry. School, Warwick. Matric. 1638; Scholar, 1638-9; B.A. 1641-2; M.A. 1645. Ord. deacon and priest (Lincoln) May 24, 1646.

DAVENPORT, HUMFREY. Adm. pens. (age 19) at ST JOHN'S, June 17, 1689. S. of William, gent. B. at Bramhall, Cheshire. School, Stockport (Mr Dobson). Matric. 1689. Adm. at Gray's Inn, Nov. 19, 1689. Called to the Bar, 1701. Bencher, 1724. Buried at Stockport, June 21, 1726. Brother of William (1681). (*Al. Oxon.*)

DAVENPORT, HUMFREY. Adm. pens. (age 17) at ST JOHN'S, Jan. 29, 1693-4. S. of Edward, gent. B. at Stockport, Cheshire. School, Manchester. Matric. 1695. Adm. at Gray's Inn, Jan. 31, 1693-4.

DAVENPORT, ISAAC. Adm. sizar at CLARE, Mar. 15, 1664-5. Matric. 1665.

DAVENPORT, JOHN. Matric. pens. from QUEENS', Lent, 1597-8. Of London.

DAVENPORT, JOHN. Matric. pens. from QUEENS', Easter, 1605. Of London. Perhaps s. of Sir William, of Bramhall, Cheshire. Bapt. at Stockport, Aug. 5, 1586. B.A. 1607-8; M.A. 1611. R. of Didsbury, Lancs., 1612-39. Buried there Mar. 18, 1638-9. Father of Edward (1650). (*Earwaker*, I. 438.)

DAVENPORT, JOHN. Adm. pens. at EMMANUEL, Feb. 9, 1642-3. Of Leicestershire. B. at Wigston. Matric. 1643; B.A. 1646-7; M.A. 1650. Fellow, 1649-54 (ejected). R. of West Rasen, Lincs. V. of Wigston, Leics., 1693-1706. Buried Mar. 9, 1708, aged 81. M.I. at Wigston. Will, Leicester. Brother of George (1646).

DAVENPORT, RALPH. Matric. pens. from TRINITY, Lent, 1581-2. Of Cheshire. Scholar, 1580; B.A. 1581-2; M.A. 1585; B.D. from QUEENS', 1593. Fellow of Queens', 1585-1605. R. of Barton Mills, Suffolk, 1592-1604. R. of Toppesfield, Essex, 1604-5. Will proved (V.C.C.) 1605; and (P.C.C.) 1606.

DAVENPORT, RICHARD. Adm. pens. (age 18) at ST JOHN'S, Feb. 17, 1724-5. S. of George, gent., of Calveley, Cheshire, Esq. B. at Whitmore, Staffs. Schools, Chester and Westminster. Matric. 1725. Adm. at the Inner Temple, Aug. 16, 1725. Of Davenport and Calveley, Esq. Died May, 1771. (For his connexion with J. J. Rousseau, *see Scott-Mayor*, III. 380.)

DAVENPORT, RICHARD. Adm. sizar at QUEENS', Apr. 12, 1726. Of Cheshire.

DAVENPORT, SHARINGTON. Adm. Fell.-Com. at CLARE, Apr. 21, 1728. Migrated to Trinity, Feb. 21, 1728-9. S. and h. of Henry, of Salop, Esq. Adm. at Lincoln's Inn, Feb. 23, 1727-8. Died 1744.

DAVENPORT, WILLIAM. Adm. pens. at JESUS, Mar. 21, 1677-8. S. of John, of Woodford, Cheshire, Esq. Died in College. Buried at All Saints', Cambridge, 1678. (A. Gray).

DAVENPORT, WILLIAM. Adm. Fell.-Com. (age 17) at SIDNEY, c. June, 1681. 1st s. of William, gent. B. at Bramhall, Cheshire, 1663. Schools, Nottingham, Chester and Manchester. Matric. 1681. Buried at Stockport, Apr. 21, 1706. Brother of Humfrey (1689). (*Earwaker*, I. 439.)

DAVENPORT, WILLIAM. Adm. sizar at ST CATHARINE'S, Nov. 7, 1716.

DAVERS, HENRY. Matric. pens. from TRINITY, Michs. 1623. One of these names M.P. for Devizes, 1640.

DAVERS, JEROME. Matric. pens. from CLARE, Michs. 1568; B.A. 1571-2; M.A. 1575. Buried at St Benet's, Cambridge, Oct. 8, 1622. Will proved (V.C.C.) 1622.

DAVYDE, GILES. Matric. pens. from ST JOHN'S, Easter, 1557.

DAVID, RICHARD. Fellow of CORPUS CHRISTI, 1477. R. of St Benet's, Cambridge.

DAVYD, ROGER. Of JESUS, when ord. priest (Ely) Mar. 23, 1566-7.

DAVID, SAMUEL. Scholar of TRINITY, 1602; B.A. 1603-4.

DAVYD, THOMAS. Matric. sizar from MAGDALENE, Michs. 1565.

DAVID, ——. A friar. *Cautio* for degree, 1460.

DAVID, ——. Fellow of CLARE, Apr. 27, 1467; M.A.; B.D.

DAVID, ——. B.Can.L. 1482 (or 1488).

DAVID, ——. Incorp. B.A. 1482.

DAVID, ——. Adm. at CORPUS CHRISTI, 1559.

DAVIDSON, CHARLES. Matric. sizar from TRINITY, Easter, 1631; B.A. 1634-5; M.A. 1638.

DAVIE, ALEXANDER. Adm. Fell.-Com. (age 17) at SIDNEY, July 4, 1712. S. of Alexander, Esq., of Salford, Lancs. School, Lichfield (Mr Hunter). Matric. 1713; M.A. 1717 (*Com. Reg.*). Adm. at the Inner Temple, 1714.

DAVY, CHARLES. Adm. sizar (age 16) at CAIUS, May 3, 1739. S. of Charles, gent., of Ipswich. B. in Norwich. Schools, Market Rasen, Lincs. (Mr Haslehurst), Watton (private; Mr Pigge) and Scarning, Norfolk (Mr Brett). Matric. 1739; Scholar, 1739-46; B.A. 1742-3; M.A. 1748. Ord. deacon (Norwich) Sept. 23, 1744; priest, Sept. 20, 1747. Usher of the Perse School, Cambridge, 1747. R. of Topcroft, Norfolk, 1764-97. R. of Benacre, Suffolk, 1766-76; of Onehouse, 1776-97. Died Apr. 8, 1797. Buried at Onehouse. (*D.N.B.*; *Venn*, II. 46.)

DAVIE, CHRISTOPHER. Adm. pens. (age 19) at CAIUS, Dec. 31, 1582. S. of John, gent. B. in London. Schools, Holt, Norfolk and Brentwood, Essex. Matric. 1582-3. Readm. as Fell.-Com. 1585.

DAVIE, CHRISTOPHER. Adm. pens. (age 16) at CAIUS, June 7, 1615. S. of Henry (1580), gent., steward of Norwich. School, Norwich. Matric. 1615; B.A. 1618-9. Brother of Henry (1613). (*Vis. of Norfolk.*)

DAVY, EDMUND. B.A. 1481-2; M.A. 1486. Proctor, 1489-90.

DAVY or DAVID, FRANCIS. Adm. sizar at CORPUS CHRISTI, 1647. Of Suffolk. Matric. 1649; B.A. 1651-2. R. of Frostenden, Suffolk, 1660.

DAVEY, GEOFFRY. Adm. pens. at EMMANUEL, Apr. 12, 1617. Perhaps s. of William, of King's Lynn. Bapt. Sept. 15, 1602. Matric. 1617. Migrated to Corpus Christi, 1617. B.A. 1620-1, as Davys; M.A. 1624. Ord. priest (Peterb.) Dec. 19, 1624.

DAVIE, GREGORY. Adm. sizar at CAIUS, May 3, 1595. S. of Christopher, gent., of Norfolk. B. at Brinton. Schools, Fakenham and Creake. Matric. c. 1595; Scholar, 1595-1602; B.A. 1598-9; M.A. 1602. Fellow, 1603-5. Will proved (V.C.C.) 1605. (*Venn*, I. 156; *Vis. of Norfolk*, 1563.)

DAVEY, HENRY. B.Can.L. 1505-6. Probably R. of Boldon, Durham, 1525. Died 1541.

DAVIE, HENRY. Adm. pens. (age 16) at CAIUS, June 27, 1580. S. of Richard, gent., of Norwich. School, Norwich. Matric. 1580. Adm. at Lincoln's Inn, June 21, 1580. Steward of Norwich, 1613-8. Father of Christopher (1615) and Henry (1613). Died 1618. Will (P.C.C.) 1619. (*Vis. of Norfolk*; *Venn*, I. 107.)

DAVIE, HENRY. Matric. sizar from PEMBROKE, c. 1593; B.A. 1595-6; M.A. 1599. One of these names R. of Dengie, Essex, 1606-13. Died 1613.

DAVY, HENRY. Adm. Fell.-Com. (age 15) at CAIUS, Apr. 17, 1613. Eldest s. of Henry (1580), gent., of Norwich. School, Norwich. Brother of Christopher (1615). (*Vis. of Norfolk.*)

DAVY, JAMES. Adm. pens. at TRINITY, Mar. 26, 1662. Perhaps s. of James, of Lynn, hatter. Bapt. Aug. 15, 1647. Matric. 1662; B.A. 1665-6; M.A. 1672. R. of Watlington, Norfolk, 1670-1710. Died 1710. (Carthew, *Launditch*, III. 282.)

DAVY, JOHN. B.Can.L. 1470-1.

DAVY, JOHN. B.Can.L. 1481-2.

DAVY or DAVID, JOHN. B.A. 1520-1.

DAVYE, JOHN. Matric. sizar from TRINITY, Michs. 1555 (*impubes*).

DAVIE, JOHN. Matric. sizar from CAIUS, Easter, 1582.

DAVIE, JOHN. Matric. sizar from EMMANUEL, Michs. 1589.

DAVIE, JOHN. Adm. pens. (age 16) at CAIUS, Apr. 10, 1597. S. of Robert, citizen of Norwich. School, Norwich. Migrated to Corpus Christi, 1597. B.A. 1600-1; M.A. 1604. Licensed to practise medicine, 1609. Of Maidstone, Kent, M.D. Died May 11, 1649. Buried at Maidstone. (*Vis. of Norf.*; *Venn*, I. 162.)

DAVY, JOHN. Adm. (age 16) at CAIUS, June 19, 1616. S. of John, gent., of Kenninghall, Norfolk. School, Roydon (Mr Hall). Matric. 1616; Scholar, 1617-20; B.A. 1619-20; M.A. 1623. Ord. priest (Norwich) 1622. V. of Kenninghall, 1634-45; sequestered. Buried at Kenninghall, July 12, 1684. (*Venn*, I. 233.)

DAVY, JOHN. Adm. sizar (age 15) at CAIUS, June 20, 1629. S. of James, attorney-at-law, of Lynn, Norfolk. School, Lynn (Mr Labourne and Mr Woodmansey). Matric. 1629; Scholar, 1629-36; B.A. 1632-3; M.A. 1636. Ord. deacon (Lincoln); priest (Norwich) June 12, 1642. Probably C. of Wormegay, Norfolk, 1637. R. of Heydon, 1645. Buried there Apr. 18, 1651. Will (Norwich) 1651. (Died 1647, aged 39; according to *Blomefield*, III. 534.) (*Venn*, I. 290.)

DAVIE, JOHN. Matric. sizar from TRINITY, Lent, 1634-5; Scholar, 1638; B.A. 1638-9. Fellow, 1645. Ord. deacon (Peterb.) Sept. 19, 1641.

DAVYE, JOHN. M.A. from JESUS, 1667. Matric. from Brasenose, Oxford, July 15, 1652; B.A. (Oxford) 1655-6. Perhaps V. of Frodsham, Cheshire, 1663. (*Al. Oxon.*)

DAVY, JOHN. Adm. sizar at ST CATHARINE'S, July 11, 1685. Matric. 1687. Possibly the same who matric. from St Mary Hall, Oxford, Dec. 17, 1684; s. of Laurence, of Cheriton, Devon.

DAVY, JOHN. Adm. sizar (age 18) at CAIUS, May 22, 1700. S. of Samuel, harness maker, of Ipswich. B. there. School, Ipswich. Matric. 1700; Scholar, 1700; B.A. 1704-5. Ord. deacon (Norwich) Sept. 1706; priest, June, 1721. C. of Halvergate, Norfolk. One of these names R. of St Mary, Whitechapel, 1750-6. Admon. (P.C.C.) 1756. (*Venn*, I. 505.)

DAVY, JOHN. Adm. sizar (age 16) at CAIUS, July 3, 1739. S. of John, surgeon, of Lowestoft, Suffolk. B. at Yarmouth. School, Beccles (Mr Symonds). Scholar 1739-45; Matric. 1740; B.A. 1742-3; M.A. 1746. Fellow, 1747-63. Ord. deacon (Norwich) Sept. 22, 1745; priest, Dec. 21, 1746, as C. of Lowestoft. R. of Teversham, Cambs., to 1763; of Lavenham, Suffolk, 1763-92; of Bucklesham, Suffolk. Died Apr. 28, 1792. (*Venn*, II. 46.)

DAVIE, JONATHAN. Matric. pens. from ST JOHN'S, Easter, 1619; B.A. 1623-4; M.A. 1627.

DAVY, OSMUND. Matric. pens. from PETERHOUSE, Easter, 1557. Of Buckinghamshire. B.A. 1560-1; M.A. from Trinity, 1564; B.D. 1572. Fellow of Pembroke, 1560. Fellow of Trinity, 1563. University preacher, 1570. R. of Wilby, Suffolk, 1569-1609. R. of Barking, 1579-1609.

DAVY, RICHARD. B.A. 1493; M.A. 1496. Fellow of QUEENS', 1497-8. Perhaps pens. at Gonville Hall, 1500. V. of Kirkham, Lancs., 1504. R. of Norton, Norf., 1535.

DAVIE, RICHARD. Matric. pens. from GONVILLE HALL, Easter, 1553.

DAVY, RICHARD. Adm. pens. at QUEENS', Mar. 18, 1662-3. Of Norfolk. Matric. 1663; B.A. 1666-7; M.A. 1670. Perhaps of Ditchingham, Norfolk; adm. at the Inner Temple, 1667.

DAVIE, ROBERT. Matric. pens. from CORPUS CHRISTI, Easter, 1575; B.A. 1577-8.

DAVIE, ROBERT. Adm. sizar (age 16) at CAIUS, Jan. 23, 1581-2. S. of Richard. B. at Sawston, Cambs. School, Mansfield, Notts. Matric. 1582. (*Venn*, I. 113.)

DAVY, ROBERT. Adm. sizar (age 16) at ST JOHN'S, Mar. 3, 1653-4. S. of Matthew, baker, of Braintree, Essex. B. there. School, Braintree (Mr Adamson). Matric. 1653-4; B.A. 1657-8; M.A. 1661. V. of Gestingthorpe, Essex, 1661; ejected, 1662.

DAVYE, ROBERT. Adm. pens. (age 18) at ST JOHN'S, June 16, 1688. S. of Robert, merchant. B. at York. School, Newton (private; Mr Denton). Matric. 1688. Adm. at the Middle Temple, Aug. 27, 1688. Recorder of Norwich. M.P. for Norwich, 1698-1703. Died Oct. 1703.

DAVY, ROBERT. Adm. pens. at CLARE, May 2, 1700. B. at Norwich. Matric. 1700. One of these names, s. of Robert, of the Inner Temple, adm. at the Inner Temple, 1701.

DAVY, SIMON. Adm. pens. (age 16) at CAIUS, May 30, 1620. S. of Simon, citizen of Norwich. Bapt. at St Peter Mancroft, Norwich, Apr. 17, 1603. School, Norwich. Matric. 1620; Scholar, 1620-7; B.A. 1623-4; M.A. 1627. Ord. deacon and priest (Norwich) Jan. 4, 1628-9. R. of one mediety of Scarning, Norfolk, 1628. R. of Ingoldisthorpe, 1638. (*Venn*, I. 249.)

DAVIE, THOMAS. B.A. from TRINITY, 1623; M.A. 1626. Ord. deacon (Peterb.) Dec. 24, 1625. Perhaps V. of Kenninghall, Norfolk, 1634-84. Died July 12, 1684, aged 83.

DAVY, THOMAS. Adm. sizar at CORPUS CHRISTI, 1625. Of Norfolk. Matric. 1626.

DAVY, THOMAS. Adm. pens. (age 17) at CAIUS, May 20, 1679. S. of William, tanner, of Swanton Morley, Norfolk. B. there. School, Scarning (Mr Burton). Matric. 1679, as Davies; Scholar, 1679-84; M.B. 1684. Died Mar. 23, 1692-3. Buried at Swanton Morley. M.I. (*Venn*, I. 462.)

DAVY, WILLIAM. B.Can.L. 1519-20. *Gr.* for D.Can.L. 1529-30; but not admitted. Prior of St Martin's.

DAVY, WILLIAM. Fellow of KING'S HALL, 1531–43. B.Can.L. 1520–1. V. of Shepreth, Cambs., till 1536. R. of St Benet's, Cambridge, 1545. Buried at St Benet's, Feb. 8, 1545–6. Will (V.C.C.). He left a sum of money for celebrating his *exequies* at St Benet's. (*Masters*, 68.)

DAVY, WILLIAM. Matric. sizar from CHRIST'S, Easter, 1606; B.A. 1608–9.

DAVIE, WILLIAM. Adm. scholar (age 16) at CAIUS, Nov. 2, 1613. S. of Henry, gent. Bapt. at St Peter Mancroft, Norwich, Jan. 18, 1595–6. School, Thetford (Mr Jenkenson). Matric. 1614; B.A. 1617–8; M.A. 1621. Incorp. at Oxford, 1621. Adm. at Gray's Inn, Aug. 8, 1630. (*Venn*, I. 223.)

DAVY, WILLIAM. Adm. pens. (age 16) at ST JOHN'S, Oct. 23, 1648. S. of Thomas, of Beckley, Sussex. B. there. School, Tonbridge. Matric. 1648.

DAVY, WILLIAM. Adm. sizar at JESUS, Feb. 19, 1655–6. Of Suffolk. S. of William, of Isleham, Cambs., gent. School, Bury. Matric. 1657; B.A. 1659–60; Scholar, 1660; M.A. 1663. Fellow, 1662–6. Ord. priest (Ely) Sept. 19, 1663. C. of Fen Ditton, Cambs., 1664. Died Nov. 15, 1667, aged 26. Buried in the College Chapel. M.I. there. Will proved (V.C.C.). (Le Neve, *Mon.*, III. 124; A. Gray.)

DAVY, ——. B.A. 1518–9.

DAVY, ——. B.A. 1534–5.

DAVY, ——. Adm. at CORPUS CHRISTI, 1575.

DAVY, ——. Sizar at PETERHOUSE, 1599–1601.

DAVIES, CHARLES. Adm. sizar (age 17) at PEMBROKE, May 12, 1729. S. of Henry, of Buckerell, Devon, gent. Matric. 1729; B.A. 1732–3. Brother of John (1719–20).

DAVIES, EDWARD. B.A. from JESUS, 1606; M.A. 1610, as Edmund. Perhaps R. of West Clandon, Surrey, till 1625. Buried there Mar. 13, 1625. But see *Al. Oxon.* for a contemporary.

DAVIS, EDWARD. Adm. sizar (age 17) at ST JOHN'S, July 15, 1637. S. of Edward, yeoman, of Eye, Suffolk. B. there. School, Eye (Mr Hall). Matric. 1637–8; B.A. 1641–2.

DAVIES, EDWARD. Adm. sizar at EMMANUEL, July 2, 1690. Of Suffolk. Migrated to St Catharine's, Nov. 10, 1692. Matric. 1693; B.A. 1694–5. Ord. deacon (Norwich) Sept. 1695; priest, Sept. 1697.

DAVIS, EDWIN. Adm. pens. (age 18) at CHRIST'S, June 30, 1730. S. of Jeremiah. B. at Stroud, Gloucs. School, Stroud. Matric. 1730; Scholar, 1731; B.A. 1733–4.

DAVIES, FRANCIS. Adm. Fell.-Com. (age 17) at ST JOHN'S, Oct. 17, 1683. S. of John, Esq. B. at Radwell, Herts. School, Chigwell, Essex (Mr Davies). Matric. 1684. Perhaps adm. at the Middle Temple, Nov. 27, 1683.

DAVIES, GEORGE. Adm. pens. (age 16) at ST JOHN'S, Apr. 11, 1718. S. of George, druggist. B. at Beverley. School, Beverley (Mr Lambert and Mr Johnstone). Matric. 1719; B.A. 1722–3; M.A. 1726; B.D. 1733. Fellow, 1725–48. Ord. priest (Lincoln) June 4, 1732. R. of Starston, Norfolk, 1746–68. Died Nov. 5, 1768. (*Scott-Mayor*, III. 316.)

DAVIS, GEORGE. Adm. pens. (age 18) at ST JOHN'S, May 25, 1747. S. of James, gent., of Berkshire. B. at Hare Hatch, Berks. School, Westminster. Matric. from Queen's College, Oxford, July 1, 1748.

DAVIS, GERSON. B.A. 1580–1 (Incorp. from Oxford). S. of Richard, Bishop of St David's. Matric. from Brasenose College, July 20, 1578, age 19; B.A. 1579–80; M.A. 1582. Preb. of St David's, 1578; of Brecon, 1582. V. of Penbryn, Cardiganshire, 1584. (*Al. Oxon.*)

DAVIES, GRIFFITH. Adm. sizar at QUEENS', June 25, 1677. Of Carmarthen. Matric. 1677; B.A. 1680–1. Perhaps adm. at Gray's Inn, Nov. 22, 1687, as Griffin Davis, s. of Griffin, of Drasleyne, Carmarth., gent.

DAVYS, HATTON. Adm. pens. (age 19) at ST JOHN'S, Oct. 20, 1685. From Magdalene, where he had been adm. Apr. 12, 1683. S. of John, Esq. B. at Long Stanton, Cambs. School, Eton. Colleger, 1677–82. Matric. 1683. V. of Amwell, Herts., 1694–1713. Died May 31, 1713. M.I.

DAVIS, HENRY. Matric. pens. from QUEENS', c. 1596.

DAVIES, HENRY. M.A. 1631 (Incorp. from Oxford); B.A. from Exeter College, Oxford, 1617; M.A. 1620.

DAVIS, HENRY. Adm. pens. (age 18) at TRINITY, June 10, 1726. S. of Henry, of London. School, Westminster. Matric. 1726; Scholar, 1727; B.A. 1729–30; M.A. 1733; B.D. 1742; D.D. 1749. Fellow, 1732. Ord. deacon (Lincoln) Dec. 23, 1733; priest, June 1, 1740. V. of Over, Cambs., 1745. V. of Trumpington, 1747–63. R. of Fakenham, Norfolk, 1763–70. Will (P.C.C.) 1770.

DAVIS, HUGH. Adm. sizar (age 18) at ST JOHN'S, June 30, 1668. S. of Robert, deceased, of Anglesey, Wales. B. there. School, Anglesey (Mr Owen). Matric. 1668.

DAVIES, HUGH. Adm. pens. at TRINITY, Nov. 12, 1733. Matric. 1733; Scholar, 1735. Perhaps adm. at the Middle Temple, July 30, 1734, as s. and h. of Henry, clerk, of Caerhun, Carnarvonshire.

DAVIS, HUGH. Adm. sizar (age 17) at PETERHOUSE, May 7, 1748. Of Flint. B. in Anglesey. Matric. 1748; Scholar, 1748; B.A. 1752; M.A. 1763. R. of Aber, Carnarvonshire. Fellow of the Linnaean Society, 1790. Retired to Beaumaris, in 1813. Learned Botanist and author. Died Feb. 16, 1821. (*D.N.B.*)

DAVIES, HUMPHREY. Matric. sizar from QUEENS', Michs. 1567. Of Warwickshire (probably of Leamington Hastings). B.A. 1571–2; M.A. 1575. R. of Llanvyllin, Montgomery, 1571 (allowed absence at Cambridge). V. of Darwen, 1577. Founded a fellowship at Queens', 1607; but the estate was lost, 1642. (Browne Willis, *St Asaph*, I. 384; *Cooper*, II. 474.)

DAVIES, ISAAC. Adm. at CORPUS CHRISTI, 1737. Of London. Matric. 1737; B.A. 1740–1. Perhaps R. of Caldecot, Herts., 1747–89. Died 1789. Will (P.C.C.), as of Edworth, Beds.

DAVIES, JAMES. Adm. pens. (age 17) at TRINITY, June 2, 1687. S. of James, R. of Barton Mills, Suffolk. School, Westminster. Matric. 1687; Scholar, 1688; B.A. 1690–1. Ord. priest (Norwich) Sept. 1693. Doubtless V. of Cavenham, Cambs., and R. of Tuddenham, Suffolk.

DAVIES, JAMES. M.A. from KING'S, 1726. Of Jesus College, Oxford. Probably s. of Daniel, of Llanfair-ar-y-Bryn, Carmarthen. Matric. from Jesus College, Oxford, Mar. 24, 1714–5, age 19; B.A. (Oxford) 1718–9. (*Al. Oxon.*)

DAVIES, JAMES. Adm. pens. at CLARE, Apr. 18, 1730. B. at Dunchurch, Warws. Matric. 1730.

DAVIES, JOHN (1536–7), *see* DAWES.

DAVIS, JOHN. M.A. 1584 (Incorp. from Oxford). S. of John, of London. B.A. from Gloucester Hall, 1577; M.A. 1581. Knighted for his services at Cadiz, 1596. Surveyor of the Ordnance, 1598. An eminent mathematician. Implicated in the plot of the Earl of Essex; condemned, but pardoned. Died at Pangbourne, Berks., May 14, 1625. Buried at Berecourt. Will (P.C.C.; *fo.* 69, Hele) 1626. (*Al. Oxon.*)

DAVIS, JOHN. M.A. from JESUS, 1608.

DAVIS, JOHN. Matric. pens. from ST JOHN'S, Easter, 1622; B.A. 1624–5; M.A. 1628. Perhaps adm. at the Middle Temple, June, 1629, as s. and h. of Sir John, Knt., of Pangbourne, Berks. If so, s. of the last but one.

DAVIS, JOHN. B.A. 1627 (Incorp. from Oxford).

DAVIES, JOHN. Adm. sizar (age 16) at CHRIST'S, May 3, 1636. S. of Evans. B. at Thurleigh, Beds. School, Clapham, Beds. (Mr Crawley). Matric. 1636; B.A. 1639–40. One of these names R. of Pitsea, Essex, 1656–9. V. of Horndon-on-the-Hill, 1659. Died 1662.

DAVIES, JOHN. Adm. sizar (age 18) at ST JOHN'S, June 29, 1642. S. of John, R. of Garthbeibio, Montgoms. B. at Cherbury, Salop. School, Shrewsbury. Matric. 1642. Twin-brother of Peter (1642).

DAVIS, JOHN. Adm. sizar at ST JOHN'S, May 14, 1646. S. of William, of Kidwelly, Carmarthens. B. there, May 25, 1625. School, Carmarthen. Matric. from Jesus College, Oxford, June 4, 1641, age 16; B.A. (Cambridge) 1646; by incorporation from Oxford. Buried at Kidwelly, July 22, 1693. (*Al. Oxon.*; *D.N.B.*)

DAVIS, JOHN. Adm. sizar (age 18) at PETERHOUSE, June 21, 1649. Of London. School, Merchant Taylors'. Matric. 1649; Scholar, 1650; B.A. 1652–3; M.A. 1656. Perhaps R. of West Leake, Notts., 1667. One of these names V. of St James, Dover, 1656–62; ejected.

DAVIES, JOHN. Adm. sizar at TRINITY, July 3, 1651. Of Leicestershire. Matric. 1654; B.A. 1654–5. Incorp. at Oxford, 1657–8.

DAVIES, JOHN. B.D. 1668 (*Lit. Reg.*). Matric. from Balliol College, Oxford, July 25, 1655; B.A. 1665. Created D.D. (Oxford) 1670. R. of Heydon, Essex, 1676. R. of Little Chishall, 1684. Died Oct. 4, 1717, aged 82. Will, P.C.C. One of these names R. of Hunsdon, Herts., 1661–78. (*Al. Oxon.*)

DAVIES, JOHN. Adm. pens. at PEMBROKE, Jan. 13, 1681–2. (Matric. from Exeter College, Oxford, Apr. 1, 1679, age 17.) S. of John, of St Hilary, Cornwall, gent. B.A. 1682–3; M.A. 1687. One of these names V. of Wharton, Lancs., 1711–4. Died 1714.

DAVIES, JOHN (JONES). Adm. sizar at TRINITY, Nov. 8, 1684, as John Davies Jones. Matric., as John Jones. S. of David Jones. B. at Dolgelley. School, Llanigryn (Mr Owen Jones). B.A. 1688–9, as John Jones.

DAVIES, JOHN. Adm. pens. (age 17) at TRINITY, Feb. 1, 1685-6. 3rd s. of Mutton, of Gwysaney, Flints. School, Westminster. Matric. 1685-6. Adm. Fell.-Com. Apr. 27, 1688; M.A. 1690 (*Com. Reg.*); D.D. 1715. Adm. at the Inner Temple, 1686. Fellow of Peterhouse, 1690-1704. (Evidently this man, and not the last, as in *T. A. Walker*.) Ord. deacon, 1690. Presented to Cherry Hinton, Cambs., 1691, but not instituted. Preb. of St Asaph, 1697. Preb. of Hereford, 1711. R. of Kingsland, Hereford. V. of Kerry, Montgom., 1717. Precentor of St David's, 1717. Married Honora, dau. of Ralph Sneyd, Esq. Died at Bath, Dec. 14, 1732. Buried at Kingsland. M.I. there. Brother of Richard (1692), father of Sneyd (1728). (Burke, *L.G.*; Browne Willis, *St Asaph*, I. 195.)

DAVIES, JOHN. Adm. pens. at QUEENS', June 8, 1695. B. in London, 1679. School, Charterhouse. Matric. 1695; B.A. 1698-9; M.A. 1702; LL.D. 1711; D.D. 1717 (*Com. Reg.*). Fellow, 1701-12. Junior Proctor, 1709-10. President, 1717-32. Vice-Chancellor, 1725-6. Ord. deacon (Ely) Sept. 21, 1711; priest, Sept. 23, 1711. Chaplain to Bishop Moore, of Ely. R. of Fen Ditton, Cambs., 1711-32. Preb. of Ely, 1711-32. R. of Glemsford, Suffolk, 1712-9. Author. Died Mar. 7, 1731-2. Will (P.C.C.) 1735. (*Queens' Coll. Hist.*, 237; *D.N.B.*)

DAVIES, JOHN. Incorp. B.A. 1698, from Jesus College, Oxford. Probably s. of Henry, of 'Gragge,' Salop, gent. Matric. from Jesus College, Oxford, June 8, 1693, age 17; B.A. (Oxford) 1697; M.A. 1700; B.D. 1701. R. of Bucknell, Salop, 1702. R. of Pitchford. Buried at Pitchford, Mar. 2, 1741-2. (*Al. Oxon.*; *Misc. Gen. et Her.*, 2nd S., v. 188.)

DAVIES, JOHN. Adm. sizar at JESUS, Oct. 16, 1712. S. of William (1671), deceased, R. of Abington, Northants. Bapt. there, Nov. 18, 1695. Matric. 1713; Rustat Scholar; B.A. 1716-7; M.A. 1720. Ord. deacon (Lincoln) Sept. 21, 1718 priest, Dec. 20, 1719.

DAVIS, JOHN. Adm. sizar (age 17) at ST JOHN'S, Nov. 1, 1712. S. of Henry, deceased. B. in London. School, Merchant Taylors'. Matric. 1712; B.A. 1716-7; M.A. 1720. Ord. priest (London) Dec. 20, 1719. Perhaps R. of Barking and Darmsden, Suffolk, 1722. One of these names V. of Brampton, Hunts., 1737-43, and R. of Sawtry St Andrew, 1743-67. Died 1767. Will, P.C.C.

DAVIES, JOHN. Adm. sizar (age 17) at PEMBROKE, Jan. 23, 1719-20. S. of Henry, of Buckerell, Devon, gent. Matric. 1720; B.A. 1723-4; M.A. 1728. Ord. deacon (Ely) Mar. 1, 1723-4; priest (Exeter) Sept. 25, 1726. C. of Stockland *w.* Dalwood, Devon, 1726-47. Chaplain to Earl Poulet. V. of Axmouth, Devon, 1746. Brother of Charles (1729). (F. S. Hockaday.)

DAVIES, JOHN. Adm. pens. (age 17) at PETERHOUSE, June 3, 1721. Of Salop. Probably s. of John (1685-6), R. of Kingsland, Heref. School, Westminster. Scholar, 1721. Died Sept. 5, 1735, aged 31. M.I. at Kingsland. Brother of Sneyd (1728).

DAVIES, JOHN. M.A. from PEMBROKE, 1731; B.A. of Magdalen Hall, Oxford. (Probably s. of Dav. Jones, of Ystrad, Cardigan.) Matric. from Jesus College, Oxford, Mar. 19, 1713-4, age 19; B.A. from Magdalen Hall, Oxford, Mar. 18, 1718-9. (*Al. Oxon.*)

DAVIES, JOHN. Adm. pens. at QUEENS', Apr. 23, 1737. Of Wales. Matric. 1737.

DAVIES, JOHN. M.A. from KING'S, 1738. S. of David, of Trawsfynydd, Carnarvs. Matric. from Jesus College, Oxford, Mar. 18, 1718-9, age 18; B.A. from St Edmund Hall, 1722-3. One of these names (M.A.) V. of Fawsley, Northants., 1738-65. Buried there 1765. (*Al. Oxon.*)

DAVIES, JOSEPH. Adm. pens. at MAGDALENE, June 24, 1673. S. of Joseph, merchant, of Wisbech. School, Wisbech. Matric. 1673. Will proved, P.C.C., 1682.

DAVIS, JOSEPH. Adm. sizar (age 18) at TRINITY, June 16, 1721. S. of George, of 'Holford,' Cheshire. School, Macclesfield (Mr Allen). Matric. 1723; B.A. 1724-5; M.A. 1736. Ord. priest (Lincoln) Dec. 18, 1726. C. of Swaffham Bulbeck, Cambs., 1728. V. of Stoke Nayland, Suffolk, 1730-51. V. of Gt Wilbraham, Cambs., 1736. R. of Barton Mills, Suffolk, 1751. V. of Bottisham, Cambs., 1758-63. Died May 5, 1763. Buried at Dottisham. M.I. Will, P.C.C.

DAVYES, NICHOLAS. Adm. pens. at TRINITY, June 1, 1670; B.A. 1673-4.

DAVYS, OWYN. Matric. sizar from TRINITY, Michs. 1561. Of Wales. B.A. 1566; M.A. from Queens', 1569; B.D. 1577. Ord. priest (Peterb.) Oct. 10, 1576.

DAVIES, OWEN. Adm. sizar at TRINITY, Mar. 11, 1653-4. Of Wales. Matric. 1654; Scholar, 1657; B.A. 1657-8; M.A. 1662. V. of St Ippolytes, Herts., 1670-7. Died 1677. (The Preb. of Bangor was probably his Oxford contemporary.) (*Al. Oxon.*)

DAVIES, OWEN. Matric. sizar from KING'S, Michs. 1735; B.A. 1739-40. V. of South Stoneham, Hants., 1744. R. of Exton. C. of St Mary's, Southampton, 1747-94. Died Sept. 30, 1794. (*Misc. Gen. et Her.*, 3rd S., II. 20.)

DAVIES, PETER. Adm. sizar (age 18) at ST JOHN'S, June 29, 1642. S. of John, R. of Garthbeibio, Montgom. B. at Cherbury, Salop. School, Shrewsbury. Twin-brother of John (1642).

DAVIS, PETER. Adm. pens. at ST CATHARINE'S, June 20, 1741. Of Chester. Matric. 1741; B.A. 1744-5. One of these names, s. of Robert, late of Llanerch, Denbigh, deceased; adm. at Lincoln's Inn, Jan. 29, 1739-40.

DAVIES, PHINEAS. Adm. sizar at JESUS, Apr. 25, 1691. Of Salop. Matric. 1691; B.A. 1694-5.

DAVIES, RANDOLPH. Adm. pens. at JESUS, Mar. 2, 1632-3. Of Montgomeryshire. Matric. 1633; Scholar, 1634; B.A. 1636-7; M.A. 1640. V. of Meifod, Montgom., 1647-9; deprived; and 1660-97. R. of Cwm, 1661-97.

DAVYSE, RICHARD. Matric. pens. from JESUS, Easter, 1567.

DAVIES, RICHARD. Adm. pens. at TRINITY, Dec. 9, 1664. Matric. 1665.

DAVIES, RICHARD. Adm. sizar (age 20) at ST JOHN'S, June 10, 1671. S. of Randolph, clerk, of 'Peniarth,' Montgom. B. there. School, Shrewsbury. Matric. 1671.

DAVIES, RICHARD. Adm. pens. (age 17) at PETERHOUSE, July 2, 1692. Of Denbighshire. 5th s. of Mutton, of Gwysaney and Llanerch. School, Ruthin. Scholar, 1693; Matric. 1694; B.A. 1695-6; M.A. 1699. Fellow, 1699-1702. V. of Ruabon, Denbighs., 1706-46. Preb. of St Asaph, 1710. R. of Kilken, 1721-46. R. of Erbistock. Preb. of Brecon. Preb. of St David's, 1723. Archdeacon of St David's, 1737-46. Benefactor to Peterhouse, and to Ruabon School. Died May 25, 1746. Buried at Mold. M.I. Brother of John (1685-6). (Browne Willis, *St Asaph.*)

DAVIES, RICHARD. Adm. pens. at QUEENS', Aug. 19, 1726. Of Salop. Matric. 1726; B.A. 1730-1; M.A. 1734; M.D. 1748. Fellow, 1730-40. F.R.S. 1738. Practised at Shrewsbury, afterwards at Bath. Author, medical. Died at Bath. Buried there Dec. 25, 1761. Will, P.C.C. (*D.N.B.*)

DAVIS, RICHARD. Adm. sizar (age 18) at MAGDALENE, Oct. 19, 1733. S. of Richard. B. at Shrewsbury. School, Shrewsbury. Matric. 1735; B.A. 1737-8. Ord. priest (Norwich) Sept. 1740.

DAVIES, ROBERT. Adm. Fell.-Com. at TRINITY, Mar. 13, 1655-6. Of Wales. Perhaps s. of Robert, of Gwysaney, Flints., Esq. Bapt. at Mold, Apr. 15, 1639. Adm. at Gray's Inn, Nov. 26, 1658. Of the Guard of Horse to Charles II. Died Nov. 8, 1668, aged 28. (Burke, *L.G.*)

DAVYES, ROBERT. Matric. pens. from QUEENS', Jan. 20, 1661-2. Of Norfolk. Matric. 1663.

DAVIES, ROBERT. Adm. scholar at TRINITY, Apr. 23, 1680. Perhaps s. of Mutton, of Llanerch, Denbs., Esq.; adm. at the Inner Temple, 1677. High Sheriff for Flints., 1704. Died July 8, 1710. If so, brother of John (1685-6) and Richard (1692).

DAVIES, ROBERT. Adm. sizar (age 18) at ST JOHN'S, June 28, 1716. S. of Francis, collector of taxes. B. at Ruthin, Denbigh. School, Shrewsbury. Matric. 1716; B.A. 1719-20.

DAVIES, ROGER. M.A. from KING'S, 1724. S. of William, of Lampeter, Pembs., gent. B. Mar. 5, 1686-7. Matric. from Jesus College, Oxford, Jan. 16, 1702-3, age 16; B.A. (Oxford) 1706. Master of Carmarthen School, 1724. R. of Rhoscrowther, Pembs., 1724. Probably preb. of St David's, 1733. (*Al. Oxon.*)

DAVYS, SIMON. Adm. pens. (age 20) at CAIUS, June 13, 1566. S. of Thomas, of Howden, Yorks. School, Howden. Brother of Thomas (1556).

DAVIES, SNEYD. Adm. at KING'S, a scholar from Eton, 1728. S. of John (1685), R. of Kingsland, Hereford. B. at Shrewsbury, 1709. Matric. 1729; B.A. 1732-3; M.A. 1737; D.D. 1759. Fellow, 1732. Ord. priest (Ely) Dec. 1733. Chaplain to Cornwallis, Bishop of Lichfield. Canon of Lichfield; and Master of St John's hospital there. R. of Kingsland, Hereford, 1732. Archdeacon of Derby, 1755-69. Author, poetical. Died Jan. 20, 1769. M.I. at Kingsland. Probably brother of John (1721). (*D.N.B.*; Browne Willis, *St Asaph*, I. 196.)

DAVIS, STAPLETON. Adm. at CLARE, Aug. 30, 1718. Migrated to Christ's, Feb. 29, 1719-20, age 22. Previously adm. at Trinity College, Dublin, Aug. 20, 1717. S. of John. B. at Montserrat. School, Westminster. Matric. 1719; B.A. 1721-2. Incorp. at Oxford, 1723. Ord. priest (Lincoln) Mar. 17, 1727-8. Went out to the Leeward Islands, Nov. 12, 1729. (*Peile*, II. 197.)

DAVYS, THEOPHILUS. Adm. pens. at EMMANUEL, Apr. 22, 1702. Of Nottinghamshire. Matric. 1702; B.A. 1705-6. Died in College. Buried Mar. 20, 1708.

DAVYS, THOMAS. LL.D. 1548, from St JOHN'S. B. at Llanbedr-y-Cennin, Carnarvs. (B.Civ.L. at Oxford.) Perhaps B.A. (Oxford) 1515-6; M.A. 1521; B.Can.L. 1530; B.Civ.L. 1535-6. R. of Llanbedr-y-Cennin, Carnarvs., and V. of Caerhun, 1535. Chancellor of Bangor, 1546; deprived, 1554; restored, 1558. Archdeacon of St Asaph, 1558. Bishop of St Asaph, 1561-73. Benefactor to Queens' College. Died Oct. 16, 1573. Buried at Abergele. Will, P.C.C. (*D.N.B.*; *Cooper*, I. 319, and III. 82; Browne Willis, *St Asaph*, I. 104.)

DAVYS, THOMAS. Matric. sizar from TRINITY, Michs. 1556. S. of Thomas, of Howden, Yorks. Scholar; B.A. 1559-60. Migrated to Caius, as Fell.-Com. June 26, 1564, age 27. One of these names R. of Shelfhanger, Norfolk, 1579-80. Brother of Simon (1566). (*Venn*, I. 54.)

DAVIES, THOMAS. Matric. sizar from QUEENS', Michs. 1572. B. at Caerhun, Carnarvon. Ord. deacon (London) Sept. 28, 1579; priest, Dec. 21, 1579.

DAVIES, THOMAS. Adm. sizar at QUEENS', Apr. 23, 1575. Of Wales.

DAVIES, THOMAS. Matric. pens. from CHRIST'S, June, 1577. Of London. B.A. 1580-1; M.A. 1584; M.D. 1591. Licentiate R.C.P. 1593. Fellow, 1594. Censor. Lumleian Lecturer, 1607. Buried at St Dunstan-in-the-West, Aug. 20, 1615. Will, P.C.C. (*Munk*, I. 107; *Peile*, I. 141.)

DAVIES, THOMAS. Adm. pens. at TRINITY, June 24, 1651. Of London. Probably s. of John, draper, of Old Jewry, London. School, Westminster. Scholar, 1651; Matric. 1652. One of these names, of Furnival's Inn, 2nd s. of Thomas, late of Droitwich, gent., deceased, adm. at Lincoln's Inn, Feb. 21, 1653-4. Sheriff of London and Middlesex, 1667-8. Knighted, 1667. Mayor of London, 1676-7. 'Davies, the little fellow, my schoolfellow, the bookseller; and is now become sheriff, which is a strange turn methinks' (Pepys, *Diary*). Died Mar. 1679-80. Father of Thomas (1704).

DAVIES, THOMAS. Incorp. M.A. 1665, from Jesus College, Oxford. Matric. there, Nov. 7, 1650; B.A. (Oxford) 1653; M.A. 1655-6. Probably ord. priest (Brian Duppa, Sarum) Mar. 12, 1658-9; C. of St Leonard, Shoreditch, in 1664.

DAVYS, THOMAS. Adm. pens. at TRINITY, Nov. 8, 1675. Perhaps s. of Mutton, of Llanerch, Denbs., Esq.; adm. at the Inner Temple, 1677. Died 1697. If so, brother of John (1685-6), Robert (1680) and Richard (1692).

DAVIES, THOMAS. M.A. from EMMANUEL, 1704. S. of Sir Thomas (1651), sheriff of London, Knt. Matric. from Trinity College, Oxford, July 13, 1686, age 15; B.A. from Oriel College, 1690. Adm. at Lincoln's Inn, Apr. 13, 1687. Inherited the manor of Cressing, near Braintree, Essex, where he shot himself, before July 23, 1705. (*Al. Oxon.*; *Her. and Gen.*, VI. 155, 357.)

DAVIS, THOMAS. Adm. sizar (age 16) at TRINITY, July 12, 1727. S. of Thomas, of Shepton Mallet, Somerset. School, Wells (Mr Creyghton). Matric. 1727; B.A. 1731-2. Perhaps V. of Ilminster, Somerset, till 1768. Will (P.C.C.) 1768.

DAVYS, WILLIAM (1506-7), *see* DAWES.

DAVICE or DAVIS, W. Matric. sizar from St JOHN'S, 1564.

DAVYS, W. Matric. sizar from JESUS, Easter, 1565.

DAVIES, WILLIAM. Matric. sizar from QUEENS', Easter, 1577. Of Salop.

DAVYES, WILLIAM. Adm. sizar at QUEENS', Oct. 16, 1596. Of Carnarvonshire. Matric. *c.* 1596.

DAVIES, WILLIAM. Adm. sizar at TRINITY, Oct. 21, 1650. Of Denbighshire. Matric. 1654; B.A. 1654-5; M.A. 1658.

DAVIES, WILLIAM. Adm. pens. at TRINITY, Mar. 1, 1661-2. Matric. 1661-2; Scholar, 1664; B.A. 1665-6; M.A. 1669. Incorp. at Oxford, 1669. Ord. deacon (Ely) June, 1669.

DAVIES, WILLIAM. Adm. pens. at TRINITY, June 5, 1668. School, Westminster. Matric. 1668; Scholar, 1669; B.A. 1671-2; M.A. 1675. Fellow, 1674.

DAVIES, WILLIAM. Adm. sizar at TRINITY, May 19, 1671. Matric. 1671; B.A. 1675-6. Ord. priest (Peterb.) Sept. 24, 1676. One of these names R. of Papworth, Cambs., 1689. R. of Abington, Northants., 1692-1709. Died 1709. Father of John (1712).

DAVIS, WILLIAM. Adm. sizar (age 18) at St JOHN'S, Mar. 28, 1678. S. of George, deceased. B. at Beverley, Yorks. School, Beverley (Mr Lambert). Matric. 1678; B.A. 1681-2; M.A. 1685. Ord. priest (York) Sept. 1685. Perhaps V. of Beverley, 1683-92, and V. of Rudstone, 1692-1717. Died 1717.

DAVIES, WILLIAM. M.A. from KING'S, 1706. S. of Hugh, of Titley, Hereford. Matric. from Oriel College, Oxford, Feb. 28, 1699-1700, age 21; B.A. (Oxford) 1703; M.A. (Incorp. from Cambridge) 1709. One of these names R. of Aldbury, Herts., 1708-54. Died 1754. Will, P.C.C. (*Al. Oxon.*)

DAVIS, WILLIAM. Adm. sizar (age 19) at St JOHN'S, Apr. 19, 1743. S. of Richard, gent., of Lancashire. B. at Exton. School, Clitheroe.

DAVYS, ——. B.A. 1513-4.

DAVIES, ——. Adm. pens. at TRINITY, Oct. 27, 1645. From Oxford.

DAVIS, ——. Adm. Fell.-Com. at KING'S, 1734-5.

DAVILL, CHARLES. Matric. sizar from KING'S, Easter, 1623; B.A. 1627-8; M.A. from Trinity, 1631.

DAVYLL, CHRISTOPHER. Matric. pens. from JESUS, Michs. 1568.

DAVIL, HENRY. Matric. pens. from St CATHARINE'S, Easter, 1641. Probably brother of Thomas (1641) and John (1645-6).

DAVILLE, JOHN. Matric. pens. from CLARE, Easter, 1610; B.A. 1613-4.

DAVILE, JOHN. Adm. pens. (age 19) at St JOHN'S, Feb. 26, 1645-6. S. of Thomas, attorney, of Kirkby Fleetham, Yorks. B. there. School, Fleetham (Mr Smelt). Matric. 1645-6; B.A. 1646-7; M.A. 1650. (Had been a student at Edinburgh for two years before admission.)

DAVILE, JOHN. Adm. sizar at TRINITY, June 21, 1733. Matric. 1733; Scholar, 1736; B.A. 1736-7. Master of Doncaster School, 1737-43. Perhaps V. of Islington, Norfolk, 1755-1800. V. of Wiggenhall St Mary, 1755-1800. R. of Boughton, 1765-1800. Died Feb. 8, 1800, aged 90.

DAVILL, THOMAS. Matric. pens. from JESUS, Michs. 1572. S. of William, of Coxwold, Yorks. Migrated to Caius, Apr. 25, 1576, age 19. School, Newburgh. B.A. 1576-7; M.A. 1580.

DAVIL, THOMAS. Matric. pens. from St CATHARINE'S, Easter, 1641. Probably s. of Thomas, of Kirkby Fleetham, Yorks.; age 40 in 1665 and brother of Henry (1641) and John (1645-6).

DAVYLL, ——. B.D. 1482-3.

DAVINE, DANIEL. Matric. pens. from TRINITY HALL, Easter, 1652.

DAVISON, ANDREW. Incorp. at Oxford, 1544-5, as B.A. of Cambridge (degree not found). Of Christ Church, Oxford, in 1547. 'M.A. from beyond the seas.' (*Al. Oxon.*)

DAVISON, ASHTON. Matric. pens. from St JOHN'S, Michs. 1626; B.A. 1630-1; M.A. 1634. ('Anthony' in *grace*.)

DAVISON, CHRISTOPHER. Matric. Fell.-Com. from KING'S, *c.* 1595. Probably s. of William, Secretary of State; and brother of Walter of the same date, and of Francis.

DAVISON, FRANCIS. Matric. Fell.-Com. (age 12) from EMMANUEL, Easter, 1586. Doubtless s. of William, Secretary of State. B. *c.* 1575. Adm. at Gray's Inn, May 14, 1593. Travelled abroad, 1595-7. Author, *Poetical Rhapsody*, etc. Probably died in or before 1619. (*D.N.B.*)

DAVISON, GEORGE. Adm. sizar at SIDNEY, Oct. 25, 1609. Matric. pens. 1609; B.A. 1613-4.

DAVISON, GEORGE. Adm. pens. (age 18) at St JOHN'S, Mar. 21, 1723-4. S. of Thomas (1681), physician, of Durham. School, Sedbergh. Matric. 1724. Brother of Robert (1727).

DAVISON, JAMES. Adm. pens. at JESUS, June 26, 1740. Of Norton, Durham.

DAVYSON, JOHN. Matric. pens. from CHRIST'S, Mar. 1557-8. Perhaps ord. acolyte at Chester, Sept. 1557. (*Peile*, I. 65.)

DAVISON, JOHN. Resident pens. at TRINITY HALL, Aug. 1564.

DAVISON, JOHN. Matric. pens. from St JOHN'S, Easter, 1625.

DAVISON, JOHN. Adm. Fell.-Com. (age 15) at St JOHN'S, June 3, 1679. S. of Alexander, Esq., deceased. B. at Wynyard House, Durham. Bapt. at Grindon, Mar. 29, 1664. School, Coxwold. Matric. 1679. Of Blakiston, Esq. Married Mary, dau. of Sir Richard Musgrave, Bart. Died Nov. 22, 1690. Buried at Norton, Durham. M.I. Pedigree in Le Neve's *Knights*, 101. (Surtees, *Durham*, III. 166.)

DAVISON, JONATHAN. Adm. pens. (age 16) at St JOHN'S, May 30, 1665. S. of Thomas, merchant, of Newcastle, Northumberland. B. there. Bapt. at St Nicholas, Jan. 14, 1649-50. School, Newcastle (Mr Oxley). Matric. 1665; B.A. 1668-9; M.A. 1672; B.D. 1679. Fellow, 1670. Ord. priest (London) Feb. 24, 1677-8. V. of Aldworth, Berks., 1687. Died Oct. 6, 1690, aged 40. M.I. at Norton, Durham. (Surtees, *Durham*, III. 157.)

DAVISON, JONATHAN. Adm. pens. (age 17) at St JOHN'S, May 6, 1703. S. of Timothy, deceased. B. at Beamish, Durham. Bapt. Dec. 30, 1686. School, Isleworth, Middlesex (private; Mr Ellis). Matric. 1703; B.A. 1706-7. Adm. at Gray's Inn, Jan. 25, 1703-4. Living, 1732. Brother of William (1690). (H. M. Wood.)

DAVISON, JONATHAN. Adm. pens. at QUEENS', June 3, 1732. Of Durham. Matric. 1732–3. Migrated to Jesus, Feb. 15, 1734–5. Scholar. Died at Norton, Durham, Nov. 8, 1788. (G. *Mag.*)

DAVISON, JOSEPH. Adm. sizar (age 18) at ST JOHN'S, June 15, 1702. S. of William, deceased. B. at Durham. School, Durham (Mr Ross). Matric. 1702; B.A. 1705–6; M.A. 1709. Ord. deacon (Peterb.) June 19, 1709; C. of King's Cliffe, Northants. V. of Ellingham, Northumberland, 1714–59. Died Oct. 1, 1759. Buried at Ellingham.

DAVISON, MORTON. Adm. pens. (age 18) at ST JOHN'S, June 23, 1739. S. of William, Esq. (1690), of Durham. B. at Beamish. Bapt. at Tanfield, May 29, 1721. School, Durham (Mr Dongworth). Matric. 1739. Married Dorothy, dau. of Thomas Younghusband, of Budle, Durham. Died without issue. Buried at Tanfield, Durham, Feb. 21, 1774. Brother of Thomas (1740). (*Scott-Mayor*, III. 501; H. M. Wood.)

DAVISON, RALPH. Matric. pens. from ST CATHARINE'S, Michs. 1624. Doubtless s. of Sir Alexander, of Newcastle-on-Tyne, Knt. Bapt. at St Nicholas, July 11, 1609. B.A. 1628–9. Adm. at Gray's Inn, Apr. 28, 1629. Of Thornley, Durham, Esq. Married, at Houghton-le-Spring, Jan. 16, 1637–8, Timothea, dau. of Sir William Belasyse, Knt. Died Aug. 15, 1684, aged 74. M.I. at St Oswald's, Durham. Father of William (1655), brother of Thomas (1623). (Le Neve, *Mon.*, V. 56; *Vis. of Durham*, 1666; H. M. Wood.)

DAVISON, RALPH. Adm. pens. (age 18) at ST JOHN'S, June 9, 1687. S. of William (1655), Esq. B. at Layton, Durham. School, St Paul's, London. Matric. 1687; B.A. from Trinity Hall, 1690–1. Barrister-at-law. Of Elvet. Buried May 5, 1699. (Surtees, *Durham*, III. 167.)

DAVISON, RICHARD. Matric. sizar from CHRIST'S, May, 1569. One of these names R. of Holton, Suffolk, 1574–85. One R. of Kirby Cane, Norfolk, 1579–1619. (*Peile*, I. 110.)

DAVISON, ROBERT. Matric. sizar from KING'S, Michs. 1602.

DAVISON, ROBERT. Adm. sizar (age 19) at ST JOHN'S, Mar. 18, 1677–8. S. of Robert, farmer. B. at Warkworth, Northumberland. School, Warkworth (private; Mr Cogin). Matric. 1678; B.A. 1681–2; M.A. 1685. P.C. of Bamburgh, Northumberland, 1690–1702. V. of Warkworth, 1696–1702. Died 1702. Buried at Warkworth.

DAVISON, ROBERT. Adm. pens. (age 18) at ST JOHN'S, July 1, 1727. S. of Thomas (1681). B. at Durham. Bapt. at St Mary-le-Bow, Nov. 25, 1708. School, Sedbergh. Matric. 1727. Probably V. of St Giles', Durham, till 1742; and V. of Croxdale, 1742–59. Brother of George (1723–4). The V. of Ellingham, Northumberland, seems to have been an Oxford contemporary. (*Scott-Mayor*, III. 407; G. B. Routledge; H. M. Wood.)

DAVYSON, ROGER. Matric. pens. from JESUS, Easter, 1566.

DAVISON, SAMUEL. Adm. pens. at EMMANUEL, June 26, 1723. Of Salop. Matric. 1724; B.A. 1726–7; M.A. 1730. Fellow, 1727. Ord. deacon (Lincoln) Mar. 17, 1727–8; priest, Sept. 21, 1729.

DAVISON, THOMAS. Matric. pens. from ST CATHARINE'S, Lent, 1623–4. Doubtless s. and h. of Alexander, of Newcastle-on-Tyne, Esq. (afterwards Knt.). Bapt. May 14, 1607. B.A. 1627–8. Adm. at Gray's Inn, Nov. 17, 1628. Knighted, July 30, 1660. Sheriff of Durham, 1661. Died May 23, 1667. M.I. at Norton. Brother of Ralph (1624).

DAVISON, THOMAS. Adm. pens. (age 16) at ST JOHN'S, May 12, 1652. S. of Thomas, merchant, of Newcastle-on-Tyne. B. there. Bapt. at St Nicholas, Mar. 20, 1635–6. School, Houghton-le-Spring. Matric. 1652; B.A. 1655–6; M.A. 1659. Fellow, 1660. Incorp. at Oxford, 1663. V. of Norton, Durham, 1663–90; deprived, as a non-juror; afterwards conformed. Married, at Durham Cathedral, Oct. 15, 1663, Mary, dau. of Joseph Naylor, D.D. Died Dec. 15, 1715. M.I. at Norton. Father of Thomas (1681).

DAVISON, THOMAS. Adm. pens. (age 17) at ST JOHN'S, June 2, 1658. S. of William, gent., of Harrington, Lincs. B. there. School, Partney (Mr Booker), Lincs. Matric. 1658.

DAVISON, THOMAS. Adm. sizar (age 20) at ST JOHN'S, Oct. 8, 1660. S. of John, deceased, of Newcastle-on-Tyne. B. there. School, Newcastle (Mr Fretevile). Matric. 1663; B.A. 1664–5; M.A. 1668. Ord. priest, 1665. C. of Bamborough, 1665–90. Licensed, Mar. 27, 1666, to marry Elizabeth Burtown. (H. M. Wood.)

DAVISON, THOMAS. Adm. pens. (age 16) at ST JOHN'S, May 23, 1681. S. of Thomas (1652). B. at Norton, Durham. School, Durham (Mr Batterson). Matric. 1681; B.A. 1684–5; M.A. 1688. Fellow, 1689–93. Non-juror. Extra-licentiate R.C.P. 1692. Practised for many years in Durham. Died Apr. 30, 1724. Father of George (1723–4) and Robert (1727). (*Munk*, I. 496.)

DAVISON, THOMAS. Adm. pens. (age 14) at MAGDALENE, July 8, 1682. S. of Thomas, gent. B. at Utterby, Lincs. School, Alford. Matric. 1684; B.A. 1686–7. Fellow, 1688.

DAVISON, THOMAS. Adm. pens. (age 19) at ST JOHN'S, Oct. 18, 1731. S. of Thomas, Esq. B. at Blakiston, Durham. Bapt. at Norton, June 19, 1712. School, Kirk-Heaton, Yorks. (Mr Clarke). Matric. 1731. Adm. at the Middle Temple, June 11, 1730. Died Feb. 5, 1756. M.I. at Norton, Durham.

DAVISON, THOMAS. Adm. pens. (age 18) at ST JOHN'S, June 27, 1740. S. of William (1690), of Beamish, Durham. B. there. Bapt. at Tanfield, June 15, 1723. School, Durham (Mr Dongworth). Matric. 1740. Adm. at Lincoln's Inn, Dec. 8, 1743. Brother of Morton (1739).

DAVISON, WALTER. Matric. Fell.-Com. from KING'S, 1595. S. of William, secretary of State. B. in London, Dec. 17, 1581. Afterwards a soldier in the Netherlands. Probably died before Dec. 1608. Author, *Poems*. Brother of Francis (1586) and probably of Christopher (1595). (*Cooper*, III. 13; *D.N.B.*)

DAVISON, WILLIAM. B.A. 1491–2.

DAVISON, WILLIAM. Matric. sizar from TRINITY, 1634; B.A. 1641–2; M.A. 1661.

DAVISON, WILLIAM. Matric. pens. from MAGDALENE, Easter, 1636. S. and h. of Edmund, deceased. Adm. at the Inner Temple, Nov. 1637. Of Horncastle, Lincs.

DAVISON or DAVIDSON, WILLIAM. Matric. sizar from KING'S, Easter, 1655; B.A. 1658–9; M.A. 1662. One of these names lecturer at Berwick-on-Tweed. Buried there Dec. 18, 1672.

DAVISON, WILLIAM. Matric. pens. from TRINITY HALL, Michs. 1655. Doubtless s. of Ralph (1624), of Wynyard, Durham, Esq. Adm. at Gray's Inn, May 1, 1656. Barrister-at-law, 1666. Buried Apr. 29, 1696. Father of Ralph (1687).

DAVISON, WILLIAM. Adm. sizar (age 15) at MAGDALENE, Jan. 13, 1673–4. S. of John, of Cambridge. School, Perse. Matric. 1674; B.A. 1677–8. Ord. deacon (Norwich) Sept. 1679.

DAVISON, WILLIAM. Adm. pens. (age 16) at ST JOHN'S, May 22, 1690. S. of Timothy, gent. B. at Newcastle-on-Tyne. School, Houghton (Mr Stubbard). Matric. 1690. Adm. at Gray's Inn, Feb. 12, 1691–2. Barrister, 1700. Died Aug. 27, 1734. M.I. at Tanfield, Durham. Brother of Jonathan (1703), father of Morton (1739) and Thomas (1740). (Surtees, II. 227.)

DAVISON, ——. Adm. Fell.-Com. at KING'S, 1587–8.

DAVISON, ——. Adm. Fell.-Com. at ST CATHARINE'S, 1627.

DAW, GEORGE. Adm. sizar (age 16) at MAGDALENE, Apr. 28, 1666. S. of George, of Drayton, Somerset. School, Martock. Matric. 1670; B.A. 1670–1.

DAW, WILLIAM. Adm. pens. at CLARE, May 25, 1745. B. in London. One of these names, s. and h. of William, of the Inner Temple, adm. at the Inner Temple, 1744.

DAWANCE, ——. Fee for B.A. 1466–7.

DAWBER, JOSEPH. Adm. pens. (age 17) at MAGDALENE, May 31 or June 1, 1670. S. of William, deceased, of Kirton-in-Lindsey, Lincs. School, Kirton. Matric. 1670; B.A. 1673–4.

DAWBER, RICHARD. Matric. sizar from MAGDALENE, Easter, 1575.

DAWBNEY, ARTHUR. Matric. pens. (age 13) from PETERHOUSE, Michs. 1576. S. of Christopher, of Sharrington, Norfolk. B.A. 1579–80; M.A. 1583, as 'Danby.' Brother of the next, and of Robert (1581). (*Vis. of Norfolk.*)

DAWBNEY, CLEMENT. Adm. scholar (age 17) at CAIUS, July 3, 1581. S. of Christopher, gent. B. at Sharrington, Norfolk. School, Eye, Suffolk. Matric. pens. 1581. Adm. at the Middle Temple, Oct. 1602, as s. of Christopher, of Sharrington, Norfolk, late of New Inn. Buried at Swanton Morley, Oct. 8, 1638. (*Venn*, I. 111.)

DAUBNEY, ISAAC. Adm. sizar at EMMANUEL, Apr. 16, 1588. Matric. 1588, as Dawney.

DAWBNEY, JOHN. Matric. pens. from ST JOHN'S, Michs. 1551. Of Lincolnshire. B.A. 1554–5; M.A. 1561; B.D. 1569. Fellow of Magdalene, in 1561. Fellow of St John's, 1562. University preacher, 1566. Proctor, 1567–8. Ord. deacon (Ely) June 8; priest (Peterb.) Sept. 20, 1561.

DAWBNEY, JOHN. Matric. sizar from ST JOHN'S, Michs. 1588. B. at Scotter, Lincs., 1570. B.A. from Magdalene, 1592–3; M.A. as 'Dawbury,' 1598. Ord. priest (Salisbury). V. of Calverton, Notts. R. of Scotter, Lincs., 1605–10. Admon. (Lincoln) 1610.

DAUBNY, JOHN. Matric. sizar from MAGDALENE, Easter, 1631; B.A. 1634–5. Perhaps R. of Brigsley, Lincs., 1642.

D'AUBENAY, RAINOR. Fellow of PEMBROKE, c. 1360. Proctor for the College at Rome (*Loder*.)

DAWBNEY, ROBERT. Matric. pens. from PETERHOUSE, Michs. 1581. Probably s. of Christopher, of Sharrington, Norfolk. Brother of Arthur (1576) and Clement (1581).

DAWBUZ, *see* DAUBUZ.

DAWES, ABRAHAM. Matric. sizar from MAGDALENE, Easter, 1575; B.A. 1579-80; M.A. from Trinity, 1587. Ord. priest (Colchester) Apr. 6, 1602. V. of Stutton, Suffolk, 1602-15.

DAWES, DARCY. Adm. Pell.-Com. at ST CATHARINE'S, May 4, 1720. S. of Sir William (1695), Archbishop of York. Matric. 1721; M.A. 1722. Succeeded as baronet, 1724. Died Aug. 16, 1732. Will (P.C.C.) 1734. Left a son William, with whom the title became extinct in 1741. (Burke, *Ext. Bart.*)

DAWES, DORMER. Adm. pens. at QUEENS', June 4, 1694. Of Salop. Matric. 1695; B.A. 1697-8; M.A. 1701; B.D. 1710. Fellow. Ord. deacon (Lincoln) June 29, 1701; priest, Dec. 21, 1701. V. of Sawston, Cambs., 1706-13.

DAWS, ED. Matric. pens. from MAGDALENE, Lent, 1564-5. One Edward Dawes, 'preacher and blind,' was buried at Berwick-on-Tweed, June 20, 1578. A contemporary in *Al. Oxon.*

DAWES, FRANCIS. Adm. pens. (age 17) at ST JOHN'S, June 25, 1742. S. of Thomas, of Solihull, Warws. B. there. School, Solihull (Mr Mashiler). Matric. 1742; B.A. 1745-6. Ord. deacon (Ely) June, 1747; C. of Foulmere, Cambs. R. of Elmdon, Warws., 1756-89. V. of Radford Semele, 1761-89. Died Feb. 1789. (*Scott-Mayor*, III. 529.)

DAWES, FRANCIS. Adm. pens. (age 18) at PETERHOUSE, June 12, 1750. Of Middlesex. S. of Francis. Bapt. Oct. 27, 1733, at St George's, Hanover Square. School, Charterhouse. Matric. 1751; Scholar, 1751; B.A. 1754; M.A. 1757. Fellow, 1758. Assistant Master at Charterhouse, 1754. Esquire Bedell, 1755-89. Taxor, 1770. Hanged himself in the bell ropes of the College Chapel. Buried at Little St Mary's, Cambridge, Oct. 2, 1789. Will, P.C.C. (*T. A. Walker*, 299; *Al. Carthus.*)

DAWES, JOHN. B.A. 1536-7; M.A. 1540. Probably fellow of CHRIST'S (as Davys), 1540-1. One of these names Master of Ipswich School, 1567-82. R. of Stutton, Suffolk, 1570-1602. (*Peile*, I. 22.)

DAWES, JOHN. B.A. from TRINITY, 1614-5.

DAWES, JOHN. Matric. pens. from QUEENS', Michs. 1620. Of Hampshire. B.A. 1624; M.A. 1628. Licensed to cure of Martin (? Merton), Surrey, Oct. 31, 1629.

DAWES, JOHN. Matric. Fell.-Com. from KING'S, Easter, 1659. Bapt. at Putney, Feb. 1, 1643-4. Adm. at the Middle Temple, Mar. 8, 1658-9; as s. and h. of Sir Thomas, Knt., of Roehampton, Surrey. Gentleman of the Privy Chamber. Created Bart., June 1, 1663. Buried at Putney, Dec. 5, 1671. Admon. P.C.C. Father of Robert (1686) and William (1695). (Burke, *Ext. Bart.*; *G.E.C.*)

DAWES, JOSEPH. Matric. sizar from MAGDALENE, Easter, 1571; B.A. 1574-5; M.A. 1579. Usher of Ipswich School, till 1580. V. of Wycombe, Bucks., 1592. R. of Harlington, Midds., 1599-1603. R. of Luddenham, Kent, 1604.

DAWES, LANCELOT. Adm. pens. (age 16) at ST JOHN'S, May 15, 1664. S. of William, gent., of High Barton, Westmorland. B. there. School, Kendal (Mr Jackson). Matric. 1664; B.A. 1667-8. Adm. at Gray's Inn, May 13, 1665.

DAWES, OWEN. Adm. sizar at CORPUS CHRISTI, 1578. Matric. Michs. 1579.

DAWES, RICHARD. Adm. Fell.-Com. at QUEENS', Sept. 13, 1661. Of Leicestershire.

DAWES, RICHARD. Adm. sizar (age 18) at TRINITY, May 25, 1697. S. of William, of Northants. School, Winchester. Ord. deacon (Peterb.) Sept. 25, 1698 (of 'Trinity College'); priest, Sept. 22, 1711 ('B.A.'). C. of Hazelbeach, Northants., 1698; of Maidwell; and of Kelmarsh, till his death. Buried there July 17, 1719. (H. I. Longden.)

DAWES, RICHARD. Adm. sizar at EMMANUEL, Feb. 18, 1725-6. Bapt. at Market Bosworth, June 27, 1709; as s. of Richard, maltster. School, Market Bosworth. Matric. 1726; B.A. 1729-30; M.A. 1733. Incorp. at Oxford, 1735-49. Fellow, 1731. Master of Newcastle-on-Tyne Grammar School, 1738. Master of St Mary's Hospital, Newcastle, 1738-49. Retired from Newcastle school 1749, to Heworth, where he died Mar. 21, 1766, aged 57. M.I. Great Greek Scholar. Author, *Miscellanea critica*. (*D.N.B.*; Surtees' *Durham*, II. 70; H. M. Wood.)

DAWES, ROBERT. Adm. as nobleman at ST CATHARINE'S, June 22, 1686. S. of Sir John (1659). LL.D. 1690 (*Com. Reg.*). Adm. at the Middle Temple, Feb. 27, 1688-9. Succeeded as 2nd Bart., 1671. Died at Cambridge, 1690. Admon., P.C.C. Brother of William (1695). (Burke, *Ext. Bart.*; *G.E.C.*)

DAWES or DAWSON, THOMAS. B.A. 1508-9.

DAWES, THOMAS. Adm. sizar at QUEENS', Mar. 26, 1668. Of Salop. Matric. 1668; B.A. 1671-2; M.A. 1675; B.D. 1684. Incorp. at Oxford, 1678. R. of Eaton Constantine, Salop, 1673. V. of St Mary's, Shrewsbury, 1679-1715. Died Jan. 10, 1714-5, aged 63.

DAWS, WILLIAM. B.A. 1496-7.

DAWES or DAVYS, WILLIAM. M.Gram. 1506-7.

DAWES, WILLIAM. B.Civ.L. 1532-3. V. of All Hallows, Barking, 1542-65. R. of All Saints, Maldon, Essex, 1551-61. R. of Rivenhall, 1560-5. Died 1565. Will (P.C.C.) 1565.

DAWES, WILLIAM. Adm. pens. at EMMANUEL, July 7, 1591.

DAWES, WILLIAM. M.D. July, 1682 (*Lit. Reg.*). 'Student in one of our Universities.' Probably matric. from All Souls' College, Oxford, 1672. Studied at Leyden; admitted there, July 12, 1680. M.D. 1680, age 25. Candidate R.C.P. 1683. Fellow, 1685. Censor. Elect. Consiliarius. President, 1712-6. Retired and resided in Guernsey. Died Mar. 9, 1733. (*Munk*, I. 437.)

DAWES, WILLIAM. M.A. from ST CATHARINE'S, 1695. S. of Sir John (1659), of Booking, Essex, Bart. B. Sept. 12, 1671. School, Merchant Taylors'. Matric. from St John's, Oxford, July 1, 1687, age 15. Migrated to St Catharine's, 1689. D.D. 1696 (*Lit. Reg.*). Master of St Catharine's, 1697-1714. Vice-Chancellor, 1698-9. Succeeded as Bart., 1690. Chaplain to William III, 1697; and to Queen Anne. Preb. of Worcester, 1698-1708. R. and Dean of Bocking, Essex, 1699. Bishop of Chester, 1708-14. Archbishop of York, 1714-24. Married Frances, dau. of Sir Thomas d'Arcy, of Braxted Lodge, Knt. Died Apr. 30, 1724. Buried in St Catharine's Chapel. M.I. there. Father of Darcy (1720), brother of Robert (1686). (*Al. Oxon.*; *D.N.B.*)

DAWES, WILLIAM. Adm. sizar (age 18) at SIDNEY, Apr. 2, 1703. S. of Thomas, Sheriff of Kildare, Ireland. B. in London. School, Merchant Taylors'. Matric. 1703; B.A. 1706-7; M.A. 1714. Ord. deacon (Peterb.) Feb. 29, 1707-8; priest, Mar. 15, 1711-2. C. of Furthoe, Northants., 1708. One of these names, of Shalford, Essex, clerk. Will (Comm. C. Essex) 1752. (J. Ch. Smith.)

DAWES, ——. Adm. at CORPUS CHRISTI, 1576.

DAWES, WILLIAM. Adm. sizar at ST CATHARINE'S, Mar. 13, 1715-6. Of London. Matric. 1716; B.A. 1719-20. Ord. priest (London) Dec. 20, 1724.

DAWES, ——. Adm. at CORPUS CHRISTI, 1580.

DAWGHS or DAUGES, JOSEPH. Adm. pens. at QUEENS', June 5, 1654. Of Essex. Matric. 1657; B.A. 1657-8; M.A. 1661. Ord. priest (Ely) Sept. 19, 1662. Probably R. of Little Bardfield, Essex, 1665. Died 1666.

DAWGHS or DAWG, ROBERT. Adm. pens. at QUEENS', 1651. Of Essex. S. and h. of Robert, of Loughton, Essex, Esq. Matric. Lent, 1653-4; B.A. 1655-6. Adm. at Lincoln's Inn, Oct. 29, 1655.

DAWKES, THOMAS. Student of PEMBROKE. B. at Southwell, Notts. Ord. deacon (London) Jan. 24, 1559-60, age 23.

DAWKYN, EDMUND. Matric. sizar from ST JOHN'S, Easter, 1584.

DAWKYN, JEREMY. Adm. sizar (age 16) at ST JOHN'S, Oct. 16, 1690. S. of Jeremy, gent. B. at Ynysawdre, Glamorganshire. School, Swansea (Mr Davys). Matric. 1691.

DAWKINS, GEORGE. Adm. pens. (age 18) at ST JOHN'S, June 26, 1673. S. of Rowland, of Swansea, Glamorgan. B. there. School, Swansea (Mr Davys). Matric. 1673; B.A. 1676-7; M.A. 1680; B.D. 1688. Fellow, 1680-1717; ejected as non-juror.

DAWKINS, WILLIAM. Adm. sizar (age 17) at CHRIST'S, June 23, 1669. S. of Jenkins, of Co. Carmarthen. B. at Llangadock. School, 'Boxrood' (? Broxted). Matric. from Christ's, 1669. Migrated to St John's, Oct. 25, 1669. M.B. from St John's, 1674; M.D. 1679. Candidate R.C.P. 1679. Fellow, 1682. Gulstonian lecturer, 1684. Censor. Died in great poverty, Jan. 1690-1. Buried at St Catherine Cree, London. Son-in-law of Jehu Smith, M.D., who died in 1679. (*Munk*, I. 422; *Peile*, II. 24; J. Ch. Smith.)

DAWLING, JOHN. B.A. 1537-8; M.A. 1541. Fellow of ST JOHN'S, 1538.

DAULING, JOHN. Adm. at CORPUS CHRISTI, 1661. Of Kent. Matric. 1661; B.A. 1665-6; M.A. 1669. Signs for deacon's orders (London) Sept. 19, 1668; for priest's, May 25, 1670. R. of Ringwould, Kent, 1679-1727. R. of Alkham, till 1727. Died 1727. One of these names, of Westerham, Kent; adm. at the Inner Temple, 1662. (H. G. Harrison.)

DAWLINGE or DAULINGE, JOHN. Adm. pens. at EMMANUEL, June 14, 1688. Of Kent. Doubtless s. of the above. Matric. 1688; B.A. 1691-2; M.A. 1695. Ord. priest (London) July 21, 1695. V. of Ewell and Alkham, Kent, succeeding his father. Father of the next.

DAWLING, JOHN. Adm. pens. at Emmanuel, Mar. 12, 1734-5. Afterwards Fell.-Com. Of Kent. Doubtless s. and h. of John above, clerk, of Alkham. Adm. at the Middle Temple, Nov. 1734.

DAWLING or DAWLYN, RICHARD. Adm. pens. (age 17) at Christ's, Feb. 11, 1631-2. S. of Richard, mercer. Bapt. at Westerham, Kent, June 22, 1615. School, Westerham (Mr Walter). Matric. 1632; B.A. 1635-6; M.A. 1639. R. of Frinsted, Kent, 1645. R. and patron of Ringwould, Kent, till his death, 1679. Perhaps father of John (1661). (*Peile*, I. 416.)

DAWNET or DAWNYLL, ——. A friar. D.D. 1485-6. Perhaps Danet, chaplain to the King. (*See Gr. Bk*, A, 138.)

DAWNEY, CHRISTOPHER. Adm. pens. at Trinity, Oct. 6, 1637. Probably s. and h. of John, late of Womersley, Yorks., Esq. B. *c.* 1620. Matric. 1637. Adm. at Gray's Inn, Nov. 2, 1639. Succeeded to his grandfather's estates at Sessay and Cowick, Yorks., 1642. Created Bart., May 19, 1642. Died July 13, 1644. Buried at Sessay. Brother of Thomas (1634) and John (1641). (*G.E.C.*)

DAWNEY, EDWARD. Adm. pens. (age 17) at Caius, May 14, 1634. S. of Thomas (1603-4), R. of Salthouse, Norfolk. B. there. School, Salthouse (Mr Woodmansey). Matric. 1634; Scholar, 1635-9; B.A. 1637-8; M.A. 1641. Ord. priest (Norwich) Sept. 20, 1640. R. of Salthouse, Norfolk, 1643. Will proved (Norwich) 1676-7. Father of John (1667-8), brother of John (1638). (*Venn*, I. 312.)

DAWNAY, GEORGE. Adm. Fell.-Com. at St John's, Mar. 14, 1670-1. S. of Sir John (1641), Knt., of Cowick, Yorks. Bapt. at Snaith, Sept. 14, 1654. School, Cheam, Surrey (Mr Aldridge). Deputy Lieutenant, East Riding, 1687-8. Buried at Snaith, Feb. 21, 1691-2. (*Vis. of Yorks.*, 1666.)

DAWNEY, JOHN. Adm. pens. (age 18) at Caius, Nov. 8, 1638. S. of Thomas (1603-4), R. of Salthouse, Norfolk. B. there. School, Holt (Mr Tallis). Matric. 1639. Brother of Edward (1634).

DAWNEY, JOHN. Adm. pens. at Jesus, May 17, 1641. 2nd s. of John, of Cowick, Yorks., deceased. Bapt. at Hooton Pagnel, Jan. 25, 1624-5. Matric. 1641. Adm. at Gray's Inn, Mar. 16, 1640-1. Knighted, June 2, 1660. M.P. for Yorks., 1660; for Pontefract, 1661-87, 1689. Created Viscount Downe, Feb. 19, 1680-1. Sat in the Irish Parliament of James II, in 1689. Died Oct. 1, 1695. Buried at Snaith. Brother of Christopher (1637) and Thomas (1634), father of George (1670). (*G.E.C.*; A. Gray.)

DAWNEY, JOHN. Adm. sizar at Tainity, July 21, 1647. Of Radnorshire.

DAWNEY, JOHN. Adm. pens. (age 16) at Caius, Mar. 17, 1667-8. S. of Edward (1634), R. of Salthouse, Norfolk. B. there. Schools, Holt (Mr Mazey) and Norwich. Matric. 1668; Scholar, 1668-75; B.A. 1671-2; M.A. 1675. Ord. deacon (Norwich) Aug. 1675; priest (Ely) Oct. 3, 1675. R. of Roydon, Norfolk, 1675-1704; of Caston, 1691-1704. (*Venn*, I. 433.)

DAWNAY, JOHN. Adm. pens. at Queens', Jan. 12, 1690-1. Of Yorkshire. S. and h. of Thomas, late of Selby, Yorks., Esq. Bapt. there, Mar. 18, 1674. Adm. at Gray's Inn, Feb. 11, 1690-1. Perhaps M.P. for Aldborough, Yorks., 1713-15.

DAWNEY, JOHN. Adm. pens. (age 17) at Caius, *c.* Apr. 1724. S. of John, gent., of Roydon, Norfolk. B. there. Schools, Botesdale (Mr Mabourne) and Norwich (Mr Reddington). Matric. 1724; Scholar, 1724-30; B.A. 1727-8; M.A. 1731. Fellow, 1730-53. Proctor, 1746. Ord. deacon (Lincoln) Mar. 24, 1730; priest (Norwich) June 4, 1732. R. of Long Stratton, Norfolk, and St Clement's, Norwich, 1753-66. Died July 7, 1766. (*Venn*, II. 20.)

DAWNEY, THOMAS. Adm. sizar (age 16) at Caius, Mar. 23, 1603-4. S. of John, of Little Walsingham, Norfolk. Bapt. Oct. 6, 1588. School, Holt (Mr Gillott). B.A. 1607-8; M.A. 1611. Ord. priest (Lincoln) Mar. 12, 1608-9. R. of Salthouse, 1613-42. Will proved (Norwich) 1642. Father of Edward (1634) and John (1638).

DAWNEY, THOMAS. Adm. sizar at Jesus, Oct. 20, 1626. Of Lancashire. Matric. 1626, as Dawning; B.A. 1631-2.

DAWNEY, THOMAS. Adm. Fell.-Com. (age 17) at Sidney, Apr. 19, 1634. S. of John, Esq. B. at Cowick, Yorks. Bapt. at Snaith, Dec. 15, 1616. Schools, Wakefield and York. Matric. 1634. Adm. at Gray's Inn, Nov. 1, 1634. Buried at Snaith, Apr. 19, 1639. Brother of Christopher (1637) and John (1641). (*Vis. of Yorks.*, 1666; *Surtees Society*, XXXVI. 101.)

DAWNYE, ——. B.A. 1455-6.

DAWNY, ——. Matric. from Trinity, *c.* 1590.

DAWNSER or DAUSER, ANTHONY. Matric. pens. from King's, 1592-3.

DAWNSER, JOHN. Matric. pens. from Kino's, 1592-3.

DAWNSER, JOHN. Adm. at King's, a scholar from Eton, 1563. Matric. 1563; B.A. 1567-8; M.A. 1571. Fellow till 1578. Held a lease of College lands at Halstead, Essex.

DAWNCER, RICHARD. Matric. sizar from Trinity, *c.* 1592; B.A. 1594-5; M.A. 1598.

DAWNSER, ROBERT. Adm. at King's, a scholar from Eton, 1557. Matric. 1557-8. Died 1559.

DAWSON, ABRAHAM. Matric. sizar from Magdalene, Michs. 1639; B.A. 1642-3. Perhaps V. of Stannington, Yorks., 1689-96.

DAWSON, ALEXANDER. B.Civ.L. 1494-5.

DAWSON, ALEXANDER. Matric. pens. from Trinitty, Lent, 1588-9; Scholar, 1590; B.A. 1593-4; M.A. 1597.

DAWSON, AMBROSE. Adm. pens. at Christ's, July 4, 1724. S. of William (1691-2), of Langcliff Hall, Settle, Yorks. B. there. School, Giggleswick (Mr Carr). Matric. 1724; Scholar, 1725; M.B. 1730; M.D. 1735. F.R.C.P. 1737. Censor. Physician to St George's Hospital, 1745. Retired to his estate of Langcliff Hall, 1776. Author. Died at Liverpool, Dec. 23, 1794, aged 88. Buried at Bolton in Craven, Yorks. M.I. Will (P.C.C.) 1795. (*D.N.B.*; *Peile*, II. 209; M. H. Peacock.)

DAWSON, ANTHONY. Adm. pens. (age 19) at St John's, Nov. 21, 1748. S. of Anthony, attorney-at-law, of Yorkshire. B. at Azerley, near Ripon. School, Coxwold (Mr Midgeley). Matric. 1748. Adm. at Lincoln's Inn, Feb. 17, 1748-9. Barrister, 1762.

DAWSON, BENJAMIN. Adm. sizar at Clare, Apr. 14, 1720. B. at Wakefield, Yorks. School, Wakefield. Matrio. 1720; Scholar; B.A. 1723-4; M.A. 1727. Fellow, 1724-38. Received testimonial for deacon's orders, Dec. 10, 1724, by Bishop of Gloucester. R. of Fornham All Saints, Suffolk, 1738-45. R. of Burgh. Died 1745.

DAWSON, CHARLES. Adm. sizar at Clare, Oct. 2, 1634. S. of Charles, of Cambridge, bookbinder. School, Perse. Matric. 1634-5. Migrated to Cains, Feb. 21, 1641-2, age 25. B.A. 1641-2.

DAWSON, CHRISTOPHER. Adm. pens. (age 16) at Christ's, Mar. 31, 1663. S. of Josias. B. at Langcliff, Yorks. School, Giggleswick. Matric. 1663. Of Langcliff. Married Margaret, dau. of Sir Thomas Craven. M.I. in Giggleswick Church, dated 1695. Father of William (1691). (*Peile*, I. 601; *Yorks. Bibliographer*, I. 166.)

DAWSON, DAVID. Adm. sizar (age 17) at Sr John's, July 1, 1703. S. of David, husbandman. B. at Allerthorpe, Yorks. School, Sherburn (Mr Baines). Matric. 1703; B.A. 1706-7. Ord. deacon (York) May, 1708; priest, 1709. R. of Didsbury, Lancs., 1709. V. of Aberford, Yorks., 1716-33. Died 1733.

DAWSON, EDWARD. Adm. pens. at Sidney, June 18, 1613. Matric. 1613; B.A. 1616-7; M.A. 1620. Incorp. at Oxford, 1620. Licensed to practise physic, 1621. M.B. and M.D. (Oxford) 1633. F.R.C.P. 1634. Died Dec. 16, 1635. (*Munk*, I. 218.)

DAWSON, EDWARD. Adm. sizar at Corpus Christi, 1655. Of Nottinghamshire. Matric. 1655; B.A. 1658-9.

DAWSON, EDWARD COOKE. Adm. Fell.-Com. at Sr Catuarine's, Feb. 21, 1727. S. of James, of Kendal, Westmorland, gent. Matric. 1727, from Queen's College, Oxford; admitted there, Feb. 20, 1721-2, age 18; M.B. (Cambridge) 1727. Adm. at Lincoln's Inn, July 15, 1721.

DAWSON, GABRIEL. Adm. sizar (age 18) at Sr John's, May 8, 1683. S. of James, shoemaker. B. at Kendal, Westmorland. School, Sedbergh. Matric. 1683. C. of Pilling, Lancs., 1689. Died, 1692. Admon. (Archd. Richmond) 1692. (*Sedbergh Sch. Reg.*, 131.)

DAWSON, GEORGE. Adm. sizar (age 18) at St John's, Apr. 16, 1655. S. of William, of Lotherton, near Tadcaster, Yorks., yeoman. School, Sherburn (Mr Clarke). Matric. 1655, as 'Pawson'; B.A. 1658-9; M.A. 1662. Incorp. at Oxford, 1669. V. of Sunninghill, Berks., 1664-1700. Author, *Origo Legum*. Buried at Sunninghill, Oct. 5, 1700. Father of the next, Robert (1695) and Thomas (1692). (*D.N.B.*; Ashmole, *Berks.*)

DAWSON, GEORGE. Adm. sizar (age 17) at St John's, July 3, 1697. S. of George (above). B. at Sunninghill, Berks. School, Eton. Matric. 1697; B.A. 1700-1; M.A. 1704. Ord. deacon (London) Mar. 12, 1703-4; priest, Feb. 17, 1705-6. Minister of Cowshete, near Woking for 50 years. Died there 1755, aged 76. M.I. Brother of Robert (1695) and Thomas (1692). (*Manning and Bray*, I. 151.) (For another of these names *see Al. Oxon.*)

DAWSON, GEORGE. Matric. sizar from Christ's, Michs. 1735; Scholar, 1735; B.A. 1739-40. Ord. deacon (Lincoln) Mar. 2, 1739-40; priest, May 29, 1743. V. of Rushden, Herts., 1750-70. Died 1770. (*Peile*, II. 232.)

DAWSON, GILBERT. Matric. pens. from ST JOHN'S, Michs. 1616. Probably s. of Robert, of Ripon. B.A. 1620–1. Adm. at the Inner Temple, Nov. 1620.

DAWSON, GODFREY. Matric. sizar from TRINITY, Easter, 1568; B.A. 1571–2.

DAWSON, HENRY. Matric. pens. from CLARE, Lent, 1580–1.

DAWSON, HENRY. Adm. pens. at JESUS, June 13, 1710. Of Suffolk. Matric. 1710–1; Scholar, 1712; LL.B. 1715; LL.D. 1720. Fellow, 1717–37. Will (P.C.C.) 1755; of Groton, Suffolk.

DAWSON, HUTTON. Matric. pens. from ST JOHN'S, Michs. 1624; B.A. 1628–9; M.A. 1632. R. of Sowton, Devon, 1635; sequestered, *c.* 1646.

DAWSON, JAMES. Adm. pens. (age 20) at ST JOHN'S, Oct. 21, 1737. S. of William, apothecary, of Lancashire. B. in Manchester. School, Salford (Mr Clayton). Matric. 1737. Adm. at Lincoln's Inn, Jan. 23, 1733–4. Joined the Pretender's forces, becoming a captain in the 'Manchester Regiment.' Taken prisoner at Carlisle, Dec. 30, 1745. Executed on Kennington Common, July 30, 1746. (*Scott-Mayor*, III. 488; *D.N.B.*)

DAWSON, JOHN. B.Civ.L. 1483–4; D.Can.L. 1489–90. Perhaps R. of Debden, Essex, 1484–92. Died 1492. Will (P.C.C.) 1492; of St Michael's, Cambridge.

DAWSON, JOHN. Matric. sizar from PEMBROKE, Michs. 1554. One of these names, s. of Henry, of Loughborough, Leics. Bapt. May 13, 1540. Clerk. Master of Loughborough School. Buried Feb. 24, 1615. (Llew. Jewitt, *The Reliquary*, XVII. 127.)

DAWSON, JOHN. Matric. sizar from ST JOHN'S, Easter, 1617; B.A. 1620–1; M.A. 1624.

DAWSON, JOHN. Adm. at CORPUS CHRISTI, 1625. Of Norfolk. B.A. 1629–30; M.A. 1633.

DAWSON, JOHN. Adm. Fell.-Com. (age 16) at SIDNEY, Jan. 25, 1633–4, from Trinity. S. of George, Esq. B. at Ripon. School, Ripon (Mr Ri. Palmes.)

DAWSON, JOHN. Admopens. (age 16) at ST JOHN'S, Sept. 18, 1639. S. and h. of J hn, gent., of Swaby, Lincs., deceased. B. there. School, Sleaford (Mr Trevilion). Matric. 1637. Adm. at the Inner Temple, Nov. 1641.

DAWSON, JOHN. Adm. pens. at JESUS, June 30, 1662. Of Suffolk. Matric. 1662; Scholar, 1664; B.A. 1665–6; 'M.A. of a Dutch University.' P.C. of Blackley, Lancs., 1669–71. Perhaps V. of Chediston, Suffolk. Buried there Sept. 4, 1684. (A. Gray.)

DAWSON, JOHN. Adm. pens. (age 16) at PEMBROKE, June 25, 1679. S. of John, gent. (? apothecary at Framlingham; died 1687). B. at Framlingham, Suffolk. Matric. 1679.

DAWSON, JOHN. Adm. sizar (age 17) at CHRIST'S, July 7, 1693. S. of Thomas. B. in Cambridge. Matric. 1693; Scholar, 1694–5; B.A. 1696–7. Ord. deacon (London) Sept. 25, 1698.

DAWSON, JOHN. Adm. pens. at EMMANUEL, Jan. 25, 1724–5. B. in Kent, 1706. Matric. 1724–5; B.A. 1728–9. Ord. deacon (Ely) Dec. 21, 1729. Will of one of these names (P.C.C.) 1767; of Burton-on-Trent, clerk.

DAWSON, O N. Adm. sizar (age 18) at ST JOHN'S, June 16, 1738. SJ of John, of Lancashire. B. in Rochdale. School, Rochdale. Matric. 1738; B.A. 1741–2. Ord. priest (Rochester) Sept. 23, 1744. Perhaps V. of Selling, Kent, 1761–2. Died 1762. (*Scott-Mayor*, III. 494; *G. Mag.*)

DAWSON, JOSEPH. Adm. pens. (age 16) at ST JOHN'S, Apr. 26, 1653. S. of Abraham, clothier, of Leeds, Yorks. Bapt. there, July 5, 1636. School, Bradford. Matric. 1653. Previously matric. from University College, Oxford, May 29, 1652. B.A. (Cambridge) 1656–7. Ejected from Thornton Chapel, Yorks., 1662. Minister at Morley, Leeds, 1688. Died June 26, 1709. Buried at Morley. (*Calamy*, II. 577; *F.M.G.*, 97; *Al. Oxon.*)

DAWSON ('DORSON'), JOSIAS. Adm. pens. at CHRIST'S, Mar. 12, 1689–90. Doubtless s. of Christopher (1663), of Langcliff, Yorks. Died, aged 16, before coming into residence. Brother of William (1691–2).

DAWSON, JOSIAS. Adm. pens. (age 18) at CHRIST'S, Feb. 23, 1711–2. S. of William. B. at Halton Gill, Yorks. School, Giggleswick (Mr Armitstead). Matric. 1712; Scholar, 1713; B.A. 1715–6; M.A. 1719. Ord. deacon (Carlisle) Dec. 1717; priest (London) Mar. 1719–20. V. of Giggles , 1719–30. Died 1730. Father of William (1741). (*Peile*wick 178.)

DAWSON, JOSIAS. Adm. pens. at CHRIST'S, Nov. 10, 1729. S. of Josias (? V. of Giggleswick). B. at Halton Gill, near Settle. , Giggleswick (Mr Carr). Matric. 1729. (*Peile*, II. 220.)School

DAWSONE, LAMBERT. Matric. sizar from TRINITY, Michs. 1566. Probably master of Kirkby Ravensworth School, Yorks., in 1593. (M. H. Peacock.)

DAWSON, LANCELOT. Matric. pens. from ST JOHN'S, Michs. 1567; B.A. from St Catharine's, 1573–4; M.A. 1577. V. of Aspatria, Cumberland, 1578–1610. Died 1610.

DAWSON, LAURENCE. Matric. sizar from TRINITY, Easter, 1617; Scholar, 1619; B.A. 1620–1; M.A. 1624. Ord. deacon (Lichfield) June 13, 1624. V. of Uttoxeter, 1653–8. R. of Bramshall, Staffs., 1659–74. Buried there Oct. 3, 1674. (*Wm. Salt Arch. Soc.*, 1915.)

DAWSON, MARK. Adm. sizar (age 17) at CHRIST'S, May 26, 1694. S. of Godfrey. B. at Coverham, Yorks. School, Burnsall (Mr Hey). Scholar, 1694–5; Matric. 1695; B.A. 1697–8.

DAWSON, MILES. Matric. sizar from ST JOHN'S, Michs. 1584; B.A. 1588–9. V. of Burton, Westmorland, 1599–1622. V. of Bolton-le-Sands, Lancs., 1618.

DAWSON, NICHOLAS. Matric. pens. from PEMBROKE, Michs. 1589.

DAWSON, PETER, *see* **DANSON.**

DAWSON, PHILIP (1581), *see* **DAWTON.**

DAWSON, RALPH. Matric. sizar from CLARE, Easter, 1577. Of London. B.A. from Peterhouse, 1580–1; M.A. 1584; B.D. from Corpus Christi, 1591; D.D. 1601. Fellow of Corpus Christi, 1586–97. R. of Rotherhithe ('Redriffe'), Surrey, 1594–1611. R. of St Mary Abchurch, 1597; and Master of St Lawrence Pountney, London, 1597–1611. Died 1611. Will, P.C.C.

DAWSON or DOWSON, RALPH. Matric. pens. from ST CATHARINE'S, Easter, 1648. Of Yorkshire. B.A. 1651–2; M.A. 1655. Fellow. Perhaps s. of Marmaduke, of 'Suncliffe,' Yorks., gent.; adm. at Gray's Inn, Mar. 23, 1651–2.

DAWSON, RICHARD. A priest. B.Can.L. 1519–20. Will of one of these names proved (P.C.C.) 1548. 'Of Thoresway, Lincs.'

DAWSON, RICHARD. Matric. pens. from ST JOHN'S, Easter, 1570. S. of William, D.D., of Holt, Norfolk. Schools, Reepham and Aylsham. Migrated to Caius, Oct. 26, 1571. R. of Reepham, 1574–94.

DAWSON, RICHARD. Perhaps adm. at EMMANUEL, 1599, as 'Samuel'; B.A. (? 1602–3); M.A. 1606. Ord. deacon (Peterb.) Sept. 21; priest, Dec. 21, 1606. V. of Pinchbeck, Lincs., 1609–18. Will, Lincoln.

DAUSON, RICHARD. Adm. sizar at JESUS, June 10, 1630. Of Leicestershire. Matric. 1631; Scholar, 1633; B.A. 1633–4; M.A. 1637. Perhaps R. of Congerstone, Leics., 1641. Will (P.C.C.) 1652. (Nichols gives George Dawson as R. of Congerstone, 1640; sequestered.)

DAWSON, ROBERT. Matric. sizar from PEMBROKE, Easter, 1544. One of these names, V. of Roxby, Lincs., was ord. priest (Lincoln) July 27, 1560; 'bred in the schools.' (*Lib. Cler. Linc.*)

DAWSON, ROBERT. B.A. from ST JOHN'S, 1608–9. B. at Kendal, Westmorland, 1589. School, Sedbergh. M.A. 1612; B.D. 1620. Fellow, 1609. Ord. deacon (Peterb.) Sept. 24; priest, Sept. 25, 1615. Chaplain to Lord Deputy of Ireland. Dean of Dromore, 1623–7; of Down, 1623–7. Precentor of Connor, 1623–8. Preb. of Lismore, 1624–6; of Dublin, 1627–30; of Clonfert, 1630–43. Bishop of Clonfert, 1627–43. During the Rebellion retired to England. Author. Died at Kendal, Westmorland, Apr. 13, 1643. Father of Robert (1635). (Cotton, *Fast. Hibern.*)

DAWSON, ROBERT. Matric. pens. from ST JOHN'S, Michs. 1616; B.A. 1620–1.

DAWSON, ROBERT. Matric. sizar from MAGDALENE, Lent, 1620–1; B.A. 1623–4. Ord. deacon (Peterb.) Feb. 22, 1623–4; priest, May 23, 1624. Admon. 1644 (Lincoln) of one of these names; of Upper Toynton, Lincs., clerk.

DAWSON, ROBERT. Adm. pens. (age 13) at CHRIST'S, Apr. 14, 1631. S. of Robert. B. at Hertford. School, Hertford (Mr Minors). Matric. 1631; B.A. 1634–5. Died Feb. 6, 1636–7. (*Cussans*; *Chauncy* gives a different date; *Peile*, I. 408; for a contemporary see *Al. Oxon.*)

DAWSON, ROBERT. Adm. pens. (age 14) at ST JOHN'S, Sept. 10, 1635. S. of Robert (1608–9), Bishop of Clonfert. B. at 'Alderbourne Bottom,' near Uxbridge, Bucks. School, Sedbergh. Matric. 1635; B.A. 1639–40.

DAWSON, ROBERT. Adm. sizar (age 17) at ST JOHN'S, Apr. 5, 1695. S. of George (1655), clerk. B. at Sunninghill, Berks. School, Shipton (Mr Hodson). Matric. 1693; B.A. 1698–9; M.A. 1702. Ord. deacon (York) May, 1700; priest, 1701–2. Brother of George (1697) and Thomas (1692).

DAWSON, THOMAS (1508–9), *see* **DAWES.**

DAWSON, THOMAS. Matric. pens. from PETERHOUSE, Michs. 1575; B.A. from Christ's, 1579–80; M.A. 1583. Ord. priest (Peterb.) Apr. 8, 1584. C. of Kimbolton, Hunts., 1585. R. of Swineshead, 1594–1639. Perhaps R. of Tilbrook, Beds., 1616–9. Buried Dec. 2, 1639.

DAWSON, THOMAS. Matric. sizar from ST JOHN'S, c. 1594. One of these names R. of Misterton, Leics., 1599.

DAWSON, THOMAS. Adm. sizar at CORPUS CHRISTI, 1607. Of Lincolnshire. Matric. 1607; B.A. 1611-2.

DAWSON, THOMAS. B.A. from ST JOHN'S, 1628-9.

DAWSON, THOMAS. Adm. pens. at JESUS, Apr. 6, 1659. Of Hertfordshire. Matric. 1660; Scholar, 1661; M.B. 1664; M.D. 1669. Adm. candidate R.C.P. Dec. 22, 1679. Died 1682. Buried in St Alphage, Cripplegate. Will, P.C.C. (*Munk*, I. 402.)

DAWSON, THOMAS. Adm. sizar (age 18) at ST JOHN'S, June 28, 1672. S. of John, yeoman, of Farndon, Cheshire. B. there. School, Wrexham. Matric. 1672; B.A. 1675-6.

DAWSON, THOMAS. Adm. sizar (age 16) at ST JOHN'S, July 27, 1692. S. of George (1655) clerk. B. at Sunninghill, Berks. Matric. 1693; B.A. 1696-7; M.A. 1700; D.D. 1714. Fellow, 1698-1704. Incorp. at Oxford, 1699. Ord. deacon (Lincoln) June 4, 1699; priest (Winchester) Dec. 22, 1700. V. of New Windsor, Berks., 1703. V. of Wexham, Bucks., 1708-40. Prisoner in the Fleet for some years. Died 1740. Brother of George (1697) and Robert (1695). (J. Ch. Smith.)

DAWSON, THOMAS. Adm. sizar (age 18) at ST JOHN'S, Aug. 18, 1714. S. of Thomas, husbandman. B. at Blencow, Cumberland. School, Sedbergh. Matric. 1714.

DAWSON, THOMAS. Adm. pens. (age 20) at SIDNEY, June 18, 1719. S. of Thomas. B. at Hull. Schools, Sutton, Yorks., and Wakefield. Matric. 1719; B.A. 1722-3. Ord. deacon (Lincoln) June 9, 1723; priest, Sept. 20, 1724.

DAWSON, WILLIAM. B.Civ.L. 1520-1.

DAWSON, WILLIAM. B.A. 1541-2; M.A. 1545. Fellow of PETERHOUSE, 1543-55. Bursar, 1545-7.

DAWSON, WILLIAM. Matric. sizar from CHRIST'S, Nov. 1554. Perhaps R. of Town Barningham, Norfolk, 1561-70; and of Hackford, 1563-83; also of mediety of Reepham, 1563-74. (*Peile*, I. 59.)

DAWSON, WILLIAM. Matric. pens. from PETERHOUSE, Michs. 1559; B.A. 1565-6; M.A. from TRINITY, 1569. Ord. priest (Ely) Sept. 21, 1567.

DAWSON, WILLIAM. Matric. sizar from JESUS, Michs. 1584; B.A. 1587-8. One of these names V. of Dunholme, Lincs., 1592. One V. of Whitwell, Norfolk, 1601.

DAWSON, WILLIAM. Matric. sizar from QUEENS', Easter, 1605. Of Cumberland. B.A. 1608-9; M.A. 1612.

DAWSON, WILLIAM. Adm. pens. at CORPUS CHRISTI, 1626. Of Peterborough. Matric. 1627; B.A. 1630-1; M.A. 1634. Probably R. of St Michael-at-Plea, Norwich, 1638-41. Died Oct. 24, 1641, aged 31. M.I. (*Masters*.)

DAWSON, WILLIAM. Adm. sizar (age 16) at CAIUS, Feb. 21, 1630-1. S. of Ephraim, linen draper, of Aylsham, Norfolk. School, Aylsham. Matric. 1631; B.A. 1634-5; M.A. 1638. Ord. deacon (Norwich) May 24, 1635. The R. of St Michael-at-Plea, Norwich, 1638-41, was probably the above. (*Venn*, I. 296.)

DAWSON, WILLIAM. Adm. sizar (age 18) at ST JOHN'S, May 24, 1667. S. of William, deceased, of Sherburn, Yorks. B. there. School, Sherburn. Matric. 1668; B.A. 1670-1; M.A. 1674. Ord. deacon (York) Dec. 1672; priest, Sept. 21, 1673.

DAWSON, WILLIAM. Adm. sizar (age 18) at ST JOHN'S, Apr. 5, 1671. S. of Edmund, of Dent, Yorks. B. there. School, Dent. Matric. 1671, as 'Fawson'; B.A. 1674-5; M.A. 1679. Probably ord. priest (Chichester) Sept. 27, 1678. R. of Kingston-Bowley, Sussex, 1679. Buried there May 30, 1700. (W. C. Harrison.)

DAWSON, WILLIAM. Adm. pens. (age 16) at JESUS, Apr. 1, 1674. Of Suffolk. Matric. 1674; Scholar, 1676; B.A. 1677-8; M.A. 1681.

DAWSON, WILLIAM. Adm. pens. (age 15) at CHRIST'S, Jan. 28, 1691-2. S. of Christopher (1663). B. at Langcliffe, Yorks. School, Giggleswick (Mr Armitstead). Matric. 1692; B.A. 1695-6. Adm. at Gray's Inn, Oct. 25, 1693. J.P. and Major in the Yorks. militia. An able mathematician and classical scholar. A friend of Sir Isaac Newton. Married Jane, dau. of Ambrose Pudsay, 1705. Of Langcliffe. Died June 25, 1762. Father of Ambrose (1724). (*Peile*, II. 123.)

DAWSON, WILLIAM. Adm. pens. at JESUS, June 27, 1737. Of York city. Matric. 1737; Scholar, 1737; LL.B. 1744. Ord. deacon (Lincoln) May 24, 1741; priest (York) 1743.

DAWSON, WILLIAM. Adm. pens. at PETERHOUSE, Apr. 4, 1737. Of Middlesex. Matric. 1737; Scholar, 1737; B.A. 1740-1; M.A. 1744. Fellow, 1741-6. Ord. deacon (Lincoln) Sept. 20, 1741; priest, Dec. 19, 1742. Perhaps V. of Ainderby Steeple, Yorks., 1743-48. (*T. A. Walker*.)

DAWSON, WILLIAM. Adm. sizar at CHRIST'S, Dec. 5, 1741. S. of Josias (1711-2), V. of Giggleswick, Yorks. B. there. School, Giggleswick (Mr Carr). Matric. 1742; M.B. 1747.

DAWSON, ——. B.A. 1495-6.

DAWSON, ——. B.Civ.L. 1502-3.

DAWSOR, ARNOLD. Matric. pens. from ST JOHN'S, Easter, 1559.

DAWTON, GEORGE. Matric. pens. from TRINITY, Michs. 1581.

DAWTON, PHILIP. Matric. pens. from TRINITY, Michs. 1581. Perhaps ord. deacon and priest (Peterb.) Nov. 13, 1590, as Philip Dawson, M.A., of Trinity.

DAWTREY, EDWARD. Adm. at ST CATHARINE'S, 1638. Of Suffolk; probably of Ipswich.

DAWTRY or DAWTEY, NICHOLAS. M.Gram. 1525-6.

DAWTREY, RICHARD. Matric. pens. from QUEENS', Easter, 1571. S. of George, of St Michael Queenhithe, London, painter. B.A. 1574-5; M.A. from Peterhouse, 1578. Exhibitioner from Christ's Hospital. Age 11, when admitted there, May 22, 1563. (*A. W. Lockhart*.)

DAWTRYE, W. B.Can.L. 1466-7. Perhaps William Dawtre, R. of Kirkheaton, Yorks., 1479-1511. Died 1511.

DAWTRY, WILLIAM. Adm. Fell.-Com. (age 18) at PETERHOUSE, Apr. 16, 1697. S. of Thomas, High Sheriff of Essex. School, Felsted, Essex. Matric. 1699. Sheriff of Essex, 1736. Of the Moor, Petworth, Sussex, and also of Doddinghurst Place, Essex. Died 1758. (*T. A. Walker*, 199; Elwes, *W. Sussex*, 172.)

DAY or DEY, BARTHOLOMEW. Adm. pens. (ag 18) at CAIUS, Apr. 26, 1720. S. of John, weaver, of Norwich. B. there. School, Wymondham, Norfolk (Mr Sayer). Scholar, 1720-5; Matric. 1725; M.B. 1725. Fellow, 1730-79. In medical practice, at Wymondham, 1728. Died 1780. (*Venn*, II. 13.)

DAY, BENJAMIN. Adm. sizar at EMMANUEL, Nov. 13, 1675. Of Yorkshire.

DEY, EDMUND. Adm. at CORPUS CHRISTI, 1624. Of Norfolk. B.A. 1627-8; M.A. 1631. Ord. priest (Peterb.) May 27, 1632. V. of East Winch, Norfolk, 1633. R. of Mannington, 1633. R. of Bexwell, 1642. R. of Blickling, 1645. R. of Hingham, 1656-67.

DEY, EDMUND. Matric. pens. from PEMBROKE, Easter, 1629. Of Norfolk. B.A. 1632-3; M.A. from Peterhouse, 1636. Fellow of Peterhouse, 1635-42.

DAY, FRANCIS. Adm. sizar at JESUS, Mar. 30, 1695. S. of Francis, of Menwith Hill, Settle, Yorks. Matric. 1695; B.A. 1698-9. Ord. priest (York) Jan. 1700-1. V. of Topcliffe, Yorks., 1713. One of these names, B.A., V. of Holbeck, Yorks., 1721-8. Lecturer at Leeds parish church. Died at Topcliffe, Mar. 25, 1763, aged 87. (G. *Mag.*)

DAY, FRANCIS. Adm. sizar (age 16) at CHRIST'S, Feb. 21, 1695-6. S. of Samuel. B. at York. School, Shipton, near York (Mr Hodgson). Matric. 1696; Scholar, 1696-7; B.A. 1699-1700; M.A. 1703. (*Peile*, II. 135.)

DAY, GAMALIEL. Matric. pens. from PEMBROKE, Easter, 1613; B.A. 1616-7; M.A. 1620. Incorp. at Oxford, 1626. R. of Hampstead Marshall, Berks., 1663. Admon. (Archd. Berks.) 1671.

DAY, GEORGE. B.A. 1520-1. S. of Richard, of Newport, Salop. School, Cambridge. M.A. 1524; B.D. 1533; D.D. 1537. Fellow of ST JOHN'S, 1522. Ord. sub-deacon (Lincoln) Mar. 7, 1527-8. Chaplain to Bishop Fisher. Public orator, 1528-37. Master of St John's, 1537-8. Vice-Chancellor, 1537-8. Provost of King's, 1538-47. R. of All Hallows-the-Great, London, 1537-43. Bishop of Chichester, 1543-56 (deprived, 1551-4). Died Aug. 11, 1556. Will (P.C.C.). (*Cooper*, I. 156; *Masters*, 67; *D.N.B.*)

DAY, GEORGE. Adm. at KING'S, a scholar from Eton, 1538.

DAY, GEORGE. Matric. pens. from ST JOHN'S, Michs. 1601.

DAYE, HENRY. Matric. pens. from CLARE, Easter, 1579. Perhaps of Oxburgh, Norfolk; adm. at Gray's Inn, May 25, 1582. One Henry Day, of Norfolk, ignoble, knighted at Whitehall, July 23, 1603.

DAY or DEY, HENRY. Matric. pens. from PEMBROKE, Easter, 1631; B.A. 1633-4; M.A. 1637.

DAY, HENRY. Adm. pens. at TRINITY, June 29, 1665. Matric. 1665; Scholar, 1668; B.A. 1668-9; M.A. 1672.

DAY, HENRY. Adm. pens. (age 17) at CAIUS, Jan. 9, 1667-8. S. of Thomas, Esq., of Scoulton, Norfolk. B. there. School, Norwich. Matric. 1667-8; Scholar, 1667-74; B.A. 1670-1; M.A. 1674. Incorporated at Oxford, 1688. Ord. deacon (Norwich) Sept. 1674; priest, Nov. 1674. V. of Hunstanton, 1674-1703. Said to have been a non-juror, in 1690. Died July 21, 1703. M.I. at Hunstanton. (*Venn*, I. 432.)

DAY, HUMPHREY. Adm. sizar (age 15) at MAGDALENE, Jan. 14, 1656–7. S. of Humphrey, of Gedney, Lincs. School, Alford. Matric. 1657; B.A. 1660–1. Ord. priest (Ely) Mar. 1671–2.

DAYE, JACOBUS. M.A. 1625 (Incorp. from Franeker). 'Per 14 annos in exteris academiis studuerit, et ante quinquennium in Acad. Frankerensi (Franeker) in artibus sit renunciatus, et in Basiliensi et Parisiensi in ordinem Bacc. in art. cooptatus.' (*Grace Bk*, July 6, 1625.)

DAY, JAMES. Adm. pens. at EMMANUEL, Apr. 9, 1659. Of Kent. Scholar. Ejected, 1662. Afterwards a nonconformist minister in and about Cambridge; and at Wendon, Saffron Walden and Arkesden, Essex. (J. B. Peace; Davids, *Essex*, 607.))

DAY, JOHN. Adm. at KING'S, a scholar from Eton, 1452; B.D. 1469–70. Proctor, 1467–8. Ord. deacon (Ely) Apr. 1, 1469; priest, May 17, 1469.

DEY, JOHN, doctor. Adm. at CORPUS CHRISTI, 1469.

DAY, JOHN. B.A. 1479–80; M.A. 1484. Fellow of QUEENS', 1485–97.

DAY, JOHN. B.A. 1510–1. Abbot of the Cistercian House of Bordesley, Worcs.; surrendered, 1538. (*Cooper*, I. 68.)

DAY, JOHN. B.A. 1512–3.

DAYE, JOHN. Matric. pens. from JESUS, Michs. 1559; B.A. 1562–3; M.A. 1566; LL.D. 1576. Fellow, 1563–78. Taxor, 1568. Adm. Advocate, Jan. 22, 1581–2. Commissary to the Bishop of Norwich, 1576. R. of Gedney, Lincs., 1588. Will (P.C.C.) 1612. (*Cooper*, II. 383; A. Gray.)

DAY, JOHN. Adm. sizar (age 18) at CAIUS, Oct. 24, 1592. S. of Walter, husbandman. B. at Cawston, Norfolk. School, Ely (Mr Spight). He was expelled from the College for stealing a book, May 4, 1593. The dramatist and poet. Author of *The Parliament of Bees*, and many other works. (*D.N.B.*; *Venn*, I. 146; *Cooper*, II. 474.)

DEY, JOHN. Adm. at CORPUS CHRISTI, 1593. Of Norfolk.

DAY, JOHN. M.A. 1597 (Incorp. from Oxford). S. of John, of London, printer. Matric. from St Albans Hall, Oct. 11, 1583, age 17; B.A. 1586–7; M.A. 1591; B.D. 1611. Fellow of Oriel College, 1588–1628. V. of St Mary, Oxford, 1609–22. R. of Little Thurlow, Cambs., 1622–8. Died Jan. 10, 1627–8. Will, P.C.C. (*Al. Oxon.*; *D.N.B.*)

DEY, JOHN. B. at Sculthorpe, Norfolk. Described as 'B.A. of TRINITY College,' when Ord. deacon (London) Dec. 17, 1608, age 24; priest, June 3, 1610. C. of St Leonard's, Foster Lane, London.

DAYE, JOHN. Matric. pens. from MAGDALENE, Easter, 1613.

DAY, JOHN. Adm. sizar at EMMANUEL, June 22, 1675. Of Yorkshire. Ord. priest (York) Mar. 1681–2.

DAY, JOHN. Adm. pens. (age 18) at PEMBROKE, Mar. 26, 1702. S. of John, gent. B. at Fletching, Sussex. Matric. 1702; B.A. 1705–6.

DAY, JOHN. Adm. pens. (age 17) at MAGDALENE, July 20, 1703. S. of John. B. at Cambridge. School, Histon (private). Matric. 1704.

DAY, JOHN. Adm. pens. (age 19) at PEMBROKE, Apr. 20, 1734. S. of John, gent. B. at Arlington, Sussex. Matric. 1734; LL.B. 1742.

DEY, JOSEPH. Adm. pens. (age 15) at CAIUS, Apr. 14, 1629. S. of Robert, druggist. B. at Norwich. Matric. 1629; B.A. 1632–3; M.A. 1636; M.D. (Padua) 1642. Licentiate of Royal College of Physicians, 1645. Adm. candidate, 1646. (*Venn*, I. 288; *Vis. of Norfolk*, 1664.)

DAY, MARTIN. Matric. sizar from CHRIST'S, c. 1591; B.A. 1593–4; M.A. 1597; D.D. 1617. Fellow, 1595–9. Incorp. at Oxford, as M.A. 1602, and as D.D. 1618. R. of Bothal, Northumberland, 1598–1609. Chaplain in Ordinary to the King. R. of St Faith's, London, 1613–24. R. of Stokeclimsland, Cornwall, 1623. Licensed, May 16, 1606, to marry Mabel, dau. of Humphrey Green, V. of Hartburn, Durham. Author, religious. Died 1629. (*Peile*, I. 201; H. M. Wood.)

DAY, MATTHEW. Adm. at KING'S, a scholar from Eton, 1630. S. of Matthew, alderman and mayor of Windsor. Bapt. there, Feb. 24, 1610–1. B.A. 1633–4; M.A. 1637; D.D. 1661 (*Lit. Reg.*). Fellow, till 1643. Ord. priest (Peterb.) Dec. 18, 1641. R. of Everdon, Northants., 1642; ejected 1644. Master of Lewisham School, Kent, 1652–60. V. of Staines, Middlesex, 1660–3. Preb. of St Paul's, 1660. Married, at Weedon, May 7, 1645, Elizabeth, dau. of David Stokes, D.D., R. of Everdon. Died Sept. 2, 1663. Buried in St John's Church, Windsor. Will, P.C.C. Brother of William (1624). (*Harwood*; *D.N.B.*; *Vis. of Berks.*, 1623; H. I. Longden.)

DAY, MATTHEW. Matric. sizar from KING'S, Lent, 1637–8.

DEY, MATTHEW. Adm. sizar at TRINITY, May 22, 1657 (*impubes*). Of Norfolk. Matric. 1657; Scholar, 1659; B.A. 1660–1; M.A. 1664. Ord. priest (Ely) Mar. 1662–3. V. of Childerley, Cambs., 1665. V. of Lolworth, 1666. R. of Littleport, 1676.

DAY, NATHANIEL. Adm. sizar at CORPUS CHRISTI, 1654. Of Bedfordshire. Matric. 1658; B.A. 1659–60.

DAY, NICHOLAS. Of TRINITY. B.A. (? 1594–5). B. at Silsoe, Beds., 1577. Ord. priest (Lincoln) Sept. 22, 1605. V. of Lidlington, Beds., 1605. V. of Sundon, 1607. Married, at Gt Barford, Beds., June 10, 1622, Mary Bradford.

DAY or DEY, OLIVER. Adm. pens. (age 18) at CAIUS, May 21, 1603. S. of Robert, of Wymondham, Norfolk, yeoman. School, Wymondham (Mr Leverington). Matric. 1603; B.A. 1606–7. Ord. deacon (Norwich) May 22, 1608; priest, Mar. 12, 1608–9. C. of Pentney, 1620. C. of West Bilney, 1620–33 ('M.A.'). (*Venn*, I. 181.)

DEYE, OLIVER. Adm. sizar (age 17) at CAIUS, July 5, 1667. S. of Thomas, Esq., of Hoxne, Suffolk. B. there. Bapt. Mar. 26, 1648. School, Eye (Mr Brown). Matric. 1667; Scholar, 1668–70. Barrister-at-law. Died unmarried, 1686. Buried in Dublin Cathedral. (*Venn*, I. 432.)

DAYE, OSBERT. Matric. pens. from TRINITY, Easter, 1555.

DAY, R. B.Can.L. 1488–9.

DAY, RICHARD. Adm. at KING'S, a scholar from Eton, 1540.

DAY, RICHARD. Adm. at KING'S, 1571, a scholar from Eton. S. of John, the celebrated printer. B. in London, Dec. 21, 1552. Matric. 1571; B.A. 1575–6. Fellow, 1574–6. For some years worked as printer in his father's shop. Ord. deacon (London) Dec. 1, 1580, age 30. V. of Mundon, Essex, 1580. V. of Reigate, Surrey, 1583–5. Probably R. of Chipstead, 1586–1611. Died 1611. (*Cooper*, II. 476; *D.N.B.*)

DAYE, RICHARD. Matric. pens. from CHRIST'S, May, 1572. Perhaps curate in charge of Litlington, Cambs., 1605.

DAY, RICHARD. Adm. at KING'S, a scholar from Eton, 1590. S. of William (1545), Bishop of Winchester. B.A. 1594. Fellow. Left in 1594. Gave the advowson of Weedon-Pinkney, Northants., to his College. (*Harwood*.)

DAY, RICHARD. Matric. sizar from CHRIST'S, June, 1602. Ord. deacon (London) Dec. 1612; priest, Dec. 1614 (at Macclesfield, Cheshire). (*Peile*, I. 240.)

DAY, RICHARD. Adm. at KING'S, a scholar from Eton, 1622. B. at Bray, Berks. B.A. 1625–6; M.A. 1629; B.D. 1637. Fellow, till 1644. V. of Prescot, Lancs., 1642. Died there Apr. 12, 1650. Will, P.C.C. Grandson of William (1545). (*Harwood*.)

DEY, RICHARD. Matric. sizar from KING'S, Easter, 1633.

DAY, RICHARD. Adm. pens. at JESUS, May 31, 1683. S. of Thomas, of York. Scholar, 1683; B.A. 1686–7. Richard Day, gent.; age 29; had a licence, in 1698, to marry Mary Day, spinster, at St Olave's, York. (A. Gray.)

DAYE, ROBERT. Matric. pens. from PETERHOUSE, Michs. 1555.

DAYE, ROBERT. Matric. sizar from JESUS, Michs. 1560.

DAYE, ROBERT. Matric. pens. from QUEENS', Michs. 1566.

DEY, ROBERT. Matric. sizar from PETERHOUSE, Easter, 1579. One of these names R. of Cranwick, Norfolk, 1583. Buried Aug. 13, 1620.

DAY, ROBERT. Matric. sizar from JESUS, c. 1594.

DAY, ROBERT. Matric. sizar from ST JOHN'S, Lent, 1629–30; B.A. 1632–3.

DAY, ROBERT. Adm. at CORPUS CHRISTI, 1650. Of Norfolk. S. of Thomas, of Scoulton. Left by will (1700) an estate at Shipdham, Norfolk, for the foundation of scholarships. The College did not inherit. (*Masters*, 179.)

DAY, ROGER. Adm. at KING'S, a scholar from Eton, 1514; B.A. 1521–2.

DAY or DEY, STEPHEN. Adm. pens. (age 16) at CAIUS, July 2, 1650. S. of Richard, gent., of Mundford, Norfolk. B. at Feltwell. Schools, Feltwell (Mr Ward), Bury St Edmunds and Lynn (Mr Bell). Matric. 1650–1; B.A. 1653–4. Will of one of these names (Norwich Archd. C.) 1712, of St Andrew's, Norwich, gent. (*Venn*, I. 379.)

DAY, THOMAS. Matric. pens. from TRINITY, Michs. 1572. Candidate for deacon (Ely) Nov. 1577; 'of Cambridge, aged 24' (rejected).

DAYE, THOMAS. Matric. sizar from QUEENS', Michs. 1615. Of London. S. of Thomas, merchant-taylor. B. May 25, 1597. School, Merchant Taylors'. B.A. 1618–9; M.A. 1622. Ord. priest (Norwich) 1622. R. of Brundall, Norfolk, 1628–57. C. of Postwick.

DAY, THOMAS. Matric. Fell.-Com. from PEMBROKE, Easter, 1629.

DAY, THOMAS. Matric. sizar from KING'S, Easter, 1629. After some years' residence became a druggist in Cambridge. Died May 17, 1681, aged 70. M.I. at Gt St Mary's. Benefactor to the parish and town. Father of Thomas (1677). (Le Neve, *Mon.*, v. 18.)

DAY, THOMAS. Adm. sizar (age 19) at CHRIST'S, Feb. 3, 1634-5, from Magdalene (adm. and matric. there, 1632). S. of Edmund. B. at 'Merston' (? Marston), Lincs. B.A. from Christ's, 1636-7; M.A. 1640. Perhaps Head Master of Whitgift's School, Croydon, 1651-62.

DAY, THOMAS. Adm. pens. at ST CATHARINE'S, 1637. Exhibitioner from Charterhouse. Matric. Michs. 1637. Migrated to Pembroke, 1638; B.A. 1640-1.

DAY, THOMAS. Adm. sizar at TRINITY, Mar. 9, 1640-1. Matric. 1641; B.A. 1646; M.A. 1650. One of these names V. of Melbourn, Cambs., 1668.

DAY, THOMAS. Adm. Fell.-Com. (age 16) at CHRIST'S, May 23, 1641. S. of John. B. at Sausthorpe, Lincs. School, London (Mr Woodward). Matric. 1641. Adm. at the Inner Temple, Apr. 24, 1646. Died before 1671. (*Peile*, I. 476; *Lincs. Pedigrees*, 1190.)

DAY, THOMAS. Adm. pens. (age 14) at ST JOHN'S, Oct. 10, 1677. S. of Thomas (1629), druggist. B. at Cambridge. School, Thetford (Mr Keene). Matric. 1677. Migrated to Jesus, Sept. 24, 1680. Died Jan. 30, 1701-2, aged 39. M.I. at All Saints', Cambridge, to Thomas D'Aye, Esq. (Le Neve, *Mon.*, II. 25.)

DAY, THOMAS. M.A. from TRINITY HALL, 1683 (*Lit. Reg.*).

DAYE, THOMAS. Adm. pens. (age 16) at ST JOHN'S, May 19, 1688. S. of Robert, Esq. B. at Scoulton, Norfolk. School, Norwich. Matric. 1688; B.A. 1691-2. Adm. at the Middle Temple, Feb. 1694.

DAY, THOMAS. Adm. pens. (age 18) at ST JOHN'S, Oct. 20, 1713. S. of Thomas, draper, of Bedford. B. there. School, Merchant Taylors', London. Matric. 1713; B.A. 1717-8; M.A. 1721. Ord. deacon (Lincoln) Mar. 5, 1720-1; priest, Mar. 10, 1722-3.

DAY or D'EYE, THOMAS. Adm. pens. (age 18) at PEMBROKE, Feb. 6, 1750-1. S. of Nathaniel, of Eye, Suffolk, gent. Matric. 1750-1; B.A. 1755. R. of Palgrave, Suffolk, 1757-66.

DEY, VALENTINE. Adm. pens. (age 15) at CAIUS, Mar. 16, 1604-5. S. of John (1559), LL.D., of Westley, Suffolk. School, Ely (Mr Holdred). Matric. 1606; B.A. 1608-9; M.A. 1612. Ord. deacon (Peterb.) Sept. 23, 1610; priest (Lincoln) Dec. 22, 1611. R. of Homersfield, Suffolk, 1612; of Spexhall, 1628. P.C. of St Michael, South Elmham, 1636. Author, *Sermons*. (*Venn*, I. 188.)

DAY, WILFRID. Adm. sizar at TRINITY, Apr. 30, 1670. Matric. 1670.

DAY, WILLIAM. Adm. at KING'S, a scholar from Eton, 1545. S. of Richard, of Newport, Salop. B. there, 1529. B.A. 1549-50; M.A. 1553; B.D. 1562. Fellow, till 1559. Proctor, 1557-8. Ord. priest, Mar. 31, 1560. Fellow of Eton, 1560-1. Preb. of York, 1560-6. Provost of Eton, 1561-96. Archdeacon of Nottingham, 1561-65. Canon of Windsor, 1563-72. Dean of Windsor and Wolverhampton, 1572-95. R. of Hambleden, Bucks., 1575. Chancellor of St Paul's, 1587-95. Bishop of Winchester, 1595. Died Sept. 20, 1596. Will, P.C.C. Brother of George, Bishop of Chichester, father of Richard (1590). (*Cooper*, II. 219; *Harwood*; *D.N.B.*)

DAYE, WILLIAM. Matric. pens. from JESUS, Easter, 1584; B.A. 1587-8; 1st in the *ordo*.

DAYE, WILLIAM. Matric. Fell.-Com. from ST JOHN'S, Easter, 1588. Perhaps s. of William (1545), Bishop of Winchester. One of these names, of Windsor, adm. at the Inner Temple, 1590. (*Vis. of Berks.*, 1623.)

DAY, WILLIAM. Adm. at KING'S, a scholar from Eton, 1624 S. of Matthew, of Windsor. B.A. 1628; M.A. 1632. Fellow, till 1637. Incorp. at Oxford, 1635. V. of Maple Durham, Oxon., 1637-84. Divinity reader in St George's Chapel, 1660. Author, theological. Buried at Maple Durham, Dec. 20, 1684, aged 79. Admon. (Archd. Oxford). Brother of Matthew (1630). (*Harwood*; *D.N.B.*; *Vis. of Berks.*, 1623.)

DAY or DEY, WILLIAM. Adm. sizar (age 17) at CAIUS, Apr. 7, 1652. S. of Nicholas. B. at Rickinghall Inferior, Suffolk. Bapt. Nov. 19, 1633. School, Botesdale (Mr Ives and Mr Ellis). Matric. 1652; Scholar, 1652-5; B.A. 1655-6. Ord. priest (Norwich) Nov. 10, 1661. R. of Banningham, Norfolk, 1670-84. (*Venn*, I. 384.)

DAYE, WILLIAM. Adm. pens. at CLARE, May 28, 1717. B. at York, 1699. B.A. 1720-1; M.A. 1725; D.D. 1728 (*Com. Reg.*). Fellow, 1722-7. Ord. deacon (Norwich) Mar. 1722-3; priest (Ely) Dec. 20, 1724. R. of East Barnet, Herts., 1726-31. A Governor of the Barnet Grammar School, 1728. R. of Toppesfield, and of Stanford Rivers, Essex, 1731-7. Preb. of Lincoln, 1735. Perhaps Chaplain to Chelsea College. Died Aug. 16, 1737. M.I. at Stanford. (*L. Mag.*; F. C. Cass, *East Barnet*, 227.)

DAYE, WILLIAM. Adm. Fell.-Com. at CLARE, June 15, 1750. S. of William (above). B. at Toppesfield. Bapt. there, Oct. 28, 1732.

DAY, ——. B.A. 1485-6.

DAY, ——. Adm. sizar at KING'S, 1601.

DAY, ——. Adm. pens. at EMMANUEL, Easter, 1623.

DAYGES, JOSEPH. B.A. from ST JOHN'S, 1606-7; M.A. 1611. Ord. priest (Peterb.) Dec. 22, 1611, as Davyes.

DAYLEY, ROBERT. Adm. sizar at SIDNEY, Apr. 3, 1619. B. in Northamptonshire (*see* Robert Deasy).

DAYNES, FRANCIS. Adm. pens. at CORPUS CHRISTI, 1648. Of Suffolk. Matric. 1650; B.A. 1651-2; M.A. 1655, as Deynes.

DAYNES, JOHN. Matric. pens. from CORPUS CHRISTI, Easter, 1579.

DAYNES, JOHN. Adm. sizar (age 17) at CAIUS, Apr. 17, 1605. S. of John, citizen of Lynn. Bapt. there, July 30, 1588. School, Lynn (Mr Man). Migrated to Emmanuel, 1606. B.A. 1608-9; M.A. 1612. Ord. deacon (London) Sept. 22, 1611; priest, Mar. 8, 1611-2. C. of Mundon, Essex, 1611; of Boreham, 1612. Perhaps master of Maldon School, Essex, in 1621. Will of John Danes, of Maldon, clerk (Comm. C. Essex) 1639. (*Venn*, I. 189.)

DAYNES, JOHN. Matric. pens. from ST JOHN'S, Easter, 1628; B.A. 1630-1.

DAYNES, JOHN. Adm. pens. at CORPUS CHRISTI, 1634. S. of John, of Coddenham, Suffolk. Matric. 1635; B.A. 1638-9; M.A. 1642; M.D. 1649. Of Coddenham, Esq. Perhaps father of John (1670). (*Vis. of Suffolk*, 1664.)

DAINES, JOHN. Adm. pens. at EMMANUEL, Mar. 18, 1658-9. Of Suffolk. Matric. 1659 (*impubes*); B.A. 1662-3; M.A. 1668.

DEYNS, JOHN. Adm. pens. (age 17) at SIDNEY, June 4, 1664. S. of Thomas, farmer. B. at Radon, Norfolk (? Raydon, Suffolk). School, Diss, Norfolk (Mr Rayner). Matric. 1664; B.A. 1667-8; M.A. 1671. Signs for priest's orders (London) Mar. 13, 1673-4. C. of Upwell, Norfolk.

DEYNES, JOHN. Adm. pens. at ST CATHARINE'S, Apr. 17, 1670. Matric. 1670; B.A. 1673-4; M.A. 1677. Perhaps s. and h. of John (1634-5), of Coddenham, M.D.; age 10 in 1664. One of these names R. of Marsham, Norfolk, 1685. Buried Aug. 3, 1686. (*Vis. of Suffolk*, 1664.)

DAYNES, THOMAS. Adm. pens. at CORPUS CHRISTI, 1580. Matric. 1580; B.A. 1584-5. Ord. priest (Norwich) July 17, 1588. V. of Flixton St Mary, Suffolk, 1588-90.

DAYNES, THOMAS. Adm. pens. at CORPUS CHRISTI, 1645. Of Suffolk. Matric. 1646; B.A. 1649-50; M.A. 1653. One of these names R. of Gosbeck, Suffolk; ejected, 1662.

DAINES or DANES, WILLIAM. Adm. sizar at JESUS, Apr. 7, 1632. Of Essex. Matric. from Emmanuel, 1632, as 'Dands'; B.A. 1635-6; M.A. 1639. V. of Althorne, Essex, 1644.

DAYRELL, BROWNLOW. Adm. Fell.-Com. (age 19) at CHRIST'S, Dec. 1, 1736. S. of Francis (1704), of Castle Camps, Cambs. B. at Kensington, London. School, private (Mr Coxe). Matric. 1736. Adm. at Lincoln's Inn, June 2, 1738. Bencher. Died 1773. Buried at Shudy Camps. Brother of Marmaduke (1740). (*Peile*, II. 233.)

DAYRELL, FRANCIS. Adm. pens. at EMMANUEL, Apr. 13, 1663. Of Cambridgeshire. S. and h. of Sir Thomas (1622), of Lillingstone, Bucks., Knt. Matric. 1663. Adm. at Lincoln's Inn, May 8, 1665. Knighted, Feb. 29, 1671-2. Of Castle Camps, Cambs. and Lillingstone, Bucks. Married Elizabeth, dau. of Edward Lewis, of the Van, Glamorgan. Died 1675, aged 29. (Le Neve, *Knights*, 275; Le Neve, *Mon.*, IV. 135; G. B. Routledge).

DAYRELL, FRANCIS. Adm. Fell.-Com. at CHRIST'S, Oct. 14, 1704. 1st s. of Sir Marmaduke (1664), Knt. B. at Shudy Camps, Cambs. Adm. at Gray's Inn, Feb. 1, 1704-5. Of Shudy Camps, Esq. Married Elizabeth, dau. of Peter Witchcomb, of Braxted, Essex. Will of one of these names, of Cambs., Esq. (P.C.C.) 1760. Father of Brownlow (1736) and Marmaduke (1740). (*Peile*, II. 160; Burke, *L.G.*)

DAYRELL, MARMADUKE. Adm. pens. at MAGDALENE, Oct. 19, 1664. S. of Sir Thomas (1622), Knt., of Hinxton, Cambs. School, Westminster. Matric. 1644. Adm. at Gray's Inn, Nov. 21, 1668. Of Castle Camps, Cambs., Esq. Knighted, Mar. 22, 1684-5. Married (1) Mary, dau. of Sir Justinian Isham, Bart.; (2) Mary, dau. of William Glascock, of Farnham, Essex. Died 1712. Father of Francis (1704), brother of Francis (1663). (Le Neve, 275; Burke, *L.G.*; G. B. Routledge.)

DAYRELL, MARMADUKE. Adm. pens. (age 18) at CHRIST'S, Nov. 29, 1740. S. of Francis (1704). B. in Middlesex. School, Kensington (Mr Cox). Matric. 1740. Perhaps adm. at Lincoln's Inn, July 10, 1739. Succeeded his brother Brownlow (1736). Died Apr. 15, 1790. Buried at Shudy Camps, Cambs. Will, P.C.C. (G. *Mag.*; *Peile*, II. 240.)

DAYRELL, NICHOLAS, M.D., *see* DARRELL.

DAYRELL, THOMAS. Matric. Fell.-Com. from CHRIST'S, July, 1622. S. and h. of Francis, of Lillingstone-Dayrell, Bucks. Adm. at Lincoln's Inn, Oct. 21, 1620. Deputy-Lieutenant for Cambridgeshire. Knighted, Feb. 4, 1633-4. Of Hinxton, and Shudy Camps, Cambs. Married Sarah, dau. of Sir Hugh Windham, Bart., of Pilsden Court, Dorset. Died Apr. 2, 1669. Buried at Castle Camps. M.I. at Hinxton. Father of the next, of Francis (1663) and Marmaduke (1664). (*Peile*, I. 343; Le Neve, *Mon.*, IV. 233.)

DAYRELL, WINDHAM. Adm. pens. at MAGDALENE, Oct. 27, 1668. S. of Sir Thomas (above), Knt., of Castle Camps, Cambs. School, Elmdon, Essex (private). Adm. at Lincoln's Inn, Aug. 4, 1673. Died of small-pox, 1674, aged 22. Buried at St Giles', Middlesex. (Le Neve, *Mon.*, IV. 135.)

'DAYSINE,' *see* DISNEY.

DAYSON, JAMES. Adm. sizar (age by) at ST JOHN'S, Apr. 18, 1657. S. of James, furrier, of Kirk Lonsdale, Westmorland. B. there. Schoois, Kirkby Lonsdale (Mr Garthwaite) and Sedbergh. Matric. 1657, as 'Day'; B.A. 1661. V. of Wressel, Yorks., 1663-79. V. of Eastington, Gloues., 1679.

DAYSON, JAMES. Adm. sizar (age 18) at PETERHOUSE, May 15, 1686. Of Yorkshire. School, Pocklington. Matric. 1686, as John; B.A. 1689-90; M.A. 1693. V. of Ellington, Hunts., 1689-91. V. of Yaxley, 1705-14. Died 1714.

DAZILL, ISAAC. Matric. pens. from CLARE, Easter, 1616.

DEACON, DANIEL. Adm. sizar at SIDNEY, Mar. 1598-9. Of Rutland. B.A. (? 1602-3); M.A. 1607. Ord. deacon and priest (Peterb.) Sept. 23, 1604. C. of Oxendon, Northants., in 1605.

DEACON, GEORGE. Adm. pens. at QUEENS', June 27, 1595. Of Bedfordshire (probably of Elstow, s. of Thomas). Matric. 1595. Will, 1610.

DEACON, JOHN. B.A. from MAGDALENE, 1575-6. R. of Saxby, Leics., 1577. Doubtless the minister, B.A., at Nottingham, in 1586, and at Ridlington, Rutland. Author, *Sermon*; *Tobacco tortured*; and controversial writings on demoniac possession.

DEACON, JOHN. Matric. sizar from JESUS, Easter, 1616; B.A. 1619-20, as 'Deken'; M.A. 1623.

DEACON, SAMUEL. Matric. sizar from TRINITY, Easter, 1633; B.A. 1636-7; M.A. 1641. Ord. deacon (Peterb.) Dec. 18, 1641. Perhaps R. of Nettlestead, Kent, 1647.

DEACON, SAMUEL. Adm. sizar (age 16) at SIDNEY, 1691-2. S. of John, of Tansor, Northants., carpenter. School Warmington (private). Matric. 1692; B.A. 1697-8; M.A. from Corpus Christi, 1704. Ord. deacon (Lincoln) June 19, 1698 priest (Peterb.) May 27, 1700. C. of Clapton. V. of Slipton, Northants., 1705-7. Buried there July 14, 1707. M.I. (H. I. Longden.)

DEACON, THEODORE. B.A. from TRINITY, 1631.

DEAKIN, JOHN. Adm. sizar (age 17) at CHRIST'S, Mar. 21, 1710-1. S. of Francis. B. at Lichfield. School, Lichfield (Mr Shaw). Scholar, 1710-1; Matric. 1711; B.A. 1714-5. Ord. deacon (Lichfield) Sept. 1715.

DEALE, THOMAS. Matric. pens. from QUEENS', Michs. 1571.

DEALTRY, GEORGE. Matric. sizar from TRINITY, Easter, 1618. Doubtless s. of William, of Full Sutton, Yorks. Scholar, 1619; B.A. 1621-2; M.A. 1625. Ord. deacon (Peterb.) Sept. 20; priest, Sept. 21, 1623. R. of Full Sutton, Yorks., 1623. Will (P.C.C.) 1657. Father of William (1652).

DEALTARY, HENRY. Adm. sizar (age 16) at ST JOHN'S, May 26, 1660. S. of Hammond, yeoman, of High Catton, Yorks. B. . School, York (Mr Banks). Matric. 1660; B.A. 1663thereM.A. 1669. Ord. deacon (York) Sept. 1664; priest, 1665. V. of Westow, Yorks., 1666-96. Buried Sept. 4, 1696. Father of the next and brother of William (1668).

DEALTARY, HENRY. Adm. sizar (age 17) at PEMBROKE, Mar. 23, 1688-9. S. of Henry (above), V. of Westow, Yorks. School, Pocklington. Matric. 1689; Scholar of Sidney, 1690; B.A. from Sidney, 1692-3. Ord. deacon (York) Sept. 1694; priest, 1696. . of Westow, 1696-1751. R. of Halsham, 1696-1722. BuriedVSept. 6, 1751. Father of John (1726).

DEALTRY, JAMES. Adm. sizar at JESUS, June 25, 1660. Of Yorkshire. Matric. 1660.

DEALTRY, JOHN. Adm. pens. (age 18) at TRINITY, Oct. 20, 1726. S. of Henry (1688-9), V. of Westow, Yorks. School, Kirkleatham, Yorks. (Mr Clark). Matric. 1726; Scholar, 1728; B.A. 1730-1. Adm. at the Middle Temple, Nov. 30, 1726. Probably the 'M.D.' who married, at York Minster, Elizabeth, dau. of Richard Langley, of Wykeham Abbey, Yorks. 'Dr Dawtry,' of York, died there suddenly, Mar. 25, 1773, aged 65. (*G. Mag.*)

DEALTARY, JOHN. Adm. sizar at JESUS, May 15, 1727. Of Yorkshire. Doubtless 2nd s. of William (1681), R. of Skirpenbeck, Yorks. Matric. 1727; Scholar, 1729; B.A. 1730-1; M.A. 1745. Ord. deacon (Chester) Oct. 31, 1731; priest (Durham) Sept. 2, 1733. R. of Skirpenbeck, 1736-74. P.C. of Bishop Wilton, 1741; of Kilburn, 1750; of Acaster Malbis, 1758-97. V. of Bishopthorpe, 1757-97. Preb. of Southwell, 1759-85. Preb. of York, 1780-97. R. of Barnburgh, 1784-97. Died Apr. 30, 1797, aged 89. (Yorks. *Arch. and Top. Journ.*, III. 102; A. Gray.)

DEALTRY, RICHARD. Adm. sizar at TRINITY, May 1, 1649. Of Yorkshire. Matric. 1649; B.A. 1652-3; M.A. 1656. R. of Skirpenbeck, Yorks., 1660-98. R. of Full Sutton, 1672-4. Died 1698.

DEALTRYE, WILLIAM. Matric. pens. from TRINITY, Easter, 1610, as 'Vealtrye'; B.A. (? 1614); M.A. 1617. Ord. priest (York) Dec. 1620. R. of Folkton, Yorks., 1620-74. Died 1674.

DEALTRY, WILLIAM. Adm. sizar at TRINITY, Oct. 25, 1652. Of Yorkshire. S. of George (1618). Bapt. at Bishop Wilton, Dec. 15, 1636. School, Pocklington. Matric. 1652; B.A. 1656-7; M.A. 1660. R. of Full Sutton, Yorks., 1662-72. Died 1686.

DEALTRY, WILLIAM. Adm. sizar (age 17) at PEMBROKE, Apr. 4, 1668. S. of Hammond, gent. B. at High Catton, Yorks. Matric. 1668; B.A. 1671-2. Ord. deacon (York) Sept. 1672. Brother of Henry (1660).

DEALTARY, WILLIAM. Adm. sizar at QUEENS', June 10, 1681. Of Yorkshire. B.A. 1684-5; M.A. 1688. Ord. deacon (York) June, 1694; priest, 1695. V. of Filey, Yorks., 1691-6. V. of Hunmanby, 1696-1703. R. of Skirpenbeck, 1698-1736. V. of Bishop Wilton in 1730. Died 1741. Father of John (1727).

DEALTARY, WILLIAM. Adm. sizar at QUEENS', Feb. 1, 1687-8. Of Yorkshire. Matric. 1691; B.A. 1691-2.

DEALTARY, WILLIAM. Adm. sizar (age 17) at ST JOHN'S, May 13, 1710. S. of William (? 1681), clerk. B. at Muston, near Scarborough, Yorks. School, Beverley (Mr Lambert). Matric. 1710; B.A. 1713-4. Ord. deacon (York) Sept. 1715; priest, 1719. V. of Garton-on-the-Wolds, Yorks., 1722-30.

DEANE or DENNE, ANDREW. B.A. 1530-1; M.A. 1534; B.D. Fellow of GONVILLE HALL, 1532-47; and of Corpus Christi, 1558. Ord. priest (Norwich) May 24, 1532. R. of Bixton and Welborne, Norfolk, 1554. V. of Swaffham Bulbeck, Cambs., 1554-62; and of Downham, 1559-65. Preb. of Ely, 1559. Buried at Downham, Dec. 16, 1565. (*Venn*, I. 30; *Masters-Lamb*, 319; according to whom he was D.D.)

DEANE, ANDREW. Adm. sizar (age 16) at CHRIST'S, May 29, 1679. S. of Richard, of Westmorland. B. at Dufton. School, Holt, Norfolk (Mr Bainbridge). Matric. 1681; B.A. 1682-3. Ord. deacon (Norwich) Dec. 1683. Brother of Bainbridge and Leonard.

DEANE, ANTHONY. Matric. pens. from ST CATHARINE'S, Easter, 1647. S. of Sir Drue (1623-4), of Gt Maplestead, Essex, Knt. Bapt. June 1, 1630. Sold Maplestead, in 1653. A Parliamentarian. (*Vis. of Essex*, 1634.)

DEAN, BAINBRIDGE. Adm. sizar (age 18) at ST JOHN'S, May 19, 1682. S. of Richard, husbandman. B. at Dufton, Cumberland. School, Sedbergh. Matric. 1682; B.A. 1685-6; M.A. 1689. Ord. deacon (Norwich) 1686; priest, 1687. R. of Crostwick, Norfolk, 1687-94. R. of Beeston, 1693. Brother of Leonard (1687) and Andrew (1679).

DEANE, BRIAN. Matric. pens. from ST JOHN'S, Michs. 1581; B.A. 1584-5; M.A. 1588. V. of Normanton, Notts., 1590-3. V. of Gt Limber, Lincs., 1593. V. of Gt Gransden, Hunts., 1599-1603. R. of Alderton, Northants., 1599-1600.

DEANE, DREW. Adm. Fell.-Com. at JESUS, Jan. 29, 1623-4. S. of Sir John, Knt., of Castle Hedingham, Essex (and Anne, dau. of Sir Drew Drury). B. Jan. 31, 1606. Matric. 1624. Knighted, July 17, 1627. J.P. for Essex, 1634. Of Gt Maplestead, Essex. Died Sept. 24, 1638. Will (P.C.C.) 1639. Brother of John (1625), and father of Anthony (1647). (*Vis. of Essex*, 1558, 1634.)

DEANE, EDMUND. M.D. 1614, Incorp. from Oxford. S. of Gilbert, of Saltonstall, Halifax, Yorks. Matric. from Merton College, Oxford, Mar. 26, 1591, age 19; B.A. 1594; M.A. 1597. Licensed to practise medicine, 1601. M.B. and M.D. 1608. Practised physic at York. Married, 1625, Mary Boyes, of Normanton. Author. Brother of Richard, Bishop of Ossory. (*Vis. of Yorks.*, 1612; *Al. Oxon.*)

DEANE, EDWARD. Matric. pens. (age 12) from JESUS, Lent, 1563-4.

DEANE, EDWARD. Adm. pens. at CAIUS, May, 1683.

DEANE, EDWARD. Adm. at EMMANUEL, Feb. 14, 1692-3. Matric. 1693. S. of Edward, of 'Hatchbury, Wilts.' (*Al. Oxon.*). Matric. from Wadham College, Oxford, July 16, 1691, age 15; B.A. 1695-6; M.A. 1699. Ord. deacon (Lincoln) Mar. 5, 1698-9.

DEANE, GEORGE. Adm. pens. (age 19) at CAIUS, Feb. 21, 1624-5. S. of Edward, silkweaver, of London. School, Eton. Matric. 1625; Scholar, 1628-33; B.A. 1628-9; M.A. 1633. Died in Cambridge. Buried at St Benet's, Nov. 17, 1633. (*Venn*, I. 270.)

DEAN, GEORGE. Adm. pens. (age 17) at ST JOHN'S, Feb. 6, 1716-7. S. of William (1720), clerk, of Huntingdonshire. B. at Offord Darcy. School, Huntingdon (Mr Matthews). B.A. 1720-1; M.A. 1724; B.D. 1731. Fellow, 1723-35. Ord. deacon (Lincoln) May 28, 1727; priest, June 1, 1729. V. of Aldworth, Berks., 1734-82. Brother of Merritt (1712). (*Scott-Mayor*, III. 308.)

DEANE, GERARD. Adm. sizar (age 17) at JESUS, Apr. 12, 1676. Of Cheshire. Matric. 1676; B.A. 1679-80.

DEANE, GERVASE. Adm. sizar at TRINITY, June 26, 1647. Of Nottinghamshire. Matric. 1649; B.A. 1650-1. One of these names, s. of Francis, of Long Eaton, Derbs., gent., adm. at Gray's Inn, May 27, 1652.

DEAN or DENE, HENRY. Of Cambridge (according to *Cooper*, I. 6). Prior of Llanthony Abbey, 1461. Specially adm. at Lincoln's Inn, Oct. 30, 1489. Lord Chancellor of Ireland, 1494-6. Bishop of Bangor, 1496-9; of Salisbury, 1499-1501. Lord Keeper of the Great Seal, 1500-3. Archbishop of Canterbury, 1501. Died Feb. 16, 1502-3. Of Oxford, according to *Al. Oxon.* Will, P.C.C., and Dean and Chapter of Canterbury. (*D.N.B.*; *Al. Oxon.*; H. G. Harrison.)

DEAN, HENRY. Matric. sizar from QUEENS', Michs. 1547.

DEANE, HENRY. Matric. sizar from CLARE, Michs. 1626; B.A. 1629-30; M.A. 1633; D.D. 1663 (*Lit. Reg.*). Fellow. Obtained a license to travel to the Low Countries, Sept. 30, 1633.

DEANE, HENRY. Adm. sizar (age 18) at TRINITY, Apr. 22, 1746. S. of Thomas, of Coventry, Warws., doctor. Clerk at Magdalen College, Oxford, 1743-5. School, Warwick (Mr Lydiat). Matric. 1746; B.A. 1749-50. Probably matric. from Trinity College, Oxford, May 16, 1743, 'age 17.' (*Al. Oxon.*)

DENE, JOHN DE, 1261. Southern scholar, who received a royal pardon for taking part in a riot against the northern students. Brother of Richard (1261) and Walter (1261). (*Fuller*, 29.)

DEANE, JOHN. Questionist, 1491-2; but did not proceed to B.A. (*Gr. Bk*, A, 49.)

DEANE, JOHN. Licensed to practise medicine, 1569.

DEANE, JOHN. Adm. sizar at QUEENS', Mar. 19, 1581-2. Of Lincolnshire. Matric., as 'Drane,' 1582. Perhaps R. of Hawkesworth, Notts., 1585.

DEANE, JOHN. Adm. sizar at EMMANUEL, June 1, 1616. Matric. 1617; B.A. 1619-20.

DEANE, JOHN. Adm. Fell.-Com. at JESUS, June 29, 1625. S. of Sir John, Knt., of Castle Hedingham, Essex. B. there, Aug. 2, 1610. Brother of Drew (1623-4). (*Vis. of Essex*, 1558, 1634.)

DEANE, JOHN. Adm. sizar (age 18) at ST JOHN'S, May 17, 1650. S. of Richard, coachman, of Hatfield, Essex. B. there. School, Bishop's Stortford (private; Mr Lee). Matric. 1650; B.A. 1653-4. Ord. deacon (Lincoln) Feb. 22, 1661-2; priest, Sept. 21, 1662.

DEANE, JOHN. Adm. sizar at JESUS, July 1, 1689. S. of William, R. of Cotgrave, Notts. Matric. 1689; Scholar, 1689; B.A. 1692-3; M.A. 1697. Ord. deacon (London) Feb. 18, 1692-3. One of these names V. of Tibberton, Worcs., 1699-1708. V. of Kempsey, 1707-12. But *see* a contemporary in *Al. Oxon.*

DEAN, JOHN. Adm. at CORPUS CHRISTI, 1703. B. in Norwich, 1686. Matric. 1703; B.A. 1706-7; M.A. 1710. Fellow, 1709-16. Ord. deacon (Ely) Sept. 25, 1709; priest, Sept. 21, 1712. P.C. of St Benet's, Cambridge, 1711-6. V. of St Peter's, Isle of Thanet, 1715-57. Died 1757.

DEAN, JOHN. Adm. pens. (age 16) at MAGDALENE, Mar. 2, 1705-6. S. of Christopher, Esq. B. in Westminster. School, Isleworth, Middlesex. Matric. 1706; B.A. 1709-10. Adm. at the Middle Temple, July 24, 1708. One of these names P.C. of Chelford, Cheshire, 1720-72. Died June 9, 1772, aged 83. (Earwaker, *E. Cheshire*, II. 369.)

DEAN, JOHN. Adm. sizar at QUEENS', Oct. 6, 1725. Of Northamptonshire. Matric. 1726; B.A. 1729-30. Ord. deacon (Lincoln) Dec. 21, 1729; priest, Mar. 2, 1734-5. R. of Gayhurst with Stoke Goldington, Bucks., 1750-9. Married, at Quinton, Northants., Feb. 2, 1743-4, Sarah Clark; both of Courteenhall. Died July 28, 1759, aged 51. M.I. at Stoke Goldington. (H. I. Longden; *Lipscomb*, IV. 358.)

DEANE, LEONARD. Adm. pens. (age 19) at CAIUS, c. June, 1687. S. of Richard, gent., of Howell Grange, Westmorland. B. at Dufton, Cumberland. School, Sedbergh. Matric. 1687; B.A. 1690-1. Ord. deacon (Norwich), as C. of Crostwick, May 21, 1692. Brother of Bainbridge (1682) and Andrew (1679). (*Venn*, I. 483.)

DEAN, MERRITT. Adm. pens. (age 17) at ST JOHN'S, Apr. 9, 1712. S. of William (1720), clerk, D.D. B. in Sussex. School, Huntingdon (Mr Matthews). Matric. 1712; B.A. 1715-6; M.A. 1719. Fellow, 1718-23. Ord. priest (Lincoln) Sept. 23, 1722. R. of Offord Darcy, Hunts., 1722-40; succeeding his father. Buried there 1740. Brother of George (1716-7). (W. M. Noble.)

DEANE, NICHOLAS. Matric. pens. from PETERHOUSE, Lent, 1579-80; B.A. 1583-4; M.A. 1587. V. of Warcop, Westmorland, 1585-9. R. of Kirkbride, Cumberland, 1586. V. of Bromfield, 1589-1602. R. of Gt Salkeld, 1602. Archdeacon of Carlisle, 1602-4. Died c. Jan. 1603-4. (*Cooper*, II. 368.)

DEANE, PETER. Adm. sizar (age 14) at SIDNEY, May 31, 1632. S. of John. B. at Staveley, Derbs. School, Staveley (Mr Tho. Dand). Matric. 1632; B.A. 1635-6.

DEANE, PETER. Adm. sizar at JESUS, June 9, 1652. Of Cheshire. Matric. 1652. Perhaps ord. deacon (Lincoln) May 2, 1661; priest, May 4, 1661; called B.A. V. of Melling, Lancs., 1689. Will proved, 1714.

DENE, RICHARD DE, 1261. Southern student, who received a royal pardon for taking part in a riot against the northern students. Brother of John (1261) and Walter (1261). (*Fuller*, 29.)

DEANE, RICHARD. B.Can.L. 1505. Probably V. of Gt Limburgh, Lincs., till 1513. V. of St Thomas-the-Apostle, London, 1536. V. of Harrow, Middlesex, 1552-8. Perhaps R. of Abinger, Surrey, 1549. Will (P.C.C.) 1558.

DEANE, RICHARD. Matric. sizar from KING'S, Lent, 1692; B.A. 1695-6.

DENE, ROBERT. B.Can.L. 1455-6.

DENE, THOMAS DE. 'King's scholar' at Cambridge, 1328.

DEAN, THOMAS. Adm. pens. at TRINITY, May 14, 1656. School, Westminster. Scholar, 1656; Matric. 1659; B.A. 1659-60. Signs for priest's orders (London) Dec. 16, 1664; C. of St Mary, Savoy. P.C. of St James, Duke Place, London, 1667-79.

DEANE, THOMAS. Adm. pens. at KING'S, c. 1673. One of these names, s. of Thomas, of Kingston, Somerset, adm. at the Inner Temple, 1680.

DEANE, THOMAS. Adm. sizar (age 18) at PETERHOUSE, May 13, 1707. Of Yorkshire. School, Drighlington. Matric. 1707; B.A. 1710-1. Ord. deacon (York) May, 1710. Head Master of Drighlington School, 1713-6.

DEANE, W. Matric. pens. from PEMBROKE, Easter, 1565.

DEANE, W. Matric. sizar from ST JOHN'S, Easter, 1573.

DENE, WALTER DE, 1261. Southern student, who received a royal pardon for taking part in a riot against the northern students. Brother of John (1261) and Richard (1261). (*Fuller*, 29.)

DEANE, WILLIAM. Matric. sizar from MAGDALENE, Michs. 1575. S. of Thomas. B. at Grassington, Yorks. Schools, Leeds and Clitheroe, Lancs. Adm. pens. at Caius, Nov. 4, 1577, age 20. Ord. priest (R.C.) at Douay, Dec. 21, 1581. Sent to England, Jan. 25, 1581-2; banished; returned, 1585. According to the *Cath. Rec. Soc.* (v. 26) he had been a protestant minister at Monk Fryston, Yorks., before going to Douay. Executed, Aug. 28, 1588, at Mile-end Green. (*Venn*, I. 94; *D.N.B.*)

DEANE, WILLIAM. Adm. sizar at PEMBROKE, May, 1641. S. of Christopher, baker. B. at Lead Hall, Tadcaster, Yorks. Matric. 1641.

DEANE, WILLIAM. D.D. from ST JOHN'S, 1720. S. of William, of Leicester. Matric. from Brasenose College, Oxford, Mar. 10, 1680-1, age 17; B.A. (Oxford) 1684; M.A. 1687. Ord. priest (Lincoln) Mar. 11, 1687-8. R. of Thakeham, Sussex, 1688-98. R. of Offord Darcy, Hunts., 1697-1722. R. of Offord Cluny, 1706-22. Buried there Oct. 8, 1722. Father of George (1716-7) and Merritt (1712). (*Scott-Mayor*, III. 335; *Al. Oxon.*: wrong in the identification.)

DEANE, ——. Adm. Fell.-Com. at ST CATHARINE'S, Easter, 1643. Possibly John, s. and h. of Sir Drue (1623-4); adm. at Lincoln's Inn, Jan. 24, 1646-7. Died young. Brother of Anthony (1647). (*Morant*, II. 278.)

DEARDE or DEARDS, PETER. Matric. pens. from TRINITY, Easter, 1631; B.A. 1634–5; M.A. 1638. One Peter Deares, V. of Coggeshall, Essex; sequestered, 1647. Will (P.C.C.) 1654, of Peter Deards, of Sion College, London, clerk.

DEARDEN, JAMES. Adm. pen . (age 18) at TRINITY, Apr. 8, 1725. S. of John, of Warley, Halifax, Yorks. School, Wakefield, Yorks. Matric. 1725; Scholar, 1726; M.B. 1730.

DEARING, *see* DERING.

DEARLE, JOHN. Adm. sizar at EMMANUEL, July 5, 1699. Of Buckinghamshire. B. at Datchet, 1680. Colleger at Eton, 1691–8. Matric. 1699; B.A. 1702–3; M.A. 1706. Perhaps Usher of Macclesfield School, 1704–12. (Earwaker, *East Cheshire*, II. 522.)

DEARLING, WILLIAM. Adm. pens. (age 20) at ST JOHN'S, Mar. 18, 1745–6. S. of John, of Sussex. B. at Chichester. School, Bury, Lancs. (Mr Lister). Matric. 1749; B.A. 1749–50; M.A. 1753. V. of Matching, Essex, 1761–85. R. of Ashley, Wilts., 1785–90. Will (P.C.C.) 1791. (*Scott-Mayor*, III. 556.)

DEARESLEY, EDMUND. Matric. pens. from CLARE, Lent, 1579–80; B.A. 1583–4; M.A. 1587. One of these names, of Cowling, Suffolk, adm. at Gray's Inn, Mar. 1, 1591–2. Will (P.C.C.) 1592.

DEARSLEY or DIERSLY, HENRY. Adm. sizar at TRINITY, May 21, 1645. Of Essex. Matric. 1645; Scholar, 1647; B.A. 1648–9; M.A. 1652; B.D. 1660. Fellow, 1649. V. of Enfield, Middlesex, 1664–72. Died 1672. Will (Consist. C. London) 1672.

DERSLEY or DEESLEY, RICHARD. Matric. sizar from QUEENS', Easter, 1563.

DEARSLEY, RICHARD. Matric. pens. from PETERHOUSE, Michs. 1571.

DERESLEY, RICHARD. Matric. sizar from QUEENS', Easter, 1641. Of Suffolk. One of these names, of Kirtling, Cambs., died 1663.

DEARSLYE, THOMAS. Matric. sizar from CLARE, Easter, 1584. Probably R. of Edwardstone, Suffolk, 1598.

DEARSLY, THOMAS. Matric. pens. from ST JOHN'S, Easter, 1613; B.A. 1615–6; M.A. 1619, as Derisley.

DEARESLEY, THOMAS. Matric. sizar from QUEENS', Easter, 1625. Of Suffolk. B.A. 1628–9; M.A. 1632. One of these names sequestered to Wickham St Paul, Essex, *c.* 1643; ejected, 1660. V. of Little Waldingfield, 1662–4. Perhaps R. of Depden, Suffolk, 1664–85. Will proved (Bury) 1686. (*Davids*, 516.)

DEARESLEY, THOMAS. Matric. pens. from ST CATHARINE'S, Easter, 1637; B.A. 1640–1; M.A. 1644. One of these names V. of Chatteris, Cambs., 1660.

DERISLEY, THOMAS. Adm. sizar (age 17) at MAGDALENE, Sept. 27, 1708. S. of Thomas. B. at Kirtling, Cambs. School, Thurlow, Cambs. Matric. 1712; B.A. 1712–3; M.A. 1716. Ord. deacon (Ely) May 31, 1713; C. of Weston Colville, Suffolk; priest, Mar. 13, 1714–5. V. of Houghton, Norfolk, 1731–68. R. of Pensthorpe, 1731–68.

DERISLEY, THOMAS. Adm. pens. at QUEENS', May 24, 1751. Of Norfolk. Probably s. of Thomas (1708), above. Matric. 1751; B.A. 1755; M.A. 1758. Fellow, 1758–66. Taxor, 1761. Ord. deacon (Norwich) Feb. 1758; priest (Ely) Mar. 11, 1759. Probably V. of Cobham, Kent, 1762–6.

DEARSLEY, WILLIAM. Matric. pens. from JESUS, Michs. 1580. Perhaps will (P.C.C.) 1615; of Monk's Eleigh, Suffolk, gent.

DEARSLEY, ——. Adm. pens. at EMMANUEL, 1620.

DEAS, WILLIAM. B.A. from EMMANUEL, 1592–3.

DEASY, ROBERT. Matric. sizar from SIDNEY, Easter, 1619; B.A. 1622–3; M.A. 1626. (Perhaps the Robert Dayley, of Northants., of the Sidney *Admission register*.)

DEAT (?), THOMAS. Matric. sizar from KING'S, Michs. 1642.

DEATH, ANTHONY. Matric. pens. from TRINITY, Michs. 1559, as Deithe; Scholar, 1565. Perhaps father of the next.

DEATH, ANTHONY. Matric. sizar from PEMBROKE, Easter, 1617. S. of Anthony, citizen and merchant taylor (perhaps the above). School, Merchant Taylors'. B.A. 1620–1; M.A. 1624. Master of Oundle School, 1624–5; dismissed. One of these names Head Master of Carlisle Grammar School during the Commonwealth. Died Feb. 9, 1679, aged 80. Buried at All Hallows, Barking. Will (P.C.C.) 1680.

DEATH or DETHE, JOHN. Matric. pens. from TRINITY, Easter, 1609; B.A. 1611–2; M.A. from Queens', 1615.

DEATH, JOHN. Adm. pens. at CORPUS CHRISTI, 1609. Of Nottinghamshire. Matric. 1610; B.A. 1613–4; M.A. 1617.

DETHE, ——. Student at PETERHOUSE, 1559.

DEATH, ——. Adm. pens. at EMMANUEL, Easter, 1628.

DEBANK, JOHN. Matric. sizar from PEMBROKE, Michs. 1551; B.A. from Corpus Christi, 1554–5. Fellow of Corpus Christi, 1554. Summoned before the visitor for being in possession of heretical books. Perhaps Fellow of Pembroke, 1554–5; 'of Derbs.' Received the tonsure (London) 1553–4; described as a scholar of St John's. Ord. priest (Lincoln) Sept. 21, 1555. R. of Easton-by-Stamford, Northants., 1559. Chaplain to William, Earl of Pembroke. R. of Willoughby Waterless, Leicester, 1559. R. of Bradwell-Juxta-Mare, Essex, 1563. Died there 1602. M.I. Will, P.C.C.

DEBANKE, NATHANIEL. M.A. from QUEENS', 1645 (Incorp. from Oxford). S. of William, of Locksley, Warws., clerk. Matric. from Lincoln College, Dec. 12, 1634, age 16; B.A. 1638; M.A. 1641. Fellow of Queens', 1645–7. (*Al. Oxon.*)

DEBANKE, ——. Matric. sizar from PEMBROKE, Michs. 1552. Probably John (above).

DEBARY, PETER. Adm. pens. (age 18) at TRINITY, June 23, 1742. S. of Peter, of London. School, Westminster. Matric. 1742; Scholar, 1743; B.A. 1745–6; M.A. 1749. Fellow, 1748. Ord. deacon (Lincoln, *Litt. dim.* from London) Mar. 4, 1747–8; priest, Feb. 19, 1748–9. V. of Hurstbourne Tarrant, Hants. V. of Burbage, Wilts. Died Jan. 4, 1814. (*Al. Westmon.*, 327.)

DEBAT, DANIEL. Adm. pens. at QUEENS', Jan. 29, 1741–2. Of Middlesex. Matric. 1742; B.A. 1745–6; M.A. 1749. Ord. deacon (Lincoln) June 5, 1748; priest, Dec. 18, 1748. Will of one of these names (P.C.C.) 1785; of Bristol, clerk.

DEBDEN, JOHN. Matric. pens. from CAIUS, *c.* 1596.

DEBNAM, JOHN. Adm. pens. at EMMANUEL, as 'Deadman,' Mar. 19, 1616–7. B. at Braintree, Essex. Matric. 1617, as 'Dedman'; B.A. 1620–1; M.A. 1624. Ord. deacon (   ) Sept. 18, 1624; priest, Mar 13, 1624–5. V. of Chrishall, Essex, 1657–73. R. of Strethall, 1670–2. Died 1673.

DEBENHAM, SAMUEL. Matric. sizar from PEMBROKE, Lent, 1581–2.

DE BERG, CHARLES BERNARD. Adm. at TRINITY, a scholar from Westminster, May 30, 1636.

DEBNEY, JOHN. Adm. scholar (age 17) at CAIUS, June 24, 1616. S. of Robert, Alderman of Norwich. Adm. at Gray's Inn, 1618.

DEBORDES, LEWIS. Adm. pens. at TRINITY, June 15, 1704. S. of James, of Greenwich, Kent. School, Westminster. M.A. 1728 (*Com. Reg.*). V. of Nazing, Essex, 1719–21. R. of St Lawrence, Newland, 1720. V. of East Ham, 1728–33. Chaplain to Duke of Dorset. Died Sept. 3, 1733. Will, P.C.C. (*Al. Westmon.*, 245.)

DE BRÉVAL, FRANCIS DURANT. D.D. 1675 (*Lit. Reg.*). Came to England, probably, about 1669. Said to have been, originally, a Capuchin. Preb. of Rochester, 1671. Preb. of Westminster, 1675. R. of Milton by Gravesend, 1680–1708. Buried in Westminster Abbey, Jan. 29, 1707–8. (*Westminster Abbey Register.*)

DECHAIR, WILLIAM. Adm. pens. (age 18) at TRINITY, Apr. 2, 1702. S. of Edward, of London. School, St Paul's. Matric. 1702; Scholar, 1703; B.A. 1705–6; M.A. from Peterhouse, 1709. Fellow of Peterhouse, 1708–10. Ord. deacon (Lincoln) Dec. 18, 1709; priest, Dec. 24, 1710. V. of Culham, Oxon. Will (P.C.C.) 1763; of St Gregory, London, clerk.

DE CHESSOY, PAUL. Adm. sizar (age 17) at ST JOHN'S, Apr. 10, 1678. S. of Paul, M.D. B. at Peterborough, Northants. School, Long-Orton (private; Mr King). Matric. 1678; B.A. from King's, 1681–2.

DECONSON, W. Matric. Fell.-Com. from QUEENS', Easter, 1565.

DE CRITZ, HENRY. Adm. pens. (age 19) at PEMBROKE, May 25, 1646. S. of John, of London. (A Fleming, serjeant painter to the King.) Exhibitioner from Charterhouse. Migrated to Oxford. B.A. from Jesus College, as Decreete, 1649; Scholar, 1649; by Parliamentary visitors. (*Al. Oxon*; *Burrows*, 177.)

'DEDDINGFIELD,' JOHN, *see* BEDINGFIELD.

DEE, ADRIAN. Matric. pens. from TRINITY, Easter, 1623. S. of Francis (next), D.D. B. Dec. 1, 1606. Bapt. at Canterbury Cathedral, Jan. 4, 1606–7. School, Merchant Taylors'. Scholar, 1623; B.A. 1626–7; M.A. 1630. Canon of Chichester, 1633. Died May 8, 1638. Will, P.C.C. (*Robinson*, I. 100; *Vis. of Sussex.*)

DEE, FRANCIS. Adm. at ST JOHN'S, *c.* 1595. S. of David, of Salop, preb. of St Paul's. B. in London. School, Merchant Taylors'. B.A. 1599–1600; M.A. 1603; B.D. 1610; D.D. 1616. Incorp. at Oxford, 1603. Ord. deacon (London) Apr. 25; priest, May 1, 1602. R. of Trinity-the-Less, London, 1607–20; of All Hallows, Lombard Street, 1615–34. Chancellor of Salisbury, 1619–34. V. of Sutton-at-Hone, Kent, 1620–2. Dean of Chichester, 1630–4. R. of Castor, Northants., 1634–8. Bishop of Peterborough, 1634–8. Died Oct. 8, 1638. Buried in his Cathedral. Will, P.C.C. Benefactor to St John's. Father of Adrian (above). (*D.N.B.*)

DEE, JOHN. Adm. pens. at ST JOHN'S, Nov. 1542. S. of Rowland, gentleman-sewer to Henry VII. B. in London, July 13, 1527. School, Chelmsford. Matric. 1544; B.A. 1545-6; M.A. from Trinity, 1548. Fellow of St John's, 1546. Assistant Greek Reader. Original Fellow of Trinity, 1546. Studied at Louvain, 1548. Perhaps LL.D. there. Lectured on Euclid at Paris, 1550. R. of Upton-on-Severn, and Long Leadenhall, Lincs. Travelled much abroad. Perhaps Chancellor of St Paul's, 1594. Warden of Manchester College, 1595-1608. Retired, c. 1604, to Mortlake, where he died, and was buried, Dec. 1608. An excellent mathematician, but better known as an astrologer. (*Cooper*, II. 497; *D.N.B.*)

DEE, JOHN. Adm. sizar at EMMANUEL, June 4, 1640. Perhaps R. of Wexham, Bucks., 1642-83. Died 1683. (*Lipscomb*, IV. 583.)

DEE, THOMAS. Matric. sizar from KING'S, Easter, 1632; B.A. 1635-6; M.A. 1639.

DEEBLE, NICHOLAS. Adm. pens. at QUEENS', May 15, 1646; M.A. 1647. S. of Nicholas, of Calstock, Cornwall. Matric. at Oxford, Dec. 6, 1639, age 19; B.A. (Oxford) 1644-5. R. of Calstock, Cornwall, 1645.

DEEDS, JULIUS. Adm. at CORPUS CHRISTI, 1709. S. of William, physician at Canterbury. School, Canterbury. Matric. 1710; Scholar, 1711; B.A. 1713-4; M.A. 1717. Ord. deacon (Lincoln) Mar. 17, 1716-7; priest, Dec. 21, 1718. R. of Dimchurch, Kent, 1718-52. R. of Gt Mongeham, 1730-52. Preb. of Canterbury, 1739. Died Apr. 19, 1752, aged 59. Buried at Hythe, in the family vault. (Burke, *L.G.*; *Masters*.)

DEEKES, JOHN. Matric. sizar from ST CATHARINE'S, Lent, 1615-6; B.A. 1618-9; M.A. 1622.

DEEPDALE, JOHN DE. A Southern student at Cambridge who received a pardon for participation in a riot, with the Northerners, 1261. (*Fuller*, 29.)

DEERE, JOHN. Adm. sizar (age 16) at CHRIST'S, July 5, 1695. S. of Richard. B. at Ashwell, Herts. School, Buntingford (Mr England). Scholar, 1695-6; Matric. 1696; B.A. 1699-1700. Ord. deacon (Ely) July 5, 1702. C. of Croxton, Cambs. Father of the next. (*Peile*, II. 134.)

DEERE, RICHARD. Adm. sizar at JESUS, Jan. 11, 1723-4. Of Cambridgeshire. S. of the above. Matric. 1724; Scholar; B.A. 1727-8. Ord. deacon (Lincoln) Dec. 22, 1728. P.C. of St John Baptist and the Holy Sepulchre, Norwich, 1737. Minor canon of Norwich. Died July 23, 1737, aged 31. Buried in Norwich Cathedral. (A. Gray; *Blomefield*, IV. 25.)

DEER, SAMUEL (1646), *see* DYER.

DEER, ——. Fee for M.A. or higher degree, 1473-4.

DEFFORD, JOHN. Matric. sizar from TRINITY, Michs. 1565. Perhaps Destford.

DEFRIAN, GEORGE. Matric. sizar from ST JOHN'S, c. 1590; B.A. 1593-4, as Defraine.

DE GALLS, GERARD. Adm. pens. (age 17) at TRINITY, Apr. 1, 1693. S. of Philip. B. at Amsterdam. School, St Paul's. Matric. 1695. Gerard De Gols, R. of St Peter's, Sandwich, 1713-37. Also minister to the Dutch congregation at St Clement's, Sandwich. One of the persons appointed by the Corporation to support the canopies at the coronation of George II. Author, *Sermons*, etc. Died Feb. 22, 1737. Buried at St Clement's. (H. G. Harrison.)

DEGGE, HERVEY. Adm. pens. (age 17) at TRINITY, June 10, 1726. S. of Simon (1693), of Derbyshire. School, Westminster. Matric. 1726; Scholar, 1727; B.A. 1729-30. Fellow, 1732. Died May 22, 1732-3. Brother of Staunton (1722) and Simon (1715). (*F.M.G.*, 981.)

DEGGE, SIMON. Adm. pens. at EMMANUEL, Oct. 18, 1693. Of Worcestershire. S. of Simon, of Broadwater, Worcs. B. 1676. Adm. at the Inner Temple, 1693. Married (1) Selina, dau. of William Williams, of Rempston, Notts.; (2) Jane, dau. of Harvey Staunton, Esq., of Derbyshire. Father of Simon (1715), Staunton (1722) and Hervey (1726). (*Staffs. Pedigrees*; *Vis. of Derbs.*, 1662; Erdeswicke's *Survey of Staffs.*, LX.)

DEGGE, SIMON. Adm. Fell.-Com. (age 16) at ST JOHN'S, Dec. 1, 1710. S. of William, deceased. B. at Derby. School, Heydon (private; Mr Goodwin). Adm. at the Inner Temple, 1709. Perhaps F.R.S. 1723. Died Nov. 8, 1729, aged 35. M.I. at Gravely, Herts. (*F.M.G.*, 983; Lysons's *Derbs.*; Jewitt's *Reliq.*, XXII. 238.)

DEGGE, SIMON. Adm. Fell.-Com. at CLARE, Nov. 28, 1715. S. of Simon (1693). B. at Nottingham, 1697. Matric. 1716-7; M.A. 1717 (*Com. Reg.*). Adm. at the Inner Temple, 1712; s. and h. of Simon, of Derby, Esq. Of Blithebridge, Staffs. and Bowden Hall, Derbs. Probably F.R.S. 1730 (see the above: there are two elections, and two signatures, but these look alike). Died c. 1765. Brother of Staunton (1722) and Hervey (1726). (Lysons's *Derbs.*, CXXV.; Erdeswicke's *Staffs.*, LX.)

DEGGE, STAUNTON. Adm. pens. (age 16) at TRINITY, June 17, 1722. S. of Simon (1693), of Derby. School, Westminster. Matric. 1723; Scholar, 1724; B.A. 1725-6. Ord. deacon (Lincoln) Sept. 20, 1730. R. of Staunton, Notts. Brother of Hervey (1726) and Simon (1715).

DE GREY, EDMUND. Adm. pens. (age 16) at CAIUS, July 27, 1636. S. of Sir William, Knt., of Merton, Norfolk, deceased. School, Thetford (Mr Ward). Matric. 1637. Perhaps scholar of Trinity Hall, 1639. Major in the Royalist army; 'employed under Sir William Hopton.' Compounded for his estates. Went to reside at Merton Hall, 1677; afterwards at Thetford, 1686. Buried at Merton, Mar. 6, 1689-90. Will (Norw. archd. C.) 1690. (*Venn*, I. 323.)

DE GREY, JAMES. Adm. pens. (age 17) at CAIUS, Apr. 7, 1630. S. of Sir William, Knt. B. at Merton, Norfolk. School, Bury. Matric. 1631. Adm. at the Middle Temple, May 13, 1633. Died July 3, 1665. Buried at Merton. M.I. Father of William (1668), brother of Robert (1629), William (1645) and Edmund (1636). (*Venn*, I. 293.)

DE GRAY, JAMES (1700), *see* BEDINGFIELD.

DE GREY, ROBERT. Adm. Fell.-Com. (age 18) at CAIUS, Apr. 21, 1629. S. of Sir William, Knt., of Merton, Norfolk. B. at Ellingham. School, Bury. Matric. 1629. Adm. at the Middle Temple, Nov. 15, 1631. Knighted, 1641. Royalist. Buried at Merton, Oct. 21, 1644. Will (Norwich) 1645. Brother of James (1630), Edmund (1636) and William (1645). (*Venn*, I. 288.)

DE GREY, THOMAS. Adm. Fell.-Com. (age 17) at ST JOHN'S, May 18, 1697. S. of William, Esq. B. at Merton, Norfolk. School, Bury. Matric. 1697. M.P. for Thetford, 1708-10; for Norfolk, 1715-27. Of Merton, Esq. Buried at Merton, Dec. 18, 1765. Father of the next. (A. B. Beaven.)

DE GREY, THOMAS. Adm. Fell.-Com. (age 17) at CHRIST'S, Apr. 29, 1735. S. of Thomas (above), of Merton, Norfolk. School, Bury. M.P. for Norfolk, 1764-74. Lieutenant-Colonel of the Norfolk Militia, 1764. Died June 23, 1781. Buried at Merton. (*Peile*, II. 231.)

DE GREY, WILLIAM. Adm. pens. (age 17) at CAIUS, Apr. 1, 1645. S. of Sir William, Knt. B. at Merton, Norfolk. Bapt. July 22, 1626. School, Thetford (Mr Ward). Matric. 1645; B.A. from Trinity Hall, 1647-8; M.A. (*Com. Reg.*) 1671. Major in the army. Described as of Norwich, in 1656; and of Merton, in 1686. Brother of James (1630), Edmund (1636) and Robert (1629). (*Venn*, I. 357.)

DE GREY, WILLIAM. Adm. Fell.-Com. (age 16) at CAIUS, Apr. 22, 1668. S. of James (1630), Esq., deceased. B. at Merton, Norfolk. School, Thetford (Mr Keen). Matric. 1668. Adm. at the Middle Temple, May 22, 1671. M.P. for Thetford, 1685. Resided at Merton. Buried there Mar. 1, 1686-7. (*Venn*, I. 434.)

DE GREY, WILLIAM. Adm. scholar at TRINITY HALL, Feb. 23, 1736-7. S. of Thomas, Esq., of Merton, Norfolk. B. July 7, 1719. Matric. 1737; M.A. 1770 (*Lit. Reg.*). Adm. at the Middle Temple, Jan. 26, 1737-8. Called to the Bar, 1742. Reader, 1765. Treasurer, 1766. K.C. 1758. M.P. for Newport, Cornwall, 1761-70; for the University, 1770-1. Attorney-General, 1766-71. Knighted. Chief Justice C.P. 1771-80. Created Baron Walsingham, 1780. Died May 9, 1781. (*D.N.B.*; where he is wrongly assigned to Christ's.)

DEGULHON or DIGULHON, STEPHEN. Adm. sizar (age 19) at ST JOHN'S, June 20, 1739. S. of Stephen, gent., of Middlesex. B. in London. School, Canterbury. Matric. 1739; B.A. 1742-3; M.A. 1771. Ord. deacon (London) May 29, 1743; priest, June 9, 1745. R. of Ashby, Norfolk, 1746-85. R. of Carleton St Peter and V. of Claxton, 1747-85. Preacher at Berwick Street Chapel, Soho, 1755. P.C. of Marylebone, 1767. Died Sept. 10, 1785. (*Scott-Mayor*, III. 501; *G. Mag.*)

DE HAGUE, THOMAS. Adm. at CORPUS CHRISTI, 1715. Of Huguenot origin. B. in Norwich. Matric. Lent, 1718-9; B.A. 1719-20.

DEHANY, DAVID. Adm. pens. at QUEENS', July 24, 1740. Of Jamaica. S. of David, merchant, of Bristol. B. Apr. 20, 1724. Matric. 1740-1. Adm. at Lincoln's Inn, May 1, 1742. Died June 22, 1761. (Laurence-Archer, *West Indies*, 335.)

DEICROWE, BENJAMIN. Scholar of TRINITY, 1619; B.A. 1622-3.

DEIGHTON, *see* DIGHTON.

DEIKE, *see* DYKE.

DEINCOURT, OLIVER. M.A. Benefactor to the University. Chancellor, some time in the 14th century. One of these names s. of William, Baron of Blankney. Died before 1392. (*Blore*, 151; *G.E.C.*)

DEIOS or DEYOS, JOHN. B.A. from CHRIST'S, 1610-1. Of Buckinghamshire. Matric. from Magdalen Hall, Oxford, Dec. 1607, age 17; M.A. (Oxford) 1613-4. Incorp. at Cambridge, 1614. Probably R. of Wavendon, Bucks., 1636. (*Peile*, I. 266.)

DEIOS, DEIOSTE or **DYOS, LAURENCE.** Matric. pens. from ST JOHN'S, Easter, 1571. B. in Salop. B.A. 1572-3; M.A. 1576; B.D. 1583. Fellow, 1573. Afterwards a minister in London. R. of Chiddingstone, Kent, 1585-1618. R. of Brastead, 1592-1618. Author, *Sermons*. Buried at Chiddingstone, Dec. 27, 1618. (*Cooper*, II. 476; III. 83; *D.N.B.*; H. G. Harrison.)

DIOS, NICHOLAS. Matric. pens. from PEMBROKE, Easter, 1607. B. at Charing, Kent. B.A. 1610-1; M.A. 1614. Ord. deacon and priest (London) Mar. 1, 1617-8, age 26.

DEIOS, THOMAS. Adm. Fell.-Com. at KING'S, Lent, 1588-9; B.A. 1592-3; M.A. 1596.

DEKENZIE, MATTHEW. Matric. sizar from TRINITY, Michs. 1626.

DE LA CHAMBER, JOHN. Adm. pens. at EMMANUEL, May 19, 1638, as Chambers. Died whilst a student. Will (P.C.C.) 1640. Mentions his tutor and kinsman, Richard Weller, and several student friends. Uncle, William Newton, exor. (J. Ch. Smith.)

DE LA CHAMPE, *see* **DALECHAMP.**

DELACOURTE, JOHN. Matric. pens. from TRINITY HALL, Michs. 1554.

DELACRE, *see also* **DILLAKER.**

DELACRE, MICHAEL. Adm. sizar at TRINITY, May 17, 1641. One of this name ('Miles'), ord. deacon and priest (Lincoln) Jan. 8, 1660-1. R. of Paston, Northants., 1669.

DELACRE, THOMAS. Adm. pens. (age 15) at PETERHOUSE, Apr. 6, 1637. Of Huntingdonshire. School, Wisbech. Matric. 1637. Migrated to Trinity, Feb. 10, 1637-8. Scholar, 1638; B.A. 1640-1; M.A. from Trinity Hall, 1646.

DE LA CROZE, ANTHONY MARK. Incorp. LL.D. 1693, from Orleans.

DE LA DOUESPE, EZEKIEL PAUL, *see* **DOUESPE.**

DELAHAY, JOHN. Adm. sizar at TRINITY, June 25, 1646. Of Herefordshire. Matric. 1646; Scholar, 1649; B.A. 1649-50; M.A. 1653. Fellow, 1651.

DELAHAY, JOHN. Adm. pens. at TRINITY, June 27, 1682. Matric. 1682; Scholar, 1685; B.A. 1685-6; M.A. 1691. Perhaps Matric. from Balliol College, Oxford, Mar. 22, 1682-3, age 17; s. of Thomas, of Peterchurch, Hereford. No Oxford degree. Perhaps R. of Gt Greenford, Middlesex, 1689-1730. Will (Consist. C. London) 1730. (*Al. Oxon.*)

DELAHAY, PAUL. Adm. sizar at TRINITY, Mar. 31, 1651. Of Herefordshire. Matric. 1654; B.A. 1654-5.

DE LA HAYE, PETER. Adm. Fell.-Com. (age 26) at ST JOHN'S, Oct. 5, 1671. S. of Jacques, of Caen, Normandy. B. there. School, Paris. Matric. 1671; M.A. 1674 (*Lit. Reg.*).

DE LA MORE, ADAM. University Bedell, *c.* 1350. Benefactor. (Stokes, *Bedells*, 55.)

DELAMORE, JOHN. Adm. pens. (age 16) at MAGDALENE, Dec. 20, 1709. S. of William, gent. B. at Long Sutton, Lincs. School, Wisbech. Matric. 1710; B.A. 1713-4; M.A. 1717. Ord. deacon (Ely) Dec. 23, 1716; priest (Norwich) Sept. 1718. C. of Walsoken. Brother of Richard (1715). (*Lincs. Pedigrees*, 1194.)

DELAMORE, MARTIN. Adm. sizar at JESUS, Jan. 31, 1625-6. Matric. 1626; B.A. 1629-30; M.A. 1633. Ord. deacon (Norwich) June 1; priest, Sept. 21, 1634. R. of All Saints', Colchester, 1637-9. V. of Littleport, Cambs., 1639.

DELAMORE, RICHARD. Adm. pens. (age 16) at MAGDALENE, July 9, 1715. S. of William, gent. B. at Sutton, Lincs. School, Wisbech. Matric. 1716; M.B. 1721. Brother of John (1709).

DELAMOTTE, WILLIAM. Adm. sizar at ST CATHARINE'S, May 18, 1736. Of Greenwich, Kent. Matric. 1736.

DE LANCY, JAMES. Adm. at CORPUS CHRISTI, 1721. S. and h. of Stephen, merchant, of New York. B. in America, 1703. Adm. at the Inner Temple, 1723. Chief Justice and Lieutenant Governor of New York. Married Ann Heathcote. Died July 31, 1760. Father of the next. (*Masters.*)

DE LANCY, JAMES. Adm. at CORPUS CHRISTI, 1750. S. of James, above. B. in America, 1732. School, Eton. Matric. 1750. Adm. at Lincoln's Inn, June 2, 1753. Married, 1771, Margaret, dau. of William Allen, Chief Justice of Pennsylvania. Died at Bath, 1800. (E. A. Jones.)

DELANDE, ALBERT. Adm. pens. at CLARE, June 27, 1728. S. and h. of Albert, of St Giles-in-the-Fields, captain. B. in London. Matric. 1729. Adm. to the Middle Temple, Oct. 22, 1733; and to Gray's Inn, Jan. 23, 1736-7.

DE L'ANGLE ('LANGLEY'), JOHN MAXIMILIAN. Incorp. D.D. from Leyden, 1681. Probably 2nd s. of Jean Maximilian, Protestant divine, of Rouen. Huguenot refugee. V. of Ruislip, Midds., 1674-82. Preb. of Canterbury, 1678-1724. R. of Kingston, Kent, 1681-92. V. of Sibertswold, 1684. R. of St George and St Mary, Canterbury, 1686-92. R. of Chartham, Kent, 1695-1724. Died Nov. 11, 1724, aged 83. Buried at Chartham. M.I. Another of these names, s. of Dr Samuel, of Rouen, matric. at Oxford, 1684. (H. G. Harrison.)

DELAP, JOHN. Adm. pens. (age 17) at TRINITY, Mar. 30, 1743. S. of John, of Gainsborough, Lincs. B. at Spilsby. School, Beverley, Yorks. (Mr Clark). Matric. 1743. Migrated to Magdalene, Mar. 15, 1743-4. B.A. 1746-7; M.A. 1750; D.D. 1762. Fellow of Magdalene, 1748. Ord. deacon (Lincoln) May 21, 1749; priest, Dec. 23, 1750. Perhaps R. of Ousby, Cumberland, 1759-66. V. of Iford and Kingston, Sussex, 1765-1812. V. of Woolavington, Somerset, 1774-1812. Poet and dramatist. Died in London, 1812. (*D.N.B.*)

DE LA PLACE, PETER. Adm. sizar at CORPUS CHRISTI, 1647. Of France. Matric. Easter, 1649; B.A. 1649-50.

DE LA POLE, *see also* **POLE.**

DE LA POOLE, RICHARD. Adm. sizar at EMMANUEL, May 1, 1666. Of Lincolnshire. Matric. 1667; B.A. 1669-70. Ord. deacon (Lincoln) Dec. 20, 1668.

DE LA PYENDE, STEPHEN. Matric. pens. from CHRIST'S, Easter, 1606. Of Depden, Suffolk. Adm. at the Inner Temple, 1610-1.

DELAUNE or **DELAUNCE, ABRAHAM.** Adm. pens. at EMMANUEL, Mar. 17, 1610-1. S. of Gideon, of London and Sharsted, Dodington, Kent. Matric. 1611; B.A. 1614-5; M.A. 1618. Incorp. at Oxford, 1619. Married Anne, dau. of Sir Richard Sondes, of Throwley, Kent. Died Jan. 23, 1637-8. Admon. (P.C.C.) 1638. Father of William (1648). (*Le Neve*, 179; *N. and Q.*, 5th S., XII. 117; *Vis. of Kent*, 1663.)

DELAWNE, HENRY. Adm. sizar (age 18) at CAIUS, Nov. 16, 1610. S. of Isaac, M.D., a Frenchman. School, Norwich. (Pedigree in *Vis. of London*, 1634.)

DE LAWNE, NATHANIEL. Adm. scholar at CORPUS CHRISTI, July 4, 1618. Of Norwich. S. of Peter, minister of the French Congregation at Norwich. School, Norwich. Matric. pens. 1618; B.A. 1621-2; M.A. 1625. V. of Broad Hempston, Devon, 1630. Translated Du Moulin's *Logic* into English, 1624. (*Masters*, 277; *Add. MSS.*, 5867.)

DE LAWNE, PAUL. Adm. pens. at EMMANUEL, Sept. 29, 1604. S. of William (1583). B. in London. B.A. 1607-8; M.A. 1611; M.D. 1615 (Incorp. from Padua). Incorp. at Oxford (M.A.) 1611. For many years in Ireland, as physician to the Viceroy. F.R.C.P. 1618. Elect, 1642. Censor, 1643. Professor of Physic at Gresham College, 1642-52. Physician-general to the fleet, 1654. Probably died in Jamaica, Dec. 1654. Will (P.C.C.) 1657. (*D.N.B.*; *Munk*, I. 170; *Vis. of London*, 1634.)

DELAWNE or **LAWNE, PETER.** Matric. pens. from PETERHOUSE, Easter, 1588, as 'Lawe'; B.A. 1591-2; M.A. 1597; D.D. 1617. Perhaps R. of Redenhall, Norfolk, 1629.

DE LAUNE, PETER. D.D. 1635 (on visit of Charles, Count Elector Palatine). S. of William (1583). Of PETERHOUSE, where he gave £25 to the College Chapel. Dr De Lawne was pastor of the French congregation (*Add. MSS.*, 5867) at Norwich in 1647. (*Vis. of London*, 1634; *Blomefield*, II. 258.)

DELAUNE, WILLIAM. Resident at Cambridge, in 1583; but doubtful if a member of the University. L.R.C.P. 1582. A French protestant minister. Studied medicine at Paris and Montpelier for eight years. Fled to England. Practised chiefly in London. Buried at St Anne's, Blackfriars, Feb. 19, 1610. Author, an epitome of Calvin's *Institution*. Will (P.C.C.) 1611; 'preacher of the word of God and physician.' Father of Paul (above) and Peter. (*D.N.B.*; *Cooper*, I. 490; *Vis. of London*, 1634.)

DELAUNE, WILLIAM. Adm. Fell.-Com. (age 18) at SIDNEY, May 23, 1648. S. of Abraham (1610-1), Esq., deceased. B. at Throwley, Kent (his mother's home). Schools, Caen, Normandy, and Bromley, Kent (Mr Brookes). Matric. 1648. Of London, merchant, and of Sharsted, Dodington, Kent. Knighted, Jan. 10, 1663-4. Died 1667. Will, P.C.C. (*Le Neve*, 179; *N. and Q.*, 5th S., XII. 29; *Vis. of Sussex*, 1663.)

DELAUNE, WILLIAM. D.D. 1714 (Incorp. from Oxford). S. of Benjamin, of London, gent. B. Apr. 14, 1659. School, Merchant Taylors'. Matric. from St John's College, Oxford, July 2, 1675, age 16; B.A. (Oxford) 1679; M.A. 1683; B.D. 1688; D.D. 1697. President of St John's, 1698-1728. Vice-Chancellor, 1702-6. Lady Margaret Professor, at Oxford, 1715-28. Preb. of Winchester, 1702-28; of Worcester, 1715-28. R. of Chilbolton, Hants., 1689. R. of Handborough, Oxon., 1699. Died May 23, 1728. Buried in St John's College Chapel, Oxford. Admon. (P.C.C.) 1729. (*Al. Oxon.*; *D.N.B.*)

DELAVAL, EDWARD HUSSEY. Adm. Fell.-Com. (age 18) at PEMBROKE, July 4, 1747. S. of Francis Blake, of Seaton Delaval, Northumberland, Esq. Bapt. at Newburn, June 12, 1729. Matric. 1748; B.A. 1750–1; M.A. 1754. Fellow, 1751. Classical scholar and chemist. F.R.S. 1759. Author. Married, Dec. 22, 1808, Sarah, dau. of George Scott, of Methley, Yorks. Died Aug. 14, 1814, at Parliament Place, Old Palace Yard, Westminster. Buried in the Abbey. Brother of John Blake (1746). (*D.N.B.*; H. M. Wood.)

DELAVALL, JOHN. Matric. Fell.-Com. from MAGDALENE, Easter, 1637. Perhaps 2nd s. of Sir Robert, of Seaton Delaval. Of Dissington, Northumberland.

DELAVAL, JOHN. Adm. pens. at CHRIST'S, July 3, 1672. S. of Sir Ralph, Bart. B. at Seaton Delaval, Northumberland. Bapt. at Earsdon, Nov. 7, 1654. Colonel in the Guards. Succeeded as 3rd Bart., Aug. 1696. M.P. for Morpeth, 1701–5; for Northumberland, 1705–8. Buried at Earsdon, June 8, 1729. (Durham) 1729. (*G.E.C.*; *Peile*, II. 44–5; H. M. Wood.)Will

DELAVAL, JOHN BLAKE. Adm. pens. (age 18) at PEMBROKE, July 3, 1746. S. of Francis Blake, Esq., of Seaton Delaval, Northumberland. B. in London, Mar. 17, 1728. Sir John Hussey-Delaval, M.P. for Berwick, 1754–61, 1765–74, 1780–6. Created Bart., July 1, 1761. Baron Delaval of Redford, in the Peerage of Ireland, 1783. Raised to the peerage of the United Kingdom, Aug. 21, 1786. Died at Seaton, May 17, 1808. Buried in St Paul's Chapel, Westminster Abbey. Brother of Edward (1747). (*G.E.C.*; H. M. Wood; A. B. Beaven.)

DELAVALL, WILLIAM. Adm. pens. (age 17) at ST JOHN'S, July 11, 1633. S. of Sir Ralph, Knt., of Seaton Delaval, Northumberland. Bapt. at Earsdon, Apr. 28, 1616. School, Morpeth. Matric. 1633. Married Mary, dau. of Sir Peter Riddell, of Newcastle. Buried at St Nicholas, Newcastle, June 2, 1667. Father of the next. (Le Neve, *Knights*, 432; H. M. Wood.)

DELAVAL, WILLIAM. Adm. pens. (age 16) at CHRIST'S, Mar. 4, 1666–7. S. of William (above). B. at Seaton Delaval, Northumberland. School, Newcastle (Mr Oxley). Matric. 1667; B.A. 1670–1. Buried at St Nicholas, Newcastle, Jan. 28, 1675–6. (*Peile*, II. 9; H. M. Wood.)

DE LA WOODE, THOMAS. Matric. pens. from JESUS, *c.* 1596.

DELBOE, SIMON. Adm. pens. (age 18) at TRINITY, June 27, 1676. S. of Simon. B. in London. Matric. 1676; Scholar from Westminster, 1677; B.A. 1679–80; M.A. 1683. Fellow, 1682. Probably of Dutch origin. One Simon Delbo was deacon of the Dutch Church in London, 1658. (J. Ch. Smith.)

DELBRIDGE, JOHN. Adm. pens. at EMMANUEL, July 3, 1604. S. and h. of John, gent., of Barnstaple, Devon. Matric. 1604. Adm. at the Middle Temple, May 10, 1606. One of these names M.P. for Barnstaple, 1620, 1624, 1625, 1626, 1628.

DELBRIDGE, NATHANIEL. Adm. pens. at EMMANUEL, Aug. 20, 1607. Matric. 1607; B.A. 1611–2; M.A. 1615; B.D. 1622. Incorp. at Oxford, 1615. Ord. deacon (Peterb.) Dec. 22; priest, Dec. 23, 1621.

DELBRIDGE, THOMAS. Adm. pens. (age 16) at PEMBROKE, June 23, 1654. S. of ——, clerk. B. in Cornwall. Matric. 1656–7, as 'John.'

DELEMARCHE, HENRY. Matric. sizar from JESUS, Easter, 1617.

DELENE, TIMOTHY. Matric. sizar from QUEENS', Easter, 1601. Of Warwickshire. Perhaps R. of Ashow, Warws.

DELIGNE, ERASMUS. Adm. Fell.-Com. (age 17) at ST JOHN'S, June 26, 1639. S. of Sir Daniel, of Harlaxton, Lincs., Knt. B. in London. School, Nottingham (Mr Gambett). Of Harlaxton, Esq. Married twice, and had issue. Died 1683. His father (b. at Frankfort) came to England, *c.* 1613, on account of religious persecution; and was knighted 1620. (*Lincs. Pedigrees*; Turnor's *Grantham*.)

DELYNE, ROBERT. Matric. pens. from PEMBROKE, Michs. 1641.

DELKE, WILLIAM, *see* **DILKE.**

DELL, GEORGE. Adm. sizar (age 17) at CHRIST'S, May 22, 1694. S. of William. B. at Sampshill, Beds. Bapt. at Westoning, June 14, 1676. School, Buckingham (Mr Styles). Scholar, 1694–5; Matric. 1695; LL.B. 1710. Ord. deacon (Lincoln) May 26, 1700; priest (Peterb.) Dec. 30, 1705. R. of Foulness, Essex, 1706. Died unmarried, 1714. Admon. (Consist. C. London) to his brother Humphrey. Grandson of William (1623–4), Master of Caius. (*Peile*, II. 130; *Add. MSS.* 5867; J. Ch. Smith.)

DELL, HUMFREY. Adm. pens. (age 15) at ST JOHN'S, Sept. 18, 1721. S. of Humphrey, jeweller, of Middlesex. B. in London. School, St Paul's. Matric. 1723; M.B. 1727. Practised physic at Flitwick, Beds. Died Sept. 12, 1764. Said to be a descendant of William Dell, the puritan Master of Caius. (*Scott-Mayor*, III. 344; *L. Mag.*; *G. Mag.*)

DELL, JOHN. Adm. pens. (age 16) at CHRIST'S, Apr. 1, 1669. S. of William (1623–4). B. at Yelden, Beds. School, St Paul's. Matric. 1669; B.A. 1672–3; M.A. 1676. Incorp. at Oxford, 1675. Ord. deacon (Peterb.) June 4, 1674; priest (Lincoln) Sept. 1685. R. of (mediety of) Woodford, Northants., 1690–1707. R. of Tilbrook, Beds., 1691. Buried at Northill, Beds., Sept. 4, 1707. (*Peile*, II. 19; H. I. Longden.)

DELL, JOHN. M.A. from QUEENS', 1711. Of Cornwall. Matric. from Pembroke College, Oxford, Oct. 27, 1694; B.A. (Oxford) 1699. Doubtless R. of Blisland, Cornwall, 1709. R. of Ruan-Lanihorne, 1711–5. Died 1715. Admon. (Exeter) 1715. (*Al. Oxon.*)

DELL, WILLIAM. Adm. sizar at EMMANUEL, Lent, 1623–4; B.A. 1627–8; M.A. 1631. Fellow of Emmanuel. For some years chaplain in the Parliamentary army. R. of Yelden, Beds., 1641–62, where he invited John Bunyan to preach in his church. Intruded as Master of Caius, May 4, 1649. Resigned, May 11, 1660. Ejected from Yelden, 1662; and retired to a property at Westoning. Buried at Yelden. Will proved (P.C.C.) 1670. (*D.N.B.* unfortunately identifies him with the next, and gives credence to the legend of his being buried in unconsecrated ground. For a full account of his life and works *see Venn*, I. 375, and *Caius* Coll. *History*.)

DELL, WILLIAM. M.A. 1628. Incorp. from Oxford. Of Wiltshire. Matric. from St John's College, Oxford, Nov. 12, 1619, age 16; B.A. (Oxford) 1622–3; M.A. 1626. Secretary to Archbishop Laud. P.C. of St Mary Aldermanbury, 1629–31. R. of Frittenden, Kent, 1635. See the above entry. (*Al. Oxon.*)

DELL, WILLIAM (1627), *see* **DALE.**

DELME, PHILIP. Adm. pens. at EMMANUEL, June 2, 1607. Matric. 1607, as 'Delve.' Will of Philip Delme (minister of the Walloon Church, Canterbury) proved (P.C.C.) 1654. (J. Ch. Smith.)

DE LOCHES, THOMAS. Adm. pens. at CLARE, June 22, 1715. B. at Hull, Yorks. Matric. 1715; B.A. 1718–9.

DELOMENCE, HENRY AUGUSTUS; Count Montbron, M.A. 1625 (on King's visit).

DELVES, HENRY. Adm. Fell.-Com. at CLARE, Mar. 18, 1718–9. S. of Sir Thomas, of Doddington, Cheshire, Bart. B. at Chelsea, Middlesex, July 18, 1700. Matric. 1719. Died Apr. 10, 1725. (Burke, *Ext. Bart.*; D. L. Broughton, *Records of a Cheshire Family*.)

DELVES, JOHN. Adm. pens. (age 16) at CHRIST'S, June 20, 1671. S. of William. B. at Knutsford, Cheshire. School, Tamworth (Mr Antrobus). Matric. 1671; B.A. 1674–5. Brother of William (1671).

DELVES, LAURENCE. Adm. pens. (age 18) at PEMBROKE, Apr. 28, 1619. S. of Sir Thomas, of Doddington, Cheshire, Knt. (afterwards Bart.). Matric. 1619. Adm. at Lincoln's Inn, Nov. 25, 1620. Died *s.p.* (Burke, *Ext. Bart.*)

DELVES, NICHOLAS. Adm. pens. (age 18) at SIDNEY, June 22, 1668. S. of Thomas, gent., of Hastings, Sussex. B. at Bexhill. Schools, 'Boan' and Merchant Taylors'. Matric. 1668; B.A. 1671–2. Ord. deacon (Peterb.) June 14, 1674, as of Trinity College. (S. of Nicholas, Master of Merchant Taylors' Company, according to C. J. Robinson's *School Register*.)

DELVES, WILLIAM. Adm. pens. (age 18) at CHRIST'S, Sept. 29, 1671. S. of William. B. at Knutsford. School, Knutsford (Mr Turner). Matric. 1671. Brother of John (1671).

DELVIN, Lord, *see* **CHRISTOPHER NUGENT.**

DELYNE, ROBERT, *see* **DELIGNE.**

DE MOIVRE, ABRAHAM. M.A. from TRINITY, 1739 (*Lit. Reg.*). S. of a surgeon. B. at Vitry, France, May 26, 1667. Educated at Sedan, Saumur and Paris. Arrived in England, as a Protestant refugee, 1688. Distinguished mathematician and friend of Newton. F.R.S. 1697. Died Nov. 27, 1754. (*D.N.B.* as Moivre.)

DEMPSTER, THOMAS. For a time at PEMBROKE, *c.* 1589, age about 10. Tutor, Walter Whalley, M.A. Left and travelled in France. Graduated at Douay; and, in Canon Law, at Paris. Professor at Toulouse, Nismes, Paris, Pisa and Bologna. Knighted by Urban VIII. Famous as a Latin poet and as a learned ecclesiastical historian. Died at Bologna, 1625. (*D.N.B.*)

DENBAUD, WILLIAM. Adm. pens. (age 15) at SIDNEY, July 6, 1698. S. of William, R. of Oakford, Devon. B. there. School, Tiverton. Matric. 1698.

DENBIGH, *see* also **FEILDING.**

DENBIGH, WILLIAM, Earl of. M.A. 1627. S. of Basil Feilding, of Newnham Paddock, Warws. B. *c.* 1582. Knighted, Mar. 4, 1606–7. Created Viscount Feilding, Dec. 30, 1620, and Earl of Denbigh, Sept. 14, 1622. Master of the Wardrobe, 1622. An admiral in several expeditions. Volunteer in Prince Rupert's Horse, 1642. Mortally wounded in a skirmish near Birmingham. Died Apr. 8, 1643. Buried at Monk's Kirby, Warws. (*D.N.B.*; *G.E.C.*)

DENBY, MICHAEL. Matric. sizar from GONVILLE HALL, Nov. 1554. Scholar, 1556-9; B.A. 1560-1. Ord. deacon (Ely) Nov. 24, 1560. R. of Scarning, Norfolk, 1584; where he kept school. R. of Tivetshall, 1596. R. of Kempston, 'no preacher; a benefice-monger.' Will proved (Norwich), 1599; of Tivetshall. (*Venn*, I. 38.)

DENDY, THOMAS, *see* **DANDY.**

DENE, *see* **DEANE.**

DE NEUFVILLE, ROBERT. LL.D. 1709 (*Lit. Reg.*). Of the University of Leyden. Of Frankfort, Germany. Created Baronet, 1709. (Burke, *Ext. Bart.*)

DENFORD, JEREMY. Described as 'of EMMANUEL College; literate' when ord. deacon (Peterb.) Dec. 18, 1614; priest, Mar. 30, 1615. Probably adm. sizar July 6, 1613, as 'Doxford.' Signs as minister at Cranfield, Beds., 1614-5.

DENGAYNE, HENRY. Matric. pens. from QUEENS', Easter, 1586. Of Norfolk. Perhaps 1st s. of Thomas, of Brunstead, Norfolk. One of these names, of Norfolk, gent., adm. at Lincoln's Inn, Nov. 20, 1602. (*Vis. of Norfolk.*)

DENGAYNE, THOMAS. Adm. pens. at QUEENS', May 17, 1593. Perhaps 3rd s. of Thomas, of Brunstead, Norfolk. Bapt. Sept. 28, 1575. Matric. *c.* 1593; B.A. 1596-7; M.A. 1600; B.D. 1607. Fellow, 1599-1616. Ord. priest (Colchester) 1601. R. of Mautby, Norfolk, 1613. (*Vis. of Norfolk.*)

DENHAM, *see also* **DINHAM.**

DENHAM, ARTHUR. B.A. from TRINITY, 1582-3. S. of Thomas, of St Peter ad Vincula, London, provost of the mint. M.A. from Balliol College, Oxford, 1585; B.D. (Oxford) 1593. R. of Laindon, Essex, 1588-1631. Died 1631. By his will (Consist. C. London) he leaves property to his son Thomas (? 1617). (*Al. Oxon.*; J. Ch. Smith.)

DENHAM, BENJAMIN. Adm. pens. (age 17) at CHRIST'S, May 15, 1639. S. of Richard. B. in London. School, Westminster. Matric. 1639; B.A. 1642-3; M.A. 1650. Chaplain to the Levant Company. One of these names R. of East Barming, Kent, 1667-70. Died 1670. (*Peile*, I. 460.)

DENHAM, DAVID. Adm. sizar (age 18) at CHRIST'S, May 15, 1711. S. of David. B. in Sussex. School, Lewes (Mr Peirce). Matric. 1711; B.A. 1714-5. Ord. deacon (London) Mar. 1714-5; priest (Chichester) Sept. 1718. R. of Waltham, near Petworth, Sussex (? V. of Cold Waltham), 1718-31. R. of Pett, 1731-45; when he died. (*Peile*, II. 177-8.)

DENHAM, EDMUND. Adm. sizar at ST CATHARINE'S, Oct. 5, 1723. Of Coventry. Matric. 1723; B.A. 1727-8. Fellow, 1728.

DENHAM, EDWARD. Adm. at KING'S, a scholar from Eton, 1689. B. in London. Matric. 1690; B.A. 1693-4; M.A. 1697. Fellow, 1693. Master of Preston School, Lancs., 1698-1704. Afterwards of Macclesfield School, 1704. Died in Chester Castle, prisoner on a charge of murder. Buried Apr. 22, 1717. (*Harwood*; Earwaker, *E. Cheshire*, II. 522.)

DENHAM, HENRY. Matric. sizar from TRINITY, Easter, 1625; B.A. from St Catharine's, 1628. Ord. deacon (Peterb.) Sept. 21; priest, Sept. 22, 1628, as of Trinity.

DENHAM, JOHN. Adm. at KING'S, a scholar from Eton, 1541. Died in College, 1542. (*Harwood.*)

DENHAM or DINHAM, JOHN. M.A. from JESUS, 1736. S. of William, of Advent, Cornwall. Matric. from Queen's College, Oxford, Mar. 20, 1727-8, age 18; B.A. (Oxford) 1731. (*Al. Oxon.*)

DENHAM, RICHARD. Adm. at KING'S, a scholar from Eton, 1445. Proceeded to M.A. Of Durham diocese. Ord. subdeacon (Ely) Mar. 1, 1454-5; priest, Apr. 5, 1455.

DENHAM, ROBERT. B.A. 1516-7.

DENHAM, ROBERT. Adm. at KING'S, a scholar from Eton, 1671. B. at Bristol, *c.* 1656. Matric. 1672. Fellow, 1675. No degree recorded. Subscribed for deacon's orders (Bristol) July 18, 1677; for priest's, Sept. 20, 1678. C. of Hinton St Mary, Dorset. (F. S. Hockaday.)

DENHAM, THOMAS (1485-6), *see* **DENMAN.**

DENHAM, THOMAS. Franciscan friar. B.D. 1519-20; D.D. 1521-2.

DENHAM, THOMAS. Matric. pens. from QUEENS', Easter, 1617. Of Essex. B.A. 1620-1; M.A. 1624.

DENHAM, THOMAS. Adm. pens. (age 17) at ST JOHN'S, May 25, 1700. S. of David, gent. B. at Withyham, Sussex. School, Lewes (Mr Reading). Matric. 1700; B.A. 1703-4; M.A. 1717.

DENHAM, WILLIAM. M.A. from SIDNEY, 1721. S. of William, of Coventry. Matric. from Merton College, Oxford, Mar. 29, 1710, age 16; B.A. 1713. V. of Stoneleigh, Warws., 1724. (*Al. Oxon.*)

DENISON, DANIEL. Matric. sizar from KING'S, Michs. 1625, as 'David.' S. of William, of Bishop's Stortford, Herts. Bapt. there, Oct. 18, 1612. Migrated to Emmanuel, 1626. B.A. 1629-30. Went with his parents, to New England, in 1631; residing at Cambridge, 1632-5; and afterwards at Ipswich, Mass.; where he was deputy to the General Court, and Speaker. Played a prominent part in the political affairs of the Colony. Assistant Commissioner of the United Colonies, 1653-82; Commissioner, 1655-7; 1659-62. Rose to be Major-General of the Colonial forces. Married, Oct. 18, 1632, Patience, dau. of Governor Thomas Dudley. Author, *Irenicon, or Salve for New England's Sore.* Died at Ipswich, Sept. 20, 1682. Brother of the next. (J. G. Bartlett.)

DENISON, JOHN. Matric. pens. from QUEENS', Michs. 1620. Of Hertfordshire. B.A. 1623-4; M.A. 1627. Ord. deacon (Peterb.) Feb. 22, 1629-30; priest (Ely) Mar. 17, 1632-3. R. of Quendon, 1650. V. of Standon, Herts., till his death, 1670. Father of Richard (1654).

DENNISON, JOHN. Adm. sizar (age 18) at ST JOHN'S, Apr. 5, 1705. S. of Samuel, gent. B. at Furness, Lancs. School, Kendal (Mr Moor). Matric. 1705; B.A. 1708-9. Ord. deacon (Peterb.) Sept. 23, 1710; priest (Lincoln) Aug. 15, 1714.

DENISON, LANCELOT. Matric. sizar from ST CATHARINE'S, Easter, 1655; B.A. 1657-8. V. of Otley, Yorks., 1662.

DENISON, NATHANIEL. Adm. pens. (age 18) at MAGDALENE, May 15, 1672. S. of Nicholas, of Wisbech. School, Wisbech. Matric. 1673; B.A. 1675-6. Ord. deacon (Peterb.) May 21, 1676. R. of Gt Wigborough, Essex, 1680-1730. Will (P.C.C.) 1730.

DENISON, RICHARD. Adm. sizar (age 17) at ST JOHN'S, June 26, 1654. S. of John (1620), V. of Furneux Pelham, Herts. (not recorded as vicar). B. at Quendon, Essex. School, Newport (Mr Woollie). Matric. 1654.

DENISON, STEPHEN. B.A. from TRINITY, 1602-3; M.A. 1606; D.D. 1627. Ord. deacon and priest (Peterb.) Sept. 21, 1603. P.C. of St Catherine Creechurch, London, 1622-50. P.C. of St James, Duke Place, 1622-6. Died 1650. Admon. P.C.C.

DENISON, TIMOTHY. Matric. sizar from TRINITY, Easter, 1635; B.A. 1638-9.

DENMAN, ARTHUR. Matric. sizar from TRINITY, Easter, 1577.

DENMAN, RICHARD. Matric. pens. from PETERHOUSE, Lent, 1582-3.

DENMAN, DENHAM or DEYNHAM, THOMAS. M.D. 1485-6 (M.B. abroad). Fellow of PETERHOUSE, 1473. Master, 1500-1. Master of Bethlehem Hospital, 1494. Physician to the Lady Margaret. Died early in 1501. Will proved (Dean and Chapter, Canterbury) Mar 17, 1500-1; 'of Cambridge and Collyweston, Northants.' (*Cooper*, III. 83.)

DENMAN, THOMAS. Adm. pens. (age 16) at SIDNEY, July 8, 1635. S. of Nicholas, merchant, of Hull, Yorks. School, Hull.

DENMAN, THOMAS. Adm. pens. (age 16) at SIDNEY, May 29, 1671. Only s. of Thomas, gent. B. at Walcott, Alkborough, Lincs. Schools, Hull (Mr Raspin), Beverley and Cottingham (Mr Ursley). Adm. at the Middle Temple, June 9, 1673.

DENMAN, WILLIAM. Matric. pens. from ST JOHN'S, Michs. 1544. Doubtless s. of Nicholas, of Newhall Grange, Wath, Yorks. B.A. 1547-8; M.A. 1551. Fellow, 1549. R. of Ordsall, Notts., *c.* 1553; ejected, but reinstated, 1558. M.I. at Ordsall. (*Hunter*, II. 75; Thoroton's *Notts.*, III. 453.)

DENMAN, WILLIAM. Matric. sizar from QUEENS', Michs. 1562; B.A. 1565-6; M.A. 1569.

DENMAN, WILLIAM. Matric. sizar from CLARE, Michs. 1589; B.A. 1593-4; M.A. 1600. Perhaps R. of Greenstead, Colchester, 1598. Admon. (Consist. C. London) 1624. (J. Ch. Smith.)

DENNE, ANDREW, *see* **DEANE.**

DENN, CHARLES, *see* **BENN.**

DENN, CHRISTOPHER. Adm. pens. at CORPUS CHRISTI, 1592. Of Kent. S. of Thomas, of Littlebourne, gent. Matric. *c.* 1593; B.A. 1596-7; M.A. 1600. Fellow, 1601-4. Ord. deacon (Norwich) Aug. 9; priest, Aug. 23, 1601. V. of Tilton, Leics., 1607. Preb. of Lincoln, 1613. R. of Upminster, Essex, till 1638. Died 1638. Will (P.C.C.) 1639. (*Vis. of Kent*, 1619.)

DENNE, DAVID. Adm. sizar (age 15) at SIDNEY, Feb. 12, 1626-7. S. of Thomas (1585), V. of Latton, Essex. B. there. Educated by his father. Matric. 1627, as 'Pen'; B.A. 1630-1; M.A. 1634. Brother of Henry (1625) and Thomas (1618-9).

DENNE, HENRY. Adm. sizar (age 14) at SIDNEY, May, 1621. S. of David, gent. B. at Well, Ickham, Kent. School, Latton, Essex (his uncle, Tho. Denne). Matric. 1621; B.A. 1624-5; M.A. 1628. Doubtless the Puritan divine described in *D.N.B.* Ordained (St David's) 1630. R. of Pyrton, Herts. Preacher at Baldock, 1641. Imprisoned, as a baptist, in Cambridge gaol. V. of Eltisley, Cambs., 1645-6. Resigned and became a soldier in the Parliamentary army. Died *c.* 1660. (*D.N.B.*)

DENNE, HENRY. Adm. sizar (age 15) at SIDNEY, Apr. 26, 1625. S. of Thomas (1585), V. of Latton, Essex. B. there. Matric. 1625; B.A. 1628–9. Brother of David (1626–7) and Thomas (1618–9).

DENNE, HENRY. Adm. sizar (age 18) at TRINITY, Apr. 5, 1689. S. of Thomas. B. in London. School, St Paul's. Matric. 1689; Scholar, 1693; B.A. 1693–4.

DENNE or DENNY, JOHN. M.A. 1508–9. Scholar or fellow of KING'S HALL, 1514–6. Proctor, 1520–1.

DENN, JOHN. Adm. sizar at SIDNEY, Mar. 11, 1606–7. Matric. 1607; B.A. 1610–1; M.A. 1614; B.D. 1621. Fellow. Ord. deacon and priest (Peterb.) Nov. 12, 1617. Probably preb. of York, 1617–43. Perhaps R. of Dartford, Kent, 1634–44; sequestered. Buried there 1646.

DENNE, JOHN. Adm. at CORPUS CHRISTI, Feb. 25, 1708–9. S. of John, woodreve to the see of Canterbury. B. at Littlebourne, Kent, May 25, 1693. Schools, Sandwich and Canterbury. Matric. 1709; Scholar; B.A. 1712–3; M.A. 1716; D.D. 1728. Fellow, 1716–21. Incorp. at Oxford, 1728. Ord. deacon (Norwich) May 27, 1716; priest (Ely) Sept. 21, 1718. P.C. of St Benet's, Cambridge, 1720. R. of Greens Norton, Northants., 1721–6. V. of St Leonard, Shoreditch, 1723–67. Boyle lecturer, 1725–8. Preb. and Archdeacon of Rochester, 1728. V. of St Margaret, Rochester, 1729–31. R. of Lambeth, 1731–67. A diligent antiquary. Died Aug. 5, 1767. Buried in Rochester Cathedral M.I. there. Will, P.C.C. Father of the next, and of Samuel. (*Masters*; *D.N.B.*)

DENNE, JOHN. Adm. at CORPUS CHRISTI, 1743. S. of John (above). B. at Bromley, Kent, July 2, 1726. Schools, Streatham, Surrey, and King's, Canterbury. Matric. 1743; B.A. 1747–8; M.A. 1751. Fellow, 1749–52. Incorp. at Oxford, 1757. Adm. at the Inner Temple, 1741. P.C. of Maidstone, 1753, and chaplain of the gaol. R. of Copford, Essex, 1754. For many years insane (the result of being shot by prisoners escaped from gaol). Died at Maidstone, Mar. 1800, aged 73. Buried in Rochester Cathedral, Mar. 31. Will, P.C.C. Brother of Samuel (1748). (*Masters*.)

DENE, LANCELOT. Matric. sizar from ST JOHN'S, Easter, 1565.

DENNE, SAMUEL. Adm. at CORPUS CHRISTI, 1748. S. of John (1708–9). B. in Westminster, Jan. 13, 1730–1. Schools, Streatham and Canterbury. Matric. 1748; B.A. 1753; M.A. 1756. Ord. deacon (Ely) June 9, 1754. V. of Lamberhurst, Kent, 1754–1767. V. of Wilmington, 1767–99. Of Darenth, 1767–99. Antiquary. Died Aug. 3, 1799. Buried in Rochester Cathedral. Will, P.C.C. Brother of John (1743). (*D.N.B.*)

DENNE or DEANE, THOMAS. Matric. pens. from CLARE, Easter, 1585. B. at Littlebourne, Kent. B.A. 1588–9; M.A. 1592. Ord. deacon (London) Dec. 21; priest, Dec. 22, 1595, age 30. P.C. of Kingsbury. V. of Latton, Essex, 1600–32. R. of Netteswell, 1634–40. Died 1640. Will (Consist. C. London) 1640. Father of the next, of David (1626–7) and Henry (1625). (J. Ch. Smith.)

DENNE, THOMAS. Adm. sizar at EMMANUEL, Feb. 10, 1618–9. S. of Thomas (above). Matric. 1619; B.A. 1622–3; M.A. 1626. Ord. deacon (Peterb.) Sept. 24; priest, Sept. 25, 1626. V. of Latton, Essex, 1632–80. Died Dec. 14, 1680. M.I. at Latton. Will (Consist. C. London) 1681.

DENNE, THOMAS. Matric. sizar from QUEENS', Michs. 1655. Of Essex. B.A. 1658–9; M.A. 1662. Ord. priest (Ely) Mar. 1662–3.

DENNE, THOMAS. Adm. at CORPUS CHRISTI, 1676. Of Kent. Matric. 1676; B.A. 1679–80.

DENNE, VINCENT. Adm. pens. at QUEENS', 1644–5. S. of Thomas, of St Alphage, Canterbury. Matric. 1647–8. Migrated to Oxford. B.A. from Magdalen Hall, 1648; M.A. 1651. Student of Christ Church, 1648. Adm. at Gray's Inn, Apr. 19, 1648. Barrister-at-law, 1655. Serjeant-at-law, 1688. Recorder of Canterbury. M.P. for Canterbury, 1681. Of Dennhill, Kingston, Kent. Died Oct. 28, 1693, aged 65. Buried at Kingston. M.I. (*Vis. of Kent*, 1663; *Al. Oxon.*; H. G. Harrison.)

DENNE, WILLIAM. Matric. pens. from QUEENS', Lent, 1647–8. Of Kent. Migrated to Oxford. Matric. from Christ Church, Mar. 14, 1650–1; B.A. 1651. Brother of Vincent (above). (*Al. Oxon.*)

DEN, WILLIAM. Matric. from CORPUS CHRISTI, Easter, 1702.

DENNE, ——. Adm. pens. at MAGDALENE, 1658.

DENNER, EDWARD. Adm. pens. (age 17) at PETERHOUSE, Oct. 4, 1638. Of Devon. School, Cambridge. Matric. 1638; Scholar, 1638–9.

DENNET, JOHN. Adm. Fell.-Com. (age 20) at SIDNEY, Aug. 29, 1723. S. of Robert, Esq. B. in London. School, Low Leyton, Essex (Mr Carter). Matric. 1724.

DENNINGTON, RICHARD. Adm. at CORPUS CHRISTI, 1660. Of Suffolk. Matric. 1660.

DENNIS or DENNYS, ANDREW. Matric. sizar from PETERHOUSE, Easter, 1585. B. at Hatfield Broad Oak, *c.* 1570. B.A. (? 1589–90); M.A. from Trinity, 1594. Ord. priest (Colchester) Feb. 24, 1597–8. V. of St Paul's, Bedford, 1601–6. V. of St John's, Bedford, 1606. Master of St John's Hospital, Bedford, 1606. Married, at Stotfold, Beds., Dec. 8, 1607, Mary Newman. Buried in St John's Church, Oct. 25, 1633. M.I. at St Paul's. Will (Northampton) 1633.

DENNIS, ANTHONY. Adm. sizar at EMMANUEL, July 5, 1711. Of Huntingdonshire. Matric. 1713; B.A. 1714–5. Ord. deacon (Lincoln) June 22, 1718; priest, Dec. 20, 1719. R. of Wouldham, Kent, 1728–75. Died June 24, 1775. Buried at Wouldham. Will, P.C.C.

DENNIS, CHRISTOPHER. B.A. from CHRIST'S, 1603. Ord. deacon (Peterb.) May 23, 1619; priest, Mar. 12, 1619–20. Probably R. of Little Warley, Essex, 1627–32; and R. of Beelsby, Lincs., 1632. Will (Lincoln) 1648. (*Peile*, I. 234.)

DENYSE, JOHN. Adm. at KING'S, a scholar from Eton, 1466.

DENNYS, JOHN. Matric. sizar from TRINITY, *c.* 1593.

DENNIS, JOHN. Matric. pens. from CHRIST'S, 1598–9; B.A. 1601–2. Perhaps V. of Kempston, Norfolk, 1604.

DENNYS, JOHN. Matric. sizar from ST JOHN'S, Easter, 1603; B.A. 1606–7; M.A. 1610. Perhaps ord. deacon (Lincoln) Aug. 1, 1607. Schoolmaster at Market Rasen, in 1614. Or perhaps ord. deacon (Peterb.) June 4; priest, June 5, 1615. 'B.A. of St John's.'

DENNIS, JOHN. Adm. sizar (age 16) at ST JOHN'S, Oct. 13, 1671. S. of Thomas, deceased, of York. B. there. School, York. Matric. 1671; B.A. 1675–6.

DENNIS, JOHN. Adm. pens. (age 17) at CAIUS, Jan. 13, 1675–6. S. of Francis, harnessmaker. B. in London. Schools, London (Mr Ellys) and Harrow. Matric. 1676; Scholar, 1676–81; B.A. 1679–80. Migrated to Trinity Hall, 1681 (on being fined, and his scholarship forfeited, for assaulting a fellow-student). M.A. 1683. Incorp. at Oxford, 1683. Literary critic, play-writer and pamphleteer. Latterly fell into poverty. Died Jan. 6, 1734. (*D.N.B.*; *Venn*, I. 455.)

DENNIS, NATHANIEL. Adm. sizar (age 15) at JESUS, June 11, 1664. Of Cambridge. Matric. 1664; B.A. 1667–8; Scholar, 1668; M.A. 1671. Ord. priest (Ely) Sept. 1672. V. of Elmstead, Essex, 1672–4. Buried at All Saints', Cambridge, Oct. 11, 1674.

DENNIS, ROBERT. B.A. 1486–7.

DENNIS, ROBERT. Adm. sizar (age 19) at ST JOHN'S, May 28, 1697. S. of Isaac, deceased. B. at Bristol. School, Pocklington, Yorks. (Mr Dwyer).

DENNIS, ROWLAND. Adm. chorister at TRINITY, Dec. 14, 1671. Matric. 1675; B.A. 1675–6; M.A. 1679. Perhaps R. of Himbleton, Worcs.

DENYS, THOMAS. M.Gram. 1519–20.

DENNYS, THOMAS. Matric. sizar from CLARE, Michs. 1569.

DENNIS, TIMOTHY. Adm. sizar at PETERHOUSE, Jan. 20, 1634–5. Of Lincolnshire. Matric. 1634–5. Migrated to Magdalene. Adm. pens. Nov. 17, 1635. B.A. 1638–9.

DENYS, WILLIAM. B.A. 1512–3.

DENNYS, WILLIAM. Adm. pens. at CHRIST'S, Apr. 8, 1581. Matric. 1581; B.A. 1584–5; M.A. 1588. Ord. deacon (Peterb.) Mar. 10, 1587–8; priest, Oct. 5, 1589. (H. I. Longden.)

DENNIS, WILLIAM. Matric. sizar from ST JOHN'S, *c.* 1593.

DENNIS, WILLIAM. M.A. from CAIUS, 1670. Incorporated from Dublin. Adm. there Jan. 21, 1662–3; aged 22. S. of Henry. B. in Lancs. B.A. (Dublin) 1669. R. of Dodleston, Cheshire, 1673–1716. Died 1716.

DENNIS, WILLIAM. Adm. sizar (age 17) at CAIUS, Sept. 21, 1711. S. of Valentine, gent., of Glandford, Norfolk. B. at Blakeney. School, Holt (Mr Raynolds). Matric. 1711, as 'Danny'; Scholar, 1711–3.

DENYS, ——. A friar. B.D. 1498–9.

DENNY, ANTHONY. Of ST JOHN'S. S. of Sir Edmund, chief Baron of the Exchequer. B. Jan. 16, 1500–1; probably at Cheshunt, Herts. School, St Paul's. King's remembrancer. Privy Councillor Knighted, *c.* 1544. M.P. for Herts., 1547–9. Executor to Henry VIII. Died Sept. 13, 1549. Buried at Cheshunt. Will, P.C.C. Father of the next. (*Cooper*, I. 99; *D.N.B.*; *Vis of Norfolk*.)

DENNYE, ANTHONY. Matric. Fell.-Com. from PEMBROKE, Michs. 1551. 2nd s. of Sir Anthony (above), Knt. Adm. at the Middle Temple, Nov. 14, 1557. Apparently admitted at Basel University, 1555, with his brother Henry (1551). Died 1562. Admon. (P.C.C.) 1563, to brother Henry; of Cheshunt, Herts.

DENNYE, ANTHONY. Matric. Fell.-Com. from TRINITY, Michs. 1570. 1st s. of John, of Howe, Norfolk. Bapt. at Lyng, Aug. 17, 1553. Died 1610. Will, Norwich. Brother of Firmin. (*Vis. of Norfolk*.)

DENNY, ANTHONY. Adm. pens. (age 17) at Christ's, Apr. 7, 1653. S. of Anthony, of Herts. School, Bishop's Stortford (Mr Leigh). Matric. 1653. M.I. to his father at Bishop's Stortford.

DENNY, ARTHUR. Matric. Fell.-Com. from Clare, Michs. 1601. Eldest s. of Sir Edward, Knt. B. 1584. Of Tralee Castle, Kerry. Married Elizabeth, dau. of Miles Forest, Esq., of Huntingdon. Died July 4, 1619. Brother of Francis (1601). (*Vis. of Northants.*)

DENNY, ARTHUR. Matric. pens. from St Catharine's, Michs. 1646. Perhaps s. of Sir Edward. B. 1629. High Sheriff of Kerry, 1656. Knighted, Feb. 16, 1660–1. M.P. for the County, 1661–6. Died Mar. 1672. Buried in Tralee Church. Will (Dublin) 1673. (*Misc. gen. et Her.*, N.S., III. 158.)

DENNY, CHARLES. Adm. at King's, a scholar from Eton, 1616. S. of Sir Edward. B. at Bishop's Stortford. Bapt. Apr. 30, 1598. B.A. 1620–1; M.A. 1624. Fellow, till his death. Died Dec. 29, 1635. M.I. at Bishop's Stortford. (*Harwood; Vis. of Northants.*, 1681.)

DENYE, ED. Matric. sizar from St John's, Easter, 1548. One Edmund Denny R. of Watlington, Norfolk, 1556: 'satis doctus, non residet.' R. of Besthorpe.

DENNYE, EDWARD. Matric. Fell.-Com. from St John's, Michs. 1585. S. of Henry (1551), and grandson of Sir Anthony. B. Aug. 14, 1569. Knighted, 1589. High Sheriff for Herts., 1602–3. M.P. for Essex, 1604. Created Baron Denny, 1604; and Earl of Norwich, 1626. Died Sept. 27, 1630. (*D.N.B.*; *G.E.C.*; A. B. Beaven.)

DENNYE, EDWARD. Adm. sizar (age 16) at Caius, May 11, 1621. S. of Anthony, gent. B. at Lyng, Norfolk. School, North Walsham (Mr Tills). Matric. 1621; Scholar, 1623–5; B.A. 1624–5; M.A. 1628. Ord. deacon (Norwich) Dec. 23, 1627; priest, Sept. 20, 1628. C. of Haveringland, Norfolk, in 1629. Buried at Lyng, Aug. 18, 1629. (*Venn*, I. 253.)

DENNY, EDWARD. Adm. pens. at Emmanuel, Dec. 13, 1642. Probably eldest s. of John, of Howe, Norfolk. B. 1624.

DENNY, EDWARD. Adm. sizar at St Catharine's, June 12, 1667. Perhaps s. of Edward. Bapt. at Yarmouth, Sept. 3, 1649.

DENNY, EDWARD. Adm. pens. at St Catharine's, Jan. 24, 1672. Perhaps s. of Arthur (1646). B. at Castle Lyons, 1652. Matric. 1672. M.P. for Kerry, 1692 and 1695. Died 1712. (*Misc. Gen. et Her.*, N.S., III. 158, 197.)

DENNY, PIRMIN. Matric. pens. from Trinity, Michs. 1570, as 'Furmian.' 2nd s. of John, of Howe, Norfolk. Of Bunwell, Norfolk. Died 1622. Will at Norwich. (*Vis. of Norfolk.*)

DENNY, FRANCIS. Matric. pens. from Clare, Michs. 1601; B.A. from Christ's, 1604. 2nd s. of Sir Edward, Knt.; adm. at Lincoln's Inn, Mar. 20, 1605–6. Brother of Arthur (1601). (*Peile*, I. 236.)

DENNY, GEORGE. Adm. pens. at Corpus Christi, 1592. Matric. 1592. Of Norwich.

DENNY, GLOVER. Adm. pens. at Trinity, Feb. 12, 1731–2. S. of ——, of Norfolk. School, Westminster. Matric. 1732; Scholar, 1732. Perhaps s. of William, of Raveningham, Norfolk. B. Jan. 16, 1714–5.

DENNYE, HENRY. Matric. Fell.-Com. from Pembroke, Michs. 1551. Of Waltham, Herts. Eldest s. of Sir Anthony (above). B. Apr. 16, 1540. Adm. at Basel University, 1555, with his brother Anthony (1551). Adm. at the Inner Temple, Nov. 1562. Friend and correspondent of H. Bullinger. Died Mar. 24, 1573–4. Father of Sir Edward (1585), Earl of Norwich. Buried at Waltham Abbey. Will (P.C.C.) 1576.

DENNY, HILL. Adm. pens. (age 16) at Sidney, Jan. 9, 1694–5. S. of Peter (1672–3), gent. B. at Bishop's Stortford. School, Bishop's Stortford. Matric. 1695; B.A. 1698–9; M.A. 1707. Ord. deacon (Lincoln) Sept. 21, 1701; priest (London) May 23, 1703. R. of Eastwick, Herts., 1705–19. R. of Little Parndon, Essex, 1710. Buried Mar. 31, 1719. Will, P.C.C. Benefactor to Sidney. (*Vis. of Northants.*, 1681.)

DENNY, JOHN (1508–9), *see* **DENNE.**

DENNY, JOHN. Matric. pens. from Clare, Michs. 1580.

DENNY, JOHN. Matric. Fell.-Com. from Christ's, Apr. 1617. Probably eldest s. of Anthony, of Howe, Norfolk. Adm. at Gray's Inn, May 15, 1618. Died 1637.

DENNY, PETER. Adm. Fell.-Com. at Sidney, Feb. 4, 1672–3. S. of Henry, gent., deceased. B. at Bishop's Stortford, Herts. School, Bishop's Stortford. M.A. 1673. Of Bishop's Stortford. Died 1696. Father of Hill (1694–5). (*Vis. of Northants.*, 1681.)

DENNIE, PHINEAS. Adm. pens. at Christ's, May 20, 1624. S. of Thomas. B. at Thurlton, Norfolk. School, Norwich (private; Mr Stonham). Matric. 1624; B.A. 1627–8. Adm. at Lincoln's Inn, June 17, 1633. Of Toft Monks. (*Vis. of Norfolk.*)

DENNY, RICHARD. Matric. pens. from King's, Easter, 1629.

DENNY, ROBERT. Matric. sizar from Peterhouse, Lent, 1580–1; B.A. 1583–4.

DENNY, THOMAS. Matric. pens. from St Catharine's, Michs. 1622. One of these names, of Thurlton, Norfolk, adm. at Gray's Inn, Feb. 16, 1623–4. Perhaps s. of Firmian. Bapt. at Howe, Norfolk, Nov. 4, 1604. Of Burwell, Esq.

DENNEY, THOMAS. Adm. pens. at St Catharine's, 1667. Matric. 1668.

DENNY, WILLIAM. Adm. pens. (age 16) at Caius, Oct. 26, 1594. S. of John, yeoman. B. at Beccles, Suffolk. School, Beccles (Mr Darley). Scholar, 1595–6. Adm. at Gray's Inn, 1598. Ancient, 1622; autumn reader, 1625. Knighted, Oct. 31, 1627. King's Counsel. Steward of Norwich, 1618. Recorder, 1629–42. M.P. for Norwich, 1620, 1624, 1625. Died Mar. 26, 1642. Buried in Norwich Cathedral. (*Venn*, I. 154.)

DENNY, WILLIAM. Matric. pens. from Christ's, July, 1608. One of these names, s. of Thomas, of Thurlton, Norfolk, gent., adm. at Lincoln's Inn, from Thavies Inn, Aug. 8, 1612.

DENNY, WILLIAM. Adm. (age 16) at Caius, Feb. 17, 1619–20. S. or Sir William (1594), of Norwich. School, Norwich (Mr Stonham). Matric. pens. 1620. Readm. Fell.-Com. 1621. B.A. 1622–3. Adm. at Gray's Inn, Nov. 2, 1621. In 1654 it was proposed by the royalists to make him governor of Yarmouth during the Civil War. Created Bart., June 3, 1642. Poet and author. Author, *Pelecanicidium*, *The Shepherd's Holiday*, and other pieces. Died in poverty. Buried June 19, 1676, at St Giles', Cripplegate. (*D.N.B.*; *Venn*, I. 248; *G.E.C.*)

DENNY, WILLIAM. Adm. sizar at Emmanuel, June 29, 1655. Of Suffolk. Matric. 1655; B.A. 1658–9; M.A. 1662. Probably R. of East Harling, Norfolk, 1665–78. Perhaps R. of Overstone, Northants., 1680–1702; and R. of Barnack, 1687–1706. Buried at Toft Monks, Norfolk, May 24, 1707. Father of William (1690).

DENNY, WILLIAM. Adm. pens. (age 19) at Trinity, June 28, 1690. S. of William (1655). B. at Harling, Norfolk. School, Westminster. Matric. 1690; Scholar, 1691; B.A. 1693–4; M.A. 1697. Chaplain of Trinity, 1700. Ord. priest (Peterb.) Feb. 24, 1710–1.

DENNY, ——. Adm. Fell.-Com. at King's, 1663–4.

DENSON, THOMAS. Adm. sizar (age 20) at St John's, May 6, 1743. S. of Richard, husbandman, of Cheshire. B. at Wervin. School, Backford (Mr Ro. Denson). B.A. 1746–7. Ord. deacon (Chester) Mar. 15, 1746–7; priest, Nov. 8, 1748. C. of Dodleston, Cheshire. (*Scott-Mayor*, III. 535.)

DENSTON, WILLIAM. Adm. sizar (age 17) at Sidney, Mar. 17, 1719–20. S. of Christopher. B. at Newport, Salop. School, Newport (Mr Greenwood). Matric. 1720; B.A. 1723–4. Will of one of these names (P.C.C.) 1761; of Warwick, clerk.

DENT, ARTHUR. Matric. pens. from Christ's, Nov. 1571. B. at Melton, Leics. B.A. 1575–6; M.A. 1579. Ord. deacon (Peterb.) Mar. 29, 1577; priest (London) May, 1577, age 24. R. of South Shoebury, Essex, 1580. Author, *Ruin of Rome*, and other religious works. Died 1601, aged *c.* 48. (*Peile*, I. 119; *D.N.B.*; *Cooper*, II. 469; III. 83.)

DENT, CHARLES. Adm. pens. (age 16) at Trinity, July 5, 1704. S. of Dr Thomas, preb. of Westminster. School, Westminster. Matric. 1704; Scholar, 1705; B.A. 1707–8. Adm. at the Middle Temple, Feb. 12, 1704–5. Perhaps Commissioner for duties on salt, 1714–8. Died Dec. 31, 1718. Will (P.C.C.) 1719; of St Michael Bassishaw. Brother of William (1705). (*Al. Westmon.*, 239.)

DENT, CHRISTOPHER. Matric. pens. from Christ's, Feb. 1563–4; B.A. 1567–8. V. of Chawreth (Broxted), Essex, 1571.

DENT, DANIEL. Adm. at King's, a scholar from Eton, 1613. Matric. 1614; B.A. 1617–8; M.A. 1621; B.D. 1627. Fellow, till 1633. Minister of St Benet's, Cambridge, 1626. V. of Clifton, Warws. (*Harwood.*)

DENT, DIGBY. Adm. pens. (age 18) at Peterhouse, May 31, 1742. Of Suffolk. School, Ipswich. Scholar, 1742; Matric. 1743; B.A. 1745–6; M.A. 1749. Fellow, 1747–56. Probably of Suffolk, Esq. Will (P.C.C.) 1799. (*T. A. Walker.*)

DENT, GEORGE. Matric. sizar from St John's, Michs. 1587; Scholar of Christ's, in 1588–9; B.A. from Christ's, 1590–1; M.A. 1594. V. of Layston, Herts., 1603–4. Died 1604. Admon. (P.C.C.) 1604, to widow Helen.

DENT, GILES. M.A. 1460–1. *Grace* for B.D. 1469–70; not conferred. Proctor, 1464–5. R. of Pentlow, Essex, 1479–84. Died 1484.

DENTE, GILES. Scholar of Clare, 1476, age 12.

DENT, JAMES. Adm. sizar at SIDNEY, July 4, 1618. B. in Yorkshire. Matric. 1618; B.A. 1621–2; M.A. 1625. Ord. deacon (York) Sept. 1625; priest, Dec. 1625. V. of Shephall, Herts., 1640–1. One of these names P.C. of Hammersmith, Midds., 1631–47. Will (P.C.C.) 1647.

DENT, JOHN. Adm. pens. at EMMANUEL, Lent, 1619–20. Matric. 1620; B.A. 1623–4. One of these names, s. and h. of Francis, of London, Esq.; adm. at Lincoln's Inn, Nov. 13, 1624.

DENT, JOHN. Matric. sizar from QUEENS', Easter, 1645. Of Yorkshire. B.A. 1648–9.

DENT, JOHN. Matric. Fell.-Com. from KING'S, Michs. 1648. One of these names, s. of John, and Katharine, dau. of George Huxley, of Edmonton, Midds. Of Thornbury, Gloucs. Died May 14, 1659, aged 28. M.I. at Edmonton. (W. Robinson, *Edmonton*.)

DENT, JOHN. Adm. sizar (age 19) at PETERHOUSE, June 7, 1740. Of Yorkshire. Perhaps s. of Robert, V. of North Otterington. Matric. 1740; Scholar, 1740; B.A. 1743–4; M.A. 1747. Fellow, 1746–9. Ord. priest (Lincoln) May 25, 1746. V. of Ainderby Steeple, Yorks., 1748–95. R. of South Otterington, 1762–95. Died Dec. 13, 1795. M.I. (*T. A. Walker*.)

DENTE, LEONARD. B.A. 1532–3. V. of Barnham, Suffolk, *c.* 1544.

DENT, PETER. Adm. sizar at TRINITY, Feb. 19, 1649–50. Of Cambridgeshire. Perhaps s. of Peter, of Gisborough, Yorks. Of Cambridge, age 55, in 1684. Married Elizabeth, dau. of John Pleys, of Little Eversden, Cambs. Father of the next. (*Vis. of Cambs.*, 1684.)

DENT, PETER. Adm. pens. at TRINITY, 1671–2. S. of Peter (above). Matric. 1672. Incorp. M.B. 1680, from Lambeth. Practised in Cambridge. Assisted Ray in his *Historia Plantarum*. Buried in St Sepulchre's, Cambridge, Oct. 5, 1689. Will proved (V.C.C.) 1689. (*D.N.B.*)

DENT, PETER. Adm. sizar at JESUS, Nov. 13, 1700. Of Maryland, America. Matric. 1701. Probably s. of Thomas (who died in Maryland, and was brother of Peter of 1649).

DENT, PETER. Adm. sizar (age 17) at ST JOHN'S, July 1, 1723. S. of Peter, gent., of Cambs. B. in Cambridge. School, Felsted (Mr Hutchin). Matric. 1724; B.A. 1727–8. Ord. deacon (Lincoln) Sept. 22, 1728; priest, Sept. 24, 1732. C. of Husbands Bosworth, Leics. Will (P.C.C.) of one of these names, 1777; of Gt Oakley, Northants., clerk. (*Scott-Mayor*, III. 363.)

DENT, ROBERT. B.A. 1515–6; M.A. 1519. Fellow of ST JOHN'S, 1516. Fellow of Christ's, 1523–4. Proctor, 1523–4. Perhaps R. of Trinity Church, Colchester, 1530. R. of Orlingbury, Northants., 1533–54. R. of Upminster, Essex, 1554–7; deprived, 1557.

DENT, ROBERT. Adm. pens. at JESUS, May 28, 1672. S. and h. of William, gent., of Guisborough, Yorks. School, Westminster. Matric. 1672. Adm. at the Middle Temple, July, 1674.

DENT, THOMAS. Matric. Fell.-Com. from CORPUS CHRISTI, Michs. 1623.

DENT, THOMAS. Adm. sizar (age 19) at ST JOHN'S, May 9, 1723. S. of William, of Leics. B. at Hallaton. School, Uppingham (Mr Savage and Mr Reddall). Matric. 1725; B.A. 1726–7. Ord. deacon (Lincoln) Sept. 24, 1727; priest, Sept. 21, 1729; C. of Shelton, Hunts. (? Beds.). R. of Foulness, Essex, 1733–42. (*Scott-Mayor*, III. 362.)

DENT, WILLIAM. Matric. pens. from ST JOHN'S, Michs. 1562; B.A. 1564–5.

DENT, WILLIAM. Adm. pens. (age 16) at TRINITY, June 7, 1705. S. of Dr Thomas, preb. of Westminster. School, Westminster. Matric. 1705–6; Scholar, 1706; B.A. 1708–9; M.A. 1712. Fellow, 1711. Incorp. at Oxford, 1712. Brother of Charles (1704).

DENT, ——. Incorp. from Paris, 1511–2.

DENT, ——. Canonicus. B.Div. (or Law), 1519–20.

DENTALL, SAMUEL. Matric. sizar from ST JOHN'S, Easter, 1580.

DENTON, ADRIAN. Matric. pens. from ST JOHN'S, Easter, 1623.

DENTON, ANTHONY. Adm. pens. (age 18) at CAIUS, Apr. 26, 1579. S. and h. of William, Esq., of Stedham, Sussex. School, Winchester. Matric. 1579. Previously matric. from Brasenose College, Oxford, Dec. 8, 1578. Adm. at the Middle Temple, Apr. 16, 1581. Knighted, July 23, 1603. Of Tonbridge, Kent. Died Aug. 26, 1615. Buried in Tonbridge Church. Admon. (P.C.C.) granted to his widow. (*Venn*, I. 102; *Vis. of Kent*, 1619; H. I. Longden.)

DENTON, CHRISTOPHER. Adm. sizar (age 16) at MAGDALENE, Mar. 20, 1683–4. S. of Thomas, clerk, R. of Crosby Garrett, Westmorland. Bapt. there, Apr. 9, 1668. School, Newcastle-on-Tyne. Matric. 1684; B.A. 1687–8. Ord. deacon (Carlisle) June 10; [illegible], Aug. 5, 1688. R. of Gosforth, Cumberland, 1688–1738. Married, Jan. 21, 1696–7, Ischell Sherwin. Buried June 6, 1738. (B. *Nightingale*.)

DENTON, EDWARD. Adm. at KING'S, a scholar from Eton, 1518. Probably B.A. 1521–2. Fellow. Ord. sub-deacon (Lincoln) Mar. 21, 1522–3. According to *Harwood* he graduated in Canon Law, from Trinity Hall.

DENTON, GEORGE. Matric. sizar from PETERHOUSE, Michs. 1555.

DENTON, JAMES. Adm. at KING'S, a scholar from Eton, 1486; B.A. 1489–90; M.A. 1492; D.Can.L. 1505 (Incorp. from Valentia). Fellow of King's. Proctor, 1495–6. *Supp.* for incorporation at Oxford, 1505. R. of St Olave's, Southwark, 1507. Preb. of Lichfield, 1509; of Sarum and Windsor, 1509–33; of Lincoln, 1514. R. of Headbourne Worthy, Hants. Almoner and chancellor to Mary, Queen of France. Dean of Lichfield, 1522. Archdeacon of Cleveland, 1523–32. Lord-president of Wales. Died Feb. 23, 1532–3, at Ludlow. Buried there. (*Cooper*, I. 45; *Harwood*; *D.N.B.*)

DENTON, JOHN. Adm. sizar at CLARE, May 4, 1646. B. at Bradford, Yorks., *c.* 1625. Matric. 1646; B.A. 1649; M.A. 1653. Fellow. Incorp. at Oxford, 1653. V. of Oswaldkirk, Yorks., till ejected, 1662. Afterwards ordained by the Bishop of Lincoln. R. of Stonegrave, Yorks. Preb. of York, 1694–1709. Died Jan. 14, 1708–9. M.I. at Stonegrave. (*D.N.B.*)

DENTON, JOHN. Adm. pens. (age 16) at SIDNEY, *c.* Nov. 1667. S. of John, dyer, of Ipswich. School, Ipswich. Matric. 1668; B.A. 1671–2; M.A. 1675. Ord. deacon (Norwich) Dec. 1672; priest, Dec. 1674. R. of Marlesford, Suffolk, 1677. R. of Little Blakenham, 1684. R. of St Stephen, Ipswich, 1689. R. of Offton and Little Bricet, 1697. Brother of Nathaniel.

DENTON, JOHN. Adm. sizar (age 17) at SIDNEY, Apr. 24, 1673. S. of John. B. at Oswaldkirk, Yorks. Matric. 1673; B.A. 1676–7.

DENTON, NATHANIEL. Adm. sizar (age 15) at SIDNEY, Sept. 9, 1673. S. of John, dyer. B. at Ipswich. School, Dedham (Mr Edm. Sherman). Matric. 1674; B.A. 1677–8. Ord. deacon (London) May 26, 1678. Brother of John (1667).

DENTON, NICHOLAS. Adm. pens. (age 16) at SIDNEY, Jan. 19, 1630–1. S. of Matthew, Esq., of Barton, Herts. (? Barton-le-Clay, Beds.). School, Flamstead (private; Mr Plumtree). Matric. 1631. Adm. at Lincoln's Inn, Aug. 14, 1632. Probably buried at Barton, Nov. 13, 1650. Will (P.C.C.) 1651.

DENTON, NICHOLAS. Adm. pens. (age 19) at SIDNEY, July 1, 1730. S. of Matthew, of Cadwell, Beds. B. at Barton-le-Clay, Beds. Schools, Elmdon, Essex and Houghton (Mr Clark). Matric. 1731; B.A. 1733–4. Ord. deacon (Lincoln) Mar. 10, 1733–4. V. of Walden St Paul's, Herts., 1736–47. Died 1747.

DENTON, RICHARD. Matric. sizar from ST CATHARINE'S, Easter, 1621. B. 1603, in Yorkshire. B.A. 1623–4. Ord. deacon (Peterb.) Mar. 9, 1622–3; priest, June 8, 1623. C. of Coley Chapel, Halifax, for some years. Went to New England, *c.* 1638. Preacher at Stamford, Conn.; and at Hempstead, Long Island, for 15 years. Returned to England, 1659. Said to have died at Hempstead, Essex, 1663. Author, *Soliliquia Sacra*. (*Felt*, 515; J. G. Bartlett; *D.N.B.*)

DENTON, ROBERT. Adm. pens. at ST CATHARINE'S, Mar. 1, 1692–3. Of East Newton, Yorks. Matric. 1693; B.A. 1696–7. Ord. deacon (York) Sept. 1699; priest, 1700. R. of Stonegrave, Yorks., 1700–47. Buried June 4, 1747.

DENTON, SAMUEL. Matric. sizar from ST JOHN'S, Easter, 1580; B.A. 1583–4; M.A. 1587. Ord. deacon (Peterb.) Sept. 19, 1585; priest, Feb. 24, 1585–6. V. of West Haddon, Northants., 1587–1605. R. of Creaton, 1592–1626. R. of Charwelton, 1605–13. V. of Spratton, 1613–26. Buried Apr. 18, 1626, at Creaton. (*Baker*, I. 69; T. P. Dorman.)

DENTON, THOMAS. Matric. pens. from PETERHOUSE, Michs. 1559; Scholar of Trinity, 1562; B.A. from Trinity, 1563–4; M.A. 1569. R. of Wolverston, Suffolk, 1566–8.

DENTON, THOMAS. Matric. sizar from TRINITY, *c.* 1591.

DENTON, THOMAS. Matric. pens. from ST JOHN'S, Easter, 1629. Perhaps s. of Henry. B. 1612. Succeeded to the estates of his great uncle, Thomas, of Warnell Denton, 1616. Captain in the army. Died of wounds, 1645. One of these names, of Warnell, Cumberland, adm. at Gray's Inn, Nov. 1, 1631.

DENTON, THOMAS. Adm. sizar at CLARE, June 22, 1733. S. of Richard, of Wakefield, Yorks. B. there. School, Wakefield. Matric. 1733. Migrated to Trinity, Apr. 7, 1735. B.A. 1736–7. Ord. deacon (Lincoln) May 28, 1738; priest (*Litt. dim.* from York) May, 1742. C. of Kirk Bramwith. Perhaps died Aug. 1790. (M. H. Peacock.)

DENTON, WALTER. Matric. sizar from ST JOHN'S, Michs. 1573. One of these names V. of Long Benton, Northumberland, 1595-1621. Died 1621.

DENTON, WILLIAM. Adm. sizar (age 17) at ST JOHN'S, May 15, 1684. S. of Nathaniel, husbandman. B. at Darton, Yorks. School, Manchester (Mr Barrow). Matric. 1684; B.A. 1687-8; M.A. 1693. Incorp. at Oxford, 1693. Ord. deacon (York) Dec. 22, 1689; priest, Dec. 1690.

DENTON, ——. B.A. 1473.

DENTON, ——. B.Civ.L. 1476-7.

DEPDEN, GEORGE. Matric. sizar from TRINITY, Easter, 1551.

DEPDEN or DIPDEN, GEORGE. Matric. pens. (age 17) from PEMBROKE, Easter, 1632. S. of John, of Ipswich. B.A. 1634-5; M.A. 1638. Fellow, 1631. Ejected, 1644. Ord. deacon (Norwich) Oct. 6, 1643, age 25. R. of Easton, Suffolk, 1649. R. of Garboldisham, Norfolk, in the Commonwealth.

DEPDEN or DEBDEN, JOHN. Adm. pens. at EMMANUEL, Apr. 18, 1585. S. of George, of Brampton, Suffolk. Matric. 1585; B.A. 1588-9; M.A. 1592. Fellow of Caius, 1595-1600. Married Mary, dau. of Edward Hunting, of Ipswich. Of Brampton, Suffolk, gent. Died *c.* 1616. Brother of the next. (*Venn*, I. 157; *Vis. of Suffolk*, 1612.)

DEPDEN, ROBERT. Adm. pens. (age 16) at CAIUS, May 10, 1596. S. of George, gent., of Brampton, Suffolk. School, Beccles. Scholar, 1598-1600. Adm. scholar at Trinity Hall, 1600. Will of one of these names (P.C.C.) 1625; died of plague; buried at St Margaret's, Westminster, Nov. 3, 1625, as 'Dibden.' (*Venn*, I. 159; J. Ch. Smith.)

DEPIN, JAMES. Matric. sizar from QUEENS', Easter, 1670.

DEPYNG, JOHN. B.Civ.L. R. of Girton, Cambs., in 1421. Canon of Lincoln.

DEPYNG, NICHOLAS. Scholar at KING'S HALL, 1388-96.

DEPLIEDGE, JEREMIAH. Adm. sizar at JESUS, Apr. 3, 1724. Of Nottinghamshire. Matric. 1724; Scholar; B.A. 1727-8. One Depliedge was Master of Mansfield Grammar School, Notts., in 1747. (A. Gray.)

DEPUP, JOHN. Matric. pens. from TRINITY, Michs. 1559. S. of George, 'innholder,' whose will (*P.C.C.*, 1566) mentions him and his brother Richard. B. in London. Scholar, 1563; B.A. 1563-4; M.A. 1567. Adm. as Fell.-Com. at Caius, Nov. 14, 1567. Fellow and Tutor at Caius, 1573-5. R. of Hawksworth, Notts., 1585-1603. Master of Nottingham Grammar School, 1578. Died Jan. 4, 1602-3. (*Venn*, I. 62; Godfrey, *Notts.*)

DEPOOPE, RICHARD. Matric. pens. from TRINITY HALL, Easter, 1553. Doubtless elder brother of John (above), named with him in his father's will.

DEPUP, THOMAS. Adm. sizar (age 18) at ST JOHN'S, July 1, 1636. S. of Thomas, hostler, of Waltham, Leics. B. at Melton Mowbray. School, Melton Mowbray (Mr Umphrey). B.A. 1639-40; M.A. 1643. Ord. deacon (Peterb.) Dec. 17, 1641.

DERBISHIRE, *see* **DARBYSHIRE.**

DERBY, *see also* **DARBY.**

DERBY, BENJAMIN. M.A. from KING'S, 1704. S. of Jeremiah, of Sherborne, Dorset, clerk. Matric. from Wadham College, Oxford, Mar. 15, 1677-8, age 17; B.A. (Oxford) 1681. Ord. deacon (B. and Wells); priest (Sarum). R. of Bryanston, Dorset, 1688-1718. Schoolmaster of Blandford. Chaplain to Lord Conway. V. of Turnworth, 1704. R. of Wootton Glanville, 1710-18. Died 1718. Father of the next, and of William (1725). (*Al. Oxon.*; Hutchins, *Dorset*, I. 264; F. S. Hockaday.)

DERBY or DARBY, BENJAMIN. Adm. sizar at EMMANUEL, Oct. 23, 1707. S. of Benjamin (above), of Blandford, Dorset, clerk. B. in Essex. Migrated to Exeter College, Oxford. Matric. there, May 20, 1708, age 18. Returned to Emmanuel; Matric. there, 1708; B.A. 1711-2. Ord. deacon (London) Dec. 21, 1712; priest, June 16, 1717. R. of Cowley, Middlesex, 1718-71. Died Jan. 18, 1771. Buried at Cowley, 1771. M.I. Will, P.C.C. Brother of William (1725). (*Al. Oxon.*; J. B. Peace.)

DERBY, JOHN. Scholar at KING'S HALL, 1427-33; LL.B. in 1430; LL.D. in 1439. R. of West Walton, Norfolk. Perhaps preb. of Lincoln, 1445; and of St Paul's, 1443-68.

DERBY, JOHN. B.Civ.L. 1472-3. Probably of KING'S HALL, 1468-73.

DERBY, JOHN. M.A. from CAIUS, 1724. S. of Jeremiah, clerk, of Broadmayne, Dorset. Matric. from Lincoln College, Oxford, Mar. 2, 1701-2, age 17; B.A. (Oxford) 1705. Ord. deacon (Salisbury) Sept. 22, 1706; priest, Sept. 19, 1708. V. of Turnworth, Dorset, 1711-6. V. of Cerne Abbas, 1711-36. R. of Minterne Magna, 1717-36. R. of Poxwell, 1724-36. Chaplain to the Earl of Anglesey. Died at Cerne Abbas, Sept. 8, 1736. (*Venn*, II. 21.)

DERBY, JOHN. Adm. sizar (age 19) at ST JOHN'S, Nov. 1, 1739. S. of William, clerk, of Wimborne, Dorset. B. at Wimborne. School, Eton. Colleger, 1733-9. Matric. 1739; B.A. 1743-4. Ord. priest (Norwich, *Litt. dim.* from Winchester) Mar. 1747-8. Perhaps R. of Gt Kington, Dorset, 1749-61. One of these names R. of Norton, Kent, 1765-7. R. of Southfleet, 1767-78. R. of Longfield, 1774-5. Six-preacher, Canterbury. Died Oct. 6, 1778. Buried at Bromley. But *see Al. Oxon.* for a contemporary.

DERBY, WILLIAM. M.A. from KING'S, 1725. S. of Benjamin (1704), of Blandford, Dorset, clerk. Matric. from Wadham College, Oxford, July 10, 1708, age 18; B.A. from All Souls, 1712. Ord. deacon (London) Sept. 23, 1711; priest (Oxford) Dec. 19, 1714. R. of Singleton, Sussex, 1715. R. of West Parley, Dorset, 1725-53. R. of Woodsford, 1729-53. Chaplain to Charlotte, Lady Lovelace. Died 1753. Buried at Wimborne Minster. Brother of Benjamin (1707). (*Al. Oxon.*; F. S. Hockaday; *Hutchins*, III. 222; where the parentage is apparently erroneously given.)

DERBY, ——. B.Can.L. 1483-4.

DEREHAM, BALDWIN. Described as 'B.A. of CHRIST'S College; aged 62; married; ord. by Bishop of Norwich; preacher; understands Latin' (*Lib. Cler. Linc.*, 1576). Probably 2nd s. of Thomas, of Crimplesham, Norfolk. V. of Ulting, Essex, 1558-63. V. of Assington, Suffolk, 1559-68. V. of Edwardstone, 1560-3. R. of Langenhoe, 1568. V. of Goadby, Leics., 1576. Father of Roger (1588). (*Vis. of Norf.*)

DEERHAM, GEORGE. Matric. pens. from ST JOHN'S, Michs. 1544.

DEERHAM, HENRY. Adm. Fell.-Com. at PETERHOUSE, July 16, 1616. 2nd s. of Sir Thomas (1588-9), of Dereham Abbey, Norfolk, Knt. Adm. at the Inner Temple, Nov. 1620. Brother of Thomas (1616) and Robert (1623). (*T. A. Walker*, 4.)

DEREHAM, JOHN. Adm. Fell.-Com. (age 16) at CAIUS, Jan. 30, 1649-50. S. of Thomas (1616), of Dereham Grange, Norfolk. B. there. Bapt. at West Dereham, July 28, 1633. Schools, Thetford (Mr Ward) and Wisbech (Mr Frisney) Matric. 1650. Adm. at the Middle Temple, 1648. Half-brother of Richard (1660). (*Venn*, I. 377; *Vis. of Norfolk*, 1664.)

DERHAM, RICHARD. D.D. Chancellor of the University, 1390-1, 1404-8. Fellow of GONVILLE HALL, 1393. Warden of King's Hall, 1399-1413, 1415-7. R. of Middleton Cheney, Northants., 1400. Papal notary for England. Preb. of Westminster, 1401. Preb. of Chichester, 1401. P.C. of St Botolph, Aldersgate, 1403. Dean of St Martin-le-Grand, 1403-11. Preb. of Salisbury, 1407. Archdeacon of Norfolk, 1412-7. King's chaplain. Employed in State affairs. Died Aug. 10, 1417. (*Venn*, I. 4.). The *Caius MS.* (No. 2) was his *cautio* (? for D.D.) in 1394.

DERHAM, RICHARD. Adm. Fell.-Com. at QUEENS', May 29, 1660. 2nd s. of Sir Thomas (1616), Bart., of Dereham Abbey, Norfolk. Bapt. Apr. 10, 1644, at West Dereham. Adm. at Lincoln's Inn, 1661. Succeeded his brother Henry as Bart., 1682. Wasted his property, and died in Jamaica. (*G.E.C.*)

DERHAM, ROBERT. Fellow of TRINITY HALL. Ord. deacon (Ely) June 6, 1411; priest, May 28, 1412.

DEREHAM, ROBERT. Matric. pens. from PETERHOUSE, Michs. 1598. 5th s. of Baldwin (above), of Norfolk. B.A. 1601-2; M.A. 1605; B.D. 1613; D.D. 1625. Fellow, 1605. R. of Stukeley, Hunts., 1618. R. of Barnack, Northants., 1633-44. Buried there July 3, 1644. Admon. (Peterb.) granted to brother Sir Thomas. Brother of Roger (1588-9) and Thomas (1585). (*T. A. Walker*; H. I. Longden.)

DEREHAM, ROBERT. Adm. pens. at PETERHOUSE, May 20, 1623. S. of Sir Thomas (1588-9), Knt., of West Dereham, Norfolk. Matric. 1623. Adm. at Gray's Inn, May 10, 1626. Author, legal. Brother of Henry (1616) and Thomas (1616).

DEREHAM, ROGER. Matric. pens. from TRINITY, Lent, 1588-9. 2nd s. of Baldwin (above), of Norfolk. Scholar, 1589; B.A. 1592-3; M.A. 1596; B.D. from Peterhouse, 1608; D.D. 1615. Fellow of Peterhouse, 1597. Ord. deacon and priest, Feb. 20, 1602. R. of Stathern, Leics. V. of Cherry Hinton, Cambs., 1604-17. R. of Gt Casterton, Rutland, 1618-20. R. of Little Stukeley, Hunts., 1618. R. of Branstone, Leics., 1621. Will (P.C.C.) 1638; proved by brother Robert. Gave £10 to the College Chapel. Brother of Robert (1598) and Thomas (1585). (*T. A. Walker*, 4; *Vis. of Norf.*; *Nichols*, II. 359.)

DERHAM, THOMAS. Of KING'S HALL, 1403-18. Died June 3, 1418.

DERHAM, THOMAS. Pensioner at QUEENS', 1518-21.

DEERHAM or DYRHAM, THOMAS. Matric. pens. from CHRIST'S, Easter, 1585. S. and h. of Baldwin (above), of Norfolk. B.A. 1588-9. Adm. at the Inner Temple, Nov. 1589. Barrister, 1600. Succeeded to his uncle's estate at West Dereham, Norfolk. Knighted, Dec. 1, 1618. Died Apr. 20, 1645. Buried at West Dereham, May 28. Will, P.C.C. Father of the next, Henry (1616) and Robert (1623). (*Peile*, I. 181; *Vis. of Norf.*)

DEERHAM or DERHAM, THOMAS. Adm. Fell.-Com. at PETERHOUSE, July 16, 1616. S. and h. of Sir Thomas (above), Knt., of Dereham Abbey, Norfolk. Adm. at the Inner Temple, Nov. 1618. Created Baronet, June 8, 1661. Buried Mar. 30, 1668, at St Giles-in-the-Fields, London. Brother of Henry (1616) and Robert (1623). (*T. A. Walker*, 3; *G.E.C.*)

DERHAM, THOMAS. Adm. sizar at CLARE, Oct. 22, 1645. Matric. 1645; B.A. 1649.

DEREHAM, ——. Adm. Fell.-Com. at TRINITY, 1660. Possibly Richard, of 1660, at Queens'.

DEREHAUGH, FRANCIS. Adm. pens. (age 17) at CAIUS, May 26, 1604. S. of William (1575), Esq., of Markshall, Essex. School, Sawbridgeworth, Herts. Readm. Fell.-Com. 1605. Adm. at the Inner Temple, Feb. 6, 1607-8. Of Gedgrave, Suffolk, Esq. Succeeded his father, 1613. Died Dec. 15, 1615. Will (P.C.C.) 1621. (*Venn*, I. 185.)

DERAUGH, ROBERT. Matric. pens. from MAGDALENE, Easter, 1567. One of these names adm. at Gray's Inn, from Staple's Inn, 1571. Will (P.C.C.) 1613; of Gray's Inn. (J. Ch. Smith.)

DERHAUGH, SAMUEL. Adm. pens. (age 15) at CAIUS, May 7, 1611. S. of William, gent., of Badingham, Suffolk. School, Cransford (Mr Bowman). Matric. 1611; Scholar, 1611-2. Of Peasenhall, Suffolk, Esq. Will proved (Norwich) 1627. (*Venn*, I. 211.)

DERAUGH, WILLIAM. Adm. pens. (age 15) at CAIUS, Oct. 8, 1575. Of Bromley, Essex. S. of Edward, Esq., of Gedgrave, Suffolk. Matric. 1575. Adm. at Gray's Inn, 1578. Of Markshall and Gedgrave, Suffolk, Esq. Died Sept. 27, 1612. Will (P.C.C.). Father of Francis (1604). (*Venn*, I. 83.)

DEREHAUGH, ——. Fellow of PEMBROKE, 1461.

DERHAUGH, ——. Pens. at PETERHOUSE, 1608-9.

DEREWARDE, ——. Fined £5 for non-inception in some faculty, 1456-7. (Gr. *Bk*, A, p. 9.)

DERING or DERYNG, ANTHONY. Matric. sizar from QUEENS', Michs. 1548; Scholar, 1548-50.

DERING, ANTHONY. Matric. pens. from CHRIST'S, June, 1575. S. of Richard. B.A. 1578-9. Adm. at Gray's Inn, 1580. M.P. for Clitheroe, 1601. Knighted, May 11, 1603. Sir Anthony, of Surrenden-Dering, Kent, Knt. Died Mar. 1635-6, aged 78. Father of Edward (1615) and the next. (*Peile*, I. 131.)

DEARING, ANTHONY. Matric. pens. from MAGDALENE, Easter, 1618. Adm. at the Middle Temple, Feb. 9, 1619-20; as s. of Sir Anthony (above), Knt., of Pluckley, Kent. Will (Archd. London) 1661. (Pedigree of Dering in *Vis. of Kent*, 1619.)

DERING, CHRISTOPHER. Adm. pens. (age 15) at SIDNEY, June 9, 1641. S. of John, Esq. B. at Charing, Kent. Schools, Ashford (Mr Nicholls), Canterbury (Mr Lud) and Beckley, Suffolk (? Sussex). Matric. 1641. Adm. at the Inner Temple, 1648. Barrister, 1655.

DERING, EDWARD. B.A. from CHRIST'S, 1559-60 (1st in the *ordo*); M.A. 1563; B.D. 1568. S. of John, of Surrenden-Dering, Kent. Fellow, 1560-70. Ord. deacon (Ely) 1561. Proctor, 1566. Lady Margaret preacher, 1567. R. of Pluckley, Kent, 1568. Chaplain to the Duke of Norfolk, and in the Tower of London. Preb. of Sarum, 1572-6. Divinity reader at St Paul's, 1572; suspended, 1573. Distinguished as Greek scholar, and as a preacher. Author. Died at Thoby, Mountnessing, Essex, June 26, 1576, aged 36. (*D.N.B.*; *Peile*, I. 55; *Cooper*, I. 354, 563; III. 83.)

DERRING, EDWARD. Matric. sizar from TRINITY, Easter, 1608; Scholar, 1611.

DERING, EDWARD. Matric. Fell.-Com. from MAGDALENE, Easter, 1615. Eldest s. of Sir Anthony (1575), of Pluckley, Kent. B. in the Tower of London, 1598, where his father was Deputy-lieutenant. Adm. at the Middle Temple, Oct. 23, 1617. Knighted, Jan. 22, 1618-9. Created Baronet, Feb. 1, 1626-7. Lieutenant of Dover Castle. M.P. for Hythe, 1629; for Kent in the Long Parliament, 1640-2. Committed to the Tower for supporting Episcopacy, 1641. For a time in the King's army. Author. Died June 22, 1644. Brother of Anthony (1618), father of the next. (*D.N.B.*; *G.E.C.*)

DERING, EDWARD. Adm. Fell.-Com. (age 13) at SIDNEY, Jan. 30, 1639-40. S. of Sir Edward, Bart. (above). B. at Pluckley, Kent, Nov. 8, 1625. Schools, Red Cross Street, London (Mr Tho. Farneby), Throwley (Mr Jo. Cragg) and Surrenden, Kent (Mr Ro. Copping). Matric. 1640. Migrated to Emmanuel, Oct. 11, 1642. B.A. 1642-3. Adm. at the Middle Temple, Dec. 1641. Perhaps the man of these names, 'Nobilis,' adm. at Leyden, Apr. 30, 1644. Succeeded his father, 1644. M.P. for Kent, 1660; for East Retford, 1670; for Hythe, 1679 (twice), 1681. Buried at Pluckley, June 28, 1684. M.I. (*D.N.B.*)

DERING, EDWARD. Adm. sizar (age 16) at ST JOHN'S, July 4, 1692. S. of Henry (1663-4), clerk. B. at Thornham, Kent. School, Rochester (Mr Bastow). Matric. 1692; B.A. 1695-6; M.A. 1699. V. of Tudeley, Kent, 1702-15. Died Dec. 26, 1715. M.I. at Tudeley.

DERING, EDWARD. Adm. Fell.-Com. (age 18) at ST JOHN'S, Mar. 15, 1750-1. S. of Sir Edward, Bart., of Kent. B. at Pluckley, Sept. 28, 1732. School, Westminster. M.P. for New Romney, Kent, 1761-87. Succeeded his father as 6th Baronet, 1762. Died Dec. 8, 1798. (*G.E.C.*)

DERING, 'ELERAD' (1650), *see* HENRY.

DERING, FRANCIS. Matric. sizar from MAGDALENE, Easter, 1605. S. of Christopher, of Wicken, Charing, Kent. B.A. 1608; M.A. 1612. Incorp. at Oxford, 1616. Ord. deacon and priest (Peterb.) Feb. 28, 1612-3; 'Fellow of Magdalen.' R. of Ringwould, Kent, 1625. (*Al. Oxon.*)

DERING, GEORGE. Matric. sizar from MAGDALENE, Easter, 1583; B.A. 1586-7; probably M.A. 1590.

DEARING, GEORGE. Matric. pens. from JESUS, Easter, 1586; B.A. 1589-90; M.A. 1593. Fellow, 1591-1613. Senior Proctor, 1607-8.

DERING, HENEAGE. Adm. pens. at CLARE, Mar. 31, 1680. Eldest s. of Christopher, of Wickins, Kent. B. in London, 1665. School, St Albans. Matric. 1680; LL.D. 1701 (*Lit. Reg.*). Adm. at the Inner Temple, May, 1678. Called to the Bar, 1690. Ord. deacon (York) Feb. 9, 1701; priest, July 20, 1701. Archdeacon of East Riding, Yorks., 1702. R. of Scrayingham, 1704-49. Preb. of York, 1705-50. Dean of Ripon, 1711. Master of St Mary Magdalene, and at St John Baptist, Hospitals, Ripon, 1711. Died Apr. 8, 1750. Will, P.C.C. Father of the next and John (1732). (*D.N.B.*)

DERING, HENEAGE. Adm. pens. (age 17) at ST JOHN'S, Apr. 22, 1737. S. of Heneage (above). B. at Ripon. School, Ripon (Mr Stephens). Matric. 1737; B.A. 1740-1; M.A. from Peterhouse, 1744. Fellow of Peterhouse, 1742-9. Ord. deacon (Lincoln) May 29; priest (Rochester) Dec. 18, 1743. V. of Tadcaster, Yorks., 1744-52. V. of Burley-on-the-Hill, Rutland, 1752-61. P.C. of Wye, Kent, 1754. R. of Milton Keynes, Bucks., 1761-1802. Chaplain and tutor in the family of the Earl of Winchelsea. D.D., of Lambeth. Preb. of Canterbury, 1766-1802. Died May 17, 1802. Brother of John (1732). (*Scott-Mayor*, III. 484.)

DERING, HENRY. Matric. pens. from MAGDALENE, Lent, 1618-9. S. of John, of Egerton, Kent. Migrated to Oxford. Matric. from Magdalen Hall, Oxford, Jan. 21, 1620-1, age 21; B.A. 1620-1; M.A. (Cambridge) 1624. V. of Newington by Sittingbourne, Kent, 1626. V. of Halstow, 1632-44 (sequestered). Married, Sept. 5, 1633, Mary Sanders, of East Sutton, Kent. Died 1666. (*Al. Oxon.*; H. G. Harrison.)

DERINGE, HENRY. Adm. Fell.-Com. at TRINITY, June 27, 1650. S. and h. of Sir Edward, of Surrenden, Pluckley, Kent. Matric. 1650-1, as 'Elerad.' Of Pevington, Kent, Esq. (*Vis. of Kent*, 1663.)

DEERING, HENRY. Adm. sizar (age 18) at ST JOHN'S, Mar. 9, 1663-4. S. of Henry (1618-9), V. of Newington, Kent. B. there. School, Maidstone. Matric. 1664; B.A. 1667-8; M.A. 1671. Incorp. at Oxford, 1671. Adm. at the Inner Temple, 1666. Barrister, 1673. Perhaps V. of Thornham, Kent, 1673-1720; and V. of Bearstead, 1693-1720. If so, died Dec. 26, 1720, aged 74. But *see Al. Oxon.*, I. XVIII. Father of Edward (1692).

DERING, JOHN. B.A. 1514-5.

DERING, JOHN. Adm. pens. (age 17) at ST JOHN'S, June 19, 1732. S. of Heneage (1680). B. at Ripon, Yorks. School, Ripon (Mr Steevens). Matric. 1732; B.A. 1735-6; M.A. 1739. Ord. deacon (Lincoln) Feb. 14, 1737-8; priest, June 17, 1739. R. of Hilgay, Norfolk, 1740-74. Sub-dean of Ripon, 1746-74. Died June 19, 1774. Brother of Heneage (1737). (*Scott-Mayor*, III. 444.)

DERYNG, RICHARD. Matric. pens. from QUEENS', Easter, 1546; Scholar, 1548-50. Perhaps adm. at Gray's Inn, 1553.

DEERING, RICHARD. Matric. pens. from JESUS, *c.* 1596. Adm. at the Middle Temple, May 4, 1598, as 4th s. of Richard, Esq., of Pluckley, Kent.

DEERINGE, THOMAS. Matric. pens. rom MAGDALENE, Easter, 1580. Adm. at the Middle Temple, July 1, 1584, as 2nd s. of Richard, Esq., of Pluckley, Kent.

DERING, ——. Adm. at PETERHOUSE, Lent, 1555-6. Perhaps Edward (1559-60).

DERISLEY, *see* DEARSLEY.

DERKINDREN, ABRAHAM. Adm. pens. (age 17) at PEMBROKE, May 16, 1621. S. of Abraham, of London, mercer.

DERLINGE, JOHN. Matric. sizar from PEMBROKE, Michs. 1588; B.A. 1592-3, as Darling; M.A. 1596.

DERLINGTON, JOHN. Clerk, bachelor in some faculty. Scholar at KING'S HALL, 1365. Archdeacon of Norwich, 1387. Chancellor, 1399.

DERMAN, WILLIAM. Scholar at KING'S HALL, 1440-50. One of these names R. of White Roothing, Essex, 1446-50. Died 1450.

DERMAR or DERMAN, JOHN. B.A. 1506-7; M.A. 1510. Fellow of PETERHOUSE, 1510. Bursar, 1510-1. Name off, 1521.

DERNEFORD, NICHOLAS. One of the original 'KING'S Scholars' at Cambridge, Apr. 14, 1318.

DERNELL, ——. M.Gram. 1480-1.

DERRICK, CHARLES. Matric. pens. from CHRIST'S, May, 1569; B.A. 1573-4.

DERYCKE, EDWARD. Matric. pens. (age 12) from CORPUS CHRISTI, Michs. 1573. (Probably adm. 1570.)

DERRICK, DYRYCKE or DETHYCKE, FRANCIS. Matric. pens. from CHRIST'S, June, 1565; B.A. 1569; M.A. from Corpus Christi, 1578. At Antwerp as an agent of the English government in 1594. (*Peile*, I. 92; *Cooper*, II. 176.)

DERRICK, JOHN. Matric. sizar from KING'S, Easter, 1688. S. of John, blacksmith. B. at Lincoln. School, Lincoln. B.A. 1691-2. Ord. deacon (Lincoln) Feb. 21, 1691-2.

DERRY, WILLIAM. Adm. sizar (age 17) at PEMBROKE, May 21, 1674. S. of Richard, gent. B. at Grimsby, Lincs. Matric. 1674.

DERSHAM, ——. Benedictine Monk. Incorp. from Oxford, 1496. D.D. 1499. Cellarer of Bury St Edmunds.

DESAGULIERS, JOHN THEOPHILUS. Incorp. LL.D. 1726, from Hart Hall, Oxford. S. of John, protestant pastor at Altré, France. B. at La Rochelle. Matric. from Christ Church, Oxford, Oct. 28, 1705, age 22; B.A. (Oxford) 1709; M.A. 1712; D.C.L. 1719. F.R.S. 1714. R. of Little Stanmore, Middlesex, 1715-44. R. of Bridgham, Norfolk, 1717-26. R. of Little Warley, Essex, 1727-44. Scientific inventor and writer. Died Feb. 29, 1744, aged 66. Will, P.C.C. (*D.N.B.*; *Al. Oxon.*)

DESBOROUGH, *see* DISBOROUGH.

DESTFORD, JOHN (1565), *see* DEFFORD.

DE TASCHER, PETER. M.A. 1690 (*Lit. Reg.*).

DETHICKE, CHRISTOPHER. Adm. pens. (age 16) at CAIUS, Oct. 1569. S. and h. of Edmund, gent., of Beechamwell, Norfolk. School, Lynn. Matric. 1569. Succeeded his father, 1565. (*Venn*, I. 65; *Vis. of Norfolk*.)

DETHICKE, EDMUND. Adm. pens. (age 15) at CAIUS, Nov. 16, 1641. S. of Edmund, gent., of Newton, Norfolk. B. at Harpley. Schools, Rudham (Mr Robotham) and Norwich (Mr Lovering). Matric. 1641; Scholar, 1642-4. Merchant in London. Living, 1670. Brother of John (1658). (*Venn*, I. 346; *Vis. of London*, 1634.)

DETHICK, EDMUND. Adm. pens. (age 15) at ST JOHN'S, May 19, 1651. S. of John, merchant and alderman, of St Mary Axe, London (Lord Mayor, 1656). B. there. School, London (private; Mr Singleton). Matric. 1651; B.A. 1654. Adm. at Gray's Inn, June 23, 1653. Died unmarried. (Le Neve, *Knights*, 134.)

DETHICK, FRANCIS, *see* DERRICK.

DETHICK, GEORGE. Matric. Fell.-Com. from ST JOHN'S, *c.* 1593. Eldest s. of Sir William (1559), Garter King-of-Arms. B.A. 1595-6. Adm. at Gray's Inn, Apr. 25, 1594.

DETHICK, GILBERT. Matric. sizar from KING'S, *c.* 1598. S. of Sir William (1559), Garter King-of-Arms. B.A. 1601-2; M.A. 1605. A proctor of the Arches Court. Died May 22, 1639. Will, P.C.C. Brother of George. (J. Ch. Smith.)

DETHICK, GILBERT. Adm. at KING'S, a scholar from Eton, 1687. S. of Henry (1642). B. at Poplar, Middlesex, 1687. Matric. 1688; B.A. 1691-2; M.A. 1695. Fellow, 1691. Ord. deacon (Lincoln) June 19, 1698; priest (London) Sept. 22, 1706. Died young, of consumption.

DETHICK or DYRRYCKE, HENRY. Matric. sizar from GONVILLE HALL, Nov. 1554. Probably 3rd s. of Simon, of Wormegay, Norfolk. B.A. 1556-7; M.A. 1560; B.D. 1565. Fellow of Caius, by charter, 1557. Expelled by Dr Caius, 1565. University preacher, 1565. Perhaps V. of Orpington, Kent, 1566-70; and chaplain to the Archbishop. Afterwards a papist. Admon. (P.C.C.) Jan. 5, 1575-6, of Henry Dethick, 'of the University of Cambridge, clerk, dying beyond the seas' granted to his brother Christopher, of Bradenham, Norfolk. The conclusion therefore (*Venn*, I. 38; *Cath. Rec. Soc.*, II. 207) that he was received at Rome, and died there in 1594, must be wrong. There was a contemporary, LL.D., at Oxford. (J. Ch. Smith.)

DETHICKE, HENRY. Adm. at KING'S, a scholar from Eton, 1642. 3rd s. of Henry, of Poplar, Middlesex. B. at Blackwall, Middlesex. B.A. 1647-8; M.A. 1650. Fellow, till 1656. Richmond Herald. Died June 19, 1707, aged 84. Buried at Poplar, Middlesex. Father of Gilbert (1687). (Noble, *Coll. of Arms*; J. Ch. Smith.)

DETHYCK, JOHN. Matric. pens. from QUEENS', Easter, 1544; Scholar, 1543-7.

DETHICK, JOHN. Adm. pens. (age 15) at CAIUS, July 6, 1658. S. of Edmund, of West Newton, Norfolk, gent. Schools, Sandringham (Mr Wibrow) and Lynn (Mr Bell). Matric. 1659. Owned property at Walpole. Brother of Edmund (1641). (*Venn*, I. 403.)

DETHICKE, RICHARD. Matric. pens. from ST JOHN'S, Easter, 1558. Will (Lewes) of one of these names; 'of Preston, Sussex, clerk.'

DETHYCK, THOMAS. Matric. pens. from ST EDMUND'S HOSTEL, Michs. 1544.

DETHICK, WILLIAM. Matric. pens. from ST JOHN'S, Michs. 1559. S. of Sir Gilbert, Garter King-of-Arms. B.A. 1562-3. Rouge Croix pursuivant, 1567. York Herald, 1570. Garter King-of-Arms, 1586. Knighted, May 13, 1603. Often travelled professionally. Died 1612, aged 70. Buried in St Paul's Cathedral. Will, P.C.C. Father of George and Gilbert. (*D.N.B.*)

DETHYCKE, ——. Fee for M.A. or higher degree, 1479-80.

DETHICKE, ——. Sizar at TRINITY, 1567.

DETLYE, GODFREY. Matric. sizar from TRINITY, Easter, 1617.

DEUFELT, JAMES. Adm. sizar at QUEENS', Apr. 26, 1610. Of Jersey.

DEUTZ, JOHN. Adm. pens. at QUEENS', May 19, 1612. Of Lincolnshire.

DEVEILLE, HANS. Adm. pens. at EMMANUEL, June 30, 1721. Of Middlesex. Perhaps s. of Sir Thomas. Matric. 1721; B.A. 1724-5 (1st in the *ordo*). Usher at Felsted School, 1731. V. of Saling, Essex, 1732-41. V. of Felsted, 1740. Died 1741. (J. Sargeaunt, *Felsted School*.)

DEVENISH, HENRY. Adm. pens. (age 16) at ST JOHN'S, Apr. 18, 1689. S. of Henry, counsellor (of Lincoln's Inn). B. in Middlesex. School, Enfield (Mr Udal), Middlesex. Matric. 1689. Adm. at the Middle Temple, Nov. 2, 1689.

DEVENISH, THOMAS. Adm. sizar (age 18) at SIDNEY, July 4, 1695. S. of John, clerk, deceased, R. of Bickleigh, Devon. B. there. School, Tiverton. Matric. 1695; Scholar, 1697; B.A. 1698-9.

DEVENISH, WILLIAM. Matric. Fell.-Com., as a resident at MICHAEL HOUSE, Easter, 1544. Doubtless s. of Richard, of Hellingley, Sussex. B.A. (Oxford) 1526-7; M.A. 1530; B.D. 1537. Fellow of Merton, 1528. Probably fellow of St John's, Cambridge, 1534. Provost of Queen's College, Oxford, 1534-1558. V. of Westerham, Sussex, 1540-54. Chaplain to Henry VIII. Preb. of Canterbury, 1544; of Windsor; of Chichester, 1556. Died Mar. 24, 1558-9. Will (P.C.C.) 1559, as Denyson. (*Al. Oxon*; J. Ch. Smith.)

DE VERE, EDWARD (1558), *see* BULBECK, Lord EDWARD.

DEVEREUX, ARTHUR. Adm. pens. at EMMANUEL, June 28, 1665. 3rd s. of George, Esq., of Vaynor, Montgomery. Matric. 1665, as 'Deurents.' Adm. at the Middle Temple, Feb. 11, 1666-7. Died 1709. Brother of Vaughan (1660).

DEVORAXE, GEORGE. Matric. Fell.-Com. from ST JOHN'S, Easter, 1560. Doubtless s. of Sir Richard, K.B. of Hereford. M.P. for Co. Pembroke, 1588. Knighted, 1596.

DEVEREUX, JONATHAN. Adm. sizar at EMMANUEL, 1626. Matric. 1626. Perhaps V. of Foxton, Leics., 1641. R. of Gateshead, July 5, 1645. R. of Wolsingham, Durham, 1648. One of these names, 'Minister of the Gospel,' buried at St Nicholas, Newcastle, Mar. 2, 1663-4. Father of the next. (*Peile*, I. 511; H. M. Wood.)

DEVEREUX, JONATHAN. Adm. pens. (age 17) at CHRIST'S, Jan. 6, 1646-7. S. of Jonathan (above). B. at Clare, Suffolk. School, Felsted (Mr Holbeach). Matric. 1647, as 'John'; B.A. 1650-1; M.A. 1656. P.C. of St Nicholas, Durham; ejected, 1662. (*Peile*, I. 511.)

DEVEREUX, PETER. Matric. sizar from PETERHOUSE, *c.* 1597; B.A. 1600-1; M.A. 1609. R. of Rattlesden, Suffolk, 1614-44. R. of Buxhall, 1627. Married, at Rattlesden, Nov. 25, 1602, Julian Frances. Will (Bury) 1645. Father of the next and Robert (1627). (V. B. Redstone.)

DEVEREUX, PETER. Adm. sizar at PETERHOUSE, Feb. 2, 1624-5. Of Suffolk. S. of Peter (above). Bapt. at Rattlesden, Apr. 10, 1610. Matric. 1625; B.A. 1629-30. Perhaps V. of Kirby-le-Soken, Essex, 1638.

DEVEREUX, ROBERT. Adm. Fell.-Com. at TRINITY, 1577. 2nd Earl of Essex. S. of Walter, 1st Earl of Essex. B. Nov. 10, 1567. Matric. 1579; M.A. 1581. Incorp. at Oxford, 1588. The famous commander, statesman, and favourite of Queen Elizabeth. Earl-marshal of England, 1597. Chancellor of the University, Aug. 10, 1598. Executed, Feb. 25, 1600-1. Will (P.C.C.) 1616. (*Al. Oxon.*; *D.N.B.*; *Cooper*, II. 296.)

DEVEREUX, ROBERT. Adm. sizar at PETERHOUSE, Feb. 6, 1626-7. S. of Peter (1597), R. of Rattlesden, Suffolk. Bapt. there, Feb. 4, 1611-2. Matric. 1627; B.A. 1630-1; M.A. 1634. Ord. priest (Norwich) Sept. 22, 1638. R. of Hepworth, Suffolk, 1644-60. R. of Little Stonham, 1660-86. Died 1686. Will, Bury.

DEVEREUX, SIMEON. Adm. pens. at TRINITY, June 10, 1675. School, Westminster. Scholar, 1676; Matric. 1677; B.A. 1678-9; M.A. 1682. Chaplain of Trinity College, 1681-9. P.C. of Nackington, Kent, 1686-1733. Minor canon of St Paul's, 1692-8. R. of Harbledown, 1731. V. of Brookland, 1731-3. Minor Canon of Canterbury. Died July 6, 1733.

DEVOREUX, VAUGHAN. Adm. pens. (age 18) at ST JOHN'S, June 14, 1660. S. of George, Esq., of Berriew, Montgomeryshire. B. there. School, Newport (Mr Chaloner). Matric. 1660. Of Nantcribba. Married and had issue. Died 1700. Brother of Arthur (1665). (W. H. Cooke, *Herefordshire*, 70.)

DEVEREUX, WILLIAM. Matric. Fell.-Com. from PEMBROKE, c. 1596.

DEVEROS, JOHN. M.A. Fellow of CORPUS CHRISTI, 1400.

DEVEY, JAMES. M.A. from TRINITY, 1724. S. of Henry, of Pattingham, Staffs., clerk. Matric. from Pembroke College, Oxford, May 13, 1700, age 19; B.A. (Oxford) 1703-4. R. of Beckbury, Salop, 1724. (*Al. Oxon.*)

DEVEY, JAMES. Adm. pens. at EMMANUEL, Mar. 2, 1740-1. B. at Kemberton, Salop. Matric. 1742; B.A. 1744-5; M.A. 1748; B.D. 1755. Fellow, 1747. Ord. deacon (Ely) Oct. 23, 1748; priest, Oct. 29, 1749. R. of Stanground, Hunts., 1766-1809. Died Jan. 31, 1809.

DEVIS, EDMUND. Adm. sizar (age 20) at PEMBROKE, Nov. 14, 1688. S. of John, gent. B. in Warwickshire.

DEVONSHIRE, Duke of, *see* CAVENDISH.

DEVYAS, WILLIAM. Matric. sizar from CLARE, Michs. 1552.

DEW, JOHN. B.A. 1484-5; M.A. 1490-1. Fellow of GONVILLE HALL, 1488-1500. President of Physwick Hostel, 1499. V. of Mattishall, Norfolk, 1500, till his death, in 1517. (*Venn*, I. 13.)

DEW, JOHN. Adm. pens. (age 16) at CAIUS, July 6, 1657. S. of Arthur, merchant, of London. B. there. School, St Paul's. Matric. 1657.

DEWE, THOMAS. B.A. from MAGDALENE, 1575-6.

DEWE, WILLIAM. Adm. pens. (age 17) at TRINITY, July 28, 1687. S. of William. B. in London. School, St Paul's. Matric. 1688. Migrated to Trinity Hall, Aug. 14, 1690. LL.B. from Trinity Hall, 1693.

DEW, WILLIAM. Adm. at CORPUS CHRISTI, 1702. Of Norwich. B.A. 1705-6.

DEW, ——. Scholar at GONVILLE HALL, 1532-3.

DEWBANK, JOHN. 'B.A. of ST CATHARINE'S; aged 45; ordained by Bishop of Lincoln,' when instituted V. of Willoughby, Leics., and Willey, Warws., 1576. (*Lib. Cler. Linc.*, 1576.)

DEWBERY, JOHN. Adm. sizar at ST JOHN'S, Feb. 18, 1706-7. S. of Thomas, of Walton, Bucks., clerk. Matric. 1707. Previously adm. at Merton College, Oxford, Nov. 21, 1704, age 18. (*Al. Oxon.*)

DEWBERRY, THOMAS. Adm. sizar (age 16) at TRINITY, Apr. 16, 1678. Of Leicestershire. S. of William. School, Market Harborough (Mr Berry). Matric. 1681; Scholar, 1681; B.A. 1681-2; M.A. 1685. Perhaps R. of Crawley, Bucks., 1686-1717. Died Aug. 14, 1717.

DEWER, *see* DUER.

D'EWES or DEWCE, PAUL. Matric. pens. from PEMBROKE, Easter, 1584. S. of Gerrard, printer, of London. Of Upminster, Essex. B. 1567. Previously Matric. from Magdalen College, Oxford, Dec. 1, 1581, age 13. Adm. at the Middle Temple, July 3, 1585. One of the six clerks in Chancery. Of Stowlangtoft, Suffolk. Married (1) Cecilia, dau. and h. of Richard Symonds, of Coxden, Dorset; (2) Elizabeth, dau. of Thomas Isham. Died in London. Buried at Stowlangtoft, Apr. 26, 1631 (*Parish Reg.*). Will (P.C.C.) 1631. Father of the next and Symonds. (*D.N.B.*; J. Ch. Smith; H. I. Longden.)

D'EWES, RICHARD. Matric. Fell.-Com. from ST CATHARINE'S, Easter, 1632. S. of Paul (above), of Suffolk. Bapt. at Stowlangtoft, Suffolk, Oct. 31, 1615. School, Bury. Adm. at the Middle Temple, Apr. 1632. Lieutenant-Colonel, quartered at Reading in Dec. 1642. Probably killed there. Will (P.C.C.) 1643; 'deceased at Reading.' (Bury School, *S.H.A.H.*)

D'EWES, SYMONDS. Adm. Fell.-Com. at ST JOHN'S, May 20, 1618. S. of Paul (1584), of Milden, and Stowlangtoft, Suffolk. B. Dec. 18, 1602, at Coxden, Dorset (his mother's home). School, Bury. Matric. 1618. Resided till Sept. 22, 1620. M.A. 1635-6 (on visit of Prince of Wales). Adm. at the Middle Temple, July 2, 1611. Barrister, 1623. Knighted, Dec. 6, 1626. High Sheriff for Suffolk, 1639-40. M.P. for Sudbury, 1640-8. Created baronet, July 15, 1641. Antiquarian writer. Buried at Stowlangtoft, June 7, 1650. Will, P.C.C. (*D.N.B.*; *G.E.C.* Extracts from his Diary are given in *College Life in the Time of James I*, 1851.)

DEWS, THOMAS. B.A. from KING'S, 1592-3.

DEWES, THOMAS. Adm. Fell.-Com. at TRINITY, May 28, 1647. Of Cheshire.

D'EWES, WILLOUGHBY. Adm. pens. (age 17) at ST JOHN'S, Mar. 31, 1690. S. of Sir Willoughby, Bart. B. at Stowlangtoft, Suffolk. Bapt. there, Sept. 19, 1672. School, Bury. Matric. 1690; B.A. 1693-4. Died of small-pox, Oct. 1698, age 26. Buried at Stowlangtoft. (H. I. Longden.)

D'EWES, WILLOUGHBY. Adm. pens. at QUEENS', Dec. 17, 1706. S. of Sir Simonds, Bart., of Suffolk. School, Bury. Matric. 1706. Died 1710, aged 19.

DEUES (? DENES), ——. B.A. 1485-6.

DEWES, ——. Adm. Fell.-Com. at TRINITY HALL, Sept. 30, 1692.

DEWHURST, JAMES. Adm. sizar at QUEENS', Apr. 1, 1574. Of Lancashire. One of these names R. of Congham, Norfolk, 1580-95.

DEWHURST, JOHN. Adm. sizar (age 18) at ST JOHN'S, June 26, 1718. S. of John. B. at Colne, Lancs. Schools, Wakefield (Mr Clarke) and Threshfield (Mr Marshall). Matric. 1718. Died in College. Buried at All Saints', Cambridge, Nov. 21, 1718.

DEWHURST, ROBERT. Matric. pens. from TRINITY, 1595. Scholar from Westminster. Perhaps of Cheshunt, Herts. Adm. at Gray's Inn, June 9, 1600. Died May 4, 1645, aged 68. Will, P.C.C.

DEWHURST or DUHURST, THOMAS. Adm. sizar at PETERHOUSE, Jan. 10, 1628-9. Matric. 1629.

DEWHURST, WILLIAM. Adm. sizar (age 19) at ST JOHN'S, Aug. 13, 1723. S. of Clayton, husbandman, of Lancashire. B. at Ribchester. School, Houghton (Mr Northcross). Matric. 1724; B.A. 1727-8. P.C. of St Mary, Eccleston, Lancs., 1728-33. Buried at Ormskirk, Feb. 9, 1733-4.

DEWING, THOMAS. Adm. sizar June 27, 1726. Of Essex. Matric. 1726.

DEWY, JAMES. Matric. sizar from QUEENS', Michs. 1562.

DEY, *see* DAY.

DEYMAN or DYMAN, PETER. Adm. pens. (age 17) at SIDNEY, Aug. 4, 1634. S. of William, clothier. B. at Tiverton, Devon. School, Tiverton. Matric. 1634-5, as 'Dimond.' Brother of William.

DEYMAN, WILLIAM. Adm. pens. (age 16) at SIDNEY, Oct. 13, 1632. S. of William, weaver. B. at Tiverton, Devon. Bapt. Apr. 9, 1615. School, Tiverton. Matric. 1634-5, as 'Dimond'; B.A. 1636-7. Brother of Peter.

DEYMAN, WILLIAM. Adm. sizar (age 18) at SIDNEY, Aug. 18, 1691. 2nd s. of William, of Devon. B. at Tiverton. School, Tiverton. Matric. 1691; B.A. 1695-6; M.A. 1699. Fellow, 1699. Ord. deacon (Lincoln) May 30, 1697. V. of Uffculme, Devon. Died Feb. 23, 1738-9.

DEYMAN, WILLIAM. Adm. pens. (age 18) at SIDNEY, July 5, 1748. S. of John, attorney, of Uffculme, Devon. Bapt. Apr. 20, 1731. Schools, Winchester and Tiverton. Matric. 1748. (Kirby, *Winchester Scholars*.)

DEYNELL, ROBERT. B.A. 1505.

DEYNE, THOMAS. Matric. sizar from TRINITY, Michs. 1567.

DEYNES, *see* DAYNES.

DEYNHAM, THOMAS, M.D., *see* DENMAN.

DEYWOOD, GEORGE. Matric. pens. from KING'S, Michs. 1564.

DIASON, HENRY. Adm. sizar at CORPUS CHRISTI, 1617. Of Essex. Matric. Lent, 1618-9; B.A. 1621-2. V. of Grays Thurrock, Essex.

DIASON, JOHN. Matric. sizar from ST JOHN'S, Michs. 1565. Ord. deacon (Ely) Aug. 24, 1566; priest, Sept. 21, 1567. V. of Tadlow, Cambs., 1567; resigned, 1575. V. of East Hatley, 1569. V. of Gt Hormead, Herts., 1575-84. Died 1584. Will (Consist. C. London) 1584.

DIBBEN, JAMES. M.A. from KING'S, 1730. S. of Richard, of Manston, Dorset, Esq. Matric. from Oriel College, Oxford, Jan. 23, 1720–1, age 17; B.A. (Oxford) 1724. R. of Fifehead Neville, Dorset, 1731–76. R. of Fontmell, 1741–76. Died 1776. (*Al. Oxon.*; Hutchins, *Dorset*, I. 271; F. S. Hockaday.)

DIBBEN, THOMAS. Adm. pens. (age 18) at TRINITY, June 17, 1696. S. of Richard. Bp in St Martin's, London. School, Westminster. Scholar, 1697; Matric. 1699, as Debben; B.A. 1699–1700; M.A. 1703; D.D. 1721. (He was not a fellow, as stated in *D.N.B.*) Ord. deacon (London) June 16, 1700; dispensation for priest, July 12, 1701. R. of Gt Fontmell, Dorset, 1701–41. Chaplain to Bishop Robinson, of Bristol, with whom he attended the Congress of Utrecht. Precentor of St Paul's, 1714–41. Latin poet. Became deranged; lost his fortune and died in the Poultry Compter, Apr. 5, 1741. (*D.N.B.*; *Al. Westmon.*)

DIBBLE, THOMAS. M.A. from KING'S, 1721. S. of John, of Abinger, Surrey, Esq. Matric. from St John's College, Oxford, Jan. 19, 1713–4, age 18; B.A. (Oxford) 1717. Ord. deacon (Winchester) June 8, 1718; priest, Dec. 21, 1719. V. of Upper Swell, Gloucs., 1719. R. of Woodchester, 1723. Chaplain to Lord Darcie. Died 1755. (*Al. Oxon.*; F. S. Hockaday.)

DICER, ROBERT. Adm. Fell.-Com. (age 18) at CAIUS, May 28, 1662. S. of Sir Robert, Bart., citizen of London. B. there. Schools, Hampstead, Middlesex (private; Mr Wagoner) and Charterhouse. Matric. 1662. Adm. at Gray's Inn, Jan. 24, 1664–5. Succeeded his father as second Bart., Aug. 26, 1667. Of Braughing, Herts. Sheriff of Suffolk, 1669–70. Buried at Braughing, Aug. 16, 1672. Will (P.C.C.) 1673. (*Venn*, I. 416; *Vis. of Midds.*, 1664; G.E.C.)

DICEY, EDWARD. Adm. pens. at TRINITY, June 28, 1739. S. of William, of Northampton, printer. Bapt. at All Saints', Mar. 6, 1721–2. School, Ely (Mr Gunning). Matric. 1739; Scholar, 1740; B.A. 1742–3; M.A. 1746. Ord. deacon (Peterb.) May 15, 1744; priest, Aug. 3, 1746. R. of Maidwell, Northants., 1746–59. R. of Walton, Bucks., 1751–90. R. of Horton, 1759–71. R. of Marsh-Gibbon, 1771. Preb. of Bristol, 1773–90. R. of St Bartholomew-by-the-Exchange, London, 1778–90. Buried there, Mar. 31, 1790. Will, P.C.C. (*Lipscomb*, IV. 386; H. I. Longden.)

DICK or DYCKE, JOHN. Matric. sizar from KING'S, Michs. 1548. Lay clerk of King's.

DICKERSON, NICHOLAS. Adm. sizar (age 17) at CAIUS, Apr. 26, 1600. S. of Nicholas, yeoman, of Wymondham, Norfolk. School, Wymondham. Of Dickelburgh. Married Elizabeth, dau. of John Roberts, of Billingford. (*Venn*, I. 172.)

DICKINS, AMBROSE. Adm. scholar at TRINITY HALL, Jan. 1, 1733–4. Of Harrow. Matric. 1733; LL.B. 1738. Fellow, 1738–48. Perhaps s. and h. of Ambrose, of Covent Garden, Esq.; adm. at Lincoln's Inn, Dec. 20, 1731.

DICKONS, BRIAN. B.A. from MAGDALENE, 1584–5; M.A. 1588. Ord. deacon (Lincoln) Nov. 9; priest, Nov. 10, 1593. C. of Grayingham, Lincs., in 1614.

DICKENS, CHARLES. Adm. scholar at TRINITY HALL, Jan. 7, 1739–40. S. of Samuel (1719). Bapt. at Hemingford Abbots, Hunts., June 17, 1720. Exhibitioner from Charterhouse. Matric. 1739; LL.B. 1745; LL.D. 1767. Ord. deacon (Lincoln) Nov. 13, 1743; priest, June 11, 1744. V. of Hemingford Grey, Hunts., 1744–93. R. of Hemingford Abbots, 1748–93. Preb. of Lincoln, 1778. Died Sept. 27, 1793, aged 73. Will, P.C.C. Brother of Thomas (1751). (G. *Mag.*; *Al. Carthus.*)

DICKINGS, FRANCIS. Adm. pens. (age 16) at CHRIST'S, Apr. 24, 1633. S. and h. of William, gent. B. at St Dunstan-in-the-East, London. School, Luffenham, Rutland (Mr Dallie). Matric. 1633; LL.B. from Trinity Hall, 1638. Adm. at the Middle Temple, Mar. 16, 1640–1.

DICKINS, FRANCIS. Adm. scholar at TRINITY HALL, Aug. 14, 1699. Of Ripplington, East Meon, Hants. School, Winchester. Matric. 1699; LL.B. 1705; M.A. 1711 (*Lit. Reg.*), LL.D. 1714. Fellow, Jan. 23, 1704–55. Junior Proctor, 1710, 1712. Regius Professor of Civil Law, 1714–55. Adm. at Gray's Inn, July 6, 1693; of Lyndhurst, Hants. Died June 1755. Brother of the next. (G. *Mag.*; *Lond. Mag.*)

DICKINS, GEORGE. Adm. pens. (age 18) at PETERHOUSE, June 25, 1703. Of East Meon, Hants. School, Winchester. Matric. 1703; Scholar, 1703; B.A. 1706–7; M.A. 1710; M.D. 1717 (*Com. Reg.*). Fellow, 1708. Brother of Francis (above).

DICKINS, GEORGE. Adm. scholar at TRINITY HALL, Feb. 28, 1738–9. Of London. Matric. 1743; LL.B. 1744. Ord. deacon (Lincoln) May 29, 1743; priest (Norwich) Apr. 1745. R. of Little Bradley, Suffolk, 1745–56.

DICKINS or DICKIN, JOHN. Adm. sizar at CHRIST'S, July 2, 1679. Matric. 1680; B.A. 1682–3.

DICKONS, NICHOLAS. Matric. pens. from PEMBROKE, Easter, 1613; B.A. 1616–7; M.A. 1620. Ord. deacon (York) June, 1622; priest, Sept. 23, 1632. Will of one of these names (York) 1637; of East Retford, Notts., schoolmaster.

DICKENS, NICHOLAS. Matric. pens. from ST JOHN'S, Easter, 1623; B.A. 1626–7; M.A. 1630; M.D. 1638. Admon. (P.C.C.) Aug. 1662. Died in the Fleet prison. (J. Ch. Smith.)

DICKONS, NICHOLAS. Adm. at CORPUS CHRISTI, 1635. Of Nottinghamshire. B.A. 1639–40; M.A. 1643. Ord. deacon (Lincoln) Sept. 24, 1643; priest, June 16, 1644. R. of Elsworth, Cambs., 1660–93.

DICKINS, RICHARD. Matric. pens. from CHRIST'S, July, 1619; B.A. 1622; M.A. 1626.

DICKEN, SAMUEL. M.A. from KING'S, 1719. S. of Joseph, of Birmingham. Matric. from Brasenose College, Oxford, Mar. 20, 1706–7, age 16; B.A. (Oxford) 1710. Ord. priest (Peterb.) Sept. 18, 1714. R. of Hemingford Abbots, Hunts., 1714–48. V. of Hemingford Grey, 1724–44. R. of Houghton and Witton, 1743–8. Died 1748. Father of Thomas (1751) and Charles (1739–40). (*Al. Oxon.*)

DICKEN, THOMAS. Adm. at CHRIST'S, July 2, 1679. Migrated to Sidney, Oct. 25, 1679. 1st s. of Thomas, R. of Weston, Staffs. B. at Wollaston, Salop. School, Newport, Salop (Mr Sam. Edwards). Matric. 1680; B.A. 1682–3.

DICKENS, THOMAS. Incorp. M.A. 1751, from Christ Church, Oxford. S. of Samuel (1719), of Hemingford Abbots, Hunts. B. there, Oct. 1, 1721. Matric. (Oxford) 1739; B.A. (Oxford) 1742–3; M.A. 1746. Doubtless fellow of PETERHOUSE, 1750–6. Exhibitioner from Charterhouse. Received a commission in 1745 during the Rebellion. Died at Little Fransham, Norfolk, Sept. 21, 1789. Buried there. M.I. Brother of Charles (1739–40). (*Al. Oxon.*; *Al. Carthus.*; H. G. Harrison.)

DICKONS, WILLIAM. B.A. 1509–10.

DICKENS or DYCANS, WILLIAM. Matric. pens. (age 14) from CHRIST'S, Nov. 1561. S. of John, of 'Stotfold,' Notts. Migrated to Caius, July 13, 1563. Probably ord. priest (Norwich) Oct. 21, 1570. R. of Gayton Thorpe, Norfolk, 1570–99. (*Venn*, I. 52.)

DICKYNS, WILLIAM. Adm. pens. (age 15) at CHRIST'S, June 29, 1644. S. of William, of Fleet St, London. School, Bishop's Stortford (Mr Leigh). Matric. 1646; B.A. from Trinity Hall, 1647–8; M.A. 1651. Fellow of Trinity Hall, 1649–68. Adm. at Gray's Inn, Dec. 28, 1649. Barrister-at-law, 1660. (Probably not the fellow of Balliol College, Oxford—*see Peile*, I. 487.) (*Vis. of London*, 1634.)

DICKONS, WILLIAM. Adm. at CORPUS CHRISTI, 1679. Of Cambridgeshire. Matric. 1679; B.A. 1682–3; M.A. 1686. Perhaps R. of Boxworth, Cambs., 1690.

DICKENS, WILLIAM. Adm. sizar (age 18) at TRINITY, June 19, 1687. S. of John, of Bakewell, Derbs. School, Bakewell. Matric. 1687.

DICKINS, WILLIAM. M.B. from TRINITY HALL, 1702.

DICKINSON or DICONSON, ABRAHAM. Matric. pens. from TRINITY, Lent, 1579–80; Scholar, 1582; B.A. 1583–4; M.A. 1587; D.D. 1609. Fellow, 1585. Incorp. at Oxford, 1609. R. of Hurstmonceaux, Sussex, 1590.

DIKYNSON or DICONSON, ANTHONY. Matric. sizar from ST JOHN'S, Easter, 1583; B.A. 1585–6.

DICKINSON, BERNARD. Adm. sizar (age 19) at SIDNEY, May 28, 1641. S. of Robert, yeoman. B. at Thorpe Pearth. Schools, Thorpe Pearth (Mr Proctor) and Collingham (Mr Dunwell). Matric. 1641; B.A. 1644–5.

DICKINSON, CHARLES. Adm. pens. (age 15) at TRINITY, June 16, 1676. S. of William, of London. B. there. School, London. Matric. 1676; Scholar, 1679–80; B.A. 1679–80; M.A. 1683.

DICKINSON, CHARLES. Adm. sizar (age 18) at ST JOHN'S, Nov. 2, 1737. S. of John, clerk, of Lincolnshire. B. at Harlaxton. School, Oakham, Rutland. Matric. 1737; B.A. 1741–2. Ord. deacon (Lincoln) Sept. 19, 1742; priest, May 25, 1755. V. of Ouston, and R. of Withcote, Leics., 1755–86. R. of Carlton Curlieu, 1768–86. Died Dec. 24, 1786. Will (P.C.C.) 1787. (*Scott-Mayor*, III. 490.)

DICKINSON, CHRISTOPHER. Matric. sizar from TRINITY, Easter, 1626.

DICKONSON, DANIEL. Adm. sizar (age 17) at ST JOHN'S, Dec. 27, 1653. S of Thomas, mercer, deceased, of Lancaster. B. there. School, Giggleswick. Matric. 1653–4; B.A. 1657–8; M.A. 1661; B.D. 1668. Fellow, 1660. Signs for priest's orders (London) Dec. 22, 1666.

DICKENSON, EDMUND. Adm. at KING'S, a scholar from Eton, 1613. S. of Thomas, of Eton. Matric. 1614; B.A. 1617–8; M.A. 1621. Fellow, till 1626. Incorp. at Oxford, 1623. V. of Minster Lovell, Oxon., 1631. R. of Sturminster Marshall, Dorset, 1643; sequestered, 1645–53; according to *Hutchins*. (*Al. Oxon.*)

DICKENSON, EDMUND. Adm. sizar at KING'S, Michs. 1615; B.A. 1618-9; M.A. 1624. R. of Pertenhall, Beds., 1633-53. Buried there Mar. 14, 1652-3. Father of Edmund (1650).

DICKINSON, EDMUND. Matric. pens. from MAGDALENE, Easter, 1641; B.A. 1644-5; M.A. 1648. Fellow of Magdalene. *See* Edward, fellow of Jesus (below).

DICKINSON, EDMUND. Adm. pens. at CORPUS CHRISTI, 1650. Of Bedfordshire. S. of Edmund (1615). Bapt. at Pertenhall, Mar. 25, 1634. Matric. 1650; B.A. 1656-7. One of these names ejected from Bozeat and Paston, Northants., 1662. (T. P. Dorman.)

DICKENSON, EDMUND. Adm. pens. at EMMANUEL, Dec. 8, 1682. Of Lincolnshire.

DICKENSON, EDWARD. Matric. sizar from TRINITY, Easter, 1624; Scholar, 1627; B.A. 1627-8; M.A. 1631. Probably ord. deacon (Norwich) Sept. 22, 1638 (B.A.).

DICKENSON, EDWARD. M.A. Intruded fellow of JESUS, July 10, 1648; resigned, 1655. Of Lincolnshire. He may be 'Edmund,' above. Ord. deacon and priest (Peterb.) Sept. 22, 1661. (A. Gray.)

DICKINSON, GEORGE. Matric. pens. from ST JOHN'S, Michs. 1562; B.A. 1567-8. Ord. deacon (Ely) Apr. 16, 1568; priest (Norwich) Oct. 21, 1569. V. of Buxhall, Suffolk, 1570. Will proved (C.C. Norwich) Apr. 29, 1619. (H. F. Waters, *Geneal. Gleanings*, 1412.)

DICKENSON, GREGORY. Matric. sizar from JESUS, Michs. 1617. Ord. deacon (York) June, 1625; priest, Mar. 1625-6, 'B.A.'

DICKINSON, HAMILTON. Adm. pens. (age 18) at ST JOHN'S, July 4, 1710. S. of Richard, deceased. B. at Whitehaven, Cumberland. School, Westminster. Matric. 1710.

DICKENSON, HENRY. Matric. sizar from ST JOHN'S, Easter, 1569. Of Lancashire. B.A. 1572-3; M.A. 1576. Fellow, 1574. Ord. deacon and priest (Ely) July 5, 1579. R. of Lolworth, Cambs., 1580-94. Died 1594.

DICKINSON, HENRY. Adm. sizar (age 19) at CAIUS, July 8, 1633. S. of John, husbandman. B. in Eskdale, Cumberland. School, St Bees (Mr Radcliffe). Matric. 1633; B.A. 1636-7. Ord. deacon (Norwich) Sept. 24, 1637; priest, Sept. 22, 1638. C. of Spixworth, Norfolk, 1637. V. of Stalham, 1640; of Paston, 1646. R. of Frettenham, 1659; of Felthorpe, 1665-7. He seems to have returned to Cumberland, as R. of Egremont, 1646-57. (*Venn*, I. 310; *B. Nightingale*.)

DICKINSON, HENRY. Adm. sizar (age 17) at PETERHOUSE, June 24, 1665. Of Yorkshire. School, Scarborough. Matric. 1665; B.A. 1668-9.

DICKINSON, HENRY. Adm. pens. at TRINITY, Mar. 3, 1672-3. Readm. Fell.-Com. Oct. 24, 1677. Matric. 1677-8; LL.B. 1678.

DICKINSON, JAMES. Matric. sizar from TRINITY, Easter, 1577.

DICKINSON, JAMES. Adm. pens. at JESUS, Apr. 8, 1637. Of London. Matric. 1637; Scholar, 1637; B.A. 1640-1.

DICKENSON, JOHN. Adm. at KING'S, a scholar from Eton, 1522.

DYCKYNSON, JOHN. Matric. sizar from ST JOHN'S, Michs. 1544.

DICONSON, JOHN. Matric. pens. from CLARE, Easter, 1586.

DICKINSON, JOHN. Matric. sizar from TRINITY, *c.* 1594; B.A. 1597-8; M.A. from Clare, 1602. Perhaps ord. deacon (Norwich) Mar. 25, 1597, age 23; C. of Wells, Norfolk; priest, Mar. 25, 1598.

DICKINSON, JOHN. B.A. from TRINITY, 1595-6.

DICKENSON, JOHN. Adm. sizar (age 19) at CAIUS, June 24, 1608. S. of Bryan, husbandman, of Newton, Lancs. School, Kirkby Lonsdale (Mr Hudson). Matric. 1608. Died in College. Buried at St Michael's, Cambridge, Mar. 26, 1610. (*Venn*, I. 198.)

DICCONSON, JOHN. Adm. sizar at EMMANUEL, May 21, 1681. Of Lancashire. S. of Thomas, of Ardwick. Bapt. Nov. 13, 1654. (Mumford, *Manchester School*.)

DICKONSON, JOHN. Adm. sizar (age 20) at MAGDALENE, June 24, 1704.

DICKINSON, JOHN. Adm. sizar at EMMANUEL, May 23, 1711. Of Leicestershire. Matric. 1710-1; B.A. 1714-5 (1st in the *ordo*); M.A. 1718. Ord. priest (Lincoln) Sept. 21, 1718. Perhaps R. of Oxcombe, Lincs., 1717, and R. of Haltham-on-Bain, 1717.

DICKINSON, JOHN. Adm. sizar (age 22) at ST JOHN'S, June 6, 1712. S. of John, husbandman. B. at Sedbergh. School, Sedbergh. Matric. 1712; B.A. 1715-6. Ord. deacon (Lincoln) Feb. 26, 1715-6; priest, July 14, 1717. One of these names V. of Spennithorne, Yorks., 1720-3. Died 1723.

DICKINSON, JOHN. Adm. Fell.-Com. at EMMANUEL, Dec. 3, 1713. Of Northamptonshire.

DICKINSON, JOHN. Adm. pens. (age 19) at PEMBROKE, June 9, 1719. S. of John, of London, mercer. Matric. 1719; B.A. 1723-4; M.A. 1730. Ord. deacon (Lincoln) Mar. 8, 1723-4; priest, Dec. 20, 1724. One of these names V. of Totternhoe, Beds., 1728-31.

DICKINSON, JOHN. Adm. sizar (age 17) at ST JOHN'S, Apr. 1, 1725. S. of Thomas, plumber, of Yorkshire. B. at Sheffield. School, Sheffield (Mr Robinson). Matric. 1725; B.A. 1728-9; M.A. 1732. Ord. deacon (Lincoln) Sept. 19, 1731; priest (Ely) June 23, 1732. C. of Leverington, Cambs. Assistant Minister at Sheffield, 1752-66. V. of Ecclesall, Yorks., 1752-66. Author and scholar. (*Scott-Mayor*, III. 381.)

DICKENSON, JOHN. Adm. sizar at ST CATHARINE'S, Nov. 14, 1738. Of Kellington, Lincs. Matric. 1738; B.A. 1742-3. Ord. deacon (Lincoln) June 13, 1742.

DICKINSON, JOHN MARSH. Matric. pens. from TRINITY HALL, Dec. 1750. Perhaps s. of Marshe, alderman of London, and M.P. for Brackley, Northants. Scholar.

DICKENSON, JOSEPH. Adm. sizar (age 19) at SIDNEY, Feb. 6, 1730-1. S. of Samuel, brazier. B. at Newport, Salop. School, Newport (Mr Lea). Matric. 1731; B.A. 1734-5; M.A. 1738. Will (P.C.C., 1795) of one of these names; of Stafford, clerk.

DICKINSON, LACY. Adm. at CORPUS CHRISTI, 1703. Of Nottinghamshire.

DICKINSON, LEONARD. Matric. sizar from JESUS, Easter, 1614; B.A. 1617-8; M.A. 1621. Incorp. at Oxford, 1621. V. of South Newton, Wilts., 1630.

DICKONSON, OLIVER. Adm. sizar (age 18) at ST JOHN'S, June 20, 1664. S. of Bryan, yeoman, of Newton, Lancs. B. there. School, Lancaster (Mr Holden). Matric. 1664; B.A. 1667-8; M.A. 1671. Ord. deacon (York) Sept. 1668; priest, 1670.

DICKANSON, PHILIP. Adm. pens. (age 15) at CAIUS, Apr. 28, 1617. S. of Thomas, merchant, of Norwich. Bapt. at St Peter Mancroft, Mar. 16, 1603-4. School, Norwich (Mr Stonham). Matric. 1617; Scholar, 1617-24; B.A. 1620-1; M.A. 1624. Ord. deacon (Norwich) Sept. 24; priest, Dec. 24, 1626.

DICKINSON, PICKERING. Adm. sizar (age 17) at SIDNEY, May 31, 1690. 1st s. of William, innkeeper, deceased. B. at Carlton, Notts. School, Newark-on-Trent (Mr Twelves). Matric. 1690; B.A. 1693-4. Ord. deacon (Lincoln) May 19, 1695; priest, May 30, 1697.

DICKINSON, RICHARD. Scholar of QUEENS', 1539; B.A. 1541-2; M.A. 1544; B.D. 1549, as Deconson. Fellow of Queens', 1541-51. Preb. of Lichfield, 1549. Admon. granted (V.C.C.) 1551.

DICKINSON, RICHARD. Matric. sizar from KING'S, Michs. 1621; B.A. 1625-6. Ord. deacon (York) June, 1626. Probably minister of Bishopton, Durham; married Elsie Aire, at Redmarshall, Dec. 1, 1634. (H. M. Wood.)

DICKINSON, ROBERT. Adm. sizar at ST CATHARINE'S, 1657. Matric. Easter, 1658.

DICKINSON, ROBERT. Adm. sizar at TRINITY, Apr. 1, 1668. Matric. 1668; Scholar, 1671; B.A. 1671-2.

DICKENSON, ROGER. Adm. pens. (age 16) at CAIUS, Jan. 17, 1638-9. S. of John, Head Master of Bury St Edmunds School. B. there. School, Bury. Matric. 1639.

DICKINSON, SAMUEL. Adm. pens. (age 16) at ST JOHN'S, May 18, 1749. S. of John, clerk, of Salop. B. at Newport. School, Newport (Mr Lea). Matric. 1749; LL.B. 1755. Ord. deacon (Lichfield) Sept. 21, 1755; priest (Chester) Sept. 25, 1757. R. of Blymhill, Staffs., 1777-1823. Died there May 22, 1823. (*Scott-Mayor*, III. 589.)

DICKENSON, THOMAS. Adm. at KING'S, a scholar from Eton, 1522; B.A. 1526-7; M.A. 1530-1 ('beneficiatus'). One of these names R. of St Mary, Colchester, 1556-8. Died 1558. *Edward* Dikonson was ord. deacon (Lincoln) Apr. 6, 1527 (B.A.); priest, June 15.

DICKENSON, THOMAS. Matric. sizar from ST JOHN'S, Michs. 1546; B.A. 1550-1. Received the tonsure (London) 1554. Of Brandeston, Suffolk. One of these names V. of Helpston, Northants., *c.* 1554.

DICKENSON, THOMAS. Matric. sizar from QUEENS', Michs. 1546; B.A. 1552-3.

DICKINSON, THOMAS. Matric. sizar from TRINITY, Michs. 1572; Scholar, 1578; B.A. 1578-9; M.A. 1582. One of these names V. of Gillingham, Kent, 1591-1616. Buried there Sept. 28, 1616 (*Fielding*). Will (P.C.C.) 1616.

DICKENSON, THOMAS. Matric. pens. from ST JOHN'S, Lent, 1577-8.

DICKENSON, THOMAS. Matric. sizar from ST CATHARINE'S, Easter, 1582; B.A. from King's, 1586-7. Will (P.C.C.) 1592; 'B.A.; of St Ives, Hunts.'

DICKINSON, THOMAS. Matric. sizar from TRINITY, *c.* 1595, as 'Dickshou'; B.A. 1598–9.

DICKENSON, THOMAS (1617), *see* **DIXON.**

DICENSON, THOMAS. B.A. from KING'S, 1629–30; M.A. 1637.

DICKINSON, THOMAS. Adm. at CORPUS CHRISTI, 1662. Of Lincolnshire. S. and h. of Peter, of Gainsborough, deceased. Matric. 1663. Adm. at Gray's Inn, Apr. 27, 1665.

DICKINSON, THOMAS. Adm. sizar (age 16) at ST JOHN'S, Feb. 8, 1663–4. S. of Thomas, of Cambridgeshire. School, Cambridge (Perse). Matric. 1664; B.A. 1667–8; M.A. 1671. Ord. deacon (Ely) Sept. 1670; priest, Mar. 1671–2.

DICKONSON, THOMAS. Adm. sizar at QUEENS', Apr. 13, 1705. Of Hampshire. Matric. 1705; B.A. 1709–10.

DICKENSON, THOMAS. Adm. sizar at CLARE, Jan. 6, 1732–3. B. at Manchester. Matric. 1733; B.A. 1736–7; M.A. 1740. R. of Tarvin, Cheshire, 1746–96. Died June 12, 1796, aged 82. Will, P.C.C.

DICKONSON, THOMAS. Adm. Fell.-Com. at JESUS, Apr. 15, 1732. Of West Retford, Notts.

DICKONSON, TIMOTHY. Adm. pens. (age 17) at TRINITY, June 29, 1728. S. of Timothy, of Scorton, Yorks. School, Kirkleatham, Yorks. (Mr Clark). Matric. 1728; Scholar, 1729; B.A. 1731–2. V. of Bolton-on-Swale, Yorks., 1732–82. V. of Grinton, 1742–82.

DICKONSON, WILLIAM. Matric. sizar from TAINITY, Easter, 1566; B.A. 1570–1. Will (P.C.C., 1615) of one of these names; of Oundle, Northants., clerk.

DICKENSON, WILLIAM. Matric. pens. from CHRIST'S, Easter, 1614; B.A. 1617–8; M.A. 1621; B.D. 1634. Ord. priest (York) 1622. Licensed to preach in the diocese, 1622. R. of Sessay, Yorks., 1624. Probably V. of Rotherham, 1628. Died there 1639. (*Peile*, I. 297; Whitaker, *Duc. Leod.*, 258.)

DICKENSON, WILLIAM. Adm. sizar at EMMANUEL, July 24, 1615. Matric. 1615; Scholar; B.A. 1618–9; M.A. 1622. Ord. deacon (Peterb.) Mar. 8; priest, Mar. 9, 1622–3.

DICKENSON, WILLIAM. Adm. pens. at EMMANUEL, May 10, 1638.

DICKINSON, WILLIAM. Adm. pens. (age 16) at SIDNEY, Mar. 27, 1651. S. of Thomas. B. at Aldwark, Yorks. Schools, Coxwold (Mr Smelt) and Selby (Mr Feirth). Matric. 1651; B.A. 1654.

DICKENSON, WILLIAM. Adm. sizar (age 16) at CHRIST'S, June 17, 1669. S. of Thomas. School, Boroughbridge. Matric. 1669.

DICKENSON or DICKONSON, WILLIAM. Adm. p n . (age 15) at PEMBROKE, Apr. 22, 1673. S. of Peter, of Geinsborough, Lincs., gent. Matric. 1673; B.A. 1676–7; M.A. 1680. Fellow, 1678–90. Died 1690.

DICKONSON, WILLIAM. Adm. sizar at CLARE, July 6, 1699. B. at Trentham, Staffs. Matric. 1699.

DICKENSON, ——. M.A. 1534–5. Incorp. from Oxford; of ten years' standing there. B.D. 1534–5. Perhaps Thomas, B.A. (Oxford) 1507.

DICKLEBURGH, RICHARD. Fellow of CORPUS CHRISTI, in 1402.

DICKLING, ——. Fee for M.A. (or higher degree) 1474–5.

DICKMAN, EDMUND. Adm. sizar (age 18) at MAGDALENE, Sept. 28, 1675. S. of Robert, of Cambridge. B. there. School, Cambridge. Matric. 1677; B.A. 1679–80; M.A. 1683. V. of Harston, Cambs., 1688–1735. V. of Triplow, 1690. Buried at Harston, Sept. 29, 1735.

DICKMAN, JOHN. Adm. sizar (age 17) at ST JOHN'S, June 21, 1667. S. of Francis, yeoman, of Uppingham, Rutland. B. there. School, Uppingham. Matric. 1667–8; B.A. 1670–1. Ord. deacon (Peterb.) June 2, 1672.

DICKMAN, ROBERT. Adm. pens. (age 17) at SIDNEY, June 28, 1661. S. of Robert, gent. B. at Meppershall, Beds. Schools, Clifton, Beds. (Mr Laurence) and Ketton, Suffolk (Mr Burnell). Matric. 1662; B.A. 1664–5; M.A. 1669. Ord. priest (Ely) Dec. 1669. R. of Streethall, Essex, 1672–1701. R. of Aldham, 1692–1701. Will (P.C.C.) 1703.

DICKON, ——. B.Can.L. 1478.

DICKS, *see* **DIX.**

DICKSON, *see* **DIXON.**

DICUS, JOHN. M.A. 1618 (Incorp. from Oxford). Matric. from Brasenose College, Oxford, June 19, 1610, age 18; B.A. 1611–2; *Supp.* for M.A. 1615. Ordered to officiate at Woodnesborough, Kent, in 1647 by the Westminster Assembly. Minister at St Mary's, Sandwich, till 1649. Buried at Elmstead, Essex, Apr. 22, 1649. (*Al. Oxon.*; H. G. Harrison.)

DIDSBURY, GEORGE. Matric. sizar from CLARE, Easter, 1631; B.A. 1634–5.

DIER, *see* **DYER.**

DIERIUS (*sic.*), **JOHN.** Adm. pens. at PEMBROKE, Feb. 28, 1646–7. S. of Gabriel, of London, clerk. Possibly the admission of John Duperier (whom *see*).

DIGBY, EDWARD. Adm. pens. at QUEENS', June 17, 1670. Of Essex. Matric. 1670; B.A. 1673–4; M.A. 1677. Ord. priest (London) June 6, 1680. R. of Chadwell, Essex, 1690–1735. Died June 18, 1735; in his 82nd year.

DIGBY, EVERARD. Matric. sizar from CHRIST'S, Nov. 1566. One of these names adm. at Lincoln's Inn, Oct. 30, 1571.

DIGBY, EVERARD. Matric. sizar from ST JOHN'S, Michs. 1567. S. of Kenelm, of Stoke Dry, Rutland. B.A. 1570–1; M.A. 1574; B.D. 1581. Fellow, 1573–87; deprived. Ord. deacon (Peterb.) Apr. 20, 1576. Probably R. of Barrowden, Rutland, 1576. R. of Glaston, 1584. R. of Hamstall Ridware, Staffs., 1590. Author, *De Arte Natandi*, *Theoria Analytica*, and other philosophical works. Died *c.* 1592. (*Cooper*, II. 146; *D.N.B.*)

DIGBY, FRANCIS. Adm. pens. at SIDNEY, Jan. 29, 1606–7. Matric. 1607.

DIGBY, HUMPHREY. Matric. pens. from CHRIST'S, Nov. 1555. Of Lincoln diocese. Received tonsure, London, June, 1557. Perhaps V. of Little Dalby, Leics., 1566. (*Peile*, I. 60.)

DYGBYE, JOHN. Matric. sizar from PETERHOUSE, Michs. 1544.

DIGBY, JOHN. Adm. Fell.-Com. at MAGDALENE, 1595. S. of Sir George, of Coleshill, Warws. B. Feb. 1580. Adm. at the Inner Temple, 1598. Knighted, Mar. 8, 1605–6. Sent on several embassies to Spain. M.P. for Hedon, 1610. Created Baron Digby, 1618; and Earl of Bristol, 1622. Afterwards fell into disfavour. Went into exile, 1646. Died at Paris, Jan. 16, 1652–3. (*Al. Oxon.* assigns him to Magdalen College, Oxford; *D.N.B.*; *G.E.C.*)

DIGBY, JOHN. Adm. pens. (age 17) at CHRIST'S, Mar. 24, 1626–7. S. of Sir Robert, of Coleshill, Warws., Knt. School, Kingshurst, Warws. (Mr Orton). Matric. 1627; B.A. 1630–1; M.A. 1634. Recommended by the King for a fellowship at St John's, 1633. One of these names V. of Higham Ferrers, Northants., 1635–45; ejected. Brother of Simon (1626–7). (*Peile*, I. 380.)

DIGBY, JOHN. Adm. pens. at ST CATHARINE'S, 1636. Of Essex.

DIGBY, JOHN. Adm. Fell.-Com. (age 17) at CHRIST'S, Feb. 5, 1646–7. S. of Sir John, Knt. B. at Mansfield Woodhouse, Notts. School, Mansfield (Mr Stacy). Matric. 1647. Married Frances Pinckney, of Mansfield Woodhouse. (*Peile*, I. 511.)

DIGBY, JOHN. Adm. sizar (age 18) at CAIUS, Oct. 13, 1669. S. of John, gent., of Newport, Essex. B. there. Schools, Bardfield (Mr Trot) and Newport (Dr Edwards). Matric. 1670; Scholar, 1670; B.A. 1673–4. Ord. deacon (London) June, 1674; priest (Lincoln) Dec. 18, 1681. Signs as minister at Streatley, 1690–1715. V. of Harlington, Beds., 1692–1716. (*Venn*, I. 439.)

DIGBY, JOHN. Adm. Fell.-Com. at JESUS, May 6, 1684. S. of John, of Mansfield Woodhouse, Notts., Esq. Matrie. 1684. M.P. for Newark, 1705–8; for Retford, 1713–22.

DIGBY, JOSEPH. Adm. sizar at EMMANUEL, Apr. 14, 1735. Of Rutland. Matric. 1735; LL.B. 1741. Ord. deacon (Lincoln) Dec. 18, 1737; priest, Dec. 23, 1739. R. of Thistleton, Rutland, 1740–54. R. of Tinwall, 1754–86; of Barrowden, 1754–86. R. of Pilton, 1767. Died Apr. 23, 1786, aged 68. (Blore, *Rutland*, 86.)

DIGBY, KENELM. Matric. sizar from TRINITY, Michs. 1552. One of these names R. of Old Romney, Kent, 1568–1603. Died 1603.

DIGBY, Sir KENELM. M.A. 1624; on the King's visit; at that time Fell.-Com. at PETERHOUSE. S. of Sir Everard, of Dry Stoke, Rutland, Knt. B. July 11, 1603. Adm. at Gloucester Hall, Oxford, 1618. Adm. at Gray's Inn, Aug. 11, 1619; of Seton, Rutland. Knighted, Oct. 28, 1623. Commanded a fleet in the Levant, 1628, where he took many prizes. Imprisoned by the Parliament, 1642. Banished to France, 1643–54. One of the original members of the Royal Society. Distinguished for his philosophical and scientific writings. Died in Covent Garden, June 11, 1665. Buried in Christ Church, Newgate. (*Al. Oxon.*; *D.N.B.*; *Vis. of Rutland.*)

DIGBY, ROGER. Matric. pens. from JESUS, Easter, 1550. Perhaps s. of Simon, of North Luffenham. Of Luffenham. Married Mary Cheyney of Agmondesham, Bucks. Died 1582. M.I. at North Luffenham. (*Nichols*, II. 261.)

DIGBY, ROLAND. B.Can.L. 1515–6. Doubtless 3rd s. of Sir John, of Eye, Leics. R. of Barrowden, Rutland. Died Apr. 18, 1546. M.I. at Barrowden. Will (P.C.C.) 1546; 'of Barrowden, Rutland, Melsonby, Yorks.' (*Nichols*, II. 261.)

DIGBY, ROLAND. Matric. pens. from TRINITY, Michs. 1547. Perhaps scholar of Christ's, 1548–50.

DIGBY, SIMON. Matric. sizar from TAINITY, 1598; B.A. 1601–2.

DIGBY, SIMON. Adm. pens. (age 16) at CHRIST'S, Mar. 24, 1626-7. 4th s. of Sir Robert, Knt., of Coleshill, Warws. School, Kingshurst, Warws. (Mr Orton). Matric. 1627. Adm. at the Middle Temple, Nov. 21, 1631. M.P. for Philipstown, 1639. Died c. 1645. Brother of John (1626-7). (*Peile*, I. 380.)

DIGBY, SIMON. Matric. pens. from QUEENS', Easter, 1636. Of Essex.

DIGBY, WILLIAM. Matric. pens. from QUEENS', Easter, 1577. Of Leicestershire. Doubtless s. of John, of Welby, Leics. High Sheriff, 1598. Died 1603. (*Nichols*, II. 261.)

DIGBY, ——. Scholar of CHRIST'S, 1549-50.

DIGGES, DUDLEY. M.A. 1638 (Incorp. from Oxford). 3rd s. of Sir Dudley, of Chilham, Kent, Knt., Master of the Rolls. Matric. from University College, Oxford, June 18, 1630, age 16; B.A. 1631-2; M.A. 1635. Fellow of All Souls', 1632. Adm. at Gray's Inn, 1641. Political writer. Died at Oxford, Oct. 1, 1643. Buried in All Souls' Chapel. Will (P.C.C.) 1647. (*Al. Oxon.*; *D.N.B.*; *Vis. of Kent*, 1619.)

DIGGES, EDWARD. Incorp. M.A. 1702, from All Souls', Oxford. S. of E., of Chilham, Kent, gent. Matric. from Wadham College, Dec. 8, 1682, age 17; B.A. (Oxford) 1686; M.A. 1690. Fellow of All Souls'. V. of Elmley, Kent, 1699. R. of Welwyn, Herts., 1700. (*Al. Oxon.*)

DYGGES or DEGGE, THOMAS. Matric. pens. from QUEENS', Easter, 1546. Of Leicestershire. B. at Ashby (according to the ordination record). B.A. 1550-1; M.A. 1557. Fellow of St Catharine's, c. 1552. Fellow of Peterhouse, 1556. Ord. deacon (London) May 15, 1552; and again, 1557. Identified by *Cooper* and *D.N.B.*, with the eminent mathematician, and astronomer; but the county origin is different.

DYGGES, WILLIAM. Matric. pens. from QUEENS', Easter, 1546.

DIGGLE, EDMUND. B.A. from PETERHOUSE, 1593-4. B. at Wells, Norfolk, 1574. M.A. 1597. Ord. deacon and priest (Peterb.) Dec. 2, 1599. V. of Sutterton, Lincs., 1604-30. Will (Lincoln C.C.) 1630; and P.C.C. Father of the next.

DIGGLE or DIGLY, EDMUND. M.A. 1637 (Incorp. from Oxford). S. of Edmund, above, of Sutterton, Lincs. Matric. from Magdalen College, Oxford, Oct. 26, 1627, age 17; B.A. (Oxford) 1629-30; M.A. 1632; B.D. 1640-1; D.D. 1661. Fellow of Magdalen College, 1631-48 (ejected); and 1660-8. Treasurer of Lichfield, 1660-88. Preb. and Archdeacon of York, 1663-88. R. of Slymbridge, Dorset, 1667-88. Preb. of Ripon, 1667-88. Died Aug. 1, 1688, aged 78. Buried at Slymbridge. (*Al. Oxon.*)

DIGGLE or DIGGLES, JOHN. Matric. pens. from MAGDALENE, Lent, 1626-7; B.A. 1630-1; M.A. 1634. Perhaps R. of Chiddingford, Surrey, June 5, 1648-c. 1662. One of these names R. of Thorp Mandeville, Northants., 1662.

DIGGONS, JOSEPH. Matric. pens. from CLARE, Michs. 1607, as Diggny. Of Liss. Benefactor to Clare College.

DIGHTON or DEIGHTON, 'EDWARD.' Mistake for Everard. Adm. pens. at SIDNEY, July 4, 1619. B. in Lincolnshire. S. of Gilbert, V. of Croft, Lincs. V. of East Kirkley, Lincs., 1626. V. of Croft, 1630. R. of Bucknall. Died c. 1677. Father of William (1659). (*Lincs. Pedigrees.*)

DEIGHTON, EVERARD. B.A. from MAGDALENE, 1627; M.A. 1631. (Perhaps same as the above.)

DIGHTON, JOHN. B.A. 1526-7.

DIGHTON, JOHN. Matric. pens. from TRINITY, Michs. 1562. S. of Christopher, of Worcestershire. B.A. 1567-8; M.A. from Queens', 1571. Perhaps preb. of Lincoln, 1565. (*Vis. of Worcs.*, 1569.)

DIGHTON, JOHN. Matric. pens. from MAGDALENE, Michs. 1564.

DEIGHTON, JOHN. Adm. sizar at JESUS, Sept. 4, 1697. Of London. School, St Paul's. Scholar, 1697; Matric. 1698; B.A. 1701-2; M.A. 1705; D.D. 1717 (*Com. Reg.*). Ord. deacon (Norwich) June, 1704; priest, Dec. 22, 1706. V. of Wood Ditton, Cambs., 1714-52. R. of Newmarket, 1717-52. Died at Newmarket, Oct. 6, 1752. Admon., P.C.C. (G. *Mag.*)

DIGHTON, RICHARD. Adm. scholar (age 17) at CAIUS, Apr. 19, 1580. Of Hutton Wandsley, Yorks. School, York. Matric. 1580.

DIGHTON, ROGER. Matric. sizar from QUEENS', Michs. 1566. Ord. priest (Carlisle), Oct. 8, 1570. V. of Helpringham, Lincs., 1577. V. of Horkstow, 1581. V. of Hainton, 1586-1607.

DIGHTON, THOMAS. Matric. Fell.-Com. from ST CATHARINE'S, Easter, 1573. One of these names; born, c. 1556; 1st s. of Edmund, of Sturton, Lincs., Esq. Of Sturton, Esq. Perhaps adm. at Gray's Inn, 1577. (*Lincs. Pedigrees.*)

DIGHTON, TIMOTHY. Adm. sizar (age 23) at MAGDALENE, June 15, 1661. S. of George, of Pudsey, Yorks. School, Bradford. Matric. 1661. V. of Stannington, Yorks., 1668-73.

DIGHTON, W. Matric. sizar from PETERHOUSE, Easter, 1586.

DIGHTON, WILLIAM. B.A. 1521-2; M.A. 1525. Fellow of PEMBROKE, 1525. V. of Tilney, Norfolk, 1541.

DIGHTON, WILLIAM. Matric. pens. from CHRIST'S, May, 1550.

DITON, WILLIAM. Matric. pens. from TRINITY, Easter, 1622.

DIGHTON, WILLIAM. Adm. pens. (age 18) at ST JOHN'S, Mar. 17, 1659-60. S. of Everard (above). B. at Croft. School, Wainfleet. Matric. 1660; B.A. 1663-4; M.A. 1667. Ord. priest (Lincoln) Sept. 20, 1668. R. of Donington-on-Bain, Lincs. R. of Bucknall. Died 1702. (*Lincs. Pedigrees.*)

DIGTON, ——. B.A. 1475-6.

DEIGHTON, ——. M.A. 1501.

DIGLANDE or DIGLEN, GILBERT. Matric. pens. from CHRIST'S, June, 1588. Of Warwickshire, gent. Migrated to St Edmund's Hall, Oxford, Oct. 22, 1591, age 21; B.A. from St Alban's Hall, Oxford, 1592, as Diglen. (*Al. Oxon.*)

DIGLEN, EZECHIEL. Adm. at CORPUS CHRISTI, 1624. Of Northamptoushire. B.A. 1628; M.A. 1632. Ord. deacon (Peterb.) Jan. 20, 1627-8; priest, Oct. 21, 1628. V. of Orston, Notts., 1661.

DIGON, ——. Paid fee for M.A. or higher degree, 1473-4.

DIGULHON, *see* DEGULHON.

DIKE, DIKES, *see* DYKE, DYKES.

DILKE, SAMUEL. Adm. Fell.-Com. (age 16) at PETERHOUSE, May 7, 1650. S. of Fisher, of Shustoke, Warwick. School, private. Matric. 1650. A strong puritan. Married and had issue. Died 1701. (*Vis. of Warws.*, 1682; *T. A. Walker*, 90.)

DILKES, THOMAS. Matric. pens. from PETERHOUSE, Easter, 1584. S. of Richard Dilke, of Kirkby Mallory, Leics. Of Maxstoke Castle, Warws., Knt. Half-brother of the next. (*Misc. Gen. et Her.*, I. 7.)

DILKES, W. Matric. pens. from PETERHOUSE, Easter, 1576. Of Kirkby Mallory, Leics.; adm. at the Inner Temple, Nov. 1584. Died 1596. Half-brother of the above.

DILKE, WILLIAM. Adm. sizar at EMMANUEL, Sept. 11, 1676, as Delke; B.A. 1680. Ord. deacon (Norwich) July, 1681; priest, Oct. 1682. R. of Bisley, Norfolk, 1690. R. of Necton, 1693-1718. Died 1718.

DILKE, ——. Adm. sizar at PETERHOUSE, Feb. 16, 1576-7.

DILLAKER, *see also* DELACRE.

DILLAKER or DELACRE, EDWARD. Matric. pens. from TRINITY, Michs. 1601; B.A. 1605-6; M.A. 1609. Incorp. at Oxford, 1611. Ord. deacon (Peterb.) July 11; priest, Sept. 19, 1613. C. of Wilburton, Cambs., 1614. R. of Houghton, Hunts., 1618-42; deprived.

DILLAKER, ROBERT. Matric. pens. from TRINITY, Michs. 1601.

DILLAN or DILLAND, PETER. Adm. pens. at CORPUS CHRISTI, 1584. Of Norfolk. Matric. 1584; B.A. 1588-9; M.A. 1592. Ord. priest (Peterb.) Mar. 20, 1613-4, as Dillon.

DILLINGHAM, BENJAMIN. Adm. pens. at EMMANUEL, July 2, 1651. S. of Thomas (1609), R. of Barnwell, Northants. School, Oundle; adm. there, 1644, age 9. Matric. 1653; B.A. 1654-5; M.A. 1658. Fellow, 1657. V. of Oundle, 1663-79. Buried there Nov. 15, 1679. Father of the next.

DILLINGHAM, EDWARD. Adm. pens. at EMMANUEL, June 26, 1679. Of Northamptonshire. S. of Benjamin (above), V. of Oundle. Bapt. there, Aug. 16, 1663. Adm. at Oundle School, Dec. 9, 1670, age 7. Matric. 1680; B.A. 1683-4. Ord. priest (Peterb.) Sept. 23, 1694. R. of Stretton, Rutland, 1699-1719. Died 1719. (*Rutland Mag.*, I. 109.)

DILLINGHAM, FRANCIS. Matric. pens. from CHRIST'S, June, 1583. B. at Deane, Beds. B.A. 1586-7; M.A. 1590; B.D. 1599. Fellow, 1594-1601. Ord. priest by Bishop of Lincoln. R. of Wilden, Beds., 1600-25. One of the translators of the Authorized Version of the Bible, 1611. Buried at Wilden, Feb. 24, 1624-5. Will (Lincoln C.C.) 1625. (*D.N.B.*; *Peile*, I. 175.)

DILLINGHAM, GILBERT. Matric. sizar from CHRIST'S, June, 1585; B.A. 1588-9; M.A. 1592. R. of Sandon, Essex, 1601. ... of St Giles-in the Fields, London, 1635. Died same year. Will proved (Consist. C. London) Dec. 15, 1635. Probably father of Samuel (1624), Henry (1625) and William (1628). (F. C. Cass, *Monken Hadley*.)

DILLINGHAM, HENRY. Matric. pens. from CHRIST'S, May, 1570; B.A. 1574-5; M.A. 1578. Ord. deacon and priest (Lincoln) Apr. 1581. R. of Cotesbach, Leics., 1581. Died there Dec. 1625.

DILLINGHAM, HENRY. Adm. pens. at EMMANUEL, Easter, 1625. Probably 2nd s. of Gilbert (1585). Matric. 1625; B.A. 1629-30; M.A. 1633.

DILLINGHAM, JOHN. Adm. pens. (age 16) at SIDNEY, Sept. 1, 1631. S. of Thomas (1585), R. of Deane, Beds. Bapt. there, Oct. 9, 1614. School, Deane (Mr Kemp). Matric. 1631; B.A. 1635–6; M.A. 1639; B.D. 1646. Fellow. Incorp. at Oxford, 1657. Ord. priest (Peterb.) Dec. 18, 1641. Brother of Theophilus (1629).

DILLINGHAM, SAMUEL. Adm. pens. at EMMANUEL, Easter, 1624. S. of Gilbert (1585), R. of Sandon, Essex. Matric. 1624; B.A. 1627–8; M.A. 1631. R. of St Pancras, Soper Lane, London, 1662–72. R. of Monken Hadley, Middlesex, 1669–72. Buried July 2, 1672, at Hadley. (F. C. Cass, *Monken Hadley*.)

DILLINGHAM, SAMUEL. Adm. sizar at EMMANUEL, Jan. 10, 1642–3. Of Northamptonshire. S. of Thomas (1609), who makes a bequest for his maintenance at Cambridge. Matric. 1643; B.A. 1646–7; M.A. 1650. Brother of Benjamin (1651) and William (1636).

DILLINGHAM, THEOPHILUS. Adm. at EMMANUEL, Sept. 13, 1629. S. of Thomas (1585), R. of Deane, Beds. Bapt. there, Oct. 18, 1612. School, Upper Deane. Matric. 1629; B.A. 1633–4; M.A. 1637; B.D. from Sidney, 1644; D.D. from Clare, 1655. Fellow of Sidney, 1638. Master of Clare, 1654–60 and 1661–78. Vice-Chancellor, 1655–6, 1656–7, 1662. Ord. deacon (Peterb.) Mar. 10, 1638–9. R. of Offord Cluny, Hunts., 1654–78. Preb. of York, 1662. Archdeacon of Bedford, 1667–78. Died in Cambridge, Nov. 22, 1678. Buried in St Edward's. M.I. there. Will (V.C.C.) 1678. Brother of John (1631), father of Thomas (1677). (*D.N.B.*)

DILLINGHAM, THEOPHILUS. Adm. pens. at CLARE, May 31, 1720. B. in London. Matric. 1720; B.A. 1723–4; M.A. 1727. Fellow, 1726–30. Grandson of the Master. Adm. at Lincoln's Inn, Apr. 3, 1721; s. and h. of Theophilus, woollen draper, of London. Buried at Hampton, Middlesex, 1743. (One of these names, of Hampton, Middlesex, died May 26, 1769; age 93; probably the father.) (G. *Mag.*; H. G. Harrison.)

DILLINGHAM, THOMAS. Matric. pens. from JESUS, Easter, 1585; B.A. 1588–9; M.A. 1592. Ord. deacon (Lincoln) Oct. 19; priest, Oct. 27, 1594. Signs as minister of Deane, Beds., 1603–32. Buried there Dec. 10, 1647. Will (P.C.C.) 1648. Father of John (1631) and Theophilus (1629). (W. M. Noble.)

DILLINGHAM, THOMAS. Matric. pens. from CHRIST'S, Easter, 1609; B.A. 1612–3; M.A. 1616. Incorp. at Oxford, 1616. Ord. deacon (Peterb.) Mar. 16; priest, Mar. 17, 1616–7. R. of Barnwell All Saints', Northants., 1618; and of Barnwell St Andrew, 1639. Will (P.C.C.) 1647. Father of William (1636), Benjamin and Samuel (1642). (*Peile*, I. 272; *Nichols*, IV. 615; J. H. Hill, *Langton*.)

DILLINGHAM, THOMAS. Adm. sizar at TRINITY, Apr. 27, 1641. Matric. 1641.

DILLINGHAM, THOMAS. Adm. sizar at EMMANUEL, Mar. 25, 1648. Of London. Matric. 1648; B.A. 1651–2; M.A. 1655. Doubtless s. of William (1617), R. of St Dunstan-in-the-West, London; adm. at Oundle School, Aug. 9, 1641, age 12. R. of Barnwell All Saints', Northants., 1658–1702. Buried there Sept. 26, 1702, aged 72. M.I. Father of William (1677). (*Nichols*, IV. 615; *Bridges*, II. 214.)

DILLINGHAM, THOMAS. Adm. pens. at CLARE, Sept. 14, 1677. S. of Theophilus (1629), master of Clare. Of Much Hadham, Herts. School, Oundle. Matric. 1678; B.A. 1681–2; M.A. 1685. Fellow, 1683–1722. Incorp. at Oxford, 1693. Senior Proctor, 1719–20. Taxor, 1703. Ord. deacon (London) Mar. 4, 1704–5; priest, Sept. 24, 1705. V. of Everton, Beds., with Tetworth, Hunts., 1705–22. Died in College, Dec. 19, 1722. M.I. at St Edward's, Cambridge. (*Al. Oxon.* seems to confuse him with the next.)

DILLINGHAM, THOMAS. Adm. pens. at EMMANUEL, Apr. 16, 1678. S. of William (1636), D.D., of Odell, Beds. B. in Cambridge. Adm. at Oundle School, Apr. 26, 1675, age 15. Matric. 1678; B.A. 1681–2; M.A. 1685. R. of Harrington, Lincs., 1699. R. of Barnwell All Saints', Northants., 1702. Buried at Barnwell, Aug. 20, 1704, aged 46. M.I. there. (*Bridges*, II. 214–5; J. H. Hill, *Langton*, 47.)

DILLINGHAM, WILLIAM. Matric. pens. from CHRIST'S, May, 1576; B.A. 1579–80. Ord. deacon and priest (Lincoln) Apr., 1582. Will of one of these names (P.C.C.) 1621; 'of Cranford, Northants., clerk.' Instituted, 1583.

DILLINGHAM, WILLIAM. Matric. pens. from CHRIST'S, July, 1617; B.A. 1620–1; M.A. 1624. Ord. deacon (Peterb.) Sept. 19; priest. Sept. 20, 1624. Perhaps R. of Barton Seagrave, Northants. Buried Jan. 29, 1646–7. Will (P.C.C.) 1647. Uncle of William (1636). (J. Ch. Smith.)

DILLINGHAM, WILLIAM. Adm. sizar at EMMANUEL, 1628. Probably s. of Gilbert (1585). Matric. 1628; B.A. 1631–2. (F. C. Cass, *Monken Hadley*.)

DILLINGHAM, WILLIAM. Adm. sizar at EMMANUEL, Apr. 22, 1636. S. of Thomas (1609), R. of Barnwell, Northants. School, Oundle. Matric. 1637; B.A. 1639–40; M.A. 1643; B.D. 1650; D.D. 1655. Fellow, 1642. Master, 1653–62 (deprived). Vice-Chancellor, 1659. Retired to Oundle, 1662–72. R. of Odell, Beds., 1672–89. Latin poet and controversialist. Buried at Odell, Nov. 28, 1689. Father of Thomas (1678). (*D.N.B.*; *Emmanuel Coll. Hist.*)

DILLINGHAM, WILLIAM. Adm. sizar at EMMANUEL, May 14, 1677. 1st s. of Thomas (1648), R. of Barnwell All Saints', Northants. Adm. at Oundle School, Feb. 28, 1671–2, age 12.

DILLON, RICHARD. Adm. pens. at EMMANUEL, June 24, 1595. Matric. 1595.

DILWORTH, JAMES. Adm. sizar (age 17) at CAIUS, June 16, 1620. S. of John, husbandman, of Lancashire. School, Blackburn (Mr Collinson). Matric. 1620; B.A. 1623–4; M.A. 1627. Ord. deacon (Norwich) Mar. 13, 1624–5; priest, Sept. 24, 1626. R. of Thrigby, Norfolk, 1649; when he signed Bishop Hall's subscription book, Apr. 20, 1649. Buried Sept. 29, 1652. Will (P.C.C.) 1653. Brother of Thomas (1629). (*Venn*, I. 249.)

DILWORTH, JOHN. Matric. pens. from ST JOHN'S, Michs. 1602; B.A. 1606–7; M.A. 1610. Ord. deacon (Peterb.) June 11; priest, Sept. 24, 1609. V. of Totternhoe, Beds., 1609–13. Buried there Mar. 24, 1612–3. (W. M. Noble.)

DILWORTH, THOMAS. Adm. sizar (age 18) at CAIUS, Apr. 18, 1629. S. of John, gent. B. in Chipping, Lancaster. School, Blackburn (Mr Halstead). Matric. 1629. Brother of James (1620).

DIMBLEBY, THOMAS. Adm. at CORPUS CHRISTI, 1705. Of Surrey. Matric. 1705–6; B.A. 1709–10; M.A. 1713.

DIMBLEBY, WILLIAM. Matric. sizar from CHRIST'S, June, 1584. Probably of Northamptonshire. B.A. 1587–8; M.A. 1591. Ord. deacon and priest (Peterb.) Aug. 5, 1592. V. of Kingston by Lewes, Sussex, 1611–39. Buried there May 16, 1639. Will at Lewes. (W. C. Harrison.)

DIMOCK, *see* **DYMOCKE.**

DIMOND or DYMAN, PETER, *see* **DEYMAN.**

DYMOND, THOMAS. Adm. pens. (age 17) at TRINITY, Apr. 12, 1677. S. of James, of London. School, St Paul's.

DYMOND, TRISTRAM. Matric. sizar from CLARE, Easter, 1605 B.A. 1608–9; M.A. 1612. Ord. deacon (London) Sept. 23, 1610. Perhaps V. of Foleshill, Warws., 1612–62; ejected. Marriage license (Archd. Hunts., July 13, 1614); Tristram Diamond, clerk, of Bluntisham, and Helen Edgar, of St Ives. (*Calamy*, II. 487.)

DIMOND, TRISTRAM. Matric. sizar from ST JOHN'S, Michs. 1608; B.A. 1611–2; M.A. 1615. Ord. deacon (Peterb.) Sept. 20; priest, Sept. 21, 1618.

DIMOND, TRISTRAM. Matric. pens. from ST JOHN'S, Michs. 1621.

DIMOND, TRISTRAM. Adm. pens. at EMMANUEL, Apr. 29, 1634. Of Cambridgeshire. Matric. 1634; B.A. 1637–8; M.B. 1642.

DIMOND, WILLIAM (1632), *see* **DEYMAN.**

DIMSDALE, JOHN. Adm. at CORPUS CHRISTI, 1566. S. of John, merchant, of Lynn, Norfolk. B.A. 1569–70. Incorp. at Oxford, 1573, as 'Thomas.' M.A. (Oxford) 1573. Ord. deacon (Norwich) June 11, 1568. R. of Gaywood, Norfolk, 1577–8, when he died. (*Venn*, I. 67.)

DIMSDALE, JOHN. Matric. pens. from ST JOHN'S, Easter, 1560.

DIMSDALL, ROBERT. Adm. . at ST CATHARINE'S, Mar. 5, 1678–9. Matric. 1679; M.B. 1684; M.D. 1696. Died Jan. 7, 1724–5, aged 65. M.I. at All Saints', Hertford.

DINELEY, FRANCIS. Adm. sizar (age 16) at CHRIST'S, June 6, 1649. S. of William. B. at Richmond, Yorks. School, Richmond (Mr Parvin). Matric. 1649.

DINELIE, GEORGE. Adm. pens. (age 15) at CAIUS, Nov. 18, 1583. Eldest s. of William, gent., of Swillington. Matric. 1583. One of a family of Popish recusants. Probably admon. (York) 1629; of Whitwell. (*Vis. of Yorks.*, 1585.)

DINLEY, JOHN. Matric. pens. from CHRIST'S, July, 1606; B.A. 1609–10; M.A. 1613. Incorp. at Oxford, 1614, as Dyneley. Ord. deacon (Peterb.) Sept. 24, 1615. M.A. of Christ's. Gave £20 to the new buildings at Christ's. *Peile* (I. 258) assumes his identity with the secretary to the Queen of Bohemia; who was knighted July 31, 1615, and died at Richmond, Surrey, Dec. 1671. He was of Oxford. (*Al. Oxon.*)

DYNELEY, JOHN. Adm. pens. at JESUS, Feb. 21, 1736–7. Of Bramhope, Yorks. S. and h. of John, of Bramhope, Esq. Matric. 1737; Scholar. Adm. at Lincoln's Inn, Oct. 26, 1738. Died *s.p.* Mar. 17, 1767. Will, York. (A. Gray.)

DINELEY, NICHOLAS. Adm. sizar at EMMANUEL, Feb. 9, 1637–8. Of Lincolnshire. Matric. 1637–8; B.A. 1641–2. probably the 'minister of God's Word at Kingston, Kent' mentioned in the will of his 'cozen' John (P.C.C.; 1668).

DYNELEY, ROBERT. Adm. pens. (age 17) at SIDNEY, May 21, 1716. 2nd s. of John, Esq., deceased. B. at Bramhope, Yorks. Schools, Bradford and York. Matric. 1716; B.A. 1721-2; M.A. 1727. Ord. deacon (York) Mar. 1722-3. V. of Bramhope, Yorks., 1728-40. Buried there Jan. 14, 1747.

DINELEY, THOMAS. Adm. pens. at CORPUS CHRISTI, 1605. Of Kent. Matric. 1607.

DINGE or DYNNS, FRANCIS. Matric. pens. from JESUS, Michs. 1608.

DINGLEY, JAMES. Matric. sizar from PEMBROKE, Easter, 1682; B.A. 1685-6; M.A. 1691. One of these names, s. of John, of Cubert, Cornwall, clerk, matric. from Exeter College, Oxford, Apr. 22, 1684, age 18. No degree there. Will of James Dingly, clerk, of South Petherwin, Devon, proved (Exeter) 1695. (*Al. Oxon.*)

DINGLEY, THOMAS. B.A. 1608 (Incorp. from Oxford). Of Worcestershire. Perhaps s. of Francis, of Charlton, Worcs. Matric. from St John's College, Oxford, Mar. 18, 1604-5, age 18; B.A. 1608; B.C.L. from All Souls', 1614. R. of Monks Risborough, Bucks., 1618-24. Died 1624. (*Al. Oxon.*; *Vis. of Worcs.*, 1569.)

DINGLEY, WILLIAM. Fellow of PETERHOUSE, 1393. Ord. deacon (Ely) Mar. 14, 1393-4; priest, Apr. 4, 1394. Fellow, till 1433, and perhaps till 1442. (*T. A. Walker.*)

DINGLEY, WILLIAM. B.A. 1515-6; Scholar or fellow of KING'S HALL, 1516-28. One of these names was R. of Stow-on-the-Wold, Gloucs., 1532; non-resident, in 1551; 'he hath 4 benefices.' (*Bishop's Visitation*; F. S. Hockaday.)

DINGLEY, WILLIAM. Matric. sizar from KING'S, Easter, 1623; B.A. 1623-4; M.A. 1627.

DINGLEY, WILLIAM. Incorp. M.A. 1679, from New College, Oxford. S. of John, of the Isle of Wight, gent. Matric. from Hart Hall, Dec. 8, 1665; B.A. from New College, 1671; M.A. 1674-5. Proctor, 1682. V. of Chesterton, Oxon., 1678. The Winchester scholar, who died 1683. (*Al. Oxon.*)

DINHAM, *see also* DENHAM.

DINHAM or DENHAM, GEORGE. B.A. from ST JOHN'S, 1654; and licensed to practise medicine (Incorp. from Oxford). S. of Francis, of Allington, Kent. B.A. of Magdalen College, Oxford, 1642. Practised medicine at Stamford, Lincs. Will (P.C.C.) 1701; of Stamford, M.D. Father of Henry (next) and John (1677). (Jewitt's *Reliq.*, XXIV. 75.)

DINHAM or DENHAM, HENRY. Adm. at ST CATHARINE'S, Nov. 29, 1683. Probably 5th s. of George (1654), of Stamford, Lincs., M.D. Living in 1694. Brother of John (1677). (*Lincs. Pedigrees.*)

DINHAM or DENHAM, JOHN. Adm. at ST CATHARINE'S, Apr. 18, 1677. S. of George (1654), of Stamford, Lincs., doctor. M.A. 1679. Matric. from Magdalen College, Oxford, Nov. 15, 1672, age 18. Chorister there. B.A. 1676. Buried at All Saints', Stamford, Dec. 27, 1682. Brother of Henry (1683). (*Lincs. Pedigrees*, 1199.)

DINHAM, JOHN. Adm. pens. (age 17) at ST JOHN'S, June 12, 1712. S. of Samuel, M.D. B. at Stamford, Lincs. School, Stamford (Mr Turner). Probably adm. at Leyden, Sept. 17, 1715. Of Spalding and Stamford, M.D. Buried at Spalding, May 21, 1752. Father of the next, and of Samuel (1742). (*Lincs. Pedigrees*, 1199.)

DINHAM, JOHN. Adm. pens. at EMMANUEL, Apr. 7, 1743. S. of John, above, M.D., of Spalding. Bapt. Sept. 24, 1725. School, Eton. Matric. 1743; B.A. 1746-7; M.A. 1750. Ord. deacon (Rochester) Mar. 6, 1746-7; priest (Lincoln) Sept. 24, 1749. P.C. of Spalding. Died Apr. 2, 1782. Brother of the next. (*Lincs. Pedigrees*, 1199.)

DINHAM, SAMUEL. Adm. pens. (age 18) at ST JOHN'S, July 3, 1742. S. of John (1712), of Lincolnshire. B. at Spalding. School, Eton. Matric. 1743. Of Spalding, M.D. Buried there Apr. 12, 1761. Brother of John, above. (*Lincs. Pedigrees.*)

DINNE, *see* DYNNE.

DINNEY, JOHN. B.A. 1504-5.

DINSDALL, ROBERT. Adm. at CORPUS CHRISTI, 1683. Of Yorkshire. Matric. 1683; B.A. 1686-7. Ord. priest (York) May, 1700. V. of Kinoulton, Notts., in 1706. Married Hannah Birch, of St Mary, Nottingham, Jan. 2, 1704-5. (Godfrey, *Notts.*)

DIODATI, CHARLES. M.A. 1629 (Incorp. from Oxford). S. of Theodore, of London, M.D. Matric. from Trinity College, Oxford, Feb. 7, 1621-2, age 13; B.A. 1625; M.A. 1628. Practised physic; first at Chester, afterwards in Blackfriars. Lifelong friend of Milton, with whom he had been at school at St Paul's. Buried at St Anne's, Blackfriars, Aug. 27, 1638. (*D.N.B.*)

DIONYSIUS, ——. Augustinian friar. D.D. 1472-3.

DIOS, *see* DEIOS.

DIPDEN, GEORGE (1632), *see* DEPDEN.

DIPTFORD, THOMAS. Adm pens. at EMMANUEL, Mar. 30, 1627. Matric. 1627; B.A. 1630-1; M.A. 1634. One of these names R. of Jacobstow, Cornwall. Will (Exeter) 1640.

DIRE (?), WILLIAM. Matric. pens. from TRINITY, *c.* 1596.

DISBEROWE or DUISBURGH, ANTHONY. Adm. sizar (age 17) at CAIUS, Sept. 8, 1586. S. of Anthony, of Chevington, Suffolk. School, Bury. Matric. 1586; Scholar, 1586-92; B.A. 1590-1; M.A. 1594; B.D. 1610. Fellow, 1592-1615. Proctor, 1608. Ord. deacon and priest (Norwich) 1596. R. of Risby, Suffolk, 1613-40. Father of Oliver (1641). (*Venn*, I. 128.)

DISBOROUGH, BRUNO. Matric. sizar from TRINITY, Michs. 1623. Of Cambridgeshire. Migrated to Queens', 1626. B.A. 1626-7; M.A. 1630. Ord. deacon (Peterb.) June 13; priest, June 14, 1630. P.C. of St James, Duke's Place, London, 1640, till perhaps 1658.

DISBOROUGH, GEORGE. Matric. sizar from CHRIST'S, *c.* 1592

DISBOROWE, HENRY. Matric. sizar from TRINITY, Easter, 1571; Scholar, 1575; B.A. 1576-7. R. of Boughton Monchelsey, Kent, 1585.

DISBOROUGH, JAMES. Adm. pens. at QUEENS', Mar. 31, 1645. Of Cambridgeshire. Perhaps same as the next.

DISBROWE, JAMES. M.A. 1675 (*Lit. Reg.*). Perhaps s. of Samuel, of Elsworth, Cambs. M.D. of Stepney, Middlesex and of Elsworth, Cambs. Will dated Nov. 26, 1690. Another of these names, clerk, buried at Eltisley, Cambs., Dec. 25, 1703. Cousin of James, M.D. (*Munk*, I. 477; H. F. Waters, *Geneal. Gleanings*, I. 244.)

DISBOROWE, JOHN. Scholar of TRINITY, 1562; B.A. 1564-5 M.A. 1568. Master of Saffron Walden School, 1573-1607. Buried there Dec. 5, 1607.

DISBOROUGH, JOHN. Matric. pens. from QUEENS', Michs. 1587. Of Essex.

DESBOROUGH, NATHANIEL. Adm. pens. at CHRIST'S, Sept. 12, 1626. S. of James, of Eltisley, Cambs. School, St Ives. Matric. 1626; B.A. 1630-1. (*Peile*, I. 377.)

DESBOROUGH, NICHOLAS. Matric. pens. from ST JOHN'S, Easter, 1627.

DISBEROWE or DUISBOROUGH, OLIVER. Adm. sizar (age 15) at CAIUS, July 6, 1641. S. of Anthony (1586), B.D. B. at Risby, Suffolk. Bapt. there, July 18, 1626. School, Bury. Readm. as pens. Dec. 24, 1641. Matric. 1641; Scholar, 1642-7; B.A. 1644-5. Adm. at Lincoln's Inn, Apr. 14, 1658. Will (P.C.C.) 1659; leaves lands in Stradishall, Suffolk. (*Venn*, I. 345.)

DESBOROW, ——. Adm. Fell.-Com. at TRINITY, 1656. Perhaps James Desborowe, '2nd s. of Right Honorable John Lord Desborowe,' who was adm. at Gray's Inn, July 8, 1658.

DESBROW, ——. Adm. pens. at ST CATHARINE'S, 1664.

DISCIPLINE, THOMAS. Matric. pens. from ST JOHN'S, Michs. 1618. Of Norfolk. B.A. 1622-3; M.A. 1626. Fellow, 1624. Ord. deacon (Peterb.) Feb. 21; priest, Feb. 22, 1629-30. R. of Anmer, Norfolk, 1662.

DISCIPLINE, THOMAS. Adm. pens. (age 18) at CAIUS, June 13, 1715. S. of Robert, gent., of Burnham Overy, Norfolk. B. at Stanhoe. School, Walsingham (Mr Harding). Scholar, 1715-20; Matric. 1716; LL.B. 1720. Of Bury St Edmunds, gent. J.P. for Suffolk. Buried at Pakenham, Apr. 21, 1752. (*Venn*, II. 4.)

DISEROTUS, ISAAC. Adm. Fell.-Com. (age 30) at TRINITY, May 6, 1698, from the University of Saumur. S. of Isaac, of 'Grolais, Beauarnais.' Perhaps matric. from Balliol College, Oxford, Apr. 9, 1690, age 18, as Isaac Dismaritz, s. of Isaac, of Middlesex; B.A. (Oxford) 1693. (*Al. Oxon.*)

DISHER, ROBERT. B.A. 1507-8; M.A. 1511.

DISSHER, ROBERT. Adm. sizar at CORPUS CHRISTI, 1570. Matric. 1572.

DISHFIELD, ——. B.A. 1494-5.

DISNEY, EDWARD. Matric. pens. from TRINITY, Michs. 1575. Perhaps s. of Thomas, of Carlton, Lincs. Died Sept. 7, 1595, aged 40. (Hutchins, *Dorset*, I. 100.)

DISNEY, EDWARD. Adm. pens. at TRINITY, June 10, 1647. Of London. Migrated to Oxford. Matric. from Corpus Christi College, Mar. 15, 1650-1; B.A. 1651. Incorp. at Cambridge, 1654. (*Al. Oxon.*)

DISNEY, GERVASE. Adm. sizar (age 17) at MAGDALENE, May 9, 1728. 6th s. of John (1720), V. of St Mary's, Nottingham. B. Aug. 18, 1709. School, Nottingham. Matric. 1728; M.B. 1734. Adm. at Leyden, June 9, 1732. Of Pontefract, Yorks. Married, at St Mary's, Nottingham, May 20, 1736, Mary Thorpe. Died at Pontefract, Nov. 4, 1786. Buried there. Brother of Henry (1720), John (1716) and Samuel (1724). (*Lincs. Pedigrees*, 310.)

DISNEY, HENRY. Adm. at King's, a scholar from Eton, 1719. Probably s. of Matthew, clerk. B. at Bletchley, Bucks. Matric. 1720. Died in College, 1720, of small-pox. (*Harwood*.)

DISNEY, HENRY. Adm. pens. at Queens', Dec. 13, 1720. Of Lincolnshire. 2nd s. of John (1720), V. of St Mary's, Nottingham. Matric. 1721. Migrated to Magdalene, Mar. 23, 1721–2. M.B. 1727. Probably adm. at Leyden, Aug. 5, 1727. Of Newark-on-Trent, Notts. Died Nov. 4, 1760. Brother of Gervase (1728), John (1716) and Samuel (1724). (*Lincs. Pedigrees*, 311; *Essex Pedigrees*.)

DISNYE, HUMPHRY. Matric. pens. from Christ's, Nov. 1548. Probably s. of Richard, of Norton Disney, Lincs. Died without issue. Brother of the next. (*Peile*, I. 44; *Lincs. Pedigrees*, 306.)

DISNYE, JOHN. Matric. pens. from Christ's, Michs. 1548. Probably s. of Richard, of Norton Disney, Lincs. Brother of Humphrey (above).

DISNEY, JOHN. Adm. pens. (age 17) at Magdalene, Dec. 1, 1716. 1st s. of John (1720). B. at Lincoln. School, Lincoln. Matric. 1717. Adm. at the Middle Temple, Apr. 7, 1719. J.P. for Lincs. and Notts. Sheriff of Notts., 1733. Of Swinderby, Esq. Died at Lincoln, Nov. 26, 1771. Brother of Gervase (1728), Henry (1720) and Samuel (1724). (*Lincs. Pedigrees*, 312.)

DISNEY, JOHN. Adm. Fell.-Com. (age 40) (*sic*) at Magdalene, Nov. 29, 1720. S. of Daniel, of Swinderby, Lincs., Esq. B. at Lincoln, Dec. 26, 1677. M.A. 1728 (*Com. Reg.*). Adm. at the Middle Temple. Ord. deacon and priest (London) 1719. V. of Croft, and Kirkby-on-Bain, Lincs. V. of St Mary's, Nottingham, 1723–30. Author. Buried at Nottingham, Feb. 6, 1729–30. M.I. at Wakefield. Father of Gervase (1728), Henry (1720), John (1716) and Samuel (1724). (*D.N.B.*; Hutchins, *Dorset*, II. 100.)

DISNEY, JOSEPH. M.A. from King's, 1724. S. of Matthew, R. of Bletchley, Bucks. Matric. from Christ Church, Oxford, Jan. 19, 1713–4, age 18; B.A. (Oxford) 1717. C. of Lambeth, 1722–5. V. of Cranbrook, Kent, 1725–77. V. of Appledore, 1726–77. Married, 1727, Ann Ross, of Biddenden, Kent. Died Aug. 3, 1777. M.I. at Appledore. Admon. (P.C.C.) 1778. Father of William (1749). (*Al. Oxon.*; *Lincs. Pedigrees*; H. G. Harrison.)

DISNEY, SAMUEL. Adm. at Corpus Christi, 1724. 4th s. of John (1720), V. of St Mary's, Nottingham. B. in Lincoln, 1705. Matric. 1724; B.A. 1727–8; M.A. 1731. Fellow, 1729–32. Ord. deacon (Peterb. *Litt. dim.* from York) Sept. 22, 1728; priest (Lincoln) Dec. 21, 1729. Cambden lecturer at Wakefield Parish Church, Yorks. Died July 22, 1741, aged 36. M.I. at Wakefield. Brother of Gervase (1728), Henry (1720) and John (1716). (*Lincs. Pedigrees*, 311; M. H. Peacock.)

DISNEY, SIRAC. Matric. pens. from Jesus, Michs. 1561, as 'Daysine,' resident, Aug. 1564. Doubtless Sirach, 4th s. of Richard, of Norton Disney, Lincs. Adm. at Lincoln's Inn, Mar. 6, 1567–8. Married Bridget, dau. of Richard Skepper, Esq., of East Kirby. Brother of Zachary (1561). (*Lincs. Pedigrees*, 306.)

DISNEY, THOMAS. Adm. pens. at Trinity, June 16, 1637. Matric. 1637. One of these names, s. and h. of Thomas, of Hinckley, Leics., Esq., adm. at Gray's Inn, Nov. 2, 1639.

DISNEY, WILLIAM. Adm. pens. at Trinity, June 27, 1638; Scholar, 1641; B.A. 1642–3; M.A. 1646. Fellow, 1645–62; Vice-Master, 1654–5. Senior Proctor, 1655–6.

DISNEY, WILLIAM. Adm. pens. at Trinity, Jan. 26, 1749. S. of Joseph (1724), V. of Cranbrook, Kent. B. Sept. 29, 1731. School, Merchant Taylors', London. Matric. 1749; Scholar, 1749; B.A. 1753 (Senior Wrangler); M.A. 1756; B.D. 1768; D.D. 1789. Fellow, 1754. Ord. deacon (Ely) Dec. 22, 1754; priest, Feb. 19, 1757–8. Regius Professor of Hebrew, 1757–71. R. of Paston, Northants., 1771–7. V. of Pluckley, Kent, 1777–1807. Died there Mar. 28, 1807. (*D.N.B.*; *Lincs. Pedigrees*.)

DISNEY, ZACHARY. Matric. pens. from Jesus, Michs. 1561, as 'Daysine.' Resident Aug. 1564. 3rd s. of Richard, of Norton Disney, Lincs. Died young. Brother of Sirac (1561). (*Lincs. Pedigrees*, 306; *Hutchins*, II. 99.)

DISON, JOHN. Adm. sizar (age 17) at Christ's, Apr. 1, 1667. S. of John. B. at Leeds. School, Leeds. Matric. 1667; B.A. 1670–1; M.A. 1674. Ord. deacon (York) June, 1671; priest, May, 1692. Doubtless the man of these names, schoolmaster of Drighlington for 24 years; buried at Birstal, Nov. 2, 1701. (*Peile*, II. 10.)

DISON or DYZON, WILLIAM. Matric. sizar from Trinity, Easter, 1567; Scholar, 1570; B.A. 1571–2; M.A. 1575. Master of Southwell Grammar School, *c.* 1589.

DISSE, JOHN. Fellow of Corpus Christi, 1399. Perhaps R. of Melton by Woodbridge, Suffolk, 1420. Buried in the Priory there, and left benefactions to the Church of Diss, Norfolk. (*Masters*.)

DISSE, THOMAS. Franciscan friar. B.D. 1532–3; D.D. 1535–6. Warden of the Cambridge House. V. of Necton, Norfolk, 1546. V. of Swaffham, 1554. R. of Bradwell, Suffolk, 1554–7. R. of Southery, Norfolk, 1557–9. Died 1559.

DISS, WALTER. Carmelite friar. D.D. of Cambridge. Papal legate to Pope Urban VI. Prior of Carmelite Friary at Norwich, 1376. Theological author. Died Aug. 22, 1404. (*D.N.B.*; *Pits*; H. G. Harrison.)

DYSSE, ——. Friar. D.D. 1469–70.

DISTER, *see* DYSTER.

DISTING, TIMOTHY. Incorp. at Oxford, July 14, 1607, as 'M.A. of Cambridge.' No such degree found.

DITCHELL, JOHN. Adm. pens. (age 20) at Caius, June 30, 1641. S. of John, gent., of Little Walsingham, Norfolk. B. there. Matric. 1641; Scholar, 1643–5; B.A. 1644–5.

DITCHFIELD, EDWARD. Adm. pens. at Emmanuel, Apr. 12, 1619. S. and h. of Edward, gent., of St Mary Woolchurch, London. Matric. 1619; B.A. 1622–3. Adm. at the Middle Temple, July, 1623; and perhaps at Gray's Inn, Mar. 5, 1628–9.

DICHFIELD, JOHN. Incorp. M.A. 1664, from Trinity College, Oxford. Matric. there, May 12, 1651; B.A. (Oxford) 1654–5; M.A. 1657. R. of Grove, Bucks., 1674. V. of Wingrave, 1678. (*Al. Oxon.*)

DITCHFIELD, ROBERT. M.A. from Emmanuel, 1674. Matric. from St Mary's Hall, Oxford, July 2, 1658; B.A. (Oxford) 1662. V. of Garstang, Lancs., 1663. Will (Archd. Richmond) 1683. (*Al. Oxon.*)

DITTON, JOHN. Adm. sizar (age 19) at Pembroke, July 4, 1733. S. of Humphrey, gent. B. in London. School, Christ's Hospital. Matric. 1733; B.A. 1736–7. Ord. deacon (Lincoln) May 28, 1738. Lecturer, for 35 years, at St Mary's, Islington; where he died Mar. 16, 1776. M.I. there. The father (for whom *see* *D.N.B.*) was mathematical master at Christ's Hospital; and Presbyterian minister at Tunbridge Wells. (*A. W. Lockhart*; Nelson, *Islington*, 322.)

DYTTON, RICHARD (or HENRY). Scholar at King's Hall, 1328. Henry de Ditton died Aug. 15, 1331.

DIVE, JOHN. Matric. pens. from Christ's, Nov. 1559. One of these names of Ridlington Park, Rutland, gent. Will (P.C.C.) 1601. (J. Ch. Smith.)

DIX, CHARLES. Adm. sizar (age 16) at Christ's, Mar. 31, 1737. S. of Charles. B. at Norwich. School, Norwich (Mr Reddington). Matric. 1737; Scholar, 1737; B.A. 1740–1; M.A. 1744. Fellow, 1742–52. Ord. deacon (Norwich) Feb. 19, 1742–3. R. of Gateley, Norfolk, 1751–1801. R. of Little Ringstead, 1751. Died May 1, 1801, at Bath. M.I. at Brisley. Will, P.C.C. (*Peile*, II. 234.)

DIXE, EDMUND. Matric. pens. from St John's, Michs. 1555.

DICKS, EDWARD. Matric. sizar from Queens', Easter, 1629. Of Northamptonshire. B.A. 1632–3; M.A. 1636.

DIX, JOHN. Adm. pens. at Corpus Christi, 1570. Of Norwich. Matric. Easter, 1575; B.A. 1577–8; M.A. 1581; B.D. 1588; D.D. 1598. Fellow, 1580–91. University preacher, 1588. Ord. deacon (Peterb.) Sept. 22; priest, Sept. 24, 1580. R. of St Bartholomew Exchange, London, 1591. Preb. of Bristol, 1596. R. of St Andrew Undershaft, 1597–1613. Sub-almoner to the Queen. Preb. of St Paul's, 1599–1613. Died 1613. Will (P.C.C.) 1614; mentions father-in-law, Edward Grant, D.D. and brothers Gabriel and John Grant. (J. Ch. Smith.)

DICKES, JOHN. Adm. pens. at Queens', Apr. 28, 1595. Of Norfolk. Matric. 1596. One of these names V. of Horning, Norfolk, 1613.

DIX, JOHN. Adm. pens. at Peterhouse, Mar. 9, 1620–1. Of Norfolk. Matric. 1621; B.A. 1624–5; M.A. 1628. Adm. at Gray's Inn, Feb. 9, 1623–4, as of Wickmere, Norfolk. Ord. deacon (Peterb.) Mar. 1, 1628–9; priest, May 22, 1630. C. of West Winch, Norfolk, in 1635. Perhaps R. of Dunham Magna, 1635. He was a s. of John Ramsey, of Hitcham, Bucks., who took, 1604, the name and arms of Dix, as heir of his relative William Dix, of Wickmere, Norfolk. Buried at Wickmere, Feb. 10, 1679–80. (*T. A. Walker*, 19.)

DICKS, JOHN. Matric. sizar from St Catharine's, Easter, 1647. Will (Exeter, 1689) of one of these names; of Crediton, Devon, clerk.

DIX, MAURICE. Adm. pens. at Clare, Jan. 5, 1669–70. S. of John and Sarah, of Gt Bowden, Leics. Bapt. there, June 20, 1653. Matric. 1670; B.A. 1673–4; M.A. 1677. Incorp. at Oxford, 1679. Ord. deacon (Peterb.) Sept. 24, 1676; C. of Ecton, Northants.; priest, Sept. 19, 1680. R. of Hargrave, Northants., 1684–9. Will (Archd. Northants.) 1689; proved by his half-brother, John Ventris, scholar of Clare. Died in London. (H. I. Longden.)

DIX, RICHARD. Adm. pens. (age 17) at St John's, June 21, 1677. S. of Edward, clerk, deceased. B. at Kirkby-Laythorpe, Lincs. School, Belton, Lincs. (private; Mr Siston). Matric. 1677; B.A. 1680-1; M.A. 1685. Ord. priest (Norwich) May, 1684. R. of Rackheath, Norfolk, 1686. R. of Markshall, 1687. V. of Wroxham, 1692-1711.

DICKS, ROBERT. Matric. pens. from Pembroke, Easter, 1584. Perhaps same as next.

DIX, ROBERT. Adm. pens. (age 19) at Caius, Feb. 6, 1584-5. S. of Henry, yeoman (died 1597). B. at Wickmere, Norfolk. Bapt. Jan. 18, 1567-8. Pedigree in *Vis. of Norfolk*, 1563. (*Venn*, I. 123.)

DIX, SAMUEL. Adm. sizar (age 18) at Sidney, Mar. 18, 1642-3. S. of Richard. B. at Arthingworth, Northants. Matric. 1644. Migrated to Oxford. B.A. from Lincoln College, 1648. Fellow of Oriel College, 1649-57. Ord. deacon (Lincoln) Dec. 12; priest, Dec. 13, 1660. R. of Horsenden, Bucks., 1650. R. of West Wycombe, 1660. V. of Winslow, 1663-81. Died 1680-1. (*Al. Oxon.*)

DIX, THOMAS. Adm. sizar at Corpus Christi, 1591. Of Norwich. Matric. c. 1592; B.A. 1595-6.

DIX or DICKS, THOMAS. Adm. pens. at Emmanuel, Apr. 7, 1659. Of Norfolk. Matric. 1659.

DIXIE, BEAUMONT. Matric. Fell.-Com. from Trinity Hall, Michs. 1647. S. and h. of Sir Wolstan, Bart. (1619). B. 1629. Succeeded his father as 2nd baronet, 1682. Died May, 1692. Buried at Market Bosworth. Will (Leicester) 1692. Father of Wolston (1675) and John (1678). (*Nichols*, IV. 506; *G.E.C.*)

DIXIE, BEAUMONT. Adm. pens. at Emmanuel, Jan. 30, 1722-3. Of Leicestershire. 2nd s. of Sir Wolstan, Bart. (1675). Matric. 1724; B.A. 1726-7; M.A. 1731. Ord. deacon (Lincoln) Dec. 22, 1728; priest, June 1, 1729. R. of Market Bosworth, Leics., 1729-40. Died at Bath, Feb. 22, 1739-40. (*Nichols*, IV. 506.)

DIXIE, JOHN. Adm. pens. at Emmanuel, Easter, 1624. S. of Wolstan, of Market Bosworth, Leics., Knt. Matric. 1624. Adm. at Gray's In , May 21, 1628. Living in 1681, age 77. Brother of Thomas (1624). (*Nichols*, IV. 506.)

DIXIE, JOHN. Adm. pens. at Clare, May 28, 1678. 3rd s. of Beaumont (1647), of Market Bosworth, Leics. Matric. 1678; B.A. 1681-2; M.A. 1685. Ord. priest (Lincoln) Aug. 6, 1685. R. of Market Bosworth, 1685-1720. Died Dec. 6, 1719-20, aged 58. Brother of Wolstan (1675). (*Nichols*, IV. 502.)

DIXIE, RICHARD. Adm. pens. at Emmanuel, Apr. 27, 1637. Matric. 1637; B.A. 1640-1. Will proved (Leicester) 1642.

DIXIE, THOMAS. Matric. pens. from Peterhouse, Michs. 1569; B.A. 1573-4; M.A. 1577; B.D. 1585. Fellow, 1576. University preacher, 1581. Ord. priest (Peterb.) May 11, 1581. Buried at Little St Mary's, Cambridge, Sept. 23, 1585.

DIXIE, THOMAS. Adm. . at Emmanuel, Easter, 1624. 3rd s. of Sir Wolstan of Market Bosworth, Leics., Knt. Matric. 1624; B.A. 1627-8; M.A. from Trinity Hall, 1631. Adm. at Gray's Inn, Oct. 25, 1633. Died unmarried. Brother of John (1624). (*Nichols*, IV. 506.)

DIXIE, THOMAS. Adm. pens. at Emmanuel, Dec. 15, 1647. Matric. 1648. Dixie scholar as 'one of the blood' of Sir Wolstan Dixie.

DIXIE, WOLSTAN. Matric. pens. from Peterhouse, Michs. 1576. Probably s. of John, of Royston, Herts. One of these names V. of Brampton St Mary, Hunts., 1603-27. (*Vis. of Northants.*, 1618.)

DIXIE, WOLSTAN. Adm. Fell.-Com. at Emmanuel, Apr. 13, 1619. Probably s. of Richard, of Catworth, Hunts., s. of Sir Wolstan, Knt. B. 1602. Matric. 1619. Created baronet, July 14, 1660. Sheriff of Leics., 1661-2. Probably M.P. for Dundalk, 1661-6. Died at Grendon, Warwa., Feb. 13, 1682, aged 80. Buried at Market Bosworth. Will, Leicester. Father of Beaumont (1647). (*Nichols*, IV. 506; *G.E.C.*)

DIXIE, WOLSTON. Adm. Fell.-Com. at Emmanuel, May 26, 1675. Of Leicestershire. S. and h. of Beaumont (1647). Bapt. at Bosworth, Mar. 25, 1657. Matric. 1675. Lieutenant-Colonel in the Leicestershire Militia, 1681. Succeeded as 3rd baronet, 1692. Died Dec. 10, 1713. Buried at Bosworth. Father of Beaumont (1722), brother of John (1678). (*Nichols*, IV. 507; *G.E.C.*)

DIXIE, YOUNG. Adm. sizar at Emmanuel, June 14, 1616. S. of Wolstan (1576), V. of Brampton St Mary, Hunts. Matric. 1617; B.A. 1619-20; M.A. 1631. Ord. deacon (Peterb.) July 11; priest, July 12, 1624. R. of Cadeby, Leics., 1628. Sequestered to Tewin, Herts., July 27, 1643. Minister of St Margaret's, Leicester, 1659. Will (Leicester) 1664. (*Vis. of Northants.*, 1618; *Shaw*, I. 314.)

DICKSON or DIXON, ABRAHAM. Adm. pens. (age 18) at Trinity, Oct. 16, 1742. S. of Abraham, of Newcastle-on-Tyne. Bapt. at St John's, Mar. 10, 1723-4. School, Fulham, London (Mr Croft). Matric. 1742; Scholar, 1746. Adm. at Lincoln's Inn, July 6, 1744. F.R.S. 1748. Of Belford Hall, Esq. Sheriff of Northumberland, 1759. (Brand's *Newcastle*, II. 575.)

DICKSON, ANTHONY. 'Of Jesus, aged 26.' Applied for ordination as deacon (Ely) Dec. 18, 1568 (rejected).

DICKSON, ANTHONY. Matric. pens. from Trinity, 1595; B.A. 1597-8.

DICKSON, BRIAN. Matric. sizar from King's, Easter, 1581.

DICKSON, BRIGHT. Adm. pens. at Jesus, Apr. 7, 1683. S. of Thomas, of Little Woodhouse, Yorks. (twice mayor of Leeds). Matric. 1683; Scholar, 1684; B.A. 1686-7; M.A. 1690. Ord. priest (York) Dec. 1689. V. of St John, Leeds, 1696-1709. Died June 13, 1710. His mother was Ruth, dau. of John Bright, V. of Sheffield.

DIXON, DAVID. Fee for M.A. or higher degree, 1482-3.

DICKSON, EDMUND. Matric. sizar from Queens', Michs. 1639. Of Lincolnshire.

DIXON, EDWARD. Adm. sizar at Clare, Apr. 9, 1717. S. of John (1681), V. of Buckminster. B. at Buckminster, Leics. School, Oakham. B.A. 1720-1. Ord. deacon (Lincoln) Sept. 25, 1720; priest, Dec. 18, 1720. Succeeded his father. Died 1763.

DIXON or DICKSON, EDWARD. Adm. sizar (age 19) at St John's, Oct. 5, 1731. S. of James, trunk maker, of Lancashire. B. at Kirkham. School, Kirkham (Mr Taylor). Matric. 1731; B.A. 1735-6. Ord. deacon (Lincoln) Mar. 21, 1735-6; priest (Chester) Dec. 19, 1736. C. of Kirkham. Will (Archd. Richmond) 1741; proved by his father. (*Scott-Mayor*, III. 438; J. Ch. Smith.)

DIXON, GEORGE. Matric. sizar from St John's, Michs. 1569.

DYCKSON, HENRY. Matric. sizar from Christ's, Nov. 1554.

DIX, HENRY. Adm. sizar at Sidney, Jan. 1611-2. Of Leicestershire. Migrated to Corpus Christi, 1612. B.A. 1615; M.A. 1619. Ord. deacon (Peterb.) May 31; priest, June 1, 1618. R. of Market Deeping, Lincs., 1619-25.

DIXON, HENRY. Adm. sizar (age 18) at Peterhouse, Apr. 18, 1672. Of Leicestershire. School, Grantham. Matric. 1672; Scholar, 1672; B.A. 1675-6; M.A. 1679. Ord. deacon (Peterb.) Sept. 24, 1676. Perhaps R. of Bloxholm, Lincs., 1680-9.

DICKSON, HUGH. Adm. sizar at Jesus, Apr. 25, 1654. Of Norfolk. Matric. 1654; B.A. 1657.

DIXON, JAMES. Adm. pens. (age 14) at St John's, Mar. 1, 1661-2. S. of Robert (1630-1), of Tunstall, Kent. B. there. School, Rochester (Mr Yardley). Matric. 1661-2. Adm. at the Middle Temple, May 20, 1663. Brother of Robert (1661).

DIXON, JAMES SAUL. Adm. sizar at Trinity, June 10, 1734. Matric. 1734.

DYXON, JOHN. Matric. sizar from Jesus, Easter, 1544.

DIXON, JOHN. Matric. sizar from Jesus, Michs. 1573.

DIXON, JOHN. Adm. pens. at Sidney, June, 1602. Of Leicestershire. Matric. 1602; B.A. 1605-6; M.A. 1609. Incorp. at Oxford, 1612. Ord. deacon (Peterb.) Sept. 20, 1615; priest, Feb. 25, 1615-6. R. of Scrivelsby, Lincs., 1615. Will (P.C.C.) 1652. (*Al. Oxon.*)

DIXON, JOHN. Adm. pens. at Corpus Christi, 1619. Of Leicestershire. Matric. 1620; B.A. 1623-4; M.A. 1627. Ord. deacon (Peterb.) June 7; priest, June 8, 1628. Perhaps R. of Offord Darcy, Hunts., 1641-71; or R. of Glenfield, Leics., 1630; sequestered, 1646. Died 1671.

DICKSON, JOHN. Adm. Fell.-Com. at Emmanuel, May 30, 1627. Of Whitechapel, Middlesex. Adm. at the Inner Temple, 1630.

DIXON, JOHN. Matric. sizar from Magdalene, Easter, 1659; B.A. 1662-3.

DIXON, JOHN. Adm. sizar (age 18) at St John's, Feb. 21, 1667-8. S. of William, of Beverley, Yorks. B. there. School, Brandesburton, Yorks. Matric. 1667-8.

DICKSON, JOHN. Adm. sizar (age 16) at Sidney, Apr. 24, 1669. 1st s. of Richard, clothier, deceased. B. at Sutton-in-Craven. School, Kildwick. Matric. 1669.

DIXON, JOHN. Adm. sizar (age 18) at Trinity, May 6, 1681. S. of Samuel (1633). School, Oakham (Mr Love). Matric. 1681; B.A. 1684-5; M.A. 1688. Ord. priest (Lincoln) May 22, 1687. V. of Buckminster, Leics., 1695-1718. Buried there Nov. 23, 1718. Admon., Leicester. Father of Edward (1717).

DIXON, JOHN. Matric. pens. from Christ's, Michs. 1730. Adm. as Fell.-Com. Easter, 1735; LL.B. 1737. One of these names 'emigrant minister to Virginia,' c. 1748. (*Peile*, II. 223.)

DIXON, JOSEPH. Adm. pens. (age 17) at ST JOHN'S, June 30, 1715. S. of Oliver, gent. B. at Dudley, Worcs. School, Rugby. Matric. 1715; B.A. 1718-9; M.A. 1722. Ord. deacon (Lincoln) Dec. 23, 1722. R. of West Felton, Salop, and Wistanstow, till 1764. Died June 27, 1764. Will, P.C.C., as of Dudley.

DIXON, JOSHUA. Adm. pens. (age 19) at JESUS, May 9, 1669. Of Ringley, Lancs. Matric. 1670; B.A. 1672-3. P.C. of Ringley, Lancs., 1691. P.C. of Rivington, 1701. Father of the next.

DIXON, JOSHUA. Adm. sizar (age 17) at ST JOHN'S, Mar. 16, 1699-1700. S. of Joshua (above), P.C. of Ringley, Lancs. B. at Ringley. School, Manchester (Mr Barrow). B.A. 1703-4. Ord. deacon(Ely) Sept. 23, 1705; priest (York) June, 1707. Assistant master at Manchester Grammar School, 1724. (Mumford, *Hist. of Manchester School*.)

DIXON, NICHOLAS. Matric. sizar from TRINITY, Michs. 1568, as Dickson; Scholar, 1575.

DIXON, OLIVER. Adm. sizar (age 16) at SIDNEY, Apr. 8, 1635. S. of Oliver, Esq. B. at Ketharpe House. Schools, Tugby (Mr Hill) and Melton Mowbray (Mr Si. Humphrey). Matric. 1635.

DIXON, PIERCE. Adm. pens. at QUEENS', Jan. 18, 1730-1. Of Kent. Matric. 1731; B.A. 1734-5; M.A. 1738; B.D. 1747. Fellow, 1735. Taxor, 1739. Master of the Mathematical School, Rochester. V. of Hartlip, Kent, 1756-9. V. of Stockbury, 1759-66. Died 1766. Will, P.C.C.

DIXON, RICHARD. Adm. at KING'S, a scholar from Eton, 1551; B.A. 1555-6. Fellow, till 1557. R. of Horstead, Norfolk, 1556. R. of Stanninghall, 1560.

DIXON, RICHARD. Adm. pens. at EMMANUEL, Oct. 18, 1693. Of Essex.

DIXON, RICHARD. Adm. sizar (age 18) at ST JOHN'S, July 1, 1732. S. of William, gent., of Lancashire. B. at Satterthwaite-in-Furness Fells. School, Hawkshead (Mr Broxholme). Matric. 1732; B.A. 1735-6; M.A. 1739. Head Master of Hawkshead School, 1736-45.

DIXON, ROBERT. Matric. sizar from ST JOHN'S, Michs. 1566; B.A. from St Catharine's, 1570-1; M.A. 1574. V. of Holy Trinity, Cambridge, 1570-8. One of these names R. of Cockfield, Durham, 1575-1616. Perhaps V. of Haltwhistle, Northumberland, 1616-23.

DIXON, ROBERT. Matric. sizar from CHRIST'S, Easter, 1577. Town Exhibitioner from Ipswich School. Scholar; B.A. 1579-80; M.A. 1583. Licensed to teach grammar in Norwich diocese, 1582. Perhaps V. of Birstall, Yorks., 1587-1614. R. of Darfield, 1600-14. Died Oct. 14, 1614, aged 59. (*Peile*, I. 142; Hunter, S. *Yorks*.)

DIXON, ROBERT. Matric. pens. from ST JOHN'S, Easter, 1605. School, Sedbergh. B.A. 1608-9; M.A. 1612. Perhaps adm. at the Middle Temple, Aug. 14, 1606, as s. and h. of Robert, gent., of Hemmington, Hants.

DIXON, ROBERT. Adm. sizar (age 16) at ST JOHN'S, Mar. 22, 1630-1. S. of James, of Aldersgate, London, cutler, deceased. School, Cambridge (Perse). Matric. 1631; B.A. 1634-5; M.A. 1638; D.D. 1668 (*Lit. Reg.*). Incorp. at Oxford, 1653. Ord. deacon and priest, Sept. 21, 1639. R. of Tunstall, Kent, 1647; sequestered, and restored, 1660-76. Preb. of Rochester, 1660. V. of St Nicholas, Rochester, 1660-88. Died May, 1688. Admon. P.C.C. Father of James (1661-2) and the next. (*Al. Oxon.*; *D.N.B.*; *Vis. of Kent*, 1663.)

DIXON, ROBERT. Adm. pens. (age 15) at ST JOHN'S, June 26, 1661. S. of Robert (1630-1), clerk, of Frindsbury, Kent. B. there. School, Rochester (Mr Yardley). Matric. 1661-2; B.A. 1664-5; M.A. 1668; LL.D. 1682 (*Com. Reg.*). Ord. deacon (Lincoln) Feb. 17, 1667-8; priest (Ely) Dec. 1668. V. of Stockbury, Kent, 1670-1711. R. of Tunstall (succeeding his father), 1676-1711. Died Mar. 1711. Brother of James (1661-2). (*Vis. of Kent*, 1663.)

DIXON, ROBERT. Adm. sizar (age 18) at PETERHOUSE, Apr. 16, 1734. Of Northumberland. School, Durham. Matric. 1734; Scholar, 1734.

DIXON, ROBERT. Adm. sizar (age 18) at CAIUS, Feb. 17, 1749-50. S. of Humphrey, of Steeple Bumpstead, Essex. B. at Gazeley, Suffolk. School, Bishop's Stortford (Mr Mawle). Scholar, 1750-5; B.A. 1754. College testimonial for deacon's orders, 1754. (*Venn*, II. 64.)

DIXON or DICKSON, SAMUEL. Adm. at EMMANUEL, June 5, 1633. Of Leicestershire. Matric. 1634; B.A. 1636-7; M.A. 1640. Ord. priest (Lincoln) Oct. 17, 1641. V. of Buckminster, Leics., 1641-95. Buried Apr. 16, 1695, aged 80. Father of John (1681). (*Nichols*, II. 125.)

DIXON, STEPHEN. Adm. sizar (age 16) at PETERHOUSE, Dec. 23, 1635. Of Leicestershire. School, Peterborough. Matric. 1636; B.A. 1639-40. Ord. priest (Lincoln) May 24, 1646. V. of Barkestone, Leics., 1646-66.

DIXON, THOMAS. B.Can.L. 1505.

DICKSON, THOMAS. Matric. pens. from ST JOHN'S, Michs. 1565; B.A. from Magdalene, 1570-1, as Dixon.

DIXON, THOMAS. Matric. pens. from CHRIST'S, June, 1602. Perhaps adm. at the Middle Temple, May 17, 1609, as s. and h. of James, gent., of London. Of Braughing, Herts. (*Vis. of Herts.*, 1634.)

DIXON, THOMAS. Matric. pens. from CHRIST'S, Easter, 1617, as Dickenson. S. of Robert, of Sherburn, Durham. B.A. 1620-1; M.A. (Oxford) 1624. C. of Winston. Buried at Whitburn, June 8, 1631. Father of the next. (*Peile*, I. 317; H. M. Wood.)

DIXON, THOMAS. Adm. pens. (age 18) at SIDNEY, Apr. 16, 1650. S. of Thomas (above), late of Whitburn, Durham. B. there. Bapt. Oct. 6, 1631. Schools, Mitford (Mr Ro. Lever) and Barwick (Mr Webb). Matric. 1650; B.A. 1653. Intruded V. of Kelloe, Durham; ejected, 1660. Perhaps P.C. of Whitworth, 1662-1703. Died 1703.

DIXON, THOMAS. Adm. sizar (age 18) at ST JOHN'S, Apr. 3, 1701. S. of Thomas, gent. B. at Leeds, Yorks. School, Sedbergh. Matric. 1701; B.A. 1704-5; M.A. 1708. Master of Leeds Grammar School, 1706-12. Died July 6, 1712. (*Sedbergh School Register*, 146.)

DIXON, THOMAS. Adm. pens. (age 17) at TRINITY, Sept. 19, 1717. S. of Joseph, gent., of Islington, Norfolk. School, St Paul's, London. Matric. 1717. Adm. at Gray's Inn, May 30, 1718; and at the Middle Temple, Mar. 1726. Buried Jan. 24, 1743-4. (Burke, *L.G.*)

DICKSON, TOBIAS. Adm. pens. (age 17) at ST JOHN'S, Apr. 23, 1651. S. of Gervase, of Darfield, Yorks., 'Medicus.' B. at Bentley. School, Hemsworth (Mr Horncastle). Matric. 1651; B.A. 1654-5; M.B. 1656; M.D. 1661. Incorp. at Oxford, 1661.

DICKSON, WILLIAM. Adm. pens. at CORPUS CHRISTI, 1596. Of Norfolk. Matric. 1596. Ord. deacon (Norwich) Sept. 29, 1601, age 24, as C. of Ashwicken and Leziate; priest, Sept. 29, 1604. V. of Snettisham, 1604. (He is described at his ordination as student of Caius.)

DIXON, WILLIAM. Matric. pens. from ST JOHN'S, Easter, 1605. One of these names, of Ramshaw, Durham, adm. at Gray's Inn, Feb. 3, 1607-8.

DICKSON, WILLIAM. Matric. sizar from CHRIST'S, Dec. 1622.

DIXON, WILLIAM. Adm. sizar (age 17) at CAIUS, Mar. 28, 1638. S. of Thomas, weaver, of Norwich. B. in parish of St Edmunds, Fishergate. School, Norwich (Mr Briggs and Mr Lovering). Matric. 1638; Scholar, 1640-5; B.A. 1641-2; M.A. 1645. Usher at Ipswich grammar school, in 1657. Licensed to teach grammar and writing, in Norwich diocese, 1662. Ord. deacon (Norwich) Sept. 1662; priest, Mar. 14, 1662-3. Will proved (Norw. Archd. C.) 1669. (*Venn*, I. 331.)

DIXON, WILLIAM. Adm. sizar (age 20) at SIDNEY, Apr. 28, 1677. S. of William, clothier, deceased. B. at Leeds, Yorks. School, Leeds (Mr Gilbert). Matric. 1677, as Richard; B.A. 1680-1. Ord. deacon (York) Feb. 1680-1; priest, Dec. 1683. V. of Marske, Yorks., 1685-1717. Married, Nov. 27, 1688, at Marske, Ann Pott, of Redcar. Buried at Marske, June 24, 1717. Father of the next.

DIXON, WILLIAM. Adm. sizar (age 19) at SIDNEY, Feb. 25, 1709-10. Only s. of William (above), V. of Marske, Yorks. Bapt. at Marske, Oct. 22, 1691. School, Guisborough (Mr Jaques). Matric. 1710; B.A. 1714-5. Ord. priest (York) Dec. 1715.

DIXON, WILLIAM. Adm. sizar (age 17) at ST JOHN'S, Mar. 1, 1721-2. S. of Edward, husbandman, of Lancashire. B. at Hawkshead. School, Hawkshead (Mr Hunter). Matric. 1721-2; B.A. 1725-6. Ord. deacon (London) Mar. 16, 1725-6; priest, Sept. 25, 1726. R. of Greenstead by Colchester, 1728-30. (*Scott-Mayor*, III. 347.)

DIXON, WILLIAM. Adm. sizar at JESUS, July 5, 1743. Of Barton, Yorks.

DYXON, ——. Matric. pens. from CHRIST'S, Easter, 1544.

DICKSON, ——. Adm. at CORPUS CHRISTI, 1577.

DIXWELL, BASIL. Adm. Fell.-Com. at CORPUS CHRISTI, Apr. 4, 1657. S. of Mark, of Bromehouse, Barham, Kent, Esq. B. June 22, 1640. Created Bart., June 19, 1660. Died in London, May 7, 1668. Brother of the next. (*Vis. of Kent*, 1663; *G.E.C.*; *Masters*, 279.)

DIXWELL, HERDSON. Adm. Fell.-Com. at CORPUS CHRISTI, Apr. 4, 1657. B. in Kent. Brother of Basil, above.

DOBBE, THOMAS. B.A. 1539-40; M.A. 1543. Fellow of ST JOHN'S, 1542. Of Coventry and Lichfield diocese. Ord. deacon (Norwich) Mar. 8, 1543-4; priest, Apr. 1544. Committed to prison by Archbishop Cranmer, for disturbing the mass in St Paul's Cathedral. Died there 1546-7. (*Cooper*, I. 91.)

DOBBS, EDWARD. Adm. sizar (age 17) at CAIUS, June 14, 1631. S. of Thomas, gent., of Guist, Norfolk. B. at Watton. School, Westfield. Matric. 1631; Scholar, 1634–8; B.A. 1634–5; M.A. 1638. Ord. deacon (Norwich) Sept. 25, 1636; priest, Sept. 24, 1637. C. of Yaxham, Norfolk, 1636; of Snoring, in 1637. R. of Gt Snoring, 1639. (*Venn*, I. 301.)

DOBBS, EDWARD. Adm. sizar at CLARE, Jan. 11, 1670–1. Matric. 1671; B.A. 1674–5; M.A. 1679. Ord. deacon (Peterb.) Dec. 26, 1676; priest (London) Mar. 11, 1676–7.

DOBBES, JOHN. Matric. pens. from QUEENS', Easter, 1575; B.A. 1578–9; M.A. 1582. Licensed to practise medicine, 1587.

DOBBS, PETER. Adm. pens. (age 16) at SIDNEY, Jan. 26, 1630–1. S. of John, baker, of Oundle, Northants. School, Oundle. Matric. 1631, as 'Doblon'; B.A. 1634–5; M.A. 1638. Ord. deacon (Peterb.) Mar. 10, 1638–9; priest, June 9, 1639. R. of West Walton, Norfolk, 1644.

DOBBES or DOBB, THOMAS. Matric. sizar from TRINITY, Easter, 1616; B.A. 1619–20; M.A. 1623. Ord. priest (Norwich) 1621. V. of Kempston, Norfolk, 1625.

DOBBS, WILLIAM. Matric. sizar from QUEENS', Easter, 1611. Of Northamptonshire. B.A. 1614–5; M.A. 1619. Ord. deacon (Peterb.) Sept. 17; priest, Dec. 17, 1620.

DOBBES, ——. Pens. at GONVILLE HALL, 1500–8; M.A. 1502–3 (Incorp. from Oxford). Perhaps John Dobbs, priest, R. of Warboys, Hunts., 1526. Of All Hallows, Barking. Died 1546. Will (P.C.C.) 1546. (*Venn*, I. 15.)

DOBIE, JOHN. Adm. pens. (age 19) at PETERHOUSE, Dec. 15, 1743. S. of John, of Bury St Edmnuds, gent., deceased. School, Bury. Matric. 1743–4; Scholar, 1743; B.A. 1747–8. Ord. deacon (Norwich) Mar. 1747–8; priest (Rochester) Sept. 21, 1748. C. of Greenwich.

DOBBYE, TOBIAS. Matric. sizar from ST JOHN'S, Michs. 1614; B.A. 1617–8. Perhaps, as Tobias Dobbin, R. of Prenze, Norfolk, 1651–73. Died 1673.

DOBBI (? DOBB), ——. A monk. Fee for M.A. or higher degree 1467–8. Perhaps 'Edmund Dobbs,' R. of Strumpshaw, Norfolk, till 1483. Died 1483.

DOBBINS, JOSEPH. Matric. pens. from KING'S, Michs. 1668. S. and h. of Joseph, of Rotherhithe, Surrey, gent. Adm. at Lincoln's Inn, July 4, 1671. Age 11, in 1662. (The father was a sea captain; of Fordhall, Warws.) (*Vis. of Surrey*, 1662.)

DOBINS, WILLIAM. Adm. pens. (age 15) at CHRIST'S, June 12, 1661. S. of William. B. in London. School, Westminster. Probably adm. at Lincoln's Inn, May 11, 1663, as s. of William, of Warmington, Gloucs. Acted as solicitor for the College. (*Peile*, I. 597.)

DOBYNSON, JOHN. Matric. sizar from PEMBROKE Michs. 1559.

DOBBINSON or DOBYSON, THOMAS. B.A. 1541–2; M.A. 1544. V. of Gt Shelford, Cambs., in 1543. Probably V. of Orwell, 1550. V. of Bassingbourne, 1557–64 (presented by the Abbey of Westminster). V. of Barley, Herts., 1559–64. Died 1564.

DOBYNSON, ——. A monk, apparently resident in 1463–4. (*Gr. Bk*, A, 42.)

DOBBINSON, ——. B.Can.L. 1470–1. Possibly Richard, R. of East Horndon, Essex, 1473–80. R. of North Ockendon, 1480–3.

DOBLE, ——. Matric. Fell.-Com. from ST CATHARINE'S, Michs. 1645.

DOBLON, PETER (1630), *see* **DOBBS.**

DOBREY, SAMUEL. Adm. sizar at JESUS, Feb. 27, 1619–20. Probably s. of John, of Guernsey. Matric. 1620; B.A. 1623–4; M.A. 1627. Chaplain to the Swedish Embassy. Died unmarried. (Burke, *L.G.*; A. Gray.)

DOBSON, *see also* **DODSON.**

DOBSON, ANTHONY. Matric. pens. from ST JOHN'S, Michs. 1565; B.A. 1568–9; M.A. 1572.

DOBSON, BARTHOLOMEW. Matric. pens. from ST JOHN'S, Easter, 1620; B.A. 1623–4; M.A. 1627. Ord. deacon (York) J e, 1625; priest, Dec. 1625. One of these names R. of Hasilton, Gloucs., 1660.

DOBSON, BUSHELL. Matric. sizar from TRINITY HALL, Easter, 1665. S. of John, clerk, of Heslerton, Yorks. School, Pocklington. Ord. deacon (York) June, 1667. Brother of John (1655).

DOBSON (? DODSON), CHRISTOPHER. Matric. sizar from ST JOHN'S, Michs. 1602.

DOBSON, CHRISTOPHER. Matric. pens. (age 16) from PETERHOUSE, Michs. 1649. Of Yorkshire. School, Coxwold. Scholar; B.A. 1652–3. Incorp. at Oxford, 1663 (as M.A.). R. of Ludborough, Lincs., 1661–80. Buried there Oct. 4, 1680. (*Lincs. Pedigrees.*)

DOBSON, EDWARD. Adm. sizar at EMMANUEL, May 28, 1642. Of Newcastle-on-Tyne. Perhaps s. of George, merchant. Bapt. at All Saints', Sept. 12, 1624. Matric. 1642. (H. M. Wood.)

DOBSON, EDWARD. Adm. Fell.-Com. at ST JOHN'S, June 30, 1662. S. of Robert, of Liverpool. B. there. Probably adm. at Gray's Inn, Nov. 23, 1657.

DOBSON, EDWARD. Adm. pens. (age 17) at ST JOHN'S, June 13, 1715. S. of Thomas, hatter. B. at Newcastle-on-Tyne. Bapt. at St Nicholas, Feb. 2, 1697–8. School, Newcastle. Matric. 1715; B.A. 1718–9.

DOBSON, FITZHERBERT. Matric. from CLARE, Michs. 1720; B.A. 1724–5; M.A. 1728.

DOBSON, ISAAC. Matric. sizar from CORPUS CHRISTI, Easter, 1620. Of Norfolk. B.A. 1623–4; M.A. 1627; B.D. 1635. Fellow, 1628–63. University librarian, 1661–8. V. of Grantchester, Cambs., 1644 (instituted, 1660). Presented to Little Wilbraham, 1653; resigned, 1654. Buried at St Benet's, Cambridge, Dec. 16, 1678. Will (V.C.C.) 1678. (*Masters.*)

DOBSON, JOHN. Matric. sizar from PETERHOUSE, 1581; B.A. 1583–4. Ord. deacon and priest (Peterb.) Sept. 27, 1587. Probably P.C. of Hexham, Northumberland, 1587–1603. V. of Corbridge, 1588. One of these names V. of Pocklington, Yorks., 1603–19. Buried Jan. 11, 1619.

DOBSON, JOHN. Adm. pens. at EMMANUEL, May 10, 1608. Matric. 1608 (as 'Dodson'); B.A. from St John's, 1613–4; M.A. 1617. Ord. deacon (Peterb.) May 1, 1619; priest (York) Sept. 1619. Licensed C. of Warter, Yorks., Jan. 1619–20. Perhaps V. of Gt Edstone, Yorks., 1619.

DOBSON, JOHN. Adm. sizar (age 18) at ST JOHN'S, June 23, 1655. S. of John, clerk, of Heslerton, Yorks. B. there. School, Pocklington. Matric. 1655; B.A. 1658–9. Perhaps R. of West Heslerton, Yorks., 1661–8. V. of Yeddingham, 1662–8. Brother of Bushell (1665).

DOBSON, JOHN. Incorp. M.A. 1663, from Magdalen College, Oxford. Matric. there, Dec. 9, 1653. B. in Warwickshire, 1633. B.A. (Oxford) 1656; M.A. 1659; B.D. 1667. Fellow of Magdalen, 1661–71. Ord. deacon (Lincoln) Dec. 21, 1661; priest (Peterb.) Sept. 24, 1665. V. of Easton Neston, Northants., 1668–71. R. of Corscombe, Dorset, 1670–81. R. of Cold Higham, Northants., 1674–81. Author, theological. Died June 9, 1681, at Corscombe. M.I. (*Al. Oxon.*; *D.N.B.*).

DOBSON, JOHN. Adm. sizar (age 17) at MAGDALENE, Apr. 22, 1669. S. of Robert, deceased, of New Malton, Yorks. School, Malton. Matric. 1669; B.A. 1672–3. Ord. priest (York) June, 1674. V. of Kirby-Grindalythe, Yorks., 1674–1722. Perhaps V. of Garton-on-the-Wolds, 1679–1722. Died 1722.

DOBSON, JOHN. Adm. pens. (age 17) at TRINITY, Feb. 8, 1728–9. S. of Thomas, of Yorkshire. School, Bingley, Yorks. (Mr Leach). Matric. 1729; Scholar, 1730. Adm. at Lincoln's Inn, Feb. 5, 1730–1; s. of Thomas, of Bingley Vicarage, Yorks.

DOBSON, LANCELOT. Adm. sizar (age 16) at CAIUS, Apr. 11, 1656. S. of George, gent., of Brancepeth, Durham. B. at Burniston, Yorks. Schools, Bedale, Yorks., Brancepeth and Auckland. Matric. 1656; Scholar, 1656–60; B.A. 1659–60; M.A. 1663. Probably V. of Ellingham, Northumberland, 1665; and of Chillingham, 1679. Died 1692. Buried at Chillingham, Nov. 25, 1692. (*Venn*, I. 394.)

DOBSON, ROBERT. Matric. pens. from ST JOHN'S, Michs. 1561. One of these names ord. deacon (York) Mar. 30, 1572; priest (Lincoln) July 26, 1577. R. of Wroot, Lincs., 1577. Perhaps minister at St Nicholas, Durham, in 1591.

DOBSON, ROBERT. Matric. sizar from TRINITY, *c.* 1591.

DOBSON, SAMUEL. Matric. sizar from ST JOHN'S, *c.* 1590. Perhaps B.A. 1594–5. Ord. deacon and priest (Peterb.) Oct. 28, 1598. V. of Reepham, Lincs., 1613.

DOBSON, SAMUEL. Matric. pens. from CORPUS CHRISTI, Michs. 1629; B.A. 1632–3; M.A. 1636. Ord. deacon (Norwich) Sept. 24, 1637, as C. of St Clement, Norwich; priest, Sept. 22, 1638. V. of Horsford, Norfolk, 1647.

DOBSON, SAMUEL. Adm. at CORPUS CHRISTI, 1665. Of Norfolk. Matric. 1665; B.A. 1668–9; M.A. 1672. V. of Besthorpe, Norfolk, 1679–81. Died Apr. 26, 1681, aged 35.

DOBSON, THOMAS. Matric. Fell.-Com. from TRINITY, Easter, 1647.

DOBSON, TIMOTHY. Adm. sizar at JESUS, Feb. 21, 1673. Of Lancashire. Matric. 1673; Scholar, 1676; B.A. 1676–7; M.A. 1690. Master of Stockport Grammar School, 1683–93. Master of Macclesfield, 1694. Died *c.* 1704. (Earwaker, *E. Cheshire*, I. 418.)

DOBSON, WILLIAM. B.A. 1531–2.

DOBSON, WILLIAM. B.A. 1537-8. Probably at CHRIST'S, 1538-41. One of these names V. of Torpenhow, Cumberland; deprived, 1568. Another V. of Ixning, Suffolk. Will (P.C.C.) 1573.

DOBSON, WILLIAM. Matric. sizar from MAGDALENE, Michs. 1642.

DOBSON, WILLIAM. Adm. sizar (age 16) at MAGDALENE, Apr. 27, 1652. S. of Simeon, of Keighley, Yorks. School, Bingley. Matric. 1652.

DOBSON, WILLIAM. Adm. pens. at ST CATHARINE'S, 1675. Matric. 1677; B.A. 1678-9. Ord. priest (Chichester) Sept. 25, 1682. V. of Hellingly, Sussex, 1682-1707. Buried there Apr. 7, 1707. Admon. at Lewes. (W. C. Harrison.)

DOBSON, WILLIAM. Matric. sizar from CHRIST'S, July, 1714; Scholar, 1715; B.A. 1717-8.

DOBSON, ——. B.Can.L. 1475-6. A John Dobson was V. of Melbourn, Cambs., 1489.

DOBSON, ——. B.A. 1496-7; M.A. 1500.

DOBTON, RALPH. Matric. sizar from TRINITY, Lent, 1578-9.

DOBULL, LAWRENCE. B.Civ.L. 1474-5; B.Can.L. 1476-7.

DOBYLL, ——. Incorp. 1477-8, from abroad.

DOCKER, HENRY. Adm. sizar (age 18) at ST JOHN'S, May 22, 1684. S. of Henry, clerk, deceased. B. at Shap, Westmorland. School, Ravenstonedale. Matric. 1684; B.A. 1687-8. V. of Willerby, Yorks., 1691-1721. V. of Scarborough, 1708-21.

DOCKERILL, JOHN. Adm. sizar (age 20) at ST JOHN'S, June 20, 1705. S. of John, barber. B. at Cambridge. School, King's, Cambridge. Matric. 1705-6; B.A. 1708-9. R. of Handley, Cheshire, 1709-30. Died 1730. (*Ormerod*, II. 397.)

DOCKET or DOGET, ANDREW. M.A. Vicar of St Botolph, Cambridge, *c.* 1435-70 (Rector from 1444). Principal of ST BERNARD'S HOSTEL, 1446. First president of Queens' College, of which he was the main founder, 1448-84. Preb. of St Stephen, Westminster, till 1479. Preb. of Lichfield, 1467-70; chancellor, 1470-7. Died Nov. 4, 1484. Buried in the College Chapel. (W. G. Searle, *Hist. of Queens'*; *D.N.B.*)

DOCKET or DUCKET, CHRISTOPHER. B.A. 1503-4; M.A. 1507-8; B.D. 1520-1. Proctor, 1511-2. Will proved (V.C.C.) 1521.

DOCKET or DOGET, THOMAS. B.A. 1509-10. Perhaps identical with Tho. Dagett, R. of Wendon Parva, Essex, 1517-22; called Dockett in the Act. Bk of the Vic. Gen., Bishop of London, 1521. (J. Ch. Smith.)

DOCKET or DOGET, WILLIAM. B.A. 1480-1; M.A. 1484; B.D. 1491. Fellow of QUEENS', 1484-8. Of York diocese. Ord. deacon (Lincoln) Apr. 3, 1484.

DOCKINGE, THOMAS. Adm. sizar (age 18) at CAIUS, July 16, 1628. S. of Robert. B. at Bury, Suffolk. School, Bury. Migrated to King's. B.A. 1630-1. Ord. priest (Lincoln) Sept. 25, 1631. C. of Charsfield, Suffolk, in 1636. R. of Dallinghoe, 1646. Head Master of Woodbridge School, 1663-4. Buried June 10, 1664. (*Venn*, I. 285.)

DOCKLEY, JOHN. Matric. sizar from TRINITY, Easter, 1625; B.A. 1628-9; M.A. 1632. R. of Little Easton, Essex, 1639-63. Died 1663.

DOCRELL, EDWARD. Matric. sizar from QUEENS', Easter, 1563 (*famulus* of the proctor).

DOCKSEY, HENRY. Adm. pens. at TRINITY, Feb. 17, 1725-6. S. of Ralph, of Mayfield, Staffs. School, Stockport, Cheshire (Mr Dale). Readm. as Fell.-Com. Feb. 18, 1754. Matric. 1754; LL.B. 1754. P.C. of St Olave, Chester, 1771-8. Died 1778.

DOCKSEY, HOPE. Adm. pens. at EMMANUEL, Apr. 26, 1732. S. and h. of Robert, Esq., of Snelston, Derbs. Matric. 1732. Adm. at the Middle Temple, July, 1731.

DOCWRA, EDWARD. Matric. pens. from TRINITY, Easter, 1571. Probably 4th s. of Thomas, of Putteridge, Lilley, Herts. Of Hitchin, gent. Died June 18, 1610, aged 57. Buried at Hitchin. Brother of Thomas (1564). (*Clutterbuck*, I. 83.)

DOCWRAY, HENRY. Adm. Fell.-Com. at EMMANUEL, Easter, 1623. Matric. 1623. 2nd s. of Thomas (1564), late of 'Osley' (? Offley), Herts., deceased; adm. at Lincoln's Inn, Feb. 8, 1624-5. Of North Mimms. Brother of Periam (1618). (*Vis. of Herts.*, 1634.)

DOCWRA, JAMES. Matric. pens. from TRINITY, Michs. 1606. Doubtless 1st s. of Ralph, of Fulbourn, Cambs. Of Fulbourn, Esq. Brother of Thomas (1606).

DOCKWRAY, JOSIAS. Adm. sizar at CHRIST'S, Apr. 9, 1652. S. of Robert, headmaster of Giggleswick School. B. there. School, Giggleswick. Matric. 1652; B.A. 1655-6; M.A. 1665; LL.D. 1673. P.C. of Lanchester, Durham, 1663-8. V. of Newburn, Northumberland, 1668-83. Married, at Lanchester, Nov. 23, 1658, Mary, dau. of Samuel Sanderson, of Hedleyhope, Durham. Buried July 31, 1683, at Newburn. Brother of Thomas (1645). (*Peile*, I. 547; H. M. Wood.)

DOCKWRAY, PERIAM. Matric. Fell.-Com. from TRINITY, Easter, 1618. S. of Thomas (1564), of Putteridge Park, Herts. Adm. at Gray's Inn, June 18, 1621. Of Putteridge, Herts., Esq. Died 1643. (*Vis. of Herts.*, 1634; *Cussans*, I. 90.)

DOCWRAY, PERIAM. Adm. pens. (age 16) at CAIUS, June 7, 1658. S. of Thomas, gent., of Putteridge Park, Lilley, Herts. B. there. Schools, Hitchin, Hexton, Herts. and St Paul's, London. Matric. 1658; Scholar, 1658-60. Probably died young. (*Venn*, I. 402.)

DOCKWREY, STEPHEN. Adm. pens. at EMMANUEL, July 4, 1615. Matric. 1615. Ord. deacon (York) Dec. 21; priest, Dec. 22, 1622. V. of Waghen, Yorks., 1622-3. R. of Harswell, 1623-60.

DOCKRAY, STEPHEN. Adm. sizar (age 14) at SIDNEY, May 26, 1665. 3rd s. of Thomas (1645), chaplain in the Navy. B. at Newburn, Northumberland. School, Morpeth (Mr Thomas Spink). Matric. 1665; B.A. 1668-9; M.A. 1672. Ord. deacon (York) *c.* 1670. V. of Tynemouth, 1673-81. Married, at Tynemouth, Aug. 11, 1674, Jane Lawson. Died at Tynemouth, Sept. 20, 1681. Brother of Thomas (1673). (H. M. Wood.)

DOCURAYE, THOMAS. Matric. pens. from TRINITY, Michs. 1564. Doubtless 1st s. of Thomas, of Putteridge, Lilley, Herts. Adm. at Gray's Inn, 1570. Died at Putteridge, Mar. 6, 1620-1, aged 72. Buried at Lilley. Father of Henry (1623) and Periam, and brother of Edward (1571). (*Clutterbuck*, III. 83.)

DOCWRA, THOMAS. Matric. pens. from TRINITY, Michs. 1606. Doubtless 2nd s. of Ralph, of Fulbourn, Cambs. Of Cherry Hinton, Cambs., Esq. Brother of James (1606).

DOCWRA, THOMAS. Adm. pens. at TRINITY, Mar. 29, 1636. Probably s. and h. of Periam (1618); age 19 in 1643. Matric. 1636; Scholar, 1640; B.A. 1641-2. Perhaps M.P. for St Albans, 1685. (*Clutterbuck*, III. 83.)

DOCKWRAY, THOMAS. Adm. sizar (age 16) at CHRIST'S, May 19, 1645. S. of Robert, R. of Giggleswick and Head Master of the school. B. there. School, Giggleswick. Matric. 1645; B.A. 1647-8; D.D. 1667 (*Lit. Reg.*). Chaplain of the Fleet. V. of Newburn, Northumberland, 1662-3. R. of Whitburn, Durham, 1667-72. R. of Tynemouth, 1669-72. Married (2) at St John's, Newcastle, May 31, 1669, Katharine, dau. of Thomas Naylor, V. of Newcastle. Died on board the *Royal James*, May 28, 1672, in the battle with the Dutch in Southwold Bay. Admon. (P.C.C.) 1672. Brother of Josias (1652), father of Stephen (1665) and Thomas (1673). (*Peile*, I. 495; H. M. Wood.)

DOCKWRAY, THOMAS. Adm. pens. (age 16) at ST JOHN'S, Apr. 14, 1673. S. of Thomas (above), deceased, of Newburn, Northumberland. B. there. School, 'Morthale.' Matric. 1673; B.A. 1676-7; M.A. 1680. Incorp. at Oxford, 1680. Ord. priest (Durham) Sept. 20, 1679. V. of Wallsend, Northumberland. V. of Tynemouth, 1681-1725. Married, at Tynemouth, June 4, 1689, Elizabeth Love. Died at Tynemouth, Feb. 21, 1724-5. Father of Thomas (1706), brother of Stephen (1665).

DOCKWRA, THOMAS. Adm. pens. (age 15) at PETERHOUSE, July 25, 1690. Of Hertfordshire. School, Hertford. Matric. 1691; Scholar, 1691; B.A. 1696-7. Ord. deacon (Norwich) Sept. 19, 1697; priest, May 26, 1700. Preacher at Yarmouth, 1700. V. of Martham, Norfolk, till 1719. Licensed by the bishop to practise surgery, 1713. Died 1719. M.I. at Martham. (*T. A. Walker*, 188.)

DOCKWRAY, THOMAS. Adm. pens. (age 16) at ST JOHN'S, May 23, 1706. S. of Thomas (1673). B. at Tynemouth. Bapt. Apr. 1, 1690. School, Newcastle. Matric. 1706; B.A. 1709-10. M.A. 1713. Ord. deacon (Durham) Sept. 1712; priest (York) Sept. 1715. V. of Wallsend, 1718-60. Lecturer at St Nicholas, Newcastle, 1724-52. Married (1) at St Nicholas, May 8, 1729, Mary Grey; (2) at St John's, Oct. 26, 1732, Mary Maynard. Buried at St Nicholas, Newcastle, May 17, 1760. (H. M. Wood.)

DOCKWRAY, THOMAS. Adm. pens. (age 18) at ST JOHN'S, Apr. 30, 1744. S. of Josiah, fish curer, of Durham. B. at Wolviston. School, Newcastle. Matric. 1744; B.A. 1747-8; M.A. 1751; D.D. 1766. Fellow, 1749-57. Ord. deacon (Ely) May 24, 1752; priest, Mar. 18, 1753. Lecturer at St Nicholas, Newcastle, 1753-83, succeeding his uncle (above). V. of Stamfordham, Northumberland, 1761-82. Married, at Otterburn, Feb. 12, 1757, Hannah, dau. of Robert Ellison. Will (P.C.C.) 1784. (*Scott-Mayor*, III. 541.)

DOCKWRA, ——. B.Can.L. 1501. Perhaps Thomas Dockwra; proctor of the Consistorial Court. Will (P.C.C.) 1559. 'Master Thomas Dockwray, notary, proctor of the Arches died June 23, 1559'; M.I. in old St Paul's Cathedral. (H. G. Harrison.)

DOCKWRAY, ——. Adm. pens. at ST CATHARINE'S, Easter, 1644.

DOD, ANDREW. Adm. sizar at QUEENS', July 2, 1603. Of Nottinghamshire.

DOD, ANTHONY. Adm. sizar at PETERHOUSE, Mar. 13, 1631-2. Of London. Matric. 1632; Scholar, 1635; B.A. 1635-6; M.A. 1639.

DOD, BENJAMIN. Adm. sizar at QUEENS', May 21, 1622. Of Bedfordshire. Migrated to Clare, 1623; B.A. 1625-6; M.A. 1629. V. of Weekley, Northants., 1631-3. R. of Luddington-in-the-Brook, 1633. Perhaps V. of Hartford, Hunts., in 1642. Died Sept. 2, 1670, aged 65. Buried at Luddington. M.I. there. Father of Thomas (1659). (H. I. Longden.)

DOD, VI . Matric. pens. from TRINITY, Easter, 1578; B.A. 158[illegible]2. D

DOD, EDMUND or EDWARD. Adm. pens. (age 15) at CAIUS, Feb. 25, 1649-50. S. of Thomas, gent., of Whittlesford, Cambs. B. there. Schools, Felsted and Newport, Essex. Matric. 1650. Of Hinxton, Cambs Died 1677-8. Buried at Whittlesford, Mar. 12, 1677-8. (*Venn*, I. 376; *Vis. of Cambs.*, 1684.)

DODD, EDWARD. Matric. pens. from JESUS, Michs. 1579; B.A. 1582-3; M.A. 1586; B.D. 1593 Fellow, 1585-97. R. of Little Canfield, Essex, 1598. Chaplain to Sir Julius Cæsar, Master of the Rolls. Brother of St Katharine's Hospital. V. of Hinxton, Cambs., till 1626. Married, 1598, Ellen, widow of David Price, R. of Little Canfield, who presented him to the living. Buried at Hinxton, Oct. 20, 1626. Will, P.C.C. (A. Gray; J. Ch. Smith.)

DOD, EDWARD. Adm. sizar (age 17) at CAIUS, Feb. 4, 1633-4. S. of Ralph, of Shocklach, Cheshire, gent., deceased. B. at Bennington, Herts. School, Bennington. Matric. 1634; Scholar, 1635-6. Died, in College, of the plague. Buried at St Michael's, Cambridge, Sept. 30, 1636. M.I. at St Michael's. (*Venn*, I. 313.)

DODD, HUGH. Adm. at KING'S, a scholar from Eton, 1518. Expelled.

DODD, HUGH. Matric. sizar from JESUS, Easter, 1587. Of Cheshire. Died July 6, 1644, aged 67. M.I. at Bennington, Herts. (Chauncey, *Herts.*, II. 83; *Urwick*; A. Gray.)

DOD, JAMES. Matric. sizar from KING'S, Michs. 1715. B. in Cambridge. B.A. 1719-20. Ord. deacon (Peterb.) June 4, 1721; priest, May 31, 1724. C. of Easton by Stamford, Northants., 1721; of St Martin by Stamford, 1724.

DOD, JOHN. Matric. sizar from JESUS, Michs. 1572 S. of John, of Shotlidge (? Shocklach), Cheshire. B. there, 1555. School, Westchester. B.A. 1575-6; M.A. 1579. Fellow, 1578-85. Ord. deacon (London) Apr. 16, 1579; priest (Ely) Apr. 15, 1580. University preacher, 1585. Incorp. at Oxford, 1585. R. of Hanwell, Oxon., 1585; suspended for puritanism, 1604. Preached at Fenny Compton, Warws., and Canons Ashby, Northants. V. of Fawsley, Northants., *c.* 1637-45. Also V. of Geddington. Author, *Sermons*, etc. Buried at Fawsley, Aug. 19, 1645. Father of Timothy (1612). (Baker, *Northants.*, I. 388; *D.N.B.*; T. P. Dorman.)

DODD, JOHN. Matric. sizar from QUEENS', Easter, 1575. Of Cheshire. B.A. 1577-8; M.A. 1582. Ord. priest (Chester) May 23, 1584. V. of Melchbourne, Beds., 1586-1624. Perhaps also R. of Drayton, Leics., 1592. Buried July 31, 1624. Will proved by widow Anne. Father of Paul (1607). (W. M. Noble; H. I. Longden.)

DODD, JOHN. Described as 'late of EMMANUEL College' when ord. deacon (London) Dec. 21, 1592, age 24. (Not in the College register.) B. in London. C. of Stepney. Perhaps V. of Coggeshall, Essex, 1609-39. Buried there Apr. 18, 1639. (G. F. Beaumont, *Coggeshall*.)

DOD, JOHN. Adm. pens. at JESUS, 1598-9. S. of Peter, of 'Shotlidge' (? Shocklach), Cheshire. B.A. 1602; M.A. 1606. Fellow, 1603-31. Junior proctor, 1614-5. V. of St Clement's, Cambridge, 1622-7. Buried in the College Chapel, May 17, 1632. Will proved (V.C.C.) 1632. Brother of Thomas (1592). (A. Gray.)

DOD, JOHN. Adm. sizar at EMMANUEL, June 23, 1608. Of Oxfordshire. Matric. 1608; Scholar; B.A. 1611-2; M.A. 1615; B.D. 1622. Fellow, 1616-26. R. of North Cadbury, Somerset, 1626-43. Died 1643. Father of John (1654).

DODD, JOHN. Matric. pens. from CHRIST'S, July, 1609; B.A. 1612-3; M.A. 1616. (*Peile*, I. 273, whose account seems erroneous.)

DOD, JOHN. Adm. Fell.-Com. at JESUS, June 29, 1627. Perhaps s. of Thomas (1592), former fellow, dean of Ripon. Matric. 1627. Buried in the College Chapel, Jan. 14, 1629-30. (A. Gray.)

DODD, JOHN. Adm. pens. at ST CATHARINE'S, May 3, 1644. S. of Nehemiah (1613), of Coggeshall, clerk, and his wife Elizabeth. Bapt. Dec. 4, 1625. School, Westminster. Migrated to St John's, Oct. 17, 1645. B.A 1647-8. Incorp. at Oxford, 1648-9; M.A. (Oxford) 1649. Fellow of Corpus Christi College, Oxford, 1648. (*Al. Oxon.*)

DOD, JOHN. Adm. sizar (age 17) at SIDNEY, Sept. 10, 1646. S. of Paul (1607), clerk. B. at Riseley, Beds. Bapt. Mar. 12, 1628-9. School, Wymington, Beds. (Mr Anderson). Matric. 1647; B.A. 1650-1; M.A. 1654. One of these names (M.A.), ord. deacon (Lincoln) Mar. 12, 1661-2. Possibly R. of Belchford, Lincs., 1662.

DOD, JOHN. Matric. sizar from KING'S, Easter, 1651; B.A. 1654-5; M.A. 1660. See *Al. Oxon.* for a contemporary.

DOD, JOHN. Adm. pens. at EMMANUEL, Feb. 2, 1654-5. Of Somerset. S. of John (1608).

DOD, JOHN. Adm. sizar (age 15) at TRINITY, Apr. 21, 1692. S. of John. B. at Combroke, Warws. School, Combroke (Mr John Fancourt). Matric. 1693; Scholar, 1695; B.A. 1695-6. C. of Wilmslow, Cheshire, 1719. Buried there Apr. 28, 1729. (Earwaker, *E. Cheshire*, II. 85.)

DODD, JOHN. Matric. from KING'S, Michs. 1735. Fell.-Com.; perhaps colleger at Eton. Intimate friend of H. Walpole. M.P. for Reading, 1740, 1755, 1761, 1768, 1774, 1780. Colonel, Berks. militia. Died, at Swallowfield, Berks., Feb. 10, 1782. (G. *Mag.*; *Add. MSS.*, 5867, 63.)

DOD, JONAS. Adm. sizar (age 16) at MAGDALENE, Sept. 28, 1730. S. of Edward. School, Shrewsbury. Matric. 1731.

DOD, NATHANIEL. Adm. sizar at JESUS, 1617. S. of Ralph (1583), of Wiggenhall St Mary Magdalen, Norfolk. School, Lynn. Matric. 1617. Migrated to Caius, Aug. 1, 1618, age 18. Scholar, 1618-24; B.A. 1620-1; M.A. 1624; B.D. 1631. Fellow of Caius, 1625-37. C. of Bennington, Herts., 1629-36. V. 1636-82. Died 1682. M.I. at Bennington. Father of the next. (*Venn*, I. 240.)

DOD, NATHANIEL. Adm. pens. (age 17) at CAIUS, May 6, 1660. S. of Nathaniel (above). B. at Bennington. School, Bishop's Stortford. Scholar, 1660-1; Matric. 1660. (*Venn*, I. 408.)

DODD, NEHEMIAH. Matric. sizar from CLARE, Easter, 1613. S. of John, clerk. B. in St Mary Aldermary, London. Bapt. there, Apr. 11, 1596. School, Merchant Taylors'. B.A. 1616-7; M.A. 1620. Ord. deacon (London) May 31, 1618, age 23; C. of Coggeshall, Essex; priest, June 18, 1623. Minister of Knightsbridge Chapel, Westminster, 1640-47. Perhaps R. of St Alphage, Cripplegate, 1643. R. of Doddinghurst, Essex, 1647-52. Died 1652. Father of John (1644).

DOD, PAUL. Matric. sizar from QUEENS', Easter, 1607. Of Bedfordshire. S. of John (1575), V. of Melchbourne. B.A. 1609-10; M.A. 1613. Ord. deacon (Peterb.) Oct. 31; priest, Dec. 19, 1613. V. of Riseley, Beds., *c.* 1622-38. Married, at Luton, June 8, 1620, Susan Spurling. Will (P.C.C.) 1647. Father of John (1646).

DOD, PETER. Adm. sizar at EMMANUEL, *c.* 1626. Matric. 1626.

DODD, PHILIP. Matric. sizar from CHRIST'S, *c.* 1592.

DODD, RALPH. Matric. pens. from JESUS, Michs. 1583; B.A. 1585-6; M.A. 1589. Ord. priest (Norwich) July 2, 1593. V. of Wiggenhall St Mary Magdalene, Norfolk, 1597; there in 1618. V. of Snettisham, 1597-8. Father of Nathaniel (1617).

DOD, RALPH. Matric. sizar from QUEENS', Easter, 1604; B.A. 1606-7.

DOD, RICHARD. Adm. sizar (age 18) at ST JOHN'S, June 21, 1721. S. of Theophilus, innkeeper, of Salop. B. at Shrewsbury. School, Shrewsbury. Matric. 1721; B.A. 1725-6. Ord. deacon (Hereford) Sept. 11, 1726; priest (Rochester) Sept. 19, 1731.

DODD, RICHARD. Adm. sizar (age 19) at PETERHOUSE, Oct. 21, 1732. Of Cambridgeshire. School, King's College, Cambridge. Matric. 1732; Scholar, 1732.

DOD, ROBERT. Adm. sizar at ST JOHN'S, as 'Thomas,' 'July 2,' 1722. S. of Thomas, cook of the College. B. at Witzer. School, King's College. Matric. 1723; B.A. 1725-6. Master of Kelvedon School, Essex, 1734.

DOD, ROBERT. Adm. pens. (age 19) at ST JOHN'S, May 13, 1746. S. of J., of Ireland. School, Wem, Salop. Matric. 1746. Ord. deacon (Norwich) Sept. 1745; priest (London) June, 17, 1753.

DODD, ROGER. Matric. pens. from PEMBROKE, Michs. 1575; B.A. 1578-9; M.A. 1582; B.D. 1589; D.D. 1594. Fellow, 1581. V. of Isleham, Cambs., 1587. R. of Scartho, Lincs., 1595. Archdeacon of Salop, 1598-1606. R. of Gt Parndon, Essex, 1603-4. V. of Epping, 1603-4. Bishop of Meath, 1605. Wife, Margaret, buried at Epping, Aug. 31, 1604. Died July 27, 1608. (*Cooper*, II. 494.)

DOD, SAMUEL. Adm. pens. at QUEENS', Apr. 11, 1660. Of London. Migrated to Clare, Mar. 29, 1661. B.A. 1663–4; M.A. 1667. Fellow of Clare, 1664. Ord. deacon and priest (Peterb.) Sept. 20, 1668. V. of Chigwell, Essex, 1672–90; ejected as non-juror. Will (P.C.C.) 1694. Father of Samuel (1697).

DOD, SAMUEL. Adm. pens. (age 15) at SIDNEY, Sept. 11, 1691. 1st s. of John, R. of Lighthorne, Warwa. School, 'Swakelight' (Mr Mayo). Matric. 1692. One of these names barrister, serjeant-at-law, knighted Oct. 11, 1714.

DOD, SAMUEL. Adm. sizar at CLARE, July 9, 1697. S. of Samuel (1660), of Chigwell, Herts. (Essex). Matric. 1698; B.A. 1701–2; M.A. 1705. Fellow, 1707–14. Ord. deacon (Peterb.) Feb. 4, 1704–5. Lecturer at St Catherine Coleman, London, 1713.

DODD, THOMAS. Matric. pens. from TRINITY, Lent, 1577–8. Scholar from Westminster, 1578. B.A. 1581–2; M.A. 1585. Ord. deacon and priest (Lincoln) Dec. 16, 1586. R. of Eastwell, Leics., 1586. One of these names signs as minister of Studham, Beds., 1603–9.

DODD, THOMAS. Matric. sizar from JESUS, *c.* 1592. S. of Peter, of Shocklach, Cheshire; nephew of John (1572). Bapt. Dec. 4, 1576. B.A. 1595–6; M.A. 1599; B.D. 1626. Fellow, 1597–1603. Incorp. at Oxford, 1600. R. of Eastwell, Leics., 1606–15. R. of Astbury, Cheshire, 1607–26. Preb. of Chester, 1607–13. Archdeacon of Richmond, 1607–47. Preh. of Lichfield, 1619. Chaplain to the King. R. of Malpas, 1623. Dean of Ripon, 1635. Buried at Malpas, Feb. 10, 1647–8. Broth of John (1598–9), perhaps father of John (1627). (A. Gray.)

DOD, THOMAS. Adm. sizar (age 16) at SIDNEY, May 4, 1659. S. of Benjamin (1622), of Luddington, Northants. Schools, Peterborough (Mr Francis Standish), Bulwick (Mr William Hicks) and Northampton (Mr Wilham Taylour). Matrie. 1659; B.A. 1662–3; M.A. 1666. Incorp. at Oxford, 1669. R. of Denton, Hunts., 1667–82. Died 1682. Father of Thomas (1693).

DOD, THOMAS. Adm. pens. (age 18) at PETERHOUSE, Apr. 20, 1669. Of Hertford. School, Hertford. Matric. 1669; Scholar, 1669. B.A. 1672–3; M.A. 1676. Fellow, 1675–7. Ord. deacon (Norwich) May, 1675. Died 1677.

DOD, THOMAS. Adm. sizar (age 20) at PEMBROKE, Mar. 30, 1693. S. of Thomas (1659), R. of Denton, Hunts. School, Oundle. Matrie. 1693; B.A. 1696–7; M.A. 1700. Ord. deacon (Lincoln) Mar. 20, 1697–8; priest, June 4, 1699. R. of Conington, Hunts., 1699–1754. Died Apr. 6, 1754. (*G. Mag.*)

DOD, THOMAS. Adm. sizar (age 18) at PEMAROKE, July 10, 1713. S. of Thomas, of Cambridge, gent. B. at Whittlesford, Cambs. Matric. 1713–4; B.A. 1717–8; M.A. 1721. Ord. deacon (Ely) June 4, 1721. R. of Billockby, Norfolk, 1730–75. V. of Upton, 1752–75. Buried at Billockly Mar. 19, 1775.

DOD, THOMAS (1722). Mistake for Robert, whom *see*.

DOD, TIMOTHY. Adm. pens. at EMMANUEL, June 6, 1612. S. of John (1572), V. of Fawsley, Northants. Matrie. 1612; Scholar; B.A. 1615–6; M.A. 1619. One of these names adm. at Leyden, June 3, 1620. 'Ordained' at Daventry, Northants. Lecturer there; ejected, 1662. Married, before 1655, Jane, widow of Richard Combes, of Daventry. Died Dec. 12, 1665. Buried at Everdon. M.I. Admon. (Archd. Northants.) 1666. (*Calamy*, II. 218; Le Neve, *Mon.*, III. 63; *D.N.B.*; H. I. Longden.)

DODD, WILLIAM. Matric. sizar from PEMBROKE, c. 1595. Of Cheshire. B.A. from St John's, 1598–9; M.A. 1602. Fellow of St John's, 1602. *Supp.* for Incorp. at Oxford, 1602.

DOD, WILLIAM. Adm. pens. at TRINITY, Apr. 17, 1657. Matric. 1659; B.A. 1660–1.

DOD, WILLIAM. Adm. pens. at QUEENS', Jan. 29, 1666–7. Of Cambridgeshire. Matrie. 1667; B.A. 1670–1.

DOD, WILLIAM. Adm. pens. (age 18) at ST JOHN'S, Mar. 22, 1704–5. S. of William, clerk. B. at Malpas, Cheshire. School, Madeley, Staffs. Matric. 1705. Sheriff of Cheshire, 1735. Of Edge, Cheshire, Esq. Buried at Malpas, Jan. 16, 1739.

DOD, WILLIAM. Adm. scholar at TRINITY HALL, Jan. 4, 1721–2. Of Cambridgeshire. Matrie. 1720; B.A. 1723–4. Ord. deacon (Lincoln) May 31, 1724; priest, Sept. 24, 1727. V. of Bourne, Lincs., 1727. Died Aug. 7, 1756. Father of William (1745).

DODD, WILLIAM. M.A. from KING'S, 1725. S. of Henry, of Cricket, Somerset, clerk. Matrie. from Wadham College, Oxford, Nov. 26, 1711 (age 17); B.A. (Oxford) 1715. R. of Charlton Mackrell, Somerset, 1718. V. of Northover, 1731. Preb. of Wells, 1735–60. Died Mar. 18, 1760. (*Al. Oxon.*)

DODD, WILLIAM. Adm. sizar at CLARE, Oct. 2, 1745. S. of William (1721–2), V. of Bourne, Lincs. B. there, May 29, 1729. Matric. 1746; B.A. 1749–50; M.A. 1759; LL.D. 1766. Ord. deacon (Ely) Oct. 18, 1751; priest (London) June 17, 1753. Lecturer at West Ham, and elsewhere in London. Chaplain at the Magdalen House, 1758. Chaplain to the King, 1763–74. Preh. of Brecon, 1763. R. of Hockliffe, Beds., with Chalgrave, 1772. V. of Wing, Bucks., 1775–7. A popular preacher in London. For forging a bond on his patron Lord Chesterfield, he was convicted and hanged at Tyburn, June 27, 1777. Author, *Beauties of Shakespeare*, and of many sermons and other religious works. Dr Johnson keenly interested himself in attempting to secure his reprieve. (*D.N.B.*)

DODD, ——. B.A. 1469–70.

DOD, ——. Matric. sizar from QUEENS', Michs. 1606.

DODD, ——. Adm. pens. at EMMANUEL, 1614.

DODING or DODYNG, BENEDICT. Adm. at KING'S, a scholar from Eton, 1467; B.A. 1470–1; M.A. (? 1474). Fellow. Ord. sub-deacon (Lincoln) Mar. 9, 1475–6; deacon, Mar. 29, 1476; priest (Ely) Apr. 13, 1476. V. of Witham, Lincs.

DODDYNG, EDWARD. Matrie. pens. from TRINITY, Michs. 1558. B. in Westmorland. Scholar, 1560; B.A. 1562–3; M.A. 1566; Lic.Med. 1573; M.D. 1576. Fellow, 1563. F.R.C.P. 1584. Practised for a time at Bristol. Buried at St Dunstan-in-the-West, Apr. 11, 1592. (*Munk*, I. 86.)

DODDING, GEORGE. Adm. Fell.-Com. at EMMANUEL, July 4, 1623. S. and h. of Miles, of Conishead, Lanes., Esq. Matric. 1623. Adm. at Gray's Inn, Aug. 15, 1628. Of Conishead, Esq. Married Sarah, dau. of Rowland Backhouse. Died *c.* 1651. Father of Miles (1659). (*Vis. of Lancs.*, 1664.)

DODDYNG, MILES. Matric. pens from ST JOHN'S, Lent, 1557–8. Of Conishead, Lancs. Died 1588. (*Vis. of Lancs.*, 1664.)

DODDING, MILES. Adm. Fell.-Com. (age 17) at ST JOHN'S, May 23, 1659. S. of George (1623), Esq., deceased, of Conishead, near Ulverstone, Lancs. B. there. School, Urswick, Lancs. Matric. 1659. J.P. for Lancashire. Of Conishead, Esq. Married Margaret, dau. of Roger Kirkby, of Kirkby, Lancs. Will (Archd. Richmond) 1683. (*Vis. of Lancs.*, 1664.)

DODDS, GREGORY. B.D. 1535. Prior of the Dominicans, Cambridge, till the surrender. Banished about 1546. V. of Tannington, Suffolk, 1539–55. R. of Tattingstone, 1539–55. Preb. of Lincoln, 1547–55. R. of Smarden, Kent, 1551–6. Dean of Exeter, 1560. Died 1570. (*Cooper*, I. 291.)

DODENHO, GEOFFREY DE. Scholar at KING'S HALL, 1350. Died Aug. 13, 1361. Probably a victim of the Black Death.

DODGE, RALPH. Matric. pens. from KING'S; Michs. 1583. Of Cheshire. B.A. from St Catharine's, 1585–6; M.A. from Queens', 1589. Ord. priest (Norwich) Apr. 7, 1590. R. of Mannington, Norfolk, 1589. R. of Marsham, 1590–1610.

DODGSON, *see* **DODSON.**

DODGWORTH, MATTHEW (1565), *see* **DODSWORTH.**

DODINGTON, BARTHOLOMEW. Matrie. pens. from ST JOHN'S, Michs. 1547. B. in Middlesex. Scholar; B.A. 1551–2; M.A. 1555. Fellow, 1552. Fellow of Trinity, 1560. Senior Proctor, 1559–60. Regius Professor of Greek, 1562–85. Died Aug. 22, 1595. Buried in Westminster Abbey. (*Cooper*, II. 184; *D.N.B.*)

DODINGTON, RICHARD. Matrie. pens. from TRINITY, Easter, 1573.

DODINGTON or DUDINGTON, ROBERT. A friar. B.D. 1508–9; D.D. 1514.

DODINGTON, ROBERT. Matric. sizar from PEMBROKE, Lent, 1577–8, as 'Dorington'; B.A. 1581–2; M.A. from Corpus Christi, 1585.

DODINGTON, SIMON DE. B.Can.L. Fellow of PEMBROKE, in 1367. (*Loder*, 212.)

DODINGTON, WILLIAM. Matrie. pens. from ST JOHN'S, Easter, 1545. One of the original fellows of Trinity, 1546. B.A. from Trinity, 1547–8. Practised as a solicitor and held an office in the Court of Exchequer. Died 1600. (*Cooper*, II. 164.)

DODINGTON, WILLIAM. Adm. pens. (age 18) at ST JOHN'S, July 10, 1668. S. of Christopher, Esq., of Middlesex. B. there. Matric. 1669.

DODDINGTON, ——. Fee for M.A. or higher degree, 1478–9.

DODKIN, THOMAS. Matric. sizar from CORPUS CHRISTI, Easter, 1577; B.A. 1582–3. V. of Studham, Beds., 1591.

DODSLEY, ALVERY. Adm. pens. at JESUS, Apr. 27, 1728. S. of Robert, of Mansfield, Notts. Matrie. 1728; Scholar, 1729; M.B. 1734. Adm. student at Leyden, Dec. 19, 1731. Practised medicine at Nottingham. Recorder of Nottingham. Died Apr. 19, 1765. (A. Gray.)

DODSLEY, GERVASE. Matric. sizar from Queens', Easter, 1657. Of Nottinghamshire. B.A. 1660–1; M.A. 1678. V. of Laxton, Notts., 1663–75. R. of Bilborough with Strelley, 1674.

DODSON, *see also* **DOBSON.**

DODSON, BERRY. Adm. sizar (age 18) at Christ's, May 30, 1741. B. at Swavesey, Cambs. School, St Neots. Matric. 1741; B.A. 1744–5. Ord. deacon (Lincoln, *Litt. dim.* from Ely) June 9, 1745; priest (Norwich) May, 1746. R. of Thelveton, Norfolk, 1750–74. P.C. of Metfield, Suffolk, Mar. 6, 1764. (*Peile*, II. 242.)

DODGSON, CHARLES. Adm. sizar (age 18) at St John's, June 3, 1741. S. of Christopher (1707), clerk, of Yorkshire. B. at Howden. School, Sherburn. Matric. 1742; B.A. 1746–7; M.A. 1758. Ord. deacon (Hereford, for Norwich) Mar. 15, 1746–7; priest (Hereford) Dec. 25, 1749. Kept a school at Stanwix, Cumberland. R. of Kirby Wiske, Yorks., 1755–62. R. of Elsden, Northumberland, 1761–5. Chaplain to the Duke of Northumberland, when Lord Lieutenant of Ireland. F.R.S. 1762. Bishop of Ossory, 1765; and of Elphin, 1775–95. Died in Dublin, Jan. 21, 1795. Will, Dublin. (*Scott-Mayor*, III. 519.)

DODSON or DOBSON, CHRISTOPHER (1602), *see* **DOBSON.**

DODSON, CHRISTOPHER. Matric. sizar from Trinity, Easter, 1628; B.A. from Trinity, 1631; M.A. 1635.

DODGSON, CHRISTOPHER. Adm. sizar (age 18) at St John's, May 26, 1707. S. of Christopher, husbandman. B. at Paythorn, Settle, Yorks. School, Bolton (private). Matric. 1707; B.A. 1710–1. Ord. deacon (London) Feb. 25, 1710–1; priest, Sept. 25, 1715. V. of Gargrave, Yorks., 1717–37. Buried there, June 1, 1737. Father of Charles (above).

DODGSON, CHRISTOPHER. Adm. sizar at St John's, May 19, 1716. S. of Robert, husbandman, of Yorkshire. B. at Gisburn. School, Threshfield. Matric. 1716; B.A. 1719–20. Ord. deacon (York) Feb. 25, 1719–20; priest, June 4, 1721. One of these names V. of Airmin, Yorks., in 1750. Possibly of Hurstpierpoint, Sussex, clerk. Will (P.C.C.) 1784.

DODSON, CHRISTOPHER. Adm. pens. at Clare, May 28, 1724. B. in London. Matric. 1724. Colleger at Eton, 1719–23.

DODSON, EDWARD. Adm. pens. (age 16) at Christ's, May 16, 1629. S. of John. B. at Sandiacre, Derbs. School, Addley (? Adderley, Salop). Matric. 1629. Migrated to King's. B.A. from King's, 1632–3. (*Peile*, I. 400.)

DODSON or DOBSON, GERVASE. Adm. at Corpus Christi, 1602; B.A. 1602–3; M.A. 1606. Ord. deacon (Peterb.) June 2; priest, July 25, 1616. Perhaps Master of Wycombe Grammar School, Bucks., till 1646. One of these names V. of Attenborough, Notts., 1625.

DODGSON, JAMES. Adm. sizar (age 19) at Christ's, May 26, 1710. S. of Edmund, of Casterton, Westmorland. B. in Lancashire. School, Kirkby Lonsdale. Scholar, 1710–1; Matric. 1711; B.A. 1713–4; M.A. 1717. Fellow, 1714 (election invalid). Ord. deacon (Ely) 1713; priest (Norwich) Dec. 1714. Chaplain to Earl Stanhope. V. of St Ives, Hunts., 1717–35. R. of Yelling, 1722–35. Died Oct. 1735. (*Peile*, II. 174.)

DODSON, JEREMIAH. Adm. pens. at Clare, May 22, 1689. Of London. Matric. 1689; B.A. 1692–3; M.A. 1696. Ord. deacon (London) Sept. 19, 1697; priest, June 19, 1698.

DODSON, JEROME or JEREMY. Adm. sizar (age 22) at Sidney, Jan. 1, 1647–8. S. of Gervase (? 1602), clerk, of Minting, Lincs. School, Repton. Probably R. of St Catherine Coleman, London, 1665–92. Died 1692. Will (P.C.C.) 1695; as Jeremiah.

DODGSON, JOHN. M.A. 1534–5.

DODGSON, JOHN. Matric. sizar from Christ's, July, 1614; B.A. 1617–8; M.A. 1621.

DODSON or DOBSON, JOHN. Adm. sizar (age 17) at St John's, Sept. 16, 1640. S. of Robert, of Cammeringham, Lincs. B. there. School, Saxby, Lincs. (private).

DODSON, JOHN. Adm. sizar at Trinity, Apr. 12, 1672. Matric. 1672; B.A. 1673–4. V. of Gt Stukeley, Hunts., 1675–90. Died 1690.

DODGSON, JOHN. Adm. Fell.-Com. at Christ's, May 16, 1728. Matric. 1728; M.A. 1728 (*Lit. Reg.*).

DODSON, MILES. Matric. pens. from Clare, Lent, 1607–8. S. and h. of Richard, of Kirkby Overblow, Yorks. Adm. at Gray's Inn, Nov. 1608. Died Sept. 19, 1657. Will (P.C.C.) 1658; of Kirkby Overblow, Esq. Father of Peter (1636). (J. Ch. Smith.)

DODSON, MILES. Adm. pens. (age 16) at Peterhouse, June 2, 1646. Of London. School, St Saviour's. Scholar, 1647; Matric. 1649; B.A. 1649–50.

DODSON, NATHANIEL. Adm. sizar at Emmanuel, 1628. Matric. 1628, as 'Matthew'; B.A. 1631–2; M.A. 1635.

DODSON, PETER. Adm. pens. (age 16) at Sidney, Apr. 29, 1636. S. of Miles (1607–8), Esq., of Kirkby Overblow, Yorks. B. at Leathley, Yorks. School, Ripon. Matric. 1636. Adm. at Gray's Inn, Aug. 13, 1638. Died before his father. (*F.M.G.*; M. H. Peacock.)

DODSON, RICHARD. Matric. pens. from St John's, Michs. 1581; B.A. from Peterhouse, 1583–4; M.A. 1587. Ord. priest (Peterb.) Dec. 12, 1585. Doubtless R. of Kirkby Overblow, Yorks., 1589–1613. Died 1613. Will (York) Jan. 1612–3.

DODGSON, SAMUEL. Adm. sizar (age 19) at Christ's, Mar. 8, 1725–6. S. of John. B. at York. School, Leeds. Matric. 1726; Scholar, 1729; B.A. 1729–30; M.A. 1734. Incorp. at Oxford, 1734. Ord. deacon (York) July, 1731; priest, Aug. 1733. V. of Headingley, 1732–51. V. of Calverley, Yorks., Apr. 5, 1742–7. (*Peile*, II. 211.)

DODSON, THOMAS. Adm. at King's, a scholar from Eton, 1520; B.A. 1524–5. Died fellow of the College.

DODSON, THOMAS. Adm. sizar at Queens', Easter, 1585. (Perhaps adm. at Peterhouse, 1584.) Of Lancashire. B.A. 1586–7; M.A. 1590. R. of Goodmanham, Yorks., 1592–1612. Author, *Sermon*. Admon. (York) 1612. Brother of Richard (1581). (*Cooper*, III. 15.)

DODSON, THOMAS. Adm. sizar at Christ's, June 30, 1623. S. of Edward. B. at Cambridge. School, Perse. Matric. 1623; B.A. 1626–7; M.A. 1630. Probably C. of Fen Drayton, Cambs., 1638–40. Leased the rectory of Hapton, Norfolk, 1642–56. Resided and served the cure there. Probably died about 1656. (*Peile*, I. 353.)

DODSON, THOMAS. Adm. pens. at Trinity, May 13, 1658; afterwards Fell.-Com. 1658. One of these names M.P. for Liskeard, 1701–7; died Sept. 11, 1707. Or he may be a s. of Peter (1636), of Kirkby Overblow, gent. Will Feb. 7, 1706–7.

DODSWORTH, ANTHONY. Adm. pens. (age 16) at Christ's, Apr. 22, 1654. S. of Anthony, of Stranton, near Hartlepool, Durham. B. there. Bapt. there, Oct. 11, 1638. School, Cheeseburn Grange, near Newcastle. Matric. Fell.-Com. 1656. Adm. at Gray's Inn, June 28, 1656. Married, at St Nicholas, Newcastle, Apr. 15, 1662, Elizabeth, dau. of Henry Maddison, merchant. Mayor of Hartlepool, 1672. Living in St Oswald's parish, Durham, 1684. Buried there, Nov. 13, 1685. (Surtees' *Durham*, III. 123; *Vis. of Durham*, 1666; *Peile*, I. 562; H. M. Wood.)

DODSWORTH, ANTHONY. Adm. sizar (age 16) at Christ's, Apr. 12, 1665. S. of John. B. at Dunsforth, Yorks. School, Ripon. Matric. 1665.

DODSWORTH, CHRISTOPHER. Adm. pens. at Sidney, May 18, 1618. Probably s. of John, of Well, Yorks. B. in Yorkshire. Matric. 1618; B.A. 1621–2; M.A. 1625. Master of Well Hospital. Buried there July 20, 1650. Brother of John (1612). (M. H. Peacock.)

DODSWORTH, EDWARD. Matric. pens. from St John's, Easter, 1615. S. of Matthew (1565). Bapt. at Holy Trinity, Goodramgate, York, Feb. 3, 1595–6. B.A. 1618–9; M.A. 1622. Ord. deacon (York) Sept. 1622; priest, Dec. 1625. R. of Badsworth, Yorks., 1625–55. Married Isabel, dau. of Thomas Wood, R. of Badsworth. Father of Matthew (1671). (*F.M.G.* 419; *Vis. of Yorks.*, 1666.)

DODSWORTH, FRANCIS. Matric. pens. from Jesus, Michs. 1571. 3rd s. of John, gent, of Thornton Watlass, Yorks. School, Newburgh. Migrated to Caius, July 15, 1573, age 18. Adm. at Gray's Inn, from Staple's Inn, 1575. Died *s.p.* Admon. (P.C.C.) 1577; granted to his father. (*Venn*, I. 73; *Vis. of Yorks.*, 1585.)

DODSWORTH, FRANCIS. Adm. at King's, a scholar from Eton, 1714. B. in London, 1698. Matric. 1715; B.A. 1718–9; M.A. 1722. Fellow, 1718. Ord. deacon (Ely) Mar. 10, 1722–3; priest (Lincoln) Sept. 22, 1723. Died in College, Dec. 3, 1726. (*Harwood.*)

DODSWORTH, FRANCIS. Adm. pens. (age 17) at St John's, June 1, 1748. S. of John Henry (1712). B. at Thornton Watlass, Yorks. Bapt. there, June 6, 1731. Schools, Beverley and Sedbergh. Matric. 1748; B.A. 1752; M.A. 1755. Ord. priest (York) Sept. 21, 1755. Preb. of York, 1755–1806. V. of Silkstone, Yorks., 1756–7. R. of Hollingbourne, Kent, 1757–74. V. of Minster, 1757–88. Treasurer of Salisbury, 1760–1806. V. of Dodington, Kent, 1773–1806. Died Oct. 18, 1806. Buried at Dodington. (*Scott-Mayor*, III. 578; M. H. Peacock.)

DODSWORTH, GEORGE. Adm. sizar (age 19) at Trinity, May 5, 1739. S. of Thomas, of Scarborough, Yorks. School, Beverley (Mr Clark). Matric. 1739; Scholar, 1742; B.A. 1742–3. Ord. deacon (Lincoln) Dec. 19, 1742; priest (York) May 20, 1744. R. of Cowlam, Yorks., 1757–64. V. (or C.) of Scalby. Married, at St Mary's, Scarborough, Dec. 30, 1749, Dorothy Bell. Died at Scarborough, Aug. 1, 1791. Will, P.C.C. (*G. Mag.*; H. G. Harrison.)

DODSWORTH, JOHN. Matric. pens. from Christ's, *c.* 1590–1.

DODSWORTH, JOHN. Adm. pens. at SIDNEY, Jan. 23, 1612-3. Probably s. and h. of John, of Thornton Watlass, Yorks., Esq. Bapt. there, Mar. 4, 1595-6. Matric. 1613. Adm. at Gray's Inn, Mar. 24, 1623-4. Of Thornton Watlass, Esq.; age 70 in 1665. Married, at Richmond, Yorks., Frances, dau. of Sir Timothy Hutton, of Marsk. Buried at Thornton, June 20, 1670. Father of the next, and of Timothy (1637). (*Vis. of Yorks.*, 1665.)

DODSWORTH, JOHN. Adm. pens. (age 16) at SIDNEY, May 8, 1635. S. of John (above). B. at Thornton Watlass, Yorks. Bapt. there, June 15, 1617. Schools, Barton (Mr Taylor) and Osmotherly (Mr Walker), Lancs. Matric. 1635. Adm. at Gray's Inn, May 19, 1637. Married Frances, dau. of Sir John Lowther, of Lowther, Westmorland. Died in his father's lifetime. Buried at Thornton Watlass, Jan. 29, 1661-2. Will (York) 1661-2. Brother of Timothy (1637). (*Vis. of Yorks.*)

DODSWORTH, JOHN. Adm. Fell.-Com. (age 14) at CHRIST'S, Feb. 10, 1664-5. Elder s. of John (above). B. at Thornton Watlass, Yorks. School, Bedale. Matric. 1665. Buried at Thornton Watlass, May 3, 1673. Will, York. Father of John Henry. (*Vis. of Yorks.*, 1665; *Peile*, I. 615; *F.M.G.*)

DODSWORTH, JOHN. Adm. pens. (age 16) at ST JOHN'S, June 10, 1672. S. of George, yeoman, of Aysgarth, Yorks. B. there. School, Sedbergh. Matric. 1672; B.A. 1675-6. Ord. deacon (York) June, 1680.

DODSWORTH, JOHN. Adm. scholar at TRINITY HALL, Jan. 7, 1737-8. Of Thornton Watlass, Yorks. S. of John Henry (1712). Bapt. Jan. 2, 1719-20. Died *v.p.*

DODSWORTH, JOHN HENRY. Adm. pens. (age 18) at TRINITY, June 18, 1712. S. of John (1664-5), of Thornton Watlass, Yorks. School, Westminster. Scholar, 1713. Will (York) 1762. Father of John (1737-8). (M. H. Peacock.)

DODSWORTH, MATTHEW. Matric. pens. from ST JOHN'S, Easter, 1565, as Dodgworth. LL.B. from Trinity Hall, 1573. S. of Simon, of Settrington, Yorks. Lived in S. Belfrey's, York. Chancellor to Toby Matthew, Archbishop of York. Died at Slingsby, *c.* 1628. Admon. (York) 1631. Father of Edward (1615). (*F.M.G.* 419; *Vis. of Yorks.*, 1666.)

DODSWORTH, MATTHEW. Adm. pens. (age 17) at ST JOHN'S, Mar. 30, 1671. S. of Edward (1615), R. of Badsworth, Yorks. B. there. Bapt. Nov. 8, 1653. School, Wakefield. Matric. 1671; B.A. 1674-5; M.A. 1678. Incorp. at Oxford, 1675. Ord. deacon (London) Feb. 20, 1675-6; priest (York) Sept. 1682. R. of Sessay, Yorks., 1690-7. Died 1697. (*J. Foster*.)

DODSWORTH, RALPH. Matric. sizar from CHRIST'S, Dec. 1618.

DODSWORTH, RALPH. Matric. sizar from ST JOHN'S, Easter, 1628.

DODSWORTH, RAMSDEN. Adm. sizar at JESUS, July 8, 1709. Of Yorkshire. Matric. 1709; Rustat Scholar; B.A. 1712-3; M.A. 1716. Fellow, 1716-42. Ord. priest (York) June, 1718. R. of Harlton, Cambs., 1722. V. of All Saints', Cambridge, 1729. R. of Trowbridge, Wilts., 1741. Chaplain to the Duke of Somerset. Died 1763. (A. Gray.)

DODSWORTH, ROBERT. Adm. sizar (age 20) at CHRIST'S, Apr. 16, 1634. S. of Roger the antiquary. B. at Preston. Schools, Preston and Westminster. Matric. 1634; B.A. 1637-8. V. of Barton-on-Humber, Lincs., 1642. R. of Burton by Lincoln, 1642. Buried at Fishlake, Yorks., Jan. 7, 1645-6. (*Vis. of Yorks.*, 1666; *Peile*, I. 431.)

DODSWORTH, ROBERT. Adm. sizar (age 17) at ST JOHN'S, June 21, 1666. S. of Rowland, deceased, of Barton, Yorks. B. there. School, Brignall. Matric. 1667; B.A. 1669-70. Ord. deacon (York) 1670-1; priest, Dec. 1674.

DODSWORTH, ROBERT. Adm. sizar (age 15) at PEMBROKE, June 28, 1673. S. of Robert, of Burton, Lincs., clerk. Matric. 1674. One of these names, of St Clement Danes, London, adm. at the Inner Temple, 1674. (*Vis. of Yorks.*, 1666.)

DODSWORTH, THOMAS. Adm. Fell.-Com. at CLARE, Feb. 18, 1664-5. Perhaps s. and h. of Robert, of Barton, Yorks. Adm. at Gray's Inn, Dec. 9, 1667. Age 19 in 1666. Died *s.p.* Sept. 28, 1680. Buried at Barton St Cuthbert's. (*Vis. of Yorks.*, 1666.)

DODSWORTH, TIMOTHY. Adm. pens. (age 15) at SIDNEY, May 6, 1637. S. of John (1612), Esq. B. at Thornton Watlass, Yorks. Bapt. there, Jan. 1, 1621-2. School, Ripon (Mr Palmes). Matric. 1637. Adm. at Gray's Inn, Jan. 23, 1639-40. Of Masham, Yorks. Servant to the Lord Deputy Wandesford in Ireland. Died before 1673. Brother of John (1635).

DODSWORTH, WILLIAM. Adm. sizar (age 17) at ST JOHN'S, Jan. 17, 1638-9. S. of Robert, maltster, of Richmond, Yorks. B. there. School, Richmond. Matric. 1639; B.A. 1642-3; M.A. 1646. One of these names licensed schoolmaster at Bassingbourne, Cambs., Oct. 1662.

DODSWORTH, WILLIAM. Adm. sizar (age 17) at TRINITY, May 9, 1726. S. of James, druggist, of York. School, York (Mr Herbert). Matric. 1726; Scholar, 1728; B.A. 1729-30; M.A. 1733. Incorp. at Oxford, 1733. Ord. deacon (Lincoln) Ju 13, 1731; priest (York) Aug. 5, 1733. V. of All Saints Pavement, York; and P.C. of St Olave's, 1733.

DODYCH or DODYKE, WILLIAM. B.A. 1511-2.

DOE, *see* DOO.

DOELL, THOMAS. Matric. pens. from GONVILLE HALL, Easter, 1544.

DOFFY, WILFRID. Adm. pens. at EMMANUEL, May 24, 1597.

DOGGE, EDWARD. B.A. from CHRIST'S, 1628.

DOGGET, *see also* DOCKET *and* DUCKET.

DOGGET, BENJAMIN. Adm. sizar (age 18) at ST JOHN'S, Jan. 27, 1654-5. S. of William, woollendraper, of Ipswich. B. there. School, Westminster (private; Mr Crouch). Matric. 1655; B.A. 1658-9; M.A. 1662. C. and schoolmaster at Stoke, Suffolk, 1662.

DOGGET, JOHN. Adm. at KING'S, a scholar from Eton, 1451. B. at Sherborne, Dorset; a nephew of Cardinal Bourchier. B.A. 1455; M.A. 1459; B.D. 1462-3; D.D. 1471-2; LL.D. (Bologna); grace for incorporation at Cambridge, 1489; D.D. (Oxford). Fellow of King's. Provost, 1499-1501. Ord. subdeacon (Ely) Dec. 22, 1459; priest, Mar. 29, 1460. Preb. of Sarum, 1474-86. Preb. of Lincoln, 1474-1501. Preb. of Southwell, 1475-89. R. of Eastbourne, Sussex, 1478. Ambassador to the pope, 1479. Treasurer of Chichester, 1479-1501. Missioner to the King of Denmark, 1480. Chancellor of Sarum, 1486-1501; and of Lichfield, 1489-1501. Died Apr. 1501. Buried in Salisbury Cathedral. Will (P.C.C.) 1501; left all his books of canon and civil law to King's College. (*Cooper*, I. 5; *D.N.B.*; H. G. Harrison; A. B. Beaven.)

DOGGET, RICHARD. Adm. pens. at EMMANUEL, Apr. 3, 1626. Perhaps s. of William, of Boxford, Suffolk, gent. B. 1608. Matric. 1626; B.A. 1629-30; M.A. 1633. (*Suff. Man. Fam.*, I. 344.)

DOGGIT, THOMAS. Matric. pens. from ST JOHN'S, Michs. 1611. One of these names s. and h. of William, late of Boxford, Suffolk, gent.; adm. at Lincoln's Inn, Mar. 26, 1614. Of Boxford, gent.; married and had issue. Probably father of the next. (*Suff. Man. Fam.*, I. 344.)

DOGGETT, WILLIAM. Matric. sizar from QUEENS', Easter, 1636. Of Suffolk. Probably s. of Thomas, above. B. at Groton, Suffolk, 1618. Bapt. there, Jan. 5, 1618-9. B.A. 1639-40; M.A. 1643.

DOGET, ——. Fee for M.A. or higher degree, 1475-6.

DOGETT, ——. B.A. 1513-4; M.A. 1522-3. Probably Thomas; will proved (V.C.C.) 1529.

DOGMANTON, ——. M.A. or higher degree, 1476-7.

DOGYN or DOGION, GEORGE. B.A. 1525-6; M.A. of Paris. Incorp. at Oxford, 1542. Preb. of Bristol, 1542. Precentor of Wells, 1543. R. of Long Langton, Dorset, 1546-9. R. of Welford, Berks., 1547. V. of Chew Magna, Somerset, 1552. Died Dec. 14, 1552. (*Al. Oxon.*)

DOILLONEUS, DANIEL (1682-3), *see* DAILLONIUS.

DOLBEN, DAVID. Matric. sizar from ST JOHN'S, Easter, 1602. S. of Robert Wynn Dolben. B. at Llanrhaiadr, Denbigh. B.A. 1605-6; M.A. 1609; D.D. 1627. Ord. deacon (London) Sept. 23; priest, Dec. 23, 1610. V. of Hackney, Middlesex, 1619-33. V. of Llangernyw, Denbigh, 1621. Preb. of St Asaph, 1625. Bishop of Bangor, 1631-3. Died Nov. 27, 1633, in London. Buried at Hackney. M.I. there. Will, P.C.C. (*D.N.B.*)

DOLBEN or DOULBEN, DAVID. Adm. sizar (age 18) at MAGDALENE, Dec. 16, 1704. S. of Hugh. B. at Llanganaval, Denbigh. School, Ruthin. Matric. 1705; B.A. 1708-9; M.A. 1712.

DOULBEN, ROBERT. B.A. 1612.

DOLBEN, THOMAS. M.A. from KING'S, 1748. S. of Thomas, V. of Wendover, Bucks. Colleger at Eton, 1707-11. Matric. from Lincoln College, Oxford, Jan. 14, 1712-3, age 18; B.A. (Oxford) 1716. V. of Stoke Poges, Bucks., 1726-54. Perhaps minor canon of Windsor. Died Sept. 5, 1754. (*Al. Oxon.*; according to *Lipscomb*, IV. 563, the father's original name was Dally.)

DOLBEN, WILLIAM. M.A. 1614. Incorp. from Oxford. S. of John, of Haverfordwest, Pembs. School, Westminster. Matric. from Christ Church, Feb. 10, 1603-4, age 16; B.A. 1607; M.A. from All Souls', 1610; B.D. 1617; D.D. 1619. R. of Stackpole Elidor, Pembs., 1616; of Lawrenny, 1620; of Llanynys, Denbigh, 1623; of Stanwick and Benefield, Northants., 1623. Preb. of Lincoln, 1629-31. Married Elizabeth, dau. of Hugh Williams, of Co. Carnarvon. Buried at Stanwick, Sept. 19, 1631. Will, P.C.C. Father of John, Archbishop of York. (*Al. Oxon.*; *D.N.B.*)

DOLBY, *see also* DALBY.

DOLBY, CHAPMAN. Adm. sizar at CLARE, Sept. 23, 1693. Of Ilston, Leics. Matric. 1697; B.A. 1697-8; M.A. 1727. Ord. deacon (Lincoln) Sept. 22, 1700; priest (Peterb.) June 3, 1705. R. of Burton Overy, Leics., 1710-42. R. of Arthingworth, Northants., 1727-42. Died May 10, 1742, aged 68. M.I. at Burton. (*Nichols*, II. 534; H. I. Longden.)

DOLITTLE, THOMAS. Adm. sizar (age 17) at PEMBROKE, June 7, 1649. S. of Anthony, of Kidderminster, Worcs., glover. Matric. 1649; B.A. 1652-3; M.A. 1656. Received presbyterian orders. R. of St Alphage, London Wall, 1653-62; ejected. Afterwards kept a school at Bunhill Fields, and elsewhere. Licensed preacher from 1689. Author. Died May 24, 1707. (*Calamy*, I. 82; *D.N.B.*)

DOELITTLE, ——. Adm. pens. at ST CATHARINE'S, 1677.

D'OLIVE or DOLLEFE, JOHN. B.A. (? 1602-3); M.A. from KING'S, 1606. Ord. deacon and priest (Peterb.) Feb. 28, 1612-3. R. of Ruckland with Worlaby, Lincs., 1614-25.

DOLLEG, JOHN. Matric. sizar from PEMBROKE, Easter, 1616; B.A. 1618-9.

DOLLIN, JOHN. Adm. at KING'S, a scholar from Eton, 1580; B.A. 1584-5; M.A. 1588. Fellow, till 1590. Conduct of the College.

DOLLYNG, ——. B.A. 1523-4.

DOLLOND, SIMON (1584), *see* DALLAND.

DOLMAN, *see also* DOWMAN.

DOLMAN or DOWLMAN, ALBAN. Matric. pens. from TRINITY, Easter, 1554; Scholar, 1554. Ord. acolyte (London) 1557-8.

DOLMAN, CHRISTOPHER. Matric. pens. from ST JOHN'S, Michs. 1564.

DOLMAN, JOHN (1488), *see* DOWMAN.

DOLMAN, JOHN. Matric. pens. from ST JOHN'S, Lent, 1577-8. S. of Thomas (1544), of Pocklington, Yorks., J.P. Probably adm. at Gray's Inn, from Staple Inn, 1580. Died Oct. 20, 1623. Brother of Robert (1575) and Peter (1581). (*Vis. of Yorks.*, 1612; Burke, *L.G.*, whose account of this family differs from that of the *Surtees Soc.* where two generations are apparently confused.)

DOLMAN, JOHN. Incorp. M.A. 1716, from New Inn Hall, Oxford. S. of Nathaniel, of Aldridge, Staffs., clerk. Matric. from New Inn Hall, Oxford, June 1, 1703, age 16; B.A. (Oxford) 1706-7; M.A. 1710. R. of Aldridge, Staffs., 1718-46. Preb. of Lichfield, 1721-4. Married Margaret, dau. of William Bendy, of Short End. Died Nov. 19, 1746. Buried at Aldridge. (H. G. Harrison.)

DOLEMAN, MARMADUKE. Matric. pens. from ST JOHN'S, Easter, 1616. One of these names s. of Marmaduke. Of Bottesford, Lincs., gent. Royalist. Estates confiscated in 1652. Buried at Bottesford, Dec. 20, 1654. (*Lincs. Pedigrees*.)

DOLMAN, PETER. Matric. pens. from ST JOHN'S, Michs. 1581. S. of Thomas (1544), of Kilpin and Pocklington, Yorks., Esq. Adm. at Gray's Inn, Feb. 10, 1584-5. Barrister, 1591. Succeeded to his father's estates. Married Elizabeth, dau. of archdeacon Richard Remington. Died Dec. 13, 1621. M.I. at Howden. Brother of John (1577-8) and Robert (1575). (*Vis. of Yorks.*, 1612, 1665; Hunter, S. *Yorks.*, II. 437; M. H. Peacock.)

DOLMAN or DOMAN, RALPH. Matric. sizar from ST JOHN'S, *c.* 1590. Doubtless s. of Robert Dolman, of Pocklington. Bapt. Jan. 7, 1570-1. V. of Everingham, Yorks., 1601-18. Buried there Dec. 26, 1618. (*Vis. of Yorks.*, 1612.)

DOLMAN, RO. Matric. pens. from ST JOHN'S, Michs. 1550.

DOLMAN, ROBERT. Matric. pens. from ST JOHN'S, Michs. 1575. S. of Thomas (1544), of Pocklington, J.P. Adm. at Gray's Inn, from Staple Inn, 1579. Knighted, 1604. Died Mar. 15, 1627-8. Brother of John (1577-8) and Peter (1581). (Burke, *L.G.*; Hunter, *S. Yorks.*, II. 437.)

DOLMAN, THOMAS. Matric. sizar from CLARE, Michs. 1544. Doubtless s. of William, of Pocklington, Yorks.; age 23 in 1546-7. J.P. 1584. Buried at Pocklington, Mar. 31, 1589. M.I. Father of Peter (1581), John (1577-8) and Robert (1575). (M. H. Peacock.)

DOLPHIN, JOHN. Adm. Fell.-Com. at TRINITY HALL, Oct. 24, 1751. Doubtless s. of Henry, of Stafford, Esq. School, Eton. High Sheriff of Staffs., 1760. Of Shenstone, Staffs. and of Eyford, Glones. (Shaw, *Staffs.*, II. 49.)

DOLSTON, *see* DALSTON *and* DALTON.

DOMELAW, JOHN. Matric. pens. from CHRIST'S, Easter, 1609. S. of John, vintner. B. in St Dunstan-in-the-East, London. B.A. 1612; M.A. from Corpus Christi, 1616; B.D. 1624; D.D. 1636. Fellow of Corpus Christi, 1617-31. Incorp. at Oxford, 1617. Ord. deacon and priest (London) Dec. 20, 1618, age 25. R. of Hambledon, Bucks., 1631-40. Will (P.C.C.) 1640.

DOMETT, PHILOBETH. Adm. sizar (age 19) at SIDNEY, Jan. 27, 1727-8. S. of John, gent. B. at 'Coust,' Dorset. School, Crewkerne, Somerset (Mr Smith). Matric. 1728; B.A. 1731-2; M.A. 1767. V. of Axminster, Devon. V. of Bovey Tracy. Admon. (P.C.C.) 1780.

DOMMETT, SAMUEL. Adm. sizar at CHRIST'S, July 4, 1682. S. of John. B. at Hawkhurst, Kent. School, Hawkhurst. Matric. 1684; B.A. 1685-6. Subscribed for deacon and priest (Bristol) 1690-1. R. of Burstock, Dorset, 1690-6. R. of Combe St Michael, Somerset, 1695-9. Died 1699. (F. S. Hockaday; *Peile*, II. 89.)

DOMINIS, MARCO ANTON DE. Incorp. from Padua, 1617. B. in the Isle of Arbe, Dalmatia, in 1566. Professor of mathematics at Padua. Bishop of Segni, Venice. Late Archbishop of Spalato. Fled to England, in 1616. Dean of Windsor and Wolverhampton, 1618-22. Master of the Savoy. V. of West Ilsley, Berks. Left England in 1622. Imprisoned by the Inquisition, and died in 1624. His body was burned as that of a relapsed heretic. Author. (*D.N.B.*; J. M. Neale, *Notes on Dalmatia*.)

DOMVILE, *see also* DUMVELL.

DOMVILE, EDWARD. Adm. pens. (age 17) at CHRIST'S, Aug. 4, 1648. S. of Richard, of Lymm, Cheshire. B. there. School, Anderton. Matric. 1648; M.B. 1654. Adm. at Gray's Inn, June 23, 1648. Died Dec. 1663. (*Peile*, I. 523.)

DOMVILL, EDWARD. Adm. pens. (age 16) at CAIUS, Mar. 30, 1665. S. of William, gent., of Lymm, Cheshire. Bapt. there, Feb. 8, 1648-9. School, Lymm. Matric. 1665. Buried Oct. 24, 1688. (*Venn*, I. 425; *Ormerod*, I. 582.)

DONATT, MATTHEW, *see* DANNETT.

DONATT, ——. Matric. pens. from ST JOHN'S, Easter, 1544.

DONELLAN, NEHEMIAH, *see* DANIEL.

DONER, CHRISTOPHER. Adm. sizar (age 22) at MAGDALENE, May 27, 1670. S. of Henry, surgeon, of Wakefield. School, Edinburgh. Matric. 1670; B.A. 1673-4; M.A. 1677. Ord. deacon (York) Sept. 21, 1673; priest, June, 1674.

DONGWORTH, RICHARD. Adm. sizar (age 19) at MAGDALENE, Sept. 28, 1722. S. of Richard, R. of Burton-Coggles, Lincs. School, Eton. Colleger, 1718-22. Matric. 1723; B.A. 1726-7; M.A. 1730. Fellow, 1728. Master of Durham Grammar School, 1732. V. of Gillingham, Durham, 1733-60. P.C. of Whitworth, 1755-60. Married Catherine, dau. of John Cosens, of Waltham Cross, Herts. Died Feb. 24, 1761. Buried in Durham Cathedral. (G. *Mag.*; H. M. Wood.)

DUNGWORTH, ——. Adm. at MAGDALENE, July 5, 1680.

DONHALT or DOWNHALL, HENRY. Matric. pens. from TRINITY, Easter, 1608. Of Northamptonshire. B.A. 1611-2; M.A. from St John's, 1615; B.D. 1622; D.D. 1660 (*Lit. Reg.*). Fellow of St Jobu's, 1614. Ord. deacon (Peterb.) June 14, 1620. R. of Toft, Cambs., 1622. V. cf St Ives, Hunts., 1631-43; sequestered. Archdeacon of Huntingdon, 1667-9. Died Dec. 1669. Will (P.C.C.) 1670.

DONMOW, *see* DUNMOW.

DONNE, *see also* DUNN.

DONNE, DANIEL. B.A. from ST JOHN'S, 1613-4; M.A. from Christ's, 1617. Ord. deacon (Peterb.) Sept. 22; priest, Sept. 23, 1616. R. of Ickburgh, Norfolk, 1626-7. V. of Besthorpe, 1630-46. R. of Caldecot, 1636. Died 1646. (*Peile*, I. 282.) Perhaps R. of St Benet, Gracechurch St, 1637-45; and s. of John (1574-5). Buried there Sept. 29, 1645. (J. Ch. Smith).

DONNE, EDWARD. Matric. pens. from ST JOHN'S, Easter, 1623. S. of Marmaduke, clerk. B. in London (Gracechurch Street, Little St Benet's). Migrated as pens. to Christ's, Oct. 18, 1624. Exhibitioner from Charterhouse. B.A. 1625-6. Ord. deacon (London) May, 1627, age 24. (*Peile*, I. 362.)

DONNE, EDWARD. Adm. pens. at QUEENS', June 28, 1682. S. and h. of Edward, of Place Court, Salop, Esq. Adm. at the Inner Temple, 1682. Father of the next.

DONNE, EDWARD. Adm. pens. at QUEENS', May 14, 1705. Of Place Court, Salop. S. of the above. Matric. 1705; LL.B. 1711; LL.D. 1722. Adm. at the Inner Temple, 1705. Preb. of Canterbury, 1734. R. of All Hallows, Lombard Street, 1738-46. Married Ann, dau. of Thomas Mulso. Died Jan. 15, 1745-6, aged 58. Buried in Canterbury Cathedral. M.I. there. (H. G. Harrison.)

DONNE, GABRIEL. Cistercian monk. Studied at TRINITY HALL. B.D. of Oxford, 1521. S. of Angel Dun, alderman, of London; whose will (P.C.C.) 1506. Of the house of Stratford Langthorne, Essex. Author of the plot to arrest Tyndale at Louvain. Returned to England, June, 1535, and was made abbot of Buckfastleigh, Devon, 1536; surrendered, 1539 and received a pension of £120 *per annum*. Preb. of St Paul's, 1541. R. of Stepney, 1544. Official of Archbishop Cranmer, 1549. Died Dec. 5, 1558. Buried in St Paul's Cathedral. Benefactor to Trinity Hall, by the foundation of a scholarship. Will (P.C.C.). (H. G. Harrison; J. Ch. Smith; *Cooper*, I. 186.)

DONNE, GEORGE. B.A. 1484-5.

DONNE, JOHN. B.A. from MAGDALENE, 1574-5. One of these names, 'M.A.', R. of St Olave, Silver St, London, 1590-2. R. of St Benet's, Gracechurch St, 1592-1636. Died 1636. Will (Cons. C. London) 1636. Probably father of Daniel (1613-4). (J. Ch. Smith.)

DONNE, JOHN. D.D. 1615 (*Lit. Reg.*; degree not recorded. Said to have been urged by the King on his visit, but refused. Afterwards enforced by mandate. *See* Cooper, *Annals*, III. 74.). Matric. from Hart Hall, Oxford, Oct. 23, 1584, age 11. S. of John, citizen of London. Created M.A. 1610. Adm. at Lincoln's Inn, 1592. After a gay life in London he was ordained *c.* 1615. Chaplain to James I. R. of Keyston, Hunts., 1616. R. of Sevenoaks, 1616-31. Preacher of Lincoln's Inn, 1616-22. Dean of St Paul's, 1621-31. R. of Blunham, Beds., 1622. V. of St Dunstan-in-the-West, 1624-31. Celebrated preacher and poet. Died Mar. 31, 1631. Buried in St Paul's Cathedral. M.I. there. Will, P.C.C. (*D.N.B.*)

DONNE, JOHN. Matric. sizar from QUEENS', Lent, 1618-9. Of Salop. B.A. 1622-3. Perhaps R. of Pertenhall, Beds.; ejected, 1662. (*Calamy*, I. 223.)

DONNE, JOHN. Matric. pens. from MAGDALENE, Michs. 1696; B.A. 1696-7. One of these names, s. of John, of Yeddingham, Yorks., clerk, matric. from University College, Oxford, Feb. 25, 1692-3, age 17. Ord. deacon (York) Jan. 1700-1; priest, 1701. V. of Yeddingham, 1701. (*Al. Oxon.*)

DONN, RICHARD. Adm. sizar (age 17) at SIDNEY, June 30, 1707. S. of William (1662), V. of Seaton, Yorks. B. at Pocklington, Yorks. School, Pocklington. Matric. 1707; B.A. 1710-1. Ord. priest (London) Dec. 21, 1718. Usher of Pocklington School, 1710-45. (M. H. Peacock.)

DONN, ROBERT. Adm. sizar at QUEENS', July 1, 1695. Of Yorkshire. Matric. 1695; B.A. 1698-9. Ord. deacon (York) May, 1700; priest, 1700-1.

DONNE, ROBERT. Adm. pens. (age 17) at CAIUS, Oct. 9, 1725. S. of Thomas (1695), of Sculthorpe, Norfolk. B. there. Schools, Thelnetham (private) and Norwich. Scholar, 1725-9; Matric. 1726; B.A. from Pembroke, 1730-1. Ord. deacon (Norwich) Sept. 23, 1733; priest, Mar. 10, 1733-4. R. of Thornham, Norfolk, 1733-9; of Titchwell, 1734; and of Sculthorpe, 1739-65. Buried at Isleworth, Midds., Oct. 11, 1765. M.I. Will, P.C.C. (*Venn*, II. 24; J. Ch. Smith.)

DONNE, ROGER. Adm. pens. (age 17) at CAIUS, Mar. 24, 1718-9. S. of Roger, gent., of Waxham, Norfolk. B. in Yarmouth. Bapt. Apr. 23, 1702. School, Norwich. Matric. 1719; Scholar, 1719-21; B.A. 1722-3; M.A. 1730. Ord. priest (Norwich) Mar. 1727-8. R. of Catfield, Norfolk, 1732-73. P.C. of Ingham, 1732-73. V. of Happisburgh, 1759-73. Died July 13, 1773. His sister, Anne, was mother of the poet Cowper. (*Venn*, II. 11.)

DONNE, THOMAS. 'B.A. Cambridge,' *supp.* for incorporation at Oxford, 1543-4.

DONNE, THOMAS. Ord. deacon and priest (Peterb.), as B.A. of ST JOHN'S College, June 29, 1603.

DONNE, THOMAS. Adm. pens. (age 16) at CAIUS, Oct. 12, 1695. S. of Robert, attorney, of South Creake, Norfolk. B. at Edgefield. Schools, Holt and Lynn. Scholar, 1695-1703; Matric. 1696; B.A. 1699-1700; M.A. 1703. Ord. deacon (Norwich) June, 1704; priest, Sept. 23, 1705. R. of Sculthorpe, 1705-39; and of Tittleshall. R. of South Creake, 1710-39. Died June 5, 1739. M.I. at Sculthorpe. Father of Robert (1725). (*Venn*, I. 497.)

DONE, THOMAS. Adm. Fell.-Com. at CLARE, Oct. 13, 1703. B. in London. Probably s. and h. of Thomas, late of Gray's Inn, Esq., adm. at the Inner Temple, 1705.

DONNE, WILLIAM. Matric. sizar from ST JOHN'S, Easter, 1624.

DONN, WILLIAM. Adm. sizar (age 24) at ST JOHN'S, June 6, 1662. S. of William, of Lockton, near Pickering, Yorks. B. there. School, Levisham. B.A. 1665-6; M.A. 1670. Ord. deacon (York) June, 1667; priest, June, 1669. V. of Seaton Ross, Yorks. Usher of Pocklington School, 1662-1710. Buried Oct. 2, 1710. Father of William (1692) and Richard (1707). (*Yorks. Arch. Journal*, XIV. 113; M. H. Peacock.)

DONNE, WILLIAM. Adm. sizar at EMMANUEL, Dec. 17, 1683. Of Durham. B.A. 1687-8; M.A. 1691. V. of Frampton-upon-Severn, Gloucs., 1692-7.

DONNE, WILLIAM. Adm. at KING'S, a scholar from Eton, 1686. B. at Ness, Salop. Matric. 1687; B.A. 1690-1; M.A. 1694. Fellow, 1690. Proctor, 1715. Died May 19, 1737.

DONNE, WILLIAM. Adm. sizar (age 18) at ST JOHN'S, May 23, 1692. S. of William (1662), clerk. B. at Pocklington, Yorks. Matric. 1692; B.A. 1695-6. Ord. deacon (Lincoln) Mar. 20, 1697; priest (York) June, 1699. Brother of Richard (1707).

DONNELL, JOHN. Adm. sizar (age 16) at CAIUS, Sept. 1590. S. of Robert (next). B. at Birdbrook, Essex. School, Haverhill, Suffolk. Scholar, 1591; Matric. *c.* 1593, as 'Dontrell'; B.A. 1594-5; M.A. 1598. Probabl V. of Bulmer, Essex, 1603.

DONNELL, ROBERT. Matric. sizar from ST CATHARINE'S, Michs. 1564; B.A. from Caius, 1568-9. Perhaps M.A. from St Catharine's, 1572, as 'Dunning.' Ord. deacon (Ely) Apr. 21, 1570. R. of Birdbrook, Essex, 1572-1601. Admon. (P.C.C.) Aug. 1601. Father of John, above.

DONNELL, THOMAS. Probably scholar of CHRIST'S, 1539; B.A. 1540-1; M.A. (Oxford) 1544-5. Incorp. at Cambridge, 1546. B.D. (Cambridge) 1549. An original fellow of Trinity, 1546. R. of Toppesfield, Essex, 1551; deprived, 1554; reinstated, 1558. An exile at Frankfort under Queen Mary. R. of Birdbrook, Essex, 1559. Died Feb. 1571-2. Will (Cons. C. London) 1572. (*Cooper*, II. 532.)

DONNELL, THOMAS. Adm. pens. at PETERHOUSE, Aug. 3, 1594.

DONNING, LANCELOT, *see* **DUNNING.**

DONNINGTON, ——. A friar. D.D. 1482.

DONNISON, JAMES. Adm. sizar (age 18) at CHRIST'S, Feb. 4, 1722-3. S. of William. B. at Gateshead, Durham. School, Sedbergh. Scholar, 1723 till 1724; Matric. 1723.

DONNITHORNE, ISAAC. Adm. pens. (age 17) at PEMBROKE, Feb. 8, 1727-8. S. of Nicholas, of St Agnes, Cornwall, gent. Matric. 1728; B.A. 1731-2; M.A. 1735. Ord. deacon (Norwich) June, 1734; priest, Oct. 1735. Of St Agnes, where he succeeded his brother Joseph, 1762. Died May, 1782. Will, P.C.C. (Burke, *L.G.*)

DONSTON, *see also* **DUNSTAN.**

DONSTON, GEORGE. Adm. pens. (age 18) at EMMANUEL, July 5, 1742. Of Worksop, Notts. S. of George (? Henry). School, Eton. Matric. 1742; B.A. 1745-6.

DONSTON, JAMES. Adm. pens. (age 16) at ST JOHN'S, May 3, 1672. S. of John, yeoman, of Worksop, Notts. B. there. School, Worksop. Matric. 1672; B.A. 1675-6; M.A. 1679. Ord. deacon (York) Dec. 1680.

DONWICH, JOHN. D.Can.L. Master of CLARE, 1371-92. Chancellor, 1371, 1374. V. of Duxworth St John, Cambs., 1391. Preb. of St Paul's. Collector of the King's Tithes. Resolute in supporting the privileges of the University against the Bishop of Ely. Died Apr. 1392. Will, P.C.C.

DOO or DOE, GEORGE. Adm. Fell.-Com. at JESUS, June 28, 1661. S. of John, citizen of London. Matric. 1661; B.A. 1663. Obtained a grant of Arms, May 8, 1662. Adm. at Lincoln's Inn, May 7, 1663.

DOO, JOHN. B.A. 1516-7; M.A. 1520-1. V. of North Collingham, Notts., 1521-7. Died 1527.

DOE or DOO, JOHN. Adm. sizar (age 17) at PEMBROKE, Jan. 15, 1675-6. S. of John, gent. B. at Harling, Norfolk. Matric. 1679; B.A. 1679-80; M.A. 1683. Ord. deacon (Norwich) May, 1684. V. of Chrishall, Essex, 1689-1712. V. of Elmdon, 1704-12. Died 1712. Father of the next.

DOO, THOMAS. Adm. sizar (age 17) at PEMBROKE, July 7, 1710. S. of John (above), V. of Chrishall, Essex. Matric. 1711; B.A. 1714-5; M.A. 1718. Fellow, 1718. Ord. deacon (London) June 12, 1715; priest, June 16, 1717. R. of Little Hormead, Herts., 1719-30. R. of Gt Hormead, 1721-30. Died 1730. Will (Commis. C. Essex) 1730.

DOODY, SAMUEL. Adm. pens. (age 17) at TRINITY, June 30, 1711. S. of Joseph, of Stafford. Exhibitioner from Charterhouse. Matric. 1711; Scholar, 1713; B.A. 1714-5; M.A. 1718. College librarian, 1717-21. Ord. deacon (Lincoln) Mar. 5, 1720-1. Chaplain, 1722-7.

DOOLE, NICHOLAS. Licensed to practise medicine, 1648.

DOOLE, VALESIUS. Adm. pens. at EMMANUEL, May 25, 1670. Of Suffolk.

DOOLITTLE, *see* **DOLITTLE.**

DORANT, HENRY. B.Can.L. 1487-8.

DORCHESTER, Viscount, *see* **CARLETON, DUDLEY.**

DORE, JOHN. Adm. at KING'S, a scholar from Eton, 1448. Fellow. M.A. Ord. deacon (Ely) May 23, 1467.

DORE, JOHN. Adm. sizar (age 15) at CAIUS, Mar. 17, 1592-3. S. of William. B. at Cornard, Suffolk. Schools, Sudbury and Bures. Matric. *c.* 1593.

DOR, ROBERT. B.A. 1490-1; M.A. 1494.

DOREWARD, RALPH. Resident graduate in 1454.

DORINGTON, AMBROSE. B.A. from CHRIST'S, 1573-4; M.A. 1577. S. of Richard, of Spaldwick, Hunts. Ord. deacon (Peterb.) Apr. 8, 1577; priest (Ely) Dec. 21, 1580. V. of Godmanchester, Hunts., 1579-87. R. of Brington, 1582-99. R. of Houghton, 1588-99. Died 1599. (*Cambs. and Hunts. Archaeol. Soc.*, II. 182.)

DORYNGTON, EDWARD. Matric. sizar from ST CATHARINE'S, Michs. 1571; B.A. 1574-5.

DORINGTON, FRANCIS. Scholar of TRINITY, 1548. S. of Robert, of Stafford. B.A. 1555-6; M.A. from St Catharine's, 1559; B.D. from Caius, 1565; D.D. 1575. Fellow of St Catharine's, c. 1557. Fellow of Caius, 1562-5. Ord. deacon (London) Mar. 1557-8; priest (Lincoln) Mar. 26, 1558. R. of Saham Toney, Norfolk, 1563-89. R. of Warboys, Hunts., 1565-1611. Buried there Apr. 13, 1611. Will, P.C.C. Benefactor to the College. Brother of John (1559) and William (1564). (*Venn*, I. 50.)

DORINGTON, FRANCIS. Matric. pens. from TRINITY, Easter, 1602. Perhaps s. of John (1559). Probably Matric. afterwards from Trinity College, Oxford, Mar. 15, 1604-5, age 18. Adm. at Gray's Inn, May 6, 1607. Of Staffs., Esq.

DORINGTON, JOHN. Matric. sizar (age 13) from ST CATHARINE'S, as 'Darington,' Michs. 1559. S. of Robert, gent., of Stafford. School, Stafford. Migrated to Caius, Dec. 19, 1561, 'age 14.' M.P. for Hunts., 1584. One of these names knighted, 1603. Of Spaldwick, Hunts. Will proved, 1604. Brother of Francis (1548) and William (1564). (*Venn*, I. 48.)

DORINGTON, JOHN. Matric. pens. from TRINITY, Michs. 1559. (Apparently distinct from the above; if so, wrongly indicated in *Matric. and Degrees*.)

DORINGTON, JOHN. Adm. at KING'S, a scholar from Eton, 1623; B.A. 1627. Fellow, till 1628. Graduated M.D. at Leyden; adm. there, Feb. 16, 1629-30.

DORINGTON or DODINGTON, MARMADUKE. Matric. pens. from TRINITY, Michs. 1587, scholar from Westminster. Perhaps s. of Francis (1548). B.A. 1591-2; M.A. 1595. Fellow, 1593-1602. (One of these names incorp. M.A. at Oxford from Lambeth, 1617; *see Al. Oxon.*)

DORINGTON, RICHARD. Matric. pens. from TRINITY, Easter, 1606, scholar from Westminster, 1605. Perhaps s. of John (1559). B. in Holborn, London. B.A. 1609-10; M.A. 1613. Ord. deacon (London) Sept. 19, 1613, age 26.

DORINGTON, ROBERT (1577-8), *see* **DODINGTON.**

DORRINGTON, THEOPHILUS. Adm. sizar (age 16) at SIDNEY, Dec. 19, 1670. 1st s. of Theophilus, clothier. Bapt. at St Mary-le-Bow, London, Nov. 23, 1654. Schools, Merchant Taylors', Newington (Mr Horrax) and Bearden, Essex (Mr Beard). Presbyterian preacher. Afterwards of Magdalen College, Oxford, June 16, 1686. M.A. (Oxford) by decree, 1711. R. of Hopton Castle, Salop, 1687. R. of Wittersham, Kent, 1699-1715. Author, theological. Died Apr. 30, 1715. (*D.N.B.*; *Al. Oxon.*)

DORINGTON, THOMAS. Matric. sizar from ST CATHARINE'S, Lent, 1578-9; B.A. 1581-2; M.A. 1585. Ord. priest (Norwich) Oct. 18, 1582. R. of Homersfield, Suffolk, 1594-1612. R. of South Cove, 1595-7.

DORRINGTON, THOMAS. Adm. pens. (age 18) at TRINITY, Oct. 18, 1726. S. of Luke, of St Martin's, London (? and of Hillingdon, Midds.; M.I. 1743). School, Eton. Adm. at Lincoln's Inn, Nov. 30, 1726.

DORYNGTON, WILLIAM. Matric. sizar from ST CATHARINE'S, Lent, 1557-8.

DORINGTON, WILLIAM. Adm. pens. (age 18) at CAIUS, May 13, 1564. S. of Robert, gent., of Stafford. Resided at Caius for a year with his brother Francis (1548). Adm. at King's, a scholar from Eton, 1565. Matric. 1565; B.A. 1569-70; M.A. from St Catharine's, 1573. Fellow of King's, till 1573. Brother of John (1559) and Francis (1548).

DORISLAUS (DORESLAWE), ISAAC. Incorp. LL.D. at Cambridge from Leyden, 1631. S. of Isaac, minister at Hensbrock, Holland. B. at Alkmaar, Holland, 1595. Greville lecturer on history at Cambridge, 1627. Admitted advocate, Nov. 4, 1645. Judge of the Admiralty Court, 1648; prepared the charge of treason against Charles I, 1648. British envoy at the Hague, 1649; assassinated there by a royalist party, May 12, 1649. Admon. (P.C.C.) May 25, 1649. (*D.N.B.*)

DORLING, JOHN. Adm. sizar (age 17) at PEMBROKE, Jan. 19, 1724-5. S. of John (? Thomas), of Isleham, Cambs. School, Bury. Matric. 1724-5; B.A. 1728-9. Ord. priest (Norwich). Nov. 1735.

DORMAN, FRANCIS. Matric. pens. from TRINITY, Lent, 1577-8.

DORMAN, JOHN. Adm. at KING'S, a scholar from Eton, 1445.

DORMAN, SIMON. Matric. pens. from CORPUS CHRISTI, c. 1596. Of Cambridgeshire. B.A. 1599-1600; M.A. 1603.

DORMER, Sir CLEMENT COTTRELL, *see* **COTTERELL.**

DORMER, FLEETWOOD. Adm. Fell.-Com. at CLARE, Nov. 25, 1713. S. and h. of Robert, Justice Queen's Bench. B. in London. Adm. at Lincoln's Inn, July 1, 1710. M.P. for Malmesbury, Wilts., 1719-22. Of Lee, Bucks. Died June 21, 1726. (Burke, *Ext. Bart.*)

DORMER, JOHN. M.A. 1632 (Incorp. from Oxford). S. of Sir Fleetwood, of Shipton Lee, Bucks., Knt. Bapt. at Quainton, Bucks., Jan. 6, 1611-2. Matric. from Magdalen Hall, Oxford, Jan. 25, 1627-8, age 16; B.A. 1627-8; M.A. 1630. Adm. at Lincoln's Inn, Feb. 7, 1628-9. Barrister, 1636. M.P. for Buckingham, 1646-53 and 1660. Of Lee Grange, Bucks., Esq. Died May 22, 1679, aged 67. M.I. at Quainton. (*Al. Oxon.*; *Lipscomb*, I. 430.)

DORMAR, MICHAEL. Adm. Fell.-Com. at KING'S, Easter, 1574. Doubtless s. of Ambrose, of Gt Milton and Ascott, Oxon. Knighted, Apr. 1604. Of Buckinghamshire. Buried at Gt Milton, Sept. 24, 1624. (*Her. and Gen.*, I. 338.)

DORMER, WALTER. B.A. 1530-1; M.A. 1534; B.D. 1543. R. of Reed, Herts., 1536-54. R. of Crawley, Bucks., 1545-66. Buried there, Apr. 1, 1566. (*Lipscomb*, IV. 128.)

DORMER, WILLIAM. B.A. from TRINITY, 1605-6. Ord. deacon (Lincoln) Sept. 22, 1611. V. of Olney, Bucks., 1611-24.

DORMER, WILLIAM. Adm. sizar (age 15) at ST JOHN'S, May 26, 1697. S. of William, gent. B. at Sheerness, Kent. School, Southwark. Matric. 1697; B.A. 1700-1; M.A. 1723. Ord. deacon (London) Sept. 21, 1707; priest, Sept. 19, 1708. Minor canon of Rochester, 1716-9. V. of Hoo St Werburgh, Kent, 1717-29. Head Master of King's School, Rochester, 1718-29. Died June 24, 1729. Buried in Rochester Cathedral. M.I. (*Fielding*.)

DORMER, ——. Matric. Fell.-Com. from CLARE, Michs. 1544.

DORRAM, JOHN. Matric. sizar from JESUS, Michs. 1550.

DORRELL, *see also* **DARRELL.**

DORRELL, ROBERT. Matric. pens. from PEMBROKE, Easter, 1631; B.A. 1633; M.A. from Trinity Hall, 1637.

DORRELL, SAMUEL. Matric. Fell.-Com. from ST CATHARINE'S, Michs. 1641. Of Kent.

DORRELL, WALTER. Adm. at KING'S, a scholar from Eton, 1577. Matric. 1577-8. Fellow, but died before graduation.

DARRELL, ——. Adm. Fell.-Com. at CORPUS CHRISTI, 1563.

DORSET, Earl of, *see* **SACKVILLE, THOMAS.**

DORSETT, JOHN. Matric. pens. from TRINITY, Easter, 1632.

DORSETT, MICHAEL. Adm. sizar (age 17) at PEMBROKE, June 30, 1740. S. of Michael. B. in London. 'Grecian' from Christ's Hospital. Matric. 1740; B.A. 1743-4; M.A. 1747. His father was a citizen and joiner of St Botolph's, Bishopsgate, London. Probably Inc. of Ford, Sussex. (*A. W. Lockhart.*)

DORSON, JOSIAS, *see* **DAWSON.**

DORVILLE, FREDERICK. B.D. 1616. Incorp. from Oxford. Of Aix-la-Chapelle. B.D. from Exeter College, Oxford, 1615-6. (*Al. Oxon.*)

DORVILL, JAMES. Matric. pens. from ST CATHARINE'S, Easter, 1644; B.A. 1647-8.

DOSSIE or DOSIE, JOHN. Adm. sizar at QUEENS', July 6, 1694. Of Yorkshire. Matric. 1695; B.A. 1697-8. Ord. deacon (York) Sept. 1698; priest, 1700. V. of Sheffield, Yorks., 1713-53. Died Dec. 24, 1753, aged 77. M.I. at Sheffield.

DOSSEY, JOHN. Adm. sizar (age 17) at PETERHOUSE, Apr. 23, 1703. S. of Richard, of Little Smeaton, Yorks. School, Richmond, Yorks. (Mr Thompson). Migrated to Trinity, June 28, 1703. Matric. 1703; Scholar, 1706; B.A. 1706-7. Ord. deacon (York) June, 1707; priest, 1709.

DOTCHIN or DOCHEN, THOMAS. M.A. 1578 (Incorp. from Oxford); B.A. from Magdalen College, Oxford, 1568; M.A. 1571-2; *supp.* for M.B. 1580; M.D. 1592. Fellow of Magdalen College, 1568-82. Proctor, 1577. Linacre lecturer, 1604. Died Jan. 20, 1604-5. Will, P.C.C. (*Al. Oxon.*)

DOTHARAM, THOMAS. Matric. pens. from PETERHOUSE, Easter, 1618.

DOUBLEDAY, FRANCIS. Adm. pens. at EMMANUEL, Apr. 27, 1639. Matric. 1639. Afterwards Fell.-Com.

DOUBLEDAY, THOMAS. Adm. pens. at CORPUS CHRISTI, 1693. Of London. Matric. 1694.

DOUESPE, EZECHIEL PAUL DE LA. Adm. pens. at CLARE, Apr. 24, 1745. B. in London, Sept. 29, 1727. School, Merchant Taylors'. Matric. 1746; B.A. 1748-9; M.A. 1752. Ord. deacon (London) Sept. 22, 1751; priest (Peterb.) Feb. 23, 1752. R. of East Farleigh, Kent, 1752-94. Died Dec. 24, 1794. Buried at East Farleigh. M.I. Will (P.C.C.) 1795. (*Robinson*, II. 93; *Fielding*.)

DOUGHTON, ARTHUR. Adm. pens. at JESUS, June 4, 1633. Of London. Matric. 1633.

DOUGHTIE, ANDREW. Adm. sizar (age 18) at CAIUS, Mar. 26, 1609. S. of William, gent., of Bacton, Norfolk. School, North Walsham. Matric. 1609; B.A. 1612-3; M.A. 1616. Ord. priest (Norwich) June 19, 1619. R. of Cranwich, Norfolk, 1620-6. Of Wilton, 1613-44. Buried at Cranwich, Jan. 3, 1665-6. (*Venn*, I. 201.)

DOUGHTY, CHARLES. Adm. pens. (age 17) at ST JOHN'S, May 31, 1667. S. of Charles, gent., of Worlaby, Lincs. B. there. School, Oxcombe, near Louth. Matric. 1667. Adm. at the Middle Temple, Nov. 17, 1673. (*Lincs. Pedigrees*.)

DOUGHTY, EDMUND. Adm. Fell.-Com. (age 20) at TRINITY, May 12, 1719. S. of Edmund, of Herts. For another of these names *see Al. Oxon*.

DOUGHTY, EDWARD. Matric. pens. from ST JOHN'S, Michs. 1564. Of Derbyshire. Scholar, 1564; B.A. 1568-9; M.A. 1572. R. of Holy Trinity, Dorchester, 1580-5. V. of Banwell, Somerset, 1584-96. V. of Loxton, 1586-91. V. of Chard, 1597-1603. R. of Hawkchurch, Dorset, 1605. In 1596 he went as chaplain with the expedition to Cadiz, whence he brought away 17 books from the Jesuit College. These are now in Hereford Cathedral Library, some inscribed 'E. Doughtie, June 23, 1596: jure belli.' Dean of Hereford, 1607-16. R. of Hampton Bishop, Hereford, 1609. V. of Badenham. Chaplain to James I. R. of Stockport, Cheshire, 1615-6. Buried there, Oct. 17, 1616. Inventory at Chester. (Dean of Hereford; *Earwaker*, I. 334.)

DOUGHTY, EDWARD. Matric. pens. from SIDNEY, Easter, 1618.

DOUGHTY, EDWARD. Adm. sizar (age 18) at ST JOHN'S, Feb. 5, 1675-6. S. of Charles, yeoman, of Louth, Lincs. B. there. School, Grantham.

DOUGHTY, GEORGE. Adm. sizar (age 19) at ST JOHN'S, Dec. 1, 1677. S. of George, draper. B. at Haverhill, Suffolk. School, Sudbury. Ord. deacon (Norwich) June, 1679, as B.A.; priest, May, 1684. R. of Martlesham, Suffolk, 1699-1724. Died Mar. 14, 1724, aged 69. Buried at Martlesham. (Burke, *L.G.*)

DOUGHTY, GREGORY. Adm. at KING'S, a scholar from Eton, 1706. B. in London. Matric. 1707; B.A. 1710-1; M.A. 1714; D.D. 1736. Fellow, 1710. Ord. deacon (Lincoln) May 20, 1722; priest, Sept. 1722. V. of Fordingbridge, Hants. Author, *Sermon*. Died Mar. 1742. Will (P.C.C.) 1743. (*Harwood*.)

DOUGHTY, HENRY. Adm. sizar at EMMANUEL, 1640. Of Yorkshire. S. of Robert (1611-2), master of Wakefield School. Matric. 1640; B.A. 1649. Master of Kirkham School, Lancs., 1644. Usher of Wakefield School, 1646-9. Probably buried at Wakefield, Apr. 30, 1698. Brother of Thomas (1653). (M. H. Peacock; J. Parker.)

DOUGHTY, HENRY. Adm. sizar at CLARE, June 26, 1651. Matric. 1651; B.A. 1654-5; M.A. 1658. Ord. deacon (Lincoln) Feb. 21; priest, Feb. 24, 1661-2. R. of Elton, Durham, 1668-1708. Married (? 2nd marriage) July 19, 1672, at Roxby, Lincs., Mary Wixman. Buried Dec. 25, 1708. Father of the next. (H. M. Wood.)

DOUGHTY, HENRY. Adm. sizar (age 19) at ST JOHN'S, May 25, 1683. S. of Henry, above. B. at Elton, Durham. School, Durham. Matric. 1683; B.A. 1686-7. Probably the nonjuror who was Chaplain to the Archbishop of York. Ordained by Wm Lloyd, May 23, 1694. C. of Robin Hood's Bay, Yorks. Consecrated Bishop by Nathaniel Spinks, and others, at Edinburgh, Mar. 30, 1725. Died July 14, 1730. (*N. and Q.*, 1863, I. 243.)

DOUGHTY, JAMES. Adm. sizar (age 19) at ST JOHN'S, June 25, 1715. S. of Thomas, parish clerk. B. at Shrewsbury. School, Shrewsbury. Matric. 1715; B.A. 1718-9. Appointed 3rd master at Shrewsbury, 1728.

DOUGHTIE, JOHN. Adm. pens. (age 16) at CAIUS, Feb. 12, 1578-9. S. of William, yeoman, of Hanworth, Norfolk. Schools, Suffield and Aylsham. Matric. 1578-9; B.A. 1582-3; Scholar to 1586; M.A. 1586; B.D. 1593. R. of Alphington, Devon, 1593-1637. Preb. of Exeter, 1602-31. Died 1637. Will (Exeter). (*Venn*, I. 100.)

DOUGHTY, JOHN. Adm. pens. at QUEENS', June 26, 1594. Of Norfolk. Matric. *c.* 1594; B.A. 1597-8; M.A. 1601. Ord. priest (Norwich) 1610. R. of Wood Norton, Norfolk, 1616.

DOUGHTIE, JOHN. Adm. pens. at EMMANUEL, Apr. 23, 1607. Matric. 1607. Perhaps s. of Robert, of Hoveton St John, Norfolk; adm. at Gray's Inn, Feb. 13, 1610-1.

DOUGHTY, JOHN. Matric. pens. from TRINITY, Michs. 1634.

DOUGHTY, JOHN. Adm. sizar (age 17) at ST JOHN'S, July 1, 1652. S. of Henry, of Gt Stainton, Durham. B. in Warwickshire. School, Sedbergh. Matric. 1652. Probably ord. deacon (Lincoln) Sept. 30, 1661, as 'literate.'

DOUGHTY, JOHN. . pens. (age 16) at CAIUS, May 10, 1660. S. of William (16[illegible]) of Aylsham, Norfolk. B. there. Schools, Aylsham (private) and Norwich. Matric. 1660; Scholar, 1660-7; B.A. 1663-4; M.A. 1667. Ord. deacon (Norwich) Dec. 23, 1665; priest, June 2, 1667, as R. of Oxnead. R. of Earsham, 1671. R. of Lyng, 1672. Chaplain to the Earl of Northampton. Died 1702. Buried at Earsham. Admon. (Norwich C.C.) 1702. (*Venn*, I. 408; *Vis. of Norfolk*, 1664.)

DOUGHTY, JOHN. Adm. sizar (age 17) at SIDNEY, June 3, 1675. S. of Samuel, of Mancetter, Warws. B. at Sibstone, Leics. Schools, Bosworth (Mr Thomas Chapman) and Ashby-de-la-Zouch (Mr Samuel Shaw.)

DOUGHTY, MICHAEL. Incorp. M.A. 1673, from Trinity College, Dublin. Perhaps s. of Thomas, of Osgodby Park, Yorks. B.A. (Dublin) 1660. Ord. deacon (York) June 14, 1663; priest, May 21, 1665. V. of Hemingbrough, Yorks., 1667-70. Married, at Hemingbrough, May 9, 1667, Anne, dau. of Edward Kirlew, of Hagthorpe. (J. Parker; Thos. Burton, *Hemingborough*, 111.)

DOUGHTY, NATHANIEL. Adm. sizar at EMMANUEL, Mar. 19, 1645-6. Matric. 1647; B.A. 1649-50; M.A. 1653. Will (P.C.C.) 1654; of Sibstone, Leics., clerk. Proved by brother Samuel (1637) and Thomas (1629).

DOUGHTY, ROBERT. B.A. from ST JOHN'S, 1611-2; M.A. 1615. Doubtless s. of John, of Ovenden, Halifax. Bapt. Nov. 9, 1589. Scholar of St John's, Nov. 1607, from Halifax School. Ord. deacon (York) Sept. 1614. Master of Gisburn School, Yorks. Headmaster of Wakefield, 1623-63. Died 1663. Buried in choir of Wakefield Church, Feb. 24, 1662-3. Father of Henry (1640) and Thomas (1653). (M. H. Peacock.)

DOUGHTY, 'ROBERT.' Matric. Fell.-Com. from CAIUS, Easter, 1632. (Doubtless a mistake for William whom *see*.)

DOUGHTY, ROBERT. Adm. at CORPUS CHRISTI, 1635. Of Norfolk. Perhaps s. and h. of William, of Hanworth, Norfolk, Esq., adm. at Gray's Inn, Oct. 10, 1634.

DOUGHTY, ROBERT. Adm. sizar (age 18) at JESUS, June 14, 1671. Of Lincolnshire. Matric. 1671; Scholar, 1674; B.A. 1674-5. Ord. deacon (York) Sept. 1677; priest, Sept. 1678. C. of Comberton, Cambs., 1685.

DOUGHTY, ROBERT. Adm. Fell.-Com. (age 17) at CAIUS, May 28, 1674. S. of William, gent., of Hanworth, Norfolk. B. in Norwich. Matric. 1674. Of Hanworth, Esq. Died 1742. Will (P.C.C.) 1742. (*Venn*, I. 450.)

DOUGHTY, SAMUEL. Adm. sizar at EMMANUEL, May 6, 1637. Of Hereford, Matric. 1637; B.A. 1640-1; M.A. 1644. R. of Bringhurst, Leics., 1644. R. of Sibstone; ejected, 1662. Afterwards preacher at Ashby. Brother of Nathaniel (1645-6) and Thomas (1629). (*Calamy*, II. 128.)

DOUGHTY, SAMUEL. Adm. sizar (age 18) at CHRIST'S, July 2, 1661. S. of Henry, minister of Gt Stainton, Durham. B. there. School, Brignall. Matric. 1661; B.A. 1664. Ord. deacon (London) Feb. 1664-5; priest, Mar. 1665-6. V. of Boxted, Essex, 1669-73. (*Peile*, I. 597.)

DOUGHTY, SAMUEL. Adm. pens. at EMMANUEL, Apr. 5, 1672. B. at Fitz, Salop. Matric. 1674; B.A. 1675-6; M.A. 1679; B.D. 1686. Fellow, 1678-90. Ord. priest (London) Dec. 19, 1680. R. of Stanground, Hunts., 1690-1720. Died Nov. 14, 1720. (Burke, *L.G.*)

DOUGHTY, THOMAS. Matric. sizar from ST JOHN'S, Michs. 1588; B.A. 1592-3; M.A. 1597.

DOUGHTY, THOMAS. Matric. pens. from CORPUS CHRISTI, Easter, 1623. Of Norfolk. B.A. 1626-7. Buried at St Botolph's, Cambridge, Aug. 30, 1628.

DOUGHTY, THOMAS. Adm. at EMMANUEL, July, 1629. Of Herefordshire. B.A. 1632-3; M.A. 1636. Ord. priest (Peterb.) June 4, 1637. Perhaps V. of Medbourne, Leics., 1646; ejected, 1661 Brother of Samuel (1637) and Nathaniel (1645-6).

DOUGHTY, THOMAS. Adm. sizar (age 15) at MAGDALENE, Apr. 23, 1653. S. of Robert (1611-2), master of Wakefield School. School, Wakefield. Matric 1653; B.A. 1656-7; M.A. 1660; D.D. 1671 (*Lit. Reg.*). Incorp. at Oxford, 1664. Chaplain to the Duke of York. V. of Romsey, Hants., 1662. R. of Bishopstoke, 1666-98. Canon of Windsor, 1673. R. of Clewer, Berks., 1680. Died Dec. 2, 1701. M.I. at Windsor. Brother of Henry (1640). (*Al. Oxon.*)

DOUBTY, THOMAS. Adm. sizar at TRINITY, Mar. 21, 1667-8.

DOUGHTY, THOMAS. Adm. sizar at JESUS, Apr. 30, 1696. S. of William, of Wakefield, Yorks. Bapt. Nov. 5, 1677. School, Wakefield. Matric. 1696; B.A. 1699-1700. Ord. priest (York) May 31, 1702. R. of Waddingworth, Lincs., 1707. V. of Wispington, 1707.

DOUGHTY, THOMAS. Adm. sizar (age 16) at MAGDALENE, Jan. 21, 1705-6. S. of ——, citizen of London. B. there.

DOUGHTY, WILLIAM. Perhaps B.Civ.L. 1480-1; and, as 'Dowting,' D.Can.L. 1494. Of York diocese. Chaplain to Bishop Alcock. Ord. deacon, Apr.; priest, May, 1488. R. of Terrington, Norfolk, 1489. Chancellor of Ely, 1490. R. of Wisbech St Peter, 1494. R. of Newton, Isle of Ely, till 1498. R. of Elm, Cambs., and Emneth, Norfolk, 1500. Died *c.* 1503. (*Cooper*, I. 8.)

DOUGHTY, WILLIAM. A priest. B.Can.L. 1520-1. V. of Caldecot, Cambs., 1520-38. Died 1538.

DOUGHTIE, WILLIAM. Adm. Fell.-Com. (age 17) at Caius, June 9, 1609. S. and h. of Robert, gent., of Hanworth, Norfolk. B. at Norwich. School, Aylsham. Matric. 1609. Adm. at Lincoln's Inn, May 10, 1610. Of Hanworth, gent. Possibly Alderman and M.P. for King's Lynn, 1624, 1628 and 1640. Will of one of these names (P.C.C.) 1656; of Lincoln's Inn. Father of the next. (*Venn*, I. 202; *Vis.* o *Norfolk*.)

DOUGHTY, WILLIAM. Adm. Fell.-Com. (age 16) at Caius, Nov. 20, 1631. S. of William (above), gent. B. at Hanworth, Norfolk. School, Aylsham. Probably matric. as 'Robert,' 1632. Of Norwich, gent. Will (P.C.C.) 1654; mentions sons Robert and William. (*Venn*, I. 304.)

DOUGHTY, WILLIAM. Adm. pens. (age 17) at Caius, May 20, 1637. S. of Robert, gent., of Aylsham, Norfolk. Schools, Aylsham and Ashmanhaugh. Of Hanworth, gent. Buried at Aylsham, Aug. 10, 1678. Will (Norw. C.C.) 1678. Father of John (1660). (*Venn*, I. 326; *Vis. of Norfolk*, 1664.)

DOUGHTY, WILLIAM. Adm. pens. (age 18) at Caius, May 2, 1696. S. of Robert (1674), gent., of Hanworth, Norfolk. B. in Norwich. School, Bury. Matric. 1696. Fell.-Com. Mar. 20, 1696-7. Died 1698. Buried at Hanworth. (*Venn*, I. 498.)

DOWTY, ——. B.Civ.L. 1480-1. Perhaps William Dowting; whom *see*.

DOUGHTIE, ——. Adm. sizar at Trinity, 1570.

DOUGLAS, JAMES. Matric. Fell.-Com. from King's, Easter, 1720; M.A. 1722. Grandson of William, Earl of Morton. One of these names R. of Enmore, Somerset, 1729-36. (The prebend of Durham seems to have been an Oxford contemporary.)

DOUGLAS, JOHN. Adm. pens. (age 18) at Trinity, Apr. 29, 1732. S. of John, of Leeds. School, Leeds (Mr Bernard). Matric. 1732; Scholar, 1732; B.A. 1735-6; M.A. 1740. Ord. deacon (Lincoln) June 1; priest, June 29, 1740. R. of Eccleston, Lancs., 1741-66. Buried there Mar. 4, 1766.

DOUGLAS, JOHN ST LEGER. Adm. Fell.-Com. (age 17) at Trinity, Oct. 22, 1748. S. of John, of St Christopher's, West Indies. School, Westminster. M.P. for Hindon, Wilts., 1768-74; for Weobley, Herefordshire, 1774-83. Died May 23, 1783. (A. B. Beaven.)

DOUGLASTE, ROBERT. Matric. sizar from Trinity, Easter, 1635.

DOWGLASSE, WILLIAM. Adm. sizar (age 17) at Caius, Apr. 13, 1630. S. of William, clothier, of Yorkshire. B. at Leeds. Bapt. at St Peter's, Feb. 2, 1614-5. School, Leeds. Matric. 1631; Scholar, 1633-7; B.A. 1633-4; M.A. 1637. Probably V. of Threckingham, Lincs., 1642. Perhaps minister of Yoxford, Suffolk, in 1646; one of the *classis*. (*Venn*, I. 293.)

DOUKER or DOWKER, CHRISTOPHER. Adm. pens. (age 20) at Sidney, Dec. 6, 1677, as 'Douser.' From Edinburgh University. Only s. of William, mercer, deceased. B. at Malton, Yorks. School, Pickering (Mr Grey). B.A. 1677-8; M.A. 1681. Ord. deacon (Peterb.) Feb. 27, 1680.

DOULSON, ——. Adm. pens. at Emmanuel, 1637.

DOUNCER, THOMAS. Pens. at Peterhouse, Aug. 1594.

DOUTH (?) WILLIAM. Matric. pens. from Trinity, *c.* 1596.

DOUTHAM, WILLIAM, *see* DUNTHORN.

DOUTHWAITE, CUTHBERT. Adm. sizar (age 19) at Magdalene, June 17, 1729. S. of Timothy. B. at Bishop Auckland, Durham. School, Bishop Auckland. Matric. 1729; B.A. 1732-3; M.A. 1736. Fellow, 1735. Tutor. Ord. priest (Ely) June, 1734. R. of Stoke St Mary, Ipswich. V. of Rushmere, Suffolk. Died at Ipswich, Dec. 29, 1781. Will (P.C.C.) 1782; of Ipswich. (G. *Mag.*)

DOUTHWAITE, JOHN. Matric. pens. from Trinity, Michs. 1623.

DOWTHWAITE, JOSEPH. Student at Christ's, as Westmoreland scholar, Michs. 1720-3. Ord. deacon (York) June, 1721; priest, June, 1723; as literate. R. of Feliskirk, Yorks., 1739-65. Died Aug. 23, 1765. (*Peile*, II. 202; G. *Mag.*)

DOUGHTWATE, NICHOLAS. Matric. sizar from Trinity, Easter, 1636.

DOVE or DOWE, BARJONAS. Adm. sizar at Emmanuel, June 30, 1609. Matric. 1609; Scholar; B.A. 1612-3; M.A. 1616. Master of Boston Grammar School, 1613-6. Ord. deacon (Peterb.) Sept. 25; priest, Sept. 26, 1614. V. of Aslackby, Lincs., 1627. Father of Timothy (1650).

DOVE, BARJONAS. Adm. sizar at Emmanuel, Oct. 6, 1692; afterwards pensioner. Of Lincolnshire. Perhaps s. of Timothy (1650), R. of Rippingale. Matric. 1693; B.A. 1696-7. Ord. deacon (Lincoln) June 19, 1698; priest, Sept. 22, 1700. V. of Croxton-Keyrial, Leics., 1701. Admon. (Leicester) 1702. (*Misc. Gen. et Her.*, IV. 424.)

DOVE or DOWE, BARJOSHUA. Adm. sizar at Emmanuel, June 17, 1614.

DOVE, CHARLES. Adm. Fell.-Com. at St Catharine's, June 12, 1708. Matric. 1708.

DOVE, CHRISTOPHER. Matric. pens. from St John's, Lent, 1564-5; B.A. 1568-9.

DOWE, CHRISTOPHER. Matric. pens. from Christ's, July, 1613; B.A. 1616-7; M.A. 1620; B.D. 1627; D.D. 1638. Incorp. M.A. at Oxford, 1621. V. of Battle, Sussex, 1629. R. of All Saints', Hastings, 1636. Author, theological. (*Peile*, I. 291.)

DOVE, EDMUND. Matric. sizar from Trinity, Michs. 1639.

DOVE, EDMUND. Adm. pens. at Clare, Apr. 17, 1689. Probably s. of Simon (1650), of Hadleigh, Suffolk. Adm. at Woodbridge School, 1682. Died before his father. (*V. B. Redstone*; Copinger, *Manors of Suffolk*, IV. 312.)

DOVE, EDWARD. Adm. pens. (age 18) at Sidney, Apr. 4, 1649. S. of Sir William, Knt., deceased. B. at Upton, Northants. School, Oundle. Matric. 1649. Brother of Nevill (1647-8).

DOVE, FRANCIS. Matric. pens. from Corpus Christi, Easter, 1628. Of Northamptonshire. B.A. 1631-2; M.A. 1635.

DOVE, FYNN. Adm. pens. (age 18) at Peterhouse, May 19, 1725. Doubtless s. of Simon, of Marlesford, Suffolk, and grandson of Simon (1650). School, Ipswich. Matric. 1725; Scholar, 1725; B.A. 1728-9; M.A. 1732. Fellow, 1730-5. Ord. deacon (Lincoln) Sept. 19, 1736; priest, Mar. 6, 1736-7. Died 1770. (Copinger, *Manors of Suffolk*, IV. 312.)

DOVE, HENRY. Adm. pens. at Trinity, May 29, 1658; scholar from Westminster, 1659. Matric. 1660; B.A. 1661-2; M.A. 1665; D.D. 1677. Fellow, 1664. Incorp. at Oxford, 1669. Ord. deacon (Ely) Mar. 1664-5; priest, June, 1672. V. of St Bride's, Fleet Street, London, 1674-95. Archdeacon of Richmond, Yorks., 1678-95. Chaplain to Charles II, James II, and William and Mary. Died Mar. 11, 1694-5. Will (P.C.C.) 1695. M.I. at St Bride's, with arms of Dove of East Bergholt, Suffolk. (*D.N.B.*)

DOVE, JAMES. Adm. sizar at Emmanuel, May 20, 1717. Of Lincolnshire. Matric. 1717; B.A. 1721-2. Ord. deacon (Lincoln) Feb. 18, 1721-2; priest (Peterb.) Sept. 25, 1726. C. of Tickencote, Rutland. V. of Exton, 1735. V. of Burton Pedwardine, Lincs., 1737-8.

DOVE, JOHN. B.Can.L. before 1459. Custos of Hospital of St John, Bedford. V. of Turvey, Beds.

DOVE, JOHN. Adm. at King's, a scholar from Eton, 1506. One of these names R. of Borley, Essex. Will (Comm. C. Essex) 1551.

DOVE, JOHN. Matric. pens. from Pembroke, Michs. 1549.

DOWE, JOHN. Matric. sizar from St John's, Michs. 1606. S. of Robert, R. of Upper Rickinghall, Suffolk. School, Botesdale. Migrated to Caius, Apr. 20, 1608, age 22.

DOVE, JOHN. Adm. pens. at Jesus, Mar. 1620-1.

DOVE, JOHN. Adm. sizar at Clare, Apr. 26, 1650. Matric. 1650; B.A. 1660-1; M.A. 1664. V. of Burstwick, Yorks., 1665-70. V. of Welton, Howden, 1670-82.

DOVE, JOHN. Adm. pens. at Trinity, June 18, 1661. Matric. 1661. Perhaps adm. at the Middle Temple, Aug. 4, 1663, as s. of Thomas, of Upton, Northants., Esq.

DOVE, NEVILL. Adm. pens. (age 18) at Sidney, Jan. 4, 1647-8. S. of Sir William, Knt., deceased. B. at Peterborough. Schools, Stamford (Mr Jackson) and Oundle. Matric. 1647-8; B.A. 1651. Licensed to practise medicine, 1661. Brother of Edward (1649), grandson of Thomas (1571).

DOVE, PHILIP. Matric. pens. from St John's, Michs. 1559.

DOVE or DOWE, RICHARD. Matric. sizar from Corpus Christi, Michs. 1566. S. of Henry, of Attleborough, Norfolk. School, Wymondham. B.A. 1569-70; M.A. 1573. Ord. priest (Norwich) Dec. 2, 1572. V. of Elm, Cambs., and Emneth, Norfolk, in 1576. V. of Stratford St Mary, Suffolk, 1587-1606. (*Venn*, I. 70.)

DOVE, ROBERT. Matric. pens. from Magdalene, *c.* 1595; B.A. from Clare, 1599-1600; M.A. from Magdalene, 1603. One of these names V. of St Neots, Hunts., 1616-22. Buried at Hail Weston, Oct. 25, 1625.

DOVE, ROBERT. M.A. 1640 (Incorp. from Oxford). S. of Henry, of Salisbury. Matric. from Magdalen Hall, Oxford, Oct. 31, 1623, age 17; B.A. 1626-7; M.A. 1629. V. of Ilsington, Devon, 1634-45. R. of Elm, Cambs., and Emneth, Norfolk, 1641-5. Died Sept. 14, 1645. Buried at Ilsington. Brother of Thomas (1650). (*Al. Oxon.*; Randolph's *Walker*.)

DOVE, ROBOSHER. Ord. deacon (London) Dec. 19, 1619; 'literate, late of Emmanuel College; born at Stratford. Sussex (? Essex); aged 23,' as C. of Manningtree, Essex; priest, Dec. 24, 1620 ('B.A.'). C. of Weeks, Essex. R. of Foulness, *c.* 1632-9.

DOVE or DOWE, SAMUEL. Adm. sizar at EMMANUEL, May 12, 1651. Of Lincolnshire. Matric. 1651; B.A. 1654-5; M.A. 1658.

DOVE, SIMON. Adm. at CORPUS CHRISTI, 1650. Of Suffolk. Probably Lord of the Manor of Marlesford, 1687. Died before 1717. Perhaps father of Edmund (1689).

DOVE, SIMON. Adm. pens. at ST CATHARINE'S, Jan. 17, 1722-3. Of Barham, Ipswich. Doubtless s. of Simon, of Marlesford, Suffolk (and grandson of the above). Matric. 1723. Of Stowmarket. Died Oct. 22, 1757. (Copinger, *Manors of Suffolk*, IV. 312.)

DOVE, THOMAS. Matric. pens. from CHRIST'S, Nov. 1566.

DOVE, THOMAS. Matric. pens. from PEMBROKE, Michs. 1571. S. of William. B. in London, 1555. School, Merchant Taylors'. B.A. 1574-5; M.A. 1578. Nominated one of the first scholars at Jesus College, Oxford. Elected 'tanquam socius,' 1575. Ord. deacon and priest (Ely) Dec. 21, 1578. V. of Saffron Walden, Essex, 1580-1607. R. of Framlingham, Suffolk, 1584-1630. R. of Heydon, Essex, 1586-8. Chaplain to the Queen. Dean of Norwich, 1589. Bishop of Peterborough, 1601-30. V. of Polebrooke, Northants., 1608. Buried at Peterborough, Aug. 30, 1630. Will, P.C.C. Father of the next. (*D.N.B.*)

DOVE, THOMAS. Scholar of TRINITY, 1605. S. of Thomas (above). Bapt. at Saffron Walden, Aug. 29, 1587. B.A. 1606-7; M.A. 1610. Ord. deacon (Peterb.) Feb. 10, 1610-1; priest, Sept. 22, 1611. R. of Scotter, Lincs., 1611. R. of Castor, Northants., 1613-29. V. of West Mersea, Essex. Archdeacon of Northampton, 1612-29. Preb. of Peterborough, 1614. Buried in Peterborough Cathedral, July 25, 1629. Admon. (Peterb.) 1629. (*D.N.B.*; H. I. Longden.)

DOVE, THOMAS. Adm. pens. at SIDNEY, June 25, 1609. Matric. 1609.

DOVE, THOMAS. Matric. pens. from QUEENS', Michs. 1618. Of Surrey. B.A. 1621-2; M.A. 1625. Perhaps R. of Pattiswick, Essex, till 1641; sequestered. V. of W. Mersea.

DOVE, THOMAS. Adm. at CORPUS CHRISTI, 1623. Of Northamptonshire. S. and h. of Sir William, Knt., of Upton, Northants. B. at Peterborough, 1606. Adm. at the Middle Temple, May 11, 1626. Married in 1633, Frances, dau. of William Becke, of Castleacre, Norfolk, Esq. Buried at Castor, Apr. 26, 1654. (*N. and Q.*, 6th S., IX. 417.)

DOVE, THOMAS. M.A. 1650 (Incorp. from Oxford). S. of Henry, of Salisbury. Matric. from Magdalen Hall, Oxford, Oct. 22, 1630, age 18; B.A. 1632; M.A. 1634-5. R. of Elm, Cambs., and Emneth, Norfolk, 1646, on his brother Robert's sequestration. (*Al. Oxon.*)

DOVE, THOMAS. Adm. at CORPUS CHRISTI, 1652. Of Northamptonshire.

DOVE, THOMAS. Adm. sizar at TRINITY HALL, June 26, 1746. Matric. 1747; Scholar, 1747. Perhaps LL.B. 1766. Ord. deacon (Lincoln) June 10, 1750; priest, Mar. 18, 1753. V. of Gazeley, Cambs., 1766-1808. R. of Rattlesden, Suffolk. 1798-1808. One of these names R of Caldecote, Herts., 1789.

DOVE or DOWE, TIMOTHY. Adm. sizar at EMMANUEL, June 6, 1650. S. of Barjonas (1609), V. of Aslackby, Lincs. B. there. Matric. 1653. Migrated to St John's, Jan. 21, 1654-5, age 20. B.A. 1654-5; M.A. 1670. Ord. in Ireland by the Bishop of Ardfert and Agbadoe. R. of Rippingale, Lincs., 1660. (*Lincs. Pedigrees*, 390.)

DOVE, WILLIAM. Matric. pens. from QUEENS', Michs. 1570.

DOVE or DOWE, WILLIAM. Adm. scholar (age 18) at CAIUS, Jan. 11, 1580-1. S. of William. B. at Debenham, Suffolk. Schools, Botesdale, Bungay, and Fressingfield. Matric. 1580-1.

DOVE, WILLIAM. Adm. pens. (age 17) at SIDNEY, June 2, 1638. S. of Thomas, yeoman. B. at Newton-on-Rawcliffe, Yorks. Schools, Pickering (Mr Edward Bright) and Coxwold (Mr William Smelt). Matric. 1638; B.A. 1641-2; M.A. 1646.

DOVE, WILLIAM. Adm. sizar at ST CATHARINE'S, Mar. 3, 1695-6. Matric. 1696; B.A. 1699-1700. Ord. deacon (York) May, 1700; priest, 1700.

DOWE, ——. Adm. at CORPUS CHRISTI, 1563.

DOVE, ——. Adm. pens. at ST CATHARINE'S, Easter, 1636. Of Suffolk.

DOVER, Earl of, *see* **CAREY, HENRY.**

DOVER, JAMES. Adm. pens. (age 17) at CAIUS, Apr. 8, 1685. S. of James, citizen of Norwich. B. there. School, Norwich. Matric. 1685; Scholar, 1685-92; B.A. 1688-9; M.A. 1692. Incorp. at Oxford, 1694. Ord. priest (Lincoln) Sept. 20, 1691. V. of Limpenhoe and Southwood, 1693-1727. R. of Burlingham St Peter, Norfolk, 1697-1727. R. of Blofield, 1727-35. Died July 18, 1735. M.I. at Blofield. Will (Norw. C.C.) 1735. (*Venn*, I. 478.)

DOVER, JOHN. Adm. sizar at QUEENS', Jan. 29, 1599-1600. B. at Bassenthwaite, Cumberland. B.A. 1602-3; M.A. 1606. Ord. deacon (London) May 26, 1605, age 24. C. of Barne Elms; priest, Dec. 20, 1606. C. of St Andrew Wardrobe. Perhaps R. of Cranford St John, Northants., 1621-4. Died 1624.

DOVER, RICHARD. Adm. sizar at QUEENS', Feb. 1593-4. Of Norfolk. Matric. *c.* 1594.

DOVER, ROBERT. Adm. sizar at QUEENS', June 15, 1595. Of Norfolk. Matric. *c.* 1595. One of these names, of Gt Ellingham, Norfolk, adm. at Gray's Inn, Feb. 27, 1604-5.

DOVER, ROBERT. Sizar at QUEENS', Aug. 25, 1613. Of Cumberland.

DOVER, THOMAS. Adm. pens. at CAIUS, Nov. 4, 1686; M.B. 1687. S. of John, of Barton-on-the-Heath, Warws., gent. Bapt. there, May 6, 1662. Matric. from Magdalen Hall, Oxford, Dec. 1, 1680, 'aged 16'; B.A. 1684. Practised at Bristol. Sailed thence in 1708, on a privateering expedition round the world for three years, where they took many prizes, and captured Guayaquil, Ecuador. Licentiate, R.C.P. 1721. Practised afterwards in London and elsewhere. Known as the inventor of 'Dover's powder.' Author, *The Ancient Physician's Legacy*. Buried at Stanway, Gloucs., Apr. 15, 1742. (*D.N.B.*; *Vis. of Warws.*, 1682; and Venn, *Early Collegiate Life*.)

DOVER, WILLIAM. Adm. sizar at TRINITY, May 6, 1653. Of Yorkshire. Scholar, 1655; B.A. 1656-7; M.A. 1660. College Chaplain, 1658-1660. V. of Appleton, Yorks., 1662.

DOVEY, JOHN. B.A. from ST JOHN'S, 1588-9. Of Worcestershire. M.A. 1592. Fellow, 1591-2.

DOWBIGGIN, DAVID. Adm. sizar at ST CATHARINE'S, Jan. 23, 1751. Of Horton, Yorks. B.A. 1755.

DOWBIGGIN, JOHN. Adm. sizar (age 22) at ST JOHN'S, Apr. 16, 1718. S. of Christopher, husbandman, of Lancashire. B. at Tatham. School, Sedbergh. Brother of Thomas (1718).

DOWBIGGIN, THOMAS. Adm. sizar (age 20) at CHRIST'S, June 9, 1671. S. of Thomas. Probably b. at Ince, Lancs. School, Thirsk. B.A. 1674-5. Ord. deacon (York) Sept. 1675; priest, June, 1680. R. of Birkby, near Northallerton, Aug. 14, 1701. Buried there July 14, 1721. (*Peile*, II. 36.)

DOWBIGGIN, THOMAS. Adm. sizar at ST JOHN'S, Apr. 14, 1718. S. of Christopher, husbandman, of Lancashire. B. at Tatham, near Lancaster. School, Sedbergh. Matric. 1718; B.A. 1721-2. Ord. deacon (York) May 20, 1722; priest, June 9, 1723 V. of Garton-on-the-Wolds, Yorks., before 1750. V. of Hutton Cranswick, 1750-67. Brother of John (1718). (*Scott-Mayor*, III. 316.)

DOWDESWELL, CHARLES. Elected scholar at TRINITY, from Westminster, 1704; but entered at Christ Church, Oxford. S. of William, of Ashton, Gloucs., clerk. Died July 22, 1705.

DOWDESWELL, GEORGE. Adm. pens. at CLARE, Sept. 20, 1731. B. in London. Matric. 1732; B.A. 1735-6. Ord. deacon (Lincoln) Mar. 21, 1735-6. R. of Bradeston, Norfolk, 1758-63. R. of Strumpshaw, 1758-63. Died Nov. 25, 1763.

DOWDING, JOSEPH. Adm. pens. (age 17) at PETERHOUSE, June 29, 1706. 2nd s. of Joseph, gent., of Stower Provost, Dorset. School, Eton. Matric. 1706; Scholar, 1706. Adm. at the Middle Temple, June, 1706.

DOWE, *see also* **DOVE.**

DOWE or DOWS, JOHN. B.Can.L. 1506-7.

DOWELL, JOHN. Adm. pens. (age 18) at CHRIST'S, May 29, 1645. S. of Peter. B. at Leicester. School, Leicester. Matric. 1645; B.A. 1648-9; M.A. 1656. Incorp. at Oxford, 1658. V. of Melton Mowbray, 1660-90. Author, theological. Buried, Oct. 5, 1690, at Melton Mowbray. Will, Leicester. (*Peile*, I. 496; *Nichols*, II. 249.)

DOWELL, SAMUEL. Adm. pens. at TRINITY, Jan. 27, 1648-9. Of Warwickshire. One of these names C. of Weeley, Essex, in 1650. R. 1654-60.

DOWELL, WILLIAM. Matric. sizar from QUEENS', Michs. 1622. Of Dorset.

DOWGLASS, *see* **DOUGLAS.**

DOWKE, JOHN. Matric. pens. from ST JOHN'S, Michs. 1555. Of Yorkshire. B.A. 1559-60. Fellow, 1560.

DOWKER, *see* **DOUKER.**

DOWLE, NATHANIEL. Matric. pens. from ST CATHARINE'S, Michs. 1622.

DOWLMAN, ——. D.D. 1523-4.

DOWLY, PETER. Adm. sizar at ST CATHARINE'S, June 19, 1680.

DOWLY, ——. Adm. Fell.-Com. at CORPUS CHRISTI, 1552.

DOWMAN, *see also* **DOLMAN.**

DOWMAN, EDWARD. Matric. pens. from TRINITY, Michs. 1582.

DOWMAN, FRANCIS. Adm. pens. (age 18) at ST JOHN'S, Jan. 29, 1639–40. S. of William, gent., of Uffington, Lincs. B. at Clipsham, Rutland. School, Stanford. Matric. 1640. Brother of Mildmay (1648). (*Lincs. Pedigrees.*)

DOWMAN, ISAAC. Adm. pens. (age 16) at ST JOHN'S, July 8, 1681. S. of Mildmay (1648), Esq. B. at Soham, Cambs. School, Bury St Edmund's. Matric. 1681. Father of the next.

DOWMAN, ISAAC. Adm. pens. (age 18) at PEMBROKE, May 26, 1708. S. of Isaac (above), of Soham, Cambs., gent. Matric. 1709.

DOWMAN, JAMES. Matric. pens. from ST JOHN'S, Michs. 1553.

DOWMAN, DOWLMAN or DOLMAN, JOHN. B.Civ.L. 1488; D.Civ.L. 1494. S. of William, of Pocklington, Yorks. Incorp. at Oxford, 1514. R. of All Saints', Fulbourn, Cambs., c. 1475. R. of Pocklington, Yorks. Preb. of Sarum, 1505. R. of St Nicholas Acons, London, 1506. Archdeacon of Suffolk, 1507–26. Preb. of St Paul's, 1507–26. Preb. of Lichfield, 1509–25. Founder of Pocklington School, 1514. Benefactor to St John's. Died Nov. 11, 1525. Will (P.C.C.) 1526. To be buried in the Chapel of St Catharine in St Paul's. (*Cooper*, I. 33; *Al. Oxon.*; M. H. Peacock.)

DOWMAN, MILDMAY. Adm. pens. (age 17) at ST JOHN'S, Apr. 5, 1648. S. of William, gent., of Uffington, near Stamford, Lincs. B. there. School, Botolph Bridge, near Peterborough. Matric. 1650. Adm. at Gray's Inn, June 14, 1651. Brother of Francis (1639–40), father of Isaac (1681).

DOWMAN or DOLMAN, RICHARD. Adm. pens. (age 18) at ST JOHN'S, Apr. 25, 1657. S. of Richard, gent., of Hayton, Yorks. B. there. School, Pocklington. Matric. 1658. Probably R. of North Newbald, Yorks., 1680.

DOWMAN, ROGER. Adm. scholar (age 19) at CAIUS, Mar. 26, 1582. S. of Thomas, gent. B. at 'Havere' (? Hathern), Leics. School, Kegworth. Probably drowned in the Cam. Buried at Grantchester, May 4, 1583. (*Venn*, I. 114.)

DOWNALL, WILLIAM. Matric. Fell.-Com. from PEMBROKE, Michs. 1602.

DOWNE, ANTHONY. Matric. sizar from PEMBROKE, Michs. 1628, as Ambrose; B.A. 1631–2; M.A. 1635. V. of Northam, Devon; ejected, 1662. Died at the age of 80. Will (Exeter) 1690; of Exeter. Brother of Mark (1629) and Thomas (1625), father of John (1677) and Thomas (1670). (*Calamy*, I. 386.)

DOWNE, HENRY. Adm. pens. at EMMANUEL, May 14, 1631. Matric. 1631. Of Devon. Perhaps s. of John (next), of Instow, Devon. Matric. from Exeter College, Oxford, June 21, 1633, age 20; B.A. (Oxford) 1634–5; M.A. 1637. M.D. from Caen, 1647–8. Incorp. at Oxford. Practised at Barnstaple. (*Al. Oxon.*)

DOWNE, JOHN. Adm. pens. at EMMANUEL, July 1, 1586. S. of John (and Joan, sister of Bishop Jewell). B. at Holdsworthy, Devon, c. 1570. Matric. 1586; Scholar; B.A. 1589–90; M.A. 1593; B.D. 1600. Fellow, 1594. Incorp. at Oxford, 1600. V. of Winsford, Somerset, 1602–5. R. of Instow, Devon, 1604–31. Author, religious. Buried at Instow, 1631. Will, P.C.C. Perhaps father of Henry (above). (*D.N.B.* According to *Misc. Gen. et Her.*, 3rd S., I. 200, he was s. of Henry.)

DOWNE, JOHN. Adm. sizar (age 17) at CAIUS, July 6, 1603. S. of William, R. of Gidleigh, Devon. School, Clanaborough, Devon. Matric. 1603. One of these names R. of Nymet Rowland; will proved (Exeter) 1619. (*Venn*, I. 182.)

DOWNE, JOHN. Adm. sizar (age 16) at SIDNEY, May 9, 1677. S. of Anthony (1628), clerk. B. at Northam, Devon. School, Tiverton. Matric. 1677; B.A. 1680–1; M.A. 1684. Fellow, 1689. Died in College, of small-pox, c. 1689. Will proved (V.C.C.) 1689. Brother of Thomas (1670).

DOWNE, MARK. Adm. sizar at QUEENS', Apr. 6, 1629. Of Devon. B.A. 1631–2; M.A. 1635. Ejected from St Petrock's, Exeter, 1662. Died Oct. 1680. Brother of Anthony (1628) and Thomas (1625). (*Calamy*, I. 370.)

DOWNE, NICHOLAS. Adm. sizar at PEMBROKE, Aug. 30, 1662. S. of Walter, of Devon, farmer. Matric. 1663. Previously matric. from Exeter College, Oxford, July 13, 1660. B.A. 1663–4. V. of St Bruard, Cornwall, 1691–1703. Will proved (Exeter) 1723.

DOWNE, RICHARD. M.A. 1626 (Incorp. from Oxford). Perhaps s. of John, of Pilton, Devon. Matric. from Exeter College, Dec. 13, 1615, age 18; B.A. 1619; M.A. 1621–2; B.D. 1630; D.D. 1633. R. of Tawstock and Marwood, Devon, 1636. (*Al. Oxon.*; *Vis. of Devon*, 1620.)

DOWNE, THOMAS. Matric. sizar from ST JOHN'S, Easter, 1598; B.A. 1601–2; M.A. 1605. Incorp. at Oxford, 1605. Ord. deacon and priest (Peterb.) June 29, 1603. V. of Stratton, Cornwall, 1606; of Buckland Bruere, Devon, 1611. Will (Exeter) 1630; of Stratton.

DOWNE, THOMAS. Matric. sizar from ST JOHN'S, Easter, 1625. Of Cornwall. Migrated to Queens', June 8, 1625. B.A. 1628–9; M.A. 1632. Ejected from St Edmund's, Exeter, 1662. Probably brother of Anthony (1628) and Mark (1629). (*Calamy*, I. 369.)

DOWNE, THOMAS. Adm. pens. (age 24) at ST JOHN'S, June 25, 1670; B.A. 1670–1. S. of Anthony (1628), V. of Northam, Devon. B. there. Matric. from Exeter College, Oxford, Dec. 17, 1663. R. of Sutcombe, Devon, 1670. Will (Exeter) 1702. Brother of John (1677). (*Al. Oxon.*)

DOWNE, Viscount, *see* DAWNAY, JOHN.

DOWNER, THOMAS. M.A. 1608 (Incorp. from Oxford); B.A. (Oxford) 1604; M.A. 1608; B.D. 1614. Ord. deacon (Oxford) Sept. 25; priest, Dec. 18, 1608. R. of Radnage, Bucks., 1613. V. of Kirtlington, Oxon., 1616. V. of Charlbury, 1623. (*Al. Oxon.*)

DOWNES, ANDREW. Scholar of ST JOHN'S, 1567. Of Salop. School, Shrewsbury. B.A. 1570–1; M.A. 1574; B.D. 1582. Fellow, 1571. Regius Professor of Greek, 1585–1624. Ord. deacon (Peterb.) June 25, 1575. One of the translators of the Authorized Version. Died Feb. 2, 1627–8. Will (P.C.C.) 1628. (*D.N.B.*)

DOWNES, ANDREW. Matric. sizar from KING'S, Michs. 1641. One of these names R. of Coppenhall, Cheshire, 1653. Buried there June 3, 1674.

DOWNES, CHARLES. Adm. pens. (age 17) at ST JOHN'S, June 25, 1743. S. of Joseph (1714), clerk, of Manchester. B. at Stockport. School, Manchester. Matric. 1743; LL.B. 1749. Ord. deacon (Norwich) Sept. 24, 1749; priest (Rochester) Sept. 23, 1750. Fellow of the Collegiate Church of Manchester, 1760–3. R. of St Mary's, Manchester, 1761–3. Died Oct. 31, 1763. (*Scott-Mayor*, III. 537.)

DOWNES, CHRISTOPHER. B.A. 1534–5; M.A. 1538–9; B.D. 1546. One of the original fellows of TRINITY, 1546. V. of Enfield, Middlesex, 1550–5. Died 1555.

DOWNES, EDMUND. LL.B. from TRINITY HALL, 1600.

DOWNES, EDWARD. Adm. Fell.-Com. at JESUS, May 14, 1709. S. and h. of Edward, of Shrigley, Cheshire, Esq. Matric. 1709. Adm. at the Middle Temple, Oct. 18, 1711. Succeeded his father at Shrigley. Died Aug. 4, 1748. Buried at Prestbury. (A. Gray.)

DOWNES, ELKANAH. Adm. sizar (age 17) at CAIUS, Apr. 10, 1630. S. of Robert, carpenter, of Yorkshire. B. at Pudsey. Bapt. at Calverley, Aug. 4, 1611. School, Bradford. Matric. 1631; B.A. 1633–4; Scholar, 1634–7; M.A. 1637; D.D. 1661 (*Lit. Reg.*). Ord. deacon (Peterb.) Sept. 24, 1637; priest, May 20, 1638. V. of Ashstead, Surrey, till 1683. R. of Digswell, Herts., 1647 (when he subscribed the Bishop of London's book, Mar. 18, 1646–7). P.C. of St Mary's, Chatham, 1661–2. P.C. of Trinity Minories, London, 1661–6. R. of St Leonard, Eastcheap, 1661–6. Preacher at St Bartholomew's, 1662. Died 1683. Will (Comm. C. Surrey) 1683. (*Venn*, I. 293.)

DOWNES, FRANCIS. Matric. pens. from CHRIST'S, Easter, 1550. One of these names adm. at Lincoln's Inn, Feb. 19, 1552–3.

DOWNES, FRANCIS. Adm. Fell.-Com. at QUEENS', Nov. 5, 1644. Of Cheshire. Doubtless s. of Francis, of Chorley, Cheshire, Esq. Adm. at Oundle School, Mar. 4, 1637–8; then living at Pytchley. One of these names, of Northamptonshire, adm. at Gray's Inn, Feb. 1, 1646–7.

DOWNES, GEOFFREY. B.A. 1485–6; M.A. 1489. Fellow of QUEENS', 1490–4. Died 1529; *see* next.

DOWNES, GEOFFREY. Of Lichfield diocese. B.A. 1511–2; M.A. 1515; B.D. 1521; D.D. 1526. S. of Roger, of Shrigley, Cheshire. Fellow of JESUS, 1512. University preacher, 1520. Ord. deacon (Ely) Oct. 20, 1516; priest, Dec. 20, 1516. Preb. of York, 1532. Preb. of Southwell, 1535. Chancellor of York, 1537–60. Died July, 1561. Will (Dean and Chapter of York) 1561. From will of James Downes, R. of Wickham Breux, Kent, 1529: 'Mr Geoffrey Downes, D.D., of Jesus College to pray for my soul and the soul of Mr Geoffrey Downes.' (*Cooper*, I. 210; A. Gray.)

DOWNES, GEOFFREY. Matric. pens. from CHRIST'S, May, 1554. B. at Shrigley, Cheshire. B.A. 1557–8; M.A. 1561. Fellow of St John's, 1558. B.D. (Oxford) 1572. Ord. deacon (London) June, 1568. R. of Chadwell, Essex, 1568–75; of St Margaret Lothbury, 1572–3; deprived. V. of Gillingham, Kent, 1572–91. R. of Bishopsbourne, 1576–9; of Little Thurrock, Essex, 1579. Buried at Gillingham, Nov. 16, 1591. (*Al. Oxon.*; *Peile*, I. 55; *Cooper*, II. 182.)

DOWNES, GEORGE. Matric. pens. from ST JOHN'S, Michs. 1564. Perhaps R. of Higham-on-the-Hill, Leics., 1579–83. Died Apr. 22, 1583.

DOWNES, HENRY. Adm. sizar (age 19) at ST JOHN'S, June 30, 1740. S. of John (1708), clerk, of Derbyshire. B. at Derwent (his mother was of Derwent Hall, Derby). School, Rotherham. Matric. 1740; B.A. 1743-4. Ord. priest (York) Feb. 19, 1743-4. C. of St Paul's, Sheffield, 1745-75. Master of Shrewsbury (or Talbot's) Hospital, Sheffield. V. of Ecclesfield, 1768-75. Died July 1, 1775. Buried at St Paul's, Sheffield. (*Scott-Mayor*, III. 508; *F.M.G.*, 694; M. H. Peacock.)

DOWNES, JAMES. Matric. pens. from ST JOHN'S, Easter, 1579. One of these names subscribed for deacon's and priest's orders (Lincoln) Mar. 26, 1586. V. of Hainton, Lincs., 1586.

DOWNES, JAMES. Adm. sizar (age 19) at ST JOHN'S, June 25, 1715. S. of Richard, clerk, deceased. B. at East Meon, Hants. School, Cambridge (Mr Foster). Matric. 1715; B.A. 1718-9. Brother of Marmaduke (1715) and John (1701). Will (P.C.C.) 1766, of one of these names, 'of Petersfield, Hants., clerk.'

DOWNES, JAMES. Adm. sizar at JESUS, Oct. 31, 1727. Of Yorkshire. Matric. 1728. Ord. deacon (Lincoln) Sept. 20, 1730. One of these names R. of North Burlingham, Norfolk, in 1737.

DOWNES, JOHN. Matric. pens. from CHRIST'S, May, 1551.

DOWNES, JOHN. Matric. pens. from ST JOHN'S, Michs. 1568; B.A. 1571-2. Ord. deacon (Lincoln) Feb. 24, 1576-7; priest, Aug. 27, 1577. R. of Benniworth, Lincs., 1576-7. R. of Lusby, 1582. R. of Manby, 1583.

DOWNES, JOHN. Matric. sizar from TRINITY, c. 1597.

DOWNES or DOWNE, JOHN. Incorp. M.A. from Oxford, 1629. Of Wiltshire. Matric. from Magdalen Hall, Oxford, June 26, 1621 (age 17); B.A. (Oxford) 1625-6; M.A. 1629. Ord. deacon (Peterb.) Feb. 28; priest, Mar. 1, 1628-9. One of these names R. of Brockley, Suffolk, 1635-70. (*Al. Oxon.*)

DOWNES, JOHN. Adm. Fell.-Com. (age 18) at CHRIST'S, June 29, 1633. S. of Roger (reader of Gray's Inn). B. at Wardley, Lancs. School, Wardley (private). Matric. 1633. Adm. at Gray's Inn, Nov. 6, 1635. Married Penelope, dau. of Sir Cecil Trafford. Of Wardley Hall, Esq. An ardent royalist. Died May, 1648. Brother of Roger (1618-9). (*Peile*, I. 428; Hart-Davis, *Wardley Hall*.)

DOWNES, JOHN. Adm. pens. (age 17) at ST JOHN'S, July 3, 1701. S. of Richard, clerk. B. at East Meon, Hants. Matric. 1701; B.A. 1705-6; M.A. 1709. One of these names C. of Rothwell, Yorks. Buried there Dec. 6, 1715. Brother of Marmaduke (1715) and James (1715).

DOWNES, JOHN. Adm. sizar (age 17) at ST JOHN'S, Oct. 12, 1708. S. of John, goldsmith. B. in London. School, Merchant Taylors'. Matric. 1708; B.A. 1712-3. Ord. deacon (Bishop of Llandaff, in Hereford Cathedral) Aug. 16, 1713. V. of St Paul's, Sheffield, 1739-45. R. of St Michael, Wood St, London, 1745-60. Lecturer at St Mary-le-Bow. Married Ann, dau. of Henry Balguy, of Darwent Hall. Died 1760. Father of Henry (1740). (*F.M.G.*, 694; M. H. Peacock.)

DOWNES, JOHN. Adm. sizar (age 19) at ST JOHN'S, Oct. 21, 1710. S. of Richard, gent. B. at Melverley, Salop. School, Oswestry. Matric. 1711; B.A. 1714-5; M.A. 1721. Ord. deacon (Ely) Mar. 13, 1714-5.

DOWNES, JONATHAN. Adm. pens. (age 18) at ST JOHN'S, Oct. 5, 1748. S. of John, counsellor, of America. B. at Spring. School, Shrewsbury. Matric. 1748; B.A. 1753-4; M.A. 1756. Fellow, 1755-62. Ord. deacon (Chester) June 13; priest (Bangor) Sept. 19, 1756. The father was of Barbados; barrister of the Middle Temple. (*Scott-Mayor*, III. 583.)

DOWNES, JOSEPH. Adm. sizar (age 17) at ST JOHN'S, Apr. 16, 1714. S. of John, cutler. B. at Sheffield, Yorks. School, Sheffield. Matric. 1714; B.A. 1717-8; M.A. 1722. Ord. deacon (London) Feb. 22, 1718-9; priest (York) June, 1721. Chaplain of the Collegiate Church of Manchester. Died 1739. Father of Charles (1743).

DOWNES, MARLUS. Matric. sizar from ST JOHN'S, Easter, 1628.

DOWNES, MARMADUKE. Adm. sizar (age 17) at ST JOHN'S, June 25, 1715. S. of Richard, clerk, deceased. B. at East Meon, Hants. School, Cambridge (Mr Foster). Matric. 1715; B.A. 1718-9; M.A. 1722; B.D. 1730. Fellow, 1722-38. Taxor, 1727. Ord. deacon (London) June 12, 1720; priest, Sept. 1722. Brother of John (1701) and James (1715).

DOWNES, PETER. B.A. 1525-6.

DOWNES, RICHARD. Matric. sizar from TRINITY, Easter, 1616.

DOWNES, RICHARD. Matric. pens. from ST JOHN'S, Easter, 1626; B.A. 1629-30. One of these names R. of Ashdon, Essex, 1659.

DOWNES, RICHARD. Adm. pens. (age 19) at ST JOHN'S, June 21, 1714. S. of Richard, clerk. B. at Chichester. School, Cambridge. Matric. 1714; B.A. 1717-8.

DOWNES, ROBERT. Matric. pens. from CHRIST'S, May, 1550.

DOWNES, ROBERT. Matric. pens. from JESUS, Easter, 1552; B.A. 1561-2; M.A. from Peterhouse, 1565. Fellow, 1563. Probably R. of Homersfield, Suffolk, 1565-6. R. of Stanstead, 1574. Preb. of Norwich, 1577-87. R. of Shimpling, Norfolk, 1586.

DOWNES, RO. Matric. pens. from ST JOHN'S, Michs. 1559. One Robert Downes adm. at Lincoln's Inn, Apr. 19, 1564.

DOWNES, ROBERT. Matric. pens. from CHRIST'S, May, 1563. B. at 'Westchester.' Scholar, in 1564. Ord. priest (London) Feb. 15, 1569-70, age 26. R. of Panfield, Essex, 1569-75. (*Peile*, I. 79.)

DOWNES, ROGER. Adm. Fell.-Com. at EMMANUEL, Feb. 22, 1618-9. Matric. 1618-9. Doubtless s. and h. of Roger, reader of Gray's Inn; adm. at Gray's Inn, Aug. 6, 1615. Of Wardley, Lancs., Esq. Died before 1638. Brother of John (1633). (*Vis. of Lancs.*, 1613, 1664; Hart-Davis, *Wardley Hall*.)

DOWNES, SAMUEL. Matric. pens. from PETERHOUSE, Michs. 1616. Of Lincolnshire. B.A. from St Catharine's, 1619-20. M.A. from St John's, 1623. Ord. deacon (Peterb.) Feb. 18; priest, Feb. 19, 1626-7. R. of Manby, Lincs., 1627.

DOWNES, SAMUEL. Adm. sizar at KING'S, Sept. 1662. Of Cheshire. Matric. 1663. Migrated to Pembroke (age 18) Jan. 2, 1663-4. B.A. 1666-7; M.A. 1671. Ord. deacon (Lincoln) May 17, 1668; priest (London) Sept. 1668. Schoolmaster at Coggeshall, Essex.

DOWNES, SAMUEL. Adm. pens. at ST CATHARINE'S, 1665-6. Matric. 1667; B.A. 1669-70; M.A. 1673; M.D. 1680.

DOWNES, THOMAS. Matric. sizar from PEMBROKE, c. 1595. One of these names adm. at Gray's Inn, Feb. 4, 1595-6.

DOWNES, THOMAS. B.A. from ST JOHN'S, 1609-10; M.A. 1613.

DOWNES, THOMAS. Adm. sizar (age 16) at PEMBROKE, Apr. 21, 1664. S. of Thomas. B. at Stowlangtoft, Suffolk. Matric. 1664; B.A. 1667-8; M.A. 1671. One of these names buried at Newton-by-Wisbech, Cambs., 1683. (*Ely Dioc. Reg.*, 342.)

DOWNES, WILLIAM. B.A. (? 1508-9); M.A. 1514-5. Perhaps R. of Gt Warley, Essex, 1522-34.

DOWNS, WILLIAM. Adm. sizar (age 19) at TRINITY, Feb. 25, 1709-10. S. of Robert, of Newby, Yorks. School, Guisborough, Yorks. (Mr Jacques). Matric. 1710; B.A. 1714-5. Ord. priest (Norwich) Dec. 1714. V. of Over, Cambs., 1714.

DOWNHALL, *see* DONHALT.

DOWNHAM or DOWNAME, GEORGE. Matric. pens. from CHRIST'S, Nov. 1581. S. of William, Bishop of Chester. B.A. 1584-5; M.A. 1588; B.D. 1595; D.D. 1601. Fellow, 1587-96. Incorp. at Oxford, 1591. One of the earliest teachers of the Logic of Ramus. Chaplain to James I. Preb. of St Paul's, 1593-1616. Preb. of Chester, 1594-9. R. of St Margaret, Lothbury, 1596-1601. R. of Gt Munden, Herts., 1601-16. R. of St Michael-le-Querne, 1614-7. Preb. of Wells, 1615. Bishop of Derry, 1616-34. Famous as a logician. Author, *Sermons*, etc. Died at Derry, Apr. 17, 1634. Buried in the Cathedral there. Brother of John (1589), father of Samuel (1615). (*Peile*, I. 166; *D.N.B.*)

DOWNHAM or DOWNAME, GEORGE. Adm. pens. (age 18) at CHRIST'S, Jan. 15, 1626-7. S. of John (1589), of All Hallows, Thames Street. B. in London. At school under Mr Harnebie. Matric. 1627; B.A. 1630-1; M.A. 1634. C. of St Stephen Walbrook, London, c. 1637-9. Perhaps R. of South Repps, Norfolk, 1638-47. Author, *Sermon*. (*Peile*, I. 379.)

DOWNHAM, GREGORY. Matric. pens. from PEMBROKE, Easter, 1572. Greek scholar, from Merchant Taylors' School. Perhaps B.A. 1575. Incorp. B.A. at Oxford (as Downhall) 1577-8. A master in chancery.

DOWNAME, JOHN. Matric. pens. from CHRIST'S, Michs. 1589. S. of William, Bishop of Chester. B.A. 1592-3; M.A. 1596; B.D. 1603. Ord. deacon and priest (London) July, 1598, age 27. V. of St Olave Jewry, 1599-1602. R. of St Margaret, Lothbury, 1602-18. R. of All Hallows, Thames Street, 1630-52. Lecturer at St Bartholomew Exchange. Licenser of the Press, 1643. Appointed to examine and ordain ministers in London, 1644. Author. Died 1652. Will (P.C.C.). Brother of George (1581), father of George (1626). (*Peile*, I. 196; *D.N.B.*)

DOWNHAM, MILES. Matric. sizar from PEMBROKE, Michs. 1565. B. in Cambridgeshire. Ord. deacon (Ely) Mar. 23, 1566-7; priest, Dec. 21, 1568. V. of Hinxton, Cambs., 1568. Aged 38 in 1572. (W. M. Noble.)

DOWNHAM, SAMUEL. Matric. pens. from CHRIST'S, July, 1615. S. of George (1581), Bishop of Derry. Bapt. at St Margaret, Lothbury, Jan. 21, 1598-9. (*Peile*, I. 302.)

DOWNHAM, ——. Resident as sizar at CHRIST'S, in 1564.

DOWNING, CALIBUTE. Adm. pens. at EMMANUEL, Easter, 1623. S. of Calibute, of Shennington, Gloucs. (?). Matric. 1623. Migrated to Oxford. B.A. from Oriel College, 1626. Incorp. at Cambridge, 1629. M.A. from Peterhouse, 1630; LL.D. 1637. R. of Ickford, Bucks., 1632-6; and of West Ilsley, Berks., 1632-7. V. of Hackney, Middlesex, 1637-43. Chaplain in the Earl of Essex's assembly of divines. Author, religious. Died 1644. Will, P.C.C. His s. George, created Bart. (*Al. Oxon.*; *D.N.B.*; *Vis. of Norfolk.*)

DOWNEING, CHARLES. Adm. Fell.-Com. (age 15) at ST JOHN'S, Apr. 10, 1683. S. of Sir George, Bart., of Gamlingay, Cambs. B. in Middlesex. School, Eton. Matric. 1683. Comptroller of the Customs at Salem, New England. Adm. at the Middle Temple, Apr. 11, 1687. Died Apr. 15, 1740. Brother of George (1668-9) and William (1678), father of Jacob Garrard (1734). (*Suff. Man. Fam.*, I. 99.)

DOWNING, EDMUND. Matric. sizar from CHRIST'S, July, 1619; B.A. 1622-3; M.A. 1626. Ord. deacon (Peterb.) Dec. 22; priest, Dec. 23, 1627. *Peile* (I. 330) suggests that he was brother of Calibute (1623). One of these names R. of Mablethorpe, Lincs., 1669.

DOWNING, EMMANUEL. Adm. scholar at TRINITY HALL, Dec. 16, 1602. S. of George (1569), of Ipswich. Bapt. at St Laurence, Ipswich, Aug. 12, 1585. Of the Inner Temple. For some years in Dublin. Emigrated to New England, 1638. Settled in Salem, Mass. Took a prominent part in Colonial affairs. After one or two trips to England he returned permanently in 1654. Died at Edinburgh, *c.* 1660. His son George was created Bart., 1663. Perhaps brother of Joseph (1610). (J. G. Bartlett.)

DOWNING, FRANCIS. Matric. pens. from PEMBROKE, Easter, 1629; B.A. 1631; M.A. 1635.

DOWNING, GEORGE. Matric. pens. from QUEENS', Michs. 1569. S. of George, of Beccles, Suffolk. B.A. 1573-4; M.A. from Corpus Christi, 1577. Master of Ipswich Grammar School, 1589-1610. Will proved, 1610. Father of Emmanuel (1602) and perhaps of Joseph (1610). (*Suff. Man. Fam.*, I. 99.)

DOWNINGE, GEORGE. Adm. sizar (age 15) at CAIUS, Feb. 18, 1636-7. S. of George, weaver. B. in Norwich. School, Saham Toney. Matric. 1637; Scholar, 1637-44; B.A. 1640-1; M.A. 1644. Fellow of Sidney, 1661 (by royal mandate). Ord. deacon (Lincoln) Aug. 20; priest, Aug. 22, 1662. V. of Chicheley, Bucks., 1662. Archdeacon of Coventry, 1673-84. Chancellor of Lichfield, 1676-84. Died 1684. (*Venn*, I. 324.)

DOWNING, GEORGE. Adm. Fell.-Com. at CLARE, Feb. 1668-9. Of East Hatley, Cambs. S. of Sir George, Bart., of Gamlingay. B. *c.* 1656. Adm. at Lincoln's Inn, Oct. 5, 1669. Teller of the Exchequer, 1680-9. Succeeded as Bart., 1684. Sheriff of Cambs. and Hunts., 1686-7 Father of the founder of Downing College. Benefactor to Clare. Died June, 1711. Brother of Charles (1683) and William (1678).

DOWNING, GEORGE. Adm. sizar at CLARE, Apr. 3, 1684. Probably s. of Richard, of Grendon, Northants. Adm. at Oundle School, Jan. 15, 1682-3, age 16. Matric. 1684; B.A. 1687-8; M.A. 1691. Ord. deacon (London) Feb. 24, 1688-9; priest, Dec. 21, 1690. R. of Hinxworth, Herts., 1697. Father of the next.

DOWNING, GEORGE. Adm. pens. (age 17) at ST JOHN'S, Jan. 21, 1719-20. S. of George (above), clerk, of Hertfordshire. B. at Hinxworth, near Biggleswade. School, Bishop's Stortford. Matric. 1720; B.A. 1723-4; M.A. 1727. Ord. deacon (Lincoln) May 23, 1725; priest (Canterbury) Mar. 6, 1725-6. C. of St Mary Magdalene, Canterbury, 1725-7. Perhaps V. of Little Wakering, Essex, 1748-79. (*Scott-Mayor*, III. 329.)

DOWNING, JACOB GARRARD. Adm. Fell.-Com. at EMMANUEL, Oct. 11, 1734, as 'James.' S. of Charles (1683). Succeeded as 4th Bart., June, 1749. Of Gamlingay Park, Cambs. M.P. for Dunwich, Suffolk, 1741-7, 1749-61 and 1763-4. Died in Hill Street, Berkeley Square, Feb. 6, 1764. Will, P.C.C. By his death the will of Sir George, for the foundation of Downing College, came into effect. (Burke, *Ext. Bart.*; *G.E.C.*)

DOWNING, HENRY. M.A. from QUEENS', 1719. Adm. at Trin. Coll., Dublin, July 1, 1712, age 16. S. of Adam, of Rocktown, Derry. B.A. (Dublin) 1716. (*Al. Dublin.*)

DOWNINGE, JOHN. Matric. pens. from CLARE, Michs. 1608.

DOWNING, JOHN. M.A. from KING'S, 1715. S. of James, of Halesowen, Worcs., gent. Matric. from University College, Oxford, Nov. 7, 1707, age 17; B.A. (Oxford) 1711. R. of Enville, Staffs., 1718. Preb. of Lincoln, 1736. Died 1737. (*Al. Oxon.*)

DOWNINGE, JOSEPH. B.A. from TRINITY, 1610-1; M.A. from Queens', 1614. S. of George (? 1569), of Ipswich, clerk. R. of St Stephen's, Ipswich, 1626. R. of La Marney, Essex, 1628-46. Perhaps brother of Emmanuel (1602).

DOWNING, RICHARD. Matric. pens. from QUEENS', Easter, 1573; B.A. from Magdalene, 1576-7; M.A. (Oxford) 1579-80. Ord. deacon (Ely) Apr. 1, 1578. R. of Burrough-on-the-Hill, Leics., 1578-83. V. of Finedon, Northants., 1582-1606. Buried there Jan. 8, 1605-6. Father of Thomas (1603).

DOWNING, RICHARD. Adm. at CHRIST'S, 1689. From Trinity College, Dublin. (Adm. there Oct. 6, 1684; aged 19. S. of John, of Middletown, Cork.) Matric. 1689; B.A. 1689-90; B.A. (Dublin) 1691; M.A. 1692. Will of one of these names (Dublin) 1723; V. of Tubbrid, Tipperary.

DOWNING, ROBERT. Matric. sizar from MAGDALENE, Easter, 1624; B.A. 1631-2. Ord. deacon (Peterb.) Feb. 26, 1631-2.

DOWNING, SAMUEL. Matric. sizar from ST JOHN'S, *c.* 1595.

DOWNING, THOMAS. Matric. sizar from CHRIST'S, Easter, 1603. B. at Thingden (near Finedon), Northants. Ord. deacon (Lichfield); priest (London) Mar. 1609-10, age 24. R. of St Helen's, London, 1613-7. P.C. of St Mary Aldermanbury, 1617-25. Died Sept. 1625. Admon. (Cons. C. London) 1625. (*Peile*, I. 244.)

DOWNING, WILLIAM. Matric. pens. from CORPUS CHRISTI, Easter, 1556.

DOWNING, WILLIAM. Adm. Fell.-Com. at CLARE, Oct. 16, 1678. S. of Sir George, of Gamlingay, Cambs., Bart. B. at the Hague, Holland, 1663. Matric. 1678. Buried at St James, Bury St Edmunds, July 25, 1704. Brother of Charles (1683) and George (1668). (*Suff. Man. Fam.*, I. 99.)

DOWSE, BENJAMIN. Adm. sizar (age 16) at CHRIST'S, May 8, 1704. S. of William. B. at Huntingdon. School, Huntingdon. Scholar, 1704; Matric. 1705-6; B.A. 1707-8; M.A. 1711. Fellow, 1711. Ord. deacon (Lincoln) Sept. 23, 1710. Died 1723. (*Peile*, II. 159.)

DOWSE, EDWARD. M.A. 1616 (Incorp. from Oxford). Of Wiltshire. Matric. from Hart Hall, Oct. 14, 1597, age 15; B.A. 1601; M.A. 1604. M.P. for Cricklade, 1625; for Chichester, 1640; for Portsmouth, 1640-8, in the Long Parliament. Died 1648. Will (P.C.C.) as of Petworth, Sussex. (*Al. Oxon.*)

DOWSE, HAMPTON. Matric. Fell.-Com. from ST JOHN'S, Easter, 1617.

DOWSE or DOWFFE, JOHN. B.A. 1509-10.

DOWSE, PETER. B.A. 1525-6. Probably fellow of CHRIST'S, 1528-9, as 'Dawys.' V. of Duxford St John, Cambs., *c.* 1529.

DOWSE, RICHARD. Adm. sizar at EMMANUEL, Easter, 1649.

DOWSE, ROBERT. Adm. pens. (age 17) at ST JOHN'S, Mar. 19, 1677-8. S. of John, bookseller, deceased. B. in London. School, Felsted. Matric. 1677-8; B.A. 1681-2.

DOWSE, ROBERT. Adm. sizar at QUEENS', July 1, 1701 Of Wiltshire. Matric. 1701; B.A. 1704-5; M.A. 1721. Ord. deacon (Peterb.) June 8, 1707; C. of Wilby, Northants.; priest, Mar. 20, 1708-9. V. of Lufton, Somerset, 1709.

DOWSE or DOWSETT, WILLIAM. Matric. sizar from ST JOHN'S, Easter, 1554. Of Lincolnshire. B.A. 1556-7; M.A. 1560. Fellow, 1557. One of these names V. of Heybridge, Essex.

DOWSE, ——. B.Civ.L. 1532-3.

DOWSEY or DOWSING, CHRISTOPHER. Matric. sizar from CLARE, Easter, 1575; B.A. 1578-9; M.A. 1582. R. of Ripple, Kent, 1599-1616, as Dowsing. P.C. of Walmer, 1616. Died 1616.

DOWSEY, GEORGE. Matric. sizar from KING'S, Lent, 1559-60.

DOWSING, DANIEL. Adm. pens. (age *c.* 18) at PEMBROKE, June 2, 1653. S. of ——, of Framlingham, Suffolk. Matric. 1656; B.A. 1656-7.

DOWSING, JOHN. Matric. sizar from TRINITY, Easter, 1575.

DOWSING, JOHN. Adm. sizar at EMMANUEL, Jan. 24, 1605-6. Matric. 1606.

DOWSING, JOHN. Adm. pens. (age 15) at ST JOHN'S, Mar. 3, 1669-70. S. of Thomas, gent., of Cottenham, Cambs. B. there. School, Cambridge (Mr Ralfe). Matric. 1670; B.A. 1673-4; M.A. 1677. Incorp. at Oxford, 1683. Ord. deacon (London) Mar. 16, 1678-9. R. of Ampthill, Beds., 1680. V. of Isleham, Cambs., 1684. Minor Canon of St Paul's, 1688. R. of Stisted, Essex, 1704-6. R. of Monk's Eleigh, Suffolk, 1706. R. of Cottenham, Cambs., 1715-22. Buried at Cottenham, Nov. 9, 1722. Father of the next. (*E. Anglian*, VIII. 103.)

DOWSING, JOHN. Adm. sizar (age 18) at TRINITY, Apr. 28, 1733. S. of John (above), R. of Cottenham, Cambs. School, Ely (Mr Gunning). Matric. 1733; LL.B. from Trinity Hall, 1739. Ord. deacon (Lincoln, *Litt. dim.* from Ely) Sept. 25, 1737; priest (Ely) July, 1739. R. of Wentworth, Cambs., 1740-2. Died Nov. 28, 1742. M.I. in Ely Cathedral.

DOWSING, JOHN. Adm. at CORPUS CHRISTI, 1736. Of Bedfordshire. Matric. 1737; B.A. 1739-40; M.A. 1743. Ord. deacon (Lincoln) June 1, 1740; priest, June 13, 1742. R. of South Wootton, Norfolk, 1743-89. V. of Middleton, 1758-97. Perhaps R. of Mannington, 1761-79; and R. of East Barsham, 1762-88. R. of Gunthorpe *w.* Bale, 1783.

DOWSING, PHILIP. Matric. sizar from Trinity, Easter, 1577; Scholar, B.A. 1580–1; M.A. 1584, as Dowsey Ord. deacon a 1578 priest (Peterb.) Nov. 13, 1590, as 'Dawson.'

DOWSING, ROBERT (1507), *see* **DUSSING.**

DOWSING, ROBERT. Adm. pens. at Corpus Christi, 1608. Of Norfolk. Matric. Easter, 1611; B.A. 1612–3; M.A. 1616.

DOWSING, SAMUEL. Adm. pens. at Emmanuel, Feb. 28, 1647–8. Of Suffolk. Matric. 1648; B.A. 1651–2; M.A. 1655.

DOWSING, THOMAS. Matric. sizar from Trinity, Easter, 1623; B.A. 1625–6; M.A. 1629. Probably V. of Long Buckby, Northants., 1629.

DOWSING, THOMAS. Matric. sizar from St John's, Michs. 1627; B.A. 1630–1; M.A. 1634.

DOWSING, WILLIAM. Adm. pens. at Emmanuel, Oct. 13, 1629. Of Suffolk. Matric. 1629–30, as 'Dowsett.' Probably not the iconoclast who was s. of Wolfran Dowsing, of Laxfield, Suffolk.

DOWSON, JAMES. Matric. sizar from Magdalene, Easter, 1569.

DOWTING, WILLIAM. D.Can.L. 1494–5.

DOXFORD, JEREMY, *see* **DENFORD.**

DOYLE or DOYELL, EDMUND. Matric. pens. from Christ's, Nov. 1566. One of these names, of Suffolk, adm. at Lincoln's Inn, Mar. 15, 1570.

DOYLE or DOYELL, EDWARD. Matric. pens. from Christ's, Nov. 1566. One of these names, of Norfolk, adm. at Lincoln's Inn, June 15, 1573.

DOYLL, H. Matric. Fell.-Com. from Queens', Michs. 1565.

DOYLE or DOYLEY, ROBERT. M.A. 1632 (Incorp. from Oxford). Of Oxfordshire. Matric. from Magdalen College, Oxford, June 5, 1618, age 18; B.A. 1618; M.A. 1621; B.D. 1640. V. of Goring, Sussex, 1628; and R. of Combes, 1640. (*Al. Oxon.*)

DOYLE, ——. Matric. Fell.-Com. from Trinity, Easter, 1608.

DOYLY, BERTRAM. Matric. pens. from Christ's, July, 1615; B.A. 1618–9; M.A. 1622. Ord. priest (Norwich) June, 1623. V. of Hickling, Norfolk, till 1625. R. of Brunstead, 1625. R. of Sutton, 1625–40. Father of Edward (1649–50). (*Peile*, I. 302.)

DOYLIE, CHRISTOPHER. Adm. pens. (age 17) at Christ's, June 12, 1637. S. of Charles B. at Trowse, Norwich. Schools, Poringland and Buckenham. Matric. 1637 Brother of Henry (1632) and Thomas (1636–7). Will of one of these names (Norw. C.C.) 1693; of Garboldisham.

D'OYLY, Sir EDMUND, Bart. Adm. Fell.-Com. (age 17) at St John's, Mar. 7, 1681–2. S. of Sir William (1655), Bart., deceased, of Shotesham, Norfolk. B. there. School, St Paul's, London. Succeeded as Bart., 1680. Buried at Shotesham, Oct. 24, 1700. (*Burke.*)

DOYLY, EDWARD. Adm. pens. (age 16) at St John's, Feb. 25, 1649–50. S. of Bertram (1615), clerk, of Sutton, Norfolk. School, Bury. Matric. 1650; B.A. 1653–4; M.A. 1657. Fellow, 1654

DOYLEY, FRANCIS. Adm. at King's, a scholar from Eton, 1657. Perhaps 6th s. of Robert, of Turville. B. in Buckinghamshire. B.A. 1661–2; M.A. 1665. Fellow, till his death, 1667. Died in London, of small-pox. (*Vis. of Bucks.*, 1634; *Harwood.*)

DOYLY, HENRY. Adm. pens. (age 17) at Caius, May 3, 1632. S. of Charles, gent., of Shotesham. B. at Trowse Newton, Norfolk. School, Ameringhall. Matric. 1632. Adm. at Lincoln's Inn, Nov. 11, 1639. Will proved (as of Brooke, Norfolk) 1679. Brother of Christopher (1637) and Thomas (1636–7). (*Venn*, I. 305.)

DOYLEY, OLIVER. Adm. at King's, a scholar from Eton, 1634. S. of John, of Buckinghamshire. B. at Henley-on-Thames. B.A. 1638; M.A. 1642; LL.D. 1690 (*Lit. Reg.*). Fellow. Senior Proctor, 1659–60. Vice-provost, 1664. Died Aug. 25, 1693. Will proved (King's College) 1693. Father of Oliver (1693). (*Harwood.*)

DOYLEY, OLIVER. Adm. at King's, a scholar from Eton, 1693. S. of Oliver (1634). No degree recorded. Fellow. Resigned on marriage. According to *Harwood* he was B.A. in 1697.

DOYLY, PEREGRINE. Adm. pens. (age 18) at St John's, Feb. 13, 1642–3. S. of Thomas, Esq., deceased, of Layham, Suffolk. B. at Springfield, Essex (his mother's home). School, Bury. Of Overbury Hall, Layham, Esq. Married Anne, dau. of Edward Wymine, Esq., of Suffolk. Died 1667. (*Vis. of Suff.*, 1664; Davy, *Suff. MSS.*)

D'OYLEY, ROBERT. Adm. pens. at Jesus, Oct. 8, 1657. Of Norfolk.

DOYLEY, SAMUEL. Adm. pens. at Trinity, June 5, 1700. School, Westminster. Scholar, 1701; Matric. 1703; B.A. 1703–4; M.A. 1707. Fellow, 1706. V. of St Nicholas, Rochester, 1710–48. Author, *Translations*, etc. Buried in Rochester Cathedral, May 9, 1748. (*D.N.B.*; *Al. Westmon.*, 237.)

DOYLY, THOMAS. Matric. pens. from St John's, Easter, 1624; B.A. 1627–8; M.A. 1631.

DOYLY, THOMAS. Adm. Fell.-Com. (age 18) at Caius, Feb. 1636–7. S. of Charles, gent., of Trowse Newton, Norfolk. Schools, Norwich and Ameringhall. Probably of Toftrees, Fakenham. Brother of Christopher (1637) and Henry (1632). (*Venn*, I. 324; *Vis. of Norfolk*, 1664.)

DOILEY, WILLIAM. Adm. Fell.-Com. at Jesus, Nov. 7, 1655. Of Norfolk. S. and h. of Sir William, of Shotesham, Norfolk (afterwards Bart.). B. *c.* 1637. Matric. 1656. Adm. at Gray's Inn, Jan. 23, 1652–3. Knighted, 1664. Teller of the Exchequer, 1666–77. Succeeded his father as 2nd Bart., 1677. Died 1680. Admon. July, 1680. Father of Sir Edmund (1681–2). (A. Gray; *G.E.C.*)

D'OYLY or DOYLE, ——. Matric. Fell.-Com. from Christ's, July, 1603. Probably s. of Edmund, of Shotesham, Norfolk. (*Peile*, I. 244.)

D'OYLY or DOYLE (*junior*). Matric. Fell.-Com. from Christ's, July, 1603. Probably s. of Edmund, of Shotesham, Norfolk. (*Peile*, I. 244.)

DOYLEY, ——. Adm. pens. at St Catharine's, 1631.

DRACKET, *see* **DRAKETT.**

DRACKLEY or DRAKELEY, HENRY. Adm. sizar at Emmanuel, June 7, 1609. Matric. 1609; B.A. 1612–3; M.A. 1616. Ord. deacon (Peterb.) June 4, 1615; priest (Lincoln) Feb. 21, 1618–9. V. of Gt Peatling, Leics., 1618.

DRAGSWERD, WILLIAM. Scholar at King's Hall, 1319–27.

DRAKE, FRANCIS. Matric. sizar from Christ's, July, 1603. Probably s. of John, of Horley Green, Yorks. B.A. 1606–7; M.A. 1610. Ord. deacon (York) May, 1611; priest, Feb. 1612–3. C. at Wakefield Church, 1611. V. of Kildwick, Yorks., 1613. Probably brother of Thomas (1596). (*Peile*, I. 244; *F.M.G.*, 506.)

DRAKE, FRANCIS. Matric. pens. from Christ's, Mar. 1613. B. at Sedgeford, Norfolk. B.A. 1616–7; M.A. 1620. Ord. priest (London) 1622, age 25. One of these names V. of Shernborne, Norfolk, 1626.

DRAKE, FRANCIS. Adm. pens. at Emmanuel, Mar. 17, 1626–7; B.A. 1630–1; M.A. 1634. Perhaps s. of Francis, of Esher, Surrey; and M.P. for Surrey, 1654–5 and 1656–8.

DRAKE, FRANCIS. Adm. pens. (age 17) at St John's, July 2, 1658. S. of Francis (? above), Esq., of Walton-on-Thames, Surrey. B. there. School, Clapham, Surrey. Adm. at the Middle Temple, Feb. 12, 1669–70. Of Woodstock, Oxon.

DRAKE, FRANCIS. Adm. pens. (age 14) at St John's, Oct. 24, 1670. S. of Samuel (1637), D.D., of South Kirkby, Yorks. Bapt. there, June 11, 1654. School, Sedbergh. Matric. 1670; B.A. 1674–5; M.A. 1678. Ord. priest (London) Feb. 20, 1675–6. V. of Pontefract, 1678–1713. V. of Hemsworth, Yorks., 1688–1713. Preb. of York, 1688–1713. Buried at Pontefract, July 3, 1713. Father of Francis, author of *Eboracum*, John (1696–7), Samuel (1704) and brother of Nathan (1681). (*F.M.G.*, 511.)

DRAKE, FRANCIS. Adm. sizar (age 19) at St John's, Apr. 17, 1714. S. of Thomas, deceased. B. at Halifax, Yorks. School. Beighton, Derbs. Matric. 1714; B.A. 1717–8; M.A. 1722. Ord. deacon (London) Dec. 21, 1718. Perhaps Usher at Uppingham School, 1737. C. of Kirk Smeaton. Died unmarried. Buried at Halifax. (*F.M.G.*, 1159.)

DRAKE, FRANCIS HENRY. Adm. Fell.-Com. at Corpus Christi, Nov. 19, 1740. S. of Sir Francis, Bart., of Buckland, Devon. B. at Meavy, Devon, Aug. 29, 1722. School, Eton. Student at Lincoln's Inn, July 19, 1740. Succeeded as Bart., 1740. M.P. for Beeralston, Devon, 1747–71 and 1774–80. Ranger of Dartmoor. Clerk of the Board of Green Cloth, 1753. Master of the Household to King George III, 1771. Died, unmarried, Feb. 22, 1794. M.I. at Buckland. (*Masters*; Elliott-Drake, *Family of Sir Francis Drake*; *G.E.C.*)

DRAKE, HUMPHREY. Incorp. M.A. 1711, from Brasenose College, Oxford. S. of John, sub-dean of Ripon, Yorks. Matric from University College, Oxford, May 11, 1677; B.A. (Oxford) 1680–1; M.A. 1683. V. of Gillingham, Kent, 1691–8. R. of Grafton Regis, Northants., 1698–1721. R. of Agmondesham, Bucks., 1702–21. Buried there Nov. 18, 1721. (*F.M.G.*, 507; *Al. Oxon.*; *Vis. of Yorks.*, 1665.)

DRAKE, JAMES. Adm. pens. (age 18) at Caius, Mar. 20, 1684–5. S. of Robert, attorney, of Cambridge. B. there. Schools, Wivelingham and Eton. Matric. 1685; Scholar, 1685–90; M.B. 1690; M.D. 1694. F.R.S. 1701. F.R.C.P. 1706. Best known as a Tory political pamphleteer. Died at Westminster, Mar. 2, 1706–7 Father of the next. (*D.N.B.*; *Venn*, I. 478.)

DRAKE, JAMES. Adm. pens. (age 17) at St John's, July 8, 1720. S. of James (above), M.D., of Middlesex. B. in London. School, Westminster. Matric. 1720; M.D. 1728 (*Com. Reg.*). Will of James Drake, M.D. (P.C.C.) 1736; of Sarum. (J. Ch. Smith.)

DRAKE, JOHN. Matric. sizar from CORPUS CHRISTI, Michs. 1568. S. of Thomas, of East Dereham, Norfolk. School, East Dereham. Migrated as pens. to Caius, Nov. 20, 1570, age 18; B.A. from Magdalene, 1571-2. Perhaps R. of All Saints', Southampton, 1600. (*Venn*, I. 67.)

DRAKE, JOHN. M.A. from CORPUS CHRISTI, 1602; (? B.A. 1598-9). Will of one of these names, M.A., of St Giles' parish, Cambridge, proved (V.C.C.) 1617.

DRAKE, JOHN. Adm. Fell.-Com. at PETERHOUSE, Jan. 29, 1618-9. Of Surrey.

DRAKE, JOHN. Matric. sizar from KING'S, Lent, 1623-4; B.A. 1627-8. Ord. deacon (Peterb.) Sept. 20, 1629; priest, July 9, 1630. Will of one of these names (Chichester) 1682; of Oving, Sussex, clerk.

DRAKE, JOHN. Adm. sizar at EMMANUEL, Apr. 17, 1655. Of Suffolk.

DRAKE, JOHN. Adm. sizar at EMMANUEL, Jan. 2, 1660-1. Of Lincolnshire. Matric. 1661; B.A. 1665-6; M.A. 1675.

DRAKE, JOHN. Adm. sizar (age 17) at CHRIST'S, May 1, 1667. S. of Michael (1639). B. at Pickworth, Lincs. School, Gainsborough. Matric. 1668. Buried Mar. 24, 1668-9, at Great St Andrew's, Cambridge.

DRAKE, JOHN. M.B. from CHRIST'S, 1681. First appears before Michs. 1679.

DRAKE, JOHN. M.A. from CORPUS CHRISTI, 1689. Matric. from All Souls', Oxford, Apr. 3, 1674; B.A. from St Edmund Hall, 1677. Perhaps V. of Isleham, Cambs., 1707-10. Master of Ashford School, Kent, 1679-1712. (*Al. Oxon.*)

DRAKE, JOHN. Adm. sizar (age 18) at ST JOHN'S, Mar. 18, 1696-7. S. of Francis (1670), clerk. B. at York. Bapt. at St Mary Bishophill Junior Jan. 9, 1677-8. School, Sedbergh. Matric. 1697; B.A. 1700-1; M.A. 1704; B.D. 1711. Fellow, 1701-15. Head Master of Pocklington School, 1709-14. V. of Pontefract, 1713. Preb. of York, 1716-42. R. of Kirk Smeaton, 1725-42. Died Nov. 17, 1742. Buried at Pontefract. (*F.M.G.*, 512; G. *Mag.*)

DRAKE, JOHN. Adm. sizar at EMMANUEL, Mar. 23, 1716-7. Of Lincolnshire. Matric. 1716-7; B.A. 1721-2; M.A. 1731. Ord. deacon (Lincoln) Sept. 23, 1722; priest, Sept. 19, 1725.

DRAKE, JOHN. Adm. sizar (age 17) at ST JOHN'S, May 21, 1724. S. of Marmaduke (1695), V. of Beighton, Derbs. Bapt. there, July 25, 1706. School, Bradford. Matric. 1724; B.A. 1727-8; M.A. 1731. Succeeded his father as V. of Beighton, 1733-63. Died Feb. 4, 1763. Buried at Beighton. Brother of William (1727). (*Scott-Mayor*, III. 367; *F.M.G.*, 509.)

DRAKE, JOHN. Adm. Fell.-Com. at ST CATHARINE'S, May 22, 1746. S. of John, of Collaton, Devon, gent. Matric. from Queen's College, Oxford, Mar. 27, 1740, age 20; M.B. (Cambridge) 1747.

DRAKE, JOSEPH. Adm. pens. (age 17) at ST JOHN'S, Apr. 17, 1714. S. of Nathan (1676), V. of Sheffield, Yorks. Bapt. there, May 12, 1697. School, Sedbergh. Matric. 1714; B.A. 1717-8; M.A. 1721. Fellow, 1721-30. Ord. deacon (York) May, 1719; priest (Peterb.) Mar. 6, 1725-6. R. of Burley-on-the-Hill, Rutland, 1727-44. Preb. of Southwell. R. of Middleton-Keynes, Bucks., 1744-51. Died Oct. 21, 1751. Father of Nathan (1749).

DRAKE, JOSHUA. Adm. sizar (age 18) at CHRIST'S, Sept. 10, 1684. S. of John. B. at Pickworth, near Folkingham, Lincs. Matric. 1685; B.A. 1688-9. Ord. deacon and priest (Lincoln) Jan. 6, 1690-1. V. of Swinderby, Lincs., 1692. P.C. of Thurlby.

DRAKE, MARMADUKE. Adm. sizar (age 18) at ST JOHN'S, June 22, 1695. S. of Marmaduke, husbandman. B. at Pennigant Hill, near Settle, Yorks. Bapt. there, Dec. 1677. School, Threshfield. Matric. 1695; B.A. 1698-9; M.A. 1702. Ord. deacon (York) Nov. 1700. V. of Beighton, Derbs., until 1733. Died Oct. 30, 1741. Buried at Beighton. Father of William (1727) and John (1724). (*F.M.G.*, 509.)

DRAKE, MICHAEL. Adm. pens. at EMMANUEL, May 3, 1611. Matric. 1611; B.A. 1614-5, as Nathan; M.A. from St Catharine's, 1618. Fellow of St Catharine's, 1616-22. Buried at St Botolph's, Cambridge, Apr. 25, 1622. Will proved (V.C.C.) 1622.

DRAKE, MICHAEL. Matric. sizar from MAGDALENE, Easter, 1639. Migrated to St John's, Nov. 26, 1639, age 17. S. of John, yeoman, of 'Pikeley' (? Ilkley), near Bradford, Yorks. School, Halifax (private). B.A. 1642-3; M.A. 1647. R. of Pickworth, Lincs., 1646-62; ejected. Afterwards preacher in Lincolnshire. Father of John (1667). (*Calamy*, II. 155.)

DRAKE, MORRIS. Adm. Fell.-Com. (age 18) at TRINITY, June 8, 1714. S. of Robert, recorder of Cambridge. School, Bishop's Stortford, Herts. (Dr Tooke).

DRAKE, NATHAN. Adm. sizar (age 16) at ST JOHN'S, Nov. 27, 1676. S. of Joseph, yeoman, of Pennigant, near Settle, Yorks. B. there, Nov. 19, 1660. School, Wakefield. Matric. 1676; B.A. 1680-1; M.A. 1684. Incorp. at Oxford, 1684. Ord. deacon (York) Sept. 1681; priest, Dec. 1684. Master of Snaith School, Yorks., 1681-9. Official of the peculiar of Snaith. V. of Market Weighton, Yorks., 1689-95. V. of Sheffield, 1695-1713. Preb. of York, 1703-29. R. of Kirkby Overblow, 1713-29. Author, *Sermons*. Died Apr. 1729. Father of Joseph (1714). (E. Trollope, *Sleaford*; *Al. Oxon.*; *F.M.G.*, 508; R. J. Wood.)

DRAKE, NATHAN. Adm. sizar (age 17) at ST JOHN'S, Apr. 27, 1681. S. of Samuel (1637). B. at Pontefract, Yorks., Mar. 31, 1663. School, Pontefract. Matric. 1681; B.A. 1684-5; M.A. 1691. Ord. priest (Lincoln) Dec. 14, 1686. Master of Pontefract School, 1685-9. R. of South Leasingham, Lincs., 1687. Preb. of Southwell, 1695-1705. R. of St Peter's, Nottingham. Died Aug. 1705. Brother of Francis (1670), father of the next. (*Vis. of Yorks.*, 1665.)

DRAKE, NATHAN. M.A. from KING'S, 1720. S. of Nathan (above), R. of St Peter's, Nottingham. Matric. from Magdalen College, Oxford, June 28, 1712, age 15; B.A. (Oxford) 1716. Ord. deacon (York) Dec. 1717. R. of South Leasingham, Lincs., 1721. (*Al. Oxon.*)

DRAKE, NATHAN. Adm. sizar (age 16) at ST JOHN'S, June 16, 1749. S. of Joseph (1714), clerk, of Rutland. B. at Burley-on-the-Hill. School, Oakham. Matric. 1749. Ord. deacon (Lincoln) Sept. 21, 1755; priest, Feb. 19, 1758. C. of Moulsoe, Bucks., in 1760. Usher at Aspley School. R. of Little Woolston, Bucks., 1764. Minister of Thorney, Ely. Died Sept. 13, 1765. M.I. at Middleton-Keynes, Bucks. (*Scott-Mayor*, III. 590; *Lipscomb*, IV. 248; *F.M.G.*, 1160.)

DRAKE, NATHANIEL. Student of EMMANUEL; perhaps adm. as Fell.-Com. Easter, 1634. Buried at St Andrew's, Cambridge, Feb. 19, 1636-7.

DRAKE, RICHARD. B.A. 1498-9; M.A. 1506-7. R. of Gt Moulton, Norfolk, 1516-26, 'LL.B.' Perhaps R. of Griston, 1521.

DRAKE, RICHARD. Matric. pens. (age 15) from PEMBROKE, Easter, 1625. Of London. S. of Roger. B. Apr. 21, 1609. B.A. 1627-8; M.A. 1631; B.D. 1639; D.D. 1661 (*Lit. Reg.*). Fellow, 1630. Taxor, 1637. R. of Radwinter, Essex, 1638-45, 1660-7. Preb. of Sarum, 1660-81. Chaplain to the King, 1660. Chancellor of Sarum, 1663. R. of Wyke Regis, Dorset, 1667-81. Died 1681. Will, P.C.C. Benefactor to Pembroke. Brother of Roger (1624). (*F.M.G.* makes him s. of 'Timothy,' of London; *Vis. of London*, 1634; J. Ch. Smith.)

DRAKE, RICHARD. Adm. sizar (age 18) at CAIUS, Feb. 13, 1688-9. S. of Robert, innkeeper, of Norwich. B. there. School, Norwich. Matric. 1688; Scholar, 1689-94; B.A. 1692-3; M.A. 1696. Ord. deacon (Norwich) June 3, 1694; priest, Sept. 1696. Incorp. at Oxford, 1712. R. of Gt Oakley, Essex, 1704-38. Married Elizabeth, dau. of Henry Cole, R. of Gt Oakley. Died 1738. Benefactor to Oakley parish. (*Venn*, I. 486; J. Ch. Smith.)

DRAKE, RICHARD. Adm. sizar (age 17) at CAIUS, June 7, 1746. S. of Richard, grocer, of Aylsham, Norfolk. B. there. School, Aylsham. Scholar, 1746-53; Matric. 1747; B.A. 1749-50; M.A. 1753. Ord. deacon (Ely, *Litt. dim.* from Norwich) June 2, 1751; priest (Norwich) June 17, 1753. R. of Mileham, Norfolk, 1753-1802; of Little Fransham, 1774-1802; and of Eccles, 1775-1802. Died Dec. 24, 1802. (*Venn*, II. 58.)

DRAKE, ROGER. Matric. pens. from CORPUS CHRISTI, Easter, 1577.

DRAKE, ROGER. Adm. pens. (age 16) at PEMBROKE, June 24, 1624. S. of Roger, of London, mercer. Matric. 1625; Scholar, 1626; B.A. 1627-8; M.A. 1631. Entered at Leyden, Aug. 2, 1638; M.D. there 1639. Candidate R.C.P. 1643. Involved in Love's plot, 1651. Minister of St Peter's Cheap, 1653. Author, religious and medical. Died at Stepney, 1669. In his will (P.C.C.) he mentions his brother Richard (1625). (*D.N.B.*; *Munk*, I. 239; *Vis. of London*, 1634; H. G. Harrison.)

DRAKE, SAMUEL. Adm. pens. (age 15) at ST JOHN'S, June 26, 1637. S. of Nathan, gent., of Godley, Halifax, Yorks. B. there. Bapt. Sept. 29, 1622. School, Pocklington. Matric. 1637; B.A. 1640-1; M.A. 1644; D.D. 1662 (*Lit. Reg.*). Fellow, 1643-4; ejected. Joined the Royal Army at the siege of Newark. R. of South Kirkby, Yorks., 1650-61. V. of Pontefract, 1661-79. Preb. of Southwell, 1670-1. R. of Handsworth, Yorks., 1671-8. Died Apr. 3, 1679 (*Hunter*). Buried at All Saints', Pontefract. M.I. Father of Francis (1670) and Nathan (1681). (*D.N.B.*; *F.M.G.*, 511; *Vis. of Yorks.*, 1665.)

DRAKE, SAMUEL. Adm. sizar (age 16) at ST JOHN'S, May 4, 1704. S. of Francis (1670). B. at Pontefract, Yorks. Bapt. Apr. 23, 1688. School, Sedbergh. Matric. 1704; B.A. 1707-8; M.A. 1711; B.D. 1718; D.D. 1724. Fellow, 1710-35. Ord. deacon (London) Mar. 5, 1709-10; priest, June 16, 1717. V. of Hutton Buscel, Yorks., 1722-8. R. of Treeton, 1728-53. R. of Holme-on-Spalding-Moor, 1733-53. Married Elizabeth, dau. of Darcy Dalton. Author. Died Mar. 5, 1753. Buried at Treeton. (*Scott-Mayor*; *F.M.G.*, 512; *D.N.B.*)

DRAKE, THOMAS. Matric. Fell.-Com. from CORPUS CHRISTI, Michs. 1566.

DRAKE, THOMAS. Adm. sizar (age 18) at CAIUS, Feb. 6, 1587-8. S. of Thomas, V. of Sedgeford, Norfolk. Bapt. there, Nov. 26, 1570. School, Norwich. Matric. 1588; Scholar, 1591-2; B.A. 1591-2; M.A. 1596. Ord. priest (Norwich) June 24, 1598. V. of Snettisham, Norfolk, 1598-1608. R. of Ingoldisthorpe, 1609-38. (*Venn*, I. 133.)

DRAKE, THOMAS. Matric. pens. from CLARE, c. 1596. Probably s. of John, of Horley Green, Yorks. B. at Halifax, 1578. B.A. 1599-1600; M.A. 1603. Ord. deacon (Lincoln) May 31, 1607; priest (York) June, 1609. R. of Thornton-in-Craven, 1623-45. Married, 1625, Mary Foster, of Guisborough. Probably brother of Francis (1603). (*F.M.G.*, 506; M. H. Peacock.)

DRAKE, THOMAS. Matric. sizar from TRINITY, Easter, 1612; Scholar, 1614; B.A. 1615-6. Ord. deacon (Peterb.) Nov. 13; priest, Nov. 14, 1625.

DRAKE, THOMAS. Matric. pens. from KING'S, Easter, 1676. Perhaps adm. at Gray's Inn, May 29, 1682, as s. of Robert, of Cambridgeshire.

DRAKE, THOMAS. Adm. sizar at CHRIST'S, June 19, 1682.

DRAKE, THOMAS. Adm. pens. at EMMANUEL, Apr. 10, 1699. Of Rutland. Matric. 1701; B.A. 1702-3; M.A. 1706. Ord. deacon (Peterb.) Sept. 23, 1705; priest, Aug. 8, 1708. V. of Bozeat, Northants., 1708-29. C. of Strixton, in 1711. C. of Easton Maudit, in 1727. Married, at Strixton, June 5, 1711, Margaret Chowne, of Newport-Pagnell, Bucks. (H. I. Longden.)

DRAKE, THOMAS. M.A. from KING'S, 1751. S. of Thomas, of Felkington, Durham, clerk (*i.e.* of Thomas, V. of Norham-on-Tweed, and Jane, dau. of Thomas Orde, of Felkington). Bapt. at Norham, Sept. 5, 1723. Matric. from Corpus Christi, Oxford, Apr. 16, 1741, age 17; B.A. (Oxford) 1744-5. R. of St Mary-le-Bow, Durham, 1751-88. P.C. of Dalton-le-Dale, Durham, 1761-74. V. of Bedlington, 1774-88. Married, at St Mary, Durham, Apr. 11, 1758, Jane Clark. Died at Durham, July, 1788. Brother of William (1748). (H. L. L. Denny; H. M. Wood.)

DRAKE, WILLIAM. Adm. pens. (age 21) at SIDNEY, July 18, 1635. S. of William, R. of St Just, Cornwall. School, Bodmin (Mr Vincent). B.A. 1635-6. Previously matric. from Exeter College, Oxford, Sept. 9, 1634, age 20.

DRAKE, WILLIAM. Adm. pens. (age 17) at CHRIST'S, Apr. 20, 1669. S. of William, of Coates Hall, Barnoldswick, Yorks. B. there School, Earby, near Skipton. Matric. 1669. Adm. at Gray's Inn, Feb. 9, 1669-70. Buried at Thornton, Oct. 13, 1687. Father of William (1700). (*Peile*, II. 21.)

DRAKE, WILLIAM. Adm. pens. at ST CATHARINE'S, June 14, 1670. Matric. 1672-3; B.A. 1673-4; M.A. 1677. Ord. priest (Durham) Sept. 23, 1677. V. of St Andrew, Newcastle-on-Tyne, 1688. C. of St Nicholas. Buried there May 24, 1693. (H. M. Wood.)

DRAKE, WILLIAM. Adm. Fell.-Com. at JESUS, Apr. 6, 1700. S. of William (1669), of Coates Hall, Barnoldswick, Yorks. B. Sept. 21, 1682. Adm. at Gray's Inn, May 13, 1699. Died unmarried, Feb. 13, 1757. (*F.M.G.*, 507; A. Gray; M. H. Peacock.)

DRAKE, WILLIAM. Adm. sizar (age 17) at ST JOHN'S, June 17, 1727. S. of Marmaduke (1695), clerk, V. of Beighton, Derbs. B. at Beighton. Bapt. Sept. 27, 1709. School, Kirk Leatham, Yorks. Matric. 1727; B.A. 1730-1; M.A. 1734. Ord. deacon (Lincoln) Sept. 19, 1731; priest, Sept. 23, 1733. R. of Full Sutton, Yorks., 1739-57. V. of Hatfield, 1744-57. Died Feb. 8, 1757. Buried at Hatfield. Brother of John (1724). (*Scott-Mayor*, III. 406; *G. Mag.*; *F.M.G.*)

DRAKE, WILLIAM. Matric. sizar from KING'S, Easter, 1748. S. of Thomas, V. of Norham, Northumberland. Bapt. there, July 21, 1729. B.A. 1752. Ord. deacon (London) Sept. 24, 1752; priest, June 9, 1754. Usher at Felsted School, 1752. V. of Good Easter, Essex. Brother of Thomas (1751).

DRAKE, ——. Adm. sizar at TRINITY HALL, Oct. 2, 1718.

DRAKEFORD, MATTHEW. Adm. sizar (age 15) at ST JOHN'S, May 19, 1669. S. of Richard, attorney, of Forebridge, Staffs. B. there. School, Stafford. Matric. 1669; B.A. 1672-3; M.A. 1676. Preb. of Lichfield, 1698-1704.

DRAKETT or DRACKET, MARK. Adm. pens. (age 16) at CAIUS, Aug. 7, 1576. S. of Matthew, of Fulbourn, Cambs. School, Ely.

DRAXYS, JOHN. B.A. 1558-9, *see* DRAX.

DRANE, JOHN (1582), *see* DEANE.

DRANSFIELD, SAMUEL. Adm. sizar (age 19) at ST JOHN'S, June 6, 1707. S. of Francis, blacksmith. B. at Wakefield, Yorks. School, Wakefield. Matric. 1707; B.A. 1710-1. Usher of Wakefield Grammar School, 1711-7. Ord. deacon (York) Sept. 1717; priest, May, 1719. V. of Hooton-Pagnell, Yorks., 1723-54. Died 1754. Buried at Hooton-Pagnell.

DRANT, THOMAS. Matric. pens. from ST JOHN'S, Lent, 1557-8. S. of Thomas. B. at Hagworthingham, Lincs. B.A. 1560-1 as Draunt; M.A. 1564; B.D. 1569. Fellow, 1561. Chaplain to Bishop Grindal. Preb. of St Paul's, 1569-70. V. of St Giles', Cripplegate, London, 1569-78. Preb. of Chichester, 1570-2. R. of Slinfold, Sussex, 1570. Archdeacon of Lewes, 1570-8. R. of East Hatley, Cambs., 1575. Author, religious, etc. Admon. (P.C.C.) Apr. 15, 1578. (*Cooper*, I. 384; *D.N.B.*)

DRAPER, CHRISTOPHER. Adm. sizar at EMMANUEL, Mar. 29, 1676. Of Essex. Matric. 1676.

DRAPER, CRESHELD. Adm. Fell.-Com. (age 15) at ST JOHN'S, June 13, 1661. S. of William, Esq., deceased, of Crayford, Kent, and Mary, dau. of Richard Cresheld, Justice C.P. B. at Bexley. School, Sevenoaks, Kent. Matric. 1661. Colonel in the army. Lord of the manor of Crayford, Kent. M.P. for Winchelsea, 1678-81, 1685-7. Died *c.* 1694. (*Hasted*, I. 206; A. B. Beaven.)

DRAPER, DANIEL. Adm. sizar at EMMANUEL, May 29, 1682. Of Hertfordshire. Matric. 1683; B.A. 1685-6. Doubtless V. of Royston, Herts., 1692-1731. Died 1731. Father of Edward (1713).

DRAPER, EDMUND. Matric. sizar from CORPUS CHRISTI, Easter, 1613. Of Nottinghamshire. B.A. 1616-7; M.A. 1621. R. of Riddlesworth, Norfolk, 1632. Doubtless nephew of George (1584). (J. Ch. Smith.)

DRAPER, EDWARD. Adm. scholar (age 15) at SIDNEY, June 29, 1665. 2nd s. of Edmund, Esq. B. at Hitchin, Herts. School, Hitchin (Mr Samuel Luke). Matric. 1667.

DRAPER, EDWARD. Adm. sizar (age 18) at ST JOHN'S, Sept. 15, 1713. S. of Daniel (1682), clerk. B. at Royston, Herts. School, Heydon, Essex. Matric. 1715; B.A. 1717-8. Ord. deacon (Ely) Mar. 13, 1719-20; priest, Dec. 24, 1721. Died Sept. 20, 1724. M.I. at Royston.

DRAPER, FRANCIS. Adm. sizar (age 18) at PEMBROKE, Apr. 30, 1678. S. of Giles, gent. B. at 'Voluba,' Cornwall. Matric. 1678; B.A. 1681-2; M.A. 1685. Fellow, 1683. Senior proctor, 1699-1700. R. of Framlingham, Suffolk, 1703-4. Died 1704.

DRAPER, GEORGE. Matric. sizar from PEMBROKE, Easter, 1584. B. at Gt Markham, Notts. B.A. 1587-8; M.A. 1591. Ord. deacon (London) Mar. 15, 1591-2, age 26, C. of Thaxted; priest, May 12, 1597. V. of Lindsell, Essex, 1596-1631. Died 1631. Will (Consist. C. London).

DRAPER, GEORGE. Adm. pens. at EMMANUEL, Apr. 4, 1627. S. of Timothy, of Co. Durham. Bapt. at St Nicholas, Newcastle, Sept. 25, 1611; his father being sheriff. Matric. 1627. Buried at Gt St Andrew's, Cambridge, Mar. 16, 1629-30.

DRAPER, HENRY. Matric. pens. from TRINITY, Lent, 1580-1.

DRAPER, HENRY. Adm. pens. (age 16) at CAIUS, Feb. 12, 1604-5. S. of Nicholas, gent., of Bromley, Kent. School, Lynn, Norfolk. Matric. 1605; Scholar, 1606-12; B.A. 1608-9; M.A. 1612. Ord. deacon (London) Feb. 22, 1623-4. R. of Worlingham, Suffolk, 1623-8. Died 1657. Father of Henry (1641). (*Venn*, I. 188.)

DRAPER, HENRY. Adm. pens. at EMMANUEL, Easter, 1624. S. and h. of Timothy, of Newcastle-on-Tyne, deceased. Bapt. at St Nicholas, Apr. 30, 1609. Matric. 1624. Adm. at Gray's Inn, Aug. 3, 1626. Married, Apr. 28, 1636, Eleanor, dau. of Henry Birkbeck. Brother of George (1627). (H. M. Wood.)

DRAPER, HENRY. Adm. pens. (age 18) at CAIUS, June 22, 1641. Readm. as Fell.-Com. Oct. 27, 1641. S. of Henry (1605), clerk. B. in the parish of St Sepulchre, London. School, Bishopsgate St (Mr Perse). Matric. 1642. Will (P.C.C.) 1645; of Cambridge; property in Essex and Kent. (J. Ch. Smith.)

DRAPER, JOHN. Matric. Fell.-Com. from QUEENS', Michs. 1573. Of Middlesex.

DRAPER, JOHN. B.A. from TRINITY, 1595-6. Perhaps M.A. 1599. Adm. licentiate R.C.P. July 4, 1617.

DRAPER, JOHN. Adm. pens. (age 16) at CHRIST'S, May 18, 1653. S. of Richard. B. at Bicker, Lincs. School, Sleaford. Matric. 1653; B.A. 1656-7. One of these names, ord. priest (Chester) Sept. 1670, was V. of Milton Ernest, Beds., 1676-7. V. of Stagsden, 1677; and V. of Steventon, 1677; deprived, 1712. Another R. of Rothersthorpe, Northants., 1676-86. *See* a contemporary in *Al. Oxon.* (*Peile*, I. 553.)

DRAPER, JOSEPH. Adm. sizar at EMMANUEL, June, 1658. Of Hertfordshire. Matric. 1658 (*impubes*); B.A. 1661-2; M.A. 1665.

DRAPER, JOSHUA. Adm. pens. at EMMANUEL, Aug. 12, 1631. Of Essex. Matric. 1631; M.B. 1638.

DRAPER, MARMADUKE. M.A. from EMMANUEL, 1741. S. of William, of Beswick, Yorks., Esq. Matric. from St John's College, Oxford, July 10, 1733, age 20; B.A. (Oxford) 1737. R. of Barton-le-Street, Yorks., 1744-50. R. of Thwing, 1747-50. Died 1750. (*Al. Oxon.*)

DRAPER, ROBERT. Studied at Cambridge. B.A. (Oxford) 1451; M.A. 1454-5. Perhaps R. of Wimbish, Essex, 1459-61; and V. of Henham, 1466.

DRAPER, ROBERT. Matric. pens. from TRINITY, Easter, 1557; Scholar, 1560, as 'Drapa.' One of these names, of London, adm. at Lincoln's Inn, June 18, 1564.

DRAPER, ROBERT. Adm. pens. at KING'S, 1563; scholar from Eton. Matric. Lent, 1563-4; B.A. 1567-8; M.A. 1571. Fellow, till 1576. Ord. deacon and priest (Lincoln) Apr. 10, 1574. Probably R. of Trim, Meath Diocese. Bishop of Ardagh and Kilmore, 1604-12. Died Aug. 1612.

DRAPER, ROBERT. Matric. pens. from CHRIST'S, Nov. 1569; B.A. 1572-3; M.A. 1576. Fellow of Caius, in 1577. Probably ord. deacon and priest (Lincoln) Apr. 1574. R. of Corringham, Essex, 1578-95. 'An unpreaching minister,' in 1585. Licensed to marry Ellen Cotton, of South Weald, Essex, Feb. 26, 1578-9. Died Dec. 18, 1595. Buried at Corringham. M.I. (*Peile*, I. 112; *Venn*, I. 92; J. Ch. Smith.)

DRAPER, ROBERT. Adm. pens. (age 16) at CAIUS, July 10, 1591. S. of William, yeoman. B. at Bottesford, Leics. School, Bottesford. Scholar, 1592-8; B.A. 1594-5; M.A. 1598. Brother of Thomas (1594).

DRAPER, ROBERT. Matric. pens. from PEMBROKE, Easter, 1609.

DRAPER, ROBERT. Adm. pens. (age 17) at ST JOHN'S, July 3, 1673. S. of Edmund, gent., of Edmonton, Middlesex. B. there. School, Herts. (Mr Lovell).

DRAPER, THOMAS. B.A. 1533-4; M.A. 1537; B.D. 1545-6. V. of Barrington, Cambs., 1546-56; of Barton, 1554- .

DRAPER, THOMAS. Matric. pens. from QUEENS', Michs. 1579. Of London.

DRAPER, THOMAS. Adm. pens. (age 14) at CAIUS, July 1, 1594. S. of William, gent. B. at Bottesford, Leics. School, Bottesford. Matric. c. 1594. One of these names R. of Willingham St Mary, Suffolk, 1634. Brother of Robert (1591). (*Venn*, I. 152.)

DRAPER, THOMAS. Matric. pens. from ST CATHARINE'S, Easter, 1641. Of Essex. Perhaps s. and h. of Robert, late of Islington, Middlesex, Esq., deceased; adm. at Lincoln's Inn, Nov. 18, 1644.

DRAPER, THOMAS. Adm. sizar (age 17) at CAIUS, Apr. 12, 1642. S. of William, gent. B. at Wentworth, Isle of Ely. School, Ely. Matric. 1642; Scholar, 1644-6; B.A. 1645-6. One of these names R. of Little Gaddesden, Herts., in 1650-5. Perhaps R. of Speldhurst, Kent, 1653-60. (*Venn*, I. 346.)

DRAPER, WILLIAM. Adm. sizar at EMMANUEL, Jan. 18, 1654-5. S. of Paul. B. Apr. 15, 1635, in All Saints', Hereford. School, Merchant Taylors'. Matric. 1655; B.A. 1658. (*Robinson*, I. 170.)

DRAPER, WILLIAM. Adm. pens. at EMMANUEL, May 17, 1697. B. at Lutterworth, Leics. Matric. 1698; B.A. 1701-2; M.A. 1705. Fellow, 1702. Ord. deacon (Lincoln) Sept. 20, 1702; priest, Sept. 19, 1703. R. of Sibstone, Leics., 1715-27.

DRAPER, WILLIAM. Adm. pens. (age 17) at ST JOHN'S, June 1, 1726. S. of Edmund, gent., of Suffolk. B. in Bury. School, Bury. Matric. 1726.

DRAPER, WILLIAM. Adm. at KING'S, a scholar from Eton, 1740. S. of Ingleby, officer of customs, Bristol. B. there, 1721. Matric. 1740; B.A. 1744-5; M.A. 1749. Fellow, 1743. Entered the army. Served at Culloden and in Flanders. Afterwards in India, with Clive. Aided in the expedition against Manila, 1763; the colours taken were presented to King's Chapel. K.B. 1765. Lieutenant-General, 1777. Lieutenant-Governor of Minorca, 1779. Died at Bath, Jan. 8, 1787. M.I. in the Abbey Church. (*Harwood*, 328; *D.N.B.*; A. B. Beaven.)

DRAPER, ——. A friar. D.D. 1459.

DRAPER, ——. B.A. 1462-3; (? M.A. 1472-3).

DRAPER, ——. B.A. 1498-9. One William Draper, Chaplain of Newark, Notts., 1503-23. Died 1523.

DRAPER, ——. B.A. 1524-5; M.A. 1528-9. One Laurence Draper, V. of Bourn, Cambs., 1555.

'DRATSAB,' THOMAS (1556), *see* ALABLASTER.

DRAWER, RICHARD. Matric. sizar from TRINITY HALL, Easter, 1549.

DRAX, HENRY. Adm. Fell.-Com. (age 16) at MAGDALENE, May 15, 1710. S. of 'Shakston,' Esq. B. at 'Poper,' Herts. School, Eton. Matric. 1710-1. Henry Shetterden, *alias* Drax; s. of Thomas, of 'Popes Common,' Herts. and Barbados. M.P. for Wareham, 1718-22, 1734-48, 1751-5; for Lyme Regis, 1727-34. Died May 24, 1755. (Le Neve, *Knights*; A. B. Beaven.)

DRAX, JOHN. Adm. pens. at ST CATHARINE'S, 1558.

DRAX or DRAKYS, JOHN. B.A. 1558-9. One of these names, a clerk, s. of Thomas, of Wood Hall, Darfield, Yorks., in 1585. Perhaps the same who received holy orders (London) Oct. 1554. R. of Darfield, Yorks. Perhaps R. of Stanford-on-Soar, Notts., 1572-1615. Died 1615. (*Vis. of Yorks.*)

DRAX, THOMAS. Matric. pens. from CHRIST'S, Dec. 1588. B. at Stoneleigh, near Coventry. Probably B.A. 1594-5; B.D. 1609. Doubtless V. of Tetney, Lincs., 1591-6 and V. of Dovercourt, Essex, 1601-19. V. of Colwich, Staffs., 1613-5. Returned to Dovercourt, and died there. Buried at Harwich, Jan. 29, 1618-9. Author, theological and classical. (*D.N.B.*; *Peile*, I. 193; *Wm. Salt Arch. Soc.*, 1915.)

DRAX, *alias* SHETTERDEN, THOMAS. Adm. Fell.-Com. (age 17) at ST JOHN'S, June 2, 1687. S. of Thomas Shetterden and Elizabeth Drax. B. at Pope's Field, Herts. School, St Albans. Matric. 1687. Assumed the name Drax.

DRAY, JOHN. Adm. sizar at JESUS, Oct. 24, 1726. Of Kent. S. of Thomas, of St Mary's, Kent. (Apparently had been at Oxford for a short time: Matric. from University College, Nov. 2, 1725, age 17.) Matric. 1726; B.A. 1729-30; M.A. 1733. Fellow, 1731-3. Ord. priest (Ely) Oct. 24, 1732. Held a living in Ireland. Died soon after. (A. Gray.)

DRAYCOTT or DRACOT, JASPER. Matric. pens. from CHRIST'S, June, 1582. Probably s. of Richard, of Loscoe, Derbs. Living, 1611. (*Vis. of Derbs.*, 1669; *Peile*, I. 170.)

DRAYCOTT, JOHN. Adm. sizar (age 16) at ST JOHN'S, May 30, 1640. S. of Thomas, registrar of the diocese of Bangor. B. at York. School, Bangor. B.A. 1643-4.

DRAKOTTE, ROBERT. B.Civ.L. 1495-6. Of Coventry and Lichfield diocese. Ord. sub-deacon (Ely) Sept. 24, 1496.

DRAYCOTT, WILLIAM. Adm. sizar at EMMANUEL, July 8, 1696. Matric. 1696.

DRAYCOTT, ——. Adm. sizar at TRINITY HALL, Jan. 19, 1698-9.

DRAYNER, EDMUND. Adm. pens. (age 17) at ST JOHN'S, June 11, 1659. S. of Robert, gent., of Biddenden, Kent. B. there. School, Biddenden. Matric. 1659. Adm. at Gray's Inn, June 9, 1659. Called to the Bar, 1671. Ancient, 1680.

DRAYNER, EDWARD. Matric. sizar from PEMBROKE, Easter, 1603. Perhaps the same who was B.A. at Magdalene, 1613-4. R. of Addington, Kent, 1615-36. V. of West Peckham, 1624-36. Buried at West Peckham, Jan. 15, 1635-6. (*Fielding*.)

DRAYNER, THOMAS. Matric. Fell.-Com. from KING'S, Lent, 1577-8.

DRAYTON, BASIL. Adm. sizar (age 19) at ST JOHN'S, May 28, 1659. S. of Francis (next), clerk, of Barham, Kent. B. there. Matric. 1659; B.A. 1662-3. R. of Little Chart, Kent, 1669-1715. Buried at Little Chart, Dec. 7, 1715.

DRAYTON, FRANCIS. Matric. sizar from CORPUS CHRISTI, Easter, 1620. Of Kent. S. of David, of Westgate, Canterbury. B.A. 1623-4; M.A. 1628. V. of Little Chart, Kent, 1645. Married, 1633, Mary, dau. of Silas Johnson, of Canterbury. Buried at Little Chart, Apr. 9, 1669. Father of Basil (above) and the next.

DRAYTON, FRANCIS. Adm. sizar at CORPUS CHRISTI, June 30, 1651. S. of Francis (above), of Little Chart, Kent. B. at Hide (?Hythe), Kent. School, Canterbury. Matric. 1651. Migrated to St John's, Aug. 20, 1652. B.A. 1654-5; M.A. from Corpus Christi, 1658. V. of Appledore, Kent, 1660-97. R. of Wittersham, 1668-97. Died Nov. 1697, at St Stephen's, near Canterbury.

DRAYTON, JOHN. M.A. 1493, as R. of Barnston, Essex. R. there, 1470-99. Will (P.C.C.) 1499; 'of West Deeping, Lincs.'

DRAYTON, JOHN. Adm. sizar (age 18) at CHRIST'S, May 30, 1700. S. of George. B. at Burton-on-Trent. School, Burton. Scholar, 1700-1; Matric. 1701; B.A. 1703-4. Ord. deacon (Lichfield) June, 1704. V. of Newton Solney, Derbs. (*Peile*, II. 148.)

• DRAYTON, NATHANIEL. Matric. sizar from QUEENS', Easter, 1610. Of Warwickshire. B.A. 1613-4. Ord. deacon (Peterb.) June 4; priest, June 5, 1615.

DRAYTON, NICHOLAS. B.C.L. Warden of KING'S HALL, 1363-4. Imprisoned for heresy, 1369. R. of St Martin Vintry till 1375. Exchequer baron, 1376-84. R. of Ware, Herts., 1384-5. Died 1385. (*D.N.B.*; where he is wrongly assigned to King's College.)

DRAYTON, PETER. B.A. 1498-9 M.A. 1503; B.D. 1510-1; D.D. 1512-3. R. of St Michael's, Cornhill, 1515-7. Will (P.C.C.) 1518.

DRAYTON, RICHARD. B.A. 1460-1; M.A. 1465.

DRAYTON, ROBERT DE. Scholar at KING'S HALL, 1347; left Jan. 12, 1350-1.

DRAYTON or DREATON, ROBERT. Adm. at PEMBROKE, scholar from Merchant Taylors' School, 1613. B. Apr. 10, 1604.

DRAYTON, SILAS. Adm. at CORPUS CHRISTI, 1709. Of Kent. Matric. 1710; B.A. 1713-4; M.A. 1720. R. of Crundale, Kent, 1729-51. V. of Postling, 1751-67. Died Jan. 31, 1767. Buried at Crundale. Will, P.C.C. (G. *Mag.*; H. G. Harrison.)

DRAYTON, THOMAS. Matric. sizar from PEMBROKE, Easter, 1608; B.A. 1611-2; M.A. 1615; D.D. 1632 (on King's visit). Ord. deacon (York) Sept. 1614. R. of Bletsoe, Beds., 1618. R. of Abbots Ripton, Hunts., 1630-(?) 56. Perhaps V. of Terrington, Norfolk, 1638. Will (P.C.C.) 1658; as of Chilmark, Wilts.; alludes to tithes owing at Ripton. (J. Ch. Smith.)

DRAITON, THOMAS. Adm. at CORPUS CHRISTI, 1691. Of Kent.

DRAYTON, WILLIAM. Adm. pens. at CLARE, June 13, 1640. Matric. 1640.

DRAYTON, ——. D.D. 1474-5.

DRAYTON, ——. B.Can.L. 1474-5. Studied at Oxford.

DREELY, THOMAS. Matric. pens. from TRINITY, Michs. 1589.

DREMAR, RICHARD. Matric. pens. from CHRIST'S, June, 1573; B.A. 1576-7; M.A. 1580.

DRENAR, ALEXANDER. Incorp. B.D. 1683, from Paris.

DRENTALL, THOMAS. M.A. 1460. Fellow of GONVILLE HALL. R. of Michael Coslany, Norwich, 1464-1501. Benefactor to Gonville Hall. Died 1501. Will proved (Norwich) Dec. 2, 1501. (*Venn*, I. 9.)

DRESSER, JOSEPH. Adm. sizar at ST CATHARINE'S, May 6, 1671. Matric. 1671; B.A. 1674-5. V. of Batheaston, Somerset, 1682-1707. R. of Walcot, 1688-1707. Died 1707.

DRESSER, THOMAS. Adm. pens. at JESUS, Feb. 9, 1646-7. Of Staffordshire. P.C. of Thursfield, Staffs., 1651-7. V. of Dilhorne, 1660-1700. 'A godly and able preacher.' Died 1700. (*Wm. Salt Arch. Soc.*, 1915.)

DRESSOR, THOMAS. Adm. sizar at ST CATHARINE'S, June 16, 1672. Matric. 1672; B.A. 1675-6; M.A. 1679. R. of Westley Waterless, Cambs., 1683-92. Non-juror. Father of the next.

DRESSER, THOMAS. Adm. pens. (age 15) at ST JOHN'S, Feb. 19, 1699-1700. S. of Thomas (above). B. at Westley Waterless, Cambs. School, ury. Matric. 1704; B.A. 1705-6; M.A. from King's, 1709. Ord. deacon (Lincoln) May 19, 1706; priest (London) May 30, 1708. Chaplain at King's College, 1708.

DREW, JOHN. B.A. from TRINITY, 1584-5.

DREW, JOHN. Matric. sizar from QUEENS', Easter, 1612; B.A. 1615-6; M.A. 1619. Ord. deacon (Peterb.) Feb. 21; priest, Feb. 22, 1618-9. Will (P.C.C.) 1655, of oue of these names, of Barrowby, Lincs., clerk.

DREW, JOHN. Adm. sizar (age 16) at SIDNEY, Mar. 3, 1640-1. S. of John, grazier. B. at Knossington, Leics. Schools, Knossington (Mr Griffin), Somerby (Mr Twigge) and Oakham. Matric. 1641; B.A. 1644-5; M.A. 1648.

DREW, JOHN. M.A. from CHRIST'S, 1706. S. of John, clerk, of Stourton, Wilts. Bapt. there, Mar. 10, 1673-4. Matric. from Oriel College, Oxford, Oct. 30, 1690; B.A. (Oxford) 1694. R. of Kingston Deverill, Wilts., 1706. (*Al. Oxon.*; *Peile*, II. 146.)

DREW, JOHN. Adm. Fell.-Com. at TRINITY, Oct. 30, 1738. S. of John, of London. School, Westminster.

DREW, ROBERT. Matric. sizar from KING'S, Michs. 1707. B. Feb. 5, 1688. School, Merchant Taylors'. B.A. 1710-11; M.A. 1719. Ord. deacon (London) Feb. 25, 1710-1; priest, Dec. 21, 1712. Chaplain to St Thomas's Hospital. R. of St Margaret Pattens, London, 1727-46. Preb. of St Paul's, 1729-46. Died 1746.

DREWE, ——. B.A. 1523-4.

DREWETT, PETER. M.A. 1511-2. Incorp. from Oxford.

DRIFFIELD, CHRISTOPHER. Adm. pens (age 16) at CHRIST'S, Mar. 30, 1681. S. of Christopher (of Gray's Inn). B. at Ripon. School, Ripon. Adm. at Gray's Inn, June 21, 1682. Of Ripon, in 1697 and 1702. Died 1724. Will, York. (*Peile*, II. 82.)

DRIFFIELD, JOSEPH. Adm. sizar (age 17) at TRINITY, Aug. 19, 1731. S. of Lancelot, of Escrick, Yorks. School, York (Dr Jackson). Matric. 1732; Scholar, 1735; B.A. 1735-6; M.A. 1765. Ord. deacon (Lincoln) Mar. 6, 1736-7; priest (Norwich, *Litt. dim.* from Chester) Mar. 1741-2. Perhaps V. of Sedbergh, 1741-6. R. of Chellesworth, Suffolk, 1754-81.

DRIFFIELD, NICHOLAS. A friar. B.D. 1483-4.

DRIFFIELD, ROBERT DE. M.A. A northern student engaged in the riot against southern students, 1261. (*Hare*, I. xxx.)

DRIFFIELD, ZACHARIAH. Adm. sizar (age 17) at SIDNEY, July 24, 1671. 2nd s. of Simon, yeoman, of Crayke, Yorks. B. at Easingwold, Yorks. Schools, Sheriff Hutton (Mr Newsham), Cawood and Snaith. Matric. 1671; B.A. 1675-6.

DRIFT, ADRIAN. Adm. pens. (age 17) at ST JOHN'S, Apr. 1726. S. of Matthew (next), clerk, of Suffolk. B. at Lavenham. School, Westminster. Matric. 1726; B.A. 1730-1. Ord. deacon (Norwich) June, 1731.

DRIFT, MATTHEW. Adm. at KING'S, a scholar from Eton 1688. B. in London. Matric. 1689; B.A. 1692-3; M.A. 1696. Fellow, 1692. Ord. deacon (London) Dec. 23, 1694; priest, Dec. 22, 1700. Master of Lavenham School, 1696-1723. R. of Dunton Waylett, Essex, 1700-26. Died 1726. Father of Adrian (above). (*Harwood*, 273.)

DRIGG, REGINALD. B.A. (? 1604-5); M.A. from ST JOHN'S, 1608.

DRING, EDMUND. Adm. pens. (age 18) at TRINITY, Feb. 22, 1719-20. S. of Edmund, of Malton, Yorks. School, Wakefield (Mr Clark). Matric. 1720; Scholar, 1721; B.A. 1723-4; M.A. 1727. Fellow, 1726. Ord. deacon (Lincoln) June 16; priest, Oct. 5, 1728. Afterwards took the name Garforth.

DRINKWATER, PETER. Adm. pens. at TRINITY, Mar. 14, 1635-6. Perhaps of Irwell House, Restwick, Lancs. School, Westminster. Matric. 1635; Scholar, 1636; B.A. 1638-9; M.A. 1642.

DRINKWATER, WILLIAM. Matric. sizar from JESUS, Easter, 1588; B.A. (? 1591-2); M.A. 1595.

DRISIUS or DRUSIUS, JOHN. Matric. (amongst the *famuli*) Aug. 3, 1569. S. of Clement. B. at Oudenarde, Flanders. B.A. from Merton College, Oxford, 1572; M.A. 1573. Professor of Hebrew at Leyden, 1577. Professor at Franeker. Died Feb. 12, 1615. (*Al. Oxon.*)

DRISIUS, SAMUEL. M.A. 1628. Incorp. from Edinburgh. M.A. there, 1627. Probably Samuel Dries. S. of Samuel, of London, pleb., matric. from St John's College, Oxford, Feb. 14, 1622-3, age 20. R. of North Mundham, Sussex (sequestered), 1645.

DRIVER, ALEXANDER Matric. pens. from QUEENS', Lent, 1577-8; B.A. 1581-2. Died in College. Buried at St Botolph's, Oct. 25, 1585 ('1575' in register).

DRIVER, FRANCIS. Matric. pens. from TRINITY, Easter, 1615; B.A. 1618-9; M.A. 1622. Ord. deacon (Peterb.) Dec. 22; priest, Dec. 23, 1622.

DRIVER, HUGH. Adm. pens. at EMMANUEL, Oct. 23, 1638. Of Suffolk. Matric. 1639; B.A. 1642-3.

DRIVER, JOHN. Adm. pens. at EMMANUEL, 1588-9. Matric. 1588-9; B.A. from Clare, 1592-3; M.A. 1596. One of these names V. of Pampisford, Cambs., 1616-38. Buried there Aug. 25, 1638.

DRIVER, JOHN. B.A. (? 1602); M.A. from CLARE, 1605.

DRIVER, JOSEPH. Matric. from ST JOHN'S, 1627. Adm. sizar (age 17) at Caius, July 4, 1628. S. of John, blacksmith. B. at Docking, Norfolk. Scholar, 1630; B.A. 1630-1. Ord. deacon (Norwich) Sept. 23, 1632; priest, Sept. 22, 1633. (*Venn*, I. 285.)

DRIVER, NICHOLAS. Scholar of TRINITY HALL, 1605; LL.B. 1609-10. Ord. deacon and priest (Peterb.) Jan. 27, 1620-1.

DRIVER, ROBERT. B.A. 1504-5; perhaps M.A. 1511-2. One of these names chantry priest at Rowell, Northants., in 1526. (H. G. Harrison.)

DRIVER, ROBERT. Adm. sizar (age 16) at ST JOHN'S, Apr. 30, 1669. S. of Richard, of Wells, Norfolk. B. there. School, Walsingham. Matric. 1669; B.A. 1672-3; M.A. 1678. Ord. deacon (Norwich) Sept. 1675. R. of North Creake, Norfolk, 1686-7.

DRIVER, THOMAS. Matric. pens. from CORPUS CHRISTI, Michs. 1580; B.A. 1583-4.

DRYVER, WILLIAM. Matric. sizar from JESUS, Michs. 1546.

DRIVER, ——. B.Can.L. 1472-3; D.Can.L. 1482. One Simon Driver, R. of Tibenham, Norfolk, until 1484.

DRIVER, ——. B.A. 1492; M.A. 1495-6.

DRIVER, ——. B.Can.L. 1508-9.

DROPE, FRANCIS. Incorp. M.A. 1663 from Magdalen College, Oxford. Chorister and demy there. S. of Thomas, V. of Cumnor, Berks. B. there. B.A. (Oxford) 1647. Created M.A. 1660; B.D. 1667. Fellow of Magdalen, 1661-71. Preb. of Lincoln, 1670. Died Sept. 26, 1671. Buried at Cumnor. (*D.N.B.*; *Al. Oxon.*)

DROPE or DROOP, JOHN. Matric. pens. from TRINITY, Michs. 1561; Scholar, 1565; B.A. 1565-6.

DROPE, JOHN. M.A. 1616 (Incorp. from Oxford). S. of Thomas, of Northamptonshire, clerk. Adm. at Magdalen College, Oxford, 1601, age 13; B.A. 1608-9; M.A. 1612; B.D. 1619. Fellow of Magdalen, 1608-29. Proctor, 1618. R. of Grindon, Staffs., 1626; and of Norbury, Derbs., 1628-9. Died Sept. 29, 1629. M.I. at Norbury. Will, P.C.C. (*Al. Oxon.*)

DROPE, THOMAS. M.A. 1579 (Incorp. from Oxford); B.A. (Oxford) 1572; M.A. 1575; B.D. 1583. Fellow of Magdalen, 1571. Preb. of Wells, 1583-1632. V. of Cumnor, Berks., 1586. R. of Aynhoe, Northants., 1588-1633. Buried there Nov. 19, 1633, aged 83. Will (P.C.C.) 1634. (*Al. Oxon.*; Le Neve, *Mon.*, I. 148.)

DROUGHT, GEORGE. Matric. pens. from TRINITY, Michs. 1567; B.A. from Christ's, 1571-2; M.A. 1575.

DROWTE, JOHN. Matric. sizar from TRINITY, Michs. 1567.

DRUELL, HUMPHREY. Matric. Fell.-Com. from JESUS, Lent, 1577-8. Probably knighted, 1596. Buried in Winchester Cathedral, Jan. 8, 1630-1.

DRUELL, JOHN. Of KING'S HALL, 1428-33 (then LL.B.); LL.D. Perhaps fellow of Queens'. Preb. of Sarum, 1441-69. R. of Fulham, Middlesex, 1452-8. Preb. of St Paul's, 1457-67; treasurer, 1458-67. Died 1469. Buried in St Botolph's, Cambridge. Benefactor to Queens', where he founded two fellowships and a scholarship. Brother of the next. (*Hennessy* identifies him with the archdeacon of Exeter, 1444-53, whose will was proved at Lambeth in 1453.)

DRUELL, NICHOLAS. Succeeded his brother, John Druell, as scholar at KING'S HALL, 1433-54. Will (P.C.C.) 1455.

DRUMM, DROME or DROWME, MICHAEL. Student at Cambridge according to Dr Caius (*De Ant. Cant.*, 150). B.A. (Oxford) 1527; M.A. 1531; B.D. 1539. Appointed to Cardinal College, Oxford. Six preacher at Canterbury, 1541. (*Cooper*, I. 83; who seems to confound him with Thos. Durham, fellow of St John's.)

DRURY, ANTHONY. Matric. pens. from CORPUS CHRISTI, Lent, 1557-8. Of Besthorpe, Norfolk, Esq. Will proved (P.C.C.) 1616. Father of the next.

DRURY, ANTHONY. Adm. pens. at EMMANUEL, Oct. 20, 1591. S. of the above. Of Besthorpe, Norfolk. Matric. *c.* 1591. Knighted, July 23, 1603. High Sheriff of Norfolk, 1617. M.P. for Norfolk, 1625. Died Oct. 1638. Buried at Besthorpe. Will (Norwich) 1638.

DRURY, CHARLES. Adm. pens. (age 17) at TRINITY, Apr. 11, 1681. S. of William. B. at Nottingham. School, Derby. Matric. 1681; Scholar, 1683; B.A. 1684-5; M.A. 1688. Ord. priest (York) Dec. 22, 1689.

DRURY, CHRISTOPHER. Adm. at KING'S, a scholar from Eton, 1552; B.A. 1556-7. Fellow, till 1559.

DRURY, DRUE. Matric. pens. from ST EDMUND'S HOSTEL, Michs. 1544. Probably s. of Robert, of Edgerly, Bucks. Sheriff of Norfolk. Knighted, 1579. M.P. for Camelford, 1562; for Norfolk, 1584. Died Apr. 29, 1617, at Riddlesworth, Norfolk, aged 99. (Le Neve, *Mon.*, I. 58.)

DRURY, DRUE. Adm. Fell.-Com. at PETERHOUSE, 1606-7. S. of Drue (above). B Oct. 7, 1588. Created Bart. May 7, 1627. M.P. for Norfolk, 1620; for Thetford, 1624. Of Riddlesworth. Died 1632. Father of the next. (*T. A. Walker*).

DRURY, DRUE. Adm. Fell.-Com. (age 17) at CHRIST'S, Mar. 21, 1628-9. S. of Sir Drue, of Riddlesworth (above). B. in London, June 17, 1611. School, Bury. Matric. 1629. Adm. at Gray's Inn, Feb. 15, 1623-4. Of Riddlesworth, Bart. Succeeded as Bart., 1632. Died July 13, 1647. Admon. P.C.C. Father of the next, of Isaac (1657) and of Robert (1654). (*Peile*, I. 398; *Suff. Man. Fam.*, I. 357; *G.E.C.*)

DRURY, DRUE. Adm. pens. (age 16) at MAGDALENE, July 5, 1654. S. of Sir Drue, above, Bart., of Riddlesworth, Norfolk. School, Grendon, Northants. Matric. 1654; B.A. 1657-8. Died *s.p.* Brother of Isaac (1657) and Robert (1654).

DRURY, ED. Matric. pens. from ST EDMUND'S HOSTEL, 1544.

DRURY, EDMUND. Matric. pens. from CORPUS CHRISTI, Michs. 1564. 4th s. of William, of Besthorpe, Esq. B. at Besthorpe, Norfolk. Ord. deacon (London) Oct. 6, 1578, age 26. R. of Yelverton and Beeston, Norfolk, 1579-86; called D.D. Living, 1612. Brother of Henry (1559).

DRURY, EDMUND. Matric. Fell.-Com. from CHRIST'S, July, 1625. Probably s. of Francis (1594), of Swaffham Prior, Cambs. B. 1607. Died 1668. Buried at Swaffham. (*Peile*, I. 377.)

DRURY, EDWARD. Matric. pens. from PETERHOUSE, 1555.

DRURY, FRANCIS. Matric. pens. from ST JOHN'S, *c.* 1594. Probably s. of John, of Swaffham Prior, Cambs. B. 1577. Of Swaffham, Esq. Will (P.C.C.) 1633. (*Vis. of Cambs.*, 1619.)

DRURY, FRANCIS. Adm. pens. (age 17) at CAIUS, Jan. 21, 1663-4. Of Gt Dunham, Norfolk. S. of Richard, gent. School, Lynn. Matric. 1664. Buried at Dunham, Mar. 18, 1686-7. Brother of Richard (1660-1). (*Venn*, I. 420.)

DRURY, GEORGE. Adm. sizar (age 18) at PETERHOUSE, June 5, 1707. Of Huntingdonshire. Perhaps s. of Richard, High Sheriff of Cambs. and Hunts., 1676. School, Huntingdon. Matric. 1707; Scholar, 1708; B.A. 1710-1; M.A. 1714. Ord. deacon (Norwich) Mar. 16, 1711-2; priest, May 31, 1713. R. of Whitton and Claydon, Suffolk, 1711. V. of Henley, 1732. Buried at Claydon, May 26, 1761. Father of the next.

DRURY, GEORGE. Adm. pens. (age 17) at EMMANUEL, Aug. 11, 1737. S. of George (above), R. of Claydon, Suffolk. Matric. 1738; B.A. 1741-2; M.A. 1761. Ord. deacon (Norwich) Sept. 19, 1742; priest, May 20, 1744. R. of Akenham, Suffolk, 1744. V. of Wherstead, 1744-61. R. of Overstone, Northants., 1761. R. of Little Billing, 1761-1807. R. of Claydon, 1761. Buried there Feb. 24, 1807. (H. I. Longden.)

DRURY, HENRY. Matric. Fell.-Com. from CHRIST'S, May, 1554. S. of Sir William, of Hawstead, Suffolk, Knt. B. Apr. 6, 1539. Adm. at Lincoln's Inn, May 16, 1557. Of Hawstead, Esq. Died 1586. Will, P.C.C. (*Peile*, I. 54.)

DREWRY, HENRY. Adm. pens. at CORPUS CHRISTI, 1559. Doubtless s. of William, of Besthorpe, Norfolk, Esq. Matric. Michs. 1559; B.A. 1563-4; M.A. 1567. Fellow, 1563. Ord. deacon (Ely) 1566; priest (London) June 4, 1566, age 24. R. of High Roothing, Essex, 1568-1601 and 1607-13. R. of Tendring, 1584-1613. Will proved (P.C.C.) 1613. Doubtless father of the next and brother of Edmund (1564).

DRURY, HENRY. Adm. pens. at CORPUS CHRISTI, 1602. Of Essex. Doubtless s. of Henry (above), R. of High Roothing, Essex. Matric. Michs. 1602; B.A. 1605-6; M.A. 1609. Of Essex, gent.

DRURY, HENRY. Adm. sizar at TRINITY, Oct. 29, 1628. Of Norfolk. Matric. 1629. Migrated to Peterhouse, Jan. 28, 1629-30. B.A. 1633-4; M.A. 1637. R. of South Runcton, Norfolk, 1661-72. Died 1672. Will, P.C.C. (*T. A. Walker*.)

DRURY, HENRY. Adm. pens. at TRINITY, Apr. 12, 1637. Perhaps s. of Thomas, of Fincham, Norfolk. B. 1622. Matric. 1637; Scholar, 1641; B.A. 1641-2; M.A. 1645. Of Beswell, and after of Holme, clerk. Will (P.C.C.) proved, 1672. (*Suff. Man. Fam.*, I. 364.)

DRURY, ISAAC. Adm. pens. (age 15) at MAGDALENE, July 10, 1657. 3rd s. of Sir Drue, Bart. (1628-9), of Riddlesworth, Norfolk. School, Grendon. Matric. 1657. Adm. at the Middle Temple, Feb. 19, 1656-7. Brother of Drue (1654) and Robert (1654).

DRURY, JOHN. Scholar of QUEENS', 1537-43; B.A. 1541-2.

DRURY, JOHN. Matric. pens. from CORPUS CHRISTI, Michs. 1552. One of these names adm. at Lincoln's Inn, Apr. 28, 1562.

DRURIE, JOHN. Adm. Fell.-Com. (age 17) at CAIUS, Apr. 15, 1590. S. of William (1545), LL.D., of Essex. School, London. B.A. 1592-3. Adm. at the Middle Temple, 1594. Of Tendring, Essex. Knighted, Nov. 6, 1604. Died Dec. 18, 1619. Will (P.C.C.) 1622. He and his family were Popish recusants. (*Vis. of Bucks.*, 1634, 159; *Venn*, I. 139.)

DRURY or DREWRY, JOHN. Adm. pens. (age 19) at PETERHOUSE, July 7, 1668. Of Leicestershire. School, Market Bosworth. Scholar, 1668.

DRURY, JOHN. Adm. pens. (age 17) at ST JOHN'S, July 6, 1716. S. of William, gent., of Nottinghamshire. B. at Nottingham. School, Nottingham.

DRURY, NICHOLAS. Adm. at ST CATHARINE'S, Oct. 18, 1660. Of Norfolk. S. and h. of Anthony, of Intwood, Norfolk, Esq. Matric. 1661-2. Adm. at Lincoln's Inn, Nov. 26, 1662. Of Intwood, Norfolk, and Southwold, Suffolk, Esq. (*Suff. Man. Fam.*, I. 355.)

DRURY, RICHARD. Adm. pens. (age 16) at CAIUS, Jan. 12, 1660-1. S. of Richard, gent., of Gt Dunham, Norfolk. B. there. School, Lynn. Matric. 1661; Scholar, 1661. Migrated to Trinity, Mar. 10, 1664-5. Adm. at Lincoln's Inn, June 27, 1664. Of Gt Dunham, gent. Died there. Buried Feb. 8, 1666-7. Brother of Francis (1663-4). (*Venn*, I. 410.)

DRURY, RO. Matric. pens. from TRINITY HALL, Michs. 1558.

DRURY, ROBERT. Probably at one time pens. of GONVILLE HALL. S. of Roger, of Hawstead, Suffolk. Barrister of Lincoln's Inn. M.P. for Suffolk. Speaker of the House of Commons, 1496. Knighted, 1497. Attended on the King in France, 1520, and held many important offices. Died Mar. 2, 1535-6. Buried at St Mary's, Bury St Edmunds. M.I. Will P.C.C. (*Cooper*, I. 56; *D.N.B.*)

DRUREY, ROBERT. Adm. pens. (age 11) at CAIUS, Dec. 14, 1564. S. of Robert, Esq., of Hawstead, Suffolk. Died young. Brother of Thomas (1564) and William (1564).

DRURY, ROBERT. Matric. pens. from TRINITY HALL, Easter, 1575.

DRURY, ROBERT. Matric. Fell.-Com. (age 13) from CORPUS CHRISTI, Easter, 1588. S. of Sir William (1564), of Hawstead, Suffolk. M.A. 1599 (*special grace*). Knighted, Sept. 1591. M.P. for Suffolk, 1604-11; for Eye, Suffolk, 1614. Died Apr. 2, 1615, aged 40. Buried at Hawstead. Will (P.C.C.) 1615. (Le Neve, *Mon.*; *Suff. Man. Fam.*, VII. 39.)

DRURY, ROBERT. Adm. pens. at EMMANUEL, June 30, 1631. Of Essex. Matric. 1631; B.A. 1634.

DRURY, Sir ROBERT, Bart. Adm. Fell.-Com. (age 17) at MAGDALENE, July 5, 1654. S. of Sir Drue (1628-9), Bart., of Riddlesworth, Norfolk. School, Grendon, Northants. Matric. 1655. Succeeded as Bart., 1647. Died Apr. 27, 1712, aged 77. M.I. at Riddlesworth. Brother of Drue (1654) and Isaac (1657). (Le Neve, *Mon.*, III. 244; *G.E.C.*)

DRURY, ROGER. B.Can.L. 1478.

DRURY, ROGER. Matric. pens. from TRINITY, Easter, 1560. Perhaps s. of William, of Besthorpe, Norfolk, Esq. Scholar, 1560; B.A. 1564-5. Of Rollesby, Norfolk, Esq. M.P. for Yarmouth, 1588. Will proved (P.C.C.) 1599. Father of the next.

DRURIE, ROGER. Adm. Fell.-Com. (age 17) at CAIUS, Sept. 30, 1605. S. of Roger (above), of Rollesby, Norfolk. School, Oby, Norfolk. Living in 1618. Of Drury Lane, Esq. Will proved (P.C.C.) Jan. 1632. (*Venn*, I. 191; *Suff. Man. Fam.*, I. 356.)

DRURY, ROGER. Matric. pens. from CLARE, Easter, 1625; B.A. 1628-9; M.A. 1632.

DREWRY, THOMAS. Matric. sizar from CORPUS CHRISTI, Michs. 1545.

DRURY, THOMAS. Adm. pens. (age 12) at CAIUS, Aug. 4, 1564. S. of Robert, Esq. B. at Hawstead, Suffolk, May 8, 1551. Matric. 1564. Died 1602. Brother of Robert (1564) and William (1564). (*Venn*, I. 54.)

DRURYE, THOMAS. Matric. pens. from JESUS, Michs. 1571. Perhaps of Maids Moreton, Bucks.; adm. at the Inner Temple, 1577.

DRURIE, THOMAS. Matric. sizar from MAGDALENE, Easter, 1589.

DRURY, THOMAS. Adm. pens. at EMMANUEL, Mar. 1597-8. Perhaps 4th s. of Sir Robert, of Rougham, Suffolk. Barrister, 1607. Died *s.p. vita patris*. Will (P.C.C.) 1616. (*Suff. Man. Fam.*, I. 347.)

DRURY, THOMAS. Matric. pens. from QUEENS', Easter, 1617. Of Norfolk. Perhaps s. and h. of Thomas, late of Fleningham (? Framingham), Norfolk, gent., deceased; adm. at Lincoln's Inn, Apr. 22, 1619.

DRURY, THOMAS. Adm. pens. at EMMANUEL, Easter, 1624. Of Suffolk. Matric. 1624; B.A. 1627-8.

DRURY, THOMAS. Adm. Fell.-Com. at ST CATHARINE'S, 1632. Of Suffolk.

DRURY, THOMAS. Adm. pens. (age 16) at CAIUS, June 23, 1635. S. of Thomas, brewer. B. at Downham, Norfolk. Bapt. June 9, 1618. School, Wisbech. Matric. 1635; Scholar, 1637-9; B.A. 1638-9. Adm. at Lincoln's Inn, June 17, 1640. Died *s.p.* Admon. (P.C.C.) 1672. (*Suff. Man. Fam.*, I. 368.)

DRURY, THOMAS. Matric. pens. from ST CATHARINE'S, Easter, 1637. Of Norfolk. Perhaps s. and h. of Thomas, of Fincham, Norfolk, Esq.; adm. at Lincoln's Inn, June 6, 1640. Lord of Talbot's in Fincham, 1674. Dead 1697. (*Suff. Man. Fam.*, I. 364.)

DRURY, WALTER. Adm. pens. at EMMANUEL, June 11, 1621. S. of William (1585). Matric. 1622; B.A. 1625-6; M.A. 1629. R. of Sandhurst, Kent, 1632-80. Died 1680.

DRURY, WATERS. Adm. sizar (age 17) at CAIUS, Apr. 25, 1666. S. of William, gent., of Downham Market, Norfolk. B. there. Schools, Downham and Lynn. Scholar, 1666-73; Matric. 1667; B.A. 1669-70; M.A. 1673. Ord. deacon (Peterb.) Dec. 22, 1672; priest (Chichester) Dec. 21, 1673. V. of Stow Bardolph, Norfolk, 1674-1722. R. of Wimbotsham, 1674-1722. Died 1722. (*Venn*, I. 427.)

DRURY, WILLIAM. Adm. at KING'S, a scholar from Eton, 1511. Left before graduation.

DRURY, WILLIAM. Educated at GONVILLE HALL. S. of Sir Robert, of Hedgerley, Bucks. B. Oct. 2, 1527. Knighted, 1570. A distinguished commander, by land and sea. At the siege of Edinburgh, 1573. President of Munster, 1575. Lord Deputy of Ireland, 1578. Died Sept. 30, 1579. One of these names (knight) M.P. for Suffolk, 1553-5. (*Cooper*, I. 412; *D.N.B.*)

DRURY, WILLIAM. Matric. sizar from TRINITY HALL, Easter, 1545. S. of John, of Rougham, Suffolk. LL.B. 1553; LL.D. 1559. Regius Professor of Civil Law, 1559-61. Admitted advocate, May 5, 1561. Secretary to Archbishop Parker. Judge of the Prerogative Court, till 1575. Will (P.C.C.) 1575. (*Cooper*, II. 74; *D.N.B.*)

DRURY, WILLIAM. Adm. (age 15) at CAIUS, Aug. 4, 1564. S. of Robert, Esq., of Hawstead, Suffolk. B. Mar. 30, 1550. School, Groton. Perhaps specially adm. at Lincoln's Inn, May 7, 1569. Knighted, 1570. High Sheriff of Suffolk, 1583. M.P. for Suffolk, 1584. Commander of a regiment in France sent in aid of Henry IV. Fought a duel there with Sir John Borough. Died in consequence of his wound, Jan. 18, 1589-90. Buried at Hawstead. M.I. there. Will (P.C.C.) 1595. Brother of Robert (1564) and Thomas (1564). (*Venn*, I. 54.)

DRURY, WILLIAM. Adm. sizar at EMMANUEL, 1585. Matric. Michs. 1585; Scholar; B.A. 1589-90; M.A. 1593. Incorp. at Oxford, 1593. B.D. (Oxford) 1600. R. of Leybourne, Kent, 1602-40. R. of Merstham, Surrey, 1625-32. Died 1640. Will (P.C.C.) proved by s. Walter (1621).

DRURY, WILLIAM. Matric. pens. from TRINITY, *c.* 1592.

DRURY, WILLIAM. Adm. Fell.-Com. at EMMANUEL, Oct. 12, 1614. Matric. 1614. One of these names, s. and h. of Sir Anthony, of Besthorpe, Norfolk, Knt. Adm. at Gray's Inn, Aug. 16, 1611. Knighted, Sept. 30, 1618. Died Nov. 8, 1639. Probably the same man who subscribed at Oxford, May 7, 1613. (*Al. Oxon.*)

DREWRY, WILLIAM. Matric. Fell.-Com. from CORPUS CHRISTI, Lent, 1618-9. Of Suffolk.

DRURIE, WILLIAM. Matric. Fell.-Com. from ST CATHARINE'S, Michs. 1633.

DRURY, WILLIAM. Adm. pens. (age 20) at CHRIST'S, Nov. 28, 1645. S. of William of Walsoken, Norfolk. School, Wisbech.

DRURYE, WILLIAM. Adm. pens. at TRINITY, Apr. 14, 1657. Of Huntingdonshire.

DRURY, WILLIAM. Adm. pens. (age 18) at TRINITY, June 26, 1679. S. of Thomas. B. at Nottingham. School, Westminster. Scholar, 1680; Matric. 1682; B.A. 1682-3; M.A. 1686. Fellow, 1685. Senior Proctor, 1706-7. Buried in Trinity College Chapel, Nov. 16, 1713.

DRURY, ——. Adm. pens. at PETERHOUSE, 1600.

DRUSIUS, *see* DRISIUS.

DRY, ISAAC. Adm. sizar at QUEENS', July 27, 1644. Of Dorset.

DRYE, JOHN. B.A. 1499-1500.

DRY, RALPH. Matric. sizar from ST JOHN'S, Lent, 1610-1; B.A. 1614-5; M.A. 1618. Ord. deacon (York) Sept. 1616; priest, Dec. 1616. V. of Sheriff Hutton, Yorks., 1628-38. Died 1638.

DRY, RICHARD. Adm. sizar at QUEENS', Apr. 23, 1687. Of Middlesex. Matric. 1687.

DRYANDER, *see* ENCINAS.

DRYDEN, CHARLES. Adm. pens. (age 17) at TRINITY, June 26, 1683. S. of John (1650), the Poet Laureate. B. at Charlton, Wilts., 1666. School, Westminster. Matric. 1683; Scholar, 1684. Went to Italy, 1692. Chamberlain to the Pope. Returned, 1698. Drowned in the Thames at Datchet, Aug. 20, 1704. Buried at Windsor. (*D.N.B.*; *Al. Westmon.*, 200.)

DRYDEN, ERASMUS. Adm. pens. at EMMANUEL, June 18, 1618. S. of Sir Erasmus, of Canons' Ashby, Northants. Bart. (created, 1619). Matric. 1618. Adm. at Gray's Inn, Feb. 11, 1621-2. Of Titchmarsh, Northants., Esq. Died 1654. Will (P.C.C.) 1655. (Burke, *Ext. Bart.*; *G.E.C.*; Baker, *Northants.*, II. 5.)

DRYDEN, JOHN. Adm. pens. at TRINITY, May 18, 1650. S. of Erasmus, of Canons' Ashby, Northants. B. at Aldwincle, Aug. 9, 1631. School, Westminster. Matric. 1650; Scholar, 1650; B.A. 1653-4. Discommuned for contumacy to the Vice-Master. F.R.S. 1663. Poet Laureate, 1670-88. Married, Dec. 1, 1663, Elizabeth Howard, dau. of the Earl of Berkshire. Died in Gerrard Street, London, May 1, 1700. Buried in Westminster Abbey. Father of Charles (1683). (*D.N.B.*)

DRYDEN, JONATHAN. Adm. pens at EMMANUEL, Oct. 24, 1617. S. of Nicholas, of Norton Pinckney, Northants. Matric. 1617; Scholar; B.A. 1621-2; M.A. 1625, as 'Briden.' Preb. of Hereford, 1627. Will of one of these names (P.C.C.) 1654; of Camberwell, minister. (Baker, *Northants.*, II. 5.)

DRYDEN, JONATHAN. Matric. pens. from TRINITY, Lent, 1656-7. Scholar from Westminster, 1656. S. of Jonathan, above. B. in Herefordshire. B.A. 1659-60; M.A. 1663. Fellow, 1661. Incorp. at Oxford, 1665. Ord. deacon (Ely) Sept. 19, 1663; priest (London) May, 1665. R. of Cheriton, Kent, 1668-76. R. of Keighley, Yorks., 1676-9. R. of Scrayingham, Yorks., 1680-1702. R. of Londesborough, 1680-1702. Preb. of York, 1682. Died Aug. 25, 1702, aged 63. Buried in York Minster. Father of the next.

DRYDEN, JONATHAN. Adm. sizar at JESUS, June 23, 1716. S. of Jonathan (above), deceased, Canon of York. Bapt. in the Minster, Apr. 2, 1700. Matric. 1717; Rustat scholar; B.A. 1720-1; M.A. 1729. Ord. deacon (York) Sept. 23, 1722. P.C. of Bolton Percy, Yorks., 1727. R. of St Cuthbert, York. Died Apr. 13, 1740, aged 39.

DRYFIELD, RICHARD. Chancellor of the University, 1261.

DRYLAND, JOHN. Matric. sizar from MAGDALENE, Easter, 1625; B.A. 1629-30.

DRYWOOD, GEORGE. Adm. at KING'S, a scholar from Eton, 1564. Probably s. of John. B. at Dunton Waylett, Essex, *c.* 1547. Fellow, but left without a degree, 1568. 'Farmer at Dunton Waylett.' Author, Latin poems. Died May 22, 1603. (*Harwood*; *Vis. of Essex*, 1634; *Cooper*, II. 354.)

DRYWOOD, GEORGE. Matric. pens. from TRINITY, Michs. 1570. Scholar from Westminster, 1570. B.A. 1573-4; M.A. 1577; B.D. 1586. Fellow, 1576-94. Ord. deacon and priest (Peterb.) May 28, 1583. Deputy Public Orator, 1582. R. of Mistley, Essex, 1586-90. R. of South Ockendon, 1590-1611. R. of Trinity-the-Less, London, 1603-5. R. of Chadwell, Essex, 1605-11. Died 1611. Will (P.C.C.) 1612. (*Cooper*, III. 43; *Vis. of Essex*, 1634.)

DRYWOOD, GEORGE. Matric. pens. from TRINITY, Michs. 1618. Scholar from Westminster, 1619; B.A. 1622-3; M.A. 1626. Fellow, 1624.

DRYWOOD, JOHN. Matric. pens. from TRINITY, Easter, 1575. One of these names, of Staple Inn, adm. at Gray's Inn, 1580.

DRYWOOD, JOHN. Adm. pens. at KING'S, Michs. 1579. Licensed to practise medicine from Trinity, 1587.

DRYWOOD, JOHN. Matric. Fell.-Com. from KING'S, Michs. 1609.

DRYWOOD, WILLIAM. Matric. sizar from TRINITY, Michs. 1570. Ord. priest (Ely) Apr. 17, 1575, age 25. R. of Downham, Essex, 1574-1608. Died 1608. Admon. (P.C.C.) June 18, 1608.

DRYWOOD, WILLIAM. Matric. pens. from TRINITY, Michs. 1588; Scholar, 1589.

DUBBER, ——. B.A. 1465-6.

DUBORDIEU, ARMAND. Adm. sizar at CHRIST'S, Jan. 31, 1690-1. A Frenchman; protestant exile from Montpelier. Matric. 1691; B.A. 1694-5; M.A. 1716. Ord. deacon (London) Feb. 17, 1694-5; priest (Peterb.) June 6, 1696. V. of Desborough, Northants., 1696-1727. V. of North Weald, Essex, 1715-33. V. of Sawbridgeworth, Herts., 1716-33. Died Aug. 25, 1733, aged 61. Buried at Sawbridgeworth. M.I. His contemporary, John Armand Dubordieu, was of Oxford. (*Peile*, II. 120; H. I. Longden.)

DUBORDIEU, JOHN. Adm. sizar at ST CATHARINE'S, June 29, 1716. Matric. 1716; B.A. 1719-20; M.A. 1734. Ord. deacon (London) June 10, 1722. C. of St Michael-le-Querne, London, c. 1726-35. V. of Sawbridgeworth, Herts., 1734-52 (resigned). Preb. of St Asaph, 1737-54; chancellor, 1743-54. R. of Newington, Surrey, 1752-4. Died 1754. Father of the next.

DUBORDIEU, JOHN. Adm. pens. at QUEENS', May 17, 1749. Of London. S. of John (above), C. of St Michael-le-Quern, and Isabella. Bapt. there, May 21, 1733. Matric. 1749. Brother of William (1751).

DUBORDIEU, PETER. Adm. sizar at CLARE, June 25, 1689. Of Montpelier, France. Matric. 1689; B.A. 1692-3; M.A. 1697. Ord. deacon (York) 1693; priest, Sept. 1693. R. of Kirby Misperton, Yorks., 1707-55. Author.

DUBORDIEU, WILLIAM. Adm. sizar (age 17) at PETERHOUSE, June 1, 1751. Of London. S. of John (1716). B. Mar. 21, 1734-5. School, Merchant Taylors'. Matric. 1751; Scholar. Migrated to Oxford. Matric. from Merton College, May 30, 1754, age 19. Brother of John (1749). (*T. A. Walker*, 301.)

DUCANE, JOHN. B.A. from TRINITY, 1623-4; M.A. 1627. Incorp. at Oxford, 1624. S. of John, of London. Died at Battersea, Apr. 22, 1684, aged 83. (*Essex Pedigrees*; Burke, *L.G.*)

DU CAREL, ANDREW COLTEE. LL.B. from TRINITY HALL, 1739 (Incorp. from Oxford). S. of James, of Greenwich. B. in Normandy. School, Eton. Matric. from Trinity College, Oxford, July 2, 1731, age 18. B.C.L. from St John's, 1738. D.C.L. 1742. Adm. at Gray's Inn, June 13, 1732; and at the Inner Temple, 1735. Admitted advocate, 1743. Official of the Diocese of Canterbury, 1758. F.S.A. 1737. F.R.S. 1762. Librarian at Lambeth, 1757. A devoted antiquary. Author, antiquarian. Died May 29, 1785. Buried at St Katharine's-by-the-Tower. Will, P.C.C. Brother of the next. (*D.N.B.*)

DU CAREL, JAMES COLTEE. Adm. Fell.-Com. (age 19) at CAIUS, Feb. 1, 1734-5. Previously matric. from Trinity College, Oxford, 1733. S. of James Coltee, Esq., of Paris. B. there, at Neuilly. Schools, Eton and Greenwich. Of Greenwich, Esq., when adm. at the Inner Temple, 1738. Of Ayot St Lawrence, Herts. Living at St Germain, France, in 1785. Brother of Andrew, above. (*Venn*, II. 40.)

DUCIE-MORETON, MATTHEW. Adm. Fell.-Com. at QUEENS', June 27, 1681. S. of Edward Moreton, Esq., of Moreton, Staffs. M.A. 1682 (*Com. Reg.*). Served under William III in Flanders. M.P. for Gloucestershire, 1710-3, 1715-20. Created Lord Ducie, Baron of Moreton, Staffs., June 9, 1720. Died May 2, 1735, in London. Buried at Tortworth, Gloucs.; aged 72.

DUCIE, WILLIAM. Adm. Fell.-Com. (age 17) at MAGDALENE, Sept. 12, 1669. S. of Sir Hugh, Knt., of Islington, Middlesex. School, Richmond. Succeeded his uncle Sir William, as 4th Bart., Sept. 9, 1679. Died in the Fleet Prison, c. 1691. (Burke, *Ext. Bart.*; *Vis. of Sussex*; *G.E.C.*)

DUCK, JOHN. Matric. pens. from PETERHOUSE, Michs. 1565. B. in Shoreditch, Middlesex. Migrated to Trinity, 1568; Scholar; B.A. 1569-70; M.A. 1573; B.D. 1584. Fellow, 1571. Ord. deacon (London) June 19; priest, June 20, 1580, age 30. V. of Marsworth, Bucks., 1584. Died 1596.

DUCKE, JOHN. Adm. at KING'S, a scholar from Eton, 1711. B. at Dunchideock, Devon. Matric. 1712; B.A. 1715-6; M.A. 1719. Fellow, 1715, till his death. Died at Exeter.

DUCKELL, THOMAS. Matric. pens. from CLARE, Easter, 1579; B.A. 1582-3.

DUCKET, CHRISTOPHER (1503-4), *see* DOCKET.

DUCKETT, FRANCIS. Matric. pens. from ST JOHN'S, Michs. 1580. Perhaps s. and h. of Richard, of Grayrigg, Westmorland. B. 1564. Knighted, 1603. Died Oct. 24, 1636. Probably father of William (1607). (G. F. Ducket, *Duckettiana*, 24.)

DUCKETT, FRANCIS. Adm. sizar at CLARE, Dec. 30, 1725. S. of Francis, R. of Little Ashby, Leics. B. there. Matric. 1726; B.A. 1729-30. Ord. deacon (Lincoln) Feb. 22, 1729-30, C. of Haselbeech, Northants. Buried there Oct. 9, 1749, aged 44. M.I. Admon. granted to brother Zacheus (1732).

DUCKETT, GABRIEL. Scholar of TRINITY, 1560. Of Westmorland. S. of Anthony, of Grayrigg, and Dorothy Bellingham. B.A. 1562-3; M.A. from St John's, 1566. Fellow, of St John's, 1563. Keeper of the University Library. Buried at All Saints', Cambridge, Aug. 28, 1623. Will proved (V.C.C.) 1624. Brother of Lionel. (J. Parker.)

DUCKET, GILES. Matric. sizar from CLARE, Michs. 1559. One of these names, student at Trinity Hall, Aug. 1564.

DUCKET, GREGORY. Matric. pens. from TRINITY, Easter, 1587; Scholar, 1588; B.A. 1590-1, as 'George'; M.A. 1594; D.D. 1613. Fellow, 1591. University Librarian, 1594. V. of Trumpington, Cambs., 1606-11. R. of Girton, 1609. R. of St Andrew's, Holborn, 1611-24. Married, at St Dunstan-in-the-East, London, May 2, 1615, Margaret, dau. of Sir John Watts, Knt. Died Dec. 29, 1624. Buried in St Andrew's, Holborn. Admon. (P.C.C.) 1625. (J. Ch. Smith.)

DUCKETT, HENRY. Adm. pens. at EMMANUEL, 1586. Matric. 1586; Scholar; B.A. 1589-90; M.A. from Clare, 1593. Perhaps R. of Cotgrave, Notts., 1595-1603. Buried there Dec. 18, 1603. (Godfrey, *Notts.*)

DUCKETT, HENRY. Matric. pens. from ST JOHN'S, c. 1596; B.A. 1600-1; M.A. 1606. Perhaps V. of Conisborough, Yorks., 1611-5.

DUCKETT, JOHN. Matric. sizar from ST EDMUND HOSTEL, Michs. 1544 (*impubes*).

DUCKETT, JOHN. Adm. at KING'S, a scholar from Eton, 1583; B.A. 1587-8. Fellow. Died in College, 1588.

DUCKET, JOHN. Matric. pens. from PETERHOUSE, Michs. 1583; B.A. 1586-7; M.A. 1599. V. of Caistor, Lincs., 1592-1593.

DUCKET, JOHN. Adm. pens. at TRINITY, June 29, 1635, Exhibitioner from Charterhouse. Matric. 1636; Scholar, 1638; B.A. 1638-9. Subscribed for deacon's orders (London) Feb. 16, 1664-5; for priest's, May 19, 1665. C. of Rettendon, Essex.

DUCKET, JOHN. Adm. pens. at EMMANUEL, Jan. 12, 1654-5. Of Cambridgeshire. S. and h. of Thomas, of Steeple Morden, Cambs., Esq.; adm. at Lincoln's Inn, July 10, 1657.

DUCKET, LIONEL. Matric. pens. from ST JOHN'S, Easter, 1579. S. of Anthony, of Grayrigg. B. in Westmorland. B.A. 1582-3; M.A. from Jesus, 1586; B.D. 1597. Fellow of Jesus, 1585-1603. Proctor, 1595-6. Ord. deacon and priest (Peterb.) Sept. 23, 1589. V. of All Saints', Cambridge, 1592-1603. Died Apr. 5, 1603. Buried in Jesus College Chapel. Benefactor to Jesus and St John's. Will (V.C.C.) 1603. Brother of Gabriel. (*Cooper*, II. 354; A. Gray.)

DUCKETT, MANSEL. Adm. Fell.-Com. at EMMANUEL, Mar. 27, 1677. Matric. 1677. S. of Thomas (1651), of Steeple Morden, Cambs., and Anne, dau. of Sir Edward Mansell, Bart., of Muddlescombe, Co. Carmarthen. (G. F. Duckett, *Duckettiana*, 53.)

DUCKET, MATTHEW. Adm. sizar (age 19) at CAIUS, June 15, 1608. S. of Robert, husbandman, of Gt Burdon, Durham. School, Darlington. Matric. 1608. One of these names V. of Bradfield, Yorks., 1617-28.

DUCKET, NATHANIEL. Matric. pens. from CLARE, Easter, 1584; B.A. 1589-90; M.A. 1593.

DUCKET, NATHANIEL. Matric. sizar from TRINITY, Easter, 1617; Scholar, 1619; B.A. 1619-20; M.A. 1623. Ord. deacon (Peterb.) Sept. 27; priest, Sept. 28, 1624. V. of Stanwell, Middlesex, 1630-2. V. of North Elmham, Norfolk, 1631. Will dated Aug. 7, 1659. Father of Nathaniel (1665) and Peter (1665). (*Her. and Gen.*, VI. 320.)

DUCKET, NATHANIEL. Adm. sizar at TRINITY, June 7, 1665. S. of Nathaniel (above), V. of North Elmham, Norfolk. Bapt. there, June 1, 1648. School, Woodbridge. Matric. 1666-7; B.A. 1668-9; M.A. 1672. Ord. deacon (Norwich) Mar. 19, 1670-1. R. of Tittleshall, Norfolk, 1679-1721. R. of Wellingham, till 1721. Died Oct. 29, 1721, aged 73. Buried at Tittleshall. M.I. Brother of Peter (1665). (*Her. and Gen.*, VI. 320.)

DUCKET, NOAH. Matric. pens. from TRINITY, Michs. 1568; B.A. 1572-3. Doubtless of Broughton-Astley, Leics. Admon. (Leicester) 1613. Father of Peter (1615).

DUCKET, PAUL. Adm. pens. at TRINITY, June 3, 1638. Scholar from Westminster; B.A. 1642-3. R. of Grinstead, Essex, 1660-2. R. of St Leonard, Colchester, 1661-2. V. of Boreham, Essex, 1662-70. R. of Rettendon, 1662-70. Died 1670. Will (Cons. C. London) 1670.

DUCKETT, PETER. Matric. sizar from TRINITY, Easter, 1615. Probably of Staple Inn. S. of Noah (1568). Will (P.C.C.) 1652; proved by brother William, of Gray's Inn.

DUCKET, PETER. Adm. sizar at TRINITY, June 7, 1665. S. of Nathaniel (1617). Bapt. at North Elmham, May 24, 1650. School, Woodbridge. Matric. 1666-7; B.A. 1668-9; M.A. 1674. Ord. deacon (Norwich) Jan. 1672-3; priest, Sept. 1675. R. of Cookley, Suffolk, 1676-9. R. of Huntingfield, 1695-1709. Died 1709. Brother of Nathaniel (1665). *See Al. Oxon.* for a contemporary.

DUCKET, RICHARD. At ST JOHN'S for three years. Migrated as sizar (age 18) to Christ's, Nov. 6, 1626. S. of James, of Yorkshire. School, Sedbergh. Ord. deacon (Peterb.) May 22, 1630. (*Peile*, I. 378.)

DUCKET, ROBERT. Probably of ST JOHN'S; founded scholarships there, 1521. R. of Chevening, Kent, 1493-1522. Died 1522. (*Cooper*, I. 26)

DUCKETT, THOMAS. Adm. pens. (age 16) at ST JOHN'S, Oct. 27, 1634. S. of Nathaniel, gent., of Albury, Herts. B. at Tring, Herts. School, Bishop's Stortford, Herts. (private; Mr Lea). Matric. 1634-5. Migrated to Trinity, Oct. 30, 1637.

DUCKETT, THOMAS. Adm. pens. at EMMANUEL, June 28, 1651. S. of Thomas, of Steeple Morden, Cambs. Matric. 1651. Afterwards Fell.-Com. Adm. at Lincoln's Inn, May 12, 1655. Of Steeple Morden; donor to the Chapel, 1667. Father of Mansel (1677) and brother of John (1654).

DUCKET, TINKLER. Adm. sizar (age 16) at CAIUS, Oct. 9, 1727. S. of Henry, farmer, of Spixworth, Norfolk. B. there. Schools, Norwich (private; Mr Brand) and Wymondham. Scholar, 1727-35; Matric. 1728; B.A. 1731-2; M.A. 1735. Fellow, 1736-9. Ord. deacon (London) Sept. 23, 1733; priest, Mar. 2, 1734-5. C. of Little Horkesley, Essex. Expelled from the University for atheism and immorality, 1738. Living 1773, when he is described as at Venice, lately residing in Constantinople. (*Venn*, II. 28; *Her. and Gen.*, VI. 320.)

DUCKET, WILLIAM. Matric. pens. from ST JOHN'S, Easter, 1607. Doubtless s. of Sir Francis (1580), Knt., of Grayrigg, Westmorland. Adm. at the Inner Temple, Nov. 1609.

DUCKET, ZACHEUS. Adm. sizar at EMMANUEL, June 12, 1732. School, Oakham. Matric. 1732-3; B.A. 1735-6. Ord. deacon (Lincoln) Mar. 21, 1735-6; priest, Dec. 19, 1736. Of Gedling, Notts., clerk, in 1749. Brother of Francis (1725).

DUCKFIELD, DANIEL. B.A. from CHRIST'S, 1604-5; M.A. 1608. V. of Childerditch, Essex, 1611-53. Died Jan. 1653. Will, P.C.C.

DUCKFIELD, DANIEL. Matric. pens. from ST CATHARINE'S, Easter, 1632. Of Essex. B.A. 1635-6; M.A. 1639. Fellow, 1637-45. Buried at St Botolph's, Cambridge, May 3, 1645. Will proved (V.C.C.) 1645.

DUCKFIELD, DANIEL. Adm. pens. (age 16) at CHRIST'S, May 22, 1683. S. of John (1642), R. of Aspeden, near Buntingford. B. at Buntingford. School, Bishop's Stortford. Matric. 1683; B.A. 1686-7; M.A. 1690. Fellow, 1688-1702. Incorp. at Oxford, 1700. Ord. deacon (Lincoln) May, 1689. V. of Hauxton, Cambs., 1700. Died between Mar. 25 and May 1, 1702. Will proved (V.C.C.). (*Peile*, II. 92.)

DUCKFIELD, GEORGE. Matric. pens. from CHRIST'S, May, 1562. Perhaps s. of John, of Harston, Cambs., adm. at the Middle Temple, Oct. 20, 1566.

DUCKFIELD, JOHN. Matric. pens. from ST CATHARINE'S, Michs. 1642. Of Essex. B.A. 1645-6; M.A. 1649. Fellow. Incorp. at Oxford, 1649-50. Ord. priest (Ardfert) Nov. 27, 1656. V. of Layston, Herts., 1663-70; of Aspeden, 1670-85. Died 1685. Father of Daniel (1683).

DUCKFIELD, JOHN. Adm. pens. at ST CATHARINE'S, Jan. 18, 1677-8. Matric. 1678; B.A. 1681-2; M.A. 1685.

DUCKLING, JOHN. Adm. sizar (age 18) at CAIUS, Mar. 8, 1631-2. S. of Thomas, of Hopton, Suffolk, husbandman. Bapt. Jan. 23, 1613-4. School, Hopton. Matric. 1633; B.A. 1636-7; M.A. 1640. Ord. deacon (Peterb.) June 9, 1639; priest, Mar. 1, 1639-40. V. of Heckington, Lincs., 1646. (*Venn*, I. 303.)

DUCKRING, THOMAS. Adm. sizar at TRINITY, Nov. 18, 1675. Matric. 1675.

DUCKWORTH, CHRISTOPHER. Matric. sizar from QUEENS', Easter, 1571. Of Lancashire. B.A. 1576-7. Ord. deacon (Peterb.) Aug. 16, 1582; priest, an. 9, 1582-3. V. of Empingham, Rutland, 1582-1628.

DUCKWORTH, CHRISTOPHER. Matric. sizar from ST JOHN'S, c. 1594; B.A. 1597-8; M.A. 1601. Ord. deacon (Norwich) Mar. 25, 1602, age 31. C. of Barmer. Perhaps V. of Walton-le-Soken, Essex, 1609-41. Died 1641.

DUCKWORTH, HENRY. Matric. sizar from ST JOHN'S, Michs. 1627; B.A. 1630-1. Ord. priest (Norwich) Dec. 23, 1632.

DUCKWORTH, JOHN. Matric. sizar from ST JOHN'S, Lent, 1615-6; B.A. 1619-20; M.A. 1623. Perhaps R. of Beighton, Norfolk, c. 1622.

DUCKWORTH, JOHN. Adm. sizar (age 18) at ST JOHN'S, Mar. 24, 1669-70. S. of James, yeoman, of Haslingden, Lancs. B. there. School, Blackburn. Matric. 1670; B.A. 1673-4; M.A. 1677. R. of Haslingden, 1680. Died 1695. (*Manning and Bray*, II. 682.)

DUCKWORTH, RALPH. Proctor, 1430-1.

DUCKWORTH, RICHARD. Matric. sizar from ST JOHN'S, Easter, 1616; B.A. 1619-20; M.A. 1623. V. of Brent Pelham, Herts., 1630-44. Died 1644.

DUCKWORTH, ROBERT. Matric. sizar from ST JOHN'S, Lent, 1615-6.

DUCY, JOHN (1659), *see* DACY.

DUDINGTON, *see* DODDINGTON.

DUDLEY, AMBROSE, Earl of Warwick. M.A. 1564, on the Queen's visit. S. of John (1551), Duke of Northumberland. B. c. 1528. Knighted, Nov. 17, 1549. Adm. at the Inner Temple, 1561. Succeeded as Earl of Warwick, 1561. K.G. 1563. D.C.L. (Oxford) 1566. Commanded in the expedition to Havre, 1563. Commissioner for the trial of Mary, Queen of Scots, 1568. Privy Councillor, 1573. Lieutenant of the order of the Garter, 1575. Died Feb. 20, 1589-90. Buried at Warwick. Brother of Robert (1564). (*D.N.B.*; *Al. Oxon.*; *G.E.C.*)

DUDELEY, AUGUSTINE. Student at JESUS, 1543-4. (A. Gray.)

DUDLEY, AUGUSTINE. Adm. pens. at EMMANUEL, Apr. 4, 1627. 6th s. of Edward (1587), of Clapton, Northants. Matric. 1627; B.A. 1630-1; M.A. 1634. Ord. deacon (Peterb.) Sept. 25, 1636. Brother of the next, Edward (1617) and Gamaliel (1627). (*Vis. of Northants.*, 1618.)

DUDLEY, CHARLES. Adm. pens. at EMMANUEL, Nov. 8, 1620. 2nd s. of Edward (1587), of Clapton, Northants. Matric. 1621; B.A. 1624-5; M.A. 1628. Ord. deacon (Peterb.) Mar. 21; priest, Mar. 22, 1629-30. Brother of Edward (1617), Gamaliel (1627) and of Augustine (above). (*Vis. of Northants.*, 1618.)

DUDLEY, EDWARD. Matric. pens. from CHRIST'S, Dec. 1587. Eldest s. of Edward, of Clapton, Northants. B.A. 1590-1. Adm. at the Inner Temple, Nov. 1591; formerly of Clement's Inn. Died May 6, 1632, aged 62. Brother of Thomas (1587), father of the next, Gamaliel (1627), Charles (1620) and Augustine (1627). (*Peile*, I. 190; *G.E.C.*; *Vis. of Beds.*, 1634; *Vis. of Northants.*, 1618.)

DUDLEY, EDWARD. Matric. Fell.-Com. from CHRIST'S, Easter, 1617. 1st s. of Edward (above), of Clapton, Northants., Esq. B. 1603. Resided, till 1619. Adm. at the Middle Temple, Feb. 11, 1620. Died Nov. 13, 1641. Brother of the next, of Charles (1620) and Augustine (1627). (*Peile*, I. 316; *G.E.C.*; *Vis. of Northants.*, 1618.)

DUDLEY, GAMALIEL. Adm. pens. at EMMANUEL, Apr. 4, 1627. 5th s. of Edward (1587), of Clapton, Northants. Adm. at the Middle Temple, June, 1634. Adm. student at Leyden, May 30, 1642. Knighted, 1646. Brother of Edward (above), Charles (1620) and Augustine (1627).

DUDLEY, JOHN, Duke of Northumberland. Chancellor of the University, 1551. S. of Edmund, privy councillor to Henry VII. B. c. 1502. Knighted, in France, 1523. Created Viscount Lisle, 1542; Earl of Warwick, 1547; and Duke of Northumberland, 1551. Earl Marshal, 1551. K.G. 1543. Governor of Boulogne, 1544. Ambassador to France, 1546. A very distinguished military commander. Supported the claims of his daughter-in-law, Lady Jane Grey, to the throne. Executed on Tower Hill, Aug. 22, 1553. Father of Ambrose and Robert (1564). (*Cooper*, I. 112; *D.N.B.*; *G.E.C.*)

DUDLEY, JOHN. Matric. sizar from JESUS, Easter, 1566.

DUDLEY, JOHN. Adm. sizar at JESUS, Aug. 29, 1711. S. of Samuel (1660), R. of Braddon, Northants. B. there, 1694. Matric. 1711; B.A. 1715; M.A. 1719. Ord. deacon (Ely) Dec. 22, 1717; priest (Lincoln) Dec. 20, 1719. V. of Watford, Northants., 1719. Preb. of Lincoln, 1723-45. Archdeacon of Bedford, 1731-45. R. of Winwick, 1743. Perhaps V. of Aylesbury, Bucks., 1729. Died 1745.

DUDLEY, MONTAGU. Adm. pens. (age 16) at SIDNEY, Sept. 11, 1620. S. of Thomas (1587), gent. B. at Harrold, Beds. School, Ravensden (Mr Guest). Matric. 1620. Buried at Harrold, Dec. 18, 1621. (*Vis. of Beds.*, 1634; *Vis. of Northants.*, 1618.)

DUDLEY, PETER. Scholar at KING'S HALL, 1504-5.

DUDLEY, ROBERT. M.A. 1564, on the Queen's visit. 5th s. of John (1551), Duke of Northumberland. M.P. for Norfolk, c. 1549-52 and 1553. Sentenced to death for participation in the attempt to place Lady Jan Grey on the throne, 1553; but pardoned. K.G. 1559. High Steward of the University, 1563-88. Created Earl of Leicester, 1564. Chancellor of Oxford, 1564-85. Married, June 4, 1550, Amy, dau. of Sir John Robsart. Died at Cornbury, Oxon., Sept. 4, 1588. Buried in the Beauchamp Chapel, Warwick. Brother of Ambrose (1564). (*D.N.B.*; *Cooper*, II. 30; *Al. Oxon.*; *G.E.C.*)

DUDLEY, ROGER. Matric. pens. from CHRIST'S, Nov. 1566.

DUDLEY, SAMUEL. Adm. pens. at EMMANUEL, Easter, 1626. S. of Thomas, manager to the Earl of Lincoln. Bapt. at Northampton, Nov. 30, 1608. Matric. 1626. Went to New England, with his father and family, 1630. Lived at Cambridge, Ipswich and Salisbury, Mass., as planter and farmer. Minister at Exeter, New Hampshire, 1650. Died there, Feb. 10, 1682-3. He had a large family by his three wives. His father went out as assistant of the Massachusetts Bay Company, and rose to be Governor of the Colony. (J. G. Bartlett.)

DUDLEY, SAMUEL. Adm. pens. at JESUS, July 6, 1660. Of Buckinghamshire. Matric. 1661; Scholar, 1664; B.A. 1666-7. R. of Alderton, Northants., 1684-1710. V. of St Giles', Northampton, 1691-7. R. of Braddon, 1697. Father of John (1711). (A. Gray.)

DUDLEY, THOMAS. Matric. pens. from CHRIST'S, Michs. 1587. S. of Edward, of Clapton, Northants. Adm. at the Inner Temple, Apr. 22, 1592, from Clement's Inn. Of Harrold, Beds., Esq. Died 1632, aged 62. M.I. at Clapton. Father of Montagu (1620), brother of Edward (1587). (*Peile*, I. 190; *Vis. of Beds.*, 1634; *Vis. of Northants.*, 1618.)

DUDLEY, THOMAS. Adm. pens. at EMMANUEL, 1623. Matric. 1624; B.A. 1626-7; M.A. 1630.

DUDLEY, TOBIAS. Matric. pens. from JESUS, Michs. 1615. S. of Ambrose, of Chopwell, Durham. Bapt. at Ryton, Jan. 21, 1598-9. Of Chopwell, Esq. Married Jane, dau. of Sir William Blakiston, Knt. Buried at Ryton, May 24, 1661. Brother of the next. (*Vis. of Durham*, 1615; *Surtees*, II. 280; H. M. Wood.)

DUDLEY, WILLIAM. Matric. pens. from JESUS, Easter, 1616. 2nd s. of Ambrose, of Chopwell, Durham. Bapt. at St Nicholas, Newcastle, Nov. 9, 1600. B.A. 1619-20. Brother of the above. (*Vis. of Durham*, 1615.)

DUDLEY, WILLIAM. Adm. sizar at JESUS, May 21, 1622. Matric. 1622; B.A. 1625-6; Scholar, 1626; M.A. 1629. Ord. deacon (Peterb.) July 1; priest, July 2, 1629. R. of Broughton, Bucks., 1632-48; reinstated, 1660-77. R. of Simpson, 1634-6. Married, at Aspley Guise, Nov. 11, 1656, Sarah Sadler. Buried at Broughton. (*Lipscomb*, IV. 80.)

DUDLEY, WILLIAM. Adm. Fell.-Com. at EMMANUEL, May 13, 1681. Of Northamptonshire. 2nd s. of Sir William, of Clapton, Knt. and Bart. School, Oundle. M.A. 1682 (*Com. Reg.*). Adm. at the Middle Temple, Apr. 24, 1683; and at the Inner Temple, 1685. Ord. deacon (Peterb.) Dec. 23, 1710; priest, Feb. 24, 1710-1. R. of Clapton, 1711. Died May, 1726. (Burke, *Ext. Bart.*)

DUDLEY, ——. Matric. pens. from ST EDMUND'S HOSTEL, Easter, 1546.

DUDLEY, ——. Adm. Fell.-Com. at EMMANUEL, 1636.

DUDSON, SAMUEL. Adm. sizar (age 18) at CHRIST'S, July 7, 1669. S. of William. B. at Hopton, Derbs. School, Wirksworth (Mr Crosedale). Matric. 1670; B.A. 1672-3. Ord. deacon (Lichfield) Sept. 1673; priest, June, 1679. V. of Alfreton, Derbs., until 1733. Buried there Feb. 11, 1732-3. Father of the next. (*Peile*, II. 25.)

DUDSON, WILLIAM. Adm. sizar (age 18) at ST JOHN'S, June 22, 1709. S. of Samuel (above). B. at Barwick-in-Elmet, Yorks. School, Chesterfield, Derbs. Matric. 1709; B.A. 1712-3; M.A. 1718. Master of Repton School, 1723-4. Died 1724.

DUELL, EDWARD. Matric. sizar from TRINITY, Lent, 1581-2.

DUER, EDWARD. Adm. pens. at CLARE, Apr. 2, 1742. S. of John, of Antigua, and of Fulham, Middlesex. B. in London. Matric. 1742. Lieutenant in the army, 1750-61. Of Chichester, Esq. Will proved, Nov. 11, 1788. (*N. and Q.*, 3rd S., II. 379; Oliver's *Antigua*, III. 421.)

DUERDEN, *see* **DURDEN.**

DUFFE, ARTHUR. Adm. pens. (age 17) at ST JOHN'S, Oct. 17, 1715. S. of Patrick, deceased, of Ireland. School, Kidderminster. B.A. of Trinity College, Dublin. Matric. 1715-6; M.A. 1724.

DUFFIELD, ANDREW. Scholar of QUEENS', 1498; B.A. 1498-9. Probably fellow of Peterhouse; died 1501.

DUFFIELD, FRANCIS. Adm. pens. at ST CATHARINE'S, Feb. 28, 1728-9. Of Sherburn, Yorks. Matric. 1729.

DUFFIELD, JOHN. Matric. pens. from TRINITY, Easter, 1565. Of London. B.A. from St John's, 1568-9; M.A. from Peterhouse, 1572; B.D. 1578-9. Fellow of St John's, 1572. Incorp. at Oxford, 1580. Ord. priest (Peterb.) Oct. 6, 1574. R. of Lopham, Norfolk, 1576-8. Preb. of St Paul's, 1579-85. R. of Acle, 1580. R. of Dengie, Essex, 1586-9. Died 1589. Admon. P.C.C.

DUFFIELD, JOHN. Matric. pens. from ST JOHN'S, Easter, 1582. Perhaps adm. at the Middle Temple, May, 1585, as s. of Richard, gent., of London. Ord. deacon (Lincoln) May 3, 1594; priest, Nov. 2, 1600. Probably V. of Stoke Poges, Bucks., 1601-15.

DUFFIELD, JOHN. Adm. sizar (age 17) at CAIUS, Jan. 12, 1621-2. S. of John, woollen-draper, of Wymondham, Norfolk. Schools, Wymondham (Mr Peechod) and Norwich (Mr Stonham). Matric. 1622; B.A. 1625-6. Ord. deacon (Norwich) 1626; priest, June 1, 1634. (*Venn*, I. 255.)

DUFFIELD, LEONARD. Licensed to practise surgery, 1559-60. Will proved (V.C.C.) 1576.

DUFFIELD, SAMUEL. Adm. pens. (age 19) at ST JOHN'S, June 21, 1686. S. of Huan, attorney-at-law. B. at Sherburn, Yorks. School, Sherburn (Mr Payn). Matric. 1686; B.A. 1689-90. Ord. priest (York) June, 1694. V. of Church Fenton, Yorks., 1689-1732. V. of Sherburn, 1695-1732. Died Apr. 2, 1732. (Wheater, *Sherburn and Cawood*, 90.)

DUFFIELD, THOMAS. Fellow of PETERHOUSE, 1422 (B.A.).

DUFFIELD, THOMAS. Fellow of QUEENS', c. 1458; D.D. (? 1463). Died 1483. Benefactor to the College. (Searle, *Hist. of Queens'*, I. 94.)

DUFFIELD, THOMAS. Matric. sizar from TRINITY, Michs. 1549; Scholar, 1554. Fellow, 1555. No degree recorded. One of these names ord. deacon (Lincoln) Sept. 10, 1574; priest, Sept. 16, 1575.

DUFFIELD, WILLIAM. B.A. 1469-70; M.A. 1472.

DUFFIELD, WILLIAM. B.Can.L. 1470-1; D.Can.L. 1479. R. of Rattlesden, Suffolk, 1484. R. of Mistley, Essex, 1488-9. R. of Holy Trinity-the-less, London, 1490-2. Probably archdeacon of Stafford, 1497-1501.

DUFFYLD, WILLIAM. Franciscan friar. D.D. 1521-2.

DUFFING, ROBERT. Adm. at KING'S, a scholar from Eton, 1529.

DUGARD, CHARLES. Adm. pens. at JESUS, Feb. 10, 1709-10. Of Staffordshire. Probably s. of Samuel, R. of Forton, Staffs. Matric. 1710; Rustat scholar, 1710; B.A. 1713-4; M.A. 1719. Ord. priest (London) Feb. 26, 1715-6. (A. Gray.)

DUGARD, HENRY. Adm. sizar at EMMANUEL, Aug. 9, 1588. Matric. 1588. Perhaps s. of William, of Grafton Fliford, Worcs. Of Lickey, Bromsgrove. Died 1635. Father of Thomas (1626) and William (1622). (*Vis. of Warws.*, 1682; *Misc. Gen. et Her.*, 3rd S., v. 161.)

DUGARD, RICHARD. Adm. sizar at SIDNEY, May 14, 1606. Matric. 1606; B.A. 1609-10; M.A. 1613; B.D. 1620. Fellow. For some years a famous College tutor. Ord. deacon (London) Feb. 25, 1615-6; priest (Peterb.) May 26, 1616. R. of Fulletby, Lincs., 1636-54. Intimate friend of Milton. Buried at Fulletby, Feb. 4, 1653-4.

DUGARD, RICHARD. Adm. sizar (age 15) at SIDNEY, Sept. 1, 1649. S. of William (1622), Head Master of Merchant Taylors' School, London. B. at Stamford, Lincs. Died unmarried. (*Vis. of Warws.*, 1682.)

DUGARD, THOMAS. Adm. sizar (age 17) at SIDNEY, Mar. 28, 1626. S. of Henry (1588). B. at Bromsgrove, Worcs. School, Worcester (Mr Henry Bright). Matric. 1626; B.A. 1629-30; M.A. 1633. Master of Warwick School, 1633-48. R. of Barford, Warws., 1648. Living, 1682. Brother of the next. (*Vis. of Warws.*, 1682; *Misc. Gen. et Her.*, 3rd S., v. 161.)

DUGARD, WILLIAM. Adm. sizar (age 15) at SIDNEY, Sept. 13, 1622. S. of Henry (1588). B. at Bromsgrove. School, Worcester (Mr Henry Bright). B.A. 1626–7; M.A. 1630. Usher at Oundle. Master of Stamford School, *c.* 1630. Master of Colchester, 1637–43. Master of Merchant Taylors', 1644. Removed and imprisoned for printing some loyal verses, 1649; reinstated, 1650. Dismissed, 1661. Kept a private school in Coleman Street. Author, classical. Died Dec. 3, 1662. Father of Richard (1649), brother of Thomas (1626). (*Vis. of Warws.*, 1682; *D.N.B.*)

DUGDAYLE, JOHN. Adm. sizar at JESUS, Mar. 24, 1626–7. Of Lancashire. Matric. 1627. Ord. deacon, 1629; priest (Chester) 1630. V. of St Helen, York, 1632–44; of St Margaret, 1660–9; of St Dionisius, 1660–7.

DUGDALE, JOHN. Incorp. M.A. 1664, from Oxford. S. of Sir William, Garter King of arms, of Shustoke, Warws. Created M.A. (Oxford) 1661. Adm. at Gray's Inn, Feb. 25, 1664–5. Windsor herald, 1676. Norroy King of arms, 1686. Knighted, 1686. Died Aug. 3, 1700. (*Al. Oxon.*; *D.N.B*; *Vis. of Warws.*, 1682; Burke, *L.G.*)

DUGSON, ——. Fee for B.A. 1468–9.

DUISBURGH, ANTHONY, *see* **DISBEROWE.**

DUJON, JOHN. Adm. sizar at ST CATHARINE'S, June 29, 1723. Of Doncaster, Yorks. S. of Patrick, V. of Doncaster. Matric. 1723; B.A. 1726–7. Ord. priest (York) June 4, 1732.

DUKE, ANDREW. Adm. pens. at QUEENS', May 17, 1650. Of Wiltshire.

DUKE or DUCKE, ARTHUR. M.A. 1610 (Incorp. from Oxford). S. of Richard, of Heavitree, Devon. Matric. from Exeter College, Oct. 24, 1595, age 15; B.A. 1599; M.A. from Hart Hall, 1602; B.C.L. 1607; D.C.L. 1612. Fellow of All Souls, 1604. Admitted advocate, 1614. Chancellor of London diocese, 1627–37. Advocate and promoter of causes in the Military Court of the Earl Marshal and Constable of England, Oct. 30, 1631. Master in Chancery, 1645–8. M.P. for Minehead, 1624, 1640. Died at Chelsea, Dec. 16, 1648. (*Al. Oxon.*; *D.N.B.*; H. G. Harrison.)

DUKE or DUKES, BENJAMIN. Adm. sizar at EMMANUEL, Michs. 1648; B.A. 1652–3.

DUKE, EDWARD. Matric. Fell.-Com. from CHRIST'S, May, 1553. Perhaps s. of George, of Brampton, Suffolk; adm. at Gray's Inn, 1555. Married Dorothy, dau. of Sir Ambrose Jermyn. Died Apr. 2, 1598. Buried at Benhall, Suffolk. Will, P.C.C. (*Peile*, I. 53; Copinger, *Manors of Suffolk*, II. 28.)

DUKE, EDWARD. Matric. pens. from PEMBROKE, Michs. 1585. Perhaps adm. at the Inner Temple, Nov. 1587; of Aylesford, Kent. One of these names, of Kent, knighted Aug. 20, 1607.

DUKE, EDWARD. Adm. pens. (age 13) at CAIUS, May 7, 1606. S. of Edward, gent. B. at Worlingham, Suffolk. Bapt. Apr. 23, 1593. School, Hedenham, Norfolk. Matric. 1606. Buried at Ubbeston, May 27, 1625. Brother of John (1606). (*Venn*, I. 192.)

DUKE, EDWARD. Matric. pens. from ST CATHARINE'S, Easter, 1633. Of Suffolk. B.A. 1636–7; M.A. 1640. Perhaps M.D. (Oxford) Aug. 9, 1660; if so, s. of George, of Wandsworth. Honorary fellow of College of Physicians, 1664. Married Elizabeth, dau. of Robert Talmach, of Helmingham. (*Munk*, I. 336; *Al. Oxon.*; *Suckling*, II. 186.)

DUKE, GEORGE. Adm. Fell.-Com. at ST CATHARINE'S, 1635. S. and h. of Sir Edward, Knt., of Maidstone. Adm. at the Middle Temple, Oct. 1635.

DUKE, GILBERT. B.A. 1528–9. Fellow of QUEENS', 1530–2.

DUKE, GILBERT. Matric. pens. from CHRIST'S, May, 1553. S. of George, of Brampton, Suffolk. Brother of Edward (1553).

DUKE, HENRY. M.A. 1631 (Incorp. from Oxford). S. of Richard, of Maidstone. Matric. from Magdalen Hall, Oxford, Jan. 31, 1622–3, age 19; B.A. 1624; M.A. 1627. R. of Midley, Kent, 1629–69. Died 1669. (*Al. Oxon.*)

DUKE, JOHN. Matric. pens. from TRINITY, Easter, 1568; B.A. from Corpus Christi, 1569–70; M.A. 1573.

DUKE, JOHN. Matric. sizar from TRINITY, Michs. 1581; B.A. from Emmanuel, 1584–5; M.A. 1588; M.D. from Clare, 1598. Fellow of Emmanuel, 1588 (one of the original scholars in 1584). Practised physic at Colchester. Married Anna, dau. of John Snelling, of Boxford, 1596. Died May 16, 1629. Will (P.C.C.) (*Suff. Man. Fam.*, I. 82.)

DUKE, JOHN. Adm. pens. (age 14) at CAIUS, May 7, 1606. S. of Edward, g . B. at Worlingham, Suffolk. School Hodenham, Norfolk (Mr Selby). Matric. 1606. Readm. Fell.-Com. 1608. B.A. 1608–9 (1st in the *ordo*). Adm. at the Middle Temple, Feb. 8, 1609–10. Of Worlingham, q., and Lord of the Manor of Diss. Died 1649. M.I. at Worlingham. Brother of Edward (1606). (*Venn*, I. 192; Copinger, *Manors of Suffolk*, VII. 224.)

DUKE, JOHN. Matric. pens. from CHRIST'S, July, 1619; B.A. 1622–3; M.A. 1626. R. of High Roding, Essex, 1628; sequestered; restored 1660; died before Feb. 1663–4. (*Peile*, I. 329.)

DUKE, JOHN. Adm. Fell.-Com. at EMMANUEL, May 15, 1649. Of Suffolk. S. of Sir Edward, of Benhall and Brampton, Suffolk (afterwards Bart.). Bapt. at Benhall, Jan. 3, 1632–3. Succeeded as Bart., 1671. M.P. for Orford, Suffolk, 1678–80, 1688, 1696 and 1698. Married Elizabeth, dau. of Edward Duke (1633). Buried at Benhall, July 24, 1705. (Burke, *Ext. Bart.*; Davy, *Suff. MSS.*; *G.E.C.*)

DUKE or DUK, RICHARD. Scholar at KING'S HALL, 1362. Died July 26, 1369.

DUKE, RICHARD. Adm. pens. at EMMANUEL, Nov. 28, 1645. S. and h. of Robert, of Otterton, Devon. Adm. at the Inner Temple, Nov. 1645. Perhaps M.P. for Ashburton, 1679, 1695, 1698, 1701.

DUKE, RICHARD. Adm. Fell.-Com. (age 18) at SIDNEY, June 10, 1675. Only s. of Richard, Esq. B. at Maidstone, Kent. Schools, Sutton, Kent (Mr Ben. Nichols) and Westerham (Mr Samuel Hoadly). Matric. 1675. Adm. at the Middle Temple, June 14, 1676.

DUKE, RICHARD. Adm. pens. at TRINITY, June 25, 1675. S. of Richard, citizen of London. B. June 13, 1658 School, Westminster. Scholar, 1676; Matric. 1678; B.A. 1678–9; M.A. 1682. Fellow, 1688. Preb. of Gloucester, 1688–1711. Chaplain to Queen Anne. Chaplain to the Bishop of Winchester. R. of Blaby, Leics., 1688–1708. R. of Witney, Oxon., 1710. Author, poems and sermons. Died Feb. 10, 1710–1; in St Andrew's, Holborn. Will (P.C.C.) 1711. (*D.N.B.*; *N. and Q.*, 3rd S., XII. 21.)

DUKE, ROBERT. B.A. 1557–8.

DUKE, ROBERT. Matric. pens. from PEMBROKE, Michs. 1585. One of these names, of Kelshall, Suffolk, adm. at Gray's Inn, Nov. 21, 1588.

DUKE, ROBERT. Adm. pens. (age 17) at PEMBROKE, Apr. 21, 1663. S. of Sir Edward, Knt. and Bart. B. at Benhall, Suffolk. Matric. 1663.

DUKE, THOMAS. B.Can.L. 1520–1.

DUKE, THOMAS. Matric. Fell.-Com. from CHRIST'S, May, 1559.

DUKE, TOLLEMACHE. Adm. Fell.-Com. (age 18) at PEMBROKE, July 3, 1707. S. of Tollemache, of Bentley, Suffolk, Esq. Died Apr. 26, 1713. M.I. at Bentley. (Le Neve, *Mon.*, V. 264.)

DUKE, WILLIAM. Adm. Fell.-Com. at QUEENS', Michs. 1595. Of Kent. Matric. as 'Tuke.' Perhaps of Cossington, Kent, gent.; adm. at Gray's Inn, July 3, 1598.

DUKE, WILLIAM. Incorp. at Oxford, as 'M.A. of Cambridge,' July 11, 1611. No such degree found.

DUKE, WILLIAM. Adm. sizar (age 17) at ST JOHN'S, Dec. 15, 1750. S. of William, lawyer, of America. School, Shrewsbury. Matric. 1750–1; LL.B. 1758. Ord. priest (Rochester, for London) May 21, 1758.

DUKE, ——. Matric. Fell.-Com. from ST JOHN'S, Easter, 1620.

DUKYS, ——. B.A. 1504–5.

DUKESON, RICHARD. B.A. from TRINITY, 1616–7; M.A. 1620; B.D. 1627; D.D. 1637. Incorp. at Oxford, 1645. B. in Lancaster. Ord. deacon (London) Dec. 20, 1618, age 25. R. of Fiskerton, Lincs., 1630. R. of St Clement Danes, London, 1634–47; sequestered; restored, 1660. R. of Ledbury, Heref., 1660–4. Chaplain to the King. Obtained a Grant of Arms, 1666. Died Sept. 17, 1678. (*Al. Oxon.*)

DUKINFIELD, Sir WILLIAM, Bart. Adm. nobleman (age 18) at TRINITY, Dec. 1, 1743. Of Over Tabley, Cheshire. S. of Sir Charles, Bart. School, Newport, Shrops. (Mr Lea). Matric. 1743. Succeeded as 3rd Bart., Feb. 23, 1741–2. Took the additional name Daniell, in 1746. Sheriff of Cheshire, 1750. Died Jan. 12, 1758. (*G.E.C.*)

DUKINSON, THOMAS. Matric. pens. from ST JOHN'S, Easter, 1626.

DULANY, DANIEL. Adm. pens. at CLARE, Jan. 22, 1738–9. S. and h. of Daniel, Esq., of Maryland, America. B. at Annapolis, Maryland. Adm. at the Middle Temple, Mar. 16, 1741–2.

DULMOHEY, THOMAS. M.A. 1641–2 (on King's visit).

DUMARESQUE, ELIAS (CÆSAR). Adm. at CORPUS CHRISTI, 1708. Of Jersey. Matric. 1709; B.A. 1712–3. Ord. deacon (London) Dec. 21, 1712.

DU MOULIN, *see* **MOLINEUS.**

DUMVELL, *see also* **DOMVILE.**

DUMVELL, ROBERT. Matric. sizar from TRINITY, *c.* 1601; B.A. from St Catharine's, 1607–8, as Dumvile. *See* the next.

DUMVILLE, ROBERT. B.A. from ST CATHARINE'S, 1611–2; M.A. 1617. Ord. deacon (York) Sept. 1610, as of Trinity; priest, Feb. 1612–3, of St Catharine's. V. of Leyton, Essex. Buried there June 18, 1638.

DUNBABIN, NATHAN. Adm. pens. (age 16) at Christ's, May 9, 1645. S. of John. B. at Warrington, Lancs. School, Warrington (Mr Ashworth). Matric. 1645; B.A. 1647-8, as 'Donboom'; M.A. at Oxford, 1651. Student of Christ Church by Visitors' mandate, 1649. Adm. at Gray's Inn, Feb. 21, 1654-5. (*Peile*, I. 495.)

DUNBAR, WILLIAM. Incorp. M.A. 1684, from St Andrews. Probably matric. from Balliol College, Oxford, June 4, 1674, age 16. S. of Alexander, of Whittington, Gloucs., clerk. Ord. deacon and priest (Lincoln) Dec. 23, 1660. R. of Little Burstead, Essex, 1682. R. of Ramsden Crays, 1684-1723. (*Al. Oxon.*)

DUNCALFE, JOHN. Adm. pens. (age 17) at St John's, Feb. 21, 1633-4. S. of John, gent., of Pattrington-in-Holderness. B. there. School, Pocklington (Mr Siggeswick). Matric. 1634.

DUNCALF, WILLIAM. Adm. sizar (age 22) at Peterhouse, Mar. 19, 1719-20. Of Cheshire. School, Congleton. Ord. deacon (Peterb., *Litt. dim.* from Chester) Mar. 13, 1719-20. (*T. A. Walker*, 244.)

DUNCALFE, ——. Of Newmarket Hostel. Fee for B.A. 1456-7.

DUNCAN, *see* DUNCON.

DUNCH, FRANCIS. Matric. pens. from Queens', Easter, 1627. Of Cambridgeshire. B.A. 1630-1; M.A. 1634, as Dench. Ord. priest (Peterb.) May 20, 1638.

DUNCH, JOHN. Matric. sizar from Queens', Lent, 1584-5. Of Lancashire. B.A. from St John's, 1587-8, as Duntch; M.A. from Queens', 1593; B.D. 1606. V. of Lakenheath, Suffolk, 1592-8. V. of Dullingham, Cambs., 1598-1639. Buried there Dec. 16, 1639.

DUNCH or DUNCK, JOHN. Adm. Fell.-Com. (age 18) at Christ's, Oct. 1644. S. of John. B. at Hastings, Sussex. School, Whatlington, near Battle (Mr Sarse). One of these names M.P. for Berks., 1654 and 1658.

DUNCH, ROBERT. LL.B. Fellow of Trinity Hall. Ord. deacon (Ely) Mar. 12, 1406-7; priest, Mar. 26, 1407.

DUNCH, THOMAS. Adm. at Corpus Christi, 1703. Of Cambridgeshire. Matric. 1703; B.A. 1706-7. Ord. deacon (Ely) Sept. 19, 1708; priest (Norwich) Oct. 28, 1709. R. of Antingham, Norfolk, 1710-18. R. of Bergh Apton, 1717-9.

DUNCH or DUNECHE, WALTER. LL.B. 1633 (Incorp. from Oxford). S. of Edmund, of Berkshire. Matric. (Exeter College) May 14, 1602 (age 18); B.C.L. (Gloucester Hall) 1631. Adm. at Gray's Inn, Oct. 29, 1605, as of Little Wittenham, Berks. Sheriff of Oxfordshire, 1625. Died Jan. 6, 1644-5. Buried at Newington, Oxon. M.I. (*Al. Oxon.*; Le Neve, *Mon.*, I. 216; *Misc. Gen. et Her.*, 3rd S., II. 45.)

DUNCON, EDMUND. Matric. pens. from Trinity Hall, Michs. 1624. S. of Eleazer (1571). LL.B. 1630. Fellow 1628-31. Ord. priest (St David's) 1630. V. of Wood Dalling and R. of Swannington, Norfolk, 1630-(?) 63. R. of Friern Barnet, Middlesex, 1663-73. Friend of Nicholas Ferrar and George Herbert. Died Oct. 4, 1673, aged 72. M.I. at Friern Barnet. Father of John (1666), brother of Eleazar (1613) and John (1620). (*D.N.B.*)

DUNCOMBE, EDWARD. Matric. pens. from St John's, Michs. 1580. One of these names, s. of William, of Battlesden, Beds., adm. at Gray's Inn, Jan. 27, 1583-4. Perhaps M.P. for Tavistock, 1604 and 1614. Knighted, July 23, 1603 (Dunton). (*Vis. of Beds.*, 1634.)

DUNCON, EDWARD. Adm. pens. (age 18) at Pembroke, May 11, 1661. S. of Edward. B. at Sproughton, Suffolk. B.A. 1664-5; M.A. 1668. Fellow, 1667. Taxor, 1679. Ord. priest (Ely) June, 1669. R. of Waresley, Hunts., 1679. Died 1680.

DUNCON, ELEAZER. Matric. sizar from Pembroke, Michs. 1571. Of Suffolk. B.A. 1574-5; M.A. 1578, as Dunckon; M.D. from Queens', 1590. Of Ipswich, in 1614; and Gipping, 1620. Father of Edmund (1624), Eleazar (next) and John (1620).

DUNKON, ELEAZAR. Adm. pens. (age 16) at Caius, Feb. 24, 1613-4. S. of Eleazar, M.D. (above). School, St Paul's, London. Matric. 1614; Scholar, 1614-9; B.A. 1617-8; M.A. from Pembroke, 1621; B.D. 1628; D.D. 1633. Fellow and tutor of Pembroke, 1619. Ord. deacon (London) Mar. 13, 1624-5; priest (Durham) Sept. 24, 1625. University preacher, 1627. Preb. of Durham, 1628; of Winchester, 1629. R. of Wyke Regis, Dorset, 1631. R. of Haughton le Skern, Durham, 1633. V. of Powick, Worcs., in 1635; of Alne, Yorks., 1640-50. Preb. of York, 1640. Chaplain to the Levant Company, at Leghorn, 1650. Probably died there soon after. (*Venn*, I. 224; *D.N.B.*)

DUNCOMBE, FRANCIS. M.A. 1621 (Incorp. from Oxford). Of Buckinghamshire. Matric. from Oriel College, Dec. 4, 1612, age 16; B.A. (Oxford) 1616; M.A. 1620. R. of Souldrop, Beds., 1626-30. Buried there Oct. 24, 1630. (*Al. Oxon.*; W. M. Noble.)

DUNCOMBE, FRANCIS. Adm. at King's, a scholar from Eton, 1632. Perhaps s. of the above. B.A. 1636; M.A. 1640. Fellow of King's, till 1648. Ord. deacon (Lincoln) Feb. 22; priest, Feb. 23, 1661-2. V. of Ivinghoe, Bucks., 1663-82.

DUNCOMBE, JOHN. Matric. pens. from Clare, Michs. 1589.

DUNCOMBE, JOHN. Matric. Fell.-Com. from King's, Easter, 1611. 2nd s. of Sir Edward (1580), of Battlesden, Beds., Knt.; adm. at Lincoln's Inn, Nov. 2, 1613. Of Battlesden. Knighted, 1646. Brother of William (1609). (*Vis. of Beds.*, 1634.)

DUNCON, JOHN. Matric. pens. (age 17) from Pembroke, Michs. 1620. S. of Eleazar (1571), of Gipping, Suffolk. B.A. 1623-4; M.A. 1627; B.D. 1634. Fellow, 1625. Incorp. at Oxford, 1628. V. of Barton, Cambs., 1636-7. R. of Stutton and Stoke St Mary, Suffolk, 1637; of Bexwell, Norfolk, 1641; and of Rettenden, Essex, 1642. (*D.N.B.*)

DUNCOMBE, JOHN. Matric. sizar from Trinity, Easter, 1632; Scholar, 1634; B.A. 1635-6; M.A. 1639. Fellow, 1637. Taxor, 1647. Probably ord. priest (Lincoln) June 5, 1642.

DUNCOMBE, JOHN. M.A. 1633 (Incorp. from Oxford). S. of John, of Claydon, Bucks. Matric. from Oriel College, Dec. 6, 1622, age 13; B.A. 1626. Fellow of Oriel, 1628-46 and 1660-9. R. of Belleau, Lincs., 1638. Preb. of Wells, 1661-8. Died Jan. 18, 1669. (*Al. Oxon.*; *Vis. of Bucks.*, 1634.)

DUNCOMBE, JOHN. Adm. Fell.-Com. (age 16) at Christ's, Jan. 18, 1637-8. S. of William. Bapt. at Battlesden, Beds., July 20, 1622. School, Eton. Matric. 1637. Knighted, 1646. M.P. for Bury St Edmunds, 1660 and 1661. Buried at Battlesden, Mar. 6, 1686-7. (*Peile*, I. 452; *Vis. of Beds.*, 1634.)

DUNCON, JOHN. Adm. sizar at Jesus, May 22, 1666. S. of Edmund (1624), R. of Friern Barnet, Middlesex. B. in Norfolk. Matric. 1667; Scholar, 1669; B.A. 1669-70; M.A. 1673. Ord. deacon (Ely) June, 1672; priest (London) Dec. 1672. R. of Friern Barnet, Middlesex, 1673. Died Oct. 4, 1673, at Cambridge. Admon. (P.C.C.) 1674.

DUNCOMBE, JOHN. Adm. at Corpus Christi, July 1, 1745. S. of William, Esq., of St Anne's, Soho. Matric. 1745; B.A. 1748-9; M.A. 1752. Fellow, 1751-8. Ord. in Kew Chapel, 1753, by Bishop of Peterborough. C. of Sundridge, Kent, 1753. V. of West Thurrock, Essex. Preacher at St Anne's, Soho. R. of St Andrew and St Mary Bredman, Canterbury, 1757-86. Six preacher, 1766. V. of Herne, Kent, 1773. Chaplain to the Archbishop. Master of Harbledown and St John's Hospital. Friend of William Cowper. Author. Died at Canterbury, Jan. 19, 1786, aged 56. Buried in St Mary Bredman. (*D.N.B.*; *Masters*; Stokes, *Cowper Memorials*.)

DUNCAN or DUNKYN, PETER. Matric. sizar from Queens', Michs. 1570. Migrated to Oxford. B.A. (Oxford) 1574; M.A. 1576. Incorp. at Cambridge, 1578. R. of Lidford, Devon, 1580. V. of Crediton, 1584. R. of Kenn, 1595. Will (Exeter) 1605. (*Al. Oxon.*)

DUNCAM, PETER. Adm. pens. (age 19) at Caius, Feb. 27, 1601-2. S. of Peter, gent., of Devon. School, Crediton, Devon (Mr Wilton). B.A. 1602-3; Scholar, 1602-4.

DUNCOMB, ROGER. Adm. pens. at Trinity, Feb. 27, 1649-50. Of Surrey. S. of John, of Weston, Albury, Surrey. Matric. 1650. Sheriff of Surrey, 1662. Died Nov. 12, 1678. (*Vis. of Surrey*, 1662.)

DUNCOMB, SAMUEL. Adm. pens. (age 15) at Sidney, Mar. 1685-6. S. of Giles, lawyer (of the Inner Temple). B. at Newton Green, Suffolk. School, Holborn, London (Mr Smith). Adm. at the Inner Temple, 1681.

DUNCOMB, STINT. Adm. pens. at Emmanuel, Sept. 23, 1674. Of Surrey. S. of John, of Shelford, Surrey, and Jane, dau. of John Stynt, of London. Buried July 29, 1690. (*Vis. of Surrey*, 1662; Burke, *Ext. Bart.*)

DUNCOMBE, THOMAS. Matric. pens. from Peterhouse, c. 1601. Of Bedford. B.A. 1604-5; M.A. 1608. Fellow, 1607-18. Incorp. at Oxford, 1614.

DUNCOMBE, THOMAS. Adm. Fell.-Com. at Clare, June 6, 1637. S. and h. of Thomas, of Broughton, Beds. (? Bucks.). B. 1618. Matric. 1637. Adm. at the Inner Temple, 1638. Died 1672.

DUNCOMBE, WILLIAM. Matric. Fell.-Com. from King's, Michs. 1609. S. and h. of Sir Edward, of Battlesden, Beds., Knt.; adm. at Lincoln's Inn, Nov. 2, 1611. Brother of John (1611). (*Vis. of Beds.*, 1634.)

DUNCON, WILLIAM. Adm. sizar (age 16) at St John's, Apr. 30, 1634. S. of John, husbandman, of Cockfield, Suffolk. B. there. School, Bury. Matric. 1634; B.A. 1637-8; M.A. 1641. Ord. deacon (Norwich) Sept. 25, 1642; C. of Cockfield.

DUNCOMBE, WILLIAM. Adm. at King's, a scholar from Eton, 1646. B. in London. B.A. 1651-2; M.A. 1655. Fellow, till 1662; ejected. Afterwards conformed, and was master of a school in Devon. Admon. of one of these names (Exeter) 1717; of Broad Clist, Devon.

DUNCOMB, WILLIAM. Adm. pens. at CLARE, July 3, 1697. Matric. 1697; B.A. 1697-8.

DUNE, *see* DUNN.

DUNGARVAN, Viscount, *see* BOYLE, RICHARD.

DUNGWORTH, *see* DONGWORTH.

DUNHAM, JOHN. Scholar and fellow at KING'S HALL, 1449-52; LL.B. 1464-5. Ord. acolyte (Ely) Apr. 17, 1473. V. of Fulbourn All Saints', Cambs., 1476-8. R. of East Wretham, Norfolk, till 1482.

DUNKERON, Viscount JAMES. Adm. Fell.-Com. at TRINITY, Nov. 13, 1729. S. of Henry Petty, Earl of Shelburne. B. *c.* 1708. Died *v.p.* Sept. 17, 1750. Buried at High Wycombe. (*G.E.C.*)

DUNKYN, JAMES. Adm. sizar (age 15) at ST JOHN'S, Sept. 9, 1637. S. of Thomas, gent., of Canterbury. B. there. School, Uppingham (Mr Johnson). Matric. 1637; B.A. 1641-2.

DUNKIN, WILLIAM. Matric. sizar from TRINITY, Easter, 1616; B.A. from Clare, 1619-20; M.A. 1623. Incorp. at Oxford, 1628. Ord. deacon (Peterb.) Dec. 17, 1620; priest, June 8, 1623. V. of St Laurence, Isle of Thanet, 1629-44. Preb. of Canterbury, 1639-44. Died 1644.

DUNLEE, EDWARD. Adm. pens. at EMMANUEL, Apr. 28, 1617.

DUNLOP, ALEXANDER. Incorp. M.A. 1698, from Aberdeen. R. of Nunnington, Yorks., 1699-1722. Buried June 24, 1722.

DUNLOP, LEWIS. Adm. sizar at ST CATHARINE'S, Mar. 21, 1719-20. Of Nunnington, Yorks. (? S. of above.) Matric. 1720; B.A. 1722-3. Ord. deacon (Lincoln) Dec. 22, 1723; priest, Mar. 17, 1727-8. C. of Odell, Beds., 1726; also signs as minister at Turvey.

DUNMOLE, JAMES. Matric. pens. from CLARE, Easter, 1623.

DUNMOLL, ROBERT. Adm. pens. at TRINITY, June 18, 1638. Matric. 1639; Scholar, 1641; B.A. 1641-2; M.A. from Peterhouse, 1645. Fellow of Peterhouse, Mar. 29 to May 30, 1645. Fellow of Trinity, 1645. (*T. A. Walker.*)

DONMOWE, JOHN. Scholar at KING'S HALL, 1395. Bachelor in 1409. Died Mar. 6, 1411-2. Left £20 to found a 'chest.'

DUNMOW, RICHARD. Fellow of PEMBROKE, *c.* 1376. Ord. subdeacon (Ely) May, 1383; deacon, Mar. 26; priest, Sept. 1384. Will (P.C.C.) 1414; 'of Cheveley, Cambs., clerk.'

DUNMOW, WILLIAM. Resident student at TRINITY HALL, Aug. 1564.

DUNMOW, ——. B.Can.L. 1476-7.

DUNN, *see also* DONNE.

DUN or DONNE, DANIEL. LL.D. 1604 (Incorp. from Oxford). S. of Robert. B.C.L. 1572; D.C.L. 1580. Fellow of All Souls. Principal of New Inn Hall, 1580. Admitted advocate, 1582. Dean ol the Arches, 1598-1615. Adm. at Gray's Inn, Aug. 9, 1599. Knighted, July 23, 1603. M.P. for Taunton, 1601; for Oxford University, 1604, 1614. Judge of the Admiralty Court, 1608. Died Sept. 15, 1617. (*D.N.B.*; *Al. Oxon.*; *Essex Pedigrees.*)

DUNN, FIELDAN or FIELD. M.A. from JESUS, 1701. S. of Field, of Weston, Yorks. Matric. from University College, Oxford, Mar. 5, 1693-4, age 18; B.A. (Oxford) 1697. V. of St Mary's, Hull, 1702-13. Preb. of York, 1720-38. Died 1738. Father of the next. (*Al. Oxon.*)

DUN, FIELD. Adm. pens. at CLARE, May 25, 1719. S. of Field (above). B. in Hull. 'B. at Leeds, Yorks.' School, Hull. Matric. 1719. Migrated as sizar to St John's, Oct. 30, 1720, age 18. Ord. deacon (Lincoln) May 24, 1730; priest, June 4, 1732. V. of Horkstow, Lincs., 1735-59. R. of South Ferriby, 1744-59. (*Scott-Mayor*, III. 336.)

DUNN, HENRY. Adm. sizar (age 18) at CHRIST'S, May 9, 1684. B. at Richmond, Yorks. School, Northallerton (Mr Smelt). Matric. 1684; B.A. 1687-8. Ord. priest (York) Mar. 12, 1692-3. (*Peile*, II. 96.)

DUNNE, HUMPHREY. B.A. 1489-90.

DUN or DUNN, JERMAN. Adm. pens. at ST CATHARINE'S, June 14, 1670. Matric. 1673; B.A. 1673-4; M.A. 1677. Adm. at the Inner Temple, 1673; of 'Hogesden,' Middlesex. Ord. priest (London) Dec. 19, 1680. R. of Orlestone, Kent, 1685-6. Died 1686.

DUNNE, JOHN. Matric. sizar from JESUS, Easter, 1568. One of these names, of All Saints' parish, Cambridge (age 30), applied for ordination as deacon at Ely, Dec. 20, 1574; rejected. He was C. of West Wratting.

DUNE, JOHN. Matric. pens. from QUEENS', Easter, 1570.

DUNNE, JOHN. Matric. sizar from TRINITY, Easter, 1579. B. at Atherstone, Warws. B.A. 1582-3. Ord. deacon (London) Apr. 15, 1584, age 24; priest, Apr. 16, 1585. V. of King's Langley, Herts., 1587.

DUNNE, JOHN. Adm. sizar (age 17) at SIDNEY, May 26, 1627. S. of William, farmer. B. at Ainderby Steeple, Yorks. Schools, Ainderby Steeple and Bedale (Mr Smelt). Matric. 1627; B.A. 1630-1.

DUNNE, JOHN. Adm. sizar (age 17) at SIDNEY, Sept. 22, 1639. S. of George, farmer. B. at Ainderby Steeple, Yorks. Schools, Floteham (Mr Thomas Smelt) and Durham (Mr Richard Smelt). Matric. 1639; B.A. 1643-4. Perhaps V. of Pickhill, Yorks., 1660. Buried Dec. 29, 1697. One of these names V. of Sherburn, Yorks., 1662-70. (McCall, *Richmondshire Churches.*)

DUNNE, JOHN. Adm. sizar (age 19) at SIDNEY, May 14, 1650. S. of Ralph, yeoman. B. at Tuddoe, Durham. Migrated to Caius, Nov. 1650. Matric. 1650; Scholar, 1650-3; B.A. 1652-3. One of these names V. of North Lydbury, Salop, 1686-99. Buried Jan. 28, 1699.

DUNN, JOHN. Adm. Fell.-Com. at CHRIST'S, June 4, 1706. (Probably a mistake for Joshua, whom *see.*)

DUNN, JOHN. Adm. sizar (age 17) at ST JOHN'S, July 1, 1714. S. of John, gent. B. at Middridge, near Bishop Auckland, Durham. School, Sedbergh. Matric. 1714.

DUNN, JOSHUA. Adm. Fell.-Com. at CHRIST'S, 1709. S. of Joshua, of Halifax, Yorks. B. at Stannery, Halifax, Sept. 28, 1684. Probably first adm. in 1706, as 'John.' Brought his friend Nicholas Sanderson, the blind mathematician, with him to Cambridge. Died Sept. 13, 1709. Buried in Halifax Church. M.I. (*Peile*, II. 164; *F.M.G.*, 250.)

DUNNE, THOMAS. Matric. pens. from PEMBROKE, Easter, 1565.

DUNNE, THOMAS. Matric. sizar from CLARE, Easter, 1571; B.A. 1575-6; M.A. 1579.

DUNN, WILLIAM. Adm. sizar at CHRIST'S, June 23, 1625. S. of Richard, of Cheshire. School, Halton (Mr Piggot). B.A. 1628-9; M.A. 1632. One of these names, minister of Ormskirk, Lancs., in 1643; transferred to Bromborough, Cheshire, 1657. (*Peile*, I. 370; *Vict. Hist. of Lancs.*, IV. 244.)

DUNN, WILLIAM. Matric. sizar from EMMANUEL, Lent, 1683-4. Of Durham. One of these names, but M.A., R. of Redmarshall, Durham, 1694-1737. Buried there Feb. 11, 1736-7.

DUNN, WILLIAM. Adm. pens. (age 18) at ST JOHN'S, May 5, 1705. S. of Robert, gent., of Coatham, Durham. B. there. School, Durham (Mr Ross). Migrated to Peterhouse, Oct. 13, 1705. Scholar, 1705; Matric. 1706; B.A. 1708-9; M.A. 1715. Ord. priest (Durham) Sept. 23, 1711. V. of Bywell St Andrew, Durham, 1711. V. of Dalton-le-Dale, 1740. R. of Easington, 1740-61. Buried there Feb. 16, 1761. (D. S. Boutflower; *T. A. Walker*, 214; H. M. Wood.)

DUNN, WILLIAM. Adm. sizar (age 18) at TRINITY, Apr. 16, 1743. S. of Thomas, of Fishburn, Durham. School, Kepier, Durham (Mr Griffiths). Matric. 1743; Scholar, 1746; B.A. 1746-7; M.A. 1754. Ord. deacon (Ely) Mar. 1746-7; Priest (Durham) Nov. 1, 1747. Probably C. of Easington, Durham, 1746-61.

DUNNAGE, THOMAS. B.A. 1522-3.

DUNNAN, EDMUND. Matric. sizar from KING'S, Michs. 1601.

DUNNING, EDWARD. Adm. sizar (age 14) at CHRIST'S, Apr. 28, 1666. S. of Shadrach. B. at Northallerton, Yorks. School, Sigglesthorne, near Hornsea (Mr Smelt). Matric. 1667; B.A. 1669-70. Ord. deacon (York) June, 1671; priest, June, 1672. C. of Givendale, Pocklington, 1674. V. of Givendale *w.* Millington, 1684-95. (*Peile*, II. 3.)

DUNNING, JOHN. Matric. sizar from KING'S, Michs. 1575.

DUNNING, JOHN. Adm. sizar at QUEENS', July 12, 1659. Of Dorset.

DUNNING, JOHN. Adm. sizar (age 17) at CHRIST'S, June 13, 1683. S. of John. B. at Netherbury, Dorset. School, Frampton (Mr Slade). Matric. 1683; M.B. 1688.

DUNNING, LANCELOT. Matric. sizar from TRINITY, Easter, 1555. S. of Christopher, of Yorkshire. Scholar, 1560, as Donnynge; B.A. 1560-1; M.A. 1564. Fellow, 1562-5. Migrated as Fell.-Com. to Caius, Sept. 14, 1568, age 26. Ord. priest (Norwich) Nov. 8, 1570. R. of Grundisburgh, Suffolk, 1566-1617. Buried Nov. 30, 1617. (*Venn*, I. 63.)

DUNNING, LANCELOT. Adm. sizar (age 16) at SIDNEY, June 4, 1623. S. of Francis, grazier. B. at Thirsk, Yorks. Schools, Kilvington and Coxwold. B.A. 1626-7; M.A. 1630.

DUNNING, MICHAEL. B.Civ.L. 1540-1; D.Civ.L. 1555. R. of Knapwell, Cambs., 1546. R. of Gissing, Norfolk, 1549-54. Vicar-general of Norwich, 1554. R. of Bluntisham, Cambs., 1554-8. Principal of St Nicholas' Hostel, Cambridge, 1556. Preb. of Lincoln, 1557-8. R. of North Tuddenham, Norfolk, 1557. Archdeacon of Bedford, 1558; deprived same year. Will (P.C.C.) 1558; 'of Lincoln Cathedral, and Knapwell, Cambs.' (*Cooper*, I. 203.)

DUNNING, RICHARD. B.Can.L. 1554-5. R. of Lyng, Norfolk, 1555-7.

DUNNING, ROBERT. Adm. at KING'S, a scholar from Eton, 1564; B.A. 1568-9; M.A. 1572. Fellow, till 1577. Expelled for slandering the Provost. 'Very skilfull in mathematics.' (*Cooper*, I. 363; *Harwood*.)

DUNNING, THOMAS. B.A. 1522-3; B.Can.L. 1531-2. R. of North Tuddenham, Norfolk, 1538-57. R. of Sculthorpe, 1538-55.

DUNSCOMBE, GEORGE. Adm. at KING'S, a scholar from Eton, 1629-30; B.A. 1633-4; M.A. 1637. Fellow, till 1644. V. of Waves Wotton, Warws., till 1652. Died there Sept. 12, 1652. M.I. (*Harwood*.)

DUNCSCOMB, THOMAS. M.A. 1587 (Incorp. from Oxford). Adm. at Christ Church, 1577; B.A. (Oxford) 1580-1; M.A. 1583-4. R. of St Thomas Apostle, London, 1587-9. R. of Kingsnorth, Kent, 1591. R. of Willesborough, 1592. (*Al. Oxon.*)

DUNSFORD, ROBERT. Scholar at KING'S HALL, 1398. 'Bachelor,' 1409. Died May 20, 1416.

DUNSTALL, GAMALIEL. Adm. sizar at PETERHOUSE, June 20, 1651. Of Derbyshire. From Oriel College, Oxford, where he entered as servitor, Apr. 1649. B.A. (Cambridge) 1653.

DUNSTALL, JOHN. M.A. from CORPUS CHRISTI, 1686. S. of Thomas, of Hurst, Sussex. Matric. from Oriel College, Oxford, Feb. 15, 1677-8, age 16; B.A. (Oxford) 1681. R. of Newtimber, Sussex, 1686-1733. R. of South Stoke, 1706. (*Al. Oxon.*)

DUNSTALL, ——. Adm. at CORPUS CHRISTI, 1544.

DUNSTAN (*alias* KITCHIN), ANTHONY. Said to have studied at Cambridge, as well as at Gloucester Hall, Oxford. Perhaps pens. at GONVILLE HALL, 1525-7. A monk from Westminster Abbey. B.D. (Oxford) 1525; D.D. 1538. Abbot of Eynsham, Oxon., 1532-9. Bishop of Llandaff, 1545-63. Died Oct. 31, 1563. Buried in Matherne Church, Monmouth. (*Cooper*, I. 238; *D.N.B.*; *E. H. Pearce*.)

DUNSTAN, JOSEPH. Adm. sizar (age 17) at ST JOHN'S, Mar. 1, 1679-80. S. of Thomas. B. in London. School, St Paul's. Matric. 1680; B.A. 1683-4. Probably Master of St Olave's School, Southwark, and father of the next.

DUNSTAN, JOSEPH. Adm. pens. (age 17) at PEMBROKE, July 3, 1707. S. of Joseph, clerk, headmaster of St Olave's School, Southwark. Matric. 1709. Lecturer at St Ann's, Blackfriars.

DUNSTON, WILLIAM. Adm. pens. (age 18) at PETERHOUSE, Jan. 18, 1664-5. Of Suffolk. School, Cambridge. Matric. 1664-5. Perhaps s. of William, of Bramfield, Suffolk, who entered at Gray's Inn, in 1647. (*T. A. Walker*.)

DUNSTONE, ——. B.A. 1510-1; M.A. 1514.

DUNSTER, CHARLES. Adm. pens. at CLARE, Apr. 3, 1736. B. in London. Matric. 1736; B.A. 1739-40; M.A. 1743. Preb. of Salisbury, 1748-50. R. of Oddingley, Worcs., 1776-81. V. of Naunton, 1776.

DUNSTOR, HENRY. Matric. sizar from MAGDALENE, Easter, 1627, as 'John.' S. of Henry, of Bolholt, Bury, Lancs. Bapt. there, Nov. 26, 1609. B.A. 1630-1; M.A. 1634. For some years taught school at Bury, Lancs. C. of Bury, 1634. Went to America, 1640. First president of Harvard College, 1640-54, when he was removed for his views on baptism. Went to Scituate in Plymouth Colony where he preached till his death, Feb. 27, 1658-9. (*D.N.B.*; J. G. Bartlett.)

DUNSTER, HENRY. Adm. sizar at EMMANUEL, July 2, 1636. Of Lancashire. Matric. 1637; B.A. 1639-40; M.A. 1643. R. of Northenden, Cheshire, 1644-61. Died Mar. 17, 1661. M.I. at Northenden. (Earwaker, *E. Cheshire*, I. 294.)

DUNSTAR, SAMUEL. Adm. pens. (age 17) at TRINITY, June 26, 1693. S. of James. B. at Westminster. School, Westminster. Matric. 1693; Scholar, 1694; B.A. 1696-7; M.A. 1700; D.D. 1713. Ord. deacon (London) Nov. 2, 1698; priest, June 11, 1700. Chaplain to the Earl of Shrewsbury, and to the Duke of Marlborough. R. of Chinnor, Oxon., 1716. V. of Paddington. Preb. of Salisbury, 1717. Preb. of Lincoln, 1720. V. of Rochdale, Lancs., 1722-54. Author, *Anglia Rediviva*. Translation of Horace, poems, etc. Buried at Rochdale, July 22, 1754. (*D.N.B.*; *Al. Westmon.*; *Robinson*, I. 320.)

DUNTHORN or DOUTHAM, WILLIAM. B.A. (? 1451-2); M.A. 1454-5. Fellow of PETERHOUSE, 1435 69. Proctor, 1457-8. Town clerk of the city of London, Oct. 2, 1461-89. Author of the *Liber Dunthorn* (a vellum folio of charters and records of the city of London). Died in St Alban's, Wood St, London. Will (P.C.C.) 1490. (*D.N.B.*)

DUNTON, ANDREW. Matric. sizar from CHRIST'S, June, 1565. Applied for ordination as deacon (Ely) Dec. 18, 1568, age 25 (rejected).

DUNTON, JOHN. B.A. 1514-5; M.A. 1517. Perhaps scholar at KING'S HALL, 1515-6.

DUNTON, JOHN. Matric. pens. from CORPUS CHRISTI, Michs. 1569.

DUNTON, JOHN. Matric. sizar from KING'S, Lent, 1634-5.

DUNTON, JOHN. Adm. pens. at TRINITY, July 5, 1645. Of Buckinghamshire. Scholar, 1647; B.A. 1648-9. R. of Grafham, Hunts., in 1650. Went to Ireland, 1660, where he was chaplain to Sir Henry Ingoldsby. R. of Aston Clinton, Bucks., 1668-76. Married Lydia, dau. of Daniel Carter, of Chesham, Bucks. Died Nov. 1676, aged 48. For his s. John, the bookseller, *see D.N.B.*

DUNWELL or DUMVELL, RICHARD. Matric. sizar from PEMBROKE, Lent, 1563-4. Resident, Aug. 1564.

DUNWELL, RICHARD. 'B.A. of EMMANUEL' when ord. priest (York) May, 1624. V. of Strensall, Yorks., 1644.

DUNWELL, THOMAS. Adm. pens. at ST CATHARINE'S, July 11, 1723. Of Yorkshire. Matric. 1724.

DUPAISY, DANIEL WALTER. Adm. pens. (age 15) at PETERHOUSE, June 29, 1694. 'Natus Genabi in Galliâ' (? Genappe, in Brabant). S. and h. of James, of Winton, Hants., clerk. School, Winchester. Scholar, 1694; Matric. 1696; B.A. 1697-8; M.A. 1701. Fellow, 1702. Ord. deacon (Ely) June 5; priest, Sept. 23, 1705. V. of Cherryhinton, Cambs., 1705-12. V. of Cuckfield, Sussex, 1713-61. Died 1761. (*T. A. Walker*, 195.)

DUPAISY, JAMES WALTER. Adm. sizar (age 19) at PETERHOUSE, June 21, 1692; afterwards pens. B. at 'Genabi in Galliâ' (? Genappe, in Brabant). School, Winchester. Scholar, 1692; Matric. 1694. Brother of the above.

DUPAQUEER, WILLIAM. Adm. sizar (age 17) at ST JOHN'S, June 17, 1714. S. of Abraham, husbandman. B. at Stamford, Lincs. School, Stamford (Mr Turner). Matric. 1715.

DUPERIER, JOHN. Matric. sizar from PEMBROKE, Michs. 1650; B.A. 1650-1; M.A. 1654.

DUPLAK, WILLIAM. B.A. 1512-3; M.A. 1516. Fellow of CORPUS CHRISTI, 1515. Proctor, 1526-7. University preacher.

DUPONT, JOHN. Adm. pens. (age 20) at TRINITY, Apr. 1, 1725. S. of Caesar, gent., of Middleham, Yorks. School, Kirkleatham, Yorks. (Mr Clark). Matric. 1724-5; Scholar, 1726; B.A. 1728-9. Adm. at the Middle Temple, Apr. 1725. Ord. deacon (Ely) May 24, 1730; priest, Sept. 24, 1732. V. of t , Yorks., 1733-68. Died Dec. 22, 1768, aged 65ysgar h

DUPORT, HENRY. Matric. pens. from JESUS, Michs. 1564. Probably s. of Thomas, of Groby, Leicester. Adm. at the Inner Temple, Nov. 1564. Seated at Sheepshead, Leics. Employed as counsel in Jesus College business. Brother of John (1564). (A. Gray; *Nichols*, III. 1023.)

DUPORT, JAMES. Matric. pens. from TRINITY, Michs. 1622; a scholar from Westminster, 1623. S. of John, D.D., Master of Jesus. B. 1606, in Jesus Lodge. B.A. 1626-7; M.A. 1630. B.D. 1637; D.D. 1660 (*Lit. Reg.*). Fellow, 1627. Regius Professor of Greek, 1639-54. Preb. of Lincoln, 1641. Archdeacon of Stow, 1641. Restored to his stall, and made King's chaplain, 1660. Lady Margaret preacher, 1660. Dean of Peterborough, 1664. R. of Boxworth, Cambs., 1668. Master of Magdalene, 1668. Vice-Chancellor, 1669-70. An eminent scholar and author. Benefactor to Magdalene College, and Peterborough Grammar School. Died July 17, 1679. Buried in Peterborough Cathedral. (*D.N.B.*)

DUPORT, JOHN. Matric. pens. from JESUS, Michs. 1564. S. of Thomas, of Sheepshead, Leics. B.A. 1569-70; M.A. 1573; D.D. 1590. Fellow, 1574-82. Proctor, 1580-1. Master, 1590-1618. Vice-Chancellor, 1593-5, 1601-2, 1609-10. Ord. deacon (Ely) Nov. 17, 1577; priest, Apr. 17, 1580. Master of the Free School, Wotton-under-Edge, Gloucs., Apr. 25, 1578. R. of Harlton, Cambs., 1580-4. R. of Medbourne, Leics. R. of Husband's Bosworth. R. of Fulham, Middlesex, 1583-1617. Precentor of St Paul's, 1585-1617. Preb. of Ely, 1609-17. One of the translators of the Bible. Married Rachel, dau. of Richard Cox, Bishop of Ely. Died 1617. Will (P.C.C. and V.C.C.) 1618. Father of James (1622) and Richard (1614), brother of Henry (1564). (*D.N.B.*)

DUPORT, JOHN. Matric. sizar from JESUS, Easter, 1614. Probably s. of Jaques, brother of John, the master. B.A. 1617-8; M.A. 1621. Ord. deacon (Peterb.) Mar. 8; priest, Mar. 9, 1622-3. V. of Empingham, Ruts., 1631-54. Buried there Apr. 14, 1654. (A. Gray.)

DUPORT, RICHARD. Matric. pens. from JESUS, Easter, 1614. 1st s. of John, Master of the College. Bapt. Sept. 4, 1597. B.A. 1617-8. Married, at Shelford, Cambs., Nov. 12, 1621, Mrs Martha Lund. (A. Gray.)

DUPPA, BRIAN. D.D. 1641 (Incorp. from Oxford). S. of Jeffrey, V. of Lewisham, Kent. Bapt. there, Mar. 18, 1588-9. Matric. from Christ Church, Oxford, July 9, 1605, age 16; B.A. 1609; M.A. 1614; B.D. and D.D. 1625. Fellow of All Souls', 1612. Proctor, 1619. Vice-Chancellor, 1632. V. of Hailsham, Sussex, 1625; of Westham, 1626; of Withyham, 1627; and Petworth, 1628. Chaplain to Prince Palatine. Dean of Christ Church, 1629-38. Canon and Chancellor of Salisbury, 1634. Bishop of Chichester, 1638; of Salisbury, 1641; and of Winchester, 1660. Died Mar. 16, 1662, at Richmond, Surrey. Buried at Westminster. (*Al. Oxon.*; *D.N.B.*)

DUPPA, HENRY. Matric. pens. from QUEENS', Lent, 1579-80. B. at Storrington, Sussex. B.A. 1583-4. Ord. deacon (London) May 22, 1584, age 25; C. of Blatchington, Sussex. R. of Barlavington, 1587-1616. Died 1616.

DUPPA, THOMAS. Matric. pens from QUEENS', Easter, 1549. One of these names M.P. for Truro, 1554.

DUPPLIN, Viscount. M.A. 1749. *See* HAY, THOMAS.

DUPRÉ, JOHN. Adm. pens. at CLARE, Mar. 28, 1743. B. in London. Matric. 1743-4. One of these names, s. of John, of Jersey, adm. at Pembroke College, Oxford, Apr. 4, 1744, age 18; B.A. (Oxford) 1748.

DUPSON, RICHARD. Matric. sizar from TRINITY, Michs. 1613.

DUPUIS, TOSSANUS (?). Adm. pens. at EMMANUEL, Feb. 3, 1658-9. Of Paris. M.A. from Sorbonne, Paris.

DU QUESNE, THOMAS ROGER. Adm. at KING'S, a scholar from Eton, 1737. Matric. 1738; B.A. 1742-3; M.A. 1746. Fellow, 1741. Ord. deacon (Norwich) May, 1744; priest, Apr. 1745. R. of Scole, Norfolk, 1756-93. V. of Horningham and East Tuddenham, 1763-93. Preb. of Lichfield, 1765-93. Died at East Tuddenham, Sept. 14, 1793. (*Harwood.*)

DURANCE, WILLIAM. Adm. sizar (age 18) at MAGDALENE, Feb. 4, 1744-5. S. of John, citizen of Lincoln. B. there. School, Lincoln. Matric. 1745-6; B.A. 1748-9; M.A. 1752. Fellow, 1750. Ord. deacon (Lincoln) Sept. 23, 1750; priest, May 24, 1752.

DURBAN, RICHARD. Adm. pens. at ST CATHARINE'S, June 3, 1697.

DURDEN or DUREDEN, ABEL. Adm. pens. (age 18) at MAGDALENE, Mar. 28, 1672. S. of Joseph, of Rochdale, Lancs. School, Manchester. Matric. 1672; B.A. 1675-6; M.A. 1679. Ord. deacon (London) June 10, 1677. Incorp. at Oxford, 1681.

DURDEN, DANIEL. Adm. pens. at PETERHOUSE, June 29, 1594. Of Essex. Migrated to Queens', July 8, 1596. B.A. 1597-8; M.A. 1601. Ord. deacon (London) Sept. 29; priest, Oct. 1, 1598. R. of North Bemfleet, Essex, 1612-41. Master of Chelmsford School, till 1633. Died 1641.

DURDAYN, DANIEL. Matric. sizar from ST CATHARINE'S, Easter, 1640. Of Essex. B.A. 1643-4.

DURDEN, JOHN. Matric. sizar from ST JOHN'S, Michs. 1566. One of these names V. of Stebbing, Essex, 1568-1600.

DURDEN, JOHN. Adm. pens. at PETERHOUSE, Feb. 16, 1592-3. Scholar. B.A. 1596-7; M.A. 1600. R. of Frating, Essex, 1607-28. R. of Panfield, 1619-28. Died 1628. (*T. A. Walker.*)

DURDEN, JOHN. Matric. sizar from QUEENS', Easter, 1631; B.A. 1634.

DURDEN, MATTHEW. Matric. sizar from TRINITY, Easter, 1631; B.A. 1634-5. R. of Beaumont *c.* Mose, Essex, 1644.

DURDEN, RALPH. Matric. sizar from PEMBROKE, Michs. 1578; B.A. 1581-2. Minister in Essex. Imprisoned in the Tolbooth, Cambridge, by the Vice-Chancellor, for disorderly preaching. Author, *Prophecies.* (*Cooper*, II. 22.)

DURDEN, ROBERT. Matric. sizar from CORPUS CHRISTI, Lent, 1579-80; B.A. 1583-4; M.A. 1587, as Dardon. Ord. deacon and priest (Peterb.) Mar. 5, 1586-7. R. of Runwell, Essex, 1604-29.

DURDEN, WILLIAM. Matric. sizar from ST JOHN'S, Michs. 1566; B.A. from Peterhouse, 1569-70.

DURELL, NICHOLAS. Adm. Fell.-Com. at CLARE, May 22, 1669; M.A. 1669 (*Lit. Reg.*). Of St Hilary, Jersey. French tutor to G. Downing. Studied at Caen and Sedan.

DURHAM, FRANCIS. Adm. sizar at CHRIST'S, June 28, 1624. S. of Robert. B. at Richmond, Yorks. School, Richmond (Mr Bathurst). Matric. 1624; B.A. 1627-8; M.A. 1631. V. of Melbourn, Cambs., 1634-44; sequestered; reinstated, 1660.

DURRAM, RICHARD. Ord. deacon (Peterb.) Mar. 9, 1627-8; priest, June 8, 1628, as 'B.A. of MAGDALENE College.'

DURHAM, ROBERT. Adm. sizar at JESUS, Feb. 23, 1700-1. Of Yorkshire. Matric. 1701; B.A. 1704-5. Ord. deacon (York) Dec. 1715.

DURHAM, THOMAS. Fellow of ST JOHN'S, 1528. Of Durham. Probably B.A. 1524-5; M.A. 1528.

DURHAM, WILLIAM. Adm. pens. (age 19) at CAIUS, May 3, 1598. S. of Ralph. B. in London. School, Ely (Mr Lucke). Matric. 1598.

DURHAM, WILLIAM. Adm. sizar at CHRIST'S, Aug. 23, 1672. S. of Robert. B. at Hucklow, Derbs. School, Wirksworth (Mr Crosedale). Matric. 1673; B.A. 1676-7. Ord. deacon (Lichfield) Sept. 1677; priest (Lincoln) May, 1689. C. of Brampton, Derbs. (Contemporary at Oxford.) (*Peile*, II. 45.)

DURHAM, WILLIAM. D.D. 1676 (*Lit. Reg.*). S. of William, R. of Tredington, Worcestershire. School, Charterhouse. Matric. from Corpus Christi, Oxford, Dec. 12, 1654; B.A. (Oxford) 1657; M.A. 1660-1; B.D. 1669. Fellow of Corpus. Proctor, 1668. R. of Beddington, Surrey, 1672. R. of Letcombe Bassett, Berks., 1674. Canon of Lincoln, 1675. Chaplain to the Duke of Monmouth. Author, *Sermons.* Died June 18, 1686. Buried at Letcombe Bassett. Will, P.C.C. (*Al. Oxon.*; *D.N.B.*)

DURHAM, ——. B.A. 1524-5; M.A. 1528. Probably Thomas, fellow of ST JOHN'S, whom *see.* (Confused by *Cooper* with Michael Drumm.)

DURNFORD, JOSEPH. M.A. from ST CATHARINE'S, 1671. S. of Richard, of Salisbury. Matric. from Gloucester Hall, Oxford, Mar. 26, 1664, age 17; B.A. (Oxford) 1667. R. of Orchardleigh, Somerset, 1674. V. of Whitsbury, Hants., 1676. Perhaps the 'J. Durnford of Whitsbury' whose name occurs in the Registry of Wills for Hants., 1714. (*Al. Oxon.*; *N. and Q.*, 3rd S., II. 57.)

DURRAND or DURANT, ARTHUR. Adm. pens. at SIDNEY, Feb. 1601-2. Probably of Devon. Matric. from Exeter College, Oxford, Mar. 9, 1603-4, age 20; B.A. 1606. (*Al. Oxon.*)

DURRANT, DAVY. Adm. pens. (age 16) at CAIUS, May 28, 1720. S. of Daniel, mercer, of Norwich. B. there. School, Loddon, Norfolk (Mr Conold). Matric. 1724; B.A. 1724-5; M.A. 1729. Fellow, 1726-32. Adm. at the Inner Temple, Feb. 15, 1721-2. Of Scottow, Norfolk, Esq. His s. Thomas, was created Bart., 1784. Died Sept. 22, 1759, aged 57. M.I. at Scottow. (*Venn*, II. 14; *G.E.C.*)

DURANT, JOHN. 'Curate of Jesus Church' (Cambridge), in 1543. Occupied chambers in the College as a fellow, 1535-50. Possibly the same as Robert. (A. Gray.)

DURRANT, JOHN. B.A. from CHRIST'S, 1607-8; M.A. 1611. Doubtless of the family of Bodmin, Cornwall. One of these names lecturer at St Peter's, Sandwich, 1642. Puritan. Probably minister of St George's, Canterbury. Six preacher. Author, religious. (*Peile*, I. 251; *D.N.B.*)

DURRANT, JOHN. Matric. sizar from PETERHOUSE, Easter, 1612; B.A. 1615-6; M.A. 1619. Ord. deacon (Peterb.) Dec. 22, 1616; priest (York, for Lincoln) Mar. 1616-7. V. of Potton, Beds., 1618. R. of Cokayne Hatley, 1621. Buried at Cokayne Hatley, May 13, 1625.

DURRANT, MAURICE. Dominican friar. B.D. 1520-1.

DURANT, NATHANIEL. Adm. sizar at JESUS, June 20, 1621. Of Middlesex. Matric. 1622; Scholar, 1624; B.A. 1624-5; M.A. 1628. One of these names chaplain to the English merchants at Smyrna, in 1635. Perhaps R. of Abinger, Surrey, 1645; and ejected from Cheriton, Hants., 1662. (A. Gray; H. G. Harrison.)

DURRANT, RICHARD. Matric. sizar from ST JOHN'S, Easter, 1555.

DURANDE or DURRANT, ROBERT. B.A. 1531-2; M.A. 1534. R. of Graveley, Cambs., 1545. Will proved (Archd. Hunts.) 1559.

DURAND, SIMON. Adm. sizar at EMMANUEL, May 12, 1729; afterwards pens. Of Middlesex. Matric. 1729; B.A. 1732-3; M.A. 1736.

DURRANT, THOMAS. Matric. pens. from CHRIST'S, June, 1602.

DURRANT, THOMAS. Matric. pens. from PETERHOUSE, Easter, 1612. B. in Cambridge. B.A. 1615-6; M.A. 1619. Fellow of Trinity, 1617. Incorp. at Oxford, 1619. Ord. deacon and priest (London) May 23, 1624, age 25. R. of West Rasen, Lincs., 1624. Will proved (V.C.C.) 1624.

DURANT or DURAND, THOMAS. Adm. sizar (age 17) at CAIUS, May 4, 1641. S. of Edmund, gent., of Brumstead, Norfolk. B. there. School, Norwich (Mr Lovering). Matric. 1641; Scholar, 1643-8; B.A. 1644-5. Probably B.D. 1661 (*Lit. Reg.*). R. of Handsworth, Yorks., 1662-71.

DURANT, WILLIAM. Adm. pens. at EMMANUEL, Apr. 13, 1593. Matric. 1596; B.A. 1596-7; M.A. 1600; B.D. 1615. Ord. deacon (London) Apr. 5; priest, Apr. 8, 1601. R. of Harlington, Middlesex, 1603-28. R. of Cranford, 1615-28. Died 1628.

DURANT, WILLIAM. Adm. sizar at ST CATHARINE'S, July 4, 1728. Of Kent. Matric. 1729; M.B. 1732.

DURRAND (? DURAM), ——. Canonicus. B.D. 1503-4.

DUSGATE, JOHN. B.A. 1520–1; M.A. 1524, as Dusgatt. Probably scholar of CHRIST'S, as B.A. (*Peile* and *Grace Bk*, p. 265, wrongly call him Thomas; but see *Gr. Bk*, I. 188.)

DUSGATE, JOHN. Adm. pens. (age 16) at CHRIST'S, Dec. 10, 1685. S. of Francis. B. at Anmer, Norfolk. Schools, Burnham Thorpe (Mr Tubing) and Norwich (Mr Burton). Matric. 1686; Scholar, 1689. Adm. at the Middle Temple, Nov. 1687. Probably died before 1699. (*Peile*, II. 101.)

DUSGATE, [THOMAS]. B.A. 1522–3 (*Grace Bk*, B², 105). Doubtless Thomas, fellow of CORPUS CHRISTI, 1523–5. There is little doubt that this is the Exeter martyr. On leaving Cambridge he went to Germany to consult Luther. Changed his name to Bennet (? suggested by the popular name of his College, 'Benet'). Settled as schoolmaster at Torrington, Devon; and afterwards at Exeter. Convicted as a heretic, and burnt at Heavitree, near Exeter, Jan. 15, 1531–2. There is much confusion between the two Dusgates and John Bennet, in *Cooper* (I. 43) and *Peile* (I. 13), but the above seems the most probable view. There seems no foundation for *Masters'* belief that he proceeded to D.D. (*D.N.B.*; H. P. Stokes; *Masters-Lamb.*)

DU SOUL, MOSES. M.A. 1701 (*Lit. Reg.*). Studied at Groningen, Utrecht and Franeker. M.A. at one of these. Spent two years at Cambridge.

DUSSING, ROBERT. B.A. 1487–8; M.A. 1491; B.D. 1503–4.

DUSSING or DOWSING, ROBERT. Scholar and fellow of KING'S HALL, 1507–22; (? B.D. 1507–8); D.D. 1512–3 (Incorporated). Vice-Chancellor, 1516–7. Died *c.* 1542. Left 20s. to King's Hall. (*Cooper*, I. 82.)

DUSSING, WILLIAM. Adm. at KING'S, a scholar from Eton, 1506; B.A. 1510–1; M.A. 1514. D.Civ.L. 1528–9. Fellow. Ord. deacon (Lincoln) Sept. 21, 1521. V. of Fordingbridge, Hants. An excellent astronomer. (*Harwood.*)

DUSTE, THOMAS. Fellow of PETERHOUSE, *c.* 1437. Of Norwich diocese. Ord. sub-deacon (Norwich) Dec. 21, 1443; deacon (Ely) Mar. 7, 1443–4; priest (Ely) May 28, 1444. R. of Gt Massingham, Norfolk, 1459–72. R. of Bridgham, 1454.

DUTTON, GEORGE. Matric. sizar from PEMBROKE, Easter, 1579; B.A. 1581–2.

DUTTON, THOMAS. Adm. sizar at EMMANUEL, Apr. 5, 1588. B. in Lancs., *c.* 1572. Matric. 1588; B.A. (? 1591–2); M.A. 1595. Afterwards at King's. Ord. deacon and priest (Lincoln). Oct. 2, 1595. R. of Eversholt, Beds., 1602. Perhaps Master of the Free School, Buckingham, 1638.

DUTTON, WILLIAM. Adm. pens. at JESUS, June 1, 1626. Of London. Matric. 1626; B.A. 1629–30; M.A. 1632 (on King's visit). One of these names 5th s. of Sir Thomas, late of Isleworth, Midds., Knt., deceased; adm. at Lincoln's Inn, Aug. 5, 1635. But *see Al. Oxon.* for a contemporary.

DUTTON, WILLIAM. Adm. Fell.-Com. at JESUS, Apr. 22, 1629. Of London. Perhaps the same as above.

DUTTON, ——. Matric. Fell.-Com. from KING'S, Lent, 1598–9.

DUTYNG, ——. B.A. 1523–4.

DUVAL, PHILIP. Adm. pens. at TRINITY, May 25, 1749. S. of Philip, of London. School, Westminster. Matric. 1749; Scholar, 1750; LL.B. 1756; D.D. (? Lambeth). F.R.S.; F.S.A. Preb. of Worcester, 1767–72. R. of Broadwas, Worcs., 1768. Chaplain to the Duke of Gloucester. V. of Twickenham, 1792–1808. Married Anna, dau. of Dr William George, Provost of King's. Died Mar. 14, 1808, in Newman St, Oxford St.

DUXBURY, JOHN. Adm. sizar (age 15) at ST JOHN'S, July 11, 1663. S. of Laurence, gent., of Deane Height, near Burnley, Lancs. B. there. School, Greenhead, near Haltwhistle, Northumberland (Mr Moore). Matric. 1663; B.A. 1667–8; M.A. 1671.

DUXFORD (Cambs.), vicar of. D.Can.L. 1458–9.

DWARRIS, FORTUNATUS. Adm. Fell.-Com. (age 20) at ST JOHN'S, June 23, 1748. S. of Thomas, of America. B. in Jamaica. Schools, Uxbridge and Eton. Matric. 1748. Adm. student at Leyden, Sept. 28, 1750. M.D. of Leyden. Practised in Jamaica. Died Feb. 5, 1790. M.I. in Jamaica Cathedral. (*Scott-Mayor*, III. 579.)

DWYER, THOMAS. Adm. sizar (age 23) at ST JOHN'S, Oct. 25, 1689. S. of William. B. at Charleville, Cork. B.A. of Trinity College, Dublin. M.A. 1692; B.D. 1700. Fellow, 1692–1710. Ord. deacon (London) May 23, 1692; priest (Ely) Sept. 25, 1692. Head Master of Pocklington School, 1693–8; of Leeds, 1698–1706; of Sedbergh, 1706–9. R. of Medbourne, Leics., 1706–17. Buried May 26, 1717. M.I. at Medbourne. (*Scott-Mayor.*)

DYBALD, JOHN. Matric. sizar from TRINITY, Easter, 1618 B.A. 1621–2. Ord. deacon (Peterb.) Mar. 3; priest, Mar. 4, 1625–6.

DYCER, *see* **DISTER.**

DYDE, WILLIAM. Adm. sizar at QUEENS', June 28, 1686. Of London. Matric. 1686; B.A. 1689–90; M.A. 1693. Fellow, 1690–8. Ord. deacon (London) Sept. 24, 1692.

DYE, CHARLES. Matric. sizar from MAGDALENE, Easter, 1618; B.A. 1621–2; M.A. 1625. Ord. deacon (Peterb.) May 23; priest, May 24, 1624.

DIE, FRANCIS. Matric. pens. from ST JOHN'S, *c.* 1596.

DYE, JOHN. B.A. from TRINITY, 1605–6; M.A. 1609. Perhaps ord. priest (Peterb.) Sept. 22, 1616.

DYE, ROBERT. Matric. sizar from CLARE, Michs. 1578.

DYER, EDWARD. Matric. Fell.-Com. from CHRIST'S, July, 1611. S. of Richard, of Gt Staughton, Hunts. Adm. at the Middle Temple, June 25, 1613.

DYER, GEORGE. B.A. 1525–6.

DYER, GEORGE. Matric. sizar from CHRIST'S, Michs. 1582. 'M.A. of Clare [not recorded] where he resided 7 years; born at Pilton, Devon; aged about 36; ord. priest (Colchester) July 1, 1599; late schoolmaster at Milton by Gravesend, six years; married' (*Linc. Presentation Deed*, 1602). V. of Gosberton, Lincs., 1602–4. V. of Anthorpe, 1603.

DYER, Sir JAMES. According to Sherman, the JESUS fellow and historian, he was a member of that college. S. of Richard, of Wincanton, Somerset. B. 1512. Barrister, Middle Temple, where he was reader, 1552. M.P. for Cambs., 1547, 1553. Serjeant-at-law, 1552. Knighted, 1552. Speaker of the House of Commons, 1553. Recorder of Cambridge; and counsel to the University. Judge of the Common Pleas, 1556; of the Queen's Bench, 1557. Died, Mar. 24, 1581–2, at Gt Staughton, Hunts. Will (P.C.C.) 1582. (*D.N.B.*; C. A. Bedwell.)

DIER, JAMES. Matric. Fell.-Com. from CLARE, Easter, 1570. 5th s. of John, gent., of Wincanton, Somerset. Adm. at the Middle Temple, July 4, 1571. One of these names M.P. for Warwick, 1588.

DYER, JAMES. Matric. sizar from ST JOHN'S, *c.* 1595; B.A. 1599–1600; M.A. 1603. P.C. of Bromley, Kent, 1604–7. V. of St Nicholas, Rochester, 1614–8. V. of Gillingham, 1616–28.

DYER, JAMES. Adm. sizar (age 15) at PEMBROKE, June 20, 1654. B. at Ipswich. B.A. 1657. R. of Bromeswell, Suffolk, 1661.

DYER, JAMES. M.A. from PEMBROKE, 1745. S. of John, of St Martin's, Cornwall. Previously matric. from Hart Hall, Oxford, May 20, 1724, age 19; B.A. (Oxford) 1727–8. (*Al. Oxon.*)

DYER, JOHN. Adm. pens. (age 17) at ST JOHN'S, Aug. 6, 1711. S. of Robert, woollendraper. B. at Combe, Somerset. School, Tiverton. Matric. 1711; B.A. 1715–6. R. of Combe, St Nicholas, Somerset, 1725–30. Died 1730.

DYER, LEWIS. Adm. pens. at EMMANUEL, Easter, 1585. Matric. 1585.

DEYER, LEWIS. Adm. Fell.-Com. (age 16) at SIDNEY, June, 1623. S. and h. of Sir William, Knt., of Gt Staughton, Hunts., deceased. B. there, 1595. School, Sutton, Beds. Adm. at the Middle Temple, Apr. 1624. Created Bart., June 8, 1627. Buried at Colmworth, Beds., Nov. 15, 1669. (*Vis. of Hunts.*, 1613; *G.E.C.*)

DYER, NICHOLAS. Adm. sizar at TRINITY, Apr. 3, 1671. Matric. 1671; B.A. 1674–5. Signs for deacon's orders (London) June 13, 1674.

DYER, RICHARD. Matric. Fell.-Com. from KING'S, Michs. 1572. Perhaps adm. at the Middle Temple, Nov. 1576, as s. and h. of Laurence, of Wincanton, Somerset.

DYER, RICHARD. M.A. from TRINITY, 1650. Of Essex. S. of Gower, of Aldermanbury, London. Matric. from Magdalen Hall, Oxford, Jan. 25, 1638–9, age 16; B.A. 1642. Student of Christ Church, till ejected, 1660. Chaplain to the Lord Mayor. Kept a grammar school near St Katherine's-by-the-Tower. Died 1695. Brother of Simon (1643) and the next. (*Al. Oxon.*; *Calamy*, I. 220.)

DYER, SAMUEL. Adm. sizar at JESUS, Aug. 31, 1646, as 'Deer.' S. of Gower or Gawen, of Aldermanbury, London. Matric. 1646; B.A. 1650–1. R. of St Nicholas Olave, London, 1654. R. of All Hallows, London Wall, 1655; ejected, 1660; also from a lectureship at Lothbury. Afterwards kept school at Mile End. Died 1700, aged 67. Brother of Richard (above) and Simon (1643). (*Calamy*, I. 80; who calls him 'M.A. of Peterhouse.')

DYER, SIMON. Adm. at CORPUS CHRISTI, 1643. S. of Gower or Gawen, of London. Matric. from Magdalen Hall, Oxford, Jan. 31, 1639–40, age 15; B.A. (Cambridge) 1643–4; M.A. 1650. Perhaps R. of Gravesend, Kent, in 1650. Brother of Richard (1638–9) and Samuel (1646).

DYER, SWYNERTON. Adm. Fell.-Com. (age 17) at Caius, June 8, 1669. S. of William, gent., of Tottenham High Cross, Middlesex. B. in London. School, Felsted. Matric. 1669. Adm. at Lincoln's Inn, Apr. 13, 1670. Died 1677. (*Venn*, I. 438; *Vis. of Midds.*, 1664.)

DYER, Sir SWYNERTON, Bart. Adm. at Corpus Christi, July 15, 1705. Of Essex. S. and h. of Sir John Swynnerton Dyer, Bart., late of Dunmow, deceased. Matric. 1705–6. Adm. at Lincoln's Inn, June 29, 1705. Succeeded as 3rd Bart., 1701. Died at Kensington, Mar. 4, 1735–6. (*Masters*; *Vis. of Midds.*, 1664.)

DIER, THOMAS. Matric. pens. from Trinity, Easter, 1550.

DYER, WILLIAM. Adm. at King's, a scholar from Eton, 1568; B.A. 1572–3; M.A. 1576. Fellow, till 1582. 'Died at the Earl of Rutland's.' (*Harwood*.)

DYER, WILLIAM. Adm. Fell.-Com. at Christ's, Apr. 20, 1708. Probably s. of Sir William, Bart., of Newnham, Herts. Adm. at Lincoln's Inn, July 4, 1707. High Sheriff of Herts.

DYER, ——. Matric. pens. from St John's, Easter, 1546.

DYER, ——. B.A. (? 1591–2); M.A. from Clare, 1595.

DIER, ——. Matric. Fell.-Com. from Christ's, *c.* 1597. Perhaps James, s. and h. of Sir Richard, of Staughton, Hunts.; adm. at the Middle Temple, Nov. 5, 1598. If so, brother of Edward (1611). (*Peile*, I. 227.)

DYKE, AUGUSTINE. Adm. at King's, a scholar from Eton, 1563. Matric. 1563–4; B.A. 1567–8; M.A. 1571. Fellow, till 1573. Adm. at Lincoln's Inn, Feb. 13, 1572–3; of Gloucestershire.

DYKE, DANIEL. Matric. pens. from St John's, *c.* 1593. S. of William, clerk (perhaps V. of Hemel Hempstead; and preacher at Coggeshall). B. at Hemel Hempstead, Herts. B.A. 1595–6; M.A. from Sidney, 1599; B.D. 1606. Fellow of Sidney. Incorp. at Oxford, 1602. Brother of Jeremy (1598) and Nathaniel (1608). (*D.N.B.*)

DYKE, DANIEL. Adm. pens. at Emmanuel, Apr. 1629. S. of Jeremy (1598), V. of Epping. B. at Epping, Essex, 1617. Matric. 1629; B.A. 1632–3; M.A. 1636. R. of Eastwick, Herts., *c.* 1636. R. of Gt Hadham, Herts., *c.* 1650, till 1660; ejected. Chaplain to Cromwell. One of the Triers for the approval of ministers. Baptist minister in London. Died 1688. Buried in Bunhill Fields. Brother of Jeremy (1629). (*Calamy*, II. 42; *D.N.B.*)

DYKE, GEORGE. Matric. pens. from St John's, Michs. 1567. B. at Glemsford, Suffolk. B.A. 1571–2; M.A. 1575. Ord. deacon (London) Sept. 25, 1608, age about 50; priest, Dec. 17, 1608. C. of Withyham, Sussex.

DYKE, HUMPHREY. Adm. at King's, a scholar from Eton, 1535.

DYKE, JEREMY. Adm. sizar at Emmanuel, May 28, 1598; migrated to Sidney, Oct. 1598. S. of William, preacher at Coggeshall, Essex. Bapt. there, Oct. 13, 1584. Matric. 1598; B.A. 1601–2; M.A. 1605. Fellow of Sidney. R. of Toft, Cambs., during 1609. V. of Epping, Essex, 1609–39. Preacher. Author, theological. Died 1639. Buried at Epping. By will (P.C.C.) he leaves to his s. Jeremy 'my silver tankard bestowed upon me by the honourable House of Commons.' Father of the next, and of Daniel (1629), brother of Daniel (1593) and Nathaniel (1608). (J. Ch. Smith.)

DYKE, JEREMY. Adm. pens. at Emmanuel, Apr. 1629. Of Essex. S. of Jeremy (above), V. of Epping. Matric. 1629; B.A. from St Catharine's, 1632–3; M.A. 1636. Ord. deacon (Peterb.) May 20, 1638; priest, Mar. 10, 1638–9. V. of Stanstead Abbots, Herts., 1640–5. R. of Gt Parndon, Essex, 1645–50. Brother of Daniel (1629). (Davids, *Essex*, 439.)

DYKE, JOHN. Adm. pens. at Emmanuel, Oct. 28, 1630. Of Frant, Sussex. S. and h. of William. Adm. at the Inner Temple, Nov. 1631.

DIKE, JOSEPH. Matric. pens. from Christ's, July, 1616. Doubtless s. of William, preacher at Coggeshall, Essex. B.A. 1619–20.

DIKE, NATHANIEL. Matric. sizar from Christ's, July, 1608. S. of William, preacher at Coggeshall and Hemel Hempstead. B.A. 1611–2; M.A. 1615. Brother of Daniel (1593) and Jeremy (1598). One of these names died V. of Axmouth, Devon, before 1647. (*Peile*, I. 270.)

DYKE, NATHANIEL. Adm. pens. at Emmanuel, May 30, 1636. Of Surrey. Matric. 1636. Died in College. Buried at St Andrew's, Cambridge, Feb. 18, 1636–7.

DYKE, RICHARD. Adm. pens. at Emmanuel, June 4, 1633. Of Middlesex. Matric. 1633; B.A. 1636–7; M.A. 1640.

DIKE, ROBERT. Matric. pens. from Trinity, Easter, 1636.

DIKE or DIKES, SAMUEL. Matric. pens. from Queens', Easter, 1617. B. at Heydric (? Hardwick), Norfolk. B.A. 1620–1; M.A. 1624. Fellow of Corpus Christi, 1627–8. Ord. deacon and priest (London) Mar. 13, 1624–5, age 24. R. of Sloley, Norfolk, 1628.

DIKE, SAMUEL. Adm. pens. at Emmanuel, Apr. 1, 1637. Matric. 1637.

DYKE, THOMAS. Adm. Fell.-Com. (age 16) at St John's, Apr. 29, 1635. S. of Thomas, Esq., of Horsham, Waldron, Sussex. B. at Ninfield, Sussex. Matric. 1635. Adm. at the Inner Temple, 1636; of Horsham, Sussex. Knighted, June 19, 1641. M.P. for Seaford. Died Dec. 13, 1669. Father of William (1672).

DYKE, THOMAS. Adm. Fell.-Com. at Peterhouse, May 15, 1655. Of Sussex. School, Maidstone. Matric. 1655. (*T. A.* 108; but *see Al. Oxon.*, for another of these names.)

DIKE, WILLIAM. Matric. pens. from St John's, *c.* 1594; B.A. 1597–8, as Dikes; M.A. 1601. Perhaps ord. deacon (London) Mar. 6; priest, Mar. 13, 1602–3. R. of Frant, Sussex, 1603. Buried there Sept. 9, 1659. (W. C. Harrison.)

DYKE, WILLIAM. Adm. pens. at Queens', May 17, 1672. 2nd s. of Sir Thomas, Knt., of Waldron, Sussex. Adm. at the Middle Temple, Nov. 1673.

DYKES or DIKES, DANIEL. Matric. sizar from St John's, *c.* 1593; *impubes*.

DIKES or DIKE, JOHN. Matric. pens. from St John's, Michs. 1622; B.A. 1626–7.

DYKES, OSWALD. Matric. sizar from Jesus, Michs. 1567; B.A. from St John's, 1570–1; M.A. 1574. R. of Asby, Westmorland, 1593–1618.

DIKES, THOMAS. B.Can.L. 1486–7. (Perhaps the 'rector Dikes' who obtained a *grace* for same degree, 1483–4.)

DYKES, THOMAS. Matric. pens. from Pembroke, Easter, 1603.

DYKLYNG, ——. B.A. 1468–9.

DYKMAN, ——. Fee for M.A. or higher degree, 1468–9.

DYLCOCKE, HENRY. Matric. pens. from Christ's, Easter, 1544; B.A. 1544–5; M.A. 1547. Fellow, 1547–51. Died 'in the time of the Sweat.' Buried at Toft, Cambs., Oct. 26, 1551. Will (V.C.C.). (*Peile*, I. 29.)

DYMES, ROBERT. Adm. at Corpus Christi, 1692. Of Norwich. Matric. 1692; B.A. 1695–6. Ord. deacon (Norwich) Aug. 1698; priest, May, 1700. R. of Swanton Abbot, Norfolk, 1700.

DYMOCK, CHARLES. Adm. Fell.-Com. (age 14) at Magdalene, Feb. 6, 1681–2. S. of Sir Charles, King's Champion. B. at Scrivelsby-in-Lindsey, Lincs. M.A. 1682 (*Com. Reg.*). M.P. for Co. Lincoln, 1698, 1701 (twice), 1702, till his death in 1702–3. (*Lincs. Pedigrees*, 1207.)

DYMOCK, EDWARD. Adm. pens. (age 16) at St John's, June 28, 1673. S. of Edward, gent., of Kirkby-upon-Bain, Lincs. B. there. Educated at home. Captain in the army. Of Waddingworth, Esq. Died Apr. 29, 1729. Brother of Robert (1673). (*Lincs. Pedigrees*, 1211.)

DYMOCKE, FRANCIS. Matric. pens. from Trinity, Michs. 1562. S. and h. of Humphrey, Esq., of Castle Over, Warws. Adm. at the Middle Temple, Feb. 1566.

DYMOCKE, HENRY. Matric. pens. from Trinity, Lent, 1564–5.

DIMOCKE, JOHN. Matric. sizar from Trinity, Michs. 1602; B.A. from St John's, 1605–6; M.A. 1609.

DYMOCK, JOHN. M.A. from King's, 1677. S. of Edmund, of Sontley, Denbs., clerk. Matric. from Jesus College, Oxford, May 27, 1669, age 17; B.A. (Oxford) 1672–3. (*Al. Oxon.*)

DYMOCK, ROBERT. Adm. pens. (age 18) at St John's, June 28, 1673. S. of Edward, gent., of Kirkby-upon-Bain, Lincs. B. there. Educated at home. Matric. 1673. Adm. at Gray's Inn, Dec. 1, 1674, as s. of Edward, of Tumby, Lincs. Of Grebby Hall, Esq. Died 1714. Father of the next. Brother of Edward (1673). (*Lincs. Pedigrees*, 1211.)

DYMOKE, ROBERT. Adm. pens. (age 18) at Magdalene, Apr. 20, 1719. S. of Robert (above), of Grebby Hall, Lincs., deceased. School, Lincoln. Matric. 1721; B.A. 1722–3. Ord. deacon (Lincoln) Sept. 22, 1723. Drowned at Lincoln, Jan. 27, 1735. (*Lincs. Pedigrees*, 1211.)

DIMMOCKE, WILLIAM. Adm. sizar (age 18) at Christ's, July 1, 1628. S. of John. B. at Wicken, Cambs. School, Ely (Mr Hitch). B.A. 1631.

DYMOKE, WINDUS. Adm. pens. (age 17) at Trinity, Apr. 12, 1677. S. of James, of London. School, St Paul's.

DYMOND, THOMAS, *see* **DIMOND.**

DYMSDALE, JOHN, *see* **DIMSDALE.**

DYNELEY, *see* **DINELEY.**

DYNNE, HENRY. Adm pens. at Corpus Christi, 1552. Matric. Easter, 1554. Perhaps of Heydon, Norfolk. Buried there Dec. 30, 1586. (*Vis. of Norfolk*.)

DYNNE, WILLIAM. Matric. pens. from QUEENS', Lent, 1579-80.

DYRHAM, THOMAS, *see* DEREHAM.

DYRKIN, JAMES. B.A. from TRINITY, 1548-9; M.A. 1552. Fellow, 1551.

DYSART, Earl of, *see* HUNTINGTOWER.

DYSON, *see also* DISON.

DYSON, EDWARD. Adm. pens. (age 17) at PETERHOUSE, June 25, 1711. Of Worcestershire. School, Stourbridge. Matric. 1710-1; Scholar, 1711; B.A. 1714-5; M.A. 1718. Fellow, 1716-41. Ord. deacon (Ely) Mar. 17, 1716-7; priest, June 8, 1718. Died Mar. 24, 1740-1. (*T. A. Walker.*)

DYSON, JEREMIAH. Adm. sizar at CLARE, May 29, 1732. B. at Greetland, Yorks. B.A. 1735-6. Ord. deacon (Lincoln) Mar. 21, 1735-6.

DYSON, JOHN. Adm. scholar at TRINITY HALL, Jan. 2, 1723-4. Of Huddersfield, Yorks. Matric. 1724. Doubtless s. and h. of John, of Westwood, Huddersfield, Esq.; adm. at Lincoln's Inn, Feb. 1, 1722-3.

DISTER, BENJAMIN. Adm. pens. at ST JOHN'S, Sept. 6, 1648. S. of John, gent., of Glemsford, Suffolk. B. there. School, St Paul's, London. Matric. 1648-9.

DYSTER, JOHN. Matric. pens. from JESUS, Easter, 1552.

DISTER or DYCER, WILLIAM. Adm. pens. (age 16) at PETERHOUSE, Oct. 9, 1639. Of Suffolk. School, Thurlow, Suffolk, where he was instructed in music. Matric. 1639; Scholar, 1639; B.A. 1644-5. Will of one of these names (Bury) 1661. (*T. A. Walker.*)

DYVE, ——. B.A. 1462-3.

E

EACHARD, ABRAHAM. Adm. sizar at CHRIST'S, Sept. 1, 1692. S. of Thomas (1660). Matric. 1693; Scholar, 1694-5. Buried at Gt St Andrew's, Cambridge, Aug. 3, 1696. Brother of Lawrence (1688) and Christopher (1689). (*Peile*, II. 127.)

EACHARD, BENJAMIN. Matric. sizar from TRINITY, Easter, 1620; B.A. 1622-3. Ord. deacon and priest (Norwich) Mar. 3, 1624-5.

EACHARD, CHRISTOPHER. Adm. pens. at ST CATHARINE'S, Sept. 17, 1667. S. of Lawrence (1625-6). Matric. 1668; B.A. 1671-2; M.A. 1675. Ord. deacon (Norwich) Sept. 1673; priest, Mar. 1673-4. R. of Frostenden, Suffolk, 1674-93. R. of Benacre, 1677-90. R. of Somerleyton, 1690-1706. R. of Blundeston, 1692-1706. V. of Cransford, 1696. Buried at Somerleyton, Dec. 1, 1706. (*Davy MSS.*)

EACHARD, CHRISTOPHER. Adm. sizar (age 16) at CHRIST'S, May 9, 1689. S. of Thomas (1660). B. at Barsham, Suffolk. Educated at home. Matric. 1689; B.A. from St Catharine's, 1692-3; M.A. 1696. Ord. deacon (Norwich) June, 1696; priest, Dec. 1696. V. of Debach, Suffolk, 1710. V. of Cransford. Brother of Abraham (1692) and Lawrence (1688). (*Peile*, II. 113.)

ECHARD, JOHN. Matric. sizar from JESUS, Michs. 1556. Perhaps adm. at Lincoln's Inn, Oct. 8, 1561. Will (P.C.C.) 1589.

ECHARD, JOHN. Matric. Fell.-Com. from PETERHOUSE, Lent, 1597-8.

EACHARD, JOHN. Matric. pens. from TRINITY, Easter, 1607; B.A. 1610-1; M.A. 1614. V. of Darsham, Suffolk, 1617-44.

EACHARD, JOHN. Adm. sizar at ST CATHARINE'S, May 10, 1653. Of Suffolk. S. of Lawrence (1625-6). Bapt. at Yoxford, Jan. 26, 1636-7. Matric. 1654; B.A. 1656-7; M.A. 1660; D.D. 1676 (*Lit. Reg.*). Fellow, 1658. Master, 1675-97. Vice-Chancellor, 1679-80, 1695-6. R. of Widdington, Essex, 1681-4. R. of Dennington, Suffolk, 1683-97. Sinecure R. of Llanynys, Denbighs., 1684-97. Supposed to be the author of *Grounds of the Contempt of the Clergy*. Died July 7, 1697, aged 61. Will (P.C.C.) dated July 1, 1697; proved 1718-9 (*sic*). Buried in the College Chapel. Brother of Lawrence (1656). (*D.N.B.*; J. Ch. Smith.)

EACHARD, JOHN. Adm. pens. at ST CATHARINE'S, Apr. 22, 1678. Matric. 1680-1; B.A. 1681-2; M.A. 1685. Perhaps R. of Edwardston, Suffolk, 1690-5. R. of Wreningham, Norfolk, 1695-1734. R. of Wicklewood, 1701-34. Died 1734.

EACHARD, LAURENCE. Matric. pens. from TRINITY, Lent, 1625-6; B.A. 1625-6; M.A. 1629. Ord. deacon (Norwich) Dec. 3, 1627; priest, Dec. 23, 1632. V. of Yoxford, Suffolk, 1632; there in 1650. Father of Christopher (1667), John (1653) and the next.

EACHARD, LAURENCE. Adm. sizar at ST CATHARINE'S, 1656. Of Suffolk. S. of Lawrence (above). Matric. Michs. 1659; B.A. 1659-60; M.A. 1663. R. of Henstead, Suffolk, 1662-1714. R. of Rushmere, 1663-1714. R. of North Cove, 1678-96. R. of Willingham St Mary, 1678. Will (P.C.C.) 1718-9. Brother of John (1653) and Christopher (1667).

EACHARD, LAURENCE. Adm. sizar (age 17) at CHRIST'S, May 26, 1688. S. of Thomas (1660), of Suffolk. Bapt. at Barsham, Mar. 23, 1671-2. Matric. 1688; Scholar, 1689; B.A. 1691-2; M.A. 1695. Ord. priest (Norwich) May 2, 1696. R. of Welton by Louth, Lincs., 1696. Chaplain to the Bishop of Lincoln. Preb. of Lincoln, 1697-1730. V. of South Elkington, Lincs., 1709. Archdeacon of Stowe, 1712-30. R. of Sudborne, Suffolk, 1722. V. of Rendlesham, 1722-30. Author, historical, classical, etc. Died at Lincoln, Aug. 16, 1730. Buried there at St Mary Magdalen's. Brother of Abraham (1692) and Christopher (1689). (*Peile*, II. 109; *D.N.B.*)

EACHARD, PETER. B.A. from TRINITY, 1573-4.

EACHARD, THOMAS. B.A. from ST CATHARINE'S, 1660; M.A. 1664. S. of John (1607). R. of Gisleham, Suffolk, 1663-93. V. of Kessingland, 1663-93. Perhaps V. of Arkesden, Essex, 1663-4. Married Sarah Ox, of Aldborough, 1664. Buried at Barsham, Oct. 26, 1693. Father of Abraham (1692), Christopher (1689) and Laurence (1688). (H. G. Harrison.)

EACHARD, THOMAS. Adm. pens. at ST CATHARINE'S, Apr. 22, 1678. Matric. 1680-1; B.A. 1681-2; M.A. 1685.

EADE or EDE, AMBROSE. B.Can.L. 1466-7. R. of Capel, Suffolk, 1479-1502. Master of Thompson College, Norfolk, 1490-1503. Chancellor of Norwich diocese, 1500-1. R. of Oxburgh.

EADE, EDMUND. Adm. pens. (age 16) at CAIUS, July 11, 1615. S. of George, husbandman, of Mundford, Norfolk. School, Onehouse, Suffolk (Mr Godley). Matric. 1615-6; Scholar, 1617-22; B.A. 1618-9; M.A. 1622; B.D. 1632. Fellow, 1622-32. University preacher, 1631. Ord. deacon (Peterb.) Aug. 21; priest, Aug. 22, 1628. R. of South Pickenham, Norfolk, 1631. R. of Ovington, 1632-55, where he kept a school. Author. Will proved, 1657. (*Venn*, I. 230; H. I. Longden.)

EADE, EDMUND. Adm. sizar (age 17) at PEMBROKE, Oct. 7, 1719. S. of Zephaniah (1686), R. of Blaxhall, Suffolk. Bapt. there, June 11, 1702. School, Woodbridge. Matric. 1720; B.A. 1724-5. Ord. priest (Norwich) Sept. 1726. C. of Saxmundham, Suffolk.

EADE, GEORGE. Adm. pens. (age 15) at ST JOHN'S, Jan. 13, 1667-8. S. of Robert (1627), M.D., of Cambridge. B. there. School, Cambridge. Matric. 1668. Brother of Robert (1657).

EADE or EIDE, JOHN. Adm. (age 15) at CAIUS, May 9, 1565. S. of Robert, of Burnham Westgate, Norfolk. School, Burnham Will of one of these names (Ipswich) 1610; of Laxfield, Suffolk.

EADE, REYNOLD. Adm. sizar at EMMANUEL, Apr. 22, 1652. Of Suffolk (probably Kelsale). Matric. 1652; B.A. 1655-6; M.A. 1659. R. of Stratford St Andrew, Suffolk, 1689-1703. One of these names, clerk, of Benhall, 1675; of Iken, 1696. (V. B. Redstone.)

EADE, REGINALD. Adm. sizar at ST CATHARINE'S, Mar. 26, 1696. B. in Suffolk. Matric. 1696; B.A. 1702-3. Ord. priest (Ely, *Litt. dim.* from Norwich) Mar. 13, 1714-5. Doubtless R. of Chesilford, Suffolk, 1720.

EADE, ROBERT. Adm. pens. (age 24) at CAIUS, July 27, 1627. S. of George, of Norfolk. B. at Mundford. School, Foulden (Mr Taylor). Matric. 1627; Scholar, 1628-33; B.A. 1630-1; M.A. 1635; M.D. (*Lit. Reg.*) 1642. Fellow, 1633-42. Licensed to practise medicine, 1637. Practised in Cambridge. Lord of the Manor of Herringswell, Suffolk. Will (P.C.C.) Sept. 1672. Father of the next and George (1667-8). (*Venn*, I. 281.)

EADE, ROBERT. Adm. pens. (age 14) at CAIUS, Mar. 11, 1657-8. S. of Robert (above). B. in Cambridge. Bapt. at Gt St Mary's, Feb. 26, 1643-4. School, Cambridge (Mr Whybro). Matric. 1658; B.A. 1661-2; M.A. from Trinity Hall, 1665. Fellow of Trinity Hall, 1665 (by royal mandate: *see Coll. Hist.*, 153, where he is wrongly described). In holy orders.

EADE, ROBERT. Matric. from QUEENS', Easter, 1720; B.A. 1722-3; M.A. 1726. Ord. deacon (London) May 28, 1727.

EDE, W. Matric. pens. from ST JOHN'S, Lent, 1563-4.

EADE, ZEPHANIAH. Adm. sizar at QUEENS', May 27, 1686. Of Suffolk. Matric. 1686; B.A. 1689–90. Ord. priest (Norwich) Sept. 1703. R. of Blaxhall, Suffolk, 1685–1737. R. of Stratford St Andrew, 1703–37. C. of Butley. Father of Edmund (1719).

EADES, *see* **EDES.**

EADMONDSON, JOSEPH. Adm. sizar (age 17) at SIDNEY, June 12, 1669. 1st s. of John, clothier. B. at Leeds, Yorks. School, Leeds. Matric. 1669; B.A. 1672–3.

EADON, *see* also **EDEN.**

EADON, RICHARD. Adm. sizar (age 19) at PETERHOUSE, May 17, 1726. Of Yorkshire. School, York. Matric. 1726; Scholar, 1726; B.A. 1729–30. *Litt. dim.* (York) for priest, July, 1731.

EAGLES, *see* **EGLES.**

EAGLESTON, ALEXANDER. Adm. pens. (age 17) at PETERHOUSE, Apr. 29, 1676. Of Durham. Perhaps s. of Joseph, of Huntsanworth, Durham. Matric. 1676; Scholar, 1676; B.A. 1679–80; M.A. 1684. P.C. of Lanchester, Durham, 1682–6. Licensed as schoolmaster at Boldon, 1686. (*T. A. Walker*, 156; Surtees, *Durham*, II. 367.)

EALAND, *see* **ELAND.**

EALES, *see* **ELES.**

EARBERY, MATTHIAS. Adm. sizar (age 18) at TRINITY, Mar. 2, 1675–6. S. of Edward, of London. School, Charterhouse. Matric. 1676; B.A. 1679–80. Ord. deacon (London) June 6, 1680; priest (Norwich) Dec. 1685. R. of Gt Greenford, Middlesex, 1686–8. V. of Hoveton, Norfolk, 1687–1730. V. of Neatishead. R. of Barsham, Suffolk, 1730–5. R. of Woodton, Norfolk, 1730–5. A non-juror. Author, theological. Perhaps died Oct. 3, 1740. Father of the next. (G. *Mag.*)

EARBERY, MATTHIAS. Adm. sizar (age 15) at ST JOHN'S, Jan. 16, 1705–6. S. of Matthias (above). B. at Hoveton, Norfolk. Matric. 1705–6; B.A. 1710–1. Ord. deacon (Ely) Mar. 16, 1711–2; priest (London) Sept. 19, 1714.

EARBERY or ERBURY, WILLIAM. B.A. from QUEENS', 1624 (Incorp. from Oxford). M.A. 1626. Of Glamorganshire. Matric. from Brasenose College, Nov. 2, 1621, age 17; B.A. (Oxford) 1623. Subscribed for deacon's orders (Bristol) Dec. 23, 1626. V. of St Mary, Cardiff, 1633. Chaplain in the Parliamentary army under Lord Essex; and to a regiment at Oxford, 1646. Died Apr. 1654. (*Al. Oxon.*; *D.N.B.*)

EARDLEY, ANDREW, *see* **YARDLEY.**

EARDLEY, ——. Matric. Fell.-Com. from CHRIST'S, 1597–8. Probably of Yardley or Eardley, Staffs. (*Peile*, I. 227.)

EARLE, CHRISTOPHER. Adm. at CORPUS CHRISTI, 1640. Probably s. of Christopher, of Sturminster Marshall, Dorset, and Elisabeth, dau. of Edward Denny, of Hertfordshire. B. in Hertfordshire. Adm. at Gray's Inn, June 2, 1641. Age 10 in 1634. Married and had issue. (*Hutchins*, III. 503.)

EARLE, DANIEL. Adm. pens. at TRINITY, Apr. 24, 1669. One of these names, of Normanton, Notts., Esq., buried there Dec. 15, 1676.

EARLE, EDWARD. Adm. pens. (age 17) at CAIUS, Apr. 9, 1649. S. of Erasmus (1609), serjeant-at-law. B. at Salle, Norfolk. Schools, Corpusty (Mr Watts) and Norwich (Mr Lovering). Adm. at Lincoln's Inn, Nov. 4, 1648. Of Salle, Cawston and Heydon. Buried at Salle, Oct. 3, 1697. Father of Erasmus (1685). (*Venn*, I. 374; *Blomefield*, VI. 246.)

EARLE, ERASMUS. Matric. pens. from PETERHOUSE, Easter, 1609. S. of Thomas, of Salle, Norfolk, gent. B. there, 1590. School, Norwich. Adm. at Lincoln's Inn, Apr. 16, 1611. Bencher, 1635. Reader, 1639. M.P. for Norwich, 1647. Serjeant-at-Law, 1648 and 1660. Recorder of Norwich, 1649–63. Died Sept. 7, 1667, aged 77. M.I. at Heydon, Norfolk. Father of Edward (above) and John (1640). (*D.N.B.*)

EARLE, ERASMUS. Adm. Fell.-Com. (age 17) at PEMBROKE, Sept. 18, 1684. S. of John (1640), late of Wood Dalling, Norfolk, Esq. Matric. 1686. High Sheriff of Norfolk, 1690. Died Mar. 5, 1721, aged 55. M.I. at Heydon, Norfolk. Brother of Ralph (1672). Father of Erasmus (1708). (*Blomefield*, VI. 247.)

EARLE, ERASMUS. Adm. pens. (age 17) at PEMBROKE, Apr. 29, 1685. S. of Edward (1649), of Salle, Norfolk. B. at Thurling (? Thurning), Norfolk. Died Mar. 1, 1695–6, aged 28. M.I. at Salle. (Le Neve, *Mon.*, IV. 170.)

EARLE, ERASMUS. Adm. pens. at PEMBROKE, Mar. 16, 1708–9. S. of Erasmus (1684), of Heydon, Norfolk, Esq. Matric. 1709. Of Heydon Hall. Died at Bath, Oct. 19, 1728, aged 35. M.I. at Heydon where he was buried.

EARLE, ERASMUS. Adm. Fell.-Com. (age 16) at PEMBROKE, Jan. 2, 1743–4. S. of Augustine, of Heydon, Norfolk. B. at Whitehaven. Matric. 1743–4; B.A. 1747–8. Fellow of Peterhouse, 1748–51. Adm. at Lincoln's Inn, Dec. 19, 1743. Of Heydon, Norfolk. Died May, 1768. Buried at Heydon, May 18. (*T. A. Walker*, 290; *G. Mag.*)

EARLE, GEORGE. Matric. pens. from CLARE, Michs. 1587.

EARLE, GILES. Adm. Fell.-Com. (age 18) at PETERHOUSE, June 15, 1750. Of Middlesex. School, Eton.

EARLE, JOHN. Adm. pens. (age 16) at PEMBROKE, July 31, 1640. S. of Erasmus (1609), of Salle, Norfolk, Esq. Matric. 1641. Adm. at Lincoln's Inn, Jan. 30, 1646–7. Married Sarah, dau. of Sir John Hare, of Stow Bardolf, Knt. Buried at Wood Dalling, 1697. Father of the next and of Erasmus (1684).

EARLE, RALPH. Adm. Fell.-Com. (age 16) at PEMBROKE, Mar. 28, 1672. S. of John (above), of Heydon, Norfolk, Esq. M.A. 1675 (*Lit. Reg.*). Incorp. at Oxford, 1675. Adm. at Lincoln's Inn, Jan. 5, 1675–6. Buried at Heydon, May 9, 1679. Brother of Erasmus (1684). (*Blomefield*, VI. 245.)

EARLE, RICHARD. Adm. Fell.-Com. (age 16) at CHRIST'S, Jan. 11, 1624–5. S. of Augustine, of Stragglethorpe, Lincs. Schools, Southwell (Mr Bayes) and Grantham (Mr Wilkinson). Matric. 1625. Adm. at Gray's Inn, Jan. 27, 1626–7. Created Baronet, 1629. Sheriff of Lincolnshire, 1647. Died Mar. 25, 1667, aged 60. Buried at Stragglethorpe. M.I. (*Peile*, I. 363; *Lincs. Pedigrees*; *G.E.C.*)

EARL, Sir RICHARD. Adm. Fell.-Com. at EMMANUEL, Jan. 31, 1688–9. Of Lincolnshire. S. of Sir Richard, of Stragglethorpe, Bart. B. *c.* 1673. Succeeded as baronet, *c.* 1680. Adm. at the Middle Temple, Jan. 12, 1690–1. Died Aug. 13, 1697, aged 24. M.I. at Stragglethorpe. (*Lincs. Pedigrees*; Le Neve, *Mon.*, V. 182; *G.E.C.*)

EARLE, ROBERT. Adm. pens. (age 17) at SIDNEY, June 28, 1666. 1st s. of [Christopher], Esq. B. at Topsfield, Essex. School, Felsted. Adm. at Gray's Inn, Nov. 27, 1666.

EARLE, THOMAS. Adm. at CORPUS CHRISTI, 1690. Of Norfolk. Matric. 1690; B.A. 1693–4.

EARLE, WALTER. Adm. Fell.-Com. (age 16) at CHRIST'S, Nov. 20, 1658. Eldest s. of Thomas. B. in London. School, St Paul's. Matric. 1658.

EARLE, WILLIAM. Matric. from ST JOHN'S, Easter, 1586; B.A. 1589–90. Ord. deacon (Peterb.) June 13, 1591.

EARLE, WILLIAM. Matric. Fell.-Com. from CHRIST'S, July, 1618. S. of Augustine, of Stragglethorpe, Lincs. Died at Cambridge. Buried at Gt St Andrew's, Apr. 2, 1620. Brother of Richard (1624).

EARL, ——. Adm. Fell.-Com. at ST CATHARINE'S, 1665.

EARLEY, JOHN. Matric. sizar from CLARE, 1601; B.A. 1605–6. Probably ord. priest (York) Sept. 1607, as John Earle.

EARNSHAW, JOSHUA. Adm. sizar (age 17) at CHRIST'S, Apr. 9, 1743. S. of James. B. at Midhope, Penistone, Yorks. School, Midhope (Mr Haigh). Matric. 1743; B.A. 1746–7. Ord. deacon (York) June, 1748; priest, Sept. 1749. V. of Ossett, Yorks., 1753–98. (*Peile*, II. 244.)

EARTHLEY, EDWARD. Probably a member of the University. Author of *Verses* on the death of the Dukes of Suffolk in 1551. (*Cooper*, I. 109.)

EARTON, JOHN. Adm. pens. (age 15) at CAIUS, Mar. 4, 1621–2. S. of John, gent., of London. School, Perse, Cambridge. Matric. 1622, as 'Carton.'

EASDALL, WILLIAM. LL.B. from TRINITY HALL, 1614; LL.D. 1620. Vicar-General to the Archbishop of York. Gave £20 to Peterhouse Chapel. Will (York) 1644. (*Coles MSS.*; J. Ch. Smith.)

EASDAY, HENRY. Matric. pens. from PETERHOUSE, Michs. 1638.

EASINGTON, JOHN. Matric. pens. from TRINITY, Easter, 1603.

ESYNGTON, ROBERT. Canonicus. B.Can.L. 1517–8.

ESYNGWOLD, RICHARD. A monk. B.D. 1458–9.

ESYNGWOLD, RICHARD. B.D. 1464–5 (perhaps the above).

ESYNGWOLD, ——. B.A. 1465–6.

EASON *and* **EASTON,** *see also* **ESTON.**

EASON or EASTON, EDWARD. Adm. Fell.-Com. at EMMANUEL, Oct. 28, 1597. Matric. 1597.

EASON, JOHN. Matric. pens. from CORPUS CHRISTI, Michs. 1598. Of Kent.

EASON, JOHN. Adm. pens. at EMMANUEL, May 19, 1634. Of Middlesex. Matric. 1634; B.A. 1637–8; M.A. 1641. Perhaps ejected from Pett, Sussex, in 1662; and father of the next.

EASTON or ESTON, JOHN. Adm. pens. (age 14) at ST JOHN'S, Sept. 17, 1673. S. of John (? above), of Pett, Sussex. B. there. School, Peterborough. Matric. 1677; B.A. 1677–8; M.A. 1681.

EASON or ESSON, SAMUEL. Adm. sizar at EMMANUEL, June 18, 1636. Of Sussex. Matric. 1636; B.A. 1639–40.

EAST, *see also* **EST.**

EAST, HENRY. Matric. sizar from TRINITY HALL, July, 1714. B. at Wingham, Kent, 1693. Migrated to Clare, Mar. 21, 1714-5. B.A. 1716-7. Fellow of Clare, 1718 Ord. deacon (Ely) June 8, 1718. Minister at Elstow, Beds. Buried there Jan. 15, 1719-20. (W. M. Noble.)

EAST, JOHN. Adm. pens. (age 15) at MAGDALENE, May 23, 1665. S. of Edward, deceased, of Orton, Northants. School, Kettering. Matric. 1665.

EAST, NICHOLAS. Adm. pens. at QUEENS', Dec. 28, 1627. Of Bedfordshire.

EAST, NICHOLAS. Adm. pens. (age 15) at SIDNEY, May 19, 1636. S. of Nicholas, yeoman. B. at Stanford, Beds. School, (private, Mr Bedford). Matric. 1636; B.A. 1639-40; M.A. 1643. Ord. deacon (Peterb.) Dec. 28, 1641. Minister of Bromham, Beds., and Houghton Conquest, in 1646. Married Lucia, dau. of Lewis Conquest, Esq.

EAST, THOMAS. Adm. pens. (age 17) at CAIUS, July 7, 1575. Of Wimpole, Cambs. S. of Alexander, gent. Schools, Godmanchester and Ely. Matric. 1575.

EAST, THOMAS. Adm. pens. (age 16) at SIDNEY, Aug. 13, 1628. S. of Thomas, Esq. B. at Hitchin, Herts. School, St Ives.

EAST, WILLIAM. Matric. Fell.-Com. from KING'S, Lent, 1713-4. S. of William, of the Middle Temple. Adm. at the Middle Temple, Feb. 23, 1713-4. Of Hall Place, Hurley, Berks. One of the Commissioners of the Wine Licence Office, 1720-7. M.P. for St Mawes, 1728. Married Anne, dau. of Sir George Cook, of Middlesex. Died Nov. 7, 1737, aged 42. (Burke, *Ext. Bart.*; *Misc. Gen. et Her.*, 2nd S., IV. 152; A. B. Beaven.)

EAST, WILLIAM. Adm. at CORPUS CHRISTI, 1715. Of London. Perhaps s. of Thomas, of Southwark, gent.; adm. at the Inner Temple, 1715.

EAST, WILLIAM. Adm. pens. at EMMANUEL, May 11, 1725. Surgeon in London.

EAST, ——. Resident student at CHRIST'S, 1556-7.

EASTBURNE, THOMAS. Adm. sizar at EMMANUEL, May 1, 1676. Of Yorkshire. Matric. 1676, as Isburn.

EASTCHURCH, HENRY. Adm. pens. (age 18) at SIDNEY, May 27, 1669. 1st s. of John, gent., of Bishopsteignton, Devon. B. at St Giles', Devon. School, Ashburton (Mr Tidball). Matric. 1669.

EASTERBY, JOHN. Matric. pens. from MAGDALENE, Easter, 1613; B.A. 1616-7; M.A. 1620. Ord. deacon (Peterb.) Mar. 12; priest, Mar. 13, 1619-20, as 'fellow of Magdalene.' R. of Hatcliffe, Lincs., 1621-9.

EASTERBY or ESTERBIE, JOHN. Adm. sizar at SIDNEY, May 25, 1621. S. of Robert, gent. B. at Seaham, Durham. School, Newcastle. B.A. 1624-5. Ord. deacon (York) June, 1625; priest, June, 1626. Probably the 'Preacher of God's Word at Seaham.' Buried there May 20, 1661.

EASTFIELD, WILLIAM. Scholar and fellow of KING'S HALL, 1472-98; B.Can.L. 1475-6. R. of Wimpole, Cambs., 1474.

EASTGATE, JOHN. A friar. B.Civ.L. 1482-3.

ESTGATE, ——. Scholar at KING'S HALL, 1538-42.

EASTHORPE or ESTHORPE, BRIAN. Adm. at KING'S, a scholar from Eton, 1471; M.A. 1478-9. Chaplain to the Bishop of Winchester. (*Harwood*.)

EASTHORPE or ESTROP, REUBEN. Matric. pens. from CHRIST'S, Michs. 1615; B.A. 1617-8; M.A. 1621. Ord. deacon (Peterb.) May 7; priest, May 27, 1621. R. of Holme Pierrepont, Notts., 1625-9. R. of Brant Broughton, Lincs., 1629. One of these names minister of the Durham *classis*, 1645; appointed to Houghton-le-Spring. (*Peile*, I. 303; H. I. Longden.)

EASTLAND, JOHN. Adm. pens. (age 18) at PEMBROKE, June 26, 1710. S. of John, of Bransby, Lincs., gent. Matric. 1710-1; B.A. 1714-5. Ord. deacon (Lincoln) Sept. 25, 1715; priest, May 27, 1716. R. of Hanworth, Lincs., 1716. C. of Hackthorn, 1716.

EASTLAND, THOMAS. Adm. sizar at JESUS, Dec. 30, 1731. Of Nottinghamshire. Matric. 1735; Scholar; LL.B. 1738. Ord. deacon (Lincoln) June 17, 1739; priest, Feb. 22, 1740-1.

EASTOFT, *see* ESTOFT.

EASTON, *see* EASON *and also* ESTON.

EASTWICK or ESTWICK, JOHN. Adm. pens. at EMMANUEL, May 5, 1652. Of London. B.A. 1655-6; M.A. (University College, Oxford) 1658-9.

ESTWICKE, NICHOLAS. Matric. sizar from CHRIST'S, June, 1602. B. at Harrowden, Northants. B.A. 1605-6; M.A. 1609; B.D. 1616. Fellow, 1609-18. R. of Barnwell All Saints', Northants., 1617. R. of Warkton, 1617-58. Author, *Sermons*. Buried at Warkton, Sept. 9, 1658. (*Peile*, I. 241.)

ESTWICK, RICHARD. Matric. Fell.-Com. from QUEENS', Easter, 1580. Of Bedfordshire.

EASTWICK, WESTERNE (*alias* WEAVER). Adm. sizar at QUEENS', July, 1613.

EATON, *see also* EYTON *and* HEATON.

EATON, BYROM. D.D. 1671 (Incorp. from Oxford). S. of Samuel, R. of Grappenhall, Cheshire. Bapt. there, Feb. 6, 1613. Matric. from Brasenose, Oxford, Feb. 21, 1633-4, age 20; B.A. 1635; M.A. 1641; B.D. 1648; D.D. 1660. Fellow of Brasenose, 1641. Proctor, 1646. Principal of Gloucester Hall, 1662-92. R. of Nuneham Courtney, Oxon., 1660. Archdeacon of Stow, Lincs., 1677-83; and of Leicester, 1683. Died 1703. Will proved (Oxford) 1704. (*Vis. of Yorks.*, 1666; *Al. Oxon.*)

EATON, CENRICKE. Matric. pens. from ST JOHN'S, Michs. 1564.

ETON, CHRISTOPHER. Adm. (age 19) at KING'S, a scholar from Eton, May 17, 1532. Of Atherstone, Warws. Left before 1534.

EATON, EDWARD. Adm. sizar (age 19) at ST JOHN'S, Apr. 16, 1729. S. of Peter, of Derbyshire. B. at Raynor. School, Chesterfield (Mr Burrow). Matric. 1729; B.A. 1732-3.

ETON, GILBERT. B.Can.L. 1515-6.

EATON, HENRY. Adm. sizar (age 18) at ST JOHN'S, May 16, 1715. S. of Henry. B. in Cheshire. School, Northwich. Matric. 1715; B.A. 1718-9.

EATON, JOHN. 'B.A. Cambridge; 24 years in theology'; Incorp. at Oxford, 1572. (No such graduate found.) B.D. Oxford, 1572. (*See Al. Oxon.*)

EATON, JOHN. Matric. pens. from QUEENS', Easter, 1580. B. in St Laurence, Old Jewry. B.A. 1583-4; M.A. 1587. Ord. deacon (London) Jan. 12, 1591-2, age 26. C. of St Christopher-le-Stocks, London. R. of South Hanningfield, Essex, 1598-1638. Died 1638. Will (Consist. C. London) 1639. (A contemporary in *Al. Oxon.*)

EATON, JOHN. Matric. sizar from TRINITY, Michs. 1628; B.A. 1632-3. One of these names C. of Ravensden, Beds., in 1640; and V. of Old Warden, 1665-73. Buried there Jan. 18, 1672-3. (W. M. Noble.)

EATON, JOHN. Adm. pens. at ST CATHARINE'S, 1666; B.A. 1670-1. Signs for deacon's orders (London) Mar. 13, 1673-4; C. of Dagenham, Essex.

EATON, JOHN. Adm. Fell.-Com. at QUEENS', Nov. 2, 1721. Of Cheshire. Perhaps s. of Richard, of Budworth, Cheshire. Matric. at Brasenose College, Oxford, May 11, 1724, age 18; B.A. (Oxford) 1727-8; M.A. 1730. Incorp. at Cambridge, 1737. (*Al. Oxon.*)

EATON, JOHN. Matric. sizar from KING'S, Michs. 1730. S. of John. B. at Amersham, Bucks., 1711. Colleger at Eton, 1728-30. One of these names (M.A.) R. of Amersham, Bucks., 1746-53; resigned. Perhaps admon. (P.C.C.) 1761; of Steeple Aston, clerk.

EATON, JONATHAN. Adm. sizar at EMMANUEL, Mar. 1630-1. Of Cheshire. Doubtless 6th s. of Richard (? 1566), V. of Gt Budworth, Cheshire. Matric. 1633; B.A. 1633-4. Brother of Samuel (1620-1) and Nathaniel (1629-30).

EATON, JOSEPH. Adm. sizar (age 19) at PEMBROKE, May 25, 1675. S. of John, of Eaton, Cheshire, gent. Matric. 1675. Adm. student at Leyden, Oct. 9, 1685. M.D. of Leyden, 1686. Previously a nonconformist minister. Adm. Licentiate R.C.P. 1713. Practised at Macclesfield and elsewhere. (*Munk*, II. 38.)

EATON, LAURENCE. 'B.A. of CHRIST'S,' when ord. deacon (Peterb.) June 11, 1620; and priest, Mar. 17, 1621-2 (not found in our records).

EATON, MATTHEW. 'B.A. of TRINITY,' when ord. deacon (Peterb.) Sept. 21, 1585; priest, Mar. 27, 1586. Probably V. of Old Warden, Beds. Buried there Oct. 22, 1639. Not found in our records. (H. I. Longden.)

EATON, MATTHEW. Matric. pens. (age 17) from PEMBROKE, Michs. 1657. S. of John, farmer. B. at Congleton, Cheshire. B.A. 1658-9; M.A. 1662. Fellow, 1662-7. Ord. deacon (Lincoln) Mar. 10, 1660-1. R. of Shipdham, Norfolk, 1667-1673.

EATON, NATHANIEL. Matric. pens. from TRINITY, Lent, 1629-30. Scholar from Westminster, 1630. 5th s. of Richard (? 1566), V. of Gt Budworth, Cheshire. B. 1609. Obtained a license to pass to Leyden, 1632; 'age 22; resident in the house of Mr Theophilus Eaton in London.' After a visit to Franeker, in Holland, he went to New England, 1637. First Master of the School at Cambridge, Mass., which was afterwards organized as Harvard College, 1638-9; dismissed for cruelty. Absconded to England. Ph.D. and M.D. Padua, 1647. V. of Bishop's Castle, Salop, 1661. R. of Bideford, Devon, 1668. Died a prisoner for debt, 1674. Brother of Jonathan (1630-1), of Samuel (1620-1) and of Theophilus, the founder of New Haven. (*Al. Westmon.*; *D.N.B.*; *Fell*, 388.)

ETON or HETTON, RALPH. B.A. 1484-5; M.A. 1488. Fellow of CLARE, 1486. V. of Linton, Cambs., 1490. R. of Duxford St Peter, 1526.

EATON, REGINALD. Adm. pens. (age 17) at CAIUS, Oct. 25, 1577. S. of John, of Southwell, Notts. Chorister at Southwell. Matric. 1577-8, as Aeton. Went to Douay College, 1586. Ord. priest (Rheims) 1587. Entered the Jesuit Society, 1610. Missioner in St Francis Xavier College, 1637-41. Died there Mar. 23, 1641. (*Venn*, I. 93; Foley, *Records*, VII. 218.)

EATON, RICHARD. Matric. sizar from CLARE, Michs. 1566. Will of one of these names (P.C.C.) 1617. He was of Budworth, Cheshire, clerk; sons Theophilus, Samuel, Nathaniel, Jonathan. (J. Ch. Smith.)

EATON, RICHARD. Adm. pens. at EMMANUEL, July 27, 1725. Of Bedfordshire. S. of Alderman Eaton, of Derby. School, Derby. Matric. 1726; B.A. 1729-30. Ord. priest (Lincoln) July 1, 1733. R. of Downham, Norfolk, 1733-79. Will (P.C.C.) 1779. (*Derby School Reg.*)

ETON, ROBERT. Matric. pens. from PEMBROKE, Easter, 1545.

EATON, ROBERT. Adm. pens. (age 22) at CHRIST'S, Apr. 10, 1646. S. of Thomas. B. at High Walton, Cheshire. School, Prescott (Mr Tyrer). Matric. 1646. Resided seven years. Created M.A. at All Souls, Oxford, 1653. Master of Dedham School, Essex, in 1649. Perhaps R. of Inworth, Essex, 1654. Removed to Walton, Lancs.; ejected, 1660. Chaplain to Lord Delamere. Preacher at Prestwich. Died in Manchester, Aug. 1, 1701. (*Calamy*, II. 108; *Peile*, I. 504; *Al. Oxon.*)

EATON, ROBERT. Adm. pens. (age 16) at JESUS, Apr. 19, 1671. Of Lancashire. Matric. from St Edmund Hall, Oxford, July 27, 1672, age 16; B.A. (Oxford) 1674-5. (*Al. Oxon.*)

EATON, ROBERT. Adm. pens. (age 17) at JESUS, June 22, 1674. Of Cheshire. Probably s. of Robert, V. of Daresbury, Warrington. Matric. 1674.

EATON, SAMUEL. Matric. sizar from MAGDALENE, Lent, 1620-1. S. of Richard (? 1566), V. of Gt Budworth, Cheshire. B.A. 1624-5; M.A. 1628. Ord. deacon (Peterb.) Dec. 18; priest, Dec. 19, 1625. Went to New England, 1637, with his brother Theophilus, as pastor at New Haven, Connecticut; returned, 1640. Assistant to the Parliamentary commissioners of Cheshire. Afterwards a minister at Dukinfield, Cheshire. Died at Denton, Lancs., Jan. 9, 1664-5. Buried in the Chapel there. Brother of Nathaniel (1629-30) and Jonathan (1630-1). (*D.N.B.*; *F.M.G.*, 1152; J. G. Bartlett.)

EATON, SIMON. Matric. pens. from TRINITY, Easter, 1632.

EATON, THOMAS. Matric. sizar from CLARE, Michs. 1573.

EATON, THOMAS. Matric. pens. from QUEENS', Easter, 1584. Of London. Probably B.A. 1589-90. Ord. deacon (Lincoln) Mar. 7; priest, Mar. 8, 1595. R. of Brocklesby, Lincs., 1604-19. ('B.A.')

EATON, THOMAS. Matric. sizar from CLARE, Easter, 1613; B.A. 1616-7; M.A. 1620. Ord. deacon (Peterb.) Oct. 30; priest, Dec. 21, 1617. V. of Goxhill, Lincs., 1619. R. of Brocklesby. One of these names V. of Maxey, Northants., 1645. Buried there May 7, 1678.

EATON, THOMAS. M.A. 1632 (Incorp. from Oxford). S. of Thomas, of London. Matric. from Christ Church, July 2, 1624, age 19; B.A. (Hart Hall) 1627; M.A. 1630. Perhaps R. of Westenhanger, Kent, 1636. (*Al. Oxon.*)

ETON, WILLIAM. R. of Bletchley, Bucks., 1420. Resident pensioner at PETERHOUSE, 1425-6. Pays 13*s*. 4*d*. for his chamber. (*T. A. Walker.*)

EATON, WILLIAM. Matric. sizar from TRINITY, Easter, 1633; B.A. 1635-6; M.A. from Peterhouse, 1639. Ord. deacon (Norwich) Mar. 9, 1638-9; priest, Dec. 22, 1639. V. of Happishurgh, Norfolk, 1638-9. V. of Framsden, Suffolk, 1639-41. R. of Catfield, Norfolk, 1640. R. of Drayton, 1640-1662.

EATON, WILLIAM. Adm. sizar (age 17) at ST JOHN'S, Dec. 23, 1663. S. of William, farmer, of Littleport, Cambs. B. there. School, Little Wratting. Matric. 1664; B.A. 1667-8; M.A. 1675. Ord. deacon (Ely) Sept. 24, 1670.

EATON, ——. Adm. at CORPUS GHRISTI, 1569.

EBOT, BENJAMIN (1696), *see* **IBBOT.**

EBBOOTS, JOHN. Adm. pens. at PETERHOUSE, July 2, 1592.

EBDEN, *see also* **HEBDEN.**

EBDEN, GEORGE. Matric. pens. from TRINITY, Michs. 1576.

EBDEN, JOHN. B.A. 1543-4; M.A. from PETERHOUSE, 1547; D.D. 1564. Fellow of Peterhouse, 1547-54. Junior Proctor, 1550-1. Ord. priest (Ely) July 7, 1560, as Hebden. Preb. of Sarum. Preb. of York, 1552. Preb. of Ely, 1559-60. Archdeacon of Durham, 1560-2. Preb. of St Paul's, 1562-96. Preb. of Winchester, 1562-1612. Archdeacon of Winchester, 1571-75. Died Nov. 16, 1614, aged 98. M.I. in Magdalen Hospital, Winchester. (H. M. Wood.)

EBDEN, ROBERT. Matric. pens. from CLARE, 1565; B.A. 1568-9.

EBDON, ROBERT. Matric. pens. from TRINITY, Easter, 1571.

EBDEN, THOMAS. Matric. sizar from CAIUS, Lent, 1580-1.

EBDYN, ——. Sizar at PETERHOUSE, 1546-7.

EBRALL, WILLIAM. Adm. sizar at CLARE, Mar. 14, 1683-4. Of Gayton, Northants. Matric. 1683-4; B.A. 1687-8.

EBURNE, *see also* **HEBBURN.**

EBURNE, JOHN. Matric. pens. from MAGDALENE, Easter, 1580; B.A. 1583-4. V. of 'Freston,' Lincs., 1595.

EBURNE, SAMUEL. Adm. pens. (age 18) at ST JOHN'S, Oct. 3, 1663. S. of Richard, of St Antholin's, London. B. there. School, Merchant Taylors'. Signs for deacon's orders (London) Mar. 1, 1666-7; for priest's, June 1, 1667. R. of Stocking Pelham, Herts., 1667.

ECCLES, GEORGE. Adm. pens. at QUEENS', Mar. 13, 1732-3. Of Lancashire. Matric. 1732-3; B.A. 1736-7; M.A. 1740.

ECCLES, JOSEPH. Adm. sizar (age 18) at ST JOHN'S, Apr. 29, 1723. S. of Joseph, farmer, of Yorkshire. B. at Coley, near Halifax. School, Hipperholme (Mr Sharpe). Matric. 1723; B.A. 1726-7. V. of Rotherham, Yorks., 1733-4. Died 1734.

ECCLES or EGLES, THOMAS. Matric. sizar from TRINITY, Michs. 1582; B.A. from St John's, 1586-7. Ord. deacon and priest (Peterb.) Apr. 9, 1587. Will of one of these names (York) 1612; of Adwick-le-Street, Yorks., clerk. (J. Ch. Smith.)

ECCLESHALL, JOSEPH. Adm. sizar at EMMANUEL, June 21, 1650. Of Staffordshire. Matric. 1650; B.A. 1653-4. Lecturer at Dudley, Staffs., 1654. V. of Sedgley, 1657-62; ejected. Afterwards preached in Staffordshire. Buried at Sedgley, Dec. 22, 1692. (*Calamy*, II. 401; *Wm. Salt Arch. Soc.*, 1915.)

ECCLESTON, *see also* **EGLESTON.**

ECCLESTON or EGLYSTON, ALEXANDER. Adm. at KING'S, a scholar from Eton, 1490. According to *Harwood* he was D.D. Cole seems to identify him with John (1493-4).

ECCLESTON, EDWARD. Adm. pens. at EMMANUEL, May 17, 1662. Of Lancashire. S. of William, of Charnock Richards. School, Manchester. Migrated to Oxford. B.A. (Lincoln College) 1665. R. of Old Sevenford, Worcs., 1673. (*Al. Oxon.*; Mumford, *Manchester Gr. School.*)

ECCLESTON, HENRY. Adm. at KING'S, a scholar from Eton, 1477; B.A. 1480-1; M.A. 1485, as Egleston.

ECCLESTON, JOHN. B.A. 1493-4; M.A. 1497-8; B.D. 1503-4; D.D. 1505-6. Master of JESUS College, 1506-16. Appointed by the crown (Bishopric of Ely being vacant). Vice-Chancellor, 1506, 1514, 1515. R. of Gt Shelford, Cambs., in 1505. Chancellor of Ely. Died Feb. 1515-6. (*Cooper*, I. 17; A. Gray.)

ECCLESTON, JOHN. Adm. pens. (age 17) at CHRIST'S, Apr. 23, 1629. S. of Robert. B. in London. School, London. Matric. 1629. Resided four years. Probably s. and h. of Robert, of Laundon, Bucks., Esq.; adm. at Lincoln's Inn, May 28, 1633. (*Peile*, I. 399.)

ECCLESTON, ROBERT. Adm. pens. (age 16) at SIDNEY, May 2, 1632. S. of Robert, Esq., of Laundon Grange, Bucks. School, Aldermanbury (Mr Ezek. Woodward). Matric. 1632; B.A. from Magdalene, 1635-6; M.A. 1639.

ECCLESTON, THOMAS. Adm. at KING'S, Lent, 1564-5.

ECKERSHALL, ELIAS. Adm. sizar at EMMANUEL, Mar. 3, 1595-6. Matric. 1596; B.A. 1603-4.

ECKERSALL, JAMES. Matric. pens. from ST JOHN'S, Lent, 1577-8.

ECKARSALL, PETER. Adm. sizar at EMMANUEL, Michs. 1584. Matric. 1584; B.A. 1588-9; M.A. 1593. Incorp. at Oxford, 1591. Ord. deacon and priest (Peterb.) Sept. 5, 1595.

ECKLEY, BENJAMIN. M.A. from PETERHOUSE, 1728. S. of Richard, of Worcestershire. Matric. at Merton College, Oxford, Feb. 28, 1720-1, age 17; B.A. (Exeter, Oxford) 1724-5.

ECOPPE, GEORGE. Adm. sizar at CHRIST'S, July 7, 1623. S. of William. B. at Mansfield, Notts. School, Richmond, Yorks. (Mr Bathurst). Matric. 1624; B.A. 1627-8; M.A. 1637. R. of St Pancras, Soper Lane, London, 1636-43; sequestered. (*Peile*, I. 354.)

ECOPPE, WILLIAM. B.Can.L. *c.* 1464; resident before 1454.

EDBOROUGH, RICHARD. Adm. sizar at QUEENS', Apr. 18, 1712. Of Kent. Matric. 1712; B.A. 1715-6. Ord. deacon (Lincoln) Mar. 5, 1720-1. Doubtless V. of Waldershare, Kent, 1738-9. Died Oct. 1739. (L. *Mag.*)

EDDEY or EDDYE, WILLIAM. Matric. sizar from TRINITY, Michs. 1579. B. at Bristol. B.A. from Trinity Hall, 1582-3; M.A. from Trinity, 1586. V. of Cranbrook, Kent, 1591-1616, Married (1) Mary Fosten, Nov. 20, 1587, (2) Sarah Tayler, widow, Feb. 22, 1613-4. Buried at Cranbrook, Nov. 23, 1616. (H. G. Harrison.)

EDDOWES, RICHARD. Adm. sizar (age 18) at ST JOHN'S, May 18, 1750. S. of William, box maker. B. at Dillon. School, Dillon (Mr Slade). Matric. 1750; B.A. 1754. Ord. deacon (Lichfield) June 9, 1754; priest, Sept. 21, 1755. C. of Ravenstone, Derbs. (*Scott-Mayor*, III. 596.)

EDDOWES, ROGER. Matric. sizar from KING'S, Easter, 1688; B.A. 1691-2.

EDEN, ALEXIUS. Adm. pens. (age 17) at CHRIST'S, June 25, 1651. S. of Colonel Robert, of West Auckland and Windlestone. B. in Co. Durham. School, Gisborne, Yorks. (Mr Smelt). Matric. 1651. Adm. at Gray's Inn, June 23, 1653. Married Eleanor, dau. of John Hodgson, of Manor House, Co. Durham. Died *s.p.* (*Peile*, I. 544; *Vis. of Durham*, 1666; H. M. Wood.)

EDEN, CHARLES. Adm. pens. at PETERHOUSE, July 8, 1618. Of Thetford, Suffolk. Matric. 1618-9; Scholar, 1619; B.A. 1621-2; M.A. from Trinity Hall, 1625. Fellow of Trinity Hall, 1624-42. Senior Proctor, 1645-6. V. of Wood Dalling and Swannington, Norfolk. Commissary, 1638. V. of Wethersfield, Essex, till 1642. Buried at St Edward's, Cambridge, Feb. 26, 1647-8. Will proved (V.C.C.) 1647. (*T. A. Walker*, 10.)

EDEN, HENRY. Adm. pens. (age 16) at MAGDALENE, June 22, 1659. S. of Henry, Esq., of Shincliffe. Bapt. at St Oswald's, Durham, Mar. 25, 1642. School, Newcastle. Matric. 1659; B.A. 1662; M.D. 1669 (*Lit. Reg.*) as 'Edes.' Buried at St Oswald's, Durham, July 29, 1702. Father of the next. (H. M. Wood.)

EDEN, HENRY. Adm. pens. (age 16) at TRINITY, May 3, 1693. S. of Henry (above). B. at Durham. Bapt. at St Oswald's, Sept. 1676. School, Durham (Mr Tho. Rudd). Matric. 1693; Scholar, 1695; B.A. 1696-7; M.A. 1700; B.D. 1708. Fellow, 1699. Taxor, 1702. Ord. deacon (Lincoln) June 29, 1701; priest, Apr. 12, 1702. Buried at St Oswald's, Durham, June 9, 1711. Will proved (V.C.C.) 1711. (H. M. Wood.)

EDEN, JOHN. Adm. pens. at QUEENS', June 13, 1611.

EDEN, JOHN. Adm. Fell.-Com. at EMMANUEL, 1624. Matric. pens. 1624. Doubtless s. and h. of Sir Thomas (1587), of Sudbury and of Ballingdon, Essex, Knt. Age 4 in 1611. Adm. at Lincoln's Inn, Apr. 26, 1626. Of Ballingdon, Esq. Married Anne, dau. of Richard Harlakenden, Esq., 1629. Buried in Sudbury Church. Probably brother of William (1632). (*Vis. of Essex*, 1634; J. J. Howard, *Vis. of Suffolk*.)

EDEN, JOHN. Adm. pens. at QUEENS', Apr. 12, 1635; readm. as Fell.-Com. July 8, 1635. Of Durham. Probably s. of Robert, of Windlestone, Durham. B. Aug. 17, 1616. Of West Auckland. Married Catharine, dau. of Sir Thomas Layton, Knt. Buried at St Helen's, Auckland, 1675. Father of Layton (1670). (*Vis. of Durham*, 1666; H. M. Wood.)

EDEN, LAYTON. Adm. pens. (age 16) at PETERHOUSE, Apr. 30, 1670. S. of John (above), of West Auckland, Durham. B. at Layton, Yorks. (his mother's home). School, Brignall. Matric. 1670; Scholar, 1670; B.A. 1673-4; M.A. 1677. Ord. deacon (Durham) Sept. 19, 1675. V. of Hartburn, Northumberland, 1685-1735. Buried there Dec. 11, 1735. Father of the next and William (1698). (*T. A. Walker*, 141; *Vis. of Durham*, 1666.)

EDEN, RALPH. Adm. pens. (age 17) at PETERHOUSE, Apr. 11, 1705. Of Northumberland. S. of Layton (above). Bapt. at Hartburn, June 11, 1687. School, Houghton-le-Spring, Durham. Scholar, 1705; Matric. 1705-6. Ord. deacon (York) June, 1718; priest, May, 1719. P.C. of St Margaret, Durham, 1722-32; deprived. Died in Yorkshire. (*T. A. Walker*; Pedigree in Hutchinson, *Durham*, III; H. M. Wood.)

EDEN, RICHARD. B.Can.L. 1519-20; D.Can.L. (on Wolsey's visit) 1520. Possibly of KING'S HALL, 1508-14. R. of Gt Waldringfield, Suffolk, 1508-45. R. of Gestingthorpe, Essex, 1514-6. V. of St Gregory and St Peter, Sudbury, Suffolk, 1516-51. Archdeacon of Middlesex, 1516-51. Preb. of Sarum, 1518-51. R. of Dickleburgh, Norfolk, 1531-51. Warden of the College of St Gregory, Sudbury, till the surrender, 1544. Preb. of Tettenhall, Staffs., 1533-48. Died 1551. Will (P.C.C.) printed in Howard's *Vis. of Suffolk*. (*Cooper*, I. 104.)

EDEN or IDEN, RICHARD. Studied at QUEENS', under Sir Thomas Smith. B. in Herefordshire, *c.* 1521. Scholar of Christ's, 1535-7; B.A. 1538-9; M.A. 1544. Held a position in the Treasury, 1544-6. Secretary to Sir W. Cecil. In France and Germany, 1562-9. Returned to England, 1569. Perhaps M.P. for Sudbury, 1572. Distinguished as a translator of travels and other historical works. Died in 1576. (*D.N.B.*)

EDEN, RICHARD. Matric. pens. from TRINITY HALL, Lent, 1557-8; Scholar, June 1, 1561. Doubtless of Hanningfield, Essex. S. of Thomas, of Sudbury. Will proved (Consist. C. London) 1604; leaves plate to Dr Cowell, Master of Trinity Hall. Brother of Thomas (1551), father of Thomas (1593). (*Vis. of Essex*, 1634; J. Ch. Smith.)

EDEN, ROBERT. Matric. pens. from QUEENS', Easter, 1610. Of Durham. Perhaps Colonel Ro. Eden buried at St Helen's, Auckland, 1662. (H. M. Wood.)

EDEN, ROBERT. M.A. 1734 (Incorp. from Oxford). S. of Robert, of Newcastle, merchant. Bapt. at All Saints', Newcastle, Aug. 26, 1701. Matric. from Brasenose College, Feb. 21, 1716-7, age 15; B.A. (Lincoln College) 1720; M.A. (University) 1723; B.D. 1734-5; D.D. 1754. Proctor, 1733. Archdeacon of Winchester, 1743-9. Preb. of Worcester, 1747-56. Preb. of Winchester, 1749-59. Died July 11, 1759. Buried in Winchester Cathedral. Admon. (P.C.C.) 1759. (*Al. Oxon.*)

EDEN, THOMAS. Matric. Fell.-Com. from TRINITY HALL, Easter, 1551. S. and h. of Thomas, of Sudbury, Suffolk. Of Sudbury, Knt. High Sheriff, 1596. Knighted, July 23, 1603. Died June 30, 1614. Will (P.C.C.) 1614. Brother of Richard (1557-8), father of the next. (*Vis. of Essex*, 1634; J. J. Howard, *Vis. of Suffolk*.)

EDEN, THOMAS. Matric. Fell.-Com. from JESUS, Michs. 1587. S. and h. of Thomas (above), of Sudbury, Suffolk, Esq. Adm. at Gray's Inn, Apr. 23, 1589. Knighted, June 29, 1604. Married Mary, dau. of Bryan Darcy, of Essex, Esq. Died Jan. 12, 1616. Will (P.C.C.) 1616. Perhaps father of John (1624) and William (1632). (*Vis. of Essex*, 1634.)

EDEN, THOMAS. Adm. at PEMBROKE, *c.* 1593. S. of Richard (1557-8), of South Hanningfield, Essex. Scholar of Trinity Hall, 1596; LL.B. 1600; LL.D. 1614. Fellow, 1599-1626. Master, 1626-45. Professor of Law, Gresham College, 1613-40. Admitted advocate, Nov. 4, 1615. Master in Chancery, 1625. M.P. for the University, 1626, 1628, 1640 (twice). Chancellor of diocese of Ely, 1630. Member of the Admiralty Committee, 1645. Died in London, July 18, 1645. Buried in Trinity Hall Chapel. Benefactor. Will, P.C.C. (*D.N.B.*; *Trin. Hall. Coll. Hist.*, 135; *Vis. of Essex*, 1634.)

EDEN, THOMAS. Adm. scholar at TRINITY HALL, Jan. 9, 1700-1. S. of Sir Robert, Bart., of West Auckland. Bapt. at St Helen's, Sept. 27, 1682. School, Newcastle. Matric. 1699; LL.B. 1705; LL.D. 1711. Ord. deacon (Durham) June 8, 1707; priest, Sept. 21, 1707. R. of Winston, Durham, 1709-54. Preb. of Durham, 1711-54. R. of Brancepeth, 1749. Married, at St Mary-le-Bow, Durham, Aug. 19, 1731, Dorothy Shafto, widow of Robert, of Whitworth. Died Mar. 3, 1754, aged 71. Buried in Durham Cathedral. (*Burke*; H. M. Wood.)

EDEN, WILLIAM. Adm. pens. at EMMANUEL, Aug. 22, 1590.

EDEN, WILLIAM. Matric. sizar from QUEENS', Michs. 1619. Of Northamptonshire. B.A. 1624. Ord. deacon (York) June, 1626; priest, Feb. 1626-7.

EDEN, WILLIAM. Adm. pens. at EMMANUEL, Apr. 10, 1632. Of Suffolk. Matric. 1633. Probably s. of Sir Thomas (1587), of Sudbury, Knt.; adm. at Lincoln's Inn, June 2, 1635. Probably brother of John (1624).

EDEN, WILLIAM. Adm. pens. (age 19) at PETERHOUSE, July 7, 1698. Of Durham. S. of Layton (1670), V. of Hartburn. School, Ryton. Scholar, 1698. M.A. 1702 (Incorp. from Glasgow). Student at Glasgow for four years. B.A. (Glasgow) 1697; M.A. 1702. Ord. deacon (Durham) Sept 21, 1701; priest, Sept. 19, 1703. P.C. of St Helen, Auckland, 1703-14. V. of Stockton, 1714-5. R. of Elwick, 1715-41. V. of St Nicholas, Durham, 1720-2. Died 1741. (*T. A. Walker*, 201.)

EDEN, ——. Adm. sizar at KING'S, Lent, 1576-7.

EDEN, ——. Pens. at PETERHOUSE, 1587-8.

EDENHAM, JOHN, *see* EDIMAN.

EDERMAN, FRANCIS. Licensed to practise surgery, 1562.

EEDES, FRANCIS. Adm. at CORPUS CHRISTI, 1687. Of Warwickshire. M.B. 1694.

EDES, HENRY. M.D. 1669 (*Lit. Reg.*), *see* EDEN.

EDES, HENRY. Matric. pens. from QUEENS', Easter, 1646. Of Suffolk. Migrated to Oxford B.A. (Magdalen Hall) 1648-9; M.A. 1651; D.D. (Cambridge) 1669 (*Lit. Reg.*). Fellow of Lincoln College, Oxford. R. of Chinnor, Oxon., 1660. V. of Amport, Hants., 1661. Canon and Precentor of Chichester, 1662-1703. R. of Felpham, Sussex, 1670-96. Supporter of the Duke of Monmouth; committed to prison, 1685. Chaplain to the King. Died 1703. Will, P.C.C. (*Al. Oxon.*; Le Neve, *Mon.*, v. 73.)

EDES, JOHN. Matric. pens. from ST JOHN'S, Easter, 1607; B.A. 1610-1; M.A. 1614. Incorp. at Oxford, 1619. Perhaps R. of Lawford, Essex, 1615-58. Died Apr. 12, 1658. Will, P.C.C. (J. Ch. Smith.)

EDES, JOHN. Matric. sizar from ST CATHARINE'S, Easter, 1647; B.A. 1650-1; M.A. 1654. Incorp. at Oxford, 1655. V. of Lillington, Warws., 1662. (*Al. Oxon.*)

EADES or EEDES, WILLIAM. Adm. pens. (age 16) at CHRIST'S, June 1, 1657. S. of Francis. B. at Warwick. Schools, Warwick (Mr Glover) and (exhibitioner from) Charterhouse. Matric. 1657; B.A. 1660-1; M.A. 1664. Fellow, 1662-8. C. of Fen Drayton, Cambs. R. of Horseheath, 1669-1709. Buried there Apr. 29, 1709. Will (P.C.C.). (*Peile*, I. 578; C. E. Parsons, *Horseheath*.)

EDESBURIE, FRANCIS, *see* EDISBURY.

EDGAR, BENJAMIN. Matric. sizar from ST JOHN'S, *c.* 1594.

EDGAR, EZECHIEL. Adm. sizar at EMMANUEL, Apr. 2, 1594-5. S. of Mark. B. at Dalston, Cumberland. Bapt. there, Oct. 7, 1575. Scholar; Matric. *c.* 1595; B.A. 1598-9; M.A. 1602. Incorp. at Oxford, 1603. Ord. deacon (London) May 26, 1605. C. of Bromley, Kent. Ord. priest, Dec. 22, 1605. R. of Hawstead, Suffolk, 1608-48. Died 1648. Father of the next, with whom *Al. Oxon.* seems to confuse him. (G. B. Routledge.)

EDGAR, EZECHIEL. Adm. pens. at EMMANUEL, Feb. 7, 1637-8. Of Suffolk. S. of Ezechiel (above). Matric. 1637-8; B.A. 1641-2. Perhaps R. of Gt Stanmore, Middlesex, 1662-3 ('M.A.'). Died 1663.

EDGAR, FRANCIS. Matric. pens. from PETERHOUSE, Michs. 1598; B.A. 1601-2. Perhaps s. of William, of Glemham, Suffolk. If so, died 1605. (*Manors of Suffolk*, v. 139.)

EDGAR, FRANCIS. Adm. sizar at EMMANUEL, 1608. Matric. 1608; B.A. 1612-3; M.A. 1616. Ord. priest (York) Feb. 1612-3 Doubtless V. of Aldborough, Yorks., 1613; of Preston-in-Holderness, 1622-4; of Winestead, 1624-54. Buried there May 16, 1654.

EDGAR, HENRY. Adm. sizar (age 15) at CAIUS, Nov. 25, 1564. S. of Edward, of Battisford, Suffolk. School, Stowmarket. Matric. 1564; Scholar of Trinity, 1568; B.A. from Trinity, 1569-70. Of Dennington, Suffolk, gent. Lord of the Manor of Pyezalls, Brockdish. Died May 7, 1619. M.I. at Dennington. Will, P.C.C. (*Venn*, I. 56.)

EDGAR, HENRY. Adm. Fell.-Com. (age 20) at CHRIST'S, June 16, 1647. S. of Miles, of Eye, Suffolk, Esq. B. there. Bapt. Apr. 23, 1628. School, Eye (Mr Echard). Adm. at Gray's Inn, Feb. 8, 1647-8. (*Peile*, I. 515; *Vis. of Suffolk*, 1664.)

EDGAR, HENRY. Adm. Fell.-Com. at EMMANUEL, June 13, 1710, from Clare. Of Suffolk.

EDGAR, MILESON. Adm. Fell.-Com. at QUEENS', Dec. 27, 1693. S. of Mileson, of Norton and Ipswich. School, Woodbridge. Adm. at the Middle Temple, Feb. 20, 1694-5. Of Ipswich. Died Nov. 8, 1713, aged 37. M.I. at St Mary-le-Tower. (Le Neve, *Mon.*, II. 264.)

EDGAR, MILESON. Adm. pens. (age 18) at EMMANUEL, Oct. 10, 1747. S. of Mileson, Esq. B. in Ipswich. School, Kingston-on-Thames. Died Mar. 29, 1770. (*L. Mag.*)

EDGAR, NICHOLAS. Matric. pens. from CORPUS CHRISTI, Easter, 1610. Of Suffolk. Probably s. of Nicholas. Bapt. at Gt Glemham, Suffolk, Sept. 13, 1591. Killed at the Isle of Rhé, 1627. Brother of Thomas (1611). (*Davy MSS.*)

EDGAR, PHILIP. Adm. pens. at TRINITY, May 30, 1653. Of Suffolk.

EDGAR, PLAYTERS. Adm. pens. (age 17) at CAIUS, July 9, 1680. S. of Thomas, gent., of Gt Glemham, Suffolk. B. there. Bapt. Apr. 14, 1663. Schools, Kelsale (Mr Barton) and Eye. Matric. 1680-1. Of Gt Glemham, Esq. Buried at Sotterley, Sept. 10, 1728. (*Venn*, I. 465; *Vis. of Suffolk*, 1664.)

EDGAR, ROBERT. Adm. pens. at QUEENS', Feb. 22, 1700-1. Of Suffolk. Doubtless s. and h. of Devereux, of Ipswich, Esq. Bapt. July 28, 1682. Matric. 1701. Adm. at Gray's Inn, May 31, 1701. High Sheriff of Suffolk, 1747. (Burke, *L.G.*)

EDGAR, ROBERT. Adm. pens. (age 19) at EMMANUEL, June 7, 1751. S. of Robert, Esq. B. at Ipswich. School, Dedham. Matric. 1751. Adm. at the Middle Temple, May 15, 1751.

EDGAR, THOMAS. M.A. 1566 (after 12 years' study in arts).

EDGAR, THOMAS. Matric. pens. from CHRIST'S, Michs. 1572. Perhaps s. of Nicholas, of Glemham, Suffolk. One of these names adm. at Lincoln's Inn, Aug. 20, 1579. Of Suffolk. Barrister, from Furnival's Inn. (*Peile*, I. 123; *Vis. of Suffolk.*)

EDGAR, THOMAS. Adm. at CORPUS CHRISTI, 1611. Of Suffolk. Doubtless s. of Nicholas, of Gt Glemham, Suffolk. Buried there . 10, 1628-9. Brother of Nicholas (1610). (*Davy MSS.*)Mar

EDGAR, THOMAS. Adm. pens. (age 16) at CAIUS, Apr. 13, 1661. S. of Stephen, gent., of Wallington, Norfolk. B. there. School, Lynn (Mr Bell). Matric. 1661. Lord of the Manor of Wereham Hall. (*Venn*, I. 411.)

EDGAR, THOMAS. Adm. pens. at QUEENS', Oct. 27, 1662. Of Suffolk. S. and h. of Thomas, of Ipswich, reader of Gray's Inn. Bapt. at St Mary-le-Tower, May 20, 1646. Matric. 1662. Adm. at Gray's Inn, Nov. 19, 1658. Barrister-at-law. Age 19 in 1664. Died of small-pox. Buried at St Mary-le-Tower, Dec. 7, 1677. (*Vis. of Suffolk*, 1664; *E. Anglian*, x. 118.)

EDGAR, THOMAS. M.A. from EMMANUEL, 1709. S. of John, of Marten, Dorset. Matric. from St Mary Hall, Oxford, Feb. 18, 1680-1, age 18; B.A. (Oxford) 1684. V. of Charlton Canfield, Somerset, 1693-1736. R. of Stowell, 1709-36. P.C. of Seaburrow, 1720. (*Al. Oxon.*; F. S. Hockaday.)

EDGAR, WILLIAM. Adm. pens. (19) at MAGDALENE, Apr. 17, 1730. S. of John, Esq. Bapt. at Gt Glemham, Suffolk. School, Monk Soham. Died at Little Bealings. Buried at Glemham, Mar. 22, 1765. (*Davy MSS.*)

EDGAR, ——. Adm. pens. at TRINITY HALL, Dec. 18, 1702.

EDGBASTON or EGBASTIAN, THOMAS. Matric. pens. from TRINITY HALL, Easter, 1624; B.A. 1628; M.A. 1633. Ord. deacon (Norwich) Sept. 20, 1628; priest, Jan. 4, 1628-9.

EDGE, FANE. Adm. sizar at EMMANUEL, Dec. 16, 1710. Of Sussex. S. of Peter, clerk. B. Dec. 20, 1692. Of founder's kin. Exhibitioner from Charterhouse. Matric. 1712. Ord. deacon (Ely) Mar. 13, 1714-5; priest (London) June 12, 1720. R. of Stow Maries, Essex. C. of Lavenham, Suffolk. Married Apr. 26, 1722, Margaret Fiske, of Shimplingthorne, Suffolk. Buried at Lavenham, Nov. 6, 1727. Father of Peter (1742).

EDGE, GILES. Matric. pens. from ST JOHN'S, Easter, 1567. *Sup.* for incorporation at Oxford, as B.A. 1574.

EDGE, ISAAC. Adm. sizar at TRINITY, Apr. 22, 1682. Matric. 1682; Scholar, 1685; B.A. 1685-6. Ord. deacon (Gloucester) May 21, 1687. C. of Somersall, Derbs.

EDGE, MICHAEL. Adm. sizar at CLARE, June 12, 1651. Matric. 1651; B.A. 1654-5; M.A. 1658. Perhaps ord. deacon (Lincoln) Mar. 10, 1660-1; priest, Mar. 13, 1660-1. V. of Uttoxeter, Staffs., 1658-82. R. of Yoxall, 1682-83. Married, July 5, 1659, Jane Pierce. Buried at Yoxall, June 1, 1683. (*Wm. Salt. Arch. Soc.*, 1915.)

EDGE, PETER. Adm. sizar (age 17) at EMMANUEL, July 22, 1740. S. of Fane (1710), clerk. B. at Lavenham, Suffolk. School, Lavenham. Matric. 1740-1; B.A. 1744-5; M.A. 1748. Ord. deacon (Norwich) Mar. 1744-5; priest, Mar. 1746-7. C. of Rattlesden, Suffolk. Chaplain to the Earl of Westmorland, Lord-Lieutenant of Ireland. Preb. of Raphoe and R. of Drimholme. Married, 1746, Anne Truelove, of Ipswich. Afterwards C. of Drinkstone, Suffolk. Died Dec. 29, 1782. Buried at Rushmere. Will (P.C.C.) 1783; of Ipswich. (H. G. Harrison; *Davy MSS.*)

EDGE, RALPH. Adm. pens. at JESUS, June 30, 1705. Of Nottinghamshire. Doubtless s. of Richard Conway (who assumed the name of Edge, 1684). B. Aug. 24, 1689. Matric. 1705. Of Strelley Hall, Notts., Esq. High Sheriff of Notts., 1760. Died Oct. 26, 1766. Brother of the next. (Burke, *L.G.*)

EDGE, RICHARD. M.A. from SIDNEY, 1726. S. of Richard Edge (formerly Conway), of Strelley, Notts., gent. Matric. from Magdalen Hall, Oxford, Apr. 30, 1719, age 17; B.A. 1722. Ord. deacon (Lincoln, *Litt. dim.* from York) Sept. 20, 1724. Died young. (*Al. Oxon.*)

EDGE, THOMAS. Adm. sizar (age 17) at CHRIST'S, Nov. 25, 1645. From King James' College, Edinburgh. S. of Oliver. B. at Withington, Lancs. School, Newton (Mr Hulme). Matric. 1645. Minister at Gostree, Middlewich. R. of Gosworth, till 1662; ejected. Afterwards preacher at Withington. Died Feb. 21, 1678-9 (or June 21, 1678). (*Peile*, I. 500; *Calamy*, I. 263.)

EDGE, ——. Adm. at CORPUS CHRISTI, 1544.

EDGECOMBE, JOSEPH. Adm. pens. at EMMANUEL, Nov. 1646. Of Devon. Migrated to Oxford. B.A. from New Inn Hall, 1650.

EDGECOMBE, PEARSE. Matric. Fell.-Com. from ST JOHN'S, Easter, 1626. S. and h. of Sir Richard, of Edgcombe, Knt. B. 1609. M.P. for Newport, Cornwall, 1628 and 1662-7; for Camelford, 1640 (twice). Died Jan. 6, 1666-7. Will (P.C.C.) 1667. One 'Perseus Edsgaimb' adm. student at Leyden, June 25, 1629. (*Vis. of Devon*, 1620; *Al. Oxon.*; Jacob's *Peerage*, II. 553.)

EDGSCOMB, RICHARD. Matric. Fell.-Com. from ST JOHN'S Easter, 1627.

EDGCUMBE, RICHARD. Adm. Fell.-Com. (age 17) at TRINITY, May 25, 1697. S. of Sir Richard, K.B., of Mount Edgcumbe, Devon. B. there, 1680. Matric. 1697; M.A. 1698. M.P. for Cornwall, 1701; for St Germans, 1701; for Plympton, 1702-34, 1741; for Lostwithiel, 1734-41. Created Lord Edgcumbe, 1742. Lord Lieutenant of Cornwall, 1742-58. Chancellor of the Duchy of Lancaster, 1743. Privy Councillor for Ireland, 1734; for England, 1744. Died Nov. 22, 1758. (*D.N.B.*; Jacob's *Peerage*, II. 553; A. B. Beaven.)

EDGCOMBE, ROBERT. Adm. pens. at SIDNEY, June 28, 1622. S. of Matthew, gent. B. at South Tavistock, Devon. School, South Tavistock (Mr Tho. Cole). Matric. 1622; B.A. 1625-6.

EDGECOMBE, WILLIAM. Adm. (age 17) at KING'S, a scholar from Eton, Aug. 13, 1547. Of Milton, Devon. Matric. 1547. Left in 1549. Will of one of these names (Exeter) 1577, R. of Stowford, Devon.

EDGEWORTH, EDWARD. Matric. sizar from ST JOHN'S, Easter, 1595; B.A. 1599-1600.

EDGEWORTH, EDWARD. Studied at Cambridge; but not found in the records. Preb. of St Patrick's, Dublin, 1565. V. of Kirby Green, Lincs., 1571. Preb. of Lincoln, 1575. R. of St Anne, Aldersgate St, 1579–80 and 1581–7. V. of St Albans, Herts., 1579. V. of Barking, Essex, 1584–7. Vicar-choral, Christ Church, Dublin, 1586. R. of Carrickfergus, 1590. Bishop of Down and Connor, 1593–5. Died 1595, at Dublin. Buried at St Michan's. (*Cooper*, II. 176.)

EDGLEY or EDGELEY (*alias* ALLEN), FRANCIS. Adm. pens. (age 17) at CHRIST'S, Oct. 2, 1661. S. of Thomas. B. at Gretton, Northants. School, Uppingham (Mr Meres). Matric. 1661–2. Adm. at Gray's Inn, Aug. 3, 1663; as s. of Thomas Edgeley (*alias* Allen).

EDGELY, GEORGE. Matric. sizar from TRINITY, Easter, 1620; B.A. 1623–4; M.A. 1627. Created D.D. (Oxford) Feb. 22, 1643–4. Preb. of Chichester, 1629. V. of Donnington, Sussex, 1630; and of Lymister, 1634. R. of Nuthurst, 1642–7. (*Al. Oxon.*)

EDGERLY, JOHN. Adm. sizar (age 18) at TRINITY, Mar. 19, 1724–5. S. of Charles, of Bedford. School, Bedford (Mr Priaulx). Matric. 1725; B.A. 1728–9. Ord. deacon (Lincoln) Mar. 2, 1728–9. V. of Stanford, Norfolk, 1730–51. R. of Little Dunham, 1741–7.

EDGELEY, SAMUEL. Adm. pens. at CLARE, May 2, 1651; B.A. 1654; M.A. 1659. Chaplain to Sir Thomas Wilbraham, till 1675. V. of Acton, Cheshire, 1675–1721. Died Dec. 18, 1721, aged 89.

EDGELEY, SAMUEL. Adm. pens. at ST CATHARINE'S, 1675. Matric. 1675; B.A. 1678–9; M.A. 1682. Ord. deacon (London) Dec. 24, 1682. R. of Wandsworth, Surrey, 1688–1732. Preb. of St Paul's, 1705–32. Died Mar. 20, 1732. Buried at Wandsworth, aged 72. (*Manning and Bray*, III. 357.)

EDGLY, THOMAS. Matric. pens. from JESUS, Easter, 1565.

EDGLY, THOMAS. Adm. pens. at EMMANUEL, July, 1664. Matric. 1665; B.A. 1667–8; M.A. 1671. Ord. deacon (Peterb.) May 29, 1670.

EDGLEY, WILLIAM. Adm. sizar (age 16) at CHRIST'S, Nov. 1, 1673. S. of William. B. at Newmarket. School, Bradley, Suffolk (Mr Billingsley). Matric. 1674; B.A. 1677–8; M.A. 1682. Ord. deacon (Lincoln) Dec. 1679; priest (Norwich) Mar. 1682–3. R. of Stradishall, Suffolk, 1701–33. Died 1733. Buried at Stradishall. (*Peile*, II. 49.)

EDGUARD, DAVID, *see* **EDWARDS.**

EDIMAN or EDNAM, JOHN. B.A. 1468, as Ednam; B.D. 1479–80; D.D. 1488. Of Norwich diocese. Probably fellow of CLARE, 1473. R. of St Vigors, Fulbourn, Cambs., 1487. R. of Foulmire, 1487. R. of Toppesfield, Essex, 1492–1504. Dean of Stoke-by-Clare, Suffolk, 1497. R. of Wimbish, Essex, 1504. Archdeacon of Taunton, 1505–9. Archdeacon of Norwich, 1508–16. Precentor of St Paul's, 1509–10. Treasurer of St Paul's, 1509. Doubtless the Master of Corpus, 1515–6. (*Masters* and *Lamb* doubt between him and Thomas.) Will (P C.C.) 1517.

EDIMAN, T. M.Gram. 1489–90.

EDIMAN, THOMAS. B.A. 1489–90; M.A. 1492; B.D. 1503; D.D. 1508–9. Of Norwich diocese. Fellow of CORPUS CHRISTI, *c.* 1493. Proctor, 1502–3. Precentor of the College of St Mary-in-the-Fields, Norwich, 1508. R. of Winterton, Norfolk, 1505–15. Will proved (P.C.C.) 1515; of Winterton.

EDISBURY, FRANCIS. Adm. pens. (age 15) at MAGDALENE, Mar. 5, 1657–8. S. of Richard, citizen of London. School, Wem, Salop. Matric. 1658.

EDISBURY or EDYSBURY, JOSEPH. Adm. Fell.-Com. at PEMBROKE, Nov. 15, 1652. Of Wales.

EDLYN or EDELEN, CHRISTOPHER. Adm. pens. at TRINITY, Nov. 4, 1648. Of Buckinghamshire. S. of Philip (1614), B.D. B. in London (St Andrew Undershaft). School, Denham, Bucks. (Mr Leigh). Matric. 1648; Scholar, 1651; B.A. 1652–3. Migrated to Sidney, 1655. M.A. 1656. Fellow of Sidney. Incorp. at Oxford, 1657.

EDLYNE, EDMUND. Adm. pens. at QUEENS', Nov. 4, 1745. Of Jamaica. Matric. 1745.

EDLIN, EDWARD. Adm. at KING'S, a scholar from Eton, 1697. B. at Silchester, Hants., Jan. 7, 1679–80. Matric. 1698; B.A. 1701–2; M.A. 1705. Fellow, 1701–15. Barrister-at-Law. Steward to the Dean and Chapter of St Paul's. Baron of the Exchequer in Scotland, 1730–60. Married Mary, dau. of John Harding, fellow of Eton. Died Dec. 10, 1760. (*Harwood*, 281; J. Ch. Smith.)

EDLIN, PHILIP. Adm. pens. at EMMANUEL, June 28, 1614. B. at Pinner, Middlesex. Scholar; B.A. 1617–8; M.A. 1621; B.D. 1628. Incorp. at Oxford, 1617. R. of North Cray, Kent, 1628; of Alverstoke, Hants., 1631; and of St John Zachary, London, 1635–57. R. of Bushey, Herts., 1642–3. R. of St Michael Bassishaw, 1656. Died Mar. 22, 1656–7. Will, P.C.C. Father of Christopher (1648). (*Al. Oxon.*; J.Ch. Smith.)

EDLIN, SAMUEL. Adm. pens. (age 16) at MAGDALENE, June 20, 1653. S. of Samuel, of Pinner, Middlesex, gent. School, Watford, Herts. Matric. 1653; B.A. 1656–7; M.A. 1660. Fellow. Ord. deacon and priest (Peterb.) Aug. 17, 1662. Incorp. at Oxford, 1669. R. of Silchester, Hants., 1667. Married Mary, dau. of Edward Hawtrey. Buried at Silchester, June 4, 1698. Admon., P.C.C.

EDLIN, SAMUEL. Adm. sizar (age 17) at MAGDALENE, Feb. 22, 1660–1. S. of John, of Watford, Herts. School, Eton.

EDELEN, WILLIAM. Adm. pens. (age 18) at SIDNEY, June 19, 1656. S. of Richard, brewer. B. at St Giles', Cripplegate, London. School, Merchant Taylors'. Matric. 1656; B.A. 1659; M.A. 1663.

EDMER, ——. Perhaps LL.B. 1516–7. (*Gr. Bk*, B[1], 52.)

EDMONDS, ANDREW. Matric. sizar from PEMBROKE, Lent, 1582–3.

EDMONDS, ANTHONY. Adm. sizar at CHRIST'S, Mar. 16, 1648–9. S. of Robert, of Middlesex. School, St Paul's. Matric. 1649; B.A. 1652–3. Head Master of Otley School, Yorks., 1653–5. Probably R. of Pitsea, Essex, 1659–64, when he died. (*Peile*, I. 524.)

EDMONDS, EDWARD. Matric. sizar from PEMBROKE, Lent, 1582–3.

EDMUNDS, ELEAZAR. Matric. sizar from TRINITY, Easter, 1625. Subscribed for deacon's orders (Bristol) Sept. 22, 1627, as 'B.A.' (F. S. Hockaday.)

EDMONDS, GIDEON. Matric. sizar from TRINITY, Easter, 1618. 3rd s. of Robert, C. of Faxton, Northants. Bapt. there, Mar. 29, 1600. Ord. deacon (Peterb.) Dec. 17, 1620, as 'B.A.'; priest, Sept. 15, 1622. Brother of Zachary (1615). (H. I. Longden.)

EDMONDS, HENRY. Matric. pens. from ST JOHN'S, Michs. 1583. One of these names matric. from Broadgates Hall, Oxford, Feb. 22, 1582–3.

EDMUNDS, HENRY. Adm. (age 17) at KING'S, a scholar from Eton, June 4, 1627. Of London. Matric. 1627; B.A. 1630–1; M.A. 1634. Fellow, 1630–44 (ejected). Afterwards Master of Cranbrook School, Kent. One of these names adm. student at Leyden, July 7, 1643. (*Harwood.*)

EDMUNDS, HENRY. Said to have been Fell.-Com. at TRINITY, *c.* 1641; but no record found. Of Worsborough, Yorks. B. Aug. 2, 1627. Lieutenant of Trained Band Horse. Buried at Worsborough, Mar. 26, 1708. Brother of Thomas (1647). (J. Foster, *Yorks. Pedigrees.*)

EDMUNDS, HENRY. Adm. sizar (age 17) at TRINITY, Aug. 18, 1692. S. of Thomas (1650). B. at Worsborough, Yorks., Apr. 23, 1675. School, Worsborough (Mr Ant. Farrer). Matric. 1693; Scholar, 1695; B.A. 1696–7; M.A. 1700. Died Sept. 6, 1724. Buried at Worsborough. Brother of John (1689) and Thomas (1686).

EDMUNDS, JOHN. LL.B. 1499–1500 (Incorp. from Oxford); D.Can.L. 1500.

EDMUNDS, JOHN. B.A. 1504–5; M.A. 1508; B.D. 1516–7; D.D. 1519–20. Fellow of ST JOHN'S, 1516. Fellow of Jesus, 1517–22. Lady Margaret preacher, 1521. Master of Peterhouse, 1522–44. Vice-Chancellor, 1522–3, 1527–8, 1528–9, 1533–4, 1540–1, 1541–2. V. of Harmondsworth, Middlesex, 1511–5. Preb. of St Paul's, 1510–7; Chancellor, 1517–29. V. of Alborne, Wilts., 1530. Chancellor of Sarum, 1538. Died Nov. 1544. Buried at Little St Mary's. Will (V.C.C. and P.C.C.) 1544. (*Cooper*, I. 86; *D.N.B.*)

EDMONDS, JOHN. Matric. pens. from PETERHOUSE, Easter, 1576; B.A. 1579–80; M.A. 1583.

EDMUNDS, JOHN. Adm. sizar (age 16) at TRINITY, Sept. 9, 1689. S. of Thomas (1650), of Worsborough, Yorks. B. Oct. 29, 1672. School, Worsborough (Mr Ant. Farrer). Matric. 1689; Scholar, 1693; B.A. 1693–4; M.A. 1697. Beneficed in the Isle of Wight. Brother of Henry (1692) and Thomas (1686).

EDMONDS, JOHN. Matric. sizar from QUEENS', Easter, 1690; B.A. 1693–4; M.A. 1703.

EDMONDS, PETER. Adm. pens. (age 17) at CAIUS, Apr. 12, 1631. S. of Peter, gent. B. at Saxthorpe, Norfolk. School, Holt (Mr Tallis). Matric. 1631; Scholar, 1633–7; B.A. 1634–5; M.A. 1638. Ord. deacon (Norwich) Sept. 22, 1639; priest, Sept. 25, 1642, as C. of Barningham, Norfolk. V. of Middleton, 1661. Licensed schoolmaster, in 1662. Will proved (Norwich Archd. C.) 1664–5. (*Venn*, I. 297.)

EDMUNDS, RICHARD. Adm. sizar at EMMANUEL, Jan. 28, 1668–9. S. of Richard, of Newport Pagnell, Bucks. Matric. 1669. Previously matric. from Oriel College, Oxford, July 17, 1668, age 17. (*Al. Oxon.*)

EDMUNDS, RICHARD. M.A. from Caius, 1733. Matric. at New Inn Hall, Oxford, June 23, 1715, age 16. S. of John, gen . B. at Llandegai, Carnarvon. B.A. (Oxford) 1719. Ord. deacon (Norwich) Sept. 22, 1723; priest, June 1, 1729. V. of Longstock, Hants., 1733; and of King's Somborne. Chaplain to the Marquis of Annandale. (*Venn*, II. 37.)

EDMONDS, SIDRACH. Matric. sizar from Trinity, Easter, 1604. B. at Faxton, Northants. B.A. from Sidney, 1609–10. Ord. deacon (London) Mar. 4, 1609–10, age 23. C. of Laindon, Essex.

EDMONDS, SIMON. Adm. pens. (age 14) at Caius, Mar. 1680–1. S. of Simon, gent., citizen of London. Schools, Hempstead (Mr Carter) and Hertford (Mr Howarth). Matric. 1681; Scholar, 1681–4. Adm. at the Middle Temple, June 28, 1682. (*Venn*, I. 466.)

EDMUNDS, THOMAS. Matric. pens. from Pembroke, Lent, 1588–9; B.A. from St John's, 1592–3; M.A. from Pembroke, 1596. One of these names V. of Llantillio-Pertholey, Co. Monmouth. Will (P.C.C.) 1609. (J. Ch. Smith.)

EDMONDS, THOMAS. Adm. Fell.-Com. at Trinity, Aug. 24, 1647. Of Yorkshire. Brother of Henry (1641).

EDMUNDES, THOMAS. Adm. pens. at Trinity, May 30, 1650. Of Yorkshire. Doubtless 2nd s. of Thomas, of Worsborough, Yorks. B. at York, Apr. 2, 1632. Matric. 1650; Scholar, 1651. Died Mar. 22, 1708–9. Will at York. Father of the next, of John (1689) and Henry (1692). (Hunter, S. *Yorks.*, II. 290.)

EDMUNDS, THOMAS. Adm. pens. (age 16) at St John's, Feb. 12, 1686–7. S. of Thomas, gent. B. at Worsborough, Yorks. Bapt. Apr. 21, 1670. School, Wakefield (Mr Clark). Matric. 1687. Of Worsborough, Esq. Married Jane, dau. of Francis Foljambe, of Aldwark, Esq. Buried at Worsborough, Feb. 9, 1726–7. Will, York. Brother of Henry (1692) and John (1689). (J. Ch. Smith.)

EDMONDS, WILLIAM. Adm. sizar (age 18) at Caius, Apr. 10, 1610. Previously adm. at Trinity College, Oxford, May, 1609. S. of William, V. of Rickmansworth, Herts. School, Eton. Matric. 1610; Scholar, 1610–3; B.A. 1612–3; M.A. 1616. R. of Rickmansworth, till 1644; again, 1660–70. Perhaps also R. of Taplow, Bucks., 1625–70. Died 1670. Will, P.C.C. (*Venn*, I. 207; *Al. Oxon.*; *Lipscomb*, III. 298.)

EDMUNDS, ZACHARY. Matric. sizar from Trinity, Michs. 1615. S. of Robert, C. of Paxton, Northants. Bapt. there, May 8, 1597. Ord. deacon (Peterb.) Dec. 19, 1619, as literate; priest, Dec. 17, 1620, as 'B.A.' Brother of Gideon (1618). (H. I. Longden.)

EDMUNDS, ——. Resident pensioner at Peterhouse, 1445–8.

EDMUNDS, ——. Adm. at Corpus Christi, 1478; B.A. (*Masters*.)

EDMONDS, ——. Sizar at Peterhouse, Sept. 1542.

EDMONDES, ——. Matric. pens. from Christ's, Easter, 1544. Perhaps scholar of Trinity, 1548.

EDMUNDSON, ALEXANDER. Adm. pens. (age 18) at St John's, Apr. 29, 1716. S. of William, gent., of Lancashire. B. at Manchester. School, Sedbergh. Matric. 1716; B.A. 1719–20; M.A. 1723; B.D. 1730. Fellow, 1722–33. Ord. deacon (Lincoln) Dec. 23, 1721; priest, Dec. 27, 1722. V. of Humberstone, Lincs., 1722–6. V. of Burwell, Cambs., 1725. Died Jan. 30, 1732–3.

EDMUNDSON, BENJAMIN. Adm. sizar (age 18) at St John's, May 20, 1674. S. of Christopher (next), R. of Garstang, Lancs. B. there. School, Kendal. Matric. 1674; B.A. 1677–8. V. of Chorley, Lancs., 1684. Buried there Apr. 22, 1713. (*Vict. Hist. Lancs.*, VI. 147.)

EDMUNDSON, CHRISTOPHER. Adm. pens. at Emmanuel, May 5, 1632. Of Yorkshire. C. at Croston, Lancs., 1642. Minister at Garstang, 1646–54; and again, 1657. V. of Hawkshead, 1657–75. Died there, 1675. Will (Archd. Richmond). Father of Benjamin (above) and Hiet (next). (*Vict. Hist. Lancs.*, VII. 298.)

EDMONDSON, HIET or HYET. Adm. sizar (age 17) at St John's, Mar. 11, 1660–1. S. of Christopher, clerk, of Oldham, Lancs. B. there. School, Sedbergh. Matric. 1661; B.A. 1664–5; M.A. 1668. V. of Deeping, Lincs. Father of the next.

EDMUNDSON, JAMES. Adm. pens. (age 17) at St John's, Mar. 7, 1691–2. S. of Hyet (above), clerk. B. at Deeping, Lincs. School, Peterborough (Mr Waring). Matric. 1692.

EDMONDSON, ROBERT. Matric. sizar from St John's, Michs. 1610; B.A. 1614–5; M.A. 1620.

EDMONDSON, THOMAS. Matric. pens. from Magdalene, Michs. 1629. One of these names (aged one year in 1612), s. and h. of Thomas, of the city of York. (*Vis. of Yorks.*)

EDMUNDSON, THOMAS. Adm. pens. (age 17) at St John's, June 27, 1663. S. of Richard, yeoman, of Overton, Lancs. B. there. School, Sedbergh.

EDMUNDSON, THOMAS. Adm. at Corpus Christi, 1748. Of Middlesex. Matric. 1748. One of these names V. of Rodmersham, Kent, 1776.

EDMUNDSON, WILLIAM. Adm. sizar (age 19) at St John's, May 6, 1692. S. of Alan, husbandman. B. at Coates Flat, Skipton, Yorks. School, Sedbergh. Matric. 1692; B.A. 1695–6; M.A. 1699; B.D. 1706; D.D. 1714. Fellow, 1698–1736. Ord. priest (Lincoln) Sept. 24, 1699. C. of Fen Ditton, Cambs. R. of Thorington, Essex, 1708–36. Died Nov. 1736. Will proved (V.C.C.) 1736.

EDMONDSON or EDMONTON, ——. A friar. Doctor, 1467.

EDMONTON, J. B.A. 1462–3; M.A. 1466. Perhaps V. of Duxford St Peter, Cambs., till 1500.

EDNAM, JOHN, *see* EDIMAN.

EDNAM, ——. A friar. D. (Div. or L.) 1462–3. One Hugh Ednam, *alias* Vivall, was R. of Boxford, Suffolk, 1462–91. Will (P.C.C.) 1491; of Stoke-by-Clare, Suffolk.

EDONE, ——. B.Civ.L. 1498–9; D.Civ.L. 1506–7.

EDRIDGE, WILLIAM. Adm. pens. at Trinity, June 28, 1669. Matric. 1669; Scholar, 1670; B.A. 1672–3; M.A. 1676. Ord. deacon (Peterb.) May 21; priest (London) Dec. 24, 1676. V. of Baton Bray, Beds., 1677–95. Buried Apr. 12, 1696. (W. M. Noble.)

EDRIDGES, JOHN. Matric. pens. from Trinity Hall, Easter, 1609.

EDRINGHAM, ——. Resident pens. at Christ's, in 1564.

EDSAW, JOHN. Matric. pens. from Queens', Easter, 1611; B.A. 1614–5; M.A. 1618. Incorp. at Oxford, Aug. 12, 1645. Will (P.C.C.) 1648; of Chailey, Sussex, clerk. (*Fast. Oxon.*, II. 46.)

EDWARD, WILLIAM. B.A. 1517–8. Perhaps Everard.

EDWARDS, ANDREW. B.A. from Trinity Hall, 1658–9.

EDWARDS, ANDREW. Adm. sizar (age 17) at St John's, Nov. 2, 1730. S. of Richard, husbandman, of Denbighs. B. at Ruthin. School, Ruthin (Mr Vaughan). Matric. 1730; B.A. 1734–5; M.A. 1743. Ord. deacon (St David's) Aug. 15, 1736; priest (Chester) May 28, 1738. R. of Llangefni, Anglesey, 1741–53. R. of Edern, Carnarv., 1750–5. R. of Aber, 1753–62. Chancellor of Bangor, 1754–62. R. of Dolgelly, 1755–9. R. of Llanllechid, 1759–62. Died 1762. (*Scott-Mayor*, II. 432.)

EDWARDS, BARTHOLOMEW. Adm. pens. (age 16) at Peterhouse, Dec. 17, 1643. Of Wisbech, Cambs. Scholar, 1643–4. (*T. A. Walker*.)

EDWARDS, BARTHOLOMEW. Adm. pens. (age 18) at Caius, May 9, 1750. S. of Bartholomew, gent., of Sporle, Norfolk. B. at Swaffham, Norfolk. School, Swaffham (Mr Quartus and Mr Ri. Hest). Matric. 1750; Scholar, 1750–4; B.A. 1754; M.A. 1757. Fellow, 1755–82. Ord. deacon (London) May 26, 1771; priest, Mar. 15, 1772. R. of Hethersett, Norfolk, 1782–1820. R. of Finningham, 1789–1805. Died 1820. (*Venn*, II. 64.)

EDWARDS, BENJAMIN. Adm. sizar at Jesus, June 15, 1689. Of Flintshire. Matric. 1689; Scholar, 1691; B.A. 1692–3. Ord. priest (London) Sept. 19, 1697. Perhaps Chaplain of the East India Co., 1698; and of St Bartholomew's Hospital. Died Oct. 12, 1715. Buried at St Bartholomew-the-Less. (Le Neve, *Mon.*, V. 315.)

EDWARDS, CLEMENT. Adm. sizar at Corpus Christi, 1616. Of Leicestershire. Matric. 1616; B.A. 1619. Ord. deacon (Peterb.) May 23, 1619. R. of Wetherley, Leics., 1623–4. Will of one of these names (P.C.C.) 1631; of Hartshorne, Derbs., clerk.

EDWARDS, DANIEL. Adm. sizar at Jesus, Mar. 14, 1697–8. Of Staffordshire. Matric. 1699.

EDWARDS or EDGUARD, DAVID. M.D. 1528–9; M.A. of Oxford. Of Northamptonshire. Adm. at Corpus Christi, Oxford, 1517; B.A. 1522; M.A. 1525. Fellow of Corpus. Author, medical. Admon. (V.C.C.) 1542, to wife Alice. (*Cooper*, I. 46; *Al. Oxon.*; *D.N.B.*)

EDWARDS, DAVID. Adm. pens. at Queens', Oct. 16, 1596. Of Wales. Matric. 1596; B.A. 1600–1. One of these names adm. at Lincoln's Inn, Nov. 12, 1601; of Co. Carmarthen.

EDWARDS, DAVID. Matric. pens. from Queens', Michs. 1631. Of Carmarthenshire. Probably brother of Thomas (1635) and father of the next.

EDWARDS, DAVID. Adm. pens. at Queens', Apr. 18, 1664. Of Carmarthen. S. and h. of David, of Rhydgorse, Carmarthen, Esq. Matric. 1664. Adm. at Gray's Inn, Oct. 27, 1668.

EDWARDS, EDMUND. Matric. sizar from Corpus Christi, Easter, 1544; B.A. 1544–5; M.A. 1549. Fellow, 1547. President, *c.* 1557. R. of St Benet's, Cambridge, 1548–61. Suspected of popery, and his chambers searched, 1568. Protected by Archbishop Parker. Probably went to Flanders. Supposed to have been residing at the R. C. College of Douay in 1591. (*Cooper*, II. 119.)

EDWARDS, EDWARD. Matric. pens. from CHRIST'S, 1593-4; B.A. 1596-7. One of these names, of Lwyndu, Merioneth, adm. at the Inner Temple, Oct. 14, 1598. (*Peile*, I. 212.)

EDWARDS, EDWARD. Adm. pens. (age 18) at ST JOHN'S, Aug. 19, 1650. S. of Ellis, gent., of Lloyndu, Merioneths. (? Monmouths.). B. there. School, Ruthin, Denbighs. (Mr Thelwell). Matric. 1650.

EDWARDS, EDWARD. M.A. from EMMANUEL, 1712. S. of John, of Carmarthen. Matric. from Jesus College, Oxford, May 21, 1703-4, age 17; B.A. (Oxford) 1707. One of these names signs as R. of Holwell, Beds., 1721-3. (*Al. Oxon.*)

EDWARDS, EDWARD. Adm. sizar (age 20) at ST JOHN'S, June 30, 1733. S. of Thomas, gent. B. at Llanilar, St David's. School, Carmarthen (Mr Davies). Matric. 1733; B.A. 1736-7. Ord. deacon (Lincoln) Mar. 6, 1736-7. C. of Little Stukeley, Hunts.

EDWARDS, EDWARD. Adm. sizar (age 18) at SIDNEY, June 10, 1748. S. of Edward, of Wheaton, Staffs. School, Newport, Salop. Matric. 1748-9; B.A. 1752. Ord. priest (Lincoln) Sept. 22, 1754. Will of one of these names (Archd. Richmond) 1796; of Ashton, Lancs., clerk. (J. Ch. Smith.)

EDWARDS, FRANCIS. Matric. sizar from QUEENS', Easter, 1583; B.A. 1586-7; M.A. 1590. A teacher at Cambridge; *see* Raphael (1604).

EDWARDES, FRANCIS. Adm. sizar at QUEENS', May 19, 1677. Of Cornwall. Matric. 1677; B.A. 1680-1.

EDWARDS, GEORGE. Matric. pens. from JESUS, Michs. 1564.

EDWARDS, GEORGE. Adm. pens. at EMMANUEL, June 24, 1633. Of Middlesex. Matric. 1633.

EDWARDS, GEORGE. Adm. sizar at JESUS, Jan. 4, 1694-5. S. of ——, clerk, deceased. Of Wales. Matric. 1695; Rustat Scholar; B.A. 1698-9. V. of Bettws-yn-Rhos, Denbighs.

EDWARDS, GILES. Matric. pens. from TRINITY, Easter, 1549; *impubes*.

EDWARDS, GODOLPHIN. Adm. Fell.-Com. at QUEENS', Apr. 19, 1717. Of Middlesex. M.A. 1717 (*Com. Reg.*). Fellow, 1719. One of these names, of Froddesley, Salop, died Nov. 6, 1772. (*Lond. Mag.*)

EDWARDS, H. Resident pens. at JESUS, Aug. 1564.

EDWARDS, HENRY. Adm. sizar at PEMBROKE, Nov. 18, 1622. S. of Thomas, of London. Matric. 1623; B.A. 1626-7; M.A. 1631 (*Lit. Reg.*).

EDWARDS, HENRY. Adm. pens. at QUEENS', June 12, 1663. Of Cambridgeshire. Matric. 1663.

EDWARDS, HUGH. Matric. sizar from JESUS, Easter, 1575; B.A. 1578-9; M.A. 1582. Ord. deacon (St Asaph); priest (Ely) Apr. 17, 1580. C. of March, Cambs. V. of Chatteris, 1584-92. Died 1592.

EDWARDS, HUGH. Matric. pens. from ST CATHARINE'S, Michs. 1638. Of Flintshire. B.A. 1641-2. Perhaps s. and h. of Nicholas, late of Holywell, Flints., gent., deceased; adm. at Lincoln's Inn, July 3, 1649.

EDWARDS, ISRAEL. Matric. pens. from QUEENS', Easter, 1604. B. in St Laurence, Old Jewry. B.A. 1606-7; M.A. 1610. Incorp. at Oxford, 1610. Ord. deacon (London) Mar. 1612-3; priest, Sept. 23, 1615, age 27. R. of East Mersey, Essex, 1615-67. V. of Gt Bentley, 1615. Died 1667. (*Al. Oxon.*)

EDWARDS, JAMES. Adm. Fell.-Com. (age 16) at PETERHOUSE, June 22, 1650. S. and h. of William, of Wisbech, gent. School, Wisbech, Cambs. Matric. 1650. Adm. at Lincoln's Inn, June 29, 1652. Bailiff of Wisbech, 1658, 1659, 1663-65. (*T. A. Walker*, 95.)

EDWARDS, JAMES. Adm. sizar at QUEENS', Jan. 12, 1682-3. Migrated to Sidney, Oct. 25, 1683. S. of Richard, hatter. B. in London. Schools, Merchant Taylors' and St Olave's, Southwark. Matric. 1683; B.A. 1686-7; M.A. 1690.

EDWARDS, JAMES. Adm. pens. (age 17) at PEMBROKE, May 24, 1693. S. of Nicholas (? 1632), M.D., of Fakenham, Norfolk. Matric. 1693.

EDWARDS, JASPER. Adm. pens. at CLARE, June 21, 1637. Doubtless 4th s. of Richard, of Arlesey, Beds. B. *c.* 1618. School, Westminster. Matric. 1637. Of Little Barford, Beds. Married Joan Devenysh. Died 1680. Brother of Richard (1620). (Burke, *L.G.*)

EDWARDS, JOHN. M.B. 1537-8.

EDWARDS, JOHN. Matric. pens. from KING'S, Lent, 1582-3.

EDWARDS, JOHN. Adm. sizar at CORPUS CHRISTI, 1584. Matric. Lent, 1584-5.

EDWARDS, JOHN. Adm. pens. at EMMANUEL, Sept. 9, 1592. Matric. 1593.

EDWARDS, JOHN. Matric. pens. from PEMBROKE, Michs. 1606 B.A. 1610-1; M.A. 1614. Incorp. at Oxford, 1617. Perhaps R. of Pakefield (med.), Suffolk, 1617; and R. of Oxwick, Norfolk, 1623. (*Al. Oxon.*)

EDWARDS, JOHN. Adm. Fell.-Com. (age 18) at ST JOHN'S, Aug. 14, 1649. S. of John, gent. B. at Iden, Sussex. School, Horton, near Canterbury. Matric. 1649.

EDWARDS, JOHN. Adm. sizar (age 16) at ST JOHN'S, Mar. 10, 1653-4. S. of Thomas, clerk, of Hertford. B. there. School, Merchant Taylors'. Matric. 1654; B.A. 1657-8; M.A. 1661; B.D. 1668; D.D. 1699. Fellow, 1659. Ord. deacon (Lincoln) Sept. 11; priest, Sept. 21, 1662. V. of Holy Trinity, Cambridge, 1664. V. of St Sepulchre's. V. of St Peter's, Colchester, 1683-98. For a time Fell.-Com. at Trinity Hall. Resided latterly at Cambridge. Author, theological. Died Apr. 16, 1716. (*D.N.B.*)

EDWARDS, JOHN. Adm. pens. at EMMANUEL, June 19, 1657. Of Salop. S. of William (s. of Edward), of Gwyddelwern, Merioneth. Matric. 1657; B.A. 1660-1; M.A. 1665; LL.D. 1683. R. of Knockin, Salop, 1666. R. of Llan-y-myneck, 1666. Preb. of St Asaph, 1675. Buried at Llan-y-myneck, 1695. (Browne Willis, *St Asaph*.)

EDWARDS, JOHN. Adm. at KING'S, a scholar from Eton, 1658. B. at White Waltham, Berks., 1642. B.A. 1662-3; M.A. 1666. Fellow, 1662-8. Ord. priest (Lincoln) Dec. 20, 1668. V. of Hambledon, Ruts., 1669-71.

EDWARDES, JOHN. Adm. sizar at QUEENS', Apr. 7, 1677. Of Wales. B. at Llanfyllin. Matric. 1677; B.A. 1680-1; M.A. 1684. Fellow. Incorp. at Oxford, 1710. V. of Nannerch and Rhuddlan, Flints., 1686; and R. of Newtown, Montgom., 1688. R. of Llanfyllin and Llanfihangel-yn-gwnfa, 1691-1711. Preb. of St Asaph, 1705-11. Chaplain to Bishop Lloyd. (*Al. Oxon.*)

EDWARDS, JOHN. Adm. at CORPUS CHRISTI, 1683. Of Norfolk. Matric. 1683; B.A. 1686-7.

EDWARDS, JOHN. Adm. sizar (age 19) at TRINITY, Apr. 1, 1691. S. of John. B. at Clun, Shropshire. School, Leominster, Heref. (Mr Arch. Lane). Matric. 1691; B.A. 1694-5. Perhaps s. of John, of Lincoln's Inn, Esq.; adm. at Lincoln's Inn, May 14, 1692.

EDWARDS, JOHN. Adm. sizar at EMMANUEL, May 20, 1698. Of Suffolk. Matric. 1698; B.A. 1701-2. Ord. deacon (Norwich) July, 1702; priest, Sept. 1703. One of these names V. of Darsham, Suffolk, 1706-20; and R. of Uggeshall, 1720.

EDWARDS, JOHN. M.A. from TRINITY, 1718. S. of Lewis, of Towin, Montgom. Matric. from Jesus College, Oxford, Apr. 12, 1709, age 17; B.A. (Oxford) 1712. Perhaps V. of Banstead, Surrey, 1714-54. (*Al. Oxon.*)

EDWARDS, JOHN. M.A. from MAGDALENE, 1730; B.A. of Jesus College, Oxford (not found in *Al. Oxon.*). One of these names R. of Horton, Bucks., 1734-50. Died 1750. (*Lipscomb*, IV. 512.)

EDWARDES, JOHN. Incorp. LL.B. 1734, from Trinity College, Dublin. Adm. there, July 6, 1714; LL.B. 1722.

EDWARDS, JOHN. Adm. pens. (age 19) at ST JOHN'S, Apr. 30, 1736. S. of Nathaniel, doctor, of Derbyshire. B. at Derby. School, Repton (Mr Fletcher). Matric. 1736; B.A. 1739-40; M.A. 1743. Ord. deacon (Lincoln) Dec. 21, 1740; C. of Bosworth, Leics. P.C. of Repton. V. of Marston-on-Dove, Derbs., 1750-1804. Died Mar. 1, 1804. (*Scott-Mayor*, III. 472; Glover, *Derbs.*, II. 570.)

EDWARDS, JOHN. M.A. from EMMANUEL, 1751. S. of Henry, of Cornwall, gent. Matric. from Exeter College, Oxford, May 12, 1729, age 17; B.A. (Oxford) 1734-5. (*Al. Oxon.*)

EDWARDS, JONATHAN. M.A. 1668 (Incorp. from Oxford). B. at Wrexham, N. Wales, 1629. Matric. from Christ Church, Oxford, June 15, 1657; B.A. 1659; M.A. (Jesus) 1662; B.D. 1669-70; D.D. 1686. Fellow of Jesus College, Oxford, 1662. Principal, 1686-1712. Vice-Chancellor, 1689. R. of Kidlington, Oxon., 1666. R. of Hinton-Ampner, Hants., 1681. R. of Llandyssil, Cardigan, 1687. Treasurer of Llandaff, 1687-1712. Preb. of Sarum, 1691. Author. Died July 20, 1712. Buried in the Chapel of Jesus College, Oxford. Will, P.C.C. (*Al. Oxon.*; *D.N.B.*)

EDWARDS, JOSEPH. Adm. at CORPUS CHRISTI, 1682. Of Norwich. Matric. 1682; B.A. 1685-6. Ord. priest (London) June 7, 1691. R. of Thurlton, Norfolk, 1694-1713. Died May 27, 1713, aged 47. M.I. at Thurlton. (*E. Anglian*, I. 282.)

EDWARDS, MORRIS. Matric. sizar from QUEENS', Michs. 1587. Of Wales. B.A. 1590-1; M.A. 1595. Perhaps R. of Snodland, Kent, 1608-13.

EDWARDS, MORRIS. Matric. pens. from ST CATHARINE'S, Easter, 1605.

EDWARDS, NATHANIEL. Adm. at CORPUS CHRISTI, 1606. Of Essex.

EDWARDS, NATHANIEL. Adm. Fell.-Com. (age 16) at PEMBROKE, May 17, 1716. S. of Sir James, of Parke Hall, Reedham, Norfolk, Bart. B. at Hackney, Middlesex. Matric. 1716. Ord. deacon (London) June 5, 1726. V. of Weybridge, Surrey, 1736-64. Succeeded as Bart., 1744. Died Mar. 10, 1764. M.I. at Weybridge. Admon. (P.C.C.) 1765. (Burke, *Ext. Bart.*; *Surrey Arch. Soc.*, XVII. 62.)

EDWARDS, NICHOLAS. Matric. sizar from CORPUS CHRISTI, Michs. 1560; *impubes*; B.A. 1566-7. Fellow, till Oct. 1569. Fellow of Caius. One of these names R. of Herringswell, Suffolk, 1574.

EDWARDS, NICHOLAS. Adm. (age 18) at KING'S, a scholar from Eton, Dec. 3, 1563. Of Peterborough. Matric. 1563-4; B.A. 1567-8; M.A. 1571. Fellow, 1566-72. Ord. deacon (Ely) Sept. 21, 1570. R. of Courteenhall, Northants., 1571-1627. Buried there Apr. 9, 1627. Will (Archd. Northants.) 1627. (H. I. Longden.)

EDWARDS, NICHOLAS. Matric. sizar from QUEENS', Easter, 1632. Of Norfolk. One of these names M.D. 1664 (*Lit. Reg.*): 'owing to the troublous times could not graduate in the ordinary way.' Probably his will (P.C.C.) 1686; of Fakenham, Norfolk, M.D. If so, father of James (1693).

EDWARDS, OWEN. Matric. sizar from TRINITY HALL, Easter, 1655; B.A. 1658-9.

EDWARDS, PIERCE. Adm. pens. at ST CATHARINE'S, Feb. 11, 1730-1. Of Nandrek, Flints. Matric. 1731.

EDWARDS, RAPHAEL. Adm. sizar (age 16) at CAIUS, Apr. 9, 1604. S. of Thomas (1575), of Cambridge. Bapt at St Benet's, Apr. 19, 1588. School, Cambridge (Mr Francis Edwards (1583), his uncle). Scholar, 1608-10; B.A. 1608-9; M.A. 1613. Ord. priest (Peterb.) Feb. 28, 1615-6. V. of Swineshead, Lincs., 1615-9. V. of Bicker, 1619-31. Will proved (Lincoln) May, 1631. (*Venn*, I. 184.)

EDWARDS, RICHARD. Matric. pens. from PETERHOUSE, Easter, 1575.

EDWARDS, RICHARD. Matric. sizar from CHRIST'S, c. 1593. B. at Bitchfield, Lincs., c. 1575. B.A. 1597-8. Ord. priest (Bishop of Colchester) July 25, 1599. R. of Frieston, Lincs., 1600-14. (*Linc. Presentation Deeds.*)

EDWARDES, RICHARD. Matric. sizar from CHRIST'S, Michs. 1607; B.A. 1614-5.

EDWARDS, RICHARD. Matric. pens. from ST JOHN'S, Easter, 1620. Doubtless s. of Richard, of Arlesey, Beds. B. 1604. Adm. at the Inner Temple, 1628. Senior Registrar in Chancery. Died 1657. Buried at Arlesey, Sept. 3, 1657. Brother of Jasper (1637) and father of Richard (1647-8). (*Vis. of Beds.*, 1634; *Coll. Top. et Gen.*, VI. 291.)

EDWARDS, RICHARD. Adm. pens. (age 16) at CAIUS, July 3, 1625. S. of Richard, merchant, of London. School, St Paul's. Matric. 1626.

EDWARDS, RICHARD. Adm. sizar (age 16) at CHRIST'S, Apr. 19, 1634. S. of Richard. B. at Stamford, Lincs. School, Stamford (Mr Dugard). Matric. 1634; B.A. 1637; M.A. 1641. Ord. priest (Peterb.) June 5, 1642. One of these names R. of Christleton, Cheshire, 1660-2 (ejected). Afterwards V. of Oswestry, till 1680. Died 1680. (*Peile*, I. 432.)

EDWARDS, RICHARD. Adm. pens. at EMMANUEL, May 10, 1634. Of Middlesex. Matric. 1634; B.A. 1637; M.A. 1641. Ord. deacon (Lincoln) Sept. 25, 1642. V. of Boughton, Northants., 1646. Probably appointed to St Nicholas Acons., London, 1646; but died before institution.

EDWARDS, RICHARD. Adm. pens. (age 17) at ST JOHN'S, Mar. 22, 1647-8. S. of Richard (1620), Esq., of Arlesey, Beds. (Registrar in Chancery). B. there. Bapt. May 20, 1630. School, Hitchin (Mr Kemp). Matric. 1648. Adm. at the Inner Temple, 1648. Barrister, 1655. Bencher, 1673. Buried Oct. 25, 1691. (*Vis. of Beds.*, 1634.)

EDWARDS, RICHARD. Adm. at KING'S, a scholar from Eton, 1647. B. in London, 1631. Left in 1648, and married.

EDWARDS, RICHARD. Adm. sizar at JESUS, Dec. 14, 1681. Of Denbighshire. School, St Paul's. Matric. 1681; B.A. 1685-6; M.A. 1689. One of these names R. of Ruthin, Denbigh; died Oct. 1740. (L. *Mag.*)

EDWARDS, RICHARD. Adm. pens. at TRINITY, June 28, 1682. Probably s. of Sir John, of Heath House, Salop, Knt. School, Westminster. Matric. 1682-3; Scholar, 1683. Adm. at the Inner Temple, Jan. 24, 1684-5.

EDWARDS, RICHARD. Adm. pens. (age 16) at ST JOHN'S, Mar. 27, 1714. S. of Timothy, gent., of Nanhoran, Carnarvon. School, St Paul's, London. Matric. 1714. Adm. at Lincoln's Inn, Nov. 30, 1713. Master in Chancery, 1732-67. Died June 19, 1770. Brother of William (1727). (Burke, *L.G.*)

EDWARDS, RICHARD. Adm. sizar (age 20) at TRINITY, July 8, 1731. S. of John, of Wells, Somerset. School, Wells (Mr Gayland). Matric. 1731; B.A. 1734-5.

EDWARDS, RICHARD SWINFEN. Adm. pens. (age 16) at ST JOHN'S, Oct. 27, 1748. S. of Grif. (? Griffith), tailor, of Middlesex. B. in London. School, Westminster. Matric. 1748; B.A. 1753; M.A. 1756. Ord. deacon (Ely) June 11, 1756; priest (Chichester) July 30, 1758. (*Scott-Mayor*, III. 583.)

EDWARDS, ROBERT. Adm. pens. at EMMANUEL, Apr. 13, 1598. Matric. 1596; B.A. 1601-2.

EDWARDS, ROBERT. B.A. from CHRIST'S, 1607-8; M.A. 1611. B. at Bitchfield, Lincs. Ord. deacon and priest (London) Dec. 1611. One of these names R. of Langdon Hills, Essex. Died 1637. Admon. (Consist. C. London) 1637. Perhaps brother of Richard (1593). (*Peile*, I. 251; J. Ch. Smith.)

EDWARDS, ROBERT. Adm. sizar at JESUS, Jan. 24, 1637-8. Of Wales. Scholar, 1640; B.A. 1641-2; M.A. 1665. Perhaps V. of Whitford, Flints. If so, father of Thomas (1671-2).

EDWARDS, ROBERT. Adm. sizar at CLARE, Apr. 6, 1638. Matric. 1639.

EDWARDS, ROBERT. Adm. sizar (age 17) at ST JOHN'S, June 21, 1651. S. of Ellice, gent., of Llanaber, Barmouth, Merioneth. B. there. School, Ruthin (Mr Thelwell). Matric. 1651; B.A. 1654-5; M.A. 1658. Fellow, 1664. Perhaps ord. priest (Lincoln) July 5, 1661; and R. of Barling, Essex, 1661-8.

EDWARDS, SAMUEL. Adm. sizar (age 14) at ST JOHN'S, Mar. 5, 1659-60. S. of Samuel, gent., of Elmdon, Essex. B. there. School, Elmdon. Matric. 1660; B.A. 1663-4; M.A. 1667. Incorp. at Oxford, 1669. Signs for deacon's orders (London) June 1, 1667. Perhaps R. of Gt Saxham, Suffolk, 1676-86; V. of Eye, 1682; R. of Troston, 1686.

EDWARDS, SAMUEL. M.A. from TRINITY, 1665. Matric. from Jesus College, Oxford, Mar. 21, 1658-9; B.A. (Oxford) 1662. Perhaps R. of Weston-under-Lizard, Staffs., 1687-1704; and R. of Donington, Salop, 1705. (*Al. Oxon.*)

EDWARDS, SAMUEL. Adm. pens. (age 20) at TRINITY, May 25, 1722. S. of Samuel, of Salop. School, Westminster. Matric. 1722; Scholar, 1723; B.A. 1725-6; M.A. 1729.

EDWARDS, SAMUEL. Adm. pens. at QUEENS', Nov. 3, 1735. Of Montgomery. Matric. 1736; B.A. 1739-40; M.A. 1744, as 'Samuel D'Elbeof.'

EDWARDS, SAMUEL. Adm. sizar at ST CATHARINE'S, Dec. 4, 1738. Of Water Newton, Hunts. Matric. 1739; B.A. 1742-3. Ord. deacon (Lincoln) Sept. 25, 1743.

EDWARDS, SAMUEL. Adm. sizar at QUEENS', July 11, 1744. Of Middlesex.

EDWARDS, SIMON. Adm. pens. at JESUS, May 18, 1672. S. of Edward, clerk, deceased, of Salop. Matric. 1672; B.A. 1675-6; M.A. 1679 (as s. of Edward, of Bettws, Salop, clerk; he matric. at Queen's College, Oxford, Mar. 27, 1672, age 16) R. of Lydham, Salop, 1686. (*Al. Oxon.*)

EDWARD, THOMAS. B.D. (1458-9 or) 1465-6; D.D. 1474-5. Augustinian canon. Abbot of Waltham Abbey, Essex, 1475. Deprived 'for dilapidation,' in 1488. (H. G. Harrison.)

EDWARDS, THOMAS. LL.B. from TRINITY HALL, 1562. Fellow, 1559. Will proved (V.C.C.) 1568.

EDWARDS, THOMAS. Matric. sizar from QUEENS', Easter, 1575. Of Huntingdonshire. B.A. 1578-9; M.A. 1582. Buried St Benet's, Cambridge, Oct. 3, 1592. Father of Raphael (1604).

EDWARDS, THOMAS (*senior*). Matric. sizar from TRINITY, Easter, 1602; Scholar, 1605; B.A. 1605-6; M.A. 1609. One of these names R. of Kirkby Overblow, Yorks., 1613-39. Died 1639.

EDWARDS, THOMAS (*junior*). Matric. sizar from TRINITY, Easter, 1602; B.A. 1605-6; M.A. 1609. One of these names R. of Langenhoe, Essex, 1618.

EDWARDS, THOMAS. Matric. pens. from ST JOHN'S, Easter, 1613.

EDWARDS, THOMAS. Adm. sizar at SIDNEY, Oct. 16, 1614. B. at Huntingdon. School, Huntingdon. Matric. 1614.

EDWARDS, THOMAS. Matric. pens. from QUEENS', Michs. 1618. Of London. B. 1599. B.A. 1621-2; M.A. 1625. Incorp. at Oxford, 1623. Ord. deacon (Peterb.) Jan. 18, 1625-6. University preacher. A zealous puritan. Forced to recant at St Andrew's, Cambridge. Licensed to preach at St Botolph's, Aldersgate, London. Suspended by Archbishop Laud. An active preacher under the Parliamentary rule. Author, *Gangrena*. Retired to Holland; where he died Aug. 24, 1647. Will (P.C.C.) 1648. (*Al. Oxon.*; *D.N.B.*)

EDWARDS, THOMAS. Matric. pens. from QUEENS', Easter, 1635. Of Carmarthen. B.A. 1638-9; M.A. 1642; LL.D. 1660 (*Lit. Reg.*). Fellow (elected, 1642; admitted, 1660), till 1683. Master of Newport Grammar School, 1657. Will (P.C.C.) 1683. Probably brother of David (1631).

EDWARDS, THOMAS. Matric. sizar from TRINITY, Easter, 1637.

EDWARDS, THOMAS. Adm. pens. (age 16) at PETERHOUSE, June 28, 1653. Of Wisbech, Cambs. School, private. Bailiff of Wisbech, 1670. High Bailiff of the Isle of Ely, 1698. D.L. and J.P. for Isle of Ely. Died July 15, 1705. M.I. at Wisbech. (*T. A. Walker*, 102.)

EDWARDS, THOMAS. Adm. sizar (age 18) at ST JOHN'S, Mar. 16, 1669-70. S. of Edward, of Llanllechyd, near Bangor. B. there. School, Bangor. Matric. 1670; B.A. 1673-4; M.A. 1677. Incorp. at Oxford, 1685. Chaplain at Christ's Church, Oxford. V. of Badby, Northants., 1690-1708. R. of Aldwincle All Saints', 1708-21. A learned Orientalist. Left a Coptic Lexicon ready for the Press. Died Sept. 5, 1721. (*D.N.B.*; H. I. Longden.)

EDWARDS, THOMAS. Adm. pens. at JESUS, Feb. 8, 1671-2. S. of Robert, V. of Whitford, Flints. B. there. Matric. 1672; Scholar, 1675; B.A. 1675-6.

EDWARDS, THOMAS. Adm. pens. (age 17) at ST JOHN'S, June 13, 1673. S. of Richard, of Llangian, Carnarvon. B. there. School, Chester. Matric. 1673.

EDWARDS, THOMAS. Adm. sizar at TRINITY, July 7, 1673.

EDWARDS, THOMAS. Adm. pens. at CLARE, Sept. 17, 1674. Of London. Matric. 1674.

EDWARDS, THOMAS. Adm. sizar (age 19) at CAIUS, July 15, 1674. S. of William, clerk. B. at Taplow, Bucks. School, Harrow. Matric. 1674; Scholar, 1674-80; B.A. 1678-9; M.A. 1683. One of these names V. of Newnham, Herts., 1680-4. (*Venn*, I. 451; apparently not the orientalist, as in *Al. Oxon.*)

EDWARDS, THOMAS. Adm. pens. (age 15) at ST JOHN'S, Sept. 11, 1678. S. of Thomas, gent. B. at Wisbech, Cambs. School, Wisbech (Mr Friskney). Matric. 1678; B.A. 1682-3. One of these names, joint clerk of the Hanaper, died at Wisbech, Oct. 5, 1725. (*Musgrave.*)

EDWARDS, THOMAS. Adm. pens. (age 17) at TRINITY, May 8, 1718. S. of John, of Lichfield, Staffs. School, Lichfield (Mr Hunter). Matric. 1718; Scholar, 1720; B.A. 1722-3; M.A. 1726. Died at West Coppice, Shropshire, Aug. 8, 1730, aged 30.

EDWARDS, THOMAS. M.A. from CLARE, 1723. S. of T., of Coventry. Matric. from St John's College, Oxford, Mar. 5, 1710-1, age 19; B.A. (Oxford) 1714. Perhaps V. of St Michael's, Coventry, 1722; and father of Thomas (1746). (*Al. Oxon.*)

EDWARDES, THOMAS. M.A. from KING'S, 1734. S. of Jonathan, of Marton, Salop, clerk. Matric. from Balliol College, Oxford, Apr. 9, 1715, age 17; B.A. (Oxford) 1718. (*Al. Oxon.*)

EDWARDS, THOMAS. Adm. sizar (age 17) at ST JOHN'S, Nov. 22, 1746. S. of Thomas (? 1723), clerk, V. of Coventry, Warws. B. there, Aug. 1729. School, Coventry (Dr Jackson). Migrated to Clare, Nov. 24, 1746 Matric. 1747; B.A. 1750-1; M.A. 1754; D.D. 1766. Fellow of Clare, 1752-9. Ord. deacon (Lichfield) 1751; priest, 1753. Master of Coventry Grammar School, 1758; and R. of St John-the-Baptist, till 1779. V. of Bablake, 1758. V. of Nuneaton, 1770. Author, theological. Died June, 1785. Buried at Foleshill, Warws. Will, P.C.C. (*D.N.B.*)

EDWARDS, TIMOTHY. Adm. sizar at QUEENS', June 1, 1702. Of Cornwall. Matric. 1702; B.A. 1705-6; M.A. 1709. Incorp. at Oxford, 1709. V. of Okehampton, Devon, 1717. Author. Will (Exeter) 1745. (*Al. Oxon.*)

EDWARDS, TUDER. Matric. pens. from JESUS, Michs. 1575.

EDWARD, WILLIAM. Graduate in Can.L., before 1454; D.Can.L. V. of Holy Trinity, Cambridge, 1471.

EDWARDS, WILLIAM. Matric. pens. from TRINITY, Easter, 1549 (*impubes*).

EDWARDS, WILLIAM. Adm. at KING'S, a scholar from Eton, 1552. Left in 1555. Presented to R. of West Wretham, Norfolk, 1559. Died 1579.

EDWARDS, WILLIAM. Matric. pens. from ST JOHN'S, Lent, 1557-8.

EDWARDS, WILLIAM. Scholar of TRINITY, 1571; B.A. 1571-2; M.A. 1575. One of these names R. of Witherley, Leics., 1595-1600.

EDWARDS, WILLIAM. Adm. pens. at PETERHOUSE, June 29, 1594. Matric. 1594.

EDWARDS, WILLIAM. Adm. pens. at QUEENS', Mar. 9, 1593-4. Of London. Matric. *c.* 1593; B.A. 1597-8.

EDWARDES, WILLIAM. Matric. sizar from TRINITY, Michs. 1609; B.A. 1612-3; M.A. 1616. One of these names V. of Tetbury, Glones., 1614-58.

EDWARDS, WILLIAM. Matric. from TRINITY, Michs. 1622; B.A. 1625-6. Ord. deacon (York) May, 1627.

EDWARDS, WILLIAM. Adm. pens. at EMMANUEL, 1623. Matric. 1623; B.A. 1625-6; M.A. 1629.

EDWARDS, WILLIAM. Matric. sizar from EMMANUEL, Lent, 1625-6.

EDWARDS, WILLIAM. M.A. 1627 (Incorp. from Oxford). Perhaps of Middlesex, *cler. fil.* Matric. from Christ Church, Oxford, Nov. 16, 1621, age 18; B.A. 1624; M.A. 1627. But *see Al. Oxon.* for another of these names.

EDWARDS, WILLIAM. Adm. sizar (age 15) at ST JOHN'S, June 18, 1666. S. of Samuel, of Walden, Essex. B. there. School, Elmdon (Mr Howarth). Matric. 1667; B.A. 1669-70. Perhaps R. of Bicknor, Kent, 1674-1704; and V. of Borden, 1690-1704. Died 1704.

EDWARDS, WILLIAM. M.A. 1671 (Incorp. from Oxford). S. of Edward, of Conanyan, Salop. Matric. from St Edmund's Hall, Oxford, Apr. 1, 1664, age 19; B.A 1667; M.A. 1670; B.D. 1677. One of these names R. of Saddington, Leics., 1677-95. Admon (Leicester) 1695. (*Al. Oxon.*)

EDWARDS, WILLIAM. Adm. pens. (age 19) at PETERHOUSE, June 17, 1685. Of Cambridgeshire. School, Wisbech. Matric. 1685; Scholar, 1685.

EDWARDS, WILLIAM. Adm. sizar (age 16) at ST JOHN'S, Feb. 16, 1688-9. S. of Samuel, clerk. B. at Denham. School, Eye, Suffolk (Mr Browne). Matric. 1689. Ord. deacon (London) Sept. 23, 1694; priest, May 26, 1700.

EDWARDS or EDWARD, WILLIAM. Adm. sizar (age 17) at ST JOHN'S, June 28, 1707. S. of George, currier, of Barnard Castle, Yorks. Bapt. there, Aug. 14, 1690. School, Sedbergh. Matric. 1707; B.A. 1710-1; M.A. 1714; D.D. from Christ's, 1728. Fellow of Christ's, 1715-26. Ord. deacon (Ely) Sept. 20, 1713; priest (London) Dec. 19, 1714. V. of Burley-on-the-Hill, Ruts., 1725-7. R. of Middleton Keynes, Bucks., 1727-44. Preb. of Lincoln, 1739-44. Died 1744. Will, P.C.C. (*Peile*, II. 169.)

EDWARDS, WILLIAM. Adm. sizar at JESUS, July 4, 1712. S. of John, of Ashford, Kent. Previously matric. from Corpus Christi, Oxford, Nov. 9, 1709, age 14. Matric. 1712; B.A. (Cambridge) 1715-6. Perhaps R. of Tarvin, Cheshire, 1724-46. If so, died Aug. 26, 1746.

EDWARDS, WILLIAM. Adm. pens. (age 18) at CAIUS, May 14, 1725. S. of William, gent., late of Troston, Suffolk. B. there. Schools, Gislingham (Mr Sparrow) and Bury (Mr Kinsman). Scholar, 1725-9; Matric. 1726; B.A. 1728-9; M.A. 1734. Ord. deacon (Norwich) Sept. 21, 1729; priest, Sept. 20, 1730. R. of Finningham, Suffolk, 1730-89. Died at Finningham, Apr. 1789. Will, P.C.C. (*Venn*, II. 23.)

EDWARDS, WILLIAM. Adm. sizar (age 18) at ST JOHN'S, Apr. 17, 1727. S. of Timothy, gent., of Carnarvon. B. at Aberdaron. School, Whitchurch, Salop (Mr Hughes). Matric. 1727. In holy orders. Brother of Richard (1714). (Burke, *L.G.*)

EDWARDS, WILLIAM. Adm. pens. at EMMANUEL, Dec. 3, 1743. S. of Nathaniel, M.D., of Derby. B. July 23, 1726. School, Repton. Matric. 1745-6. Lieutenant of Marines. Mayor of Derby in 1773, 1785 and 1798. Died at Derby, 1800. Buried in St Michael's Church. Brother of John (1736). (Glover, *Derbs.*, II. 570.)

EDWARDS, ——. Adm. at CORPUS CHRISTI, 1558.

EDWARDS, —— Adm. sizar at TRINITY HALL, Feb. 24, 1731-2.

EDWYNE, ——. Matric. pens. from PEMBROKE, Michs. 1548.

EDYLL, ANTHONY. Scholar of TRINITY, as Anthony Idyll; *see* Ithell, Thomas.

EDYLL or IDLE, RICHARD. Matric. pens. from CHRIST'S, 1544. Of Cumberland. B.A. 1546-7; M.A. 1549; B.D. 1556. Fellow of Pembroke, 1547. Fellow of Jesus, 1558-9. Received tonsure (London) 1554. Will proved (V.C.C.) 1559. Benefactor to Jesus. (A. Gray.)

EDYN, ——. B.Civ.L. 1488.

EDYSBURY, JOSEPH, *see* EDISBURY.

EFFORD, JOHN. Matric. pens. from JESUS, Easter, 1569.

EFFORD, NICHOLAS. Matric. pens. from JESUS, Easter, 1569; B.A. at Oxford, 1575.

EFFORD, THOMAS. Matric. pens. from PETERHOUSE, Michs. 1586.

EGAR, *see* EGGER.

EGBASTIAN, *see* EDGBASTON.

EGERTON, CHARLES. 'Of ST JOHN'S College, Cambridge,' but not found in our records. S. of Sir Charles, of Newborough, Staffs., Knt. B. in Ireland, 1586. Of Lincoln's Inn. Principal ranger of Needwood Forest. Knighted. Died May 3, 1662, *s.p.* M.I. in Hanbury Church. (Shaw, *Staffs.*, I. 93.)

EGERTON or EGGESTON, JOHN. Probably scholar at KING'S HALL, 1508–17; B.Can.L. 1511–2. Studied also at Oxford. R. of Gt Billing, Northants., 1512–32. R. of Farthingston, 1519. R. of Weston Favell. Died 1532. Will dated Mar. 22, 1532–3 (Archd. Northants.); parson of Gt Billing. (H. I. Longden; Baker's *Northants.*, I. 23, 373.)

EGERTON, JOHN. Adm. pens. (age 17) at MAGDALENE, Jan. 10, 1727–8. S. of John, Esq., deceased. B. at Tatton, Cheshire, Oct. 14, 1710. School, Sandbach. Matric. 1728. Married Christian, dau. of John Ward, Esq., 1735. Died 1738. (Burke, *L.G.*)

EGERTON, LEONARD. Adm. pens. (age 17) at ST JOHN'S, Apr. 22, 1686. S. and h. of Peter, of Shaw, Lancs., Esq. B. at Boughton, Cheshire. School, Manchester. Matric. 1686. Adm. at Gray's Inn, Apr. 24, 1686. Buried at Flixton, 1688. (Mumford, *Manch. Gr. School*; *Vis. of Lancs.*, 1664.)

EGERTON, PETER. Matric. Fell.-Com. from PETERHOUSE, Michs. 1602. Doubtless s. of Sir John, of Egerton, Cheshire, Knt. B. Dec. 7, 1582. Adm. at Gray's Inn, Aug. 4, 1612. Brother of Philip (1589). (*T. A. Walker.*)

EDGERTON, PHILIP. Matric. Fell.-Com. from JESUS, Michs. 1589. Of Cheshire. Perhaps adm. at Lincoln's Inn, June 30, 1592. 1st s. of Sir John, of Egerton, and Oulton, Lancs. B. 1574. Died 1592. Brother of Peter (above). (Foster, *Lancs. Pedigrees.*)

EGERTON, STEPHEN. B.A. from PETERHOUSE, 1575–6. S. of Thomas, mercer, of London. M.A. 1579. Fellow, 1579–85. Incorp. at Oxford, 1583. Ord. priest (Peterb.) May 11, 1581. Adm. at Gray's Inn, Aug. 18, 1588. As a puritan he was suspended by Whitgift, and imprisoned in the Fleet for three years. Minister of St Anne's, Blackfriars, 1598–1622. Author, theological. Buried at St Anne's, Blackfriars, May 7, 1622. Will (P.C.C.) 1622. Brother of the next and Timothy. (*D.N.B.*)

EGERTON, THOMAS. Matric. pens. from PETERHOUSE, Michs. 1564; B.A. 1567–8; M.A. 1571. Incorp. at Oxford, 1583. Ord. deacon and priest (Peterb.) July 24, 1572. R. of Adstock, Bucks., 1569 (?)–1622. Will (P.C.C.) 1622. Brother of Stephen, above, and Timothy. (*T. A. Walker.*)

EGERTON, Sir THOMAS. University Counsel, 1586. Adm. at Brasenose College, Oxford, 1556, age 17. Adm. at Lincoln's Inn, Oct. 31, 1560. Barrister, 1572. Solicitor-General, 1581–92; M.P. for Cheshire, 1586–7. Attorney-General, 1592–4. Master of the Rolls, 1594–1603. Lord Keeper, 1596–1603. Knighted, 1597. Created Baron Ellesmere, 1603. Lord Chancellor, 1603. Chancellor of Oxford University, 1610–7. Created Viscount Brackley, 1616. Died Mar. 15, 1617. (*Al. Oxon.*; *D.N.B.*; A. B. Beaven.)

EGERTON, TIMOTHY. Matric. pens. from PETERHOUSE, Easter, 1563. S. of Thomas, mercer, of London. Brother of Thomas (1564) and Stephen.

EGGER or EGAR, WILLIAM. Adm. sizar (age 16) at CAIUS, Oct. 7, 1625. S. of William, husbandman, of Bentley, Hants. School, Saham Toney, Norfolk (Mr Hammont). Matric. 1625; Scholar, 1628–33; B.A. 1629–30; M.A. 1633. Died in College. Buried at St Michael's, June 28, 1633. (*Venn*, I. 273.)

EGGINTON, JOHN. Adm. sizar (age 16) at SIDNEY, Feb. 19, 1673–4. 1st s. of Brownlow. B. at Nottingham. School, Nottingham (Mr Birch and Mr Cudworth).

EGINTON, JOHN. Adm. pens. at ST CATHARINE'S, May 16, 1707. Perhaps s. of the above.

EGLES, GEORGE. Adm. pens. (age 18) at EMMANUEL, Nov. 22, 1740. S. of George, Esq. B. at Framfield, Sussex. School, Tonbridge. Matric. 1741. Adm. at the Inner Temple, Nov. 18, 1740; s. and h. of George, of Wadhurst, Sussex.

EGLES, THOMAS (1582), *see* ECCLES.

EGLESFIELD or EGLISFYLD, CHRISTOPHER. Matric. Fell.-Com. from CLARE, Easter, 1569. One of these names adm. at Gray's Inn, 1571, from Staple Inn. Perhaps s. of Thomas, of East Ham, Essex. (*Vis. of Essex*, 1612.)

EGLESFIELD, JOHN. M.A. 1614 (Incorp. from Oxford). Of Bristol. Matric. from Queen's College, Oxford, Oct. 16, 1601, age 17; B.A. 1605; M.A. from All Souls', 1608–9; B.D. 1617–8. V. of Congresbury, Somerset, 1614; of Worle, 1618–28; of Chew Magna, 1628. R. of Loxton, 1631; sequestered and imprisoned, 1647. (*Al. Oxon.*)

EGLESFIELD, MILES. B.A. 1537–8; M.A. 1540. Fellow of CHRIST'S, 1538, till his death, 1545. Will proved (V.C.C.) 1546.

EGLEFIELD, SAMUEL. Adm. pens. at EMMANUEL, Feb. 27, 1625–6. One of these names, s. of John, of Stratford-at-Bow, matric. from Queen's College, Oxford, Oct. 15, 1624.

EGYLSFELD, ——. B.Can.L. 1504–5.

EGLESTON, *see* also ECCLESTONE.

EGLESTON, PETER. Matric. sizar from TRINITY, *c.* 1596.

EGLESTON, WILLIAM. Matric. pens. from TRINITY, Michs. 1582; Scholar, 1586; B.A. 1586–7; M.A. 1590. Fellow, 1589. Incorp. at Oxford, 1591.

EGLYSTOM, ——. B.Can.L. 1511–2. Had studied nine years at Oxford.

EGLINTON or EAGLENTON, ANTHONY. Adm. pens. (age 17) at CAIUS, June 19, 1666. S. of Henry, gent., of Bawdeswell, Norfolk. School, Searning (Mr Burton). Matric. 1667; Scholar, 1667–72; B.A. 1669–70; M.A. 1673. Ord. deacon (Norwich) Mar. 16, 1673–4, as C. of Foxley, Norfolk. (*Venn*, I. 427.)

EGLINTON, RICHARD. Adm. sizar (age 18) at CAIUS, Oct. 13, 1744. S. of Richard, attorney, of North Elmham, Norfolk. B. at Sparham. School, Searning (Mr Brett). Scholar, 1744; Matric. 1745; B.A. 1748–9; M.A. 1752. Ord. deacon (Norwich) May 21, 1749, as C. of Sharrington, Norfolk; priest, Sept. 23, 1750, as C. of Scarning. R. of Saxlingham, 1758–86; of Sharington, 1758; of Themelthorpe, 1774–86. Died Aug. 26, 1786. M.I. at Saxlingham. (*Venn*, II. 56.)

EGLINTON, THOMAS. Adm. sizar (age 17) at CAIUS, Feb. 22, 1722–3. S. of Henry, gent., of Bawdeswell, Norfolk. B. there. Schools, Walsingham (Mr Harding), Norwich, Wymondham (Mr Sayer) and Bury. Matric. 1724; Scholar, 1724–8; B.A. 1726–7; M.A. 1730; D.D. 1745. Fellow, 1728–45. Ord. deacon (Lincoln) Mar. 2, 1728; priest, May 24, 1730. R. of Scarning, Norfolk, 1739–41. R. of Hockwold, 1744–6. R. of Elsing, 1745–6. Died Apr. 14, 1746. Will proved (Norwich) 1746. (*Venn*, II. 17.)

EGLIONBY, *see also* AGLIONBY.

EGLYONBYE, BARTHOLOMEW. Matric. sizar from CLARE, Michs. 1546.

EGLYONBYE, EDMUND. Matric. pens. from MICHAEL HOUSE, Michs. 1546; *impubes*. Scholar of Trinity College, in 1548. Brother of Thomas (1546).

EGLONBY, EDWARD. Adm. pens. at QUEENS', Dec. 17, 1600. Of Cumberland. Probably s. of Edward, of Carlisle. Married Jane, dau. of Henry Brougham. Died 1648. (G. B. Routledge; *Vis. of Cumberland*, 1665.)

EGLYONBY, THOMAS. Matric. pens. from MICHAEL HOUSE, Michs. 1546; *impubes*. Scholar of Trinity College in 1548. Brother of Edmund (1546).

EGMANTON, WILLIAM. Fellow of KING'S HALL. Resided there, 1414–34. B.A. in 1420. Received the tonsure (Ely) May 25, 1415. Went with FitzHugh's Mission to Rome, 1429. R. of Hackney, 1434–63. (*Trin. Coll. Adm.*, I. 114.)

EGTON, HENRY, *see* EYTON.

EISTEADE, RICHARD. Matric. pens. from MAGDALENE, Michs. 1585.

EKINS, ALEXANDER. Adm. pens. at CLARE, Feb. 14, 1644–5. Of Northamptonshire. Migrated to Trinity, Jan. 22, 1645–6. Matric. 1646; Scholar, 1647; B.A. 1648–9; M.A. 1652. Fellow of Trinity, 1649. R. of Orlingbury, Northants., 1656–99. Married, Oct. 5, 1658, at Kettering, Martha Sawyer. Died June 14, 1699, aged 70. M.I. at Orlingbury. Father of John (1683) and probably of the next. (*Bridges*, II. 119.)

EKINS, ALEXANDER. Adm. pens. at CLARE, Mar. 21, 1671–2. S. of Alexander, of Raunds, Northants. Bapt. there, May 6, 1655. Matric. 1672; B.A. 1675–6; M.A. 1679. Incorp. at Oxford, 1684. V. of Weekley, Northants., 1682–6. R. of Barton Seagrave, 1686–1703. Buried there June 3, 1703. M.I. Will (Archd. Northants.) 1703. Probably brother of John (1683), father of Geoffrey (1717). (*Al. Oxon.*)

EKINS, EDWARD. Matric. sizar from SIDNEY, Easter, 1622.

EKINS, GEOFFREY. Adm. pens. at JESUS, June 24, 1717. S. of Alexander (above), clerk, deceased. Bapt. at Barton Seagrave, Jan. 17, 1698–9. Colleger at Eton, 1710–6. Rustat Scholar at Jesus. Matric. 1717; B.A. 1720–1; M.A. 1725. Incorp. at Oxford, 1733. Ord. deacon (Peterb.) Sept. 23, 1722. R. of Barton Seagrave, Northants., 1723–73. R. of Doddershall and Quainton, 1732. Executor to Lady Lamington, grand niece of Isaac Newton: by her will be came into possession of several of his MSS. Died at Barton, Aug. 23, 1773. Father of Geoffrey (1749) and John (1750). (H. M. Wood.)

EKINS, GEOFFREY. Adm. at KING'S, a scholar from Eton, 1749. S. of Geoffrey (above). B. at Barton Seagrave, Northants. Bapt. July 2, 1731. Matric. 1750; B.A. 1755; M.A. 1758; D.D. 1781. Fellow, 1753. Assistant Master at Eton. Chaplain to the Lord Lieutenant in Ireland. R. of Quainton, Bucks., 1761–75. R. of Morpeth, 1775. R. of Sedgefield, Durham, 1777. Dean of Carlisle, 1782–91. Poet and classical author. Died at Parson's Green, Fulham, Nov. 20, 1791. Buried at Fulham. Will, P.C.C. Brother of John (1750). (*D.N.B.*; *Harwood*, 338; H. I. Longden.)

EKINS, GEORGE. Adm. pens. (age 16) at ST JOHN'S, June 7, 1748. S. of George, attorney-at-law, of Northamptonshire. B. at Wellingborough. Schools, Oakham and Wellingborough (Mr Holme).

EKINS, JOHN. Matric. sizar from ST JOHN'S, Easter, 1610; B.A. 1613-4; M.A. 1617. Ord. deacon (Peterb.) May 26, 1616. *See* a contemporary in *Al. Oxon.*

EKINS, JOHN. Adm. pens. at EMMANUEL, May 13, 1641. Matric. 1641; B.A. 1644-5; M.A. 1648. One of these names presented to Weekley, Northants., Oct. 23, 1647. Probably R. of Weldon, 1663-81. Died Aug. 2, 1681, aged 58. M.I. at Weldon. Perhaps father of John (1673). (*Bridges*, II. 357.)

EKINS, JOHN. Adm. sizar at TRINITY, July 1, 1653. Of Northamptonshire. Scholar, 1655; B.A. 1656-7; M.A. 1660. Fellow, 1658, Taxor, 1679. Senior Proctor, 1683-4. V. of Barrington, Cambs., 1672.

EKINS, JOHN. Adm. pens. at TRINITY, Apr. 11, 1662. Matric. 1662. Buried at St Michael's, Cambridge, July 8, 1664.

EKINS, JOHN. Adm. pens. at CORPUS CHRISTI, 1671. Of Northamptonshire. S. and h. of Alexander, gent., of Chelveston-*cum*-Caldecott. Matric. 1671. Adm. at Gray's Inn, May 23, 1671.

EKINS, JOHN. Adm. sizar (age 16) at ST JOHN'S, Apr. 22, 1673. S. of John, clerk, of Weldon, Northants. B. there. School, Oundle. Matric. 1673; B.A. 1676-7; M.A. 1680. Ord. deacon (Peterb.) Sept. 19, 1680; priest, Dec. 18, 1681.

EKINS, JOHN. Adm. pens. (age 16) at TRINITY, May 29, 1683. S. of Alexander (1644), R. of Orlingbury, Northants. School, Eton. Matric. 1683-4; Scholar, 1687; B.A. 1687-8. Buried at St Michael's, Cambridge, Dec. 29, 1689. Probably brother of Alexander (1671-2).

EKINS, JOHN. Adm. pens. (age 17) at TRINITY, Oct. 29, 1695. S. of Thomas, of Rushden, Northants. Bapt. there, Oct. 25, 1678. School, Eton. Adm. at the Middle Temple, Feb. 2, 1696-7. Brother of Thomas (1700).

EKINS, JOHN. Adm. at KING'S, a scholar from Eton, 1750. S. of Geoffrey (1717), R. of Barton Seagrave, Northants. Bapt. there, Sept. 8, 1732. Matric. 1751; B.A. 1755; M.A. 1758. Fellow, 1754. Assistant Master at Eton. Chaplain to the Duke of Rutland, Lord Lieutenant of Ireland. R. of Trowbridge, Wilts., 1774-1808. R. of Newton Toney, 1776. Dean of Salisbury, 1786. Died Sept. 18, 1808. Buried at Higham Ferrers. Brother of Geoffrey (1749).

EKINS, LAWRENCE. Adm. sizar at TRINITY, Apr. 4, 1651. Of Northamptonshire. Matric. 1651; B.A. 1654-5.

EKINS, RANDOLPH. Adm. pens. at EMMANUEL, Oct. 21, 1696. S. of Thomas, of Chester. Bapt. at Irchester, Northants., Feb. 11, 1678-9. Matric. 1697; B.A. 1700-1; M.A. 1704. Ord. deacon (Lincoln, *Litt. dim.* from Peterb.) Mar. 14, 1702-3; priest (Norwich) Sept. 23, 1705. V. of Dallington, Northants., 1706-17. R. of Holcot, 1716-45. R. of Rushden, 1721-45. Buried at Holcot, May 9, 1745. (*Baker*, I. 134; H. I. Longden.)

EKINS, RANDOLPH. Adm. pens. (age 19) at ST JOHN'S, June 19, 1740. S. of Robert, gent., of Middlesex. B. in London. School, Merchant Taylors'. Matric. 1745; LL.B. 1746. R. of Pebmarsh, Essex, 1746-87. Died Dec. 24, 1787. Will (P.C.C.) 1788. (*Scott-Mayor*, IV. 506; *G. Mag.*)

EKINS, ROBERT. Matric. pens. from CLARE, Easter, 1623. S. of Thomas, of Twywell, Northants., Esq. Bapt. there, May 12, 1605. B.A. 1626-7; M.A. 1630. Ord. deacon (Peterb.) June 8; priest, June 9, 1623. R. of Barton Seagrave, Northants., 1632-41; sequestered. (*Vis. of Northants.*, 1618.)

EKINS, ROBERT. Adm. sizar at TRINITY, June 20, 1655. Of Northamptonshire. Matric. 1656; Scholar, 1657; B.A. 1658-9. Excluded from a fellowship for nonconformity. Afterwards preacher at Oakham, Ruts. (*Calamy*, I. 218.)

EKINES, THOMAS. Adm. pens. at TRINITY, Mar. 31, 1665.

EKINS, THOMAS. Adm. pens. (age 16) at TRINITY, July 6, 1700. S. of Thomas, of Rushden, Northants. School, Guilsborough. Matric. 1701; Scholar, 1703; B.A. 1704-5. Brother of John (1695).

EKLES, THOMAS, *see* **ECCLES.**

BLAME or ELAND, EDWARD. Matric. pens. from ST JOHN'S, Easter, 1572.

ELAM, JOHN. Adm. sizar (age 21) at ST JOHN'S, June 21, 1727. S. of Thomas, husbandman, of Yorkshire. B. at Hutton Panel. School, Sedbergh. Matric. 1727; B.A. 1730-1. Ord. deacon (York) Aug. 5, 1733; priest (Lincoln) June 1, 1740. V. of Tickhill, Yorks., 1740-74. Died Apr. 29, 1774. Buried in Tickhill Church. (*Scott-Mayor*, III. 407.)

ELAM, ROBERT. Matric. sizar from TRINITY, Michs. 1581; B.A. from Pembroke, 1584-5. Ord. deacon (Peterb.) Mar. 21, 1587-8.

ELAND, BRIAN. Matric. pens. from ST JOHN'S, Easter, 1563.

ELAND, EDMUND. Matric. pens. from MAGDALENE, Easter, 1626; B.A. 1629; M.A. 1633.

ELAND, GABRIEL. Matric. pens. from PEMBROKE, Lent, 1585-6. V. of Cratfield, Suffolk, 1602. There in 1650.

ELAND or ELAM, GEORGE. B.A. from JESUS, 1584-5. B. at Hatcliffe, Lincs., 1565. M.A. 1588; B.D. 1596. Fellow, 1590-5. R. of Foston, Leics., 1594. R. of Kettlethorpe, Lincs., 1598-1600. University preacher. Chaplain to the Bishop of Lincoln, 1598-1600. Preb. of Lincoln, 1598. R. of Tempsford, Beds., 1600. Archdeacon of Bedford, 1600-31. Chancellor of Lincoln Cathedral, 1606-31. R. of Washingborough, Lincs., 1607. Died 1631. (A. Gray.)

ELAND, MARMADUKE. Matric. pens. from ST JOHN'S, Easter, 1571. Perhaps s. and h. of Robert, of Carlinghow, Yorks. Buried Dec. 4, 1615. Will (York) 1617. (*Vis. of Yorks.*; M. Sheard, *Batley*, 73.)

ELBOROUGH, HENRY. Matric. sizar from ST JOHN'S, Easter, 1611; B.A. 1614-5; M.A. 1618. Incorp. at Oxford, 1617. Ord. priest (Peterb.) May 31, 1618. V. of Scraptoft, Leics., 1620-39. V. of Stainton-by-Langworth, Lincs., 1626. Will (P.C.C.) 1653.

ELBOROUGH, JEREMIAH. Matric. pens. from ST JOHN'S, Michs. 1614; B.A. 1617-8; M.A. 1621. R. of Throcking, Herts., 1623-6. One of these names 'preacher to the English merchants at Hamburg' licensed to pass to the Low Countries May 28, 1634.

ELBOROWE, JOHN. Matric. sizar from ST JOHN'S, Easter, 1606; B.A. 1609-10; M.A. 1613. R. of Birkby, Northallerton, 1616-9. V. of St Pancras, London, 1625-31. V. of Rainham, Essex, 1628-44. R. of Wennington, 1643. Admon. (P.C.C.) May 4, 1653; of Dagenham, clerk.

ELBOROUGH, ROBERT. Adm. pens. at EMMANUEL, Mar. 1, 1650-1. B. in Hamburg. School, St Paul's; exhibitioner thence, 1650. Matric. 1652; B.A. 1655; M.A. 1659. Signs for priest's orders (London) June 8, 1664. P.C. of St Laurence Poultney, London, 1664. Schoolfellow of Pepys; who pronounced him 'a fool, as he ever was, or worse' (1662).

ELBOROUGH, ROGER. Matric. sizar from ST JOHN'S, Easter, 1617. B. in Trinity parish, Cambridge. B.A. 1620-1; M.A. 1624. Ord. deacon (London) June 18, 1623, age 31. C. of Buntingford, Herts. R. of Widford, 1636-70. Died 1670.

ELBOROWE, THOMAS. Adm. sizar (age 17) at ST JOHN'S, Apr. 30, 1639. S. of John, farmer, of Haselbeech, Northants. B. there. School, Peterborough (Mr Wildbore). Matric. 1639; B.A. 1642-3. V. of Chiswick, Middlesex, 1662-75. M.I. there. Will, P.C.C. (J. Ch. Smith.)

ELBOROUGH, WILLIAM. Matric. sizar from ST JOHN'S, *c.* 1593; B.A. 1595-6; M.A. 1599.

ELBOROW, WILLIAM. B.A. from ST JOHN'S, 1615-6. Ord. deacon (Peterb.) May 31, 1618.

ELBURNE, ROBERT. Matric. sizar from QUEENS', Michs. 1569.

ELCOCKE, ANTHONY. Matric. pens. from CHRIST'S, Oct. 1567. Probably s. of Alexander, of Stockport. B.A. 1571-2; M.A. 1575. Ord. priest (Norwich) Jan. 31, 1579-80. R. of Hamerton, Hunts., 1579-1606. Will (P.C.C.) 1606. (*Peile*, I. 101.)

ELCOCKE, EPHRAIM. Adm at CHRIST'S, 1677; B.A. 1680.

ELCOCK, FRANCIS. Matric. pens. from ST JOHN'S, Easter, 1613. One of these names, s. of Alexander, of Whitepoole. Age 17 in 1613. (*Ormerod*, III. 188.)

ELCOCKE, FRANCIS. Matric. pens. from ST JOHN'S, Easter, 1621.

ELCOKE, GEORGE. Matric. pens. from ST JOHN'S, Michs. 1565.

ELCOCK, JOHN. Matric. sizar from ST JOHN'S, Michs. 1622. Probably s. of Alexander, of Whitepoole. B.A. from Christ's, 1626-7. (*Peile*, I. 355.)

ELCOCK, JOHN SYMONDS. Adm. sizar (age 17) at ST JOHN'S, June 14, 1686. S. of Seth. B. at Kirby Wiske, Yorks. School, York (Mr Tomlinson). Matric. 1686; B.A. 1689-90. Ord. deacon (Durham) Sept. 20, 1691; priest (York) Feb. 1694-5.

ELCOCK, RICHARD. B.A. from ST JOHN'S, 1609. Of Cheshire. B. at Stockport. M.A. 1612. Fellow, 1611. Ord. priest (Peterb.) July 16, 1611. Master of Pocklington Grammar School, 1613-24. V. of Pocklington, 1619-22. R. of Westhorpe, Suffolk, 1622-30. Died July 21, 1630. Buried there. M.I. (Le Neve, *Mon.*, I. 119.)

ELCOCK, RICHARD. Adm. sizar (age 17) at ST JOHN'S, Apr. 30, 1709. S. of Alexius, mercer, deceased. B. at York. School, York (Mr Tomlinson). Matric. 1709; B.A. 1712-3. Took the surname of Weddell, pursuant to his uncle's will, 1748. Died at Newby, Yorks., 1762. (Whitaker, *Richmondshire*, II. 122.)

ELCOCKE or ALCOCK, ROBERT. Adm. pens. (age 18) at ST JOHN'S, June 28, 1633. S. of Alexander, gent., of Whitepoole, in Acton, Cheshire. B. there. School, Wrenbury, Cheshire (private; Mr Harwar). Matric. 1633; B.A. 1636-7; M.A. 1640.

ELCOCKE, SETH. Adm. sizar (age 17) at ST JOHN'S, June 24, 1637. S. of Richard, clerk, of Beverley. B. at Pocklington. School, Beverley (Mr Pomroy). Matric. 1637; B.A. 1640-1; M.A. 1644. Ord. priest (Lincoln) Sept. 24, 1643. R. of Kirkby-Wiske, Yorks., 1661.

ELCOCK, THOMAS. Adm. sizar (age 13) at ST JOHN'S, Sept. 11, 1686. S. of Thomas. B. at Beverley, Yorks. School, Beverley (Mr Lambert). Ord. deacon (York) May, 1695; priest, 1697.

ELCOCKS, THOMAS. M.A. from KING'S, 1725. S. of William, of St Swithin's, Worcester. Matric. from Oriel College, Oxford, Mar. 31, 1718, age 19; B.A. (Oxford) 1721-2. (*Al. Oxon.*)

ELCOCK, THOMAS. Adm. sizar (age 17) at ST JOHN'S, May 18, 1727. S. of T., clerk, of Derbyshire. B. at South Normanton. School, Beverley (Mr Jefferson). Matric. 1727; B.A. 1730-1; M.A. 1741. Assistant Master at Tonbridge School, 1731-42. V. of Pembury, Kent, 1738-52. Buried at Pembury, Dec. 21, 1752. (*Scott-Mayor*, III. 403.)

ELDE, JOHN. Adm. pens. (age 17) at TRINITY, June 30, 1721. S. of Francis, of Seighford, Staffs. School, Stafford (Mr Dearle). Of Dorking, Surrey, and Seighford, Staffs. Married Catherine, widow of Rowland Cotton, Esq., of Etwall. Died Apr. 16, 1796. (*Staffs. Pedigrees*; Burke, *L.G.*)

ELDER, ARTHUR. Incorp. at Oxford, as M.A. of Cambridge, 1561, *see* Yeldert.

ELDER, JOHN. 'M.A. of Cambridge'; incorp. at Oxford, July 30, 1560. Had studied 12 years at Aberdeen, Glasgow, and St Andrews. His incorporation at Cambridge is not recorded. Author. (*Cooper*, I. 208; *D.N.B.*)

ELDER, ROGER. A scholar. Buried in St Benet's, Cambridge, May 27, 1616. Perhaps Roger Eltye, whom *see*.

ELDERKAR, ROBERT. Matric. pens. from TRINITY, Michs. 1566.

ELDERSON, CLEMENT. Matric. pens. from CLARE, Easter, 1569.

ELDERTON, THOMAS, *see* **ELRINGTON.**

ELDRED, JOHN. B.A. from EMMANUEL, 1610-1. One of these names, s. of John, of London, gent., adm. at Lincoln's Inn, June 26, 1611. Bencher. Of Newington Butts. Died Jan. 1649. Buried at Mitcham. (*Davy MSS.*)

ELDRED, JOHN. Adm. Fell.-Com. at PETERHOUSE, Sept. 6, 1621. S. of John, of Colchester, afterwards of Little Birch Hall, and of Olivers, Essex. Adm. at Lincoln's Inn, May 7, 1623. Succeeded his father at Olivers, in 1645. Collector of the Sequestrations for the County, 1645. Died Nov. 16, 1682. Father of the next. (*T. A. Walker*, 21; *Morant*, II. 193.)

ELDRED, JOHN. Adm. pens. (age 16) at CAIUS, July 2, 1646. S. and h. of John (above), gent., of 'Bourls' (? Bures), Essex. B. at Colchester, Oct. 2, 1629. Schools, Colchester (Mr Dugard), Bishop's Stortford (Mr Lea) and Merchant Taylors'. Matric. 1646. Adm. at Lincoln's Inn, May 2, 1648. Lord of the Manor of Olivers, Stanway. M.P. for Harwich, 1689. Died Sept. 2, 1717. Buried at Earle's Colne. (*Venn*, I. 364; *Vis. of Essex*, 1634.)

ELDRED, JOHN. Adm. sizar at ST CATHARINE'S, Apr. 11, 1659. Of Huntingdonshire. Matric. 1661; B.A. 1662-3. Ord. priest (Chichester) Feb. 9, 1662-3. R. of Watlington, Sussex, 1663-85. Buried there Apr. 6, 1685. (W. C. Renshaw.)

ELDRED, JOSEPH. Adm. sizar at TRINITY, May 31, 1658. Matric. 1660; B.A. 1661-2. Signs for deacon's orders (London) Dec. 19, 1663; Chaplain to Sir Heneage Fetherstone, Bart. Licensed schoolmaster, by Bishop of Norwich, Apr. 1667. C. of Antingham, Norfolk, 1673. Father of Robert (1691).

ELDRED, MARTIN. Matric. pens. from CLARE, Easter, 1631. Of London. B.A. 1634-5. Migrated to Jesus; adm. Fell.-Com. there, Oct. 6, 1637. M.A. 1638. Committed to the Gatehouse by the House of Commons, 1642, as author of a mock petition from the University. (Cooper, *Annals*, III. 318.)

ELDRED, ROBERT. Adm. sizar (age 18) at CAIUS, June 2, 1691. S. of Joseph (1658), of North Walsham, Norfolk. B. there. School, North Walsham (Mr Harvey). Matric. 1691; Scholar, 1691-6; B.A. 1694-5. Ord. deacon (Norwich) 1695; priest, May 31, 1697. (*Venn*, I. 490.)

ELDRED, SAMUEL. Adm. sizar at TRINITY, Sept. 9, 1656. Matric. Michs. 1657; and again, Michs. 1658; B.A. 1660-1. V. of Peasmarsh, Sussex, 1662-94.

ELDRED, THOMAS. Matric. pens. from JESUS, Easter, 1572; B.A. 1575-6. One of these names licensed as schoolmaster at Duxford, Cambs., 1581.

ELDRINGTON, *see* **ELRINGTON.**

ELENDEN, THOMAS. B.A. from CORPUS CHRISTI, 1575-6.

ELES or EALES, EDWARD. Incorp. M.A. 1668, from Corpus Christi College, Oxford. S. of Edward, of Hatford, Berks. Matric. at Trinity College, Oxford, Dec. 16, 1640, age 14; B.A. (Oxford) 1644; M.A. 1647-8. Chaplain of Corpus Christi, Oxford; ejected, 1648; restored, 1660. Died 1683. (*Al. Oxon.*)

EELES, ISAAC. Adm. sizar at ST CATHARINE'S, Jan. 24, 1671-2. Matric. 1672.

ELES, LUKE. Adm. sizar at EMMANUEL, June 30, 1649. Of Runcton Holme, Norfolk. Matric. 1649; M.B. 1654; M.D. 1661 (*Lit. Reg.*). Physician to the King. Received a grant of Arms, 1670. Father of the next.

EALES, LUKE. Adm. pens. (age 16) at ST JOHN'S, Nov. 2, 1687. S. of Luke, M.D. (above). B. at Welwyn, Herts. School, Berkhampstead. Matric. 1693; M.B. 1693.

EELES, NATHANIEL. Adm. pens. at EMMANUEL, June 12, 1633. S. of John. B. at Aldenham, Herts. Bapt. there, Oct. 19, 1617. Matric. 1633; B.A. 1636-7. Studied at Leyden (Utrecht?). Ord. presbyter there. Minister at Harpenden Chapel, Wheathampstead, Herts., 1643-61; ejected. Died Dec. 18, 1678. (*Calamy*, II. 44; Cussans, *Herts.*)

ELES, ROBERT. B.Can.L. 1467.

ELES, STEPHEN. M.Gram. 1480-1.

ELES, THOMAS. B.A. 1454-5; M.A. 1458.

EALES, THOMAS. Adm. sizar at QUEENS', May 6, 1616. Of Warwickshire. B.A. 1620-1; M.A. 1624; B.D. 1631 (*Lit. Reg.*). Fellow, 1624-34. R. of South Runcton, Norfolk, 1631-61.

ELES, ——. Fee for B.A. 1463-4.

ELFORD, HUGH. Matric. pens. from CLARE, Michs. 1579. Migrated to Oxford. Matric. from Exeter College, Nov. 17, 1581, age 20. Adm. at the Middle Temple, 1582, as s. of John, of Sheepstor, Devon, gent.

ELFORD, HUGH. Adm. pens. (age 19) at SIDNEY, June 18, 1625. S. of Walter, Esq., of Shipstor, Devon. B. at Buckland. Schools, Exeter (Mr Periman) and Plymouth (Mr Horsman). Matric. 1625; B.A. 1628-9; M.A. 1632. Admon. of one of these names (Exeter) 1645; V. of Walkhampton, Devon. (*Vis. of Devon*, 1620.)

ELFORD, JEREMIAH. Adm. pens. at PEMBROKE, 1682, as B.A. S. of Thomas, R. of Acton, Middlesex. Matric. from Trinity College, Oxford, May 31, 1677, age 16; B.A. (Oxford) 1680-1. Subscribed for priest's orders (Bristol) Dec. 24, 1682. R. of Pilsdon, Dorset, 1683-1709. R. of Rampisham, till 1709. Died 1709. M.I. at Rampisham. (*Al. Oxon.*; *Hutchins*, II. 695.)

ELFORD, JOHN. M.A. 1608 (Incorp. from Oxford). Of Devon. Matric. from Exeter College, Mar. 28, 1595, age 16; B.A. 1598; M.A. 1601. Adm. at Lincoln's Inn, 1602. One of these names M.P. for Tiverton, 1646.

ELFORD, JOHN. Matric. pens. from ST JOHN'S, Easter, 1620.

ELGAR, EDMUND. Matric. pens. from CORPUS CHRISTI, Michs. 1569; B.A. 1574-5.

ELGAR, THOMAS. Matric. pens. from CHRIST'S, Easter, 1621; B.A. from Trinity Hall, 1624-5; M.A. 1628. Ord. deacon (Peterb.) May 31; priest, June 1, 1629.

ELGIN, Earl of, *see* **AILESBURY, ROBERT.**

ELHAM, JOHN. Adm. pens. at EMMANUEL, July 7, 1619. Matric. 1619.

ELIN or HELIN, JOHN. Of Norfolk, Carmelite friar at Lynn. D.D. of Cambridge. Prior of the Carmelite Convent in London. Died *c.* 1379. (*Pits*, 519.)

ELING or EELYNGE, ROBERT. Matric. pens. from TRINITY, Easter, 1578. B. at Leighton Buzzard, *c.* 1563. Scholar, 1582; B.A. 1582-3; M.A. 1586. Ord. priest (Lincoln). V. of Keysoe, Beds., 1599.

ELING, THOMAS. Matric. sizar from CORPUS CHRISTI, 1597. Of Cambridgeshire.

ELKIN, GEORGE. Matric. pens. from JESUS, Michs. 1552. Perhaps B.A. Oxford, 1559, as 'A priest, with cure of souls.' One of these names V. of Lyme Regis, Dorset, 1573.

ELKIN, JOHN. Matric. pens. from ST JOHN'S, *c.* 1590; B.A. 1593-4. One of these names, of London, was adm. at Gray's Inn, Nov. 18, 1594.

ELKYN, RICHARD. Matric. pens. from ST JOHN'S, Michs. 1587; B.A. 1590-1; M.A. 1594.

ELKINTON, THOMAS. Matric. pens. from PETERHOUSE, Michs. 1580.

ELLA, JOHN. Adm. sizar at JESUS, May 21, 1746. Of Rampton, Notts. S. of ——, clerk, deceased. Matric. 1746; Scholar; B.A. 1749-50; M.A. 1754.

ELLAY, WILLIAM. Adm. sizar (age 15) at SIDNEY, June 20, 1702. S. of William, of Thirsk, Yorks. School, Thirsk (Mr Midgley). Matric. 1704; B.A. 1705-6. Ord. deacon (York) Nov. 1710; priest, 1711.

ELLERKER or ELLAKAY, EDWARD. Adm. pens. (age 18) at CAIUS, Oct. 28, 1584. S. of Edward, gent., of Risby, Beverley, Yorks. School, Hull. Readm. as Fell.-Com. 1587. B.A. 1587-8.

ELLECAR, FRANCIS. Matric. pens. from TRINITY, Easter, 1584. Perhaps of Youlton, Easingwold, Yorks. (M. H. Peacock.)

ELARKAR, ——. Matric. pens. from ST JOHN'S, Easter, 1544.

ELLERKER, ——. Adm. Fell.-Com. at JESUS, 1598-9.

ELLERKER, ——. Adm. Fell.-Com. at ST CATHARINE'S, Easter, 1646.

ELLERSHAW, JOHN. Adm. sizar (age 19) at CHRIST'S, Mar. 26, 1720. S. of Richard (1679), V. of Giggleswick, Yorks. School, Giggleswick (Mr Carr). Matric. 1720; Scholar, 1721; B.A. 1723-4. Ord. priest (Norwich) June, 1726. V. of Ubbeston St Peter, Suffolk, 1748. Died 1760. (*Peile*, II. 197.)

ELLERSHAW, RICHARD. Adm. sizar at CLARE, May 21, 1679. Of 'Bentham Ewcross,' Yorks. School, Wakefield. Matric. 1679; B.A. 1682-3; M.A. 1688. Temporary Head Master of Giggleswick in 1685. Ord. priest (York) Mar. 1684-5. V. of Giggleswick, 1686-1719. Died 1719. Father of John (above).

ELLERTON, JOHN. Matric. sizar from QUEENS', Easter, 1577. Of Salop. B.A. 1580-1; M.A. 1584. Ord. priest (Lichfield) Nov. 1, 1582. C. of Therfield, Herts. Perhaps V. of Barling, Essex, 1586-1601. Buried there 1601.

ELLERTON, ——. M.Gram. 1482.

ELLESLEY, CHRISTOPHER. Matric. sizar from ST JOHN'S, Easter, 1581.

ELLESMERE, Lord, *see* EGERTON, Sir THOMAS.

ELLETSON, ANTHONY. Adm. pens. (age 18) at ST JOHN'S, Feb. 23, 1663-4. S. of Robert, of Furness Fell, Lancs. B. there. School, Sedbergh. Matric. 1664; B.A. 1667-8; M.A. 1671. Ord. deacon (Ely) June 2, 1672. Brother of Laurence (1663-4).

ELLETSON, JOHN. Matric. sizar from TRINITY, Michs. 1584; Scholar, 1588; B.A. 1588-9; M.A. 1592. R. of Chignal Smely, Essex, 1597-1617. Died 1617.

ELLETSON or ELLOTSON, JOHN. Adm. pens. (age 15) at PEMBROKE, May 6, 1658. S. of John, currier. B. at Fairsted, Essex. Matric. 1660; B.A. 1661-2.

ELLETSON, LAURENCE. Adm. pens. (age 17) at ST JOHN'S, Feb. 23, 1663-4. S. of Robert, of Furness Fell, Lancs. B. there. School, Sedbergh. Matric. 1664; B.A. 1667-8; M.A. 1671. Incorp. at Oxford, 1671. Ord. deacon (London) Sept. 1669; priest (Ely) Dec. 18, 1669. V. of Winterton, Lincs., 1671. V. of Aukborough, Yorks., 1685-6. Brother of Anthony (1663-4). (*Al. Oxon.*)

ELLETSON, ROGER. Adm. pens. (age 18) at ST JOHN'S, Feb. 14, 1660-1. S. of Robert, gent., of Broughton, Lancs. B. there. School, Urswick, Lancs. Matric. 1661. Adm. at Gray's Inn, Apr. 29, 1662.

ELLETSON, ROGER HOPE. Adm. pens. (age 18) at TRINITY, June 5, 1745; and Fell.-Com. 1746. S. of Richard, of Jamaica. School, Eton. Matric. 1746. One Roger Elletson adm. at Lincoln's Inn, July 6, 1744. [According to *Burke* he was s. of Roger, of Jamaica.] Lieutenant-Governor of Jamaica, 1766. Died Nov. 28, 1775. (G. *Mag.*; Burke, *L.G.*)

ELLINGHAM, JOHN. Fellow of PEMBROKE. Ord. priest (Ely) Sept. 1376.

ELLINGHAM or ELMHAM, ——, *see* ELMAN.

ELLINGTON, THOMAS. Adm. sizar (age 16) at PETERHOUSE, May 20, 1658. Of Northamptonshire. School, Peterborough. Migrated to Emmanuel, 1659. Matric. 1661; B.A. 1661-2. Ord. priest (Peterb.) Aug. 2, 1664.

ELLINGTON or ELKINGTON, ——. Adm. at PEMBROKE, Dec. 31, 1657-8.

ELLIOT or ELYOTT, ADAM. Adm. sizar (age 18) at CAIUS, Nov. 10, 1664. S. of Henry, clerk, of Jedburgh, Scotland. B. there. Scholar, 1666; B.A. 1668-9. Travelled on the continent for two years. On the voyage home captured by a Sallee rover, and sold as a slave in Morocco. Escaped to England. Ord. deacon (Ely) 1671; priest (London) Dec. 1672, as C. of Allington, Kent. Chaplain to Lord Grey, of Werke. Officiated in Dublin. P.C. of St James, Duke Place, London, 1685-1700. His *Modest Vindication* contains an account of his travels, and of his quarrel with his fellow collegian Titus Oates, who had accused him of being a Jesuit priest. Died 1700. (*Venn*, I. 423; *D.N.B.*)

ELLIOTT, ADAM. Adm. at KING'S, a scholar from Eton, 1709. B. in London. Matric. 1710; B.A. 1713-4; M.A. 1717. Fellow, 1713. Ord. deacon (London) Apr. 11, 1721. R. of Milton, Cambs., 1727. Assistant Master at Eton. Died at Eton, 1735. (*Harwood.*)

ELIOT, ALEXANDER. Adm. pens. (age 17) at ST JOHN'S, Apr. 23, 1737. S. of Griffith, gent., of Tenby, Pembs. School, Tenby. Matric. 1737. Adm. at the Middle Temple, Apr. 21, 1737. High Sheriff of Pembs., 1754.

ELLIOTT, BENJAMIN. B.D. 1634 (Incorp. from Oxford) S. of Laurence, of Busbridge, Surrey. Matric. from Corpus Christi College, Oxford, Oct. 18, 1616, age 19; B.A. 1616; M.A. 1620; B.D. 1627. R. of Trent, Somerset, 1640. Brother of Joshua (1616). (*Al. Oxon.*; *Vis. of Surrey*, 1623.)

ELIOT, CHARLES. Matric. sizar from CLARE, Easter, 1625; B.A. 1627-8; M.A. 1632. Ord. deacon (Peterb.) Sept. 19, 1629.

ELIOT, DANIEL. Adm. Fell.-Com. (age 17) at CHRIST'S, July 17, 1663. S. of John, of Port Eliot, Cornwall, Esq. B. at Portsmouth. School, Thurston (? Suffolk). Adm. at Lincoln's Inn, Nov. 3, 1668. M.P. for St Germans, Cornwall, 1678-1701. Died Oct. 1702. (*Peile*, I. 606.)

ELYOTT, EDMUND. Adm. pens. (age 17) at ST JOHN'S, July 8, 1741. S. of Thomas, doctor, of Middlesex. B. in London. School, Bury, Suffolk. Matric. 1742; B.A. 1744-5; M.A. 1748. Ord. deacon (Norwich) Dec. 20, 1748; priest (York) June 10, 1750. One of these names R. of Litchfield, Hants., 1757-81. (*Scott-Mayor*, III. 522.)

ELIOT, EDWARD. Matric. pens. from CHRIST'S, Dec. 1582. Probably of Newlands, Essex; s. of John, of Bishop's Stortford, Herts. B.A. (St Catharine's, according to the *Grace*) 1584-5. Probably M.A. Ord. deacon and priest (Peterb.) Sept. 29, 1587. V. of Sawston, Cambs., 1587. (*Vis. of Essex*, 1612.)

ELIOTT, EDWARD. Adm. sizar at ST JOHN'S, Apr. 2, 1638. S. of John, gent., of Writtle, Essex. B. there. Educated at Lord Maynard's private school by Mr Morris. Matric. 1638; B.A. 1641-2.

ELLIOTT, EDWARD. Adm. at CORPUS CHRISTI, 1692. Of Surrey. S. of Sir William, of Busbridge, Knt. Matric. 1693; B.A. 1696-7; M.A. 1700. Incorp. at Oxford, 1703. V. of Buttermere, Wilts., 1700-22. R. of Dunsfold, Surrey, 1722-39; perhaps of Hambledon also. Died Mar. 26, 1740. Father of the next, of William (1726-7) and Lawrence (1743). (*Manning and Bray*, II. 63.)

ELIOT, EDWARD. Adm. sizar (age 18) at MAGDALENE, Dec. 19, 1749. S. of Edward (above), clerk, of Hambledon, Surrey. B. there. School, Eton. Matric. 1750; B.A. 1754; M.A. 1764. Fellow, 1754. V. of Hambledon, 1756. R. of Alfold, 1764. Died Aug. 7, 1790. Brother of Lawrence (1743) and William (1726). (G. *Mag.*; *Manning and Bray*, II. 58.)

ELYOTT, GEORGE. Adm. (age 19) at KING'S, a scholar from Eton, Aug. 28, 1587. Of Guildford, Surrey. Matric. 1587; B.A. 1591-2; M.A. 1595. Fellow, 1590-98. Perhaps R. of Hopton, Suffolk, 1599-1601. 'Esteemed a good poet.' (*Harwood.*)

ELIOT, HENRY. Adm. sizar at JESUS, Mar. 24, 1679-80. Of Yorkshire. Matric. 1680; Scholar, 1683; B.A. 1683-4. Ord. priest (York) Sept. 1689. One of these names V. of Olney, Bucks., 1701-18. R. of Haversham, 1717-35. Buried at Haversham, Dec. 2, 1735. (*Lipscomb*, IV. 191.)

ELLIOTT, JAMES. Adm. pens. at KING'S, Michs. 1602. B. at Hunsdon, Essex. B.A. 1601-2; M.A. 1606. Ord. deacon (London) Mar. 1, 1606-7; priest, Sept. 25, 1609. R. of Rayleigh, Essex, 1609.

ELLIOTT, JAMES. Adm. pens. at CORPUS CHRISTI, Easter, 1636. Of Essex. Probably migrated to King's, 1637. Donor to King's library.

ELIOT, JAMES. Adm. Fell.-Com. (age 18) at EMMANUEL, Jan. 17, 1738-9. Of London. S. of Edward, Esq. School, Winchester. Matric. 1739.

ELLIOTT, JOHN. Matric. pens. from ST JOHN'S, Easter, 1567.

ELLIOTT, JOHN. Matric. sizar from KING'S, Michs. 1608; B.A. 1612-3; M.A. 1616. Ord. deacon (Peterb.) Dec. 23, 1615.

ELLIOTT, JOHN. Matric. pens. from JESUS, Lent, 1618-9. S. of Bennet. Bapt. at Widford, Herts., Aug. 5, 1604. B.A. 1622. Probably in Holy Orders. Lived for a time at Nazing, Essex; and, as assistant at Mr Thos. Hooker's school at Little Baddon, 1629. Went to Holland, 1630; and to New England, 1631. Minister at Boston, 1631; and at Roxburgh, Mass., 1632-90. Best known for his labours amongst the Indians, and his translation of the Scriptures into the language of the Massachusett Indians. Died May 20, 1690. (D.*N.B.*; J. G. Bartlett.)

ELLIOTT, JOHN. Matric. sizar from JESUS, Easter, 1621; B.A. 1624-5.

ELLIOT, JOHN. Adm. sizar (age 17) at TRINITY, July 2, 1679. Of Gloucestershire. S. of John. Exhibitioner from St Paul's School when he received a grant of £5. Matric. 1679; B.A. 1682-3. One of these names, B.A., V. of St John, Yeovil, Somerset, 1683-90. Died 1690.

ELLIOTT, JOHN. M.D. 1681 (*Lit. Reg.*). Incorp. at Oxford, 1683. Fellow, R.C.P. June 25, 1687. Censor. Impeached for high treason for his attack on William III, and committed to Newgate, 1689. Died c. 1691. (*Munk*, I. 477; *D.N.B.*)

ELLIOTT, JOHN. Adm. sizar at CLARE, July 9, 1689. Of Countesthorpe, Leics. Matric. 1689; B.A. 1693-4; M.A. 1713. Ord. priest (Lincoln) Mar. 20, 1697-8. V. of Welham, Leics., 1700-34. V. of Slawston, 1712-27. Perhaps R. of Langton, 1727. Died May 28, 1734, aged 61. M.I. at Welham. (*Nichols*, II. 867.)

ELLIOT, JOHN. Adm. pens. (age 17) at SIDNEY, Feb. 24, 1690-1. S. of Samuel, yeoman. B. at St Ives, Hunts. School, Huntingdon (Mr Jo. Matthews). Matric. 1691.

ELLIOTT, JOHN. Adm. scholar at TRINITY HALL, Jan. 9, 1703-4. Matric. 1703; LL.B. 1709.

ELLIOTT, JOSHUA. M.A. 1616 (Incorp. from Oxford). S. of Laurence, of Busbridge, Surrey. Matric. from Queen's College, Oxford, Oct. 26, 1604, age 15; B.A. 1608; M.A. 1614. R. of Woolston, Glocs., 1618. V. of Leigh, 1619; and of Cold Aston, 1629. Brother of Benjamin (1634). (*Al. Oxon.*; *Vis. of Surrey*, 1623.)

ELIOT, LAWRENCE. Adm. sizar (age 17) at MAGDALENE, Oct. 8, 1743. S. of Edward (1692), clerk. B. at Hambledon, Surrey. School, Basingstoke, Hants. Matric. 1743; B.A. 1747-8; M.A. 1751. Fellow, 1749. Taxor, 1752. Proctor, 1761-2. Ord. priest (Ely) Oct. 7, 1750. V. of Steeple Ashton, Wilts. Died Sept. 17, 1784. Brother of Edward (1749) and William (1726).

ELLIOTT or ELLET, LUKE. Adm. sizar at EMMANUEL, May 29, 1667. Of Derbyshire. Matric. 1668.

ELLIOTT, ORLANDO. B.A. from MAGDALENE, 1631-2; M.A. 1635. Licensed to practise medicine, 1639.

ELLIOTT, PETER. B.A. 1639 (Incorp. from Oxford). S. of Edward, of Newton Ferrers, Devon, clerk. Matric. from Corpus Christi, Oxford, Aug. 28, 1634, age 17; B.A. 1638; M.A. 1640-1; M.B. 1645-6; M.D. 1652. Sometime chaplain of Corpus College (Oxford), and preacher. Practised medicine in and near Oxford. Died Mar. 5, 1681. M.I. at St Peter-in-the-East, Oxford. (*Al. Oxon.*; Le Neve, *Mon.*, V. 31.)

ELLIOTT, PHILIP. Matric. pens. from KING'S, Easter, 1637; B.A. 1640-1; M.A. 1644. Ord. priest (Lincoln) Oct. 22, 1645. R. of Hunsdon, Herts., 1644-61 and 1666-c. 1686. Father of the next. (*Cussans*, I.)

ELIOT, PHILIP. Adm. pens. (age 16) at CHRIST'S, May 17, 1666. S. of Philip (above), R. of Hunsdon, Herts. B. there. School, Bishop's Stortford (Mr Leigh). B.A. 1669-70. Ord. deacon (Lincoln) Dec. 18, 1670. (*Peile*, II. 4.)

ELLIOTT, RICHARD. Adm. pens. at EMMANUEL, May 12, 1592. Matric. 1592.

ELLIOTT, RICHARD. Adm. at KING'S, a scholar from Eton, 1666. B. in London. Matric. 1667; B.A. 1669-70; M.A. 1674. Fellow, 1669. Chaplain to the East India Company, 1677. Died in India, Oct. 18, 1696. Benefactor to the College. (*Harwood*, 257.)

ELLIOTT, RICHARD. Adm. at CORPUS CHRISTI, 1746. Of Devon. Matric. 1746; B.A. 1749-50. A dissenting minister.

ELLIOTT, ROBERT. B.Civ.L. 1538-9.

ELLIOTT, ROBERT. Adm. sizar (age 22) at TRINITY, Jan. 4, 1717-8. S. of Robert, of Southwark, London. Exhibitioner from Charterhouse. Matric. 1718. Ord. priest (Lincoln) Feb. 21, 1724-5, as B.A. R. of Dunsby, Lincs., 1724-39. Buried there Aug. 9, 1739.

ELIOT or ELLOT, ROGER. Matric. pens. from CHRIST'S, June, 1575, as 'Hellot'; B.A. 1578-9; M.A. 1582.

ELLIOT, ST JOHN. M.A. from KING'S, 1748. S. of John, of Liskeard, Cornwall, gent. Matric. from Exeter College, Oxford, May 17, 1738, age 17; B.A. (Oxford) 1741-2. (*Al. Oxon.*)

ELYOTT, THOMAS. Of Jesus College. S. of Sir Richard, Justice C.P. M.A. 1507 (according to *Cooper*). Clerk of the Council. Knighted, c. 1527. Sheriff of Cambs., 1532 and 1543. Employed on foreign missions. For a list of his works see *Cooper*, I. 89. Died at his estate at Carlton, Cambs. Buried there Mar. 25, 1546.

ELLIOTT, THOMAS. Matric. Fell.-Com. from KING'S, Easter, 1572. One of these names adm. at Lincoln's Inn, Oct. 30, 1575.

ELLIOTT, THOMAS. Matric. Fell.-Com. from CHRIST'S, Michs. 1589. One of these names adm. at the Middle Temple, July 7, 1592; s. and h. of Edward, of Newlands (Writtle), Essex. Knighted, July 23, 1603. (*Vis. of Essex*, 1612.)

ELIOT, THOMAS. Adm. sizar at JESUS, July 6, 1620. (Perhaps already adm. at Emmanuel, May 22, 1619.) B.A. 1623-4; M.A. 1627. Ord. deacon (Peterb.) June 4; priest, June 5, 1626. Of Wimpole, Cambs., in 1627. Perhaps C. of Wisbech, in 1635. (A. Gray.)

ELIOTT, THOMAS. Adm. pens. at JESUS, June 13, 1660. Of Cambridgeshire.

ELYOTT, THOMAS. Adm. pens. at EMMANUEL, May 19, 1740. S. of Thomas, of Westminster, Esq. School, Kensington. Matric. 1740. Adm. at Lincoln's Inn, Apr. 23, 1740.

ELIOTT, THURSTAN. Adm. sizar (age 19) at SIDNEY, Feb. 17, 1637-8. S. of Simon, clerk, deceased. B. at Stony Middleton, Derbs. Matric. 1637-8. Head Master of Pontefract School, 1650.

ELIOT, WALTER. Matric. sizar from ST JOHN'S, Easter, 1578.

ELLIOTT, WALTER. Matric. sizar from EMMANUEL, Lent, 1620-1; B.A. 1624-5; M.A. 1628. Ord. deacon (Peterb.) Sept. 25; priest, Sept. 26, 1625.

ELLOT, WILLIAM. Fellow of KING'S HALL. Adm. 1423, resided till 1437. LL.B. in 1430. Ord. priest (Norwich) Dec. 18, 1428. Of York diocese.

ELLIOTT, WILLIAM. Pens. of CORPUS CHRISTI, 1464. R. of Bampton, Devon. *Masters* suggests that he was LL.B., and preb. of Lincoln.

ELLIOTT, WILLIAM. Matric. pens. from ST CATHARINE'S, Easter, 1640; B.A. 1643-4; M.A. from St John's, 1647. Fellow of St John's, 1644 (intruded). Perhaps Master of Aldenham School, Herts., 1653-63. One of these names R. of Shenley, Herts., 1663-86.

ELIOT, WILLIAM. Adm. sizar at JESUS, July 2, 1650. Of Suffolk. S. of a minister at Bury. School, Bury. Matric. 1651; B.A. 1653-4; Scholar, 1654; M.A. 1657. Usher of Bury School, 1655-60. R. of West Stow, Suffolk, 1660-2. V. of Pakenham, 1661-4. Schoolmaster there. R. of Fornham All Saints', 1663-1705. Died Oct. 1705, aged 72. M.I. at Fornham.

ELLIOT, WILLIAM. Adm. sizar (age 17) at MAGDALENE, Mar. 22, 1726-7. S. of Edward (1692), clerk. B. at Hambledon, Surrey. School, Guildford. Matric. 1728; B.A. 1730-1; M.A. 1734. Fellow, 1734. Ord. deacon (Lincoln) Sept. 24, 1732. R. of Dunsfold, Surrey, 1739-55. V. of Hambledon, 1742-55. Died Oct. 7, 1755. Brother of Edward (1749) and Lawrence (1743). (*Manning and Bray*, II. 58.)

ELLIOTT, WILLIAM. M.A. from KING'S, 1734. S. of William, of Gloucester. Matric. from Oriel College, Oxford, May 15, 1712, age 17; B.A. (Oxford) 1715-6. V. of Elmstone Hardwick, Gloucs., 1721. R. of St John Baptist, Gloucester, 1733.

ELYOT, ——. Sizar at PETERHOUSE, 1592.

ELLIS, ANTHONY. Matric. pens. from CHRIST'S, Michs. 1547, as Elys or Elye. Scholar in 1546.

ELLYS, ANTHONY. Adm. pens. at CLARE, June 7, 1709. S. of Anthony, merchant, and mayor of Yarmouth. B. at Yarmouth. Bapt. June 8, 1690. Matric. 1709; B.A. 1712-3; M.A. 1716; D.D. 1728 (*Com. Reg.*). Fellow, 1714-22. Ord. deacon (Ely) Sept. 22, 1717; priest, Sept. 21, 1718. Minister of St George's, Yarmouth, 1719-21. R. of St Michael, Wood St, London, 1721-4. Chaplain to the Lord Chancellor. F.R.S. 1723. Preb. of Gloucester, 1724. V. of Gt Marlow, Bucks., 1729. Bishop of St David's, 1752-61. Died Jan. 16, 1761. Buried in Gloucester Cathedral. (*D.N.B.*; F. S. Hockaday.)

ELLIS, AUGUSTUS. Matric. pens. from ST JOHN'S, Easter, 1559. Perhaps Augustine, of Barnard's Inn, adm. at Gray's Inn, 1568.

ELLYS, BARTHOLOMEW. Adm. sizar at CORPUS CHRISTI, 1587. Matric. 1588. Of Yorkshire.

ELLIS, BENJAMIN JOSEPH. Adm. at CORPUS CHRISTI, 1702. S. of Joseph (1674), of Norwich. B. 1688. Matric. 1704; B.A. 1706-7; M.A. 1710; D.D. 1725. Ord. deacon (Ely) Sept. 23, 1711; priest (Norwich) July, 1712. Lecturer at St Andrew's, Norwich, 1712. Minister of St Peter Hungate. R. of Hassingham and Buckenham Ferry, Norfolk, 1722-67. R. of Melton St Mary, till 1723. Died June 2, 1767. (G. *Mag.*)

ELLIS, BERNARD. B.A. 1533-4.

ELLIS, BERNARD. Adm. pens. (age 16) at ST JOHN'S, May 2, 1661. S. of Robert, merchant, of London. B. there. Matric. 1661; B.A. 1664-5. Adm. at Gray's Inn, June 17, 1664, as s. and h. of Robert, of Greenwich. Lieutenant-Governor of Guernsey. Died in London. Buried at St Dionis Backchurch, Dec. 22, 1703. (*Scott-Mayor*, I. xxxvi.)

ELLIS, CHARLES. Adm. pens. (age 18) at TRINITY, May, 1681. S. of John (1630), R. of Waddesdon, Bucks. B. there. School, Westminster. Matric. 1681; Scholar, 1682; B.A. 1684-5; M.A. from Christ's, 1688. Fellow of Christ's, 1686. Ord. deacon (Lincoln) May 22; priest, May 29, 1687. Died before 1700. Brother of William (1671) and of Samuel (1669). (*Peile*, II. 86.)

ELLIS, EDMUND. Matric. pens. from ST JOHN'S, Easter, 1611. One of these names (age 22 in 1617), s. of William, recorder of Lincoln. Adm. at Gray's Inn, May 6, 1607. Of Wellingore, Esq. Buried Nov. 7, 1659. (*Lincs. Pedigrees*, 323.)

ELLIS, EDMUND. Matric. pens. from CHRIST'S, July, 1622. S. of Sir Thomas (1586), of Grantham. Adm. at Gray's Inn, Oct. 26, 1622. Brother of Thomas (1620), William (1623) and John (1631). (*Lincs. Pedigrees*, 325.)

ELLIS, EDMUND. M.A. 1632 (Incorp. from Oxford). Of Devon, *fil. cler.* Matric. from Balliol College, Nov. 16, 1621, age 17; B.A. 1624-5; M.A. 1627. R. of East Allington, Devon, 1631-59. (*Al. Oxon.*)

ELLIS, EDMUND. Adm. Fell.-Com. (age 17) at MAGDALENE, June 21, 1672. S. of Thomas, Esq., of Wellingore, Lincs. School, Colesworth. Buried at Wellingore, July 7, 1681. (*Lincs. Pedigrees*, 323.)

ELLIS, EDWARD. Matric. pens. from CHRIST'S, Nov. 1562. S. of Lyon, mayor of Lincoln. B.A. 1565-6; M.A. from St John's, 1569. Fellow of St John's, 1567. Incorp. at Oxford, 1572. One of these names adm. at Gray's Inn, 1574. Barrister, 1577. Of Chesterton, Cambs. Died Nov. 20, 1595. Father of Edward (1605) and probably of Lion (1606). (*Lincs. Pedigrees*, 322.)

ELLIS, EDWARD. Counsel to the University, 1586. Perhaps the fellow of ST JOHN'S (above).

ELLIS, EDWARD. Adm. pens. (age 16) at CAIUS, Apr. 12, 1605. S. of Edward (1562) gent., of Chesterton, Cambs. School, Huntingdon (Mr Brand). Scholar, 1605-9; Matric. 1606; B.A. 1608-9. Of Buckden, Hunts., and of New Windsor. Died 1656. Buried in Westminster Abbey, Oct. 14, 1656. Perhaps brother of Lion (1606). (*Lincs. Pedigrees*, 322.)

ELLIS, EDWARD. Matric. sizar from ST JOHN'S, Easter, 1619; B.A. 1622-3; M.A. 1626; B.D. 1633. Perhaps Canon of St Asaph, 1660.

ELLIS, EDWARD. Adm. pens. (age 16) at CAIUS, June 14, 1647. S. of John, gent., of Milton, Cambs. Schools, King's College (Mr Hammond) and Chishall, Essex (Mr Hanchett). Matric. 1647; Scholar, 1647-9. Adm. at Gray's Inn, Sept. 3, 1649. (*Venn*, I. 368.)

ELLIS, EDWARD. Adm. pens. (age 18) at CHRIST'S, Feb. 10, 1708-9. S. of Thomas. B. at Holbeck, Lincs. School, Wisbech (Mr Carter). Scholar, 1708-9; Matric. 1709; B.A. 1712-3; M.A. 1716. Fellow, 1716-9. Ord. deacon (Ely) Sept. 1716; priest, Dec. 22, 1717. Buried in the College chapel, Nov. 23, 1719. Will, V.C.C. (*Peile*, II. 171.)

ELLIS, EDWARD. Adm. sizar at EMMANUEL, May 13, 1731. B. at Enfield, Middlesex. School, Westminster. Matric. 1731; B.A. 1734-5. Ord. priest (Norwich) July, 1736. R. of Osgathorpe, Leics., 1749-64. V. of Ledsham, Yorks., 1765-70. R. of Leake, Notts., 1770-95. Died Mar. 17, 1795, aged 84. (G. *Mag.*; *Nichols*, III. 921.)

ELLIS, FRANCIS. Adm. sizar at PETERHOUSE, Aug. 19, 1593; B.A. 1596-7; M.A. 1600. Ord. deacon (Peterb.) Dec. 21; priest, Dec. 23, 1604. V. of Owthorne, Yorks., 1604-42.

ELLIS, GEORGE. Matric. from TRINITY, Michs. 1615, as 'Elwis'; B.A. 1617-8; M.A. 1621.

ELLIS, GEORGE. Matric. pens. from CLARE, Michs. 1617; B.A. 1620-1. Ord. priest (Peterb.) Feb. 22, 1623-4.

ELLIS, GEORGE. Adm. pens. at CHRIST'S, June 14, 1625. S. of George, of Yorkshire. School, Beverley (Mr Pomeroy).

ELLIS, GEORGE. Adm. sizar at TRINITY, May 30, 1671. Matric. 1671; Scholar, 1674; B.A. 1674-5; M.A. 1680. Incorp. at Oxford, 1680. Ord. priest (London) Apr. 23, 1678. R. of Over Worton, Oxon., 1683.

ELLYS, GILBERT. Matric. sizar from PETERHOUSE, Michs. 1565.

ELLIES, GRIFFITH. Adm. Fell.-Com. (age 17) at ST JOHN'S, Apr. 9, 1641. S. of Ellis Jones, yeoman, of Llanllyfny, Carnarvon. B. there. School, Bangor. Matric. 1641.

ELLYS, HENRY. Adm. (age 14) at CAIUS, Dec. 19, 1560. Of Thorpe, Norfolk. S. of Hugh (1560), gent. School, Norwich.

ELLIS, HENRY. Matric. sizar from TRINITY, Easter, 1602; B.A. 1605-6, as Ellice.

ELYS, HUGH. Adm. Fell.-Com. at CAIUS, Dec. 19, 1560. Of Thorpe, Norfolk, gent. Probably came to accompany his s. Henry (1560). Buried at Martham Jan. 6, 1564-5. Will (Norwich) 1565.

ELLYS, JAMES. Matric. sizar from QUEENS', Michs. 1554; B.A. 1557-8; M.A. 1561; LL.D. 1568. 'Priest, M.A., parson of Llanfwrog, Carnarvon, and of Llandwrog: student in Cambridge.' (*Return of Bishop of Bangor*, 1561.) Resident in Trinity Hall, Aug. 1564. Adm. advocate, Jan. 21, 1571-2. Chancellor and preb. of Peterborough. Treasurer of Bangor. R. of Llanvoroc, Denbigh. Died 1596. (*Cooper*, II. 208; Browne Willis, *Bangor*, 266.)

ELLIS, JEREMIAH. Adm. at KING'S, a scholar from Eton, 1705. B. at Swaffham, Norfolk. Matric. 1705; B.A. 1709-10; M.A. 1713. Fellow, 1708. Ord. deacon (London) Dec. 18, 1709; priest, May 27, 1711. Usher at Grantham School. R. of Charleton, Lincs. R. of Harston, Leics., 1721.

ELLIS, JOHN. B.A. 1507-8.

ELLIS, JOHN. Of JESUS. B.A. 1532-3. Preb. of Rochester, 1551-4 and 1559-76. V. of St Nicholas, Rochester, 1551. Preb. of Hereford, 1552. R. of Cegidog, Denbigh, 1553; deprived, 1554; restored, 1559. Dean of Hereford, 1560-76. Preb. of Worcester, 1570. Died 1576. (*Cooper*, I. 363; A. Gray.)

ELLIS, JOHN. Matric. sizar from PETERHOUSE, Michs. 1554.

ELLIS, JOHN. Adm. scholar at CLARE, 1562.

ELLYS, JOHN. Adm. sizar at KING'S, Easter, 1564. Sizar to Lord Henry Howard.

ELLYS, JOHN. Matric. pens. from ST JOHN'S, Michs. 1581. Perhaps ord. deacon and priest (Peterb.) Oct. 1, 1587, as 'B.A.' Probably R. of Fletton, Hunts., 1588-1635. Died 1635.

ELLIS, JOHN. Matric. sizar from ST JOHN'S, Easter, 1586; B.A. 1589-90; M.A. 1593. Ord. deacon and priest (Peterb.) July 11, 1591.

ELLIS, JOHN. Matric. sizar from ST JOHN'S, Michs. 1618; B.A. 1622-3; M.A. 1626. Ord. deacon (Peterb.) Sept. 19; priest, Sept. 20, 1624.

ELLIS, JOHN. Matric. sizar from ST JOHN'S, Easter, 1626. Of Wales. B.A. 1629-30; M.A. from St Catharine's, 1633. Fellow of St Catharine's, 1631.

ELLIS, JOHN. Matric. pens. from ST CATHARINE'S, 1630. Of Yorkshire. B.A. 1634; M.A. 1638. Fellow, 1634. Doubtless the author of *Vindiciae Catholicae*, described in the *D.N.B.* (but not B.D., as stated by *Lipscomb* and *D.N.B.*, or proctor). Sided at first, with the Parliament, and preached before the House of Commons, 1644. Appointed to the third portion of Waddesdon, Bucks., before 1660. Changed sides, and was appointed to the other two-thirds, in 1661. Married Susanna, dau. of William Welbore, of Cambs. Died Nov. 3, 1681, aged 75. Buried at Waddesdon. M.I. there. Father of William (1671), Charles (1681) and Samuel (1669). (*Lipscomb*, I. 508; *D.N.B.*)

ELLYS, JOHN. Adm. pens. (age 17) at CHRIST'S, June 15, 1631. S. of Sir Thomas (1586), Knt. B. at Grantham. Bapt. July 26, 1614. School, Grantham (Mr Wilkinson). Matric. 1631; B.A. 1634-5; M.A. 1638. One of these names V. of South Kyme, Lincs., 1648; another R. of Toft, Cambs., till 1656. Brother of Thomas (1620) and William (1623). (*Peile*, I. 412.)

ELLIS, JOHN. D.D. 1635 (Incorp. from St Andrews). Of Llandegwin, Merioneth. Matric. from Hart Hall, Oxford, 1617, age 18; B.A. (Oxford) 1621-2; M.A. 1625; B.D. 1632; D.D. St Andrews, 1634. Fellow of Jesus College, Oxford, 1628. R. of Wheatfield, Oxon., 1629-47. R. of Chinnor, *c.* 1646. R. of St Mary, Dolgelley, 1646-66. Died 1666. (*Al. Oxon.*)

ELLIS, JOHN. Adm. Fell.-Com. at ST CATHARINE'S, 1637. Of Lincolnshire.

ELLIS, JOHN. Matric. sizar from ST CATHARINE'S, Easter, 1647.

ELLYS, JOHN. Adm. sizar (age 14) at CAIUS, Feb. 15, 1647-8. S. of John, of Raveningham, Norfolk, gent. B. at Huntingfield, Suffolk. Schools, Wingfield, Suffolk (Mr Jermey), Hoxne (Mr Hall) and Wrentham (Mr Batho and Mr Poliard). Matric. 1647-8; Scholar, 1648-55; B.A. 1651-2; M.A. 1655. Fellow, 1659-1703. Incorp. at Oxford, 1661. Master of Caius, Jan. 1, 1702-3. Knighted, 1705, whilst Vice-Chancellor, on the visit of Queen Anne. An eminent tutor, but as master in bitter strife with the fellows. Died Nov. 29, 1716. Buried at Swaffham Prior, Cambs. M.I. there. (*Venn*, I. 370.)

ELLIS, JOHN. Adm. sizar (age 18) at ST JOHN'S, May 26, 1655. S. of Evan, clerk, of Pennant, Montgomeryshire. B. there. School, Shrewsbury. Matric. 1655; B.A. 1658-9. Perhaps fellow of Clare, 1662.

ELLIS, JOHN. Incorp. M.A. 1663, from New College, Oxford. Matric. from Wadham, Oxford, July 25, 1655; B.A. 1658-9; M.A. 1661; D.D. 1678, from St John's College, Oxford. Chaplain at New College. R. of Llanddyfnan, Anglesea, and of Llanfawr, 1658. Precentor of St David's, 1667. Preb. of St Asaph, 1670-93. Died Oct. 15, 1693. Buried at St Chad's, Shrewsbury. (*Al. Oxon.*)

ELLYS, JOHN. Adm. pens. (age 16) at CAIUS, Apr. 13, 1664. S. of Edward, gent., of Henstead, Suffolk. Schools, Northcove (Mr Nuttall), Henstead (Mr Utting) and Barsham (Mr Nuttall). Matric. 1664; Scholar, 1664–8; M.B. 1669; M.D. 1704. One of these names adm. at Leyden, Apr. 27, 1688. (*Venn*, I. 421.)

ELLIS, JOHN. Adm. sizar (age 17) at PETERHOUSE, Apr. 18, 1673. Of Norfolk. School, Cambridge. Matric. 1673; B.A. 1676–7. Ord. deacon (Norwich) Sept. 1677; priest, Mar. 12, 1681–2. V. of Didlington, Norfolk, 1685–1720. R. of Mundeford, 1699–1720.

ELLIS, JOHN. B.A. 1678 (Incorp. from Oxford). S. of Andrew, of Hanmer, Flints. Matric. from Brasenose, May 13, 1673, age 17; B.A. (Oxford) 1676–7; M.A. (from Hart Hall) 1709. Perhaps V. of Willesford, Wilts., 1686. (*Al. Oxon.*)

ELLYS, JOHN. Adm. pens. at CLARE, Oct. 20, 1679. Of Wyham, Lincs. S. of Sir Thomas (1645), of Wyham. Matric. 1680. Adm. at the Inner Temple, Jan. 21, 1681–2. Died May 2, 1686, aged 22. Buried in the Temple. Probably brother of William (1673). (*Lincs. Pedigrees*, 326; Burke, *Ext. Bart.*)

ELLYS, JOHN. Adm. pens. (age 16) at CAIUS, Jan. 20, 1682–3. S. of Anthony, woollen-draper, of Yarmouth. B. there. School, Yarmouth. Matric. 1683; Scholar, 1683–90; B.A. 1686–7; M.A. 1690. Fellow, 1690–1716. Ord. deacon (Rochester) Sept. 20, 1696; priest, Feb. 28, 1696–7. R. of Burgh Castle and Belton, Suffolk, 1714–28. Died Jan. 13, 1728–9. Buried at Burgh Castle. M.I. there. Nephew of John, the master. (*Venn*, I. 472.)

ELLIS, JOHN. Adm. at CORPUS CHRISTI, 1686. Of Norfolk. Matric. 1686; B.A. 1689–90; M.A. 1693. Ord. priest (Norwich) Dec. 20, 1696. R. of Igborough, Norfolk, 1696. R. of Cranwich, 1713, and R. of Langford.

ELLIS, JOHN. Adm. pens. (age 17) at CAIUS, Apr. 5, 1692. S. of Thomas, gent., of Cotton, Suffolk. B. there. Schools, Gislingham (Mr Sparrow) and Bury. Matric. 1692; Scholar, 1692–6. A medical student. Died Aug. 18, 1696. M.I. at Bury. Uncle of John (1727). The father was a medical doctor. (*Venn*, I. 490.)

ELLIS, JOHN. Adm. sizar (age 22) at ST JOHN'S, June 29, 1696. S. of Joseph, husbandman. B. at Llanvihangel, Montgom. School, Shrewsbury. Matric. 1696; B.A. 1699–1700.

ELLIS, JOHN. Adm. pens. (age 17) at ST JOHN'S, May 17, 1697. S. of John, gent. B. at Burton Agnes, Yorks. School, Beverley. Matric. 1697; B.A. 1700–1; M.A. 1704. Ord. deacon (York) May 1703; priest, 1704.

ELLIS, JOHN. Adm. at CORPUS CHRISTI, 1701. Of Norfolk. Matric. 1702.

ELLIS, JOHN. M.A. 1714 (Incorp. from Oxford). S. of John, clerk, of Llanbeblig, Carnarvon. Matric. from Jesus College, Oxford, June 23, 1707, age 16; B.A. (Oxford) 1711; M.A. 1714. (*Al. Oxon.*)

ELLIS, JOHN. Matric. pens. from PEMBROKE, 1717 (s. of John). Migrated to Trinity, as sizar, Apr. 21, 1719 (s. of William). Age 17. School, St Paul's, London. Scholar, 1722; B.A. 1722–3. One of these names V. of Westbury, Bucks., 1735–40.

ELLIS, JOHN. Adm. p . (age 18) at MAGDALENE, May 18, 1723. B. at Newark, Notts. School, Brigg, Lincs. Matric. 1723, as William.

ELLIS, JOHN. Adm. Fell.-Com. (age 18) at CAIUS, Feb. 14, 1726–7. S. of William, Esq., of Westhorpe, Suffolk. B. there. School, Botesdale (Mr Mabourn). Matric. 1727. Of Cotton, Suffolk, Esq. Died Nov. 1, 1739. Buried at Cotton. M.I. there. (*Venn*, II. 26.)

ELLIS, JOHN. Adm. pens. at JESUS, June 15, 1738. S. of ——, clerk, deceased. Matric. 1738; Rustat Scholar; LL.B. 1745. Ord. deacon (Norwich) June, 1745. Perhaps R. of Runcton, Norfolk. Died Nov. 4, 1787, aged 65. (*G. Mag.*)

ELLIS, JOHN. Adm. at CORPUS CHRISTI, 1740. Of Norfolk. Matric. 1741; B.A. 1743–4; M.A. 1747. Ord. deacon (Norwich) Dec. 1745; priest, May, 1746. R. of Runton, Norfolk, 1746–88. R. of Beeston Regis, 1746–56. R. of South Repps, 1756–88.

ELLIS, JOHN. Adm. sizar at TRINITY HALL, Dec. 3, 1750; Scholar, 1752; LL.B. 1759.

ELLIS, JOSEPH. Adm. at CORPUS CHRISTI, 1674. Of Norwich. Matric. 1675; B.A. 1678–9; M.A. 1682. Ord. deacon (Norwich) Sept. 1679; priest, Feb. 1680–1. V. of Earlham, Norwich, 1683–1712. Lecturer of St Edmund's, Norwich, 1681; of St Andrew's, 1694–1712. Died 1712, aged 55. Father of Benjamin Joseph (1702). (*Masters*.)

ELLIS, JOSEPH. B.A. of TRINITY HALL, when ord. deacon (London) Dec. 4, 1721; priest (York) Mar. 1722–3. Doubtless the man who was LL.B. from Trinity Hall, 1728.

ELLYS, LANCELOT. Matric. sizar from CLARE, Easter, 1570; B.A. 1574–5; M.A. 1581. Ord. deacon (Peterb.); priest (Ely) Apr. 15, 1576. V. of Wimbish, Essex, 1581–1634.

ELLIS, LION. Matric. pens. from ST JOHN'S, Michs. 1606. Probably 4th s. of Edward (1562). B.A. 1610–1; M.A. 1614. Ord. deacon (Peterb.) June 4; priest, June 5, 1615. R. of Fulbeck, Lincs. Preb. of Lincoln, 1615–35. Died May 27, 1635. Buried in Lincoln Cathedral. Probably brother of Edward (1605). (*Lincs. Pedigrees*, 324.)

ELLIS, NICHOLAS. B.Civ.L. 1536–7 (Incorp. from Oxford). A Nicholas Ellys was R. of Catwick, Holderness, in 1526.

ELLIS, PETER. Matric. pens. from ST CATHARINE'S, Easter, 1647; B.A. 1649–50.

ELLYS, RALPH. B.A. from ST JOHN'S, 1592–3. One of these names, of Spinkhall, Yorks., gent., adm. at Gray's Inn, Nov. 26, 1594. Perhaps of York, Esq.; b. at Bradfield, Yorks.; buried in York Minster. Will Jan. 3, 1622. (*F.M.G.*, 798.)

ELLIS, RICHARD. Matric. sizar from TRINITY, c. 1595.

ELLIS, RICHARD. B.A. from MAGDALENE, 1608–9. B. at Lavenham, Suffolk. Ord. deacon (Coventry and Lichfield); priest (London) Dec. 23, 1610, age 24. C. of Gt Wigborough, Essex. R. of Beaumont *with* Mose, 1616–28. Perhaps R. of Thornton-le-Moor, Lincs., 1623–8. Died 1628.

ELLIS, ROBERT. B.D. 1523–4; D.D. 1530–1. Dominican friar. Prior of the house at Stafford. (*Cooper*, I. 528.)

ELLIS or ALLIS, ROBERT. Adm. sizar at CHRIST'S, Feb. 3, 1624–5. S. of Robert, of Essex. Schools, Linton (Mr Leinitz) and Ashdon (Mr Britten). Matric. 1625; B.A. 1629–30; M.A. 1634. One of these names V. of Burham, Kent, 1647.

ELLIS, ROBERT. Adm. pens. (age 17) at ST JOHN'S, May 1, 1652. S. of Robert, gent., of Rudstone, Bridlington, Yorks. B. there. School, Sneaton, Yorks.

ELLIS, ROBERT. Adm. .. (age 16) at CHRIST'S, Mar. 19, 1654–5. S. of Robert. B. at Ipswich. School, Felsted (Mr Glascock). Matric. 1655; B.A. 1658–9. Ord. deacon (London) July, 1677; priest, Sept. 1677. R. of Ramsden Crays, Essex, 1677. Died 1678. (*Peile*, I. 565.)

ELLIS, ROBERT. Adm. pens. at JESUS, May 8, 1689. Of Yorkshire. Matric. 1689; B.A. 1692–3; M.B. 1694.

ELLIS, ROGER. Matric. sizar from CLARE, Michs. 1579.

ELLIS, ROGER. Adm. sizar at CHRIST'S, Apr. 8, 1665; B.A. 1668. Ord. deacon (York) Mar. 1668–9; priest, Sept. 1669. V. of Brompton, Yorks., 1671. Died before Sept. 1685. (*Peile*, I. 615.)

ELLYS, ROWLAND. Matric. pens. from CHRIST'S, Nov. 1581; B.A. 1584–5. One of these names, of Carnarvon, adm. at the Inner Temple, Dec. 11, 1586.

ELLIS, SAMUEL. Matric. sizar from QUEENS', Michs. 1629. Of Lincolnshire. B.A. 1633–4.

ELLIS, SAMUEL. Adm. pens. at TRINITY, May 21, 1669. Doubtless s. of John (1630), R. of Waddesdon, Bucks. From Westminster School. Marshal of the King's Bench, 1688. Left the country after the Revolution. Brother of Charles (1681) and William (1671). (*Al. Westmon.*)

ELLIS, SETH. Adm. sizar (age 18) at ST JOHN'S, May 12, 1690. S. of William, cutler. B. at Sheffield, Yorks. School, Sheffield. Matric. 1690; B.A. 1693–4; M.A. 1697. Ord. priest (York) Sept. 1703. P.C. of Brampton, Chesterfield. Died 1747. Father of the next. (*F.M.G.*, 827.)

ELLIS, SETH. Adm. sizar (age 19) at ST JOHN'S, June 24, 1734. S. of Seth (above), P.C. of Brampton, Derbs. School, Chesterfield (Mr Burrow). Matric. 1735; B.A. 1737–8. Ord. deacon (Lincoln) June 17, 1739; priest, Sept. 20, 1741. C. of Claxby. C. of Gt Hale, Lincs., 1765–91. He was suspended by the Bishop, 1748–58. Died Jan. 20, 1791 (*Scott-Mayor*, III. 457; *F.M.G.*, 827.)

ELLIS, THEOPHILUS. Adm. sizar (age 18) at ST JOHN'S, July 3, 1663. S. of Edward, clerk, of Guilsfield, near Welshpool, Montgom. B. there. School, Shrewsbury. Matric. 1664; B.A. 1666–7.

ELLIS, THOMAS. Adm. at KING'S, a scholar from Eton, c. 1460.

ELLYS, THOMAS. Matric. pens. from JESUS, Easter, 1545.

ELLIS, THOMAS. Matric. pens. from CHRIST'S, May, 1562. One of these names V. of Darton, Yorks., 1578–1625. Another, R. of Gt Carlton, near Louth, 1603–26. (*Peile*, I. 77.)

ELLYS, THOMAS. Matric. pens. from CHRIST'S, Nov. 1586. This, or the next, was s. of Thomas, of Witham, Lincs. Adm. at Gray's Inn, May 9, 1589. Barrister. Ancient, 1608. Bencher, 1618. Knighted at York, Apr. 15, 1617. One of the King's Council in the North. Died 1627. Buried at Grantham, Sept. 7, 1627. Father of Thomas (1620), John (1631), William (1623) and Edmund (1622). (*Peile*, I. 185; *Lincs. Pedigrees*, 325.)

ELLIS, THOMAS. Matric. pens. from TRINITY, Easter, 1589.

ELLIS, THOMAS. Matric. Fell.-Com. from Christ's, July, 1620. Eldest s. of Sir Thomas (1586), of Grantham, Knt. Adm. at Gray's Inn, May 22, 1622. Of Witham and Northill, Beds. Died Apr. 6, 1640. Brother of John (1631) and William (1623). Father of Thomas (1645-6). (*Lincs. Pedigrees*, 325.)

ELLIS, THOMAS. Adm. pens. at Christ's, Apr. 26, 1623. S. of William (1587-8), minister, of Brinkley, Cambs. Schools, Brinkley (Mr Ashwell) and Perse, Cambridge. Migrated to Magdalene. B.A. 1626-7; M.A. 1630. One of these names R. of Lopham, Norfolk. Deprived, 1663. Another ejected from Hempstead, Essex, 1662. (*Peile*, I. 350.)

ELLIS, THOMAS (1631), *see* ELWIS.

ELLIS, THOMAS. Adm. sizar (age 17) at Sidney, Apr. 14, 1635. S. of Allen, weaver. B. at Hinderclay, Suffolk. School, Botesdale (Mr Eaton). Matric. 1635; B.A. 1638-9; M.A. 1642. Ord. deacon (Norwich) Dec. 22, 1639.

ELLIS, THOMAS. Matric. sizar from St Catharine's, Michs. 1638. Of Yorkshire.

ELLIS, THOMAS. Adm. Fell.-Com. at Jesus, Jan. 30, 1645-6. Of Bedfordshire. S. of Thomas (1620), of Northill, Beds. and Wyham, Lincs. Bapt. at Northill, Oct. 8, 1627. Adm. at the Inner Temple, Nov. 1646. Created baronet, June 30, 1660. Of Gt Ponton, Lincs. Died before Nov. 1670. Father of John (1679) and probably of William (1673). (*Lincs. Pedigrees*, 325; *G.E.C.*)

ELLIS, THOMAS. Adm. Fell.-Com. at Emmanuel, May 20, 1647. Of Lincolnshire. Perhaps the same as the last.

ELLIS, THOMAS. Adm. sizar at Trinity, May 17, 1662. Matric. 1662; B.A. 1665-6. Ord. deacon (York) *c.* 1667.

ELLIS, THOMAS. B.A. from Christ's, 1674. S. of Thomas, of Bridport, Dorset. No matriculation found. Possibly matric. from University College, Oxford, Feb. 8, 1669-70, age 18. Ord. deacon (York) Dec. 1674; priest, Feb. 1680-1.

ELLIS, THOMAS. Adm. pens. (age 17) at Trinity, Feb. 8, 1699-1700. S. of Thomas, of Brome, Suffolk. School, Brome. Matric. 1700; Scholar, 1703; B.A. 1703-4; M.A. 1707.

ELLYS, THOMAS. Adm. sizar (age 18) at St John's, as 'William,' May 29, 1724. S. of Thomas, cutler, of Yorkshire. B. in Sheffield. School, Sheffield (Mr Robinson). Matric. 1724; B.A. 1727-8; M.A. 1733. Ord. deacon (Ely) July 12, 1728; priest, Sept. 19, 1729; title, minor canon of Ely. Died 1764.

ELLIS, TIMOTHY. Student at St John's, when ord. deacon (Lincoln) Sept. 20, 1607.

ELLYS, TOBIAS. Adm. sizar at Trinity, Feb. 3, 1650-1. Of Yorkshire. Matric. 1651; B.A. 1655-6. Licensed preacher at Belton and Burgh Castle, Suffolk, 1661.

ELLIS, WALTER. Adm. pens. at Peterhouse, Mar. 7, 1638-9. Matric. 1639. Previously matric. from New Inn Hall, Oxford, Mar. 11, 1635-6, age 16. S. of Richard, of London. B.A. from Emmanuel, 1639-40; M.A. 1643. Fellow of Peterhouse, 1644-53. V. of Cherryhinton, Cambs. (*T. A. Walker*, 68.)

ELLYS, WILLIAM. Matric. sizar from Queens', Easter, 1548.

ELLYS, WILLIAM. Matric. sizar from St John's, Michs. 1554.

ELYS, WILLIAM. Matric. sizar from Jesus, Michs. 1555.

ELLYS, WILLIAM. B.A. from St John's, 1572.

ELLYS, WILLIAM. B.A. from Magdalene, 1587-8; M.A. 1591; B.D. 1598. Ord. deacon and priest (Peterb.) Sept. 21, 1589. R. of Brinkley, Cambs., 1602-25. Buried there July 29, 1625. Father of Thomas (1623).

ELLIS, WILLIAM. Matric. sizar from Peterhouse, Michs. 1598; B.A. 1601-2; M.A. 1605. One of these names, M.A., V. of St Mary, Beverley, 1608-37. Preb. of Ripon, 1626-37. (*N. and Q.*)

ELLIS, WILLIAM. Matric. pens. from St John's, Michs. 1601.

ELLIS, WILLIAM. Matric. pens. from King's, Easter, 1618.

ELLIS, WILLIAM. Adm. pens. at Christ's, May 26, 1623. S. of Sir Thomas (1586), Knt., of Grantham. B. at Lincoln. Bapt. at Grantham, July 19, 1607. School, Lincoln (Mr Phipps). Matric. 1623; B.A. 1626-7. Adm. at Gray's Inn, Nov. 6, 1627. Barrister, Feb. 9, 1634-5. Bencher, 1654. Treasurer, 1658. M.P. for Boston, 1640 (twice), 1649-53, 1655 and 1679; for Grantham, 1656, 1660. Solicitor-General, 1654. Created Baronet by Cromwell, Aug. 13, 1658. Bencher, Gray's Inn, 1659. Reader, 1664. Serjeant-at-law, 1669. King's serjeant, and knighted, Apr. 30, 1671. Justice C.P. 1672-6 and 1679-80. Died in Serjeant's Inn, Dec. 17, 1680. Buried at Nocton, Lincs. Brother of Thomas (1620) and John (1631). (*D.N.B.*; *Peile*, I. 350; *Lincs. Pedigrees*; *G.E.C.* *D.N.B.* is wrong in making him M.A. at Caius.)

ELLIS, WILLIAM. Matric. pens. from Queens', Easter, 1627. Of Lincolnshire. Perhaps s. and h. of George, of Wyham, Lincs., gent., adm. at Gray's Inn, Mar. 6, 1628-9; age 23 in 1634. (*Lincs. Pedigrees*, 325.)

ELLIS, WILLIAM. Adm. pens. (age 16) at Caius, Mar. 19, 1627-8. S. of John, cook, of King's College. B. in Cambridge. School, Cambridge (Perse). Matric. 1628; Scholar, 1628-34; B.A. 1631-2; M.A. 1636. Fellow, 1634-74. V. of Foulden, Norfolk, May 8, 1648; by the Parliamentary Committee. (He subscribed in the Bishop of London's book, May 11, 1648. (*Venn*, I. 283.)

ELLIS, WILLIAM. Matric. Fell.-Com. from St Catharine's, Michs. 1638. Of London. One of these names s. and h. of Edmund, of Wellingore, Lincs., Esq., adm. at Gray's Inn, May 4, 1638.

ELLIS, WILLIAM. Adm. pens. (age 16) at St John's, July 2, 1670. S. of Sidney, deceased, of Lledrode in Llansilin, near Chirk, Denbigh. B. there. School, Ruthin. Matric. 1670.

ELLIS, WILLIAM. M.A. 1671 (*Lit. Reg.*). S. of John (1630), R. of Waddesdon, Bucks. Elected to Christ Church, Oxford, from Westminster, 1665. B.A. (Oxford) 1669. Comptroller for Leinster and Munster, 1678. Knighted, 1686. Privy Councillor to James II in Ireland, 1690. Attainted, 1691. Secretary to James II at St Germain. Died at Rome, 1732. Brother of Charles (1681) and of Samuel (1669). (*D.N.B.*; *Al. Westmon.*; *Al. Oxon.*)

ELLIS, WILLIAM. Adm. Fell.-Com. at Trinity, Jan. 21, 1673-4. Probably s. of Sir Thomas (1645-6), of Wyham, Lincs., Bart. Succeeded as Bart. Died Oct. 6, 1727, aged 74. Probably brother of John (1679). (Burke, *Ext. Bart.*; *Lincs. Pedigrees*, 326.)

ELLIS, WILLIAM. M.A. from Emmanuel, 1674. S. of William, of Coventry, clerk. Matric. from Magdalen College, Oxford, Mar. 15, 1666-7, age 18; B.A. (Oxford) 1670. (*Al. Oxon.*)

ELLIS, WILLIAM. Adm. pens. (age 17) at Trinity, Mar. 21, 1683-4. S. of William, of Kiddall, Yorks. Bapt. at Barwick-in-Elmet, Sept. 27, 1665. School, Grantham. Matric. 1684. Of the Inner Temple; adm. Apr. 14, 1684. High Sheriff of Yorks. Buried at Kellington, Oct. 27, 1729. (*Thoresby Soc.*, II. 57.)

ELLIS, WILLIAM. Adm. pens. (age 19) at St John's, Oct. 30, 1724, from Magdalene. S. of Timothy, gent., of Yorkshire. B. at Doncaster. School, Brigg, Lincs. (Mr Waterworth).

ELLIS, WILLIAM. Adm. sizar (age 17) at St John's, June 11, 1733. S. of John, of Yorkshire. B. at Clifton. School, Sherburn (Mr Young). Matric. 1734; B.A. 1737-8; M.A. 1741. Ord. deacon (London) Feb. 26, 1737-8; priest, Mar. 13, 1738-9. V. of Kirby and Broughton, Yorks., 1745-80. V. of Lastingham, 1771-89. Chaplain to Lord Grantham. (*Scott-Mayor*, III. 447.)

ELLIS, WILLIAM. Adm. sizar (age 17) at St John's, Nov. 19, 1747. S. of Henry, alehouse-keeper, of Middlesex (brewer of Wapping). B. at Wapping, May 19, 1730. School, Merchant Taylors'. Matric. 1748; B.A. 1752; M.A. 1755. Fellow, 1753-60. Ord. deacon (Ely) Mar. 18, 1753; priest (Chester) Nov. 17, 1754. Master of Aldenham Grammar School, 1757-68. R. of All Hallows, Steyning, 1758-1801. Master of Alford School, Lincs., 1775-1801. Author, classical, etc. Buried at Alford, Nov. 29, 1801. (*Scott-Mayor*, III. 573; *Genealogist*, N.S., XIV. 109.)

ELLIS, ——. B.Can.L. 1502-3.

ELLIS, ——. D.Civ.L. before 1535-6.

ELLYS, ——. Adm. Fell.-Com. at King's, 1693-4.

ELLIS, ——. Adm. Fell.-Com. at Trinity Hall, Nov. 9, 1720. Resided, till 1726.

ELLISON or ELYSON, ANTHONY. Matric. sizar from Christ's, Nov. 1545. Of Northumberland. B.A. 1549-50. Fellow of St John's, 1555. Doubtless Master of Pocklington School, till 1581. Buried Sept. 27, 1581.

ELLISON, CUTHBERT. Adm. pens. (age 17) at St John's, Apr. 22, 1654. S. of Robert, merchant, of Newcastle-on-Tyne (M.P. for Newcastle). B. there. School, Houghton-le-Spring (Mr Caunt). Matric. 1654; B.A. 1657-8. Adm. at Gray's Inn, Mar. 27, 1655. Married, at St Nicholas, Newcastle, July 2, 1663, Jane, dau. of William Carr. Died Aug. 1685. Brother of Robert (1666) (*Surtees Soc.*, II. 280.)

ELLISON, DAVID. Matric. sizar from St John's, Easter, 1626; B.A. 1629-30; M.A. 1633. P.C. of Chelford, Cheshire, 1635. R. of Childwall, Lancs., *c.* 1645.

ELLYSON, GEORGE. Adm. sizar (age 20) at St John's, Mar. 8, 1666-7. S. of Thomas, husbandman, of Pocklington, Yorks. B. at Easington, Durham [? E. Riding, Yorks.]. School, Pocklington. Matric. 1667; B.A. 1670-1. Ord. deacon (York) Sept. 1671; priest, Sept. 1672. V. of Ellerton, Yorks., 1691-1703.

ELLISON, JOHN. Adm. sizar (age 17) at ST JOHN'S, May 19, 1652. S. of John, draper, of Altham, Lancs. B. in Upper Darwen, Lancs. School, Burnley (Mr Asplin). Matric. 1652; B.A. 1655-6.

ELLISON, JOHN. Adm. pens. at EMMANUEL, May 23, 1663. Of Yorkshire. Matric. 1663. One of these names, s. and h. of James, of Skircoat, Yorks., gent., adm. at Gray's Inn, June 1, 1663.

ELLISON, JOHN. M.A. from KING'S, 1719. S. of Nathaniel, of Newcastle-on-Tyne, D.D. Matric. from University College, Oxford, Mar. 22, 1710-1, age 16; B.A. (Oxford) 1715. V. of Bedlington, Northumberland, 1719-73. Lecturer at St Andrew's, Newcastle. Married at St John's, Newcastle, Sept. 29, 1719, Mary Bates. Buried at St Nicholas, Newcastle, Dec. 30, 1773. (*Al. Oxon.*)

ELLISON, ROBERT. Adm. pens. at CHRIST'S, June 23, 1666. S. of Robert, of Newcastle (Sheriff and M.P.). B. there. School, Berwick. Brother of Cuthbert (1654).

ELLISON, SAMUEL. Adm. pens. (age 16) at ST JOHN'S, June 7, 1652. S. of Henry, yeoman, deceased, of Wavertree, Lancs. B. there. School, Much Woolton. Matric. 1655; B.A. 1655-6; M.A. 1659. V. of Hale Chapel, Lancs., 1659. R. of Warrington, 1663-4. Brother of William (1652).

ELISON, THEOPHILUS. Adm. pens. at CAIUS, May 14, 1625. S. of John, minister of the Flemish Church, Norwich. B. there. Matric. 1625; Scholar, 1626-9; B.A. 1628-9. Adm. student at Leyden, 1630. Succeeded his father as minister of the Flemish Church, Norwich, *c.* 1639-76. Died June 1, 1676. M.I. in the Dutch Church. Will, P.C.C. (*Venn*, I. 270.)

ELLISON, THOMAS. Adm. sizar (age 16) at ST JOHN'S, June 22, 1655. S. of Thomas, husbandman, of Hutton, Yorks. B. there. School, Wearmouth. Matric. 1655; B.A. 1658-9; M.A. 1667. Head Master of Pocklington School, 1664-93. Stated to be 'de Heldon in Com. Dunelm.' Buried May 6, 1693.

ELLISON, THOMAS. M.A. from PEMBROKE, 1668. Matric. from Wadham College, Oxford, Mar. 28, 1655; B.A. (Oxford) 1665. R. of Ashton-under-Lyne, Lancs., 1662. Buried in Dukinfield Nonconformist Chapel, Feb. 26, 1700. (*Al. Oxon.*; *Vict. Hist. Lancs.*, IV. 348.)

ELLISON, THOMAS. Adm. pens. at EMMANUEL, June 13, 1685. Of Lancashire. Matric. 1685; B.A. 1688-9; M.A. 1692. Probably R. of Pulford, Cheshire, 1694.

ELLISON, THOMAS. Adm. sizar (age 18) at TRINITY, May 15, 1699. S. of John, of Bingley, Yorks. School, Bingley (Mr Hoyle). Matric. 1699; B.A. 1702-3.

ELLYSON, THOMAS. Adm. sizar (age 19) at CHRIST'S, June 10, 1720. S. of Thomas, R. of Ashton, Cheshire. B. at Pulford, Cheshire. Matric. 1720; Scholar, 1721; LL.B. 1725. R. of Hoole, Lancs., 1732-63. P.C. of Chorley, 1733-63. Buried there Aug. 13, 1763. (*Vict. Hist. Lancs.*, VI. 147.)

ELLISON, TIMOTHY. Adm. pens. (age 16) at CAIUS, June 21, 1670. S. of William (? 1652), of Wavertree, Lancs. School, Toxteth Park (Mr Ursely). Matric. 1670; Scholar, 1670. Ord. deacon (Chester) June 17, 1673; priest (Lincoln) June 13, 1676. R. of Market Bosworth, 1676. P.C. of Coley, Halifax, 1682-*c.* 1702. V. of Haworth, 1702-3; and V. of Otley. R. of Wattisfield, Suffolk, 1714-33. Chaplain to Lady Anne Cheek. Died Jan. 29, 1732-3. M.I. at Wattisfield. (*Venn*, I. 441; Turner's *Haworth*.)

ELLISON, WILLIAM. Matric. sizar from ST JOHN'S, Easter, 1604; B.A. 1607-8. Ord. deacon (York) Mar. 1611-2; priest, June, 1612. Licensed to preach.

ELLISON, WILLIAM. Adm. pens. (age 20) at ST JOHN'S, June 7, 1652. S. of Henry, yeoman, deceased, of Wavertree, near Liverpool, Lancs. B. there. School, Much Woolton. Matric. 1652. Brother of Samuel (1652). Perhaps father of Timothy (1670).

ELLISON, WILLIAM. Adm. pens. (age 18) at ST JOHN'S, Jan. 31, 1658-9. S. of John, gent., of Silkstone, Yorks. B. there. School, Worsborough, Yorks. (Mr Hanson). Adm. at Gray's Inn, Jan. 25, 1660-1.

ELLISTON, *see also* ALLISTON.

ELLISTON, EDWARD. Matric. sizar from CHRIST'S, Michs. 1584; B.A. 1590-1. Probably ord. priest (Norwich) Sept. 1595. R. of Wetherden, Suffolk, 1597. Perhaps V. of Acton, 1597.

ELLISTON, JOHN. Matric. pens. from CORPUS CHRISTI, Easter, 1616. Of Essex. B.A. 1619.

ELLISTON, JOHN. Adm. pens. at EMMANUEL, Easter, 1641. S. of Joseph Alliston (1595). Matric. 1642. One of these names adm. student at Leyden, Sept. 1646. Brother of Matthew (1642).

ELLISTON, JOHN. Adm. at CORPUS CHRISTI, 1727. Of Suffolk. Matric. 1727; B.A. 1730-1; M.A. 1734. Fellow, 1732-4. Died in College, Feb. 6, 1734-5. Buried in the Chapel. (*G. Mag.*)

ELLISTON, JOSEPH. M.D. from ST JOHN'S, 1662. Possibly Joseph Allistone (1625).

ELLISTON, MATTHEW. Adm. pens. at EMMANUEL, Apr. 22, 1642. Of Essex. S. of Joseph Alliston (1595). Matric. 1642. Died of small-pox, in College, May 14, 1644. Brother of John (1641).

ELLISTON, WILLIAM. Adm. sizar (age 17) at ST JOHN'S, June 6, 1750. S. of William, farmer, of Suffolk. B. at Bardfield. School, Dedham (Mr Grimwood). Matric. 1750; B.A. 1754; M.A. 1757; B.D. from Sidney, 1764; D.D. 1764 (*Lit. Reg.*). Fellow of Sidney, 1758. Master, May 8, 1760-1807. Vice-Chancellor, 1763-4, 1786-7. Ord. deacon (Ely) May 21, 1758; priest (Ely) Dec. 21, 1759. R. of Keystone, Hunts., 1764-1807. Died Feb. 11, 1807. Buried in Sidney College Chapel. (*Scott-Mayor*, III. 598.)

ELLITHORPE, JOSEPH. Adm. sizar (age 17) at ST JOHN'S, Apr. 24, 1673. S. of Thomas, yeoman, of Holme, Yorks. B. there. School, Pocklington. Matric. 1673; B.A. 1676-7; M.A. 1681. Ord. priest (York) Sept. 1680.

ELLOTSON, JOHN, *see* ELLETSON.

ELLWALL, THOMAS. Adm. sizar at CLARE, Oct. 16, 1644. Matric. 1644.

ELLY, *see* ELY.

ELMAN, ELMHAM or HELMAN, JOHN. Adm. at KING'S, a scholar from Eton, 1502. B.A. 1506-7, 1st in the *ordo*; M.A. 1510; B.D. 1517-8; D.D. 1520-1. Ord. sub-deacon (Lincoln) Mar. 7, 1511-2. Will proved (P.C.C.) 1533. 'Of Norwich diocese.'

ELMAR, JOHN. A monk. B.D. 1529-30; D.D. 1535-6.

ELMER, *see also* AYLMER.

ELMER, LEVENTHORPE. Matric. pens. from ST JOHN'S, Easter, 1616. Buried at All Saints', Cambridge, Nov. 19, 1619.

ELMES, EDWARD. Adm. pens. (age 20) at CAIUS, Sept. 18, 1573. S. of Henry, of Cransley, Northants. School, Peterborough.

ELMES, JOHN. Adm. (age 18) at KING'S, a scholar from Eton, Oct. 1, 1556. 4th s. of John, of Lilford, Northants. Matric. 1556. Left, in 1559. Adm. at the Inner Temple, 1560. Inherited from his father lands in Swinestead and Swayfield, Lincs. Buried at Swinestead. Will proved at Grantham, Aug. 8, 1622. Brother of the next.

ELMES, LEWIS. Matric. Fell.-Com. from QUEENS', Michs. 1559. 5th s. of John, of Lilford, Northants. In Holy Orders. Confrater of Browne's Hospital, Stamford, 1573. Buried at Stamford, Oct. 19, 1576. Brother of John (above).

ELMES, SPINKES. Adm. pens. at CLARE, Jan. 1713-4. B. in London.

ELMS, THOMAS. Adm. Fell.-Com. (age 16) at CHRIST'S, Sept. 9, 1641. S. of Anthony, of Greens-Norton, Northants., Esq. School, Adstone (Mr Cotton). Sheriff of Northants., 1669. Knighted, July 19, 1688. Died at Lilford, 1690. M.I. there; since removed to Achurch Tower. (*E. H. Elmes*; *Peile*, I. 478.)

ELMES, WILLIAM. Adm. pens. at EMMANUEL, Apr. 13, 1646. Of Northamptonshire. 2nd s. of Thomas, of Lilford and Green's Norton. B. 1625. School, Oundle. Died 1653. M.I. at Warmington Church. (*E. H. Elmes.*)

ELMESMORE or ELSMERE, JAMES. Adm. sizar (age 17) at CAIUS, June 3, 1585. S. of William, of Diss, Norfolk. School, Diss (Mr Pickering). B.A. 1588-9.

ELMHAM, THOMAS. Scholar at KING'S HALL, 1389-94. Probably the Benedictine monk of St Augustine's, Canterbury. Prior of Lenton, Notts., 1414. Vicar-general for England and Scotland, 1416. Author, historical. Died *c.* 1440. (*D.N.B.*)

ELMHAM, WILLIAM. Fellow of GONVILLE HALL, when ord. acolyte by Bishop of Ely, Mar. 29, 1376.

ELMHIRST, WILLIAM. Adm. pens. at CLARE, Apr. 15, 1665. Of Yorkshire. S. of Richard, of Houndhill, Doncaster. B. 1645. Matric. 1665; M.B. 1670. Lived at Houndhill. Died unmarried, Dec. 23, 1715, aged 71. Will dated 1702. (Burke, *L.G.*; *Vis. of Yorks.*, 1665.)

ELMORE, JOHN. Adm. sizar (age 15) at ST JOHN'S, Mar. 11, 1655-6. S. of William, carrier, of London. B. there. School, St Paul's. Matric. 1656; B.A. 1659-60.

ELMSAL, HENRY. Adm. pens. (age 18) at ST JOHN'S, Apr. 13, 1710. S. of William, gent. B. July 31, 1691. Bapt. at Thornhill, Yorks., Aug. 12, 1691. Exhibitioner from Charterhouse. Matric. 1710; B.A. 1713-4; M.A. 1717. Ord. priest (York) May, 1716. V. of East and West Ardsley, Yorks., in 1721-50. Chaplain to the Duke of Leeds. R. of Thornton-in-Craven, 1730-5. R. of Thornhill, 1732-58. Died June 18, 1758. Buried at Thornhill, June 20. Father of the next. (*F.M.G.*, 905; *Al. Carthus.*)

ELMSAL, HENRY. Adm. pens. (age 17) at ST JOHN'S, June 29, 1750. S. of Henry (above), clerk, of Yorkshire. B. at Thorpe, near Wakefield. School, Bradford (Mr Butler). Matric. 1750; B.A. 1754; M.A. 1757; B.D. from Emmanuel, 1764. Fellow of Emmanuel, 1758. Chancellor's medallist, 1754. Ord. deacon (York) Sept. 21, 1755; priest (Lincoln) June 14, 1767. Inc. of East Ardsley, Yorks., 1772-97. V. of Batley, 1772-97. R. of Emley, 1772-97. Died Dec. 6, 1797. Buried at Thornhill, Dec. 10. (*Scott-Mayor*, III. 600; *F.M.G.*, 905.)

ELMESALL, JOHN. Adm. pens. (age 16) at ST JOHN'S, May 11, 1665. S. of Thomas, deceased, of Purston Jaglin, near Pontefract, Yorks. B. there. School, Sedbergh. Matric. 1665.

ELMSALL, THOMAS. Matric. pens. from TRINITY, Easter, 1586.

ELMESTON, JAMES. Adm. sizar at EMMANUEL, Apr. 5, 1660. Of Devon. Previously matric. from Exeter College, Oxford, June 15, 1657. Matric. 1660; B.A. 1660-1. R. of Harford, Devon, 1666. (*Al. Oxon.*)

ELMSTONE, THOMAS. Adm. pens. at EMMANUEL, Apr. 2, 1622. Matric. 1622; B.A. 1625-6; M.A. 1629.

ELMSLEY, ——. B.A. 1473-4; M.A. 1477, as Helmsley. Probably William, V. of Longstanton, Cambs., till his death, 1506.

ELMY, EDWARD. Adm. sizar at QUEENS', Michs. 1604.

ELMY, THOMAS. Adm. pens. at EMMANUEL, Jan. 19, 1629-30. Of Suffolk. Matric. 1631; B.A. 1633-4; M.A. 1637. One of these names, of Rumburgh, Suffolk, s. of Jeremy; bapt. there, 1612. (*Suff. Man. Fam.*, I. 196.)

ELMY, WILLIAM. Adm. pens. at EMMANUEL, 1625; B.A. 1628-9. ('Elinge' in *grace*.)

ELPHICKE, GEORGE. Adm. pens. (age 18) at CHRIST'S, Apr. 22, 1653. S. of John. B. at Worth, Sussex. School, Eton. Matric. 1653, as 'Uphicke'; B.A. 1656-7. Adm. at Gray's Inn, Nov. 28, 1656. Barrister, 1664. (*Peile*, I. 552.)

ELRINGTON, EDWARD. Matric. pens. from TRINITY, Easter, 1586. Perhaps s. and h. of Edward, of Widdington, Essex. Age 7 in 1578. Died Aug. 3, 1618. (*Morant*, II. 566.)

ELDRINGTON, EDWARD. Adm. pens. (age 18) at CAIUS, Nov. 8, 1600. S. of Edward, of Withersfield, Suffolk. School, Bishop's Stortford (Mr Bedwell), Herts. Died in College. Buried at St Michael's, Cambridge, May 5, 1605. Brother of Thomas (1600). (*Venn*, I. 174.)

ELRINGTON, EDWARD. Matric. sizar from TRINITY, Easter, 1617.

ELRINGTON, EDWARD. Adm. sizar (age 18) at ST JOHN'S, Mar. 13, 1705-6. S. of William, deceased. B. at Molescroft, near Beverley, Yorks. School, Merchant Taylors'. Matric. 1705-6. Ord. deacon (York) Sept. 1710; priest, 1711. V. of Ottringham, Yorks., 1719-39.

ELRINGTON, JOHN. Matric. pens. from TRINITY HALL, Lent, 1618-9; B.A. 1621; M.A. 1624.

ELRINGTON or ELDERTON, THOMAS. Matric. pens. from CHRIST'S, June, 1566. Probably of Essex. B.A. 1569-70; M.A. 1574. Fellow, 1571-4. (*Peile*, I. 93.)

ELDRINGTON, THOMAS. Adm. pens. (age 16) at CAIUS, Nov. 8, 1600. S. of Edward, of Withersfield, Suffolk. School, Bishop's Stortford (Mr Bedwell), Herts. Brother of Edward (1600).

ELRYNGTON, WILLIAM. Adm. (age 16) at CAIUS, Feb. 13, 1562-3. S. of Edward, gent., of London. School, Elmdon, Essex. Matric. 1562, as Elderton. (*Venn*, I. 50.)

ELDRINGTON, ——. Adm. pens. at PETERHOUSE, 1599-1600.

ELSAM or ELSHAM, JOHN. B.A. from MAGDALENE, 1603-4. Ord. deacon (Peterb.) Sept. 16, 1604; priest, Sept. 18, 1608. C. of Waddington, Lincs., 1609. Schoolmaster there.

ELSAM or ELSHAM, JOHN. Adm. pens. at JESUS, Sept. 16, 1639. Of Nottinghamshire. Matric. 1640. Migrated to Emmanuel, 1642. B.A. 1643-4.

ELSAM, ROBERT. Adm. sizar (age 16) at MAGDALENE, June 25, 1679. S. of William, fuller. B. at Little Steeping, Lincs. School, Alford. Matric. 1679; B.A. 1682-3; M.A. 1686.

ELSBIE, JAMES. Adm. sizar (age 17) at PEMBROKE, July 2, 1662. S. of James, of Huntingdonshire. Matric. 1662; B.A. 1665-6; M.A. 1669. V. of Chiswick, Middlesex.

ELSEY, SAMUEL, *see* **AILESBY.**

ELSEY, ——. Adm. at CORPUS CHRISTI, 1576.

ELSE, THOMAS. Adm. pens. at EMMANUEL, June 4, 1640. Of Northamptonshire. Matric. 1640; B.A. 1643-4; M.A. 1649.

ELSING or ELSYN, HENRY. Adm. pens. (age 17) at CAIUS, Oct. 14, 1595. S. of Henry, gent., of London. School, St Albans. Probably barrister of law of the Middle Temple, 1605. Clerk of the House of Lords. Will proved (P.C.C.) Mar. 7, 1635-6; 'of Cornwell, Oxon.' Father of Henry, clerk of the House of Commons. (*Venn*, I. 157.)

ELSLEY, CHARLES. Adm. pens. (age 18) at ST JOHN'S, May 15, 1718. S. of William (1689), clerk, of Ryther, Yorks. School, York (Mr Foster). Matric. 1718. Adm. at Gray's Inn, July 10, 1718.

ELSLEY, CHARLES. Adm. pens. (age 18) at SIDNEY, Oct. 24, 1732. 1st s. of Gregory, gent., of Yorkshire. School, Coxwold. Matric. 1732-3. Brother of the next.

ELSLEY, GREGORY. Adm. pens. (age 20) at ST JOHN'S, Apr. 23, 1737. S. of Gregory, gent., of Yorkshire. B. at Patrick Brompton. School, Kirk Heaton (Mr Clarke). Matric. 1737; B.A. 1740-1; M.A. 1744. R. of Patrick Brompton, 1740-66. V. of Burneston, 1765-89. J.P. for North Riding, in 1758. Died May 24, 1789. Brother of Charles (above).

ELSLEY, WILLIAM. Adm. sizar (age 16) at ST JOHN'S, May 6, 1689. S. of Samuel, husbandman. B. at Kirby Malzeard, Yorks. School, Sedbergh. Matric. 1689; B.A. 1692-3; M.A. 1698. Incorp. at Oxford, 1703. Ord. deacon (York) May, 1697; priest, 1697. R. of Ryther, Yorks., 1704-43. Preb. of York, 1721-40. R. of Throckington, Northumberland, 1721-40. Sub-dean of Ripon, 1723-43. Preb. of Ripon. Died May, 1743. Father of Charles (1718).

ELSMERE, JAMES, *see* **ELMESMORE.**

ELSMER, ROBERT. B.A. 1475-6; M.A. 1479-80. Will (P.C.C.) 1512; 'of Watton, Herts.; St Thos. Acres, London; Fordingbridge, Hants.'

ELSTOB, CHARLES. Adm. pens. (age 16) at PETERHOUSE, May 29, 1665. 3rd s. of Charles, of Foxton, near Sedgefield, Durham. School, Durham. Matric. 1665; Scholar, 1665; B.A. 1668-9; M.A. 1672; D.D. 1705 (*Lit. Reg.*). Ord. deacon (London) June, 1671. V. of Merrington, Durham, 1676-80. V. of Hartburn, Northumberland, 1680-3. Preb. of Canterbury, 1686-1721. R. of Tillington, Sussex, 1697-1721. Died Nov. 18, 1721. Father of the next, brother of John (1665). (*Vis. of Durham*, 1666; *T. A. Walker*, 128.)

ELSTOB, CHARLES. Adm. pens. (age 16) at ST JOHN'S, May 22, 1714. S. of Charles, D.D. (above). B. at Canterbury. School, Westminster. Matric. 1714.

ELSTOB, JOHN. Adm. pens. at PETERHOUSE, May 30, 1665. S. and h. of Charles, of Foxton, near Sedgefield, Durham. School, Durham. Of Foxton, Durham. Died 1701. Brother of Charles (1665). (*T. A. Walker*, 129.)

ELSTOB, WILLIAM. Adm. sizar at ST CATHARINE'S, June 23, 1691. S. of Ralph, of Newcastle-on-Tyne, gent. B. there, 1673. Colleger at Eton, 1687-90. Matric. 1691. Migrated to Oxford. Matric. at Queen's, Dec. 15, 1691, age 17; B.A. (Oxford) 1694; M.A. 1697. Fellow of University College, Oxford, 1696. Incorp. at Cambridge, 1698. R. of St Swithin and St Mary Bothaw, London, 1703-15. Author. Died Mar. 3, 1714-5. (*Al. Oxon.*; *D.N.B.*)

ELSTON, HENRY, *see* **OLSTEN.**

ELSTON, JOHN. B.A. from ST JOHN'S, 1570-1. Ord. priest (Lincoln) Oct. 1586. V. of Redbourne, Lincs., 1585.

ELSTON, MICHAEL. Adm. sizar (age 18) at PEMBROKE, July 6, 1669. S. of Michael, of Shipton, Yorks. Matric. 1669; B.A. 1672-3.

ELSTON, ——. B.Civ.L. 1477-8.

ELSWOOD, CLEMENS. M.A. from KING'S, 1751. S. of Richard, of Wayford, Somerset. Matric. from Wadham College, Oxford, Dec. 17, 1726, age 19; B.A. (Oxford) 1730. Ord. deacon (Bath and Wells) Sept. 20, 1730; priest, Sept. 24, 1732. R. of Ibberton, Dorset, 1752-75. Chaplain to Earl of Berkeley. R. of Corton Dinham, Somerset, 1755. Died Nov. 9, 1775. M.I. at Ibberton. (*Al. Oxon.*; *Hutchins*, IV. 361.)

ELSWORTH, JOHN. Matric. pens. from ST JOHN'S, Easter, 1577.

ELSWORTH, JOHN. Adm. pens. at KING'S, *c.* 1665.

ELTAME, JOHN. Matric. sizar from JESUS, Michs. 1587.

ELTHAM, ——. Incorp. 1482-3.

ELTISLEY, ROBERT. Fellow of CORPUS CHRISTI, 1366. Brother of the Master, Thomas Eltisley. R. of Lolworth, Cambs. R. of St Andrew's, Holborn, 1394-6; of St Bartholomew-by-the-Exchange, 1398-9. R. of Shering, Essex, 1399-1407. R. of Twerne, Dorset; of Stower Provost. (*Masters.*)

ELTISLEY, THOMAS. B.Can.L. First Master of CORPUS, *c.* 1350. Probably of Eltisley, Cambs. R. of Lambeth. Chaplain to J. Stratford, Archbishop of Canterbury. R. of Longstanton, Cambs. R. of Grantchester, 1364-75. R. of Landbeach, 1375. Died Aug. 21, 1376. (*Masters.*)

ELTISLEY, THOMAS (*junior*). B.Can.L. Probably a member of CORPUS CHRISTI, as he succeeded the above at the College living of Grantchester, 1375. R. of Bletchley, Bucks., 1358. R. of Landbeach, 1374-5. (*Masters.*)

ELTOFT, THOMAS. Adm. sizar (age 19) at ST JOHN'S, June 27, 1743. S. of Thomas, husbandman. B. at Kippax, Yorks. School, Wath (Mr Parnther). Matric. 1743. Died in College. Buried at All Saints', Aug. 19, 1745.

ELTON, ANTHONY. Matric. pens. from TRINITY, Easter, 1576. Perhaps s. of William, of Ledbury. Of the Hazle. Buried Sept. 3, 1587. (C. J. Robinson, *Mansions of Herefordshire*, 165.)

ELTON, CHARLES. Adm. at KING'S, a scholar from Eton, 1675. B. at Ledbury, Herefordshire. Matric. 1675-6. Died as a student, of small-pox, Apr. 7, 1676. (*Harwood*.)

ELTON, EDWARD. Matric. pens. from CHRIST'S, Dec. 1585. Doubtless of Shropshire. B.A. 1588-9; M.A. 1592; B.D. from Magdalene, 1599. R. of Thorpe-in-Glebis, Notts., 1601-6. R. of St Mary Magdalene, Bermondsey, 1605-24. Buried there Sept. 6, 1624. Will (P.C.C.) mentions late brother Anthony: leaves books and a legacy to Magdalene College. Perhaps brother of Anthony (1576) and Richard (1581). (*Peile*, I. 183; *Manning and Bray*, I. 214; J. Ch. Smith.)

ELTON, JOHN. Adm. at KING'S, a scholar from Eton, 1452; B.A. 1459-60. Fellow. Ord. acolyte (Ely) Apr. 5, 1455. Perhaps R. of St Bartholomew-by-the-Exchange, London, 1466-70 ('B.D.'). V. of Fulham, 1466-7.

ELTON, JOHN. B.Civ.L. 1494. Of Yorkshire. Ord. sub-deacon (Ely) Apr. 4, 1495; priest, Apr. 18, 1495. R. of Staunton-in-le-Vale, Notts., 1528-35. Died 1535.

ELTON, JOHN. B.Can.L. 1504-5.

ELTON, JOHN. Matric. sizar from MAGDALENE, Easter, 1605; B.A. 1608-9; M.A. 1612.

ELTON, JOHN. Adm. sizar at JESUS, May 9, 1705. B. in Leicestershire, 1686. Matric. 1705; B.A. 1708-9; M.A. 1712. Ord. deacon (Ely) Sept. 25, 1709; priest, Dec. 23, 1711. C. of Lolworth, Cambs. Probably V. of St Charles, Tunbridge Wells, 1723-44. R. of Speldhurst, 1727-8. R. of Trottiscliffe, 1744-7. V. of Tonbridge, 1747. Died 1747.

ELTON, RICHARD. Adm. pens. at CHRIST'S, Apr. 11, 1581. Of Shropshire. Perhaps brother of Edward (1585).

ELTON, THOMAS. B.A. 1505-6.

ELTON, THOMAS. Adm. sizar at PETERHOUSE, 1605. B.A. 1608-9. Ord. deacon (Peterb.) Mar. 19, 1608-9; priest, Sept. 25, 1614. Minister of Melbourn, Cambs.

ELTON, ——. Fee for M.A. or higher degree, 1469-70.

ELTONHEAD, GEORGE. Chorister of KING'S when ord. deacon (Ely) Mar. 22, 1561-2, age 24.

ELTONHEADE, JOHN. Matric. sizar from CHRIST'S, Dec. 1602. Doubtless s. of William, of Eltonhed, Lancs., gent. B.A. 1605-6. Adm. at the Middle Temple, Mar. 1, 1607-8. Barrister-at-Law. (*Vis. of Essex*, 1634; *Vis. of Lancs.*, 1664.)

ELTONHEAD, THOMAS. Scholar of PETERHOUSE. Buried at Little St Mary's, Dec. 24, 1603.

ELTONHED, WILLIAM. Adm. pens. (age 16) at ST JOHN'S, Jan. 21, 1631-2. S. of John, Esq., of London. School, Charlton, Kent (private; Mr Pemberton). Matric. 1632. (*Vis. of Essex*, 1634.)

ELTYE, ROGER. Matric. sizar from TRINITY, Easter, 1615.

ELVEDON, WALTER. LL.D. Early member, and probably fellow, of GONVILLE HALL. R. of Icklingham St James, Suffolk, till 1347. R. of Elveden, 1347. Precentor of Hereford, 1349-58. R. of Snetterton, Norfolk, 1352-9. R. of Shropham, 1358-60. Archdeacon of Sudbury, 1349. Vicar-general to Bishop Bateman, 1355. Benefactor to Gonville Hall. An astronomer: his astrolabe is still in possession of the College. (*Venn*, I. 2.)

ELVEN, JOHN. Matric. pens. from QUEENS', Easter, 1573. Ord. deacon (Lincoln) Mar. 28, 1577; priest, Aug. 24, 1577. R. of Hareby, Lincs.

ELVERED, JOHN. Adm. sizar at CORPUS CHRISTI, 1618. Of Suffolk. Matric. Easter, 1619; B.A. 1622-3 (as 'Elured'); M.A. 1628.

ELVIE, SAMUEL. Adm. pens. (age 16) at CAIUS, July 1, 1622. S. of George, husbandman, of Reymerstone, Norfolk. School, Reymerstone (Mr Chapman). Matric. 1623; Scholar, 1623-4.

ELVIN, ISAAC. Adm. pens. at SIDNEY, Apr. 19, 1615. Matric. 1615; B.A. 1618-9.

ELWALD, WILLIAM. Adm. pens. (age 18) at SIDNEY, Nov. 7, 1635. S. of William, Esq. B. at Middleton-on-the-Wolds, Beverley, Yorks. School, Beverley (Mr Pomeroy).

ELWES, *see also* HELWYS.

ELWES, GAWFRED (? JEFFREY). Adm. at CORPUS CHRISTI, 1712. Of Hertfordshire. Doubtless s. of Robert (1681-2), of Throcking, Herts. Bapt. there, Jan. 16, 1696. Matric. 1713-4. Knighted, 1744. Died Feb. 5, 1776. (*Misc. Gen. et Her.*, N.S., IV. 135.)

ELWES or HELWYS, GERVASE. Matric. pens. from ST JOHN'S, June, 1573. S. of John, of Worlaby, Lincs. Bapt. at Askham, Notts., Sept. 1, 1561. Studied law at Lincoln's Inn. Knighted, May 7, 1603. Lieutenant of the Tower. Hanged on Tower Hill for complicity in the murder of Sir Thomas Overbury, Nov. 20, 1615. (*D.N.B.*; *D'Ewe's Diary*.)

ELWES, GERVASE. M.A. 1675 (*Lit. Reg.*). 1st s. of Sir Gervase, of Stoke College, Bart. M.P. for Sudbury, 1679 (Feb. and Sept.) and 1681. Died before his father. Father of Hervey (below). (Burke, *Ext. Bart.*; *G.E.C.*)

ELWES, HENRY. Matric. pens. from TRINITY, Michs. 1629. S. and h. of Edward, of Grove House, Fulham, London, deceased. Adm. at the Inner Temple, 1632. Died 1678. (*Misc. Gen. et Her.*, IV. 133.)

ELWES, HERVEY. Adm. pens. at QUEENS', June 22, 1702. Fell.-Com. Apr. 17, 1703. Of Suffolk. S. of Gervase (1675). Succeeded his grandfather as Bart., 1706. M.P. for Sudbury, 1706, 1708, 1713, 1715. Died, at Stoke, unmarried, Sept. 18, 1763. (Burke, *Ext. Bart.*; *G.E.C.*)

ELWES, JAMES. Adm. pens. at TRINITY, June 30, 1650. Doubtless 2nd s. of Jeremy, of Broxbourne, Herts., and Roxby, Lincs., to whom his father bequeathed Ellerbeck, Yorks. Brother of Jeremy (next). (*Misc. Gen. et Her.*, IV. 134.)

ELWES, JEREMY. Adm. Fell.-Com. at TRINITY, Sept. 6, 1649. Of Hertfordshire. S. of Jeremy, of Throcking, Herts., and Roxby, Lincs. Succeeded his father, 1654. Died 1678-9. Father of the next and of Robert, brother of James (above).

ELWES or ELLWAYS, JEREMY. Adm. Fell.-Com. at TRINITY, Oct. 16, 1678. Eldest s. of Jeremy (above). Matric. 1678. Succeeded his father, 1678. Died 1683. Brother of Robert (1681-2). (Burke, *L.G.*)

ELWYS, JOHN. M.Gram. 1490-1.

ELWES, ROBERT. Adm. pens. (age 19) at PETERHOUSE, Jan. 11, 1681-2. Fell.-Com. Mar. 31, 1683. S. of Jeremy (1649), of Throcking, Herts., and of Roxby and Bigby, Lincs. School, St Paul's. Matric. 1682. Adm. at Gray's Inn, July 30, 1682. Succeeded his elder brother Jeremy (1678) in the family estates. Died June 10, 1731. Buried at Throcking. (*T. A. Walker*, 170; Burke, *L.G.*)

ELWES, SILVIUS. Scholar of TRINITY, 1596. S. of Geoffrey, of Woodford, Essex. Bapt. at St Mary Bothawe, London, Sept. 26, 1576. B.A. 1596-7; M.A. 1600. Chaplain of Trinity, 1601-37. Died Dec. 14, 1638. (*Misc. Gen. et Her.*, IV. 133.)

ELWES or ELWAES, THOMAS. Matric. pens. from ST JOHN'S, *c.* 1590. Scholar of Trinity, 1590.

ELWICK, GEORGE. Adm. sizar at CLARE, May 12, 1721. B. at Bredgar, Kent. Matric. 1721.

ELWICK, ROBERT. Adm. sizar at CLARE, May 27, 1692. Of Doncaster. Matric. 1692; B.A. 1695-6. V. of Bredgar, Kent, 1699-1722. Died 1722.

ELWYN, EDWARD. Matric. pens. from CORPUS CHRISTI, Lent, 1597-80. Of Norfolk. B.A. 1583-4; M.A. 1587; M.D. 1595. Fellow, 1586-98. Taxor, 1591. L.R.C.P. 1602. Fellow, R.C.P. 1605. Physician to the royal household. (*Cooper*, II. 528; *Munk*, I. 122.)

ELWYN, JOHN. Of GONVILLE HALL. B.A. 1521-2; M.A. 1525. S. of Peter, of Wood Dalling. Chantry priest of St Michael Coslany, Norwich; afterwards rector, 1561-8. Benefactor to Gonville Hall. Will (Norw. C. C.) 1569. (*Venn*, I. 26.)

ELWYN or ELVIN, JOHN. Matric. sizar from CLARE, Easter, 1569; B.A. 1572-3. V. of Westwell, Kent, 1580; suspended, 1583. Died *c.* 1592. (*Cooper*, II. 145.)

ELWIN, PETER. Adm. pens. at EMMANUEL, Mar. 3. 1641-2. Of Norfolk. S. and h. of Peter, of Thurning, Norfolk. B. *c.* 1623. Matric. 1642. Adm. at the Inner Temple, 1643. Died July 7, 1695. Buried at Thurning. M.I. Will (Norwich) 1695. Father of the next.

ELWIN, PETER. Adm. Fell.-Com. (age 16) at CAIUS, July 25, 1678. S. of Peter, gent. (above), of Thurning, Norfolk. B. there. Schools, Wood Dalling (Mr Hutton) and Scarning (Mr Burton). Of Tuttington, Esq. Bought the Manor of Booton, 1713. Died Feb. 5, 1721. M.I. at Tuttington. Father of the next, and of Thomas (1705). (*Venn*, I. 460.)

ELLWYN, PETER. Adm. pens. (age 18) at CAIUS, May 8, 1703. S. of Peter (1678), of Tuttington, Norfolk. B. at Hevening-ham. Schools, North Walsham (Mr Harvey) and Norwich. Matric. 1703; Scholar, 1703-6. Adm. at the Middle Temple, May 15, 1702. Sheriff of Norfolk, 1720. Died *s.p.* Sept. 15, 1731. Buried at Tuttington. M.I. (Will P.C.C.) 1731. Brother of Thomas (1705). (*Venn*, I. 510.)

ELWYN, PETER. Adm. Fell.-Com. (age 18) at CAIUS, June 3, 1748. S. of Peter, of Booton, Norfolk and grand-nephew of Peter (1703). B. at Thurning, Jan. 20, 1729-30. Schools, Norwich (Mr Bullimer) and Scarning (Mr Brett). Matric. 1748. Of Booton and Thurning, Esq. Died June 22, 1798. Buried at Booton. M.I. Will, P.C.C. (*Venn*, II. 61.)

ELWYN or ELVYN, THOMAS. Adm. sizar at CORPUS CHRISTI, 1575. Matric. Easter, 1576; B.A. 1578-9. Perhaps s. of John, of Heigham, Norfolk, tanner. R. of Lammas, Norfolk, 1581-1609. Buried there Aug. 11, 1609. (J. H. Holley.)

ELWIN or ELVIN, THOMAS. Adm. pens. (age 15) at CAIUS, Feb. 24, 1617-8. S. of Simon, attorney, of Hevingham Park, Norwich. School, 'St Edward's Church, Cambridge,' and King's, Cambridge (Mr Leveringe). Scholar, 1618-22; B.A. 1620-1; M.A. 1625. Fellow, 1622-8.

ELWYN, THOMAS. Adm. pens. (age 17) at CAIUS, Mar. 31, 1705. S. of Peter (1678), Esq., of Tuttington, Norfolk. B. there. School, Norwich (Mr Burton and Mr Hoadley). Matric. 1705. Adm. at the Middle Temple, Nov. 27, 1706. Apparently died young. Brother of Peter (1703). (*Venn*, I. 513.)

ELWIS, THOMAS. Matric. sizar from TRINITY, Michs. 1631, as 'Ellis'; B.A. 1635-6.

ELWYS, ——. B.Can.L. 1500-1.

ELWOOD or ELLWOOD, GEORGE. Adm. sizar (age 17) at SIDNEY, Apr. 12, 1654. 4th s. of Thomas, farmer, of 'Dereding,' Cumberland. Schools, Calbeck (Mr Waterson) and Sebergham (Mr Hecsteter). Matric. 1654. Migrated to Clare, Nov. 28, 1654, with Dr Dillingham, the Master. B.A. 1657-8; M.A. 1661. Fellow of Clare. Ord. deacon (Lincoln) July 15; priest, July 18, 1661. Brother of John (1648).

ELWOOD, HENRY. Matric. sizar from QUEENS', Easter, 1588 Of Cambridgeshire.

ELWOOD, HENRY. Adm. pens. (age 17) at TRINITY, Feb. 13, 1716-7. S. of Henry, of Dartford, Kent. School, Charterhouse.

ELLWOOD, JOHN. Adm. sizar (age 18) at SIDNEY, Sept. 27, 1648. S. of Thomas, farmer. B. at 'Deridding,' Grastak (Greystoke), Cumberland. Schools, Sowerby (Mr Priestman) and Crosthwaite (Mr Sanderson). Matric. 1648-9; B.A. 1652-3; M.A. 1656. V. of East Riston, Norfolk, 1661. V. of Happisburgh, 1661. R. of Ridlington, 1668-70. Married, Apr. 1655, Mary Drew, widow. Brother of George (1654).

ELWOOD, MATTHEW. Matric. sizar from TRINITY, Michs. 1611; B.A. 1614-5. Ord. deacon (York) Feb. 1615-6; priest, Dec. 1618.

ELWOOD, MUNGO. Adm. sizar at CLARE, Oct. 7, 1661. Matric. 1661-2; B.A. 1665-6.

ELWOOD, SAMUEL. Adm. sizar (age 15) at ST JOHN'S, June 13, 1635. S. of Francis, farmer, deceased, of Hull. B. at Marfleet, Yorks. School, Hull. Matric. 1635. One of these names V. of West Malling, Kent, 1660-2.

ELWOOD, THOMAS. Matric. pens. from QUEENS', Easter, 1587. Of Dover, Kent. Adm. at the Inner Tempie, 1589.

ELWOOD, THOMAS. Matric. pens. from ST JOHN'S, Michs. 1588.

ELWOOD, W. Matric. pens. from ST JOHN'S, Easter, 1567. A William Elwood living at Nafferton, East Riding, Yorks., in 1572.

ELY, ANTHONY, *see* ELLIS.

ELY, BENJAMIN. Matric. sizar from JESUS, Easter, 1617; B.A. 1619-20; M.A. 1623. Incorp. at Oxford, as 'Ellis,' 1622 (as 'B.A.', and s. of John, of Gt Carlton, Lincs.). Ord. deacon (Peterb.) Dec. 19; priest, Dec. 20, 1624. V. of Utterby, Lincs., 1631.

ELIE, CHRISTOPHER. Matric. sizar from ST JOHN'S, Easter, 1575. One of these names 'chapter-messenger' at Lincoln, 1580.

ELEY, HENRY. Matric. pens. from PEMBROKE, Easter, 1617; B.A. 1619-20; M.A. 1623.

ELY, JOHN. M.A. 1485-6; B.D. 1499-1500. Fellow of CLARE, 1486.

ELLY, JOHN. Adm. (age 16) at KING'S, a scholar from Eton, Sept. 4, 1641. Of Lapworth, Warws. S. of John, D.D., Canon of Windsor. Matric. 1641; B.A. 1645-6, as 'Ellis.' Fellow, 1645-8.

ELY, JOHN. Matric. pens. from QUEENS', Michs. 1657. Of Lincolnshire. Doubtless 1st s. of Thomas, of Utterby, Lincs. Of Utterby, Esq. Married Sarah, dau. of John Vesey, about 1670. (*Lincs. Pedigrees*.)

ELY, NATHANIEL. Matric. pens. from ST JOHN'S, *c*. 1590; B.A. 1593-4; M.A. 1597. Incorp. at Oxford, 1605.

ELYE, ROBERT. Matric. pens. from PEMBROKE, Lent, 1582-3; B.A. 1586-7; M.A. 1590. Fellow, *c*. 1588. Incorp. at Oxford, 1593. V. of Charing, Kent, 1595. R. of Dimchurch, 1605-19. R. of Smarden, 1619-44. Died 1644.

ELYE, SAMUEL. Matric. sizar from CLARE, *c*. 1592.

ELY, SAMUEL. Adm. sizar at EMMANUEL, 1641. Matric. 1641; B.A. 1644-5; M.A. 1648. V. of Henham, Essex, till 1662 (ejected). Died 1681, at Bishop's Stortford. Buried Dec. 14. Father of William (1675). (*Calamy*, I. 508.)

ELLY, SAMUEL. Adm. sizar (age 17) at ST JOHN'S, July 8, 1699. S. of John, druggist. B. at Hinkly, Leics. School, Kibworth (Mr Dand). Matric. 1700; B.A. 1703-4. Ord. priest (Lincoln) June 19, 1709.

ELY, SAMUEL. Adm. pens (age 17) at TRINITY, Apr. 8, 1741. S. of Thomas, of Thorley, Herts. School, St Paul's. Exhibitioner from thence. Matric. 1742; Scholar, 1742; B.A. 1744-5. Under-Master, St Paul's School, 1748-61. Died July 28, 1761. (G. *Mag*.)

ELY, STEPHEN. Matric. sizar from KING'S, Easter, 1651; B.A. 1654-5.

ELY, STEPHEN. Adm. sizar at EMMANUEL, July 6, 1674. Of Suffolk. Matric. 1675; B.A. 1677-8. Ord. deacon (Norwich) Sept. 1678; priest, May, 1681.

ELY, THOMAS. D.D. Augustinian friar. Licensed to hear confessions in the Ely diocese, Nov. 15, 1466.

ELIE, THOMAS. Adm. sizar (age 17) at CAIUS, May 16, 1605. S. of Walter, gent., of Scarning, Norfolk, deceased. School, East Dereham (Mr Alstone). Matric. 1605; Scholar, 1606-12; B.A. 1608-9.

ELEY, THOMAS. Matric. pens. from MAGDALENE, Michs. 1632. S. and h. of Thomas. Perhaps of Louth, Lincs.; adm. at the Inner Temple, 1633.

ELY, WILLIAM. Adm. sizar (age 17) at SIDNEY, May 28, 1675. S. of Samuel (1641). B. at Henham, Essex. School, Bishop's Stortford. V. of Henham, Essex.

ELYN, ——. Fee for B.A. 1543-4.

ELYSDON, ——. B.A. 1504-5.

EMAN, JOHN. Adm. at KING'S, a scholar from Eton, 1677. S. of Timothy. B. in Windsor. Matric. 1679; B.A. 1682-3; M.A. 1687. Fellow. Married whilst B.A. Drowned soon after. (*Harwood*; *Vis. of Berks*., 1665.)

EMANUEL, ——. Adm. Fell.-Com. at CORPUS CHRISTI, 1548.

EMBERSON, LAURENCE. Adm. pens. at CORPUS CHRISTI, 1583, as Emmerson. Matric. 1583.

EMBLING, *see* EMLYN.

EME, ——. A friar. D.D. 1468-9.

EMERSON, ALEXANDER. Adm. pens. (age 16) at SIDNEY, May 6, 1658. S. of Alexander, barrister, of Lincoln's Inn. B. at Caistor, Lincs. School, Caistor (Mr Jo. Garthwait). Matric. 1658. Adm. at Lincoln's Inn, May 18, 1658. Brother of Michael (1668). (*Lincs. Pedigrees*.)

EMERSON, ALEXANDER. Adm. pens. (age 17) at SIDNEY, June 11, 1668. S. of Thomas (1644), gent., of Caistor, Lincs. B. 1651. School, Grimsby (Mr Beatniffe). Married Alice Wharton.

EMERSON, CHRISTOPHER. Matric. pens. from ST JOHN'S, Easter, 1546. S. of Cuthbert. B.A. 1548-9. R. of Furthoe, Northants., 1561-92. R. of Cosgrave, 1563-92. Buried there Jan. 5, 1592. Aged 68. M.I. (*Baker*, II. 133.)

EMERSON, CHRISTOPHER. Matric. pens. from ST JOHN'S, Easter, 1610. S. of Roger, of Pickering, Yorks. B.A. 1613-4; M.A. 1617. Ord. deacon (Peterb.) Sept. 24; priest, Sept. 25, 1615. R. of Barton-le-Street, Yorks., 1620-33. Will proved, Mar. 13, 1657-8. (H. M. Wood.)

EMERSON, GEOFFREY. Adm. (age 18) at KING'S, a scholar from Eton, Aug. 6, 1540. Of Hanslope, Bucks. B.A. 1544-5; M.A. 1548. Fellow, 1543-51. Presented to R. of Haddiscoe, Norfolk, 1550; resigned, 1554.

EMERSON, JOHN. Adm. sizar at EMMANUEL, Michs. 1629. Matric. 1629. One of these names R. of Shoreham, Sussex, in 1634. Perhaps V. of Ryarsh, Kent, 1653-60.

EMMERSON, JOHN. Adm. sizar (age 18) at ST JOHN'S, June 27, 1719. S. of Ralph, clerk. B. in Newcastle-on-Tyne. Exhibitioner from Charterhouse. Matric. 1720; LL.B. 1728 (*Com. Reg*.). Ord. deacon (London) Dec. 22, 1723; priest, May 23, 1725. R. of Wixoe, Suffolk, 1728-66. R. of Little Halingbury, Essex, 1734-66. Married, Sept. 1734, Mary Kemble. Died 1766. Will, P.C.C. (*Scott-Mayor*, III. 327; *Al. Carthus*.)

EMMERSON, LAURENCE, *see* EMBERSON.

EMERSON, MICHAEL. Adm. pens. (age 17) at SIDNEY, Aug. 29, 1668. Of Barnetby, Lincs. S. of Alexander, barrister, deceased, of Barnaby, Lincs. School, Caistor (Mr Tho. Waters). Matric. 1668; Fell.-Com. 1670. Adm. at Lincoln's Inn, Aug. 29, 1666; and at Gray's Inn, June 19, 1673. Brother of Alexander (1658).

EMMERSON, MORDECAI. Adm. sizar (age 19) at ST JOHN'S, June 6, 1674. S. of Richard, carpenter. B. at Hull. School, Hull. Matric. 1674; B.A. 1677-8. Ord. deacon (York) Sept. 22, 1678.

EMMERSON, NICHOLAS. Adm. sizar at JESUS, July 5, 1692. Of Brotherbee, Durham. Matric. 1692; B.A. 1695-6. Ord. deacon (York) Sept. 1697; priest (Durham) Sept. 24, 1699.

EMERSON, PETER. Adm. sizar (age 19) at JESUS, May 9, 1669. Of Lancashire. Matric. 1669; B.A. 1672-3; M.A. 1691. V. of Buckden, Hunts., 1674-82. V. of Diddington, 1682-98. Died 1698.

EMERSON, RALPH. Matric. sizar from JESUS, Michs. 1584; B.A. 1585-6. Matric. from Queen's College, Oxford, Nov. 17, 1581, age 17. Of Co. Durham.

EMERSON, THOMAS. Matric. pens. from ST JOHN'S, Michs. 1566.

EMERSON, THOMAS. Adm. pens. at QUEENS', Feb. 22, 1644-5. Of Lincolnshire. S. and h. of Alexander, of Caistor, Lincs., Esq. B. 1628. Adm. at Lincoln's Inn, Oct. 27, 1645. Married Mildred Saunderson. Buried at Searby, Nov. 9, 1667. Father of Alexander (1668). (*Lincs. Pedigrees.*)

EMERSON, THOMAS. Adm. at CLARE, Jan. 18, 1683-4. Exhibitioner from Charterhouse. Matric. 1683-4; B.A. 1687-8; M.A. 1691. Fellow, 1689. V. of Litlington, Cambs., 1711. Died 1715.

EMERSON, WILLIAM. Adm. pens. (age 14) at ST JOHN'S, June 20, 1683. S. of James, merchant. B. at Dunston, near Durham. School, Durham. Matric. 1683; B.A. 1686-7. Said to have refused the M.A. as a non-juror. One of these names adm. student at Leyden, Oct. 22, 1691. (*Kettlewell's Life.*)

EMERSON, WILLIAM. Adm. sizar at ST CATHARINE'S, June 26, 1701. Matric. 1701; B.A. 1704-5. Ord. deacon (York) June, 1705; priest, 1706.

EMMERTON, JOHN. Adm. pens. at EMMANUEL, Nov. 3, 1674. Of Hertfordshire.

EMERTON, RICHARD. Adm. pens. at EMMANUEL, June 22, 1672. Of Hertfordshire. Probably of North Mimms. (*Clutterbuck*, I. 149.)

EMERTON, SAMUEL. Adm. pens. at EMMANUEL, June 22, 1672. Of Hertfordshire.

EMERY, MARK. Scholar at KING'S HALL, 1440; last appearance, 1454.

EMERY, RICHARD. Adm. Fell.-Com. (age 17) at ST JOHN'S, Oct. 29, 1639. S. of Thomas, yeoman, of Stone, Staffs. B. there. School, Shrewsbury. Matric. 1639. Minister at Shareshill, Staffs., 1651-2. Ord. deacon and priest (Lichfield) Dec. 20, 1663. V. of Brewood, 1664-77. Called B.A. Died Jan. 1, 1677-8. (*Wm. Salt Arch. Soc.*, 1915.)

EMERY, ROBERT. B.Can.L. 1501-2. Perhaps R. of Stambridge, Essex, till his death, 1519.

EMERYE, ROBERT. Matric. pens. from PETERHOUSE, Easter, 1568; B.A. 1571-2.

EMERE, THOMAS. Matric. pens. from ST JOHN'S, Michs. 1569.

EMERY, W. Matric. pens. from CHRIST'S, June, 1587. One William Emery was R. of Giffield, Northants. Buried there Feb. 2, 1616. (*Baker*, II. 309.)

EMERY, ——. A friar. B.D. 1468-9; D.D. 1470-1.

EMERY, ——. B.A. 1469-70.

EMERY, —— (*junior*). Pens. at PETERHOUSE, 1568-9.

EMES, DANIEL. Matric. pens. from ST JOHN'S, Easter, 1582.

EMES, SAMUEL. Adm. sizar (age 21) at TRINITY, June 17, 1728. S. of John, of Worcester. School, Greenwich, Kent (Mr Jeffries). Matric. 1728.

EMES, WILLIAM. M.A. 1670 (Incorp. from Oxford). S. of Thomas, of East Tisted, Hants., clerk. Matric. from New College, Oxford, Jan. 29, 1661-2, age 19; B.A. (Oxford) 1665; M.A. 1668-9. R. of Ashe, Surrey, 1677-1703. Canon of Chichester, 1679. (*Al. Oxon.*)

EMILEY, ANDREW. Adm. pens. at TRINITY, Sept. 27, 1645. Matric. 1645.

EMYLEY, HENRY. Matric. sizar from TRINITY, Michs. 1572.

EMILY, HENRY. Adm. scholar at TRINITY, 1646. Of Northamptonshire. B.A. 1648; M.A. 1651.

EMLIN, THOMAS. Adm. pens. at EMMANUEL, May 20, 1679. S. of Silvester, of Stamford, Lincs. B. there, May 27, 1663. School, Walcot (Mr George Boheme). Chaplain to Letitia, Countess of Donegal, a presbyterian lady, 1683-8. Chaplain to Sir Robert Rich, 1688-91. Colleague to Joseph Boyse at Dublin, 1691-1702. Accused of heresy, 1702. Returned to London. Fined and imprisoned for publishing *An Humble Inquiry into the Scripture Account of Jesus Christ*. Released, 1705. Preached occasionally at the Baptist Church in the Barbican. The first preacher who described himself as a Unitarian. Author of unitarian pamphlets. Died July 30, 1741. Buried in Bunhill Fields. (*D.N.B.*)

EMLYN, THOMAS. Adm. pens. at TRINITY HALL, Oct. 21, 1751. Perhaps s. and h. of Sollom, barrister; adm. at Lincoln's Inn, Feb. 25, 1748-9. A chancery barrister. Died 1796. For the father *see D.N.B.*

EMLING or EMBLING, WILLIAM. Matric. sizar from CORPUS CHRISTI, Michs. 1621. Of Lincolnshire. B.A. 1624-5; M.A. 1628 (Emlyn). Ord. deacon (Peterb.) Sept. 24; priest, Sept. 25, 1626.

EMLING or EMBLIN, WILLIAM. Adm. sizar (age 20) at ST JOHN'S, Jan. 22, 1654-5. S. of Daniel, gent., of Tinwell, Rutland. B. there. Bapt. May 2, 1633. School, Stamford. (*Scott-Mayor*, XXIX.)

EMLYN, ——. B.A. 1485-6.

EMMETT, ——. B.A. 1474-5.

EMMYSSON, ——. B.A. 1477-8.

EMMYSSON, ——. M.A. 1477-8.

EMNYTH, NICHOLAS. B.D. 1459-60.

EMONT, JOHN. B.A. from KING'S, 1637-8; M.A. 1641.

EMONT, MICHAEL. B.A. from KING'S, 1603-4; M.A. 1607, as Emott. R. of Little Saxham, Suffolk, 1618. Died Aug. 14, 1661.

EMOTT or EMOD, ALEXANDER. Matric. sizar from ST JOHN'S, Easter, 1566. Applied for priest's orders (Ely) Dec. 20, 1569, age 23. R. of Bolton-by-Bolland, Yorks., inst. June 8, 1598. Died there before Apr. 1624.

EMOT, JOHN. Matric. sizar from ST JOHN'S, Michs. 1567.

EMMOT, LAURENCE. Adm. sizar (age 17) at ST JOHN'S, May 19, 1654. S. of John, of Colne, Lancs., yeoman. School, Colne. Matric. 1654. Migrated to Oxford. Matric. from Christ Church, July 31, 1658. B.A. 1660.

EMOT or EMONT, RICHARD. Matric. sizar from QUEENS', Michs. 1581. Of Yorkshire. B.A. 1585-6; M.A. 1589.

EMMOTT, WILLIAM. Adm. sizar at CLARE, June 24, 1662. Matric. 1662; B.A. 1671-2. Ord. deacon (York) *c.* 1667. R. of Folkton, Yorks., till 1687.

EMMOTT, WILLIAM. Adm. Fell.-Com. at JESUS, Apr. 29, 1682. S. of William, of Emmott, Lancs., Esq. Matric. 1683. Died *s.p.* May 13, 1720, aged 51. (Burke, *L.G.*; Whitaker, *Whalley*, II. 257.)

EMPRINGHAM, JOHN. Adm. pens. at QUEENS', July 3, 1603. Of Nottinghamshire.

EMPSON, EDWARD. Matric. pens. from ST CATHARINE'S, Easter, 1635. S. and h. of Francis, of Boston, Lincs., gent. Adm. at Gray's Inn, May 4, 1638. Buried at Boston, Dec. 12, 1648. Brother of the next. (*Lincs. Pedigrees.*)

EMPSON, FRANCIS. Adm. pens. at EMMANUEL, May 21, 1647. S. of Francis, of Boston, deceased. Matric. 1647. Adm. at Gray's Inn, May 21, 1650. Buried Apr. 4, 1664. Brother of Edward, above. (*Lincs. Pedigrees.*)

EMPSON, GEORGE. Adm. Fell.-Com. at JESUS, June 26, 1691. Of Yorkshire. S. and h. of George, late of Goole, gent. Matric. 1692. Adm. at Gray's Inn, Feb. 17, 1690-1. Married Jan. 19, 1708-9, Margaret Webster, widow of Francis Nevile, Esq. Buried at Horbury, Yorks., Dec. 24, 1733. (*Goole Hall, Yorks.*; *see 'Lister' in Burke*; A. Gray.)

EMPSON, JOHN. Adm. sizar (age 18) at CAIUS, May 18, 1682. S. of Thomas, grocer, of Aylsham, Norfolk. School, Clitheroe, Lancs. Matric. 1682; Scholar, 1682-3. (*Venn*, I. 470.)

EMPSON, JOHN. Adm. sizar at ST CATHARINE'S, June 4, 1736. Of Reedness, Yorks. Matric. 1736; B.A. 1739-40; M.A. 1743. Ord. deacon (Lincoln) May 24, 1741; priest (*Litt. dim.* from York) Jan. 1742-3.

EMPSON, RICHARD. High Steward of the University, 1504. S. of Peter. B. at Towcester. The notorious minister of Henry VII. M.P. for Co. Northants., 1491. Speaker, 1491. Recorder of Coventry. Knighted, Feb. 18, 1503-4. Chancellor of the Duchy of Lancaster, 1504. Tried and convicted on a charge of treason. Executed, Aug. 17, 1510. (*Cooper*, I. 14; *D.N.B.*)

EMPSON or AMPSON, RICHARD. Adm. pens. (age 18) at JESUS, Mar. 23, 1672. Of Middlewich, Cheshire. Matric. as Amson (whom *see*); Scholar, 1675.

EMSON, THOMAS. B.D. 1488-9; D.D. 1492.

EMPSON, THOMAS. Adm. pens. at TRINITY, June 20, 1721. S. of ——, of York. School, Kirkleatham, Yorks. (Mr Thos. Clark).

ENCINAS, FRANCIS (*alias* **DRYANDER** or **VAN EYCK**). Resident at Cambridge, in 1549. Reader in Greek to the University. B. at Burgos, Spain, *c.* 1520. Pupil of Melancthon. Imprisoned at Brussels, 1543. Left for Basel. Died at Strasburg, Dec. 21, 1552. (*Cooper*, I. 292 and III. 85.)

ENDERBY, GEORGE. Adm. pens. at SIDNEY, June 23, 1604. Matric. 1604. Perhaps s. of Thomas, of Lincoln, attorney. Of Donington in 1634. (*Lincs. Pedigrees.*)

ENDERBY, RICHARD. Matric. pens. from TRINITY, Easter, 1610. S. of Richard, of Metheringham, Lincs. Scholar, 1611; B.A. 1612-3; M.A. 1616. Ord. deacon (Peterb.) Dec. 20; priest, Dec. 21, 1616. R. of Potter Hanworth, Lincs. V. of Ashby Puerorum, 1624. (*Lincs. Pedigrees.*)

ENDERBY, WILLIAM. B.D. of Cambridge. Dominican friar. *Sup.* for D.D. at Oxford, 1449-50.

ENDON, LAURENCE. Adm. pens. (age 21) at ST JOHN'S, Dec. 9, 1637. S. of Thomas, of Rudyard, Leeke, Staffs. School, Macclesfield. Previously matric. at Brasenose, Oxford, Feb. 13, 1634-5.

ENFIELD, RICHARD. Matric. pens. from CLARE, Easter, 1584.

ENGHAM, *see also* INGHAM.

ENGHAM, EDWARD. Matric. pens. from QUEENS', Michs. 1581. Of Kent. B.A. 1584-5; M.A. 1588. Fellow, 1586-92.

ENGHAM, EDWARD. Matric. Fell.-Com. from QUEENS', Easter, 1587. Of Kent. S. and h. of Thomas, of Goodnestone, Kent, Esq. Adm. at Gray's Inn, Jan. 30, 1589-90. Contributor towards building the gate of the Inn, 1593. Knighted, July 15, 1619. Sheriff of Kent, 1629. (*Vis. of Kent*, 1619; *Hasted*.)

ENGHAM, ROWLAND. Matric. Fell.-Com. from CLARE, *c.* 1597. Perhaps 2nd s. of Thomas, of Goodnestone, Esq. B.A. 1600-1. (*Vis. of Kent*, 1619.)

ENGHAM, THOMAS. Matric. pens. from CORPUS CHRISTI, Easter, 1659. Of Kent. Doubtless 1st s. of Edward, and grandson of Thomas, of Goodnestone. B.A. 1662-3. Adm. at the Inner Temple, Dec. 7, 1669. (*F.M.G.*)

ENGLAND, CHRISTOPHER. Matric. pens. from CHRIST'S, May, 1567; Scholar; B.A. 1571-2. Ord. priest (Norwich, by Suff. Bishop of Dover) Nov. 8, 1573. R. of Weston, Norfolk, 1577-1631. R. of Helmingham, 1599-1631. Chaplain to the Bishop of Gloucester, 1603. V. of Goodnestone, Kent, 1575.

ENGLAND, GEORGE. Adm. pens. at EMMANUEL, June 6, 1660. Of Norfolk. Doubtless s. and h. of George, of Yarmouth, merchant. Bapt. Sept. 22, 1643. Matric. 1660. Adm. at Gray's Inn, Nov. 12, 1661. Barrister, 1668. Recorder of Yarmouth. M.P. for Yarmouth, 1679-1701. Died 1702, aged 59. M.I. at Yarmouth. Brother of John (1668).

ENGLAND, GEORGE. Adm. pens. at CAIUS, Feb. 14, 1693-4. S. of Thomas, merchant. B. at Yarmouth, Dec. 1679. School, Yarmouth (Mr Reynolds and Mr Pate). Scholar, 1694-7; Matric. 1695. Adm. at Gray's Inn, Apr. 21, 1696. M.P. for Yarmouth, 1710, 1713, 1715. Mayor of Yarmouth, 1715. Of Stokesby, Norfolk. Buried there June 12, 1725. M.I. Father of Thomas (1726). (*Venn*, I. 494.)

ENGLAND, JOHN. Adm. pens. at CORPUS CHRISTI, 1668. Of Norfolk. S. of Sir George, Knt., of Yarmouth. Matric. 1668. Died in London, July 11, 1688. Buried at St Mary Woolnoth. Brother of George (1660). (Dawson Turner, *Yarmouth*, III.)

ENGLAND, RICHARD. Adm. sizar at CHRIST'S, June 12, 1667. S. of George. B. at Thornton, Yorks. School, South Dalton (Mr Callis). Matric. 1668; B.A. 1670-1. Master of Buntingford School before 1691; still there, 1721. Father of the next.

ENGLAND or INGLAND, THOMAS. Matric. sizar from ST JOHN'S, Easter, 1556.

ENGLAND or INGLAND, THOMAS. Matric. pens. from JESUS, Michs. 1579; B.A. 1582-3; M.A. 1586.

ENGLAND, THOMAS. Adm. sizar (age 16) at CHRIST'S, June 20, 1698. S. of Richard (above). B. at Buntingford. Educated there by his father. Matric. 1698; Scholar, 1698-9; B.A. 1701-2; M.A. 1705. Ord. deacon (London) Mar. 12, 1703-4; priest (Norwich) Dec. 1706. V. of Westwell, Kent, 1711-29. V. of Wennington, 1729. Chaplain to the Countess of Salisbury. Died Oct. 1729. (*Peile*, II. 142.)

ENGLAND, THOMAS. Adm. pens. (age 15) at CAIUS, July 26, 1726. S. of George (1694), of Stokesby, Norfolk. B. at Yarmouth. Bapt. June 11, 1711. School, Yarmouth (Mr Welham). Matric. 1726; Scholar, 1726; B.A. 1730-1; M.A. 1738. Adm. at the Inner Temple, June 21, 1726. (*Venn*, II. 26.)

ENGLEIS or INGLES, JOHN DE. 'King's scholar,' 1332.

ENGLESBY, WILLIAM. Adm. sizar at CLARE, Aug. 27, 1664; B.A. 1668-9.

ENGLISH or INGLISH, EDMUND. Matric. sizar from MAGDALENE, Lent, 1564-5.

ENGLISH, FRANCIS. Adm. sizar at CORPUS CHRISTI, 1644. Of Norfolk. Matric. Easter, 1645; B.A. 1648-9; M.A. 1655. Perhaps R. of St Laurence, Norwich, till 1657.

ENGLISH, HENRY. Adm. Fell.-Com. at EMMANUEL, June 28, 1637. Matric. 1637. Perhaps 2nd s. of Henry, of Maidstone, Kent, Esq.; adm. at Lincoln's Inn, Nov. 20, 1639.

ENGLISH, JOHN. B.A. 1502-3; M.A. 1506-7. One of these names V. of Abeley, Essex, 1532-6. Died 1536.

ENGLISH, JOHN. Dominican friar. B.D. 1517-8; D.D. 1521-2.

ENGLISH, JOHN. B.A. 1527-8. One of these names V. of Washbrook, Suffolk, 1550-4.

ENGLISH, JOHN. M.A. 1617 (Incorp. from Oxford). Of Worcestershire. Matric. from Balliol College, June 16, 1610, age 17; B.A. (Oxford) 1612; M.A. 1615; B.D. 1624; D.D. 1630. R. of Riseholme, Lincs., 1620-32; of Sherborne St John, Hants., 1634; and of Rudford, Glouces., 1634. P.C. of Cheltenham; sequestered, 1646. Buried there Nov. 26, 1647.

ENGLISH or INGLISH, JOHN. Adm. pens. (age 15) at PEMBROKE, Mar. 24, 1647-8. S. of Robert, of London, mercer. B. at Edinburgh. Matric. 1648. (*Vis. of London*, 1634.)

ENGLISH, MAURICE. A friar. B.D. 1458-9.

ENGLISH, NICHOLAS. Adm. scholar (age 18) at CAIUS, June 30, 1609. S. of Simon (1560), deceased. B. at Peterborough. School, Monk Soham (Mr Wm Smith), Suffolk. Matric. 1609; B.A. 1612-3. One of these names R. of Dowlishwake, Somerset, 1619. Brother of Simon (1604). (*Venn*, I. 202; *Vis. of London*, 1633.)

ENGLISH, ROBERT. Matric. sizar from MAGDALENE, Easter, 1567; B.A. 1570-1; M.A. 1575. Entered the College of Douay, 1579. Ord. priest there, 1580 ('Norvicencis'). Sent to England, 1580. (*Douay Diary*.)

ENGLISH, ROBERT. Adm. sizar (age 17) at EMMANUEL, June 30, 1739. S. of Thomas, of Ipswich. School, Ipswich. Matric. 1739; B.A. 1742-3; M.A. 1754. Master of Bungay School. Ord. deacon (Norwich) June, 1745; priest (Ely, *Litt. dim.* from Norwich) Dec. 25, 1753. Usher at Ipswich Grammar School. V. of St Andrew's, Ilketshall, Suffolk, 1754-84. V. of Horsford, Norfolk, 1770-84. P.C. of Horsham St Faith, 1781-4. Died May 10, 1784. (*G. Mag.*)

ENGLISH, SIMON. Matric. pens. from ST JOHN'S, Michs. 1560. B. in Yorkshire. S. of John, of Grimsby. School, Peterborough. B.A. 1564-5; M.A. 1568. Master of the Cathedral Grammar School, Peterborough. Died Jan. 6, 1592-3. Father of the next and of Nicholas (1609). (*Cooper*, II. 140; *Vis. of London*, 1634.)

ENGLISH, SIMON. Adm. pens. at EMMANUEL, Apr. 11, 1604. S. of the above. Matric. 1604. Of the Middle Temple, barrister. (*Vis. of London*, 1634.)

ENGLISH, THOMAS. Adm. pens. at EMMANUEL, Oct. 19, 1640. Of Kent. Perhaps 3rd s. of Henry, of Ewhurst, Sussex, Esq. Matric. 1641. Adm. at Lincoln's Inn, Feb. 8, 1644-5.

ENGLISH, ——. M.A. 1500. Perhaps Richard, University preacher, 1515.

ENNEW, HENRY. Adm. pens. at EMMANUEL, July 4, 1654. Of Essex.

ENEW, STEPHEN. B.A. 1453-4.

ENNEWES, EDMUND. Matric. pens. from JESUS, Lent, 1563-4; B.A. from Pembroke, 1568-9.

ENOWES, JOHN. Matric. pens. from SIDNEY, Easter, 1606; B.A. 1609-10. Ord. deacon (Peterb.) Dec. 22, 1611; priest, Dec. 26, 1614.

ENOCH, RICHARD. M.A. 1686 (Incorp. from Oxford). S. of George, of Sibford, Oxon., gent. Matric. from Trinity College, Oxford, May 5, 1673, age 15; B.A. (Oxford) 1677; M.A. 1680. R. of Erwarton, Suffolk, 1682-4. R. of Stutton, 1684. (*Al. Oxon.*)

ENSING, DAVID. Adm. pens. at EMMANUEL, Apr. 2, 1622. B. at Rye, Sussex. Matric. 1622; B.A. 1625-6; M.A. 1629. Fellow, 1629. R. of Preston, Northants. Father of the next.

ENSINGE, EDWARD. Adm. sizar (age 15) at MAGDALENE, Jan. 8, 1657-8. S. of David (above), clerk, of Northamptonshire. School, Daventry. Matric. 1660; B.A. 1661-2.

ENSOR, JOHN. Adm. sizar (age 19) at PEMBROKE, June 3, 1669. S. of John, farmer, of Wilnecote, Warws. Ord. priest (York) Sept. 1690.

ENSOR, JOHN. Adm. pens. at CLARE, June 9, 1686. Of Polesworth, Warws. B.A. from St Catharine's, 1691-2. P.C. of Long Stow, Hunts., 1698-1724. P.C. of Spaldwick. Buried there Jan. 4, 1723-4.

ENSOR, RICHARD. Adm. pens. (age 17) at MAGDALENE, Mar. 22, 1660-1. S. of John, of Tissington, Derbs. School, Ashbourne. Matric. 1661; B.A. 1664-5; M.A. 1668. V. of Ilam, Staffs., 1669-1714. Died Nov. 6, 1714. Father of the next. (*Wm. Salt Arch. Soc.*, 1915.)

ENSOR, RICHARD. Adm. sizar (age 18) at ST JOHN'S, Apr. 27, 1689. S. of Richard (above), clerk. B. at Ilam, Staffs. School, Ashbourne. Matric. 1689.

ENSTABLE, ——. Adm. Fell.-Com. at CORPUS CHRISTI, 1569.

ENT, GEORGE. Adm. pens. (age 18) at SIDNEY, July 8, 1624. S. of John (Josias, in *D.N.B.*), merchant in Flanders. B. at Sandwich, Kent, Nov. 6, 1604. Educated 'in Wallachia' and at Rotterdam. Scholar, 1624; B.A. 1627; M.A. 1631. Studied at Padua, where he graduated M.D. 1636. Incorp. at Oxford, 1638. Fellow, R.C.P. 1639. F.R.S. 1663. Knighted, Apr. 15, 1665. Gulstonian lecturer. President, 1670-5, 1682, 1684. Author, medical. Died in London, Oct. 13, 1689. Buried in St Lawrence Jewry. Father of the next. (*Munk*, I. 223; *D.N.B.*)

ENT, GEORGE. Adm. pens. (age 16) at SIDNEY, Sept. 9, 1660. S. of George (above), M.D. B. at Sandwich. School, Enfield, Middlesex (Mr Martn. Millington). Matric. 1661. Adm. at Gray's Inn, Mar. 9, 1662-3. Barrister, 1670. Perhaps of the Middle Temple. Died Aug. 1679. Buried in the Temple Church. (Le Neve, *Knights*, 191.)

ENTENSE, ——. Adm. at CORPUS CHRISTI, 1578.

ENTWISTLE, EDWARD. Matric. pens. from MAGDALENE, Easter, 1639.

ENTWISTLE, JOHN. Matric. pens. from MAGDALENE, Michs. 1642; B.A. 1645-6.

ENTWHISTLE, JOSEPH. Matric. sizar from TRINITY, Michs. 1581; B.A. from Magdalene, 1584-5.

EPHRON, SAMUEL, *see* **BENEDICTUS.**

EPISCOPUS, *see* **L'EVESQUE.**

EPS, ALLEN. Adm. pens. at EMMANUEL, Aug. 26, 1594. Matric. c. 1594; B.A. 1597-8. One of these names s. of Thomas, of New Romney, Kent, grandfather of the next. (*Vis. of Kent*, 1663.)

EPES, ALAN. Adm. Fell.-Com. (age 20) at CAIUS, Apr. 23, 1679. M.B. 1680. From Lincoln College, Oxford. Matric. there, July 2, 1675, age 17. S. of Paul, of Wye, Kent. B. at Canterbury. Adm. at Gray's Inn, June 17, 1675. (*Venn*, I. 462.)

EPPES, WILLIAM. Adm. pens. at EMMANUEL, May 20, 1594. Matric. c. 1593.

EPPS, ——. Adm. pens. at ST CATHARINE'S, 1641.

EPWORTH, CHRISTOPHER. Adm. pens. (age 18) at MAGDALENE, Apr. 5, 1676. S. of Christopher. Bapt. Spilby, Lincs. School, Kirton, Lincs. B.A. 1679-80.

EPWORTH, CHRISTOPHER. Adm. pens. at JESUS, Apr. 13, 1705. Matric. 1705; Scholar, 1707; B.A. 1708-9; M.A. 1723. Ord. deacon (Lincoln) June 19, 1709; priest (York) Sept. 1710. V. of Wrawby, Lincs., 1715.

EPWORTH, CHRISTOPHER. Adm. sizar at JESUS, July 7, 1732. Of Yorkshire. S. of ——, clerk, deceased. Matric. 1735; B.A. 1735-6; M.A. 1776. Ord. deacon (Lincoln) June 20, 1736; priest, May 28, 1738. R. of Croxton, Lincs. V. of Killingholme. V. of Keelby. Died May, 1792, aged 79.

ERASMUS, DESIDERIUS. B. at Rotterdam, Oct. 28, 1465. The illegitimate s. of Gerrit, of Gouda. Educated at the school of Deventer, where he learned Greek. Ord. priest, 1492. Private secretary to the Bishop of Cambrai who gave him the means to go to Paris. Studied there, 1496-7. Came to England; studied at St Mary Hall, Oxford, and visited Cambridge, where he was made D.D. 1506. Went to Rome in 1506, and was dispensed from his monastic vows; also visited Venice and Bologna. Returned to England in 1510, and resided in Queens' College, 1510-5. For a time Public Orator. Lady Margaret Professor of Theology, 1511-5. Visited Flanders in 1514, and became a Councillor of Charles V. Latterly resided at Basel, where his great work, the first edition of the New Testament in Greek, was published, in 1516. Offered a Cardinalate by Paul III, in 1535. Died July 11, 1536, at Basel. (*Cooper*, I. 57; *The New Calendar of Great Men*.)

ERASTUS, DANIEL. Matric. pens. from ST CATHARINE'S, Easter, 1633, as 'Brastus.' A Pole. B.A. 1636-7.

ERAT, WILLIAM. Adm. sizar (age 16) at ST JOHN'S, May 4, 1672. S. of William, deceased, of Warter, Yorks. B. there. School, Pocklington. Matric. 1672; B.A. 1675-6; M.A. 1696. Ord. deacon (York) May, 1676; priest, Dec. 1683. C. of Sykehouse, Yorks., 1676. V. of Hatfield, Yorks., 1689. Buried there, Mar. 30, 1702.

ERATT, WILLIAM. Adm. pens. at JESUS, Dec. 26, 1705. S. of ——, clerk (? the above), deceased, of Yorkshire. Matric. 1706; B.A. 1709-10; Rustat Scholar. Practised at Doncaster. Died Mar. 13, 1727, aged 41. Called 'M.D.' (Abr. de la Pryme's *Diary*, 179.)

ERBERY, WILLIAM, *see* **EARBERY.**

ERBY, *see* **IRBY.**

ERDISWICK, RICHARD. Adm. Fell.-Com. (age 15) at CAIUS, Jan. 29, 1608-9. S. and h. of Sampson, Esq., historian, of Sandown, Staffs. School, Eton. Adm. at Lincoln's Inn, May 19, 1612. M.P. for Staffordshire, 1625. For the father *see D.N.B.* (*Staffs. Pedigrees*.)

ERDNAM, RICHARD. Matric. sizar from JESUS, Easter, 1548.

ERESBY, DANIEL. Adm. sizar (age 17) at MAGDALENE, May 8, 1672. S. of John, of Caistor, Lincs. School, Caistor. Matric. 1672; B.A. 1675-6. Ord. deacon (Peterb.) Sept. 24, 1676. Brother of John (1675).

ERSBY, JOHN. Matric. pens. from ST JOHN'S, c. 1592. Probably s. of Richard, of Somercotes, Lincs. Of Somercotes, Esq. (*Lincs. Pedigrees*.)

ERESBY, JOHN. Adm. sizar (age 18) at MAGDALENE, June 19, 1675. S. of John, ostler (stabularius). B. at Caistor, Lincs. School, Caistor. Matric. 1675; B.A. 1678-9. Ord. deacon (Lincoln) Feb. 27, 1679-80; priest, Sept. 18, 1680. R. of St Thomas-at-Cliffe, Lewes, 1682. V. of West Firle, Sussex, 1690-1740. Buried there June 26, 1740. Brother of Daniel (1672). (W. C. Renshaw.)

ERSBYE, RICHARD. Matric. pens. from TRINITY, Easter, 1562. 1st s. of Thomas, of Spilsby. Probably adm. at Gray's Inn, 1568, from Staple Inn. One of these names of Somercotes, Lincs. (*Lincs. Pedigrees*.)

ERFIELD, THOMAS. Matric. Fell.-Com. from TRINITY, Easter, 1615.

ERICKE, JAMES. Matric. sizar from ST JOHN'S, Easter, 1620; B.A. 1623-4; M.A. 1627. V. of Thornton *with* Bagworth, Leics., 1627. Doubtless father of the next.

ERRICK, THOMAS. Adm. sizar (age 17) at CHRIST'S, May 29, 1645. S. of James. B. at Thornton, Leics. School, Leicester (Mr Knightley). Matric. 1645; B.A. 1647-8. Ord. deacon (Lincoln) Aug. 7, 1662; priest (London) Dec. 1663. C. of Bourne, Lincs., 1662. Perhaps V. of Fisby-on-the-Wreak, Leics., 1664-81. Buried there Aug. 23, 1681. His sister Abigail was mother of Jonathan Swift. (*Peile*, I. 496; *Nichols*, III. 177.)

ERISEY, HENRY. Adm. . at EMMANUEL, June 21, 1645. Of Cornwall. 4th s. of Richard, of Erisey, Cornwall, Esq. Adm. at Lincoln's Inn, May 27, 1647.

ERLHAM or ERLOUN, JOHN. B.D. Fellow of CORPUS CHRISTI, 1440. President and bursar of the College.

ERLAM, NICHOLAS. Scholar at KING'S HALL, 1385. Died Aug. 16, 1386.

ERLWIN, MARMADUKE. Matric. pens. from PEMBROKE, Lent, 1656-7.

ERLYCH or ARLICH, JOHN. Adm. at KING'S, a scholar from Eton, 1497. S. of John, burgess and mayor of Cambridge. B.A. 1501-2; M.A. 1505. Fellow, till 1514. Died 1551. Will proved (V.C.C.) 1551. (*Cooper*, I. 57 and III. 85; where he is confused with his father).

ERMITAGE, *see* **ARMITAGE.**

ERNE, JOHN. Adm. sizar at KING'S, 1551-2.

ERNESBY, GRIFFIN. Matric. pens. from TRINITY, Michs. 1584; Scholar, 1586.

ERNESTUS, JOACHIM. M.A. 1619. S. of Hans, Duke of Plöen. B. 1595. Succeeded his father as Duke of Plöen, 1622 (*i.e.* not as described in the *grace*, heir to the crown of Norway). Died 1671. (E. Magnússon.)

ERRINGTON or ERYNGTON, CLEMENT. B.A. 1507-8; M.A. 1511-2. Fellow of ST JOHN'S, 1516. V. of Weston-by-Bath, Somerset, 1525-41. R. of Lee, Essex, 1531-3. V. of St Olave Jewry, 1545-58. Will (P.C.C.) 1558.

ERINGTON, GERARD. M.A. 1690 (Incorp. from Oxford). S. of G[erard], of Salisbury. Matric. from Magdalen Hall, July 14, 1676, age 16; B.A. (Oxford) 1680; M.A. 1683. V. of East Garston, Berks., 1686. R. of Little Layer, Essex, 1690. Brother of Samuel (1690). (*Al. Oxon.*)

ERRINGTON, RICHARD. Adm. sizar (age 17) at CHRIST'S, June 1, 1650. S. of Richard. B. at Shadforth, Durham. School, Guisborough (Mr Smelt). Matric. 1650, as 'Orrington.'

ERINGTON, SAMUEL. Adm. sizar (age 17) at ST JOHN'S, June 31, 1690. S. of Gerard, deceased. B. at Salisbury. School, Salisbury. Matric. 1690, as 'Herrington'; B.A. 1693-4; M.A. 1697. Ord. deacon (London) Sept. 19, 1697. Brother of Gerard (1690).

ERRINGTON, THOMAS. Adm. sizar at CHRIST'S, June 25, 1685. S. of Richard. B. at Modbury, Devon. Educated by his father. Matric. 1685. Resided till Lady Day, 1686. (*Peile*, II. 99.)

ERSBY, *see* **ERESBEY.**

ERSKINE, CHARLES. Adm. at CORPUS CHRISTI, 1733. Of Edinburgh. Probably s. of Charles, Solicitor-General for Scotland. B. Oct. 21, 1716. Matric. 1733. Adm. at the Middle Temple, Aug. 24, 1733; and at Lincoln's Inn, 1743. Barrister-at-Law. Died prematurely. Buried in the Chapel of Lincoln's Inn. (*Masters*; *Collins*, v. 427.)

ERSKINE, JOHN. M.A. 1638. S. of the Earl of Mar. Married Margaret Inglis, dau. of William, of Otterstown, Fife, 1640. Died before 1668. (Wood's *Peerage of Scotland*, v. 622.)

ERSKINE, WILLIAM. M.A. of St Andrews. Incorp. at Oxford, 1632; and at Cambridge, 1635. B.D. from Magdalene College, Cambridge, 1640. Created D.D. (Oxford) 1642. Fellow of Magdalene; ejected, 1644. R. of Cwm, Flints., 1644-53. Preb. of St Asaph, 1644-60. R. of the sinecure of Cwm, St Asaph. Died 1660. (Browne Willis, *St Asaph*.)

ERSON, JOHN (1535–6), *see* ARSON.

ERSWELL, ROBERT. Adm. sizar at Queens', Apr. 29, 1595. Of Huntingdonshire. Matric. c. 1596.

ERYVAN or ERYUM, HENRY. M.A. of Cambridge. Incorp. at Oxford, 1457–8.

ESCOLME, JOHN. Adm. sizar (age 18) at Trinity, Apr. 13, 1715. S. of Richard, of London. School, St Paul's. Exhibitioner. Matric. 1715; Scholar, 1718; B.A. 1718–9. Ord. deacon (Lincoln) Sept. 23, 1722; priest, Sept. 22, 1723. R. of Covenham St Mary, Lincs., 1723.

ESCOSCE (?), W. Matric. pens. from St John's, Lent, 1563–4.

ESCOTT or ESTCOTE, DANIEL. M.A. 1615 (Incorp. from Oxford). Of Devon. Matric. from Exeter College, Oct. 14, 1608, age 18; B.A. 1611; M.A. 1614. Created D.D. 1636. Fellow of Wadham College, 1613–34. Proctor, 1624. V. of Southrop, Gloucs., 1633–41. Warden of Wadham, 1635–44. R. of Beverstone *with* Kingscote, Gloucs., 1638. Died Apr. 1644. (*Al. Oxon.*)

ESCOTT, DANIEL. M.A. 1659 (Incorp. from Oxford). Matric. from Wadham College, Oct. 24, 1645, age 18; B.A. 1648; M.A. 1650; B.D. 1662. Fellow of Wadham, 1651. R. of Dunchideock, Devon, 1663. Canon of Exeter, 1663; Archdeacon, 1665. V. of Totnes, 1664. Died Mar. 28, 1668. Will (Exeter) 1668. (*Al. Oxon.*)

ESDALL, BALDWIN. Matric. sizar from Pembroke, Easter, 1560. B. at Hornchurch, Essex. B.A. 1562–3; M.A. 1566; B.D. 1573. Fellow, c. 1565. Ord. priest (London) June 12, 1569, age 26. R. of Orton Waterville, Hunts., 1569–99. V. of Bottisham, Cambs., 1573. R. of Creeton, Lincs., 1574–7. R. of Chesterton, Hunts., 1580–8. R. of Rollesby, Norfolk, 1586–9. R. of Haddon, 1589–99. Died 1599.

ESDAY, HENRY. Adm. pens. (age 16) at Peterhouse, June 6, 1638. Doubtless s. of Henry, of Saltwood, Kent. Scholar, 1641; B.A. 1641–2; M.A. 1646. Minister at Gingrave, Essex. R. of Pentlow, 1650–60; ejected. Afterwards preacher in Essex. Died in St Leonard's, Shoreditch. (*Davids*, 442.)

ESH, *see also* ASH.

ESHE, CHRISTOPHER. Matric. sizar from Trinity, Easter, 1575. Perhaps of Woodhall, Yorks. Adm. at the Inner Temple, 1581. Barrister, 1590.

ESH, EDMUND. Adm. sizar at Trinity, July 7, 1658. Matric. 1658; B.A. 1661–2, as 'Ash'; M.A. 1670.

ESHE, JOHN. Matric. sizar from Trinity, Easter, 1618. Ord. deacon (York) Mar. 1624–5; priest, Dec. 1625.

ESHE, W. Matric. sizar from Trinity, Michs. 1575.

ESKRIGG, ROBERT. Adm. sizar (age 17) at Christ's, Mar. 16, 1674–5. S. of Robert. B. at Eskrigg, Lancs. (? Escrick, Yorks.). School, Kirkby Lonsdale. Matric. 1674–5; B.A. 1678–9; M.A. 1682. Ord. priest (Peterb.) Dec. 18, 1680. V. of Ravenstone, Bucks., 1680. P.C. of Weston Underwood, 1684–92. Buried at Ravenstone, Sept. 27, 1721. (*Peile*, II. 57.)

ESQUIRE, WILLIAM. Matric. sizar from Trinity Hall, Easter, 1647.

ESSEX, Earl of, *see* CROMWELL, THOMAS (1535).

ESSEX, EDWARD. Matric. pens. from King's, Michs. 1572. 3rd s. of Thomas, of Lamborne, Berks. Knighted, Aug. 5, 1599. Brother of Robert (1573), Scipio (1572) and William (1572).

ESSEX, JOHN. Scholar at King's Hall, 1379. Died Sept. 8, 1397.

ESSEX, ROBERT. Adm. pens. at King's, 1573. 5th s. of Thomas, of Lamborne. Brother of the next, Edward (1572) and William (1572).

ESSEX, SCIPIO. Matric. pens. from King's, Michs. 1572. 2nd s. of Thomas, of Lamborne, Berks., Esq. Brother of Edward (1572), Robert (above) and William (1572). (*Vis. of Berks.*, 1665, II. 125.)

ESSEX, THOMAS. Fellow of King's Hall. Ord. acolyte (Ely) May 20, 1402.

ESSEX, THOMAS. Adm. sizar at Jesus, Apr. 27, 1637. Of Cambridgeshire. Matric. 1637; B.A. 1640– ; M.A. 1644. Ord. deacon (Peterb.) June 5, 1642; priest (Lincoln) Sept. 19, 1645. R. of Wickhampton, Norfolk, 1651–69. R. of Moulton, 1658–68. R. of Rockland St Andrew, 1661, and of Reedham. Father of the next.

ESSEX, THOMAS. Adm. sizar (age 16) at Caius, June 22, 1668. S. of Thomas, R. of Reedham, Norfolk. B. at Wickhampton. Schools, Norwich, Sisland (Mr Bell), Beccles (Mr Wells) and Thetford (Mr Keen). Matric. 1668; Scholar, 1668–70; B.A. 1672–3; M.A. 1677. Ord. deacon (Norwich) Sept. 1673; priest, Sept. 1674. R. of Moulton, 1675; of Beighton, 1675–8. Will proved (Norwich C.C.) 1689. (*Venn*, I. 435.)

ESSEX, WILLIAM. Matric. pens. from King's, Michs. 1572. 4th s. of Thomas, of Lamborne, Berks., Esq. Brother of Edward (1572), Robert (1573) and Scipio (1572). One of these names M.P. for Arundel, 1597; for Stafford, 1601. But *see Al. Oxon.* for a contemporary.

ESSON, *see* EASON.

EST, *see also* EAST.

EST or EAST, FRANCIS. Matric. sizar from Christ's, Lent, 1581–2. One of these names, 'of Cambs.', adm. at Gray's Inn, Feb. 2, 1594–5 (but entry erased). (*Peile*, I. 168.)

EST or EAST, GEORGE. B.A. 1507–8; M.A. 1511.

EST or EAST, SIMON. Matric. sizar from Queens', Lent, 1581–2. Of Lincolnshire.

ESTE, THOMAS. Scholar at King's Hall, 1458–65.

ESTE, THOMAS. Matric. sizar from St John's, Easter, 1549. One of these names ord. priest (Suffragan Bishop of Thetford) Dec. 8, 1556. V. of Owersby, Lincs. Died 1585.

ESTE, THOMAS. Matric. sizar from Queens', Michs. 1556.

EST, WILLIAM. Matric. sizar (age 12) from Caius, May, 1559.

ESTCOURT, EDMUND. Adm. sizar (age 19) at Sidney, Apr. 15, 1627. S. of John, Esq. B. at Tetbury, Gloucs. Schools, Tetbury (Mr Lake, Mr Workman) and Berkeley. One Edward Escourt student at Leyden, Jan. 3, 1624–5 and Aug. 28, 1627. Adm. at Gray's Inn, May 4, 1632. (*Vis. of Gloucs.*, 1623.)

ESTERBIE, *see* EASTERBY.

ESTEY, BENJAMIN. Adm. pens. at Emmanuel, Apr. 2, 1614 S. of George (next). Matric. 1615; Scholar; B.A. 1617–8; M.A. 1621. Ord. deacon and priest (Norwich) Dec. 18, 1625. V. of West Bradenham, Norfolk, in 1625. Father of John (1649).

ESTEY, GEORGE. Adm. pens. (age 16) at Caius, Feb. 10, 1576–7. S. of John. B. in Cambridge. School, Cambridge. B.A. 1580–1; Scholar, till 1584; M.A. 1584; B.D. 1591. Fellow, 1584–1600. Scrutator, 1598. Ord. deacon and priest (Lincoln) Oct. 25, 1587. V. of St Mary, Bury St Edmunds, 1598–1601. Author. Died Aug. 2, 1601. Buried at St Mary's. M.I. Father of Benjamin (1614). (*Venn*, I. 90; *D.N.B.*; *Cooper*, II. 319.)

ESTEY, JOHN. Adm. sizar (age 17) at Caius, Apr. 6, 1649. S. of Benjamin (1614), V. of West Bradenham, Norfolk. B. there. School, Lynn (Mr Bell). Of Gaywood, Norfolk, (*Venn*, I. 374.)

ESTHAM, THOMAS. Resident pensioner at Peterhouse, c. 1403–4. (*T. A. Walker.*)

ESTMAN, JOHN. Matric. pens. from Jesus, Michs. 1578.

ESTHORPE, ——. Excused from Regency, 1478–9.

ESTOFFE, CHRISTOPHER. Matric. pens. from Magdalene, Michs. 1567. Perhaps s. of Christopher Estoft, Esq. 'one of the Quenes Majestic Honorable Council established in the North,' who married Isabel, widow of Sir John Ellerker. Died May 14, 1566.

EASTOFTE, JOHN. Matric. pens. from St John's, Easter, 1569. S. of Thomas, Esq., of Eastoft, near Thorne, Yorks. School, Merchant Taylors', London. Migra to Caius, Oct. 9, 1571. Of Eastoft. Alive in 1604. Father of Thomas (1617). (*Venn*, I. 68; *Lincs. Pedigrees.*)

EASTOFT, JOHN. Adm. Fell.-Com. (age 15) at Sidney, June 29, 1655. S. of Thomas, Esq. B. at Rockcliffe, Yorks. School, Howden, Yorks. (Mr Jo. Thompson). Matric. 1656; B.A. 1657–8. Of Eastoft, Esq. Deputy Lieutenant, East Riding, 1687–8. Married and had issue. (*Lincs. Pedigrees.*)

EASTOFT, JOHN. Adm. pens. (age 16) at Sidney, Apr. 1691. 1st s. of John, Esq. B. at Etton, Yorks. School, Beverley (Mr Jos. Lambert). Matric. 1692.

ESTOFT, THOMAS. Matric. pens. from St John's, Easter, 1555.

ESTOFT, THOMAS. Matric. Fell.-Com. from Corpus Christi, Easter, 1617. Of Yorkshire. 1st s. of John (1569), of Eastoft. Age 30 in 1634. (*Lincs. Pedigrees.*)

ESTOFTE, W. Matric. pens. from St John's, Lent, 1563–4.

ESTON, *see also* EASTON *and* EASON.

ESTON, EDMUND. Adm. sizar at Emmanuel, as Eason, Feb. 1, 1596–7. Matric. c. 1596; B.A. 1600–1; M.A. 1604. Fellow of Sidney. Ord. deacon (Peterb.) Sept. 20; priest, Sept. 27, 1607.

ESTON, HENRY. Matric. pens. from Christ's, May, 1570.

ESTON, JOHN. Matric. pens. from Clare, Easter, 1580.

ESTON, JOHN. Adm. pens. (age 15) at Caius, June 24, 1613. S. of Nicholas (1593), schoolmaster of Norfolk. School, Beeston (under his father). Matric. 1613; Scholar, 1614; B.A. 1617–8; M.A. from Corpus Christi, 1621; B.D. 1629. Fellow of Corpus Christi, 1619–38. Incorp. at Oxford, 1627. Ord. priest (Peterb.) Sept. 14, 1627. R. of Raynham St Mary, Norfolk, 1638. (*Venn*, I. 221.)

ESTON, JOHN. Adm. sizar (age 15) at SIDNEY, June 3, 1641. S. of William, Esq. B. at Deane, Beds. Schools, Deane (Mr Taylor) and Sutton (Mr Kempe). B.A. 1644–5; M.A. 1648. Incorp. at Oxford, 1648. Fellow of Oriel College, Oxford, 1648. R. of Pertenhall, Beds., 1660–89. Buried there Jan. 2, 1689–90. (*Al. Oxon.*; W. M. Noble.)

ESTON, JOHN (1673), *see* EASON or EASTON.

ESTON, NICHOLAS. Matric. pens. from PEMBROKE, Michs. 1586; B.A. 1589–90; M.A. 1593. Master of Ipswich Grammar School, 1616–31. Master of Botesdale, 1631. Father of John (1613).

ESTON, THOMAS. Matric. pens. from CLARE, Easter, 1581.

ESTON, WALTER. Fellow of TRINITY HALL. Ord. acolyte (Ely) Sept. 14, 1412. Preb. of Hereford, 1421. Resident in 1434.

ESTON, WILLIAM. B.A. 1491–2; M.A. 1494.

EASTON, WILLIAM. LL.B. from TRINITY HALL, 1641–2.

ESTON, ——. M.A. or higher degree, 1467–8. Resident at CORPUS CHRISTI, in 1471. *Masters* suggests that he may be Thomas, chaplain to the altar of St Christopher, York. Buried there 1493.

EASTON, ——. B.A. 1476–7; M.A. 1482.

ESTUBY, WILLIAM. B.A. 1515–6. V. of Lindsell, Essex, 1551. Died 1566. (*Ess. Arch. Soc.*, 2nd S., II. 237.)

ESTWICK, *see* EASTWICK.

ESYNGWOLD, *see* EASINGWOLD.

ETHERIDGE, JAMES. Adm. pens. at TRINITY, May 7, 1674. S. of James, of London. B. there, Feb. 9, 1657. Schools, Hitchin and Bishop's Stortford. Adm. at the Inner Temple, June 28, 1676. Knighted, Feb. 17, 1681–2. J.P. for Bucks., 1684. Recorder of Chipping Wycombe, 1687. M.P. for Gt Marlow, 1695–1713. Deputy-Lieutenant for Bucks., 1712. Buried June 23, 1730, at Marlow. (*Miscell. Gen. et Her.*, N.S., I. 211.)

ETHERIDGE, JOHN. Adm. sizar at QUEENS', May 16, 1609 Of Hertfordshire. B.A. 1612–3; M.A. 1616; B.D. 1623 Fellow, 1615–26. Ord. deacon and priest (Peterb.) Dec. 21, 1617. V. of Oakington, Cambs., 1622–7. R. of Fairstead, Essex, till 1643; and of Halstead, till 1641.

ETHERIDGE, WILLIAM. 'Of TRINITY; incorp. M.A. at Oxford, 1676' (*Al. Oxon.*). Not found in the Cambridge lists.

ETHERINGTON, *see also* HETHERINGTON.

ETHERINGTON, AMBROSE. Matric. sizar from MAGDALENE, Michs. 1545; B.A. 1550–1; M.A. 1554; B.D. 1562; D.D. 1583. Fellow of Trimity, 1552. Ord. deacon (Ely) June 8, 1561; priest, June 8, 1561. V. of Kendal, Westmorland, 1562–91.

ETHRINGTON, CHRISTOPHER. Adm. sizar (age 15) at SIDNEY, Apr. 6, 1647. S. of Christopher, shoemaker. B. at Hull. Yorks. School, Hull (Mr Stephenson). Matric. 1647; B.A, 1650–1. Perhaps V. of Sowerby, Yorks., 1676–8. Died 1678. Father of Joseph (1678).

ETHERINGTON, GEORGE. Matric. pens. from TRINITY, Michs. 1588.

ETHERINGTON, GEORGE. Matric. pens. from ST JOHN'S, Michs. 1607; B.A. 1611–2; M.A. 1615. Ord. deacon (York) May, 1616; priest, Sept. 1617. R. of Middleton-on-the-Wolds, 1617–27. Father of Richard (1640).

ETHERINGTON, GEORGE. Adm Fell.-Com. at EMMANUEL, Sept. 12, 1612. Matric. 1612. Knighted, Feb. 16, 1618–9. Probably brother of Richard (1612).

ETHERINGTON, GEORGE. Adm. sizar at TRINITY HALL, May 2, 1741. Matric. 1743–4; LL.B. 1748. V. of Collingham, Yorks., 1762–1802. Died Oct. 28, 1802, aged 79.

ETHERINGTON, JOHN. Adm. sizar at TRINITY, June 12, 1663. Matric. 1664; B.A. 1667–8. Perhaps P.C. of Trentham, Staffs., *c.* 1677–82.

ETHERINGTON, JOSEPH. Adm. sizar (age 17) at SIDNEY, May 8, 1678. S. of Christopher (1647), clerk. B. at 'Morlaynat' (? Morley), Yorks. School, Sowerby, Yorks. Matric. 1678; B.A. 1681–2; M.A. 1688. Ord. deacon (York) Sept. 1681; priest, June, 1682.

ETHERINGTON, LAYTON. Adm. sizar at TRINITY, Aug. 30, 1675. Matric. 1675; B.A. 1679–80; M.A. 1683. Ord. deacon (York) May, 1681. V. of Washington, Durham, 1685–1718. V. of Heighington, 1705–18. Married Mary Sparrow, Feb. 10, 1690–1. Buried Oct. 11, 1718, at Washington. M.I. (H. M. Wood.)

ETHERINGTON, LEWIS. Adm. pens. at QUEENS', July 7, 1658. Fell.-Com. 1659. Of Rillington, Yorks., Esq.

ETHERINGTON, NICHOLAS. Adm. pens. at EMMANUEL, Apr. 23, 1638. Matric. 1639; B.A. 1641–2.

ETHERINGTON, PETER. Adm. pens. (age 18) at CAIUS, July 5, 1578. S. of Robert, yeoman, of Saltfleetby All Saints, Lincs. Bapt. there, Nov. 1558. Schools, Boston and Louth (Mr Goodale and Mr Woodroffe). Matric. 1578; B.A. 1581–2.

ETHERINGTON, RICHARD. Adm. Fell.-Com. at EMMANUEL, Sept. 12, 1612. Matric. 1612. Adm. at Gray's Inn, June 3, 1614, as s. and h. of George, of Newton Garth, Yorks.; or Aug. 10, 1616, as s. of Richard, of Eberston, Yorks. Probably brother of George (1612).

ETHERINGTON, RICHARD. Adm. pens. at EMMANUEL, Aug. 4, 1632. Of Yorkshire. S. and h. of Thomas, deceased, of Dunsley, Yorks. Adm. at the Inner Temple, 1633. Barrister, 1641. Bencher. Perhaps Recorder of York.

ETHERINGTON, RICHARD. Adm. pens. (age 17) at ST JOHN'S, June 13, 1640. S. of George (1607), R. of Middleton-on-the-Wolds, Yorks. B. there. School, Beverley. Matric. 1640.

ETHERINGTON or HETHERINGTON, ROBERT. Matric. sizar from ST JOHN'S, Easter, 1582; B.A. from Trinity, 1586–7; M.A. 1590. R. of Salthouse, Norfolk, 1592.

ETHERINGTON, WILLIAM. Adm. pens. at EMMANUEL, May, 1604. Matric. 1604; Scholar; B.A. 1608–9; M.A. 1612. Ord. priest (Peterb.) Mar. 12, 1619–20. V. of Langton-by-Wragby, Lincs., 1620. Father of William (1640).

ETHERINGTON, WILLIAM. Matric. sizar from TRINITY, Easter, 1634; B.A. 1637–8.

ETHERINGTON, WILLIAM. Adm. sizar (age 17) at ST JOHN'S, May 28, 1640. S. of William (1604), V. of Langton-by-Wragby, Lincs. B. there. School, Sleaford. Matric. 1640; B.A. 1643–4. Probably ord. deacon (York) Nov. 1664.

ETKINS, RICHARD. B.D. 1609 (Incorp. from Oxford). Of Worcestershire. Matric. from Christ Church, Apr. 26, 1593, age 17; B.A. (Oxford) 1597; M.A. 1600; B.D. 1609; D.D. 1618. V. of Kensington, Middlesex, 1608–41. (*Al. Oxon.*)

ETON, *see* EATON.

ETONY, GEORGE. Matric. sizar from QUEENS', Easter, 1631, as 'Stoney.' Of Essex. B.A. 1634–5. Nominated to Greenstead, Essex, Apr. 29, 1648. (*Shaw*, I. 355.)

ETOUGH, HENRY. M.A. 1717 (*Com. Reg.*). V. of Cringleford, Norfolk. R. of Caldecot, 1717. V. of Eaton, Norwich, 1728–35. R. of Therfield, Herts., 1735–57. Died Aug. 10, 1757, age 69. M.I. at Therfield.

ETOUGH, RICHARD. Adm. pens. at ST CATHARINE'S, May 29, 1740. Bapt. at St Mary's, Warwick, Dec. 24, 1721. Exhibitioner from Charterhouse. Matric. 1740; B.A. 1743–4; M.A. 1753. Subscribes for deacon and priest (Peterb.) Feb. 23, 1743–4. C. of Islip. R. of Lowick, Northants. Will (P.C.C.) 1779. (*Al. Carthus.*)

ETTY, LEWIS. Adm. sizar (age 17) at ST JOHN'S, May 19, 1725. S. of William, clerk ('builder' in St Mary's Reg.), of Yorkshire. B. at York. School, Ely (Mr Tennant). Matric. 1725; B.A. 1728–9; M.A. 1749. Ord. deacon (York) July 18, 1731; priest, June 4, 1732. R. of Knaresdale, Northumberland, 1732–42. R. of St Mary Castlegate, 1742–73. R. of St Michael's, Spurriergate, York, 1742–73. Preb. of York, 1754–73. Died, in Castlegate, July 7, 1773. Buried in St Mary's, Castlegate; 'long affiieted with palsy.' (*Scott-Mayor*, III. 386.)

EUCHERSTER, GILBERT. B.Can.L. 1463–4.

BUGGEN, EDWARD. Matric. pens. from ST JOHN'S, Michs. 1570.

EULESTONE, JOHN. Matric. pens. from ST JOHN'S, Easter, 1565.

EURE, *see also* EVERS.

EURE, JOHN. Adm. sizar (age 18) at ST JOHN'S, as 'Eare,' Jan. 26, 1729. S. of John, grocer, of Lincolnshire. B. in Lincoln. School, Lincoln (Mr Goodall). Matric. 1729; B.A. 1732–3.

EURE, WILLIAM. *Cautio* for degree, 1467. Perhaps s. of Sir William, Knt. R. of Brompton, Yorks., Jan. 31, 1447–8. Master of St Mary's, Bootham, York, 1453 to death. Precentor of York, 1460. V. of Leeds, 1470–1482, where he founded Chantry of St Mary Magdalen. Died before Mar. 1482. Buried in York Minster. One of these names archdeacon of Sarum, 1471–6. (M. H. Peacock.)

EURIDGE, *see* URIDGE.

EURIE, THOMAS. Matric. pens. from MAGDALENE, Easter, 1625. Probably same as Thomas Evers, or Eureus.

EUSDEN, JOHN. Adm. sizar at TRINITY, Apr. 11, 1671. Matric. 1671; B.A. 1674–5; M.A. 1678. Ord. priest (London) Sept. 21, 1679. V. of Shillington, Beds., 1683–95. Buried there Sept. 17, 1695.

EWSDEN, LAWRENCE. Adm. sizar at KING'S, 1595. Probably lay clerk of the Chapel.

EWSDEN, LAWRENCE. Adm. sizar at JESUS, Jan. 14, 1660–1. Of Cambridgeshire. Matric. 1661. Migrated to Trinity, May 13, 1662. Scholar, 1664; B.A. 1664–5; M.A. 1668; D.D. 1688. Fellow of Trinity, 1667. Signed for deacon and priest (London) May 28, 1670. R. of Spofforth, Yorks., 1677–99. Buried in York Minster, Feb. 14, 1699. Father of the next.

EUSDEN, LAURENCE. Adm. pens. (age 16) at TRINITY, Mar. 24, 1704-5. S. of Dr Laurence (above), of Spofforth, Yorks. School, York (Mr Thompson). Matric. 1705; Scholar, 1706; B.A. 1708-9; M.A. 1712. Fellow, 1711. Ord. deacon (Lincoln) Sept. 20, 1724; priest, Mar. 25, 1729. Chaplain to Richard, Lord Willoughby de Broke. R. of Coningsby, Lincs., 1730. Poet Laureate, 1718-30. Author of poems and poetical translations. Died at Coningsby, Sept. 27, 1730. (*D.N.B.*)

EWSDEN, WILLIAM. Matric. sizar from KING'S, Easter, 1671; B.A. 1673-4; M.A. 1677. Ord. priest (Peterb.) Sept. 23, 1677.

EUSTANCE, EVANS. M.A. from KING'S, 1721. S. of How, of Llanbithion, Glamorgan. Matric. from Jesus College, Oxford, Apr. 6, 1709, age 16; B.A. (Oxford) 1712-3. Ord. deacon (St David's) Sept. 21, 1714; priest (Llandaff) Sept. 22, 1717. V. of Abergavenny, Monmouth. Chaplain to Countess Strafford. V. of Newland, Gloucs., 1740-5. (F. S. Hockaday.)

EVANS, ADAM. Matric. sizar from ST JOHN'S, c. 1590.

EVANS or EVANCE, ARTHUR. Matric. pens. from CHRIST'S, May, 1567; B.A. from Queens', 1571-2.

EVANS, BEZALEEL. Matric. sizar from ST JOHN'S, Easter, 1631.

EVANCE, DANIEL. Adm. pens. (age 16) at SIDNEY, Sept. 17, 1629. S. of Hugh, mercer, of London. B. at St Michael-le-Querne. Matric. 1629; B.A. 1633-4; M.A. 1637. One of these names R. of Calbourne, Isle of Wight, Jan. 31, 1647-8. One, lecturer at Lichfield Cathedral, July 22, 1646. (But *see Al. Oxon.*)

EVANS, DANIEL. Adm. sizar at JESUS, May 19, 1660. B. at Monk Moor, Shrewsbury. School, Shrewsbury. Matric. 1660. Left, as nonconformist, in 1662. Chaplain to Chancellor Smith at Norwich. Minister of a dissenting congregation at Woolwich for 16 years. Died at Bethnal Green, July, 1698, age 58. (*Calamy*, I. 205.)

EVANS, DAVID. Matric. pens. from ST JOHN'S, Michs. 1552; B.A. 1555-6; M.A. 1559. One of these names R. of Surville, Bucks., c. 1582. 'Parson of Melteirne, Carnarvon; student in Cambridge; M.A.' (Return of Bishop of Bangor, 1561.) (Browne Willis, *Bangor*, 265.)

EVANS, DAVID. Adm. sizar at JESUS, Sept. 8, 1623. School, Shrewsbury. Matric. 1623; B.A. 1626-7; Scholar, 1627; M.A. 1630. 3rd master, Shrewsbury School, 1627; 2nd master, 1638-58. Died May 26, 1658, aged 61. M.I. at St Mary's, Shrewsbury. (G. W. Fisher, *Shrewsbury*.)

EVANS, DAVID. Adm. sizar (age 22) at ST JOHN'S, July 7, 1680. S. of Evan Davis, husbandman. B. at Carno, Montgom. School, Bangor. Previously matric. from Jesus College, Oxford, July 10, 1679, age 19.

EVANS, EDMUND. B.A. from ST CATHARINE'S, 1605-6. Ord. priest (Norwich) Dec. 18, 1608, age 24. V. of Brundish and Tannington, Suffolk, 1609-45.

EVANS, EDMUND. Adm. sizar (age 19) at ST JOHN'S, June 5, 1731. S. of Edmund, gent., of Derbyshire. B. at Bonsall. School, Chesterfield (Mr Burrow). Matric. 1731; B.A. 1734-5. Ord. deacon (Lincoln) June 1, 1735; priest, June 20, 1736. V. of Mayfield, Staffs., 1736-91. V. of Alveton, 1752-91. Died 1791. (*Scott-Mayor*, III. 437; Glover, *Derbs.*, II. 18.)

EVANCE, EDWARD. Matric. sizar from ST JOHN'S, Michs. 1571.

EVANS, EDWARD. Adm. sizar at JESUS, Mar. 19, 1628-9. Of Wales. Matric. 1629; Scholar, 1632; B.A. 1632-3; M.A. 1636. One of these names s. and h. of David, of Neath, Glamorgan, adm. at Lincoln's Inn, June 25, 1631.

EVANS, EYTON. Matric. pens. from ST JOHN'S, Michs. 1627. Probably s. and h. of Thomas, of Watstane, Denbigh. Age c. 13 in 1623. (*Misc. Gen. et Her.*, 2nd Ser., I. 175.)

EVANS, GEORGE. Adm. sizar at JESUS, June 26, 1646. Of Hertfordshire. Matric. 1648-9; B.A. 1649-50; Scholar, 1650; M.A. 1653; D.D. 1665. Fellow, 1650-8. Incorp. at Oxford, 1654. Canon of Windsor, 1660-1702. V. of New Windsor, 1663. R. of St Benet Fink, London, 1663-93. R. of Hitcham, Bucks., 1667. Antiquary; his collections on the history of St George's Chapel printed in Ashmole's *Berkshire*. Died Mar. 2, 1701-2, aged 72. M.I. at Hitcham. Father of the next and John (1677). (*D.N.B.*)

EVANS, GEORGE. Adm. pens. at JESUS, July 1, 1675. Of Berkshire. S. of George (above), D.D., Canon of Windsor. Matric. 1675; Scholar, 1677; B.A. 1678-9; M.A. 1683. Fellow, 1683-92. Incorp. at Oxford, 1703. R. of St Benet Fink, London, 1693-1702. Died Mar. 2, 1725-6. Brother of John (1677). (*Musgrave; Hennessy.*)

EVANS, HENRY. Matric. sizar from ST JOHN'S, Michs. 1579. B. at Aber, Carnarvon, c. 1563. B.A. 1583-4; M.A. 1587. Ord. priest (Bangor). Tutor in the family of Sir Henry Cromwell. C. of Ramsey, Hunts., c. 1590-2. V. of East Rasen, Lincs., 1599-1603. R. of Preston Bagot, Warws. V. of Fiskney, Lincs., 1607-10.

EVANS, HENRY. M.A. from TRINITY, 1747. S. of Evan, of Machynlleth, Montgom., clerk. Matric. from Christ Church, Oxford, Mar. 15, 1732-3, age 19; B.A. (Oxford) 1736. One of these names minor canon of St Paul's, 1739-58. Perhaps died at Byletts, Heref., Aug. 22, 1793, aged 80. (*G. Mag.*; *Al. Oxon.*)

EVANCE, HUGH. Matric. sizar from MAGDALENE, Michs. 1565. Ord. deacon (Ely) May 26, 1566.

EVANS, HUGH. M.A. from KING'S, 1720. S. of Evan, of Llanfihangel, Cardigan. Matric. from New Inn Hall, Oxford, July 5, 1686, age 18; B.A. (Corpus Christi College, Oxford) 1690. (*Al. Oxon.*)

EVANS, JAMES. Adm. sizar (age 16) at TRINITY, July 18, 1720. S. of Richard, of Westminster. School, Westminster. Matric. 1721; B.A. 1724-5. Lower Master at King's School, Canterbury, 1731-43. C. of Washington, Kent, 1734-42. Died Oct. 2, 1743. M.I. in Canterbury Cathedral.

EVANS, JOHN. Matric. sizar from ST JOHN'S, Michs. 1562. One of these names V. of Wickham Skeith, Suffolk, 1566-8; and R. of Poslingford, till 1585. Died 1585.

EVANS, JOHN. Adm. sizar at TRINITY, Feb. 23, 1662-3. Exhibitioner from St Paul's School. Matric. 1663; B.A. 1666-7; M.A. 1670. One of these names R. of St Ethelburga, London, 1677-85.

EVANS, JOHN. M.A. from JESUS, 1674. Of Carnarvonshire. S. of David, of Trowerth, Denbighs., clerk. Matric. from Jesus College, Oxford, July 5, 1667, age 19; B.A. (Oxford) 1671. One of these names ord. priest (Chester) Mar. 25, 1675; R. of Uffington, Lincs., till 1718. Preb. of Peterborough, 1696-1718. Died Nov. 22, 1718, aged 73.

EVANS, JOHN. Adm. pens. at JESUS, Sept. 21, 1677. S. of George (1646), Canon of Windsor. Matric. 1680; Scholar, 1681; B.A. 1681-2; M.A. 1685. Doubtless of Gt Budworth, Cheshire. Died Oct. 7, 1743, aged 84. Brother of George (1675). (*G. Mag.*)

EVANS, JOHN. Adm. sizar at TRINITY, June 24, 1682. Matric. 1682; B.A. 1685-6.

EVANS, JOHN. Adm. at KING'S, a scholar from Eton, 1713. B. in London. Matric. 1713-4; B.A. 1717-8; M.A. 1721. Fellow, 1717. Senior proctor, 1733-4. Barrister, Middle Temple. Died 1741. (*Harwood*, 294.)

EVANS, JOHN. Adm. pens. at TRINITY, May 21, 1720. S. of John, of Ewell, Surrey, clerk. Matric. 1720; Scholar, 1722; B.A. 1723-4.

EVANS, JOHN. Adm. at KING'S, a scholar from Eton, 1745. S. of John. B. at Shrewsbury, 1726. Matric. 1745-6; B.A. 1749-50; M.A. 1753. Fellow, 1749. Owned an estate at Shrewsbury. Died young. (*Harwood.*)

EVANS, LEWIS. M.A. from PEMBROKE, 1728. S. of Daniel, of Llanegwad, Carmarthen. Matric. from Jesus College, Oxford, Mar. 17, 1717-8, age 17; B.A. (from St Edmund Hall) 1721. (*Al. Oxon.*)

EVANS, MICHAEL. Matric. pens. from ST JOHN'S, Easter, 1624. Migrated to Oxford. Matric. from Magdalen College, Feb. 16, 1627-8, age 20; B.A. (Oxford) 1627-8; M.A. 1630. Incorp. at Cambridge, 1642. B.D. (Cambridge) 1642. R. of Tarrant Rawston, Dorset, 1628. Preb. of Bangor, 1636. R. of Llanllyfni, Carnarv., 1639. R. of Llanbeulan and Llanddensant, Anglesey. Preb. of Chester, 1660-2. Preb. of Brecknock. Treasurer of Bangor, 1660-70. Died 1670. (*Al. Oxon.*; Browne Willis, *Bangor*, 157.)

EVANS, MORRICE. Matric. sizar from ST JOHN'S, Easter, 1616. Probably the scholar buried at All Saints', Cambridge, Mar. 4, 1617-8.

EVANS, OWEN. Matric. sizar from ST JOHN'S, Easter, 1603. B. 1583. B.A. 1607-8; M.A. 1611. Ord. deacon (Peterb.) Sept. 25; priest, Dec. 18, 1608. V. of Spaldwick, Hunts., 1613. V. of Easton, 1613.

EVANS, OWEN. Adm. sizar (age 21) at ST JOHN'S, June 26, 1673. S. of Maurice, of Standwomoch, Bangor. B. there. School, Bangor. Matric. 1673; B.A. 1676-7; M.A. 1680.

EVANS, OWEN. Adm. sizar at TRINITY HALL, July 7, 1676. Migrated to Jesus, Aug. 13, 1677. Matric. 1677; B.A. 1679-80; Scholar, 1680; M.A. 1683. One of these names V. of St Paul's, Canterbury, 1681. R. of Elmstone, Kent, 1691-1742. R. of St Martin's, Canterbury, 1693-1742. Died 1742.

EVANS, OWEN. Adm. sizar (age 15) at ST JOHN'S, Mar. 3, 1701-2. S. of Owen, clerk. B. at Llangoedmore, Cardigan. School, Carmarthen. Matric. 1702; LL.B. 1707. Perhaps ord. priest (London) Mar. 9, 1706-7.

EVANCE, RICHARD. B.A. from ST JOHN'S, 1580-1. Possibly Incorp. at Oxford, 1585, as 'Thomas.'

EVANS, RICHARD. Matric. pens. from PETERHOUSE, Easter, 1604.

EVANS, RICHARD. Adm. sizar (age 25) at CAIUS, c. May, 1668. S. of Richard, tailor, of Battersea. B. there. School, Eton. Matric. 1668.

EVANS, RICHARD. Adm. pens. (age 18) at CHRIST'S, July 5, 1748. S. of William (of Treveilor, and Mary, dau. of Wm Morton, Chancellor of Bangor). B. at Bangor. School, Lucton, Heref. Matric. 1748; Scholar, 1748; B.A. 1752; M.A. 1755. Fellow, 1754-66. R. of Kingsland, Herefordshire. Preb. of Bangor, 1779-97. Died 1797. (Peile, II. 253.)

EVANS, ROBERT. B.D. 1544. Already B.A. and B.Can.L. (1534) at Oxford. S. of Evan ap Riaulte. R. of Llantrissant, Anglesey, 1526-34. Dean of Bangor, 1534 and 1557. R. of Llaneingan-in-Llyn, 1534. V. of Terrington St John, Norfolk, 1540; and of Llanllechid, Carnarv., 1555. First master of Magdalene College, 1542-6. Deprived of his preferments under Queen Mary, but restored under Elizabeth. Died about 1570. Buried at Bangor. (Cooper, I. 284; Al. Oxon.)

EVANCE, ROBERT. M.A. 1615 (on King's visit).

EVANCE, ROBERT. Matric. sizar from KING'S, Easter, 1618.

EVANS, ROBERT. Adm. pens. (age 18) at ST JOHN'S, May 20, 1633. S. of Evan, gent., of Festiniog, Merioneth. B. there. School, Denbigh (private). Matric. 1633.

EVANS, ROBERT. Adm. sizar (age 19) at ST JOHN'S, Apr. 13, 1672. S. of Robert, of Llandrinio, St Asaph. B. there. School, Oswestry. Matric. 1672; B.A. 1675-6.

EVANS, RODERIC. Adm. sizar (age 19) at ST JOHN'S, Mar. 22, 1675-6. S. of John, of Penmachno, Bangor. Born there. School, Wrexham. Matric. 1676; B.A. 1679-80.

EVANS, ROGER. Adm. pens. at TRINITY, Feb. 20, 1668-9. Matric. 1669. Adm. at the Inner Temple, July 28, 1669. Of Trevelech, Salop.

EVANS, ROWLAND. Matric. sizar from ST JOHN'S, Michs. 1612. Ord. deacon (Peterb.) Mar. 20, 1613-4; priest, Sept. 25, 1614.

EVANS, SAMUEL. LL.B. 1635 (Incorp. from Oxford). S. of David, V. of Bierton, Bucks. Matric. from New College, Mar. 11, 1624-5, age 18; B.C.L. 1632. R. of Syresham, Northants., 1637. (Al. Oxon.)

EVANS, SIMON. M.A. from MAGDALENE, 1729. S. of 'Ev. Sym,' of Clocaenog, Denbigh. Matric. from Jesus College, Oxford, Mar. 27, 1710, age 21; B.A. from St Edmund's Hall, 1713. R. of Llandegla, Denbigh, 1718-31. V. of Llanarmon, 1731-53. (Al. Oxon.)

EVANS, THOMAS. Matric. sizar from PEMBROKE, Lent, 1581-2. B. in St Andrew's, Holborn. B.A. 1584-5; M.A. 1588. Ord. deacon (London) Dec. 21, 1588, age 26; priest (Lichfield) Aug. 18, 1589. R. of Easton Bavent, Suffolk, 1597-1608.

EVANS, THOMAS. Adm. sizar at QUEENS', Feb. 20, 1587-8. Of Salop.

EVANS, THOMAS. Scholar of TRINITY HALL, 1601.

EVANS, THOMAS. Matric. pens. from ST JOHN'S, Michs. 1608; B.A. from Corpus Christi, 1612-3; M.A. 1616; B.D. 1628. R. of St Helen's, Bishopgate St, 1618-9. R. of Little Holland, Essex, 1618-33. Author of *Oedipus*, one of the rarest poetical works in the English language. Died 1633. (D.N.B.)

EVANS, THOMAS. Matric. sizar from ST JOHN'S, Easter, 1618; B.A. 1621-2; M.A. 1627.

EVANCE, THOMAS. Matric. sizar from ST JOHN'S, Easter, 1631.

EVANS, THOMAS. Adm. sizar (age 18) at ST JOHN'S, June 14, 1636. S. of David, husbandman, of Llanerfyl, Montgom. B. there. School, Shrewsbury. B.A. 1639-40.

EVANCE, THOMAS. Matric. pens. from ST CATHARINE'S, Easter, 1640. Of London. B.A. 1643-4; M.A. from Magdalene, 1647. Fellow of Magdalene. R. of Caldecote, Warws.; ejected, 1662. (Calamy, II. 482)

EVANS, THOMAS. Adm. pens. at EMMANUEL, Apr. 2, 1655. Of London. Matric. 1657; B.A. 1658-9.

EVANS, THOMAS. Adm. pens. (age 16) at PETERHOUSE, May 14, 1670. Of Flintshire. School, Newport, Salop. Scholar, 1670.

EVANS, THOMAS. Adm. at KING'S, a scholar from Eton, 1686. B. in Windsor, 1667. Matric. 1687; B.A. 1690-1; M.A. 1694; M.D. 1701. Fellow, 1690. Fellow of Eton, 1716. Travelled much. Perhaps adm. student at Leyden, Nov. 21, 1697. Ord. deacon (Ely) May 27; priest, May 28, 1716. Died 1733. (Harwood, 85.)

EVANS, THOMAS. Adm. pens. (age 18) at ST JOHN'S, June 4, 1716. S. of William, gent., of Montgomeryshire. B. at 'Landvinium.' School, Shrewsbury. Matric. 1716; B.A. 1719-20.

EVANS, THOMAS. Matric. pens. from CHRIST'S, July, 1718; Scholar, 1719-21.

EVANS, THOMAS. M.A. from KING'S, 1732. S. of Morgan, of Weobley, Heref., gent. Matric. from Merton College, Oxford, May 4, 1725, age 17; B.A. (Oxford) 1728-9. Preb. of Hereford. V. of Dilwyn, King's Pyon, Weobley; and of Bromyard (all in Heref.). Died Mar. 27, 1767. (Al. Oxon.)

EVANS, THOMAS. M.A. from CLARE, 1738. S. of John, of Lampeter, Pembs. Matric. from Jesus College, Oxford, June 12, 1719, age 21; B.A. (from All Souls') 1724-5. (Al. Oxon.)

EVANS, THOMAS. Adm. sizar at JESUS, Apr. 20, 1745. S. of ——, clerk, deceased, of Bangor. Matric. 1745; Rustat scholar; B.A. 1748-9; M.A. 1752; D.D. 1777. Ord. priest (London) May 24, 1752. V. of Gt Finborough, Suffolk, 1753-64.

EVANS, THOMAS. Adm. Fell.-Com. (age 18) at PETERHOUSE, Jan. 14, 1747-8. S. of Thomas, of Bury St Edmunds (Recorder of Bury). School, Bury. Matric. 1748. Died Apr. 1767. Buried in St James', Bury. (T. A. Walker.)

EVANCE, W. Matric. sizar from ST JOHN'S, Michs. 1583.

EVANS, WALTER. M.A. from ST JOHN'S, 1734. S. of David, of Caron, Cardigan. Matric. from Jesus College, Oxford, Apr. 2, 1726, age 18; B.A. (Oxford) 1729. One of these names held several livings in Monmouthshire. (Scott-Mayor, III. 458.)

EVANCE, WILLIAM. Matric. pens. from ST JOHN'S, Michs. 1586.

EVANS, WILLIAM. Matric. sizar from ST JOHN'S, Michs. 1626; B.A. 1629-30; M.A. 1634. One of these names C. of Whittlesford, Cambs., in 1634. Perhaps R. of St George, South Elmham, Suffolk, 1639; ejected. V. of Bramfield, 1661-95.

EVANS, WILLIAM. Adm. pens. at QUEENS', July 4, 1681. Of Wales. B.A. 1684-5.

EVANS, WILLIAM. Adm. pens. at QUEENS', May 13, 1685. Of Gloucestershire. (See Al. Oxon. for a contemporary.)

EVANS, WILLIAM. Adm. sizar (age 18) at ST JOHN'S, Feb. 26, 1685-6. S. of John, weaver. B. at Llanelltyd, Merioneth. School, Llanegryn. Matric. 1686; B.A. 1689-90; M.A. 1693. Ord. deacon (London) June 11, 1693. One of these names R. of Barthomley, Cheshire, 1726-39. Buried Apr. 18, 1739.

EVANS, WILLIAM. Adm. sizar (age 19) at TRINITY, July 5, 1748. S. of William, of Bodfaen, Carnarv. School, Bangor (Mr Bennet). Matric. 1748; B.A. 1752. Ord. deacon (London) Mar. 18, 1753. V. of Hockham, Norfolk, 1754-72. R. of Wortham, Suffolk, 1761-72. Died 1772.

EVANS, ——. Adm. at CORPUS CHRISTI, 1556.

EVANSON, EDWARD. Adm. pens. (age 14) at EMMANUEL, 1746. S. of Thomas, mercer, of Warrington. B. there. School, Mitcham. Matric. 1746; B.A. 1749-50; M.A. 1753. Ord. priest (London) Sept. 21, 1755. V. of South Mimms, Middlesex, 1766-70. V. of Tewkesbury, 1769. P.C. of Tredington, Worcs., 1769. V. of Longdon, 1770-8. Chaplain to Wedderburne, the Solicitor-General, 1775. Prosecuted in the Consistory Court for Unitarianism. Retired to Mitcham and established a school there, 1778. His works include *The Dissonance of the four...Evangelists*, 1792. Died Sept. 25, 1805, at Coleford, Devon. (D.N.B.)

EVANSON, JOHN. Adm. pens. at CAIUS, Oct. 14, 1736.

EVARD, ——. Resident B.A. at CORPUS CHRISTI, 1472.

EVART, THOMAS. Matric. pens. from CLARE, Easter, 1612.

EVASTON, WILLIAM. Matric. pens. from MAGDALENE, Easter, 1636.

EVAT, ANTHONY. Matric. pens. from CLARE, Michs. 1618; B.A. 1620-1. R. of Whepstead, Suffolk, 1629-42. Died 1642.

EVATT, EDWARD. Adm. pens. at TRINITY, Mar. 31, 1665. One of these names, s. of Edward, of Northop, Flint., gent., matric. from Jesus College, Oxford, Apr. 1, 1664, age 15. (Al. Oxon.)

EVATT, RICHARD. Matric. sizar from CORPUS CHRISTI, Easter, 1583; B.A. 1585-6; M.A. 1589; B.D. 1599. Ord. deacon and priest (Lincoln) July 31, 1589. V. of Burton Pedwardine, Lincs., 1589-1603. R. of St John's, Stamford, 1603-15. R. of St Mary's, 1615-33.

EVAT, ROBERT. Matric. sizar from JESUS, Michs. 1569. One of these names R. of Little Ellingham, Norfolk, 1580.

EVE, HENRY. Adm. sizar (age 16) at CAIUS, May 31, 1634. S. of Robert, draper, of Wye, Kent. School (Mr Nichols). Matric. 1634. Migrated to Clare in 1635. B.A. 1638-9; M.A. 1642. Created D.D. (Oxford) 1661. V. of Lynsted, Kent, 1647-86; of Buckland, 1663-81. V. of Teynham, 1663-86. R. of Midley, 1681-6. Died Mar. 4, 1685-6. Buried at Lynsted. Father of the next. (Venn, I. 314.)

EVE, HENRY. Adm. pens. (age 17) at ST JOHN'S, Oct. 13, 1669. S. of Henry (above), D.D., V. of Lynsted, Kent. B. there. School, Well (Mr Parris). Matric. 1670; M.B. 1673. Said to have been M.D. Died 1686. Buried at Lynsted. Father of the next.

EVE, JAMES. Adm. pens. at ST CATHARINE'S, June 5, 1700. S. of Henry (above), 'M.D.', of Kent. Matric. 1702; B.A. 1703-4; M.A. 1708. Ord. deacon (London) June 4, 1704. R. of Buckland, Kent, 1707-43. V. of Teynham, 1708-43. R. of Midley, 1719-43. Died Mar. 1743. (L. Mag.)

EVE, THOMAS. Matric. pens. from QUEENS', Easter, 1624. Of Essex.

EVELEIGH, JOHN. M.A. 1585 (Incorp. from Oxford). Of Devon. Perhaps s. of John, of Holcombe. Matric. from Exeter College, Dec. 3, 1575, age 16; B.A. (Oxford) 1581; M.A. 1584. Fellow of Exeter, 1578–93. Proctor, 1590. Principal of Hart Hall, 1599–1604. Buried in Magdalen Chapel, Aug. 10, 1604. (*Al. Oxon.*)

EVELEGH, JOHN. Adm. pens. at JESUS, May 26, 1640. Of Devon. Matric. 1640; Scholar, 1640. For a contemporary *see Al. Oxon.*

EVELEIGH, RICHARD. Adm. sizar (age 18) at CAIUS, July 3, 1606. S. of Robert, yeoman, of Clist-Hydon, Devon. School, Tiverton (Mr Butler). Matric. 1606; Scholar, 1608–12; B.A. 1609–10; M.A. 1613. Incorp. at Oxford, 1611. R. of St Peter Tavy, Devon, 1615–37; and of Bratton, 1616. Preb. of Exeter, 1616–37. Admon. (Exeter) 1637. (*Venn*, I. 193.)

EVELEIGH, ROGER. Adm. sizar (age 17) at SIDNEY, Feb. 4, 1677–8. 1st s. of Robert. B. at Exeter. School, Tiverton. Matric. 1678; B.A. 1681–2.

EVELYN, FREDERIC. Adm. Fell.-Com. at CLARE, May 5, 1750. S. of Sir John, of Wotton, Surrey, 2nd Bart. B. in London, 1734. Matric. 1750. Served in Elliot's Horse at Minden, 1759. Succeeded as Bart. 1767. A member of the Jockey Club. Died Apr. 1, 1812. Buried at Wotton. (*Misc. Gen. et Her.*, 2nd S., V. 211; *G.E.C.*)

EVELIN, GEORGE. Adm. Fell.-Com. at EMMANUEL, Mar. 8, 1593–4. Probably s. of John, of Godstone, Surrey. Matric. 1593; B.A. 1596–7. Adm. at Lincoln's Inn, May 1, 1599; of Surrey, gent. Of West Deane, Wilts. One of the six clerks of Chancery and J.P. Died Jan. 19, 1636–7. (*Misc. Gen. et Her.*, 2nd S., I. 2.)

EVELIN, GEORGE. Matric. pens. from QUEENS', Easter, 1652; B.A. 1652. Perhaps s. and h. of George, of Hammersmith, Esq.; adm. at Gray's Inn, Aug. 2, 1652.

EVELYN, JOHN. Adm. pens. at EMMANUEL, Mar. 13, 1605–6. Probably 2nd s. of John, of Godstone, Surrey. Bapt. at Kingston, Oct. 20, 1591. Matric. 1606. Knighted, Aug. 8, 1623. M.P. for Bletchingley, 1627, 1628 and 1640. Buried at Godstone, Jan. 18, 1663–4. Doubtless brother of George (1593–4). (*Misc. Gen. et Her.*, 2nd S., IV. 329.)

EVELYN, JOHN. Adm. pens. at EMMANUEL, July 4, 1615. Fell.-Com. 1616. Matric. 1615; B.A. 1618–9. Doubtless s. of Thomas, of Long Ditton. Bapt. there, Dec. 14, 1597. Died young. If so, brother of William (1621). (*Cooper* identifies him with Sir John, of Godstone, who was b. Aug. 11, 1601; but this is improbable.)

EVELYN, RICHARD. Adm. pens. at ST CATHARINE'S, Oct. 13, 1703. Matric. 1704. One of these names adm. at the Inner Temple and settled in Tipperary, Ireland, 1718. (*Misc. Gen. et Her.*, 2nd S., IV. 328.)

EVELIN, THOMAS. Matric. Fell.-Com. from ST CATHARINE'S, Easter, 1636. Perhaps s. of Thomas, of Long Ditton, Surrey. B. 1618. Died Jan. 18, 1649–50. (*Misc. Gen. et Her.*, 2nd S., IV. 313.)

EVELYN, THOMAS. Adm. pens. (age 17) at CAIUS, Apr. 29, 1681. S. of Arthur, merchant, of Lynn. B. there. School, Lynn (Mr Horne and Mr Bell). Matric. 1681; Scholar, 1681–4.

EVELYN, WILLIAM. Adm. pens. at EMMANUEL, Easter, 1621. Perhaps s. of Thomas, of Long Ditton. Bapt. there, Aug. 31, 1604. B.A. 1624; M.A. from Trinity, 1628. Incorp. at Oxford, 1627. R. of Tarrant Keynston, Dorset, 1636. Died 1652. Perhaps brother of John (1615). (*Al. Oxon.*; *Misc. Gen. et Her.*, 2nd S., IV. 312.)

EVELYN, ——. Adm. Fell.-Com. at TRINITY HALL, Nov. 15, 1751.

EVENSON, THOMAS. Matric. sizar from TRINITY, Easter, 1626; B.A. 1631.

EVER or EWER, RICHARD. Studied at Cambridge. B.A. (Oxford) 1520–1; M.A. 1525; B.D. 1534. R. of Hornsey, Middlesex, 1536–57. V. of Bishopscleeve, Clones. V. of South Weald, Essex, 1537. Preb. of Worcester, 1542–58. R. of Ripple, Worcs., 1543–54. Will (P.C.C.) 1559. (*Al. Oxon.*)

EVER, WILLIAM. Matric. pens. from ST JOHN'S, Easter, 1579.

EVERARDE, ALDROVANDUS. Adm. pens. (age 18) at TRINITY, July 2, 1677. S. of John, of London. School, Westminster. Scholar, 1678.

EVERARDE, ANDREW. Matric. sizar from ST JOHN'S, Easter, 1611. B. at High Easter, Essex. B.A. 1614–5; M.A. 1618; B.D. 1631–2 (*Lit. Reg.*). Ord. deacon (London) Sept. 1, 1617; priest, Sept. 20, 1618, age 24. R. of Kirk Bramwith, Yorks., 1627–8. R. of Kirby Underdale, 1631–9. Buried Aug. 29, 1639.

EVERARD, ANTHONY. Matric. Fell.-Com. from JESUS, Easter, 1575. S. of Richard, of Langley, and Much Waltham, Essex. Adm. at the Inner Temple, 1578. M.P. for East Looe, 1588. Knighted, July 23, 1603. Died 1615. Brother of Hugh (1585) and Matthew (1576). (*Vis. of Essex.*)

EVARARD, BARRINGTON. Adm. pens. at JESUS, Apr. 13, 1646. Of Essex. 2nd s. of Sir Richard (1617), of Much Waltham, Essex, Bart. (Mother, Joan Barrington.) Adm. at Gray's Inn, Aug. 2 1647. Died unmarried. Brother of Hugh (1651). (Burke, *Ext. Bart.*; *Vis. of Essex*, 1634.)

EVERARD, CHARLES. Adm. sizar (age 17) at TRINITY, Feb. 3, 1698–9. S. of Charles, of Somerford, Cheshire. School, Sandbach (Mr Jenkyns). Matric. 1699; B.A. 1703–4; M.A. 1707. Ord. deacon (Norwich) May, 1706. V. of King's Langley, Herts., 1711–9. Perhaps V. of Westwell, Kent, till 1711. R. of Brereton, Cheshire, 1719–31. Died Apr. 28, 1731. M.I. at Brereton. (*Ormerod*, III. 53.)

EVERARD, GEORGE. Adm. sizar at EMMANUEL, Jan. 30, 1711–2. Of Heather, Leics. Matric. 1712; B.A. 1715–6; M.A. 1720. Fellow, 1716. Ord. priest (Lincoln) Sept. 21, 1718. Doubtless father of the next and brother of Thomas (1700) and John (1707–8).

EVERARD, GEORGE. Adm. sizar (age 18) at EMMANUEL, June 21, 1744. Of Loughborough, Leics. S. of George, clerk. School, Hartshorn, Derbs. Matric. 1744; LL.B. 1750. Ord. deacon (Lincoln) Dec. 18, 1748; priest, Sept. 23, 1750. V. of Capesthorne, Cheshire, 1750–75. R. of Heather, Leics. Died July 9, 1775, aged 52. M.I. at Capesthorne. (Earwaker, *E. Cheshire*, II. 410.)

EVERARDE, HENRY. Matric. pens. from ST JOHN'S, Easter, 1545. Perhaps of Shotteshall, Norfolk; adm. at the Inner Temple, 1549.

EVERARD, HUGH. Matric. pens. from JESUS, Michs. 1585, as 'Henry.' S. of Richard, of Waltham, Essex. B.A. 1587–8; M.A. 1591. Of Much Waltham, Esq. Sheriff of Essex, 1626. Died 1637. Brother of Anthony (1575) and Matthew (1576). Father of Richard (1617). (*Vis. of Essex*; A. Gray.)

EVERET, HUGH. Matric. sizar from PEMBROKE, Easter, 1608; B.A. 1611–2. Licensed to preach (Archbishop of York) 1615. 'Clerk, of Worsborough,' Yorks., in 1625.

EVERARD, HUGH. Matric. pens. from ST CATHARINE'S, Easter, 1651. S. of Sir Richard (1617), of Much Waltham, Essex, Bart. B.A. 1654; M.A. 1658. Fellow, 1658. Ejected from Hickleton, Yorks., 1662. Died 1665. Brother of Barrington (1646). (*Calamy*, II. 563.)

EVEROT, HUMPHREY. Matric. pens. from CHRIST'S, Easter, 1559.

EVERARD, HUMPHREY. Matric. pens. from ST JOHN'S, Easter, 1570; B.A. from Peterhouse, 1571–2.

EVERARD, J. B.A. 1470–1.

EVERARD, JAMES. Adm. pens. (age 15) at CHRIST'S, Jan. 3, 1687–8. S. of James, of Cambridge. B. there. School, Ashwell, Cambs. (Mr Backler). Matric. 1688; Scholar, 1689; B.A. 1691–2; M.A. 1695. Ord. deacon (Norwich) June 11, 1693; priest (Lincoln) Sept. 22, 1700. V. of East Winch, Norfolk, 1716–22; of Middleton, 1721–2. Died 1722. (*Peile*, II. 107.)

EVERARDE, JOHN. Matric. pens. from JESUS, Michs. 1547. Probably B.A. 1547–8; first appears in the College books in 1542. (A. Gray.)

EVERED, JOHN. Matric. pens. from TRINITY, Easter, 1560.

EVERARD, JOHN. Resident student at TRINITY HALL, Aug. 1564.

EVERARD, JOHN. B.A. from CLARE, 1600–1; M.A. 1607; B.D. 1619. Reader at St Martin-in-the-Fields, London, *c.* 1618. R. of Fairstead, Essex, till 1636; deprived. R. of Hinton Martell, Dorset, 1621–2. Previously imprisoned for censuring Spanish outrages in the Indies. Scholar and philosopher. His works include a translation of the *Poemander* of Hermes Trismegistus. Died *c.* 1650. (*D.N.B.*)

EVERARD, JOHN. Adm. at CLARE, *c.* 1603. B. at Deane, Northants., *c.* 1586. Became R.C., and entered the English College at Rome, 1610; but owing to illness did not stay long. Returned to England and published an account of his experiences as a student. Nothing certain is known of his subsequent career. Possibly identical with the Jesuit father John Everard. If so, died Dec. 6, 1649, at Antwerp. (*Records, S.J.*, IV. 611; *D.N.B.*)

EVERARD, JOHN. Adm. pens. at EMMANUEL, 1628; B.A. 1631; M.A. 1635.

EVERARD, JOHN. Matric. pens. from QUEENS', Easter, 1637. Of Leicestershire.

EVERARD, JOHN. Matric. pens. (age 16) from PEMBROKE, Michs. 1642. S. of Richard. B. at Hawkedon, Suffolk.

EVERARD, JOHN. Adm. Fell.-Com. at St Catharine's, Easter, 1659.

EVERARD, JOHN. Adm. sizar at Emmanuel, Mar. 3, 1707-8. Of Leicestershire. S. of Thomas, of Heather, Leics., Esq. Matric. 1708; B.A. 1711-2; M.A. 1715. Ord. priest (Lincoln) July 5, 1713. V. of Thornton-by-Bagworth, Leics., 1718-23. R. of Heather, 1730-51. Buried there July 29, 1751. (*Nichols*, IV. 522.)

EVERARD, JOSEPH. Adm. sizar at Trinity, Apr. 24, 1651. Of Yorkshire. Matric. 1651.

EVERARDE, MATTHEW. Adm. pens. (age 16) at Caius, Nov. 16, 1576. S. of Richard, of Gt Waltham, Essex. School, Braintree. Matric. 1576. Of Rettendon, Essex. Died *s.p.* Brother of Anthony (1575) and Hugh (1585). (*Venn*, I. 88.)

EVERERD, NICHOLAS. Matric. pens. from Trinity, Easter, 1570.

EVERARD, NICHOLAS. Matric. pens. from Queens', Michs. 1571. One of these names adm. student at Leyden, June 8, 1585.

EVERARD, NICHOLAS. Adm. sizar at Christ's, June 18, 1686. Matric. 1686; Scholar, 1689; B.A. 1689-90; M.A. 1694. Ord. deacon (Lincoln) Sept. 1690; priest, Sept. 1691. C. of Clifton, Beds. Probably s. of James, manciple of Christ's; and brother of James (1687-8). (*Peile*, II. 102.)

EVERAT, OWYN. Matric. pens. from Jesus, Michs. 1572.

EVERARD or EVERED, RALPH. Matric. pens. from Christ's, June, 1577. Probably 5th s. of Henry, of Linstead, Suffolk. (*Peile*, I. 141; *Vis. of Suffolk*, 1561.)

EVERARD, RALPH. Adm. pens. (age 16) at St John's, May 27, 1631. S. of Ralph, gent., of Mashbury, Essex. B. at Marlesford, Suffolk. School, Felsted. Matric. 1631. (*Vis. of Essex*, 1634.)

EVERET or EVEROD, RICHARD. Matric. sizar from Corpus Christi, Michs. 1578; B.A. 1582-3.

EVERARD, RICHARD. Matric. Fell.-Com. from Jesus, Easter, 1617. S. and h. of Hugh (1585), of Gt Waltham, Essex, Esq. Adm. at Lincoln's Inn, June 10, 1619. Created Bart., Jan. 29, 1628-9. Parliamentarian. Sheriff of Essex, 1644-5. Died *c.* 1680. Will (Archd. C. Essex) 1680. Father of Barrington (1646) and Hugh (1651). (*G.E.C.*)

EVERARD, RICHARD. Adm. Fell.-Com. (age 15) at Sidney, Apr. 27, 1629. S. of John, Esq. B. at Gt Baddow, Essex. School, Baddow (Mr Hooker). Matric. 1628. (*Vis. of Essex*, 1612.)

EVERARD, RICHARD. Adm. pens. (age 16) at Pembroke, Nov. 4, 1634. S. of Richard. B. at Hawkedon, Suffolk. Matric. 1634-5. (*Vis. of Suffolk*, 1664.)

EVERARD, RICHARD. Adm. Fell.-Com. at St Catharine's, 1659.

EVERARD, RICHARD. Adm. pens. at St Catharine's, July 2, 1660. Perhaps same as last.

EVERARDE, SIMON. Matric. pens. from St John's, Easter, 1614.

EVEREDE, THOMAS. Matric. pens. from Magdalene, Michs. 1547.

EVERARD or EVERAT, THOMAS. Matric. sizar from Clare, Michs. 1572; B.A. 1575-6. Ord. deacon (Ely) Apr. 29, 1576; priest, Nov. 17, 1577. C. of Northwold, Norfolk. R. of Southery, 1583-8. Died 1588.

EVERAT, THOMAS. Matric. pens. from Jesus, Michs. 1572. Doubtless the Jesuit priest, Thomas Everard or Everet. S. of Henry, of Linstead, Suffolk. B. *c.* 1560. Spent a year and a half at Cambridge. Adm. at Rheims, 1592. Ord. priest (R.C.) Sept. 18, 1592. Entered the Society of Jesus, 1593. Master of novices at Louvain. Missioner in England, 1603-4, and again, in 1617. Banished, 1620-1. Author and translator. Died in London, May 16, 1633. (*Records, S.J.*, II. 399; *D.N.B.*)

EVERIT or EVERED, THOMAS. Adm. sizar at Emmanuel, Apr. 12, 1597; afterwards pensioner. Matric. *c.* 1597; B.A. 1600-1; M.A. 1604. One of these names V. of Borden, Kent, 1611-9. Died 1619.

EVERITT, THOMAS. Adm. (age 17) at King's, a scholar from Eton, Sept. 5, 1639. Of London. Matric. 1639; B.A. 1642-3. Fellow, 1642-4. Died 1644.

EVERARD, THOMAS. Adm. pens. at Trinity, Sept. 14, 1654. Of Bedfordshire. S. of John and Mary. Bapt. at Sandy, Mar. 8, 1638-9. Scholar, 1657; B.A. 1658-9; M.A. 1662. C. at Sandy, Beds., 1665. Buried there Apr. 29, 1673.

EVERARD, THOMAS. Adm. pens. at Clare, May 25, 1700. B. at Heather Temple, Leics. Matric. 1700; B.A. 1703-4; M.A. from Emmanuel, 1710. Doubtless brother of George (1712) and John (1707-8).

EVERED, VALENTINE. Matric. Fell.-Com. from Queens', Lent, 1578-9. Of Kent. B.A. 1581-2.

EVERARD, VALENTINE. Matric. pens. from Trinity, Easter, 1606. Doubtless s. and h. of Valentine, of Canterbury, gent.; adm. at Gray's Inn, Apr. 26, 1613.

EVERARD, WILLIAM. Scholar of Trinity Hall, 1596.

EVERED, WILLIAM. Adm. sizar (age 20) at Caius, Apr. 28, 1632. S. of Geoffray, yeoman. B. at Pilsdon, Dorset. School, Rampesham (private, Mr Hallet). Matric. 1632. Drowned in the Cam. Buried at Grantchester, June 16, 1633.

EVERARD, WILLIAM. Adm. pens. (age 16) at Peterhouse, June 20, 1687. Of Suffolk. School, Bury St Edmunds. Scholar, 1687; Matric. 1688; B.A. 1690-1. Ord. deacon (Norwich) June, 1693; priest, Sept. 1695. R. of Syderstone, Norfolk, 1695-1708. Will (Norw. C. C.). (*T. A. Walker*, 181.)

EVERARD, WILLIAM. Adm. pens. at Queens', Mar. 28, 1721. Of Norfolk. Matric. 1721; B.A. 1724-5; M.A. 1728; B.D. 1737. Fellow, 1730-46. Taxor, 1732. V. of St Botolph's, Cambridge, 1732. R. of Walpole St Peter, Norfolk, 1743-80.

EVERARD, ——. B.Can.L. 1487-8. Perhaps Philip, abbot of Croyland, 1497-1503; or Thomas, V. of Whaplode, Lincs., till 1505.

EVERET, ——. B.Can.L. 1497-8.

EVERARD, ——. B.A. 1517-8.

EVERDALL, THOMAS. Matric. pens. from Trinity, Easter, 1586.

EVERDEN or EVERENDEN, HUMPHREY. Adm. sizar at Emmanuel, May 7, 1603. Matric. 1603. Migrated to Oxford, after 10 terms. B.A. (St John's College, Oxford) 1607.

EVERENDEN, JOHN. Adm. pens. at Jesus, Mar. 9, 1653-4. Of Sussex. Scholar, 1655; M.B. 1659.

EVERENDEN, ROBERT. Adm. sizar at Emmanuel, Nov. 8, 1630. Of Kent. Probably lecturer at Woodchurch, Kent, 1642. One of these names ejected from Brighton, 1662.

EVERDEN, ——. M.Gram. 1485-6.

EVERFOLD, JOHN (1548), *see* EVERSFIELD.

EVERILL, EDWARD. Matric. sizar from Peterhouse, Michs. 1613; B.A. 1616-7; M.A. 1620. Incorp. at Oxford, 1618. Ord. deacon (Peterb.) June 15, 1617; priest, Dec. 9, 1624.

EVERELL, EDWARD. Adm. pens. (age 14) at Sidney, Mar. 27, 1650. S. of Robert, clothier. B. at Oundle, Northants. School, Oundle (Mr Hicks). Matric. 1650; B.A. 1653-4.

EVERING, JOHN. Matric. pens. from Corpus Christi, Easter, 1604. Of Kent. Perhaps s. of John, of Lymynge. Adm. at Gray's Inn, Feb. 17, 1607-8. (*Vis. of Kent*, 1663.)

EVERING, WILLIAM. Matric. pens. from Queens', Lent, 1577-8. Of Kent.

EVERINGHAM, JOHN. Adm. pens. (age 15) at Magdalene, May 23, 1667. S. of Thomas, gent., of Womersley, Yorks. School, Kirton, Lincs. Matric. 1667; B.A. 1670-1; M.A. 1674.

EVERINGHAM, WILLIAM. Adm. sizar at Emmanuel, June 16, 1684. Of Lincolnshire. Matric. 1685; B.A. 1687-8. Ord. priest (Lincoln) Sept. 20, 1691. V. of Anwick, Lincs., 1691-1717. R. of Braunswell, 1703-17.

EVERS, *see also* EURE.

EVERS or EURE, CHARLES. Adm. Fell.-Com. at Queens', Dec. 3, 1591. Of Malton, Yorks. Doubtless 5th s. of William, Lord Eure, adm. at Gray's Inn, Oct. 23, 1598. Brother of Francis (1583) and Ralph (1568).

EVERS, EDWARD. Matric. Fell.-Com. from Queens', *c.* 1592.

EVERS or EURE, FRANCIS. M.A. 1583 (*fil. nob.*). 2nd s. of William, Lord Eure. Adm. at Gray's Inn, Oct. 23, 1598. Barrister, 1603. Reader, 1610. M.P. for Scarborough, 1604-14. Knighted, May 12, 1604. Chief Justice of North Wales, 1610. Of Heyford Warren, Co. Oxon., and Porkington, Salop. Died May 1, 1621. Buried at Selattyn, Salop. Brother of Charles (1591) and Ralph (1568). (*Vis. of Yorks.*)

EVERS, HENRY. Matric. sizar from St John's, Easter, 1576.

EVERS or EURE, Sir RALPH. Matric. Fell.-Com. (age 10) from St John's, Michs. 1568. Eldest s. of William, Lord Eure. B. in Berwick Castle, Sept. 24, 1558. Bapt. on Sept. 26, 1558, at Berwick Parish Church, by the Earl of Northumberland. Adm. at Gray's Inn, 1575. Succeeded as 3rd Lord Eure. Warden of the Middle Marches, 1586. Sheriff of Yorks., 1594. Lord President of Council in Principality and Marches of Wales. Ambassador extraordinary to Emperor Rudolph II, in 1603, and to King of Denmark, 1603. Died Apr. 1, 1617. Coat of Arms, in east window of Gray's Inn Hall. Brother of Francis (1583) and Charles (1591).

EVERS or EUREUS, THOMAS. Adm. pens. (age 18) at CHRIST'S, May 19, 1627. S. of Charles (1591). B. in Goodnestone, Kent. Schools, Sandwich (Mr Cholfin and Mr Brett), Gt Brisett (Mr Ray) and Honington, Suffolk (Mr Ray). Probably same as Thomas Eurie, whom *see*. (*Peile*, I. 384.)

EVERS, WILLIAM. Adm. pens. (age 16) at PEMBROKE, May 10, 1678. S. of John, gent. B. in Kent. Matric. 1678.

EVERS, ——. *Cautio* for M.A. or higher degree, 1484–5.

EVERSDEN, HENRY. Matric. pens. from CHRIST'S, July, 1622; B.A. 1624–5.

EVERSFIELD, ANTHONY. Matric. pens. from CLARE, Michs. 1581; B.A. 1583–4; M.A. 1587. Incorp. at Oxford, as 'Erffield,' 1598.

EVERSFIELD or EVERFOLD, JOHN. Matric. sizar from CORPUS CHRISTI, Michs. 1548.

EVERSFIELD, NICHOLAS. Matric. Fell.-Com. from TRINITY, *c.* 1595; B.A. 1598–9. Doubtless of Uckfield, Sussex, gent.; adm. at Gray's Inn, May 3, 1602. Probably s. of Thomas. Of Grove, Hastings. High Sheriff for Sussex, 1619. M.P. for Hastings, 1624, 1625, 1626, 1628. (Burke, *L.G.*)

EVERSFIELD, RICHARD. Adm. pens. at EMMANUEL, Easter, 1641; afterwards Fell.-Com. Of Sussex. Matric. 1641.

EVERSFYLD, THOMAS. Matric. Fell.-Com. from CLARE, Michs. 1571.

EVERSHAM, ——. B.Civ.L. 1470–1.

EVERSHED, JOHN. Adm. pens. (age 17) at CHRIST'S, Apr. 17, 1647. S. of John. B. at Ockley, Surrey. School, Horsham (Mr Smith).

EVERSOLL, WILLIAM. B.A. from EMMANUEL, 1603–4.

EVERSON, THOMAS. Adm. sizar (age 18) at CAIUS, July 4, 1726 S. of Thomas, grazier, of Langford, Norfolk. B. there. Schools, Tottington (Mr Rutland) and West Ham, Essex (Mr Phipps). Matric. 1727; Scholar, 1727–33; B.A. 1729–30; M.A. 1733. Ord. deacon (Norwich) June 13, 1731; priest, July 18, 1736. Master of Thetford School, 1738–48. Will (Norwich Archd. C.) 1748. (*Venn*, II. 25.)

EVERY, HENRY. Adm. Fell.-Com. (age 16) at CHRIST'S, Apr. 24, 1646. S. of Sir Simon, Bart. B. at Egginton, Derbs. Bapt. there, Nov. 15, 1629. School, Repton. Succeeded as Bart., *c.* 1647. Royalist. Died Sept. 29, 1700. M.I. in Egginton Church. Brother of John (1648), father of Simon (1680). (*Peile*, I. 505; *Staffs. Pedigrees*; *Vis. of Derbs.*, 1662; *G.E.C.*)

EVERY, HENRY. Adm. pens. (age 18) at CHRIST'S, June 30, 1726. S. of Sir Simon (1680), Bart. B. at Navenby, Lincs., Oct. 25, 1708. School, Repton. Matric. 1726; Scholar, 1727–8. Of Egginton, Derbs. High Sheriff for Derbs., 1749. Succeeded as Bart., 1753. Died May 31, 1755. Buried at Egginton. Brother of John (1726) and Simon (1730). (*Peile*, II. 213; *G.E.C.*)

EVERY, JOHN. Adm. pens. (age 16) at CHRIST'S, Oct. 14, 1648. S. of Sir Simon, Bart. B. at Egginton, Derbs. School, Repton. Matric. 1648. Migrated to St Mary Hall, Oxford, Nov. 26, 1650. B.A. (Oxford) 1651–2. Adm. at Gray's Inn, Nov. 26, 1652. Of Chardstock, Dorset. J.P. for Staffs., in 1680. Died without issue. Brother of Henry (1646). (*Peile*, I. 524; *Staffs. Pedigrees*.)

EVERY, JOHN. Adm. pens. (age 17) at CHRIST'S, June 30, 1726. S. of Sir Simon (next). B. at Navenby, Lincs., Oct. 17, 1709. School, Repton. Matric. 1726; Scholar, 1727; B.A. 1729–30; M.A. 1733. Ord. deacon (Lincoln) Feb. 18, 1732–3; priest, Dec. 23, 1733. R. of Waddington, Lincs., 1733. V. of Bracebridge, 1737. Succeeded as Bart., May 31, 1755. Died June 29, 1779. Buried at Egginton. Brother of Henry (1726) and Simon (1730). (*Peile*, II. 213; G.E.C.)

EVERY, SIMON. Adm. pens. (age 17) at CHRIST'S, Apr. 26, 1680. S. of Sir Henry (1646), Bart. B. at Egginton, Derbs. School, Repton. Matric. 1680; B.A. 1683–4; M.A. 1687. Fellow, 1687–1704. Proctor, 1699. Ord. deacon (Lincoln) June, 1688; priest, Aug. 12, 1688. R. of Navenby, Lincs., 1703–53. Succeeded as Bart., July 1, 1729. Died Jan. 12, 1753. Buried at Egginton. Brother of William (below), father of Henry (1726), John (1726) and Simon (next). (*Peile*, II. 78; *Staffs. Pedigrees*; G.E.C.)

EVERY, SIMON. Adm. pens. (age 18) at CHRIST'S, May 28, 1730. S. of Sir Simon (above), Bart., R. of Navenby. B. there. School, Peterborough (Mr Bradfield). Matric. 1730; Scholar, 1731; M.B. 1740. Adm. student at Leyden, Oct. 19, 1734. Ord. deacon (Lincoln) May 24, 1741; priest, Sept. 20, 1741; C. of Navenby. R. of Egginton, 1747. Buried there 1758. Brother of Henry (1726) and John (1726). (*Peile*, II. 222.)

EVERY, WILLIAM. 'Of CHRIST'S College' (according to the *Repton School Reg.*). 6th s. of Sir Henry (1646). B. 1662. Captain, 1st Regiment of Marines. Killed at the siege of Cork, 1690. Brother of Simon (1680).

EVERY, ——. Adm. Fell.-Com. at TRINITY, 1656. One William Every adm. at the Inner Temple, 1657.

EVES, GEOFFREY. Adm. sizar (age 19) at PEMBROKE, June 5, 1671. Exhibitioner from Tonbridge School. S. of George (next), clerk. B. at Hartley, Kent. Matric. 1671; B.A. 1674–5. Ord. deacon and priest (London) Dec. 19, 1680.

EVES, GEORGE. Adm. sizar (age 18) at PEMBROKE, June 16, 1632. S. of George. B. at Croydon, Surrey. Matric. 1632; B.A. 1635–6; M.A. 1639. R. of Hartley, Kent, 1642–67. Died 1667. Father of the above.

EVES, THOMAS, *see* IVES.

EVINGTON, FRANCIS. Adm. pens. at TRINITY, June 19, 1637. Matric. 1637; Scholar, 1638; B.A. 1641–2.

EVINGTON, JOHN. Matric. pens. from PEMBROKE, Michs. 1609. S. of Francis, merchant taylor, and alderman of London. School, Merchant Taylors'. Migrated to Sidney, Sept. 13, 1611. B.A. 1612–3. Of Enfield, Middlesex, and King's Walden, Herts. Married Dorothy, dau. of —— Forth, of Enfield. (*Vis. of Midds.*, 1663.)

EVINGTON, JOHN. Matric. pens. from QUEENS', Easter, 1635. Of Lincolnshire. B.A. 1638–9; M.A. 1642.

EVINGTON, MAURICE. Adm. Fell.-Com. at QUEENS', July 4, 1632. Of Lincolnshire. S. and h. of Nicholas, of Halstead and Spalding. Bapt. Oct. 2, 1615. Died Oct. 21, 1636. (*Lincs. Pedigrees*, 1220.)

EVINGTON, RICHARD. Matric. pens. from PEMBROKE, Easter, 1625. One of these names 1st s. of Nicholas, of Spalding. Bapt. Jan. 24, 1607–8. Buried June 27, 1626. (*Lincs. Pedigrees*, 1220.)

EVYNGTON, ROBERT. Matric. sizar from CHRIST'S, Nov. 1571. Perhaps s. of Francis, of Houghton-on-the-Hill, Leics. B.A. 1575–6; M.A. 1579. Incorp. at Oxford, 1577. R. of Normanton-on-Soar, Notts., 1586. (*Peile*, I. 121.)

EWBANKE, FRANCIS. Matric. sizar from TRINITY, Easter, 1612.

EWBANK, GEORGE. Matric. sizar from TRINITY HALL, Easter, 1654, as 'Orbanke'; B.A. 1656–7.

EWBANCKE, HENRY. Adm. pens. (age 15) at ST JOHN'S, Apr. 28, 1638. S. of Toby, gent., of Staindrop, Durham. B. there. School, Durham. Matric. 1639. (*Vis. of Durham*, 1615.)

EWBANKE, JOHN. Adm. pens. at SIDNEY, June 7, 1617. B. in Durham. Matric. 1617.

EUBANK, MICHAEL. Adm. pens. at SIDNEY, Oct. 28, 1610. B. at Stansmore, Westmorland. Matric. 1611; B.A. 1614–5; M.A. 1618. Ord. deacon (London) Mar. 16, 1616–7, age 27; pries , 15, 1617. V. of Braughing, Herts., 1616–20. Diedt16June

EUBANCKE, ROBERT. Matric. pens. from ST JOHN'S, Easter, 1617.

EUBANCKS, WILLIAM. B.A. from TRINITY, 1595–6; M.A. 1602, as 'Ubankes.' One of these names R. of Simonburn, Northumberland, till 1604.

EWELL, HENRY. Matric. pens. from CORPUS CHRISTI, Michs. 1626. Of Kent. B.A. 1629–30.

EWLE, JOHN. Student at ST CATHARINE'S, 1558.

EWELL, ROBERT. Adm. at CORPUS CHRISTI, 1587. Of Kent. Perhaps s. of Robert, R. of Orlestone. B.A. 1590–1; M.A. 1594; B.D. 1599, as 'Evall.' R. of Barfriston, Kent, 1601–38. R. of Knolton, 1608–38. Died 1638.

EWELL, SAMUEL. Adm. pens. at JESUS, June 23, 1634. Of Kent.

EWELL, ——. Adm. at CORPUS CHRISTI, 1587 (not Robert, above).

EWELLS, FRANCIS. Adm. sizar at EMMANUEL, July 4, 1657. Of Suffolk.

EWEN, *see* EWIN.

EWER, HENRY. Matric. pens. from QUEENS', Easter, 1632. Fell.-Com. Jan. 1632–3. Of Hertfordshire. Doubtless s. of Henry, of Lees Langley, Herts.; age 20 in 1634. Died Jan. 31, 1653–4. M.I. at Watford. (*Vis. of Herts.*, 1634; Le Neve, *Mon.*, IV. 26.)

EWER, JOHN. Adm. pens. at EMMANUEL, Mar. 24, 1619–20. Matric. 1620.

EWER, JOHN. Adm. sizar at QUEENS', Oct. 24, 1650. Of London. Probably s. of William, of St Stephen Walbrook. Bapt. there, Sept. 10, 1632. School, Merchant Taylors'. Matric. from St John's, Oxford, Dec. 11, 1651; B.A. 1654–5; M.A. 1658. For a time in the State service of the Navy. C. of Sawbridgeworth, 1658. R. of Ingatestone, 1662–1716. Buried there Dec. 23, 1716. (*Al. Oxon.*; J. Ch. Smith.)

EWER, JOHN. Adm. at KING'S, a scholar from Eton, 1723. S. of Edward. B. at Belchamp St Paul, Essex. Matric. 1724; B.A. 1728-9; M.A. 1732; D.D. 1756. Fellow, 1727. Assistant Master at Eton. Ord. priest (Lincoln) June 1, 1735. R. of Bottesford, Leics., 1735-52. R. of Dengie, Essex, 1749. Preb. of Hereford, 1751. Canon of Windsor, 1752. R. of West Ilsley, Berks. Bishop of Llandaff, 1761. Bishop of Bangor, 1768. Died Oct. 28, 1774. (*Harwood*; *D.N.B.*)

EWER, JOSEPH. Matric. sizar from TRINITY, Easter, 1618. Of London. Migrated to Corpus Christi. B.A. 1621-2.

EWER, RICHARD, *see* EVER.

EWER, ROGER. M.A. 1597 (Incorp. from Oxford). Of Hertfordshire. Matric. (Christ Church, Oxford) Jan. 27, 1586-7, age 18; B.A. 1590; M.A. 1593. R. of Wendlebury, Oxon., 1605. (*Al. Oxon.*)

EWER, WILLIAM. Adm. pens. (age 17) at ST JOHN'S, Feb. 29, 1635-6. 1st s. of William, of Cheshunt, Herts., Esq. B. there. School, Hertford. Matric. 1636. Adm. at Lincoln's Inn, June 13, 1638. (*Vis. of Herts.*, 1634.)

EWERD, WILLIAM. B.D. 1458-9.

EWIN, JOSEPH. Adm. pens. (age 17) at MAGDALENE, May 13, 1654. S. of John, alderman and mayor of Cambridge. School, Huntingdon. Matric. 1654; B.A. 1657-8; M.A. 1661. License to practice medicine, 1662. Died *c.* 1667. (*Vis. of Cambs.*, 1684.)

EWEN, RICHARD. M.A. R. of Elsworth, Cambs., 1456. R. of Porlock, Somerset. R. of Cleeve, Gloucs. Preb. of St Paul's, 1459-64. Will (P.C.C.) 1464.

EWEN, RICHARD. Adm. pens. at EMMANUEL, June 13, 1633. Of Northamptonshire. Matric. 1633.

EWIN, THOMAS. Adm. pens. at JESUS, Apr. 28, 1736. Of Cambridgeshire. S. of William, of Cambridge. Bapt. at All Saints', Cambridge, Nov. 17, 1717. Matric. 1737; B.A. 1739-40. Ord. deacon (Lincoln) May 24, 1741; priest, Mar. 28, 1742. R. of Swanton Morley, Norfolk, 1744-79. P.C. of Belaugh. Died June 14, 1779, aged 61. (A. Gray.)

EWEN, EUYN or EWING, WILLIAM. B.A. 1486-7; M.A. 1489-90.

EWIN, WILLIAM. Adm. pens. (age 16) at SIDNEY, May 24, 1704. Eldest s. of Thomas, alderman of Cambridge. B. there. School, Bishop's Stortford (Mr Tho. Tooke). Matric. 1704; B.A. 1707-8; M.A. 1711. Ord. priest (Peterb.) Dec. 23, 1711. R. of Ovington, Norfolk, 1711-49. Died July 9, 1749.

EWEN, WILLIAM HOWELL. Adm. pens. (age 16) at ST JOHN'S, Mar. 15, 1748-9. S. of Thomas, gent., grocer and brewer, of St Sepulchre's, Cambridge. B. in Cambridge. School, Colne, Essex (Mr Stringer). Matric. 1749; B.A. 1753; M.A. 1756; LL.D. 1766. Deprived of his degrees, 1778, and expelled the University. Restored by mandamus. Carried on the business of a brewer in the town. Died Dec. 20, 1804. Buried at New Brentford. M.I. (For personal character *see Scott-Mayor*, III. 586; *D.N.B.*)

EWENS or EWINGS, CHRISTOPHER. Adm. sizar (age 16) at CHRIST'S, Feb. 13, 1683-4. S. of Christopher. B. at Broadwindsor, Dorset. School, Ilminster (Mr Hunt). Matric. 1684; B.A. 1687-8. Ord. deacon (Oxford) Mar. 1689-90; priest (Bristol) Mar. 1690-1. R. of East Stoke, Dorset, 1693-6. (*Peile*, II. 94.)

EWINGS, CHRISTOPHER. Adm. scholar (age 16) at SIDNEY, May 1, 1710. S. of John, sea-captain, of Topsham, Devon. School, Tiverton. Matric. 1710; B.A. 1713-4; M.A. 1717. Incorp. at Oxford, 1741. Ord. priest (Ely) June 16, 1717.

EWSDEN, *see* EUSDEN.

EXCESTRE, PETER. Scholar at KING'S HALL, 1393. Died Nov. 8, 1399.

EXCESTRE or EXETRE, ROBERT. Scholar at KING'S HALL, 1437-40.

EXELBY, MILES. B.A. from TRINITY, 1621-2; M.A. 1625. Doubtless s. of Miles, of Stoke Nayland, Suffolk and grandson of Miles, citizen and merchant taylor, of St Dunstan-in-the-West, London. Ord. deacon (Peterb.) Sept. 25; priest, Sept. 26, 1625. V. of St Keverne, Cornwall, 1626-41 (inst. Apr. 20, 1629). Died 1641.

EXLEY, SAMUEL. Adm. sizar (age 19) at CHRIST'S, Feb. 9, 1707-8. S. of John. B. at Rawdon, Yorks. School, Bradford (Mr Tho. Clapham). Matric. 1708; B.A. 1711-2. Ord. deacon (York) Sept. 1712; priest, Sept. 1713. V. of Bramley, Yorks., 1713-29. V. of Farnley, 1728-9. Died 1729. (*Peile*, II. 169.)

EXLEY, TRISTRAM. Adm. sizar (age 19) at ST JOHN'S, Oct. 27, 1742. S. of John, woolspinner, of Yorkshire. B. at Guiseley. School, Threshfield (Mr Knowles). Matric. 1743; B.A. 1747-8. Ord. priest (Lincoln) May 21, 1749. R. of Trowell, Notts., 1753-92. Died Apr. 19, 1792. (*Scott-Mayor*, III. 533.)

EXMEUSE or EXMEW, WILLIAM. Educated at CHRIST'S. B. *c.* 1507. A Carthusian monk; vicar and steward of the Charterhouse. Hanged at Tyburn, June 19, 1535, for denying the King's supremacy. (*Cooper*, I. 52; *D.N.B.*)

EXON, JOSEPH. Adm. sizar (age 17) at CHRIST'S, June 4, 1679. S. of John. B. at Diseworth. School, Repton. Matric. 1679. Buried at Gt St Andrew's, Cambridge, May 1, 1682.

EXTON, BRIAN. Adm. pens. at CORPUS CHRISTI, 1571. Matric. 1572; B.A. 1575-6; M.A. 1579. Ord. priest (Lincoln) Oct. 22, 1591. V. of Hanbury, Staffs., 1585 (*sic.*). Preb. of Lichfield, 1585. R. of North Darley, Derbs., 1590. (*Wm. Salt Arch. Soc.*, 1915.)

EXTON, EDWARD. M.A. 1664 (Incorp. from Oxford). S. of Robert, of Chichester. Matric. from Magdalen College, Oxford, Apr. 30, 1643, age 15; B.A. (Oxford) 1646; M.A. 1660; B.D. and M.D. 1666. Fellow of Magdalen College. Died Oct. 26, 1683. (*Al. Oxon.*)

EXTON, JOHN. Matric. pens. from CHRIST'S, July, 1617. Migrated to Trinity Hall, Mar. 1618-9. B.A. 1619-20; M.A. 1623; LL.D. 1634. Admiralty Judge, 1649 and 1661. Author of *The Maritime Dicaeologie*. Buried at St Benet, Paul's Wharf, Oct. 22, 1668. Father of Thomas (1647). (*Peile*, I. 316; *D.N.B.*)

EXTON, JOHN. Matric. pens. from QUEENS', Easter, 1640. Of Huntingdonshire. Perhaps s. of John (above). B. Apr. 4, 1624. School, Merchant Taylors'.

EXTON, JOHN. Matric. Fell.-Com. from EMMANUEL, Easter, 1689. S. of Thomas, Master of Trinity Hall. M.A. 1690 (*Com. Reg.*); LL.D. 1697. Fellow of Trinity Hall, 1690-1716. Died 1716.

EXTON, RICHARD. Adm. at CORPUS CHRISTI, 1715. Of Northamptonshire. School, Charterhouse. Matric. 1716; B.A. 1719-20; M.A. from Peterhouse, 1723. Ord. deacon (Peterb.) Sept. 23, 1722; priest (Norwich) Mar. 1722-3. V. of Codicote, Herts., 1725-31. R. of Chilbolton, Hants. Preb. of Winchester, 1748-59. Chaplain to the Earl of Portsmouth. Died 1759.

EXTEN, RICHARD. Adm. pens. at CLARE, Mar. 26, 1716. B. at Sulton, Wilts. Matric. 1717; B.A. 1719-20; M.A. 1723. Incorp. at Oxford, 1723. Doubtless R. of Piddletrenthide, Dorset, 1734.

EXTON, SAYER. Matric. pens. from TRINITY HALL, July, 1709.

EXTON, THOMAS. Matric. pens. from TRINITY HALL, Easter, 1647. S. of John (1617), LL.D. School, Merchant Taylors'. LL.B. 1652; LL.D. 1662. Fellow, 1651-63. Master, 1676-88. Adm. at Gray's Inn, Dec. 28, 1649. Barrister, 1659. Ancient, 1676. Adm. advocate, June 22, 1664. Knighted, Nov. 23, 1675. M.P. for the University, 1679, 1681, 1685. Judge of the Admiralty, 1686. Advocate-general. Dean of the Arches, 1686. Died 1688. Buried at St Peter's, Paul's Wharf, Nov. 8. Father of John (1689). (*D.N.B.*; *Hist. of Trin. Hall.*, 161.)

EXUNO, THOMAS DE. Fellow of PETERHOUSE, in 1339.

EXWORTH, ROBERT, *see* SKUT.

EYE, STEPHEN DE. University Bedell, *c.* 1324. Benefactor. (Stokes, *Bedells*, 53.)

EYES, JOHN. Adm. pens. (age 17) at CHRIST'S, Apr. 15, 1646. S. of Alexander, yeoman. B. at Standish, Lancs. School, Wigan (Mr Barrow). Migrated to St John's, Oct. 30, 1648. One of these names R. of Whitby, Yorks., 1654-9.

EYLES, FRANCIS. Adm. at CORPUS CHRISTI, 1727. Of London. Doubtless s. of Sir John, alderman of London. Matric. 1728. F.R.S. 1742. Succeeded his father as Baronet, 1745. Assumed the additional surname of Haskin-Styles, on inheriting the estate of his uncle. Died at Naples, Jan. 26, 1762. (Burke, *Ext. Bart.*; *G.E.C.*)

EYLES, JOSEPH. Adm. at CORPUS CHRISTI, 1737. Of London. Matric. 1737. Adm. at the Inner Temple, Dec. 7, 1737. S. of Sir Joseph, of London, Knt.

EYLES, ROBERT. Adm. sizar (age 18) at ST JOHN'S, July 1, 1715. S. of John, maltster. B. at Hambledon, Hants. School, Corhampton, Hants. (Mr Sone). Matric. 1715; B.A. 1718-9; M.A. 1722. Fellow, 1720-3.

EYRE, *see also* AYRE.

EYRE, AMBROSE. Adm. pens. (age 17) at CHRIST'S, Apr. 6, 1703. S. of William. B. in London. Exhibitioner from Charterhouse. Matric. 1704. Adm. at the Middle Temple, Nov. 18, 1702, as s. and h. of William, of Chelsea, Esq. Receiver of Charterhouse, 1719-39. Adm. a poor brother, 1755. Died Apr. 21, 1756. Buried at Fulham. Father of Venn (1728-9). (*Peile*, II. 156; *Al. Carthus.*)

EYRE, ANTHONY. Matric. Fell.-Com. from KING'S, Easter, 1709. Doubtless s. of Gervase, of Rampton, Notts., deceased. Of Adwick-le-Street, Yorks., and Rampton, Esq. Sheriff of Notts., 1729. Married Margaret, dau. of Charles Turner, of Kirk Leatham, Esq., 1717. Died 1748. (*F.M.G.*, 559.)

EYRE or EYER, EDWARD. M.A. from ST JOHN'S, 1612. One of these names ord. deacon (Chichester) Oct. 26, 1610; priest, Nov. 7, 1610. R. of St Thomas-at-Cliffe, Lewes, 1610. Perhaps V. of Haverhill, Suffolk, 1615. (W. C. Renshaw.)

EYRE, GERVASE. Matric. Fell.-Com. from QUEENS', Michs. 1565. B. at Rampton, Notts. Probably s. of Anthony, of Kiveton, Yorks.; age 28 in 1575. Married Mary, dau. of George Nevile, of Ragnal, Esq. Buried at Laughton, Oct. 28, 1625. (Burke, *L.G.*; *Vis. of Yorks.*; *Hunter*, I. 288.)

EYRE, HENRY. Adm. pens. (age 17) at ST JOHN'S, May 12, 1638. S. of Nathaniel, gent., of Bramley Hall, Yorks. Bapt. at Braithwell, Jan. 30, 1621-2. School, Laughton (Mr Seton). Matric. 1638; B.A. 1641-2; M.A. 1645; M.D. 1658. Fellow, 1647. Taxor, 1649. Died 1686. (*Vis. of Yorks.*, 1665.)

EYR, JOHN. Fellow of PETERHOUSE, 1420-1443-.

EYRE or EYRES, JOHN. Matric. pens. from ST CATHARINE'S, Easter, 1637. Of London. B.A. 1640-1; M.A. (Oxford) 1652. Perhaps V. of Marston St Laurence, Northants., 1647. R. of Little Ashby, Leics., 1647-53. Died 1653.

EYRE or AYRE, JOHN. Adm. sizar (age 17) at MAGDALENE, Nov. 4, 1664. S. of John, clerk, of East Farndon, Northants. School, Winchester. Matric. 1666-7; B.A. 1666-7; M.A. 1672. Incorp. at Oxford, 1676. Ord. priest (Ely) Mar. 19, 1670-1. Perhaps R. of Howe, Norfolk, 1684.

EYRE, JOHN. Incorp. M.A. 1675, from Christ Church, Oxford. ('Syre' in the *grace*). Not found in *Al. Oxon.*

EYRE, JOSEPH. Adm. sizar (age 20) at ST JOHN'S, June 30, 1729. S. of Thomas, husbandman, of Yorkshire. B. at Ecclesfield. School, Sheffield (Mr Robinson). Matric. 1730; B.A. 1734-5. Ord. deacon (Lincoln) Sept. 22, 1734; priest, June 20, 1736. R. and V. of Ruskington, Lincs., 1739. Held the rectory till 1780, and the vicarage till 1781. (*Scott-Mayor*, III. 424.)

EYRE, JOSEPH. Adm. Fell.-Com. (age 20) at SIDNEY, May 20, 1732. Only s. of Joseph, gent., of Richmond, Surrey. Schools, Richmond and Colchester. Matric. 1733.

EYRE or AYRE, REARSBY. Matric. sizar from ST JOHN'S, Easter, 1618. 2nd s. of William, of Bramley Hall, Yorks. Bapt. Oct. 9, 1601. B.A. 1621-2; M.A. 1625. Ord. deacon (York) June, 1623; priest, Sept. 1623. V. of Darton, Yorks., 1628-41. Died Sept. 14, 1641. (*Vis. of Yorks.*, 1665.)

EYRE, RICHARD. Matric. pens. from CLARE, *c.* 1590.

EYRE, RICHARD. Adm. pens. at TRINITY, June 9, 1656. Of Derbyshire. 3rd s. of Robert, of Highlow, Derbs. Adm. at Gray's Inn, June 19, 1656. Died *s.p.* Brother of the next and of Thomas (1656). (*F.M.G.*, 553.)

EYRE, ROBERT. Adm. pens. at TRINITY, June 9, 1656. Of Derbyshire. S. and h. of Robert, of Highlow, Derbs. Adm. at Gray's Inn, June 19, 1656. Died in College, June 26, 1656. M.I. at Hathersage. Brother of Richard (above), Thomas (1656) and William (1660). (*F.M.G.*, 553.)

EYRE, ROBERT. Adm. pens. (age 19) at ST JOHN'S, Apr. 6, 1739. S. of John, Esq., of Surrey. B. at Putney. School, Guilsborough, Northants. (Mr Horton). Matric. 1739. Died in College Buried at All Saints', Cambridge, Aug. 10, 1739.

EYRE, SAMUEL. M.A. 1679 (Incorp. from Oxford). S. of Reginald, of Nether Seale, Leics. Matric. from Lincoln College, Oxford, Mar. 17, 1664-5, age 15; B.A. (Oxford) 1668; M.A. 1671; B.D. 1680; D.D. 1687. R. of Neenton, Salop, 1676. R. of Whitburn, Durham, 1686. Preb. of Durham, 1690. Died 1694. (*Al. Oxon.*)

EYRE, SAMUEL. LL.D. 1728 (*Com. Reg.*). Probably s. of Sir Robert, of London, Knt. Matric. from New College, Oxford, Sept. 26, 1716, age 18; B.C.L. (Oxford) 1723. Preb. of Salisbury, 1729. Died Dec. 2, 1742. (*Al. Oxon.*)

EYRE, THOMAS. Scholar of CLARE, 1513.

EYRE, THOMAS. Adm. pens. at EMMANUEL, May 28, 1640. Of Suffolk. Matric. 1641; B.A. 1643-4. Perhaps nominated to Ashby Parva, Leics., 1647.

EYRE, THOMAS. Adm. pens. (age 19) at ST JOHN'S, June 6, 1649. S. of Roger, Esq., of Birchover, and Rowter Hall, Youlgreave, Derbs. B. at Birchover. School, Repton. Matric. 1650. Adm. at Gray's Inn, Feb. 8, 1647-8. Called to the bar, 1657. Reader elect of Barnard's Inn, 1673; fined £30 for not reading. (*Repton Sch. Register.*)

EYRE, THOMAS. Adm. pens. at TRINITY, June 9, 1656. Of Derbyshire. 2nd s. of Robert, of Highlow, Derbs. Adm. at Gray's Inn, June 19, 1656. Barrister, 1657. Died without issue. Brother of Richard (1656), Robert (1656) and William (1660). (*F.M.G.*, 553.)

EYRE, THOMAS. Adm. pens. (age 16) at PEMBROKE, July 9, 1668. S. of Christopher, gent. B. at Manuden, Essex. Matric. 1669; B.A. 1671-2; M.A. 1675. Ord. deacon (Norwich) Dec. 1675; priest (London) Mar. 11, 1676-7. V. of Staines, Middlesex, 1696-1713. Died 1713. Admon. (P.C.C.) 1717.

EYRE, THOMAS. Adm. pens. at TRINITY, June 18, 1733. S. of Thomas, of Stockport, Cheshire. School, Chester (Mr Dale). Matric. 1733. Ord. deacon (Lincoln) Sept. 25, 1737.

EYRE, URBAN. Adm. pens. (age 16) at PETERHOUSE, Apr. 21, 1673. S. of Samuel, of Hartlebury, Worcs. School, Hartlebury. Scholar, 1673. Previously matric. from Trinity College, Oxford, Nov. 4, 1672, age 16.

EYRE, VENN. Adm. pens. (age 17) at ST JOHN'S, Mar. 22, 1728-9. S. of Ambrose (1703), gent., of Middlesex. B. in London, Sept. 21, 1712. Exhibitioner from Charterhouse. Matric. 1729. Migrated to St Catharine's, Oct. 23, 1730. B.A. 1732-3; M.A. 1736. Fellow of St Catharine's, 1736-9. Ord. priest (Lincoln) June 5, 1737. R. of Gt Stambridge, Essex, 1737-77. R. of Stambourne, 1741-77. Preb. of St Asaph, 1754. Archdeacon of Carlisle, 1756-77. R. of Gt Salkeld, Cumberland, 1756-77. Lecturer at Lynn, Norfolk. Died there May 18, 1777. (*Scott-Mayor*, III. 430; *Al. Carthus.*)

EYRE, WILLIAM. Adm. pens. (age 15) at CHRIST'S, May 28, 1642. Eldest s. of Robert, of Royton, near Worksop, Notts. B. there. Schools, Staveley (Mr Dand) and Laughton-en-le-Morthen (Mr Seton). Adm. at the Inner Temple, 1647. Died without issue. One of these names knighted, Feb. 28, 1662-3. (*Peile*, 481.)

EYRE, WILLIAM. Adm. Fell.-Com. (age 18) at ST JOHN'S, June 23, 1660. S. of Robert, Esq., of Highlow, Derbs. B. there. School, Buxton (Mr Ogden). Of Highlow and Holme Hall, Derbs., Esq. Sheriff of Derbs., 1691. Buried at Hathersage, Aug. 9, 1706. Brother of Richard (1656), Thomas (1656) and Robert (1656). (*F.M.G.*, 553.)

EYRE, WILLIAM. Adm. pens. at QUEENS', July 6, 1663. Matric. 1663; B.A. 1666-7; M.A. 1670. Ord. deacon (Ely) Dec. 20, 1668; priest (London) May, 1670. R. of Mile End, Colchester, 1673-86.

EYRE, ——. Fee for M.A. or higher degree, 1467-8.

EYRE, ——. Adm. at CORPUS CHRISTI, 1583.

EYRE, ——. Adm. sizar at SIDNEY, Apr. 1599.

EYRE, ——. Adm. scholar at TRINITY HALL, Jan. 23, 1704-5.

EYRE, ——. Adm. Fell.-Com. at KING'S, 1715-6.

EYRES, *see also* AYRES.

EYRES, DANIEL. Matric. sizar from EMMANUEL, Easter, 1615; B.A. from Magdalene, 1618-9; M.A. 1622. Ord. deacon (Peterb.) Sept. 21; priest, Sept. 22, 1623, as 'fellow of Magdalene College.'

EYRES, NATHANIEL. Adm. sizar (age 19) at ST JOHN'S, Mar. 26, 1647. S. of Edward, V. of Haverhill, Suffolk. B. there. School, Bumsted (Mr French). Matric. 1647; B.A. 1650-1; M.A. 1654. V. of North Weald, Essex, 1660-9.

EYERS or AIRES, ROBERT. Matric. sizar from QUEENS', Easter, 1621. Of London. B.A. 1624-5; M.A. 1634.

EYRES or AIERS, WILLIAM. Adm. sizar at EMMANUEL, Mar. 25, 1592. Of Rampton, Notts. Matric. *c.* 1592; Scholar; B.A. 1595-6; M.A. 1599; B.D. 1606. Fellow, 1599-1611. R. of Gt Horkesley, Essex, 1617-42. Preb. of Ely, 1629. Died Jan. 1670.

EYTON, DAVID. Adm. sizar at TRINITY, June 28, 1641. Matric. 1641, as Eaton. Migrated to Clare. B.A. 1644-5. One of these names R. of Bodfari, Flints., 1666-8.

EYTON, HENRY. Adm. sizar at TRINITY, Apr. 27, 1654. Matric. 1656, as Eaton; B.A. 1657-8. Ord. deacon (Lincoln) June 25; priest, June 29, 1661. V. of Ashby Folville, Leics., 1661-2.

EYTON, KENRICK. Adm. Fell.-Com. (age 18) at TRINITY, May 18, 1689. S. of Kenrick, of Eyton, Denbigh. B. at Hackney. School, Eton. Matric. 1689. (For a different man, apparently, of the same date and names, *see Al. Oxon.*) (Le Neve, *Knights*, 298.)

EYTON, ROBERT. Adm. pens. (age 17) at ST JOHN'S, Mar. 11, 1699-1700. S. of Philip, Esq. B. at Shrewsbury. School, Llanvair, Denbigh. (Mr Price). B.A. 1703-4; M.A. 1718. Ord. deacon (Ely) Dec. 23, 1705. R. of Wem, Salop. Preb. of Hereford. Archdeacon of Ely, 1742-51. Died Oct. 18, 1751. (G. *Mag.*)

F

FABBE, JOHN. M.A. Will proved (V.C.C.) 1504; left legacies to God's House (Christ's College). Will also (P.C.C.) 1505; 'clerk, of Burwell, Cambs.'

FABER, JOHN. Adm. pens. at EMMANUEL, Easter, 1623. Matric. 1623; B.A. 1626; M.A. (Oxford) 1629. (*Al. Oxon.*)

FABER, THOMAS. Adm. sizar (age 19) at ST JOHN'S, Mar. 15, 1748-9. S. of William, currier, of Yorkshire. B. at Leeds. School, Linton-in-Craven (Mr Hewitt). Matric. 1749; B.A. 1753; M.A. 1757. Ord. deacon (London) June 17, 1753; C. of Gt Braxted, Essex. P.C. of Bramley, Leeds, 1757-1821. V. of Calverley, Yorks., 1770-1821. Died Nov. 28, 1821. (*Scott-Mayor*, III. 585.)

FABIAN, JOHN. Matric. pens. from TRINITY, Lent, 1581-2. (He had resided for four years.) Scholar, 1580; B.A. 1581-2; M.A. from Balliol College, Oxford, 1585. R. of Sapcote, Leics., 1588. R. of Gt Warley, Essex, 1589. R. of Houghton Regis, Beds., 1591. Suspended, 1597: resigned before Aug. 10, 1600. Admon. (Cons. C. London) July 6, 1626, to s. John. Father of the next. (*Al. Oxon.*; *Cooper*, II. 288.)

FABIAN, JOHN. Matric. pens. from PEMBROKE, Michs. 1618. S. of John (above), of Gt Warley, Essex, clerk. B.A. 1621-2; M.A. 1625. Ord. deacon (London) May 20, 1627. Probably R. of Chew Magna, Somerset, 1628-43. But *see* a contemporary in *Al. Oxon.*

FABYON, THOMAS. B.Can.L. 1519-20. Perhaps R. of Polstead, Suffolk, till 1542. Will (P.C.C.) 1542.

FABIAN, THOMAS. Matric. sizar from ST JOHN'S, *c.* 1601.

FABIAN, THOMAS. Matric. sizar from CLARE, Easter, 1631; B.A. 1634-5; M.A. 1638. Fellow, 1642-4; ejected. Licensed to practise medicine, 1648. Will of one of these names (P.C.C.) 1651-2; of Hastings, physician.

FABIAN, ——. B.A. 1489-90; M.A. 1493.

FACER, CLEMENT. Matric. sizar from KING'S, Michs. 1601. S. of John, R. of Grove, Bucks. B.A. from Clare, 1605-6. Ord. deacon (Lincoln) June 15, 1606; priest, May 31, 1607; C. to his father at Grove.

FACON or FAUCON, ROBERT. Matric. sizar from TRINITY, Easter, 1607. S. of Robert, R. of Bainton, Yorks. Bapt. at Hadleigh, Suffolk, Dec. 14, 1589. Scholar, 1608; B.A. 1610-1; M.A. not recorded. Fellow, 1612-21. R. of Bainton, Yorks. 1620-44; sequestered and imprisoned: restored, 1660-1. Minister of Coxwold, 1649-51; of St Crux, York, 1652-60. Married, at St Michael Belfry, York, May 4, 1620, Ann Staincliff. Buried at Bainton, Sept. 7, 1661. M.I. (M. H. Peacock.)

FACY, HUMFREY. Adm. sizar (age 16) at CAIUS, Mar. 16, 1615-6. S. of Humfrey, gent., of Landkey, Devon. School, Barnstaple. B.A. 1619-20; M.A. 1623. R. of Uphill, Somerset, 1639-40.

FAGE, ANTHONY. Matric. pens. from MAGDALENE, Lent, 1598-9. Migrated to Emmanuel, Aug. 9, 1600.

FAGE or PHAGE, FRANCIS. Matric. pens. from PETERHOUSE, Easter, 1584.

FAGE, GEORGE. B.Civ.L. 1520-1.

FAGE, GEORGE. Adm. pens. at CORPUS CHRISTI, 1691. Of London. Matric. 1692; B.A. 1695-6; M.A. 1699. Fellow, 1698-1702. Ord. deacon (Lincoln) Sept. 24, 1699; priest, Mar. 16, 1700-1. V. of Hougham, Kent, 1701. R. of Hunton, 1701-28. V. of Marden, 1707-28. Preb. of Lichfield, 1709-28. Died Sept. 8, 1728, aged 53. Buried at Hunton. M.I. Executor of Archbishop Tenison. (*Masters*.)

FAGE or FAGGE, ROBERT. Matric. sizar from ST CATHARINE'S, Easter, 1621; B.A. 1623-4; M.A. 1627. V. of Fulbourn, Cambs., 1632. V. of Wilburton. Buried there Dec. 6, 1669. (*Misc. Gen. et Her.*, 3rd S., II. 142.)

FAGE, THOMAS. B.A. from CHRIST'S, 1603-4; M.A. 1607. B. about 1582. Ord. deacon (Ely) 1608; priest (Lincoln) Mar. 12, 1608-9. V. of Old Hurst, Hunts., 1612. R. of Langton-by-Horncastle, Lincs., 1613-22. V. of St Neots, Hunts., 1622-51. (*Peile*, I. 233, erroneously reads the name 'Faye.')

FAGE, ——. B.Can.L. 1534-5.

FAGGE, EDWARD. Matric. pens. from ST JOHN'S, Michs. 1576; B.A. 1579-80; M.A. 1583. Incorp. at Oxford, 1584.

FAGG, JOHN. Matric. Fell.-Com. from PEMBROKE, Michs. 1617 ('phrenesi correptus,' paulo post hinc recedit') (*Coll. register*). Perhaps s. and h. of John, of Brensett, Kent; adm. at Gray's Inn, Nov. 1, 1619. If so, died July 25, 1646. (Burke, *L.G.*; *Hasted*, III. 492.)

FAGG, JOHN. Adm. Fell.-Com. at ST CATHARINE'S, Oct. 28, 1663. S. of Sir John, of Wiston, Sussex, Bart. Matric. 1664. Adm. at the Inner Temple, Dec. 16, 1664. M.P. for Shoreham, 1667-72. Died 1672. Brother of Robert (1663). (*Vis. of Kent*, 1663; Dallaway's *Sussex*, II. 151; *Kimber*, II. 125.)

FAGGE, JOHN MERES. Adm. scholar at TRINITY HALL, Jan. 5, 1743-4. Of Chichester. S. and h. of John Meres, of Glinley, Sussex. Matric. 1748; LL.B. 1749. Fellow, 1748-50. Adm. at the Middle Temple, Feb. 23, 1739-40. Barrister-at-Law. Died May 18, 1750. (G. *Mag.*)

FAGG, ROBERT. Adm. Fell.-Com. at ST CATHARINE'S, Oct. 28, 1663. S. of Sir John, of Wiston, Sussex, Bart. Matric. 1664. Adm. at the Inner Temple, Dec. 16, 1664. M.P. for Shoreham, 1679 and 1681; for Steyning, 1690-5, Feb.-Apr. 1701, 1701-2. Succeeded as 2nd Bart., 1701. Died Aug. 26, 1715. Buried at Albourne, Sussex. M.I. Brother of John (1663). (*G.E.C.*; A. B. Beaven.)

FAGG, THOMAS. Adm. pens. at CLARE, Oct. 29, 1751. 2nd s. of Charles. B. at Mystole, Chartham, Kent. Matric. 1751. Adm. at the Middle Temple, May 2, 1752. Brother of the next.

FAGG, Sir WILLIAM, Bart. Adm. Fell.-Com. at CLARE, Mar. 24, 1743-4. S. of Charles, of Mystole, Kent. B. at Canterbury, *c.* 1726. Succeeded his cousin, Robert, as 5th Bart., Sept. 14, 1740. Adm. at the Middle Temple, Jan. 25, 1741-2. Died Nov. 14, 1791. Brother of the above. (*G.E.C.*)

FAGGE, ——. Adm. Fell.-Com. at EMMANUEL, July 2, 1644. Not improbably John, s. and h. of John, of Rye, Sussex. Adm. at Gray's Inn, July 1, 1644. Of Mystole, Kent. M.P. for Rye, 1645-53; for Sussex, 1654-9 and 1681; for Steyning, 1660-81 and 1685-1701. Parliamentarian. Created Bart. Dec. 11, 1660. Died Jan. 18, 1700-1. (*G.E.C.*)

FAGIUS (BÜCHLEIN), PAUL. Hebrew lecturer at Cambridge, 1549. S. of Peter, schoolmaster at Rheinzabern. B. there, 1504. Preacher at Isne, Strassburg and Heidelberg. Came to England, 1549; appointed to lecture in Cambridge, but died soon after. Buried at St Michael's, Cambridge, Nov. 25, 1549. Will proved (V.C.C.) 1549. Under Queen Mary, his body was exhumed, Feb. 6, 1556-7, and burnt as that of a heretic. His degree and titles were restored, 1560. Father of the next. (*Cooper*, I. 95, III. 85; *D.N.B.*)

FAGIUS, PAUL. Matric. pens. from TRINITY, Easter, 1550. S. of the above. Scholar, 1550. (*Cooper*, III. 85.)

FAIDE, ——. B.Can.L. 1500-1.

FAIRBARN, JOHN. Matric. sizar from KING'S, Easter, 1623.

FAIRBARN or FAIRBURN, WILLIAM. Adm. pens. (age 16) at MAGDALENE, Mar. 7, 1656-7. S. of John, of Woodhouse, Yorks. School, Leeds. Matric. 1657; B.A. 1660-1; M.A. 1664. Incorp. at Oxford, 1664. V. of Rothwell, Yorks., 1664-81.

FAIRBEARD, ROBERT. Adm. pens. at EMMANUEL, Mar. 24, 1658-9. Of Essex. Perhaps s. and h. of Robert, of Gray's Inn, deceased; adm. at Gray's Inn, Apr. 25, 1668; if so, father of the next.

FAIRBEARD, ROBERT. Adm. sizar (age 17) at CAIUS, Mar. 29, 1716. S. of Robert, barrister of Gray's Inn. B. at Epsom, Surrey. School, Marlborough (Mr Hildrop). Matric. 1716; Scholar, 1716-22. Ord. deacon (Lincoln, *Litt. dim.* from Norwich) Mar. 5, 1720-1. (*Venn*, II. 5.)

FAIRBRASS or FIREBRACE, HENRY. Matric. pens. from ST JOHN'S, Michs. 1568; B.A. 1571-2; M.A. 1575. R. of Ightham, Kent, 1574-86; of Halstead, 1594-1601; and of Farningham, 1594-1601. Died Feb. 21, 1601-2. M.I. at Farningham. (*Cooper*, II. 321; H. G. Harrison.)

FAIRBROTHER, WILLIAM. Adm. at KING'S (age 17) a scholar from Eton, Apr. 19, 1630. Of London. Matric. 1631; B.A. 1633-4; M.A. 1637; LL.D. 1660 (*Lit. Reg.*). Fellow, 1633-81. Vice-provost, 1653. Senior Proctor, 1654-5. Incorp. at Oxford, 1669. Served in the Royal army. Prisoner at Naseby, 1645. Died Aug. 10, 1681. (*Harwood*.)

FAIRBY, ——. B.A. 1473.

FAIRECHILD, EDWARD. Adm. pens. (age 17) at ST JOHN'S, Oct. 3, 1678. S. of Edward, gent. B. at Pilton, Devon. School, Shirwell, Devon (Mr 'Rumphry'). Matric. 1678; B.A. 1682-3. Will of one of these names (Exeter) 1710 and 1714; 'clerk, of Goodleigh, Devon.'

FAIRCHILD, JOHN. Adm. sizar at EMMANUEL, June 25, 1602. Matric. 1602; B.A. 1605-6; M.A. 1609. Ord. deacon (Norwich) Sept. 21, 1606, age 23; priest, Sept. 21, 1607; C. of Hedenham, Norfolk.

FAIRCHILD, THOMAS. Adm. pens. (age 16) at Trinity, Apr. 21, 1740. S. of Thomas, of London. School, St Paul's. Matric. 1740; Scholar, 1741; B.A. 1743-4. Ord. priest (Peterb.) Dec. 20, 1747. Doubtless R. of Pitsea, Essex. Died June 7, 1782. Will (P.C.C.); of St Paul's, Deptford, Kent. (*G. Mag.*)

FAIRCLOUGH, *see also* **FEATLEY.**

FAIRCLOUGH or FORKCLOWE, ALEXANDER. Fellow of Queens', 1446; living, 1472.

FAIRCLOUGH, EDWARD. Adm. pens. at Queens', July 2, 1594. Of Hertfordshire. Perhaps s. of John, of Weston, Esq. Matric. *c.* 1594, as Partlow. B.A. 1597-8. Adm. at Lincoln's Inn, from Furnival's Inn, Feb. 7, 1599-1600. (*Vis. of Herts.*, 1634.)

FAIRCLOUGH, FRANCIS. Matric. pens. from St John's, Easter, 1621.

FAIRCLOUGH or FERKLOW, GEOFFREY. Fellow of Pembroke, 1444. Proctor, 1450.

FAIRCLOUGH, GEORGE. Adm. pens. at Queens', Mar. 10, 1674-5. Of Leicestershire.

FAYRCLOGH, HENRY. Fellow of Peterhouse, 1405-22.

FAIRCLOUGH, HENRY. Adm. pens. (age 17) at Caius, June 21, 1682. S. of James (1651-2), M.D., of London. B. there. Schools, Islington and Eton. Matric. 1682; Scholar, 1682-4. Adm. at the Middle Temple, Feb. 13, 1681; migrated to the Inner Temple, Mar. 14, 1683-4. Admon. (P.C.C.) 1710; of the Inner Temple. Died at Carlisle. (*Venn*, I. 471; J. Ch. Smith.)

FAIRCLOUGH, JAMES. Adm. pens. (age 21) at St John's, Feb. 6, 1651-2; readm. Fell. Com. Sept. 8, 1654. S. of Thomas, gent., of Upholland, Lancs. B. there. School, Winwick, Lancs. Matric. 1654; B.A. 1654-5; M.A. from Caius, 1658. Licensed to practise medicine, 1658. M.D. 1661 (*Lit. Reg.*). Fellow of Caius, 1655-9. Practised in London. Will (P.C.C.) 1685; of the Inner Temple. Father of Henry, above. (*Venn*, I. 391.)

FAIRCLOUGH or FAYRECLOTH, JOHN. Adm. pens. (age 17) at Caius, May 5, 1651. S. of Samuel (1608), minister, of Kedington, Suffolk. B. there. Schools, Bury St Edmunds (Mr Leigh) and Dedham, Essex (Mr Oddy). Matric. 1651; Scholar, 1651-5; B.A. 1654-5; M.A. 1658. R. of Kennett, Cambs., 1662-96. Buried there Feb. 1, 1695-6. Father of Richard (1686) and Samuel (1696), brother of Nathaniel (1641), Richard (1637) and Samuel (1643). (*Venn*, I. 382; where he is confused with James, above.)

FAIRCLOUGH, JOHN. Adm. sizar (age 17) at Trinity, Mar. 8, 1716-7. S. of Richard (1686-7), R. of Kennett, Cambs. School, Bury St Edmunds (Mr Kynnesman). Scholar, 1719; Matric. 1720; B.A. 1720-1. Ord. deacon (Norwich) May, 1722; priest, May, 1724. R. of Colton, Norfolk, 1728-30. Died Aug. 14, 1730. M.I. at Colton.

FAIRCLOUGH, NATHANIEL. Adm. pens. at Emmanuel, May 11, 1641. S. of Samuel (1608). B.A. 1644-5; M.A. 1648. R. of Stalbridge, Dorset. Died Oct. 11, 1656. M.I. at Long Burton. Father of Samuel (1664) and of the next. (*Hutchins*, IV. 133.)

FAIRCLOUGH, NATHANIEL. Adm. sizar at St Catharine's, Feb. 1, 1669-70. S. of Nathaniel (above). Matric. 1670; B.A. 1673-4. Ord. deacon (Norwich) Sept. 1673. Master of Sudbury School, Suffolk, *c.* 1677. V. of Cornard Magna and Parva, Suffolk, 1682-91; deprived. Brother of Samuel (1664). (*Suff. Man. Fam.*, III. 74.)

FAIRCLOUGH, RICHARD. M.A. 1581 (Incorp. from Oxford). Of Bedford. School, Winchester. Age 12, in 1565. Scholar of New College, Oxford, 1570; B.A. 1573-4; M.A. 1577-8. R. of Bucknell, Oxon., 1592-1638. Died at Weston, Herts. Will (P.C.C.) 1638. (*Al. Oxon.*; J. Ch. Smith.)

FAIRCLOUGH, RICHARD. Adm. pens. at Emmanuel, Easter, 1637. S. of Samuel (1608), of Ashdon, Essex. B. 1621. Matric. 1637; B.A. 1640-1; M.A. 1644. Fellow, 1644. R. of Mells, Somerset, 1647-1662; ejected. Afterwards minister in Bristol. Died in London, July 4, 1682, aged 61. Buried in Bunhill Fields. M.I. there. Brother of Samuel (1643), John (1651) and Nathaniel (1641). (*D.N.B.*; *Calamy*, II. 371.)

FAIRCLOUGH, RICHARD. Adm. sizar (age 17) at Caius, Jan. 22, 1686-7. S. of John (1651), R. of Kennett, Cambs. School, Bury St Edmunds. Matric. 1687; Scholar, 1687-94; B.A. 1690-1; M.A. 1694. Ord. deacon (Norwich) June 11, 1693; priest, Sept. 23, 1694. C of Quiddenham, 1694. R. of Kennett, Cambs., 1696-1751. Died Sept. 12, 1750-1. Buried at Kennett. Father of John (1717). (*Venn*, I. 482; *Suff. Man. Fam.*, III. 75.)

FAIRCLOUGH, SAMUEL. Matric. sizar from Queens', Easter, 1608 ('Fetloe,' in College register). 4th s. of Lawrence, V. of Haverhill. B. at Haverhill, Suffolk. Bapt. May 22, 1594. B.A. 1615. Lecturer at Lynn, 1619. R. of Barnardiston, Suffolk, 1623-9. R. of Kedington, 1629-62; ejected. Nominated one of the Assembly of Divines, 1643, but excused himself from attending. Published *The Pastor's Legacy* and other works. Died Dec. 14, 1677, at the residence of his son-in-law, Richard Shute, V. of Stowmarket. Father of Richard (1637), Samuel (1643) and Nathaniel (1641). (*D.N.B.*; *Calamy*, II.)

FAIRCLOUGH, SAMUEL. Adm. pens. at Emmanuel, May 23, 1643. S. of Samuel (1608), R. of Barnardiston, Suffolk. Matric. 1644; B.A. 1646-7; M.A. 1650. Intruded fellow of Caius, 1650-6. R. of Houghton Conquest, Beds.; ejected, 1662. Afterwards licensed as minister at Chippenham, Cambs., 1672. Married, at Ketton, Oct. 25, 1655, Frances, dau. of —— Folkes. Benefactor to Caius, by foundation of an exhibition. Author, *Sermons*. Died Dec. 21, 1691. Buried at Heveningham, Suffolk. M.I. there. Will (P.C.C.) 1692. Brother of Richard (1637) and John (1651). (*Venn*, I. 379; *D.N.B.*; *Davy MSS.*)

FAIRCLOUGH, SAMUEL. Adm. sizar (age 14) at Christ's, Oct. 28, 1664. S. of Nathaniel (1641). B. at Long Burton, near Sherborne, Dorset. School, Wratting, Suffolk (Mr Burwell). Matric. 1668; B.A. 1668-9; M.A. 1672. Signed for priest's orders (London) Mar. 13, 1673-4; C. of Boxted, Suffolk. Described as 'M.A. of Magdalene.' R. of Hawkchurch, Dorset, 1673-6. Died Aug. 23, 1676. Brother of Nathaniel (1669-70).

FAIRCLOUGH, SAMUEL. Adm. sizar (age 17) at Caius, June 22, 1696. S. of John (1651), R. of Kennett, Cambs. B. there. Schools, Kennett and Bury. Scholar, 1696-1700; Matric. 1698; B.A. 1699-1700; M.A. 1724. Ord. deacon (Norwich) May 26, 1700; priest, Mar. 15, 1700-1. R. of Lidgate, Suffolk, 1701-40; of Little Bradley, 1724-40. R. of Barnardiston, 1724-40. Buried at Lidgate, Jan. 20, 1740-1. Brother of Richard (1686-7). Father of the next. (*Venn*, I. 498; *Suff. Man. Fam.*, III. 75.)

FAIRCLOUGH, SAMUEL. Adm. sizar (age 18) at Caius, Feb. 1726-7. S. of Samuel (above), R. of Lidgate, Suffolk. B. there. School, Bury. Matric. 1727; Scholar, 1727-32; B.A. 1730-1. Ord. deacon (Norwich) Sept. 19, 1731; priest, June 9, 1734. R. of Little Bradley, Suffolk, 1740. R. of Barnardiston, 1740-3. Buried at Little Bradley, Dec. 14, 1743. (*Venn*, II. 26.)

FARCLOGH, THOMAS. Gilbert Worthington, R. of St Andrew's, Holborn (*q.v.*) by will (P.C.C., 1477), left eight marks to Thomas Farclogh, of Cambridge University, to pray for his soul, etc. (Strype's *Stow*, III. 248; J. Ch. Smith.)

FARCLOUGH, WILLIAM. Adm. sizar (age 19) at Sidney, July 7, 1680. 1st s. of Thomas, yeoman. School, Holland, Lancs. Perhaps C. of Little Staughton, Beds., 1684. R. of Graffham, Hunts., 1689-1713; called 'B.A.' Died 1713. Father of the next.

FAIRCLOUGH, WILLIAM. Adm. sizar at Clare, May 30, 1715. S. of William, above. B. at Graffham, Hunts. Matric. 1715; B.A. 1719-20. Ord. deacon (Lincoln) June 12, 1720; priest, June 4, 1721. R. of Graffham, 1721-62. P.C. of Barham, Hunts., till 1762. Died 1762.

FAIRFAX, ARTHUR. Matric. pens. from Queens', Easter, 1615.

FAIRFAX, BARWICK. Adm. pens. (age 18) at Trinity, June 11, 1687. S. of Henry, 4th Baron Fairfax, and Francis, dau. of Sir Robert Barwick. B. at Denton, Yorks. Bapt. at Bramham, Oct. 18, 1667. School, Westminster. Matric. 1687; Scholar, 1689; B.A. 1690-1; M.A. 1694. Fellow, 1693. Incorp. at Oxford, 1700. Of Tadcaster, Yorks. Will proved at York, July 1, 1734. (*Al. Oxon.*)

FAIRFAX, BENJAMIN. Adm. at Corpus Christi, 1673. S. of John (1640), R. of Barking, Suffolk. School, Woodbridge. Adm. student at Leyden, May 27, 1676. Brother of Thomas (1674).

FAIRFAX, BLACKERBY. Adm. pens. at Corpus Christi, 1686. S. of Nathaniel (1655), of Woodbridge, Suffolk. Bapt. Feb. 16, 1668-9. School, Woodbridge. Matric. 1686; B.A. 1689-90; M.A. 1693; M.D. 1728 (*Com. Reg.*). Adm. medical student at Leyden. M.D. (Leyden) 1696. Appointed physician in the Navy. Author, miscellaneous. (*D.N.B.*)

FAIRFAX, BRIAN. Adm. pens. at Trinity, Apr. 8, 1648. 2nd s. of Henry (1602), R. of Bolton Percy. B. at Newton Kyme, Yorks., Oct. 6, 1633. School, Coxwold. Matric. 1648; Scholar, 1650; B.A. 1651-2; M.A. 1655. Incorp. M.A. (Oxford) 1663. Created D.C.L. (Oxford) 1677. Adm. at Gray's Inn, May 10, 1654. Barrister, 1661. Ancient, 1680. In 1658 he went to France with the Earl of Kildare. In 1659 he was sent on a mission to Monk, then in Scotland. Private Secretary to his cousin Lord Fairfax. Appointed equerry to Charles II, 1670-85; and afterwards to William III, 1689-94. Secretary to Archbishop Tillotson, till 1694; when he retired into private life, and devoted himself to literary work. Married, at Westminster Abbey, Apr. 22, 1675, Charlotte, dau. of Sir Edmund Carey. Author, *Iter Boreale*. Died Sept. 20, 1711. Father of Brian (1693) and Ferdinando (1694). (*D.N.B.*; M. H. Peacock.)

FAIRFAX, BRIAN. Adm. pens. (age 17) at TRINITY, June 28, 1693. S. of Brian (1648). B. in the Mews at Westminster, London, Apr. 11, 1676. School, Westminster. Scholar, 1694; Matric. 1695; B.A. 1696–7; M.A. 1700. Fellow, 1699. Commissioner of Customs, 1723–50. Lived in Panton Square, London. Antiquary. Died Jan. 7, 1749–50. Will, P.C.C. Brother of Ferdinando (1694). (*Misc. Gen. et Her.*, VI. 399; *D.N.B.*)

FAIRFAX, CECIL JACQUES. Adm. pens. (age 18) at ST JOHN'S, Ju 19, 1745. S. of George, clerk, of Lincolnshire. B. at Washingborough, Lincs. School, Beverley, Yorks. Matric. 1745; B.A. 1748–9; M.A. 1752. Fellow, 1752. Ord. deacon (York) June 10, 1750; priest (Lincoln) Dec. 22, 1751. V. of Marton and Grafton, Yorks., 1755–90. Died Oct. 22, 1790. Brother of George (1735). (*Scott-Mayor*, III. 552.)

FAIRFAX, CHARLES. Matric. pens. from CLARE, Easter, 1584. Probably s. of Sir Thomas, of Denton, Yorks. Knighted, May 11, 1603. Will (P.C.C.) 1604. (*Vis. of Yorks.*, 1665.)

FAIRFAX, CHARLES. Adm. pens. at TRINITY, Oct. 5, 1611. Of Menston, Yorks. 7th s. of Thomas (1577), 1st Baron Fairfax. B. at Denton, Mar. 5, 1597–8. Adm. at Lincoln's Inn, Oct. 27, 1611. Barrister, 1618. Appointed steward of the courts at Ripon, 1646. Colonel in Monk's army in Scotland. Governor of Kingston-upon-Hull, 1660. Antiquary and genealogist. Married, 1627, Mary Brearey, of Scow Hall. Died at Menston. Buried Dec. 22, 1673, at Otley. Brother of Henry (1602) and Peregrine (1618–9), father of Henry (1662). (*D.N.B.*; M. H. Peacock.)

FAIRFAX, CHARLES. Adm. pens. at CORPUS CHRISTI, 1690. Of Norfolk. Matric. Easter, 1691.

FAIRFAX, CHRISTOPHER. Adm. pens. at TRINITY, Apr. 2, 1640. Migrated to Trinity Hall. M.A. 1641–2 (on King's visit)

FAYRFAXE, EDWARD. Adm. pens. (age 15) at CAIUS, Oct. 6, 1580. 2nd s. of Henry, of Streetthorpe. Of Bilborough, Yorks. Schools, Coxwold, Yorks., and Pocklington. Brother of Gabriel (1579). (*Vis. of Yorks.*, 1584; *Venn*, I. 107.)

FARFAX, EDWARD. Matric. Fell.-Com. from CLARE, Lent, 1580–1.

FAIRFAX, FERDINANDO. Adm. pens. (age 16) at TRINITY, June 21, 1694. S. of Brian (1648). B. in the Mews at Westminster, June 11, 1678. School, Westminster. Matric. 1695; Scholar, 1695; B.A. 1697–8. Died Feb. 12, 1748–9. Brother of Brian (1693). (*D.N.B.*)

FAYRFAXE, GABRIEL. Adm. Fell.-Com. (age 16) at CAIUS, Oct. 17, 1579. Of Streetthorpe. Eldest s. of Henry, of Bilborough, Yorks. Schools, Copmanthorpe and Coxwold. Of Streetthorpe, Esq. Married Frances, dau. of Sir Brian Palmes, of Naburn. Brother of Edward (1580). (*Venn*, I. 104; *Vis. of Yorks.*, 1584.)

FAIRFAXE, GEORGE. Matric. pens. from CHRIST'S, Nov. 1553.

FARFAX, GEORGE. Matric. pens. from TRINITY, Michs. 1583; Scholar, 1586; B.A. 1587–8; M.A. 1591. Fellow, 1589.

FAIRFAX, GEORGE. Matric. Fell.-Com. from TRINITY HALL, Easter, 1667. Perhaps s. and h. of Joseph, late of Moulton, Lincs., Esq.; adm. at Gray's Inn, May 7, 1670.

FAIRFAX, GEORGE. Adm. sizar at JESUS, May 26, 1735. Of Yorkshire. S. of George, clerk, deceased, R. of Washingborough, Lincs. Matric. 1738; Scholar; B.A. 1738–9; M.A. 1745. Ord. deacon (Lincoln) Sept. 21, 1740. V. of Cropwell Bishop, Notts., 1744–50. R. of Elton, 1745–50. Brother of Cecil Jacques (1745). (A. Gray.)

FAIREFAX, HENRY. Matric. pens. from TRINITY, Lent, 1578–9.

FAIRFAX, HENRY. Matric. pens. from TRINITY, Michs. 1602. 4th s. of Thomas (1577). B. at Denton, Yorks., Jan. 14, 1588–9. Scholar, 1605; B.A. 1606–7; M.A. 1610. Fellow, 1608–16. Incorp. at Oxford, 1611. Ord. deacon (York) Sept. 1614; priest, Sept. 1616. R. of Ashton-under-Lyne, Lancs., 1619–33. R. of Newton Kyme, Yorks., 1633–46. Preb. of York, 1645–65. R. of Bolton Percy, 1646–60. Married, at St Helen's, York, Feb. 4, 1626–7, Mary, dau. of Sir Hugh Cholmey. Antiquary and genealogist. Retired to Oglethorpe, 1662. Died Apr. 6, 1665. Buried at Bolton Percy. Brother of Peregrine (1618–9) and Charles (1611), father of Brian (1648). (*Al Oxon.*; *D.N.B.*; M. H. Peacock.)

FAIRFAX, HENRY. Incorp. M.A. 1662, from Magdalen College, Oxford. S. of Charles (1611), of Menston, Yorks. Bapt. at Otley, Oct. 28, 1634. Matric. from Exeter College, Oxford, July 21, 1653; B.A. (Oxford) 1656–7; M.A. 1659, B.D. 1666; D.D. 1681. Fellow of Magdalen College, 1659–87, when he was ejected by James II; and 1688. R. of Tubney, Berks., 1683. Dean of Norwich, 1689–1702. Died Dec. 1702, aged 68. Buried in Norwich Cathedral. M.I. there. (*D.N.B.*; *Al. Oxon.*; Le Neve, *Mon.*, IV. 39.)

FAIRFAX, ISAAC. Adm. pens. at CLARE, July 29, 1650. Matric. 1650. Doubtless s. of Thomas, of Dunsley, near Whitby, Yorks.; age 32 in 1665. Succeeded at Dunsley. Of Thornton-in-Pickering, Esq. Married Catherine, dau. of James Herbert, of London. Buried at Ellerburn-in-Pickering, Aug. 1, 1687. (*Vis. of Yorks.*, 1665; M. H. Peacock.)

FAIRFAX, JOHN. Matric. sizar from CORPUS CHRISTI, Easter, 1640. Of Norfolk. S. of Benjamin, clerk, of Rumburgh, Suffolk. B.A. 1643–4; M.A. 1647. Fellow, 1645–50. V. of Barking, Suffolk, 1650; ejected, 1662. Suffered imprisonment in Bury gaol. Afterwards a preacher at Ipswich. Author, *Life of Owen Stockton*; *Sermons*, etc. Died at Barking, Aug. 11, 1700, aged 77. Father of Benjamin (1673) and Thomas (1674), brother of Nathaniel (1655). (*Calamy*, II. 409; *D.N.B.*; *Masters*, 281.)

FERFEX, MARK. Matric. pens. from TRINITY, Michs. 1611.

FAIRFAX, NATHANIEL. Matric. sizar from CORPUS CHRISTI, Easter, 1655. Of Suffolk. 3rd s. of Benjamin, clerk, of Rumburgh, Suffolk. B.A. 1657–8: M.A. 1661. Ord. deacon (Norwich) Sept. 1661. Ejected from Willisham, Suffolk, 1662. Studied medicine as a means of livelihood. M.D. (Leyden) 1670. Practised at Woodbridge, Suffolk. Married (1) Eliza Blackerby, (2) Elizabeth, widow of Francis Wade, and dau. of Nathaniel Bacon, of Ipswich. Author. Died June 12, 1690. Buried at Woodbridge. Brother of John (1640), father of Blackerby (1686). (*Calamy*, II. 442; *D.N.B.*; *Masters*, 283; V. B. Redstone.)

FAIRFAX, PEREGRINE. B.A. from TRINITY, 1618–9. S. of Thomas (1577), of Denton, Yorks. B. May 31, 1599. Secretary to the Earl of Carlisle, when Ambassador in France. Killed at Monslack, near Montauban, Sept. 1621. Brother of Henry (1602) and Charles (1611). (*Her. and Gen.*, VI. 401.)

FAIRFAX, ROBERT. Mus.Bac. 1500–1; Mus.Doc. 1504. Incorp. at Oxford, 1511. Of Acaster Malbis, Yorks. 4th s. of Sir Thomas, of Walton. Gentleman of the King's Chapel, 1509. Poor Knight of Windsor, 1514. Author of musical works, as early as 1485. Lived at Bayford, Herts. Organist or sacrist at St Albans Abbey. Buried there. Died 1529. Will (Archd. St Albans) 1529. (*Cooper*, I. 15; *D.N.B.*; J. Ch. Smith; M. H. Peacock.)

FAYREFAX, THOMAS. Matric. pens. from PEMBROKE, Michs. 1551. Ord. priest (Lincoln) Oct. 21, 1560; 'aged 41; married. resides; knows Latin competently' (*Lib. Cleri Linc.*, 1576). 'Bred in the Schools.' Doubtless R. of Hagworthingham, Lincs., 1571; and R. of Thorpe, till 1568.

FAIRFAX, THOMAS. Matric. sizar from QUEENS', Lent, 1557–8. B. at Bury, Suffolk. B.A. 1560–1; M.A. 1564; B.D. from St Catharine's, 1574–5. Fellow of St Catharine's, 1561. University preacher, 1569. V. of Sutton, Cambs., 1571–8. Preb. of Carlisle, 1578–95. R. of Gt Asby, Westmorland, 1578–93. R. of Lowther, 1579–86. R. of Caldbeck, Cumberland, 1583. Afterwards Chaplain to Dr Mathew, Bishop of Durham. (*Cooper*, II. 176.)

FAIRFAX, THOMAS. Matric. Fell.-Com. from QUEENS', Easter, 1577. Of Yorkshire. Probably s. of Sir Thomas, of Denton. B. 1560, at Bilborough, Yorks. Perhaps adm. at Lincoln's Inn, Oct. 22, 1579. Served in the Low Countries. Knighted at Rouen, 1591. M.P. for Yorks., 1625. Created Baron Fairfax of Cameron, in the Scotch Peerage, May 4, 1627. Died May 2, 1640. Buried at Otley, Yorks. Father of Henry (1602), Charles (1611), Peregrine (1618–9) and Thomas (1612–3). (*D.N.B.*; A. B. Beaven.)

FAIRFAX, THOMAS. Matric. pens. from QUEENS', Michs. 1587. Of Cambridgeshire. Probably s. of Thomas (1557–8). B.A. 1590–1; M.A. 1594. Succeeded his father as R. of Caldbeck, Cumberland; and died there, 1640. (B. *Nightingale*.)

FARFFAX, THOMAS. Adm. Fell.-Com. (age 15) at CAIUS, Dec. 8, 1590. Of Walton and Gilling, Yorks. S. of Sir William, Knt. B. at Gilling, Yorks. Bapt. Feb. 5, 1576–7. School, Gilling. Matric. *c.* 1591. Knighted, Apr. 17, 1603. M.P. for Boroughbridge, 1601; for Hedon, Yorks., 1624, 1625, 1626. Sheriff of Yorks., 1627–8. Created Viscount Fairfax of Emley in the peerage of Ireland, 1634. Died at Howsham, Yorks., Dec. 23, 1636. Buried at Scrayingham. M.I. there. Will (York) 1637. (*Venn*, I. 142; *G.E.C.*)

FAIRFAX, THOMAS. B.A. 1612–3 (on visit of Prince Charles). Perhaps s. of Thomas, 1st Baron Fairfax. If so, born at Denton, Aug. 4, 1594. Merchant adventurer. Died at Scanderoon, July 4, 1621. Brother of Peregrine (1618–9), Charles (1611) and Henry (1602). (*D.N.B.*; M. H. Peacock.)

FAIRFAX, THOMAS. Matric. sizar from CORPUS CHRISTI, Easter, 1621. Of Norfolk. B.A. 1624–5; M.A. 1628. Fellow, 1629–32. Ord. deacon (Peterb.) Dec. 21; priest, Dec. 22, 1627.

FAIRFAX, THOMAS. Adm. Fell.-Com. at ST JOHN'S, c. 1626. S. of Ferdinando, 2nd Lord Fairfax. B. at Denton, Yorks., Jan. 17, 1611-2. Matric. 1626; M.A. 1647; D.C.L. (Oxford) 1649. Adm. at Gray's Inn, May 26, 1628. Sent to the Low Countries under Sir Horace Vere. Present at the siege of Bois-le-Duc, 1629. Held a command during the first Scottish war. Knighted, Jan. 1640-1. Supported the parliament and became commander-in-chief of the parliamentary army, 1645-50. Defeated Charles I at Naseby, 1645. Remodelled the army. Succeeded his father as 3rd Baron Fairfax of Cameron, 1648. State Councillor, 1649-51 and 1659-60. M.P. for Cirencester, 1649; for West Riding of Yorkshire, 1654; for Co. Yorks., 1660. During the Protectorate, he lived in retirement at Nun Appleton, Yorks., and devoted himself to literature. Headed the commission sent to Charles II at The Hague, 1660. Author of poems, translations, and two autobiographical works. Died at Nun Appleton, Nov. 12, 1671. Buried at Bilborough. M.I. (*D.N.B.*)

FAIRFAX, THOMAS. Adm. pens. at TRINITY, Oct. 27, 1645. Of Yorkshire. Matric. 1646; Scholar, 1647; B.A. 1649-50. Incorp. at Oxford, 1651. M.A. (Oxford) 1652. Fellow of New College, 1650. Perhaps s. and h. of Charles (1611), of Menston, Yorks., adm. at Gray's Inn, Mar. 16, 1640-1. If so, born at Otley, July 26, 1628. J.P. for West Riding. Died 1716. (*Vis. of Yorks.*, 1666; *Al. Oxon.*; *Her. and Gen.*, VI. 400.)

FAIRFAX, THOMAS. Educated at ST JOHN'S. S. of Henry, 4th Baron Fairfax. B. at Bolton Percy, Feb. 16, 1657. Succeeded as Baron, Apr. 9, 1685. Colonel 5th Foot, 1690; 3rd Dragoons, 1694. Brigadier-General, 1702. M.P. for Malton, 1685; for Yorks., 1689-1702; Jan.-Dec. 1707. Benefactor to St John's. Died Jan. 6, 1709-10. Buried in St Martin-in-the-Fields. Brother of Barwick (1687). (*Founders and Benefactors*, 52; *Her and Gen.*, VI. 406; A. B. Beaven; *G.E.C.*)

FAIRFAX, THOMAS. Adm. at CORPUS CHRISTI, 1674. S. of John (1640), R. of Barking, Suffolk. School, Woodbridge. Brother of Benjamin (1673).

FAIRFAX, THOMAS. Adm. sizar (age 18) at ST JOHN'S, May 16, 1717. S. of William, husbandman, of Yorkshire. B. at Ruswarp. School, Thornton. Matric. 1717; B.A. 1721-2. Ord. deacon (London) June 4, 1721; priest, June 9, 1723. V. of Gt Canfield, Essex, 1723-31. R. of Little Easton, 1731-44. (*Scott-Mayor*, III. 311.)

FAIRFAX, WILLIAM. B.Can.L. 1516-7.

FAIRFAX, WILLIAM. Adm. Fell.-Com. (age 15) at CAIUS, May 19, 1576. S. of Gabriel, of Steeton, Yorks. School, Pickering. Adm. at Gray's Inn, 1578. Of Steeton, Esq. Knighted, Apr. 23, 1603. Died at Finningley, July 7, 1603. Buried at Bolton Percy. (*Venn*, I. 85.)

FAREFAX, WILLIAM. Matric. sizar from JESUS, Easter, 1611. Perhaps s. of Thomas, of Caldbeck, Cumberland. B.A. 1614-5; M.A. 1622; D.D. 1631-2 (on the King's visit). Perhaps incorp. at Oxford, 1622. Ord. deacon (York) Sept. 1620; priest, Sept. 1621. Probably V. of Castle Sowerby, Cumberland, 1623-46; and 1660-4. R. of Bolton Mealsgate, Carlisle, 1629-55, ejected; reinstated, 1660-5. Buried there May 2, 1665. (B. *Nightingale*; *Her. and Gen.*, vii. 149.)

FAIRFAX, WILLIAM. Matric. pens. from TRINITY, Easter, 1616; B.A. from St John's, 1620-1; M.A. 1624. Perhaps ord. deacon (Carlisle) Jan. 18, 1623-4. Dean of Sion College, London. Chaplain to Charles I. R. of St Peter Cornhill, London, 1626-55; sequestered and imprisoned during the Commonwealth. V. of East Ham, Essex, till 1642. Buried at Peter's, Cornhill, Nov. 20, 1655. Admon. (P.C.C.) 1656; as of St Martin-in-the-Fields. (J. Ch. Smith.)

FAIRFAX, WILLIAM. Matric. pens. from QUEENS', Michs. 1616. Of Cambridgeshire. B.A. from Clare, 1619-20. Perhaps incorp. at Oxford, 1624. (*Al. Oxon.* seems to confound him with the D.D., who was certainly of Jesus.)

FAIRFAX, WILLIAM. Matric. sizar from ST JOHN'S, Easter, 1625; B.A. 1627-8; M.A. 1633.

FAIRFAX, WILLIAM. Adm. pens. (age 17) at CHRIST'S, May 21, 1679. S. of William, of Steeton, Yorks. B. there. Bapt. in Steeton Chapel, Nov. 21, 1664. School, Wakefield (Mr Baskerville). Resided for a year. Buried at Bolton Percy, Yorks., July 20, 1694. M.I. (*Peile*, I. 72; *Her. and Gen.*, VI. 615.)

FAIRLIE, WILLIAM. Matric. sizar from CHRIST'S, c. 1593.

FAIRMEDOW, THOMAS. Adm. pens. (age 16) at CHRIST'S, Oct. 26, 1660. S. of Edward. B. at Molesworth, Hunts. School, Huntingdon (Mr Taylor). Matric. 1660; B.A. 1664-5; M.A. 1668. Fellow, 1668-94. Taxor, 1677. Senior Proctor, 1684-5. Incorp. at Oxford, 1680. R. of Anstey, Herts., 1694-1711. R. of Clapton, Northants., 1700-11. Died in Cambridge, June 15, 1711. Buried at Gt St Andrew's. M.I. (*Peile*, I. 594; Le Neve, *Mon.*, IV. 225.)

FAIRSIDE, *see* FARSIDE.

FAIRWEATHER, *see also* FAWETHER.

FAIRWEATHER, THOMAS. Adm. pens. (age 15) at SIDNEY, May 13, 1676. 1st s. of Edward, yeoman, of Barton, Hull. B. at Ferriby, Lincs. School, Cottingham, Yorks. (Mr Clerke). Matric. 1676; B.A. 1679-80. Ord. priest (Lincoln) June 11, 1682. V. of Gt Grimsby, 1690. R. of Scartho, 1711.

FAIRWELL, *see* FARWELL.

FAKE, JOHN. B.A. 1494-5; M.A. 1498.

FALCONBRIDGE, *see* FAUCONBERG.

FALCONER, *see* FAWCONER.

FALDER, JOHN. Adm. sizar (age 18) at QUEENS', Feb. 15, 1624-5. Perhaps s. of Thomas, of Alnwick, Northumberland, clerk. B.A. 1629-30. V. of Shilbottle, 1636-48 and 1660-73. V. of Leshury, 1666-73. Married Jane Forster, of Alnwick, 1635. Buried at Alnwick, Jan. 13, 1673. Probably brother of the next. (H. M. Wood.)

FALDER, THOMAS. Matric. sizar from QUEENS', Easter, 1621. Of Northumberland. B.A. 1624-5.

FALDO, ABRAHAM. Adm. sizar (age 24) at JESUS, Dec. 16, 1674. Of Bedfordshire. Matric. 1674-5; B.A. 1678-9. V. of Harrold, Beds., 1689-96. Buried there Dec. 4, 1696. M.I.

FALDO, CHARLES. Matric. pens. from KING'S, Michs. 1624; B.A. 1626-7; M.A. 1630. Master of Dulwich College, 1633. R. of Titchwell, Norfolk, 1642.

FALDOE, DAVID. Matric. sizar from TRINITY, Michs. 1571.

FALDO, DAVID. Matric. sizar from KING'S, Lent, 1660; B.A. 1663-4; M.A. 1667. Probably buried at Biddenham, Beds., Apr. 8, 1680; as David Faldoe, clerk.

FALDOWE, FRANCIS. Matric. pens. from ST CATHARINE'S, Easter, 1631.

FALDOE, JOHN. Matric. sizar from TRINITY, c. 1596; Scholar 1599; B.A. 1600-1; M.A. 1604. Fellow, 1602.

FALDOE, JOHN. Matric. sizar from KING'S, Michs. 1615.

FALDO, OSBERT. Matric. sizar from QUEENS', Michs. 1631. Of Bedfordshire. Doubtless s. of John, of Oakle ; bapt. June, 1611. B.A. 1634-5; M.A. 1638. Ord. priest (Peterb.) Sept. 19, 1641. Signs as minister of Odell, Beds., 1665-87. Buried at Oakley, July 22, 1687.

FALDO, PAUL. Adm. pens. (age 17) at SIDNEY, c. July, 1680. S. of William, tobacconist. B. at Bedford. Bapt. at St Paul's, Bedford, Feb. 22, 1662-3. School, Newmarket Street, Bedford (Mr Welburn and Mr Thomas). Matric. 1681; B.A. 1684-5; M.A. 1689. V. of Ravensden, Beds., 1688-1711. R. of St John the Baptist, Bedford, 1713; also Master of the Hospital. Died Apr. 12, 1714. M.I. in St John's Church. (*Victoria Co. Hist. Beds.*, III. 27.)

FALDOE, ROBERT. Matric. sizar from TRINITY, Easter, 1575.

FALDOE, ROBERT. Matric. pens. from PEMBROKE, Michs. 1583. Doubtless s. of Richard, of Maulden, Beds. Bapt. Jan. 22, 1566-7. Of 'Marledon' (Maulden), Beds., when adm. at Gray's Inn, Apr. 27, 1586. Ancient, 1603. Reader, 1620. (*Vis. of Beds.*, 1634.)

FALDOE, THOMAS. Matric. pens. from PEMBROKE, Easter, 1623. S. of Robert (? above), of Maulden, Beds. Of North Mymms, Herts. Adm. at Gray's Inn, Aug. 5, 1624. (*Vis. of Beds.*, 1634.)

FALDO, THOMAS. Adm. sizar at JESUS, Oct. 19, 1660. Of Bedfordshire. S. of Thomas, merchant taylor. B. at Byusham, Oxon., Aug. 12, 1646. School, Merchant Taylors'. Matric. 1661; B.A. 1664-5; M.A. 1668. Incorp. at Oxford, 1673. V. of Harrold, Beds., 1666-87. C. of Biddenham. Of Wymondley, Herts., in 1697. Buried at Biddenham, Oct. 21, 1716. (*Al. Oxon.*)

FAWLDO, WILLIAM. Matric. sizar from QUEENS', Easter, 1546.

FALDO, WILLIAM. Adm. at KING'S (age 17) a scholar from Eton, Aug. 24, 1590. Of Cardington, Beds. (Probably s. of Thomas.) B.A. 1594-5; M.A. 1598. Fellow, 1593-1601. Registrar to the Bishop of London. (*Harwood*.)

FALDO, WILLIAM. Adm. pens. (age 18) at CHRIST'S, June 10, 1624. S. and h. of William (1590), of Islington. B. at Essendon, Herts. School, Islington (Mr Dukeson). Matric. 1624. Adm. at Gray's Inn, May 7, 1624. Barrister, 1633. Ancient, 1654. He wrote a long Latin epitaph on Sir Thomas Adams, founder of the Arabic lectureship, for the Guildhall. (*Peile*, I. 360; *Vis. of Beds.*, 1634; Stow's *Strype*, I. 276.)

FALE, JAMES. Adm. scholar (age 17) at CAIUS, Mar. 31, 1619. S. of John (1584), minister. B. at Harleston, Norfolk. Matric. 1619; Scholar, 1622-3; B.A. 1622-3; M.A. 1627. Ord. deacon (Norwich) Dec. 18, 1625; priest, Sept. 20, 1628. C. of Spexhall, Suffolk, in 1627. V. of Fressingfield, 1629-43 and 1660-71. Married, at Fressingfield, June 18, 1632, Anne, dau. of Francis Woolnough. Buried there, Aug. 19, 1678. Father of John (1643-4). (*Venn*, I. 244.)

FALE, JOHN. Matric. pens. from CORPUS CHRISTI, Easter, 1584; B.A. 1587-8; M.A. 1591. R. of Roydon, Essex, 1585-1615. Probably R. of Stockton, Norfolk, 1610. Died 1615. Father of James (1619). (*Masters*.)

FALE, JOHN. Adm. pens. at CAIUS, Jan. 16, 1643-4. S. of James (1619), V. of Fressingfield, Suffolk. B. at Spexhall. School, Norwich (Mr Lovering). Matric. 1644; Scholar, 1644-8; B.A. 1647-8.

FALE, THEODORE. Adm. at CORPUS CHRISTI, 1609. Of Hertfordshire.

FALE, THOMAS. Adm. pens. (age 17) at CAIUS, Feb. 16, 1578-9. S. of James, yeoman, of Redgrave, Suffolk. School, Botesdale (Mr Bartholomew and Mr More). Matric. 1578-9; B.A. from Corpus Christi, 1582-3; M.A. 1586; B.D. 1597. Ord. deacon (London) Nov. 5, 1585; C. of Roydon, Essex. Licensed to practise medicine, 1604. Author, *Art of Dialling*. (*Venn*, I. 101; *Cooper*, II. 176; *D.N.B.*)

FALE, ——. B.D. from CHRIST'S, 1611. (*Peile*, I. 167.)

FALEYS, JOHN DE. Scholar at KING'S HALL, 1327-8.

FALHETT, *see* **FAWLET.**

FALKE, THOMAS, *see* **FAWKES.**

FALKENBRIDGE, *see* **FAUCONBERG.**

FALKER, HENRY. Fee for M.A. or higher degree, 1468-9. One of these names V. of Aylsham, Norfolk, 1484-9.

FALKES, ——, *see* **FAWKE, FAWKES** *and* **FOLKES.**

FALKINGHAM, *see also* **FOLKINGHAM.**

FALKINGHAM or FOLKINGHAM, ARTHUR. Matric. sizar from CHRIST'S, 1597-8. (Wrongly given as 'Anthony' by *Peile*.)

FALKINGHAM, ——. Fee for B.A. 1473-4.

FALKLAND, Viscount, *see* **CAREY, LUCIUS.**

FALL, JAMES. Incorp. D.D. from St Andrews, 1698. Canon residentiary and Precentor of York, 1691-1711. Principal of Glasgow University. Archdeacon of Cleveland, 1700-11. R. of Londesborough, Yorks., 1707-8. Buried June 13, 1711, in York Minster, aged 64. (M. H. Peacock.)

FALL, MICHAEL. Matric. sizar from TRINITY, Easter, 1582; B.A. 1586-7, as Faule. Will of one of these names (P.C.C.) 1648; of Eglaton, Rutland, clerk.

FALLE, PHILIP. M.A. 1687 (Incorp. from Oxford). S. of Thomas, of Jersey. Matric. from Exeter College, Oxford, Dec. 10, 1669, age 14; B.A. (Oxford) 1675-6 (?); M.A. 1676. R. of Holy Trinity, Jersey, 1681-7; of St Saviours, 1689-1709. Preb. of Brecon, 1689. Chaplain to the Duke of Portland, 1691. R. of Shenley, Herts., 1699-1742. Preb. of Durham, 1700-42. Author, *Accounts of Jersey*. Died May 7, 1742. (*D.N.B.*; *Al. Oxon.*)

FALL, THOMAS. Matric. sizar from ST JOHN'S, Easter, 1566. Perhaps V. of Flitton *with* Silsoe, Beds., 1580.

FALL, ——. Adm. sizar at ST CATHARINE'S, 1649.

FALLAN, WILLIAM. Resident pensioner at CORPUS CHRISTI, *c.* 1458. Third proctor, or master, of God's House, 1462. One of these names R. of Sible Hedingham, Essex, 1433-8. (*Peile*, I. 2.)

FALLAND, ——. Adm. at CORPUS CHRISTI, *c.* 1688. Of Nottinghamshire. B.A. 1691. (*Masters*.) Not found in the University records.

FALLOWFIELD, HENRY. Matric. sizar from ST JOHN'S, Easter, 1626. Of Westmorland. B.A. 1629-30; M.A. 1633. Fellow, 1633. R. of Uldale, Cumberland, 1647-65. Died 1665. Buried at Temple Sowerby, Westmorland, June 25. (*B. Nightingale*.)

FALLOWFIELD, ROBERT. Matric. sizar from QUEENS', Easter, 1606. Of Yorkshire.

FALLOWFYLDE, THOMAS. Matric. pens. from ST JOHN'S, Michs. 1554. B. in Westmorland. School, Sedbergh. Usher at Pocklington School, Yorks., 1577. Buried there Dec. 6, 1606. (*Sedbergh Sch. Register*.)

FALOWFYLD, THOMAS. Matric. pens. from ST JOHN'S, Michs. 1561.

FALMOUTH, Viscount, *see* **BOSCAWEN, HUGH.**

FALTER, WILLIAM. Adm. at CORPUS CHRISTI, 1690. Of Norwich.

FALTHROP, THOMAS. Matric. sizar from PETERHOUSE, Easter, 1610. B. at Giggleswick, Yorks. B.A. 1613-4; M.A. 1620. Ord. deacon (London) Dec. 2; priest, Dec. 22, 1616, age 25. C. of St Margaret Moses, London. R. of Little Berkhampstead, Herts., 1624-60. Died 1660.

FAME, EDMUND, *see* **FENN.**

FANCOURT, CHARLES. Adm. sizar (age 13) at TRINITY, Aug. 23, 1711. S. of John (? next), of Combroke, Warws., clerk. School, Combroke (Mr Gibbs). Matric. 1714. Brother of Richard (1706).

FANCOURT, JOHN. Adm. pens. (age 16) at MAGDALENE, Feb. 2, 1670-1. S. of Richard, gent., of Glaston, Rutland. School, Uppingham. Matric. 1671; B.A. 1674-5. Ord. deacon (Peterb.) Sept. 24, 1676; priest, Sept. 22, 1678. R. of Kimcote, Leics., 1713-25. Chaplain to Lord Willoughby. Perhaps R. of Combroke, Warws.; and father of the next and the above.

FANCOURT, RICHARD. Adm. sizar (age 15) at TRINITY, May 9, 1706. S. of John (? above), of Combroke, Warws., clerk. School, Combroke (Mr John Fancourt). Matric. 1709; B.A. 1714-5. Ord. priest (Lincoln) June 12, 1720. V. of Caxton, Cambs., 1728. Brother of Charles (1711).

FANCOURT or FANCOTES, THOMAS. Adm. pens. at EMMANUEL, June 1, 1627. Of Lincolnshire. Matric. 1627; B.A. 1630-1; M.A. from Peterhouse, 1634. Will (P.C.C.) 1655, of Thos. Fancourt, of Grantham, Lincs., clerk.

FANCOURT, WILLIAM. Adm. sizar at EMMANUEL, Apr. 18, 1727. Of Rutland. Matric. 1731; B.A. 1731-2. Ord. deacon (Lincoln) Sept. 24, 1732; priest, May 19, 1734. R. of South Luffenham, Ruts., 1734.

FANE, ANTHONY. Adm. Fell.-Com. at EMMANUEL, June 23, 1632. Of Kent. 3rd s. of Francis (1595), Earl of Westmorland. Matric. 1632; M.A. 1635 (*fil. nob.*). Elected M.P. for Peterborough, 1640, but return disallowed. Colonel in the Parliamentary Army; killed at the taking of Farnbam Castle, 1643; in the thirtieth year of his age. Brother of Francis (1631) and George (1632). (Collins' *Peerage*, III. 294.)

FANE, CHARLES (Lord DE LA SPENCER). Adm. Fell.-Com. at EMMANUEL, Sept. 18, 1649. S. of Mildmay (1618), Earl of Westmorland. B. Jan. 6, 1634-5. M.P. for Peterborough, 1660, 1661-6. Succeeded as 3rd Earl of Westmorland, 1666. Died Sept. 22, 1691. Half-brother of Henry (1662-3). (*G.E.C.*; J. B. Peace.)

FANE, EDWARD. Adm. pens. (age 18) at ST JOHN'S, June 11, 1695. 7th s. of Sir Francis (1653), K.B. B. at Henbury, near Bristol. Bapt. there, Nov. 13, 1676. School, Eton. Matric. 1695; B.A. 1698-9; M.A. 1702. Ord. deacon (Lincoln) May 26, 1700; priest, Mar. 16, 1700-1. R. of Fulbeck, Lincs., 1703-37. Preb. of Lincoln, 1731-7. Buried at Fulbeck, Feb. 19, 1736-7. Father of the next. (*Lincs. Pedigrees*; Collins' *Peerage*, III. 302; H. I. Longden.)

FANE, EDWARD. Adm. pens. at EMMANUEL, June 19, 1727. S. of Edward (above), R. of Fulbeck, Lincs. B. May 13, 1709. Matric. 1727; B.A. 1730-1; M.A. 1734. Ord. deacon (Lincoln) Mar. 5, 1731-2; priest, May 20, 1733. R. of Fulbeck, 1737-60. Died Feb. 23, 1760. (*Lincs. Pedigrees*.)

FANE, FRANCIS. Matric. Fell.-Com. from QUEENS', *c.* 1595. S. of Sir Thomas. Adm. at Lincoln's Inn, Nov. 19, 1597. M.P. for Kent, 1601; for Maidstone, 1604, 1614 and 1620; for Peterborough, 1624. K.B. 1603. Created Baron Burghersh and Earl of Westmorland, 1624. Died Mar. 23, 1628-9. M.I. in Mereworth Church, Kent. Father of the next, Anthony (1632) and George (1632). (Collins' *Peerage*, III. 294; *D.N.B.* under 'Thomas'; *G.E.C.*)

FANE, FRANCIS. M.A. from ST JOHN'S, 1631 (*fil. nob.*). Of Fulbeck, Lincs. 3rd s. of Francis (above), 1st Earl of Westmorland. K.B. 1636. Governor of Doncaster. F.R.S. 1663. Died 1680, aged 68. M.I. at Fulbeck. Father of Francis (1653) and brother of Anthony (1632) and George (1632). (Collins' *Peerage*, III. 291; *Vis. of Yorks.*, 1666.)

FANE, FRANCIS. Adm. Fell.-Com. at EMMANUEL, May 27, 1653. Of Yorkshire. S. and h. of Sir Francis (1631). Adm. at Gray's Inn, Nov. 18, 1655. K.B. 1661, at the Coronation of Charles II. Of Henbury, Gloucs. Dramatist. Buried at Westbury, Gloucs., Apr. 8, 1691. Will proved, 1691. Father of Edward (1695), brother of Henry (1657-8). (*Vis. of Yorks.*, 1666; *D.N.B.*)

FANE, FRANCIS. Adm. Fell.-Com. at ST JOHN'S, June 17, 1714. S. of Francis, Esq., of Fulbeck, Lincs. B. there. Matric. 1714. Died at Cressy Hall, Lincs., Oct 19, 1758. (*Lincs. Pedigrees*; *G. Mag.*)

FANE, FRANCIS. Matric. Fell.-Com. from KING'S, Easter, 1715. Doubtless s. of Henry, and grandson of Sir Francis, of Fulbeck. Adm. at the Middle Temple, Apr. 8, 1714. One of His Majesty's Counsel at law, 1725; and standing Counsel to the Board of Trade and Plantations. M.P. for Taunton, 1727-41; for Petersfield, 1741-7; for Ilchester, 1747-54; for Lyme Regis, 1754-7. Died May 28, 1757, aged 59. Buried at Lewknor, Oxon. (Collins' *Peerage*, III. 303; A. B. Beaven.)

FANE, GEORGE. Matric. Fell.-Com. from QUEENS', c. 1595. Of Burston, Kent. 2nd s. of Sir Thomas. Adm. at Lincoln's Inn, Nov. 19, 1597. Knighted, July 23, 1603. M.P. for Dover, 1601 and 1614; for Sandwich, 1604-11; for Kent, 1620-2; for Maidstone, 1624, 1626, 1628 and 1640. Died June 26, 1640, aged 59. Will, P.C.C. (Collins' *Peerage*, III. 293.)

FANE, GEORGE. Adm. Fell.-Com. at EMMANUEL, June 23, 1632. Of Northamptonshire. 5th s. of Francis (1595), Earl of Westmorland. Matric. 1632; M.A. 1635 (*fil. nob.*). M.P. for Callington, 1640; for Wallingford, Berks., 1661. Died 1663.

FANE or VANE, HENRY. M.A. 1612-3 (on visit of Prince Charles). Of Raby Castle, Durham. S. of Henry, of Hadlow, Kent. Matric. from Brasenose College, Oxford, June 15, 1604, age 15. Adm. at Gray's Inn, Mar. 15, 1605-6. Knighted. Mar. 14, 1610-1. M.P. for Lostwithiel, 1614 (also elected 1620, 1625); for Carlisle, 1620-2 and 1624-6; for Thetford, 1628; for Wilton, 1640; and for Kent, 1654-5. Secretary of State, 1640. Died May, 1655. (*Al. Oxon.*)

FANE, HENRY. Adm. pens. at EMMANUEL, Feb. 9, 1657-8. Of Northamptonshire. 3rd s. of Sir Francis (1631). Adm. at Gray's Inn, Jan. 10, 1656-7. Barrister, 1667. Ancient, 1680. Died Nov. 27, 1686. M.I. at Fulbeck. Brother of Francis, 1653. (*Lincs. Pedigrees.*)

FANE, HENRY. Adm. Fell.-Com. at EMMANUEL, Feb. 1662-3. S. of Mildmay (1618), Earl of Westmorland. His brother Vere had arranged to come up with him, but the plan fell through. Half-brother of Charles (1649). (J. B. Peace.)

FANE, HENRY. Adm. pens. at EMMANUEL, July 23, 1691. Of Northamptonshire.

FANE, HENRY. Adm. Fell.-Com. at EMMANUEL, Apr 20, 1732. Of Middlesex.

FANE, JOHN. Matric. pens. from CLARE, Michs. 1580; B.A. 1584-5; M.A. 1588.

FANE, JOHN. M.A. 1612-3 (on visit of Prince Charles).

FANE, JOHN. Adm. Fell.-Com. at EMMANUEL, Mar. 10, 1703-4. Of Mereworth Castle, Kent. S. of Vere, 4th Earl of Westmorland. Matric. 1704. Adm. at Lincoln's Inn, June 21, 1703. M.P. for Hythe, 1708-11; for Kent, 1715-22; for Buckingham, 1727-34. Created Baron Catherlough (Ireland), 1733. Succeeded as 7th Earl, July, 1736. High Steward of Oxford University, 1754; Chancellor, 1759-62. General in the Army, 1761. Died Aug. 26, 1762. (*D.N.B.*; Collins' *Peerage*, III. 299.)

FANE, MILDMAY. Matric. Fell.-Com. from EMMANUEL, Michs. 1618. S. of Francis (1595), Earl of Westmorland. M.A. 1619 (*fil. nob.*). Adm. at Lincoln's Inn, Aug. 7, 1622. M.P. for Peterborough, 1620-2, 1626, 1628-9; and for Kent, 1625. K.B. Feb. 1, 1625-6. Succeeded as 2nd Earl, 1629. Fined and sequestered by Parliament, 1642. Lord Lieutenant of Northamptonshire, 1660. Died Feb. 12, 1665. Left manuscript poems. Father of Charles (1649) and Henry (1662). (*D.N.B.*)

FANE, RALPH. Matric. pens. from CHRIST'S, Dec. 1606, as 'Phenne.' Adm. Fell.-Com. 1606-7. (*Peile*, I. 262.)

FANE, ROBERT. Adm. Fell.-Com. at EMMANUEL, Apr. 30, 1639. 7th s. of the Earl of Westmorland. Matric. 1639; M.A. 1640 (*fil. nob.*).

FANE, THOMAS. Adm. at CHRIST'S, 1618; B.A. 1619-20; M.A. 1623; D.D. 1640. Of Kent. Previously matric. from Jesus College, Oxford, 1616. Ord. deacon (Peterb.) Apr. 22; priest, Apr. 23, 1621. One of these names R. of Albourne, Sussex, 1622-9; R. of Crayford, Kent, 1626-43. Died Sept. 1692, aged 90. (*Peile*, I. 312; H. I. Longden.)

FANE, WILLIAM. Adm. Fell.-Com. at EMMANUEL, 1636. Matric. 1637; B.A. 1639-40.

FANE, WILLIAM. Adm. Fell.-Com. at QUEENS', Apr. 11, 1642. 6th s. of Francis, Earl of Westmorland. M.A. 1642; D.D. 1662. Ord. priest (Peterb.) Sept. 25, 1642. Preb. of Wells, 1661-79. R. of Huntspill, Somerset, 1662-79. Died 1679.

FAN or FAMME, EDWARD. B.A. 1522-3; M.A. 1526; B.D. 1546-7. Fellow of CORPUS CHRISTI, in 1547 (perhaps from 1531). Minister of St Benet's, Cambridge, 1551-70. Will proved (V.C.C.) 1570.

FAN, JOHN. B.A. 1468-9; M.A. 1471.

FANN, JOHN. Matric. pens. from ST JOHN'S, Easter, 1551.

FANN, NICHOLAS. Matric. pens. from PEMBROKE, Michs. 1589.

FANN, OWEN. Adm. pens. (age 16) at ST JOHN'S, May 7, 1675. S. of Owen, of Bodsey, near Ramsey, Hunts. B. there. School, Offord-Cluny. Matric. 1675; M.B. 1680-1.

FANNYNGE, THOMAS. Matric. sizar from MAGDALENE, Easter, 1548.

FANSHAWE, CHARLES. Adm. Fell.-Com. (age 17) at CHRIST'S, Apr. 26, 1663. S. of Thomas, Viscount Fanshawe of Dromore. School, Westminster. Matric. 1663; M.A. 1665 (*fil. nob.*). Adm. at the Inner Temple, Mar. 17, 1663-4. Succeeded as 4th Viscount, 1688. M.P. for Michael, Cornwall, 1689. Died Mar. 28, 1710. Buried at Ware. (*D.N.B.*; *Peile*, I. 602; *Cussans*, I. 139; *G.E.C.*)

FANSHAWE, HENRY. Matric. Fell.-Com. from PETERHOUSE, Michs. 1581. S. of Thomas (of Jesus), of Ware, Herts. B.A. from Jesus, 1584-5; 1st in the *ordo*. Adm. at the Inner Temple, 1586. M.P. for Westbury, Wilts., 1588 and 1593; for Boroughbridge, Yorks., 1597. King's Remembrancer of the Exchequer, 1601-16. Inherited Ware Park, Herts., 1601. Knighted, May 7, 1603. Horticulturist and Italian scholar. Buried at Ware, Mar. 12, 1615-6. Will (P.C.C.) 1616. Father of Richard (1623) and Simon (1620), and brother of Thomas (1589-90). (Burke, *Ext. Bart.*; *Vis. of Essex*; *D.N.B.*)

FANSHAWE, JOHN. Matric. Fell.-Com. from QUEENS', Easter, 1618. Of London. Perhaps s. of William, of Dagenham, Essex, Esq. B.A. 1620-1; M.A. 1624. Incorp. at Oxford, 1624. (*Vis. of Essex*, 1612.)

FANSHAWE, LIONEL. Matric. pens. from QUEENS', Easter, 1616. Of Derbyshire. Will of one of these names (P.C.C.) 1656; of Dronfield, Derbs., Esq.

FANSHAWE, RICHARD. Adm. Fell.-Com. at JESUS, Nov. 12, 1623. 5th s. of Sir Henry (1581), of Ware Park, Herts. B. there, 1608. School, Cripplegate. Adm. at the Inner Temple, Jan. 22, 1626. Appointed secretary to Lord Aston, English Ambassador to Spain, 1635-8. A zealous royalist. Treasurer of the Royalist Navy, 1648. Created Baronet, 1650. Taken prisoner at the battle of Worcester, 1651. Master of Requests and Latin secretary to Prince Charles at the Hague, 1660. Knighted, Apr. 1660. M.P. for Cambridge University, 1661-6. Privy Councillor of Ireland, 1662. Ambassador to Portugal, 1662-3. Privy Councillor, 1663. Ambassador to Spain, 1664-6. An accomplished linguist and scholar; his works include poems and translations. Died at Madrid, June 16, 1666. Buried in St Mary's Chapel, Ware. (*D.N.B.*; *G.E.C.*)

FANSHAWE, SIMON. Adm. pens. at JESUS, Sept. 23, 1620. Matric. Fell.-Com. 1621. Of London. 3rd s. of Sir Henry (1581), of Ware Park, Herts. Adm. at Lincoln's Inn, Oct. 18, 1623. Knighted, Feb. 11, 1640-1. Died Mar. 1680. Buried at Ware. Brother of Richard (1623). (Burke. *Ext. Bart.*; Cussans, *Pedigree*, I. 135.)

FANSHAWE, THOMAS. Of JESUS College. S. of John, of Dronfield, Derbs. Adm. at the Middle Temple, Jan. 23, 1570-1. Queen's Remembrancer of the Exchequer, 1568. Of Ware Park, Herts., and Jenkins, Barking, Essex. M.P. for Arundel, 1572, 1584, 1588, 1593; for Much Wenlock, 1597-8. Established the Free Grammar School of Dronfield, 1579. Author, legal. Died Feb. 19, 1600-1. Will, P.C.C. Father of Henry (1581) and Thomas (1589-90). (*Cooper*, II. 295; *D.N.B.*; *Cussans*, I. 135.)

FANSHAWE, THOMAS. Adm. pens. at QUEENS', Mar. 2, 1589-90. Of London, and of Jenkins, Barking. 2nd s. of Thomas (above), of Ware Park. B.A. 1595-6. Adm. at the Inner Temple, 1595. Barrister, 1606. Bencher, 1614. Knighted, Sept. 19, 1624. K.B. Feb. 1, 1625-6. Surveyer-General of Crown Lands. M.P. for Bedford, 1601; for Launceston. 1604-11, 1614, 1620-2, 1624-5, 1626, 1628-9. Died Dec. 12, 1631. Brother of Henry (1581), father of the next. (*D.N.B.*; *Vis. of Essex*, 1612; A. B. Beaven.)

FANSHAWE, THOMAS. Matric. Fell.-Com. from TRINITY, Easter, 1622. 1st s. of Thomas (above), of Jenkins, Barking, Essex. B. 1607. M.A. 1624 (*Lit. Reg.*). Adm. at the Inner Temple, 1620. Barrister, 1630. Bencher. M.P. for Preston, 1626; for Launceston, 1640-2. Died 1651. Will (P.C.C.) 1652. (*Cussans*, I. 139; A. B. Beaven.)

FANSHAWE, THOMAS. 2nd Viscount Fanshawe of Dromore. M.A. of TRINITY (according to *D.N.B.*; probably a confusion with the above).

FANSHAWE, WALTER. Adm. Fell.-Com. at EMMANUEL, Mar. 9, 1587-8. S. of Thomas. B. 1575. His mother, Mary Bourchier, was a niece of Sir Walter Mildmay, founder of Emmanuel. Matric. 1588. Adm. at the Middle Temple, Nov. 25, 1590. Died before 1593. (J. B. Peace.)

FANT, WILLIAM Matric. Fell.-Com. from JESUS, c. 1594.

FARAM or PHARAM, RICHARD. Matric. sizar from ST JOHN'S, c. 1596; B.A. 1600-1. Ord. deacon (Lincoln) Sept. 23, 1604 priest, Sept. 21, 1606. V. of Legsby, Lincs., 1612-9.

FARBECK, CUTHBERT. B.A. from PETERHOUSE, 1593-4; M.A. 1600; M.D. 1616.

FARBECKE, WILLIAM. Matric. pens. from PETERHOUSE, Michs. 1572; B.A. 1576-7; M.A. 1580; M.D. 1589. Fellow, 1580. Taxor, 1584-5.

FARBOCK, THOMAS. Matric. sizar from ST JOHN'S, Easter, 1607; B.A. 1610-1; M.A. 1614. V. of Ketton, Rutland, 1614.

FARDYN, JOHN. Matric. sizar from TRINITY, Michs. 1579.

FARELES, WILLIAM. Adm. sizar (age 18) at SIDNEY, Apr. 1621. S. of John. B. at Sedgefield, Durham. Bapt. May 3, 1602. School, Durham Cathedral. Matric. 1621. Buried at Sedgefield, Sept. 20, 1624.

FAREWELL, *see* **FARWELL.**

FARLEY, EDMUND. B.Civ.L. 1533-4.

FARLEY, RICHARD. LL.B. 1534; LL.D. 1547. (*Grace Bk.* Δ, 44.)

FARLEY, SAMUEL. Adm. at KING'S (age 18), a scholar from Eton, June 26, 1637. Of Cambridge. B.A. 1641; M.A. 1644. Fellow, 1640-51. Buried at St Edward's, Cambridge, Aug. 23, 1651. Will proved (V.C.C.).

FARLOW, HUMPHREY. Adm. pens. at PETERHOUSE, June 2, 1595; Ferrely.

FARM, JOHN. Resident pensioner at CORPUS CHRISTI, 1481.

FARMAN, THOMAS. B.A. 1511-2. *See* Forman.

FARMAR, ANTHONY. Adm. sizar (age 15) at SIDNEY, June 25, 1650. S. of Laurence, Esq. B. at Uppingham, Rutland. School, Stamford (Mr Humphry). Matric. 1650; B.A. 1653-4. R. of Morborn, Hunts., 1661-70. Died 1670.

FARMER, ANTHONY. Adm. pens. (age 14) at ST JOHN'S, Aug. 14, 1672. S. of John, of Frolesworth, Leics. B. there. Matric. 1673. Migrated to Trinity, Dec. 27, 1675. Scholar, 1676; B.A. 1676-7; M.A. 1680. Incorp. at Magdalen Hall, Oxford, 1680. The papist, intruded as Master at Magdalen College, Oxford, but rejected by the fellows. Brother of Henry (1672). (*D.N.B.*)

FARMER, BENJAMIN. Adm. sizar (age 20) at ST JOHN'S, Feb. 15, 1682-3. Colleger at Eton, 1672-81. S. of Hatton, attorney, deceased. B. at Northampton. Matric. 1683.

FARMER, EDWARD. Adm. pens. (age 18) at CAIUS, Oct. 8, 1650. S. of George, of Holbeach, protonotary of the Common Pleas. B. in London. Schools, Cobham, Surrey (Mr Goldwyre) and Cheam (Mr Aldrich). Matric. 1650. Adm. at the Inner Temple, June 24, 1652. Knighted, July 14, 1660. Died before May 30, 1706. Father of Edward (1685-6). (*Venn*, I. 379; *Lincs. Pedigrees*; Le Neve, *Knights*.)

FARMER, EDWARD. Matric. pens. from ST CATHARINE'S, Easter, 1658; B.A. 1663; M.A. 1667. Signed for deacon's orders (London) Sept. 19, 1668; C. of Nursling, Hants. One of these names P.C. of Codsall, Staffs., in 1676.

FARMER, EDWARD. Adm. pens. (age 16) at CAIUS, Jan. 9, 1685-6. S. of Sir Edward (1650), Knt., and Lady Margaret, of Gt Parndon, Essex. B. there, Dec. 21, 1669. Schools, Ware and St Paul's. Matric. 1686-7. Adm. at the Inner Temple, Dec. 4, 1685. Living in London, 1700. (*Venn*, I. 480; *Lincs. Pedigrees*.)

FARMER, EDWARD. Adm. pens. at EMMANUEL, Apr. 1, 1692. Of Middlesex. One of these names, s. and h. of Edward, of Oldbury, Warws., Esq., deceased, adm. at the Inner Temple, June 11, 1695. (*See Al. Oxon.* for a contemporary.)

FARMER, EDWARD. Adm. at CORPUS CHRISTI, 1716. Of Middlesex. B.A. 1719-20; M.A. 1723. Ord. deacon (Lincoln) Mar. 5, 1720-1; priest (Norwich) May, 1722. R. of Gt Ryburgh, Norfolk, 1722. R. of Twyford, 1730-40.

FARMER, GEORGE. Adm. pens. (age 17) at TRINITY, Oct. 31, 1683. S. of George, of Ratcliffe, near Atherstone, Warws. B. at Westhorpe, Lincs. School, Coventry (Mr Samuel Frankline). In 1684 he became for a short time a member of Pembroke. Matric. from Trinity, 1685; Scholar, 1687; B.A. 1687-8; M.A. 1691. Ord. priest (Lincoln) Sept. 21, 1689. V. of Heversham, Westmorland, 1691-1724. Buried at Heversham, Feb. 7, 1723-4. (*Vis. of Warwickshire*, 1682; B. *Nightingale*.)

FARMER, HENRY. Adm. pens. (age 16) at ST JOHN'S, Aug. 14, 1672. S. of John, gent., of Slatemore, Bucks. B. there. Educated at home. Matric. 1673. Brother of Anthony (1672).

FARMER, HENRY MAIDSTONE. Adm. sizar at QUEENS', Apr. 11, 1751. Of Essex.

FARMER, JAMES. Adm. sizar (age 17) at ST JOHN'S, Oct. 27, 1634. S. of James, gent., of Aston, Leics. B. at Hugglescote Grange, Leics. School, Coventry (Mr White). Matric. 1634; B.A. 1638-9; M.A. 1642. V. of Leire, Leics., 1659; ejected, 1662; survived but a few years. (*Nichols*, IV. 243.)

FARMER, JOHN. Adm. pens. at CAIUS, Oct. 23, 1652. S. of Ralph, of Baddesley, Warws. Schools, Alveston (Mr Perkins) and Coventry (Dr Bryan). Matric. 1652. Already adm. at Peterhouse, July 2, 1652. Ord. deacon and priest (Lichfield) July 13, 1662. V. of Hanbury, Staffs., 1672-6; 'B.A.' Buried there Apr. 6, 1676. (*Wm. Salt Arch. Soc.*, 1915; *Vis. of Warws.*, 1684.)

FARMER, JOHN. Adm. at CORPUS CHRISTI, 1667. Of Northamptonshire.

FARMER, JOHN. Adm. sizar at CLARE, May 16, 1683. Of Leicestershire. Matric. 1686; B.A. 1686-7. Ord. priest (Lincoln) Mar. 5, 1698-9. Will of one of these names (Leicester) 1730; of Stoke Golding, Leics., clerk. Probably father of the next.

FARMER, JOHN. Adm. sizar (age 19) at MAGDALENE, June 29, 1710. S. of John (? above), clerk. B. at Bedston, Salop. School, Shrewsbury. Matric. 1710.

FARMER, JOHN. Adm. sizar at MAGDALENE, Mar. 24, 1738-9. S. of John, clerk. School, Shrewsbury. Matric. 1739; B.A. 1742-3.

FARMER, JOSEPH. Matric. pens. from QUEENS', Michs. 1615. Of Leicestershire. B.A. 1618-9; M.A. 1622. Ord. deacon (Peterb.) Sept. 20; priest, Sept. 21, 1623. R. of Glenfield, Leics., 1630.

FARMER, RALPH. Matric. Fell.-Com. from QUEENS', Easter, 1594. Of Norfolk. Probably brother of William (1594).

FARMER, RALPH. Licensed to practise medicine, 1638.

FARMER, RICHARD. Matric. pens. from PETERHOUSE, Easter, 1558.

FARMER, RICHARD. Matric. sizar from TRINITY, Easter, 1573; Scholar, 1578; B.A. 1578-9; M.A. 1582. Will of one of these names (P.C.C. 1619); R. of Holt, Worcs.

FARMER, RICHARD. Matric. pens. from PEMBROKE, c. 1593; B.A. 1596-7; M.A. 1600. Elected 'tanquam socius,' 1601. Incorp. at Oxford, 1600. Master of Nuneaton Grammar School, 1610. R. of Charwelton, Northants., 1613. V. of Daventry. Buried there, Feb. 27, 1648-9. (Henry Farmer of Daventry; will, P.C.C. 1608; had a s. Richard.) (J. Ch. Smith; *Al. Oxon.*)

FARMER, RICHARD. M.A. of CORPUS CHRISTI, 1609. (*Masters.*) Not found in the records.

FARMOR, RICHARD. Adm. sizar (age 17) at CHRIST'S, June 23, 1670. S. of Richard. B. at Repton, Derbs. School, Repton (Mr Sedgwick). Matric. 1673; B.A. 1673-4. Ord. deacon (Lichfield) Sept. 1675. (*Peile*, II. 30.)

FARMAR, ROBERT. Matric. sizar from ST JOHN'S, Easter, 1578. One of these names R. of Sutton Bonnington, St Anne, Notts., 1593.

FARMER, ROGER. Adm. sizar at EMMANUEL, Apr. 13, 1633. Of Leicestershire. Scholar from Market Bosworth School. Matric. 1633; B.A. 1636-7; M.A. 1640. V. of Alstonefield, Staffs., 1675-83. Buried Mar. 17, 1682-3. (*Wm. Salt Arch. Soc.*, 1915.)

FARMER, SAMUEL. Adm. sizar (age 17) at MAGDALENE, June 30, 1687. S. of John, gent. B. at Westlope, Salop. School, Knighton, Radnor. Matric. 1687.

FARMER, SETH. Adm. sizar at EMMANUEL, 1623. Matric. Michs. 1623.

FARMER, THOMAS. B.A. from ST JOHN'S, 1575-6.

FARMER, THOMAS. Adm. pens. at EMMANUEL, June 2, 1647. Of Leicestershire. School, Market Bosworth. Matric. 1647; Scholar; B.A. 1650. One of these names V. of Ashby Ledgers, Northants., 1665-84.

FARMER, THOMAS. Adm. pens. at EMMANUEL, Apr. 9, 1660.

FARMER, THOMAS. Mus.Bac. 1684. Originally one 'of a company of musitians in London and played in the waytes' (Wood, *MS. Notes*, Bodleian). Contributed to musical collections; published 'consorts,' 1686, 1690. Purcell wrote an elegy upon him. Died before Nov. 1695. (*D.N.B.*)

FARMER, WILLIAM. Matric. sizar from CHRIST'S, Easter, 1546. One of these names minor canon of St Paul's, 1561; sub-dean, 1576-80. (*Peile*, I. 39.)

FARMER, WILLIAM. Matric. Fell.-Com. from QUEENS', Easter, 1594. Of Norfolk. Probably brother of Ralph (1594).

FARMER, WILLIAM. Matric. pens. from CHRIST'S, Easter, 1610; B.A. 1612-3; M.A. 1616. One of these names R. of West Deeping, Lincs., 1618-32.

FARMER, ——. Adm. pens. at ST CATHARINE'S, Easter, 1656.

FARMERYE, FRANCIS. Matric. pens. from PETERHOUSE, Easter, 1566.

FARMERY, GEORGE. Matric. pens. from MAGDALENE, Easter, 1637; B.A. 1640-1. Ord. deacon (Peterb.) Sept. 19, 1641.

FARMERRY, GEORGE. Adm. pens. at EMMANUEL, May 16, 1678. Of Lincolnshire. Perhaps s. of George, of Northope. Bapt. there, Aug. 12, 1660. Buried Oct. 14, 1696. (*Lincs. Pedigrees*, 348.)

FARMERY, JOHN. Scholar of QUEENS', 1533-8; B.A. 1536-7; M.A. 1540; B.D. 1560. B. c. 1506. Ord. priest (Philadelphia, Suffragan of Lincoln) 1538. R. of Blyborough, Lincs. R. of Grayingham.

FARMERY, JOHN. Matric. pens. from KING'S, Michs. 1561. Of Lincolnshire. B.A. 1564-5; M.A. 1568. Candidate of College of Physicians, 1587; fellow, 1589. M.D. of Leyden. Assisted in drawing up formulae for the 'Pharmacopoeia.' Died 1590. Will, P.C.C.; of Alderbert St, London. His widow, Ann, married Edward Lister, M.D. (*Cooper*, II. 98; *D.N.B.*; *Munk*, I. 96.)

FARMERIE or FURMERY, JOHN. Matric. sizar from CHRIST'S, Easter, 1565. Perhaps s. of William, of Northrop, Lincs. B.A. 1568-9; M.A. 1572; B.D. 1579. Fellow of St Catharine's, c. 1572. University preacher, 1575. Preb. of Lincoln, 1580-1610. Archdeacon of Stow, 1582-1610. Probably V. of Aylsham, Norfolk; and R. of Beeston, 1590-1603. Died Aug. 4, 1610. Buried in Aylsham Church. M.I. there. Will (P.C.C.) 1610; Furmary. Probably father of the next. (*Cooper*, III. 25; *Peile*, I. 92.)

FARMERY or FURMARY, JOHN. Matric. sizar from PETERHOUSE, Easter, 1607, as Furman. Probably s. of John (above). B.A. 1610-1; M.A. 1614; B.D. 1621. R. of Beeston Regis, Norfolk, 1622.

FARMERY, JOHN. Matric. pens. from ST JOHN'S, Easter, 1607. S. of William (1577-8), R. of Heapham. Bapt. at Springthorpe, Feb. 24, 1590-1. B.A. 1610-1; M.A. 1614; LL.D. 1620. Admitted advocate, May 6, 1637. Incorp. at Oxford, 1618; and, as LL.D., 1624. Chancellor of Lincoln Diocese. M.P. for Lincoln, Apr. 1640. Died 1647. Will proved, Feb. 1647-8. Probably brother of William (1611). (*Lincs. Pedigrees*, 346.)

FARMERIE, JOHN. Adm. pens. (age 15) at MAGDALENE, May 11, 1667. S. of William, gent. School, Lincoln. Matric. 1667; B.A. 1670-1; M.A. 1674. Incorp. at Oxford, 1674. V. of Kingerby, Lincs., 1674. R. of Broxholme, 1690. Preb. of Lincoln, 1700-14. Died 1714. (*Al. Oxon.*)

FARMERY, JOHN. Adm. sizar at JESUS, Oct. 27, 1737. Of Normanton, Notts. Matric. 1737.

FARMERY, ROBERT. Adm. sizar (age 17) at ST JOHN'S, Feb. 13, 1716-7. S. of William (1681), R. of Heapham and Blyton, Lincs. B. at Blyton. School, Westminster. B.A. 1720-1; M.A. 1739. Ord. deacon (Lincoln) June 4, 1721; priest (York) Dec. 22, 1723. R. of Heapham, Lincs., 1727-66. R. of Broxholme, 1739-66. Chaplain to Lord Monson. (*Scott-Mayor*, III. 308; *Lincs. Pedigrees*, I. 345.)

FARMARIE, WILLIAM. Adm. scholar (age 16) at CAIUS, Feb. 12, 1577-8. S. of Nicholas, husbandman. B. at Burton Gate, Lincs. School, Kettlethorpe. B.A. 1581-2; M.A. 1585. Ord. deacon and priest (Lincoln) Sept. 6, 1586. R. of Springthorpe, Lincs., 1586-1624; of Heapham, 1588-1633. Chaplain to Bishop of Lincoln. Perhaps V. of West Saltfleetby. Buried at Heapham, Nov. 11, 1633. (*Venn*, I. 95; *Lincs. Pedigrees*, where the father, Nicholas, is called 'Standard-bearer to Lord Willoughby of Parham' and said to be buried at Heapham, 1617.)

FARMERIE, WILLIAM. Matric. sizar from PETERHOUSE, c. 1601; Scholar, 1607-9; B.A. 1605-6; M.A. 1609. Ord. deacon (York) Dec. 1609.

FARMERY, WILLIAM. Matric. sizar from ST JOHN'S, Easter, 1611. Doubtless s. of William, R. of Heapham (1577-8); bapt. at Springthorpe, May, 1594. Ord. priest (Peterb.) Aug. 18, 1627; 'of St John's College, B.A.' R. of Ludborough, Lincs., 1627. (*Lincs. Pedigrees.*)

FARMERY, WILLIAM. Adm. sizar (age 18) at MAGDALENE, Jan. 28, 1681-2. S. of John, gent. B. at Heapham, Lincs. School, Grantham. Matric. 1682; B.A. 1685-6; M.A. 1690. Ord. priest (Lincoln) Feb. 20, 1686-7. V. of Blyton, Lincs., 1686. R. of Heapham, 1690. Buried at Heapham, Nov. 29, 1726. Father of Robert (1716-7). (*Lincs. Pedigrees*, I. 346.)

FURMERY, ——. Adm. Fell.-Com. at CORPUS CHRISTI, 1583.

FARMLIE, W. Matric. pens. from ST JOHN'S, Michs. 1584.

FARMORE, JOHN. Matric. sizar from ST JOHN'S, Easter, 1572.

FARNABY, JOHN. Adm. pens. at EMMANUEL, Jan. 23, 1677-8. Of Kent. Perhaps 2nd s. of John, of Canterbury. Matric. 1678. Student at Leyden, June 4, 1680. M.B. 1683. (*Vis. of Kent*, 1663.)

FARNABY, THOMAS. Matric. (age 15) from Merton College, Oxford, June 26, 1590. S. of Thomas, of London. Studied at a Jesuit College in Spain. Afterwards at Cambridge, and incorp. at Oxford, 1616, as 'M.A. Cambridge' (degree not recorded). Minor canon of St Paul's, 1626-9. Commissioned by Charles I to prepare a new Latin Grammar, 1641. An eminent scholar and schoolmaster; at Martock, Somerset, in Cripplegate, and at Sevenoaks, Kent. Friend of Ben Jonson. Edited most of the classical authors. Died June 12, 1647. (*Al. Oxon.*; *D.N.B.*)

FARNHAM, HUMPHREY. Matric. Fell.-Com. from QUEENS', Easter, 1573. Of Rutland. S. and h. of Matthew, of Cottesmore, Rutland. Adm. at the Middle Temple, Jan. 14, 1575-6.

FARNAM, JOHN. Matric. sizar from TRINITY, c. 1595; Scholar, 1599; B.A. 1599-1600; M.A. 1603, as 'Farman.' V. of Gt Wilbraham, Cambs., 1609-16.

FARNHAM, THOMAS. Matric. pens. from ST JOHN'S, Michs. 1612.

FARNSFIELD, THOMAS. Adm. pens. at CLARE, Apr. 22, 1668. Of Sleaford, Lincs. B.A. 1671-2. Signed for deacon's orders (London) Dec. 20, 1673. C. of Westham, Essex.

FARNWORTH, ELLIS. Adm. sizar (age 19) at MAGDALENE, Mar. 20, 1661-2. S. of Ellis, late of Prestolee, Lancs. School, Ringley, Lancs. Matric. 1659; B.A. 1661; M.A. 1665. V. of Rotherham, Yorks., 1666-70. V. of Mickleover, Derbs., 1669-91. Father of the next.

FARNEWORTH, ELLIS. Adm. sizar at JESUS, July 4, 1693. Of Derbyshire. S. of Ellis (above), V. of Rotherham. Matric. 1693; Rustat Scholar; B.A. 1696-7; M.A. 1709. R. of Bonsall, Derbs., 1708-16. R. of Mugginton, 1709-13. Father of the next.

FARNEWORTH, ELLIS. Adm. sizar at JESUS, Nov. 10, 1730. S. of Ellis (above), deceased, R. of Bonsall. B. at Ashbourne, Derbs. Schools, Chesterfield and Eton. Matric. 1730; Rustat Scholar; B.A. 1734-5; M.A. 1738. V. of Rostherne, Cheshire, 1758-62. R. of Carsington, Derbs., 1762-3. Author, translations, etc. Died Mar. 25, 1763. (*D.N.B.*)

FARNWORTH, JOHN. Matric. sizar from KING'S, Easter, 1643.

FARNWORTH, THOMAS. Matric. sizar from QUEENS', Michs. 1568. One of these names ord. priest (Peterb.) Oct. 24, 1582. (H. I. Longden.)

FARR or FAR, EDWARD. Adm. sizar (age 15) at PEMBROKE, June 29, 1662. S. of Edward, of Warwick, butcher. Matric. 1662; B.A. 1664-5.

FARRE, FRANCIS. M.A. 1631 (*fil. nob.*).

FARRE, HENRY. Matric. pens. from PEMBROKE, Easter, 1566. 2nd s. of Walter, of Gt Burstead, Essex. B.A. 1569-70; M.A. 1573. Fellow, 1570. Incorp. at Oxford, 1576. Junior Proctor, 1586-7. Benefactor to the College. Brother of Richard, etc. (*Cooper*, II. 22; *Vis. of Essex*, 1634.)

FARR, HENRY. Matric. Fell.-Com. from ST JOHN'S, Easter, 1620. Perhaps s. of Henry, of Gt Burstead, Essex. Succeeded his father. (*Vis. of Essex*, 1634.)

FARRE, JOHN. Matric. pens. from CHRIST'S, Michs. 1558.

FARRE, JOHN. Adm. pens. at QUEENS', Sept. 9, 1580. Of Lincolnshire.

FARR, RICHARD. Matric. pens. from CHRIST'S, Michs. 1562. Eldest s. of Walter, of Gt Burstead, Essex. Scholar, 1564. Succeeded his father, 1590. Died May 3, 1595. Brother of Henry (1566), Samuel (1573) and Walter (1573). (*Vis. of Essex*, 1634; *Peile*, I. 78; *Morant*, I. 240.)

FARRE, SAMUEL. Matric. pens. from PEMBROKE, Easter, 1573. S. of Walter, of Gt Burstead, Essex. B.A. 1576-7; M.A. 1580. Fellow, c. 1580. Brother of Richard, etc. (*Vis. of Essex*, 1634.)

FARR, SAMUEL. Adm. sizar (age 17) at EMMANUEL, Apr. 13, 1667. Migrated to Caius, Oct. 15, 1667. S. of Ellis, farmer, of Ovington, Essex. B. at Ashen. School, Felsted. Matric. 1668; Scholar, 1668-71; B.A. 1670-1; M.A. 1674. Ord. deacon (Norwich) June, 1674; priest, Feb. 27, 1680-1. V. of Little Waldingfield, Suffolk, 1680-7; of Stowmarket, 1688-1710; of Gt Finborough, 1706. Died Mar. 13, 1709-10. Buried at Stowmarket. M.I. there. Admon. (Norw. C.C.). His account of the injury to Stowmarket Church, in the great gale of 1703, is given in De Foe's narrative. (*Venn*, I. 433.)

FARR, THOMAS. Adm. scholar at TRINITY HALL, May 30, 1721. Of London. Matric. 1719.

FARRE, WALTER. Matric. pens. from PEMBROKE, Easter, 1573. Doubtless 3rd s. of Walter, of Gt Burstead, Essex. B.A. 1576-7; M.A. from Peterhouse, 1580. Fellow of Peterhouse, 1579-87. Died Sept. 20, 1604. Brother of Richard, etc. (*Vis. of Essex*, 1634; *Morant*, II. 50.)

FARRAND, *see also* **FERRAND.**

FARRAND, CHARLES. Matric. pens. from TRINITY, Easter, 1575. Scholar from Westminster, 1575. B.A. 1578-9; M.A. 1582. Fellow, 1581. Incorp. at Oxford, 1584. Ord. deacon (Peterb.) Apr. 3; priest, Apr. 11, 1584. V. of Blyth, Notts., 1588. V. of Gainford, Durham, 1589-93. Master of St John's Hospital, Barnard Castle, 1590. R. of Aston Clinton, Bucks., 1597.

FARRAND, EDMUND. Matric. pens. from TRINITY, Easter, 1571. Adm. at the Inner Temple, 1574. Of London.

FARRAND, GEORGE. Matric. pens. from TRINITY, Michs. 1559.

FARRAND, GEORGE. Matric. sizar from TRINITY, Michs. 1633, as Ferrand; B.A. 1636-7.

FARRAND, RICHARD. Matric. pens. from Trinity, Michs. 1564; B.A. 1569–70; M.A. 1573. Fellow, 1572.

FARRANT or FERRAND, RICHARD. Adm. pens. at Emmanuel, Sept. 6, 1646. Of Manchester. Matric. 1647; Scholar, 1648; B.A. 1650. Incorp. at Oxford, 1652, as Ferrand. M.A. from Brasenose, Oxford, 1652. Fellow of Brasenose. Adm. student of the Middle Temple, 1649, as 's. of Richard, of Mitcham, Surrey.' (*Al. Oxon.*)

FARRAND or FEROND, STEPHEN. B.A. 1505–6; M.A. 1509; B.D. 1530–1. Probably R. of Wendon Parva, Essex, 1522–33; V. of Chishall Magna, 1527–31. (J. Ch. Smith.)

FARRAND, THOMAS. Matric. pens. from Trinity, Michs. 1587.

FARRAND, WILLIAM. Matric. pens. from Trinity, Michs. 1559. S. of Richard. Scholar, 1562; B.A. 1562–3; M.A. 1566; LL.D. 1580. Fellow, 1563. Proctor, 1578–9. Adm. advocate, Jan. 27, 1581–2. Commissary of the deaneries of Shoreham and Croydon. Married, at Mitcham, Surrey, Oct. 9, 1592, Mary, widow of Edward Orwell, of Christ Church, London. Buried at Mitcham, July 1, 1615. Will (P.C.C.) 1615. (*Cooper*, II. 16; *Vis. of Surrey*; J. Ch. Smith.)

FARREN, ANTHONY. Matric. pens. from Christ's, July, 1608. Doubtless s. and h. of Thomas, of Lutterworth, Leics., gent. Adm. at Gray's Inn, June 15, 1612.

FARRAN, GEORGE. Adm. sizar (age 18) at Trinity, May 21, 1738. S. of Richard, of Dublin. School, St Andrew's, London (Mr Quig). Matric. 1739; Scholar, 1739; B.A. 1741–2; M.A. 1747. Ord. deacon (Lincoln) Dec. 19, 1742; priest (Bath and Wells) 1744–5.

FARREN, JAMES. Adm. pens. (age 15) at Sidney, May 9, 1629. S. of Thomas, of Lutterworth, Leics., gent. Schools, Lutterworth (Mr Cox) and Oakham (Mr Whitaker). Migrated to Oxford. Matric. from Oriel, Jan. 25, 1632–3, 'aged 21'; B.A. (Oxford) 1632–3; M.A. 1638. Fellow of Oriel, 1634. Proctor, 1646. V. of St Mary's, Oxford, 1649. (*Al. Oxon.*)

FARREN, JOHN. Adm. pens. (age 17) at St John's, Oct. 23, 1706. S. of Thomas, gent. B. at Coton, near Market Bosworth, Leics. School, Atherstone, Warws. (Mr Shaw). Matric. 1707, as 'Thomas.'

FARREN, THOMAS. Adm. pens. at St Catharine's, Feb. 18, 1735–6. Of Farthingstone, Northants. Matric. 1736.

FARRER, *see also* FERRAR.

FARRAR, DENNIS, Adm. at Corpus Christi, 1717. Of Buckinghamshire. S. of William, of Cold Brayfield, Bucks. Adm. at the Inner Temple, Nov. 29, 1717. Married Elizabeth, dau. of William Hillersdon, 1725. Died 1746. Father of William (1743–4). (*Victoria* Co. *Hist. Beds.*, III. 304.)

FARRER or FERROUR, EDMUND. Adm. pens. (age 14) at Caius, Nov. 10, 1595. S. of Henry, gent., of Wendling, Norfolk. Bapt. there, Sept. 3, 1581. School, Scarning (Mr Denby). Scholar, 1597–1602; B.A. 1598–9; M.A. 1602. Fellow, 1604–7. Buried at Wendling, Apr. 6, 1607. (*Venn*, I. 157; *Carthew*, III. 228.)

FARRER, EDWARD. Adm. pens. at Trinity, Dec. 5, 1647. Of St Andrews University. S. of John, of Ewood, Halifax, Yorks. Migrated to Oxford. B.A. from Magdalen Hall, 1650–1; M.A. 1653; B.D. and D.D. 1689. Fellow of University College. Master, 1688–91. Died Feb. 13, 1698–9. (*Al. Oxon.*)

FARRAR, FRANCIS. Matric. pens. from Clare, Lent, 1564–5. Probably s. of Ralph, grocer, of London. Of Harrold, Beds. Buried there Aug. 11, 1616. Perhaps brother of Paul (1564–5). (*Victoria Co. Hist. Beds.*, III. 66.)

FARRER, GEORGE. Matric. sizar from Queens', Easter, 1576. ('John' in College register.) Of Suffolk. B.A. 1579–80.

FARRER, GEORGE. Adm. pens. at Queens', Mar. 15, 1624–5. Of Herefordshire.

FARRAR, HENRY. Matric. pens. from St John's, Michs. 1568. One of these names J.P. for West Riding, Yorks., 1601.

FARRER, HENRY. Matric. pens. from Peterhouse, Michs. 1578, as Ferrard; B.A. 1581–2.

FARRER, HENRY. Matric. pens. from Christ's, Easter, 1676. S. of William, of Ewood, Halifax, Yorks. B.A. 1679–80; M.A. 1683. Incorp. at Oxford, 1682. Ord. deacon (York) Dec. 1683; priest, May, 1684. R. of Hemsworth, Yorks., 1685. Died before July, 1718. (*Peile*, II. 61.)

FARRER, JAMES. Matric. pens. from Corpus Christi, Easter, 1577; B.A. 1579–80.

FARRAR, JAMES. Adm. at Corpus Christi, 1661. Of Norwich. Matric. 1663; B.A. 1666–7. Perhaps R. of Ridlington, Norfolk, 1670–1709. Will (Norwich C.C.) 1709.

FARRER, JEREMY. Incorp. M.A. 1678, from Edinburgh. Adm. at Emmanuel, June 23, 1679. R. of Nunburnholme, Yorks., 1695–1735. Buried July 1, 1735. Father of William (1714–5).

FARRAR, JOHN. B.A. 1513–4; M.A. 1517.

FARRER or FERRER, JOHN. Matric. pens. from Jesus, *c.* 1595; B.A. 1597–8; M.A. 1601. Ord. deacon (London) May 7, 1598; priest, Apr. 7, 1601. R. of Holton, Norfolk, 1601. R. of Witnesham, Suffolk, 1606–20. Perhaps R. of Langham, Essex, 1607–47. Will (P.C.C.) 1649. Thomas Farrer, R. of Langham, Essex (will, Consist. C. London) had a s. John, clerk; and a brother George (? 1576). (J. Ch. Smith.)

FARRER, JOHN. Adm. Fell.-Com. at Trinity, 1660. Perhaps s. and h. of John, of Durham, and brother of Thomas (1666). Matric. 1661–2. Of Sedgefield, 1674, afterwards of Bradbury. Buried Aug. 28, 1704. (*Surtees*, III. 43.)

FARRAR, JOHN. Adm. sizar (age 18) at Caius, Sept. 10, 1683. B. at Shalford, Essex. School, Felsted. Scholar, 1684–7.

FARRER, MARMADUKE. Matric. pens. from St John's, Michs. 1568; B.A. 1572–3. Perhaps V. of Luddenden, Yorks., 1606–34. Buried at Halifax.

FARRAR, PAUL. Matric. pens. from Clare, Lent, 1564–5. Perhaps brother of Francis (1564–5).

FARRER, RICHARD. Matric. sizar from Trinity, Michs. 1575.

FARRER, RICHARD. Adm. pens. at Trinity, July 2, 1652. Of London.

FARRER, RICHARD. Adm. sizar at Christ's, May 27, 1680. S. of Joseph. B. at Kirkby Lonsdale, Westmorland. School, Kirkby (his brother, Miles Farrer). Matric. 1680. Resided, till 1682. Usher, under his brother, in 1678. (*Peile*, II. 79.)

FARROR, THOMAS. Matric. sizar from Pembroke, Lent, 1580–1; B.A. from Peterhouse, 1583–4. One of these names R. of St James', Colchester, 1591–1610.

FARRAR, THOMAS. Matric. sizar from King's, Easter, 1623; B.A. 1627–8.

FARRER, THOMAS. Adm. pens. (age 16) at Christ's, Feb. 4, 1638–9. S. of William. B. in London. School, Hertford (Mr Minors). Matric. 1639.

FARRER, THOMAS. Adm. pens. (age 16) at Sidney, May 12, 1666. S. of John, gent., of Durham. Bapt. at Bishop Middleham, Nov. 1, 1647; as s. of Captain John Farro, of the Navy. School, Bishop Auckland (Mr Holand). Living, 1699. (H. M. Wood.)

FARRER, THOMAS. Adm. pens. (age 15) at Trinity, May 13, 1685. S. of Thomas. B. at Warmington, Warws. School, Lavendon, Bucks. (Mr John Warburton). Matric. 1685; Scholar, 1687; B.A. 1688–9; M.A. from Peterhouse, 1692. Fellow of Peterhouse, 1693–7.

FARRER, THOMAS. Adm. pens. at Emmanuel, May 10, 1728. Of Lincolnshire. S. of Thomas, M.D. B. at Market Harborough, Leics., *c.* 1710. Matric. 1731; B.A. 1731–2; M.A. 1735. Ord. deacon (Peterb.) May 19, 1733. C. of Brampton, Northants., 1733; R. 1734. R. of Warmington, Warws. Buried there Sept. 1, 1764. (H. I. Longden.)

FARRAR, TIMOTHY. Matric. pens. from Trinity, Michs. 1561.

FARRER, WILLIAM. *Cautio* for degree, 1487–8.

FARRER, WILLIAM. Matric. sizar from Trinity, *c.* 1595; B.A. 1598–9. Ord. deacon (Colchester) Oct. 12; priest, Oct. 19, 1600. C. of Ramsholt, Suffolk, 1604. R. of Campsea-Ashe, 1607. R. of Hasketon, 1620–37. Died 1637.

FARRER, WILLIAM. Matric. Fell.-Com. from Jesus, Easter, 1604.

FARRER, WILLIAM. Adm. Fell.-Com. at Trinity, May 13, 1685. S. of William, of Stagsden, Beds. B. at Brayfield, Bucks. School, Lavendon (Mr John Warburton). Matric. 1685. M.P. for Bedford, 1695–8, 1701, 1705, 1708, 1710, 1715, 1722. Clerk of the Pipe, 1710–37. Master of St Katharine's Hospital, 1715–37. Died Sept. 22, 1737. (A. B. Beaven.)

FARRER, WILLIAM. Adm. pens. (age 18) at St John's, Mar. 2, 1714–5. S. of Jeremy (1679), clerk. B. at York. School, Pocklington (Mr Drake). Matric. 1715; B.A. 1718–9; M.A. 1722. Ord. deacon (York) Sept. 1719; priest, Dec. 1720. R. of Burnby, Yorks., 1720–35. Married Ann Collins, of Londesborough, Nov. 16, 1732. Buried July 5, 1735. (M. H. Peacock.)

FARRER, WILLIAM. Adm. sizar at Jesus, June 29, 1720. S. of William, of Hatfield, Yorks. Matric. 1721; Scholar; LL.B. 1728. Ord. deacon (York) Sept. 22, 1723; priest, July 21, 1728.

FARRAR, WILLIAM. Matric. sizar from Christ's, Michs. 1736. Of Lancashire. Scholar, 1737; B.A. 1739–40; M.A. 1743. Ord. deacon (Lincoln) June, 1740; priest, Sept. 20, 1741. C. of Gt Munden, Herts. (*Peile*, II. 232.)

FARRER, WILLIAM. Adm. pens. (age 17) at Trinity, Feb. 9, 1743–4. S. of Dennis (1717), of Brayfield, Bucks. Bapt. there, July 9, 1726. School, Hackney, London (Mr Newcombe). Matric. 1744. Of Cold Brayfield, Esq. (Burke, *L.G.*)

FARRER, ——. Adm. sizar at St Catharine's, Easter, 1649.

FARRER, ——. Adm. pens. at TRINITY HALL, Nov. 21, 1739. Probably resided till 1741.

FARRINGTON, GEORGE. Matric. sizar from TRINITY, Easter, 1625; B.A. 1627-8. Perhaps s. of John, of Sussex. A priest. (*Vis. of London*, 1568.)

FARRINGTON, HENRY. Adm. pens. (age 15) at ST JOHN'S, Feb. 2, 1720-1. S. of Valentine, M.D., of Lancashire. B. at Preston. School, Manchester. Matric. 1721; B.A. 1724-5; M.A. from Sidney, 1728. Guild-Mayor of Preston, 1741-2. (*Scott-Mayor*, III. 337; *Baines*, IV. 172.) An Oxford contemporary was ord. priest at Norwich, 1739.

FARINGTON, HUGH. Adm. sizar (age 16) at ST JOHN'S, June 16, 1703. S. of Alexander, clerk. B. at Kendal, Westmorland. School, Kendal. Matric. 1703; B.A. 1706-7; M.A. 1710. Fellow, 1711-8. Ord. deacon (London) Mar. 5, 1709-10. R. of Elsdon, Northumberland, 1715-39. Married, at St John's, Newcastle, Aug. 8, 1717, Jane, dau. of Nathaniel Ellison. Died Sept. 4, 1739. Buried at St Nicholas, Newcastle. (H. M. Wood.)

FARRINGTON, RICHARD. M.A. from KING'S, 1738. S. of Robert, of Carnarvon. Matric. from Jesus College, Oxford, Nov. 23, 1720, age 18; B.A. (Oxford) 1724-5. Chancellor of Bangor, 1762-72. Buried at St James', Bath, Oct. 19, 1772. (*Al. Oxon.*)

FARRINGTON, ROBERT. B.Civ.L. 1530-1 (similar grace, 1526-7). 3rd s. of Sir Henry. R. of North Meols, Lancs., 1530-7, 'became weary of holy orders,' resigned his living and married. (*Vict. Hist. Lancs.*, III. 228; *Baines*, IV. 172.)

FARRINGTON, ROBERT. Matric. pens. from ST JOHN'S, c. 1594; B.A. (?) 1596-7; M.A. 1600.

FARRINGTON, ROBERT. Adm. sizar (age 18) at ST JOHN'S, Apr. 12, 1652. S. of Robert, husbandman, of Stanthorne, near Middlewich, Cheshire. B. there. School, Northwich. Matric. 1652; B.A. 1655-6.

FARRYNGTON, ROGER. Matric. pens. from ST JOHN'S, Michs. 1567; B.A. 1570-1.

FARRINGTON, THOMAS. Adm. Fell.-Com. (age 18) at PEMBROKE, May 19, 1693. S. of Sir John, Knt., of Chichester, J.P. B. in Bow, Middlesex. Bapt. May 10, 1677. Adm. at the Inner Temple, May 9, 1693. Died unmarried, 1697. (Le Neve, *Knights*, 350; Burke, *Ext. Bart.*)

FARRINGTON, WILLIAM. Matric. pens. from ST JOHN'S, Michs. 1628. Probably s. of William, of Worden, Lancs., age 1 in 1613. Named as a knight of the Royal Oak. Captain of the Militia under Earl Derby. Will (Chester) 1673. (*Vis. of Lancs.*, 1613; *Baines*, IV. 171.)

FARRINGTON, WILLIAM. Adm. Fell.-Com. (age 19) at ST JOHN'S, July 21, 1740. S. of George, Esq., of Worden, Lancs. B. at Shawe Hall, Leyland. School, Chesterfield. Matric. 1740. High Sheriff of Lancs., 1761-2. Knighted, Mar. 6, 1761. Died 1781. (*Baines*, IV. 171.)

FARRINGTON, ——. Adm. sizar at EMMANUEL, July 3, 1675. Of Lancashire.

FARROLD, DANIEL. Matric. sizar from CHRIST'S, Nov. 1558.

FARROW, BENJAMIN. Adm. sizar at EMMANUEL, May 19, 1681. Of Lincolnshire. Matric. 1681. Ord. deacon (Lincoln) June 4, 1699; priest, May 23, 1703. C. of Bennington, Lincs.

FARROW, CHRISTOPHER. Adm. sizar at EMMANUEL, June 27, 1661. Of Durham.

FARROW, FRANCIS. Adm. sizar at EMMANUEL, Feb. 15, 1632-3. Of Northamptonshire. Matric. 1633; B.A. 1636-7; M.A. 1640.

FARROW, JOSEPH. Adm. sizar (age 16) at MAGDALENE, May 25, 1669. S. of Thomas, of Boston, Lincs., deceased. B. there. School, Boston. Matric. 1669; B.A. 1672-3; M.A. 1677. Episcopally ordained. At Boston, till 1683. Chaplain to Sir William Ellys, of Nocton, 1683-92. Died unmarried, July 22, 1692, at Newark-upon-Trent, Notts. (*Calamy*, II. 169; *D.N.B.*)

FARROW, SAMUEL. Adm. sizar at EMMANUEL, June 13, 1665. Of Northamptonshire. Matric. 1665; B.A. 1668-9; M.A. 1672. Signed for deacon's orders (London) Sept. 18, 1669. Ord. priest (Peterb.) June 18, 1671. V. of Rothwell with Orton, Northants., 1673-5. Buried at Broughton, Northants., Dec. 8, 1675. (H. I. Longden.)

FARROWE, WILLIAM. Adm. sizar at EMMANUEL, Apr. 10, 1619. Matric. 1619; B.A. 1622-3; M.A. 1626; B.D. 1637. Ord. deacon (Peterb.) July 22; priest, July 23, 1627. Probably R. of Strixton, Northants., 1628-80. R. of Knaptoft, Leics., 1638. Died Dec. 1, 1680.

FARROW (1590), *see* FERROUR, JOHN.

FARSFIELD, THOMAS. Matric. pens. from CLARE, Easter, 1668.

FARSIDE, JOHN. Adm. sizar (age 20) at ST JOHN'S, Dec. 29, 1662. S. of James, deceased, of Fotheringay, Northants. B. there. School, Fotheringay. Matric. 1663; B.A. 1666-7; M.A. 1670. Ord. deacon (Ely) Sept. 20, 1668; priest (Peterb.) May 25, 1673.

FARSIDE or FAIRSIDE, THOMAS. Adm. sizar (age 17) at ST JOHN'S, June 27, 1712. S. of John, gent. B. at Fylingdales, Yorks. School, Scalby (Mr Houls). Matric. 1712; B.A. 1715-6. Ord. deacon (York) Sept. 1717; priest, May, 1719. V. of Willerby, Yorks., 1723.

FARSIDE, THOMAS. Adm. sizar (age 18) at SIDNEY, Apr. 4, 1748. S. of Thomas, clerk. B. at Hinderwell, Yorks. School, Thornton (Mr Ward). Matric. 1748-9; B.A. 1752; M.A. 1762. Ord. priest (Lincoln) Sept. 23, 1753.

FARTHING, JOHN. Matric. pens. from QUEENS', Easter, 1635. Of Norfolk. B.A. 1638-9.

FARTHING, RALPH. Adm. sizar at QUEENS', Feb. 21, 1705-6. S. of John, of Crocombe, Somerset. Matric. 1706. Migrated to Oxford. Matric. from University College, May 17, 1708, age 18; B.Civ.L. from New Inn Hall, 1719. V. of Ottery St Mary, Devon, 1722. (*Al. Oxon.*)

FARTHING, ROBERT. Adm. pens. (age 16) at PETERHOUSE, May 14, 1650. Of Wisbech. School, Wisbech. Matric. 1650. Scholar, 1650; B.A. 1653-4; M.A. 1657. Probably V. of Winsford, Somerset, 1664-1714. Buried there June 2, 1714.

FARWELL or FAERWELL, ARTHUR. M.A. 1682 (*Lit. Reg.*). Perhaps matric. from Magdalen College, Oxford, 1658. Adm. at the Inner Temple, 1660. M.P. for Dartmouth, 1685-7.

FARWELL, CHARLES. Matric. pens. from ST CATHARINE'S, Michs. 1648. One of these names s. and h. of Sir John, of Nuthall, Somerset, Knt., deceased; adm. at Lincoln's Inn, June 9, 1650.

FAREWELL, GEORGE. Adm. pens. at QUEENS', Feb. 2, 1647-8. Of Kent. Doubtless s. and h. of George, barrister of the Inner Temple. Adm. at the Inner Temple, 1648. Barrister, 1656.

FAREWELL, GEORGE. M.A. from KING'S, 1706. S. of Thomas, of Horsington, Somerset, gent. Matric. from Hart Hall, Oxford, Dec. 26, 1696, age 20; B.A. from Wadham College, 1700. Ord. priest (Bath and Wells) Sept. 21, 1707. Chaplain to Baroness Haversham. R. of South Cadbury, Somerset, 1709-17. Preb. of Wells, 1709-17. R. of Portland, Dorset, 1712-7. Died Apr. 6, 1717. Buried at South Cadbury. (*Al. Oxon.*; F. S. Hockaday.)

FAIRWELL, GEORGE. Adm. at CORPUS CHRISTI, 1711. Perhaps s. and h. of George, of Brenchley, Kent, Esq. B. in London. Matric. 1711. Adm. at the Inner Temple, Jan. 7, 1712-3. Died Mar. 21, 1750, aged 57. (*Hasted*, III. 3.)

FAREWEL, JAMES. Adm. pens. at ST CATHARINE'S, Apr. 24, 1689. Matric. 1691. Probably s. and h. of James, of the Inner Temple, Esq. Adm. there, July 3, 1690.

FAREWELL, JOHN. Canonicus. B.Can.L. 1464-5. Perhaps same as the next.

FAREWELL, JOHN. D.Can.L. 1474-5. Prior of Walsingham in 1474. Studied at Cambridge and Bologna.

FAREWELL, JOHN. B.A. 1486-7; M.A. 1489-90; B.D. 1505-6. Pens. at GONVILLE HALL, 1495-9. One of these names V. of Bermondsey, Surrey, 1523-37. V. of Camberwell, 1526-56. R. of Rotherhithe, 1537. Preb. of Llandaff, 1537. Died 1556. Will (P.C.C.); to be buried in the Chancel of Camberwell. (*Venn*, I. 14.)

FAREWELL, JOHN. Adm. pens. (age 17) at SIDNEY, May 1, 1660. S. of John, deceased. B. in London. School, Merchant Taylors'. Matric. 1660. Perhaps buried at All Saints', Cambridge, Oct. 21, 1662, as 'Harwell.'

FARWELL, JOHN. Adm. pens. at EMMANUEL, Oct. 26, 1660.

FAREWELL, JOHN. Adm. pens. at JESUS, May 15, 1723. S. of Robert, gent., of Nottingham. Matric. 1723; Scholar, 1724; LL.B. 1728.

FAREWELL, PHILLIPS. Adm. pens. (age 18) at TRINITY, May 28, 1706. S. of Phillips, of Ware, Herts. School, Westminster. Matric. 1706; Scholar, 1707; B.A. 1709-10; M.A. 1713; D.D. 1730. Fellow, 1712-30. Taxor, 1717. Resided mostly at Lambeth with Archbishop Wake. Ord. deacon (Peterb.) Feb. 2; priest, Feb. 8, 1729-30. R. of Clipsham, Ruts., 1730. Buried at St Michael's, Cambridge, Dec. 12, 1730. Admon. P.C.C. (*Al. Westmon.*, 247.)

FAREWELL, PHILLIPS. Adm. pens. (age 17) at CAIUS, May 28, 1741. S. of John, Esq., of Hadleigh, Suffolk. B. there. Schools, Dedham, Essex (private) and Eton. Matric. 1741; Scholar, 1741-6; B.A. 1744-5. Ord. deacon (Norwich) Dec. 22, 1745, as C. of Witnesham, Suffolk; priest, Sept. 24, 1769. (*Venn*, II. 49.)

FARWELL or FAYREWELL, WILLIAM. Adm. sizar at JESUS, Apr. 17, 1624. Of Norfolk. Matric. 1624; B.A. 1627-8; Scholar, 1628; M.A. 1631.

FARY, JOHN. Adm. sizar (age 16) at CAIUS, Feb. 23, 1630-1. S. of Israel, citizen of Norwich, deceased. B. there. School, Norwich (Mr Stonham and Mr Briggs). Matric. 1631; Scholar, 1631-8; B.A. 1634-5; M.A. 1638. Ord. deacon (Norwich) Sept. 24, 1637; priest, Mar. 9, 1638-9. C. of Gunton, 1637; R. 1638-61. Author, sermon. (*Venn*, I. 296.)

FASEDA ——. D.Can.L. 1497-8.

FASCETT, JOHN (1624), *see* FAWCETT.

FASCETT, FAUSETT or **FASECK, RICHARD.** Adm. sizar at EMMANUEL, Easter, 1626. Matric. 1626; B.A. 1629-30.

FASSET, THOMAS. Adm. sizar (age 20) at EMMANUEL, June 29, 1743. S. of Jeremy, of Norwich, schoolmaster. School, Bungay. Matric. 1743; B.A. 1746-7; M.A. 1751. Ord. deacon (Norwich) Sept. 1747; priest, Sept. 1748. R. of Beeston St Laurence, Norfolk, 1756-72. P.C. of Ashmanhaw, 1768-72.

FALCONBRIDGE, CHRISTOPHER. Matric. pens. from CHRIST'S, July, 1612. Doubtless s. and h. of Robert, of Otterington, Yorks.; age 17 in 1612. (*Vis. of Yorks.*; *Peile*, I. 286; where he is wrongly named.)

FAUCON, *see* FACON.

FAUCONBERG, *see also* BELLASSIS.

FAUCONBERG or **FALKENBRIDGE, HENRY.** Matric. pens. from TRINITY HALL, Easter, 1652. Doubtless s. of John, of Westminster; adm. at Gray's Inn, June 2, 1655. LL.B. 1658; LL.D. 1665. Fellow, 1656-73. Founder of the Fauconberg School, Beccles. Chancellor of the diocese of St David's. Registrar of the Faculty Office. Official of the Archdeaconry of Suffolk. Benefactor to the College, 1713. Died at Beccles, Oct. 29, 1713, aged 78. M.I. there. (*Warren*, 305; *Suckling*, I. 32.)

FAUDEN, EDWARD, *see* FAWDEN.

FAUNCE, ZACHARIUS. Adm. pens. at PETERHOUSE, June 13, 1618. Of Leicester. Matric. 1618; B.A. 1621-2; M.A. 1625.

FAUNE, JOHN. Matric. pens. from PETERHOUSE, Michs. 1566.

FAWNE or **FOWNES, JOHN.** Matric. Fell.-Com. from KING'S, Michs. 1657 (*impubes*).

FAUNT, JOSHUA. Matric. pens. from EMMANUEL, Easter, 1609. Perhaps s. of Nicholas, below. (*Middlesex Pedigrees*.)

FAUNT, NICHOLAS. Adm. pens. (age 18) at CAIUS, Jan. 29, 1571-2. S. of John, of Canterbury. School, Canterbury. Matric. 1572; Scholar, 1572; B.A. from Corpus Christi, 1575-6. In Paris during the Bartholomew Massacre. Secretary to Sir Francis Walsingham, *c.* 1580. M.P. for Boroughbridge, 1584-6. Clerk of the Signet, 1603. (*Venn*, I. 69; *Middlesex Pedigrees*; *D.N.B.*; *Cooper*, II. 477.)

FAWNT, ROBERT. B.A. 1459-60; M.A. as Fawtt, 1464-5.

FAUNT, WILLIAM. Adm. Fell.-Com. at TRINITY, Sept. 28, 1673. One of these names s. of George, of Claybrooke, Leics. Of Foston, Leics., Esq. (*Nichols*, IV. 175.)

FAUNTLEROY, JOHN. Adm. Fell.-Com. at TRINITY, Mar. 8, 1674-5. One of these names, of Isleworth, Middlesex; died Feb. 6, 1732-3, aged 77. Will (P.C.C.) 1733. (J. Ch. Smith.)

FAUQUIER, FRANCIS. Adm. pens. at QUEENS', July 3, 1750. Of Suffolk. Matric. 1750. Probably s. of Francis, Esq., who took up the freedom of Ipswich, 1733. (V. B. Redstone.)

FAUQUIER, WILLIAM. Adm. pens. at QUEENS', July 3, 1750. Of Suffolk. Matric. 1750. Doubtless brother of the above. Took up the freedom of Ipswich, 1766.

FAUSCOT or **FOSCOT, JOHN.** Matric. sizar from QUEENS', Easter, 1586. Of Bedfordshire.

FAUTRART, DANIEL. Adm. sizar at EMMANUEL, June 7, 1606.

FAUTRART, PETER. Adm. sizar at EMMANUEL, July 29, 1609. B. at St Martin, Guernsey. Matric. 1609; B.A. 1612-3; M.A. 1619. Ord. deacon (London) June 15, 1617; priest, Sept. 1, 1617, age 23. Incorp. at Oxford, 1621. C. of Burnham, Bucks. R. of Paulerspury, Northants., 1630-1. (H. I. Longden.)

FAUX, *see* FAWKES.

FAUWTT, *see* FAWNT.

FAVELL, ANTHONY. Adm. sizar (age 16) at MAGDALENE, June, 1666. S. of Lawrence, clerk, of Sutton-on-Lound, Notts. School, Burn (? Burnsall), Yorks. Matric. 1667; B.A. 1669-70, as 'Favile.'

FAVEL, GEORGE. Adm. sizar (age 17) at MAGDALENE, Apr. 12, 1710. S. of Robert. B. at Gt Barford, Beds. School, Bedford. Matric. 1710; B.A. 1714-5. Ord. deacon (Peterb.) June 7, 1718; priest (Lincoln) Sept. 20, 1719. C. of Wilden, Beds., 1718-26. C. of Roxton, 1726. V. of Gt Barford, 1726.

FAVELL, HENRY. Adm. sizar (age 16) at ST JOHN'S, Nov. 27, 1635. S. of John, husbandman, of Burnsall, Yorks. Bapt. there, Jan. 7, 1620-1. School, Burnsall. Matric. 1635; B.A. 1639-40. Will of one of these names (York) 1664; of Altoftes, Yorks., gent.

FAVELL, JAMES. Adm. pens. (age 17) at TRINITY, July 29, 1726. 4th s. of James, of Normanton, Yorks. Bapt. there, June 12, 1708. School, Wakefield, Yorks. (Mr Wilson). Matric. 1727; Scholar, 1728; B.A. 1730-1; M.A. 1734; D.D. 1746. Fellow, 1733. Incorp. at Oxford, 1734. Ord. deacon (Lincoln) Mar. 14, 1730-1; priest, Dec. 19, 1736. R. of Houghton, Hunts., 1748-77. Preb. of Lincoln, 1755-77. Married the widow Bridge, eldest dau. of Dr Richard Bentley. Died Sept. 25, 1777. Buried at Normanton, Yorks. M.I. Will (P.C.C.). (*F.M.G.*, 909.)

FAVELL, JAMES. Adm. sizar (age 17) at TRINITY, Mar. 24, 1739-40. 3rd s. of Redman, of Normanton, Yorks. School, Wakefield, Yorks. (Mr Wilson). Matric. 1740; Scholar, 1742; B.A. 1743-4; M.A. 1747. Ord. priest (Lincoln) Sept. 20, 1747. P.C. of Bury, Hunts., in 1750. V. of Alconbury, 1750-1803. Died 1803.

FAVELL, JOHN. Adm. sizar (age 17) at PEMBROKE, June 22, 1678. S. of Lawrence, of Sutton, Notts., clerk. Matric. 1678; B.A. 1681-2. Ord. deacon (York) June 11, 1682.

FAVELL, ——. B.A. 1469-70.

FAVOUR, JOHN. Adm. pens. at CLARE, July 29, 1645. Matric. 1645; B.A. 1649. Probably R. of Bainton, Yorks., 1661.

FAWCETT, CHRISTOPHER. Matric. pens. from ST JOHN'S, Easter, 1550.

FAWCETT, CHRISTOPHER. Adm. at CORPUS CHRISTI, 1708. B. in London, 1690. Matric. Michs. 1708; B.A. 1711-2; M.A. 1715; B.D. 1723. Fellow, 1716-34. Ord. deacon (Ely) Feb. 21, 1713-4; priest, Mar. 13, 1714-5. R. of St Mary Abchurch, and St Laurence Poultney, London, 1733-48. Died 1748.

FAWCETT, CHRISTOPHER. Adm. scholar at TRINITY HALL, Dec. 30, 1734. Of Boldon, Durham. Only s. of William, of Boldon, Esq. Bapt. at Boldon, May 9, 1715. Matric. 1734. Adm. at Gray's Inn, Feb. 1, 1733-4; and at the Middle Temple, Dec. 21, 1736. Died in the West Indies. *See Al. Oxon.* for another. (H. M. Wood; *Surtees*, II. 60.)

FAWCET, EDWARD. Matric. pens. from ST JOHN'S, Michs. 1570. B. in Yorkshire. School, Sedbergh. B.A. 1574-5; M.A. 1578. V. of Higham, Kent, 1580-91. Died 1591. (*Sedbergh Sch. Register*, 82.)

FAWCET, EDWARD. Adm. sizar (age 15) at ST JOHN'S, Mar. 17, 1672-3. S. of Anthony, yeoman, of Dent, Yorks. B. there. School, Sedbergh. Matric. 1672-3; B.A. 1676-7. Ord. deacon (York) Sept. 1679. A doctor. Died 1687. M.I. at Dent. (*Sedbergh Sch. Register*, 118.)

FAWCETT, FRANCIS. Adm. sizar (age 26) at SIDNEY, June 11, 1658. 3rd s. of Giles, scrivener, deceased. B. at Rufforth, Yorks. Schools, Poppleton (private; Mr Dan. Sherwood) and York (Mr Young). Matric. 1658; B.A. 1662.

FAWCETT, GEORGE. Matric. sizar from ST JOHN'S, Michs. 1568.

FAWCETT, GEORGE. Matric. pens. from CHRIST'S, Michs. 1583; B.A. from St John's, 1587-8. Probably buried at St Edward's, Cambridge, Apr. 6, 1588, as 'of Clare.'

FAWCET or **FASSETT, GEORGE.** Adm. sizar at EMMANUEL, Feb. 20, 1609-10. Matric. 1610; B.A. 1613-4; M.A. 1617; B.D. 1626. Doubtless V. of Roughton, Norfolk. Father of Robert (1641).

FAWCETT, GEORGE. Adm. sizar (age 18) at ST JOHN'S, June 11, 1703. S. of William, gent. B. at Brearton, Knaresborough, Yorks. School, Sedbergh. Matric. 1703; B.A. 1706-7. Ord. deacon (York) May, 1708; priest, 1709. V. of Myton, Yorks., 1716. R. of Nunnington, 1723.

FAWCETT, HORACE. Adm. sizar (ag 18) at ST JOHN'S, Apr. 3, 1717. S. of Robert (1685), clerk, of Norfolk. B. at Rackheath. School, Wymondham (Mr Sayer). B.A. 1720-1; M.A. 1724. Ord. priest (Norwich) June, 1723. V. of Moulton St Mary, Norfolk, 1723-6. R. of Watlington, 1726-64. Brother of Thomas (1715). (*Scott-Mayor*, III. 309.)

FAWKETT, JAMES. Adm. pens. at TRINITY, May 29, 1673. School, Westminster. Scholar, 1674; Matric. 1676; B.A. 1676-7; M.A. 1680. Fellow, 1679. Ord. priest (London) Sept. 2, 1681.

FAUCET, JOHN. Matric. pens. from ST JOHN'S, Michs. 1565. Of Yorkshire. B.A. 1568-9; M.A. 1572; B.D. 1579. Fellow, 1571. V. of Stanstead Abbots, Herts., 1575. Perhaps also R. of Little Hormead, 1578-80. Died 1580.

FAWCET, JOHN. Matric. pens. from ST JOHN'S, Michs. 1571.

FAWCET, JOHN. Matric. pens. from ST JOHN'S, Michs. 1578; B.A. 1582-3; M.A. 1586; B.D. 1593. Ord. deacon and priest (Peterb.) Apr. 10, 1586.

FAWCETT, JOHN. Matric. sizar from ST JOHN'S, Easter, 1583; B.A. 1586-7; M.A. 1590. Ord. deacon and priest (Peterb.) Mar. 22, 1589-90.

FAWCETT, JOHN. B.A. from ST JOHN'S, 1588-9; M.A. 1592.

FAWCETT or FASSET, JOHN. Adm. sizar at MAGDALENE, May 28, 1624. Migrated to Christ's, Sept. 20, 1624. S. of Richard, taylor. B. at 'Kingston' (King's Lynn), Norfolk. B.A. 1627-8; M.A. 1631. Ord. deacon (Peterb.) June 8, 1628; priest, May 31, 1629. R. of Twyford, Norfolk, 1631.

FAUCET, JOHN. Adm. pens. (age 18) at ST JOHN'S, Sept. 8, 1649. S. of Hugh, yeoman, of Laytham, Howden, Yorks. B. there. School, Wheldrake, Yorks. (private; Mr Tomlinson). Matric. 1649; B.A. 1653-4.

FAWCET, JOHN. Adm. sizar (age 18) at CHRIST'S, June 5, 1674. S. of Giles. B. at Marrick Abbey, near Richmond, Yorks. School, Marske (Mr Sedgwick). Matric. 1674; B.A. 1677-8; M.A. 1681. Ord. deacon (York) July, 1677; priest, May, 1681. (*Peile*, II. 54.)

FAWCETT, MILES. Matric. sizar from GONVILLE HALL, 1554.

FAWCETT, RICHARD. B.A. from ST JOHN'S, 1536-7; M.A. 1540; B.D. 1549; D.D. 1554. Fellow, 1536. Of York diocese. Ord. deacon (Norwich) Mar. 13, 1540-1; priest, Apr. 16, 1541. Preb. of Canterbury, 1554-60. Preb. of Lincoln, 1559. Deprived as a Papist, 1559. Will of one of these names (York) 1575; clerk, b. at Sedbergh. (*Cooper*, I. 209, III. 86; J. Ch. Smith.)

FAUCET, RICHARD. Matric. pens. from ST JOHN'S, Michs. 1560. Of Bedfordshire. B. in Westmorland. School, Sedbergh. B.A. 1563-4; M.A. 1567; B.D. 1574. Fellow, 1564. Ord. priest (Ely) Nov. 5, 1564. R. of Gravenhurst, Beds., till 1573. R. of Boldon, Durham, 1575-1610. Preb. of Durham, 1576-1610. Died Feb. 5, 1609-10. Buried at Boldon. (*Cooper*, II. 526.)

FAWCET, RICHARD. Matric. pens. from ST JOHN'S, *c.* 1593; B.A. 1597-8. One of these names V. of Catterick, Yorks., 1603-60. Perhaps father of Timothy (1624).

FAWCET, RICHARD. Adm. sizar (age 15) at ST JOHN'S, Jan. 25, 1630-1. S. of John, farmer, of Sedbergh. B. there. School, Sedbergh. Matric. 1631.

FAUCETT, RICHARD. Adm. sizar (age 16) at ST JOHN'S, Oct. 7, 1639. S. of Oswel, yeoman, of Darlington, Durham. B. there. School, Durham (Mr Smelt). Matric. 1639.

FAWCETT, RICHARD. Adm. sizar (age 17) at PEMBROKE, May 23, 1687. S. of John, of Ravenstonedale, Westmorland. Matric. 1687; B.A. 1690-1. Ord. priest (York) May, 1695. C. of H. Trin., Hull.

FAWCETT, RICHARD. Adm. sizar (age 21) at ST JOHN'S, Mar. 5, 1724-5. S. of James, fuller, of Yorkshire. B. at Dent. School, Sedbergh. Matric. 1725; B.A. 1728-9; M.A. 1734. Incorp. at Oxford, 1734. Ord. deacon (Ely) Sept. 21, 1729; priest (York) June 4, 1732. Reader at Leeds, 1732. V. of Holbeck, 1754-5. V. of St John's, Leeds, 1768-83. Died June 7, 1783. (*Scott-Mayor*, III. 380.)

FAUCET, ROBERT. Matric. sizar from ST JOHN'S, Michs. 1576; B.A. 1580-1; M.A. 1584. V. of Kilwick Percy, Yorks., 1593-8. R. of Huggate, 1598-1602. Died 1602.

FAWCET, ROBERT. M.A. from PEMBROKE, 1631. Of Westmorland. Matric. from Queen's College, Oxford, Nov. 3, 1620, age 18; B.A. (Oxford) 1624. One of these names P.C. of Denton, Durham, 1640-57. Buried there Nov. 28, 1657. (H. M. Wood.)

FAWCETT, ROBERT. Matric. pens. from PEMBROKE, Easter, 1632.

FAUCET, ROBERT. Adm. sizar (age 17) at PEMBROKE, 1641. S. of George (1609-10), clerk. B. at Roughton, Norfolk. Matric. 1641; B.A. 1646. V. of Cromer, Norfolk, with Roughton, 1662-74. (W. Rye, *Cromer*.)

FAWCETT, ROBERT. Adm. sizar (age 18) at ST JOHN'S, July 23, 1685. S. of Thomas, husbandman. B. in Ilketshall, St Andrew's parish, Suffolk. School, Bungay. Matric. 1686; B.A. 1689-90; M.A. 1693. R. of Markshall, Norfolk, 1695. R. of Poringland, 1696-1736. V. of Aylsham, 1699. R. of Caistor St Edmund, 1695. Buried there. Father of Horace (1717) and Thomas (1715).

FAWCET, ROGER. Matric. sizar from CLARE, Easter, 1587.

FAWCET, SAMUEL. M.A. 1632 (Incorp. from Oxford). Of London. Matric. from Queen's College, Oxford, July 3, 1618, age 17; B.A. 1621; M.A. 1624. R. of St Mary Staining, London, 1628-62. R. of Whipsnade, Beds., 1642. R. of St Alphage, London, 1643-7. (*Al. Oxon.*)

FAWCET, THOMAS. Matric. sizar from ST JOHN'S, Michs. 1584; B.A. from St Catharine's, 1588-9. Incorp. as M.A. at Oxford, 1594. V. of Awre, Gloucs., 1604-36. R. of Aston-sub-Edge, 1607-36. Will (Gloucester) 1636. (*Al. Oxon.*; F. S. Hockaday.)

FAWCET, THOMAS. Adm. sizar (age 19) at CAIUS, June 6, 1589. Of Russendale (? Ravenstondale), Westmorland. S. of Cuthbert. School, Appleby. B.A. 1592-3; Scholar, 1593-4; M.A. 1596. Ord. deacon and priest (Peterb.) Feb. 1, 1594-5. R. of Aldham, Suffolk, 1595-1602.

FAWCETT or FOSSETT, THOMAS. Matric. pens. from CORPUS CHRISTI, Michs. 1625. Of Norwich. B.A. 1628-9; M.A. 1632; B.D. 1640. Pre-elected fellow, 1636, but not admitted. Preb. of Lincoln, 1660-7. R. of Yelling, Hunts., 1660. Died 1667. (*Masters*.)

FAWCETT, THOMAS. Adm. at CORPUS CHRISTI, 1694. Of London. School, St Paul's. Matric. 1695, as Fosset; B.A. 1697-8; M.A. 1701; B.D. 1709. Fellow, 1700-17. Ord. deacon (Norwich) Sept. 1699; priest, Mar. 1700-1. Presented to Monk Eleigh, Suffolk, 1717; but died before leaving College. Buried in the Chapel. (*Masters*.)

FAUCET, THOMAS. Adm. sizar (age 18) at CAIUS, May 25, 1715. S. of Robert (1685), clerk, of Caistor, Norfolk. B. at Rackheath. Schools, Holt (Mr Reynolds) and Norwich (Mr Pate). Matric. 1715; Scholar, 1715-20; LL.B. 1720. Died Aug. 23, 1726. Buried at Caistor. M.I. there. Brother of Horace (1717). (*Venn*, II. 3.)

FAUCITT, TIMOTHY. Matric. sizar from ST JOHN'S, Easter, 1624. Perhaps of Catterick, Yorks., gent. Age 58 in 1666. S. of Richard (? 1593), V. of Catterick. (M. H. Peacock.)

FAWCET, WILLIAM. B.A. 1517-8; M.A. 1521. Perhaps R. of St Rumbald's, Colchester, 1525-44.

FAWCOT, ——. M.A. 1497-8.

FAWCONER or FAWKNER, ANTHONY. Adm. pens. at EMMANUEL, July 1, 1671. Of Rutlandshire. Matric. 1672-3; B.A. 1675-6; M.A. 1679. Ord. deacon (Peterb.) Dec. 21, 1679; priest, Mar. 10, 1679-80.

FAWKNER or FALCONER, DANIEL. Matric. pens. from CHRIST'S, Dec. 1615; B.A. 1618-9; M.A. 1622. Ord. deacon (Peterb.) May, 1621; priest, Dec. 21, 1623. One of these names R. of Ackworth, Yorks., in 1634. Perhaps R. of Hinxworth, Herts., 1636-57. Died May 29, 1657. (*Peile*, I. 306.) For an Oxford contemporary, probably confused with the above, *see Al. Oxon.*

FAWKENER, EDWARD. Adm. pens. at TRINITY, May 8, 1674. Matric. 1674. One of these names M.P. for Rutland, 1681.

FAWKENER or FALKNER, EDWARD. Adm. sizar at EMMANUEL, Nov. 27, 1674. Matric. 1675; B.A. 1678-9.

FAWKNER, GEORGE. Matric. sizar from TRINITY, Easter, 1631. Of Rutland. Migrated to Queens', 1633. B.A. 1634-5.

FAWKNER or FALCONER, GERVASE. Matric. sizar from TRINITY, Easter, 1628; Scholar, 1631; B.A. 1631-2; M.A. 1635. Chaplain of Trinity, 1637. V. of Keysoe, Beds., *c.* 1640.

FAULKNER, HENRY. Matric. sizar from QUEENS', Easter, 1606, as 'Fautherner.' Of Sussex. Perhaps of Balcombe; adm. at the Inner Temple, 1610. Barrister, 1620.

FAWKENER, HENRY. Adm. Fell.-Com. at CHRIST'S, Jan. 19, 1705-6. S. of Edward, Esq. B. at Uppingham. School, Eton. Adm. at the Middle Temple, June 17, 1707. (*Peile*, II. 163.)

FAULKNER, ISAAC. Adm. pens. (age 17) at CHRIST'S, Sept. 21, 1631. S. of Abraham. B. at Stamford, Lincs. School, Oakham. Matric. 1632; B.A. 1635-6; M.A. from Magdalene, 1639. Ord. deacon (Peterb.) June 9, 1639; priest, Mar. 1, 1639-40.

FAUKENER, JOHN (1502), *see* **FEWTERER.**

FAWLKNER, JOHN. Matric. pens. from ST JOHN'S, Michs. 1544. One of these names V. of Gt Staughton, Hunts., 1558-67. Buried Dec. 13, 1567.

FAWCONER, JOHN. Matric. sizar from CORPUS CHRISTI, Michs. 1572.

FAUCKNER, JOHN. Matric. pens. from TRINITY, Easter, 1606; B.A. 1610-1, as 'Faulcon'; M.A. 1614, as 'Fawken.'

FAULCONER, JOHN. Adm. pens. at JESUS, June 10, 1635. Of Sussex. S. of John, of Balcombe. Matric. 1635. Migrated to Trinity, Nov. 30, 1638. Scholar; B.A. 1638-9. Adm. at the Inner Temple, 1638.

FAWKENER, MAURICE. Matric. sizar from MAGDALENE, Michs. 1561. Of London. B.A. 1564-5; M.A. from St John's, 1568; B.D. 1575. Fellow of St John's, 1568. University preacher, 1575. R. of Eversholt, Beds., 1575-8. Died 1578. Will, P.C.C. (*Cooper*, I. 383.)

FALKNER, RICHARD. Adm. pens. at CLARE, July 6, 1722. B. at Boston, Lincs. Matric. 1723; B.A. 1726-7; M.A. 1730. Ord. deacon (Lincoln) Sept. 21, 1729; priest, Feb. 22, 1729-30. R. of Leverton, Yorks., 1730. Preb. of Lincoln, 1753-80. Died 1780. Will, P.C.C.

FAWKNER, ROBERT. Matric. sizar from CHRIST'S, Apr. 1606; B.A. 1608-9; M.A. 1612. Incorp. at Oxford, 1616.

FALCONER, ROBERT. Adm. Fell.-Com. at MAGDALENE, June 1, 1700. M.A. of St Andrews. One of these names ord. deacon (Peterb.) Dec. 23, 1710. Perhaps V. of Gt Dunmow, Essex, 1711-29. Died 1729.

FALKNER, THOMAS. Adm. sizar at JESUS, Feb. 7, 1700–1. Of Staffordshire. Matric. 1702.

FALKNER, THOMAS. Adm. pens. at CLARE, Mar. 10, 1718–9. Matric. 1719; B.A. 1722–3; M.A. 1726. Ord. deacon (Lincoln) Dec. 19, 1725; priest, July 10, 1726. R. of Biscathorpe, Lincs., 1726.

FALCONAR, WILLIAM. M.A. 1622; Incorp. from King's College, Aberdeen; student there, 1613–7.

FALKNER or FAULKENER, WILLIAM. Adm. sizar at ST CATHARINE'S, Dec. 20, 1648. Matric. 1649. Migrated to Peterhouse, July 6, 1650. Scholar, 1652–3; B.A. 1652–3; M.A. 1656; D.D. 1680. Fellow of Peterhouse, 1654. Ord. deacon (Lincoln) June 8; priest, June 10, 1661. R. of Glemsford, Suffolk, 1679–82. Preacher at St Nicholas Chapel, King's Lynn. Married Susan, dau. of Thomas Greene, of Lynn. Author of works in defence of the Church of England. Died at Lynn, Apr. 9, 1682. Father of William (1681). (*T. A. Walker*, 96; *D.N.B.*)

FAWKNER, WILLIAM. Adm. sizar at EMMANUEL, Apr. 26, 1667. Of Rutlandshire. Matric. 1668. Buried at St Andrew's, Cambridge, July 21, 1670.

FAWCONAR, WILLIAM. Adm. pens. at QUEENS', Sept. 12, 1678. Of Wiltshire. Matric. 1679; B.A. 1682–3; M.A. 1686. Ord. priest (London) Dec. 20, 1685. One Wm Fawconar R. of Stratford Tony, Wilts. Admon. (Consist. C. Sarum) 1719.

FALKNER, WILLIAM. Adm. pens. (age 15) at PETERHOUSE, Sept. 12, 1681. Migrated to Jesus, May 5, 1683. S. of William (1649), D.D. School, Lynn. Rustat Scholar, 1684; B.A. 1685–6; M.A. from Clare, 1689. Fellow of Clare, 1688–92. Ord. priest (Lincoln) June 7, 1691. R. of Leverton, Lincs., 1691–1727. Died 1727.

FAWKENER, WILLIAM. Adm. Fell.-Com. (age 17) at CHRIST'S. May 8, 1704. S. of William, of Christ Church, London, treasurer of the Turkey Company. School, Tottenham High Cross (Mr Baxter). Adm. at the Middle Temple, Aug. 1, 1704. (*Peile*, II. 159.)

FAWCONER, WILLIAM. Adm. sizar (age 18) at PEMBROKE, June 30, 1740. S. of Edward, of St Dunstan-in-the-West, London, citizen and cutler. 'Grecian' from Christ's Hospital. Matric. 1740; B.A. 1743–4; M.A. 1747. Ord. priest (Peterb.) Dec. 20, 1747. (*A. W. Lockhart.*)

FALCONAR, ——. B.A. 1477–8; M.A. 1482.

FAWCUS, HENRY. Matric. sizar from CHRIST'S, Dec. 1573; B.A. 1576–7; M.A. 1580.

FAWCUS, JOHN Matric. sizar from CHRIST'S, Apr. 1579.

FAWDEN or FAUDEN, EDWARD. Adm. sizar at EMMANUEL, May 2, 1671. Of Suffolk. Matric. 1671; B.A. 1674–5. Ord. deacon (Norwich) Sept. 1677; priest, Mar. 1679–80. R. of Sotterley, Suffolk, 1679–1727.

FAWDON, GERARD. Matric. sizar from CHRIST'S, 1592–3.

FAWDEN, JOHN. Matric. sizar from PETERHOUSE, Michs. 1581.

FAWDEN, NICHOLAS. Matrie. pens. from TAINITY, Easter, 1572; B.A. from Clare, 1575–6. Ord. deacon and priest (Lincoln) Jan. 15, 1577–8. R. of Fordley, Suffolk, 1584–1612.

FAWDEN, THOMAS. B.A. 1537–8; M.A. 1541; B.D. 1549. Fellow of ST JOHN'S, 1537. Fellow of Eton, 1552. R. of Buxted, Sussex, 1559. Buried there Mar. 19, 1573–4. (*Cooper*, I. 320; called 'Richard' by *Baker-Mayor*.)

FAWDES, THOMAS. Matric. pens. from PEMBROKE, Michs. 1561.

FAWELL, MICHAEL. M.A. from MAGDALENE, 1726. S. of Edward, of Durham city (butcher). Bapt. at St Margaret's, Durham, Mar. 18, 1701–2. Matric. from Lincoln College, Oxford, Mar. 18, 1718–9, age 17; B.A. (Oxford) 1722. (*Al. Oxon.*)

PAWEN or FAWCON, JOHN. Franciscan friar. B.D. 1535–6.

FAWETHER, JAMES. Adm. sizar at EMMANUEL, Apr. 14, 1585. Matric. 1585; B.A. 1588–9; M.A. 1592.

FAWETHER, JOHN. B.A. from CHRIST'S (probably 1602–3). Ord. deacon (York) Sept. 1607; priest, Feb. 21, 1607–8. V. of Wissett St Andrew, Suffolk, 1627. (*Peile*, I. 233.)

FAWETHER, JOSIAS. Matric. pens. from ST JOHN'S, Michs. 1580. Probably of Talmach Hall, Bricet, Suffolk. S. of Thomas, of Hull, Yorks. Married (1) Martha, dau. of Philip Smith, of Wiltshire, (2) Elizabeth, dau. of Thomas Kemp, of Beccles. (Davy, *Suff. MSS.*)

FAWETHER, SAMUEL. Adm. Fell.-Com. at BMMANUEL, 1641. Of Suffolk. One of these names, s. of Josias (? above), of Talmach Hall, Bricet, Suffolk, J.P. for Suffolk. (Davy, *Suff. MSS.*)

FAWKE or FAWXE, ANTHONY. B.A. 1505–6.

FAWLKE, JOHN. Matrie. pens. from CLARE, Easter, 1583.

FAWKE or FALKE, THOMAS. B.Civ.L. 1511–2. Scholar and fellow of KING'S HALL, 1505–44.

FAWKES, EDWARD. Matric. sizar from NICHOLAS HOSTEL, Michs. 1548.

FAUX, EDWARD. Matric. sizar from CHRIST'S, July, 1617; B.A. 1620–1. Possibly s. of Henry (1572). (*Peile*, I. 319.)

FAWKES, FRANCIS. Adm. Fell.-Com. at JESUS, Oct. 6, 1690. Of Yorkshire. S. and h. of Thomas, of Farnley, Esq. B. June 18, 1674. Matric. 1690. Adm. at Gray's Inn, Nov. 8, 1692. Barrister, 1699. Bencher, 1724. Succeeded his father at Farnley, in 1707. M.P. for Knaresborough, 1714. J.P. for Yorkshire. Married Margaret, dau. of John Ayscough, Esq., May 7, 1700. Died Nov. 11, 1747. Buried at Otley. M.I. Brother of Thomas (1685). (Whitaker, *Loidis*; M. H. Peacock.)

FAWKES, FRANCIS. Adm. sizar at JESUS, Mar. 16, 1737–8. S. of Jeremy (1704), R. of Warmsworth, Yorks. Bapt. Apr. 4, 1720. Schools, Leeds and Bury, Lancs. Matric. 1738; Scholar; B.A. 1741–2; M.A. 1745. Ord. deacon (Lincoln) June 13, 1742; C. of Bramham, Yorks. C. of Croydon, Surrey. P.C. Orpington, Kent, 1755–74. V. of St Mary Cray, 1755. V. of Knockholt, 1755. R. of Hayes, 1774–7. R. of Downe, 1774–7. Chaplain to the Princess Dowager of Wales. Poet and translator. Died Aug. 26, 1777. Will, P.C.C. (*D.N.B.*)

FAWKES, GUY. Of the Gunpowder Plot. S. of Edward of York, proctor and advocate. Bapt. at St Michael-le-Belfry, York, Apr. 15, 1570. School, St Peter's, York. Afterwards (his own statement) at Cambridge. Can he be our 'Egrimon Fox'? (*D.N B.*; *Facsimile of National MSS.*, Sir H. James, 1868, P. IV.)

FAUX, HENRY. Matric. sizar from CHRIST'S, May, 1572; B.A. 1576–7; M.A. 1580. R. of Mepal, Isle of Ely, 1583–97. V. of Sutton, 1592–1617. Buried there Oct. 29, 1617. Will (P.C.C.).

FAWKS, JEREMY. Adm. sizar (age 18) at ST JOHN'S, June 15, 1704. S. of Nicholas, husbandman. B. at Farnley, Yorks. School, Threshfield (Mr Marshall). Matric. 1704; B.A. 1707–8. Ord. deacou (York) Sept. 1708; priest, 1710. R. of Warmsworth, Yorks., 1716–44. Buried there June 26, 1744. Father of Francis (1737–8). (*F.M.G.*, 494.)

FAULKES or FALKE, THOMAS. Matric. sizar from PETERHOUSE, Easter, 1623. Ord. deacon (Peterb.) Mar. 1; priest, Mar. 2, 1628–9.

FAWKES, THOMAS. Adm. Fell.-Com. (age 15) at MAGDALENE, July 15, 1685. S. of Thomas, Esq. B. at Farnley, Yorks., Feb. 13, 1669–70. Bapt. at Adel. School, Otley. Matric. 1685. Adm. at Lincoln's Inn, Mar. 17, 1687–8. Died while a student there. Buried under the Chapel. Brother of Francis (1690). (Whitaker, *Loidis*, 191.)

FAWLEY, RICHARD. Adm. at KING'S, a scholar from Eton, 1444; D.Can.L. Died in College, 1457. (*Harwood.*)

FAWLIAT or FAWLET, ROBERT. B.A. 1504–5. Of London. M.A. 1508. Fellow of PEMBROKE, 1505. V. of Tilney, Norfolk, 1510–19.

FAWNE, JOHN. B.A. 1493; M.A. 1496–7; B.D. 1503; D.D. 1510. Fellow of QUEENS', 1495–1513. Lady Margaret preacher, 1504. Vice-Chancellor, 1512–4. Lady Margaret Professor, 1515. Died *c.* 1519. (*Cooper*, I. 22; *Baker-Mayor*, I. 56.)

FAWNES, WILLIAM. Matric. sizar from PETERHOUSE, 1551.

FAWNT, *see* **FAUNT.**

FAYERMAN, FRANCIS. Adm. sizar (age 17) at PEMBROKE, May 19, 1698. S. of Andrew, weaver. B. in Norwich. Matric. 1698; B.A. 1701–2; M.A. 1705. Ord. deacon (Norwich) June 11, 1704; priest, Sept. 24, 1704. R. of Thurlton, Norfolk, 1713–56. R. of Geldeston, 1732–54. Married Margaret, dau. of Captain Thomas Bayspole, of Haddiscoe, Nov. 2, 1718. Author. Died Nov. 7, 1756, aged 77. Buried at Hardley. M.I. Father of the next and of Richard (1741).

FAYERMAN, JOHN. Adm. sizar (age 17) at CAIUS, July 6, 1743. S. of Francis (above), R. of Thurlton. B. at Chedgrave. Bapt. Oct. 8, 1724. School, Chedgrave (private; Mr Conold). Matric. 1743–4; Scholar, 1743–7; B.A. 1747–8. Ord. deacon (Norwich) Sept. 20, 1747; priest, May 21, 1749. R. of Geldeston, Norfolk, 1754–1816; and of Chedgrave, 1759–1816. C. of Langley-by-Carlton, 1772–1816. Married, July 14, 1760, Mary, dau. of John Fox, Sacrist of Norwich Cathedral. Died at Norwich, Aug. 1, 1816. Buried at Loddon. M.I. Brother of Richard (1741). (*Venn*, II. 53.)

FAYERMAN, RICHARD. Adm sizar (age 18) at CAIUS, Oct. 12, 1741. S. of Francis (1698), R. of Geldeston. B. at Chedgrave. Bapt. Feb. 23, 1722–3. Scholar, 1741–5; Matric. 1742; B.A. 1745–6; M.A. 1752. Ord deacon (Norwich) Sept. 22, 1745. R. of Ashby and Oby, Norfolk, 1747–1800. V. of Repps and Bastwick, 1753–1800. R. of Littlebury, Essex, 1754. Author, poetical. Died Feb. 4, 1800. Will, P.C.C. Brother of John (1743). (*Venn*, II. 50.)

FAYLE, JOHN. M.A. from CHRIST'S, 1747. Matric. from Brasenose College, Oxford, Mar. 17, 1730–1. S. of John, of Poulton, Lancs. B.A. (Oxford) 1734; D.D. from St John's (Cambridge), 1768. Will (P.C.C.) 1778; of Beckbury, Salop.

FAYR or FAIRY, JOHN. M.A. Fellow of PETERHOUSE, 1400-33. Chaplain of Little St Mary's, Cambridge, 1414-26. Donor of books to College library. (*T. A. Walker*.)

FAYRHARE, JOHN. B.Can.L. 1554-5.

FAYRHARE, WILLIAM. LL.D. V. of Swaffham Prior, Cambs., 1497-1519. Vicar-general of Ely Diocese, 1515. R. of Kirby Sigston, Yorks., 1519-23. (*Cooper*, I. 22.)

FAYTING, GEORGE. M.A. from EMMANUEL, 1669. S. of Thomas, of Bromsgrove, Worcs. Matric. from Magdalen Hall, Oxford, May 10, 1662, age 17; B.A. (Oxford) 1665. R. of All Saints', Worcester, 1668. R. of St Andrew's, 1692-1726. (*Al. Oxon.*)

FAYTING, NICHOLAS. Adm. sizar (age 19) at ST JOHN'S, Sept. 30, 1721. S. of John, factor at Blackwall Hall, Basinghall St, Middlesex. B. Jan. 22, 1700-1. School, Merchant Taylors'. Matric. 1721; B.A. 1725-6; M.A. 1729. Ord. deacon (London) Dec. 19, 1725; priest, Dec. 18, 1726. Under-Master at Merchant Taylors', 1726-53. R. of St Martin Outwich, 1748-89. Preb. of Lincoln, 1756-89. Chaplain to the Duchess of Devonshire. R of Hawkeswell, Essex, 1757-89. Died Feb. 22, 1789. Buried in St Martin's, Outwich. Will, P.C.C. (*Scott-Mayor*, III. 345.)

FAZAKERLEY, NICHOLAS. University Counsel, 1738-57. Of Prescot, Lancs. S. of Henry, of Fazakerley, near Liverpool. Matric. from Brasenose College, Oxford, Mar. 12, 1701-2, age 17. Adm. at the Middle Temple, May 13, 1700. Barrister, 1707. M.P. for Preston, 1732, 1734, 1741, 1747, 1754, 1761-7. Recorder of Preston, 1742-67. An authority on Constitutional Law. Died in London, Feb. 1767. Will, P.C.C. (*D.N.B.*; *Al. Oxon.*)

FEAKE, CHARLES. Adm. pens. (age 16) at CAIUS, Nov. 5, 1732. S. of Samuel. B. at 'Cossimbazar' (? Cossipur), India. Schools, Newington and Hackney (private). Matric. 1732; Scholar, 1733-8; M.B. 1738; M.D. 1743. Candidate of the Royal College of Physicians, 1744. Fellow, 1745. Censor, 1747. F.R.S. 1748. Harveian orator, 1749. Consiliarius, 1761. Physician to Guy's Hospital. Died Aug. 2, 1762. Will, P.C.C. (*Venn*, II. 36.)

FEAKE, CHRISTOPHER. Adm. pens. at EMMANUEL, 1628. S. of Edward, of Godstone, Surrey; age 11 in 1623. Matric. 1628; B.A. 1631-2; M.A. 1635. 'Fifth Monarchy' man. V. of Elsham, Lincs. V. of All Saints', Hertford, 1646. Perhaps V. of Christ Church, Newgate, 1649. Lecturer at St Anne's, Blackfriars. Imprisoned for denouncing Cromwell, 1653, but subsequently released. Published millenarian writings. (*D.N.B.*, which makes no reference to his University career; *Vis. of Surrey*, 1623.)

FEAKE, HENRY. Matric. pens. from EMMANUEL, Lent, 1584-5. Of Norfolk. Migrated to Caius. B.A. 1588-9. Ord. priest (Norwich) Jan. 1, 1595-6. R. of Warham St Mary and St Margaret, Norfolk.

FEAKE, JOHN. Adm. pens. (age 17) at TRINITY, June 19, 1676. S. of William. B. at Stanbrooke Hall, Staffordshire. Educated there. Matric. 1678. Migrated to Jesus, May 30, 1679. Scholar, 1679; B.A. 1679-80; M.A. 1683. (*Staffs. Pedigrees*.)

FEAKE, SAMUEL. Adm. pens. at EMMANUEL, Apr. 1629. Of Hertfordshire. S. of John, goldsmith, of London and Elstree, Herts. Matric. 1631; B.A. 1632-3; M.A. 1636. V. of Staindrop, Durham, 1652-60. One of these names R. of Fosell, Warws., and of St Michael's, Coventry, 1662. (*Vis. of Surrey*, 1623.)

FEAKE, THOMAS. Adm. pens. at EMMANUEL, Lent, 1584-5. S. of Robert, of Witchingham, Norfolk, mercer. School, Norwich. Matric. 1584-5. Migrated to Caius, Dec. 20, 1587, age 21. B.A. 1589-90. Ord. priest (Norwich) Jan. 1, 1595-6. C. of Oby and Ashby, Norfolk. (*Venn*, I. 132; where he is confused with Henry.)

FEAKE, THOMAS. Matric. pens. from TRINITY, Easter, 1589. S. of William, of London, goldsmith. Scholar, 1590; B.A. 1592-3; M.A. 1596. Mentioned in his father's will (P.C.C.) 1595. (*Vis. of Surrey*, 1623.)

FEARON, *see also* FERON.

FEARON, JOSEPH. Adm. pens. (age 17) at TRINITY, Feb. 18, 1740-1. S. of Joseph, of London. School, St Paul's. Matric. 1741; Scholar, 1742; B.A. 1744-5; M.A. from Sidney, 1748; B.D. 1755. Fellow of Sidney, 1748. Ord. priest (Ely) Oct. 29, 1749.

FEASOR, ROGER. Matric. sizar from TRINITY, c. 1594; B.A. 1597-8, as Peyzor.

FEAST, EDWARD. Matric. sizar from KING'S, Easter, 1664. Adm. at Clare, May 19, 1666; B.A. 1667-8.

FEAST, EDWARD. Adm. pens. (age 16) at PEMBROKE, July 7, 1668. S. of William, mercer. B. at Ipswich. Matric. 1668; B.A. 1671-2; M.A. 1675. Fellow, 1674. Taxor, 1686. President, 1703. Ord. deacon (London) Aug. 12; priest, Aug. 14, 1679. V. of Elmeden, Essex, 1679. R. of Framlingham, Suffolk, 1694. Died at Elmeden, Jan. 25, 1703.

FEATHERSTON, *see* FETHERSTON.

FEATHERSTONHAUGH, *see* FETHERSTONHAUGH.

FEATLEY, *see also* FAIRCLOUGH.

FEATLEY, HENRY. Adm. sizar at CHRIST'S, June 28, 1677. Matric. 1679; B.A. 1680-1. Ord. deacon (York) Sept. 1681; priest, Dec. 1689. Perhaps s. of John Fairclough or Featley, of Newark. Bapt. there, Sept. 7, 1660. Buried there Apr. 23, 1711. (*Peile*, II. 65; *Lincs. Pedigrees*.)

FECHER, ——. B.A. or M.A. 1501-2.

FEE, ISAAC. Matric. pens. from CORPUS CHRISTI, Michs. 1580.

FEEFER, WILLIAM. Adm. pens. at TRINITY, Oct. 8, 1642.

FEELER, JOHN. Matric. pens. from CHRIST'S, Dec. 1615.

FEELER, ROBERT. Matric. pens. from CHRIST'S, Dec. 1615.

FEEZER, RICHARD. Adm. sizar (age 15) at ST JOHN'S, Nov. 9, 1664. S. of William, deceased, of Catwick-in-Holderness, Yorks. B. there. School, Brandesburton (Mr Steele). Matric. 1664; B.A. 1668-9; M.A. 1672. Ord. deacon (York) June, 1669; priest (Peterb.) Sept. 20, 1674. R. of Croydon, Cambs., 1675-83. V. of Wendy, 1683-1718. Buried there Nov. 23, 1718, as 'Fearer.'

FEHER, ——. Fee for M.A. or higher degree, 1478-9.

FEILDING, *see* FIELDING.

FEIST, *see* FISTE.

FELDHAM, WILLIAM, *see* FELTHAM.

FELGATE, WILLIAM. Adm. sizar (age 17) at ST JOHN'S, Apr. 18, 1681. S. of Samuel, V. of Mitton-in-Craven, Yorks. B. there. School, Clitheroe (Mr Cockroft). Matric. 1681. C. at Ribchester, Lancs., 1686-90. Buried there Dec. 1, 1690. Doubtless same as next.

FELGATE, WILLIAM. Adm. sizar (age 17) at JESUS, Apr. 15, 1681. Of Yorkshire. Perhaps same as above.

FELIX (? FELIP), ——. Two years at Oxford; three at Cambridge. B.Civ.L. 1503-4. (*Gr. Bk.* Γ, 24.)

FELL, CHARLES. Adm. at CORPUS CHRISTI, 1667 Of Suffolk. Matric. 1668. Probably of Gt Wenham.

FELL, EDWARD. Matric. pens. from CHRIST'S, Nov. 1547.

FELL, EDWARD. Adm. sizar (age 20) at ST JOHN'S, June 5, 1657. S. of Richard, yeoman, of Aldingham, Lancs. B. there. School, Sedbergh. Matric. 1657; B.A. 1660-1; M.A. 1664. Head Master of Sedbergh School, 1662-74. R. of Bentham, Yorks., 1670-4. Died Oct. 25, 1674.

FELL, GEORGE. Matric. sizar from PEMBROKE, Lent, 1588-9; B.A. 1592-3; M.A. 1596.

FELL, GEORGE. Adm. Fell.-Com. (age 15) at CHRIST'S, July 6, 1655. S. of Thomas, judge, of Swarthmoor Hall, Lancs. School, Little Urswick (Mr Iugman). Matric. 1655. Adm. at Gray's Inn, Feb. 9, 1652-3, as s. of Thomas, of Swarthmore, Lancs. Died 1670. (*Peile*, I. 569; *Vict. Hist. of Lancs.*, VIII. 354.)

FELL, HENRY. Fellow of CORPUS CHRISTI, 1400. (*Masters*.)

FELL, JOHN. Matric. sizar from MAGDALENE, Michs. 1588; B.A. 1593-4. One of these names 'B.A.,' V. of Kirkharle, Northumberland, 1613-6.

FELL, JOHN. Adm. sizar (age 19) at PEMBROKE, Oct. 7, 1620. S. of Thomas (? 1571), of Tydd, Lincs. Matric. 1620; B.A. 1623-4. Schoolmaster at Wiggenhall St German's (*apud Pontem Ste Germane*), Isle of Ely, 1623.

FELL, SPENCER. Matric. sizar from CORPUS CHRISTI, Easter, 1620. Of Norwich. B.A. 1623-4; M.A. 1627. R. of Flixton, Suffolk, 1633-5. R. of Gt Wenham, 1635-76. Died 1676, aged 77. M.I. at Wenham. (*E. Anglian*, VIII. 221.)

FELL, THOMAS. Scholar of TRINITY, 1571; B.A. 1571-2. Ord. deacon (Lincoln) Nov. 7, 1576; priest (London) Dec. 1, 1579. Perhaps V. of East Tilbury, Essex, 1586. One of these names R. of Tydd St Mary, Lincs., 1593-1614. Preb. of Lincoln, 1593-5. Perhaps father of John (1620).

FELL, WILLIAM, D.D. Probably of Furness, Lancs. Archdeacon of Nottingham, 1516-28. Perhaps R. of Theydon Mount, Essex, 1499-1514. Benefactor to ST JOHN'S. Died, 1528. Will (P.C.C.); of Charterhouse, London, and Leicester. (*Cooper*, I. 37.)

FELL, WILLIAM. Matric. sizar (age 16) from PEMBROKE, Michs. 1623. S. of Thomas (? 1571), of Tydd St Mary, Lincs. B.A. 1627-8; M.A. 1631. Ord. deacon (Peterb.) Mar. 1, 1628-9; priest, May 31, 1629. V. of St Mary Castlegate, York. Resided at Clementthorpe Hall. (*F.M.G.*, 902.)

FELL, ——. Incorp. from Sienna, 1497-8.

FELLOWE, EDWARD. Matric. sizar from QUEENS', Michs. 1615. Of Leicestershire. B.A. 1618-9; M.A. 1622. Ord. deacon (Peterb.) May 23, 1619; priest, Mar. 12, 1619-20. R. of St Alphage, Canterbury, 1661-3. R. of Stonar, Kent, till his death, in 1663. Buried at St Alphage's, May 18, 1663. (H. G. Harrison.)

FELLOWE, JOHN. Matric. pens. from TRINITY, 1557-8; Scholar, 1560.

FELLOWES, WILLIAM. Adm. pens. (age 15) at TRINITY, Apr. 19, 1676. S. of William, of London. B. there, Oct. 4, 1660. School, Eufield (Mr Robert Udall). Matric. 1677. Adm. at Lincoln's Inn, Nov. 2, 1678. Barrister-at-law, 1686. Bencher, 1708. Treasurer, 1718. Master in Chancery, 1707-24. F.R.S. 1708. Of Eggesford, Devonshire, Esq. Died Jan. 19, 1723-4. Buried at Eggesford.

FELLOWS, WILLIAM. Adm. sizar at ST CATHARINE'S, July 1, 1692. Matric. 1694; B.A. 1696-7. Ord. deacon (London) Sept. 24, 1699. R. of Broughton Hacket, Worcs., 1702. V. of Tibberton, 1708.

FELLOWES, WILLIAM. Adm. Fell.-Com. (age 17) at ST JOHN'S, June 26, 1744. S. of Coulson, gent., of Ramsey Abbey, Hunts. School, Dalston, near Hackney, Middlesex (Mr Graham). Matric. 1744. High Sheriff of Cambs. and Hunts., 1779. M.P. for Andover, 1784-96. Died Feb. 3, 1804, in London. Will, P.C.C. (*Scott-Mayor*, III. 544.)

FELMINGHAM, ——. A friar. B.D. *c.* 1492; D.D. 1495-6. One Dr Felmingham was Prior of the Black Friars at Norwich in 1499. (Will of Tho. Caryngton, P.C.C.)

FELMINGHAM, ——. B.A. 1499-1500.

FELSTED, RICHARD. Adm. pens. at EMMANUEL, June 15, 1620. S. of Thomas, of Audley End, Essex. Died *s.p.* (*Vis. of Cambs.*, 1684.)

FELSTEAD, SAMUEL. Adm. pens. (age 16) at CAIUS, Mar. 27, 1646. S. of Thomas, merchant and bailiff of Yarmouth, Norfolk. B. there. Bapt. at St Nicholas, Nov. 6, 1629. School, Hoxne, Suffolk (Mr Hall). Matric. 1646; Scholar, 1647-50; B.A. 1649-50. Probably buried at Yarmouth, Jan. 10, 1651-2. (*Venn*, I. 361.)

FELSTED, THOMAS. Matric. sizar from ST JOHN'S, Easter, 1605. S. of Thomas, of Audley End, Essex. B.A. 1608-9; M.A. 1612. Died beyond sea, unmarried. (*Vis. of Cambs.*, 1684.)

FELSTEAD, THOMAS. Adm. sizar (age 15) at CHRIST'S, Dec. 18, 1671. S. of Thomas, alderman of Cambridge. B. there. School, Perse (Mr Griffith). B.A. 1675-6; M.A. 1679. Ord. deacon (London) June 10, 1677; priest (Norwich) June, 1680. R. of Bodney, Norfolk, 1681-90. Preb. of St Paul's, 1691-1711. R. of Christ Church, Southwark, 1691-1711. Died 1711. (*Vis. of Cambs.*, 1684; *Peile*, II. 39.)

FELT, JONATHAN. Adm. sizar at TRINITY, May 1, 1658.

FELTHAM, RALPH. Adm. Fell.-Com. (age 16) at TRINITY, Jan. 28, 1706-7. S. of Charles, of London. School, Eufield, Middlesex (Dr Uvedale). Matric. 1707. Adm. at the Middle Temple, Nov. 21, 1710; and at Gray's Inn, May 2, 1722. Bencher, 1736. Treasurer, 1747. Died Sept. 13, 1751. (*G. Mag.*)

FELTHAM, THOMAS. Adm. sizar (age 17) at TRINITY, May 1, 1660. Of Norfolk. School, Norwich. Migrated to Peterhouse, Feb. 13, 1660-1. Matric. 1661; Scholar, 1661; B.A. 1663. Probably buried in Norwich Cathedral, Oct. 2, 1668. In Holy Orders.

FELTHAM, WILLIAM. Adm. pens. (age 16) at PETERHOUSE, Feb. 4, 1650-1. Matric. Easter, 1651. Of Norfolk. S. of Robert, of Sculthorpe, Norfolk. School, Norwich. Scholar, 1651; B.A. 1654. Adm. at Gray's Inn, June 27, 1654. Of Rougham, Suffolk. Died 1664. (*T. A. Walker*, 97.)

FELTON, ANTHONY. Matric. sizar from QUEENS', Michs. 1570. One of these names, of Newcastle-on-Tyne, Queen's Escheator, Surveyor of Crown Land, etc. M.P. for Morpeth, 1586. Lord of the Manor of Ovington, Northumberland, 1591. Said to have died near London, *c.* 1612. (H. M. Wood.)

FELTON, GEORGE. Matric. pens. from CHRIST'S, Easter, 1559. Perhaps s. of George, of Glemsford, Suffolk. (*Vis. of Suffolk*; *Peile*, I. 68.)

FELTON, GEORGE. Adm. sizar (age 19) at SIDNEY, Apr. 1, 1702. S. of George, farmer, of Turnhill, Salop. School, Wem (Mr Williams). Matric. 1704; B.A. 1705-6; M.A. 1711. Incorp. at Oxford, 1711. Died Nov. 27, 1721. M.I. at St Anne's, Manchester. Perhaps father of William (1735). (*Scott-Mayor*, III. 469.)

FELTON, HENRY. Matric. Fell.-Com. from TRINITY, Easter, 1607. Doubtless s. and h. of Sir Anthony, of Playford, Suffolk, Knt.; adm. at Gray's Inn, Nov. 3, 1609. Succeeded his father, 1614. Created Bart., 1620. Died Sept. 18, 1624. (*G.E.C.*, I. 154.)

FELTON, HENRY. Adm. pens. (age 17) at ST JOHN'S, Nov. 1, 1673. S. of Sir Henry, Knt. Of Suffolk; and grandson of Henry (1607). Bapt. at Gt Fakenham, Jan. 2, 1654-5. School, Thetford. Matric. 1677; B.A. 1677-8; M.A. from Peterhouse, 1681; LL.D. 1688. Fellow of Peterhouse, 1681-98. Public Orator, 1689-98. College testimonial for deacon's orders, 1690. R. of Long Melford, Suffolk, 1690-1701. Married Isabella, dau. of Baptist May, Esq. Buried at Playford, Apr. 26, 1701. Will (P.C.C.) 1702. (Burke, *Ext. Bart.*; *Davy MSS.*)

FELTON or FELTHAM, JOHN. B.A. 1519-20.

FELTON, JOHN. Adm. pens. at EMMANUEL, June 25, 1596. Matric. 1596.

FELTON, JOHN. Adm. sizar (age 15) at CAIUS, Apr. 28, 1648. S. of Robert (1608). B. at Little Gransden, Cambs. School, Hitchin (Mr Kempe). Matric. 1648; Scholar, 1650-2; B.A. 1651-2; M.A. 1655; B.D. 1662. Fellow, 1652-6. Usher of the Perse School, Cambridge, 1653-6. Author. Died in College. Will proved (V.C.C.) Sept. 20, 1667. Brother of William (1641). (*Venn*, I. 371.)

FELTON, JOHN. Adm. pens. at TRINITY, Mar. 7, 1659-60. Probably 2nd s. of Timothy, of Ovington, Essex, gent. Matric. 1660. Adm. at Lincoln's Inn, May 8, 1662. Brother of Timothy (1656-7) and father of the next.

FELTON, JOHN. Adm. pens. (age 18) at TRINITY, June 20, 1699. S. of John (above), of Ovington, Essex. School, Westminster. Matric. 1700; Scholar, 1700; B.A. 1702-3; M.A. 1706. Fellow, 1705. Adm. at Lincoln's Inn, Oct. 22, 1698. Died Apr. 1735. (A. B. Beaven.)

FELTON, NICHOLAS. Matric. pens. from QUEENS', Easter, 1577. Of Norfolk. S. of John, merchant, of Yarmouth (will, P.C.C., 1602). B. 1556, at Yarmouth. Migrated to Pembroke. B.A. 1580-1; M.A. 1584; B.D. 1591; D.D. 1602. Fellow of Pembroke, *c.* 1582. Greek lecturer, 1586. Master of Pembroke, 1617-9. Ord. deacon and priest (Peterb.) Aug. 15, 1589. R. of St Helen's, London, 1592. R. of St Anthony, 1592-5. R. of St Mary-le-Bow, London, 1596-1617. R. of Gt Easton, Essex, 1616-26. Preb. of St Paul's, 1616-8. Bishop of Bristol, 1617-9. Bishop of Ely, 1619-26. V. of Blagdon, Somerset. An eminent scholar and theologian. Compiled statutes for Merchant Taylors' School, in reference to the annual probation days. Appointed one of the translators of the Bible Died Oct. 5, 1626. Buried in St Antholin's Church, London. Will, P.C.C. Father of the next and Robert (1608). (*Loder*; *D.N.B.*; J. Ch. Smith.)

FELTON, NICHOLAS. Matric. pens. from PEMBROKE, Easter, 1610. S. of Nicholas (above), D.D. Migrated to Oxford. B.A. (Christ Church) 1612; M.A. 1615. Incorp. at Cambridge, 1621. R. of Streatham, Cambs., 1622-42.

FELTON, NICHOLAS. Matric. sizar (age 15) from PEMBROKE, Easter, 1634. S. of Robert (1608). B.A. 1637-8; M.A. 1641. Fellow, 1633; ejected, 1644. Ord. deacon (Lincoln) Dec. 23, 1660, as 'M.A.' R. of Hardwick, Cambs., 1670. R. of Rettenden, Essex, 1670-2. R. of Newton, Cambs., 1672. Brother of William (1641).

FELTON, RICHARD. Matric. sizar from CHRIST'S, Nov. 1581. Probably of Suffolk. B.A. 1584-5; M.A. 1588. Ord. deacon and priest (Lincoln) Dec. 18, 1588. V. of Patcham, Sussex, 1598. Died before Nov. 1608. (W. C. Renshaw; *Peile*, I. 167.)

FELTON, ROBERT. Matric. pens. from PEMBROKE, Michs. 1608. S. of Nicholas (1577). B.A. 1612-3. Fellow, 1613-8. Incorp. M.A. (Oxford) 1617. Ord. deacon (Peterb.) Aug. 5; priest, Aug. 6, 1619, as M.A. R. of Glemsford, Suffolk, 1619; of Little Gransden, Cambs., 1623-42. Father of William (1641) and John (1648).

FELTON, THOMAS. Pensioner at GONVILLE HALL, 1519. One of these names chaplain at Wyton, in Holderness, Yorks., in 1526. (M. H. Peacock.)

FELTON, THOMAS. Adm. pens. at CORPUS CHRISTI, 1601. Of Essex. Matric. Easter, 1602; B.A. 1605-6; M.A. 1609. R. of Little Bromley, Essex, 1611. Will (P.C.C.) 1656.

FELTON, TIMOTHY. Adm. pens. at TRINITY, Feb. 24, 1656-7. Probably s. and h. of Timothy, of Ovington, Essex, gent. Matric. 1657. Adm. at Lincoln's Inn, Apr. 25, 1659. Brother of John (1659-60).

FELTON, WILLIAM. Adm. sizar at PEMBROKE, May 25, 1641. S. of Robert (1608). B. at Little Gransden, Cambs. Matric. 1641; B.A. 1644-5; M.A. 1652. Brother of John (1648).

FELTON, WILLIAM. Adm. sizar (age 19) at ST JOHN'S, June 26, 1735. S. of George (? 1702), clerk, of Salop. B. at Drayton. School, Manchester (Mr Brooke). Matric. 1735; B.A. 1738-9; M.A. 1745. Probably R. of Wendon Lofts and Elmdon, Essex, 1740-81. Master of the Grammar School, Highgate. Died Jan. 9, 1781. Will, P.C.C.

One of these names (identified by *D.N.B.* with the above) was ord. priest (Hereford) Aug. 11, 1742. Vicar-choral in the choir of Hereford, 1741; custos of the Vicars-choral, 1769; and chaplain to the Princess Dowager of Wales. A skilled performer on the harpsichord and other instruments. Died Dec. 6, 1769. Buried in Hereford Cathedral. Admon. (P.C.C.) 1770. (*Scott-Mayor*, III. 469; *D.N.B.*)

FELTON, ——. Adm. student at PETERHOUSE, Aug. 2, 1567.

FELTWELL, ROBERT. Adm. sizar (age 15) at CAIUS, July 5, 1626. S. of Robert, gent. B. at Fenteney, Norfolk. Matric. 1626; B.A. 1630–1. Ord. priest (Norwich) Sept. 23, 1632. C. of Barningham, Norfolk, in 1636. V. of East Walton, in 1660. V. of Ormesby, 1662–9. Buried there Nov. 2, 1669. Author, *David's Recognition*, a sermon; from which he seems to have suffered during the Rebellion. (*Venn*, I. 278.)

FELTWELL, ——. *Cautio* for degree, 1487–8.

FELYS, —— (rector). B.Can.L. 1487–8.

FEMERS, WILLIAM. Matric. pens. from MAGDALENE, Michs. 1586; B.A. 1589–90; M.A. 1593. Ord. deacon and priest (Peterb.) Oct. 15, 1592. R. of Cavendish, Suffolk, 1609–10. V. of Newton, 1609.

FENBY, WILLIAM. Matric. sizar from ST JOHN'S, Easter, 1605; B.A. 1608–9.

FENBY, WILLIAM. Matric. sizar from ST JOHN'S, Easter, 1606 (perhaps a repetition of the above).

FENBY, WILLIAM. Adm. at CORPUS CHRISTI, 1648. Of Yorkshire.

FENDER, GEORGE. M.A. from KING'S, 1733. B.A. from Trinity College, Dublin. Adm. there June 13, 1722, age 22. S. of William. B.A. 1726. Incorp. at Oxford, 1733. Of St Stephen's, Cornwall, clerk. Will (Exeter), 1771.

FENEY, GILES. Matric. pens. from TRINITY, Easter, 1571. Probably s. of William, of Almondbury, Yorks. Will, 1616; of York. (M. H. Peacock.)

FENNY, JOHN. Matric. pens. from ST JOHN'S, *c.* 1593; B.A. 1596–7.

FEYNEY, NICHOLAS. Matric. pens. from TRINITY, Michs. 1560.

PENYE, ROGER. Matric. pens. from ST JOHN'S, Michs. 1559.

FENAY, THOMAS. Adm. pens. (age 16) at SIDNEY, May 17, 1625. S. of Thomas. B. at Fenay (near Huddersfield). Bapt. June 24, 1608. School, Fenay (Mr Bellwood). Matric. 1625. Of Fenay Hall. Succeeded to the estate, 1644. Married Mary dau. of Richard Horsfall, of Storthes Hall. Died before 1649. (C. Hulbert, *Almondbury*, 155; *F.M.G.*)

FENGE, JOHN. Fellow of GONVILLE HALL, *c.* 1460–80.

FENHOUSE, DELIVERANCE. Adm. pens. at QUEENS', Apr. 30, 1625. S. of Richard, minister of Barby, Northants. B. in Bedfordshire. Matric. from Exeter College, Oxford, 1622, age 18; B.A. (Oxford) 1626–7; M.A. 1634. Ord. deacon (Lichfield) Sept. 19, 1629; priest, Feb. 20, 1629–30. P.C. of Stone, Staffs., 1642–6. R. of Leigh, 1646–66. Will of Richard Fennyhouse, of Stone, Staffs. (P.C.C.) 1618. (*Wm. Salt Arch. Soc.*, 1915.)

FENNE (or FAME), EDMUND. B.A. 1522–3; M.A. 1526.

FENN, EDWARD. Adm. pens. (age 18) at CAIUS, Mar. 14, 1694–5. S. of William, gent., of Houghton, Norfolk. B. at Swanton Novers. Schools, Walsingham (Mr Green) and Barsham (Mr Tompson). Matric. 1695; Scholar, 1695–1702; B.A. 1698–9. Ord. deacon (Norwich) Mar. 1701–2; priest, Sept. 1702. C. of Gt Snoring, 1702. Died Feb. 21, 1710–1. M.I. at Snoring. Will (Norwich Archd. C.) 1711. (*Venn*, I. 496.)

FENNE, GEORGE. Ord. priest (Peterb.) June 11, 1620, as 'late of CORPUS CHRISTI.' No matriculation or degree found. V. of Mendham, Suffolk, 1631.

FENNE, GILES. Matric. pens. from ST JOHN'S, Michs. 1548.

FEN, HENRY. Adm. sizar at SIDNEY, Sept. 24, 1608. Matric. 1608.

FENN, HUGH. Founder of a 'chest' for the benefit of poor scholars, *c.* 1480. Probably a member of the University.

FENN, HUMPHREY. Matric. sizar from QUEENS', Michs. 1568; B.A. 1572–3; M.A. from Peterhouse, 1576. V. of Holy Trinity, Coventry, 1578. Suffered suspension and imprisonment as a puritan. Returned to Coventry, 1592. Appointed lecturer at St John the Baptist's, 1624. Buried Feb. 8, 1634, in Holy Trinity Churchyard, Coventry. (*Cooper*, II. 150; *D.N.B.*)

FENN, JOHN. Matric. sizar from CORPUS CHRISTI, Easter, 1640. Of Norfolk. B.A. 1642–3. Probably Master of Holt Grammar School, Norfolk, 1644–6. (L. B. Radford, *Holt School*, p. 123; but see p. 105.)

FENN, JOHN. Adm. pens. at QUEENS', 1651. Probably s. of William, of Essex. Matric. Lent, 1653–4; B.A. 1654–5; M.A. 1658. C. of Barsham, 1662. Perhaps R. of Shipmeadow, Suffolk, 1667–70; and R. of Theberton. Buried there Oct. 22, 1678. (*E. Anglian*, I. 243.)

FENN, NICHOLAS. Matric. pens. from JESUS, Lent, 1557–9. One of these names adm. at Lincoln's Inn, Oct. 11, 1561.

FEN, RICHARD. B.Civ.L. 1502–3; B.Can.L. 1506–7.

FENN, RICHARD. Adm. Fell.-Com. at EMMANUEL, Apr. 25, 1646. Of Middlesex.

FENN, ROBERT. B.A. from TRINITY, 1600–1; M.A. from King's, 1605. Incorp. at Oxford, 1605. Author, *Verses*. (*Cooper*, II. 445.)

FENN, ROBERT. Adm. pens. at TRINITY, June 11, 1637. Matric. 1637.

FENN, SAMUEL. Adm. sizar at ST CATHARINE'S, June 3, 1680; B.A. 1683–4. Perhaps R. of Campsea Ashe, Suffolk.

FENN, SIMON. Matric. pens. from JESUS, Lent, 1582–3.

FENN, STEPHEN. Adm. pens. (age 17) at CAIUS, Apr. 17, 1646. S. of Thomas, gent., of Houghton, Norfolk. B. there. School, Norwich (Mr Cushing and Lovering). Matric. 1646; Scholar, 1648–9; B.A. 1649. One of these names minister of Walberswick; and of Southwold, Suffolk, till his death, in 1654. (*Venn*, I. 362.)

FEN, THOMAS. Adm. at KING'S (age 17) a scholar from Eton, Aug. 25, 1595. B. at Old Windsor, Berks. Matric. *c.* 1595; B.A. 1599; M.A. 1603. Fellow, 1598–1604. A physician. Will (P.C.C.) 1608; practitioner in physic, Leicester. (*Harwood*.)

FENN, THOMAS. Adm. pens. at CLARE, July 5, 1634. Matric. 1635. Ord. deacon (Norwich) Mar. 17, 1643–4, age 26, as B.A. C. of Watlington, Norfolk.

FENNE, WILLIAM. Student at Cambridge, *c.* 1500–1. A monk from Westminster Abbey. (Pearce, *Monks of Westminster*.)

FENNE, WILLIAM. Adm. sizar at EMMANUEL, Feb. 20, 1609–10. Matric. 1610; B.A 1613. R. of Theberton, Suffolk, 1626.

FENNE, WILLIAM. Adm. pens. (age 17) at CAIUS, Apr. 11, 1646. S. of Edward, gent., of Harrow-on-the-Hill. B. in London. School, Harrow. Matric. 1646; Scholar, 1646–50; B.A. 1649–50; M.A. 1653. Adm. at Gray's Inn, June 6, 1649. Barrister, 1660. Governor of Harrow School, 1683. (*Venn*, I. 362; *Vis. of London*, 1634.)

FEN, —— (rector). B.Can.L. 1467–8.

FENNEL, GEORGE. Adm. sizar (age 16) at ST JOHN'S, June 18, 1640. S. of Mathew, husbandman, of Bumsted, Essex. B. at Birdbrooke, Essex. School, Bumsted (private; Mr Thornbeck). Matric. 1640, as 'Fennie.'

FENNELL, JOHN. Matric. pens. from CLARE, Easter, 1579. B. at Bourne, Sussex. B.A. 1582–3; M.A. from King's, 1586. Ord. deacon (London) May 22, 1584, age 23; priest (Lincoln) 1586. R. of Cattistock, Dorset, 1588.

FENNELL, RICHARD. Adm. sizar at QUEENS', June 5, 1673. Of Sussex. Matric. 1673. Exhibitioner from Tonbridge School; B.A. 1676–7.

FENNELL, ROBERT. Matric. pens. from CLARE, Michs. 1569.

FENNER, DUDLEY. Matric. Fell.-Com. from PETERHOUSE, Easter, 1575. B. in Kent. Minister at Marden and Cranbrook, Kent, 1575–6 and 1583–4. Afterwards a reformed minister at Antwerp, and later chaplain to the English merchants at Middelburg. Author, *Arts of Logic and Rhetoric*; and various theological treatises. Died at Middelburg, *c.* 1587. (*D.N.B.*; *Cooper*, II. 72.)

FENNER, EDWARD. Matric. Fell.-Com. from ST JOHN'S, *c.* 1593. One of these names s. of Sir Edward. Died 1614. (Dallaway, *Sussex*, I. 16.)

FENNER, NICHOLAS. Matric. sizar from PETERHOUSE, Easter, 1578. Admon. of Nicholas Farmer (P.C.C.) 1636; of Mells, Suffolk, clerk. (J. Ch. Smith.)

FENNER, THOMAS. Adm. sizar (age 18) at PEMBROKE, May 18, 1627. S. of John, verger, of Rochester Cathedral. B. at Rochester. Matric. 1627; B.A. 1630–1.

FENNER, WILLIAM. Matric. pens. (age 13) from PETERHOUSE, Michs. 1576.

FENNER, WILLIAM. Matric. sizar from PEMBROKE, Easter, 1612; B.A. 1615–6; M.A. 1619; B.D. 1627. Fellow, 1618. Incorp. at Oxford, 1622. V. of Sedgley, Staffs., 1625–7; ejected. V. of Harston, Cambs., 1625. Minister of St Peter's, Ipswich. R. of Rochford, Essex, 1629–40. Puritan author. Died 1640, aged 40. (*Fast. Oxon.*; *D.N.B.*; P. Benton, *Rochford*, 860.)

FENNETT, JOHN. Matric. Fell.-Com. from ST JOHN'S, Easter, 1588.

FENNING, JEREMY. Adm. pens. at EMMANUEL, Feb. 20, 1609–10. Matric. 1610; B.A. 1613–4.

FENNYNGE, JOHN. Adm. pens. (age 18) at CAIUS, Aug. 5, 1567. S. of John. Of Braintree, Essex. School, Braintree. Matric. 1567, as 'Josias.' Ord. deacon (London) Feb. 24, 1569–70. V. of Henham, Essex, 1575–1609, as Josias. Will (Consist. C. London) 1609.

FENNY, *see* FENEY.

FENOUR, ANDREW. Matric. Fell.-Com. from ST JOHN'S, Michs. 1622.

FENTON, ANTHONY. Matric. sizar from ST JOHN'S, Easter, 1625; B.A. 1629-30; M.A. 1633. Ord. deacon (Peterb.) Apr. 25; priest, Apr. 26, 1630. P.C. of Wix, Essex, 1632. Perhaps V. of Wickham Skeith, Suffolk, 1664-70.

FENTON, ANTHONY. Adm. sizar at JESUS, July 4, 1663. Of Suffolk. Matric. 1663; B.A. 1666-7; M.A. 1670. Ord. priest (Norwich) Feb. 1674-5; C. of St John Maddermarket, Norwich. R. of Little Thornham, Suffolk, 1702-12.

FENTON, BUTLER. Adm. pens. at JESUS, June 28, 1732. B. in the West Indies. Matric. 1732; LL.B. 1740. In the will of S. Dunbar, late of Isle of Nevis (P.C.C., 1759) is allusion to Rev. Butler Fenton. (J. Ch. Smith.)

FENTON, CHARLES. Matric. sizar from PETERHOUSE, Lent, 1582-3.

FENTON, ELIJAH. Adm. sizar at JESUS, July 1, 1700. S. of John, attorney. Of Staffordshire. B. at Shelton, near Newcastle-under-Lyme, May 25, 1683. Matric. 1701; Scholar, 1701; B.A. 1704-5; M.A. from Trinity Hall, 1726. Secretary to the Earl of Orrery, in Flanders. Master of Sevenoaks Grammar School. Poet. Translated part of the *Odyssey* for Pope. Died July 16, 1730. Buried at East Hampstead, Berks. (*D.N.B.*; W. W. Lloyd, *Elijah Fenton*, 1894.)

FENTON, HENRY. Matric. pens. from JESUS, Michs. 1568.

FENTON, HENRY. Matric. pens. from PEMBROKE, Easter, 1606.

FENTON, HENRY. Adm. sizar (age 17) at PEMBROKE, June 20, 1670. S. of Thomas, farmer. B. at Copmanthorpe, Yorks. Matric. 1671; B.A. 1673-4. Ord. deacon (York) Dec. 1674; priest, Sept. 1676. V. of Ilketshall St Mary, Suffolk, 1679-94. V. of Mettingham, 1681-94.

FENTON, JAMES. Adm. pens. at JESUS, Sept. 12, 1649. Of Suffolk. Matric. 1650; Scholar, 1651; B.A. 1653-4; M.A. 1657. University Librarian, 1655. R. of Waldingfield, Suffolk, 1661. V. of Mildenhall, 1662. V. of Dovercourt and Harwich, 1663-78. Died 1678. Admon. (P.C.C.) Nov. 1678.

FENTON, JAMES. LL.B. from MAGDALENE, 1690. S. of John, of Garthes, Westmorland, clerk. Matric. from Queen's College, Oxford, May 23, 1672, age 18; B.A. (Oxford) 1675-6. Incorp. at Cambridge. M.A. 1696-7; B.D. and D.D. 1696-7. V. of Lancaster, 1685-1714. Died 1714. Will (Archd. Richmood). Father of the next. (*Al. Oxon.*)

FENTON, JAMES. LL.B. from CHRIST'S, 1711. S. of James (above), of Lancaster. Matric. from Corpus Christi, Oxford, Mar. 13, 1704-5, age 17; B.A. (Oxford) 1708; D.C.L. 1721. V. of Lancaster, 1714-67. Died 1767. (*Al. Oxon.*; *Whitaker*, II. 236.)

FENTON, JOHN. Matric. pens. from PETERHOUSE, Michs. 1568; B.A. 1571-2. One of these names R. of Newton Flotman, Norfolk, 1570-76; R. of Swainsthorpe, 1571-98. Perhaps R. of Cole Orton, Leics., 1572. R. of Smallburgh, 1596-1602.

FENTON, JOHN. Adm. sizar at EMMANUEL, Mar. 1607-8. Matric. 1608; B.A. 1611-2; M.A. 1615. Perhaps R. of Witnesham, Suffolk, 1632.

FENTON, JOHN. Adm. pens. (age 15) at CAIUS, Mar. 1, 1633-4. S. of John. B. at Wetheringsett, Suffolk. Bapt. Apr. 14, 1619. School, Ipswich. Matric. 1634; B.A. 1637-8. Ord. deacon (Bishop Hall) Mar. 31, 1650; priest, Apr. 1, 1650. V. of Terrington St John in 1677. One of these names V. of Soham, Cambs., 1644. Another, minister of Thelnetham, Suffolk, 1647. (*Venn*, I. 311; Norwich Consign. Bk, 1677.)

FENTON, JOHN. Matric. sizar from ST CATHARINE'S, Easter, 1655. Of Staffordshire.

FENTON, JOSEPH. Adm. sizar at JESUS, 1613-4; B.A. 1617.

FENTON, MATTATHIAS. B.A. from PEMBROKE, 1620 (Incorp. from Oxford). S. of Joseph, of London, surgeon. Matric. from Trinity College, Oxford, Dec. 13, 1616, age 17. Probably of St Bartholomew's-the-Less. Will (P.C.C.) 1634. The father Joseph was Master of the Barber-Surgeons' Company, 1624. Colleague of Dr William Harvey, at St Bartholomew's. (J. Ch. Smith.)

FENTON, MATTHEW. Matric. sizar from JESUS, Lent, 1563-4.

FENTON, RALPH. Adm. pens. at JESUS, Apr. 11, 1646. S. of Thomas, of Fenton, Staffs. Matric. from All Souls', Oxford, July 1, 1642, age 15. Probably R. of Ludlow, Salop, 1661.

FENTON, RICHARD. Adm. sizar at EMMANUEL, Mar. 16, 1736-7. Of Staffordshire. Matric. 1737; B.A. 1740-1; M.A. 1745. Ord. deacon (Lincoln) June 13, 1742.

FENTON, ROBERT. Fellow of PETERHOUSE, 1460-83. Probably M.A. 1460-1. Chaplain of Little St Mary's, Cambridge. V. of Terrington, Norfolk, 1474. (*T. A. Walker.*)

FENTON, ROGER. Matric. sizar from PEMBROKE, Michs. 1585. B. in Lancashire, 1565. B.A. 1588-9; M.A. 1592; B.D. 1602; D.D. 1613. Fellow, 1590. Preacher at Gray's Inn, 1598. R. of St Stephen, Walbrook, 1601-16. R. of St Benet Sherehog, 1603-6. V. of Chigwell, Essex, 1606-16. Preb. of St Paul's, 1609-16. Died Jan. 16, 1615-6. Buried at St Stephen, Walbrook, aged 49. M.I. Will (Consist. C. London) 1616. (*D.N.B.*)

FENTON, SAMUEL. Adm. pens. (age 19) at TRINITY, June 18, 1720. S. of Timothy (1708), R. of St Peter's, Nottingham. School, Westminster. Matric. 1720; Scholar, 1721; B.A. 1723-4; M.A. 1728. Ord. deacon (Lincoln) June 5, 1726; priest, Sept. 25, 1726. C. of Keysoe, Beds., 1726; of Little Staughton, 1726.

FENTON, THOMAS. Adm. sizar at ST CATHARINE'S, 1642. Of Suffolk. Matric. 1644. Migrated to Jesus, June 12, 1645. B.A. 1645-6; Scholar, 1646; M.A. 1649. Fellow of Jesus, 1647. Taxor, 1652. One of these names R. of St Olave, Hart St, London, 1655. Died same year. Will, P.C.C. (A. Gray; J. Ch. Smith.)

FENTON, THOMAS. Adm. sizar (age 18) at TRINITY, June 5, 1699. S. of Thomas, of Dorlington, Staffs. School, Stone, Staffs. (Mr Stebbin). Matric. 1699; B.A. 1702-3; M.A. 1706. Ord. priest (Lincoln) Sept. 22, 1706. V. of Pulloxhill, Beds., 1706. C. of Sundon, 1707.

FENTON, TIMOTHY. M.A. from KING'S, 1708. S. of Samuel, of Hunslet, Yorks. Matric. from University College, Oxford. Mar. 30, 1694, age 17; B.A. (Oxford) 1697-8. V. of Arnall, Notts., 1701-4. R. of St Peter, Nottingham, 1704-21. Preb. of Southwell, 1714-24. R. of Barnold-le-Beck, Lincs., 1721. R. of Hatcliffe, 1721. Married, at St Mary's, Nottingham, Dec. 15, 1698, Martha Chadwick. Died Aug. 12, 1724. Father of Samuel (1720). (*Al. Oxon.*)

FENTON, WILLIAM. Matric. pens. from CHRIST'S, Michs. 1556; B.A. 1561-2; M.A. from Pembroke, 1567; B.D. 1576. Fellow of Pembroke. V. of Stoke Nayland, Suffolk, 1555-6. V. of Coddenham, 1571-7. Preb. of Norwich, 1574-7. R. of Ling, Norfolk, 1576-7. Admon. (P.C.C.) Aug. 5, 1577; to a creditor. (J. Ch. Smith.)

FENTON, WILLIAM. Adm. sizar (age 17) at CHRIST'S, Apr. 25, 1674. S. of William, of Hunslet, Leeds. B. at Leeds. School, Leeds. Matric. 1674. Resided, till 1675. Of Underbank, Esq. Grandfather of the next. (M. H. Peacock.)

FENTON, WILLIAM. Adm. pens. (age 19) at TRINITY, May 17, 1745. S. of William, of Dodworth, and Underbank, Penistone, Yorks. School, Beverley, Yorks. (Mr Clark). Scholar, 1746. Barrister-at-law. Died Apr. 11, 1792. (M. H. Peacock.)

FENTON, ZACHARIAH. Adm. sizar at CLARE, Apr. 13, 1666; B.A. 1671-2. Ord. priest (Lincoln) Sept. 24, 1671.

FENTON, ——. Adm. at CORPUS CHRISTI, 1569.

FENTON, ——. Adm. Fell.-Com. at TRINITY HALL, May 26, 1726; resided a year.

FENTYMAN, JOHN. Adm. sizar (age 17) at MAGDALENE, Oct. 13, 1656. S. of John, late of Barwick-in-Elmet, Yorks. School, Barwick. Matric. 1656; B.A. 1660-1. Ord. priest (Durham) Sept. 22, 1661. V. of Bardsey, Yorks., 1661. R. of Irby-on-Humber, Lincs., 1679-1721.

FENWELL or FANWELL, ——. Adm. pens. at ST CATHARINE'S, Sept. 24, 1664.

FENWICK, AMBROSE. Matric. sizar from CHRIST'S, July, 1707. S. of Edward, V. of Stamfordham. Scholar, 1707; B.A. 1710-1; M.A. 1714. Ord. deacon (Norwich) Sept. 1714; priest (York) Sept. 1716. C. of All Saints', Newcastle. V. of Stamfordham, 1719-32. Died Feb. 1, 1731-2. Buried at St Mary's, Gateshead. Brother of Edward (1711). (*Peile*, II. 166; H. M. Wood.)

FENWICKE, BARTHOLOMEW. Adm. sizar (age 19) at CAIUS, Apr. 24, 1621. S. of Bartholomew, R. of Hockering, Norfolk. B. there. School, private (Mr Castleton). Matric. 1621. Ord. deacon (Norwich) Sept. 23, 1632; priest, June 16, 1633. V. of Rudham, Norfolk, 1635. Died during the rebellion. (*Venn*, I. 253.)

FENWICK, BURGIS. Adm. sizar (age 19) at MAGDALENE, Nov. 28, 1726. S. of William, shoemaker. B. at Wisbech, Cambs. School, Wisbech. Matric. 1728; B.A. 1731-2. Ord. deacon (Lincoln) Dec. 24, 1732.

FENWICK, CLAUDIUS. Matric. pens. from ST CATHARINE'S, Lent, 1634-5; B.A. 1636-7. S. of George, of Brinkburn, Northumberland. Doubtless entered at Leyden, 1638, 1642, 1647. M.D. there. Buried at St Nicholas, Newcastle, June 24, 1669. Brother of George (1619). Father of William (1673). (H. M. Wood.)

FENWICK, CUTHBERT. Adm. sizar at CHRIST'S, Apr. 19, 1687. S. of Ralph (1662), V. of Stamfordham, Northumberland. B. there. Bapt. Sept. 15, 1668. School, Morpeth (Mr Step. Jackson). Matric. 1687; Scholar, 1689; B.A. 1690-1; M.A. 1694. Fellow, 1691-2. Ord. deacon and priest (Lincoln) Sept. 1691. R. of Morpeth, 1691-1745. Buried there Oct. 22, 1745. (*Peile*, II. 104-5.)

FENWICK, EDWARD. Adm. sizar (age 18) at CHRIST'S, Sept. 19, 1711. S. of Edward, V. of Stamfordham, Northumberland. Bapt. there, July 26, 1694. School, Stamfordham (Mr Salkeld). Matric. 1711; Scholar, 1712; B.A. 1716-7. Ord. deacon (York) Sept. 1716; priest, Sept. 1718. V. of Kirk Whelpington, 1721. Married Ann, dau. of Thomas Newton, of Hawkwell. Died 1734. Buried at Stamfordham, July 22. (*Peile*, II. 178.)

FENWICK, FREDERICK. Adm. pens. at ST CATHARINE'S, 1633. Of Cumberland.

FENWICK, GEORGE. Matric. Fell.-Com. from QUEENS', Easter, 1619. Of Northumberland. S. and h. of George, of Brinkburn, Esq., deceased. B. *c.* 1602. Adm. at Gray's Inn, Feb. 11, 1621-2. Barrister, 1631. Ancient, 1650. Secured a patent in Connecticut, New England, and lived there, 1636-45. Returned to England, 1645. Colonel in the Parliamentary Army. Governor of Leith Garrison. M.P. for Morpeth, 1645-53; for Berwick-on-Tweed, 1654-6. One of the Commissioners appointed for the Government of Scotland, 1651. Married (1) Alice, dau. of Sir Edward Apsley, of Worminghurst, Sussex, widow of Sir John Butler; (2) Catherine, dau. of Sir Arthur Heselrigg, of Naseby, Leics. There is a M.I. at Berwick-on-Tweed; but his will is dated at Worminghurst, Feb. 2, 1656-7; and proved at Lewes, Apr. 27, 1657. (J. G. Bartlett; *D.N.B.*; H. M. Wood.)

FENWICK, GEORGE. Adm. pens. (age 15) at ST JOHN'S, May 4, 1705. S. of William (1673), R. of Hallaton, Leics. B. there. School, Winchester. Matric. 1705; B.A. 1708-9; M.A. 1712; B.D. 1720. Fellow, 1710-22. Ord. deacon (London) Dec. 21, 1712; priest (Lincoln) Dec. 20, 1713. R. of Hallaton, 1723-60. Author of devotional works. Died Apr. 10, 1760. M.I. at Hallaton. Father of George (1746). (*Nichols*, II. 606; *D.N.B.*)

FENWICK, GEORGE. Adm. sizar (age 16) at CHRIST'S, June 6, 1706. S. of George. B. at Morpeth. School, Morpeth (Mr Meggison). Matric. 1706; Scholar, 1706-7; B.A. 1709-10. Ord. deacon (Durham) Sept. 1712; priest (London) Sept. 25, 1715. V. of Bolam, Northumberland, 1722-70. Died Apr. 27, 1770. Buried at Morpeth. (*Peile*, II. 164.)

FENWICK, GEORGE. Adm. pens. (age 17) at ST JOHN'S, Apr. 9, 1746. S. of George (1705), clerk, of Northamptonshire. B. at Carlton. School, Oakham, Rutland (Mr Adcock). Matric. 1747; B.A. 1749-50. Died in College, May 20, 1750. Buried at All Saints', Cambridge.

FENWICK, JOHN. Matric. sizar from CHRIST'S, Dec. 1617. Of Northumberland. S. of John, of Butterlawe. B.A. 1621-2; M.A. 1625; B.D. 1639. Fellow, 1628. Taxor, 1633. R. of Chignal St James, Essex, 1639; an 'able preaching minister,' in 1650. V. of Corbridge, Northumberland, 1665-74. Buried there Mar. 28, 1674. Brother of Martin (1614). (*Peile*, I. 322.)

FENWICKE, JOHN. Matric. Fell.-Com. from TRINITY, Easter, 1628. Doubtless s. and h. of Sir John, of Wallington, Northumberland, Knt. and Bart. Adm. at Gray's Inn, Apr. 28, 1630. M.P. for Morpeth, 1640-4. Colonel of Dragoons, Married Mary, dau. of Sir George Selby, of Whitehouse, Durham. Killed at Marston Moor, July 2, 1644. Brother of William (1633). (Burke, *Ext. Bart.*)

FENWICKE, JOHN. Matric. sizar from ST CATHARINE'S, Easter, 1644; B.A. 1646-7; M.A. 1650. One of these names V. of Humbleton, Yorks., 1665-86.

FENWICK, JOHN. Adm. pens. at TRINITY, July 1, 1647. S. of John, of Newcastle-on-Tyne, Esq. Bapt. at All Saints', Dec. 3, 1628. B.A. 1650; M.A. 1654. Incorp. at Oxford, 1654. Adm. at Gray's Inn, Nov. 6, 1648. R. of Somerton, Oxon., till 1662; ejected. Died at Crayford, Kent, 1665, aged 42. (*Al. Oxon.*; *Calamy*, II. 311.)

FENWICKE, JOHN. Adm. Fell.-Com. (age 18) at ST JOHN'S, June 2, 1716. S. of Roger, of Stanton, Northumberland, Esq. B. at Stanton, Feb. 24, 1698-9. Educated at home (Mr Lisle). Matric. 1716. High Sheriff for Northumberland, 1727-8. M.P. for the county, 1741, 1747. Married Margaret, dau. of Wm Fenwick, of Bywell. Died Dec. 19, 1747. (*Scott-Mayor*, III. 302.)

FENWICK, LANCELOT. Adm. pens. (age 16) at CHRIST'S, July 7, 1640. S. and h. of Martin (below), of Ellingham, near Alnwick. B. at Kenton, Northumberland. School, Durham. Matric. 1640.

FENWICK, MARTIN. Matric. pens. from CHRIST'S, Apr. 1614. S. and h. of John, of Butterlaw, Northumberland. Of Ellingham, Alnwick, Esq. Age 18, in 1615. Father of Lancelot, and brother of John (1617). (*Peile*, I. 295.)

FENWICK, MICHAEL. Adm. sizar (age 19) at ST JOHN'S, Apr. 24, 1682. S. of Thomas, shipwright. B. at Newcastle-on-Tyne. Bapt. at All Saints', Apr. 14, 1663. School, Newcastle (Mr Garthwait). Matric. 1682; B.A. 1685-6; M.A. 1700. Reader at St Nicholas, Newcastle. R. of Long Newton, Durham, 1706-12. Buried there June 27, 1712. (H. M. Wood.)

FENWICK, RALPH. Incorp. M.A. 1662, from Christ Church, Oxford. Matric. there, Apr. 21, 1656; B.A. (Oxford) 1658-9; M.A. 1661-2. V. of Stamfordham, Northumberland, 1662. R. of Morpeth, 1669-72. Buried at Stamfordham, Feb. 17, 1674-5. Father of Cuthbert (1687). (*Al. Oxon.*)

FENWICK, RICHARD. Adm. sizar at CHRIST'S, Apr. 18, 1681. S. of Arthur. B. at Appleby, Westmorland. Matric. 1681.

FENWICK, RICHARD. Matric. sizar from CHRIST'S, July, 1719. Perhaps s. of Richard (1681). Buried at Gt St Andrew's, Cambridge, Mar. 11, 1719-20. (*Peile*, II. 195.)

FENWICK, ROBERT. Adm. pens. (age 17) at ST JOHN'S, Nov. 13, 1658. S. of Edward, Esq., of Stanton, in Long Horsley, Northumberland. B. there. School, Berwick. Matric. 1658. According to Hodgson (*Northumb.*, II. 114) he was born June 8, 1646; and died at Morpeth, June 23, 1693.

FENWICK, ROBERT. Adm. pens. (age 17) at ST JOHN'S, June 19, 1706. S. and h. of John, lawyer, of Burrow Hall, Westmorland, Esq. B. at Burrow, Lancs. School, Lowther (Mr Lodge). Matric. 1708. Adm. at Gray's Inn, Nov. 28, 1703. Died Nov. 9, 1736. (G. *Mag.*)

FENWICKE, THOMAS. Matric. pens. from PETERHOUSE, Lent, 1582-3; B.A. 1587-8.

FENWICK, THOMAS. Adm. pens. (age 17) at ST JOHN'S, June 5, 1751. S. of T., gent., of Northumberland. B. at Newcastle. School, Eton. Matric. 1751; B.A. 1755.

FENWICKE, WILLIAM. Matric. Fell.-Com. from TRINITY, Michs. 1609.

FENWICK, WILLIAM. Adm. Fell.-Com. (age 16) at CHRIST'S, June 26, 1633. S. of Sir John, Bart., of Wallington. B. at Blanchland, Northumberland. School, Morpeth (Mr Oxley). M.A. 1636 (*Lit. Reg.*). Adm. at Gray's Inn, Feb. 10, 1635-6. Member of the Long Parliament, 1645. M.P. for Northumberland, 1645-8, 1654-8, 1659, 1660-76. Succeeded as Baronet, 1658. Married Jane, dau. of Henry Stapylton, of Wighill, Yorks., 1637. Died *c.* 1682. Brother of John (1628). (*Peile*, I. 427; *G.E.C.*; A. B. Beaven.)

FENWICK, WILLIAM. Adm. pens. (age 16) at ST JOHN'S, June 9, 1673. S. of Claudius (1634), of Newcastle-on-Tyne. B. there. Bapt. at St Nicholas, Aug. 16, 1657. School, Hexham. Matric. 1674; B.A. 1676-7; M.A. 1680. Fellow, 1679. Ord. priest (London) Mar. 4, 1682-3. R. of Hallaton, Leics., 1688-1723. R. of Carlton Curlieu, 1722-33. R. of Thakeham, Sussex. Married Cecily, dau. of Gilbert Coles, D.D., fellow of Winchester. Died Oct. 8, 1733. M.I. at Carlton Curlieu. Father of George (1705). (*Nichols*, II. 546.)

FENWICK, WILLIAM. Incorp. M.A. at CHRIST'S, from Edinburgh, 1674; and at Oxford same year. M.A. (Edinburgh) 1671. V. of Shilbottle, Northumberland, 1673-8. R. of Cliburn, Westmorland, 1673-87. V. of Lesbury, Northumberland, 1673-87. Married Jane Shafto, of Ponteland, Dec. 1674. Died Sept. 30, 1688. Buried at Cliburn. (*Peile*, I. 427; *Al. Oxon*; H. M. Wood.)

PENNICK, WILLIAM. Adm. sizar (age 17) at PETERHOUSE, May 13, 1680. Of Lincolnshire. School, Louth, Lincs. Buried at Little St Mary's, Cambridge, Aug. 25, 1680.

FENWICK, WILLIAM. Adm. pens. at CHRIST'S, July 4, 1704. B. in the Barbados. Scholar, 1704-5. Resided one year.

FENWICK, ——. Adm. sizar at PETERHOUSE, Aug. 8, 1585.

FERDINAND, PHILIP. Matric. Dec. 16, 1596 (amongst the college servants and other privileged persons). Polish Jew. B. *c.* 1555. For some time a student at Oxford. For some years a teacher of Hebrew in Cambridge. 'Professor privatus in omnibus fere collegiis, Hebraicae, Chaldaicae, et Syriacae Linguae.' Died, probably at Leyden, 1598. (*Cooper*, II. 239; *Al. Oxon.*)

FERENTS, THOMAS. Colonel. M.A. 1635-6 (*Lit. Reg.*).

FERILL, TADD. Matric. sizar from MAGDALENE, Michs. 1562.

FERREMAN, HARBERT. 'Of ST JOHN'S College,' when ord. deacon (York) *c.* 1666; priest, June, 1667.

FERMAN, JAMES. Matric. sizar from CHRIST'S, Dec. 1714; Scholar, 1715. Resided a year.

FERMENT, JOHN (*Gallus*). Matric. pens. from TRINITY, Easter 1589.

FERMOR, WILLIAM. Matric. pens. at TRINITY, 1642. Of Sussex. Doubtless s. and h. of Alexander, of Rotherfield, Sussex, Esq. Scholar, 1646; B.A. 1646-7. Adm. at Gray's Inn, Nov. 6, 1647. Barrister-at-law, 1655. Of Welches, Sussex, Esq. (Burke, *Ext. Bart.*)

FERMORE, WILLIAM. Matric. pens. from KING'S, Michs. 1680.

FERN, FRANCIS. Adm. sizar (age 19) at ST JOHN'S, June 17, 1667. S. of George, clerk, of Whitwell, near Chesterfield, Derbs. B. there. School, Merchant Taylors'. Matric. 1670; B.A. 1670-1; M.A. 1674. Fellow, 1672. Signed for deacon's orders (London) Sept. 29, 1672. Head Master of Wisbech School, Cambs. Preb. of Ely, 1690-1713. R. of Downham, Cambs., 1690. Buried at Ely, Aug. 24, 1713.

FERNE, GEORGE. Scholar of TRINITY, 1608. S. of Sir John (1572), of Temple Belwood, Yorks. B.A. 1608-9; M.A. 1612. Incorp. at Oxford, 1618. Ord. deacon (York) Sept. 1614; priest, Dec. 1614. R. of St Mary Somerset, London, 1617. R. of Barkstone, Lincs., 1618. Admon. (Lincoln) 1620; of Geo. Ferne, of Barkstone, clerk. Brother of Henry (1620). (J. Ch. Smith.)

FERNE, GEORGE. Adm. sizar (age 16) at ST JOHN'S, Oct. 13, 1702. S. of George, M.D. B. at Cheshunt, Herts. School, King's, Cambridge (Mr Thackham). Matric. 1702; B.A. 1706-7. Ord. priest (Lincoln) May 27, 1711. V. of Stevington, Beds., 1712-6.

FERN, GEORGE. Adm. sizar (age 17) at ST JOHN'S, Jan. 8, 1728-9. S. of Giles (1696), clerk, of Cambridgeshire. B. at Ely. School, Ely (Mr Gunning). Matric. 1729; B.A. 1732-3; M.A. 1738. Ord. deacon (Peterb.) Sept. 23, 1733; priest, Sept. 21, 1735. Usher of Peterborough School. V. of Wigtoft, Lincs., 1737-90. Chaplain to the Earl of Kilmarnock. V. of Burgh and Winthorpe, 1739-90. (*Scott-Mayor*, III. 419.)

FERN, GILES. Adm. sizar (age 16) at TRINITY, July 3, 1696. S. of Francis (1667), of Ely. B. at Wisbech, Apr. 20, 1680. School, Merchant Taylors'. Matric. 1698; Scholar, 1699; B.A. 1699-1700; M.A. 1703. Ord. deacon (Ely) May 30, 1703; priest, June 11, 1704. Father of the above.

FERN, GODFREY. Adm. sizar at JESUS, June 29, 1720. S. of Joseph (1673), late R. of Matlock, Derbs. Matric. 1721; B.A. 1723-4; M.A. 1728. Ord. priest (Lincoln) Mar. 10, 1733-4.

FERNE, HENRY. Matric. pens. from TRINITY, Easter, 1620. Previously adm. at St Mary's Hall, Oxford, 1618. 8th s. of Sir John (1572), of Temple Belwood, Yorks. B.A. 1622-3; M.A. 1626; B.D. 1631-2 (*Lit. Reg.*); D.D. 1641. Fellow, 1624. Incorp. at Oxford, 1643. Master of Trinity, 1660-2. Vice-Chancellor, 1660-1. V. of Masham, Yorks., 1638-9. R. of Medburn, Leics., 1639-47. Archdeacon of Leicester, 1641. Chaplain to Charles I, 1643. Ejected from his preferments. Dean of Ely, Feb. 1660-1. Bishop of Chester, Feb. 1661-2. Author of theological pamphlets. Died Mar. 16, 1661-2, aged 59. Buried in Westminster Abbey. Will (P.C.C.) 1663. Brother of George (1608). (*Al. Oxon.*; *D.N.B.*)

FERN, JAMES. Adm. pens. at JESUS, July 29, 1728. Of the Isle of Ely. Matric. 1728; B.A. 1732-3. Ord. deacon (Ely) June 1, 1735.

FERNE, JAMES. Adm. pens. at TRINITY, Dec. 1, 1729. Matric. 1729; Scholar, 1731; B.A. 1733-4.

FERN or FERON, JASPER. Adm. at KING'S (age 17) a scholar from Eton, Aug. 11, 1521. Of Ruislip, Middlesex. B.A. 1525-6; M.A. 1529. Fellow, 1524. Probably brother of Stephen (1522).

FERNE, JOHN. Matric. pens. from ST JOHN'S, Easter, 1572. Perhaps s. of William, of Temple Belwood, Yorks. Said to have studied at Oxford. Adm. at the Inner Temple, 1576. Appointed Deputy Secretary of the Council of the North, at York, 1595. Knighted, Aug. 5, 1603. Joint Secretary and keeper of the signet in the North, 1604. M.P. for Boroughbridge, 1604-9. Of Temple Belwood. Author, *Blazon of Gentry*. Died June 20, 1609. Father of Henry (1620) and George (1608). (*Lincs. Pedigrees*; *D.N.B.*; A. B. Beaven.)

FERNE, JOHN. Adm. pens. at CLARE, Apr. 13, 1724. B. in London. Matric. 1724.

FERNE, JOSEPH. Adm. sizar (age 19) at CHRIST'S, May 29, 1673. S. of George. B. at Fairfield, Derbs. School, Ashby-de-la-Zouch (Mr Shaw). Matric. 1674; B.A. 1676-7; M.A. 1680. Ord. deacon (Lichfield) Sept. 1677; priest, June, 1679. Married Jane, dau. of Godfrey Walkinson. R. of Matlock, 1688-1716, where he died and was buried. Father of Godfrey (1720). (*F.M.G.*; *Peile*, II. 48.)

FEARNE, ROBERT. Adm. pens. at EMMANUEL, June 27, 1671. Of Derbyshire. Matric. as sizar, 1672; B.A. 1674-5.

FERN or FERON, STEPHEN. Adm. at KING'S (age 18), a scholar from Eton, Aug. 9, 1522. Of Ruislip, Middlesex. B.A. 1526-7; M.A. 1530; B.D. 1537. Fellow, 1525-36. R. of Horstead, Norfolk, 1536-54. Probably brother of Jasper (1521).

FERN, THOMAS. Adm. Fell.-Com. at ST CATHARINE'S, Nov. 22, 1688, from Exeter College, Oxford, having resided three years there. S. of John, of London. Matric. 1689; M.B. 1691; M.D. 1698.

FEARNE, WILLIAM. Adm. sizar (age 20) at MAGDALENE, July 1, 1661. S. of Richard, of Mildale, Staffs. School, Alstonfield. Matric. 1661-2.

FERNE, WILLIAM. Adm. sizar (age 17) at ST JOHN'S, May 31, 1672. S. of George, clerk, of Tickhill, Yorks. B. there. Matric. 1672.

FERN, WILLIAM. Adm. sizar (age 17) at PETERHOUSE, Oct. 27, 1703. Of the Isle of Ely. School, Ely. Matric. 1704; Scholar, 1705; B.A. 1707-8. C. at Melchbourne, Beds., 1710-4.

FERN, ——. Adm. Fell.-Com. at KING'S, 1724-5.

FERNELY, EDMUND. Matric. sizar from ST JOHN'S, Easter, 1626; B.A. 1629-30. Bapt. at West Creeting, 1609. One of these names, s. of John, of West Creeting, Suffolk, adm. at Gray's Inn, May 1, 1630. Barrister, 1640. Bencher, 1654. Died 1664. (Davy, *Suff. MSS.*)

FERNELY, GEORGE. Matric. pens. from TRINITY, Easter, 1616; B.A. 1619; M.A. 1623. Ord. deacon (York) Dec. 1622.

FERNELEY, JOHN. Matric. sizar from ST JOHN'S, Michs. 1578. B. at Wakefield, Yorks. Ord. deacon (London) May 14, 1585; 'aged 24; late scholar of Peterhouse'; priest (London) Mar. 26, 1586. C. of Newmarket, Cambs. Probably V. of Eaton, Norwich, 1586.

FERNELEY, JOSEPH. Matric. sizar from CLARE, Easter, 1617. Ord. deacon (Peterb.) June 8, 1623; priest, Dec. 20, 1625.

FERNIERS, S. Adm. at CORPUS CHRISTI, 1544.

FERNIHOUGH, JOHN. Adm. sizar (age 20) at TRINITY, Apr. 13, 1710. S. of John, of Marton, Cheshire. School, Macclesfield (Mr Dobson). Matric. 1710; B.A. 1714-5. Ord. deacon (London) May 23, 1714; priest (York) Sept. 1714. V. of Flintham, Notts., 1714-42. Married, at Flintham, Apr. 27, 1721, Elizabeth Smith. Died Mar. 10, 1742-3. Buried at Flintham. (Godfrey, *Notts.*)

FERNYHOUGH, JOHN. Adm. pens. at QUEENS', July 4, 1748. Of Staffordshire. Matric. 1748; B.A. 1752; M.A. 1755; B.D. 1764. Fellow, 1756-73. Ord. priest (Lincoln) Sept. 6, 1757.

FERNYHOUGH, WILLIAM. M.A. 1734 (Incorp. from Oxford). S. of Philip, of Gt Fenton, Staffs., gent. Matric. from Balliol College, Oxford, 1724, age 19; B.A. (Oxford) 1727; M.A. 1731.

FEARNISIDE, ADAM. Matric. pens. from CHRIST'S, Easter, 1664; B.A. 1667-8; M.A. 1671.

FERNESIDE, JAMES. B.A. from ST JOHN'S, 1611-2. Perhaps V. of Long Benton, Northumberland, 1621-8. Died 1628.

FERNISIDE, JOHN. Adm. sizar at EMMANUEL, June 25, 1593. Matric. c. 1596; B.A. 1596-7.

FERNESLEY, SAMUEL. Adm. (age 16) at CAIUS, Mar. 15, 1561-2. S. of John, of Reed, Herts. School, Elmdon, Suffolk.

FERNSLAY, WILLIAM. Matric. sizar from ST JOHN'S, Easter, 1545 (*impubes*). One of these names adm. at Lincoln's Inn, Oct. 16, 1560.

FERON, HENRY. B.A. 1493-4; M.A. 1497; B.D. 1504-5. Fellow of PEMBROKE, 1494. Of Cumberland.

FERON, ROBERT. B.A. 1520-1; M.A. 1524. Fellow of CHRIST'S, till 1531. Perhaps V. of St Ethelburga, London, 1554-69. Admon. (P.C.C.) 1570.

FERON, ROBERT. Matric. sizar from ST JOHN'S, Easter, 1572. One of these names V. of Skipsea, Yorks., 1575-1615. Died 1615.

FEROW, ——. D.Civ.L. 1499-1500.

FERRABOSCO, JOHN. Mus.Bac. 1671 (*Lit. Reg.*). Probably s. of either Alfonso the younger, or Henry, musicians in ordinary. Organist of Ely Cathedral, 1662-82. Died 1682. (*D.N.B.*)

FERRAND, *see also* **FARRAND.**

FERRAND, BENJAMIN. Adm. sizar (age 17) at ST JOHN'S, Mar. 8, 1707-8. S. of Samuel (1679), clerk, R. of Todwick, Yorks. B. at Calverley, near Leeds, Yorks. Bapt. there, Apr. 24, 1689. School, Sherburn (Mr Baine). Matric. 1708; B.A. 1711-2; M.A. 1721. Incorp. at Oxford, 1723. Ord. deacon (York) Sept. 1712; priest, May 27, 1716. V. of Gt Peatling, Leics., 1716. V. of Attercliffe, Yorks., 1719-29. Married Elizabeth, dau. of Thomas Diston, of Sheffield Park, Apr. 25, 1725. Died Feb. 27, 1728-9. Buried at Attercliffe. (M. H. Peacock.)

FERRAND, BRADGATE. Adm. sizar (age 17) at TRINITY, May 15, 1699. S. of Robert, of Harden Grange, Bingley, Yorks. Bapt. May 8, 1682. School, Bingley (Mr Hoyle). Matric. 1699; B.A. 1702-3; M.A. 1707. Ord. deacon (York) Nov. 1704; priest, 1706. V. of Bradford, Yorks., 1706-9. Died May 3, 1709. Buried at Bradford.

FERRAND, JOHN. Adm. sizar (age 18) at TRINITY, Mar. 20, 1724. S. of Thomas (1698), of Bingley, Yorks., clerk. Bapt. there, Nov. 5, 1706. School, Bingley (Mr Ellison). Matric. 1724; Scholar, 1727; B.A. 1727-8; M.A. 1731. Ord. deacon (Lincoln) Dec. 22, 1728. V. of Messingham, Lincs. Married Mary, dau. of Thomas Hatchett, of Edwinstow, Notts. Died 1759. Brother of Thomas (1726). (M. H. Peacock.)

FERRAND, SAMUEL. Adm. pens. (age 18) at MAGDALENE, Dec. 27, 1648. S. of Francis, of Harwill (?), Suffolk, gent. School, Halstead. Matric. 1648-9; B.A. 1652-3; M.A. 1656. Fellow. Ord. deacon (Lincoln) Feb. 22; priest, Feb. 23, 1661-2.

FERRAND, SAMUEL. Adm. pens. (age 14) at TRINITY, June 27, 1679. S. of Benjamin, of Harden Beck, Bingley, Yorks. Bapt. there, Nov. 24, 1664. School, Bingley (Mr Murgatroyd). Matric. 1679; B.A. 1682-3; M.A. 1686. R. of Todwick, Yorks., 1685-7. V. of Calverley, 1688-93. V. of Rotherham, 1704-33. Died 1733. Father of Benjamin (1707-8). (Burke, *L.G.*)

FERRAND, THOMAS. Adm. pens. at EMMANUEL, Jan. 15, 1700-1; Fell.-Com. Apr. 7, 1701. Of Essex.

FERRAND, THOMAS. Adm. sizar (age 18) at TRINITY, June 11, 1698. S. of Stephen, deceased, of Bingley, Yorks. Bapt. there, June 9, 1680. School, Bingley (Mr Hoyle). Matric. 1698; B.A. 1701-2. Ord. deacon (York) Sept. 1702; priest, June, 1704. V. of Cross Stone, Yorks., 1703-6. V. of Thornton, Bradford, 1706-14. V. of Bingley, 1718-40. Buried there Dec. 15, 1740. Father of the next and of John (1724).

FERRAND, THOMAS. Adm. sizar (age 18) at TRINITY, Mar. 10, 1726-7. S. of Thomas (above), of Bingley, Yorks., clerk. Bapt. there, Dec. 21, 1709. School, Kirkleatham, Yorks. (Mr Clark). Matric. 1727; Scholar, 1730; B.A. 1730-1; M.A. 1734. Fellow, 1733. Ord. deacon (Lincoln) June 13, 1731; priest, Mar. 10, 1733-4. Died unmarried, 1741. Brother of John (1724).

FERRAND or FARRAND, TIMOTHY. Adm. sizar at TRINITY, June 2, 1668. Matric. 1668; B.A. 1673-4; M.A. 1677. Ord. deacon (York) June, 1674; priest, May, 1676. R. of Bolton Abbey, Yorks., 1680-3. R. of Skipton, 1683-5. Buried Nov. 12, 1685.

FERRANT, EDMUND. Matric. Fell.-Com. from JESUS, Michs. 1615. Perhaps Edm. Ferrand, s. and h. of Thomas, of Carlton-in-Craven, Yorks.; age 14 in 1612. (*Vis. of Yorks.*)

FERRAR, *see also* FARRAR.

FERRAR, ABRAHAM. Matric. sizar from TRINITY, Easter, 1571.

FERRER, ANTHONY. Adm. sizar (age 22) at ST JOHN'S, Sept. 11, 1685. S. of Anthony, husbandman. B. at Grayrigg, near Kendal, Westmorland. School, Rotherham (Mr Ferrer). Matric. 1685. Of Worsborough, clerk, schoolmaster. Buried there Nov. 7, 1704. Cousin and executor of Edmund (1668).

FERRERS, CHARLES. M.A. 1675 (*Lit. Reg.*).

FERRAR or FARRER, EDMUND. Adm. sizar (age 18) at ST JOHN'S, June 1, 1668. S. of Joseph, yeoman, of Killington, Westmorland. B. there. School, Sedbergh. Matric. 1668; B.A. 1672-3; M.A. 1687. Head Master of Rotherham School, 1678-93. Afterwards Head Master of Wakefield, 1693-1703. Married Martha, dau. of Walker Fowke, of Staffordshire. Died at Wakefield, Apr. 7, 1703. M.I. in the parish Church. (*Scott-Mayor*, II. 16; M. H. Peacock.)

FERRER, EDMUND. Adm. pens. (age 17) at TRINITY, Mar. 28, 1704. S. of William, of Norwich. School, St Paul's, London. Matric. 1704; Scholar, 1705; B.A. 1707-8. (*Vis. of Norfolk.*)

FERRERS, GEORGE. B.Can.L. 1530-1, as 'William.' S. of Thomas, of St Albans. B. *c.* 1500. Adm. at Lincoln's Inn, Nov. 22, 1534, as Ferres. M.P. for Plymouth, 1541-4, 1544-7, 1553; for Brackley, 1554-5; for St Albans, 1571. Served under the Protector, Somerset, in Scotland. 'Master of the King's pastimes,' 1551 and 1552. Assisted in suppressing Wyatt's Rebellion, 1554. Escheator for Essex and Herts., 1567. Author. Of Hamstead, Herts. Buried there Jan. 11, 1578-9. (*Cooper*, I. 387; *D.N.B.*)

FERRER, JOHN. Adm. at CORPUS CHRISTI, 1645. Of Derbyshire.

FERRER or FARRER, JOHN. Adm. sizar (age 18) at ST JOHN'S, May 22, 1676. S of Joseph, deceased, of Firbank, Westmorland. B. there. School, Sedbergh. Matric. 1676; B.A. 1680-1.

FERRAR, JOHN. Adm. pens. (age 17) at PEMBROKE, June 29, 1677. S. of John, of Little Gidding, Hunts., Esq. B. Mar. 8, 1659-60. Matric. 1677. Married, Nov. 23, 1714, Elizabeth Goddard. He was a great-nephew of Nicholas (1609), and brother of Thomas (1679).

FERRAR, JOHN. Adm. pens. at CLARE, May 28, 1718. S. of Thomas (1679). B. at Little Gidding, Hunts. Matric. 1717; B.A. 1721-2; M.A. 1725. Fellow, 1722-39. Junior Proctor, 1736-7. Ord. deacon (Lincoln) Aug. 17; priest, Sept. 21, 1735. V. of Everton and Tetworth, Hunts., 1735-9. Buried at Little Gidding, Mar. 6, 1738-9. According to his friend, Wm Cole, he was 'little inferior to an idiot.'

FERRAR or FARRER, MILES. Adm. sizar (age 18) at ST JOHN'S, July 1, 1671. S. of George, yeoman, of Firbank, Westmorland. B. there. School, Sedbergh. Matric. 1671. Head Master of Leeds School, 1694-8. Head Master of Pocklington School, 1698-1704. Died Apr. 17, 1704. (*Scott-Mayor.*)

FERRER or FERRIER, NATHANIEL. Adm. sizar at EMMANUEL, Apr. 22, 1673. Of Norfolk. Matric. pens. Easter, 1674; B.A. 1677-8.

FERRAR, NICHOLAS. B.A. from CLARE, 1609-10. S. of Nicholas, merchant. B. in London, Feb. 22, 1592-3. School, Enborne, near Newbury, Berks. Fellow, 1610. Perhaps created M.A. 1613. Attended the Queen of Bohemia (Princess Elizabeth) to Holland, 1613. Devoted himself to the affairs of the Virginia Company, 1619. Travelled much. Refused Professorship at Gresham College. M.P. for Lymington, 1624-5. Retired to Little Gidding, Hunts., 1625. Ord. deacon (Westminster) 1626. Head of the Anglican Community at Little Gidding; for a full account of his activities there, *see Life* by his brother John, edited by J. E. B. Mayor. Died Dec. 4, 1637. Admon. (P.C.C.) 1638. (*D.N.B.*)

FERRER, RICHARD. Matric. pens. from CORPUS CHRISTI, Easter, 1631; B.A. 1633-4; M.A. 1637. Ord. deacon (Norwich) Feb. 15, 1634-5. Usher of Norwich Grammar School. S. of Richard. Bapt. at St Michael at Plea, Norwich, Apr. 9, 1619. Probably buried there Feb. 9, 1671-2.

FERRAR or FERRER, RICHARD. Matric. sizar from ST CATHARINE'S, Easter, 1650.

FERROR, ROBERT. B.A. 1529-30. Scholar of GONVILLE HALL, 1531-3. Ord. priest (Norwich) 1532, as 'Francis, *alias* Ferror.' Perhaps V. of Althorne, Essex, 1556. Died 1557.

FERRAR, ROBERT. Augustinian Canon. Of Halifax, Yorks. Studied at Cambridge, whence he proceeded to Oxford B.D. (Oxford) 1533. Last Prior of Nostel, Yorks. Preb. of York, 1540. Appointed Bishop of Sodor and Man, 1545 (but *D.N.B.* disputes this). Bishop of St David's, 1548. Deprived, 1554. Condemned as a heretic and burnt at Carmarthen, Mar. 30, 1555. (*Cooper*, I. 125; *D.N.B.*)

FERRER, THOMAS. Matric. pens. from ST JOHN'S, Easter, 1555.

FERRAR, THOMAS (1555), *alias* OXFORD, *see* OXFORD.

FERRAR, THOMAS. Adm. pens. at TRINITY, May 7, 1661, as Farrer. Matric. 1661; Scholar, 1664; B.A. 1664-5; M.A. 1668.

FERRAR, THOMAS. Adm. pens. (age 15) at PEMBROKE, June 13, 1679. S. of John, Esq. B. in Huntingdonshire. Matric. 1680; B.A. 1682-3; M.A. 1686. Ord. priest (Lincoln) May 22, 1687. R. of Little Gidding, Hunts., 1691-1707. R. of Steeple Gidding, 1691-1739. R. of Sawtry St Andrew's, 1706-39. Died 1739. Brother of John (1677), father of the next and John (1718).

FERRAR, THOMAS. Adm. pens. at CLARE, July 2, 1725. S. of Thomas (above). B. at Little Gidding, Hunts. Matric. 1725; B.A. 1728-9; M.A. 1732. Ord. deacon (Lincoln, *Litt. dim.* from Peterb.) June 9, 1734. Buried July 6, 1748, at Little Gidding, of which he was Lord of the Manor. Will proved, Aug. 31, 1748.

FERRAR, WILLIAM. Matric. pens. from CLARE, Easter, 1607. Probably brother of Nicholas (1609); adm. at the Middle Temple, May 10, 1610.

FERRARI, DOMINICK. Incorp. LL.D. 1710, from Naples. Will (P.C.C.) 1744; as Dominico Antonio Ferrari. (J. Ch. Smith.)

FERRIBY, NICHOLAS. Scholar at KING'S HALL, 1365. Graduate in Civil Law. Beneficed, 1369.

FERREBY, RICHARD. Scholar at KING'S HALL, 1455-7. One of these names R. of Cold Norton, Essex, 1458-66; of Shenfield, 1466.

FERYBY, ROBERT. Scholar at KING'S HALL, 1439-44. One of these names, D.D., R. of Holland Magna, Essex, 1455-66. (J. Ch. Smith.)

FERRIER, NATHANIEL (1673), *see* FERRER.

FERRIER, RICHARD. Adm. pens. (age 15) at SIDNEY, Apr. 22, 1685. Only s. of Richard, mercer. B. at Yarmouth. School, Yarmouth (Mr Reynolds). M.P. for Yarmouth, 1708, 1710, 1713-5. Died Oct. 1728. Buried at Yarmouth. Father of the next. (Davy, *Suff. MSS.*)

FERRIER, RICHARD. Adm. pens. (age 14) at CAIUS, July 26, 1710. S. of Richard (above), mercer, of Yarmouth. B. there. School, Yarmouth. Matric. 1710; Scholar, 1710-6. Mayor of Yarmouth, 1724. Receiver-general for Norfolk, 1730. Died 1739. Buried at Yarmouth. M.I. (*Venn*, I. 524.)

FERRIN or FERIAN, NATHANIEL. Matric. pens. from CORPUS CHRISTI, Easter, 1613. Of Essex. B.A. 1614-5; M.A. 1618.

FERRIS, BENJAMIN. Adm. sizar (age 17) at CHRIST'S, Mar. 7, 1671-2. S. of Samuel. B. at Beverley, Yorks. School, Felsted (Mr Glascock). Matric. 1672; B.A. 1675-6. Ord. deacon (London) May 21, 1676; priest, May 30, 1678. V. of Prittlewell, Essex, 1678. Died Apr. 1683. Will, P.C.C. (*Peile*, II. 40.)

FERRIS, SAMUEL. Adm. pens. at ST JOHN'S, July 10, 1663. One of these names V. of Good Easter, Essex, 1668-71. R. of Little Lees, 1671-9. Will (Comm. C. Essex) 1679. (J. Ch. Smith.)

FERRIS, ——. B.A. 1477-8; M.A. 1481. *Cautio* for further degree, 1484-5.

FERROUR, HENRY. Adm. pens. (age 17) at CHRIST'S, Mar. 4, 1636–7. S. of Henry. B. at Emneth, Norfolk. School, Wisbech (Mr Friskney). Adm. at Lincoln's Inn, Feb. 15, 1640–1, as 's. and h. of Henry, of Wisbech, gent.' Probably died Dec. 11, 1686. Buried in St Nicholas, Lynn. Will (P.C.C.) 1687.

FERROUR, JOHN. Adm. at CORPUS CHRISTI, as 'Farrow,' 1590. Of Norfolk. B.A. 1593–4.

FERROUR, JOHN. B.A. from CHRIST'S, 1607–8; M.A. 1611. Probably ord. priest (Norwich) Dec. 1612. R. of Trimley St Mary, Suffolk, 1627–45; sequestered. (*Peile*, I. 251.)

FERROR, ——. B.Can.L. 1509–10.

FERRYAN, RICHARD. Matric. sizar from CLARE, Easter, 1580. B. at Ickleford, Herts. B.A. 1583–4; M.A. 1587. Ord. deacon (London) Feb. 24, 1585–6, age 24; priest (Lincoln) Dec. 1586. R. of Horham, Suffolk, 1606.

FERYE, ROBERT. Matric. pens. from ST JOHN'S, Easter, 1571.

FERYMAN, THOMAS. Matric. pens. from QUEENS', Easter, 1566; B.A. 1568–9. Incorp. at Oxford, 1573. R. of Fladbury, Worcs., 1597–1617. R. of Harvington, 1618.

FESTING, MICHAEL. Adm. pens. (age 19) at TRINITY, June 29, 1743. S. of Michael Christian, musician, of London (for whom *see D.N.B.*). B. in St Giles', London, 1725. School, Eton. Matric. 1743–4; Scholar, 1744; B.A. 1746–7; M.A. 1750; D.D. 1762. Fellow, 1749. Ord. deacon (Ely) June, 1747. R. of Wyke Regis, Dorset, till his death, 1765.

FETHAM, THOMAS. Matric. pens. from ST JOHN'S, Michs. 1608.

FETHEON, GILBERT, *see* **PHITHEON.**

FETHERSTONE or FEATHERSTONHAUGH, CHRISTOPHER. B.A. from ST JOHN'S, 1603–4; M.A. 1607. S. of Alexander, of Featherstonhaugh, Northumberland. School, Sedbergh. R. of Bentham, Yorks., 1616–53. Died there Oct. 8, 1653. Will (P.C.C.) 1655. (*Staffs. Pedigrees*; Hodgson, *Northumberland*; *Genealogist*, II. 254.)

FETHERSTONHAUGH, GEORGE. Adm. sizar (age 16) at CHRIST'S, July 8, 1674. S. of William. B. at Alston, Cumberland. School, Holt, Norfolk. Matric. 1676; B.A. 1677–8; M.A. 1682. Ord. deacon (Norwich) Sept. 1678; priest, June, 1680. R. of Bintree, Norfolk, 1688–1721. R. of North Creake. Died 1721. (*Peile*, II. 55.)

FEATHERSTON, LEONARD. Adm. sizar (age 19) at TRINITY, Apr. 16, 1681. S. of George. B. in Co. Durham. School, Durham (Mr Battersby). Matric. 1681; B.A. 1684–5. Ord. deacon (Durham) Apr. 13, 1685; priest, Sept. 29, 1685. P.C. of St Andrew's, Auckland, 1685–9.

FETHERSTON, THOMAS. B.A. 1532–3; M.A. 1540.

FETHERSTON, WILLIAM. Matric. pens. from TRINITY, Easter, 1610; B.A. 1614–5; M.A. 1619.

FEATHERSTONHAUGH, HENRY. Adm. pens. (age 17) at ST JOHN'S, July 2, 1712. S. of Timothy, gent. B. at Kirk Oswald, Cumberland. Bapt. there, Apr. 1, 1695. School, Kendal. Matric. 1712; B.A. 1715–6; M.A. 1719; B.D. 1727. Fellow, 1717–29. Ord. deacon (London) Mar. 13, 1719–20. Lecturer at St Jobu's, Newcastle, 1724–31; at All Saints' 1731–79. Buried there Apr. 15, 1779. (H. M. Wood.)

FETHERSTONHALGH, JOHN. Matric. Fell.-Com. from MAGDALENE, Easter, 1617. Probably s. and h. of Ralph, of Stanhope Hall, Durham; age 17, in 1615. (*Vis. of Durham.*)

FETHERSTONHAUGH, RICHARD. B.A. 1499–1500; M.A. 1506–7 (Incorp. from Oxford).

FETHERSTONHAUGH or FETHERSTON, UTRICK. M.A. from ST JOHN'S, 1747. S. of Matthew, of St Magnus, London (mayor of Newcastle). B. in Middlesex. Matric. from Trinity College, Oxford, Nov. 11, 1735, age 17; B.A. (Oxford) 1739. Ord. deacon (London) Dec. 21, 1740; priest, Dec. 19, 1742. R. of Oxted, Surrey, 1746–88. R. of Stauford-le-Hope, Essex, 1747–73. R. of Harting, Sussex, 1757–73. Chaplain to the Bishop of Hereford. Died Dec. 26, 1788. M.I. at Oxted. Admon. (P.C.C.) 1789. (*Scott-Mayor*, III. 565.)

FETTIPLACE, EDMUND. M.A. 1614 (Incorp. from Oxford). Of Childrey and Lambourne, Berks. S. of Sir Edmund. Bapt. Sept. 8, 1590. Matric. from Queen's College, Oxford, Nov. 15, 1605, age 15; B.A. 1608–9; M.A. 1612. Buried at Lambourne, Apr. 3, 1661. (*Vis. of Berks.*, 1623; *Misc. Gen. et Her.*, 5th S., II. 206.)

FETYPLACE, FRANCIS. Matric. sizar from PETERHOUSE, Michs. 1544. Perhaps s. of Anthony, of Berkshire. Died Nov. 9, 1557. Inq. p.m. (*Misc. Gen. et Her.*, 5th S., II. 186.)

FETTIPLACE, THOMAS. Adm. pens. (age 15) at PETERHOUSE, Mar. 23, 1617. Of London. Matric. 1618. Licensed to practise medicine, 1650. M.D. 1663. Probably killed by a fall from his horse. Buried at Pangbourne, Berks., Apr. 5, 1670. (J. Ch. Smith.)

FEVER, ROBERT. B.Can.L. 1476–7.

PEVERELL, BARNARD. Matric. sizar from PEMBROKE, Michs. 1608. Will of one of these names (P.C.C.) 1655; of Stratford, Suffolk.

FEVERSHAM, Abbot of. B. and D.Can.L. 1479–80. Walter Gore or Goore, abbot, 1458–99. (*Dugdale*, IV. 570.)

FEVERYEARE, JOHN. Adm. sizar (age 17) at CAIUS, June 11, 1631. S. of John, gent., of Claxton, Norfolk. B. at 'Barrow.' School, Norwich (Mr Stonham). Matric. 1631; B.A. 1634–5; M.A. 1638. Ord. deacon (Norwich) Sept. 24, 1637; priest, Sept. 23, 1638. C. of Claxton, Norfolk, 1637. R. of Ashby and Hellington, 1662–85. (*Venn*, I. 301.)

FEWELL, LAWRENCE. Adm. sizar at TRINITY, May 24, 1642.

FEWELL, ROBERT. B.A. 1539–40; M.A. 1543. R. of Withersfield, Suffolk, 1558–84.

FEWSTER, NICHOLAS. Adm. sizar (age 18) at PETERHOUSE, May 17, 1671. Of Durham. School, Durham. Matric. 1671; B.A. 1675–6; M.A. 1679. Ord. deacon (Durham) Sept. 19, 1675. Minor canon of Durham. Under Master of Durham School. Married, at St Oswald's, Durham, Feb. 8, 1675–6, Dorothy, dau. of John Martin, of Elvet. Died 1680. Buried Apr. 13, in the Cathedral. (H. M. Wood.)

FEWTERER, JOHN. B.A. 1502–3; M.A. 1506; B.D. 1515. Fellow of PEMBROKE, 1505. Ord. deacon (Lincoln) Feb. 27, 1506–7; priest, Apr. 3, 1507. Confessor-general of Syon Monastery. Benefactor to Pembroke. Doubtless 'John Fewter, LL.D., St Faith, London,' whose will (P.C.C.) 1532. Caller 'Faukener' by Wm Cole. (*Cooper*, I. 57.)

FEWTRELL, THOMAS. Adm. sizar at QUEENS', June 26, 1727. Of Salop. Matric. 1727; B.A. 1730–1.

PEYNEY, NICHOLAS, *see* **FENEY.**

FICKES or FYKES, ——. B.A. 1461–2; M.A. 1464.

FICKES or FYKES, ——. M.Gram. 1515–6.

FIDCOCK, HENRY. B.Can.L. 1494–5.

FIDDIS, CHRISTOPHER. Matric. sizar from ST JOHN'S, Easter, 1607; B.A. 1610–1; M.A. 1614. Ord. deacon (York) May, 1613; priest, Dec. 1613. V. of Nafferton, Yorks., 1617–37. Died 1637.

FIDDES, RICHARD. Incorp. D.D. 1720, from University College, Oxford. S. of John, of Hunmanby, Yorks. Matric. from Corpus Christi, Oxford, Oct. 21, 1687, age 17; B.A. from University College, 1691; B.D. 1714; D.D. 1718. R. of Halsham-in-Holderness, Yorks., 1696–1725. R. of Redenhall, Norfolk, 1724. Chaplain to the Earl of Oxford. Author theological. Died July 8, 1725. (*Al. Oxon.*; *D.N.B.*)

FIDDIS, THOMAS. Matric. sizar from QUEENS', Easter, 1637. Of Yorkshire. B.A. 1641–2; M.A. 1645; B.D. 1661 (*Lit. Reg.*). Ord. deacon and priest (Lincoln) May 24, 1646. V. of Barkway, Herts., 1648–66. V. of Wyddial, 1664–6. R. of Brightwell, Oxon., 1666.

FIDLER, THOMAS. Adm. sizar (age 18) at ST JOHN'S, Nov. 29, 1723. S. of Jasper, farmer, of Derbyshire. B. at Chesterfield. School, Chesterfield (Mr Burronghs). Matric. 1723; B.A. 1727–8; M.A. 1731. R. of Shirland, Derbs., 1754–92.

FIDLING, RICHARD. Matric. sizar from ST JOHN'S, Michs. 1567; B.A. 1571–2; M.A. 1575. R. of Loughton, Essex, 1576.

FIDOE, ANTHONY. Adm. sizar at TRINITY, June, 1658. S. of Robert, of Stamford-on-Teme, Worcs. B. Aug. 20, 1640. Matric. 1658. Ejected from Hemingborough, Yorks., 1662. Afterwards a preacher in London. Died Jan. 17, 1715, aged 75. Brother of the next. (*Calamy*, II. 588.)

FIDOE, JOHN. Adm. sizar at TRINITY, Nov. 28, 1645. Previously matric. from New Inn Hall, Oxford, May 6, 1642. S. of Robert, of Stamford-on-Teme, Worcs. B.A. 1647–8; M.A. 1651. Fellow, 1651. V. of Hardwick, Cambs., 1652. V. of Whittlebury, Northants.; ejected, 1662. Died in London, *c.* 1667. Brother of the above. (*Calamy*, II. 233.)

FIDYON, WILLIAM. Student of Canon Law in Cambridge. R. of 'Wytlingworth' (? Whitlingham), Norwich diocese. Received a Papal dispensation to hold other livings, June 15, 1442. One of these names R. of Chelsea, Middlesex, 1451–4. (*Cal. Papal Letters.*)

FIELD, ANTHONY. Matric. sizar from JESUS, Michs. 1579. B. at Gt Waltham, Essex. B.A. 1582–3; M.A. 1586. Ord. deacon (London) June 27, 1587, age 25. R. of 'Milles,' Norfolk. One of these names R. of Chillenden, Kent, 1588–1607; deprived. R. of Knolton, 1591–1608; deprived. P.C. of Nonington, till his death, 1626.

FIELD, BENJAMIN. M.A. from ST JOHN'S, 1750. S. of Nicholas, of Evesham, Worcs., gent. Matric. from Balliol College, Oxford, June 26, 1731, age 19. Exhibitioner from Charterhouse. B.A. (Hart Hall) 1735. Ord. deacon (Worcester) June 1; priest, Sept. 21, 1735. V. of Mickleton, Gloucs., 1746–81. Chaplain to Lord Olyphant. R. of Aston-under-Edge, 1750–81. Died at Mickleton, Aug. 17, 1781. Will, P.C.C. (*Scott-Mayor*, III. 600; G. *Mag.*)

FIELD, EDMUND. Matric. Fell.-Com. from EMMANUEL, Easter, 1637. Of 'Mardon,' Herts., Esq. Adm. at the Inner Temple, 1639. Barrister, 1652. Of Stanstead-Bury, Herts., Esq. M.P. for Hertford, 1675-6. Died June 3, 1676, aged 56. Buried at Shephall. Father of Thomas (1671-2). (Le Neve, *Knights*, 354.)

FEILD, EDMUND. Adm. Fell.-Com. (age 18) at PETERHOUSE, Mar. 6, 1722-3. S. of Edmund, of Stanstead-Abbots, Herts. School, Eton. Matric. 1725. Of Stanstead-Bury. Died Aug. 1729. Brother of Thomas (1719) and James (1730-1).

FYLD or FELD, EDWARD. Matric. sizar from CORPUS CHRISTI, Michs. 1571.

FEILD, FRANCIS. Adm. pens. (age 16) at ST JOHN'S, May 14, 1664. S. and h. of Francis, gent., of Watton Abbey, near Gt Driffield, Yorks. B. there. School, Pocklington (Mr Clarke). Matric. 1664. Adm. at the Middle Temple, Aug. 6, 1664.

FEILD, GEORGE. Matric. sizar from TRINITY, Easter, 1578; Scholar, 1582; B.A. 1582-3.

FIELD, HENRY. M.A. from CHRIST'S, 1645. Fellow of Christ's, 1645-8. Matric. from Pembroke College, Oxford, Oct. 26, 1638, age 17. B. at King's Norton, Worcs. B.A. 1641. R. of Uffington, Lincs., 1645. Imprisoned after the Restoration. Died in the Gatehouse, Westminster. (*Peile*, I. 457; *Calamy*, II. 637.)

FIELD, JAMES. Matric. sizar from KING'S, Easter, 1688; B.A. 1691-2. Ord. deacon (London) June 11; priest, June 23, 1693.

FEILDE or FIELDE, JAMES. Adm. pens. (age 17) at PETERHOUSE, Mar. 6, 1730-1. S. of Edmund, Esq., of Stanstead, Herts. School, Westminster. Matric. 1731; Scholar, 1731; B.A. 1734-5; M.A. 1738. Fellow, 1735-41. Ord. deacon (Lincoln) Mar. 18, 1738-9; priest, June 17, 1739. Chaplain to the East India Co., 1743. Died at Fort St George, Oct. 1745. Brother of Edmund (1722-3) and Thomas (1719). (*T. A. Walker*, 262.)

FIELD, JOHN. Matric. pens. from PEMBROKE, Easter, 1587. Probably from Merchant Taylors' School; s. of Humphrey, clothier. Migrated to Oxford after four years. B.A. from St John's College, Oxford, 1590-1; M.A. (Cambridge) 1594. Fellow of Pembroke, 1593.

FEILDE, JOHN. Matric. pens at TRINITY, Easter, 1613.

FIELD, JOHN. Matric. sizar from TRINITY, Micha. 1617; Scholar, 1619; B.A. 1620-1. Ord. deacon (Peterb.) Mar. 4; priest (as M.A.), Mar. 5, 1625-6. Perhaps Incorp. at Oxford, 1628, as 'Jonathan, M.A.' V. of Penbryn, Cardigan, 1632. Preb. of St David's. V. of Llangammerch, Brecon, 1634. C. of St Margaret, Wiggenhall, Norfolk, in 1635. Preb. and treasurer of Brecon. (*Al. Oxon.*)

FEILD, JOHN. Adm. pens. at TRINITY, June 25, 1662. Matric. 1662; B.A. 1665-6; M.A. 1669. Adm. at the Inner Temple, May 25, 1664.

FIELD, JOHN. Adm. Fell.-Com. (age 18) at SIDNEY, Aug. 15, 1751. Eldest s. of John, gent., of Campton, Beds. School, Market Street, Beds. (Dr William Pitman). Matric. 1751. Adm. at the Middle Temple, July 2, 1753.

FEILD, PLAYFORD. Adm. pens. (age 14) at PEMBROKE, June 10, 1632. S. of Theophilus (1591-2), Bishop of St David's. B. at Westminster. Matric. 1632; B.A. 1635-6; M.A. 1639. V. of Caerwent, Monmouth, 1660.

FIELD, RICHARD. M.A. 1683 (Incorp. from Oxford). Of London. S. of Nathaniel, of Stourton, Wilts., clerk. Bapt. June 3, 1648. Matric. from Trinity College, Oxford, Apr. 10, 1663, age 15; B.A. 1667; M.A. 1670. M.D. from Sidney, 1683. Candidate R.C.P. 1685. Fellow by charter of James II, 1687. (*Munk*, I. 446.)

FIELD or FEYLDE, ROWLAND. Matric. pens. from TRINITY, Easter, 1608; Scholar, 1608; (? B.A. 1609-10, or in *ordo*, 1608-9, of Christ's); M.A. 1613. Ord. deacon (Peterb.) Sept. 18; priest, Sept. 19, 1613. Licensed to cure of Kilnwick, Yorks.; and to preach, Apr. 1616.

FIELD, THEOPHILUS. Adm. sizar at EMMANUEL, Jan. 1591-2. S. of John, clerk (will, P.C.C. 1588). B. in St Giles', Cripplegate. Matric. 1592; B.A. from Pembroke, 1595-6; M.A. 1599; B.D. 1605; D.D. 1611. Fellow of Pembroke, 1598. Incorp. at Oxford, 1600. Ord. deacon and priest (Peterb.) Sept. 25, 1603. Chaplain to James I. R. of Cotton, Suffolk, 1607. V. of Mashfield (? Mayfield), Sussex, 1610. V. of Lydd, Kent, 1611-27. Bishop of Llandaff, 1619-27. V. of Bassaleg, Monmouth, 1623. Bishop of St David's, 1627-35; of Hereford, 1635-6. Died June 2, 1636. Buried in Hereford Cathedral. (*Al. Oxon.*; *D.N.B.*; Browne Willis, *St David's*.)

FEYLDE, THOMAS. Said to have graduated M.A. in 1508. No such degree found. Poetical writer. (*Cooper*, I. 24.)

FIELD, THOMAS. Matric. sizar from CORPUS CHRISTI, Easter, 1584. B. at Weston, Herts., *c.* 1568. B.A. 1587-8; M.A. 1591. Ord. priest (Bishop of Colchester) 1595. V. of Bengeo, Herts., 1595. V. of Babraham, Cambs., 1595-7. Preacher (London) 1598. R. of Wormley, Herts., 1598-9. R. of St Andrew and St Nicholas, Hertford, 1598-1623. Will, P.C.C.

FIELD, THOMAS. Adm. pens. (age 17) at PETERHOUSE, Jan. 24, 1671-2. Of Stanstead. S. and h. of Edmund (1637), of Marden and Stanstead-Bury, Herts. School, Hitchin. Matric. 1672. Afterwards Fell.-Com. M.A. 1675 (*Lit. Reg.*). Knighted at Windsor, July 29, 1681. Died Jan. 13, 1689-90. Father of the next. (*T. A. Walker*, 146.)

FIELD, THOMAS. Adm. pens. (age 19) at ST JOHN'S, June 1, 1699. S. of Sir Thomas (1671-2), Knt. B. at Stanstead, Herts. School, Eton. Matric. 1699; B.A. 1702-3; M.A. 1706; B.D. 1714. Fellow, 1704-18. Junior Proctor, 1712-3. Ord. deacon (London) May 30, 1708; priest, Dec. 24, 1710. R. of Sutton-in-the-Dale, Derbs., 1710-6; and R. of Malpas, Cheshire, 1716-9. Father of Thomas (1747).

FIELD, THOMAS. Adm. pens. at EMMANUEL, Feb. 3, 1710-1. Of Hertfordshire. Doubtless s. and h. of John, of Hitchin, Herts., gent. Matric. 1712; B.A. 1714-5. Adm. at Gray's Inn, Aug. 2, 1712.

FIELD, THOMAS. Adm. Fell.-Com. (age 18) at PETERHOUSE, Nov. 21, 1719. S. of Edmund, of Stanstead-Abbots, Herts. School, Enfield. Matric. 1719. Died of small-pox, Mar. 1719-20. M.I. at Stanstead. Brother of Edmund (1722-3) and James (1730-1). (*T. A. Walker*, 241.)

FIELDE, THOMAS. Adm. pens. (age 17) at ST JOHN'S, June 5, 1747. S. of Thomas (1699), clerk, of Derbyshire. B. at Wingfield, near Chesterfield. School, Tipshall. Matric. 1747; B.A. 1750-1; M.A. 1754. Ord. deacon (Lichfield) 1753; priest, Sept. 22, 1754. R. of Eastwick, Herts., 1764-81. V. of Stanstead-Abbots, 1767-81. Died 1781. (*Scott-Mayor*, III. 567.)

FEILD, TURPIN. Adm. sizar (age 18) at PETERHOUSE, May 12, 1669. Of Lincolnshire. School, Stamford.

FIELD, WALTER. Adm. at KING'S, a scholar from Eton, 1445. B. at Winchester. B.A. 1449; D.D. Provost of King's, 1479-99. Chaplain to the King. Chancellor of Wells, 1496-9. Will (P.C.C.) 'of King's College, and St Elizabeth, Winchester.'

FIELD, WALTER. Adm. at KING'S, a scholar from Eton, 1486.

FIELD, WILLIAM. B.A. 1469-70; M.A. 1471; B.D. 1484-5. One of these names Master of the College of Fotheringhay, Northants., 1496-9.

FIELD, WILLIAM. Adm. sizar (age 16) at MAGDALENE, Apr. 16, 1646. S. of Edmund, of Market Rasen, Lincs. School, Market Rasen. Matric. 1646.

FIELDEN, *see also* FIELDING.

FIELDEN, GEORGE. Adm. at CORPUS CHRISTI, 1658. Of Norfolk.

FIELDEN, JOHN. Adm. sizar (age 18) at MAGDALENE, June 29, 1670. S. of Henry, of Wigan, Lancs. School, Wigan.

FYLDEN, ROBERT. Matric. sizar from ST JOHN'S, Easter, 1586; B.A. 1589-90. Ord. priest (Norwich) Mar. 10, 1591-2; 'B.A.' V. of St Mary Wiggenhall, Norfolk, 1591-2. V. of Appleton, 1591-1620. V. of West Newton, 1595-1608. Perhaps R. of Thorpe by Norwich, 1607.

FILDEN, SAMUEL. Matric. sizar from MAGDALENE, Easter, 1633.

FEILDER, JOHN. Adm. sizar (age 16) at TRINITY, June 28, 1683. S. of Thomas, of Andover, Hants. School, Southampton (Mr Samuel Man). Matric. 1683; Scholar, 1685; B.A. 1686-7. R. of Little Thorpe, Norfolk, 1700.

FIELDHOUSE, JOHN. M.A. from EMMANUEL, 1748. S. of John, of Kinnersley, Salop, clerk. Matric. from Pembroke College, Oxford, May 20, 1737, age 20; B.A. (Oxford) 1740-1. (*Al. Oxon.*)

FIELDHOUSE, WILLIAM. B.A. from MAGDALENE, 1637-8. Perhaps matric. 1635, as 'James.' Ord. deacon (Peterb.) May 20, 1638; priest, June 9, 1639.

FIELDING, *see also* FIELDEN.

FEILDING, BASIL. Matric. Fell.-Com. from KING'S, Lent, 1581-2. Doubtless s. of Sir William, Knt., and sheriff of Warws. Sheriff of Warws., 1611-2. Father of William (1603), Roger (1606) and Edward (1606). (*Vis. of Warws.*, 1682; *Vis. of London*, 1634; Collins, III. 270.)

FEILDING, BASIL. Matric. Fell.-Com. from QUEENS', Easter, 1621. Of Warwickshire. S. and h. of William (1603), first Earl of Denbigh. B. *c.* 1608. M.A. 1622 (*fil. nob.*). K.B. 1626. Summoned to the House of Lords as Baron Feilding, of Newnham Paddock, Warws., 1628. Served as a volunteer at the siege of Bois-le-Duc, 1629. Travelled in Germany. Entered at Basel University, 1631. Ambassador extraordinary to the Venetian Republic, 1634–9. Commanded a regiment in the Parliamentary Army at Edgehill, 1642. Appointed commander-in-chief of the Parliamentary forces in the associated counties of Warwick, Worcester, Stafford, and Salop, 1643. Lord-Lieutenant of Warws., 1643. Succeeded as 2nd Earl of Denbigh, 1643. Suspected of disaffection and relieved of his command, 1644. Employed as commissioner for the Treaty of Uxbridge, 1645. State-councillor, 1649–51. Gradually went over to the Royalist party. Created Baron St Liz, 1664. Died at Dunstable, Nov. 28, 1675, *s.p.* Buried at Monk's Kirby. (*D.N.B.*; *G.E.C.*)

FEILDING, EDWARD. Matric. pens. from QUEENS', Michs. 1606. Of Warwickshire. S. of Basil (1581–2). Died of wounds at Newbury, Sept. 2, 1643. Buried at St Mary's, Oxford. M.I. Brother of William (1603) and Roger (1606). (*Collins*, III. 270.)

FEILDING, EUSTACE. Matric. sizar from TRINITY, Easter, 1636; B.A. 1639–40. Ord. priest (Lincoln) June 5, 1642. R. of Ashby Folvile, Leics., 1647–53. (*Shaw*, I. 343.)

FYLDYNGE, FAWSTEN. Matric. pens. from ST JOHN'S, Michs. 1551.

FYLDINGE, FERDINAND. Matric. pens. from GONVILLE HALL, Michs. 1555. Perhaps 2nd s. of Basil, of Newnham, Warws., Esq. If so, married Isabel, dau. of George Ashley, of Wolvey, Warws. Adm. at Lincoln's Inn, Aug. 21, 1560. (*Nichols*, IV. 292.)

FIELDING, GEORGE. Adm. Fell.-Com. at QUEENS', July 3, 1660. Of Middlesex. S. of George, Earl of Desmond. Matric. 1661. Of Bury, Suffolk; age 40, in 1682. Married a daughter of Sir John Lee. Will of the father proved (Bury) 1666. Brother of John (1668). (*Vis. of Warws.*, 1682.)

FIELDING, GEORGE. Adm. sizar at ST CATHARINE'S, June 23, 1737. S. of Colonel Edmond Fielding. Bapt. at St James', Westminster, Oct. 29, 1719. Exhibitioner from Charterhouse. Matric. 1737. Died young. Half-brother of the novelist. (*Al. Carthus.*)

FIELDING, JOHN. Adm. pens. at QUEENS', Mar. 25, 1668. Of Suffolk. S. of George, Earl of Desmond. B. about 1650. Matric. 1668; M.A. 1671; D.D. 1690 (*Lit. Reg.*). Fellow by mandate, 1671–2. V. of Puddletown, Dorset, 1675–91. Preb. of Salisbury, 1677–82. Chaplain to William III. Died 1697. Buried at Salisbury. Grandfather of the novelist and father of the next, brother of George (1660). (*Vis. of Warws.*, 1682; *Collins*, III. 276; F. S. Hockaday.)

FEILDING, JOHN. Adm. pens. (age 15) at CHRIST'S, Feb. 21, 1688–9. S. of John, D.D. (above). B. at Puddletown, Dorset. School, Salisbury (Mr Hardwick). Matric. 1689; Scholar, 1689; B.A. 1692–3. Secretary to Henry, Duke of Portland, and Governor of Jamaica. Died June 24, 1725, in Jamaica. (*Vis. of Warws.*, 1682; *Peile*, II. 112.)

FIELDING, JOHN. Matric. sizar from KING'S, Lent, 1740.

FIELDING or FELDING, MARTIN. B.A. 1478–9.

FIELDING, MICHAEL. Matric. Fell.-Com. from KING'S, Lent, 1581–2.

FEILDING, PHILIP. Adm. sizar (age 17) at ST JOHN'S, June 13, 1657. S. of Israel, deceased, of Startforth, Richmond, Yorks. B. there. School, Bishop Auckland (Mr Robinson). Matric. 1657; B.A. 1660–1; M.A. 1664. Ord. deacon and priest (Carlisle) Feb. 2, 1662–3. V. of Brampton, Cumberland, 1662–92. V. of Crosby-on-Eden, 1666–70. V. of Irthington, 1666–92. Buried at Brampton, June 25, 1692. Brother of William (1640). (*Vis. of Yorks.*, 1665; *B. Nightingale.*)

FEILDING, RICHARD. Matric. sizar from QUEENS', Michs. 1619. B. at Pythorne, Lancs. B.A. 1623–4; M.A. 1627. Ord. deacon (London) May 23, 1624, age 24; priest (Norwich) Sept. 24, 1626. R. of Beighton, Norfolk, 1632. R. of Stokesby, till 1652. Buried there Oct. 17, 1652. Will (P.C.C.) 1653.

FEILDING, RICHARD. M.A. 1641–2 (on King's visit). Possibly Sir Richard, of Lisbon, Knt. Will (P.C.C.) 1651.

FEILDING, ROBERT. Adm. sizar at QUEENS', July 8, 1627. Of Lancashire. B.A. 1630–1; M.A. 1634. Ord. priest (Norwich) 1631.

FEILDING, ROGER. Matric. pens. from QUEENS', Michs. 1606. Of Rutlandshire. S. of Basil (1581–2), of Newnham Paddock, Warws. Knighted, June 5, 1641. Died *c.* 1648. Brother of William (1603) and Edward (1606). (*Vis. of Warws.*; *Collins*, III. 270.)

FEILDEN, ROGER. Matric. pens. from TRINITY HALL, Michs. 1609; Scholar, 1610; LL.B. 1616. R. of Horton, Gloucs., 1618. R. of Newington Bagpath, 1620. (F. S. Hockaday.)

FYLDYN, WILLIAM. Matric. pens. from ST JOHN'S, Easter, 1551.

FEILDING, WILLIAM. Adm. Fell.-Com. at QUEENS', July 1, 1603. Of Warwickshire. S. of Basil (1581–2), of Newnham Paddock, Monk's Kirby, Warws. M.A. 1627. Knighted, Mar. 4, 1606–7. Created Viscount Feilding, 1620; and subsequently Earl of Denbigh, 1622. Became master of the great wardrobe, 1622. Followed Buckingham and Prince Charles to Spain, 1623. Commanded the Fleet sent to relieve Rochelle, 1628. A member of the Council of Wales, 1633. Served as a volunteer under Prince Rupert, 1643. Married Susan, dau. of Sir George Villiers, of Leicestershire. Died of wounds received at a skirmish near Birmingham, Apr. 8, 1643. Buried at Monk's Kirby, Warws. Father of Basil (1621), brother of Edward (1606) and Roger (1606). (*D.N.B.*; *G.E.C.*)

FEILDING, WILLIAM. Adm. pens. (age 16) at ST JOHN'S, June 16, 1640. S. of Israel, of Startforth, Yorks. School, Lartington (Mr Rose). Matric. 1640. Will (York) 1708. Brother of Philip.

FIELDING, WILLIAM. LL.D. 1705 (*Com. Reg.*).

FIENNES or FINES, CHARLES. Adm. pens. (age 16) at CHRIST'S, Apr. 9, 1624. S. of Sir Edward, Knt. B. at Sturton, Lincs. Educated at home. Matric. 1624. (*Peile*, I. 359.)

FIENNES, EDWARD, *see* **CLINTON.**

FINES, HENRY. Adm. pens. at EMMANUEL, May 21, 1635. Of Hertfordshire. Matric. 1635; B.A. 1638–9.

FIENNES, HENRY, *alias* **CLINTON.** Adm. pens. at EMMANUEL, July 3, 1660. Of Lincolnshire. Matric. 1660; B.A. 1663–4.

FINES, JAMES. Matric. Fell.-Com. from QUEENS', Easter, 1618. Of Oxfordshire. S. of William, Lord Saye and Sele. Migrated to Emmanuel, Oct. 12, 1622. Adm. at Lincoln's Inn, Mar. 11, 1627–8. Succeeded as 2nd Viscount, Apr. 14, 1662. M.P. for Banbury, 1625; for Oxfordshire, 1626, 1628–9, 1640–9, 1660. Married Frances, dau. of Sir Edward Cecil, Viscount Wimbledon. Lord Lieutenant of Oxfordshire. Died Mar. 15, 1673–4. Buried at Broughton. (*Collins*, VII. 22; *G.E.C.*)

FYNES, RALPH. Matric. pens. from CLARE, Michs. 1565.

FINES, ROBERT. Adm. pens. at TRINITY, May 10, 1639. Matric. 1639.

FIENNES, THEOPHILUS. Adm. Fell.-Com. at EMMANUEL, Feb. 9, 1632–3. Of Oxfordshire.

FIENNES, WILLIAM. Adm. Fell.-Com. at EMMANUEL, Feb. 9, 1632–3. Of Oxfordshire.

FIENNES, ——. Adm. Fell.-Com. at EMMANUEL, Easter, 1625.

FIFEFIT, JOHN. Fellow of PEMBROKE. Ord. priest (Ely) Mar. 29, 1376. Probably R. of Ramsden Bellhouse, Essex, 1394–6. Will (P.C.C.) 1411, as 'of Bright well; St Clement's, Cambridge; St Nicholas, Cole Abbey, London.'

FIFIELD, JOHN. Adm. pens. at CLARE, Oct. 14, 1674. S. of John, of Richmond, Surrey. Bapt. there, July 19, 1658. Matric. 1674; M.A. 1675 (*Lit. Reg.*). Adm. at the Inner Temple, May 12, 1677, from Clement's Inn.

FIFIELD, LEONARD. Adm. pens. (age 16) at JESUS, May 29, 1667. S. of Leonard. B. at East Drayton, Notts. Matric. 1667; B.A. 1670–1. Ord. deacon (Lincoln) Sept. 24, 1671; priest (Peterb.) Mar. 3, 1671–2.

FIGG, THOMAS. Adm. scholar at TRINITY HALL, Mar. 30, 1698.

FILBECKE, JOSEPH. Matric. sizar from TRINITY, 1610, as 'Fulbeach.' B. at Muncaster, Cumberland. B.A. 1614–5. Ord. deacon (London) Dec. 21, 1617, age 24; C. of Little Hallingbury, Essex.

FILBECKE, ROGER. Matric. sizar from TRINITY, Lent, 1580–1.

FILBIE, JOHN. Matric. pens. from CORPUS CHRISTI, Lent, 1615–6. Of Suffolk. B.A. 1618–9.

FILAY, JOHN, *see* **FYLAY.**

FILEY, WILLIAM. B.A. 1505–6; M.A. 1509; B.D. 1516; D.D. 1522. Of MICHAEL HOUSE. R. of Somersham, Hunts., 1525. Benefactor to Trinity College. Died 1549. Will (Archd. Hunts.) 1551. (*Cooper*, I. 97.)

FILOLL, JOHN. Adm. pens. at EMMANUEL, Sept. 9, 1600. One of these names s. of Anthony, of Old Hall, Rayne, Essex. Another s. of William, of Dorset. Will proved, Feb. 2, 1636–7. (*Vis. of Essex*, 1612; *Misc. Gen. et Her.*, 2nd S., II. 191.)

FILMER, EDWARD. Adm. Fell.-Com. (age 18) at CAIUS, Apr. 30, 1584. S. of Robert, Esq. B. at East Sutton, Kent. School, East Sutton. Knighted, July 23, 1603. Of East Sutton. Sheriff of Kent, 1614. Died 1629. Father of the next and of Robert (1604) and probably of Henry (1624), and Richard (1620), brother of Robert (1586). (*Vis. of Kent*; *Venn*, I. 119.)

FILMER or FILMORE, EDWARD. Matric. pens. from TRINITY, Easter, 1606. 2nd s. of Sir Edward, above. Scholar, 1608. Brother of Robert (1604), Henry (1624) and Richard (1620). (*Vis. of Kent.*)

FILMER, HENRY. Matric. pens. from QUEENS', Easter, 1624. Of Kent. Doubtless 6th s. of Sir Edward (1584), of East Sutton. B.A. 1627-8; M.A. 1631. (*Vis. of Kent.*)

FILMER, RICHARD. Matric. pens. from ST JOHN'S, Easter, 1620. Doubtless 5th s. of Sir Edward (1584), of East Sutton. (*Vis. of Kent*, 1619.)

FILMER, ROBERT. Adm. pens. (age 17) at CAIUS, Nov. 4, 1586. S. of Robert, Esq. B. at East Sutton, Kent. School, Sutton. Adm. at Gray's Inn, July 3, 1598, from Staple Inn. Brother of Edward (1584). (*Venn*, I. 128.)

FILMER, ROBERT. Matric. p . from TRINITY, Easter, 1604. Eldest s. of Sir Edward (1584), of East Sutton, Kent. Knighted, Jan. 24, 1618-9. An ardent Royalist. Imprisoned in Leeds Castle, Kent, 1644. Author of *Patriarcha* and other political treaties. Died May 26, 1653. (*D.N.B.*)

FILMER, ——. Matric. pens. from ST JOHN'S, Easter, 1604.

FINCHE, ANDREW. Matric. pens. from TRINITY, Michs. 1575.

FINCH, CHRISTOPHER. Matric. pens. from JESUS, Michs. 1559; B.A. 1566-7; M.A. from Trinity Hall, 1571. Probably adm. at Gray's Inn, 1573.

FINCH, DANIEL. LL.D. 1728 (*Com. Reg.*). Matric. from Christ Church, Oxford, June 23, 1704, age 15. S. of Daniel, Earl of Nottingham. School, Westminster. M.P. for Rutland, 1710-29. Succeeded as 3rd Earl of Nottingham, and as 8th Earl of Winchelsea, 1730. First Lord of the Admiralty, 1742. K.G. 1752. Lord president of the Council, 1765. Died at Fulham, Aug. 2, 1769. Buried at Ravenstone. Brother of Edward (1713) and Henry (1712). (*Al. Oxon.*; *G.E.C.*)

FINCH, EDWARD. Adm. at KING'S (age 18) a scholar from Eton, Sept. 4, 1581. Of Appledore, Kent. Matric. 1581. Left in 1582, 'and was never afterwards heard of.' (*Harwood.*)

FINCH, EDWARD. Adm. pens. at EMMANUEL, May 14, 1631. Of Kent. Matric. 1631; B.A. 1634.

FINCH, EDWARD. B.D. 1631-2 (*Lit. Reg.*). Probably the Royalist V. of Christ Church, Newgate, London, 1630-41; ejected; s. of Sir Henry (1572). Died c. 1642-3. Brother of John (1596). (*D.N.B.*)

FINCH, EDWARD. Adm. nobleman (age 14) at CHRIST'S, June 8, 1677. 5th s. of Heneage, Baron Finch, of Daventry, afterwards Earl of Nottingham. Matric. 1677; M.A. 1679. Fellow, 1680-4. Adm. at the Inner Temple, Apr. 23, 1683. M.P. for the University, 1690-5. Afterwards took holy orders. Ord. deacon (York) Sept. 8; priest, Sept. 15, 1695. Preb. of York, 1704. R. of Kirkby-in-Cleveland, 1705-37. R. of Wigan, 1707-14. Preb. of Canterbury, 1711-38. R. of Eyam, Derbs. Chaplain to the Queen. Composer. A 'Te Deum' and anthem by him are to be found in Dr Tudwa 's Manuscript Collection. Died Feb. 14, 1737-8, at York.y Buried there with his brother Henry. M.I. in the Minster. Brother of Henry (1679). (*Peile*, II. 64; *D.N.B.*)

FINCH, The Hon. EDWARD. Adm. Fell.-Com. (age 16) at TRINITY, Oct. 10, 1713. 5th s. of Daniel, Earl of Nottingham. School, Isleworth (Mr Ellis). Matric. 1713-4; M.A. 1718. Fellow of Christ's, 1728-46. M.P. for the University, 1727-68. Ambassador in Holland, Sweden, Poland and Russia. Groom of the royal bedchamber, 1742. Master of the Robes, 1757. Surveyor of the King's Private Roads, 1760. Took the name Finch-Hatton, 1764. One of the originators of the 'Members' Prizes.' Died May 16, 1771. Brother of Daniel (1728) and Henry (1712). (*D.N.B.*; *Peile*, II. 190.)

FINCH, FRANCIS. Matric. pens. from TRINITY, Easter, 1612, a scholar from Westminster. 5th s. of Sir Moyle, of Eastwell, Kent, and Elizabeth, dau. of Sir Thomas Heneage. B.A. 1615-6; M.A. 1629, as *fil. nob.*; his mother being created Countess of Winchelsea, 1628. M.P. for Eye, 1624-5, 1626, 1628-9. (*Vis. of Kent*, 1619; *Vis. of Midds.*, 1663.)

FINCH, GEORGE. D.D. 1499-1500.

FYNCHE, GEORGE. Matric. pens. from ST JOHN'S, Michs. 1544.

FINCH, HENEAGE. Matric. Fell.-Com. from TRINITY, c. 1592. 4th s. of Sir Moyle, of Eastwell, Kent. B.A. 1595-6. Adm. at the Inner Temple, Nov. 1597. Barrister, 1606. M.P. for Rye, 1607-11; for West Looe, 1620-2; for London, 1624-6. Recorder of London, 1621-31. Knighted, June 22, 1623. Serjeant-at-law, 1623. Speaker of the House of Commons, 1626. Died Dec. 5, 1631. Buried at Ravenstone, Bucks. Will, P.C.C. Father of John (1645) and brother of Thomas (1592) and Francis (1612). (*D.N.B.*; *Vis. of Midds.*, 1663.)

FYNCHE, HENRY. Matric. pens. from JESUS, Easter, 1548. One of these names V. of Rickmansworth, Herts., 1559-62. Died 1562.

FYNCHE, HENRY. Matric. pens. from CHRIST'S, May, 1572. Doubtless 2nd s. of Sir Thomas, of Eastwell, Kent. B.A. 1575-6. Adm. at Gray's Inn, Nov. 25, 1577. Barrister, 1585. Ancient, 1593. M.P. for Canterbury, 1592-3, 1597-8; for St Albans, 1614. Recorder of Sandwich, 1613. Serjeant-at-law, 1614. Knighted, June 20, 1616. Employed upon the attempted codification of Statute laws. Published a valuable treatise on common law, 1613. Another work entitled *The World's Great Restauration or Calling of the Jews* was suppressed. Died Oct. 1625. Buried at Boxley, Kent. Father of John (1596) and perhaps of Edward (B.D. 1631-2). (*Peile*, I.122; *Vis. of Kent*, 1619; *D.N.B.*)

FINCH, HENRY. Matric. sizar from TRINITY, Easter, 1576; B.A. 1579-80.

FYNCHE, HENRY. Matric. pens. from TRINITY, Michs. 1580.

FINCH, HENRY. Adm. pens. at CLARE, Oct. 16, 1651; B.A. 1652. B. at Standish, 1633. Schools, Wigan and Standish. Probably matric. from St Mary Hall, Oxford, Nov. 26, 1650. V. of Walton-on-the-Hill, Lancs., 1654-62; ejected. Afterwards minister at Birch Hall, in Lancs., 1672. Imprisoned at Chester, 1685. Aided Calamy in the history of the silenced ministers. Died Nov. 13, 1704, aged 71. (*D.N.B.*; *Calamy*, II. 106.)

FINCH, HENRY. Adm. Fell.-Com. (age 15) at CHRIST'S, June 9, 1679. S. of Heneage, Baron Finch, of Daventry. B. at Kensington. Matric. 1679; M.A. 1682. Fellow, 1683-92. Ord. deacon (Lincoln) Dec. 1689. Preb. of Ely, 1690-1714. R. of Winwick, Lancs., 1692-1725. Preb. of York, 1695-1704. Dean of York, 1702-28. Died Sept. 8, 1728. Buried in the Minster. M.I. there. Will, P.C.C. Brother of Edward (1677). (*Peile*, II. 74.)

FINCH, HENRY. Adm. Fell.-Com. (age 17) at CHRIST'S, Aug. 19, 1712. 4th s. of Daniel, Earl of Nottingham. B. at Exton, Ruts. School, Eton. M.A. 1714. Fellow, 1713-49. M.P. for Malton, 1724-61. H.M. Receiver-General at Minorca, 1729. Died May 27, 1761, aged 66. (*Baker*, I. 308; *Peile*, II. 180.)

FINCH, ISAAC. Adm. sizar at ST CATHARINE'S, June 23, 1714. Of Bradley, Suffolk. Matric. 1715; B.A. 1717-8; M.A. 1721. Ord. deacon (Ely) Sept. 20, 1719. V. of Stockbury, Kent, 1725-37. V. of Goudhurst, 1737-59.

FYNCHE, JOHN. Matric. sizar from PEMBROKE, Michs. 1569. One of these names V. of East Tilbury, Essex, 1575-84. Died 1584. Will (Consist. C. London).

FYNCHE, JOHN. Matric. pens. from TRINITY, Easter, 1577.

FYNCH, JOHN. Matric. pens. from PEMBROKE, Easter, 1584.

FINCH, JOHN. Adm. Fell.-Com. at EMMANUEL, Aug. 26, 1594. Perhaps 3rd s. of Sir Moyle, Bart. Matric. 1594. Adm. at the Inner Temple, 1597-8. Barrister, 1606. Died 1624.

FINCH, JOHN. Matric. pens. from JESUS, c. 1595. *Peile* (I. 219) seems wrong in assigning him to Christ's and in identifying him, probably, with the Emmanuel man of 1596.

FINCH, JOHN. Adm. pens. at EMMANUEL, Apr. 15, 1596. Doubtless s. of Sir Henry (1572), of Eastwell, Kent. Matric. c. 1596. Adm. at Gray's Inn, Feb. 5, 1600-1, as 's. and h. apparent of Henry Finch of the City of Canterbury, Esq.' Barrister, 1611. Recorder of Canterbury, 1619. M.P. for Canterbury, 1620-2, 1625-6, 1628-9; for Winchelsea, 1624-5. Knighted, June 15, 1625. King's Counsel, 1626. Speaker of the House of Commons, 1628-9. Serjeant-at-law, 1634. Chief Justice of Common Pleas, 1634-40. Lord Keeper, 1640. Created Baron Finch of Fordwich, 1640. Impeached and his estates sequestered. Retired to Holland, 1640, but returned at the Restoration. Died Nov. 27, 1660. Buried at Canterbury. Probably brother of Edward (1631-2). (*D.N.B.*; *Peile*, I. 219; A. B. Beaven.)

FINCH, JOHN. Adm. sizar at EMMANUEL, Apr. 16, 1607. Matric. 1607; B.A 1610-1; M.A. 1614.

FINCH, JOHN. Adm. Fell.-Com. at QUEENS', July 25, 1644. Of Kent.

FINCH, JOHN. Adm. pens. (age 18) at CHRIST'S, Apr. 11, 1645. 3rd s. of Sir Heneage (1592), Speaker of the House of Commons. B. in London, 1626. Schools, Eton and Oxford. Adm. at the Inner Temple, 1644. Removed to Balliol College, Oxford. B.A. 1647. Incorp. at Cambridge, 1647. M.A. (Cambridge) 1649; M.D. (Padua) 1660. Incorp. at Cambridge, 1660. Became English Consul at Padua and Syndic of the University; afterwards professor at Pisa. Returned to England and was elected extraordinary fellow of the College of Physicians, 1661. Knighted, June 10, 1661. F.R.S. 1663. Minister to the Grand Duke of Tuscany, 1665. Ambassador at Constantinople, 1672-82. Went on special mission to Adrianople, 1675. Died in London, Nov. 14, 1682. Buried, in the same vault in Christ's College Chapel, with his friend Sir Thomas Baines. Benefactor to the College. (*Peile*, I. 492; *D.N.B.*)

FINCH, JOHN. Adm. pens. (age 16) at St John's, Mar. 15, 1665–6. S. of John, deceased, of London. B. there. School, Maidstone, Kent (Mr Lawe).

FINCH, JOHN. Adm. pens. (age 16) at Sidney, July, 1690. S. of John, barber, of Cambridge. B. there. School, private. Matric. 1691; B.A. 1694–5; M.A. 1698. Ord. priest (Lincoln) Mar. 20, 1697–8. V. of Brampton, Hunts., 1712–36. Died 1736.

FINCH, JOHN. Adm. scholar (age 17) at Sidney, Oct. 15, 1715. Only s. of John, deceased. B. in London. School, Wrestlingworth, Beds. (Mr Bristow). Matric. 1715; LL.B. 1721. Ord. deacon (Norwich) Dec. 1721. Probably lecturer at St Peter-le-Poer, London: 'officiated more than 20 years at West Ham, Essex.' Died May 6, 1748. M.I. at West Ham. Will, P.C.C. (J. Ch. Smith.)

FINCH, LAURENCE. Adm. sizar at Queens', Oct. 11, 1624. Of Sussex. B.A. 1628–9.

FINCH, MARTIN. Adm. pens. at Trinity, Jan. 23, 1645–6. Of Norfolk. B.A. 1646–7; Scholar, 1647. Ejected from Tetney, Lincs., 1662. Afterwards a minister at Norwich, where the Old Meeting House was built for him. Died Feb. 13, 1697–8, aged 69. (*Calamy*, II. 162; *D.N.B.*)

FINCH, PETER. M.Gram. 1537–8.

FINCH, RALPH. Matric. pens. from Queens', Easter, 1549. Perhaps s. of Thomas, of Kingsdown, Kent. Succeeded his father at Kingsdown, 1555. Died Mar. 9, 1591. (*Hasted*, II. 592.)

FYNCHE, RALPH. Matric. pens. from Magdalene, Michs. 1567.

FINCHE, RICHARD. Matric. sizar from Trinity, Easter, 1577; B.A. 1581–2. One of these names, of London, adm. at Gray's Inn, 1583.

FINCH, RICHARD. Adm. at Corpus Christi, 1591. Of Kent. B.A. 1594–5; M.A. 1598.

FINCH, RICHARD. Adm. sizar at Emmanuel, Apr. 10, 1702. Of Hertfordshire. Matric. 1703; B.A. 1705–6. Ord. deacon (Ely, *Litt. dim.* from Lincoln) Dec. 19, 1708; priest, Sept. 25, 1709. Probably V. of Gt Wymondley, Herts., 1710–51. V. of St Ippolyt's, 1710–51. But *see Al. Oxon.* for a contemporary.

FINCH, RICHARD. M.A. from Pembroke, 1714. Matric. from Christ Church, Oxford, Apr. 4, 1696, age 18; B.A. (Oxford) 1699. One of these names signs as C. of Holwell, Beds., 1726–31.

FINCH, ROBERT. Adm. Fell.-Com. (age 16) at Christ's, Mar. 8, 1686–7. S. of Heneage, Lord Nottingham. B. at Kensington, Middlesex. School, Felsted (Mr Glascock). Matric. 1687; M.A. 1693. Fellow, 1692–6. Died 1696, in College. Buried at Gt St Andrew's, Cambridge, July 16. (*Peile*, II. 104.)

FINCH, ROBERT POOLE. Adm. sizar (age 16) at Peterhouse, Oct. 31, 1739. Of Kent. S. of Richard, clerk. B. at Greenwich, Mar. 3, 1723–4. School, Merchant Taylors'. Scholar, 1739; Matric. 1740; B.A. 1743–4; M.A. 1747; D.D. 1772. Ord. deacon (Ely) Sept. 23, 1744; priest (Rochester) Mar. 1747–8. Chaplain of Guy's Hospital for 37 years. Lecturer of St Bartholomew's behind the Exchange, London, 1755. R. of Gt Tay, Essex, 1763. R. of St Michael's, Cornhill, 1771–83. Preb. of Westminster, 1781–1803. R. of St John's, Westminster, 1782. Treasurer of the S.P.C.K. Author, sermons, etc. Died May 18, 1803. Buried in Westminster Abbey. Admon. (P.C.C.) 1803. (*D.N.B.*; *Peile*, II. 250; *T. A. Walker*, 277.)

FINCHE, SILVANUS. Adm. sizar at Trinity, June 4, 1664. Matric. 1664; B.A. 1667–8; M.A. 1671. Ord. deacon (Ely) May 29, 1670; priest, Dec. 24, 1671. C. of Sawston, Cambs., 1683.

FINCHE, THOMAS. Matric. Fell.-Com. from Clare, Easter, 1578.

FINCH, THOMAS. Matric. pens. from Pembroke, Easter, 1584.

FYNCH, THOMAS. Matric. Fell.-Com. from Trinity, *c.* 1592. S. of Sir Moyle, of Eastwell, Kent, Bart. B. *c.* 1575. Knighted, Jan. 8, 1608–9. Succeeded as Bart., *c.* 1619. M.P. for Winchelsea, 1620–2; and for Kent, 1628. Succeeded his mother as Earl of Winchelsea, Mar. 12, 1633–4. Died Nov. 4, 1639. Buried at Eastwell. Brother of Heneage (1592) and Francis (1612). (*G.E.C.*, I. 36; *Baker*, I. 307.)

FINCHE, THOMAS. Matric. pens. from Magdalene, Easter, 1614.

FINCH, THOMAS. Incorp. M.A. 1734. S. of William, of Headington, Oxon. Matric. from Trinity College, Oxford, Feb. 23, 1721–2, age 16; B.A. (Oxford) 1725; M.A. 1728. (*Al. Oxon.*)

FYNCHE, W. Matric. sizar from Trinity, Michs. 1571.

FINCH, WILLIAM, *see* BARLOW.

FYNCHE, WILLIAM. Matric. pens. from Jesus, Lent, 1557–8.

FINCH, WILLIAM. Adm. pens. at Christ's, July 2, 1625. S. of William, of Bedfordshire. School, Bishop's Stortford (Mr Leigh). Matric. 1625; B.A. 1628–9; M.A. 1632.

FINCH, WILLIAM. Adm. pens. (age 20) at St John's, June 12, 1662. S. of Roger, yeoman, of Manchester. B. there. Schools, Rivington (Mr Feilding) and Manchester. Probably M.A. 1673 (*Lit. Reg.*), as 'of St John's.' One of these names R. of Saunderton, Bucks., 1685–9.

FINCH, WILLIAM, Viscount MAIDSTONE. Adm. Fell.-Com. at St John's, Nov. 28, 1664. S. of Heneage, Earl of Winchelsea. Matric. 1664; M.A. 1666. Killed in the sea-fight with the Dutch, May 28, 1672.

FINCH, WILLIAM. Adm. sizar (age 17) at St John's, Apr. 4, 1716. S. of Henry, husbandman, of Staffordshire. B. at Brewood. School, Brewood (Mr Hillman). B.A. 1719–20.

FYNCHE, WULFRAM. Matric. sizar from Christ's, Easter, 1576.

FINCH, ——. Adm. at Corpus Christi, 1578.

FINCHAM or FYNCHAM, JOHN. B.Civ.L. 1455–6. Early monuments to Fincham family at Fincham, Norfolk. (*Blomefield*, VII. 349.)

FINCHAM, RICHARD, *see* CORNWALLIS.

FINCHAM, RICHARD. Matric. pens. from Queens', Lent, 1615–6. Of Cambridgeshire. Perhaps s. of John, of Outwell. B. 1597. Died 1681. One of these names adm. at the Inner Temple, 1618, as s. and h. of Edward. Possibly a mistake for 'Thomas,' *see* below. Resided at Outwell, Isle of Ely. (Wm Blyth, *Fincham*.)

FINCHAM, RICHARD. Adm. pens. (age 16) at St John's, Aug. 18, 1671. S. of Richard, deceased, of Elme, Norfolk. B. there. School, Bradley. Matric. 1671. Adm. at the Inner Temple, Feb. 10, 1672–3. Married and had issue. Will dated 1680.

FINCHAM, ROBERT. Matric. pens. (age 16) from Pembroke, Lent, 1623–4. 2nd s. of Edward, of Outwell, Isle of Ely, Esq. Brother of Thomas (1620). (*Vis. of Cambs.*)

FINCHAM, SIMON. B.A. 1481–2; M.A. 1485–6; B.D. 1503–4. Probably s. of Simon, of Fincham, Norfolk. Fellow of Corpus Christi, 1486. R. of St Benet, Cambridge, 1498. Afterwards R. of Landbeach, Cambs. Died 1512. (*Masters*.)

FINCHAM, [THOMAS]. B.Civ.L. 1466–7. Scholar and fellow of King's Hall, 1465–1517. May have taken another degree, 1468–9. Preb. of Lincoln, 1485–1517. Of Hockwold, Norfolk. Will proved (P.C.C.) 1517. (*E. Anglian*, I. 95.)

FINCHAM, THOMAS. Adm. Fell.-Com. (age 19) at Pembroke, Apr. 5, 1620. 1st s. of Edward, of Outwell, Cambs., Esq. Matric. 1620. Of Outwell, and Norwich. Died 1666, at Norwich. Brother of Robert (1623–4). (*Vis. of Cambs.*; Wm Blyth, *Fincham*.)

FINCHAM, WILLIAM. Adm. sizar (age 15) at Christ's, Sept. 18, 1629. S. of William. B. at Thurlow, Suffolk. School, Thurlow. Matric. 1629; B.A. 1633–4; M.A. 1637. Ord. deacon (Peterb.) Sept. 24, 1637; priest, May 20, 1638. C. of Mendlesham, Suffolk, 1637. R. of Wortham, 1644–80. Married at Mendlesham, Jan. 23, 1639–40, Jane, dau. of Chr. Wragge, V. of Mendlesham. Buried at Wortham, Mar. 25, 1680. One of these names minister of the Tower Church, Ipswich, in Sept. 1649. R. of Wortham Everard, 1656–80. (*Peile*, I. 402; Wm Blyth, *Fincham*, 130.)

FINCHAM, ——. B.A. 1458–9; M.A. 1462–3.

FINCHAM, ——. B.Can.L. 1487–8.

FINCHAM, ——. B.D. 1496.

FINCHER or FINCKER, RICHARD. Adm. pens. at Emmanuel, Oct. 29, 1646. Matric. 1647; B.A. 1650. R. of All Saints', Worcester, till 1662, ejected. Afterwards minister in London. Perhaps s. of John, of Hanbury, Worcs.; age 56 in 1682. Died Feb. 10, 1692. (*Calamy*, II. 549; *Vis. of Worcs.*)

FYNCKLE, THOMAS. Matric. pens. from St John's, Easter, 1567.

FYNDERYN, WILLIAM. Scholar at King's Hall, 1397–9.

FINEUX or FENNIS, JOHN. Matric. pens. from Trinity, *c.* 1593, as Fennis. Perhaps 2nd s. of Thomas, of Hougham, Kent. B.A. 1596–7; M.A. 1600. (*Vis. of Kent*, 1619.)

FINEUX, THOMAS. Matric. pens. from Corpus Christi, Easter, 1587. Perhaps s. of Thomas, of Hougham, Kent. (*Vis. of Kent*, 1619.)

FINETT, JOHN. M.A. 1612–3 (on visit of Prince Charles). Probably of Kent; Master of the Ceremonies. Knighted at Whitehall, Mar. 21, 1615–6. Author, on the Etiquette of Embassies. Died July 12, 1641, aged 70. M.I. at St Martin-in-the-Fields. Will (P.C.C.). (*D.N.B.*; J. Ch. Smith.)

FINNETT, THOMAS. Matric. pens. from St John's, *c.* 1591.

FINET or FINIT, WILLIAM. Adm. Fell.-Com. at EMMANUEL, Feb. 23, 1640-1. Matric. 1641. One of these names student at Leyden, Aug. 28, 1643.

FING, ——. B.Can.L. 1475-6. Probably John Fyn. Will (P.C.C.) 1506; 'of Hereford Cathedral, and Madingley, Cambs.' (J. Ch. Smith.)

FINGLEY or FINGLOW, JOHN. Matric. sizar from CAIUS, Dec. 1573. B. at Barnby, Yorks., about 1554. Butler (*promus*) of the College, for three or four years; where he became the subject of bitter complaints against the Master. Seminary priest and martyr. Adm. at Douay, Feb. 13, 1579-80. Ord. priest at Rheims, Mar. 25, 1581. Sent to England, Apr. 24, 1581. Committed to York gaol; executed, Aug. 8, 1586. (*Venn*, I. 76; *D.N.B.*; which makes no reference to his college career.)

FINLAY, JAMES. Adm. Fell.-Com. at CAIUS, July 1, 1720. Adm. at Dublin (age 16) July 26, 1698. S. of Robert, merchant. B. at Cavan, Ireland. B.A. (Dublin) 1703; M.A. (Dublin) 1706; D.D. (Cambridge) 1720. Incorp. at Oxford, 1720. Ord. deacon (Dublin) Mar. 12, 1703; priest (Kilmore) Mar. 4, 1704. V. of Christchurch, Surrey, 1713-51. R. of Little Ilford, Essex, 1736-51. Chaplain to the Earl of Abercorn. Died Jan. 29, 1750-1. Will (P.C.C.) 1752. (*Venn*, II. 14.)

FINLEY, JUSTICE. Adm. pens. at CLARE, June 5, 1734. B. at York. Matric. 1735; B.A. 1737-8; M.A. 1773. Ord. deacon (Lincoln) June 17, 1739; priest, June 1, 1740. Will (P.C.C.) 1787; 'formerly of Burton-upon-Stater, Lincs.; late of Louth, clerk.' (J. Ch. Smith.)

FINLOW or FINDLOW, REGINALD. Matric. pens. from JESUS, Easter, 1646. Migrated to Clare, Jan. 25, 1649-50. B.A. 1649-50. Sequestered to Stottesdon, Salop; ejected, 1660. (*Calamy*, II. 338.)

FINLOW, THOMAS. Adm. pens. at JESUS, June 26, 1646. Of Cheshire. (No matriculation. Perhaps a mistake for Reginald, above.)

FINLOW, THOMAS. Adm. sizar (age 20) at TRINITY, Mar. 29, 1714. S. of Thomas, of Congleton, Cheshire. School, Macclesfield (Mr Denham)

FINNEMORE, ELIAS. Matric. pens. from MAGDALENE, Michs. 1583; B.A. 1586-7. V. of Stickford, Lincs., 1588.

FINIMORE, JOHN. B.A. at Oxford, 1538-9, as a student from Cambridge. V. of Dagenham, Essex, 1557. R. of Loughton, 1558. Will (Consist. C. London) 1576. (*Al. Oxon.*)

FYNNIMORE, WILLIAM. Matric. pens. from TRINITY, Easter, 1570; Scholar, 1575; B.A. 1575-6; M.A. 1579. Doubtless Master of Louth Grammar School, 1587-91. Buried Dec. 8, 1591.

FINNY, CHRISTOPHER. Adm. at CORPUS CHRISTI, 1670. Of Yorkshire.

FINNAY, JOHN. B.Can.L. 1487-8. Archdeacon of Sudbury, 1497-1514.

FINNAY, ROGER. B.Can.L. 1493-4. Of KING'S HALL. Scholar and Fellow, 1494-1509. One of these names R. of Easthorp, Essex, 1493-5.

FINNEY or FINNE, THOMAS. Adm. sizar at EMMANUEL, Feb. 23, 1611-2. Matric. 1612; B.A. 1614-5. Probably will (Exeter) 1672; of Perranzabuloe, Cornwall, clerk.

FINNEY, THOMAS. Adm. pens. (age 18) at PETERHOUSE, June 14, 1750. Of Rutland. School, Tiverton, Devon. Matric. 1750; Scholar, 1750; B.A. 1754; M.A. 1763. (*T. A. Walker*, 300.)

FYNNEY, W. Matric. sizar from PETERHOUSE, Michs. 1560.

FYNNYE, W. Matric. pens. from ST JOHN'S, Easter, 1584.

FIRBANKE, JOHN. Adm. sizar (age 19) at ST JOHN'S, Feb. 16, 1668-9. S. of Thomas, yeoman, of Ingleton, Yorks. B. there. School, Sedbergh. Matric. 1669; B.A. 1672-3. Ord. deacon (York) Feb. 1675-6.

FIRBANK, ROBERT. Matric. sizar from TRINITY, Michs. 1551; Scholar, 1552; B.A. 1553-4; M.A. 1557. Fellow, 1555. Ord. sub-deacon (Norwich) Sept. 21, 1555. Perhaps V. of Thirkleby, Yorks., 1584-1621. Died 1621.

FIRBY, JOHN. B.A. 1473-4; M.A. 1477; B.D. 1483-4; D.D. 1486-7. Fellow of PEMBROKE, 1474. Scrutator, 1478. R. of Orton Waterville, Hunts., 1490.

FIREBRACE, CHARLES. Adm. Fell.-Com. (age 15) at TRINITY, June 12, 1695. S. of Sir Basil, Knt. and Bart., merchant of London. Bapt. June 18, 1680. Matric. 1695. Succeeded as Bart., 1724. Died Aug. 2, 1727. Buried at Long Melford, Suffolk. Brother of the next. (G.E.C.)

FIREBRACE, GEORGE. Adm. Fell.-Com. (age 14) at TRINITY, June 12, 1695. 2nd s. of Sir Basil, Knt. and Bart. B. at Richmond, Surrey. Bapt. there, Sept. 3, 1681. School, Enfield (Dr Robert Udall). Matric. 1695. Died young, without issue. Brother of Charles. (Burke, *Ext. Bart.*)

FIREBRACE, HENRY. Adm. pens. at TRINITY, June 11, 1668. S. of Sir Henry, of Stoke Golding, Leics., Knt. School, Westminster. Matric. 1668; Scholar, 1669; B.A. 1671-2; M.A. 1675; D.D. 1688 (*Lit. Reg.*). Fellow, 1674. Will proved (V.C.C. and P.C.C.) 1708. For the father *see D.N.B.*

FIRMAN or FIRMIN, ROBERT. Adm. pens. at EMMANUEL, Lent, 1623-4. Matric. 1623-4; B.A. 1627-8; M.A. 1631. Ord. deacon (Peterb.) Sept. 20; priest, Sept. 21, 1629. R. of Shotley, Suffolk, 1638-44. Buried there, Mar. 29, 1644. (V. B. Redstone.)

FIRMAN, ——. Sizar at PETERHOUSE, Mar. 1, 1583-4.

FIRMIN, EDWARD. Adm. sizar at EMMANUEL, Apr. 8, 1614. B. at Bocking, Essex. Matric. 1615; B.A. 1617-8; M.A. 1621. Ord. deacon (London) Sept. 24, 1620, age 22; priest, Dec. 23, 1621. C. of Black Notley, Essex.

FIRMIN, GILES. Adm. pens. at EMMANUEL, Sept. 24, 1629. S. of Giles and Martha (Dogget) Firmin, apothecary of Sudbury, Suffolk. B. *c.* 1615. Matric. 1629. Went to New England, 1632, with his father and family. Returned to England, 1633, and studied medicine four years. Physician at Ipswich, Mass. Ord. deacon of the first church at Boston, Mass. V. of Shalford, Essex, 1648-62, ejected. Afterwards practised medicine at Ridgewell, Essex; and from 1672, had a congregation there. Married, in New England, 1639, Susan, dau. of Nathanial Ward, of Ipswich, Mass. Author, *A serious question stated, A vindication of Mr Stephen Marshall*, and other religious works. Died Apr. 1697. Father of the next and of Nathaniel (1664). (*D.N.B.*; *Calamy*, I. 517; J. G. Bartlett.)

FIRMIN, GILES. Adm. sizar (age 18) at SIDNEY, June, 1668. S. of Giles (above), of Ridgewell, Essex. School, Ridgewell. Matric. 1668; B.A. 1671-2; M.A. 1675. V. of Little Walding-field, Suffolk, 1679-80. R. of Tilbury-by-Clare, Essex, 1680. R. of Ovington, 1684. Died 1725. Will (P.C.C.) 1725. Father of the next, brother of Nathaniel (1664).

FIRMIN, GILES. Adm. sizar at CLARE, May 16, 1704. S. of Giles, above. B. at Ovington, Essex. Matric. 1704; B.A. 1707-8. Ord. deacon (London) Sept. 19, 1708.

FERMYN, JOHN. Matric. sizar from PEMBROKE, Michs. 1579. R. of Brockley, Suffolk, 1589. R. of Foxearth, Essex, 1596-1638. Died 1638. Will (Consist. C. London) 1638. Father of the next.

FIRMIN, JOHN. Matric. sizar from CLARE, Easter, 1605. S. of John, above. B. at Brockley, Suffolk. Bapt. at Brockley, May 4, 1589. B.A. 1608-9; M.A. 1612. Ord. deacon (London) Mar. 1612-3; priest, June 18, 1614, age 25. C. of Gt Henney, Essex. Succeeded his father as R. of Foxearth, Essex, 1638-56.

FIRMIN, JOHN. Matric. sizar from CLARE, Easter, 1621; B.A. 1624-5; M.A. 1628. One of these names V. of Caddington, Beds., 1641. Will (P.C.C.) 1651.

FIRMIN, JOHN. Matric. sizar from PEMBROKE, Michs. 1638. Perhaps s. of John, of 1605; bapt. at Romford, 1620. B.A. 1641-2; M.A. 1646. R. of Hawkedon, Suffolk, 1651. Licensed schoolmaster at Long Melford, Suffolk, 1662. R. of Stanstead, 1666-87. Will at Bury. Father of Thomas (1679).

FIRMIN, MARK. Adm. pens. (age 17) at ST JOHN'S, June 30, 1715. S. of Thomas, registrar ('tabellarius'). B. at Sudbury, Suffolk. School, Lavenham. Matric. 1715; B.A. 1719-20.

FIRMIN, NATHANIEL. Adm. sizar (age 16) at CAIUS, June 10, 1664. S. of Giles, gent. (1629). B. at Shalford, Essex. Schools, Braintree (Mr Adamson), Wethersfield (Mr Fish) and Felsted (Mr Glascock). Scholar, 1664; Matric. 1664-5; B.A. 1667-8; M.A. 1671. Licentiate of the Royal College of Physicians, 1676. Brother of Giles (1668). (*Venn*, I. 422.)

FIRMIN, THOMAS. Adm. sizar (age 18) at CHRIST'S, June 3, 1679. S. of John (1638), R. of Hawkedon, Suffolk. B. there. Bapt. July, 1660. School, Bury (Mr Leeds). Matric. 1679; B.A. 1682-3; M.A. 1686. Ord. deacon (Norwich) Dec. 1683. R. of Sudbourne All Saints with Orford St Bartholomew, Suffolk. Died 1720. (*Peile*, II. 73.)

FIRTH, HUMPHREY. Matric. sizar from CLARE, Easter, 1607.

FEIRTH, JOHN. Adm. sizar (age 16) at SIDNEY, June 25, 1644. S. of John, farmer. B. at Barton, Yorks. Schools, Womersley (Mr Thurstan Elliott) and Kellington. Matric. 1645; B.A. 1647-8; M.A. 1651. Probably V. of Mansfield, Notts., 1654-99. Called 'B.D.' Married Sara, dau. of Wm Staniforth, of Rotherham. Died May 25, 1699, aged 74. M.I. at Mansfield. (Prior, *Mansfield Church*; M. H. Peacock.)

FIRTH, MICHAEL. Adm. sizar (age 18) at TRINITY, Feb. 22, 1724–5. S. of Richard (? below), of Ripponden, Yorks. School, Bingley, Yorks. (Mr Ellison). Matric. 1724–5; Scholar, 1728; B.A. 1728–9. *Litt. dim.* from York for deacon, Sept. 1729. V. of Felmersham, Beds., 1733–55. Buried Nov. 6, 1755.

FIRTH, PETER, *see* FRITH.

FIRTH, RICHARD. Adm. pens. (age 16) at TRINITY, June 22, 1689. S. of Michael, of Ripponden, Yorks. School, Bingley (Mr William Hustler). Matric. 1689. Probably father of Michael (above).

FEIRTH, WILLIAM. Adm. pens. (age 17) at SIDNEY, Apr. 3, 1652. S. of John, farmer, of Yorkshire. B. at Barton. School, Selby. Matric. 1652; B.A. 1655; M.A. 1659. Ord. deacon (Lincoln) Apr. 26; priest, May 25, 1662.

FIRTUN, JOHN. Mus.Bac. 1515–6. V. of St Stephen's Chapel, Westminster.

FISH, AMBROSE. B.A. from CHRIST'S, 1608–9; M.A. 1612. B. at Gt Bowden, Leics. Ord. deacon (Peterb.) Dec. 18, 1614; priest (London) Mar. 1616–7, age 27. V. of Raunds, Northants., 1619–23. R. of Carlton-Curlieu, Leics., 1627. (*Peile*, I. 254.)

FISH, ANTHONY. Adm. sizar (age 18) at SIDNEY, May 28, 1647. Eldest s. of Jerome (1615), clerk. B. at Little Bytham, Lincs. School, Uppingham, Ruts. (Mr Meeres). Matrie. 1647; B.A. 1650–1; M.A. 1654. Died soon after, 1654. Brother of Robert (1648) and Jeremiah (1652).

FISH, AUGUSTINE. Adm. pens. (age 17) at ST JONN'S, July 12, 1660. S. of Robert (? 1611), clerk, of Little Bytham, Lincs. B. there. School, Uppingham. Matrie. 1660; B.A. 1664–5; M.A. 1668. V. of Gedney, Lines., 1681. Father of James (1701).

FISH, AUGUSTINE. Adm. pens. (age 17) at SIDNEY, June 1, 1725. S. of Augustine, hatter, of Weldon, Northants. B. in London. School, Oundle. Matric. 1725; B.A. 1728–9; M.A. 1733. Ord. deacon (Peterb.) Sept. 19, 1731; priest, May 20, 1733. R. of Luddington, Northants., 1737–42. V. of Sywell, 1742–94. Buried there Sept. 23, 1794. Admon. to son George, 1795. (G. *Mag.*; H. I. Longden.)

FYSHE, CORNELIUS. Matric. pens. from ST JOHN'S, Easter, 1565. Doubtless Chamberlain of the City of London. Buried at St Mary Woolchurch, Sept. 16, 1626. Will, P.C.C. (J. Ch. Smith.)

FISH, EDWARD. Matrie. Fell.-Com. from CHRIST'S, 1595–6. *Peile* (I. 218) identifies this man with the s. of Sir John Fish.

FISH, EDWARD. Scholar of CAIUS, 1595–1600; B.A. 1598–9.

FISH, GEORGE. Adm. pens. at CAIUS, July 6, 1602. Of Hertford. Matrie. 1602; Scholar, 1602–7; B.A. 1605–6. Perhaps of New Inn, gent.; adm. at the Middle Temple, Mar. 4, 1611–2, as s. and h. of Leonard, of Hatfield.

FISH, GEORGE. Adm. sizar (age 16) at CHRIST'S, Feb. 28, 1638–9. S. of Hanby. B. in London. Schools, Merchant Taylors' and Bishop's Stortford (Mr Leigh). Matric. 1639; B.A. 1642–3; M.A. 1647. R. of Illington, Norfolk. R. of Brockdish, 1663–8. Buried there Oct. 29, 1686. (*Peile*, I. 458.)

FISH, HENRY. Adm. sizar (age 16) at CHRIST'S, May 25, 1658. S. of Phatuel (1637), R. of Staveley, Yorks. B. there. School, York (Mr Wallis). Matrie. 1658; B.A. 1661–2; M.A. 1665. Perhaps R. of Foston, Yorks., 1667–93. Brother of Thomas (1666). (*Peile*, I. 582.)

FISH, HENRY. Adm. pens. (age 16) at CHRIST'S, Apr. 25, 1672. S. of Humphry (1645), of Ickwell, Beds. B. at Northill, Beds. School, Sutton All Saints, near Potton (Mr Spalding). Adm. at Gray's Inn, Mar. 25, 1674. Buried at Northill, Nov. 9, 1677. (*Peile*, II. 43.)

FISH, HENRY. Adm. sizar (age 17) at CHRIST'S, Oct. 18, 1703. S. of Thomas (1666). B. at Lynn. School, Lynn (Mr Horne). Scholar, 1704–5; Matric. 1705; B.A. 1707–8; M.A. 1711. Ord. deacon (Norwich) Sept. 1709; priest, Dec. 1710. R. of Irstead, Norfolk, 1711. V. of Scottow, 1713. Chaplain to the Earl of Kintoul. V. of Middleton, 1722–37. R. of Walpole, 1726–43. Author, *Sermon*. (*Peile*, II. 158.)

FISH, HUMPHRY. Adm. pens. (age 16) at CHRIST'S, July 14, 1645. S. of Thomas (perhaps of Southill, Beds.). B. at Hunsdon, Herts. School, Bishop's Stortford (Mr Leigh). Matrie. 1645–6. Adm. at Gray's Inn, June 1, 1647. Of Ickwell Green, Northill, Beds. Sheriff of Beds., 1684. Died Apr. 3, 1720. M.I. at Northill. Father of Henry (1672). (*Beds. N. and Q.*, III. 366; *Peile*, I. 498; *Vis. of Beds.*, 1634.)

FISH, HUMPHREY. Adm. sizar at TRINITY, Nov. 7, 1650.

FYSH, HUMPHREY. Adm. pens. at QUEENS', Jan. 7, 1685–6. Of Bedfordshire. 1st s. of Humphrey, of Ickwell Bury, Northill, Beds. Matrie. 1686. Adm. at Gray's Inn, Mar. 4, 1688–9.

FISH, JAMES. Adm. pens. at EMMANUEL, 1619. Matric. 1619; B.A. 1622–3; M.A. 1626. Ord. [illegible] (Peterb.) Mar. 2, 1622–3; priest, Dec. 21, 1623. V. of Biggleswade, Beds., 1627. R. of Radwell, Herts., 1629–46. V. of Norton, 1635. Died 1646. Perhaps will (P.C.C.) 1647; of Conington, Hunts., clerk.

FISH, JAMES. Adm. pens. (age 15) at ST JOHN'S, Apr. 9, 1701. S. of Augustine (1660), V. of Gedney, Lincs. B. there. School, Uppingham. Matric. 1701; B.A. 1704–5; M.A. 1708. Ord deacon (Peterb.) June 8, 1707; priest (Lincoln) Mar. 5, 1709–10. C. of Collyweston, Northants. (H. I. Longden.)

FISH, JAMES Adm. pens. (age 19) at TRINITY, Oct. 19, 1705. S. of James, of Twickenham, Middlesex. Bapt. there, Aug. 27, 1686. School, Westminster. Matric. 1705–6; Scholar, 1707.

FISH, JEROME. Adm. pens. at EMMANUEL, May 30, 1615. 5th s. of Robert, of Aldwincle, Northants. Matrie. 1615; B.A. 1618–9; M.A. 1622. Ord. deacon (Peterb.) June 16; priest, June 17, 1622. R. of Little Bytham, Lincs., 1624. Married, at Stoke Doyle, Northants., Sept. 29, 1624, Grace, dau. of Anthony Wells, clerk. Will (P.C.C.) 1658. Father of the next, of Robert (1648) and Anthony (1647). (H. I. Longden.)

FISH, JEREMIAH. Adm. sizar (age 18) at CAIUS, Oct. 27, 1652. 3rd s. of Jerome (above), R. of Little Bytham, Lincs. B. there. Schools, Stamford (Mr Humphreys) and Uppingham (Mr Meres). Scholar, 1652–8; B.A. 1656–7; M.A. 1660. Ord. deacon (Lincoln) May 24; priest, May 25, 1662. R. of Alphamstone, Essex, 1662–92. V. of Ridgewell, 1662. Married Amy Brewer, of Wethersfield, Essex. Will (Consist. C. London) May 14, 1692. Brother of Robert (1648) and Anthony (1647). (*Venn*, I. 386.)

FISH, JOHN. Adm. sizar at KING'S, 1554–5.

FISHE, JOHN. Matrie. pens. from PETERHOUSE, Michs. 1582.

FISH, JOHN. Matric. pens. from CHRIST'S, 1597–8. S. of William, of Southill, Beds. B.A. 1601–2; M.A. 1605; B.D. 1613; D.D. 1639. Ord. priest (Ely) Dec. 20, 1607. R. of Little Hallingbury, Essex, 1610; sequestered, 1646. Brother of William (1593). (*Peile*, I. 228; *Vis. of Beds.*, 1634.)

FISH, JOHN. Matrie. pens. from KING'S, Easter, 1622; B.A. 1625–6. Ord. deacon (York) Sept. 1626; priest (Peterb.) Dec. 21, 1628.

FYSCH, NICHOLAS. Resident graduate in 1448.

FISH, PHATUEL. M.A. 1637. Incorp. from Glasgow. R. of Staveley, Yorks., 1638–76. Died 1676. Father of Henry (1658) and Thomas (1666).

FYSHE, ROBERT. Matric. pens. from TAINITY, Michs. 1570. One of these names B.A. (Oxford) 1575–6; M.A. 1579. R. of Bentham, Yorks., 1582. (*Al. Oxon.*)

FISH, ROBERT. Adm. pens. at EMMANUEL, Apr. 2, 1611. Matric. 1611; B.A. from Trinity, 1614–5. Ord. deacon (Peterb.) Mar. 5; priest, Mar. 6, 1614–5. V. of Clopham, Beds., 1615. Probably R. of Little Bytham, Lincs.; and father of Augustine (1660).

FISH, ROBERT. Adm. pens. at CLARE, Mar. 9, 1640–1. Matrie. 1641. Migrated to Trinity, June 29, 1641. B.A. 1644–5; M.A. 1648. Chaplain of Trinity, 1647. Incorp. at Oxford, 1648. Fellow of Magdalen College, Oxford, 1648. R. of Nuthurst, Sussex, till 1662, ejected. Retired to Ockley, Surrey. Died, aged about 70. (*Calamy*, II. 466.)

FISH, ROBERT. Adm. sizar (age 18) at SIDNEY, Aug. 2, 1648. S. of Jerome (1615), clerk. B. at Little Bytham, Lincs. School, Stamford (Mr Humphrey). Matric. 1648–9. Migrated to Caius, June 14, 1652. Scholar, 1652; B.A. 1652–3; M.A. 1656. Fellow, 1653–8. Ord. priest (Ardfert and Aghadoe) Aug. 17, 1660. R. of Little Bytham, 1669. R. of Gt Coates, 1675–96. Chaplain to Earl of Lichfield. Father of Robert (1683), brother of Jeremiah (1652) and Anthony (1647). (*Venn*, I. 385.)

FISH, ROBERT. Matric. sizar from ST JOHN'S, Easter, 1683. Perhaps same as the next.

FISH, ROBERT. Adm. scholar (age 17) at SIDNEY, May 12, 1683. 1st s. of Robert, clerk (1648). B. at Ennis, Ireland. School, Oakham. Matrie. 1683; B.A. 1686–7. Curate to his father, 1687, whom he succeeded as R. of Gt Coates, Lincs., 1696–1706. Died *c.* 1706.

FISH, ROBERT. Adm. pens. (age 17) at CHRIST'S, July 14, 1685. 2nd s. of Robert, of Finedon, Northants. Bapt. there, July 2, 1668. Schools, Kimbolton (Mr Trot) and Oundle. Matric. 1685; B.A. 1689–90. Ord. deacon (Lincoln, *Litt. dim.* from London) Feb. 12, 1692–3; priest (Lincoln) June 19, 1698. Lecturer at All Hallows, London. R. of Awnsby, Lincs., 1693–1694. (*Peile*, II. 100.)

FISH, ROBERT. Adm. pens. (age 16) at Christ's, Feb. 1, 1710–1. S. of Phatuel. B. at Stokesley, Yorks. School, Stokesley (Mr Jo. Forster). Matric. 1710–1; Scholar, 1713; B.A. 1714–5; M.A. 1718. Ord. deacon (York) Sept. 1717; priest, Sept. 1718. R. of Slingsby, Yorks., 1718. V. of Hovingham, 1719–39. R. of Kirby-Underdale, 1730–9. Preb. of York, 1731–9. Died 1739. (*Peile*, II. 177.)

FISH, THOMAS. B.A. 1482–3. Fellow of Queens', 1498–9. R. of St Botolph, Cambridge, 1499–1528.

FISH, THOMAS. Adm. sizar at Clare, Dec. 22, 1638. Matric. 1639.

FISH, THOMAS. Adm. sizar at Christ's, Mar. 26, 1666. S. of Phatuel (1637). B. at Staveley, Yorks. School, York (Mr Langley). Matric. 1667; B.A. 1669–70; M.A. 1673. Ord. deacon (London) Sept. 1670; priest (Chichester) 1673. R. of Ringstead St Andrew, Norfolk, 1673–87. R. of Staveley, Yorks., 1677. R. of Foston, 1686–91. Died Dec. 31, 1701. Buried at Ringstead. Brother of Henry (1658). (*Peile*, II. 2.)

FISH, THOMAS. Adm. sizar at Emmanuel, Jan. 8, 1695–6. Of Lincolnshire. Matric. 1696; B.A. 1699–1700; M.A. 1728. Ord. deacon (Lincoln) Mar. 16, 1700–1; priest, Sept. 20, 1702.

FISH, THOMAS. Adm. pens. (age 17) at Trinity, Apr. 30, 1712. S. of Robert, of Enfield, Middlesex. School, Enfield (Dr Uvedale). Matric. 1712. Adm. at the Inner Temple, June 20, 1711; s. of Robert, of the Inner Temple.

FYSH, TIMOTHY. Adm. scholar at Trinity Hall, Jan. 14, 1712–3; LL.B. 1718.

FYSSH, WILLIAM. Of King's Hall; 'petit clerk de notre chapelle,' 1382. Expelled, May 12, 1385; at a Visitation of the Bishop of Ely. (*Trinity Admissions*, I. 106.)

FISH, WILLIAM. Matric. pens. from Christ's, Lent, c. 1593. Doubtless s. and h. of William, of Southill, Beds. Adm. at Gray's Inn, Oct. 22, 1595. Barrister, 1600. Reader, 1613, 1621. Of Biggleswade, Knt. Married Elizabeth, dau. of Sir Thomas Barnardiston. Will (P.C.C.) 1646. Brother of John (1597). (*Peile*, I. 214; *Vis. of Beds.*, 1634; *Cussans*, II. 244.)

FISH, WILLIAM (1631), *see* FISK.

FISHE, WILLIAM. Adm. pens. (age 16) at Sidney, Dec. 2, 1637. S. of Oliver, Esq. B. at Biggleswade, Beds. Schools, Holme, Beds. (Mr Bond), Biggleswade (Mr Scarlett) and Sutton (Mr Kemp). Matric. 1637; B.A. 1641–2. (*Vis. of Beds.*, 1634.)

FISH, WILLIAM. Adm. sizar (age 17) at Caius, June 20, 1706. S. of Robert (1683), clerk, of Gt Coates, Lincs. B. there. School, Gt Coates (Mr Thompson). Matric. 1706; Scholar, 1706–13; B.A. 1709–10; M.A. 1713. Incorp. at Oxford, 1712. Fellow, 1713–6. Ord. deacon (Ely) Sept. 23, 1711. R. of Swarraton, Hants., 1715; of Nately-Scures, 1719. (*Venn*, I. 515.)

FISH, ——. B.Can.L. 1475–6.

FISHENDEN, GEORGE. Adm. sizar (age 20) at St John's, June 19, 1665. S. of George, clerk, of Brenchley. B. in Kent. School, Canterbury. Matric. 1665. Buried at All Saints', Cambridge, Jan. 18, 1668–9.

FISHER, AMBROSE. B.A. from Trinity, 1597–8; M.A. 1601. R. of Holy Trinity, Colchester, 1610–17. Tutor in the family of Dr Gabriel Grant, preb. of Westminster. He was blind all his life. Author, *Defence of the Liturgy*. The preface gives a sketch of his life. Died 1617. Buried in Cloisters of Westminster Abbey, Nov. 21, 1617.

FISHER, ANTHONY. Adm. pens. at Trinity, Mar. 16, 1646–7. Of the Isle of Ely. S. and h. of William, of Wisbech, Esq. Matric. 1647. Adm. at Lincoln's Inn, June 5, 1649. Married Anne, dau. of Sir Tho. Willis, of Fen Ditton, Cambs. Died June 9, 1679. M.I. at Pickenham, Norfolk. Father of the next. (Le Neve, *Mon.*, III. 141.)

FISHER, ANTHONY. Adm. pens. at Trinity, June 12, 1672. S. and h. of Anthony (above), of Lincoln's Inn, Esq. Matric. 1672. Adm. at Lincoln's Inn, Jan. 27, 1675–6.

FISHER, BARDSEY. Adm. pens. (age 16) at Sidney, Feb. 17, 1673–4. 2nd s. of George (1648), R. of Hickling, Notts. B. at Nottingham. Matric. 1674; B.A. 1677–8; M.A. 1681; D.D. 1704. Perhaps fellow. Master, 1704–23. Vice-Chancellor, 1705–6. Ord. deacon (London) Mar. 12, 1681–2. R. of Newmarket. R. of Withersfield, Suffolk, 1717. Died Feb. 18, 1722–3. Brother of Robert (1672).

FISHER, CHARLES. Adm. sizar at Magdalene, May 8, 1652. S. of Thomas. B. at Rotherham, Yorks. School, Rotherham. Matric. 1652. Migrated to Pembroke, Dec. 9, 1652. B.A. 1657. V. of Blyth, Notts. Admon. granted to his mother, Isabel Fisher, June 5, 1668. (J. Raine, *Blyth*.)

FISHER, CHARLES. Adm. pens. at St Catharine's, July 6, 1711. S. of Peter (1661), D.D. Matric. 1712.

FISHER, CHRISTOPHER. Matric. pens. from Peterhouse, Easter, 1615. Probably licensed, as 'literate,' to teach at Thornton-le-Moor, Yorks., Aug. 12, 1619. Ord. deacon (Peterb.) Sept. 21; priest, Sept. 22, 1623 (as B.A.). C. of Terrington St John, Norfolk, in 1635 (as M.A.). Perhaps V. of Holme-by-the-Sea, 1662. V. of Sowthowram, Yorks., 1665–6.

FISHER, CORNELIUS. Matric. sizar from Emmanuel, Easter, 1616; B.A. 1620; M.A. 1625. Probably will (P.C.C.) 1641; of East Bergholt, Suffolk, clerk.

FISHER, EDMUND. Adm. at Corpus Christi, 1749. B. in Norfolk, 1729. Matric. Michs. 1749; B.A. 1753; M.A. 1756. Fellow, 1754–64. Ord. deacon (Ely) May 25, 1755; priest, Mar. 7, 1756. R. of Duxford St Peter, Cambs., 1761. V. of Linton, 1789–1819. Died Mar. 29, 1819.

FISHER, EDWARD. Matric. pens. from Christ's, Nov. 1569; B.A. 1573–4. One of these names ord. priest (Gloucester) 1571–3. Perhaps R. of Witton, Norfolk, 1580–91.

FISHER, EDWARD. Adm. sizar at Queens', May 16, 1593. Of Cumberland. Matric. 1593; B.A. 1596–7. Probably V. of Beetham, Westmorland, 1614–42. Buried there Apr. 5, 1642. (*B. Nightingale*.)

FISHER, EDWARD. Matric. sizar from Queens', Michs. 1609. Of Cumberland. B.A. 1612–3; M.A. 1616.

FISHER, EDWARD. Matric. sizar from Christ's, Michs. 1620; B.A. 1624–5; M.A. 1628. Ord. deacon (Peterb.) June 11, 1625; priest, Dec. 17, 1625. (*Peile*, I. 336.)

FISHER, EDWARD. Adm. sizar (age 18) at St John's, June 27, 1670. S. of John, surgeon, of Wye, Kent. B. there. School, Wye. Matric. 1670; B.A. 1673–4; M.A. 1683. Signs for deacon's orders (London) June 11, 1674. V. of Sellinge, Kent, 1680–1710. R. of Buckland, 1688–1707. Died Feb. 2, 1709–10. Buried at Sellinge. (H. G. Harrison.)

FISHER, EDWARD. Adm. sizar (age 16) at Caius, Apr. 16, 1673. S. of Robert, merchant, deceased, of Shernbourn, Norfolk. B. there. School, Lynn (Mr Bell). Matric. 1673; Scholar, 1673–80; B.A. 1676–7. Ord. deacon (Norwich) June, 1680; priest, May, 1681. One of these names V. of Thrussington, Leics.; admon. (Leicester) 1692 and 1698. (*Venn*, I. 448.)

FISHER, GEORGE. B.A. 1537–8.

FISHER, GEORGE. Matric. sizar from Trinity, Michs. 1586; Scholar, 1590; B.A. 1594–5. Ord. deacon and priest (Peterb.) Sept. 6, 1595 (as M.A.). V. of Stotfold, Beds., 1595–7. Buried there Aug. 18, 1597. (*Beds. N. and Q.*, III. 306.)

FISHER, GEORGE. Adm. sizar at Queens', Apr. 6, 1648. Of Essex. B.A. 1651; M.A. 1655. Incorp. at Oxford, 1666–7. Ord. priest (Lincoln) Nov. 19, 1665. Minister at Hickling, Notts., in 1653; R. 1662–1716. R. of North Claypole, Lincs., 1668. Father of Robert (1672) and Bardsey (1673–4). (Godfrey, *Notts.*)

FISHER, HENRY. B.A. 1534–5; M.A. 1538–9. R. of Fulbourn St Vigors, Cambs., 1551–4.

FISHER, HENRY. Matric. pens. from Trinity Hall, Easter, 1553.

FISHER, HENRY. Adm. sizar at Christ's, between Jan. 21 and Feb. 20, 1642–3, from Trinity College, Dublin. Adm. there, June 8, 1640, age 17. S. of Richard. B. at Geggin, Co. Cork. School, Cork (Mr Godinch). Matric. 1643. One of these names V. of Wartling, Sussex, 1664; and of Hove, 1664. (*Al. Dub.*; *Peile*, I. 484; *see* a contemporary in *Al. Oxon.*)

FISHER, JAMES. Incorp. from Oxford, 1493–4.

FISHER, JAMES. Matric. sizar from Magdalene, Easter, 1622; B.A. 1625–6; M.A. 1629. Ord. deacon (Peterb.) Dec. 18; priest, Dec. 19, 1628. Probably at Clipsham, Rutland, in 1640. V. of Sheffield, 1646–62. After his ejection he retired to Hatfield, Doncaster. Died c. 1666. Father of James (1659). (*F.M.G.* 1056; Gatty, *Hallamshire*, 88; *Calamy*, II. 573.)

FISHER, JAMES. Matric. sizar from Emmanuel, Easter, 1625; B.A. 1627–8; M.A. 1631. Ord. deacon (Peterb.) Aug. 14, 1628. R. of Fetcham, Surrey, 1643; ejected, 1662. Afterwards kept school, at Dorking. Died 1691, aged 86. (*Calamy*, II. 448.)

FISHER, JAMES. Adm. pens. (age 15) at Magdalene, Apr. 29, 1659. S. of James (1622), clerk, of Sheffield, Yorks. School, Sheffield. Matric. 1659.

FISHER, JAMES. Adm. sizar at Clare, Feb. 16, 1667–8. Of Grantham, Lincs. Matric. 1668. Ord. deacon (Peterb.) Dec. 24, 1671; priest, Sept. 21, 1673, as B.A. V. of West Wratting, Cambs., 1685–95. Buried there Apr. 19, 1696. (*See Al. Oxon.* for a contemporary.)

FISHER, JASPER. M.A. 1629 (Incorp. from Oxford). S. of William, of Carleton, Beds. Matric. from Magdalen Hall, Oxford, Nov. 13, 1607, age 16; B.A. (Oxford) 1610–1; M.A. 1613–4; D.D. (Magdalen) 1638. R. of Wilden, Beds., 1624–43. Will proved, Oct. 27, 1643. (*Al. Oxon.*; *D.N.B.*; *Vis. of Beds.*, 1634.)

FISHER, JASPER. Adm. pens. at EMMANUEL, Mar. 21, 1659–60. Afterwards Fell.-Com. Of Bedfordshire. Doubtless s. of the above; b. at Wilden. One of these names married at Pertenhall, Beds., to Mary Gray, widow, 1670. Buried there Oct. 21, 1680. (*Beds. N. and Q.*, III. 362.)

FISSHER, JOHN. Scholar at KING'S HALL, 1417–32.

FYSHER, JOHN. Resident member of PETERHOUSE, 1445–6; perhaps fellow. (*T. A. Walker.*)

FISHER, JOHN. B.A. 1487–8; M.A. 1491; D.D. 1501. S. of Robert, mercer, of Beverley Minster. B. at Beverley. Fellow; and afterwards, 1497, Master, of MICHAELHOUSE. Proctor, 1494–5. Vice-Chancellor, 1501. Lady Margaret Professor of Divinity, 1502–3. Chancellor of the University, 1504–35. President of Queens' College, 1505–8. V. of Northallerton, Yorks., 1491–4. Bishop of Rochester, 1504–35. Created Cardinal, 1535. Adviser of the Lady Margaret in the foundation of Christ's and St John's. Author of theological works in English and Latin. Condemned of treason, for denying the King's supremacy. Executed, June 22, 1535. (*Cooper*, I. 52; *D.N.B.*)

FISHER, JOHN. Scholar of QUEENS', 1517; B.A. 1520–1; M.A. 1524. Fellow, 1521–6. Incorp. at Oxford, 1533. B.D. (Oxford) 1533. R. of Leigh, Essex, 1535–45. V. of Roydon, 1541–3. R. of Stisted, Essex. Admon. (Lambeth) 1564. (J. Ch. Smith.)

FISHER, JOHN. Adm. sizar at CORPUS CHRISTI, 1567. Of Cambridgeshire. Matric. Michs. 1568; B.A. 1571–2; M.A. 1575. Perhaps ord. priest (Peterb.) Sept. 23, 1575; on recommendation of Clare Hall. Buried at St Benet, Cambridge, June 4, 1578.

FISHER, JOHN. Matric. pens. from JESUS, Easter, 1577. Migrated to Trinity. Scholar, 1580; B.A. 1580–1; M.A. 1584. Fellow, 1583. Ord. deacon and priest (Lincoln) Feb. 10, 1587–8. R. of Ingoldsby, Lincs., 1590. Will proved (Lincoln) 1634.

FISHER, JOHN. Matric. sizar from KING'S, Easter, 1578.

FISHER, JOHN. Matric. pens. from PEMBROKE, Michs. 1618. S. of William, of Bures, Essex.

FISHER, JOHN. M.A. 1631 (Incorp. from Oxford). S. of John, of Formarke, Derbs. Matric. from Lincoln College, Oxford, Apr. 30, 1624, age 18; B.A. 1626–7; M.A. 1629.

FISHER, JOHN. Adm. pens. (age 15) at CAIUS, Oct. 10, 1632. S. of John, gent. B. at Croxton, Fulmodeston, Norfolk. Schools, Aylsham (Mr Knolles) and North Walsham (Mr Acres). Matric. 1632.

FISHER, JOHN. Matric. pens. from MAGDALENE, Easter, 1633; B.A. 1636–7. One of these names, s. of Anthony, of the Isle of Ely, adm. at Lincoln's Inn, May 3, 1637.

FISHER, JOHN. Adm. pens. at CORPUS CHRISTI, 1640. Of Essex. Matric. Easter, 1642; B.A. 1644. One of these names R. of Ashingdon, Essex, 1654–5. Died 1668. (J. Ch. Smith.)

FISHER, JOHN. Adm. pens. at QUEENS', June 20, 1644. S. of Richard, of Northamptonshire. Previously matric. from New Inn Hall, Oxford, Dec. 4, 1640, age 16; B.A. (Cambridge) 1644. Perhaps V. of Kirkham, Lancs., 1650–66. Died Mar. 17, 1666.

FISHER, JOHN. Adm. pens. at TRINITY, June 22, 1649. Of Yorkshire. Matric. 1649; B.A. 1652–3. One of these names, of Staple Inn, adm. at Gray's Inn, Nov. 20, 1652.

FISHER, JOHN. Described as 'M.A. Cambridge' when created M.D. at Oxford, Mar. 12, 1660–1. Hon. fellow, R.C.P. 1664. Died 1682. Will (P.C.C.) 'to be buried near his wife, at Everton, Hunts.' (*Munk*, I. 347; *Al. Oxon.*)

FISHER, JOHN. Adm. sizar (age 17) at TRINITY, Apr. 1, 1696. S. of William, of Holborn. B. there. School, St Paul's. Matric. 1696; Scholar, 1699; B.A. 1699–1700. Ord. deacon (London) Dec. 20, 1702; priest, Feb. 21, 1702–3. One of these names R. of Bringhurst, Leics., 1729–43. Died Apr. 1743, at Bath.

FISHER, JOHN. M.A. from KING'S, 1725. S. of Tristram, of Stowe, Somerset. Matric. from Wadham College, Oxford, Dec. 11, 1717, age 21; B.A. (Oxford) 1721. V. of St John the Baptist, Peterborough, 1748–66. (*Al. Oxon.*)

FISHER, JOHN. Adm. sizar at CLARE, May 27, 1728. B. at Kilby, Leics. Matric. 1728. One of these names, s. of Humphrey, of Melton Mowbray, Leics., clerk, matric. from Pembroke College, Oxford, June 22, 1730, age 19.

FISHER, JOSEPH. Adm. pens. at EMMANUEL, Mar. 18, 1643–4. Probably s. of Thomas, of Stratford-on-Avon. B.A. 1644–5; M.A. 1652. Matric. from Queen's College, Oxford, Apr. 1, 1642, age 20. Perhaps V. of Tarvin, Cheshire, 1662. (*Al. Oxon.*)

FISHER, MATTHEW. Adm. sizar at CORPUS CHRISTI, 1577. Matric. Lent, 1577–8; B.A. 1581–2. R. of North Cove-*cum*-Willingham, Suffolk, 1599–1625.

FISHER, MILES. B.A. 1541–2; M.A. 1544.

FISHER, NICHOLAS. Matric. sizar from TRINITY, Easter, 1589. B. at Edmunthorp, Leics., 1573. Scholar, 1592; B.A. 1592–3; M.A. 1595. Ord. deacon (Peterb.) Oct. 31; priest, Nov. 20, 1596. Preacher at Lincoln. R of Lowesby, Leics., 1601–2. V. of Scraptoft, 1604–10. V. of Wymeswold, 1619.

FYSSHER, OCTAVIUS. Matric. pens. from PEMBROKE, Michs. 1554. One 'Octavian' Fisher, of Threckingham, Lincs., buried Dec. 4, 1610, aged 69. (*Lincs. Pedigrees.*)

FISHER, PAYNE. B.A. from MAGDALENE, 1637–8. S. of Payne, of Nettleton, Dorset. B. at Warnford, Dorset. Matric. from Hart Hall, Oxford, Sept. 10, 1634, age 18. Served in the wars in Brabant; and afterwards in the Royal Army in Scotland and Ireland, and at Marston Moor. Deserted the Royalist cause and retired to London. Author, poetical, etc. Made poet-laureate to Oliver Cromwell. Died in a coffee-house, in the Old Bailey. Buried in St Sepulchre's, Apr. 2, 1693. (*Al. Oxon.*; *D.N.B.*; *Ath. Oxon.*)

FISHER, PETER. Adm. pens. at ST CATHARINE'S, Mar. 27, 1661. Of Suffolk. Matric. 1661–2; B.A. 1664–5; M.A. 1668; D.D. 1690 (*Lit. Reg.*). Fellow, 1672–7. Incorp. at Oxford, 1671. Elected Master of St Catharine's, July 12, 1697; but resigned, Aug. 11. V. of Shephall, Herts., 1679–91. R. of Bennington, 1683–1718. Died 1718. Will (P.C.C.) 1718. Father of Charles (1711). (*See* a contemporary at Oxford.)

FISHER, PHILIP. Adm. sizar at EMMANUEL, Mar. 25, 1587. Matric. 1587; Scholar; B.A. 1590–1; M.A. from Clare, 1594.

FISHER, RICHARD. M.A. 1633 (Incorp. from Oxford). Of Cumberland. Matric. from Queen's College, Oxford, Nov. 21, 1628, age 18; B.A. (Trinity, Oxford) 1632; M.A. (Queen's, Oxford) 1633. V. of Sulgrave, Northants., 1646–83, resigned. Buried at Sulgrave, Mar. 23, 1686–7. (*Al. Oxon.*)

FISHER, RICHARD. Licensed to practise surgery, 1643. One Richard Fisker student at Leyden, June 10, 1650.

FISHER, RICHARD. Matric. pens. from TRINITY HALL, Lent, 1650–1; B.A. 1653–4; LL.B. 1656.

FISHER, RICHARD. Adm. pens. at TRINITY HALL, Apr. 10, 1696. Matric. 1696.

FISHER, ROBERT. Matric. sizar from QUEENS', Michs. 1616. Of Leicestershire. B.A. 1620–1; M.A. 1624. Ord. deacon (Peterb.) Apr. 15; priest, Apr. 16, 1621.

FISHER, ROBERT. Adm. sizar at EMMANUEL, Apr. 20, 1619. Matric. 1619; B.A. 1622–3. Ord. deacon (Peterb.) Apr. 24, 1624; priest, Sept. 25, 1625.

FISHER, ROBERT. Adm. sizar at CLARE, June 29, 1659. Matric. 1659; B.A. 1662. Ord. deacon (Carlisle) Feb. 1, 1662–3. V. of Penrith, Cumberland, 1664–5. Died 1665. (B. *Nightingale.*)

FISHER, ROBERT. Adm. sizar at JESUS, May 14, 1666. Of Yorkshire. School, Wakefield. Matric. 1667; B.A. 1669–70. Ord. deacon (York) May, 1670.

FISHER, ROBERT. Adm. pens. (age 16) at SIDNEY, Apr. 11, 1672. 1st s. of George (1648), clerk. B. at Hickling, Notts. Schools, Claxton, Notts. (Mr Reay) and Nottingham (Mr Birch). Matric. 1672; B.A. 1675–6; M.A. 1679. Ord. deacon (London) Dec. 23, 1677; priest (York) June, 1679. Brother of Bardsey (1673–4).

FISHER, SAMUEL. Matric. pens. from CLARE, Michs. 1615.

FISHER, SAMUEL. Adm. sizar at TRINITY, May 27, 1650. Of Rutland. Matric. 1650; Scholar, 1651; B.A. 1653–4.

FISHER, THOMAS. D.D. Fellow of CORPUS CHRISTI, *c.* 1437. R. of Gestingthorpe, Essex, 1450–64. Will (P.C.C.) 1464.

FISHER, THOMAS. Matric. Fell.-Com. from QUEENS', Easter, 1606; B.A. 1609. Possibly s. of Thomas, of St Giles, Middlesex. Knighted, Mar. 12, 1616–7. Created Bart., July 19, 1627. Died May 22, 1636. Buried at Islington, Middlesex. (*G.E.C.*)

FISHER, THOMAS. Matric. sizar from QUEENS', Easter, 1610. Of Huntingdonshire. B.A. 1613. Ord. deacon (Peterb.) Sept. 18; priest, Sept. 19, 1614.

FISHER, THOMAS. Adm. at KING'S (age 15) a scholar from Eton, Aug. 25, 1622. Of London. Matric. 1623; B.A. 1627. Fellow, 1625–30. Left, and died insane. (*Harwood.*)

FISHER, THOMAS. Adm. pens. at CORPUS CHRISTI, 1633. Of Suffolk. Matric. Easter, 1634; B.A. 1637–8; M.A. 1641.

FISHER, TIMOTHY. Matric. sizar from ST JOHN'S, Michs. 1568. Perhaps ord. deacon and priest (Lincoln) May 23, 1575. But *see* a contemporary in *Al. Oxon.*; who may possibly be the same man.

FISHER, TIMOTHY. Matric. pens. from CLARE, Easter, 1612. B. 1594. School, Merchant Taylors'. B.A. 1615-6.

FISHER, TIMOTHY. Matric. pens. from TRINITY HALL, Mar. 1710-1.

FISHER, WILLIAM. B.Civ.L. 1502-3. Ord. deacon (Lincoln) Apr. 6, 1504; title, 'House of St Edmund'; priest, June 1, 1504; 'of Ludburgh' (? Ludburgh Lane, Cambridge).

FISHER, WILLIAM. Matric. pens. from TRINITY, *c.* 1591; B.A. (? 1593-4); M.A. 1601.

FISHER, WILLIAM. Matric. sizar from ST JOHN'S, Easter, 1609; B.A. 1611-2.

FISHER, WILLIAM. Adm. pens. at CLARE, Mar. 30, 1742. B. at Irchester, Northants. Matric. 1742; B.A. 1745-6. Ord. deacon (Lincoln) Sept. 20, 1747; priest (Peterb.) Feb. 19, 1748-9. R. of Newton Bromswold, Northants., 1749-78. Will (Archd. Northants.) Aug. 13, 1778. (H. I. Longden.)

FISHER, ——. B.Can.L. 1472-3.

FISHER, ——. M.Gram. 1482-3.

FISHER, ——. M.A. 1500-1.

FISHER, ——. Adm. Fell.-Com. at KING'S, 1597-8.

FISHER, ——. Matric. pens. from ST JOHN'S, Michs. 1608.

FISHER, ——. Adm. Fell.-Com. at TRINITY, Michs. 1645.

FISHER, ——. Adm. pens. at TRINITY HALL, Feb. 7, 1699-1700; Fell.-Com. 1701.

FISHER, ——. Adm. Fell.-Com. at TRINITY HALL, Mar. 25, 1702.

FISHPOOL, THOMAS. Adm. pens. (age 17) at SIDNEY, Sept. 9, 1681. 2nd s. of Joseph, gent. B. at Billericay, Essex. School, Felsted. Matric. 1682.

FISHWICK, *see also* PHYSWICK.

FISHWICK, JAMES. Adm. sizar at EMMANUEL, June 15, 1732. S. of James, of Bulsnape, Goosnargh, Lancs. B. there, Feb. 14, 1711. Matric. 1732. Minister of the Chapelry of Padiham, Lancs., 1740. Buried there Apr. 26, 1793. Brother of Thomas (1742-3). (H. Fishwick, *Goosnargh*.)

FISHWEEK, JOHN. Adm. pens. (age 18) at ST JOHN'S, May 4, 1664. S. of John, deceased, of Chorley, Lancs. B. there. School, Rivington.

FISHWICK or FISWICK, THOMAS. Adm. pens. (age ? 18) at PETERHOUSE, Feb. 12, 1742-3. Of Lancashire. S. of James, of Bulsnape, Goosnargh. B. there, June 23, 1721. School, Clitheroe. Matric. 1743; Scholar, 1745; B.A. 1746-7. Chaplain of St George's, Liverpool, 1772. Died Jan. 5, 1781. Brother of James (1732).

FISKE, AMBROSE. Matric. pens. from CHRIST'S, July, 1581; B.A. 1584-5; M.A. from Clare, 1588. V. of Cavenham, Suffolk, 1590. C. of Feltwell, Norfolk, 1603-4. Probably V. of Gayton, Lynn, 1604-14.

FISKE, JAMES. Adm. pens. at CORPUS CHRISTI, 1669. 5th s. of John, of Clopton Hall, Suffolk. School, Bury. Matric. 1670; B.A. 1672-3; M.A. 1677. Ord. deacon (Norwich) June, 1674; priest, Feb. 1674-5. R. of Whepstead, Suffolk, 1678-1711. Married, 1682, Mary, dau. of Ambrose Salusbury, R. of Whepstead. Died Sept. 11, 1711, aged 60. Buried at Whepstead. Brother of William (1658).

FISKE, JOHN. B.A. 1492-3; B.D. 1502-3.

FISKE, JOHN. Matric. pens. from ST JOHN'S, Michs. 1623; B.A. 1626-7.

FISKE, JOHN. Adm. sizar at PETERHOUSE, July 2, 1625. S. of John, of St James, South Elmham, and Stadhaugh, Laxfield, Suffolk. B. *c.* 1606. Matric. 1625; B.A. 1628-9. Emigrated to New England, 1637. Preacher and schoolmaster at Salem, Mass., for four years. Went to Wenham, 1641; pastor there, 1644-56. Pastor at Chelmsford, 1656-77. Also practised medicine. Married (1) 1635, Anne Cippes, of Prenze, Norfolk; (2) Elizabeth Hincksman, widow. Died Jan. 14, 1676-7. (J. G. Bartlett.)

FISKE, JOHN. Matric. pens. from ST JOHN'S, Easter, 1627.

FISKE, JOHN. Adm. pens. at QUEENS', Feb. 15, 1710-1. Of Suffolk. Matric. 1710-1; B.A. 1715-6. Ord. deacon (Norwich) Dec. 20; priest (Lincoln) Dec. 25, 1719. R. of Thorpe Morieux, Suffolk, 1719. Father of John (1744).

FISKE, JOHN. Adm. pens. (age 17) at PEMBROKE, Jan. 8, 1719-20. S. of John, of Mildenhall, Suffolk, gent. Matric. 1720.

FISKE, JOHN. Adm. pens. (age 19) at CAIUS, Nov. 28, 1744. S. of John (1710-1), R. of Thorpe Morieux, Suffolk. B. there. School, Bury. Matric. 1744; B.A. 1748; M.A. 1756. Ord. deacon (Ely) May 21, 1749; priest (Norwich, *Litt. dim.* from Ely) Sept. 1749, as 'C. of Weston Colville.' R. of Thorpe Morieux, 1753. V. of Haughley, 1758-63; of Little Waldingfield, 1773. R. of Shimplingthorne, 1773. Died Apr. 10, 1778. M.I. at Thorpe Morieux. Will, P.C.C. (*Venn*, II. 56.)

FISKE, ROBERT. Adm. Fell.-Com. (age 17) at CAIUS, Feb. 25, 1685-6. S. of William, gent., of Stiffkey, Norfolk. B. there. School, Norwich. Matric. 1686.

FISKE, ROBERT. Adm. pens. (age 17) at CAIUS, Apr. 19, 1731. S. of Robert (?), grazier, late of Norton, Suffolk. B. there. (? S. of John and Martha Fiske; bapt. at Norton, Jan. 2, 1713-4.) School, Bury. Matric. 1731; Scholar, 1731-8; B.A. 1734-5; M.A. 1738. Fellow, 1739-42. Ord. deacon (London) Sept. 24, 1738, as 'C. of Ashdon, Essex'; priest (Norwich) June 1, 1740. V. of Wendens Ambo, Essex, 1741. Died July, 1783. Will, P.C.C. (*Venn*, II. 34; V. B. Redstone.)

FISKE, SAMUEL. Adm. pens. at QUEENS', June 12, 1728. Of Suffolk. Matric. 1728.

FYSKE, THOMAS. Matric. pens. from ST JOHN'S, Michs. 1569.

FISKE, THOMAS. Adm. sizar (age 16) at ST JOHN'S, Mar. 19, 1686-7. S. of Zachary, deceased. B. at Hinderclay, Suffolk. School, Bury St Edmunds. Matric. 1687; B.A. 1690-1; M.A. 1697. Ord. priest (Norwich) May, 1695. Perhaps R. of Gt Bromley, Essex and R. of Shimplingthorne, Suffolk. Buried at Bath, Aug. 27, 1763. (G. *Mag.*) But *see* the next.

FISK, THOMAS. Adm. sizar at QUEENS', Feb. 2, 1694-5. Of Suffolk. Matric. 1697; B.A. 1698-9; M.A. 1710. Ord. deacon (Norwich) Mar. 1700-1. Perhaps R. of Old Newton, Suffolk. If so, died Mar. 11, 1765, but *see* the above. (*G. Mag.*)

FISKE, THOMAS. Adm. sizar at ST CATHARINE'S, June 24, 1735. S. of Thomas (1694-5). Matric. 1736; B.A. 1738-9. Ord. deacon (Norwich) July, 1739, 'C. to his father at Old Newton'; priest, June, 1747.

FISKE, WILLIAM. Adm. pens. at CORPUS CHRISTI, 1631, as Fish. Of Suffolk. Matric. Easter, 1631.

FISKE, WILLIAM. Adm. pens. at CORPUS CHRISTI, 1658. Of Suffolk. S. of John, of Clopton Hall, Esq. Bapt. at Rattlesden, Sept. 29, 1638. Matric. 1658. At Bury school, in 1656. Died at Stiffkey, Norfolk, Jan. 1670. Brother of James (1669).

FISKE, ZACHARY. Adm. sizar at QUEENS', Oct. 4, 1664. Of Suffolk. Matric. 1664-5; B.A. 1668-9; M.A. 1673. V. of Westleton, Suffolk, 1672. Possibly R. of Hadleigh, 1691-1709.

FISK, ——. B.A. 1479-80; M.A. 1483.

FISON, GEORGE. Adm. sizar at QUEENS', Mar. 2, 1648-9. Of London.

FISONE, JOHN. Matric. pens. from CLARE, *c.* 1596.

PISON, PRATT. Adm. sizar at CLARE, July 9, 1696. Of Ely.

FISON, RICHARD. Ord. deacon and priest (Peterb.) Jan. 31, 1590-1, as 'B.A. of CLARE HALL.' Perhaps B.A. 1589-90, in which year the records are defective.

FYSEN, RICHARD. Adm. sizar (age 16) at PETERHOUSE, Oct. 23, 1671. Of Cambridge. School, Cambridge. Matric. 1671; B.A. 1675-6; M.A. 1679.

FYSON, RICHARD. Adm. sizar at JESUS, June 10, 1693. Of Norfolk. School, Charterhouse. Matric. 1695; Rustat Scholar; B.A. 1696-7; M.A. from King's, 1700. Chaplain at King's, 1699.

FISSON, THOMAS. Adm. pens. (age 16) at CAIUS, Aug. 26, 1598. S. of George. B. at Bury St Edmunds. School, Bury. Scholar, 1598-1604; B.A. 1601-2.

FYSEN, THOMAS. Adm. sizar at PETERHOUSE, Mar. 30, 1630. Matric. 1631; Scholar, 1632; B.A. 1633-4; M.A. 1637. Perhaps R. of Woolpit, Suffolk, 1647.

FYSON or POYSON, THOMAS. Adm. sizar (age 17) at PETERHOUSE, July 9, 1663. Of Cambridge. School, Cambridge. B.A. 1667-8; M.A. 1671. Ord. priest (Ely) June 6, 1669.

FYSEN, THOMAS. Adm. sizar (age 16) at PETERHOUSE, July 7, 1694. Of Norfolk. School, King's College School, Cambridge. Matric. 1696; B.A. 1698-9; M.A. 1702. Ord. priest (London) Feb. 17, 1705-6. Chaplain to Lord Paget. V. of West Drayton, Middlesex, 1714-27. V. of Harmondsworth, 1714-27. Died Feb. 1726-7. (*T. A. Walker*, 196.)

FISON, WALTER. Matric. pens. from JESUS, *c.* 1596; B.A. 1599-1600.

FISYON, WILLIAM. Student of Canon Law at Cambridge, in 1442. R. of 'Wytlingworth,' Norfolk. (*Cal. of Papal Letters.*)

FISTE, MARTIN. Matric. sizar from ST JOHN'S, Easter, 1620; B.A. 1623-4; M.A. 1627.

FYST, WILLIAM. Matric. sizar from ST JOHN'S, Michs. 1616; B.A. 1620-1; M.A. 1624.

FIST or FEIST, ——. Adm. sizar at SIDNEY, May, 1601.

FYTCHE, BARROW. Adm. Fell.-Com. at QUEENS', 1665. S. of Charles, of Woodham Walter, Essex. B. in Surrey. Knighted, Apr. 5, 1670. Adm. at the Middle Temple, Feb. 9, 1671–2. Of Woodham Walter. Father of William (1689). (Le Neve, *Knights*, 232.)

FITCHE, JAMES. Matric. pens. from JESUS, Michs. 1576. B. at East Tilbury, Essex. Migrated to Queens', June, 1577. B.A. 1579–80; M.A. 1583; B.D. 1590; D.D. 1597. Incorp. at Oxford, 1605. Ord. deacon (London) July 16; priest, July 17, 1585. R. of Hanworth, Middlesex, 1587–1607. V. of Kingston, Surrey, 1598–1607. V. of Newchurch, Kent, 1607–11; and of Elham, 1607–12. Preb. of Rochester, 1611. Died July, 1612. Will, P.C.C. (*Al. Oxon.*)

FITCHE, JOHN. Matric. pens. from ST JOHN'S, Michs. 1552. One of these names V. of Upton, Norfolk, 1556–9.

FITCH, JOSEPH. Adm. pens. (age 16) at CAIUS, Oct. 7, 1603. S. of George, yeoman, of Braintree, Essex. School, Boxford, Suffolk (Mr Huggen). Scholar, 1604–6.

FITCHE, OSWALD. Matric. pens. from TRINITY, Easter, 1559. Will of one of these names (P.C.C.) 1613; of Bocking, Essex, gent. M.I. there.

FITCHE, RICHARD. Adm. sizar at QUEENS', Mar. 29, 1581. Of Suffolk. B.A. 1584–5; M.A. 1588.

FITCH or FITZ, ROBERT. Adm. sizar at EMMANUEL, Jan. 1654–5. Matric. 1658; B.A. 1658–9; M.A. 1662.

FITCH, SAMUEL. Adm. sizar at TRINITY, Apr. 27, 1647. Of Essex. Matric. 1646.

FITCH, THOMAS. B.A. from ST JOHN'S, 1621–2; M.A. 1625.

FITCH, THOMAS. Adm. pens. at PEMBROKE, Sept. 13, 1652. S. of Thomas, of Wolvey, Warws. One of these names s. of Gilbert, of Wolvey; died 1658, aged 24. (Pedigree in *Vis. of Warws.*, 1682.)

FITCH, WILLIAM. Matric. pens. from PEMBROKE, Easter, 1579.

FITCH, WILLIAM. Adm. sizar (age 17) at CAIUS, Nov. 19, 1675. S. of Samuel, grocer, deceased. B. at Wethersfield, Essex. School, Felsted (Mr Glascock). Matric. 1675; Scholar, 1679–80; B.A. 1679–80. Ord. priest (London) June 3, 1681. R. of Hazeleigh, Essex, 1681–1708. Died 1708. Buried at Southminster, Dec. 2, 1708. (*Venn*, I. 455.)

FYTCH, WILLIAM. Adm. Fell.-Com. at QUEENS', June 4, 1689. Of Essex. S. of Sir Barrow (1665), of Woodham Walter, Knt. B. *c.* 1673. Matric. 1689. M.P. for Malden, 1701–8, 1711–2. Comptroller of Lotteries, 1712. Died Sept. 21, 1728. (Le Neve, *Knights*, 233; A. B. Beaven.)

FITCH, ZACHARY. Adm. pens. at EMMANUEL, Feb. 15, 1631–2. Of Essex. Matric. 1632; B.A. 1635–6; M.A. 1639. Minister at Twinstead, Essex, 1647. R. of Shelley, 1650–62, ejected. Died at Cockerells, Havering. Buried at Romford, Feb. 10, 1686–7. (Davids, *Essex*, 461.)

FICHE or FISH, ——. Pens. at PETERHOUSE, 1576.

FITCHETT, JOHN. Adm. sizar at CLARE, Apr. 3, 1701. B. at Bawtry, Yorks. Matric. 1701; B.A. 1704–5. Ord. deacon (Peterb.) Sept. 23, 1705; priest (York) June 9, 1709. V. of Everton, Notts.; and C. of Bawtry, 1709–11. Died 1711.

FITLING, EDWARD. Adm. pens. (age 15) at CAIUS, Apr. 11, 1618. S. of John, husbandman, of Hingham, Norfolk. School, Reymerstone (Mr Chapman). Matric. 1618–9; Scholar, 1620–3; B.A. 1621–2; M.A. 1625. Incorp. at Oxford, 1627. Fellow, 1628–42. Ord. deacon (Norwich) Dec. 18, 1625; priest (Peterb.) July 16, 1628. C. of West Bilney, Norfolk, in 1627. V. of Stainton, Lincs. (University presentation) 1636. V. of Mattishall, Norfolk, 1641–50. R. of East Lexham, 1649 (subscribes Bishop Hall's book, Jan. 30, 1649–50). R. of West Lexham, 1661. Buried at East Lexham, Aug. 26, 1671. (*Venn*, I. 239.)

FITLING, RICHARD DE. Scholar at KING'S HALL, 1337. Died Feb. 3, 1348–9. Perhaps a victim of the Black Death.

FITTS, HUGH. Adm. pens. at TRINITY, Sept. 8, 1675.

FITZALAN, HENRY, Lord MALTRAVERS. Matric. from QUEENS', Easter, 1549. S. of Henry, Earl of Arundel. K.B. 1547. Despatched on a mission to the King of Bohemia. Died at Brussels, July 31, 1556. (*Cooper*, I. 548.)

FITZEDWARDS, FRANCIS. Adm. pens. (age 18) at ST JOHN'S, June 25, 1717. S. of Francis, gent., of Surrey. B. at Lambeth. School, Sutton Coldfield, Warws. Matric. 1717; B.A. 1720–1; M.A. 1724. Ord. deacon (Peterb.) Mar. 16, 1727–8; priest (London) Sept. 22, 1728; (he obtained a dispensation from the Archbishop, in consequence of his illegitimate birth). R. of Bishop's Cleeve with the Chapel of Stoke Orchard, Glouces., 1737–53. Died 1753. (*Scott-Mayor*, III. 313.)

FITZ-GERALD, THOMAS. Adm. pens. (age 19) at TRINITY, May 27, 1714. S. of Gerald, of Westminster. School, Westminster. Scholar, 1715; B.A. 1717–8; M.A. 1721. Fellow, 1720. Ord. deacon (Rochester) Mar. 9, 1717–8; priest, Dec. 18, 1718. Lecturer at St John the Evangelist, Westminster. Usher of Westminster School. V. of Brigstock, Northants., 1737. R. of Wotton, Surrey, 1739–52. R. of Abinger, 1743–52. Author, poetical. Died Aug. 15, 1752. (*Al. Westmon.*, 263.)

FITZGERALD-VILLERS, *see* **VILLERS.**

FITZHERBERT, DOBSON. Adm. pens. at CLARE, Dec. 12, 1720. B. at Durham. School, Westminster.

FITZHERBERT, GEORGE. Adm. at KING'S, a scholar from Eton, 1475; B.A. 1478–9. Probably B.Can.L. 1483–4 and D.Can.L. 1491–2. Fellow of King's. 'R. of Stanford Rivers, Essex; and of North Swinfield.' (So *Harwood*; but *Newcourt* gives other names.)

FITZHERBERT, HUGH. B.A. 1523–4; M.A. 1527; B.D. 1536–7. Fellow of ST JOHN'S, 1528. Tutor to Roger Ascham. Died 1537. (*Cooper*, I. 64.)

FITZHERBERT, JOHN. B.A. 1501–2. Probably V. of Dovebridge, Derbs., 1520–51; R. of Norbury, 1535. Died 1551. (Cox, *Churches of Derbs.*, III. 231.)

FITZHERBERT, JOHN. Adm. Fell.-Com. (age 18) at ST JOHN'S, Sept. 7, 1677. S. of John, Esq. B. at Somershall-Herbert, Derbs. School, Repton. Matric. 1677.

FITZHERBERT, JOHN. Adm. pens. (age 18) at ST JOHN'S, June 19, 1736. S. of William, lawyer, of Tissington, Derbs. B. in Derby. School, Appleby. Matric. 1736; B.A. 1739–40. Migrated to Emmanuel, Aug. 19, 1740. M.A. 1743. Dixie Fellow of Emmanuel, 1740. Ord. deacon (Lincoln) June 13, 1742; priest, May 29, 1743. R. of Doveridge, Derbs., 1741–85. V. of Ashbourne, 1750–72. Appointed Master of Ashbourne School, 1752. Married Susanna Peacock. Died *c.* July, 1785. Brother of William (1731–2). (*Scott-Mayor*, III. 474; *F.M.G.*, 252.)

FITZHERBERT, MICHAEL. One of the original fellows of TRINITY, Dec. 19, 1546. Resided till 1549. No degree found. (*Trin. Coll. Adm.*)

FITZHERBERT, RICHARD. Adm. pens. (age 16) at ST JOHN'S, Nov. 8, 1706. S. of John, Esq. B. at Mansfield Woodhouse, Notts. (Perhaps s. of John, of Somershall, Derbs.) School, Ashbourne. Matric. 1707.

FITZHERBERT, THOMAS. B.Can.L. 1483–4; D.Can.L. 1491–2. S. of Sir Ralph, of Norbury, Derbs. R. of Stanford Rivers, Essex, 1482–1532. R. of Norbury and North Wingfield, Derbs., 1500. Preb. of Southwell, 1501–28. Preb. of Lichfield, 1513. Precentor, 1519–32. Died Nov. 20, 1532. (Cox, *Churches of Derbs.*, III. 237.)

FITZHERBERT, WILLIAM. Adm. pens. at EMMANUEL, Jan. 17, 1731–2. S. and h. of William, of Tissington, Derbs. Matric. 1732. Adm. at the Inner Temple, Jan. 18, 1731–2. F.R.S. 1762. Succeeded his father at Tissington. M.P. for Derby. Friend of Dr Sam. Johnson. Died, by his own hand, Jan. 2, 1772. Brother of John (1736). (*F.M.G.*, 252.)

FITZHERBERT, —— B.A. 1504, 1st in the *ordo*; M.A. 1507. Probably fellow of JESUS.

FITZHUGH, GEORGE. B.A. 1478–9. S. of Henry, Lord Fitzhugh. M.A. 1479; grace for B.D. and D.D. 1484. Master of PEMBROKE, 1488–1505. Chancellor of the University, 1496–9 and 1502. Preb. of York, 1475–1505. Preb. of Lincoln, 1475–7. R. of Wintringham, Lincs., 1479; of Bingham, Notts., 1482–1505; of Kirkby Ravensworth and Bedale, Yorks. Dean of Lincoln, 1483–1505. Died Nov. 20, 1505. Buried in Lincoln Cathedral. Will (York) 1506. (*Cooper*, I. 10.)

FITZHUGH, ROBERT. LL.D. 3rd s. of Henry, Lord Fitzhugh. Warden of KING'S HALL, 1424–31. Chancellor of the University, 1424–6. Ord. sub-deacon (Ely) 1417; deacon (1418). Preb. of Lincoln, 1417–31. Preb. of York, 1418–31. Archdeacon of Northampton, 1419–31. Preb. of Lichfield, 1420–8. Ambassador to Rome and Venice, 1429. Bishop of London, 1431–6. Delegate at Council of Basel, 1434, and while there was elected Bishop of Ely, 1435. Died at St Osyth, Essex, Jan. 15, 1435–6. Buried in St Paul's. Will (Lambeth). (*D.N.B.*)

FITZJAMES, RICHARD. D.D. 1496–7 (Incorp. from Oxford). S. of John, of Redlynch, Somerset. Fellow of Merton College, Oxford, 1465. Proctor, 1473. Warden, 1483. Vice-Chancellor, 1481. Chancellor, 1502. Preb. of Wells, 1474. Treasurer of St Paul's, 1483–97. V. of Minehead, Somerset, 1484. Preb. of St Paul's, 1485–97. R. of Aller, Somerset, 1485. Bishop of Rochester, 1497–1503; of Chichester, 1503–6; of London, 1506–22. Died Jan. 15, 1521–2. Buried in St Paul's. Will (P.C.C.) 1522. (*Cooper*, I. 25.)

FITZJEFFREY, ALEXANDER. Matric. pens. from QUEENS', Michs. 1560; B.A. 1562–3, 1st in the *ordo*; M.A. 1566. Fellow, 1562–8. Ord. priest (Ely) July 29, 1565, as 'H. Fitzfarren, B.A.' University preacher, 1571. Preacher at Lostwithiel, Cornwall, in 1584. Father of Charles (below). (*Cooper*, II. 86.)

FITZJEFFREY, CHARLES. M.A. 1618 (Incorp. from Oxford). Of Cornwall. S. of Alexander (above). B. at Fowey, Cornwall. Matric. from Broadgates Hall, Oxford, July 6, 1593, age 17; B.A. 1596-7; M.A. 1600. R. of St Dominick, Cornwall, 1603-38. Author, poetical, etc. Died Feb. 24, 1637-8. Buried at St Dominick. Father of John (1622). (*Al. Oxon.*; *D.N.B.*)

FITZJEFFERIE, GEORGE. Matric. Fell.-Com. from CHRIST'S, Easter, 1607. Of Creaken-in-Barford, Beds. Adm. at the Inner Temple, 1609. Doubtless s. of Sir George, of Barford, Beds. Buried there Sept. 2, 1616. (*Vis. of Beds.*, 1634; *Vis. of Northants.*, 1618.)

FITZ-JEFFREY, HENRY. Matric. pens. from TRINITY, Michs. 1611, scholar from Westminster, 1612. Doubtless 2nd s. of Sir George, of Barford, Beds. Adm. at Lincoln's Inn, Nov. 5, 1614. *D.N.B.* suggests that he may be a s. of Charles, above, and author of *Satires*, published 1617.

FITZ JEFFREY, JOHN. Matric. pens. from ST JOHN'S, Easter, 1622. S. of Charles (1618), R. of St Dominick, Cornwall. B.A. 1624-5. Incorp. at Oxford, 1628. M.A. (Gloucester Hall, Oxford) 1628. R. of St Dominick, 1637. Will (P.C.C.) 1653. (*Al. Oxon.*)

FITZ-JEFFRYE, THOMAS. Matric. pens. from JESUS, Michs. 1618. Perhaps bapt. at Gt Barford, Beds., Apr. 27, 1602. One of these names buried there Apr. 11, 1651.

FITZJOHN, FRANCIS. Adm. pens. at KING'S, Michs. 1564.

FITZJOHN, JOHN. B.D. 1492-3. Eight years study after M.A.

FITZJOHN, ROBERT. Adm. sizar at PETERHOUSE, 1595-6. Matric. *c.* 1596.

FITZJOHN, THOMAS. Adm. sizar (age 17) at CAIUS, June 24, 1642. S. of Thomas, tanner, of Swaffham, Norfolk. Bapt. there, Apr. 16, 1624. School, Swaffham. Matric. 1642. Probably buried at Swaffham, Aug. 16, 1684. (*Venn*, I. 347.)

FITZJOHN, WILLIAM. B.A. 1478-9; M.A. 1482; B.D. 1490-1. Fellow of QUEENS', 1484-98. Proctor, 1485-6.

FITZ-JOHN, WILLIAM. Adm. pens. (age 18) at CHRIST'S, July 5, 1631. S. of William. B. at Braintfield, near Hertford, Herts. School, Hertford (Mr Minors). Matric. 1634.

FITZJOHN or FYDYON, ——. University stationer, in 1483-4. (*Gr. Bk.* A, 187; Bk. B[1], 11.)

FITZRANDOLPH, THOMAS. Matric. pens. from TRINITY, Michs. 1606, scholar from Westminster, 1607; B.A. 1610-1; M.A. 1614. Fellow, 1612.

FITZROY, AUGUSTUS HENRY. Adm. Fell.-Com. (age 16) at PETERHOUSE, Oct. 26, 1751. S. of Lord Augustus, and grandson of the Duke of Grafton. B. Oct. 9, 1735. School, Hackney (Dr Newcome). M.A. 1753. Chancellor of the University, 1768-1811. M.P. for Bury St Edmunds, 1756. Succeeded as 3rd Duke of Grafton, 1757. Lord Lieut. of Suffolk, 1757-63, and again, 1769-90. Secretary of State, 1765-6. First Lord of the Treasury, 1766. Prime Minister, 1767-70. K.G. 1769. Lord Privy Seal, 1771-5 and 1782-3. Author. Died Mar. 14, 1811. Buried at Euston. (*D.N.B.*; *T. A. Walker*, 303.)

FITZROY, CHARLES, *see* GRAFTON, Duke of.

FITZROY, JAMES, *see* MONMOUTH, Duke of.

FITZ-SIMMONS, RICHARD. Matric. pens. from MAGDALENE, Lent, 1615-6. Perhaps s. of Richard, of Gt Yeldham, Essex, gent.; adm. at Lincoln's Inn, June 27, 1615.

FITZWALTER, CHARLES. Adm. at KING'S (age 17) a scholar from Eton, Aug. 14, 1548. Of Canterbury. Matric. 1548; B.A. 1552-3 (1st in the *ordo*); M.A. 1556. Fellow, 1551-9. Fellow of Eton, 1559. R. of Piddlehinton, Dorset, 1562.

FITZWALTERS, HENRY. Matric. Fell.-Com. from TRINITY, Michs. 1610.

FITZ-WHITE, *see* WHITE.

FITZWILLIAM, CHARLES. Adm. (age 17) at MAGDALENE, Jan. 21, 1663-4. S. of William, Lord Lifford. School, Westminster. Matric. 1664; M.A. 1665. Adm. at the Middle Temple, Dec. 11, 1661. M.P. for Peterborough, 1685-7, 1689. Died 1689.

FITZWILLIAM, HUMPHREY. (? B.A. 1482-3); B.D. 1489-90; D.D. 1501. S. of Sir Richard, of Ecclesfield. Fellow of PEMBROKE. Vice-Chancellor, 1502. Preb. of York, 1498. Died 1503. (*Cooper*, I. 8.)

FITZWILLIAM, HUMPHREY. Adm. Fell.-Com. at EMMANUEL, Feb. 24, 1634-5. Of Bedfordshire. S. of Sir John. Bapt. at Kempston, Beds., Sept. 21, 1617. Matric. 1635.

FITZWILLIAMS, JOHN. Adm. Fell.-Com. at KING'S, Easter, 1563. Perhaps brother of William (1564).

FITZWILLIAM, JOHN. Matric. Fell.-Com. from CHRIST'S, Michs. 1570. Perhaps adm. at the Inner Temple, Apr. 12, 1573, as s. of Sir William, of Milton, Northants., Lord Deputy of Ireland. If so, bapt. at St Benetfink, London, Feb. 4, 1553-4. Afterwards captain in the army in Scotland. Will (P.C.C.) of one of these names, 1612. (*Peile*, I. 115.)

FITZWILLIAMS, JOHN. Matric. pens. from ST JOHN'S, Easter, 1582. One of these names, s. and h. of Charles, of Staple Inn, adm. at Gray's Inn, Nov. 1, 1587.

FITZWILLIAMS, JOHN. Adm. pens. (age 17) at PETERHOUSE, Oct. 14, 1628. Of London. S. of John, merchant taylor. 'Grecian' from Christ's Hospital. Matric. 1628; Scholar, 1628; B.A. 1632-3; M.A. 1636. Ord. priest (Lincoln) Sept. 19, 1641. (*A. W. Lockhart.*)

FITZWILLIAM, JOHN. Incorp. M.A. 1664; also B.D. 1675; and D.D. 1679; from Magdalen College, Oxford. Matric. there, July 15, 1652; B.A. (Oxford) 1655-6; M.A. 1658; B.D. 1666; D.D. 1677. Fellow of Magdalen College, 1661-70. R. of Brightstone, Isle of Wight, 1669. R. of Cottenham, Cambs., 1674. Canon of Windsor, 1688-90; deprived as non-juror. Died Mar. 26, 1699. Buried in St Dunstan-in-the-West. (*D.N.B.*; *Al. Oxon.*)

FITZWILLIAM, ROBERT. Matric. Fell.-Com. from QUEENS', Michs. 1589. Of Lincolnshire. Probably s. and h. of William, of Mablethorpe, Lincs. Age 19 in 1592. Buried at Withern, Sept. 5, 1602. Brother of William (1589). (*Vis. of Lincs.*; *Lincs. Pedigrees*, 358.)

FITZ-WILLIAM, THOMAS. Adm. pens. (age 15) at SIDNEY, May 13, 1657. S. of Thomas, Esq. B. at Doncaster. School, Doncaster (Mr Marmaduke Cooke). Matric. 1657; B.A. 1660. Adm. at the Inner Temple, 1656.

FITZWILLIAMS, W. Matric. pens. from ST JOHN'S, Easter, 1582.

FITZWILLIAM, WALTER. Adm. Fell.-Com. at EMMANUEL, Sept. 29, 1591. S. of Sir William, of Gaynes Park, Essex, and Winifred, dau. of Sir Walter Mildmay. Matric. *c.* 1593. M.P. for Peterborough, 1620-2. Brother of William (1591). (*Vis. of Essex*, 1612.)

FITZWILLIAMS, WILLIAM. Matric. Fell.-Com. from KING'S, Michs. 1564. Perhaps brother of John (1563).

FITZWILLIAM, WILLIAM. Matric. Fell.-Com. from QUEENS', Michs. 1589. Of Lincolnshire. Probably 2nd s. of William, of Mablethorpe, Lincs. Admon. granted to Augustine Pearson, a creditor, Oct. 27, 1646. Brother of Robert (1589). (*Lincs. Pedigrees*, 359.)

FITZWILLIAM, WILLIAM. Adm. at EMMANUEL, May 19, 1591. S. of Sir William, of Gaynes Park, Essex, Knt., and Winifred, dau. of Sir Walter Mildmay. Matric. 1591. Of Gaynes Park, Esq. Created Baron FitzWilliam, of Lifford, 1620. Died in London, Jan. 6, 1643-4. Buried at Marholm, Northants. Father of the next. Brother of Walter. (*Vis. of Essex*, 1612; *G.E.C.*)

FITZWILLIAM, WILLIAM. Adm. Fell.-Com. at EMMANUEL, Aug. 23, 1621. Doubtless s. of William (1591). B. *c.* 1609. Matric. 1622. Succeeded his father as Baron Fitzwilliam, of Lifford, 1644. Died in London, Feb. 21, 1658. Buried at Marholm, Northants. (*Vis. of Essex*, 1612; *Hunter*, II. 94; *G.E.C.*)

FITZWILLIAM, WILLIAM. Adm. Fell.-Com. at CLARE, Feb. 12, 1728-9. Doubtless 2nd s. of Richard, 5th Viscount. B. in Ireland. Bapt. Sept. 11, 1712. Matric. 1729; B.A. 1732-3; M.A. from Trinity, 1735. Appointed Usher of the Black Rod in Ireland, 1747. (*Lodge*, IV. 320.)

FITZWILLIAMS, ——. Adm. at CORPUS CHRISTI, 1571.

FLACK, GEORGE. Adm. pens. (age 16) at PETERHOUSE, Sept. 17, 1675. Of Essex. S. of Thomas, of West Wickham, Cambs. School, Merchant Taylors'. Matric. 1675; Scholar, 1675. Attendant at Gray's Inn. Barrister, 1686. Brother of Thomas (1682-3). (*Vis. of Cambs.*, 1684.)

FLACK, RICHARD. Adm. pens. (age 16) at PEMBROKE, Mar. 2, 1691-2. S. of Samuel (1661), R. of Sall, Norfolk. Matric. 1692; B.A. 1695-6; M.A. 1699. Fellow, 1698-1704. Ord. deacon (Lincoln) June 4, 1699; priest, Dec. 24, 1699. R. of Gt Fransham, Norfolk, 1703. R. of Congham, 1706-15. Buried Mar. 29, 1715. Father of Thomas (1726) and Samuel (1730). (*Carthew*, II. 180.)

FLACK, ROBERT. Adm. at CORPUS CHRISTI, 1598. Of Suffolk.

FLACK, ROBERT. Adm. pens. (age 17) at PETERHOUSE, July 2, 1678. Of Cambridgeshire. S. of Thomas, of West Wickham, Cambs. School, Hertford. Scholar, 1678. Died in College, July 2, 1679. M.I. at Linton. (Le Neve, *Mon.*, IV, 195.)

FLACKE, SAMUEL. Adm. pens. (age 17) at PEMBROKE, May 18, 1661. S. of Richard. B. at Chattisham, Suffolk. Matric. 1661; B.A. 1664-5; M.A. 1668. Fellow, 1668-71. Ord. deacon (Peterb.) Sept. 20, 1668; priest (Ely) Sept. 24, 1670. R. of Sall, Norfolk, 1670-1708. V. of Saxthorp, 1671-1708. Died 1708. Father of Richard (1691-2).

FLACK, SAMUEL. Adm. pens. (age 16) at CAIUS, Apr. 17, 1730. S. of Richard (1691-2), late R. of Congham St Ann, Norfolk. B. there. School, Lynn. Scholar, 1730-5; Matric. 1731; B.A. 1734-5. Brother of Thomas (1726). (*Venn*, II. 32.)

FLACK, THOMAS. Adm. pens. (age 17) at PETERHOUSE, Mar. 21, 1682-3. Of Cambridgeshire. S. of Thomas, of West Wickham, Cambs. School, St Paul's. Died July 3, 1683. Brother of George (1675).

FLACK, THOMAS. Adm. pens. (age 17) at CAIUS, June 1, 1726. S. of Richard (1691-2), R. of Congham St Ann, Norfolk. B. there. School, Darsingham, Norfolk (private). Scholar, 1726-30; Matric. 1727; B.A. 1730. Ord. deacon (Norwich) Sept. 25, 1748, as C. of Hindringham; priest, May 21, 1749, as C. of Briningham. R. of Waterden, Norfolk, 1750-80; of Twyford, 1779-80. Died Oct. 28, 1780. M.I. at Briningham. Brother of Samuel (1730). (*Venn*, II. 25.)

FLACKE, WILLIAM. Adm. sizar (age 17) at CAIUS, Mar. 27, 1579. Of Mellis, Suffolk. S. of Walter, husbandman. Schools, Eye and Botesdale. Matric. 1579. Afterwards a Jesuit priest. Entered Douay, Feb. 22, 1581-2. Received minor orders from the Archbishop of Rheims. Entered the English College at Rome, Oct. 20, 1584. Ord. deacon and priest at Valladolid, 1591. Rector of St Omer two years and Ghent three years. Died at St Omer, Dec. 13, 1637. (*Venn*, I. 201.)

FLACKE, WILLIAM. B.A. from CLARE, 1588-9.

FLACK, WILLIAM. Adm. sizar at QUEENS', Apr. 9, 1595. Of Suffolk. Matric. *c.* 1595; B.A. 1599-1600; M.A. 1603. Perhaps V. of West Wratting, Cambs., 1615.

FLACK, WILLIAM. Adm. pens. at JESUS, Sept. 6, 1645. Of Suffolk. Matric. 1645-6.

FLAMANK, CHARLES. Matric. pens. from MAGDALENE, *c.* 1593. S. of William, of Boscarne, Cornwall. Bapt. at Bodmin, 1572. B.A. 1596-7; M.A. from Jesus, 1600; B.D. from Peterhouse, 1606. Fellow of Peterhouse, 1602-6. Incorp. at Oxford, 1600. Minister at Haddenham, Cambs., 1602. V. of Little St Mary's, Cambridge, 1604. R. of Burgh St Margaret, Norfolk, 1609. Died at Yarmouth, Norfolk. Probably brother of William (1596). (Maclean, *Trigg.*, I. 283; *Walker*, 28; *Al. Oxon.*)

FLAMANK, CHARLES. Matric. pens. from PETERHOUSE, Easter, 1624; Scholar, 1626. Buried at St Botolph's, Cambridge, Sept. 3, 1626.

FLAMMANKE, WILLIAM. Matric. sizar from MAGDALENE, *c.* 1596. Probably 5th s. of William, of Boscarne, Cornwall. Bapt. 1576; and brother of Charles (1593).

FLAMSTEED, JOHN. Adm. pens. (age 24) at JESUS, Dec. 21, 1670. S. of Stephen, maltster, of Derby. School, Derby. M.A. 1674 (*Lit. Reg.*). Ord. (Bishop of Ely) Easter, 1675. Astronomer-Royal, 1675-1719. F.R.S. 1677. V. of Burstow, Surrey, 1684. His observations gave great help to Newton in writing his *Principia*. In 1707 the first volume of his Catalogue and Observations of the stars was printed. His *Historia Coelestia Brittannica* was finally completed in 1725 by his assistant Joseph Crosthwait. Died Dec. 31, 1719. Will (P.C.C.) 1720. (*D.N.B.*)

FLAMSTED, ——. M.A. or higher degree, 1460-1. (*See* Gr. *Bk.* A, 53.)

FLANDEN, BENEDICT. Matric. pens. from JESUS, Michs. 1602.

FLANDON, PHILIP. Matric. pens. from JESUS, Easter, 1603.

FLANNER, HUBERSTED. Adm. pens. at CORPUS CHRISTI, 1645. Of Norfolk. Matric. Lent, 1645-6; B.A. 1648-9.

FLANNER, JOHN. Adm. at CORPUS CHRISTI, 1649. Of Norfolk. Migrated to Emmanuel, Feb. 2, 1651-2. Matric. 1653; B.A. 1654-5; M.A. 1658. R. of Kilverstone, Norfolk, 1656-8. Perhaps buried at St Cuthbert's, Thetford, Oct. 4, 1658. Will proved (P.C.C.) 1658; by son John.

FLANNER, PHILIP. Matric. pens. from TRINITY HALL, Easter, 1647; B.A. 1650; M.A. from King's, 1654. One of these names s. of Thomas, of Withersfield, Suffolk, gent., adm. at Gray's Inn, Feb. 12, 1657-8.

FLASBY, EDWARD. Adm. sizar (age 17) at CHRIST'S, Mar. 30, 1715. S. of Francis. B. at Leck, Kirkby Lonsdale. School, Kirkby Lonsdale (Mr Gibson). Matric. 1715; Scholar, 1716; B.A. 1718-9; M.A. 1722. Ord. deacon (London) Mar. 13, 1719-20; priest (Norwich) Sept. 1722. R. of Groton, Suffolk, 1736-42. Buried at Groton, Oct. 27, 1742. (*Peile*, II. 187.)

FLASBY, JOHN. Adm. sizar (age 16) at CHRIST'S, June 9, 1698. S. of Thomas. B. at Overtown, Lancs. School, Kirkby Lonsdale. Matric. 1698; B.A. 1701-2; M.A. 1706. Incorp. at Oxford, 1712. Ord. deacon (Worcester) 1702; priest (Lincoln) Mar. 14, 1702-3. R. of Groton, Suffolk, 1704-36. V. of Edwardstone, 1706-36. Buried at Groton, Dec. 7, 1736. Father of the next. (*Peile*, II. 142.)

FLASBY, JOSEPH. Adm. pens. (age 17) at ST JOHN'S, Mar. 23, 1726-7. S. of John (above), R. of Groton, Suffolk. B. at Groton. School, Bury St Edmunds. Matric. 1727; B.A. 1730-1. Adm. at the Middle Temple, Jan. 22, 1730-1. Died June, 1731. Buried at Groton.

FLATHERS, MARMADUKE. Adm. sizar (age 17) at ST JOHN'S, June 21, 1667. S. of Robert, clerk, V. of Lastingham, Yorks. B. there. School, York. Matric. 1667; B.A. 1670-1; M.A. 1675. Ord. deacon (York) June, 1671; priest, Sept. 1672.

FLATHERS, THOMAS. Adm. pens. (age 16) at SIDNEY, Nov. 7, 1623. S. of Martin, R. of Leathley, Yorks. B. there. Schools, Burnsall and Coxwold. Matric. 1623-4; B.A. 1627-8; M.A. 1631. Brother of William (1620).

FLATHERS, THOMAS. Adm. pens. (age 15) at SIDNEY, May 14, 1631. S. of Marmaduke, R. of Hemsworth, Yorks. Schools, Wakefield and Coxwold (Mr Smelt). Matric. 1631; B.A. 1635-6. Perhaps V. of Lastingham, Yorks., 1662-86. Died 1686.

FLATHERS, WILLIAM. Adm. pens. (age 15) at SIDNEY, May 3, 1620. S. of Martin, R. of Leathley, Yorks. B. there. School, Burnsall. Matric. 1620; B.A. 1623-4; M.A. 1627; B.D. 1634. Fellow. Ord. deacon (York) Sept. 1627. R. of Howick, Northumb., 1636-8. V. of Hartburn, in 1636. Archdeacon of Northumberland, 1636-8. License, 1637, to marry Ursula Staveley, of Ripon. Brother of Thomas (1623). (H. M. Wood.)

FLATMAN, ROBERT. Adm. sizar at PETERHOUSE, July 3, 1621. Matric. 1623.

FLATMAN, THOMAS. Matric. pens. from CHRIST'S, Nov. 1554.

FLATMAN, THOMAS. M.A. from ST CATHARINE'S, 1667 (*Lit. Reg.*). B. in London. School, Winchester. Matric. from New College, Oxford, July 25, 1655. 'B.A. of Oxford' according to the Cambridge mandate. Adm. at the Inner Temple, 1654. Barrister, 1662. F.R.S. 1668. Poet and miniature painter. Died in London, Dec. 8, 1688, aged 53. Buried in St Bride's. (*Al. Oxon.*; *D.N.B.*)

FLAUNCE, EDMUND. Fellow of CORPUS CHRISTI, 1544.

FLAWELL, ——. Adm. at CORPUS CHRISTI, 1568.

FLAXMAN, HENRY. B.A. 1480-1; M.A. 1484-5. V. of Long Stow, Cambs., 1487. V. of Caxton, till 1520.

FLEAR, RICHARD. Matric. sizar from CHRIST'S, Lent, 1597-8. Probably B.A. 1602-3. Ord. deacon (Colchester) Jan. 15; priest, Jan. 22, 1603-4. C. of Cranwell, Lincs., 1604. R. of Leasingham. Father of Samuel (1647).

FLEARE, RICHARD. Adm. pens. (age 18) at PETERHOUSE, July 6, 1636. Of Lincolnshire. School, Sleaford.

FLEAR or FLEARD, SAMUEL. Adm. pens. (age 22) at CAIUS, Apr. 30, 1647. S. of Richard (1597-8), R. of Leasingham, Lincs. School, Digby (Mr Harkley). Matric. 1647.

FLECKNOWE, RICHARD (? ROGER). Adm. at KING'S, a scholar from Eton, 1445; B.A. 1449.

FLECKNOWE, WILLIAM. Adm. at KING'S, a scholar from Eton, 1450. Proceeded to M.A. (*Harwood*.)

FLEET, ANTHONY. Matric. sizar from ST CATHARINE'S, Easter, 1636. Of Huntingdonshire. B.A. 1639-40; M.A. 1643.

FLEETE, CHRISTOPHER. Matric. sizar from ST CATHARINE'S, Easter, 1636. Of Huntingdonshire. B.A. 1639-40; M.A. 1643. Ord. deacon and priest (Lincoln) Feb. 23, 1644. V. of Sawston, Cambs., 1645-58. V. of Ashdon, Essex, 1664-97.

FLEET, SAMUEL. Adm. sizar at CORPUS CHRISTI, 1647. Of Suffolk. Matric. Michs. 1649; B.A. 1652-3; M.A. 1660. R. of Bromley Parva, Essex, 1657-8. R. of Belton, Suffolk, 1660-94. R. of Burgh Castle, 1660.

FLETE, THOMAS. Matric. pens. from PETERHOUSE, Michs. 1560.

FLETE, W. Matric. pens. from PETERHOUSE, Michs. 1560. V. of Selworthy, Somerset, 1570-1617. Perhaps V. of Hawkridge, 1574-86. Will (Taunton) 1617.

FLEETWOOD, ARTHUR. B.A. 1608 (Incorp. from Oxford). S. of Sir George, of the Vache, Chalfont St Giles, Bucks. Matric. from Trinity College, Oxford, May 24, 1606, age 17; B.A. 1607. Adm. at Gray's Inn, Mar. 12, 1608-9. Brother of James (1622). (*Al. Oxon.*)

FLEETWOOD, ARTHUR. Matric. sizar from KING'S, Easter, 1655. Of Salop. B.A. 1658-9; M.A. from Queens', 1662. Fellow of Queens', 1661-3.

FLEETWOOD, CHARLES. Adm. Fell.-Com. at EMMANUEL, July 8, 1635. S. of Sir Miles, of Wood Street, London, Knt. Matric. 1637; B.A. 1638. Adm. at Gray's Inn, Jan. 16, 1638-9. Barrister, 1645. Served in the army under the Earl of Essex; wounded at Newbury, 1643. Appointed Receiver of the Court of Wards, 1644. Commanded a regiment at Naseby, 1645. M.P. for Marlborough, 1646-53; also elected, 1654, 1656; for Co. Oxford, 1654-5, 1656-8. Joint Governor of the Isle of Wight, 1649. Lieut.-general of horse at Dunbar, 1650. Member of the Council of State, 1651. Commander-in-chief in Ireland, 1652-7; also Lord-deputy, from 1654. A member of the House of Lords, 1656. Commander-in-chief, 1659. Deprived of his post, Dec. 1659, and incapacitated for life from holding office. Married (1) Frances, dau. of Thomas Smith, of Winston, Norfolk, Esq.; (2) Cromwell's daughter, Bridget, the widow of Ireton, 1652. Died Oct. 4, 1692. Buried in Bunhill Fields. Brother of William (1618) and Roger (1632), father of Smith (1659-60). (*D.N.B.*)

FLEETWOOD, CHARLES. Adm. at KING'S, a scholar from Eton, 1711. S. of William (1675), Bishop of Ely. B. in London, 1693. Matric. 1712; B.A. 1716–7; M.A. 1717 (*Com. Reg.*); LL.D. 1726. Fellow, 1715. Ord. deacon (Ely) Mar. 9; priest, Mar. 16, 1717–8. Preb. of Ely, 1718–37. R. of Barley, Herts., 1719–22. R. of Cottenham, Cambs., 1722–37. Preb. of Exeter, 1726–37. Archdeacon of Cornwall, 1732–7. Died July 27, 1737. Buried at Ely. (*Harwood*, 292; *Coll. Hist. King's*, 199.)

FLEETWOOD, CHARLES WILLIAM. Adm. pens. (age 17) at ST JOHN'S, Feb. 16, 1714–5. S. of William, deceased. B. at Aldwincle, Northants. School, Northampton. Matric. 1715; B.A. 1718–9; M.A. 1722. Ord. deacon (Lincoln) Dec. 24, 1721; priest (Peterb.) Feb. 18, 1721–2. R. of Aldwincle, 1722. Died at Finchley, Middlesex, Aug. 29, 1763. Buried at Aldwincle. Will (P.C.C.) 1763. (*Northants. N. and Q.*, N.S., I. 110.)

FLEETWOOD, JAMES. Adm. at KING'S (age 17) a scholar from Eton, 1622. S. of Sir George, of the Vache, Bucks. Matric. 1622; B.A. 1627; M.A. 1631. Fellow, 1626–34. Provost, 1660–75. D.D. (Oxford) 1642; for services to the King at Edgehill. Incorp. as D.D. at Cambridge, 1660. Vice-Chancellor, 1663–4, 1667–8. Ord. deacon (Peterb.) Sept. 23, 1632. R. of Shaw, Berks.; and V. of Prees, Salop. Preb. of Lichfield, 1636; sequestered, 1647. Chaplain in the Royal army, during the rebellion. R. of Sutton Coldfield, Warws. R. of Anstey, Herts., 1662–71; and of Denham, Bucks., 1669. Chaplain to Charles II. Bishop of Worcester, 1675–83. Died July 17, 1683. Buried in Worcester Cathedral. Father of the next and brother of Arthur (1608). (*Al. Oxon.*; *D.N.B.*)

FLEETWOOD, JOHN. Adm. at KING'S, a scholar from Eton, 1660. S. of James (above), Bishop of Worcester. B. at Prees, Salop. Matric. Easter, 1661; B.A. 1663–4; M.A. 1668. Fellow, 1663–8. Ord. deacon (Peterb.) Dec. 19, 1668; priest (Ely) Sept. 24, 1670. R. of Willian, Herts., 1673–5. Archdeacon of Worcester, 1676–1705. Died Dec. 8, 1705, aged 64. (*N. and Q.*, N.S., VII. 303.)

FLEETWOOD, MILES. Adm. Fell.-Com. at QUEENS', Sept. 7, 1646. Of Middlesex. S. and h. of Sir William, of Aldwincle, Northants., Knt. Adm. at Gray's Inn, June 23, 1648. M.P. for New Woodstock, 1659; for Northants., 1679–81. Died July 28, 1688. Buried at Aldwincle. Father of William (1669). (*Lipscomb*, III. 227; *Northants. N. and Q.*, N.S., I. 110.)

FLEETWOOD, RICHARD. Matric. pens. from QUEENS', Easter, 1622. Of London. B.A. 1624–5. R. of Stratford St Andrew, Suffolk, 1630–42.

FLEETWOOD, ROGER. B.A. 1632–3 (Incorp. from Oxford); M.A. from ST CATHARINE'S, 1634. S. of Sir Miles, of Thrapston, Northants. Matric. from Lincoln College, Oxford, Oct. 24, 1628, age 14; B.A. (Oxford) 1631. Preb. of Lichfield, 1640. V. of Hanbury, Staffs. Joi the Royalist army. Brother of William (1618) and Charles (1635). (*Al. Oxon.*; Pedigree in *Northants. N. and Q.*, N.S., I. 110.)

FLEETWOOD, SMITH. Adm. Fell.-Com. (age 14) at ST JOHN'S, Jan. 27, 1659–60. Eldest s. of Charles (1635), Esq., of Feltwell, Norfolk. B. at Feltwell. Matric. 1660. Died Jan. 1708; 'of Newington, Midds.' Buried at Stoke Newington. (*Le Neve, Mon.*, IV. 164.)

FLEETWOOD, WILLIAM. Adm. Fell.-Com. at EMMANUEL, Dec. 3, 1618. S. of Sir Miles, of Aldwincle, Northants. Bapt. at Cardington, Beds., July 20, 1603. Matric. 1618–9. Incorp. at Oxford, 1633, as M.A. of Cambridge (degree not recorded). Comptroller of Woodstock Park. Knighted, July 20, 1624. M.P. for New Woodstock, Mar. 1640, 1640 (L.P.), 1661–74. Died 1674, aged 71. Brother of Roger (1632) and Charles (1635). (*Al. Oxon.*)

FLEETWOOD, WILLIAM. Adm. Fell.-Com. (age 17) at SIDNEY, July 13, 1669. 1st s. of Miles (1646), of Aldwincle, Northants. B. at Woodstock, Oxon. Adm. at the Middle Temple, Nov. 13, 1668. Of Aldwincle. Will proved, Dec. 14, 1698. (*Northants. N. and Q.*, N.S., I. 110.)

FLEETWOOD, WILLIAM. Adm. at KING'S, a scholar from Eton, 1675. S. of Captain Geoffrey, of Hesketh, Lancs. B. in the Tower of London. Matric. Michs. 1675; B.A. 1679–80; M.A. 1683; D.D. 1705 (*Com. Reg.*). Fellow, 1678. Fellow of Eton College, 1691. Lecturer of St Dunstan-in-the-West, London, 1689. Chaplain to King William. R. of St Augustine, London, 1689–1706. Canon of Windsor, 1702. R. of Wexham, Bucks., 1705–23. Bishop of St Asaph, 1708. Bishop of Ely, 1714–23. A zealous Whig. Author, theological. Died at Tottenham, Middlesex, Aug. 4, 1723, aged 67. Buried in Ely Cathedral. (*Hist. of King's*, 161; *D.N.B.*)

FLEETWOODE, WILLIAM. Adm. pens. (age 17) at TRINITY, Jan. 24, 1706–7. S. of William, of Missenden, Bucks. School, Enfield, Middlesex (Dr Uvedale). Matric. 1707. Adm. at Lincoln's Inn, Jan. 18, 1706–7. Died 1737.

FLEETWOOD, WILLIAM. Adm. sizar (age 16) at TRINITY, May 18, 1739. S. of Miles, of London. School, Stand, Lancs. (Mr Walker). Matric. 1739. An Apothecary, of the parish of St Luke, Middlesex. Married, in 1745. Buried in Bunhill Fields, Oct. 23, 1747. (*Northants. N. and Q.*, N.S., I. 110.)

FLEMYNG, ABRAHAM. Matric. sizar from PETERHOUSE, Michs. 1570. B. in London, c. 1552. B.A. 1581–2. Ord. deacon and priest (Peterb.) Aug. 2, 1588. Chaplain to the Countess of Nottingham. R. of St Pancras, Soper Lane, 1593–1607. Poet and antiquary. Died at Bottesford, Leics., Sept. 18, 1607. Buried there. M.I. Brother of Samuel (1565). (*Cooper*, II. 459; *D.N.B.*)

FLEMYNG, AVERY. Matric. sizar from PEMBROKE, Michs. 1554.

FLEMING, BRIAN. Matric. sizar from ST JOHN'S, c. 1595.

FLEMING, DAVID. Adm. pens. (age 19) at TRINITY, May 28, 1703. S. of David, of London. School, Westminster. Matric. 1704; Scholar, 1704; B.A. 1706–7; M.A. 1710. Fellow, 1709. Ord. deacon (Ely) May 27, 1711; priest, May 31, 1713. R. of Bixley, Norfolk. R. of Framlingham Earl. R. of Marlingford, 1723–8. Died 1747.

FLEMING, GILES. Matric. sizar from ST JOHN'S, Lent, 1618–9; B.A. 1622–3; M.A. 1626. Ord. deacon (Peterb.) Mar. 5; priest, Mar. 6, 1625–6. R. of Gautby, Lincs., 1626. R. of Waddingworth, 1629–65. Buried in Beverley Minster, Jan. 23, 1664–5. Will (York) 1665. (M. H. Peacock.)

FLEMING, JOHN. M.A. Fellow of PEMBROKE, 1450. Proctor, 1453–4.

FLEMING, JOHN. B.Civ.L. 1520–1.

FLEMING, JOHN. Adm. pens. at EMMANUEL, Apr. 3, 1630. Of Essex. Matric. 1631. Perhaps s. and h. of Giles, of Warley, Essex, Esq.; adm. at Lincoln's Inn, June 13, 1632. Of Warley Place, 'Captain.' (*Vis. of Essex*, 1634.)

FLEMING, JOHN. Adm. sizar (age 17) at ST JOHN'S, Mar. 14, 1722–3. S. of William, barrister, of Yorkshire. B. at Kippax. Bapt. May 22, 1706. Schools, Sherburn and Wakefield. Matric. 1723; B.A. 1726–7. Ord. priest (York) Aug. 16, 1730; C. of Monk Fryston, Yorks. V. of Thorner, 1731–69. Died Nov. 1769. (*Scott-Mayor*, III. 359.)

FLEMMING, JOSEPH. Matric. sizar from ST JOHN'S, Easter, 1602; B.A. 1605–6; M.A. 1609. R. of Ellough, Suffolk, 1610–18. R. of Barsham, 1617–36. Buried there June 6, 1636. (*Genealogist*, N.S., 23, 14.)

FLEMMING, NICHOLAS. Adm. pens. at PEMBROKE, June 13, 1683. Matric. from Exeter College, Oxford, Dec. 17, 1679, age 18. S. of Thomas, of Madren, Cornwall, gent. Bapt. there, Apr. 21, 1663. V. of Sancreed, Cornwall, 1692–1708. Buried Oct. 20, 1708. (*Al. Oxon.*; *Vis. of Cornwall.*)

FLEMIN, RICHARD. Matric. sizar from MAGDALENE, Easter, 1589; B.A. 1592–3; M.A. 1598.

FLEMING, RICHARD. Matric. sizar from ST JOHN'S, c. 1594. Ord. deacon (Peterb.) May 19, 1611; priest, June 7, 1612, as M.A. Perhaps R. of Gt Orton, Cumberland, 1625–39. Buried there June 13, 1639. But *see Al. Oxon.* for another of the names.

FLEMING, ROGER. Adm. sizar (age 20) at ST JOHN'S, July 1, 1676. S. of John, of Newfield, Lancs. B. there. School, 'S. Byram.' Matric. 1676.

FLEMING, SAMUEL. Adm. at KING'S (age 17) a scholar from Eton, Aug. 27, 1565. Of London. Matric. 1565; B.A. 1569–70; M.A. 1573; B.D. 1580. Fellow, 1568–81. Ord. deacon and priest (Lincoln) Oct. 25, 1576. R. of Bottesford, Leics., 1581. R. of Cottenham, Cambs., 1581. Chaplain to the Earl of Rutland. Preb. of Southwell, 1609–20. Died at Cottenham, 1620. Admon. (P.C.C.) 1620. Brother of Abraham. (*Harwood.*)

FLEMYNG, THOMAS. Matric. pens. from EMMANUEL, 1586.

FLEMING, WILLIAM. B.Civ.L. 1508–9.

FLEMING, WILLIAM. Matric. sizar from ST JOHN'S, Easter, 1569; B.A. 1572–3; M.A. 1576. Fellow, 1577. Perhaps R. of Endgate, Beccles, 1580–1613. R. of Beccles, 1580. Deprived for nonconformity, 1584. (*Cooper*, I. 508.)

FLEMING, WILLIAM. Matric. pens. from TRINITY, c. 1591; B.A. 1595–6; M.A. 1599. Ord. deacon (Norwich) Oct. 3, 1596, age 24; priest, Mar. 25, 1597. C. of Morley, Norfolk. V. of Worstead, in 1603. R. of South Runcton, 1603–14. R. of Beeston Regis, 1612–22.

FLEMING, WILLIAM. Adm. sizar (age 19) at ST JOHN'S, Feb. 12, 1711–2. S. of William, glover. B. at Gt Urswick, near Ulverstone, Lancs. School, Little Urswick. Matric. 1712. Died in College. Buried at All Saints', Cambridge, May 4, 1712.

FLEMING, ——. Matric. Fell.-Com. from ST JOHN'S, c. 1594.

FLENT, OLIVER. Matric. pens. from CLEMENT HOSTEL, Easter, 1544.

FLENTON, GEORGE. B.Civ.L. 1520–1.

FLESHWAR, BERNARD. B.A. (? 1616–7); M.A. from St John's, 1620. R. of Saddington, Leics., 1628–46, sequestered.

FLESHER, JOHN (1685), *see* FLETCHER.

FLESHWAR or FLUSHWAR, RICHARD. Matric. sizar from Trinity, Easter, 1606.

FLETCHER, BARTHOLOMEW. Adm. pens. (age 18) at Caius, Apr. 23, 1645. S. of Thomas (1609), reader at Lincoln's Inn. B. at Braconash, Norfolk. Schools, Bury and London (Mr Ridley). Matric. 1645; Scholar, 1645–7. Adm. at Lincoln's Inn, May 8, 1647. Brother of John (1644) and William (1638). (*Venn*, I. 357.)

FLETCHER, BASIL. Adm. sizar at Trinity, June 22, 1665. Matric. 1665; B.A. 1668–9. Ord. deacon (Peterb.) Sept. 24, 1670; priest, Sept. 21, 1673.

FLETCHER, CARTER. Adm. sizar (age 17) at St John's, May 20, 1749. S. of Henry (1717), V. of Spondon, Derbs. B. at Spondon. School, Mansfield, Notts. Matric. 1749; B.A. 1753. Ord. deacon (Lichfield) Sept. 22, 1754; priest, Sept. 19, 1756. V. of Boylestone, Derbs., 1761–1808. Died July 11, 1808. M.I. at Boylestone. (*Scott-Mayor*, III. 589.)

FLETCHER, CHARLES. Adm. at Clare, Feb. 22, 1682–3. Of Harrold, Beds. Matric. 1683; B.A. 1686–7; M.A. 1690. Fellow, 1689. Ord. priest (Lincoln) July 27, 1690. R. of Clophill, Beds., 1690–1731.

FLETCHER, CHRISTOPHER. Matric. sizar from Magdalene, *c.* 1596.

FLETCHER, DAKINS. Matric. sizar from Trinity, Easter, 1617; B.A. 1619–20. Ord. deacon (York) Sept. 1622; priest, Sept. 1623.

FLETCHER, EDWARD. Adm. at Corpus Christi, 1591. Of London.

FLETCHER, EDWARD. Matric. pens. from Pembroke, Easter, 1626. S. of Henry, of Cumberland. B.A. 1629–30; M.A. 1633. Fellow, 1631.

FLETCHER, EDWARD. Adm. pens. (age 16) at Christ's, July 6, 1648. S. of Anthony, merchant, of York and Dordrecht. B. at Delft. School, York (Mr Wallis). Matric. 1648; B.A. 1651–2. Incorp. at Oxford, 1654. Adm. at Gray's Inn, Nov. 6, 1649. One of these names R. of Distington, Cumberland; died before Apr. 1669. (*Peile*, I. 523.)

FLETCHER, FRANCIS. Matric. sizar from Pembroke, Michs. 1564. One of these names adm. at Gray's Inn, 1567. Married, 1605, Margaret Gallard, of Tickhill, widow. Perhaps R. of Bradenham, Bucks., 1579–92; or V. of Tickhill, Yorks., 1596–1619.

FLETCHER, FRANCIS. Matric. sizar from Trinity, Michs. 1622; B.A. from St Catharine's, 1625. Ord. deacon (Peterb.) Sept. 25; priest, Sept. 26, 1625. V. of Husborne Crawley, Beds., 1625–8. Buried there, June 30, 1628. (W. M. Noble.)

FLETCHER, FRANCIS. Matric. pens. (age 17) from Pembroke, Easter, 1631. S. of Henry. B. at Moresby, Cumberland. B.A. 1634–5; M.A. 1638.

FLETCHER, GEORGE. Matric. pens. from Pembroke, Michs. 1606. Buried at Little St Mary's, Cambridge, Oct. 10, 1608.

FLETCHER, GEORGE. Adm. sizar (age 18) at St John's, June 1, 1747. S. of George, clerk, of Derbyshire, Head Master of Repton. B. at Repton. School, Repton. Matric. 1747; B.A. 1750–1; M.A. 1762. Ord. deacon (Lichfield) June 30, 1751; priest, June 17, 1753. R. of Cubley, Derbs., 1753–1800. R. of Barton Blount, 1762–76. Chaplain to George, Lord Vernon. R. of Sudbury, Derbs., 1776–80. R. of Mavesyn Ridware, Staffs., 1780–1800. Died Oct. 11, 1800. (*Scott-Mayor*, III. 567.)

FLETCHER, GILES. Adm. at King's (age 17) a scholar from Eton, 1565. S. of Richard, V. of Bishop's Stortford. B. at Watford. Matric. 1565; B.A. 1569–70; M.A. 1573; LL.D. 1581. Fellow, 1568–81. Deputy Public Orator, 1577–82. Chancellor of diocese of Chichester, 1582. M.P. for Winchelsea, 1584–6. Remembrancer for London, 1587–1605. Envoy to Russia, 1588. Treasurer of St Paul's, 1597–1611. Poet and traveller. Died Feb. 16, 1610–1. Will (P.C.C.) 1611; of St Catherine Coleman, London. Father of Phineas (1600) and Giles (1601), brother of Richard (1562). (*Cooper*, III. 35; *D.N.B.*)

FLETCHER, GILES. Matric. pens. from Trinity, Michs. 1601. S. of Giles (1565). Scholar, 1605; B.A. 1605–6; M.A. 1609; B.D. 1619. Fellow, 1608. Reader in Greek Grammar, 1615; and in Greek Language, 1618. Ord. deacon (Peterb.) Sept. 18; priest, Sept. 19, 1613. R. of Helmingham, Suffolk, 1617. R. of Alderton, till 1623. Poet. Died at Alderton, 1623. Brother of Phineas. (*D.N.B.*)

FLETCHER, HENRY. B.A. 1508–9; M.A. 1512; B.D. 1520–1. Fellow of Christ's, 1519–23. One of these names V. of Aylesford, Kent, 1521–4. V. of West or Town Malling, 1524. Will (P.C.C.) 1561.

FLETCHER, HENRY. Scholar of Christ's, 1518–9. (*Peile*, I. 13; where he seems confused with John, of 1517–8.)

FLETCHER, HENRY. Scholar of Trinity, 1560. S. of Henry, of Cockermouth, Cumberland. B. there *c.* 1539. B.A. 1560–1. Migrated as Fell.-Com. to Caius, Apr. 22, 1569; aged 26. Ord. deacon (London) Oct. 28, 1562; priest, Mar. 14, 1562–3. V. of St James, Clerkenwell, 1585–1607. Minor canon of St Paul's, 1595–1606. Buried there July 14, 1607. (*Venn*, I. 64.)

FLETCHER, HENRY. Matric. pens. from Jesus, Easter, 1565; B.A. from Clare, 1569–70; M.A. 1573; B.D. 1580. R. of Barnston, Essex, 1579–1610. R. of Little Easton, 1582–1634. Died 1634. Admon. (Consist. C. London) 1634. (J. Ch. Smith.)

FLETCHER, HENRY. Matric. pens. from Trinity, Michs. 1582. Will (York) of one of these names; of Chesterfield, clerk.

FLETCHER, HENRY. Adm. sizar at Emmanuel, Apr. 8, 1717. Of Derbyshire. S. of Samuel (1681–2), V. of Spondon. Exhibitioner from Derby School. Matric. 1717. V. of Spondon, 1723–61. Brother of Samuel (1708–9), father of Carter (1749).

FLETCHER, ISAAC. Adm. pens. at Peterhouse, May 27, 1592. Matric. *c.* 1592.

FLETCHER, JAMES. Scholar of Queens', 1555–7. One of these names V. of Yoxford, Suffolk, 1554–7.

FLETCHER, JAMES. Adm. sizar (age 16) at Caius, Mar. 24, 1587–8. S. of Henry, yeoman, of Leeds. School, Leeds. Matric. 1587.

FLETCHER, JAMES. Adm. sizar (age 18) at St John's, May 14, 1655. S. of John, of Bury, Lancs., chapman. B. at Bury. School, Bolton. Matric. 1655; B.D. 1669 (*Lit. Reg.*). Incorp. at Oxford, 1675. Perhaps V. of Chipping Walden, Essex, 1664–74. Probably father of James (1676).

FLETCHER, JAMES. Adm. pens. (age 16) at Jesus, Oct. 17, 1676. S. of James (? 1655), clerk, of Essex. Matric. 1676; Scholar, 1680; B.A. 1680–1. R. of Mobberley, Cheshire, 1690–1733. Died 1733.

FLETCHER, JAMES. Adm. sizar at Emmanuel, Apr. 29, 1717. Of Gloucester. Matric. 1719; B.A. 1720–1.

FLETCHER, JOHN. B.A. 1517–8; M.A. 1521. Probably fellow of St John's, 1520. Ord. sub-deacon (Ely) Apr. 23, 1519.

FLETCHER, JOHN. B.Civ.L. 1524–5. A priest.

FLETCHER, JOHN. Adm. pens. (age 18) at Caius, Oct. 3, 1569. S. of Robert, of Tivetshall, Norfolk. School, Tivetshall. Migrated to Corpus Christi, 1569. Matric. 1569; B.A. 1572–3.

FLETCHER, JOHN. Adm. pens. (age 21) at Caius, Feb. 5, 1577–8. S. of Thomas, husbandman. B. at Hebden, Yorks. School, Leeds (Mr Hargraves). Scholar, till 1584; B.A. 1580–1; M.A. 1584. Fellow, 1587–1613. Mathematician and astrologer. Benefactor to Caius. Died in College, Oct. 14, 1613. Buried in the Chapel. Will proved (V.C.C.). (*Venn*, I. 95; Venn, *Early College Life*.)

FLETCHER, JOHN. Adm. at Corpus Christi, 1591. S. of Richard (1562), Bishop of London. B. at Rye, Dec. 20, 1579. B.A. 1594–5; M.A. 1598. The dramatist. For an account of his works *see D.N.B.* Buried Aug. 29, 1625, at St Saviour's, Southwark, in the same grave with Philip Massinger. Brother of Nathaniel (1590). (*D.N.B.*)

FLETCHER, JOHN. Matric. pens. from Trinity, *c.* 1595; Scholar, 1599; B.A. 1599–1600. Ord. deacon (Colchester) Nov. 16; priest, Nov. 23, 1600. V. of Kirton, Suffolk, 1603.

FLETCHER, JOHN. B.A. (? 1602–3); M.A. from Queens', 1606.

FLETCHER, JOHN. Adm. pens. at Queens', July 7, 1604. Of Sussex.

FLETCHER, JOHN. Matric. pens. from Pembroke, Michs. 1613. S. of Thomas, skinner, of London (will, P.C.C. 1617). B. July, 1596. School, Merchant Taylors'. B.A. 1617–8. Adm. at Lincoln's Inn, May 14, 1617.

FLETCHER, JOHN. Matric. pens. from Christ's, Dec. 1614.

FLETCHER, JOHN. Adm. pens. (age 15) at Christ's, May 15, 1644. 3rd s. of Thomas (1609), of Bury, bencher of Lincoln's Inn. B. at Bracon-Ash, Norfolk. Schools, Bury (Mr Stephens) and Pakenham (Mr Wright). Adm. at Lincoln's Inn, May 8, 1647. Brother of Bartholomew (1645) and William (1638).

FLETCHER or FLESHER, JOHN. Matric. sizar from Trinity Hall, Easter, 1685.

FLETCHER, JOHN. Adm. sizar (age 19) at St John's, July 4, 1737. S. of John, gent., of Cumberland. B. at Westward. School, Appleby. Matric. 1737; B.A. 1740–1.

FLETCHER, JOSEPH. Matric. sizar from CORPUS CHRISTI, 1595. Of Yorkshire. Perhaps the same who graduated B.A. from St Catharine's, 1605–6; M.A. 1609. The religious poet, R. of Wilby, Suffolk, was probably an Oxford contemporary (*see D.N.B.*).

FLETCHER, JOSEPH. Adm. sizar at EMMANUEL, Dec. 26, 1664. Of Derbyshire. Matric. 1665; B.A. 1668–9.

FLETCHER, LANCELOT. Matric. pens. from TRINITY, Lent, 1580–1. Perhaps s. of Henry, of Cockermouth, Cumberland. B.A. 1584–5; M.A. 1588. R. of Dean, Cumberland, 1593–1635. Died 1635. Father of the next.

FLETCHER, LANCELOT. Adm. pens. (age 18) at PEMBROKE, Dec. 20, 1624. S. of Lancelot (1580), of Cumberland, clerk. Matric. 1626; B.A. 1627–8; M.A. 1631. R. of Plumbland, Cumberland, 1628–47. R. of Dean, 1635–64. Died Feb. 7, 1663–4. Buried at Dean. Admon. (Archd. Richmond) 1664. Father of William (1651). (*B. Nightingale.*)

FLETCHER, NATHANIEL. Adm. pens. at QUEENS', Oct. 1590. Of Sussex. S. of Richard (1562), Bishop of London. B. at Rye, 1575. Matric. 1590; B.A. 1592–3; M.A. 1597; B.D. 1606. Fellow, 1594–1611. R. of Barking and Darmsden, Suffolk, 1609. Father of Toby (1645), brother of John (1591).

FLETCHER, PHILIP. Matric. sizar from TRINITY HALL, Easter, 1629. One of these names R. of Todwick, Yorks. Buried there 1660. Admon. (York) 1661.

FLETCHER, PHINEAS. Adm. at KING'S, a scholar from Eton, 1600. S. of Giles (1565). Bapt. at Cranbrook, Kent, Apr. 8, 1582. B.A. 1604–5; M.A. 1608. Fellow, 1603–16. Chaplain to Sir Henry Willoughby. R. of Hilgay, Norfolk, 1620–50. Poet. Died 1650. Brother of Giles (1601), father of William (1645). (*D.N.B.*)

FLETCHER, RICHARD. M.A. of Cambridge. Adm. *c.* 1540. Of the Province of York. Ord. by Bishop Ridley, *c.* 1548. V. of Bishop's Stortford, Herts., 1551–5. At Frittenden, Kent, in 1557. V. of Cranbrook, Kent, 1559–86. R. of Smarden, 1566–86. Died Feb. 12, 1585–6, aged 63. Buried at Cranbrook. M.I. there which states his Cambridge connection, and mentions, Richard (next) and Giles (1565). (H. G. Harrison.)

FLETCHER, RICHARD. Matric. pens. from TRINITY, Michs. 1562. S. of Richard (above), V. of Cranbrook, Kent. B. at Watford, Herts. Scholar, 1563; B.A. 1565–6; M.A. from Corpus Christi, 1569; B.D. 1576; D.D. 1580. Fellow of Corpus Christi, 1569–73. Incorp. at Oxford, 1572. Ord. deacon (London) Sept. 19, 1569. Preb. of St Paul's, 1572–89. Chaplain to the Queen. V. of Rye, Sussex, 1574. Preacher in Chichester diocese. Dean of Peterborough, 1583–89. Attended Mary, Queen of Scots, at her execution, Feb. 18, 1586–7. Preb. of Lincoln, 1586–92. R. of Barnack, Northants., 1586. R. of Alderkirk, Lincs. Bishop of Bristol, 1589–92; of Worcester, 1593–4; and of London, 1594–6. Adm. at Gray's Inn, Feb. 20, 1593–4. Suspended by the Queen for some time on account of his second marriage. Died June 15, 1596. Buried in St Paul's Cathedral. Will, P.C.C. Father of John (1591) and of Nathaniel (1590), brother of Giles (1565). (*Cooper*, II. 205; *D.N.B.*; *N. and Q.*, S. I., VI. 511.)

FLETCHER, RICHARD. Adm. at CORPUS CHRISTI, 1592. Of Yorkshire. B.A. 1596.

FLETCHER, RICHARD. B.A. from ST JOHN'S, 1607–8; M.A. 1611. B. in Bangor. Fellow of Jesus, 1611–7. Died at Saffron Walden. Buried there June 12, 1617. Will (V.C.C.). (A. Gray.)

FLETCHER, RICHARD. Adm. sizar (age 19) at ST JOHN'S, July 2, 1631. S. of Thomas, of Bilsdale (? Billesdon), Leics. B. there. School, Winchester. Matric. 1631; B.A. 1634–5.

FLETCHER, RICHARD. Adm. sizar at TRINITY, Apr. 29, 1661. Migrated (age 16) to St John's, June 26, 1662. S. of William, deceased, of Aston, Yorks. B. there. School, Doncaster. B.A. 1664–5; M.A. 1668. Ord. deacon (Ely) Dec. 22, 1667; priest (York) Feb. 1675–6.

FLETCHER, RICHARD. Adm. sizar (age 18) at TRINITY, Feb. 18, 1686–7. 'Grecian' from Christ's Hospital. S. of Francis, citizen and grocer, of St Stephen, Walbrook, London. Matric. 1686–7; Scholar, 1689; B.A. 1690–1; M.A. 1694. Ord. priest (London) Feb. 17, 1694–5. Will of one of these names (P.C.C.) 1697; of London, chaplain of H.M. ship *Cambridge*.

FLETCHER, RICHARD. Adm. sizar at EMMANUEL, Mar. 4, 1719–20. Of Kent. Matric. 1720; B.A. 1723–4; M.A. 1728. Incorp. at Oxford, 1728. Ord. deacon (London) Mar. 16, 1725–6. V. of Bobbing, Kent, 1726. R. of St Mary, Hoo, 1753–62. R. of High Halstow, 1753–62. Buried at Milton-by-Sittingbourne, Dec. 22, 1762. Will (P.C.C.) 1763.

FLETCHER, ROBERT. Resident student at TRINITY HALL, Aug. 1564. Will of one of these names (P.C.C.) 1606; R. of Mawgan-in-Kerrier, Cornwall.

FLETCHER, SAMUEL. Adm. sizar at EMMANUEL, Feb. 9, 1681–2. Of Derbyshire. School, Derby. Matric. 1683; B.A. 1685–6; M.A. 1689. V. of Spondon, Derbs., 1695–1719. Father of the next and of Henry (1717).

FLETCHER, SAMUEL. Adm. sizar at EMMANUEL, Jan. 8, 1708–9. S. of Samuel (above), V. of Spondon, Derbs. School, Derby. Matric. 1710; Scholar; B.A. 1713–4; M.A. 1717. Fellow, 1716. Ord. deacon (Peterb.) Sept. 22, 1716. V. of Fressingfield, Suffolk. Brother of Henry (1717).

FLETCHER or FLETHAR, THOMAS. B.A. 1503–4.

FLETCHER, THOMAS. B.A. 1513–4.

FLETCHER, THOMAS. Adm. pens. (age 18) at CAIUS, June 21, 1585. S. of John, of North Elmham, Norfolk. Bapt. there, Sept. 7, 1567. Schools, Norwich (Mr Limbert) and East Dereham (Mr Paynter). Scholar, 1585; B.A. 1588–9. Died in College. Buried in St Michael's, Mar. 7, 1588–9. (*Venn*, I. 125.)

FLETCHER, THOMAS. Matric. pens. from CHRIST'S, July, 1609. S. of Bartholomew, of Campsall, Yorks. Bapt. there, Dec. 4, 1594. B.A. 1612–3. Incorp. at Oxford, as 'M.A.' 1618. Adm. at Lincoln's Inn, May 20, 1615. Barrister, 1622. Bencher, 1639. Reader, 1640. Treasurer, 1652. Sergeant-at-Law, 1654. Died Feb. 4, 1656–7. Buried at Croxton, Norfolk. M.I. there. Father of William (1638), of Bartholomew (1645) and of John (1644). (*Peile*, I. 272; *Vis. of Yorks.*, 1665; Le Neve, *Mon.*, III. 29.)

FLETCHER, THOMAS. Matric. pens. from PEMBROKE, Michs. 1615; B.A. 1618.

FLETCHER, THOMAS. Adm. sizar (age 14) at CAIUS, July 17, 1625. S. of Roger, gent., of St Ives. B. at Ely. School, St Ives (Mr Smith). Matric. 1625; B.A. 1629–30; M.A. 1635. C. of Stratford-le-Bow, in 1663. In a petition, Oct. 1663, he states that he 'has been constant, 22 years, in preaching and reading the Book of Common Prayer. Buried Abp. Laud, with that book, when others dared not; kept Christmas Day at St Giles Cripplegate, when others were shut, etc.' Will (Consist. C. London) 1672. (*Venn*, I. 271; *Cal. State Papers*.)

FLETCHER, THOMAS. Matric. sizar from CAIUS, Michs. 1627. Perhaps repetition of above.

FLETCHER, THOMAS. Matric. pens. from QUEENS', Easter, 1655. Of Yorkshire. B.A. 1658–9; M.A. 1662. Ord. deacon (Lincoln).

FLETCHER, THOMAS. Adm. pens. (age 18) at ST JOHN'S, Oct. 29, 1680. S. of Thomas, gent. B. at Bangor, Carnarv. School, Bangor. Matric. 1680–1.

FLETCHER, THOMAS. Adm. sizar (age 17) at PEMBROKE, June 19, 1728. S. of John, citizen and haberdasher of London. 'Grecian' from Christ's Hospital. Matric. 1728; B.A. 1731–2; M.A. 1735. Master of the Grammar School, Halstead, Essex, 1734–5. Died same year. (*A. W. Lockhart.*)

FLETCHER, THOMAS. Adm. sizar (age 18) at CHRIST'S, Apr. 9, 1743. S. of Joseph. B. at 'Stearndale,' Derbs. School, Tideswell (Mr Goddard). Matric. 1743; Scholar, 1744; B.A. 1746–7.

FLETCHER, TOBY. Adm. sizar (age 18) at CHRIST'S, June 12, 1645. S. of Nathaniel (1590). B. at Barking, Suffolk. School, Ipswich (Mr Woodseat). Matric. 1645; Scholar, 1648; B.A. 1648–9.

FLETCHER, WILLIAM. Matric. pens. from PETERHOUSE, Easter, 1584. Migrated to Oxford after four years. B.A. (Broadgates Hall) Dec. 1587; M.A. 1590. Perhaps R. of Martlesham, Suffolk, 1608.

FLETCHER, WILLIAM. Adm. pens. at CORPUS CHRISTI, 1592. B. at Monk Fryston, Yorks. Matric. *c.* 1593; B.A. 1596–7. Ord. deacon (London) Nov. 22; priest, Nov. 29, 1601, age 28. One of these names V. of Shackerstone, Leics., 1628. Perhaps father of William (1646).

FLETCHER, WILLIAM. Matric. pens. from ST JOHN'S, Easter, 1613. One of these names, s. and h. of Henry, of 'Morsbie,' Cambs., adm. at Gray's Inn, May 17, 1615.

FLETCHER, WILLIAM. Matric. sizar from ST JOHN'S, Easter, 1622; B.A. from Clare, 1626; M.A. 1630. Ord. deacon (Peterb.) June 5, 1631.

FLETCHER, WILLIAM. Matric. sizar from QUEENS', Easter, 1622. Of Leicestershire. B.A. 1625–6. Ord. deacon (Peterb.) May 23; priest, Sept. 19, 1624. One of these names R. of Aston, Yorks., 1631–51.

FLETCHER, WILLIAM. Adm. pens. (age 16) at CHRIST'S, Apr. 11, 1638. S. and h. of Thomas (1609), of Bury St Edmunds, Esq., bencher of Lincoln's Inn. B. at Tharston, Norfolk. Schools, Bury (Mr Dickenson) and Pakenham (Mr Wright). Adm. at Lincoln's Inn, Nov. 16, 1639. Brother of Bartholomew (1645) and John (1644).

FLETCHER, WILLIAM. Adm. sizar (age 16) at ST JOHN'S, June 24, 1645. S. of Phineas (1600), R. of Hilgay, Norfolk. Bapt. there, Oct. 12, 1628. School, Ely. Matric. 1646. Buried at Hilgay, Dec. 14, 1695. (*N. and Q.*, 6th S., I. 511.)

FLETCHER, WILLIAM. Adm. pens. (age 17) at PEMBROKE, June 27, 1646. S. of William (? 1592), clerk. B. in Leicestershire. Matric. 1646.

FLETCHER, WILLIAM. Adm. sizar (age 16) at ST JOHN'S, June 16, 1651. S. of Lancelot (1624), clerk, of Dean, near Cockermouth, Cumberland. B. there. School, Dean. Matric. 1651.

FLETCHER, WILLIAM. Adm. sizar at ST JOHN'S, Jan. 4, 1711-2. S. of John, deceased. B. at Hunslet, Leeds, Yorks. School, Sedbergh. Migrated to Trinity (age 22) Feb. 21, 1716-7. Scholar, 1717; B.A. 1717-8; M.A. 1721; B.D. 1728. Fellow, 1720. Ord. deacon (Ely) Sept. 21, 1718. V. of Hitchin, Herts., 1728-31. Died 1731.

FLETCHER, WILLIAM. Adm. at KING'S, a scholar from Eton, 1732. S. of John, R. of Wappenham, Northants. Bapt. there, Apr. 7, 1715. Matric. 1732-3; B.A. 1736-7; M.A. 1740. Fellow, 1736. Ord. deacon (Lincoln) June 5, 1737; priest, June 17, 1739. R. of Dunton, Essex. R. of Leire, Leics., 1741-7. Buried at Wappenham, Mar. 11, 1779; of Weedon Loys, Northants., clerk. Will (P.C.C.) 1780. (H. I. Longden.)

FLETE, *see* FLEET.

FLICKE, ANTHONY. Adm. pens. at EMMANUEL, 1640. Of Suffolk. Matric. 1640. One of these names, in 1652, proved the will (P.C.C.) of his father Robert, of Creeting St Peter, Suffolk. (J. Ch. Smith.)

FLICK, NATHANIEL. Adm. pens. at CORPUS CHRISTI, 1610. Of Suffolk. S. of Robert and Margaret. Bapt. at West Creeting, Suffolk, May 9, 1594. Matric. Easter, 1611; B.A. 1613-4; M.A. 1617; B.D. 1624. Fellow, 1616-24. Junior Proctor, 1622-3. Ord. deacon (Peterb.) Aug. 27; priest, Aug. 28, 1620. R. of Creeting St Peter, Suffolk, 1625-50, ejected. R. of Hardingham, Norfolk, 1632-41, ejected.

FLICK, SAMUEL. Adm. pens. at CORPUS CHRISTI, 1633. Of Suffolk. Probably s. of Samuel, and Sarah, of Creeting St Peter. Matric. Easter, 1634; B.A. 1637. Samuel and Nathaniel Flick were nephews of John Flick, of St Clement's, Ipswich, whose will (P.C.C.) 1631. (V. B. Redstone.)

FLIGHT, PHILIP. Adm. sizar at CORPUS CHRISTI, 1630. Matric. Easter, 1631; B.A. 1634-5; M.A. 1638. Ord. deacon (Norwich) Sept. 24, 1637; priest, Mar. 9, 1638-9. C. of Gt Fransham, Norfolk. R. of Winfarthing, 1641-3. Died 1643.

FLIGHT, ROBERT. Adm. pens. (age 16) at CAIUS, Sept. 28, 1606. S. of William, of Suffield, Norfolk. School, North Walsham (Mr Tilles). Scholar, 1606-10; Matric. 1607; B.A. 1609-10; M.A. 1613. R. of Gunton, Norfolk, 1614-20.

FLIGHT, W. Adm. pens. at CORPUS CHRISTI, 1566. Matric. Michs. 1567.

FLIGHT, ——. Fellow of GONVILLE HALL, 1454.

FLINT, ANTHONY. Adm. pens. (age 16) at CAIUS, May 29, 1623. S. of Robert, Esq., of Stuston, Suffolk. School, Stuston (Mr Hall). Matric. 1623; Scholar, 1624-8; B.A. 1626-7.

FLINTE, GEORGE. Matric. sizar from JESUS, Easter, 1617; B.A. 1620-1; M.A. 1629. Ord. deacon (York) Sept. 1621; priest, Dec. 1621. V. of Askham Richard, Yorks., 1625-69. Married, 1629, Elizabeth Scatcherd, of Wakefield. Died 1669. (*Yorks. Arch. and Top. Journal*, XV. 226.)

FLINT, HENRY. Adm. sizar at JESUS, July 2, 1631. Of Yorkshire. Matric. 1631; Scholar, 1634; B.A. 1634-5; M.A. 1638. Perhaps R. of Cowthorpe, Yorks., 1638-71. If so, died Mar. 8, 1671, aged 64. But one of these names, b. at Matlock, Derbs., emigrated to New England, in 1653. Teacher of the church at Braintree, Mass. Died there Apr. 27, 1668. (*Felt*, 387; J. G. Bartlett.)

FLINT, JAMES. Adm. sizar at CHRIST'S, May 20, 1625. S. of Stephen, of Northamptonshire. School, Tichmarsh (Mr Woolfall). Matric. 1625; B.A. from Jesus, 1628-9; M.A. 1636. Ord. deacon (Peterb.) May 23, 1630; priest, Sept. 20, 1635. Buried at Wellingborough, Northants., Dec. 30, 1642; Jacob Flint, minister of Haroden. (*Peile*, I. 367.)

FLINT, JOHN. Matric. pens. from CHRIST'S, Mar. 1582-3; B.A. 1586-7; M.A. 1590. R. of St Olave, Silver Street, London, 1592-(?) 1610. Mentioned by Andrew Willet, of Christ's, as one of the great preachers of the College.

FLINT, JOHN. Matric. sizar from TRINITY, *c.* 1595.

FLINT, JOHN. Matric. sizar from JESUS, Lent, 1618-9; B.A. 1623-4; M.A. 1629. Ord. deacon (York) Dec. 1625; priest, Mar. 1625-6. V. of Guilden Morden, Cambs., in 1625. V. of Hunsingore, Yorks., 1626. R. of Cowthorpe, 1632-8. Died 1638.

FLINT, LUKE. Adm. sizar (age 18) at CHRIST'S, June 3, 1693. S. of Francis. B. at Chesterfield. Schoolmaster, Mr Brown. Matric. 1693; Scholar, 1694-5; B.A. 1696-7. Ord. deacon (Lichfield) Sept. 1697. R. of Somershall Herbert, Derbs., 1705-21. Married Margaret, dau. of Robert Dale, of Parwick, Derbs. Died Oct. 30, 1721. Buried at Somershall. M.I. Father of Robert (1724). (*Peile*, II. 128; *F.M.G.*; Cox, *Churches of Derbs.*, III. 288.)

FLINT, ROBERT. Adm. pens. at CORPUS CHRISTI, 1557. Matric. Easter, 1559. One of these names adm. at Gray's Inn, 1565.

FLINT, ROBERT. Adm. sizar at JESUS, May 27, 1724, as 'George.' Of Derbyshire. S. of Luke (1693), deceased, R. of Somershall Herbert, Derbs. B.A. 1727-8; M.A. 1758. Ord. deacon (Chichester) 1728; priest, 1731. V. of Westbourne, Sussex, 1733-66. V. of Stoughton, 1734-66. Buried at Westbourne, Feb. 7, 1766. Admon. (P.C.C.) 1766. (A. Gray.)

FLINT, ROGER. Matric. pens. from CORPUS CHRISTI, Michs. 1632. B. in St Laurence, Norwich. B.A. 1636-7; M.A. 1640. Elected fellow, but not admitted. Ord. deacon (Norwich); priest, Dec. 18, 1642, age 25. R. of Gt Canfield, Essex, 1642. R. of Beeston Regis, Norfolk, 1661-85. R. of Runcton, till 1685. Author, sermon. Died Jan. 1685, aged 69. Buried at St Peter's, Hungate, Norwich. M.I. (*Masters*.)

FLINT, THOMAS. Adm. pens. at QUEENS', July 3, 1593. Of Warwickshire. Matric. from King's, *c.* 1593.

FLINT, THOMAS. Adm. pens. (age 18) at TRINITY, Jan. 9, 1688-9. S. of Thomas. B. at Allesley, Warws. School, Tamworth.

FLINT, WILLIAM. Adm. sizar at EMMANUEL, Easter, 1625; B.A. 1629-30; M.A. 1633.

FLINT, ——. Adm. pens. at ST CATHARINE'S, 1629.

FLINTOFT, LUKE. Adm. sizar at QUEENS', July 9, 1697. Of Yorkshire. Matric. 1697; B.A. 1700-1. Chaplain at King's College, 1700. Ord. deacon (Lincoln) June 29, 1701; priest, Dec. 20, 1702. Minor canon of Westminster. V. of Inkberrow, Yorks., 1713. Sworn a Gentleman of the Chapel Royal, Dec. 1715. Reader in Whitehall Chapel, 1719. Musical composer. Died Nov. 3, 1727. Buried in Westminster Abbey. Admon. (P.C.C.) 1727. (*D.N.B.*)

FLIXTON, ADAM DE. Capellanus of the University, 1293. (Stokes, *Chaplains*.)

FLOOD, *see* FLOYD *and* LLOYD.

FLORENCE, GARRET. Matric. pens. from JESUS, Easter, 1573.

FLOTE, JOHN. Matric. sizar from QUEENS', Easter, 1631. Of Sussex. B.A. 1634-5.

FLOTER, GILBERT. Fined for not proceeding in Grammar, 1431.

FLOTTER or FLOWTER, JOHN. M.A. 1473-4. Ord. subdeacon (Lincoln) Feb. 21, on title of HOUSE OF ST EDMUND, Cambridge; deacon, Mar. 11; priest, Mar. 24, 1474-5; 'of Gosberkirk.' Probably the 'J. Flottar' who left money to the University, 1479-80. (*Gr. Bk.* A, 136.)

FLOWE, EDWARD. Matric. sizar from JESUS, Michs. 1626.

FLOWER, ANTHONY. Matric. sizar from TRINITY, Easter, 1603.

FLOWER, BENJAMIN. Adm. pens. (age 19) at CHRIST'S, May 11, 1646. S. of Roger (1609), R. of Castle Combe, Wilts. B. there. School, Wotton-under-Edge (Mr Woodward). Matric. 1646. Ejected from Cardiff; then assisted his father at Castle Combe. Minister at Chippenham. Died Aug. 1709, 'aged 86.' (*Calamy*, II. 501; *Peile*, I. 506.)

FLOWER, CHRISTOPHER. Adm. at EMMANUEL, 1642. S. of Ralph, of London, gent. (Already matric. from Merton College, Oxford, Oct. 11, 1639, age 17.) Matric. 1642; B.A. 1643-4; M.A. 1647; D.D. 1660 (*Lit. Reg.*). Incorp. at Oxford, 1653. V. of Boldre, Hants., 1649. R. of St Margaret Lothbury, London, 1652-99. V. of St Peter-in-the-East, Oxford, 1667. R. of Naunton Beauchamp, Worcs., 1668. Married, July 21, 1653, at St Bartholomew-the-Great, Dorothy Hill. Died 1698-9. Buried in St Margaret's, Lothbury. (H. G. Harrison.)

FLOWER, EDWARD. Adm. pens. at EMMANUEL, Apr. 1607. S. of Thomas. B. at Hucknall Torkard, Notts. Matric. 1607; B.A. 1610-1; M.A. 1614; B.D. from Jesus, 1621. Fellow of Jesus, 1614-26. Ord. deacon (London) Dec. 24, 1620, age 28. V. of Elmstead, Essex, 1624-33. Chaplain to the Lord Treasurer. (*Vis. of Notts.*, 1614; A. Gray.)

FLOWER, FRANCIS. Adm. Fell.-Com. at KING'S, Easter, 1574. Ord. deacon (Lincoln) Sept. 20, 1577; priest, Sept. 30, 1579. R. of Langar, Notts., 1580-8. Died 1588. (Contemporary in *Al. Oxon.*) (Godfrey, *Notts.*, 290.)

FLOWER, GEORGE. Matric. pens. from CHRIST'S, Nov. 1544.

FLOWER, GEORGE. Matric. pens. from TRINITY, Michs. 1551; Scholar, 1555. Perhaps B.A. (Oxford) 1558. R. of Tetford, Lincs., 1571; and of Wickenby, 1573. Preb. of Carlisle, 1577–82. Admon. (Lincoln) 1583. (*Al. Oxon.*) Perhaps the 'priest,' s. of Henry, of Langar, Notts. (*Vis. of Notts.*, 1614.)

FLOWER, GEORGE. Adm. sizar at JESUS, Apr. 17, 1719. Of Yorkshire. Matric. 1719; B.A. 1722–3. R. of Skelton, Yorks., 1727–30. Died 1730.

FLOWER, HENRY. Matric. pens. from QUEENS', Michs. 1579. Of Nottinghamshire. S. of Thomas, of Langar, Notts., adm. at Gray's Inn, June 7, 1581.

FLOWER, 'JAY.' Matric. pens. from CHRIST'S, Lent, 1584–5. Doubtless Jayre Flower, s. of John, of Edith-Weston, Rutland; adm. at Gray's Inn, May 19, 1587. Will (P.C.C.) 1625; of Whitwell, Rutland. (*Peile*, I. 181.)

FLOWER, JOHN. M.A. 1574 (Incorp. from Oxford). B. *c.* 1535. B.A. (Oxford) 1553; M.A. 1557–8. *Supp.* for B.D. 1565. Fellow of Magdalen College, Oxford. Ord. priest (Salisbury) 1561. Perhaps R. of Beckingham, Lincs.; and R. of Offord Darcy, Hunts., 1571–85. Preb. of Lincoln, 1572–85. Warden of Mere Hospital. Died 1585. Admon. (Lincoln) 1585. (But *see Al. Oxon.*)

FLOWER, JOHN. Matric. pens. from PEMBROKE, Easter, 1568; B.A. 1571–2; M.A. 1575. Fellow, 1572. Incorp. at Oxford, 1578. Probably preb. of St Paul's, 1579–99. R. of Stourmouth, Kent, 1580–99. Buried there May 22, 1599. Will, P.C.C.

FLOWER, JOHN. Matric. sizar from ST JOHN'S, Michs. 1601.

FLOWER, JOHN. Adm. pens. (age 18) at CAIUS, Apr. 9, 1607. Previously matric. from Gloucester Hall, Oxford, Jan. 17, 1600–1, age 9. S. of John, Esq., of Whitwell, Rutland. School, Billesdon, Leics. (Mr Cade). Matric. 1607. Of Whitwell, Esq. Married Jane, dau. of Ralph Sheldon, Esq. Perhaps adm. at Gray's Inn, Feb. 26, 1604–5. Brother of Ralph. (*Venn*, I. 195; *Vis. of Ruts.*, 1618.)

FLOWER, JOSHUA. Matric. sizar from JESUS, Michs. 1567; B.A. 1572–3. Ord. deacon (Peterb.) July 16, 1574; priest, Feb. 9, 1574–5. V. of Sutterton, Lincs., 1575.

FLOWER, RALPH. Adm. pens. (age 17) at CAIUS, Apr. 9, 1607. S. of John, Esq., of Whitwell, Ruts. School, Billesdon, Leics. (Mr Cade). Matric. 1607. Probably died young; not mentioned in the Rutland *Visitation*. Brother of John (1607).

FLOWER, RICHARD. B.A. 1522–3.

FLOWER, RICHARD. Adm. pens. at PETERHOUSE, Mar. 6, 1621–2. S. of James, of Ely. Matric. 1623; B.A. 1625–6; M.A. 1629. (*Vis. of Cambs.*, 1619.)

FLOWER, ROGER. B.A. 1609 (Incorp. from Oxford). Of Wiltshire. Matric. from Magdalen Hall, Oxford, Mar. 1, 1604–5, age 18; B.A. 1609; M.A. from PEMBROKE, 1611; elected 'tanquam socius.' R. of Castle Combe, Wilts., 1613; and of Little Cheverell, 1625. Father of Benjamin (1646). (*Al. Oxon.*).

FLOWER, ROGER. Matric. pens. from ST JOHN'S, Michs. 1617. One of these names, s. of John, of Whitwell, Yorks., adm. at the Middle Temple, Feb. 11, 1619–20. (*Add. Pedigrees*; *Vis. of Yorks.*, 1612.)

FLOWER, STEPHEN. Adm. sizar (age 18) at PETERHOUSE, June 26, 1669. Of Yorkshire. School, Allerton. Matric. 1669; Scholar, 1670; B.A. 1672–3; M.A. 1676. Incorp. at Oxford, 1676. Ord. deacon (London) June, 1672; priest (Lincoln) Mar. 23, 1672–3. V. of Barnby-in-the-Willows, Notts., 1675.

FLOWER, THOMAS. M.A. from JESUS, 1617 (Incorp. from Oxford); B.D. 1621. Already B.A. from Magdalen Hall, Oxford, 1613–4. Incorp. M.A. at Oxford, 1617.

FLOWER, WILLIAM. Adm. sizar (age 16) at CHRIST'S, May 21, 1658. S. of Thomas. B. at Northallerton, Yorks. School, Northallerton (Mr Smelt). B.A. 1661–2; M.A. 1665. Ord. deacon (Salisbury) Sept. 27, 1664; priest (London) June 9, 1666; C. of Radwinter, Essex. Perhaps V. of Leake, Northallerton, 1667. Died before Oct. 1683. (*Peile*, I. 581.)

FLOWER, ——. B.A. 1467–8. Perhaps John 'Pflore,' M.A.; fellow of CLARE, 1475.

FLOUR, ——. B.A. 1498–9.

FLOWER, ——. Adm. pens. at EMMANUEL, 1586.

FLOWERDAY, EDWARD. Matric. pens. from ST JOHN'S, Easter, 1585.

FLOWERDEW, EDWARD. Studied at Cambridge. 4th s. of John, of Hethersett, Norfolk. Adm. at the Inner Temple, Oct. 11, 1552. Autumn reader, 1569. Counsel to the Dean and Chapter of Norwich, 1571; and to the town of Yarmouth, 1573. M.P. for Castle Rising, 1572–84. Recorder of Gt Yarmouth, 1580. Serjeant-at-law, 1580. Baron of the Exchequer, 1584–86. Died on circuit of gaol-fever at Exeter, Mar. 31, 1586. Buried at Hethersett. Will, P.C.C. (*Cooper*, II. 5; *D.N.B.*; A. B. Beaven.)

FLOWERDEW, NATHANIEL. Adm. sizar (age 17) at CAIUS, Feb. 1, 1647–8. S. of Nathaniel, gent., of Farnham, Suffolk. B. there. Schools, Benhall (Mr Whight), Sternfield (Mr Bartlet) and Glemham (Mr Turner). Matric. 1647–8; Scholar, 1651–2; B.A. 1651–2. Probably the 'minister' buried at Walberswick, Dec. 31, 1659. (*Venn*, I. 370.)

FLOWERDEW, SAMUEL. Matric. pens. from CORPUS CHRISTI, Easter, 1654. Of Suffolk. B.A. 1657–8; M.A. 1661. Ord. deacon (Norwich) Sept. 1661; priest, Sept. 1679. C. of Lopham, Norfolk, 1675.

FLOWERDEW, STANLEY. Matric. pens. from TRINITY, Michs. 1612. S. and h. of Anthony, of Hethersett, Norfolk, Esq., and Martha, dau. of John Stanley, of Scotway, Norfolk. Adm. at Gray's Inn, Feb. 25, 1615–6. Will of one of these names (P.C.C.) 1620; of Scottow, Norfolk.

FLOWERDUE, WILLIAM. Matric. sizar from PEMBROKE, *c.* 1593; B.A. from Trinity, 1597–8. Ord. deacon (Norwich) June 29; priest, Sept. 29, 1599. R. of Brampton, Suffolk, 1601–6. R. of Ashby, Norfolk, 1606–18. R. of Helhoughton, 1606–18.

FLOWERY or FLOURY, WOOLSTONE. Adm. pens. at EMMANUEL, Sept. 10, 1595. Matric. *c.* 1595.

FLOYD or FLUD, ABIEL. Adm. sizar at EMMANUEL, 1618. S. of William, of Northampton, clerk. Bapt. there, at All Saints', June 29, 1600. Matric. Michs. 1618; B.A. 1621–2. Ord. deacon (Peterb.) June 8; priest, June 9, 1623. (H. I. Longden.)

FLUID, BRYAN. Matric. sizar from MAGDALENE, Easter, 1571. One of these names preb. of Lincoln, 1572–5. R. of Sudbrooke, Lincs., 1572–3. R. of East Hatley, Cambs., 1574–5.

FLOODE, DAVID. Matric. pens. from CHRIST'S, Michs. 1558. Perhaps ord. deacon (Ely) Dec. 19, 1563. Will (P.C.C.) 1621, of one of these names; V. of Cudham, Kent.

FLOODE, DAVID. Matric. pens. from CHRIST'S, Easter, 1561.

FLUDD, DAVID. Matric. pens. from QUEENS', *c.* 1591.

FLOYD, DAVID. Matric. pens. from MAGDALENE, *c.* 1594; B.A. from Jesus, 1599–1600. One of these names, of Llwydiarth, Anglesey, adm. at Gray's Inn, Feb. 20, 1601–2.

FLUED, DAVID. Adm. pens. at JESUS, Oct. 4, 1627.

FLOYD or FLUDD, EDWARD. Matric. pens. from JESUS, Michs. 1575; B.A. 1579–80; M.A. 1583. Incorp. at Oxford, 1586.

FLOOD or LLOYD, EDWARD. Adm. pens. at QUEENS', June 22, 1594. Of Salop. Matric. *c.* 1593.

FLOOD, EDWARD. Matric. pens. from ST JOHN'S, Michs. 1614; B.A. 1618–9, as Floyd; M.A. 1621, as Lloyd. The fellow, of 1618, was Edw. Lloyd, whom *see*.

FLUDD, EDWARD. Matric. pens. from MAGDALENE, Michs. 1639; B.A. 1639–40. One of these names, a 'preaching minister,' was V. of Yaxley, Hunts., in 1651. Apparently instituted in 1664.

FLUDD or LLOYD, GEORGE (1579), *see* LLOYD.

FLOYD or LLOYD, GEORGE. Matric. sizar from QUEENS', Easter, 1610. B. at Cherbury, Salop. B.A. from St John's, 1613–4; M.A. from Queens', 1617. Ord. deacon (London) Dec. 24, 1615, age 24.

FLUED, HENRY. Matric. sizar from JESUS, Michs. 1546.

FLUDD, HENRY. Adm. at CORPUS CHRISTI, 1557.

FLOODE, HENRY. Matric. pens. from CHRIST'S, Easter, 1561; B.A. 1563–4.

FLUED, HENRY. Matric. pens. from QUEENS', Easter, 1576. B. in Cambridgeshire. Perhaps ord. deacon at the College of Douay, 1588; sent to Valladolid, 1589. Became a Jesuit. Died in London, Mar. 7, 1640–1. (*Records S.J.*, I. 503.)

FLUDE, HERBERT. Matric. pens. from PETERHOUSE, Easter, 1562.

FLOYD, HUGH. B.A. from JESUS, 1601–2; M.A. 1605; D.D. 1617. Fellow, 1602–11. B. at Llwydiarth, Anglesey. R. of Woodford-by-Thrapston, Northants., 1609. R. of Barton Seagrave, 1610. Chaplain to James I. Archdeacon of Worcester, 1623–9. Buried at Barton Seagrave, July 18, 1629. Will, P.C.C. Father of the next. (A. Gray.)

FLOYD or LLOYD, HUGH. Adm. pens. at JESUS, June 5, 1628. Of Northamptonshire. S. of Hugh (above), R. of Barton Seagrave. Bapt. there, Sept. 22, 1611. Scholar, 1628; B.A. 1631–2; M.A. 1635; B.D. 1642. Incorp. at Oxford, 1634. Ord. priest (Peterb.) Mar. 10, 1638–9. Perhaps V. of Iver, Bucks., 1634. V. of Fordham, Cambs., 1661–89. R. of Cheveley, 1663–89.

FLOOD, HUMPHREY. Matric. pens. from JESUS, Michs. 1562.

FLUDD, JAMES. B.A. (? 1602-3); M.A. from CLARE, 1606; D.D. from Sidney, 1618. Fellow of Sidney. R. of Carlton *with* Willingham, Cambs., 1610. Perhaps V. of Swinstead, Lincs., 1618-26. Will (P.C.C.) 1626; of Newington, Surrey, D.D. Probably father of the next. (*Vis. of Cambs.*)

FLUDD, JAMES. Matric. pens. from TRINITY, Easter, 1628. Probably s. of the above. Scholar; B.A. 1631-2; M.A. 1635.

FLOWDE, JOHN. B.Civ.L. 1537-8.

FLUDE, JOHN. Matric. sizar from CHRIST'S, Feb. 1564-5. One of these names, of London, late of Clifford's Inn, was adm. at the Inner Temple, June 16, 1574. (*Peile*, I. 90.)

FLUDD, JOHN. Matric. sizar from JESUS, Michs. 1565.

FLUDD, JOHN. Matric. pens. from JESUS, Easter, 1566.

FLUDE, JOHN. Matric. pens. from QUEENS', Michs. 1567. One of these names adm. at the Inner Temple, 1574.

FLOYD or LLOYD, JOHN. Matric. sizar from JESUS, Michs. 1602. Ord. deacon (Peterb.) Dec. 22, 1605, as 'B.A.'

FLOUDE, JOHN. Matric. sizar from ST JOHN'S, Easter, 1607; B.A. 1610-1, as 'Flord.'

FLUD, JOHN. Adm. sizar (age 17) at CAIUS, July 25, 1626. S. of John, gent., of Cockley Cley, Norfolk. B. at Wells. School, Lynn (Mr Robinson). Matric. 1626. One of these names adm. at Leyden, 1649. (*Venn*, I. 278.)

FLUDD or LLOYD, JOHN. Adm. pens. (age 18) at ST JOHN'S, Nov. 6, 1637. S. of Evan, R. of Rhoscolyn, Anglesey. B. there. School, Bangor. Matric. 1637.

FLOYD or LLOYD, JOHN (1646), *see* LLOYD.

FLOYD or FLUDE, JOSEPH. Adm. sizar at EMMANUEL, May 23, 1684. Of Leicestershire. Matric. 1686; B.A. 1687-8.

FLOOD or FLOWD, LANCELOT. Matric. pens. from CHRIST'S, Nov. 1561.

FLUD, LEWIN. Matric. pens. from TRINITY, Easter, 1629; Scholar, 1631; B.A. 1631-2. Perhaps student at Leyden, July 25, 1634, as Levinus Fluvius.

FLUD, MEREDITH. Matric. pens. from ST JOHN'S, Michs. 1588; B.A. 1592-3; M.A. 1596.

FLUD, MICHAEL. Adm. at TRINITY, a scholar from Westminster, 1593; B.A. 1597-8; M.A. 1601. Ord. priest (Peterb.) Apr. 13, 1600. Minister at Stretham, Cambs., in 1629. P.C. of Knockholt, Kent. Buried Feb. 20, 1644.

FLOYD or LLOYD, PETER (1681), *see* LLOYD.

FLOOD, RALPH. Adm. at KING'S, a scholar from Eton, June 30, 1619. Of Hitcham, Bucks. Matric. 1619; B.A. 1622. Fellow, 1622-4. Drowned. Buried in the College Chapel. (*Harwood*.)

FLUDD, RALPH. Adm. pens. at TRINITY, June 27, 1663. Matric. 1663; Scholar, 1664; B.A. 1666-7.

FLUDE, RICHARD. Matric. pens. from CHRIST'S, May, 1571; B.A. 1574-5; M.A. 1578.

FLUDE, RICHARD. Matric. pens. from JESUS, Easter, 1574; B.A. 1577-8.

FLUDD, RICHARD. Matric. sizar from ST JOHN'S, Easter, 1586; B.A. 1589-90; M.A. 1593.

FLOUDE, RICHARD. Matric. sizar from ST JOHN'S, Lent, 1597-8; B.A. 1601-2.

FLOOD or LLOYD, ROBERT. Matric. sizar from ST JOHN'S, Michs. 1623; B.A. 1627-8; M.A. 1631.

FLUDD or LLOYD, ROBERT. Adm. pens. (age 16) at ST JOHN'S, Nov. 6, 1637. S. of Nathaniel, gent., deceased, of Chirk, Denbigh. B. at Llanrhaiadr, Denbigh. School, Bangor. Matric. 1637.

FLUD, ROGER. Matric. pens. from ST JOHN'S, Easter, 1588.

FLUD, ROGER. Matric. pens. from ST JOHN'S, *c.* 1593; B.A. 1596-7.

FLUD, SAMUEL. Adm. pens. at EMMANUEL, Apr. 30, 1597.

FLUED, SPLENDIAN. Matric. pens. from QUEENS', Easter, 1576. Probably of Enfield, Herts.; adm. at the Middle Temple, Jan. 27, 1582-3.

FLUDD, THOMAS. Licensed to practice medicine by the R.C.P. Oct. 17, 1595. 'Born in London; M.D. of Cambridge.' Not found in our records. (*Munk*, I. 107.)

FLOYD, FLUDD or LLOYD, THOMAS. Matric. sizar from JESUS, Easter, 1604. Ord. deacon (Peterb.) Feb. 21, 1607-8; priest, May 22, 1608. V. of Renhold, Beds., 1612, as 'B.A.' V. of Thurleigh, 1616-30. Married, at Renhold, Aug. 8, 1614, Elizabeth Pecke.

FLUED, WILLIAM. Esquire Bedell, 1549-*c.* 1550. Apparently not a graduate. (Stokes, *Bedells*, 81.)

FLUDE, WILLIAM. Matric. pens. from TRINITY HALL, Michs. 1556. R. of Ufford, Northants., 1559-74. R. of Stilton, Hunts., 1560-5. Preb. of Lincoln, 1569-74. One of these names, 'LL.B.,' was R. of Offord Cluny, Hunts., 1563-74. Died 1574. Will (P.C.C.) 1575. (T. P. Dorman.)

FLUDE, WILLIAM. Matric. pens. from PETERHOUSE, Michs. 1567. Ord. priest, Mar. 4, 1568-9. One of these names V. of Buckminster, Leics., in 1576. 'Aged 30; married; ord. by Bishop of Peterborough.' (*Lib. Cleri, Lincoln.*)

FLOYD, WILLIAM. Matric. pens. from ST JOHN'S, Easter, 1609.

FLOYD, WILLIAM. Matric. sizar from ST JOHN'S, Easter, 1613; B.A. 1616-7; M.A. 1620. One William Fludd, M.A., V. of Dorney, Bucks., 1633.

FLOYD, WILLIAM. Incorp. M.A. 1660, from Oxford. (Identification uncertain.)

FLUDE, ——. Matric. sizar from QUEENS', *c.* 1591.

FLOYER, SACHEVEREL. Adm. Fell.-Com. (age 20) at ST JOHN'S, May 29, 1719. S. of Ralph, gent., of Staffordshire. B. at Sutton. School, Tamworth. Matric. 1719. Of Hints Hall, Staffs. Married Susanna, dau. of John Floyer, of London, Esq. Died *s.p.* Aug. 6, 1735. (Burke, *L.G.*).

FLOYER, WILLIAM. Adm. pens. (age 18) at CHRIST'S, June 16, 1702. S. of Samuel. B. in London. Exhibitioner from Charterhouse. Scholar, 1702-3; Matric. 1704; B.A. 1705-6. V. of Belgrave *cum* Birstall and Thurmaston, Leics., 1720-49.

FLUCODE, THOMAS. Adm. at CORPUS CHRISTI, 1604. Of Cambridgeshire.

FLUETT, GILES. Matric. pens. from ST JOHN'S, Easter, 1555.

FLUSHWAR, RICHARD, *see* FLESHWAR.

FLY, JOHN. Adm. pens. at EMMANUEL, Aug. 11, 1635.

FLYER, FRANCIS. Matric. Fell.-Com. from TRINITY HALL, Easter, 1667. Doubtless s. and h. of Thomas (1638). Sheriff of Herts., 1688. Married Elizabeth, dau. of Edward Chester, of Cockenhatch, near Barkway. Died Jan. 12, 1722, aged 72. Brother of Thomas (1669), father of the next. (*Clutterbuck*, III. 446.)

FLYER, FRANCIS. Adm. pens. (age 17) at ST JOHN'S, Nov. 5, 1707. S. of Francis (above), Esq. B. at Cockenhatch, near Barkway, Herts. School, Bishop's Stortford. Matric. 1708. Died before 1722.

FLYER, RALPH. Adm. at KING'S, a scholar from Eton, 1645. S. of Francis, of Brent Pelham, Herts. B. in London, *c.* 1627. Matric. 1645; B.A. 1649; M.A. 1653; M.D. 1665. Fellow, 1648-84. Travelled in France and Italy. Died Jan. 20, 1683-4. Buried in the College Chapel. M.I. Brother of the next. (Le Neve, *Mon.*, v. 49.)

FLYER, THOMAS. Adm. at CORPUS CHRISTI, 1638. S. of Francis, of Hertfordshire. Died Jan. 1, 1658-9. Buried at Brent Pelham. Father of the next and of Francis (1667). (*Cussans*, VII. 1; *Vis. of London*, 1634.)

FLYER, THOMAS. Adm. at KING'S, a scholar from Eton, 1669. S. of Thomas (above). B. at Pelham, Herts. Matric. 1670; B.A. 1673; M.A. 1677. Fellow, *c.* 1672. Died 1680. Brother of Francis (1667). (*Harwood*.)

FOBERY, *see also* FOLBERY.

FOBERYE, ANTHONY. Matric. pens. from ST JOHN'S, Easter, 1583.

FOBERYE, ROBERT. Matric. pens. from ST JOHN'S, Easter, 1583.

FOCHE, HENRY. Adm. sizar at CLARE, Apr. 18, 1709. S. of William (1678). B. at Herne, Kent. Matric. 1709; B.A. 1712-3; M.A. from St John's, 1716; B.D. 1723. Fellow of St John's, 1713-26. Junior proctor, 1721-2. Ord. deacon (Ely) May 27, 1716; priest, Sept. 21, 1718. V. of Higham, Kent, 1725-32. Minor canon of Rochester, 1728-32. Died Feb. 6, 1731-2, aged 58. Buried at Higham. M.I. (*Scott-Mayor*; H. G. Harrison.)

FOOCHE, THOMAS. Adm. pens. at EMMANUEL, Apr. 16, 1630. Of Kent. Matric. 1631.

FOCHE, WILLIAM. Adm. pens. at CLARE, Apr. 17, 1678. Of Canterbury. 2nd s. of Henry, of Canterbury, Esq. Matric. 1678; B.A. 1681-2; M.A. 1685. Fellow, 1685. V. of Herne, Kent, 1689-1713. Died 1713. Buried at Herne. Father of Henry (1709). (*Vis. of Kent*, 1663.)

FOCKWELL, PHILIP, *see* FOXWELL.

FODEN, SAMUEL. Adm. pens. at JESUS, May 20, 1676. Of Staffordshire. Matric. 1676; B.A. 1679-80; M.A. 1683. Died Mar. 1688. ('Foden, of Fulford,' in *Staffs. Pedigrees*.)

FODEN, WILLIAM. Adm. pens. at JESUS, Apr. 30, 1703. Of Staffordshire. Matric. 1703; Scholar, 1704; B.A. 1706–7; M.A. 1722. Ord. deacon (Lichfield) May 30, 1708; priest (London) Sept. 24, 1710. R. of Market Overton, Rutland, 1725–40. R. of Deene, Northants., 1727–49. R. of Thorpe Achurch, 1743–8. R. of Easton-on-the-Hill, 1748–9. Died June 4, 1758. Will, P.C.C. (*G. Mag.*)

FOE, EDWARD. Matric. sizar from ST JOHN'S, Easter, 1575.

FOGG, ARTHUR. Adm. pens. (age 17) at ST JOHN'S, Apr. 22, 1686. S. of Laurence (1644), D.D. B. at Heaton-Norris (or Heaton-Mersey), Lancs. School, Eccles, Lancs. Matric. 1686; B.A. 1690–1; M.A. 1694; D.D. 1709. V. of St Oswald, Chester, 1699–1739. R. of Heswall, 1702–16. Preb. of Chester, 1702–39. R. of Doddleston, 1716–39. Died Jan. 8, 1739. Buried in Chester Cathedral. Father of John (1718), Orlando (1723) and Robert (1718). (*G. Mag.*)

FOGG, DANIEL. D.D. from JESUS, 1703. S. of D., of Oxford city, gent. Matric. from St Edmund's Hall, Oxford, July 12, 1670, age 13; B.A. (Queen's College, Oxford) 1674; M.A. 1676–7. P.C. of All Hallows, Staining, 1688–1728. Died May 5, 1728. Will, P.C.C. (*Al. Oxon.*)

FOGGE, JOHN. Adm. pens. (age 16) at ST JOHN'S, Apr. 26, 1718. S. of Arthur (1686), D.D. B. at Chester. School, Chester. Matric. 1718; B.A. 1721–2; M.A. 1725; B.D. 1733; D.D. 1745. Fellow, 1724–49. Ord. deacon (Lincoln) Sept. 19, 1725; priest, June 5, 1726. R. of Haselbury Bryan, Dorset, 1729–47. R. of Spofforth, Yorks., 1747–74. Preb. of Ripon, 1750–74. Preb. of York, 1756–74. Died in York, Apr. 20, 1774. Will, P.C.C. Brother of Orlando (1723) and Robert (1718). (*Scott-Mayor*, III. 317.)

FOGGE, LAURENCE. Adm. at EMMANUEL, Sept. 28, 1644. Migrated (age 16) at St John's, Aug. 2, 1645. S. of Robert (1612), clerk. B. at Preston, Lancs. School, Bolton. Matric. 1645; B.A. 1648–9; M.A. 1652; B.D. 1659; D.D. 1679. Fellow of St John's, 1650. Taxor, 1657. Approved for presbyterian orders, June 16, 1658. R. of Hawarden, till 1662. Afterwards conformed. R. of Wicken Bonant, Essex, 1668–71. V. of St Oswald, Chester, 1672–99. V. of Plemondstall, 1673. Preb. of Chester, 1673–91. Dean, 1691–1718. Author, theological. Died Feb. 27, 1717–8. Buried in Chester Cathedral. Father of Arthur (1686). (*D.N.B.*)

FOGGE, ORLANDO. Adm. pens. at EMMANUEL, Sept. 28, 1644. Migrated (age 19) at St John's, Aug. 2, 1645. S. of Robert (1612), R. of Hoole. B. at Preston, Lancs. School, Wigan. Matric. 1645; B.A. 1648–9; M.A. 1652. Received presbyterian ordination, and afterwards episcopal. R. of Hawarden, Cheshire, 1662–6. Died at Shrewsbury, c. Nov. 10, 1666. M.I. at St Mary's, Shrewsbury.

FOGG, ORLANDO. Adm. pens. (age 17) at ST JOHN'S, Oct. 26, 1723. S. of Arthur (1686), D.D. B. in Chester. School, Chester. Matric. 1723; B.A. 1727–8; M.A. 1731. Ord. deacon (Chester) June 16, 1728; priest, Sept. 31, 1729. C. of Halton, Cheshire, 1736. Brother of Robert (1718) and John (1718). (*Scott-Mayor*, III. 364.)

FOGGE, ROBERT. Adm. pens. at SIDNEY, June 25, 1612. Matric. 1612; B.A. from St John's, 1615–6; M.A. 1619. Incorp. at Oxford, 1616. Ord. deacon (Peterb.) Mar. 1; priest, Mar. 2, 1617–8. (Perhaps, as in *Al. Oxon.*, R. of Moresby, Cumberland, 1618; and of Grasmere, Westmorland, 1627. But Robert Fogge, of Longthorpe, Northants., clerk, was licensed, Apr. 22, 1624, to marry Ann Robinson.) Chaplain to Col. Myttou, of the Parliamentary army. R. of Hoole, Lancs., 1641–7. R. of Bangor-is-Coed, Flints., 1646–62, ejected. Died at Nantwich, Cheshire, 1676, aged 80. Father of Laurence (1644) and Orlando (1644). (*Calamy*, II. 605; Phillips' *Civil War in Wales*.)

FOGGE, ROBERT. Adm. pens. (age 17) at ST JOHN'S, Apr. 26, 1718. S. of Arthur (1686), D.D. B. at Chester. School, Chester. Matric. 1718; B.A. 1721–2; M.A. 1725. Ord. deacon (Chester) July 28, 1723; priest, June 20, 1725. Minor canon of Chester. R. of Handley, Cheshire, 1730–5. Died 1735. Brother of John (1718) and Orlando (1723). (*Scott-Mayor*, III. 317.)

FOGG, TIMOTHY. Adm. sizar (age 15) at ST JOHN'S, June 29, 1676. S. of John, deceased, of Liverpool. B. there. School, Chester. Matric. 1676.

FOGGERTHWAITE, GEORGE. Adm. sizar (age 18) at MAGDALENE, May 5, 1670. S. of John, of Richmond, Yorks. School, Richmond. Matric. 1670; B.A. 1673–4. Ord. deacon (York) June, 1674; priest, Dec. 1674.

FOLBERY, *see also* **FOBERY.**

FOLBERY, GEORGE. B.A. 1514–5; M.A. 1517; B.D. 1524; D.D. (Montpelier). Fellow of CLARE, 1515. Fellow of Pembroke. University preacher, 1519. Master of Pembroke, 1537–40. R. of Maidwell St Mary, Northants., 1534–7. Poet, orator, and epigrammatist. Died c. Oct. 1540. Buried at St Mary-the-less, Cambridge. Will (V.C.C.) 1540. Of the family of Fowbery, of Fowbery, Chatton, Northumberland. (*Cooper*, I. 76; *D.N.B.*; *Vis. of Yorks.*, 1585; H. M. Wood.)

FOLBERY, JOHN. B.A. 1538–9. Of Northumberland. M.A. 1542. Fellow of PEMBROKE, 1539.

FOLCHAM or FOLSAM, THOMAS. B.Can.L. 1504–5.

FOLCHIER, *see also* **FULCHER.**

FOLCHIER, FRANCIS. M.A. 1690 (*Com. Reg.*). Perhaps V. of Calton and of Lakenham, Norfolk, 1692–1715, deprived.

FOLCHIER, JOHN. Adm. pens. at CLARE, May 22, 1707. B. at Norwich. Matric. 1707. Perhaps adm. student at Leyden, Apr. 10, 1710, as Folkier.

FOLDINGTON, JOHN. Matric. sizar from ST JOHN'S, c. 1597. *See* **FOLKINGHAM.**

FOLDS, THOMAS. Adm. sizar at CHRIST'S, Feb. 25, 1642–3. S. of William. B. at Loughborough, Leics. School, Loughborough (Mr Laughtonhouse). Matric. 1645; B.A. 1646–7.

FOLDS or FOWLDS, WILLIAM. Adm. sizar (age 22) at ST JOHN'S, May 9, 1705. S. of John, deceased. B. at Burnley, Lancs. School, Burnley. Matric. 1705; B.A. 1708–9. Ord. deacon (London) July 4, 1710; priest, Sept. 23, 1711.

FOLE, ROBERT. Matric. sizar from PEMBROKE, Michs. 1564; B.A. 1570–1.

FOLEY, EDWARD. Matric. pens. from CLARE, Easter, 1631.

FOLEY, JOHN. Incorp. M.B. 1681, from Trinity College, Dublin. Adm. there, Aug. 6, 1673, age 14; B.A. 1677; M.B. 1680. 2nd s. of Samuel, of Clonmel and Dublin. Incorp. at Pembroke College, Oxford, 1687. M.D. (Oxford) 1687. Of Cheshire. Buried at Stockport. Brother of Samuel (1681). (Burke, *Ext. Bart.*)

FOLEY, PHILIP. Adm. pens. (age 18) at CAIUS, Apr. 7, 1703. S. of Robert, Esq., of Stourbridge, Worcs. B. in London. Schools, Hartlebury, Worcs. (private; Mr Perse) and Charterhouse. Matric. 1703; Scholar, 1703–5. Migrated to Peterhouse, Mar. 31, 1705. Scholar there, 1705; B.A. 1706–7; M.A. 1710. Fellow of Peterhouse, 1707–16. Moderator, 1712. Incorp. at Oxford, 1712. Ord. deacon (Peterb.) June 3, 1710; priest (Ely) Feb. 25, 1710–1. Died June 12, 1716. M.I. in Old Swinford Church. (*Venn*, I. 510.)

FOLEY, PHILIP. Adm. sizar (age 18) at TRINITY, Nov. 23, 1739. S. of Robert, of Stourbridge, Worcs. School, Newport, Shrops. (Mr Lea). Matric. 1740; Scholar, 1740; B.A. 1743–4; M.A. 1747. Ord. deacon (Lincoln) June 11, 1744; priest, Dec. 22, 1745. Chaplain of Trinity, 1746–57. V. of Barrington, Cambs., 1750. R. of Shelsley Beauchamp, Worcs., 1764–75. Admon. P.C.C.

FOLEY, ROBERT. Adm. pens. (age 18) at TRINITY, Apr. 11, 1737. S. of Thomas (1711), of Stoke Edith, Heref. School, Bury, Suffolk (Mr Kyunesman). Matric. 1738; Scholar, 1738; B.A. 1740–1; M.A. 1744; D.D. 1756. Fellow, 1743. Adm. at the Inner Temple, Dec. 17, 1734. Ord. priest (Norwich) June, 1745. V. of Newent, Gloucs., 1762. R. of Kingham, Oxon. Dean of Worcester, 1778–83. Died Jan. 8, 1783. Buried at Worcester. Will, P.C.C. Brother of Thomas (1732). (F. S. Hockaday.)

FOLEY, SAMUEL. M.A. 1681 (Incorp. from Trinity College, Dublin). Adm. there, June 8, 1672, age 16; B.A. 1675; M.A. 1678; D.D. 1691. Fellow. 1st s. of Samuel, of Clonmel, and Dublin. Chancellor of St Patrick's, Dublin, 1689–94. Dean of Achonry, 1691–4. Bishop of Down and Connor, Ireland, 1694–5. Died May 22, 1695. Will, Dublin. Brother of John (1681). (Burke, *Ext. Bart.*; A. B. Beaven.)

FOLEY, THOMAS. Adm. Fell.-Com. (age 16) at PEMBROKE, July 4, 1657. S. of Thomas, Esq., of Whitley, Worcs. B. at Stourbridge, Worcs. Matric. 1659; B.A. 1659–60. Adm. at the Inner Temple, 1657. M.P. for Co. Worcs., 1679–81, 1689–98; for Droitwich, 1699–1701. Died Feb. 1, 1701–2. Will (P.C.C.) 1702. (A. B. Beaven.)

FOLEY, THOMAS. Adm. Fell.-Com. (age 16) at TRINITY, Sept. 18, 1711. S. of Thomas, of Stoke Edith, Heref. School, Hereford (Mr Rodd). Matric. 1712; M.A. 1728 (*Com. Reg.*). M.P. for Hereford, 1734–41; for Co. Hereford, 1742–7. Died Apr. 3, 1749. Father of the next and of Robert (1737). (*Nash*, II. 465.)

FOLEY, THOMAS. Adm. Fell.-Com. (age 16) at TRINITY, Sept. 27, 1732. S. of Thomas (above), of Stoke Edith, Heref. School, Westminster. Matric. 1732; B.A. 1735–6; M.A. 1739. M.P. for Droitwich, 1741–7, 1754–67; for Co. Hereford, 1767–75. Heir to Thomas, Lord Foley. Succeeded to his estate, 1766. Recorder of Droitwich. Created Baron Foley of Kidderminster, 1776. Died Nov. 14, 1777. Brother of Robert (1737). (*Nash*, II. 465.)

FOLJAMBE, FRANCIS. Adm. pens. (age 18) at ST JOHN'S, June 27, 1661. S. of Peter, Esq., of Milford-in-Sherburn, Yorks. B. there. Bapt. Feb. 26, 1643–4. School, Sherburn. Matric. 1661. Adm. at Gray's Inn, Dec. 2, 1664. Of Aldwark and Steeton, Yorks., Esq. Married, at Westow, Sept. 17, 1668, Elizabeth, dau. of George Montague, of Westow. Died at Aldwark, May 15, 1707. Buried at Ecclesfield, May 19. M.I. there. Father of the next, brother of Godfrey (1661). (Hunter, S. *Yorks.*, II. 61; Burke, *L.G.*; *Vis. of Yorks.*, 1665; M. H. Peacock.)

FOLJAMBE, FRANCIS. Adm. pens. (age 17) at ST JOHN'S, Sept. 7, 1692. 3rd s. of Francis, gent. (1661). B. at Westow, near Malton, Yorks. (mother's home), Aug. 9, 1675. School, Worsbrough. Matric. 1693. Adm. at the Inner Temple, Apr. 30, 1695. Succeeded his father at Aldwark. Died Dec. 6, 1752. Buried at Ecclesfield. Father of the next. (Hunter, S. *Yorks.*, II. 61; M. H. Peacock.)

FOLJAMBE, FRANCIS. Adm. Fell.-Com. (age 18) at ST JOHN'S, Apr. 20, 1723. S. of Francis (1692), Esq., of Aldwark, Yorks. B. at Aldwark. Bapt. Oct. 24, 1704, at Ecclesfield. School, Kirk Leatham. Adm. at the Inner Temple, Feb. 23, 1724–5. Died at St Germains, France, Jan. 19, 1726–7. Buried at Ecclesfield, Apr. 1, 1727. (*Scott-Mayor*, III. 361.)

FOLJAMBE, GODFREY. Matric. Fell.-Com. from MAGDALENE, Michs. 1567. S. of Godfrey, of Morehall, Derbs. B.A. 1568–9. Married Jane, dau. of Richard Trentham. Died Nov. 15, 1591. Buried at Brampton, near Chesterfield. Will, P.C.C. (*Cooper*, II. 274; *Hunter*, II. 60.)

FOLJAMBE, GODFREY. Matric. Fell.-Com. from JESUS, Easter, 1572. S. of Sir Godfrey, Knt. B. at Walton, Chesterfield, Derbs., Nov. 21, 1558. M.P. for Co. Derbs.; for Dunwich, Suffolk, 1580–1. Owned large estates in Derbs. and Yorks. Sheriff of Derbs., 1589. Benefactor to Jesus and Magdalene. Buried at Chesterfield, June 14, 1595. M.I. Will, P.C.C. (*Cooper*, II. 273; *Lincs. Pedigrees*, 363; M. H. Peacock.)

FOLJAMBE, GODFREY. Adm. pens. (age 17) at ST JOHN'S, June 27, 1661. S. of Peter, Esq., of Hope, Derbs. B. there. Bapt. Oct. 16, 1645. School, Sherburn, Yorks. Matric. 1661. Died at Steeton, 1665. Buried at Ledsham. Brother of Francis (1661). (*Vis. of Yorks.*, 1665; M. H. Peacock.)

FULJAMBE ('FOOLYAMS'), H. Matric. pens. from MAGDALENE, Michs. 1562.

FULJAMBE, JOHN. Matric. pens. from PETERHOUSE, Easter, 1574; B.A. 1577–8; M.A. 1581.

FOLJAMBE, ——. Matric. Fell.-Com. from MICHAEL HOUSE, Easter, 1544. Perhaps 'Godfrey,' s. of Sir James, of Walton, Derbs., and Aldewark, Yorks. B. 1528. Sheriff of Derbs., 1578. Knighted (as Geoffrey of Derbs.), Jan. 24, 1579–80. Died Dec. 22, 1584–5. Father of Godfrey (1572). (*Hunter*, II. 58; *Lincs. Pedigrees*.)

FOLKARD, FRANCIS. Adm. pens. (age 17) at PEMBROKE, July 3, 1706. S. of Francis, of Parham, Suffolk. B. at East Bergholt, Suffolk. Matric. 1706; B.A. 1709–10; M.A. 1737. Ord. deacon (Norwich) Mar. 1711–2; priest, Dec. 1714. R. of Clopton, Suffolk, 1722. R. of Hasketon, 1736–53. Died Nov. 26, 1753. (G. *Mag.*)

FOLCARD, THOMAS. Adm. at CORPUS CHRISTI, 1665. Of Suffolk.

FOLCARD, THOMAS. Adm. sizar at ST CATHARINE'S, Apr. 18, 1669. Matric. 1670; B.A. 1672–3; M.A. 1676. Ord. deacon (Norwich) Sept. 1675. R. of Sotherton, Suffolk, 1675. R. of Uggeshall, 1678.

FOLKELEN, ROBERT. B.A. 1459–60; M.A. 1464.

FOLKES or FOWKES, BARTHOLOMEW. Adm. (age 15) at CAIUS, July 2, 1594. S. of Richard, citizen of London. B. there. School, London, under Dr Grant (Westminster). Scholar, 1595–9. Perhaps knighted, July, 1603. (*Vis. of Herts.*, 1634.)

FOWKE, BARTHOLOMEW. Adm pens. at TRINITY, Mar. 11, 1645–6. Doubtless 2nd s. of John, alderman of London (Lord Mayor, 1653). B.A. 1649–50. Adm. at the Inner Temple, 1650. (*Staffs. Pedigrees.*)

FOWKE, EDWARD. M.Gram. 1503–4. (Identified with the next in *Gr. Bk.* Γ.)

FOWKE, EDWARD. B.A. 1503–4 (one year at Oxford); M.A. 1508; B.D. 1519–20. Of GOD'S HOUSE. One of the first fellows of Christ's. R. of Navenby, Lincs., 1513–29. V. of Newark, 1521. Died 1529. Admon. (V.C.C.) 1529, to brother Roger. (*Peile*, I. 5.)

FOLKES, EDWARD. Matric. pens. from CHRIST'S, Nov. 1561.

FOULKES, EDWARD. Adm. sizar (age 17) at MAGDALENE, 1714. S. of John, grocer. B. at Denbigh. School, Ruthin, Denbigh. Matric. 1714; B.A. 1718–9; M.A. 1722. Fellow, 1719. Perhaps R. of Caerwys, Flints., 1730–40; of Llanvwrog, Denbs., 1740. Died same year. Brother of Robert (1713).

FOLKES, FRANCIS. B.A. from MAGDALENE, 1593–4; M.A. 1597. Ord. priest (Colchester) Sept. 2, 1594. R. of Earl Soham, Suffolk, 1600.

FOULKE, FRANCIS. Adm. Fell.-Com. (age 16) at MAGDALENE, Oct. 29, 1661. S. of Francis, gent., of Camphaire, Waterford, Ireland. School, Shrewsbury. Matric. 1661. Adm. at Gray's Inn, May 9, 1663.

FOULKE, FRANCIS. From Trinity College, Dublin. Adm. there, May 26, 1685, age 17. S. of Robert. B. at Carraghnehiney, Cork, Ireland. School, Charleville. Matric. Michs. 1689; B.A. 1689–90; M.A. 1694. Incorp. at Dublin, 1702. (*Al. Dub.*)

FOLKE, HENRY. B.Civ.L. 1459–60.

FOLKES, JAMES. Adm. p . at CORPUS CHRISTI, 1577. Matric. Lent, 1577–8; B.A. 1580–1; M.A. 1584.

FOKES, JOHN. Matric. pens. from ST JOHN'S, *c.* 1593.

FOWKE, JOHN. Adm. sizar at TRINITY, July 2, 1674. Matric. 1674; Scholar, 1676; B.A. 1677–8.

FOULKES, JOHN. Adm. sizar (age 16) at ST JOHN'S, Oct. 24, 1689. S. of John, clerk. B. at St Michael's, Llanfihangel-Glyn-Myfyr, Denbigh. School, Ruthin. Matric. 1689; B.A. 1693–4; M.A. 1697; B.D. 1705. Fellow, 1696–1719. Proctor, 1702–3. Ord. deacon (Lincoln) May 26, 1700; priest, Mar. 16, 1700–1. Head Master of Pocklington School, 1704–9. R. of Medbourne-*cum*-Holt, Leics., 1717–48. Died May 16, 1748. Buried at Holt. M.I. there. Will, Leicester. (*Scott-Mayor*; *Nichols*, II. 729.)

FOWKES, JOHN. Adm. pens. (age 16) at PETERHOUSE, Apr. 1, 1718. Of Middlesex. School, Bishop's Stortford. Scholar, 1718; B.A. 1722–3. Ord. deacon (Norwich) May, 1724; priest, Dec. 1725. V. of North Walsham, Norfolk, 1730.

FOULKES, JOHN. Adm. Fell.-Com. (age 17) at MAGDALENE, May 3, 1718. S. of Peter, Esq., deceased, of Eriviat, Henllan, Denbighs. and Margaret Betton. School, Cotesbach, Leics. (private). Matric. 1719. Succeeded to his father's estate. Married, Sept. 25, 1729, at Henllan, Catherine, dau. of Henry Roberts, of Rhydonen. Buried at Henllan, May 1, 1758.

FOLKES, MARTIN. Matric. sizar from ST CATHARINE'S, Michs. 1619; B.A. 1623–4; M.A. 1627. Ord. deacon (Peterb.) Sept. 19; priest, Sept. 20, 1624. Minister at Haddenham, Cambs., 1629. Father of Robert (1655).

FOLKES, MARTIN. Adm. pens. (age 16) at PEMBROKE, Dec. 23, 1698. S. of John, of Cheveley, Cambs., Esq. Matric. 1699. Of Cheveley, Esq. Married Frances, dau. of Robert Pennyng, Esq. Died 1746, aged 65. M.I. at Cheveley. Father of Martin (1729–30). (*Suff. Man. Fam.*, II. 113; Le Neve, *Mon.*, II. 108.)

FOLKES, MARTIN. Adm. Fell.-Com. at CLARE, July 31, 1706. S. of Martin. B. in London, 1690. Matric. 1709; M.A. 1717 (*Com. Reg.*). Studied at Saumur. D.C.L. (Oxford) 1746. Incorp. at Cambridge, 1749. F.R.S. 1741. President of the Royal Society, 1741–52. Member of the French Academy, 1742. President of the Society of Antiquaries, 1750–4. Author, antiquarian, etc. Died June 28, 1754. Buried in Hillington Church, Norfolk. A monument erected to him in Westminster Abbey, in 1792. Father of Martin (1737) and brother of William (1717). (D.*N*.B.)

FOLKES, MARTIN. Adm. pens. (age 17) at PEMBROKE, Mar. 3, 1729–30. S. of Martin (1698), of Cheveley, Cambs. Matric. 1729–30. Adm. at the Middle Temple, Oct. 15, 1731.

FOLKES, MARTIN. Adm. Fell.-Com. at CLARE, Oct. 29, 1737. S. of Martin (1706). B. in London. Matric. 1737. Sent to study at Caen, Normandy. Killed there by a fall from his horse, during his father's lifetime.

FOWKE, PHINEAS. Matric. pens. from QUEENS', Easter, 1655. S. of Walter, of Little Wirley, and Brewood, Staffs., Esq. B. in Yorkshire. B.A. 1657–8; M.A. 1661; M.D. 1668. Fellow, 1660–84. F.R.C.P. 1680. Practised in London for some years. Afterwards lived at Little Wirley Hall. Died Jan. 1710, aged 72. Admon. (P.C.C.) 1711. (*Munk*, I. 417.)

FOWKE, RICHARD. Adm. pens. at TRINITY, June 28, 1669. School, Westminster. Matric. 1669; Scholar, 1670; B.A. 1672–3; M.A. 1676. Fellow, 1674. Signs for deacon's and priest's orders (London) June 11, 1674. R. of Stanmore, Midds., 1677–86. R. of Greystoke, Cumberland, 1686–93. Buried there Feb. 19, 1692–3.

FOLKES, ROBERT. Matric. pens. from CHRIST'S, May, 1560. Perhaps s. of Robert, citizen and merchant of London. Adm. at the Middle Temple, Mar. 4, 1564–5. Of Mountnessing, Essex. (*Peile*, I. 72.)

FOULKES or FOWKES, ROBERT. Adm. pens. (age 14) at MAGDALENE, Apr. 7, 1655. S. of Martin (1619), clerk, of Haddenham, Cambs. School, Lincoln. Matric. 1655; B.A. 1658–9; M.A. 1662. Fellow. Adm. at Lincoln's Inn, June 4, 1663.

FOULKES, ROBERT. Adm. sizar (age 18) at MAGDALENE, June 23, 1670. S. of Peter, gent., of Eriviat, Henllan, Denbigh. Matric. 1670; B.A. 1673-4; M.A. 1677. Probably R. of Llanfair, Denbighs., 1675. R. of Llanbedr, 1683. Precentor of Bangor, 1685-1728. Died c. 1728. One of these names adm. at Gray's Inn, Apr. 16, 1668, as 's. and h. of Peter, late of Llanasaph, Flints., Esq., deceased.' (*Misc. Gen. et Her.*, N.S., II. 28.)

FOULKES, ROBERT. Adm. pens. (age 18) at MAGDALENE, Mar. 27, 1713. S. of John, grocer. B. at Denbigh. School, Ruthin, Denbigh. Matric. 1713; B.A. 1716-7; M.A. 1720. Fellow, 1719. Proctor, 1731-2. Ord. priest (Ely) Sept. 25, 1720. V. of Stow-*cum*-Quy, Cambs., 1725. V. of St Catherine Cree, London, 1732-52. V. of Steeple Ashton, Wilts. Will (P.C.C.) 1771. Brother of Edward (1714).

FOULKES, ROBERT. Adm. pens. (age 19) at TRINITY, June 5, 1724. S. of Edward, of Cheshire. School, Westminster. Matric. 1724; Scholar, 1725.

FOAKES or FOOKES, ROGER. Matric. sizar from CLARE, c. 1595; B.A. 1598-9; M.A. 1602. Ord. deacon and priest (Norwich) Feb. 24, 1604-5. C. of Saxted, Norfolk. R. of Belaugh, c. 1628.

FOWKE, ROGER. Adm. pens. at TRINITY, June 4, 1672. School, Westminster. Scholar, 1673; Matric. 1675; B.A. 1675-6. Ord. priest (London) May 21, 1676.

FOLKES, SIMON. Matric. pens. from CHRIST'S, June, 1587. Perhaps s. of John, of Swaffham Bulbeck, Camb. Of Cheveley, Cambs., and of Burtons, Freckenham, Suffolk. Died 1642, aged 76. Will dated, Feb. 20, 1641. (Copinger, *Manors of Suffolk*, IV. 164; *Suff. Man. Fam.*, II. 113.)

FOLKES, THOMAS. Matric. pens. from CHRIST'S, Nov. 1561 Scholar. Adm. at Lincoln's Inn, Mar. 11, 1564-5, as of London.

FOLKES or FALKES, THOMAS. Matric. pens. from CLARE, Michs. 1579.

FOLKES, THOMAS. Matric. sizar from ST CATHARINE'S, Easter, 1617; B.A. 1620-1; M.A. 1624. Ord. priest (Peterb.) Feb. 18, 1626-7. One of these names V. of North Clifton, Notts., 1629-61. Died 1661.

FOWKES, THOMAS. Incorp. M.A. 1664; and B.D. 1671, from New College, Oxford. Matric. there, Dec. 1, 1642, age 18; B.A. (Oxford) 1647; M.A. 1660; B.D. 1667. Fellow of New College, 1645-8 and 1660. (*Al. Oxon.*)

FOULKS, THOMAS. M.A. from EMMANUEL, 1675. S. of Thomas, of Llanfechan, Montgom. Matric. from Hart Hall, Oxford, May 14, 1662, age 19; B.A. (Jesus, Oxford) 1665. (*Al. Oxon.*)

FOLKES, WILLIAM. Matric. sizar from ST CATHARINE'S, Michs. 1642. Of the Isle of Ely. B.A. 1645-6; M.A. 1649. Ejected from Sudbury, Suffolk, 1662. Afterwards a preacher at Colchester. (*Calamy*, II. 438.)

FOLKES, WILLIAM. Adm. pens. at CLARE, Nov. 1, 1717. B. in London. Matric. 1717. Adm. at Gray's Inn, June 20, 1717, as 2nd s. of Martin, late of Gray's Inn; and at the Middle Temple, Oct. 22, 1720. Of Hillington, Norfolk. Registrar of the Alienation Office. Died Apr. 9, 1773. Brother of Martin (1706). (*G.E.C.*; *G. Mag.*)

FOLKE, ——. B.D. 1519-20, *see* FOWKE, EDWARD.

FOLKINGHAM, JOHN. Matric. pens. from CHRIST'S, Nov. 1550.

FOLKINGHAM, JOHN. Matric. from ST JOHN'S, c. 1597; B.A. 1600-1; M.A. 1604. V. of Weston, Lincs., 1604. P.C. of Burton-on-Trent, 1611-56. Died June 12, 1656, aged 78. M.I. at Burton. Father of Thomas (1647) and William (1642).

FOLKINGHAM, NICHOLAS. B.A. from MAGDALENE, 1637-8. Lecturer at Greenwich, 1643. V. of South Weald, Essex, Aug. 6, 1646. V. of St Mary, Nottingham, Feb. 24, 1647-8. P.C. of Sneinton. Died at Nottingham, Mar. 1648-9. Father of the next. (*Shaw*, I. 352, 330; *Peile*, I. 597.)

FOLKINGHAM, NICHOLAS. Adm. sizar (age 17) at CHRIST'S, May 29, 1661. S. of Nicholas (above), V. of South Weald, Essex. B. there. School, Nottingham (Mr Pitts). Matric. 1661; B.A. 1664-5; M.A. 1668 (*Lit. Reg.*). Ord. deacon and priest (York) June, 1668. R. of Sutton Bonington, Notts., 1668-1701. R. of Glenfield, Leics., 1671. Died 1701. Admon. (Leicester) 1701. (*Peile*, I. 597.)

FOLKINGHAM, THOMAS. Adm. sizar (age 18) at MAGDALENE, May 13, 1647. S. of John (1600-1), clerk, of Burton-on-Trent. School, Burton. Matric. 1647; B.A. 1650-1. Brother of the next.

FOLKINGHAM, WILLIAM. Matric. sizar (age 16) from PEMBROKE, Michs. 1642. S. of John (1600-1), clerk. B. at Burton, Staffs. B.A. 1644-5; M.A. 1649. Incorp. at Oxford, 1649. R. of North Piddle, Worcs., 1660. Brother of Thomas (above).

FOLKLYNG, ——. Pens. at GONVILLE HALL, 1535-8.

FOLLENSBY, WILLIAM. Matric. pens. from SIDNEY, Easter, 1612. B. at Akeley, Durham. Migrated to Christ's. B.A. 1615-6; M.A. 1619. Ord. deacon (London) 1618, age 24; priest, Feb. 1618-9. (*Peile*, I. 289.)

FOLLIOTT, EDWARD. LL.B. 1635 (Incorp. from Oxford). S. of Sir John, of Naunton, Worcs., Knt. Matric. from Hart Hall, Oxford, Apr. 13, 1632, age 22; B.C.L. (Oxford) 1632. R. of Alderton, Northants., 1634, sequestered. Restored, c. 1660. R. of Foots Cray, Kent, 1634. Probably died 1684. (*Al. Oxon.*; H. I. Longden.)

FOLLIOT, RICHARD. Matric. pens. from JESUS, Lent, 1618-9.

FOLSER or FULSER, ——. B.A. 1464.

FOLSER or PULSER, ——. M.A. 1503-4.

FOLSHAM, JOHN. D.D. of Cambridge. Carmelite friar of Norwich. Provincial of the Carmelites. Died at Norwich, Apr. 18, 1348. (*Pits*, 459; *Weever*, 806.)

FOLTON, ——. M.A. 1481.

FOLVILLE, WILLIAM. D.D. of Cambridge. Of Lincolnshire. Franciscan friar. Buried at Stamford, 1384. (*Pits.*)

FONES, HUMPHREY. Adm. pens. at PETERHOUSE, 1597. Scholar, 1599-1600.

FONS, JOHN. Scholar of QUEENS', 1521-4.

FONES, THOMAS. Adm. pens. (age 17) at CHRIST'S, July 3, 1660. S. of Samuel, minister, of Woodbury, near Exeter (ejected, 1662). B. at Exeter. School, Exeter (Mr Hyter). Matric. 1660. Student at Leyden, Aug. 28, 1668. Practised as a physician at Ipswich. Died there 1679.

FONNEREAU, CLAUDIUS. Adm. pens. at QUEENS', Feb. 10, 1717-8. 2nd s. of Claude, of Christchurch, Ipswich, and Wicks-Ufford, Suffolk, Hamburgh merchant. B. in Middlesex, Apr. 14, 1701. B.A. 1721-2; M.A. 1725; LL.D. 1734. Incorp. at Oxford, 1726. Ord. deacon (Norwich) May 31, 1724; priest (Peterb.) Sept. 25, 1726. R. of Clapton, Northants., 1726-84. Died Dec. 1, 1785, at Christchurch. Buried at St Margaret's, Ipswich. Will, P.C.C. Father of the next. (Burke, *L.G.*; Cussans' *Herts.*, III.; *Misc. Gen. et Her.*, 2nd S., V. 281; H. I. Longden.)

FONNEREAU, WILLIAM. Adm. pens. at TRINITY HALL, July 3, 1748. S. of Claudius (above). B. Sept. 11, 1732. Scholar, 1749; Matric. 1750; LL.B. 1755. In holy orders. R. of Gt Munden, Herts., 1773. Died Feb. 23, 1817, aged 84, at his seat, Christchurch, Ipswich. Will, P.C.C. (Burke, *L.G.*; T. P. Dorman; Corder, *Christchurch*.)

FONT (? FANT), HENRY. Matric. pens. from TRINITY, c. 1598.

FOOCHE, *see* FOCHE.

FOOKS or FOWKS, THOMAS. Matric. pens. from JESUS, Easter, 1586.

FOOKS, ——. Matric. pens. from CHRIST'S, July, 1609.

FOORT, *see* FORT.

FOOTE, DANIEL. Adm. sizar at TRINITY, July 8, 1645. Matric. 1645; B.A. 1649-50; M.A. 1653; M.D. 1664. Perhaps V. of Little Swaffham, Cambs.; ejected, 1662. Afterwards in London. (*Calamy*, I. 254.)

FOOTT, FRANCIS. Adm. pens. (age 16) at PEMBROKE, Jan. 7, 1697-8. S. of John, of Saint Veryan, Cornwall, gent. Matric. 1698; B.A. 1701-2; M.A. 1714. Adm. at Gray's Inn, Feb. 17, 1712-3. Barrister, Nov. 26, 1714. Perhaps died June 27, 1730. (*H.R.C.*, 48.)

FOOTS, JOHN. Matric. pens. from ST JOHN'S, Lent, 1557-8. (Contemporaries at Oxford.)

FOOT, JOSHUA. Adm. pens. at TRINITY, May 29, 1648. Of London. B.A. 1651.

FOOT, WALTER. M.A. from KING'S, 1719. S. of George, of Madley, Heref. Matric. from Brasenose College, Oxford, May 8, 1707, age 18; B.A. (Oxford) 1710-1. Ord. priest (Ely) Dec. 21, 1712. V. of Chalgrave, Beds., 1712-43. V. of Harlington, 1718-50. R. of Halstead, Kent, 1725-42. R. of Hockliffe, Beds., 1743-50. Buried there Apr. 4, 1750. (*Al. Oxon.*; *Beds. N. and Q.*, II. 343.)

FOOT, ——. B.A. 1485-6.

FORAKER, JOHN. B.A. from TRINITY, 1610-1. Ord. deacon (Peterb.) Sept. 20, 1612.

FORBY, FELIX. Adm. at CORPUS CHRISTI, 1591. Of Norfolk. Matric. c. 1593; B.A. 1595-6.

FORBYE, JOHN. Adm. pens. (age 19) at CAIUS, Jan. 29, 1582-3. S. of John, of Beeston, Norfolk. Schools, Beeston and Rougham. Matric. 1582-3; Scholar, 1585-90; B.A. 1586-7; M.A. from St Catharine's, 1590; B.D. 1598. Fellow of St Catharine's. Ord. deacon and priest (Lincoln) Nov. 9, 1590. R. of Beeston, Norfolk, 1598; and of Attleborough, 1614-38. Author. Buried at Attleborough, Dec. 29, 1638. Father of the next. (*Venn*, I. 117.)

FORBY, JOHN. Adm. pens. (age 16) at CAIUS, July 1, 1634. S. of John (1582–3), R. of Attleborough, Norfolk. B. there. School, Botesdale (Mr Nich. Eston). Matric. 1634; Scholar, 1636–41; B.A. 1637–8. Ord. priest (Chichester) Oct. 9, 1660. C. of Hopton, Suffolk, in 1667. Master of Leman's School, Beccles, 1667–72. (*Venn*, I. 314.)

FORBIE, JOHN. 'B.A. of ST CATHARINE's' when ord. deacon, Dec. 23, 1671 (Gloucester) and licensed chaplain to Lord Tracy, of Toddington, Gloucs. Probably adm., 1668, as Forsby. (F. S. Hockaday.)

FORBY, JOSEPH. Adm. pens. (age 17) at CHRIST'S, 1716–7. S. of Thomas. B. at Saham Toney, Norfolk. School, Wymondham (Mr Sayer). Scholar, 1717; LL.B. 1722. Ord. deacon (Norwich) June, 1723; priest, Dec. 1723. R. of Fincham, Norfolk, 1723–45. R. of Barton St Andrew, 1741–5. Died 1745. Father of the next. (*Peile*, II. 191.)

FORBY, JOSEPH. Adm. pens. (age 18) at CHRIST'S, Oct. 23, 1751. S. of Joseph (1716), R. of Fincham, Norfolk. B. there. School, Lynn (Mr Daville). Matric. 1751; Scholar, 1751; B.A. 1756; M.A. 1764. Ord. priest (Norwich) May, 1758. C. of Threxton. (*Peile*, II. 256.)

FORBIE, SAMUEL. Adm. sizar at ST CATHARINE'S, Oct. 19, 1678. Ord. deacon (Norwich) May, 1684.

FORCET or FORSETT, EDWARD. Matric. pens. (age 10) from CHRIST'S, Feb. 1563–4. S. of Richard, of Gray's Inn. Migrated to Trinity. Scholar, 1571; B.A. 1571–2; M.A. 1575. Fellow of Trinity, 1574–81. M.P. for Wells, Somerset, 1606–11. J.P. for Middlesex, 1620. Author, political and poetical. Buried at Marylebone Church. Will proved (P.C.C.) May 25, 1630. Brother of Henry (1563–4) and William. (*Peile*, I. 82.)

FORCET, GEORGE. Matric. pens. from TRINITY, Lent, 1578–9.

FORCET or FORSETT, HENRY. Matric. pens. (age 11) from CHRIST'S, Feb. 1563–4. S. of Richard, of Gray's Inn. B.A. from St John's, 1571–2. Brother of Edward and William (1563–4). (*Peile*, I. 82.)

FORCET, JOHN. Adm. at KING'S (age 17) a scholar from Eton, Aug. 25, 1559. Of London. Matric. 1559. Fellow, 1562–3. V. of All Saints', Edmonton, 1572–5. 'A good poet.' (*Cooper*, I. 349; *Harwood*.)

FORSET, RICHARD. Matric. pens. from ST JOHN'S, Michs. 1567.

FORSETT, ROBERT. Adm. Fell.-Com. at TRINITY, Apr. 1670. Matric. 1671, as Fossett; M.A. 1675 (*Lit. Reg.*).

FORCET or FORSETT, WILLIAM. Matric. pens. from CHRIST'S, Feb. 1563–4. S. of Richard, of Gray's Inn. Of Stonham Parva, Suffolk, gent. Brother of Edward and Henry (1563–4). (*Peile*, I. 82.)

FORD, *see also* **FORTH.**

FORD, ANTHONY. Matric. pens. from CHRIST'S, Michs. 1554. B. at Cundall, Yorks. Migrated to Trinity. Scholar, 1555; B.A. 1559–60; M.A. 1563; B.D. 1570. Fellow of Trinity, 1562. Incorp. at Oxford, 1565. Ord. deacon (Ely) Mar. 23, 1566–7; priest (London) Apr. 6, 1567. R. of Richmond, Yorks., 1569. V. of Masham and Kirkhy Malzeard, 1570–8. R. of Keighley, 1572–8. Succentor of York Minster. Died 1578. (*Al. Oxon.*; *Peile*, I. 58.)

FORD, CORNELIUS. Adm. pens. at QUEENS', June 6, 1679. Of Worcestershire. (*See* JOSEPH FOORD.)

FORD, CORNELIUS. Adm. pens. (age 16) at ST JOHN'S, Mar. 6, 1709–10. S. of Joseph, doctor (Medicus). B. at Stourbridge, Worcs. School, Mansfield. Matric. 1710; B.A. 1713–4; M.A. from Peterhouse, 1720. Fellow of Peterhouse, 1720–4. Ord. deacon (Peterb.) Jan. 1, 1724–5; priest, Jan. 1, 1726–7. R. of South Luffenham, Rutland, 1727. Died Aug. 22, 1731.

FORD, EDWARD. Adm. pens. at JESUS, July 3, 1620. Matric. 1620–1; B.A. 1623–4; M.A. 1627. Ord. deacon (Peterb.) Sept. 24; priest, Sept. 25, 1626. C. of Rochford, Essex. V. of Gt Warley, Essex. Died there July 10, 1659. Admon. (P.C.C.) 1661. Father of the next.

FORD, EDWARD. Adm. pens. (age 18) at CAIUS, Apr. 30, 1646. S. and h. of Edward (above), V. of Gt Warley, Essex. B. at Rochford. Schools, Billericay (Mr Long), Little Warley (Mr Holden) and Brentwood (Mr Lathum). Matric. 1646. Adm. at Lincoln's Inn, May 4, 1647; and at the Inner Temple, 1647. Barrister, 1654.

FOURD, EMANUEL. Matric. sizar from TRINITY, Lent, 1584–5. Presumably the Romance writer, author of *Parismus*, etc. (*D.N.B.*)

FORD, FRANCIS. Adm. sizar at ST JOHN'S, Oct. 27, 1630. S. of Richard, farmer, of Kingsly, Staffs. School, Repton. Matric. 1631; B.A. 1634–5; M.A. 1689.

FORD, HARRISON. Adm. pens. (age 18) at EMMANUEL, June 7, 1743. S. of John, of Wallington, Herts. School, Bury. Matric. 1743; B.A. 1746–7; M.A. 1750. Fellow, 1749. Ord. deacon (Ely) Oct. 23, 1748; priest, Dec. 25, 1751. V. of Twyford, Hants., 1753–6. One of these names V. of Barnby Dun, Yorks., *c.* 1775. R. of Kirkbramwith. (M. H. Peacock.)

FORD, HECTOR. Adm. sizar at PETERHOUSE, May 2, 1626, from Trinity. Of London. Not recorded in *Trin. Coll. Register*.

FORD or FOORTH, HENRY. B.A. 1501–2; M.A. 1504; B.D. 1511–2. Fellow of JESUS. V. of All Saints', Cambridge, 1511–24. V. of St Stephen, Coleman Street, London, 1517–24. Died before Nov. 18, 1524. (A. Gray.)

FORD, JAMES. M.A. 1701 (Incorp. from Oxford). S. of William, of Oxford city. Matric. from New College, Oxford, Mar. 18, 1686–7; B.A. (Oxford) 1690; M.A. 1693. Fellow of New College. Died at Oxford, Aug. 13, 1743. (*Al. Oxon.*; G. *Mag.*)

FORD or FORTH, JOHN. Matric. sizar from ST JOHN'S, Michs. 1572; B.A. 1576–7; M.A. 1580. R. of Goodnestone, Kent, 1584–93. V. of Eltham, 1597–1627. Married, at Eltham, Oct. 4, 1602, Mary Courteus. Died Mar. 19, 1627. Buried at Eltham. (*Cooper*, II. 160.)

FORDE, JOHN. Matric. sizar from MAGDALENE, Easter, 1618; B.A. 1621.

FORD, JOHN. Adm. pens. at PETERHOUSE, Mar. 24, 1645–6. S. of Emanuel, of Honiton, Devon. Matric. from Wadham College, Oxford, Apr. 16, 1641, age 18; B.A. (Oxford) 1644. One of these names V. of Totnes, Devon, 1663–4.

FORD, JOHN. M.A. 1651 (Incorp. from Oxford). Perhaps B.A. from Magdalen Hall, Oxford, 1624–5; M.A. 1630.

FORD, JOHN. Adm. sizar (age 19) at ST JOHN'S, May 18, 1748. S. of Richard, metal founder, of Lancashire. B. at Cansery, near Hawkshead. School, Sedbergh, Yorks. Matric. 1748; B.A. 1752; M.A. 1755. Ord. deacon (Lincoln) June 17; priest (Ely) Dec. 25, 1753. C. of Girton, Cambs. Perhaps V. of Colwich, Staffs., 1760–71; and R. of Gratwick, 1761–71. (*Scott-Mayor*, III. 575.)

FOORD, JOSEPH. Matric. pens. from QUEENS', Michs. 1679. (*See* CORNELIUS.)

FORD, PHILIP. Matric. sizar from TRINITY, *c.* 1594. Of Yorkshire. Migrated to Queens', June 14, 1596; B.A. 1597–8; M.A. 1601. R. of Nunburnholme, Yorks., 1601–43. Preb. of York, 1605. Will (P.C.C.) 1657.

FOURD, RICHARD. Matric. sizar from QUEENS', Easter, 1559; B.A. 1564–5.

FORD, RICHARD. Matric. sizar from CLARE, *c.* 1596.

FOURD, ROBERT. Matric. sizar from QUEENS', Easter, 1557.

FORDE, ROBERT. Adm. p s. (age 16) at ST JOHN'S, Apr. 19, 1682. S. of William, M.A. (? 1618). B. at Charlton, Kent. School, Oundle. (In the Oundle School register the father is described as 'Londinensis.') Matric. 1682; B.A. 1685–6. Ord. priest (London) Feb. 24, 1688–9, as 'M.A.'

FORD, SAMUEL. Adm. sizar at EMMANUEL, May 11, 1738. (Already matric. from Trinity College, Oxford, Mar. 11, 1735–6, age 18.) Of Lincolnshire. S. of Samuel, of Erdington, Warws., gent. B. at Strawston, Lincs. Bapt. there, Aug. 25, 1717. School, Sutton Coldfield (Mr Paul Lowe). Matric. 1739; B.A. 1740–1; M.A. 1744. R. of Brampton Abbotts, Heref., 1742–93. V. of Monkland, 1754–80. Died May 6, 1793, in Hereford. Will (P.C.C.) 1793. His father was an uncle of Dr Samuel Johnson. (A. L. Reade.)

FORD, SIMON. B.D. 1650 (Incorp. from Oxford). S. of Richard, of East Ogwell, Devon. B. at East Ogwell. Schools, Exeter and Dorchester. Matric. from Magdalen Hall, Oxford, Nov. 4, 1636, age 17; B.A. (Oxford) 1641. Student of Christ Church, 1648–51. M.A. 1648; B.D. 1649–50; D.D. 1665. Expelled from Oxford for puritanism, 1641; restored by the parliamentary visitors, 1647. At one time minister at Puddletown, Dorset. V. of St Laurence, Reading, 1651–9; and of All Saints', Northampton, 1659–70. Ord. deacon and priest (Norwich) Aug. 28, 1661. Chaplain to the King. P.C. of St Mary Aldermanbury, 1671–7. R. of Old Swinford, Worcs., 1676–99. R. of Llansannan, Denbs., 1685. Author, *Sermons*. Married (1) Mrs Ann Thackham, of St Mary's, Reading; (2) Martha Stamp, of Reading. Died Apr. 7, 1699. Buried at Old Swinford. (*Al. Oxon.*; *D.N.B.*; J. Ch. Smith.)

FORD, THOMAS. Adm. sizar at TRINITY, June 24, 1651. B. at Willington, Derbs. School, Repton. Matric. 1651; Scholar, 1652; B.A. 1654; M.A. 1658. C. of Clifton Campville, Staffs., 1650–60. Lecturer at Gresley, Derbs.; ejected, 1662. Afterwards, as preacher, in prison at Stafford and Derby. Died 1677. (*Calamy*, I. 322.)

FORD, THOMAS. Adm. sizar (age 18) at CHRIST'S, Mar. 20, 1668–9. S. of William. B. at Ford-green, Staffs. Bapt. Feb. 19, 1652–3. School, Audlem, Cheshire (Mr Coulton). Matric. 1669; B.A. 1672–3; M.A. 1676. Ord. deacon (London) Sept. 1673; priest, Sept. 24, 1676. V. of Wymondley, Herts., 1676. V. of St Ippolyt's, 1686–1710. Died *c.* 1710. (*Peile*, II. 19; Foster, *Lancs. Pedigrees*.)

FORD, THOMAS. Adm. sizar at Christ's, June 30, 1690. Matric. 1690; Scholar, 1690; B.A. 1693-4; M.A. 1697. Incorp. at Oxford, 1703. Ord. deacon (Lincoln) June 19, 1698; priest, Feb. 17, 1705-6. Perhaps V. of Banwell, Somerset, 1713. Preb. of Wells, 1721-46. Died Aug. 29, 1746. One of these names 'B.A.' Master of the Free School, Buckingham, 1696. (*Peile*, II. 118.)

FORD, THOMAS. Adm. pens. (age 18) at St John's, June 26, 1723. S. of Thomas, innkeeper, of Hereford. B. there. School, Hereford. Matric. 1723. Died in College. Buried at All Saints', Cambridge, Dec. 6, 1724.

FOARD, TIMOTHY. Adm. pens. (age 18) at St John's, May 1, 1652. S. of William, gent., of Scarborough, Yorks. B. there. School, Sneaton. Matric. 1652.

FOURD, W. Matric. pens. from Peterhouse, Michs. 1559.

FOURDE, WILLIAM. Matric. sizar from Queens', Easter, 1557; B.A. 1561-2.

FORD, WILLIAM. Scholar of Trinity, 1578. B. at Bury, Suffolk, 1559. B.A. 1578-9; M.A. 1582; B.D. 1591. Fellow, 1581. Ord. deacon and priest (Lincoln) Feb. 21, 1587-8. University preacher. Chaplain to the Levant Company at Constantinople, 1611; returned to England, 1614. One of these names ('B.D.') V. of Thurleigh, Beds., 1594-1615; of Keysoe, 1596-7; and afterwards V. of Bristow, Herefs., 1615. (*D.N.B.*; Marsh Harvey, *Beds.*, 531.)

FORD, WILLIAM. Matric. pens. from St John's, Easter, 1618; B.A. 1621-2. Migrated to Oxford, 1622. M.A. from Broadgate Hall, 1624; M.B. and M.D. from Pembroke College, 1631. Admon. (York) 1635; of Newark, Notts., M.D. (*Al. Oxon.*)

FORD, WILLIAM. Adm. pens. (age 17) at Magdalene, Jan. 3, 1690-1. S. of William, citizen of London. B. there. School, Newington. Matric. 1691. Adm. at the Middle Temple, Jan. 24, 1694-5.

FORDE, WILLIAM. Adm. sizar at St Catharine's, Feb. 26, 1696-7. Matric. 1697.

FOORD, WILLIAM. Adm. scholar (age 16) at Sidney, Apr. 24, 1724. 2nd s. of William, gent., deceased, of Scarborough, Yorks. B. there. Schools, Thornton and Kirk Leatham, Yorks. (Mr Clark). Matric. 1724; B.A. 1727-8; M.A. 1731; D.D. 1753. Fellow, 1729. Taxor, 1734. Ord. deacon (Lincoln) Sept. 22, 1728. R. of Foxholes, Yorks., 1736. Perhaps R. of Weaverthorpe, in 1753. Died June 12, 1762. Will (P.C.C.) 1763. (*G. Mag.*)

FORDE, WILLIAM. Adm. pens. (age 18) at Christ's, May 22, 1735. S. of John. B. at Stone Hall, Pembrokeshire. School, St Petrox (Mr Rowe). Matric. 1735; Scholar, 1736; B.A. 1738-9.

FORDE or FOORDE, ——. B.A. 1521-2.

FORD, ——. Adm. at Corpus Christi, 1557.

FORDAM, EDMUND. Matric. pens. from Clare, Michs. 1610.

FORDHAM, JOHN. Adm. sizar at Clare, July 20, 1681. Of Cambridgeshire. S. of Richard, of Royston, Herts. Matric. 1681; B.A. 1685-6. Died at Bedford. Buried at Therfield, Herts. (*Cussans*, I. 149; where the date of his death is apparently confused with that of William (1713), *see Clutterbuck*, III. 593.)

FORDAM, ROBERT. Degree in Divinity or Law, 1458-9. A monk.

FORDHAM, ROBERT. B.A. 1534-5. One of these names R. of Brome, Suffolk, 1549. R. of Stuston, 1566-70.

FORDHAM, ROBERT. Adm. sizar (age 19) at Caius, July 3, 1622. S. of Philip, husbandman, of Sacomb, Herts. School, Watton (Mr Ro. Porter). Matric. 1623; B.A. 1625-6; M.A. 1629. V. of Flamstead, Herts., 1628-38. Licensed preacher in Lincoln diocese, 1634. Went to New England, 1638. One of the founders of Sudbury, Mass. Resided there, 1639-43. Afterwards at Hempstead, Long Island. Minister at Southampton, L. I., 1649-74. Married, in England, *c.* 1631, Elizabeth Benning. Died *c.* Nov. 1674. (*Venn*, I. 259; J. G. Bartlett.)

FORDHAM, WILLIAM. Adm. pens. ('age 30' *sic.*) at St John's, June 8, 1665. S. of Edward, deceased, of Kelshall, Herts. B. there, 1643. B.A. 1671-2. Of Therfield. Will proved, May 30, 1678. (*Cussans*, I. 148.)

FORDHAM, WILLIAM. Adm. pens. at Emmanuel, Dec. 30, 1713. Of Hertfordshire. Doubtless s. of Richard, of Royston. Matric. 1714; B.A. 1717-8; M.A. 1721. Taxor, 1725. Conduct of King's, 1727. Ord. deacon (London) Oct. 9, 1720. V. of Royston, Herts. Died Sept. 16, 1747, aged 51. Buried at Therfield. M.I. Admon., P.C.C. (*Clutterbuck*, III. 593.)

FORDYNGHAM, ED. Matric. pens. from St John's, Michs. 1566.

FOREBENCH, CHARLES. Matric. pens. from Magdalene, Michs. 1612; B.A. 1616; M.A. 1620. Ord. deacon (Peterb.) June 11; priest, June 12, 1620. R. of Hennay Magna, Essex; sequestered, 1642; restored. Died 1666. (J. Ch. Smith.)

FORER, W. Matric. sizar from Trinity, Easter, 1575.

FORGE, ELIAS. Adm. sizar (age 16) at St John's, Apr. 27, 1688. S. of John (? 1663), clerk, Master of Beverley School. B. at Beverley, Yorks. School, Beverley. Matric. 1688; B.A. 1691-2. Ord. deacon (York) Sept. 1692. V. of Beverley Minster, 1692-1703.

FORGE, JOHN. Adm. sizar (age 18) at St John's, June 13, 1663. S. of Thomas (? 1631), clerk, of Ellington-in-Masham, Yorks. B. there. School, South Dalton. Matric. 1663; B.A. 1666-7. Ord. deacon (York) June, 1668. Probably Master of Beverley School, 1669-74; and father of the above.

FORGE, THOMAS. Matric. sizar from St John's, Easter, 1631, as 'Frogg'; B.A. 1633-4; M.A. 1637. Ord. deacon (Peterb.) Sept. 21, 1634; priest, June 12, 1636. V. of North Cave, Yorks., 1646-81. Died 1681.

FORGON, JOHN. Adm. pens. (age 15) at Sidney, June 30, 1621. S. of Samuel, yeoman. B. at Gipping Stow, Suffolk. School, Bacton. Matric. 1622; B.A. 1624-5; M.A. 1628. Ord. deacon (Peterb.) May 31; priest, June 1, 1629.

FORKELOWE, *see* FAIRCLOUGH.

FORMAN, ABRAHAM. M.A. 1626 (Incorp. from Oxford). Of Yorkshire. Matric. from University College, Oxford, Nov. 8, 1611, age 17; B.A. (Oxford) 1614-5; M.A. 1618; B.D. 1627; *Supp.* for D.D. 1644. Fellow of University College, 1619-48; ejected; restored, 1660-7. Died July 6, 1667. (*Al. Oxon.*)

FORMAN, ADEODATUS. Matric. pens. from St John's, Easter, 1609; B.A. 1612-3. Ord. deacon (York) Sept. 1613; priest, Dec. 1613. V. of Whitton, Lincs., 1615. V. of Roxby, 1627.

FORMAN, CHRISTOPHER. B.A. 1489-90; M.A. 1493.

FORMAN, CHRISTOPHER. Matric. sizar from Peterhouse, Easter, 1578; B.A. 1581-2. Ord. deacon and priest (Lincoln) 1586. C. and schoolmaster at Bawdeswell, Norfolk, 1585. R. of Eastwood, Notts., 1589. R. of Gedling, 1603-40. Buried May 8, 1640.

FOREMAN, GERVASE. Adm. sizar (age 17) at Sidney, Mar. 22, 1668-9. S. of Gervase, farmer, deceased. B. at Castleton, Notts. School, Gedling, Notts. (Mr Palmer). Matric. 1669; B.A. 1672-3; M.A. 1676. Ord. deacon (Peterb.) May 25, 1673.

FORMAN, HENRY. Matric. sizar from Christ's, July, 1606; B.A. 1608-9. One of these names V. of Roxby, Lincs., in 1646; another R. of Redmile, Leics., 1613. (*Peile*, I. 260.)

FORMAN, JOHN. B.A. from Jesus, 1588-9. One of these names was ord. deacon and priest (Norwich) Sept. 21, 1606; but described as age 26 and M.A. He was C. of Illington, Norfolk.

FORMAN, JOHN. Adm. sizar (age 16) at Sidney, July 3, 1679. 2nd s. of John, grocer, of Kent. B. at Elham, Kent. Schools, Elham (Mr Perne, Crew and Cross) and Merchant Taylors'. Matric. 1680, as 'Thomas.' Migrated to Christ's, Mar. 3, 1681-2. B.A. 1682-3; M.A. 1686. Incorp. at Oxford, 1691. (*Peile*, II. 86.)

FORMAN, JOHN. M.A. from Queens', 1725 (Incorp. from Oxford). S. of John, of Devizes, Wilts. Matric. from Hart Hall, Oxford, Apr. 9, 1717, age 18; B.A. (Queen's College, Oxford, 1720); M.A. 1725. R. of Bishopstrow, Wilts. (*Al. Oxon.*)

FORMAN, RICHARD. Matric. pens. from St John's, Michs. 1582; B.A. 1585-6; M.A. 1589. R. of West Halton, Lincs., 1591-1612.

FORMAN, SIMON. Of Jesus. Licensed to practise medicine, 1604. S. of William, of Wiltshire. B. at Guidhampton (?), Dec. 30, 1552. School, Salisbury. Entered Magdalen College, Oxford, 1573, as servitor. Usher in small schools at Wilton, Ashmore and Salisbury, 1574-8. Practised astrology and medicine in London, where he was frequently in trouble with the authorities. Author. Buried at Lambeth, Sept. 12, 1611. (*D.N.B.*)

FORMAN, THOMAS. B.A. 1485.

FORMAN or FARMAN, THOMAS. B.A. 1511-2; M.A. 1515; B.D. 1521-2; D.D. 1524. Fellow of Queens', 1514-25. President of Queens', 1525-8. An early reformer. R. of All Hallows, Honey Lane, London, 1525-8. Died 1528. Referred to in will of Wm Gybbons (P.C.C., 1526) as Farman. (*Cooper*, I. 37.)

FOREMAN, THOMAS. Matric. pens. from St John's, Easter, 1559.

FORMAN, THOMAS. Matric. pens. from Clare, Michs. 1566.

FORMAN, THOMAS. Matric. pens. from ST JOHN'S, Michs. 1576; B.A. 1580–1; M.A. 1584. Perhaps B.D. Ord. deacon and priest (Peterb.) Nov. 30, 1585. R. of South Ferriby, Lincs., 1591–3. R. of Wintringham, 1592–1623. R. of Gt Coates, 1592. V. of Little Coates, 1605–6. V. of Haynton, 1607.

FORMAN, WATSON. Adm. sizar (age 19) at ST JOHN'S, June 20, 1665. S. of Parmeridry, of Middleton. B. in Northamptonshire. School, Melton, Leics. B.A. 1668–9. Ord. deacon (Lincoln) Feb. 17, 1668–9; priest, June 6, 1669. R. of Swallow, Lincs., 1670–1717.

FORMAN, ——. B.A. 1478–9; M.A. 1482.

FORMAN or FARMAN, ——. M.A. 1489.

FORMLEY, ——. Adm. pens. at TRINITY HALL, Apr. 22, 1740. Name removed, 1743.

FORNHAM, PETER. Fellow of CORPUS CHRISTI, 1400.

FORREST, ANTHONY. Adm. Fell.-Com. at EMMANUEL, Sept. 8, 1591. Of Morborne, Hunts. Matric. 1591. Adm. at Gray's Inn, July 8, 1595. Knighted, Aug. 20, 1604. M.P. for Wallingford, 1624–5, 1626. Father of the next.

FORREST, ANTHONY. Matric. Fell.-Com. from MAGDALENE, Easter, 1618. S. and h. of Sir Anthony (above), of Morborne, Hunts., Knt. Adm. at Gray's Inn, Aug. 8, 1620.

FOREST, HENRY. Matric. pens. from ST CATHARINE'S, Easter, 1550. Perhaps adm. at Lincoln's Inn, Nov. 2, 1555.

FORREST, HENRY. Matric. pens. from TRINITY, Lent, 1579–80; B.A. from Clare, 1584–5; M.A. from Magdalene, 1588. Ord. deacon (Lincoln) May 25, 1585; priest, Jan. 31, 1585–6. R. of Morborne, Hunts., 1585–(?) 1626.

FORREST, JOHN. Adm. pens. at QUEENS', Sept. 7, 1590. Of Rutland. Matric. 1590; B.A. 1593–4; M.A. 1597; B.D. 1604. Fellow, 1597–1607. Incorp. at Oxford, 1602 and 1606. Buried at St Botolph's, Cambridge, Sept. 1, 1607.

FORREST, JOHN. Matric. pens. from ST JOHN'S, c. 1597.

FORREST, MILES. Matric. Fell.-Com. from CHRIST'S, June, 1565.

FORREST, MILES. Adm. pens. at EMMANUEL, Apr. 12, 1595. Matric. 1595. Migrated to Trinity; Scholar, as Emilius Forrest, 1599; B.A. 1599–1600. One of these names adm. at the Middle Temple, 1602, as s. of Miles, of Morborne, Hunts.

FORREST, MILES. Adm. pens. at PETERHOUSE, June 5, 1619. Of Northamptonshire. Matric. 1619.

FORREST, SAMUEL. Matric. sizar from TRINITY, Michs. 1575.

FOREST, THOMAS. B.Can.L. 1454–5.

FOREST, WALCOTT. Matric. pens. from MAGDALENE, Michs. 1586.

PORRESTER, ABRAHAM. Adm. pens. at CAIUS, Mar. 17, 1608–9. S. of William, M.D., of London. School, London (Mr Slater). Matric. 1610; B.A. 1612–3; M.A. 1616. Incorp. at Oxford, 1616. R. of Folke, Dorset, 1614–45; sequestered; reinstated, 1660–5. R. of Whatley, Somerset, 1664–8. Married, Nov. 2, 1660, Joane Pawlet, widow. Buried at Folke, Oct. 1668. (*Venn*, I. 201; F. S. Hockaday.)

FORESTER, CHARLES. Adm. pens. (age 17) at TRINITY, May 28, 1695. S. of Adam. B. at Westminster. School, Westminster. Matric. 1695; Scholar, 1696; B.A. 1698–9; M.A. 1702. Ord. deacon (Norwich) Apr. 1702; priest (Lincoln) May 31, 1702. V. of Monks Kirby, Warws., 1702–6. Died 1706.

FORRESTER, FRANCIS. Adm. Fell.-Com. at EMMANUEL, May 17, 1615. Matric. 1615.

FORESTER, HENRY. Matric. pens. from TRINITY, Easter, 1631. Scholar from Westminster, 1630.

FORESTER, JAMES. Matric. sizar from CLARE, Easter, 1576. B. in Cambridge, 1561. B.A. 1579–80; M.A. 1583. Ord. deacon (London) July 21, 1585, age 25; priest, 1586. Held curacies in London diocese. Chaplain to the Earl of Lincoln. R. of Mavis-Enderby, Lincs., 1606–22. (In the Bishop's register he is described as 'of Corpus,' but there is no other graduate of these names.) According to *Cooper*, III. 58, and *D.N.B.*, he practised physic; and was indicted in 1593, with H. Barrow, for an attack on the Church. Logical and medical writer.

FORRESTER, JOHN. Adm. sizar (age 16) at SIDNEY, July 27, 1749. S. of William. B. at Newport, Salop. School, Newport. Matric. 1750; B.A. 1754; M.A. 1764.

FORESTER, MATTHEW. Adm. pens. (age 18) at TRINITY, June 18, 1712. S. of Matthew, of Wandsworth, Surrey. B. 1692. School, Westminster. Matric. 1713; Scholar, 1713; B.A. 1715–6; M.A. 1721. Ord. deacon (Ely) Feb. 22, 1718–9.

FORESTER, PULTER. Adm. at CORPUS CHRISTI, 1706. Of Hertfordshire. S. of James, of Cottered, Herts. B. there, Mar. 30, 1690. Matric. 1706; B.A. 1709–10. Adm. at the Middle Temple, Feb. 12, 1704–5. Of Broadfield, Herts., Esq. Sheriff of Herts., 1717. Married Agnes, dau. of William Harvey, of Chigwell, Essex. Buried at Cottered, Dec. 6, 1753. Father of the next and Richard (1744) and perhaps William (1731). (*Clutterbuck*, III. 516.)

FORESTER, PULTER. Adm. pens. at PETERHOUSE, June 20, 1737. 4th s. of Pulter (above), of Broadfield, Herts. School, Bury St Edmunds. Matric. 1737; Scholar, 1737; B.A. 1740–1; M.A. 1744; D.D. 1757. Fellow, 1741. Ord. deacon (Norwich) Sept. 19, 1742; priest (London) Dec. 23, 1744. R. of Knapwell, Cambs., 1745. R. of Cosgrave, Northants., 1752–78. Preb. of St Paul's, 1756–78. Preb. of Salisbury, 1759–78. R. of Gayhurst with Stoke Goldington, Bucks., 1759–66. Chancellor of diocese of Lincoln, 1766–78. R. of Passenham, Northants., 1769–78. R. of Skinnand, Lincs. Chaplain to the King. Archdeacon of Buckingham, 1769–78. J.P. for Northants. Died July 20, 1778. Buried at Cosgrave. M.I. Will, P.C.C. (*T. A. Walker*; H. I. Longden; T. P. Dorman.)

FORESTER, RICHARD. Adm. pens. (age 17) at PEMBROKE, July 6, 1744. 5th s. of Pulter (1706), of Broadfield, Herts., Esq. Matric. 1744; B.A. 1747–8; M.A. 1751. Fellow, 1749. Ord. deacon (Ely) Feb. 19, 1748–9; priest (Norwich) Mar. 1750–1. R. of Easton, Essex. V. of Ashwell, Herts., 1756–69. R. of Passenham, Northants., 1762–9. Died Apr. 19, 1769. Buried at Passenham. Will, P.C.C. (*Baker*, II. 192.)

FORESTER, THOMAS. Adm. pens. at EMMANUEL, Aug. 24, 1708. Of Dorset. Matric. 1708; B.A. 1712–3; M.A. 1716. Ord. deacon (London) Sept. 21, 1712.

FORESTER, WILLIAM. Adm. pens. at QUEENS', July 12, 1607. Of Cambridgeshire. Licensed to practise Medicine and Surgery, 1608. He obtained his medical license after being prosecuted by the College of Physicians for unlawfully practising in London. Described as M.A. and a clergyman. (*Cooper*, II. 495.)

FORRESTER, WILLIAM. Adm. Fell.-Com. at TRINITY, June 13, 1673. Of Shropshire. B. Dec. 1655. M.A. 1675 (*Lit. Reg.*). M.P. for Wenlock, 1689–1718. Knighted, Aug. 1689. Died Mar. 4, 1717–8. (A. B. Beaven.)

FORESTER, WILLIAM. Adm. Fell.-Com. (age 17) at PEMBROKE, May 12, 1731. 1st s. of William (? Pulter, 1706), of Broadfield, Herts., Esq. B. in London. Matric. 1731; B.A. 1735–6. Married Anne, dau. of Francis Mundy, of Markeaton Park, Derbs. Died Feb. 9, 1768, aged 53. Buried at Mackworth, Derbs. Brother of Pulter (1737) and Richard (1744). (*Clutterbuck*, III. 516; *Glover*, II. 591.)

FORRET, GEORGE. Matric. pens. from ST JOHN'S, Easter, 1604.

FORSET, *see* FORCET.

FORSHEDE, JOHN. Proctor, 1433–4.

FORSITH, BENJAMIN. Adm. pens. (age 15) at ST JOHN'S, June 12, 1634. S. of James, R. of Old or Wold, Northants. B. in London. School, Harborough, Leics. Matric. 1634; B.A. 1637–8; M.A. 1641. Ord. deacon (Peterb.) Sept. 19, 1641.

FORSITH, ROBERT. 'Of PEMBROKE HALL, Cambridge' (not recorded there or in University records). Subscribed for priest's orders (Bristol) May 24, 1662. R. of St Mary Port, Bristol, 1662–4. R. of St Peter, Bristol, 1664–7. R. of Winterbourne Abbas, Dorset, 1667–1717. Died Apr. 17, 1717, aged 85. (F. S. Hockaday.)

FORT or FOORT, FRANCIS. Adm. sizar (age 19) at SIDNEY, Apr. 4, 1717. S. of Hugh. B. at Huntsham, Devon. School, Tiverton. B.A. 1720–1. Will (P.C.C.) 1761; of Huntsham, clerk.

FORTE, JOHN. Scholar at KING'S HALL, 1321–5. Referred to as a sick clerk in London, July 1 to Sept. 29, 1327. R. of Holy Trinity-the-less, 1323. (*Trin. Coll. Adm.*, I. 84.)

FORT, WILLIAM. Adm. sizar (age 18) at CHRIST'S, Apr. 13, 1639. S. of William. B. at Haxey-in-Axholme, Lincs. School, Laughton-en-le-Morthen (private; Mr Seaton). Matric. 1639; B.A. 1642–3; M.A. 1646. Ord. deacon and priest (Lincoln) July 1, 1646. (*Peile*, I. 459; where he seems confused with W. Forth, LL.D.)

FORTESCUE, FRANCIS. Matric. pens. from ST JOHN'S, Easter, 1555. Probably adm. at Gray's Inn, 1562; eldest s. of Henry, of Faulkborne, Essex; and brother of the next. (J. Ch. Smith.)

FORTESCUE, GEORGE. Matric. pens. from CHRIST'S, Michs. 1564; B.A. 1566–7 (1st in the *ordo*); M.A. from Pembroke, 1570. Fellow of Pembroke, 1567. Probably s. of Henry, of Faulkborne, Essex. Named, with his brother Francis, in the father's will (P.C.C., 1576). rri Sarah, dau. of Nicholas Williams, of Burghfield. (J. Ch. Smith.)

FORTESCUE, JOHN. Adm. pens. (age 18) at CHRIST'S, June 29, 1672. S. of Thomas. B. at Spernall, Warws. School, Spernall (Mr Grove).

FORTESCUE, WILLIAM. Matric. Fell.-Com. from King's, Lent, 1629-30. One of these names s. of John, of Faulkborne, Essex; age 18 in 1634. (*Vis. of Essex*, 1634.)

FORTH, *see also* **FORD.**

FORTH, AMBROSE. Adm. at King's, a scholar from Eton, 1560. B. in London, *c.* 1545. Matric. 1560; B.A. from Jesus, 1564-5 (1st in the *ordo*); M.A. 1568; LL.D. from Trinity, 1581. Fellow of Jesus, 1568-73. Master in Chancery in Ireland, 1579-1610. Knighted, Aug. 1604. Died Jan. 13, 1609-10. (*Cooper*, II. 525; *Midds. Pedigrees*.)

FORTH, CLEMENT. Matric. pens. from Jesus, Easter, 1569; B.A. 1572-3; M.A. 1576. Licensed to practise medicine, 1587. Ord. deacon (Peterb.) June 9, 1582.

FORTH, EDWARD. Adm. Fell.-Com. at Queens', 1601. Of Essex. Probably s. and h. of Edward, of Kelvedon, Essex. Of New Windsor, Berks. Will proved, July 27, 1612. (*Suff. Man. Fam.*, I. 131.)

FORTH or FORD, JOHN. Adm. pens. (age 16) at Caius, June 24, 1599. S. of Thomas, of Suffolk. School, Hadleigh. Matric. 1599; Scholar, 1600-4; B.A. 1602-3; M.A. from St Catharine's, 1606. Ord. deacon (Norwich) Sept. 24, 1609; priest, May 30, 1613. C. of Belaugh. C. of Burwell, Lincs., 1614. R. of Swainsthorpe, Norfolk, 1620-45; ejected; re-instituted, 1660. Will proved (Norwich) 1671. (*Venn*, I. 170.)

FOURTH or FOORD, PHILIP. Matric. pens. from Trinity, *c.* 1592. Perhaps s. and h. of William, of Hadleigh, Suffolk. Bapt. there, 1572. Scholar, 1592; B.A. 1596-7. Married Joan Walton. Will proved, Aug. 31, 1646. Probably father of William (1616). (*Suff. Man. Fam.*, I. 119.)

FORTH, PHILIP. Adm. pens. at Trinity, July 31, 1672. Matric. 1675; Scholar, 1676; B.A. 1676-7; M.A. 1680. Perhaps of Cranworth, Norfolk, gent.; adm. at Gray's Inn, May 31, 1681.

FOURTH, PHILOLOGUS. Matric. pens. from St John's, Easter, 1559. S. of William, of Hadleigh, Suffolk. Of Witnesham, gent. Married Mary, dau. of John Wiseman, of Thornham, Suffolk. (*Suff. Man. Fam.*, I. 119.)

FORTHE or FURTH, RICHARD. Matric. sizar from Pembroke, Easter, 1577; B.A. 1577-8. One of these names R. of Frinton, Essex, 1585-1616; R. of Gt Holland, 1589-1618. Died 1618. Admon. (Consist. C. London) 1619.

FORTH, ROBERT. Matric. pens. from Trinity Hall, Easter, 1552. Of Streatham, Surrey. S. of Robert, clerk of the Privy Seal. B. in St Dunstan-in-the-East. LL.B. 1556-7; LL.D. 1562. Incorp. at Oxford, 1567. Adm. advocate, Jan. 20, 1562-3. Master in Chancery, 1579. One of the council of the Lord High Admiral. Died Oct. 3, 1595. Buried at St Gregory's by St Paul's. Will, P.C.C. (*Cooper*, II. 187; *Midds. Pedigrees*.)

FOURTH, ROBERT. Matric. pens. from St John's, Easter, 1559.

FOARTH, THOMAS. Matric. pens. from Trinity, Michs. 1589.

FORTH, THOMAS. Adm. pens. (age 18) at Magdalene, May 30, 1651. S. of Thomas, alderman, of Chesterfield, Derbs. School, Chesterfield. Matric. 1651; B.A. 1654-5.

FOURTH, VALENTINE. Matric. pens. from Pembroke, Easter, 1606.

FORTH, W. Matric. sizar from Queens', Michs. 1562.

FORTH, WILLIAM. Matric. pens. from Pembroke, Easter, 1606.

FOURTH, WILLIAM. Matric. pens. from Pembroke, Easter, 1616. Doubtless 1st s. of Philip (? 1592), of Hadleigh, Suffolk; adm. at the Inner Temple, 1618. Died before 1643.

FORTH, WILLIAM. Adm. Fell.-Com. at Emmanuel, Feb. 16, 1626-7. Perhaps s. and h. of Sir William, of Butley Abbey, Suffolk. Age 5, in 1615. Matric. 1626-7. Of Butley, Esq. Will proved, May 10, 1645. (*Suff. Man. Fam.*, I. 120.)

FORTH, WILLIAM. Matric. pens. from Trinity, Easter, 1632, a scholar from Westminster, 1633. S. of William, of Nayland, Suffolk. Scholar of Trinity Hall, 1635; LL.B. 1638; LL.D. 1646. Fellow of Trinity Hall, 1639-49. Adm. advocate, Jan. 29, 1646-7. Of St Giles-in-the-Fields, London. Will proved (P.C.C.) 1671. (*Suff. Man. Fam.*, I. 119.)

FORTH, WILLIAM. Adm. pens. (age 17) at Caius, Feb. 17, 1675-6. S. of Thomas, brewer, citizen of London. B. there. Schools, St Paul's and Dorking (Mr Fisher). Matric. 1676; Scholar, 1676-81; LL.B. 1681. Ord. deacon (London) Mar. 4, 1682-3; priest (Norwich) Apr. 1683. R. of Eriswell, Suffolk, 1683-1715. Died 1715. (*Venn*, I. 456.)

FORTH, YOUNG ('Junius'). Matric. pens. from Queens', Easter, 1643. Of Suffolk.

FORTHO, *see* **FURTHO.**

FORTIUS, JOHN. B.A. from Pembroke, 1598-9.

FORTREY, ISAAC. Matric. pens. from Trinity, Easter, 1622. Probably 2nd s. of John, of All Hallows, Lombard St, London. B.A. 1624-5; M.A. from Emmanuel, 1628. R. of Northolt, Middlesex, 1647. V. of Godalming, Surrey, 1648. Buried Feb. 28, 1661, at Godalming. Will (Archd. Surrey) 1661. (*Manning and Bray*, I. 646; *Vis. of London*, 1634.)

FORTRY, JAMES. Adm. at Corpus Christi, 1649. Of London. Probably s. and h. of Peter, of St Dionis Backchurch. (*Vis. of London*, 1634.)

FORTREY, JAMES. Adm. Fell.-Com. at Queens', Apr. 29, 1691. Of Cambridgeshire. S. of Samuel, of Mepal, Cambs., and of Kew, Surrey. In the service of James II. Retired at the Revolution and resided in Queens'. Died 1719. His house at Kew is now the 'Palace,' and has his initials over the door. (*Searle*, 318; J. Ch. Smith.)

FORTRYE, JAMES. Adm. pens. (age 17) at Pembroke, June 9, 1735. Of Kent. Matric. 1736. One of these names, commissioner for victualling; died June 15, 1767. (G. *Mag.*)

FORTREY, SAMUEL. Adm. pens. (age 15) at Christ's, July 2, 1666. S. of Samuel, of Richmond, Surrey. B. at Oakington, Cambs. Bapt. there, Mar. 2, 1651-2. School, Oakington (Mr Shafto). Matric. 1667. Adm. at the Inner Temple, Jan. 23, 1669-70. Of Byall Fen, in Mepal, Esq. J.P. for Hunts. and Isle of Ely. Capt. of Militia. Died Feb. 10, 1688, aged 38. Buried at Mepal. Brother of the next. (*Peile*, II. 8.)

FORTREY, WILLIAM. Adm. pens. (age 14) at Christ's, July 2, 1666. S. of Samuel, of Richmond, Surrey. B. at Oakington, Cambs. School, Oakington (Mr Shafto). Matric. 1667. Married Anne Whalley, of Norton, Leics. Died 1722. Buried at Norton. Father of the next, brother of the above. (*Peile*, II. 8.)

FORTREY, WILLIAM. Adm. pens. (age 16) at Pembroke, Apr. 4, 1715. S. of William (above), of Norton, Leics., Esq. Matric. 1715; LL.B. 1720. Died Dec. 11, 1783. (G. *Mag.*)

FORTUNE, JOHN. M.A. from St John's, 1740. S. of William, of North Nibley, Gloucs., gent. Matric. from Pembroke College, Oxford, Mar. 26, 1729, age 19; B.A. (Oxford) 1732. Ord. deacon (Peterb.) Sept. 23, 1733; priest (Rochester) May 19, 1734. R. of Wickwar, Gloucs., 1734-77. R. of Tretire and Michaelchurch, Hereford, 1740-77. Chaplain to Lord Willoughby de Broke. Died 1777. Will, P.C.C. (*Scott-Mayor*, III. 508; F. S. Hockaday.)

FORTUNE, ROBERT. Matric. sizar from Queens', Easter, 1618. Of Cambridgeshire.

FORTUNE, STEPHEN. Matric. sizar from Jesus, Michs. 1582.

FORWARD, JOHN. Adm. sizar at Emmanuel, July 11, 1645. Of Devon. Matric. 1645. Migrated to Jesus College, Oxford, 1648. B.A. 1648-9. Fellow of Jesus, Oxford, 1648. Ord. deacon (Chichester) Mar. 10, 1665-6; priest, Aug. 18, 1666. Probably a minister at Bassenthwaite, Cumberland, 1655; at Lamplugh, 1655-6; and at Bolton, Mealsgate, 1656-60. V. of Kingston-by-Lewes, Sussex, 1665-6. V. of Iford, 1666-90. Buried at Iford, July 12, 1690. (*Al. Oxon.*; W. C. Renshaw; B. *Nightingale*.)

FORWARD, JOHN. Adm. pens. (age 16) at Pembroke, July 5, 1681. S. of John, of Sowton, Devon, 'medicus.' M.B. 1686.

FORWARD, NICHOLAS. Adm. sizar (age 17) at Pembroke, June 11, 1685. S. of John, of Sowton, Devon, 'medicus.' Student at Leyden, Oct. 29, 1688. Admon. of one of these names (Exeter) 1709 and 1711; of Sowton.

FORWARD, ROBERT. M.A. 1623 (Incorp. from Oxford); B.A. from Oriel College, 1611-2; M.A. 1617; B.D. 1628. Fellow of Oriel. V. of Eltham, Kent, 1628-35. Precentor of St Patrick's, Dublin, 1635; and of Lismore, 1636. V. of North Aston, Kent, 1637. Dean of Dromore, 1639. R. of Loughgilly, Armagh. Died 1641. (*Al. Oxon.*)

FOSBROKE, ELEAZER. Adm. sizar at Emmanuel, Apr. 15, 1596. S. of Ralph (1571), R. of Cranford St Andrew, Northants. Matric. 1596. Migrated after nine terms, to Oxford. B.A. from New College, 1601-2; M.A. 1605. Perhaps of Hambledon, Hants., clerk. (*Al. Oxon.*; H. I. Longden.)

FOSBROOK, JOHN. Adm. pens. at Sidney, Lent, 1599-1600. S. of John, of Cranford, Northants. B.A. 1603-4; M.A. 1607; B.D. from King's, 1615. Ord. priest (Peterb.) Sept. 24, 1609. R. of Cranford St Andrew, Northants., 1609-41. R. of Cranford St John, 1640-1. Married Susan, dau. of George Lynne, of Southwick, Northants. (*Vis. of Northants.*, 1618; H. I. Longden.)

FOSBROOK, JOHN. Adm. sizar at Pembroke, Sept. 3, 1651.

FOSBROCKE, RALPH. Matric. pens. from St John's, Michs. 1571. 3rd s. of John, of Cranford St Andrew, Northants., Esq. B.A. 1575-6. Ord. priest (Peterb.) Mar. 29, 1577. R. of Cranford St Andrew, 1576-91. Will proved (Archd. Northants.) Oct. 29, 1591, by widow Mary. (H. I. Longden.)

FOSBROOK, RICHARD. Adm. sizar at Clare, Jan. 9, 1656-7.

FOSBROKE, W. Matric. pens. from CHRIST'S, May, 1568. One William Fosbroke, of Cranford, Northants., and of Barnard's Inn, adm. at Gray's Inn, May 1, 1588.

FOSCRAFTE, WILLIAM. Matric. sizar from ST JOHN'S, c. 1594.

FOSCROFT, RICHARD. Matric. pens. from ST JOHN'S, Michs. 1569.

FOSDYKE, LAMBERT. B.Can.L. 1476-7. A monk; doubtless from Croyland. Abbot of Croyland, Jan. 12, 1483-4. Died of the sweating sickness, Nov. 14, 1487.

FOSS, GEORGE. Adm. pens. (age 17) at SIDNEY, May 25, 1736. 2nd s. of John, gent., deceased, of Chumleigh, Devon. B. there. School, Tiverton. Matric. 1739; B.A. 1739-40. Ord. deacon (Lincoln) Nov. 8, 1741. Admon. (P.C.C.) 1789, of George Foss, clerk, of Lerling, Norfolk.

FOSS, JOHN. Adm. pens. at JESUS, Oct. 14, 1698. Of Yorkshire. Matric. 1699; Scholar, 1700; B.A. 1702-3; M.A. 1718. Ord. priest (York) June, 1707. R. of Castleford, Yorks., 1729-53.

FOSSE, THOMAS. Matric. sizar from ST JOHN'S, Michs. 1568.

FOSSAN, THOMAS. Adm. pens. (age 16) at MAGDALENE, June 27, 1651. S. of Thomas, citizen and skinner of London. School, St Mary Axe, London. Matric. 1651; B.A. 1654. Adm. at Gray's Inn, Feb. 13, 1654-5. R. of Little Gaddesden, Herts., 1660-82. Master of Berkhampstead School, 1666-70. Licence to marry, Apr. 20, 1666, Elizabeth Field, of Battersea, dau. of Henry, of Lyon's Inn, gent. (J. C. Smith.)

FOSSET, THOMAS (1694), *see* FAWCETT.

FOSTER or FORSTER, ALEXANDER. Adm. scholar (age 16) at CAIUS, Dec. 14, 1618. S. of George, gent. B. at Lyham, Northumberland. School, Berwick (Mr Knowsley). Matric. 1618-9.

FOSTER, ANDREW. Matric. sizar from QUEENS', c. 1591. Of Cambridgeshire. B.A. (? 1594-5). Ord. deacon (Lincoln) Feb. 13, 1595-6. C. of Warboys, Hunts., 1613; also schoolmaster there.

FOSTER, AUGUSTUS or AUGUSTINE. Matric. pens. from CHRIST'S, Nov. 1562. Perhaps of Nassington, Northants.; and father of John (1597).

FOSTER, CHARLES. Adm. at KING'S, a scholar from Eton, 1700. B. in London. Matric. 1701; B.A. 1705-6; M.A. 1709. Fellow, 1704. Ord. deacon (London) Aug. 13, 1708; priest, Sept. 25, 1709. R. of Gt Fransham and Congham, Norfolk, 1715-23. Died 1723.

FOSTER, CHRISTOPHER, *see* COLEMAN.

FOSTER, CHRISTOPHER. Matric. sizar from ST JOHN'S, Easter, 1585. Perhaps s. of Christopher, of Darlington. B.A. 1588-9; M.A. 1592; B.D. 1599. Fellow, 1590. R. of St John's, Watling St, London, 1608-14. R. of Graffham, 1614. Probably brother of George (1579).

FOSTER, CUTHBERT. Matric. pens. from QUEENS', Michs. 1569. Perhaps adm. at Gray's Inn, from Staple Inn, 1574-5. Will (P.C.C.) 1582; has reference to Hexham, Northumberland, so perhaps s. of Thomas. (*Vis. of Northumberland*, 1615.)

FOSTER, EDMUND. Adm. at CHRIST'S, Nov. 29, 1670; M.A. 1671 (*Lit. Reg.*). Described as M.A. of Queen's College, Oxford. B. at Hoddesdon, Herts. One of these names V. of Elmdon, Essex, 1669-79. Died 1679. (*Peile*, II. 32.)

FOSTER, EDWARD. Adm. at KING'S (age 16) a scholar from Eton, Aug. 21, 1535. Of 'Hollington, Oxon.' B.A. 1539-40. Fellow, 1538-c. 1544. Perhaps preb. of Chichester; will (P.C.C.) 1568.

FORSTER, EDWARD. Adm. pens. at CHRIST'S, June 5, 1627. 3rd s. of Mark, town clerk of Durham. B. there. Bapt. at St Nicholas, Feb. 14, 1612-3. Schools, Durham and Haughton. Matric. 1627; B.A. 1630-1; M.A. 1634. Master of Hexham School, 1634. V. of Bourn, Cambs., 1639. Chosen by Emmanuel College as V. of Winsford, Somerset, 1656. Adm. at Emmanuel, Mar. 31, 1656, in order to be appointed to Winsford. V. of Ringstead St Andrew, Norfolk, 1661-73. Died 1673. M.I. at Ringstead. Brother of John (1619), father of Mark (1668). (*Peile*, I. 384; *Vis. of Durham*, 1666.)

FOSTER, EDWARD. Adm. sizar at QUEENS', May 4, 1686. Of Middlesex. Matric. 1686; B.A. 1689-90; M.A. 1693. Perhaps V. of Gt Finborough, Suffolk, 1700-4.

FOSTER, ELLIS. Adm. sizar (age 24) at PEMBROKE, Apr. 10, 1716. Of Blackrod, Lancs. B. at Anderton, Lancs.

FOSTER or FORRESTER, FERDINAND. Adm. pens. (age 15) at ST JOHN'S, June 28, 1686. S. of Sir William (1653), Knt. B. at Bamborough, Northumberland, Feb. 14, 1669-70. School, Durham. Matric. 1686. Adm. at Gray's Inn, May 13, 1687. M.P. for Northumberland, 1700-1. Murdered at Newcastle, Aug. 22, 1701. M.I. at Bamborough. Brother of William (1682) and John (1686). (Jos. Foster, *Pedigree of the Fosters*; H. M. Wood.)

FOSTER, FRANCIS. Matric. sizar from PETERHOUSE, Easter, 1576; B.A. 1579-80; M.A. 1583.

FOSTER, GEORGE. B.Civ.L. 1530-1.

FOSTER, GEORGE. Matric. sizar from ST JOHN'S, Easter, 1579; B.A. 1582-3. Probably s. of Christopher, of Darlington, Durham; and brother of Christopher (1585). (*Surtees*, III. 357.)

FOSTER, GEORGE. Matric. sizar from MAGDALENE, Easter, 1619.

FOSTER, GEORGE. Matric. pens. from QUEENS', Easter, 1632. Of Northumberland. B.A. 1635-6. Perhaps V. of Bolam, Northumberland, 1640; ejected, 1646; restored, 1660-94. Died 1694, aged 81. Will mentions eldest s. John (? 1671). (H. M. Wood.)

FORSTER, GEORGE. Adm. Fell.-Com. (age 17) at ST JOHN'S, July 17, 1731. S. of George, Esq. B. at Little Bristol, Barbadoes. School, St James, Barbadoes. Matric. 1731. Brother of Richard (1738) and Thomas (1741).

FOSTER, GILES. B.A. from PETERHOUSE, 1612-3. One of these names, s. of Giles, of Dymock, Gloucs., adm. at the Inner Temple, 1607. Another, 'M.A.' was C. of Barnard Castle, in 1627, age about 38. V. of Hamsterley, Durham. Buried there Aug. 18, 1661. Admon. of his goods, Dec. 1661, as late C. of Witton-le-Wear. (H. M. Wood.)

FOSTER, HENRY. Adm. sizar at QUEENS', May 9, 1681. Of London. B.A. 1684-5; M.A. 1688. Ord. deacon (London) Mar. 16, 1684-5.

FOSTER, JAMES. Matric. sizar from TRINITY, Easter, 1617; B.A. 1620-1; M.A. 1628. Ord. deacon (York) Sept. 1621; priest, Mar. 1621-2.

FOSTER, JAMES. Adm. pens. (age 17) at CHRIST'S, Apr. 3, 1663. S. of Christopher. B. in London. School, London (private; Mr Perkins).

FORSTER, JAMES. Adm. sizar at CHRIST'S, Apr. 25, 1681. S. of George (? 1632). B. at Bolam, Northumberland. Matric. 1681; B.A. 1684-5. Ord. deacon (Carlisle) Feb. 1685-6. V. of Lesbury and of Shilbottle, Northumberland, 1688-1712. Buried Aug. 27, 1712, at Lesbury. (*Peile*, II. 82; *New Hist. of Northumberland*, II. 442; V. 435.)

FOSTER, JAMES. Adm. sizar (age 16) at TRINITY, May 18, 1701. S. of Roger, of Lancashire. School, Mercers' (Mr Barrow). Matric. 1701; B.A. 1704-5; Scholar, 1705. Perhaps V. of Turnworth, Dorset, 1725-6; also V. of Osmington, 1726-45. Died 1745.

FORSTER, JAMES. Adm. pens. (age 18) at TRINITY, June 23, 1730. S. of Clement, of Alnwick, Northumberland. Bapt. there, Feb. 6, 1711-2. School, Alnwick (Mr Wilson). Matric. 1730; Scholar, 1731; B.A. 1733-4. Ord. deacon (Durham) 1735; priest, Aug. 29, 1736. C. of Ingram, Northumberland. Married, at Berwick, Apr. 28, 1747, Isabel Collingwood. One of these names V. of Brantingham, Yorks., 1768-93. (H. M. Wood.)

FORSTER, JAMES. Adm. pens. (age 17) at MAGDALENE, Oct. 31, 1735. S. of John, gent. B. at Enfield, Middlesex. School, Caddington, Herts. Matric. 1735. Adm. at Gray's Inn, Oct. 25, 1735. Barrister, 1742. Probably Chief Justice of Ely. Died Jan. 2, 1781.

FORSTER, JOHN. M.A. Fellow of CORPUS CHRISTI, 1437.

FOSTER, JOHN. Exhibitioner at Cambridge, 1478. (*Harl. MS.*, 58, G. 11.)

FOSTER, JOHN. M.A. 1501-2. Probably V. of Barrington, Cambs., 1505.

FOSTER, JOHN. Matric. sizar from QUEENS', Easter, 1576. Of Cambridgeshire. B.A. 1580-1; M.A. from Peterhouse, 1584. Ord. priest (Lincoln) Sept. 20, 1587. R. of Dembleby, Lincs., 1588-1614. R. of South Kelsey, 1589-1600. V. of Hotoft, 1600. V. of Wigtoft, 1602-4. Perhaps also R. of Creeton, 1603-31.

FOSTER, JOHN. Matric. pens. from TRINITY, Lent, 1579-80. One of these names, of Salop, adm. at Lincoln's Inn, from Furnival's Inn, May 3, 1582.

FOSTER, JOHN. Ord. deacon (London) Mar. 5; priest, Mar. 6, 1592-3, age 30, as 'of KING'S College.' B. at Eton, Bucks. V. of Datchet, Bucks., 1598. Perhaps V. of Masworth, 1598.

FOSTER, JOHN. Matric. Fell.-Com. from CLARE, c. 1597. Perhaps s. of Augustin (1562), of Nassington, Northants., gent.; adm. at Gray's Inn, Oct. 24, 1599.

FOSTER, JOHN. Matric. sizar from ST JOHN'S, Easter, 1611; B.A. 1614-5.

FORSTER, JOHN. Matric. pens. from ST JOHN'S, Easter, 1619. 2nd s. of Mark, town clerk, of Durham. Bapt. at St Nicholas, Dec. 2, 1604. Migrated to Christ's. B.A. 1622-3; M.A. 1626. Fellow of Christ's, 1626-40. Taxor, 1633. Ord. deacon and priest (Norwich) Feb. 18, 1626-7. Died Sept. 3, 1640. Brother of Edward (1627). (*Peile*, I. 326; *Vis. of Durham*, 1666.)

FOSTER, JOHN. Matric. pens. from MAGDALENE, Michs. 1638.

FOSTER, JOHN. Adm. pens. (age 14) at CAIUS, Jan. 31, 1664-5. S. of Samuel (1634), B.D., of Redgrave, Suffolk. B. there. School, Thetford (Mr Keen). Scholar, 1666-9; Matric. 1667; B.A. 1668-9. Died 1669. Buried at Redgrave, May 3. M.I. there. (*Venn*, I. 424.)

FOSTER, JOHN. Adm. sizar (age 16) at CHRIST'S, May 1, 1671. S. of George. B. at Holbeck, Yorks. School, Leeds (Mr Gilbert). Matric. 1671; B.A. 1674-5. Ord. deacon (York) Feb. 1675-6; priest, Dec. 1680. Perhaps C. of Stokesley, Yorks. Buried there 1718 or 1719. (*Peile*, II. 35.)

FOSTER or FORRESTER, JOHN. Adm. pens. (age 16) at ST JOHN'S, June 28, 1686. S. of Sir William (1653), Knt. B. at Bamborough, Northumberland, Sept. 29, 1668. School, Durham. Matric. 1686, as Foster. Adm. at Gray's Inn, May 13, 1687. Died Nov. 15, 1699. M.I. at Bamborough. Brother of Ferdinand (1686) and William (1682).

FORSTER, JOHN. Adm. pens. at JESUS, Oct. 17, 1702. Of Yorkshire. Perhaps s. of Richard, R. of Kirk Ella, Yorks.; who died in 1700. Matric. 1703; Rustat Scholar; B.A. 1706-7; M.A. 1714. Ord. deacon (York) Dec. 1712; priest, 1713. R. of Elvington, Yorks., 1728-42. Preb. of Ripon, 1733-42. R. of Skelton, till 1742. Died May 24, 1742, aged 56. (*See Al. Oxon.* for a contemporary.)

FOSTER, JOHN. Adm. pens. at QUEENS', Mar. 7, 1708-9. Of Essex. Matric. 1709; B.A. 1712-3; M.A. 1728. Ord. deacon (London) May 23, 1714. Perhaps R. of Tatsfield, Surrey. Died 1720.

FORSTER, JOHN. Adm. pens. (age 16) at ST JOHN'S, July 4, 1717. S. of William (1682), V. of Stamford Baron, Northants. B. there. School, Stamford. Matric. 1717; B.A. 1720-1; M.A. 1742. One of these names R. of Walsoken, Norfolk, 1742.

FORSTER, JOHN. Adm. pens. at EMMANUEL, Apr. 7, 1729. Of Middlesex. Matric. 1731; B.A. 1732-3; M.A. 1736; D.D. 1777. R. of Elton, Hunts., 1739-87. Died 1787. Will, P.C.C.

FOSTER, JOHN. Adm. at KING'S, a scholar from Eton, 1748. S. of Henry. Bapt. at Windsor, Jan. 7, 1730-1. Matric. 1748; B.A. 1753; M.A. 1756; D.D. 1766 (*Lit. Reg.*). Fellow, 1751. Ord. deacon (Ely) Mar. 18, 1753. Assistant Master at Eton. Head Master, 1765-73. Canon of Windsor, 1772-4. Author, *Critical Scholarship*. Died July, 1774, in Germany. Buried at Windsor. M.I. there. Will, P.C.C. (*D.N.B.*; *Harwood*.)

FOSTER, JONATHAN. Matric. sizar from TRINITY, Michs. 1635; B.A. 1638-9; M.A. 1642. (The V. of Welton, Northants., was probably of Oxford.)

FOSTER or FORSTER, JOSEPH. Adm. pens. (age 16) at PETERHOUSE, Jan. 12, 1692-3. Of Durham. School, Houghton-le-Spring. Scholar, 1693; Matric. 1694; B.A. 1696-7; M.A. 1700. Ord. deacon (York) June, 1697. V. of Norton, Durham, 1712-46 (previously C., 1700-12). Married, Dec. 29, 1707, Mary Davison. Died Jan. 23, 1746. Father of the next. (*Surtees*, III. 357.)

FORSTER, JOSEPH. Adm. sizar at QUEENS', Apr. 10, 1729. Of Durham. S. of Joseph (above). Matric. 1729; B.A. 1732-3; M.A. 1736. Ord. deacon (Ely) Dec. 1733; priest (Durham) Sept. 1735. C. to his father, at Norton.

FOSTER, JOSIAH. M.A. from PEMBROKE, 1692. S. of J., of Birmingham, Warws. Matric. from Brasenose College, Oxford, May 22, 1685, age 16; B.A. (Oxford) 1688-9. Master of Solihull Grammar School, Warws., 1690-2. V. of Aston, Warws., 1716. (*Al. Oxon.*)

FOSTER, LEONARD. Matric. sizar from CLARE, Lent, 1579-80; B.A. 1583-4; M.A. 1587. V. of Boseford, Notts., 1595-1604. R. of Screveton, 1602. Buried there June 27, 1652. (Godfrey, *Notts.*)

FOSTER, LIONEL. Matric. sizar from TRINITY, Easter, 1578. B. at Giggleswick, Yorks. B.A. 1581-2. Ord. priest (London) Nov. 30, 1585, age 25. V. of Gt Tey, Essex, 1585-92. R. of Little Tey, 1588-97. R. of Lammarsh, 1597. Will (Consist. C. London) 1622.

FORSTER, MARK. Adm. sizar (age 18) at CHRIST'S, June 2, 1668. S. of Edward (1627). B. at Bourn, Cambs. School, Wainfleet, Lincs. (Mr Gibbs). Matric. 1668; B.A. 1671-2. Ord. deacon (Norwich) 1673-4; priest, Feb. 1674-5. Usher at Lynn School, and C. of St Nicholas. R. of Clenchwarton, near Lynn, 1675. R. of North Lynn, 1712. Died 1719-20, aged 70. (*Peile*, II. 16.)

FOSTER, MARTIN. Adm. sizar (age 14) at PETERHOUSE, Aug. 4, 1635. Of Durham. Matric. 1636. A Martin Foster was in 1673 Comptroller of the Customs at Newcastle-on-Tyne. Died 1678. (*T. A. Walker*, 54.)

FORSTER, MATTHEW. Adm. pens. (age 16) at PETERHOUSE, Feb. 9, 1693-4. S. of Francis, of the South Bailey, Durham. Bapt. at St Mary's, Dec. 12, 1678. School, Houghton-le-Spring. Scholar, 1694; Matric. 1695; B.A. 1697-8; M.A. 1701. Fellow, 1698. Ord. priest (Lincoln) June 29, 1701. Lecturer of St John's, Newcastle-on-Tyne, from 1710. R. of Whalton, Northumberland, 1710-23. Married, Oct. 12, 1710, at Houghton-le-Spring, Elizabeth Fawcett, of Newcastle. Died Oct. 23, 1723. Buried at St John's, Newcastle. (H. M. Wood.)

FOSTER, MICHAEL. Matric. sizar from TRINITY, Michs. 1555.

FOSTER, MICHAEL. Matric. sizar from CORPUS CHRISTI, Michs. 1598. Of Norfolk. B.A. 1601-2; M.A. 1605. Ord. deacon (Norwich) Dec. 23, 1604; priest, Feb. 24, 1604-5. C. of Gt Snoring, Norfolk. R. of Kelling, 1608.

FOSTER, NATHANIEL. Adm. sizar (age 17) at CHRIST'S, Apr. 19, 1634. S. of Nathaniel. B. at Billingborough, Lincs. Schools, Boston (Mr Winter) and Bradford, Yorks. Matric. 1634; B.A. 1637-8. R. of Allington, Wilts.; ejected, and kept school at Salisbury. Restored, 1660. Father of Samuel (1682). (*Peile*, I. 432.)

FOSTER, NATHANIEL. Adm. sizar (age 16) at PETERHOUSE, May 4, 1646. Of Middlesex. School, St Saviour's. One of these names licensed by the Bishop of Ely, as schoolmaster in Cambridge, Nov. 1684.

FOSTER, NICHOLAS. Matric. pens. from ST JOHN'S, Lent, 1564-5; B.A. 1568-9; M.A. 1572.

FORSTER, NICHOLAS. Adm. at KING'S (age 18) a scholar from Eton, Aug. 24, 1570. Of Harlaxton, Lincs. Matric. 1570; B.A. 1574-5; M.A. 1578. Fellow, 1573-85. Vice-provost, 1584-5. R. of Ditchingham, Norfolk, 1585-7.

FOSTER, NICHOLAS. Matric. sizar from PETERHOUSE, Michs. 1584.

FOSTER, OUDART. Adm. pens. (age 18) at TRINITY, June, 1695. S. of William, and Barbara, dau. of Nicholas Oudart. B. at Bedford. Bapt. at St Paul's, Aug. 23, 1678. School, Bedford (Mr Nicholas Aspinal). Buried at Gt Barford, Beds., Apr. 25, 1698.

FOSTER, PETER. Matric. sizar from PEMBROKE, Michs. 1546. Of Durham. B.A. 1549-50 (1st in the *ordo*); M.A. from St John's, 1553. Fellow of St John's, 1552. University preacher, 1560.

FORSTER, PEXALL. Adm. pens. (age 17) at PETERHOUSE, Apr. 17, 1680. Eldest s. of Pexall, of Durham. Bapt. at St Nicholas, Mar. 29, 1663. School, Durham. Migrated to St Catharine's, 1681. Matric. 1681; B.A. 1683-4; M.A. 1687. V. of St Oswald's, Durham, 1690-1711. Minister of St Giles'; and minor canon of the Cathedral. R. of Egglescliffe, 1711-40. Died Feb. 27, 1739-40. Buried at Egglescliffe. Father of the next. (H. M. Wood.)

FORSTER, PEXALL. M.A. from KING'S, 1718. S. of Pexall (above), of Durham city, clerk. Bapt. at St Oswald's, Mar. 30, 1693. Matric. from Lincoln College, Oxford, Mar. 22, 1709-10, age 17; B.A. (Oxford) 1713. V. of Lakenham, Norfolk, 1718-9. Precentor of Norwich Cathedral. Died Oct. 4, 1719. (*Al. Oxon.*; H. M. Wood.)

FORSTER, RALPH. Adm. at CORPUS CHRISTI, 1648. Of London.

FORSTER, RALPH. Adm. pens. (age 18) at ST JOHN'S, May 25, 1750. S. of Joseph, gent., of Newton-by-the-Sea, Northumberland. B. at Newton. Bapt. Jan. 19, 1730-1, at Embleton. School, Durham. Matric. 1750; B.A. 1754; M.A. 1757; B.D. 1765. Fellow, 1754-74. Proctor, 1763-4. Ord. deacon (Chester) Mar. 6, 1757. C. of Horningsea, Cambs., 1766-73. R. of Gt Warley, Essex, 1772-1804. Buried there Dec. 2, 1804. Brother of William (1750). (*Scott-Mayor*, III. 596.)

FORSTER, REYNOLD. 'Of ST JOHN'S.' Ord. deacon and priest (Norwich, *Litt. dim.* from London) Mar. 1741-2.

FOSTER, RICHARD. Matric. sizar from PETERHOUSE, Michs. 1549; B.A. 1552-3; M.A. 1556.

FOSTER, RICHARD. Matric. sizar from TRINITY, Michs. 1552; Scholar, 1551; B.A. 1552-3; M.A. 1556. Fellow, 1553. V. of Gainford, Durham, 1559-62. Perhaps R. of Cheadle, Staffs., 1562-74. R. of Kingsley, 1565. Preb. of Lichfield, 1574. Buried at St Nicholas, Durham, Sept. 14, 1575. Will, Durham.

FOSTER, RICHARD. Adm. sizar at CORPUS CHRISTI, 1571. Matric. 1573; B.A. 1576-7; M.A. 1580. One of these names R. of Kirkby-on-Bain, Lincs., 1586-96. One, V. of Horncastle, 1587-93; R. of Scremby, 1591-1612; V. of Skendelby, 1593-1606.

FOSTER, RICHARD. Matric. sizar from ST JOHN'S, Easter, 1575; B.A. 1578-9; M.A. 1582. R. of Alderford, Norfolk, 1591-4; and perhaps R. of Melton Constable, 1593.

FOSTER, RICHARD. Matric. sizar from ST JOHN'S, Easter, 1604. B. in St Michael-le-Querne, London. B.A. 1607–8. Ord. deacon (London) June 3, 1610, age 26; priest, Mar. 8, 1611–2. C of St Leonard, Shoreditch.

FOSTER, RICHARD. Matric. sizar from KING'S, Easter, 1605.

FOSTER, RICHARD. Matric. pens. from CHRIST'S, Easter, 1618. One of these names (called M.A.) was P.C. of Buttsbury, Essex, 1637–45, sequestered. (*Peile*, I. 323.)

FOSTER, RICHARD. Matric. pens. from TRINITY, Easter, 1629.

FORSTER, RICHARD. Adm. pen. at TRINITY, June 29, 1667. School, Westminster. Matric. 1667; Scholar, 1668.

FORSTER, RICHARD. M.A. 1676 (Incorp. from Oxford). S. of Clement, of Chester. Matric. from Brasenose College, Mar. 30, 1666, age 15; B.A. (Oxford) 1669; M.A. 1673. Usher of Tonbridge School. Master of Town Sutton School, Kent. Ord. priest (Chichester) Nov. 3, 1682. R. of Beckley, Sussex, 1682–99. R. of Crondal, Kent, 1698–1729. V. of Eastchurch, Isle of Sheppy, 1699–1729. Died at Crondal, Jan. 8, 1728–9, aged 79. Buried there. (*Al. Oxon.*)

FOSTER or FORSTER, RICHARD. Adm. sizar (age 15) at CHRIST'S, July 7, 1699. S. of Richard. B. at Cambridge. School, King's College (Mr Rosewell). Scholar, 1702–3; B.A. 1703–4; M.A. 1716. Ord. deacon (Norwich) Sept. 22, 1706; priest (Peterb.) May 30, 1708. V. of Halvergate, Norfolk, 1709. R. of Bexwell, 1711–39. Father of Richard (1732).

FORSTER, RICHARD. Adm. pens. (age 18) at ST JOHN'S, June 17, 1714. S. of Thomas (? 1662) clerk, deceased. B. at Nassington, Northants. School, East Carlton. Matric. 1714.

FOSTER, RICHARD. Adm. sizar (age 19) at CHRIST'S, Mar. 26, 1717. S. of Robert. B. at Stainforth, Yorks. School, Giggleswick (Mr Jo. Carr). Scholar, 1719–20; B.A. 1720–1. Ord. deacon (York) June, 1723; priest (Peterb.) Sept. 19, 1725. C. of Easton Maudit, Northants. (*Peile*, II. 191.)

FOSTER, RICHARD. Adm. sizar (age 17) at ST JOHN'S, May 31, 1732. S. of Richard (1699), V. of Bexwell, Norfolk. B. at Bexwell. Schools, Wisbech and Ely. Matric. 1733. Doubtless succeeded his father at Bexwell, 1739–69. (*Scott-Mayor*, III. 442.)

FORSTER, RICHARD. Adm. pens. (age 21) at ST JOHN'S, Nov. 4, 1738. S. of George, Esq. B. in the parish of St Joseph, Barbadoes. School, Hackney, Middlesex. Matric. 1738. Brother of George (1731) and Thomas (1741).

FOSTER, ROBERT. Matric. pens. from TRINITY, Easter, 1565.

FOSTER, ROBERT. Matric. sizar from ST JOHN'S, Michs. 1615.

FOSTER, ROBERT. Matric. pens. from QUEENS', Easter, 1622. Of Kent. B.A. 1625–6; M.A. 1629.

FOSTER, ROBERT. Adm. sizar (age 20) at CHRIST'S, Sept. 29, 1637. S. of Richard. B. at Kirkby Lonsdale, Westmorland. School, Kirkby. Matric. 1637.

FOSTER, ROBERT. Matric. sizar from CHRIST'S, Michs. 1678. Exhibitioner from Charterhouse. B.A. 1681–2. One of these names V. of Norham, Northumberland, 1714–20; buried there June 19, 1720. (H. M. Wood.)

FOSTER, ROBERT. Adm. sizar at JESUS, May 3, 1700. Of Lancashire. Matric. 1700; Scholar, 1703; B.A. 1703–4. Perhaps Master of Blackburn Grammar School, 1704–5. Died 1705.

FOSTER, ROBERT. Adm. pens. at CLARE, Oct. 18, 1742. B. at Woodborough, Notts. Matric. 1742.

FOSTER, ROGER. Matric. pens. from ST JOHN'S, Lent, 1557–8. Of Norfolk. B.A. 1559–60; M.A. 1563. Fellow, 1560. Ord. priest (Dover) July 2, 1573, age 36. V. of St Bride's, London, 1574–92. Died Feb. 4, 1591–2. Admon. (Consist. C. London) June 30, 1592.

FOSTER, ROWLAND. Adm. pens. (age 17) at CAIUS, Apr. 10, 1580. S. of John, yeoman, and Margaret Burton. B. at Gislingham, Suffolk. School, Botesdale. B.A. 1583–4; M.A. 1587; Scholar.

FOSTER, SAMUEL. Adm. sizar at EMMANUEL, Apr. 23, 1616. Of Northamptonshire. Matric. 1616; Scholar; B.A. 1619–20; M.A. 1623. Gresham professor of astronomy, 1637 and 1641–52. One of the original fellows of the Royal Society. Author, on Dialling. Died May, 1652. Will (P.C.C.); as of St Peter-le-Poer. Brother of Walter (1614). (*D.N.B.*)

FOSTER, SAMUEL. Matric. sizar from MAGDALENE, Michs. 1623. Ord. deacon (Peterb.) July 15, 1626.

FOSTER, SAMUEL. Adm. pens. (age 13) at CAIUS, July 2, 1634. S. of Michael (1598), R. of Kelling, Norfolk. B. there. Schoolmaster, Mr Holt. Matric. 1634; Scholar, 1635–41; B.A. 1637–8; M.A. 1641; B.D. 1649. Fellow, 1644–50. Ord. deacon (Norwich) Sept. 22, 1644; priest (Lincoln) Aug. 24, 1646. C. of Kelling, 1644. R. of Redgrave, Suffolk, 1649 (instituted by Bishop Joseph Hall, Feb. 16, 1648–9). R. of Hinderclay, 1662. Died Mar. 24, 1680–1. M.I. at Redgrave. Father of John (1664). (*Venn*, I. 314.)

FOSTER, SAMUEL. Adm. sizar (age 16) at PEMBROKE, Feb. 28, 1637–8. S. of William, farmer. B. at Overton Waterville, Hunts. Matric. 1637–8; B.A. 1641–2; M.A. 1646. R. of Woodstone, Hunts., 1653–61. Buried there Oct. 13, 1661.

FOSTER, SAMUEL. Adm. sizar at EMMANUEL, Oct. 25, 1645. Matric. 1647; B.A. 1648–9.

FORSTER, SAMUEL. Adm. sizar at CHRIST'S, Apr. 1, 1682. S. of Nathaniel (1634), R. of Allington, Wilts. School, Salisbury. Matric. 1682; B.A. 1686–7; M.A. 1690. Ord. priest (Salisbury) June 15, 1690. R. of Welby, Lincs., 1692–1730. P.C. of Ancaster. Buried June 4, 1730, at Welby. (*Peile*, II. 86.)

FOSTER, SAMUEL. Adm. sizar (age 19) at PEMBROKE, June 26, 1751. S. of Caseley, citizen and barber-surgeon, of St Mary-le-Bow. ('Of Hackney, Midds., mercer,' in College Register.) Grecian from Christ's Hospital. Matric. 1751; B.A. 1755; M.A. 1759. Ord. deacon (Ely) Mar. 7, 1756; priest, Sept. 19, 1756. One of these names R. of Eastbridge, Kent, 1757–65. Died at Chelmsford, 1765. Admon. (P.C.C.) Feb. 1771. (*A. W. Lockhart.*)

FOSTER, THOMAS. B.A. 1505–6; M.A. 1509. Principal of ST MARY'S HOSTEL, 1510. Died *c.* 1518.

FOSTER, THOMAS. Described as 'B.A. (Oxford); M.A. (Cambridge); B.D. (Louvain)' when incorp. as M.A. and B.D. at Oxford, 1526. (Not found in Cambridge records.)

FOSTER, THOMAS. Matric. sizar from TRINITY, Michs. 1550.

FOSTER, THOMAS. Matric. pens. from CHRIST'S, Dec. 1560; Scholar, 1561–2. One of these names R. of Luddesdown, Kent, 1569–70. Perhaps R. of Runwell, Essex, 1570; later also of Easthorpe; died before May, 1579. (*Peile*, I. 73.)

FORSTER, THOMAS. Adm. at KING'S (age 17) a scholar from Eton, Aug. 26, 1562. Of Balsall, Warws. Matric. 1562; B.A. 1566–7. Fellow, 1565–9.

FOSTER, THOMAS. Matric. from PETERHOUSE, Easter, 1579; B.A. 1583–4; M.A. 1587.

FOSTER, THOMAS. Matric. sizar from MAGDALENE, Michs. 1587. B. at Barnoldby, Lincs., 1572. B.A. (? 1589–90); M.A. 1597. Ord. deacon and priest (Peterb.) May 4, 1593. V. of Gt Stukeley, Hunts., 1595–1607. R. of Hamerton, 1606–9. R. of Thurning, 1609–27. Father of Thomas (1624).

FOSTER, THOMAS. Adm. pens. at EMMANUEL, June 15, 1609. Matric. 1609.

FORSTER, THOMAS. Matric. pens. from CHRIST'S, Dec. 1617; B.A. 1620–1. One of these names V. of South Witham, Lincs., ejected. (*Peile*, I. 320.)

FOSTER, THOMAS. Adm. sizar (age 16) at CAIUS, Aug. 13, 1619. S. of Randolph, husbandman, of Kirby-Bellars, Leics. School, Melton Mowbray (Mr Humfrey). Matric. 1620; B.A. 1623–4. Ord. deacon (Peterb.) Dec. 19; priest, Dec. 20, 1624. One of these names V. of Horton and Piddington, Northants., 1641. (*Venn*, I. 247.)

FOSTER, THOMAS. Adm. sizar (age 16) at CAIUS, July 9, 1624. S. of Thomas (1587), R. of Thurning, Hunts. Taught by his father. Matric. 1625; B.A. from Magdalene, 1627–8; M.A. 1634. Ord. deacon (Peterb.) Mar. 9; priest, Mar. 10, 1627–8. One of these names sequestered from Hawkhurst, Kent, 1645. (*Venn*, I. 269.)

FOSTER, THOMAS. Matric. pens. from MAGDALENE, Easter, 1627; B.A. 1630–1; M.A. 1634.

FORSTER, THOMAS. Adm. sizar (age 16) at ST JOHN'S, Apr. 9, 1640. S. of Thomas, gent., deceased. B. at Ely. School, Ely.

FORSTER or FORRESTER, THOMAS. Adm. pens. at EMMANUEL, July 1, 1662. Of Northamptonshire. Matric. 1663; B.A. 1665–6; M.A. 1670. Ord. deacon (Peterb.) Sept. 19, 1669; priest, May 25, 1673. One of these names (Foster), R. of Tempsford, Beds., –1684–7. Perhaps father of Richard (1714).

FORSTER, THOMAS. Adm. Fell.-Com. (age 18) at ST JOHN'S, June 16, 1677. S. of Thomas, Esq., deceased, of Adderston, Northumberland. B. there, Aug. 9, 1659. School, Durham. Matric. 1677. Sheriff of Northumberland, 1703. M.P. for Northumberland, 1705. Buried at Bamburgh, Oct. 25, 1725. Father of Thomas (1700). (H. M. Wood.)

FOSTER or FORSTER, THOMAS. Adm. pens. at EMMANUEL, May 13, 1689. Of Lincolnshire. S. of Thomas, of Dowsby and Pointon. Bapt. Aug. 2, 1672. Matric. 1690; B.A. 1692–3; M.A. 1696. Ord. deacon (Lincoln) Mar. 16, 1700–1; priest, Mar. 14, 1702–3. Warden of Browne's Hospital, Stamford, 1708–19. Died Dec. 16, 1719. Buried at St Michael's, Stamford. (*Lincs. Pedigrees*, 1227; *F.M.G.*, I. 404.)

FORSTER, THOMAS. Adm. pens. (age 18) at CHRIST'S, July 2, 1691. S. of John, of Crookletch, Northumberland, Esq. Bapt. at Bamburgh, May 9, 1672. School, Morpeth. Scholar, 1693; B.A. 1694-5; M.A. 1701. Ord. deacon (London) June 16, 1701; perhaps priest (Durham) Sept. 24, 1704. C. of All Saints', Stamford, 1702. V. of Leek, near Thirsk, 1704. Died 1726. (*Peile*, II. 122; H. M. Wood.)

FORSTER, THOMAS. Adm. Fell.-Com. (age 18) at ST JOHN'S, July 3, 1700. S. of Thomas, Esq. (1677). B. at Adderston, Northumberland. Bapt. Mar. 29, 1683. School, Newcastle. Died in exile at Boulogne. Buried at Bamburgh, Dec. 7, 1738.

FOSTER, THOMAS. Adm. pens. at EMMANUEL, June 11, 1720. S. of Thomas (1689), of Dowsby and Pointon. B. at Stamford, Lincs. Bapt. Sept. 17, 1702. Matric. 1720; B.A. 1723-4; M.A. 1727. Ord. deacon (Lincoln) Mar. 6, 1725-6; priest (Peterb.) Dec. 24, 1727. C. of Preston, Northants., 1727. Died Feb. 24, 1735-6. (*Lincs. Pedigrees*.)

FORSTER, THOMAS. Adm. sizar at QUEENS', June 25, 1728. Of Durham. Matric. 1728; B.A. 1731-2; M.A. 1735. Ord. deacou (Lincoln) June 9, 1734; priest, June 1, 1735. Perhaps V. of Tunstead, Norfolk, 1746-76; and R. of Halesworth, Suffolk, 1746-85. Died in London, Oct. 23, 1785. (Davy, *Suff. MSS.*)

FORSTER, THOMAS. Adm. sizar (age 19) at ST JOHN'S, Oct. 12, 1741. S. of George, Esq. B. in the Barbadoes. School, Streatham, Surrey. Matric. 1741. Brother of George (1731) and Richard (1738).

FOSTER, VERE. Adm. pens. (age 16) at ST JOHN'S, 1713-4. S. of William, clerk. B. at Cuddington, Bucks. School, Ditton, near Datchet, Bucks. (private; Mr Churchley). Matric. 1714; B.A. 1718-9; M.A. 1722; B.D. 1730. Fellow, 1720-32. Ord. deacon (Peterb.) Mar. 17, 1727-8; priest (Lincoln) Mar. 25, 1728. R. of Barrow-on-Soar, Leics., 1730-57. Died 1757. (*Scott-Mayor*.)

FOSTER, W. Matric. pens. from ST JOHN'S, Michs. 1561.

FOSTER, W. Matric. pens. from ST JOHN'S, Easter, 1565.

FOSTER, WALTER. Adm. at EMMANUEL, May 24, 1614 (previously at Oxford); Scholar; B.A. 1617-8; M.A. 1621; B.D. 1628. Fellow, 1622-32. Ord. deacon (Peterb.) June 8; priest, June 9, 1628. R. of Aller, Somerset, 1633- , ejected. Living at Sherborne, Dorset, in 1652. Mathematician. Brother of Samuel (1616). (*D.N.B.*)

FOSTER, WILLIAM. Fellow of CLARE, in 1494.

FOSTER, WILLIAM. Adm. at KING'S (age 18) a scholar from Eton, Aug. 20, 1526. Of Hatfield, Herts. B.A. 1530-1; M.A. 1534; B.D. 1544. Fellow, 1529-44.

FOSTER, WILLIAM. Matric. sizar from JESUS, Michs. 1565. Ord. deacon (Ely) May 26, 1566.

FOSTER, WILLIAM. Matric. sizar from PEMBROKE, Michs. 1567. B. in Craven, Yorks. B.A. 1571-2. Ord. deacon (London) Oct. 6, 1577; priest, Mar. 25, 1578, age 27. Perhaps V. of South Mimms, Middlesex, 1586-1618. V. of Ridgewell, Essex, 1598-1604. Will (P.C.C.) 1618.

FOSTER, WILLIAM. Adm. pens. (age 15) at CAIUS, Mar. 29, 1577. S. of Thomas, gent., of Bridgham, Norfolk. School, Lynn. Matric. 1576; B.A. from St Catharine's, 1580-1; M.A. 1584. (*Venn*, I. 91.)

FOSTER, WILLIAM. Matric. sizar from ST CATHARINE'S, Lent, 1588-9. Of Cambridgeshire. B.A. 1593-4; M.A. 1595; D.D. 1618 (*Lit. Reg.*). Fellow. King's preacher at Garstang, 1609. Preb. of Chester, 1618. Bishop of Sodor and Man, 1633-5. Buried at Barrow, Feb. 26, 1634-5. (*Hist. Cath. Coll.*, 88; *Ormerod*, I. 222.)

FOSTER, WILLIAM. Matric. pens. from PETERHOUSE, Easter, 1609. Perhaps Fellow of Trinity Hall, as 'LL.B.', 1615-24. Buried at St Edward's, Cambridge, Feb. 17, 1624-5. Will proved (V.C.C.).

FOSTER, WILLIAM. M.A. 1618 (Incorp. from Oxford). Of London. S. of William, barber-surgeon. Matric. from St John's College, Oxford, Dec. 8, 1609, age 18, from Merchant Taylors' School. B.A. 1613; M.A. 1617. R. of Hedgerley, Bucks., 1618. Chaplain to the Earl of Carnarvon. Killed, 1643. (*Al. Oxon.*; *D.N.B.*)

FOSTER, WILLIAM. Adm. pens. (age 17) at PEMBROKE, June 25, 1622. S. of Francis, of London, weaver. Matric. 1623; B.A. 1625-6; M.A. 1629. Ord. priest (St David's) 1629. One of these names V. of Watton, Norfolk, 1632-60.

FOSTER, WILLIAM. Matric. sizar from MAGDALENE, Easter, 1625; B.A. 1628-9; M.A. 1633. Ord. deacon (Peterb.) June 5, 1631. One of these names R. of Eastwick, Herts., 1662-4. Died 1664.

FOSTER, WILLIAM. Matric. pens. from TRINITY, Easter, 1627; B.A. 1630-1; M.A. 1634.

FORSTER or FORESTER, WILLIAM. Adm. sizar at CHRIST'S, Apr. 11, 1648. S. of William. B. at Newcastle. Bapt. at All Saints', Feb. 20, 1630-1. School, Halifax. B.A. 1651-2; M.A. 1655; B.D. from Emmanuel, 1662. Fellow of Emmanuel, 1655. V. of Stanground, Hunts., 1662-70. Died Dec. 8, 1679. (*Peile*, I. 518.)

FORSTER, WILLIAM. Adm. Fell.-Com. at CHRIST'S, May 31, 1653. S. of Nicholas. B. at Bamborough, Dec. 13, 1636. School, Bamborough (private; Mr Shaw). Adm. at Gray's Inn, 1653. Knighted, Dec. 3, 1660. Of Bamborough Castle. Married Dorothy, dau. of Sir William Selby, Knt., of Thornton. Buried Nov. 12, 1674. Father of William (1682), John (1686) and Ferdinand. (*Peile*, I. 554; *Pedigree of Foster*.)

FOSTER, WILLIAM. LL.B. from CLARE, 1663 (*Lit. Reg.*); LL.D. 1672. Of Bedford. Chancellor of the diocese of Lincoln. Buried at Gt Barford, Beds., Apr. 5, 1708. (*Beds. N. and Q.*, I. 275.)

FOSTER, WILLIAM. Adm. sizar (age 17) at ST JOHN'S, May 12, 1666. S. of Robert, of Standish, Lancs. B. there. School, Sedbergh. Matric. 1667; B.A. 1669-70; M.A. 1673. Head Master of Heskin Grammar School, Lancs., 1670. R. of Sudborough, Northants., 1682-1704. Died Apr. 6, 1704, aged 57. Father of William (1700).

FOSTER, WILLIAM. M.A. from KING'S, 1673. S. of John, of Leicester, clerk. Matric. from Lincoln College, Oxford, Apr. 21, 1665, age 16; B.A. (Oxford) 1668-9. Ord. priest (Peterb.) May 29, 1670. R. of Elmsthorpe, Leics., 1672. (*Al. Oxon.*; H. I. Longden.)

FOSTER, WILLIAM. Matric. pens. from TRINITY HALL, Michs. 1673; LL.B. 1677. Buried at Gt Barford, Beds., Dec. 31, 1688.

FOSTER or FORSTER, WILLIAM. Adm. sizar at EMMANUEL, June 2, 1673. Of Yorkshire. Matric. 1674; B.A. 1676-7.

FORSTER, WILLIAM. Adm. sizar at EMMANUEL, June 22, 1674. Of Yorkshire. Matric. 1674. Perhaps same as the above.

FORSTER, WILLIAM. Adm. Fell.-Com. (age 14) at ST JOHN'S, July 4, 1682. S. of Sir William (1653), Knt., deceased. B. July 28, 1667, at Bamborough, Northumberland. School, Durham. Married Elizabeth, dau. of William Pert, Esq. Died *s.p.* Sept. 1, 1700. M.I. at Bamborough. Brother of Ferdinand (1686) and John (1686).

FORSTER, WILLIAM. Adm. sizar at EMMANUEL, July 5, 1682. Of Huntingdonshire. Matric. 1683-4; B.A. 1686-7; M.A. 1690. One of these names R. of Sculthorpe, Norfolk, 1697-1700. V. of Stamford Baron, 1700-9. R. of St Clement Danes, London, 1708-19. Died Dec. 11, 1719. Father of John (1717).

FOSTER, WILLIAM. Adm. pens. at CLARE, June 10, 1689. Of Acrise, Kent. Matric. 1689; B.A. 1692-3; M.A. 1696. Ord. deacon (London) Dec. 19, 1697; priest, Oct. 6, 1698. R. of Eythorne, Kent, 1698-1708. Died 1708.

FOSTER, WILLIAM. Adm. pens. (age 16) at SIDNEY, June 25, 1700. S. of William (1666), R. of Sudborough, Northants. B. at Rushton, Northants. School, Oundle. Matric. 1700; Scholar; B.A. 1703-4; M.A. 1708. Ord. deacon (Peterb.) May 19, 1706; priest (Lincoln) Sept. 19, 1708. R. of Tilbrook, Beds., 1708.

FORSTER, WILLIAM. Adm. sizar (age 18) at SIDNEY, May 22, 1704. 4th s. of Ralph, gent., deceased. B. at Doxford, Ellingham, Northumberland. Schools, Durham and Newcastle. Matric. 1704; B.A. 1709-10. Ord. deacon (Durham) Sept. 25, 1709; priest, Sept. 24, 1710. For a contemporary *see Al. Oxon.*, also *Surtees*, IV. 152.

FOSTER, WILLIAM. Adm. sizar (age 19) at CHRIST'S, Feb. 7, 1708-9. Of Yorkshire. School, Giggleswick (Mr Armitstead). Matric. 1709; B.A. 1713. Ord. deacon (York) Dec. 1712; priest, Sept. 1713. P.C. of Holbeck, Leeds., 1718-21. Died Apr. 29, 1721. Buried at Holbeck. (*Peile*, II. 171; R. J. Wood.)

FOSTER, WILLIAM. Adm. sizar (age 19) at ST JOHN'S, July 7, 1726. S. of William, R. of Hampreston, Dorset. B. at Hampreston. Educated at home. Matric. 1726; B.A. 1729-30; M.A. 1733. Ord. deacon (Ely) Feb. 21, 1729-30; priest (York) July 18, 1731. R. of Holy Trinity, Goodramgate, York, 1739-68. V. of Ferry Friston, Yorks., 1761-8. (*Scott-Mayor*, III. 401.)

FORSTER, WILLIAM. Adm. pens. (age 17) at ST JOHN'S, June 16, 1740. S. of William, clerk, V. of Aycliffe, and Precentor of Durham Cathedral. B. there, 1723. School, Durham. Matric. 1740; B.A. 1743-4; M.A. 1747. Ord. deacon (Durham) Nov. 1, 1747; priest, Oct. 1748. C. of Embleton, Northumberland. V. of Heighington, Durham, 1750-63. Lecturer at St Nicholas, Durham, 1754-63. Buried at St Oswald's, Dec. 9, 1763. (*Pedigree of Foster of Durham*; H. M. Wood.)

FORSTER, WILLIAM. M.A. from St John's, 1750. S. of Joseph, of Newton, Northumberland, Esq. Bapt. at Warkworth, Mar. 27, 1722. Matric. from Lincoln College, Oxford, Mar. 19, 1740-1, ge 18; B.A. (Oxford) 1744; M.A. 1750. Ord. deacon (Norwich) Dec. 18, 1748; priest (Gloucester) Oct. 8, 1750. V. of Long Houghton, Northumberland, 1752-84. V. of Lesbury, 1775-84. Died at Lesbury, Aug. 31, 1784, aged 61. Buried at Embleton. Brother of Ralph (1750). (*Scott-Mayor*, III. 598.)

FOSTER, ZEATH. Matric. pens. from Trinity, Easter, 1573.

FOSTER, ——. B.Can.L. 1477-8.

FOSTER, ——. Vicar of Ware. Incorp. 1480-1.

FOSTER, ——. B.A. 1524-5.

FOSTER, ——. B.A. 1538-9.

FOSTER, ——. Adm. Fell.-Com. at King's, Michs. 1569.

FOSTER, ——. Adm. at Corpus Christi, 1580.

FOSTER, ——. Adm. sizar at Trinity, Easter, 1645.

FOSTER, ——. Adm. Fell.-Com. at Trinity Hall, Apr. 29, 1743. Name off, Aug. 1744.

FOSTON, PETER. B.Can.L. 1482-3; D.Can.L. 1494-5 (? 1505-6). Official of Norwich diocese. R. of Attleborough, Norfolk, 1486. R. of Papworth St Agnes, Cambs., 1495.

FOTARE, ——. *Cautio* for M.A. 1489. Possibly William Fostere; 'regent M.A.,' when elected fellow of Clare, in 1494; whom *see*.

FOTEHEDE, JOHN. M.A. 1481-2; B.D. 1491; D.D. 1497-8, as Futede. Master of Michaelhouse, 1507-15. R. of Simondsbury, Dorset, 1494. Preb. of Lincoln, 1505-12. University preacher, 1509. Died *c.* 1520. (*Cooper*, I. 23.)

FOTHER, ——. M.A. 1503-4.

FOTHERBY, CHARLES. Matric. sizar from Trinity, Easter, 1573. S. of Martin, of Grimsby (in Walbran's *History of Gainford* the father is called Maurice). Scholar, 1575; B.A. 1576-7; M.A. 1580; B.D. 1587. Fellow, 1579. Incorp. at Oxford, 1579. V. of Chislet, Kent, 1587-92; of Deal, 1587; of Aldington, 1592-1619. V. of Teynham, 1595-1600. Archdeacon of Canterbury, 1595-1619. Preb. of Canterbury, 1595-1604. R. of Bishopsbourne, Kent, 1600-19. Dean of Canterbury, 1615-19. Married Cecilia, dau. of Ralph Walker, of Cambridge. Died Mar. 29, 1619, aged 70. Buried in Canterbury Cathedral. Brother of Martin (1576). (*Vis. of Kent*, 1619; *Al. Oxon.*; *Lincs. Pedigrees*; H. M. Wood.)

FOTHERBIE, CHARLES. Matric. pens. from Trinity, Lent, 1618-9. 1st s. of Martin (1576), Bishop of Salisbury. (By his will Bishop Martin left his books to this son, and provided for his maintenance at Cambridge.) Bapt. in Canterbury Cathedral, Oct. 21, 1603. Scholar, 1619; B.A. 1621-2; M.A. 1625. Fellow, 1621-2. R of Southill and Callington, Cornwall, 1637. R. of St Ives, 1639. Preb. of Exeter, 1639; ejected, but restored, 1660-77. Died Oct. 1677. Brother of Thomas (1625). (Walker, *Sufferings*; *Lincs. Pedigrees*; where he is apparently confused with the next.)

FOTHERBY, CHARLES. Matric. pens. from Trinity, Easter, 1627; B.A. 1631; M.A. from Jesus, 1634. Fellow of Jesus, 1632-37. Adm. at Gray's Inn, Mar. 5, 1630-1; s. and h. of Sir John, of Kent, Knt. Age 9, in 1619. V. of Guilden Morden, Cambs., 1637. Married Elizabeth Beckingham. (*Vis. of Kent*, 1619; A. Gray.)

FOTHERBY, EDMUND. Adm. pens. at Trinity, June 4, 1645. S. of Sir John, of Barham, Kent. Scholar from Westminster, 1645. Matric. 1648; B.A. 1648-9; M.A. 1652. Fellow, 1651. V. of Gainford, Durham, 1660-1701. Died Mar. 12, 1700-1, aged 76. Buried at Gainford. M.I. Father of the next. (*Al. Westmon.*)

FOTHERBY, EDMUND. Adm. pens. (age 18) at Trinity, May 7, 1680. S. of Edmund (above), R. of Gainford, Durham. B. at Gainford. Bapt. there, Mar. 10, 1661-2. School, Durham (Mr Battersby). Matric. 1680; Scholar, 1683; B.A. 1683-4. Ord. deacon (London) Feb. 24; priest, Mar. 1, 1683-4. 'Parson of Chalwick, Essex, 1683-90. Died 1690.' (Walbran, *Gainford*, 88.)

FOTHERBYE, EDWARD. Matric. pens. from Clare, Easter, 1583.

FOTHERBYE, FRANCIS. Matric. pens. from Pembroke, Michs. 1560.

FOTHERBY, FRANCIS. Matric. pens. from Trinity, Easter, 1610; Scholar, 1611; B.A. 1612-3; M.A. 1616. Fellow, 1614. Ord. deacon (Peterb.) June 15; priest, June 16, 1617. V. of St Clement's, Sandwich, 1618-42, ejected. V. of Linsted, 1618-49.

FOTHERBY, GEORGE. Matric. sizar from St John's, Easter, 1628; B.A. 1631-2. Perhaps s. of George. C. of Stow, Lincs., 1634. Buried there Oct. 1, 1644. (*Lincs. Pedigrees.*)

FOTHERBY, JOHN. Matric. sizar from Queens', Easter, 1577. Of Gt Grimsby, Lincs. S. of Robert, of Kent, clerk. B.A. 1580-1; M.A. from Trinity, 1584. V. of Headcorn, Kent, 1584-1602. R. of Smarden, 1586-1619. R. of Little Chart, 1602-19. Married, at Headcorn, May 8, 1587, Amia Kelsham. Died Apr. 9, 1619. Buried at Little Chart. Will (Consist. C. Cant.) 1619. (*Lincs. Pedigrees.*)

FOTHERBY, MARTIN. Matric. sizar from Trinity, Michs. 1576. 2nd s. of Martin, of Grimsby, Lincs. Scholar, 1580; B.A. 1580-1; M.A. 1584; B.D. 1591; D.D, 1607. Fellow, 1583. V. of Chislet, Kent, 1592-4. R. of St Mary-le-Bow, London, 1594-5. Preb. of Canterbury, 1596-1618. R. of Gt Mongeham, Kent, 1596-1603. R. of Chartham, 1596-1618. R. of Adisham, 1601-18. Fellow of Chelsea College, 1610. Bishop of Salisbury, 1618-20. Married Margaret, dau. of John Winter, D.D., Preb. of Canterbury. Died Mar. 11, 1619-20 (*D.N.B.* wrong here). Buried in All Hallows Church, Lombard Street. Will, P.C.C. Brother of Charles (1573), father of Charles (1618-9) and Thomas (1625). (*Vis. of Kent*, 1619; *Lincs. Pedigrees*; *D.N.B.*)

FOTHERBY, SIDNEY. Adm. pens. at Emmanuel, Nov. 25, 1695. 3rd s. of Sir John Fotherby, of Barham, by his wife Elizabeth, only dau. of Sir Anthony Coke, of Gideon Hall, Essex. B. at Barham, Kent, 1677. Colleger at Eton, 1689-94. Matric. 1695; B.A. 1699-1700; M.A. 1703.

FOTHERBY, THOMAS. Matric. pens. from Trinity, Easter, 1625. 2nd s. of Martin (above), Bishop of Salisbury. (Bishop Martin Fotherby's will provided that this son Thomas was 'to be brought up to law or divinity.') B. Nov. 9, 1609. Bapt. in Canterbury Cathedral. School, Merchant Taylors'. Scholar, 1627; B.A. 1628-9; M.A. 1632. Buried in Canterbury Cathedral, Dec. 1, 1674. Brother of Charles (1618-9), probably father of the next. (*Robinson*, I. 101; *Vis. of Kent*, 1619.)

FOTHERBYE, THOMAS. Adm. pens. at Trinity, May 28, 1674. Matric. 1674; Scholar, 1676; B.A. 1677-8. Probably s. of Thomas (above). B. 1659. Married Elizabeth, dau. of Manwaring Hamond, Esq. Buried in Canterbury Cathedral, 1710. M.I. (J. R. Walbran, *Gainford.*)

FOTHERBY, WILLIAM. Matric. pens from Pembroke, *c.* 1593.

FOTHEREY, ——. M.Gram. 1482-3.

FOTHERGILL, FRANCIS. Adm. sizar (age 17) at St John's, Apr. 26, 1704. S. of Thomas (1663). B. at Warsop, Notts. School, Southwell. Matric. 1704; B.A. 1707-8. Ord. deacon (Ely) Dec. 18, 1709; priest (York) Sept. 1711. P.C. of Norton Disney, Lincs., 1714. V. of Ossington, Notts. Brother of George (1696).

FOTHERGILL, GEORGE. Matric. sizar from St John's, Michs. 1623. B. in Westmorland. School, Sedbergh. B.A. 1627-8; M.A. 1631. V. of Pontefract, 1641. V. of Orton, Westmorland, 1643-63. R. of Warsop, Notts., 1663-83. Died Aug. 23, 1683. M.I. at Warsop. (*B. Nightingale.*)

FOTHERGILL, GEORGE. Adm. pens. (age 17) at St John's, May 21, 1696. S. of Thomas (1663). B. at Warsop, Notts. School, Newark. Matric. 1696. Adm. at Lincoln's Inn, June 17, 1697. Barrister. Died Oct. 1741. Brother of Francis (1704). (*Lond. Mag.*)

FOTHERGILL, HENRY. Matric. pens. from Trinity, Easter, 1551. Will of one of these names (P.C.C.) 1586; of the Inner Temple.

FOTHERGILL, JOHN. Matric. pens. from St John's, Easter, 1626; B.A. 1629-30; M.A. 1633. Probably R. of Epperstone, Notts., 1640; and Preb. of Southwell, 1660-76. Died 1676.

FOTHERGILL, MARK. Adm. pens. (age 17) at Sidney, Apr. 8, 1650. S. of John, yeoman. B. at Aiskew, Bedale, Yorks. School, Aiskew (Mr Rawlins). Matric. 1650; B.A. 1653-4; M.A. 1657. R. of Culmington, Salop, 1660-91. Preb. of Hereford, 1685-91. Died 1691.

FOTHERGILL, MARMADUKE. Adm. sizar (age 15) at St John's, June 18, 1669. S. of Thomas, dyer, of York. B. there. Bapt. at St Dionys, June 2, 1654. School, Pocklington. Matric. 1669; B.A. 1673-4; M.A. 1677. Incorp. at Oxford, 1677. Qualified as D.D., but, declining the oath, was not admitted. Ord. deacon (York) Mar. 1679-80; priest, Feb. 1680-1. V of Skipwith, Yorks., 1681-9, resigned as non-juror. Liturgical scholar. Died at Westminster, 1731. (*Mag. Coll. Hist.*, 141.)

FOTHERGILL, STEPHEN. Adm. pens. (age 17) at St John's, June 8, 1661. S. of John (1626), R. of Epperstone, Notts. B. there. School, Repton. Chorister at Southwell. Matric. 1661.

FOTHERGILL, THOMAS. Adm. pens. (age 18) at Caius, Nov. 23, 1610. Of Yorkshire. S. of William, tanner. School, Well, Yorks. Matric. 1610; Scholar, 1610-4; B.A. (in the *ordo*) 1614, as 'Soddergill.' One Thomas Fothergill was V. of Holme-on-Spalding-Moor, Yorks., 1640-62 (he signed the Bishop of London's subscription book, June 2, 1648). Preb. of York, 1660. (*Venn*, I. 208; where the degree of the next is assigned to him.)

FOTHERGILL, THOMAS. B.A. from ST JOHN'S, 1616–7. Of Westmorland. M.A. 1620; B.D. 1627. Fellow, 1618. Ord. deacon (Peterb.) May 15; priest, May 16, 1625. Perhaps R. of Hardwick, Cambs., 1630–2; and R. of Thorington, Essex, 1643; sequestered, 1644.

FOTHERGILL, THOMAS. Adm. sizar (age 16) at ST JOHN'S, Apr. 6, 1663. S. of George (1623), V. of Orton, Westmorland. B. there. School, Kirkby Stephen. Matric. 1663; B.A. 1666–7; M.A. 1670. Ord. deacon (Ely) June 6, 1669; priest, May 29, 1670. R. of Warsop, Notts., –1703. Died 1703. M.I. Father of Francis (1704) and George (1696).

FOTHERGILL, THOMAS. Adm. pens. (age 17) at ST JOHN'S, Apr. 3, 1673. S. of Abraham, gent., of Chancery Lane, London. B. there. School, in Surrey (Mr Aldrich). Matric. 1673. Adm. at Lincoln's Inn, Dec. 21, 1674.

FOTHERGILL, THOMAS. Adm. Fell.-Com. (age 17) at SIDNEY, June 27, 1706. Only s. of Richard, Esq. B. at York. School, Westminster. Matric. 1706. Adm. at Gray's Inn, June 22, 1706.

FOTHERGILL, THOMAS. Adm. sizar (age 20) at ST JOHN'S, June 14, 1707. S. of Thomas, deceased. B. at Sedbergh, Yorks. School, Sedbergh. Matric. 1707; B.A. 1710–1. One of these names R. of Bridlington, Yorks., 1715–9; R. of Rise, 1719–22.

FOTHERGILL, TIMOTHY. Matric. pens. from TRINITY, Easter, 1605. Migrated, as scholar, to Trinity Hall, Dec. 22, 1606. One of these names, of York, gent., adm. at Gray's Inn, Nov. 3, 1615. Perhaps of St Margaret, Yorks., licensed to marry Mary Haddlesey, of Beeford, in 1627. (M. H. Peacock.)

FOTHERLEY, JOHN. Adm. Fell.-Com. (age 16) at CAIUS, Oct. 13, 1638. Eldest s. of Thomas (1597), Esq., of Rickmansworth, Herts. B. in parish of St Margaret, Westminster. Matric. 1639. Of Rickmansworth, Esq. Sheriff of Herts., 1652. An earnest Royalist. Died Jan. 4, 1702–3. Buried at Rickmansworth. (*Venn*, I. 332.)

FOTHERLY, THOMAS. Adm. pens. at KING'S, Lent, 1565–6.

FOTHERLEY, THOMAS. Adm. sizar at CAIUS, July 28, 1597. S. of Thomas, of Rickmansworth, Herts. School, Rickmansworth. Matric. 1597; Scholar, 1598–9. A devoted Royalist. Gentleman of the Privy Chamber to Charles I. M.P. for Rye, 1625–6, 1628–9. Knighted, Mar. 31, 1640. Buried at Rickmansworth, Dec. 13, 1649. M.I. there. Will (P.C.C.) 1650. Father of John (1638). (*Venn*, I. 163; A. B. Beaven.)

FOTYCHYDE, *see* FOTEHEDE.

FOTYTT, ——. B.A. 1477–8.

FOULCE, THOMAS. B.A. (? 1589–90); M.A. from JESUS, 1593.

FOULCHIER, JOHN, *see* FOLCHIER.

FOULDEN, HENRY. Probably member of GONVILLE HALL; executor to the Master, William Somersham, 1416.

FOULIS, *see also* FOWLES.

FOULIS or FOWLES, Sir DAVID. M.A. 1608 (Incorp. from Oxford). S. of James, of Colinton, Edinburgh. Came to England with James I. Adm. at Gray's Inn, 1603. Created M.A. (Oxford) Aug. 30, 1605. Gentleman of the King's Privy Chamber. Knighted, May 13, 1603. Created baronet, 1619–20. Purchased the estate of Ingleby, Cleveland, Yorks. Died 1642. at Ingleby, Aug. 24. (*Al. Oxon.*; *D.N.B.*; *G.E.C.*)Buried

FOULIS or FOWLE, DAVID. M.A. 1615 (Incorp. from Oxford). B. in Scotland. M.A. of Glasgow; Incorp. at Oxford, Jan. 22, 1610–1. Ord. deacon (London) Dec. 18, 1614, age 27. R. of Sudbrook, Lincs., 1619. Perhaps R. of Nevendon, Essex, 1654–62. V. of St James', Paddington, 1664–9. (*Al. Oxon.*)

FOWLIS, DAVID. Adm. Fell.-Com. at KING'S, 1672–3. Doubtless s. of Sir David, of Ingleby Manor, Yorks. Bapt. there, Apr. 18, 1656. M.A. 1675 (*Lit. Reg.*). Doubtless brother of John (1672). (*Vis. of Yorks.*, 1665.)

FOULIS, HENRY. Incorp. from Oxford, as B.A. 1658; and as M.A. 1664. S. of Sir Henry, Bart. Bapt. at Ingleby, Yorks., Apr. 5, 1635. Matric. from Queen's College, Oxford, Nov. 10, 1654; B.A. (Oxford) 1656–7; M.A. 1659; B.D. 1667. Fellow of Lincoln College, 1660. Historian and divine. Buried at St Michael's, Oxford, Dec. 26, 1669. (*Al. Oxon.*; *D.N.B.*)

FOULIS or FOWLES, JOHN. Matric. Fell.-Com. from KING'S, Michs. 1672. Probably s. of Sir David, of Ingleby Manor, Yorks.; and brother of David (1672–3).

FOULIS, WILLIAM. Adm. Fell.-Com. (age 15) at TRINITY, July 2, 1705. S. of Sir William, Bart., of Ingleby, Cleveland, Yorks. School, Enfield, Middlesex (Dr Uvedale). Matric. 1705. Succeeded as Bart. Oct. 1741. Buried at Ingleby, Dec. 11, 1756. Will (York) 1757. (*G.E.C.*)

FOULKE, FOULKES, *see* FOLKES.

FOULSAM or FALSAM, RICHARD. Matric. pens. from ST JOHN'S, Easter, 1583; B.A. 1586–7.

FOULSON, ROBERT. Matric. sizar from CORPUS CHRISTI, Easter, 1577.

FOULTHORPE, *see* FULTHORPE.

FOUNSTONE, EDMUND. Matric. pens. from PEMBROKE, Lent, 1579–80.

FOUNTAYNE, ANDREW. Adm. pens. at ST CATHARINE'S, Apr. 20, 1738. Of Melton, Yorks. S. of John, of Melton. B. July 10, 1721. Matric. 1739. Buried at Melton, Apr. 4, 1741. (Hunter, *S. Yorks.*, 367.)

FOUNTAINE, BRIGGE. Adm. pens. at CHRIST'S, Mar. 22, 1683–4. S. of James (1650). B. at Salle, Norfolk. School, St Paul's. Adm. at the Inner Temple, July 7, 1685. Probably of Salle. Died Apr. 1729, at Norwich. (*Peile*, II. 95; *Blomefield*, VIII. 271.)

FOUNTAIN, HARRINGTON. Adm. Fell.-Com. at CLARE, June 18, 1665. S. of John (1613), of Salle, Norfolk, Esq. Adm. at Lincoln's Inn, June 30, 1666.

FOUNTEYNE, JAMES. Adm. pens. at EMMANUEL, June 6, 1650. Of Norfolk. Doubtless s. of Brigge Fountaine, of Salle. Of Salle, Esq. Died Nov. 2, 1690. Buried at Salle. Father of Brigge (1683). (Le Neve, *Knights*, 472; *Blomefield*, VIII. 271.)

FOUNTAIN, JAMES. Adm. at CORPUS CHRISTI, 1688. Of London. Matric. 1688; B.A. 1691–2; M.A. 1695.

FOUNTEYNE, JOHN. Matric. pens. from CORPUS CHRISTI, Easter, 1573. One of these names, of Salle, Norfolk, adm. at the Inner Temple, 1578. Died 1621.

FUNTAYNE, JOHN. Matric. pens. from CLARE, Easter, 1620.

FOUNTAIN, JOHN. Matric. pens. from PEMBROKE, Michs. 1613. Doubtless s. of Arthur, of Wood Dalling, Norfolk. B.A. 1617–8; M.A. from Trinity Hall, 1621. Incorp. at Oxford, 1621. Adm. at Lincoln's Inn, Oct. 30, 1622. Barrister, 1629. University Counsel, 1641. Imprisoned for refusing to pay the Parliament's war tax, 1642; pardoned, 1652, and placed upon Parliamentary commissions. Serjeant-at-Law, 1658. Married Theodosia, dau. of Sir Edward Harrington. Died June 14, 1671, aged 70. M.I. at Salle, Norfolk. Will, P.C.C. Father of John (1653), Thomas (1657) and Harrington. (Le Neve, *Mon.*, IV. 147; *D.N.B.*)

FOUNTAIN, JO N. Adm. Fell.-Com. at EMMANUEL, May 11, 1636. Of Somerset. Matric. 1637.

FOUNTAINE, JOHN. Adm. Fell.-Com. at EMMANUEL, July 1, 1653. Of London. S. and h. of John (1613), of St Clement Danes, bencher. Adm. at Lincoln's Inn, Jan. 23, 1654–5. Of Melton, Yorks. Married Elizabeth, dau. of John Monkton, of Melton-on-the-Hill, Yorks. Died Sept. 1680. Brother of Thomas (1657). (Hunter, *S. Yorks.*, 367; M. H. Peacock.)

FOUNTAINE, JOHN. Adm. pens. (age 16) at SIDNEY, June 23, 1664. 2nd s. of Thomas, gent. B. in London. Schools, Merchant Taylors' and Oundle. Matric. Easter, 1665.

FOUNTAIN, JOHN. Adm. Fell.-Com. at CLARE, May 19, 1701. S. of Thomas (1657), of Melton, Yorks. B. at Cockenhatch, Barkway, Herts. (his mother's home). Of Melton, Esq. Died Oct. 30, 1736, aged 52. Buried at Melton. Brother of Thomas (1707). (Burke, *L.G.*)

FOUNTAYNE, JOHN. Adm. pens. at ST CATHARINE'S, Mar. 28, 1732. S. of John, of Melton, Yorks., Esq. Matric. 1732; B.A. 1735–6; M.A. 1739; D.D. 1751. Fellow, 1736–41. Ord. deacon (Lincoln) Feb. 26, 1737–8; priest, Mar. 1738–9. Preb. of Salisbury, 1739–1802. Canon of Windsor, 1741–8. Dean of York, 1747–1802. Owner of Melton. Died Feb. 14, 1802, aged 87. Buried at Melton. Will, P.C.C. (Hunter, *S. Yorks.*, 367; *D.N.B.*)

FOUNTAIN, JOHN. M.A. from KING'S, 1738. S. of Robert, of Easingwold, Yorks. Matric. from University College, Oxford, Apr. 2, 1726, age 20; B.A. from Christ Church, Oxford, 1729–30. Ord. priest (Lincoln) June 1, 1740. R. of Folkingham, Lincs.; and perhaps of North Tidmouth, Wilts. Died Oct. 1787. Will (P.C.C.) as of St Mary-le-Bone, Middlesex; where he seems to have kept a school. (*Al. Oxon.*; *G. Mag.*)

FOUNTAIN, MARTIN. Matric. pens. from CLARE, Easter, 1629. S. of Arthur, of Salle, Norfolk. B.A. 1631–2; M.A. 1635. Ord. deacon (Norwich) June 1, 1634; priest, May 24, 1635. R. of Burgh, Norfolk, 1634. Martin, s. of Arthur, of Salle, seems to have resided at Kempston, Beds. Will (P.C.C.) 1656; as of Burgh St Margaret. (*Vis. of Norfolk.*)

FOUNTAINE, ROBERT. Adm. sizar (age 19) at ST JOHN'S, May 5, 1732. S. of William, gent., of Yorkshire. B. at Linton-in-Craven. Schools, Threshfield and Burnsall. Matric. 1732; B.A. 1736–7; M.A. 1740. Ord. deacon (Lincoln) Mar. 6, 1736–7; priest (Norwich) Oct. 12, 1744. R. of Wells, Norfolk, 1744–55.

FOUNTAIN, THOMAS. Adm. Fell.-Com. (age 17) at MAGDALENE, Jan. 12, 1646-7. S. and h. of Thomas, of Hulcote, Bucks. Matric. 1647. Adm. at the Inner Temple, 1645. Died 1656. Will, P.C.C.

FOUNTAIN, THOMAS. Adm. at KING'S, a scholar from Eton, 1657. 2nd s. of John (1613), Serjeant-at-Law. B. in London, c. 1641. B.A. 1660-1. Fellow, 1660-3. Adm. at Lincoln's Inn, Apr. 30, 1661. Barrister, Lincoln's Inn. Succeeded his brother John (1653) at Melton, Yorks. Married Anne, dau. of Edward Chester, of Barkway, Herts. Died Feb. 5, 1709-10, aged 70. (Burke, *L.G.*; Le Neve, *Mon.*, II. 170.)

FOUNTAYNE, THOMAS. Adm. pens. (age 17) at ST JOHN'S, Oct. 25, 1707. S. of Thomas (1657), of Melton-on-the-Hill, near Doncaster. B. at Barkway, Herts. (his mother's home). Educated at Barkway. Matric. 1707. Died of small-pox, Sept. 26, 1708. Buried at Barkway. M.I. there. Brother of John (1701). (Hunter, *S. Yorks.*, I. 367; Le Neve, *Mon.*, II. 152.)

FOUNTAYNE, THOMAS. Adm. pens. at ST CATHARINE'S, Aug. 26, 1731. S. of John, of Melton, Yorks., Esq. B. Dec. 4, 1713. Matric. 1731. Died Jan. 18, 1739. Buried at Melton. Brother of John (1732). (Hunter, *S. Yorks.*, 367.)

FOURDEN, WILLIAM. Matric. pens. from ST JOHN'S, Michs. 1610.

FOURNESSE, *see* FURNESS.

FOWLBERYE, GEORGE. Matric. pens. from ST JOHN'S, Michs. 1552. Perhaps of Newbold, Yorks. If so, his will is dated Oct. 6, 1592, proved Dec. following, at York. (*Vis. of Yorks.*, 1584.)

FOWBRAY, ROBERT. Adm. at TRINITY, Apr. 25, 1619. S. of Robert, Head Master of Hull, 1593-1613. B. at Hull. School, Newcastle (under his father). Matric 1619. Migrated (age 16) to Sidney, July 7, 1620. B.A. 1622-3. Ord. deacon (York) June, 1623. Master of Northallerton Grammar School, 1623-38. (M. H. Peacock.)

FOWBERY, THOMAS. Adm. sizar at EMMANUEL, May 15, 1617. Of Yorkshire. Matric. 1617. Migrated to Queens', Sept. 12, 1617. B.A. from St John's, 1620-1; M.A. 1627. Ord. deacon (York, for Durham) Sept. 1622.

POWELL, Sir JOHN, Bart. Matric. Fell.-Com. from KING'S, Michs. 1681. S. of Sir John, of Fowellscombe, Devon, Bart. Bapt. at Ashprington, Dec. 12, 1665. M.A. 1682. Succeeded as Bart. Jan. 1676-7. M.P. for Totnes, 1688-92. Died 1692, aged 27. Buried at Ugborough, Devon, Nov. 26, 1692. (Burke, *Ext. Bart.*; *G.E.C.*)

FOWKES, *see* FOLKES.

FOWLE or 'FEWELL,' CHRISTOPHER. Matric. sizar from PEMBROKE, Easter, 1560. Of Yorkshire. B.A. 1562-3; M.A. from St John's, 1566. Fellow of St John's, 1563. V. of Whaddon, Cambs., 1565, as 'Fewell.' Perhaps P.C. of Easington, Durham (? Yorks.) 1572-98.

FOWLE, HENRY. *Grace* for M.A. from CLARE, 1630.

FOWLE, JOHN. B.A. from QUEENS', 1550-1. Fellow. Probably matric. pens. at St John's, Michs. 1548.

FOWLE, JOHN. Matric. sizar from TRINITY, Michs. 1570; B.A. 1573-4. Will (P.C.C.) 1622; pastor of St Ives, Cornwall. Mentions sons Nathaniel (1612) and Joseph (1617). (J. Ch. Smith.)

FOWLE, JOHN. Adm. pens. at EMMANUEL, June 18, 1609. Matric. 1609; Scholar; B.A. 1612-3. Doubtless buried at St Andrew's, Cambridge, Nov. 3, 1613, as 'Fowke.'

FOWLE, JOHN. Adm. at CORPUS CHRISTI, 1610. Of Suffolk.

FOWLE, JOHN. Matric. pens. from TRINITY, Michs. 1621. S. of Thomas (1584). Bapt. at Redgrave, Suffolk, Sept. 28, 1599. Scholar, 1625; B.A. 1625-6; M.A. 1629. Fellow, 1627.

FOWLE, JOHN. Adm. pens. at EMMANUEL, Sept. 11, 1641. Of Essex. Matric. 1642; B.A. 1645-6. Perhaps of Castle Hedingham, Essex; adm. at Gray's Inn, Nov. 7, 1644. Barrister, 1651.

FOWLE, JOHN. Adm. pens. (age 16) at CAIUS, Apr. 23, 1663; shortly afterwards, on his father's death, sizar. S. of Thomas (1624), clerk, of Monewden, Suffolk. B. there. Schools, Coddenham (Mr Candler), Wickham Market (Mr Whitcraft) and Stowmarket (Mr Colston) (all private). Matric. 1663; Scholar, 1663-7; B.A. 1667-8. Probably ord. deacon (Lincoln) May 17, 1668; priest (Norwich) Mar. 19, 1670-1, as C. of Boyton. R. of Creeting St Peter, Suffolk, 1670-1724. Buried there July 23, 1724. Will (Norwich C. C.) 1724. (*Venn*, I. 418.)

FOWLE, JOHN. Adm. pens. (age 18) at TRINITY, June 7, 1686. S. of Edward. B. at Stanton Barnet, Marlborough. School, Piccadilly, London (Mr John Goad). Matric. 1687-8; Scholar, 1689; B.A. 1689-90; M.A. 1693. Ord. deacon (Peterb.) Sept. 20, 1696; C. of Clipsham, Rutland.

FOWLE, JOHN. Adm. pens. at ST CATHARINE'S, July 6, 1707. Matric. 1708. One of these names, s. of John, of Broomhall, Norfolk, Esq., adm. at Gray's Inn, Feb. 25, 1706-7. Barrister, 1714. Bencher, 1732. Sub-steward of Yarmouth, 1735-44. Recorder, 1744-61. Auditor of Excise, 1750-72. Died Oct. 2, 1772. (A. B. Beaven.)

FOWLE, JOSEPH. Adm. pens. at EMMANUEL, May 30, 1617. S. of John (1570). Matric. 1617; Scholar; B.A. 1620-1; M.A. 1624. Brother of the next.

FOWLE, NATHANIEL. Adm. pens. at EMMANUEL, June 14, 1612. Of Cornwall. S. of John (1570). Scholar; B.A. 1615-6; M.A. 1620; B.D. 1627. Fellow, 1621. Ord. deacon (Peterb.) Mar. 25; priest, Mar. 26, 1627. Probably R. of St Ives, Cornwall. Will (Exeter) 1630. Brother of Joseph, above. (J. Ch. Smith.)

FOWLE, NICHOLAS. Matric. pens. from QUEENS', Easter, 1580. Of Suffolk. S. of Thomas (1547), R. of Redgrave. B.A. 1583-4; M.A. 1588. Licensed schoolmaster at Redgrave, Suffolk, 1592. Perhaps father of Thomas (1624).

FOWLE, ROBERT. Adm. pens. at QUEENS', Jan. 2, 1585-6. Of Essex.

FOWLE, ROBERT. Matric. sizar from EMMANUEL, Easter, 1609.

FOWLE, THOMAS. Matric. pens. from ST JOHN'S, Michs. 1547; B.A. 1549-50; M.A. 1553. Fellow, 1550; deprived under Queen Mary, but restored, 1558. R. of Redgrave *with* Botesdale, Suffolk, 1561-97. R. of Hinderclay, 1561-6. R. of Aldham, Essex, 1562-3. Preb. of Norwich, 1563-81. Chaplain to Sir Nicholas Bacon. Perhaps Master of Botesdale School, 1586. Will (Norwich C. C.) mentions sons Nicholas (1580) and Thomas (1584-5). (*Cooper*, I. 452; V. B. Redstone.)

FOULE, THOMAS. Adm. scholar (age 20) at CAIUS, Apr. 25, 1578. S. of Robert, of Kirton-in-Lindsey, Lincs. School, Kirton.

FOWLE, THOMAS. Matric. pens. from QUEENS', Lent, 1584-5. Of Suffolk. S. of Thomas (1547); and brother of Nicholas (1580) and father of John (1621).

FOWLE, THOMAS. Matric. sizar from CLARE, Easter, 1614; B.A. 1617-8; M.A. 1621. Fellow. Ord. deacon (Peterb.) Sept. 22, 1622; priest, May 23, 1624.

FOULE, THOMAS. Matric. pens. from ST CATHARINE'S, Easter, 1624; B.A. 1627. Perhaps Thomas, s. of Nicholas (? 1580); bapt. at Redgrave, Nov. 16, 1609. One of these names, ordained 1662, R. of Monewdon, Suffolk, 1647-63. Father of John (1663). Died 1663.

FOWLE, THOMAS. Adm. pens. (age 16) at CAIUS, July 5, 1712. S. of John, Esq., of Broome, Norfolk. B. at Gt Melton. School, Norwich. Scholar, 1712-7; Matric. 1713; LL.B. 1718; LL.D. 1727. Fellow, 1719-22. Commissary to the Dean and Chapter of Norwich, and to the Archdeacon of Norfolk, 1731. Married, at Burlingham St Peter, Mar. 27, 1722, Mary Goose, of Yarmouth. Died Nov. 22, 1755. (*Venn*, I. 527.)

FOWLL, ——. B.A. 1522-3. Perhaps the Richard Flower in *Gr. Bk.* Γ.

FOWLE, ——. Adm. Fell.-Com. at EMMANUEL, June 17, 1618. Matric. 1618.

FOWLE, ——. Adm. Fell.-Com. at TRINITY HALL, June 22, 1694. Resided till Sept. 1696.

FOWLER, ABRAHAM. Adm. pens. at EMMANUEL, June 20, 1640. Of Cheshire. Matric. 1640; B.A. 1643-4; M.A. from Pembroke, 1647. Fellow of Pembroke, *c.* 1645.

FOWLER, BRIAN. Adm. pens. (age 18) at CHRIST'S, Apr. 8, 1631. S. of Rowland (1593). B. at Bromhill, Norfolk. School, Chesterford (private) under Mr Adams. Matric. 1631. (*Peile*, I. 408.)

FOWLER, CHAPPEL. Adm. sizar (age 17) at ST JOHN'S, Oct. 14, 1721. S. of George, mercer, of Nottinghamshire. B. in Southwell. Schools, Southwell and Newark. Matric. 1722; B.A. 1725-6; M.A. 1729; B.D. 1737. Fellow, 1727-47. Junior Proctor, 1735-6. Ord. deacon (Lincoln) May 28, 1727; priest, June 1, 1729. R. of Thorington, Essex, 1746-81. R. of Frating, 1746-81. Died at Colchester, Dec. 24, 1781. Will, P.C.C.; of Colchester. (*Scott-Mayor*, III. 346.)

FOWLER, CHARLES. Adm. sizar (age 17) at ST JOHN'S, May 23, 1746. S. of Francis, mercer, of Nottinghamshire. B. at Southwell. School, Southwell. Matric. 1746; B.A. 1749-50; M.A. 1761. Ord. deacon (York) June 10, 1750; priest, May 24, 1752. Perhaps R. of Hatcliffe, Lincs., 1760-78. R. of Claypole, June-July, 1778. (*Scott-Mayor*, III. 559.)

FOWLER, DANIEL. Adm. pens. at CORPUS CHRISTI, 1607. Of York. S. of Moses (1569). Matric. 1608; B.A. 1609-10; M.A. 1613. Ord. priest (York) Mar. 613-4. M.I. to him and his father at Ripon.

FOWLER, DAVID. Adm. sizar (age 20) at MAGDALENE, Mar. 7, 1729-30. S. of David. B. at Stanefield, Lincs. School, Brigg. Matric. 1731; LL.B. 1736. Ord. deacon (Lincoln) Mar. 2, 1734-5; priest, June 1, 1735. V. of Hanslape, Bucks., 1742.

FOWLER, EDWARD. M.A. from TRINITY, 1656. S. of William, V. of Westerleigh, Gloucs. B. there, 1632. School, Gloucester. Matric. from Corpus Christi, Oxford, Nov. 22, 1650; B.A. (Oxford) 1653; M.A. (Incorp. from Cambridge) 1656; B.D. and D.D. (Oxford) 1681. Presbyterian chaplain to Amabel, dowager countess of Kent. R. of Northill, Beds., 1656-73. R. of All Hallows, Bread St, London, 1673-81. Preb. of Gloucester, 1676-91. V. of St Giles', Cripplegate, 1682-1714. Chaplain to the King, 1689. Member of the commission for revising the Prayer Book, 1689. Bishop of Gloucester, 1691-1714. Author, theological. Died at Chelsea, Aug. 26, 1714, aged 82. Buried at Hendon. Will, P.C.C. Father of Richard (1710). (*Al. Oxon.*; *D.N.B.*)

FOWLER, ELISHA. Adm. sizar (age 19) at ST JOHN'S, Mar. 24, 1667-8. S. of Robert, clerk, of 'Leekfrith,' Staffs. B. there. School, Shrewsbury. Matric. 1668; B.A. from King's, 1671-2. Brother of John, of same date.

FOULER, FRANCIS. Adm. sizar (age 16) at CAIUS, June 26, 1626. S. of Richard, husbandman. B. at Beighton, Norfolk. Bapt. Aug. 20, 1609. School, Norwich. Matric. 1626; B.A. 1630-1. Ord. priest (Norwich) Sept. 23, 1632. Marie, wife of Francis Fowler, clerk, was buried at Beighton, Mar. 10, 1652-3. (*Venn*, I. 277.)

FOWLER, GEORGE. Matric. pens. from JESUS, Michs. 1553.

FOWLER, GEORGE. Matric. pens. from CHRIST'S, c. 1595. S. of George, of Bromhill, Norfolk. Brother of Rowland (1593). (*Peile*, I. 219.)

FOWLER, GERVASE. Adm. sizar (age 17) at CHRIST'S, Feb. 5, 1696-7. S. of Samuel. B. at Stonegravel, Derbs. School, Chesterfield. Matric. 1697; B.A. 1701. Ord. deacon (Lichfield) June, 1705; priest, May, 1711. Usher of Chesterfield School. C. of Staveley, Derbs. R. of Langwith, 1719. Died Feb. 1, 1719-20. Buried at Chesterfield. M.I. (*F.M.G.*, I. 165; *Peile*, II. 138.)

FOWLER, ISAAC. Matric. sizar from KING'S, Easter, 1616.

FOWLER, ISAAC. Adm. pens. at EMMANUEL, June 20, 1640. Of Cheshire. Matric. 1640; B.A. 1643-4; M.A. from Clare, 1647. Fellow of Clare, Apr. 25, 1645, by visitor's warrant. Will proved (V.C.C.) 1659.

FOWLER, JAMES. Matric. pens. from GONVILLE HALL, Easter, 1544. One of these names adm. at the Inner Temple, Feb. 5, 1546-7; perhaps buried at Weeting, Norfolk, 1585. (*Venn*, I. 32.)

FOWLER, JAMES. Adm. sizar (age 18) at MAGDALENE, June 23, 1748. S. of James. B. at Horncastle, Lincs. School, Horncastle. Matric. 1748. Ord. deacon (Lincoln) June 2, 1751; priest, June 17, 1753.

FOWLER, JOHN. B.A. 1526-7; M.A. 1529. One 'Mr John Fowler, vir doctus,' was V. of Bisley, Gloucs., 1543-53. Will (Gloucester) 1553. (But *see Al. Oxon.*)

FOWLER, JOHN. Matric. pens. from QUEENS', Easter, 1625. Of Leicestershire.

FOWLER, JOHN. Adm. pens. (age 19) at ST JOHN'S, Mar. 15, 1629-30. S. of William, R. of Kedleston, Derbs. B. there. School, Repton. Matric. 1629-30.

FOWLER, JOHN. Adm. sizar (age 17) at ST JOHN'S, Mar. 24, 1667-8. S. of Robert, clerk, of Leek Frith, Staffs. B. there. School, Shrewsbury. Matric. 1668; B.A. 1671-2. Brother of Elisha (1667-8).

FOWLER, JOHN. Adm. Fell.-Com. (age 16) at ST JOHN'S, June 21, 1669. S. of Thomas, gent., of Aislaby, Durham. B. there. Bapt. at Egglescliffe, Sept. 28, 1652. School, Northallerton. Matric. 1669.

FOWLER, MATTHEW. M.A. from QUEENS', 1641; D.D. 1660 (*Lit. Reg.*). S. of Walter, of Penford, Staffs. Matric. from Christ Church, Oxford, Sept. 1, 1634, age 16; B.A. (Oxford) 1637-8. R. of Willey, Warws., 1648 and 1660. R. of St Paul's, Hammersmith, 1661-2. R. of St Alphage, Cripplegate, 1662-3. R. of Whitchurch, Salop, 1667. Preb. of Lichfield, 1667-83. Died Dec. 26, 1683. Buried at Whitchurch. M.I. there. (*Al. Oxon.*; *Staffs. Pedigrees*; J. Ch. Smith.)

FOWLER, MATTHEW. Matric. sizar from QUEENS', Easter, 1641. S. of John, of Billesdon, Leics. Migrated to St John's, 1644. B.A. 1644-5. Ord. deacon (Lincoln) Sept. 19, 1645; priest, May 22, 1646.

FOWLER, MATTHEW. Matric. pens. from QUEENS', Jan. 26, 1670-1. Of Middlesex. Probably s. of Matthew (M.A. 1641). Matric. 1671; M.B. 1676. Died Jan. 31, 1677-8, aged 24. M.I. at Whitchurch, Salop. (*Vis. of Staffs.*, 1663; J. Ch. Smith.)

FOWLER, MOSES. Matric. pens. from CORPUS CHRISTI, Michs. 1569. Of Kent. B.A. 1572-3; M.A. 1576; B.D. 1583. Fellow, 1576-86. Scrutator, 1585. University preacher, 1585. V. of Aylsham, Norfolk, 1584. R. of Brandsburton, Yorks., in 1591. R. of Sigglesthorne, 1591-3. Dean of the Collegiate Church of Ripon, 1604-8. Married, 1586, Catharine Raye, of Landbeach, Cambs. Died Mar. 1608-9. Buried at Ripon. M.I. Father of Daniel (1608). (*Cooper*, II. 480.)

FOWLER, NATHANIEL. Adm. sizar at EMMANUEL, Feb. 24, 1668-9. Of Northamptonshire. Matric. 1669; B.A. 1672-3; M.A. 1682. Ord. deacon (London) May 21; priest, May 26, 1676.

FOWLER, RICHARD. B.A. 1508-9. Will (P.C.C.) 1558, of one of these names; of Clipsham, Rutland, clerk.

FOWLER, RICHARD. Matric. pens. from ST JOHN'S, Michs. 1607; B.A. 1611-2; M.A. 1615. Ord. deacon (London) Dec. 20, 1612; priest, Mar. 1612-3. Will (Exeter) 1669, of one of these names; of Zennor, Cornwall, clerk.

FOWLER, RICHARD. Matric. sizar from MAGDALENE, Easter, 1618; B.A. 1620-1. Ord. deacon (Peterb.) Mar. 17; priest, Mar. 18, 1621-2.

FOWLER, RICHARD. M.A. 1626 (Incorp. from Oxford). S. of Richard, of Harnage Grange, Salop. Matric. from St Mary's Hall, Oxford, Oct. 22, 1619, age 19; B.A. 1619; M.A. from Oriel, 1625. (*Al. Oxon.*; Pedigree in Burke's *Ext. Bart.*)

FOWLER, RICHARD. LL.B. from TRINITY HALL, 1710. S. of Edward (1656), of Northill, Beds., D.D. Matric. from Exeter College, Oxford, May 3, 1689, age 17; B.A. (Oxford) 1691-2. (*Al. Oxon.*)

FOWLER, RICHARD. Adm. sizar (age 18) at SIDNEY, June 7, 1723. S. of John, gent. B. at Sutton, Yorks. School, Coxwold. Matric. 1723.

FOWLLER, RICHARD. Adm. sizar (age 19) at PEMBROKE, June 24, 1736. S. of Richard, of Helland, Cornwall, clerk. Matric. 1736; B.A. 1741-2. Ord. deacon (Ely) Feb. 26, 1742-3; priest (Norwich) Feb. 1742-3. Probably R. of Dallinghoe and Easton, Suffolk. Died Apr. 5, 1784, aged 67. M.I. at Framlingham. Will (P.C.C.) 1785.

FOWLER, ROBERT. Adm. sizar (age 17) at TRINITY, July 1, 1729. S. of Samuel, of Wainfleet, Lincs. School, Wainfleet (Mr Younge). Matric. 1729; Scholar, 1733; B.A. 1733-4. Ord. deacon (Lincoln) Mar. 10, 1733-4. Perhaps of Skendlethorpe, Lincs.; died June 11, 1759. (*Musgrave.*)

FOWLER, ROBERT. Adm. pens. (age 18) at TRINITY, May 24, 1744. S. of George, of Skendleby Thorpe, Lincs. School, Westminster. Matric. 1744; Scholar, 1745; B.A. 1747-8; M.A. 1751; D.D. 1764. Fellow, 1750. Ord. deacon (Ely) Feb. 23, 1752; priest, Dec. 25, 1752. Chaplain to the King, 1758-71. Preb. of Westminster, 1765-71. Bishop of Killaloe, 1771-9. Archbishop of Dublin, 1779-1801. Died at Bassingbourne Hall, Essex, Oct. 10, 1801. (*D.N.B.*; *Al. Westmon.*, 332; *Lincs. Pedigrees.*)

FOWLER, ROLAND. Matric. pens. from JESUS, Lent, 1557-8.

FOWLER, ROWLAND. Matric. Fell.-Com. from CHRIST'S, 1593. Probably s. of George, of Bromhill, Norfolk. Had a lease from the College of the Priory of Bromhill, 1613. Probably buried at Weeting, Norfolk, Oct. 21, 1637. Brother of George (1595), father of Brian (1631). (*Peile*, I. 208; where he is wrongly called Brian.)

FOWLER, SAMUEL. Adm. sizar (age 18) at ST JOHN'S, as 'Foulis,' May 4, 1687. S. of William, gent. B. at Repton, Derbs. School, Repton. Matric. 1687; B.A. 1690-1. One of these names R. of Blunham, Beds.; buried there Dec. 1, 1704.

FOWLER, SAMUEL. Adm. pens at ST CATHARINE'S, June 28, 1695. Matric. 1697; B.A. 1699-1700; M.A. 1717. Ord. deacon (Gloucester) May 4, 1704; priest, Mar. 6, 1708. V. of Standish, Gloucs., 1709-24. Chaplain to Bishop of Coventry and Lichfield. R. of Cowley, Gloucs., 1717-24. Died 1724. (F. S. Hockaday.)

FOWLER, STEPHEN. Adm. at EMMANUEL, Sept. 22, 1645. S. of Richard, clerk, of Sodbury, Gloucs. Matric. from Lincoln College, Oxford, Dec. 10, 1641, age 16; B.A. (Cambridge) 1645-6; M.A. (Oxford) 1648-9. Ord. deacon and priest (Norwich) Aug. 28, 1661. R. of Crick, Northants., 1650; ejected, 1662. (*Al. Oxon.*)

FOWLER, THOMAS. R. of Sausthorpe, Lincs., 1596. Described as 'M.A. of Cambridge; ord. priest by Wykeham, Bishop of Lincoln.' (*Lib. Cler. Linc.*)

FOWLER, THOMAS. Matric. sizar from TRINITY, Lent, 1620-1.

FOWLER, THOMAS. Adm. pens. at EMMANUEL, Feb. 3, 1626-7. Of Ely. B.A. 1630-1; M.A. from Jesus, 1634.

FOWLER, THOMAS. Adm. sizar (age 15) at ST JOHN'S, Oct. 2, 1640. S. of Thomas, stonemason, of Barley, Derbs. B. there. School, Dronfield, Derbs. Matric. 1642.

FOWLER, THOMAS. Adm. scholar (age 15) at SIDNEY, Mar. 18, 1662-3. S. of Daniel, deceased. B. in the Isle of Ely. School, Ely (Mr Hitche). Matric. 1663; B.A. 1666-7; M.A. 1670; B.D. 1677. Fellow, 1668-80. Incorp. at Oxford, 1675. Ord. deacon (Gloucs., at Holborn) Feb. 17, 1669-70; priest (Ely) Mar. 19, 1670-1. Buried at St Edward's, Cambridge, Sept. 13, 1680. Will (V.C.C.) 1680.

FOWLER, THOMAS. Adm. pens. (age 17) at CHRIST'S, Apr. 12, 1672. S. of Thomas. B. at Faringdon, Berks. Matric. 1672; B.A. 1675-6. Probably ord. priest (Lincoln) 1678-9. R. of Sheepy, Leics., 1679-1710. (*Peile*, II. 41.)

FOWLER, WILLIAM. Matric. sizar from TRINITY, Michs. 1580; B.A. 1584-5. One of these names R. of Kelleston, Derbs. R. of Radborne, 1626. *See* John (1629-30). (Contemporary in *Al. Oxon.*)

FOWLER, WILLIAM. B.A. from TRINITY, 1597-8; M.A. 1601. Adm. at the Middle Temple, Aug. 4, 1604. Secretary and Master of Requests to the Queen of James I, 1603. Author, *Sonnets*, *Letters*. Will (P.C.C.) 1613. (*Cooper*, II. 528.)

FOWLER, WILLIAM. Matric. pens. from TRINITY, Easter, 1632.

FOWLER, WILLIAM. Adm. sizar at QUEENS', July 3, 1660. Of Leicestershire. Matric. 1660; B.A. 1663-4. Incorp. at Oxford, July 11, 1676, as M.A. Ord. deacon (Peterb.) May 21, 1665; priest, Mar. 3, 1666-7. R. of Kettering, Northants., 1670-80. R. of Cranford St Andrew, 1680-1714. R. of Woodford, 1707-14. Buried at Cranford, Oct. 12, 1714. Admon. (Archd. Northants.) 1715. (H. I. Longden; T. P. Dorman.)

FOWLER, WILLIAM. M.A. from QUEENS', 1708. Assumed, in the *Graduati*, to be identical with the above.

FOWLER, ——. B.A. 1476-7.

FOWLES, *see also* FOULIS.

FOWLES, JOHN. Adm. sizar at EMMANUEL, June 29, 1704. Of Kent. Matric. 1705-6.

FOWNES, GEORGE. Adm. pens. at EMMANUEL, Feb. 1, 1650-1. Of Salop. School, Shrewsbury. Matric. 1651; B.A. 1654-5; M.A. 1659. V. of High Wycombe, till about 1660. Preacher at Bristol and elsewhere. Died in prison at Gloucester, Dec. 1685. (*Calamy*, I. 243.)

FOWNES, THOMAS. Adm. Fell.-Com. at Trinity, Dec. 10, 1646. Of Devon.

FOWNES, WILLIAM. Adm. pens. (age 18) at TRINITY, June 1, 1683. S. of Thomas, of Dorchester. School, Westminster. Scholar, 1684; Matric. 1685-6; B.A. 1686-7; M.A. from Peterhouse, 1690. Fellow of Peterhouse (by mandate) 1687. Junior Proctor, 1706-7. Ord. deacon (Ely) 1692; priest, 1694. R. of Wimpole, Cambs., 1695-1713. Buried at Little St Mary's, Cambridge, May 20, 1713. (*T. A. Walker*, 182.)

FOWSERE, EDMUND. Scholar of CLARE, Dec. 18, 1495, age 13.

FOXE, CHARLES. Matric. pens. from ST JOHN'S, Easter, 1576.

FOX, CHRISTOPHER. Matric. sizar from JESUS, Michs. 1582.

FOXE, CHRISTOPHER. Matric. sizar from KING'S, Michs. 1618; B.A. 1621-2; M.A. 1625.

FOX, CHRISTOPHER. Adm. sizar (age 17) at ST JOHN'S, Jan. 18, 1681-2. S. of Christopher, yeoman. B. at Deane, Beds. Schools, Newton, Northants. (private, Mr Trot) and Oundle. Matric. 1682; B.A. 1685-6; M.A. 1693. Ord. deacon (London) Feb. 24, 1688-9; priest, Mar. 20, 1697-8. V. of Kimpton, Herts., 1698-1722. R. of Pirton. Died Nov. 15, 1722.

FOXE, DANIEL. Matric. sizar from TRINITY HALL, Easter, 1554.

FOX, DANIEL. Matric. pens. from TRINITY, Easter, 1631; B.A. 1634-5. One of these names s. and h. of Thomas, of St Andrew, Holborn, citizen; adm. at Gray's Inn, Nov. 1, 1635. Barrister, 1642.

FOX, EDMUND. Matric. pens. from ST JOHN'S, Easter, 1585. One of these names, 1st s. of Edmund, of Ludford, Heref.; adm. at the Inner Temple, 1586.

FOX, EDMUND. Adm. sizar (age 16) at CAIUS, June 19, 1667. B. at Saxthorpe, Norfolk. Schools, Holt and Walsingham. Matric. 1667; Scholar, 1668-70. Buried at St Michael's, Cambridge, Dec. 27, 1670. (*Venn*, I. 431.)

FOX, EDWARD. Adm. at KING'S (age 18) a scholar from Eton, Mar. 27, 1512. B. at Dursley, Gloucs. B.A. 1515-6; M.A. 1519-20; D.D. (by 1532). Fellow, 1515. Provost of King's, 1528-38. Secretary to Wolsey. Master of Sherburn Hospital, Durham, 1527. Preb. of York, 1527. R. of Combemartin, Devon, 1528. Archdeacon of Leicester, 1531-5; of Dorset, 1533-5. Bishop of Hereford, 1535-8. Preb. of Wells, 1537. Much employed on foreign missions and state affairs. Died May 8, 1538. Will (P.C.C.). (*Cooper*, I. 66; *D.N.B.*)

FOX, EGREMOND. Matric. pens. from PEMBROKE, Easter, 1586. Can this be Guy Fawkes, whom *see*?

FOXE, FRANCIS. Matric. pens. from MAGDALENE, Easter, 1623.

FOXE, FRANCIS. Adm. pens. at TRINITY, May 27, 1661. School, Westminster. Matric. 1661; Scholar, 1662; B.A. 1664-5; M.A. 1668. Fellow, 1667. Ord. deacon (Ely) May 29, 1670; priest, Sept. 24, 1670. Undermaster at St Paul's, 1673-85. Died Apr. 28, 1686, aged 43. Buried at Chislehurst, Kent. M.I. there; 'of Co. Hereford.' (*Al. Westmon.*)

FOX, FRANCIS. M.A. 1707 (Incorp. from Oxford). S. of Francis, of Brentford, Middlesex. Matric. from St Edmund's Hostel, Oxford, Apr. 14, 1698, age 22; B.A. (Oxford) 1701; M.A. 1704. R. of Boscombe, Wilts., 1708. V. of Potterne, 1711. Preb. of Sarum, 1713-38. R. of Woodford, 1717. V. of St Mary, Reading, 1726-38. R. of Stratton, 1730. Died Ju 6, 1738. Buried at St Mary, Reading. (*Al. Oxon.*; *D.N.B.*)y

FOX, GEORGE. Adm. at KING'S (age 16) a scholar from Eton, Aug. 14, 1534. Of Ludlow, Salop. Left about 1537. Perhaps brother of William (1537).

FOXE, HENRY. Adm. pens. (age 18) at CAIUS, Mar. 14, 1582-3. S. of William, of Kendal, Westmorland. School, Skelsmergh, Westmorland. Matric. 1582-3; B.A. from St John's, 1586-7.

FOX, HENRY. Matric. sizar from QUEENS', Michs. 1638. Of Cambridgeshire. B.A. 1641-2. Ord. deacon (Norwich) Sept. 22, 1644.

FOX, HUGH. Matric. pens. from ST JOHN'S, Easter, 1579.

FOX, ISAAC. Adm. sizar (age 17) at ST JOHN'S, June 27, 1672. S. of Robert, innkeeper. B. at Warwick. School, Burbrooke. Matric. 1672; B.A. 1675-6; M.A. 1680. Incorp. at Oxford, 1683. V. of St Michael, Coventry, 1684. V. of Foleshill, Warws., 1704. (*Al. Oxon.*)

FOX, JOHN. B.A. 1509-10. One of these names V. of Collingham, Yorks., in 1524.

FOXE, JOHN. Matric. pens. from CHRIST'S, May, 1549.

FOX, JOHN. Matric. sizar from TRINITY, Easter, 1550; Scholar, 1550; B.A. 1550-1. Fellow, 1552. R. of South Cove, Suffolk, 1554-66, as 'M.A.' Perhaps V. of Reydon and Southwold, 1555-66.

FOXE, JOHN. Matric. sizar from ST CATHARINE'S, Michs. 1552.

FOXE, JOHN. Matric. sizar from TRINITY, Lent, 1563-4; B.A. 1567-8; M.A. 1572. V. of Holy Trinity, Cambridge, 1578.

FOXE, JOHN. Matric. pens. from CHRIST'S, Feb. 1564-5; B.A. 1567-8.

FOXE, JOHN. Matric. pens. from ST JOHN'S, Easter, 1573. S. of John, citizen and goldsmith, of London. B.A. 1573-4; M.A. 1577; B.D. from St Catharine's, 1584. Fellow of St Catharine's, *c.* 1575. University preacher, 1582. R. of Linwood, Lincs. Preb. of St Paul's, 1591-1623. R. of Hanwell and Brentwood, Middlesex, 1596-1623. Preb. of Westminster, 1603-23. Preb. of Wolverhampton, 1620-3. Buried in Westminster Abbey, Sept. 27, 1623. Will (P.C.C.) 1623. (*Westminster Abbey Registers.*)

FOX, JOHN. Matric. pens. from CLARE, *c.* 1591. S. of William. B. at Gt Missenden, Bucks., 1572. B.A. (? 1594-5). Ord. priest (Colchester) Nov. 16, 1600. V. of Streatley, Beds., 1605; signs till 1611. (*Vis. of Bucks.*, 1634.)

FOXE, JOHN. M.A. 1635-6 (*Lit. Reg.*). Possibly the nonconformist divine; V. of Pucklechurch, Gloucs., 1657-62, ejected. Afterwards pastor of a congregation at Nailsworth. Author. (But no one of these names took a B.A. degree from Clare in 1624, as stated in the *D.N.B.*)

FOX, JOHN. Adm. pens. (age 16) at SIDNEY, Mar. 1, 1663-4. 1st s. of Anthony, Esq. B. at Syleham, Suffolk. Schools, Eye (Mr Browne) and Starston (Mr Coppen). B.A. 1666-7.

FOX, JOHN. Adm. sizar (age 17) at PEMBROKE, May 16, 1668. S. of William, clerk. B. at Ilkeston, Derbs. Matric. 1668; B.A. 1671-2. Ord. deacon (Lincoln) June 2, 1672; C. of Hatherne; priest (York) Dec. 1674.

FOX, JOHN. Adm. sizar at CLARE, June 28, 1704. B. at Holt, Norfolk. Matric. 1704; B.A. 1707-8; M.A. 1712. Ord. deacon (Lincoln) June 15, 1712; priest (Norwich) July 4, 1714. V. of Lakenham, Norfolk, 1719. V. of Catton. Preb. of Norwich.

FOX, JOHN. Adm. sizar (age 20) at ST JOHN'S, June 25, 1709. S. of Alexander, dyer. B. at Thwaites, Cumberland. School, Kendal. Matric. 1709; B.A. 1712-3. Ord. deacon (York) Sept. 1715; priest, 1716-7. V. of Cantley, Yorks., 1717.

FOX, JOHN. Adm. sizar (age 17) at ST JOHN'S, May 19, 1746. S. of J., clerk, of Yorkshire. B. at Doncaster. School, Beverley. Matric. 1746; B.A. 1749-50. Ord. deacon (Lincoln) May 24; priest, June 11, 1752. V. of Uffculme, Devon, till 1756. V. of Kilnwick Percy, Yorks., 1756-*c.* 1775.

FOXE, LAURENCE. M.A. from ST JOHN'S, 1624. Of Somerset. Matric. from Exeter College, Oxford, Dec. 16, 1608, age 18; B.A. 1611-2. R. of Lenham and Royton, Kent, 1620. (*Al. Oxon.*)

FOX, NATHANIEL. Adm. at EMMANUEL, Sept. 7, 1622. Matric. from Magdalene, Easter, 1623. Perhaps R. of Poyntington, Somerset, 1643–78; but called M.A. Died 1678.

FOXE, NICHOLAS. Matric. pens. from JESUS, Michs. 1571. S. of Thomas, gent., of Thorpe, Yorks. School, Newburgh, Yorks. Migrated to Caius, July 17, 1573, age 18. Fell.-Com. 1574. Probably ord. priest at Douay, in 1581. (*Venn*, I. 73.)

FOX, OBADIAH. Incorp. M.A. 1671, from Exeter College, Oxford. Matric. there, June 28, 1662, age 17. S. of Thomas, of Davidstowe, Cornwall. B.A. (All Souls') 1666; M.A. (Exeter) 1669. R. of Stockleigh Pomeroy, Devon, 1668. Will (Exeter) 1710. (*Al. Oxon.*)

FOX (*alias* RAGHAT), PATRICK. Clerk, of Ossory diocese. Of the household of the bishop of Tusculum. For many years studied civil and canon law at Cambridge and Oxford. (*Cal. of Papal Letters*, 1406.)

FOX, RICHARD. Probably of PEMBROKE. Perhaps fellow. Master, 1507–18. S. of Thomas, of Ropesley, Lincs. First at Oxford. Said to have graduated D.Can.L. at Paris. Preb. of St Paul's, 1485–7. Preb. of Wells, 1485. Preb. of Sarum, 1485. V. of Stepney, Aug.–Sept., 1485. Master of the Hospital of St Cross, Winchester. Bishop of Exeter, 1487–92; and Lord privy-seal, 1487–1516. Bishop of Bath and Wells, 1492. Bishop of Durham, 1494–1501. Chancellor of the University, 1500–1. Bishop of Winchester, 1501–28. Founder of Corpus Christi College, Oxford. Died Sept. 14, 1528. Buried in Winchester Cathedral. (*Cooper*, I. 35; *D.N.B.*)

FOXE, RICHARD. Adm. pens. (age 16) at CAIUS, Nov. 12, 1588. S. of Henry, yeoman, of Sprowston, Norfolk. Schools, Norwich and Wood Dalling. Scholar, 1588–94; Matric. 1589. Probably B.A. 1593–4. One of these names V. of Folkton, Yorks. Will (York) 1614.

FOX, RICHARD. Adm. pens. (age 16) at ST JOHN'S, Sept. 21, 1714. S. of Thomas, gent. B. at Cambridge. School, Merchant Taylors'. Matric. 1715; B.A. 1722–3. Ord. deacon (Ely) Sept. 23, 1722; priest (Lincoln) Mar. 8, 1723–4. C. of Longstow, Cambs.

FOX, ROBERT. Fined and imprisoned, 1467–8. (*Gr. Bk.* A, 69.)

FOX, ROBERT. Matric. sizar from ST JOHN'S, Easter, 1604.

FOX, ROWLAND. Adm. pens. at JESUS, June 28, 1694. Of Cambridgeshire. Scholar, 1695; B.A. 1698–9; M.A. 1702. Ord. deacon (Norwich) Mar. 1700–1; priest (Lincoln) Dec. 20, 1702. R. of Evedon, Lincs., 1702–23.

FOX, SIMEON. Adm. at KING'S, a scholar from Eton, 1583. S. of John, the Martyrologist. B. 1568. Matric. 1583; B.A. 1587–8; M.A. 1591. Fellow, 1586, till 1592. M.D. (Padua). Fought in Ireland and the Netherlands. F.R.C.P. 1608. Censor; treasurer, etc. President, 1634–41. Died Apr. 20, 1642. Buried in St Paul's. Will (P.C.C.) 1642. (*D.N.B.*; *Munk*, I. 147.)

FOX, SIMON. Matric. sizar from ST JOHN'S, Michs. 1608; B.A. 1612–3; M.A. 1616. Ord. priest (York) Sept. 1619.

FOXE, THOMAS. Matric. pens. from PEMBROKE, Michs. 1546.

FOXE, THOMAS. Matric. sizar from TRINITY, Michs. 1575.

FOX, THOMAS. Adm. pens. at SIDNEY, Feb. 11, 1604–5. Matric. 1605.

FOX, THOMAS. M.A. 1615 (Incorp. from Oxford). S. of Samuel, of Essex. B. at Havering-atte-Bow. Matric. from Magdalen Hall, Oxford, July 19, 1607, age 15; B.A. 1611; M.A. 1614. Fellow of Magdalen College, 1613–30. Proctor, 1620–1. Candidate, R.C.P. 1623. Died at Warlies, Essex, Nov. 20, 1662. Buried in Waltham Abbey. Will, P.C.C.; of Waltham-Holy-Cross. (*Munk*, I. 185; *D.N.B.*; *Al. Oxon.*)

FOX, THOMAS. Adm. pens. at SIDNEY, July 4, 1664. S. of James, clerk, deceased. B. at South Dalton, Yorks. Schools, Hull and Beverley. B.A. (Dublin) 1658; M.A. (Cambridge) 1665. Doubtless V. of Hessle, Yorks., 1670–89. Died Oct. 26, 1689.

FOX, THOMAS. Adm. sizar (age 16) at ST JOHN'S, Feb. 8, 1674–5. S. of Thomas, of Hastings, Sussex. B. there. School, Chichester. Matric. 1674–5; B.A. 1678–9.

FOX, THOMAS. Adm. sizar (age 18) at CHRIST'S, May 13, 1679. S. of Cornelius. B. at Corpusty, Norfolk. School, Holt. Matric. 1679; B.A. 1682–3; M.A. 1686. Ord. deacon (Norwich) 1683–4; priest, May, 1686. Probably R. of Aldby, Norfolk, where he was buried Oct. 17, 1715. He held it with Wickmere. (*Peile*, II. 72.)

FOX, THOMAS. Adm. sizar (age 17) at MAGDALENE, June 23, 1681. S. of William. B. at Louth, Lincs. School, Louth. Matric. 1681; B.A. 1684–5.

FOXE, TIMOTHY. Adm. pens. (age 17) at CHRIST'S, Mar. 32, 1646–7. S. of Edward. B. at Birmingham. Schools, Aston and Birmingham. Matric. 1647–8. R. of Drayton Bassett, Staffs., 1651–62, ejected. Preached, and held meetings in his own house at Caldwell, Derbs. Imprisoned in Derby gaol, 1684; and at Chester, on Monmouth's rising. Died May 30, 1710. (*Peile*, I. 512; *D.N.B.*)

FOXE, TOBIAS. Matric. pens. from ST JOHN'S, *c.* 1596; B.A. 1599–1600.

FOXE, WILLIAM. Adm. at KING'S (age 19) a scholar from Eton, Aug. 23, 1537. Of Ludlow, Salop. Fellow, 1540–1. Perhaps brother of George (1534).

FOX, WILLIAM. B.A. from JESUS, 1573–4. Perhaps ord. priest (Coventry) Sept. 29, 1581. C. of Keystone, Hunts., 1585.

FOX, WILLIAM. Matric. pens. from JESUS, Easter, 1611; B.A. 1613–4.

FOX, WILLIAM. B.A. from TRINITY, 1629–30; M.A. 1634. One of these names R. of Bilborough *with* Strelley, Notts., till 1674. Died 1674.

FOX, WILLIAM. Adm. pens. (age 17) at SIDNEY, June 10, 1632. S. of Ulysses, gent. B. at Fulwood, Sheffield, Yorks. Schools, Bradfield and Sheffield. Matric. 1632.

FOX, WILLIAM. Adm. sizar at EMMANUEL, June 3, 1672. Of Leicestershire. S. of Richard, of Thornton, Leics. Migrated to Trinity, Oxford. Matric. there, Dec. 6, 1672, age 19; B.A. 1676; M.A. 1682. V. of St Mary-de-Castro, Leicester, 1689. (*Al. Oxon.*)

FOX, WILLIAM. Adm. sizar at CLARE, Jan. 10, 1707–8. S. of John, of Stilton, Hunts. B. there. Matric. 1709. Migrated to Oxford. Matric. from Balliol College, Oct. 13, 1711, age 20; B.A. from Pembroke, Oxford, 1712. Perhaps V. of Crowle, Lincs., 1718. (*Al. Oxon.*)

FOX, ——. B.Can.L. or B.Civ.L. 1458–9.

FOX, ——. Fee for M.A. or higher degree, 1468–9.

FOX, ——. B.A. 1513–4.

FOXCROFT, EDWARD. Matric. pens. from ST JOHN'S, Lent, 1579–80. Migrated to Oxford. B.A. from Brasenose, 1583–4; M.A. 1588; B.D. 1600. Fellow of Brasenose, 1583. Will (Oxford) 1608. (*Al. Oxon.*)

FOXCROFT, EZECHIEL. Adm. at KING'S (age 16) a scholar from Eton, May 5, 1649. S. of George, of London, merchant. Matric. 1649; B.A. 1652–3; M.A. 1656. Fellow, 1652–75. Senior Proctor, 1673–4. (*Harwood*; *Vis. of London*, 1634.)

FOXCROFT, GEORGE. Matric. sizar from ST JOHN'S, *c.* 1601.

FOXCROFT, GEORGE. Adm. at CORPUS CHRISTI, 1732. Of Hampshire. Matric. 1732–3; B.A. 1736–7.

FOXCROFT, JOHN. Adm. pens. at EMMANUEL, Apr. 6, 1611. Eldest s. of George, of Sowerby, Halifax, Yorks. B. Jan. 1594–5. Matric. 1611; Scholar; B.A. 1614–5; M.A. from Magdalen Hall, Oxford, 1617. R. of Gotham, Notts., 1619–62. One of the Westminster assembly. Died 1662. Father of Moses (1644). (*Al. Oxon.*)

FOXCROFT, JOHN. Adm. pens. at CLARE, Mar. 6, 1671–2. Of Gotham, Notts. Matric. 1672; B.A. 1675–6; M.A. 1679. Probably C. of Sutton, Beds. Buried there Nov. 10, 1720. Father of the next. (W. M. Noble.)

FOXCROFT, JOHN. Adm. pens. (age 16) at ST JOHN'S, Aug. 27, 1703. S. of John (above), clerk. B. at Wilford, Notts. School, Nuneaton. Matric. 1703; LL.B. 1710.

FOXCROFT, MOSES. Adm. pens. at EMMANUEL, May 27, 1644. Of Nottinghamshire. S. of John (1611), R. of Gotham. B. June 26, 1627. Matric. 1644; B.A. 1647–8. Incorp. at Oxford, 1648. M.A. (Oxford) 1650. Fellow of Queen's College, Oxford, 1648–60, ejected. R. of Gotham, Notts., 1663–73. Died 1673.

FOXCROFT, NATHANIEL. Adm. pens. at EMMANUEL, June 29, 1653. Of London.

FOXCROFT, RICHARD. B.A. from ST JOHN'S, 1572–3. Of Yorkshire. Perhaps 2nd s. of James, of Sowerby, Halifax. M.A. 1576. Fellow, 1577. Will proved (V.C.C.) 1609. (M. H. Peacock.)

FOXCROFT, RICHARD. Adm. pens. (age 16) at CHRIST'S, May 29, 1673. S. of Edward. B. at Thornton, Yorks. School, Kirkby Lonsdale. Matric. 1673; B.A. 1677–8. Ord. deacon (York) June, 1679; priest, Feb. 1680–1. R. of Hoole, Lancs., 1686–1701. (*Peile*, II. 48.)

FOXCROFT, SAMUEL. Matric. pens. from ST CATHARINE'S, Easter, 1633. Of Yorkshire.

FOXCROFTE, THOMAS. Adm. sizar at CORPUS CHRISTI, 1584. Matric. Lent, 1584–5; B.A. 1588–9. Perhaps schoolmaster at Bedford, 1612. C. of Metfield, Suffolk, 1613–20. R. of Withersdale, 1620–5. Married Agnes Brown, widow, at Metfield, Sept. 16, 1613.

FOXCROFT, WILLIAM. Matric. sizar from St John's, Easter, 1579; B.A. from Corpus Christi, 1582-3. Ord. priest (Lincoln) May 17, 1586, as 'M.A.' R. of St Cuthbert's, Bedford, 1585. Admon. (Lincoln) 1625.

FOXCROFT, WILLIAM. B.A. from St Catharine's, 1597-8; M.A. 1601. Probably V. of Angersleigh, Somerset, 1606.

FOXLEY, JOHN. Adm. pens. at Emmanuel, July 1, 1597.

FOXELEY, JOHN. Adm. sizar (age 15) at St John's, June 1, 1682. S. of Isaac, husbandman. B. at Ashton, Lancs. School, Stockport. Matric. 1682. Perhaps V. of Farnworth, Lancs., till 1705. Will proved at Chester, 1705. (*Vict. Hist. of Lancs.*, III. 391.)

FOXLEY, THOMAS. Adm. pens. at Emmanuel, July 1, 1597.

FOXLEE, WILLIAM DE. Scholar at King's Hall, 1358. A John Foxle (probably the same) was there, Sept. 23, 1370.

FOXLEY, WILLIAM. Adm. pens. at Emmanuel, Mar. 4, 1622-3. Matric. 1623; B.A. 1626-7. One of these names s. of Michael, of Blakesley, Northants.; age 8 in 1618. (*Vis. of Northants.*, 1618.)

FOXLEY, WILLIAM. Adm. sizar (age 17) at Sidney, May 16, 1673. S. of Thomas, farmer. B. at Tallington, Derbs. (? Lincs.). School, Tideswell (Mr Bell and Mr Wray).

FOXLOWE, WILLIAM. M.A. from Sidney, 1691 (*Lit. Reg.*).

FOXON, JOHN. Matric. pens. from St John's, Easter, 1570.

FOXTON, ANTHONY. Matric. pens. from St John's, Easter, 1616. S. of Francis (1588), of Kent. B. at Milton. School, Canterbury. Migrated to Caius, Oct. 29, 1618, age 17, as Archbishop Parker's scholar. Scholar, 1618-23; B.A. 1619-20; M.A. 1623. R. of Burmarsh, Kent, 1623-31. Buried in Canterbury Cathedral, Aug. 29, 1631. Brother of Francis (1623). (*Venn*, I. 241.)

FOXTON, ELIAS. Adm. pens. at Emmanuel, Michs. 1584. S. of William, alderman of Cambridge. Matric. 1584; B.A. 1588-9. Adm. at Gray's Inn, Feb. 11, 1589-90. Will (P.C.C.) 1632; of St Olave St, London. (*Vis. of Cambs.*, 1619; J. Ch. Smith.)

FOXTON, FRANCIS. Matric. sizar from St John's, Easter, 1588; B.A. 1591-2; M.A. 1595; B.D. 1603; D.D. 1619. Incorp. at Oxford, 1624. V. of Sittingbourne, Kent, 1603-23. R. of Rucking, 1610. R. of Little Bitham, Lincs., 1610; and of Marsham, 1613-26. Died 1626. Will (P.C.C.). Father of the next, and of Anthony (1616).

FOXTON, FRANCIS. Adm. pens. (age 15) at Caius, June 2, 1623. S. of Francis (1588), V. of Sittingbourne. B. there. School, Canterbury. Matric. 1623; Scholar, 1623-8; B.A. 1626-7; M.A. 1631. C. of Maidstone, 1634. Brother of Anthony (1616). (*Venn*, I. 262.)

FOXTON, RICHARD. Adm. pens. at Emmanuel, Oct. 3, 1590. S. of William, alderman of Cambridge. Matric. *c.* 1592. Adm. at the Middle Temple, Apr. 19, 1597. Mayor of Cambridge, 1619-21. Elected M.P. for the borough, 1621; but, being mayor, the election was declared void. Parliamentarian member of the Eastern Counties Association. Commissioner for the collection of taxes in Cambridge. Died 1648. Buried Dec. 8, in Gt St Mary's. Will (P.C.C.) 1649. He left £40 to the University Library. Brother of Elias. (*Vis. of Cambs.*, 1619.)

FOXTON, ROBERT. Matric. sizar from St John's, Easter, 1621. V. of Gt Shelford, Cambs., 1632-7. Buried there Nov. 6, 1637. Will proved (Ely) 1637.

FOXTON, THOMAS DE. LL.D. Chancellor of the University, 1329-31. Vicar-general of Norwich, 1316. Benefactor.

FOXWELL, JOHN. Adm. sizar at Emmanuel, Apr. 24, 1704. Perhaps first adm. Sept. 12, 1700. S. of Philip (1673), R. of Tostock, Suffolk. Matric. 1705-6; B.A. 1707-8. Ord. deacon (Norwich) Sept. 1708; priest, Mar. 5, 1709-10. C. to his father at Tostock. R. of Rattlesden, Suffolk, 1711-31. Died Apr. 11, 1731. Buried at Rattlesden. (G. *Mag.*)

FOXWELL or FOCKWELL, PHILIP. Adm. pens. at Trinity, May 29, 1673. School, Westminster. Scholar, 1674; Matric. 1676; B.A. 1676-7. Ord. priest (Norwich) Nov. 1679. R. of Tostock, Suffolk, 1679-1736. R. of Norton, 1708-10. Father of John (above).

FOXWIST, LLOYD. Adm. sizar (age 19) at Trinity, June 28, 1751. S. of William, of Carnarvon. School, Beaumaris, Anglesey (Mr Vincent). Matric. 1751; B.A. 1754. Ord. deacon (Norwich) Feb. 1755.

FOY, JOHN. Matric. pens. from Clare, Easter, 1621; B.A. 1624-5; M.A. 1628.

FOYKE, ——. B.A. 1514-5.

FOYSTER or FUSTER, MICHAEL. B.A. 1533-4.

FOYSTER, NICHOLAS. Matric. pens. from Corpus Christi, Michs. 1549.

FOYSTER or FUSTER, ROBERT. B.A. 1532-3.

FRAIGNEAU, WILLIAM. Adm. pens. (age 19) at Trinity, June 24, 1736. S. of John, of London. B. there, 1717. School, Westminster. Matric. 1736; Scholar, 1737; B.A. 1739-40; M.A. 1743. Fellow, 1742. Regius Professor of Greek, 1744-50. Tutor to the family of Frederick, Lord Bolingbroke. V. of Battersea, Surrey, 1758-78. R. of Beckenham, Kent, 1765-78. Died Sept. 12, 1778. Will (P.C.C.) 1778; of Battersea. (*D.N.B.*; *Al. Westmon.*, 314.)

FRAKE, ROBERT, *see* **FREAKE.**

FRAME, RICHARD. Adm. sizar (age 16) at Pembroke, June 26, 1700. S. of Richard, glover, of All Hallows, Barking, London. B. in London. Matric. 1700; B.A. 1703-4; M.A. 1707. Ord. deacon (Ely) Sept. 21, 1707; priest (London) Feb. 1707-8. Will of one of these names (P.C.C.) 1718; of Fulham, and St Catherine Creechurch, London, late of Hoxton, clerk. (J. Ch. Smith.)

FRAMINGHAM, CHARLES. Matric. pens. from St John's, Easter, 1556.

FRAMINGHAM, EDMUND. Adm. scholar at Trinity Hall, Jan. 15, 1607-8; B.A. 1612-3. Fellow, 1612-20. Will (P.C.C. 1651) of one of these names; of Little Walsingham, Norfolk.

FRAMINGHAM, JOHN. Adm. pens. at Emmanuel, June 26, 1733, as Fremingham; afterwards Fell.-Com. Of Norfolk. Matric. 1734. Probably the barrister-at-law who died May 28, 1763, aged 47. M.I. at Little Walsingham, Norfolk. (*G. Mag.*)

FRAMINGHAM, LANCASTER. Adm. sizar (age 18) at Caius, May 26, 1746. S. of John, druggist, of Swaffham, Norfolk. B. there. Bapt. Sept. 23, 1727. Schools, Swaffham (private; Mr Hest) and Charterhouse (exhibitioner). Matric. 1746; Scholar, 1746-53; B.A. 1749-50; M.A. 1753. Fellow, 1754. Ord. deacon (Norwich) Dec. 22, 1751, as C. of Raydon, Suffolk; priest, July 7, 1754. V. of Castleacre, Norfolk, 1756-71; of Hindringham, 1768-83; of East and West Rudham, 1771-85; of Rougham, 1783-1800. R. of West Walton, 1785-1800. Died May, 1800. (*Venn*, II. 58.)

FRAMINGHAM, ROBERT. Adm. pens. at Jesus, Oct. 16, 1657. Of Norfolk. Matric. 1657; Scholar, 1658; B.A. 1661-2; M.A. 1666. Perhaps V. of Helhoughton, Norfolk, 1662-78.

FRAMINGHAM, ROGER. *Grace* for B.D. 1458-9. A monk from Norwich.

FRAMINGHAM, WILLIAM. Of Pembroke and Queens'. S. of Richard. B. in Norwich. School, Norwich. B.A. 1530-1; M.A. 1533. Fellow of Queens', 1530-7. A learned man, and intimate friend of Dr Caius, who undertook to publish his works. Sept. 25, 1537. Will, V.C.C. (*Cooper*, I. 63; *D.N.B.*)Died

FRAMISHAM, RICHARD. M.A. 1481.

FRAMLINGHAM, CLEMENT. Adm. Fell.-Com. (age 16) at Caius, Jan. 8, 1580-1. S. of Charles. B. at Debenham, Suffolk. Schools, Botesdale, Bungay and Fressingfield, Suffolk. Adm. at Lincoln's Inn, Mar. 16, 1582-3. The father, Sir Charles, died 1595. The son died *c.* 1585. (*Venn*, I. 109.)

FRAMLINGHAM, ——. B.Can.L. 1477-8.

FRAMPTON, ALGERNON. Adm. pens. (age 16) at St John's, July 7, 1736. S. of Thomas, clerk, of Wiltshire (V. of Shrewton and Broad Hinton). B. at Marlborough. School, Marlborough. Matric. 1737; B.A. 1740-1; M.A. 1744; B.D. 1752. Fellow, 1743-65. Incorp. at Oxford, 1745. Ord. deacon (Lincoln) Apr. 17, 1743; priest (Salisbury) Mar. 10, 1744-5. R. of Tokenham Week, Wilts., 1745-88. Died Apr. 22, 1788. Will, P.C.C. Brother of Thomas (1742-3). (*Scott-Mayor*, III. 477.)

FRAMPTON, JAMES. Adm. Fell.-Com. (age 17) at Peterhouse, Mar. 8, 1728-9. S. of William, of Moreton, Dorset, deceased. B. Oct. 1711. Succeeded his father at Moreton. Sheriff of Dorset, 1744. Died Oct. 28, 1784. (*T. A. Walker*, 259; *Hutchins*, I. 145.)

FRAMPTON, RICHARD. Matric. pens. from Trinity, Easter, 1606.

FRAMPTON, THOMAS. Adm. pens. (age 18) at St John's, Mar. 17, 1742-3. S. of Thomas, clerk, of Wiltshire (V. of Shrewton and Broad Hinton). B. at Marlborough. School, Marlborough. Matric. 1743; B.A. 1747-8; M.A. 1751; B.D. 1759; D.D. 1769. Fellow, 1751-71. Taxor, 1754. Ord. deacon (Lincoln, *Litt. dim.* from Salisbury) Mar. 4, 1747-8; priest (Salisbury) Sept. 24, 1749. R. of Ousden, Suffolk, 1762-1803. R. of Starston, Norfolk, 1769-1803. Died June 18, 1803, at Newmarket. Will, P.C.C. M.I. at Ousden. Brother of Algernon. (*Scott-Mayor*, III. 534; *Add. MS.* 5869, 112.)

FRAMPTON, WILLIAM. M.A. 1668 (Incorp. from Oxford). Matric. from Pembroke College, Oxford, Mar. 18, 1657-8; B.A. (Oxford) 1661; M.A. 1664-5. Proctor, 1674. R. of Llanfair-Kilgeddin, Monmouth. (*Al. Oxon.*)

FRANCE or FRAUNCE, ABRAHAM. Matric. pens. from St John's, Easter, 1576. Of Salop. Sent to college by Sir Philip Sidney. B.A. 1579-80; M.A. 1583. Fellow, 1580. Adm. at Gray's Inn, June 5, 1583. Barrister. Practised in the court of the Marches of Wales. Poet. Living, 1633. (*Cooper*, II. 119; *D.N.B.*)

FRANCE, THOMAS. Matric. pens. from Trinity, Michs. 1570.

FRANCE, THOMAS. Adm. at Corpus Christi, 1671. Of Nottinghamshire. Matric. 1671; B.A. 1674-5. Ord. deacon (York) Sept. 1675; priest, Mar. 1679-80. Will (Dublin) 1721, of one of these names; precentor of Waterford Cathedral.

FRANCE, PRAWNS, ——. B.A. 1478-9; M.A. 1482.

FRAUNCEIS, ALAN; le clerk. Of Durham bishopric. When a scholar at Cambridge (c. 1270-80) used to hunt hares with his greyhound in Cambridge Warren. (*Pleas of the Forest. See* preface.)

FRANCIS, ALBAN. Received a Royal mandate for M.A. 1685-6; refused by the Vice-Chancellor, Dr Peachell, who was removed in consequence. A native of Middlesex. A Benedictine of St Adrian's Abbey, Lansperg, Hanover. After the Revolution withdrew to Lansperg, and thence to Douay. Missioner in the South Province of England. Died July 27, 1715. (*D.N.B.*)

FRANCIS, ARTHUR. Matric. sizar from Queens', Michs. 1644. Of Nottinghamshire.

FRANCIS, CLEARE. M.A. from Christ's, 1598. Of London. Matric. from Magdalen College, Oxford, June 26, 1591, age 14; B.A. (Oxford) 1594-5.

FRANCIS, EDMUND. Adm. at Trinity Hall, July 23, 1624. S. of Edmund, of London, mercer. Migrated to Pembroke, Nov. 23, 1625. Perhaps adm. student at Leyden, Apr. 29, 1622.

FRANCES, EDWARD. Matric. pens. from St John's, Michs. 1582.

FRAUNCES, EDWARD. Matric. pens. from Trinity, Lent, 1623-4; Scholar, 1627; B.A. 1628-9; M.A. 1632. Perhaps R. of Elmswell, Suffolk, 1637. Head Master of Bury School, 1637-46.

FRANCES, EDWARD. Adm. sizar at Emmanuel, Apr. 3, 1676. Of Norfolk. Matric. 1676.

FRANCIS, FRANCIS, *see* **SAMUEL.**

FRAUNCIS, HENRY. Adm. sizar (age 17) at Pembroke, Sept. 29, 1620. Of London. Matric. 1620; B.A. 1623-4.

FRANCIS, HENRY. Adm. pens. at Caius, May 16, 1676. S. of Henry, gent., of Mattishall, Norfolk. B. at Welborne. Matric. 1676; Scholar, 1676-81; B.A. 1679-80. Ord. deacon (Norwich) May, 1681; priest, Mar. 1681-2. V. of Baotou, Norfolk, 1681-1711. R. of Witton, 1694-1711. Died Sept. 3, 1711. M.I. at Bacton. Will (Norwich C. C.) 1711. (*Venn*, I. 456.)

FRANCIS or FRANCEYS, HENRY. Adm. sizar at Emmanuel, May 29, 1706. S. of William, of Derby, apothecary, mayor of Derby. Matric. 1706; B.A. 1709-10; M.A. 1713. Ord. deacon (London) Sept. 21, 1712; priest (Ely) Jan. 11, 1712-3. Perhaps R. of Caldecote, Herts., 1712-9. (*Derby School Reg.*)

FRANCIS, JOHN. B.A. 1527-8.

FRANCES, JOHN. Matric. pens. from St John's, Easter, 1571.

FRANCIS, JOHN. Matric. sizar from Clare, Easter, 1583; B.A. 1586-7. Ord. deacon (London) Dec. 21, 1588; priest (Norwich) Mar. 20, 1589-90. V. of Langford, Beds., 1593-1623. Buried there July 8, 1623. Father of Jonathan (1610).

FRANCIS, JOHN. Matric. sizar from Trinity, Easter, 1584 (perhaps same as the next).

FRANCIS, JOHN. Adm. pens. at Queens', June 14, 1585. Of Essex. B.A. 1588-9; M.A. 1592. V. of Southminster, Essex, 1597-1615. Died 1615.

FRANCYS, JOHN. Matric. sizar from Pembroke, Michs. 1586; B.A. 1590-1.

FRANCIS, JOHN. B.A. (? 1602-3); M.A. from Trinity, 1606. V. of Lympne, Kent, 1610-6. R. of Ripple, 1616.

FRANCIS, JOHN. Matric. sizar from Jesus, Michs. 1607; B.A. 1610-1; M.A. 1614. Ord. deacon (York) May, 1611; priest, Dec. 1611. V. of Lund, Yorks., 1616.

FRANCIS, JOHN. Matric. sizar from Clare, Lent, 1629-30; B.A. 1633-4.

FRANCES, JOHN. Adm. sizar at Emmanuel, June 7, 1666. Of Derbyshire. Matric. 1667; B.A. 1669-70.

FRANCIS, JOHN. Adm. sizar (age 17) at Magdalene, June 11, 1678. S. of John, citizen of Chester. B. there. School, Chester. Matric. 1678; B.A. 1681-2; M.A. 1685. Fellow, 1684.

FRANCIS, JOHN. Adm. pens. at Jesus, May 31, 1680. S. of John, of Horncastle, Lincs., Esq. Matric. 1680; Scholar, 1682; B.A. 1683-4; M.A. 1687. Ord. priest (Rochester) Sept. 29, 1686. R. of Stickney, Lincs., 1686. V. of Sibsey, 1689. (*Lincs. Pedigrees.*)

FRANCIS, JOHN. Adm. sizar (age 16) at Caius, July 3, 1711. S. of Thomas, attorney, of North Elmham, Norfolk. B. there. School, Walsingham. Matric. 1711; Scholar, 1711-7; B.A. 1714-5. Ord. deacon (Norwich) Mar. 9, 1717-8; priest, Dec. 20, 1719. Probably R. of Billingford and Brisley, Norfolk, 1727-42. Will (Norwich Archd. C.) 1749. (*Venn*, I. 526.)

FRANCIS, JOHN. Adm. scholar at Trinity Hall, Jan. 5, 1719-20. Of Norwich. Matric. 1718; LL.B. 1723; LL.D. 1729. Ord. deacon (Norwich) Mar. 1725-6; priest, June, 1726. R. of Morley St Botolph, Norfolk, with St John, Maddermarket, Norwich, 1726. Minister at St Peter Mancroft.

FRANCIS, JOHN. Adm. scholar at Trinity Hall, Jan. 5, 1720-1. Of Lincolnshire. Matric. 1720; LL.B. 1725. Ord. deacon (Lincoln) June 5, 1726; priest, Sept. 25, 1726.

FRANCES, JOHN. Adm. sizar (age 16) at Pembroke, June 26, 1725. S. of William, of Canterbury. Matric. 1725; B.A. 1728-9; M.A. 1732. Fellow, 1733. Ord. deacon (Lincoln) Dec. 19, 1731. V. of Waresley, Hunts., 1745-6. V. of Soham, Cambs., 1746-82. Admon. (P.C.C.) 1783.

FRANCES, JONATHAN. Adm. sizar (age 14) at Caius, July 4, 1610. S. of John (1583), V. of Langford, Beds. Schools, Ely, and Clifton, Beds. Matric. 1610; Scholar, 1613-4; B.A. 1613-4; M.A. 1617. Licensed to practise physic and medicine in diocese of Lincoln, 1630. V. of Langford, Beds., 1631. V. of Norton, Herts., 1633-5. V. of Biggleswade, 1640. (*Venn*, I. 208.)

FRANCIS, MARTIN. Matric. pens. (age 18) from Pembroke, Michs. 1648, exhibitioner from Charterhouse. Of Middlesex. S. of Richard, of Brentford. B.A. 1651-2; M.A. 1655. Fellow, 1650; re-elected, 1660. Incorp. at Oxford, 1657. Taxor, 1657. R. of Castle Camps, Cambs., 1657-9. Approved for presbyterian ministry, at Cambridge, June 16, 1658. Buried there Feb. 9, 1668-9.

FRANCIS, MELCHIZEDEC. Adm. at Corpus Christi, 1593; B.A. 1593-4. Of London. P.C. of All Hallows, Staining, 1598-1607. One of these names, of Little Hinton, Wilts., clerk. Will (Consist. C. Sarum) 1635.

FRANCIS, RICHARD. Adm. sizar at Corpus Christi, 1645. Of Norwich. Matric. Easter, 1646; B.A. 1649-50; M.A. 1661. R. of Flordon, Norfolk, 1661.

FRANCIS, ROBERT. Secular chaplain. Studied at Cambridge. B.Can.L. at Oxford, 1535.

FRANCIS, ROBERT. Matric. sizar from Peterhouse, Michs. 1580; B.A. 1583-4; M.A. 1587. Perhaps R. of North Pickenham, Norfolk, 1585; and R. of Houghton, 1585-7.

FRANCIS, SAMUEL. Adm. sizar at Emmanuel, May 29, 1667, as 'Francis Francis.' Of Derbyshire. Matric. 1668; B.A. 1670-1.

FRANCIS, THEOPHILUS. Adm. pens. at Trinity, Apr. 14, 1664. Matric. 1664; B.A. 1667-8; M.A. 1671.

FRANCIS, THOMAS. B.Can.L. 1531-2.

FRANCIS, THOMAS. Matric. pens. from Jesus, Easter, 1572; B.A. 1575-6; M.A. 1579. R. of Morborn, Hunts., 1581. The R. of Little Tey, Essex, 1597-1601, was perhaps an Oxford contemporary.

FRANCIS, THOMAS. Adm. pens. (age 14) at Caius, June 20, 1653. S. of Thomas, of Boxted, Suffolk. School, Dedham. Matric. 1654; Scholar, 1654-60; B.A. 1657-8. (*Venn*, I. 389.)

FRAUNCEYS, WILLIAM. Chaplain of King's Hall, in 1402. Died May 26, 1406.

FRAUNCIS, WILLIAM. Scholar at King's Hall, in 1404. Resigned May 10, 1424.

FRANCIS, WILLIAM. Matric. sizar from Queens', c. 1596. Will of one of these names (P.C.C.) 1617; of Harlow, Essex, clerk.

FRANCIS, WILLIAM. Matric. sizar from St John's, Lent, 1626-7; B.A. 1630-1; M.A. 1634. One of these names P.C. of Leeds, Kent, 1641-3.

FRAUNCIS, WILLIAM. Adm. pens. (age 16) at Sidney, Apr. 1, 1724. S. of William, Esq., deceased. B. at Combe Flory, Somerset. School, Taunton (Mr Upton). Matric. 1724. Of Combe Flory, Esq. Married Johanna Whittock, of Old Cleeve, Somerset. Died 1739. (*Hutchins*, IV. 528.)

FRANCIS, WYATT. Adm. pens. at Emmanuel, May 20, 1725. S. of James, of Lincoln. Matric. 1725; B.A. 1728-9. Ord. deacon (Lincoln) Mar. 14, 1730-1; priest, Nov. 7, 1731. V. of Heckington, Lincs., 1741. R. of Wilsford, Lincs., 1744. R. of Burton-by-Lincoln. Preb. of Lincoln, 1764-80. Buried Mar. 18, 1780. (*Lincs. Pedigrees.*)

FRANCIS, ——. M.A. 1514.

FRANCIS, ——. Adm. at CORPUS CHRISTI, 1571.

FRANCISCANS, Warden of. B.D. 1495–6.

FRANCIUS or FRANSSEUS, GODFREY. D.D. from PETERHOUSE, 1581 (Incorp. from Douay).

FRANCIUS, JOHN. Ph.D. 1628 (Incorp. from Frankfort): signs as 'M.A.' Of Silesia. Licensed to practise medicine, 1644. M.D. 1647. Fellow of PETERHOUSE (by mandate) 1628–65. Senior Proctor, 1640. President, tutor, bursar, etc. Buried at Little St Mary's, Cambridge, June 11, 1665. Will proved (V.C.C.). (*T. A. Walker*, 37.)

FRANCIUS, JOHN. Adm. sizar at PETERHOUSE, July 23, 1655. Of the Province of Drenthe, Holland (Drentanus). Matric. 1655. 'In schola Campensi Trans-Isulaniorum educatus' (Kampen on the Yssel) (age 18). Perhaps nephew of Dr John Francius (above). (*T. A. Walker*, 109.)

FRANE, DANIEL. Matric. sizar from TRINITY, Easter, 1636.

FRANFELD, JOHN. Scholar at KING'S HALL, 1385–7.

FRANCKE, ABRAHAM. Matric. sizar from CLARE, c. 1595; B.A. 1598–9; M.A. 1604. Probably of Ashburnham, Sussex.

FRANKE, ABRAHAM. Matric. sizar from QUEENS', Michs. 1635. Of Sussex. Probably s. of Abraham (above), of Ashburnham, Sussex. B.A. 1639–40. Buried at St Botolph's, Cambridge, May 26, 1642. (*Vis. of Sussex*.)

FRANK, ANTHONY. Adm. sizar at EMMANUEL, July 3, 1666. Of Suffolk. Matric. 1669; B.A. 1669–70. V. of Methwold, Norfolk, 1673–90. R. or C. of Ickburgh, 1673.

FRANK, CHARLES. Matric. pens. from CLARE, Easter, 1631; B.A. 1634–5; M.A. 1638. Ord. priest (Norwich) Sept. 24, 1637; C. of Syleham, Suffolk.

FRANKE, CHARLES. Adm. sizar (age 18) at ST JOHN'S, June 7, 1723. S. of Richard, mercer, of Nottinghamshire. B. at Southwell. School, Southwell. Matric. 1723; B.A. 1726–7; M.A. 1735. Ord. deacon (York) July 21, 1728; C. of Popplewick, Notts. V. of Whitwick, Leics., 1736–67. Died Aug. 1, 1767. (*Scott-Mayor*, III. 362; *Nichols*, III. 1120.)

FRANCK, EDMUND. Matric. sizar from CORPUS CHRISTI, Easter, 1614. B. at Maldon, Essex. B.A. 1617–8; M.A. 1621. Incorp. at Oxford, 1621. Ord. deacon (London) Sept. 19, 1619, age 23; priest, Dec. 24, 1621. C. of Friern Barnet, Middlesex. R. of Bonsall, Derbs., 1628.

FRANK, FRANCIS. Adm. pens. at JESUS, Aug. 18, 1716. Of Campsall, Yorks. 2nd s. of Matthew Ashton, who took the name Frank. Scholar; LL.B. from Trinity Hall, 1722. Official and commissary of the archdeacon of Suffolk. Married Elizabeth, dau. of Waller Bacon, of Earlham, Norfolk. Died May 1, 1773. Brother of Richard (1714). (A. Gray; *Burke*, II. 576.)

FRANCK, HUMPHREY. Adm. sizar at EMMANUEL, July 15, 1594. B. in Iremonger Lane, London. Matric. 1594; B.A. 1597–8. Migrated to Sidney, Sept. 1598. M.A. 1601. Ord. deacon (Chester) Feb. 11, 1608–9; priest (London) Mar. 19, 1608–9, age 34. V. of Little Brickhill, Bucks., 1609. Schoolmaster at Sevenoaks. Will (Archd. Surrey) 1637; as Master of St Saviour's Southwark School. Father of Mark. (J. Ch. Smith.)

FRANCKE, ISAAC. Matric. pens. from TRINITY, Easter, 1574; B.A. from Clare, 1576–7.

FRANKE, JOHN. Adm. pens. (age 17) at ST JOHN'S, May 12, 1653. S. of Charles, gent., of Pontefract. B. in Hertfordshire. School, Wakefield. Matric. 1653. (*Vis. of Yorks.*, 1665.)

FRANKE, JOHN. Adm. sizar at JESUS, June 16, 1656. Of Norfolk. Matric. 1656.

FRANKE, JOHN. Adm. sizar at CLARE, Oct. 30, 1661. Of Kent. Matric. 1661–2; B.A. 1665–6. Perhaps V. of Leatherhead, Surrey, 1671–9. Died 1679.

FRANK or FRANKES, JOHN. Adm. pens. at EMMANUEL, May 3, 1669, as Franks. Of Leicester. Matric. sizar, Easter, 1669; B.A. 1672–3. Ord. deacon (Peterb.) Sept. 19, 1675; priest, Feb. 20, 1675–6. V. of Queniborough, Leics., 1680. Admon. (Leicester) 1715. (H. I. Longden; J. Ch. Smith.)

FRANKE, JOHN. Adm. sizar (age 15) at TRINITY, June 20, 1676. S. of Richard. B. at Cottingley, Yorks. School, Bingley (Mr Murgatroyd). Matric. 1676.

FRANK, JOHN HILLERSDEN. Adm. at KING'S, a scholar from Eton, 1746. Matric. Easter, 1747; B.A. 1750–1; M.A. 1754. Fellow, 1750. Lived in Cambridge for some time. Retired to Bath. Died there Jan. 28, 1780. (G. *Mag.*; *Harwood*.)

FRANKE, LEVIT. Adm. pens. at EMMANUEL, June 23, 1716. Of Leicestershire. Matric. 1716; B.A. 1720–1. Ord. deacon (Lincoln) Sept. 20, 1724; priest, Sept. 19, 1725. Admon. (Leicester) 1735; of Caythorpe, Lincs.

FRANCK, MARK. Matric. sizar from PEMBROKE, Easter, 1627. S. of Humphrey (1594). Bapt. at Little Brickhill, Bucks., Dec. 29, 1612. B.A. 1630–1; M.A. 1634; B.D. 1641; D.D. 1661 (*Lit. Reg.*). Fellow, 1634; ejected, 1642; restored, 1660. Elected Master, Aug. 23, 1662. Chaplain to Archbishop of Canterbury. Archdeacon of St Albans, 1660–4. Treasurer of St Paul's, 1660–4. Preb. of St Paul's, 1662–4. R. of Barley, Herts., 1662–4. Author, sermons. Died 1664, aged 51. Buried in St Paul's Cathedral. Will, P.C.C. (*D.N.B.*)

FRANK, NATHANIEL. Adm. pens. (age 19) at ST JOHN'S, Mar. 28, 1717. S. of John, of Lancashire. B. at Preston. School, Sedbergh. B.A. 1720–1; M.A. 1724.

FRANKE, RICHARD. B.A. 1508–9; M.A. 1512; B.D. 1522–3. Fellow of PETERHOUSE, 1512. Bursar, 1518. Proctor, 1521–2. A Richard Francks, deceased, is named as brother, in will of John Francs, *alias* Ferror, R. of Hinderclay, Suffolk, 1559.

FRANKE, RICHARD. Matric. pens. from QUEENS', Michs. 1567. One of these names, of Cambridge, ord. deacon (Ely) Mar. 22, 1561–2, age 40. Perhaps V. of Silverley, Suffolk, 1563; and R. of Ashley, 1563–74.

FRANCKE, RICHARD. Matric. pens. from ST JOHN'S, Easter, 1611. Probably s. of John, alderman of Pontefract. Bapt. there, Feb. 20, 1591–2. Recorder of York. Buried at Campsall, Dec. 1661. Will, York. Perhaps father of Richard (1648). (Burke, *L.G.*; J. Ch. Smith.)

FRANKE, RICHARD. Matric. pens. from QUEENS', Easter, 1627. Of Sussex. Perhaps s. of Abraham (1595), of Ashburnham, Sussex. B.A. 1630–1; M.A. 1635.

FRANKE, RICHARD. Adm. pens. (age 18) at ST JOHN'S, May 10, 1648. S. of Richard (? 1611), Esq., of Campsall, Yorks. Bapt. July 31, 1627. School, Laughton, Rotherham. Matric. 1648. Adm. at Gray's Inn, Dec. 28, 1649. Buried at Campsall, Dec. 7, 1657.

FRANK, RICHARD. Adm. pens. (age 16) at ST JOHN'S, Apr. 2, 1692. S. of John, gent. B. at Pontefract, Yorks. School, Pontefract. Matric. 1692; B.A. 1695–6. Ord. deacon (Peterb.) Feb. 21, 1702–3; priest, Sept. 24, 1704. C. of Fotheringay, Northants. V. of Searby w. Owmby, Lincs., 1705.

FRANK, RICHARD. Adm. pens. at JESUS, July 2, 1714. 1st s. of Matthew, gent., of Campsall, Yorks. (Matthew Ashton, grandson of Richard Frank, of 1611, assumed the name Frank.) School, Doncaster. Matric. 1714. Adm. at Gray's Inn, Apr. 30, 1715. Of Campsall, Esq. Recorder of Pontefract, 1735; and Doncaster, 1756. One of the earliest members of the Society of Antiquaries. Married Margaret, dau. of Robert Frank, of Pontefract. Died *s.p.* May 22, 1762, aged 64. Brother of Francis (1716). (Burke, *L.G.*; A. Gray.)

FRANKE, ROBERT. Scholar and fellow of KING'S HALL, 1456–92. B.Can.L. 1459–60; D.Can.L. 1465–6. R. of Little Stukeley, Hunts., 1463–1505. Preb. of Southwell, 1480–6. V. of Chesterton, Cambs., 1491. Will (P.C.C.) 1505.

FRANKE, ROBERT. Adm. pens (age 16) at ST JOHN'S, Sept. 22, 1676. S. of John, gent., of Pontefract, Yorks. Bapt. there, Feb. 2, 1659–60. School, Pontefract. Matric. 1676. Adm. at Gray's Inn, May 16, 1678. Barrister, 1685. Ancient, 1704. M.P. for Pontefract, 1710–6. Buried there Sept. 6, 1738. (*Vis. of Yorks.*, 1665; *Hunter*, II. 465.)

FRANKE, THOMAS. Matric. pens. from QUEENS', Easter, 1569. One of these names (no degree; but 'bred in the schools'), was ord. priest (Lincoln) Sept. 21, 1565. V. of Morton, Lincs., in 1585.

FRANKE, THOMAS. Adm. sizar at EMMANUEL, May 23, 1706. Of Leicestershire. Matric. 1706; B.A. 1711–2. Ord. deacon (Peterb.) May 26, 1711; priest, June 14, 1712. V. of Oadby, Leics., 1714.

FRANK, THOMAS. M.A. from KING'S, 1724. S. of Thomas, R. of Cranfield, Beds., clerk. Bapt. there, Jan. 24, 1698–9. Matric. from Merton, Oxford, Apr. 6, 1717, age 17; B.A. (Oxford) 1720. P.C. of Loose, Kent, 1722–31. R. of Cranfield, Beds., 1731. Brother of Walter (1742). (*Al. Oxon.*)

FRANCK, THOMAS. Adm. sizar (age 19) at ST JOHN'S, July 19, 1732. S. of T., farmer, of Leicestershire. B. at Queniborough. School, Loughborough. Matric. 1732; B.A. 1736–7. Ord. deacon (Lincoln) Sept. 25, 1737; priest, Mar. 2, 1739–40. C. of Appleby, Leics. Doubtless V. of Gt Glen and Gt Stretton, Leics., 1739–44. Will (Leicester) 1744. (*Scott-Mayor*, III. 445.)

FRANK, THOMAS. Adm. sizar (age 18) at ST JOHN'S, June 6, 1748. S. of Walter (1742), clerk, of Kent. B. at Chatham. School, King's, Rochester. Matric. 1748; LL.B. 1754. Ord. deacon (Rochester) Sept. 24, 1752; priest, Sept. 22, 1754. V. of Darenth, Kent, 1759–66. Minor canon of Rochester, 1759. V. of Stockbury, 1766–94. V. of Borden, 1768–94. Died 1794. Will (P.C.C.). (*Scott-Mayor*, III. 578.)

FRANCKE, WALTER. Matric. sizar from ST JOHN'S, Easter, 1579. One of these names s. of Henry, of Knighton, Yorks.; age c. 16, in 1576. (*Add. Pedigrees*; *Vis. of Yorks.*)

FRANKE, WALTER. Matric. sizar from CORPUS CHRISTI, Easter, 1619. Of Essex. One of these names, 'M.A.,' was V. of Gwinear, Cornwall, 1636, sequestered; another was R. of Onehouse, Suffolk.

FRANK, WALTER. M.A. from QUEENS', 1742. S. of Thomas, R. of Cranfield, Beds. Matric. from Merton College, Oxford, Mar. 23, 1720-1, age 18; B.A. (Oxford) 1724-5. Ord. deacon, 1727; priest (Lincoln) 1728. V. of Hartlip, Kent, 1729-47. Minor canon of Rochester, 1733-84. P.C. of Chatham, 1747. R. of Cranfield, Beds., 1782-4. Died Mar. 29, 1784. M.I. in Rochester Cathedral. Admon. P.C.C. Father of Thomas (1748), brother of Thomas (1724). (*Al. Oxon.*; G. *Mag.*)

FRANK, ——. M.A. 1473-4.

FRANCK, ——. Adm. at CORPUS CHRISTI, 1580.

FRANK, —— (*senior*). Adm. Fell.-Com. at KING'S, Lent, 1613-4.

FRANK, —— (*junior*). Adm. Fell.-Com. at KING'S, Lent, 1613-4.

FRANCKLAND, ANTHONY. Adm. pens. at JESUS, June 2, 1664. Of Yorkshire. 1st s. of Henry, of Aldwarke, Esq. Matric. 1664; Scholar, 1665. Adm. at the Inner Temple, Sept. 12, 1664. (*Vis. of Yorks.*, 1665.)

FRANKLAND or FRANKLIN, CHRISTOPHER. Adm. sizar at PETERHOUSE, June 13, 1621. Of Yorkshire. Matric. 1621; B.A. 1624-5. (*T. A. Walker*, 21.)

FRANKLAND, FREDERIC MEINHARDT. Adm. pens. at JESUS, Apr. 9, 1711. 6th s. of Sir Thomas, Bart., of Thirkleby, Yorks. Matric. 1710-1. Adm. at Middle Temple, Apr. 3, 1711. Barrister-at-Law, May 23, 1718. M.P. for Thirsk, 1734-49. Commissioner of revenues in Ireland, 1749; and of Excise in England, 1753-63. Died Mar. 8, 1768. Brother of Thomas (1699-1700) and Richard (1709). (A. Gray; G. *Mag.*)

FRANKLAND, HENRY. Adm. pens. (age 17) at CHRIST'S, May 10, 1626. Eldest s. of William. B. at Thirkleby, Yorks. Schools, Rye, Herts., and York. Matric. 1626, as Franklin. Adm. at Gray's Inn, Nov. 25, 1628. Knighted, at Dublin, Nov. 27, 1636. Of Thirkleby. Buried there Feb. 27, 1672-3. Brother of John (1626), of Matthew (1637) and Thomas (1641). (*Peile*, I. 373; *Vis. of Yorks.*, 1665; M. H. Peacock.)

FRANKLAND, HENRY. Adm. pens. (age 17) at SIDNEY, May 17, 1684. 2nd s. of Sir William, Knt. and Bart. B. at Thirkleby, Yorks. School, Coxwold. Matric. 1684. Adm. at Lincoln's Inn, Dec. 2, 1685. Of Sowerby, Yorks., Esq. Clerk of the Peace for the North Riding. Died unmarried, 1716. Brother of John (1691). (*Burke.*)

FRANKLAND, JOHN. Adm. pens. at CHRIST'S, May 10, 1626. S. of William. B. at Thirkleby, Yorks. Schools, Rye, Herts., and York. Matric. 1626, as Prankling. Of Barnard's Inn. Died unmarried. Brother of Henry (1626), Matthew (1637) and Thomas (1641).

FRANKLAND or FRANKLIN, JOHN. Adm. scholar (age 16) at SIDNEY, c. May, 1691. S. of Sir William, Bart., of Thirkleby, Yorks. Schools, Coxwold and Eton. Matric. 1691; B.A. 1694-5; M.A. 1698; D.D. 1712. Fellow, 1700. Incorp. at Oxford, 1700. Senior Proctor, 1703-4. Master of Sidney, 1728-30. Vice-Chancellor, 1728-9. Ord. deacon (Lincoln) May 31, 1702; priest, Dec. 20, 1702. R. of Oswaldkirk, Yorks., 1700-14. R. of St Stephen's, Bristol, 1707. Chaplain to the King. Dean of Gloucester, 1724-9. Dean of Ely, 1729-30. Died Sept. 3, 1730. M.I. at St Stephen's, Bristol. Father of the next and brother of Henry (1684). (F. S. Hockaday.)

FRANKLAND, JOHN. Adm. pens. (age 14) at SIDNEY, Feb. 4, 1729-30. Only s. of John (above), Dean of Ely. B. at Bristol. School, Bristol. Matric. 1731; B.A. 1733; M.A. from St John's, 1737. Fellow of St John's, 1736-42. Ord. deacon (Lincoln) Dec. 24, 1738; priest, June 1, 1740. V. of Eastbourne, Sussex. R. of Sundridge, Kent, 1753-7. Preb. of Chichester, 1742-77. Died 1777. Will, P.C.C.

FRANKLAND, MATTHEW. Adm. pens. (age 16) at CHRIST'S, June 21, 1637. S. of William, of Thirkleby. B. at Punsborn, Herts. Schools, Coxwold and Ripon, Yorks. Matric. 1637, as Franklin. 'Brought up to the sea: drowned.' Brother of Henry and John (1626) and Thomas (1641). (*Peile*, I. 449.)

FRANKLAND or FRANKLIN, RICHARD. Matric. sizar from ST JOHN'S, Michs. 1575; B.A. 1579-80; M.A. 1583. Ord. deacon and priest (Peterb.) July 6, 1583, as Franklin.

FRANCKLAND, RICHARD. B.A. from PETERHOUSE, 1593-4; M.A. 1597; B.D. 1606. Perhaps V. of Haslingfield, Cambs., 1599.

FRANCKLAND, RICHARD. Adm. pens. (age 17) at CHRIST'S, May 18, 1648. S. of John. B. at Rathmell, Giggleswick, Yorks. School, Giggleswick. Matric. 1648; B.A. 1651-2; M.A. 1655. V. of St Andrew, Auckland, Durham, 1653-62. Appointed by Cromwell tutor at his college at Durham. Set up an 'Academy' for divinity and medical students, at Rathmell, 1670; removed to Natland, Kendal, 1674, and afterwards to Attercliffe, Yorks., and other places. Returned to Rathmell, 1689. Died Oct. 1, 1698. Buried at Giggleswick. M.I.; 'of the Franklands of Thirkleby.' (*Peile*, I. 520; *D.N.B.*)

FRANKLAND, RICHARD. Adm. pens. at JESUS, June 29, 1709. 5th s. of Sir Thomas, Bart., of Thirkleby, Yorks. B. in London. Matric. 1709; Scholar; B.A. 1712-3; M.A. 1716. Fellow, 1714-49. Commissioner of Taxes, 1749-61; and Comptroller of the Post Office. Died Sept. 21, 1761. Brother of Frederic Meinhardt (1711) and Thomas (1699-1700). (*Lipscomb*; *Pedigrees*, II. 196.)

FRANCKLAND or FRANKLIN, SAMUEL. Adm. sizar at PETERHOUSE, Apr. 5, 1639. Of Warwickshire. Migrated to St Catharine's. Matric. 1640; B.A. 1642-3; M.A. 1646. Master of Coventry Grammar School, 1651-91. Founded a fellowship at St Catharine's for Coventry School, and a scholarship from Tamworth. Died July 22, 1691. (*Vict. Hist. of Warws.*, II.)

FRANKLAND, THOMAS. Adm. Fell.-Com. at TRINITY, Apr. 13, 1618. Perhaps of Aldwark, Yorks. S. of Sir Henry, Lieut.-Colonel in the Civil War, under Sir William Pennyman. Died unmarried. (M. H. Peacock.)

FRANKLAND, THOMAS. Adm. pens. (age 17) at CHRIST'S, Sept. 27, 1641. 7th s. of William, of Thirkleby, Yorks. B. there. School, York. Matric. 1642. Of Silverdale. Brother of Henry and John (1626) and Matthew (1637). (*Peile*, I. 478.)

FRANKLAND, THOMAS. M.A. 1656 (Incorp. from Oxford). Of Lancashire. Matric. from Brasenose College, Oxford, June 14, 1649; B.A. (Oxford) 1652-3; M.A. 1655; B.D. 1663. Proctor, 1662. Fellow of Brasenose, 1654. F.R.C.P. 1675-82, ejected. Incorp. M.D. at Cambridge, 1678. Married Ruth, dau. of Thomas Newcombe, King's printer. Died c. 1690, in the Fleet prison. Buried in St Vedast's. 'Imposter and annalist.' Admon. (P.C.C.) 1692. (*Munk*, I. 382; *D.N.B.*; *Al. Oxon.*)

FRANKLAND, THOMAS. Adm. Fell.-Com. at JESUS, Jan. 12, 1699-1700. 1st s. of Sir Thomas, Bart., of Yorkshire. Matric. 1700. Held various public offices. M.P. for Harwich, 1708-13; for Thirsk, 1715-47. Succeeded as 3rd Bart., 1726. Lord of the Admiralty, 1730-41. Commissioner of Revenue (Ireland) etc. Died Apr. 17, 1747. Brother of Frederic Meinhardt (1711) and Richard (1709). (*G.E.C.*; A. Gray.)

FRANKLAND, THOMAS. Adm. pens. (age 19) at TRINITY, Nov. 30, 1716. S. of Cornelius, of Glaisdale, Yorks. School, Wakefield, Yorks. (Mr Clark). Matric. 1716; B.A. 1720-1. Ord. deacon (York) Mar. 1720-1.

FRANKLAND, WILLIAM. Adm. sizar (age 17) at SIDNEY, Apr. 11, 1668. S. of William, Esq., deceased, of Lincolnshire. School, Coxwold. Matric. 1668; B.A. 1671-2; M.A. 1675. Ord. deacon (York) Sept. 11; priest, Sept. 28, 1673. R. of Kirkby Knowle, Yorks., 1673-1731. R. of Oswaldkirk, 1714-31. Died 1731.

FRANKLAND or FRANKLIN, WILLIAM. Adm. pens. (age 17) at ST JOHN'S, Mar. 4, 1679-80. S. of Hugh, attorney-at-law. B. in London. School, Mercers'. Matric. 1680, as Franklin.

FRANKLAND, WILLIAM. Adm. pens. (age 18) at TRINITY, July 1, 1735. S. of William, of Bedale, Yorks. School, Durham (Mr Dongworth). Matric. 1735; Scholar, 1736; B.A. 1738-9; M.A. 1742. Fellow, 1741.

FRANKLIN, CHRISTOPHER. Matric. sizar from ST JOHN'S, Michs. 1573.

FRANKLIN, EDMUND. Matric. pens. from ST JOHN'S, Easter, 1563. Of Norfolk. B.A. 1566-7; M.A. 1570. Fellow, 1567. Ord. deacon (Lincoln); priest (Ely) Apr. 15, 1568. V. of Holy Trinity, Cambridge, 1568-70. V. of Shernborne, Norfolk, 1572. R. of Gosbeck, Suffolk, 1572-5. R. of West Winch, Norfolk, 1573. Will (P.C.C.) 1612; of West Winch.

FRANKLYN, EDWARD. Matric. pens. from QUEENS', Easter, 1566. Of Bedfordshire. S. of John. B. 1548. B.A. 1569-70; M.A. from St Catharine's, 1573. Fellow of St Catharine's, 1573. Ord. deacon (Peterb.); priest (Ely) Apr. 1576. R. of Kelshall, Herts., 1580-1617. Buried there Sept. 4, 1617. Father of Edward (1604). Will (P.C.C.) 1617. (*Cooper*, II. 85; Burke, *L.G.*)

FRANKLIN, EDWARD. Adm. at TRINITY, a scholar from Westminster, 1603; B.A. 1607-8; M.A. 1611. Fellow, 1610. Doubtless ord. priest (Coventry and Lichfield) 1615. R. of Bawdeswell, Norfolk, 1614. R. of Billingford, 1630.

FRANKLIN, EDWARD. B.A. from CHRIST'S, 1604. S. of Edward (above), R. of Kelshall, Herts. M.A. 1608; B.D. 1616; D.D. 1630. Fellow, 1610–23. Ord. priest (London) Dec. 1610. Chaplain to Lord Chancellor Bacon. Held the rectory of St Laurence Dengie, Essex, with vicarage of Kelvedon, Essex, 1620. R. of Little Cressingham, Norfolk, 1622; and of Gt Cressingham, 1627–44, ejected. Died *c.* 1644. Father of John (1646). (*Peile*, I. 236.)

FRANCKLIN, EDWARD. Adm. sizar (age 15) at CAIUS, July 7, 1713. S. of John (1682), R. of Gressenhall, Norfolk. B. at Mileham. School, Wisbech. Scholar, 1713–8; Matric. 1714; B.A. 1717–8; M.A. 1731. Ord. deacon (Ely) June 4, 1721; priest (Norwich) June 29, 1723. R. of Raynham, Norfolk, 1730. R. of Toftrees, 1732–66. Died unmarried, Jan. 3, 1766. (*Venn*, I. 531; Burke, *L.G.*)

FRANKLEYNE, GEORGE. Matric. pens. from TRINITY, Lent, 1588–9. One of these names P.C. of Little Horkesley, Essex, 1612. Probably brother of Thomas (1588–9).

FRANCLIN, GEORGE. Adm. pens. at TRINITY, Feb. 13, 1654–5. Of London. Matric. 1656; Scholar, 1657.

FRANKLYN, GREGORY. Adm. sizar at CORPUS CHRISTI, 1590. Of Norfolk. Matric. *c.* 1591; B.A. 1593–4; M.A. 1597. V. of Swaffham, Norfolk, 1628.

FRANCKLIN, HENRY. Adm. pens. (age 16) at CAIUS, Apr. 30, 1629. S. of William (? 1603), R. of St Margaret-at-Cliffe, Kent. School, Rochester. Matric. 1629; Scholar, 1632–3; B.A. 1632–3; M.A. 1636. R. of Ickburgh, Norfolk, 1645; and of Shelfhanger, 1646. 'A godly and orthodox divine.' (*Venn*, I. 289.)

FRANKLIN, JAMES. Adm. pens. (age 16) at CHRIST'S, Mar. 11, 1651–2. S. of Sir John (1614), of Willesden, Middlesex. Bapt. there, Mar. 27, 1636. School, Bishop's Stortford. Matric. 1652. Adm. at Gray's Inn, July 21, 1655. Buried at Willesden, Dec. 16, 1656. Brother of Richard and John (1646–7). (*Peile*, I. 546.)

FRANKELEYN, JOHN. Scholar at KING'S HALL, 1379. Died Aug. 10, 1390.

FRANCKLYNE, JOHN. Matric. sizar from ST CATHARINE'S, Easter, 1574.

FRANKLIN, JOHN. Matric. sizar from TRINITY, Easter, 1602 (entry erased).

FRANKELIN, JOHN. Matric. Fell.-Com. from PETERHOUSE, Easter, 1614. Doubtless s. of Richard, of Willesden, Middlesex; age 23, in 1619. Of Willesden. Knighted, Oct. 1614. M.P. for Middlesex, 1625, 1640–8; for Wootton Bassett, 1626, 1628–9. Died Mar. 24, 1647–8, aged 48. Buried at Willesden. Father of James (1651–2) and of John and Richard (1646–7). (*Midds. Pedigrees*; A. B. Beaven.)

FRANKLIN, JOHN. Matric. sizar from PEMBROKE, Easter, 1629; B.A. 1631–2; M.A. 1635. One of these names R. of Kelshall, Herts., 1660–3.

FRANKLIN, JOHN. Adm. pens. (age 16) at CAIUS, Apr. 7, 1646. S. of Edward (1604), R. of Gt Cressingham, Norfolk. B. there. Schools, Saham Tony, Hertford and Norwich. Matric. 1646; Scholar, 1647–50; B.A. 1649–50; M.A. 1653. Ord. deacon (Chichester) Sept. 22; es (Bath and Wells) Sept. 23, 1660. R. of Tattingstone, Norfolk, 1660. C. of Wissingset, 1662. R. of Godwick and Tittleshall, 1662–78. R. of Wellingham, 1676–8. Buried at Tittleshall, 1678. Will (Norwich Archd. C.) 1678. Father of John (1682). (*Venn*, I. 361.)

FRANKLIN, JOHN. Adm. Fell.-Com. at EMMANUEL, Mar. 6, 1646–7. Of Middlesex. 2nd s. of Sir John (1614), of Willesden, Middlesex. Bapt. Nov. 30, 1631. Brother of Richard (1646–7) and James (1651).

FRANKLIN, JOHN. Adm. pens. (age 19) at SIDNEY, June, 1660. 1st s. of John, gent. B. at Ampthill, Beds. Bapt. May 18, 1641. Schools, Roxton, Beds., Hexton, Herts. (Mr Jo. Davis) and Bedford. Matric. 1661.

FRANKLIN, JOHN. Adm. sizar (age 18) at ST JOHN'S, Feb. 21, 1665–6. S. of William, husbandman, of Castle Bytham, Lincs. B. there. School, Oakham. Matric. 1667. Ord. deacon (Peterb.) May 29, 1670, as B.A.

FRANKLIN, JOHN. Adm. pens. (age 15) at CAIUS, Apr. 15, 1682. S. of John (1646), R. of Tittleshall, Norfolk. B. there. Schools, Scarning and Lynn. Matric. 1682; Scholar, 1682–9; B.A. 1685–6; M.A. 1692. Ord. priest (Norwich) Sept. 1694. R. of Sculthorpe, Norfolk, 1700–3. R. of Stanfield, 1703–5. R. of Brisley, 1703–5. R. of Gressenhall, 1704–10. R. of Testerton, 1709. Lecturer at Wisbech. Died Nov. 26, 1710. (*Venn*, I. 470.)

FRANKLYN, JOHN. Adm. at CORPUS CHRISTI, 1702. Of Suffolk. B.A. 1705–6. Ord. priest (London) Dec. 24, 1710.

FRANKLIN, JOHN. Adm. sizar (age 16) at PEMBROKE, Feb. 18, 1716. S. of John, of Flitcham, Norfolk. B.A. 1720–1; M.A. 1726. Ord. deacon (Norwich) June, 1723; priest, Sept. 1726. Doubtless P.C. of Weasenham, Norfolk, 1729–82. Will, P.C.C.

FRANKLIN, MATTHEW, *see* FRANKLAND.

FRANKLYN, NICHOLAS. Matric. pens. from CLARE, Michs. 1553. One of these names adm. at Gray's Inn, 1556.

FRANKLYN, NICHOLAS. Matric. pens. from JESUS, Michs. 1564.

FRANKLYN, NICHOLAS. Matric. sizar from CHRIST'S, July, 1612; B.A. 1615–6; M.A. 1619. Ord. deacon (Peterb.) Sept. 19; priest, Sept. 20, 1619. R. of West Barkwith, Lincs., 1623–41. Married, Oct. 20, 1625, Grace, dau. of Ro. Williamson, R. of Titchmarsh, Northants. (*Peile*, I. 287; H. I. Longden.)

FRANKLYN, NICHOLAS. Matric. pens. from CHRIST'S, July, 1613. S. of George, of Bolnhurst, Beds. Adm. at Lincoln's Inn, 1615. Barrister. Subscriber to the New Buildings of Christ's. (*Peile*, I. 291.)

FRANCKLIN, PETER. Adm. sizar at SIDNEY, Oct. 1601. Matric. 1601, as Frankland; B.A. 1604–5; M.A. 1608.

FRANCKLIN or FRANKLAND, PETER. Adm. pens. (age 17) at PETERHOUSE, Oct. 13, 1638. Of Haddenham, Cambs. Schools, Wisbech and Cambridge. Matric. 1639. One Peter Frankland R. of Wood Rising, Norfolk, 1665. (*T. A. Walker*, 66; *Vis. of Cambs.*, 1619.)

FRANKLIN, PHILIP. Adm. sizar at EMMANUEL, Aug. 21, 1686. Of Norfolk. Matric. 1687. Perhaps s. of John (1646). B. 1668. Died 1689. Brother of John (1682). (Burke, *L.G.*)

FRANKLIN, RICHARD. Matric. sizar from MAGDALENE, Easter, 1606; B.A. 1608–9; M.A. 1612. Incorp. at Oxford, 1612. R. of Elsworth, Cambs., 1612–32. Buried there Feb. 15, 1631–2.

FRANKLIN, RICHARD. Adm. pens. at JESUS, May 27, 1645. Of Wiltshire. Matric. 1645.

FRANKLIN, RICHARD. Adm. Fell.-Com. at EMMANUEL, Mar. 6, 1646–7. Of Middlesex. S. and h. of Sir John (1614), of Willesden, Middlesex, Knt. Bapt. at Willesden, July 20, 1630. Adm. at Gray's Inn, June 23, 1648. Perhaps matric. from Balliol, Mar. 19, 1648–9. Knighted, July 14, 1660. Created Bart., Oct. 16, 1660. M.P. for Herts., 1661–79. Buried at Willesden, Sept. 16, 1685. Father of Robert (1676). (*G.E.C.*)

FRANKLIN, RICHARD. M.A. 1652 (Incorp. from Oxford). Described as 'B.A. Cambridge' on taking his B.A. at Magdalen Hall, Oxford, 1648 (can he be the matriculant at Jesus, 1645?). M.A. (Oxford) 1651. Fellow of Merton, 1648. Proctor, 1655. Died 1674. (*Al. Oxon.*)

FRANKLYN, RICHARD. Adm. at KING'S, a scholar from Eton, 1670. S. of William (1635). B. at Eton. Matric. 1671. Fellow, 1674. Died as junior fellow. (*Harwood.*)

FRANKLYN, RICHARD FAREWELL. Adm. pens. (age 17) at ST JOHN'S, June 30, 1737. S. of Thomas, attorney, of Wiltshire. B. at Marlborough. School, Marlborough. Matric. 1737. Died in College. Buried at All Saints', Cambridge, Jan. 5, 1738–9.

FRANCKLIN, ROBERT. Adm. sizar at JESUS, Mar. 4, 1646–7. B. in London, July 16, 1630. School, Woodbridge, Suffolk. Migrated to Queens'. Matric. 1647. R. of Kirton, Suffolk. V. of Westhall, 1659–62, ejected. V. of Blythburgh, till 1659. Afterwards a preacher in London. Suffered imprisonment. Died 1684. (*Calamy*, II. 439; *D.N.B.*)

FRANKLYN, ROBERT. Adm. at KING'S, a scholar from Eton, 1676. S. of Sir Richard (1646–7), of Moor Park, Herts., Bart. B. at Rickmansworth. Matric. 1677; B.A. 1680. Fellow, 1680. Died in College, July 2, 1683.

FRANCKLYN, SAMUEL. M.A. 1675 (*Lit. Reg.*).

FRANKLIN, THOMAS. Adm. at KING'S, a scholar from Eton, 1496.

FRANKLIN, THOMAS. B.Can.L. 1527–8. Dean of the Collegiate Church of St Cuthbert at Darlington. Died 1528. (*Cooper*, I. 527.) In the *Gr. Bk*, B[a], he is described as 'Cardinalis cancelarius.'

FRANKLEYNE, THOMAS. Matric. pens. from TRINITY, Lent, 1588–9. Probably brother of George (1588–9).

FRANKLIN, THOMAS. Matric. sizar from JESUS, Easter, 1609; B.A. from Peterhouse, 1612–3; M.A. 1616. Ord. deacon (Peterb.) Dec. 17, 1615. V. of Frampton, Lincs., 1619–29.

FRANKLIN, THOMAS. Matric. sizar from QUEENS', Easter, 1631. Of Cambridgeshire. B.A. 1633–4.

FRANCKLIN, THOMAS. Adm. pens. (age 18) at TRINITY, June 21, 1739. S. of Richard, bookseller, of London. School, Westminster. Matric. 1739; Scholar, 1740; B.A. 1742–3; M.A. 1746; D.D. 1770. Fellow, 1745–58. Regius Professor of Greek, 1750–9. Ord. deacon (Ely) May, 1746; priest (Rochester) Mar. 6, 1746–7. V. of Ware and Thundridge, Herts., 1759–77. V. of Brasted, Kent, 1777–84. Preacher at St Paul's, Covent Garden. Classical scholar. Died Mar. 15, 1784. Will (P.C.C.) 1784; of St Giles-in-the-Fields. (*Al. Westmon.*, 320; *D.N.B.*)

FRANKLYN, WILLIAM. Adm. at KING'S, a scholar from Eton, 1496. B. at Bledlow, Bucks. B.Can.L. 1504. Archdeacon of Durham, 1515; also Chancellor. Preb. of Lincoln, 1518. R. of Houghton-le-Spring, 1522. Preb. of York, 1526–56. President of Queens', 1526–8. Dean of Windsor, 1536–52. Dean of Wolverhampton, 1536–48. R. of Chalfont St Giles, 1540. Died Jan. 1555–6. (*Cooper*, I. 141; *D.N.B.*)

FRANKLIN, WILLIAM. Matric. pens. from ST JOHN'S, Lent, 1563–4; B.A. 1566–7. Ord. deacon (Ely) Aug. 24, 1566; priest (Norwich) June 11, 1568.

FRANCKLYN, W. Matric. pens. from CLARE, Easter, 1582.

FRANKLIN, WILLIAM. Scholar of EMMANUEL, 1603; B.A. 1604–5; M.A. 1608. One of these names V. of Shorne, Kent, 1617–24. V. of St Margaret, Rochester, 1625–7. Head Master, King's School, Rochester, 1608–17 and 1624–7. (J. Ch. Smith.)

FRANCKLIN, WILLIAM. Matric. sizar from CLARE, Easter, 1612; B.A. 1615–6; M.A. 1619. Ord. deacon (Peterb.) June 4, 1615; priest, Mar. 16, 1616–7. R. of Flowton, Suffolk, 1624–44, ejected.

FRANKLIN, WILLIAM. Adm. pens. at QUEENS', Mar. 16, 1630–1. Of Bedfordshire. Matric. 1631; B.A. 1633–4.

FRANKLIN, WILLIAM. Adm. at KING'S (age 16) a scholar from Eton, Aug. 28, 1635. B. at Eton. Matric. 1635; B.A. 1639; M.A. 1642; M.D. 1661 (*Lit. Reg.*). Fellow, 1638; deprived, but 'apostatised, took the Covenant and was restored, 1647, by Parliament.' Left, 1650. (*Harwood.*)

FRANKLYN, WILLIAM. Matric. pens. from PEMBROKE, Easter, 1641. S. of John, of Metfield, Suffolk. B.A. 1642–3. Doubtless B.D. 1664 (*Lit. Reg.*). Ord. deacon (Norwich) May 28, 1643. C. of Forncett. R. of Burnham Sutton, Norfolk; 'late chaplain in the King's army.' R. of Burnham Norton, 1660.

FRANKLYN, WILLIAM. Adm. sizar (age 15) at CHRIST'S, Apr. 13, 1683. S. of William. B. at Fring, Norfolk. School, Cawston. Matric. 1684; B.A. 1686–7.

FRANKLIN, ——. Adm. at CORPUS CHRISTI, 1553.

FRANCKLYN, ——. Adm. Fell.-Com. at KING'S, Easter, 1576.

FRANCKLIN, ——. Adm. sizar at KING'S, Michs. 1590.

FRANKS or FRANK, ABRAHAM. Adm. pens. (age 17) at TRINITY, June 6, 1702. S. of John, of Preston, Lancs. School, Westminster. Matric. 1702; Scholar, 1703; B.A. 1705; M.A. 1709; D.D. 1728 (*Com. Reg.*). Fellow, 1708. Ord. deacon (Ely) May 23; priest, June 11, 1714. Chaplain to George II. R. of West Dene, Wilts., -1733. Preb. of Sarum, 1720–33. Died Oct. 2, 1733. Will, P.C.C. (*Al. Westmon.*, 240.)

FRANCS, ROBERT. Matric. sizar from ST JOHN'S, Michs. 1569.

FRANKS, WILLIAM. M.A. from CHRIST'S, 1739. S. of John, of Loughborough. Matric. from Lincoln College, Oxford 1723, age 17; B.A. (Oxford) 1726. Ord. deacon (Lincoln) June 16, 1728; priest (Ely) Feb. 22, 1729–30. R. of Gt Oxendon, Northants., 1738–51. R. of Hardwick, 1739–51. R. of Market Harborough, 1739–51. Died Dec. 30, 1751. Buried at Oxendon. Will (Archd. Northants.) 1752. (*Al. Oxon.*; *Peile*, II. 227; H. I. Longden.)

FRANKWELL, NICHOLAS. B.A. from ST CATHARINE'S, 1603–4; M.A. 1607. V. of Bexley, Kent, 1609–58. R. of Gravesend, 1615–7. Died Oct. 11, 1658. Buried at Bexley. M.I.

FRANKYSCH, ROBERT. Scholar at KING'S HALL, 1446–54.

FRANKYSSHE, ROBERT. M.A. 1501–2 (Incorp. from Oxford). V. of All Hallows, Hoo, Kent, 1525–41. Died 1541.

FRANSSEUS, *see* FRANCIUS.

'FRAYER,' WILLIAM, *see* ARMINE, WILLIAM.

FRASER or FRAIZER, ALEXANDER. M.D. 1637 (Incorp. from Montpelier). B. in Scotland, *c.* 1610. Fellow, R.C.P. 1641. F.R.S. 1663. Elect, 1666. Physician to Charles II. Knighted (according to *Munk*). Died May 3, 1681. Will, P.C.C. Father of Charles (1667). (*D.N.B.*; *Munk*, I. 232.)

FRASER or FRAIZER, CHARLES. Adm. pens. at TRINITY, June 28, 1667. S. of Alexander (1637). School, Westminster. Matric. 1667; Scholar, 1668; B.A. 1670–1; M.A. 1674; M.D. 1678 (*Lit. Reg.*). Fellow, 1673. F.R.C.P. 1684. Physician to Charles II, James II, and William III. (*Munk*, I. 432.)

FRASSENDEN, ROBERT DE. Southern scholar, who received a royal pardon for taking part in a riot against the northern students, 1261. (*Fuller*, 29.)

FRAUNCEYS, *see* FRANCIS.

FREAKE, EDMUND. M.A. *c.* 1550; D.D. 1570. B. in Essex, *c.* 1516. Augustinian Canon of Waltham, till the surrender, 1540. Ord. deacon (London) 1544; p , June 18, 1545. R. of Foulmire, Cambs., 1562–71. Archdeacon of Canterbury, 1564–76. Preb. of Westminster, 1564–72. Canon of Windsor, 1565–72. R. of Purleigh, Essex, 1567–75. Dean of Rochester, 1570–2. Dean of Sarum, 1570–2. Bishop of Rochester, 1572–5; of Norwich, 1575–84; of Worcester, 1584–91. Died Mar. 21, 1590–1. Buried at Worcester. Father of John (1562). (*Cooper*, II. 96; *Al. Oxon.*; *D.N.B.*)

FREAKE, EDMUND. Matric. pens. from PEMBROKE, Easter, 1569; B.A. 1572–3; M.A. 1576. Fellow, 1574.

FREAKE, JOHN. Matric. pens. from CHRIST'S, Nov. 1562. S. of Edmund (above), Bishop of Norwich. Scholar, 1564; B.A. 1565–6; M.A. from Pembroke, 1569; B.D. 1576. Fellow of Pembroke, 1567. R. of Foulmire, Cambs., 1570. R. of Purleigh, Essex, 1575–1604. Archdeacon of Norwich, 1581–1604. Preb. of Norwich, 1581. Died Sept. 4, 1604. Buried at Purleigh. M.I. there. Will (P.C.C.) 1604. Father of the next. (*Peile*, I. 78; *Cooper*, II. 393.)

FREAKE, JOHN. Matric. pens. from TRINITY, *c.* 1596. S. of John (1562). Scholar, 1599; B.A. 1600–1; M.A. 1604. Fellow, 1602. R. of Watlington, Norfolk, 1606–28. Died Jan. 20, 1628–9.

FREKE, JOHN. M.A. 1664 (Incorp. from Oxford). S. of Richard. B. at Chard, Somerset. Matric. from Wadham College, Oxford, May 31, 1655, age 18; B.A. (Oxford) 1658–9; M.A. 1661. Fellow of Wadham. V. of Hannington, Wilts., 1668–85. C. of Okeford Fitzpaine, Dorset, 1683; R. 1685–1712. V. of Belchalwell, 1692–1712. Died Jan. 19, 1711–2. M.I. at Okeford. (*Al. Oxon.*; F. S. Hockaday.)

FREKE, RICHARD. M.A. from KING'S, 1736. S. of Francis, of Loddiswell, Devon, clerk. Matric. from Exeter College, Oxford, May 22, 1729, age 18; B.A. from Christ Church, 1732–3. Brother of Thomas (1735). (*Al. Oxon.*)

FRAKE, ROBERT. Matric. pens. from TRINITY, Michs. 1587.

FREAKE, THOMAS. Matric. pens. from CLARE, Michs. 1579.

FREKE, THOMAS. M.A. from KING'S, 1735. S. of Francis, V. of Loddiswell, Devon. Matric. from Wadham College, Oxford, Apr. 6, 1723, age 18; B.A. (Oxford) 1726. Probably succeeded his father as V. of Loddiswell, 1744–77. Will (Exeter) 1777. Brother of Richard (1736). (*Al. Oxon.*)

FREBOLD, HUMPHREY. Matric. pens. from ST JOHN'S, Easter, 1560.

FRECKINGHAM, *see* FREKINGHAM.

FREKLETON, MARTIN. Matric. pens. from JESUS, Michs. 1598.

FRECKLETON, ROGER. Adm. sizar at EMMANUEL, Mar. 20, 1741–2. Of Freckleton, Lancs. S. of Henry, gent. School, Clitheroe. Matric. 1742; B.A. 1745–6; M.A. 1749. V. of Bispham, Lancs., 1753.

FRECKLETON, SAMUEL. Adm. sizar at CLARE, Apr. 21, 1679. Of Statherne, Leics. Matric. 1680; B.A. 1682–3. R. of West Lydford, Somerset, 1690.

FRECYE, RICHARD. Matric. pens. from ST JOHN'S, Easter, 1602. (Perhaps Frerye.)

FRECYE, TOBIAS. Matric. pens. from ST JOHN'S, Easter, 1605.

FREDERICK, JOHN. Adm. Fell.-Com. (age 18) at SIDNEY, Nov. 12, 1695. 1st s. of Thomas, Esq. B. at St Olave's, London. Bapt. there, Mar. 10, 1677–8. Schools, Croydon (Mr Jo. Caesar) and Mercers'. Matric. 1695. Created Bart. June 18, 1723. Died Oct. 3, 1755. (*G.E.C.*)

FREE, NATHANIEL. Adm. pens. (age 15) at CHRIST'S, June 1, 1650. S. of Thomas. B. in London. School, Bishop's Stortford. Matric. 1650. Migrated to Oxford. B.A. from Christ Church, 1653–4; M.A. 1656. (*Peile*, I. 536; *Al. Oxon.*)

FREE, ——. B.A. 1465–6.

FREE, ——. Fee for M.A. (?) 1491–2.

FREEBODY, WILLIAM. Adm. pens. at QUEENS', May 17, 1595. Of Northamptonshire.

FREEBONE or FREEBORN, JOHN. Adm. sizar at CHRIST'S, May 19, 1582. Of Dorset. Migrated to Queens', Oct. 25, 1583; and to Emmanuel, 1585. B.A. from Emmanuel, 1586–7; M.A. 1590. One of these names had license from Lambeth to teach boys in the province of Canterbury, 1592. (*Peile*, I. 169.)

FREEBORNE, JOHN. Matric. sizar from KING'S, Easter, 1624.

FREEBORNE, PATRICK. Matric. pens. from MAGDALENE, Easter, 1572.

FREEBORNE, SAMUEL. Matric. pens. from KING'S, Easter, 1627.

FREEBORNE, ——. Adm. pens. at ST CATHARINE'S, 1628.

FREEBURN, ——. Adm. pens. at ST CATHARINE'S, Easter, 1653.

FREEMAN, AUBREY. Adm. pens. (age 15) at CHRIST'S, June 18, 1700. S. of Ralph and Elizabeth, dau. of Sir John Aubrey. B. at Aspeden Hall, Herts. School, Bishop's Stortford. Scholar, 1700–1; Matric. 1701. Died young. (*Peile*, I. 148.)

FREEMAN, BARTHOLOMEW. Matric. pens. from ST JOHN'S, *c.* 1601.

FREEMAN, CHARLES. Adm. pens. at CORPUS CHRISTI, 1695. Of London. Matric. 1695; B.A. 1699–1700; M.A. 1703. Ord. deacon (Peterb.) Sept. 21, 1701; priest, May 31, 1702. Probably P.C. of St Botolph's, Aldersgate, 1714–22. Will (P.C.C.) 1722. (H. I. Longden; J. Ch. Smith.)

FREEMAN, EDWARD. Matric. pens. from TRINITY, 1598. S. of Edward, gent. B. at Caldecote, Herts. Schools Southhill, Beds. (Mr Carter) and Stotfold (Mr Gammon). Migrated to Caius, Nov. 14, 1599, age 16. Scholar; B.A. 1601–2; M.A. 1605. (*Venn*, I. 170.)

FREEMAN, EDWARD. Matric. pens. from CORPUS CHRISTI, Lent, 1623–4; B.A. 1625–6; M.A. 1631.

FREEMAN, EDWARD. Adm. at KING'S, a scholar from Eton, 1645. B. at Betchworth, Surrey, *c.* 1630. Matric. 1645–6; B.A. 1649; M.A. 1653. Fellow, 1649–66. One of these names, s. of Edward, of Gray's Inn, adm at Gray's Inn, Nov. 12, 1650.

FREEMAN, EDWARD. Adm. pens. at CLARE, May 30, 1648. Matric. 1648.

FREMAN, ESAY. Matric. sizar from QUEENS', Easter, 1584.

FREEMAN, GEORGE. Matric. pens. from TRINITY, *c.* 1592; scholar from Westminster, 1591; B.A. 1594–5; M.A. 1598. Incorp. at Oxford, 1600.

FREEMAN, GEORGE. Matric. pens. from SIDNEY, Easter, 1610. Not in the College register. One of these names, of Higham Ferrers, Northants., gent., adm. at Gray's Inn, Mar. 9, 1614–5.

FREEMAN, GEORGE. Matric. pens. from KING'S, Lent, 1618–9; B.A. 1621–2.

FREEMAN, HENRY. Adm. pens. at CLARE, July 6, 1633. Matric. 1634.

FREEMAN, HENRY. Adm. at CORPUS CHRISTI, 1673. Of Northamptonshire.

FREEMAN, HOUSELY. Adm. pe . (age 18) at TRINITY, May 14, 1730. S. of Housely, of Housely Hall, Yorks. Bapt. Apr. 28, 1712. School, Greasborough (near Rotherham), Yorks. Adm. at the Middle Temple, Nov. 28, 1730. Captain of militia. Died *s.p.* Buried at Ecclesfield, Mar. 5, 1783. (M. H. Peacock.)

FREEMAN, JAMES. Matric. sizar from CORPUS CHRISTI, Easter, 1654. Of Suffolk.

FREEMAN, JOHN. Adm. at KING'S, a scholar from Eton, 1445; B.A. 1449. Clerk of the Privy Seal.

FREEMAN, JOHN. Matric. sizar from TRINITY HALL, Easter, 1549 (*impubes*).

FREEMAN, JOHN. Matric. sizar from TRINITY, Michs. 1575; Scholar, 1580; B.A. 1580–1; M.A. 1584. Fellow, 1583. Preacher at Lewes, Sussex. Author, sermons. Will proved (V.C.C.) 1596. (*Cooper*, III. 59; *D.N.B.*)

FREEMAN, JOHN. Matric. sizar from PETERHOUSE, Easter, 1578. One of these names V. of Felsted, Essex. Will (P.C.C.) 1614.

FREEMAN, JOHN. Adm. scholar (age 18) at CAIUS, May 7, 1616. S. of John, gent., of Wendling, Norfolk. School, Norwich. Matric. 1616; B.A. 1619–20; M.A. 1629. Ord. priest (Norwich) Sept. 21, 1623. C. of Thorington, Suffolk, in 1627 and 1633. Will (Norwich Archd. C.) between 1653–60. (*Venn*, I. 232.)

FREEMAN, JOHN. Adm. pens. (age 15) at CHRIST'S, Mar. 20, 1623–4. S. of Richard, barrister. B. at Chelmsford. School, Maldon. Matric. 1623–4; B.A. 1627. Adm. at the Middle Temple, Oct. 19, 1626. Brother of Richard (1626–7) and Thomas (1631). (*Peile*, I. 359; *Vis. of Essex*, 1634.)

FREEMAN, JOHN. Adm. sizar at EMMANUEL, Mar. 22, 1629–30. Of Northamptonshire. Matric. 1631.

FREEMAN, JOHN. Adm. at KING'S, a scholar from Eton, 1650. B. in London, *c.* 1636. Matric. Easter, 1651; B.A. 1654–5; M.A. 1658. Fellow, 1654–8. Died in London of small-pox, July 15, 1658. (*Harwood.*)

FREEMAN, JOHN. Adm. sizar at CLARE, June 10, 1671. Of Irchester, Northants. Matric. 1671; B.A. 1674–5; M.A. 1678. Fellow, 1678. Ord. deacon (Peterb.) Sept. 24, 1676. One of these names signs as minister of Deane, Beds., 1680–7. Buried there Dec. 12, 1688. (W. M. Noble.)

FREEMAN, JOHN. Adm. sizar (age 16) at CHRIST'S, May 6, 1675. S. of John. B. at Wilby, Northants. School, Strixton. Matric. 1675.

FREEMAN, JOHN. Adm. sizar at JESUS, May 26, 1677. Of Yorkshire. Matric. 1677.

FREEMAN, JOHN. Adm. pens. (age 16) at TRINITY, Feb. 23, 1709. S. of Samuel (1661), Dean of Peterborough. School, Bishop's Stortford (Mr Tooke). Matric. 1709; Scholar, 1711; M.B. 1714; M.D. 1719. Probably adm. student at Leyden, Aug. 24, 1713. Doubtless of St Thomas the Apostle, London. Died Jan. 19, 1775. (G. *Mag.*)

FREEMAN, JOHN. Adm. sizar (age 18) at SIDNEY, May 11, 1731. S. of John, farmer. B. at Ringstead, Northants., Sept. 29, 1712. School, Oakham. Matric. 1731; B.A. 1734–5; M.A. 1738; B.D. 1745. Fellow, 1736. Ord. deacon (Lincoln) Oct. 12, 1735. Died Dec. 30, 1746. Buried at Ringstead. M.I. (H. I. Longden.)

FREEMAN, JOHN. Adm. pens. at EMMANUEL, Mar. 15, 1731–2. Of Norfolk. Matric. 1732; B.A. 1735–6; M.A. 1739. Ord. priest (Norwich) July, 1739. P.C. of Horsham St Faith, Norfolk, 1739–66. R. of Rackheath, 1739. R. of Caistor. V. of Little Melton, 1743–6. Will (P.C.C.) 1797; as of Caistor.

FREEMAN, LAURENCE. Adm. sizar at CORPUS CHRISTI, 1589. B. at Gt Stukeley, Hunts., *c.* 1572. Matric. *c.* 1591; B.A. 1593–4; M.A. 1598. Ord. priest (Lincoln) Mar. 19, 1596–7. V. of Toynton All Saints', Lincs., 1601.

FREEMAN, MARTIN. Adm. at KING'S, a scholar from Eton, 1613. B. in London, *c.* 1596. Matric. Easter, 1614; B.A. 1617–8; M.A. 1621. Fellow, 1616–30. Proctor, 1625. Declaimed before King James and the French ambassadors on philosophy. Died Apr. 7, 1630. Buried in the College Chapel. (*Harwood*; Le Neve, *Mon.*, I. 119.)

FREEMAN, RALPH. Adm. pens. at SIDNEY, Mar. 1602–3. Matric. 1603.

FREEMAN, RALPH. Matric. pens. from KING'S, Easter, 1605; B.A. 1607–8. Perhaps same as last.

FREEMAN, RALPH. Matric. Fell.-Com. from KING'S, Easter, 1618; B.A. 1619–20. Doubtless s. and h. of William, of Aspeden Hall, Herts., Esq. Bapt. at St Michael, Cornhill, Aug. 31, 1600. Adm. at Gray's Inn, Oct. 24, 1620. Died July 28, 1665, aged 65. Buried in Aspenden Church. M.I.

FREEMAN, RALPH. Adm. pens. at TRINITY, May 25, 1639. Matric. 1639.

FREMAN, RALPH. D.D. 1746 (Incorp. from Oxford). S. of Ralph, of Ecton, Northants., Esq. Matric. from Magdalen College, Oxford, June 21, 1723, age 16; B.A. (Trinity College, Oxford) 1727; M.A. (All Souls') 1732–3; B.D. 1738; D.D. 1741–2. R. of Aspenden, Herts., 1743–70. Preb. of Salisbury, 1746. Died June 29, 1772. Will, P.C.C. (G. *Mag.*; *Al. Oxon.*)

FREEMAN, RICHARD. Adm. Fell.-Com. at CORPUS CHRISTI, 1577. Of Hertfordshire. Matric. Lent, 1577–8; B.A. 1580–1. One of these names, 'ord. deacon (Coventry) Sept. 29, 1581; bred in the schools,' was C. of Hugglescote, Leics., in 1585.

FREEMAN, RICHARD. Matric. sizar from CHRIST'S, Dec. 1615.

FREEMAN, RICHARD. Adm. pens. (age 14) at CHRIST'S, Mar. 27, 1626–7. S. of Richard (barrister). B. at Chelmsford. Schools, Chelmsford and Maldon. Matric. 1627; B.A. 1630–1; M.A. 1634; D.D. 1660 (*Lit. Reg.*). Ord. priest (Lincoln) May 20, 1642. R. of St James, Garlickhithe, London, 1642. R. of Springfield Boswell, Essex, till 1645; again R. in 1661. Died in Dec. 1661. Brother of John (1624) and Thomas (1631). (*Peile*, I. 380; *Vis. of Essex*, 1634.)

FREEMAN, ROBERT. B.A. 1507–8.

FREEMAN, ROBERT. Matric. sizar from CORPUS CHRISTI, Easter, 1623. Of Norfolk. B.A. 1626–7; M.A. 1630. Petitioned the Chancellor for a Norfolk fellowship, without success. (*Masters.*)

FREEMAN, SAMUEL. Adm. sizar at CLARE, June 10, 1661. Matric. 1661–2; B.A. 1664–5; M.A. 1668; D.D. 1685. Ord. priest (Peterb.) Sept. 22, 1667. V. of Olney, Bucks., 1668–71. R. of St Paul, Covent Garden, 1689–1707. Preb. of Canterbury, 1691–1704. Dean of Peterborough, 1691–1707. Married, May 21, 1674, Susanna, dau. of John Palmer, R. of Ecton, Northants. Died Oct. 14, 1707, aged 63. Buried at Ecton, Northants. M.I. Will, P.C.C. Father of John (1709). (Le Neve, *Mon.*, II. 143; *Lipscomb*, IV; H. I. Longden.)

FREEMAN, SAMUEL. Adm. pens. at CLARE, Aug. 3, 1706. B. in London. Migrated to Trinity Hall. Matric. July, 1711; LL.B. 1712. Ord. deacon (Ely) Dec. 20, 1713; priest (London) June 16, 1717.

FREEMAN, STEPHEN. Matric. pens. from CORPUS CHRISTI, Easter, 1571. (Probably adm. 1569.)

FREEMAN, STEPHEN. Adm. pens. at PETERHOUSE, Mar. 1, 1594–5; B.A. 1598–9; M.A. 1602. R. of Occold, Suffolk, 1602. Living there, 1639. Will (P.C.C.) 1655; of Topcroft, Norfolk, clerk.

FREMAN, THOMAS. Matric. pens. from ST JOHN'S, Michs. 1556. One of these names R. of Woodchester, Gloucs., 1560–85. R. of Boxwell, 1561–76. R. of Minchinhampton, 1576–85. Chaplain to Sir Ambrose Dudley. Died 1585. He is called 'M.A.' (F. S. Hockaday.)

FREEMAN, THOMAS. Adm. pens. (age 16) at CAIUS, Jan. 26, 1618-9. S. of Isaiah, of Wymondham, Norfolk. School, Wymondham. Matric. 1618-9; Scholar, 1619-20.

FREEMAN, THOMAS. Matric. sizar from CLARE, Easter, 1621; B.A. 1624-5; M.A. 1628. Ord. deacon (Peterb.) Mar. 13, 1624-5; priest, Feb. 18, 1626-7. One of these names V. of Cold Ashby, Northants., 1662-86. Buried there May 21, 1686. (T.bP. Dorman.)

FREEMAN, THOMAS. Adm. pens. (age 15) at CHRIST'S, Apr. 18, 1631. S. of Richard, barrister. B. at Chelmsford, Essex. School, Maldon. Matric. 1631. One of these names minister of Barley, Herts., 1645-7. Brother of John (1624) and Richard (1626-7). (*Peile*, I. 409; *Vis. of Essex*, 1634.)

FREEMAN, THOMAS. Adm. pens. (age 15) at CHRIST'S, May 11, 1636. S. of Thomas, escheator for the County of Essex. B. at Chelmsford. School, Chelmsford. Matric. 1636. Adm. at the Middle Temple, Nov. 18, 1641. Of Springfield, Essex. Married Thomasine, dau. of Thomas Manwood, of Bromfield, Essex. (*Peile*, I. 443; *Vis. of Essex*, 1664.)

FREEMAN, THOMAS. Matric. pens. from TRINITY HALL, Easter, 1647.

FREEMAN, THOMAS. Adm. pens. (age 16) at SIDNEY, Jan. 11, 1654-5. S. of Abraham. B. at Stotfold, Beds. Schools, Hitchin (Mr Kemp) and Sutton (Mr Bancks). Matric. 1655; B.A. 1658-9; M.A. 1662. Fellow (by royal mandate) 1661. One of these names V. of Penn, Bucks., 1663-76.

FREEMAN VINCENT. Adm. pens. at EMMANUEL, June 13, 1622. Matric. 1622; B.A. 1625-6.

FREEMAN, WILLIAM. B.A. 1459-60.

FREEMAN, WILLIAM. Adm. pens. (age 21) at ST JOHN'S, Feb. 12, 1649-50. S. of John, clerk, of Kippax, Yorks. School, Leeds.

FREEMAN, WILLIAM. Adm. pens. at QUEENS', June 30, 1718; Fell.-Com. Oct. 6, 1719. Of London. Matric. 1718-9; B.A. 1722-3. Ord. deacon (London) June 9, 1723.

FREEMAN, ——. B.A. 1466-7.

FREEMAN, ——. Adm. at CORPUS CHRISTI, 1580.

FREEMAN, ——. Matric. pens. from SIDNEY, Michs. 1609.

FREEMAN, ——. Adm. pens. at CLARE, July 1, 1695.

FREEMAN, ——. Adm. pens. at TRINITY HALL, Feb. 25, 1708-9; Fell.-Com. 1711-2.

FREEMIS, JOHN. B.A. 1459-60.

FREEMOULT, JOHN. Adm. pens. (age 17) at CAIUS, July 10, 1701. S. of Joel, attorney, of Norwich. B. at Canterbury. Schools, Norwich and Reepham. Scholar, 1701-7; Matric. 1702; M.B. 1707; M.D. 1712. Fellow, 1709-11. Died Jan. 23, 1717. Buried at St Saviour's, Norwich. M.I. at St Michael's, Coslany. Brother of Robert (1720). (*Venn*, I. 507.)

FREMOULT, ROBERT. Adm. pens. (age 18) at CAIUS, Apr. 26, 1720. S. of Joel, attorney, of Norwich. B. there. School, Wymondham. Matric. 1720; Scholar, 1720; LL.B. 1725. Adm. at the Inner Temple, July 1, 1721. The Freemoults belonged to the Walloon Church at Norwich. (*Venn*, II. 14.)

FREMOULT, SAMUEL. Adm. at CORPUS CHRISTI, 1727. Of Kent. Matric. 1727; B.A. 1730-1. Ord. deacon (Ely) Sept. 19, 1731. R. of Wootton, Kent, 1739-79. Died Sept. 28, 1779.

FREESTON, *see* FRESTON.

FREISE, JOHN. Matric. Fell.-Com. from MAGDALENE, Easter, 1608.

FREKINHAM, CLEMENT. Matric. sizar from TRINITY, Michs. 1564. B. 1548. B.A. 1569-70. Ord. priest (Peterb.) Dec. 2, 1569; 'well versed in sacred learning.' Preacher. V. of Whaplode, Lincs., 1570. Admon. (Leicester) 1613.

FREKYNGHAM, EDWARD. Matric. sizar from QUEENS', Michs. 1565.

FREKYNGHAM, GODFREY. Adm. sizar at EMMANUEL, June, 1588. Matric. 1588-9.

FREMINGHAM, JOHN (1733), *see* FRAMINGHAM.

FRENCH, ANTHONY. Matric. sizar from TRINITY, 1555.

FRENCH, ANTHONY. Adm. at TRINITY, a scholar from Westminster, May 24, 1637; Scholar, 1638 (assigned to St John's in the matriculation register). Died in College. Buried at St Michael's, May 16, 1639.

FRENCH, ARTHUR. Adm. Fell.-Com. at EMMANUEL, June 3, 1734. From the West Indies. Matric. 1735.

FRENCH, CLEMENT. Matric. pens. from QUEENS', Easter, 1584. Of Suffolk. B.A. 1588-9; M.A. 1592; B.D. 1599. Fellow, 1592-1601. Ord. deacon and priest (Peterb.) Sept. 3, 1593. V. of Stradishall, Suffolk, 1594. R. of Castle Camps, Cambs., 1605. Father of Henry (1617).

FRENCH, EDMUND. Adm. pens. at EMMANUEL, June 14, 1659. Of Lancashire. S. of Edward, of Preston, age 22, in 1664. Matric. 1659; LL.B. from Trinity Hall, 1664. Signs for deacon's orders (London) Feb. 18, 1664-5. R. of Campsey Ash, Suffolk, 1677. (*Vis. of Lancs.*, 1664.)

FRENCH, EDWARD. Adm. sizar (age 19) at CHRIST'S, June 8, 1637. S. of Thomas, yeoman, of Steeple Bumpstead, Essex. B. there. Schools, Bishop's Stortford, Herts. and Bumpstead. B.A. 1640-1. Probably died before 1661. One of these names was an original settler of Salisbury, Massachusetts, in 1650. (*Peile*, I. 448.)

FRENCH, GEORGE. Matric. pens. from CHRIST'S, July, 1617; B.A. 1620-1; M.A. 1624. Ord. deacon (Peterb.) Mar. 24, 1624-5; priest, Mar. 25, 1625. Perhaps V. of Cockfield, Durham, 1629. (*Peile*, I. 318.)

FRENCH, GEORGE. Matric. sizar from CLARE, Easter, 1631; B.A. 1634-5; M.A. 1638.

FRENCH, GEORGE. Adm. sizar (age 18) at PETERHOUSE, June 20, 1643. Of Peterborough. B.A. 1646-7.

FRENCH, GEORGE. Adm. sizar at CHRIST'S, Jan. 4, 1737-8. S. of John (1708-9), R. of Gt Saxham, Suffolk. Exhibitioner from Bury School. Matric. 1738; B.A. 1741-2; M.A. 1745. Ord. deacon (Norwich) June, 1742. C. of Gedding, Suffolk, 1743-58. Died 1762. Will (P.C.C.) as of Rougham. Brother of Robert (1745-6). (*Peile*, II. 236.)

FRENCH, GREGORY. Adm. pens. (age 16) at PEMBROKE, Mar. 18, 1621-2. S. of Thomas, of Cambridge, alderman. Migrated to Magdalene. Matric. there, 1623. Ord. deacon (Peterb.) July 20, 1640; priest, Sept. 19, 1641. R. of Cowbit, Lincs., 1641.

FRENCH, HENRY. Adm. sizar (age 16) at PEMBROKE, Oct. 12, 1617. S. of Clement (1584), of Castle Camps, Cambs. Bapt. July 5, 1601. Matric. 1618. Died 1618-9.

FRENCH, JEREMIAH. Adm. pens. (age 16) at CAIUS, Apr. 28, 1641. S. of Thomas, gent., of Knettishall, Suffolk. B. at Saxmundham. School, Benhall. Matric. 1641; Scholar, 1643-5; B.A. 1644-5; M.A. 1648. Minister of Newport, Isle of Wight. Imprisoned in Carisbrook Castle for his comments upon the treatment of Charles I, and tried for his life. Afterwards minister at Yeovil; and South Perrott, Dorset, 1652-62. After his ejection he preached in the neighbourhood of Bradford Abbas, Dorset. Died *c.* May 10, 1685. (*Venn*, I. 343; *Calamy*, II. 375.)

FRENCH, JOHN. Matric. from ST JOHN'S, *c.* 1592; perhaps same as the next.

FRENCH, JOHN. Adm. pens. at QUEENS', 1592. Of Suffolk. B.A. 1595-6; M.A. 1599. Ord. deacon (Norwich) June 24, 1600; priest, Jan. 1, 1600-1. C. of Ameringhall, Norfolk. R. of Stradishall, Suffolk, 1604.

FRENCH, JOHN. Adm. sizar (age 19) at ST JOHN'S, Apr. 3, 1639. S. of John, husbandman, of Gt Budworth, Cheshire. B. there. School, Northwich. Matric. 1639; B.A. 1642-3; M.A. 1646. R. of Wenvoe, Glamorgan; ejected, 1662. Died Feb. 28, 1691.

FRENCH, JOHN. Adm. at CORPUS CHRISTI, 1647. Of Essex.

FRENCH, JOHN. M.A. from EMMANUEL, 1699. S. of Thomas, of Shute, Devon, clerk. Matric. from New Inn Hall, Oxford, Apr. 6, 1677, age 19; B.A. from Exeter College, 1680. R. of Seaborough, Somerset, 1684. V. of Ilminster, 1685-1729. R. of Earnshill, 1694-1729. R. of Cricket Malherbe, 1699-1729. Died 1729. (*Al. Oxon.*)

FRENCH, JOHN. Adm. sizar (age 18) at CHRIST'S, Jan. 23, 1708-9. S. of John. B. at Gazeley, Suffolk. School, Bury. Scholar, 1708-9; Matric. 1709; B.A. 1712-3; M.A. 1716. Ord. deacon (Peterb.) Sept. 19, 1713; priest (Ely) Sept. 1717. Reader at St Mary's, Bury. R. of Gt Saxham, Suffolk, 1721-67. R. of Horningsheath, 1758-67. Buried at Saxham, Jan. 3, 1767. Father of George (1737-8) and Robert (1745-6). (*Peile*, II. 171.)

FRENCH, JOHN. Adm. pens. at ST CATHARINE'S, May 15, 1727. Of Sudbury, Suffolk. Matric. 1728; B.A. 1730-1; M.A. 1735. Ord. deacon (Lincoln) Feb. 18, 1732-3; priest, June 20, 1736. One of these names R. of Creeting All Saints', Suffolk, 1737-43.

FRENCHE, PETER. Matric. sizar from ST JOHN'S, Michs. 1578; B.A. from Magdalene, 1581-2; M.A. 1585. One of these names P.C. of Weston-on-Trent, Staffs., 1619-21.

FRENCH, PETER. Adm. sizar at EMMANUEL, Apr. 12, 1632. Of Oxfordshire. Perhaps s. of Thomas French, of Wonderton, Oxon., and cousin of William (1633). Matric. 1632; B.A. 1635-6; M.A. 1639; B.D. 1646. Incorp. at Oxford, 1650. Canon of Christ Church, 1651-5. D.D. (Oxford, by diploma) 1653. R. of Cottenham, Cambs., 1644. Married Robina, sister of Oliver Cromwell. Died June 17, 1655. Will, P.C.C. (*Al. Oxon.*)

FRENCH, RICHARD. Adm. sizar at Jesus, May 24, 1637. Of Norfolk. Matric. 1637. Buried in the College Chapel, July 13, 1640.

FRENCH, RICHARD. Adm. pens. (age 17) at Caius, July 5, 1712. S. of Robert, gent., of Hempnall, Norfolk. B. there. School, Norwich. Matric. 1712; Scholar, 1712–8; B.A. 1716–7; M.A. 1734. Ord. deacon (London) June 8, 1718; priest (Peterb., *Litt. dim.* from Norwich) Sept. 20, 1719. R. of Framingham-Pigot, Norfolk. R. of Bergh Apton, 1719–64. Chaplain to Sir Robert Walpole. Died Nov. 4, 1764. Will, P.C.C. (*Venn*, I. 527; A. B. Beaven.)

FRENCH, ROBERT. Adm. pens. at Sidney, July 3, 1613. Matric. 1613; B.A. 1616–7; M.A. 1620.

FRENCH, ROBERT. Adm. sizar (age 15) at Christ's, June 26, 1623. S. of Thomas. B. at Halstead, Essex. School, Halstead. Matric. 1623–4; B.A. 1626–7; M.A. 1630. One of these names V. of Gt Hockham, Norfolk, 1634–6. (*Peile*, I. 352.)

FRENCH, ROBERT. Adm. sizar (age 20) at Christ's, June, 1706. S. of John. B. at Chilton, Suffolk. School, Sudbury. Matric. 1706. Ord. deacon (Ely) June, 1712, as B.A. (*Peile*, II. 164.)

FRENCH, ROBERT. Adm. sizar (age 18) at Christ's, Jan. 1, 1745–6. S. of John (1708–9). B. at Bury St Edmunds. School, Bury. Matric. 1745–6; Scholar, 1745–6; B.A. 1749; M.A. 1753. Fellow, 1750–71. Ord. deacon (Ely) Dec. 1750; priest, Sept. 1752. C. of Cockfield, Suffolk, 1754–71. Died at Cockfield, June 30, 1771. Buried at Gt Saxham. Brother of George (1737–8). (*Peile*, II. 248.)

FRENCH, ROGER. Adm. at King's (age 16) a scholar from Eton, Aug. 13, 1525. B. at Eton. Left *c.* 1526.

FRENCHE, SAMUEL. Matric. pens. from Trinity, *c.* 1592; Scholar, 1593; B.A. 1596–7.

FRENCH, THOMAS. M.A. 1635 (Incorp. from Oxford). B.A. from Merton College, 1628; M.A. 1631. Doubtless R. of Threxton, Norfolk, 1642.

FRENCHE, WILLIAM. Matric. sizar from Trinity Hall, Easter, 1549 (*impubes*).

FRENCH, WILLIAM. Adm. pens. at Emmanuel, July 2, 1633. Of Broughton, Oxon. S. of John. Matric. 1633; B.A. 1636–7; M.A. 1640; M.D. from Caius, 1647. Fellow of Caius, 1644–51. Licensed to practise medicine, 1640. Physician to the Parliamentary army in Scotland. Died there 1650. Will dated Dec. 1650; proved (P.C.C.) Feb. 20, 1650–1; by brother John, M.D. (*Venn*, I. 354; J. B. Peace.)

FRENCH, WILLIAM. M.A. from St John's, 1749. S. of William, of Merriott, Somerset. Matric. from Wadham College, Oxford, Oct. 22, 1736, age 19; B.A. (Oxford) 1740. V. of Thorncombe, Devon, 1748–61. R. of Wambrook, Dorset, 1749–61. Chaplain to Edward Lord Stawell. Died Mar. 10, 1761. Will, P.C.C. (*Scott-Mayor*, III. 588.)

FRENCH or FRANK, ——. Pens. at Peterhouse, Feb. 24, 1581–2.

FRENCH, ——. Adm. pens. at St Catharine's, 1644.

FRENCHAM, BARNABAS. Matric. pens. from Pembroke, Easter, 1613. S. of Henry, R. of Walpole St Peter, Norfolk. B.A. 1616–7; M.A. 1620. Incorp. at Oxford, 1622. Ord. deacon (Peterb.) June 7; priest, June 8, 1623. R. of Walpole St Peter, Norfolk, 1629–61. Father of the next.

FRENCHAM, BARNABAS. Adm. pens. (age 16) at Peterhouse, May 14, 1650. S. of Barnabas (above). School, Wisbech. Scholar, 1650. Died Aug. 25, 1652. Buried at Walpole St Peter. M.I. thare. (*T. A. Walker*, 94.)

FRENCHAM, EDWARD. Matric. pens. from St Catharine's, Easter, 1552.

FRENCHED, THOMAS. Adm. at Corpus Christi, 1606.

FRENT, JOHN. Adm. scholar (age 18) at Caius, Apr. 25, 1587. S. of John, of 'Hauston,' Suffolk (? Hunston). School, Bury St Edmunds. Licensed to teach grammar at Whittlesford, Cambs., 1596. Curate there.

FRERE, *see also* **FRYER.**

FRYER, ALEXANDER. Matric. sizar from Gonville Hall, Michs. 1548; Scholar, 1551. Perhaps 2nd s. of John Frere, of Wickham Skeith, Suffolk. (Horace Frere, *Parentalia*; *Vis. of Norfolk*, 1563.)

FREER, ANTHONY. B.A. from St John's, 1611–2, as 'Friery'; M.A. 1615. S. of Richard, of Occold, Suffolk. R. of Mulbarton, Norfolk, 1616–60. Married Elizabeth, dau. of Henry Hartstongue. Buried Dec. 27, 1660. Father of Richard (1636) and Thomas (1647). (Le Neve, *Mon.*, III. 46.)

FRERE, EDWARD. Adm. pens. (age 16) at Trinity, Apr. 6, 1697. S. of John (1662), of Finningham, Suffolk. School, Bury (Mr Leeds). Matric. 1697; Scholar, 1699; B.A. 1700–1; M.A. 1704. Fellow, 1703. Resided at Thwaite Hall, Suffolk. Married Eleanor, dau. of Thomas Smith, of Thrandeston, Suffolk. Died May, 1766. Buried at Finningham. Father of Sheppard (1732). (*Frere Pedigree*.)

FRERE, FRANCIS. B.A. from Clare 1582–3. Doubtless V. of Gt Totham, Essex, 1587–98; 'M.A.' Died 1598. Will (Cons. C. Lond.) 1598.

FREER, FRANCIS. Adm. sizar at Emmanuel, Jan. 16, 1677–8. Of Leicestershire. Matric. 1678; B.A. 1681–2.

FREER, GEORGE. Adm. pens. (age 14) at Sidney, June 25, 1646. S. of George, yeoman, deceased. B. at Carleton, Yorks. School, Coxwold. Matric. 1646; B.A. 1649–50.

FREER, HENRY. Matric. sizar from Trinity, 1636; Scholar, 1638; B.A. 1639–40; M.A. 1643. Fellow, 1640.

FREERE, HENRY. Adm. sizar (age 16) at Sidney, June 12, 1655. S. of Thomas, clerk. B. at Whitwell, Rutland. School, Oakham (Mr Freere). Matric. 1656; B.A. 1658–9; M.B. from Queens', 1660. Ord. deacon (Peterb.) Sept. 19; priest, Sept. 20, 1663. R. of Tickencote, Rutland, 1663–82. R. of Whitwell, 1668–82. Died 1682. Brother of Michael (1666–7). (T. P. Dorman.)

FRERE, ISRAEL. Deputy High Steward of the University, 1609.

FREER or FREIER, JAMES. Matric. sizar from Magdalene, Easter, 1613; B.A. 1616–7; M.A. 1620. Ord. deacon (Peterb.) June 15; priest, Sept. 21, 1617. Incorp. at Oxford, 1628.

FRERE, JOHN. Adm. pens. at Corpus Christi, 1662. Of Suffolk. S. of John, of Finningham. Bapt. Jan. 30, 1645–6. Matric. Easter, 1662. Migrated to Trinity, Apr. 22, 1663. Age 17, in 1664. Married Anne, dau. of George Pretyman, of Bacton, Suffolk. Buried at Finningham, Jan. 14, 1709–10. Father of Edward (1697). (*Vis. of Suffolk*, 1664; *Cussans*, I. 103.)

FREER, JOHN. Adm. sizar (age 18) at Sidney, June 17, 1664. 2nd s. of Deliverance, butcher. B. at Wigston, Leics. School, Oakham, Rutland (Dr Freer). Matric. 1664; B.A. 1667–8. Ord. deacon and priest (Peterb.) Aug. 2, 1668. R. of Knossington, Leics., 1668–1718. Buried there, Aug. 10, 1718. M.I. Will (Leicester) 1718. (*Nichols*, II. 658.)

FREER, MICHAEL. Matric. sizar from Queens', Michs. 1629. Of Leicestershire. B.A. 1633–4; M.A. 1637; M.D. 1660 (*Lit. Reg.*). Fellow, 1636–44, ejected. Probably Master of Oakham Grammar School, *c.* 1649. Died 1660–1.

FREERE, MICHAEL. Adm. sizar (age 17) at St John's, Feb. 13, 1666–7. S. of Thomas, clerk, of Whitwell, Rutland. B. there. Exhibitioner from Charterhouse. Matric. 1667; B.A. 1670–1; M.A. 1676. Ord. deacon (Peterb.) Dec. 22, 1672; priest (London) Sept. 24, 1676. V. of Cromer, Norfolk, 1676. V. of Roughton, till 1719. R. of Metton. Brother of Henry (1655).

FRERE, RICHARD. D.D. 1486–7. Proctor, 1476–7.

FRERE, RICHARD. Adm. at Corpus Christi, 1636. Of Norfolk. S. and h. of Anthony (1611–2), R. of Mulbarton. Migrated to Emmanuel, Sept. 12, 1637. Adm. at Gray's Inn, July 7, 1641. Probably died before 1660. Brother of Thomas (1647).

FRERE, SHEPPARD. Adm. Fell.-Com. (age 17) at Trinity, Oct. 18, 1732. S. of Edward (1697), of Thwaite Hall, Suffolk. B. Dec. 1712. School, Bury (Mr Kynnesman). Matric. 1732. Adm. at Lincoln's Inn, June 25, 1734. Purchased an estate at Roydon, Norfolk. Married Susanna, dau. of John Hatley, Esq. Died at Roydon, July 14, 1780. Buried at Finningham. (*Burke*; G. *Mag.*)

FREER, THOMAS. B.A. 1466–7.

FRERE, THOMAS. B. at Godmanchester. Ord. deacon and priest (London) Mar. 25, 1604, as 'B.A. late of Jesus College' (? B.A. 1602–3; when the records are missing).

FRERE, THOMAS. Adm. pens. (age 17) at St John's, May 18, 1647. S. of Anthony (1611–2), R. of Mulbarton, Norfolk. School, Moulton. Matric. 1647; B.A. 1650–1; M.A. 1654. Incorp. at Oxford, 1654. Adm. at Gray's Inn, Nov. 14, 1654. Brother of Richard (1636).

FRERE, THOMAS. Adm. sizar at Queens', Jan. 11, 1659–60. Of Rutland. Matric. 1660; B.A. 1663–4; M.A. 1667. Ord. deacon (Peterb.) May 21, 1665; priest, June 10, 1666. R. of Whitwell, Rutland, 1682–7. R. of Tickencote, 1682–7. Died 1687.

FRERE, TOBY. Adm. pens. (age 17) at St John's, Mar. 4, 1645–6; afterwards Fell.-Com. S. of Toby, gent., of Harleston, Norfolk. B. there. School, Norwich. Adm. at Lincoln's Inn, Feb. 12, 1647–8. Of Harleston and Redenhall. Married Sarah, dau. of Robert Longe, of Foulden, Norfolk, 1653. Will (Norwich) 1666. One of these names adm. student at Leyden, May 14, 1640.

FREER, WILLIAM. Adm. pens. (age 15) at Sidney, Apr. 12, 1651. S. of John, Esq., deceased, of Yorkshire. B. at Carlton. School, Coxwold (Mr Thornton). Matric. 1652; B.A. 1654–5; M.A. 1658; B.D. 1665. Fellow. Will proved (V.C.C.) 1682.

FREER, WILLIAM. Adm. pens. (age 18) at Sidney, June 20, 1656. S. of William, Esq., of Craike, Yorks. B. at 'Conney Street' (? Coneysthorpe), Yorks. Schools, York (Mr Dent) and Northallerton (Mr Smelt). Matric. 1656.

FRERE, ——. B.A. 1465–6.

FRERE, ——. Incorp. from Oxford, 1482–3.

FRERY, JOHN. Matric. pens. from ST JOHN'S, Michs. 1579, as 'Frieris'; B.A. 1582–3.

FRERYE, RICHARD. Matric. pens. from ST JOHN'S, Easter, 1602.

FRESHEWELL, RALPH. Matric. pens. from ST JOHN'S, Michs. 1586.

FRESHWATER, EDWARD. Adm. pens. at CHRIST'S, Mar. 8, 1624–5. S. of Richard, of Essex. School, Maldon. Matric. 1625. Adm. at Lincoln's Inn, Oct. 19, 1626. Donor to the New Buildings at Christ's. (*Vis. of Essex*, 1634; *Peile*, I. 365.)

FRESHWATER, THOMAS. Matric. pens. from TRINITY, Easter, 1585. Of Bocking, Essex. Perhaps s. of John, of Heybridge Hall, Essex. Will (P.C.C.) 1639. (*Vis. of Essex*, 1634.)

PRESSON, JOHN. Adm. pens. (age 18) at PEMBROKE, Jan. 16, 1621–2. S. of John, of Norwich. Matrie. 1623, as Freston; B.A. 1624–5; M.A. 1628. Will of one of these names (P.C.C.) 1653; of Cambridge, clerk.

FRESSON, THOMAS. Matric. pens. from CHRIST'S, Dec. 1615. *Peile* (I. 307) suggests Thomas *Freeston*, s. of Richard, of Mendham, Norfolk. Died 1635.

FREESTON, ABRAHAM. Adm. sizar (age 15) at SIDNEY, Apr. 1, 1669. 1st s. of Abraham, deceased. B. in Holborn, London. School, Preston, Northants. Matrie. 1669; B.A. 1672–3. Ord. priest (Lincoln) 1678. Master of Beachampton School, Bucks., 1678. R. of Mavis Enderby, Lincs., 1685. R. of West Keal, 1698.

FRESTON, COOKE. Adm. pens. at CLARE, June 8, 1744; afterwards Fell.-Com. B. at Mendham, Suffolk. Died at Mendham, Dec. 1760. (*G. Mag.*)

PRESTON, HUGH. Scholar at KING'S HALL, 1410. Died Oct. 1, 1420.

FREESTON, JOHN. Adm. pens. at MAGDALENE, June 9, 1679. S. of Thomas, Esq. B. at Horncastle, Lincs. School, Merchant Taylors', London. Matrie. 1679; B.A. 1682–3.

FREESTON, JOHN. Adm. pens. (age 18) at CAIUS, Apr. 16, 1751. S. of Thomas (1708), V. of Cratfield, Suffolk. B. there. Schools, Dedham and Woodbridge. Scholar, 1751–3. Afterwards took the name of Scrivener. (His mother was Ann, dau. and heiress of Charles Scrivener, of Sibton.) Sheriff of Suffolk, 1771. Married Dorothea, dau. of Roger Howman, M.B. Died Sept. 8, 1797. (*Venn*, II. 65.)

PRESTON, MICHAEL. B.A. 1518–9. One of these names, B.A., V. of Yeddingham, Yorks., in 1525.

FREESTON, MICHAEL. Matrie. Fell.-Com. from PEMBROKE, Michs. 1571.

PRESTON, RICHARD. Matric. pens. from PETERHOUSE, Michs. 1564. One of these names of Mendham, Norfolk, Esq. Will (P.C.C.) 1617. M.I.

PRESTON, ROBERT. Adm. pens. at EMMANUEL, May 14, 1603. Matric. 1603; B.A. 1606–7; M.A. 1610.

PRESTON or FREESTON, ROBERT. Adm. Fell.-Com. at EMMANUEL, 1608. Of Thimbleby, Lincs. S. of Robert, of Brinkhill, Lincs. B. 1586. B.A. 1609–10; M.A. (? 1613); M.D. 1628. Died 1638. Buried at Horncastle. (*Lincs. Pedigrees.*)

PRESTON, ROBERT. Adm. pens. at TRINITY, May 6, 1641. Doubtless s. of Robert, M.D. (above). Age 11, in 1634. Matric. 1641. Inherited lands at Thimbleby and Horncastle. (*Lincs. Pedigrees.*)

PRESTON or FREESTONE, ROBERT. Adm. pens. (age 18) at MAGDALENE, May 23, 1688. S. of Thomas, gent. B. at Horncastle, Lincs. School, Lincoln. Matrie. 1688; B.A. 1691–2, as 'Freston.' Buried at Horncastle, Mar. 4, 1691–2. (*Lincs. Pedigrees.*)

PRESTON, THOMAS. Adm. pens. (age 16) at PEMBROKE, June 9, 1639. S. of Thomas. B. at Mendham, Suffolk. Adm. at the Middle Temple, May 12, 1640.

FREESTONE, THOMAS. Adm. pens. (age 16) at CAIUS, *c.* June, 1708. S. of Richard, Esq., of Mendham, Norfolk. B. at Broome, Norfolk. School, Bury St Edmunds. Scholar, 1708–12; Matric. 1709. Migrated to Trinity Hall, Mar. 10, 1711–2. LL.B. 1713. Ord. deacon (Norwich) Mar. 9; priest (Ely) Mar. 16, 1717–8. V. of Cratfield and Laxfield, Suffolk, 1718–43. Married Ann, dau. of Charles Scrivener, R. of Wilby, Suffolk. Died Oct. 26, 1743. M.I. at Cratfield. Father of John (1751). (*Venn*, I. 518.)

PRESTON, WILLIAM. Adm. pens. at EMMANUEL, Feb. 16, 1594–5. Matrie. *c.* 1595.

PRESTON, ——. M.A. 1456–7.

FRESTON, ——. Incorp. as doctor, 1458–9.

FREESTONE, ——. Adm. Fell.-Com. at ST CATHARINE'S, Nov. 16, 1670.

FRETCHWELL or FRETCHVILLE, PETER. Matrie. Fell.-Com. from ST JOHN'S, Michs. 1587. Doubtless M.A. 1612–3 (on visit of Prince Charles). Sir Peter, of Staveley, Derbs. Knighted, 1603. M.P. for Co. Derby, 1601, 1620–2. Died Apr. 7, 1634. Will, P.C.C. (*Vis. of Derbs.*, 1662; A. B. Beaven.)

FRETHORNE, FERDINAND. Adm. sizar at EMMANUEL, June 17, 1616, as 'Fretheren.' B. in St Dunstan-in-the-East parish, London. Matric. 1616, as 'Frederic'; B.A. 1619–20. Ord. deacon (London) Dec. 23, 1621, age 24.

FRETON, NICHOLAS. Student apparently at GONVILLE HALL, in 1385. (*See* his *Cautio*; *Caius MSS. Calendar*, 9.)

FRETWELL, JOHN. Matrie. pens. from ST JOHN'S, Easter, 1624; B.A. 1627–8; M.A. 1634.

FRETWELL, RALPH. Matric. pens. from ST JOHN'S, Michs. 1579. Doubtless s. of Roger, of Hellaby, South Yorks.; bapt. Sept. 21, 1558. Married and had issue. Will (York) 1647. (*Surtees Soc.*, LXV. 330.)

FRETWELL, ROGER. Matric. sizar from TRINITY, Lent, 1580–1. Subscribed for deacon's orders (Lincoln) July 14, 1586, as 'of Lincoln diocese.' R. of Dinnington, Yorks., 1591–1609. Died 1609.

FRETWELL, WILLIAM. Matrie. pens. from CORPUS CHRISTI, Easter, 1622. Of York. B.A. 1625–6. Ord. deacon (York) June, 1626; priest (Peterb.) Feb. 21, 1629–30. V. of Stainton, Yorks., 1629–59.

PREVEN, LATON. Adm. pens. at CLARE, July 2, 1724. B. at 'Bratterton' (? Brotherton), Yorks. Matrie. 1724.

FREVILLE, GEORGE. Studied at Cambridge. S. of Robert, of Shelford, Cambs. Of the Middle Temple, barrister. M.P. for Preston, 1547–52. Deputy High Steward of the University, 1549. Recorder of Cambridge, 1553. Baron of the Exchequer, 1559–79. Married, at St Pancras, Soper Lane, London, Jane, widow of Edward Banckes. Died May, 1579. Admon. (P.C.C.) 1580. (*Cooper*, I. 407; *D.N.B.*; J. Ch. Smith.)

FREVILLE, GEORGE. Matrie. Fell.-Com. from CLARE, Lent, 1577–8. Adm. at Gray's Inn, Nov. 21, 1580. One of these names, of Durham, knighted, Apr. 17, 1603. Buried at Sedgefield, Nov. 25, 1619.

FREVILL or FRYVEL, HUMPHREY. Mus.Doc. 1504–5.

FREVELL, HUMPHREY. Matric. pens. from ST JOHN'S, Michs. 1654 (not recorded in College register).

FREVYLL, JASPER. Matric. sizar from JESUS, Michs. 1573. V. of Dorney, Bucks., 1580–3; called 'B.A.' R. of Gt Leighs, Essex, till 1588.

PREVILE, JOHN. Adm. pens. (age 18) at ST JOHN'S, May 22, 1640. S. of Gilbert, gent., of Durham. B. at Bolton Garths, Bishop Auckland. School, Durham. Matric. 1640.

FREVELL, RICHARD. Matrie. pens. from ST JOHN'S, Michs. 1610. Doubtless 3rd s. of Richard, of Bishop Middleham, Durham. Bapt. there, Oct. 21, 1592. B.A. 1614–5; M.A. 1618. Living at Cambridge, in 1630. Brother of Thomas (1610). (Surtees, *Durham*, III. 36.)

FREVELL, ROBERT. Matrie. Fell.-Com. from CLARE, Michs. 1544.

FRYVELL, ROBERT. Matric. sizar from PETERHOUSE, Easter, 1549 (*impubes*).

FREVELL, ROBERT. Scholar of QUEENS', 1555–8.

FREVILL or FRETWELL, THOMAS. B.A. 1524–5.

FREVELL, THOMAS. Matrie. pens. from ST JOHN'S, Michs. 1610. Doubtless 2nd s. of Richard, of Bishop Middleham, Durham. Bapt. there, Sept. 16, 1591. B.A. 1614–5; M.A. 1618. Died before 1630. Brother of Richard (1610).

FREVILL, WILLIAM. Resident pens. at PETERHOUSE, 1438–9. Paid 3*s.* 4*d.* for his chamber. Lord of the Manor of Little Shelford. Buried Jan. 19, 1460–1. (*T. A. Walker.*)

FREVYLL, WILLIAM. Matrie. pens. from ST JOHN'S, Michs. 1555.

FREWEN, ACCEPTED. M.A. 1616 (Incorp. from Oxford). S. of John, R. of Northiam, Sussex. B. there. Matric. from Magdalen College, Oxford, June 8, 1604, age 16; B.A. (Oxford) 1608–9; M.A. 1612; B.D. 1619; D.D. 1626. Fellow of Magdalen College, Oxford, 1612–26. President, 1626–44. Vice-Chancellor, 1628, 1638. Chaplain to Lord Digby, in Spain, 1621. Chaplain to the King, 1625. Preb. of Canterbury, 1625. R. of Warnford, Hants., 1626–45, sequestered. Dean of Gloucester, 1631–43. R. of Stanlake, Oxon., 1635. Bishop of Lichfield, 1643. Archbishop of York, 1660–4. Died at Bishopsthorpe, Mar. 28, 1664. M.I. in York Minster. (*D.N.B.*; *Al. Oxon.*; Le Neve, *Mon.*, IV. 101.)

FREWEN, JOHN. Adm. Fell.-Com. at St John's, May 24, 1720. S. of Thanckfull (1685), R. of Northiam, Sussex. B. there. School, Northiam. Matric. 1720; B.A. 1723-4; M.A. 1728 (*Com. Reg.*). Ord. deacon (Chichester) May 23, 1725; priest, Aug. 21, 1726. V. of Fairlight, Sussex, 1726-43. R. of Guestling, 1736-43. Chaplain to the Earl of Lincoln. Died Apr. 1743. (*Scott-Mayor*, III. 334; *L. Mag.*)

FREWEN, RICHARD. Incorp. M.A. from Oxford, 1707. S. of Ralph, of London, gent. Matric. from Christ Church, July 4, 1698, age 17; B.A. (Oxford) 1702; M.A. 1705; M.B. 1707; M.D. 1721. Physician at Oxford. Camden Professor of Ancient History. Died May 29, 1761. Buried at St Peter-in-the-East, Oxford. (*Al. Oxon.*)

FREWEN, STEPHEN. Adm. pens. (age 18) at St John's, May 17, 1695. S. of Richard, R. of Northiam, Sussex. B. there. School, Tonbridge. Matric. 1695; B.A. 1698-9; M.A. 1702. Fellow, 1700-4. Ord. deacon (Lincoln) June 29, 1701; priest (Chichester) Sept. 21, 1701. V. of Fairlight, Sussex, 1701-26. Buried there June 22, 1726. (W. C. Renshaw.)

FREWIN, THANCKFULL. Adm. pens. (age 16) at St John's, May 13, 1685. S. of Thomas, deceased, R. of Northiam, Sussex. School, Northiam. Matric. 1685; B.A. 1688-9. Ord. deacon (London) June 7, 1691; priest (Lincoln) Feb. 12, 1692-3. R. of Northiam, Sussex, 1693. Died Sept. 2, 1749. Father of John (1720). (*Scott-Mayor*, III. 333; G. *Mag.*)

FREWEN, THOMAS. M.A. from Emmanuel, 1738. S. of Thomas, of Brackley, Northants., gent. School, Oakham. Matric. from Magdalen College, Oxford, May 24, 1715, age 17; B.A. from Lincoln College, 1718-9. Perhaps V. of Ivinghoe, Bucks., 1729. V. of Moreton Pinkney, Northants., 1746-57. (*Al. Oxon.*)

FRICKEWELL, JOHN. Matric. Fell.-Com. from St John's, *c.* 1594.

FRICKLEYE, JOHN. Matric. sizar from Jesus, Easter, 1572. B. at South Kirkby, Yorks., *c.* 1554. Notary public in Cambridge, 1594. Died 1612. (*See* abstract of his inventory in *Camb. Ant. Soc.*, LVIII. 188.)

FRIDAY, THOMAS. Adm. sizar at Emmanuel, Easter, 1604. B. at Winscombe, Somerset. Matric. 1604; B.A. 1607-8; M.A. 1611. Ord. deacon (Bath and Wells); priest (London) Sept. 22, 1611, age 25. C. of St Bartholomew-the-Great, London. Chaplain to the East India Co., 1617-23 and 1624-30. Died at Suratt, 1630. Will (P.C.C.) 1631. (*F. Penny.*)

FRIEND or FRENDE, JOHN. M.A. 1612-3 (on visit of Prince Charles).

FRIEND, JOHN. Adm. pens. at Emmanuel, June 11, 1644. Of Middlesex. Matric. 1644; B.A. 1647. Incorp. at Oxford, 1648. M.A. (Oxford) 1650. Incorp. M.A. at Cambridge, 1658. Fellow of New College, Oxford, 1650. Afterwards fellow of Balliol. Admon. (Oxford) June 8, 1659. (*Al. Oxon.*)

FRIEND, WILLIAM. M.A. 1609 (Incorp. from Oxford). Of Nottinghamshire. Matric. from Magdalen College, July 6, 1593, age 15; B.A. (Oxford) 1595-6; M.A. 1599.

FRIEND, WILLIAM. M.A. 1664 (Incorp. from Oxford). Matric. from Christ Church, Mar. 18, 1656-7; B.A. (Oxford) 1659-60; M.A. 1662. R. of Croughton, Northants., 1663-89. Died Sept. 20, 1689. Buried at Croughton, Sept. 23, 1689. Father of the next. (*Al. Oxon.*)

FRIEND, WILLIAM. M.A. 1714 (Incorp. from Oxford). S. of William (above), R. of Croughton, Northants. Matric. from Christ Church, Oxford, July 15, 1687, age 18; B.A. (Oxford) 1691; M.A. 1694. Proctor (Oxford) 1698. R. of Turvey, Beds., 1705-45. R. of south moiety of Woodford-by-Thrapston, 1711-5. Died Apr. 15, 1745. (*Al. Oxon.*; T. P. Dorman.)

FRIENDSHIP, JOHN. Adm. at King's (age 18) a scholar from Eton, May 24, 1507. Of Lamerton (?Tamerton), Devon. Died 1509.

FRIES or FREIS, JAMES. M.D. 1460-1.

FRISBY, JOHN. B.A. 1468-9, as 'Frosby'; M.A. 1472-3. Fellow of King's Hall, 1469. Of Lincoln diocese. Ord. sub-deacon (Lincoln) Mar. 9, 1475-6; priest, Mar. 29, 1476. Scrutator, 1478-9. Will proved (V.C.C.) 1504. Left money to King's Hall.

FRISBY, JOHN. Adm. pens. (age 15) at Caius, Jan. 16, 1659-60. S. of William, druggist, of Cambridge. Bapt. at Gt St Mary's, Aug. 26, 1644. School, Perse, Cambridge. Matric. 1660. (*Venn*, I. 408.)

FRISKNEY or FRISNEY, GEORGE. Adm. pens. at Magdalene, Lent, 1657-8. S. of William (next). School, Wisbech. Matric. 1658; B.A. 1662-3; M.A. 1666. Fellow.

FRISKNEY, WILLIAM. Matric. sizar from Magdalene, Easter, 1614; B.A. 1617-8; M.A. 1621. Master of Wisbech School. Father of the above.

FRISLE or FIRSELL, THOMAS. Matric. sizar from King's, Easter, 1631; B.A. 1633-4.

FRITH or FRETHE, ARTHUR. M.Gram. 1520-1.

FRITH, GEORGE. Matric. pens. from Christ's, July, 1622; B.A. 1625-6 (1st in the *ordo*). One of these names s. of Thomas, of Upminster, Essex. (*Vis. of Essex*, 1612.)

FRITH or FRETHE, JOHN. Scholar at Queens', 1523-4. S. of Richard, of Westerham, Kent. School, Eton. B.A. from King's, 1525-6. Canon of Cardinal College, Oxford, 1526; where he was imprisoned for heresy. Assisted Tyndal in translating the New Testament into English. Afterwards wandered abroad for some years, residing chiefly at Marburg. Returned to England, 1532. Condemned as a heretic, and burnt at Smithfield, July 4, 1533. (*Cooper*, I. 47; *D.N.B.*; *Al. Oxon.*)

FRITH, JOHN. Matric. pens. from Queens', Lent, 1577-8; B.A. 1581-2; M.A. 1585. R. of Hawkeswell, Essex, 1587-1617. R. of Langdon Hills, 1589-92. Died 1617. Will (Consist. C. London) 1617.

FRITH, JOHN. Adm. sizar (age 18) at Sidney, Feb. 23, 1707-8. S. of James, shoemaker. B. at Newport, Salop. School, Newport (Mr Jo. Greenwood). Matric. 1711; B.A. 1711-2. Ord. deacon (Lichfield) June 5, 1712; priest, Sept. 20, 1713. C. of Gt Thurlow, Suffolk. R. of Little Thurlow, till 1765. Died Oct. 3, 1768.

FRITH, JOHN. Adm. sizar (age 17) at Trinity, Jan. 29, 1739-40. S. of John, of Thurlow, Suffolk. School, Lavenham, Suffolk (Mr Smith). Matric. 1740; Scholar, 1743.

FRITH, JOSIAS. Matric. sizar from St John's, *c.* 1601. R. of St Alphage, London, 1619-37; 'M.A.' Died Sept. 27, 1637. Will, P.C.C. 1638.

FRITH, NATHANIEL. Adm. sizar (age 19) at Trinity, Mar. 1, 1694-5. S. of Nathaniel, citizen and glazier, of St Olave, Hart St, London. Bapt. Dec. 5, 1675. 'Grecian' from Christ's Hospital. Matric. 1695; Scholar, 1697; B.A. 1698-9; M.A. 1702. Ord. deacon (Lincoln) Sept. 22, 1700; priest (Norwich) Sept. 1701. C. of Gt Barford, Beds., in 1700. V. of Hoxne, Suffolk, 1706.

FRITH, NICHOLAS. Licensed to practise surgery, 1612.

FRITH, PETER. Adm. sizar (age 20) at Magdalene, Apr. 5, 1667. S. of Robert, shoemaker, of Eckington, Derbs. School, Wales, Yorks. (private). Matric. 1667; B.A. 1670-1; M.A. 1674. Ord. deacon (Peterb.) June 2, 1672.

FRYTH, ROBERT. Matric. Fell.-Com. from St Catharine's, Easter, 1614. One of these names s. and h. of Thomas, of Upminster, Essex. (*Vis. of Essex*, 1612.)

FRITH, THOMAS. Matric. sizar from Queens', Easter, 1618.

FRITH, THOMAS. Adm. sizar at Christ's, May 4, 1624. S. of John, whitesmith. B. at Mansfield Woodhouse, Notts. School, Repton. Matric. 1624; B.A. 1627-8; M.A. 1631.

FRITH, THOMAS. Adm. sizar (age 18) at Trinity, Oct. 16, 1751. S. of John, of Thurlow, Suffolk. School, Langham, Suffolk (Mr Coulter). Matric. 1751; Scholar, 1755; B.A. 1756; M.A. 1768. Ord. deacon (Norwich) Sept. 1757. R. of Thurlow. Died Oct. 3, 1768. (G. *Mag.*)

FRITHE, WILLIAM. Matric. sizar from Clare, c. 1591. Probably the man described in Porah's *Hist. of St Olave's, Hart St.* A notary. Died 1648, aged 74. M.I. in All Hallows, Staining. Will (P.C.C.) 1648. Father of the next. (J. Ch. Smith.)

FRITHE, WILLIAM. Adm. pens. (age 18) at Sidney, 1627-8, from St Catharine's. S. of William (? above). B. at All Hallows, Staining, London. School, private (Mr Drake). B.A. 1629-30. Adm. at the Middle Temple, Oct. 25, 1630.

FRODSHAM, JOHN. Adm. at King's, a scholar from Eton, 1654. B. at Plymouth, *c.* 1637. Matric. 1655; B.A. 1658-9; M.A. 1663. Fellow, 1658-68. Incorp. at Oxford, 1663. V. of Modbury, Devon, 1668. Will (Exeter) 1686.

FROGGE, HENRY. Matric. sizar from Trinity, Michs. 1581; B.A. 1586-7; Scholar, 1587; M.A. 1590. University librarian, 1583-7. Ord. deacon and priest (Lincoln) Apr. 14, 1589. V. of Sh[illegible] Camps, Cambs., 1590. R. of Little Wendon, Essex, 1598-1600. V. of Walton and Trimley, Suffolk, 1600. V. of Felixstowe, 1600-19. Chaplain to Lord Exeter, 1603.

FROGGE, OLIVER. Matric. pens. from Queens', Michs. 1544.

FROGATT, GODFREY. Adm. pens. at Queens', Feb. 2, 1690-1. Of Derbyshire. S. of John, of Staveley. Bapt. there, Sept. 7, 1673. Married Helen Burton, of Dronfield. Died *s.p.*, (*F.M.G.*, 446.)

FROGGAT, JOHN. Adm. pens. (age 15) at Peterhouse, May 18, 1691. S. of George, merchant, deceased. B. at Hull. Schools, Hull and Northallerton. Matric. 1691; Scholar, 1691; B.A. 1694-5. Adm. scholar at Sidney, Feb. 9, 1695-6. M.A. from Sidney, 1698. Ord. deacon (London) Sept. 19, 1697; priest (York) Sept. 1699. R. of Kirk Deighton, Yorks., 1703-47. Died 1747.

FROGGOTT, THOMAS. Adm. sizar (age 18) at ST JOHN'S, May 10, 1701. S. of George, merchant, alderman of Hull. B. at Hull, Yorks. School, Threshfield. Matric. 1701; B.A. 1704-5; M.A. 1710. Ord. deacon (Peterb.) Mar. 20, 1702-3; priest (York) Sept. 22, 1706. P.C. of Cawood, Yorks., 1700-21. V. of Riccall, 1706-21. Died 1721.

FROHOCK, GEORGE. Adm. sizar at QUEENS', June 9, 1710. Of Cambridgeshire. B. 1692. Matric. 1710; B.A. 1713-4; M.A. 1717; B.D. 1726. Fellow, 1719-31. Junior proctor, 1723-4. Ord. deacon (Ely) Sept. 25, 1715; priest, Mar. 17, 1716-7. V. of Barton, Cambs., 1721. Died July 2, 1731.

FROHOCK, JOHN. Adm. sizar at ST CATHARINE'S, Apr. 12, 1712. S. of George, of Cambridge. Matric. 1712; B.A. 1715-6. Perhaps the minister who died at Ipswich, Apr. 25, 1733.

FROHOCK, NATHANIEL. Matric. pens. from TRINITY, Michs. 1620.

FROMANTEEL, DANIEL. Adm. at CORPUS CHRISTI, 1733. Of Norwich. Matric. 1733; LL.B. 1739. Ord. deacon (Norwich) June, 1739; priest, Sept. 1739. R. of Thwaite, Norfolk, 1739. V. of Calthorpe, 1739-55. R. of Alby, 1755-90. R. of Wolterton, 1755-90. P.C. of St Michael-at-Thorn, Norwich, 1762-90. Died Sept. 4, 1790. Will, P.C.C.

FRONTIN, JAMES. Adm. Fell.-Com. at CLARE, July 2, 1711. B. in London.

FROSSELL, THOMAS, *see* FROYSELL.

FROST, BENJAMIN. Adm. sizar (age 16) at CAIUS, Jan. 26, 1724-5. S. of Benjamin, grazier, of Waldingfield, Suffolk. B. there. Schools, Lavenham and Bury. Matric. 1724-5; Scholar, 1725-30; B.A. 1728-9; M.A. 1732. Fellow, 1730-7. Ord. priest (Lincoln) June 4, 1732. C. of Glemsford, Suffolk, 1741. R. of Topcroft, Norfolk; and of Shipmeadow, Suffolk, 1758-64. Died Jan. 12, 1764. (*Venn*, II. 22.)

FROST, GEORGE. Matric. sizar from TRINITY, 1640.

FROST, GEORGE. Adm. sizar at EMMANUEL, July 8, 1726. Of Suffolk. Matric. 1729; M.B. 1732.

FROST, JAMES. Adm. sizar (age 15) at ST JOHN'S, Nov. 3, 1652. S. of John (1618), clerk, R. of Fakenham, Suffolk. B. there. School, Bury. Matric. 1653; B.A. 1656-7; M.A. 1660. R. of Langham, Suffolk, 1660-91. Father of the next, and John (1680), brother of John (1641-2) and Thomas (1643).

FROST, JAMES. Adm. sizar (age 18) at ST JOHN'S, Apr. 28, 1693. S. of James (above). B. at Langham, Suffolk. School, Bury. Matric. 1693; B.A. 1696-7; M.A. 1700. Ord. deacon (Lincoln, *Litt. dim.* from Norwich) May 26, 1700. V. of Cherry Marham, Norfolk, 1700. Died 1730. Brother of John (1680).

FROST, JOHN. M.A. 1479-80; B.D. 1490. Fellow of QUEENS', 1484-96. V. of Lythe, Yorks., 1511-8. Died 1518.

FROST, JOHN. Adm. sizar (age 17) at CAIUS, July 20, 1587. S. of Thomas. B. at Chevington, Suffolk. School, Bury. Probably ord. deacon and priest (Norwich) Oct. 3, 1596. R. of Fornham St Genevieve, Suffolk, 1596-*c.* 1646. Signed the petition in favour of Presbyterianism, 1646. Will proved (Norwich) 1646. Father of William (1609-10). (*Venn*, I. 130.)

FROSTE, JOHN. Matric. pens. from ST JOHN'S, Michs. 1618; B.A. from Trinity Hall, 1621-2; M.A. 1625. R. of Langham, Suffolk, 1623. R. of Gt Fakenham, 1632. Father of James (1652), John (1641-2) and Thomas (1643).

FROST, JOHN. Matric. sizar from MAGDALENE, Easter, 1633.

FROST, JOHN. Adm. pens. (age 16) at ST JOHN'S, Feb. 21, 1641-2. S. of John (1618). B. at Langham, Suffolk. Schools, Thetford, Norfolk and Bury. Matric. 1644; B.A. 1645-6; M.A. 1649; B.D. 1656. Fellow, 1647. Taxor, 1652. Preached regularly at St Benedict's, Cambridge, and elsewhere in the town and county. R. of St Olave, Hart St, London, in 1655. Author, sermons. Died of small-pox, Nov. 2, 1656. Buried at St Olave's. Will, P.C.C. Brother of James (1652) and Thomas (1643). (*D.N.B.*; J. Ch. Smith.)

FROST, JOHN. Adm. pens. (age 15) at ST JOHN'S, Sept. 15, 1671. S. of Thomas (1643), LL.D., of Tacolneston, Norfolk. B. there. School, Bury. Matric. 1671; B.A. 1675-6.

FROST, JOHN. Matric. pens. from ST JOHN'S, Lent, 1675-6. Probably s. of William (1645), 'Minister of Great Ashfield, Suffolk for 26 years'; bapt. there, Nov. 27, 1660.

FROST, JOHN. Adm. sizar (age 18) at ST JOHN'S, Nov. 4, 1680. S. of James (1652), R. of Langham, Suffolk. B. there. School, Bury. Matric. 1680-1; B.A. 1684-5; M.A. 1688; B.D. 1696. Fellow of Clare, 1691-2. Fellow of St John's, 1692-1705. Ord. deacon (Norwich) Aug. 1688. R. of Cley, Norfolk, 1701. R. of Sheringham, 1701. Brother of James (1693).

FROST, JOHN. Adm. sizar at CLARE, Oct. 11, 1706. B. at Harpole, Northants. Matric. 1708; M.B. 1712. Ord. deacon (Lichfield) May 27, 1711; priest, Sept. 20, 1713. V. of Weedon, Northants., 1734-6. Married, at St Sepulchre's, Northampton, July 4, 1715, Elizabeth, dau. of Henry Rushton, of Flore, Esq. Buried at Weedon, Apr. 8, 1736. M.I. Will, Archd. Northants. (*Baker*, I. 454; H. I. Longden.)

FROST, JOSEPH. Adm. pens. at EMMANUEL, May 4, 1647. Matric. 1647-8.

FROST, NICHOLAS. Matric. sizar from QUEENS', Easter, 1632. Of Suffolk. B.A. 1635-6. Incorp. at Oxford, 1637. M.A. from Balliol College, 1638. Ord. deacon (Norwich) Sept. 20; priest, Dec. 20, 1640. R. of Westhorpe, Suffolk, 1660. V. of Wyverton, 1662. (*Al. Oxon.*)

FROST, ROBERT. Scholar at KING'S HALL, 1480-7. Probably and s. of Thomas, of Aketon, Pontefract, Yorks. B.Can.L. (Oxford); D.Can.L. 1506-7. Chancellor to Arthur, Prince of Wales. R. of Thornhill, Yorks., 1482-98. R. of Tankersley, 1486. Preb. of York, 1491-1507. Archdeacon of Stow, Lincs., 1497-1506. Archdeacon of Winchester. Preb. of Lichfield, 1500-7. V. of Sandal Magna, Yorks., 1511-34. Buried in Wakefield Church. (*Yorks. Arch. Journal*, XXIV; M. H. Peacock.)

FROST, ROBERT. Matric. sizar from TRINITY, Easter, 1620.

FROST, THOMAS. Adm. sizar (age 15) at CAIUS, Apr. 13, 1643. S. of John (1618), clerk, R. of Fakenham, Suffolk. B. at Langham, Suffolk. School, Bury. Migrated to St John's. Matric. there, as pens., Easter, 1644; B.A. 1646-7; M.A. from Trinity Hall, 1650; LL.D. 1665. Fellow of Trinity Hall, 1649-56. R. of Poringland, Norfolk, 1672-4. Died 1674. Brother of James (1652) and John (1641-2), father of John (1671).

FROST, THOMAS. Adm. sizar (age 18) at CHRIST'S, Apr. 6, 1670. S. of Thomas. B. at Cowlinge, Suffolk. School, Bury. Matric. 1670; B.A. 1673-4. Ord. deacon (Norwich) June, 1674; C. at Rougham, near Bury. Usher of Lynn Grammar School, Michs. 1675. Buried there Oct. 5, 1675. (*Peile*, II. 28.)

FROST, WALTER. Adm. pens. at EMMANUEL, Aug. 3, 1636. Of Suffolk. Matric. 1637.

FROST, WALTER. Adm. p . (age 18) at ST JOHN'S, Sept. 27, 1704. S. of Walter, deceased. B. at Lancaster. School, Sedbergh. Of Cockerham, Lancs. Died May 31, 1713. (*Sedbergh Sch. Reg.*)

FROST, WALTER. B.A. from QUEENS', 1720-1; M.A. 1724. Fellow, 1721.

FROST, WARINE. Scholar of CLARE (age 14) in 1476. Of Lytlyngston (? Litlington, Cambs.).

FROSTE, WILLIAM. Adm. at CAIUS (age 16) Aug. 4, 1564. S. of Richard, of Brockley, Suffolk. School, Groton.

FROST, WILLIAM. Adm. sizar (age 16) at CAIUS, Jan. 12, 1609-10. S. of John (1587), R. of Fornham, Suffolk. School, Bury. Matric. 1610; Scholar, 1612-4; B.A. 1613-4; M.A. 1617. Ord. priest (Norwich) Sept. 25, 1614. C. of Ashfield Magna, Suffolk, in 1617. R. of Middleton, Essex, 1624-44. (*Venn*, I. 206; *Davids*, 244.)

FROST, WILLIAM. Matric. pens. from QUEENS', Easter, 1645. Of Suffolk. Perhaps the 'Minister of Gt Ashfield, Suffolk' who was father of John (1675-6).

FROSWELL, THOMAS. Matric. sizar from TRINITY, Easter, 1612; B.A. 1615-6; M.A. 1619. Ord. deacon (Peterb.) May 23; priest, May 24, 1619.

FROTHINGHAM, CHRISTOPHER. Adm. (age 17) at CAIUS, June 5, 1589. Eldest s. of Edward, gent., of York. School, York. Adm. at the Middle Temple, Nov. 10, 1591. (*Vis. of Yorks.*, 1584.)

FROTHINGHAM, EDWARD. B.A. from TRINITY, 1568-9. Probably s. of Edmund, of Frothingham, Yorks. Escheator in Yorks., in 1591. One of these names adm. at Gray's Inn, 1572. (M. H. Peacock.)

FROWYK, THOMAS. Studied at Cambridge. S. of Thomas, of Gunnersbury, Middlesex. B. there. Of the Inner Temple; serjeant-at-law, 1494. Lord Chief Justice, C.P. 1502. Knighted, 1502. Died Oct. 17, 1506. Buried at Finchley. Will (P.C.C.) 1506. (*Cooper*, I. 10; *D.N.B.*; Weaver, *Mon.*)

FROYSELL or FROSSELL, THOMAS. Matric. sizar from CLARE, Michs. 1623; B.A. 1626-7; M.A. 1631. V. of St Margaret, Fish St, London, 1643. Lecturer at St Dunstan-in-the-West. V. of Clun, Salop; ejected, 1662. Died *c.* 1672. Perhaps s. and executor of Edward, of Downton, Herefs., clerk, whose will (P.C.C.) 1623. (*Calamy*, II. 324; *Shaw*, I. 305.)

FRY, JOHN. Adm. at KING'S, a scholar from Eton, 1466. 'Died a monk at Canterbury.' (*Harwood*.)

FRY, JOHN. M.A. from EMMANUEL, 1733. S. of Edward, of West Pennard, Somerset, gent. Matric. from Balliol College, Oxford, Apr. 8, 1717, age 19; B.A. (Oxford) 1720. Adm. at the Middle Temple, Feb. 24, 1721-2. (*Al. Oxon.*)

FRY, JOSEPH. Adm. sizar (age 19) at ST JOHN'S, Mar. 29, 1737. S. of Walter, stonemason, of Salisbury. B. there. School, Salisbury. Matric. 1737. (Previously matric. from Wadham College, Oxford, June 23, 1736.) B.A. 1746–7. Ord. deacon (Norwich) Dec. 20, 1741; priest, Mar. 14, 1741–2. R. of Uphavon, Wilts., 1742–59. Died 1759. Admon. (Archd. Wilts.) 1759.

FRYE, ROWLAND. Adm. pens. (age 18) at CHRIST'S, Nov. 6, 1714. S. of John, of Antigua (member of the Council, and Colonel of Militia). B. there. School, Eton. Matric. 1714. Graduated at Leyden, 1717. Merchant of London. Purchased Banstead Manor, Surrey, 1762. Died Oct. 20, 1777. M.I. at Banstead. (*Peile*, II. 185.)

FRY, ——. B.A. 1482–3.

FRYER, *see* also **FRERE.**

FRIER, HENRY. Matric. pens. from CHRIST'S, May, 1571.

FRYER, HENRY. Matric. pens. from ST JOHN'S, Michs. 1572.

FRYER or FREARE, JOHN. Adm. at KING'S, a scholar from Eton, 1517. B. at Balsham, Cambs., *c.* 1499. B.A. 1521–2; M.A. 1525. Fellow, 1520–5. Incorp. at Oxford, 1525. Afterwards of Cardinal College, Oxford. M.D. (Padua) 1535. Perhaps incorp. at Cambridge. Attended his friend and patron Edward Fox to the Diet at Smalcalde, Saxony, 1535. F.R.C.P. 1536; president, 1549. Imprisoned as a Catholic, 1561. Died Oct. 21, 1563, of the plague. Buried in St Martin Outwich. Will (P.C.C.). (*Cooper*, I. 225; *Munk*, I. 31; *D.N.B.*)

FRYER or FRERE, JOHN. Matric. pens. from JESUS, Easter, 1544. B. at Godmanchester, Hunts. B.A. 1544–5; M.A. 1548; M.D. 1555. Disputed in the Physic Act before the Queen, at her visit to Cambridge, in 1564. Afterwards settled at Padua. A Romanist. Perhaps brother of Thomas (1544). (*Cooper*, I. 302; *Vis. of London*, 1568; *D.N.B.*, according to which *Cooper* is wrong in the parentage.)

FRYER, JOHN. Matric. pens. from ST JOHN'S, Easter, 1567; B.A. 1570–1; M.A. 1574.

FRYER, JOHN. Matric. sizar from KING'S, *c.* 1594. Perhaps s. of Thomas (1553). Died Nov. 12, 1672, aged 96. Will, P.C.C. (*Munk*, I. 72.)

FRYER, JOHN. Matric. sizar from KING'S, *c.* 1597; B.A. 1600–1; M.A. 1605. Ord. deacon (Colchester) Sept. 9; priest, Sept. 16, 1604. C. of Risborough, Bucks., 1609.

FRYER or FRIAR, JOHN. Adm. pens. at TRINITY, July 13, 1664. S. of William, of London. M.B. from Pembroke, 1671 (*Lit. Reg.*); M.D. 1683. Incorp. at Oxford, 1683. In 1672 he undertook a tour in India and Persia in the interests of the East India Company, returning to England, in 1682. He subsequently published an account of his travels. F.R.S. 1698. Died Mar. 31, 1733. Buried at All Hallows, Bread St, London. Admon. P.C.C. (*D.N.B.*)

FRYER, RICHARD. Matric. pens. from KING'S, *c.* 1595.

FRIER, RICHARD. Matric. sizar from QUEENS', Easter, 1617. Of Cheshire. B.A. 1620–1. C. of Hayfield, 1629. R. of Taxal, Cheshire, 1631–3. Probably V. of Glossop, Derbs., 1645–8.

FRYER, ROBERT. Adm. pens. (age 16) at CAIUS, Ap. 3, 1573. S. of John, of Gravesend, Kent. School, Canterbnry. B.A. 1576–7; M.A. 1580. Ord. deacon (London) Dec. 21, 1581; priest (Lincoln) Dec. 13, 1582. Licensed as preacher by Archbishop of Canterbury, 1581. V. of West Thurrock, Essex, 1584–93. Died 1593. (*Venn*, I. 72.)

FRYER, ROBERT. Matric. sizar from TRINITY, Easter, 1586.

FRYER, THOMAS. Excused regency, 1476–7.

FRYAR, THOMAS. Matric. pens. from JESUS, Easter, 1544.

FRYER or FREARE, THOMAS. Matric. pens. from TRINITY, Michs. 1553. S. of John, M.D. Scholar, 1554, as Freer; B.A. 1557–8. Fellow, 1560. Incorp. at Oxford, 1560. M.A. (Oxford) 1562; M.D. (Oxford) 1623. M.D. of Padua. F.R.C.P. 1572. Censor, Elect, etc. Buried in St Botolph, London, 1623. M.I. at Harlton, Cambs. Will (P.C.C.) 1623. (*Munk*, I. 72; *Vis. of London*, 1568; Foster (*Al. Oxon.*) makes two men of him.)

FRIER, THOMAS. Matric. sizar from TRINITY, Easter, 1577. Perhaps the 'Thos. Frier, Scholar,' who was preb. of Lincoln, 1581–1619.

FRYERE, THOMAS. Matric. sizar from JESUS, Easter, 1614; B.A. 1617–8. Ord. deacon (York) May, 1618; priest, Sept. 1618.

FRYER, THOMAS. Matric. sizar from MAGDALENE, Easter, 1617; B.A. 1620–1; M.A. 1625. Ord. deacon (Peterb.) Sept. 19, 1619; priest, Sept. 16, 1621. R. of Whitwell, Rutland, 1627–68. (T. P. Dorman.)

FRIER, W. Matric. sizar from TRINITY, Lent, 1581–2.

FRYER, WILLIAM. Adm. at KING'S (age 16) a scholar from Eton, Aug. 23, 1552. B. at Eton. B.A. 1556–7. Fellow, 1555–8. Master of the school at Stevenage, Herts. (*Harwood.*)

FRYER or FRERE, ——. B.A. 1525–6.

FRYER, ——. Adm. sizar at SIDNEY, Feb. 1598–9.

FRYERS, JOHN. Matric. sizar from TRINITY, *c.* 1596, as 'Frearor'; B.A. 1600–1.

FUELL, ROBERT. Matric. sizar from ST JOHN'S, Michs. 1573.

FUGAYLE, THOMAS. Matric. sizar from KING'S, Michs. 1554. Conduct of King's. Will (P.C.C.) 1580; of Tho. Pugale, of St Alphage, London, clerk.

FUGILL, CHRISTOPHER. Adm. sizar (age 19) at SIDNEY, July 6, 1633 (*sic*). S. of William, gent., of Trinity parish, Hull. B. at Hessle, Yorks. School, Hull (James Burney, M.A.). Matric. 1633. Migrated to Caius, May 17, 1636, age 18; B.A. 1636–7; M.A. 1640. Ord. priest (York) Sept. 20, 1663. V. of Garton-in-Holderness. V. of Barrow-on-Humber, Lincs., 1659–80. Buried there Nov. 24, 1680. (*Venn*, I. 321.)

FUGILL, WILLIAM. Matric. sizar from PETERHOUSE, Easter, 1584; B.A. 1588–9. Ord. deacon (Norwich) Dec. 1598; priest, Feb. 24, 1598–9. V. of Catton, Norfolk, 1598.

FUGELL, ——. M.A. 1556 (no B.A.).

FULBECK or FILBECKE, JOSEPH. Matric. sizar from TRINITY, Easter, 1610. *See* Filbeck.

FULBERY, JOHN. M.A. (? Cambridge). Ord. priest (Ely) July 7, 1560. V. of Witcham, Cambs.

FULBOURN, ROGER DE. Chancellor of the University, 1276.

FULBOURNE, ——. A friar. B.D. 1485–6.

FULBY, WILLIAM. B.A. 1505–6.

FULCHER, *see also* **FOLCHIER.**

FULCHER, EDWARD. Adm. pens. at EMMANUEL, May 20, 1647. Of Suffolk. Matric. 1647; B.A. 1650–1.

FULCHER, JOHN. Adm. pens. at EMMANUEL, Apr. 25, 1612. Matric. 1612; B.A. 1615–6.

FULCHER, SIMON. Adm. pens. at CORPUS CHRISTI, 1571. Matric. Michs. 1573.

FULCIS, JOHN. Adm. sizar (age 15) at PEMBROKE, Oct. 1, 1645. S. of Henry. B. at Norwich. Matric. 1646.

FULFORD, JOHN. M.A. from MAGDALENE, 1637. S. of Sir Francis, of Whitchurch, Dorset, Knt. Matric. from Wadham College, Oxford, Apr. 22, 1631, age 19; B.A. (Oxford) 1634. V. of Toller Porcorum, Dorset, 1640. Buried at Dunsford, Apr. 28, 1655. (*Al. Oxon.*)

FULGER, RICHARD. Adm. pens. (age 16) at CAIUS, Jan. 20, 1608–9. S. of Nicholas, gent., of Mellis, Suffolk. School, Eye.

FULHAM, EDWARD. M.A. 1632 (Incorp. from Oxford). S. of Edward, of Westminster, gent. Matric. from Christ Church, May 9, 1628, age 20; B.A. 1628; M.A. 1631; B.D. 1642–3; D.D. 1660. Whyte's Professor of Moral Philosophy, 1634–8. Proctor, 1639. R. of Wootton, Oxon., 1638; and of Hampton Poyle. Chaplain at Leghorn, during the Interregnum. V. of Bray, Berks., 1660. Canon of Windsor, 1660–94. V. of West Ilsley, Berks., 1662. Preb. of Lichfield, 1673. Chaplain to the King, 1676. Died Dec. 9, 1694. Buried at Compton, Surrey. M.I. Will (P.C.C.) 1695. (*Al. Oxon.*; *Manning and Bray*, II. 5.)

FULLAM, JAMES. Adm. sizar at CHRIST'S, May 22, 1624. S. of William. B. at Waltham. School, Waltham.

FULHAM, JOHN. M.A. from MAGDALENE, 1736. S. of John, of Compton, Surrey, Esq. School, Eton. Matric. from Christ Church, Mar. 26, 1717, age 18; B.A. (Oxford) 1720. R. of Compton, 1722–77. R. of Merrow, 1736–52. Preb. of Chichester, 1745–73. Chaplain to the House of Commons, 1746. Archdeacon of Llandaff, 1749–77. Canon of Windsor, 1750–77. V. of All Saints', Isleworth, 1751–77. Died July 13, 1777. M.I. at Compton. Will, P.C.C. (*Al. Oxon.*; *Manning and Bray*, II. 5.)

FULHAM, WILLIAM. Adm. sizar at EMMANUEL, Easter, 1624. Matric. 1624; B.A. 1627–8.

FULKE, THOMAS. Matric. pens. from MAGDALENE, Michs. 1572. One of these names V. of Chigwell, Essex, 1571–89. R. of Tolleshunt Knights, 1579. Died 1589.

FULKE, THOMAS. Adm. sizar at PETERHOUSE, Apr. 29, 1623. Of Suffolk.

FULKE, WILLIAM. Matric. pens. from ST JOHN'S, Michs. 1555. S. of Christopher. B. in London, 1538. B.A. 1557–8; M.A. 1563; B.D. 1568; D.D. 1572. Fellow, 1564. Incorp. at Oxford, 1566. University preacher, 1563. Master of Pembroke, 1578–89. Vice-Chancellor, 1581–2. R. of Gt Warley, Essex, 1571–89. R. of Dennington, Suffolk, 1573–89. Author, religious. Died Aug. 28, 1589. M.I. at Dennington. Will proved (V.C.C.). (*Cooper*, II. 57.)

FULKE, WILLIAM. Matric. pens. from TRINITY, Easter, 1606.

'FULLER, ABRAHAM' (*Cooper*, II. 383; mistake for Puller).

FULLER, BENJAMIN. Adm. sizar at EMMANUEL, June 23, 1614; B.A. 1617-8; M.A. 1621. Doubtless of Syleham, Suffolk, gent., in 1646. Will proved 1648. Father of the next and of William (1646). (*Vis. of Suffolk.*)

FULLER, BENJAMIN. Adm. pens. (age 17) at CAIUS, June 18, 1647. Doubtless s. of Benjamin (1614), gent., of Syleham, Suffolk. Schools, Hoxne, Suffolk and Yoxford. Matric. 1647; Scholar, 1648-50. Will proved (Norwich C.C.) 1670; as of Wingfield. Brother of William (1646). (*Venn*, I. 369.)

FULLER, DANIEL. Adm. pens. at JESUS, Jan. 6, 1652-3. Of Essex. Matric. 1653; Scholar, 1655; B.A. 1656-7; M.A. 1660.

FULLER, EDMUND. B.A. 1500-1.

FULLER, EDWARD. B.A. 1521-2.

FULLER, EDWARD. Adm. sizar at CORPUS CHRISTI, 1607. Matric. Lent, 1607-8; B.A. 1610-1.

FULLER, EDWARD. Adm. at KING'S, a scholar from Eton, 1671. B. at Colnbrook, Bucks. Matric. Michs. 1672. Did not graduate. Died as junior fellow. (*Harwood.*)

FULLER, FRANCIS. Adm. p . at QUEENS', Apr. 18, 1653. S. of John (1618), V. of Stebbing, Essex. B.A. from Pembroke 1656; M.A. from Queens', 1660. Incorp. at Oxford, 1663. C. of Warkworth, Northants.; ejected for nonconformity. Afterwards preacher at Bath, Bristol, etc. Died in London, July 21, 1701, aged 64. Father of the next. Brother of Thomas (1645) and Samuel (1650). (*Calamy*, II. 234; *D.N.B.*)

FULLER, FRANCIS. Adm. pens. (age 17) at ST JOHN'S, July 8, 1687. S. of Francis (1653). B. at Bristol. School, Eton. Matric. 1688; B.A. 1691-2; M.A. 1704. Author of *Medicina Gymnastica*. Died June, 1706. (*D.N.B.*)

FULLER, GEORGE. Perhaps adm. at CORPUS CHRISTI, 1553; B.A. from Christ's, 1553-4; M.A. 1556; B.D. 1561. Fellow of Christ's, 1554-61. Junior Proctor, 1559. Received tonsure (London) Sept. 1554. R. of Little Shelford, Cambs., 1560. R. of Hildersham, 1561-91. Will (P.C.C.) 1591; 'parson of Hildersham.' (*Peile*, I. 43.)

FULLER, GERVASE. Adm. pens. at TRINITY, July 15, 1640. S. of William (1596), D.D. B. Oct. 10, 1623. School, Merchant Taylors'. Matric. 1640; Scholar, 1641; B.A. 1643-4. Probably M.A. 1647, as 'Richard.' Adm. at Gray's Inn, Nov. 6, 1647.

FULLER, HENRY. Adm. pens. (age 19) at TRINITY, Feb. 3, 1731-2. S. of John, of Brightling, Sussex. School, Charterhouse, London. Matric. 1732; Scholar, 1732; B.A. 1735-6; M.A. 1739. R. of North Stoneham; and of Stoneham Abbots, 1749-64. Buried at North Stoneham. Will, P.C.C. Brother of John (1723), Rose (1732) and Stephen (1734).

FULLER, IGNATIUS. Adm. pens. at EMMANUEL, Apr. 6, 1643. Of Buckinghamshire. Matric. 1645; B.A. 1646-7; M.A. 1650. R. of Sherrington, Bucks., 1647. Reputed to be a Socinian. Died Oct. 21, 1711, aged 86. M.I. at Sherrington. Father of Thomas (1669). (*Lipscomb*, IV. 335.)

FULLER, ISAAC. Adm. pens. at EMMANUEL, Apr. 1629. Of Essex. Matric. 1629.

FULLER, JAMES. *Cautio* for degree, 1482-3.

FULER, JAMES. Adm. sizar (age 18) at ST JOHN'S, July 9, 1680. S. of Mark, baker. B. at Pocklington, Yorks. School, Pocklington. Matric. 1681.

FULLER, JOHN. B.A. 1474-5; M.A. 1478-9. Fellow of CORPUS CHRISTI, 1477.

FULLER, JOHN. Adm. at KING'S (age 18) a scholar from Eton, Aug. 12, 1528. Of Bury, Suffolk. Left about 1530. One of these names V. of Bentley, Suffolk, 1539.

FULLER, JOHN. LL.D. 1558 (Incorp. from Oxford). B. in Gloucestershire. Of All Souls', Oxford. B.C.L. (Oxford) 1533; D.C.L. 1546. Admitted advocate, 1546. R. of Hanwell, Middlesex, 1548-51. Vicar-general of Norwich diocese, 1550. R. of North Creake; and V. of Swaffham, Norfolk. Canon of Ely, 1554. R. of Little Wilbraham, Cambs., 1555. Master of JESUS College, Feb. 23, 1556-7, till 1558. R. of Fen Ditton, Cambs., 1557-8; and Hildersham, of East Dereham, Norfolk, 1557. Preb. of St Paul's, 1558. Benefactor to Jes College. Died July 30, 1558. Will proved (P.C.C.) and (V.C.C.); to be buried in St Paul's. (*Cooper*, I. 188; *D.N.B.*; *Al. Oxon.*)

FULLER, JOHN. Matric. pens. from ST JOHN'S, *c.* 1593; B.A. 1596-7.

FULLER, JOHN. Matric. pens. from PEMBROKE, Easter, 1618; B.A. 1621-2; M.A. 1625. Doubtless V. of Stebbing, Essex, 1633. Father of Francis (1653), Samuel (1650) and Thomas (1645).

FULLER, JOHN. Adm. pens. (age 16) at SIDNEY, Feb. 7, 1631-2. S. of Thomas (1584), B.D. Schools, Oundle, Aldwinkle (Mr Archibald Simmers) and Sutton, Beds. Matric. 1632; B.A. 1635-6; M.A. 1639. Brother of Thomas (1622).

FULLER, JOHN. Adm. pens. at EMMANUEL, May 2, 1635. Of Sussex. Will (P.C.C.) 1660, of one of these names, R. of St Martin, Iremonger Lane, 1654-60.

FULLER, JOHN. Adm. pens. (age 16) at SIDNEY, July 8, 1657. S. of Thomas (1622), R. of Waltham, Essex. B. at Broad Windsor, Dorset. School, St Paul's. Matric. 1658; B.A. 1660; M.A. 1664. Fellow. Signs for deacon and priest (London) June 7, 1666. V. of Gt Wakering, Essex, 1667-87. V. of Little Wakering, till 1687. Died 1687.

FULLER, JOHN. Adm. pens. (age 17) at ST JOHN'S, Apr. 23, 1674. S. of William, deceased, of Caldecote, Hunts. B. there. Schools, Peterborough and Oundle. Matric. 1674. Migrated to Emmanuel, 1677; B.A. 1677-8; M.A. 1681.

FULLER, JOHN. Adm. pens. (age 15) at CAIUS, May 14, 1695. S. of Samuel, merchant, of Yarmouth. B. there. Schools, Colchester and Yarmouth. Matric. 1695; Scholar, 1695-6. Consul at Leghorn, till 1722. M.P. for Plympton, 1728-34. Died 1744. Brother of Samuel (1691) and Richard (1698). (*Venn*, I. 496; A. B. Beaven.)

FULLER, JOHN. Adm. pens. (age 16) at TRINITY, May 15, 1696. S. of John, of Walton, Suffolk. B. there. School, St Paul's. Matric. 1696-7; Scholar, 1699; B.A. 1699-1700.

FULLER, JOHN. Adm. pens. (age 16) at TRINITY, Dec. 22, 1696. S. of Thomas. B. at Cambridge. School, King's, Cambridge (Mr Rawson). Matric. 1696; B.A. 1700-1; M.A. from King's, 1704. Ord. deacon (Peterb.) May 31, 1702. Chaplain at King's, 1702. V. of Pampisford, Cambs., 1706. One of these names V. of Linton, Kent, 1729-51; and V. of Yalding, 1738-51. Died 1751.

FULLER, JOHN. Adm. pens. at TRINITY, July 4, 1723. S. of John, of Brightling, Sussex. Bapt. there, Feb. 8, 1705-6. School, Lewes, Sussex. Matric. 1724. Adm. at the Middle Temple, Dec. 1, 1724. F.R.S. 1726. M.P. for Boroughbridge, 1754-5. Of Rosehill, Brightling, Esq. Buried at Waldron, Feb. 12, 1755. Brother of Henry (1732) and Rose (1732).

FULLER, JOHN. Adm. sizar (age 18) at TRINITY, July 6, 1727. S. of Robert, of Cambridge. School, Cambridge (Mr Heath). Matric. 1727.

FULLER, JOHN. Adm. pens. (age 17) at TRINITY, June 6, 1743. S. of Thomas, of Sussex. School, Hackney, London (Mr Newcombe). Matric. 1743.

FULLER, NICHOLAS. Matric. pens. from CHRIST'S, Dec. 1560. Doubtless s. of Nicholas, merchant, of London. B. 1543. B.A. 1562-3. Adm. at Gray's Inn, 1563. Barrister. Reader. Treasurer, 1591. Common Pleader, City of London, 1584-1611. M.P. for St Mawes, 1592-3; for London, 1604-11. Of Thatcham, Berks. Died in prison, Feb. 23, 1619-20, aged 76. Buried at Thatcham. Will (P.C.C.) 1620. (*Peile*, I. 73; *Ath. Oxon.*; *Gray's Inn Pension Book*, 237; S. Barfield, *Thatcham*; A. B. Beaven.)

FULLER, PETER. Matric. pens. from ST JOHN'S, Easter, 1575. Ord. deacon (Ely) Dec. 21, 1578, age 25; priest, Apr. 17, 1579. C. of Outwell, Norfolk; R. 1582-95.

FULLER, RICHARD. Matric. pens. from CLARE, Easter, 1576.

FULLER, RICHARD. Adm. pens. (age 13) at CAIUS, July 8, 1698. S. of Samuel, merchant, of Yarmouth. B. there. School, Yarmouth. Scholar, 1698-1703; Matric. 1699; LL.B. 1704; LL.D. 1709. Fellow, 1704-26. Adm. at Gray's Inn, Nov. 16, 1702. Admiralty Advocate, 1715-26. Died Oct. 5, 1726. Buried at St Nicholas, Yarmouth. Admon. (P.C.C.) 1727. Brother of Samuel (1691) and John (1695). (*Venn*, I. 501.)

FULLER, RICHARD. Adm. pens. (age 16) at CAIUS, Feb. 23, 1725-6. S. of Samuel (1691), merchant, of Yarmouth. B. there. Schools, Yarmouth and Harleston (private; Mr D'Oyley). Matric. 1726; Scholar, 1726-33. Adm. at the Inner Temple, Feb. 14, 1725-6. Owned an estate at Fritton, Suffolk; and was repeatedly a candidate for Parliament. Sheriff for Norfolk, 1759. Died unmarried at Yarmouth, June 13, 1770. M.I. at St Nicholas. (*Venn*, II. 24; *G. Mag.*)

FULLER, ROBERT. B.A. 1454-5; M.A. 1458-9; grace for B.D. 1469-70. Incorp. B.D., from abroad, 1480-1. Fellow of CORPUS CHRISTI, 1454. V. of Swaffham, Norfolk, 1465.

FULLER, ROBERT. B.A. 1499-1500.

FULLER, ROBERT. Adm. pens. at EMMANUEL, May 24, 1639. Matric. 1639; B.A. 1642-3; M.A. 1646. One of these names R. of Tillingham, Essex, in 1650. V. of Ghignai St James, *c.* 1655.

FULLER, ROBERT. Adm. pens. at EMMANUEL, Feb. 12, 1712-3. B. at Lynn. B.A. 1716-7; M.A. 1720. Fellow, 1719-26. Ord. deacon (London) Mar. 13, 1719-20; priest (Peterb.) Sept. 22, 1723, age 28. R. of Water Newton, Hunts., 1732-5. Died 1735. (*Emmanuel Coll. Hist.*, 129.)

FULLER, ROBERT. Mus.Bac. from KING'S, 1724. Lay clerk and organist at King's, 1700. Will proved (V.C.C.) 1728.

FULLER, ROSE. M.D. (*Com. Reg.*) 1728: not adm. until 1732. S. of John, of Brightling, Sussex, Esq., and Elizabeth, dau. of Fulke Rose, Esq., of Jamaica. Student at Leyden, Apr. 26, 1729. F.R.S. 1732. M.P. for New Romney, 1756–61; for Maidstone, 1761–8; for Rye, 1768–77. Died May 7, 1777. Buried at Waldron. Brother of Henry (1732), John (1723) and Stephen (1734).

FULLER, SAMUEL. Adm. pens. (age 15) at ST JOHN'S, Sept. 9, 1650. S. of John (1618), clerk, of Stebbing, Essex. Scholar; B.A. 1654–5; M.A. 1658; B.D. 1665; D.D. 1679. Fellow, 1656. Incorp. at Oxford, 1663, as Fullerton. V. of Elmdon, Essex, 1663–8. R. of Tinwell, Rutland, 1669–1700. Chancellor of Lincoln, 1670. R. of Knaptoft, Leics., 1671–1700. Chaplain to the King, 1677. Preb. of Lincoln, 1695. Dean of Lincoln, 1695–1700. Benefactor to St John's. Died Mar. 4, 1699–1700. Buried in Lincoln Cathedral. M.I. there. Will, P.C.C. Brother of Thomas (1645) and Francis (1653). (Le Neve, *Mon.*, V. 209; *Al. Oxon.*; *D.N.B.*; T. P. Dorman.)

FULLER, SAMUEL. Adm. pens. (age 16) at CAIUS, Apr. 9, 1691. S. of Samuel, merchant, of Yarmouth. B. there. School, Yarmouth. Matric. 1691; Scholar, 1691–4. Adm. at the Inner Temple, Oct. 26, 1694. Alderman of Yarmouth. Buried at St Nicholas, Dec. 16, 1720. Brother of John (1695) and Richard (1698), father of Richard (1725–6). (*Venn*, I. 489.)

FULLER, STEPHEN. Adm. pens. (age 18) at TRINITY, Nov. 4, 1734. S. of John, of Brightling, Sussex. School, Charterhouse, London. Matric. 1734; Scholar, 1735; B.A. 1738–9; M.A. 1742. Fellow, 1741. Brother of Henry (1732), John (1723) and Rose (1732).

FULLER, THOMAS. B.Civ.L. 1463–4.

FULLER, THOMAS. B.A. 1484–5.

FULLER, THOMAS. Adm. at KING'S (age 17) a scholar from Eton, Aug. 11, 1521. B. in London. B.A. 1525–6; M.A. 1529. Fellow, 1524–35. Ord. deacon (Lincoln) Apr. 6; priest, Apr. 20, 1527. V. of Willoughton, Lincs., 1533.

FULLER, THOMAS. Adm. at KING'S (age 17) a scholar from Eton, 1538. Of Clewer, Berks. B.A. 1541–2. Fellow, 1541–2. Assistant Master at Eton. Afterwards Master at Fotheringay. Took the name Hurland. (*Harwood.*)

FULLER, THOMAS. Matric. pens. from PETERHOUSE, Easter, 1582; B.A. 1585–6; M.A. 1589. Ord. deacon and priest (Peterb.) Nov. 2, 1589. V. of Hatfield Peverel, Essex, 1590–6. Perhaps V. of Little Baddow, 1596.

FULLER, THOMAS. Matric. pens. from TRINITY, Easter, 1584; Scholar, 1586; B.A. 1587–8; M.A. 1591; B.D. 1598. Fellow, 1589. R. of Aldwincle St Peter's, Northants., 1602. Preb. of Salisbury, 1622–32. Admon. granted to his s. Thomas, Apr. 10, 1632. Father of Thomas (1622) and John (1631).

FULLER, THOMAS. Matric. pens. from PEMBROKE, *c.* 1590; B.A. from Corpus Christi, 1593–4; M.A. 1597. One of these names, s. and h. of William, of Coggeshall, Essex, adm. at Gray's Inn, Feb. 9, 1596–7.

FULLER, THOMAS. Matric. pens. from PEMBROKE, Easter, 1609; B.A. 1612–3. Chaplain to the East India Co., at Swally, 1628–32. (*F. Penny.*)

FULLER, THOMAS. Matric. pens. from QUEENS', Michs. 1622. S. of Thomas (1584), and nephew of John Davenant, Bishop of Salisbury. B. at Aldwincle, 1608. B.A. 1624–5; M.A. 1628; B.D. from Sidney, 1635; D.D. 1660. Ord. deacon (Peterb.) June 5, 1631. V. of St Benet's, Cambridge, 1631. Preb. of Sarum, 1631. R. of Broadwindsor, Dorset, 1634. Lecturer at the Savoy Chapel, 1640. P.C. of Waltham Abbey, Essex, *c.* 1649. Chap to Sir Ralph Hopton during the war. R. of Cranford, Middlesex, 1658–61. Went to the Hague, 1660, to meet Charles II. Chaplain to the King, 1660. Author, *Church History*, *History of Cambridge*, *Worthies of England*, etc. Died Aug. 15, 1661. Admon. Archd. (Middlesex) 1661. M.I. at Cranford. Father of John (1657) and probably of Thomas (1672). (D.*N.B.*)

FULLER, THOMAS. Matric. pens. from ST CATHARINE'S, Lent, 1645–6. S. of John (1618), V. of Stebbing, Essex. B.A. 1647–8; M.A. from Christ's, 1651; B.D. 1659; D.D. 1665. Fellow of Christ's, 1649–61. Taxor, 1656. R. of Navenby, 1659–1701. R. of Willingale Doe, Essex, 1670. Will (P.C.C.) 1702. Brother of Francis (1653) and Samuel (1650). (*Peile*, I. 490.)

FULLER, THOMAS. Adm. sizar (age 18) at CAIUS, July 11, 1664. S. of Anthony, gent., of Downham Market, Norfolk. Schools, Downham Market and Scarning. Scholar, 1664–72; Matric. 1665; B.A. 1668–9; M.A. 1672. Fellow, 1673–7. Went beyond the seas. (*Venn*, I. 423.)

FULLER, THOMAS. Adm. pens. (age 15) at CHRIST'S, July 7, 1669. S. of Ignatius (1643). B. at Sherrington, Bucks. School, Strixton. Matric. 1670; B.A. 1672–3; M.A. 1676; D.D. 1689. R. of St Margaret Pattens, London, 1683–5. R. of Bishop Hatfield, Herts., 1685–1712. Author, sermon. Died May 21, 1712, aged 60. Will, P.C.C. (Le Neve, *Mon.*, II. 239; *Peile*, II. 25.)

FULLER, THOMAS. Adm. sizar at QUEENS', May 19, 1671. B. at Rosehill, Sussex, June 24, 1654. M.B. 1676; M.D. 1681. Extra licentiate R.C.P. 1679. Practised at Sevenoaks, Kent. Died Sept. 17, 1734, aged 80. Will, P.C.C. (*D.N.B.*; *Munk*, I. 376.)

FULLER, THOMAS. Adm. sizar (age 16) at JESUS, Apr. 1672. S. of Thomas (? 1622), D.D. Matric. 1672; Rustat Scholar.

FULLER, THOMAS. Matric. from CORPUS CHRISTI, Easter, 1707. B. in Norfolk, 1689. B.A. 1710–1. Ord. deacon (Norwich) Sept. 1712; priest (Ely) Sept. 20, 1713. C. of Heynford. R. of All Souls', South Elmham, Suffolk, 1737–43. R. of St James', 1737–43.

FULLER, THOMAS. Adm. pens. (age 18) at ST JOHN'S, June 14, 1711. S. of Stephen, gent. B. at Waldron, near Hurst Green, Sussex. School, Merchant Taylors'. B.A. 1714–5. Adm. at the Middle Temple, Aug. 24, 1714. R. of Waternewton, Hunts., 1732–5. Buried there 1735.

FULLER, THOMAS. Matric. from EMMANUEL, Easter, 1713. Perhaps a mistake for Robert (1712–3).

FULLER, WILLIAM. Matric. sizar from PEMBROKE, *c.* 1590.

FULLER, WILLIAM. Matric. sizar from TRINITY, *c.* 1596. S. of Andrew, of Hadleigh, Suffolk. B.A. 1599–1600; M.A. 1603; B.D. from St Catharine's, 1610; D.D. 1627–8 (*Lit. Reg.*). Fellow of St Catharine's. Incorp. at Oxford, 1645. Chaplain to James I and Charles I. R. of Weston, Notts., 1616. R. of St Giles', Cripplegate, 1628–59. Dean of Ely, 1636–45; and of Durham, 1646. Died May 12, 1659, aged 79. Buried at St Vedast, Foster Lane. M.I. there. Will, P.C.C. Father of Gervase (1640). (*D.N.B.*; Le Neve, *Mon.*, IV. 66.)

FULLER, WILLIAM. Adm. pens. at EMMANUEL, July 2, 1639. Matric. 1639.

FULLER, WILLIAM. Adm. pens. (age 18) at CAIUS, Apr. 23, 1646. S. of Benjamin (1614), gent., of Syleham, Suffolk. B. there. Schools, Wingfield and Hoxne. Matric. 1646. Of Syleham and Bradwell, Suffolk, gent. Died Oct. 1668. Will (Archd. Sudhury) 1668. Brother of Benjamin (1647). (*Venn*, I. 362; *Vis. of Essex*, 1664.)

FULLER, WILLIAM. Bishop of Lincoln, 1667. Said by *D.N.B.* to have been D.D. 1660. Not found in our records. (*See Al. Oxon.*)

FULLER, WILLIAM. Adm. pens. at ST CATHARINE'S, Mar. 26, 1661. Of Suffolk. Matric. 1661; B.A. 1664–5; M.A. 1668. Perhaps R. of Chatgrave, Norfolk, 1670.

FULLER, WILLIAM. Adm. sizar (age 18) at PETERHOUSE, June 30, 1680. Of Hertford. School, Hertford. Matric. 1681; Scholar, 1681; B.A. 1683–4.

FULLER, WILLIAM. Adm. sizar at JESUS, Sept. 28, 1694. Of Huntingdonshire. Matric. 1695; B.A. 1698–9; Scholar, 1699.

FULLER, WILLIAM. Adm. sizar (age 16) at ST JOHN'S, Jan. 22, 1700–1. S. of William, pewterer. B. at Cambridge. School, Histon (Mr Scaife). Matric. 1701; B.A. 1704–5; M.A. 1708. Ord. deacon (Peterb.) May 19, 1706; priest, Dec. 19, 1708. C. of Etton, Northants. Perhaps V. of Farningham, Kent, 1720–38. Buried there Feb. 18, 1737–8.

FULLER, ——. B.A. 1489–90.

FULLER, ——. M.A. 1523–4.

FULLER, ——. Perhaps B.A. 1526–7; and pens. at GONVILLE HALL, 1532.

FULLERTON, JOHN. Adm. pens. (age 18) at EMMANUEL, Jan. 11, 1748–9. S. of John, of St George's, Middlesex, Esq. School, Westminster. Matric. 1748–9; LL.B. 1755. Died unmarried. The father was of Craighall. (*Her. and Gen.*, VIII. 196.)

FULMAN, WILLIAM. M.A. 1668 (Incorp. from Oxford). B. at Penshurst, Kent. Scholar at Corpus Christi, Oxford, 1647; ejected, 1648; restored, 1660. Fellow of Corpus Christi; and created M.A. (Oxford) 1660. R. of Meysey Hampton, Gloucs., 1669–88. Died June 28, 1688. Buried at Meysey Hampton. (*Al. Oxon.*; *D.N.B.*)

FULMERSTON, JOHN. Matric. pens. from QUEENS', Easter, 1611. Of Norfolk. B.A. 1613–4. (Pedigree of Fulmerston in *Vis. of Norfolk.*)

FULMISTON, EDWARD. Adm. scholar at TRINITY HALL, July 7, 1604.

FULNEBIE, ROBERT. Matric. pens. from PETERHOUSE, Lent, 1577–8.

FULNETBYE, CHRISTOPHER. Matric. pens. from PETERHOUSE, *c.* 1601.

FULNETBYE, JOHN. Matric. pens. from CLARE, Easter, 1583; B.A. 1586–7; M.A. 1590; B.D. 1597. Preb. of Lichfield, 1605; precentor, 1608–36. R. of Handsworth, Staffs., 1608–36. Archdeacon of Stafford, 1614–36. R. of Aldridge, 1622–36. Buried at Handsworth, Sept. 4, 1636, aged 71. Will (Lichfield, and P.C.C.) 1636. (*Wm Salt Arch. Soc.*, 1915.)

FULTHORPE, CHRISTOPHER. Adm. pens. (age 16) at ST JOHN'S, May 18, 1650. 3rd s. of Clement, Esq., of Tunstall, Bishop Wearmouth, Durham. B. there. Bapt. at Stranton, June 11, 1633. School, Guisborough. Matric. 1650; B.A. 1653-4; M.A. 1657; B.D. 1665. Fellow, 1654. R. of Siggleschorne, Yorks., 1661-1709. Married, at Pocklington, May 14, 1667, Mary Robinson. Died Sept. 5, 1709, aged 75. Will dated, June 13, 1707. Father of the next, and brother of John (1648) and William (1661). (*Vis. of Yorks.*, 1665; *Vis. of Durham*; M. H. Peacock.)

FULTHORP, CHRISTOPHER. Adm. pens. (age 17) at ST JOHN'S, Mar. 25, 1697. S. of Christopher (above), clerk. B. at Sigglesthorne, near Hull, Yorks. Bapt. July 3, 1679. School, Beverley. Matric. 1697. Adm. at Lincoln's Inn, Mar. 10, 1700-1. Buried May 3, 1702. (*Vis. of Yorks.*, 1665.)

FULTHORPE, JOHN. Matric. sizar from CLARE, Easter, 1589.

FULTHORPE or FOULTHORPE, JOHN. Adm. pens. (age 16) at CHRIST'S, Sept. 20, 1648. 1st s. of Clement, 'vir melancholicus.' B. at Tunstall, Durham. Bapt. Apr. 11, 1630, at Stranton. Schools, Durham and Guisborough. Matric. 1648. Married Mary, dau. of George Trotter, of Skelton Castle, Yorks. Buried at Stranton, Feb. 8, 1698-9. Brother of Christopher (1650) and William (1661). (*Peile*, I. 523.)

FULTHORPE, WILLIAM. B.A. 1521-2. Fellow of ST JOHN'S, 1524. Of Richmondshire, Yorks.

FULTHORPE, WILLIAM. Adm. pens. (age 17) at ST JOHN'S, Apr. 5, 1661. 6th s. of Clement, Esq., of Tunstall, Durham. B. there. Bapt. at Stranton, Jan. 9, 1641-2. School, Allerton. Matric. 1661. Brother of Christopher (1650) and John (1648). (*Vis. of Durham*, 1666.)

FULTON, THOMAS. D.Can.L. 1478-9. Already B.Can.L. of Oxford.

FULTON, THOMAS. Adm. pens. at JESUS, Sept. 18, 1712. S. of Robert, clerk, of Guanabo, Jamaica. Matric. 1712; Scholar. Migrated to Christ Church, Oxford, Oct. 13, 1715, age 19. B.A. (Oxford) 1716; M.A. 1718. Obtained the grant of £20 as emigrant minister to Jamaica, 1720.

FULWELL, GEORGE. Matric. pens. from QUEENS', Easter, 1566.

FULWELL, STEPHEN. Matric. sizar from PEMBROKE, Michs. 1544.

FULWELL, WILLIAM. Adm. Fell.-Com. at QUEENS', June 30, 1621. Of Oxfordshire. Ord. deacon and priest by Bishop Laud, Mar. 1623-4.

FULWER, DANIEL. Adm. pens. at CHRIST'S, Apr. 7, 1584. Matric. Fell.-Com. 1584. B. in London.

FULWER, SAMUEL. Adm. Fell.-Com. at CHRIST'S, Apr. 7, 1584. Matric. 1584. B. in London.

FULLWOOD, ANTHONY. Matric. pens. from CHRIST'S, July, 1606; B.A. (? 1609-10); M.A. 1613. Doubtless of Newark-on-Trent, Notts., Esq.; adm. at Gray's Inn, Nov. 15, 1613. (*Peile*, I. 259.)

FULWOOD, DICKENSON. Adm. sizar at PETERHOUSE, June 15, 1624. Of Lincolnshire. Matric. 1625; B.A. 1627-8.

FULWOOD, FRANCIS. Adm. pens. at EMMANUEL, Mar. 14, 1643-4. Exhibitioner from Charterhouse. Matric. 1644; B.A. 1647; D.D. 1660 (*Lit. Reg.*). Archdeacon of Totnes, 1660-93. Preb. of Exeter, 1662-93. Died Aug. 27, 1693. Will (P.C.C.) 1693. Father of James (1682).

FULWOOD, GERVASE. Adm. pens. at ST CATHARINE'S, 1649. Of Huntingdonshire. Matric. Lent, 1649; B.A. 1653-4; M.A. 1657. Fellow, 1655-72. Licensed to practise medicine, 1649. R. of Coton, Cambs., 1662.

FULWOOD, HENRY. Matric. sizar from JESUS, Easter, 1548 (*impubes*).

FULWOOD, JAMES. LL.D. 1682 (*Lit. Reg.*). S. of Francis (1643-4), Archdeacon of Totnes. Matric. from Exeter College, Oxford, Apr. 14, 1671, age 16; B A. (Oxford) 1674; M.A. 1677. Incorp. D.C.L. at Oxford, 1682. Adm. at Gray's Inn, 1682. (*Al. Oxon.*)

FULWOODE, JOHN. Matric. pens. from TRINITY, Michs. 1566.

FULWOOD, PETER. Adm. sizar (age 18) at ST JOHN'S, June 14, 1636. S. of Edmund, barrister, of Bilsthorpe, Notts. B. at Newark-on-Trent. School, Newark. Matric. 1636; B.A. 1639-40. Settled at Stamford; benefactor to the poor there. Will proved (P.C.C.) Mar. 15, 1644-5; by nephew Gervase. (*Scott-Mayor*.)

FULWOOD, PETER. Matric. pens. from ST CATHARINE'S, Michs. 1658; B.A. 1658-9; M.A. 1662. Licensed to practise medicine, 1662. M.D. 1669.

FULWOOD, THOMAS. Adm. at KING'S (age 18) at scholar from Eton, Aug. 17, 1510. Of Tanworth, Warws. Left about 1513. Probably B.A. 1513-4.

FULWOOD, THOMAS. B.A. 1536-7. Doubtless the conduct of KING'S, who was ord. deacon (Lincoln) Mar. 31; priest, Sept. 22, 1537; title, Barnwell priory.

FULWOOD, VINCENT. Matric. sizar from TRINITY, Michs. 1571.

FULWOOD, WILLIAM. Adm. sizar (age 27) at CAIUS, Feb. 5, 1612-3. S. of Thomas, of Mansfield, Notts. School, Mansfield. Matric. 1614.

FULWOOD, WILLIAM. Matric. pens. from ST CATHARINE'S, Easter, 1646; B.A. 1647-8; M.A. 1651; M.D. 1659. Perhaps brother of Gervase (1649).

FULWOOD, WILLIAM. Adm. pens. at EMMANUEL, June 29, 1649. Of Lincolnshire.

FULWOOD, WILLIAM. Adm. pens. at ST CATHARINE'S, 1695. Matric. Easter, 1695; M.D. 1717 (*Com. Reg.*). Adm. extra-licentiate R.C.P. Feb. 21, 1710-1. Died Mar. 25, 1751.

FUNSTON, CHRISTOPHER. Adm. at TRINITY HALL. Migrated to Pembroke, 1626. Matric. there, sizar, Easter, 1627, as 'Fuston.' After a year he returned to Trinity Hall.

FUNSTON, PHILIP. Matric. sizar from JESUS, Michs. 1569.

FUNSTONE, THOMAS. Matric. pens. from QUEENS', Easter, 1606. Of Norfolk. B.A. from St John's, 1606-7; M.A. 1610.

FUNSTON or FENSTONE, ——. Pens. at PETERHOUSE, May 13, 1581. Scholar till 1584.

FURBISHON, JOHN. Fellow of GONVILLE HALL, 1429-34. Ord. sub-deacon (Norwich) Mar. 1432-3; on the title of Westacre Priory, Norfolk.

PURD, ROBERT. Matric. pens. from CHRIST'S, Mar. 1586.

FURLEY or FARLEY, ROBERT. Matric. sizar from KING'S, Michs. 1601; B.A. 1605-6.

FURMARY, *see* FARMARY.

FURNISS, ADAM. Matric. sizar from ST JOHN'S, Easter, 1573; B.A. from Clare, 1576-7; M.A. 1580. Ord. deacon (Ely) Dec. 21, 1580, age 26. Schoolmaster at Depden, Suffolk. V. of North Wootton, Norfolk, 1582. Will (P.C.C.) 1616.

FURNISE, EDWARD. Adm. sizar (age 16) at CHRIST'S, May 29, 1628. S. of Edward. B. at Harborough, Leics. School, Harborough. Matric. 1628; B.A. 1631-2; M.A. 1635. Ord. deacon (Peterb.) May 27, 1632. Perhaps R. of Wisbech St Mary and St Peter, Cambs., 1637-45, ejected. One of these names V. of Harmondsworth, Middlesex, till 1664. V. of Staines, 1663, till his death, 1671. (*Peile*, I. 391.)

FURNESS, JOHN. B.Can.L. 1505-6.

FURNESS, RALPH. Matric. pens. from ST JOHN'S, Michs. 1575. Of Yorkshire. B.A. 1579-80; M.A. 1583; B.D. 1590. Fellow, 1583. Ord. deacon (Peterb.) Mar. 28; priest, July 9, 1583. R. of Merston, Norfolk, 1596. Will (P.C.C.) 1639.

FURNESS, RICHARD. B.A. 1467-8; M.A. 1472-3. Fellow of KING'S; probably therefore a scholar from Eton. Ord. deacon (Lincoln) Sept. 19, 1479.

FURNESS, ROBERT. Adm. at KING'S, a scholar from Eton, 1474; B.A. 1476-7; M.A. 1480.

FURNESS or FURNACE, SAMUEL. Matric. pens. from CORPUS CHRISTI, Easter, 1617, as 'Furnar.' Of Norfolk. B.A. 1620-1; M.A. 1624. Ord. deacon (Peterb.) Dec. 22; priest, Dec. 23, 1622. R. of Aunsby, Lincs., 1627.

FOURNESSE, SAMUEL. Adm. pens. (age 18) at CHRIST'S, Feb. 26, 1680-1. S. of Joseph. B. at Ovenden, near Halifax, Yorks., Dec. 7, 1662. Resided, till the summer of 1682. Buried at Ovenden, Feb. 23, 1687-8. M.I. (*Peile*, II. 81; O. Heywood, *Diary*, 72.)

FURNESS, ——. B.Can.L. 1502-3.

FURNIVAL, JOHN. Adm. sizar at JESUS, May 28, 1705. Of Cheshire. Matric. 1705; B.A. 1708-9. Presumably brother of the next.

FURNIVALL, WILLIAM. Adm. sizar at JESUS, May 18, 1706. Of Cheshire. Matric. 1706.

FURSSE, JOSEPH. Adm. sizar (age 17) at CAIUS, Mar. 24, 1718-9. S. of Joseph, R. of Brandeston, Norfolk. B. at Cawston. School, Norwich. Matric. 1719; Scholar, 1719-24; LL.B. 1724.

FURTHO, JOHN. Adm. scholar at TRINITY, 1584; B.A. 1586-7; M.A. 1590; M.D. 1606. Fellow, 1589. Senior Proctor, 1602. Buried at St Botolph, Cambridge, Feb. 13, 1632-3. Will proved (V.C.C.) and (P.C.C.) 1633.

FURTHO, THOMAS. Matric. pens. from TRINITY, Easter, 1578; Scholar, 1582; B.A. 1582-3. Fellow, 1585. Ord. deacon and priest (Peterb.) June 10, 1593. V. of Chesterton, Cambs., 1602-28. Buried Apr. 24, 1628.

FURTHOE, WILLIAM. Matric. pens. from TRINITY, Easter, 1578.

FURYE, PEREGRINE. Adm. pens. (age 18) at TRINITY, May 25, 1749. S. of Peregrine, of London, secretary to Chelsea Hospital. School, Westminster. Matric. 1750; Scholar, 1750. Gentleman of his Majesty's Privy Chamber, 1779-92. Died Feb. 1792. Will, P.C.C. (*Al. Westmon.*, 350; G. *Mag.*)

FUSTER, *see* FOYSTER.

FUTEDE, *see* FOTEHEDE.

FUTTER, HENRY. Matric. pens. from JESUS, Easter, 1568. (Pedigree of Futter in *Vis. of Norfolk.*)

FUTTER, RICHARD. Adm. pens. at JESUS, May 14, 1623. Matric. 1623; B.A. 1626-7; M.A. 1630.

FUTTER, ROBERT. Adm. pens. at JESUS, May 14, 1623. Of Norfolk. Scholar, 1624; B.A. 1626-7; M.A. 1630. Fellow, 1629-32.

FYCHELER, WILLIAM. Scholar at KING'S HALL, 1359. S. of Peter.

FYDELL, RICHARD. Adm. pens. (age 16) at TRINITY, July 9, 1726. S. of Robert, of London. School, Charterhouse. Matric. 1727. Adm. at the Middle Temple, Nov. 4, 1727. M.P. for Boston, 1734-41. Doubtless of Boston. Died Apr. 11, 1780, aged 70. (*G. Mag.*)

FYDYON, *see* FITZJOHN.

FYFE, THOMAS. Adm. pens. at EMMANUEL, July 6, 1670. O Lancashire. Doubtless s. of William, of Weddaker, Lancs.; M.D. Age 13, in 1665. Probably matric. from Trinity, Oxford, July 14, 1671, age 16, as s. of William, of Garstang. Adm. at Gray's Inn, Mar. 7, 1673-4; s. of William, late of Hackensall, Lancs. (*Vis. of Lancs.*, 1664; *Al. Oxon.*)

FYGE, THOMAS. Adm. pens. (age 15) at CHRIST'S, June 3, 1675. S. of Thomas, druggist. B. in London. School, Stafford. Matric. 1675. (*Peile*, II. 58.)

FYGE, VALENTINE. Adm. pens. (age 16) at PEMBROKE, July 3, 1645. S. of Valentine, of London, druggist. Matric. 1645; B.A. 1648-9.

FYKES, *see* FICKS.

FYLAND, CORNELIUS. Matric. sizar from MAGDALENE, Michs. 1562.

FYLAY, JOHN. Scholar of KING'S HALL, 1446-76.

FYLAY, JOHN. Scholar and fellow of KING'S HALL, 1475-92. Ord. sub-deacon (Lincoln) 1477-8; deacon, June 15, 1478.

FYLER, SAMUEL. Adm. sizar at QUEENS', June 30, 1683. S. of Samuel, R. of Stockton, Wilts. Matric. 1683. (Previously matric. at Trinity College, Oxford, Mar. 17, 1681-2, age 17.) B.A. (Cambridge) 1686-7; M.A. 1690. Incorp. at Oxford, 1693. R. of Orcheston St George, Wilts., 1711. Father of the next. (*Al. Oxon.*)

FYLER, SAMUEL. M.A. from EMMANUEL, 1742. S. of John (above), of Stockton, Wilts., clerk. Matric. from Magdalen Hall, Oxford, May 19, 1721, age 18; B.A. (Oxford) 1724-5. Will (P.C.C.) 1761; C. of Dunstable, Beds. (*Al. Oxon.*; Burke, *L.G.*)

FYNDERN, WILLIAM. S. of Sir Thomas, of Carlton, Cambs., Knt. Sheriff of Cambs. Was a knight in 1477. Resided at Carlton. Benefactor to CLARE, of which he is said to have been a member. Died 1517. Will (P.C.C.) 1517; of Carlton, Cambs., Little Horkesley, Essex, etc. (*Cooper*, I. 19.)

FYNKELL, EDMUND. Matric. sizar from CLARE, Michs. 1572.

FYNKELL, EDWARD. Matric. pens. from CHRIST'S, 1595-6.

FYNKELL, ROBERT. Adm. pens. at CORPUS CHRISTI, 1560. Matric. Michs. 1561; B.A. 1565-6; M.A. 1569. Perhaps C. and schoolmaster at Walsingham, Norfolk; licensed, 1583.

FYNKYLL, ——. B.A. 1498-9.

FYNNE or FYNE, JOHN. B.Can.L. 1474-5; D.Can.L. 1478-9. R. of Boxworth, Cambs., till 1478. R. of Elsworth, 1492-8. Master of St Mary Magdalen Hospital, Cambridge, 1494. R. of Tydd St Giles, Cambs., 1495.

FYNNE or FYNNIE, ROBERT. Matric. pens. from CAIUS, Michs. 1559. Perhaps adm. at Gray's Inn, 1564.

FYNNE, ROBERT. Adm. sizar at TRINITY, May 1, 1667. Matric. 1667; B.A. 1670-1. Ord. deacon (Norwich) Sept. 1673; priest, June, 1675. R. of Bradfield, Suffolk, 1675.

FYNN, THOMAS. Adm. pens. at EMMANUEL, May 25, 1704. B. at Leake, Lincs. Matric. 1705; B.A. 1707-8; M.A. 1711. Fellow, 1710-5. Ord. deacon (London) Sept. 23, 1711; priest, (Norwich) Oct. 1714. Head Master of Lewisham School, 1705. R. of Henstead, Suffolk, 1714-27. R. of Little Hallingbury, Essex. R. of Raydon, Suffolk, 1723. R. of Dennington, 1727-40. Died Mar. 8, 1740, aged 53. M.I. at Dennington.

FYN, ——. Adm. at CORPUS CHRISTI, 1544.

FYRMAGE, WILLIAM. Adm. pens. at EMMANUEL, May 6, 1602.

G.

GABATHUS, THOMAS. B.Civ.L. 1541-2.

GABBET, HENRY. Matric. pens. from TRINITY, Lent, 1579-80; scholar from Westminster, 1580. Doubtless s. of Robert, citizen and haberdasher, of St Mary Bothaw, London. Will (Consist. C. London) 1610; of Rainham, Essex. (J. Ch. Smith.)

GABRY, SAMUEL. Adm. at TRINITY, 1621. S. of John, citizen of London; of French extraction. School, in St Mary's Street (private; Mr Reynolds). Migrated to Christ's, as Fell.-Com. June 12, 1623. B.A. 1623-4.

GABREY, SAMUEL. Matric. sizar from CORPUS CHRISTI, 1649. Of Surrey. Perhaps s. of the above. M.B. 1654. Incorp. at Oxford, 1655. Probably created M.A. (Oxford) 1661.

GABRIELL, *see* SYLVESTER.

GACE, EDWARD. Adm. sizar at JESUS, July 5, 1680. Of Lincolnshire. Matric. 1680; B.A. 1683-4.

GACE, LANGLEY. Matric. sizar from ST JOHN'S, Easter, 1628. S. of Thomas, of Worksop, Notts. Bapt. Apr. 1, 1610. R. of Sotby, Lincs., 1644-58. (*Lincs. Pedigrees*, 382.)

GACE, MILES. B.A. 1531-2.

GACE or GASE, WILLIAM. Matric. sizar from CLARE, Michs. 1568; B.A. 1572-3. Author, theological. (*Cooper*, II. 22; *D.N.B.*)

GACHES, DANIEL. Adm. at KING'S, a scholar from Eton, 1751. S. of John. Bapt. at Glapthorn, Northants., Feb. 13, 1732-3. B.A. 1756; M.A. 1759. Fellow. Ord. deacon (Ely) Mar. 7, 1756; priest, Dec. 21, 1758. V. of Wootton Wawen, Warws. V. of Long Compton.

GADLYNGTON, ——. Fell.-Com. at JESUS, 1568-9.

GADSDEN or GAYDSDEN, JOHN. Matric. pens. from CHRIST'S, Nov. 1568. Doubtless schoolmaster at Hitchin, in 1613; appointed, 1577.

GADDESDEN, THOMAS. Adm. sizar at PETERHOUSE, Mar. 28, 1632. Of Hertfordshire. Matric. 1633; B.A. 1636-7.

GAFORTH, JOHN. Incorp. at Oxford, 1521-2, as 'M.A. of Cambridge.' (No University or College record. One Garforth was B.A. 1522-3.)

GAGE, EDWARD. Matric. pens. from NICHOLAS HOSTEL, Michs. 1555.

GAGE, FREEMAN. Adm. pens. (age 18) at TRINITY, Nov. 8, 1751. Of Holton, Oxon. S. of Thomas, of Little Marlow, Bucks. School, Oxford. Matric. 1751; Scholar, 1752; LL.B. 1758. Previously matric. from Magdalen College, Oxford, Mar. 21, 1750-1. Ord. deacon (Lincoln) Sept. 21, 1755; priest, Dec. 18, 1757. Died Mar. 11, 1794. Will, P.C.C. (*Al. Oxon.*; G. *Mag.*)

GAGE, GEORGE. Matric. pens. from CHRIST'S, *c.* 1597 (entry erased).

GAGE, JOHN. Matric. pens. from CLARE, Easter, 1628; B.A. 1631-2; M.A. 1635.

GAGE, JOHN. Adm. at CORPUS CHRISTI, 1732. Of Nottinghamshire. S. of John, of Bentley, Sussex. B. 1711. Matric. Michs. 1732; B.A. 1736-7; M.A. 1740. Ord. deacon (Lincoln) May 28, 1738. R. of Colwick, Notts., 1749. V. of Rowston, Lincs., 1760. R. of West Bridgeford, Notts., 1764. Died unmarried, Jan. 14, 1770, aged 59. Buried at Nottingham. (*Nichols*, III. 149.)

GAGE or GADGE, MAURICE. Matric. pens. from TRINITY, *c.* 1593; B.A. 1596-7. Ord. deacon and priest (Peterb.) May 25, 1598. C. of Gt Bytham, Lincs., 1603. Will (Lincoln) 1647-8; of Swineshead, Lincs., clerk.

GAGE, ROBERT. Matric. pens. from CHRIST'S, Dec. 1589. Doubtless s. and h. of Robert, of Northamptonshire; adm. at the Middle Temple, June 2, 1592; formerly of New Inn. Married Mary, dau. of Robert Pemberton, of Rushden, Northants. Died Feb. 23, 1616-7. M.I. at Raunds. (*Peile*, I. 196; *Bridges*, II. 188.)

GAGE, ROBERT. Adm. pens. at CHRIST'S, Apr. 21, 1626. S. of John, of Raunds, Northants. School, Higham (Mr Frier). Matric. 1626. Adm. at the Middle Temple, Nov. 20, 1629. (*Peile*, I. 373.)

GAGE, THOMAS. Matric. pens. from CHRIST'S, *c.* 1593.

GAGE, WILLIAM, *see* GEDGE.

GAGE, ——. Matric. pens. from CHRIST'S, *c.* 1597. (Probably George, above.)

GAGE, ——. D.Can.L. 1481–2.

GAGER, JOHN (1650), *see* GAYER.

GAGER, WILLIAM. M.A. 1581 (Incorp. from Oxford). LL.D. 1601 (*do.*). Adm. at Christ Church, Oxford, 1574, from Westminster School; B.A. (Oxford) 1577; M.A. 1580; B.C.L. and D.C.L. 1589. Vicar-general of Ely, and Chancellor of the diocese. Eminent Latin poet and dramatic author. Buried at All Saints', Cambridge, Sept. 1, 1622. Will proved (V.C.C.) 1622. (*D.N.B.*; *Al. Oxon.*)

GAGES, THOMAS. Adm. pens. at EMMANUEL, Mar. 16, 1630–1. Of Suffolk. Matric. 1631.

GAGNIER, JOHN. M.A. 1703 (*Lit. Reg.*). B. in Paris, *c.* 1670. Of the College of Navarre, Paris University. Priest and canon. Became a Protestant and retired to England. Chaplain to William Lloyd, Bishop of Worcester. Hebrew teacher at Oxford. Professor of Arabic there, 1724–40. Author, oriental. Died at Oxford, Mar. 21, 1740. (*D.N.B.*)

GAINES, *see also* GAYNES.

GAINES, DUNHAM. Adm. sizar (age 17) at PEMBROKE, July 2, 1734. S. of Samuel, of Stalham, Norfolk, mercer. Matric. 1735; B.A. 1738–9. Ord. deacon (Norwich) July, 1739; priest, Feb. 1748–9. R. of East Wretham, Norfolk, 1753–90; and of West Wretham, 1754–90. Died May 21, 1790. Will, P.C.C. (*G. Mag.*)

GAINSBOROUGH, EDWARD. Adm. sizar at EMMANUEL, May 7, 1629. Of Lincolnshire. Matric. 1629; B.A. 1632–3.

GAINSFORD, *see* GAYNSFORD.

GAISKELL or GATESKELL, RICHARD. Adm. sizar (age 18) at ST JOHN'S, June 3, 1667, as 'Gatesbell.' S. of Thomas, yeoman, of Furness Fells, Lancs. B. there. School, Sedbergh. Matric. 1667; B.A. 1670–1.

GALARD, *see* GALLARD *and* GAYLARD.

GALASIUS, *see* GELASIUS.

GALE, ARTHUR. Matric. pens. from CHRIST'S, Lent, 1577–8; B.A. 1581–2; M.A. 1585. Probably ord. priest (Bishop of Colchester, at Norwich) Feb. 1597–8. Master of Dedham School, Essex, 1588–97. R. of Semer, Suffolk, 1598–1622. Will (P.C.C.) 1623; of Semer. (*Peile*, I. 145.)

GALE, CHARLES. Matric. sizar from MAGDALENE, Easter, 1631; B.A. 1634–5; M.A. 1638. Fellow; ejected *c.* 1645.

GALE, CHARLES. Adm. pens. (age 17) at TRINITY, Mar. 26, 1695. S. of Thomas (1655), D.D. B. in London. Bapt. at St Faith's, Aug. 6, 1677. School, St Paul's. Matric. 1695; Scholar, 1697; B.A. 1698–9; M.A. 1702. Ord. deacon (Lincoln) Sept. 20, 1702; priest, Mar. 14, 1702–3. Chaplain of Trinity, 1703–6. R. of Scruton, Yorks., 1705–38. V. of Kirkby Fleetham, 1719–28. R. of Barningham, 1728–38. Married Cordelia, dau. of Thomas Thwaits, of Burrel. Died 1738. Brother of Roger (1691), father of Thomas (1726). (M. H. Peacock.)

GAELL, ELDRED. Adm. at KING'S, a scholar from Eton, 1687. B. at Hadleigh, Suffolk, Aug. 29, 1670. Matric. Michs. 1687; B.A. 1691–2; M.A. 1695. Fellow, 1690. Assistant Master at Eton. Died of small-pox in King's, May 3, 1702, aged 33. M.I. in King's Chapel. (Le Neve, *Mon.*, II. 48.)

GALE, HENRY. Matric. sizar from CORPUS CHRISTI, *c.* 1593. Of Bedfordshire. B. 1578. B.A. from Queens', 1596–7; M.A. 1600. Ord. deacon and priest (Lincoln) July 19, 1601. V. of Renhold, Beds., 1603–12. R. of Little Staughton, 1612–39. Buried there Aug. 16, 1639. Will (P.C.C.) 1639. Doubtless father of Simon (1635).

GALE, HENRY. Adm. pens. (age 15) at MAGDALENE, Mar. 30, 1654. S. of Robert (1609), R. of Epworth. School, Westminster. Matric. 1654; B.A. 1657–8; M.A. 1661. Signed for deacon's orders (London) Sept. 19, 1663.

GALE, ISAAC. Adm. Fell.-Com. at QUEENS', Oct. 13, 1743. Of Jamaica. Matric. 1743; B.A. 1747–8.

GALE, JOHN. Matric. pens. from CHRIST'S, Apr. 1582. Perhaps brother and executor of Arthur.

GALE or GAEL, JOHN. Matric. pens. from PEMBROKE, Easter, 1607. S. of John, first mayor of Hadleigh, Suffolk. B.A. 1610–1; M.A. 1614. Fellow, 1612. Perhaps R. of High Hoyland, Yorks., 1614–5. Died same year. (*Peile*, I. 168.)

GALE, JOHN. M.A. from CLARE, 1668. S. of Thomas, of Taunton, Somerset. Matric. from Balliol College, Oxford, Mar. 14, 1662–3, age 19; B.A. (Hart Hall) 1666. V. of Creech St Michael, Somerset, 1666–96. Buried there July 7, 1696. Will, at Taunton. Father of the next. (*Al. Oxon.*)

GALE, JOHN. Adm. pens. (age 19) at SIDNEY, Mar. 3, 1696–7. S. of John (above), V. of Creech St Michael, Somerset. B. there. Schools, Taunton and Tiverton. Matric. 1697; B.A. 1700–1. V. of Creech St Michael, 1704–38. Buried there May 5, 1738.

GALE, JOSIAS. M.A. 1626 (Incorp. from Oxford). Of Devon. Matric. from Pembroke College, Oxford, May 9, 1626, age 30; M.A. same day. (? where B.A.) R. of West Buckland, Devon, 1635; ejected, 1662. Admon. (Exeter) 1662. (*Al. Oxon.*; *Calamy*, I. 346.)

GALE, LEONARD. Matric. sizar from CHRIST'S, Dec. 1602. Ord. deacon (Lincoln) . 20, 1607; priest, Feb. 21, 1607–8. B. at Hemingby, 1578. [illegible] Honington, Lincs., 1607. (*Peile*, I. 242.)

GALE, MILES. Adm. sizar at TRINITY, Mar. 5, 1662–3. S. of John, of Farnley Hall, near Leeds. B. there, June 19, 1647. Matric. 1663; B.A. 1666–7; M.A. 1670. Ord. deacon (Peterb.) Sept. 20, 1668. R. of Keighley, Yorks., 1680–1721. Antiquary and author. Married Margery, dau. of Dr Christopher Stone, Chancellor of York. Died Jan. 3, 1720–1, aged 74. Buried at Keighley. M.I. Father of Thomas (1705). (*D.N.B.*; M. H. Peacock.)

GALE, PETER. Matric. sizar from ST JOHN'S, Easter, 1617.

GALE, RICHARD. Adm. pens. (age 18) at PEMBROKE, Oct. 11, 1707. S. of Thomas, of Whitehaven, Cumberland, gent. Matric. 1708, as 'Gate.'

GALE, ROBERT. Matric. pens. from CHRIST'S, Easter, 1609; B.A. 1612–3; M.A. 1616. Ord. deacon (Peterb.) Sept. 22; priest, Sept. 23, 1616. Chaplain to the Countess of Devonshire. R. of Brindle, Lancs., 1637–40. V. of Buckminster, Leics., 1639. R. of Epworth, Lincs., 1641–60. (*Peile*, I. 273.)

GALE, ROBERT. Adm. pens. at QUEENS', Apr. 10, 1711. Of Bedfordshire. Probably s. of Simon (1671–2), V. of Oakley. Bapt. there, Nov. 28, 1693.

GALE, ROBERT. Adm. pens. (age 18) at TRINITY, Apr. 20, 1726. S. of Benjamin, of Abbot's Langley, Herts. School, Charterhouse, London. Matric. 1726. Died Oct. 7, 1738. Buried at Abbot's Langley. M.I. (*Clutterbuck*, I. 177.)

GALE, ROGER. Adm. pens. ('age 16') at TRINITY, Apr. 15, 1691. S. of Thomas (1655), D.D., Dean of York. B. at Impington, Cambs. (his mother's home). School, St Paul's (under his father). Matric. 1691; Scholar, 1693; B.A. 1694–5; M.A. 1698. Fellow, 1697. Incorp. at Oxford, 1699. M.P. for Northallerton, 1705–13. Commissioner of Excise, 1715–35. F.R.S. 1717. Treasurer, Royal Society. Vice-President of the Society of Antiquaries. Left manuscripts to Trinity College, and his collection of coins to the University Library. Married Henrietta, dau. of Henry Raper, Esq. Died at Scruton, Yorks., June 25, 1744. Brother of Charles (1695), father of the next. (*D.N.B.*; *Al. Oxon.*)

GALE, ROGER HENRY. Adm. pens. (age 20) at SIDNEY, Oct. 20, 1729. S. of Roger (above), gent., of Scruton, Yorks. B. at Bedford Row, London. School, Eton. Matric. 1729. Adm. at Lincoln's Inn, Feb. 4, 1724–5. Married Catherine, dau. of Christopher Crow, of Kipling, Esq. Died 1768. (Thoresby, *Duc. Leod.*, 203.)

GALE, SIMON. Matric. pens. from QUEENS', Michs. 1635. Of Bedfordshire. Doubtless s. of Henry (1593), R. of Little Staughton, Hunts. Bapt. there, Mar. 25, 1619. School, Oundle; adm. there, Oct. 8, 1632, age 13. B.A. 1639. C. of Basildon, Essex, 1650. V. of Horndon-on-the-Hill, 1662–8. Died 1668. Will, P.C.C. (H. Smith.)

GALE, SIMON. Adm. sizar at QUEENS', Feb. 29, 1671–2. Of Bedfordshire. Matric. 1672; B.A. 1675–6; M.A. 1679. Ord. deacon (London) Mar. 11, 1676–7. V. of Oakley, Beds., 1687–1712. V. of Bromham, 1688–1712. Died Aug. 1, 1712, aged 57. Buried in Oakley Church. (Harvey, *Willey Hundred, Beds.*)

GALE, THEOPHILUS. B.D. 1619 (Incorp. from Oxford). Of Devon. Matric. from Exeter College, Oxford, Oct. 11, 1605, age 17; B.A. (Oxford) 1609; M.A. 1611–2; B.D. 1619; D.D. 1624. Fellow of Exeter, 1611–21. V. of King's Teignton, Devon, 1620. Preb. of Exeter, 1629. Died May, 1639. Will (Exeter) 1639. Father of the next. (*Al. Oxon.*)

GALE, THEOPHILUS. M.A. 1656 (Incorp. from Oxford). S. of Theophilus (above). B.A. (Magdalen College, Oxford) 1649; M.A. 1652. Fellow of Magdalen, 1650–60. Preacher at Winchester Cathedral, 1657–60, ejected. Became tutor in the family of Philip, Baron Wharton, 1662–5. Afterwards kept a school at Newington. Author, theological. Died Mar. 1678, aged 49. Buried in Bunhill Fields. M.I. (*Calamy*, I. 243; *D.N.B.*; *Al. Oxon.*)

GALE, THOMAS. Adm. pens. at TRINITY, May 23, 1655. S. of Christopher, of Scruton, Yorks. B. there, *c.* 1636. Scholar from Westminster, 1655. B.A. 1658–9; M.A. 1662; B.D. and D.D. 1675. Fellow, 1659. Taxor, 1670. Incorp. at Oxford, 1669. Regius Professor of Greek, Apr.–Oct. 1672. Signed for priest's orders (London) Sept. 22, 1666. V. of Barrington, Cambs., 1667. High Master of St Paul's, 1672–97. Preb. of St Paul's, 1676–1702. F.R.S. 1677; and first secretary to the Royal Society. Dean of York, 1697–1702. Married Barbara, dau. of Roger Pepys, of Impington, Cambs. Died Apr. 8, 1702. Buried in York Minster. M.I. Father of Roger (1691 and Charles (1695). (*Al. Oxon.*; *D.N.B.*)

GALE, THOMAS. Adm. pens. at QUEENS', June 27, 1695. Of Somerset. Probably of Taunton Deane. Will (Taunton) 1717.

GALE, THOMAS. Adm. pens. at TRINITY, July 2, 1705. S. of Miles (1662-3), R. of Keighley, Yorks. School, Sedbergh. Matric. 1705; Scholar, 1706; B.A. 1708-9. Ord. deacon (York) Sept. 1710; priest, 1711. V. of Withernwick, Yorks., 1715-6. R. of Linton, 1716-50. Died 1750. Perhaps father of William (1736-7). (G. *Mag.*; Whittaker, *Craven*, 539.)

GALE, THOMAS. Adm. pens. (age 18) at TRINITY, June 23, 1726. S. of Charles (1695), R. of Scruton, Yorks. School, Darlington (Mr Marshall). Matric. 1726; Scholar, 1727; B.A. 1729-30; M.A. 1733. Fellow, 1732. Ord. deacon (Lincoln) Sept. 22, 1734; priest, June 5, 1737. Succeeded his father as R. of Scruton, 1738-56. R. of West Rounton, 1742-56. Died July 7, 1756. (Nichols, *Lit. Anecdotes*, IV. 550; Thoresby, *Duc. Leod.*, 203.)

GALE, WILLIAM. Probably of GONVILLE HALL, to which he was a benefactor. A priest. Of Eye, Suffolk. Founded scholarships, 1506. Will (P.C.C.) 1508: bequest to the High altar of Hatfield Peverell, Essex. (*Venn*, I. 17.)

GALE, WILLIAM. Adm. pens. at TRINITY, May 8, 1649, a scholar from Westminster, 1650. Of Northamptonshire. Probably s. of Robert (1609). Bapt. at All Saints', Northampton, Dec. 25, 1630. (H. I. Longden.)

GALE, WILLIAM. Adm. sizar (age 20) at ST JOHN'S, Jan. 24, 1736-7. S. of Thomas (? 1705), clerk, of Yorkshire. B. at Keighley. School, Threshfield. Matric. 1737; B.A. 1740-1; M.A. 1744. Ord. deacon (Lincoln) Oct. 28, 1740; priest, May 24, 1741. R. of Careby, Lincs., 1752-89. R. of Braceborough, 1753-89. Chaplain to the Earl of Wigton. Died Mar. 1789. Will (P.C.C.) 1789. (*Scott-Mayor*, III. 482.)

GALFRIDE, STEPHEN. Matric. pens. from TRINITY HALL, Michs. 1558.

GALFRIDUS, ——. M.A. 1463.

GALHAMPTON, OLIVER. M.A. from TRINITY, 1631. S. of Francis, of Bridgewater, Somerset, gent. Matric. from Magdalen Hall, Oxford, Oct. 20, 1626, age 19; B.A. (Oxford) 1628. R. of All Hallows, Exeter, 1637. R. of Enmore, Somerset, 1639-77. Preb. of Wells, 1661-77. Will (Taunton) 1677. (*Al. Oxon.*)

GALIAN, WILLIAM. B.D. 1485-6; D.D. 1488. A friar.

GALION, ——. B.Can.L. 1491-2. Perhaps John, R. of Broughton, Hunts., 1500-20. Died 1520.

GALIMORE, THOMAS. Matric. sizar (probably from JESUS), *c.* 1595; B.A. from Jesus, 1598-9; M.A. 1602.

GALLE, EDWARD. Matric. pens. from EMMANUEL, Easter, 1611.

GALL, JOHN. Matric. pens. from MAGDALENE, Michs. 1623.

GALL, SAMUEL. Adm. sizar at QUEENS', July 11, 1713. Of Suffolk. S. of Robert and Martha Fiske, of Norton. Bapt. there, July 18, 1695. School, Bury. Matric. 1714; B.A. 1717-8. Ord. deacon (London) June 8, 1718; priest (Norwich) Dec. 1719. R. of Langham, Suffolk, 1725-8. R. of Elmswell, 1726-8.

GALL, ——. Fee for B.A. 1468-9.

GALL, ——. B.Can.L. 1476-7.

GALL, ——. B.D. 1506-7. A friar.

GALL, ——. B.Can.L. 1506-7.

GALLANT, ARTHUR. Adm. sizar (age 15) at PEMBROKE, Oct. 18, 1672. S. of John, of Wood Dalling, Norfolk. Matric. 1673; B.A. 1676-7; M.A. 1680. Ord. deacon (Norwich) June, 1680; priest, June, 1682. R. of Thurning, Norfolk, 1688-1706. R. of Brinton, 1693-1713. R. of Heydon and Irmingland, 1693-1713. Died July 3, 1713. Buried at Heydon. M.I. Brother of John (1665).

GALLANT, HENRY. Matric. pens. from TRINITY, Michs. 1559, as 'Galoue'; Scholar, 1563; B.A. 1563-4; M.A. 1568. V. of Yaxley, Hunts., 1573-83. Died 1583.

GALLANT, JOHN. Adm. pens. (age 15) at PEMBROKE, Mar. 30, 1665. S. of John, gent., of Wood Dalling, Norfolk. Matric. 1665. Adm. at Lincoln's Inn, Feb. 10, 1669-70; from Thavies Inn. Brother of Arthur (1672).

GALLANT, JOHN. Adm. at CORPUS CHRISTI, 1707. Of Norwich. Matric. 1707; B.A. 1710-1. Ord. deacon (Ely) Sept. 23, 1711; priest (Norwich) Jan. 18, 1712-3. R. of Swanton Abbots, Norfolk. R. of Bradfield, 1716-55. Died Apr. 6, 1755, aged 67.

GALLANT, ROBERT. Adm. pens. (age 16) at CAIUS, Oct. 20, 1707. S. of Henry, grocer, of Aldborough, Norfolk. B. there. Schools, Alby (Mr Fox) and Aylsham (Mr Wrench). Scholar, 1707-11; Matric. 1708; M.B. 1713. Practised as physician at Yarmouth. Died June 27, 1746. M.I. at St Nicholas, Yarmouth. Brother of the next. (*Venn*, I. 517.)

GALLANT, THOMAS. Adm. sizar (age 17) at CAIUS, Sept. 13, 1712. S. of Henry, clothier, of Aldborough, Norfolk. B. there. School, Aylsham (Mr Wrench). Matric. 1712; Scholar, 1712-8; B.A. 1716-7; M.A. 1721. Ord. deacon (Winchester) June 16, 1717; priest (Ely) Mar. 13, 1719-20. R. of Matlask, Norfolk, 1719-41; of Blickling, 1732-61; of Burgh-by-Aylsham, 1741-61. Buried at Blickling, Nov. 20, 1761. Will (Norwich Archd. C.) 1762. Brother of Robert (above). (*Venn*, I. 528.)

GALLARD, *see also* **GAYLARD.**

GALLARD, JOHN. Matric. pens. from CHRIST'S, Michs. 1576.

GALLARD, JOHN. Adm. at CORPUS CHRISTI, 1600. Of Norfolk.

GALLARD, JOHN. Matric. pens. from CHRIST'S, July, 1616. S. of Richard, of Bunwell, Norfolk. B.A. 1619-20. Died 1621. Will proved (P.C.C.) Apr. 18, 1622. (*Misc. Gen. et Her.*, 2nd S., I. 158; *Peile*, I. 309.)

GALLARD, ROBERT. B.A. (? 1602-3); M.A. from CHRIST'S, 1606. Ord. priest (Norwich) Sept. 1607. Chaplain of St Andrew, Norwich, 1614-5. R. of Beeston St Andrew, Norfolk, 1615-39. V. of Sprowston, 1616-39. Perhaps father of Samuel (1622). (*Peile*, I. 233.)

GALLARD, ROBERT. Adm. pens. (age 15) at CAIUS, Apr. 8, 1656. S. of Roger (below), R. of Wreningham, Norfolk. B. there. School, Wymondham. Matric. 1656; Scholar, 1656; B.A. 1659-60; M.A. 1663. Ord. deacon (Norwich) July, 1662; priest Dec. 23, 1665. Schoolmaster at Wymondham, 1662. R. of Cranwich, Norfolk, 1665-7. Buried there Aug. 15, 1667. (*Venn*, I. 394.)

GALLARD, ROGER. Matric. pens. from CHRIST'S, Apr. 1617; B.A. 1620-1; M.A. 1624. Ord. priest (Norwich) Sept. 1622. R. of Wreningham, Norfolk, 1625-72. R. of Ashwellthorpe, 1627. Died 1672, aged 74. Father of Robert (above). (*Peile*, I. 313.)

GALLARD, SAMUEL. Matric. pens. from CHRIST'S, July, 1622. Perhaps s. of Robert (? 1602-3). B.A. 1625-6; M.A. 1629. Ord. priest (Norwich) 1630. C. of Beeston St Andrew, 1634; R. 1639-60.

GALLARD, WILLIAM. Matric. pens. from CHRIST'S, July, 1620.

GALLATINE, DAVID. B.A. from CORPUS CHRISTI, 1600-1; M.A. 1605. Of Geneva.

GALLET, HENRY. Adm. sizar at ST CATHARINE'S, Easter, 1645. S. of William, labourer, of Mayfield, Sussex. School, Tonbridge, Kent. Migrated to St John's, July 14, 1645, age 16.

GALLIS, RICHARD. Adm. at KING'S (age 16) a scholar from Eton, Aug. 13, 1533. Of Windsor. B.A. 1536-7. Fellow, 1536-7. Student at Barnard's Inn. Afterwards settled at Windsor, where he was landlord of the Garter Inn. Mayor of Windsor. M.P. for Windsor, 1563-7, 1572-4. Died Nov. 30, 1574. (*Cooper*, I. 561.)

GALLOWAY, EDMUND. Matric. sizar from ST JOHN'S, Michs. 1582; B.A. 1585-6; M.A. 1594. R. of Stanton All Saints, Suffolk, 1602-13. R. of Westhorp, 1613-22.

GALOWAYE, GEORGE. Matric. pens. from PETERHOUSE, Easter, 1579.

GALLOWAY, JAMES. Adm. sizar (age 17) at CAIUS, July 4, 1628. S. of Humfrey, husbandman. B. at Newbald, Yorks. School, Stainton (Mr Simpson). Matric. 1628; B.A. 1631-2. C. of Old Malton, Yorks., 1634-49. Buried there Oct. 29, 1669. (*Venn*, I. 285.)

GALLOWAY, THOMAS. Adm. pens. at CAIUS, *c.* Apr. 7, 1646. Matric. 1646. Probably licensed schoolmaster of Bildeston, Suffolk, Feb. 12, 1662-3; there in 1677.

GALLOWAY, WILLIAM. Matric. pens. from TRINITY, Michs. 1571. Will of one of these names (P.C.C.) 1611; of Creeton, Lincs., gent.

GALLY, HENRY. Adm. at CORPUS CHRISTI, 1714. S. of Peter, a Huguenot refugee. B. at Beckenham, Kent, Aug. 1696. Matric. 1714; B.A. 1717-8; M.A. 1721; D.D. 1728 (*Com. Reg.*). Ord. deacon (Lincoln) Nov. 13; priest, Dec. 18, 1720. R. of Wavendon, Bucks., 1721. Chaplain to Lord Chancellor King, 1725. Preb. of Gloucester, 1728. R. of Ashton, Northants., 1731-2. Preb. of Norwich, 1731-69. Lecturer at St Paul's, Covent Garden. R. of St Giles-in-the-Fields, 1732-69. Chaplain in ordinary to George II, 1735-60. Married Elizabeth, dau. of Isaac Knight, Esq., of Langold, Yorks. Author. Died Aug. 7, 1769. Will, P.C.C. (*Masters*; *D.N.B.*)

GALLY, JOHN. Matric. sizar from ST JOHN'S, Easter, 1584; B.A. from St Catharine's, 1587-8. One of these names R. of Hoyland, Yorks., 1614-5. Died 1615.

GALLY, SAMUEL. Adm. sizar (age 19) at ST JOHN'S, May 31, 1680. S. of Richard, husbandman. B. at 'Birtson,' Cheshire. School, Wrexham, Denbighshire. Matric. 1681, as 'Gales'; B.A. 1683-4. V. of Helpringham, Lincs.; and V. of Sempringham.

GALT, OLIVER. Probably B.A. 1473; M.A. 1476; B.D. 1490–1.

GALTHORP (? CALTHORPE), JAMES. Matric. Fell.-Com. from St CATHARINE's, Easter, 1644.

GALWAY, Viscount, *see* MONCKTON, JOHN.

GALWYS, ROBERT. B.Can.L. 1464–5.

GAMAGE, GAMYDGE or GAMINGE, ANTHONY. Matric. pens. from ST JOHN'S, Michs. 1559.

GAMAGE or GAMINE, ANTHONY. Matric. Fell.-Com. from QUEENS', Easter, 1602. Of London. Adm. at Lincoln's Inn, Mar. 11, 1605–6.

GAMAGE, JOHN. Adm. sizar at EMMANUEL, May 21, 1739. Of Derbyshire. S. of John, V. of Lullington. School, Derby. Matric. 1739; B.A. 1742–3; M.A. 1746. Fellow, 1745. Taxor, 1746. Ord. deacon (Lincoln) May 25; priest, Sept. 21, 1746. Died in College, 1751. Will, P.C.C.

GAMAGE or GAMADGE, ROGER. Matric. pens. from TRINITY, 1608. Scholar from Westminster, 1607. B.A. 1611–2.

GAMMAGE, WILLIAM. Matric. Fell.-Com. from CLARE, Michs. 1572. Perhaps s. and h. of William, alderman of London. (*Vis. of London*, 1568.)

GAMBLE, ALGERNON. Adm. sizar at EMMANUEL, Jan. 8, 1712–3. Of Middlesex. Matric. 1713–4; B.A. 1716–7. Ord. deacon (Peterb., *Litt. dim.* from Norwich) Sept. 20, 1719; priest (Norwich) Sept. 1720.

GAMBELL, EDWARD. Adm. sizar at PETERHOUSE, Aug. 14, 1626. Of Leicester. Matric. 1626–7; B.A. 1630–1; M.A. 1634. Head Master of Newark Grammar School, till 1642.

GAMBLE, JOHN. Adm. scholar at TRINITY HALL, Jan. 23, 1723–4. Of Whittlesey, Cambs. Matric. 1724; B.A. 1728–9. Ord. deacon (Lincoln) June 5, 1726; priest, Feb. 26, 1726–7. C. of Elstow, Hunts., 1728–32. V. of Felmersham, Beds., 1732–3. R. of Little Barford, 1732.

GAMBLE, LINCOLNE. Adm. pens. at CLARE, May 5, 1679. Of Kirk Sandal, Yorks. Matric. 1679.

GAMBLE, PETER. Matric. sizar from TRINITY, Michs. 1627 B.A. 1630–1. R. of Frisby-on-the-Wreak, Leics., 1635.

GAMBLE, RICHARD. Matric. pens. from QUEENS', Michs. 1566.

GAMBLE, RICHARD. Adm. at CORPUS CHRISTI, 1667. Of Bedfordshire. Matric. 1667; B.A. 1670–1. Ord. deacon (Peterb.) Dec. 22, 1672.

GAMBLE, ROBERT. Adm. sizar (age 19) at CAIUS, May 29, 1747. S. of John, surgeon, of Bungay, Suffolk. B. there. Schools, Bungay (Mr Smee), Norwich and Bury. Matric. 1747; Scholar, 1747–54; B.A. 1750–1. Ord. deacon (London) Sept. 22, 1751; priest (Norwich) Mar. 18, 1753. P.C. of Wingfield, Suffolk, 1753–4. Died May 21, 1754. M.I. at St Mary's, Bungay. (*Venn*, II. 59.)

GAMBLE, SAMUEL. Matric. sizar from TRINITY, *c.* 1595.

GAMBLE, THOMAS. Adm. scholar at TRINITY HALL, Jan. 6, 1711–2. Matric. 1710–1; B.A. 1715–6. Ord. deacon (Norwich) Oct. 1715; priest, Sept. 1716. V. of Wroxham, Norfolk, 1719–31. R. of Helhoughton, 1723–31. (*Blomefield*, x. 137.)

GAMBLE, W. Matric. sizar from CAIUS, May 8, 1580. Resident in 1581.

GAMDE, THOMAS. Matric. pens. from CORPUS CHRISTI, Lent, 1629–30.

GAMER or GAIMER, ROBERT. Matric. Fell.-Com. from KING'S, Easter, 1575.

GAMES, WILLIAM LANGHORNE. Adm. at CHRIST'S, July 19, 1720. Adm. at Lincoln's Inn, Apr. 14, 1720. Lord of the manor of Hampstead, Middlesex. Died Jan. 27, 1732. (*G. Mag.*)

GAMLIN, JOHN. Matric. Fell.-Com. from MAGDALENE, Easter, 1634; M.A. 1641–2 (on King's visit). Doubtless s. and h. of Sir John, Knt., of Pulney Hall, Spalding. Bapt. there, July 20, 1615. Colonel in the King's army. Compounded for his estates under the Protectorate. Of St Giles-in-the-Fields, Middlesex, in 1666. Brother of Matthew (1636). (*Geneal.*, II. 386.)

GAMLIN, JOHN. Adm. sizar at QUEENS', May 29, 1665. Of Middlesex. Matric. 1665; B.A. 1668–9; M.A. 1672. Signed for deacon's orders (London) Sept. 15, 1668; for priest's, Sept. 18, 1669. C. of Wootton, Kent. V. of Herne Hill, 1676–81. V. of Preston, 1684–1715. V. of Faversham, till 1715. Married, 1700, Catherine Bunce, of Faversham. Died 1715. (H. G. Harrison.)

GAMLYN, MATTHEW. Matric. sizar from TRINITY, Michs. 1562. Probably of Lincolnshire. S. of John, of Fulney Marsh, Spalding. Bapt. there, Sept. 21, 1546. Adm. at Lincoln's Inn, Nov. 5, 1565. Attorney-at-law. Knighted, July 23, 1603. Died Oct. 25, 1617. Buried at Spalding. (*Geneal.*, II. 386.)

GAMLYN, MATTHEW. Adm. pens. (age 15) at PEMBROKE, Apr. 28, 1636. 3rd s. of Sir John, Knt. B. at Spalding, Lincs. Matric. 1636, as 'Gramlin'; B.A. 1639–40. Brother of John (1634).

GAMMON, JOHN. Matric. sizar from PEMBROKE, Michs. 1586; B.A. 1590–1; M.A. 1594. Fellow of Sidney. Ord. deacon and priest (Lincoln) Dec. 21, 1596. R. of Aston, Herts., 1601–29. Will (P.C.C.) 1629. Father of John (1628), Robert (1626–7) and Richard (1636–7).

GAMMON, JOHN. Adm. pens. (age 16) at CAIUS, Jan. 14, 1625–6. S. of Richard, B.D., minister of St Giles', Norwich. B. in the parish of St Laurence, Norwich. School, Norwich. Matric. 1626; Scholar, 1626–8. Probably C. of Blofield, Norfolk, in 1634. Brother of Richard (1626) and Roger (1640).

GAMON, JOHN. Adm. pens. (age 14) at SIDNEY, June 28, 1628. S. of John (1586), R. of Aston, Herts. B. there. School, London, Red Cross St (Mr Farnaby). Matric. 1628; B.A. 1631–2; M.A. 1635. Brother of Robert (1626–7) and Richard (1636–7).

GAMON, RICHARD (1531–2), *see* BARKWAY.

GAMMON, RICHARD. Adm. pens. (age 17) at CAIUS, July 4, 1626. S. of Richard, B.D. (of Oxford), R. of St Laurence, Norwich. B. there. Scholar, 1628–34; Matric. 1629; B.A. 1630–1; M.A. 1634. Ord. deacon (Norwich) Dec. 22, 1633; priest, Sept. 1, 1634. C. of St Saviour's, Norwich, 1636. R. of Barford, 1637. Died same year. Brother of John (1625–6) and Roger (1640). (*Venn*, I. 277.)

GAMON, RICHARD. Adm. pens. (age 18) at SIDNEY, Jan. 17, 1636–7. S. of John (1586). B. at Aston, Herts. School, Westminster. Matric. 1637. Adm. at Gray's Inn, Feb. 2, 1637–8, as 's. and h. of John, late of Thetchworth, Herts.' Barrister, 1645. Ancient, 1658. Brother of the next, and of John (1628).

GAMON, ROBERT. Adm. pens. (age 13) at SIDNEY, Feb. 1626–7. S. of John (1586). School, Red Cross St, London (Mr Thomas Farnaby). Matric. 1627. Brother of Richard (above) and John (1628).

GAMMON, ROGER. Adm. sizar (age 17) at CAIUS, Apr. 16, 1640. S. of Richard, R. of St Laurence, Norwich. B. there. School, Norwich. Matric. 1640. Brother of John (1625–6) and Richard (1626). (*Venn*, I. 338.)

GAMSON (? GAINSON), WILLIAM. Matric. sizar from CHRIST'S, *c.* 1597.

GAMULL, FRANCIS. Adm. sizar (age 21) at ST JOHN'S, Dec. 23, 1664. S. of Leonard, deceased, of Alton, Staffs. B. there. School, Sedbergh. Matric. 1665; B.A. 1668–9. Perhaps V. of Kirk-Whelpington, Northumberland. Buried there Sept. 30, 1720. (*Staffs. Pedigrees*; H. M. Wood.)

GAMUL, GEORGE. Matric. pens. from TRINITY, Michs. 1598; Scholar, 1602; B.A. 1602–3; M.A. 1606.

GAMULL, STEPHEN. B.A. 1486–7; M.A. 1491.

GANDY, HENRY. M.A. from KING'S, 1735. S. of William, of St Paul's, Exeter. Matric. from St John's College, Oxford, Oct. 13, 1715, age 18; B.A. (Oxford) 1719. Admon. of one of these names (Exeter) 1766. (*Al. Oxon.*)

GANDY, JOHN. Adm. pens. (age 18) at ST JOHN'S, Oct. 26, 1692. S. of William, grocer. B. at Reading, Berks. School, Reading. Previously matric. from St John's College, Oxford, Jan. 23, 1691–2.

GANE, JOHN. Adm. pens. at CLARE, Apr. 9, 1703. S. of Thomas, of Watерslip, Somerset. B. at Deane, Somerset. Matric. 1703; B.A. 1705–6; M.A. 1711. Previously matric. from Hart Hall, Oxford, Apr. 3, 1700, age 16. Probably V. of Turnworth, Dorset, 1727–8. V. of Winterborne Whitchurch, 1728–38. (*Al. Oxon.*; F. S. Hockaday.)

GANGE, ——. D.D. 1463.

GANNING, NATHANIEL. Adm. at CORPUS CHRISTI, 1676. Of Norfolk. Matric. 1676; B.A. 1679–80; M.A. 1683. Ord. deacon (Norwich) Dec. 1681; priest, Dec. 1683. R. of Reymerston; and of Thurston, Norfolk, till 1728. Died 1728. (*Blomefield*, x. 242.)

GANNING, NICHOLAS. Matric. pens. from CORPUS CHRISTI, Easter, 1617. Of Norwich. B.A. 1620–1; M.A. 1624; B.D. 1631. Fellow, 1623–50; ejected, 1654. Ord. deacon (Peterb.) June 4; priest, June 5, 1626. R. of Barnham Broom and Bixton, Norfolk, *c.* 1645. Died 1687. Father of the next.

GANNING, SAMUEL. Adm. at CORPUS CHRISTI, 1666. Of Norfolk. S. of Nicholas (above), R. of Barnham Broom. Matric. Lent, 1667–8; B.A. 1669–70; M.A. 1675. Ord. deacon (Norwich) Sept. 1673; priest, Sept. 1679. R. of Barnham Broom and Bixton, Norfolk, 1680–1708.

GANNING, SAMUEL. Adm. at CORPUS CHRISTI, 1703. Of Norwich. Matric. 1704; B.A. 1707-8; M.A. 1711. Fellow, 1710-9. Ord. deacon (London) Dec. 21, 1712. V. of Swardeston, Norfolk, until 1726. R. of Earsham, 1718-40. Minister of St Peter Mancroft, Norwich. Probably R. of St Laurence, Norwich, 1728-40. R. of Gedney, Lincs. Died Nov. 1740. Will (P.C.C.) 1741. M.I. in St Peter Mancroft.

GANNING, SAMUEL. Adm. at CORPUS CHRISTI, 1715. Of Norwich. Matric. 1715; B.A. 1718-9. Ord. deacon (Norwich) June, 1720; priest, Sept. 1720. R. of Bracon-Ash, Norfolk, 1728-46. Died there 1746. Buried in the chancel.

GANNOCK, EDWARD. Matric. pens. from CORPUS CHRISTI, c. 1596. Of Lincolnshire. Probably s. of Edward, of Skirbeck. Will proved, 1633. (*Lincs. Pedigrees*, 384.)

GANNOCKE, WILLIAM. Matric. sizar from TRINITY, Michs. 1639. Doubtless s. of William, of Sibsey, Lincs. Living, 1647. (*Lincs. Pedigrees*, 384.)

GANNOT, W. Matric. pens. from CLARE, Michs. 1576.

GANSELETT, ——. Matric. sizar from ST JOHN'S, Michs. 1544.

GANT, *see also* **GAUNT.**

GANT or GAUNT, GEORGE. Matric. pens. from CLARE, 1612; B.A. 1615-6; M.A. 1619. Apparently adm. at Corpus Christi, 1619; of Kent. Ord. deacon (Peterb.) Dec. 22; priest, Dec. 23, 1622; of Corpus Christi.

GANT, JONATHAN. Matric. sizar from TRINITY, 1636.

GANTON, ROBERT. Adm. pens. (age 19) at ST JOHN'S, May 17, 1742. S. of William (1698), clerk, of Yorkshire. B. at Hessle. School, Sedbergh. Matric. 1742; B.A. 1745-6 (allowed one term during which he had fought in the King's army against the rebels); M.A. 1749. Ord. deacon (York) May 25, 1746; priest (London) Sept. 20, 1747. C. of Radwinter, Essex, 1747. C. of Saffron Walden, 1759-89. (*Scott-Mayor*, III. 525.)

GANTON, WILLIAM. Adm. pens. (age 13) at SIDNEY, June 4, 1698. S. of Robert, druggist. B. at Hull. School, Hull (Mr Pell). Matric. 1698, as 'John'; B.A. 1701-2; M.A. 1705. Ord. deacon (York) Sept. 1708; priest, 1709. V. of Kirk Ella, Yorks., 1713-22. V. of N. Ferriby, 1718-31. V. of Hessle, 1722-31. Father of Robert (above).

GANTON, ——. M.A. 1456.

GAPE, JOHN. Adm. Fell.-Com. (age 17) at TRINITY, Jan. 18, 1699-1700. S. of John, of St Albans, Herts. School, St Albans (Mr Fothergell). M.P. for St Albans, 1701-13, 1714-5. Died May 7, 1734. Will, P.C.C. Brother of the next. (*G. Mag.*)

GAPE, THOMAS. Adm. Fell.-Com. (age 17) at TRINITY, May 31, 1703. S. of John, of St Albans, Herts., and of Lincoln's Inn. School, Canterbury. Matric. 1703. Adm. at Lincoln's Inn, June 19, 1703. M.P. for St Albans, 1730-2. Died Dec. 11, 1732. Admon. (P.C.C.) 1733. Brother of the above. (*G. Mag.*)

GAPPER, HENRY. Adm. pens. at EMMANUEL, July 10, 1730. Of Somerset. S. and h. of Abraham, of Balsome, Wincanton. Adm. at Lincoln's Inn, Feb. 10, 1729-30. Barrister-at-Law. Died May 15, 1772. M.I. at Wincanton.

GARAWAY, *see* **GARWAY.**

GARBET, SAMUEL. Adm. pens. at EMMANUEL, Feb. 11, 1675-6. Of Salop. Matric. 1675-6; B.A. 1679-80.

GARBRAND, EDWARD. Adm. Fell.-Com. at QUEENS', May 16, 1721. Of London. Matric. 1721.

GARBRAND (*alias* HERKS), JOHN. M.A. 1568 (Incorp. from Oxford). S. of Garbrand Herks, Dutch bookseller, of Oxford. B. there, c. 1542. School, Winchester. B.A. (Oxford) 1563; M.A. 1567; D.D. 1582. Fellow of New College, 1562. Proctor, 1565. Preb. of Salisbury, 1564-89. R. of North Crawley, Bucks., 1566-89. Preb. of Wells, 1571-8. R. of Farthingstone, Northants., 1572. Edited works of his patron, Bishop Jewel. Author, religious. Died at North Crawley, Nov. 17, 1589, aged 47. Will (P.C.C.) 1589. Brass at Crawley. (*Cooper*, II. 64; *D.N.B.*; J. Ch. Smith.)

GARBRAND, THOMAS. Adm. pens. (age 16) at PETERHOUSE, June 30, 1729. Of Jamaica. Perhaps s. of Thomas, of Jamaica, who was B.A. (Oxford) 1704. (*Al. Oxon.*)

GARBSLYE, THOMAS. Adm. Fell.-Com. at EMMANUEL, May 5, 1593.

GARBUT, JAMES. Adm. sizar at SIDNEY, June 3, 1616. B. in Yorkshire. Matric. 1616; B.A. 1619-20; M.A. 1623; B.D. 1630. Fellow. Ord. deacon (Peterb.) Sept. 19; priest, Sept. 20, 1624. Buried at All Saints', Cambridge, Jan. 1, 1648-9. Will proved (V.C.C.).

GARBUT, RICHARD. Adm. sizar at SIDNEY, June 10, 1606. Matric. 1606, as Garbought; B.A. 1609-10; M.A. 1613; B.D. 1620. Fellow. Lecturer of Leeds Parish Church, 1624-31. Died Mar. 7, 1630-1. Will (York) 1631. (M. H. Peacock.)

GARBUT or GARBOT, WILLIAM. Matric. sizar from ST JOHN'S, Michs. 1584; B.A. 1588-9. One of these names a schoolmaster at Kildwick, Yorks., in 1592.

GARDE, GEORGE (*alias* PERCY). B.Can.L. 1486-7. V. of Rainham, Essex, 1482. V. of Ruislip, Middlesex, 1483-92. R. of Ickenham, 1486. R. of Lee, Essex, 1488-1506. R. of Chelsea, 1492. V. of South Benfleet, Essex, till 1506. (*Newcourt*, II. 384.)

GARDEMAN, BALTHAZAR. Incorp. M.A. 1696, from Saumur. B. at 'Pouctiers,' France. V. of Coddenham, Suffolk, 1690-1739. V. of Ashbocking, 1692. Married Lady Catherine Bacon, dau. of the Earl of Sandwich. Died Dec. 19, 1739, aged 84. M.I. at Coddenham. (*E. Angl.*, N.S., IV. 51.)

GARDEN, JAMES. M.A. 1728 (*Com. Reg.*). One of these names R. of Slingsby, Yorks., and V. of Hovingham, about 1745.

GARDINER, BARKELEY. Matric. pens. from PETERHOUSE, Lent, 1577-8. 2nd s. of Thomas, of Coxford Abbey, Norfolk. Adm. at Gray's Inn, Feb. 6, 1582-3. Brother of Humphrey (1575). (*Vis. of Norfolk*; *Vis. of Cambs.*)

GARDNER, CHARLES. Adm. pens. (age 17) at PEMBROKE, Apr. 17, 1679. S. of Thomas, gent. B. in Cheshire. Matric. 1679. Adm. at Gray's Inn, Apr. 28, 1682; 's. and h. of Thomas, of Southley, Cheshire.' Barrister, 1689. Ancient, 1704. Brother of Thomas (1680).

GARDINER, CHARLES. Adm. pens. (age 18) at ST JOHN'S, Sept. 7, 1750. S. of Robert (1720), clerk, of Lincolnshire. B. at Evedon. School, Beverley (Mr Clarke). Matric. 1750

GARDINER, CHRISTOPHER. Adm. Fell.-Com. at SIDNEY, July 8, 1613. Doubtless 1st s. of Christopher, of Dorking, Surrey, and of the Inner Temple. Adm. at the Inner Temple, 1614. Married Elizabeth, dau. of Sir Edward Onslowe, Knt., of Knole, Surrey. Father of Onslow (1637-8) and nephew of Richard (1587).

GARDINER, CHRISTOPHER. B.A. from TRINITY, 1624-5; M.A. 1628.

GARDINER, CHRISTOPHER. Adm. sizar at ST JOHN'S, July 7, 1693. S. of Christopher, painter. B. at Salisbury. School, Charterhouse; exhibitioner, 1693. Matric. 1695; B.A. 1696-7. Ord. priest (London) Mar. 6, 1700-1.

GARDINER, CHRISTOPHER. Adm. pens. at ST CATHARINE'S, Feb. 13, 1696-7.

GARDNER, DANIEL. Matric. pens. from CLARE, Easter, 1561; B.A. 1564-5; M.A. 1568; B.D. 1575. Ord. priest (Ely) May 26, 1566. Canon residentiary of Chichester, 1578. Preacher in Chichester diocese. Will (P.C.C.) 1592.

GARDINER, DANIEL. Matric. pens. from ST CATHARINE'S, Michs. 1642. Of Bedfordshire. S. of Daniel. Bapt. at St Paul's, Bedford, Oct. 4, 1624. B.A. 1644; M.A. 1648. R. of Fincham, Norfolk, 1653. Died 1682.

GARDINER, EDMUND. Matric. pens. from CORPUS CHRISTI, Michs. 1578.

GARDINER, EDMUND. Adm. pens. at CORPUS CHRISTI, 1653. Matric. Easter, 1654. Of Cambridgeshire.

GARDENER, EDMUND. Adm. pens. at TRINITY, Apr. 16, 1661. Matric. 1661; Scholar, 1664; B.A. 1664-5. Doubtless 2nd s. of William, of the City of London, gent.; adm. at Lincoln's Inn, June 22, 1664.

GARDINER, EDMUND. Adm. pens. (age 6) at CHRIST'S, June 9, 1712. S. of Edmund. B. at Stoke Ash, Suffolk. School, Eye (Mr Bridge). Matric. 1712; Scholar, 1713; B.A. 1715-6.

GARDINER, EDWARD. Matric. sizar from PEMBROKE, Michs. 1584.

GARDNER, EDWARD. Matric. pens. from QUEENS', Michs. 1624.

GARDNER, EDWARD. M.A. from ST CATHARINE'S, 1715. S. of Edward, of Oxford, clerk. Matric. from University College, Oxford, Mar. 28, 1707, age 16; B.A. (Brasenose) 1710. (*Al. Oxon.*)

GARDINER, FRANCIS. Matric. pens. from TRINITY, Easter, 1560. One of these names, of Suffolk, adm. at Lincoln's Inn, Aug. 4, 1566.

GARDYNER, FRANCIS. Matric. sizar from TRINITY, Lent, 1593-4; B.A. 1597-8; M.A. 1601; B.D. 1608. Fellow, 1599. R. of Girton, Cambs., 1609. V. of Kendal, Westmorland, 1627-40.

GARDINER, FRANCIS. Adm. pens. at CAIUS, Oct. 27, 1618, from St John's College, Oxford. S. of Christopher, of Tinhead, Wilts., gent. B. at Edmondsham, Dorset. School, London (Mr Tho. Farnaby). Matric. 1618; B.A. 1619-20; M.A. 1623. Incorp. at Oxford, 1623. Adm. at the Middle Temple, Oct. 27, 1624. (*Venn*, I. 242.)

GARDINER, FRANCIS. Adm. pens. at QUEENS', Jan. 14, 1662-3. Of Wiltshire. Matric. 1663; B.A. 1666-7; M.A. 1670. Ord. deacon (Ely) Dec. 18, 1669; priest, Sept. 24, 1670. R. of Wickham St Paul, Essex, 1672. V. of Acton, Suffolk, 1690-1700.

GARDINER, FRANCIS. Adm. at CORPUS CHRISTI, 1697. Of Norwich. Matric. Easter, 1698; B.A. 1701-2; M.A. 1705. Ord. deacon (Norwich) Sept. 1703. Doubtless R. of Antingham, Norfolk, 1705-10; and R. of Bradfield, 1709-16.

GARDINER, GEORGE. Matric. pens. from CHRIST'S, Michs. 1552. B. at Berwick-on-Tweed. S. of George (Cuthbert). B.A. 1554-5; M.A. from Queens', 1558; B.D. 1565; D.D. 1569. Fellow of Queens', 1557-61. Ord. priest (London) Mar. 1557-8. Chancellor of diocese of Norwich, 1558-79. Preb. of Norwich, 1565; Archdeacon, 1573; Dean, 1573. R. of West Stow, Suffolk, 1566-72. R. of St Martin, Outwich, London, 1572-4. R. of St Michael, Bassishaw, 1572. Chaplain to the Queen, 1573. V. of Swaffham, Norfolk, 1575. R. of Badingham, Suffolk, 1575-6. R. of Heylesdon, Norfolk, 1579. R. of Blofield, 1580. R. of Ashill, 1583. R. of Forncet, 1584. Admon. (Norwich Cons. C.) 1589. Buried in Norwich Cathedral. Brother of German (1561). (*Cooper*, II. 55; *D.N.B.*)

GARDINER, GEORGE. Matric. pens. from MAGDALENE, c. 1594; B.A. from Caius, 1598-9; M.A. from Magdalene, 1602. One of these names R. of Gunton, Suffolk, 1639.

GARDINER, GERMAN. Probably of TRINITY HALL. Cousin and secretary of Stephen Gardiner, Bishop of Winchester. A zealous Romanist. Convicted of denying the King's supremacy: executed at Tyburn, Mar. 7, 1543-4. (*Cooper*, I. 83.)

GARDINER, GERMAN. Adm. (age 21) at CAIUS, Nov. 14, 1561. S. of Cuthbert, gent. Of Berwick-on-Tweed. School, Durham. R. of Thorpe, Norfolk, 1569-86. R. of Kirby Kane, 1570-1. R. of St Simon and St Jude, Norwich, 1579-82. R. of Beighton, Suffolk, 1583. V. of Eglingham, Northumberland, 1587-90. Brother of George (1552). (*Venn*, I. 47.)

GARDINER, GODFREY. Adm. at CORPUS CHRISTI, 1681. Of Derbyshire. Matric. 1681; B.A. 1684-5; M.A. 1688. Ord. priest (Lincoln) Dec. 23, 1683. R. of Walkern, Herts., 1686-1722. Married Deborah Willymot, of Kelshall. Died 1722. Father of Willimot (1712).

GARDYNER, HENRY. Matric. pens. from ST JOHN'S, Michs. 1550. One of these names adm. at Lincoln's Inn, Oct. 13, 1555.

GARDENER, HENRY. Matric. pens. from ST JOHN'S, c. 1595.

GARDINER, HENRY. Adm. sizar (age 15) at CAIUS, May 19, 1599. S. of William, citizen of Norwich. School, Norwich. Matric. 1599; Scholar, 1599-1605; B.A. 1602-3; M.A. 1606. Perhaps V. of Elmdon, Essex, till 1645, when he died.

GARDNER, HENRY. Adm. sizar at JESUS, May 11, 1621. Matric. 1621; Scholar, 1624; B.A. 1624-5; M.A. 1628. Ord. deacon (Peterb.) Dec. 18; priest, Dec. 19, 1625. V. of Welford, Northants., 1630.

GARDNER, HENRY. Adm. Fell.-Com. (age 16) at CHRIST'S, June 27, 1646. S. of Henry, of Jenningsbury, Herts. B. at Hertford. School, Hertford (Mr Minors). Matric. 1646. Died 1646. (*Vis. of Herts.*, 1634; *Clutterbuck*, II. 183.)

GARDINER, HENRY. Adm. pens. (age 17) at SIDNEY, Mar. 30, 1709. S. of Thomas. B. at Little Baddow, Essex. School, Bishop's Stortford (Mr Tooke). Matric. 1710; B.A. 1712-3; M.A. 1716. Ord. deacon (London) Dec. 21, 1718; priest, Feb. 22, 1718-9. R. of Woodham Ferrers, Essex, 1718-36. Died 1736. (*Morant*, I. 412.)

GARDINER, HUMPHREY. Matric. pens. from QUEENS', Michs. 1575; M.A. 1615 (on King's visit). Doubtless s. and h. of Thomas, of Coxford Abbey, Norfolk. Of Histon, Cambs., Esq. Brother of Barkeley (1577-8). (*Vis. of Norfolk*; *Vis. of Cambs.*)

GARDINER, HUMPHREY. M.A. 1635-6 (*Lit. Reg.*). One of these names, of Co. Cambs., married, at Canterbury Cathedral, Jan. 18, 1640-1, Helen Wyld, of the Archbishop's Palace.

GARDINER, HUMPHRE. Adm. pens. (age 14) at CHRIST'S, July 5, 1660. S. of Humphry, gent. B. at Histon, Cambs. School, Newark. Matric. 1661; B.A. 1663; M.A. from Magdalene, 1667. Fellow of Magdalene, 1664.

GARDINER, JAMES. Adm. pens. (age 17) at ST JOHN'S, Apr. 19, 1637. S. of Edward, Esq., of Wadesmill, Herts. B. at Thundridgebury, Herts. School, Hertford. Matric. 1637. Afterwards Fell.-Com. (*Vis. of Herts.*, 1634.)

GARDINER, JAMES. Adm. pens. at EMMANUEL, May 9, 1649, as Garner. S. of Adrian, of Nottingham, apothecary. Matric. 1649; B.A. 1652-3; M.A. 1656; D.D. 1669. Incorp. at Oxford, 1665. Chaplain to the Duke of Monmouth. Preb. of Lincoln, 1661-98; and of Salisbury, 1666-71. R. of Epworth, Lincs., 1668. Sub-dean of Lincoln, 1671-95. Bishop of Lincoln, 1695-1705. Antiquary. Died Mar. 1, 1704-5, aged 68. Will (Dean and Chapter of Westminster) 1705. Father of James (1695) and William (1698). Perhaps brother of Joseph (1649). (*Al. Oxon.*; *D.N.B.*; Le Neve, *Mon.*, II. 77.)

GARDINER, JAMES. Adm. sizar at EMMANUEL, Oct. 10, 1683. Of Nottinghamshire.

GARDINER, JAMES. Adm. pens. at EMMANUEL, Nov. 7, 1695. S. of James (1649), Bishop of Lincoln. School, Westminster. Matric. 1695; B.A. 1699-1700; M.A. from Jesus, 1702. Fellow of Jesus, 1700-5. Incorp. at Oxford, 1703. Ord. deacon (Lincoln) May 31, 1702. Preb. of Lincoln, 1704-32. Master of St John's Hospital, Northampton, 1704; and of Bedford Hospital, Nottingham. Sub-dean of Lincoln, 1704-32. Author, *Sermons*. Died Mar. 24, 1731-2. Buried in Lincoln Cathedral. Brother of William (1698). (*D.N.B.*) According to *Hennessy* he was R. of St Michael, Crooked Lane, London, 1690-1723. Died 1723.

GARDENER, JEREMY. Matric. Fell.-Com. from EMMANUEL, Easter, 1589. Doubtless Jerome Gardiner, s. of Thomas, of St Peter's, Cornhill, London. Bapt. there. Adm. at Gray's Inn, May 30, 1592. Buried at St Peter's, Cornhill, Feb. 5, 1640-1. Will (P.C.C.) 1641. (J. Ch. Smith.)

GARDENER, JOHN. Matric. sizar from JESUS, Michs. 1559.

GARDYNER, JOHN. Matric. pens. from CHRIST'S, Oct. 1567. Doubtless s. of Henry, of Thundridge, Herts. One of these names (of Bucks.) adm. at Lincoln's Inn, Oct. 27, 1568. Brother of Michael (1569). (*Peile*, I. 102.)

GARDINER, JOHN. Scholar of TRINITY HALL, 1571; LL.B. 1576; LL.D. 1583. Fellow, 1574-84. Adm. advocate, Oct. 3, 1590. Will (P.C.C.) 1594; of Hertford. (*Cooper*, II. 98.)

GARDINER, JOHN. Adm. at CORPUS CHRISTI; perhaps 1579. Minister at Malden, Essex; silenced and imprisoned for non-conformity, c. 1586. (*Cooper*, II. 10.)

GARDINER, JOHN. Matric. pens. from PETERHOUSE, Lent, 1582-3.

GARDINER, JOHN. Adm. pens. (age 18) at CAIUS, Sept. 22, 1604. S. of William, gent., of Badingham, Suffolk. School, Stradbroke (Mr Clayton). Matric. 1604-5; Scholar, 1605-8. Adm. at Gray's Inn, May 26, 1609.

GARDNER, JOHN. B.A. 1632 (Incorp. from Oxford). Probably B.A. from Magdalen College, Oxford, 1622. R. of Hardwick, Cambs., 1630. One of these names R. of Mursley, Bucks., 1644-82. Buried there Mar. 4, 1682. One was R. of Farnham Royal, Bucks., 1658-60, ejected. (*Lipscomb*, III.)

GARDINER, JOHN. Matric. pens. from CORPUS CHRISTI, Easter, 1647. Of Hertfordshire. B.A. 1649-50; M.A. 1653; B.D. 1661; D.D. 1666. Fellow, 1650-63. Junior Proctor, 1659-60. Incorp. at Oxford, 1661. R. of St Mary Abchurch and St Laurence Pountney, London, 1661-81. R. of Cottered, Herts., 1662-81. Died there 1681.

GARDINER, JOHN. Adm. sizar (age 16) at CAIUS, Apr. 10, 1660. S. of Edward, tailor. B. at Glemsford, Suffolk. Bapt. there, May 23, 1641. School, Bury. Scholar, 1660-3; Matric. 1661. Adm. at Lincoln's Inn, Feb. 17, 1675-6, as s. and h. of Edmund, of Glemsford. (*Venn*, I. 408.)

GARDINER, JOHN. Adm. Fell.-Com. at QUEENS', Feb. 12, 1661-2. Of Hertfordshire. Doubtless s. of Edward, of Thundridge, Herts. Bapt. there, Mar. 16, 1642-3. Matric. 1663. Died Oct. 29, 1693. (*Clutterbuck*, III. 279.)

GARDINER, JOHN. Adm. pens. (age 15) at SIDNEY, May 31, 1675. Only s. of John, late R. of Bridgewater, Somerset (ejected, 1662). B. at Staplegrove, Somerset. School, Staplegrove.

GARDNER, JOHN. M.A. 1676 (Incorp. from Lincoln College, Oxford). S. of John, of Guilsborough, Northants. Matric. (Oxford) Apr. 2, 1669, age 18; B.A. 1672; M.A. 1675. One of these names signs as minister of Little Staughton, Beds., 1694-7. (*Al. Oxon.*)

GARDINER, JOHN. Adm. pens. at ST CATHARINE'S, Apr. 19, 1686.

GARDNER, JOHN. Adm. pens. (age 18) at TRINITY, June 25, 1686. S. of Samuel. B. at Buckland, Glouc. School, Westminster. Matric. 1686; Scholar, 1687; B.A. 1689-90.

GARDNER, JOHN. Adm. sizar at ST CATHARINE'S, Sept. 16, 1718; afterwards pensioner. Of Aldborough, Suffolk. Matric. 1720; LL.B. 1724; LL.D. 1731. Ord. deacon (Norwich) Sept. 1724; priest, June, 1726. R. of Little Moulton, Norfolk, 1725. V. of Hickling, 1728-30. R. of Brunstead, 1729. R. of Gt Massingham. R. of St Giles'; and P.C. of St Gregory, Norwich, 1731-71, as 'D.D.' Died Nov. 15, 1770. Father of Richard (1741-2). (*G. Mag.*)

GARDNER, JOSEPH. Adm. pens. at EMMANUEL, May 9, 1649. Of Nottinghamshire. Doubtless s. of Adrian, apothecary, of Nottingham. Matric. 1649; M.B. 1654; M.D. 1659. Practised physic at Nottingham. Buried at St Mary's, Nottingham, Mar. 5, 1669-70. M.I. there. Brother of James (1649).

GARDINER, LAURENCE. Adm. pens. (age 16) at PETERHOUSE, July 1, 1700. Of Salop. School, Shrewsbury. Matric. 1700; Scholar, 1700; B.A. 1703–4; M.A. 1707. Preb. of Lichfield, 1720. R. of Coppenhall, Cheshire, 1721–50. Died 1750.

GARDINER, MICHAEL. Matric. pens. from CHRIST'S, Nov. 1569. S. of Henry, of Thundridge, Herts. B.A. 1573–4; M.A. 1577. Fellow, 1574–83. R. of Littlebury, Essex, 1583–1618; of Gt Greenford, Middlesex, 1584–1630. Buried Aug. 24, 1630. Will (P.C.C.) 1630. Brother of John (1567), grandfather of the next. (*Peile*, I. 112; *Vis. of Herts.*, 1634.)

GARDINER, MICHAEL. Adm. pens. at TRINITY, June 1, 1652. Of Middlesex. School, Westminster. Scholar, 1652; B.A. 1655–6. Doubtless s. and h. of Michael, citizen and vintner, of London, deceased; adm. at the Inner Temple, 1651. Barrister, 1659. (Le Neve, *Knights*.)

GARDYNER, ONSLOW. Adm. Fell.-Com. (age 16) at SIDNEY, Mar. 14, 1637–8. S. of Christopher (1613), Esq., of Haling, Croydon, Surrey. School, Croydon (Mr John Webbe). Matric. 1637–8. Married Susan, dau. of Sir John Ogle, Knt. (*Vis. of Surrey*, 1623.)

GARDINER, PETER. Adm. at CORPUS CHRISTI, 1594. Of Essex.

GARDNER, PHILIP. Adm. pens. (age 16) at ST JOHN'S, July 7, 1647. S. of Francis, Esq., of Cheshunt, Herts. B. there. Matric. 1647.

GARDINER, RALPH. B.Can.L. 1524–5.

GARDINER, RICHARD. Matric. Fell.-Com. from PETERHOUSE, Michs. 1564; B.A. 1564–5; M.A. 1568. Perhaps R. of St Mary, Whitechapel, 1570–1617. Died 1617, aged 76. Will (P.C.C.) 1617.

GARDINER, RICHARD. Matric. pens. from TRINITY, Easter, 1587. Doubtless s. of William, of Bermondsey, Surrey; adm. at the Inner Temple, 1587. Probably brother of William (1588–9) and uncle of Christopher (1613).

GARDINER, RICHARD. M.A. 1620 (Incorp. from Oxford). Of Christ Church, 1607. Matric. 1610; B.A. 1611; M.A. 1614; B.D. and D.D. 1630. Canon of Christ Church, 1629–48 and 1660. Chaplain to Charles I, 1630. V. of Flore, Northants., 1632–46, sequestered. R. of Westwell, Oxon., 1632. Died Dec. 20, 1670, aged 79. Buried in Christ Church Cathedral, Dec. 22. (*Al. Oxon.*; *D.N.B.*)

GARDINER, RICHARD. Adm. sizar at ST CATHARINE'S, Jan. 15, 1741–2; afterwards pensioner. S. of Dr John Gardiner (1718). Bapt. at Saffron Walden, Essex, Oct. 3, 1724. School, Eton (colleger). Matric. 1742. Travelled abroad. Returned to England, 1748. Took Holy Orders, but resigned clerical functions in 1751. Entered the army and served abroad. Finally settled at Ingoldisthorpe, Norfolk. Author of *The History of Pudisa*, in which the character named 'Dick Merryfellow' was intended for himself. Died Sept. 11, 1781. Buried at Ingoldisthorpe. (*D.N.B.*)

GARDINER, ROBERT. Adm. at KING'S (age 18) a scholar from Eton, Aug. 24, 1580. Of Cambridge. Matric. 1580; B.A. 1584–5; M.A. 1588. Fellow, 1583–92.

GARDINER, ROBERT. Matric. Fell.-Com. from KING'S, Lent, 1623–4; B.A. 1626–7. Doubtless s. and h. of Thomas, of Shimpling, Suffolk, gent.; adm. at Lincoln's Inn, May 11, 1628.

GARDINER, ROBERT. Adm. Fell.-Com. (age 13) at SIDNEY, Apr. 25, 1632. S. of Jeremy, Esq., of Stratford-le-Bow. B. at Hawstead, Essex. School, Isleworth (Mr Thomas Willis). Matric. 1632. Adm. at Gray's Inn, Apr. 16, 1634.

GARDINER, ROBERT. M.A. from CHRIST'S, 1672. S. of Richard, of Kellet, Lancs. Matric. from Queen's College, Oxford, Mar. 18, 1664–5, age 17; B.A. (Oxford) 1668. One of these names R. of Ridley, Kent, till 1688. Died Aug. 8, 1688, aged 39. Buried at Crayford. M.I. (*Al. Oxon.*; *Peile*, II. 1.)

GARDINER, ROBERT. Adm. pens. (age 17) at ST JOHN'S, Oct. 5, 1720. S. of Robert, gent., of Lincolnshire. B. at Sleaford. School, Lincoln. Matric. 1720; B.A. 1726–7 (according to the *Graduati*). Ord. deacon (Lincoln) June 5, 1726; priest, Sept. 22, 1728 (described as LL.B.). R. of Brauncewell and Anwick, Lincs., 1730–60. R. of Stubton, 1733–60. R. of Washingborough, 1760–3. Died May 7, 1763. Perhaps father of Charles (1750). (*Scott-Mayor*, III. 336.)

GARDINER, SAMUEL. Adm. at KING'S (age 17) a scholar from Eton, Sept. 4, 1581. Of Norwich. Matric. 1581; B.A. 1585–6; M.A. 1589; B.D. 1596; D.D. 1601. Fellow, 1584–8. R. of Rainham, Norfolk, 1581. V. of Ormesby, 1588–1631. R. of Gt Dunham, 1599–1616. Lecturer at St Peter Mancroft, Norwich, 1620–32. Father of Thomas (1611). Possibly the author of *A Book of Angling*, *The Scourge of Sacriledge*, and other theological works, of whom the *D.N.B.* says that nothing is known but that he was D.D. and chaplain to Abp. Abbot. (*Harwood*.)

GARDINER, SAMUEL. Adm. at CORPUS CHRISTI, 1624; B.A. 1627–8; M.A. 1631. Ord. deacon (Norwich) Dec. 22, 1633; priest, Sept. 22, 1638. R. of Winfarthing, Norfolk, 1643. R. of Reepham and Kerdiston, till 1672. Died Mar. 16, 1671–2, aged 65. M.I. at Reepham. (Le Neve, *Mon.*, III. 95.)

GARDINER, SAMUEL. Adm. at CORPUS CHRISTI, 1636. Of London. B.A. 1639–40; M.A. 1643; D.D. 1657. Fellow, 1642–50. Junior Proctor, 1649. Ord. deacon (Lincoln) Sept. 22, 1644. R. of Eckington, Derbs., 1650–86. Preb. of Lichfield, 1666–86. Author. Died Mar. 8, 1685–6, aged 66. Father of the next. (*F.M.G.*, 840; *Masters*.)

GARDINER, SAMUEL. Adm. at CORPUS CHRISTI, 1671. S. of Samuel (above), D.D. B. at Eckington, Derbs. Matric. Easter, 1671; B.A. 1674–5; M.A. 1678. Fellow, 1675–80. Succeeded his father as R. of Eckington, Derbs., 1686–1721. Preb. of Lichfield, 1701–21. Married Elizabeth, dau. of William Revel, of Ogston. Died 1721. Buried at Eckington. Father of William (1707). (*F.M.G.*, 840; *Masters*.)

GARDINER, SAMUEL. Adm. sizar at EMMANUEL, Mar. 29, 1676. Of Nottinghamshire.

GARDNER, SAMUEL. D.D. 1682 (*Lit. Reg.*). Matric. from Christ Church, Oxford, Feb. 23, 1653–4; B.A. (Oxford) 1653–4; M.A. 1656. Perhaps R. of Walkern, Herts., 1679–86. (*Al. Oxon.*; *Clutterbuck*, II. 468.)

GARDENER, SILVESTER. Adm. at KING'S (age 18) a scholar from Eton, Aug. 13, 1533. Of Maidenhead, Berks. B.A. 1537–8. Fellow, 1536–9. Probably brother of Thomas (1542).

GARDINER, STEPHEN. Of TRINITY HALL. S. of John, of Bury St Edmunds (clothworker; will at Bury, 1506). B. *c.* 1495 (*Cooper*). B.Civ.L. 1517–8; D.Civ.L. 1520; D.Can.L. 1521. Incorp. at Oxford, 1531. Secretary to Wolsey, and chaplain to the King. Master of Trinity Hall, 1525–49. Chancellor of the University, 1539, and again, 1553–6. Archdeacon of Norfolk, 1529–31; of Leicester, 1531. Much employed by the King in the matter of the divorce. Bishop of Winchester, 1531–51 and 1553–5. Deprived of his offices, and imprisoned under Edward VI, 1551. Liberated and restored to his bishoprick under Mary. Lord Chancellor, 1553–5. Adm. at Gray's Inn, 1555. Died Nov. 12, 1555. Will (P.C.C.) (*Cooper*, I. 139; *D.N.B.*; *College History of Trinity Hall*.)

GARDINER, STEPHEN. Matric. sizar from CLARE, Michs. 1581.

GARDINER, STEPHEN. Adm. pens. (age 14) at CAIUS, May 19, 1681. S. of Francis, citizen of Norwich. B. at Mendham, Suffolk. School, Norwich. Matric. 1681; Scholar, 1681–4. Adm. at the Middle Temple, May 6, 1684. Of Mendham, Esq. Recorder of Norwich, 1703–27. Died June 7, 1727. Perhaps father of the next. (*Venn*, I. 467.)

GARDINER, STEPHEN. Adm. scholar at TRINITY HALL, Jan. 6, 1725–6. Perhaps s. of Stephen (above), of Norwich. Matric. 1725. Died Sept. 27, 1768.

GARDINER, THOMAS. Student at Cambridge, *c.* 1500. A monk from Westminster Abbey. Prior of Blythe, 1507–11. Returned to Westminster. Resident till *c.* 1530. (Pearce, *Monks of Westminster*.)

GARDINER, THOMAS. Adm. at KING'S (age 16) a scholar from Eton, Aug. 13, 1542. Of Maidenhead, Berks. Matric. 1544; B.A. 1546–7; M.A. 1550. Fellow, 1545–55. Proctor, 1553–4. Public Orator, 1554–7. M.P. for Midhurst, 1557. Died 1585, after several years' imprisonment for debt. Probably brother of Silvester. (*Cooper*, I. 515.)

GARDINER, THOMAS. Matric. Fell.-Com. from PETERHOUSE, Michs. 1581. Probably s. of William, of Peckham, Surrey. Knighted, 1603. (*T. A. Walker*.)

GARDNER, THOMAS. Adm. Fell.-Com. at EMMANUEL, Mar. 22, 1587–8. Matric. 1588.

GARDNER, THOMAS. Matric. sizar from PETERHOUSE, Easter, 1587; B.A. 1590–1; M.A. 1594. Perhaps V. of Elmdon, Essex, 1602. Will (Archd. Colchester) 1646; of Elmdon, clerk.

GARDINER, THOMAS. Matric. pens. from MAGDALENE, *c.* 1589.

GARDINER or GARNER, THOMAS. M.A. 1608 (Incorp. from Oxford). B.A. (Magdalen Hall, Oxford) 1603; M.A. (Magdalen College) 1608.

GARDINER, THOMAS. Adm. pens. (age 16) at CAIUS, July 8, 1611. S. of Samuel (1581), D.D., R. of Gt Rainham, Norfolk. B. at South Walsham. School, Norwich. Matric. 1611; Scholar, 1611–4; B.A. 1618–9; M.A. 1622. One of these names ord. priest (Peterb.) July 22, 1619. R. of Shereford, Norfolk, 1624. Probably R. of Cottered, Herts., 1627–62. Licensed as Presbyterian minister in 1672. (*Venn*, I. 214.)

GARDINER, THOMAS. Matric. sizar from CLARE, Easter, 1613; B.A. 1616–7; M.A. 1620. Ord. deacon (Peterb.) June 11; priest, June 12, 1620. One of these names V. of Sutton-on-the-Forest, Yorks., 1635–52.

GARDINER, THOMAS. Adm. pens. at EMMANUEL, Jan. 23, 1612-3. B. in St Botolph's, Aldersgate Street. Matric. 1613; B.A. 1616-7; M.A. 1620. Ord. priest (London) Sept. 24, 1620, age 24. One of these names V. of St Mary, Sandwich, Kent, 1624-35. Died 1635.

GARDINER, THOMAS. Matric. sizar from SR JOHN'S, Easter, 1615; B.A. 1618-9; M.A. 1622.

GARDINER, THOMAS. Matric. pens. from PEMBROKE, Easter, 1615; B.A. 1618-9; M.A. 1622.

GARDINER, THOMAS. Adm. Fell.-Com. at EMMANUEL, July 11, 1646. Of Essex. Doubtless s. and h. of Francis, of Tollesbury; adm. at Gray's Inn, June 26, 1648. Knighted, 1660. Married Jane, dau. of Sir Robert Kempe.

GARDINER, THOMAS. Adm. pens. (age 15) at PETERHOUSE, Oct. 18, 1678. Of Bedfordshire. School, Potton, Beds. Matric. 1679; Scholar, 1679; B.A. 1683-4; M.A. 1687. Fellow, 1685-1704. Barrister-at-Law. Buried at Little St Mary's, Cambridge, Mar. 6, 1703-4. Will proved (V.C.C.). (*T. A. Walker*, 163.)

GARDNER, THOMAS. Adm. pens. at ST CATHARINE'S, July 2, 1680. S. of Thomas, gent. B. in Cheshire. Migrated to Pembroke, June 30, 1681. Matric. 1681; B.A. 1683-4; M.A. 1687. Brother of Charles (1679).

GARDINER, THOMAS. Adm. pens. (age 17) at SR JOHN'S, June 30, 1682. S. of Thomas, gent. B. at Bristol, Gloucs. School, Lewisham, Kent (Mr Newman). Matric. 1682; B.A. 1685-6; M.A. 1690. Fellow, 1688-1705.

GARDNER, THOMAS. Adm. pens. (age 16) at SIDNEY, June 8, 1697. 1st s. of John, gent., of Sansaw, Salop. B. at Drayton, Salop. Schools, Wem (Mr Williams) and Shrewsbury (Mr Lloyd). Adm. at the Inner Temple, Dec. 2, 1698. Probably succeeded his father at Sansaw.

GARDNER, W. Matric. sizar from PEMBROKE, Michs. 1558.

GARDINER, W. Matric. pens. from TRINITY, Easter, 1560.

GARDINER, WALTER. Scholar of TRINITY, 1548; B.A. 1551-2; M.A. 1555. Fellow, 1553.

GARDINER, WALTER. Adm. Fell.-Com. at KING'S, Michs. 1575.

GARDNER, WILLIAM. Matric. pens. from TRINITY, Lent, 1588-9. Probably s. of William, of Bermondsey, Surrey; adm. at the Inner Temple, 1591. M.P. for Lostwithiel, 1588-9; for Helston, 1592-3. Knighted, May 13, 1603. Died Feb. 16, 1621. Buried at Godstone, Surrey. Will (P.C.C.) 1622. Brother of Richard (1587).

GARDINER, WILLIAM. Matric. pens. from TRINITY, Michs. 1602. Migrated to Oxford, after keeping seven terms. B.A. from St John's College, Oxford, 1611; M.A. 1613-4. (*Al. Oxon.*)

GARDINER, WILLIAM. Adm. pens. at EMMANUEL, July 7, 1656. Of Cheshire. Matric. 1656; B.A. 1659-60. One of these names V. of Eccleshall, and minister at Sheffield, Yorks., 1662-89.

GARDINER, WILLIAM. Adm. pens. at EMMANUEL, Oct. 17, 1696. Of Middlesex. Matric. 1698.

GARDINER, WILLIAM. Adm. scholar at TRINITY HALL, Feb. 6, 1698-9. S. of James (1649), Bishop of Lincoln. LL.B. 1702. Preb. of Lincoln, 1705-50. V. of Hambledon, Rutland, 1709-50. Brother of James (1695).

GARDINER, WILLIAM. Adm. sizar at QUEENS', Jan. 5, 1699-1700. Of Essex. Matric. 1700; B.A. 1703-4.

GARDINER, WILLIAM. Adm. pens. at CHRIST'S, 1707. Matric. Michs. 1707. Resided till Christmas, 1708. Perhaps adm. at the Middle Temple, Dec. 20, 1709; and at the Inner Temple, Nov. 26, 1713, as 's. of William of Pishiobury, Herts.' (*Peile*, II. 167.)

GARDINER, WILLIAM. Adm. at CORPUS CHRISTI, 1707. Of Derbyshire. Doubtless s. of Samuel (1671). Matric. Michs. 1707; B.A. 1711-2; M.A. 1715. V. of Scarcliffe, Derbs. V. of Ault Hucknall. Died 1765, aged 75. (*F.M.G.*, 840.)

GARDINER, WILLIAM. Adm. at CORPUS CHRISTI, 1707. Of London.

GARDINER, WILLIMOT. Adm. at CORPUS CHRISTI, 1712. Of Hertfordshire. S. of Godfrey (1681), R. of Walkern. Colleger at Eton, 1706-10. Matric. Lent, 1713-4; B.A. 1715-6; M.A. 1719. Ord. deacon (Lincoln) Mar. 1717-8; priest, May 25, 1719. C. of Walkern, Herts.

GARDNER, ——. B.A. 1473; M.A. 1478.

GARDNER, ——. D.D. 1476-7.

GARDINER, ——. Pens. at PETERHOUSE, 1605-6.

GARDINER, ——. Matric. pens. from PEMBROKE, Easter, 1623.

GARDNER, ——. Adm. pens. at SR CATHARINE'S, June 16, 1672.

GARDUM, JOHN. Adm. sizar (age 18) at PETERHOUSE, Oct. 10, 1651. Of Derbyshire. School, Baslow (Barslovencis), Derbs.

GARE, JOHN. M.A. when ord. deacon (Ely) Dec. 21, 1420; priest, May 17, 1421. Of Yorkshire.

GARENCIERES, DUDLEY. Adm. pens. at TRINITY, June 28, 1669. Matric. 1669; Scholar, 1670; B.A. 1672-3; M.A. 1676. Incorp. at Oxford, 1676. R. of Handley, Cheshire, 1684-1702. Preb. of Chester, 1696. R. of Waverton, 1696-1702. Died Apr. 8, 1702. Buried in Chester Cathedral. (*Al. Westmon.*, 169.)

GARESEED, JAMES, *see* GARTHSIDE.

GAREY, *see also* GEARY.

GARY or GEARY, BENJAMIN. Adm. sizar (age 17) at CAIUS, July 5, 1652. S. of Thomas, of Bedingfield, Suffolk. B. there. School, Eye (Mr Browne). Matric. 1653; Scholar, 1655-8; B.A. 1655-6; M.A. 1659.

GAREY, NATHANIEL. Matric. sizar from TRINITY, Michs. 1602; B.A. 1606-7. Ord. deacon (Norwich) Dec. 18, 1608, age 23; priest, June 11, 1609. C. of Easton Bavent, Suffolk. Will of one of these names (P.C.C.) 1655, of St Michael Coslany, Norwich, clerk.

GAREY, SAMUEL. Adm. pens. (age 15) at CAIUS, July 4, 1598. S. of Christopher, minister. B. at Wicklewood, Norfolk. School, Kimberley (Mr Rosier). Matric. 1598; Scholar of Trinity Hall, 1600; LL.B. from Trinity Hall, 1606. Ord. deacon (Norwich) Sept. 21, 1605; priest, Sept. 18, 1607. R. of St Peter's, Denver, 1608-17; of Easton Bavent, Suffolk, 1608-20; of Winfarthing, 1610-21; and of Icklingham St James, 1621-46. Preb. of Norwich, 1620-46. Author, *Sermons*. Buried in Norwich Cathedral, Aug. 25, 1646. Father of the next. (*Venn*, I. 166.)

GAREY, SAMUEL. Adm. pens. (age 16) at CORPUS CHRISTI, J 6, 1646, as 'Carey.' S. of Samuel (above), minister, of Norfolk. B. in Norwich. Migrated to Caius, Sept. 19, 1646. Matric. 1646; Scholar, 1646-9.

GAREY or GEARY, THOMAS. Adm. sizar at PETERHOUSE, Nov. 30, 1611. Matric. 1612; Scholar; B.A. 1616-7; M.A. 1620. Ord. deacon (Peterb.) Sept. 23; priest, Sept. 24, 1621. Of Bedingfield, Suffolk, in 1633.

GARFIELD, ABRAHAM. B.A. from ST CATHARINE'S, 1612. S. of Ralph, of Kilsby, Northants., Esq., citizen and dyer, of London. Will (P.C.C.) 1616; of Cambridge University. (*Vis. of Midds.*, 1663.)

GARFIELD, JOHN. Matric. sizar from JESUS, Easter, 1615. B. in St Olave's, Southwark. School, St Paul's. Scholar, 1618; B.A. 1618-9; M.A. 1622. Ord. deacon (London) Dec. 23, 1621, age 23; priest (York) Sept. 1623. V. of Tickhill, Yorks., 1623-65. Died 1665.

GARFIELD, THOMAS. Matric. sizar from TRINITY, Easter, 1618; Scholar, 1619.

GARFIELD, WILLIAM. Matric. sizar from CHRIST'S, Easter, 1576; B.A. 1579-80; M.A. 1583. Ord. deacon (London) Dec. 21, 1582; priest (Lincoln) Mar. 26, 1583. R. of Denton, Hunts., 1591-1624. R. of Sawtry St Andrew's, 1592-1624. Died 1624. (*Peile*, I. 136.)

GARFIELD, WILLIAM. Matric. sizar from TRINITY, Easter, 1620; B.A. 1623-4; M.A. 1627. Ord. deacon (Peterb.) Sept. 19; priest, Sept. 20, 1624.

GARFOOTE, THOMAS. Matric. pens. from TRINITY, Easter, 1629. S. and h. of William, of Ingatestone, Essex. Scholar, 1631. Adm. at the Inner Temple, 1630. Barrister, 1639. Brother of William (1629). (*Vis. of Essex*, 1634.)

GARFOOT, THOMAS. Adm. pens. at TRINITY, Apr. 18, 1659. (? s. of the above.) Matric. 1660. Perhaps of the Middle Temple, gent. Will (P.C.C.) 1686.

GARFOOTE, WILLIAM. Matric. pens. from TRINITY, Easter, 1629. 2nd s. of William, of Ingatestone, Essex. Adm. at the Inner Temple, 1632. Will (P.C.C.) 1682. Brother of Thomas (1629).

GARFORTH, DIONYSIUS. Matric. sizar from QUEENS', Michs. 1568. R. of Folkton, Yorks., 1589-1620. Died 1620.

GARFORTHE or GARFOOT, EDMUND. Adm. sizar (age 17) at SR JOHN'S, May 8, 1648. S. of William, yeoman, of Steeton Hall, Yorks. B. there. School, Bingley (Mr Watkins). Matric. 1648; B.A. 1651-2; M.A. 1660. V. of Haworth, Yorks., 1654-5. V. of Gargrave, 1660-73. V. of Lancaster, 1672-82. Buried there Jan. 8, 1681-2.

GARFORTH, THOMAS. Adm. sizar (age 17) at SR JOHN'S, June 19, 1668. S. of Matthew, of 'Holden' (? Holdenclough), near Dewsbury, Yorks. B. there. School, Ilkley. Matric. 1668; B.A. 1671-2. Ord. deacon (York) Sept. 1673; priest, Dec. 1674. Minister of Gressingham, Lancs., 1677. V. of Bolton-le-Sands, 1688-90. Died in prison at York for debt. (*Vict. Hist. Lancs.*, VIII. 130.)

GARFORTH, THOMAS. Adm. at MAGDALENE, June 17, 1639. S. of John. B. at Scrafton (? Scruton), Yorks. Matric. 1639. Migrated as sizar (age 18) to Christ's, Dec. 3, 1640. Ord. deacon (Lincoln) Dec. 24, 1643; 'B.A.' Perhaps V. of Gill Church, Barnoldswick, Yorks., 1671–8. (*Peile*, I. 473.)

GARFORTH, WILLIAM. Adm. sizar (age 18) at CHRIST'S, May 5, 1721. Of Yorkshire. Matric. 1721; Scholar, 1721; B.A. 1724–5. Ord. deacon (Chester) Aug. 1, 1725; C. of Leck in Lonsdale; priest (Norwich) Mar. 2, 1728–9. V. of Helpstone, Northants., 1731–4. V. of Wiggenhall St Mary Magdalen, Norfolk, 1733–56. R. of Bacton, 1744–55.

GARFORTH, ——. B.A. 1522–3. (*See* GAFORTH.)

GARGE, RICHARD. B.Can.L. 1512–3. A priest.

GARGRAVE, FRANCIS. Matric. pens. from TRINITY, Lent, 1597–8. 5th s. of Sir Cotton, of Hemsworth, Yorks. B.A. 1601–2. Adm. at the Inner Temple, 1611. Steward to the Earl of Mulgrave. Married, at Wragby, May 12, 1605, Mary Sissope. Brother of the next and of Richard (1591). (*Vis. of Yorks.*, 1612; *Hunter*, II. 214.)

GARGRAVE, JOHN. Matric. pens. from TRINITY, Lent, 1597–8. 4th s. of Sir Cotton, of Yorkshire. Adm. at the Inner Temple, 1600. Living, 1614. Died unmarried. Brother of Francis (above) and of the next. (*Vis. of Yorks.*, 1612.)

GARGRAVE, RICHARD. Matric. Fell.-Com. from PETERHOUSE, c. 1591. S. of Sir Cotton, of Nostell, Hemsworth and Kinsley, Yorks. Bapt. at Nostell, July 12, 1573. Adm. at the Inner Temple, 1591. M.P. for Aldeburgh, 1597–8; for Yorks., 1605–11. Knighted, Apr. 17, 1603. Sheriff of Yorks., 1604. Married Catherine, dau. of Sir John Danvers. Sold Nostell in 1613. 'Living in a low condition, 1634.' Died insolvent. Brother of John (above) and of Francis (1597–8). (*Vis. of Yorks.*, 1612; *Hunter*, II. 214; M. H. Peacock.)

GARGRAVE, THOMAS. Matric. Fell.-Com. from ST JOHN'S, Michs. 1573. S. of Sir Cotton, of Nostell and Hemsworth, Yorks. B. 1561. Executed for murder at York, June 16, 1595. Half-brother of Richard (1591). One of these names, of Yorkshire, adm. at Lincoln's Inn, Feb. 12, 1581–2; 'barrister, Thavies Inn.' (Hunter, *S. Yorks.*, II. 214.)

GARLACUS or GARLICK, ——. (*Frisius.*) B.A. from TRINITY, 1551–2; Scholar, 1552. Fellow, 1553. Charles Garlich was R. of Rainham, Kent, 1571.

GARLAND, AUGUSTIN. Adm. pens. at EMMANUEL, Easter, 1618. S. and h. of Augustin, attorney, of London. Matric. 1618. Adm. at Lincoln's Inn, June 14, 1631. M.P. for Queenborough, 1648–53, 1654–5. One of the regicides. Imprisoned, 1660, and condemned to death; but the sentence was not carried out. A warrant was issued for his conveyance to Tangiers, Mar. 31, 1664, but whether he was transported is uncertain. (D.*N.B.*)

GARLAND, EDWARD. Matric. pens. from JESUS, Michs. 1612; B.A. 1615–6; M.A. 1619. V. of Sittingbourne, Kent, 1623. One of these names presented to Tunstall, Sept. 26, 1647. V. of Hartlip.

GARLAND, JAMES. Adm. Fell.-Com. at CLARE, Sept. 17, 1734. B. in London. Probably migrated to Trinity, Nov. 9, 1736. Adm. at the Inner Temple, Nov. 13, 1741; s. of Nathaniel, of St Christopher's, London, Esq.

GARLAND, JOHN. Scholar and fellow at KING'S HALL, 1422–70. B.Can.L. V. of All Saints', Cambridge, 1444.

GARLAND, JOHN. Matric. sizar from PEMBROKE, Easter, 1582. Of Todwick, Yorks. B.A. from St Catharine's, 1584–5; M.A. 1588. Ord. deacon and priest (Oxford) Dec. 1, 1585. R. of Willingham, Lincs., 1591. (*F.M.G.*)

GARLAND, JOHN. Matric. sizar from ST JOHN'S, Michs. 1617. Of Lincolnshire. B.A. 1621–2; M.A. 1625. Fellow, 1626. Ord. deacon (Peterb.) Jan. 7, 1625–6.

GARLAND, JOHN. Matric. sizar from TRINITY, Easter, 1635. Perhaps of Todwick, Yorks. S. of William. Father of the next.

GARLAND, JOHN. Adm. pens. (age 16) at ST JOHN'S, May 21, 1657. S. of John (? 1635), gent., of Todwick Hall, Yorks. B. there. School, Hemsworth. Matric. 1657. Adm. at Gray's Inn, May 18, 1658. Barrister, 1664. Ancient, 1680. Died Jan. 9, 1691–2, aged 51. M.I. at Todwick. (*Hunter*, II. 159; *F.M.G.*)

GARLAND, NATHANIEL. Matric. sizar from TRINITY, Easter, 1633; B.A. 1636–7.

GARLAND, ROBERT. Matric. pens. from ST JOHN'S, Michs. 1614. Of Lincolnshire. Probably s. of John (1582). B.A. 1618–9; M.A. 1622; B.D. 1629. Fellow, 1623. Ord. deacon (Peterb.) May 27, 1621; priest, Sept. 16, 1621. R. of Kirkby St Denis and St Peter, Lincs., 1626. Will (P.C.C.) 1655. Father of the next.

GARLAND, ROBERT. Adm. pens. (age 16) at ST JOHN'S, Apr. 22, 1651. S. of Robert (above), R. of Long Kirkby, Lincs. B. there. School, Sleaford (Mr Gibson). Matric. 1651.

GARLAND, SAMUEL. Adm. at QUEENS', June 9, 1652. S. of Francis, of Mansfield, Notts. School, Mansfield. Migrated to Caius, Mar. 28, 1655. Matric. 1656.

GARLAND, THOMAS. Matric. pens. from ST JOHN'S, Michs. 1626. Probably s. of William, of Todwick Hall, Yorks., Esq. B.A. 1629–30; M.A. 1633. Brother of John (1635). (*F.M.G.*)

GARLEY, ANTHONY. Matric. pens. from MAGDALENE, Easter, 1631; B.A. 1634–5; M.A. 1638. R. of Walkern, Herts., 1660–79. Perhaps of Bilsby, Lincs.; *see* the next. Died 1679. (*Clutterbuck*, II. 469.)

GARLEY, ANTHONY. Adm. sizar (age 15) at MAGDALENE, June 23, 1669. S. of Anthony, of Bilsby, Lincs. School, Alford. Matric. 1669; B.A. 1672–3; M.A. 1676. Ord. deacon (Peterb.) Sept. 19, 1675; priest (Lincoln) Nov. 1, 1678. V. of Bilsby, Lincs., 1680.

GARLICKE, GEORGE. Adm. sizar (age 18) at CHRIST'S, Feb. 19, 1628–9. S. of John. B. at Preston Patrick, Westmorland. School, Heversham. Matric. 1629; B.A. 1632–3; M.A. 1636. One of these names had a private school at Hastings, in 1638. Will (Lewes) 1638; as of Rye, Sussex, clerk. (*Peile*, I. 398.)

GARLICK, JOHN. Adm. pens. (age 16) at ST JOHN'S, June 5, 1651. S. of William, of Dinting, Glossop, Derbs. Bapt. at Glossop, Oct. 12, 1634. School, Littleborough, Notts. (private). Matric. 1651; B.A. 1654–5; M.A. 1658; B.D. 1665. Fellow, 1655. R. (sinecure) of Aberdaron, Carnarv., 1670–1717. R. of Wells, Norfolk, 1670–1717. Died Oct. 17, 1717. Buried at Wells. (*F.M.G.*, 652.)

GARLICK, JOHN. Adm. sizar at ST CATHARINE'S, May 20, 1724. Of Wolverhampton, Staffs. Matric. 1724; B.A. 1727–8; M.A. 1732. Ord. priest (Lincoln) Sept. 24, 1732.

GARLICK, JOHN. Adm. sizar at CLARE, June 2, 1737. S. of James, of Wakefield. Bapt. there, Oct. 14, 1719. School, Wakefield. Matric. 1737; Scholar, 1738; B.A. 1740–1; M.A. 1744. Fellow, 1743–70. Usher of Wakefield School, 1741–51. Ord. priest (York) June, 1745. V. of Kirkthorpe, Wakefield, 1763–70. Died May 21, 1770, aged 51. M.I. at Kirkthorpe. (M. H. Peacock.)

GARMSTON, JOHN. Adm. sizar (age 17) at MAGDALENE, Jan. 25, 1696–7. S. of Thomas, farmer. B. at Dowles, Salop. School, Lincoln. Matric. 1698; B.A. 1700–1; M.A. 1704. Ord. priest (Lincoln) May 23, 1703. V. of St Benedict, Lincoln. Schoolmaster in Lincoln. R. of Salmonby, 1711–22. R. of Tetford, 1711. Father of Thomas (1723–4).

GARMSTON, LANDON. Adm. sizar at JESUS, Dec. 17, 1747. Of Hanslope, Bucks. S. of Shadrach, clerk, deceased. School, Rugby. Matric. 1747; Rustat Scholar; B.A. 1752. Ord. deacon (Lincoln) Sept. 21, 1755.

GARMSTON, THOMAS. Adm. sizar (age 17) at MAGDALENE, Feb. 28, 1723–4. S. of John (1696–7), clerk. B. at Lincoln. School, Lincoln. Matric. 1725; B.A. 1728–9; M.A. 1732. Fellow, 1730. Ord. priest (Lincoln) Sept. 19, 1731.

GARNER or GARNERS, CHRISTOPHER. Matric. sizar from TRINITY, Easter, 1633; B.A. 1637. Ord. deacon (Peterb.) Dec. 22, 1639.

GARNER, JAMES. M.A. from EMMANUEL, 1691. S. of Stephen, of Nottingham. Matric. from St Mary Hall, Oxford, May 6, 1687, age 20; B.A. (Oxford) 1687–8. (*Al. Oxon.* seems to confound him with James Gardiner, 1695.)

GARNER, ROBERT. Matric. sizar from MICHAELHOUSE, Easter, 1545.

GARNER, WILLIAM. Matric. sizar from MICHAELHOUSE, Easter, 1544.

GARNETT, BARNARD. Adm. pens. (age 18) at SIDNEY, Apr. 30, 1733. S. of John (1689), R. of Sigglesthorne, Yorks. Schools, Beverley and Coxwold. Matric. 1734; B.A. 1736–7; M.A. 1740; D.D. 1753. Fellow, 1738. Proctor, 1744. Incorp. at Oxford, 1741; and at Dublin, 1765. Ord. deacon (Lincoln) Mar. 6, 1736–7. Preb. of Ely, 1754. R. of Snailwell, Cambs., 1754–68. R. of Feltwell, Norfolk, 1754. P.C. of Haddenham and Wilburton, Isle of Ely, 1754. V. of Wilhampstead, Beds. Died Jan. 1768. Brother of Henry (1725) and John (1725).

GARNET, BRIAN. Matric. pens. from ST JOHN'S, Lent, 1564–5.

GARNETT, CHRISTOPHER. Adm. at QUEENS', Oct. 4, 1596. Of Westmorland. Matric. 1596.

GARNET, EDWARD. Matric. from ST JOHN'S, Michs. 1609. B.A. 1613–4; M.A. 1617. Ord. deacon (Norwich) Dec. 19, 1618.

GARNET, FRANCIS. Matric. sizar from CHRIST'S, Oct. 1583.

GARNETT, HENRY. Adm. pens. (age 17) at ST JOHN'S, May 21, 1725. S. of John (1689), clerk, of Surrey. B. at Lambeth. School, Beverley. Matric. 1725; B.A. 1729–30. Ord. deacon (Lincoln) May 24, 1730; priest, June 4, 1732; C. of Little Stoughton, Beds. Buried Nov. 13, 1732. Brother of John (1725) and Barnard (1733). (*Scott-Mayor*, III. 386; *Poulson*, I. 420.)

GARNET, HUGH. B.A. 1491-2; M.A. 1494; B.D. 1503-4. Chaplain of St Thomas the Martyr, Eynesbury, Hunts., 1504-33. V. of Triplow, Cambs., 1521-33. Benefactor to St Catharine's. Died 1533.

GARNET, JAMES. Matric. sizar from St John's, Lent, 1581-2.

GARNET, JOHN. Matric. pens. from St John's, Easter, 1569; B.A. 1577-8; M.A. 1581.

GARNET, JOHN. Adm. sizar (age 18) at Sidney, Apr. 5, 1689. 1st s. of John (? Henry), V. of Kilham, Yorks., deceased. B. there. Schools, Moulton and Kilham. Matric. 1689; B.A. 1692-3; M.A. 1696. Ord. deacon (York) June, 1693; priest, 1694. R. of Cowlam, Yorks., 1699-1735. R. of Sigglesthorne, 1710-35. R. of Barmston, 1719-35. Buried Feb. 24, 1734-5. Father of the next, of Henry (1725) and Barnard (1733). (*Poulson*, I. 420.)

GARNETT, JOHN. Adm. pens. (age 16) at St John's, May 21, 1725. S. of John (above), R. of Sigglesthorne, Yorks. B. in Lambeth, Surrey. School, Beverley. Matric. 1725. Migrated to Sidney, Sept. 13, 1728. Scholar; B.A. 1728-9; M.A. 1732; B.D. 1739; D.D. 1752 (*Lit. Reg.*). Fellow of Sidney, 1730. Incorp. at Oxford, 1738. Lady Margaret preacher, 1744-52. Incorp. at Dublin, 1752. Ord. deacon (Lincoln) May 24, 1730; priest, Apr. 8, 1733. Whitehall preacher. R. of Lockington, Yorks., 1748. Chaplain to the Lord Lieutenant of Ireland, 1751. Bishop of Ferns, 1752. Bishop of Clogher, 1758-82. Died Mar. 1, 1782, in Dublin. Will, Dublin. Brother of Henry (1725) and Barnard (1733). (*D.N.B.*)

GARNETT, JOHN. M.A. from King's, 1728. S. of Thomas (? 1668), of Farthingstone, Northants., clerk. Matric. from Queen's College, Oxford, Mar. 22, 1709-10, age 17; B.A. (Oxford) 1713. V. of Fawsley, Northants., 1720-38. Died Apr. 14, 1738. M.I. at Fawsley. Will (Archd. Northants.) 1738. (*Al. Oxon.*; *Baker*, I. 393.)

GARNET, RICHARD. Matric. sizar from Trinity, Michs. 1578. One of these names R. of Rougham, Suffolk, 1583-1620.

GARNETT, RICHARD. Adm. at Trinity, *c.* 1598. S. of William. B. at Cansfield, Lancs., *c.* 1581. Schools, Tunstall and Kirklandsdale, Lancs. B.A. (? 1602-3). College tutor, Robert Cheke. Entered the English College at Rome, June 13, 1605. Ord. priest, Dec. 23, 1606. (*Records S. J.*, IV. 183. College and University entries missing.)

GARNET, RICHARD. Matric. pens. from Peterhouse, Easter, 1608; B.A. 1611-2.

GARNET, ROBERT. Adm. sizar (age 17) at Christ's, June 19, 1660. S. of William. B. at Kendal, Westmorland. School, Leeds (Mr Garnet). Matric. 1660; B.A. 1663; M.A. 1667. Master of the Grammar School at Leeds. Died Nov. 10, 1700. M.I. at Leeds. (M. H. Peacock.)

GARNET, THOMAS. Ord. deacon (Peterb.) Dec. 20, 1629, as 'of St John's, literate.'

GARNET, THOMAS. Adm. sizar (age 17) at Christ's, July 9, 1668. S. of Edward. B. at Kirkby Lonsdale. School, Kirkby Lonsdale (Mr Garthwaite). Matric. 1668; B.A. 1671-2. Ord. deacon (York) Sept. 1672; priest, Sept. 1673. (*Peile*, II. 17; *see Al. Oxon.* for a contemporary.)

GARNET, THOMAS. Adm. sizar at St Catharine's, Sept. 2, 1689. Of Tamworth. Matric. 1689; B.A. 1693-4.

GARNETT, WILLIAM. Matric. sizar from Christ's, July, 1718; Scholar, 1719. Resided till 1720.

GARNET, ——. B.Can.L. 1534-5.

GARNETT, ——. B.A. 1540-1. Perhaps John, V. of Gamlingay, Cambs., 1545.

GARNEYS, CHARLES. Adm. pens. (age 18) at Christ's, June 10, 1640. S. of Clere, of Kenton, Esq. B. at Redisham, Suffolk. School, Kenton (Mr Jeffray). Matric. 1640. Of Kenton, gent. Married Margaret, dau. of John Richmond, of Hedenham. Buried at Morningthorpe, Norfolk, June 25, 1678. Father of Clere (1676). (*Peile*, I. 472; *Suff. Man. Fam.*, I. 193; *Davy MSS.*)

GARNEYS, CHARLES. Adm. pens. (age 17) at Christ's, Apr. 23, 1706. S. of Nathaniel. B. at Kenton, Suffolk. School, Ipswich. Matric. 1706-7; Scholar, 1706-7. Migrated to St Catharine's, Nov. 7, 1709. Died *s.p.* 1711. Brother of Wentworth John (1702). (*Suff. Man. Fam.*, I. 192; *Peile*, II. 164.)

GARNEYS, CHARLES. Adm. Fell.-Com. (age 17) at Pembroke, July 1, 1743. S. of Richmond (1713), of Hedenham, Norfolk, Esq. Of Hedenham, Esq. Died *s.p.* June, 1808. (*Suff. Man. Fam.*, I. 193))

GARNEYS, CLERE. Adm. at Corpus Christi, 1676. S. of Charles (1640), of Kenton, Suffolk, Esq. B. in Norfolk. Matric. Easter, 1677; B.A. 1680-1; M.A. 1684. Lord of the Manor of Hedenham, Norfolk. Married Margaret, dau. of John Watts, of Burnham Market. Died at Bungay, Norfolk, Sept. 1, 1730. Will (Norwich) 1730. Father of Richmond (1713). (*Suff. Man. Fam.*, I. 193.)

GARNISHE, JOHN. Matric. sizar from Gonville Hall, Easter, 1556. Perhaps of Gt Bealings, Suffolk. Will (Norwich C.C.) 1583. One of these names adm. at Gray's Inn, 1562.

GARNISH, RICHARD. Matric. sizar from Corpus Christi, Michs. 1547. Perhaps s. of John, of Mendlesham, Suffolk. Of Boyland Hall, Norfolk. Will (Norwich C. C.) 1586.

GARNEYS, RICHMOND. Adm. pens. (age 15) at Caius, June 10, 1713. S. of Clere (1676), of Hedenham, Norfolk, gent. B. there. Schools, Beccles (Mr Leeds) and Woodbridge. Matric. 1713. Adm. at Gray's Inn, Nov. 3, 1713. Of Hedenham, Esq. Died 1762. Father of Charles (1743). (*Venn*, I. 530.)

GARNISHE, THOMAS. B.D. 1534-5. S. of Richard, of Mendlesham, Suffolk. Will proved (P.C.C.) 1542.

GARNYSHE, THOMAS. Matric. pens. from Trinity, Michs. 1552. Will of one of these names (P.C.C.) 1567; of Kenton, Suffolk.

GARNEYS, THOMAS. Adm. Fell.-Com. (age 17) at Caius, May 14, 1659. S. of John, gent. of Somerleyton, Suffolk. B. at Felmingham, Norfolk (his mother's home). School, Yoxford, Suffolk (Mr Eachard). Matric. 1659. Succeeded his father at Somerleyton. Of Boyland Hall, Morningthorpe, Norfolk. Died Oct. 25, 1701. (*Venn*, I. 406; *Vis. of Norfolk*, 1664.)

GARNEIS, WENTWORTH. Adm. Fell.-Com. at Clare, June 8, 1670. Of Somerleyton, Suffolk. S. of John, of Boyland, Morningthorpe. Adm. at the Middle Temple, Jan. 27, 1672-3. Married Anne, dau. of Sir Charles Gawdy, of Crow's Hall, Suffolk. Died *s.p. c.* 1684. (*Suckling*, 64.)

GARNIES, WENTWORTH JOHN. Adm. pens. (age 17) at Christ's, Apr. 7, 1702. S. of Nathaniel, of Mickfield, Suffolk. B. at Kenton, Suffolk (his mother's home) 1684. School, Stonham (Mr Sam. Stevenson). Of Kenton, gent. Died July 28, 1728. Buried at Kenton. Will proved (Norwich) 1728. Brother of Charles (1706). (*Suff. Man. Fam.*, I. 192; *Peile*, II. 152.)

GARNIS, ——. Matric. pens. from St John's, *c.* 1594.

GARNISH, ——. Adm. Fell.-Com. at Emmanuel, Easter, 1625.

GARNHAM, ROBERT. Adm. sizar (age 18) at Trinity, Apr. 16, 1734. S. of Robert, of Shakerland Hall, Badwell-Ash, Suffolk. School, Bury (Mr Kynnesman). Matric. 1734; Scholar, 1737; B.A. 1737-8; M.A. 1741. Fellow, 1740. Ord. deacon (Norwich) July, 1739; priest, Apr. 1745. Head Master of Bury School, 1745-67. R. of Hargrave, Suffolk, 1755-98. R. of Nowton, 1757-98. Died Nov. 8, 1798, aged 82. Admon. (P.C.C.) 1799.

GARNHAM, THOMAS. Adm. sizar (age 16) at Caius, Sept. 25, 1620. S. of Thomas, citizen of Norwich. B. in Norwich. School, Norwich. Matric. 1620; B.A. 1625; M.A. 1629. Ord. deacon (Peterb.) Sept. 25, 1625; priest, Feb. 15, 1626-7. C. of Barnham, Suffolk, 1638, and in 1662. C. of Radwinter, Essex, 1642. (*Venn*, I. 250.)

GARNHAM, WILLIAM. Matric. pens. from Trinity Hall, *c.* 1593; Scholar, 1594; LL.B. 1600. Ord. deacon and priest (Norwich) Sept. 29, 1600. C. of Linstead, Suffolk.

GARNIER, JOHN. Adm. at Clare, Apr. 18, 1750. B. at Chelsea, Middlesex.

GARNON, RICHARD. Adm. sizar (age 17) at St John's, May 10, 1642. S. of William, of Brant Broughton, Lincs. B. there. School, Brant Broughton (private; Mr Walker). Matric. 1642; B.A. 1645-6; M.A. 1649. R. of Thistleton, Rutland, 1653-89. R. of North Witham, Lincs. Died Feb. 5, 1688-9. Probably father of the next. (*Lincs. Pedigrees*, 387.)

GARNON, RICHARD. Adm. pens. at Emmanuel, Apr. 16, 1684. Of Lincolnshire. Matric. 1686; B.A. 1687-8; M.A. 1698. Ord. deacon (London) Feb. 24, 1688-9; priest (Lincoln) May 26, 1689. R. of North Witham, Lincs., 1689-1717. R. of Gumby, 1698-1718. Father of the next.

GARNON, RICHARD. Adm. pens. (age 17) at St John's, July 5, 1712. S. of Richard (above), R. of North Witham, Lincs. B. there. Matric. 1713-4; B.A. 1716-7. Ord. deacon (York) Sept. 1717.

GARNON or GERNON, WILLIAM. Adm. pens. at Corpus Christi, 1628. Of Suffolk. Matric. Easter, 1629; B.A. 1631; M.A. 1635. Ord. deacon (Norwich) Dec. 23, 1632; priest, Dec. 22, 1633. V. of Haughley, Suffolk, 1661.

GARNONS, ABRAHAM. Adm. pens. at Emmanuel, Apr. 2, 1646. Of Suffolk. Matric. 1649; B.A. 1649-50; M.A. 1653. R. of South Ockendon, Essex, 1656. R. of Little Thurrock, 1658-61. R. of Stifford, 1658-61. Buried there, Mar. 3, 1660-1. (W. Palin, *Stifford.*)

GARNONS, JOHN. Adm. pens. at Emmanuel, June, 1608. Of Bedfordshire. Matric. Easter, 1609; Scholar; B.A. 1611-2; M.A. 1615; B.D. 1622; D.D. 1631. Fellow, 1616. Incorp. at Oxford, 1612 and 1617. R. of Glemsford, Suffolk, 1624. Father of Luke (1666).

GARNONS, JOHN. B.A. from Emmanuel, 1621-2.

GARNONS, JOHN VAUGHAN. Adm. sizar at QUEENS', Aug. 23, 1746. Of Carmarthen. Matric. 1747; B.A. 1752; M.A. 1756.

GARNONS, LUKE. Adm. sizar at JESUS, Mar. 30, 1666. S. of John (1608), D.D., late R. of Glemsford, Suffolk. Matric. 1667; B.A. 1669-70; Scholar, 1670; M.A. 1673. Ord. deacon (Ely) Sept. 24, 1670; priest, Sept. 24, 1671. V. of Pagham, Sussex, 1678-81. V. of Ringmer, 1680-1. Buried there, Apr. 13, 1681.

GARNONS, RALPH. Adm. pens. at TRINITY, Apr. 1, 1646. Of Suffolk. Matric. 1646; Scholar, 1647; B.A. 1649-50; M.A. 1653. Ord. priest (Bp Brownrigg, Exeter) Aug. 9, 1654. R. of Tilbury-by-Clare, Essex, 1654-80. R. of Little Yeldham, 1662-4. R. of Weston Colville, Cambs., 1663-80. Buried there Sept. 17, 1680. (J. Ch. Smith.)

GARNONS, WILLIAM. Matric. pens. from EMMANUEL, Michs. 1649.

GARNONSE, ——. Adm. pens. at EMMANUEL, Apr. 26, 1600.

GARRAD, SAMUEL. Adm. sizar (age 17) at PEMBROKE, Apr. 16, 1632. Of London. Matric. 1632; B.A. 1635-6; M.A. 1639. Ord. deacon (Lincoln) Apr. 20, 1642. V. of Sutton, Isle of Ely, 1662-3. R. of Ramsden Bellhouse, Essex, 1663-86. Admon. (P.C.C.) 1686.

GARRARD, *see also* GARRETT *and* GERRARD.

GARRARD, EDWARD. Adm. Fell.-Com. (age 17) at ST JOHN'S, Feb. 22, 1655-6. S. of Benedict, Esq., of Malden, Essex. B. there. School, Braintree (Mr Adamson). Matric. 1656. (Pedigree in Burke, *Ext. Bart.*)

GARRARD, EDWARD. Adm. pens. at QUEENS', June 5, 1678. Of Wiltshire. Matric. 1679; B.A. 1681; M.A. (Balliol College, Oxford) 1684. V. of Mere, Wilts., 1691-1734. (*Al. Oxon.*)

GARRARD, GEORGE. M.A. 1607 (Incorp. from Oxford). S. of Sir William, of Dorney, Bucks. Matric. from Merton College, Oxford, Nov. 8, 1594, age 14; B.A. (Oxford) 1597; M.A. 1602-3. Fellow of Merton, 1598. Master of Sutton's Hospital (*i.e.* Charterhouse). Chaplain to the Earl of Northumberland. Of Buckinghamshire, Esq. Married Margaret, dau. of George Dacres, of Cheshunt, Herts. (*Al. Oxon.*; *Vis. of Bucks.*, 1634.)

GARRARD or GERRARD, JACOB. Adm. Fell.-Com. at ST CATHARINE'S, Apr. 9, 1669. Doubtless s. and h. of Sir Thomas, of Langford, Norfolk, Bart. Died before his father. (Burke, *Ext. Bart.*; *G.E.C.*)

GARRARD, JAMES. Matric. sizar from CHRIST'S, May, 1546. Probably of Langford, Norfolk. (*Peile*, I. 39.)

GARRARD or GARRETT, JOHN. Matric. Fell.-Com. from KING'S, Michs. 1634. Probably s. of Sir John, of Lamer, Wheathampstead, Herts., Bart. Succeeded as Bart., 1637. Sheriff of Herts., 1643-5. Died Mar. 11, 1685-6. Brother of Nethermill (1637). (*G.E.C.*, I. 189.)

GARRARD or GARRAD, JOHN. Adm. pens. at EMMANUEL, July 5, 1640. Matric. 1640; B.A. 1643-4; M.A. 1647. V. of Wiston, Suffolk, 1662-84.

GARRARD or GERARD, NATHANIEL. Adm. at CORPUS CHRISTI, 1671. Of Norwich. Matric. 1671; B.A. 1674-5; M.A. 1678. Fellow, 1677-85. Incorp. at Oxford, 1680. Ord. deacon (London) Sept. 22, 1678.

GARRARD, NEHIMILLAS (? NETHERMILL). Matric. Fell.-Com. from KING'S, Easter, 1637. Nethermill Garrard, s. of John, of Lamer, Wheathampstead, Herts., Knt. and Bart., was adm. at Gray's Inn, May 8, 1639. Brother of John (1634).

GARRARD or GARRET, PETER. Adm. pens. (age 16) at CAIUS, Oct. 27, 1570. Readm. Fell.-Com. Jan. 20, 1570-1. S. of Sir William, Knt., and Lord Mayor. B. in London. School, London. (*Venn*, I. 66; *Vis. of Herts.*)

GARRARD or GARRETT, WILLIAM. Adm. pens. at EMMANUEL, 1639. Of Suffolk. Matric. Easter, 1639; B.A. 1642-3; M.A. from Jesus, 1646. Fellow of Jesus, 1644-57. Died 1657.

GARARD, ——. D.Can.L. 1479-80.

GARRARD or GARROD, ——. Adm. pens. at EMMANUEL, Mar. 1631-2.

GARRETT or GARARD, EDWARD. Pens. at GONVILLE HALL, 1503 onwards. B.A. 1499-1500; M.A. 1503-4; B.D. 1511-2. 'Knight's priest,' *i.e.* preacher, at Gonville Hall. Presented to Pattisley, Norfolk, 1522. Died 1544. (*Venn*, I. 16.)

GARRETT, EDWARD. Matric. pens. from QUEENS', Michs. 1570. Of Northumberland. B.A. 1574-5; M.A. 1578; B.D. 1585. Fellow, 1577-85. Ord. deacon (Peterb.) Sept. 28, 1577; priest (Ely) Nov. 17, 1577.

GARRATT, FRANCIS. Adm. pens. (age 20) at CHRIST'S, May 3, 1733. S. of Thomas. B. at Uttoxeter, Staffs. School, Burton-on-Trent (Mr Jackson). Matric. 1733; Scholar, 1734; LL.B. from Magdalene, 1739. Ord. deacon (Lincoln) June 17, 1739; priest, Dec. 21, 1740. Probably C. of Navenby, Lincs., 1739-41. Died 1772. (*Peile*, II. 228; *F.M.G.*, 466.)

GARRETT or GARRARD, HUMPHREY. Matric. sizar from CHRIST'S, July, 1604; B.A. 1607-8; M.A. 1611. Ord. deacon and priest (Peterb.) June 7, 1612. V. of Mumby, Lincs., 1614. (H. I. Longden.)

GARRETT, JOHN. B.A. from PEMBROKE, 1603-4; M.A. 1607.

GARRET, JOHN. M.A. from ST CATHARINE'S, 1631. Probably B.A. from New Inn Hall, Oxford, 1628. R. of St Bartholomew-the-Great, London, 1644. (But *see Al. Oxon.*)

GARRETT, JOHN. M.D. 1680 (*Lit. Reg.*). Licentiate R.C.P. 1679. Hon. fellow, 1680. Died Aug. 8, 1683, aged 50. M.I. at St Dunstan-in-the-East. Will, P.C.C. (*Munk*, I. 412.)

GARRETT, PETER. Adm. at KING'S (age 17) a scholar from Eton, Aug. 13, 1517, as Clason *alias* Garrett. Of Cambridge. B.A. 1521-2; M.A. 1525. Fellow, 1520-9.

GARRETT or GARARD, ROBERT. Scholar of QUEENS', 1496; B.A. 1498-9; M.A. 1501-2. Fellow, 1505-56. Probably first in the *ordo*, *i.e.* the earliest of what would subsequently have been called 'senior wranglers.' Will proved (V.C.C.) 1557.

GARRET, ROBERT. Matric. pens. from CHRIST'S, Michs. 1559; B.A. 1561-2; M.A. from Queens', 1565; B.D. 1571. Fellow of Queens', 1562-76. V. of St Botolph's, Cambridge, 1566. University preacher, 1568. R. of Little Eversden, Cambs., 1574-6. Will proved (V.C.C.) 1576.

GARRETT, ROBERT. Adm. sizar at CORPUS CHRISTI, 1630. Matric. Easter, 1631; B.A. 1637-8. Ord. deacon (Norwich) Sept. 22, 1638; priest, Dec. 22, 1639. R. of Thurning, Norfolk, 1641.

GARRAT, ROBERT. Adm. pens. at CORPUS CHRISTI, 1660. Of Canterbury. Matric. 1660; B.A. 1663; M.A. 1669. C. of Kingston, Kent, 1679-82. R. of Wootton, Kent, 1680-1712. Married, at Beakesbourne, Kent, Sept. 14, 1686, Susanna Copping, of Canterbury. Died at Wootton, July, 1712, aged 70. Admon., 1712. (H. G. Harrison.)

GARRET, ROGER. Adm. at KING'S (age 18) a scholar from Eton, Aug. 26, 1562. Of Uxbridge, Middlesex. Matric. 1562. Left in 1563.

GARRETT, SAMUEL. Adm. sizar at EMMANUEL, May 11, 1683. Matric. 1683-4; B.A. 1686-7. Perhaps M.A. 1724. One of these names Archdeacon of Salop, 1726-32.

GARRET, SAMUEL. Adm. sizar at EMMANUEL, June 26, 1723. Of Cheshire. Matric. 1724; B.A. 1726-7.

GARRET, W. Matric. pens. from JESUS, Michs. 1568.

GARRET, WALTER. Adm. pens. at TRINITY, Oct. 16, 1660. Matric. 1660, as 'William'; Scholar, 1660; B.A. 1664-5; M.A. 1668. Fellow, 1667. Ord. deacon and priest (Peterb.) Sept. 20, 1668. Perhaps R. of Everley, Wilts. Admon. (Cons. C. Sarum) 1716. (H. I. Longden; J. Ch. Smith.)

GARRETT, ——. M.A. 1503-4.

GARROOD, WILLIAM. Adm. sizar at JESUS, May 31, 1720. Matric. 1721; Scholar, 1722; B.A. 1723-4. Ord. deacon (Norwich) Dec. 1726; priest, Dec. 1727. R. of Belstead, Suffolk, 1733-85. Died Aug. 19, 1785, aged 83. M.I. Will, P.C.C. (*G. Mag.*)

GARROD, WILLIAM. Adm. at CORPUS CHRISTI, 1731. Of Norfolk. Matric. 1731; B.A. 1734-5; M.A. 1738. V. of Woodbastwick, Norfolk, 1736-76. V. of Wroxham, 1736-76. R. of Panxworth, 1736.

GARROOD, WILLIAM. Adm. sizar at ST CATHARINE'S, Mar. 24, 1746. Of Sproughton, Suffolk. Matric. 1747; LL.B. 1752. Ord. deacon (Norwich) May, 1752; priest, June, 1753. R. of Stoke Ash, Suffolk, 1755-89. Died Apr. 1, 1789, aged 62. M.I. (*G. Mag.*; *E. Ang.*, VII. 268.)

GARRYNGTON, EDWARD. Matric. pens. from TRINITY, Easter, 1572; B.A. from Clare, 1576-7.

GARSET, RALPH, *see* GARTHSIDE.

GARSETT, SAMUEL. Matric. pens. from ST JOHN'S, Michs. 1589.

GARSET, THOMAS. Matric. sizar from ST JOHN'S, Easter, 1572.

GARSHE, NICHOLAS. Matric. pens. from ST JOHN'S, Easter, 1560.

GARTEN, CLEARE. Matric. pens. from CHRIST'S, May, 1569.

GARTEN, GILES, *see* GARTON.

GARTH, CHARLES. Matric. pens. from CHRIST'S, 1592-3. Probably s. of Richard, of Headlam, Durham. Nephew of Barwell, the Master of Christ's. B.A. 1597-8; M.A. 1604. R. of Holton-in-Beckering, Lincs., 1605. R. of Bradley, 1611-25. R. of Wickenby, 1630. (*Peile*, I. 208, where he is wrongly called Christopher.)

GARTH, GEORGE. Adm. Fell.-Com. at EMMANUEL, 1638. Matric. 1639; B.A. 1641-2. Doubtless s. and h. of Richard (1611), late of Morden, Surrey, Esq., deceased; adm. at Lincoln's Inn, June 13, 1642. Married Anne, sister and co-heir of Sir George Carlton, Bart. Died Nov. 30, 1676, aged 53. (Pedigree in *Vis. of Surrey*; *Manning and Bray*, II. 488.)

GARTH, GREGORY. Matric. sizar from PEMBROKE, Easter, 1545. Of Richmondshire, Yorks. B.A. 1548–9; M.A. 1552; B.D. 1562. Fellow, 1548. Proctor, 1554–5. Lady Margaret preacher, 1562. Incorp. at Oxford, 1565–6. Ord. priest (Suffragan bishop, Shaxton) 1555. R. of St Andrew's, Cambridge, 1561. R. of Chalfont St Giles', Bucks., 1562–85. R. of Glatton, Hunts., 1563–5. Preb. of Lincoln, 1564–74; Chancellor, 1568–1605. R. of Warboys, Hunts., 1565. V. of Hemel Hempstead, Herts., 1566–71. R. of Holton-in-Beckering, Lincs., 1571. R. of Springthorpe, 1573–6. Adm. at Gray's Inn, Aug. 14, 1600. Died 1608. (*Cooper*, II. 481; *Al. Oxon.*)

GARTH, JOHN. Adm. pens. at CLARE, Oct. 24, 1719. Matric. 1719. One of these names, s. of Thomas, of London, Esq., adm. at Lincoln's Inn, May 7, 1718, and at the Inner Temple, May 5, 1727.

GARTH, JONATHAN. Adm. pens. (age 17) at TRINITY, May 18, 1681. S. of William, of Headlam, Durham. Bapt. at Gainford, Sept. 12, 1665. Matric. 1681. Of Headlam. Married and had issue. Buried at Gainford, Nov. 14, 1690. (*Surtees*, IV. 28.)

GARTH, RICHARD. Matric. pens. from PETERHOUSE, Easter, 1611. Doubtless s. and h. of George, of Morden, Surrey, Esq.; adm. at Lincoln's Inn, Oct. 23, 1615. Died Nov. 23, 1639, aged 44. Will (P.C.C.) 1640. If so, father of George (1638). (*Vis. of Surrey*, 1623.)

GARTH, RICHARD. Adm. pens. at CHRIST'S, June 1, 1625. S. of Charles (? 1592), of Lincolnshire. School, Brocklesby (private; Mr Acton). Matric. 1625; B.A. 1628–9; M.A. 1632. Probably V. of Bromfield St Mungo, Cumberland, 1663–73.

GARTH, RICHARD. Adm. pens. at TRINITY, Jan. 10, 1667–8.

GARTHE, ROBERT. Matric. Fell.-Com. from TRINITY, Michs. 1569. Perhaps s. of Richard, of Morden, Surrey. Died Apr. 25, 1613. One of these names, of Middlesex, adm. at Lincoln's Inn, May 16, 1575; of Clifford's Inn.

GARTH, SAMUEL. Adm. pens. (age 16) at PETERHOUSE, May 27, 1676. Eldest s. of William, of Bolam, Durham. School, Ingleton, Durham. Matric. 1676; Scholar, 1676; B.A. 1679–80; M.A. 1684; M.D. 1691. Incorp. at Oxford, 1694. Gulstonian lecturer, 1694. Harveian orator, 1697. F.R.C.P. June 26, 1693. F.R.S. 1706. Physician in ordinary to George I, and physician-general to the army. Knighted, Oct. 10, 1714. A member of the Kitcat club. Author of the *Dispensary*. Married Martha, dau. of Sir Henry Beaufoy, of Emscote, Warws. Died Jan. 18, 1718–9. Buried at Harrow, Middlesex. (*T. A. Walker*, 157; *D.N.B.*; *Al. Oxon.*)

GARTH, WILLIAM. B.A. 1527–8. Probably of QUEENS' College, in 1525.

GARTH, WILLIAM. Adm. pens. at JESUS, June 21, 1625. Of Surrey. Matric. 1625; B.A. from Corpus Christi, 1628; M.A. 1635.

GARTHFORD, ANTHONY. Matric. sizar from ST JOHN'S, Michs. 1568.

GARTHORNE, JOHN. Matric. sizar from TRINITY HALL, July, 1716; Scholar, 1716; B.A. 1719–20; M.A. 1734. Ord. deacon (London) Oct. 9, 1720.

GARTHESYDE, FRANCIS. Matric. pens. from CHRIST'S, Nov. 1559; B.A. 1562–3; M.A. 1566; B.D. from St John's, 1576. Fellow of St John's, 1563, and again 1570. Ord. acolyte at Chester, 1558–9. V. of Bassingbourne, Cambs., 1564. University preacher, 1571. R. of Burrough Green, 1572. Buried there June 30, 1619. (*Peile*, I. 71.)

GARTHSIDE, FRANCIS. Adm. sizar at EMMANUEL, Feb. 23, 1676–7; pensioner, 1679. Of Lincolnshire. Matric. 1677; B.A. 1680–1; M.A. 1689. Ord. priest (Lincoln) Dec. 20, 1685. R. of Partney, Lincs., 1685. R. of Claxby, 1689.

GARTHSIDE or GARSED, JAMES. Matric. sizar from TRINITY, c. 1592. B. at Prestwick, Lancs., c. 1578. B.A. 1596–7; M.A. 1600. Ord. deacon and priest (Peterb.) Oct. 4, 1601. V. of Witham, Lincs., 1603. Will (Lincoln) 1617, of one of these names, of Witham, clerk.

GARTHSIDE, JOHN. Matric. sizar from TRINITY, Michs. 1583. V. of Wigtoft, Lincs., 1592, as 'B.A.' One of these names R. of Willoughby-in-the-Marsh, Lincs., 1609.

GARTSIDE or GARSET, RALPH. Scholar at KING'S HALL, 1471–91; B.Can.L. 1484–5. Doubtless R. of St Andrew's, Holborn, 1478–1531.

GARTHWAITE, EPHRAIM. Adm. sizar (age 16) at CHRIST'S, Apr. 26, 1664. S. of Ephraim, R. of Barkston, Lincs. B. there. School, Grantham (Mr Siston). Matric. 1664; B.A. 1667–8; M.A. 1671. Ord. deacon (Lincoln) Sept. 1668; priest, Sept. 24, 1671. R. of Harston, Leics., 1672–1719. V. of Croxton Keyril, 1680–92. R. of Ropsley, Lincs., 1692–1719. Will proved, Oct. 5, 1719. (*Peile*, I. 609; *Lincs. Pedigrees*, 391.)

GARTHWAITE, HENRY. Matric. sizar from CHRIST'S, July, 1621; B.A. 1624; M.A. 1628. Ord. deacon (Peterb.) Dec. 18; priest, Dec. 19, 1625. Probably master of a private school at Yeldham, and afterwards at Bocking. R. of Kirby Bain, Lincs., 1640–59. Author, theological. (*Peile*, I. 341; *Misc. Gen. et Her.*, IV. 418.)

GARTHWAITE, JEREMY. Adm. at CORPUS CHRISTI, June 24, 1633. Of Yorkshire. Migrated to Jesus, June 14, 1634. B.A. 1636–7; Scholar, 1637. Minister of Barnaby (? Barnby-on-the-Moor), 1655. R. of Kirby Underdale, Yorks., 1662–71. Died Mar. 1671–2. (A. Gray.)

GARTHWAIT, JEREMIAH. Adm. sizar at JESUS, Mar. 25, 1708. S. of John (1665–6), V. of Bonby, Lincs. Matric. 1708; B.A. 1711–2. Ord. deacon (York) Sept. 1712; priest, Aug. 16, 1730.

GARTHWAITE, JOHN. Matric. pens. from CHRIST'S, July, 1604; B.A. 1607–8; M.A. 1611. Ord. priest (York) Dec. 1618. Perhaps Head Master of Beverley School, 1614. Head Master of York, about 1623. Possibly R. of Rothbury, 1661; exchanged this for Catwick-in-Holderness, 1665. Preb. of Southwell, 1665–78. Preb. of York, 1666–78. Died 1678. (*Peile*, I. 248.)

GARTHWAITE, JOHN. Matric. pens. from CHRIST'S, July, 1605. Perhaps licensed to practise medicine, 1628. (*Peile*, I. 252.)

GARTHWAITE, JOHN. Adm. sizar (age 15) at CHRIST'S, June 22, 1633. S. of John (1604), schoolmaster, of York. B. there. School, York. Matric. 1633. One of these names V. of Beverley Minster, 1665–71. (But *see* above.) (*Peile*, I. 427.)

GARTHWAIT, JOHN. Adm. sizar (age 18) at ST JOHN'S, Mar. 24, 1665–6. S. of William, furrier, of Beverley, Yorks. B. there. School, Beverley. Matric. 1667; B.A. 1669–70. Ord. deacon (York) May, 1670; priest (Lincoln) Sept. 21, 1673. V. of Bonby, Lincs., 1681. Father of Jeremiah (1708).

GARTHWAITE, MILES. Matric. sizar from ST JOHN'S, Michs. 1588. B. c. 1576. B.A. 1592–3; M.A. 1596. Ord. deacon and priest (Peterb.) Feb. 15, 1596–7. R. of Fulbeck, Lincs., 1598–1616. Buried there Jan. 12, 1616. Will proved (Lincoln) 1616. Brother of Thomas (1596). (*Lincs. Pedigrees*, 389.)

GARTHWAYTE, RICHARD. Adm. sizar (age 18) at ST JOHN'S, Apr. 30, 1640. S. of Philip, husbandman, of Dent, Yorks. B. there. Schools, Dent (Mr Battersby) and Sedbergh. Matric. 1640; B.A. 1643–4; M.A. 1647. Master of the Grammar School, Sedbergh, 1646–8. Afterwards Master of Kirkby Lonsdale; and of St Mary's Hospital, Newcastle-on-Tyne, 1671–90. Master of Newcastle Grammar School. Buried at St Nicholas, Sept. 17, 1690. (H. M. Wood.)

GARTHWAITE, THOMAS. Matric. sizar from ST JOHN'S, c. 1596; B.A. 1600–1; M.A. 1604. Incorp. at Oxford, 1612. R. of Copdock, Suffolk, 1617. R. of Blaxhall, 1621. Will (P.C.C.) 1653. Brother of Miles (1588). (*Lincs. Pedigrees*, 389; *Al. Oxon.*)

GARTON, GILES. Matric. pens. from ST JOHN'S, Easter, 1614, as Garten. S. of Peter (1583), of Woollavington, Sussex. 'Died at Cambridge.' Perhaps his will (P.C.C.) 1645–6. (*Vis. of Sussex*; D. G. C. Elwes, *Western Sussex*.)

GARTON, MATTHEW. Matric. pens. from QUEENS', Easter, 1576.

GARTON, PETER. Matric. Fell.-Com. from ST JOHN'S, Michs. 1583. Doubtless s. of Giles, ironmonger, of London. Adm. at Gray's Inn, Oct. 21, 1584. Knighted, Mar. 14, 1603–4. Of Woollavington, Sussex, Knt. Died Aug. 21, 1606. Will (P.C.C.) 1607. Father of Giles (1614). (*Vis. of Sussex*; D. G. C. Elwes, *Western Sussex*.)

GARWAY, JONAS. Adm. at KING'S (age 17) a scholar from Eton, Dec. 8, 1610. Of London. Matric. 1610; B.A. 1614. Fellow, 1613–5. 'Became a merchant.' Lord Mayor of London. Died c. 1646. (*Harwood*.)

GARWAY, PHILIP. Adm. at KING'S (age 18) a scholar from Eton, Oct. 4, 1610. Of Iver, Bucks. Left in 1613. 'Afterwards a captain under Count Mansfield.' Will of one of these names (P.C.C.) 1625; of Acton, Middlesex, Esq. (*Harwood*.)

GARWAY or GARAWAY, THOMAS. Matric. pens. from CORPUS CHRISTI, Easter, 1623. Of London. B.A. 1625–6; M.A. 1629. R. of Snodland, Kent, 1631. Buried there Feb. 21, 1666–7. (F. S. Hockaday.)

GARWAY or GARAWAY, WILLIAM. Matric. pens. from TRINITY, Easter, 1573. S. of Walter, merchant. B. in London. Schools, Mercers', London and Tonbridge. Migrated to Caius, Aug. 4, 1574, age 20; B.A. 1575–6. One of these names, of London, knighted, July 16, 1615. (*Venn*, I. 80.)

GARWAY, WILLIAM. Adm. Fell.-Com. (age 17) at SIDNEY, Apr. 25, 1629. S. of William, Esq. B. at Lothbury, London. Schools, Hertford (Mr Thomas Wright) and Mercers', London. Matric. 1629. One of these names, of London, adm. student at Leyden, Dec. 4, 1642.

GARWAY or GARRAWAY, WILLIAM. Adm. Fell.-Com. (age 16) at PEMBROKE, June 22, 1632. S. of Henry, of London (Lord Mayor, 1639–40; *D.N.B.*, 'Garraway'). Matric. 1632. Of Ford, Sussex. Gentleman of the Privy Chamber to Charles II, 1662. M.P. for Chichester, 1661–79; for Arundel, 1679–81, 1685–7, 1689–90. Died Aug. 4, 1701. (*Dallaway*, II. i. 48; A. B. Beaven.)

GARWOOD, ROBERT. Adm. pens. (age 17) at PEMBROKE, Apr. 19, 1707. S. of John, of Ipswich, gent. Matric. 1707; B.A. 1710–11; M.A. 1715. Ord. priest (London) Apr. 13, 1721. Will (P.C.C.) 1765; of Pentlow, Essex.

GARYNG or CARYNG, JOHN. B.A. 1521–2; M.A. 1524.

GARYNER (? WARENER). *Cautio* for degree, 1488. A friar. Author. (*London and Middlesex Arch. Soc.*, II. 138.)

GASCARTH, JOHN. Adm. sizar at PEMBROKE, Mar. 26, 1667. S. of John, of Cumberland, farmer. Matric. 1667; B.A. 1670–1; M.A. 1674; D.D. 1700. Fellow, 1674. V. of St Nicholas, Bristol, 1684. R. of Chevening, Kent, 1685–6. R. of All Hallows, Barking, London, 1686–1732. Died Dec. 10, 1732. Buried at All Hallows. M.I. there. Will, P.C.C. (J. Ch. Smith; H. G. Harrison.)

GASKARTH, JOSEPH. Adm. sizar (age 16) at PEMBROKE, Feb. 23, 1743–4. S. of Joseph, of Hill-top, Cornwall (? Cumberland), gent. Matric. 1744; B.A. 1747–8; M.A. 1751. Fellow, 1749.

GASCOIGNE or GASKYN, EDWARD. B.A. 1540–1. Of Yorkshire. Perhaps s. of Francis, of Micklefield. M.A. 1543; LL.D. 1559–60. Fellow of QUEENS', 1541. Fellow of Jesus. Proctor, 1548–9. Master of Jesus, 1560–3. Chancellor of the diocese of Norwich, 1558. Preb. of Ely, 1559. Vicar-general of Ely, 1562. Admon. (P.C.C.) 1569. (*Cooper*, I. 244.)

GASCOYNE, EDWARD. Matric. pens. from JESUS, Easter, 1577.

GASCOIGNE, GEORGE. Probably of TRINITY. S. of Sir John, of Cardington, Beds. Adm. at Gray's Inn, 1555. M.P. for Bedford, 1558; for Midhurst, 1572. Went to Holland to avoid his creditors, 1572. Served in Holland under the Prince of Orange; captured by the Spaniards; returned to England after four months' imprisonment. Accompanied the Queen to Kenilworth, 1575. Dramatic poet. Died Oct. 7, 1577, at Stamford, Lincs. Admon. (P.C.C.) Dec. 2, 1578, of George Gascoigne, gent., of Walthamstow, Essex. (*Cooper*, I. 374; *D.N.B.*) The *D.N.B.* states definitely that he was educated at Trinity, where Stephen Nevynson was his tutor. There is no College or University record of this.

GASCOIGNE, GEORGE. Matric. pens. from JESUS, *c.* 1590.

GASCOIGNE, GEORGE. M.A. from EMMANUEL, 1687. S. of George, of Market Deeping, Lincs., clerk. Matric. from Brasenose, Oxford, Oct. 26, 1678, age 16; B.A. (Oxford) 1682. Assistant Master at Peterborough School, 1683. R. of Paston, Northants., 1691–1705. Died Feb. 16, 1704–5. Buried at Paston. (*Al. Oxon.*; T. P. Dorman.)

GASCOYNE or GASWYN, HUMPHREY. B.Civ.L. 1493–4. Of Yorkshire. Ord. deacon (Ely) Apr. 2, 1496; priest, May 26, 1496. V. of Rothwell, Yorks., till 1531. Perhaps R. of Linton-in-Craven, 1521–40. Died 1540.

GASCOYNE, JOHN. Adm. pens. (age 18) at SIDNEY, June 28, 1671. S. of Robert, yeoman, deceased. B. at Bedford. School, Bedford (Mr Butler).

GASCOIGNE, JOSEPH. Adm. sizar at TRINITY, Mar. 31, 1659. Matric. 1659; Scholar, 1661; B.A. 1662–3; M.A. 1666; D.D. 1687. Fellow, 1664. Signed for deacon's orders (London) Feb. 18, 1664–5; for priest's, June 5, 1669. R. of Papworth Everard, Cambs., 1677. V. of Enfield, Middlesex, 1681–1721. Died July 11, 1721. Will, P.C.C. Father of the next and of Theobald (1706). (His Oxford contemporary is wrongly assigned in *Al. Oxon.* to these Trinity College livings.)

GASCOIGNE, JOSEPH. Adm. pens. (age 17) at TRINITY, July 1, 1712. S. of Joseph (above), V. of Enfield. School, Enfield (Dr Uvedale). Scholar, 1715; LL.B. 1717 (*Com. Reg.*). Brother of Theobald (1706).

GASCOYNE, LEONARD. Matric. pens. from JESUS, Easter, 1578. S. of George, of Kirby, Northants. Brother of Richard (1594) and the next. (*Vis. of Yorks.*, 1584.)

GASCONE, NICHOLAS. Adm. Fell.-Com. at JESUS, *c.* 1586. 1st s. of George, of Kirby, Northants. B. May 17, 1571. Matric. 1586. Adm. at the Middle Temple, Nov. 15, 1590. Knighted, July 23, 1603. Of Oldhurst, Hunts., Knt. Died Jan. 26, 1617. Brother of Richard (1594) and the above. (*Vis. of Yorks.*; A. Gray.)

GASCOINE, RICHARD. Adm. pens. (age 15) at JESUS, Oct. 21, 1594. 4th s. of George, of Kirby, Northants. Matric. 1594; B.A. 1598–9. Lived for some time at Bramham Biggin, Yorks.; later in Lincoln's Inn Fields. Died there *c.* 1663. Will proved Mar. 24, 1663–4. Left his books to Jesus College. He says that he refused a fellowship owing to ill-health. Antiquary. Brother of Nicholas (1586) and Leonard (1578). (*D.N.B.*; *Vis. of Yorks.*, 1584; *Thoresby Soc.*, 17. 172; A. Gray.)

GASCOYNE, RICHARD. Adm. pens. at EMMANUEL, Feb. 25, 1644–5. Of Northamptonshire. Migrated to King's, Lent, 1645–6. B.A. 1651; M.A. 1653. V. of Warmington, Northants., 1656–80; conformed, 1662. Ord. deacon (Peterb.) Sept. 19; priest, Sept. 20, 1663. Probably V. of St John's, Peterborough, 1667–8. Buried at Warmington, Aug. 29, 1680. (H. I. Longden; T. P. Dorman.)

GASCOIGNE, THEOBALD. Adm. pens. (age 17) at TRINITY, July 2, 1706. S. of Joseph (1659), V. of Enfield, Middlesex. School, Enfield (Dr Uvedale). Matric. 1707. Adm. at Gray's Inn, Aug. 25, 1708. Brother of Joseph (1712). Died Oct. 16, 1715. Buried at Barking. (*E. Anglian*, IV. 158.)

GASCOYNE, THOMAS. Matric. sizar from JESUS, Easter, 1573; B.A. 1576–7; M.A. 1580. Perhaps 2nd s. of John, of Partington, Yorks. If so, lived at Maidswell, Northants. Married Alice, dau. of Sir Wm Gascoigne, and widow of Edm. Hazlewood, of Maidswell. (*Vis. of Yorks.*, 1584; M. H. Peacock.)

GASCOIGNE, WADE. Adm. pens. (age 17) at TRINITY, July 7, 1750. S. of John. School, Westminster. Matric. 1750; Scholar, 1751; LL.B. 1757. Ord. deacon (Lincoln) Mar. 6, 1757; priest, Mar. 11, 1759. R. of Terrington St John, Norfolk, 1767–1801.

GASCOIGNE, Sir WILLIAM. Said to have studied at Cambridge, but not found in any of the University or College records. S. of William. B. at Gawthorpe Hall, Yorks., *c.* 1350. Reader at Gray's Inn. Advocate, 1374. King's serjeant, 1397. Justice C.P. 1399–1401. Chief-justice of the King's Bench, 1400–13. Died Dec. 1419. M.I. at Harewood. Will, York. (*D.N.B.*; M. H. Peacock.)

GASCOIGNE, ——. Adm. pens. at TRINITY HALL, Mar. 23, 1715–6; Fell.-Com. 1717. Name off, 1722.

GASE, *see* GACE.

GASELEY, ——. Doctor in some faculty, 1444. Augustinian friar.

GASLEY, ——. Probably M.A. before 1459. (Gr. *Bk*, A, 17.)

GASKYN, THOMAS. B.A. 1536–7.

GASLYNG, NICHOLAS. Matric. pens. from CAIUS, Michs. 1559.

GASSON, JOSEPH. Matric. sizar from PETERHOUSE, Easter, 1623.

GASTEIN, JAMES. Adm. pens. at QUEENS', May 30, 1717. Of Middlesex. Probably s. of Matthew, of London, merchant, deceased; adm. at the Inner Temple, Apr. 18, 1724.

GASTRELL, BENJAMIN. M.A. 1633 (Incorp. from Oxford). Of Surrey. 7th s. of Henry. Matric. from New Inn Hall, Oxford, Jan. 18, 1627–8, age 18; B.A. (Oxford) 1627–8; M.A. 1631. Will (P.C.C.) 1637. M.I. at East Garston, Berks. (*Al. Oxon.*; J. Ch. Smith.)

GASTRELL, JOSEPH. M.A. 1627 (Incorp. from Oxford). Of Surrey. Doubtless s. of Henry, of East Garston, Berks. Matric. from Magdalen Hall, Oxford, June 23, 1621, age 18; B.A. (Oxford) 1623; M.A. (New Inn Hall) 1626. Sequestered to V., of Ridge, Herts., Oct. 7, 1643. Died 1644. Will (P.C.C.) 1645; which suggests that he had been ejected, as a Royalist, from Tetsworth, Oxon. (*Al. Oxon.*; *Shaw*, I. 316; J. Ch. Smith.)

GASTRELL, PEREGRINE. Adm. Fell.-Com. at TRINITY HALL, Mar. 28, 1717. S. of Edward, of Slapton, Northants. LL.B. 1717. Chancellor of Chester diocese. Died July 23, 1748. Buried in Chester Cathedral. One of these names, s. and h. of Edward, of Slapton, Northants., adm. at Lincoln's Inn, July 2, 1702. (*Ormerod*, I. 246; *Baker*, II. 101.)

GASWELL, *see* GAWSELL.

GASWYN, *see* GASCOIGNE.

GATAKER, CHARLES. Adm. pens. (age 14) SIDNEY, Mar. 11, 1628–9. S. of Thomas (1593–4), B.D. B. at Rotherhithe, Surrey. School, St Paul's. Matric. 1629; B.A. 1632–3; M.A. (Pembroke College, Oxford) 1636. Incorp. at Cambridge, 1657. Chaplain to Viscount Falkland. R. of Hoggeston, Bucks., 1647. Died there Nov. 20, 1680. Author. Father of Thomas (1667). (*Al. Oxon.*; *D.N.B.*)

GATACKER, CHARLES. Adm. pens. at TRINITY, June 26, 1666. School, Westminster. Scholar, 1667.

GATAKER, THOMAS. At Oxford about eleven years. Then at MAGDALENE, Cambridge, four years. S. of William, of Gataker Hall, Salop. Student of the Middle Temple, *c.* 1553. The parents were strong Catholics, and sent him to Louvain. On his change of faith they cast him off. Ord. deacon and priest (London) 1568. Chaplain to the Earl of Leicester. R. of St Edmund's, Lombard St, 1572–93; and of Christ Church, Newgate St, 1578–9. Died Mar. 1592–3. Will (P.C.C.) 1593; R. of Newington, Surrey. Father of the next. (*D.N.B.*; *Vis. of Shrops.*; *Cooper*, II. 164; Burke, *L.G.*; E. J. Beck, *Rotherhithe.*)

GATAKER, THOMAS. B.A. from St John's, 1593–4; M.A. 1597; B.D. from Sidney, 1604. S. of Thomas (above). B. Sept. 4, 1574, at St Edmund's rectory. Fellow of Sidney, 1596–1600. Declined the Mastership of Trinity. Preacher at Lincoln's Inn, 1601. R. of Rotherhithe, 1611–54. One of the Westminster Assembly, 1643. Well known scholar and author. Died July 27, 1654. Will, P.C.C. Father of Charles (1629). (*D.N.B.*; F. J. Beck, *Rotherhithe*.)

GATAKER, THOMAS. Adm. pens. at Clare, June 11, 1667. S. of Charles (1628–9), R. of Hoggeston, Bucks. Matric. 1667; B.A. 1670–1; M.A. 1674. Incorp. at Oxford, 1676. R. of Hoggeston, 1680–1701. Died 1701. Will, P.C.C. (*Al. Oxon.*; Burke, *L.G.*)

GATCHELL, THOMAS. Adm. sizar (age 18) at Caius, Oct. 10, 1657. S. of Thomas, husbandman. B. at Angersleigh, Somerset. School, Pitminster (Mr Glenvill). Matric. 1657; Scholar, 1657–61. Subscribed for deacon's orders (Bristol) Dec. 21, 1662. V. of Burstock, Dorset, 1662–90. Admon. of one of these names (Exeter) 1713; of Ottery St Mary, clerk. Perhaps father of the next. (*Venn*, I. 401; F. S. Hockaday.)

GATCHELL, THOMAS. Adm. sizar (age 17) at Sidney, Apr. 27, 1714. S. of Thomas (? Vicar) of Ottery St Mary, Devon. B. there. School, Ottery St Mary (Mr Marker). Matric. 1714; B.A. 1717–8.

GATE, J. D.D. 1464.

GATE, REGINALD. B.Can.L. 1474–5.

GATTE, THOMAS. B.A. 1526–7.

GATEHOUSE, ABRAHAM. Adm. sizar (age 17) at St John's, Apr. 5, 1687. S. of William, gent. B. at Ashmoore, Dorset. School, Sherborne (Mr Curganven). Matric. 1687.

GATER, WILLIAM. Adm. sizar at Emmanuel, May 29, 1612. Matric. 1612; Scholar; B.A. 1615–6; M.A. 1619. Ord. deacon (Peterb.) July 28, 1616; priest, Mar. 16, 1616–7.

GATER, WILLIAM. Adm. sizar (age 22) at Sidney, June 15, 1732. Only s. of William, farmer, of Lapford, Devon. Schools, Morchard Bishop (Mr Dean) and Crediton (Mr John Leach). Matric. 1732; B.A. 1735–6; M.A. 1752. Will (Exeter) 1770, of William Gater, clerk, of Lapford.

GATES, ABRAHAM. Matric. pens. from Jesus, *c.* 1590. B. at Kingston-on-Thames. B.A. (? 1594–5); M.A. 1602; B.D. 1608–9. Ord. deacon (London) Dec. 30; priest, Dec. 31, 1597, age 26. C. of Leyton, Essex. R. of Weston Colville, Cambs., 1605–45. Died 1645. (A. Gray.)

GATES, EDWARD. Matric. Fell.-Com. from Pembroke, Michs. 1562. One of these names s. and h. of Sir Henry, of Seamer, Yorks., Knt. B. at Syon, Middlesex, Apr. 24, 1547. Probably adm. at Lincoln's Inn, Mar. 16, 1565–7. M.P. for Scarborough, 1571, 1588–9, 1593; for Thirsk, 1572–83. Buried at Seamer, Jan. 27, 1621–2. (*Vis. of Yorks.*, 1665; A. B. Beaven.)

GATES, FRANCIS. Matric. pens. from Jesus, Lent, 1577–8. B. at Walton, Hunts. B.A. 1581–2. Ord. deacon (London) age 29. V. of Whittlesey St Mary and St Andrew, Isle of Ely, 1589. V. of Wisbech St Peter's, 1607. Buried at Whittlesey, Oct. 22, 1622. (A. Gray.)

GATES, GEORGE. Scholar of Trinity, 1634; B.A. 1635–6; M.A. 1639. Ord. deacon (Peterb.) June 9, 1639; priest, Mar. 1, 1639–40. C. of Bletsoe, Beds., in 1640. R. of Bolnhurst. Buried at Bolnhurst, July 16, 1661. Perhaps father of William (1658).

GATES, HENRY. Matric. Fell.-Com. from Trinity, Easter, 1571. One of these names 3rd s. of Sir Henry, of Seamer, Yorks., Knt. Of Gosberton, Lincs. (*Surtees Soc.*, XXXVI. 76; *Vis. of Yorks.*, 1665.)

GATES, JOHN. Matric. sizar from Jesus, Easter, 1582; B.A. 1585–6.

GATES, JOHN. Adm. at Corpus Christi, 1627. Of Suffolk. B.A. 1631–2; M.A. 1635. V. of Sawston, Cambs., 1639–44.

GATES, THOMAS. Matric. pens. from Christ's, Easter, 1544; Scholar, 1542–3; B.A. 1544–5.

GATES, THOMAS. Matric. pens. from Pembroke, Easter, 1584. One of these names knighted, 1596.

GATES or GATIS, THOMAS. Adm. pens. (age 17) at St John's, June 16, 1729. S. of George, of Northumberland, skinner and glover. Bapt. at St John's, Newcastle, Apr. 3, 1712. School, Sedbergh. Matric. 1729; B.A. 1732–3; M.A. 1736. Ord. deacon (Lincoln) Sept. 22, 1734; priest, Dec. 19, 1736. C. of All Saints', Newcastle, 1741. Buried at St John's, Newcastle, Mar. 26, 1745. (*Scott-Mayor*, III. 423; H. M. Wood.)

GATES, WILLIAM. Adm. sizar at Trinity, May 6, 1658. Perhaps s. of George (1634). Matric. 1658. Migrated to Emmanuel, June 26, 1661. B.A. 1661–2. Ord. deacon (Lincoln) Aug. 12, 1661. R. of Bolnhurst, Beds., 1661–1709.

GATES, WILLIAM. Adm. sizar at Clare, June 12, 1695. Of Woodford, Northants. Matric. 1697. Ord. deacon (Lincoln) Dec. 22, 1700; C. of Bolnhurst, Beds.; and of Houghton Conquest, 1702. Perhaps V. of Meopham, Kent, 1711–3.

GATESCALL, RICHARD. Matric. sizar from Trinity, Easter, 1614; B.A. 1615–6.

GATFORD, LIONEL. Matric. pens. from Jesus, Michs. 1618. Of Sussex. Scholar, 1618; B.A. 1621–2; M.A. 1625; B.D. 1633; D.D. 1660 (*Lit. Reg.*). Fellow, 1625–38. Junior proctor, 1631–2. Ord. deacon (Peterb.) Dec. 24, 1626. V. of St Clement's, Cambridge, 1633. R. of Dennington, Suffolk, 1641–4 and 1660–5. Imprisoned, 1643. Minister in Jersey, 1647. Chaplain to Sir Edward Hyde, 1647. Nominated V. of Plymouth, 1661, but never had possession. Died of the plague, 1665, while acting as C. of Yarmouth, pending his installation as vicar. Father of the next. (*D.N.B.*; A. Gray.)

GATFORD, LIONEL. Adm. sizar at Jesus, July 2, 1660. Of Suffolk. S. of Lionel (above). School, Bury. Matric. 1661; B.A. 1663–4; Scholar, 1664; M.A. 1671; D.D. 1705 (*Com. Reg.*). Incorp. at Oxford, 1706. R. of Laceby, Lincs., 1670. R. of Clewer, Berks., 1677. R. of St Dionis Backchurch, 1680–1715. Archdeacon of St Albans, 1713–5. Precentor and treasurer of St Paul's, 1714–5. Died Sept. 15, 1715. Buried at St Dionis. Will, P.C.C. Benefactor to Jesus College. (Le Neve, *Mon.*, II. 304; *Al. Oxon.*)

GATFORDE, WILLIAM. Adm. pens. at Jesus, May 17, 1632. Of Sussex. Matric. 1632; B.A. 1635–6; M.A. 1639.

GATFOULD, RICHARD. Matric. sizar from Trinity, Easter, 1565.

GATIFER (? GATIKER), GEORGE. Matric. sizar from Trinity, *c.* 1595.

GATLEY, JAMES. Adm. sizar (age 16) at Christ's, May 6, 1646. S. of James, V. of Leigh, Lancs. B. there. School, Leigh (Mr Battersby). Matric. 1646. Migrated to Brasenose College, Oxford, 1647.

GATLIFFE, SAMUEL. Adm. sizar (age 20) at Magdalene, May 25, 1670. S. of Humphrey, of Knutsford, Cheshire. School, Manchester. Matric. 1672; B.A. 1674–5. Subscribed for deacon's orders (Bristol) Dec. 20, 1673.

GATON, ROBERT, *see* **CATON.**

GATS, JOHN. Matric. sizar from Peterhouse, Michs. 1609.

GATWARD, JOHN. Matric. pens. from Trinity Hall, Easter, 1557.

GATWARD, PELL. Adm. pens. at Jesus, May 3, 1728. Of Cambridge. S. of Samuel (next), Recorder of Cambridge. Matric. 1728. Adm. at the Middle Temple, July 10, 1728. His father married him, when a lad at Eton, to his wealthy ward Sarah Rowlands Marsh. Died *s.p.* Oct. 27, 1741, aged 32. Buried in Trinity Church, Ely. (A. Gray.)

GATTWARD, SAMUEL. Adm. pens. at Jesus, Jan. 10, 1690–1. S. of ——, of Steeple Morden, Cambs. Matric. 1691; Scholar, 1693. Adm. at the Middle Temple, Dec. 7, 1698. Recorder of Cambridge, 1713–41. Died in the Middle Temple, Apr. 20, 1742. Will, P.C.C. Father of Pell (above). (*G. Mag.*)

GATWARD, STEPHEN. Matric. pens. from Jesus, Michs. 1566; B.A. 1569–70; M.A. 1573.

GATTWELL, JOHN. Adm. sizar at Trinity, June 21, 1658. Matric. 1658 (*impubes*).

GAUDEN, CLERKE. Adm. (age 17) at Caius, Feb. 17, 1673–4. S. of Sir Dennis, Knt., of Clapham, Surrey. School, Eton. Matric. 1674; M.A. 1675 (*Lit. Reg.*). Adm. at the Inner Temple, July 26, 1676. (*Venn*, I. 450.)

GAUDEN or GAWDING, JOHN. Matric. sizar from St John's, Michs. 1587. B. at Dorchester. B.A. (? 1591–2); M.A. 1595; B.D. 1602. Fellow, 1594. Ord. deacon and priest (London) Dec. 31, 1597, age 26. V. of Mayland, Essex, 1598. Will (P.C.C.) 1625. Father of the next.

GAUDEN, JOHN. Matric. sizar from St John's, Michs. 1619. S. of John (above), V. of Mayland, Essex. B. there. School, Bury. B.A. 1622–3; M.A. 1626; B.D. (Wadham College, Oxford) 1635; D.D. (Oxford) 1641. V. of Chippenham, Cambs., 1640–2. Chaplain to the Earl of Warwick. Dean of Bocking, Essex, 1642. One of the Assembly of Divines, 1643. Retained his benefices during the commonwealth, though writing against the army and in defence of the church of England. Preacher at the Temple, 1660. Chaplain to Charles II, 1660. Bishop of Exeter, 1660–2; of Worcester, 1662. Reputed author of *Eikon Basilike*. Married Elizabeth, widow of Edward Lewknor, of Denham, Suffolk. Died Sept. 20, 1662, aged 57. Buried in Worcester Cathedral. Will, P.C.C. Father of Lewknor (1661) and perhaps of the next. (*D.N.B.*; *Al. Oxon.*)

GAUDEN, JONATHAN. Adm. pens. at Trinity, June 29, 1661. Perhaps s. of the above, and brother of the next.

GAUDEN, LEWKENOR. Adm. pens. at TRINITY, June 29, 1661. S. of John (1619). Matric. 1661; M.A. 1664 (*Lit. Reg.*).

CAWDEN or GAWDING, MORGAN. Matric. sizar from ST JOHN'S, Easter, 1580. Of Dorset. B.A. 1583–4; M.A. 1587; B.D. 1594. Fellow, 1587. V. of Asheldham, Essex, 1596–1604. Died 1604. Admon. (Cons. C. London) 1605. (J. Ch. Smith.)

GAWDEN, ——. Adm. Fell.-Com. at TRINITY, July 1, 1664.

GAUDERN, EDWARD. M.A. from PETERHOUSE, 1710. S. of Stephen, of Earl's Barton, Northants., gent. Matric. from Queen's College, Oxford, July 14, 1702, age 15; B.A. (Oxford) 1706. Ord. deacon (Peterb.) Sept. 25, 1709; priest, June 3, 1710. R. of Sywell, Northants., 1710–38. Died Apr. 28, 1738. Buried at Sywell. Admon. 1738 (Northampton). (*Al. Oxon.*; H. I. Longden.)

GAUDY, ANTHONY. Adm. pens. (age 18) at CAIUS, Mar. 21, 1620–1. S. of Philip, gent., of Norfolk. Schools, Botesdale, Suffolk (Mr Foule) and Blo Norton, Norfolk (Mr Wright). Matric. 1622; Scholar, 1622–7; B.A. 1625–6; M.A. 1629. Ord. priest (Norwich) Feb. 21, 1629–30. C. or V. of Aspall, Suffolk, 1632–52. R. of Garboldisham, Norfolk, 1634–7; of Sternfield, Suffolk, 1652. Buried at Aspall, Mar. 8, 1652–3. Will (P.C.C.) 1652–3. (*Venn*, I. 252; *Gawdy Letters*, Brit. Mus.)

GAWDY, BASSINGBORNE. Matric. pens. from TRINITY HALL, Easter, 1545, *impubes*. 2nd s. of Thomas, of West Harling, Norfolk. Adm. at the Inner Temple, 1551. Sheriff of Norfolk, 1578. Died Jan. 20, 1589–90. Brother of Thomas (1545).

GAWDY, BASSINGBOURNE. Adm. pens. (age 17) at CAIUS, Apr. 19, 1632. 3rd s. of Framlingham, Esq., of West Harling, Norfolk. B. there. School, Bury. Matric. 1632. Inherited, by his father's will, lands in Sternfield, Suffolk. Will (Bury) 1692. Brother of Charles (1637), Robert (1638–9), Thomas (1636), William (1629) and Framlingham (1630–1). (*Venn*, I. 304.)

GAUDY, BASSINGBOURNE. Adm. pens. (age 16) at CAIUS, Jan. 22, 1648–9. S. of Bassingbourne, gent., of West Harling, Norfolk. B. in Gelderland. Schools, Bury and Gressenhall (Mr Greene). Matric. 1648–9. Probably went to France, 1657. (*Venn*, I. 374.)

GAUDY, BASSINGBOURN. Adm. Fell.-Com. (age 17) at CHRIST'S, Mar. 3, 1653–4. S. of Sir William (1629), Bart., of West Harling, Norfolk. School, Bury. Matric. 1654. Died of small-pox, Feb. 23, 1660–1. Buried in the Temple Church. (*Peile*, I. 558.)

GAWDEY, CHARLES. Adm. pens. (age 17) at CAIUS, July 1, 1637. 5th s. of Framlingham, Esq., of West Harling, Norfolk. B. there. School, Thetford (Mr Ward). Probably died *c.* 1686. Brother of Bassingbourne (1632), etc. (*Venn*, I. 329.)

GAWDY, CLIPSBY. Adm. Fell.-Com. at EMMANUEL, Feb. 17, 1592–3. S. of Thomas. Matric. *c.* 1593. Adm. at the Inner Temple, 1594. M.P. for Dunwich, 1597–8. Knighted, July 23, 1603. Sheriff of Norfolk, 1611. Of Redenhall, Knt. Died 1619. Buried at Redenhall. Will (P.C.C.) 1621. Father of Thomas (1626). (*Vis. of Norfolk.*)

GAUDY, EDWARD. Adm. pens. (age 13) at CHRIST'S, June 24, 1656. S. of Sir Charles, of Crow's Hall, Debenham, Suffolk, Knt. B. in London. School, Bury. Matric. 1656. Brother of Framlingham (1656).

GAUDY, FRAMLINGHAM. Adm. pens. (age 17) at CAIUS, Jan. 31, 1630–1. 2nd s. of Framlingham, Esq. B. at West Harling, Norfolk. School, Bury. Matric. 1631. Adm. at the Inner Temple, May 3, 1634. Lived at Bury. Of Crow's Hall, Debenham, Esq. Will proved (Norwich C.C.) Sept. 5, 1673. (*Venn*, I. 295.)

GAUDY, FRAMLINGHAM. Adm. pens. (age 15) at CHRIST'S, June 24, 1656. S. of Sir Charles, of Crow's Hall, Debenham, Suffolk. B. in London. School, Bury. Matric. 1656. Adm. at the Inner Temple, Feb. 4, 1657–8. Buried in the Temple Church, Feb. 27, 1660–1. Brother of Edward (1656). (*Peile*, I. 573.)

GAWDIE, HENRY. Matric. pens. from TRINITY HALL, Easter, 1571. Of Claxton, Norfolk. 1st s. of Sir Thomas (1545), Justice Q.B. Adm. at the Inner Temple, 1571. Sheriff for Norfolk, 1592, 1608. M.P. for Norfolk, 1597–1603. K.B. 1603. Died 1620. Will (P.C.C.) 1621. Brother of Thomas 1571), father of the next, of Robert (1593) and Thomas (1596). (*Vis. of Norfolk.*)

GAWDIE, HENRY. Matric. Fell.-Com. from EMMANUEL, *c.* 1596. S. of Sir Henry (above), of Claxton, Norfolk. Bapt. Swardeston, Norfolk, Apr. 29, 1580. Adm. at the Imiat Temple, 1594. Brother of Robert (1593) and Thomas (1596). (G. H. Holley.)

GAWDEY, HENRY. Adm. Fell.-Com. at PETERHOUSE, May 1, 1619. Of Norfolk. S. and h. of Sir Robert (1593), Knt., of Claxton Hall, Norfolk. Matric. 1619. Adm. at Gray's Inn, Jan. 31, 1620–1. Died before 1632. (*T. A. Walker*, 12.)

GAUDY, HENRY. Adm. pens. (age 16) at PEMBROKE, Mar. 23, 1637–8. S. of George, of Plumstead, Norfolk. Bapt. at Norwich Cathedral, Jan. 3, 1620–1. Matric. 1638; B.A. 1641–2. R. of Cantley, Norfolk, 1650–63, as 'M.A.' Brother of Robert (1631) and Thomas (1631).

GAWDY, HENRY. Adm. pens. at QUEENS', Mar. 28, 1665. Of Essex. Matric. 1665. One of these names, of Crowe Hall, Suffolk, adm. at the Inner Temple, Jan. 25, 1667–8.

GAWDY, ROBERT. Adm. Fell.-Com. at EMMANUEL, May 5, 1593. S. of Sir Henry (1571), of Claxton, Norfolk. Matric. *c.* 1593. M.P. for East Looe, 1597–8. Sheriff of Norfolk, 1628–9. Married Winifred, dau. of Sir Nathaniel Bacon. Died 1638. Will (Norwich C.C.) 1639. Brother of Thomas (1596), father of Henry (1619). (*Vis. of Norfolk.*)

GAUDY, ROBERT. Adm. pens. (age 15) at CAIUS, June 10, 1631. S. of George, Esq., barrister. B. at Claxton, Norfolk. School, Claxton (Mr Chapman). Matric. 1631; Scholar, 1631–6; B.A. 1634–5. Brother of Thomas (1631) and Henry (1637–8).

GAWDY, ROBERT. Adm. pens. (age 16) at CAIUS, Feb. 4, 1638–9. 6th s. of Framlingham, Esq. B. at East Harling, Norfolk. School, Thetford (Mr Smith and Mr Ward). Matric. 1639; Scholar, 1639–45; B.A. 1642–3; M.A. 1646. Brother of Bassingbourne (1632), etc.

GAWDY, THOMAS. Matric. pens. from TRINITY HALL, Easter, 1545. S. of Thomas, of Harleston, Esq., of the Inner Temple, barrister. M.P. for Arundel, 1553. Treasurer of Lincoln's Inn, 1562. Recorder of Norwich, 1566–76. Serjeant-at-law, 1567. Justice Q.B. 1574–88. Knighted, Aug. 26, 1578. Buried Dec. 12, 1588, at Harleston. Will, P.C.C. Father of Henry (1571) and Thomas (1571). (*Cooper*, II. 36; *D.N.B.*; *Vis. of Norfolk.*)

GAWDY, THOMAS. Matric. pens. from TRINITY HALL, Easter, 1571. 2nd s. of Sir Thomas (above), Justice Q.B. Adm. at the Inner Temple, 1571. Brother of Henry (1571).

GAWDY, THOMAS. Matric. Fell.-Com. from EMMANUEL, *c.* 1596. S. of Sir Henry (1571), of Claxton, Norfolk. Adm. at the Inner Temple, 1594. Buried at St Dunstan-in-the-West, 1596. Brother of Robert (1593) and Henry (1596).

GAWDY, THOMAS. Matric. Fell.-Com. from CORPUS CHRISTI, Easter, 1626. Of Norfolk. S. and h. of Sir Clipsby (1592–3), of Gawdy Hall, Norfolk, Knt., deceased. Adm. at Gray's Inn, Nov. 29, 1627. Knighted, Dec. 9, 1629. Father of William (1647). (*Vis. of Norfolk.*)

GAUDY, THOMAS. Adm. pens. (age 16) at CAIUS, June 10, 1631. S. of George, Esq., barrister. B. at Claxton, Norfolk. School, Claxton (Mr Chapman). Matric. 1631. Adm. at the Inner Temple, Feb. 10, 1632–3. Succeeded to the estates of his uncle Sir Robert (1593), at Claxton. Brother of Robert (1631) and Henry (1637–8). (*Venn*, I. 300.)

GAWDY, THOMAS. Adm. pens. (age 18) at CAIUS, May 16, 1636. 4th s. of Framlingham, Esq. B. at East Harling, Norfolk. School, Bury. Matric. 1636. Inherited property at Sternfield, Suffolk. Died unmarried. Brother of Bassingbourne (1632), etc. (*Venn*, I. 321.)

GAUDY, WILLIAM. Adm. Fell.-Com. (age 17) at CAIUS, Apr. 30, 1629. Eldest s. of Framlingham, Esq., of West Harling, Norfolk. B. there. School, Bury. Matric. 1629; B.A. 1631–2. Adm. at the Inner Temple, Feb. 4, 1633–4. M.P. for Thetford, 1661–9. Created Baronet, 1663. Died Aug. 1669. Will (P.C.C.) 1670. Brother of Bassingbourne (1632), etc., father of Bassingbourn (1653–4) and William (1657–8). (*Venn*, I. 289.)

GAWDY, WILLIAM. Adm. at CORPUS CHRISTI, 1647. Of Norfolk. S. and h. of Sir Thomas (1626), Knt., of West Harling, Norfolk. Adm. at the Inner Temple, 1650.

GAWDY, WILLIAM. Adm. pens. at JESUS, Mar. 13, 1657–8. Of Norfolk. 3rd s. of William (1629), of Framlingham and West Harling, Esq.; afterwards Bart. Matric. 1658. Adm. at the Inner Temple, May 11, 1660. Died in London, of small-pox. Buried in the Temple Church, Feb. 21, 1660–1. (A. Gray.)

GAUDY, WILLIAM. Adm. sizar (age 17) at ST CATHARINE'S, Aug. 31, 1728. Of Ipswich, Suffolk. Matric. 1729; B.A. 1732–3.

GAUGE (? GANGE), ——. *Cautio* for degree, 1465–6. (Perhaps William; ord. acolyte at Ely, 1452–3.)

GAULE, EDMUND. Adm. pens. (age 15) at MAGDALENE, May 14, 1672. S. of John, of Spilsby, Lincs. School, Alford. Matric. 1672.

GAULE, JOHN. B.A. from MAGDALENE, 1623–4. Probably matric. (Gall) from Magdalen College, Oxford, Nov. 16, 1621, age 17, of Lincolnshire. Ord. deacon (Peterb.) June 11; priest, June 12, 1625. Chaplain to Lord Camden, *c.* 1629. V. of Gt Staughton, Hunts., 1632. Author, theological. Died 1687. (*D.N.B.*; where it is said that he did not graduate.)

GAUNT, *see also* GANT.

GAUNT, JOSHUA. Adm. pens. at EMMANUEL, Mar. 20, 1608-9.

GAVELL, ROBERT. Adm. Fell.-Com. at ST JOHN'S, Feb. 19, 1658-9. S. of Vincent, Esq., deceased, of Cobham, Surrey. B. there. School, Guildford (Mr Graile). Matric. 1659. Of Cobham, gent. Living, 1719. (*Vis. of Surrey*, 1662; *Manning and Bray*, II. 734.)

GAVELL, W. Matric. sizar from ST JOHN'S, Lent, 1579-80.

GAWBAR, JOHN. Matric. pens. from PEMBROKE, Michs. 1564; B.A. 1568-9; M.A. 1572; M.D. 1583.

GAWEN, EDWARD. Matric. sizar from ST CATHARINE'S, c. 1597. Probably B.A. 1602-3. Ord. priest (Peterb.) Nov. 27, 1603, as B.A. R. of Thrussington, Leics., 1605.

GAWEN, WILLIAM. Matric. sizar from JESUS, c. 1595; B.A. 1598-9; M.A. 1602. Ord. priest (Chichester) 1600. C. of Biddenham, Beds., 1606-11. R. of Hainford, Norfolk, 1619.

GAWYN, ——. M.A. 1458-9; B.D. 1468-9.

GAWEN, ——. B.D. 1531-2. A friar.

GAWKRODGER, JOHN. Adm. sizar (age 17) at CHRIST'S, May 25, 1710. S. of Joseph. B. at Heaton, Bradford, Yorks. School, Bradford (Mr Clapham). Matric. 1710; Scholar, 1710; B.A. 1713-4. (*Peile*, II. 174.)

GAWKROGER, RICHARD. Adm. sizar at CLARE, Feb. 25, 1660-1. Matric. 1661; B.A. 1664-5; M.A. 1670. Ord. priest (York) Nov. 1664.

GAWNSLER, ——. Matric. sizar from MAGDALENE, Easter, 1544.

GAWSELL or GAUSSELL, GREGORY. Adm. pens. at SIDNEY, Apr. 1602. S. of Thomas, of Watlington, Norfolk. B. there. Matric. 1602. Succeeded to his father's estate, 1600. Died Mar. 5, 1656, aged 70. (*Blomefield*, VII. 480.)

GAWSELL, ROBERT. Adm. pens. at CORPUS CHRISTI, 1577, as Gasweil. Probably of Norfolk. Perhaps s. of Thomas, of Denver. Matric. Lent, 1577-8. Adm. at Lincoln's Inn, Nov. 23, 1580. Died c. 1628. (*Vis. of Norfolk*.)

GAWSELL, ROBERT. Adm. Fell.-Com. at EMMANUEL, Easter, 1624. Matric. 1624. Doubtless s. and h. of Sir Edmund, late of Denver, Norfolk, Knt., deceased; adm. at Lincoln's Inn, Nov. 4, 1626. Of Shottesham, Esq. (*Vis. of Norfolk*, 1664.)

GAWTHROP, LEONARD. Adm. sizar at EMMANUEL, June 12, 1620; B.A. 1623-4. Ord. deacon (York) Dec. 1624; priest, Mar. 1624-5.

GAWTHROP, THOMAS. Adm. sizar (age 20) at ST JOHN'S, July 1, 1721. S. of Christopher, of Yorkshire. B. at Dent, Yorks. Schools, Dent (Mr Nelson) and Sedbergh. Matric. 1721; B.A. 1724-5; M.A. 1736.

CAWTON, THOMAS. M.A. 1720 (Incorp. from Oxford). S. of Thomas, of Hightington, Worcs., gent. Matric. from Christ Church, Oxford, Oct. 12, 1704, age 18; B.A. (Oxford) 1708; M.A. 1711. Probably Head Master of Repton, 1714. (*Al. Oxon.*; A. B. Beaven.)

GAWTON, THOMAS. Adm. pens. (age 19) at TRINITY, May 20, 1732. S. of Thomas, of Long Ditton, Surrey. School, Westminster. Matric. 1732; Scholar, 1733; B.A. 1735-6; M.A. from King's, 1739. *Litt. dim.* from York for deacon, Jan. 1737-8; for priest, Feb. 1737-8. R. of Bisley, Surrey, 1739-48. V. of Godalming, 1757-61. V. of Shalford, 1760-1. Buried at Godalming, Oct. 21, 1761. Will (P.C.C.) 1762. (*Al. Westmon.* 304; *Manning*, I. 648.)

GAYE, EDMUND. Adm. pens. (age 17) at CAIUS, June 30, 1623. S. of Philip, husbandman, of Matlask, Norfolk. School, North Walsham (Mr Tilles). Matric. 1623; Scholar, 1624-8. Ord. deacon (Peterb.) May 19; priest, May 20, 1627. R. of Bradfield, Norfolk, 1629. Brother of Richard (1614). (*Venn*, I. 263.)

GAY, GEORGE. Adm. pens. (age 17) at CAIUS, Jan. 2, 1702-3. S. of Edward, gent., of Yarmouth. B. at Ormesby. Schools, Norwich and Yarmouth. Matric. 1702-3; Scholar, 1703-6; B.A. 1707-8; M.A. 1714. Ord. deacon (Norwich) Mar. 1, 1712-3; priest, Dec. 11, 1715. C. of Buckenham and Hassingham, Norfolk. R. of Mulbarton, 1721-8. Married Elizabeth, dau. of Bovill Wimberley, of Lincs. Died 1728. M.I. at Mulbarton. Will (Norwich C. C.) 1728. (*Venn*, I. 509; G. H. Holley.)

GAY, JAMES. Adm. sizar (age 18) at ST JOHN'S, Feb. 7, 1673-4. S. of John, yeoman, of Frithelstock, Devon. B. there. Bapt. Nov. 20, 1655. School, Torrlugton. Matric. 1674; B.A. 1677-8. Ord. deacon (London) Mar. 16, 1678-9. Buried at Upton Pyne, Devon, June 3, 1720. Will, Exeter. Father of John (1717) and Nicholas (1718).

GAY, JOHN. Adm. pens. (age 17) at CAIUS, Mar. 15, 1627-8. S. of Thomas (1602), R. of Gestingthorpe, Essex. School, Bury. Matric. 1628; Scholar, 1629-35; B.A. 1631-2; M.A. 1635. Ord. deacon (Norwich) Sept. 22, 1638; priest, Sept. 22, 1639. V. of Gt Barton, Suffolk, 1639. Married, at East Lexham, Norfolk, June 22, 1641, Anne, dau. of Edward Shene, R. of East Lexham. Probably will (P.C.C.) 1656; of Ampton, Suffolk, clerk. (*Venn*, I. 282.)

GAY, JOHN. Adm. pens. (age 18) at ST JOHN'S, Feb. 7, 1697-8. S. of John, gent. B. at Frithelstock, Devon. Bapt. July 30, 1678. School, Gt Torrington (private; Mr Cory). Buried at Frithelstock, June 20, 1720. Cousin of John Gay, the poet. Probably brother of Richard (1721).

GAY, JOHN. Adm. pens. (age 18) at SIDNEY, Nov. 7, 1717. S. of James (1673-4). B. at Meath, Devon. Schools, Torrington (Mr Reynolds) and Tiverton. B.A. 1721-2; M.A. 1725. Fellow, 1724-32. Probably ord. deacon (York) Sept. 23, 1722, as 'William'; priest, Dec. 22, 1723. V. of Wilshampstead, Beds., 1732-45. V. of Hawnes, 1739. Author, philosophical. Died July 18, 1745. Buried at Wilshampstead. (*D.N.B.*)

GAY, JOHN. Adm. pens. (age 16) at PEMBROKE, Feb. 9, 1733-4. S. of John, ge . B. at Calthorne, Norfolk (his mother's home). Matricnt735. Succeeded his father at Aldborough. Married Frances, dau. of the Rev. Francis Copeman, Nov. 1741. (Burke, *L.G.*)

GAY, NICHOLAS. D.D. Fellow of PETERHOUSE, 1437. Bursar, 1455-67. P.C. of Little St Mary's, Cambridge, 1446-8. Vice-Chancellor, 1454-5. An active member of the syndicate for building the south side of the University Library, 1458. R. of Pulham, Norfolk, 1468-74. Died July 4, 1474. Brass in Pulham Church. Will, P.C.C. (*T. A. Walker*; H. P. Stokes.)

GAY, NICHOLAS. Adm. sizar (age 17) at SIDNEY, Oct. 20, 1718. S. of James (1673-4). B. at Meath, Devon. School, Tiverton. Matric. 1717; B.A. 1722-3; M.A. 1731. V. of Newton St Cyres, near Exeter. Died 1775. Brother of John (1717). (*N. and Q.*, 1 S. v. 36.)

GAYE, RICHARD. Matric. pens. from ST JOHN'S, Michs. 1608.

GAY, RICHARD. Adm. pens. (age 16) at CAIUS, Apr. 27, 1614. S. of Philip, husbandman, of Matlask, Norfolk. School, North Walsham (Mr Tilles). Matric. 1613; Scholar, 1614-20; B.A. 1616-7; M.A. 1620. Ord. priest (Norwich) Mar. 11, 1623-4. R. of Barningham, Norfolk, in 1636. R. of Thimblethorpe. Will (P.C.C.) 1655. Brother of Edmund (1623). (*Venn*, I. 225.)

GAY, RICHARD. M.A. from KING'S, 1721. S. of John, of Frithelstock, Devon, gent. Bapt. Apr. 18, 1682. Colleger at Eton, 1696-9. Matric. from Merton College, Oxford, Mar. 23, 1699-1700, age 16; B.A. (Oxford) 1703-4. R. of Frithelstock. R. of St Leonard, Exeter, 1708-55. Buried there Jan. 21, 1755. Will (Exeter) 1755. Probably brother of John (1697-8). (*Al. Oxon.*)

GAY, ROBERT. M.A. 1629 (Incorp. from Oxford). Of Somerset. Matric. from Magdalen Hall, Oxford, Nov. 16, 1621, age 19; B.A. (Oxford) 1624; M.A. 1627. R. of Nettlecombe, Somerset, 1631-72. Died 1672. (*Al. Oxon.*)

GAY, ROBERT. Adm. pens. at JESUS, June 20, 1693. Of London. Probably F.R.S. 1718. Treasurer of Christ's Hospital. M.P. for Bath, 1720-2, 1727-34. Died Oct. 31, 1738. M.I. at Wanstead, Essex. (*G. Mag.*; *E. Anglian D. S.*, IV. 17.)

GAY, ROBERT. Matric. pens. from CLARE, Lent, 1710-1.

GAYE, THOMAS. Matric. pens. from QUEENS', Michs. 1571.

GAYE, THOMAS. Adm. pens. (age 16) at CAIUS, July 7, 1602. Of Norfolk. School, 'Southwick' (? South Creake), Norfolk (Mr Hooke). Matric. 1602; B.A. 1605-6; M.A. 1609. Ord. priest (London) Dec. 17, 1608. R. of Gestingthorpe, Essex, 1609; of Southacre, 1624-51. Died Jan. 27, 1651-2. Will, P.C.C. Father of John (1627-8). (*Venn*, I. 179.)

GAY, THOMAS. Adm. pens. (age 16) at ST JOHN'S, June 23, 1665. S. of Jeremy, gent., of Goddington, near Ashford, Kent. B. there. School, Canterbury (Mr Paris). (*Vis. of Kent*, 1663.)

GAY, WILLIAM. B.A. from ST JOHN'S, 1606-7. One of these names, B.A., R. of Bagendon, Gloucs., 1622-33. Probably preb. of Wells, 1617. R. of Buckland, Gloucs., 1633-47, ejected. Will (P.C.C.) 1656, as of Buckland. (F. S. Hockaday.)

GAY, WILLIAM. Adm. sizar (age 18) at CAIUS, Apr. 28, 1685. S. of Henry, gent., of Lyng, Norfolk. B. there. Schools, Norwich and Lynn. Matric. 1685; Scholar, 1685-90; B.A. 1688-9. Probably V. of Snettisham, 1697. R. of Anmer, 1705-7. Will proved (Norwich C.C.) 1707-8. (*Venn*, I. 479.)

GAYER, JAMES. Adm. pens. (age 15) at ST JOHN'S, Apr. 27, 1709. S. of Sir Robert (1651), K.B. B. in London. School, London (private). Matric. 1709.

GAYER or GAYRE, JOHN. Adm. Fell.-Com. at EMMANUEL, July 20, 1650, as 'Gager.' S. of Sir John, Lord Mayor of London. Matric. 1651. Adm. at Gray's Inn, June 15, 1649; and at the Middle Temple, 1652. Knighted, Mar. 18, 1692-3. (*See Al. Oxon.*)

GAYER or GAYRE, ROBERT. Adm. Fell.-Com. at EMMANUEL, June 3, 1651. S. of Sir John, Lord Mayor of London. K.B. 1661. Married Mary, dau. of Sir Thomas Rich, of Sonning, Berks. Gave £1040 towards the building of the College Chapel in 1670. Died June 14, 1702. (*Lipscomb*, IV. 554; J. B. Peace.)

GAYER, ROBERT. Adm. Fell.-Com. (age 17) at MAGDALENE, May 24, 1717. Doubtless s. of Sir Robert, Knt., of Stoke Poges. B. at Stoke Poges, Bucks. School, Eton. (Le Neve, *Knights*, 24.)

GAYRE or GEARE, THOMAS. Adm. pens. at CLARE, July 29, 1650. Matric. 1650.

GAYER, WILLIAM. Adm. sizar (age 18) at ST JOHN'S, May 6, 1686. Of Dowland. S. of Roger, clerk. B. at North Tawton, Devon. School, Crediton. Matric. 1686; M.A. 1691. Died Jan. 29, 1722. (*Misc. Gen. et Her.*, 2nd S., IV. 126.)

GAYLARD, *see also* **GALLARD.**

GAYLARD or GALARD, JOHN. Adm. pens. (age 22) at CHRIST'S, June 10, 1670. Of Devon. School, Exeter. Matric. 1672; B.A. 1673–4; M.A. 1677. Doubtless V. of Selworthy, Somerset, June 16, 1692. Died before June, 1724. (*Peile*, II. 30.)

GAYLARD, JOHN. Adm. sizar at EMMANUEL, Nov. 8, 1707. Of Sherborne, Dorset. Matric. 1708; B.A. 1711–2; M.A. 1715. Fellow, 1713. Ord. deacon (London) June 15, 1712. V. of Winsford, Somerset, 1714–43. Head Master of Sherborne School, 1733–43. Died June, 1743. (*Lond. Mag.*)

GAYLARD, JOSEPH. Incorp. M.D. 1693, from Leyden. B. in Exeter, *c.* 1657. Adm. at Leyden, May 6, 1688. M.D. there, 1688. Candidate R.C.P. 1694. Surgeon to the Duke of Monmouth in 1685. (*Munk*, I. 504.)

GAYNES, *see also* **GAINES.**

GAYNES, FRANCIS Adm. pens. (age 15) at PETERHOUSE, May 21, 1636. S. of Christopher, of School Aycliffe, Durham. Bapt. at Heighington, Aug. 23, 1618. Matric. 1637. Of School Aycliffe, Durham, Esq. Married, at Merrington, June 20, 1649, Sarah, dau. of Ferdinando Morecraft. (*T. A. Walker*, 56; J. Ch. Smith.)

GAYNES, OLIVER. Adm. pens. (age 18) at ST JOHN'S, June 29, 1639. S. of Oliver, 'Medicus,' of Wellingborough, Northants. B. at Stratford, Bucks. School, Wellingborough (Mr Jones)Fenny

GAYNSFORD, JOHN. Matric. sizar from QUEENS', Michs. 1571. Probably s. of Thomas. School, Merchant Taylors'. B.A. 1575–6. Incorp. at Oxford, 1579. Ord. priest (London) Oct. 6, 1577, age 25. R. of St Laurence, Brentford, 1583. V. of Feltham, Middlesex, 1584–93. R. of Littleton, 1592–1616. V. of Gt Dunmow, Essex, 1593; and of Heston, Middlesex, 1593–1616. Will (Cons. C. London) 1616; to be buried at Heston. (*Al. Oxon.*; J. Ch. Smith.)

GAINSFORD, JOHN. Adm. Fell.-Com. at QUEENS', Aug. 13, 1605. Of Surrey. Probably s. of Sir William, of Ford, Surrey, Knt. Matric. from Gloucester Hall, Oxford, Feb. 16, 1598–9, age 14. Adm. at Gray's Inn, Aug. 11, 1608. (*Vis. of Surrey*; *Al. Oxon.*)

GAYNSFORD, THOMAS. Matric. pens. from PETERHOUSE, Easter, 1582. One of these names s. of William, of Lingfeld, Surrey. Died *s.p.* 1587. (*Vis. of Surrey*; *Vis. of London.*)

GAYTFIELD, ——. Scholar of CHRIST'S, 1540–1.

GAYTON, JAMES. Matric. pens. from ST JOHN'S, Michs. 1566; B.A. 1569–70; M.A. 1573. Ord. deacon and priest (Peterb.) Jan. 21, 1572–3. R. of Rowley, Yorks., 1583–93. Admon. (Lincoln) 1596, of one of these names; of Lincoln, clerk.

GAYTON, JOHN. Fellow of PETERHOUSE, 1339.

GAYTON, JOHN. Matric. pens. from EMMANUEL, Easter, 1602.

GAYTON, PAUL. Adm. at CORPUS CHRISTI, *c.* 1452. Pens. at Gonville Hall, 1505; probably M.A. Preb. of the College of St Mary-in-the-Fields, Norwich, 1492. (*Venn*, I. 16; *Masters*.)

GAYTON, RALPH. B.D. 1464–5; D.D. 1467–8 (perhaps adm. 1472–3). Fellow of CORPUS CHRISTI, 1452.

GAYTON, THOMAS. Matric. sizar from QUEENS', Michs. 1626. Of Yorkshire. B.A. 1630–1; M.A. 1634. Ord. deacon and priest (Norwich) Dec. 23, 1632. Perhaps of Cherry Burton, Yorks., 1664–81.

GAYTON, WILLIAM. D.D. 1458. Prior of Watton.

GAYTON, ——. B.D. 1501–2. Prior canonicorum.

GAYWOOD, THOMAS. Matric. pens. from PETERHOUSE, Easter, 1579.

GEAGE, *see* **GEDGE.**

GEARE, *see* **GEERE.**

GEARING, ALEXANDER. Matric. Fell.-Com. from CLARE, Easter, 1577. Of Winterton, Lincs., Esq. S. and h. of Peter, of Winterton. Father of Peter (1604). (*Vis. of Lincs.*, 1592.)

GERING, GEORGE. Matric. Fell.-Com. from TRINITY, Michs. 1622.

GEARING, JOHN. Adm. pens. at EMMANUEL, June 27, 1622. Matric. 1622.

GEERING, NATHANIEL. M.A. 1734 (Incorp. from Oxford). S. of Gregory, of Denchworth, Berks., Esq. Matric. from Trinity College, Oxford, June 30, 1725, age 13; B.A. (Oxford) 1729; M.A. 1732; B.D. 1742. Perhaps R. of Farnham, Essex, 1756. Died at Bishop's Stortford. Will (P.C.C.) 1784. (*Al. Oxon.*; J. Ch. Smith.)

GERING, PETER. Adm. pens. at QUEENS', Oct. 14, 1604. Of Lincolnshire. S. and h. of Alexander (1577), of Winterton, Lincs., gent. Adm. at Gray's Inn, Nov. 20, 1605.

GEARING, RICHARD. Adm. pens. at ST CATHARINE'S, 1627.

GEARING, THOMAS. Adm. at KING'S, a scholar from Eton, Aug. 23, 1631. Of London. Matric. 1631; B.A. 1635; M.A. 1639. Vice-provost for twenty-eight years. Fellow, 1634, till his death, Oct. 17, 1694, aged 84. (*Harwood*; Le Neve, *Mon.*, V. 156.)

GEARING, WILLIAM. Adm. sizar (age 16) at TRINITY, July 4, 1685. S. of Richard. B. at Stourbridge, Worcs. School, Stourbridge. Matric. 1685; Scholar, 1687; B.A. 1688–9; M.A. 1692. Fellow, 1691.

GEARY, *see also* **GAREY.**

GERY, BENJAMIN. Matric. sizar from EMMANUEL, Easter, 1622. One of these names R. of Little Stukeley, Hunts., 1657–99. Died 1699.

GERY, GEORGE. Adm. pens. at QUEENS', May 5, 1681. Of Leicestershire. S. of John (1672), R. of Swepstone, Leics. Matric. 1681; B.A. 1684–5; M.A. 1688. Fellow (by mandate), 1688; not admitted. Ord. deacon (London) Feb. 24, 1688–9.

GEARY or GERY, JOHN. M.A. from PEMBROKE, 1672; LL.D. 1684. S. of John, of Coventry. Matric. from Magdalen College, Oxford, 1653; and incorp. at Cambridge, as 'Jery, B.A. of Oxford,' 1672. Ord. priest (Lincoln) May 1, 1661. R. of Swepstone, Leics., 1662–1722. R. of Stony Stanton, 1676–22. Archdeacon of Stow, 1683. Archdeacon of Buckingham, 1684–1722. Preb. of Lincoln, 1687–1722. Died Aug. 9, 1722, aged 85. M.I. at Swepstone. Father of George (1681). (*Nichols*, III. 1041.)

GERY, RICHARD. Adm. Fell.-Com. at EMMANUEL, May 5, 1597. Of Bushmead, Beds. S. of William, of Bushmead Priory, Eaton Socon, deceased. Adm. at Gray's Inn, Jan. 28, 1599–1600. Sheriff of Beds., 1636. Died 1638. Buried at Little Staughton, Hunts. Will proved, June 14, 1638. Father of William (1628) and Richard (1631), brother of William (1603). (*Vict. Co. Hist. Beds.*, III. 197; *Beds. N. and Q.*, III. 49.)

GERY, RICHARD. Matric. pens. from CLARE, Michs. 1601. Doubtless previously matric. from University College, Oxford, Apr. 30, 1601; 'of Cambs., gent.,' age 17.

GEREY, RICHARD. Adm. pens. at CORPUS CHRISTI, 1631. S. of Richard (1597), of Bushmead Priory, Eaton Socon, Beds., Esq. B. there. Schools, Hertford and Westminster. Matric. 1631. Migrated to Sidney, Sept. 16, 1634, age 18. B.A. from Sidney, 1635–6; M.A. 1639. Will (P.C.C.) 1652; as of Sidney College. Brother of William (1628).

GERY, ROBERT. Adm. pens. at TRINITY, June 10, 1671. S. of William (1635), D.D. School, Westminster. Scholar, 1672; Matric. 1674–5; B.A. 1674–5; M.A. 1678. Ord. deacon (London) Dec. 24, 1676. P.C. of Northaw, Herts., 1677–83. R. of Abinger, Surrey, 1685–90. R. of All Hallows-the-Great, London, 1690–1707. V. of Islington, 1691–1707. Preb. of Lincoln, 1701–7. Died Oct. 1, 1707, aged 55. Buried at Islington. M.I. Father of Thomas (1708). (*Al. Westmon.*, 172.)

GEREE or GERVIE, SAMUEL. Adm. sizar at EMMANUEL, Feb. 19, 1652–3. Of Gloucestershire. Matric. 1656; B.A. 1656–7; M.A. 1660. Ord. deacon (Lincoln) July 2, 1661; priest, July 4, 1661. Appointed Head Master of Wakefield Grammar School by Emmanuel College, July 21, 1663. Resigned, Oct. 24, 1665. (M. H. Peacock.)

GERRYE, THOMAS. Adm. sizar at KING'S, Lent, 1565–6.

GEARYE, THOMAS. Scholar of PETERHOUSE, 1601–5; B.A. 1602–3; M.A. 1606; B.D. from Emmanuel, 1613. Dixie fellow of Emmanuel, 1607. R. of Barwell, Leics., till 1662. Will (Leicester) 1670. Father of William (1635).

GERY, THOMAS. Adm. at ST CATHARINE'S, 1676.

GERY, THOMAS. Adm. sizar (age 16) at CAIUS, Oct. 10, 1678. S. of Thomas, attorney-at-law, of Harleston, Norfolk. B. there. School, Earl Stonham (Mr Wilson). Scholar, 1678–83; Matric. 1679; B.A. 1682–3. Ord. deacon (Norwich) May 30, 1686. C. of Needham, Norfolk. Probably R. of St Mary, Bedford, 1724. V. of Buckden, Hunts., 1727–37; of Wigtoft and Quadring, Lincs., 1729. Preb. of Lincoln, 1733–7. Will proved (Buckden peculiar) 1737. (*Venn*, I. 460.)

GERY, THOMAS. Adm. sizar at SIDNEY, Mar. 1694–5. S. of Benjamin (? 1622), R. of Little Stukeley, Hunts. B. there. School, Uppingham. Matric. 1698; B.A. 1698–9; M.A. 1718. Ord. deacon (Peterb.) Sept. 24, 1699. C. of Harrington, Northants. R. of Aldwincle St Peter, 1717–8. V. of Quilsborough, 1718–21. Died 1721. (H. I. Longden.)

GEREY, THOMAS. Adm. pens. at JESUS, June 3, 1708. Of Islington, Middlesex. S. of Robert (1671), clerk, deceased. Matric. 1708.

GERY, THOMAS. Adm. sizar (age 17) at ST JOHN'S, June 22, 1734. S. of Thomas, clerk, of Cambridgeshire. B. at Chatteris. School, King's, Cambridge. Matric. 1735.

GERYE, WILLIAM. Matric. pens. from ST JOHN'S, Lent, 1587–8.

GERAY, WILLIAM. Adm. at CORPUS CHRISTI, 1603. Of Bedfordshire. S. of William, of Bushmead Priory, Eaton Socon, Beds. Adm. at Gray's Inn, Mar. 17, 1602–3. Counsellor-at-law. Brother of Richard (1597). (*Vis. of Beds.*, 1634.)

GEREY, WILLIAM. Matric. Fell.-Com. from CORPUS CHRISTI, Easter, 1628. Of Bedfordshire. S. and h. of Richard (1597), of Bushmead, Eaton Socon, Beds., Esq. Adm. at Lincoln's Inn, May 10, 1630. Of Bushmead, Esq. Married Anna, dau. of Sir William Dyer. An ardent Royalist. Compounded for delinquency in arms and fined, 1647; subsequently lost his whole estate. Died before 1660. Brother of Richard (1631). (*Vis. of Beds.*, 1634; *Vict. Co. Hist. Beds.*, III. 197.)

GERY, WILLIAM. Adm. pens. (age 17) at ST JOHN'S, Apr. 29, 1635. S. of Thomas (1602–3), R. of Barwell, Leics. B. there. School, Bosworth (Mr Chawney). Matric. 1635; B.A. 1638–9; M.A. from Emmanuel, 1642; D.D. 1661. Dixie fellow of Emmanuel, 1641. Ord. priest (Lincoln) Sept. 24, 1643. R. of Braunstone, Leics., 1649–68. Archdeacon of Norwich, 1660–8. Preb. of Southwell, 1660–8. Preb. of Lincoln, 1661–8. R. of Market Bosworth, 1661. Died Mar. 31, 1668. (*Nichols*, II. 108; J. B. Peace.)

GEARY, WILLIAM. Adm. pens. at EMMANUEL, Mar. 31, 1725. Of Northamptonshire. Matric. 1726; B.A. 1728–9; M.A. 1733. Ord. deacon (Lincoln) Dec. 21, 1729; priest, Sept. 24, 1732. V. of Burton Hussey, Lincs. R. of Gt Billing, Northants., *c.* 1748–87. Preb. of Peterborough, 1759–87. Died Aug. 26, 1787, aged 79. M.I. in the Cathedral. Will, P.C.C. (H. I. Longden; Baker's *Northants.*, I. 20.)

GERY, ——. Fee for B.A. 1478–9.

GEYNEY, ——. B.Can.L. 1480–1.

GEAST or GHEAST, *see also* GUEST.

GEAST or GHEAST, EDWARD. Adm. sizar (age 18) at ST JOHN'S, June 13, 1681. S. of William, gent., deceased. B. at 'Knaveston,' in Gartrey Hundred, Leics. School, Oakham (Mr Love). Matric. 1681; LL.B. 1686. V. of Heckington, Lincs., 1686.

GEAST, WILLIAM. Matric. sizar from MAGDALENE, Michs. 1615; B.A. 1619–20; M.A. 1623. Ord. deacon (Rochester); priest (Norwich) Dec. 18, 1624. R. of Westerfield, Suffolk, 1630–8. R. of Garboldisham, Norfolk, 1637.

GEBON, *see also* GIBBON.

GEBON, JOHN. Fellow of CORPUS CHRISTI, 1378.

GEDDES, MICHAEL. M.A. 1671 (Incorp. from Edinburgh). S. of Robert. Matric. from Gloucester Hall, Oxford, Dec. 13, 1669, age 22. M.A. (Edinburgh) 1668. Incorp. at Oxford (as M.A.) 1671. LL.D. (Lambeth) 1695. Chaplain to the English Factory in Portugal, 1678–87. R. of Farmington, Gloucs., 1688–93. Chancellor of Salisbury, 1691–1713. R. of Compton Bassett, Wilts., 1693. R. of East Hendred, Berks., 1710–3. Author and translator of Portuguese and Spanish works. Died 1713. M.I. at East Hendred. Will, P.C.C. (*Al. Oxon.*; *D.N.B.*)

GEDDING, BARTHOLOMEW DE. Adm. fellow of PETERHOUSE, 1347. B.A. Clerk.

GEDGE, GAGE or GEAGE, WILLIAM. M.A. 1482; B.D. 1493–4. Of Norwich diocese. Fellow of PETERHOUSE, 1481–1500. Proctor, 1484–5. Ord. priest (Norwich) Apr. 6, 1482. Chaplain at Little St Mary's, Cambridge. Died 1500.

GEGH, ——. D.Can.L. 1479–80.

GEDLING, ROBERT. B.A. 1491. Ord. sub-deacon (Ely) Mar. 17, 1491–2, as 'Richard.'

GEDNEY, JOHN DE. Scholar of UNIVERSITY HALL (afterwards Clare) when ord. acolyte (Ely) Apr. 1342.

GEDNEY, JOHN. Matric. pens. from QUEENS', Lent, 1579–80. Of Lincolnshire. Doubtless s. of John, of Bag Enderby, Lincs. Adm. at Lincoln's Inn, Feb. 4, 1582–3. Married Mary Arden, 1587. Buried at Bag Enderby, Oct. 6, 1603. (*Lincs. Pedigrees*, 396.)

GEDNEY, JOHN. Adm. pens. at CORPUS CHRISTI, 1582. Matric. Michs. 1583.

GEDNEY, JOHN. Adm. at CORPUS CHRISTI, 1666. Of Norfolk. Matric. Lent, 1667–8; B.A. 1669–70. Ord. deacon (Peterb.) May 29, 1670. R. of Boughton, Northants., 1670–88. Died Jan. 18, 1688–9, aged 42. Buried at Pitsford Church Northants. Admon. (Archd. Northants.) 1689. (*Baker*, I. 33 H. I. Longden.)

GEDNEY, NICHOLAS. Matric. pens. from CHRIST'S, Nov. 1554.

GEDNEY, NICHOLAS. Matric. sizar from ST JOHN'S, Easter, 1576; B.A. 1579–80; M.A. 1583. Ord. deacon (Ely) Dec. 1580, age 25. V. of Gt Stukeley, Hunts., 1581–5. Died 1585.

GEDNEY, R. DE. M.A. Chancellor of the University in 1260. Benefactor. There is a letter from him to King Henry III, about University privileges. (*See Letters of Henry III*, II. 165.)

GEDNEY, RICHARD. Matric. pens. from TRINITY, Michs. 1568. Probably of Lincolnshire; adm. at Lincoln's Inn, Nov. 29, 1570.

GEDNEY, RICHARD. Matric. sizar from CLARE, Michs. 1584.

GEDNEY, RICHARD. Matric. pens. from MAGDALENE, *c.* 1595 B.A. 1601–2; M.A. 1605. Fellow. Will proved (V.C.C.) 1606.

GEE, ALEXANDER. Matric. sizar from PEMBROKE, Michs. 1581. Ord. deacon (Lincoln) Aug. 10, 1583; priest, Apr. 30, 1585. R. of Thorpe-on-the-Hill, Lincs., 1594; 'B.A.'

GEE, EDWARD. Matric. pens. from MAGDALENE, Easter, 1640.

GEE, EDWARD. Adm. sizar (age 17) at ST JOHN'S, May 9, 1676. S. of George, shoemaker. B. at Manchester. School, Manchester. Matric. 1676; B.A. 1679–80; M.A. 1683. Incorp. at Oxford, 1684. D.D. (Lambeth) 1695. V. of Gt Wilbraham, Cambs., 1685–8. R. of St Benet, Paul's Wharf, 1688–1707. Chaplain to William III, 1688. Preb. of Westminster, 1701–30. R. of Chevening, Kent, 1707–30. Dean of Peterborough, 1721–2. Dean and preb. of Lincoln, 1722–30. R. of St Margaret, Westminster, 1724–30. Died Mar. 1, 1729–30. Buried in Westminster Abbey. Will, P.C.C. (*Al. Oxon.*; *D.N.B.*)

GEE, EDWARD. Adm. pens. at QUEENS', Apr. 26, 1724; afterwards Fell.-Com. Of Middlesex. Matric. 1724; M.A. 1728 (*Com. Reg.*).

GEE, GEORGE. Scholar at CHRIST'S, *c.* 1522.

GEE, JAMES. Adm. pens. at QUEENS', Apr. 28, 1702. Of Yorkshire. 2nd s. of William (1664), of Beverley, Esq. Matric. 1702 Adm. at the Inner Temple, Nov. 23, 1704. Probably Receiver-General for Yorks. Married Constantia Moyser, 1727. Died Sept. 8, 1751. Will (P.C.C.) 1751. (G. *Mag.* G. Poulson, *Beverley*, I. 398.)

GEE, JOHN. Matric. Fell.-Com. from CHRIST'S, July, 1620. S. of Sir William, of Bishop Burton, Yorks. Bapt. there, Feb. 19, 1603–4. Adm. at the Inner Temple, 1622. Married Frances, dau. of Sir John Hotham. Buried at Bishop Burton, May 12, 1627. Admon. (York) 1627. Brother of Thomas (1621) and William (1621), father of William (1640). (M. H. Peacock.)

GEE, JOHN. M.A. from ST JOHN'S, 1670. S. of Thomas, of Warrington, Lancs., clerk. B. there. Matric. from Brasenose College, Oxford, July 16, 1661, age 17; B.A. (Oxford) 1665. R. of Lofthouse, Yorks., 1676. R. of Plumtree, Notts., 1683–1713. Preb. of Southwell, 1704–13. Chaplain to William III, and Anne. Died 1713. Buried at Plumtree. (*Al. Oxon.*; J. T. Godfrey, *Lenton*.)

GEE, JOHN. Adm. pens. (age 17) at PETERHOUSE, July 10, 1719. Of Cambridgeshire. School, Bishop's Stortford. Matric. 1719; Scholar, 1719; B.A. 1723–4; M.A. 1727. Fellow, 1726–8. Ord. deacon (Ely) Dec. 19, 1725; priest, Mar. 17, 1727–8. V. of Stapleford, Cambs., 1726. V. of Burwell, 1729. V. of Moulton, Suffolk, 1734. Died Feb. 9, 1772. Will, P.C.C. (*T. A. Walker*, 241.)

GEE, ROBERT. Matric. sizar from CORPUS CHRISTI, Easter, 1606. Of Derbyshire. Probably B.A. 1609–10. One of these names P.C. of Kingsley, Staffs., 1609.

GEE, THOMAS. Matric. pens. from TRINITY, Michs. 1616; Scholar, 1619; B.A. 1621–2; M.A. 1625.

GEE, THOMAS. Matric. pens. from CHRIST'S, July, 1621. 3rd s. of Sir William, of Bishop Burton, Yorks. B.A. 1624–5. Of Killingreaves, Yorks. Married, at St Michael Belfry, York, Sept. 24, 1633, Katherine, dau. of Philip Constable, Esq. Brother of John (1620) and William (1621). (*Peile*, I. 340; *Vis. of Yorks.*, 1665.)

GEE, THOMAS. Adm. sizar (age 15) at SIDNEY, Apr. 21, 1625. S. of William, farmer. B. at Exon, Ruts. School, Odcombe (Mr Jeremiah Whitaker). Matric. 1625; B.A. 1628–9. One of these names V. of Saxby, Lincs., 1647. (*Shaw*, I. 339.)

GEE, THOMAS. Adm. pens. (age 16) at ST JOHN'S, July 2, 1690. S. of William (1664), Esq. B. at Bishop Burton, Yorks. Bapt. Nov. 4, 1673. School, Sedbergh. Matric. 1692; B.A. 1693-4. Adm. at the Middle Temple, Feb. 24, 1695-6. Buried at Bishop Burton, July 28, 1750. Will (York) 1750. Half-brother of James (1702). Doubtless father of the next and of William (1715). (*Sedbergh Sch. Reg.*, 132.)

GEE, THOMAS. Adm. pens. (age 15) at ST JOHN'S, Apr. 9, 1716. S. of Thomas (above), gent., of Yorkshire. B. at Bishop Burton. Bapt. Oct. 3, 1700. School, Beverley (Mr Lambert). Matric. 1716; B.A. 1719-20; M.A. 1723. Ord. deacon (London, *Litt. dim.* from York) Feb. 21, 1724-5; priest, Dec. 18, 1725-6. R. of Foxholes, Yorks., 1726-36. R. of Cherry Burton, 1727-36. Chaplain to the Earl of Alhemarle. Admon. (York) Mar. 5, 1735-6. Brother of William (1715). (*Scott-Mayor*, III. 299.)

GEE or **JEE, W.** Matric. pens. from ST JOHN'S, Easter, 1577.

GEE, WALTER. Matric. pens. from TRINITY, Easter, 1583. S. of William, merchant, of Hull, Yorks. B. there. B.A. 1586-7; M.A. 1590; B.D. 1597. Ord. priest (York). V. of Fen Drayton, Cambs., 1599-1605. R. of Maids Morton, Bucks., 1603. R. of Bainton, Yorks., 1617.

GEE, WILLIAM. Matric. pens. from CHRIST'S, July, 1621. 2nd s. of Sir William, of Bishop Burton, Yorks. Bapt. July 25, 1605. B.A. 1623-4. Adm. at the Inner Temple, Nov. 27, 1627. Of Bentley, Yorks. Died 1657. Will (P.C.C.) 1657. Brother of John (1620) and Thomas (1621). (*Peile*, I. 340.)

GEE, WILLIAM. Adm. Fell.-Com. (age 15) at CHRIST'S, May 19, 1640. S. of John (1620), of Bishop Burton, near Beverley. B. at Scorborough (his mother's home). School, Helton (? Dalton), Yorks. (Mr Suffden). Matric. 1640. Of Bishop Burton, Esq. Married (1) Rachel, dau. of Sir Thomas Parker, of Willingdon, Sussex. Buried at Bishop Burton, Aug. 30, 1678. M.I. Father of the next. (*Vis. of Yorks.*, 1666; *Peile*, I. 471.)

GEE, WILLIAM. Adm. Fell.-Com. (age 15) at CHRIST'S, Apr. 15, 1664. S. of William, Esq. (1640), of Bishop Burton, Yorks. B. 1648, at Willingdon, Sussex (his mother's home). School, Westminster. M.P. for Beverley, 1679-81, 1689-90; for Hull, 1690-5, 1701-5. Married (1) Elizabeth, dau. of Sir John Hotham, of Scorborough, Yorks.; (2) Elizabeth Ellerker. Buried at Bishop Burton, Oct. 18, 1718. Father of James (1702) and Thomas (1690). (*Vis. of Yorks.*, 1666; *Peile*, I. 608; A. B. Beaven.)

GEE, WILLIAM. M.A. from SIDNEY, 1710. S. of Nathaniel, of Tavistock, Devon. Matric. from Exeter College, Oxford, May 20, 1697, age 18; B.A. (Oxford) 1700-1. 'Astronomer, at Maristor, Tamerton, Devon.' V. of Walkhampton, Devon, 1713. V. of St Winnow, Cornwall, 1728-39. Will (Exeter) 1739. (*Al. Oxon.*)

GEE, WILLIAM. Adm. pens. (age 16) at ST JOHN'S, Apr. 7, 1715. 1st s. of Thomas (1690), gent., of Bishop Burton, Yorks. B. at Edwinstowe, Notts. Bapt. there, Apr. 13, 1699. School, Beverley (Mr Lambert). Matric. 1715. Colonel, 20th Foot. Killed at Fontenoy, Apr. 30, 1745. Brother of Thomas (1716). (G. Poulson, *Beverley*; M. H. Peacock.)

GEE, WILLIAM. Adm. pens. (age 17) at PETERHOUSE, June 29, 1749. Of Cambridgeshire. Matric. 1749; Scholar, 1749; B.A. 1753. Ord. deacon (Norwich) Mar. 1753; priest (Lincoln) Dec. 18, 1756. V. of Wherstead, Suffolk, 1761-1815. V. of Bentley. R. of St Stephen's, Ipswich, 1772-1815. Died Apr. 19, 1815. Buried at St Stephen's, Ipswich. M.I. there. (*T. A. Walker*, 294.)

GEEKIE, JOHN. Adm. pens. at QUEENS', Nov. 15, 1742. Of the East Indies. 1st s. of John, of Bombay. Matric. 1743. Adm. at the Middle Temple, Feb. 12, 1741-2.

GEEKIE, WILLIAM. Adm. pens. (age 16) at ST JOHN'S, Oct. 19, 1706. S. of Alexander, surgeon. B. in London. School, Tottenham High Cross. Matric. 1706; B.A. 1710-1; M.A. 1714; B.D. from Queens', 1723; D.D. 1729. Fellow of Queens'. Incorp. at Oxford, 1716. Ord. priest (Ely) Dec. 23, 1722. Chaplain to the Duke of Somerset, and afterwards to Archbishop Wake. R. of Southfleet, Kent, 1729-67. R. of Chevening, 1729-32. R. of Woodchurch, 1729-30. R. of Deal, 1730-53. Preb. of Canterbury, 1731-67. R. of All Hallows, Barking, 1733-67. Archdeacon of Gloucester, 1738-67. R. of Dursley, Glouc., 1738-67. Died July 22, 1767. Buried at Canterbury. Will, P.C.C.

GEERE, DIONES. Adm. sizar (age 18) at CHRIST'S, June 2, 1726. S. of Dionis. B. at Rottingdean, Sussex. School, Battle. Matric. 1726; Scholar, 1727; B.A. 1729-30; M.A. 1746. Ord. deacon (Chichester) June, 1731; priest (Ely) Dec. 1732. R. of South Heighton, Sussex, with Tarring Neville, 1738. Also R. of Pett. Will (P.C.C.) 1765; of South Heighton. (*Peile*, II. 212; J. Ch. Smith.)

GERE or **GIER, NICHOLAS.** Matric. pens. from CLARE, Easter, 1566; B.A. 1569-70.

GEERS, FRANCIS. M.B. from ST CATHARINE'S, 1682. S. of Thomas, of Bridge Sollers, Heref., gent. Matric. from Brasenose College, Oxford, Apr. 10, 1663, age 18. Of Garnons, Heref. Died July 17, 1721, aged 76. M.I. at Mansell Gamage. Father of Timothy (1711-2). (*Al. Oxon.*; Robinson, *Mansions of Herefordshire*, 194.)

GEERES, JOHN. Mus.Doc. from KING'S, 1623.

GEERS, TIMOTHY. Adm. pens. (age 17) at ST JOHN'S, Mar. 3, 1711-2. S. of Francis (1682), M.D. B. at Hereford. School, Hereford (Mr Trahern). Matric. 1712; B.A. 1715-6; M.A. 1720. R. of Whitney, Heref. Died Nov. 10, 1746. M.I. at Mansell Gamage.

GEFFORNE, ——. B.Can.L. 1502-3.

GEGGYS, WILLIAM. B.Civ.L. 1516-7.

GELASIUS or **GALASIUS, JOHN.** Matric. pens. from TRINITY, Easter, 1563; B.A. 1563-4; Scholar, 1564.

GELDART, ROBERT. Adm. pens. (age 18) at TRINITY, June 18, 1688. S. of John. B. at Wiganthorpe, Yorks. Bapt. at Terrington, Oct. 17, 1670. School, Wakefield. Matric. 1688. Adm. at Gray's Inn, May 15, 1690. Of Wiganthorpe and Askham Bryan, Yorks. (M. H. Peacock.)

GELDAR, CHRISTOPHER. Matric. pens. from TRINITY, Michs. 1579. One of these names, of Bridlington, Yorks., licensed to marry Bridget Hobman, of Hutton Cranswick, in 1592.

GELDER, HUGH. Matric. pens. from ST JOHN'S, Easter, 1584; B.A. 1587-8. Perhaps M.A. Ord. deacon (Lincoln) Nov. 12, 1590; priest, June 30, 1591. V. of Horkstow, Lincs., 1590, as M.A.

GELDER, JOHN. Matric. sizar from PEMBROKE, Easter, 1605. Probably buried at St Botolph's, Cambridge, Nov. 1, 1620, as 'subcoquus' of Queens'.

GELDER, JOHN. Adm. sizar (age 17) at ST JOHN'S, Mar. 29, 1707. S. of Richard, deceased. B. at Barton-on-Humber, Lincs. School, Beverley (Mr Lambert). Matric. 1707; B.A. 1710-1. Ord. deacon (York) Sept. 1711; priest, 1713. V. of Barton-on-Humber, 1713. Preb. of Lincoln, 1720-52.

GELDER, WILLIAM. Matric. sizar from ST JOHN'S, Easter, 1583. B. at Hull, Yorks. B.A. 1586-7. Ord. deacon (London) Sept. 26, 1589; priest (York) Aug. 1, 1600, as M.A. R. of the mediety of Westborough, Lincs., 1610. V. of Farndon and Balderton, Notts.

GELL, GEORGE. Adm. sizar at EMMANUEL, May 24, 1693. Of Middleton, Derbs. S. of Thomas. B. 1674. Matric. 1695; B.A. 1696-7; M.A. 1723. Ord. priest (Ely) Mar. 1, 1701-2. V. of Castle Donington, Leics., 1704-23. R. of Appleby Magna, 1731-43. Will (Leicester) 1744. Father of the next.

GELL, GEORGE. Adm. sizar at EMMANUEL, May 26, 1726. Of Middleton, Derbs. S. of George (above). Matric. 1726; B.A. 1729-30; M.A. 1733. Dixie fellow, 1731. Ord. deacon (Lincoln) June 4, 1732; priest, June 20, 1736. R. of Thurning, Hunts., 1739-40. Died 1780.

GELL, JOHN. B.A. from ST JOHN'S, 1742 (according to the *Graduati*).

GELL, MATTHEW (1607), *see* GILL.

GELL, PHILIP. Adm. pens. at EMMANUEL, Juue 26, 1732. Of Middleton, Derbs. S. of Thomas, of Wirksworth. B. 1714. Matric. 1733; M.B. 1737. Adm. at Leyden, Sept. 17, 1737. Died Sept. 8, 1776. Probably brother of Thomas (1743). (J. B. Peace.)

GELL, PHILIP. Adm. Fell.-Com. (age 17) at PEMBROKE, Sept. 28, 1741. S. of John, Esq. B. at Holme, Derbs. Matric. 1741. Of Hopton, Derbs., Esq. Sheriff, 1755. Married Dorothy, dau. of William Milnes, Esq., of Aldercar Park. Died Aug. 5, 1795. The father, John Eyre, took his mother's name Gell, on inheriting Hopton. (Burke, *Ext. Bart.*; F.M.G., 46.)

GELL, ROBERT. Adm. sizar at QUEENS', Nov. 26, 1594. Of Norfolk. Ord. deacon (London) Feb. 22; priest, Feb. 27, 1600-1, as B.A. C. of Oxnead, Norfolk, 1605-35.

GELL, ROBERT (1601), *see* GILL.

GELL, ROBERT. Matric. sizar from CHRIST'S, Apr. 1615. S. of William, V. of Frindsbury, Kent. B. at Pampisford, Cambs. School, Westminster. B.A. 1617-8; M.A. 1621; B.D. 1628; D.D. 1641. Fellow, *c.* 1623. Chaplain to Sheldon, Archbishop of Canterbury. R. of St Mary Aldermary, London, 1641-65. Author and critic; his works include an essay towards the Amendment of the last English Translation of the Bible. Perhaps C. of Pampisford, Cambs. Died Mar. 25, 1665, aged 70. Buried at Pampisford. M.I. there. Will (P.C.C.) 1665. (*Peile*, I. 301; D.N.B.)

GELL, THOMAS. Adm. at Corpus Christi, 1743. Of Wirksworth, Derbs. S. of Thomas. B. 1723. Matric. Michs. 1743; B.A. 1746-7; M.A. 1750. Attorney-at-law. Died Jan. 26, 1767. Probably brother of Philip (1732).

GELLIBRAND, ANDREW. Adm. sizar at Emmanuel, Apr. 27, 1671. S. of John, V. of Leigh, Lancs., and Mary, dau. of Andrew Chorlton, of Tearne, Salop. B. in Salop. Age 12 in 1664. Matric. 1671; B.A. 1674-5; M.A. 1678. Ord. deacon (Peterb.) Sept. 19, 1675. (*Vis. of Lancs.*, 1664.)

GELLIBRAND, EDWARD. B.D. from Emmanuel, 1585 (Incorp. from Oxford). Of Kent. Matric. from Magdalen College, Oxford, 1571, age 18; B.A. (Oxford) 1573; M.A. 1577; B.D. 1584. Fellow, 1573-88. Specially adm. at Lincoln's Inn, May 6, 1587. A strong Puritan. Minister at the English church at Middleburg, Holland. Died there 1601. *See* an account of his troubles with the Archbishop in 1586, in *Part of a Register*, II. 36. Will (P.C.C.) 1601. (*Al. Oxon.*)

GILLIBRAND, THOMAS. Adm. sizar at Trinity, May 10, 1659. Matric. 1660, as Gellibrand.

GELOWE or JELOWE, HENRY. B.Can.L. 1460.

GELSON, ANDREW. Adm. pens. (age 19) at St John's, May 2, 1639. S. of John, yeoman, of Kirton, Lincs. B. there. School, Spalding (Mr Heaton). Matric. 1639.

GELSTHORPE, EDWARD. Adm. pens. (age 17) at Caius, Feb. 20, 1642-3. S. of William, gent., of Edingthorpe, Norfolk. B. at East Ruston. School, Norwich. Matric. 1643; Scholar, 1644-9; B.A. 1646-7; M.A. 1651; M.D. 1663 (*Lit. Reg.*). Fellow, 1655-77. Proctor, 1662. Incorp. at Oxford, 1663. Hon. Fell. R.C.P. 1664. Physician to the Duke of Monmouth, 1668. Benefactor to Caius. Died Mar. 6, 1676-7. Will proved (Dean and Chapter, Norwich) June 20, 1677. (*Venn*, I. 349; *Vis. of Norfolk*, 1664.)

GELTHORPE or GELSTROP, FRANCIS. Matric. pens. from Trinity, Michs. 1582; B.A. 1585-6; M.A. 1589. R. of Gt Ponton, Lincs., 1592-1602. Died 1602.

GELSTHORPE, PETER. Adm. pens. (age 18) at Caius, May 16, 1679. S. of Peter, druggist, of London. B. there. Schools, Uxbridge (Mr Robinson) and Felsted. Matric. 1679; Scholar, 1679-84; M.B. 1684; M.D. (Utrecht) 1688. Candidate of the College of Physicians, 1688. F.R.C.P. 1691. Practised at Deal. Died in Hatton Garden, London. Buried at St Andrew's, Holborn, June 18, 1719. Will (P.C.C.) 1723. Father of the next. (*Venn*, I. 461; Munk's *Roll*.)

GELSTHORPE, ROBERT. Adm. pens. (age 17) at Caius, May 6, 1713. S. of Peter (1679), M.D. School, Charterhouse. Matric. 1713; Scholar, 1713-5; M.B. 1718. Resided at Welwyn, Herts. Died Jan. 8, 1731-2. Buried at St Andrew's, Holborn. M.I. at Welwyn. (*Venn*, I. 529.)

GEM, RICHARD. Adm. pens. (age 19) at St John's, June 12, 1735. S. of Richard, gent., of Worcestershire. B. at Barnsley Hall, Bromsgrove. School, Worcester (private; Mr Phillips). Matric. 1735. Doubtless V. of Crowle, Worcs. Died Dec. 1769. (*G. Mag.*)

GENAYS, BARNABAS. Adm. sizar (age 18) at St John's, June 23, 1683. S. of Elias, Esq. B. at Fontaine, in Lower Poitou. Privately educated under Dr Walker. Matric. 1683; B.A. 1686-7; M.A. 1690. Ord. deacon (London) Sept. 21, 1690.

GENNA (?), ANDREW. Matric. sizar from Jesus, Michs. 1583.

GENNY, *see also* JENNEY.

GENNYE, CHRISTOPHER. Matric. pens. from Gonville Hall, Easter, 1557. Perhaps s. of John Jenney, of Cressingham, Norfolk; adm. at Lincoln's Inn, Oct. 7, 1560. (*Venn*, I. 40.)

GENYE, W. Matric. sizar from Caius, Easter, 1559. Perhaps brother of Christopher; adm. at Lincoln's Inn, Aug. 6, 1565.

GENTE or GEINT, EDWARD. Matric. sizar from Corpus Christi, *c.* 1593. Of Essex. B.A. 1596-7; M.A. 1600. Fellow, 1597-1606. Junior Proctor, 1605-6. Taxor, 1606. Incorp. at Oxford, 1606.

GENT, GEORGE. Adm. scholar at Trinity Hall, Jan. 6, 1660-1. Probably s. of George, of Moyns, Essex. Matric. 1661; B.A. 1664-5. Died 1713, aged 72. (Wright, *Essex*, I. 633.)

GENT, GEORGE. Adm. Fell.-Com. at Trinity Hall, Mar. 12, 1746-7 (name off, 1749). Doubtless s. of George, of Moyns Park, Essex. Adm. at Lincoln's Inn, Jan. 23, 1746-7. Succeeded his father. Died 1818. (*Vis. of Essex*, 1634.)

GENT, HENRY. Matric. Fell.-Com. from Queens', Michs. 1581. S. of Thomas (below), Baron of the Exchequer. Of Steeple Bumpstead, Essex, Esq. High Sheriff of Essex, 1632, and J.P. Married Dorothy, dau. of Sir John Dalston. Died June 15, 1639. Father of John (1622) and Nicholas (1628). (*Vis. of Essex*, 1634; *Morant*, II. 354.)

GENT or GEINT, JOHN. Adm. at Corpus Christi, 1562. Resident pensioner in 1564. Possibly same as the next.

GENT or JENTE, JOHN. Matric. sizar from Magdalene, Michs. 1564; B.A. 1567-8.

GENT, JOHN. Matric. pens. from St John's, Michs. 1622. S. of Henry (1581), of Steeple Bumpstead, Essex, Esq. B.A. 1625-6; M.A. 1629. R. of Birdbrook, Essex, 1632-51. Buried Jan. 13, 1650-1. Will (P.C.C.) 1651. Brother of the next. (*Vis. of Essex*, 1634; H. Smith.)

GENT, NICHOLAS. Matric. pens. from St John's, Michs. 1628. S. of Henry (1581), of Steeple Bumpstead, Essex. B.A. 1631-2; M.A. 1635. Ord. priest (Rochester) Sept. 23, 1633. R. of Shadoxhurst, Kent, 1639. R. of Sturmer, Essex, 1645-77. R. of Birdbrook, 1670-7. Died 1677. Brother of the above. (*Vis. of Essex*, 1634.)

GENT, THOMAS. Educated at Cambridge. S. of William, of Moyns, Essex. Barrister, of the Middle Temple. Recorder of Maldon. M.P. for Maldon, 1572-83. Serjeant-at-law, 1584. Baron of the Exchequer, 1586-94. A member of the high commission in causes ecclesiastical. Died Jan. 1593-4. Buried at Steeple Bumpstead. Admon., P.C.C. Father of Henry (1581). (*Cooper*, II. 163; *Vis. of Essex*, 1634; *D.N.B.*)

GENT, ——. B.Civ.L. 1477-8.

GENT, ——. Matric. pens. from Christ's, Easter, 1548. (*See Peile*, I. 44, who identifies him with Thomas, above.)

GENTLE, GEORGE. Matric. sizar from Corpus Christi, 1606. Of Lincolnshire. Probably B.A. 1609-10. V. of Timberland, Lincs. V. of Dunston, 1611-32, 'B.A.'

GENTLE, JOHN. Adm. pens. at Jesus, Apr. 23, 1623. Matric. 1623; B.A. 1626-7. Ord. deacon (Peterb.) Sept. 7; priest, Sept. 8, 1627.

GENTREY, NATHANIEL. Adm. sizar (age 17) at St John's, Dec. 13, 1704. S. of John, shopkeeper. B. in London. School, St Paul's. Matric. 1705. Ord. deacon (London) Sept. 19, 1708; priest, Mar. 20, 1708-9. R. of Hazeleigh, Essex, 1709; deprived, 1724.

GEORDIUS, ——. Of St Mary's Hall or Hostel, 1464. (*Gr. Bk*, A, 44.)

GEORGE, JOHN. Adm. sizar (age 15) at Pembroke, Mar. 23, 1692-3. S. of John, of Thetford, Norfolk. Matric. 1693; B.A. 1696-7. Ord. deacon (Norwich) June 15, 1701; priest, Sept. 1702. R. of East and West Lexham, Norfolk, 1702-41. F.R.S. 1719.

GEORGE, SAMUEL. Adm. sizar at St John's, Apr. 11, 1665. S. of Thomas, butcher, of Titchmarsh, Northants. B. there. Schools, Kimbolton (Mr Taylor) and Oundle. Matric. 1667; B.A. 1668-9; M.A. 1673. Ord. deacon (Peterb.) Sept. 19, 1669; priest (Ely) Sept. 24, 1670. V. of Staverton, Northants., 1674-7. Buried there Dec. 9, 1677.

GEORGE, THEOBALD. M.A. 1612 (on visit of Prince Charles).

GEORGE, THOMAS. Adm. pens. (age 18) at St John's, Apr. 16, 1678. S. of Thomas. B. at Chartham, Kent. School, Canterbury. Matric. 1678.

GEORGE, WILLIAM. Adm. at King's, a scholar from Eton, 1715. B. in London, 1697. Matric. Easter, 1716; B.A. 1719-20; M.A. 1723; D.D. 1728 (*Com. Reg.*). Fellow, 1719. Provost of King's, 1743-56. Vice-Chancellor, 1743-4. Ord. priest (Ely) July 17, 1726. Assistant Master at Eton; Head Master, 1728-43. Chaplain to the King, 1728-56. Canon of Windsor, 1731-48. Preb. of Lincoln, 1748-56. Dean of Lincoln, 1748-56. R. of Whittington, Derbs., till 1748. Author, sermons. Died Sept. 22, 1756. Admon., P.C.C. (*D.N.B.*; *Harwood*.)

GEORGES, DAVID. 'Student at Trinity, Cambridge. B. at Charbury, Salop'; so described when ord. deacon (London) Feb. 23, 1566-7.

GEREY, WILLIAM. Scholar of Clare, 1503.

GERDON, PAUL. Grace for incorporation and for B.D. 1473-4. V. of Mildenhall, Suffolk.

GERE, NICHOLAS, *see* GEERE.

GERMIN, *see also* JERMIN.

GERMIN or GERMAN, DANIEL. Matric. pens. from King's, Easter, 1603; B.A. 1605-6; M.A. 1613. Incorp. at Oxford, 1615. R. of Woollavington, Sussex, 1609; and of Up Waltham, 1614.

GERMYN, GERVASE. Adm. pens. (afterwards Fell.-Com.) at Jesus, June 9, 1621. Of Huntingdonshire. Matric. 1621; B.A. 1626. One of these names was s. of Edward Jermyn (? 1564), D.D., J.P. of Hunts.

GERMYN, JOHN. Matric. sizar from Gonville Hall, Michs. 1548. Perhaps s. of Edmund Jermyn, of Sturston, Norfolk; adm. at Gray's Inn, 1552. (*Venn*, I. 35.)

GERMAN or JERMAN, JOHN. Adm. sizar at Jesus, July 5, 1625. Matric. 1626, as Jerman; B.A. 1629-30; M.A. 1633, as German.

GERMYN, THOMAS. Matric. sizar from Gonville Hall, Michs. 1548. Perhaps s. of Edmund Jermyn, of Sturston, Norfolk; and brother of John.

GERMAIN, WILLIAM. Adm. pens. at CLARE, June 24, 1710. S. of Paschal, of Paris, Esq. B. in Holland. Matric. 1710. Adm. at the Inner Temple, July 15, 1714.

GERNEA, JOHN BAPTIST. Incorp. M.D. from Pisa, 1669.

GERNINGHALL, REGINALD. Chancellor of the University, 1256.

GERNAYS, JOHN. B.D. 1460-1. Canonicus.

GERNON, WILLIAM, *see* GARNON.

GERRARD, *see* also GARRARD.

GERRARD or GERARD, CHARLES. Adm. Fell.-Com. at CORPUS CHRISTI, Jan. 15, 1609-10. Of Lancashire. S. and h. of Radcliffe, Esq. Matric. 1610. Adm. at Gray's Inn, Feb. 28, 1612-3. Knighted, Aug. 12, 1617. Of Halsall, Lancs. Married Penelope, dau. of Sir Edward Fitton. Buried at Halsall. (Foster, *Lancs. Pedigrees*; *Masters*, 293.)

GERRARD, CHARLES. Adm. pens. at QUEENS', Sept. 14, 1647. Of Cheshire.

GERRARD, CHARLES. Adm. Fell.-Com. at EMMANUEL, Sept. 18, 1649. S. of Dutton, 3rd Baron Gerard. Succeeded as 4th Baron Gerard, 1640. Died in London, Dec. 28, 1667. Buried at Ashley, Staffs. (Baines, *Lancs.*, IV. 374; *Collins*, IX. 420; *G.E.C.*)

GERRARD, FELIX. Adm. scholar (age 17) at CAIUS, Mar. 10, 1577-8. S. of William, of Harrow-on-the-Hill. Schools, Harrow and Eton. Scholar to 1582. Probably adm. at Gray's Inn, Feb. 2, 1591-2. Will (P.C.C.) 1637; proved by nephew, Sir Gilbert, Bart. Brother of Philip (1581). (*Midds. Pedigrees*; *Venn*, I. 96.)

GERRARD, FRANCIS. Matric. pens. from CHRIST'S, Dec. 1615; B.A. from Balliol College, Oxford, 1618-9; M.A. (all Souls') 1621-2; B.C.L. 1625; D.C.L. 1631-2. Died July 3, 1643. (*Peile*, I. 304; *Al. Oxon.*)

GERHARD, FRANCIS. Matric. Fell.-Com. from ST CATHARINE'S, Easter, 1632. Of Hertfordshire. Probably s. of Sir Gilbert, of Harrow, Middlesex. B. *c.* 1620. M.P. for Seaford, 1641-8; for Middlesex, 1659; and for Bossiney, 1660. Knighted, June 8, 1660. Succeeded as Bart., 1670. Died before 1685. (*G.E.C.*)

GERARD, GILBERT. Studied at Cambridge (*Cooper*, II. 141). S. of James, of Holcroft, Lancs. Adm. at Gray's Inn, 1537. Barrister, 1539. Treasurer, 1555. M.P. for Liverpool, 1545-7; for Wigan, 1552, 1553 and 1555; for Steyning, 1554; and for Co. Lancs., 1584-6. Attorney-general, 1559-81. Counsel of the University, 1561. A member of the Ecclesiastical Commission, 1567. Knighted, 1579. Master of the Rolls, 1581-93. Chief Commissioner of the Great Seal, 1591-2. Died Feb. 4, 1592-3. Will (P.C.C.) 1593. Father of Thomas (1579). (*Midds. Pedigrees*; *D.N.B.*)

GERRARD, GILBERT. Matric. pens. from TRINITY, Easter, 1602.

GERRARD, GILBERT. Adm. Fell.-Com. at CORPUS CHRISTI, Jan. 15, 1609-10. S. of Thomas (1579), Lord Gerard, of Gerard's Bromley. Matric. 1610. Adm. at Gray's Inn, Feb. 1612-3. K.B. 1610. M.P. for Wigan, 1614. Succeeded as 2nd Baron, 1618. Married Eleanor, dau. of Thomas Dutton, of Dutton, Cheshire. Died 1622. (Foster's *Lancs. Pedigrees*; *Ormerod*, I. 482; G.*E.C.*)

GERARD, GILBERT. Adm. pens. at EMMANUEL, Aug. 20, 1634. Of Essex. Matric. 1634.

GERARD, JOHN. Matric. pens. from TRINITY, Easter, 1582; Scholar, 1582; B.A. 1585-6; M.A. 1589. Fellow, 1588.

GERRARD, JOHN. Matric. pens. from JESUS, Easter, 1615; B.A. 1618-9; M.A. 1622. Contributed to the new buildings at Jesus, 1638. One of these names R. of Drayton Beauchamp, Bucks., 1630. Perhaps R. of Necton, Norfolk, 1630; and R. of East Bradenham, 1632. Will (P.C.C.) 1650; proved by brothers Sir Gilbert and William (1602). (J. Ch. Smith.)

GERARD, JOHN. Licensed to practise medicine, 1643.

GERARD, JOHN. Adm. at KING'S, a scholar from Eton, Aug. 13, 1656. S. of Sir Gilbert, Bart. B. at Harrow, 1638. Matric. 1656; B.A. 1660; M.A. 1664. Fellow, 1659-90. Died 1690. Buried in King's Chapel. (Le Neve, *Mon.*, V. 121.)

GERARD, JOHN (1661), *see* JARRAT.

GERARD, JOHN. Adm. pens. (age 17) at CHRIST'S, June 30, 1677. S. of Joshua. B. at Stockport, Cheshire. School, Stockport (Mr S. Needham). Matric. 1677; B.A. 1680-1. Brother of the next and of Joshua.

GERARD, JOSEPH. Adm. pens. (age 19) at CHRIST'S, May 5, 1677. S. of Joshua. B. at Stockport, Cheshire. School, Stockport (Mr Sam. Needham). Matric. 1677; B.A. 1680-1. V. of Tarvin, Cheshire, 1680-1708. Died Jan. 8, 1708-9. M.I. at Tarvin. Brother of John (above) and Joshua (next). (*Peile*, II. 63.)

GERARD, JOSHUA. Adm. pens. (age 18) at CHRIST'S, June 9, 1688. S. of Joshua. B. at Stockport, Cheshire. School, Tarvin (Mr Radley). Matric. 1688; Scholar, 1689; M.B. 1693. Brother of John (1677) and Joseph. (*Peile*, II. 110.)

GERARD, NATHANIEL. Adm. sizar (age 18) at PEMBROKE, Dec. 15, 1727. S. of Peter, gent. B. at Hinckley, Leics. Matric. 1728; B.A. 1731-2; M.A. 1752. Ord. deacon (Peterb.) June 4, 1732; priest (Lincoln, *Litt. dim.* from Peterb.) June 1, 1735. Master of the Free School at Clipston, Northants., 1732. V. of Palling, Norfolk, 1769-98. R. of Waxham, 1769-98. Married, May 14, 1735, Elizabeth, widow of John Oakley, of Clipston, clerk. (H. I. Longden.)

GERRARDE, PHILIP. Adm. (age 18) at CAIUS, Feb. 9, 1581-2. S. of William, gent. B. at Harrow, Middlesex. School, Harrow. Scholar, 1582-5. Adm. at Gray's Inn, Feb. 2, 1583-4. Barrister, 1593. Ancient, 1603. Reader, 1611. Will (P.C.C.) 1637. Brother of Felix (1577) and the next. (*Venn*, I. 113.)

GERARD, RICHARD. Adm. pens. (age 15) at CAIUS, Nov. 4, 1567. Of Harrow, Middlesex. S. of William, Recorder of Chester. Matric. 1568. Migrated to Trinity. Scholar, 1569; B.A. 1571-2; M.A. from Caius, 1575; B.D. 1582. Fellow of Caius, 1574-82. Incorp. at Oxford, 1578. R. of Stockport, Cheshire, 1577-1614. Chaplain to the Queen. Preb. of Southwell, 1580. Buried at Stockport, May 17, 1614. Brother of the above and Felix. (*Venn*, I. 61.)

GERARD, RICHARD. Matric. pens. from PETERHOUSE, Easter, 1611; B.A. 1614-5; M.A. 1618. Doubtless s. of William, late reader at Gray's Inn; adm. at Gray's Inn, June 26, 1617. Barrister, 1633. Will (P.C.C.) 1641; as of Drayton Beauchamp, Bucks.; proved by brothers John and Francis. (J. Ch. Smith.)

GERARD, THOMAS. B.Can.L. 1467-8.

GERARD, THOMAS. M.A. and B.D. (Cambridge) according to *Cooper*. B.A. (Oxford) 1517. An early reformer. R. of All Hallows, Honey Lane, London, 1537. Chaplain to Cranmer, 1537. Distributed Lutheran books, and Tyndall's translation of the New Testament. Convicted of heresy, and burnt at Smithfield, July 30, 1540. (*Cooper*, I. 75; *D.N.B.*)

GERRARDE, THOMAS. Adm. Fell.-Com. (age 16) at CAIUS, Feb. 1, 1579-80. S. of Sir Gilbert, Knt., Attorney-general, of Harrow-on-the-Hill. Perhaps specially adm. at Gray's Inn, 1577. Knighted, 1591. Knight Marshal of the Royal Household, 1597. Governor of Harrow School, 1597. Created Baron Gerard, of Gerard's Bromley, Staffs., July 21, 1603. Lord President of Wales. Died Jan. 15, 1617-8. Buried at Ashley, Staffs. , P.C.C. Father of Gilbert (1610). (*Venn*, I. 105; *G.E.C.*)Will

GERRARDE, THOMAS. Adm. pens. (age 16) at CAIUS, Sept. 24, 1603. S. of William, Esq., late reader Gray's Inn, of London. Scholar, 1604-9; B.A. 1606-7. Adm. at Gray's Inn, Feb. 2, 1609-10. Of Barnwell, Kent. (*Venn*, I. 183.)

GERARD, Sir THOMAS. M.A. 1612 (on King's visit). Probably s. of Sir Thomas, of Bryn, Lancs. Knighted, 1603. Created Bart., 1611. M.P. for Liverpool, 1597-8; for Lancaster, 1614; for Wigan, 1620-1. Died Feb. 1620-1. Buried at St Margaret's, Westminster. (*G.E.C.*)

GERRARD, THOMAS. Adm. pens. at EMMANUEL, June 11, 1622. Matric. 1622.

GERRARD, THOMAS. Adm. pens. at QUEENS', June 24, 1665. Matric. 1665. Doubtless s. and h. of Francis, of Leatherhead, Surrey; adm. at Lincoln's Inn, Feb. 13, 1666-7.

GERARD, WILLIAM. Matric. pens. (age 13) from TRINITY, Easter, 1565; B.A. 1568-9; M.A. 1572.

GERARD, WILLIAM. Matric. pens. from TRINITY, Easter, 1602. S. of William, of Flambards. B. at Harrow, Middlesex. Scholar, 1605; B.A. 1605-6; M.A. 1609. Incorp. at Oxford, 1615. Ord. deacon (London) June 15, 1617, age 28; priest, Dec. 24, 1620. R. of Aston Clinton, Bucks., 1631 (patron, Sir Gilbert Gerard, Bart.); deprived, 1662. (*Vis. of Bucks.*, 1634; *Midds. Pedigrees*; *Al. Oxon.*)

GERARD, WILLIAM. Adm. pens. at EMMANUEL, May 21, 1603. Matric. 1603.

GERARD, ——. B.D. 1463-4; D.D. 1468-9.

GERARD, ——. *Cautio* for degree, 1487-8.

GERARD, ——. B.A. 1500-1.

GERRARD, ——. Adm. Fell.-Com. at JESUS, Dec. 24, 1622.

GERRARD, ——. Adm. pens. at ST CATHARINE'S, 1675.

GERRATT, WILLIAM. Matric. Fell.-Com. from JESUS, Easter, 1615.

GERTH, JONATHAN, *see* GARTH.

GERVASE or GERVYS, *see also* JERVIS.

GERVASE or JARVIS, G. (? GULIELMUS). D.D. 1661 (*Lit. Reg.*).

GERVEYS or JERVEYS, JOHN. B.D. 1501-2. Canonicus.

GERVASE or GWARVES, JOHN. Adm. at KING'S (age 16) a scholar from Eton, 1500. Of Bradfield, Suffolk. B.A. 1504. Fellow, 1503. R. of Horstead, Norfolk, 1505-20. (*Harwood.*)

GERVIE, SAMUEL, *see* GEARY.

GERY, *see* GEARY.

GESLINGE, NICHOLAS. Matric. pens. from CHRIST'S, July, 1612; B.A. 1615-6; M.A. 1620.

GETHYN, GEOFFREY. M.Gram. 1547-8. Possibly the 'M.A.; canon of St Asaph, 1548. R. of Llanbrynmair; schoolmaster at Denbigh.' (Browne Willis, *St Asaph*, 254.)

GETHIN, JOHN. Matric. sizar from QUEENS', Easter, 1626. Of Denbighshire. B.A. 1629-30; M.A. 1637. R. of Llanvoroc, Denbigh. R. of Aberdaron, Carnarvon. Preb. of Bangor, 1661-6. (Browne Willis, *Bangor.*)

GETSIUS (GOETZ), DANIEL. Adm. sizar at QUEENS', Nov. 29, 1621. B. at Odenheim in the Palatinate, 1592. Incorp. at Oxford, 1628, as 'John Daniel, B.A. from Cambridge'; though this degree is not recorded. Studied at Marburg University, where he took the degree of doctor of philosophy, 1618. Religious difficulties forced him to fly from Hesse, and he finally proceeded to Cambridge. V. of Stoke Gabriel, Devon, 1636-72. Imprisoned, 1643, for a royalist sermon, but released. R. of Bigbury Devon, 1660. Author. Died Dec. 24, 1672. Will (Exeter) 1672. (*D.N.B.*)

GEURDAIN, AARON. Matric. pens. from PEMBROKE, Easter, 1619. S. of Michael, of Jersey. B.A. 1622-3; M.A. from Queens', 1627. Licensed to practise medicine, 1632. Fellow of Queens', 1628-31. M.D. at Rheims, Apr. 1634. Practised in London. Hon. fellow R.C.P. Dec. 1664. Will of one of these names (P.C.C.) 1657; of Bevis Marks, London: property in Jersey. (*Munk*, I. 328.)

GEURDON, DENNIS. Matric. pens. from QUEENS', Easter, 1632. 'Of Hants.' Probably of Jersey; *see* Michael Geurdon in *Al. Oxon.*, 1677.

GEVE, ——. Adm. at CORPUS CHRISTI, 1584.

GEYNEY, ——. B.Can.L. 1480-1.

GEYSTE or GOYSTE, JOHN. University chaplain, 1276. (Stokes, *Chaplains*, 81.)

GEYTON, *see* GAYTON.

GHENAYE, ——. Fee for degree, 1539-40.

CHILT, WILLIAM. 'Of CLARE.' Ord. deacon (York) Sept. 1610; priest, Feb. 1610-1.

GIBART or GIBERT, HENRY. Adm. Fell.-Com. (age 26) at TRINITY, Mar. 10, 1722. S. of Henry, 'Auliensis,' France. Protestant refugee. School, Geneva (Dr Morrice). M.A. 1728 (*Com. Reg.*). Perhaps of Rotton, Lincs. Died May, 1770. (G. *Mag.*)

GIBB, FREDERIC. M.A. from PETERHOUSE, 1618 (Incorp. from St Andrews). Fellow of Peterhouse, 1619. Ord. deacon and priest (London) Feb. 22, 1623-4. R. of Hartest and Boxted, Suffolk, 1627-42, ejected. Probably uncle of Frederick Gibb, the author. (*D.N.B.*)

GIBBE or GYBBE, ——. B.A. 1510-1.

GIBBENSON, HUGH. Matric. sizar from ST JOHN'S, *c.* 1593; B.A. 1596-7; M.A. 1600. R. of Nevendon, Essex, 1609-15. Will (Cons. C. London) 1615.

GIBBEX, JOHN. Matric. sizar from CLARE, Easter, 1653.

GIBBIN, PETER, *see* GIBBONS.

GIBBINS, MICHAEL. Matric. sizar from QUEENS', Easter, 1637. Of Suffolk. B.A. 1640-1. R. of Hollesley, Suffolk, 1662.

GIBBINS, VINCENT. Adm. pens. at EMMANUEL, Nov. 27, 1683. Of Salop.

GIBBINSON or GIBSON, ——. B.Can.L. 1511-2. Perhaps John Gibbinson, chaplain to the Bishop of Ely. R. of Doddington, Cambs., 1527.

GIBBON or GIBBONS, ANTHONY. Matric. pens. from MAGDALENE, Michs. 1633. Doubtless s. of John, of Tealby, Lincs.; age 18, in 1634. Captain in the army, 1646. Died 1649. Brother of John (1634). (*Lincs. Pedigrees*, 400.)

GIBBON, ARTHUR. Matric. sizar from TRINITY, Easter, 1587, as 'Gibball'; Scholar, 1588; B.A. 1590-1. Fellow, 1591.

GIBBON, CHRISTOPHER. Adm. sizar at EMMANUEL, June 11, 1733. Matric. 1733; B.A. 1736-7. Ord. deacon (Lincoln) June 5, 1737. Master of Cavendish School, Suffolk, 1741.

GIBBON, EDMUND, *see* GUYBON.

GIBBONS, EDWARD. Incorp. at Oxford, 1592, as 'Mus.Bac. from Cambridge' (degree not recorded). S. of William, of Cambridge. Organist at King's; afterwards at Bristol Cathedral, about 1600; and Exeter, 1611-44. Priest-vicar and precentor at Exeter; ejected, *c.* 1644. Died before the Restoration. Brother of Orlando (1598). (*D.N.B.*; Walker, *Sufferings.*)

GIBBON, EDWARD. Adm. pens. at EMMANUEL, Oct. 3, 1723. Afterwards Fell.-Com. Of Middlesex. S. of Edward, army contractor, of London. B. 1707. School, Westminster. Alderman of London. M.P. for Petersfield, 1734-41; for Southampton, 1741-7. Retired to Buriton, near Petersfield, 1747. Married Judith, dau. of James Porten. Died Nov. 12, 1770. Admon., P.C.C. Father of the historian. (*D.N.B.*; *G. Mag.*)

GYBBONS, FRANCIS. Matric. Fell.-Com. from TRINITY, Easter, 1578.

GIBBONS, GEORGE. Adm. pens. (age 18) at ST JOHN'S, May 8, 1695. S. of Peter, clerk. B. at Moreton Corbet, Salop. School, Shrewsbury. Matric. 1695; B.A. 1698-9; M.A. 1709. R. of Nantwich, Cheshire, 1711-20. Buried Feb. 29, 1720. Brother of Henry (1698). (*Ormerod*, III. 225.)

GYBBONS, GERVASE. Matric. Fell.-Com. from PETERHOUSE, Lent, 1584-5. Adm. at Gray's Inn, Oct. 12, 1586. Will of one of these names (P.C.C.) 1595; of Benenden, Kent.

GIBBON, HENRY. Matric. pens. from TRINITY HALL, Easter, 1544; LL.B. 1548-9, as Gibbons.

GIBBON or GIBBONS, HENRY. Matric. sizar from PEMBROKE, Michs. 1586; B.A. 1589-90; M.A. 1593. Incorp. at Oxford, 1593.

GIBBONS, HENRY. Matric. sizar from EMMANUEL, *c.* 1596.

GIBBONS, HENRY. Adm. pens. (age 18) at ST JOHN'S, June 4, 1698. S. of Peter, clerk. B. at Moreton Corbet, Salop. School, Shrewsbury. Matric. 1698; B.A. 1701-2; M.A. 1709. Brother of George (1695).

GYBBONS or GUYBON, HUMPHREY. Matric. pens. from GONVILLE HALL, Easter, 1552. Of Stradset, Norfolk. S. of Thomas Guybon, of Lynn, Norfolk. Sheriff of Norfolk. Married Alice, dau. of Thomas Dereham, of Crimplesham. Died Aug. 6, 1601. Buried at Castleacre, Norfolk. Will (P.C.C.) 1601. (*Venn*, I. 36; G. H. Holley.)

GYBBON, HUMPHREY. Matric. Fell.-Com. from MAGDALENE, Easter, 1607. Probably s. of Thomas, of Lynn, and grandson of the above. Pedigree in *Vis. of Norfolk*. (G. H. Holley.)

GIBBONS, JAMES. Adm. sizar (age 19) at TRINITY, Jan. 4, 1735. S. of Colonel Geoffrey, of Middlesex. School, Eton. Matric. 1735. Perhaps ord. priest (Norwich) Aug. 1738.

GIBBON or GYBON, JOHN. B.A. 1478-9; M.A. 1482. Of CORPUS CHRISTI. Perhaps ord. priest (Norwich) 1499.

GYBBONS, JOHN. Matric. sizar from ST JOHN'S, Michs. 1545.

GIBBON, JOHN. B.A. (? 1602-3); M.A. from JESUS, 1606. B. at Bury, Suffolk. Ord. deacon (London) Mar. 19, 1608-9, age 23. C. of Halstead, Essex. Perhaps R. of Wordwell, Suffolk, 1619-29.

GIBBON, JOHN. Scholar of EMMANUEL, 1603. Of Rolvenden, Kent. B.A. 1604-5; M.A. 1608; B.D. 1615. Fellow, 1609-17. Preacher at West Waltham, Essex, in 1637; and at Bury. Father of John (1643). (J. Ch. Smith.)

GIBBON, JOHN. Adm. pens. at EMMANUEL, July 6, 1620. Matric. 1620-1. Probably s. of Thomas, of Lynn; bapt. at Oby, Sept. 1602; adm. at Gray's Inn, Oct. 26, 1622; of Oby, Norfolk, gent.; married Katherine, dau. of Francis Mapes, of Rollesby; buried at Oby, Aug. 19, 1650. (*Vis. of Norfolk*, 1664; G. H. Holley.)

GIBBON, JOHN. Adm. pens. (age 16) at CHRIST'S, Oct. 21, 1634. S. of John, of Tealby, Lincs. B. there. Schools, Wold Newton (Mr Petley) and Lincoln (Mr Clarke). Matric. 1634; B.A. 1642. One of these names V. of Hinton Blewett, Somerset, 1640. Brother of Anthony (1633). (*Peile*, I. 433, 480; *Lincs. Pedigrees*, 400.)

GIBBON, JOHN. Adm. pens. at EMMANUEL, May 10, 1643. S. of John (1603), B.D., of Waltham, Essex. Matric. 1645; B.A. 1646-7; M.A. 1650; B.D. 1657. Fellow, 1649. Proctor, 1652-3. Ejected, 1662, from Blackfriars. Died soon after. Will (P.C.C.) 1663; of Waltham Abbey, late minister of Blackfriars. (*Calamy*, I. 93; J. Ch. Smith.)

GIBBON, JOHN. Adm. pens. (age 15) at MAGDALENE, Sept. 17, 1644. S. of Anthony, of Langton-by-Wragby, Lincs., gent. School, Islington. Matric. 1645. Adm. at the Middle Temple, Nov. 20, 1648. Died 1661. (*Lincs. Pedigrees*, 400.)

GIBBON, JOHN. Adm. pens. at JESUS, May 7, 1645. S. of Robert, woollen-draper, of London. Bapt. at St Mary Aldermary, Nov. 15, 1629. School, Merchant Taylors'. Matric. 1645. Went as a soldier to France and the Netherlands. Afterwards travelled to America. Bluemantle Pursuivant, 1668-1718. Author, heraldic and political. Died Aug. 2, 1718. (*D.N.B.*; *Vis. of London*, 1634.)

GIBBON, JOHN. Adm. Fell.-Com. (age 17) at MAGDALENE, Nov. 6, 1649. S. of William, of Bourne, Kent, gent. School, Camberwell.

GIBBON, JOHN. Adm. Fell.-Com. at EMMANUEL, Oct. 29, 1652. Of Kent.

GIBBON, JOHN. Adm. sizar (age 17) at ST JOHN'S, Apr. 6, 1676. S. of Francis, of Eresby and Horsington, Lincs. B. there. School, Louth. Matric. 1677; B.A. 1679-80. C. of Stainfield, in 1688. (*Lincs. Pedigrees*, 400.)

GIBBON, JOHN. Adm. at CORPUS CHRISTI, 1715. Of Suffolk. Matric. Easter, 1715; B.A. 1718-9; M.A. 1722. Ord. deacon (Norwich) Dec. 1723. R. of Roydon, Suffolk, 1730.

GIBBONS, MARMADUKE. Matric. sizar from PETERHOUSE, Easter, 1611; B.A. 1614-5; M.A. 1618. Ord. deacon and priest (York) Dec. 1618. V. of St Martin, York, 1618-32. V. of St Mary Bishophill, 1620-32.

GIBBON, MELCHIOR. Matric. pens. from PEMBROKE, Michs. 1578; B.A. 1581-2; M.A. 1593.

GIBBONS, NICHOLAS. Matric. pens. from CLARE, Easter, 1585; B.A. 1588-9; M.A. 1592. Incorp. at Oxford, 1592. Perhaps of Hickford, in Canford, Dorset. Author, theological. Namesake at Oxford. (*Cooper*, II. 430; *D.N.B.*)

GIBBONS, ORLANDO. Matric. sizar from KING'S, Easter, 1598. S. of William, of Cambridge. B. there, 1583. Chorister at King's. Mus.Bac. 1606. Incorp. at Oxford, 1607. *Supp.* for Mus.D. at Oxford, 1622. Organist at Westminster Abbey, and the Chapel Royal. Musical composer. Summoned to Canterbury to attend the wedding of Charles I, for which he had composed an ode: seized with small-pox there. Died June 5, 1625. Buried in Canterbury Cathedral. Brother of Edward (1592). (*D.N.B.*, where he is wrongly supposed to be an 'M.A.' of Cambridge; *Al. Oxon.*)

GIBBONS, PETER. Ord. deacon (Peterb.) Dec. 20; priest, Dec. 21, 1629, as 'of MAGDALENE College, literate.' V. of Holton-le-Clay, Lincs., 1632. R. of Brigsley, 1660.

GIBBONS, PETER. Matric. sizar from KING'S, Easter, 1653; B.A. 1656-7; M.A. 1660.

GIBBONS, RICHARD. Matric. sizar from CLARE, Easter, 1585.

GIBBON, RICHARD. Adm. pens. at EMMANUEL, Jan. 18, 1639-40. S. of Thomas, of Westcliffe, Kent. Matric. 1640; M.D. (Padua) 1645. Perhaps adm. at Leyden, May, 1646. Incorp. at Oxford, 1652. Adm. candidate R.C.P. June 25, 1652. Lord of the Manor of Kingston, Kent. Married Anne, dau. of Joseph Taylor, 1647. Buried at St Olave's, Hart St, London, Aug. 26, 1652. Admon. (P.C.C.) to widow Ann. Brother of Thomas (1637). (*Munk*, I. 266; *Hasted*, III. 749; J. Ch. Smith.)

GIBBONS, SAMUEL. Adm. pens. (age 17) at MAGDALENE, Sept. 27, 1682. S. of John, mercer. B. at Shrewsbury. School, Shrewsbury. Matric. 1682.

GIBBON or GEBON, T. B.D. 1492-3. Doubtless Thomas; M.A.; fellow of CORPUS CHRISTI. V. of Gamlingay, Cambs., 1477. Chaplain of Holme Hall Chantry, Quy, Cambs., 1490.

GIBBONS, THOMAS. Matric. sizar from QUEENS', Easter, 1611. Of Lincolnshire. B.A. 1614-5; M.A. 1618. V. of Oakington, Cambs., 1614. C. of St Botolph, Cambridge, 1620-9.

GIBBON, THOMAS. Adm. pens. at EMMANUEL, Oct. 24, 1637. S. and h. of Thomas, of Westcliffe, Kent. Matric. 1637. Adm. at Gray's Inn, June 26, 1640. Married Mary, sister of Sir William Rooke, Knt., of Westcliffe. Alienated the estate, 1660. Brother of Richard (1639-40). (*Hasted*, IV. 29.)

GIBBONS, THOMAS. Matric. sizar from QUEENS', Easter, 1645. Of London. B.A. 1647-8; M.A. (Oxford) 1651. Fellow of Oriel, 1649-57. One of these names R. of Pulham, Dorset, 1657-88. (*Al. Oxon.*; F. S. Hockaday.)

GIBBON, THOMAS. Adm. pens. (age 16) at ST JOHN'S, Feb. 23, 1684-5. S. of Matthew, draper. B. in London. School, St Paul's. Matric. 1685; B.A. 1688-9; M.A. 1692; D.D. 1714. Fellow, 1692-8. R. of Greystoke, Cumberland, 1693-1716. Dean of Carlisle, 1713. Died Oct. 24, 1716. Buried in St Mary's, Carlisle. Father of William (1717). (B. *Nightingale*.)

GIBBON, THOMAS. Adm. sizar (age 17) at PEMBROKE, Mar. 30, 1717. S. of Thomas, of Bury St Edmunds, grocer. School, Bury. B.A. 1720-1; M.A. 1724. Incorp. at Oxford, 1740. Ord. deacon (Norwich) June, 1725; priest, Mar. 1725-6. V. of Thurston, Suffolk, 1726-62. R. of Beyton, 1734-62.

GIBBONS, THOMAS. M.A. from SIDNEY, 1731. S. of Benjamin, of Worfield, Salop, *pleb.* Matric. from Pembroke College, Oxford, July 16, 1720, age 19; B.A. (Oxford) 1724-5. Perhaps will (P.C.C.) 1767; of Crowell, Oxon., clerk. (*Al. Oxon.*; J. Ch. Smith.)

GYBBON, W. Matric. pens. from PEMBROKE, Lent, 1564-5.

GYBBON, W. Matric. pens. from CLARE, Easter, 1566.

GIBBONS or GIBBINS, WILLIAM. Adm. sizar at EMMANUEL, Jan. 12, 1590-1. Matric. 1591; Scholar; B.A. (? 1594-5). V. of Little Bealings, Suffolk, 1601.

GIBBINS, WILLIAM. B.D. 1608-9 (Incorp. from Oxford); D.D. from PETERHOUSE, 1609. Adm. at Christ Church, Oxford, a scholar from Westminster, 1586; B.A. (Oxford) 1590; M.A. 1593; B.D. 1600. Ord. deacon and priest (Rochester) Oct. 28, 1597. V. of All Saints', Lynn, 1601-5. R. of Glemsford, Suffolk, 1608-19; of Rettendon, Essex, 1611. Will (P.C.C.) 1619; D.D., of Glemsford. Father of the next. (*Al. Oxon.*)

GIBBONS, WILLIAM. Adm. pens. (age 17) at PEMBROKE, Apr. 23, 1633. S. of William (above), D.D. B. at Glemsford, Suffolk.

GIBBONS, WILLIAM. Adm. pens. (age 17) at CHRIST'S, Feb. 5, 1634-5. S. of William. B. at Coventry. School, Coventry (Mr White). Matric. 1635. Probably adm. at the Middle Temple, Nov. 4, 1637. Captain in the King's army. Died 1646. (*Vis. of Warws.*, 1682; *Peile*, I. 435.)

GIBBONS, WILLIAM. M.A. 1678 (Incorp. from Oxford). S. of John, of London. School, Merchant Taylors'. Matric. from St John's, Oxford, July 3, 1668, age 18; B.A. (Oxford) 1672; M.A. 1675-6; M.D. 1683. F.R.C.P. 1692. Died Mar. 25, 1728. Will, P.C.C. (*Munk*, I. 490; *D.N.B.*; *Al. Oxon.*)

GIBBON, WILLIAM. Adm. pens. (age 18) at ST JOHN'S, July 2, 1717. S. of Thomas (1684-5), Dean of Carlisle. B. at Greystoke, Cumberland. School, Sedbergh. Matric. 1717; B.A. 1720-1; M.A. 1724. Fellow of Pembroke, 1736. Ord. deacon (Norwich) May 31, 1724; priest (London) Dec. 19, 1725. R. of Dufton, Westmorland, 1730-6. Probably V. of St Dunstan-in-the-West, London, 1736-57. Preacher at Bridewell. R. of St Martin, Ludgate, 1741-3. Died Jan. 22, 1758. Buried at St Dunstan's. Admon. (P.C.C.) 1758. (*Scott-Mayor*, III. 314; the name is given as 'Gibson' in *Hennessy*.)

GIBBON, ——. B.A. 1475-6. Perhaps Thomas, fellow of CORPUS CHRISTI.

GIBBON or GYBON, ——. B.D. 1488-9.

GIBBON, ——. B.Civ.L. 1514-5.

GIBBON or GYBON, ——. Pens. at PETERHOUSE, Dec. 9, 1581.

GIBBON, ——. Adm. pens. at TRINITY HALL, Nov. 3, 1735.

GIBBS, CHARLES. Adm. sizar at CORPUS CHRISTI, 1691. Of Norfolk. Matric. 1693; B.A. 1694-5; M.A. 1698. Ord. deacon (Norwich) Sept. 1697; priest, Mar. 1701-2. R. of Tivetshall, Norfolk, 1701. R. of Redgrave, Suffolk, 1709-42. Probably father of John (1727).

GIBBS, EDMUND. Adm. sizar (age 18) at PETERHOUSE, Feb. 28, 1666-7. Of Ely. School, Peterborough. Matric. 1667; B.A. 1671-2. Ord. priest (Peterb.) Sept. 19, 1675, as B.A. of St John's. P.C. of Ramsey, Hunts., 1675-86. Perhaps V. of Mazey, Northants., 1691-1701. Buried July 14, 1701. (*Misc. Gen. et Her.*, 2nd S., v. 82.)

GIBBS, EDWARD. Adm. sizar (age 18) at TRINITY, Aug. 28, 1707. S. of Edward, of London. School, London. Matric. 1707.

GIBBS, HENRY. Matric. pens. from ST JOHN'S, Michs. 1576; B.A. 1578-9; M.A. 1582.

GIBBS, HENRY. Adm. at CORPUS CHRISTI, 1669. Of Norfolk.

GIBBS, JAMES. Adm. pens. at ST CATHARINE'S, Mar. 4, 1678-9. Migrated to Trinity Hall, 1683, as Fell.-Com. Matric. there Easter, 1683; LL.B. 1684.

GIBBS, JAMES. Adm. pens. (age 16) at TRINITY, July 1, 1689. S. of James, of Truro, Cornwall. School, Gerrans (Mr John Bedford). Matric. 1689; M.B. 1695. Father of William (1727-8).

GIBBES, JOHN. B.A. V. of Holy Trinity, Cambridge. Licensed to hear confessions by the Bishop of Ely, 1457.

GYBBES, JOHN. Matric. pens. from ST JOHN'S, Michs. 1564.

GIBBS, JOHN. Adm. sizar at EMMANUEL, Easter, 1625. Matric. 1625; B.A. 1628-9; M.A. 1632. Ord. deacon (Norwich) Dec. 22, 1633; priest, Mar. 2, 1633-4. R. of Frenze, Norfolk, 1642-51. Brother of Thomas (1624). Perhaps father of John (1660).

GIBBS, JOHN. Adm. pens. at TRINITY, June 9, 1640.

GIBBS, JOHN. Adm. sizar (age 17) at SIDNEY, June 26, 1645. S. of Samuel, cooper. B. at Bedford. School, Bedford (Mr Varnill). Matric. 1645; B.A. 1647-8.

GIBBS, JOHN. Adm. pens. at CORPUS CHRISTI, 1660. Of Norfolk. (? s. of John, 1625.) Matric. Michs. 1660; B.A. 1663-4; M.A. 1667. Incorp. at Oxford, 1669. R. of Gissing, Norfolk, 1668-90. R. of Banham, 1671, ejected as non-juror. Probably brother of Thomas (1660).

GIBBS, JOHN. Adm. pens. (age 17) at ST CATHARINE'S, June 14, 1727. Of Tivetshall, Norfolk. (? s. of Charles, 1691.) Matric. 1728; B.A. 1730-1; M.A. 1734. Ord. priest (Norwich) Dec. 1738. R. of Burgate, Suffolk, 1738-43. R. of Billingford, Norfolk, 1739-42. R. of Redgrave, Suffolk, 1742-8.

GIBBS, RICE. Adm. sizar (age 16) at CAIUS, July 8, 1718. S. of John, husbandman, of Hindolvestone, Norfolk. B. there. School, Yarmouth. Matric. 1718-9; Scholar, 1718-9. Died in College. Buried at St Michael's, Cambridge, May 14, 1719. (*Venn*, II. 10.)

GIBBS, ROBERT. Adm. sizar (age 18) at CAIUS, May 15, 1703. S. of Stephen, gent., of Wymondham, Norfolk. B. there. Bapt. June 17, 1685. School, Wymondham. Matric. 1703. Perhaps father of Stephen (1729). (*Venn*, I. 511.)

GIBBS, SAMUEL. Adm. pens. at PETERHOUSE, May 19, 1617. Doubtless s. of Henry, and cousin of William (1617). Matric. 1617. Migrated to Trinity. B.A. 1620-1; M.A. 1627. Chaplain of Trinity, 1636. (*T. A. Walker*, 5.)

GIBBS, SAMUEL. Adm. pens. (age 18) at CAIUS, Jan. 27, 1729-30. S. of Samuel, of Gt Horkesley, Essex. B. there. Schools, Boxford (Mr Tatham) and Bury. Matric. 1729-30; Scholar, 1730-3. Adm. at the Inner Temple, Dec. 14, 1730. Of Nayland and Horkesley Park, Colchester, Esq. Died Feb. 29, 1740-1. (*Venn*, II. 32.)

GIBBS, SIMON. Adm. at CORPUS CHRISTI, 1551. B. 1533. B.A. 1551-2; M.A. 1555. Fellow, 1552. University preacher, 1561. R. of Stowe-Nine-Churches, Northants., 1557-72. R. of Boddington, 1559-96. R. of Church Brampton, 1572-1603. R. of Wicken, 1596-1603. Buried at Wicken, Nov. 23, 1603. (*Baker*, I. 481; H. I. Longden.)

GIBBES, SIMON. Resident pens. at TRINITY HALL, Aug. 1564.

GIBBS, STEPHEN. Adm. sizar (age 17) at CAIUS, May 27, 1729. S. of Robert (? 1703), farmer, of Wymondham, Norfolk. B. there. School, Wymondham. Matric. 1729; Scholar, 1729-36; B.A. 1732-3; M.A. 1736. Fellow, 1737-47. Ord. deacon (Norwich) Mar. 10, 1733-4. (*Venn*, II. 30.)

GIBBES, THOMAS. Matric. sizar from TRINITY, Easter, 1611; Scholar, 1614; B.A. 1615-6; M.A. 1619.

GIBBS, THOMAS. Adm. sizar at EMMANUEL, Easter, 1624. Matric. 1624; B.A. 1628-9; M.A. 1632. Ord. deacon (Peterb.) July 18; priest, July 19, 1630.

GIBBS, THOMAS. Adm. pens. at CORPUS CHRISTI, 1660. Of Norfolk. Matric. Lent, 1660; B.A. 1663-4; M.A. 1667. Buried in St Benet's, Cambridge, Aug. 21, 1669. Will (V.C.C.) 1669. Probably brother of John (1660).

GIBBS, THOMAS. Adm. sizar (age 16) at MAGDALENE, Mar. 26, 1671. S. of Thomas, college cook. School, Perse, Cambridge. Matric. 1671; B.A. 1674-5; M.A. 1678. Ord. deacon (London) Dec. 23, 1677; priest, Nov. 17, 1680.

GYBES, WILLIAM. Matric. pens. from TRINITY, Michs. 1578.

GIBBS, WILLIAM. Adm. pens. (age 17) at PETERHOUSE, May 19, 1617. S. of William, of Elmeston, Kent, Esq. Matric. 1617; B.A. from Corpus Christi, 1619-20. Adm. at Gray's Inn, Nov. 1, 1617. Married Anna, dau. of William Thomas, of Selling, Kent. (*T. A. Walker*, 5; *Vis. of Kent*, 1619.)

GIBBS, WILLIAM. Matric. pens. (age 17) from PEMBROKE, Lent, 1653-4. Of London. S. of Robert, citizen. B.A. 1657-8; M.A. 1661. Fellow, *c*. 1660-7. R. of St John, Wapping, 1662-5. P.C. of St Clement's, Cambridge, 1664. V. of Hitchin, Herts., 1665-89. V. of St Neots, Hunts., 1707-13. Died 1713. (Gorham, *St Neots*, 171.)

GIBBS, WILLIAM. LL.B. from MAGDALENE, 1670.

GIBBS, WILLIAM. Adm. sizar (age 19) at CHRIST'S, Mar. 23, 1721-2. S. of Thomas. B. at Ludlow, Salop. School, Whitchurch (Mr Hughes). Scholar, 1722; Matric. 1723; B.A. 1725-6. Ord. deacon (Hereford) Sept. 1726; priest (Lincoln) Mar. 5, 1731-2. V. of Shackerstone, Leics., 1732-57. R. of Baxterley, Warws., 1733. R. of Congeston, Leics., 1740. Died Oct. 12, 1757. M.I. at Congeston. (*Nichols*, IV. 521; *Peile*, II. 206.)

GIBBS, WILLIAM. Adm. sizar (age 18) at PEMBROKE, Mar. 1, 1727-8. S. of James (1689), M.B., of Tregony, Cornwall. Matric. 1728; B.A. 1731-2. One of these names received the £20 bounty for the voyage, as emigrant minister to New England, Oct. 11, 1744. (*Fothergill*, 29.)

GIBERNE, DANIEL GABRIEL. Adm. pens. at TRINITY HALL, Feb. 16, 1710-1. S. of Reginald, of London, gent. Matric. 1711. Previously matric. from Gloucester Hall, Oxford, Nov. 9, 1706, age 19; B.A. (Oxford) 1710; M.A. (Cambridge) 1713. Taxor, 1714. Ord. deacon (Ely) June 12, 1715; priest (Lincoln) Sept. 23, 1716. Preb. of Lincoln, 1722. R. of Ashley, Staffs., 1731. (*Al. Oxon.*)

GIBSON, ABRAHAM. Matric. sizar from ST JOHN'S, Easter, 1603. B. at Ridlington, Rutland. B.A. 1606-7; M.A. 1610; B.D. 1617; D.D. 1624 (on the King's visit to Cambridge). Incorp. at Oxford, 1615 and 1617. Ord. deacon (London) Sept. 22, 1611, age 24; priest, Dec. 22, 1611. C. of Witham, Essex. V. of Little Waldingfield, Suffolk, 1612-29. R. of Kedington, 1618. Chaplain in ordinary to the King. Preacher in the Temple Church. Buried there Jan. 5, 1629. Will (P.C.C.) 1630. Father of Samuel (1644).

GIBSON, ABRAHAM. Adm. sizar (age 16) at CHRIST'S, Feb. 6, 1638-9. S. of Thomas (1596). B. at Ridlington, Rutland. Schools, Uppingham and Ridlington (Mr Stackhouse). Matric. 1639; B.A. 1642-3. Brother of Thomas (1631), Edward (1633) and John (1644).

GIBSON, ABRAHAM. Matric. sizar from ST CATHARINE'S, Easter, 1639. Of Suffolk. B.A. 1642; M.A. 1646.

GIBSON, ALEXANDER. Incorp. as M.A. from Glasgow, 1644-5. Matric. there, 1638; graduated, 1642. Intruded fellow of CAIUS, 1644-8. Examined and approved by the Westminster Assembly. Died *c*. 1648. Admon. granted (V.C.C.) 1648. (*Venn*, I. 354.)

GIBSON, CHARLES. Matric. sizar from TRINITY, Lent, 1626-7; Scholar, 1631; B.A. 1631-2; M.A. 1635. Fellow, 1633.

GIBSON, CHARLES. Adm. pens. at JESUS, Apr. 19, 1653. B. at Little Stonham, Suffolk. Matric. 1653; Scholar, 1655; B.A. 1656-7; M.A. 1660. Fellow, 1662-74. V. of Comberton, Cambs., 1660-2. C. of Teversham, 1671. Died in College, Aug. 13, 1674. Left £100 to the College. Will proved (V.C.C.) 1674.

GIBSON, CHARLES. Adm. pens. at JESUS, Apr. 26, 1675. S. of Barnabas, of Little Stonham, Suffolk, Esq. Matric. 1675; B.A. 1678-9; M.A. 1682. Ord. deacon (Norwich) Dec. 1683; priest, May, 1684.

GIBSON, CHRISTOPHER. B.Can.L. 1524-5.

GIBSON, CHRISTOPHER. Adm. sizar (age 18) at ST JOHN'S, Apr. 7, 1703. S. of John, butcher. B. at Lancaster. School, Sedbergh. Matric. 1703; B.A. 1706-7. Ord. deacon (Peterb.) June 8, 1707. C. of St Mary, Lancaster, 1713-8. V. of Ormskirk, 1718-27. Buried there Aug. 16, 1727. (*Sedbergh Sch. Reg.*, 147.)

GIBSON, DANIEL. 'Of —— College, Cambridge; aged 53, in 1612.' Ord. deacon (Lincoln) Sept. 23, 1599; priest, June 22, 1600 (Reg. of Bishop of Lincoln). R. of Braunston, Leics., 1612. Perhaps R. of Gt Casterton, Rutland, 1622-35. Died 1635.

GIBSON, EDGAR. Adm. sizar at JESUS, Sept. 9, 1707. S. of ——, clerk, deceased, of Suffolk. Matric. 1708; Rustat Scholar, 1710; B.A. 1711-2; M.A. 1715. Fellow, 1714-6. Ord. deacon (Ely) Mar. 13, 1714-5; priest (Lincoln) June 12, 1715. R. of Wetheringsett, Suffolk, 1715. R. of Finningham, 1728-30. R. of Occold, 1736-45.

GIBSON, EDMUND. B.A. 1540-1.

GIBSON, EDWARD. Matric. pens. from TRINITY, Easter, 1612; B.A. from St Catharine's, 1618. Probably V. of Cottingham, Yorks., 1622-53. Died 1653.

GIBSON, EDWARD. Adm. sizar (age 14) at SIDNEY, Apr. 11, 1633. S. of Thomas (1596), R. of Ridlington, Rutland. B. there. School, Uppingham. Matric. 1633; B.A. 1636-7; M.A. 1640. Fellow, ejected 1644. Ord. priest (Lincoln) May 28, 1643. V. of Hawnes, Beds. Died Apr. 22, 1690, aged 73. Brother of Abraham (1638-9), Thomas (1631) and John (1644), father of the next.

GIBSON, EDWARD. Adm. sizar at CLARE, Nov. 15, 1677. Of Hawnes, Beds. S. of Edward (above), V. of Hawnes. Bapt. there, Aug. 14, 1661. Matric. 1678; B.A. 1681-2; M.A. 1685. Fellow, 1684. Ord. priest (Lincoln) Sept. 20, 1685. V. of Hawnes, 1692-1732. C. of Warden. Married Mary, dau. of Laurence Washington, of Luton and Virginia. Died May 11, 1732, aged 71. Buried at Hawnes. M.I. Will (P.C.C.). Father of William (1720). (H. I. Longden.)

GIBSON, ERASMUS. Matric. sizar from JESUS, *c*. 1596.

GIBSON, FRANCIS. Matric. pens. from TRINITY, Lent, 1563-4.

GIBSON, FRANCIS. Adm. sizar at SIDNEY, May 13, 1606. Matric. 1606; B.A. 1609-10; M.A. 1613. Ord. deacon and priest (Peterb.) Feb. 28, 1612-3.

GIBSON, GEORGE. Adm. at KING'S (age 17) a scholar from Eton, Aug. 16, 1529. Of Windsor. B.A. 1533-4; M.A. 1537. Fellow, 1532-40. R. of Thorpe-by-Haddiscoe, Norfolk, 1559-67.

GYBSON, GEORGE. Matric. sizar from JESUS, Easter, 1568. One of these names V. of Grindon, Durham, 1579. One V. of Castle Eden, 1577-82.

GIBSON, GEORGE. Adm. sizar (age 17) at ST JOHN'S Mar. 11, 1663-4. S. of Roger, husbandman, of Seaton, in Holderness, Yorks. B. there. School, Sedbergh. Matric. 1664; B.A. 1667-8; M.A. 1671. Ord. deacon (York) Sept. 1668. V. of Withernwick, Yorks., 1669-1715. Died May 14, 1715. Brother of Samuel (1663-4).

GIBSON, GEORGE. Adm. sizar (age 18) at ST JOHN'S, May 14, 1690. S. of John, husbandman. B. at Aycliffe, Durham. School, Sedbergh. Matric. 1690; B.A. 1693-4; M.A. 1697. Ord. deacon (London) Feb. 17, 1694-5; priest (Durham) Sept. 20, 1695. C. of Hamsterley, Durham, 1695-1712. C. of Witton-le-Wear, 1695-1712. V. of Stockton, 1712-4. Died June 17, 1714. M.I. at Stockton. (D. S. Boutflower.)

GIBSON, GODFREY. Adm. pens. at JESUS, Sept. 20, 1641. Of Middlesex. Matric. 1641; Scholar, 1644; B.A. 1644-5. Doubtless s. of Richard, of Westminster, gent.; adm. at Gray's Inn, Nov. 22, 1642.

GIBSON, HENRY. Adm. sizar at EMMANUEL, Apr. 1592. S. of Henry, yeoman. B. at Darsham, Suffolk. School, Westleton (Mr Oughtred). Matric. 1592. Migrated as pens. to Caius (age 18) Aug. 9, 1594. Scholar, 1594-8; B.A. 1595-6; M.A. 1599. V. of Wadsworth, Yorks., 1634-6. Presumably the same who obtained letters testimonial from the University in 1636. (*Venn*, I. 153.)

GIBSON, HUGH. B.Civ.L. 1515-6. Doubtless V. of Gt Bursted, Essex, 1512-54, deprived. R. of Eynesbury, Hunts., 1523-46. R. of South Church, Essex, 1556-9. Died 1559.

GYBSON, ISAAC. Matric. sizar from JESUS, Michs. 1570. One of these names a 'notorious recusant' in Yorkshire, *c.* 1590.

GIBSON, JEREMY. Matric. sizar from CLARE, *c.* 1590. S. of Richard, of Southowram, Yorks. Bapt. at Halifax, Sept. 23, 1571. B.A. 1593-4; M.A. 1597. Head Master of Wakefield Grammar School, June-July, 1607; appointed to draw up statutes for the school. C. of Coley, Halifax, 1611-6. Died Oct. 9, 1616. Buried at Halifax. Will (York) 1617. (M. H. Peacock.)

GIBSON, JOHN. M.A. 1460-1.

GIBSON, JOHN. Matric. sizar from CLARE, Lent, 1557-8. S. of Thomas, of Ireby, Lancs. Scholar, 1560; B.A. from Trinity, 1560-1; M.A. 1564; LL.D. 1571. Fellow of Trinity, 1561. Adm. advocate, June 12, 1572. Judge of the Prerogative Court of York. Obtained a graut of Arms, 1574. Preb. of York, 1571-5. Precentor of York, 1575-1612. Archdeacon of East Riding, 1578-88. Master in Chancery, 1578-1611. Knighted, July 23, 1603. Of Welburn Hall. Died Feb. 28, 1612-3. Buried at Kirkdale. Will (York) 1613. Brother of Robert (1571) and Thomas (1572). (M. H. Peacock; A. B. Beaven; J. Parker.)

GIBSON, JOHN. Adm. at KING'S, a scholar from Eton, 1568. B. at Sawston, Cambs., 1550. Matric. Michs. 1568; B.A. 1572-3. Assistant Master at Lynn School. Perhaps ord. priest (Lincoln) Dec. 23, 1573. V. of Hemel Hempstead, Herts., 1578-9. R. of Eversholt, Beds., 1579-1602. Buried there Nov. 17, 1602. (*Cooper*, II. 282.)

GIBSON, JOHN. Matric. sizar from Sr JOHN'S, Easter, 1583. Of Scotland. Migrated to Queens', Mar. 3, 1584-5. B.A. 1585-6. One of these names V. of Foxton, Cambs., till 1613. Another V. of Kilham, Yorks., 1592-1602-.

GIBSON, JOHN. Matric. sizar from CLARE, Michs. 1583.

GIBSON, JOHN. Matric. sizar from TRINITY, *c.* 1591; Scholar of Trinity Hall, Apr. 16, 1591; LL.B. 1598. Fellow of Trinity Hall, 1597-1609. R. of Swanington, Norfolk, 1609. V. of Wood Dalling, 1610-6.

GIBSON, JOHN. Matric. sizar from CHRIST'S, *c.* 1593; B.A. 1597-8; M.A. 1601. V. of Warmington, Northants., till *c.* 1605. Perhaps also V. of Higham Ferrers, 1605. (*Peile*, I. 210.)

GIBSON, JOHN. Matric. pens. from TRINITY, Easter, 1622; B.A. 1625-6.

GIBSON, JOHN. Matric. pens. from CLARE, Easter, 1627; B.A. 1629-30; M.A. from Trinity Hall, 1633.

GIBSON, JOHN. Matric. sizar from TRINITY, Easter, 1633; B.A. from Emmanuel, 1636-7; M.A. 1641. One of these names R. of Ashingdon, Essex, 1644-9. Buried there Apr. 7, 1649.

GIBSON, JOHN. Adm. sizar (g 17) at CHRIST'S, Dec. 17, 1644. S. of Thomas (1596), R. of Ridlington, Rutland. B. there. Schools, Uppingham and Oakham. Matric. 1645. Migrated to St John's, Nov. 4, 1647. Doubtless the 'literate, of Ridlington,' ord. deacon (Peterb.) May 21, 1665. Brother of Abraham (1638-9), Edward (1633) and Thomas (1631).

GIBSON, JOHN. Matric. sizar from QUEENS', Easter, 1645. Of Lincolnshire.

GIBSON, JOHN. Adm. pens. at TRINITY, June 25, 1647. Of Yorkshire. Probably s. and h. of Sir John, of Welburn, Yorks., Knt. B. u . 4, 1630. Matric. 1646. Adm. at Gray's Inn, Nov. 29, 1648. Of Welburn, Esq. Married, at Ormesby, Sept. 3, 1650, Joan, dau. of James Pennyman, of Ormesby, Yorks. Died Nov. 28, 1711. Probably father of John (1668). (*Vis. of Yorks.*, 1665; M. H. Peacock.)

GIBSON, JOHN. Matric. pens. from TRINITY HALL, Easter, 1648; B.A. 1651; M.A. from King's, 1661. One of these names ord. priest (Ely) Dec. 22, 1661. V. of Ringland, Norfolk. R. of West Winch, 1663-7. R. of Helmingham. R. of Swanington, 1667-1702.

GIBSON, JOHN. Adm. pens. at TRINITY, Apr. 4, 1655. S. of John, gent., of North Runcton, Norfolk. B. there. School, Lynn (Mr Bell). Matric. 1656. Migra to Caius, Sept. 1, 1657. Scholar of Caius, 1657-60; B.A. 1658-9; M.A. 1662. Ord. deaeou (Norwich) Nov. 10, 1661; priest, Apr. 25, 1662. R. of Caistor, Norfolk, 1662-1708. C. of Yarmouth, in 1678. R. of Rollesby, 1684. Chaplain to Lord Morley. Married Martha, dau. of William Crow. Died Dec. 9, 1708. M.I. at Caistor. Admon. (Norw. Cons. C.) 1708. (*Venn*, I. 399; G. H. Holley.)

GIBSON, JOHN. Adm. sizar (age 20) at ST JOHN'S, June 9, 1658. S. of William, yeoman, of Yanwath, Penrith, Cumberland. B. there. School, Bampton, Westmorland. Matric. 1658. Perhaps brother of Thomas (1671).

GIBSON, JOHN. Adm. sizar at EMMANUEL, May 21, 1664. Of Staffordshire.

GIBSON, JOHN. Adm. pens. (age 17) at ST JOHN'S, Apr. 13, 1667. S. of John, husbandman, deceased. B. at Habton, Pickering, Yorks. School, Pocklington (Mr Ellyson). Matric. 1667; B.A. 1670-1; M.A. 1674. Ord. deacon (York) June 18, 1671; priest, Sept. 22, 1672. Assistant Master at Pocklington School. V. of Thorp Arch, Yorks., 1673-1727. V. of South Kirkby, 1675-1727. R. of Folkton, 1718-27. Buried Dec. 13, 1727, at South Kirkby. (*Scott-Mayor*.)

GIBSON, JOHN. Adm. pens. at TRINITY, Apr. 30, 1668. Doubtless s. of John (1647). B. Jan. 25, 1651-2. Matric. 1668. Adm. at Gray's Inn, Nov. 29, 1669. (*Vis. of Yorks.*, 1665.)

GIBSON, JOHN. Adm. sizar (age 18) at ST JOHN'S, May 21, 1686. S. of William, husbandman. B. at Cantsfield, Lancs. School, Sherburn (Mr Bane). Matric. 1689; B.A. 1689-90; M.A. 1693. Ord. deacon (York) Mar. 1689-90.

GIBSON, JOHN. Adm. sizar (age 16) at CHRIST'S, May 27, 1704. S. of John. B. at Lancaster. School, Lancaster (Mr Bordley). Matric. 1704; Scholar, 1704-5; B.A. 1707-8; M.A. 1711. Fellow, 1709-12. Will proved (V.C.C.) 1714. (*Peile*, II. 160.)

GIBSON, JOHN. Adm. pens. at JESUS, June 22, 1705. Of Doncaster, Yorks. Matric. 1705; Scholar, 1707; B.A. 1708-9.

GIBSON, JOHN. Adm. sizar (age 20) at ST JOHN'S, Feb. 25, 1711-2. S. of Richard, deceased. B. at Kellet, near Lancaster. School, Sedbergh. Matric. 1713; B.A. 1715-6. Ord. deacon (York) May, 1716; priest, June, 1720. Perhaps R. of Folkton, Yorks., 1718. (R. J. Wood.)

GIBSON, JOHN. Adm. at CORPUS CHRISTI, 1717. Of London. Matric. Easter, 1719. Will proved (V.C.C.) 1722.

GIBSON, JOHN. Adm. sizar at EMMANUEL, June 29, 1723. Of Yorkshire. Matric. 1724; B.A. 1726-7.

GIBSON, JOHN. Adm. pens. at CLARE, Nov. 3, 1726. S. of Edmund, Bishop of London. B. at Lambeth. Matric. 1726; M.A. 1729 (as *fil. nob.*). Fellow, Dec. 12, 1730. Died 1731.

GIBSON, JOHN. Adm. sizar (age 19) at ST JOHN'S, May 15, 1739. S. of Richard, husbandman, of Lancashire. B. at Hollinghead. School, Manchester (Mr Brook). Matric. 1739; B.A. 1742-3.

GIBSON, JOHN. Adm. sizar at TRINITY HALL, Nov. 11, 1747; Scholar, 1749; Matric. 1750. Ord. deacon (Lincoln) Feb. 23, 1752; priest, June 17, 1753. One of these names V. of Fishlake, Yorks., 1755-68. Died 1768.

GIBSON, JOSEPH. Matric. sizar from CLARE, Easter, 1575; B.A. 1577-8; M.A. 1581. Ord. deacon (Ely) 1580; priest, Dec. 21, 1580. C. of Barley, Herts., 1580. R. of Swaby, Lincs., 1582-3.

GIBSON, KENNETT. Adm. pens. (age 18) at CHRIST'S, May 7, 1748. S. of Thomas, R. of Paston, Northants. and nephew of Bishop Kennett. B. there. School, Eton (colleger). Matric. 1748; Scholar, 1748; B.A. 1752. Ord. deacon (Peterb.) Sept. 24, 1752; priest, Dec. 23, 1753. R. of Marholm, Northants., 1756-71. Author and antiquary. Died 1771. Buried at Paston. (*Peile*, II. 252; *D.N.B.*)

GIBSON, NATHANIEL. Adm. sizar at EMMANUEL, Jan. 8, 1639-40. Of Suffolk. Matric. 1640; B.A. 1643-4; M.A. from Pembroke, 1647. Fellow of Pembroke, *c.* 1645. R. of Orton Waterville, Hunts., 1652; ejected, 1662. Ord. deacon and priest (Peterb.) June 2, 1667. R. of Sawtry St Andrew, 1670-4. Died 1674. (*Calamy*, II. 52; H. I. Longden.)

GIBSON, NATHANIEL. Matric. sizar from KING'S, Easter, 1672; B.A. 1675-6; M.A. 1679. Ord. deacon (Peterb.) July 23; priest, Sept. 23, 1677. R. of Denton, Hunts., 1682-9. Preb. of Lincoln, 1683-1706. R. of Sawtry St Andrew's, 1689-1706. C. of Lilford, Northants., 1696. C. of Luddington, 1702. Died 1706.

GIBSON, NICHOLAS. Adm. pens. at EMMANUEL, Feb. 12, 1695-6. Of Norfolk. Matric. 1699; B.A. 1699-1700.

GYBSON, PERSE. Matric. pens. from ST CLEMENT'S HOSTEL, Easter, 1544. Perhaps 'Percival Gibson,' R. of Reed, Herts., 1554-6. Died 1556.

GIBSON, PETER. Adm. sizar at SIDNEY, Apr. 1600. S. of [Thomas (1572)], R. of Ridlington, Rutland. B.A. 1603-4; M.A. 1607. Incorp. at Oxford, 1624. Ord. deacon (Peterb.) Dec. 22, 1605; priest, Dec. 20, 1607. Perhaps R. of Goodleigh, Devon; and V. of Sonning, Berks., 1633. Brother of Thomas (1596). (*Al. Oxon.*)

GIBSON, PETER. Matrie. pens. from TRINITY, Easter, 1634; B.A. 1635-6.

GYBSON, RICHARD. Matric. pens. from PEMBROKE, Michs. 1555.

GIBSON, RICHARD. Adm. sizar at CORPUS CHRISTI, 1571. Matric. Michs. 1573; B.A. 1576-7; M.A. 1580. Ord. deacon and priest (Ely) Mar. 30, 1581, as M.A. Perhaps V. of Brockdish, Norfolk, 1586. Died 1625.

GIBSON, RICHARD. Matric. sizar from PEMBROKE, Easter, 1575.

GIBSON, RICHARD. Matric. sizar from TRINITY, Easter, 1577; Scholar, 1578; B.A. 1580-1; M.A. 1584. One of these names V. of Skipton, Yorks., 1587-91. R. of Marton, 1591-1631. Died 1631. (M. H. Peacock.)

GIBSON, RICHARD. Adm. pens. at EMMANUEL, June 20, 1627. Of Yorkshire. Matric. 1627. One of these names, clerk, was brought as minister, by Robert Trelawney, Esq., to his colony at Richmond Island, Maine, New England, in 1636. Returned to England in a few years, being out of sympathy with the views of the colonists. Married about 1638, Mary, dau. of Thomas Lewis, of Saco, Maine. (J. G. Bartlett.)

GIBSON, RICHARD. Adm. sizar at TRINITY, June 7, 1656. Of Yorkshire. Matric. 1656; B.A. 1661-2; M.A. 1665. Ord. deacon (Lincoln) Nov. 2; priest, Nov. 5, 1661. One of these names preb. of Southwell, 1688-90. Died 1690.

GIBSON, RICHARD. Adm. sizar (age 19) at ST JOHN'S, June 3, 1742. S. of Abraham, gent., of Yorkshire. B. at Midgley. School, Rishworth (Mr Wadsworth). Matric. 1742; B.A. 1745-6. Ord. deacon (Lincoln) June 5, 1748; priest, Dec. 18, 1748. C. at Holbeach, Lincs., 1751-82. Master of the Grammar School, Holbeach, 1751. R. of Fleet, 1782-3. Buried at Holbeach, Oct. 4, 1783. (*Scott-Mayor*, III. 526.)

GIBSON, ROBERT. A student of TRINITY, 1571. 2nd s. of Thomas, of Ireby, Lancs. B.A. 1572-3; M.A. 1576. Ord. priest (Peterb.) Sept. 28, 1577. Preb. of Southwell, 1576-88. Perhaps R. of Kirkheaton, Yorks., 1577-88. Died 1588. Brother of John (1557-8) and Thomas (1572).

GIBSON, ROBERT. B.A. from ST CATHARINE'S, 1590-1; M.A. 1595.

GIBSON, ROBERT. Adm. sizar (age 20) at ST JOHN'S, June 16, 1708. S. of Marmaduke, deceased. B. at Seaton Ross, Yorks. School, Pocklington (Mr Foulks). Matric. 1708; B.A. 1711-2. Ord. deacon (York) June, 1712; priest, 1713.

GIBSON, ROBERT. Adm. Fell.-Com. (age 17) at TRINITY, Nov. 1, 1742. S. of Charles, of Preston, Lancs. School, Chesterfield, Derbs. (Mr Burroughs). Matric. 1742. Died 1790. (Fishwick, *Goosnargh*, 159.)

GIBSON, SAMUEL. Adm. sizar at EMMANUEL, Apr. 10, 1596. Matric. 1596; Scholar; B.A. 1599-1600; M.A. 1603. Ord. priest (Peterb.) Sept. 23, 1610. Perhaps V. of Burley-on-the-Hill, Rutland, 1618.

GIBSON, SAMUEL. Matric. sizar from EMMANUEL, Easter, 1624; B.A. 1627-8; M.A. 1631. Ord. priest (Peterb.) June 5, 1631.

GIBSON, SAMUEL. Matric. sizar from TRINITY, Easter, 1634; B.A. 1637-8; M.A. 1642. Ord. priest (Peterb.) June 9, 1639.

GIBSON, SAMUEL. Adm. sizar (age 17) at ST JOHN'S, June 25, 1644. S. of Abraham (1603), D.D., V. of Little Waldingfield, Suffolk. School, Felsted (Mr Holbeach). Matric. 1645; B.A. 1647-8; M.A. 1651.

GIBSON, SAMUEL. Adm. sizar (age 15) at ST JOHN'S, Mar. 11, 1663-4. S. of Roger, husbandman, of Seaton, Yorks. B. there. School, Sedbergh. Matric. 1664; B.A. 1667-8; M.A. 1671. Ord. deacon (York) Dec. 1668. Brother of George (1663-4).

GIBSON, SAMUEL. Adm. scholar at TRINITY HALL, Feb. 13, 1670-1. Of Suffolk. Matric. 1670; B.A. 1672-3.

GIBSON, SAMUEL. Adm. sizar at CLARE, Jan. 15, 1674-5. Matric. 1677; B.A. 1678-9; M.A. 1684. V. of Frindsbury, Kent, 1690-1725. Died Feb. 10, 1724-5, aged nearly 70. Buried at Strood. M.I. there.

GIBSON, SIMON. Adm. sizar (age 18) at TRINITY, May 30, 1726. S. of Gervase, surgeon, of Radford, Notts. School, Glamford Bridge, Lincs. (Mr Waterworth). Matric. 1726. Readm. as pens. Nov. 11, 1728. Scholar, 1729; B.A. 1729-30. Ord. deacon (Lincoln) June 13, 1731; priest, Mar. 5, 1731-2.

GIBSON, THOMAS. Licensed to practise medicine, 1559. Of Morpeth, Northumberland. An early reformer; for some years a printer in London, and in this capacity recommended by Bishop Latimer to Cromwell. Also known for his skilful medical practice. Author, religious, medical, etc.; his works were printed by himself. In the reign of Queen Mary he fled to Geneva. Returned to England on the accession of Elizabeth. Died in London, 1562. (*Cooper*, I. 217; *D.N.B.*)

GIBSON, THOMAS. Matric. sizar from TRINITY, Easter, 1572. 3rd s. of Thomas, of Ireby, Lancs. B.A. 1576-7. Ord. priest (London) Apr. 16, 1579. V. of Wendover, Bucks., 1579-95. R. of Ridlington, Rutland; deprived, 1586. Father of Thomas (1596) and Peter (1600), brother of John (1557) and Robert (1571). (*Cooper*, II. 10.)

GIBSON, THOMAS. Adm. pens. (age 17) at CAIUS, Jan. 20, 1584-5. Readm. Fell.-Com. 1586. S. of Robert, gent., of Norwich School, Norwich. B.A. 1587-8. Probably adm. at Gray's Inn, from Barnard's Inn, Nov. 6, 1590. One of these names C. of Wicklewood, Norfolk, 1594.

GIBSON, THOMAS. Adm. sizar at EMMANUEL, Apr. 10, 1596. S. of Thomas (1572), R. of Ridlington, Rutland. Matric. 1596. Migrated to Sidney, Oct. 1598. Scholar, 1598; B.A. 1599-1600; M.A. 1603. Ord. deacon and priest (Peterb.) Feb. 24, 1604-5. R. of Ridlington, Rutland, 1605. Brother of Peter (1600), father of Abraham (1638-9), Edward (1633), John (1644) and Thomas (1631).

GIBSON, THOMAS. Adm. sizar (age 17) at CHRIST'S, May 24, 1631. S. of Thomas (above), R. of Ridlington, Rutland. B. there. School, Uppingham. Matric. 1631; B.A. 1634-5; M.A. 1638. Ord deacon (Peterb.) May, 1638; priest, June, 1639. Perhaps preb. of Lincoln, 1661-79. Brother of Abraham (1638-9), Edward (1633) and John (1644). (*Peile*, I. 410.)

GIBSON, THOMAS. Adm. sizar at EMMANUEL, Jan. 9, 1638-9. Matric. 1639; B.A. 1642-3; M.A. 1646.

GIBSON, THOMAS. M.A. 1660 (Incorp. from Edinburgh). Of Lincolnshire. M.A. (Edinburgh) 1653. One of these names V. of East Rudham, Norfolk; also V. of West Rudham, 1669-93.

GIBSON, THOMAS. Adm. sizar (age 19) at CHRIST'S, Apr. 24, 1661. S. of John. B. at Giggleswick. School, Giggleswick (Mr Walker).

GIBSON, THOMAS. Adm. pens. (age 22) at ST JOHN'S, June 26, 1671. S. of William, yeoman, of Bampton, Westmorland. B. there. School, Bampton. M.D. 1671 (Incorp. from Lambeth); M.D. of Leyden, 1675. Hon. fellow R.C.P. Sept. 30, 1680. Physician-general to the army, 1719-22. Died July 16, 1722. Will, P.C.C. Perhaps brother of John (1658). (*Munk*, I. 413; *D.N.B.*)

GIBSON, THOMAS. Adm. sizar at JESUS, May 17, 1679. S. of ——, clerk, deceased, of Warwickshire. Matric. 1679; Rustat scholar, 1680; B.A. 1682-3; M.A. 1686. One of these names R. of Greystoke, Cumberland, 1692-1717. But *see Al. Oxon.* for a contemporary.

GIBSON, THOMAS. Matric. pens. from TRINITY HALL, Dec. 1696.

GIBSON, THOMAS. M.A. from EMMANUEL, 1736. S. of Thomas, of Flyford, Worcs., clerk. Matric. from Balliol College, Oxford, Jan. 26, 1716-7, age 16; B.A. (Oxford) 1720. Will of one of these names (P.C.C.) 1797; of Ipswich, clerk. (*Al. Oxon.*)

GYBSON, W. Matric. sizar from ST JOHN'S, Michs. 1567.

GYBSON, W. Matric. sizar from PEMBROKE, Easter, 1569.

GYBSON, WILLIAM. B.A. 1542-3; M.A. 1546. One of the original fellows of TRINITY, 1546. Perhaps V. of Kinolton, Notts., 1565-71; and V. of Lakenheath, Suffolk, 1579-87.

GYBSON, WILLIAM. Matric. pens. from ST JOHN'S, Michs. 1547. One of these names, 'bred in the schools,' ord. priest (Lincoln) Sept. 19, 1563. V. of Barkby, Leics. Perhaps V. of Bahraham, Cambs., 1568.

GIBSON, WILLIAM. Matric. sizar from CLARE, Easter, 1571, as 'Jebson'; B.A. 1573-4; M.A. 1577. Ord. deacon (Ely) Apr. 24, 1576.

GIBSON, WILLIAM. Adm. at PETERHOUSE, 1599. Scholar; B.A. 1602-3; M.A. 1606. Fellow, 1605. Buried in Little St Mary's, Cambridge, Sept. 18, 1613. Will proved (V.C.C.).

GIBSON, WILLIAM. Matric. sizar from TRINITY, Easter, 1607.

GIBSON, WILLIAM. Adm. sizar (age 17) at SIDNEY, Aug. 1622. S. of William, attorney, deceased. B. at Sevenoaks, Kent. School, Sevenoaks. Matric. 1622; B.A. 1626-7; M.A. 1633. Perhaps V. of West Malling, Kent, 1637-59. V. of Meopham, 1646 (again inducted, 1661). R. of Lullingstone, 1663-70. Buried there Dec. 7, 1670.

GIBSON, WILLIAM. Matric. sizar from TRINITY HALL, Michs. 1628; B.A. 1630-1; M.A. 1639.

GIBSON, WILLIAM. Adm. sizar (age 16) at CHRIST'S, Sept. 11, 1677. S. of Robert. B. at Laughton, Lincs. School, Kelham, near Newark (Mr Gibson). Matric. 1678; B.A. 1681-2; M.A. 1685. Ord. deacon (York) June 11, 1682. Perhaps V. of Cameringham, Lincs., 1695. Buried there Feb. 1, 1704-5. (*Peile*, II. 66; where father's name is wrongly given as William.)

GIBSON, WILLIAM. Adm. pens. at CLARE, May 20, 1719. B. at Grantham, Lincs. Matric. 1719. Migrated to Magdalene, as sizar, Nov. 18, 1720. LL.B. 1724. Ord. deacon (Lincoln) Feb. 21, 1724-5. One of these names R. of Gilston, Herts., 1741-3; also R. of Thorley, 1742-5. Died July 28, 1791. (*G. Mag.*; *Cussans*, I.)

GIBSON, WILLIAM. Adm. sizar (age 19) at Pembroke, June 21, 1720. S. of Edward (1677), V. of Hawnes, Beds. Bapt. there, July 4, 1701. Buried there Oct. 16, 1720.

GIBSON, WILLIAM. Adm. sizar at Jesus, Oct. 19, 1731. B. at Slead Hall, Halifax, Yorks. Matric. 1731; B.A. 1735–6; Scholar, 1736; M.A. 1739; M.D. 1746. Professor of Anatomy, 1746–53. Practised at Brighouse, Yorks. Died Feb. 16, 1753, aged 39. (A. Gray; Whitaker, *Loidis*.)

GIBSON, WILLIAM. Adm. sizar (age 18) at Sidney, Mar. 24, 1732–3. S. of William, ironsmith, of Yorkshire. School, Coxwold. Matric. 1733; B.A. 1736–7. Perhaps ord. deacon (Lincoln) Sept. 23, 1750; priest, Dec. 22, 1751. Canon of Windsor, 1746. R. of Saltfleetby St Clement, Lincs., 1751.

GIBSON, WILLIAM. Adm. sizar at Jesus, May 26, 1746. Of Westborough, Lincs. Matric. 1746.

GIBSON, ——. B.A. 1463–4; M.A. 1467.

GIBSON, ——. Matric. sizar from Trinity, c. 1595.

GIBSON, ——. Matric. sizar from Christ's, July, 1603.

GIDDING, WILLIAM, *see* WILLIAMS, WILLIAM.

GIDDINGS, JOHN. Adm. sizar (age 18) at St John's, May 3, 1656. S. of John, husbandman, of Urchfont, Wilts. School, Devizes. Matric. 1656; B.A. 1659–60.

GIFFORD or GYFFORD, ANTHONY. Adm. pens. (age 16) at St John's, Sept. 8, 1659. S. of John, hosier, mayor of Northampton. B. at Northampton. Bapt. there, at All Saints', Dec. 6, 1643. School, Northampton. Matric. 1660; B.A. 1663–4; M.A. 1667. Signed for deacon's orders (London) June 2, 1672. V. of Hardingstone, Northants., 1676–90. R. of Nuffield, Oxon. Married, at Hardingstone, May 30, 1686, Mary, dau. of Wm Kilpin, V. of Hardingstone. (H. I. Longden.)

GIFFORD, CHARLES. Adm. sizar (age 19) at St John's June 10, 1741. S. of John, clerk, of Surrey. B. at Stoke-by-Guildford, 1722. School, Eton (colleger). Matric. 1741; B.A. 1744–5.

GIFFORD, DANIEL. Adm. pens. at Emmanuel, Mar. 27, 1600; Scholar; B.A. 1603–4; M.A. 1607. Perhaps s. of George, and brother of John (1597).

GIFFARD, EMMANUEL. Matric. pens. from Christ's, 1596–7. S. of Anthony, of Milton Damerell, Devon. B.A. 1599–1600; M.A. 1603. Incorp. at Oxford, 1605. M.P. for Rye, 1621–2; for Bury St Edmunds, 1626. Of Tapley, Devon. Will proved Dec. 7, 1633. (*Al. Oxon.*)

GIFFORD, FRANCIS. Matric. pens. from Trinity, Michs. 1585, a scholar from Westminster, 1585; B.A. 1589–90; M.A. 1593.

GIFFORD, FRANCIS. Matric. pens. from Queens', Lent, 1647–8. Of Northamptonshire. 1st s. of Richard (1625), clerk. B.A. 1650–1; M.A. 1654. Incorp. at Oxford, 1660. Ord. deacon (Lincoln) Feb. 10; priest, Mar. 10, 1660–1. V. of Pattishall, Northants. (Godstone moiety), 1661–83; (Dunstable moiety), 1663–90. R. of Rushall, Wilts., 1682–1703. Admon. (Cons. C. Sarum) 1708. Brother of Samuel (1667–8). (*Al. Oxon.*)

GIFFARD or GIFFORD, GEORGE. B.A. from Christ's, 1569–70; M.A. 1573. (He had probably been a student at Hart Hall, Oxford, for several years before 1568.) Ord. deacon and priest (London) Dec. 1578, age 30, as of 'Deston,' Cambs. V. of All Saints', Malden, Essex, 1582; ejected before 1585. Lecturer and preacher at St Paul's Cross, 1591. Engaged in controversy with the Brownists. A leader of the Puritan party in Essex. Author, theological. Buried at Malden, May 10, 1600. Will (Consist. C. London) 1600. Father of John (1597) and haps of Daniel. (*Peile*, I. 98; *Al. Oxon.*; *D.N.B.*; J. Ch. Smith.)

GIFFORD, HANANIAH. Matric. sizar from Queens', Easter, 1642. Of St Ives, Hunts. B.A. from Magdalene, 1646–7. Ord. deacon (Lincoln) Dec. 23, 1660; priest (London) Mar. 5, 1663–4. Preb. of Salisbury, 1684. R. of Raydon, Suffolk, 1693. Probably of Calne, Wilts., and father of the next.

GIFFORD, HENRY. Adm. sizar (age 17) at St John's, Apr. 30, 1672. S. of Ananias (? Hananiah, above), clerk, of Calne, Wilts. B. there. School, Calne. Matric. 1672; B.A. 1675–6; M.A. 1684. Incorp. at Oxford, 1684. Ord. deacon (London) Feb. 20, 1675–6. V. of Montacute, Somerset, 1677–1708.

GIFFORD, HOPE. Matric. sizar (age 15) from Pembroke, Easter, 1623. S. of Daniel, of London. B.A. 1626–7; M.A. 1630.

GYFFURD, JOHN. Matric. sizar from Trinity, Michs. 1569.

GIFFORD, JOHN. Matric. pens. from Pembroke, c. 1597. S. of George (1569), of Malden, Essex. Migrated to Emmanuel, Apr. 27, 1598. B.A. 1600–1; M.A. 1604; D.D. 1616. R. of St Michael Bassishaw, London, 1607–43, sequestered. R. of Hoxton. R. of Eynsford, Kent, 1629. Author, ecclesiastical. Father of John (1637). Perhaps brother of Daniel. (*Vis. of London*, 1634; *D.N.B.* (under George), where he is apparently confused with a contemporary at Oxford.)

GIFFORD, JOHN. Matric. sizar from Queens', Easter, 1618–9. Of Derbyshire. B.A. 1622–3. Perhaps R. of Burton Joyce, Notts., 1627.

GIFFORD, JOHN. Matric. pens. from Pembroke, Easter, 1637. S. of John (1597), D.D. B. at Hoxton, Middlesex. B.A. 1640–1. (*Vis. of London*, 1634.)

GIFFARD, JOHN. Adm. pens. at St Catharine's, July 6, 1734. Of London. Matric. 1737; B.A. 1738–9.

GIFFORD, NATHANIEL. Matric. pens. from Pembroke, Easter, 1586; B.A. 1589–90; M.A. 1593; D.D. 1613. Fellow, 1590. Senior Proctor, 1604. Chaplain to the Bishop of London. R. of Ashingdon, Essex, 1601–2. V. of St Bride's, London, 1603–16. R. of Stone, Dartford, Kent, 1607–15. Archdeacon of Huntingdon, 1612–6. Died 1616. Admon. (P.C.C.) 1616.

GIFFORD, NICHOLAS. Matric. pens. from Pembroke, Easter, 1586; B.A. 1592–3; M.A. 1596.

GIFFORD, NICHOLAS. Matric. sizar from St John's, Easter, 1586. Perhaps scholar of Trinity, 1588.

GIFFORD, RICHARD. Matric. pens. from Trinity, Easter, 1625. 3rd s. of Francis, of St James's Abbey, Northants. Bapt. at Hanslope, Bucks., Feb. 1, 1606–7. Scholar, 1627; B.A. 1627–8; M.A. 1631. Ord. deacon (Peterb.) Sept. 20; priest, Sept. 21, 1629. V. of Olney, Bucks., 1638–40. R. of Gayton, Northants., 1648–56. Buried there Mar. 2, 1655–6. Will (P.C.C.) 1656. Father of Francis (1647–8) and Samuel (1667–8). (*Baker*, I. 151; H. I. Longden.)

GIFFARD, RICHARD. Adm. pens. at Clare, July 9, 1689. (Previously matric. from Trinity College, Oxford, June 12, 1686, age 18.) S. of William, of Ealing, Middlesex. Matric. 1689; B.A. 1690–1. (*Al. Oxon.*)

GIFFORD, ROBERT. B.A. from St John's, 1583–4; M.A. 1587. Probably s. of John, V. of Laughton, Yorks., 1569–1603. V. of Laughton, 1603–49. Buried there July 10, 1649.

GIFFORD, ROBERT. Adm. sizar at Queens', 1610. Of Cambridgeshire. Matric. Easter, 1612; B.A. 1614–5; M.A. 1618; B.D. 1637. Ord. deacon (Peterb.) Dec. 22, 1616; priest (Lincoln) Mar. 1, 1617–8. V. of Biddenham, Beds., 1618. V. of Harrold, 1625–32. R. of Chellington, 1642. R. of Ellisfield, Hants., 1648.

GIFFORD, SAMUEL. B.A. from Clare, 1667–8. 5th s. of Richard (1625), of Gayton, Northants. Bapt. at Gayton, Mar. 28, 1647. Matric. from Wadham College, Oxford, 1663–4. Ord. deacon (Lincoln) June 6, 1669. V. of Little Houghton, Northants., 1676. V. of Brafield, 1686–1732. Buried there June 29, 1732, aged 85. Brother of Francis (1647–8). (Baker, *Northants.*, I. 151; *Al. Oxon.*; H. I. Longden.)

GIFFORD, THOMAS. B.A. from St John's, 1593–4. Perhaps adm. at Lincoln's Inn, Mar. 23, 1591–2; of London.

GIFFORD, THOMAS. Matric. pens. from Trinity, c. 1595, a scholar from Westminster, 1594. 3rd s. of Roger, of St James's Abbey, Northants. B.A. 1598–9; M.A. 1602. Ord. deacon (Peterb.) Sept. 20; priest, Dec. 20, 1607. R. of Braybrook, Northants., 1607–19. R. of Ashley, 1611. Will (P.C.C.) 1653. (Baker, *Northants.*, I. 151.)

GIFFORD, THOMAS. Adm. pens. at Emmanuel, Easter, 1611. School, Merchant Taylors'. Scholar; B.A. 1612–3; M.A. 1616. Incorp. at Oxford, 1616. One of these names, B.A., V. of Willesden, Middlesex, 1615.

GIFFORDE, THOMAS. Adm. Fell.-Com. (age 18) at Caius, c. May, 1625. S. of John, Esq., of Landcross, Devon. School, Torrington (Mr Salisbury). Matric. 1625.

GIFFORD, THOMAS. Adm. pens. at Emmanuel, Apr. 2, 1627. Matric. 1627; B.A. 1630–1; M.A. 1634.

GUIFFARD, THOMAS. Adm. pens. at Clare, Apr. 22, 1672. Of Wiveton, Norfolk. Matric. 1672.

GIFFORD, WILLIAM. Matric. sizar from St John's, Easter, 1628; B.A. 1631–2.

GIFFARD, WILLIAM. Adm. pens. at Queens', June 29, 1670. Of London. Matric. 1670; B.A. 1673–4; M.A. 1677. Ord. deacon (Norwich) Dec. 1677; priest, Dec. 1679. R. of Gt Bradley, Suffolk, 1679–90.

GIFFORD, ——. Pens. at Peterhouse, 1599–1600.

GIFFORD, ——. Matric. pens. from Christ's, July, 1609.

GIGAR or GYGUR, JOHN. Incorp. from Oxford, 1480. Warden of Merton College. Warden of Tattershall College, Lincs. Fellow of Eton College, 1453. Died c. 1510. *See* the laudatory letter from the University printed in *Gr. Bk*, A, 137.

GIGGIS, SIMON. Fellow of ST JOHN'S (B.A.) 1516. Perhaps M.A. 1517-8.

GIGGES, ——. B.A. 1464-5.

GILBANKE or GILLANT, JOHN. B.A. 1501-2; M.A. 1505-6.

GILBER, ——. M.A. or higher degree, 1476-7.

GILBERSON, THOMAS. B.Civ.L. 1511-2.

GILBERT, AMBROSE. Matric. pens. from ST JOHN'S, Easter, 1610. S. of Ambrose. B.A. 1613-4; M.A. 1617; B.D. 1624. Incorp. at Oxford, 1617. Benefactor to St John's. Died 1649. Will (P.C.C.) 1650; of Orsett, Essex. Brother of William (1612). (*Vis. of Essex*, 1634.)

GILBERT, AMBROSE. Matric. pens. from ST JOHN'S, Easter, 1629; B.A. 1632-3. Ord. deacon (Peterb.) Sept. 22; priest, Sept. 23, 1632, as M.A. (H. I. Longden.)

GILBERT, BLASE. Matric. sizar from ST CATHARINE'S, Michs. 1572.

GILBERT, CHARLES. Adm. p . at CLARE, Sept. 12, 1733. B. at Tiffield, Northants. Matric. 1733.

GILBERT, CLAUDIUS. Adm. pens. at ST CATHARINE'S, Michs. 1642; B.A. 1647-8. Doubtless the minister, under the Commonwealth, of the precinct of Limerick, 1652. Active against the Quakers. Minister of St Michael's, Dublin, 1658-9. After the Restoration settled in Belfast. Preb. of Ballymore (Armagh) 1666-8. V. of Belfast, 1668. In 1683, under the designation of 'Minister of Belfast,' he published a translation of Pierre Jurien's reply to Bossuet, under the title of *A Preservative against the Change of Religion.*' Author, theological. Died *c.* 1696. (*D.N.B.*; H. B. Swanzy.)

GILBERT, 'DOMINUS.' Adm. Fell.-Com. at ST JOHN'S, Jan. 18, 1711-2.

GILBERT or GILBERD, EDWARD. Matric. sizar from TRINITY, Easter, 1563; Scholar, 1565; B.A. 1566-7; M.A. 1570. Fellow, 1569. Incorp. at Oxford, 1572. Ord. deacon and priest (Lincoln) Apr. 15, 1576. V. of Brading, Isle of Wight, 1579.

GILBERT, EDWARD. M.A. from QUEENS', 1676. Of Warwickshire. Matric. from Magdalen Hall, Oxford, Mar. 18, 1657-8; B.A. (Oxford) 1658. R. of Barton-on-Dunsmore, Warws., 1660. (*Al. Oxon.*)

GYLBERT, GREGORY. Matric. sizar from ST JOHN'S, Easter, 1568; B.A. 1571-2, as 'George.'

GILBERT, HENRY. Adm. sizar at EMMANUEL, Jan. 14, 1735-6. Of Derbyshire.

GILBERT, ISAAC. Adm. pens. at TRINITY, Apr. 12, 1638. Matric. 1638.

GILBERT, JOHN. Scholar of QUEENS', 1525-8.

GILBERT, JOHN. Matric. sizar from KING'S, Easter, 1548.

GILBERT, JOHN. Matric. pens. from QUEENS', Easter, 1549.

GILBERT, JOHN. Adm. pens. (age 23) at CAIUS, July 26, 1602. S. of Robert. B. at North Walsham, Norfolk. School, North Walsham (Mr Fen). Matric. 1602. Inherited property in North Walsham from his father. Perhaps benefactor to the Boys' Hospital in Norwich; died 1641. (*Venn*, I. 180.)

GILBERT, JOHN. Adm. sizar at EMMANUEL, July 1, 1616. Matric. 1616; B.A. 1619-20; M.A. 1631. R. of Downham Market, Norfolk, 1640. Will dated Aug. 1650. Father of Robert (1648) and of the next.

GILBERT, JOHN. Adm. sizar (age 17) at CAIUS, July 3, 1642. S. of John (above), R. of Downham, Norfolk. B. at Bedingham. Educated by his father. Matric. 1642. Brother of Robert (1648). (*Venn*, I. 347.)

GILBERT, JOHN. Adm. pens. (age 17) at ST JOHN'S, June 12, 1672. S. of William, yeoman, of Withstow, Warws. B. there. School, Barwell. B.A. 1675-6. Ord. priest (York) Sept. 1684. Brother of William (1672).

GILBERT, JOHN. Adm. pens. (age 15) at CHRIST'S, Aug. 20, 1687. S. of Henry. B. at Locko, Derbs. School, Nottingham (Mr Cudworth). Matric. 1688; Scholar, 1689; B.A. 1691-2; M.A. 1695. Buried at Gt St Andrew's, Cambridge, Mar. 10, 1697-8. Perhaps brother of Thomas (1707). *See Al. Oxon.* for a contemporary. (*Peile*, II. 106; family pedigree in *F.M.G.*)

GILBERT, JOHN. M.A. 1687 (Incorp. from Oxford). S. of John, of Salisbury, gent. Matric. from Hart Hall, Oxford, Apr. 9, 1674, age 15; B.A. (Oxford) 1677; M.A. 1680. Author, theological. (*Al. Oxon.*; *D.N.B.*)

GILBERT, JOHN. Adm. pens. at EMMANUEL, Oct. 8, 1710. Of Lincolnshire. School, Winchester. Matric. 1710; B.A. 1714-5. Ord. priest (Norwich) Dec. 1714. V. of Long Parish, Hants., 1714. R. of Whippingham, Isle of Wight, 1717. Died 1724.

GILBERT, JOSHUA. Adm. sizar (age 20) at CHRIST'S, Apr. 28, 1668. S. of Michael (1621), V. of Aldborough, near Boroughbridge, Yorks. B. there. School, Leeds (Mr Michael Gilbert). Matric. 1668; B.A. 1671. Ord. deacon (York) June; priest (Peterb.) Dec. 24, 1671. Brother of Michael (1658). (*Peile*, II. 15.)

GILBERT, MICHAEL. Matric. sizar from CHRIST'S, July, 1621; B.A. 1624 (on the King's visit). V. of Aldborough, Yorks., 1629-77. Buried there Dec. 10, 1677. Father of the above and the next. (*Peile*, I. 341.)

GILBERT, MICHAEL. Adm. sizar (age 16) at CHRIST'S, May 25, 1658. S. of Michael (above), V. of Aldborough, Yorks. B. there. School, York (Mr Wallis). B.A. 1661-2; M.A. 1665. Ord. deacon (Lincoln) May 24; priest (York) 1662. C. of Boroughbridge. Head Master of Leeds School, 1662-90. Brother of Joshua (1668), father of the next. (*Peile*, I. 582.)

GILBERT, MICHAEL. Adm. sizar at JESUS, Apr. 12, 1684. S. of Michael (above), of Leeds, clerk. Matric. 1684; B.A. 1687-8. Perhaps C. of Spexhall, Norfolk, non-juror.

GILBERT, NICHOLAS. Adm. Fell.-Com. (age 18) at ST JOHN'S, May 16, 1691. S. of Thomas, lawyer. B. at Eastbourne, Sussex. School, Horsham. Matric. 1691.

GILBERT, RALPH. Adm. scholar at TRINITY HALL, Jan. 28, 1692-3; probably from Westminster School. Matric. 1693; LL.B. 1698; LL.D. 1705. Fellow, 1698-1711. Adm. licentiate R.C.P. Apr. 17, 1707. Died 1711. (*Munk*, II. 18.)

GILBERT, RICHARD. Ord. deacon (London) Dec. 24, 1615, age 31, as 'late of TRINITY College.' B. at Wellingborough, Northants.

GILBERT, ROBERT. Probably of PETERHOUSE. R. of Wing, Rutland, till his death, Dec. 11, 1503. Benefactor to Peterhouse. (*Cooper*, I. 8.)

GILBERT, ROBERT. Matric. sizar from PEMBROKE, Easter, 1618. S. of William (1579-80), R. of Melford, Suffolk. B.A. from Trinity Hall, 1621-2; M.A. 1625. Ord. deacon (London) June 4, 1626, age 23. Brother of William (1610).

GILBERT, ROBERT. Adm. sizar (age 16) at CAIUS, Jan. 14, 1627-8. S. of John, husbandman, of Norfolk. B. at Flordon. School, Norwich (Mr Stonham). Matric. 1628; B.A. 1632-3. Ord. deacon (Norwich) June 16, 1633; priest, Mar. 2, 1634. R. of Flixton, Suffolk, 1639-45, sequestered. Perhaps V. of Stradset, Norfolk, 1656-62; and V. of Wiggenhall St Germans, 1661. Died 1662. (*Venn*, I. 282.)

GILBERT, ROBERT. Adm. sizar (age 16) at CAIUS, Apr. 4, 1648. S. of John (1616), R. of Downham Market, Norfolk. B. at Saham Tony, Norfolk. Matric. 1648; B.A. 1651-2; M.A. 1655. One of these names C. of Reedham, 1662. Brother of John (1642). (*Venn*, I. 370.)

GILBERT, ROBERT. Adm. pens. (age 17) at ST JOHN'S, June 10, 1662. S. of Robert, gent., of Melton Mowbray, Leics. B. there. School, Melton Mowbray.

GILBERT, ROBERT. Adm. pens. (age 18) at CAIUS, May 30, 1682. S. of John, gent., of Moulton, Norfolk. B. at Gissing. Schools, Flordon and Norwich. Matric. 1682. Died in College. Buried Nov. 21, 1682, at St Michael's, Cambridge. (*Venn*, I. 470.)

GILBERT, ROBERT. Adm. sizar (age 18) at CAIUS, June 3, 1695. S. of Robert, furrier, of Uttoxeter, Staffs. B. there. Schools, Uttoxeter (Mr Bladen) and Dilhorne, Staffs. (Mr Pointon). Matric. 1695; B.A. 1699-1700. Ord. priest (Lichfield) Sept. 27, 1709, as C. of Sharshill. (*Venn*, I. 496.)

GILBERT, ROBERT. Adm. sizar at CLARE, Dec. 30, 1725. B. at Little Ashby, Leics. Matric. 1726; B.A. 1729-30. Ord. deacon (Lincoln) May 24, 1730; priest, June 9, 1734. One of these names R. of Dunnington, Yorks., in 1779.

GILBERT, SIMON. B.A. 1511-2. Perhaps preb. of Hereford, 1558. Died Aug. 1568. Will (P.C.C.) 1568, of Simon Gilbert, parson of Kentchurch, Hereford.

GILBERT, SIMON. Adm. sizar (age 16) at ST JOHN'S, May 4, 1682. S. of Thomas, gent. B. at Uttoxeter, Staffs. School, Uttoxeter (Mr Smithson). Matric. 1682. Probably brother of Thomas (1678-9).

GILBERT, THEODORE. Adm. pens. at CORPUS CHRISTI, 1631. Of Cambridgeshire. Matric. Easter, 1631.

GILBERT, THOMAS. B.A. 1517-8; M.A. 1522. Fellow of PETERHOUSE, 1521-6.

GILBERT, THOMAS. Matric. sizar from TRINITY, Michs. 1620; B.A. 1623-4. One of these names V. of Tollesbury, Essex, 1646-50-.

GILBERT, THOMAS. Adm. pens. (age 16) at PETERHOUSE, June 17, 1637. Of Kent. Doubtless s. of Thomas, of Westbere, Kent, gent. School, Canterbury. Matric. 1637; Scholar, 1638; B.A. 1640-1. V. of Loose, Kent, 1643. (*T. A. Walker*; *Vis. of Kent*, 1619.)

GILBERT, THOMAS. Adm. pens. (age 16) at TRINITY, Feb. 1, 1678-9. S. of Thomas, of Uttoxeter, Staffs. School, Uttoxeter (Mr Smythson). Matric. 1679; B.A. 1682-3; M.A. 1686. Probably brother of Simon (1682).

GILBERT, THOMAS. M.A. 1682 (*Com. Reg.*).

GILBERT, THOMAS. Adm. pens. (age 16) at ST JOHN'S, Mar. 4, 1707-8. S. of Henry, of Locko, Derbs., gent. B. at Derby. School, Westminster. Matric. 1708; B.A. 1711-2; M.A. 1715. Ord. deacon (Ely) May 21; priest, May 27, 1716. Of Boylston, Lincs. Perhaps brother of John (1687). Died Sept. 11, 1733. (*F.M.G.*, 870.)

GILBERT, THOMAS. Adm. at PETERHOUSE, Apr. 12, 1735. S. of Thomas, of London, gent. Matric. from Trinity College, Oxford, Oct. 29, 1729, age 16; B.A. (Oxford) 1733; M.A. (Cambridge) 1737. Fellow of Peterhouse, 1736-44. Author, poetical. Died Nov. 23, 1766. Buried at Petersham, Surrey. M.I. there. Will (P.C.C.); as of St James's Square, London. (*D.N.B.*; *Walker*, 270.)

GILBERT, WILLIAM. Matric. pens. from ST JOHN'S, Easter, 1558. S. of Jerome, recorder of Colchester. B. at Clare, Suffolk, 1540. B.A. 1560-1; M.A. 1564; M.D. 1569. Fellow, 1561. Physician in London for thirty years. F.R.C.P. Censor. Treasurer. President, 1600. Physician to Elizabeth and James I. The distinguished physicist. Author, scientific. Died Nov. 30, 1603, aged 63. Buried at Colchester. Will (P.C.C.) 1604. Half-brother of the next. (*Cooper*, II. 356; *D.N.B.*; *Munk*, I. 77; *Vis. of Essex*, 1634.)

GILBERT, WILLIAM. Matric. pens. from ST JOHN'S, Lent, 1579-80. S. of Jerome, recorder of Colchester, and Jane (2nd wife), dau. of Robert Wingfield, of Suffolk. B. at Boughton, Suffolk (? Norfolk). B.A. 1583-4; M.A. 1587. Ord. deacon (London) Sept. 7, 1590, age 25; priest, May 12, 1591. V. of Fingringhoe, Essex, 1590-7. R. of Long Melford, Suffolk, 1599-1618. Owner of Badley Hall, Essex. Will (P.C.C.) 1618. Father of the next and of Robert (1618). (*Essex Archaeol. Soc.*, N.S., IX. 200.) (Contemporary at Oxford.)

GILBERT, WILLIAM. Matric. pens. from ST JOHN'S, Easter, 1610. S. of William (above). B.A. 1613-4; M.A. from Trinity Hall, 1617. Incorp. at Oxford, 1621. Of Long Melford, Suffolk, when adm. at Lincoln's Inn, May 11, 1616. Barrister, 1623. Counsellor of Colchester and Bury St Edmunds. Of Badley Hall, Essex. Father of William (1647), brother of Robert (1618).

GYLBERT, WILLIAM. Matric. pens. from ST JOHN'S, Michs. 1612. S. of Ambrose, of Colchester. B.A. 1616-7; M.A. 1620; B.D. 1627; D.D. 1632. Ord. deacon (Peterb.) Sept. 23; priest, Sept. 24, 1621. R. of Orsett, Essex, 1626-40. Died Dec. 18, 1640, aged 43. M.I. Will, P.C.C. Brother of Ambrose (1610). (*Vis. of Essex*, 1634; J. Ch. Smith.)

GILBERT, WILLIAM. Adm. pens. (age 15) at ST JOHN'S, May 13, 1647. S. of William (1610), counsellor, of Bury St Edmunds. B. there. Schools, Bury and Colchester. Matric. 1647-8; B.A. 1650-1; M.A. 1654. Of Brent Eleigh, clerk. Perhaps lecturer at Witney, Oxon.; ejected, 1662; but *see Al. Oxon.* for another.

GILBERT, WILLIAM. Adm. pens. (age 17) at ST JOHN'S, Feb. 24, 1647-8. S. of Robert, attorney-at-law, of Melton, Leics. B. there. School, Melton (Mr Stokes). Matric. 1647-8. Adm. at Gray's Inn, July 6, 1650.

GILBERT, WILLIAM. Adm. pens. (age 19) at ST JOHN'S, June 12, 1672. S. of William, yeoman, of Withstow, Warws. B. there. School, Barwell. Matric. 1672; B.A. 1675-6. Brother of John (1672).

GILBERT, WILLIAM. Adm. sizar (age 16) at ST JOHN'S, Oct. 27, 1675. S. of Faustin, deceased. B. at Leicester. School, Leicester. Matric. 1676; B.A. 1679-80; M.A. 1683. Ord. priest (Lincoln) Dec. 9, 1686. R. of Cadeby, Leics., 1688. R. of Newbold, 1693-1719. Died Apr. 7, 1719. Admon. (Leicester) 1720. (*Nichols*, IV. 824.)

GILBERT, WILLIAM. Adm. pens. at CORPUS CHRISTI, 1690. Of Norfolk. Matric. 1691.

GILBERT, WILLIAM. Adm. at CORPUS CHRISTI, 1707. Of Staffordshire. Matric. Michs. 1707.

GILBERT, WILLIAM. Adm. sizar at EMMANUEL, June 25, 1713; afterwards pens. Of Leicestershire. School, Derby. Matric. 1713; B.A. 1716-7.

GILBERT, WILLIAM. Adm. sizar (age 18) at PEMBROKE, July 5, 1731. S. of Arthur, of London, fish merchant. Matric. 1731. Grecian from Christ's Hospital. B.A. 1734-5; M.A. 1738. Fellow, 1735. Ord. deacon (Norwich) June, 1735; priest (Lincoln) Feb. 26, 1737-8.

GILBERT, ——. Fee for M.A. or higher degree, 1460-1.

GILBERT, ——. D.D. 1463-4. Carmelite friar.

GILBERT, ——. B.A. 1474-5; M.A. 1478-9.

GILBERT, ——. Of TRINITY HOSTEL. B.Civ.L. 1477-8.

GILBERT, ——. B.Can.L. 1482-3.

GILBERT, ——. B.A. 1507-8.

GILBY, ANTHONY. B.A. from CHRIST'S, 1531-2. Of Lincolnshire. B. c. 1510. M.A. 1535. A fugitive at Frankfort and Geneva, under Queen Mary. Adm. at Basel University, 1555. Pastor of the English Church at Geneva. V. of Ashby-de-la-Zouch, c. 1564-83, when he resigned. A strong puritan. Author, religious. Assisted in the Geneva translation of the Bible. Died 1585. Will (Leicester) 1585. Father of Nathaniel (1582). (*Cooper*, I. 516; *D.N.B.*)

GILBY, CHARLES. Matric. pens. from MAGDALENE, Easter, 1620. Probably 3rd s. of Sir George, of Stainton, Lincs., Knt. B.A. 1623-4; M.A. 1627. V. of Appleby, Lincs., 1631. Mentioned in the will of his brother Emanuel (1660), as then deceased. (*F.M.G.*, 1228.)

GILBEY, GEORGE. Adm. pens. at EMMANUEL, Oct. 23, 1592. Doubtless 2nd s. of John (below). Matric. 1593; B.A. 1596-7; M.A. 1600. Fellow of Magdalene, 1608. Ord. deacon (Peterb.) Mar. 7; priest, Mar. 8, 1611-2. Brother of Thomas (1589).

GYLBYE, JOHN. Matric. pens. from ST JOHN'S, Michs. 1565. Doubtless 1st s. of George, of Stainton-le-Hole, Lincs. Married Magdalen, dau. of William White, of Louth, 1570. Died *vita patris* Nov. 15, 1580, aged 30. Brother of Tristram (1577-8), father of George (above) and Thomas (1589). (*Lincs. Pedigrees*, 402.)

GYLBY, NATHANIEL. Matric. pens. from ST JOHN'S, Easter, 1579.

GILBEY, NATHANIEL. Matric. Fell.-Com. from CHRIST'S, Jan. 1582-3. S. of Anthony (1531), V. of Ashby-de-la-Zouch. B. at Hinckley, Leics. B.A. 1582-3; M.A. from Emmanuel, 1596; B.D. 1593. Fellow of Emmanuel, 1585. Preacher at Bedford; and Master of the Hospital of St John, 1599-1600. (*Peile*, I. 173.)

GILBY, THOMAS. Adm. at KING'S (age 17) a scholar from Eton, Aug. 6, 1540. Left about 1543-4.

GILBY, THOMAS. Matric. pens. from MAGDALENE, c. 1589. Doubtless 1st s. of John (1565). Married Elizabeth, dau. of Charles Bolle, of Haugh, 1596. Living, 1611. Brother of George (1592). (*Lincs. Pedigrees*, 402.)

GILBY, THOMAS. Adm. sizar (age 17) at ST JOHN'S, Apr. 16, 1687. S. of John, gent. B. in London. School, Hatfield, Yorks. (private; Mr Wm Yarret). Matric. 1687. Migrated to Trinity Hall. B.A. 1691-2; M.A. 1708. Ord. deacon (York) May 22, 1692; priest, 1693. Perhaps R. of West Retford, Notts.; and minister of East Retford, 1709. (*F.M.G.*, 1230.)

GYLBY, THOMAS. Matric. from TRINITY HALL, Easter, 1714; Scholar, 1716; LL.B. 1719. Ord. priest (Lincoln) June 20, 1736.

GYLBIE, TRISTRAM (or THURSTAN). Matric. pens. from ST JOHN'S, Lent, 1577-8. 3rd s. of George, of Stainton-le-Hole, Lincs. Buried at Waltham, June 8, 1611. Brother of John (1565). (*Lincs. Pedigrees*, 402; *Vis. of Lincs.*, 1592.)

GILBURNE, EDWARD. Matric. pens. from CHRIST'S, 1593-5. Doubtless of Charing, Kent; adm. at the Inner Temple, June 30, 1595. Perhaps knighted, July 17, 1617. (*Peile*, I. 214; *Vis. of Kent*, 1619.)

GILDER, EDWARD. Matric. pens. from ST JOHN'S, Easter, 1620; B.A. 1623; M.A. 1627.

GILDER, RICHARD. Adm. sizar (age 17) at ST JOHN'S, Mar. 11, 1674-5. S. of Richard, yeoman, of Bardwell, Suffolk. B. there. School, Bury. Matric. 1675. Died Sept. 1676. Buried at Bardwell.

GILDERD, GYLDARD or GYLDAR, GEORGE. Matric. pens. from PEMBROKE, Michs. 1562; B.A. 1566-7. Ord. deacon (Ely) Sept. 21, 1567. Probably followed John Gildered who was instituted to Collingtree, Northants., 1559. (H. I. Longden.)

GILDON, MICHAEL. Matric. pens. from JESUS, Easter, 1611. 2nd s. of Martin, of Upper Toynton, Lincs. Bapt. Feb. 18, 1593-4. B.A. 1614-5. Will (P.C.C.) 1617; of Jesus College. (*Lincs. Pedigrees*, 404.)

GYLDON or GYLDYNE, RICHARD. Matric. pens. from CHRIST'S, Nov. 1544. Doubtless 1st s. of John, Lord of the Manor of Burton-by-Lincoln. B.A. 1548-9. Fellow of Jesus, c. 1550. He left a number of Hebrew books. Will proved (V.C.C.) 1551. (A. Gray; *Camb. Ant. Soc.*, LXIII. 192.)

GILES, ABRAHAM. Adm. pens. (age 16) at ST JOHN'S, Apr. 16, 1666. S. of Abraham, deceased, of Shrewsbury. B. there. School, Shrewsbury. Matric. 1667; B.A. 1669-70. Signs for deacon's orders (London) Sept. 24, 1670.

GILES, ALEXANDER. Adm. sizar at PETERHOUSE, 1592-3. B.A. 1596-7.

GYLES, EDWARD. Matric. sizar from PEMBROKE, Lent, 1563-4.

GILLES, EDWARD. Matric. sizar from PEMBROKE, Lent, 1597-8. Doubtless buried at Little St Mary's, Cambridge, July 6, 1600.

GILES, GEORGE. B.A. 1514-5; M.A. 1518. Fellow of ST JOHN'S, 1520. V. of Little Eversden, Cambs., 1525-37.

GILES, HENRY. Matric. pens. from ST JOHN'S, Michs. 1620.

GILES, JOHN. Adm. sizar at SIDNEY, Dec. 1602. B. at Eastbourne, Sussex. Matric. 1602; B.A. 1606-7; M.A. 1610. Incorp. at Oxford, 1622. Ord. deacon (Chichester) Dec. 8; priest, Dec. 22, 1611. R. of Ninfield, Sussex, 1611-54. Died Nov. 5, 1654, aged 67. Will (P.C.C.) 1655. (W. C. Renshaw.)

GILES, JOHN. Adm. pens. at EMMANUEL, Easter, 1623. Matric. 1623; B.A. 1626-7; M.A. 1630. Ord. priest (Gloucester) Sept. 23, 1632. V. of Arlingham, Gloucs., 1633; there, as 'an able minister,' in 1650. Conformed and subscribed, 1662. (F. S. Hockaday.)

GYLES, JOHN. Adm. pens. at TRINITY, June 15, 1648. Of Worcestershire. Matric. 1649; Scholar, 1650; B.A. 1651; M.A. 1655. R. of Gt Fakenham, Suffolk, 1661-78. One of these names, s. of the V. of Lindridge, Worcs., silenced, 1662. Minister at Henley-on-Thames. Died there. (*Calamy*, II. 543.)

GILES, MASCALL. Matric. sizar from PEMBROKE, Michs. 1611. B. at Lewes, Sussex. B.A. 1618-9. Ord. deacon (London) Mar. 12, 1619-20, age 24. C. of Hamsey, Sussex. V. of Ditchling, 1621-44. V. of Wartling, 1648-52. Buried there Aug. 14, 1652. Will (P.C.C.) 1653. (*Shaw*, I. 352; *D.N.B.*)

GILES, NATHANIEL. M.A. 1614 (Incorp. from Oxford). Of Berkshire. S. of Nathaniel, Mus.D. (will, P.C.C. 1634; of Windsor Castle). Matric. from Magdalen College, Oxford, Dec. 16, 1608, age 19; B.A. (Oxford) 1609; M.A. 1612; B.D. 1622; D.D. 1625. Fellow of Magdalen College, 1608-19. R. of Newbury, Berks., 1619; of Newton Longueville, Bucks., 1620. Canon of Windsor, 1624. Preb. of Worcester, 1627; R. of Chinnor, Oxon., 1628; sequestered, 1644. Afterwards V. of Ruislip, Middlesex, 1648. Father of the next. (*Al. Oxon.*; *Vis. of Berks.*, 1665, II. 135.)

GILES, NATHAN. M.A. 1651 (Incorp. from Oxford). S. of Nathaniel (above), D.D. Matric. from Queen's College, Oxford, July 23, 1641, age 16; B.A. (Oxford) 1644-5; M.A. 1647. Fellow of Magdalen College, 1645-8, 1660-1. Adm. at the Middle Temple, Feb. 12, 1656-7. Barrister, 1664. (*Al. Oxon.*)

GYLES, RICHARD. Adm. sizar (age 18) at ST JOHN'S, Apr. 11, 1648. S. of Jerome, yeoman, of Tenterden, Kent. B. there. School, Mayfield (Mr Hilder). Matric. 1648; B.A. 1651-2. R. of Rolvenden, Kent, till 1662; ejected, 1662.

GILES, STEPHEN. Adm. pens. at EMMANUEL, Easter, 1623. Matric. 1623; B.A. 1626-7; M.A. 1630. C. of Stone, Gloucs., in 1642: 'an able minister' there, in 1650. Subscribed in 1662. (F. S. Hockaday.)

GYLES, THOMAS. Matric. sizar from TRINITY, Michs. 1564; Scholar, 1567.

GILES, THOMAS. Adm. pens. at CAIUS, Mar. 5, 1587-8. Of Sheldwich, Kent. S. of Gabriel. School, Sheldwich (Mr Lankishire). Matric. 1588; Scholar, 1588-93; B.A. 1591-2; M.A. 1595. R. of Thursford, Norfolk, 1604-11. (*Venn*, I. 134.)

GILES, THOMAS. Adm. sizar at EMMANUEL, Easter, 1613. Matric. 1613.

GILES, THOMAS. Adm. pens. at PETERHOUSE, May 17, 1634. Of Northampton. Matric. 1636; B.A. 1637-8; M.A. 1641.

GYLES, THOMAS. Matric. pens. from TRINITY, Easter, 1642, a scholar from Westminster. Of Worcestershire. B.A. 1644-5; M.A. 1648. Fellow, 1647-51. R. of Downham, Cambs., 1653. Father of the next.

GYLES, THOMAS. Adm. pens. (age 17) at TRINITY, Jan. 17, 1686-7. S. of Thomas (above), former fellow of Trinity. B. at Wicken, Cambs. School, Bury St Edmunds. Matric. 1688; Scholar, 1689; B.A. 1690-1.

GILES or GYLYS, WILLIAM. B.D. 1523; D.D. 1528. Franciscan friar. Last Warden of the House at Leicester; surrendered, Nov. 10, 1539. (*Cooper*, I. 69; *Dugdale*.)

GYLES, WILLIAM. Matric. sizar from ST JOHN'S, c. 1593. B. at Dublin. B.A. 1596-7; M.A. 1600. Ord. deacon (London) Nov. 25, 1599; priest, Nov. 16, 1600. C. of Staines, Middlesex. V. of Elm and Emneth, Cambs., 1600-40.

GILES, WILLIAM. Matric. sizar from CLARE, Michs. 1620; B.A. 1623-4. Ord. deacon (Peterb.) Dec. 18; priest, Dec. 19, 1625. V. of Waldershare, Kent, 1627.

GILES, ——. Adm. at CORPUS CHRISTI, 1569.

GILHAM, ——. B.A. 1489-90.

GILL, ALEXANDER. M.A. 1623 (Incorp. from Oxford); B.D. 1636. S. of Alexander, of London, Master of St Paul's School. School, St Paul's. Matric. from Trinity College, Oxford, June 26, 1612, age 15; B.A. 1615-6; M.A. 1619; B.D. 1627; D.D. 1636-7. Usher of St Paul's School, 1621. High Master, 1635-40. Dismissed for excessive severity. Author, poetical. One of Milton's chief friends. Died 1642. Buried at St Botolph, Aldersgate. Brother of George (1629). (*Al. Oxon.*; *D.N.B.*)

GILL, CHARLES. Adm. pens. at CORPUS CHRISTI, 1570. Matric. Easter, 1571.

GYLL, EDWARD. Matric. pens. from ST JOHN'S, Lent, 1557-8. S. of George, of Wyddial, Herts. B.A. 1561-2. Adm. at the Middle Temple, Mar. 10, 1564-5. Of Anstey and Littlecourt, Layston and Bandon, Herts. Died May, 1616. Buried at Buntingford. Will, P.C.C. Grandfather of the next, brother of Thomas (1557-8), George (1567) and John (1551). (*Cussans*, I. 83, 119; *Peile* (I. 65) for some reason assigns him to Christ's.)

GILL, EDWARD. Matric. pens. from TRINITY, Easter, 1631. S. of Edward, of Bandons, Anstey, Herts. Bapt. at Anstey, Mar. 9, 1614-5. Buried Dec. 19, 1658, at Anstey. (*Cussans*, I. 119.)

GILL, FRANCIS. Matric. pens. from ST JOHN'S, c. 1592.

GYLL, GEORGE. Matric. pens. from CHRIST'S, Michs. 1567. S. of George, of Wyddial, Herts. Of Swaffham, Cambs. Brother of John (1551), Edward (1557-8) and Thomas (1557). (*Misc. Gen. et Her.*, II. 27; *Cussans*, I. 118.)

GYLL, GEORGE. Matric. pens. from CLARE, Easter, 1582. S. of John (1551), High Sheriff of Herts. Of Wyddial. Engaged in the expedition under the Earl of Essex against Cadiz, 1597. Knighted, July 3, 1603. Died Nov. 17, 1619. Buried at Wyddial. Admon., P.C.C. Father of the next and brother of John (1582). (*Cussans*, I. 118.)

GILL, GEORGE. Matric. pens. from CHRIST'S, Michs. 1615. S. of Sir George (above), of Wyddial. Of Walton, Northants. Living at Buntingford, Herts., 1659. (*Cussans*, I. 119; *Misc. Gen. et Her.*, II. 29.)

GILL, GEORGE. Matric. pens. from QUEENS', Easter, 1616. Of Derbyshire. Probably s. of Philip, of Lightwood, Derbs. Bapt. at Norton, Mar. 10, 1600-1. Married Ann, dau. of Darcy Washington, Esq., of Adwick, Yorks., July 25, 1638. (M. H. Peacock.)

GILL, GEORGE. M.A. 1629 (Incorp. from Oxford). Of London. Matric. from Trinity College, Oxford, Dec. 13, 1616, age 14; B.A. (Oxford) 1620; M.A. 1623-4. Under usher at St Paul's School, 1628-37. Sur-master, 1637. Died 1639-40. Brother of Alexander (1623).

GYLL, HENRY. Matric. pens. from CLARE, Michs. 1578. S. of Francis, of Heydon, Essex. Adm. at the Inner Temple, 1579. Of Peldon, Essex. Brother of Thomas (1579). (*Lipscomb*, IV. 606.)

GILL, HENRY. Adm. sizar (age 17) at ST JOHN'S, Mar. 22, 1651-2. S. of Thomas, gent., of Conisborough, near Rotherham, Yorks. B. at Preston, Pontefract. School, Doncaster. Matric. 1652.

GILL, HENRY. Adm. sizar at TRINITY, Dec. 18, 1660, from Magdalene. Matric. 1661; Scholar, 1661; B.A. 1662-3; M.A. 1666. R. of Hargham, Norfolk, 1666-77. V. of Roudham, till 1677. Master of Bradford School, 1671-2. V. of Collingham, Yorks., 1672. Died Feb. 23, 1676-7.

GILL, HENRY. Adm. pens. (age 17) at SIDNEY, June 12, 1672. S. of William, yeoman. B. at Threshfield, Yorks. School, Sedbergh. Matric. 1672; B.A. 1675-6. Ord. deacon (York) May, 1676. Perhaps P.C. of Farlam, Cumberland, 1674-95. Buried there June 25, 1695. (*Sedbergh Reg.*; *B. Nightingale*.)

GILL, JAMES. Adm. sizar (age 16) at PEMBROKE, July 3, 1679. S. of Robert, of Cambridge. Matric. 1680; B.A. 1682-3; M.A. 1686.

GILL, JOHN. B.Civ.L. 1495-6. Of Carlisle diocese. Ord. deacon (Lincoln) Mar. 11, 1496-7; priest (?) 1496-7; title, 'Hospital of St John,' Cambridge.

GYLL, JOHN. Matric. sizar from JESUS, Easter, 1544.

GYLL, JOHN. Matric. pens. from CHRIST'S, May, 1551. S. and h. of George, of Buckland and Wyddial, Herts. B. 1538. Adm. at the Middle Temple, Oct. 27, 1555. Sheriff of Herts., 1575-6. Died Oct. 22, 1600, aged 62. Will, P.C.C. Brother of Edward (1557-8), Thomas (1557-8) and George (1567), father of George (1582) and of John (1582). (*Peile*, I. 48; *Misc. Gen. et Her.*, II. 29.)

GYLL, JOHN. Matric. pens. from ST JOHN'S, Easter, 1568. One of these names V. of Weston Favell, Northants., 1574-9.

GYLL, JOHN. Matric. pens. from CLARE, Easter, 1582. Doubtless 2nd s. of John (1551). Of Little Buntingford Court, Herts. Knighted, Nov. 26, 1613. M.P. for Minehead, Somerset, 1625. Will proved, May 20, 1651. Brother of George (1582).

GILL, JOHN. Matric. pens. from CLARE, c. 1593, *impubes*. One of these names, s. and h. of Francis, of Tempsford, Beds., Esq., adm. at Gray's Inn, Oct. 22, 1595.

GILL, JOHN. Matric. sizar from JESUS, Michs. 1611. B. at Liverpool. B.A. 1614; M.A. 1619. Ord. deacon (London) June 18, 1614, age 26; priest, June 4, 1615. C. of Whittlesford, Cambs.

GILL, JOHN. Adm. pens. at CLARE, June 30, 1652. Matric. 1652.

GILL, JOHN. Adm. Fell.-Com. (age 17) at CHRIST'S, Mar. 4, 1660-1. S. of Edward. B. at Norton, Yorks. Bapt. at Rotherham, May 14, 1643. Matric. 1661. Of Carhouse, Yorks. Sheriff of Yorks., 1692. Married, at Huddersfield, Jan. 31, 1664-5, Elizabeth, dau. of Joshua Brooke. Died Jan. 24, 1705-6. Buried at Rotherham. His father was the Parliamentary Governor of Sheffield Castle, and M.P. for the West Riding, 1653. Father of Westby (1695). (*Peile*, I. 595; *Vis. of Yorks.*, 1666.)

GILL, JOHN. Adm. sizar (age 19) at ST JOHN'S, Feb. 2, 1744-5. S. of Peter, butcher, of Kent. B. at Canterbury. School, King's, Canterbury. Matric. 1745. Ord. deacon (Peterb.) June 2, 1751; priest, June 17, 1753 (*Litt. dim.* from Canterbury). Perhaps of Minster, Kent; died Oct. 3, 1771. (*G. Mag.*)

GILL, JOSHUA. Adm. sizar at TRINITY, July 11, 1662. Matric. 1662.

GILL or GYLL, LEONARD. B.Civ.L. 1522-3. Doubtless s. of William, of Buckland, Herts. Fellow of Jesus, c. 1535-47. Died c. Apr. 1547. Buried in St Edward's Church, Cambridge. Will proved (V.C.C.) July 14, 1547; described as priest. (*Lipscomb*, IV. 606; *Cussans*, I. 118; A. Gray.)

GILL or GELL, MATTHEW. Matric. sizar from CORPUS CHRISTI, Easter, 1607. Of Cambridgeshire. B.A. 1610-1; M.A. 1614. R. of Tolleshunt Knights, Essex, 1628-c. 1658. Will (P.C.C.) 1658.

GILL, NICHOLAS. B.A. from TRINITY, 1612-3; M.A. 1616. Ord. priest (Peterb.) May 23, 1619. C. of Bottisham, Cambs., 1633. V. of Shopland, Essex, 1639. V. of Tolleshunt Major, in 1650.

GILL, PETER. Matric. pens. from ST JOHN'S, Michs. 1585.

GILL, RALPH. Adm. Fell.-Com. at EMMANUEL, May 29, 1587. S. of Thomas, of Mucking, Essex, and lion keeper at the Tower of London. Matric. 1587. Doubtless adm. at Gray's Inn, Nov. 6, 1590, as of St Peter-ad-vincula, London. Married Anne, dau. of Michael Heneage, Esq. Died Feb. 12, 1620. Buried at St Peter's-in-the-Tower. Will (P.C.C.) 1621. (*Coll. Top. et Gen.*, VIII. 280; *Lincs. Pedigrees*.)

GYLL, RICHARD. 'Of CAIUS College.' S. of John, and nephew of Leonard (1522-3). A minor in 1547. (*Misc. Gen. et Her.*, II. 27.) Not found in the College records.

GILL, RICHARD. Adm. sizar at EMMANUEL, May 30, 1670. Of Cheshire. Matric. 1670; B.A. 1673-4.

GILL or GELL, ROBERT. Matric. sizar from CORPUS CHRISTI, Michs. 1601. Of Cambridgeshire. B.A. 1605-6; M.A. 1609. Perhaps V. of Stalham, Norfolk, 1624-30.

GILL (? SILL), ROWLAND. Matric. sizar from ST CATHARINE'S, c. 1596.

GYLL, THOMAS. Matric. pens. from CHRIST'S, Mar. 1557-8. S. of George, of Buckland and Wyddial, Herts. Of Chancery Lane. Will proved, Mar. 4, 1611. Brother of Edward (1557-8), George (1567) and John (1551). (*Peile*, I. 65; *Misc. Gen. et Her.*, II. 29.)

GYLE, THOMAS. Matric. pens. from CHRIST'S, May, 1579. S. of Francis, of Heydon, Essex. Scholar. Adm. at the Inner Temple, Feb. 4, 1586-7. Married Joan, dau. of Henry Hopper. Brother of Henry (1578). (*Peile*, I. 153; *Misc. Gen. et Her.*, II. 27.)

GILL, THOMAS. Matric. pens. from CHRIST'S, Dec. 1615. Perhaps s. of the above. Bapt. at Heydon, Essex, Apr. 25, 1602.

GILL, THOMAS. Matric. pens. from ST CATHARINE'S, Michs. 1619. One of these names R. of Nunburnholme, Yorks., 1656. Conformed, and reinstituted, 1662-85. Buried July 22, 1685. (M. H. Peacock.)

GILL, THOMAS. Adm. sizar (age 15) at ST JOHN'S, Apr. 19, 1672. S. of Thomas (? above), clerk, of Nunburnholme, Yorks. Bapt. there, Sept. 25, 1656. School, Pocklington (Mr Elletson). Matric. 1672; B.A. 1675-6. Ord. deacon (Norwich) Sept. 1678. R. of Knapton, Norfolk, 1683-1705. R. of Antigham, 1701-5. R. of Dersingham, 1705-29. R. of West Newton, 1705-29. Licensed to practise medicine by the Bishop, 1705.

GILL, THOMAS. Adm. pens. at QUEENS', July 2, 1673. Of Middlesex. S. of Philip, M.D., of Edmonton. M.A. 1675 (*Lit. Reg.*); M.D. 1681. Candidate R.C.P. 1683. Fellow, R.C.P. 1685. Censor. Registrar, 1692-1701. Died July 4 or 5, 1714. (*Munk*, I. 437.)

GYLL, THOMAS. Adm. scholar at TRINITY HALL, Jan. 5, 1719-20. S. of Thomas, of Barton, North Riding, Yorks. Matric. 1718. Adm. at Lincoln's Inn, Jan. 24, 1718-9. Solicitor-general of the Palatinate of Durham, 1733. Recorder of Durham, 1767. Died at Barton, Mar. 12, 1780, aged 79. M.I. there. His *Diary* in the *Surtees Soc.*, No. 118. (H. M. Wood.)

GILL, WESTBY. Adm. pens. at JESUS, Apr. 21, 1695. 1st s. of John (1660), of Car-house, Rotherham. Bapt. at Rotherham, Mar. 21, 1678-9. Matric. Fell.-Com. 1695; B.A. 1698-9; M.A. 1702. Candidate for the represeutation of the University, in 1710. F.R.S. 1740. Died Oct. 1746. (Hunter, *Sheffield*; L. *Mag.*)

GILL, WILLIAM. Matric. sizar from CLARE, Easter, 1606; B.A. 1609-10. Admon. (York) 1615, of one of these names; C. of Thorne, Doncaster.

GILL, WILLIAM. Matric. sizar from CHRIST'S, Dec. 1609; B.A. 1613-4; M.A. 1618. Ord. deacon (Peterb.) May 31; priest, June 1, 1618.

GILL, WILLIAM. Adm. at CORPUS CHRISTI, 1707. Of Hertfordshire. Doubtless s. and h. of John, of Bishop's Stortford, Herts., gent.; adm. at Lincoln's Inn, Feb. 15, 1709-10. Living, 1714; had property at Clavering, Essex. (*Misc. Gen. et Her.*, II. 31.)

GILL, WILLIAM. Adm. sizar (age 19) at ST JOHN'S, May 25, 1727. S. of Stephen, husbandman, of Yorkshire. B. at Church Fenton. School, Sherburn (Mr Lowther). Matric. 1727; B.A. 1730-1. Ord. deacon (Norwich) June 13, 1731; priest (*Litt. dim.* from York) Mar. 1731-2. V. of Church Fenton, Yorks., 1733-56. V. of Sherburn, 1733-56. Died Feb. 2, 1756. Father of William (1751).

GILL, WILLIAM. Adm. pens. at ST CATHARINE'S, Oct. 21, 1749. Of Surrey. Doubtless of Eashing, Godalming, Surrey, Esq. S. of Ezra, of Eashing, Esq. Matric. 1749. Adm. at Lincoln's Inn, Jan. 24, 1753. Died 1813. (J. Ch. Smith.)

GILL, WILLIAM. Adm. sizar (age 18) at ST JOHN'S, May 22, 1751. Probably s. of William (1727), V. of Sherburn, Yorks. B. at Sherburn. Schools, Beverley (Mr Clarke) and Wakefield. Matric. 1751; B.A. 1755; M.A. 1758. Ord. deacon (Chester) Dec. 21, 1755; priest (Peterb.) Sept. 25, 1757.

GILL, ——. B.A. 1509-10.

GILL, ——. B.A. 1526-7; M.A. 1530. Fellow of CHRIST'S, 1530-4.

GILLEAT, DAVID. Matric. sizar from TRINITY, Easter, 1612.

GILLET, *see also* GILLOTT.

GILLET, JOHN. Adm. pens. (age 17) at CHRIST'S, Jan. 28, 1635-6. S. of John. B. at Cambridge. School, Perse. Matric. 1636. One, John Gillott, V. of Stainton, Yorks., 1664-67. Died 1667. (*Peile*, I. 440.)

GILLETT, THOMAS. Grace for B.A. from CHRIST'S, 1631-2.

GILLEY, JOHN. B.A. from MAGDALENE, 1618-9; M.A. 1622. Will (P.C.C.) 1660, of one of these names, V. of Hornby, Yorks.

GILLIE, MARTIN. Matric. pens. from CAIUS, Michs. 1559; B.A. 1562-3. Fellow, about 1564. Probably s. of John, and nephew of Martin, of Lincoln's Inn, whose will (P.C.C. 1564) mentions him.

GILLIAM, JOHN. Adm. pens. at JESUS, Mar. 6, 1675-6. S. of John, of Manchester, Esq. Matric. 1675-6. Adm. at Gray's Inn, Apr. 18, 1678.

GILLIBRAND, *see* GELLIBRAND.

GILLING, JOHN. A scholar and fellow of KING'S HALL, 1388-92. Ord. deacon (Ely) Dec. 18, 1389; priest, Feb. 26, 1389-90.

GILLINGHAM, RICHARD. Adm. sizar (age 16) at CAIUS, Aug. 31, 1629. S. of Richard, R. of Lillington, Dorset. B. there. School, Rampisham (Mr Hartwell and Mr Hallet). Matric. 1629; Scholar, 1634-7; B.A. 1634-5; M.A. 1638. Probably R. of Lillington, 1640. (*Venn*, I. 292.)

GILLINGHAM, RICHARD. Adm. sizar at EMMANUEL, June 10, 1687. Of Norfolk. Matric. 1687; B.A. 1691-2; M.A. 1695. Ord. deacon (London) May 23, 1692; priest (Lincoln) Feb. 12, 1692-3. Probably reader to the Temple. V. of Chigwell, Essex, 1701-21. Will (P.C.C.) 1721: leaves £1600 to found a scholarship at EMMANUEL. (J. Ch. Smith.)

GILLINGHAM, ROGER. Adm. pens. (age 17) at SIDNEY, May 7, 1702. S. of John, mercer. B. at Southampton. School, Wimborne (Mr Loyd). Matric. 1705; B.A. 1705-6; M.A. 1709. Ord. deacon (Ely) June 19; priest, June 24, 1709. R. of Little Shelford, Cambs., 1709.

GILLINGHAM, ROGER. Adm. pens. at EMMANUEL, Aug. 24, 1724. Of Cambridgeshire. Perhaps of Shelford Hall.

GILLIOTT, THOMAS. B.A. 1474-5.

GILLOTT, *see also* GILLET.

GILLOTT, HENRY. Matric. sizar from CLARE, Easter, 1575. B. at Burton, Yorks. B.A. 1577-8; M.A. 1581. Ord. deacon (London) Dec. 21, 1583, age 26. Curate and schoolmaster at Walsingham, Norfolk. Ord. priest (Norwich) Apr. 8, 1587. V. of Houghton-le-Dale, Norfolk, 1587 (Gillett).

GILLOTT or GILLETT, HENRY. Matric. sizar from ST JOHN'S, Easter, 1612; B.A. 1615-6. Ord. deacon (Peterb.) Sept. 22, 1616; priest, Mar. 1, 1617-8.

GILLOT, MATTHEW. Matric. sizar from ST CATHARINE'S, Easter, 1649. Probably brother of Samuel (1652).

GILLOT, ROBERT. Scholar at KING'S HALL, 1410-20; vacated on marriage. Clerk in the Chapel Royal. (*Trin. Coll. Admissions*, I. 113.)

GILLOT, SAMUEL. Matric. sizar from ST CATHARINE'S, Easter, 1652; B.A. 1655. Probably brother of Matthew (1649).

GILLOTT, WILLIAM. B.A. 1503-4; M.A. 1507.

GILLOTT, ——. B.Can.L. 1490.

GILLOTT, ——. B.Can.L. or B.Civ.L. 1518-9.

GILMAN, HENRY. M.A. 1693 (Incorp. from Oxford). S. of John, of Withington, Gloucs., clerk. School, Winchester. Matric. from Queen's College, Oxford, May 17, 1675, age 17; B.A. (Magdalen College, Oxford) 1678-9; M.A. 1681. Preb. of Rochester, 1689. R. of Kingsdown, Kent, 1690-1710. V. of St Nicholas, Rochester, 1701-10. Died Nov. 17, 1710, aged 49. Buried in the Cathedral. (H. G. Harrison.)

GILMAN, JOHN. Adm. sizar (age 16) at CHRIST'S, May 12, 1704. S. of William. B. at Norwich. School, Norwich. Scholar, 1704-5; Matric. 1705. Buried at Gt St Andrew's, Cambridge, June 16, 1707. (*Peile*, II. 159.)

GILLMAN, REUBEN. Adm. pens. (age 16) at CAIUS, May, 1727. S. of Reuben, attorney, late of Loddon, Norfolk. B. there. Schools, Loddon (private; Mr Lann), Norwich (Mr Pykaring) and Chedgrave (Mr Conold). Scholar, 1727-32; Matric. 1728; B.A. 1730-1. (*Venn*, II. 27.)

GILLMAN, SAMUEL. Adm. sizar (age 18) at CAIUS, Mar. 27, 1695. S. of Samuel, brewer, of Hingham, Norfolk. B. there. Schools, Norwich and Wymondham (Mr Clarke). Matric. 1695; Scholar, 1695-1700; B.A. 1698-9. Lived at Hingham. Married Hester, dau. of Wm Le Neve, of Wymondham, Norfolk. Died Nov. 28, 1741. Buried at Hingham. M.I. (*Venn*, I. 496; G. H. Holley.)

GILMAN, SAMUEL. Adm. sizar at PETERHOUSE, May 23, 1705. Migrated to King's, a scholar from Eton, 1705. S. of Samuel, of New Windsor. B. there. Matric. Michs. 1705; B.A. 1709-10; M.A. 1713. Fellow, 1708. Assistant Master at Eton. Ord. deacon (London) Dec. 19, 1714; priest (Ely) Dec. 18, 1715. R. of Avington, Oxon. Chaplain to the Bishop of Exeter. R. of Ickenham, Middlesex, Apr.-Aug. 1725. Died 1725.

GILLMAN, ——. Matric. pens. from CHRIST'S, July, 1609.

GILLMAN, ——. Adm. Fell.-Com. at TRINITY HALL, June 28, 1698.

GILPYN, ALAN. Matric. sizar from ST JOHN'S, Michs. 1575; B.A. 1579-80.

GYLPYN, BERNARD. Adm. sizar (age 16) at CAIUS, Feb. 7, 1563-4. Of Lancaster. S. of Randall. School, Lancaster. Scholar, 1564. Nephew of the 'Apostle of the North.' (*Venn*, I. 52; *F.M.G.*)

GILPIN or GUILPIN, EVERARD. Adm. pens. at EMMANUEL, June 1, 1588. Matric. 1588.

GYLPIN, FRANCIS. Adm. sizar (age 17) at MAGDALENE, June 24, 1665. S. of Nicholas, of Hornby, Yorks. School, Bedale. Matric. 1665; B.A. 1668-9. Ord. deacon (York) Mar. 1670-1; priest, Sept. 1671.

GYLPINE, GEORGE. Matric. sizar from TRINITY, c. 1596; Scholar, 1599. One of these names student at Leyden, Feb. 11, 1591.

GILPIN, GODFREY or GEOFFREY. B.A. 1532-3; M.A. 1535; B.D. 1544. Fellow of CHRIST'S, 1532-47. Proctor, 1538-9. One of the original fellows of Trinity, 1546. Lady Margaret preacher, 1547. V. of Pinchbeck, Lincs., 1548. Will proved (V.C.C.) Sept. 12, 1550. (*Peile*, I. 16; *Cooper*, I. 97.)

GILPIN, JOHN. B.Can.L. 1529-30. Fellow of JESUS, c. 1527. Principal of Borden Hostel. V. of Swavesey, Cambs., 1527-30. Died Dec. 27, 1530. Will (V.C.C.). (*Cooper*, I. 41.)

GYLPYN, JOHN. Matric. sizar from TRINITY, Easter, 1551; Scholar, 1552.

GILPIN, LUKE. A scholar of TRINITY, 1560. B. at Kentmoor, Westmorland. B.A. 1561-2; M.A. 1565; B.D. 1576. Fellow, 1562. Proctor, 1574-5. Ord. priest (London) Apr. 3, 1569. V. of Chesterton, Cambs., 1571. R. of Bebington, Cheshire, 1573. Archdeacon of Derby, 1577-87. Preb. of Southwell, 1581-7. Died 1587. (*Cooper*, II. 17.)

GYLPYN, OWEN. Matric. pens. from ST JOHN'S, Michs. 1550. At Trinity, in 1552.

GILPIN, RANDALL. Adm. at KING'S (age 17) a scholar from Eton, July 4, 1611. Of Aldingham, Lancs. Matric. 1611; B.A. 1614-5; M.A. 1618; D.D. 1661 (*Lit. Reg.*). Fellow, 1614, till 1629. Chaplain of the fleet which sailed to the relief of Rochelle. Minister of St Benet, Cambridge, 1625-6. R. of Barningham, Suffolk, 1629. R. of Worlingham, 1661. Author. Died Nov. 1661. (*D.N.B.*)

GILPIN, SIMON. Adm. sizar (age 17) at PETERHOUSE, Nov. 12, 1638. Probably s. of Isaac, of Leatherhead, Cumberland. Matric. 1638; B.A. 1642-3. V. of Staindrop, Durham, 1660-99. R. of Cockfield, 1690-9. Buried Jan. 19, 1698-9, at Staindrop. Father of the next. (H. M. Wood; *T. A. Walker*, 67.)

GILPIN, SIMON. Adm. sizar (age 17) at PETERHOUSE, Apr. 22, 1667. S. of Simon (above), V. of Staindrop, Durham. School, Brignall, Durham. Matric. 1667; Scholar, 1670; B.A. 1670-1; M.A. 1675. Ord. deacon (York) Feb. 1674-5; priest (Durham) Sept. 20, 1679. V. of Staindrop, Durham, 1700-17. R. of Cockfield, 1714-7. Buried at Staindrop, Sept. 5, 1717. (*T. A. Walker*, 133; D. S. Boutflower.)

GILLS, RICHARD. Adm. sizar at TRINITY, Nov. 27, 1647.

GILLES, (?) WILLIAM. Adm. sizar at ST CATHARINE'S, July 1, 1692.

GILSON, DANIEL. Adm. pens. (age 16) at SIDNEY, July 17, 1673. S. of Thomas (? 1645), clerk. B. at Brentwood, Essex. School, Brentwood (Mr Barnard). Of Colchester. Died Feb. 8, 1727, aged 71. (*Musgrave*.)

GILSON, EDMUND. Matric. sizar from CLARE, Michs. 1560. S. of John, of Stapleford, Cambs. School, Ely. Migrated as pens. (age 23) to Caius, Jan. 29, 1571-2, being then in deacon's orders. Ord. deacon (Norwich); priest (Ely) Dec. 1569. R. of Caston, Norfolk, 1575-9. Will proved (Norwich) 1579. (*Venn*, I. 69.)

GYLSON (? GYBSON), EDWARD. Matric. sizar from ST JOHN'S, Easter, 1579.

GYLSON, GEORGE. Matric. pens. from ST JOHN'S, Michs. 1561. Will of one of these names (P.C.C.) 1617; of St Dunstan-in-the-West, London, Esq.

GYLSON, THOMAS. Matric. sizar from TRINITY, Michs. 1572.

GILSON, THOMAS. Adm. sizar at EMMANUEL, June 18, 1645. Probably s. of Sir Thomas, of St Peter's. B. at Sudbury, Suffolk. School, Dedham. Migrated to Oxford, after residing four years; B.A. (Magdalen Hall, Oxford) 1648; M.A. 1649-50. Fellow of Corpus Christi, Oxford, 1649. V. of Little Baddow, Essex, c. 1657; ejected, 1662. Afterwards a minister at Stepney, Middlesex. Died May 6, 1680, aged 50. Buried at Stepney. M.I. Perhaps father of Daniel (1673). (*Al. Oxon.*; *Calamy*, I. 496; J. Ch. Smith.)

GIMLING, WILLIAM. B.A. 1534-5.

GINBED or GYNNEBY, ——. Pens. at PETERHOUSE, 1570-1. Probably B.A. 1571-2.

GINDER, JOHN. Matric. pens. from TRINITY, c. 1595; Scholar, 1599; B.A. 1599-1600; M.A. 1603.

GYNNE, JAMES. Matric. sizar from JESUS, Lent, 1577-8.

GYNNER, JOHN. Matric. pens. from CLARE, Michs. 1589.

GYNNER, ROBERT. Matric. sizar from CAIUS, Mar. 8, 1579-80. Of Suffolk. B.A. 1583-4; M.A. 1588. V. of Stetchworth, Cambs., 1591-1648. Buried there Jan. 26, 1648-9. (*Venn*, I. 105.)

GINNER, THOMAS, *see* JENNER.

GINNER, WILLIAM. Matric. pens. from CLARE, Lent, 1588-9.

GYNNINGE, RICHARD. Matric. sizar from CLARE, Michs. 1564.

GINNINGS, THOMAS. Matric. sizar from QUEENS', Easter, 1646. Of Hertfordshire.

GIPPES, GEORGE. Matric. pens. from ST JOHN'S, Michs. 1606. Of London. B.A. 1610-1; M.A. 1614. Adm. Fell.-Com. at Queens', 1618-9. Incorp. at Oxford, 1621. Preb. of Lichfield, 1624, ejected. R. of St Andrew's, Hertford, 1624-33. R. of Aylestone, Leics., 1633. R. of Bottesford, Leics., 1646. Died May, 1654. Father of John (1651). (*Al. Oxon.*)

GIPPS, GEORGE. M.A. 1675 (Incorp. from Oxford). S. of Roger, of Newington, Kent, gent. Matric. from Magdalen Hall, Oxford, July 6, 1666, age 17; B.A. (Oxford) 1669-70; M.A. 1672-3. V. of Lympne, Kent. V. of Brenzett, 1677-1707. P.C. of Wye, 1679-1707. Died Jan. 3, 1707. Buried at Wye. (*Al. Oxon.*; H. G. Harrison.)

GIPPS, JOHN. Adm. pens. at EMMANUEL, Apr. 10, 1596. Matric. 1596.

GIPPES, JOHN. Adm. pens. at EMMANUEL, Sept. 16, 1641. Of Suffolk. Became a Fell.-Com. 1644. Perhaps of Whelnetham, Suffolk. If so, doubtless father of John (1676) and Richard (1675). (*E. Anglian*, IV. 207.)

GIPPES, JOHN. Adm. pens. at EMMANUEL, May 20, 1651. Of Leicestershire. S. of George (1606), R. of Aylestone, Leics. B. there. Schools, Wormley, Herts. (Mr Lovelass) and St Paul's, London. Migrated to Sidney, adm. pens. there (age 18) Apr. 14, 1652. Matric. 1652. Migrated to Oxford (Magdalen Hall). Matric. there, Dec. 9, 1653; B.A. (Oxford) 1654. Chaplain at Magdalen College. Member of the Westminster Assembly. Died 1666. (*Al. Oxon.*; *Calamy*, I. 246.)

GIPPS, JOHN. Adm. pens. (age 14) at CAIUS, July 7, 1676. S. of John (? 1644), gent. of Gt Whelnetham, Suffolk. B. there. School, Bury St Edmunds. Scholar, 1676–82; Matric. 1677–8; LL.B. 1682. Fellow, 1683–7. Ord. deacon (Lincoln) Dec. 20, 1685; priest (Norwich) Nov. 19, 1686. R. of Brockley, Suffolk, 1685–90, deprived as a non-juror. Brother of Richard (1675). (*Venn*, I. 456.)

GIPPS, JOHN GILES. Adm. pens. (age 18) at CAIUS, Dec. 17, 1711. S. of Sir Richard (1675), Knt., of Gt Whelnetham, Suffolk. B. there. School, Bury. Matric. 1712; Scholar, 1712–6; B.A. 1715–6. Ord. deacon (Ely) June 16, 1717; priest (Norwich) July 13, 1718. R. of Brockley, Suffolk, 1726–34; of Chevington, 1727–34. Died 1734. Buried at Whelnetham. (*Venn*, I. 526.)

GIPPS, RICHARD. Adm. pens. at EMMANUEL, Apr. 10, 1596. Doubtless of London, gent.; adm. at Gray's Inn, July 3, 1598. One of these names, 'of London,' judge of the sheriffs' court. Married Margaret, dau. of Valentine Pell, of Norfolk. Perhaps father of Richard (1635). (Gage, *Suffolk*, 522.)

GIPPES, RICHARD. Adm. pens. at EMMANUEL, Sept. 8, 1627. Of Suffolk. S. of Richard, of Bury, gent., deceased. Adm. at Gray's Inn, Feb. 2, 1628–9.

GIPPES, RICHARD. Adm. Fell.-Com. at EMMANUEL, May 21, 1635. Of Middlesex. One of these names s. of Richard, of London. Of Horningsheath, Suffolk. Buried there Feb. 8, 1663.

GIPPS, RICHARD. Adm. pens. (age 16) at CAIUS, Sept. 24, 1675. S. of John (? 1644), gent., of Gt Whelnetham, Suffolk. B. there. Bapt. Sept. 15, 1659. School, Bury. Matric. 1675. Adm. at Gray's Inn, Feb. 5, 1675–6. Knighted, Nov. 27, 1682. Antiquarian writer. Died Dec. 21, 1708. Buried at Whelnetham. Will (P.C.C.) 1709. Brother of John (1676), father of John Giles (above). (*D.N.B.*; *Venn*, I. 454.)

GIPPS, RICHARD. Adm. Fell.-Com. at QUEENS', Jan. 18, 1694–5. Of Suffolk. Doubtless s. of Sir Richard, of Horringer (Horningsheath). Bapt. Dec. 27, 1677. School, Bury. Adm. at the Middle Temple, Aug. 28, 1695. Major in the army. Living at Badley, 1722. (*Bury School*; *S.H.A.H.*; Gage, *Suffolk*, 522.)

GIPPES, SYLLARD (SULYARD). Adm. pens. (age 17) at CHRIST'S, Apr. 1677. S. of Valentine, of Horningsheath, Suffolk. B. there. Bapt. Mar. 20, 1659–60. School, Bury. Matric. 1677. Adm. at the Middle Temple, Dec. 8, 1677. Buried at Horningsheath, June 3, 1680. (*Peile*, II. 63.)

GIPPES, THOMAS. Adm. sizar at TRINITY, Feb. 23, 1654–5. Of Leicestershire. School, St Paul's. Matric. 1656; Scholar, 1657; B.A. 1658–9; M.A. 1662. Fellow, 1661. Ord. deacon and priest (Peterb.) Sept. 22, 1667. C. of Bottisham, Cambs., 1668. Chaplain to the Earl of Derby. R. of Bury, Lancs., 1675–1710, 'B.D.' Author, sermons. Died Mar. 11, 1709–10. Will proved at Chester, 1710. (*Vict. Hist. of Lancs.*, V. 126; *D.N.B.*)

GIPPES, THOMAS. Adm. pens. (age 16) at CHRIST'S, June 18, 1667. S. of Richard. B. at Horningsheath, Suffolk. Bapt. Mar. 26, 1650. School, Bury St Edmunds. Matric. 1667.

GYPPES, WILLIAM. B.A. 1525–6; M.A. 1529. Perhaps V. of Arkesden, Essex, 1529–54. R. of Salcott-Virley, 1554–7.

GIRALDUS or GIRAUD, WILLIAM HENRY. Adm. sizar at CAIUS, Jan. 21, 1712–3. S. of John, a Waldensian minister, of Torre Pellice. B. there. School, Chigwell, Essex (Mr Nobilet). Matric. 1713; Scholar, 1713–20; B.A. 1716–7. Ord. deacon (London) Feb. 22, 1718–9; priest, Mar. 13, 1719–20. V. of Graveney, Kent, 1727–69. Master of Faversham School. Died Mar. 18, 1769. (*Venn*, I. 528.)

GIRARD, JOHN. Adm. Fell.-Com. at QUEENS', Jan. 19, 1698–9. Of Nevers, France. Matric. 1698; B.A. of the Academy of Die; M.A. 1700. Protestant refugee.

GIRDLESTON, JOHN. Adm. sizar (age 17) at CAIUS, Apr. 25, 1728. S. of Thomas, farmer, of Letheringsett, Norfolk. B. there. School, Norwich (Mr Redington). Matric. 1728; Scholar, 1728–35; B.A. 1731–2; M.A. 1735. Ord. deacon (Norwich) June 17, 1733; priest, Oct. 19, 1735. R. of Cley-next-the-Sea, Norfolk, 1734–61. Died Jan. 24, 1761. M.I. (*Venn*, II. 29.)

GIRDLESTONE, ZURISHADDAI. Adm. sizar (age 18) at CAIUS, Apr. 1, 1738. S. of John, grazier, of Kelling, Norfolk. B. there. School, Holt (Mr Holmes). Scholar, 1738–42; Matric. 1739; B.A. 1741–2. Ord. deacon (Norwich) Mar. 14, 1741–2; priest, June 26, 1743, as C. of Scarning. R. of Bodham, 1744–67. R. of Baconsthorpe, 1746–67. Died at Mattishall, Mar. 18, 1767. M.I. at Baconsthorpe. (*Venn*, II. 44.)

GIRLING or GURLYN, EDMUND. Adm. pens. (age 18) at JESUS, Jan. 18, 1681–2. Of King's Lynn, Norfolk. S. of Edmund, of Sedgeford, Norfolk. Matric. 1682; Scholar, 1683; M.B. 1687. Died July 10, 1688. Buried in St Nicholas, Lynn. M.I. Will (Norw. Archd. C.) 1688. (Carthew, *Launditch*, III. 436.)

GIRLING, GEORGE. Matric. pens. from CORPUS CHRISTI, Easter, 1626. Of Suffolk. S. and h. of William, of Stradbrook, Suffolk, deceased. Adm. at Gray's Inn, Nov. 21, 1627. Died 1627. (*Copinger*, IV. 88.)

GIRLING, HENRY. Matric. Pell.-Com. from CLARE, Easter, 1577. Of Stradbrook, Suffolk. Adm. at the Inner Temple, 1579.

GIRLING, ISAAC. Adm. sizar (age 16) at CAIUS, June 29, 1664. S. of Lionel, citizen of Norwich. B. there. Schools, Norwich (private; Mr Stinnet and public). Matric. 1664; B.A. 1667–8; Scholar, 1670–1; M.A. 1671. Ord. deacon (Norwich) Dec. 20, 1668, as C. of Bradeston, Norfolk; priest Dec. 24, 1670. V. of West Barsham, Norfolk, 1672; of Westhall, Suffolk, 1685–1705. Chaplain of St Giles', Norwich, 1690. Died Mar. 8, 1704–5. (*Venn*, I. 422.)

GIRLING, JOHN. Adm. pens. at EMMANUEL, Apr. 10, 1678. Of Suffolk.

GIRLING or GURLING, NATHANIEL. Adm. pens. (age 15) at CAIUS, June 10, 1612. S. of William, gent. (mayor of Lynn), deceased. B. at Terrington, Norfolk. School, Lynn (Mr Allston). Matric. 1614; B.A. 1614–5. Incorp. M.A. at Oxford, 1618, as 'Nathan Gwyn.' Perhaps M.P. for Castle Rising, 1626–8. Died May 1, 1638. Brother of William (1604). (*Venn*, I. 217.)

GURLING, NICHOLAS. Adm. sizar (age 17) at CHRIST'S, Feb. 20, 1693–4. S. of Nicholas. B. at Bury St Edmunds. School, Bury. Scholar, 1694–5; Matric. 1695; B.A. 1697–8. Ord. deacon (Norwich) Sept. 1702; priest (York) May, 1703. V. of Tadcaster, May 23, 1703; also Master of Tadcaster School. R. of Newton Kyme, near Tadcaster, for 42 years. Died Sept. 9, 1767. (*Peile*, II. 129.)

GURLIN, RAYMOND. Matric. pens. from QUEENS', Easter, 1665; B.A. 1668–9.

GURLYNG, THOMAS. Matric. sizar from CLARE, Michs. 1567.

GIRLING, THOMAS. Adm. pens. (age 17) at CAIUS, Apr. 25, 1649. S. of Thomas, of Wisbech, Cambs., gent. School, Wisbech (Mr Frisney). Matric. 1649. Migrated to Peterhouse, June 22, 1650. Scholar, 1650; B.A. 1652. Adm. at Lincoln's Inn, May 14, 1655. Doubtless of Horham, Suffolk. Died Dec. 16, 1694, aged 63. Buried at Horham. Father of the next. (*Venn*, I. 375.)

GIRLING, THOMAS. Adm. pens. (age 16) at PEMBROKE, June 19, 1678. S. of Thomas (above), gent. B. at Cockerington, Lincs. Matric 1678. Adm. at Gray's Inn, Nov. 13, 1680, as 's. and h. of Thomas, of Horham, Suffolk, gent.'

GURLING, WILLIAM. Adm. pens. (age 14) at CAIUS, Apr. 27, 1604. S. of William, alderman of Lynn. Bapt. there, Dec. 14, 1589. School, Lynn. Matric. 1604; B.A. 1607–8; M.A. 1611. Ord. priest (Norwich) Dec. 18, 1614. R. of Sandringham, and of Babingly, Norfolk, 1614; sequestered, 1646. Married Elizabeth, dau. of John Dethick, of Newton, Norfolk. Died Dec. 13, 1649. Brother of Nathaniel (1612). (*Venn*, I. 185; *Vis. of Norfolk*, 1664.)

GIRLINGE, WILLIAM. Matric. pens. from TRINITY, Easter, 1606; B.A. from Emmanuel, 1609–10; M.A. 1613. Perhaps R. of Kirkley, Suffolk, 1613–34.

GURLING, ——. Adm. at CORPUS CHRISTI, 1568.

GIRLINGTON, ANTHONY. Matric. pens. from TRINITY, Michs. 1548. Of Richmond, Yorkshire. Perhaps s. of Randall, of Girlington Hall, Wycliffe, Yorks. Migrated to Pembroke; thence, B.A. 1551–2; M.A. 1555. Fellow of Pembroke, 1552. Proctor, 1560–1. Public orator, 1560–1. R. of Tilney, Norfolk, 1558. (Cooper, I. 212; *Coll. Top. et Gen.*, VI. 190.)

GIRLINGTON or JYRLYNGTON, JOHN. Scholar at KING'S HALL, 1481–7.

GIRLINGTON, JOHN. Matric. pens. from JESUS, Easter, 1573. S. of Nicholas, gent., of Hutton, Yorks. Schools, Heighington, Kirkby and Barnard Castle. Migrated to Caius, July 15, 1573, age 16. Of Thurland Castle, Lancs., and Hutton, Yorks., Esq. A popish recusant, in 1604. Died 1612. Father of the next and brother of Thomas (1572). (*Venn*, I. 73; *Vis. of Yorks.*)

GIRLINGTON, NICHOLAS. Matric. Fell.-Com. from MAGDALENE, c. 1595. Doubtless s. and h. of John (1573), of Thurland Castle, Lancs. Succeeded his father, 1612. Died 1628. (*Vis. of Lancs.*, 1613; *Vict. Co. Hist. Lancs.*, VIII. 234.)

GIRLYNGTON, THOMAS. Matric. Fell.-Com. from JESUS, Easter, 1572. Doubtless s. and h. of Nicholas, of Yorkshire. Brother of John (1573). (*Vis. of Yorks.*)

GYRLINGTON, WILLIAM. Adm. sizar (age 16) at CAIUS, Mar. 15, 1609-10. S. of Ninian, Esq., of Wycliffe, Yorks. School, Aldborough (Mr Nicholson). Matric. 1610; Scholar, 1613. Adm. at Lincoln's Inn, Oct. 8, 1612. (*Venn*, I. 206.)

GYRLINGTON, ——. A scholar at KING'S HALL, 1517-8.

GERLINGTON, ——. Matric. Fell.-Com. from MAGDALENE, c. 1597.

GIRTON, FRANCIS. Adm. pens. at JESUS, July 4, 1696. Of Nottinghamshire. Scholar, 1696.

GIRTON, JOHN. A scholar at KING'S HALL, c. 1461; B.A. 1462; M.A. 1468-9. Fellow, till 1494. Will proved (P.C.C.) 1494.

GIRTON, THOMAS, *see* GORTON.

GIRTON, ——. D.Can.L. 1482-3.

GIRTON, Rector of. Excused congregations, etc., 1469-70.

GISBIE, ABRAHAM. Adm. pens. at QUEENS', July 8, 1687. Of Middlesex. Matric. 1688.

GISBYE, GEORGE. B.A. 1631 (Incorp. from Oxford). S. of Michael, of Stepney, Middlesex. B. Mar. 10, 1610. School, Merchant Taylors'. Matric. from St John's College, Oxford, Nov. 13, 1629, age 18; B.A. (Oxford) 1631; M.A. 1635; B.D. 1646. Fellow of St John's, 1630-48. White's reader in Moral Philosophy, 1638-43. Preb. of Lincoln, 1660-4. Died May 13, 1664. Will (Oxford) 1664. (*Al. Oxon.*)

GISBOROUGH, PAUL. Adm. sizar at QUEENS', May 11, 1604. Of Norfolk.

GISBROUGH, FRANCIS. Adm. sizar (age 18) at ST JOHN'S, June 19, 1638. S. of Robert, attorney, of Beverley. B. there. School, Beverley (Mr Pomeroy). Matric. 1638; B.A. 1641-2; M.A. 1645. Probably R. of Middleton, Essex, 1645-7.

GYSBROUGH, W. B.A. 1459; M.A. 1463.

GISBOURNE, FRANCIS. Adm. pens. (age 16) at PETERHOUSE, Sept. 28, 1749. S. of James (next), R. of Staveley, Derbs. B. there, Nov. 25, 1732. School, Netherthorpe (Mr Ri. Robinson). Matric. 1750; Scholar, 1750; B.A. 1754; M.A. 1757. Fellow, 1758-70. Ord. deacon (Lichfield) Sept. 23, 1759; priest (Ely) Nov. 1, 1759. R. of Staveley, 1760-1821. Died July 29, 1821. Benefactor to Peterhouse, to Sheffield and to various Derbyshire parishes. Brother of John (1746), Thomas (1744) and James (1740). (*F.M.G.*, 481; *T. A. Walker*, 295; Hunter, *Hallamshire.*)

GISBORNE, JAMES. Adm. pens. at JESUS, Apr. 6, 1705. Of Derbyshire. S. of John, of Boylston, Esq. B. 1687. School, Loughborough. Matric. 1705; Scholar, 1706; B.A. 1708-9; M.A. 1712. Fellow of Queens', 1714. Ord. deacon (Ely) Dec. 20, 1713; priest, May 23, 1714. C. of Fen Ditton, Cambs., 1713. R. of Staveley, Derbs., 1716-59. Preb. of Durham, 1742-59. Died Sept. 11, 1759. Will, P.C.C. Father of the next three and the above. (*F.M.G.*, 481.)

GISBORNE, JAMES. Adm. pens. (age 18) at ST JOHN'S, Oct. 17, 1740. S. of James (above). B. at Staveley. School, Staveley (Mr Robinson). Brother of the next, Francis (1749) and Thomas (1744).

GISBORNE, JOHN. Adm. pens. at CLARE, Oct. 15, 1746. S. of James (above), R. of Staveley, Derbs. Bapt. there, Sept. 21, 1727. Exhibitioner from Charterhouse. Matric. 1746. Died about 1748, at Clare College, Cambridge. (*F.M.G.*, 481; *Al. Carthus.*)

GISBORNE, THOMAS. Adm. pens. (age 18) at ST JOHN'S, June 28, 1744. S. of James (1705), R. of Staveley, Derbs. B. at Staveley. School, Staveley (Mr Robinson). Matric. 1744; B.A. 1747-8; M.A. 1751; M.D. 1758. Fellow, 1753-1806. Gulstonian lecturer, 1760. Physician to St George's Hospital, 1757-81. F.R.S. 1758. President R.C.P. 1791-2, 1794-5, 1796-1804. Physician to the King, 1794. Benefactor to the College library. Died Feb. 24, 1806. Will, P.C.C. (*Founders and Benefactors*, 81; *D.N.B.*; *Munk*, II. 227.)

GISBRIMER, ELIAS. Matric. pens. from SIDNEY, Easter, 1611. Not found in the College register.

GISLAND, TRISTRAM. Matric. pens. from MAGDALENE, Easter, 1639.

GISLEHAM, ANDREW DE. M.A. Chancellor of the University, 1283. Benefactor.

GISLING, JOHN. M.A. from PEMBROKE, 1683. S. of Thomas, of London, gent. Matric. from Queen's College, Oxford, Apr. 6, 1666, age 17; B.A. (Oxford) 1669. R. of St Michael's, Penkeville, Cornwall, 1680. V. of Tregoney, 1690. (*Al. Oxon.*)

GISSING, JOHN. B.A. 1480-1.

GISSING, RICHARD. Matric. sizar from CORPUS CHRISTI, Easter, 1659. Of Suffolk. B.A. 1661-2; M.A. 1665.

GISSING, WILLIAM. B.A. 1480-1.

GISTE, DANIEL. Adm. pens. at EMMANUEL, Nov. 1586. B. at Kilkhampton, Cornwall, 1563. Matric. 1586, as 'Gerte'; Scholar; B.A. 1590-1; M.A. 1594. Ord. deacon and priest (Exeter) Aug. 25, 1601. V. of Ravensden, Beds., 1603-26. Married, Aug. 16, 1595, at St Peter's, Northampton, Martha, dau. of Richard Potter. Buried at Ravensden. Sept. 20, 1626, as 'Gych.' Will (Bedford) 1626. (H. I. Longden.)

GITTINS, DANIEL. Adm. sizar at CLARE, Apr. 8, 1727. B. at Goring, Sussex. Matric. 1727; Scholar at Trinity Hall, Jan. 3, 1728-9; LL.B. 1742. R. of South Stoke, Sussex, 1733-61. V. of Lyminster, 1742-61. Died 1761. (H. G. Harrison.)

GYTTONS, DAVID. Matric. sizar from CORPUS CHRISTI, Michs. 1569.

GYTTINGS, EDWARD. Matric. pens. from PETERHOUSE, Michs. 1580.

GITTONS, GEORGE. Adm. pens. at QUEENS', June 10, 1599. Of London.

GYTTONS, HENRY. B.A. from PEMBROKE, 1572-3.

GITTINS, JAMES. Adm. sizar (age 18) at ST JOHN'S, July 1, 1632. S. of Griffith, V. of Kinnar, Carnarvon (? Kenarth, Carmarthen). B. in London, Aug. 22, 1614. School, Merchant Taylors'. Matric. 1633; B.A. 1636-7.

GITTINS, RALPH. Matric. pens. from ST JOHN'S, Easter, 1589. Of Shrewsbury. S. of a burgess. Adm. at Shrewsbury School, 1578. B.A. 1592-3; M.A. 1596. Third Master of Shrewsbury School, 1594; second Master, 1612-3 and 1631-8. Retired to Middle, Salop, where he died. (G. W. Fisher, *Shrewsbury.*)

GITTENS, RICHARD. Adm. pens. (age 19) at ST JOHN'S, June 11, 1716. S. of Thomas, goldsmith, of Salop. B. at Shrewsbury. School, Eton. Matric. 1716; B.A. 1719-20; M.A. 1723. Ord. deacon (Hereford) June 12, 1720. C. of Wollaston, Hereford (? Worcs.).

GITTINGS, ——. B.A. 1520-1; M.A. 1523. Perhaps Maurice, R. of St Mary-le-Bow, 1554-9. Will (P.C.C.) 1559.

GLACTON, ROGER. D.D., Cambridge. Of Huntingdonshire. Augustinian friar. Died at Huntingdon, c. 1340. (*Pits*, 441.)

GLADHILL, THOMAS, *see* GLEDHILL.

GLADMAN, BAANAH. Adm. sizar at SIDNEY, Michs. 1598; B.A. 1609. Ord. deacon and priest (Ely) June 11, 1609. C. of Flamstead, Herts., 1613.

GLADMAN, ELIAS. Adm. sizar at CLARE, Apr. 5, 1643.

GLADMAN, ELKANAH. M.A. 1626 (Incorp. from Oxford). Of Hertfordshire. Matric. from Trinity College, Oxford, Nov. 27, 1618, age 16; B.A. (Oxford) 1620-1; M.A. 1623; B.D. 1631. V. of Chesham (Woburn), Bucks., 1626-60. V. of Wing, 1648-78. Married, at Chesham, Dec. 5, 1626, Abigail Bredon. (*Al. Oxon.*; *Lipscomb*, III. 264.)

GLADMAN, NAARIAH (or NAZARIAH). Matric. sizar from TRINITY, c. 1598. Migrated to Sidney, Oct. 1598. B.A. 1601-2; M.A. 1605. Incorp. at Oxford, 1605. V. of Ridge, Herts., 1608-18. R. of South Mimms, 1618-42. Buried there June 25, 1642. (*Al. Oxon.*; F. C. Cass, *S. Mimms.*)

GLADMAN, NICHOLAS. B.A. 1530-1; M.A. 1534. V. of Fingringhoe, Essex, 1534-51. Died 1551. (*See Gr. Bk*, A, 227.)

GLADSTAINS, ALEXANDER. M.A. 1609-10 (Incorp. from St Andrews).

GLADWIN, LEMUEL. Adm. sizar (age 20) at ST JOHN'S, Oct. 11, 1733. S. of Lemuel, Esq., of Tupton, Derbs. B. at Tupton. School, Chesterfield (Mr Burrows). Matric. 1733. Died *s.p.* (*F.M.G.*, 616.)

GLANVILL, JOHN. Adm. pens. at EMMANUEL, Feb. 10, 1586-7. Matric. 1587; B.A. (? 1591-2); M.A. 1595. Will (Exeter), of one of these names, 1632, of St German's, Cornwall.

GLANVILE, JOHN. Adm. pens. at EMMANUEL, Jan. 15, 1638-9. One of these names, 3rd s. of John, serjeant-at-law, of Broad Hinton, Wilts., adm. at Lincoln's Inn, June 29, 1639.

GLANVILLE, JOHN. Adm. pens. at PETERHOUSE, May 7, 1661. Of Suffolk. Matric. 1661; Scholar, 1661; B.A. 1664-5; M.A. 1668. Fellow, 1665-83. Signed for deacon's orders (London) Dec. 22, 1666. R. of Elmsett, Suffolk, 1668-9. V. of Barton, Cambs., 1673-83. Buried at Little St Mary's, Cambridge, May 30, 1683. Will (V.C.C.) 1683. (*T. A. Walker.*)

GLANVILL or GLANFIELD, JOSEPH. Adm. pens. (age 17) at PETERHOUSE, June 16, 1638. Of Suffolk. School, Hadleigh. Matric. 1638; Scholar, 1641; B.A. 1641-2; M.A. 1646. Ord. deacon (Lincoln) May 24; priest, May 25, 1662. C. of Ingham, 1662. R. of Wimbish, Essex, 1660-80 (*D.N.B.* assigns this to his Oxford contemporary). Died 1680. (*T. A. Walker.*)

GLANVILLE, MAURICE. Adm. pens. (age 17) at PETERHOUSE, May 12, 1674. Of Suffolk. S. of Joseph, R. of Wimbish, Essex (above). School, Walden, Essex. Matric. 1674; Scholar, 1674; B.A. 1677-8; M.A. 1681. Ord. deacon and priest (London) Feb. 19, 1680-1. R. of Wimbish, 1680-95. R. of Walton, Bucks., 1687-1695. Died 1695. Will (P.C.C.) 1695. (*T. A. Walker.*)

GLANVILE or GLANFEILD, RICHARD. Adm. pens. (age 16) at PEMBROKE, May 22, 1624. S. of Richard, of Hadleigh, Suffolk, clothier. Matric. 1624; B.A. 1627-8; M.A. 1631; B.D. 1638. R. of Somersham, Suffolk, 1647. R. of Elmsett, 1650. Died Dec. 15, 1667, 'aged 63.' Buried at Elmsett. Will, P.C.C. (G. R. Woodward.)

GLANVILLE, RICHARD. Adm. sizar (age 15) at PETERHOUSE, Apr. 12, 1671. Of Suffolk. School, Hadleigh. Matric. 1671; Scholar, 1672; B.A. 1674-5; M.A. 1678.

GLANVILE, WILLIAM. Adm. pens. (age 16) at PEMBROKE, Oct. 24, 1710. S. and h. of William, of the Isle of Antigua, mercer. Matric. 1712. Adm. at the Inner Temple, Mar. 1, 1710-1. Married Elizabeth Allison, at Gray's Inn Chapel, Nov. 5, 1713. Buried Nov. 22, 1734, at St Jobu's, Antigua. His son was adm. at Gray's Inn, June 12, 1733, as s. and h. of William, of Antigua. (Oliver's *Antigua*, II. 18.)

GLANVILLE, ——. B.A 1511-2; M.A. 1515. A Robert Glanville or Glanfeld, was V. of Trumpington, Cambs., 1520. Will proved, 1527. (*Baker MS.*, XVI. 171.)

GLAPTHORNE, GEORGE. Adm. pens. at EMMANUEL, Oct. 16, 1607. Matric. 1607, as 'Clapthorne.'

GLAPTHORNE, HENRY. Matric. pens. from CORPUS CHRISTI, Easter, 1624. Of Cambridgeshire. Probably s. of Thomas, of Whittlesey, Isle of Ely. Perhaps, as suggested by *Masters*, the dramatist and poet. (*Cambs. Vis.*, 1619; *D.N.B.*; where no biographical particulars are given.)

GLAPTHORNE, JOHN. Adm. pens. at EMMANUEL, July 23, 1616.

GLASBROOK, JOHN. Adm. sizar (age 17) at TRINITY, May 16, 1709. S. of John, of Haigh, Lancs. B. at Wigan. School, Rivington, Lancs. (Mr Bradley). Matric. 1709; B.A. 1713-4. Ord. deacon (York) Dec. 23, 1716; priest (Peterb.) Mar. 6, 1725-6. V. of Higham Ferrers, Northants., 1726-30. Buried there Sept. 6, 1730. (H. I. Longden.)

GLASSBROOKE, SIMON PETER. Adm. pens. (age 20) at ST JOHN'S, Sept. 14, 1719. S. of Peter, M.D. (? of Oxford), of Kent. B. at Whitstable, Kent. School, Canterbury. Matric. 1719; B.A. 1723-4. Ord. deacon (Lincoln) June 9, 1723; priest, Dec. 22, 1723. C. of Creeton, Lincs.

GLASBROOK, WILLIAM. Adm. pens. at EMMANUEL, Apr. 22, 1673. Of Derbyshire. Matric. 1675; B.A. 1676-7.

GLASCOCK, ANDREW. Matric. pens. from CHRIST'S, Nov. 1554. Perhaps s. of William, of Gt Dunmow, Essex. Of Barking, and of Eltham, Kent. Died Dec. 1621. Buried at Barking. Will, P.C.C. (*Peile*, I. 58; J. Ch. Smith.)

GLASCOCKE, BARTHOLOMEW. Matric. pens. from CHRIST'S, Michs. 1571. B. at Bobbingworth, Essex (doubtless s. of John, yeoman). B.A. from St Catharine's, 1574-5; M.A. 1578. Ord. deacon (London) Nov. 1580, age 28; priest, Easter, 1581. R. of Weeley, Essex, 1580-98. R. of Bobbingworth, 1582. Died Oct. 13, 1619. Will (Consist. C. London) 1622. (*Peile*, I. 120; *Ess. Arch. Soc.*, 25, II. 231.)

GLASSCOCK, CHARLES. Adm. pens. at ST CATHARINE'S, Apr. 10, 1680. Doubtless s. of Christopher (next). School, Felsted. Matric. 1681. Buried at St Benet's, Cambridge, Apr. 19, 1682.

GLASCOCK, CHRISTOPHER. Matric. sizar from ST CATHARINE'S, Easter, 1631. Of Essex. S. of Christopher, of Much Waltham, whose will, P.C.C. 1650. B.A. 1634-5; M.A. 1638. Head Master of Ipswich School, 1644-50. Master of Felsted, 1650-89. Died Jan. 22, 1690. Will (Commis. C. Essex) 1730 (*sic*.). Father of the next, of George (1680-1) and doubtless of the above. (*Musgrave*.)

GLASSCOCK, CHRISTOPHER. Adm. pens. at EMMANUEL, Apr. 30, 1667. S. of Christopher (above), schoolmaster of Felsted, Essex. B. at Ipswich. School, Felsted. Matric. 1667. Migrated to Caius, Oct. 15, 1667, age 16; Scholar, 1667-74; B.A. 1670-1; M.A. 1674. Brother of George (1680-1). (*Venn*, I. 432.)

GLASCOCK, EDWARD. Matric. pens. from QUEENS', Michs. 1587. S. of Edward, of Castle Hedingham, Essex. B.A. 1590-1; M.A. from Corpus Christi, 1594. Incorp. at Oxford, 1597. Adm. at Gray's Inn, Oct. 16, 1594. Barrister-at-law, 1600. M.P. for Sudbury, 1601.

GLASCOCK, EDWARD. Adm. Fell.-Com. (age 16) at CHRIST'S, June 8, 1638. S. of Henry (1581), of Hartesbury, Farnham, Essex. B. at Farnham. School, Bishop's Stortford. Matric. 1639. Adm. at Gray's Inn, May 5, 1642. Of Brises, Kelvedon, Esq. Will (P.C.C.) 1667. Father of Thomas (1666) and brother of William (1626-7). (*Peile*, I. 455; *Vis. of Essex*, 1634.)

GLASCOCK, ETHAN. Adm. sizar (age 15) at SIDNEY, Apr. 16, 1627. S. of Robert, tailor. B. at Pritwell, Essex. Schools, Rochford (Mr Lone), Pritwell, and Maldon. Matric. 1627; B.A. 1630-1. Of 'Potsev' (? Portsea), Hants., in 1634: will of Richard Glascock, P.C.C.

GLASCOCK, FRANCIS. Adm. sizar (age 15) at ST JOHN'S, July 8, 1665. S. of John (1639), R. of Little Canfield, Essex. B. there. School, Felsted. Will proved (P.C.C.) Feb. 20, 1706-7.

GLASCOCKE, GEORGE. Adm. sizar (age 17) at TRINITY, Mar. 10, 1680-1. S. of Christopher (1631). B. at Felsted, Essex. School, Felsted. Matric. 1681; Scholar, 1683. Died in College. Buried at St Michael's, Cambridge, May 13, 1683. Brother of Christopher (1667).

GLASCOCK, HENRY. Matric. pens. from CHRIST'S, Nov. 1581. S. of Henry, of High Easter Parsonage, Essex. B.A. from Clare, 1585; M.A. 1589. Father of Edward (1638) and William (1626-7). (*Cooper*, II. 76; *Peile*, I. 167; *Vis. of Essex*, 1634.)

GLASCOCK, IGNATIUS. Adm. Fell.-Com. (age 16) at MAGDALENE, July 23, 1667. S. of William, of Farnham, Essex, Esq. School, Newport Pond, Essex. Matric. 1667-8. Died 'about 20 years old.' Buried at Farnham. Brother of William (1673). (Le Neve, *Knights*, 368.)

GLASCOCK, JOHN. Adm. (age 17) at KING'S, a scholar from Eton, Aug. 13, 1541. Of Bobbingworth, Essex. Matric. 1544; B.A. 1545-6. Fellow, 1544-6. Adm. at the Inner Temple, 1550. Bencher, 1568.

GLASCOCK, JOHN. Matric. pens. from CHRIST'S, Nov. 1554.

GLASCOCKE, JOHN. Matric. pens. from MAGDALENE, Easter, 1639. S. of Francis. B.A. 1642-3; M.A. 1646. Fellow. R. of Little Canfield, Essex, 1649-61. Died 1661. Will, P.C.C. Father of Francis (1665).

GLASCOCK, JOHN. Matric. pens. from ST CATHARINE'S, 1640. Probably 2nd s. of William, of Felsted, Essex, gent.; adm. at Lincoln's Inn, Jan. 12, 1641-2. Died *s.p.* Will (Comm. C. Essex) 1646. Probably brother of William (1633).

GLASCOCK, JOHN. Adm. sizar (age 16) at CHRIST'S, June 16, 1659. S. of John. B. at Chelmsford. School, Chelmsford (Mr Peake). Matric. 1660; B.A. 1662-3. Signed for deacon's orders (London) Dec. 18, 1663; for priest's, Mar. 5, 1663-4. P.C. of Blackmore, Essex, 1664-1711. Perhaps R. of Meesden, Herts., 1694-1711. Buried at Blackmore, Sept. 2, 1711. Will (Archd. Essex) 1711. (*Peile*, I. 587.)

GLASCOCK, JOHN. Adm. sizar at QUEENS', June 22, 1660. Of Essex. Matric. 1661; B.A. 1663-4; M.A. 1667. Signed for priest's orders (London) Sept. 24, 1670. Perhaps usher at Felsted School, 1664. R. of Ramsden-Crays, 1678-83. Died 1683.

GLASSCOCK, JOHN. Adm. pens. at ST CATHARINE'S, May 9, 1664. Matric. 1664. One of these names adm. at the Inner Temple, June 18, 1666; of Sevenoaks, Kent.

GLASCOCKE, PHILIP. Matric. pens. from CLARE, Michs. 1572. Perhaps s. of William, of Gt Dunmow, Essex (whose will, P.C.C. 1579).

GLASCOKE, PHILIP. Matric. sizar from CLARE, Easter, 1607. Perhaps his admon. (P.C.C.) as of the Middle Temple, Jan. 28, 1624-5; to his father Philip (? above).

GLASCOCKE, RICHARD. Adm. pens. at PETERHOUSE, 1597-8. One of these names, s. of Richard, of Hatfield Broad Oak, Essex, adm. at the Inner Temple, 1599. Barrister, 1608. Died Feb. 5, 1624. Will (Comm. C. Essex) 1624. (*Vis. of Essex*; *Morant*, II. 508.)

GLASCOCKE, RICHARD. Adm. pens. (age 18) at CHRIST'S, Jan. 16, 1654-5. Eldest s. of William (1626). B. in Essex. Schools, Bedford and Herts. (Mr Baines). Adm. at Lincoln's Inn, May 10, 1654, 's. and h. of William, of St Bartholomew-the-Great, Smithfield, bencher.' (*Peile*, I. 564.)

GLASCOCK, THOMAS. B.Civ.L. 1538-9.

GLASCOCK, THOMAS. Adm. pens. (age 16) at CHRIST'S, May 9, 1666. S. of Edward (1638), of Brises, Kelvedon, Essex. B. there. School, Brentwood (Mr Bernard). Matric. 1667; B.A. 1669-70.

GLASCOKE, W. Matric. pens. from CORPUS CHRISTI, Lent, 1564-5. One William Glascock, R. of Willingale Doe, Essex, 1570-87. Died 1587. Will (Cons. C. London). But *see* New-court.

GLASCOKE, WILLIAM. Adm. pens. at JESUS, June 5, 1626. Of Essex. Doubtless s. and h. of William, late of Felsted, Essex, Esq., deceased; adm. at Lincoln's Inn, June 26, 1628. Master in Chancery. Of St Bartholomew's, Smithfield. Father of Richard (1654-5). (A. Gray; Le Neve, *Knights*, where he is apparently confused with William (1633).)

GLASCOCK, WILLIAM. Matric. pens. from CHRIST'S, Mar. 17, 1626-7. S. and h. of Henry (1581), of Hartesbury, Farnham, Essex. B.A. 1629-30. Adm. at Gray's Inn, Feb. 7, 1630-1. Brother of Edward (1638). (*Peile*, I. 388; *Vis. of Essex*, 1634.)

GLASCOCK, WILLIAM. Matric. pens. from St Catharine's, Michs. 1633. Of Essex. Probably eldest s. of William. LL.B. from Trinity Hall, 1640. Knighted, May 12, 1661. Master of Requests. Master in Chancery. Judge of the Admiralty in Ireland. Of Wormely, Herts. Died July 14, 1688, aged 73. Buried at King's Langley, Herts. M.I. Will, P.C.C. Probably brother of John (1640). (*Clutterbuck*, III. 439; Shaw, *Knights*.)

GLASCOCK, WILLIAM. Adm. Fell.-Com. (age 17) at Magdalene, Apr. 19, 1673. S. of William, Esq., of Farnham, Essex. School, Bishop's Stortford. Adm. at Gray's Inn, Feb. 9, 1675-6. Sheriff of Essex, 1682. Knighted, Nov. 25, 1682. Died Mar. 23, 1690-1. Buried at Farnham. M.I. Will (P.C.C.) 1691. Brother of Ignatius (1667). (Le Neve, *Knights*, 368.)

GLASCOCK, ——. Matric. pens. from St John's, Easter, 1544.

GLASCOCK, ——. Adm. Fell.-Com. at Corpus Christi, 1562.

GLASIER, GEOFFREY. LL.D. 1644 (*Lit. Reg.*).

GLASYER, LAURENCE. Matric. Fell.-Com. from Trinity Hall, Michs. 1553.

GLASIER, ROBERT. Matric. sizar from Trinity, Michs. 1629; B.A. 1631-2.

GLASS or GLAS, JOHN. Adm. at Corpus Christi, 1547.

GLASS, JOHN. Adm. pens. at Emmanuel, Easter, 1624. Matric. 1624.

GLASSE, JOHN. Adm. pens. (age 18) at Trinity, Mar. 27, 1749. S. of John, of London. School, Westminster. Matric. 1750. Adm. at Lincoln's Inn, Nov. 20, 1746; as s. of John, of Cary St, gent. Author, *Poems*.

GLASSE, RICHARD. M.A. from King's, 1737. S. of Richard, of Winterbourne Basset, Wilts., clerk. Matric. from Magdalen Hall, Oxford, Apr. 11, 1717, age 17; B.A. (Oxford) 1720. Will probably (Archd. Wilts.) 1748; of Purton, Wilts., clerk. (*Al. Oxon.*; J. Ch. Smith.)

GLASSE, THOMAS. Adm. pens. at Jesus, Apr. 5, 1624. Matric. 1624; Scholar, 1625; B.A. 1627-8; M.A. 1631.

GLASTON, JOHN DE. 'King's scholar' at Cambridge, 1328; afterwards at King's Hall. Beneficed, Mar. 10, 1358.

GLATTON, ROBERT DE. Fellow of Peterhouse, 1339.

GLAVEN, ——. Fee for B.A. 1469-70.

GLEADALL, RICHARD. Matric. sizar from St John's, c. 1596; B.A. from Christ's, 1600-1. Ord. priest (York) July, 1607.

GLEANE, JOHN. Adm. pens. (age 16) at Caius, June 27, 1609. 3rd s. of Peter (1582-3), gent., citizen and alderman (afterwards knight), of Norwich. School, Norwich (Mr Townley). Matric. 1610. M.I. at Sandcroft (South Elmham), Suffolk, to John Gleane, gent., who died Feb. 11, 1664-5, aged 72. Brother of Thomas (1603). (*Vis. of Norfolk*; *Venn*, I. 205.)

GLEANE, JOHN. Adm. at Corpus Christi, 1647. Of Norfolk. Perhaps s. of Thomas, of Hardwick, Norfolk; brother of Sir Peter, 1st Bart.

GLEAN, LEONARD. Adm. pens. (age 17) at Caius, c. June, 1700. S. of Leonard, woollen draper, of Norwich. B. there. Bapt. at St George Tombland, Aug. 19, 1683. School, Norwich. Scholar, 1700-6; Matric. 1701; LL.B. 1706. Died 1720. Buried in St George Tombland, Norwich, July 19, 1720. M.I. (*Venn*, I. 506.)

GLEANE, PETER. B.A. from Clare, 1582-3. S. of Thomas. Bapt. at St Peter Mancroft, Norwich, June 27, 1564. Sheriff of Norwich, 1610. Mayor, 1615. Knighted, June 13, 1624. M.P. for Norwich, 1628. Married Maud, dau. of Robert Suckling, of Norwich. Buried at St Peter Mancroft, May 10, 1633. Father of Thomas (1603) and John (1609). (*Blomefield*, v. 218; G. H. Holley.)

GLEANE, PETER. Adm. pens. (age 16) at Caius, Feb. 12, 1688-9. S. of Thomas (1667), Esq. (afterwards Bart.), of Hardwick, Norfolk. B. there. School, Wymondham. Matric. 1689; Scholar, 1689-96; B.A. 1692-3. Proctor in the Court at Canterbury. Succeeded as Baronet, c. 1700. (*Venn*, I. 486; *G.E.C.*)

GLEEN, RODNEY. Adm. pens. (age 16) at Caius, Feb. 10, 1668-9. S. of Sir Peter, Bart., of Hardwick, Norfolk. B. at Pilton, Somerset. Bapt. at Hardwick, Sept. 23, 1653. School, Moulton, Norfolk (Mr Wickham). Matric. 1669. Died unmarried. Buried at Hardwick. Brother of Thomas (1667). (*Venn*, I. 436.)

GLEANE, THOMAS. Matric. pens. from Peterhouse, Easter, 1603. S. of Peter (1582-3). Of Hardwick Hall, Norfolk. Married Elizabeth, dau. of Thomas Brewse, Esq. Died Jan. 27, 1660, aged c. 74. M.I. at Hardwick. Brother of John (1609). (*Blomefield*, v. 218.)

GLEANE, THOMAS. Adm. at Corpus Christi, 1667. Of Somerset. 1st s. of Sir Peter, of Hardwick, Norfolk. Bapt. at Hardwick, Mar. 28, 1652. Succeeded as Bart. Married Ann, dau. of Leonard Mapes, of Rollesby, Norfolk, at Oby, Oct. 24, 1671. Ruined his estate: imprisoned in the Fleet. Died c. 1703. Brother of Rodney (1668-9). (*G.E.C.*; G. H. Holley.)

GLEAVE, JOHN. Adm. sizar (age 18) at Trinity, Apr. 27, 1717. S. of John, of Hulme, Cheshire. School, Peover, Cheshire (Mr Allen). Matric. 1717; B.A. 1720-1. R. of Swettenham, Cheshire, 1735-83. Died 1783. (*Ormerod*, III. 44.)

GLEAVE, JOHN. Adm. sizar (age 16) at Peterhouse, June 18, 1748. Of Cheshire. School, Nantwich. Matric. 1748; Scholar, 1748; B.A. 1752; M.A. 1756.

GLEDELL, JOHN. Matric. pens. from St John's, Michs. 1622. Probably s. of Thomas Gledhill, of Barkisland, Yorks. Bapt. at Elland, Sept. 15, 1605. Buried there May 28, 1656. Will (P.C.C.) 1657. (J. Ch. Smith.)

GLEDHILL, RICHARD. Adm. pens. (age 17) at Sidney, June 9, 1634. S. of Thomas, Esq. B. at Barkisland, Yorks. School, Leeds (Mr Samuel Pullen). Matric. 1634. Adm. at Lincoln's Inn, Jan. 11, 1637-8; '2nd s. of Thomas, deceased.' Captain of Horse. Slain at Marston Moor. Buried at St Martin's, Micklegate, York, July 8, 1644. Admon. (P.C.C.) 1658. (M. H. Peacock.)

GLEDHILL, THOMAS. Adm. Fell.-Com. at Clare, Apr. 26, 1656. Doubtless s. and h. of John (1622), of Barkisland, Yorks., gent. Bapt. at Elland, Sept. 5, 1637. Matric. 1656. Adm. at Gray's Inn, Dec. 14, 1655. Executor of his father's will, but died before proving. Buried at Elland, Mar. 30, 1657. (*Yorks. Arch. Record Series*, IX. 108.)

GLADHILL, THOMAS. Adm. pens. at Emmanuel, Oct. 26, 1672. Of Yorkshire. Matric. 1673; B.A. 1676-7. Ord. deacon (York) Dec. 1677; priest, June, 1679. V. of Mirfield, Yorks., 1678-87. Buried there Dec. 20, 1687.

GLEDSTONE, FRANCIS. Adm. sizar at Trinity, June 21, 1662. Matric. 1662; B.A. 1665-6; M.A. 1669. Ord. deacon (York) c. 1666. C. of Hamsterley, Durham, 1666-73.

GLEGG, JOHN. Adm. pens. (age 18) at Pembroke, June 12, 1751. S. of John, of Irby, Cheshire, gent. Matric. 1751; B.A. 1755; M.A. 1758. Fellow, 1756. Married Betty, dau. of John Baskervyle Glegg, of Gayton. Died Mar. 6, 1804, aged 72. Buried at St Mary's, Chester. (*Ormerod*, II. 200.)

GLEGG, WILLIAM. Matric. pens. from Christ's, July, 1607. Probably s. and h. of William, of Caldey Grange, Cheshire, gent.; adm. at Gray's Inn, May 26, 1609. Of Caldey Grange, Esq. Died Dec. 15, 1644, aged 57. (*Ormerod*, II. 492.) Or perhaps, s. of Edward, of Gayton, Cheshire. (*Ormerod*, II., 519.)

GLEMHAM, CHARLES. Adm. pens. (age 15) at Caius, Apr. 20, 1675. S. of Sir Sackville, Knt., of Glemham, Suffolk. B. there. Schools, Campsey Ash (Mr Stubbing) and Woodbridge. Matric. 1675; Scholar, 1675-82; B.A. 1678-9; M.A. 1682. Ord. deacon (Norwich) Dec. 1682. V. of Little Glemham, 1684. (*Venn*, I. 452.)

GLEMHAM, HENRY. B.A. 1620-1 (Incorp. from Oxford). S. of Sir Henry, of Glemham, Suffolk. Matric. from Trinity College, Oxford, Oct. 15, 1619, age 16; B.A. (Oxford) 1621; M.A. 1623-4; B.D. 1631; D.D. 1633. R. of Symondsbury, Dorset, 1631-45 and 1660-70. Dean of Bristol, 1660-7. Bishop of St Asaph, 1667-70. R. of Llandrinio. Died Jan. 17, 1669-70, at Glemham Hall. Buried at Little Glemham. Admon. and will (P.C.C.) 1671. (*Al. Oxon.*)

GLEMAM, JOHN. Matric. pens. from Gonville Hall, Easter, 1557. Perhaps s. of Edward, of Sternfield and Benham, Suffolk.

GLEMHAM, THOMAS. Adm. Fell.-Com. (age 17) at Christ's, Feb. 1, 1703-4. S. of Thomas. B. near Ipswich. School, Bury. Served in the army. Captain of Dragoons. Died at Valladolid, 1711. (*Peile*, II. 158.)

GLEN, ANDREW. Adm. pens. (age 15) at Jesus, May 31, 1680. S. of George, of Donbridge, Derbs., lately deceased. Matric. 1680; Rustat scholar; B.A. 1683-4; M.A. 1687. Fellow, 1687-95. Ord. priest (Lincoln) Sept. 25, 1687. R. of St Clement's, Cambridge, 1690-4. V. of Gt Shelford, Cambs., 1694. R. of Hathern, Leics., 1694-1732. V. of Dishley. Resided some time in Turin, c. 1692. Botanist. Friend of Ray. Died Sept. 1, 1732. Buried at Hathern. (A. Gray; *D.N.B.*)

GLENDALL or GLENDOLE, JOHN. Adm. pens. at Emmanuel, Feb. 16, 1646-7. S. of John, V. of St Oswald, and St Peter, Chester. Matric. 1647; B.A. 1650-1; M.A. (Oxford) 1653. Fellow of Brasenose College, Oxford, 1654. Incorp. at Cambridge, 1654. Died 1660. Buried at St Mary's, Oxford (so *Al. Oxon.* where the father is apparently confused with the son). But perhaps minister of St Peter's, Chester, 1654 and 1659; of Bangor, 1657. Buried at Coley, Halifax, Yorks., 1674, aged 48. (*Al. Oxon.*)

GLESON, JOHN. Matric. sizar from TRINITY, Easter, 1579; Scholar, 1582; B.A. 1582–3; M.A. 1586 (as Gledson). Fellow, 1585. V. of Lowestoft, Suffolk, 1603–10.

GLESON, THOMAS. Matric. sizar from TRINITY, Easter, 1587. One of these names V. of Boxted, Essex, 1596: but he may have been R. of Little Wigborough by 1573. (*Newcourt*.)

GLESYN, ——. Student at PETERHOUSE, 1542.

GLEWE or GLUE, HENRY. M.A. from MAGDALENE, 1636. B.A. from Balliol College, Oxford, 1633. 'A minister; changed his religion for that of Rome, and was made priest.' (*Al. Oxon.*; *Fasti Oxon.*, I. 468.)

GLINESTER, EDMUND. Adm. pens. (age 16) at CHRIST'S, Apr. 25, 1715. S. of Edmund, Esq., of Royston, Herts. B. there. School, Chesfield, Herts. (Mr Goodwin). Matric. 1715. Migrated to Caius, as fell.-com., July 11, 1717. Adm. at the Inner Temple, Nov. 27, 1716. (*Venn*, II. 9.)

GLINTON, NICHOLAS. B.A. 1514–5; M.A. 1519–20. Fellow of ST JOHN'S, 1516. R. of Rushden, Northants., 1520–30.

GLISSON, FRANCIS. Adm. pens. (age 18) at CAIUS, June 28, 1617. 2nd s. of William, gent., of Rampisham, Dorset. School, Rampisham (Mr Allot). Matric. 1617; Scholar, 1617–24; B.A. 1620–1; M.A. 1624; M.D. 1634. Fellow, 1624–34. Incorp. at Oxford, 1627. Regius Professor of Physic, Cambridge, 1636–77. Gulstonian lecturer, 1640. Fellow of the College of Physicians, 1635; President, 1667–70. One of the first fellows of the Royal Society, 1663. Living in Colchester at the time of the siege, 1648; afterwards went to London. Very distinguished physiologist; for an account of his works *see D.N.B.* Died in London, Oct. 14, 1677. Buried in St Bride's, Fleet Street. Will (P.C.C.) 1677. Brother of Henry (1625), Humphrey (1636), John (1633) and Paul (1627). (*Venn*, I. 237; *Vis. of Dorset*, 1623; *D.N.B.*)

GLISSON, HENRY. Adm. pens. (age 17) at CAIUS, July 1, 1625. 6th s. of William, gent., of Rampisham, Dorset. School, Rampisham. Matric. 1625; Scholar, 1626–32; B.A. 1628–9; M.A. 1632; M.D. 1639. Fellow, 1632–40. Hon. fellow R.C.P. 1664. Brother of Francis, above, etc. (*Venn*, I. 272.)

GLISSON, HUMPHREY. M.A. 1636 (Incorp. from Oxford). 9th s. of William, of Rampisham, Dorset. Matric. from Christ Church, Feb. 24, 1631–2; B.A. (Oxford) 1632; M.A. 1635; B.D. 1642–3. R. of Fleet Marston, Bucks., 1642–3. Died Aug. 7, 1643. (*Al. Oxon.*)

GLISSON, JOHN. M.A. 1633 (Incorp. from Oxford). 5th s. of William, of Rampisham, Dorset. Matric. from Trinity College, Oxford, Oct. 22, 1624, age 17; B.A. (Oxford) 1627; M.A. 1631; B.D. 1639. Proctor (Oxford) 1637. R. of Marnhull, Dorset, 1639–76; and of Woodsford, 1662–76. Died 1676. Brother of Francis, etc. (*Al. Oxon.*; Hutchins, *Dorset*, IV. 323.)

GLISSON, JOHN. Adm. scholar (age 16) at SIDNEY, Apr. 24, 1697. 1st s. of Gilbert, R. of Marnhull, Dorset. B. there. School, Dorset (Mr Place). Matric. 1697; B.A. 1700–1. Brother of William (1703).

GLISSON, PAUL. Matric. pens. from TRINITY HALL, Michs. 1627. 8th s. of William, of Rampisham, Dorset. LL.B. 1634. Fellow, 1633–46. Ord. deacon (Peterb.) June 9, 1639. Brother of Francis, etc.

GLISSON, WILLIAM. Adm. scholar (age 17) at SIDNEY, Apr. 24, 1703. S. of Gilbert, R. of Marnhull, Dorset. School, Dorchester (Mr Place). Matric. 1703. Migrated to Trinity, Feb. 3, 1703–4. Brother of John (1697).

GLOSSE, CHARLES. Adm. sizar (age 17) at MAGDALENE, Mar. 18, 1668–9. S. of John, of Upton, Lincs. School, Nottingham. Matric. 1670; B.A. 1672–3. Ord. deacon (Lincoln) Mar. 23, 1672–3.

GLOSS, CRISPUS. Adm. sizar (age 18) at ST JOHN'S, June 15, 1665. S. of John (? 1622), clerk, of Saxelby, Lincs. B. there. School, Lincoln. Matric. 1665; B.A. 1668–9. Ord. priest (Lincoln) Sept. 24, 1671.

GLOSSE, JOHN. Matric. sizar from QUEENS', Michs. 1622. Of Leicestershire. B.A. 1626–7. Ord. deacon (Peterb.) Mar. 5; priest, Mar. 6, 1625–6. Probably minister at Saxelby, Lincs.; and father of Crispus.

GLOSSOPPE, WILLIAM. Matric. pens. from CHRIST'S, Easter, 1549.

GLOUCESTER, JOHN. Scholar at KING'S HALL, 1369–80. S. of Thomas, of Gloucester.

GLOUCESTER, RICHARD (*alias* BRISLEY). B.Can.L. 1519–20; D.Can.L. 1522–3. Perhaps also B.D. and D.D. of Oxford, in 1510. Pens. at GONVILLE HALL, 1521–5. A Cistercian from Lewes; prior of their cell at Horton, Kent. Surrendered the priory in 1538, when he received a pension of £15. Preb. of Chichester. R. of All Saints', Purleigh, Essex, 1527. R. of Stoke-by-Guildford, Surrey, 1530–8. Archdeacon of Lewes, 1551. Will proved (P.C.C.) 1558. (*Venn*, I. 25.)

GLOUCESTRE, ROBERT. A scholar at KING'S HALL, 1432–6.

GLOUCESTRE, THOMAS. A scholar at KING'S HALL, 1365. Probably B.C.L. and Commissary to Bp Arundel. Died July 14, 1389. (A. Gray.)

GLOVER, ALEXANDER. Matric. sizar from CHRIST'S, 1591–2.

GLOVER, BENJAMIN. Adm. at KING'S, a scholar from Eton, 1710. S. of William, V. of Burnham, Bucks. B. there. Matric. Easter, 1711. Fellow, 1713; no degree recorded. Ord. deacon (London) Sept. 19, 1714. Died in London, of small-pox, 1714, aged 23. Buried at Burnham. (*Harwood*.)

GLOVER, CHRISTOPHER. Matric. pens. from MAGDALENE, Easter, 1619; B.A. 1622; M.A. from Clare, 1627. Ord. deacon (Peterb.) Sept. 3; priest, Sept. 4, 1624. R. of Stapleford, Herts., 1626. R. of Saxby, Leics., 1633.

GLOVER, CORNELIUS. Matric. sizar from CORPUS CHRISTI, Easter, 1618. Of Yorkshire. B.A. 1621–2.

GLOVER, DANIEL. Adm. sizar at CHRIST'S, Feb. 18, 1715–6. S. of John. B. at Royston, Herts. School, Chesfield (Mr Goodwin). Matric. 1716; Scholar, 1716. Resided two years.

GLOVER, EDWARD. M.A. 1617 (Incorp. from Oxford). Of Essex. Matric. from Trinity College, Oxford, Apr. 15, 1603, age 16; B.A. (Oxford) 1606; M.A. 1609. R. of Lamarsh, Essex, 1622–37. Buried there July 28, 1637. Admon. (Consist. C. London) Aug. 4, 1637. (J. Ch. Smith.)

GLOVER, EDWARD. M.A. from TRINITY, 1679. S. of William, of Tenbury, Worcs. Matric. from Christ Church, Oxford, Apr. 15, 1671, age 16; B.A. (Oxford) 1674. R. of Burford (1st portion), Salop, 1679. (*Al. Oxon.*)

GLOVER, FRANCIS (B.A. 1611–2), *see* GOWER.

GLOVER, FRANCIS. Adm. pens. at QUEENS', Apr. 13, 1648. Of London. Perhaps s. and h. of John, late of Water Newton, Hunts., Esq., deceased; adm. at Lincoln's Inn, Oct. 25, 1649.

GLOVER, HENRY. Matric. pens. from PEMBROKE, Michs. 1564–5. B. at Cranborne, Dorset. B.A. 1567–8; probably at Christ's. Ord. deacon (London) Nov. 6, 1569, age 22, as 'a scholar of Christ's.'

GLOVER, HENRY. Matric. sizar from ST JOHN'S, Easter, 1618; B.A. from King's, 1622–3; M.A. 1626. Ord. deacon (Peterb.) Mar. 5; priest, Mar. 6, 1625–6. R. of Lower Isham, Northants., 1642–53. R. of Conington, Hunts., till 1658. Sub-dean of Lincoln, 1645. Will (P.C.C.) 1658.

GLOVER, HUGH. Matric. pens. from PEMBROKE, Michs. 1561. Perhaps 1st s. of Robert (1533); age 10 in 1555. B.A. 1564–5. Doubtless R. of Snoreham, Essex, 1570–83. R. of St Laurence Dengie, 1570. (*N. and Q.*, 3rd S., I. 182.)

GLOVER, HUGH. M.A. 1608 (Incorp. from Oxford). Of Worcestershire. Matric. from Exeter College, Oxford, Apr. 6, 1593, age 18; B.A. (Oxford) 1596; M.A. (St Edmund Hall) 1599. V. of Inkberrow, Worcs., 1612. (*Al. Oxon.*)

CLOVER, HUGH. Adm. sizar at EMMANUEL, Easter, 1627. Of Leicestershire. School, Market Bosworth. Matric. 1627; Scholar; B.A. 1630–1; M.A. 1634. C. of Finchingfield, Essex, 1637. R. of Debden, 1644–52. V. of Finchingfield, 1653; ejected, 1662. Afterwards preacher in Essex. Died at Bishop's Stortford, *c.* 1670. (*Calamy*, I. 505; *Davids*, 391.)

GLOVER, HUGH. Adm. pens. (age 14) at PETERHOUSE, July 2, 1652. Of Warwickshire. School, Coventry.

GLOVER (*alias* CAMBRYDGE), JOHN. Matric. sizar from CHRIST'S, Michs. 1555. Ord. sub-deacon (London) Dec. 1555; priest (Bishop of Sidon) Feb. 9, 1555–6. R. of Little Woolston, Bucks., 1562–75. R. of Gt Woolston, 1576–93. Died 1593. (*Peile*, I. 62.)

GLOVER, JOHN. Adm. at KING'S (age 16) a scholar from Eton, Aug. 25, 1604. Of London. B.A. 1607–8; M.A. 1612; B.D. 1626. Fellow, 1607–11. Incorp. at Oxford, 1612. R. of Exhall, Warws., 1610; and of Dallinghoe, Suffolk, during 1613. R. of Shottesham, 1618. R. of Laughton, Leics. Will (P.C.C.) 1653. (*Al. Oxon.*; *Harwood*.)

GLOVER, JOHN. Adm. pens. (age 18) at CAIUS, Feb. 6, 1604–5. S. of William, gent., of Ash-Booking, Suffolk. School, Sutton (Mr Ferrer). Adm. at Gray's Inn, Oct. 29, 1611. Buried at Ash-Bocking, Apr. 6, 1625. (*Venn*, I. 188.)

GLOVER, JOHN. Adm. sizar at PETERHOUSE, June 30, 1624. Of Suffolk. Matric. 1625.

GLOVER, JOHN. Adm. pens. at EMMANUEL, Sept. 9, 1632. Of Essex. Matric. 1633; B.A. 1636–7.

GLOVER, JOHN. Adm. pens. at TRINITY, Feb. 17, 1664–5. Matric. 1665; Scholar, 1668; B.A. 1668–9; M.A. 1672; D.D. 1689. Fellow of Peterhouse, 1672–81. Incorp. at Oxford, 1680. Signed for deacon's orders (London) Sept. 19, 1673; ord. priest (Ely) Oct. 2, 1675. R. of Ickenham, Middlesex, 1686–1714. Died June 23, 1714, aged 53. M.I. at Ickenham. Will, P.C.C. (Le Neve, *Mon.*, III. 257.)

GLOVER, JOHN. Adm. sizar (age 19) at CHRIST'S, May 2, 1710. S. of John. B. at Mansergh, Westmorland. School, Kirkby Lonsdale (Simon Atkinson). Matric. 1710; Scholar, 1710–1; B.A. 1713–4. Perhaps C. of Bothal, Northumberland. Buried there Aug. 31, 1716. (H. M. Wood; *Peile*, II. 174.)

GLOVER, NICHOLAS. Matric. sizar from JESUS, Easter, 1584; B.A. 1587–8; M.A. 1591. C. of Elstow, Beds., *c.* 1607–9. Perhaps the 'Mr Clover,' preacher in Beds. and Hunts., who went to Virginia, 1611. Died soon after.

GLOVER, PETER. Matric. pens. from ST JOHN'S, Easter, 1631; B.A. 1634–5.

GLOVER, RICHARD. Matric. sizar from ST JOHN'S, Michs. 1576.

GLOVER, RICHARD. Matric. pens. from CHRIST'S, Dec. 1602. One of these names, of Salop, gent., adm. at Lincoln's Inn, Feb. 22, 1610–1. (*Peile*, I. 242.)

GLOVER, RICHARD. Matric. sizar from TRINITY, Easter, 1636.

GLOVER, RICHARD. Adm. pens. at TRINITY, June 24, 1659. Matric. 1660; Scholar, 1661; B.A. 1662–3. One of these names, 4th s. of John, of Water Newton, Hunts., Esq., adm. at Lincoln's Inn, Jan. 30, 1664–5.

GLOVER, ROBERT. Adm. at KING'S, a scholar from Eton, 1533. S. of John, of Baxterley, afterwards of Mancetter, Warws. B.A. 1537–8; M.A. 1541. Fellow, 1533–43. An early reformer. Married a niece of Bishop Latimer. Condemned for heresy and burnt at Coventry, Sept. 20, 1555. Perhaps father of Hugh (1561). (*Cooper*, I. 129; *D.N.B.*)

GLOVER, SAMUEL. Matric. sizar from ST CATHARINE'S, Easter, 1637. Of Northamptonshire. B.A. 1640–1; M.A. 1644. Fellow of Queens', 1644. R. of East Farndon, Northants., 1649–59. Married, at All Saints', Northampton, Nov. 20, 1648, Elizabeth Hill. Buried Jan. 6, 1658–9, at Farndon. (H. I. Longden.)

GLOVER, SAMUEL. M.A. 1656 (Incorp. from Oxford). Not found in *Al. Oxon.*

GLOVER, THOMAS. Matric. sizar from CHRIST'S, Dec. 1588. B. at Kirkby Lonsdale, Westmorland, *c.* 1571. B.A. 1592–3. M.A. 1596. Ord. priest by Bishop of Colchester. Chaplain to the Countess of Warwick. P.C. of Northaw, Herts., 1599–1604. R. of Malden, Beds., 1604–11. Buried at Malden, Dec. 30, 1611. (*Peile*, I. 194.)

GLOVER, THOMAS. Matric. pens. from ST JOHN'S, *c.* 1591.

GLOVER, THOMAS. Matric. pens. from ST JOHN'S, Easter, 1618. Of Lancashire. B.A. 1621–2; M.A. 1625. Fellow, 1622. Ord. deacon (Peterb.) May 23, 1624; priest, May 23, 1630. Perhaps R. of Kirby (diocese Chester) 1631–46, deprived.

GLOVER, THOMAS. M.A. from TRINITY, 1642 (*grace* passed).

GLOVER, THOMAS. Adm. pens. (age 18) at CAIUS, Oct. 30, 1706. S. of Thomas, gent., of Yarmouth, Norfolk (of the Campsea Ash and Frostenden family). B. at Lowestoft. Schools, Beccles (Mr Leeds) and Norwich (Mr Pate). Matric. 1706; Scholar, 1706–11; B.A. 1710–1. Ord. deacon (London) June 16, 1728. Father of William (1732–3). One of these names R. of Hawkhurst, Kent, 1729–37. (*Venn*, I. 515.)

GLOVER, WILLIAM. Adm. Fell.-Com. at EMMANUEL, June 7, 1627. Matric. 1627.

CLOVER, WILLIAM. Adm. Fell.-Com. (age 16) at CAIUS, Nov. 2, 1637. S. and h. of William, gent., of Ash-Bocking, Suffolk. B. at Pettistree. Bapt. Jan. 6, 1620–1. School, Westleton (Mr Pollerd). Adm. at Gray's Inn, Jan. 16, 1638–9. Of Frostenden, Esq. Died Mar. 11, 1660–1. M.I. at Frostenden. (*Venn*, I. 329; *Vis. of Norfolk*, 1664.)

CLOVER, WILLIAM. Matric. sizar from QUEENS', Michs. 1648. Of Northamptonshire. B.A. 1652–3; M.A. 1656. Probably R. of Steppingley, Beds., 1667.

GLOVER, WILLIAM. Adm. pens. (age 17) at SIDNEY, Mar. 24, 1690–1. S. of William, gent. B. at Bozeat, Northants. School, Bozeat (Mr Benford). Matric. 1691; M.B. 1696.

GLOVER, WILLIAM. Adm. pens. (age 18) at CAIUS, Feb. 13, 1732–3. S. of Thomas (1706), gent., late of Yarmouth. B. at Burgh Castle, Suffolk. School, Monk Soham (private; Mr Ray). Matric. 1732–3; Scholar, 1733–4. Died Oct. 20, 1742, aged 28. M.I. at Frostenden, Suffolk. (*Venn*, II. 36.)

GLOVER, ——. *Cautio* for degree, 1483–4.

GLOVER, ——. Matric. pens. from CLARE, Easter, 1613.

GLUE, *see* GLEWE.

GLYD, RICHARD. LL.B. 1659 (Incorp. from Oxford). School, Winchester. Matric. from New College, Oxford, 1650, *cler. fil.*; B.C.L. (Oxford) 1654. Fellow of New College, 1650–60, ejected. V. of West Hoathley, Sussex, 1661. Preb. of Chichester, 1661–76. V. of Newton Valence, Hants., 1662. (*Al. Oxon.*)

GLYDELL, GEORGE. Matric. sizar from ST JOHN'S, Easter, 1573. Probably R. of Buers Gifford, Essex, 1588. Will (P.C.C.) 1607; as Glidwell. (J. Ch. Smith.)

GLYNN, GEOFFREY. Of TRINITY HALL. S. of John, R. of Heneglwys, Anglesey. B.A. 1526–7; M.A. 1530; B.Civ.L. 1534–5; D.Civ.L. 1538–9. Advocate of the Arches, 1544. Preb. of Lichfield, 1550–7. Founded the grammar school at Bangor. Died July, 1557. Will (P.C.C.). Brother of William (1526) and Hugh (1544). (*Cooper*, I. 166.)

GLYNN, HUGH. Matric. sizar from QUEENS', Easter, 1544. Of Anglesey. S. of John, R. of Heneglwys, Anglesey. B.A. 1548–9; M.A. 1552; M.D. 1558. Fellow of St Catharine's, *c.* 1550. Proctor, 1556–7. Appointed fellow of Gonville and Caius in the charter, 1557. Practised physic at Chester. Brother of William (1526) and Geoffrey (1526). (*Venn*, I. 42; *Cooper*, I. 209.)

GLYNNE, Sir JOHN. University Counsel, 1647–60. S. of Sir William. B. 1603, at Glynllifon, Carnarvon. School, Westminster. Matric. from Hart Hall, Oxford, Nov. 9, 1621, age 18. Adm. at Lincoln's Inn. Barrister, 1628. Bencher, 1641. King's serjeant, 1660. M.P. for Westminster, 1640–8; for Carnarvonshire, 1654 and 1660; for Flint, 1655–8. Recorder of London, 1645–8. Chief Justice of the Upper Bench, 1655–9. Knighted, Nov. 16, 1660. As King's serjeant acted for the crown in the prosecution of Sir Henry Vane, 1662. Of Henley Park, Surrey. Died Nov. 15, 1666. Buried in St Margaret's, Westminster. Father of Thomas (1657). (*D.N.B.*; *Al. Oxon.*)

GLYNN, NICHOLAS. Adm. Fell.-Com. at CLARE, Aug. 11, 1730. S. and h. of William, of Cornwall. Bapt. at Cardynham, Cornwall, Jan. 22, 1713. Sheriff of Cornwall, 1743. Died June 22, 1744. (Maclean, *Trigg Minor*, II. 70.)

GLYNN, OWEN. M.A. 1581 (Incorp. from Oxford). Of Carnarvon. Adm. commoner of University College, 1572, age 20; B.A. (Oxford) 1573–4; M.A. 1576; B.D. 1583; D.D. 1590. R. of Litchborough, Northants., 1580. Canon of Bangor, 1593. R. of Eglwysail, Anglesey, 1601. R. of Rhoscolyn, 1613–5. Died 1615. (*Al. Oxon.*; Browne Willis, *Bangor*, 177.)

GLYNN, RICHARD. B.A. 1635 (Incorp. from Oxford). S. of Thomas, of Nantlle, Carnarvon. Matric. from Hart Hall, Oxford, Apr. 13, 1632, age 18; B.A. (Oxford) 1634; M.A. 1637. R. of 'Llan Ederne,' Carnarvon, 1637. (*Al. Oxon.*)

GLYNN, ROBERT. Adm. at KING'S, a scholar from Eton, 1737. S. of Robert, of Helland, Bodmin. B. there, Aug. 5, 1719. B.A. 1741–2; M.A. 1745; M.D. 1752. Seatonian prize, 1757. Fellow. Practised physic at Richmond and afterwards in Cambridge. F.R.C.P. 1763. Took the name Clobery on inheriting an estate. Died Feb. 8, 1800. Buried in King's College Chapel. M.I. there. Will, P.C.C. Friend of Thomas Gray and William Cowper. 'A solitary savage' according to Wm Cole. (*Hist. of King's College*, 218; *D.N.B.*; *Munk*, II. 247.)

GLYN, ROGER. B.A. 1516–7.

GLYNN, THOMAS. Adm. Fell.-Com. (age 17) at ST JOHN'S, Dec. 19, 1657. S. of John (1647), chief justice, of Henley Park, Surrey. B. there. School, Westminster. Matric. 1658. Adm. at Lincoln's Inn, Nov. 25, 1658.

GLYN, WILLIAM. Adm. at KING'S (age 16) a scholar from Eton, Nov. 9, 1523. Of the parish of St James-ex-Portis, London. Name off *c.* 1526.

GLYNN, WILLIAM. B.A. 1526–7; M.A. 1530; B.D. 1538; D.D. 1544. S. of John, of Glynn, Heneglwys, Anglesey. Fellow of QUEENS', 1530. Lady Margaret Professor, 1544–9. One of the original fellows of Trinity, 1546. Vice-Master, 1546–51. President of Queens', 1553–6. Vice-Chancellor, 1554. Incorp. D.D. at Oxford, 1554. Archdeacon of Anglesey, 1537. R. of St Martin, Ludgate, London, 1550–3. R. of Heneglwys, 1552. Ambassador to Rome, 1555. Bishop of Bangor, 1555–8. Died May 21, 1558. Buried in the Cathedral. M.I. there. Will (P.C.C.). Brother of Geoffrey (1526) and Hugh (1544). (*Cooper*, I. 175; *D.N.B.*)

GLYNNE or GLENNE, WILLIAM. Matric. sizar from QUEENS', Michs. 1576. Of Leicestershire. Ord. priest (London) Dec. 21, 1579.

GLYN, ——. D.Can.L. 1460–1.

GLYN, ——. B.Can.L. 1478.

GOAD, *see also* GOOD.

GOADE, CHRISTOPHER. Adm. at KING'S, a scholar from Eton, 1569. B. at Windsor, 1552. Matric. 1569; B.A. 1573–4. Fellow, 1572–7. Adm. at Gray's Inn, from Staple Inn, 1577. Will of one of these names (P.C.C.) 1596; of New Windsor, Berks., gent.

GOAD, CHRISTOPHER. Adm. at KING'S, a scholar from Eton, Nov. 9, 1607. 5th s. of Roger (1555), provost of King's. B.A. 1611–2. Fellow, 1610, till his death, 1613. Buried in the College Chapel. Brother of Matthew (1591), Richard (1610), Robert (1594), Roger (1601) and Thomas (1592).

GOAD, CHRISTOPHER. Adm. at King's (age 15) a scholar from Eton, Aug. 14, 1613. Of Windsor. Matric. 1614; B.A. 1617-8; M.A. 1621; B.D. 1630. Fellow, 1616, till 1637. Ord. priest (Peterb.) May 31, 1618. R. of Broughton. Sequestered to St Pancras, Soper Lane, London, 1643-44. Will (P.C.C.) 1653; of Broughton, Oxon. Brother of Thomas (1611) and George (1620). (*Harwood*; *Shaw*, I. 317.)

GOAD, CHRISTOPHER. Adm. at King's, a scholar from Eton, 1669. S. of George (1620). B. at Eton. Matric. Easter, 1670; B.A. 1672-3; M.A. 1677. Fellow, 1671. Died in College. Brother of George (1662) and Thomas (1668).

GOAD or GOOD, FRANCIS. Adm. at King's (age 18) a scholar from Eton, June 28, 1616. Of Hatley, Cambs. Matric. 1616; B.A. 1619-20; M.A. 1623. Fellow, 1619, till 1635. Died in College. (*Harwood*.)

GOAD, FRANCIS. Matric. pens. from Clare, Michs. 1626. Of Norfolk. Probably s. of Matthew. B.A. from Peterhouse, 1630-1; M.A. 1634.

GOAD, GEORGE. Adm. at King's, a scholar from Eton, 1620. B. at Windsor. B.A. 1623-4; M.A. 1627. Fellow, till 1647. Proctor, 1637-8. Fellow of Eton, 1648-58. R. of Horstead and Coltishall, Norfolk, 1646. Chaplain to Judge Banks. Head Master of Eton, 1647-8. Buried at Eton, Oct. 10, 1671. Will, P.C.C. Brother of Thomas (1611) and Christopher (1613), father of George (1662), Christopher (1669) and Thomas (1668). (*Harwood*; *D.N.B.*)

GOAD, GEORGE. Adm. at King's, a scholar from Eton, 1662. S. of George (1620). B. at Eton. Matric. Easter, 1663; B.A. 1666-7; M.A. 1670. Fellow, 1666. Died in College, June 13, 1678. Brother of Christopher (1669) and Thomas (1668). (*Harwood*.)

GOAD, HENRY. Matric. sizar from Queens', Lent, 1564-5. Of Berkshire. B.A. 1568-9; M.A. 1572; B.D. 1579. Fellow, 1572-80. Ord. deacon and priest (Peterb.) July 25, 1572. University preacher, 1579.

GOAD, MATTHEW. Adm. at King's, a scholar from Eton, 1591. 1st s. of Roger, provost of King's. B. 1575. Matric. Michs. 1591; B.A. 1595-6; M.A. 1599. Fellow, 1594-1600. Adm. at Gray's Inn, Aug. 4, 1600. Lived on his estate in Suffolk, and enjoyed a place in the Court of Chancery. Will (P.C.C.) 1638; of St Andrew, Holborn, London, and Hadleigh, Suffolk. Brother of Christopher (1607), etc. (*Harwood*.)

GOADE or GOODE, RICHARD. Adm. at King's (age 18) a scholar from Eton, Aug. 25, 1578. Of London. Matric. 1578; B.A. 1582-3.

GOAD, RICHARD. Adm. at King's, a scholar from Eton, 1610. 6th s. of Roger (1555), the provost. B. in Cambridge. B.A. 1613-4. Fellow 1613, till 1615. Lived on his estate. Died in London. Buried at St Mary-le-Bow, Apr. 13, 1625. Will (P.C.C.) 1625; of Milton, Cambs. Brother of Christopher (1607), etc. (*Harwood*.)

GOAD or GOOD, ROBERT. Adm. pens. at King's, Lent, 1569-70; afterwards Fell.-Com.

GOAD, ROBERT. Adm. at King's, a scholar from Eton, 1594. 3rd s. of Roger (1555), the provost. B. in Cambridge, 1577. Died in College, 1596. Brother of Christopher (1607), etc.

GOAD, ROGER. Adm. at King's, a scholar from Eton, 1555. B. at Horton, Bucks. Matric. Michs. 1555; B.A. 1559-60; M.A. 1563; B.D. 1568-9; D.D. 1576. Fellow, 1558. Provost, 1570-1610. Lady Margaret preacher, 1572-7. Vice-Chancellor, 1576-7, 1595-6, 1607-8. Ord. pr (Ely) July 29, 1565. Master (? usher) of Guildford Grammar School, till 1569. Chancellor of the diocese of Wells, 1577. R. of Milton, Cambs., 1597. Chaplain to the Earl of Warwick. Died Apr. 25, 1610. Buried in the College Chapel. M.I. there. Will (P.C.C.) 1610. Father of Christopher (1607), Matthew (1591), Richard (1610), Robert (1594), Roger (1601) and Thomas (1592). (*Cooper*, III. 19; *D.N.B.*; *Harwood*.)

GOAD, ROGER. Adm. at King's, a scholar from Eton, 1585. B. at Streatham, Cambs., 1567. Matric. Michs. 1585; B.A. 1589; M.A. 1593. Fellow, 1588-94. Conduct of King's, 1599. Ord. deacon (Lincoln) Oct. 14, 1599; priest (Colchester) July 1, 1604. C. of Therfield, Herts., 1613. Afterwards went to Ireland. Doubtless will proved, P.C. Dublin, 1643, as of 'Schoolhouse Lane, clerk.' (H. B. Swanzy.)

GOAD, ROGER. Adm. at King's, a scholar from Eton, 1601. 4th s. of Roger (1555). B. at Cambridge, 1585. Matric. Michs. 1601; B.A. 1605-6. Fellow, 1604, till his death in College, 1608-9. Brother of the next and of Robert (1594), etc.

GOADE, THOMAS. Adm. at King's, a scholar from Eton, 1592. 2nd s. of Roger (1555), provost of King's. B. 1576. B.A. 1596; M.A. 1600; B.D. 1607; D.D. 1615. Fellow, 1595-1611. Incorp. at Oxford, 1600. Ord. priest (Lincoln) June 15, 1606. R. of Milton, Cambs., 1600. Adm. at Gray's Inn, Feb. 21, 1615-6. R. of Merstham, Surrey, 1617. Precentor of St Paul's, 1618-38. R. of Hadleigh, Suffolk, 1618-38. Employed at the Synod of Dort, 1619. Preb. of Wolverhampton, 1620-38. Chaplain to Archbishop Abbot. Preb. of Winchester, 1621-38. R. of Black Notley, Essex, 1623. Co-dean of Bocking, 1633-8. Preb. of Canterbury, 1636. Author, theological. Died at Hadleigh, Aug. 8, 1638. Buried in the Chancel. Will (P.C.C.) 1640. (*D.N.B.*; *Harwood*.)

GOAD, THOMAS. Adm. at King's (age 15) a scholar from Eton, Aug. 24, 1611. Of Windsor. Matric. 1611; B.A. 1613; M.A. 1619; LL.D. 1630. Fellow, 1614-34. Senior proctor, 1629. Incorp. at Oxford, 1617. Regius Professor of Civil Law, 1635-66. Adm. advocate, May 7, 1631. Buried at Grantchester, June 11, 1666. Brother of Christopher (1613) and George (1620). (*D.N.B.*)

GOAD, THOMAS. Matric. pens. from Clare, 1626. Of Norfolk. Migrated to Peterhouse, July 16, 1628. Scholar, 1628; B.A. 1629-30; M.A. 1633. One of these names V. of Grinton, Yorks., 1637-73. (*T. A. Walker*, 37.)

GOAD, THOMAS. Adm. at King's, a scholar from Eton, 1668. S. of George (1620). B. at Eton. Matric. Michs. 1669; B.A. 1672-3; M.A. 1677. Fellow, 1671. Died in College. Brother of George (1662) and Christopher (1669).

GOAD, WILLIAM. B.D. (*Lit. Reg.*) 1631-2. *See* GOOD.

GOAT, EDWARD. Adm. pens. at Caius, Dec. 18, 1683. S. of Edward, attorney, of Botesdale, Suffolk. School, Bury. Matric. 1684; Scholar, 1684-6. Adm. at the Middle Temple, Dec. 6, 1686. (*Venn*, I. 475.)

GOAT, ROBERT. Adm. pens. (age 17) at Caius, Apr. 6, 1719. S. of John, gent., of Thrandeston, Suffolk. B. there. School, Botesdale (Mr Maybourne). Scholar, 1719-23; Matric. 1720; B.A. 1722-3. Fellow, 1723-5. Died Nov. 1725. (*Venn*, II. 11.)

GOATER, *see also* GOTER.

GOATER, GEORGE. Adm. sizar (age 16) at Jesus, Nov. 10, 1673. Of Sussex. Scholar from St Paul's School. Matric. 1673; B.A. 1677-8; M.A. 1681. Buried in the College Chapel, Sept. 15, 1681.

GOBERT, JOHN. B.A. from Trinity, 1622-3; M.A. 1628.

GOBET, ——. M.A. 1462. Perhaps Robert Gobert, V. of Orwell, Cambs., 1462.

GOBSBORGE, JOHN. Adm. pens. at Trinity, Feb. 5, 1641-2.

GOCCHINGA, SCATHO À. LL.D. 1593. Incorp. from Frankfort. A Frisian.

GODBED, GORBETT or GOTOBED, AUGUSTINE. Adm. sizar at Peterhouse, Jan. 4, 1620-1. Matric. 1621; Scholar, 1621; B.A. 1624-5; M.A. 1628. R. of Gt Thornham, Suffolk, 1641-60.

GOTOBED, EDWARD. Matric. sizar from Jesus, *c.* 1596. B. in the Isle of Ely. B.A. from Peterhouse, 1600-1. Ord. deacon (Peterb.) Oct. 23, 1601; priest (London) Mar. 18, 1603-4, age 26. C. of Gt Hadham, Herts. V. of Gt Canfield, Essex, 1604-8. Licensed, Sept. 15, 1604, to marry Ann, dau. of William Squire, of London. Will perhaps (P.C.C.) 1653; of St Giles', Cripplegate, clerk. (J. Ch. Smith.)

GODBED, HENRY. Matric. pens. from Jesus, Easter, 1544.

GODBED, JOHN. Matric. sizar from Peterhouse, Michs. 1560. Ord. deacon (Ely) Mar. 23, 1566-7; priest, Apr. 16, 1568, age 25; 'petty canon of Ely.'

GOTOBED, RICHARD. Adm. sizar at Jesus, May 6, 1664. Of the Isle of Ely. Matric. 1664; B.A. 1667-8. Ord. deacon (Lincoln) May 17, 1668. C. of Ravensden, Beds., in 1687; of Tempsford, 1688-9- .

GODBED or GOTOBED, THOMAS. Matric. sizar from Jesus, Easter, 1578; B.A. 1581-2; M.A. 1585.

GOTOBET, THOMAS. Adm. sizar (age 18) at Caius, Mar. 3, 1640-1. S. of Tobias, butcher, of Ely, Cambs. B. there. School, Ely (Mr Hitch). Matric. 1641; Scholar, 1643-8; B.A. 1644-5; M.A. 1648. V. of Manea, Cambs., 1661. R. of Coveney, 1663-1703. Buried there, Oct. 20, 1703. (*Venn*, I. 341.)

GOTOBED or GODBED, THOMAS. Adm. sizar (age 19) at Caius, June 6, 1699. S. of William, husbandman, of Coveney, Cambs. B. there. School, Peterborough (Mr Waring). Matric. 1699; Scholar, 1699-1704; B.A. 1702-3. Ord. priest (Ely) Dec. 1709. C. of Wieken, Cambs., 1709. R. of Wentworth, 1709. Master of the Grammar School at Sutton, 1722. R. of Coveney, 1723-36. (*Venn*, I. 502.)

GODEED, WILLIAM. Matric. pens. from Clement Hostel, Easter, 1544.

GOTOBED, WILLIAM. Matric. sizar from Trinity, Easter, 1631; B.A. 1632-3; M.A. 1636. R. of South Pickenham, Norfolk, 1651; ejected, 1658; restored, 1660. Died 1674.

GODBED, WILLIAM. Adm. pens. at Trinity, Apr. 24, 1672.

GODBOLD, ANTHONY. Adm. pens. at JESUS, Oct. 31, 1651. Of Essex. S. and h. of John, of Hatfield Peverill, Essex. Brother of John (1651) and Richard (1652). (*Vis. of Essex*, 1634.)

GODBOLD, HENRY. B.A. 1515-6; M.A. 1519; B.D. 1527-8. Fellow of PETERHOUSE, 1517-40. Ord. priest (Ely) Apr. 23, 1519. Will (V.C.C.) 1540.

GODBOULD or GODBOLT, JOHN. Adm. pens. (age 17) at CAIUS, June 29, 1599. S. of Thomas, of Tannington, Suffolk. School, Worlingworth. Scholar, 1600-2. Adm. at Gray's Inn, Nov. 16, 1605. Serjeant-at-law, 1636. Chief Justice of the Isle of Ely, 1638. M.P. for Bury St Edmunds, in 1640. Judge of Common Pleas, 1647. Died Aug. 3, 1648. (*Venn*, I. 169; *D.N.B.*)

GODBOLD, JOHN. Adm. pens. at JESUS, Oct. 31, 1651. Of Essex. 2nd s. of John, of Hatfield Peverill, Essex. Brother of Richard (1652) and Anthony (1651). (*Vis. of Essex*, 1634.)

GODBOLD, JOHN. Adm. Pell.-Com. at QUEENS', Aug. 20, 1684. Of Essex. Matric. 1685. Probably brother of Richard (1685).

GODBOLT, JOHN. Adm. sizar (age 19) at MAGDALENE, May 5, 1729. S. of James, gent., deceased. B. at Worlingworth, Suffolk. School, Monk Soham. Matric. 1729.

GODBOLD, RICHARD. Adm. pens. at JESUS, July 4, 1652. Of Essex. 3rd s. of John, of Hatfield Peverill, Essex, gent. Matric. 1653; B.A. 1655-6. Adm. at Gray's Inn, Feb. 12, 1655-6. Brother of John (1651) and Anthony (1651). (*Vis. of Essex*, 1634.)

GODBOLD, RICHARD. Adm. pens. at QUEENS', May 23, 1685. Of Essex. Matric. 1685. Probably brother of John (1684).

GODBOLD, RICHARD. Adm. sizar at CLARE, Aug. 2, 1710. S. of John, of Terling Hall, Essex. School, Felsted. Matric. 1711; B.A. 1714-5; M.A. 1718. Ord. deacon (London) Sept. 22, 1717; priest (Ely) Mar. 13, 1719-20. V. of All Saints', Sudbury, 1720-47. V. of Margaret Roding, Essex, 1733-47. Died 1747.

GODBOLD, THOMAS. Adm. pens. at TRINITY, June 27, 1645. Readm. June 23, 1646. Of Suffolk. One of these names 2nd s. of John, serjeant-at-law, of Southland, Suffolk, adm. at Gray's Inn, Feb. 2, 1640-1.

GODBOLD, WILLIAM. Adm. pens. (age 16) at PEMBROKE, Jan. 22, 1639-40. S. of Thomas. B. at Mendham, Suffolk. Adm. at Gray's Inn, Feb. 2, 1640-1.

GODDARD, BENJAMIN. Adm. pens. (age 16) at CHRIST'S, Sept. 17, 1649. S. of Edward. B. at Upham, Wilts. School, St Paul's. Matric. 1649; B.A. 1653.

GODDARD, EDWARD. Matric. pens. from ST JOHN'S, Easter, 1622. Perhaps s. of Edward, of Hartham, Wilts.; age 18 in 1623. B.A. 1625-6; M.A. 1629. (*Vis. of Wilts.*)

GODDARD, EDWARD. M.A. from KING'S, 1687. S. of John, of Twyford, Dorset (? Hants.), clerk. Matric. from Magdalen College, Oxford, July 10, 1668, age 17; B.A. (Oxford) 1680 (?). Ord. deacon (Bristol) Feb. 27, 1674-5, as B.A. R. of Fifehead Neville, Dorset, 1685-1706. R. of Stock Gaylard, 1686-1703. Chaplain to the House of Commons, 1705. (*Al. Oxon.*; F. S. Hockaday.)

GODDART, GUYBON. Adm. pens. (age 17) at PETERHOUSE, Jan. 22, 1628-9. S. of Thomas, of Stanhow, Norfolk (and Mary, dau. of William Guybon). Matric. 1629. Adm. at Lincoln's Inn, Feb. 5, 1630-1. Recorder of Lynn, 1651-60. M.P. for Lynn, 1654-5, 1656-8; for Castle-Rising, 1659. Lord of the Manor of Swanton Morley, Norfolk, 1659. Serjeant-at-law, 1669. An active antiquary. Died May 29, 1671. Buried at Brampton. Admon. (P.C.C.) 1671. Father of Thomas (1659-60). (*T. A. Walker*, 38; A. B. Beaven.)

GODDARD, HENRY. Adm. pens. (age 17) at ST JOHN'S, Jan. 20, 1724-5. S. of Edward, gent. B. at Richmond, Yorks. School, Kirkleatham (Mr Clark). Matric. 1725; B.A. 1728-9; M.A. 1732; M.D. 1753. Fellow, 1730-5. Practised as physician at Foston, Yorks. Benefactor to Addenbrooke's Hospital. Died Nov. 24, 1767. (*Scott-Mayor*, III. 379.)

GODDARD, JOHN. Adm. sizar (age 15) at ST JOHN'S, Feb. 9, 1637-8. S. of Thomas (*c.* 1594), R. of Hopton, Suffolk. School, Botesdale (Mr Eston). Matric. 1638; B.A. 1641-2; M.A. 1645. Incorp. at Oxford, 1655. R. of Caister St Edmund, and Markshall, Norfolk, 1657. R. of Little Poringland, 1663-95. Died 1695. Will, P.C.C.

GODDARD, JOHN. Adm. sizar (age 15) at CAIUS, Apr. 23, 1675. S. of Amos, deceased, of Wiggenhall St Mary, Norfolk. B. there. School, Lynn (Mr Bell). Matric. 1675; Scholar, 1675-80; B.A. 1678-9; M.A. 1682. Fellow, 1680-1710. Moderator, 1686. Incorp. at Oxford, July 10, 1690. Ord. priest (Norwich) Sept. 1683. R. of Pattesley, Norfolk, 1687. Buried at All Saints', South Lynn, Apr. 3, 1710. Will (V.C.C.) 1710. (*Venn*, I. 453.)

GODDARD, JOHN. Adm. at KING'S, a scholar from Eton, 1726. S. of Thomas, canon of Windsor. B. at Cricklade, Wilts. Matric. Easter, 1727; B.A. 1730-1; M.A. 1738. Fellow, 1730-1. Assistant Master at Eton. Afterwards became insane. (*Harwood*.)

GODDARD, JOHN. Adm. pens. (age 18) at CAIUS, Mar. 23, 1729-30. S. of John, grazier, of West Wretham, Norfolk. B. there. Bapt. at All Souls', Lynn. Schools, Brandon (Mr Knowles) and Eton (colleger). Scholar, 1730-1. Migrated to Emmanuel, Mar. 23, 1730-1. Matric. 1731; B.A. 1733-4; M.A. 1737. Ord. deacon (Norwich) June 9, 1734; priest, Nov. 23, 1735. R. of Wreningham, All Souls' and St Mary, Norfolk, 1735-49. (*Venn*, II. 32.)

GODDARD, JONAS. Adm. pens. (age 17) at PETERHOUSE, Mar. 28, 1733. Of Norfolk. School, Wymondham, Norfolk. Scholar, 1733; Matric. 1734. Buried at Little St Mary's, Cambridge, June 25, 1735.

GODDARD, JONATHAN. Adm. pens. (age 21) at CHRIST'S, June 26, 1637. Previously adm. at Magdalen Hall, Oxford, Feb. 20, 1632. Matric. 1632. S. of Henry, shipbuilder, of Deptford. B. at Chatham. Schools, Chatham (Mr Chapman and Mr Spencer) and London (private; Mr Dier). M.B. from Christ's, 1638; M.D. from St Catharine's, 1642-3. Incorp. at Oxford, 1651-2. Gulstonian lecturer, 1648. Warden of Merton College, Oxford, 1651-60. F.R.C.P. 1646. Censor, 1660-72. Physician to the Parliamentary army, 1649-50. M.P. for Oxford University, 1653. Professor of Physic at Gresham College, 1655-75. F.R.S. and member of the Council of the Royal Society, 1663. Author, medical. Died Mar. 24, 1674-5. Buried at St Helen's, Bishopsgate. (*D.N.B.*; *Peile*, I. 449; *Al. Oxon.*)

GODARD, PETER STEPHEN. Adm. sizar at CLARE, June 23, 1721. S. of a French refugee; a barber by trade. B. at Cambridge, Aug. 28, 1705. School, Merchant Taylors'. Matric. 1721; B.A. 1724-5; M.A. 1728; D.D. 1761. Fellow, 1727. Senior proctor, 1745-6. Master, Sept. 25, 1762-81. Vice-Chancellor, 1762-3. Ord. deacon (Lincoln) Sept. 24, 1727; priest, May 24, 1730. V. of Gt Gransden, Hunts., 1742-7. R. of Fornham All Saints', Suffolk, 1747. R. of Westley, 1749. Preb. of Peterborough, 1761-81. Preb. of St Paul's, 1770-81. R. of Whepstead, Suffolk, 1774-81. Author, sermons. Died Oct. 25, 1781. Will, P.C.C. (*Clare Coll. Hist.*, 162.)

GODDARD, THOMAS. Adm. pens. (age 18) at CAIUS, May 5, 1565. S. of Thomas, of Stowmarket. School, Stowmarket. Readm. Aug. 12, 1573.

GODDARD, THOMAS. Matric. pens. from CLARE, Easter, 1577; B.A. 1580-1; M.A. 1584. Ord. deacon and priest (Lincoln) Sept. 24, 1585. R. of Sandon, Essex, 1588-1601. Will (Consist. C. London) 1601; to be buried at Sandon.

GODDARD, THOMAS. Matric. sizar from ST JOHN'S, *c.* 1594; B.A. 1598-9; M.A. 1602. Incorp. at Oxford, 1604. R. of Hopton, Suffolk, 1606. Will proved (Norw. C. C.) 1639. Father of John (1638).

GODDARD or GODWARD, THOMAS. Adm. pens. at CORPUS CHRISTI, 1605. Of Suffolk. Matric. Easter, 1607.

GODDARD, THOMAS. Adm. pens. at EMMANUEL, Sept. 24, 1606.

GODDARD, THOMAS. Adm. Fell.-Com. (age 17) at CHRIST'S, Feb. 21, 1659-60. Eldest s. of Gibbon (Guybon, of 1628-9), Esq. B. in London. School, Westminster. Matric. 1660. Married Mary, dau. of Sir Henry Crofts, of Saxham, Suffolk. (*Vis. of Norfolk*, 1664.)

GODDARD, THOMAS. Adm. sizar at JESUS, Mar. 9, 1686-7. Of Dorset. Matric. 1687. Died in College. Buried in the Chapel, Feb. 13, 1688. (A. Gray.)

GODDARD, THOMAS. Adm. at CORPUS CHRISTI, 1724. Of Norwich. Matric. Michs. 1724; B.A. 1727-8. R. of Honing, Norfolk, 1730-2. V. of Dilham, 1730-2. V. of Halvergate, 1731-68. R. of Wickhampton, 1731-85.

GODARD, WILLIAM. Matric. sizar from MICHAELHOUSE, Michs. 1544.

GODDART, WILLIAM. Matric. pens. from TRINITY, Easter, 1578. One of these names V. of Mendham, Suffolk, 1588. R. of St Margaret, South Elmham, 1599.

GODDARD, WILLIAM. Adm. scholar (age 16) at CAIUS, Oct. 25, 1617. S. of Thomas, gent., of Rudham, Norfolk. School, Holt. Matric. 1617. M.D. of Padua. Incorp. at Oxford, 1634. Fellow of the College of Physicians, 1634-49. Censor, 1638, 1641, 1644. Dismissed from his fellowship, Nov. 23, 1649. Buried at St James, Clerkenwell, Jan. 13, 1669-70. Will, P.C.C. (*Munk*, I. 216; J. Ch. Smith.) The 'satirist' (for whom *see D.N.B.*) must have been a different man.

GODDELL, ZACHARIAS. Matric. pens. from QUEENS', Michs. 1582. Of Lincolnshire. B. at Brasbridge. B.A. (? 1589-90); M.A. from St Catharine's, 1605. Ord. deacon (London) Sept. 3, 1590; priest, Mar. 30, 1591. V. of Enderby *with* Weston, Lincs., 1595-6. One of these names preb. of St Paul's, 1590.

GODDEN, ROBERT. Matric. sizar from TRINITY, Lent, 1623-4; Scholar, 1625; B.A. 1627-8; M.A. 1631. Perhaps V. of Ryarsh, Kent, 1660-1. R. of Reculver, 1663-72. Died 1672.

GODDEN, THOMAS, *see* TYLDEN.

GODDEN, GOODEN or GOODWIN, WILLIAM. Matric. sizar from CORPUS CHRISTI, *c.* 1593. Of Kent. B.A. 1597-8; M.A. 1601.

GODDING, RICHARD. Matric. sizar from CLARE, Easter, 1621; B.A. 1623-4; M.A. 1627. Ord. deacon (Peterb.) Sept. 20, 1623; priest, Dec. 16, 1627.

GODEALE, ——. B.A. 1463-4.

GODELYNE, WILLIAM. Scholar of CLARE, 1458, age 13.

GODERICH, *see also* GOODRICKE, GOODRICH.

GODERICH, JOHN. A scholar at KING'S HALL, 1361; 'left to be made an esquire,' 1368. (*Trin. Coll. Adm.*, I. 101.)

GODERICH, ROBERT. A scholar at KING'S HALL, 1364-81.

GODERICH, SIMON. A scholar at KING'S HALL, 1361-87.

GODERICH, WILLIAM. Scholar at KING'S HALL, 1375-83. S. of John, the King's cook.

GODFREY, ANTHONY. Matric. pens. from TRINITY, Easter, 1609; Scholar, 1611; B.A. 1612-3; M.A. 1616. Fellow, 1614. Ord. deacon (Peterb.) Sept. 7; priest, Sept. 8, 1622. R. of Broughton, Hunts., 1623-68. Buried at Somersham, 1668. Father of Henry and Richard (1641). (H. I. Longden.)

GODFREY, ARTHUR. Adm. (age 16) at CAIUS, Apr. 7, 1589. Readm. Fell.-Com. 1589. S. of Richard, serjeant-at-law, of Hindringham, Norfolk. School, Walsingham (Mr Dallington). Adm. at the Inner Temple, 1592, from Clifford's Inn. One of these names adm. at Douay College, 1606. (*Venn*, I. 136.)

GODFREY, DANIEL. Adm. pens. at CORPUS CHRISTI, 1570. Of Norwich. Matric. Michs. 1571; B.A. 1575-6; M.A. 1579.

GODFRAY, FRANCIS. Adm. at CORPUS CHRISTI, 1599. Of Suffolk. B.A. 1602-3; M.A. 1606. Ord. deacon (Norwich) Dec. 21, 1603; priest, June 15, 1606. C. of Thompson, Norfolk. C. of Caston. One of these names R. of Euston, Suffolk.

GODFRAY, FRANCIS. Matric. sizar from CORPUS CHRISTI, Easter, 1608. Of Suffolk. B.A. 1610-1.

GODFREY, FRANCIS. Adm. pens. at PETERHOUSE, Jan. 27, 1624-5. Of Suffolk. Matric. 1625; B.A. 1628-9.

GODFREY, FRANCIS. Adm. pens. at TRINITY, Aug. 31, 1672. Matric. 1673. Buried at All Saints', Cambridge, Mar. 24, 1674-5.

GODFREY, HENRY. Adm. pens. (age 15) at CAIUS, June 21, 1641. S. of Anthony (1609), R. of Broughton, Hunts. Schools, Upwood (Mr Harvey) and Perse, Cambridge. Matric. 1641; Scholar, 1642-8; B.A. 1644-5; M.A. 1648. Brother of Richard (1641).

GODFRAY, JOHN. Matric. pens. from CORPUS CHRISTI, Easter, 1589. Of Suffolk. B.A. (? 1591-2); M.A. 1595. Ord. deacon (Norwich) May 18; priest, Aug. 1, 1592. R. of Newbourne and Hemley, Suffolk, 1597-1607. One of these names, R. of Lackford, Suffolk, died 1630.

GODFREY, JOHN. Adm. pens. at QUEENS', Apr. 1709. Of Middlesex. Matric. 1709; B.A. 1712-3. Ord. deacon (London) May 23, 1714; priest, May 27, 1716.

GODFREY, JOSEPH. Matric. pens. from PEMBROKE, Michs. 1588. One of these names (*alias* Cowper), s. of William, of Thaxted, Essex, adm. at Gray's Inn, Feb. 23, 1593-4.

GODFREY, JOSEPH. Adm. pens. at ST CATHARINE'S, May 9, 1664.

GODFREY, JOSEPH. Adm. pens. at QUEENS', Apr. 21, 1686. Of Essex. S. of William, of Ongar, practitioner in physic. Matric. 1686; M.B. 1691. Of Starnbrooke, Beds., M.B. Admon. (P.C.C.) 1740, to his sister, wife of Sir Charles Gresham, Bart. (J. Ch. Smith.)

GODFREY, LAMBARD. B.A. 1628 (Incorp. from Oxford). S. of Thomas, of Selling, Kent, Esq., by his 1st wife, Margaret Lambard. Matric. from Hart Hall, Oxford, May 4, 1627, age 16; B.A. (Oxford) 1627-8. Adm. at Gray's Inn, May 18, 1625. Barrister-at-law, 1636. M.P. for Kent, 1654-5, 1656-8; for New Romney, 1659. Buried in Westminster, Apr. 1671. M.I. to his father at Selling. (*Al. Oxon.*; *Vis. of Kent*, 1619; Le Neve, *Mon.*, IV. 104.)

GODEFRIDUS, MICHAEL. Incorp. in theology and law (on King's visit) 1624.

GODFRAYE, OLIVER. Matric. pens. from TRINITY, Easter, 1563. Adm. at the Inner Temple, 1565. Of London.

GODFRAY, OWEN. D.Can.L. 1502-3.

GODFRAY, PETER. Matric. Fell.-Com. from ST JOHN'S, Michs. 1628. Doubtless 2nd s. of Peter, of Lydd, Kent, Esq. Bapt. Feb. 14, 1609. Knighted, July 21, 1641. Brother of Thomas (1625). (*Vis. of Kent*, 1619; *Archaeol. Cantiana*, VI. 260.)

GODFREY, RICHARD. B.A. from ST JOHN'S, 1554-5. Fellow, 1556. Of Norfolk. Perhaps V. of Wicklewood, Norfolk, 1564.

GODFREY, RICHARD. Matric. sizar from MAGDALENE, Lent, 1637-8; B.A. 1641-2. One of these names Master of Camberwell Grammar School, 1644-6. (*See* a contemporary at Oxford.)

GODFREY, RICHARD. Adm. pens. (age 16) at CAIUS, July 5, 1641. S. of Anthony (1609), R. of Broughton, Hunts. B. there. School, King's, Cambridge (Mr Younge). Matric. 1641. Brother of Henry (1641). (*Venn*, I. 344.)

GODFREY, RICHARD. Adm. Fell.-Com. (age 19) at ST JOHN'S, Sept. 20, 1644. S. of Richard, gent., deceased, of Wye, Kent. School, Wye (Mr Nichols).

GODFREY, RICHARD. Adm. pens. at EMMANUEL, Jan. 6, 1735-6. S. of John, of Brinkley, Cambs. School, Bury. Matric. 1736; Scholar; B.A. 1739-40; M.A. 1743. Ord. deacon (Lincoln) June 13, 1742; priest (Norwich) Sept. 1743. V. of Poslingford, Suffolk, 1750-66. Died 1766.

GODFREYE, ROBERT. Matric. sizar from ST JOHN'S, Easter, 1555. One of these names adm. at Gray's Inn, 1556.

GODFREY, ROBERT. B.A. from QUEENS', 1578-9; M.A. 1582. Ord. deacon and priest (Lincoln) Apr. 5, 1583. R. of Layton, Essex. Will (P.C.C.) 1617.

GODFRY, ROBERT. Matric. pens. from PEMBROKE, *c.* 1596; B.A. from Trinity, 1599-1600. One of these names adm. at Lincoln's Inn, Jan. 25, 1597-8; of Norfolk, gent.

GODFREY, ROBERT. M.A. 1617 (Incorp. from Oxford). Of Worcestershire. Matric. from Balliol College, Oxford, June 22, 1610, age 18; B.A. (Oxford) 1612; M.A. 1615. Perhaps R. of Patching, Sussex, 1618; and of Nuffield, Oxon., 1624. (*Al. Oxon.*)

GODFREY, THOMAS. Adm. Fell.-Com. at CHRIST'S, Feb. 20, 1625-6. 1st s. of Peter, of Lydd, Kent. Age 11 in 1619. School, London, under Mr Farnaby. Matric. 1626. Knighted, July 21, 1641. Of Heppington, Kent. Married Hester, dau. of Sir John Wilde. Died 1684. Buried at Nackington. Brother of Peter (1628). (*Vis. of Kent*; Burke, *L.G.*)

GODFREY, THOMAS. Matric. pens. from ST JOHN'S, Lent, 1626-7; B.A. 1630-1.

GODFRAY, WILLIAM. B.A. 1518-9.

GODFREY, WILLIAM. Adm Fell.-Com. at TRINITY, Aug. 8, 1661. Matric. 1661-2.

GODFREY, WILLIAM. Adm. sizar (age 18) at TRINITY, June 26, 1742. S. of William, of Hook, Howden, Yorks. School, Beverley (Mr Clark). Matric. 1743; B.A. 1746-7. Ord. deacon (Norwich) Sept. 1747; priest (Lincoln) Dec. 24, 1749. C. of Battisford, Suffolk.

GODLINGTON, RICHARD DE. M.A. Chancellor some time in the 14th century. Benefactor to the University.

GODLY, BEVIS. Matric. sizar from QUEENS', Easter, 1597. Of Huntingdonshire.

GODLY, BLASTUS. Adm. sizar at TRINITY, Jan. 18, 1668-9. Exhibitioner from Charterhouse. Matric. 1672; B.A. 1672-3; M.A. 1676. Ord. deacon (Ely) 1675; priest (London) Mar. 11, 1676-7. V. of Shillington, Beds., 1677-82. V. of Flempton and Hengrave, Suffolk, 1682-1719. Buried at Flempton, Oct. 29, 1719. M.I. there. Father of William (1705). (Gage, *Suffolk*, 67.)

GODLEY, BRIAN. B.A. from CHRIST'S, 1603-4; M.A. 1607. B. at Worksop, Notts. Ord. deacon (London) Mar. 1608-9; priest, Dec. 23, 1610. C. of Tortington, Sussex, 1608-9. V. of Donington, Lincs., 1612. (*Peile*, I. 235.)

GODLEY, HENRY. Matric. pens. from QUEENS', Easter, 1576; B.A. 1579-80; M.A. 1583; B.D. 1592. Fellow, 1582-1601. Ord. priest (Norwich) Feb. 28, 1584-5. V. of Onehouse, Suffolk, 1598-1623.

GODLY, MICHAEL. Adm. sizar (age 17) at ST JOHN'S, June 12, 1722. S. of Joseph, of Yorkshire. B. at 'Trimmingham,' near Halifax. School, Halifax (Mr Lister). Matric. 1722; B.A. 1725-6. Ord. priest (York) Aug. 16, 1730. V. of Cross Stone, Yorks., 1728-32. V. of Farndon St Peter, Notts., 1731-66. (*Scott-Mayor*, III. 350.)

GODLY, WILLIAM. Adm. scholar (age 15) at SIDNEY, Apr. 21, 1705. Only s. of Blastus (1668-9), R. of Flempton, Suffolk. B. there. Schools, Bury and Wrestlingworth (Mr Brestow). Matric. 1705; B.A. 1708-9; M.A. 1712; B.D. 1719. Fellow, 1712. Ord. deacon (Peterb.) May 30, 1713; priest, Sept. 19, 1713. R. of Lockinton, Yorks. Died Oct. 26, 1748. M.I. at Hitchin, Herts.

GODLUCK, ——. B.A. 1475-6; M.A. 1479.

GODMAN, HENRY. Adm. pens. (age 17) at PETERHOUSE, Apr. 17, 1647. Of Sussex. B. at Lewes. School, Mercers', London. Scholar, 1647; B.A. 1650-1. R. of Rodmell, Sussex; intruded; ejected, 1660. Afterwards minister at Deptford, where he died Jan. 29, 1702, aged 72. (*T. A. Walker*; *Calamy*, II. 471.)

GODMAN, JOHN. Adm. pens. (age 17) at MAGDALENE, May 7, 1660. S. of Richard, farmer, of Chanson (?), Beds. School, Huntingdon. Matric. 1660.

GODMAN, JOHN. Adm. sizar at JESUS, July 2, 1734. Of Uckfield, Sussex. S. of Francis, of Hemel Hempstead. Bapt. at Framfield, Sussex, Sept. 1, 1715. Matric. 1735; B.A. 1737-8. C. of Waldron, Sussex, 1742-7. V. of Mayfield, 1747-50. Died 1750. (A. Gray.)

GODMAN, THOMAS. Matric. sizar from PETERHOUSE, Easter, 1586.

GODMAN, THOMAS. Adm. pens. at EMMANUEL, c. 1588. Matric. 1589. One of these names, of London, adm. at Gray's Inn, Mar. 1, 1596-7.

GODMAN, WILLIAM. Adm. at KING'S, a scholar from Eton, 1642. B. at Windsor, 1625. Matric. 1642; B.A. 1646; M.A. 1650; B.D. 1659. Fellow, 1645-72. V. of Ringwood, Hants., 1671. Author, *Sermons*.

GODOLPHIN, FRANCIS. Adm. Fell.-Com. at KING'S, 1695. S. of Sidney, Earl of Godolphin. B. in Whitehall, Sept. 3, 1678. School, Eton. Matric. Easter, 1695; M.A. 1705. M.P. for East Looe, 1701; for Helston, 1701-8; for Oxon., 1708-10; for Tregony, 1710-2. Cofferer of the household, 1704-11 and 1714-23. Lord Lieutenant of Oxfordshire, 1715-35. Privy councillor, 1723. Acted as Lord Chief Justice, 1723, 1725 and 1727. Governor of the Scilly Islands, 1728. Lord Privy Seal, 1735-40. Created Baron Godolphin of Helston, 1735. Died Jan. 17, 1766, aged 87. Buried at Kensington. M.I. (*D.N.B.*; *G.E.C.*)

GODOLPHIN, WILLIAM. Matric. Fell.-Com. from EMMANUEL, Lent, 1584-5. Doubtless s. of Sir Francis, Knt., M.P. for Cornwall. Adm. at Lincoln's Inn, Jan. 29, 1586-7. Knighted, July 13, 1599. M.P. for Cornwall, 1603. Died 1613. (Burke, *Ext. Bart.*)

GODOLPHIN, WILLIAM (Viscount RIALTON). Adm. Fell.-Com. (age 18) at PEMBROKE, May 1, 1712. S. of Francis. Matric. 1712; D.C.L. Oxford, 1730 and Cambridge, 1730. M.P. for Penrhyn, 1720-2; for Woodstock, 1727-31. Marquess of Blandford, 1722. Died Aug. 24, 1731. Buried at Blenheim. (*Lipscomb*, IV. 560; *G.E.C.*)

GODS, ——. Adm. at CORPUS CHRISTI, 1547.

GODSALVE, EDWARD. B.A. 1543-4; M.A. 1546; B.D. 1554. One of the original fellows of TRINITY, 1546. Ord. sub-deacon (London) 1553. R. of Fulbourn St Vigors, Cambs., 1554. Preb. of Chichester, 1558. Deprived on the accession of Elizabeth, and retired to Antwerp, where he was Professor of Divinity at the Monastery of St Michael, c. 1560. Author. Died (?) 1568. (*Cooper*, I. 275; *D.N.B.*)

GODSALVE, HENRY. Adm. pens. at EMMANUEL, Nov. 1594. Matric. c. 1595.

GODSALVE, HENRY. Adm. pens. (age 19) at CAIUS, Jan. 21, 1595-6. S. of Thomas (1552), of Buckenham, Norfolk, gent. School, Norwich. Probably died young. Not in the pedigree in *Vis. of Norfolk*. Brother of Roger (1584). (*Venn*, I. 158.)

GODSALVE, HENRY. Matric. pens. from CORPUS CHRISTI, Michs. 1614. Of Norfolk.

GODSALVE, JOHN. B.A. from TRINITY, 1549-50; Scholar, 1550.

GODSALVE, JOHN. Adm. Fell.-Com. at EMMANUEL, July 3, 1607. Matric. 1607. Perhaps s. of Roger (1584), of Buckenham Ferry, Norfolk, Esq.; adm. at Lincoln's Inn, Feb. 14, 1609-10. (*Vis. of Norfolk.*)

GODSALVE, RICHARD. Adm. sizar (age 17) at ST JOHN'S, July 4, 1656. S. of James, of Newton-in-Whittington, Lancs., husbandman. School, Sedbergh. Matric. 1656-7; B.A. 1659-60; M.A. 1663. Incorp. at Oxford, 1663. R. of Richmond, Yorks., 1664-99. V. of Gt Smeaton, 1668-99. Died 1699.

GODSALVE, ROGER. Adm. Fell.-Com. (age 15) at CAIUS, May 2, 1584. Eldest s. of Thomas (1552), Esq., of Buckenham Ferry, Norfolk. Schools, Buckenham Ferry and Bungay. Adm. at Gray's Inn, 1588. Of Buckenham Ferry, Esq. Married Barbara, dau. of Richard Cutts, Esq., of Arkesden, Essex. Brother of Henry (1595-6). (*Venn*, I. 119; *Vis. of Norfolk.*)

GODSHALFE, THOMAS. Matric. pens. from TRINITY, Michs. 1552. Doubtless s. of Sir John, attorney-general to Queen Mary. Of Buckenham Ferry, Norfolk, Esq. Married Elizabeth, dau. of Richard Townsend, of Rainham. Father of Roger (above) and Henry (1595-6). (*Vis. of Norfolk.*)

GODSAVE or GODSAWFF, WILLIAM. Matric. sizar from CHRIST'S, June, 1582. B. in Yorkshire. B.A. 1585-6.

GODSCALE, JAMES. B.A. from TRINITY, 1599-1600. '7 years study at Leyden, Basle and Heidelberg.' Also at Geneva. M.A. 1600. Incorp. at Oxford, 1602. Author. (*Cooper*, II. 396.)

GODSONE or GOTSON, THOMAS. B.Civ.L. 1500; D.Civ.L. 1507-8.

GODWICK, JOHN. Studied at Cambridge and Oxford. Of Norfolk. Augustinian friar at Lynn. Died at Lynn, c. 1360. (*Pits*, 485.)

GODWICK, ——. B.D. 1462-3. A friar.

GODWIN, *see also* GOODWIN.

GODWYN, CHARLES. M.A. 1734 (Incorp. from Oxford). S. of Samuel, of Thornbury, Gloucs., clerk. Matric. from Balliol College, Mar. 20, 1717-8, age 17; B.A. (Oxford) 1721; M.A. 1724; B.D. 1740. (*Al. Oxon.*)

GODWIN, EDMUND. Matric. sizar from QUEENS', Easter, 1635. Of Kent. B.A. 1638-9; M.A. 1642. V. of Docking, Norfolk, 1644-62. V. of Eastwick, Herts., 1658-62. Perhaps R. of Cowley, Middlesex, 1679-1705. Died 1705.

GODWIN, EDMUND. Adm. pens. at QUEENS', Apr. 29, 1696. Of Hertfordshire. Matric. 1696; B.A. 1699-1700. Ord. deacon (London) Oct. 12, 1701; priest (Peterb.) Oct. 18, 1702. V. of Bozeat, Northants., 1702-8. Buried there Feb. 12, 1707-8. (H. I. Longden.)

GODWIN, EDWARD. Adm. pens. (age 17) at CHRIST'S, Apr. 14, 1629. S. of Richard. B. in London. School, Ropley, Worcs. Matric. 1629; B.A. 1632-3. Brother of the next.

GODWIN, JOHN. Adm. pen . (age 18) at CHRIST'S, Apr. 14, 1629. S. and h. of Richard. B. in London. School, Ropley, Worcs. Matric. 1629. Adm. at the Middle Temple, June 20, 1629. Brother of the above. (*Peile*, I. 399.)

GODWYN, THOMAS. 'KING'S scholar,' 1330.

GODYNOW, WILLIAM. B.A.; B.Can.L. 1502-3.

GOETZ, *see* GETSIUS.

GOFELL, THOMAS. D.D. 1462-3.

GOFFALAR, *see* GOPFERLER.

GOFFE, *see* GOUGH.

GOFTON, FRANCIS. Matric. pens. from ST JOHN'S, Easter, 1577. Of Surrey. Knighted, Feb. 2, 1618-9. Benefactor to Lambeth. M.I. at Lambeth. Will (P.C.C.) 1628; of St Giles', Cripplegate. Father of the next. (*Vict. Co. Hist. Surrey*, IV. 59; J. Ch. Smith.)

GOFTON, FRANCIS. Adm. at PEMBROKE, 1627. S. of Sir Francis (above), of Lambeth, Surrey, Knt. Perhaps matric. from Christ Church, Oxford, June 22, 1632, age 16. Died 1642, in France. Perhaps father of the next. (*Manning and Bray*, III. 498.)

GOFTON, FRANCIS. Adm. Fell.-Com. (age 18) at PETERHOUSE, Nov. 7, 1654. Of Surrey. Doubtless s. of Fraucis (above). Of Awbridge, Mottisfont, Hants. Buried at Mottisfont, Sept. 1684, aged 48. M.I. (J. Ch. Smith.)

GOGGES, JOHN. Adm. sizar at CLARE, c. 1585-6. S. of Robert. B. at Harpley, Norfolk. School, Harpley. Matric. Easter, 1586. Migrated as pens. to Caius, Jan. 28, 1587-8. Scholar, 1588-9; B.A. 1588-9. V. of Hickling, Norfolk, 1595-1613. Will proved (Norwich) 1613. (*Venn*, I. 133.)

GOGGLE or GOGILL, JOHN. Adm. sizar (age 16) at CAIUS, Feb. 26, 1729-30. S. of John, of Norwich. B. there. School, Norwich (Mr Reddington). Matric. 1729-30; Scholar, 1730-6; B.A. 1733-4. Ord. deacon (Norwich) Oct. 19, 1735. R. of Brundall, Norfolk, 1737-75. P.C.C. of Lingwood, 1747. R. of St Edmund, Norwich, 1751-7; of Lammas, 1754. V. of Ranworth, 1762-71. Died Jan. 7, 1775. Buried at Brundall. M.I. there. Will proved (Norw. C. C.) 1775. (*Venn*, II. 32.)

GOGMAN or GOKEMAN, WILLIAM. B.A. 1539-40; M.A. 1546; B.D. 1554. Fellow of ST JOHN'S, 1547. Will proved (V.C.C.) 1558.

GOGNEY, JOHN. B.Can.L. 1478-9.

GOGNEY, SIMON. Matric. pens. from TRINITY HALL, Easter, 1553.

GOGNEY, THOMAS. B.A. 1483-4; M.A. 1487. Proctor, 1495-6.

GOGOYN or GOGYN, ——. B.A. 1493-4; M.A. 1497.

GOLBORNE or GOLDISBORNE (? GOLDSBOROUGH), THOMAS. Adm. at KING'S (age 16) a scholar from Eton, Aug. 30, 1527. Of Bolton, Yorks. B.A. 1530-1.

GOLD, *see* GOULD.

GOLDBORN, *see* GOULBORNE.

GOLDEN, ROBERT. Matric. sizar from PEMBROKE, Lent, 1563-4.

GOLDFINCH or GOULDFINCH, THOMAS. Matric. pens. from TRINITY, Michs. 1606. Scholar from Westminster, 1607. B.A. 1610-1; M.A. 1614. Fellow, 1612. V. of Marsworth, Bucks., till 1630.

GOLDFINCH, WILLIAM. Adm. pens. (age 16) at TRINITY, June 22, 1719. S. of William, lawyer, of Wells, Somerset. School, Taunton (Mr Upton). Matric. 1719.

GOLDHAM or GOLDUM, THOMAS. Adm. sizar at EMMANUEL, Easter, 1640. Matric. 1640; B.A. 1643-4; M.A. 1647. Perhaps V. of Burwash, Sussex, till 1662, ejected. (*Calamy*, II. 459.)

GOULDHAM, THOMAS. Adm. sizar at ST CATHARINE'S, Apr. 9, 1669. Matric. 1669.

GOLDING, AMBROSE. Matric. sizar from TRINITY, Michs. 1573. Ord. deacon (Peterb.) Sept. 21, 1576; priest, Feb. 27, 1576-7. Minor canon of St Paul's, 1582; sub-dean, 1604-6. R. of St Gregory-by-St Paul's, 1591-1606. Buried there Nov. 29, 1606. Will, P.C.C. (J. Ch. Smith.)

GOLDING, AMBROSE. Adm. sizar at PEMBROKE, 1627. Of Suffolk. Matric. 1627; B.A. 1630-1; M.A. 1634. Ord. deacon (Norwich) Sept. 22; priest, Dec. 22, 1633.

GOLDING, ARTHUR. Matric. Fell.-Com. from JESUS, Easter, 1552. S. of John, of Belchamp St Paul, Essex. B. *c.* 1536. A member of the Elizabethan Society of Antiquaries. A friend of Sir Philip Sidney, whose translation of De Mornay's *Truth of Christianity* he completed in 1589. Died (?) 1605. (*Cooper*, II. 431; *D.N.B.*; *Vis. of Essex*, 1558.)

GOLDING or GOLDEN, BARTHOLOMEW. Adm. sizar at EMMANUEL, June 23, 1614. Matric. 1614; B.A. 1617-8; M.A. 1621. Ord. deacon (Norwich) Dec. 19, 1619. Probably V. of Ilketshall, Suffolk, *c.* 1626. Sequestered to South Elmham St Peter, Suffolk, 1645.

GOLDING, EDMUND. Matric. Fell.-Com. from PETERHOUSE, Michs. 1564. Perhaps s. of John, of Halstead, Essex. B.A. 1565-6; M.A. 1569. Ord. deacon (Ely) May 26, 1566; priest, Mar. 23, 1566-7. R. of Gt Dunham, Norfolk, 1566-72. R. of Birdbrook, Essex, 1571. Will proved (P.C.C.) 1572. Half-brother of Arthur. (*Vis. of Essex*, 1558.)

GOLDYNGE, EDWARD. Matric. sizar from GONVILLE HALL, Easter, 1548.

GOLDING, EDWARD. Matric. pens. from PEMBROKE, Easter, 1613; B.A. 1615-6; M.A. 1619. Ord. deacon and priest (Peterb.) Feb. 25, 1620-1. Incorp. at Oxford, 1621.

GOLDING, EDWARD. M.A. from JESUS, 1750. Doubtless s. of George, of Middlesex. Matric. from St John's College, Oxford, May 15, 1732, age 17; B.A. (New College) 1736, as 'Goldwin.' (*Al. Oxon.*)

GOLDING, GEORGE. Adm. pens. (age 16) at ST JOHN'S, Sept. 26, 1687. S. of Thomas (1652), gent. B. at Poslingford, Suffolk. School, Bury. Matric. 1688. Adm. at the Inner Temple, Jan. 29, 1690-1. Succeeded his father at Poslingford, 1702. Married Anne, dau. of William Colmore. Died May, 1739. Brother of Thomas (1675). (Davy, *Suff. MSS.*)

GOLDING, HENRY. Matric. pens. from ST JOHN'S, Michs. 1567; B.A. 1571-2. One of these names adm. at Gray's Inn, 1573.

GOLDING, HENRY. Adm. pens. at CORPUS CHRISTI, 1571. Matric. Michs. 1572; B.A. 1575-6; M.A. 1579. Perhaps ord. priest (Norwich) Jan. 25, 1579-80. V. of Carlton St Mary, 1579. Died June 2, 1628. Buried at Carlton.

GOLDING, HENRY. Matric. sizar from QUEENS', Easter, 1613. B. in St Leonard's parish, Colchester. B.A. 1616-7; M.A. 1620. Ord. deacon (London) May 23, 1619, age 23. C. of Copford, Essex. V. of Marks Tey, 1633.

GOLDING, JOHN. B.A. 1479-80; M.A. 1484-5.

GOULDING, JOHN. Matric. pens. from CORPUS CHRISTI, Easter, 1587.

GOLDING, JOHN. Adm. sizar at EMMANUEL, Feb. 20, 1609-10. Matric. 1610; Scholar; B.A. 1613-4.

GOLDING, MICHAEL. B.Can.L. 1483-4.

GOULDING, PETER. Adm. pens. at QUEENS', Dec. 4, 1647. Of Middlesex.

GOULDING, RICHARD. Matric. pens. from ST JOHN'S, Easter, 1606; B.A. 1609-10; M.A. 1613.

GOLDING, RICHARD. Matric. sizar from QUEENS', Easter, 1632. Of Suffolk. B.A. 1635-6; M.A. 1639. Perhaps P.C. of Little Maplestead, Essex, 1646-64-. R. of Middleton, 1650-7.

GOULDING, ROBERT. Matric. sizar from GONVILLE HALL, Easter, 1548.

GOLDING, ROBERT. Matric. pens. from CHRIST'S, Michs. 1549; B.A. 1554-5. One of these names adm. at the Inner Temple, 1556. Bencher and reader.

GOULDING, ROBERT. Matric. pens. from QUEENS', Easter, 1575.

GOLDING, ROBERT. Matric. pens. from CLARE, Michs. 1602; B.A. 1606; M.A. 1610. Ord. deacon (Lincoln) May 19, 1611. V. of Wigtoft, Lincs., 1612-5.

GOLDNYGE, ROGER. Adm. at KING'S (age 17) a scholar from Eton, Aug. 24, 1571. Of Cavendish, Suffolk. Fellow, 1574. No degree recorded. Will (P.C.C.) 1610, of one of these names, of Clare, Suffolk, gent.

GOLDING, THOMAS. Matric. pens. from GONVILLE HALL, Easter, 1551. One of these names adm. at the Middle Temple, Nov. 15, 1559; s. of Richard, of Henny, Essex.

GOLDING, THOMAS. Matric. pens. from JESUS, Michs. 1554.

GOLDING, THOMAS. Adm. Fell.-Com. at CAIUS, Apr. 15, 1652. Eldest s. of Thomas, Esq., of Poslingford, Suffolk. B. at Darsham. School, Yoxford (Mr Eacher). Matric. 1652. Adm. at Lincoln's Inn, May 18, 1653. Of Poslingford, Esq. Buried Aug. 11, 1702, at Poslingford. M.I. Father of Thomas (1675) and George (1687). (*Venn*, I. 384.)

GOLDING, THOMAS. Adm. sizar at CORPUS CHRISTI, 1671. Of Norfolk. Matric. 1672; B.A. 1674-5; M.A. 1679. Ord. deacon (Norwich) Feb. 1675-6; priest, Dec. 1677.

GOLDING, THOMAS. Adm. pens. (age 15) at ST JOHN'S, June 8, 1675. S. of Thomas (1652), gent., of Poslingford, Suffolk. B. there. School, Bradley. Matric. 1675. Buried at Poslingford, Sept. 7, 1676. M.I. Brother of George (1687).

GOULDING, THOMAS. Adm. sizar (age 18) at MAGDALENE, Apr. 19, 1697. S. of Thomas, doctor (medicus). B. at Askrigg, Yorks. School, Richmond, Yorks. Matric. 1698; B.A. 1700-1.

GOLDING or GOLDWIN, WILLIAM. Adm. at KING'S (age 18) a scholar from Eton, Aug. 16, 1515. Of Windsor. B.A. 1519-20; M.A. 1522-3. Fellow, 1518-25. Master of Cardinal Wolsey's School, Ipswich. Fellow of Eton, *c.* 1540.

GOLDING, WILLIAM. Scholar of GONVILLE HALL, 1540; B.A. 1544-5; M.A. 1548. Fellow of Trinity Hall, in 1557. Proctor, 1557-8. Fellow of Gonville Hall, 1559. Preb. of Hereford, 1548-60. Ord. deacon (Norwich) Mar. 1554-5; priest (London) Apr. 1558. Will (Norwich) 1579; 'of Fakenham, Norfolk.' (*Venn*, I. 31; *Cooper*, I. 421.)

GOLDING, W. Matric. sizar from TRINITY, Michs. 1582. One William Golding, V. of St Andrew's, Ilketshall, Suffolk, 1593.

GOLDING, WILLIAM. Adm. sizar at EMMANUEL, Easter, 1626. Matric. 1626; B.A. 1629-30; M.A. 1633.

GOULDING, ——. Fell.-Com. at PETERHOUSE, 1560.

GOLDINGHAM, ANTHONY. Matric. pens. from GONVILLE HALL, Easter, 1551. No B.A. M.A. 1562. 'In priest's orders; had studied 10 years at Cambridge and abroad.' (Gr. *Bk*, Δ, 154.) Probably V. of Little Belstead, Suffolk, 1561-3. Certified as a fugitive abroad, 1576; a recusant. (*Venn*, I. 36.)

GOLDINGHAM, CHRISTOPHER. Matric. pens. from TRINITY HALL, Easter, 1575; B.A. from Magdalene, 1577-8. One of these names, s. of John, of Banham, Norfolk, V. of Tolleshunt Major, Essex, 1579-81. R. of Tendring, 1580-3. Died 1583. (*Vis. of Norfolk.*)

GOULDINGHAM, EDWARD. Scholar of TRINITY, 1601; B.A. 1605-6; M.A. 1609. Fellow, 1608. Will proved (V.C.C.) 1614.

GOLDINGHAM, FRANCIS. Matric. pens. from GONVILLE HALL, Easter, 1544. Perhaps s. of John, of Banham, Norfolk. Ord. deacon and priest (Ely) Sept. 1575, as 'of Northborough, Norfolk, aged 46.' Doubtless V. of Narborough, Norfolk, 1577. Buried there Sept. 10, 1607. (*Venn*, I. 33.)

GOLDINGHAM, JOHN. Adm. at KING'S (age 18) a scholar from Eton, Aug. 13, 1542. Of Belstead, Suffolk. Matric. 1544. Left in 1545. Perhaps R. of Finningham, Suffolk, in 1555. (*Vis. of Suffolk.*)

GOLDINGHAM, WILLIAM. Matric. Fell.-Com. from MAGDALENE, Lent, 1564-5; B.A. from Trinity Hall, 1567-8; M.A. 1571; LL.D. 1579. Fellow of Trinity Hall, 1571-81. Adm. advocate, June 15, 1579. Adm. at Gray's Inn, Feb. 2, 1583-4. Will (P.C.C.) 1589. (*Cooper*, II. 10.)

GOLDINGHAM, WILLIAM. Matric. pens. from QUEENS', Easter, 1602. Of Suffolk. B.A. 1605-6; M.A. 1609. Incorp. at Oxford, 1621. Probably adm. at Gray's Inn, May 11, 1609, as 'of Dedham, Essex, gent.' Barrister-at-law, 1617. Doubtless father of the next.

GOLDINGHAM, WILLIAM. Adm. at EMMANUEL, May 28, 1651. Of Essex. Doubtless s. of William (above), of Gray's Inn; adm. at Gray's Inn, Feb. 1, 1646-7.

GOULDINGHAM, ——. Matric. Fell.-Com. from PETERHOUSE, Michs. 1602.

GOLDKNOPPE or GOODKNAPPE, THOMAS. B.A. 1493; M.A. 1496. R. of Alphamstone, Essex, 1511-29. Died 1529.

GOLDMAN or GOULDMAN, FRANCIS. Adm. pens. at CHRIST'S, Apr. 26, 1623. S. of Richard (*sic*), of Norfolk. School, London (private). Matric. 1623; B.A. 1626-7; M.A. 1630. R. of South Ockendon, Essex, 1634 (succeeding George (1582) Gouldman whom *D.N.B.* wrongly makes his father); sequestered, 1644; and 1660-88. Compiled an English-Latin and Latin-English Dictionary. Died 1688. Will, P.C.C. (*Peile*, I. 350; *D.N.B.*)

GOULDMAN, GEORGE. Adm. pens. (age 16) at CAIUS, July 2, 1582. S. of Robert, citizen of Norwich. Bapt. at St Peter Mancroft, Jan. 28, 1565–6. School, Norwich. Matric. 1582; Scholar of Caius, 1582–9; B.A. 1585–6; M.A. 1589; B.D. from St John's, 1597; D.D. 1608. Fellow of St John's, 1590. R. of Patching, Sussex, to 1605. V. of Stepney, 1605–33. Archdeacon of Essex, 1609–33. R. of South Ockendon, Essex, 1611–33. Died Jan. 1, 1633–4. Will, P.C.C. (*Venn*, I. 114.)

'GOLDREN,' FRANCIS, *see* GOLDWELL, FRANCIS (1639).

GOLDSBOROW, ANTHONY. Adm. at KING'S, a scholar from Eton, 1493; B.A. 1496–7; M.A. 1500–1. Fellow, till *c.* 1506. Ord. deacon (Ely) June 9, 1498; priest, Mar. 13, 1499–1500.

GOLDSBOROUGH, CHARLES. Adm. sizar (age 17) at PEMBROKE, Sept. 14, 1716. S. of Thomas, of Chipping Ongar, Essex, Esq. Bapt. there, Apr. 16, 1700. B.A. 1720–1.

GOULDSBOROUGH, EDWARD. Scholar of TRINITY, 1602; B.A. 1603–4; M.A. 1607.

GOLDSBOROUGH, GODFREY. Matric. pens. from TRINITY, Michs. 1560. S. of John, of Goldsborough, Yorks. B. in Cambridgeshire. Scholar, 1562; B.A. 1565–6; M.A. 1569; B.D. 1577; D.D. 1583. Fellow, 1567. Incorp. at Oxford, 1579. Archdeacon of Worcester, 1579–98; of Salop, 1580. Preb. of Hereford, 1580; of Worcester, 1581; and of St Paul's, 1581–98. R. of Stockton, Salop, 1580–98. Bishop of Gloucester, 1598–1604. Died May 26, 1604. Buried in Gloucester Cathedral. M.I. there. Will (P.C.C.) 1604. (*Cooper*, II. 388; *D.N.B.*; *Vis. of Yorks.*, 1585.)

GOLDESBURGE, JOHN. Matric. pens. from CHRIST'S, Michs. 1611. Probably s. of John, one of the Protonotaries of the King's Bench (*q.v. D.N.B.*). Adm. at the Middle Temple, Mar. 11, 1613–4. (*Peile*, I. 284.)

GOLDISBOROUGH, NICHOLAS. Matric. pens. from QUEENS', Easter, 1571; B.A. 1573–4; M.A. 1577; B.D. 1595, as 'Glosborow.' Incorp. at Oxford, 1578. Ord. deacon (Peterb.) Sept. 28, 1577. Sacrist of Corpus Christi, Oxford. Head Master of King's School, Canterbury, 1580–4. R. of Norton, Kent, 1581–1610. V. of Linsted, 1585–9. R. of Knowlton, 1589. R. of Buckland, 1592–1610. Buried Sept. 26, 1610.

GOLDSBOROUGH, THOMAS. Matric. pens. from ST JOHN'S, Lent, 1563–4; B.A. 1567–8, as Goldisborowe. Doubtless of Little Shelford, Cambs. Married Alice, dau. of Thomas Pythen (?), of Trumpington. Will (P.C.C.) 1598. Father of the next.

GOLDSBOROW, THOMAS. Adm. pens. at QUEENS', May 16, 1595. Of Cambridgeshire. Adm. at Gray's Inn, Mar. 21, 1605–6; 'late of Little Shelford, Cambs., from Barnard's Inn.'

GOLDSBOROUGH, ——. D. (Div. or L.) *c.* 1462. A friar.

GOULDSMYTHE, CHARLES. Adm. pens. (age 16) at PEMBROKE, Sept. 9, 1619. S. of Henry, of Norfolk. Matric. 1619; M.B. 1627. Adm. at Gray's Inn, Nov. 1, 1618; 's. and h. of Henry, of Gray's Inn.' Probably will (P.C.C.) 1656; of St Andrew's, Holborn, M.D. Father of the next and Mathias (1654–5).

GOLDSMITH, CHARLES. Adm. pens. (age 18) at PEMBROKE, Feb. 27, 1654–5. S. of Charles (above), M.B., 'sometime fellow.' B. in Middlesex. Matric. 1656–7; B.A. 1658–9. Brother of Mathias (1654–5).

GOULDSMITH, DANIEL. Matric. sizar from TRINITY, Michs. 1627. S. of William (1599), R. of Campton, Beds. Bapt. there, Feb. 8, 1612–3. Scholar, 1631; B.A. 1631–2; M.A. 1635. V. of Gt Barford, Beds., 1635–40. R. of Wootton, Northants., 1665–7. R. of Campton, Beds., 1667. Buried there Oct. 2, 1685. Will (Bediord) 1685. (H. I. Longden.)

GOLDSMITH, FRANCIS. Scholar of CHRIST'S, 1532–3; B.A. 1534–5; M.A. 1538–9. Fellow of Peterhouse, 1536, till 1543.

GOLDSMITH, GEORGE. Matric. pens. from QUEENS', Michs. 1588. Of Suffolk. B.A. (? 1591–2); M.A. 1595. R. of Carlton and Willingham, Cambs., 1597–1610. Perhaps licensed, May 31, 1597, to marry Hester, dau. of Wm Fulke, D.D. Will (P.C.C.) 1610; parson of Carlton, Cambs. (J. Ch. Smith.)

GOLDSMITH, GEORGE. Adm. pens. (age 15) at SIDNEY, Dec. 27, 1623. S. of Thomas, gent., deceased. B. at Wrexham. School, Whitechurch, Salop. Matric. 1623–4; B.A. 1627–8.

GOLDSMITH, JOHN. Adm. at KING'S, a scholar from Eton, 1444. Of Exton, Hants., M.A. Died in College. (*Harwood*.)

GOLDSMITH, JOHN. B.A. from TRINITY, 1620–1. V. of Reydon and Southwold, Suffolk, 1627–45. Probably V. of Westhall, Dec. 4, 1647. (*Shaw*, I. 348.)

GOLDSMITH, MATHIAS. Adm. pens. (age 17) at PEMBROKE, Feb. 27, 1654–5. S. of Charles (1619), M.B., 'sometime fellow.' B. in Middlesex. Matric. 1656–7; B.A. 1658–9; M.A. 1662. Brother of Charles (1654–5).

GOLDSMITH, THOMAS. Adm. pens. at EMMANUEL, Easter, 1623. Matric. 1623.

GOLDSMITH, WILLIAM. Scholar of TRINITY, 1599; B.A. 1599–1600; M.A. 1603. Fellow, 1602. Ord. deacon and priest (Lincoln) Jan. 22, 1603–4. R. of Campton, Beds., 1603. Buried there Jan. 14, 1666–7. Father of Daniel (1627).

GOLDSMITH, ——. M.A. 1499–1500.

GOULDSMITH, ——. Matric. Fell.-Com. from TRINITY, Easter, 1626.

GOLDSTON, *see also* GOULDSTONE *and* GULSTON.

GOLDSTONE or GOULDESTONE, HUGH. Adm. pens. (age 17) at SIDNEY, July 10, 1635. S. of German (next), deceased. B. at Stoke Damarell, Devon. Schools, Stoke Damarell (Mr Atkins), Awtrey (Mr Beirou) and Maristow (Mr Williams).

GOULSTON, JERMAN or GERMAN. Adm. pens. at CHRIST'S, Jan. 1580–1. Of Devon. B.A. 1584–5; M.A. from Magdalene, 1588. R. of Stoke Damarell, Devon, in 1594. Will (Exeter) 1623. Father of the above. (*Peile*, I. 161; *Cooper*, II. 40.)

GOLDSTON, JOHN. Matric. sizar from PETERHOUSE, 1544.

GOLSTONE, RAPHAEL. Matric. pens. from PETERHOUSE, Michs. 1570. S. of Gabriel Colston (*sic*), of London, grocer. Adm. at Gray's Inn, 1573. (*Vis. of London*, 1568.)

GOLDSTON or GOLDSON, ROBERT. B.A. 1525–6 (1st in the *ordo*); M.A. 1529. Fellow of PETERHOUSE, 1526. Ord. deacon (Lincoln) June 6; priest, Sept. 19, 1528 (*see Gr. Bk*, A, 223). V. of Higham Ferrers, 1534. Preb. of Canterbury, 1544–54. (*T. A. Walker*.)

GOLDSTONE, THOMAS. Matric. sizar from QUEENS', Michs. 1646; B.A. 1650–1; M.A. 1654. R. of Finchley, Middlesex, 1657; ejected, 1662. (*Calamy*, II. 172.)

GOLDSTON, WILLIAM. B.A. Fellow of PETERHOUSE, 1400.

GOLDSWORTH (*alias* PORTER), THOMAS. Adm. pens. (age 18) at CAIUS, Oct. 7, 1631. S. of Thomas, gent., of Bungay, Suffolk. B. at Thurton, Norfolk. School, Bungay (Mr Smith). Matric. 1631. Living at Thurton in 1661. (*Venn*, I. 302.)

GOLDWELL, CHARLES. Matric. pens. from QUEENS', Easter, 1606. Of Hampshire. B.A. 1610–1; M.A. 1614. Ord. deacon (Peterb.) Apr. 16; priest, Apr. 21, 1611.

GOLDWELL, FRANCIS. Adm. sizar at EMMANUEL, July 2, 1639. Of Middlesex. Matric. 1639, as 'Goldren.' Probably ord. priest (Lincoln) Feb. 8, 1660–1. Doubtless R. of Bridgham St Mary, Norfolk, 1663–91; and R. of Upwell and Outwell, 1666–91.

GOLDWELL, FRANCIS. Adm. sizar (age 17) at ST JOHN'S, May 8, 1674. S. of Francis (? above), clerk, of Stoke, Norfolk. B. there. School, Thetford. Matric. 1674; B.A. 1677–8.

GOLDWELL, J. Resident pens. at JESUS, Aug. 1564.

GOLDWELL, JAMES. LL.D. 1462 (Incorp. from Oxford). Of All Souls, Oxford. B.C.L. 1449; D.C.L. 1452. R. of St John, Watling St, London, 1455–6. R. of Rivenhall, Essex, 1456. Preb. of St Paul's, 1457–61. Canon of Windsor, 1458–60. Preb. of Hereford, 1461–4. Archdeacon of Essex, 1461–72. Dean of Salisbury, 1463–72. R. of Charing, Kent, to which he was a benefactor. Secretary of State under Edward IV. Negotiated peace with France, 1471. Master of the Rolls, 1472. Bishop of Norwich, 1472–99, where he completed the tower, etc. Benefactor of All Souls, Oxford, and Gonville Hall. M.I. in Norwich Cathedral. Will (P.C.C.) 1499. (*D.N.B.*; *Weever*, 795.)

GOLDWELL, JOHN. B.A. 1537–8; M.A. 1541. Fellow of QUEENS', 1538–42. One of these names adm. at Gray's Inn, 1543.

GOLDWELL, JOHN. Matric. pens. from ST JOHN'S, Easter, 1544; B.A. 1544–5. Nominated an original fellow of Trinity, 1546, but doubtful if he accepted nomination.

GOLDWELL, JOHN. Matric. Fell.-Com. from QUEENS', 1567.

GOLDWELL, NICHOLAS. Grace for degree (? M.A.) 1479–80; 'had studied at Oxford.' Ord. deacon (Norwich) Mar. 27; priest, Sept. 18, 1479. R. of St Mary, Gt Massingham, Norfolk, 1475–8. R. of Worlingworth, Suffolk (as sub-deacon). Archdeacon of Sudbury, 1479. Vicar-general, 1482–3. Archdeacon of Norwich, 1483–97. Archdeacon of Suffolk, 1497–1505. Will proved (P.C.C.) 1505; of Blofield, Norfolk.

GOLDWELL, RICHARD. B.A. from CLARE, Feb. 10, 1645–6. S. of James, of Rochester. Matric. 1645–6. Previously matric. from University College, Oxford, May 13, 1640, age 16: 'Gunsley scholar; expelled for non-appearance, 1648.' (*Al. Oxon.*)

GOLDWELL, THOMAS. Adm. at KING'S, a scholar from Eton, 1449. Of Bodicote, Oxon.

GOLDWELL, THOMAS. Matric. pens. from TRINITY, Michs. 1559. One of these names adm. at Gray's Inn, 1563.

GOLDWELL, WILLIAM. Matric. pens. from QUEENS', Easter, 1616. (Coldwell in College register.)

GOLDWIN, WILLIAM. Perhaps of KING'S HALL, 1479–80. Incorp. M.D. 1479–80, from Oxford. Doubtless of St Thomas Acon and St Stephen Walbrook, 'bachelor of physic'; will proved (P.C.C.) 1482. Leaves bequests to All Souls, Oxford.

GOLDWIN, WILLIAM (1515), see GOLDING.

GOLDWIN, WILLIAM. Adm. at KING'S, a scholar from Eton, 1700. B. at Windsor. Matric. Michs. 1700; B.A. 1704–5; M.A. 1708. Fellow, 1703. Ord. deacon (London) May 19, 1706; priest, May 30, 1708. Master of the Grammar School at Bristol, 1710–7. V. of St Nicholas, Bristol, 1717–47. Fellow of Eton College, 1733–47. Author, sermons. Died June 1, 1747. (*Harwood*; F. S. Hockaday.)

GOLDWYER, GEORGE. Adm. pens. (age 18) at ST JOHN'S, May 30, 1749. S. of George, surgeon, of Wiltshire. B. at Marlborough. School, Marlborough (Mr Stone). B.A. 1753. Ord. deacon (London) Mar. 18, 1752; priest (Lincoln, *Litt. dim.* from Sarum) Feb. 23, 1755. V. of Letcombe Regis, Berks., 1761–83. Perhaps the 'Rev. Mr Goldwyer famous for his surgical knowledge' (*G. Mag.*) who died at Hatton St, London, May 31, 1783. (*Scott-Mayor*, III. 589.)

GOLDWYRE, HENRY. Adm. pens. at TRINITY, Apr. 3, 1656. One of these names V. of Christchurch, Hants., 1673–89.

GOLDWYRE, JOHN. Adm. pens. at QUEENS', Michs. 1647. S. of John, V. of Arundel, Sussex. Migrated to Oxford. Matric. from New Inn Hall, June 20, 1651; B.A. 1651; M.A. 1654. Ejected from Felpham, Sussex, 1662. Afterwards lived at Romsey, Hants. Died Dec. 9, 1713, aged 83. (*Calamy*, II. 462; *Al. Oxon.*)

GOLDWYER, ROGER. Adm. pens. at EMMANUEL, Easter, 1628. Matric. Michs. 1628.

GOLLAND, ROBERT. Adm. pens. at EMMANUEL, July 2, 1614; B.A. 1617–8. Ord. deacon (York) Dec. 1619.

GOLLIFORD, ROBERT. B.A. from ST JOHN'S, 1576–7. One of these names, of Holy Trinity, Gloucester, preb. of Bristol, 1596–1613. Will, P.C.C.

GOLLOP, HENRY. Adm. pens. at CLARE, June 22, 1705. S. of Henry, of Barbados. Matric. 1705. Adm. at the Inner Temple, May 17, 1708.

GOLSYLL, ——. Probably B.Can.L. 1470–1, as Gowsill. Fee for M.A. or higher degree, 1473–4. Perhaps Richard Golsyll, or Golfyll, R. of Carlton and Willingham, Cambs., till 1489.

GOLTY, EDWARD. Adm. pens. (age 16) at CAIUS, Apr. 17, 1607. S. of George, gent., of Aylsham, Norfolk. School, Aylsham (Mr Eston). Matric. 1607; Scholar, 1608–13; B.A. 1610–1; M.A. 1614. R. of Little Steeping, Lincs., 1618. (*Venn*, I. 195.)

GOLTEY, MILES. Matric. sizar from PEMBROKE, Easter, 1626. S. of Edmund, of Gipping, Suffolk, mercer (and Susan Collins, of Ipswich). B. at Woodbridge. Bapt. Feb. 27, 1606–7. B.A. 1629–30; M.A. 1633. Ord. priest (Norwich) Sept. 20, 1640. V. of Felixstowe and Walton, Suffolk, 1639–44, ejected.

GOLTY, RICHARD. Matric. pens. from PEMBROKE, Easter, 1613. S. of Edmund, of Ipswich. B.A. 1615–6; M.A. 1619. R. of Framlingham, Suffolk, 1626–43 and 1660–78. Married Deborah, dau. of Samuel Ward, town preacher of Ipswich. Died 1678. Father of Richard (1671).

GOLTY, RICHARD. Matric. pens. from ST CATHARINE'S, Michs. 1646; B.A. 1649–50; M.A. 1653. R. of Hutton, Essex, 1654–97. Perhaps R. of Bradwell-by-sea, 1673–97. V. of Bacon's portion, Dengie, 1680. Died 1697. Father of Samuel (1674).

GOLTY, RICHARD. Adm. pens. at ST CATHARINE'S, May 29, 1671. S. of Richard (1613), R. of Framlingham, Suffolk (and Deborah). School, Woodbridge. Matric. 1671; B.A. 1674–5; M.A. 1678. Fellow, 1676–81. Ord. deacon (Ely) Sept. 24, 1676; priest, Dec. 1679. R. of Dennington, Suffolk, until 1723. R. of Hutton, Essex. Author, *Sermon*, 1688. Buried Mar. 25, 1723. Father of Richard (1707) and Samuel (1702).

GOLTY, RICHARD. Adm. pens. (age 18) at PEMBROKE, July 1, 1707. S. of Richard (above), R. of Dennington, Suffolk. Matric. 1708; B.A. 1711–2; M.A. 1715. Ord. deacon (Norwich) May, 1713; priest, Dec. 1714. R. of Belstead, Suffolk, 1720. R. of Boyton, 1721. Brother of Samuel (1702).

GOLTY, SAMUEL. Matric. pens. from ST CATHARINE'S, Easter, 1641. Of Suffolk. B.A. 1644–5; M.A. 1648. Incorp. at Oxford, 1653. V. of Burnham, Essex, 1657. R. of Dennington, Suffolk, 1658. R. of St Clement's, Ipswich, 1662. (*Suff. Ch. Notes*.)

GOLTY, SAMUEL. Adm. pens. (age 16) at CHRIST'S, May 26, 1674. S. of Richard (1646). B. at Hutton, Essex. School, Brentwood (Mr Bernard). Matric. 1674; B.A. 1677–8. Ord. deacon (London) Dec. 21, 1679. (*Peile*, II. 52.)

GOLTY, SAMUEL. Adm. sizar at EMMANUEL, Apr. 6, 1702. 1st s. of Richard (1671), R. of Dennington, Suffolk. B. there, May 4, 1684. School, Merchant Taylors'. Matric. 1702–3; B.A. 1705–6; M.A. from Pembroke, 1709. Fellow of Pembroke, 1710. Ord. deacon (Lincoln) May 30, 1708; priest (Ely) Sept. 25, 1709. Died Dec. 8, 1718. Buried at Northfleet, Kent. M.I. there. (*Robinson*, I. 341.)

GOLTZ, GEORGE. M.A. 1619 (*fil. nob.*).

GOMAR, FRANCIS. B.A. from MAGDALENE, Mar. 2, 1582–3. A Fleming from Bruges. Had studied seven years at Strasburg, Neustadt and Oxford. Allowed the M.A. Mar. 22, 1582–3.

GOMARUS, FRANCIS. B.A. and M.A. 1624. A Fleming.

GONESSE, ——. B.Civ.L. 1483–4.

GONESTER, RICHARD. Matric. from KING'S, Michs. 1545. Conduct at King's in 1564.

GONISTON, EDWARD. B.A. from JESUS, 1603–4; M.A. 1607. V. of Seasalter, Kent, 1611. P.C. of Whitstable, in 1643.

GONNFELD, JOHN. B.A. 1511–2.

GONSON, ANTHONY. Matric. Fell.-Com. from ST JOHN'S, Michs. 1586.

GONVILLE, see also GUNNELL.

GONVILLE, EDMUND. S. of William, of Lerling, Norfolk, a Frenchman by birth. R. of Thelnetham, Suffolk, 1320–6; of Rushworth, Norfolk, 1326–43; and of Terrington, 1343–50. Steward to Earl Warren and the Earl of Lancaster. Commissary to the Bishop of Ely. Founder of the College at Rushworth, Norfolk, 1342 (suppressed in 1541) and of the Hospital of St John at Lynn. Founder of Gonville Hall, 1348. Dying (*c.* 1351) before completing his work, it was carried on by Bateman, Bishop of Norwich. (*Venn*, III. 1; *D.N.B.*)

GUNVIL, GEOFFREY. Adm. sizar at JESUS, Mar. 31, 1626. Of Norfolk. Matric. 1626; Scholar, 1629; B.A. 1629–30; M.A. 1633. Ord. deacon (Norwich) Mar. 2, 1633–4. Probably R. of West Walton, Norfolk, *c.* 1636. Father of Thomas (1653).

GONEVILE or GUNNELL, NICHOLAS. Adm. sizar (age 18) at CAIUS, Mar. 27, 1611. S. of Robert, of Worstead, Norfolk. School, Norwich (Mr Briggs). B.A. 1614–5; M.A. 1618. Incorp. at Oxford, 1627. Ord. priest (Norwich) Dec. 24, 1615. C. of South Repps, Norfolk, in 1617. Licensed to preach by Archbishop of Canterbury, 1619. C. of Brumstead, in 1639. Married, at Horstead, Norfolk, July 19, 1621, Jane Bert. (*Venn*, I. 210.)

GONVILE, THOMAS. Adm. pens. (age 17) at CAIUS, May 24, 1653. S. of Geoffrey (1626), clerk. B. at Walton, Norfolk. Schools, Horncastle, Withern, Lincs. and Lynn. Matric. 1653; Scholar, 1653–7; B.A. 1656–7; M.A. 1660. Perhaps of West Walton, in 1707. (*Venn*, I. 388.)

GONELL or GUNNELL (*senior*). Doubtless WILLIAM. Pens. at GONVILLE HALL, 1531–6; B.A. 1484–5; M.A. 1488. Of Landbeach, Cambs. The friend of Erasmus. Of the household of Cardinal Wolsey. Tutor to the family of Sir Thomas More. R. of Conington, Hunts., 1517–44. Author. Died *c.* 1546. (*Cooper*, I. 94; *D.N.B.*; *Venn*, I. 28.)

GONELL or GUNNELL, WILLIAM (*junior*). Pens. at GONVILLE HALL, 1533–6. Probably same as the next.

GONELL, WILLIAM. Matric. Fell.-Com. from GONVILLE HALL, Michs. 1546. Will proved (P.C.C.) 1560. (*Venn*, I. 34.)

GOOCHE or GOOGE, BARNABE. Matric. pens. from CHRIST'S, May, 1555. B. at Alvingham, Lincs., *c.* 1540. S. of Robert, recorder of Lincoln. Migrated to New College, Oxford. Removed thence to Staple Inn. A kinsman and retainer of of Sir William Cecil, who employed him in Ireland. Appointed Provost Marshal of the Presidency Court of Connaught, 1582–5. Of Lamberhurst, Kent. Poet and scholar. His works include a translation of Heresbach's *Four Books of Husbandrie*. Died Feb. 1593–4. Father of Barnabas (1582) and Henry (1596). (*Peile*, I. 56; *D.N.B.*)

GOCHE, BARNABAS. Matric. pens. from MAGDALENE, Michs. 1582. S. of Barnaby (above). B. at Alvingham, Lincs. B.A. 1586–7; M.A. 1590; LL.D. 1604. Master of Magdalene, 1604–26. Vice-Chancellor, 1611–2. Commissary of the University, 1615–25. Incorp. at Oxford, 1605. Adm. advocate, Feb. 4, 1612–3. M.P. for the University, 1620–2, 1624–5. Elected also for Truro, 1620. Chancellor of Worcester and Exeter. Benefactor to Magdalene. Died at Exeter, *c.* 1626. Will proved (V.C.C. and P.C.C.) 1626. Father of John (1611), brother of Henry (1596). (*Lincs. Pedigrees*, 408; *Magdalene Coll. Hist.*, 93.)

GOCHE, BARNABIE. Matric. pens. from MAGDALENE, Easter, 1624. Perhaps s. of Thomas. B.A. 1627–8; M.A. 1631. (*Lincs. Pedigrees*, 409.)

GOCHE, BARNABY. Adm. pens. (age 16) at PETERHOUSE, Nov. 20, 1693. Of Bedfordshire. School, Biggleswade. Scholar, 1693-4; Matric. 1694; B.A. 1697-8. Ord. deacon (London) June 19, 1698. R. of Croyland, Lincs., 1724-30. Buried there Oct. 24, 1730.

GOOCH, BENJAMIN. Adm. sizar (age 16) at CAIUS, Jan. 8, 1685-6. S. of Henry, husbandman, of Wreningham, Norfolk. B. there. School, Norwich. Matric. 1686; Scholar, 1686-90; B.A. 1689-90. Ord. priest (Norwich) May 22, 1692. R. of Ashwelthorpe, Norfolk, 1693-1728. Died Mar. 25, 1728. M.I. at Carlton Forehoe. Will (Norwich C.C.) 1728. (*Venn*, I. 480.)

GOOCH or GOOGE, HENRY. Matric. pens. from TRINITY, c. 1596. S. of Barnabe (1555). B. at Lamberhurst, Kent. Scholar, 1599; B.A. 1600-1; M.A. 1604; B.D. 1620; D.D. 1627 (*Lit. Reg.*). Fellow, 1602. Senior proctor, 1618. Ord. deacon and priest (London) Mar. 4, 1609-10, age 26. Minister of Longstanton St Michael, Cambs., 1616-26. Travelled with Sir Dodmore Cotton, on an embassy to Persia, by the Cape. Buried him at Kasbin and returned by the same route in 1629. R. of Cheadle, Staffs., 1630-45, sequestered. Died before 1660. Brother of Barnabas (1582). (Herbert, *Oriental Travels*.)

GOOCH, HENRY. Adm. pens. at EMMANUEL, May 30, 1657. Of Norfolk. Matric. 1658; B.A. 1660-1; M.A. 1668. (Compare the next.)

GOUCHE, HENRY. Adm. sizar at CORPUS CHRISTI, 1666. Of Norfolk. Probably s. of Thomas (1627). Bapt. at Hoo, Norfolk, Dec. 4, 1647. Matric. 1667-8; B.A. 1669-70. V. of Happisburgh, Norfolk, 1670-87. Perhaps R. of Crostwick, 1674-87. (*Carthew*, II. 702.)

GOOGE, JOHN. Adm. at KING'S (age 17) a scholar from Eton, Aug. 12, 1528. Of Earith, Hunts. B.A. 1532-3, as 'Gugge.' Fellow, 1531-5.

GOCHE, JOHN. Matric. sizar from TRINITY, Easter, 1578, as Googe; Scholar, 1582; B.A. 1582-3; M.A. 1585.

GOOCHE, JOHN. Matric. pens. from MAGDALENE, Easter, 1611. S. of Barnabas (1582), Master of Magdalene. B.A. 1614; M.A. 1618. Fellow, 1615. Ord. deacon and priest (Lincoln) Feb. 21, 1618-9.

GOOCHE, JOHN. Matric. pens. from MAGDALENE, Easter, 1623. Perhaps 2nd s. of Matthew, of Alvingham, Lincs. B.A. 1626-7; M.A. 1630. Ord. deacon (York) May, 1627; priest, Sept. 1627. R. of Longstanton St Michael, Cambs., 1631-50. (*Lincs. Pedigrees*.)

GOCHE, JOHN. Matric. sizar from TRINITY HALL, Michs. 1624.

GOOCHE, JOHN. Adm. pens. (age 17) at CHRIST'S, Oct. 14, 1628. S. of John. B. at Norwich. School, Eton. Matric. 1628.

GOUGE, JOHN. B.A. from PEMBROKE, 1650-1.

GOOCH, JOHN. Adm. pens. at ST CATHARINE'S, June 12, 1667.

GOOCH, JOHN. Adm. pens. (age 16) at CAIUS, May 5, 1746. S. of Thomas (1691), Bishop of Norwich. B. in Cambridge. School, Bury. Matric. 1746; Scholar, 1746-50; B.A. 1749-50; M.A. 1753; D.D. from Christ's, 1765. Fellow of Caius, 1750-1. Ord. deacon (Ely) Feb. 23, 1752; priest, Aug. 24, 1753. Sequestrator of Fen Ditton, 1753. R. of Willingham, 1753. Preb. of Ely, 1753-1804. Died at the Palace, Wells (the Bishop, Dr Beadon, was his son-in-law) Jan. 7, 1804. M.I. there. Brother of Thomas (1737). (*Venn*, II. 58; *Peile*, II. 250.)

GOOCH or GOUGE, LEONARD. Adm. pens. (age 17) at CHRIST'S, Mar. 11, 1645-6. S. of Robert, of Earsham, near Bungay. B. at Yarmouth. Bapt. there, Dec. 17, 1627. School, Bungay (Mr Creed). Adm. at Gray's Inn, June 1, 1647. Married Dorothy, dau. of Richard Catlyn, of Kirby Cane, Norfolk. Died Jan. 10, 1686-7. Buried at Earsham. M.I. there. Brother of Robert (1645-6). (*Peile*, I. 503; Davy, *Suff. MSS.*)

GOCH, MATHIAS. Matric. pens. from MAGDALENE, Easter, 1640; B.A. 1644-5.

GOOCH, MATTHEW. Adm. sizar at QUEENS', Aug. 12, 1659. Matric. 1660. Migrated to Trinity, Mar. 15, 1660-1.

GOOCH, NATHANIEL. Matric. pens. from MAGDALENE, Easter, 1607. Ord. deacon (Peterb.) June 7; priest, Sept. 20, 1612. V. of Twyford, Leics., 1630.

GOOGE, NICHOLAS. Adm. pens. at KING'S, c. 1627; B.A. from St Catharine's, 1629-30; M.A. from King's, 1633; M.D. 1645.

GOUGE, NICHOLAS. Adm. pens. at ST CATHARINE'S, Mar. 16, 1669-70; B.A. 1673-4; M.A. 1677; D.D. 1692. Fellow, 1674. R. of Coton, Cambs. R. of Westley Waterless, 1681. R. of Boddington, Northants., 1691-4. V. of St Martin-in-the-Fields, London, 1694. Admon. (P.C.C.) Dec. 1694. (H. I. Longden.)

GOUGE, NICHOLAS. Adm. pens. at ST CATHARINE'S, May 16, 1702. Matric. 1702; B.A. 1705-6; M.A. 1709; D.D. 1732. Fellow, 1710. V. of Gilling, Yorks., 1715-55. Preb. of York, 1722. Preb. of Lincoln, 1746. Died Oct. 15, 1755. Will, P.C.C. (G. *Mag.*)

GOOCH, PHILIP. Matric. sizar from ST JOHN'S, Easter, 1577; B.A. 1580-1. Ord. priest (Norwich) Oct. 20, 1583. V. of Walsham-le-Willows, Suffolk. Licensed to teach grammar.

GOCHE, ROBERT. Matric. Fell.-Com. from QUEENS', Michs. 1573. Of Nottinghamshire.

GOOCH, ROBERT. Adm. sizar at EMMANUEL, June 19, 1616. Matric. 1618; B.A. 1619-20.

GOOCH or GOUGE, ROBERT. Adm. pens. (age 16) at CHRIST'S, Mar. 11, 1645-6. S. of Robert, of Earsham, near Bungay. B. at Yarmouth. Bapt. at Yarmouth, Dec. 21, 1628. School, Bungay (Mr Creed). Matric. 1647. Adm. at Gray's Inn, June 1, 1647. Of Earsham. Died Sept. 29, 1704. M.I. at Earsham. Will (Norwich C.C.) 1704. Brother of Leonard (1645-6). (*Peile*, I. 503.)

GOUGE, ROBERT. Adm. sizar (age 17) at CHRIST'S, June 8, 1647. S. of Robert. B. at Chelmsford. School, Chelmsford (Mr Peake). Master of Maldon School, Essex. R. of St Helen's, Ipswich, 1652-62, ejected. Afterwards Congregational preacher at Coggeshall. Author. Died Oct. 1705. (*Peile*, I. 514; *Calamy*, II. 428; *D.N.B.*, where he is confused with Robert of 1645-6.)

GOCHE, SAMPSON. Matric. pens. from QUEENS', Easter, 1626 (Couch in College Register). Of Bedfordshire. Buried at St Botolph's, Cambridge, Oct. 22, 1629.

GOOCH or GOWTCH, THOMAS. Matric. pens. from CHRIST'S, Oct. 1564; B.A. 1567-8; M.A. 1571. Fellow of Corpus Christi, 1569-75. V. of Ilketshall St Margaret, Suffolk, 1567-70. One of these names R. of Bradwell-on-Sea, Essex, 1611. Will (P.C.C.) 1613; 'Geuge.' (*Peile*, I. 87.)

GOOCHE, THOMAS. Matric. sizar from TRINITY, Michs. 1570. S. of John, of Botesdale, Suffolk, deceased. School, Botesdale. Migrated to Caius, July 13, 1574, age 19. B.A. 1574-5. One of these names, of Suffolk, was M.D. (Basel) 1593. Licentiate of College of Physicians, 1599. Of Harleston in 1631. Married, at Hellesdon, Norfolk, Oct. 9, 1610, Katherine Sotherton. (*Venn*, I. 79.)

GOOCHE or GOOGE, THOMAS. Matric. sizar from TRINITY, c. 1592; B.A. 1596-7; M.A. 1600. Probably the 'M.A. of Trinity, who went to Valladolid to study.' Afterwards at Douay, Aug. 1603. Ord. deacon (R.C.) Sept. 21; priest, Sept. 28, 1603. Returned to England, 1604. Further career not known. (E. H. Burton.)

GOUGE, THOMAS. Adm. pens. at EMMANUEL, May 4, 1622. Matric. 1622; B.A. 1625-6; M.A. from King's, 1629. Ord. deacon and priest (St David's), 1627. Perhaps R. of Conington, Hunts.; deprived, 1657. V. of Atwick, Yorks., 1634.

GOUGE, THOMAS. Adm. at KING'S, a scholar from Eton, 1625. S. of William (1595). B. at Bow, Stratford, Sept. 19, 1605. Matric. Michs. 1625; B.A. 1629; M.A. 1633. Fellow 1628 till 1639. P.C. of St Anne's, Blackfriars, 1628-31. P.C. of Teddington, Middlesex, 1637-8. R. of Coulsdon, Surrey, till 1638. V. of St Sepulchre's, Holborn, London, 1638; ejected, 1662. Married in 1639, Anne, dau. of Sir Robert Darcy. Organised religious instruction in South Wales. A friend of Thomas Firmin. Author, religious. Died Oct. 29, 1681. Buried in St Anne's, Blackfriars. Difficulties between this and the last. Father of William (1658) and Thomas (1662). (*Calamy*, I. 144; *D.N.B.*; *Hennessy*.)

GOOCH, THOMAS. Adm. sizar (age 19) at CAIUS, May 10, 1627. S. of John. B. at Hargrave, Suffolk. School, Elsing, Norfolk (Mr Robinson). Matric. 1627; B.A. 1630-1; M.A. 1634. Ord. priest (Norwich) 1631. V. of Haveringland, Norfolk, 1633-62. Resided at Hoo, East Dereham. Buried there, May 13, 1662. Will (Norwich C.C.) 1662. Probably father of Henry (1666). (*Venn*, I. 280; *Carthew*, II. 704; *Vis. of Norfolk*, 1664.)

GOOCH, THOMAS. Adm. pens. at CLARE, June 2, 1659. S. of William, of Mettingham, Suffolk. Matric. 1659. Married Frances, dau. of Thomas Lone, of Worlingham, Suffolk. Of Yarmouth. Died 1688. Will (Norwich Archd. C.) 1689. Father of Sir T. Gooch (1691), Master of Caius. (*Suckling*, II. 125; *G.E.C.*)

GOUGE, THOMAS. Adm. pens. (age 17) at PEMBROKE, Apr. 5, 1662. Doubtless s. of Thomas (1625), of London, clerk. Matric. 1662. Brother of William (1658).

GOUGE, THOMAS. Adm. sizar (age 17) at MAGDALENE, Jan. 22, 1668-9. S. of Thomas (? 1622), of Conington, Hunts., deceased. School, Charterhouse. Matric. 1669; B.A. 1672-3; M.A. 1676. Fellow, 1676. Ord. deacon (London) Dec. 22; priest, Dec. 23, 1677. R. of Bramfield, Herts., 1677-1715. Died 1715.

GOOCH, THOMAS. Adm. sizar at PETERHOUSE, June 14, 1688. S. of Thomas, attorney, of Hoo, Norfolk. B. there. Bapt. Apr. 23, 1667. Schools, Scarning aud Wymondham. Migrated to Caius, 1688-9, age 22. Matric. 1688; Scholar, 1689-91. Ord. priest (Norwich) May 21, 1692. R. of St Lawrence, Norwich, 1693-1715. V. of Crostwick, Norfolk, 1700. C. of St Ethelred, Norwich, 1709. Died Apr. 28, 1715. Buried at St Lawrence. Will (Norwich C.C.) 1715. (*Venn*, I. 486.)

GOOCH, THOMAS. Adm. pens. (age 16) at CAIUS, May 5, 1691. S. of Thomas (1659), gent., of Yarmouth. B. at Worlingham, Suffolk. School, Yarmouth (Mr Reynolds). Matric. 1691; Scholar, 1691-8; B.A. 1694-5; M.A. 1698; B.D. 1706; D.D. 1711. Fellow, 1698-1714. Master of Caius, 1716-54. Vice-Chancellor, 1717-20. Ord. deacon and priest (Norwich) Mar. 1, 1698-9. R. of St Clement *with* St Martin Orgar, Eastcheap, 1713-38. Archdeacon of Essex, 1714-37. Chaplain to the King, 1715-8. Domestic chaplain to the Bishop of London. Lecturer at Gray's Inn, 1716. Preb. of Chichester, 1719-39. Preb. of Canterbury, 1730. Bishop of Bristol, 1737; of Norwich, 1738-48; ofaEly, 1748-54. Succeeded his brother as Bart., 1751. Died t Ely House, Holborn, Feb. 14, 1754. Buried in Caius College Chapel. M.I. there. Father of John (1746) and Thomas (1737). (*Venn*, I. 489; *D.N.B.*)

GOOCH, THOMAS. Adm. pens. (age 16) at CAIUS, July 9, 1737. S. of Thomas (1691), Bishop of Bristol. B. in London. Schools, Wymondham (Mr Brett) and Bury. Scholar, 1737-42; Matric. 1738; B.A. 1741-2; M.A. 1742 (*fil. nob.*). Succeeded his father as baronet, 1754. Of Benacre, Suffolk. Inherited a fortune of £150,000 from his maternal uncle, Thomas Sherlock, Bishop of London. Died at Tunbridge Wells, Sept. 10, 1781. Brother of John (1746). (*Venn*, II. 43; *G.E.C.*)

GOWCHE, W. Matric. pens. from TRINITY, Easter, 1587; B.A. 1590-1.

GOOCH or GOWCH, WILLIAM. Fee for M.A. or higher degree, 1459-60.

GOOGE or GOUCH, WILLIAM. Adm. at KING'S, a scholar from Eton, 1595. S. of Thomas, of Stratford, Middlesex (whose will, Cons. C. London, 1616). B. Dec. 25, 1578 (*D.N.B.*). B.A. 1600-1; M.A. 1603; B.D. 1611; D.D. 1628. Fellow, 1598-1604. Incorp. at Oxford, 1609. R. of St Anne's, Blackfriars, 1621-53. One of the Westminster assembly of divines, 1641. Refused the provostship of King's, 1645. Author. Died Dec. 12, 1653, 'aged 79.' 'Buried in the church at Blackfriars.' Will (P.C.C.) 1654. Father of Thomas (1625). (*Al. Oxon.*; *D.N.B.*; *Harwood*.)

GOOCHE, WILLIAM. Adm. pens. at EMMANUEL, Apr. 4, 1627. One of these names, s. of William, of Gray's Inn, adm. there, Nov. 26, 1630.

GOUGE, WILLIAM. Adm. p . (age 15) at PEMBROKE, June 8, 1658. Doubtless s. of Thomas (1625), clerk. B. in London. Died Oct. 13, 1706. Brother of Thomas (1662).

GOOD, *see also* **GOADE.**

GOODE, BARNHAM. Adm. at KING'S, a scholar from Eton, 1691. B. at Malden, Surrey. Matric. Michs. 1691; B.A. 1695-6; M.A. 1699. Fellow, 1694. For his controversy with the poet Pope and Pope's personal description of him, *see Harwood*, 275.

GOODE, EDWARD. Matric. sizar from TRINITY, *c.* 1597.

GOODE, FRANCIS. Adm. at KING'S, a scholar from Eton, 1695. B. at Northall, Middlesex. Matric. Easter, 1695; B.A. 1699-1700; M.A. 1703. Fellow, 1699. Lower Master of Eton, 1716-34. Died at Kingston-on-Thames, July 1, 1739. (*Harwood*.)

GOODE, HENRY. Adm. sizar (age 16) at EMMANUEL, June 12, 1668. S. of William, of Kettering, Northants. Bapt. there, Dec. 16, 1651. Migrated to Pembroke, Sept. 12, 1668. Matric. 1669; B.A. 1671-2; M.A. 1675. Ord. deacon (Peterb.) June 14, 1674; priest, Sept. 24, 1676. R. of Carleton Curlieu, Leics., 1676-82. R. of Weldon, Northants., 1684-1726. R. of Deane, 1690-1727. Father of William (1701-2). (H. I. Longden.)

GOOD, HENRY. Adm. pens. (age 19) at EMMANUEL, Apr. 21, 1743. S. of Henry, gent. B. at Bower Chalk, Wilts. School, Sherborne. Matric. 1743; B.A. 1746-7; M.A. 1754; D.D. 1773. Ord. deacon (Winchester) June 14, 1747; priest (Salisbury) Sept. 24, 1749. One of the ministers of Wimborne Minster, Dorset, 1763-1800. Chaplain to Bishop of Bath and Wells. R. of Shuston St Rumbold, Dorset, 1772-1800. Died June 9, 1800. Will (P.C.C.) 1800. (F. S. Hockaday.)

GOOD, JEREMIAH. Adm. pens. at EMMANUEL, May 12, 1688. Of Surrey. Matric. 1690. Probably brother of John (1683).

GOOD, JOHN. Matric. pens. from CLARE, Easter, 1573; B.A. 1576-7. One of these names V. of East Hatley, Cambs., 1577-1626; buried 1627. Another was Master of Guildford Grammar School, 1589; buried in Holy Trinity Church, Guildford, Sept. 6, 1594. (*Manning and Bray*, I. 79.)

GOOD, JOHN. Adm. sizar (age 16) at SIDNEY, May 3, 1650. S. of Thomas, farmer. B. at Islip, Northants. School, Oundle (Mr Hicks). Matric. 1650. Migrated to Trinity, June 1, 1652; B.A. 1653-4; M.A. 1657. Incorp. at Oxford, 1657. Perhaps R. of Rotherhithe, Surrey, 1654-75. Buried there May 30, 1675. Not to be confused with John Goode, B.D., for whom *see Al. Oxon.* (*Manning and Bray*, I. 237.)

GOODE, JOHN. Adm. pens. at EMMANUEL, Sept. 11, 1683. Of Surrey. Matric. 1686; B.A. 1687-8. Probably brother of Jeremiah (1688).

GOODE, NEVELL. Matric. pens. from JESUS, Michs. 1567; B.A. 1569-70. Will (P.C.C.) 1610, of one of these names, of Henley-on-Thames, gent. (J. Ch. Smith.)

GOODE, RICHARD, *see* **GOADE.**

GOOD, ROBERT. Matric. pens. from QUEENS', Easter, 1603. Of Cambridgeshire. B.A. 1606-7; M.A. 1610. Ord. deacon and priest (Lincoln) Sept. 23, 1610. C. of Barford, Beds., 1610.

GOOD, SAMUEL. Matric. pens. from CORPUS CHRISTI, Easter, 1657. S. of William (1617), R. of Denton, Norfolk. B.A. 1660-1; M.A. 1664. Pedigree in *Vis. of Norfolk*, 1664. (G. H. Holley.)

GOODE, THOMAS. Matric. pens. from CHRIST'S, Easter, 1559.

GOODE, THOMAS. Adm. at CORPUS CHRISTI, 1599. Of Cambs. (perhaps of East Hatley). B.A. 1602-3; M.A. 1606. Perhaps V. of Lowdham, Notts., 1609. Probably V. of East Hatley, Cambs., 1628-41. Will (P.C.C.) 1655.

GOOD, WILLIAM. Adm. sizar (age 17) at PEMBROKE, June 3, 1617. Probably s. of William, of Ashby, Lincs. Matric. 1617; B.A. 1620-1; M.A. 1624; B.D. 1631-2 (*Lit. Reg.*), as Goad. Perhaps R. of Clare, Suffolk, 1627, and R. of Kirk Bramwith, Yorks., 1628-38. Certainly R. of Denton, Norfolk, 1638, and father of Samuel (above).

GOODE, WILLIAM. Adm. pens. (age 16) at PEMBROKE, Mar. 4, 1701-2. S. of Henry (1668), R. of Weldon, Northants. Matric. 1702-3; Scholar at Trinity Hall, Jan. 9, 1703-4; LL.B. 1707. Ord. deacon (Peterb.) Sept. 21, 1707; priest, Sept. 24, 1710. Succeeded his father as R. of Weldon, Northants., 1727-61. Will (P.C.C.) 1761.

GOODDALL, ANDREW. Adm. sizar (age 17) at ST JOHN'S, Mar. 9, 1664-5. S. of Richard, of Uttoxeter, Staffs. B. there. School, Uttoxeter. Matric. 1665; B.A. 1668-9; M.A. 1672. Ord. deacon (Peterb.) May 29, 1670; priest, June 18, 1671. V. of Hambleton, Rutland, 1689-1706. Married at Theddingworth, Leics., May 8, 1690, Mary Jenkins. Died 1706. Father of John (1713) and Samuel (1707-8). (H. I. Longden.)

GOODALL, BENJAMIN. M.A. from CLARE, 1666. Matric. from St John's, Oxford, Mar. 18, 1657-8; B.A. (Oxford) 1663. V. of Kirtlington, Oxon., 1662. V. of Wendy, Cambs., 1664-83. Buried Jan. 27, 1682-3. (*Al. Oxon.*; *E. Anglian*, X. 138.)

GOODALL, CHARLES. Adm. pens. at EMMANUEL, Jan. 20, 1658-9. S. of Thomas, of Earl Stonham, Suffolk. Licensed to p surgery, 1665. M.D. 1670 (Incorp. from Leyden). F.R.C.P. 1680. Gulstonian lecturer, 1685. Harveian orator, 1694, 1709. Censor, etc. President, 1708-12. Physician to the Charterhouse. Died Aug. 23, 1712. Will, P.C.C. Father of Thomas (1683). (*D.N.B.*; *Munk*, I. 402; *Vis. of Suffolk*, 1664.)

GOODDELL, EDMUND. Matric. pens. from ST CATHARINE'S, Easter, 1615; B.A. 1615-6; M.A. 1619.

GOODALL, EDWARD. Matric. sizar from TRINITY, Easter, 1614; B.A. 1618-9; M.A. 1622. R. of Horton, Bucks., 1631-*c.* 52. Father of the next.

GOODALL, EDWARD. Adm. at KING'S, a scholar from Eton, 1661. S. of Edward (above), R. of Horton, Bucks. B. there, 1644. Matric. 1663; B.A. 1666-7; M.A. 1670. Fellow, 1665. Ord. deacon (Ely) Sept. 24, 1670; priest, Sept. 21, 1671. V. of Prescot, Lancs., 1677-90. Resigned his living on becoming a Roman Catholic. (*Lipscomb*, IV. 511.)

GOODALL, EDWARD. Adm. pens. at TRINITY, Apr. 19, 1662.

GOODALE, GEORGE. Matric. pens. from CLARE, Michs. 1571; B.A. 1574-5; M.A. 1578.

GOODDALL, GEORGE. M.A. 1668 (Incorp. from Oxford). Matric. from Exeter College, July 23, 1656; B.A. (Oxford) 1661; M.A. 1664; B.D. 1674. Fellow of Exeter College, 1658-89. R. of Padworth, Berks., 1683-1707. Buried there Dec. 23, 1707. Will, P.C.C. (*Al. Oxon.*; J. Ch. Smith.)

GOODALL, HENRY. Adm. sizar (age 16) at CAIUS, Feb. 24, 1723-4. S. of Thomas, butler of the College. B. in Cambridge. Schools, King's College (Mr Manning, Mr Kemys and Mr Campbell) and Histon, Cambs. (private). Matric. 1724; Scholar, 1724-30; B.A. 1727-8; M.A. 1731; D.D. 1752. Fellow, 1730-41. Ord. deacon (Lincoln) June 13, 1731; priest, Feb. 18, 1732-3. Master of the Perse School, Cambridge, 1732-51. Chaplain to Dr Gooch, Bishop of Ely. V. of Thornham, Norfolk, 1739-43. R. of Mattishall, 1743-81. R. of Bixley and Framingham Earl, 1747-81. Archdeacon of Suffolk, 1748-81. Preb. of Ely, 1752. Preb. of Norwich, 1752-81. Author. Died Feb. 23, 1781. Will, P.C.C. (*Venn*, II. 19.)

GOODALL or GOODALE, JAMES. Adm. sizar at TRINITY, June 29, 1644. Migrated to Peterhouse, Jan. 23, 1644-5, age 18. Matric. 1645-6; Scholar, 1647; B.A. 1647-8; M.A. 1651. Fellow, 1650-2. Died 1652. (*T. A. Walker.*)

GOODALL, JAMES. Adm. sizar (age 20) at TRINITY, June 28, 1726. S. of Joshua (? 1670), of Hunsingore, Yorks., clerk. School, Kirkleatham, Yorks. (Mr Clark). Matric. 1726; B.A. 1729-30. Ord. priest (Norwich) Oct. 1735. R. of South Creake, Norfolk, 1739-68. V. of Hindringham, 1745-68.

GOODALL, JOHN. Adm. at KING'S (age 17) a scholar from Eton, Aug. 1, 1519. Of Cambridge. Fellow, 1522. 'A lawyer at Windsor.' (*Harwood.*)

GOODALL, JOHN. Adm. sizar at EMMANUEL, Apr. 1627. Matric. 1627; B.A. 1630-1; M.A. 1634.

GOODDALL, JOHN. Adm. sizar (age 18) at ST JOHN'S, June 13, 1713. S. of Andrew (1664-5), clerk, deceased. B. at Hambleton, Rutland. School, Oakham (Mr Wright). Matric. 1713; B.A. 1716-7; M.A. 1721. Ord. deacon (Peterb.) Sept. 21, 1717; C. of Egleton, Rutland. Head Master of Lincoln Grammar School, 1724-42. Preb. of Lincoln, 1736-42. Died May 25, 1742. Brother of Samuel (1707-8).

GOODALL, JOSHUA. Adm. pens. (age 17) at MAGDALENE, June 3, 1670. S. of Joshua, of Idle, Bradford, Yorks. School, Church Fenton (private). Matric. 1671; B.A. 1673-4. Ord. deacon (York) June, 1674; priest, May, 1676. V. of Swine, Yorks., 1681-6.

GOODALL, MICHAEL. Adm. at KING'S (age 18) a scholar from Eton, Aug. 23, 1537. Of Cambridge. Name off *c.* 1539.

GOODHALL, ROBERT. Matric. pens. from ST JOHN'S, Easter, 1586. Probably s. of Robert, of Holywell, Lincs. Bapt. at Castle Bytham, Apr. 7, 1568. Adm. at Gray's Inn, May 29, 1590. Perhaps father of William (1612). (*Lincs. Pedigrees,* 410.)

GOODALL, ROBERT. Adm. pens. at CLARE, Oct. 14, 1691. Probably s. of William, of Holywell, Lincs. Bapt. there, Dec. 31, 1674. Matric. 1691. Married Mary, dau. of Edmund Bolsworth, of London. If so, father of William (1715-6). (*Lincs. Pedigrees,* 411.)

GOODHALL, ROBERT. Adm. pens. (age 16) at EMMANUEL, July 1, 1740. B. at Tinwell, Rutland. School, Oakham. Matric. 1740-1; B.A. 1743-4; M.A. 1747. Dixie fellow, 1745. Ord. deacon (Lincoln) Dec. 20, 1747; priest (Peterb.) Sept. 23, 1750. V. of Tickencote, Rutland, 1750-8. R. of Whitwell, 1750-84. Died Jan. 18, 1784. (A. B. Beaven.)

GOODDALL, SAMUEL. Adm. sizar (age 17) at ST JOHN'S, Feb. 24, 1707-8. S. of Andrew (1664-5), deceased. B. at Hambleton, Rutland. School, Oakham. Matric. 1708; B.A. 1712-3. Brother of John (1713).

GOODALL, THOMAS. Matric. sizar from KING'S, Easter, 1618; B.A. 1622-3. Ord. deacon (Peterb.) Dec. 21; priest, Dec. 22, 1623.

GOODALL, THOMAS. Adm. pens. (age 16) at CAIUS, Nov. 11, 1683. S. of Charles (1658-9), M.D., F.R.C.P. B. at Stonham, Suffolk. Schools, Grantham and St Paul's. Matric. 1684; Scholar, 1684-9; B.A. 1687-8; M.A. 1691. Fellow, Mids. to Michs. 1693. (*Venn,* I. 475.)

GOODHALL, WILLIAM. Matric. pens. from ST JOHN'S, Easter, 1612. One of these names, s. and h. of Robert (? 1586), of Holywell, Lincs., adm. at Gray's Inn, Feb. 25, 1615-6. Of Holywell, Esq. Married Hannah, dau. of William Panell, of London. (*Lincs. Pedigrees.*)

GOODAL, WILLIAM. Adm. sizar (age 17) at PETERHOUSE, May 30, 1649. Of Leicestershire. School, Sileby. One of these names R. of Keyworth, Notts., 1660; and perhaps of Wymondham, Leics., 1670-3.

GOODALL, WILLIAM. Adm. pens. (age 17) at PETERHOUSE, Apr. 27, 1699. Of Middlesex. School, Eton. Matric. 1699; Scholar, 1699; B.A. 1702-3; M.A. 1706. Fellow, 1704-34. Ord. deacon (Ely) Dec. 23, 1705; priest (London) Dec. 19, 1708. Buried at Little St Mary's, Cambridge, Aug. 18, 1734. Benefactor to Peterhouse. (*T. A. Walker,* 203.)

GOODHALL, WILLIAM. Adm. pens. at EMMANUEL, Feb. 29, 1715-6. Of Rutland. Only surviving s. of Robert (? 1691), Esq., deceased. B. at Holywell, Lincs. Schools, Oakham and Stamford. Migrated as scholar to Sidney, Apr. 19, 1716, age 18. Matric. 1717. Sold Holywell to Lady Mary Barnardiston, 1729. Died in great poverty. Buried at Tinwell, Rutland, Aug. 11, 1766. (*Lincs. Pedigrees,* 411.)

GOODALL, WILLIAM. Adm. at CORPUS CHRISTI, 1717. Of Yorkshire. B.A. 1721-2; M.A. 1726. Ord. deacon (York) May, 1722.

GOODALL, ——. M.A. 1489.

GOODALL, ——. Adm. sizar at EMMANUEL, Apr. 1630.

GOODANTER, THOMAS. Adm. sizar at PETERHOUSE, June 1, 1633. Of Staffordshire. Exhibitioner from Charterhouse. Matric. 1633; Scholar, 1636; B.A. 1636-7. Ord. deacon (Lincoln) June 5, 1642. Died *c.* 1651. Will (P.C.C.) Aug. 1651; of Tottenham High Cross, clerk. (J. Ch. Smith.)

GOODBORNE or GOODBARNE, JOHN. Adm. sizar at JESUS, June 3, 1622. Matric. 1622; B.A. 1625-6; M.A. 1629.

GOODCHILD, CHRISTOPHER. B.Civ.L. 1495-6.

GOODCHILD, CECIL WRAY. Adm. pens. (age 18) at TRINITY, June 17, 1747. S. of John, of London. School, Westminster. Matric. 1748; Scholar, 1748; B.A. 1750-1; M.A. 1754. Ord. priest (London) Sept. 23, 1753.

GOODCHILD, ——. 'Rev. of CLARE HALL. Died Sept. 1743.' No University or College record. (*Lond. Mag.*)

GOODCREE, (?) HENRY. Matric. pens. from ST JOHN'S, Easter, 1550.

GOODDAY, ARTHUR. Matric. pens. from CORPUS CHRISTI, 1593. Of Essex. S. of Roger (1568), of Pentlow, Essex. Adm. at Gray's Inn, Feb. 11, 1594-5. Barrister, 1601. Of Higham Ferrers, Northants., Esq. Buried there Feb. 14, 1638-9. M.I. Will (P.C.C.) 1639. (*Vis. of Essex,* 1612; *Vis. of Northants.,* 1618; H. I. Longden.)

GOODAY, GEORGE. Matric. pens. from QUEENS', Easter, 1636. Of London. 1st s. of William, of St Andrew's, Holborn. Adm. at Gray's Inn, Nov. 3, 1637. Barrister, 1645. Of Bower Hall, Pentlow, Essex. Nephew of Arthur (1593), brother of John (1637) and Roger (1640).

GOODDAY, GEORGE. Adm. Fell.-Com. (age 18) at ST JOHN'S, May 9, 1719. S. of George, Esq., of Suffolk. B. at Tostock. School, Bishop's Stortford (Dr Tooke). B.A. 1722-3; M.A. 1727. Adm. at the Middle Temple, May 30, 1719; s. and h. of George, of Fornham All Saints', Esq. High Sheriff of Suffolk, 1751-2. Buried at Fornham All Saints', Jan. 13, 1758. (*Scott-Mayor,* III. 323.)

GOODDAY, JOHN. Adm. pens. (age 15) at CHRIST'S, July 14, 1637. 2nd s. of William. B. in London. School, Higham Ferrers, Northants. (Mr Freer). Matric. 1637; B.A. 1641-2; M.A. 1645. Fellow of Pembroke, 1644. Junior Proctor, 1648. Studied physic. Died *s.p.* 1651. Brother of Roger (1640) and George (1636). (*Peile,* I. 449.)

GODDAYE, RICHARD. Matric. pens. from JESUS, Easter, 1575. Doubtless s. of John, of Braintree, Essex; adm. at the Inner Temple, 1579. Doubtless brother of the next.

GOODAY, ROGER. Matric. pens. from JESUS, Michs. 1568. Probably 1st s. of John, of Braintree, Essex. B.A. 1571-2. Of Pentlow, Essex. Buried there July 19, 1617. Will (P.C.C.) 1617; of Pentlow, Essex, gent. Doubtless brother of Richard (1575) and father of Arthur (1593). (*Morant,* II. 324.)

GOODDAY, ROGER. Adm. pens. (age 16) at CHRIST'S, June 15, 1640. S. of William, citizen and merchant taylor. B. in London. School, Higham Ferrers (Mr Taylor). Matric. 1640. Married Frances, dau. of Ralph Wiseman, of Clerkenwell. Died May 9, 1675. Buried at Chelsfield, Kent. Brother of John (1637) and George (1636). (*Peile,* I. 472; *Vis. of Northants.,* 1618.)

GOODDAY, SAMUEL. Adm. pens. (age 16) at ST JOHN'S, Jan. 14, 1651-2. S. of Forth, gent., of Preston, Suffolk (merchant tailor; imprisoned at Ipswich, as delinquent; discharged, 1644). B. at Hackney, Middlesex. School, Bury St Edmunds. Matric. 1652. Adm. at Gray's Inn, May 3, 1651.

GOODAY, THOMAS. Adm. sizar (age 16) at CAIUS, Oct. 24, 1566. Matric. 1566. Previously at St Catharine's. S. of Thomas, of Sawbridgeworth, Herts. (*Venn,* I. 59; *Vis. of Northants.,* 1618.)

GOODAY, THOMAS. Matric. sizar from QUEENS', Easter, 1626. Of Cambridgeshire. B.A. 1629-30; M.A. 1633. Fellow, 1631-5. Buried in the College Chapel, Jan. 21, 1634-5. Will proved (V.C.C.).

GOODDAY, WILLIAM. Adm. pens. (age 17) at TRINITY, July 5, 1721. S. of William, of Northampton. Bapt. at St Giles', Mar. 16, 1703-4. School, Westminster. Matric. 1721; Scholar, 1723; B.A. 1724-5; M.A. 1728. Ord. deacon (Lincoln) June 5, 1726; priest, Mar. 17, 1727-8. R. of Strelley, Notts., 1728-83. R. of Bilborough. Died May 21, 1783. Buried at Strelley. M.I. Will (P.C.C.) 1783. (*Essex Pedigrees*; H. G. Harrison.)

GOODENOUGH, ——. B.Can.L. 1482-3.

GOODENOUGH, ——. B.A. 1485-6.

GOODERE, *see also* GOODYEAR.

GOODERE, GEORGE. Adm. pens. (age 20) at ST JOHN'S, Mar. 27, 1739. S. of John, Esq., of Essex. B. at Barking. School, Eton. Matric. 1739. Brother of Richard (1739).

GOODERE, JOHN. Adm. at CORPUS CHRISTI, 1669. Of Northamptonshire. Adm. at Gray's Inn, Feb. 11, 1670–1, as s. and h. of Henry, of Northampton, Esq.

GOODDER or GOODYEAR, RALPH. Matric. sizar from TRINITY, Easter, 1623. Ord. deacon (Peterb.) May 20, 1627, as 'of Trinity College; literate.'

GOODERE, RICHARD. Adm. pens. (age 20) at ST JOHN'S, Mar. 27, 1739. S. of John, Esq., of Essex. B. at Barking. School, Eton. Matric. 1739; LL.B. 1750. Ord. deacon (London) June 13, 1742; priest (Winchester) July 18, 1742. V. of Felsted, Essex, 1742–69. R. of Wivenhoe, 1750. R. of Wanstead, 1750–69. Died July 11, 1769. Admon. (P.C.C.). Brother of George (1739). (*Scott-Mayor*, III. 499.)

GOODEVE, RICHARD. Matric. sizar from QUEENS', Easter, 1632. Of Essex. B.A. 1634–5; M.A. 1638.

GOODFELLOW, CHRISTOPHER. Adm. pens. at QUEENS', Dec. 3, 1681. Of Bedfordshire. Doubtless s. of Christopher, serjeant-at-law. Matric. 1682; B.A. 1685–6; M.A. 1689. Fellow, 1686–98. Junior Proctor, 1695–6.

GOODFELLOW, LEWIS. Matric. pens. from QUEENS', Lent, 1577–8. Of Bedfordshire. Lewis Goodfellow married Anne Downes, at Bromham, Beds., July 8, 1582.

GOODFELLOW, MATTHIAS. Adm. pens. (age 14) at MAGDALENE, Sept. 27, 1664. S. of Matthias, citizen of London. School, Mercers'. Matric. 1664; B.A. 1668–9. Probably adm. at the Inner Temple, 1669.

GOODFELLOW, THOMAS. Matric. pens. from PETERHOUSE, Michs. 1561.

GOODFELLOW, WALTER. Adm. at KING'S, a scholar from Eton, 1689. B. in Chancery Lane, London. Matric. Michs. 1690; B.A. 1693–4; M.A. 1697. Fellow, 1693. Ord. priest (Ely) May 30, 1703. R. of Ladbroke, Warws. Died 1746.

GOODFELLOW, WILLIAM. B.A. 1485–6.

GOODHAND, CHARLES. Adm. sizar (age 19) at TRINITY, May 22, 1723. S. of Thomas. B. at Binbrooke, Lincs. School, Lincoln (Mr Garington). Migrated to Magdalene, Nov. 2, 1723. Matric. 1723; B.A. 1726–7. Ord. deacon (Lincoln) Feb. 26, 1726–7; priest, Sept. 22, 1728. (Pedigree in *Lincs. Pedigrees*.)

GOODHAND, LEONARD. Adm. sizar (age 15) at PEMBROKE, May 3, 1665. S. of John, gent. B. at Algarkirk, Lincs.

GOODHAND, TRIAMOUR. Matric. pens. from ST JOHN'S, Easter, 1581. Ord. deacon (Lincoln) Sept. 23, 1585; priest, Oct. 1586.

GOODHAND, W. Matric. pens. from JESUS, Easter, 1572. Will (P.C.C.) 1617, of William Goodhand, of Binbrooke, Lincs., gent. He was a s. of John, of Market Rasen. (*Lincs. Pedigrees*.)

GOODICAR, (?) JOHN. B.A. from MAGDALENE, 1600–1.

GOODIN, GEORGE. Adm. sizar (age 17) at MAGDALENE, Feb. 21, 1742–3. B. at Alford, Lincs. School, Alford. Perhaps a mistake for John, whom *see*.

GOODDING, JAMES. Adm. pens. at EMMANUEL, May 1, 1591. Matric. *c.* 1592.

GOODING, JOHN. Matric. pens. from SIDNEY, Easter, 1610. B. at Ipswich. B.A. from Pembroke, 1613–4; M.A. 1617. Ord. priest (London) Sept. 1, 1617, age 24. C. of Copley, Kent. V. of Burton-upon-Stather, Lincs., 1626–42. (V. B. Redstone.)

GOODING, JOHN. Adm. (age 16) at PEMBROKE, 1658. S. of Robert. B. at Ardleigh, Essex. Matric. 1660; B.A. 1661–2; M.A. 1665. Fellow, 1664–5. Signed for deacon's orders (London) Mar. 5, 1663–4, as under-master at Felsted School. Buried at St Botolph, Cambridge, Apr. 2, 1665.

GOODIN, JOHN. Matric. sizar from MAGDALENE, Michs. 1743; B.A. 1746–7; M.A. 1750. Fellow, 1748. Ord. deacon (Lincoln) June 14, 1747; priest, May 21, 1749. (*See* George (above).)

GOODIN, SAMUEL, *see* **GOOKIN.**

GOODDINGE, THOMAS. Matric. pens. from CLARE, Lent, 1577–8; B.A. 1581–2; M.A. 1585, as 'Golding.' One of these names, of London, adm. at Gray's Inn, Oct. 12, 1586.

GOODKNAP, JEREMY. Adm. pens. at EMMANUEL, Mar. 21, 1653–4. Of Lincolnshire. Matric. 1654; B.A. 1657–8; M.A. 1661.

GOODKNAPE, ROBERT. B.Can.L. 1464–5; D.Can.L. 1469–70. Fellow of TRINITY HALL. Benefactor, by foundation of a fellowship, 1483. (*Coll. Hist.*, 68; *Warren*.)

GOODKNAPE, THOMAS, *see* **GOLDKNAPPE.**

GOODLADE, NICHOLAS. Matric. sizar from TRINITY, Michs. 1559; Scholar, 1562; B.A. 1563–4. One of these names R. of Tinwell, Rutland. Admon. (P.C.C.) June 20, 1575. (J. Ch. Smith.)

GOODLAD, THOMAS. Adm. sizar (age 17) at SIDNEY, May 30, 1661. S. of Thomas, clothier, deceased. B. at Tinwell, Rutland. School, Stanford (Mr Howman). Matric. 1661; B.A. 1664–5; M.A. 1668; B.D. 1675. Fellow, 1666.

GOODLET, ANDREW. Matric. sizar from MAGDALENE, Michs. 1564.

GOODLOVE, W. Matric. pens. from PEMBROKE, Easter, 1588.

GOODMAN, BENJAMIN. Adm. pens. at EMMANUEL, May 19, 1676. Of Middlesex. Matric. 1676; B.A. 1679–80. Ord. deacon (London) May 26, 1700.

GOODMAN, CARDELL. B.A. from EMMANUEL, 1625–6. S. of John, of Ware, Herts. M.A. from St John's, 1629. Fellow of St John's, 1626. Matric. from Christ Church, Oxford, Jan. 28, 1625–6, age 18. R. of Freshwater, Isle of Wight, 1641–51; deprived. Father of the next.

GOODMAN, CARDELL. Adm. pens. (age 13) at ST JOHN'S, Nov. 30, 1666. S. of Cardell, clerk (above). B. at Southampton. School, Cambridge (Mr Wyborrow). Matric. 1667; B.A. 1670–1. The notorious 'Scum Goodman'; Page of the backstairs to Charles II. Player, highwayman, spy, etc. Died in France, 1699. (*D.N.B.*)

GOODMAN, DAVID. Adm. sizar (age 18) at CHRIST'S, May 18, 1654. S. of Arthur, baker, of Weekeley, Northants. B. there. School, Gretton (Mr Hicks). Matric. 1654. Migrated to St John's, Oct. 8, 1655. B.A. 1657–8. Intruded R. of Little Oakley, Northants., 1658. (H. I. Longden.)

GOODMAN, ED. Matric. sizar from PEMBROKE, Michs. 1566.

GOODMAN, EDWARD. Matric. pens. from CHRIST'S, Mar. 1615–6.

GOODMAN, EVERARD. Matric. pens. from ST CATHARINE'S, Easter, 1629. S. and h. of William (1606). B. 1612. Of Blaston, Leics. Buried Jan. 9, 1687, at Blaston. Father of the next. Probably brother of John (1632). (*Nichols*, II. 455; *Vis. of Leics.*)

GOODMAN, EVERARD. Adm. pens. at JESUS, Nov. 11, 1658. Of Leicestershire. S. of Everard (above), of Blaston, Leics. Bapt. at Hallaton, Leics., Jan. 23, 1642–3. Matric. 1659. Died unmarried. Buried at Medbourn, Leics., Sept. 11, 1704. (A. Gray; Nichols, *Leics.*, II. 455.)

GOODMAN, FRANCIS. B.A. from PEMBROKE, 1599–1600; M.A. 1603.

GOODMAN, GABRIEL. Matric. sizar from JESUS, Michs. 1546. S. of Edward, of Ruthin, Wales. B. there. B.A. (perhaps from St Jobu's, 1549–50); M.A. from Christ's, 1553; D.D. from St John's, 1564. Fellow of Christ's, 1552–4. Fellow of Jesus, *c.* 1554–5. R. of South Luffenham, Ruts., 1558. R. of Waddesdon, Bucks., 1559–82. Preb. of St Paul's, 1559. Prob. of Westminster, 1560. Dean of Westminster, 1561–1601. Founded the Hospital and Grammar School at Ruthin. Translated the 1st Corinthians for the Bishops' Bible, 1568. Died June 17, 1601, aged 73. Buried in Westminster Abbey. Will, P.C.C. (*Peile*, I. 41; *D.N.B.*) 'Goodman was his name, and goodman his nature.' (*T. Fuller*.)

GOODMAN, GEORGE. Matric. pens. from MAGDALENE, Michs. 1613. 4th s. of Everard, of Blaston, Leics. B.A. 1616–7; M.A. 1620; B.D. 1630. Incorp. at Oxford, 1620. Ord. deacon (Peterb.) Jan. 16[illegible] priest, Jan. 17, 1620–1. R. of Croft, Leics., 1624–41. Buried there Sept. 15, 1641. Brother of John (1612) and half-brother of William (1606). (*Nichols*, IV. 585; *Vis. of Leics.*, 1619.)

GOODMAN, GEORGE. Adm. pens. at TRINITY, May 30, 1657. Of Leicestershire. Matric. 1657; Scholar, 1659; B.A. 1660–1; M.A. from Peterhouse, 1664. Fellow of Peterhouse, 1662–4. Incorp. at Oxford, 1679. Ord. deacon (Lincoln) Sept. 21, 1662. R. of Moulsoe, Bucks., 1663–95. Married, Aug. 2, 1664, Elizabeth Cave. Died Sept. 12, 1695. M.I. at Moulsoe. Father of the next. (*Lipscomb*, IV. 254; *T. A. Walker*.)

GOODMAN, GEORGE. Adm. pens. (age 16) at TRINITY, July 9, 1680. S. of George (above), of Buckinghamshire, clerk. School, Eton. Matric. 1681; Scholar, 1683; B.A. 1684–5; M.A. 1688.

GOODMAN, GODFREY Matric. pens. from CHRIST'S, May, 1553. Probably s. of Edward, of Ruthin, Denbs., and father of Godfrey, Bishop of Gloucester. Perhaps Will (P.C.C.) 1586. (*Peile*, I. 53.)

GOODMAN, GODFREY. Matric. pens. from TRINITY, Lent, 1581–2; scholar from Westminster, 1582; B.A. 1585–6.

GOODMAN, GODFREY. Adm. scholar at TRINITY, 1600, from Westminster. S. of Godfrey (? 1553). B. at Ruthin, Denbs. B.A. 1603–4; M.A. 1607; B.D. 1614; D.D. 1619. Incorp. t Oxford, 1615. Ord. deacon (Bangor); priest (London) Dec. 20, 1606, age 24. R. of Llansannan, Denbs., 1603; of Stapleford Abbots, Essex, 1607; of Llandyssil, Montgom., 1607–15. Preb. of Westminster, 1607–23. R. of Seefiog, Flints., 1617–24. Canon of Windsor, 1617. Preb. of Wolverhampton, 1617–21. R. of West Ilsley, Berks , 1620. Dean of Rochester, 1621–4. R. of Llanarmon-yn-Jal, Denbs., 1621. Bishop of Gloucester, 1625–40. R. of Kemerton, Gloues., 1631–6. Elected to Bishopric of Hereford, 1634, but refused it. V. of Kempsford, Gloucs., 1639–43. Deprived of his bishopric, 1640. Died in Westminster, Jan. 19, 1655–6. Will, P.C.C. Was a professed Roman Catholic at his death. (*Al. Oxon.*; *D.N.B.*; A. B. Beaven.)

GOODMAN, JOHN. B.Can.L. 1520–1. Principal of ST PAUL'S HOSTEL, Cambridge, 1525. Perhaps V. of Caldecot, Cambs., till 1517. Preb. of Wells, in 1549. Dean of Wells, 1548–50, 1553–60: as to which he had much litigation. Preb. of Sarum, 1552–61. Admon. (P.C.C.) Dec. 13, 1561. (*Cooper*, I. 209.)

GOODMAN, JOHN. Matric. pens. from MAGDALENE, Easter, 1612. 3rd s. of Everard, of Blaston, Leics. Died 1668. Brother of George (1613) and half-brother of William (1606). (*Vis. of Leics.*, 1619.)

GOODMAN, JOHN. Matric. sizar from ST JOHN'S, Michs. 1612. B. in Denbs. B.A. 1616–7. Ord. deacon (London) May 31, 1618, age 24; priest, Sept. 20, 1618; C. of St Nicholas Olave, London.

GOODMAN, JOHN. Matric. pens. from MAGDALENE, Easter, 1632. Probably 2nd s. of William (1606) and brother of Everard (1629).

GOODMAN, JOHN. Adm. pens. at TRINITY, Oct. 19, 1637. Matric. 1637; Scholar, 1638; B.A. 1641–2.

GOODMAN, JOHN. Adm. sizar (age 15) at SIDNEY, July 3, 1641. S. of Richard, attorney, of Rothwell, Northants. B. there. School, Kettering (Mr Seton). Matric. 1641; B.A. 1644–5; M.A. from Trinity, 1648; B.D. from Caius, 1656; D.D. 1673. Chaplain of Trinity, 1647–51. Fellow of Caius, 1650–1. Ord. deacon (Lincoln) Feb. 3; priest, Feb. 13, 1660–1. V. of Watford, 1651–74. V. of Much Hadham, Herts., 1674–90. Archdeacon of Middlesex, 1686–90. Author, sermons, etc. Died Aug. 5, 1690. Buried at Much Hadham. Will, P.C.C. (*Venn*, I. 377.)

GOODMAN, JOHN. Matric. pens. from ST CATHARINE'S, Michs. 1642. One of these names s. and h. of John, of Blaston, Leics., Esq.; adm. at Gray's Inn, July 1, 1644.

GOODMAN, JOHN. Adm. sizar (age 16) at CAIUS, Apr. 17, 1655. S. of Richard, vintner, of St Michael's, Stamford, Lincs. B. there. School, Stamford (Mr Humphrey). Matric. 1655; Scholar, 1655–61; B.A. 1658–9. Ord. deacon (Norwich) July 13, 1662: priest, Dec. 20, 1663. C. of Gt Ryburgh, Norfolk. R. of Themilthorpe, 1671. R. of Twyford, 1689. (*Venn*, I. 391.)

GOODMAN, LAU. Matric. sizar from CHRIST'S, July, 1581. Will (P.C.C.) 1605; of Laurence Goodman, of Blaston, Leics., gent.

GOODMAN, LAWRENCE. Adm. sizar (age 17) at CAIUS, Apr. 23, 1656. S. of Henry, shoemaker, of Falkingham, Lincs. B. there. Schools, Falkingham (Mr Worseley) and Sleaford (Mr Gibson). Matric. 1656; Scholar, 1656–61; B.A. 1659–60; M.A. 1663. Ord. deacon (Lincoln) May 24; priest, May 25, 1662. (*Venn*, I. 394.)

GOODMAN, RALPH. B.D. 1517–8. Franciscan friar. *Supp.* for B.D. at Oxford, 1515.

GOODMAN, RICHARD. Adm. sizar at CORPUS CHRISTI, 1579. Matric. Easter, 1581; B.A. 1585–6.

GOODMAN, RICHARD. Adm. sizar (age 18) at CAIUS, Oct. 8, 1633. S. of Henry, gent. B. at Plumpton, Northants. School, Plumpton (Mr Dickes). Matric. 1634. One of these names graduated B.A. at All Souls, Oxford, 1637–8. Ord. deacon (Peterb.) June 9, 1639. (*Venn*, I. 311.)

GOODMAN, ROBERT. Matric. pens. from JESUS, Michs. 1589; B.A. 1593–4; M.A. 1597. Ord. priest (Colchester) Oct. 7, 1597. C. of Stoke-by-Nayland, Suffolk, 1599.

GOODMAN, ROBERT. Scholar of MAGDALENE, Easter, 1612.

GOODMAN, SAMUEL. Matric. pens. from MAGDALENE, Michs. 1634.

GOODMAN, THOMAS. Matric. pens. from CHRIST'S, Nov. 1561. C. of Gt Abington, Cambs.; and V. of Little Abington, in 1567. V. of Gt Abington, 1574. Licensed preacher, 1579. Will (P.C.C.) 1607; of his widow Alice. (*Peile*, I. 76.)

GOODMAN, THOMAS. Matric. pens. from TRINITY, Easter, 1576.

GOODMAN, THOMAS. Adm. sizar (age 15) at CAIUS, Apr. 5, 1652. S. of Thomas, of Lynn. School, Lynn (Mr Bell). Matric. 1652; Scholar, 1652–5.

GOODMAN, THOMAS. Incorp. M.D. 1689, from Utrecht.

GOODMAN, W. Adm. at KING'S, a scholar from Eton, 1455. B. at Lewes, Sussex. B.A. 1459; M.A. 1463.

GOODMAN, W. B.Can.L. 1466–7. Perhaps the same as the above.

GOODMAN, WILLIAM. Matric. pens. from MAGDALENE, Easter, 1606. Doubtless s. and h. of Everard, of Blaston, Leics., gent. Adm. at Gray's Inn, Oct. 17, 1608. Died 1640. Half-brother of John (1612) and George (1613), father of Everard (1629) and John (1632). (*Vis. of Leics.*, 1619; J. H. Hill, *Langton*, 217.)

GOODMAN, ——. Adm. at CORPUS CHRISTI, 1566.

GOODMAN, ——. Adm. sizar at KING'S, Lent, 1571–2.

GOODREAD, THOMAS. Adm. sizar (age 15) at CHRIST'S, Mar. 18, 1656–7. S. of John. B. near Giggleswick. School, Giggleswick (Mr Briggs). B.A. 1660–1; M.A. 1664. Head Master of Ashbourne Grammar School, 1666–72. V. of Ashbourne, 1669–1702. Died 1702. M.I. in Ashbourne Church. (*Peile*, I. 575.)

GOODRICKE, *see also* GODERICH.

GOODRICKE, EDWARD. Adm. pens. at CORPUS CHRISTI, 1571. Matric. Easter, 1573. Will (P.C.C.) 1618, of one of these names, of South Kirkby, Lincs., Esq.

GOODRIDGE, GEORGE. Adm. sizar (age 17) at PEMBROKE, July 8, 1736. S. of George, of Broadhempston, Devon. Matric. 1736; B.A. 1739–40; M.A. 1759. Will (Exeter) 1781, of George Goodridge, of Stoke Fleming, clerk.

GOODRICH, HENRY. B.A. 1512–3. Incorp. at Oxford, Mar. 3, 1512–3. M.A. (Oxford) 1515, from Lincoln College.

GOODRICK, HENRY. Matric. pens. from TRINITY, Easter, 1579.

GOODRICK, HENRY. M.A. 1612 (on visit of Prince Charles).

GOODRICKE, HENRY. Matric. pens. from CLARE, Easter, 1614 B.A. 1617–8.

GOODRICK, HENRY. Matric. sizar from PEMBROKE, Easter, 1631; B.A. 1634–5.

GOODRICK, HENRY. Matric. sizar from QUEENS', Easter, 1640. Of Cambridgeshire. B.A. 1643–4. Probably of the Isle of Ely, Cambs., gent.; adm. at Gray's Inn, Aug. 10, 1642.

GOODRICK, HENRY. Adm. pens. (age 19) at PEMBROKE, Feb. 10, 1662–3. S. of Robert (1619), R. of Horningsheath, Suffolk. Matric. 1663; B.A. 1666–7; M.A. 1670. Adm. extra-licentiate R.C.P. Feb. 25, 1663–4; 'practising at Lewes, Sussex.' Ord. deacon (Ely) Sept. 24, 1670; priest (Norwich) Jan. 1672–3. R. of Illington, Norfolk, 1673–1712. Died 1712. Brother of Robert (1656). (*Munk*, I. 314.)

GOODRICK, HENRY. Adm. sizar at ST CATHARINE'S, June 5, 1712. Matric. 1712; B.A. 1715–6. Ord. deacon (Norwich) July, 1716; priest, July 13, 1718. C. of Risby. Perhaps V. of B , Norfolk, 1719–20. Probably brother of Robert (1712). edon

GOODRICKE, HENRY. Adm. pens. (age 18) at MAGDALENE, Feb. 19, 1736–7. S. of Sir Henry, Bart. B. at Ribston, Yorks., Oct. 20, 1719. School, Wakefield. Matric. 1737. Migrated to Jesus, Nov. 15, 1737. B.A. 1740–1; M.A. 1744. R. of Ribston and Hunsingore, Yorks. R. of Aldborough, 1750–1801. Preb. of Ripon, 1750–74. Preb. of York, 1752–1801. Sub-dean of Ripon, 1774–92. Died Oct. 24, 1801, at Sutton-in-the-Forest. Buried there. Brother of John (1725) and Thomas (1730). (M. H. Peacock.)

GOODRICKE, HENRY. Adm. sizar (age 19) at ST JOHN'S, June 22, 1741. S. of William, of Middlesex. B. in London. School, Sedbergh. Matric. 1741; M.A. 1744–5. Ord. deacon (Norwich) June 9, 1745; priest (Canterbury) Sept. 20, 1746. V. of Lingfield, Surrey, 1749–1807. V. of Godmersham, Kent, 1772–4. R. of Coulsdon, Surrey, 1774–1807. Died 1807. (*Scott-Mayor*, III. 521.)

GOODRICH or GOODRICK, JOHN. Adm. pens. at CORPUS CHRISTI, *c.* 1500. S. of Edward, of East Kirby, Lincs. B.A. 1506. Succeeded to his father's estates. Commissioner for First Fruits in Hunts. Sheriff of Lincs. Elder brother of Thomas (1500). (*Masters*, 293.)

GOODRICH, JOHN. Matric. pens. from ST JOHN'S, Michs. 1545; B.A. 1547–8; M.A. from Christ's, 1551. Fellow of Jesus, 1547–9. Fellow of Christ's, 1549–53. R. of Elm and Emneth, Cambs., 1552.

GOODRICK, JOHN. Matric. sizar from MAGDALENE, Easter, 1612.

GOODERICKE, JOHN. Adm. pens. at JESUS, Jan. 25, 1632-3. Matric. Fell.-Com. 1633. S. of Sir Henry, of Ribston, Yorks., Knt. B. Apr. 20, 1617. Succeeded his father at Ribston, July 22, 1641. Created Bart., 1641. Compounded for his estates, as a Royalist. Commander of a Troop of Horse under the Earl of Newcastle, 1642. Fined and imprisoned. M.P. for Yorks., 1661-70. Died Nov. 1670. Will, York. (*Vis. of Yorks.*, 1665; A. Gray; *G.E.C.*; M. H. Peacock.)

GOODERICKE, JOHN. Matric. sizar from QUEENS', Easter, 1635. Of Norfolk. B.A. 1637-8; M.A. 1641. Ord. deacon (Norwich); priest, Dec. 18, 1642, age 26. R. of Whissonsett, Norfolk, 1642.

GOODRICK, JOHN. Adm. sizar (age 17) at ST JOHN'S, June 20, 1655. S. of Lionel (1623), clerk, of Nazing, Essex. B. there. School, Northampton (Mr Archer). Matric. 1655; B.A. 1658-9; M.A. 1663 (*Lit. Reg.*). Chaplain in the Navy. One of these names (ord. priest by Bishop of Galloway, Aug. 27, 1660) V. of South Mimms, Middlesex, 1663-7.

GOODRIDGE, JOHN. Adm. sizar (age 20) at CHRIST'S, June 17, 1664. S. of George (not John, as in *Peile*). B. at Hathern, Leics. School, Loughborough (Mr Somerville).

GOODRICH, JOHN. Adm. pens. (age 16) at CAIUS, July 8, 1698. S. of Matthew, surgeon, of Norwich. B. there. School, Wymondham. Scholar, 1698-1700; Matric. 1699. One of these names licensed, by the Bishop, to practise surgery, Sept. 12, 1698. Brother of Matthew (1705). (*Venn*, I. 501.)

GOODRICH, JOHN. Adm. Fell.-Com. at TRINITY, July 6, 1725. S. of Sir Henry, Bart., of Ribston, Yorks. B. May 20, 1708. Matric. 1725; M.A. 1734 (*Lit. Reg.*). Succeeded as Bart., 1738. M.P. for Pontefract, 1774-80; for Ripon, 1787. Envoy Extraordinary to Stockholm. Died Aug. 3, 1789. Buried at Hunsingore. Will, York. Brother of Henry (1736-7) and Thomas (1730). (*G.E.C.*)

GOODRICK, LIONEL. Adm. pe[illegible]. at EMMANUEL, Oct. 6, 1596. Doubtless of East Kirby, Lincs., gent. S. and h. of Edward. Adm. at Gray's Inn, Feb. 9, 1597-8. Of Stickney, Lincs. Died Feb. 1624-5. Doubtless father of the next and Thomas (1630). (*Lincs. Pedigrees*, 416.)

GOODERICK, LIONEL. Adm. sizar at CAIUS, June 27, 1623. S. of Lionel (? above), gent., of North Creake, Norfolk. Bapt. Aug. 27, 1607. School, Ely (Mr Hick). Matric. 1623; B.A. from St John's, 1626-7; M.A. 1630. C. of Nazing, Essex, in 1637. V. of Little Houghton, Northants., 1638-46. R. of Overstone, 1648; appointed by the Parliamentary Committee. Ejected, 1662, but afterwards conformed. P.C. of Waltham Abbey, Essex, 1672-93. Will (Cons. C. London) 1693. Father of John (1655) and brother of Thomas (1630). (*Venn*, I. 263; H. Smith; J. Ch. Smith.)

GOODRICH, MATTHEW. Adm. pens. (age 17) at CAIUS, Oct. 11, 1705. .. of Matthew, surgeon, of Norwich. B. there. School, Norwich (private; Mr Scott). Matric. 1705; Scholar, 1705-11; B.A. 1709-10; M.A. 1713. Ord. deacon (Ely) Dec. 25, 1710; priest, Mar. 25, 1713. R. of Wangford St Denis, Suffolk, 1714-7. R. of East Harling, Norfolk, 1716-9. R. of Brandon Ferry, Suffolk, 1718-42. Buried at St Bartholomew-the-Less, London, Sept. 12, 1742. Brother of John (1698) and father of Robert (1734). (*Venn*, I. 513.)

GOODRICH, NICHOLAS. Adm. sizar (age 17) at CAIUS, May 29, 1597. S. of William, of Wyverstone, Suffolk. Bapt. Oct. 9, 1580. Matric. c. 1597; Scholar, 1597-8; B.A. 1600-1; M.A. from St Catharine's, 1604. Probably a Popish recusant in 1615. Private tutor in the family of Lady Sulyard, at Haughley, Suffolk. Brother of William (1599). (*Venn*, I. 163.)

GOODRICK, OLIVER. Adm. Fell.-Com. at EMMANUEL, Jan. 15, 1606-7. Matric. 1607.

GOODRICKE, PETER. Adm. sizar (age 18) at CHRIST'S, June 18, 1664. S. of William. B. at Leeds. School, Leeds (Mr Gilbert). Matric. 1667.

GOODRICH, RICHARD. B.A. 1496.

GOODRICH, RICHARD. Studied at JESUS. Of Yorkshire, nephew of Thomas, Bishop of Ely. Adm. at Gray's Inn, 1532. Barrister. Attorney of the Court of Augmentations, 1535. Ecclesiastical commissioner under Edward VI. M.P. for Grimsby, 1545-52. Died May, 1562. Buried at St Andrew's, Holborn. (*Cooper*, I. 214; *D.N.B.*)

GOODRICKE, RICHARD. Matric. Fell.-Com. from CHRIST'S, May, 1576. S. of Richard, of Ribston, Yorks. B. c. 1560. Adm. at Gray's Inn, 1578. High Sheriff of Yorks., 1591. Married Muriel, dau. of William Lord Eure, at Ingleby, Nov. 4, 1578. Died Sept. 21, 1601. (*Peile*, I. 135, where he is called 'Robert'; M. H. Peacock.)

GOODRICKE, RICHARD. B.A. (? 1609-10); M.A. from CLARE, 1613.

GOODRICK, ROBERT. Matric. pens. from TRINITY, 1598; Scholar, 1602.

GOODRICK, ROBERT. Adm. pens. at SIDNEY, May, 1602. Matric. 1602. Perhaps of Ipswich, and of Barnard's Inn adm. at Gray's Inn, Aug. 10, 1609.

GOODRICKE, ROBERT. Matric. sizar (age 17) from PEMBROKE, Easter, 1619. S. of Richard, of Bradfield. B.A. 1622-3; M.A. 1626. Fellow, 1627. R. of Horningsheath, Suffolk, 1629. R. of Rushbrooke, 1634, sequestered. Buried at Horningsheath, 1660. Father of the next and Henry (1662-3). (V. B. Redstone.)

GOODRICK or GOODRICH, ROBERT. Adm. sizar at CHRIST'S, Sept. 29, 1656. S. of Robert (above), R. of Horningsheath, Suffolk. B. there. School, Bury, Suffolk (private; Mr Blemmel). Matric. 1657; B.A. from Pembroke, 1660-1; M.A. 1664; B.D. 1671. Fellow of Pembroke, 1662. Ord. deacon and priest (Lincoln) July, 1666. C. of Gt St Andrew's, Cambridge, 1667. V. of Tilney, Norfolk, 1671. R. of North Barsham, 1681-6. Died 1689. Brother of Henry (1662-3). (*Peile*, I. 573.)

GOODRICK, ROBERT. Adm. sizar at ST CATHARINE'S, June 5, 1712. B. in Norfolk, 1694. Matric. 1712; B.A. 1715-6. Ord. deacon (Ely) Sept. 22, 1717; priest (Norwich) June, 1720. Probably brother of Henry (1712).

GOODRICH, ROBERT. Adm. pens. (age 16) at CAIUS, Sept. 30, 1734. S. of Matthew (1705), R. of Brandon, Suffolk. B. at Wangford. Schools, Brandon (Mr Kendall) and Botesdale (Mr Mabourn). Scholar, 1734-42; Matric. 1735; B.A. 1738-9; M.A. 1742. Fellow, 1743-54. Moderator, 1746. Taxor, 1747. Ord. deacon (Norwich) Feb. 22, 1740-1; priest (Lincoln) Sept. 25, 1743. Usher of the Perse School, Cambridge, 1740-7. R. of Bincombe and Broadway, Dorset, 1753-97. R. of Pentridge, 1780-97. Chaplain to the Bishop of St David's. Died Apr. 1797. Will, P.C.C. (*Venn*, II. 40.)

GOODRICK, ROGER. Adm. sizar (age 17) at ST JOHN'S, June 30, 1677. S. of George, of Wrangle, Lincs. B. there. School, Wainfleet (Mr Gibbs). Matric. 1677; B.A. 1680-1. Perhaps V. of Thorpe, Lincs., 1695.

GOODRICKE, SAMUEL. Adm. pens. at EMMANUEL, May 26, 1600.

GOODRICKE, THOMAS. Matric. sizar from CLARE, Easter, 1576.

GOODRICK, THOMAS. Adm. at CORPUS CHRISTI, c. 1500. S. of Edward, of East Kirby, Lincs. B.A. 1510-1; M.A. from Jesus, 1514. Fellow of Jesus, 1511. D.D. Proctor, 1515-6. R. of St Peter Cheap, London, 1529-34. Ambassador to France, 1533-5. Bishop of Ely, 1534-54. Privy Councillor and commissioner for the visitation of the University under Edward VI. A compiler of the Bishops' Book, 1537; and of the first book of Common Prayer, 1547. Lord Keeper, 1551-2; Chancellor, 1552-3. Retained his bishopric under Queen Mary. Died May 10, 1554. Buried in Ely Cathedral. Will (P.C.C.). Brother of John (1500). (*Cooper*, I. 117; *D.N.B.*; *Masters*, 293.)

GOODRICH, THOMAS. Matric. pens. from CHRIST'S, May, 1567.

GOODRICH, THOMAS. Of ST JOHN'S. Author of poems on the accession of James I. (*Cooper*, II. 297.)

GOODRICK, THOMAS. Adm. sizar (age 18) at CHRIST'S, Mar. 14, 1630-1. S. of Lionel (Lyon) (? 1596). B. at North Creake. School, South Creake (Mr Sturgis). Matric. 1631; B.A. 1634-5. Brother of Lionel (1623).

GOODRICKE, THOMAS. Adm. p ns. (age 17) at CHRIST'S, June 13, 1730. 3rd s. of Sir Henry, Bart. B. at Ribston, Yorks., Mar. 12, 1711-2. School, York. Matric. 1731. Lieut.-Colonel of the 25th regiment. Married Elizabeth, dau. of James Button, of Rochester, Esq. Died 1803. Brother of Heury (1736-7) and John (1725). (*Peile*, II. 222.)

GOODRYCKE, WILLIAM. Matric. pens. from QUEENS', Easter, 1545.

GOODERICH, WILLIAM. Adm. sizar (age 14) at CAIUS, June 14, 1599. S. of William, of Wyverstone, Suffolk. Educated by his father. Brother of Nicholas (1597).

GOODERICHE, WILLIAM. Adm. sizar (age 17) at CAIUS, Apr. 15, 1634. S. of John, draper. B. at Bury St Edmunds. School, Bury. Matric. 1634; B.A. 1637-8. Perhaps of Hessett, Suffolk, clerk. Will (Archd. Sudbury) 1678. (*Venn*, I. 313.)

GOODSON, JOHN. Adm. at KING'S (age 18) a scholar from Eton, May 17, 1532. Of Wycombe, Bucks. Name off before 1534.

GOODESON, JOHN. Adm. pens. (age 17) at CAIUS, June 25, 1586. S. of Thomas, citizen of London. B. in London. School, London (Mr Waddington). Scholar, 1586-9.

GOODWIN, *see also* GODWIN.

GOODWIN, ABRAHAM. Adm. sizar (age 18) at CHRIST'S, July 2, 1660. S. of John. B. at (?) Pigtor, Derbs. School, Dronfield (Mr Whitaker). Matric. 1660. Ord. priest (Lichfield) Dec. 6, 1665. (*Peile*, I. 593.)

GOODWIN, ANTHONY. Matric. sizar from TRINITY, Easter, 1571. S. of Humphry, of East Grinstead, Sussex. B.A. 1575-6. R. of Rawmarsh, Yorks., 1577-1628. Buried June 4, 1628. (*F.M.G.*, 604; *Vis. of Yorks.*, 1666.)

GOODWYN, BARTHOLOMEW. Matric. pens. from QUEENS', Lent, 1578-9. Of Cambridgeshire.

GOODWIN, BARTHRAM (BERTRAM). Matric. pens. from ST JOHN'S, Easter, 1618. S. of Thomas (? c. 1593), of Stonham Parva, Suffolk. Bapt. there, Dec. 6, 1601. B.A. 1621-3; M.A. 1625. R. of Earl Stonham and Stonham Parva, 1634. R. of Stanningfield, 1637. (*Suff. Man. Fam.*, I. 235.)

GOODWIN, BENJAMIN. M.A. from ST CATHARINE'S, 1715. S. of William, of London, gent. Matric. from Queen's College, Oxford, July 8, 1707, age 17; B.A. (Oxford) 1711. Ord. priest (Ely) Feb. 21, 1713-4. Minor canon of St Paul's, 1711-23. R. of Somersham, Suffolk, 1718. (*Al. Oxon.*)

GOODWYN, BLASIUS. Adm. Fell.-Com. (age 19) at CAIUS, Nov. 17, 1569. S. of William, gent., merchant, of London. School, Eton. Adm. at the Middle Temple, Dec. 14, 1572. (*Venn*, I. 66.)

GOODWIN, EDMUND. Matric. sizar from CORPUS CHRISTI, 1607. Of Kent. B.A. 1610-1; M.A. 1614, as Godwin. Presented to Herne, Kent, Feb. 29, 1647-8. (*Shaw*, I. 352.)

GOODWIN or GODWYN, EDMUND. Adm. pens. at JESUS, Feb. 6, 1655-6. Of Suffolk. Matric. 1656; Scholar, 1657; B.A. 1659-60; M.A. 1664. One of these names s. of Edmund, of Neyland, Suffolk. (*Suff. Man. Fam.*, I. 226.)

GOODWIN, EDWARD. Adm. at CORPUS CHRISTI, 1581. Of Norfolk.

GOODWIN, EDWARD. Adm. Fell.-Com. at JESUS, May 3, 1693. Of Yorkshire. 1st s. of Edward, of Rawmarsh, Esq. Matric. 1693. Married Jane, dau. of Robert Wainwright, of Middlewood. Of Rawmarsh Hall, Esq. Died *s.p.* Jan. 12, 1747, aged 70. M.I. at Rawmarsh. (Hunter, *S. Yorks.*, II. 48; *F.M.G.*; M. H. Peacock.)

GOODWIN or GOODING, EWIN. Adm. pens. at CORPUS CHRISTI, 1622. Matric. Easter, 1623; B.A. 1626-7. Ord. deacon (Peterb.) Feb. 24, 1626-7. Perhaps R. of Gedding, Suffolk, 1630-42, as 'Edwin.' Died 1642.

GOODWIN, FRANCIS. Matric. pens. at TRINITY, 1637; Scholar, 1641; B.A. 1641-2; M.A. 1645. Ord. deacon and priest (Lincoln) Jan. 5, 1645-6. Perhaps V. of Hinton Ampner, Hants., 1648.

GOODWYN, GEORGE. Matric. pens. from TRINITY, Michs. 1578; Scholar, 1582; B.A. 1582-3; M.A. 1586; B.D. 1593. Fellow, 1585. R. of Moreton, Essex, 1596-1625. Married, at Chipping Ongar, Essex, May 19, 1594, Elizabeth Morris. Buried at Moreton, Mar. 1625. (W. M. Noble.)

GOODWIN, GEORGE. Matric. sizar from CHRIST'S, Jan. 1581-2.

GOODWIN, GEORGE. Adm. at EMMANUEL, Apr. 6, 1630. S. of George, medical practitioner at Stowmarket. B. at Earl Stonham, Suffolk. School, Earl Stonham (Mr Jo. Dodson). Migrated to Caius, June 11, 1631, age 18. B.A. 1634-5; M.A. 1638. Succeeded to his father's property, and apparently to his practice. Called 'physician' in his will, proved (Ipswich) Apr. 13, 1696. (*Venn*, I. 301.)

GOODWIN, GEORGE. Adm. pens. (age 18) at TRINITY, June 18, 1685. S. of James. B. at Shirland, Derbs. School, Westminster. Scholar, 1685. Migrated to Peterhouse, Feb. 15, 1685-6. Matric. 1687; B.A. 1688-9; M.A. 1698. Doubtless R. of Methley, Yorks., 1709-51. Died 1751.

GOODWIN, HUGH. Adm. pens. at TRINITY, Mar. 29, 1669. Matric. 1669; Scholar, 1671; B.A. 1672-3. Fellow, 1674.

GOODWIN, JAMES. Adm. pens. at CLARE, Feb. 18, 1659-60. Of Teversham, Cambs. Matric. 1660; B.A. 1663-4; M.A. 1667. Fellow. Incorp. at Oxford, 1671. Ord. priest (Peterb.) Sept. 20, 1668. R. of Nowton, Suffolk, 1676-80. R. of Sundridge, Kent, 1680-5. Buried there Mar. 19, 1684-5.

GOODWYN, JOHN. Matric. pens. from MICHAELHOUSE, Easter, 1544. One of these names R. of Stanway, Essex, 1570-88. Will (Consist. C. London) 1588. (J. Ch. Smith.)

GOODWYNNE, JOHN. Matric. pens. from CORPUS CHRISTI, Michs. 1581.

GOODWYN, JOHN. Matric. sizar from ST JOHN'S, Michs. 1587. Of Staffordshire. B.A. 1591-2; M.A. 1595; B.D. 1602; D.D. 1616. Fellow, 1593. V. of Rushall, Staffs., 1599-c. 1603. R. of Lydeard St Lawrence, Somerset, 1614-28.

GOODWIN, JOHN. Matric. pens. from TRINITY, Easter, 1609, as Gooddin; B.A. 1612-3; M.A. 1616. Fellow, 1614.

GOODWYN, JOHN. Adm. pens. at SIDNEY, Apr. 14, 1610. *See* GOODING.

GOODWIN, JOHN. Matric. sizar from QUEENS', Easter, 1612. Of Norfolk. B.A. 1615-6; M.A. 1619. Fellow, 1617-27. Incorp. at Oxford, 1622. Preached for a time in Norfolk and at Dover. V. of St Stephen, Coleman St, London, 1633-45. After his ejection set up an Independent congregation. Well-known republican controversialist. Died 1665. For a list of his many works *see D.N.B.*

GOODWIN, JOHN. Matric. sizar from KING'S, Easter, 1613.

GOODWIN, JOHN. Matric. sizar from TRINITY, Easter, 1625. Doubtless s. of Thomas, of Swineshead, Lincs. Scholar, 1627; B.A. 1628-9; M.A. 1632. R. of Brauncewell, Lincs., 1634-9. R. of East Barnet, Middlesex, 1639-43; sequestered, but re-instated, 1660. Buried at East Barnet, Aug. 10, 1679. Father of John (1660). (F. C. Cass, *E. Barnet*, 223.)

GOODWIN, JOHN. Adm. pens. at EMMANUEL, Apr. 1, 1629. S. of John, of East Bergholt, Suffolk. Matric. 1629; B.A. 1632-3; M.A. 1636. In Holy Orders. Married and had issue. (*Suff. Man. Fam.*, I. 226.)

GOODWIN, JOHN. M.A. from KING'S, 1631. S. of Thomas, of Trosle Hill, Kent. Matric. from St John's College, Oxford, June 30, 1626, aged 17; B.A. (Oxford) 1627.

GOODWIN, JOHN. Adm. pens. (age 19) at CHRIST'S, July 2, 1635. S. of Thomas. B. at Thrumpton, Notts. School, Repton (Mr Whitehead).

GOODWIN, JOHN. Adm. pens. (age 17) at ST JOHN'S, May 6, 1656. S. of Philip (1623), clerk, of Watford, Herts. B. there. School, Eton. Matric. 1656; B.A. 1659-60; M.A. 1663. Usher at Felsted School, 1662-4. One of these names, B.A., ord. deacon (Lincoln) June 25; priest, June 29, 1661. Perhaps R. of Morton Bagot, Warws., 1662.

GOODWIN, JOHN. Adm. pens. at TRINITY, June 30, 1660. Doubtless s. of John (1625). Bapt. at East Barnet, July 10, 1642. Matric. 1660; Scholar, 1664; B.A. 1664-5; M.A. 1668. Fellow, 1667. Incorp. at Oxford, 1669. Succeeded his father as R. of East Barnet, Herts., 1679-81. Died 1681. Will proved (P.C.C.) July 8, 1681. (J. Ch. Smith; F. C. Cass, *E. Barnet*, 224.)

GOODWIN, JOHN. Adm. pens. at EMMANUEL, June 3, 1661. Of Lancashire. Matric. 1661; B.A. 1664-5.

GOODWYN, JOHN. Adm. sizar (age 15) at ST JOHN'S, Feb. 4, 1662-3. S. of Thomas, 'sculptor,' of Cambridge. B. there. School, Cambridge. Matric. 1663; B.A. 1666-7. Ord. deacon (Ely) Dec. 22, 1667; priest (London) Sept. 1668. V. of Gestingthorpe, Essex, 1668.

GOODWIN, JOHN. Adm. pens. (age 17) at PEMBROKE, June 19, 1701. S. of Samuel, clerk. B. at Tonbridge, Kent. School, Merchant Taylors'. Matric. 1702; B.A. 1704-5; M.A. 1708. Fellow, 1708. Ord. deacon (London) June 19, 1709; priest (Lincoln) Sept. 23, 1710. Probably R. of Market Bosworth, Leics., 1719-29; and R. of Clapham, Surrey, 1729-53. Died Jan. 22, 1753, aged 71. Father of the next. (But *see Al. Oxon.* for a contemporary.)

GOODWIN, JOHN. Adm. pens. at PEMBROKE, May 13, 1741. S. of John (above), R. of Clapham, Surrey. B. at Market Bosworth, Leics., Nov. 6, 1722. School, Winchester. Matric. 1741. Migrated to Oxford. Matric. from New College, Oxford, May 13, 1742, age 19, as s. of John, of Bosworth, Leics.; B.C.L. (Oxford) 1749. V. of Heckfield, Hants. R. of Paulersbury, Northants., 1767-75. Died Jan. 1775. (*Al. Oxon.*; J. Ch. Smith.)

GOODWIN, JOHN. Adm. sizar (age 20) at PETERHOUSE, June 18, 1748. Of Derby. School, Tideswell. Matric. 1748; Scholar, 1748.

GOODWIN, JONATHAN. Adm. sizar at JESUS, June 13, 1633. Of Derbyshire. B. 1617. School, Repton. Matric. 1633; B.A. 1636-7; M.A. 1641. Perhaps V. of Lazonby, Cumberland, 1637-45, ejected. Minister of Barton-in-Fabis, Notts.; afterwards rector, 1662-71. Died 1671. (*B. Nightingale*, 325.)

GOODWYN, MATTHEW. Adm. scholar (age 17) at CAIUS, Mar. 20, 1578-9. S. of John. B. at Godmanchester, Hunts. School, St Neots.

GOODWIN, MATTHEW. M.A. from KING'S, 1711. S. of Stephen, of Horley, Oxon., clerk. Matric. from Merton College, Oxford, July 8, 1701, age 15; B.A. (New Inn Hall) 1706. Ord. deacon (Peterb.) Sept. 23, 1705. (*Al. Oxon.*)

GOODWIN, NATHANIEL. Matric. sizar from CORPUS CHRISTI, Michs. 1619. Of Suffolk. B.A. 1623; M.A. 1627. Ord. deacon (Norwich) Dec. 18, 1625; priest, Dec. 17, 1626. Doubtless C. of Castle Camps, Cambs., 1632. R. of Cransford, Suffolk, 1635-47, sequestered. (*Al. Oxon.*, where this preferment is assigned to the next.) Admon. (Bury, 1660) of Nathaniel Goodwin, clerk, of Sapiston, to son Nathaniel, clerk, of Barningham. (V. B. Redstone.)

GOODWIN, NATHANIEL. M.A. 1633 (Incorp. from Oxford). S. of John, of Rollwright, Oxon., clerk. Matric. from Magdalen Hall, Oxford, Oct. 20, 1626, age 17; B.A. (Oxford) 1628-9; M.A. 1631. R. of Bridport, Dorset, 1661-82. Preb. of St Asaph, 1668-82. R. of Edgcote, Northants., 1674-86. Died Mar. 26, 1686. Buried at Edgcote. M.I. Will (Northampton) 1686. *See* the above. (*Al. Oxon.*; H. I. Longden.)

GOODWIN, NATHANIEL. M.A. from ST JOHN'S, 1715. S. of John, of Sherrington, Gloucs., gent. Matric. from Oriel College, Oxford, Mar. 4, 1691-2, age 15; B.A. (Oxford) 1695. Will (P.C.C.) 1756, of one of these names; of Alderbury, Wilts., clerk. (J. Ch. Smith.)

GOODWIN, PHILIP. Matric. sizar from ST JOHN'S, Easter, 1623; B.A. 1626-7; M.A. 1630. Ord. deacon (Peterb.) Mar. 16; priest, Mar. 17, 1626-7. One of Cromwell's 'triers.' Lecturer at Hemel Hempstead, 1642. V. of Watford, Herts., 1645; ejected, 1661. Afterwards conformed. Author, theological. Died 1699. Will, P.C.C. Father of John (1656). (*D.N.B.*)

GOODWIN, PHILIP. Matric. sizar from CORPUS CHRISTI, Easter, 1653. Of Suffolk. B.A. 1656-7; M.A. 1660. R. of Gt Moulton, Norfolk, 1661-73. R. of Little Wacton, 1672-1700. Perhaps R. of Liston, Essex, 1673-99. Died 1700. (*Masters.*)

GOODWIN, RALPH. Matric. pens. from TRINITY, Easter, 1608; Scholar, 1611; B.A. 1611-2; M.A. 1615. Fellow, 1614. Incorp. at Oxford, 1615.

GOODWIN, RALPH. Matric. sizar from TRINITY HALL, Easter, 1636. Of Norfolk. Migrated to Queens', Easter, 1637. B.A. 1639-40; M.A. 1643. Ord. deacon (Norwich) Sept. 20, 1640.

GOODWIN, RICHARD. Matric. sizar from MAGDALENE, Michs. 1621; B.A. 1624-5. Buried at St Giles', Cambridge, Oct. 1625.

GOODWIN, RICHARD. Adm. sizar at EMMANUEL, June 30, 1632. Of Sussex. Matric. 1632; B.A. 1635-6; M.A. 1639. Ordained by Bishop Bridgman. C. at Cockey Moor, Bolton. Sequestered to Hargrave, Northants., 1644. Assistant minister (presbyterian) at Bolton, Lancs., 1647. V. of Bolton, 1657-62, ejected. Died Dec. 12, 1685, aged 72. Buried at Bolton. (*Calamy*, II. 85; Shaw, *Bury Classis*, II. 228.)

GOODWIN, RICHARD. Adm. sizar (age 17) at TRINITY, July 27, 1685. S. of William, of Tibberton, Salop. School, Newport, Salop (Mr Sam. Edwards). Matric. 1685; Scholar, 1687.

GOODWIN, RICHARD. Adm. sizar (age 18) at ST JOHN'S, June 26, 1696. S. of Samuel, husbandman. B. at Shirland, Derbs. School, Mansfield (Mr Holcot). Matric. 1696; B.A. 1699-1700; M.A. 1703; B.D 1710; D.D. 1727. Fellow, 1701-18. Ord. deacon (Lincoln) Dec. 22, 1700; priest (London) Mar. 6, 1700-1. R. of Tankersley, Yorks., 1715-52. Preb. of York, 1720-52. R. of Prestwick, Lancs., 1732. Died 1752.

GOODWIN, ROBERT. Adm. sizar at QUEENS', July 6, 1620. Of Suffolk. B.A. 1623-4; M.A. 1627. Ord. priest (Chichester). R. of Brome, Suffolk, 1647. V. of Upton, Norfolk, 1661-79. R. of Fishley, 1672-9. Buried at Upton, Feb. 12, 1678-9.

GOODWIN, ROBERT. Adm. pens. (age 30) at PETERHOUSE, May 30, 1660. Of Middlesex. Perhaps C. of Burlingham St Peter, Norfolk, 1671, as 'B.A.' Licensed to teach grammar.

GOODWIN, ROBERT. Adm. sizar at QUEENS', Mar. 30, 1692. Of Norfolk. S. of Philip (? 1653), R. of Liston, Essex. Matric. 1692; B.A. 1695-6; M.A. 1699. Ord. deacon (London) Dec. 20, 1696; priest, June 21, 1699. Schoolmaster at Sudbury, 1698. Succeeded his father as R. of Liston, Essex, 1699-1719. Perhaps R. of Wormingford, 1701-9. R. of Borley, 1709-19. Married, at Temple Church, Feb. 16, 1701-2, Sarah Smythies. Died 1719. Father of the next and of William (1728). Perhaps brother of Thomas (1697). (*Newcourt.*)

GOODWIN, ROBERT. Adm. sizar at JESUS, Jan. 26, 1724-5. Of Essex. S. of Robert (above), clerk, deceased. Brother of William (1728).

GOODWIN, ROBERT. Adm. pens. (age 18) at CAIUS, *c.* Apr. 1735. S. of Thomas, surgeon, of Lynn. B. there. Schools, Lynn (Mr Horne and Mr Squire) and Wymondham (Mr Brett). Scholar, 1735-42; Matric. 1736; B.A. 1738-9; M.A. 1742. Ord. deacon (Norwich) Feb. 24, 1742; priest (Ely) Feb. 26, 1742-3. R. of Clippesby, Norfolk, 1743-89; of Warham St Mary Magdalene, 1749-89. Will (P.C.C.) 1789. (*Venn*, II. 41.)

GOODWIN, ROGER. Matric. sizar from QUEENS', Michs. 1569. Of Nottinghamshire. B.A. 1573-4. Ord. deacon (Durham) June 7, 1579; priest (Lincoln) July 28, 1580. V. of Prodingham, Lincs., 1579.

GOODWIN or GODWIN, SAMUEL. Adm. pens. (age 15) at CHRIST'S, Jan. 12, 1638-9. S. of Francis. B. at Derby. School, Derby (Mr Whiting). Matric. 1639. Adm. at the Inner Temple, Apr. 20, 1648. Possibly father of the next. (*Peile*, I. 457.)

GOODWIN, SAMUEL. Adm. pens. at CHRIST'S, 1673. S. of Samuel (? above). B. at Little Eaton, Derbs. School, Derby (Mr Mathews). Matric. 1674.

GOODWYNE, THOMAS. Adm. at KING'S, a scholar from Eton, 1490. Possibly Thomas Goodrich, whom *see.*

GOODWIN, THOMAS. B.Civ.L. 1541-2. Doubtless s. of Roger, of Stonham Parva, Suffolk. R. of Bressingham, Norfolk, 1547. V. of Mattishall. Commissary for the Archdeacon of Norfolk, 1556; for the Archdeaconry of Norwich, 1563. Will proved, Aug. 10, 1569. (*Suff. Man. Fam.*, I. 235.)

GOODWIN, THOMAS. Matric. pens. from ST JOHN'S, *c.* 1593. Perhaps s. and h. of Theodore, of Stonham Parva, Suffolk, and of Barnard's Inn; adm. at Gray's Inn, Nov. 20, 1595. Of Stonham Parva, Esq. Died Apr. 3, 1638. If so, father of Barthram (1618).

GOODWIN, THOMAS. Adm. pens. at EMMANUEL, Apr. 1607. S. of Francis, Bailiff of Derby. Matric. 1607; Scholar; B.A. 1610-1; M.A. 1614. Incorp. at Oxford, 1614. Ord. deacon (Peterb.) June 14; priest, June 15, 1617. Apparently the 'Thomas Goodwin, *alias* Okenden, diocesis Cantuariensis'; M.A. of Cambridge, and Oxford, who appeared at Douay, Feb. 14, 1619-20, and left Aug. 1621, rejoining the Church of England. (*Derby School Reg.*; *Douay Diary.*)

GOODWIN, THOMAS. Matric. pens. from CHRIST'S, Apr. 1614. B. at Rollesby, Norfolk, Oct. 5, 1600. B.A. 1616-7; M.A. (St Catharine's) 1620; B.D. 1630; D.D. (by diploma, Oxford) 1653. Fellow of St Catharine's, 1620. Ord. deacon (Peterb.) Mar. 2, 1621-2. Lecturer at Trinity Church, Cambridge, 1628; Vicar, 1632. Became an Independent, 1634. Went to Holland and became pastor of the English Church at Arnheim. Returned to London, 1640. Member of the Westminster Assembly, 1643. Chaplain to the Council of State, 1649. President of Magdalen College, Oxford, 1650. Deprived, 1660. Author, sermons. Died Feb. 23, 1679-80, aged 79. Will (P.C.C.) 1682; of St Bartholomew-the-Great, London. (*Peile*, I. 295; *D.N.B.*)

GOODWIN, THOMAS. Adm. pens. (age 16) at SIDNEY, May 9, 1632. S. of Richard, gent., deceased. B. at Hogsthorpe, Lincs. School, Alford (Mr William Bennet). Matric. 1632. Adm. at the Inner Temple, 1634.

GOODWIN, THOMAS. Adm. pens. (age 17) at PETERHOUSE, May 4, 1637. Perhaps s. of Thomas, of Sleaford, Lincs. School, Newark. Matric. 1637. (*T. A. Walker*, 60.)

GOODWIN, THOMAS. Matric. pens. from ST CATHARINE'S, Michs. 1639. Of Essex. B.A. 1642-3; M.A. from St John's, 1646. Fellow of St John's, 1644. V. of Weald, Essex, 1649-58. Died Sept. 4, 1658. Buried at South Weald. M.I. Will proved (P.C.C.) 1658.

GOODWIN, THOMAS. Adm. pens. at EMMANUEL, Feb. 6, 1689-90. Of Derbyshire. Matric. 1690. One of these names, s. of ——, of Derby, clothworker, adm. at Gray's Inn, Apr. 11, 1691. Barrister, 1699. Bencher, 1724.

GOODWYN, THOMAS. Adm. sizar (age 17) at ST JOHN'S, June 17, 1697. S. of Philip (? 1653), clerk. B. at Sudbury, Suffolk. School, Sudbury (Mr Hast). Matric. 1697; B.A. 1700-1; M.A. 1720. Perhaps R. of Wivenhoe, Essex, 1710. R. of Liston, 1719-49. Died *c.* 1749. Perhaps brother of Robert (1692).

GOODWIN, THOMAS. Adm. sizar (age 21) at CAIUS, July 10, 1714. S. of Edmund, husbandman, of Brisley, Norfolk. B. there. Schools, Saham Toney (Mr Sayer), Watton (Mr Berry) and Walsingham (Mr Harding). Matric. 1714; Scholar, 1714-9; B.A. 1718-9. Ord. deacon (Norwich) Dec. 20, 1719, as C. of Horningtoft. C. of Hingham, in 1723. Will of Thomas Goodwin, clerk, of Brisley (Norwich C. C.) 1768. (*Venn*, II. 3.)

GOODWIN, THOMAS. Adm. sizar (age 18) at TRINITY, Mar. 23, 1736-7. S. of Thomas, of Uttoxeter, Staffs. School, Uttoxeter (Mr Daintry). Matric. 1737; Scholar, 1739; B.A. 1740-1; M.A. 1744. Fellow, 1743. Ord. deacon (Lincoln, *Litt. dim.* from Peterb.) June 13, 1742; priest (Peterb.) May 15, 1744. C. of Addington Magna, Northants. R. of Loughton, Bucks., 1758-85. Will (P.C.C.) 1785.

GOODWIN, THOMAS. Adm. sizar (age 18) at PEMBROKE, June 1, 1745. S. of John, of Martlesham, Grundisburgh, Suffolk. B. at Woodbridge. Matric. 1745; B.A. 1748-9. Ord. deacon (Norwich) Sept. 1750; priest, Dec. 1750. R. of Martlesham, 1750-98. Died Feb. 12, 1798. Buried at Martlesham. M.I. (*Suff. Man. Fam.*, I. 214; V. B. Redstone.)

GOODWIN, TIMOTHY. Adm. at CORPUS CHRISTI, 1694. Of Norwich. Ord. priest (Norwich) Jan. 1698-9. One of these names adm. at Leyden, Nov. 22, 1691. Probably same as the next.

GOODWYN, TIMOTHY. M.A. 1697 (Incorp. from Oxford). D.D. of Utrecht, 1692. Created M.A. from St Edmund's Hall, Oxford, 1697; D.D. (Lambeth) 1714. R. of Rushock, Worcs., 1701. Chaplain to the bishop of Oxford, 1707. Archdeacon of Oxford, 1707-14. R. of Heythrop, Oxon., 1710-4. Chaplain to Charles, Duke of Shrewsbury. Bishop of Kilmore and Ardagh, 1714. Archbishop of Cashel, 1727-9. Died at Dublin, Dec. 13, 1729. Buried at St Anne's, Dublin. Will, Dublin. (*Al. Oxon.*; *D.N.B.*)

GOODWIN, VINCENT. Matric. sizar from GONVILLE HALL, Nov. 1554. Ord. priest (Lincoln) Apr. 8, 1562. R. of Oakington, Cambs., 1564. Preacher at Yarmouth, 1570-84, suspended. R. of Maltby, Norfolk, 1571. R. of Whissonsett, 1572-7. R. of Cley, 1600. Will (Norwich) 1606. Father of the next. (*Venn*, I. 39.)

GOODWIN, VINCENT. Adm. pens. (age 15) at CAIUS, Mar. 2, 1587-8. S. of Vincent (1554), R. of Cley, Norfolk. School, Holt (Mr Williams). Matric. 1588; Scholar, 1588-95; B.A. 1591-2; M.A. 1595. Ord. deacon and priest (Norwich) Sept. 29, 1604. R. of Cley, 1606. Will (Norwich Archd. C.) 1645; of Cley. (*Venn*, I. 133.)

GOODWYN, W. Matric. pens. from ST JOHN'S, Michs. 1564.

GOODWIN, WILLIAM. M.A. 1583 (Incorp. from Oxford). Student at Christ Church, 1573. B.A. (Oxford) 1577; M.A. 1580; B.D. and D.D. 1602. Dean of Christ Church, 1611-20. Vice-Chancellor, 1614-6 and 1617-9. R. of Upton Scudamore, Wilts., 1587. Preb. of Sarum, 1587-1620. Preb. of York, 1590-1605; Chancellor, 1605. R. of Stonegrave, Yorks., 1590; of Etton, 1591; of Escrick, 1603; of Wheldrake, 1606. R. of All Hallows-the-Great, London, 1614-7. Archdeacon of Middlesex, 1616-20. R. of Stanton St John, Oxon., 1616. V. of Chalgrove, 1617. Died June 11, 1620. Buried in Christ Church Cathedral, Oxford. (*Al. Oxon.*; *D.N.B.*)

GOODWIN, WILLIAM (1593), *see* GODDEN.

GODWIN, WILLIAM. Matric. sizar from QUEENS', Lent, 1620-1. Of Norfolk. B.A. 1623-4. Ord. deacon (Peterb.) May 23, 1624; priest, June 4, 1626.

GOODWIN, WILLIAM. Matric. sizar from QUEENS', Michs. 1621. Of Norfolk. B.A. 1624-5; M.A. 1628. Ord. deacon and priest (Norwich) Sept. 24, 1626.

GOODWIN, WILLIAM. Matric. sizar from ST JOHN'S, Easter, 1621.

GOODWIN, WILLIAM. Adm. pens. at EMMANUEL, Mar. 27, 1627. Matric. 1627; B.A. 1630-1.

GOODWIN, WILLIAM. Adm. sizar (age 15) at ST JOHN'S, Apr. 10, 1668. S. of Matthew, merchant, of All Saints', Lombard Street, Middlesex. B. there. School, Highgate (Mr Carter). Matric. 1668; B.A. 1671-2; M.A. 1675. Ord. priest (London) Mar. 4, 1682-3. V. of Ickleford, Herts., 1682. V. of Pirton, 1682-1732. Died Mar. 25, 1732. (*G. Mag.*)

GOODWIN, WILLIAM. Adm. sizar at EMMANUEL, July 1, 1669. Of Derbyshire.

GOODWIN, WILLIAM. Adm. sizar at JESUS, Dec. 27, 1728. S. of Robert (1692), clerk. B. at Liston, Essex. School, Bury St Edmunds. Matric. 1729; Rustat scholar, 1729. Migrated to Christ's, June 12, 1731. B.A. 1732-3. Ord. deacon (Norwich) Dec. 1733; priest (York) Mar. 1738-9. C. of West Wickham, Kent, 1738. R. of Stanstead, Suffolk, 1739-48. Died at Stanstead, Nov. 7, 1748. Buried at Liston. Brother of Robert (1724-5). (*Peile*, II. 22-4.)

GODWIN, ——. B.Can.L. 1477-8.

GOODWIN (Rector). *Cautio* for degree, 1483-4.

GOODWINE, ——. Adm. sizar (age 17) at CHRIST'S, Jan. 22, 1622-3. S. of John. B. in London. Schools, Shenley, Essex (Mr Syddall) and Havering (Mr Hampton and Mr Eyer).

GOODWIN, ——. Adm. Fell.-Com. at ST CATHARINE'S, Nov. 1683.

GOODYEAR, *see also* GOODERE.

GOODYARE, HENRY. Matric. Fell.-Com. from TRINITY, Michs. 1570. Probably s. and h. of William, of Hadley, Herts.; age 20 in 1572. Knighted, July 19, 1608. Of Newgate Street, Herts. Died June 12, 1629. Buried at Hatfield. Will, P.C.C. One of these names adm. at Gray's Inn, 1570, and another in 1572. (*Vis. of Herts.*; J. Ch. Smith; F. C. Cass, *Monken Hadley*.)

GOODYERE, HENRY. Matric. Fell.-Com. from ST JOHN'S, Michs. 1587. One of these names s. of William, of Monk's Kirby, Warws. Of Polesworth, Knt. Gentleman of the Privy Chamber to James I. Died Mar. 13, 1626-7. (F. C. Cass, *Monken Hadley*.)

GOODYERE, HENRY. Matric. pens. from TRINITY, *c.* 1595. One of these names R. of Limpenhoe, Norfolk, 1630.

GOODYEARE, HENRY. Matric. sizar from CLARE, Michs. 1626; B.A. 1630-1; M.A. 1634. Sequestered to Shenfield, Essex, 1643-7; and possibly to Hambledon, Bucks., till 1660, as Goodeen, and called the 'Parson of Hambledon.' (*Lipscomb*, III. 573.)

GOODYEAR, HUGH. Adm. sizar at EMMANUEL, Easter, 1608. Matric. 1608; Scholar; B.A. 1612-3; M.A. 1616. Adm. at Leyden, Jan. 14, 1617-8.

GOODYERE, JOHN. Adm. sizar at EMMANUEL, Jan. 11, 1590-1. Matric. 1591; Scholar; B.A. 1594-5; M.A. 1598. Ord. priest (Norwich) Mar. 25, 1598, age 25; C. of Upwell, Norfolk. R. of West Walton, 1614.

GOODYEERE, JOHN. Matric. Fell.-Com. from TRINITY, Michs. 1610. Perhaps only s. of Henry (? 1587), of Polesworth, Warws., Knt. Died Dec. 1624. (F. C. Cass, *Monken Hadley*, 151.)

GOODYEAR, JOHN. Adm. sizar at ST CATHARINE'S, July 8, 1685. Matric. 1687; B.A. 1688-9; M.A. 1695. V. of Bapchild, Kent, 1695-1709. V. of Newington, 1708-15.

GOODYEAR, ROGER. Adm. pens. at EMMANUEL, June 19, 1622. Matric. 1622; B.A. 1625-6. Adm. at Leyden, July 6, 1627.

GOODYEARE, SAMUEL. Matric. sizar from ST JOHN'S, Michs. 1576. Of Essex. Perhaps s. of Leonard, R. of Colchester. B.A. 1580-1; M.A. 1584. Fellow, 1585. Will of one of these names (P.C.C.) 1625; 'LL.D.,' Dean of St Asaph. Not found in *Le Neve* or *Browne Willis*.

GOODYER, THOMAS. Matric. pens. from ST JOHN'S, Michs. 1552.

GOODYER, WILLIAM. Matric. pens. from ST JOHN'S, Michs. 1552.

GOODYON, GEORGE. Adm. sizar (age 17) at CAIUS, May 18, 1614. S. of William, husbandman. B. at Horncastle, Lincs. School, Horncastle (Mr Mulsey). Matric. 1613; B.A. 1617-8. Ord. deacon (Peterb.) Sept. 21, 1617; priest, May 31, 1618.

GOOKIN, SAMUEL. Adm. pens. at QUEENS', Easter, 1627. S. and h. of John, of Northborne, Kent, Esq. Matric. 1627, as 'Goodin.' Adm. at Lincoln's Inn, Jan. 26, 1628-9. Proved his father's will, 1637.

GOOKYN, THOMAS. Matric. pens. from ST JOHN'S, Michs. 1588.

GOOLE, WILLIAM. Matric. sizar from TRINITY, Easter, 1575.

GOOSE, JEREMIAH. Adm. pens. (age 17) at CHRIST'S, Apr. 25, 1627. S. of Jeremiah. B. at Cambridge. School, Perse (Mr Lovering). Matric. 1627; B.A. 1630-1; M.A. 1634. Doubtless R. of St Leonard's, Colchester, 1643-61. Died before 1662. Brother of the next. (*Peile*, I. 382.)

GOOSE, JOHN. Adm. sizar (age 16) at CHRIST'S, Jan. 26, 1629-30. S. of Jeremiah. B. at Cambridge. School, Perse. Matric. 1629-30. Brother of the above.

GOOSE, JOHN. Adm. at CORPUS CHRISTI, 1674. Of Norfolk. Matric. 1675; B.A. 1677-8; M.A. 1681. Ord. deacon (Norwich) Feb. 1677-8; priest, June, 1679. R. of Reedham, Norfolk, till 1720. R. of Billockby, 1679-92. Died 1720.

GOOSE, THOMAS. Matric. pens. from QUEENS', Easter, 1575; B.A. 1577-8; M.A. 1581. Perhaps incorp. at Oxford, 1611, as 'Gootes.' One of these names V. of Twickenham, Middlesex, 1596-1640. Buried there Mar. 10, 1639-40, aged 83. Will proved (P.C.C.) 1641.

GOOSE, WILLIAM. Matric. sizar from TRINITY, Easter, 1628; B.A. 1631-2.

GOOSEY, JOHN. Matric. pens. from CLARE, Michs. 1617.

GOOSTREE, JOHN. Ord. deacon (Peterb.) Mar. 16, 1616-7, as 'late of ST JOHN'S, literate'; priest, Mar. 1, 1617-8.

GOOTES, THOMAS. B.Civ.L. 1521-2.

GOOTES, THOMAS. 'M.A. of Cambridge,' Incorp. at Oxford, 1612. (*Al. Oxon.*, perhaps a mistake for Tho. Coote.)

GOPFERLER, ——. Matric. Fell.-Com. from MICHAELHOUSE, Easter, 1544; B.D. 1543-4, as Jofferler.

GORDON, JOHN. Adm. pen. (age 19) at TRINITY, June 18, 1720. S. of John, of London, citizen and watchmaker. School, Westminster. Matric. 1720; Scholar, 1721. Adm. at Gray's Inn, Nov. 9, 1718. Barrister, 1725. Professor of music at Gresham College, 1724-39. Died Dec. 12, 1739. (*D.N.B.*; *Al. Westmon.*, 275.)

GORDON, JOHN. Adm. sizar at PETERHOUSE, Feb. 8, 1744-5. S. of John, of Whitworth, Durham. B. Nov. 6, 1724. School, Durham (Mr Dougworth). Matric. 1745; Scholar, 1745. Migrated to Emmanuel, July 15, 1747. B.A. 1748-9; M.A. 1752; D.D. 1765. Gillingham fellow of Emmanuel, 1751. Proctor, 1755. Fellow of Peterhouse, 1759. Ord. deacon (Ely) May 24, 1752; priest, Dec. 25, 1752. R. of Henstead, Suffolk, 1758-93. Chaplain to the Bishop of Lincoln, 1765. Archdeacon of Buckingham, 1766-9. Archdeacon of Lincoln, 1769-93. Preb. of Lincoln, 1769-75. Precentor of Lincoln, 1775-93. F.S.A. Married, June 14, 1762, Anne, dau. of Dr Dighton, of Newmarket, and widow of Dr Williams, public orator. Author, sermons, etc. Died at Lincoln, Jan. 5, 1793, aged 67. (*T. A. Walker*; G. *Mag.*)

GORDON, Sir ROBERT. M.A. 1615 (on King's visit). 4th s. of Alexander, Earl of Sutherland. B. May 14, 1580. Educated at St Andrews University and afterwards at Edinburgh. Travelled abroad, 1602–5. Entered the service of King James VI. Knighted, 1609. Created Knight Baronet, May 25, 1625. Tutor and guardian to his nephew John (afterwards Earl of Sutherland) 1615–30. Author of the *Genealogie of the Earls of Sutherland*. Died at Gordonstown, Mar. 1656. (The *Scots Peerage*, VIII. 345.)

GORDOUN, ROBERT. Adm. sizar (age 17) at ST JOHN'S, Mar. 29, 1721. S. of Robert, gent., of Durham. B. at Wolsingham. Bapt. there, Oct. 21, 1703. School, Durham (Mr Rosse). Matric. 1721. Adm. at the Middle Temple, Apr. 2, 1724.

GORDON, WILLIAM. Adm. at CORPUS CHRISTI, 1737. Of London. Matric. 1738; B.A. 1740–1; M.A. 1744; B.D. 1752. Fellow, 1744–54. Junior Proctor, 1748–9. Ord. deacon (Norwich) Mar. 1741–2; priest, Apr. 1743. Died June 20, 1796. For a personal description *see* Cole (*Brit. Mus.* 5870, 132.)

GORE, CHARLES. Adm. pens. at JESUS, June 29, 1678. S. of Sir John (? 1640), Knt., of Sacombe, Herts. Matric. 1678; B.A. 1681–2; Scholar, 1682. Probably brother of Ralph (1675).

GORE, CHARLES. Adm. Fell.-Com. at CHRIST'S, Mar. 30, 1744. S. of Thomas. B. at Barrow, Somerset. School, Fulham (Mr Crofts). Matric. 1744. Adm. at the Inner Temple, Aug. 17, 1742. (*Peile*, II. 246.)

GORE, EDWARD. Adm. pens. at EMMANUEL, Sept. 7, 1693. Of Kent. S. and h. of Gerard, of Chilton, Kent. Adm. at the Inner Temple, Oct. 25, 1695.

GORE, HENRY. Adm. pens. at ST CATHARINE'S, May 25, 1679. Matric. 1682; B.A. 1682–3. Probably 2nd s. of Humphrey, of Gilston, Herts., Knt.; adm. at the Inner Temple, Oct. 31, 1684.

GORE, JOHN. Matric. pens. from QUEENS', Michs. 1613. Of London. Probably s. of Sir John (Lord Mayor of London, 1625). Adm. at the Middle Temple, Mar. 10, 1617–8. Knighted, 1641. M.P. for Herts., 1656–8. Of Gilston, Herts. Died Nov. 3, 1659, aged 62. Will (P.C.C.) 1660. Father of William (1647). (Le Neve, *Knights*, 100.)

GORE, JOHN. Matric. Fell.-Com. from ST CATHARINE'S, 1640. Of Essex. Perhaps s. of Christopher, of London and Susan, dau. of Sir Kenelm Jenour, of Essex, Bart. (*Vis. of London*, 1634.)

GORE, JOHN. Adm. pens. at TRINITY, Apr. 24, 1649. Of Surrey. Matric. 1649.

GORE or GOORE, JOHN. Matric. Fell.-Com. from QUEENS', Easter, 1659. Of Hertfordshire.

GORE, JOHN. Adm. Fell.-Com. at QUEENS', Apr. 16, 1678. Of Hertfordshire. Probably 1st s. of Humphrey, of Gilston, Herts., Knt. Bapt. there, June 6, 1659. Married Sarah, dau. of Sir John Robinson, Bart. Buried at Gilston, Aug. 4, 1691. Perhaps brother of Henry (1679). (*Clutterbuck*, III. 170.)

GORE, RALPH. M.A. 1675 (*Lit. Reg.*). Probably brother of Charles (1678).

GOORE, RICHARD. Matric. sizar from CLARE, Michs. 1581.

GOORE, ROGER. Matric. pens. from TRINITY, Michs. 1566.

GORE, THOMAS. Matric. pens. from KING'S, Easter, 1625; B.A. 1628–9; M.A. 1633.

GORE, THOMAS. Adm. sizar (age 15) at ST JOHN'S, Dec. 6, 1638. S. of John, lecturer at St Peter's, Cornhill, London. B. at Wenden Lofts, Essex. School, Newport, Essex (private; Mr Woolley). Matric. 1640; B.A. 1642–3.

GORE, THOMAS. Adm. pens. at JESUS, Sept. 11, 1663. Previously matric. from Magdalen Hall, Oxford, Oct. 29, 1661, age 15. S. of Charles, draper, of Towcester, Northants. B. Mar. 12, 1645–6. School, Merchant Taylors'. Matric. 1663; Scholar, 1664; B.A. 1665–6; M.A. 1669. Signed for deacon (London) June 7, 1666. Ord. priest (*Litt. dim.* from Lincoln) May 17, 1668. R. of Maidford, Northants., 1672–89. Buried at Towcester, Aug. 31, 1689. Will (Northampton) 1689. (*Al. Oxon.*; *Baker*, II. 47.)

GORE, WILLIAM. Matric. pens. from QUEENS', Easter, 1647. S. of Sir John (1613), of Gilston, Herts. B.A. 1649; M.A. 1653. Fellow, 1657–9. Adm. at Gray's Inn, Jan. 30, 1651–2. Barrister-at-law. Of Tewin, Herts. Died Aug. 9, 1709, aged 79. M.I. at Tewin. Will, P.C.C. (Le Neve, *Knights*, 100.)

GORE, WILLIAM. Adm. pens. at QUEENS', Dec. 15, 1691. Of Hertfordshire. Doubtless of Tring. Matric. 1692. M.P. for Colchester, 1711–3, 1714; for St Albans, 1722–7; for Cricklade, 1734–9. Died Oct. 22, 1739. (A. B. Beaven.)

GORE, —— (*senior*). Matric. Fell.-Com. from TRINITY, Easter, 1623.

GORE, —— (*junior*). Matric. Fell.-Com. from TRINITY, Easter, 1623.

GORE, ——. Adm. pens. at ST CATHARINE'S, Easter, 1642.

GORGE, ——. B.Civ.L. 1482.

GORGES or GORGE, Sir FERDINAND. M.A. 1594–5. Of Ashton, Somerset. S. of Edward, of Wraxall. Naval and military commander and the father of English colonisation in America. Served under the Earl of Essex in Normandy, 1591; wounded at the siege of Rouen; knighted for his gallantry, Sept. 27 (?), 1591. M.P. for Cardigan, 1593. Joined Essex in the Island Voyage, 1597. Governor of Plymouth. Arrested along with Essex, 1601, but gave evidence against him. Formed the settlement of New Plymouth, 1628; lord proprietary of the province of Maine, 1639. Died May, 1647. (*D.N.B.*)

GORGES, FRANCIS. Adm. as nobleman at CLARE, July 16, 1635. Matric. Fell.-Com. Easter, 1635; M.A. 1635–6.

GORGES, RICHARD. Adm. as nobleman at CLARE, June 30, 1637. Matric. Fell.-Com. 1637. S. and h. of Edward, Baron Gorges. B. 1619. Succeeded his father, *c.* 1650. M.P. for Newton, Lancs., 1661–79. Died Sept. 1712. (*G.E.C.*; J. Ch. Smith.)

GORGES, ROBERT. M.A. 1652 (Incorp. from Oxford). Of Cheddar, Somerset. S. of Henry. Created M.A. (St Edmund's Hall, Oxford) Apr. 15, 1648; LL.D. (Trinity College, Dublin). Delegate of Parliamentary visitors, 1647. Fellow of St John's College, Oxford, 1648. Proctor (Oxford) 1653. Student of the Inner Temple, 1650. Secretary to Henry Cromwell, Lord Lieutenant of Ireland. General of the King's forces in Ireland. (*Al. Oxon.*)

GORGES, ROBERT. Adm. Fell.-Com. (age 18) at ST JOHN'S, June 20, 1721. S. of Henry, gent., of Eye and the Mynde, Hereford. B. at Eye. Schools, Coney Hatch (Mr Ellis) and Hereford (Mr Rodd). Matric. 1721. Died young. Buried at Eye, Dec. 22, 1727.

GORGES, THOMAS. M.A. 1628 (Incorp. from Oxford). S. of Sir Edward, of Wraxall, Somerset. Bapt. there, Feb. 13, 1602–3. Matric. from Queen's College, Oxford, Feb. 1, 1621–2, age 18; B.A. 1624; M.A. (St Alban's Hall) 1627; D.D. 1661. Fellow of All Souls, 1629. Preb. of Sarum, 1643–67. Sub-almoner to the King. R. of Wraxall, 1663–7. Archdeacon of Winchester, 1661–6. Preb. of Westminster, 1661–7. Died Dec. 12, 1667. Buried in Westminster Abbey. Will (Westminster) 1668. (*Al. Oxon.*)

GORGES, WILLIAM. Adm. Fell.-Com. at EMMANUEL, Apr. 26, 1636. Of Somerset. Perhaps s. of Sir Robert, of Redlinch, Somerset. Matric. 1636. Died in College. Buried at St Andrew's, Cambridge, Apr. 8, 1639. (Hoare, *Wilts.*, IV. ii. 30.))

GORING, ARTHUR. Adm. Fell.-Com. at EMMANUEL, Mar. 4, 1614–5. S. of Sir George (1600), of Lewes, Sussex, Knt. Matric. 1615. Adm. at Gray's Inn, Oct. 21, 1618. Brother of the next and George (1626).

GORING, CHARLES. Adm. Fell.-Com. at JESUS, Sept. 19, 1636. S. of George (1600), Baron Hurstpierpoint, of Sussex, afterwards Earl of Norwich. Bapt. at St Margaret's, Westminster, Oct. 23, 1624. Matric. 1637. Commander in the Royalist cavalry. Fought at Newbury. Succeeded his father, 1663. Died Mar. 3, 1670–1. Buried at Leyton, Essex. M.I. there. Will, P.C.C. Brother of the above and George (1626). (A. Gray.)

GORING, EDWARD. Adm. scholar at SIDNEY, Mar. 3, 1608–9. Matric. 1609. Probably brother of Henry (1608–9).

GORING, EDWARD. Adm. Fell.-Com. at TRINITY, June 1, 1660. Died June 8, 1661, aged 17. M.I. at All Saints', Cambridge. (Le Neve, *Mon.*, IV. 82.)

GORINGE, GEORGE. Adm. Fell.-Com. at SIDNEY, Sept. 1600. Previously matric. at Brasenose, Oxford, May, 1594, age 15. S. of George, of Hurstpierpoint, Sussex. Perhaps specially adm. at Lincoln's Inn, Feb. 24, 1591–2. Knighted, May 29, 1608. M.P. for Lewes, 1620–2, 1624–5, 1626, 1628. Elected also for Stamford, 1624. M.P. for Portsmouth, 1640. Accompanied Prince Charles to Spain, 1623: negotiated his marriage with Henrietta Maria of France. Privy Councillor, 1639. Ambassador extraordinary to the Hague, 1642; and to Paris, 1643–4. Created Earl of Norwich, 1644. Subsequently commanded in Kent and Essex. Sentenced to death after the capitulation of Colchester, 1648, but respited by the casting vote of the Speaker. At the Restoration be became captainmf the Yeomen of the Guard, 1660–3. Died at Brentford, J . 6, 1652–3. Buried in Westminster Abbey. Father of Asthur (1614–5), Charles (1636) and the next. (*Al. Oxon.*; *D.N.B.*; G.E.C.; A. . Beaven.)

GORING, GEORGE. M.A. 1626 (*fil. nob.*). S. and h. of George (above), Lieut.-General in the Royalist army. Married Lettice, dau. of Richard, Earl of Cork. Died at Madrid, *c.* July, 1657. Brother of Arthur (1614–5) and Charles (1636).

GORING, HENRY. Adm. scholar at SIDNEY, Mar. 3, 1608–9. Matric. 1609; B.A. 1612–3. Perhaps 3rd s. of George, and brother of George (1600). (*Vis. of Sussex*, 1633.)

GORING, LOVETT. Adm. pens. (age 17) at CHRIST'S, Apr. 13, 1664. Eldest s. of William, of Booth, Staffs. and Anne, dau. of Thomas Lovett. B. Apr. 14, 1647. School, Mackworth (Mr Ogden). Matric. 1664. (*Staffs. Pedigrees*; *Peile*, I. 608.)

GORING, THOMAS. Adm. Fell.-Com. at EMMANUEL, Sept. 22, 1616. Matric. 1616.

GORING, THOMAS. Adm. Fell.-Com. (age 15) at CHRIST'S, Feb. 8, 1663–4. Eldest s. of John, Esq., of Kingston, Staffs. B. there. School, Mackworth (Mr Ogden). Married Elizabeth, dau. of Richard Ployer, of Hints, Staffs. Died 1678. Brother of the next. (*Peile*, I. 607; *Staffs. Pedigrees*.)

GORING, WILLIAM. Adm. pens. (age 17) at CHRIST'S, June 18, 1666. S. of John. B. at Kingston, Staffs. School, Repton. Matric. 1667–8. Married and had issue. Brother of the above. (*Staffs. Pedigrees*; *Peile*, II. 5.)

GORREY, *see* TORREY, ROGER.

GORST, CHARLES. Adm. at EMMANUEL, Dec. 11, 1654. S. of John. B. in London. School, London (private; Mr Rosse). Matric. 1655. Migrated as Fell.-Com. to Christ's, Sept. 25, 1657, age 21. B.A. 1657–8. Incorp. at Oxford, 1658.

GORSTELOW, THOMAS. B.D. 1634 (Incorp. from Oxford). Of Oxfordshire. S. and h. of Richard, of Prescott House, Cropredy. Bapt. there, June 25, 1597. Matric. from Corpus Christi College, Oct. 18, 1616, age 19; B.A. (Oxford) 1616; M.A. 1620; B.D. 1628. V. of Farnborough, Warws., 1630. (*Al. Oxon.*)

GORSUCH, JOHN. Adm. Fell.-Com. (age 17) at PEMBROKE, June 18, 1617. S. of Daniel, of London and of Walkern, Herts., mercer. Matric. 1617; B.A. 1620–1; M.A. 1624; D.D. 1636. R. of Walkern, Herts., 1632: patron, his father; ejected, 1642. Following upon his ejection he is said to have been 'smothered in an Haymow.' (*Vis. of London*, 1634; *Cussans*, II. iii. 85.)

GORTON or GORDEON, JAMES. B.Can.L. 1519–20. Perhaps at KING'S HALL, 1529–35. One of these names V. of Rotherthorpe, Northants., 1528. (*Bridges*, I. 387.)

GORTON, THOMAS. Adm. sizar at TRINITY, June 10, 1647. Of Coventry. Matric. 1646, as 'Girton'; B.A. 1650–1; M.A. 1657. Incorp. at Oxford, 1658. V. of Wolston, Warws., 1665.

GOSNALD, ANTHONY. Matric. sizar from JESUS, Michs. 1550, *impubes*. One of these names adm. at Gray's Inn, 1554.

GOSNOLD, ANTHONY. Matric. pens. from TRINITY, Lent, 1578–9. Doubtless s. of Robert, of Otley, Suffolk, Esq.; adm. at Gray's Inn, May 25, 1582.

GOSNOLD, ANTHONY. Adm. pens. at CORPUS CHRISTI, 1598. Of Suffolk. Matric. 1598.

GOSNOLD, ANTHONY. Adm. pens. at ST CATHARINE'S, 1676. Perhaps s. of Henry, of Ipswich. Matric. 1679; B.A. 1679–80. Ord. deacon (Norwich) Dec. 1682; priest, May, 1684. (*Vis. of Suffolk*, 1664.)

GOSNOLD or GOSENALL, BARTHOLOMEW. Matric. pens. from JESUS, 1587. One of these names was a famous navigator and discoverer in North America. Sailed from Falmouth, Mar. 25, 1602. Discovered Cape Cod and the adjoining islands. Leader of an expedition under the auspices of Sir Ferdinando Gorges, 1606. Discovered the Capes of Virginia. Founded Jamestown. Died there Aug. 22, 1607. (*D.N.B.*)

GOSNOLD, HENRY. Matric. pens. from TRINITY, Easter, 1577. Adm. at Gray's Inn, Nov. 3, 1581; from Staple Inn.

GOSNOLD, HENRY. Adm. pens. at TRINITY, Aug. 6, 1635. Exhibitioner from Charterhouse. Matric. 1636, as Gosnole; Scholar, 1638; B.A. 1638–9; M.A. 1642.

GOSNOLD, JAMES. Matric. pens. from JESUS, Lent, 1564–5. Perhaps the same who was licensed to practise medicine, 1581.

GOSNALDE, JOHN. Matric. sizar from JESUS, Michs. 1550 (*impubes*).

GOSNALL, JOHN. Adm. pens. (age 19) at PEMBROKE, May 20, 1646. S. of Robert. B. at Dunmow, Essex. Exhibitioner from Charterhouse School. Chaplain to Lord Grey. Anabaptist preacher; silenced, in 1662. Founder of the Baptist Church in Paul's Alley, London. Died Oct. 3, 1678, aged 53. Buried in Bunhill Fields. M.I. (*Calamy*, I. 150; *D.N.B.*)

GOSNOLD, LIONEL. Adm. pens. at CORPUS CHRISTI, May, 1657. Of Swaffham Market, Norfolk. School (private). Matric. 1657. Migrated to Peterhouse, Dec. 21, 1660. Scholar, 1660–1; B.A. 1660–1; M.A. 1664. Fellow of Peterhouse, 1664. Signed for deacon's and priest's orders (London) Dec. 17, 1664. R. of Boyton, Suffolk, 1664. V. of Framsden, 1669. R. of Otley, 1674; of Barham, 1692. (*T. A. Walker*, 117.)

GOSNOLD, PAUL. Matric. pens. from CHRIST'S, 1621; B.A. 1624–5; M.A. 1628. One of these names V. of Alciston, Sussex, 1640. Perhaps also R. of Bradfield St Clare, Suffolk, 1641–4, sequestered. (*Peile*, I. 340.)

GOSNALL, PETER. Matric. sizar from PEMBROKE, Easter, 1562; B.A. from Jesus, 1568–9.

GOSNOLD, PHILIP. Matric. sizar from ST EDMUND'S HOSTEL, Michs. 1544 (*impubes*).

GOSNELL or GOSWELL, RICHARD. B.A. 1532–3; M.A. 1536–7. Fellow of PETERHOUSE, 1536. Will (V.C.C.) 1552.

GOSNELL, ROBERT. University Bedell, *c.* 1250. Benefactor. (Stokes, *Bedells*, 49.)

GOSNALD, ROBERT. Matric. sizar from JESUS, Michs. 1550. Adm. at Gray's Inn, 1553.

GOSNOLD, ROBERT. Adm. at CORPUS CHRISTI, 1597. Of Lincolnshire.

GOSNOLD, ROBERT. Adm. pens. at EMMANUEL, May 18, 1603. Matric. 1603. Doubtless s. of Robert, of Otley. Adm. at the Inner Temple, 1604. Of Otley Manor, Suffolk, Esq. Married, at Helmingham, Feb. 20, 1609–10, Anne, dau. of Sir Lionel Talmarsh, Bart. Compounded for his estates, 1646. Died 1656. Father of the next. (Copinger, *Manors of Suffolk*, III. 83.)

GOSNOLD, ROBERT. Adm. pens. at CORPUS CHRISTI, 1650. Of Suffolk. S. of Robert, above. Matric. 1654. (*Vis. of Suffolk*, 1664.)

GOSNALL, W. Matric. pens. from TRINITY, Michs. 1566.

GOSNELL or GOSNOLL, W. B.Civ.L. 1510–1.

GOSSE, JOHN. Adm. scholar (age 21) at CAIUS, May 31, 1581. S. of John, yeoman. B. at Ramsey, Essex.

GOSSE, JOHN. Adm. pens. at EMMANUEL, Apr. 27, 1612. Matric. 1612; B.A. 1615.

GOSSE, WILLIAM. Adm. at KING'S, a scholar from Eton, 1472. Ord. acolyte (Lincoln) Sept. 1473.

GOSSE, WILLIAM. Matric. pens. from ST JOHN'S, Michs. 1575; B.A. 1579–80. Ord. priest (Norwich) Sept. 21, 1584. R. of Langham, Suffolk, 1589–1623.

GOSSET, JAMES. Adm. sizar (age 16) at CHRIST'S, June 5, 1655. S. of James. B. in London. School, St Saviour's, Southwark (Mr Augur). One of these names, of London, adm. at the Inner Temple, Feb. 10, 1665–6. (*Peile*, I. 567.)

GOSSINGHILL, EDWARD. Adm. at KING'S (age 18) a scholar from Eton, Aug. 17, 1510. Of Bridgnorth, Salop. 'Went away scholar, became a Friar, and soon died.' (*Harwood*.)

GOSSIP, GREGORY. B.A. from ST JOHN'S, 1603–4.

GHOSSIP, JAMES. Matric. sizar from TRINITY, Easter, 1619; B.A. 1622–3; M.A. 1626. Ord. deacon (York) May, 1624.

GOSSOP, NATHANIEL. Incorp. from Oxford, 1584. Status not mentioned.

GOSSIPE, OBADIAH. Matric. sizar from ST JOHN'S, Easter, 1613; B.A. 1615–6; M.A. from Jesus, 1619. Ord. deacon (York) Mar. 1619–20; priest, Dec. 1620. R. of St Tudy, Cornwall, 1630. V. of Quethiock. Sequestered during the Rebellion. Died Feb. 14, 1659–60. Will (Exeter) 1661. (*Parochial Hist. of Cornwall*, IV. 264.)

GOSSIP, RICHARD. Adm. sizar (age 15) at SIDNEY, May 22, 1629. S. of Richard. B. at Beverley, Yorks. School, Beverley (Mr Pomray). Matric. 1629; B.A. 1632–3.

GOSSIP, ROBERT. Matric. sizar from TRINITY, Michs. 1567.

GOSSIP, WILLIAM. Adm. pens. (age 17) at TRINITY, June 17, 1722. S. of William, of York, gent. B. Mar. 6, 1704–5. School, Kirkleatham, Yorks. (Mr Clark). Matric. 1723; Scholar, 1723; B.A. 1725–6; M.A. 1729. College librarian, 1729. Lord of the manor of Thorparch, Yorks. Married, at York Minster, Nov. 13, 1731, Anne, dau. of Geo. Wilmer, of Helmsley, Esq. Died Mar. 25, 1772. (M. H. Peacock.)

GOSSIP, ——. Pens. at PETERHOUSE, 1580–2.

GOSSON, JAMES. Adm. Fell.-Com. at PEMBROKE, June 1, 1633. Had resided six years at Oxford. S. of Richard, goldsmith, of London. Bapt. at St Vedast, Foster Lane, Jan. 9, 1602–3. School, Winchester. B.A. (Cambridge) 1633; M.A. 1637. Not recorded in *Al. Oxon.* (J. Ch. Smith.)

GOSSON, JOSEPH. Adm. at PETERHOUSE, Sept. 18, 1622. Of London. B.A. 1626–7; M.A. 1631.

GOSTLING, HENRY. Adm. pens. (age 14) at ST JOHN'S, Apr. 2, 1660. S. of John, of Norwich. School, Yarmouth (Mr Lock). Matric. 1660; B.A. 1663–4; M.A. 1667; B.D. from Corpus Christi, 1674. Fellow of Corpus Christi, 1667–75. Taxor, 1670. Incorp. at Oxford, 1670. Died Jan. 9, 1674–5, aged 27. Buried at St Benet's, Cambridge. M.I. there. Will (V.C.C.) 1675. Benefactor to Corpus Christi. (Le Neve, *Mon.*, IV. 162; *Masters*, 161.)

GOSTLING, HENRY. M.A. from KING'S, 1708. S. of Henry, of London, clerk. B. Oct. 1672. School, Merchant Taylors'. Matric. from St John's College, Oxford, July 15, 1690, age 18; B.A. (Oxford) 1695. Minor canon of St Paul's, 1699–1730; sacrist and senior cardinal. C. of St Gregory, London, 1703–29. Died Aug. 29, 1730. (*Al. Oxon.*; *Hennessy*; J. Ch. Smith.)

GOSTLING, ISAAC. Adm. sizar (age 14) at ST JOHN'S, June 25, 1652. S. of Isaac, chandler, of East Malling, Kent. B. there. School, East Malling (Mr Whitle). Matric. 1652; B.A. 1655–6; M.A. 1659. R. of Woldham, Kent, 1667–82. Minor canon of Rochester, 1676–7. V. of Sturry, Kent, 1680. Minor canon of St Paul's, 1687. Non-juror. Brother of John (1668). (H. G. Harrison.)

GOSLIN, JAMES. Adm. pens. (age 15) at ST JOHN'S, May 21, 1716. S. of Joseph, ironmonger, of Buckinghamshire. B. at Chalfont St Peter's. School, Westminster. Matric. 1716; B.A. 1719–20.

GOSTLIN, JOHN. Adm. pens. (age 16) at CAIUS, Nov. 22, 1582. Of Norwich. S. of Robert. Bapt. at St Clement's, Mar. 12, 1568–9. School, Norwich. Matric. 1582; Scholar, 1582–90; B.A. 1586–7; M.A. 1590; M.D. 1602. Fellow, 1592–1618. Proctor, 1600. Elected Master of Caius, Feb. 26, 1618–9, till his death, 1626. Incorp. at Oxford, 1612. Practised physic at Exeter, 1607–19. M.P. for Barnstaple, 1614. Professor of Physic, 1623–5. Vice-Chancellor, 1625. Died in office, Oct. 21, 1626. Buried in the College Chapel. Will, P.C.C. (*Venn*, I. 116; *D.N.B.*)

GOSLING, JOHN. Matric. sizar from PETERHOUSE, Easter, 1582; B.A. 1585–6. Perhaps M.A. 1590. Ord. deacon (Peterb.) June 10, 1586; priest, Mar. 5, 1586–7. V. of Meldreth, Cambs., 1586–1616. Buried there Dec. 5, 1616.

GOSTLIN, JOHN. Matric. pens. from TRINITY, Michs. 1586; B.A. 1589–90. Ord. deacon (Norwich) Dec. 1, 1598, age 28. C. of Garboldisham, Norfolk.

GOSTLYN, JOHN. Adm. pens. (age 16) at CAIUS, Apr. 8, 1619. S. of Edmund. Bapt. at St Edmund's, Norwich, Jan. 27, 1604–5. School, Norwich (Mr Gammond). Matric. 1620; Scholar, 1620–6; B.A. 1622–3; M.A. 1626. Fellow, 1626–31. Of Dickleburgh. Died *c.* 1641. Father of John (1647). (*Venn*, I. 244.)

GOSTLIN, JOHN. Adm. pens. (age 16) at CAIUS, Sept. 16, 1640. S. of William, merchant and alderman, of Norwich. B. in the Parish of St Simon, Norwich. Bapt. Apr. 27, 1625. School, Norwich (Mr Briggs and Mr Lovering). Matric. 1640; Scholar, 1640–8; B.A. 1644–5; M.A. 1648. Fellow in 1649. Died before May 8, 1657. (*Venn*, I. 340.)

GOSTLIN or GOSLEN, JOHN. Adm. pens. at CAIUS, July 6, 1647. S. of John (1619), deceased. B. at Dickleburgh, Norfolk, 1632. Schools, Diss and Moulton (Mr Lancetter). Matric. 1647; Scholar, 1648; B.A. 1650–1; M.A. 1654; M.D. 1661. Fellow of Peterhouse, 1654–61. Fellow of Caius (*Lit. Reg.*) 1661–1705. President, 1679–1705. Incorp. at Oxford, July 13, 1658. His petition to the king for the fellowship states that he 'was debarred from preferment for his known loyalty.' Author, *Historiola*, a MS. history of the College. Buried in the College Chapel, Feb. 3, 1704–5. Will, V.C.C. and P.C.C. Considerable benefactor to the College. (*Venn*, I. 369; *D.N.B.*)

GOSTLING, JOHN. Adm. sizar (age 18) at CHRIST'S, Sept. 18, 1657. S. of William. B. at 'Christ Church,' Norfolk. Bapt. in Norwich Cathedral, Dec. 2, 1638. School, Norwich (Mr Lovering). Matric. 1658; B.A. 1661. Ord. deacon (Norwich) Sept. 1661. R. of Sharrington, Norfolk, 1669. R. of Swanton Morley, 1670–80. (*Peile*, I. 579; G. H. Holley.)

GOSLING or GOSTLING, JOHN. Adm. sizar (age 18) at ST JOHN'S, Oct. 21, 1668. S. of Isaac, mercer, of East Malling, Kent. B. there. School, Rochester (Mr Edwards). Matric. 1669; B.A. 1672–3. Ord. priest (Ely) May 30, 1675. Minor canon of Canterbury, 1674–1733. V. of Littlebourne, Kent, 1675–1733. R. of Hope All Saints', Kent, 1682–1709. Minor canon of St Paul's, 1683–90; sub-dean, 1689. Preb. of Lincoln, 1689–1733. R. of H. Cross, Westgate, 1716. R. of Brook and Milton. Chaplain to the King. Famous bass in the Chapel Royal, for whom Purcell wrote the Anthem, 'They that go down to the sea in ships.' Died July 18, 1733. Father of William (1712) and brother of Isaac (1652). (*D.N.B.*)

GOSTLING, JOHN. LL.B. 1671 (*Lit. Reg.*).

GOSTLING, JOHN. Adm. sizar (age 18) at PEMBROKE, July 12, 1743. S. of William (1712), minor canon of Canterbury. B. at Canterbury. Matric. 1743. Migrated to Corpus, 1746. B.A. 1747–8; M.A. 1751. R. of Brooke, Kent, 1751–1804. R. of Milton, 1770–1804. V. of Alkham, 1784–6. R. of St Peter, Canterbury, 1786–1804.

GOSLIN, NICHOLAS. Fellow of PETERHOUSE, 1432. Name off, 1474. Perhaps the D.Can.L. 1456–7. (*T. A. Walker.*)

GOSTLYN, NICHOLAS. Adm. pens. at CORPUS CHRISTI, 1630. Matric. Easter, 1631; B.A. 1634–5; M.A. 1638. Ord. deacon (Norwich) Sept. 22, 1638; priest, Sept. 22, 1639. R. of Ringsfield, Suffolk, 1639–63. Will proved (Norwich Cons. C.) 1663.

GOSLING, RICHARD. B.A. from ST JOHN'S, 1612. One of these names V. of Eckington, Worcs., 1613. Will (Worcester) 1622; of Gt Comberton, clerk.

GOSTLYN, THOMAS. Adm. sizar (age 18) at CAIUS, June 12, 1605. S. of John, gent., of Hickling, Norfolk. School, Yarmouth (Mr Hodgkins). Matric. 1605; Scholar, 1605–12; B.A. 1608–9; M.A. 1612. Fellow, 1613–51. University preacher, 1625. Taxor, 1629. Will (V.C.C.) 1651. (*Venn*, I. 189; *Vis. of Norfolk*, 1664.)

GOSLINGE, THOMAS. Matric. sizar from ST JOHN'S, Easter, 1606; B.A. 1609–10; M.A. 1617.

GOSTLIN, WILLIAM. Adm. pens. at CORPUS CHRISTI, 1625. Of Norfolk. Matric. Easter, 1626; B.A. 1629–30.

GOSTLING, WILLIAM. Adm. pens. (age 16) at ST JOHN'S, June 30, 1712. S. of John (1668) clerk. B. at Canterbury. Bapt. at the Cathedral, Jan. 30, 1695–6. School, Canterbury (Mr Jones). Matric. 1712; B.A. 1715–6; M.A. 1719. Ord. priest (Lincoln, *Litt. dim.* from Canterbury) Mar. 5, 1720–1. R. of Brook, Kent, 1722–33. Minor canon of Canterbury, 1727–77. V. of Littlebourne, 1733–53. V. of Stone-in-Oxney, 1753–77. Author, antiquarian. Died Mar. 9, 1777. Buried in Canterbury Cathedral cloisters. Admon., P.C.C. Father of John (1743). (*D.N.B.*)

GOSLYN, ——. D.Can.L. 1456–7.

GOSTLOW, WILLIAM. M.A. 1515–6. Nominated fellow of JESUS, 1517 (not elected).

GOSTWYKE, EDWARD. Matric. Fell.-Com. from CHRIST'S, Apr. 1606. S. of Sir William (1582), Bart., of Willington, Beds. Knighted, May 3, 1607. Succeeded as Bart., Sept. 19, 1615. Sheriff of Beds., 1626–7. Buried at Willington, Beds., Sept. 20, 1630. M.I. Father of Thomas (1639). (*Peile*, I. 255; *G.E.C.*, I. 100.)

GOSTWICK, GABRIEL. Adm. scholar (age 14) at SIDNEY, June 4, 1627. S. of Roger (1586), R. of Sampford Courtney, Devon. B. at North Stanton. School, Perse, Cambridge. Matric. 1627; B.A. 1630–1; M.A. 1634. R. of Sampford Courtney. Minister of North Tawton, Devon. Will (P.C.C.) 1656. Father of William (1668).

GOSTWICK, JOHN. Matric. pens. from CLARE, Michs. 1554; Scholar, 1555.

GOSTWYCK, JOHN. Adm. Fell.-Com. (age 17) at SIDNEY, June 30, 1695. 1st s. of William (1667), Bart., of Willington Park, Beds. B. there. School, Winchester. Matric. 1695. Died before his father. Buried at Willington, Mar. 8, 1715. Father of William (1717) and brother of William (1698). (Burke, *Ext. Bart.*; *G.E.C.*)

GOSTWICK, ROGER. Adm. at KING'S (age 18) a scholar from Eton, Aug. 24, 1586. Of Barkway, Herts. (his mother's home). S. of William, of Shefford, Beds. Matric. 1586; B.A. 1590–1; M.A. 1594; B.D. 1601. Fellow, 1589–1609. Vice-Provost, 1608–9. Incorp. at Oxford, 1597. Chaplain to Dr Heyton, Bishop of Ely. R. of Sampford Courtney, Devon, 1609–45. Author, religious. Will (Exeter) 1646. Father of Gabriel (1627). (*Harwood*; *Vis. of Beds.*)

GOSTWICK, THOMAS. Adm. Fell.-Com. (age 15) at CHRIST'S, Oct. 18, 1639. S. of Sir Edward (1606), of Willington, Beds. B. there. Schools, Carrington (Mr Watson) and Potton (Mr Shiers). Matric. 1640. Married Elizabeth, dau. of Mynheer Dorislaus, ambassador from Holland to Oliver Cromwell. (*Peile*, I. 463; Burke, *Ext. Bart.*)

GOSTWYCKE, WILLIAM. Matric. Fell.-Com. from CHRIST'S, June, 1582. S. of John, of Willington, Beds., Esq. Bapt. Dec. 2, 1565, at St Mary's, Bedford. High Sheriff of Beds., 1595–6. Created Bart., Nov. 25, 1611. Of Willington, Beds. Died Sept. 19, 1615. Buried at Willington. M.I. Father of Edward (1606) and probably of William, next. (*Peile*, I. 169; *G.E.C.*, I. 100.)

GOSTWICK, WILLIAM. Matric. pen. from CHRIST'S, July, 1617. Probably s. of Sir Williams (above), of Willington, Beds. B.A. 1620–1; M.A. 1624. Buried at Gt St Mary's, Cambridge, Mar. 17, 1625–6. (*Peile*, I. 317.)

GOSTWYKE, WILLIAM. Adm. Fell.-Com. (age 16) at SIDNEY, June 6, 1667. S. of Sir Edward, Bart. and grandson of Edward (1606). B. at Willington, Beds. Bapt. Aug. 21, 1650. School, Hadley, Middlesex (Mr Lowell). Succeeded as Bart. (? 1665). Perhaps knighted, Nov. 24, 1668 (*Shaw*). Sheriff of Beds., 1679–80. M.P. for Beds., 1698–1713. Wasted his estates. Died at St Martin-in-the-Fields. Buried at Willington, Jan. 24, 1719–20. Father of William (1698) and John (1695). (*G.E.C.*, I. 100.)

GOSTWYCKE, WILLIAM. Adm. pens. at Trinity, June 5, 1668. S. of William, merchant, of London. B. in St Mary Bothaw parish, July 8, 1650. Schools, Merchant Taylors' and Westminster. Matric. 1668; Scholar from Westminster, 1669; B.A. 1671–2; M.A. 1675. Fellow, 1674. Ord. deacon (London) May 26, 1678. V. of St Michael's, Cambridge, 1681. V. of Gt St Mary, 1693. V. of Bottisham, Cambs., 1693–6. Died Feb. 4, 1702–3. Buried in Trinity College Chapel. (*Al. Westmon.*, 167.)

GOSTWICK, WILLIAM. M.A. from Sidney, 1668. S. of Gabriel (1627), of North Tawton, Devon, clerk. Matric. from Exeter College, Oxford, Apr. 3, 1661, age 18; B.A. (Hart Hall, Oxford) 1664. R. of Purley, Berks., 1684–1719. Buried there, Oct. 24, 1719. (*Al. Oxon.*; J. Ch. Smith.)

GOSTWYCK, WILLIAM. Adm. pens. (age 18) at St John's, May 16, 1698; afterwards Fell.-Com. Previously matric. from Wadham, Oxford, June 26, 1697. S. of Sir William (1667), Bart. B. at Marden Hill, near Hertford. School, Lilley, Herts. (private; Mr Villar). Matric. 1698. Adm. at Lincoln's Inn, Mar. 8, 1699–1700, as 2nd s. of Sir William, of Willington, Beds., Knt. Died young. Brother of John (1695).

GOSTWICK, WILLIAM. Adm. pens. (age 17) at Pembroke, July 1, 1717. S. of John (1695), of Carrington, Beds., Esq. Grandson of Sir William, of Willington, Beds., Bart. Succeeded as Bart., Jan. 24, 1719–20. Officer in the Irish service. Buried at North Tawton, Devon, May 6, 1766. (*G.E.C.*, I. 100.)

GOSTWYKE, ——. B.Can.L. 1500–1.

GOTCH, CLEMENT. Matric. sizar from Jesus, *c.* 1592; B.A. 1595–6; M.A. 1599.

GOTER, *see also* **GOATER.**

GOTER or GOTHER, PAUL. Matric. pens. from Pembroke, Lent, 1564–5; B.A. 1567–8; M.A. 1571. Ord. deacon and priest (Lincoln) Jan. 5, 1576–7. R. of Tingrith, Beds., 1577.

GOTER, ROGER DE LA. Master of Peterhouse, 1339–49.

GOTER, SYLVESTER. M.A. 1629 (Incorp. from Oxford). S. of Sylvester, of Titherley, Hants. Matric. from Magdalen Hall, Oxford, Jan. 31, 1622–3, age 17; B.A. (Oxford) 1625; M.A. 1628.

GOTHAM, WILLIAM DE. D.D. Fellow of Peterhouse. Received all orders (Ely) Dec. 9, 1349. Master of Michaelhouse, 1359. Chancellor of the University, 1366–9, and 1376. Preb. of Lichfield, 1376. Penitentiary-general of Ely diocese, 1385. Benefactor to the University, by foundation of a chest.

GOTOBED, *see* **GODBED.**

GOTT, SAMUEL. Matric. pens. from St Catharine's, Lent, 1629–30. S. of Samuel, citizen and merchant, of London (will proved, P.C.C., 1642, by s. Samuel). B. Jan. 20, 1613–4. School, Merchant Taylors'. B.A. 1632–3; M.A. 1644. Adm. at Gray's Inn, Mar. 19, 1632–3. Barrister, 1640. Reader, 1657. Ancient, 1658. M.P. for Winchelsea, 1645–8; for Sussex, 1656–8; for Hastings, 1659. Buried at Battle, Sussex, 1671. (*Robinson*, I. 119; A. B. Beaven.)

GOTT, SIMON. Matric. sizar from Trinity, 1621, as 'Cutt'; Scholar, 1625; B.A. 1626–7.

GOUGE, *see* **GOOCH.**

GOUGH, ALEXANDER HENRY. Adm. sizar at Clare, Apr. 29, 1736. B. in London. Matric. 1736; B.A. 1739–40. Ord. deacon (Norwich) Sept. 1741. V. of Thorpe-le-Soken, Essex, 1745–74. Died July 7, 1774. Will, P.C.C. (G. *Mag.*)

GOFFE, CHRISTOPHER. Adm. sizar at Corpus Christi, 1577. B. at Norwich. Matric. Lent, 1577–8; B.A. 1580–1; M.A. 1586. Ord. deacon (London) Apr. 15, 1584, age 24; C. of Clothall, Herts. V. of Fulham, Middlesex, 1591–3. V. of Gt Waltham, Essex, 1593–1629. Died 1629. Admon., P.C.C. to a creditor.

GOFFE, EDMUND. Matric. sizar from Trinity, Michs. 1575.

GOFFE, EDWARD. Adm. Fell.-Com. (age 18) at Caius, Nov. 29, 1648. S. of Thomas, Esq., deceased. B. at Saham Tony, Norfolk. Bapt. Feb. 4, 1630–1. Educated by Messrs French and Smith. Married Frances, dau. of Edmund Eade, B.D. Buried at Saham Tony, May 10, 1659. (*Venn*, I. 374.)

GOUGH or GOAH, FRANCIS. Adm. sizar at Emmanuel, June, 1588. Matric. 1588; Scholar; B.A. 1591–2; M.A. 1595; B.D. 1602. Fellow, 1595. V. of Winsford, Somerset, 1604–29. Died there Apr. 26, 1629. Buried May 2. Will, P.C.C. Father of the next.

GOUGH, FRANCIS. Adm. pens. (age 16) at Sidney, May, 1627. S. of Francis (above), V. of Winsford, Somerset. B. there. School, Taunton (Mr Richard Mercer and Mr Henry Evans). Matric. 1627; B.A. 1630–1; M.A. 1634. Probably V. of Stockland, Dorset, in 1662.

GOUGH, FRANCIS. Adm. sizar (age 18) at Trinity, Dec. 4, 1722. S. of Francis. School, Newport, Salop. Matric. 1723; Scholar, 1724; B.A. 1726–7. Ord. priest (Lincoln) Sept. 21, 1729. V. of Swineshead, Lincs., 1729.

GOUGH, HENRY. Adm. Fell.-Com. at Corpus Christi, Nov. 1, 1725. Of Edgbaston, Warws. S. and h. of Sir Richard, Knt., merchant, of London. B. Mar. 9, 1708–9. Adm. at the Middle Temple, May 5, 1725. Created Bart., Apr. 1728. M.P. for Totnes, 1732–4; for Bramber, 1734–41. Died June 8, 1774. Buried at Edgbaston. Will, P.C.C. Brother of John (1728). (*G.E.C.*; J. Ch. Smith; *Masters*, 299.)

GOUGH, JOHN. B.A. 1524–5; M.A. 1528; B.D. 1535; D.D. 1537. Fellow of Queens', 1527–36. Preb. of Bristol, 1542–5. Died *c.* 1544–5. (*D.N.B.*; *Cooper*, I. 536.)

GOFFE, JOHN. Matric. sizar from St John's, Michs. 1617; B.A. 1620–1; M.A. 1624. Ord. priest (Peterb.) June 8, 1623. One of these names presented to Buckenhill, Salop, Sept. 28, 1647.

GOFFE, JOHN. Adm. pens. (age 17) at Pembroke, Sept. 12, 1621. S. of Richard, of Suffolk. Matric. 1623; B.A. 1624–5.

GOFFE, JOHN. M.A. 1632 (Incorp. from Oxford). S. of Stephen, R. of Stanmer, Sussex. Matric. from Merton College, Apr. 13, 1627, age 17; B.A. (Magdalen) 1628; M.A. 1631; D.D. 1660. Fellow of Magdalen College, 1629–36. R. of Rype, Sussex, 1629–45, ejected. V. of Hackington, Canterbury, 1642–5. R. of Norton-by-Sittingbourne, 1652–61. Author. Buried Nov. 26, 1661, in St Alphage's Church, Canterbury. (*Al. Oxon.*; *D.N.B.*)

GOFF, JOHN. Adm. sizar at Emmanuel, Feb. 15, 1678–9. Of Middlesex. S. of Francis, citizen and mercer of London. B. Feb. 10, 1660–1. 'Grecian' from Christ's Hospital. Matric. 1679; B.A. 1682–3; M.A. 1686. (A. W. Lockhart.)

GOUGH, JOHN. Adm. pens. at Trinity, Dec. 19, 1705. S. of Thomas, of Shrewsbury. Exhibitioner from Charterhouse. Matric. 1706; Scholar, 1707; B.A. 1709–10; M.A. 1713. Ord. deacon (Ely) Dec. 21, 1712; priest, May 23, 1714. Chaplain of Charterhouse, 1712–22. Usher, 1728–31. One of these names V. of Godmersham, Kent, 1714–31. Died Oct. 17, 1731; probably at Charterhouse.

GOUGH, JOHN. Adm. pens. at Corpus Christi, Oct. 28, 1728. Of Middlesex. S. of Sir Richard, Knt., merchant, of London. Matric. 1728. Adm. at the Middle Temple, Oct. 19, 1728. Brother of Henry (1725).

GOUGH, JOHN. Adm. sizar at Clare, Jan. 2, 1732–3. B. in London. Matric. 1732; B.A. 1735–6. Ord. deacon (Lincoln, *Litt. dim.* from Ely) Sept. 25, 1737.

GOFFE, JONATHAN. Adm. pens. at Emmanuel, Mar. 8, 1652–3. Of Suffolk. Matric. 1653, as 'John'; B.A. 1656; M.A. 1660. R. of Brantham, Suffolk, 1662. R. of Whatfield, 1662.

GOFF, JONATHAN. Adm. sizar at Emmanuel, Oct. 7, 1685. Of Suffolk. Matric. 1686; B.A. 1689–90. R. of Felsham, Suffolk, 1691.

GOUGH, MORRIS. Matric. pens. from Queens', Easter, 1578. Of Wales. B.A. from St Catharine's, 1584–5.

GOUGH, MAURICE. Adm. sizar (age 19) at Magdalene, Dec. 15, 1736. S. of John, gent. B. in London. School, Brigg, Lincs. Matric. 1737; LL.B. 1760. Ord. deacon (Norwich) Sept. 1739. Probably V. of Little Clacton, Essex, 1750–84. R. of Wrabness, 1752–84. Died Feb. 29, 1784. (G. *Mag.*, where he is styled D.D.)

GOUGH, MICHAEL. Adm. pens. at Queens', Nov. 1, 1712. Of Wilton (? Norfolk). Matric. 1712; B.A. 1716–7; M.A. 1724.

GOUGH, OWEN. M.A. from King's, 1745. S. of William, of Amlwch, Anglesey. Matric. from Christ Church, Oxford, Dec. 17, 1718, age 19; B.A. (Oxford) 1722. V. of Turnworth, Dorset, 1738–41. R. of Ampthill, Beds., 1741. (*Al. Oxon.*)

GOFFE, RICHARD. Adm. sizar at Clare, June 30, 1632. Matric. 1632; B.A. 1636–7; M.A. 1640.

GOFFES, ROBERT. Matric. sizar from St John's, Michs. 1584. B. at Lewes, Sussex. B.A. 1588–9; M.A. 1592. Ord. deacon (Chichester) Oct. 3, 1589; priest, Feb. 13, 1589–90. R. of East Blatchington, Sussex, 1605–28. Buried Nov. 10, 1628, aged 64. Will at Lewes and P.C.C. (W. C. Renshaw.)

GOFFE, THOMAS. M.A. 1617 (Incorp. from Oxford). Of Essex; *cler. fil.* School, Westminster. Matric. from Christ Church, Oxford, Nov. 3, 1609, age 18; B.A. (Oxford) 1613; M.A. 1616; B.D. 1623. R. of East Clandon, Surrey, 1620–9. Poet and orator. Buried at Clandon, July 29, 1629. M.I. (*Al. Oxon.*; *D.N.B.*)

GOUGH, THOMAS. Adm. sizar (age 19) at Christ's, Apr. 18, 1724. S. of Edward. B. at Eyton, Salop. School, Shrewsbury. Matric. 1724; Scholar, 1725; B.A. 1727–8. Ord. priest (Hereford) Oct. 1729.

GOUGH, THOMAS. Adm. pens. (age 18) at ST JOHN'S, May 26, 1738. S. of Walter, of Old Fallings and Perry Hall, Staffs., Esq. B. at Bishopberry, June 6, 1720. School, Newport, Salop (Mr Lea). Matric. 1738; LL.B. 1744. Ord. deacon (Norwich) May 20, 1744; priest, Sept. 23, 1744. R. of Fornham St Genevieve, Suffolk, 1744–86. R. of Risby, 1744–86. Died Jan. 6, 1786. Buried at Risby. Will, P.C.C. Brother of William (1738). (*Scott-Mayor*, III. 493; Davy, *Suff. MSS.*)

GOUGH, WILLIAM. Matric. pens. from ST JOHN'S, Easter, 1614; B.A. 1618.

GOUGH, WILLIAM. Matric. pens. from QUEENS', Lent, 1645–6. Previously matric. from Christ Church, Oxford, Dec. 15, 1643, age 17. S. of Edward, R. of Cheverell Magna, Wilts. B.A. 1647–8. At first kept school, and preached at Warminster, Wilts. R. of Inkpen, Berks.; ejected, 1662. Afterwards preacher at Earl Stoke, Marlborough and elsewhere. Died at Marlborough, aged 66. (*Calamy*, I. 228.)

GOUGH, WILLIAM. Adm. pens. (age 17) at CHRIST'S, Mar. 21, 1645–6. S. of Giles. B. at Bristol. School, Wotton-under-Edge, Gloucs. (Mr Woodward). Matric. 1646.

GOUGH, WILLIAM. Adm. at CORPUS CHRISTI, 1681. Of Norfolk. Matric. 1681; B.A. 1684–5; M.A. 1689. Ord. priest (Norwich) June, 1688; C. of Blickling, Norfolk. R. of Burnham Norton, 1690–1708. V. of Docking, 1699–1708. Died 1708.

GOFFE, WILLIAM. Adm. sizar at ST CATHARINE'S, Dec. 23, 1681. Matric. 1683–4; B.A. 1685–6. Ord. deacon (Norwich) Dec. 1686; priest, Dec. 1687, as C. of Shadingfield, Suffolk. V. of Edwardston, 1695–1706.

GOUGH, WILLIAM. Adm. sizar at CLARE, Mar. 30, 1709. B. at Norwich. Matric. 1709.

GOUGH, WILLIAM. Adm. pens. (age 18) at ST JOHN'S, May 26, 1738. S. of Walter, Esq., of Staffordshire. B. at Bishopberry. School, Newport, Salop (Mr Lea). Matric. 1738. Brother of Thomas (1738).

GOUGH, ——. Adm. at CORPUS CHRISTI, 1583.

GOULBOURNE, JOSEPH. Matric. sizar from ST JOHN'S, Easter, 1624; B.A. 1627–8; M.A. from King's, 1636.

GOULBORNE or GOLDBORN, NATHAN. Adm. sizar (age 18) at MAGDALENE, Mar. 25, 1682. S. of John, maltster, of Warrington, Lancs. B. there. School, Warrington. B.A. 1685–6. Ord. deacon (Chester) Feb. 20, 1686–7. C. of Wigan. V. of Billinge, 1689–92. Buried at Warrington, Mar. 12, 1691–2. Will, Chester.

GOULD or GOLD, HENRY. B.A. 1514–5; M.A. 1518. Fellow of ST JOHN'S, 1516. Of St Neots, Hunts. Ord. deacon (Lincoln) June 2, 1520; priest, Sept. 22, 1520. V. of Ospringe, Kent, 1525. R. of St Mary Aldermary, 1526–34. V. of Hayes-*cum*-Norwood, Middlesex, 1529–34. Chaplain to Archbishop Warham. Implicated in the imposture of the Maid of Kent. Executed for treason at Tyburn, Apr. 20, 1534. (*Cooper*, I. 49; in *Al. Oxon.* some of his preferment is assigned to an Oxford contemporary.)

GOULD or GOLD, HENRY. Matric. pens. from CORPUS CHRISTI, Michs. 1571 (apparently adm. 1569); B.A. 1575–6; M.A. from Pembroke, 1579; B.D. 1586. Fellow of Pembroke, 1578–81. Ord. deacon (Lincoln) Dec. 1, 1582. V. of Pitsea, Essex. Probably R. of Benacre, Suffolk, during 1588. Died at Pitsea before Aug. 12, 1588.

GOULD, HUGH. Adm. sizar (age 18) at ST JOHN'S, May 10, 1671. S. of Hugh, deceased, of Bagworth, Leics. B. there. School, Ashby-de-la-Zouch. Matric. 1671; B.A. 1674–5.

GOULDE, JOHN. Matric. from CLARE, *c.* 1592. S. of Edward, of Bury St Edmunds. School, Bury. Migrated as sizar (age 15) to Caius, Feb. 1, 1592–3. B.A. 1595–6; Scholar, 1596; M.A. 1599. Doubtless R. of Forncett, Norfolk, 1617–30. (*Venn*, I. 147.)

GOULD, JOHN. Adm. Fell.-Com. at J[illegible], June 16, 1715. Previously at Clare. Of Devon. 2nd s. of Moses. Bapt. at Crediton, Apr. 7, 1698. Died *s.p.* Buried at St Thomas-by-Exeter, Dec. 6, 1726. Will, Exeter. Brother of William (1714). (J. Ch. Smith; *Vis. of Devon.*)

GOULD, JOHN. M.A. from KING'S, 1728. S. of Henry, of London, gent. Matric. from Wadham College, Oxford, Mar. 13, 1705–6, age 18; B.A. (Oxford) 1709. (*Al. Oxon.*)

GOULD, PASTON. Adm. pens. (age 18) at TRINITY, June 1, 1749. S. of Paston, of London. School, Westminster. Colonel in the army, 1777. Brigadier-General in S. Carolina. Died Aug. 14, 1782. (*Al. Westmon.*)

GOOLDE, PAUL. Matric. pens. from CORPUS CHRISTI, Michs. 1569. S. of Peter. B. at Norwich. B.A. 1572–3; M.A. from Caius, 1576. Fellow of Caius, 1574–82. Master of a school in Norwich. Student in medicine, in 1581. Practised at Norwich. Married Bridget, dau. of Thomas Barsham, of Colkirk, Norfolk. (*Venn*, I. 78.)

GOULD, RICHARD. Matric. pens. from TRINITY, Easter, 1625, a scholar from Westminster, 1625.

GOULD or GOLD, ROBERT. Adm. pens. at CORPUS CHRISTI, 1571. Matric. Easter, 1577; B.A. 1579–80; M.A. 1583. Ord. deacon (Norwich) Sept. 26; priest, Oct. 8, 1588. R. of Benacre, Suffolk, 1588–95. R. of Thorington, 1595–1611 and 1612–20. R. of Felbrigge, Norfolk, in 1603. R. of Tittleshall, 1609–12. R. of Gt Blakenham, Suffolk, 1612. R. of Creeting St Olave, 1612.

GOULD or GOLD, SAMUEL. Matric. sizar from TRINITY, Easter, 1603; B.A. 1606–7. Ord. deacon (Norwich) Sept. 24, 1609, age 23. C. of Rockland St Peter's, Norfolk. R. of Beeston, before 1658.

GOULD, WILLIAM. Adm. pens. (age 18) at ST JOHN'S, Apr. 2, 1657. S. of James, merchant, of Dorchester. B. there. School, Dorchester (Mr Crumlum). Matric. 1657; Scholar; B.A. 1660–1; M.A. 1664; B.D. 1671. Fellow, 1664–90. P.C. of St Clement's, Cambridge, 1670. V. of Fulbourn All Saints', Cambs., 1683. Benefactor to the College. Died July 4, 1690. Will proved (V.C.C.) 1690.

GOULD, WILLIAM. Adm. Fell.-Com. at CLARE, July 30, 1714. S. of Moses. B. at Crediton, Devon. Bapt. Mar. 22, 1696–7. Matric. 1714. Buried at St Thomas-by-Exeter, Mar. 17, 1725–6. Admon., P.C.C. Brother of John (1715). (*Vis. of Devon.*)

GOULD, WILLIAM. Adm. pens at EMMANUEL, Jan. 29, 1733–4. Of Middlesex. S. of Edward, of Highgate. Bapt. July 17, 1715. Matric. 1734; Scholar; B.A. 1737–8; M.A. 1741. Ord. deacon (Lincoln) May 28, 1738; priest, Nov. 1743. V. of Hoxne, Suffolk, 1743. V. of Dedham, Essex. Buried at Hoxne, June 13, 1772. Will, P.C.C. (Vivian, *Devon Visitations.*)

GOULD or GOLD, ZEPHANIAS. Matric. sizar from QUEENS', Lent, 1620–1. Of Hertfordshire. B.A. 1623–4; M.A. 1627. Ord. deacon (Peterb.) June 12; priest, June 13, 1625.

GOULDHAM, GEORGE. Matric. sizar from TRINITY, *c.* 1596, as Goulding; B.A. 1599–1600.

GOULDAN, ROBERT. Matric. pens. from PETERHOUSE, Michs. 1583.

GOULDAN, WILLIAM. Matric. pens. from PETERHOUSE, Michs. 1583.

GOULDES, HENRY. Adm. scholar at TRINITY HALL, June 28, 1605; LL.B. 1609–10.

GOULDES, W. Matric. sizar from MAGDALENE, Easter, 1567.

GOULDSON, GOLDSON or GOLDSTONE, HUMPHREY. B.A. 1533–4; M.A. 1538–9.

GOLDSON or GOLDSTON, JOHN. Scholar of CHRIST'S; B.A. 1531–2; M.A. 1536–7. One of these names chantry priest at Drayton Basset, Staffs., *c.* 1535.

GOULDSON, JOHN. Adm. pens. at QUEENS', June 27, 1594. Of Yorkshire. Matric. 1594.

GOLDSON, ROBERT., *see* GOLDSTON.

GOULDSTONE, *see* also GOLDSTON *and* GULSTON.

GOULSTON, EDWARD. Adm. Fell.-Com. (age 15) at ST JOHN'S, June 27, 1681. S. of Edward, Esq. B. at Westfarleigh, Kent. Educated at home (Mr Burletson). Matric. 1681. Adm. at Gray's Inn, Nov. 3, 1683, as s. and h. of Edward, late of Tetham Hall, Kent. Barrister, 1689. Perhaps M.P. for Romney, 1701–2. Died Sept. 2, 1720. Buried at Westfarleigh. (*Hasted*, II. 296.)

GOULSTON, RICHARD. Adm. Fell.-Com. (age 15) at TRINITY, June 26, 1684. S. of James, of Wyddial Hall, Herts. B. at Barkway. School, Enfield. Adm. at Gray's Inn, Nov. 1, 1687. M.P. for Hertford, 1701–5, 1710–5. Died Mar. 11, 1730–1. (*Misc. Gen. et Her.*, 3rd S., I. 111; A. B. Beaven.)

GOULTON, CHRISTOPHER. Adm. scholar (age 17) at SIDNEY, Apr. 1695. 2nd s. of Christopher, attorney, of Highthorne, Husthwaite, Yorks. School, Coxwold. Matric. 1695. Died 1716. (Burke, *L.G.*)

GOULTON, CHRISTOPHER. Adm. pens. (age 16) at ST JOHN'S, May 30, 1723. S. of Thomas, gent., of Bessingby, Bridlington, Yorks. B. there. School, Beverley (Mr Tatham). Matric. 1724. Adm. at Gray's Inn, July 11, 1723. Treasurer for North Riding, 1779. Of Highthorne, Yorks., Esq. Died Mar. 17, 1792. (*Scott-Mayor*, III. 362; G. *Mag.*; M. H. Peacock.)

GOULTON, RICHARD. Matric. sizar from TRINITY, Michs. 1588; B.A. 1592–3. Ord. deacon (York) June, 1622; priest, Sept. 1622. Licensed to teach at Coxwold School, Aug. 16, 1619. Licensed to marry Barbara Thornton, of Kilburn, 1600.

GOULTRY, ——. Adm. pens. at ST CATHARINE'S, Easter, 1646.

GOURNAY, *see* GURNAY.

GOUSSET, JAMES. Adm. sizar at QUEENS', July 7, 1687. Of Poitou, France. Matric. 1688; B.A. 1690–1.

GOVE, NICHOLAS. Adm. pens. at TRINITY, Dec. 10, 1646. Of Devon.

GOWE, WILLIAM. B.Can.L. 1467.

GOWE, ——. S. of Ralph, of Beverley, Yorks.; allowed 10s. by the Corporation for his s. at Cambridge, Michs. 1605–6. (Poulson, *Beverley*, I. 453.)

GOWELL, JOSIAS. B.A. from CLARE, 1611–2.

GOWER, EWERS or EVERARD. Matric. pens. from CHRIST'S, Dec. 1622. S. of Sir Thomas, Knt. and Bart., of Stittenham, Yorks. B. at York. Educated at home. B.A. 1626–7; M.A. 1630; B.D. 1636. Fellow of Jesus, 1632–8. Archdeacon of Northumberland, 1638–44. R. of Howick, 1638–44. V. of Norton, Durham, 1640. V. of Staubope-in-Weardale, 1641–4. Chaplain to Bishop Morton, of Durham. Died May, 1644. (*Peile*, I. 347; H. M. Wood.)

GOWER, FRANCIS. Matric. sizar from CHRIST'S, Dec. 1608; B.A. 1611–2, as Glover.

GOWER, HUMFREY. Adm. pens. (age 17) at ST JOHN'S, May 21, 1655. S. of Stanley, clerk, of Brampston Brian, Hereford. B. there. Schools, Dorchester (Mr Crumlum) and St Paul's. Matric. 1655; B.A. 1658–9; M.A. 1662; B.D. 1669; D.D. 1676. Fellow, 1658. Taxor, 1667. Master of Jesus, July to Dec. 1679. Master of St John's, 1679–1711. Vice-Chancellor, 1680–1. Lady Margaret Professor, 1688–1711. R. of Hammoon, Dorset, 1663–7. R. of Paglesham, Essex, 1667–75. R. of Newton, Isle of Ely, 1675. R. of Fen Ditton, Cambs., 1677. Preb. of Ely, 1679–1711. R. of Terrington, Norfolk, 1688–1711. Died Mar. 27, 1711. Buried in the College Chapel. Will, P.C.C. (*D.N.B.*)

GOWRE, JOHN. Matric. pens. from TRINITY, Easter, 1562.

GOWER, JOHN. Matric. pens. from PEMBROKE, Michs. 1562.

GOWER, JOHN. Adm. sizar at JESUS, Aug. 9, 1628. Of Essex. Matric. 1629; B.A. 1632; M.A. 1636. Author, *Translation of Ovid's Fasti*, printed at Cambridge, posthumously, 1640. (A. Gray.)

GOWER, JOHN. Matric. pens. from ST JOHN'S, Michs. 1654. (*See* Jower.)

GOWER, NATHANIEL. Incorp. M.A. 1710, from Pembroke College, Oxford. Matric. there, Mar. 19, 1686–7, age 18. S. of Samuel, of King's Norton, Worcs., gent. B.A. (Oxford) 1690; M.A. 1693. V. of Battersea, Surrey, 1701–27. R. of West Horsley, 1711. Married Johanna, dau. of Wm Foote, of Battersea. Died Mar. 17, 1726–7. M.I. at Bath. (*Al. Oxon.*; *Manning and Bray*, III. 340.)

GOWER, PATRICK. M.A. 1519–20 (Incorp. from Paris). *Supp.* for incorporation at Oxford, 1521.

GOWER, THOMAS. Adm. pens. at CLARE, May 15, 1668. Of Hutton-on-Derwent, Yorks. Matric. 1668, as Gore.

GOWRE, W. Matric. pens. from ST JOHN'S, Michs. 1579.

GOWER, WILLIAM. 'Of TRINITY College,' when ord. deacon (London) June 8, 1718. (No University or College record.)

GOWILL, JAMES. Adm. sizar at QUEENS', June 25, 1706. Of Somerset.

GOWINGE, JAMES. Adm. sizar at CORPUS CHRISTI, 1666. Of Suffolk. Matric. 1667; B.A. 1669–70; M.A. 1673. Ord. priest (Norwich) Mar. 1672–3. V. of Swilland, Suffolk, 1676.

GOWING, JEREMY. Adm. sizar at EMMANUEL, Nov. 28, 1628. Of Norfolk. Matric. 1629; B.A. 1632–3; M.A. 1636. R. of Shimpling, Norfolk, 1642–9. Buried May 28, 1649.

GOWLAND, RICHARD. B.A. from ST CATHARINE'S, 1620. B. in the parish of St Swithin, Lincoln. M.A. 1625. Adm. at Gray's Inn, Aug. 7, 1622. Keeper of the Library, Westminster Abbey, 1626. Preb. of Lincoln, 1632. Died Nov. 10. Buried in Westminster cloisters, Nov. 15, 1659. Will (P.C.C.) 1660. (*Westm. Abbey Reg.*)

GOWNDRILL, GEORGE. Adm. sizar at JESUS, June 24, 1751. Of Yorkshire. S. of George, R. of Atwick, Yorks. School, Wakefield. Matric. 1751; B.A. 1755. Ord. priest (Peterb.) Sept. 25, 1757. V. of Easington and Kilnsea, Yorks., 1769–75. Died 1775. (M. H. Peacock.)

GOWRY, JOSEPH. Adm. pens. (age 18) at ST JOHN'S, Sept. 8, 1686. S. of Richard, gent. B. at York. School, Thornton (Mr Hunter).

GOWSILL, *see* GOLSYLL.

GRACE, CHRISTOPHER. Matric. sizar from CLARE, Easter, 1625. One of these names, of London, attorney, 1634. Another V. of Lancing, Sussex, 1645. (*Vis. of Bucks.*, 1634, 167.)

GRACE, JOB. Adm. sizar at TRINITY, June 13, 1660. S. of William (1627). Matric. 1660, as 'James'; Scholar, 1664; B.A. 1664–5; M.A. 1668. V. of Long Buckby, Northants., 1667–77. V. of Watford, 1671–1719. V. of Sawley, Derbs., 1688–1719. Treasurer of Lichfield Cathedral, 1688. Married, at Long Buckby, May 27, 1668, Bridget Vyse, of Standon, Staffs. Died Oct. 2, 1719, aged 75. M.I. at Watford. Probably brother of Robert (1660). (*Nichols*, III. 393.)

GRACE, JOHN. Matric. sizar from PETERHOUSE, Easter, 1544.

GRACE, JOHN. Matric. pens. from ST JOHN'S, *c.* 1596. Of Nottinghamshire. B.A. 1600–1; M.A. 1604; B.D. 1612. Fellow, 1602. Incorp. at Oxford, 1604. R. of Averham, Notts., 1613; of Welton-le-Wold, Lincs., 1616. V. of Aldworth, Berks., 1619. Married Millicent, dau. of Edward Needham, of Ilston, Leics. (*Al. Oxon.*)

GRACE, LANGLEY. Adm. pens. at ST CATHARINE'S, July 3, 1747. Of Edlington, Lincs. Matric. 1747.

GRACE, ROBERT. B.A. from TRINITY, 1569–70; M.A. 1573. University preacher, 1575. C. of St Andrew's, Cambridge, 1567; R. 1570–8. R. of Averham, Notts., 1576–1612. R. of Branston, Lincs., 1577. Preb. of Southwell, 1587–1612. Buried at Averham, 1612.

GRACE, ROBERT. Adm. sizar at TRINITY, June 13, 1660. Probably s. of William (1627). Matric. 1660; B.A. 1663–4; M.A. 1668. Ord. deacon (Lichfield) Dec. 18, 1664. V. of Shenstone, Staffs., 1665. Doubtless brother of Job. (*Wm Salt Arch. Soc.*, 1915; *Nichols*, III. 393.)

GRACE, WILLIAM. Matric. sizar from CLARE, Easter, 1627. Probably s. of Richard, of Ellington, Hunts.; age 2 in 1613. B.A. 1629–30; M.A. 1633. R. of Rearsby, Leics., 1659–60. V. of Shenstone, Staffs., 1661–2. Ejected and reduced to great want. Died Nov. 10, 1699. M.I. at Shenstone. Father of Job (1660) and probably of the above. (*Vis. of Hunts.*; *Nichols*, III. 392.)

GRACE, WILLIAM. Adm. sizar (age 16) at ST JOHN'S, Sept. 10, 1685. S. of William, husbandman. B. at Stony Stanton, Leics. School, Leire, Leics. (private; Mr Seagrave). Matric. 1686; B.A. 1689–90.

GRACE, ——. 'Minor.' Adm. sizar at PETERHOUSE, *c.* 1543.

GRACEBOROUGH, MARK. Matric. pens. from CORPUS CHRISTI, Easter, 1579; B.A. 1582–3; M.A. 1586. V. of Sibertswold, Kent, 1601–37. Died 1637.

GRADBADGE, WILLIAM. Matric. sizar (age 11) from TRINITY HALL, Michs. 1561. Of Tuddenham, Norfolk. Adm. at the Inner Temple, 1572.

GRAFFE, ——. D.D. 1498–9.

GRAFFENREID, CHRISTOPHER. M.A. 1682 (*Lit. Reg.*).

GRAFTON, ADAM. 'LL.D. Cambridge.' V. of St Alkmund's, Shrewsbury, 1473–87. R. of St Dionis Backchurch, London, 1491–1528. Dean of St Mary's, Shrewsbury, till 1513. Preb. of Lichfield, 1497. Archdeacon of Salop and of Staffs. Died July 24, 1530. Probably the man who graduated as 'Adam.' (H. E. Forrest, *Old Churches of Shrewsbury*.)

GRAFTON, Duke of (CHARLES FITZROY). LL.D. 1705 (*Com. Reg.*). S. of Henry, Duke of Grafton. B. Oct. 25, 1683. Served in the army in Flanders. Lord-Lieutenant of Suffolk, 1705. Lord of the Bedchamber, P.C., 1715. Viceroy of Ireland, 1720–4. Lord Justice of the Realm during the King's absence. K.G., 1721. F.R.S., 1749. Died May 6, 1757. (*G.E.C.*)

GRAFTON, GREGORY (? GEORGE). Matric. pens. from TRINITY, Easter, 1559; Scholar, 1560.

GRAFTON, MATTHEW. Matric. pens. from TRINITY, Easter, 1604; B.A. 1607–8; M.A. 1611.

GRAFTON, ROBERT. Matric. sizar from PETERHOUSE, Easter, 1550; B.A. 1553–4; M.A. 1558. Fellow, 1558–60. Adm. at the Inner Temple, 1560. Perhaps V. of Godalming, Surrey, till 1578, deprived. R. of Garboldisham, Norfolk, 1579–89. V. of Swaffham, 1580. Died 1589.

GRAHAM, DAVID. Adm. at KING'S, a scholar from Eton, 1745. S. of Dr Andrew. Bapt. at Eton, June 18, 1727. Matric. Lent, 1745–6; B.A. 1749–50; M.A. 1753. Fellow, 1749. Adm. at the Middle Temple, June 16, 1750; and at Lincoln's Inn, July 9, 1757. Barrister-at-law, 1753. Died 1764. Brother of George (1746). (*Harwood*.)

GRAHAM, GEORGE. 'M.A. of Cambridge'; incorp. at Oxford, July 12, 1603. (*Al. Oxon.*) Not found in our records.

GRAHAM, GEORGE. Adm. Fell.-Com. (age 15) at ST JOHN'S, Jan. 27, 1641–2. S. of Sir Richard, Knt. and Bart., of Norton Conyers, Yorks. B. at Netherby, Cumberland (his mother's home). School, Hadley (Mr Atkinson). Succeeded as Bart., Jan. 28, 1653–4. Died Mar. 19, 1657–8, aged 31. Buried at Arthuret, Cumberland. M.I. Brother of Richard (1652–3). (*G.E.C.*)

GRAHAM, GEORGE. Matric. pens. from KING'S, 1709–10; LL.B. 1710. S. of George. B. at Ludgershall, Wilts., 1676. Colleger at Eton, 1687–92. Matric. from Queen's College, Oxford, Feb. 11, 1692–3. V. of Dewlish with Milborne St Andrew's, Dorset, 1710–6. R. of Winterborne Clenston, 1710–6. Died at Milborne, July 17, 1716. M.I. (F. S. Hockaday.)

GRAHAM, GEORGE. Adm. at KING'S, a scholar from Eton, 1746. S. of Andrew. Bapt. at Blankney, Lincs., Oct. 30, 1728. Matric. Easter, 1747; B.A. 1750–1; M.A. 1754. Fellow, 1749. Ord. deacon (Ely) Dec. 25, 1751. Assistant Master at Eton. Author of a masque, *Telemachus*. Died Feb. 1767. Brother of David (1745). (*D.N.B.*)

GRAHAM, JAMES, Earl of Montrose. M.A. 1635–6 (*Lit. Reg.*). S. of John, 4th Earl. B. 1612. Succeeded as 5th Earl, 1626. Adm. at St Andrews University, Jan. 26, 1627. Travelled abroad, 1633–6. Joined the Covenanters, 1637; took part in the invasion of England, 1641. Joined Charles I, 1641. Created Marquis, 1644. Appointed Lieutenant-general in Scotland, 1644. Defeated at Philipshaugh, 1645. Escaped to the Continent. Made Field-Marshal by Ferdinand III. Advised Charles II against accepting the throne of Scotland from the Covenanters. Defeated at Invercarron, 1650. Author, poetical. Betrayed and hanged in the Grassmarket, Edinburgh, May 21, 1650. (*D.N.B.*)

GRAHAM or GREAM, JOHN. Adm. sizar at EMMANUEL, Apr. 19, 1671. Of Yorkshire. Matric. 1671; B.A. 1674–5. Ord. deacon (York) Sept. 1676.

GRAHAM, RICHARD. Adm. Fell.-Com. (age 19) at CHRIST'S, Mar. 19, 1652–3. 2nd s. of Sir Richard, of Norton Conyers, Yorks., Knt. and Bart. B. there. Bapt. at Wath, Mar. 11, 1635–6. Educated privately. Matric. 1653–4. Adm. at Gray's Inn, Feb. 12, 1651–2; and at the Inner Temple, 1654. Created Bart., Nov. 17, 1662. Deputy Lieutenant of North Riding, 1687–8. Of Norton Conyers. Married Elizabeth, dau. of Colonel Sir Chichester Fortescue, Knt. Buried at Norton, Dec. 21, 1711. Brother of George (1641–2) and father of the next. (*Peile*, I. 550.)

GRAHAM, RICHARD. Adm. pens. (age 13) at CHRIST'S, Sept. 27, 1675. 1st s. of Sir Richard, Bart. (above). B. at Norton Conyers, Yorks. Matric. 1675. Died before his father. Buried at Wath, Yorks., Mar. 4, 1680–1, aged 20. M.I. (*Peile*, II. 60; *Vis. of Yorks.*, 1665.)

GRAHAM, RICHARD. Adm. pens. (age 16) at TRINITY, Apr. 2, 1678. Of London. S. of Richard. 'B. Dec. 3, 1657.' School, Merchant Taylors'. Matric. 1678.

GRAYHAM, RICHARD. Adm. Fell.-Com. at TRINITY, Sept. 7, 1680. Perhaps adm. at the Middle Temple, 1682; and at the Inner Temple, Oct. 20, 1684. Probably father of the next.

GRAHAM, RICHARD. Adm. Fell.-Com. (age 18) at TRINITY, July 7, 1709. S. of Richard, of London. B. Mar. 8, 1692–3. School, Merchant Taylors'. Matric. 1709. Adm. at the Inner Temple, May 11, 1710; s. and h. of Richard (? above), of the Inner Temple.

GRAHAM, ROBERT. Adm. sizar (age 18) at MAGDALENE, July 7, 1711. S. of Samuel. B. at Boston, Lincs. School, Boston. Matric. 1712; B.A. 1715–6. Ord. deacon (Lincoln) May 27, 1716; priest, June 22, 1718. V. of Thorpe, Lincs., 1717–23. Died July 9, 1724, aged 32. M.I. at All Saints', Wainfleet. (E. Oldfield, *Wainfleet*.)

GRAHAM, WILLIAM. Adm. pens. (age 17) at ST JOHN'S, July 8, 1747. S. of Charles, clerk, of Middlesex. B. at Tottenham. Bapt. Aug. 22, 1730. Exhibitioner from Charterhouse. Matric. 1747. Ord. priest (London, *Litt. dim.* from Winchester) Sept. 22, 1754. Assumed the English Baronetcy and the Scotch Peerage of his cousin Charles, Viscount Preston. Died Sept. 21, 1774. Buried at Carmarthen. Admon. (P.C.C.) 1775. (*G.E.C.*; *Al. Carthus.*)

GRAILE or GRAYLE, JOHN. Matric. sizar from TRINITY, Easter, 1627; Scholar, 1631; B.A. 1631–2; M.A. 1635. Probably Master of Guildford Grammar School, 1645–98. Died Jan. 4, 1697–8, aged 88. M.I. in Trinity Church, Guildford.

GRAIN, *see also* **GREYN.**

GRAIN, EDMUND. B.A. 1474–5.

GRANE or GROME, HENRY. B.Can.L. 1488.

GRAYNE, ROLAND. Matric. pens. from CLARE, Easter, 1612; B.A. 1615–6; M.A. 1619.

GRAYNE, THOMAS. Matric. pens. from CLARE, Easter, 1618; B.A. 1621–2; M.A. 1625.

GRAIN, WILLIAM. B.A. 1474–5.

GRAME, ABRAHAM. Adm. sizar at EMMANUEL, Easter, 1624. Matric. 1624; B.A. from Trinity Hall, 1627; M.A. 1632 (*Lit. Reg.*). Will (P.C.C.) 1636, of one of these names, of St Olave, Southwark, clerk.

GRAME or GREAME, ARTHUR. Matric. pens. from ST JOHN'S, Michs. 1586; B.A. 1590–1; M.A. 1594.

GRANBY, Marquess of, *see* **MANNERS, JOHN.**

GRANDFELD or GLANDFIELD, GEOFFREY. D.D. of Cambridge. Augustinian friar at Northampton. Afterwards went to Rome; where he was chaplain to the Cardinal bishop of Frascati. Suffragan bishop of Lincoln, 1340. Died *c.* 1341. Buried at the monastery, Northampton. (*Pits*; H. G. Harrison.)

GRANDIDGE or GRANDISH, BENJAMIN. Matric. pens. from PEMBROKE, Easter, 1606. S. of Richard (1567), R. of Bradfield St Clare, Suffolk. B.A. 1608–9; M.A. 1612. In Holy Orders. Buried at Bradfield St Clare, Mar. 11, 1613–4.

GRANDORGE, CHARLES. Matric. pens. from ST JOHN'S, Michs. 1562. Probably 1st s. of Humphrey, of Donington, Lincs. Adm. at the Inner Temple, 1565. Of Donington, Lincs. Brother of Nicholas (1562). (*Lincs. Pedigrees*, 419.)

GRANDIDGE or GRANDORGE, CHRISTOPHER. Matric. sizar from CLARE, Easter, 1607; B.A. 1610–1; M.A. 1614. Ord. deacon (Peterb.) June 19, 1614. R. of Marton-in-Craven, Yorks., 1631–72. Died 1672. Father of the next and of Isaac (1646). (Whitaker, *Craven*.)

GRANDORGE, CHRISTOPHER. Adm. sizar (age 16) at ST JOHN'S, Feb. 14, 1658–9. S. of Christopher (above), R. of Marton. B. there. Brother of Isaac (1646).

GRANDORGE, ISAAC. Adm. sizar (age 16) at ST JOHN'S, May 22, 1646. S. of Christopher (1607), R. of Marton-in-Craven, Yorks. B. there. School, Giggleswick (Mr Lucas). Matric. 1646; B.A. 1649–50; M.A. 1653. Fellow, 1650; ejected, 1662. R. of Birdbrook, Essex, 1656; ejected, 1660. Afterwards at Black Notley. Brother of Christopher (1658–9). (*Calamy*, I. 498.)

GRANDORGE, NICHOLAS. Matric. pens. from ST JOHN'S, Michs. 1562. Probably s. of Humphrey, of Donington, Lincs. Died 1578. Will dated Sept. 5; proved Oct. 2, 1578. Brother of Charles (1562). (*Lincs. Pedigrees*, 419.)

GRANDEDGE, RICHARD. Matric. sizar from ST JOHN'S, Michs. 1567; B.A. 1571–2. Ord. priest (Ely) Apr. 17, 1579. R. of Bradfield St Clare, Suffolk, 1578–1619. Buried there Dec. 9, 1619. Father of Benjamin (1606).

GRANEBY or CRANEBY, HENRY. Master of MICHAELHOUSE, 1410–27. R. of Elsworth, Cambs. Allowed three years' absence, for study, 1405.

GRANDISON, Viscount, *see* **VILLERS, JOHN.**

GRANGE, FRANCIS. Adm. sizar (age 16) at CHRIST'S, May 20, 1671. S. of John. B. at Ripon, Yorks. School, Ripon (Mr Oxley). Matric. 1671; B.A. 1674–5; M.A. 1678. R. of Widford, Herts., 1693–5. Died 1695. (*Peile*, II. 36.)

GRAYNGE, GREGORY. Matric. sizar from JESUS, Michs. 1547, as George. R. of Gissing, Norfolk, 1554–61. R. of North Tuddenham, 1559–70. R. of Foxley, 1579. Perhaps will (P.C.C.) 1605; of Bawdswell, Norfolk, clerk (? George).

GRAYNGE, GEORGE. Matric. sizar from KING'S, Lent, 1579–80.

GRAINGE, GEORGE. Adm. pens. at TRINITY, Apr. 18, 1677. School, St Paul's. Probably of St Dunstan's, London. Adm. at the Inner Temple, Jan. 26, 1675–6.

GRANGE or GRAUNGE, JOHN. Matric. sizar from TRINITY, Michs. 1602; B.A. 1606–7; M.A. 1610. Ord. priest (Norwich) 1610. R. of Foxley, Norfolk, 1616.

GRANGE, THOMAS. Matric. pens. from TRINITY, Michs. 1586. Perhaps of East Herlesey, Yorks., gent., and of Barnard's Inn; adm. at Gray's Inn, June 3, 1589. Barrister, 1595.

GRANGE, WILLIAM. Matric. sizar from ST JOHN'S, Easter, 1571.

GRANGE, WILLIAM. Matric. sizar from ST JOHN'S, *c.* 1593. Perhaps matric. also as pens. *c.* 1593; Scholar at Trinity, 1596; B.A. from Trinity, 1597–8.

GRANGER, BENJAMIN. Adm. sizar (age 15) at CAIUS, Jan. 30, 1604–5. Of Depden, Suffolk. S. of John, husbandman. School, Depden (Mr Aldrich). Matric. 1605; Scholar, 1608–10; B.A. 1608–9; M.A. 1612. Ord. priest (Norwich) Sept. 23, 1610. R. of Somerton, Suffolk, 1622–64. Father of the next. (*Venn*, I. 188.)

GRANGER, BENJAMIN. Adm. pens. (age 17) at CAIUS, May 14, 1644. S. of Benjamin (above), R. of Somerton, Suffolk. School, Bury (Mr Stephens). Matric. 1644; Scholar, 1645–8; B.A. 1647–8; M.A. 1651. Applied to the presbyterian *classis* in London, Nov. 23, 1649. (*Venn*, I. 353.)

GRANGER, EDMUND. M.A. 1738 (Incorp. from Oxford). S. of Edmund, of Cruwys Morchard, Devon, clerk. Matric. from Exeter College, Oxford, Apr. 5, 1731, age 18; B.A. (Oxford) 1734; M.A. 1737; B.D. 1746. R. of Sowton, Devon, 1751–77. Preb. of Exeter, 1771–7. Died Aug. 25, 1777, aged 64. Will (Exeter); of Sowton, Devon. (G. *Mag.*; *Al. Oxon.*)

GRANGER, GEORGE. Adm. pens. (age 17) at ST JOHN'S, Sept. 9, 1653. S. of John. B. at Isleworth, Middlesex. School, Charterhouse. Previously matric. from Magdalen College, Oxford, Nov. 27, 1652. B.A. (Cambridge) 1655–6. Incorp. at Oxford, 1669, as M.A. B.D. (Oxford) 1670–1. R. of Halford, Warws., 1659–1707. Buried there July 10, 1707. M.I. (*Al. Oxon.*)

GRANGER, GEORGE. Adm. pens. (age 16) at TRINITY, July 28, 1708. S. of John (1684), of Shillington, Beds. Taught by Mr Goodwin. Matric 1709; Scholar, 1710; B.A. 1712–3.

GRANGER, GILBERT. Adm. pens. (age 17) at TRINITY, Aug. 10, 1702. S. of Nicholas (? 1663), of Shillington, Beds. Bapt. Aug. 25, 1685. School, Peyrton, Herts. (Mr Goodwin). Scholar, 1704; Matric. 1705; B.A. 1706–7; M.A. 1725. Ord. deacon (Ely) Sept. 25, 1709; priest (London) Oct. 21, 1709. Brother of the next.

GRANGER, JOHN. Adm. pens. (age 17) at TRINITY, Oct. 30, 1684. S. of Nicholas. B. at Shillington, Beds. School, Northill, Beds. Matric. 1685; Scholar, 1687; B.A. 1688–9. Adm. at the Inner Temple, June 23, 1688. Brother of the above and father of George (1708).

GRANGER, NICHOLAS. Adm. pens. at TRINITY, June 9, 1663. Matric. 1664; B.A. 1666–7; M.A. 1670. Perhaps father of John (1684) and Gilbert (1702).

GRANGER, THOMAS. Matric. sizar from PETERHOUSE, Michs. 1598. B. at Epworth, Lincs., 1578. B.A. 1601–2; M.A. 1605. Ord. deacon (Lincoln) Sept. 21, 1606; priest, Sept. 20, 1607. V. of Butterwick, Lincs., 1606–25. V. of Horbling, 1621–7.

GRANGER, WILLIAM. Adm. pens. at TRINITY, June 12, 1647. One of these names V. of Bromfield, Cumberland, till 1662. (*See Al. Oxon.* for a contemporary.)

GRAINGER, WILLIAM. Adm. sizar (age 20) at ST JOHN'S, Oct. 7, 1668. S. of William, yeoman, of Crosbyhill, Westmorland. B. there. School, Sedbergh. Matric. 1668; B.A. 1672–3. Ord. deacon (Carlisle) Sept. 21, 1673; priest, Sept. 15, 1674. R. of Waberthwaite, Cumberland, 1677–98. V. of Muncaster, 1686–98. Buried at Waberthwaite, May 15, 1698. (*B. Nightingale.*)

GRAINGER, WILLIAM. Adm. sizar (age 18) at ST JOHN'S, June 3, 1719. S. of Thomas, husbandman, of Cumberland. B. at Stone-raise, near Wigton. Schools, Wigton (Mr Salkeld) and Appleby (Mr Bankes). B.A. 1722–3. Ord. deacon (London) June 9, 1723; priest, Feb. 21, 1724–5. R. of St Anne's, Blackfriars and St Andrew-by-the-Wardrobe, 1736–59. Died Feb. 18, 1759. Will, P.C.C. (*Scott-Mayor*, III. 326.)

GRAINGER, WILLIAM. Adm. sizar (age 19) at CHRIST'S, May 30, 1751. Of Cumberland. School, Wigton. Matric. 1751; Scholar, 1752; B.A. 1755; M.A. 1777. Ord. deacon (London) Feb. 1755; priest (Norwich) Mar. 1756. R. of Salcott Virley, Essex, Apr. 1761. V. of Teynham, Kent, Nov. 9, 1776–8. Chaplain to Lord Cathcart. Died May, 1778. (*Peile*, II. 255.)

GRANGER, ——. M.Gram. 1528–9.

GRANSWORTH or GREENSWORTH, HENRY. Adm. pens. (age 15) at ST JOHN'S, May 9, 1653. S. of James, of Haydock, Lancs. School, Winwick (Mr Ralph Gorst). Matric. 1653; B.A. 1656–7.

GRANT, ANDREW. Matric. Fell.-Com. from MAGDALENE, Easter, 1728.

GRANT, BRIAN. Matric. pens. from ST JOHN'S, c. 1595; B.A. 1598–9; M.A. 1602. V. of Darlington, Durham, 1612–22. Buried there Jan. 26, 1621–2.

GRANT, CHARLES. Adm. sizar at CORPUS CHRISTI, 1662. Of Suffolk. Matric. 1663; B.A. 1666–7; M.A. 1670. Ord. deacon (York) Sept. 1669; priest, Sept. 1670.

GRANT, EDWARD. Matric. sizar from ST JOHN'S, Lent, 1563–4. Migrated to Oxford. B.A. 1571–2; M.A. 1572. Incorp. at Cambridge, 1573. B.D. (Cambridge) 1578–9; D.D. 1588. University preacher, 1580. Head Master of Westminster School, 1572–92. Preb. of Westminster, 1577–1601. R. of Shenley, Herts., 1581; of South Benfleet, Essex, 1584–5; of Bintree and Foulsham, Norfolk, 1586–94. Preb. of Ely, 1589. R. of East Barnet, Herts., 1591; of Algarkirk, Lincs., 1594–1602; and Toppesfield, Essex, 1598. An intimate friend of Roger Ascham. Author, classical. Died Aug. 4, 1601. Will, P.C.C. Father of Gabriel (1593) and John (1596). (*Cooper*, II. 320; *D.N.B.*; *Al. Oxon.*)

GRANT, FRANCIS. Matric. pens. from PETERHOUSE, Easter, 1619; B.A. 1622–3; M.A. 1626. Ord. deacon (Norwich) Mar. 3, 1624–5.

GRANT, FRANCIS. Adm. sizar (age 15) at ST JOHN'S, Jan. 26, 1698–9. S. of John, baker. B. at Burwell, Cambs. School, Godmanchester (Mr Allen). B.A. 1702–3. Ord. deacon (Peterb.) June 3, 1705; priest (Lincoln) June 8, 1707. R. of Laughton-by-Partney, Lincs., 1707.

GRANT, GABRIEL. Matric. pens. from TRINITY, c. 1593. S. of Edward (1563), Head Master of Westminster. Scholar from Westminster, 1593. B.A. 1596–7; M.A. 1600; D.D. 1612. Incorp. at Oxford, 1597. Adm. at Lincoln's Inn, June 15, 1598. R. of Layer Marney, Essex, 1602–4; of St Leonard's, Foster Lane, London, 1604–22. V. of Walthamstow, Essex, 1612–38. Preb. of Westminster, 1613–38. V. of Plumstead, Kent, 1618. R. of Sutton, Surrey, 1621; and of Boxford, Suffolk, 1624–38. Died 1638. Admon. (P.C.C.) Dec. 18, 1638. Brother of John (1596) and father of John (1624). (*Al. Oxon.*; *Westm. Abbey Registers.*)

GRANT, HENRY. Matric. sizar from CHRIST'S, July, 1620; B.A. 1623–4; M.A. 1627.

GRANT, JOHN. Matric. sizar from MAGDALENE, c. 1596. S. of Edward (1563), Master of Westminster. Migrated to Trinity. Scholar, 1596; B.A. 1597–8; M.A. 1601; B.D. 1608; D.D. 1614. Fellow of Trinity, 1599. R. of Benefield, Northants., 1606–23. R. of Barming, Kent, 1623–4. R. of St Bartholomew-by-the-Exchange, London, 1623. V. of South Benfleet, Essex, till 1641. Died 1653. Brother of Gabriel (1593). (J. Ch. Smith; H. I. Longden.)

GRANT, JOHN. Adm. pens. at PEMBROKE, Nov. 4, 1624. S. of Gabriel (1593), D.D. Matric. 1625; B.A. 1627–8; M.A. 1631. Perhaps V. of Holbeach, Lincs., 1632–40; and R. of Hockerton, Notts., 1640.

GRANT, JOHN. M.A. from ST JOHN'S, 1628 (Incorp. from Dublin). Probably B.D. from Trinity College, Dublin, 1618. V. of Calverley, Yorks., 1627–42. Married Ann Pease, of Leeds, 1628. Buried at Calverley, Mar. 14, 1641–2. (*Bradford Antiq.*, N.S., II. 361.)

GRANT, JOHN. Matric. sizar from ST JOHN'S, Michs. 1628; B.A. 1631–2; M.A. 1635.

GRANT, JOHN. D.D. 1631–2 (*Lit. Reg.*).

GRANT, JOHN. Adm. sizar (age 15) at SIDNEY, June, 1668. S. of Samuel, gent., deceased. B. in Hampshire. School, Guildford (Mr Gray). Matric. 1668; B.A. 1671–2; M.A. 1675; D.D. 1709. Fellow, 1673. Ord. priest (Gloucester) 1674. R. of St Dunstan-in-the-West, 1677–1736. Preb. of Rochester, 1692–1736. V. of Kingsdown, Kent, 1710–36. Died July 10, 1736. (H. G. Harrison.)

GRANT, JOHN. Adm. pens. at EMMANUEL, Jan. 6, 1735–6. Of Leicestershire. Matric. 1737. Died in College. Buried Nov. 24, 1737.

GRANT, PAUL. Matric. pens. from ST JOHN'S, Michs. 1579. Of Yorkshire. B.A. 1582–3; M.A. 1586. Fellow, 1587. Ord. deacon and priest (Peterb.) Apr. 13, 1589. R. of Weston, Suffolk, 1593–1610. Will (Bury) 1610.

GRANT, RICHARD. Adm. sizar (age 16) at ST JOHN'S, July 3, 1641. S. of Augustine, yeoman, of Allington (? Ellington, Masham), Yorks. B. there. School, Newark (Mr Gambull). Matric. 1641; B.A. 1644–5; M.A. 1648.

GRANT, THOMAS. Matric. sizar from EMMANUEL, Michs. 1601.

GRANT, THOMAS. Matric. sizar from QUEENS', Easter, 1629. Of Kent. B.A. 1632.

GRANT, WILLIAM. Matric. sizar from TRINITY, Easter, 1569; B.A. 1572–3.

GRANT, WILLIAM. Matric. pens. from TRINITY, Easter, 1627; B.A. 1630–1; M.A. from Exeter College, Oxford, 1633. V. of Isleworth, Middlesex, 1639–78, sequestered during the rebellion. Buried at Isleworth, May 8, 1678. Will (Consist. C. London). (*Al. Oxon.*; J. Ch. Smith.)

GRANT, ——. Scholar of JESUS, 1535–6.

GRANTCHESTER, ANTHONY DE. Chancellor of the University, 1352.

GRANTCHESTER, THOMAS DE. Chancellor of the University, 1348.

GRANTHAM, EDMUND. Matric. pens. from JESUS, Michs. 1559.

GRANTHAM, FRANCIS. Matric. pens. from JESUS, c. 1590. Perhaps adm. at Lincoln's Inn, Nov. 1, 1595. Of Langton, Lincs., Esq.

GRANTHAM, HENRY, Earl of, *see* AUVERQUERQUE.

GRANTHAM, LANCELOT. Matric. Fell.-Com. from KING'S, Michs. 1650. S. of Thomas, of Gotham (? Goltho), Lincs. Adm. at the Inner Temple, 1651.

GRANTHAM, ROBERT. Adm. pens. (age 18) at ST JOHN'S, Mar. 30, 1722. S. of Leonard, barrister, of Cheshire. B. at Chester. School, Chester (Mr Henchman). Matric. 1722; B.A. 1725–6.

GRANTHAM, THOMAS. M.A. from PETERHOUSE, 1634. Of Lincolnshire. (B.A. from Hart Hall, Oxford, 1630.) A nephew of Sir Thomas Grantham, of Radcliffe, Notts. C. of High Barnet. R. of Waddington, Lincs., 1646; ejected, 1656. Afterwards kept school in London. Died in St Ann's, Blackfriars, London, Mar. 1664. (*D.N.B.*; *Al. Oxon.*)

GRANTHAM, THOMAS. Adm. Fell.-Com. at TRINITY, July 3, 1650. Of Lincolnshire. S. of Thomas, of Goltho, Lincs., and Meaux, Yorks. Matric. 1650–1. Married Frances, dau. of Sir George Wentworth, of Woolley, Yorks. Died Apr. 1, 1668, aged 35. Buried at Ealand, Halifax. (*Lincs. Pedigrees*, 423.)

GRANTHAM, ——. Fee for M.A. or higher degree, 1484–5.

GRAPPE, JOHN. Adm. at KING'S (age 17) a scholar from Eton, Aug. 17, 1510. Of Coventry. B.A. 1513–4. Vacated scholarship c. 1513.

GRAPE, NICHOLAS. Incorp. from Oxford, 1479–80.

GRASBOROUGH, *see* **GRACEBOROUGH.**

GRASCOME, NATHANIEL. Adm. pens. (age 30) at PETERHOUSE, May 7, 1660. Of Warwickshire.

GRASCOMBE, SAMUEL. Adm. sizar (age 19) at MAGDALENE, June 1, 1661. S. of John, of Coventry. School, Coventry. Matric. 1661; B.A. 1664–5; M.A. 1674. Ord. deacon (Peterb.) July 30, 1664; priest, May 21, 1665. R. of Stourmouth, Kent, 1680–90, deprived. V. of Bromley, 1681. Author of controversial tracts. Died *c.* 1708. Will (P.C.C.) 1708; of St Andrew, Holborn. (*D.N.B.*; J. Ch. Smith.)

GRASKE, ——. B.D. 1468–9.

GRASTY, JOHN. Adm. sizar (age 19) at ST JOHN'S, Feb. 5, 1679–80. S. of Samuel, R. of Brougham, Westmorland. B. at Wistaston, Cheshire. School, Appleby (Mr Jackson). Matric. 1680; B.A. 1683–4; M.A. 1698. Ord. deacon (London) Feb. 24, 1683–4. P.C. of St James', Duke's Place, London, 1700–28. Master (perhaps deputy) of Aldenham School, Herts., *c.* 1700–1. Died June 29, 1728.

GRATWICK, CHARLES. Adm. pens. (age 17) at ST JOHN'S, June 27, 1690. S. of John, bailiff. B. at Horsham, Sussex. School, Horsham (Mr Wickliffe). Matric. 1690; B.A. 1693–4. R. of Curry Mallet, Somerset, 1714–35. Died 1735.

GRAVE, BARTHOLOMEW. M.A. 1650 (Incorp. from Oxford). Of London. M.A. of St Andrews, 1647. Incorp. at Oxford, 1648, from Merton College. Fellow of Wadham, by the visitors, 1648. (*Al. Oxon.*)

GRAVE, GEORGE. Matric. sizar from TRINITY, Lent, 1577–8; B.A. 1582–3. Ord. deacon and priest (Peterb.) Apr. 16, 1579; of Lincoln diocese. C. of Algarkirk, Lincs., 1579. R. of Sotby, in 1585.

GRAVE, HAMOND. B.A. 1478; M.A. 1478 (*sic*). Proctor, 1482–3. Probably fellow of QUEENS', 1484–5. Ord. priest (Norwich) June 5, 1479; of Norwich diocese. R. of Halesworth, Suffolk. Admon., 1500.

GRAVE, JAMES. Matric. pens. from ST JOHN'S, Michs. 1621; B.A. 1624–5; M.A. 1628.

GRAVE, JOHN. Matric. sizar from JESUS, Easter, 1607. Doubtless the scholar of these names buried at All Saints', Cambridge, Sept. 27, 1607.

GRAVE, ROBERT. Scholar of CHRIST'S, 1531–2; B.A. 1532–3.

GRAVE, ROBERT. Educated at Cambridge. B. in Kent. Dean of Cork, 1590. Precentor of Limerick, 1591; and of Christ Church, Dublin, 1595–1600. Bishop of Ferns, and of Leighlin, July to Oct., 1600. Drowned in Dublin Harbour, Oct. 1, 1600. (*Cooper*, II. 288.)

GRAVE, ROBERT. Matric. sizar from PEMBROKE, Easter, 1615; B.A. 1618–9; M.A. 1622. Chaplain of Thetford, Streatham, Cambs., in 1623. Minister at Witcham, 1626.

GRAVE, THOMAS. Matric. sizar from TRINITY, Michs. 1584.

GRAVE, THOMAS. Matric. sizar from TRINITY, Lent, 1584–5. (Perhaps a repetition of the above.)

GRAVE or GRAVES, THOMAS. Matric. sizar from QUEENS', Easter, 1588. B. at Wallington, Herts., *c.* 1571. B.A. (? 1591–2); M.A. 1595. Ord. priest (Lincoln) Aug. 24, 1596. V. of Winterton, Lincs., 1600–5. V. of Crowle, 1605–13.

GRAVE, THOMAS. Matric. sizar from QUEENS', Michs. 1602. Of Cumberland. B.A 1606–7; M.A. 1610. Perhaps R. of Chipping Ongar, Essex, 1617–35. Buried June 10, 1635.

GRAVE or GREAVE, WILLIAM. Scholar of TRINITY, 1596; B.A. 1596–7; M.A. 1600; B.D. 1607. Fellow, 1599. Ord. deacon and priest (Peterb.) Sept. 23, 1604. Perhaps R. of Baconsthorpe, Norfolk, 1607.

GRAVE, W. Matric. sizar from TRINITY, Michs. 1583.

GRAVE, WILLIAM. Adm. pens. (age 17) at PEMBROKE, Mar. 1, 1618–9. S. of George, of London. Matric. 1618–9; B.A. 1622–3; M.A. 1626. One of these names R. of Roos, Yorks., 1627–62.

GRAVELEY, GEORGE. Adm. sizar at KING'S, Lent, 1566–7.

GRAVELYE, JOHN. Matric. sizar from CLARE, Easter, 1558.

GRAVELEY, THOMAS. Matric. sizar from QUEENS', Michs. 1550.

GRAVELEY, THOMAS. Matric. sizar from TRINITY, Lent, 1582–3. Perhaps of Graveley, Herts.; adm. at Gray's Inn, Nov. 5, 1585; s. of Thomas. (*Vis. of Herts.*, 1572.)

GRAVELL, ——. Adm. sizar at TRINITY HALL, June 16, 1694.

GRAVENER, GODDARD. Matric. pens. from TRINITY, Michs. 1601.

GRAVENOR, HENRY. Adm. pens. (age 16) at TRINITY, June 9, 1747. S. of Thomas, of Antigua, West Indies. School, Isleworth, Middlesex (Mr Jeffreys). Matric. 1747. Not found in pedigree in Oliver's *Antigua*.

GRAVENOR, JOHN. Adm. at KING'S, a scholar from Eton, 1538. B. at Eccleston, Cheshire, *c.* 1522. B.A. 1542–3. Fellow, 1541–6. Chaplain to the Bishop of Rochester. Author, translations out of Saxon. (*Cooper*, II. 532.)

GRAVENER, RICHARD. Matric. pens. from PETERHOUSE, Michs. 1607.

GRAVENER, WILLIAM. Adm. pens. at PETERHOUSE, Nov. 21, 1631. Scholar, 1632; Matric. 1632. (For suggestions *see* *T. A. Walker*, 45.)

GRAVER, RALPH. Adm. sizar (age 17) at MAGDALENE, May 20, 1648. Perhaps s. of Henry, of Fewston, Yorks. (M. H. Peacock.)

GRAVER, WALTER. B.A. 1534–5.

GRAVES, ABRAHAM. Matric. pens. from EMMANUEL, Michs. 1649.

GREEVES, ANDREW. Matric. sizar from ST JOHN'S, *c.* 1593.

GRAVES, ANTHONY. Adm. pens. at EMMANUEL, Feb. 24, 1645–6. Of Lincolnshire. Matric. 1646; B.A. 1649–50; M.A. 1653. Ord. deacon (Peterb.) Sept. 5; priest, Sept. 20, 1663. R. of Little Casterton, Rutland, 1674–1701. Buried there May 2, 1701.

GRAVES or GREAVES, BENJAMIN. Adm. sizar at TRINITY, May 13, 1664. Matric. 1664; B.A. 1667–8; M.A. 1672. Ord. deacon (York) Sept. 1671; priest, Sept. 1672. V. of Brodsworth, Yorks., 1674–99.

GREAVE, EDWARD. B.A. from TRINITY, 1605–6; M.A. 1609. Ord. priest (York) Sept. 1607.

GREAVES, EDWARD. Matric. pens. from JESUS, Easter, 1604; B.A. 1607–8.

GRAVES, EDWARD. Adm. pens. (age 18) at ST JOHN'S, May 11, 1730. S. of John, gent., of Lancashire. B. in Manchester. School, Bradford, Yorks. Matric. 1730.

GRAVES, GAWEN. Adm. sizar (age 19) at CHRIST'S, June 14, 1712. S. of John. B. in St Martin's parish, London. School, King's College (Mr Baker). Matric. 1712; Scholar, 1713; B.A. 1715–6; M.A. 1730. Ord. deacon (London) Dec. 1721. V. of Burnham Overy, Norfolk, 1729–42. (*Peile*, II. 179.)

GREAVES, GEORGE. Adm. sizar at TRINITY, July 2, 1652. Of Yorkshire. Matric. 1652; Scholar, 1655; B.A. 1655–6; M.A. 1659. Tutor, 1660–1. Ord. deacon and priest (Peterb.) Aug. 17, 1662.

GREVES, JOHN. Matric. sizar from JESUS, Michs. 1556.

GREAVES, JOHN. Matric. sizar from ST JOHN'S, *c.* 1595.

GRAVES, JOHN. Matric. pens. from ST JOHN'S, Easter, 1624.

GREAVES, JOHN. M.A. 1633 (Incorp. from Oxford). Of Hampshire. S. of John, R. of Colmer, Hants. Matric. from Balliol College, Dec. 12, 1617, age 15; B.A. (St Mary's Hall, Oxford) 1621; M.A. 1628. Fellow of Merton, 1624. Gresham Professor of Geometry, 1631–43. Savilian Professor of Astronomy, Oxford, 1643–8, expelled. Travelled abroad, collecting coins, gems and oriental MSS., 1637–40. Died in London, Oct. 8, 1652. Will, P.C.C. Brother of Nicholas (1634). (*Al. Oxon.*; *D.N.B.*; A. B. Beaven.)

GRAVES, JOHN. Scholar of MAGDALENE, Lent, 1638–9.

GREAVES, JOHN. Adm. sizar (age 17) at CHRIST'S, June 9, 1647. S. of Humphry. B. at Nottingham School, Nottingham (Mr Leake). Matric. 1647; B.A. 1651; M.A. 1660. Perhaps R. of Whitwell, Derbs., 1673–90. (*Peile*, I. 514.)

GREAVES, JOHN. Adm. pens. (age 16) at MAGDALENE, May 7, 1667. S. of Thomas, D.D., Preb. of Peterborough. School, Oundle, Northants.

GRAYVES or GREAVES, LEONARD. Matric. sizar from ST JOHN'S, Easter, 1571; B.D. 1595. Doubtless ord. priest (Peterb.) Apr. 15, 1578. V. of Oundle, in 1583. V. of Thurston, Suffolk, 1589–1609. R. of Beeston, Norfolk, 1609.

GRAVES or GREAVES, MATTHEW. Adm. sizar at EMMANUEL, Feb. 23, 1638–9. Of Lincolnshire. Matric. 1639; B.A. 1642–3; M.A. 1647. Perhaps of Stamford, Lincs., clerk; father of Thomas (1666–7).

GREAVES, NICHOLAS. Matric. sizar from ST JOHN'S, Easter, 1610; B.A. 1613–4; M.A. 1617. Ord. deacon (Peterb.) J n 10; priest, June 11, 1620. Licensed to marry Mary Crosslande, of Almondbury, 1627. Probably R. of Holmfirth, Yorks., 1630–4. R. of Tankersley, 1634. R. of Welwyn, Herts., till 1662, ejected.

GREAVES, NICHOLAS. M.A. 1634 (Incorp. from Oxford). S. of John, of Colmer, Hants., clerk. School, Winchester. Matric. from St Mary Hall, Feb. 4, 1624–5, age 19; B.A. (Oxford) 1627; M.A. 1630–1; B.D. 1642; D.D. 1643. Fellow of All Souls, 1627. Proctor, 1640. Ord. priest (Oxford) Dec. 20, 1635. Dean of Dromore, 1642 (installed 1661)–1673. Treasurer of Connor, 1668–73. Will, 1673. Brother of John (1633). (H. B. Swanzy; *Al. Oxon.* probably confuses him with the preceding.)

GREAVES, PAUL. Matric. sizar from CHRIST'S, June, 1588; B.A. 1591-2; M.A. 1595. Fellow, 1595-8. Lecturer at St Andrew's, Norwich, 1614-6. Author, *Grammatica Anglicana*. (*Peile*, I. 192; *Cooper*, II. 174.)

GREAVES, RALPH. Adm. pens. (age 18) at CAIUS, Oct. 8, 1572. S. of Charles, of Todwick, Yorks. School, Laughton, Yorks. Matric. 1572; B.A. from Clare, 1575-6; M.A. 1579. R. of Culmerton, Salop, 1578. (*Venn*, I. 71.)

GREAVES, RICHARD. Adm. at CORPUS CHRISTI, 1610. Of Nottinghamshire. B.A. 1613-4. One of these names, of Beeley, Derbs., adm. at Gray's Inn, Mar. 9, 1614-5.

GRAVES, RICHARD. Matric. pens. (age 16) from PEMBROKE, Easter, 1626. S. of Richard, of London. B.A. 1629. Adm. at Lincoln's Inn, May 24, 1631.

GRAVES or GREAVES, RICHARD. Matric. pens. from ST JOHN'S, Michs. 1627; B.A. 1631-2; M.A. 1638.

GREAVES or GREVES, THOMAS. Matric. pens. from CHRIST'S, Easter, 1570; Scholar, 1571-2. One of these names school-master at Hinxton, Cambs., 1580. (*Peile*, I. 113.)

GRAVES, THOMAS. Matric. sizar from MAGDALENE, Michs. 1635; B.A. 1638-9; M.A. 1642. Ord. deacon (Peterb.) June 9, 1639; priest (Lincoln) Sept. 25, 1642. Perhaps V. of Minting, Lincs., 1642. But *see Al. Oxon.* for a contemporary.

GREAVES, THOMAS. Adm. sizar (age 16) at ST JOHN'S, Feb. 13, 1666-7. S. of Matthew (? 1638-9), clerk, of Stamford, Lincs. B. there. School, Oakham, Rutland. Matric. 1667; B.A. 1670-1. Ord. deacon (Peterb.) Dec. 24, 1671. Perhaps R. of Quarrington, Lincs., 1691; and father of Thomas (1713-4).

GRAVES, THOMAS. Adm. sizar at EMMANUEL, Apr. 20, 1681. Of Lincolnshire. Matric. 1681; B.A. 1685-6.

GREAVES, THOMAS. M.B. from KING'S, 1685.

GRAVES, THOMAS. Adm. pens. (age 18) at ST JOHN'S, Mar. 10, 1713-4. S. of Thomas (? 1666-7), clerk. B. at Quarrington, Lincs. School, Sleaford (Mr Smith). Matric. 1713-4; B.A. 1717-8. Ord. deacon (Lincoln) Mar. 15, 1718-9; priest, Sept. 23, 1722. C. of Crowle, Lincs., 1719.

GRAVES, WILLIAM. Matric. pens. from CORPUS CHRISTI, c. 1594. S. of William, of London, and Mary, dau. of John Gregory, of Nottingham. B. in Nottinghamshire. B.A. 1598-9; M.A. 1602; B.D. 1610. Fellow, 1603-13. Incorp. at Oxford, 1610. Ord. deacon and priest (Norwich) Sept. 29, 1604. R. of Brailsford, Derbs., 1607; sequestered, 1646. R. of Nuthall, Notts., 1612.

GRAVES, WILLIAM. Matric. sizar from TRINITY, Michs. 1585. Perhaps B.A. 1589-90. One of these names, 'B.A.,' R. of Witnesham, Suffolk, 1591-1602; and V. of Framsden, 1591-1606.

GREAVES, WILLIAM. Matric. pens. from JESUS, Easter, 1604; B.A. 1606-7; M.A. from King's, 1610. Perhaps V. of Stanford, Norfolk, 1634.

GRAVES, WILLIAM. Adm. sizar at TRINITY, Apr. 15, 1641. Matric. 1641; B.A. 1645-6; M.A. 1650. Probably Registrary of the Archdeaconry of Nottingham. Alderman and Mayor of Nottingham, 1663-70, 1677, 1692. Buried at St Mary's, Nottingham, June 1, 1697, aged 77. M.I. there. (Godfrey, *St Mary's, Nottingham*.)

GRAVES, WILLIAM. Matric. pens. from ST CATHARINE'S, Michs. 1642. Of Hertfordshire. B.A. 1645-6; M.A. 1649. One of these names R. of Little Munden, Herts., 1659.

GRAVES, WILLIAM. Matric. pens. from ST CATHARINE'S, Easter, 1647; B.A. 1647-8. One of these names intruded minister at Bishopwearmouth, 1654-61. Married, at Bishop-wearmouth, Dec. 6, 1657, Hannah, dau. of Gabriel Sangar, minister. Another, B.A., R. of St Martin Orgar, London, in 1679.

GREAVES, WILLIAM. Adm. pens. (age 17) at TRINITY, May 26, 1686. S. of William. B. at Nottingham. School, Nottingham (Mr Jer. Cudworth). Matric. 1686; Scholar, 1689; B.A. 1689-90; M.A. 1693.

GREAVES, WILLIAM. Adm. pens. at CLARE, Jan. 26, 1719-20. S. of William, of Gartside Hall. B. at Rochdale, Lancs. Matric. 1720; B.A. 1720-1; M.A. 1724. Fellow, 1722-42. Adm. at Lincoln's Inn, June 3, 1724; and at the Inner Temple, Nov. 9, 1727. Commissary of the University, 1726-79. Steward of the estates of Trinity College. Married a daughter of Beaupré Bell. Succeeded to his estates at Outwell, Norfolk, and assumed the name of Beaupré-Bell. Died at Fulbourn, Cambs., Mar. 10, 1787. (*G. Mag.*)

GREAVES, WILLIAM. Adm. sizar at CLARE, June 28, 1729. B. at Rochdale, Lancs. Matric. 1729; B.A. 1732-3; M.A. 1749. Ord. deacon (Lincoln) July 1, 1733. V. of Gt and Little Abington, Cambs., 1736. Perhaps R. of Newton, Isle of Ely, 1754. Will of one of these names (P.C.C.) 1783; of Lackford, Suffolk, clerk.

GRAVESEND (? GRANYSEND), ——. Pens. at GONVILLE HALL, 1524. A monk.

GRAVETT, HENRY. Matric. pens. from ST JOHN'S, Michs. 1548; B.A. 1551-2; M.A. 1555. Fellow of Peterhouse, 1553-5. Adm. at Lincoln's Inn, Aug. 21, 1556. Called to the Bar, 1563. Licensed Oct. 24, 1570, to marry Alice Barnard, of S. Andrews, Holborn. Will (P.C.C.) 1575, of one of these names; of Kingston-on-Thames, gent.

GRAVET, JOHN. Matric. pens. from PEMBROKE, Michs. 1559. B. at Wycombe, Bucks. B.A. 1562-3; M.A. 1566. Fellow, c. 1566. Ord. deacon (London) July 16, 1568. V. of Bishop's Stortford, 1571-5.

GRAVET, JOHN. Adm. at KING'S (age 18) a scholar from Eton, Aug. 26, 1562. Of Henley-on-Thames, Oxon. Matric. 1562; B.A. 1566-7. Fellow, 1565-9. 'Lived to a very great age.' (*Harwood*.)

GRAVETT, JOHN. Matric. sizar from PEMBROKE, Michs. 1576; B.A. 1580-1; M.A. 1584. Fellow. Incorp. at Oxford, 1586. V. of Tilehurst, Berks., 1593. R. of Bradfield. Buried there July 19, 1613. (J. Ch. Smith.)

GRAVET, JOHN. Matric. pens. from CORPUS CHRISTI, Easter, 1621. Of Sussex. B.A. 1624-5; M.A. 1628. Ord. deacon (Peterb.) July 18, 1627; priest, July 2, 1628.

GRAVETT, JOHN. M.A. 1663 (Incorp. from Oxford). Matric. from Hart Hall, July 25, 1655, *fil. cler.*; B.A. (Oxford) 1658-9; M.A. 1661-2. V. of Ditchling, Sussex, 1662. R. of Litlington, 1664. V. of East Dean, 1674. (*Al. Oxon.*)

GRAVETT, THOMAS. Adm. at KING'S (age 18) a scholar from Eton, Sept. 22, 1567. Of Wycombe, Bucks. Matric. 1567; B.A. 1571-2; M.A. 1575. Fellow, 1570-5.

GRAVETT, WILLIAM. Matric. pens. from PETERHOUSE, Michs. 1554. Of Buckinghamshire. B.A. 1557-8; M.A. from Pembroke, 1561; B.D. 1569. Fellow of Pembroke, 1558. V. of St Sepulchre, London, 1566-99. Preb. of St Paul's, 1567-99. R. of Little Laver, Essex, 1569-99. Author, *Sermons*. Died Mar. 1598-9. (*D.N.B.*; *Cooper*, II. 268.)

GRAY or GREY, *see also* DE GREY.

GRAYE, ANDREW. Matric. sizar from CLARE, Michs. 1546. Of Albury, Herts. Adm. at the Inner Temple, 1553. Bencher, 1574. Treasurer, 1585. Died Jan. 13, 1614-5, at Pulters, Herts., aged 85. Buried in Hinxworth Church. M.I. He was a contributor, £25, to the defence of the country at the time of the Armada, 1588. (*Clutterbuck*, III. 529.)

GRAY or GREY, ANTHONY, Earl of Kent. Adm. nobleman at TRINITY, May 31, 1658. S. of Henry, Earl of Kent. B. June 11, 1645. M.A. 1661. Succeeded as Earl, 1651. Married Mary, dau. of John, Lord Lucas, of Shenfield. Died at Tonbridge, Aug. 19, 1702. Buried at Flitton. Father of Henry (1705). (Collins' *Peerage*, III. 345; *G.E.C.*)

GRAY, CORNELIUS. Adm. sizar (age 16) at SIDNEY, Nov. 17, 1624. S. of Thomas, R. of Clapton, Northants. School, Uppingham. Matric. 1624; B.A. 1629-30. Ord. deacon (Peterb.) Feb. 14; priest, Feb. 15, 1629-30. R. of Wickford, Essex, 1635.

GRAYE, ED. Matric. pens. from CORPUS CHRISTI, Michs. 1572.

GRAY, EDMUND. Adm. at KING'S (age 15) a scholar from Eton, Aug. 6, 1649. Of Saffron Walden. Matric. 1649; B.A. 1653. Fellow, 1652-5.

GRAYE, EDWARD. Matric. Fell.-Com. from TRINITY, Easter, 1563.

GRAYE, EDWARD. Matric. pens. from JESUS, Easter, 1609.

GREY, EDWARD. Adm. Fell.-Com. (age 15) at CHRIST'S, May 25, 1626. (Previously matric. from University College, Oxford, Nov. 18, 1625.) 4th s. of Sir Ralph, of Chillingham, Northumberland. Educated at home. Matric. 1626; B.A. 1627-8. Adm. at Gray's Inn, Aug. 3, 1629. Of Nunnykirk. Brother of Robert (1626) and Ralph (1618). (*Peile*, I. 376.)

GRAY, EDWARD. M.A. 1640 (Incorp. from Oxford). S. of Edward, of Fordham, Cambs. Matric. from Christ Church, June 22, 1632, age 16; B.A. (Oxford) 1635; M.A. 1638. Student of Christ Church. Died July 27, 1642. Buried in Christchurch Cathedral. (*Al. Oxon.*)

GREY, EDWARD. Adm. Fell.-Com. (age 18) at ST JOHN'S, June 10, 1650. S. of Edward, gent., of Beverley, Yorks. B. there. School, Beverley. Matric. 1650; B.A. 1652. Adm. at Gray's Inn, July 7, 1652.

GREY, EDWARD. Adm. pens. (age 14) at CHRIST'S, June 7, 1654. S. of Edward, of Howick, Northumberland. B. there. Educated at home. Matric. 1654. Buried at Howick, July 19, 1667. Brother of John (1654) and Philip (1654). (*Peile*, I. 563.)

GRAY, ENOCH. Adm. sizar at EMMANUEL, Easter, 1628. Matric. 1629; B.A. 1631-2. Ord. deacon (Norwich) June 16; priest, Sept. 22, 1633. Suspended in Norwich diocese, 1634, by Bishop Wren. At Sandwich, Kent, in 1639. R. of Wickham Bishop, Essex, 1644-c. 1650. (H. Smith.)

GRAY, FRANCIS. Matric. sizar from JESUS, Easter, 1612. S. of Robert, of Nolt Market, Newcastle-on-Tyne, merchant taylor. B.A. 1615-6; M.A. 1619. Incorp. at Oxford, 1617. Ord. priest (Durham) Sept. 20, 1618. P.C. of St James', Newcastle. V. of Hartburn. V. of Ponteland. Head Master of Newcastle Grammar School, till 1637. Preacher at St Andrew's, Newcastle, 1622-41. Master of the Hospital in Westgate, Newcastle-on-Tyne, 1630. Buried at Newcastle, Jan. 1641-2. (D. S. Boutflower.)

GRAY, FRANCIS. Adm. pens. at CLARE, Jan. 31, 1639-40. Matric. 1640; B.A. 1643-4. One of these names s. and h. of Francis, of Wellingborough, Northants., gent.; adm. at Lincoln's Inn, Feb. 1, 1647-8.

GRAYE, FULK. Matric. pens. from ST JOHN'S, Michs. 1552.

GRAY, GE. Matric. sizar from CLARE, Easter, 1544.

GRAY, GEORGE. Adm. sizar at TRINITY, Apr. 6, 1667. S. of George, of Southwick, Durham (Captain in the Parliamentary army). B. there, Feb. 28, 1651-2. School, Brignall. Matric. 1667; Scholar, 1671; B.A. 1671-2; M.A. 1675. Ord. deacon (? Durham) 1676; priest, 1677. R. of Lawton, Cheshire, 1679-82. V. of Burneston, Yorks., 1682-1711. Married (1) Elizabeth, dau. of Zachary Cowdray, R. of Barthomley, Cheshire; (2) Sarah, dau. of Tho. Harrison; (3) Hannah, dau. of Tho. Bendlowes. Buried at Burneston, June 13, 1711. Father of Zachary (1704). (H. M. Wood.)

GREY, GEORGE. Adm. pens. (age 17) at ST JOHN'S, Apr. 9, 1731. S. of George, of Newcastle-on-Tyne, barrister. B. there. Bapt. at St John's, Newcastle, Aug. 24, 1713. School, Newcastle (Mr Salkeld). Matric. 1731. Adm. at Lincoln's Inn, Oct. 26, 1731. Of Southwick, Durham, Esq. Buried at St Nicholas, Newcastle, Mar. 28, 1746. (Surtees, *Durham*, II. 19; H. M. Wood.)

GRAYE, HENRY. Matric. pens. from PETERHOUSE, Michs. 1554. Doubtless s. of Henry, of Wrest, Beds., and grandson of Henry, Earl of Kent. Adm. at Gray's Inn, Feb. 22, 1568-9. Knighted, 1573. Succeeded his brother Reginald (1551) as 6th Earl of Kent. Died Jan. 31, 1614-5. Buried at Flitton. (*T. A. Walker*.)

GRAYE, HENRY. Adm. sizar at EMMANUEL, May 11, 1594. Matric. *c.* 1594; Scholar; B.A. 1597-8; M.A. 1601. Licensed to preach (York) Oct. 1607.

GRAY, HENRY. Matric. Fell.-Com. from TRINITY, Michs. 1598. One of these names, of Suffolk, gent., adm. at Lincoln's Inn, May 13, 1604.

GRAY, HENRY. Matric. pens. from JESUS, Michs. 1602.

GREY, HENRY. Adm. pens. at SIDNEY, Mar. 31, 1611. Matric. 1611; B.A. 1614-5. One of these names, s. and h. of Anthony, of Burbage, Leics., adm. at Gray's Inn, Jan. 31, 1615-6.

GRAY or GREY, HENRY. Matric. Fell.-Com. from TRINITY, Easter, 1615. S. of Sir John. M.A. 1615 (on King's visit). Succeeded his grandfather as 2nd Baron Grey of Groby, 1614. Created Earl of Stamford, 1628. Parliamentary general. M.P. for Leicestershire, 1654 (though a peer). Declared for Charles II, 1659. Married Anne, dau. of William Cecil, Lord Burghley. Died Aug. 21, 1673. Buried at Bradgate, Leics. (*D.N.B.*; *Nichols*, III. 683; *G.E.C.*)

GRAY, HENRY. Adm. pens. at EMMANUEL, June 25, 1622. Matric. 1623; B.A. 1625-6; M.A. 1629. One of these names V. of Long Stanton St Michael, Cambs., 1651-69; and of Long Stanton All Saints', 1660-73.

GRAY, HENRY. Adm. sizar at MAGDALENE, July 20, 1639. Migrated to Clare, June 19, 1640. Perhaps ord. deacon (Lincoln) Nov. 26, 1644, as 'B.A.'; priest, June 1, 1645. Possibly R. of Heyford, Northants., 1668-73; and father of the next.

GRAY, HENRY. Adm. sizar at CLARE, Apr. 23, 1663. Matric. 1663; B.A. 1666-7; M.A. 1670. Ord. deacon (Peterb.) Sept. 22, 1667; priest, Sept. 19, 1669. C. of Heyford, Northants., 1669. R. 1679-1721. Schoolmaster at Heyford, 1683. Buried there Feb. 27, 1720-1. 'Rector almost 42 years; age 75.' Will (Northampton) 1721. (H. I. Longden.)

GREY, HENRY. Adm. pens. at CLARE, Oct. 3, 1677. Of Kilworth, Leics. Matric. 1677; LL.B. 1683.

GREY, HENRY. Adm. pens. at QUEENS', Apr. 18, 1682. S. of Thomas (1639), R. of Cavendish, Suffolk. B. May 4, 1665. Matric. 1682; B.A. 1685-6; M.A. 1689; D.D. 1717 (*Com. Reg.*). Ord. deacon (London) May 26, 1689; priest, June 15, 1690. R. of Cavendish, 1705-20. Preb. of Chichester, 1718. Buried Jan. 27, 1720-1. Brother of Thomas (1670).

GREY, HENRY, Earl of Kent. LL.D. 1705 (*Com. Reg.*). S. of Anthony (1658), Earl of Kent. Bapt. Sept. 28, 1671. Succeeded as Earl, 1702. Created Duke of Kent, 1710. K.G., 1712. Died June 5, 1740. Father of the next. (*G.E.C.*)

GREY, Lord HENRY. Adm. Fell.-Com. (age 16) at TRINITY, Dec. 23, 1713. S. of Henry (above), Duke of Kent. Matric. 1714, as De Grey. Died Dec. 4, 1717.

GRAYE, HERBERT. Adm. at CLARE, Easter, 1648. Matric. sizar from Sidney, Michs. 1648.

GRAYE, HUGHYN. Matric. pens. from TRINITY, Easter, 1562.

GRAY, HUGH. LL.B. from TRINITY HALL, 1573. (Probably the above.)

GRAY, HUGH. Matric. sizar from TRINITY, Easter, 1574; Scholar, 1578; B.A. 1578-9; M.A. 1582; B.D. 1589; D.D. 1595. Fellow, 1581. Gresham Professor of Divinity, 1598-1604. Preb. of Lincoln, 1600. R. of Meon Stoke, Hants. Benefactor to Trinity and Gresham College. Died *c.* July, 1604. Will, P.C.C. (*Cooper*, II. 392; *D.N.B.*)

GRAY, HUGH. Scholar of TRINITY, 1602; B.A. 1603-4; M.A. 1607.

GRAYE, HUMPHRY. Matric. pens. from QUEENS', Michs. 1566; B.A. 1569-70; M.A. from St Catharine's, 1573. R. of St Helen's, Ipswich, 1574-95.

GRAY, JAMES. Adm. sizar at JESUS, July 9, 1640, as Cray. Of Yorkshire. Matric. 1641.

GRAY, JAMES. Adm. pens. (age 17) at MAGDALENE, Nov. 17, 1681. S. of Matthew, clerk. B. at Santa Lucia, Barbados.

GRAY, JAMES. Adm. pens. at JESUS, July 8, 1697. Of Essex. S. of Thomas (1670). Matric. 1697; Rustat scholar, 1697; B.A. 1700-1. Brother of Thomas (1706).

GRAY, Sir JAMES, Bart. Adm. as nobleman at CLARE, Apr. 8, 1727. S. of Sir James, Bart. M.A. 1729. Succeeded as Bart., 1722. Envoy to Naples, 1753-64. K.B., 1761. Ambassador to Spain, 1766-70. Privy Councillor, 1769. One of the first excavators at Herculaneum. Died Jan. 9, 1773. Buried at Kensington. Will, P.C.C. (*G.E.C.*, IV. 445.)

GRAY, JEREMIAH. Matric. sizar from CHRIST'S, July, 1616; B.A. 1619-20; M.A. 1623. Ord. deacon (Peterb.) Mar. 2, 1621-2. One of these names R. of West Tilbury, 1627; died before 1631. (*Peile*, I. 310.)

GRAY, JOB. Matric. pens. from QUEENS', Easter, 1625. Of Leicestershire. 3rd s. of Anthony, clerk, R. of Aston Flamville and Earl of Kent. B.A. 1628-9; M.A. 1632. Governor of Leicester Hospital, 1644-5. R. of South Kilworth, Leics., 1659-62. R. of Ibstock, 1662. (*Shaw*, I. 319, 348; *Nichols*, IV. 206.)

GRAY, JOHN. M.A. 1460-1. Fellow of PETERHOUSE, 1460-73. Nephew of William Gray, Bishop of Ely. Proctor, 1462-3. R. of Tydd St Giles, Cambs., 1477. At that time a scholar at Cambridge and sub-deacon. Received a licence for seven years' absence for study in the University. R. of Doddington, Cambs., 1478. Died 1519. (*Register of Bishop of Ely*; *T. A. Walker*.)

GRAY, JOHN. Scholar of QUEENS', 1529-31. One of these names V. of Foxton, Cambs., 1552-4.

GRAY, JOHN. Matric. sizar from CLARE, Michs. 1547.

GRAY, JOHN. Matric. sizar from TRINITY, Michs. 1560. One of these names ord. priest (Lincoln) May 13, 1569; 'bred in the schools'; R. of Ludborough, Lincs.

GRAYE, JOHN. Matric. pens. from JESUS, Michs. 1566.

GRAY, JOHN. Matric. pens. from QUEENS', Easter, 1580. Of London. B.A. 1583-4; M.A. from Emmanuel, 1587; B.D. 1594. Fellow of Emmanuel, 1587. R. of Snave, Kent, 1600-21. V. of Teynham, 1600. V. of Alkham, 1600-7. V. of St James', 1606-8; and of St Mary, Dover, 1608-16. R. of Deal, 1617-21. Died 1621. Will (P.C.C.).

GRAY, JOHN. Adm. sizar at CORPUS CHRISTI, 1582. Matric. Easter, 1583.

GRAY, JOHN. Adm. sizar at QUEENS', Sept. 3, 1583.

GRAY, JOHN. Adm. sizar at QUEENS', May 4, 1596. Of Lincolnshire. Matric. 1596.

GRAY, JOHN. Matric. sizar from CLARE, Easter, 1614; B.A. 1617-8; M.A. 1621. Ord. deacon (Peterb.) June 1; priest, June 2, 1618. V. of Ruskington, Lincs., 1623-7. V. of North Somercotes, 1626.

GRAYE, JOHN. Matric. Fell.-Com. from CHRIST'S, Lent, 1618-9. S. of Sir Ralph, of Chillingham, Knt. Resided till 1621. Colonel in the Parliamentary army. Killed in Ireland. Admon. Apr. 10, 1647. One of these names adm. at Gray's Inn, Aug. 6, 1621. Brother of Ralph (1618) and Robert (1626). (*Peile*, I. 327; Raine, *North Durham*.)

GRAY, JOHN. Adm. pens. at EMMANUEL, May 18, 1622. Matric. 1622.

GRAY, JOHN. Adm. sizar (age 17) at CAIUS, May 1, 1624. S. of John, of Norwich, druggist. Bapt. at St Peter Mancroft, Nov. 29, 1607. Matric. 1624; Scholar, 1624-9; B.A. 1627-8; M.A. 1631. Perhaps R. of Melton, Suffolk. If so, buried there Jan. 31, 1652-3. (*Venn*, I. 266.)

GRAY, JOHN. Adm. sizar at CLARE, June 4, 1641. Matric. 1641.

GREY, JOHN. Adm. pens. (age 13) at CHRIST'S, June 7, 1654. S. of Edward, of Howick, Northumberland. B. at Alnwick. Educated at home. Matric. 1654. Of Howick, where he succeeded his brothers, Edward (1654) and Philip (1654). Married Dorothy, dau. of Edward Lisle, of Acton. Ancestor of Earl Grey and Viscount Grey. (*Peile*, I. 563; H. M. Wood.)

GRAY, JOHN. Adm. sizar at CLARE, Easter, 1659. Matric. 1660; B.A. 1662-3. Ord. deacon (Peterb.) Aug. 17, 1662.

GREY, JOHN. Adm. sizar (age 18) at CAIUS, June 10, 1679. S. of Christopher, brewer, of Barningham, Norfolk. B. there. School, Holt (Mr Bainbrigge). Scholar, 1679-84; Matric. 1680; B.A. 1682-3; M.A. 1687. Ord. priest (Norwich) as C. of Hanworth, Norfolk, Mar. 1687-8. Perhaps R. of Little Barningham, 1692. (*Venn*, I. 462.)

GRAY, JOHN. Adm. at CORPUS CHRISTI, 1686. Of Norwich. Matric. Lent, 1687; B.A. 1690-1; M.A. 1694. Ord. deacon (Chichester) June 6, 1694; priest, Sept. 20, 1696. V. of West Tarring, Sussex, till 1700. R. of Southwick, 1700-51. Died May 13, 1751. Will (P.C.C.). (W. C. Renshaw.)

GRAY, JOHN. Adm. at CORPUS CHRISTI, 1706. S. of Matthias, alderman of Canterbury. Matric. 1706; Parker scholar; M.B. 1711; M.D. 1721. Practised at Canterbury. Died there Aug. 5, 1737. M.I. in the Cathedral. (*Masters*, 300.)

GRAY, JOHN. Adm. sizar (age 21) at CHRIST'S, May 27, 1726. S. of William. B. at Burton, Yorks. School, Morland (Mr Thompson). Matric. 1726; B.A. 1729-30; M.A. 1737. Ord. deacon (York) Aug. 1730. Perhaps R. of Rifford, Lancs., 1734-52. R. of West Tanfield, Yorks., 1744-74. Died 1774. Will (P.C.C.) 1775. (Burke, *L.G.*; *Peile*, II. 212.)

GREY, JOHN. Adm. Fell.-Com. (age 17) at EMMANUEL, June 16, 1740. 2nd s. of Henry, Earl of Stamford. B. at Enfield, Staffs. School, Westminster. Matric. 1740. Clerk Comptroller of the Board of Green Cloth, 1754-77. M.P. for Bridgnorth, 1754-68; for Tregony, 1768-74. Died Feb. 25, 1777. (A. B. Beaven.)

GRAYE, MATTHEW. Matric. pens. from CHRIST'S, June, 1585. One of these names s. of Henry, of South Middleton, Northumberland.

GREY, MATTHEW. Adm. sizar (age 17) at CHRIST'S, Feb. 10, 1644-5. S. of James. B. at Norwich. School, Norwich. Matric. 1645.

GRAYE, MICHAEL. Matric. sizar from PEMBROKE, Michs. 1580.

GRAYE, MICHAEL. Matric. pens. from MAGDALENE, *c.* 1593. Perhaps of Langton, Cheshire, and of Staple Inn; adm. at Gray's Inn, Nov. 21, 1597.

GRAY, NICHOLAS. M.A. 1614 (Incorp. from Oxford). Of London. Matric. from Christ Church, Dec. 5, 1606, age 16, scholar from Westminster; B.A. (Oxford) 1610; M.A. 1613; D.D. (Cambridge) 1631-2 (*Lit. Reg.*). First Master of Charterhouse School, 1614-25. Master of Merchant Taylors', 1625-32. R. of Castle Camps, Cambs., 1630-45; ejected; restored, 1660. R. of Saffron Walden, 1632; and Master of the Grammar School. Head Master of Eton, 1632-47. Head Master of Tonbridge, 1647-60. Fellow of Eton. Classical scholar and author. Died at Eton. Buried in the College Chapel, Oct. 5, 1660. (*D.N.B.*; *Harwood*.)

GREY, NICHOLAS. Adm. sizar (age 23) at SIDNEY, June 20, 1657. S. of Leonard, furrier. B. at Pocklington. School, Pocklington (Mr Robert Sedgwick). Matric. 1657; B.A. 1660-1; M.A. 1664. R. of Normanby, Yorks., 1671-1701.

GRAYE, OLIVER. Matric. sizar from KING'S, Easter, 1606; Scholar of Trinity, 1611; B.A. from Trinity, 1611-2.

GREY, PHILIP. Adm. pens. (age 15) at CHRIST'S, June 7, 1654. 1st s. of Edward, of Howick, Northumberland. B. at Kenton (his mother's home). Educated at home. Matric. 1654. Married Magdalen, dau. of Thomas Foster, of Adderstone. Died June 7, 1666. Buried at Howick. M.I. Brother of Edward (1654) and John (1654). (*Peile*, I. 563; H. M. Wood.)

GRAY, RALPH. Adm. Fell.-Com. at CHRIST'S, June 23, 1618. 2nd s. of Sir Ralph, of Chillingham, Northumberland. Buried, within a month, at Gt St Mary's, Cambridge, July 16. Brother of John (1618-9) and Robert (1626). (*Peile*, I. 326.)

GREY, RALPH. Adm. sizar (age 16) at CHRIST'S, June 5, 1674. School, Houghton-le-Spring, Durham (Mr Caunt). Matric. 1674; B.A. 1677-8; M.A. 1686. Ord. deacon (Durham) Sept. 20, 1679; priest (Lincoln) Feb. 1680-1. C. of All Saints', Newcastle, 1686. (*Peile*, II. 53.)

GREYE, REGINALD. Matric. pens. from ST JOHN'S, Michs. 1551. S. of Henry, of Wrest, Beds., and grandson of Henry, Earl of Kent. Adm. at Gray's Inn, Feb. 22, 1568-9. Resumed the earldom, 1571. Died at Hornsey, 1573. Brother of Henry (1554).

GRAY, RICHARD. B.Can.L. 1468-9.

GRAY, RICHARD. B.Can.L. 1480-1.

GRAY, RICHARD. B.A. 1521-2 (Incorp. from Oxford).

GRAY, RICHARD. Adm. at KING'S (age 17) a scholar from Eton, Nov. 1523. Of the City of London. B.A. 1527-8; M.A. 1531; B.D. 1536-7. Fellow, 1526-40. Ord. priest (Lincoln) Apr. 1, 1536. R. of Wythiam, Sussex, 1540-83. Died Feb. 27, 1582-3. Will (Lewes) 1583. (*Cooper*, II. 21.)

GRAYE, RICHARD. Matric. sizar from TRINITY, Easter, 1559.

GRAY, RICHARD. Matric. pens. from CORPUS CHRISTI, Easter, 1571. Probably adm. 1569.

GREY, RICHARD. D.D. 1732 (Incorp. from Oxford). S. of John, of Newcastle-on-Tyne. Matric. from Lincoln College, June 20, 1712, age 16; B.A. (Oxford) 1716; M.A. 1719-20; D.D. 1731. R. of Hinton, Northants., 1720. R. of Kilncote, Leics., 1725. Preb. of St Paul's, 1743-71. Archdeacon of Bedford, 1757-71. Died Feb. 28, 1771. Buried at Hinton. Will, P.C.C. (*Al. Oxon.*; T. P. Dorman.)

GRAY, ROBERT. B.A. 1546-7. Of Yorkshire. M.A. 1549; B.D. 1557. Fellow of PEMBROKE, 1547. Perhaps fellow of Trinity, 1555. V. of Barrington, Cambs., 1557. Possibly R. of Castle Rising, Norfolk, 1575.

GRAY, ROBERT. Matric. sizar from CLARE, Easter, 1577. One of these names V. of Ketteringham, Norfolk, 1584-6.

GRAYE, ROBERT. Matric. pens. from ST JOHN'S, Easter, 1589; B.A. 1592-3. Perhaps V. of Dunston, Lincs., 1602. One of these names (B.A.) R. of St Benet Sherehog, London, 1606-12.

GRAYE, ROBERT. M.A. 1612 (on visit of Prince Charles).

GRAY, ROBERT. Matric. pens. from TRINITY, Easter, 1622; B.A. 1625-6. Ord. deacon and priest (Norwich) May 20, 1627.

GREY, ROBERT. Adm. Fell.-Com. (age 17) at CHRIST'S, May 25, 1626. (Previously matric. from University College, Oxford, 1625.) S. of Sir Ralph, of Chillingham, Northumberland. Educated at home. Matric. 1626; B.A. 1627-8; M.A. 1631; B.D. 1638; D.D. 1660 (*Lit. Reg.*). R. of Mashbury, Essex, 1637-43 (sequestered; 'had gone to the Royal army'; restored, 1660-1). Preb. of Durham, 1643 (installed, 1660). R. of Bishop Wearmouth, 1652, ejected; and 1661-1704. Died July 9, 1704. Brother of John (1618-9) and Ralph (1618). (*Peile*, I. 376; Raine, *North Durham*.)

GRAY, ROBERT. Matric. pens. from TRINITY, 1638; Scholar, 1641; B.A. 1641-2.

GRAY, ROBERT. Adm. sizar (age 17) at ST JOHN'S, June 6, 1665. S. of Thomas, tailor, of Newcastle-on-Tyne. B. there. Bapt. at All Saints', Mar. 29, 1648. School, Newcastle (Mr Oxley). Matric. 1665; B.A. 1668-9; M.A. 1672. Perhaps M.D. Ord. deacon (York) Sept. 1672. Practised as physician at Newcastle, where he was the last 'Town's physician.' Buried at St Nicholas, Mar. 11, 1700-1. (H. M. Wood.)

GRAY, ROBERT. Adm. sizar (age 20) at MAGDALENE, July 22, 1681. S. of George. B. at Pocklington, Yorks. School, Holden (? Howden), Yorks. Matric. 1682. Migrated to Peterhouse, Jan. 11, 1682-3. B.A. 1685-6; M.A. 1689.

GRAYE, ROGER. Matric. pens. from TRINITY, Easter, 1562. Perhaps adm. at Gray's Inn from Barnard's Inn, 1570.

GREY, SAMUEL. Adm. sizar (age 17) at CAIUS, May 22, 1673. S. of Edmund, barber, of Norwich. B. there, May 8, 1656. School, Norwich (private; Mr Cushen; and public). Matric. 1673; Scholar, 1673-7; B.A. 1676-7; M.A. 1681. Ord. priest (Norwich), as C. of Winterton, Sept. 1677. R. of Rockland Tofts, 1679-1710, deprived. R. of Wood Rising, 1681-1712. (*Venn*, I. 449.)

GRAY, SIMON. Adm. pens. at TRINITY, July 17, 1640. Matric. 1640.

GRAY, THOMAS. Matric. pens. from CHRIST'S, Nov. 1550. Tho. Gray, age 60, was ord. deacon (Norwich) June 24, 1597. Called B.A. Ord. priest (Norwich) Dec. 21, 1599, age 66. C. of Pulham St Mary, Norfolk.

GRAY, THOMAS. Matric. pens. from JESUS, Lent, 1557-8.

GRAYE, THOMAS. Matric. pens. from ST JOHN'S, Michs. 1560.

GRAY, THOMAS. Adm. Fell.-Com. at CORPUS CHRISTI, 1569. Matric. Easter, 1570. One of these names adm. (specially) at Gray's Inn, 1570.

GRAYE, THOMAS. Matric. sizar from JESUS, Michs. 1578; B.A. 1583-4.

GRAYE, THOMAS. Matric. pens. from PETERHOUSE, Easter, 1582; B.A. 1585-6; M.A. 1589.

GRAYE, THOMAS. Adm. sizar at CHRIST'S, Apr. 24, 1582. B. in Hertfordshire. Matric. 1582; B.A. 1585-6; M.A. 1589. Fellow, 1589-94. Ord. deacon and priest (Peterb.) June 10, 1590. (*Peile*, I. 170.)

GRAY, THOMAS. Matric. sizar from PEMBROKE, *c.* 1591; B.A. 1593-4. Buried at Little St Mary's, May 20, 1594.

GRAYE, THOMAS. Matric. pens. from MAGDALENE, *c.* 1593.

GREY, THOMAS. Matric. sizar from CHRIST'S, July, 1617; B.A. 1620-1. Ord. deacon (Peterb.) Dec. 19; priest, Dec. 20, 1624. Probably brother of Jeremiah (1616). (*Peile*, I. 320; H. I. Longden.)

GRAY, THOMAS. Adm. sizar at CLARE, Oct. 9, 1632.

GRAY, THOMAS. Incorp. from St Andrews, 1636; probably as M.A. Perhaps ord. deacon (Durham) Sept. 1622; V. of Ponteland, Northumberland, 1627; and of Chillingham, 1636; 'M.A.' (See another in *Al. Oxon.*)

GREY (*alias* BISHOP), THOMAS. Adm. sizar (age 16) at CAIUS, June 18, 1639. S. of William, gent. B. at Aldeburgh, Suffolk. School, Eye (Mr Hall). Matric. 1640; B.A. 1642-3; M.A. 1646. Ord. deacon (Lincoln) May 28, 1643; priest, June 16, 1644. V. of Wickhambrook, Suffolk, 1645. R. of Cavendish, 1650-1705 (he signed Bishop Jos. Hall's subscription book, July 26, 1650). Founded the Grammar School at Cavendish. Died Mar. 18, 1704-5. M.I. at Cavendish. Father of the next and Henry (1682). (*Venn*, I. 335.)

GRAY, THOMAS. Adm. pens. at CLARE, May 3, 1670. S. of Thomas (above), R. of Cavendish. B. at Wickhambrook, Suffolk. Matric. 1670; B.A. 1673-4; M.A. 1677. Ord. deacon (Norwich) Dec. 1677. V. of Dedham, Essex, 1679-92. Died Jan. 9, 1691-2. M.I. at Cavendish. Father of the next.

GREY, THOMAS. Adm. pens. at JESUS, Apr. 5, 1706. S. of Thomas (above), deceased, V. of Dedham, Essex. Matric. 1707; Rustat scholar. Died Dec. 17, 1707, aged 18. M.I. at Cavendish. Brother of James (1697). (A. Gray.)

GRAY, THOMAS. Adm. pens. (age 18) at PETERHOUSE, July 4, 1734; Fell.-Com. 1742. S. of Philip, scrivener, of Cornhill. Bapt. at St Michael's, Cornhill, Dec. 26, 1716. School, Eton. Scholar, 1734; LL.B. 1744. Migrated to Pembroke, Mar. 6, 1756-7. Appointed Regius Professor of History and Modern Languages, 1768. Adm. at the Inner Temple, Nov. 22, 1735. The poet. Travelled on the Continent with Horace Walpole, 1739-40. Made Cambridge his head quarters for the rest of his life. Ill-health and nervous shyness caused him to live in great retirement. Poet, classical scholar, linguist, student of science, and a good musician. Died July 30, 1771. Buried at Stoke Poges. (*D.N.B.*)

GRAYE, W. Resident pens. at JESUS, Aug. 1564.

GRAYE, WALTER. Adm. pens. (age 17) at CAIUS, Sept. 23, 1577. S. of Robert, gent., of Eaton Socon, Beds. School, Eaton Socon (Mr Huckle). Matric. 1578. One of these names, buried at Pertenhall, Beds., Aug. 22, 1616.

GRAY, WALTER. Matric. sizar from TRINITY, 1639; B.A. 1641-2. One of these names, s. of Walter, of Pertenhall, Beds., gent., adm. at Lincoln's Inn, Feb. 13, 1640-1.

GRAY, WILLIAM. Matric. sizar from QUEENS', Easter, 1585. Of Lincolnshire. Ord. deacon (Peterb.) Mar. 13; priest, Mar. 14, 1613-4, as 'late of Queens' College.' Admon. (Leicester) 1619, of one of these names; R. of Grainthorpe, Lincs.

GRAY, WILLIAM. Matric. pens. from ST JOHN'S, Easter, 1614; B.A. 1617-8; M.A. 1621. Licensed to teach in Scarborough, Apr. 27, 1619. Ord. deacon (York) Dec. 1620; priest, Sept. 1621. Perhaps R. of Roos, Yorks., 1627.

GREY, WILLIAM. Adm. pens. at EMMANUEL, Apr. 4, 1618. Matric. 1618.

GRAYE, WILLIAM. Matric. sizar from MAGDALENE, Michs. 1639.

GREY, WILLIAM. Adm. pens. (age 16) at ST JOHN'S, May 23, 1674. S. of Ralph, alderman, of Newcastle, and Backworth, Northumberland. B. there. Bapt. Nov. 10, 1659. School, Bury St Edmunds. Adm. at Lincoln's Inn, Aug. 9, 1676. Married Anne, widow of Robert Grey, of Newcastle. Buried at St Nicholas, Newcastle, July 15, 1714. Will proved, 1716. (H. M. Wood.)

GREY, ZACHARY. Adm. pens. at JESUS, Apr. 18, 1704. S. of George (1667), of Lawton and Southwick, Durham. B. at Burneston, Yorks., May 6, 1688. Matric. 1704; Scholar, 1705. Scholar of Trinity Hall, Jan. 1706-7; LL.B. from Trinity Hall, 1709; LL.D. 1720. Ord. deacon (Lincoln) July 25; priest, Sept. 22, 1711. R. of Houghton Conquest, Beds., 1725. V. of St Peter's and St Giles', Cambridge, 1729-60. Literary critic and author. Died at Ampthill, Beds., Nov. 25, 1766. (*D.N.B.*)

GRAY, ——. B.A. 1463-4; M.A. 1467.

GRAY, ——. B.Can.L. 1480-1. Had studied abroad and in Cambridge.

GRAY, ——. B.Civ.L. 1518-9.

GRAYE, ——. Sizar at PETERHOUSE, 1542-3.

GRAYE, ——. Matric. pens. from CHRIST'S, Easter, 1544. Perhaps Robert, B.A. 1546-7.

GRAY, ——. Adm. pens. at CORPUS CHRISTI, 1569.

GRAY, ——. Adm. at EMMANUEL, Lent, 1626-7.

GRAYBARN, WILLIAM. B.D. 1463-4; D.D. 1470-1. Elected fellow of CLARE, 1459, as M.A. Proctor, 1461-2. (Wrongly indexed as 'John' in Gr. *Bk*, A.)

GRAYDON, EDWARD. Adm. scholar (age 17) at SIDNEY, Apr. 4, 1723. S. of John, sea captain. B. at Chatham. School, private. Matric. 1723.

GRAYLE, *see* GRAILE.

GREATHEAD, EDWARD. Matric. sizar from JESUS, *c.* 1593; B.A. 1597-8; M.A. 1601. Ord. deacon (Colchester) Aug. 13, 1600; priest (Ely) Feb. 8, 1606-7. R. of South Willingham, Lincs., 1610. Buried there Jan. 7, 1662-3. Father of the next. (*Lincs. Pedigrees*, 425.)

GREATHEAD, EDWARD. Adm. pens. (age 16) at SIDNEY, Apr. 2, 1631. S. of Edward (above), R. of South Willingham, Lincs. School, Bolingbroke, Lincs. (Mr Power). Matric. 1631; B.A. 1634-5; M.A. 1638. Ord. deacon (Peterb.) May 20, 1638; priest, June 9, 1639. R. of Bridgeford, Notts., 1662-73. Died 1673.

GREATHEAD, EDWARD. Adm. sizar (age 17) at ST JOHN'S, Nov. 22, 1671. S. of Thomas, deceased, of Stow, Lincs. B. there. School, Nottingham (Mr Birch). Matric. 1671; B.A. 1675-6; M.A. 1680. V. of Sibsey, Lincs. Died 1687. Will proved, Oct. 21, 1687. Father of the next.

GREATHEAD, EDWARD. Adm. sizar (age 17) at MAGDALENE, Dec. 18, 1704. S. of Edward (above), clerk. B. at Sibsey, Lincs. School, Boston. Matric. 1705; B.A. 1708-9. Ord. deacon (Lincoln) Mar. 5, 1709-10. R. of East Barkwith, Lincs., 1712. Schoolmaster at Stickney. Buried there Feb. 20, 1727-8.

GREATHED, HENRY. Adm. at CORPUS CHRISTI, 1686. Of Nottinghamshire. Matric. 1686; B.A. 1689-90. Ord. deacon (Lincoln) Feb. 21, 1691-2; priest (London) Mar. 4, 1693-4. V. of Bisbrooke, Rutland, 1694-6.

GRETHETT, JOHN. Matric. sizar from CHRIST'S, Easter, 1605.

GREATHEAD, RICHARD. Matric. sizar from TRINITY, Michs. 1570.

GREATHEED, SAMUEL. Adm. pens. (age 19) at TRINITY, May 4, 1730. S. of John, of St Christopher's, West Indies. School, Bradford, Yorks. (Mr Butler). Adm. at Lincoln's Inn, Apr. 14, 1730. M.P. for Coventry, 1747-61. Died Aug. 2, 1765. (M. H. Peacock.)

GREATING, ——. B.Can.L. 1476-7.

GREATOREX, DANIEL. Adm. sizar (age 17) at EMMANUEL, June 21, 1703. Of Derbyshire. Matric. 1704; B.A. 1706-7; M.A. 1711. Ord. priest (Ely) Mar. 5, 1709-10. R. of West Hallam, Derbs., 1716-24. Died 1724. Father of John (1736).

GREATOREX, HENRY. Adm. pens. at EMMANUEL, Jan. 25, 1658-9. Of Derbyshire. Matric. 1659; B.A. 1662-3. R. of West Hallam, Derbs., 1668-1716. Died 1716.

GREATOREX, ISAAC. Adm. sizar at CHRIST'S, July 3, 1672. Matric. 1673; B.A. 1675-6. Ord. deacon (Lichfield) May, 1676. Chaplain of Turnditch, Duffield, Derbs.

GREATOREX, JOHN. Adm. pens. (age 19) at ST JOHN'S, May 1, 1736. S. of Daniel (1703), clerk, of Derbyshire. B. at West Hallam. School, Chesterfield (Mr Burrow). Matric. 1736; B.A. 1739-40; M.A. 1756. Ord. deacon (Lincoln) June 1, 1740; priest (Lichfield) Sept. 21, 1746. V. of Gt Dalby, Leics., 1752-7. V. of Abkettleby, 1756-7. Chaplain to the Duke of Buccleugh. Died Dec. 1757. (*Scott-Mayor*, III. 472.)

GREATOREX, SAMUEL. Adm. sizar at EMMANUEL, Apr. 10, 1700. Of Derbyshire. Matric. 1701; B.A. 1703-4. R. of Holme Pierrepont and Adbolton, Notts., 1722-8. Buried at Holme, Sept. 9, 1728. Perhaps brother of the next and of Daniel (1703). (Godfrey, *Notts.*)

GREATOREX, WILLIAM. Adm. sizar at EMMANUEL, May 19, 1697. Of Derbyshire. Matric. 1698; B.A. 1700-1; M.A. 1705.

GREAVE *and* GREAVES, *see* GRAVE.

GREBBY, HENRY. Adm. pens. at PETERHOUSE, 1605-6. Matric. Michs. 1606, as (?) 'Gredmer.'

GREBY, RICHARD. Adm. sizar (age 18) at PEMBROKE, June 23, 1694. S. of Thomas, of Treviles (? Trevalga), Cornwall. Matric. 1695; B.A. 1697-8. Ord. priest (London) May 19, 1706.

GREBBIE or GREBBY, WILLIAM. Adm. sizar (age 18) at CAIUS, June 26, 1622. S. of William, husbandman, of Tumby, Lincs. School, Tattershall (Mr Male). Matric. 1622; Scholar, 1624-6; B.A. 1625-6; M.A. 1629. Ord. deacon (Peterb.) Sept. 20; priest, Sept. 21, 1629. V. of Billinghay, Lincs., 1631. Admon. (Lincoln) 1646. (*Venn*, I. 258.)

GRECHFIELD, ——. Matric. Fell.-Com. from TRINITY, Easter, 1608.

GREE, JOHN. B.A. 1472-3, as Cree; M.A. 1475-6; B.D. 1484-5. Proctor, 1482-3. Fellow of QUEENS', 1484-93. R. of St Botolph's, Cambridge, 1492.

GREEGE, RANDOLPH. Matric. pens. from ST JOHN'S, Easter, 1617.

GREEGS, W. Matric. pens. from CHRIST'S, Nov. 1575.

GREEKE, JOHN. Matric. pens. from TRINITY, Michs. 1612. S. of William (1564). B.A. 1616-7; M.A. 1620. Fellow, 1618. Will proved (V.C.C.) 1625. Brother of Thomas (1609) and William (1605). (*Vis. of Cambs.*)

GREEKE, THOMAS. 'Born in Cambridge. Studied at the University.' B. *c.* 1514. Baron of the Exchequer, 1576-7. Died Nov. 18, 1577. Buried in St Botolph, Aldersgate. Will (P.C.C.) 1577. Father of William (1564). (*Cooper*, I. 379; *Vis. of Cambs.*; Foss.)

GREEKE, THOMAS. Matric. pens. from TRINITY, Michs. 1609. S. of William (1564), of Cambridgeshire. Scholar, 1611; B.A. 1612-3; M.A. 1616. Fellow, 1614. R. of Carlton *with* Willingham, Cambs., 1619. Brother of John (1612) and William (1605). (*Vis. of Cambs.*)

GREEKE, THOMAS. Adm. pens. (age 17) at PETERHOUSE, Jan. 18, 1638-9. Of Cambridge. Doubtless s. of Thomas (above), of Cambridgeshire. Matric. 1639. (*T. A. Walker*, 67.)

GREEKE, WILLIAM. Matric. pens. from PETERHOUSE, Michs. 1564. S. of Thomas (above), Baron of the Exchequer. B.A. 1567-8; M.A. 1571. Fellow, 1569. Scrutator, 1581-2. Resided in Cambridge. Buried at Little St Mary's, July 22, 1619. Will, P.C.C. Father of William (1605), Thomas (1609) and John (1616). (*Cooper*, I. 379.)

GREKE, WILLIAM. Matric. pens. from PETERHOUSE, Easter, 1605. S. and h. of William (1564). Bapt. at Little St Mary's, Aug. 24, 1588. Adm. at Gray's Inn, May 3, 1608. Brother of John (1605) and Thomas (1609). (*Vis. of Cambs.*)

GREEN, ALEXANDER. Matric. sizar (age 16) from PEMBROKE, Michs. 1646. Of Cambridge. S. of Christopher. B.A. 1647-8; M.A. 1651. Fellow, 1650; readm. 1660. 'An holy but melancholy person.' (Calamy, *Baxter*.)

GREEN, ALEXANDER. Adm. pens. (age 16) at PETERHOUSE, Apr. 30, 1663. Of Middlesex. School, Westminster. Matric. 1663; Scholar, 1663; B.A. 1666-7. Buried at Little St Mary's, Cambridge, Mar. 11, 1666-7.

GREEN, AMBROSE. Matric. pens. from JESUS, Easter, 1580.

GREENE, ANTHONY. Matric. sizar from PEMBROKE, Lent, 1581-2. B. in Russia. B.A. 1584-5; M.A. 1588. Fellow, 1588. (*Cooper*, II. 165.)

GREENE, ANTHONY. Matric. sizar from CORPUS CHRISTI, Michs. 1628. B. at Cambridge. B.A. 1632-3; M.A. 1636. Fellow of Jesus, 1638-44, ejected. Ord. deacon (Lincoln) Feb. 22, 1645-6. Died before 1660. (A. Gray.)

GREEN, BENJAMIN. M.A. from ST CATHARINE'S, 1745. S. of Thomas, of Beckbury, Salop, clerk. Matric. from Balliol College, Oxford, May 18, 1727, age 18; B.A. (Oxford) 1731. Brother of Thomas (1714). (*Al. Oxon.*)

GREEN, CHARLES. Adm. at CORPUS CHRISTI, 1609. Of Norwich. Charles Green, junior, of St Gregory, Norwich, married Alice Framingham, of Field Dalling, at St Stephen's, Norwich, Sept. 14, 1616. (G. H. Holley.)

GREEN, CHARLES. Adm. at CORPUS CHRISTI, 1612. Of Suffolk.

GREEN, CHRISTOPHER. Matric. sizar from TRINITY, Easter, 1567. One of these names P.C. of St Giles', Durham, 1574-8.

GREEN, CHRISTOPHER. Matric. sizar from TRINITY, Easter, 1576. Ord. deacon (Peterb.) Dec. 10, 1587; priest, Feb. 18, 1587-8, as B.A. R. of Scaldwell, Northants., 1587-1611. Buried there Sept. 20, 1611. Will (P.C.C.) 1611. (H. I. Longden.)

GREEN, CHRISTOPHER. B.D. 1620 (Incorp. from Oxford). S. of Edward (? 1568), Preb. of Bristol. Matric. Jan. 1, 1595-6; B.A. from Corpus Christi, Oxford, 1599; M.A. 1603; B.D. 1610; D.D. 1622. R. of Nuthurst, Sussex, 1613. Preb. of Bristol, 1614-59. R. of Littlebury, Essex, 1618. Died Mar. 6, 1658-9, aged 79. Buried in Bristol Cathedral. Will, P.C.C. The V. of Shaftesbury St James, 1620, was probably of Wadham, Oxford. (F. S. Hockaday; F. C. Cass, *East Barnet*, 140.)

GREEN, CHRISTOPHER. Adm. sizar (age 13) at CHRIST'S, Apr. 12, 1650. S. of Edmund. B. at Cambridge. School, Perse. Matric. 1650; B.A. 1653-4; M.A. 1657.

GREEN, CHRISTOPHER. Adm. pens. (age 16) at CAIUS, Dec. 13, 1667. S. of Christopher, the college cook (his will proved, V.C.C. 1699). B. at Cambridge. Bapt. at St Botolph's, Feb. 23, 1651-2. School, Perse. Matric. 1667-8; Scholar, 1668-74; B.A. 1671-2; M.A. 1675; M.D. 1685. Fellow, 1674-88. Regius Professor of Physic, 1700-41. Married, at Hildersham, Cambs., Jan. 21, 1688-9, Susan Flack, of Linton. Died Apr. 1, 1741. Will (P.C.C.) 1741. Portrait in Caius College. Father of the next and of Robert (1708-9). (*Venn*, I. 433.)

GREEN, CHRISTOPHER. Adm. pens. at EMMANUEL, Feb. 26, 1708-9. Of Cambridgeshire. S. of Christopher (above). Matric. 1709; M.B. 1714; M.D. 1717 (*Com. Reg.*). Of St Andrew's-the-Great, Cambridge. Married Mary, dau. of Richard Fordham, of Royston, Herts. Will (P.C.C.) 1738. Brother of Robert (1708-9). (J. Ch. Smith.)

GREEN, CHRISTOPHER. Adm. pens. at CHRIST'S, July 6, 1738. S. of Christopher (above), M.D. B. at Cambridge. School, Ely (Mr Gunning). Matric. 1738; Scholar, 1739; B.A. 1741-2; M.A. 1745. Died *c.* 1773-4. (*Peile*, II. 237.)

GREEN, DANIEL. Matric. pens. from TRINITY, Easter, 1612; Scholar, 1614; B.A. 1615-6; M.A. 1619; B.D. 1627. Fellow, 1618. Ord. deacon (Peterb.) June 11, 1625. R. of Gressenhall, Norfolk, 1634. Perhaps s. of Thomas, of the Forncet family, and father of the next. Will (P.C.C.) 1656.

GREENE, DANIEL. Adm. sizar at TRINITY, Apr. 24, 1647. Of Norfolk. (? S. of Daniel, above.) Matric. 1646; Scholar, 1649; B.A. 1650-1; M.A. 1654. Fellow, 1651. R. of Fulmodeston and Croxton, Norfolk, 1655-1700. Died 1700, aged 71. M.I. at Croxton. Will (Norwich Archd. C.) 1700. (G. H. Holley.)

GREEN, EDMUND. Adm. sizar (age 15) at CHRIST'S, May 4, 1660. S. of Thomas. B. at Stainforth, near Giggleswick. School, Giggleswick (Mr Briggs). Matric. 1660. Ord. priest (London) Dec. 1666, as B.A. Chaplain to Sir George Carteret. (*Peile*, I. 591.)

CREANE, EDWARD. Matric. pens. from CHRIST'S, May, 1549.

GRENE, EDWARD. Matric. sizar from CLARE, Michs. 1568. Perhaps 2nd s. of William, of Birstall, Yorks. B.A. 1571-2; M.A. 1575. Incorp. at Oxford, 1578. Perhaps Preb. of Bristol, *c.* 1582-1627. V. of Henbury, Gloucs., 1582-1627. Died 1627. (F. S. Hockaday; *F.M.G.*, 890.)

GREEN, EDWARD. Matric. sizar from TRINITY, Easter, 1584.

GRENE, EDWARD. Adm. scholar (age 14) at CAIUS, Apr. 27, 1601. S. of Richard, yeoman. B. in Cambridge. Bapt. at Great St Mary's, Nov. 12, 1587. School, Cambridge (Mr Edwards).

GREEN, EDWARD. Matric. sizar from EMMANUEL, Easter, 1606; Scholar; B.A. 1608-9; M.A. 1612. Ord. deacon (Peterb.) May 30, 1613; priest, Sept. 23, 1621. One of these names V. of Thornton (by Horncastle), Lincs., 1618.

GREEN, EDWARD. Matric. pens. from PETERHOUSE, Easter, 1620; B.A. 1622-3; M.A. 1626. Ord. deacon (Peterb.) Dec. 19, 1624; priest, Dec. 18, 1625. This, or the next, probably R. of Shelley, Essex, 1628-50-.

GREENE, EDWARD. Matric. sizar from CHRIST'S, July, 1621; B.A. 1624-5; M.A. 1628.

GREEN, EDWARD. Matric. pens. from MAGDALENE, Easter, 1625; B.A. 1628-9; M.A. 1632; B.D. 1639. Fellow, till 1644, ejected. Perhaps presented to the rectory of Sutton, Norfolk, by the University, 1640. If so, father of John (1662).

GREEN, EDWARD. Adm. at EMMANUEL, May 2, 1646. Of Lancaster. Migrated to Oxford. B.A. (Magdalen Hall) May 1, 1649; M.A. (All Souls') 1651-2.

GREEN, EDWARD. Adm. at CORPUS CHRISTI, 1669. Of Somerset.

GREEN, EDWARD. Adm. pens. (age 17) at MAGDALENE, May 8, 1679. S. of Edward, citizen of Lincoln. B. there. School, Lincoln. Matric. 1679; B.A. 1682-3; M.A. 1686. Fellow, 1685. Doubtless R. of Alphamstone, Essex, 1692. R. of Drinkstone, Suffolk, 1692-1740. Died Jan. 3, 1740. (*E. Anglian*, V. 327.)

GREEN, EDWARD. Adm. at KING'S, a scholar from Eton, 1710. 2nd s. of William. B. at Stafford. Matric. Easter, 1711; B.A. 1714-5; M.A. 1718. Fellow. Adm. at the Middle Temple, June 19, 1713. Barrister, 1721. Bencher, 1749. Attorney-general. Died Dec. 13, 1759. (G. *Mag.*)

GREEN, FLOWER. Matric. pens. from MAGDALENE, Easter, 1629; B.A. 1632-3; M.A. 1636. Ord. deacon (Peterb.) Sept. 24, 1637; priest, Feb. 18, 1637-8. R. of Market Overton, Rutland. Father of John (1658).

GREEN, FRANCIS. Matric. pens. from CLARE, Easter, 1571. One of these names V. of Grindon, Durham, 1599-1618. Buried there May 10, 1618. (H. M. Wood; *see Al. Oxon.* for another.)

GREEN, FRANCIS. Adm. sizar (age 18) at CHRIST'S, Sept. 9, 1669. Of Bedfordshire. School, Hockliffe, Beds. (Mr Stackhouse). Matric. 1670; B.A. 1673-4; M.A. 1677. Ord. priest (Lincoln) Sept. 20, 1674. C. of Husborne Crawley, Beds., 1674-80. V. of East Claydon, Bucks., 1680-1741. Died 1741. Will (Archd. Bucks.) 1741. (*Peile*, II. 25.)

GREEN, FRANCIS. Adm. sizar (age 17) at CAIUS, Mar. 28, 1710. S. of John, weaver, of Norwich. B. there. Bapt. at St Lawrence, Norwich, Feb. 9, 1692–3. School, Norwich. Matric. 1710; Scholar, 1710–5; B.A. 1713–4; M.A. 1717. Fellow, 1715–8. Ord. deacon (London) Mar. 13, 1714–5; priest (Ely, *Litt. dim.* from Norwich) Mar. 17, 1716–7. R. of Little Dunham, Norfolk, 1716–24. R. of Erpingham, 1724–38. Perhaps R. of Coulston, Wilts. Died June 7, 1738. M.I. at Erpingham. Admon. (Consist. C. Sarum) Oct. 26, 1738. (*Venn*, I. 522.)

GREEN, GABRIEL. Matric. pens. from QUEENS', Lent, 1563–4. B. at Stafford, *c.* 1548. For a time at Brasenose, Oxford. No degree. Ord. priest (Gloucester) Apr. 10, 1566; C. at Millbrook, Beds., 1588; R. there, 1598.

GREEN, GEORGE. Adm. at CORPUS CHRISTI, 1604. Ord. deacon (Peterb.) May 19, 1611, as B.A.; priest, Sept. 15, 1611.

GREEN, GEORGE. Adm. pens. at SIDNEY, June, 1609. Matric. 1609; B.A. 1612–3; M.A. 1616. Ord. deacon (Peterb.) July 20, 1617. Perhaps V. of Thedingworth, Leics., 1620. Died 1662.

GREENE, GEORGE. Adm. pens. (age 16) at CAIUS, July 1, 1609. Of Norwich. S. of Robert, gent., attorney-at-law. School, Norwich (Mr Brigges). Matric. 1609. Readm. Fell.-Com. Dec. 1609. B.A. 1611–2. Adm. at Lincoln's Inn, from Furnival's Inn, 1610. Brother of John (1617). (*Venn*, I. 203.)

GREEN, GEORGE. Matric. sizar from MAGDALENE, Easter, 1624; B.A. 1627–8; M.A. 1631. Ord. deacon (Peterb.) Sept. 21; priest, Sept. 22, 1628. Perhaps V. of Eltisley, Cambs., 1630. One of these names lecturer at Bluntisham, Hunts., 1642; and at Sutton, Cambs., 1643. (*Shaw*, I. 303.)

GREEN, GEORGE. Adm. at CORPUS CHRISTI, 1652. Of Norwich.

GREEN, GEORGE. Adm. pens. at EMMANUEL, Feb. 23, 1671–2. Of Suffolk. S. of George, of Brundish. Matric. 1671–2; B.A. 1675–6; M.A. 1679; B.D. 1686. Fellow, 1678–88. Taxor, 1684. V. of Cliffe, Kent, 1681–1739. Died Oct. 15, 1739, aged 84. Buried at Wilby, Suffolk. M.I. there. (Burke, *L.G.*)

GRENE, GILBERT. Matric. pens. from JESUS, Michs. 1572.

GREEN, GODFREY. Matric. sizar from PETERHOUSE, Easter, 1587; Scholar, 1588–94; B.A. 1590–1; M.A. 1594; B.D. 1610. V. of Clapham, Surrey, 1604–15.

GREEN, HENRY. Adm. at CORPUS CHRISTI, 1570; B.A. 1576–7.

GREENE, HENRY. Matric. pens. from EMMANUEL, Michs. 1601; B.A. from Trinity, 1604–5; M.A. 1608. Ord. deacon (York) Dec. 1608; priest, Dec. 1609. V. of Tadcaster, Yorks., 1609–13. Perhaps V. of Walsall, Staffs., 1616–38. Buried there Oct. 23, 1638. (*Wm Salt Arch. Soc.*, 1915.)

GREENE, HENRY. Adm. pens. (age 18) at CAIUS, Oct. 1, 1623. S. of Oliver (1582), M.D., of Potton, Beds. Bapt. there, May 5, 1605. School, Perse, Cambridge (Mr Lovering). Matric. 1623; Scholar, 1623–7.

GREEN, HENRY. Adm. pens. at EMMANUEL, July 2, 1634. Of Essex. Bapt. at Gt Bromley, Essex, Jan. 20, 1618–9. Matric. 1635. Probably the emigrant adm. freeman of Massachusetts, May 13, 1642. Described by Governor Winthrop as a scholar. Ord. pastor of the church of Reading, Massachusetts, Nov. 5, 1645. Married, *c.* 1645, Frances Stone. Died at Reading, Oct. 11, 1648. (J. G. Bartlett.)

GREEN, HENRY. Adm. pens. at EMMANUEL, May 2, 1646. Of Lancaster.

GREENE, HENRY. Adm. pens. at ST JOHN'S, Mar. 29, 1665. S. of James, brewer, of St Giles', Cripplegate. B. there. School, Islington (Mr Lovejoy). Matric. 1667; M.B. 1670.

GREEN, HENRY. Adm. pens. (age 16) at PEMBROKE, June 15, 1689. S. of Henry, gent. B. in Warwickshire. Matric. 1689. Fell.-Com. Apr. 28, 1691. Probably s. of Henry, of Wyken, Coventry; adm. at the Middle Temple, May 4, 1692.

GREEN, HENRY. Adm. sizar at EMMANUEL, June 30, 1702. Of Surrey. B.A. 1705–6; M.A. 1709. Dixie fellow, 1706. Ord. deacon (London) Sept. 25, 1709; priest, Sept. 21, 1712. Probably V. of St Peter, Derby, 1715–49. Perhaps Preb. of Lincoln, 1722–49. Died 1749.

GREEN, HENRY. Adm. pens. (age 19) at TRINITY, Apr. 4, 1719. S. of William, of Thundercliffe Grange, Yorks. School, Wakefield, Yorks. (Mr Clark). Matric. 1719; Scholar, 1720; B.A. 1722–3; M.A. 1726. Ord. deacon (York) June 9, 1723; priest, Sept. 1726. V. of Brayton, Yorks., 1728. Of Hall, Pontefract, clerk. Married Grace, widow ofHague Watson, of East Hague. Brother of William (1709). (M. H. Peacock.)

GREEN, HENRY. Adm. pens. (age 18) at ST JOHN'S, June 20, 1746. S. of Richard, gent., of Rolleston, Leics. B. there. Schools, Uppingham (Mr Hubbard) and Leicester (Mr Andrews). Matric. 1747; B.A. 1749–50; M.A. 1753. O d. deacon (York) Dec. 6, 1763; priest, June 17, 1764. V.rof Feering, Essex, 1764–75. V. of Boreham, 1767–70. R. of Laingdon, 1770–7. Preb. of St Paul's, 1772–97. R. of Little Burstead, 1775–7. Chaplain to the Countess of Chedworth. Died Sept. 1797. Will (P.C.C.) as of Rolleston. (*Scott-Mayor*, III. 563.)

GREENE, HUGH. Matric. sizar from PETERHOUSE, *c.* 1601. 'Grecian' from Christ's Hospital. S. of John, goldsmith, of St Giles' parish. B. 1586. Scholar, 1603; B.A. 1605–6; M.A. 1609. Became a Roman Catholic. Received into the English College at Douay, 1609. Ord. deacon at Arras, Mar. 18; priest, June 14, 1612. Chaplain to Lady Arundell at Chideock Castle, Dorset. Executed at Dorchester, Aug. 19, 1642. (*D.N.B.*)

GREEN, JAMES. Matric. Fell.-Com. from MAGDALENE, Michs. 1586.

GREEN, JAMES. Matric. pens. (age 14) from QUEENS', 1593; B.A. 1596–7. Ord. deacon (Norwich) Mar. 25, 1601; priest, Mar. 25, 1602. C. of Stanton, Norfolk.

GREEN, JAMES. Matric. from CLARE, *c.* 1593; B.A. 1596–7; M.A. 1600.

GREENE, JAMES. Adm. pens. at SIDNEY, Apr. 1599; B.A. (? 1602–3); M.A. 1605. This, or the last, Incorp. at Oxford, 1606.

GREEN, JAMES. Adm. pens. at JESUS, 1603–4; B.A. 1607–8; M.A. 1611. Ord. deacon and priest (Peterb.) June 7, 1612. R. of Brinkhill, Lincs., 1625.

GREEN, JAMES. Adm. pens. at EMMANUEL, Apr. 6, 1630. Of Suffolk. Matric. 1631; B.A. 1633–4; M.A. 1637. Perhaps will (P.C.C.) 1655; of Bardwell, Suffolk, clerk.

GREEN, JAMES. M.A. from CLARE, 1720. S. of James, of Tiberton, Herefordshire. Matric. from Balliol College, Oxford, Mar. 28, 1702, age 17; B.A. (Oxford) 1705. (*Al. Oxon.*)

GREEN, JOHN. B.A. 1469–70.

GREEN, JOHN. D.D. Letters of Conversation, 1480–1. His 'letters of conversation' state that he had taken 'arcium sacrarum baccalaureatum et doctorale decus.' One of these names (B.D.), was Master of St Michael Royal, London, 1482. (*Newcourt.*)

GREEN, JOHN. Matric. pens. from TRINITY, Michs. 1559; Scholar, 1561; B.A. 1562–3. Fellow, 1563. One of these names R. of Alpheton, Suffolk, 1570–2. Another, R. of Beaumont, Essex; will (Consist. C. London) 1624.

GREEN, JOHN. Matric. pens. from JESUS, Michs. 1571. Of Barnby-on-Don, Yorks. S. of John, gent. Migrated to Caius, Oct. 17, 1573, age 18.

GRENE, JOHN. Adm. sizar at CORPUS CHRISTI, 1571. Matric. Easter, 1572; B.A. 1575–6. Perhaps the R. of Badsworth, Yorks.; buried there Jan. 22, 1598–9.

GRENE, JOHN. Matric. sizar from PEMBROKE, Michs. 1572.

GREENE, JOHN. Matric. pens. from CLARE, Easter, 1576. Buried at St Edward's, Cambridge, June 15, 1578.

GREEN, JOHN. B.A. from TRINITY, 1592–3; M.A. from St Catharine's, 1597. Ord. deacon (Peterb.) Sept. 9, 1599; priest, Nov. 30, 1602, as C. of Teigh, Rutland. One of these names R. of Market Overton, Rutland, 1616–49. Died 1649.

GREEN, JOHN. Adm. pens. at QUEENS', June 28, 1593. Of Suffolk. One of these names s. of Robert, of Wells, Norfolk. Comptroller of Customs at Lynn Regis. Died Dec. 4, 1618, aged 41. Perhaps father of Robert (1614) and Joshua (1622). (Carthew, *East Bradenham.*)

GREEN, JOHN. Matric. sizar from JESUS, c. 1594. B. at Howsham, Cadney, Lincs., 1573. B.A. 1597–8; M.A. 1601. Ord. deacon (Lincoln) Mar. 5, 1597–8. R. of Swinhope, Lincs., 1601–41. Perhaps R. of Rand, 1611.

GRENE, JOHN. Matric. pens. from ST JOHN'S, *c.* 1595; B.A. 1598–9; M.A. 1602. Probably s. of Thomas, of London. Judge of the Sheriffs' Court, London, 1634. Serjeant-at-law, 1640. Died May 17, 1653, aged 74. If so, father of John (1631–2). (*East Anglian*, III. 86.)

GREEN, JOHN. B.A. from ST JOHN'S, 1600–1; M.A. 1604. One of these names R. of Shelton, Norfolk. Buried there Oct. 24, 1633. (*East Anglian*, IV. 258.)

GREEN, JOHN. Licensed to practise medicine, 1615.

GREEN, JOHN. Adm. pens. (age 17) at CAIUS, Nov. 4, 1617. S. of Robert, attorney, of Norwich. School, Norwich (Mr Briggs). Matric. 1617; Scholar; B.A. 1621–2; M.A. 1625. Ord. deacon and priest (Norwich) Aug. 24, 1626. R. of Weston, Suffolk, 1626; sequestered, 1645. But *see* John (1621). Brother of George (1609). (*Venn*, I. 237.)

GREENE, JOHN. Matric. pens. from ST CATHARINE'S, Michs. 1622; B.A. 1626–7; M.A. 1630. One of these names C. of Croxdale, Durham, 1639–67.

GREENE, JOHN. Adm. sizar (age 17) at PEMBROKE, June 29, 1621. S. of John, of Stanton, Suffolk. Bapt. there, Apr. 9, 1604. Matric. 1623; B.A. 1624-5; M.A. 1628. One of these names, 'B.A.,' R. of Weston, Suffolk, 1627. With brother Richard administered his father's estate, 1640. But *see* John (1617). (V. B. Redstone.)

GREENE, JOHN. Matric. pens. from PEMBROKE, Easter, 1629; B.A. 1631-2.

GREENE, JOHN. Matric. sizar from MAGDALENE, Easter, 1631. S. of John, husbandman, of Bromyard, Herefordshire. B. there. School, Bromyard (Mr Barber). Migrated to St John's, Apr. 16, 1632, age 17.

GREENE, JOHN. Adm. Fell.-Com. (age 15) at ST JOHN'S, Mar. 6, 1631-2. S. of John (? *c.* 1595), Esq., of London (serjeant-at-law). B. in Middlesex. School, Brentwood, Essex (Mr Cartwright). Matric. 1632. Doubtless adm. at the Inner Temple, 1638; 'of Madeleys, Epping.' Recorder of London, 1658-9. Died Nov. 1, 1659. Father of John (1659) and Thomas (1664). (*East Anglian*, III. 86.)

GREENE, JOHN. Adm. sizar (age 17) at ST JOHN'S, Dec. 16, 1645. S. of Nicholas, farmer, of Sible Hedingham, Essex. B. there. Schoolmaster, Mr Abbot. Matric. 1646; B.A. 1649.

GREENE, JOHN. Adm. sizar (age 17) at CHRIST'S, Jan. 6, 1646-7. S. of John. B. at Cambridge. School, Perse, Cambridge. Matric. 1647; B.A. 1650-1. One of these names R. of Ousden, Suffolk, 1663. One (M.A.), R. of Hackney, 1664-85. Died 1685. (*Peile*, I. 511.)

GREEN, JOHN. Adm. sizar (age 14) at MAGDALENE, June 15, 1652. S. of John, of Wacton, Norfolk. School, Moulton, Norfolk (private). Matric. 1652; B.A. 1659. One of these names ord. deacon (Lincoln) Oct. 15, 1663, as B.A. Probably R. of Cumberworth, Lincs., 1660 (presented by Magdalene); and V. of Mumby, 1660.

GREEN, JOHN. Adm. pens. at EMMANUEL, Easter, 1654. Of London. Matric. 1654; B.A. 1657-8; M.A. 1663.

GREENE, JOHN. Adm. sizar (age 17) at SIDNEY, Apr. 14, 1658. S. of Flower (1629), clerk. B. at Market Overton, Rutland. School, Uppingham. Matric. 1658; B.A. 1661-2; M.A. 1665. Subscribed for priest's orders (London) May 19, 1665. C. of Bocking, Essex. Doubtless R. of Market Overton, Rutland, 1679-89. Died 1689. (T. P. Dorman.)

GREENE, JOHN. Adm. Fell.-Com. (age 16) at ST JOHN'S, Aug. 25, 1659. S. of John (1631-2), Esq., recorder of London. B. in Middlesex. School, Westminster. Matric. 1660. Perhaps matric. from Pembroke College, Oxford, Apr. 28, 1659. Adm. at Lincoln's Inn, May 2, 1659. Barrister, 1667. Treasurer, 1693. Serjeant-at-law, 1700. Died Dec. 12, 1725. Will, P.C.C. Brother of Thomas (1664) and father of John (1711). (*East Anglian*, III. 86.)

GREENE, JOHN. Adm. pens. (age 16) at CAIUS, Oct. 1661. S. of Edward, tailor, of Cambridge. B. there. School, Perse (Mr Griffith). Matric. 1662; B.A. 1665-6; M.A. 1669. Fellow, 1666-9. One of these names ord. priest (Norwich) Sept. 20, 1668. V. of Tetney, Lincs., 1670. R. of Brigsley, 1673-82. Another V. of Wickhambrook, Suffolk, 1668. (*Venn*, I. 415.)

GREENE, JOHN. Adm. sizar (age 18) at ST JOHN'S, Apr. 29, 1662. S. of Edward (? 1625), clerk, of Sutton, Norfolk. B. there. School, Oakham (Mr Brooks). Matric. 1662; B.A. 1665-6; M.A. 1669. Signed for deacon's orders (London) Dec. 22, 1666.

GREENE, JOHN. Adm. pens. at EMMANUEL, June 4, 1667. Of Lincolnshire. Perhaps s. of John, of Dunsby Hall, Lincs. Bapt. there, Oct. 24, 1650. Matric. 1667. Buried at Dunsby, June 15, 1693. M.I. Perhaps father of John (1702). (*Lincs. Pedigrees*, 1242.)

GREEN, JOHN. Adm. pens. (age 18) at TRINITY, June 18, 1685. S. of John, of Ravenstone, Bucks. B. there. School, Westminster. Scholar, 1685. Migrated to Christ's, Feb. 13, 1685-6. Matric. 1686; B.A. 1688-9. (*Peile*, II. 101.)

GREEN, JOHN. Adm. sizar (age 18) at PETERHOUSE, Apr. 17, 1690. Of Yorkshire. School, Skipton, Yorks. Matric. 1690; B.A. 1693-4. Ord. deacon (Peterb.) Sept. 22, 1695; priest (York) May, 1697.

GREEN, JOHN. Adm. sizar (age 20) at MAGDALENE, June 11, 1691. S. of James. B. at Wells, Norfolk. School, Gt Massingham. Matric. 1693; B.A. 1694-5; M.A. 1725. Ord. deacon (Norwich) May, 1695; priest, Sept. 1696.

GREEN, JOHN. Adm. Fell.-Com. at EMMANUEL Mar. 31, 1694. Of Middlesex. Matric. 1695.

GREEN, JOHN. Adm. pens. (age 15) at PETERHOUSE, Nov. 9, 1697. Of London. School, Hackney. Matric. 1697; Scholar, 1697.

GREEN, JOHN. Adm. pens. at EMMANUEL, June 8, 1702. Matric. 1702-3. Perhaps s. of John (? 1667), of Dunsby Hall, Lincs. Bapt. at Horbling, Lincs., Sept. 20, 1683. Died Aug. 23, 1709. Buried at Spalding. If so, father of John (1725). (*Lincs. Pedigrees*, 1243.)

GREEN, JOHN. Adm. Fell.-Com. (age 24) at ST JOHN'S, June 3, 1709. S. of Daniel, deceased, of Low-Leyton, Essex (and probably grandson of Daniel (1647). B. at Fulmodeston, Norfolk. Matric. 1710; M.B. 1714; M.D. 1720.

GREEN, JOHN. Adm. Fell.-Com. (age 16) at ST JOHN'S, June 28, 1711. S. of John (1659), serjeant-at-law. B. in Essex. School, Westminster. Matric. 1710. Adm. at Lincoln's Inn, June 20, 1709. Steward of the Manor of Hackney. Died Jan. 14, 1752. Left his estate to his kinsman Maurice (1730). (*East Anglian*, III. 86; *N. and Q.*, 2 S., X. 394.)

GREEN, JOHN. Adm. sizar (age 17) at ST JOHN'S, June 10, 1724. S. of J., tax-collector. B. at Beverley, Yorks. School, Beverley (Mr Jefferson). Matric. 1724; Scholar; B.A. 1727-8; M.A. 1731; B.D. 1739; D.D. 1749. Fellow, 1731-50. Master of Corpus, 1750-64. Vice-Chancellor, 1757-8. For a short time usher at Lichfield School, 1729. Ord. deacon (Lincoln) June 13; priest, Sept. 19, 1731. V. of Hinxton, Cambs., 1731-47. R. of Borough Green, 1747. Regius Professor of Divinity; and R. of Somersham, 1749-56. R. of Barrow, Suffolk, 1750-62. Chaplain to the King, 1753-6. Dean of Lincoln, 1756. Bishop of Lincoln, 1761-79. Preb. of St Paul's, 1771-9. Died at Bath, Apr. 25, 1779. (*Masters*; *D.N.B.*)

GREEN, JOHN. Adm. pens. (age 17) at ST JOHN'S, Oct. 19, 1725. S. of John (? 1702), gent., of Dunsby Hall, Lincs. B. at Spalding. Bapt. May 31, 1708. School, Spalding (Mr Neve). Matric. 1725. Adm. at Leyden, Nov. 6, 1731. Practised as physician at Spalding. Secretary and librarian to the Gentlemen's society at Spalding. Died Nov. 1, 1756. M.I. at Spalding. (*Scott-Mayor*, III. 392; *Lincs. Pedigrees*, 1243.)

GREEN, JOHN. Adm. sizar (age 25) at ST JOHN'S, May 28, 1729. S. of Richard, husbandman, of Yorkshire. B. at Wentworth. School, Risbrook (private). Matric. 1729; LL.B. 1735. Ord. deacon (St David's) Dec. 22, 1734; priest (Lichfield) Sept. 21, 1735. R. of Ashton-on-Mersey, Cheshire, 1767-74. Died 1774.

GREEN, JOHN. Adm. pens. (age 18) at ST JOHN'S, Aug. 26, 1736. S. of Maurice (1730), Professor of Music in Cambridge. B. in London. Bapt. at St Alphage, May 28, 1719. School, Eton. Matric. 1736.

GREEN, JOHN. Adm. sizar (age 18) at PETERHOUSE, Apr. 27, 1744. S. of Edward, of Walkern, Herts. School, Eton (Colleger, 1740-4). Matric. 1744; Scholar, 1744; B.A. 1747-8. Ord. deacon (Lincoln) Mar. 4, 1747-8.

GREEN, JOHN. Adm. at CORPUS CHRISTI, 1744. Of Norfolk. S. of Francis. Bapt. at St Lawrence, Norwich, Nov. 15, 1728. Colleger at Eton, 1743-4. Matric. Michs. 1745; B.A. 1748-9; M.A. 1752. Senior Wrangler. Fellow, 1749-56. Ord. deacon (Ely) Feb. 23, 1752; priest, Dec. 25, 1752. V. of St George Tombland, Norwich, 1756-86. R. of Marsham, Norfolk, 1757-86. Died Nov. 11, 1786. Will, P.C.C.

GREENE, JOHN. Adm. at CORPUS CHRISTI, 1749. Of London. Matric. 1749; B.A. 1753. One of these names s. of John, of Milman St, London, Esq.; adm. at Lincoln's Inn, Jan. 15, 1753. Ord. deacon (Norwich) July, 1755; priest, Nov. 1759. C. of Ash Wicken, Norfolk. Perhaps R. of Stody and Hunworth, Norfolk, 1761-1801. (H. G. Holley.)

GREENE, JOSHUA. Adm. pens. (age 16) at PEMBROKE, May 6, 1622. S. of John (? 1593), of Lynn, mercer. Matric. 1623; B.A. 1625; M.A. 1629. Perhaps of East Bradenham, Norfolk. Died July 9, 1659. Buried at East Bradenham. Will (P.C.C.).

GREENE, JOSHUA. Adm. pens. (age 16) at CAIUS, Mar. 6, 1659-60. S. of Joshua (? above), Esq., of East Bradenham, Norfolk. B. at Shipdham. School, Scarning (Mr Burton). Matric. 1660; Scholar, 1662, till his death, 1665. Not the man adm. at Gray's Inn, Nov. 28, 1661. (*Venn*, I. 408; Carthew, *East Bradenham*, 106, where the date of his death is apparently confused with that of a cousin.)

GREENE, JOSHUA. Adm. sizar (age 18) at PEMBROKE, Apr. 22, 1670. S. of Francis. B. at Yarmouth, Norfolk. B.A. 1673-4. One of these names R. of Gt Hormead, Herts., 1679-1714. Died 1714.

GREEN, LAURENCE. Matric. pens. from PETERHOUSE, Easter, 1578; B.A. 1581-2. Probably s. of Gabriel, of Horsforth, Yorks. Brother of Thomas (1580).

GREENE, LAURENCE. Matric. Fell.-Com. from PETERHOUSE, Michs. 1613.

GREEN, LEONARD. Matric. sizar from CORPUS CHRISTI, Michs. 1633. Of Cambridgeshire.

GREEN, LEONARD. Adm. sizar at CORPUS CHRISTI, 1689. Of Huntingdonshire. Matric. 1690; B.A. 1692-3; M.A. 1699. Incorp. at Oxford, 1699. Ord. deacon (London) Sept. 23, 1694; priest (Lichfield) Dec. 22, 1700. R. of Little Stukeley, Hunts., 1701-37. Died 1737.

GREENE, MAURICE. Mus.Doc. 1730. S. of Thomas (1664), D.D. B. in London, c. 1696. Incorp. at Oxford, 1735. Organist at St Andrew's, Holborn, 1717; at St Paul's, 1718; and at the Chapel Royal, 1727. Professor of Music, 1730–55. Assisted in founding the Royal Society of Musicians, 1738. Author of many well-known pieces. Buried at St Olave's, Jewry, Dec. 10, 1755; reinterred in St Paul's Cathedral, 1888. Will, P.C.C. Father of John (1736). (*D.N.B.*; C. F. Abdy Williams, *Degrees in Music*.)

GREEN, MICHAEL. B.A. 1532–3.

GREENE, NATHANIEL. Ord. deacon (Peterb.) Sept. 23, 1610; priest, Feb. 17, 1610–1, as 'B.A. of CLARE College.' V. of Claxby-in-the-Marsh, Lincs., 1620. Possibly s. of Thomas, clerk; bapt. at St Dionis, London, Sept. 24, 1587.

GREEN (? GREW), NEHEMIAH. Adm. pens. at ST CATHARINE'S, June 17, 1696. Matric. 1696, as Grew.

GRENE, OLIVER. Adm. pens. (age 19) at CAIUS, Apr. 23, 1582. S. of William. B. at Trumpington, Cambs. Schools, Godmanchester (Mr Braldan) and Elsworth. Scholar, 1585–9; B.A. 1585–6; M.A. 1589; Licensed to practise medicine, 1599; M.D. 1615. Mathematician. Buried at St Michael's, Cambridge, Dec. 6, 1625. Will proved (V.C.C.) 1628. Father of Henry (1623). The site of 'Green Street,' Cambridge was his Property. (*Venn*, I. 114.)

GREEN, RALPH. Matric. sizar from CLARE, Michs. 1572.

GREEN, RICHARD. B.A. 1458–9; M.A. 1463–4. Fellow of PEMBROKE, 1465. Donor of books to that College. One of these names, M.A., R. of Upper Rickinghall, Suffolk, 1496–1507.

GREEN, RICHARD. B.A. 1484–5.

GREEN, RICHARD. Matric. sizar from CLARE, Michs. 1545 (*impubes*).

GREENE, RICHARD. Adm. (age 11) at CAIUS, Oct. 20, 1564. S. of Rooke, Esq. B. at Sampford, Essex. Of a recusant family. Adm. at the Middle Temple, Nov. 10, 1573. Probably adm. at the English College at Rome, 1581. Ord. priest (R.C., Bishop of St Asaph) Nov. 1582. Drowned in the Mediterranean, between Genoa and Spain, 1590. Brother of William (1564). (*Venn*, I. 56; Foley, VI. 151.)

GREEN, RICHARD. Matric. pens. from CHRIST'S, Easter, 1576; B.A. 1579–80. *Peile* (I. 136) suggests his identity with the last named. Perhaps R. of Asterby, Lincs., 1588–1621.

GREEN, RICHARD. Matric. sizar (age 17) from PEMBROKE, Michs. 1642. S. of Christopher, of Cambridge. B.A. 1645–6; M.A. 1649. Fellow, 1652–89 (he was actually 'tanquam socius'). Died 1697.

GREEN, RICHARD. Adm. Fell.-Com. at EMMANUEL, Aug. 12, 1647. Of Lancashire.

GREEN, RICHARD. Adm. pens. at JESUS, Sept. 20, 1675. Of London. Scholar from St Paul's. Matric. 1675–6; B.A. 1679–80. Ord. priest (London) Mar. 16, 1683–4.

GREEN, RICHARD. Adm. pens. (age 17) at PETERHOUSE, Mar. 28, 1681. Of Yorkshire. School, Wakefield. Matric. 1681; Scholar, 1681; B.A. 1684–5; M.A. 1688. Fellow, 1685–9. Died 1689.

GREEN, RICHARD. Adm. sizar (age 17) at TRINITY, May 22, 1697. S. of Thomas, of Lighthorne, Warws. School, Swalcliffe, Oxon. (Mr Mayo). Matric. 1697.

GREEN, RICHARD. Adm. Fell.-Com. (age 17) at TRINITY, July 1, 1700. S. of William, of the Bank (? Banks Hall, Barnsley), Yorks. Educated by Mr Hawksworth. Matric. 1700. Died Mar. 16, 1707, aged 24. (Hunter, *S. Yorks.*, II. 234.)

GREEN, RICHARD. Matric. from EMMANUEL, Michs. 1702.

GREEN, RICHARD. Adm. pens. (age 16) at MAGDALENE, Aug. 1, 1706. S. of Richard, gent. B. at High Butling, Falkingham, Lincs. School, Charterhouse. Matric. 1707; Scholar, 1708; B.A. 1710–1; M.A. 1714. Fellow, 1712. Ord. deacon (E) June 12, 1715; priest (Peterb.) May 26, 1716. R. of Little Casterton, Rutland, 1722–49. R. of Aston-le-Walls, 1748. Died July 20, 1749. (*Lincs. Pedigrees*, 1242.)

GREEN, RICHARD. Adm. sizar (age 16) at ST JOHN'S, Apr. 29, 1706. S. of Cornelius, gent. B. at Slyne, near Bolton-le-Sands, Lancs. School, Sedbergh (Mr Wharton). Matric. 1706; B.A. 1709–10.

GREEN, RICHARD. Adm. pens. (age 17) at CLARE, Jan. 28, 1715–6. B. at Cambridge. School, Bishop's Stortford. Matric. 1715–6. Migrated to Peterhouse, Oct. 21, 1718. Scholar, 1719; LL.B. 1722. R. of Merston, Sussex, 1727–74. Preb. of Chichester, 1730–75. Died Apr. 1775. Will, P.C.C. (*T. A. Walker*, 238.)

GREEN, RICHARD. Adm. pens. (age 18) at MAGDALENE, June 24, 1746. S. of Cornelius. B. at Boulton, Westmorland. School, Heversham. Matric. 1746; B.A. 1747–8; M.A. 1759. Ord. deacon (Lincoln) Mar. 11, 1749–50. Will of one of these names (P.C.C.) 1785; of St Clement Danes, London, clerk.

GREEN, RICHARD. D.D. 1749 (Incorp. from Oxford). S. of Richard, of Bishopsgate, London, gent. B. Nov. 15, 1708. School, Merchant Taylors'. Matric. from St John's College, Oxford, July 25, 1726; B.A. (Oxford) 1730; M.A. 1734; B.D. 1739; D.D. 1743. Fellow of St John's (Oxford), 1726–86. R. of Bell Broughton, Worcs. R. of St Nicholas, Worcester. F.R.S., 1752. Died at Oxford, June, 1786. (*Al. Oxon.*; A. B. Beaven.)

GRENE, ROBERT. Matric. pens. from TRINITY, Easter, 1560; Scholar, 1562; B.A. 1564–5. One of these names V. of Tollesbury, Essex, 1584–5. Perhaps R. of Mannington and Trimingland, Norfolk; V. of Corpusty, 1577–89; and R. of Burgh, 1580–3.

GRENE, ROBERT. Matric. sizar from CORPUS CHRISTI, Easter, 1573.

GREENE, ROBERT. Matric. sizar from ST JOHN'S, Michs. 1575. B. at Norwich, c. 1560. B.A. 1579–80; M.A. from Clare, 1583. Incorp. at Oxford, 1588. The well-known dramatist and pamphleteer. Travelled in Italy and Spain, leading a dissolute life; returned to London. Died Sept. 3, 1592. The 2nd part of his *Mamillia* is issued 'from my study in Clare Hall.' He describes himself as 'M.A. and student in Physic.' (*Cooper*, II. 127; *D.N.B.*; H. P. Stokes.)

GREEN, ROBERT. Ord. deacon (Peterb.) Apr. 10, 1586, as 'B.A. of ST JOHN'S'; priest, Apr. 9, 1587. Perhaps R. of Sudborough, Northants., 1596–1617. (T. P. Dorman.)

GREEN, ROBERT. Matric. pens. from CORPUS CHRISTI, Easter, 1609. Perhaps ord. deacon (Peterb.) Mar. 20; priest, Mar. 21, 1613–4, as 'B.A. of Trinity.'

GREENE, ROBERT. Matric. pens. from CHRIST'S, Michs. 1614. Doubtless adm. at Gray's Inn, Aug. 13, 1616, as s. and h. of John (? 1593), of Lynn. If so, of Rishangles, Suffolk, Esq., afterwards of Mendham. Married Elizabeth, dau. of William Coleman, of Braiseworth, Suffolk. Died July 15, 1642. Buried at Braiseworth. M.I. there. (*Peile*, I. 298; Carthew, *East Bradenham*.)

GREENE, ROBERT. Adm. pens. (age 16) at ST JOHN'S, Mar. 24, 1652–3. S. of Robert, gent., of Forncett, Norfolk. B. there. School, Bury St Edmunds (Mr Stephens). Adm. at Gray's Inn, Feb. 4, 1656–7. Married Mary Bussy. (*Vis. of Norfolk*, 1664.)

GREEN, ROBERT. Adm. sizar at CLARE, Oct. 8, 1694. Of Tamworth. S. of Robert, mercer. Matric. 1696; B.A. 1699–1700; M.A. 1703; D.D. 1728 (*Com. Reg.*). Fellow, 1703–30. Senior proctor, 1727–8. Founded scholarships at Clare. Ord. priest (London) Sept. 24, 1705. V. of Everton, Beds.; and Tetworth, Hunts., 1723–30. An eccentric philosophical writer. Died at Tamworth, Aug. 16, 1730. Buried at All Saints', Cambridge, Aug. 16, 1730. Will proved (P.C.C.) 1743. (*D.N.B.*)

GREEN, ROBERT. Adm. pens. (age 16) at CHRIST'S, Mar. 9, 1708–9. S. of Christopher (1667), M.D., Professor of Physic. B. in Cambridge. School, Bishop's Stortford (Mr Tooke). Matric. 1709; Scholar, 1710. Adm. at the Inner Temple, Apr. 24, 1712; and at the Middle Temple, Apr. 8, 1721. Brother of Christopher (1708–9). (*Peile*, II. 172.)

GREEN, ROGER. Matric. sizar from ST CATHARINE'S, Easter, 1631. Of Norfolk. B.A. 1634–5; M.A. 1638. Ord. priest (Norwich) Mar. 9, 1638–9.

GREEN, SAMUEL. Matric. sizar from ST JOHN'S, Easter, 1618; B.A. 1621–2; M.A. 1625. Ord. deacon (Peterb.) Feb. 26; priest, Feb. 27, 1625–6. R. of Marholm, Northants., 1642–69. Buried there Dec. 14, 1669. (Sweeting, *Peterborough Churches*; H. I. Longden.)

GREENE, SAMUEL. Adm. sizar (age 17) at CAIUS, Mar. 25, 1645. S. of James, minister, of Suffolk. Schools, Bale, Norfolk (Mr Walker) and Moulton (Mr Lancetter). Matric. 1645; Scholar, 1648–9; B.A. 1648–9. Ord. priest (Bishop Jos. Hall, of Norwich) Jan. 4, 1649–50. V. of Gt and Little Hockham, Norfolk, 1661–7. Died 1667. (*Venn*, I. 356.)

GREEN, SAMUEL. Adm. pens. at JESUS, June 10, 1658. Of Cheshire. Matric. 1658; Scholar, 1660; B.A. 1661–2; M.A. 1665.

GREEN, SAMUEL. Adm. pens. (age 18) at PEMBROKE, July 3, 1708. S. of Samuel, of Warwick, gent. Matric. 1708; B.A. 1711–2; M.A. 1716. (*Vis. of Warws.*, 1682–3.)

GREEN, SAMUEL. D.D. 1735 (Incorp. from Oxford). S. of Samuel, of Heversham, Westmorland. Matric. from Queen's College, Oxford, July 3, 1703, age 16; B.A. (Oxford) 1707–8; M.A. 1711; D.D. 1733. Probably ord. deacon (Oxford) May 7, 1711; priest, Sept. 21, 1712. V. of Stanton Lacy, Salop, 1718. R. of Blisworth, Northants., 1721–3. V. of Upton Grey, Hants., 1730–47. R. of St George-the-Martyr, London, 1730–47. Preb. of Worcester, 1732–47. Died at Worcester, from a fall from his horse, Oct. 25, 1747. Will, P.C.C. (*Al Oxon.*)

GREEN, SIMON. M.A.; B.D. 1472. Fellow of CORPUS CHRISTI before 1468. Master, 1477–87. Licensed to preach by the Bishop of Ely, 1469. One of the Ediles for superintending the building of Gt St Mary's, Cambridge. Benefactor to Corpus. Died Oct. 1487. (*Masters*.)

GREEN, STEPHEN. B.A. 1530–1 (1st in the *ordo*); M.A. 1534. R. of St Dionis Backchurch, London, 1553.

GRENE, THOMAS. M.A. *c.* 1490. S. of Thomas, of Cockermouth, Cumberland. B.D. 1502–3; D.D. 1511–2. Fellow of JESUS, *c.* 1498. Master of St Catharine's, 1507–*c.* 1529. Vice-Chancellor, 1523–4. Benefactor to St Catharine's. (*Cooper*, I. 32.)

GREEN or GREYN, THOMAS. B.Can.L. 1530–1.

GRENE, THOMAS. Matrie. pens. from ST JOHN'S, Lent, 1557–8.

GRENE, THOMAS. Matric. pens. from CHRIST'S, Easter, 1568.

GRENE, THOMAS. Matric. pens. from QUEENS', Michs. 1572.

GREEN, THOMAS. Matric. pens. from TRINITY, Easter, 1579; B.A. from Magdalene, 1580–1; M.A. 1584. Probably ord. deacon (Lincoln) July 12, 1585; priest, June, 1587. V. of Thorneton, Lincs., 1587–1618. R. of Wilksby, 1588–1631. V. of Royston, Herts., till 1634, when he died.

GREEN, THOMAS. Matrie. pens. from PETERHOUSE, Easter, 1580. Probably s. of Gabriel, of Horsforth, Yorks. B.A. from Magdalene, 1585–6. Incorp. at Oxford, 1586. Brother of Laurence (1578).

GREEN, THOMAS. Matrie. sizar from TRINITY, Lent, 1580–1; B.A. 1582–3; M.A. 1586; B.D. 1597.

GREEN, THOMAS. Matrie. pens. from ST CATHARINE'S, Easter, 1631.

GREEN, THOMAS. Adm. pens. at CLARE, Feb. 25, 1636–7. Matrie. 1637; B.A. 1640–1; M.A. 1646. Ord. deaeou (Lincoln) June 16, 1644; priest, June 17, 1644.

GREEN, THOMAS. Matrie. sizar from TRINITY, Michs. 1639. Probably B.A. Ord. deacon (Peterb.) Feb. 26, 1642–3.

GREEN, THOMAS. Adm. Fell.-Com. (age 15) at PEMBROKE, June 9, 1647. S. of Giles, Esq. B. in the Isle of Purbeck, Dorset.

GREEN, THOMAS. Adm. pens. (age 16) at PETERHOUSE, Apr. 2, 1664. Of Middlesex. S. of John (1631–2). School, Hertford. Matrie. 1664; Scholar, 1664; B.A. 1667–8; M.A. 1671; D.D. 1684. Fellow, 1673–9. V. of St Olave, Jewry, 1678–1720. Preh. of Sarum, 1693–1720. Preb. of Norwieh. R. of St Martin's, Iremonger Lane, London. Died Feb. 1719–20. Will (P.C.C.) 1720. Brother of John (1659) and father of Maurice (1730).

GREENE, THOMAS. Adm. at CORPUS CHRISTI, 1674. S. of Thomas, of Norwich. B. there. Bapt. at St Peter Mancroft, Dec. 12, 1658. Matric. 1675; B.A. 1678–9; M.A. 1682; B.D. 1690; D.D. 1695. Fellow, 1680–95. Master, 1698–1716. Vice-Chancellor, 1699–1700, 1713–4. Ord. priest (Norwich) Dec. 1683. V. of St Benet's, Cambridge, *c.* 1682. V. of Minster, Thanet, Kent, 1695–1708. Preb. of Canterbury, 1701–21. R. of Adisham, 1708–17. Archdeacon of Canterbury, 1708–21. V. of St Martin-in-the-Fields, Westminster, 1717–23. Chaplain to the King. Bishop of Norwich, 1721–3. Bishop of Ely, 1723–38. Married a dau. of Bishop Trimnell. Died May 18, 1738, aged 80. Father of Thomas (1727). (*Masters*; *D.N.B.*)

GREEN, THOMAS. Adm. sizar (age 22) at CHRIST'S, May 6, 1689. S. of Samuel. B. at Skipton. School, Giggleswick (Mr Briggs). Matrie. 1689; Scholar, 1690; B.A. 1693. Ord. deacon (York) May, 1694; priest, May, 1695. Perhaps V. of Pannal, Yorks., 1694. Will proved (York) Jan. 1, 1704–5. (*Peile*, II. 112.)

GREEN, THOMAS. Adm. pens. (age 17) at CHRIST'S, Apr. 8, 1690. S. of Thomas. B. at Colchester. School, Felsted (Mr Glascock). Doubtless s. and h. of Thomas, of Easthorpe, Colchester; adm. at Lincoln's Inn, June 6, 1689. (*Peile*, II. 116.)

GREEN, THOMAS. Adm. sizar (age 18) at CHRIST'S, June 3, 1693. S. of Thomas. B. at Lighthorne, Warws. Matric. 1693; Scholar, 1694–5; B.A. 1696–7; M.A. 1733. Perhaps ord. deacon (Lincoln, *Litt. dim.* from Worcester) Sept. 26, 1698. Ord. priest (Lincoln) Dec. 21, 1701. V. of Burton Dassett, Warws., 1702. R. of Water Stratford, Bucks., 1723. Chaplain to the Bishop of St David's. Died 1747. (*Peile*, II. 128.)

GREEN, THOMAS. Adm. sizar at CLARE, May 2, 1693. Of Northamptonshire. Probably s. of James, of Northampton; bapt. at All Saints', Sept. 3, 1675. Matric. 1694; B.A. 1696–7; M.A. 1700. Fellow, 1698–1705. Ord. deacon (Lincoln) Sept. 24, 1699; priest, Mar. 16, 1700–1. C. of St Peter's, Northampton. V. of Lilbourne, Northants., 1704–23. Admon. granted to James, of Northampton, draper, his father. (H. I. Longden.)

GREENE, THOMAS. Adm. pens. (age 17) at PETERHOUSE, Mar. 23, 1701–2. Of Middlesex. Exhibitioner from St Paul's School. Scholar, 1702; Matric. 1702–3; B.A. 1705–6; M.A. 1709. Ord. deacon (London) Feb. 1707–8; priest, Mar. 20, 1708–9.

GREEN, THOMAS. Adm. pens. (age 18) at TRINITY, Apr. 2, 1714. S. of Thomas, of Beckbury, Shropshire. School, Beckbury (Mr Green). Matrie. 1715; Scholar, 1717; B.A. 1717–8. Brother of Benjamin.

GREEN, THOMAS. Adm. sizar (age 19) at TRINITY, June 16, 1722. S. of John, of Westmorland. School, Heversham, Westmorland (Mr Watson). Matrie. 1722; Scholar, 1725; B.A. 1725–6; M.A. 1729. Perhaps ord. deacon (Lincoln) Sept. 25, 1726.

GREEN, THOMAS. Adm. sizar at EMMANUEL, Apr. 19, 1722. Of Huntingdonshire. Matric. 1724; B.A. 1725–6. Ord. deacon (Lincoln) Sept. 24, 1727; priest, Sept. 22, 1728. Perhaps will (P.C.C.) 1766; of Birmingham, clerk.

GREENE, THOMAS. Adm. at CORPUS CHRISTI, 1727. S. of Thomas (1674), Master of Corpus. B. at Cambridge. Matric. 1727; B.A. 1730–1; M.A. 1734; D.D. 1749. Fellow, 1732–5. Fellow of Jesus, 1736–8. Ord. deacon (Ely) July 30, 1737. R. of Cottenham, Cambs., 1737. Preb. of Ely, 1737–80. Chancellor of Lichfield, 1751–80. Chaplain to George II, 1751–7. Preb. of Westminster, 1756–1757. Dean of Salisbury, 1757–80. Died in Gerarde St, London, Mar. 23, 1780. Buried in St Martin's Church. Will, P.C.C. (*D.N.B.*; *Masters*; G. *Mag.*)

GREENE, THOMAS. Adm. sizar (age 18) at PEMBROKE, Nov. 11, 1728. S. of Roger, of Craston, Lanes., clerk. Matrio. 1728.

GREENE, THOMAS. Adm. scholar at TRINITY HALL, Jan. 7, 1737–8. Of Westminster. Matrie. 1738.

GREEN, THOMAS. Adm. sizar (age 18) at PETERHOUSE, June 24, 1749. Of Kent. B. Feb. 10, 1730–1. School, Merchant Taylors'. Matric. 1749; Scholar, 1749; B.A. 1753; M.A. 1756. Fellow, 1756. Ord. priest (London) May 25, 1755. Assistant Master of Merchant Taylors' School, 1753; Head Master, 1778–83. Chaplain of St Thomas' Hospital, Southwark. Died Jan. 1, 1783. Buried at St Clement's, Eastcheap. Admon., P.C.C. (*T. A. Walker*.)

GRENE, WILLIAM. D.D. Fellow of GONVILLE HALL, 1434–48. V. of Mundon, Essex, 1422–7. V. of Boreham, 1429–33. R. of Salcott and Virley, 1443–7. R. of St Andrew's, Holborn, 1447–78. Donor of a window, and books, to Gonville Hall. Died May, 1478. Will (Bishop of London's C.) 1478: to be buried in St Andrew's. (*Venn*, I. 7.)

GREEN, WILLIAM. Carmelite friar. B.D. of Cambridge. Flourished *c.* 1470. (*Pits*, 662.)

GREEN, WILLIAM. B.D. 1493. Fellow of QUEENS', 1484–94. One of these names treasurer of Chichester, 1501.

GREEN, WILLIAM. B.A. 1508–9 (*Supp* for Incorp. at Oxford, 1512); M.A. 1513–4; B.D. 1519–20; D.D. 1521–2. Fellow of PEMBROKE, 1515. Vice-Chancellor, 1524–5. R. of Kettering, 1529–40. R. of Northchurch, Herts. Preb. of St Paul's, 1534–40. V. of Lancaster, 1535–40. Died 1540. Will (P.C.C. 1541. (According to *Cooper* (I. 69) the B.D. of 1519–20, was Thomas.)

GREEN, WILLIAM. B.A. 1526–7. Scholar of GONVILLE HALL, 1526.

GREEN, WILLIAM. B.A. 1539–40.

GREEN, WILLIAM. Adm. at KING'S (age 17) a scholar from Eton, Aug. 16, 1546. Of Wycombe, Bucks. Matric. 1546; B.A. 1550–1. Fellow, 1549.

GRENE, WILLIAM. Matric. pens. from MAGDALENE, Easter, 1549.

GREEN, WILLIAM. Matric. pens. from CLARE, Michs. 1554; B.A. 1558. Perhaps V. of Chesterton, Cambs., 1561.

GREENE, WILLIAM. B.A. 1560–1; M.A. 1564. One of these names V. of Barton Turf, Norfolk, 1567–71.

GREENE, WILLIAM. Adm. Fell.-Com. (age 19) at CAIUS, Oct. 20, 1564. S. and h. of Rooke, Esq. B. at Sampford, Essex. Matric. 1564–5. Of Hedingham, Little Sampford Hall and Gt Sampford Manor. Suffered as a Popish recusant in 1578. Probably will (P.C.C.) 1621. Brother of Richard (1564). (*Venn*, I. 55.)

GRENE, WILLIAM. Matric. pens. from CLARE, Michs. 1572; B.A. 1575–6; M.A. 1579. One of these names V. of Broxbourne, Herts., 1580–3. One (M.A.), V. of South Kirkby, Yorks., in 1619; and perhaps preb. of York, 1598–1640.

GREEN, WILLIAM. Matric. pens. from ST JOHN'S, Easter, 1579.

GREEN, WILLIAM. Matric. pens. from TRINITY, Easter, 1588; Scholar, 1590; B.A. 1592–3; M.A. 1596. Ord. deacon (Lichfield) Apr. 10, 1597; priest (Peterb.) Sept. 15, 1611. R. of South Lessingham, Lincs., 1613. Admon. (Lincoln) 1616.

GREEN, WILLIAM. Matric. sizar from St John's, Michs. 1588.

GRENE, WILLIAM. Matric. pens. from Trinity, c. 1592.

GREEN, WILLIAM. Matric. sizar from Christ's, Dec. 1621; B.A. 1624–5; M.A. from Magdalene, 1628; LL.D. 1636. Fellow of Magdalene; ejected, 1644. Town clerk of Newcastle. Doctor of the Arches. Chancellor of York. Will (P.C.C.) 1655.

GREENE, WILLIAM. Matric. pens. from Trinity, Easter, 1631.

GREEN, WILLIAM. M.A. 1634 (Incorp. from Oxford). S. of Richard, of Wyken, Warws., gent. Matric. from St John's, Oxford, June 30, 1626, age 15; B.A. from Oriel, 1629; M.A. from All Souls, 1633. 'Now living at Maldford (? Maidford), Northants.; aged c. 70; coelebs.' (*Vis. of Warws.*, 1682–3.)

GREENE, WILLIAM. Adm. pens. (age 15) at Caius, July 3, 1643. S. of George, Esq. B. at Langham, Norfolk. School, Norwich (Mr Lovering and Mr Gilbert). Matric. 1644. Re-adm. Fell.-Com. 1646. One of these names, of Burnham Market, Norfolk, gent., adm. at Gray's Inn, Nov. 6, 1647. (*Venn*, I. 350.)

GREEN, WILLIAM. Matric. sizar from St Catharine's, Lent, 1645–6. Of Huntingdonshire. B.A. 1648–9; M.A. 1652. Fellow, 1650; ejected, 1662 (? 1658). Afterwards preached in Cambs. Resided at Fenstanton. (*Calamy*, I. 208.)

GREENE, WILLIAM. Adm. pens. at Trinity, June 29, 1654. Of Yorkshire. Matric. 1654. Perhaps s. of Robert, of Thundercliffe Grange, Yorks.; adm. at the Inner Temple, 1655. Age c. 37 in 1674. Married Mary, dau. of Nicholas Stones, of Derbyshire, 1662. (Hunter, *Hallamshire*, 449.)

GREEN, WILLIAM. Adm. sizar (age 18) at St John's, Aug. 10, 1658. S. of William, of Swithland, Leics. B. there. School, Dort, Holland. Matric. 1659; B.A. 1662–3.

GREEN, WILLIAM. Adm. pens. (age 16) at Peterhouse, Aug. 24, 1668. Of Warwickshire. S. of William, of Coventry, gent. School, Coventry. Migrated to Oxford. Matric. from Trinity College, July 7, 1669, age 16; B.A. (Oxford) 1673; M.A. 1676. V. of Corley, Warws., 1681. R. of Foleshill, 1691. (*Al. Oxon.*)

GREEN, WILLIAM. Adm. sizar at Clare, May 22, 1673. Of Ipswich. Matric. 1673, as 'Greet'; B.A. 1676–7; M.A. 1680. Ord. deacon (Norwich) May, 1678; priest, Feb. 1680–1. R. of Chillesford, Suffolk, 1684. R. of Glemham, 1685. R. of Sweffling, 1696.

GREEN, WILLIAM. Adm. pens. at St Catharine's, Apr. 20, 1678. Of Suffolk.

GREEN, WILLIAM. Adm. pens. (age 18) at Caius, Apr. 1, 1687. S. of John, weaver, citizen, of Norwich. B. there. School, Norwich. Matric. 1687; Scholar, 1687–8. Migrated to Clare, Oct. 11, 1688. Probably adm. at Gray's Inn, July 10, 1688. Barrister, 1696. Bencher, 1720. (*Venn*, I. 482.)

GREEN, WILLIAM. Adm. pens. (age 18) at St John's, June 30, 1709. S. of William, Esq., of Thundercliffe Grange, near Rotherham, Yorks. B. there. School, Threshfield. Matric. 1709. Died Feb. 14, 1719–20. Brother of Henry (1719).

GREEN, WILLIAM. Adm. sizar at Jesus, May 31, 1720. Of Pentir, Carnarvon. Matric. 1720; Scholar; B.A. 1723–4; M.A. 1730.

GREEN, WILLIAM. Adm. sizar at Clare, Mar. 16, 1733–4. B. at Newark, Notts. Matric. 1735; B.A. 1737–8; M.A. 1741. Fellow, 1738–59. Ord. deacon (Lincoln) Sept. 24, 1738; priest (Norwich) June, 1740. R. of Hardingham, Norfolk, 1759–94. R. of Barnham Broom, 1790–4. Hebraist. Died Oct. 31, 1794. (*D.N.B.*)

GREEN, WILLIAM. Adm. sizar at Queens', Apr. 16, 1735. Of Northamptonshire. Matric. 1736.

GREEN, WILLIAM. Adm. pens. at Clare, June 29, 1749. S. of Richard. B. at Chichester. Bapt. at All Saints', Chichester, Dec. 14, 1731. Probably scholar from Charterhouse.

GREEN, WILLIAM. Adm. pens. (age 18) at Trinity, June 30, 1750. S. of Smithson, of Thundercliffe Grange, Yorks. School, Chesterfield, Derbs. (Mr Burroughs). Matric. 1750; Scholar, 1751; M.B. 1755. Sold Thundercliffe Grange, and lived near York. Described as M.D. Died 1816. (M. H. Peacock.)

GREEN, ——. M.A. 1477–8. (? William, of Queens'.)

GREEN, ——. B.A. 1481–2. Of Corpus Christi.

GREEN, ——. B.A. 1487–8; M.A. 1490.

GREEN, ——. Of St Gregory Hostel. B.A. 1490–1; M.A. 1493.

GREEN, ——. M.A. 1497–8.

GREENACARS, EDWARD. Matric. pens. from St John's, Michs. 1564.

GRENEAKERS, RICHARD. Matric. Fell.-Com. from Pembroke, Easter, 1563. 3rd s. of Richard, of Worston, Lancs. Adm. at the Inner Temple, 1564. Keeper of Clitheroe Castle, 1585. Married Frances, dau. of John Lambert, of Calton. (J. Parker.)

GRENACRE, RICHARD. Matric. pens. from Trinity, Michs. 1579. S. of John. B. 1562. Succeeded his grandfather, Richard, at Worston. Died Oct. 26, 1618. Nephew of the above.

GRENEAKERS, ——. B.A. 1528–9. One Robert Grenakers preb. of Chichester, 1564–73.

GREENAWAY, *see* **GREENWAY.**

GREENBURY, ARTHUR. Adm. sizar (age 19) at St John's, Apr. 27, 1709. S. of Arthur, deceased. B. at York. School, York (Mr Thomlinson). Matric. 1709; B.A. 1712–3. Ord. deacon (York) Nov. 1713; priest (London) May 23, 1714.

GREENBURY, TOBIAS. Matric. sizar from Trinity, c. 1598; B.A. 1602–3; M.A. 1606. Ord. deacon (Peterb.) June 15; priest, Sept. 21, 1606. V. of Lambourn, Berks., 1611; apparently retained his living during the Commonwealth. Buried at Lambourn, Oct. 14, 1664. (Jo. Footman, *Lambourn Church*.)

GREENELL, *see* **GREENHILL.**

GREENFIELD, *see also* **GRINFIELD.**

GREENFIELD, CHRISTOPHER. Matric. pens. from Trinity Hall, Apr. 1699.

GREENFIELD, DANIEL. Adm. pens. at St Catharine's, 1668. Matric. 1670; B.A. 1672–3. Signed for deacon's orders (London) June 13, 1674. C. of Ivychurch, Kent.

GREENFIELD, JOHN. Adm. sizar at Emmanuel, June 9, 1669. Of Yorkshire. B.A. 1672. Ord. deacon (York) Sept. 1672; priest, Dec. 1672. V. of Bramham, Yorks., 1682–5. V. of Tadcaster, 1684–1703. Died 1703.

GREENFEILD, JOHN. Adm. sizar at Jesus, Mar. 7, 1698–9. Of Nottinghamshire. Matric. 1701; B.A. 1702–3.

GREENFIELD, RICHARD. Adm. pens. (age 16) at Pembroke, Sept. 15, 1624. S. of Thomas. B. at Chichester. One of these names adm. at the Inner Temple, from Clements' Inn, 1628.

GRENFORD, ROGER. Adm. at King's Hall, 1411. Fellow; resigned, 1428. Received tonsure (Ely) June 6, 1412. Perhaps R. of Eastling, Kent, in 1460.

GREENGRAS, ABRAHAM. Matric. sizar from St John's, Easter, 1579; B.A. from St Catharine's, 1584–5.

GRENEGRES, JOHN. Matric. sizar from Trinity Hall, Easter, 1550.

GREENHALGH, *see* also **GREENOUGH.**

GREENAUGH, ARTHUR. B.A. from St Catharine's, 1597–8.

GREENHALGH, HENRY. Adm. pens. (age 17) at St John's, Oct. 19, 1688. S. of Thomas, Esq. B. at Chester. School, Stockport. Matric. 1688; B.A. 1692–3.

GREENHALGH, HENRY. Adm. pens. (age 19) at St John's, July 6, 1722. S. of Richard, ironmonger, of Middlesex. B. in London. S , Bury, Lancs. (Mr Rider). Matric. 1723; B.A. 1726–7chool

GREENHALGH, JAMES. Adm. pens. (age 18) at St John's, May 22, 1671. S. of John (1627), clerk, of Knowsley, Lancs. B. there. School, Manchester. Matric. 1671; B.A. 1674–5; M.A. 1678. Ord. deacon (Ely) Sept. 23, 1676. R. of Hooton Roberts, Yorks., 1692–1714. (*Vis. of Lancs.*, 1664.)

GREENEHALGH, JOHN. Adm. pens. (age 15) at Sidney, May 26, 1627. S. of John, Esq. B. at Brandleson, Bury, Lancs. School, Manchester. Matric. 1627; B.A. 1630–1; M.A. from St John's, 1634; B.D. 1641; D.D. 1672. Fellow of St John's, 1632–44, ejected. Junior Proctor, 1639–40. Ord. priest (Peterb.) Mar. 1, 1639–40. V. of Bury, Lancs., 1661–74. Chaplain to the Earl of Derby. Died Oct. 27, 1674. Father of James (1671). (Mumford, *Manch. Gr. School*; *Vis. of Lancs.*, 1664.)

GREENHALGHE, JOHN. Adm. sizar (age 17) at St John's, June 2, 1632. S. of John, farmer, of Bury, Lancs. B. there. School, Bolton (Mr Duckworth). Matric. 1632; B.A. 1635–6. Head Master of Chesham School. Antiquary. Died Dec. 1674. (C. H. Cooper.)

GREENHALH, JOHN. Adm. Fell.-Com. (age 16) at St John's, May 12, 1684. S. of Thomas, Esq. B. at Bury, Lancs. School, Bolton, Lancs. (Mr Coap). Matric. 1684.

GRENHALGH or GREENOUGH, OLIVER. Matric. sizar from Christ's, Mar. 1588–9. B. at Horwick, Deane, Lancs., c. 1569. B.A. 1592–3; M.A. 1596; B.D. 1603. Fellow, 1599–1608. Ord. priest (Colchester) Sept. 23, 1599. R. of Navenby, Lincs., 1607–42. Married, at All Saints', Cambridge, Mar. 3, 1607–8, Elizabeth Boordman, widow. Admon. (Leicester) 1642. (*Peile*, I. 196.)

GREENOUGH, OLIVER. B.A. from Christ's, 1604–5.

GREENHALGH, ORLANDO. Adm. pens. (age 14) at St John's, Oct. 19, 1688. S. of Thomas, Esq. B. at Chester. School, Stockport. Matric. 1688. Adm. at Gray's Inn, July 2, 1692, as 3rd s. of Thomas, of Brandalsome, Lancs., deceased. Brother of Henry (1688).

GREENHALGH, RICHARD. Adm. pens. (age 14) at SIDNEY, Dec. 9, 1624. Matric. Fell.-Com. S. of John, Esq. B. at Wimsley, Cheshire. School, Manchester (Mr Clayton). Matric. 1624.

GREENHALGH, THOMAS. Adm. sizar at JESUS, Dec. 17, 1663. Of Cheshire. Matric. 1664; B.A. 1667-8. Perhaps R. of Cooling, Kent, 1673-4.

GREENHALL, JOHN. Adm. at KING'S (age 17) a scholar from Eton, Aug. 27, 1576. Of Fletton, Hunts. Matric. 1576. Left, 1579. 'Took to the road, and was hanged and dissected' (*Blackwood*, Feb. 1865.)

GREENHALL, W. Matric. pens. from PETERHOUSE, Easter, 1579. One William Greenhall was R. of Oakley, Suffolk, 1628-35; and schoolmaster at Lavenham. Buried there Oct. 2, 1635. Will (Bury) 1635.

GREENHAM, BALTHAZAR. Matric. sizar from ST JOHN'S, 1626.

GREENHAM, JOHN. Adm. sizar at EMMANUEL, Apr. 16, 1599; B.A. from Christ's, 1603-4. 'A principal attorney [at Dublin] and said to be an honest man.' (Letter of Bishop Bedell to Dr Ward, Master of Sidney, 1630.)

GREENHAM, RICHARD. Matric. sizar from PEMBROKE, Easter, 1559; B.A. 1563-4; M.A. 1567. Fellow, *c.* 1566. R. of Dry Drayton, Cambs., 1570-91. Preacher at Christ Church, Newgate Street, *c.* 1590. Author, theological. Died 1594. (*Cooper*, II. 143; *D.N.B.*)

GREENHILL, CLEAVE. M.A. from SIDNEY, 1722. S. of Joseph, of Chesham, Bucks., gent. Matric. from Trinity College, Oxford, Nov. 30, 1713, age 18; B.A. (Oxford) 1718. V. of Abbots Langley, Herts., 1725-47. Died Jan. 24, 1747. Brother of Joseph (1717). (*Al. Oxon.*)

GREENELL, JOHN. Licensed to practise medicine, 1615.

GREENHILL or GREENELL, JOHN. Adm. pens. at TRINITY, Oct. 13, 1663. Matric. 1663; Scholar, 1668; B.A. 1668-9; M.A. 1672. Signed for deacon's orders (London) Sept. 23, 1671. V. of Sawston, Cambs., 1674. Probably V. of Wilbarston, Northants., 1686. V. of Weston-by-Welland, 1686-91. Died 1691. (H. I. Longden; T. P. Dorman.)

GREENHILL, JOHN. Adm. pens. (age 16) at TRINITY, May 5, 1707. S. of Richard, of Canterbury. School, Canterbury. Matric. 1707; Scholar, 1708. Adm. at the Middle Temple, Nov. 27, 1706.

GREENHILL, JOSEPH. Adm. sizar (age 16) at SIDNEY, June 17, 1715. Only s. of Newton, gent., clerk of the Ballast Office; of Hoxton, Middlesex. B. at Finsbury, London. School, Bunhill Fields, London (Mr Barron).

GREENHILL, JOSEPH. M.A. from ST CATHARINE'S, 1717. S. of Joseph, of Chesham, Bucks. Matric. from Trinity College, Oxford, Nov. 8, 1708, age 17; B.A. (Oxford) 1712. R. of Howell, Lincs., 1713. V. of Heckington, 1717. Admon. (P.C.C.) 1741. Father of Joseph (1740) and brother of Cleave (1722). (*Al. Oxon.*)

GREENHILL, JOSEPH. Adm. scholar (age 19) at SIDNEY, Feb. 12, 1722-3. S. of William, Esq. B. at Abbots Langley, Herts. School, Westminster. Matric. 1723; B.A. 1726-7; M.A. 1728 (*Com. Reg.*; adm. 1731). Ord. deacon (London) Sept. 24, 1727. R. of East Horsley, Surrey, 1727. R. of East Clandon, 1732. Author, theological. Died Mar. 10, 1788, aged 84. Will, P.C.C. (*Manning and Bray*, III. 34; *D.N.B.*)

GREENHILL, JOSEPH. Adm. pens. (age 19) at SIDNEY, July 11, 1740. S. of Joseph (1717), R. of Howell, Lincs. B. there. Schools, Appleby, Leics. (Mr Martin) and Oakham. Matric. 1742.

GREENHILL, STEPHEN. Adm. pens. at JESUS, July 7, 1724. Matric. 1724; B.A. 1727-8. Ord. deacon (Lincoln) Mar. 2, 1728-9. R. of Sevington, Kent; and P.C. of Egerton, 1731-77. Married, at Little Chart, Sept. 8, 1736, Mary Elvy. Died at Ashford, July 13, 1777. (*G. Mag.*; H. G. Harrison.)

GRENEHILL, WILLIAM. Matric. sizar from TRINITY, Easter, 1572. S. of John, of Harrow-on-the-Hill, Middlesex. School, Harrow. Migrated to Caius, Feb. 16, 1574-5, age 22. B.A. 1575-6; M.A. 1579. Ord. deacon (Ely) Dec. 21, 1576. Doubtless a governor of Harrow School, in 1586; V. of Brixworth, 1589-1621. Buried there Sept. 2, 1621. Father of the next. (*Venn*, I. 80.)

GREENHILL, WILLIAM. Adm. sizar at SIDNEY, Feb. 4, 1613-4. S. of William (above), V. of Brixworth, Northants. Bapt. there, July 1, 1598. Matric. 1614; B.A. 1617-8; M.A. 1621; D.D. 1636. Ord. deacon (Peterb.) Sept. 29, 1621; priest, Aug. 18, 1622. V. of Brixworth, 1621. R. of Peakirk, 1637-52. Married Mary, dau. of Francis Dee, Bishop of Peterborough. Buried at Peakirk, May 1, 1652. Will (P.C.C.) 1652. (H. I. Longden; T. P. Dorman.)

GREENHILL, WILLIAM. Adm. pens. (age 17) at CAIUS, June 26, 1615. S. of John, husbandman, of Harrow-on-the-Hill. School, Harlington, Middlesex (Mr Durant). Matric. 1615; Scholar, 1617-22; B.A. 1618-9; M.A. 1622. Probably appointed to Stepney, Middlesex, in 1653. Governor of Harrow School, 1653-7.

GREENEHILL, WILLIAM. Adm. pens. (age 18) at SIDNEY, June 20, 1647. S. and h. of William, of Blackfriars, gent. B. in London. School, Harrow. Matric. 1647. Adm. at Gray's Inn, Mar. 30, 1649-50.

GREENHILL, ——. Adm. Fell.-Com. at EMMANUEL, Easter, 1626.

GREENING, JOHN. Adm. sizar (age 18) at CHRIST'S, June 25, 1668. S. of Thomas. B. at Basford, Notts. School, Basford (private; Mr Harris).

GREENING, THOMAS. Adm. sizar (age 17) at SIDNEY, Apr. 1, 1637. S. of Thomas, yeoman. B. at Newton, Gloucs. Schools, Gloucester (Mr Jo. Langley) and Bristol (Mr Chr. Prior). Matric. 1637; B.A. 1640-1. Ord. deacon (Lincoln) June 5, 1642. One of these names minister of Rushden, Northants., 1648-50-.

GREENLING, ANTHONY. Matric. pens. from EMMANUEL, Easter, 1637. Of Stradbrook, Suffolk. Died Oct. 24, 1653, aged 33. M.I. at Stradbrook. (Le Neve, *Mon.*, IV. 25.)

GREENLING, RALPH. Adm. sizar at EMMANUEL, May 23, 1622. Matric. 1622; B.A. 1625-6, as 'Girling'; M.A. 1629.

GREENNOPP, JOHN. Adm. sizar (age 20) at ST JOHN'S, May 13, 1680. S. of William, husbandman. B. at Leece, near Dalton, Lancs. School, Urswick (Mr Inman).

GREENOUGH, *see also* GREENHALGH.

GREENOUGH, ROBERT. Matric. sizar from CHRIST'S, Lent, 1597-8; B.A. 1602-3; M.A. 1606. Ord. deacon (Lincoln) Dec. 21, 1606. One of these names V. of West Waltham, Essex, 1614-9. (*Peile*, I. 231.)

GREENOUGH, WILLIAM. Matric. pens. from CURIAT'S, *c.* 1592-3. B. at Rochdale, Lancs., *c.* 1576. B.A. 1595-6; M.A. 1600. Ord. deacon (Lincoln) May 25, 1599; priest (Colchester) Oct. 4, 1603. V. of Cople, Beds., 1607-8. R. of Aspley Guise, 1629-32. Licensed to marry Agnes, dau. of Geoffrey Moore, of Colmworth, May 12, 1613, at St Alban's, Wood St, London. At that time of London. Buried at Aspley Guise, 1632.

GREENOWES, ROBERT. Adm. pens. (age 16) at CHRIST'S, June 20, 1639. S. of Richard. B. in London. School, Bishop's Stortford (Mr Leigh). Matric. 1639.

GREENSHIELDS, JAMES. M.A. 1711 (Incorp. from Glasgow). Also Incorp. at Balliol College, Oxford, 1711.

GREENSIDE, JOHN. Adm. sizar (age 17) at PETERHOUSE, Feb. 18, 1733-4. Of Yorkshire. School, Kirk Levington, Yorks. Scholar, 1733; Matric. 1734; B.A. 1737-8; M.A. 1741. Ord. deacon (Lincoln) Dec. 24, 1738; priest (*Litt. dim.* from York) May, 1740. V. of Middlesbrough, Yorks., 1739-69. V. of Marton-in-Cleveland, 1749-98. R. of Crathorne, 1768-81. Died at Marton, 1798.

GRENESIDE, THOMAS. Matric. pens. from PETERHOUSE, Michs. 1576.

GREENSMITH, EDWARD. Adm. sizar at EMMANUEL, June 25, 1670. Of Nottinghamshire. Matric. 1671; B.A. 1673-4. Ord. deacon (York) Dec. 1674; priest, Sept. 1679. Perhaps R. of Rockland, Norfolk, 1684.

GRENESTED, ——. A friar. Degree, 1457-8.

GREENSTREET, PETER. Adm. pens. (age 18) at ST JOHN'S, Apr. 5, 1662. S. of Peter, of Ospringe, Kent. B. there. School, Faversham (Mr Rider). Matric. 1662; B.A. 1665-6. Adm. at Gray's Inn, May 19, 1664. Died Apr. 5, 1677, aged 33. Buried at Ospringe. Father of the next. (*Hasted*, II. 793.)

GREENSTREET, PETER. Adm. pens. at EMMANUEL, Aug. 3, 1691. Of Kent. S. and h. of Peter (above), of Ospringe, Kent, Esq., deceased. Adm. at the Inner Temple, Nov. 28, 1691. Married, at Maidstone, May 2, 1717, Anne Dering, of Thornham. Of Sellinge.

GREENSWORTH, HENRY. Adm. pens. (age 15) at ST JOHN'S, May 9, 1653. S. of James, of Haydock-in-Winwick, Lancs. B. there. School, Winwick (Mr Ra. Gost). Matric. 1653; B.A. 1656-7.

GRENWALL or GRENWELL, NICHOLAS. B.A. 1540-1; M.A. 1544. Fellow of CHRIST'S, 1541-7. Fellow of Trinity, 1547. Doubtless V. of Lenham, Kent, 1553, as 'Greenway.' (*Peile*, I. 26.)

GREENWHALL or GRENEWALD, RICHARD. Matric. pens. from KING'S, Easter, 1569; B.A. 1570-1. Probably lay clerk at King's.

GREENAWAY, DANIEL. Adm. sizar (age 17) at CAIUS, Apr. 21, 1711. S. of Joseph, grocer, of Norwich. B. there. School, Norwich (Mr Hoadley and Mr Pate). Matric. 1710-1; B.A. 1714-5; M.A. 1718. Fellow, 1716-30. Ord. deacon (London) June 16, 1717. R. of Denver, Norfolk, 1728-34. Buried there Jan. 11, 1734-5. M.I. Will, Norwich. (*Venn*, I. 525.)

GREENWAY, GEORGE. Adm. pens. (age 16) at TRINITY, Mar. 26, 1714. S. of Henry, of London. School, Merchant Taylors', London. Matric. 1714. Migrated to Corpus, 1716. B.A. 1717–8; M.A. 1721. Perhaps R. of Chilcombe, Dorset, 1722–45; and also lecturer of Berwick-on-Tweed, 1728–45. Buried there Dec. 9, 1745, as Greenaway. (*Hutchins*, II. 740.)

GREENWAY, GEORGE. Adm. sizar (age 18) at SIDNEY, July 2, 1734. S. of John, ironmonger. B. at Tiverton, Devon. School, Tiverton. Matric. 1735; B.A. 1737–8. Brother of Thomas (1726).

GREENWAY, JOHN. M.A. from KING'S, 1730. S. of William, of Butlers Marston, Warws. Matric. from Queen's College, Oxford, May 13, 1703, age 16; B.A. (Oxford) 1706–7. Ord. deacon (Peterb.) Sept. 21, 1707; priest, Sept. 1710. (*Al. Oxon.*)

GRENEWAYE, SAMUEL. Matric. sizar from CHRIST'S, June, 1577; B.A. from Magdalene, 1579–80. Ord. deacon and priest (Norwich) May, 1583. R. of Gimingham, Norfolk, 1592–1623. (*Peile*, I. 142.)

GREENWAY, THEOPHILUS. Adm. at CORPUS CHRISTI, 1601, from Trinity. Of Norfolk. B.A. 1605–6; M.A. 1609. Ord. deacon (Norwich) May 22; priest, Sept. 25, 1608, age 23. C. of Forncett, Norfolk. Doubtless R. of Framlingham Earl; and father of Timothy (1640). (*Masters*.)

GREENWAY, THOMAS. Adm. sizar at ST CATHARINE'S, 1705, from St John's College, Oxford, where he had matric. Dec. 7, 1702. S. of Robert, of Hinxill, Kent. B. June 10, 1687. School, Merchant Taylors'. (*Al. Oxon.*)

GREENWAY, THOMAS. Adm. sizar (age 18) at SIDNEY, Oct. 26, 1726. S. of John, ironmonger. B. at Tiverton, Devon. School, Tiverton. Matric. 1726; B.A. 1730–1; M.A. 1734. Ord. deacon (Lincoln) Mar. 14, 1730–1. Brother of George (1734).

GREENAWAY, TIMOTHY. Adm. pens. (age 17) at CAIUS, July 3, 1640, as 'Theophilus.' S. of Theophilus, R. of Framlingham Earl, Norfolk. B. at Framlingham Pigot. Bapt. Sept. 6, 1621 (with a twin brother Theophilus). School, Norwich (Mr Lovering). Matric. 1640; Scholar, 1642–4; B.A. 1643–4; M.A. 1647.

GREENWELL, JOHN. Matric. pens. from CHRIST'S, Nov. 1566; B.A. 1569–70. R. of Edmundbyers, Durham, 1575–1609. Died 1609.

GREENWELL, STEPHEN, *see* GRENNELL.

GREENWELL, WILLIAM. Matric. pens. from EMMANUEL, Michs. 1601; B.A. 1604–5.

GREENWELL, WILLIAM. Adm. Fell.-Com. at JESUS, June 29, 1625. Of London. S. of Robert (of Newcastle-on-Tyne), citizen, and merchant taylor, of London. B. Apr. 1610. School, Merchant Taylors'. Matric. 1625.

GREENWELL, WILLIAM. Adm. pens. at EMMANUEL, Apr. 29, 1640. Matric. 1640.

GREENWOOD, CHRISTOPHER. B.A. 1530–1.

GREENWOOD, CHRISTOPHER. Matric. sizar from CORPUS CHRISTI, Easter, 1577; B.A. 1578–9; M.A. 1582. V. of Shottesham, Norfolk, 1603. Died 1607–8. Father of Devoreux (1605). (*Misc. Gen. et Her.*, 2nd S., V. 254.)

GREENEWOOD, CHRISTOPHER. Matric. sizar from ST JOHN'S, Michs. 1601.

GREENWOOD, DANIEL. B.A. 1632 (Incorp. from Oxford). S. of Richard, of Sowerby, Yorks., pleb. Matric. from Lincoln College, Oxford, Apr. 30, 1624, age 19; B.A. (Oxford) 1626–7; M.A. 1629; B.D. 1640–1; D.D. 1649. Fellow of Brasenose. Principal, 1648–60. Vice-Chancellor, 1650–2. R. of Chastleton, Oxon., 1640–62. Died at Steeple Aston, Jan. 29, 1673–4. Will, P.C.C. (*Al. Oxon.*)

GREENWOOD, DANIEL. Adm. pens. (age 17) at CHRIST'S, June 23, 1645. S. of John. B. at Sowerby, Yorks. School, Halifax (Mr Wood). Matric. 1645; B.A. (Oxford) 1648; M.A. 1651. Fellow of Brasenose, 1648. R. of Steeple Aston, Oxon., 1653. Died at Woodstock, Oct. 14, 1679. Buried at Steeple Aston. M.I. there. (*Peile*, I. 497; Le Neve, *Mon.*, IV. 198.)

GRENEWOOD, DEVOREUX. Adm. at ST CATHARINE'S, Apr. 24, 1605. S. of Christopher (1577), V. of Shottesham. School, Hedenham (Mr Sebly). Migrated to Emmanuel, Nov. 1, 1606. Matric. 1606. Migrated to Caius, May 25, 1609, age 19. B.A. 1610–1. Buried at All Saints', Norwich, Oct. 21, 1611. (*Venn*, I. 202.)

GREENWOOD, EDWARD. Matric. pens. from ST JOHN'S, Easter, 1559; B.A. 1562–3; M.A. 1566. Fellow, 1564. Ord. deacon (Norwich) May 23, 1567; priest, Mar. 31, 1574. V. of Wood Dalling, Norfolk, 1573–80. R. of Gt Dunham, 1580. Died there 1591.

GREENWOOD, FRANCIS. Adm. sizar at JESUS, Mar. 16, 1737–8. S. of William, R. of Darfield, Yorks., deceased. Matric. 1738; B.A. 1741–2; M.A. 1745. Ord. deacon (Lincoln) Feb. 27, 1742–3; priest (Norwich) May, 1746, age 26. C. of Cockfield, Suffolk. V. of Higham Ferrers, Northants., 1752–61. V. of St Peter's, Irthlingborough, 1752–61. Buried there June 20, 1761.

GREENWOOD, HENRY. Matric. pens. from ST JOHN'S, Michs. 1564. B. at Sudbury, Yorks. (*sic*). Scholar; B.A. 1567–8; M.A. 1571. Fellow, 1570. Ord. deacon (London) Dec. 20, 1571, age 26; priest (Norwich) Oct. 22, 1572. Master of Felsted School, 1576–96. V. of Hatfield Peveril, Essex, 1596–1605. V. of Gt Sampford, 1601–34. R. of Little Leighs, 1609.

GREENWOOD, HENRY. Matric. sizar from PEMBROKE, Michs. 1598; B.A. 1601–2; M.A. 1605. Ord. deacon (Peterb.) Oct. 12, 1602.

GREENWOOD, HENRY. Adm. pens. (age 16) at PEMBROKE, July 3, 1624. S. of Henry (? above), of Hempstead, Essex. Matric. 1625; B.A. 1627–8; M.A. 1631. Minister at Willingale Doe, Essex, 1647. Probably V. of South Benfleet, 1660–3. Died Feb. 1662–3.

GREENWOOD, HENRY. Adm. pens. at TRINITY, June 4, 1645. Of Somerset. Scholar from Westminster, 1645. Matric. 1646; B.A. 1648–9; M.A. 1651. Fellow, 1649–55.

GREENWOOD, JAMES. B.A. (? 1589–90) according to *Lincoln Register*. B. at Aylsham, Norfolk, 1571. Ord. deacon (Norwich) Sept. 29, 1601, age 29, as 'late student of CORPUS CHRISTI'; priest (Colchester) Feb. 14, 1601–2. V. of Scawby, Lincs., 1604–24. Perhaps V. of Haslingfield, Cambs., 1618–39.

GRENEWOOD, JAMES. Matric. sizar from TRINITY, 1637; B.A. 1637. One of these names minister at Old Hutton, Westmorland, 1654–7.

GREENWOOD, JAMES. Adm. sizar (age 16) at JESUS, May 7, 1677. S. of Samuel, of Leeds, Yorks. Matric. 1677; B.A. 1680–1; M.A. 1685. Ord. deacon (York) Sept. 1681; priest, June, 1696. C. of Dunnington, Yorks., 1681–4. P.C. of Snaith, 1696–7. Buried there June 18, 1697. Will, York. Pedigree in Whitaker's *Leeds*.

GREENWOOD, JOHN. B.A. 1542–3; M.A. 1547. Fellow of ST JOHN'S, 1547. Perhaps V. of Orford, Suffolk, *c.* 1544.

GREENWOOD, JOHN. Matric. pens. from ST JOHN'S, Easter, 1559. Of Yorkshire. B.A. from St Catharine's, 1561–2; M.A. 1565. Fellow of St Catharine's, 1565. Ord. priest (Ely) Mar. 23, 1566–7. Master of Brentwood School, Essex, 1570–1604. Author, *Syntaxis et Prosodia*, 1590. Died 1609. Will, P.C.C. (*Cooper*, II. 98; *D.N.B.*)

GREENWOOD, JOHN. Matric. sizar from ST CATHARINE'S, Lent, 1564–5.

GREENWOOD, JOHN. Matric. sizar from CORPUS CHRISTI, Lent, 1577–8; B.A. 1580–1. Ord. deacon (London); priest (Lincoln) Aug. 8, 1582. R. of Wyham, Lincs., 1582–3. Perhaps R. of Rackheath, Norfolk, 1583–7. Afterwards a non-conforming minister in London. Associate of Henry Barrow; imprisoned and executed, with him, for sedition, Apr. 6, 1593. (*Cooper*, II. 153; *D.N.B.*)

GREENWOOD, JOHN. Matric. pens. from ST JOHN'S, Michs. 1581; B.A. 1584–5; M.A. 1588. Ord. deacon and priest (Peterb.) Mar. 25, 1587. Perhaps R. of Ingestre, Staffs., 1597. R. of Standon, 1604–44.

GRENEWOOD, JOHN. Matric. sizar from TRINITY, Michs. 1589; B.A. 1593–4; M.A. 1597. Doubtless ord. priest (Norwich) 1614. R. of Brampton, Norfolk, 1620; ejected, *c.* 1645. (Walker, *Sufferings*, where he is called D.D.)

GRENEWOOD, JOHN. Matric. sizar from ST CATHARINE'S, Easter, 1612.

GREENWOOD, JOHN. Matric. sizar from ST JOHN'S, Michs. 1622.

GREENWOOD, JOHN. Adm. sizar at TRINITY, June 11, 1675. Matric. 1675; B.A. 1678–9; M.A. 1694. Incorp. at Oxford, 1694. Preb. of Lichfield, 1704 16.

GREENWOOD, JOSEPH. Adm. pens. at EMMANUEL, June 15, 1665, as 'Josiah.' Of Derbyshire. Matric. 1665.

GREENWOOD, MILES. Adm. sizar (age 17) at SIDNEY, July 2, 1645. S. of Rowland (1616), V. of Wimbish, Essex. B. at Aldenham, Herts. Bapt. Feb. 15, 1626–7. School, Eton. Matric. 1645. Migrated to St John's, Oct. 31, 1645.

GREENWOOD, PAUL. Adm. sizar (age 16) at ST JOHN'S, June 23, 1645. S. of Ambrose, merchant, of Skircoate, Halifax, Yorks. School, Halifax (Mr Wood). Matric. 1645, as 'William'; B.A. 1648–9; M.A. 1652. Doubtless Head Master of Halifax School, 1652–64. V. of Illingworth, 1658–68. V. of Dewsbury, 1666–8. Died Feb. 1, 1668.

GREENWOOD, RICHARD. Matric. sizar from CORPUS CHRISTI, Michs. 1586. Of Norfolk. B.A. 1590–1; M.A. 1594. Will of one of these names (P.C.C.) 1614; of Playden, Sussex, clerk.

GREENWOOD, ROBERT. Matric. sizar from St John's, Michs. 1570; B.A. 1574-5. Ord. deacon and priest, Feb. 21, 1574-5. R. of Heydon, Norfolk, 1576. Died 1601.

GREENWOOD, ROWLAND. Matric. pens. from St John's, Easter, 1616. B. in Westmorland. School, Sedbergh. B.A. 1619-20; M.A. 1623; B.D. 1638. Incorp. at Oxford, 1620. Ord. deacon (Peterb.) Mar. 8; priest, Mar. 9, 1622-3. Head Master of Aldenham School, Herts., 1623-34. V. of Wimbish, Essex, 1634-57. Doubtless Head Master of Pocklington School, 1657-60. V. of Bubwith, Yorks., 1660-3. Father of Miles (1645).

GREENWOOD, THOMAS. B.A. 1510-1 (Incorp. from Oxford); M.A. 1511; B.D. 1527-8; D.D. 1532. Fellow of St John's. Doubtless Carthusian (*Harl. MS.*, 7030, 53) who suffered for denying the Royal supremacy. Died in prison, June, 1537. He was also called Green and Greenway. (Camm, *Martyrs*, I. 20; *Cooper*, I. 64.)

GREENWOOD, THOMAS. Of Clare; 'Professor.' (? D.D.) Will proved (V.C.C.) 1541. Can he be the above?

GREENWOOD, THOMAS. M.A. 1543 (Incorp. from Paris). Presumably the man of these names; pens. of Clare, M.A.; whose will was proved (V.C.C.) June 7, 1546.

GREENWOOD, THOMAS. Matric. sizar from Corpus Christi, Michs. 1581; B.A. 1584-5; M.A. 1588. R. of Castor, Norfolk, 1592-1600. R. of Clipsham, Rutland, 1601-5. R. of Beccles, Suffolk, 1608. Died Aug. 1638. (*Misc. Gen. et Her.*, 2nd S., V. 253.)

GREENWOOD, THOMAS. Adm. pens. at Trinity, May 25, 1650, a scholar from Westminster. Of Somerset. B.A. 1653-4. Probably of Gregory Stoke, Somerset; adm. at the Inner Temple, 1656.

GREENWOOD, THOMAS. Adm. sizar at Jesus, Nov. 17, 1690. Of Yorkshire. Matric. 1691; B.A. 1694-5. Doubtless V. of Lightcliffe, Yorks., 1703-6. V. of Luddenden, 1706-13. V. of Heptonstall, 1712-44. V. of Wragby.

GRENEWOOD, WILLIAM. Matric. pens. from St John's, Easter, 1570; B.A. 1573-4.

GREENWOOD, WILLIAM. Matric. pens. from Corpus Christi, Easter, 1605. Adm. as Greenward. Of Norfolk.

GREENWOOD, WILLIAM. D.D. 1728 (*Com. Reg.*). S. of John, of Newport, Salop, clerk. Matric. from Trinity College, Oxford, Oct. 21, 1703, age 15; B.A. (Oxford) 1707; M.A. 1710. R. of St Nicholas, Warwick, 1713. V. of St Mary, Warwick, 1724. R. of Solihull, 1739-69. Author. Died Jan. 5, 1769. Will, P.C.C. (*Al. Oxon.*; *G. Mag.*)

GREET, AMBROSE. Adm. sizar at Sidney, Apr. 20, 1604; B.A. 1607-8.

GRET, JOHN. Matric. from Trinity, Michs. 1559. Admon. (P.C.C.) 1570, of John Grete, of Southwark, Surrey, clerk.

GREET, THOMAS. Adm. pens. at Trinity, May 31, 1733. S. of John. B. in Jamaica. School, Westminster. Matric. 1733; Scholar, 1734; B.A. 1736-7; M.A. 1740. Fellow, 1739. Usher of Westminster School, 1740. Ord. deacon (Lincoln) Sept. 19, 1742; priest (Norwich) Apr. 1745. V. of Marsworth, Bucks., 1762-77. R. of St James', Garlickhithe, London, 1766-76. V. of Eaton Bray, Beds. Died May, 1777. Will (P.C.C.); of Chelsea, Middlesex. (*Al. Westmon.*, 308.)

GREGELL, JOHN. B.A. 1509-10; M.A. 1513. V. of Barking, Essex, 1524-59. Will (P.C.C.) 1559.

GREGG or GRIGGE, CHRISTOPHER. Adm. sizar at Caius, Apr. 28, 1620. S. of Hamlet, V. of Sotby, Lincs. School, Horncastle (Mr Hughes). Matric. 1620; B.A. 1623-4; M.A. 1627. Ord. deacon (Peterb.) May 23; priest, May 24, 1624. R. of Biscathorpe, Lincs., 1626-31. Admon., Lincoln. Brother of the next. (*Venn*, I. 249.)

GREGG, EDMUND. Adm. sizar (age 17) at Caius, Apr. 28, 1620. S. of Hamlet, minister, V. of Sotby, Lincs. School, Horncastle (Mr Hughes). Matric. 1620; B.A. 1623-4; M.A. 1627. Ord. deacon (Peterb.) May 23; priest, May 24, 1624. R. of Hatton, Lincs., 1635. Brother of Christopher (above).

GREGGE, ROBERT. A scholar of Queens', 1530-2.

GREGGE, WALTER. A priest. B.A. 1492-3; B.Can.L. 1498-9. R. of Barton, Norfolk, 1515-8.

GREGS, THOMAS. Adm. sizar at Peterhouse, Nov. 15, 1591. Pens. 1592.

GREGGS, WHICHCOTT. Adm. sizar (age 18) at Christ's, June 30, 1698. S. of William, of Spanby, Lincs., gent. B. at Pickworth, Lincs. School, Lincoln. Matric. 1698. Migrated to Pembroke, July 1, 1703. B.A. 1705-6. (*Peile*, II. 143.)

GREGOR, FRANCIS. Matric. Fell.-Com. from King's, Easter, 1705. Probably s. of John, of Trewarthenic, Cornwall, Esq. Author, legal. Father of the next. (*Bibliotheca Cornubiensis*.)

GREGOR, JOHN RATCLIFF. Adm. pens. at Peterhouse, Nov. 6, 1736. Of Cornwall. S. and h. of Francis (above), of Trewarthenic, Esq. Adm. at the Inner Temple, May 14, 1734.

GREGORY, ABRAHAM. M.A. 1665 (*Lit. Reg.*); D.D. 1677 (*Lit. Reg.*). S. of Francis, of Oxford. B. at Old Woodstock, Oxon., Apr. 23, 1643. Matric. from Oriel College, Oxford, Dec. 7, 1660, age 17. Usher of the College School, Gloucester, 1661. V. of Sandhurst, Gloucs., 1664-76. R. of Cowley, 1670-3. Preb. of Gloucester, 1671. Preb. of Lincoln, 1672-90. V. of Churcham, 1673-90. R. of St Mary-de-Crypt, Gloucester, 1675-9. Precentor of Llandaff, 1679-90. R. of Cromhall, 1679-90. Died July 29, 1690. Buried in Gloucester Cathedral. M.I. (*Al. Oxon.*; F. S. Hockaday.)

GREGORY, ANTHONY. Adm. sizar at Peterhouse, 1600. B.A. 1603-4. R. of Petrockstowe, Devon, 1614, sequestered. R. of Charles. Will (Exeter) 1663; of Anthony Gregory, of Petrockstowe. Father of Samuel (1625) and John (1625). (Walker, *Sufferings*.)

GREGORY, ANTHONY. Adm. sizar (age 18) at St John's, July 4, 1668. S. of Samuel, deceased, of Barnstaple, Devon. B. there. School, Barnstaple. Matric. 1668; B.A. 1671-2; M.A. 1675. Ord. deacon (London) Dec. 1672; priest (Ely) May 30, 1675. C. of Therfield, Herts. V. of Sutton, Isle of Ely, 1676-1735. R. of Mepal, Cambs., 1686-1733. Died May 6, 1735, aged 85. Father of the next. (*G. Mag.*)

GREGORY, ANTHONY. Adm. sizar (age 16) at St John's, May 22, 1706. S. of Anthon (above), R. of Mepal, Cambs. School, Peterborough (Mr Warring). Matric. 1706. Ord. deacon (Ely) Sept. 21, 1712. One of these names, of Halwell, Devon, clerk. Admon. (Exeter) 1758.

GREGORY, CHRISTOPHER. B.D. 1579 (Incorp. from Oxford). Of Warwickshire. B.A. from Magdalen College, Oxford, 1568; M.A. 1571-2; B.D. 1579. Fellow of Magdalen, 1567-85. Preb. of York, 1577. Preb. of Southwell, 1580-1600. R. of Cromwell, Notts., 1581. R. of Kirkby Misperton, Yorks., 1582. R. of Scrayingham, 1587. Archdeacon of West Riding, Yorks., 1597-1600. Died 1600. (*Al. Oxon.*)

GREGORY, CLEMENT. Matric. sizar from Trinity, c. 1591; B.A. 1593-4; M.A. 1597. Ord. deacon (Peterb.) Sept. 5, 1595. R. of Rushton All Saints', Northants., 1603-15.

GREGORY, CLEMENT. Adm. at Clare, July 15, 1634. Matric. 1634-5; B.A. 1638-9; M.A. 1642. Ord. deacon (Lincoln) July 15, 1643; priest (Peterb.) May, 1648. R. of Thornton, Bucks., 1651. R. of Leckhampstead, 1660. Buried there July 10, 1669.

GREGORY, EDWARD. Matric. sizar from Trinity, Michs. 1619; B.A. 1622-3; M.A. from Trinity Hall, 1626. Ord. deacon (Peterb.) June 4; priest, June 5, 1626.

GREGORY, EDWARD. Adm. at Corpus Christi, 1723. S. of George (1688). Bapt. at St Mary's, Nottingham, May 10, 1706. Matric. 1724; B.A. 1727-8; M.A. 1731. Ord. deacon (Ely) Dec. 21, 1729; priest (York) Aug. 16, 1730. P.C. of St Margaret Crosgate, Durham, 1732-53. Minor canon of Durham. Preb. of Southwell, 1733-53. R. of Ashwell, Rutland, 1743-59. R. of Widmerpool, Notts. Died July 2, 1759. (*L. Mag.*; H. M. Wood; *Lincs. Pedigrees*, 429; H. I. Longden.)

GREGORY, FRANCIS. Adm. pens. at Trinity, June 16, 1641. S. of Francis, of Woodstock, Oxon. Matric. 1642; Scholar from Westminster, 1642; B.A. 1644-5; M.A. 1648; D.D. (Oxford) 1661. Usher under Dr Busby at Westminster. Master of Woodstock School, Oxon., 1654. Head Master of Witney, Oxon. R. of Wick Rissington, Gloucs., 1670. R. of Hambledon, Bucks., 1671-1707. Author. Died June, 1707. Will, P.C.C. (*Al. Oxon.*; *D.N.B.*)

GREGORY, FRANCIS. Adm. Fell.-Com. at Christ's, Apr. 29, 1652. S. of John, gent., of Nottingham. Bapt. at St Mary's, Nov. 8, 1643 (*sic*). Married twice, but died without issue. Buried at St Mary's, Nottingham, Feb. 23, 1712-3. Brother of George (1655). (*Peile*, I. 547.)

GREGORY, GEORGE. Adm. pens. at Jesus, Apr. 28, 1620. Matric. 1620.

GREGORY, GEORGE. Adm. pens. (age 19) at St John's, May 9, 1655. S. of John, gent., of Nottingham. B. there. Bapt. at St Mary's, May 18, 1638. School, Nottingham (Mr Leeke). High Sheriff of Notts., 1666. Married Susanna, dau. of Sir Martin Lister, Knt., of Thorpe Arnold, Leics. Buried at St Mary's, Nottingham, July 10, 1688. Father of the next. Brother of Francis (1652). (J. T. Godfrey, *Notts.*)

GREGORY, GEORGE. Adm. pens. (age 18) at St John's, May 3, 1688. S. of George (above). B. at Nottingham. Bapt. at St Mary's, Feb. 2, 1669-70. School, Nottingham (Mr Cudworth). High Sheriff for Notts., 1694. M.P. for Nottingham, 1702-5, 1715-27; for Boroughbridge, 1727-46. Married Susanna, dau. of William Williams, of Rempstone Hall, Notts. Buried at St Mary's, Nottingham, Apr. 10, 1746. Father of Edward (1723) and William (1713). (J. T. Godfrey, *Notts.*)

GREGORY, JOHN. Matric. pens. from St John's, Easter, 1577. One of these names, of Hull, Yorks., adm. at Gray's Inn, June 12, 1581, from Barnard's Inn.

GREGORIE, JOHN. Adm. sizar (age 15) at CAIUS, June 26, 1625. S. of Anthony (1603–4), R. of Petrockstowe, Devon. School, Torrington (Mr Salisbury). Matric. 1625; Scholar, 1627–31; B.A. 1628–9; M.A. 1632. R. of Meeth, Devon, 1634. Married, at Huish, Feb. 2, 1641–2, Grace Cory. Admon. (Exeter) 1663; of Meeth. Brother of Samuel (1625). (*Venn*, I. 272.)

GREGORY, JOHN. Matric. pens. from PEMBROKE, Easter, 1629.

GREGORY, JOHN. Adm. sizar at TRINITY, May 25, 1646. Of Oxfordshire. Exhibitioner from Charterhouse. Matric. pens. 1646; Scholar, 1647; B.A. 1649–50; M.A. 1653. Fellow, 1650. Doubtless Master of the College School, Gloucester, 1660–73. R. of Hempstead, Gloucs., 1669–78. R. of Dursley, 1672–8. Archdeacon of Gloucester, 1672–8. Died Dec. 10, 1678. Buried at Hempstead. Will, Gloucester. (F. S. Hockaday.)

GREGORY, JOHN. Adm. sizar (age 16) at PEMBROKE, Apr. 19, 1664. S. of Edward, barber. B. at Bury St Edmunds. Matric. 1664–5; B.A. 1667–8; M.A. 1672. Incorp. at Oxford, 1672. Ord. deacon (Ely) Dec. 20, 1668. Perhaps R. of Hargrave, Suffolk, 1673–1727; and father of John (1705).

GREGORY, JOHN. Adm. pens. (age 16) at TRINITY, May 22, 1705. S. of John (? 1646), R. of Hargrave, Suffolk. School, Bury (Mr Randall). Matric. 1706.

GREGORY, JOHN. Adm. sizar (age 18) at PETERHOUSE, Apr. 24, 1728. Of Nottinghamshire. School, Risley, Derbs. Matric. 1728; Scholar, 1728; B.A. 1731–2; M.A. 1736. Ord. deacon (Lincoln) Sept. 24, 1732. Perhaps R. of Twyford, Norfolk, 1740–79.

GREGORY, OLIVER. Adm. pens. at EMMANUEL, May 21, 1670. Previously matric. from Trinity, Oxford, Apr. 2, 1669, age 19. S. of Oliver, of Battersea, Surrey, gent. Exhibitioner from Charterhouse. LL.B. from Trinity Hall, 1673. Adm. at Gray's Inn, July 7, 1674. Licensed, Jan. 4, 1683–4, of St Martin-in-the-Fields, age 30, to marry Mary Squibb, of Swinn, Dorset. (*Al. Carthus.*)

GREGORY, RICHARD. Matric. sizar from JESUS, Michs. 1615. Of Salop. Scholar, 1618; B.A. 1618–9. Perhaps R. of Upton Cressett, Salop, 1623. (But *see Al. Oxon.* for a contemporary.)

GREGORY, RICHARD. LL.B. from MAGDALENE, 1719. S. of John, of Arle, Cheltenham, Gloucs. Matric. from Balliol College, Oxford, Mar. 23, 1688–9, age 15; B.A. (Oxford) 1692. Ord. deacon (Gloucester) July 17, 1695; priest (Worcester) Sept. 20, 1696. R. of Broadway, Worcs., 1696. V. of Childs Wickham, Gloucs., 1700–18. R. of Willersey, 1701–18. R. of Dumbleton, 1718. Died 1718. (*Al. Oxon.*; F. S. Hockaday.)

GREGORY, ROBERT (1576), *see* SAYER.

GREGORIE, ROBERT. Adm. sizar at EMMANUEL, Mar. 26, 1589. Matric. 1589; B.A. 1592–3; M.A. 1596. R. of Westley Waterless, Cambs., 1599–1647. Buried there Aug. 13, 1647.

GREGORY, ROGER. Adm. Fell.-Com. at QUEENS', Mar. 2, 1608–9. B. in Suffolk. One of these names, s. of Roger, of Stockwith, Lincs., Esq., adm. at Gray's Inn, Feb. 6, 1610–1; age 18 in 1612. (*Vis. of Yorks.*)

GREGORIE, SAMUEL. Adm. pens. (age 17) at CAIUS, June 26, 1625. S. of Anthony (1603–4), R. of Petrockstowe, Devon. School, Torrington (Mr Salisbury). Matric. 1626; Scholar, 1626–32; B.A. 1628–9; M.A. 1632; B.D. 1660 (*Lit. Reg.*). R. of High Bray, Devon, 1633–63; and of Charles, 1660. Buried at High Bray, Nov. 26, 1663. Will (Exeter) 1664. Brother of John (1625). (*Venn*, I. 272.)

GREGORY, THOMAS. Matric. pens. from MAGDALENE, *c.* 1594; B.A. from St Catharine's, 1597–8.

GREGORY, THOMAS. Matric. sizar from TRINITY, Easter, 1614; B.A. 1617–8. Ord. deacon (Peterb.) Dec. 19; priest, Dec. 20, 1619.

GREGORY, THOMAS. Matric. pens. from CLARE, Easter, 1625; B.A. 1627–8; M.A. 1631. Perhaps R. of Saxelby, Leics., 1655; buried Sept. 4, 1656.

GREGORY, THOMAS. Adm. pens. at CLARE, May 21, 1656. Matric. 1656. One of these names, s. of Thomas, of Allerton, Hunts., gent., adm. at Oundle School, July 17, 1650, age 11. Perhaps V. of St Ippolyts, Herts., 1664–70. One of these names V. of Weston, Herts., 1665–8. Died 1670.

GREGORY, THOMAS. Adm. sizar at TRINITY, May 4, 1664. Matric. 1664; B.A. 1667–8. Ord. deacon (London) May 29; priest, May 30, 1681. One of these names R. of Wivenhoe, Essex, 1695–7. R. of Toddington, Beds., 1697–1713. (But *see* a contemporary in *Al. Oxon.*)

GREGORY, THOMAS. Adm. pens. (age 19) at CHRIST'S, July 4, 1706. S. of Love-is-God. B. at Stivichall, Warws. School, Coventry (Mr Greenway). Matric. 1706; Scholar, 1706–7. (*Peile*, II. 165.)

GREGORY, THOMAS. M.A. from KING'S, 1747. S. of Blagrave, of Banbury, Oxon., gent. B.A. from Trinity College, Oxford, 1737. Ord. priest (Norwich) Sept. 1740. V. of Hindolveston, Norfolk, 1740–1. V. of North Elmham, 1741–77. (*Al. Oxon.*)

GREGORY, THOMAS. M.A. from KING'S, 1751. S. of William, of Burlton, Salop. Matric. from Christ Church, Oxford, Apr. 30, 1734; B.A. (Oxford) 1737–8. (*Al. Oxon.*)

GREGORYE, W. Matric. pens. from MAGDALENE, Easter, 1585. Perhaps William, s. of William, of East Stockwith, Lincs.; adm. at Gray's Inn, July 3, 1587. Another 'William,' s. of Roger, of Stockwith; bapt. at Gainsborough, Nov. 16, 1568. Of Barnby-on-Dun, Yorks. Buried July 20, 1637. (*Lincs. Pedigrees*, 430.)

GREGORY, WILLIAM. M.A. 1617 (Incorp. from Oxford). Of Warwickshire. Matric. from Exeter College, Oxford, Oct. 16, 1607, age 16. B.A. (Oxford) 1611; M.A. 1615. Perhaps V. of All Saints', Bristol, 1618–9. R. of Chelvey, Somerset, 1619–67. (*Al. Oxon.*)

GREGORYE, WILLIAM. Matric. pens. from JESUS, Easter, 1618. One of these names, s. of Roger, of Mount St John, Yorks., adm. at Lincoln's Inn, Nov. 23, 1616.

GREGORY, WILLIAM. Adm. at CORPUS CHRISTI, 1713. Of Nottinghamshire. 1st s. of George (1688). Bapt. at St Mary's, Nottingham, Nov. 20, 1694. Matric. 1713–4. Adm. at the Middle Temple, May 2, 1715. Buried at Nottingham, Jan. 13, 1726–7. Brother of Edward (1723). (J. T. Godfrey, *Lenton*, 34.)

GREGORY, ——. B.Civ.L. 1500–1. Will (P.C.C.) 1549, of John Gregory, 'LL.B., priest, of Islington, Midds.,' formerly a brother of Mottenden Priory, Kent. (J. Ch. Smith.)

GREGORY, ——. B. and D.Can.L. 1511–2.

GREGSON or GRIGSON, EDWARD. B.A. 1489–90; B.D. 1501. Of Preston, Lancs. Original fellow of JESUS, 1498. Founded fellowships and scholarships at St John's, 1527. R. of Fladbury, Worcs. Will (P.C.C.) 1540. (*Cooper*, I. 61; A. Gray.)

GREGSON, HENRY. Adm. pens. (age 17) at CHRIST'S, Feb. 16, 1639–40. S. of Henry, escheator of Derbyshire (of Sherrow Hall, and Turnditch, Derbs.). Bapt. at Duffield, Derbs., Oct. 27, 1621. School, Repton (Mr Ward). Matric. 1640; B.A. 1643–4. Adm. at Magdalene, 1645–6. Living at Wapping in 1663. (*F.M.G.*)

GREGSON, JOHN. Adm. sizar (age 18) at ST JOHN'S, Nov. 7, 1691. S. of William, deceased. B. at Ormside, Westmorland. School, Sedbergh (Mr Wharton). Matric. 1691; B.A. 1695–6. Ord. priest (Lincoln) Sept. 20, 1696. C. of Frampton; and schoolmaster at Kirton-in-Holland, Lincs. V. of Kirton, 1702.

GREGSON, R. B.A. 1488–9; M.A. 1493. Fellow of QUEENS', 1494–7.

GREGSON, ROBERT. Adm. pens. at EMMANUEL, Nov. 7, 1719. S. of George, of Turnditch, Esq. Of Turnditch and Dronfield, Esq. Married Jane, dau. of Joseph Rogers, of Dronfield. (F.*M*.G.)

GREGSON, THOMAS. Adm. pens. at QUEENS', June 21, 1644. Previously at Oxford. Of London. Matric. 1644; B.A. 1644–5. One of these names presented to Ponton, Lincs., 1648.

GRENDON, *see* GRINDON.

GRENNELL or GRENWELL, STEPHEN. Matric. pens. from ST JOHN'S, Lent, 1582–3; B.A. from Corpus Christi, 1585–6; M.A. 1589.

GRENT, HENRY. M.A. 1626 (Incorp. from Oxford). Of Middlesex, gent. Matric. from New College, Oct. 31, 1617, age 20; B.A. (Oxford) 1621; M.A. 1624–5; B.D. 1642. R. of Church Lawford, Warws., 1635. (*Al. Oxon.*)

GRENT, THOMAS. M.D. 1628 (Incorp. from Oxford). Of Sussex, gent. Matric. from New College, Nov. 29, 1605, age 21; B.A. (Oxford) 1609; M.A. 1612–3; M.B. and M.D. 1619. F.R.C.P., 1623. Physician to St Thomas's Hospital. Died Dec. 11, 1649. (*Al. Oxon.*; *Munk*, I. 184.)

GRENT, WILLIAM. M.A. from KING'S, 1620–1 (Incorp. from Oxford). S. of John, of Deptford, Kent. B.A. from Hart Hall, Oxford, 1620–1. Adm. at the Middle Temple, July 3, 1617. (*Al. Oxon.*)

GRENVILLE, BERNARD. Matric. Fell.-Com. from KING'S, Michs. 1584. Previously matric. from University College, Oxford, 1574, age 15. Of Cornwall. Doubtless s. and h. of Sir Richard, of the 'Revenge.' M.P. for Bodmin, 1597–8. Knighted, 1608. Buried at Kilkhampton, Cornwall, June 26, 1636. Brother of John (1584).

GRENVILLE or GRANVILLE, BEVILL. Adm. as nobleman (age 12) at TRINITY, Aug. 21, 1677. S. of Bernard. B. in St Martin's, Westminster. Matric. 1677; M.A. 1679. Served in the army in Flanders. M.P. for Fowey, 1685–7, 1695–1700; for Lostwithiel, 1690–5. Knighted at Hounslow Heath, May 28, 1686. Governor of Pendennis Castle, Cornwall, 1696–1703. Appointed Governor of Barbados, 1702–6. Major-General, 1704. Died on his passage home, Sept. 15, 1706. Brother of George (1677). (D.*N.B.*)

GRENVILLE, CHRISTOPHER. Adm. scholar at TRINITY HALL, Jan. 16, 1698-9. Of Preston, Lancs. Probably s. of Sir Christopher.

GRENVILE, DENNIS. M.A. 1667 (Incorp. from Oxford). S. of Sir Bevill, of Kilkhampton, Cornwall, Knt. Bapt. Feb. 26, 1637-8. Matric. from Exeter College, Aug. 6, 1658; M.A. (Oxford) 1660; D.D. 1670-1. Ord. deacon (Lincoln) Jan. 31, 1660-1. Fellow of Eton College, 1662. Archdeacon, 1662-91; and Canon of Durham, 1662-84. R. of Kilkhampton, 1662-84. R. of Easington, 1662-91; and Elwick, 1664-7. R. of Sedgfield, Durham, 1668. Dean of Durham, 1684-91. Deprived of his preferments, as non-juror, 1691. Married Anne, dau. of Bishop Cosin, at Auckland, Dec. 16, 1662. Died in Paris, Apr. 7, 1703. Buried in the churchyard of the Holy Innocents, Paris. (*D.N.B.*; *Al. Oxon.*; A. B. Beaven; H. M. Wood.)

GRENVILLE, GEORGE, afterwards Baron LANSDOWNE. Adm. as nobleman (age 11) at TRINITY, Aug. 21, 1677. S. of Bernard (brother of John, Earl of Bath). B. in St Martin's, Westminster. Matric. 1677; M.A. 1679. M.P. for Fowey, 1702-10; for Cornwall, 1710-1. Secretary-at-war, 1710-2. Created a peer with the title of Baron Lansdowne, of Bideford, Devon, 1711. Privy-councillor, 1712; and comptroller of the household, 1712-3. Treasurer of the household, 1713. Imprisoned in the Tower on suspicion of Jacobitism, 1715-7. Created a duke by the titular King, James III, in 1721. Retired to Paris, 1722; lived there for ten years. Poet and dramatist. Died in London, Jan. 30, 1734-5. Buried at St Clement Danes. Brother of Bevill (1677). (*D.N.B.*; *G.E.C.*)

GRENVILLE, JOHN. Matric. Fell.-Com. from KING'S, Michs. 1584. Doubtless 2nd s. of Sir Richard. Killed in the Indies while serving under Sir Francis Drake. Brother of Bernard (1584). (J. Ch. Smith.)

GRESBY, GEORGE. B.Civ.L. 1540-1. V. of Gazeley, Suffolk, 1552-60. Will (Bury) 1560.

GRESHAM, EDMUND. Adm. Fell.-Com. (age 17) at CAIUS, Jan. 16, 1614-5. S. of Sir Richard, Knt., of Bury St Edmunds. Schools, Saxham, Suffolk (Mr Ward) and Wymondham, Norfolk (Mr Eston). Buried in St Luke's Chapel, Norwich, 1649. Will, Norwich. (*Misc. Gen. et Her.*, N.S., IV. 271; *Venn*, I. 228.)

GRESSAM, EDWARD. Matric. sizar from TRINITY, Easter, 1584.

GRESHAM, EDWARD. Matric. pens. from JESUS, c. 1592.

GRESHAM, EDWARD. Matric. pens. from JESUS, Easter, 1594.

GRESHAM, JAMES. Matric. pens. from ST JOHN'S, Easter, 1544. S. of Sir John, of Titsey, Surrey. B. July 18, 1526. B.A. 1545-6. Original fellow of Trinity, 1546 (doubtful if he accepted nomination). Perhaps adm. at the Inner Temple, 1549; of London. Died before 1552, *s.p.* (*Misc. Gen. et Her.*, IV. 270.)

GRESHAM, MARMADUKE. Matric. Fell.-Com. from KING'S, Michs. 1645. S. of Sir Edward, of Limpsfield and Titsey, Surrey, Knt. Bapt. at Betchworth, Jan. 24, 1627. Of Limpsfield, Surrey. Created Bart., July 31, 1660. M.P. for East Grinstead, 1660; for Bletchingley, 1685-7. Married Alice, dau. of Richard Corbet, Bishop of Norwich. Died at Gresham College, London, Apr. 14, 1696. Buried at Titsey. (*G.E.C.*)

GRESHAM, PERROT. Matric. sizar from TRINITY, Easter, 1606; Scholar, 1608; B.A. 1609-10; M.A. 1613. Chaplain, 1616-21. Ord. deacon (Peterb.) Sept. 20; priest, Sept. 27, 1615. Perhaps s. of Thomas, and Jane Parratt his wife. (Marriage licence, Oct. 27, 1579.) Will proved (V.C.C.) 1630.

GRESSUM, RICHARD. Matric. Fell.-Com. from ST JOHN'S, Michs. 1582. S. of Edward, of Thorpe Market, Norfolk. B. 1565. Adm. at the Inner Temple, 1584. Married Ann, dau. of Thomas Crofts, of Saxham Parva, Suffolk. Died in Norwich, 1627.

GRESHAM, THOMAS. Educated at GONVILLE HALL. Resident pens. for a year from Oct. 1530. S. of Sir Richard, Lord Mayor of London. Of Norfolk. Banker in London. Financial agent for the King at Antwerp, 1551; and later for Queen Elizabeth. Intimate friend of Sir William Cecil. Knighted, 1559. Established, at Osterley, Middlesex, the first English paper mills, 1565. Founder of the Royal Exchange, London. Repeatedly entertained the Queen. Died Nov. 21, 1579. Buried in Gt St Helen's, London. Will (P.C.C.) 1579. Left estates for the foundation of the Gresham lectures. (*Cooper*, I. 414; *D.N.B.*; *Vis. of London*, 1568; *Vis. of Norfolk*.)

GRESHAM, THOMAS. Matric. Fell.-Com. from PEMBROKE, 1633. Previously matric. from Queen's College, Oxford, Nov. 9, 1632, age 17. S. of Edward, of Brockham, Surrey. Died in the Fleet. Buried at St Faith's, London, Jan. 6, 1654-5. (*Al. Oxon.*)

GRESHAM, WILLIAM. Adm. pens. at QUEENS', Apr. 3, 1716. Of Middlesex. Matric. 1716.

GRESLEY, GEORGE. Resident student at JESUS, 1535-6.

GRESLEY, HENRY. M.A. 1651 (Incorp. from Oxford). S. of John, of Shrewsbury. School, Westminster. Matric. from Christ Church, Sept. 1, 1634, age 17; B.A. (Oxford) 1638; M.A. 1641. R. of Severn Stoke, Worcester, 1661-78. Preb. of Worcester, 1672-78. Translated Balsac's *Prince and Senault's Christian Man*. Died June 8, 1678.

GRESLEY, HENRY. Adm. sizar at TRINITY HALL, Apr. 29, 1749. *See Al. Oxon.* for a contemporary.

GRESLEY, JAMES. Adm. pens. at EMMANUEL, Apr. 19, 1734. S. of Thomas, of Nether Seale, Leics., Esq. Bapt. there, Aug. 13, 1715. Matric. 1734; Scholar; B.A. 1737-8. Ord. deacon (Lincoln) Sept. 20, 1741; priest, May 29, 1743. Assistant Master in the Free School, Appleby Magna, Leics., 1738. Died Oct. 23, 1745. Buried at Appleby. M.I. there. Will (Leicester) 1747. (*Nichols*, IV. 437.)

GRESWELL, ——. B.A. 1460-1; M.A. 1464. Fellow of CLARE, 1461.

GRESWOLD, BOURNE. Adm. pens. (age 16) at TRINITY, June 28, 1693. S. of Henry (next), R. of Solihull, Warws. B. there. School, Solihull. Matric. 1693. Adm. at Lincoln's Inn, July 4, 1695, as 'Bovine.' Brother of Marshall (1693) and Humphrey (1689).

GRESWOLD, HENRY. Adm. pens. at TRINITY, June 30, 1645. Of Worcester. 2nd s. of Humphrey, of Gt Yardley, Warws., gent., and Elizabeth Bourne. Matric. 1645; Scholar, 1646; B.A. 1648-9; M.A. 1652. Fellow, 1649. Adm. at Gray's Inn, May 19, 1656. V. of Gainford, Durham, till 1700. R. of Solihull, Warws., 1660-1700. Preb. of Ripon, 1660-87. Preb. of Lichfield, 1662-6. Precentor, 1666-1700. Sub-dean of Ripon, 1681-1700. Married Anne, dau. of Samuel Marshall, clerk. Died Oct. 6, 1700. Buried at Solihull. Father of Humphrey (1689), Marshall (1693) and Bourne (1693). (Le Neve, *Mon.*, II. 21; H. M. Wood.)

GRESWOLD, HUMPHREY. Adm. pens. (age 17) at TRINITY, Sept. 9, 1689. S. of Henry (above), R. of Solihull, Warws. School, Eton. Adm. at Lincoln's Inn, May 30, 1691. Built Malvern Hall, Solihull. Died *s.p.*, 1701. One of these names adm. at Leyden, Sept. 17, 1696.

GRESWOLD or GRISWOLD, JOHN. Matric. sizar from QUEENS', Michs. 1650. Of Warwickshire. B.A. 1654-5; M.A. 1658. R. of Stow Maries, Essex, 1662-70. Admon. (Commis. C. Essex) 1670.

GRESWOLD, MARSHALL. Adm. pens. (age 17) at TRINITY, June 28, 1693. S. of Henry (1645), R. of Solihull, Warws. B. there. School, Solihull. Matric. 1693; Scholar, 1695; B.A. 1696-7; M.A. 1700. Fellow, 1699. Ord. deacon (Ely) Sept. 22, 1706; priest, Mar. 9, 1706-7. R. of Beckingham, Lincs., 1721. Inherited Malvern Hall from his brother Humphrey. Died Feb. 8, 1728. M.I. at Yardley. Brother of Bourn (1693) and Humphrey (1689).

GRESWOULD, RICHARD. Adm. pens. at TRINITY, Mar. 19, 1654-5. Of Worcestershire. S. of Humphrey, of Yardley, Worcs. Matric. 1656, as Gressald; Scholar, 1657; B.A. 1658-9; M.A. 1662. Fellow, 1661. Adm. at Gray's Inn, May 19, 1656. Will proved (V.C.C.) 1664.

GRETFORD, HENRY DE. 'King's scholar' at Cambridge, 1319-33.

GRETFORD, RALPH DE. 'King's scholar' at Cambridge, 1319-27.

GRETHAM, ROBERT. B.Can.L. 1455-6; D.Can.L. 1480-1. Perhaps R. of St Dionis Backchurch, London, 1464-89. Called 'B.D.'

GRETTYNG, ——. B.A. 1506.

GRETTON, CHARLES. Adm. pens. (age 16) at TRINITY, Feb. 23, 1731. S. of Philips (1694), of Springfield, Essex. Educated at home. Scholar, 1732; Matric. 1732-3; B.A. 1735-6; M.A. 1739. Brother of Mark (1734).

GRETTON, GEORGE. Adm. sizar at ST JOHN'S, Jan. 21, 1674-5. S. of Anthony, deceased, of Boylstone, Derbs. B. there. School, Ashby. Matric. 1675; B.A. 1678-9; M.A. 1682. Ord. priest (York) Sept. 1681. R. of Seale, Leics., 1693-1705. R. of Stretton-en-le-Field, Derbs., 1705-50. V. of Marston-on-Dove, for 64 years. Father of the next. (*Nichols*, III. 999.)

GRETTON, GEORGE. Adm. sizar (age 18) at ST JOHN'S, Feb. 13, 1706-7. S. of George, clerk (above). B. at Marston, near Tutbury, Derbs. School, Appleby (Mr Wait). Matric. 1707; B.A. 1710-1; M.A. 1715. V. of Longford, Derbs., 1722-32. V. of Dalbury, 1731. Died 1732. Father of the next.

GRETTON, GEORGE. Adm. sizar at JESUS, Dec. 1, 1740. S. of George (above), deceased, V. of Longford, Derbs. Matric. 1740; Rustat scholar; B.A. 1744-5; M.A. 1748. Ord. deacon (Lincoln) Dec. 21, 1746; priest (Norwich, *Litt. dim.* from Lichfield) Mar. 1747-8. R. of Blore, Staffs., 1752-86. Died 1786. (A. Gray.)

GRETTON, JOHN. Matric. sizar at TRINITY, 1637; Scholar, 1641; B.A. 1641-2; M.A. 1645. Ord. deacon and priest (Lincoln) Mar. 18, 1645-6.

GRETTON, MARK. Adm. pens. (age 17) at PEMBROKE, Sept. 28, 1734. Of Rossing, Essex. S. of Phillips (next), D.D., R. of Springfield, Essex. Matric. 1735; B.A. 1738-9; M.A. 1742. Fellow of Peterhouse, 1742. R. of Roding, Essex. V. of Good Easter. Died Feb. 7, 1762. Brother of Charles (1731). (*G. Mag.*)

GRETTON, PHILLIPS. Adm. pens. (age 16) at TRINITY, Apr. 19, 1694. S. of Charles. B. in Fleet Street, London. School, St Paul's. Matric. 1695; Scholar, 1697; B.A. 1697-8; M.A. 1701; D.D. 1732. Fellow, 1700. Ord. deacon (Lincoln) Apr. 12, 1702; priest, Oct. 11, 1702. R. of Springfield Richards, Essex, 1703-46. R. of Springfield Bosvile, 1708-46. Author. Died Feb. 1745-6. Will (P.C.C.) 1746. Father of Charles (1731) and Mark (above). (Morant, *Essex*.)

GRETTON, ROGER. Scholar of MAGDALENE, Michs. 1604; B.A. 1605-6.

GREVE, THOMAS. Matric. pens. from ST JOHN'S, Easter, 1575.

GREVILLE, FULKE. Matric. Fell.-Com. from JESUS, Easter, 1568. S. of Sir Fulke, of Beauchamp Court, Warws. B. there. School, Shrewsbury. Created M.A. (Oxford) 1588. Adm. at the Middle Temple, Feb. 11, 1580; and at Gray's Inn, 1588. Intimate with Philip Sidney; came to Court with him, and became a favourite of Elizabeth. Accompanied Sidney to Heidelberg, 1577. Secretary for the Principality of Wales, 1583-1628. A member of Gabriel Harvey's 'Areopagus.' Entertained Giordano Bruno. 'Treasurer of the Wars,' and the Navy, 1598. K.B., 1603. Chancellor of the Exchequer, 1614-21. M.P. for Warws., 1620-1. Created Baron Brooke, 1621. Gentleman of the bedchamber. Granted Warwick Castle and Knowle Park by James I. A generous patron of poets. Friend of Spenser. Founded a lectureship in History in the University. His works include a *Life of Sidney*. Stabbed by his servant, and died of the wound, Sept. 30, 1628. (*Vis. of Warws.*, 1682; Cooper, *Ann.*, III. 209; *D.N.B.*; A. B. Beaven.)

GREVELL, JOHN. Matric. pens. from ST JOHN'S, Easter, 1545. (The entry is repeated; possibly there were two of the name.)

GREVILLE, ROBERT. M.A. 1629. 2nd Baron Brooke, of Beauchamp Court, Warws. S. of Fulke. B. 1607. Adopted by his cousin Fulke (1568) whom he succeeded in the barony of Brooke. M.P. for Warwick, 1628. A member of the Company for the plantation of Providence and Henrietta Islands, 1630. Commissioner for the Treaty of Ripon, 1640. Lord-Lieutenant of Militia for the counties of Warwick and Stafford. Speaker of the House of Lords, 1642. Served under Essex in the Midlands. Author. Killed while directing the attack on Lichfield, Mar. 2, 1642-3. (*D.N.B.*; *G.E.C.*)

GREVELL, ——. Adm. at CORPUS CHRISTI, 1584.

GREW, JONATHAN. Adm. sizar (age 17) at PEMBROKE, June 27, 1646. S. of Jonathan, of Warwickshire. B. at Atherstone, 1626. Matric. 1646; B.A. 1649-50; M.A. 1655. R. of Framlingham, Suffolk. Tutor in the family of Lady Hales, first at Coventry and afterwards at Caldecote, Warws. Kept a school at Newington Green; and finally became minister of the Presbyterian Congregation at St Albans. Buried in the Abbey Church there, 1711. (*Calamy*, II. 482; *D.N.B.*)

GREW, NEHEMIAH. Adm. pens. (age 17) at PEMBROKE, June 21, 1658. S. of Obadiah (D.D. Oxford), of Atherstone, Warws. Matric. 1659; B.A. 1661-2. Adm. at Leyden, July 6, 1671. Probably M.D. there, *c.* 1671. F.R.S., 1671. Secretary R.S., 1677-9. Honorary fellow R.C.P., 1680. Distinguished botanist. Author. Died Mar. 25, 1712. Admon. (P.C.C.) as of Christ Church, London. (*D.N.B.*; *Munk*, I. 406.)

GREYN, *see also* GRAIN.

GREYN, THOMAS. B.D. 1501-2; D.D. 1506-7. Possibly same as Thomas Coren. (*Gr. Bk*, Γ.)

GREYN or KREYN, ——. Fee for M.A. or higher degree, 1487-8. Probably Thomas, one of the earliest fellows of JESUS, 1499. A priest near Wisbech, in 1487; unable to pay subsidy ('alit matrem'). He may be the same as the last and the next. (A. Gray.)

GREYN, ——. Dr (Div. or L.) 1511-2.

GRICE or GRYSE, CHARLES. Matric. pens. at ST JOHN'S, Michs. 1548. Of Norfolk. B.A. 1551-2. Fellow, 1552. One of these names adm. at Gray's Inn, 1554. Perhaps s. of Anthony Le Grys, of Brockdish, Norfolk. Buried there Apr. 12, 1575. Will, P.C.C.

GRICE or GRYS, HENRY. Matric. pens. from TRINITY, Easter, 1574. S. of William; mentioned in will of Rose Beawe. A scholar from Westminster, 1574; B.A. 1577-8; M.A. 1581. Fellow, 1579. (P.C.C.) 1579.

GRISE or LE GRYS, JOHN. Matric. sizar from TRINITY, Easter, 1586. B. at Alphamstone, Essex. B.A. as 'William,' 1588-9. Ord. deacon (London) Apr. 15, 1590, age 24, as 'B.A.' of Trinity. C. of Alphamstone. Will (Norwich) 1631, of John Gris, of Wiston, Suffolk, clerk.

GRICE, NATHANIEL. Adm. pens. at EMMANUEL, June 10, 1637. Of London. Matric. 1637, as 'Nicholas.' Nicholas Grice, s. of Thomas, late of Littleton, Middlesex, clerk, deceased, was adm. at Lincoln's Inn, May 16, 1637. (*Vis. of London*, 1634.)

GRICE, NICHOLAS. Adm. pens. at ST CATHARINE'S, 1665-6. Previously matric. from St John's, Oxford, July 22, 1664, age 17. S. and h. of Henry, citizen and merchant taylor, of London, deceased. Adm. at Gray's Inn, May 13, 1664. (*Al. Oxon.*)

GRYCE or GRISE, ROBERT. Adm. Fell.-Com. at EMMANUEL, 1585. Matric. 1585. Perhaps s. of Charles (1548). Bapt. at Brockdish, June 12, 1571. (G. H. Holley.)

GRICE, THOMAS. Adm. sizar (age 18) at PETERHOUSE, June 17, 1674. Of St Clement's, London. School, Winchester. Scholar, 1674; Matric. 1675; B.A. 1677-8; M.A. 1689. Ord. deacon (London) May 26, 1678; priest, June 6, 1680. V. of Eye, Suffolk, 1681-90, deprived.

GRICE, WILLIAM. Adm. sizar (age 22) at PEMBROKE, Oct. 11, 1709. S. of Thomas, of Havering, Cumberland (? Essex). Matric. 1710; B.A. 1713-4; M.A. 1718. Ord. deacon (Ely) Sept. 23, 1722; priest, June 14, 1724.

GRIFFIE, THOMAS. Matric. pens. from MAGDALENE, Easter, 1640.

GRIFFIES, GEORGE. Adm. pens. (age 17) at ST JOHN'S, Oct. 8, 1733. S. of John, gent., of Iscoed. B. at Carmarthen. School, Westminster. Matric. 1733. Died in College. Buried at All Saints', Nov. 2, 1734. Brother of the next.

GRIFFIES, JOHN. Adm. pens. (age 18) at ST JOHN'S, May 5, 1740. S. of J., gent., of Iscoed. B. in Carmarthen. School, Charterhouse. Matric. 1740; B.A. 1743-4; M.A. 1758. Ord. deacon (Lincoln) June 9, 1745; priest (London) Dec. 23, 1750. R. of Chipstead, Surrey, 1753-1808. R. of Sanderstead, 1758-78, resigned. Died Apr. 1808. (*Scott-Mayor*, III. 505.)

GRIFFIN, BARTHOLOMEW. Matric. from TRINITY, Lent, 1593-4. Probably B.A. from St Mary Hall, Oxford, Feb. 5, 1598-9. Perhaps R. of Fenny Bentley, Derbs., till 1638. Buried there Jan. 12, 1638. (J. C. Cox, *Churches of Derbs.*, II. 469.)

GRIFFEN, BENJAMIN. Adm. at CORPUS CHRISTI, 1674. Of Norfolk. B. at Felmingham, 1655. Matric. 1674; B.A. 1677-8. Ord. deacon (Norwich) May, 1678; priest, June, 1679. V. of Buxton, Norfolk, 1681-91. Chaplain to the Earl of Yarmouth. Died May 8, 1691. Buried at Buxton, Norfolk. M.I. Father of Benjamin, actor and dramatist. (*D.N.B.*)

GRIFFIN, CADWALLADER. Matric. sizar from MAGDALENE, Easter, 1603; B.A. 1605-6, as Griffith. Buried at St Sepulchre's, Cambridge, June 14, 1607.

GRIFFIN, CONIERS. Adm. Fell.-Com. (age 17) at CHRIST'S, July 8, 1629. S. of Sir Edward, Knt. B. at Stoke Albany, Northants. School, Oundle. Matric. 1629. Probably died young. (*Peile*, I. 401.)

GRIFFIN, DAVID. Matric. sizar from MAGDALENE, Easter, 1571.

GRIFFIN, EDWARD. Matric. sizar from KING'S, Michs. 1588.

GRIFFIN, EDWARD. Adm. Fell.-Com. (age 16) at PETERHOUSE, Nov. 1656. Of Northampton. School, private. Perhaps s. of Sir Edward, Lord of Gumley, Northants. Created Baron Griffin of Braybrooke, 1688. Followed King James II to France and was outlawed. Taken prisoner, with others, off the coast of North Britain, by Sir George Byng, 1708. Committed to the Tower of London. Died there Nov. 10, 1710. (Burke, *Ext. Bart*; *Banks*, III. 329.)

GRIFFIN, EDWIN. Adm. pens. at ST CATHARINE'S, Oct. 14, 1663.

GRIFFIN, HUGH. B.Can.L. 1535; D.Can.L. 1556. Of PETERHOUSE, 1556. V. of Ashton-under-Lyne, 1557-64. Died 1564.

GRIFFIN, JAMES. Adm. Fell.-Com. at ST JOHN'S, Aug. 12, 1713. S. of James, Baron Griffin, of Braybrooke, Northants. Bapt. May 6, 1697, at Dingley. Matric. 1713. Died Apr. 22, 1718, aged 21. M.I. at Dallington. (*Baker*, I. 136; Banks, *Ext. Bart.*, III. 330.)

GRIFFIN, JOHN. Matric. Fell.-Com. from JESUS, Michs. 1544. Probably brother of Thomas (1544).

GRIFFIN, JOHN. Matric. sizar from QUEENS', Michs. 1566.

GRIFFIN or GRIFFITH, JOHN. Matric. sizar from JESUS, Lent, 1582-3; B.A. 1585-6; M.A. from Magdalene, 1589; B.D. 1596. Incorp. at Oxford, 1604. Probably V. of Dunston, Lincs., 1591-1611. R. of Icklingham All Saints', Suffolk, 1607-17.

GRIFFIN, JOHN. Adm. at King's (age 17) a scholar from Eton, Sept. 1, 1592. Of London. B.A. 1596–7; M.A. 1600. Fellow, 1595–1604, ejected. Ord. deacon (Lincoln) May 31, 1607; priest, Sept. 20, 1607. V. of Chrishall, Essex, 1609–57. Will (P.C.C.) 1657–8. (*Hist. of King's College*, 83; H. Smith.)

GRIFFIN, JOHN. Matric. pens. from St John's, Easter, 1613. Possibly B.A. 1624–5, as Griffith.

GRIFFIN, LANCELOT. Matric. sizar from Pembroke, Easter, 1605.

GRIFFIN or GRISTON, LANCELOT. Adm. sizar (age 18) at Caius, June 3, 1630. S. of Thomas, husbandman, of Merton, Norfolk. B. at Griston. Matric. 1631. One of these names executor and legatee of a namesake (? above), of Griston, clerk, 1633. (*Venn*, I. 295.)

GRIFFIN, LEWIS. Matric. pens. from Queens', Michs. 1652. Of Leicestershire. Master of Colchester Grammar School, 1664–71. Perhaps R. of Grinstead-by-Colchester, 1666–76. Died 1676. One of these names buried at St Benet's, Paul's Wharf, May 19, 1676; 'a minister and stranger who died suddenly.' (J. Ch. Smith.)

GRIFFIN, LEWIS. M.A. from Clare, 1700. S. of 'Royl' (? Roland), of Carlton, Notts., clerk. Matric. from Queen's College, Oxford, May 11, 1683, age 17; B.A. (Oxford) 1686–7. V. of Bisbrooke, Rutland, 1692–4. R. of Knipton, Leics., 1695–8. R. of Whitwell, Derbs., 1698–1711. R. of Bottesford, Leics., 1711–35. Died May 16, 1735. M.I. at Bottesford. Will, Leicester. (*Al. Oxon.*; *Nichols*, II. 99.)

GRIFFIN, MORRIS. Matric. sizar from Queens', Michs. 1550.

GRIFFIN, OLIVER. Adm. pens. at Peterhouse, July 6, 1616. B.A. 1616–7; M.A. 1620. Ord. priest (York) June, 1620. R. of Averham, Notts., 1624. Obtained mandate for fellowship, 1618.

GRIFFIN, PETER. B.A. from Jesus, 1611–2.

GRYFFYN, RICHARD. Matric. sizar from Queens', Michs. 1550.

GRIFFIN, RICHARD. Matric. sizar from Trinity Hall, Easter, 1639; B.A. 1642–3.

GRIFFIN, ROBERT. Matric. sizar from Queens', Easter, 1576. Of Wales.

GRIFFIN or GRIFFITH, ROBERT. Matric. pens. from St John's, c. 1597; B.A. 1601–2; M.A. 1605. Ord. deacon (Norwich) Dec. 21, 1603, age 24; priest, Sept. 29, 1604. R. of Langford, Norfolk, 1603. R. of Booton, 1611–33. R. of Hackford, 1620–33. Married, at Booton, Apr. 13, 1630, Mary Layer.

GRIFFIN, ROBERT. Matric. sizar from Pembroke, 1606; B.A. from Christ's, 1608–9.

GRIFFIN, ROBERT. Adm. pens. at Jesus, Jan. 12, 1620–1. Of Cambridgeshire. Matric. 1620–1; Scholar, 1622; B.A. 1624–5; M.A. 1628. Ord. deacon (Peterb.) Dec. 20; priest, Dec. 21, 1629.

GRYFFYN, THOMAS. Matric. Fell.-Com. from Jesus, Michs. 1544. Probably brother of John (1544).

GRIFFIN, THOMAS. Adm. at King's (age 17) a scholar from Eton, Aug. 24, 1594. Of London. Matric. c. 1594; B.A. 1598–9; M.A. 1602; B.D. 1608–9. Fellow, 1597–1621. Ord. deacon (Lincoln) Sept. 21, 1606; priest, Dec. 21, 1606. Perhaps R. of Aythorp Roothing, Essex, in 1610. R. of Stower Provost, Dorset, 1621–46. Died Sept. 1646.

GRIFFEN, THOMAS. Matric. sizar from Jesus, Easter, 1617. Of Essex. B.A. 1619–20; Scholar, 1620; M.A. 1623, as Griffith.

GRIFFIN, THOMAS. Matric. sizar from Trinity, Easter, 1636; B.A. 1638–9.

GRIFFIN or GRIFFITH, WILLIAM. Matric. pens. from Clare, Michs. 1567; B.A. from St Catharine's, 1570–1; M.A. from St John's, 1574; LL.D. 1581. Incorp. at Oxford, 1580. Ord. priest (Peterb.) Nov. 10, 1575. Adm. advocate, Feb. 2, 1582–3.

GRIFFIN, WILLIAM. Adm. pens. at Peterhouse, 1588–9. B.A. 1590–1.

GRIFFIN, WILLIAM. Matric. pens. from Peterhouse, Easter, 1618; Scholar, 1620; B.A. 1621–2; M.A. from St John's, 1625. Ord. deacon (Peterb.) Sept. 20; priest, Sept. 21, 1629. R. of Cold Overton, Leics., 1632.

GRYFFYN, ——. Matric. Fell.-Com. from Jesus, Easter, 1544.

GRIFFIN, ——. Adm. pens. at St Catharine's, 1637. Of Wales.

GRIFFENHOOF, NICHOLAS. Adm. pens. (age 20) at St John's, Oct. 31, 1737. S. of Abraham, druggist, of Essex. B. at Chelmsford. School, Chelmsford (Mr Tindall). Matric. 1737; B.A. 1741–2; M.A. 1749. Ord. deacon (London) Dec. 19, 1742; priest, May 29, 1743. V. of Mountnessing, Essex, 1748–58. R. of Woodham Mortimer, 1749–89. R. of Kelvedon Hatch, 1758–60. R. of Stow St Mary, 1761–89. Died July 7, 1789. Will, P.C.C. (*G. Mag.*)

GRIFFITH, ALBAN. B.A. from Queens', 1604–5; M.A. 1611. Of Co. Carnarvon. Matric. from St Mary Hall, Oxford, Oct. 16, 1601, age 16. R. of Letton, Hereford, 1610.

GRIFFITH, ALEXANDER. Matric. pens. from Emmanuel, Easter, 1689; M.D. 1690 (*Com. Reg.*).

GRIFFITHS, ANDREW. M.D. from Magdalene, 1686. S. of Roger, of Shrewsbury, gent. Matric. from Christ Church, Oxford, May 15, 1673, age 18; B.A. (Oxford) 1676–7; M.A. 1679. Adm. at Leyden, Mar. 29, 1680. Practised at Shrewsbury. Extra licentiate R.C.P., 1682. (*Munk*, I. 424; *Al. Oxon.*)

GRIFFITH, DANIEL. M.A. from Trinity, 1681. S. of Thomas, of Llangeler, Carmarthen, clerk. Matric. from Magdalen College, Oxford, May 21, 1672, age 16; B.A. (Oxford) 1675–6. R. of Staverton, Glouc., 1681–90. R. of Wistanstow, Salop, 1690. R. of West Felton, 1690. Will (P.C.C.) 1728. (*Al. Oxon.*)

GRIFFITHS, DANIEL. D.D. from Jesus, 1710. Perhaps same as last.

GRIFFITH, EDWARD. A student of Trinity. B. at Pen-y-Goes, St Asaph (? Montgoms.). Ord. priest (London) Sept. 29, 1568, age 24. One of these names V. of Staines, Middlesex, 1573–6.

GRIFFITHS or GRYFFES, EDWARD. Matric. sizar from Jesus, Michs. 1578; B.A. 1581–2.

GRIFFITH, EDWARD. B.A. from Clare, 1592–3; M.A. 1596. Perhaps R. of Abinger, Surrey, 1603–38.

GRIFFITH, EDWARD. Adm. pens. at Trinity, July 25, 1670. One of these names, of Standale, Sligo, Ireland, adm. at the Inner Temple, June 13, 1670. Another, of Henllion, Denbighs., adm. Aug. 10, 1670.

GRIFFITH, EDWARD. Adm. sizar at Queens', Mar. 10, 1685–6. Of Salop. Matric. 1686; B.A. 1689–90; M.A. 1693. Incorp. at Oxford, 1693. Ord. deacon (York) Sept. 1690. One of these names usher at Nottingham Grammar School; Head Master, 1691–1707. Perhaps R. of Hursley, Hants.; and preb. of Peterborough, 1723–4. Said by Willis to have died in London in 1724 and to have been 'buried obscurely in that City.' (*Northants. N. and Q.*, III. 183.)

GRIFFITH, EDWARD. Adm. scholar at Trinity Hall, Jan. 6, 1689–90. Matric. 1689; B.A. 1693–4.

GRIFFITH, EDWARD. Adm. pens. (age 19) at Peterhouse, Apr. 25, 1716. Of Nottinghamshire. School, Eton. Matric. 1716; Scholar, 1716.

GRIFFITHS, EDWARD. M.A. from Sidney, 1738. S. of Charles, of Langunider, Brecon, clerk. Matric. from Jesus College, Oxford, Mar. 30, 1726, age 19; B.A. (Oxford) 1729–30. Will (P.C.C.) 1786, of one of these names; of Monks Eleigh, Suffolk, clerk. (*Al. Oxon.*)

GRIFFITH, EMMANUEL. Adm. at St John's, 1629. S. of Thomas. B. at Aythorpe-Roothing, Essex. Matric. 1630. Migrated to Christ's, July 5, 1631, age 18. B.A. 1632–3; M.A. 1636.

GRIFFETH, GEORGE. Adm. sizar at Jesus, July 6, 1620. Received a testimonial for Holy Orders, 1624, after nine months' residence in Dublin University.

GRIFFITH, GEORGE. Adm. pens. at Emmanuel, Mar. 26, 1640. Of London. Matric. 1640; B.A. 1643–4; M.A. from Queens', 1647. Fellow of Queens', 1644. Head Master of the Perse School, Cambridge, 1652–86. Died Jan. 6, 1686, aged 64. (Le Neve, *Mon.*, v. 89.)

GRIFFITHS, GEORGE. M.A. from Emmanuel, 1645. Fellow of Trinity, 1645. Of Montgomeryshire. Matric. from Magdalen Hall, Oxford, Nov. 2, 1638, age 19; B.A. (Oxford) 1642. Independent minister. Preacher at the Charterhouse, 1648–61; silenced for nonconformity. Perhaps minister of St Bartholomew Exchange, London, 1654, May till December. (*Al. Oxon.*; *Calamy*, I. 107.)

GRIFFITHS, GRIFFITH. Adm. sizar (age 19) at St John's, July 3, 1738. S. of Maurice, gent. B. at Aberdaron, Bangor. School, Carnarvon (Mr Jones). Matric. 1738.

GRIFFITH, GUYON. Adm. pens. at Clare, July 5, 1746. S. of Moses, M.D., of Colchester. B. at Sible Hedingham, Essex. School, Felsted. Adm. student at Leyden, June 23, 1744 (*see* Moses). Matric. 1748; B.A. 1750–1; M.A. 1754; D.D. 1766. Fellow, 1752–63. Ord. deacon (Lincoln) June 9; priest, Aug. 24, 1754. R. of St Mary-at-Hill, London, 1763–84. Died Jan. 11, 1784, aged 54. Will, P.C.C. (*Al. Oxon.*; *G. Mag.*)

GRIFFITH, HENRY. Matric. sizar from Magdalene, Easter, 1575; B.A. 1577–8.

GRIFFITH, HENRY. Matric. Fell.-Com. from St John's, Easter, 1619. Perhaps s. and h. of Sir Henry, of Burton Agnes, Yorks.; age 9 in 1612. Created Bart., June 7, 1627. Sheriff of Staffs., 1633–4. Died before Oct. 1644. (*Vis. of Yorks.*; *G.E.C.*)

GRIFFITH, HENRY. Adm. pens. at EMMANUEL, June 20, 1633. Of Cheshire. Matric. 1633; B.A. 1636-7; M.A. 1640. Will (P.C.C.) 1655, of Henry Griffiths, of Bromhall, Cheshire, clerk.

GRIFFITH, JEREMIAH. Adm. sizar at CLARE, July 4, 1713. B. at Brecknock, Wales. Matric. 1713; B.A. 1717-8. Perhaps V. of Norton, Herts., 1766-82. Died May 4, 1782. Will (P.C.C.) 1784; of St Paul's, Shadwell, Middlesex, clerk.

GRIFFITH, JEROME. M.A. 1713 (Incorp. from Oxford). S. of Peter, of Disserth, Radnor. Matric. from Balliol College, Mar. 20, 1672-3, age 21; B.A. (Oxford) 1676; M.A. 1679. R. of Disserth, Co. Radnor, 1680. Preb. of St David's, 1680. V. of Llansantffraid, Radnor, 1691. (*Al. Oxon.*)

GRIFFITH, JOHN. Adm. sizar at PETERHOUSE, July 4, 1618. Of Shropshire. Matric. 1618. Died in College. Buried at Little St Mary's, Cambridge, Mar. 5, 1618-9.

GRIFFITHE, JOHN. Matric. sizar from ST JOHN'S, Michs. 1614; B.A. 1618-9; M.A. 1625. Perhaps s. of Robert, of Penrhyn. If so, precentor of Bangor, 1634. R. of Llanbeulan, Anglesey, 1635. (T. Nicholas, *County Families of Wales*, 42.)

GRIFFITH, JOHN. B.A. from ST JOHN'S, 1624-5. Perhaps matric. Easter, 1613, as Griffin.

GRIFFITH or GRIFFITHS, JOHN. Matric. sizar from QUEENS', Easter, 1627. Of Salop. B.A. 1630-1; M.A. 1634.

GRIFFITH, JOHN. Adm. pens. (age 18) at ST JOHN'S, May 19, 1632. S. of Evan, of Pengwern, Denbs., gent. School, Eton. Matric. 1632.

GRYFFYTH, JOHN. Adm. sizar (age 17) at ST JOHN'S, Feb. 22, 1633-4. S. of Robert, gent., of Carnarvon. B. there. School, Bangor (Mr Lewis). Matric. 1634.

GRIFFITH or GRIFFIES, JOHN. Adm. pens. at JESUS, May 18, 1657; 'from Oxford after 2 years residence there.' Of Salop. S. of William, of Llanfaethlu, Anglesey. Perhaps matric. from Jesus College, Oxford, Mar. 17, 1653-4. Stndent at Gray's Inn, 1654. High Sheriff of Anglesey, 1690. (*Al. Oxon.*)

GRIFFITH, JOHN. Adm. sizar (age 17) at TRINITY, Feb. 11, 1685-6. S. of John. B. in London. Exhibitioner from Charterhouse. Matric. 1689; Scholar, 1689; B.A. 1689-90; M.A. 1693. Ord. deacon (London) May 20, 1695; priest, Oct. 21, 1696. Perhaps V. of Dorney, Bucks., 1698-9.

GRIFFITHS, JOHN. Adm. pens. (age 18) at ST JOHN'S, June 5, 1712. S. of John, gent. B. at Wolverhampton, Staffs. School, Shrewsbury. Matric. 1712.

GRIFFITH, JOHN. M.A. 1715 (Incorp. from Oxford). Probably s. of Samuel, of Llannon, Carmarthen. Matric. from Jesus College, Oxford, Feb. 26, 1707-8, age 17; B.A. (Oxford) 1711. (*Al. Oxon.*)

GRIFFITH, JOHN. M.A. from CHRIST'S, 1722; D.D. 1741. S. of Edward, clerk, of Aston, Salop. Matric. from University College, Oxford, Dec. 2, 1712, age 16; B.A. (Oxford) 1718-9. R. of Eckington, Derbs., 1721-65. Preb. of Canterbury, 1738-65. R. of Whiston, Yorks., 1739-49 and 1759-65. R. of Prestwich, Lancs., 1752-63. He managed Lord Melton's Irish estates. Died Mar. 8, 1765. Father of Middlemore (1734) and John (1735). (*Al. Oxon.*; *Peile*, II. 188; *F.M.G.*, 839.)

GRIFFITHS, JOHN. M.A. from TRINITY, 1731. Already B.A. from Jesus College, Oxford. (Identification uncertain; *see Al. Oxon.*)

GRIFFITH, JOHN. Adm. pens. (age 19) at ST JOHN'S, Oct. 31, 1735. S. of John (1722), clerk, of Derbyshire. B. at Stainton. School, Chesterfield (Mr Burrow). Matric. 1736; B.A. 1739-40; M.A. 1743. Ord. deacon (Lincoln) May 6, 1739; priest, Sept. 20, 1741. V. of Leathley, Yorks., 1743-55. P.C. of Wentworth-in-Wath, about 1745. R. of Thurnscoe, 1748-64. R. of Hansworth, Derbs., 1752-84. R. of Treeton, Yorks., 1763-4. R. of Eckington, 1765-84. Died Sept. 6, 1784. Buried at Hansworth. Brother of Middlemore (1734). (*Scott-Mayor*, III. 471; *F.M.G.*, 839; M. H. Peacock.)

GRIFFITHS, JOHN. M.A. from ST CATHARINE'S, 1750 (B.A. from Jesus College, Oxford. Identification uncertain; *see Al. Oxon.*)

GRIFFITH, JOSIAS. Adm. at KING'S (age 16) a scholar from Eton, Apr. 14, 1617. Of Churton, Cheshire. Matric. 1617; B.A. 1620-1. Fellow, 1620-3. Died 1623.

GRIFFITH, LAURENCE. Matric. sizar from ST CATHARINE'S, Michs. 1654; B.A. 1657-8; M.A. 1663. Incorp. at Oxford, 1669. R. of Church Lawton, Cheshire, 1663.

GRIFFITH, MATTHEW. M.A. from CHRIST'S, 1621. B. in London. Matric. from Brasenose College, Oxford, May, 1615; B.A. (Gloucester Hall), 1618-9; D.D. (Oxford) 1643. Lecturer at St Dunstan-in-the-West. R. of St Mary Magdalen, Old Fish Street, 1625-42. R. of St Benet Sherehog, 1640-2; sequestered, 1642. Chaplain to the King, 1642. R. of Burghfield, Berks., 1645. Imprisoned in Newgate, 1660. Restored to St Mary Magdalen, Old Fish Street, 1660-5. His royalist sermon, answered by Milton, 1660. R. of Bladon, Oxon., *c.* 1661-5. Married Sarah, dau. of Richard Smith, D.D. Died at Bladon, Oct. 14, 1665. Will, P.C.C. (*Peile*, I. 300; *D.N.B.*; *Al. Oxon.*)

GRIFFITH, MIDDLEMORE. Adm. pens. (age 19) at ST JOHN'S, June 24, 1734. S. of John (1722), R. of Eckington, Derbs. B. at Stainton. School, Chesterfield (Mr Burrow). Matric. 1735; B.A. 1737-8; M.A. 1741. Ord. priest (Lincoln) Mar. 2, 1739-40. R. of St Michael, Queenhithe, 1739-46. R. of Upham, Hants., 1746-9. R. of Whiston, Yorks., 1749-63. R. of Treeton, 1753-63. Died Oct. 23, 1763. (*Scott-Mayor*, III. 456; *F.M.G.*, 839.)

GRIFFITH, MOSES. Adm. sizar (age 18) at ST JOHN'S, June 2, 1742. S. of Edward, collector of taxes, of Salop. B. at Lapidon. School, Shrewsbury (Mr Hotchkiss). Matric. 1742. Adm. at Leyden, June 23, 1744. M.D. there, Dec. 30, 1744. Adm. licentiate R.C.P., 1747. Practised in London, and afterwards in Colchester. Author, medical. Died at Colchester, Mar. 1785. Will, P.C.C. (*Munk*, II. 165; *D.N.B.*)

GRIFFITH, PEARCE. Matric. sizar from JESUS, Easter, 1608. One of these names (Peirce) buried in Westminster Abbey, Aug. 21, 1608. He equipped a privateer in the time of the Armada. (*Westm. Abbey Reg.*)

GRIFFITH, PETER. Adm. sizar at TRINITY, Mar. 19, 1655-6. Matric. 1656.

GRIFFITH, RICHARD. Adm. at KING'S (age 14) a scholar from Eton, Aug. 24, 1629. Of Abinger, Surrey. (? S. of Edward, 1592-3). Matric. 1629; B.A. 1633-4; M.A. 1637. Fellow, 1632, till 1642. Died in College, 1642. Confused by *Harwood* with Richard Griffith, M.D.

GRIFFITH, RICHARD. Elected from Eton to KING'S, 1654, but matric. at University College, Oxford, Mar. 28, 1655; B.A. (Oxford) 1657; M.A. 1660. Fellow of University College. Studied at Leyden. M.D. of Caen, 1664. Honorary Fellow R.C.P., 1664; Fellow, 1687. Censor and Registrar, 1690-1. Author, medical. Died Sept. 1691. Will, P.C.C. (*D.N.B.*; *Munk*, I. 470; *Al. Oxon.*)

GRIFFITHS or GRIFFITH, RICHARD. M.A. from ST JOHN'S, 1738. S. of Richard, of Llansawel (? Carmarthen), Glamorgan. Matric. from University College, Oxford, July 3, 1708, age 18; B.A. (Oxford) 1712. (*Al. Oxon.*)

GRIFFITH, ROBERT. Matric. sizar from MAGDALENE, Easter, 1614; B.A. 1617-8, as Griffin. One Robert Griffith, R. of Hackford, Norfolk, 1620-33. (*See* Griffin.)

GRIFFITH, ROBERT. Adm. sizar (age 18) at ST JOHN'S, June 27, 1670. S. of Hugh, yeoman, of Llanbrough, Beaumaris. B. there. Matric. 1670; B.A. 1673-4. One of these names V. of Eastham, Cheshire, 1695-1728. Died 1728.

GRIFFITH, ROBERT. Adm. sizar (age 18) at ST JOHN'S, Nov. 2, 1682. S. of John, feltmaker. B. at Shrewsbury. School, Shrewsbury. Matric. 1682.

GRIFFITH, ROGER. M.A. from EMMANUEL, 1668. Matric. from Balliol College, Oxford, Oct. 26, 1660; B.A. (Oxford) 1664. Incorp. M.A. at Oxford, 1669. Perhaps B.D. 1705 (*Com. Reg.*), but *see* the next. V. of Padbury, Bucks., 1665. Master of the Free School, Buckingham, 1665-(?) 1682. (*Al. Oxon.*)

GRIFFITH, ROGER. B.D. 1705 (*Com. Reg.*). Perhaps Archdeacon of Brecknock, 1704-8. Died Oct. 1708.

GRIFFITH, SAMUEL. Adm. Fell.-Com. (age 18) at ST JOHN'S, Feb. 26, 1749-50. S. of Leighton Owen, Esq., of Salop. B. at Preston. School, Shrewsbury. Matric. 1750. Of Dintle, Esq. High Sheriff of Salop, 1759-60. Died 1767. (J. B. Blakeway, *Sheriffs of Shropshire*.)

GRIFFITH, THOMAS. Matric. pens. from QUEENS', Easter, 1614. Of Lincolnshire. B.A. 1616-7; M.A. 1620. Ord. deacon (Peterb.) Dec. 21, 1617. V. of Sleaford, Lincs., 1627-8. Perhaps V. of Lindsell, Essex, 1632-5. Died 1635.

GRIFFITH, THOMAS. Adm. scholar at JESUS, Lent, 1620-1. Buried in the College Chapel, June 6, 1622. (A. Gray.)

GRIFFITH, THOMAS. Adm. pens. (age 16) at PEMBROKE, Oct. 12, 1652. Exhibitioner from Charterhouse. S. of Richard, of Montgomery, Wales, Esq. Matric. 1653-4; B.A. 1656-7.

GREFYTHE, WALTER. Matric. pens. from ST JOHN'S, Michs. 1546.

GREFYTHE, WILLIAM. Matric. Fell.-Com. from MAGDALENE, Michs. 1546.

GRIFFITH, WILLIAM. Matric. sizar from QUEENS', Michs. 1622. Of the Isle of Anglesey. B.A. 1625-6; M.A. 1629. One of these names R. of Dalston, Cumberland; buried there Dec. 6, 1642. Perhaps preb. of Bangor, 1634; and V. of Llanddeiniol, 1634. Died before 1660. (Browne Willis, *Bangor*, 177.)

GRIFFITH, WILLIAM. M.A. 1635 (Incorp. from Oxford). Perhaps B.A. from Hart Hall, Oxford, 1623; M.A. from Jesus, 1628.

GRIFFITH, WILLIAM. Adm. sizar at Christ's, Apr. 16, 1652. B. at Stratford Longton, Essex. School, St Paul's. Matric. 1652; B.A. 1655-6; M.A. 1659. One of these names V. of East Dean, Sussex, 1679. (*Peile*, I. 547.)

GRIFFON, JOHN. 'King's scholar' at Cambridge, 1319. Brother of the next. Left before 1332.

GRIFFON, THOMAS. 'King's scholar' at Cambridge, 1319. Left before 1332.

GRIFFOUN, WILLIAM. 'King's scholar' at Cambridge in 1332.

GRIGBY, JOSHUA. Adm. pens. at Clare, Apr. 9, 1748. S. of Joshua, of Wymondham, Norfolk, and Drinkstone, Suffolk. B. at Bury, Suffolk. Matric. 1751; LL.B. 1754. Adm. at Gray's Inn, Feb. 1, 1748-9. M.P. for Suffolk, 1784-90. Died Dec. 26, 1798, aged 67. Buried at Drinkstone. (A. B. Beaven.)

GRIGGS, BARDOLPH. B.A. from St John's, 1620-1. Ord. deacon (Peterb.) Apr. 13, 1622; priest (York) Mar. 1622-3. V. of Thorney, Notts., 1622.

GRIGG, FRANCIS. Matric. pens. (age 16) from Pembroke, Michs. 1659. S. of Roger. B. at Bassenthwaite, Cumberland. B.A. 1659-60; M.A. 1663. Fellow, 1665. Ord. deacon (Lincoln) Mar. 10, 1660-1; priest (London) Dec. 1664. R. of Rawreth, Essex, 1678-1704. Died 1704.

GRIGGE, JOHN. B.A. 1542-3. Will of one of these names (P.C.C.) 1555; of Little Birch, Hereford, clerk.

GRIGG or GRIGGS, MICHAEL. Adm. sizar at Emmanuel, Apr. 10, 1678. S. of Michael, of Little Bealings, Suffolk. Bapt. Jan. 2, 1659-60. School, Woodbridge. B.A. 1681-2; M.A. 1685; LL.D. 1690 (*Com. Reg.*). Ord. deacon (Norwich) Dec. 1683. R. of Cressingham, Norfolk, 1691. R. of Upwell, 1692-8. Admon. (P.C.C.) 1698. (*Suff. Man. Fam.*, I. 200; *Vis. of Suffolk*, 1664.)

GRIGGS, RICHARD. Adm. scholar (age 17) at Caius, July 6, 1598. S. of Edward, of Norwich. Matric. 1598. School, Norwich (Mr Limbert).

GRIGGS or GRIGGE, RICHARD. Adm. sizar at Jesus, Jan. 9, 1666-7. Of Essex. Matric. 1667; B.A. 1670-1; M.A. 1674. Ord. deacon (Ely) Sept. 24, 1671; priest, Sept. 22, 1672.

GRIGG, ROBERT. Matric. pens. from Christ's, Michs. 1615; B.A. 1618-9; M.A. 1622. R. of Houghton Conquest, Beds., 1629-36. Buried there Dec. 16, 1636.

GRIGGE or GRIGGS, STEPHEN. Matric. sizar from Queens', Easter, 1606. Of Suffolk. B.A. (? 1609-10); M.A. 1613. R. of Whitton and Thurleston, Suffolk, 1620.

GRIGGS, STEPHEN. Adm. at Corpus Christi, 1680. Of Norwich. Matric. 1680; B.A. 1683-4; M.A. 1687. Ord. deacon (Norwich) Dec. 1683; priest, May, 1686. R. of St Edward and St Julian, Norwich, 1688-91. R. of All Saints', 1688-91, deprived.

GRIGG, THOMAS. M.A. 1663 (Incorp. from Oxford). Matric. from Trinity College, Oxford, Mar. 4, 1652-3; B.A. (Oxford) 1655-6; M.A. 1658; B.D. 1665-6. Ord. deacon and priest (Norwich) Nov. 1661. R. of St Andrew Undershaft, London, 1664-70. Preb. of St Paul's, 1666-70. Died Sept. 4, 1670. Will, P.C.C. Father of William (1684). (*Al. Oxon.*)

GRIGGE, WILLIAM. Matric. pens. from Clare, Easter, 1618; B.A. 1621-2; M.A. 1625. Ord. deacon (Peterb.) Mar. 13; priest, Mar. 14, 1624-5.

GRIGGS or GRIGG, WILLIAM. Matric. sizar from Queens', Easter, 1620. Of Suffolk. B.A. 1623-4; M.A. 1627. Ord. deacon (Peterb.) Sept. 20; priest, Sept. 21, 1629.

GRIGG, WILLIAM. Adm. pens. at Jesus, Sept. 24, 1684. S. of Thomas (1663), deceased. Of Middlesex. Matric. 1685; Scholar, 1685, from St Paul's School; Rustat scholar; B.A. 1688-9; M.A. 1697; D.D. (*Com. Reg.*) 1717. Fellow, 1696-1714. Master of Clare, May 16, 1713-26; he was nominated by the Duke of Somerset, the Chancellor; the votes of the society being equally divided. Vice-Chancellor, 1716-7. Ord. priest (Lincoln) June 8, 1707. V. of Whittlesford, Cambs., 1705; of All Saints', Cambridge, 1707-17. R. of Trowbridge, Wilts., 1717-26. Chaplain to the Duke of Somerset. Died Apr. 9, 1726. Will proved (V.C.C. and P.C.C.) 1726. (A. Gray.)

GRIGMAN, STEPHEN. Adm. sizar (age 17) at St John's, Oct. 20, 1711. S. of Thomas, upholsterer. B. in London, May 30, 1694. School, Merchant Taylors'. Matric. 1711; B.A. 1715-6; M.A. 1719; D.D. 1739. Fellow, 1717-21. Ord. priest (London June 8, 1718. C. of St Botolph, Bishopsgate. Lecturer at St George, Botolph Lane. (G. R. Woodward.)

GRIGSON, EDWARD, *see* GREGSON.

GRIGSON, ROBERT. Adm. pens. (age 16) at Caius, Dec. 26, 1695. .. of William (1666), clerk, of Morley, Norfolk. B. there. School, Wymondham (Mr Clarke). Matric. 1696; Scholar, 1696-1701; M.B. 1701. Of Attleborough Hall, Norfolk. Married Frances Tawell. Died Nov. 10, 1747. M.I. at Morley St Botolph. Will (Archd. C. Norwich) 1749. (*Venn*, I. 497.)

GRIGSON, WILLIAM. Adm. pens. (age 16) at Caius, Sept. 26, 1666. S. of Robert, gent., of Hardingham. School, Scarning (Mr Burton). Matric. 1667; Scholar, 1667-74; B.A. 1670-1; M.A. 1674. Ord. deacon (Norwich) July, 1673; priest, Mar. 1673-4. R. of Morley St Botolph, Norfolk, 1674-1725. Married Susan, dau. of Miles King. Died Jan. 17, 1725-6. Buried at Morley. M.I. Will (Norwich C. C.) 1725. Father of Robert (1695). (*Venn*, I. 429.)

GRIMALDE or GRYMBOLD, NICHOLAS. A scholar of Christ's, 1536. Of Huntingdonshire. B. 1519. B.A. 1539-40. Incorp. at Oxford, 1542. M.A. (Oxford) 1544. Fellow of Merton College; afterwards of Christ Church. Chaplain to Bishop Ridley. Charged with heresy, but said to have recanted. Author, theological, etc. Died *c.* 1562. (*Cooper*, I. 230; *D.N.B.*; *Al. Oxon.*)

GRIMBALSTON, WILLIAM. Adm. sizar at Jesus, May 27, 1680. S. of John, of Tralles, Lancs. Migrated to Oxford. Matric. from Brasenose College, Oxford, July 4, 1681, age 19; B.A. (Oxford) 1685; M.A. (Cambridge) 1688; M.D. (*do.*) 1696. Adm. licentiate R.C.P., 1688. For a time physician to the Fleet in the West Indies. F.R.C.P. 1708. Died Sept. 29, 1725. Will, P.C.C. Benefactor to Jesus, and to Brasenose. (*Munk*, II. 21; *Al. Oxon.*)

GRIME or GRIMES, CHARLES. Adm. sizar (age 19) at Pembroke, 1631. S. of ——, of Ightham, Kent (? John, of 1595). Matric. 1631.

GRIMES, FERDINANDO. Adm. sizar at Trinity, May 28, 1652.

GRYME, GEORGE. Matric. Fell.-Com. from Corpus Christi, Easter, 1576. Probably s. of Thomas, of Foulsham, Norfolk. Buried at Gimmingham, Nov. 4, 1637. Will (Norwich C. C.) 1637. (G. H. Holley.)

GRIME, GEORGE. Matric. pens. from Trinity Hall, Michs. 1613. Probably s. and h. of George (? above); adm. at Gray's Inn, Mar. 15, 1619-20. Of Gimmingham, Norfolk. Buried there Oct. 31, 1647. Will (P.C.C.) 1649.

GRIME, GEORGE. Matric. pens. from St Catharine's, Lent, 1653-4. Doubtless s. of the above. Of Gimmingham, Esq. Married Dorothy, dau. of John Hobart, of Sall, Norfolk. Buried at Gimmingham, Nov. 24, 1664. Will (Norfolk Archd. C.) 1664. (G. H. Holley.)

GRYME, JOHN. Adm. at King's Hall, 1397. Bachelor in 1409. Fellow of King's Hall. Ord. deacon (Ely) Mar. 24, 1413-4; priest, Dec. 22, 1414. Beneficed, 1419.

GRIME, JOHN. Matric. pens. from Trinity, *c.* 1595. S. of Robert, yeoman. B. at Horning, Norfolk. Schools, Coltishall and Oxnead. Migrated to Caius, Jan. 25, 1596-7, age 17. Scholar, 1597-1600; B.A. 1598-9; M.A. 1602. Ord. priest (Norwich) June 13, 1605. C. of Teversham, Cambs. V. of Rainham, Kent, 1609. R. of Ightham, 1616-44. Will (P.C.C.) 1645. Probably father of Charles (1631). (*Venn*, I. 161.)

GRIMES, JOHN. Adm. pens. (age 17) at Caius, Apr. 10, 1667. S. of John, gent., of Thetford, Norfolk. B. at Norwich. School, Thetford (Mr Keene). Matric. 1667; Scholar, 1667-71; B.A. 1670-1; M.A. 1674. Ord. deacon (Norwich) Dec. 1671; signed for priest's orders (London) Dec. 20, 1673. V. of Kinoulton, Notts., 1675. (*Venn*, I. 430.)

GRYMES, JOHN. Adm. scholar at Trinity Hall, Nov. 7, 1735. Of County Middlesex, Virginia. S. and h. of John, of the Council of Virginia, Esq. Matric. 1735. Adm. at the Inner Temple, Nov. 29, 1736.

GRYME, RICHARD. Matric. sizar from Corpus Christi, Michs. 1580.

GRIM, ROBERT. B.Can.L. 1484-5. Benefactor to the University. (*Gr. Bk*, A, 191.)

GRYME, THOMAS. Matric. pens. from Christ's, Lent, 1580-1.

GRIME, WILLIAM. Adm. sizar (age 18) at Caius, June 10, 1636. S. of Edward, tailor. B. at Ingworth, Norfolk. School, Erpingham (Mr Harman). Matric. 1637. Died in College. Buried at St Michael's, Mar. 19, 1638. (*Venn*, I. 322.)

GRIMLEY, THOMAS. Matric. sizar from Clare, Easter, 1631.

GRIMMAR, ROBERT. Matric. pens. from Queens', Easter, 1620. Of Essex, or the Isle of Ely. Migrated to Jesus, July 25, 1620. Scholar, 1623; B.A. 1624; M.A. 1627. Ord. deacon (Peterb.) Mar. 6, 1624-5; priest, Mar. 5, 1625-6. Ejected from curacy of Wicken, Cambs., 1644; 'year's stipend; 20 marks and Easter Offerings, £20.' V. of Soham, 1661. R. of Borough Green, 1662. Buried there Apr. 12, 1672.

GRIMMER, THOMAS. Adm. sizar at JESUS, Apr. 29, 1624. Matric. 1627; B.A. 1628. Ord. deacon (Peterb.) Feb. 20; priest, Feb. 21, 1629-30.

GRIMSBY, JOHN DE. Scholar at KING'S HALL, 1357. Died Feb. 20, 1358-9. Perhaps, like several others, a victim of the Black Death.

GRIMSBY, JOHN. Adm. pens. (age 16) at CAIUS, Apr. 28, 1641. S. of Thomas, gent., of Benhall, Suffolk. B. there. Taught by Mr White. Matric. 1641; Scholar, 1643-5; B.A. 1644-5.

GRIMSBY, ——. Fee for M.A. or higher degree, 1479-80. Distinct from the next.

GRIMSBY, ——. Fee for M.A. or higher degree, 1479-80.

GRIMSDITCH, *see* GRYMSDITCH.

GRIMSHAW, HENRY. B.A. 1526-7. One of these names (M.A.) was V. of Gt Barton, Suffolk, 1540-54. R. of Gt Saxham, till 1554. V. of Stow Mary, 1554.

GRIMSHAWE, JAMES. Matric. pens. from TRINITY, Michs. 1560. Perhaps scholar of Christ's, *c.* 1563.

GRIMSHAWE, JOHN. Matric. sizar from CLARE, Michs. 1570.

GRIMSHAW, NICHOLAS. Matric. sizar from QUEENS', Easter, 1581.

GRIMSHAW, THOMAS. Adm. sizar (age 14) at CHRIST'S, July 6, 1635. S. of Lancelot. B. in London (probably in St Mary Aldermary). Matric. 1635; B.A. 1638-9.

GRIMSHAW, WILLIAM. B.A. from TRINITY, 1590-1; M.A. 1594. Ord. priest (Durham) 1594. R. of Castle Rising, Norfolk, in 1606.

GRIMSHAW, WILLIAM. Adm. sizar (age 17) at CHRIST'S, Apr. 2, 1726. S. of William. B. at Brindle, Lancs. Schools, Heskin (Mr Johnson) and Blackburn. Matric. 1726; Scholar, 1727; B.A. 1729-30. V. of Todmorden, Lancs., 1731. P.C. of Haworth, Yorks., 1742-63. Associated with John Wesley and the Methodists; preached with great success throughout the north of Eugland. Married a daughter of John Lockwood, of Little Ewood, Halifax. Died Apr. 8, 1763. Buried at Luddenden, near Halifax. (*Peile*, II. 212; *D.N.B.*; M. H. Peacock.)

GRIMSHAW, ——. Scholar of CHRIST'S, 1564.

GRIMSHEY, RICHARD. Matric. sizar from MAGDALENE, Easter, 1623.

GRYMSTON, CHRISTOPHER. Matric. pens. from CHRIST'S, May, 1572. Possibly a brother of Edward (1572). (*Vis. of Norfolk*; *Peile*, I. 122.)

GRYMSTON, CHRISTOPHER. Adm. pens. (age 14) at CAIUS, Dec. 17, 1578. 6th s. of Thomas, of Grimston, Yorks. B.A. 1582-3; M.A. 1586. Fellow, 1587-92. Adm. at Gray's Inn, 1593. Brother of John (1578), Thwaites and Walter. (*Venn*, I. 99; *Vis. of Yorks.*, 1584.)

GRIMSTONE, EDWARD. Said to have studied at GONVILLE HALL. B. *c.* 1528. S. of Edward, and Anne, dau. of John Garnish, of Suffolk. M.P. for Bossiney, 1553; for Ipswich, 1563-7 and 1571-83; for Eye, 1588-9; and for Orford, 1593. Comptroller of Calais, 1553. Purchased the Manor of Rishangles, Suffolk, 1557. Taken prisoner by the Duke of Guise, and sent to the Bastille, 1557-8. Escaped to London. Indicted on a charge of high treason and sent to the Tower, but was acquitted and discharged. Died Mar. 17, 1599-1600. M.I. at Rishangles. Father of Edward (1572). (*Cooper*, II. 280; *D.N.B.*; *Copinger*, III. 26, who differs as to the parentage.)

GRYMSTONE, EDWARD. Matric. pens. from GONVILLE HALL, Easter, 1554. One of these names adm. at Gray's Inn, 1559.

GRIMSTON, EDWARD. Matric. pens. from ST JOHN'S, Michs. 1555.

GRIMSTONE, EDWARD. Matric. pens. (age 13) from CHRIST'S, May, 1572. S. of Edward (1528), sometime comptroller of Calais, of Bradfield, Essex. Scholar of Trinity Hall, 1573; LL.B. 1578. Master in Chancery, 1601-10. Freeman of Ipswich, 1604. Married Joan, dau. of Thomas Risby, of Lavenham, Suffolk. Died Aug. 16, 1610. Will (P.C.C.). Probably father of Henry (1598-9). (*Cooper*, III. 26; *Vis. of Essex*, 1634; A. B. Beaven.)

GRIMSTON, EDWARD. Matric. Fell.-Com. from CLARE, Michs. 1616. S. of Sir Harbottle, of Bradfield, Essex, Knt. Migrated to Emmanuel, May 1, 1617. B.A. 1618-9. Adm. at Gray's Inn, May 7, 1619. Married Elizabeth, dau. of Thomas Massam, Esq. Died *s.p.* 1624. Brother of Harbottle (1619) and Henry (1621). (*Vis of Essex*, 1634; Burke, *Ext. Bart.*)

GRIMSTONE, GEORGE. Adm. Fell.-Com. (age 15) at SIDNEY, July 4, 1731. S. of William, Viscount Grimston, of Ireland (of Gorhambury, Herts.). B. at Gorhambury. School, St Albans. Matric. 1731; B.A. 1734-5; M.A. 1738. Died May 15, 1782. Of Gerard St. (*G. Mag.*)

GRIMSTONE, HARBOTTLE. Adm. pens. at EMMANUEL, July 28, 1619. S. of Sir Harbottle, of Bradfield, Essex, Knt. and Bart. B. Jan. 27, 1602-3, at Thorndon. Matric. 1620. Adm. at Lincoln's Inn, Nov. 1, 1621. Barrister. M.P. for Harwich, 1628; for Colchester (Apr. to May), 1640; and in the Long Parliament, 1640-8; for Essex, 1656-8; and for Colchester, 1660-81. Recorder of Harwich, 1634 and 1660; of Colchester, 1638-53. Succeeded as 2nd Bart., 1648. Appointed to th Council of State on the abdication of Richard Cromwell, 1659. Speaker of the Convention Parliament, 1660. Master of the Rolls, 1660-85. Died Jan. 2, 1684-5, aged 82. Buried at St Michael's, St Albans. Father of Samuel (1663), brother of Edward (1616) and Henry (1621). (*D.N.B.*; G.*E.C.*)

GRIMSTONE, HENRY. Scholar of CLARE, July 6, 1452. Perhaps same as next.

GRIMSTON, HENRY. B.A. 1460-1.

GRIMSTON, HENRY. Matric. pens. from CHRIST'S, 1598-9. Probably s. of Edward (1572), of Bradfield, Essex. Adm. at Gray's Inn, Aug. 19, 1597. Knighted, Oct. 19, 1619. Married ...dau. of Ralph Coppinger, of Stoke, Kent. Died Sept. 22, 1645, aged 64. Buried at Boxley, Kent. M.I. Will, P.C.C. Probably father of William (1627). (*Peile*, I. 231; *Cussans*, III. 247.)

GRIMSTON, HENRY. Matric. pens. from CHRIST'S, Dec. 1614. Probably s. of John (1578), of Fraysthorpe, Yorks. B.A. 1617-8. Ord. deacon (York) June, 1623; priest, Dec. 1623. V. of Sherburn, Yorks., 1624-33. Married Anne, dau. of William Strickland, of Eston, Yorks. Died 1645. (*Peile*, I. 299; M. H. Peacock.)

GRIMSTONE, HENRY. Adm. pens. at EMMANUEL, June 30, 1621. Matric. 1621. Migrated as Fell.-Com. (age 19) to Caius, Dec. 23, 1623. 3rd s. of Sir Harbottle, Knt., of Bradfield, Essex. Bapt. at Rishangles, Suffolk, Feb. 17, 1606-7. B.A. from Caius, 1623-4; M.A. 1626. Fellow of Caius, 1625-7. Died July 12, 1627. Buried at Islington, Middlesex. M.I. Brother of Edward (1616) and Harbottle (1619). (*Venn*, I. 264; *Vis. of Essex*, 1612.)

GRIMSTON, HENRY. Adm. pens. at EMMANUEL, Jan. 17, 1630-1. Of Kent. Matric. 1631; B.A. 1634-5; M.A. 1638. R. of Frinton, Essex, 1639. Probably V. of Aylesford, Kent, 1649-54. Buried there Sept. 20, 1654.

GRIMSTON, JAMES. Adm. pens. (age 17) at SIDNEY, May 8, 1722. S. of John, barrister-at-law. B. at Bridlington, Yorks. School, Eton. Matric. 1723. Adm. at Gray's Inn, Mar. 1, 1720-1.

GRYMSTON, JOHN. Adm. pens. (age 18) at CAIUS, Dec. 17, 1578. 3rd s. of Thomas, of Grimston, Yorks. Signed the pedigree in the *Vis. of Yorks.*, 1612. Brother of Christopher (1578), etc., father of Marmaduke (1606). (*Vis. of Yorks.*, 1584.)

GRIMSTONE, JOHN. Matric. pens. from PETERHOUSE, Michs. 1579; B.A. from Clare, 1582-3; M.A. from Peterhouse, 1586; B.D. 1595. Perhaps R. of Orleston, Kent, 1588. V. of Northfleet, 1596-1600. One of these names V. of Lyminge, 1581-1602. Died 1602.

GRIMSTON, MARMADUKE. Matric. pens. from TRINITY, Easter, 1606. S. of John (1578). Age 21 in 1612. Of Fraysthorpe, Yorks. Died *c.* 1650. Father of William (1635). (*Vis. of Yorks.*, 1612.)

GRIMSTON, SAMUEL. Adm. sizar (age 18) at PEMBROKE, June 16, 1665. S. of Daniel, chandler. B. at Coventry.

GRIMSTON, SAMUEL. Adm. Fell.-Com. at CLARE, May 27, 1663. Of Gorhambury. S. and h. of Sir Harbottle (1619), Bart. B. 1648-9. B. Jan. 7, 1643-4 (*Clutterbuck*). Adm. at Lincoln's Inn, Jan. 4, 1667-8. M.P. for St Albans, 1668-81 and 1689-1700. Succeeded as Bart., 1685. Died Oct. 1700. (*G.E.C.*; *Cussans*, III. 247-8; *D.N.B.*)

GRYMSTON, THOMAS. Will proved (V.C.C.) 1558; of KING'S.

GRYMSTONE, THOMAS. Matric. sizar from CLARE, Michs. 1573. Perhaps s. of Edmund, of Oxborough, Norfolk. B.A. 1577-8; M.A. 1581; M.D. from Caius, 1601. Fellow of Caius, 1582-95. Proctor, 1592. Probably practised in Cambridge. Buried Mar. 23, 1607-8. Will (V.C.C.) 1608. Gave books to Caius and Clare. (*Venn*, I. 115; *Cooper*, II. 480.)

GRIMSTON, THOMAS. Adm. Fell.-Com. (age 17) at SIDNEY, June 3, 1720. S. of Thomas, Esq., of Grimston, Yorks. Bapt. at York, Oct. 3, 1702. School, private. Matric. 1720. Adm. at the Middle Temple, Nov. 28, 1720. Of Grimston and Kilnwick, Yorks. Died Oct. 22, 1751. Buried at Kilnwick. M.I. (M. H. Peacock.)

GRIMSTON, THWAITES. Adm. pens. at CAIUS, Dec. 17, 1578. 4th s. of Thomas, of Grimston, Yorks., Esq. B. 1562. Matric. 1578-9. Married Bridget, dau. of Henry Mainwaring, of Carmingham, Cheshire. Brother of Christopher (1578), etc. (*Venn*, I. 99; *Vis. of Yorks.*)

GRIMSTON, WALTER. Adm. pens. at CAIUS, Dec. 17, 1578. 5th s. of Thomas, of Grimston, Yorks., Esq. B. 1563. Matric. 1578-9; B.A. 1582-3; M.A. 1586. Married Dorothy, dau. of Marmaduke Thirkeld, of Easthorpe. Brother of the above, etc. (*Venn*, I. 99; *Vis. of Yorks.*)

GRIMSTONE, WILLIAM. Adm. pens. at EMMANUEL, June 20, 1627. Of Kent. S. and h. of Sir Henry (? 1598-9), of Boughton Monchelsea, Kent, Knt. Matric. 1627. Adm. at Gray's Inn, June 28, 1630.

GRIMSTON, WILLIAM. Adm. Fell.-Com. (age 15) at CHRIST'S, Sept. 21, 1635. S. of Marmaduke (1606), of Grimston, Yorks. B. at York. Bapt. at St Michael-le-Belfrey, Dec. 18, 1619. School, York (Mr Cudworth). Matric. 1635; M.A. 1635-6 (*Lit. Reg.*). Adm. at Lincoln's Inn, Apr. 25, 1638. Of Grimston Garth and Goodmanham, Yorks., Esq. Suffered heavily as a royalist. Died Apr. 1664. Father of the next. (*Peile*, I. 439.)

GRIMSTON, WILLIAM. Adm. Fell.-Com. (age 16) at CHRIST'S, June 15, 1657. S. of William (above), of Grimston-in-Holderness. B. there, Aug. 16, 1640. School, York (Mr Wallis). Matric. 1657. Of Grimston Garth and Goodmanham, Yorks., Esq. Died Aug. 5, 1711. Buried at Garton. Will (York) 1711. (*Peile*, I. 579; M. H. Peacock.)

GRIMSTON, ——. Adm. pens. at TRINITY HALL, Apr. 19, 1744. (Name off, 1747.) Perhaps John, s. of Thomas (1720). B. Feb. 17, 1724-5. Died June 21, 1780. Buried at Kilnwick. (Poulson, *Beverley*, I. 433.)

GRIMWADE, JOB. Matric. pens. from TRINITY, *c.* 1596.

GRIMWADE, JOHN. Adm. sizar (age 15) at SIDNEY, Apr. 10, 1664. 1st s. of Thomas, gent. B. at Creeting All Saints', Suffolk. Schools, Stowmarket (Mr Coulson) and Burstall (Mr Gouge). Matric. 1664; B.A. 1667-8.

GRIMWOOD, THOMAS. Adm. sizar at ST CATHARINE'S, Sept. 11, 1722. Of Ipswich. Matric. 1723; B.A. 1726-7; M.A. 1730. R. of Newborne, Suffolk, 1730. Master of Dedham School, Essex, 1736-78. Will, P.C.C.

GRINDAL, EDMUND. Of MAGDALENE, CHRIST'S and PEMBROKE. S. of William, of Hensingham, Cumberland. B. *c.* 1519. B.A. from Pembroke, 1537-8; M.A. 1541; B.D. 1549; D.D. 1564. Fellow of Pembroke, 1538-53. Proctor, 1548-9. Lady Margaret preacher, 1549. Master of Pembroke, 1559-62. Precentor of St Paul's, 1551-4. Chaplain to Bishop Ridley. Chaplain to the King, 1551. Canon of Westminster, 1552-4. A fugitive abroad under Mary. Commissioner for revision of the liturgy. Bishop of London, 1559-70. Archbishop of York, 1570. Archbishop of Canterbury, 1576-83. Suspended 1577-82. Eulogised in Spenser's *Shepherd's Calendar*. Died July 6, 1583. Buried at Croydon. Will, P.C.C. (*Cooper*, I. 470; *D.N.B.*)

GRINDALL, JOHN. B.Can.L. 1495-6. Principal of ST THOMAS' HOSTEL. Perhaps R. of Houghton, Hunts., 1502-37. Died 1537. One of these names V. of St John-the-Baptist, Peterborough, 1497-9.

GRINDALL, JOHN. B.A. 1502-3; M.A. 1506. Of Cumberland. Fellow of ST CATHARINE'S.

GRINDALL, RALPH. Adm. pens. at JESUS, Sept. 10, 1696. Of Hertfordshire. Matric. 1698.

GRINDALL, WILLIAM. B.A. 1541-2. Fellow of ST JOHN'S, 1542-3. An excellent Greek scholar; pupil of Roger Ascham. Tutor to the princess Elizabeth. Died of the plague, 1548. (*Cooper*, I. 94; *D.N.B.*)

GRYNDON or GRENDON, LAURENCE DE. Scholar at KING'S HALL, June 1, 1350-9.

GRINDON, ——. B.Can.L. 1482.

GRINFEILD or GREENFIELD, RICHARD. Adm. pens. (age 17) at ST JOHN'S, Mar. 16, 1725-6. S. of Richard, gent., of Wiltshire. B. at Marlborough. School, Marlborough (Mr Hildrop). Matric. 1726; B.A. 1729-30. Ord. deacon (Salisbury) Sept. 20, 1730. C. of Wilsford, Wilts. (*Scott-Mayor*, III. 393.)

GRINFIELD, WILLIAM. Adm. pens. (age 17) at ST JOHN'S, Nov. 11, 1738. S. of Richard, gent., of Wiltshire. B. at Mildenhall. School, Marlborough (Mr Stone). Matric. 1738; B.A. 1742-3; M.A. 1746. Perhaps V. of Buckland, Berks., 1755-82.

GRINKIN, WILLIAM. M.A. 1629 (Incorp. from Oxford). Of Surrey, gent. Matric. from Queen's College, Oxford, Nov. 10, 1621, age 18; B.A. (Oxford) 1621; M.A. from Jesus, 1626-7.

GRYNLEY, ——. Fee for M.A. or higher degree, 1480-1.

GRINLING, LIONEL. Adm. sizar (age 15) at CAIUS, Jan. 20, 1622-3. S. of Lionel, gent., of Fressingfield, Suffolk. Taught by Mr Godfry. Will of one of these names proved 1649. (*Venn*, I. 260.)

GRINROD, LAURENCE. Matric. sizar from TRINITY, Easter, 1619.

GRINSELL, RICHARD. Adm. sizar (age 18) at TRINITY, May 11, 1714. S. of Jonathan, of London. School, Dulwich, London (Mr Hilary). Matric. 1714.

GRINSELL, WILLIAM. Adm. sizar (age 19) at CAIUS, Apr. 29, 1708. S. of William, ge ., of Drayton, Salop. B. there. School, Drayton (Mr Felton). Matric. 1708; Scholar, 1708-10. (*Venn*, I. 518.)

GRISAGRE, ——. Incorp. from Oxford, 1489-90. Will of Wm. Harvey (P.C.C.) 1503, refers to Thomas Grisacre as parish priest of Halstead, Essex. (J. Ch. Smith.)

GRISE, *see* GRICE.

GRO[··]ER (? GROCER), JOHN. Matric. pens. from CHRIST'S, *c.* 1595.

GROCER, THOMAS. Adm. pens. (age 15) at JESUS, Feb. 2, 1670-1. Of Suffolk. Probably 2nd s. of John and Elizabeth, of Walsham-le-Willows. Matric. 1671; Scholar, 1674; B.A. 1674-5. Will proved (V.C.C.) 1676; 'of St John's.'

GROMWELL or GRUMBELL, ROBERT. Adm. at KING'S, a scholar from Eton, 1494; B.A. 1497-8. Fined, as Cromwell, 1499-1500, for non-determination.

GRONOVIUS, JAMES. LL.D. 1671 (*Lit. Reg.*).

GRONOW, THOMAS. Of CLARE. B.A. 1500; M.A. 1502-3; B.D. 1515-6; D.D. 1517-8.

GRONTE, ——. Student of PETERHOUSE, Michs. 1557.

GROOBY, ANDREW. Matric. sizar from QUEENS', Easter, 1617. Of Northamptonshire. B.A. 1620-1; M.A. 1624. Ord. deacon (Peterb.) May 23; priest, May 24, 1624. C. of Warkworth, Northants., 1632. C. of Bromham, Beds., 1635-41. Married, June 27, 1632, at Gt Doddington, Elizabeth Jackman, widow. Buried at Abington, Northants., Oct. 18, 1651. (H. I. Longden.)

GROOM, JOHN. B.A. 1529-30; M.A. 1533-4.

GROOM, JOHN. B.A. 1536-7. Fellow of ST JOHN'S, 1537. Perhaps R. of St Dionis, London, 1569-74. Buried there Sept. 15, 1574.

GROOME, JOHN. Adm. sizar (age 16) at MAGDALENE, Oct. 14, 1695. S. of John. B. at Norwich. School, Norwich. Matric. 1696; B.A. 1699-1700. V. of Childerditch, Essex, 1709. Chaplain to Robert, Earl of Holderness. Married, at Gray's Inn Chapel, June 28, 1712, Mary Moor, of St James', Westminster. Author. Died July 31, 1760. Will, P.C.C. Benefactor to Magdalene. (*D.N.B.*; J. Ch. Smith.)

GROME or GROMME, REGINALD. Matric. pens. from ST JOHN'S, Michs. 1561. B. at Woodford, Northants. B.A. 1566-7. Ord. deacon (Ely) Apr. 16, 1568; priest (London) Sept. 9, 1569. R. of Monks Horton, Kent, 1570-1. R. of Theddlethorpe St Helen, Lincs., 1578.

GROME or GROWME, RICHARD. Matric. sizar from ST JOHN'S, Easter, 1584.

GROOME, RICHARD. Adm. sizar (age 22) at TRINITY, May 24, 1725. S. of Richard, of Wolverhampton, Staffs. School, Wolverhampton. Matric. 1725. Ord. deacon (London) May 28, 1727. Will of one of these names (P.C.C.) 1777; of Sedgeley, Staffs., clerk.

GROOM, SIMON. B.Civ.L. 1512-3. Of Norwich diocese. Fellow of TRINITY HALL. Ord. priest (Lincoln) June 14, 1511.

GROUME (?), THOMAS. Matric. pens. from TRINITY, Michs. 1560.

GROOME, THOMAS. Matric. sizar from ST JOHN'S, Easter, 1589.

GROOME, THOMAS. Adm. pens. at PEMBROKE, Apr. 9, 1674. S. of John, of (?) Ludham, Norfolk; age 16. Matric. 1674; B.A. 1677-8; M.A. 1681. Ord. deacon (Norwich) May, 1681; priest, Dec. 1681. R. of Burnham Deepdale, Norfolk, 1686-1749. Married, at Stanhoe, Norfolk, Sept. 21, 1695, Ann, dau. of Edmund Mott, of Caldicott, and widow of Martin Cobb, of Burnham Norton. Buried at Burnham Deepdale, Oct. 24, 1749, aged 93. Father of the next. (*G. Mag.*)

GROOME, THOMAS. Adm. sizar (age 17) at CAIUS, June 16, 1712. S. of Thomas (above), R. of Burnham Deepdale, Norfolk. B. there. Bapt. there, Sept. 18, 1694. School, Holt (Mr Reynolds). Matric. 1712; Scholar, 1712-8; B.A. 1715-6; M.A. 1725. Ord. deacon (Norwich) June 12, 1720; priest, May 20, 1722. R. of Burnham Norton, 1724; of Burnham Ulph, 1724; of Burnham Westgate, 1724-9; of Burnham Overy, 1724; of Ingoldisthorpe, 1736-42; of Tittleshall, 1739-42. Chaplain to Lady Clifford. Buried at Burnham Deepdale, Jan. 29, 1741-2. (*Venn*, I. 527; G. H. Holley.)

GROME, WILLIAM. Matric. sizar from TRINITY, Easter, 1624; B.A. 1627-8. One of these names adm. at Gray's Inn, Aug. 12, 1622.

GROOME, WILLIAM. Adm. pens. (age 18) at PETERHOUSE, Feb. 6, 1709–10. Of Sussex. School, Winchester. Scholar, 1710; Matric. 1711; B.A. 1713–4; M.A. 1724. Ord. deacon (Ely) Feb. 21, 1713–4; priest (London) Sept. 25, 1716. One of these names V. of Binstead, 1726–38. (*T. A. Walker*, 223.)

GROOM, ——. B.Can.L. 1475–6.

GROOM (? BROOM), LAURENCE. B.D. 1484–5.

GROOM, ——. Adm. pens. at ST CATHARINE'S, 1666.

GROOMBRIDGE, JOHN. Adm. pens. (age 17) at TRINITY, July 7, 1677. Of Kent. S. of Alexander. Matric. 1677; Scholar, 1681; B.A. 1681–2; M.A. 1685. Extra-licentiate R.C.P., July 22, 1697. Practised physic at Cranbrook, Kent. Buried there 1721. (*Munk*, I. 518.)

GROOMET or GROMET, WILLIAM. Matric. sizar from MAGDALENE, Easter, 1603; B.A. 1606–7.

'GROSDEN,' LAURENCE. Error in *Matriculations* for EUSDEN.

GROSSE or GROSE, ALEXANDER. Adm. sizar (age 22) at CAIUS, July 26, 1618. S. of William, husbandman, of Christow, Devon. School, Exeter (Mr Periman). B.A. from Trinity Hall, 1631. Incorp. M.A. at Exeter College, Oxford, 1632. B.D. (Oxford) 1633. Incorp. at Cambridge, 1633. Preacher at Plympton, Devon. R. of Bridford, 1639–45. V. of Ashburton, 1647; again, with Buckland and Bickington, 1652–4. Author. Buried at Ashburton, Apr. 10, 1654. Father of the next. (*Venn*, I. 240; *D.N.B.*)

GROSSE, ALEXANDER. Adm. pens. at EMMANUEL, Lent, 1640–1. Previously matric. from Exeter College, Oxford, May 4, 1638, age 15. S. of Alexander (above), of Plympton, Devon, clerk. Perhaps brother of Matthias (1643).

GROS, JOHN. 'KING'S scholar' at Cambridge, 1330. Of Hereford.

GROSSE, JOHN. Matric. Fell.-Com. from CORPUS CHRISTI, Easter, 1574.

GROSSE, JOHN. Adm. pens. at PETERHOUSE, June 27, 1595. Of Norfolk. B. at Yarmouth, 1580. Father, a merchant. B.A. from Pembroke, 1598–9; M.A. from Corpus Christi, 1602. Entered at Douay College; afterwards at the English College at Rome, Oct. 2, 1603. Ord. priest, 1606. Became a Jesuit, 1610. Died Feb. 27, 1645. (Foley's *Records*, I. 629.)

GROSSE, LUKE. Matric. sizar from JESUS, Easter, 1612. Probably of Cold Ashby, Northants. B.A. 1615–6; M.A. 1619. Ord. deacon (Peterb.) Nov. 15, 1616; priest, Sept. 19, 1619. V. of Gt Gidding, Hunts., 1619–66.

GROSSE, MATTHIAS. Adm. pens. at EMMANUEL, Apr. 1, 1643. Of Devon. Matric. 1643; B.A. 1646. Perhaps brother of Alexander (1640–1).

GROSSE, ROBERT. Adm. pens. at JESUS, June 21, 1625. Matric. 1625; Scholar, 1626; B.A. 1628–9.

GROSSE, WILLIAM. Matric. pens. from CHRIST'S, 1595–6.

GROSSMITH, GEORGE. Adm. sizar at EMMANUEL, May 9, 1720. Matric. 1723; B.A. 1723–4; M.A. 1728. Incorp. at Oxford, 1736. Perhaps V. of Dorney, Bucks., 1735. V. of Upton, 1746–54. R. of Hedgerley, 1746–54. Died 1754.

GROSTRE, JOHN. Matric. sizar from ST JOHN'S, Easter, 1603.

GROSVENOUR, JOB. Adm. sizar at TRINITY, July 29, 1673.

GROSVENOR, RICHARD. Adm. Fell.-Com. at EMMANUEL, Apr. 8, 1626. Doubtless s. of Sir Richard, of Eaton, Cheshire, Bart. Age 11 in 1613. Sheriff of Chester, 1643–4; sequestered and fined as a royalist. Succeeded as Bart., Sept. 14, 1645. Died Jan. 31, 1664–5. Buried at Eccleston. (*Vis. of Cheshire*, 1613; *G.E.C.*)

GROSWOOD, ——. *Grace* for degree (? B.D.) 1481.

GROUSE, THOMAS. Adm. pens. at QUEENS', May, 1603. Of Suffolk. Matric. 1604; B.A. 1606–7; M.A. 1610; B.D. 1617. C. of Fleet, Lincs., in 1611. V. of Oakington, Cambs., 1616–22. Perhaps R. of Walsoken, Norfolk, 1620–35. V. of Gedney, Lincs., 1622–35. Died 1635.

GROVE, BENDY. Adm. at ST CATHARINE'S, July 19, 1696. Matric. 1696; B.A. 1699–1700; M.A. 1707. Ord. deacon (Norwich) Dec. 1701.

GROVE, CHRISTOPHER. Adm. pens. at CLARE, June 26, 1701. B. at Clopton, Suffolk. Matric. 1702; B.A. 1705–6; M.A. 1709. Ord. deacon (Norwich) Mar. 1708–9; priest, Sept. 25, 1709. C. of Somerton, Suffolk. R. of Hemingstone, 1718. Died Jan. 14, 1769. Buried at Hemingstone. Will, P.C.C. (*G. Mag.*)

GROVE, EDWARD. Adm. pens. at QUEENS', Mar. 5, 1686–7. Of Suffolk. Matric. 1687; B.A. 1690–1; M.A. 1694; D.D. 1724. Ord. deacon (Winchester) Dec. 18, 1692; priest (Norwich) June, 1693. R. and patron of Chevington, Suffolk, 1693–1727. Married, June 29, 1697, Anne, dau. of John Risby, of Thorpe Morieux, Esq. Author, *Sermon*, 1702. Died Feb. 18, 1726–7, aged 59. Buried at Chevington. Perhaps father of the next. (H. G. Harrison; G. R. Woodward.)

GROVE, EDWARD. Adm. pens. at QUEENS', Nov. 10, 1716. Of Suffolk. Perhaps s. of Edward (above). Matric. 1716; B.A. 1720–1.

GROVE, GEORGE. Matric. sizar from PEMBROKE, Easter, 1588; B.A. 1591–2; M.A. 1595. Head Master of Sherborne School, Hants., 1603–39. (W. B. Wildman, *Sherborne*.)

GROVE, GREGORY. Adm. pens. (age 19) at ST JOHN'S, June 26, 1712. S. of Henry, clerk. B. at Witherley, Leics. School, Atherstone, Warws. (Mr Shaw). Matric. 1712; B.A. 1715–6; M.A. 1733. Ord. deacon (Lincoln) May 27, 1716 (as 'George'). R. of Witherley, Leics., 1746–56. Buried there May 3, 1756. Admon. (P.C.C.) 1756. (*Nichols*, IV. 1009.)

GROVE, HUGH. Adm. Fell.-Com. (age 16) at ST JOHN'S, Jan. 29, 1708–9. S. and h. of John, Esq. B. at Chisenbury, near Enford, Wilts. School, Mere, Wilts. (Mr Gouldsbury). Matric. 1709. Adm. at the Middle Temple, Nov. 25, 1708. Died *s.p.* 1765. Brother of John (1711) and William (1708). (*Hutchins*, III. 568.)

GROVE or GROVES, HUTTOFT. Adm. Fell.-Com. (age 16) at MAGDALENE, Nov. 3, 1663. S. of Thomas, Esq., of Debden, Essex. Matric. 1663. Of Birden Hall, Essex. Owned property in Dorset, which he mortgaged for a term of years, in 1685. (*Hutchins*, I. 421.)

GROVE, JOHN. Fellow of PETERHOUSE, till 1453. Perhaps the same as 'William,' who was fellow from 1433. (*T. A. Walker*.)

GROVE, JOHN. Adm. sizar at TRINITY, Mar. 31, 1665. Matric. 1665.

GROVE, JOHN. Adm. pens. (age 16) at ST JOHN'S, Oct. 25, 1711. S. of John, Esq. B. at Chisenbury, Wilts. School, Burton (Mr Gouldsbury). Matric. 1712. Migrated to Trinity College, Oxford. Matric. there, Mar. 15, 1713–4, age 18. Brother of Hugh (1708–9) and William (1708).

GROVE, PEIRCE. Adm. pens. (age 17) at ST JOHN'S, Dec. 17, 1726. S. of J., gent., of Cambridgeshire. B. at Cambridge. School, Bury St Edmunds (Mr Kinnesman). Matric. 1727.

GROVE, RICHARD. Adm. pens. (age 17) at ST JOHN'S, Dec. 17, 1735. Of Tunstall, Suffolk. S. of John, gent., of Cambridgeshire. B. at Cambridge. School, Bury, Suffolk (Mr Kinnesman). Matric. 1733; B.A. 1737–8; M.A. 1741. Fellow, 1741–61. Adm. at the Middle Temple, Dec. 6, 1735. Barrister, 1742. Bencher. Died July 18, 1791. M.I. at Tunstall. (*Scott-Mayor*, III. 449.)

GROVE, ROBERT. Adm. pens. at ST JOHN'S, Oct. 18, 1652. S. of William, of Morden, Dorset. B. in London. School, Winchester. Matric. 1652; Scholar, 1653; B.A. 1656–7; M.A. 1660; B.D. 1667; D.D. 1681. Fellow, 1659. Signed for deacon and priest (London) June 7, 1666. R. of Wennington, Essex, 1667–9. R. of Aldham, 1669–70. R. of St Andrew Undershaft, 1670–92. Preb. of St Paul's, 1679–91. Archdeacon of Middlesex, 1690–1. Chaplain to the King. Bishop of Chichester, 1691–6. Author, theological. Died Sept. 25, 1696. Will, P.C.C. (*D.N.B.*)

GROVE, ROBERT. Adm. scholar at TRINITY HALL, Feb. 13, 1664–5. Of Wiltshire. Perhaps adm. at Winchester College, 1650; age 13. Of Gillingham, Dorset.

GROVE, ROBERT. Adm. pens. (age 17) at ST JOHN'S, Oct. 20, 1687. S. of Robert, clerk. B. in London. School, Eton. Matric. 1688; B.A. 1691–2; M.A. 1695. Fellow, 1694–1726 (*see Coll. Hist.*, 210). Taxor, 1699. Registrary, 1701–26. Died Apr. 20, 1726.

GROVE, SAMUEL. Adm. Fell.-Com. (age 24) at TRINITY, Oct. 9, 1721. Matric. 1724; LL.B. 1724. From Oriel College, Oxford. S. of Isaac, of London. Ord. deacon (London) Feb. 18, 1721–2; priest (Lincoln, *Litt. dim.* from London) Mar. 10, 1722–3. R. of East Barnet, Herts., 1743–69. Died Feb. 19, 1769. Will, P.C.C. The father was a Huguenot, named Group. (*Cussans*, III.)

GROVE, THOMAS. B.A. 1514–5; M.A. 1518. Fellow of ST JOHN'S, 1516. Ord. sub-deacon (Ely) Mar. 28, 1517, title 'Jesus College' ('prefuit scholae grammaticae' there). R. of Hadstock, Essex, 1519–22. Died 1522. (A. Gray.)

GROVE, THOMAS. Adm. sizar at ST CATHARINE'S, Feb. 3, 1717–8. Of Penn, Staffs. Matric. 1717; B.A. 1721–2; M.A. 1725. One of these names V. of Bakewell, Derbs.

GROVE, WILLIAM. Fellow of PETERHOUSE, 1433. V. of Meldreth, Cambs., 1455.

GROVE, WILLIAM. Adm. pens. at QUEENS', July 7, 1629. S. of Hugh, of Buford, Wilts. Migrated to Oxford. Matric. from Wadham College, Jan. 28, 1630–1, age 18; B.A. 1634; M.A. 1637. Perhaps R. of Poulshot, Wilts. Preb. of Sarum, 1662–6. Died 1666. (*Al. Oxon.*)

GROVE, WILLIAM. Adm. sizar at ST CATHARINE'S, Apr. 11, 1680. Matric. 1680; B.A. 1683–4; M.A. 1689. Perhaps P.C. of St Catherine Cree church, London, 1696–1712.

GROVE, WILLIAM. Adm. pens. (age 16) at St John's, Nov. 29, 1708. S. of John, Esq. B. at Chisenbury, Wilts. School, Mere, Wilts. (Mr Gouldsbury). Matric. 1708; B.A. 1712-3; M.A. 1716; B.D. 1723. Fellow, 1716-30. Ord. deacon (London) Sept. 1, 1714; priest (Bristol) Apr. 9, 1716. R. of Manston, Dorset, 1716-68. R. of Wootton Rivers, Wilts., 1729-68. Died Feb. 11, 1768. Will, P.C.C.; of Zeals, Mere, Wilts. Uncle of the next, brother of Hugh (1708-9) and John (1711). (F. S. Hockaday.)

GROVE, WILLIAM CHAFIN. Adm. pens. (age 18) at St John's, Apr. 30, 1750. S. of Chafin, Esq., of Wiltshire. B. at Mere. School, Sutton (Mr Rogers). Matric. 1750; B.A. 1754. Adm. at the Middle Temple, Apr. 28, 1750. Barrister, 1756. M.P. for Shaftesbury, 1768-74; and for Weymouth, 1774-81. Of Zeals House, Wilts. Died at Bath, Jan. 17, 1793. (*Scott-Mayor*, III. 596; *G. Mag.*)

GROVER, THOMAS. Adm. sizar (age 18) at Trinity, June 11, 1714. S. of Thomas, citizen and tallow chandler, of London. 'Grecian' from Christ's Hospital, London. Matric. 1714; Scholar, 1716; B.A. 1717-8; M.A. 1721. Fellow, 1720. Senior Proctor, 1734-5. Ord. deacon (London) July 16, 1718; priest (York) Dec. 1720. 2nd Master at Morpeth School, Northumberland; elected Head Master, June 28, 1724.

GROWNE, *see* GROOM.

GROYFFE, NICHOLAS. B.A. 1469-70.

GRUBB, JOHN. Matric. sizar from Queens', Michs. 1579. Of Norfolk. B.A. 1582-3; M.A. 1587.

GRUBBE, JOHN. Adm. pens. at Emmanuel, July 4, 1642. Perhaps s. of John, of Horsenden, Bucks.; b. 1625; died June 16, 1700. (Lipscomb, *Pedigree*, II. 332.)

GRUBBE, THOMAS. M.A. 1619 (Incorp. from Oxford). S. of Thomas, of Potterne, Wilts. Matric. from Queen's College, Oxford, June 16, 1610, age 16; B.A. 1613-4; M.A. (St Edmund's Hall) 1616. Adm. at Lincoln's Inn, 1618. R. of Cranfield, Beds., 1619-52. Buried there Sept. 2, 1652. (*Vis. of Wilts.*, 1623.)

GRUCHY, LUKE. Matric. sizar from Trinity, Easter, 1616; B.A. 1620-1. Probably of Jersey.

GRUMBULL, ROBERT, *see* GROMWELL.

GRUNDON, RICHARD. Adm. sizar (age 19) at Sidney, June 4, 1668. S. of James, farmer, of Sinnington, Yorks. Taught by Mr Nich. Grey, of Sidney. Matric. 1668; B.A. 1671-2; M.A. 1675. Ord. deacon (York) Sept. 1672; priest, May, 1673.

GRUNDON, WILLIAM. Adm. sizar (age 20) at Sidney, May 26, 1744. S. of James, farmer, of Sinnington, Yorks. B. there. Schools, Kirby, Yorks. (Mr Mauset) and Thornton (Mr Ward). Matric. 1744; B.A. 1747-8; M.A. 1751.

GRUNDY, GEORGE. Matric. pens. from Queens', Michs. 1589. Of Lancashire. B.A. 1593-4; M.A. 1597. Ord. priest (Lincoln) Sept. 12, 1597. R. of Gislingham, Suffolk, 1601-26. Will (P.C.C.) 1627.

GRUNDY, GEORGE. Matric. pens. from Queens', Michs. 1625. Of Suffolk. Probably s. of George (above). Bapt. at Gislingham, July 24, 1608. B.A. 1628-9. Buried at St Botolph's, Cambridge, Apr. 10, 1629. (V. B. Redstone.)

GRUNDY, JAMES. Adm. pens. (age 19) at Pembroke, Apr. 8, 1662. Of Bolton-le-Moors. S. of Ralph, farmer. B. at Middleton, Lancs. Matric. 1662; M.B. 1667. Governor of Chetham's Library, Manchester. Died 1712. (Mumford's *Manchester School*, 115.)

GRUNDEY, JOHN. Matric. sizar from Pembroke, Lent, 1557-8. Of Lancashire. B.A. 1560-1; M.A. from St John's, 1564; B.D. 1570. Fellow of St John's, 1561. University preacher, 1567. R. of Gt Livermere, Suffolk, 1571. R. of Gt Cressingham, Norfolk, 1582-98. V. of Little Fakenham, 1582-1608. V. of Gt Barton, till 1583. Will (P.C.C.) 1608; of Gislingham, Suffolk, clerk.

GRUNDY, JOHN. Matric. pens. from Corpus Christi, Easter, 1620. Of Nottinghamshire.

GRUNDY, JOHN. Adm. at Magdalene, June 2, 1683. Matric. 1683.

GRUNDY, JOHN. Adm. pens. (age 16) at Trinity, Sept. 28, 1688. S. of John, of Bleasby, Notts. School, Bleasby (Mr Cudworth). Matric. 1688-9.

GRUNDY, JOHN. Adm. pens. at Clare, May 8, 1717. S. and h. of John (? above), of Bleasby, Notts., genty B. at Nottingham. Adm. at Lincoln's Inn, July 5, 1718.

GRUNDY, RALPH. Matric. sizar from St John's, Easter, 1622; B.A. 1625-6. Probably of Yarm-on-Tees, Yorks. Licensed, 1626, to marry Isabel Barton, of Yarm, widow.

GRUNDY, ROBERT. Matric. sizar from Queens', Easter, 1575. Of Lancashire.

GRUNDY, THOMAS. Matric. sizar from Queens', Easter, 1617. Of Staffordshire. B.A. 1620-1; M.A. 1624. Ord. deacou (Peterb.) May 19; priest, May 20, 1627.

GRUNDY, THOMAS. Adm. at Corpus Christi, 1629. Of Norfolk. B.A. 1632-3; M.A. 1636. Ord. deacon (Norwich) Mar. 2, 1633-4; priest, Sept. 25, 1636. R. of St Peter Hungate, Norwich, 1638. R. of Palgrave, 1645-62. R. of Mellis, Suffolk, 1662-8. Will proved (Norwich Cons. C.) 1668.

GRUNDY, THOMAS. Matric. pens. from Queens', Michs. 1649. Of Warwickshire. B.A. 1652-3. One of these names ejected from Denton, Sussex, 1662. (*Calamy*, II. 461.)

GRUTER, JANUS. Adm. pens. (age 19) at Caius, July 11, 1577. S. of Walter, citizen and merchant of Antwerp. B. there, Dec. 3, 1560. School, Norwich (Dr Matthias). Resided for some time, his tutor being Robert Swayle. Afterwards studied at Leyden. Professor at Wittenberg and Heidelberg. Librarian at Heidelberg, where he lost his books at the siege of 1622. There is a copy of his portrait in Caius College. Died at Heidelberg, Sept. 20, 1627. (*Venn*, I. 92.)

GRIGG, *see* GREGG.

GRYMDYTCHE, HENRY. Matric. pens. from Trinity, Easter, 1563; Scholar, 1563; B.A. 1566-7.

GRYMESDYTCHE, THOMAS. Matric. pens. from St John's, Michs. 1560.

GRIMSDITCH, WILLIAM. Of Christ's. B.A. 1542-3; M.A. 1545. Ord. deacon (London) 1552, when he is described as 'born in Chester; age 33.' R. of St Michael, Chester, 1566-74. Apparently his admon. (P.C.C.) Oct. 9, 1574; R. of Ashprington, Devon; died in London. (J. Ch. Smith.)

GRYSLEYE, EDWARD. Matric. pens. from Christ's, Easter, 1546 (*impubes*).

GRYNHAM, EDWARD. Matric. pens. from St John's, Lent, 1557-8.

GRYSWOLL, JOHN. Adm. at King's, a scholar from Eton, 1447.

GUALTER, RALPH. Adm. Fell.-Com. at Trinity, 1571; sent thither by Dr Parkhurst, Bishop of Norwich. S. of Ralph, pastor at Zurich. Migrated to Magdalen College, Oxford, 1573. M.A. there, Oct. 12, 1573. Minister at St Peter's, Zurich. Author. Died there 1577, aged 25. (*Cooper*, I. 380.)

GUALTER, WILLIAM, *see* WALTER.

GUALTIER, GEOFFREY. M.A. 1624 (on King's visit).

GUBBARD or GOBART, JOSEPH. Matric. sizar from Caius, July 2, 1645. S. of —— Gobart, clerk (probably Robert, below, R. of Marlingford, Norfolk).

GUBBARD or GOBERT, ROBERT. Matric. sizar from Corpus Christi, Michs. 1584. Of Norfolk. B.A. 1588-9; M.A. 1592. R. of Marlingford, Norfolk, 1594.

GUDFIELD, WALTER. B.D. 1507-8 (Incorp. from Oxford).

GUDHYNE, HENRY. Probably B.A. Fined 20*d.* for disturbance of the peace, 1486-7. (*Gr. Bk*, A, 205.)

GUERCYE, BALTHASAR. Matric. sizar from Clare, Michs. 1544. An Italian. Surgeon to Queen Catherine of Aragon. M.B. *c.* 1530; M.D. 1546. Surgeon to Henry VIII. F.R.C.P., 1556. Died Jan. 1556-7. Buried at St Helen's, Bishopsgate. Will (P.C.C.) Jan. 1556-7. (*Cooper*, I. 173; *D.N.B.*)

GUERDAIN, AARON, *see* GEURDAIN.

GUEROUT (? GUÉROULT), JAMES. M.A. 1624 (on the King's visit).

GUERTZ, ANDREW. Adm. pens. at Clare, June 17, 1745. B. in London. Matric. 1746; B.A. 1748-9.

GUEST or GEAST, EDMUND. Adm. at King's, a scholar from Eton, 1536. S. of Thomas, of Northallerton, Yorks. B. *c.* 1517. B.A. 1540-1; M.A. 1544; B.D. 1551. Fellow, 1539-54. Chaplain to Archbishop Parker. Archdeacon of Canterbury, 1559-64. R. of Cliffe, Kent, 1559. Bishop of Rochester, 1560. Bishop of Salisbury, 1571-7. A reviser of the liturgy. Author. Died Feb. 28, 1576-7. Buried in Salisbury Cathedral. M.I. Will (P.C.C.). (*Cooper*, I. 361; *D.N.B.*; A. B. Beaven.)

GUEST, GEORGE. Adm. sizar (age 18) at St John's, May 28, 1658. S. of Randle, clerk, of Pulford, Cheshire. B. there. Matric. 1658. One of these names R. of Pulford, Cheshire, 1661. Brother of Randolph (1661).

GUEST, JOHN. Adm. at Pembroke, Apr. 1, 1672; B.A. 1672-3. Previously matric. from Pembroke College, Oxford, May 10, 1667, age 17. S. of Richard, of Stafford, clerk. Adm. at Lincoln's Inn, Nov. 28, 1676; s. and h. of Richard, of West Bromwich. One of these names R. of Churchill, Worcs., 1678. (*Al. Oxon.*)

GUEST, JOHN. M.A. from King's, 1723. S. of Joseph, of Winforton, Hereford, clerk. Matric. from Pembroke College, Oxford, July 3, 1712, age 17; B.A. (Oxford) 1716; M.A. 1720. R. of Monnington, Hereford, 1722. V. of Bromyard, 1732-60. Died Mar. 8, 1760. (*Al. Oxon.*; *Duncomb*, II. 85.)

GUEST, JOSEPH. Adm. pens. (age 16) at St John's, June 15, 1741. S. of Joseph, V. of Weobley, Hereford. B. at Titley. School, Hereford. Matric. 1741; B.A. 1744-5; M.A. 1748. Fellow, 1748-52. Ord. deacon (Hereford) Feb. 1, 1746-7; priest, Sept. 29, 1748. Preb. of Hereford, 1753-1804. V. of Staunton-on-Arrow, Herefordshire, 1759-1804. V. of Westbury-on-Severn, Gloucs., 1763-5. V. of Weston Beggard, Heref., 1765-6. V. of Madley, 1780-2. V. of Upton Bishop, 1782-5. V. of Lugwardine, 1785-1804. Also held other preferments. Died Sept. 14, 1804. Will, P.C.C. (*Scott-Mayor*, III. 521.)

GUEST, RANDOLPH. Adm. sizar (age 16) at St John's, June 1, 1660. S. of Randolph, clerk, of Sutton, Cheshire. B. there. Brother of George (1658).

GUEST or GEST, THOMAS. Matric. pens. from Jesus, Easter, 1576. Migrated to Oxford. B.A. (Oxford) 1579. Ord. deacon (Worcester) Nov. 4, 1580; priest (Gloucester) Aug. 29, 1584. R. of Stondon, Beds., 1589. R. of South Kilworth, Leics., 1593.

GUEST or GEST, WILLIAM. Matric. pens. from Christ's, Dec. 1613; B.A. 1617-8; M.A. 1621. One of these names Chaplain to the Bishop of Norwich. R. of St John's, Garboldisham, Norfolk, 1637. (*Peile*, I. 293.)

GUEST, WILLIAM. Adm. sizar at St John's, Nov. 2, 1728. S. of John, cutler, of Yorkshire. B. at Sheffield. School, Chesterfield. Matric. 1728; B.A. 1732-3. Ord. priest (Lincoln) Sept. 19, 1736. R. of Collyweston, Northants., 1751-82. Will (P.C.C.) 1782. (*Scott-Mayor*, III. 419.)

GUETZ (? GUETTE), CHARLES DE. M.A. 1624 (on King's visit).

GUEVARA, HENRY. Matric. pens. from Magdalene, *c.* 1589. 3rd s. of Francis Velez de Guevara, of Boston, Lincs., and Stenigot. Captain in the army. Brother of John (1582) and Peregrine (1586). (*Lincs. Pedigrees*, 433, where he is called a knight.)

GUEVARA, HENRY. Matric. pens. from Magdalene, Easter, 1603.

GUEVARA, JOHN. Matric. Fell.-Com. from Magdalene, Easter, 1582. 1st s. of Francis Velez de Guevara, of Stenigot, Lincs. Adm. at Gray's Inn, Nov. 6, 1584. Knighted, Mar. 23, 1604-5. Will proved, 1607, by brother, Sir Henry. Brother of Henry (1589) and the next, father of William (1610). (*Lincs. Pedigrees*, 433.)

GUEVARA, PEREGRINE. Matric. pens. from Magdalene, Easter, 1586. 2nd s. of Francis Velez de Guevara, a Spaniard. Of Boston, Lincs. Buried at Stenigot, Lincs., May 29, 1587. Brother of John (above) and of Henry (1589). (*Lincs. Pedigrees*, 433.)

GUEVARA, WILLIAM. Matric. Fell.-Com. from Magdalene, Michs. 1610. 3rd s. of Sir John (1582), of Stenigot, Lincs., Knt. Died 1628. Will proved, May 9, 1628. (*Lincs. Pedigrees*, 433.)

GUGE, FRANCIS. Adm. at Corpus Christi, 1650. Of Essex.

GUIDE, CLAUDIUS. Adm. sizar at St Catharine's, Feb. 19, 1703-4. Matric. 1707. S. of Philip, M.D., a Frenchman, whose will (P.C.C.) 1716.

GUIDE, JOHN PAUL. Adm. pens. at Clare, Apr. 24, 1745. B. in London. Matric. 1745-6; B.A. 1748-9.

GUIDOTT, ROBERT. M.A. 1663 (Incorp. from Oxford). S. of Kellaway, of St Clement Danes, London, gent. Matric. from Exeter College, Nov. 27, 1652; B.A. (Oxford) 1655-6; M.A. 1658. Adm. at the Inner Temple, 1654. R. of Little Barford, Beds., 1661. V. of St Paul, Bedford, 1662; and of St John's, 1663. Buried at St John's, Bedford, Nov. 27, 1677. (*Al. Oxon.*)

GUILE, THOMAS. Adm. pens. at Jesus, Oct. 29, 1619; B.A. from St Catharine's, 1623-4.

GUISBOROUGH or GRYSBURGH, ——. Adm. at King's, a scholar from Eton, 1455. Of Hull.

GUISE, WILLIAM. M.A. from Magdalene, 1681. S. of Edward, of Brookworth, Gloucs. Bapt. there, Dec. 29, 1652. Matric. from Christ Church, Oxford, Dec. 18, 1671, age 18; B.A. (Oxford) 1675. Chaplain to Lord Wootton. R. of Almsford, Somerset, 1677-1719. R. of Moor Critchell, Dorset, 1681-1719. Died there May 10, 1719. M.I. (*Al. Oxon.*; F. S. Hockaday.)

GULL, WILLIAM. D.D. Master of Clare, 1421-46. Proctor, 1431-2. Living, 1455. Benefactor to the College buildings. Assisted William Bingham in the foundation of God's House, afterwards Christ's College. (*Pat. Rolls, Henry VI*; *Clare College History*.)

GULLARD, EDWARD. Adm. Fell.-Com. at Queens', Oct. 11, 1645. Of Middlesex.

GULLIFORD, ROBERT, *see* GOLLIFORD.

GULLIVER, JOHN. Adm. sizar (age 15) at Pembroke, June 3, 1661. S. of Edward, of Coventry, Warws. Matric. 1661; B.A. 1664-5; M.A. 1668. Fellow, 1667. Incorp. at Oxford, 1670. R. of Waresley, Hunts., 1680-3. Died 1683. Will proved (V.C.C.) 1683. Brother of Josias (1669).

GULLIFER, JOSEPH. Adm. at Corpus Christi, 1730. Of Suffolk. Matric. 1730; B.A. 1734-5; M.A. 1750. Ord. deacon (Norwich) Oct. 1735; priest, Aug. 1738. C. of Coggeshall, Essex, 1739; V. 1746-67. V. of Burnham. Chaplain to Lord Fitzwalter. Died Mar. 31, 1767. (G. *Mag.*)

GULLIVER, JOSIAS. Adm. sizar (age 17) at Pembroke, May 10, 1669. S. of Edward. B. at Coventry, Warws. Matric. 1669; B.A. 1672-3; M.A. 1676. Ord. priest (London) Feb. 24, 1683-4. V. of Tolleshunt Major, Essex, 1683-97. V. of Messing, 1694-1704. Died 1704. Brother of John (1661).

GULSON, ANTHONY. Matric. pens. from Queens', Michs. 1571; B.A. 1574-5; M.A. 1578. Perhaps preb. of Salisbury, 1623-6. Died 1626.

GULSON, FRANCIS. Adm. sizar at Emmanuel, Jan. 12, 1587-8. Matric. 1588; Scholar, 1588; B.A. 1591-2.

GULSON, GEORGE. Matric. sizar from Queens', Michs. 1560; B.A. 1564-5; M.A. 1568. Fellow, 1566-71. Ord. priest (Ely) Mar. 23, 1566-7. V. of Pickwell, Leics. 'Aged 29; married; ordained by Bishop of Ely, a towardly young man' (*Lib. Cler. Linc.*, 1576). Admon. (Leicester) *c.* 1580.

GULSON, HENRY. Matric. sizar from Pembroke, Lent, 1563-4. Resident, Aug. 1564.

GULSON, HENRY. Matric. sizar from Queens', Michs. 1581. Of Leicestershire.

GULSON, HENRY. Matric. sizar from Trinity, Michs. 1608. Buried at All Saints', Cambridge, Feb. 26, 1608-9.

GULSON, JOHN. Matric. sizar from Queens', Easter, 1578; B.A. 1581-2; M.A. 1585. V. of Prittlewell, Essex, 1593-1615. Died 1615. Admon. (Consist. C. London) 1615.

GULSON, JOHN. Adm. Fell.-Com. at Queens', Aug. 17, 1602. Of Northamptonshire. 2nd s. of William (1561). Bapt. at Thrapston, Jan. 1, 1576-7. Adm. at Gray's Inn, June 22, 1601, as of Wymondham, Leics., gent. Prothonotary of the Court of Common Pleas. Brother of Theodore (1590). (H. I. Longden.)

GULSON or GOLDSON, JOHN. Matric. sizar from Queens', Easter, 1622. Migrated to Emmanuel, Oct. 12, 1622. B.A. 1625-6; M.A. 1629. Ord. deacon (Peterb.) Feb. 20; priest, Feb. 21, 1629-30.

GULSON, JOSEPH. Matric. pens. from Trinity, Easter, 1619; B.A. 1622-3; M.A. 1626; B.D. 1631-2 (*Lit. Reg.*). Fellow, 1624. D.D. (Oxford) 1643. Ord. deacon (Peterb.) Oct. 3; priest, Oct. 4, 1629. V. of Bottisham, Cambs., 1633-4. R. of Ham, Wilts., 1634; of Fonthill Bishop, 1639; of Waltham Bishop, 1643. Chaplain to the King. Preb. of Winchester, 1660-9. Dean of Chichester, 1663-9. R. of Felpham, Sussex, 1668. Died Apr. 10, 1669. (*Al. Oxon.*)

GULSON, MORICE. Matric. sizar from Christ's, Lent, 1584-5. R. of Scartho, Lincs., 1595, as 'B.A.' Admon. (Lincoln) 1613. (*Peile*, I. 181.)

GULSON or GULSTON, THEODORE. Adm. sizar at Peterhouse, 1590-1. S. of William (1561), R. of Thrapston. Bapt. there, Mar. 6, 1575. Scholar, 1594; B.A. 1594-5. B.A. (Oxford) 1595; M.A. 1600; M.D. 1610. Fellow of Merton, 1596. Adm. at Gray's Inn, Mar. 8, 1605-6, as s. of William, R. of Wymondham, Leics. F.R.C.P., 1611. Censor. Author, classical. Founder of the Gulstonian lecture at the College of Physicians. Settled as a physician in the parish of St Martin-extra-Ludgate, London. Married Helena, dau. of George Sotherton. Died May 4, 1632. Will, P.C.C. Brother of John (1602). (*D.N.B.*; *Munk*, I. 157; *Vis. of Herts.*, 1634.)

GULSON or GOLDSTON, THOMAS. Adm. at King's (age 17) a scholar from Eton, Aug. 13, 1533. Of Coventry. B.A. 1537-8; M.A. 1541. Fellow, 1536-46. V. of Wootton Wawen, Warws., 1545.

GULSON, WILLIAM. Matric. sizar from Queens', Michs. 1561. B. *c.* 1542. B.A. from Christ's, 1564-5; M.A. 1569. R. of Thrapston, Northants., 1573-9. R. of Wymondham, Leics., 1584. Father of Theodore (1590) and John (1602). (*Vis. of Herts.*, 1634.)

GULSTON, *see also* GOLDSTON.

GULSTON, FRANCIS. Adm. pens. (age 17) at Pembroke, Sept. 15, 1744. S. of Francis, of Wyddial, Herts., Esq. Matric. 1744; LL.B. 1752. Ord. priest (London) Sept. 22, 1751. R. of Wyddial, Herts., 1752-97. Died July 14, 1797. Buried in Wyddial Church. Will, P.C.C.

GULSTON, JOHN. Matric. pens. from St John's, Michs. 1568.

GULSTON, JOHN. Matric. pens. from Trinity, Easter, 1644.

GULSTON, RICHARD. Scholar of Trinity, 1631; B.A. 1631-2.

GULSTON, WILLIAM. Adm. pens. at Trinity, Sept. 7, 1668.

GOULDSTON or GOLDSTON, WILLIAM. Adm. sizar (age 17) at ST JOHN'S, Oct. 4, 1653. S. of Nathaniel, D.D., deceased, of Wymondham, Leics. B. there. School, Grantham (Mr Stokes). Matric. 1653; B.A. 1657–8; M.A. 1661; D.D. 1679, as 'Gulston.' Preb. of Chichester, 1666–81. R. of Simondsbury, Dorset, 1670–84. Chaplain to the Duchess of Somerset. Bishop of Bristol, 1679–84. Died Apr. 4, 1684, at Simondsbury. Buried there. Will, P.C.C. (*Baker-Mayor*, I. 271; F. S. Hockaday.)

GULSTON, ——. Adm. sizar at SIDNEY, June, 1599.

GUMBLE, THOMAS. Adm. sizar (age 16) at CAIUS, Feb. 14, 1642–3. S. of John, of the parish of St Stephen, Norwich. School, Norwich (Mr Lovering). Matric. 1643; B.A. 1646–7; M.A. 1650; D.D. (*Lit. Reg.*) 1661. Ord. deacon and priest (Lincoln) Dec. 19, 1660. Chaplain to General Monk; entrusted by him with many delicate commissions. Preb. of Winchester, 1661–76. R. of East Lavant, Sussex, 1663. Probably chaplain of H.M.S. *Royal Charles*, in 1666. Wrote a life of General Monk, Duke of Albemarle. Died 1676. Admon. (P.C.C.) 1677. (*Venn*, I. 348; *D.N.B.*)

GUNBY, CHRISTOPHER. Adm. sizar (age 17) at ST JOHN'S, Mar. 18, 1714–5. S. of John, currier. B. at Beverley, Yorks. School, Beverley. Matric. 1715; B.A. 1719–20; M.A. 1738. Ord. deacon (London) Dec. 20, 1719; priest (York) May, 1722. V. of Sowerby, Yorks., 1736–50. V. of Hutton Cranswick, *c.* 1745. Died 1750. Brother of John (1704–5).

GUNBY, JOHN. B.A. 1482.

GUNBYE, JOHN. Adm. sizar (age 18) at PETERHOUSE, Apr. 25, 1649. Of Wisbech. School, Wisbech. Matric. 1650; B.A. 1652–3. R. of Little Dunham, Norfolk, 1660–82.

GUNBY, JOHN. Adm. pens. (age 17) at ST JOHN'S, Mar. 22, 1704–5. S. of John, currier. B. at Beverley, Yorks. School, Beverley (Mr Lambert). Matric. 1705. Brother of Christopher (1714–5).

GUNBY, THOMAS. Adm. sizar at ST CATHARINE'S, Apr. 22, 1718. Of Worlham (? Worlingham), Suffolk. Matric. 1720; B.A. 1721–2; M.A. 1730. Ord. priest (Norwich) May, 1724. V. of Flixton, Suffolk, 1727–54.

GUNDES or GUNDYS, JOHN. Adm. at KING'S, a scholar from Eton, 1480; B.A. 1483–4; M.A. 1487. Died in College.

GUNDRY, CHRISTOPHER. Adm. pens. (age 17) at TRINITY, Apr. 20, 1738. S. of Robert, of London. Bapt. at St Martin-in-the-Fields, London, Nov. 20, 1720. School, Eton. Scholar, 1738; Matric. 1739; B.A. 1741–2.

GUNN, RICHARD. Adm. pens. (age 17) at CAIUS, Mar. 26, 1672. S. of Richard, of Lewes, Sussex. School, Lewes (Mr Stafford). Matric. 1672. Adm. at the Middle Temple, July 1, 1674. Doubtless same as the next. (*Venn*, I. 446.)

GUNN, RICHARD. Adm. pens. at CLARE, Apr. 10, 1672. Of Patcham, Sussex.

GUNN or GONN, ROBERT. Matric. sizar from KING'S, Easter, 1612; B.A. 1615–6. Ord. deacon (York) Dec. 1616; priest, May, 1618.

GUNNELL, *see also* GONVILLE.

GUNNELL, BENJAMIN. Matric. pens. from ST JOHN'S, Michs. 1581; B.A. 1584–5; M.A. 1588. V. of Takeley, Essex, 1598–1629. Died 1629. Will (P.C.C.) as Goonald.

GUNNEL or GUNVYLE, ROBERT. Matric. pens. from CLARE, 1579; B.A. 1582–3; M.A. 1587. Probably P.C. of Ramsey, Hunts., 1599–1600; and of Bury, till 1620. Died 1620.

GUNNEL, THOMAS. Matric. pens. from PEMBROKE, Lent, 1580–1. One of these names V. of Newnham, Herts., 1588.

GUNNELL, WILLIAM. Matric. sizar from KING'S, Michs. 1729; B.A. 1733–4. Ord. deacon (Lincoln) Dec. 23, 1733; priest, Mar. 21, 1735–6. Will of one of these names (P.C.C.) 1771; of New Sleaford, Lincs., clerk.

GUNNELL, ——. B.A. 1474–5. Perhaps Thomas, of Papworth St Agnes, Cambs.; received letters dimissory from the Bishop of Ely, 1489.

GUNNES, ——. B.Can.L. 1502–3.

GUNNING, FRANCIS. Adm. sizar (age 16) at ST JOHN'S, Mar. 9, 1707–8. S. of William, deceased. B. at Downham, Cambs. School, Ely (Mr Tenant). Matric. 1708; B.A. 1711–2. Ord. deacon (London) Dec. 21, 1712; priest, Dec. 18, 1715. Brother of Henry (1705) and Peter (1702).

GUNNING, FRANCIS. Adm. sizar (age 17) at ST JOHN'S, June 13, 1747. S. of Henry (next). B. at Ely. Taught there by his father. Matric. 1748; B.A. 1750–1; M.A. 1754. Fellow, 1753–61. Ord. deacon (Lincoln) June 17, 1753; priest, June 9, 1754. V. of Hauxton and Newton, Cambs., 1754–88. V. of Thriplow, 1759–88. Admon. (P.C.C.) 1789. Father of the well-known Esquire Bedell, brother of Peter (1733) and Stuart (1738). (*Scott-Mayor*, III. 568.)

GUNNING, HENRY. Adm. pens. (age 15) at ST JOHN'S, July 17, 1705. S. of William, deceased. B. at Ely. School, Ely (Mr Tenant). Matric. 1705; B.A. 1709–10; M.A. 1713. Fellow, 1711–5. Ord. deacon (London) Mar. 16, 1711–2; priest (Peterb.) Sept. 18, 1714. Minor canon of Ely. Precentor of the Cathedral. Died 1764. Will (P.C.C.) 1765. Father of the above, Peter (1733), Stuart (1738) and grandfather of the well-known University Bedell.

GUNNING, PETER. B.A. from PETERHOUSE, 1605. S. of Thomas, of Ightham, Kent. Bapt. there, Aug. 28, 1585. V. of Hoo St Werbergh, Kent, 1613; and minister of Gravesend. Buried there Dec. 12, 1615. Father of the next. (*Misc. Gen. et Her.*, 5th S., II. 162.)

GUNNING, PETER. Matric. sizar from CLARE, Michs. 1629. S. of Peter (above), V. of Hoo, Kent. B. there, Jan. 11, 1613–4. School, King's, Canterbury. B.A. 1632–3; M.A. 1636; D.D. from Corpus Christi, 1660 (*Lit. Reg.*). Fellow of Corpus, 1633–44, ejected. B.D. (Oxford) 1646. University preacher, 1641. Lady Margaret Professor, 1660–1. Master of Corpus Christi (by mandate) Feb. to June, 1661. Regius Professor of Divinity, 1661–74. Master of St John's, 1661–9. Chaplain to the King, 1660. R. of Cottesmore, Rutland, 1660–70; of Stoke Bruerne, Northants., 1660–70. Preb. of Canterbury, 1660–9. Bishop of Chichester, 1670–5; and of Ely, 1675–84. An ardent royalist. Author. Died unmarried, July 6, 1684. M.I. in Ely Cathedral. (*D.N.B.*; Le Neve, *Mon.*, V. 57.)

GUNNING, PETER. Adm. pens. (age 17) at ST JOHN'S, Oct. 24, 1702. S. of William, gent. B. in London. School, Wisbech (Mr Carter). Matric. 1703; B.A. 1706–7. Ord. deacon (Ely) Dec. 21, 1707; priest (London) Mar. 5, 1709–10. Brother of Francis (1707–8) and Henry (1705).

GUNNING, PETER. Adm. sizar (age 18) at ST JOHN'S, May 9, 1733. S. of Henry (1705). B. at Ely. Educated by his father. Matric. 1733. Died Feb. 1735–6. M.I. at Ely. Brother of Francis (1747) and Stuart.

GUNNING, STUART. Adm. sizar (age 15) at ST JOHN'S, June 24, 1738. S. of Henry (1705). B. at Ely. Educated there by his father. Matric. 1739; B.A. 1741–2; M.A. 1745; B.D. 1752. Fellow, 1745–66. Ord. deacon (Ely) Mar. 1744–5. V. of Hauxton and Newton, Cambs., 1747–52. V. of Madingley, 1752–72. R. of Ufford, Northants., 1765–74. Buried there Oct. 19, 1774. Brother of Francis (1747) and Peter (1733). (*Scott-Mayor*, III. 495; *G. Mag.*)

GUNNIS, VALENTINE. Matric. sizar from MAGDALENE, Easter, 1606; B.A. 1609–10, as 'Gonnis.'

GUNSBY, ——. A monk. Grace for degree, 1464–5.

GUNSON, RALPH. Matric. pens. from JESUS, Michs. 1611.

GUNSTON, JOHN. Adm. sizar (age 17) at ST JOHN'S, June 25, 1711. S. of John, shoemaker. B. in St Clement Danes, London, Oct. 12, 1693. School, Merchant Taylors'. Afterwards became a Roman Catholic. Died June 24, 1736. (Cole, *Add. MS.*, 5870, 169.)

GUNSTON, ROBERT. Matric. sizar from PEMBROKE, Michs. 1569.

GUNSTON or GUNSON, ROGER. Matric. sizar from TRINITY, Michs. 1571; B.A. 1574–5; B.D. 1593. R. of St Michael's, Denver, Norfolk, 1577–1617. R. of Fincham, 1587–1615.

GUNTER, JAMES. Matric. pens. from KING'S, Lent, 1694. Probably s. of Robert, of the Priory, Abergavenny, Monmouth. Bapt. Aug. 8, 1676. M.P. for Co. Monmouth, 1712. Died 1712. (J. A. Bradney, *Monmouth*, II. 160.)

GUNTER, JOHN. Matric. pens. from QUEENS', Easter, 1647. Of Berkshire. Migrated to Oxford, 1648. B.C.L. there, 1649. Fellow of St John's, Oxford, 1648. Fellow of New College, 1650. Incorp. at Cambridge, 1652. R. of Waddesden, Bucks. R. of Bedale, Yorks., 1658–60. Chaplain to the factory at Hamburg. P.C. of Whittlebury, Northants; ejected, 1662. Agent for Lord Wharton. Died Nov. 27, 1688. Buried at Helaugh, Yorks., in Lord Wharton's vault. (*Calamy*, II. 584; *Al. Oxon.*)

GUNTHORPE, JOHN. Warden of KING'S HALL, 1467–75. Probably B.D. 1467–8. Proctor, 1454–5. Chaplain to Edward IV. Preb. of St Paul's, 1468–72. R. of St Mary, Whitechapel, 1471–2. Preb. of Lincoln, 1471–98. Archdeacon of Essex, 1472–5. Canon of St Stephen's, Westminster, 1472–98. Dean of Wells, 1472–98. Preb. of York, 1478–85. Keeper of the Privy Seal, 1483. Died June 25, 1498. Buried in Wells Cathedral. Will (P.C.C.) 1498. (*D.N.B.*)

GUNTHORPE, ROBERT. B.A. 1509–10; M.A. 1513; B.D. 1520–1. Fellow of CHRIST'S, 1522–3. R. of Weeting St Mary, 1524–39; and All Saints', Norfolk. Died 1539.

GUNTHORP, ROBERT. Adm. sizar (age 18) at ST JOHN'S, May 3, 1727. S. of John, gent., of Nottinghamshire. B. at Mansfield Woodhouse. School, Mansfield (Mr Hucklebridge). Matric. 1727; LL.B. 1742. Ord. deacon (Lincoln) June 4; priest, Sept. 24, 1732. C. of Cromwell and Sutton-on-Trent, Notts., 1734. (*Scott-Mayor*, III. 402.)

GUNTHORPE, WILLIAM. Adm. pens. at EMMANUEL, Jan. 24, 1619–20. Matric. 1620.

GUNTON, JOSEPH. Matric. sizar from KING'S, Easter, 1635.

GUNTON, SIMON. Matric. pens. from MAGDALENE, Lent, 1626–7. S. of William, of Peterborough. Bapt. there, Dec. 30, 1609. B.A. 1630–1; M.A. 1634. Ord. deacon (Peterh.) Sept. 20, 1635; priest, Ju 4, 1637. V. of Pytchley, Northants., 1637. Preb. of Peterborough, 1646–76. V. of Leighton Bromswold, Hunts., *c.* 1651. V. of St John the Baptist, Peterborough, 1660–6. R. of Fiskerton, Lincs., 1666–76. Author, *History of Peterborough Cathedral*. Buried at Fiskerton, May 17, 1676, aged 66. M.I. (*D.N.B.*; *Fenland N. and Q.*, VI. 160.)

GUNTON, THEODORE. Adm. pens. at JESUS, June 9, 1641. Of Cambridgeshire. Matric. 1641; B.A. 1644–5; M.A. 1648. V. of Spaldwick, Hunts., in 1651.

GUNTON or GUNSTON, THOMAS. Matric. sizar from CLARE, Easter, 1577; B.A. 1580–1.

GUNTON, WILLIAM. Matric. sizar from TRINITY, *c.* 1593.

GUNWARDBY, HENRY. Fellow of PETERHOUSE, 1380–92. B.A.

GURDON, BRAMPTON. Adm. pens. at EMMANUEL, June 2, 1614. 3rd s. of Brampton, of Assington, Suffolk, Esq. Died, unmarried, at Clifford's Inn, 1621. Buried at St Dunstan-in-the-West. Brother of John (1611) and Robert (1614). (*Suff. Man. Fam.*, I. 287.)

GURDON, BRAMPTON. Adm. Fell.-Com. at JESUS, Apr. 22, 1656. 1st s. of Brampton, of Letton, Norfolk. Bapt. at Greenford, Middlesex. Matric. 1656. Adm. at the Inner Temple, 1654. Of Letton, Esq. Married Elizabeth, dau. of Colonel Francis Thornhagh, of Penton, Notts. Died 1691. Father of the next, of John (1683) and Thornhagh (1681). (Burke, *L.G.*; J. B. Peace.)

GURDON or GOURDON, BRAMPTON. Adm. pens. (age 15) at CAIUS, July 8, 1687. S. of Brampton (above), of Letton, Norfolk. B. there. School, Wymondham. Scholar, 1686–95; Matric. 1688; B.A. 1691–2; M.A. 1695. Fellow, 1695–1721. Ord. deacon (Ely) Sept. 19, 1697; priest (Lincoln) Sept. 25, 1698. C. of St Vedast, London, in 1717. Boyle lecturer, 1721. R. of Stapleford Abbotts, Essex, 1720–4. Chaplain to the Lord Chancellor, 1723. R. of St Nicholas, London, 1724–41; of St Edmund-the-King, Lombard Street, 1724–41. Archdeacon of Sudbury, 1727–41. R. of Denham, Bucks., 1730–41. Author. Died Nov. 20, 1741. Admon. (P.C.C.) 1741. Brother of Thornhagh (1681) and of John (1683). (*D.N.B.*; *Venn*, I. 483.)

GURDON, BRAMPTON. Adm. pens. (age 18) at CAIUS, Oct. 26, 1710. S. of Thornhagh (1681), Esq., of Letton, Norfolk. B. there. School, Norwich (Mr Hoadley and Mr Pate). Matric. 1710; Scholar, 1710–2. Adm. at the Middle Temple, Dec. 18, 1710. Of Grundisburgh, Suffolk. Died before Aug. 1733. (*Venn*, I. 524.)

GURDON, BRAMPTON. Adm. pens. (age 18) at CAIUS, July 8, 1725. S. of John, Esq., of Assington, Suffolk. B. there. Schools, Boxford (Mr Tatham) and Bury (Mr Kinnesman). Matric. 1725; Scholar, 1725–30; B.A. 1728–9; M.A. 1732. Ord. deacon (Norwich) May 31, 1730; priest, June 4, 1732. V. of Assington, Suffolk, 1732–80. R. of Milden, 1751–80. Official of the Archdeacon of Sudbury. Married Anne, dau. of William Woodroofe, R. of Balsham, Cambs. Died Aug. 21, 1780. Buried at Assington. M.I. there. Will, P.C.C. (*Venn*, II. 23.)

GURDON, JOHN. Adm. pens. at EMMANUEL, Apr. 13, 1611. S. and h. of Brampton, of Assington, Suffolk, Esq. B. July 3, 1595. Matric. 1611. Adm. at Gray's Inn, Nov. 16, 1614. M.P. for Ipswich, 1639–40. M.P. for Suffolk, in the Short and Long Parliament, 1640–53; for Suffolk, 1654; for Sudbury, 1660. One of the Commissioners nominated for the trial of Charles I, but refused to attend. Member of the Council of State, 1650–3. Governor of the Charterhouse. Died Sept. 9, 1679, aged 84. Will proved (P.C.C.) 1679. Buried at Assington. Brother of Brampton (1614) and Robert (1614); father of Nathaniel (1650). (*Suff. Man. Fam.*, I. 287; *Vis. of Suff.* 1664; Burke, *L.G.*; *D.N.B.*)

GURDON, JOHN. Adm. pens. (age 17) at CAIUS, Mar. 14, 1682–3. S. of Brampton (1656), gent., of Letton, Norfolk. B. there. School, Wymondham. Matric. 1683; Scholar, 1683–5. Adm. at the Middle Temple, May 27, 1685. Died 1691. Brother of Thornhagh (1681) and Brampton (1687). (*Venn*, I. 472, error in date of death.)

GURDON, JOHN. Adm. pens. at QUEENS', Feb. 14, 1689–90; afterward Fell.-Com. S. of Nathaniel (1650), R. of Chelmsford. B. in Essex. Matric. 1690. Adm. at Lincoln's Inn, Feb. 6, 1692–3. Of Assington, Esq. . . for Sudbury, 1699–1700. Died Dec. 2, 1758, aged 86. Buried at Assington. (*Suff. Man. Fam.*, I. 287; *G. Mag.*)

GURDON, JOHN. Adm. pens. at JESUS, Nov. 1, 1744. S. of Nathaniel (1712), Esq. B. at Stowmarket (his mother's home), Feb. 23, 1726–7. Matric. 1744. Migrated to Oriel College, Oxford. Matric. thence Apr. 2, 1748, age 21; s. of Nathaniel, of Hintlesham and Assington, Suffolk; B.A. (Oxford) 1749. Of Assington, Esq. Buried there Nov. 13, 1777. (*Al. Oxon.*; *Suff. Man. Fam.*, I. 287.)

GURDON, NATHANIEL. Adm. pens. at EMMANUEL, Apr. 19, 1650. Of Suffolk. 4th s. of John (1611), of Assington, Esq. School, Colchester. Matric. 1652; B.A. 1653–4; M.A. from Queens', 1657; D.D. 1691 (*Lit. Reg.*). Incorp. at Oxford, 1657. V. of Little Abingdon, Cambs., 1660–2. R. of Woodham Ferrers, Essex, 1666–91. R. of Chelmsford, 1681–96. Died Feb. 11, 1696–7, aged 64. Buried at Assington. Will (P.C.C.) 1698. Father of John (1689–90), brother of Robert (1645). (Burke, L.G.)

GURDON, NATHANIEL. Adm. pens. at JESUS, July 4, 1712. S. of John, of Assington, Suffolk, Esq. Bapt. Jan. 13, 1696–7. Matric. 1714. Adm. at Lincoln's Inn, Oct. 22, 1714. Of Assington, Esq. Married Elizabeth, dau. of John Sayer, of Stowmarket. Buried Mar. 18, 1767. Father of John (1744). (*Suff. Man. Fam.*, I. 287.)

GURDON, PARKER. Adm. pens. at QUEENS', June 3, 1728. S. of John, of Assington, Suffolk, Esq. Matric. 1728; B.A. 1731–2; M.A. 1740. R. of South Burgh, Norfolk, 1750. R. of Cranworth, 1753–62. Died June 14, 1762. Buried at Cranworth. (*Suff. Man. Fam.*, I. 287; G. *Mag.*)

GURDON, PHILIP. Adm. pens. at EMMANUEL, Apr. 19, 1650. 3rd s. of John, of Assington, Suffolk. B. at Gt Wenham, Suffolk, 1631. B.A. 1653; M.A. from Queens', 1657. Incorp. at Oxford, 1657. M.P. for Sudbury, 1689–90. Buried at Assington, June 23, 1690. Brother of Robert (1645) and Nathaniel (1650).

GURDON, PHILIP. Adm. pens. at JESUS, Apr. 9, 1723. S. of John, Esq., of Assington, Suffolk. Bapt. there, Aug. 16, 1706. Matric. 1724; B.A. 1726–7; M.A. 1730. Ord. deacon (Ely) Sept. 22, 1728. R. of Bures, Suffolk, 1731–85. Married Rachel, dau. of Sir Thomas Abdy, Bart. Will (P.C.C.) 1785.

GURDON, ROBERT. Adm. pens. at EMMANUEL, June 2, 1614. 2nd s. of Brampton, of Assington, Suffolk, Esq. Age 13 in 1612. Adm. at the Inner Temple, 1615. Barrister, 1626. Bencher, 1646. Married Joyce, dau. of James Harvey, of Maldon, Essex. Will (P.C.C.) 1647. Brother of Brampton (1614) and John (1611). (*Suff. Man. Fam.*, I. 287.)

GURDON, ROBERT. Adm. pens. at EMMANUEL, May 6, 1645. 1st s. of John, of Assington. B. at Gt Wenham, Suffolk. School, Colchester. Of Assington, Esq. Buried there May 24, 1683, aged 68. Brother of Nathaniel (1650) and Philip (1650).

GURDON, THORNHAGH. Adm. Fell.-Com. (age 18) at CAIUS, Apr. 23, 1681. S. of Brampton (1656), gent., of Letton, Norfolk. B. there, July 28, 1663. Schools, Wymondham (Mr Clarke) and Earl Stonham (Mr Wilson). Matric. 1681; M.A. 1682 (*Com. Reg.*). Receiver-general of Norfolk. F.S.A., 1718. Author, historical. Died at Letton, Nov. 19, 1733. M.I. at Cranworth. Will, P.C.C. Brother of John (1683) and Brampton (1687), father of Brampton (1710). (*D.N.B.*; *Venn*, I. 466.)

GURDON, WILLIAM. Adm. pens. at EMMANUEL, Apr. 16, 1619. S. of Brampton, of Assington, Suffolk, Esq. Matric. 1619. Buried at Gt St Andrew's, Cambridge, Dec. 25, 1620.

GURERD, STEPHEN. Matric. pens. from PETERHOUSE, Easter, 1586. A Frenchman.

GURLEY, ——. Matric. sizar from KING'S, Michs. 1549.

GURLING, *see* **GIRLING.**

GURMESCHESTRE, JOHN. Fellow of CLARE, when ord. deacon (Ely) Apr. 13; priest, June 8, 1392.

GURNALL, JOHN. Adm. sizar (age 17) at CHRIST'S, Apr. 20, 1682. S. of William (1632), minister of Lavenham, Suffolk. School, Felsted (Mr Glascock). Matric. 1682; B.A. 1685–6. C. of Brockley, Suffolk, 1691–8. Died 1700. Brother of William (1670–1). (*Peile*, II. 87.)

GURNALL, PENNINGTON. Adm. at CORPUS CHRISTI, 1732. Of Westminster. Matric. 1732; B.A. 1735–6.

GURNELL or GYRNELL, THOMAS. B.Can.L. 1519–20. One of these names R. of Pluckley, Kent, 1519–23; of Marestone, 1528; of Mereworth, 1536–57.

GURNALL, WILLIAM. Adm. pens. at EMMANUEL, Mar. 29, 1632. S. of Thomas. B. at Walpole, near Lynn, 1617. School, Lynn. Matric. 1632; Scholar; B.A. 1635-6; M.A. 1639. Ord. priest (Norwich) Aug. 21, 1662. R. of Lavenham, Suffolk, 1644-79. Married Sara, dau. of Thomas Mott, V. of Stoke-by-Nayland. Author, theological. Died Oct. 12, 1679. Father of the next and John (1682). (*D.N.B.*; J. B. Peace.)

GURNALL, WILLIAM. Adm. pens. (age 16) at CHRIST'S, Jan. 19, 1670-1. S. of William (1632). B. at Lavenham, Suffolk. School, Felsted (Mr Glascock). Matric. 1671. Buried July 28, 1674, at Gt St Andrew's, Cambridge. Brother of John (1682).

GURNARD, RICHARD. Adm. Fell.-Com. at PETERHOUSE, Mar. 23, 1631-2. S. of Richard. Bapt. at St Vedast, London, Dec. 17, 1615. Matric. 1632, as 'Jurnard.' Died *v.p.* and *s.p.* The father, Gurnard or Gurney, was Lord Mayor of London, 1641-2. Created Bart., 1641. (*T. A. Walker*, 47.)

GURNETT, GEORGE. Adm. sizar (age 20) at TRINITY, June 26, 1716. S. of George, of Dorking, Surrey. School, Kingston, Surrey (Mr Winde). Matric. 1716; Scholar, 1719; B.A. 1719-20; M.A. 1723. Chaplain of Trinity College, 1723-46.

GURNEY, EDMUND. Matric. pens. from QUEENS', 1595. Adm. Oct. 30, 1594. S. of Henry, of West Barsham, Norfolk. B.A. 1598-9; M.A. from Corpus Christi, 1602; B.D. 1609. Fellow of Corpus Christi, 1601-14. Incorp. at Oxford, 1606. Ord. priest (Norwich) 1614. R. of Edgefield, Norfolk, 1614-20. R. of Harpley, 1620-48. Author of anti-Romanist treatises. One of Fuller's *Worthies*. Buried at St Peter Mancroft, Norwich, May 14, 1648. (*House of Gournay*, 287, 463; *Masters*, 301; *Vis. of Norfolk*, 1664.)

GURNAY, EDWARD. Adm. Fell.-Com. at CHRIST'S, Apr. 22, 1625. S. of Thomas, of Norfolk. School, Bury (Mr Dickinson). Adm. at Lincoln's Inn, May 15, 1628, as 's. of Thomas, deceased.' Of West Barsham, Esq. Died Aug. 6, 1641. M.I. Will (P.C.C.) 1642. Brother of Thomas (1627-8), father of Henry (1647-8). (*Peile*, I. 366; *House of Gournay*, 287.)

GURNEY, EDWARD. Matric. sizar from QUEENS', Easter, 1627. Of London. B.A. 1630-1; M.A. 1634.

GURNEY or GOURNEYE, GEORGE. Matric. pens. from CHRIST'S, Dec. 1573.

GURNEY or GOURNAY, H. Matric. pens. from CHRIST'S, Oct. 1564. Probably Henry, s. of Francis, of Irstead, Esq. B. 1548. Of West Barsham and Ellingham, Esq. Married Ellen, dau. of John Blennerhasset, of Barsham, Norfolk. Will proved, 1623. Grandfather of Edward (1625). (*House of Gournay*, 287, 454.)

GOURNAY, HENRY. Adm. Fell.-Com. (age 16) at CAIUS, Feb. 18, 1647-8. S. of Edward (1625), Esq., of West Barsham, Norfolk. B. at Hillington, Jan. 23, 1631-2. School, Gressenhall (Mr Greene). Matric. 1648. Adm. at Lincoln's Inn, 1651. Of West Barsham, Esq. Died 1661. M.I. at West Barsham. Will, P.C.C. (*Venn*, I. 371.)

GURNEY, JOHN. Matric. pens. from QUEENS', Easter, 1613. Of Norfolk. B.A. 1616-7; M.A. 1620.

GURNEY, JOHN. Adm. sizar (age 17) at TRINITY, Apr. 10, 1697. S. of John, of London. School, St Paul's. Matric. 1697; Scholar, 1699; B.A. 1700-1; M.A. 1705.

GURNEY, JOHN. Adm. sizar (age 16) at TRINITY, June 23, 1721. S. of John, clerk, of London. Matric. 1721; Scholar, 1725; B.A. 1725-6; M.A. 1730. Incorp. at Oxford, 1740. Ord. deacon (Lincoln) Sept. 24, 1727; priest (Ely) Sept. 19, 1731. Brother of Samuel (1733).

GOURNEY, JUSTINIAN. M.A. 1679 (Incorp. from Oxford). S. of John, of Hanging Houghton, Lamport, Northants., gent. Bapt. at Lamport, Dec. 30, 1650. Matric. from Brasenose College, Mar. 28, 1667, age 15; B.A. (Oxford) 1670; M.A. 1673. Ord. deacon (Peterb.) Sept. 21, 1673; priest, June 4, 1674. R. of Wadenhoe, Northants., 1674-1714. Buried there Feb. 25, 1713-4. (*Al. Oxon.*; H. I. Longden.)

GURNEY, SAMUEL. Adm. sizar (age 18) at TRINITY, Oct. 25, 1733. S. of John, of London, clerk. Matric. 1733; B.A. 1737. Brother of John (1721).

GURNEY, THOMAS. Matric. pens. from JESUS, Michs. 1588; B.A. 1592-3; M.A. 1596; M.D. 1608. Incorp. at Oxford, 1601.

GURNAY, THOMAS. Adm. pens. (age 16) at CHRIST'S, Mar. 4, 1627-8. S. of Thomas. B. at Barsham, Norfolk. School, Bury (Mr Dickinson). Matric. 1628; B.A. 1631-2. Adm. at Lincoln's Inn, Aug. 10, 1632, as '2nd s. of Thomas, late of Great Ellingham, Norfolk, Esq., deceased.' Barrister-at-law. Living, 1662. Brother of Edward (1625). (*Peile*, I. 389; *House of Gournay*, 476.)

GURNEY, THOMAS. Adm. sizar (age 17) at TRINITY, Jan. 4, 1728-9. Matric. 1729; B.A. 1732-3. One of these names, B.A., V. of Bapchild, Kent, 1764-5. V. of Seasalter, 1764-74. P.C. of Whitstable, 1765-74. V. of Charlton, 1770. Died June 12, 1774.

GURNEY, WILLIAM. Matric. sizar from CORPUS CHRISTI, Easter, 1613. Of Warwickshire.

GURNEY, WILLIAM. Adm. at CORPUS CHRISTI, 1716. Of Kent. S. of Thomas, of Shoulden. King's scholar from Canterbury School. Ord. priest (Norwich) Sept. 1722. C. of Dymchurch, Kent. R. of Hurst, 1726-55. V. of Westwell, 1730-55. Assistant Master of Canterbury School, 1743-55. Married, 1732, Alice Bourne, of Westwell. Died Apr. 1, 1755. (*G. Mag.*; H. G. Harrison.)

GURNEY, WILLIAM. Adm. at CORPUS CHRISTI, 1751. Of Kent. Matric. 1751; B.A. 1755; M.A. 1761. Ord. deacon (Peterb.) Sept. 19, 1756. R. of Leveland, Kent, 1763. R. of Badlesmere, 1763. R. of Selling, 1763. V. of Bredgar, 1772-80. R. of Luddenham, 1780. Died Apr. 8, 1784. (*G. Mag.*)

GURNEY, ——. Degree (? B.D.) 1474-5. A friar.

GURNAY, ——. Probably B.D. 1487-8; D.D. 1491-2, but dates uncertain. A friar.

GURNAY, ——. B.Can.L. 1499-1500.

GURREY, THOMAS. Matric. sizar from CHRIST'S, June, 1586; B.A. (? 1589-90); M.A. 1593. One of these names V. of Kenton, Suffolk, 1605-10. Possibly R. of Westfield, Sussex, 1612. Preb. of Wolverhampton, *c.* 1620. (*Peile*, I. 187.)

GURREY, WILLIAM. Matric. sizar from ST JOHN'S, Easter, 1573. One of these names ord. deacon (Peterb.) July 9, 1575. Probably C. of Everdon, Northants. Perhaps R. of Bradfield, Lincoln diocese, 1586.

GUSTARD, ROBERT. Matric. sizar from TRINITY, *c.* 1595.

GUTER, WILLIAM. 'M.A. Cambridge': Incorp. at Oxford, July 12, 1623. Not found.

GUTTER, EDWARD. Matric. sizar from CLARE, Michs. 1580; B.A. 1584-5 as 'Edmund'; M.A. 1588. V. of St Peter, Colchester, 1590-3. Died 1593. Will (Commis. C. Essex) 1593.

GUTTER, JONAS. Matric. sizar from TRINITY, Lent, 1577-8; Scholar, 1582; B.A. 1582-3.

GUTTER, THOMAS. Matric. pens. from JESUS, Michs. 1566.

GUTTERIDGE, BARTIN. Adm. sizar (age 20) at ST JOHN'S, June 25, 1734. S. of Bartin, husbandman, of Northamptonshire. B. at Thorpe Malsor. Bapt. there, Mar. 9, 1714-5. School, Oakham (Mr Adcock). Matric. 1735; B.A. 1737-8. Ord. deacon (Lincoln) Sept. 23, 1739; priest, June 13, 1742. R. of Upper Isham, Northants., 1742-4. Died, unmarried, Jan. 7, 1759. Buried at Thorpe Malsor. (*Scott-Mayor*, III. 458; *G. Mag.*)

GUTTERIDGE, BENJAMIN. M.A. from EMMANUEL, 1748. S. of Charles, of St Helen's, Abingdon, Berks. Matric. from Pembroke College, Oxford, June 30, 1725, age 17; B.A. (Oxford) 1729-30. Will of one of these names (P.C.C.) 1786; of Walcot, Somerset, clerk. (*Al. Oxon.*)

GUY, BRYAN. Adm. pens. (age 15) at ST JOHN'S, Oct. 11, 1634. S. of Edmund, yeoman, of Sedbergh. B. there. School, Sedbergh (Mr Nelson). B.A. 1638-9; M.A. 1642. Of Kirkland, Cumberland. Father of Edmund (1669).

GUY, CHARLES. M.A. from PEMBROKE, 1725. S. of C., of St Minver, Cornwall, clerk. Matric. from Exeter College, Oxford, Feb. 22, 1710-1, age 19; B.A. (Oxford) 1714. V. of Padstow, Cornwall, 1720. Admon. (Exeter) 1770. (*Al. Oxon.*)

GUY, EDMUND. Adm. sizar (age 18) at ST JOHN'S, Apr. 26, 1669. S. of Brian (1634), clerk, deceased, of Kirkland, Cumberland. B. there. School, Sedbergh. Matric. 1669; B.A. 1672-3.

GUY, EDWARD. Adm. sizar at TRINITY, Mar. 18, 1641-2. Matric. 1642; B.A. 1645-6; M.A. 1649. V. of Flintham, Notts., 1660-95. Died 1695. Buried at Flintham. M.I.

GUY, EDWARD. Adm. at CORPUS CHRISTI, 1710. Of Nottinghamshire. Matric. 1710; B.A. 1713-4. Ord. deacon (York) Sept. 1714; priest (Lincoln) Sept. 23, 1716. V. of Bennington, Lincs., 1716. Perhaps V. of Broughton, Yorks., 1741-62.

GUY, FRANCIS. 'B.A. of JESUS,' when ord. priest (Ely) Sept. 24, 1670. Not found in our records.

GUY, GEORGE. Adm. sizar at SIDNEY, Feb. 6, 1614-5. Matric. 1615; B.A. 1618-9; M.A. 1622. R. of Widford, Essex, 1637. Died 1678, aged 78. M.I. Will, P.C.C.

GUY, HENRY. M.A. 1671 (Incorp. from Oxford). S. of William, of Kendal, Westmorland. Matric. from Queen's College, Oxford, May 20, 1664, age 17; B.A. (Oxford) 1667; M.A. 1670. R. of Uldale, Cumberland, 1677-84, when he resigned. A non-juror. (*Al. Oxon.*; *B. Nightingale*.)

GUY, JOHN. Adm. pens. at TRINITY HALL, July 8, 1664. 2nd s. of Robert, yeoman. B. at Isham, Northants. Schools, Strixton, Northants. (Mr Farrow) and Eton. Migrated to Sidney, Aug. 16, 1664, age 16. Matric. 1664; B.A. 1667-8.

GUY, JOHN. Adm. at CORPUS CHRISTI, 1680. Of Nottinghamshire. Matric. 1680-1; B.A. 1684-5. V. of Whatton-in-the-Vale, Notts., 1687. Married at St Mary, Nottingham, Jan. 24, 1690-1, Mary Smith. (Godfrey, *Notts.*)

GUY or GYE, JOSEPH. Adm. sizar (age 16) at ST JOHN'S, Apr. 6, 1659. S. of Solomon, deceased, of Falkingham, Lincs. B. there. School, Grantham (Mr Stokes). Matric. 1659; B.A. 1663.

GUY, WILLIAM. Matric. from TRINITY, 1637. S. of John, draper, of Sedbergh. B. there. School, Sedbergh (Mr Nelson). Migrated as pens. to St John's, June 24, 1641, age 19. B.A. 1641-2.

GUY, WILLIAM. Adm. pens. (age 15) at ST JOHN'S, May 30, 1670. S. of John, factor, of Garsdale, Yorks. B. there. School, Sedbergh (Mr Fell). Matric. 1670; B.A. 1674-5. Ord. deacon (York) Sept. 1675; priest, May, 1676. Probably V. of Whatton-in-the-Vale, Notts., 1676-9. Buried at Flintham, June 12, 1679. (Godfrey, *Notts.*)

GUY, WILLIAM. Adm. at CORPUS CHRISTI, 1690. Of Nottinghamshire. Matric. 1691; B.A. 1694-5. Ord. deacon (York) Feb. 1694-5.

GUYBON, EDMUND. Adm. Fell.-Com. at CORPUS CHRISTI, 1692. Of Rolvendon, Kent. Matric. 1692. Brother of Philip (1692).

GUYBON, FRANCIS. Adm. at CORPUS CHRISTI, 1689. Of Norwich. S. of William, of Norwich, alderman. Bapt. at St Peter Mancroft, Sept. 7, 1673. Matric. 1689; Scholar; B.A. 1692-3; M.A. 1696; M.D. 1706. Practised for many years at Diss, Norfolk. Died there Dec. 21, 1750. Buried at Lammas. M.I. there. (*Masters.*)

GUYBON, PHILIP. Adm. Fell.-Com. at CORPUS CHRISTI, 1692. Of Rolvendon, Kent, Esq. Matric. 1692. M.P. for Rye, 1707-62. One of the Lords of the Treasury, 1741. Died Mar. 1762. Brother of Edmund (1692). (*Masters*, 300.)

GUYBON, THOMAS. Adm. Fell.-Com. at PETERHOUSE, Oct. 6, 1617. S. of William, of Watlington, Norfolk. Bapt. there, Jan. 18, 1600-1. Of Thursford, Esq. Sheriff of Norfolk, 1641. Died May 29, 1666. Father of Thomas (next) and William. (*T. A. Walker.*)

GUYBON, THOMAS. Adm. pens. (age 16) at CAIUS, Mar. 16, 1647-8. S. of Sir Thomas (above), of Thursford, Norfolk. Bapt. at Merton, Feb. 17, 1630-1. Schools, Cantley (Mr Chapman) and Norwich (Mr Lovering). Matric. 1648. Adm. at Lincoln's Inn, May 23, 1650. Died before 1666. Brother of the next. (*Venn*, I. 371; *Blomefield*, IX. 259; *Vis. of Norfolk.*)

GUYBON, WILLIAM. Adm. Fell.-Com. (age 17) at CAIUS, Mar. 16, 1647-8. Eldest s. of Sir Thomas (1617), of Thursford, Norfolk. Bapt. at Merton, Aug. 17, 1629. Schools, Cantley (Mr Chapman) and Norwich (Mr Lovering). Matric. 1647-8. Adm. at Lincoln's Inn, May 23, 1650. Will proved (P.C.C.) Feb. 14, 1664-5. M.I. at Thursford. Brother of the above.

GUYBON, WILLIAM. Adm. Fell.-Com. (age 17) at CAIUS, May 11, 1702. Eldest s. of Sir Francis, Knt., of Thursford, Norfolk. Schools, Fakenham (Mr Osborn) and Norwich (Mr Hoadley). Of Thursford, Esq. Lord of the Manor of Islington, Norfolk. Married Sarah, dau. of John Knapp, of Wells, Norfolk. (*Venn*, I. 509; *Vis. of Norfolk*, 1664.)

GUYBON, ——. Adm. pens. at PETERHOUSE, Dec. 9, 1581.

GUYON, CHARLES. M.A. from KING'S, 1729. S. of Charles, of Patteswick, Essex, gent. Matric. from Merton College, Oxford, July 9, 1711, age 17; B.A. (Oxford) 1715. V. of Cressing, Essex, 1727. R. of Cricksea, 1729. (*Al. Oxon.*)

GUYON, GEORGE. Adm. pens. (age 14) at MAGDALENE, Mar. 29, 1670. S. of George, gent., deceased, of Coggeshall, Essex. School, Felsted. Matric. 1670. Adm. at Gray's Inn, May 29, 1671. One of these names, of Hovills, Coggeshall, captain of a company of Trained Bands; buried there, Oct. 6, 1676. (V. B. Redstone.)

GUYON, ROBERT. Scholar at EMMANUEL, Dec. 1615; B.A. 1617-8; M.A. 1621. Ord. deacon (Peterb.) Sept. 29; priest, Sept. 30, 1622. P.C. of White Colne, Essex, 1634; sequestered about 1644. (*Davids*, 377; H. I. Longden.)

GUYON, WILLIAM. Adm. Fell.-Com. (age 17) at MAGDALENE, Mar. 10, 1687-8. S. of Sir Mark, Knt., of Dyne's Hall, Essex. B. at Coggeshall. School, Felsted. Matric. 1688; M.A. 1690 (*Com. Reg.*). Died in London, Aug. 21, 1691. Buried at Coggeshall. (Le Neve, *Knights*, 303; V. B. Redstone.)

GUYON, ——. Adm. at MAGDALENE, June 20, 1691.

GUYRES, ——. Probably M.A. Of Huntingdon. Cited for some cause by the University, 1458-9. (*Gr. Bk*, A, 19.)

GWAVAS, JOHN. Adm. pens. (age 18) at CHRIST'S, June, 1708. S. of William. B. at Huntingfield Hall, Suffolk. Matric. 1708; Scholar, 1710-1; LL.B. 1713. R. of Wheatacre All Saints', Norfolk, 1715. R. of Horham, Jan. 7, 1716-7. R. of Thorpe, near Haddiscoe, Norfolk, 1746-53. (*Peile*, II. 170.)

GWILLIM, JOSEPH. M.A. 1662 (Incorp. from Oxford). Matric. from Merton College, Dec. 16, 1653; B.A. from Brasenose College, 1657; M.A. 1660; B.D. 1669. Fellow of Brasenose, 1656-70. Died Sept. 10, 1670. Will (P.C.C.); of Highgate, Middlesex. (*Al. Oxon.*)

GUILLIM, LUCIUS. Matric. pens. from CORPUS CHRISTI, Michs. 1655. S. and h. of Thomas, of Holborn, London, Esq. Adm. at Gray's Inn, June 16, 1654.

GWILLIM, PETER. Adm. pens. (age 15) at ST JOHN'S, Aug. 6, 1645. S. of Peter, of St Margaret's, Westminster, brewer. Bapt. there, Feb. 11, 1629-30. School, Islington (Mr Vowell). Matric. 1645. Migrated to Oxford. B.A. from Magdalen Hall, 1648; M.A. 1651. Fellow of Magdalen College, 1648. R. of Slymbridge, Gloucs., 1656-62, ejected. (*Al. Oxon.*; *Calamy*, II. 254.)

GWINNET, ISAAC. Adm. pens. at KING'S, 1679-80. Previously matric. from Queen's College, Oxford, Mar. 21, 1677-8, age 15. S. of Isaac, of Sherrington, Gloucs. (*Al. Oxon.*)

GWYNNETT, SAMUEL. LL.B. 1728 (*Com. Reg.*).

GWYNN, ARTHUR. Adm. pens. at TRINITY, July 8, 1672.

GWIN, AUGUSTIN. Adm. at KING'S, a scholar from Eton, 1715. B. at Brentford, Middlesex. Matric. Easter, 1716; B.A. 1719-20; M.A. 1723. Fellow, 1719. Ord. deacon (London) Dec. 4, 1721. V. of Prescot, Lancs., 1730-76. Died Feb. 27, 1776.

GWYN, GEORGE. Adm. sizar (age 16) at CAIUS, May 26, 1719. S. of George, gent., of London. B. in the parish of St Olave, Surrey. School, St Olave's (Mr Rogerson). Matric. 1719; Scholar, 1719-23; B.A. 1722-3. Ord. deacon (London) Jun 1, 1729; priest, Sept. 19, 1731. Lecturer at St Mary-at-Hill, London. Died Oct. 5, 1732. (*Venn*, II. 11.)

GWYN, HUMPHREY. Adm. sizar (age 17) at MAGDALENE, June 16, 1694. S. of John. B. at Condover, Salop. Matric. 1695; B.A. 1697-8.

GWYNNE, JOHN. Matric. sizar from QUEENS', Michs. 1545. Of Carnarvon. S. of John Wynn, of Gwydir. B.A. 1547-8; M.A. (St John's) 1551; LL.D. 1560. Fellow of St John's, 1548. Proctor, 1555-6. Preb. of Bangor, 1550-74. Adm. advocate, 1560. R. (sinecure) of Llanrhaiadr-in-Kinmerch, Deubs., 1561. M.P. for Cardigan, 1563-7; for Carnarvonshire, 1572-4. Benefactor to St John's by gift of fellowships and scholarships. Died 1574. Will (P.C.C.) (*Cooper*, I. 324.)

GWYN, JOHN. Matric. sizar from ST JOHN'S, Easter, 1568. Perhaps migrated to Hart Hall, Oxford, 1571, age 16; B.A. there, 1571.

GWYN, JOHN. Matric. pens. from ST JOHN'S, Michs. 1575. Of Of Denbighshire. B.A. 1579-80; M.A. 1583. Fellow, 1584.

GWINNE, JOHN. Matric. pens. from PEMBROKE, Easter, 1583.

GWIN, JOHN. B.A. from MAGDALENE, 1673-4; M.A. 1677. Ord. deacon (Peterb.) June 18, 1671. Perhaps, as John Guin, clerk, buried at Conington, Cambs., Aug. 24, 1688.

GWYN, JOHN. Adm. sizar at JESUS, June 30, 1683. Of Carmarthenshire. Matric. 1683.

GWYNNE, JONATHAN. Adm. sizar (age 18) at MAGDALENE, June 24, 1749. S. of Evan. B. at Llanvair, Montgom. School, Shrewsbury. Matric. 1749; B.A. 1753.

GWYN, LEWIS. Matric. pens. from JESUS, Michs. 1555. Of Wales. B.A. 1556-7; M.A. 1560. Fellow, 1559-66. One of these names Archdeacon of Cardigan, 1569-84. V. of Nantmel. Preb. of St David's. Died *c.* Dec. 1584. (A. Gray.)

GWYNN, LEWIS. Matric. sizar from CHRIST'S, *c.* 1595; B.A. 1598-9; M.A. 1603. Perhaps V. of Newton, Montgom., 1614-7. V. of Llanrhiadr-yn-Mochnant, 1616; and R. of Denbigh, 1621-5.

GWYN, LEWIS. Adm. sizar (age 17) at ST JOHN'S, July 1, 1661. S. of William, clerk, of Ingoldsby, Lincs. B. there. School, Westminster. Matric. 1661; B.A. 1664-5. Ord. priest (Peterb.) Sept. 22, 1667. R. of Normanton, Lincs., 1671. V. of Honington, Lincs., 1694-1720.

GWIN, LEWIS. Adm. pens. at TRINITY, June 26, 1666. School, Westminster. Matric. 1666-7; Scholar, 1667; B.A. 1669-70. Perhaps V. of Honington, Lincs., 1720; and R. of Normanton, 1720.

GWYN, NATHAN. 'M.A. Cambridge'; Incorp. at Oxford, July 14, 1618. Name not found.

GWYNN, NICHOLAS. Adm. pens. (age 18) at MAGDALENE, Apr. 3, 1729. S. of Rice, gent., of Sutton, Lincs. B. at Long Sutton. School, Eton (colleger), 1723-8. Matric. 1729. Resided at Magdalene two years. Afterwards at Leyden University. M.D. Leyden. Married Rebecca, dau. of Richard Little, of Peterborough. Resided at Ipswich. Died there Jan. 20, 1798. Buried at Rushmere, Suffolk. M.I. at Fakenham. Will, P.C.C. Grandson of Rice (1665).

GWYN, OWEN. Matric. sizar from QUEENS', Michs. 1545.

GWYN, OWEN. Matric. pens. from ST JOHN'S, Easter, 1584. Of Denbighshire. B.A. 1587-8; M.A. 1591; B.D. 1599; D.D. 1613. Fellow, 1589. Master, May 16, 1612-33. Vice-Chancellor, 1615-6. R. of Honington (? Suffolk), 1600-5. V. of East Ham, Essex, 1605-11. R. of South Luffenham, Rutland, 1611. Archdeacon of Huntingdon, 1622-33. Preb. of Lincoln, 1622. Buried in St John's Chapel, June 5, 1633. Will proved (V.C.C.) 1633. (*Al. Oxon.* suggests another man for the above preferments.)

GWYNNE, RICE. Matric. sizar from ST JOHN'S, c. 1596; B.A. 1599-1600. Ord. deacon and priest (Peterb.) Sept. 25, 1603.

GUYNNE, RICE. Adm. Fell.-Com. (age 17) at CAIUS, May 4, 1640. S. of Rice, Esq. B. at Fakenham, Norfolk. School, Norwich (Mr Lovering). Matric. 1640. Of Fakenham, Esq. Married Alice, dau. of Robert Bacon, Esq. (afterwards Bart.), of Ryburgh, Norfolk. Will proved (P.C.C.) 1667. Father of the next. (*Venn*, I. 338.)

GUYNNE, RICE. Adm. pens. (age 17) at CAIUS, May 17, 1665. S. of Rice (above), of Fakenham. B. there. School, Botesdale, Suffolk (Mr Ives). Matric. 1665. Of Fakenham, Norfolk, Esq. Married at South Wootton, Oct. 14, 1675, Mary, dau. of Anthony Hammond, of South Wootton, Norfolk. Will proved (Archd. Norfolk) Apr. 9, 1690. (*Venn*, I. 426.)

GWYN, RICHARD. Matric. pens. from ST JOHN'S, Michs. 1571. Perhaps migrated to Hart Hall, Oxford, Dec. 17, 1576, age 19; B.A. 1575-6; M.A. 1578. Of Co. Carnarvon.

GWYN, RICHARD. Adm. pens. at TRINITY, Feb. 9, 1647-8. Of Carmarthen. Perhaps s. and h. of Charles, of Gwempa, Esq.; adm. at Lincoln's Inn, Feb. 1, 1647-8. One of these names, 'citizen of London,' died Nov. 12, 1701, aged 71. Buried at Wonersh, Surrey. (*Manning and Bray*, II. 114.)

GWYNNE, ROBERT. B.A. from ST JOHN'S, 1611-2. Of St Asaph. M.A. 1615. Fellow, 1613. Incorp. at Oxford, 1613. Ord. deacon (York, for Lincoln) May 26, 1615.

GWYN, THOMAS. Matric. pens. from ST JOHN'S, Michs. 1588.

GWYN, W. Matric. pens. from ST JOHN'S, Michs. 1567.

GWIN, WILLIAM. Matric. pens. from ST JOHN'S, Michs. 1611.

GWYN, WILLIAM. Adm. pens. (age 21) at ST JOHN'S, July 2, 1632. Previously at Brasenose College, Oxford, where he matriculated Dec. 9, 1631. Of Merioneth. S. of Lewis, gent., of Dolseran. School, Bunbury, Cheshire (Mr Cole). B.A. 1632-3; M.A. 1636. Perhaps V. of Biddenham, Beds., 1636-40-.

GWYNNE, ——. Incorporated, 1499-1500.

GYDON, ——. Fellow of GONVILLE HALL, 1423-5.

GYLFORD or GULDEFORD, HENRY. Matric. Fell.-Com. from TRINITY, Lent, 1580-1. Perhaps s. and h. of Sir Thomas, of Hemsted, Kent. If so, knighted, 1591. Married Lady Elizabeth Somerset, dau. of Edward, Earl of Worcester. (Burke, *Ext. Bart.*)

GYLGATE, WILLIAM. Matric. pens. from CLARE, Michs. 1580; B.A. 1584-5. Ord. priest (Norwich) Apr. 19, 1593. V. of Ashfield and Thorpe, Suffolk.

GYLIAN, JOHN. Matric. sizar from ST JOHN'S, Michs. 1568.

GYLMORE, JOHN. Matric. sizar from MAGDALENE, Easter, 1581.

GYLMYN, ROBERT. Matric. pens. from TRINITY, Michs. 1571.

GYLYS, *see* GILES.

GYMBER, ——. B.A. 1477-8.

GYNE, —— (1532), *see* KING.

H

HABECIUS, GASPAR. Matric. pens. from MAGDALENE, Lent, 1564-5; being M.A. from Marburg. Teacher of Hebrew in the University.

HABER, REYNOLD. Matric. pens. from CLARE, c. 1596.

HABER or HEBBER, WILLIAM. B.A. 1519-20; M.A. 1523.

HABERGHAM, JOHN. Matric. sizar from ST JOHN'S, Easter, 1566.

HABERGHAM, SAMUEL. Adm. sizar at EMMANUEL, July 1, 1641. Of Suffolk. S. of Laurence, clerk, of Framlingham. Bapt. Nov. 5, 1626. Matric. 1641; B.A. 1644-5; M.A. 1648. R. of Heveningham, Suffolk, 1650. V. of Syleham; ejected, 1662. Buried there Jan. 7, 1664-5. (*Calamy*, II. 436; V. B. Redstone.)

HABERYE, ROBERT. Matric. sizar from TRINITY, Easter, 1588.

HABINGTON, HENRY. B.Mus. 1463. (J. Hawkins, *Hist. of Music*, II. 346. Not found in the *Grace Books*.)

HACKE, RICHARD. Matric. sizar from TRINITY, Michs. 1562.

HACKE, WILLIAM. Matric. Fell.-Com. from ST JOHN'S, Easter, 1581.

HACKER, CHARLES. Adm. at ST CATHARINE'S, Mar. 9, 1693-4. Of Southwell, Notts. Matric. 1695; B.A. 1697-8. Ord. deacon (York) May, 1700; priest (London) June 16, 1701.

HACKER, FRANCIS. Adm. pens. (age 16) at PETERHOUSE, Mar. 28, 1649. Of Leicestershire. S. of Francis, Parliamentary Colonel and regicide (for whom *see D.N.B.*). School, Coventry. Held a commission in his father's regiment. (*T. A. Walker*, 92.)

HACKER, JOHN. Adm. pens. (age 17) at CHRIST'S, May 16, 1627. Eldest s. of Richard, of Sawley, Derbs. B. there. School, Repton (Mr Whitehead). Matric. 1627; B.A. 1630-1. High Sheriff of Notts., 1673-4. Father of the next. (*Peile*, I. 383.)

HACKER, RICHARD. Adm. pens. at TRINITY, Apr. 6, 1667. S. and h. of John (above), of Flintham, Notts., Esq. Adm. at Gray's Inn, May 22, 1669. Buried at Flintham, Apr. 18, 1723. (Godfrey, *Notts.*)

HACKET, ANDREW. Adm. pens. at TRINITY, June 30, 1645, a scholar from Westminster. S. and h. of John (1609), D.D., Bishop of Lichfield. B. in London, c. 1632. Matric. 1646; B.A. 1648-9; M.A. 1652. Adm. at Gray's Inn, Jan. 24, 1652-3. Barrister, 1659. Of Moxhull, Warws. Knighted, Jan. 16, 1670-1. Master in Chancery, 1670-80. M.P. for Tamworth, 1679-81. Died Mar. 19, 1709-10. Will, P.C.C. Father of the next, of John (1688) and Lisle (1683). (Le Neve, *Knights*, 244; *Vis. of Warws.*, 1682.)

HACKET, ANDREW. Adm. pens. (age 15) at TRINITY, Oct. 23, 1683. 2nd s. of Sir Andrew (above), of Moxhull, Warws. School, Solihull, Warws. (Mr George Ward). Matric. 1683. Adm. at Gray's Inn, Feb. 2, 1685-6. Of Moxhull, Esq. Married (1) Dorcas Fulwood, by whom he left issue. Died Feb. 23, 1733-4. Father of the next, and of Robert (1729), brother of John (1688) and Lisle. (Le Neve, *Knights*, 244; *Vis. of Warws.*, 1682; H. I. Longden.)

HACKET, ANDREW. Adm. pens. (age 18) at TRINITY, May 18, 1720. S. of Andrew (above), of Grantham, Leics. and Moxhull, Warws. School, Offchurch, Warws. (Mr Greenaway). Scholar, 1721; Matric. 1723-4; B.A. 1723-4; M.A. 1727. Fellow, 1726. Perhaps of Sutton Coldfield, Warws. Died Aug. 15, 1788, aged 88. Brother of Robert (1729). (*G. Mag.*)

HACKET, CONNAND. Adm. (age 17) at CAIUS, Sept. 17, 1575. S. of Richard, of Market Harborough, Leics. School, Godmanchester. Matric. sizar, 1575; B.A. from Magdalene, 1579-80. Ord. deacon (London) Nov. 28, 1583; C. of Letchworth, Herts. (*Venn*, I. 83.)

HACKETT, EDMUND. Matric. sizar from CLARE, Easter, 1626. Buried at St Edward's, Cambridge, Oct. 4, 1626.

HACKETT, JOHN. Matric. pens. from TRINITY, Easter, 1609. S. of Andrew, of Pitferran, N.B. B. in St Martin-in-the-Fields, Sept. 1, 1590. School, Westminster. B.A. 1612-3; M.A. 1616; B.D. 1623; D.D. 1628. Fellow, 1614. Incorp. at Oxford, 1616. Ord. deacon and priest (London) Dec. 20, 1618, age 26. R. of Stoke Hammond, Bucks., 1618-24. V. of Trumpington, Cambs., 1620. R. of Kirby-under-Wood, Lincs., 1621. R. of Barcombe, Sussex, 1622. Preb. of Lincoln, 1623-61. R. of St Andrew's, Holborn, 1624-62. R. of West Cheam, Surrey, 1624. Adm. at Gray's Inn, Feb. 2, 1627-8. President of Sion College, 1633. Archdeacon of Bedford, 1631-61. Preb. of St Paul's, 1642-61. Chaplain to Charles I and II. Bishop of Lichfield, 1661-70. Lichfield Cathedral was restored partly at his own expense. Built Bishop's Hostel, Trinity College, 1670. Died Oct. 28, 1670. Bequeathed his books to the University Library. Father of Andrew (1645). (*D.N.B.*; *Al. Oxon.*)

HACKETT, JOHN. Adm. pens. at CLARE, Oct. 5, 1633. Matric. 1633.

HACKET or HOCKET, JOHN. Adm. pens. at TRINITY, May 10, 1659. Of Hertfordshire. School, Westminster. Scholar, 1659; Matric. 1660; B.A. 1662-3; M.A. 1666. Fellow, 1664. Probably R. of Motson, Hants.; and father of John (1692-3).

HACKET, JOHN. Adm. pens. (age 17) at TRINITY, May 31, 1688. S. of Sir Andrew (1645). B. at Moxhull, Warws. School, Tamworth (Mr George Anthrobus). Matric. 1690; Scholar, 1691; B.A. 1691-2; M.A. 1695; B.D. 1710; D.D. 1717. Fellow, 1694. Vice-Master, 1733-4. Ord. deacon (Lincoln) Mar. 20, 1697-8; priest, Apr. 12, 1702. R. of Claydon, Suffolk, 1711. V. of Barrington, Cambs., 1715. V. of Trumpington, 1719-32. V of St Andrew, Enfield, Feb.-Oct. 1732. R. of Fakenham, Norfolk, 1732-45. Died May 4, 1745. Buried at Fakenham. Brother of Andrew (1683) and Lisle (1683). (*Vis. of Warws.*, 1682.)

HACKETT or HOCKETT, JOHN. Adm. pens. (age 19) at TRINITY, Mar. 9, 1692-3. S. of John (? 1659), R. of Motson, Hants. School, Winchester. Matric. 1693; Scholar, 1695; B.A. 1696-7.

HACKET, JOHN. Adm. Fell.-Com. (age 18) at TRINITY, Oct. 28, 1710. S. of Lisle (next), of Moxhull, Warws. B. Jan. 9, 1690-1. School, Tamworth (Mr Antrobus). Matric. 1710. Died, without issue, Sept. 10, 1718. (Pedigree in *Vis. of Warws.*, 1682; H. I. Longden.)

HACKET, LISLE. Adm. pens. (age 17) at TRINITY, Oct. 23, 1683. S. of Sir Andrew (1645), of Moxhull, Warws. B. Aug. 5, 1665. School, Solihull, Warws. (Mr George Ward). Matric. 1683. Adm. at Gray's Inn, as of Monksworth Hall, Warws. Married (1) Martha, dau. of Maurice Shelton, of Suffolk; (2) Dorothy, dau. of Sir John Bridgeman, Bart. Died Mar. 28, 1728. Father of John (above), brother of Andrew (1683) and John (1688). (Le Neve, *Knights*, 244; *Vis. of Warws.*, 1682; H. I. Longden.)

HACKET, ROBERT. M.A. 1729 (Incorp. from Oxford). S. of Andrew (1683), of Stroxton, Lincs., gent. Matric. from Lincoln College, Oxford, May 9, 1722, age 18; B.A. (Magdalen, Oxford) 1725-6; M.A. 1729. Demy of Magdalen. Brother of Andrew (1720). (*Al. Oxon.*)

HACKET, THOMAS. Adm. pens. at EMMANUEL, Apr. 18, 1600; B.A. 1603-4; M.A. 1607. Ord. deacon (Lincoln) Dec. 20, 1607. V. of Ashby-de-la-Zouch, Leics., 1611. Perhaps R. of Mersham, Kent, 1628-36.

HACKETT, THOMAS. Adm. pens. at EMMANUEL, Apr. 17, 1667. Of Leicestershire. S. of Thomas, of Derbyshire. School, Ashby-de-la-Zouch (Mr Shaw). Migrated to Christ's, Apr. 1669. B.A. from Emmanuel, 1670-1; M.A. from Queens', 1680. Ord. deacon (Lincoln) Sept. 22, 1672; priest (Lichfield) Sept. 21, 1673. R. of Whittington, Gloucs., 1678-1718. Died 1718. (*Peile*, II. 21; F. S. Hockaday.)

HACKET, ——. Adm. pens. at PETERHOUSE, July 17, 1614. Probably resided six months.

HACLUYT, EDMUND. Matric. pens. from TRINITY, Michs. 1611; a scholar from Westminster, 1612. S. of Richard, R. of Wetheringsett, Suffolk. B.A. 1615-6; M.A. 1619. Fellow, 1618. Ord. deacon (Peterb.) June 24; priest, June 25, 1626. Held Bridge Place, Coddenham, Suffolk, on the death of his father, 1616. (V. B. Redstone.)

HACKLUIT, JEREMIAH. 'S. of Henry, and Susannah; B. at Streatham, Cambs.; aged 24 in 1666. School, Westminster. Father an Anglican Minister. M.A. of Cambridge. Had fought in the Navy against the Dutch.' (Statement on admission at the English College at Rome. *Records S.J.*, v. 524.) Not found in our records.

HACKLUYT or HACKLUIT, THOMAS. Matric. pens. from TRINITY, Easter, 1570, a scholar from Westminster. B.A. 1571-2; M.A. 1575. Incorp. at Oxford, 1576.

HACMAN, ——. B.A. 1458.

HACKNEY, EDMUND. Matric. sizar from MAGDALENE, Michs. 1598.

HACKNEY or HARTNEY, THOMAS. Matric. sizar from CHRIST'S, Dec. 1586.

HACKSHAW, SAMUEL. Matric. pens. from PETERHOUSE, c. 1596; B.A. 1599-1600; M.A. 1603. Ord. deacon and priest (Peterborough) Mar. 8, 1603-4.

HACKSUPP, NICHOLAS. B.A. from CLARE, 1606-7; M.A. from Peterhouse, 1616. B. at Hadham, Herts. Ord. deacon (London) Dec. 17, 1608, age 24. C. of Snave, Kent.

HACKSUP, NICHOLAS. Adm. pens. at JESUS, June 25, 1641. Of Kent. Probably s. of the above. Matric. 1641; Scholar, 1641; B.A. 1644-5.

HACSOPE or HACKSUP, SAMUEL. Matric. sizar from KING'S, Easter, 1605; B.A. 1609-10; M.A. 1614. R. of Ravenstone, Leics. Died Feb. 20, 1666, aged 76. M.I. at Ravenstone. (*Nichols*, III. 935.)

HAXUP, SIMON. Matric. sizar from PETERHOUSE, Michs. 1576; B.A. 1579-80; M.A. 1583. V. of Weston Colville, Cambs., 1582.

HACOMBLENE, ROBERT. Adm. at KING'S, a scholar from Eton, 1472; B.A. 1475-6; M.A. 1480; B.D. 1490; D.D. 1507. Proctor, 1483-4. Provost of King's, 1509-28. Ord. acolyte (Lincoln) Sept. 1473. V. of Prescot, Lancs., 1492. Gave the brass lectern, still in use in the Chapel; and fitted up the chantry on the south side. Signed the contract for the stained glass windows, 1526. Died Sept. 8, 1528. Buried in the College Chapel. (*Cooper*, I. 34; *D.N.B.*)

HACON, *see also* HAKEN.

HACON, GAWDY. Matric. pens. from CORPUS CHRISTI, Easter, 1645. Of Norfolk. B.A. 1648-9; M.A. 1653. R. of Hedenham, Norfolk, 1661-1707.

HACON, HUBERT. Adm. pens. (age 18) at CAIUS, Jan. 26, 1563-4. Eldest s. of Francis, of Wheatacre, Norfolk, gent. School, Norwich. Matric. 1563-4. Of Wheatacre, Esq. Married Jane Lusher. Died 1598. Buried at St Michael-at-Plea, Norwich. Will (Norwich) 1598. (*Venn*, I. 52; *Vis. of Norfolk.*)

HACON, JOHN. Adm. at CORPUS CHRISTI, 1680. Of Norfolk. Matric. 1680; B.A. 1683-4; M.A. 1690. Ord. deacon (Norwich) Dec. 1686; priest, June, 1688. V. of Ilketshall St Margaret, Suffolk, 1694-1731. V. of Mettingham, 1694-1731. Died 1731.

HACON, JOSEPH. Adm. sizar at EMMANUEL, July 10, 1618. B. May 17, 1603, at Topcroft, Suffolk. Matric. 1618; B.A. 1621-2; M.A. 1625. Ord. priest (Norwich) Sept. 24, 1626. R. of Little Massingham, Norfolk, 1643-62. Died 1662. M.I. at Massingham.

HACON, ROBERT. Adm. sizar at ST CATHARINE'S, Jan. 12, 1696-7. Matric. 1698; B.A. 1700-1; M.A. 1704. Ord. deacon (Norwich) Sept. 1704; priest, May, 1706. R. of Westleton, Suffolk, 1710-37. R. of Theberton, 1730. Buried at Westleton, May 9, 1737. M.I. (*E. Anglian*, III. 314; Doughty, *Theberton.*)

HACON, THOMAS. Adm. at CORPUS CHRISTI, 1691. Of Norfolk. Matric. 1692; B.A. 1694-5. Ord. deacon (Norwich) Sept. 1695; priest, Sept. 1696. R. of Little Poringland, Norfolk, 1696. R. of Yelverton, 1698-1733.

HACON, WILLIAM. Adm. sizar at EMMANUEL, Mar. 2, 1605-6. Matric. 1606; Scholar; B.A. 1609-10; M.A. 1613.

HACTON, ——. Fee for B.A. 1473-4.

HADAMS, *see* ADAMS.

HADDES or HADDE, MATTHEW. Matric. pens. from TRINITY, Michs. 1561. Perhaps 1st s. of Henry Hadde, of Frinsted, Kent, Esq. Of Lincoln's Inn. Barrister-at-law. J.P. for Canterbury. Steward of the Cinque Ports. Died 1617, aged 72. Buried in St Alphage's Church, Canterbury. (*Hasted*, IV. 465.)

HADDE, MATTHEW. Matric. Fell.-Com. from CORPUS CHRISTI, Easter, 1624. Of Kent. S. and h. of Edward, of Canterbury, Esq. B.A. 1626-7. Adm. at Lincoln's Inn, Jan. 31, 1625-6. Age 12, in 1619. (*Vis. of Kent.*)

HADDELEYE, ROBERT. Scholar at KING'S HALL, 1380. Left before 1392.

HADDER, GEORGE. Matric. pens. from TRINITY, Michs. 1645.

HADDERTON, RALPH. Adm. sizar at ST CATHARINE'S, Mar. 28, 1709. Matric. 1709.

HADDERTON, SAMUEL. Adm. sizar (age 18) at TRINITY, May 2, 1707. S. of Abraham, of Newport, Salop. School, Newport (Mr Greenwood). Matric. 1707; Scholar, 1708; B.A. 1710-1; M.A. 1714. Fellow, 1713. University librarian, 1721-31. Ord. deacon (Lincoln) June 12, 1720; priest (Lincoln, *Litt. dim.* from Ely) Mar. 5, 1720-1. Died, probably at Cambridge, Mar. 20, 1732. (G. *Mag.*)

HADDISON, GEORGE. Adm. sizar at TRINITY, Easter, 1641.

HADDOCK, JAMES. Adm. sizar (age 16) at ST JOHN'S, June 14, 1648. S. of John, blacksmith, of Turton, near Gt Bolton, Lancs. B. there. School, Anderton (Mr Rudall). Matric. 1648.

HADDOCK or HAYDOCK, JOHN. Adm. sizar at EMMANUEL, Apr. 24, 1646. Of Lancashire. Probably migrated to Oxford. Scholar of Wadham, Sept. 7, 1649; B.A. (Oxford) 1649. (*Al. Oxon.*)

HADDOCK, JOSIAH. Adm. pens. at TRINITY, Sept. 17, 1670. Matric. 1671.

HADDOCK, RICHARD. Adm. at KING'S, a scholar from Eton, 1554; B.A. 1558-9. Died 1560. Admon. granted (King's College) Sept. 8, 1560.

HADDON, CLERE. Adm. at KING'S, a scholar from Eton, 1567. S. of Walter (1533), LL.D., and Margaret, dau. of Sir John Clere. B. at Ormesby, Norfolk. Fellow for a short time. Drowned in the Cam, May, 1571. Admon. (P.C.C.) 1571. (*Cooper*, I. 295, 558.)

HADDON, EDWARD. Adm. sizar at QUEENS', Feb. 5, 1669-70. Of Sussex. Matric. 1670; B.A. 1673-4; M.A. 1677. V. of Alconbury, Hunts., 1681-1701. R. of Little Gransden, 1701-14. Will proved (Ely Cons. C.) Aug. 26, 1714; to be buried at Alconbury.

HADDON, FRANCIS. Adm. pens. at TRINITY, Apr. 6, 1645. Matric. 1645. One of these names adm. at Leyden, Oct. 8, 1649.

HADDON, HENRY. Adm. pens. (age 18) at ST JOHN'S, Mar. 27, 1714. S. of Michael, farmer. B. at Gilston, Herts. School, Merchant Taylors'. Matric. 1715; B.A. 1717-8; M.A. 1742. Ord. deacon (London) May 24, 1719. Perhaps R. of Roding Abbas, Essex. Admon. (P.C.C.) 1784. (J. Ch. Smith.)

HADDON, JAMES. Adm. pens. at KING'S, c. 1539. 3rd s. of William, of Buckinghamshire. B.A. 1541; M.A. 1544. One of the original fellows of Trinity, 1546. Tutor to the Lady Jane Grey. Chaplain to the Duke of Suffolk. Preb. of Westminster, Aug. to Dec. 1552. Dean of Exeter, 1553-4. Deprived of his preferments, and a fugitive under Queen Mary. One of the Protestant disputants on the real presence, 1553. Left England for Strasburg, in 1554. Died there c. 1556. Brother of Walter (1533). (*Cooper*, I. 164; *D.N.B.*)

HADDON, JOHN. Adm. at QUEENS', Nov. 8, 1644. Of Northamptonshire. Previously matric. from St Alban's Hall, Oxford, May 14, 1642 (not in *Al. Oxon.*). B.A. (Cambridge) 1645-6; M.A. 1649. Fellow of Queens', 1647-51.

HADDON, ROGER. Matric. sizar from JESUS, c. 1596; B.A. 1599-1600; M.A. 1603. Ord. deacon and priest (Ely) Jan. 2, 1603-4. R. of Little Casterton, Rutland, 1605-40. Buried there Oct. 27, 1640. (*Genealogist*, I. 155.)

HADDON, WALTER. Adm. at KING'S (age 16) a scholar from Eton, Aug. 13, 1533. Of St Mary Cray, Kent. 2nd s. of William, of Buckinghamshire. B.A. 1537-8; M.A. 1541; LL.D. 1549. Fellow, 1536-52. Vice-Chancellor, 1549-50. Regius Professor of Civil Law, 1551. Master of Trinity Hall, 1552. Incorp. at Oxford, 1552. President of Magdalen College, Oxford, 1552-3. Advocate of the Court of Arches, 1555. Judge of the Prerogative Court of Canterbury, 1559. M.P. for Reigate, 1555; for Thetford, 1558; for Poole, 1559; and for Warwick, 1563-7. Employed in Commercial negotiations with Flanders, 1565-6. Defended the Reformation against Osorio da Fonseca. Married Margaret, dau. of Sir John Clere, of Ormesby. Author, classical, etc. Died in London, Jan. 24, 1570-1. Buried at Christ Church, Newgate St. Will (P.C.C.). Father of Clere (1567), brother of James (1539). (*Cooper*, I. 299; *D.N.B.*; A. B. Beaven.)

HADDRIDGE, JAMES. Adm. sizar (age 18) at SIDNEY, 1653. S. of John. B. at Halberton, Devon. School, Tiverton. Matric. Easter, 1654; B.A. 1657-8. Will (Exeter) of one of these names, 1700; of Halberton.

HADEN, FULLWOOD. Adm. sizar (age 18) at CHRIST'S, June 3, 1711. S. of Henry. B. at Haden Hill, Staffs. School, Halesowen (Mr Thorpe). Matric. 1711; Scholar, 1713; B.A. 1714-5; M.A. 1722. Ord. deacon (Worcester) June 12, 1715; priest (Peterb.) June 15, 1717. R. of Quinton, Northants., 1717-54. R. of Milton Malsor, 1746-54. Died at Birmingham, 1754. (*Peile*, II. 178; H. I. Longden.)

HADENHAM, ROGER DE. Scholar at KING'S HALL, 1378.

HADESSON, RICHARD. Fee for M.A. or higher degree, 1466-7.

HADFIELD or HARDFIELD, RALPH. Adm. at EMMANUEL, 1601; Scholar, 1603; B.A. 1604-5; M.A. 1608; B.D. 1615; D.D. 1622. C. of Wilburton, Cambs., 1606.

HADFIELD, RICHARD. B.A. 1521-2; M.A. 1526. Fellow of ST JOHN'S, c. 1523.

HADHAM, JOHN. Scholar at KING'S HALL, 1383. Expelled at the Bishop's Visitation, May 19, 1385. (*Trin. Coll. Admissions*, I. 107.)

HADLEY, GEORGE. Matric. pens. from CHRIST'S, Nov. 1578.

HADLEY, JOHN. Adm. pens. at QUEENS', May 9, 1749. S. of Henry. B. in London, 1731. Matric. 1749; B.A. 1753; M.A. 1756; M.D. 1763. Fellow, 1756-64. Professor of Chemistry, 1756-64. F.R.S. 1758. Physician to the Charterhouse, 1763. F.R.C.P. 1764. An intimate friend of the poet Gray. Died Nov. 5, 1764, aged 33. Will, P.C.C. (*D.N.B.*; *Munk*, II. 259; Cass, *East Barnet*.)

HADLEY, MILES. B.Civ.L. 1519-20.

HADLEY, THOMAS. Fellow of CLARE. Proctor, 1391-2. Ord. deacon (Ely) Sept. 1386; priest, Mar. 2, 1386-7.

HADLEY, WILLIAM. Pens. of GONVILLE HALL, 1515-9; B.D. 1518-9. Canon of Westacre priory, Norfolk. Had spent eleven years' study in arts and theology. Perhaps the last prior of Eye, Suffolk. One William Hadley, *alias* Hunt, preb. of Canterbury, 1542. (*Venn*, I. 23.)

HADSLEY, JOHN. Matric. sizar from CORPUS CHRISTI, Easter, 1640. B. at 'Ward' (? Ware), Herts., 1624. B.A. 1643-4; M.A. 1647. Minister at Poole, Dorset, 1647-c. 59. Ejected from Rockbourne, Hants., 1662. Afterwards preacher at Salisbury. Died June 11, 1699, aged 75. (*Calamy*, II. 19.)

HADSLEY, RICHARD. D.Can.L. 1471-2.

HADDLESEY, ROBERT. Matric. from ST JOHN'S, c. 1594. Probably s. of Michael Hoddlesey, merchant. B. at Hull, Yorks. B.A. 1597-8; M.A. 1601. Ord. deacon (London) Jan. 23; priest, Jan. 25, 1600-1, age 25. R. of Catwick, Yorks., 1602-21. Died 1621. (M. H. Peacock.)

HADSLEY, ROBERT. Adm. Fell.-Com. (age 19) at SIDNEY, Jan. 12, 1716-7. S. and h. of Robert, gent., of Munden, Herts. B. there. School, Charterhouse. Adm. at the Inner Temple, Nov. 21, 1716. Died Feb. 20, 1765. Buried at Gt Munden. M.I. (*Clutterbuck*, II. 396.)

HADDLESAY, SAMUEL. Matric. pens. from ST JOHN'S, Easter, 1606.

HADDLESEY, THOMAS. Matric. sizar from TRINITY, 1609; Scholar, 1614; B.A. 1614-5; M.A. 1618. Ord. deacon (Peterb.) Sept. 2; priest, Sept. 8, 1618. V. of Kirby Grindalyth, Yorks., 1618-60. Chaplain of Trinity, 1621. Licensed to marry Jane Thompson, of Wighill, Yorks., in 1625.

HADNAME, ——. B.Civ.L. 1487. Perhaps of Norwich diocese; ord. sub-deacon (Norwich) Dec. 23, 1486; title, TRINITY HALL.

HADSON, *see* ADSON.

HADWAY or HATHEWAY, THOMAS. B.A. 1516-7; M.A. 1520; B.D. 1532-3. Fellow of QUEENS', 1518-56. Ord. deacon (Ely) Apr. 7, 1520.

HADWEN, JOHN. Adm. sizar (age 20) at CHRIST'S, Oct. 29, 1705. S. of Robert. B. at Silverdale, Lancs. School, Lowther, Westmorland (Mr Lodge). Matric. 1705-6; B.A. 1709-10. One of these names incumbent of Tockhole's Chapel, near Blackburn, 1736-66. (*Peile*, II. 163.)

HAFTER, THOMAS. Adm. sizar at TRINITY, June 26, 1647. Of Staffordshire.

HAGGE, MARK. Matric. sizar from QUEENS', Easter, 1637. Of Lincolnshire. B.A. 1640-1. Ord. deacon and priest (Lincoln) July 11, 1646.

HAGG or HAGGS, MARK. Adm. pens. at EMMANUEL, Oct. 18, 1675. Of Lincolnshire. Matric. 1675.

HAGGE, RALPH. Matric. sizar from KING'S, Easter, 1633.

HAGGE, RICHARD. Matric. sizar from MAGDALENE, Easter, 1589.

HAGGAR, JAMES. Matric. sizar from CHRIST'S, July, 1619; B.A. 1623-4; M.A. 1627. C. of Barrington, Cambs., 1630. Probably s. of John, of Bourn, Cambs.; and brother of John (1613). (*Peile*, I. 330.)

HAGGAR, JOHN. Matric. sizar from TRINITY, Easter, 1577, as Hagyard; B.A. 1580-1. Perhaps ord. deacon and priest (Norwich) June 11, 1609, as 'M.A.; aged 40.'

HAGGAR or HAGER, JOHN. Adm. pens. at EMMANUEL, Easter, 1613. Matric. 1613. Probably s. of John, of Bourn, Cambs., Esq.; adm. at Gray's Inn, Nov. 3, 1615. Buried at Bourn, Jan. 6, 1616-7.

HAGGER, JOHN. Matric. pens. from CHRIST'S, July, 1621; B.A. 1624-5; M.A. from Queens', 1628. Ord. deacon (Peterb.) June 7; priest, June 8, 1628. One of these names R. of Chilcomb, Hants., 1631.

HAGGER or HAGAR, JOHN. Matric. Fell.-Com. from ST CATHARINE'S, Easter, 1640. Of Cambridgeshire. Probably of Bourn, Cambs., Esq. Adm. at Gray's Inn, May 2, 1655.

HAGGAR, JOHN. Adm. sizar (age 17) at PETERHOUSE, Jan. 11, 1697-8. Of Cambridge. School, King's College School, Cambridge. Matric. 1698; B.A. 1701-2. One of these names V. of Cropwell Bishop, Notts., 1708-35. Buried there Nov. 3, 1735. (Godfrey, *Notts.*)

HAGAR, ROBERT. Adm. Fell.-Com. at QUEENS', Nov. 10, 1688. Of Cambridgeshire. Matric. 1688.

HAGAR, ROBERT. Adm. pens. at CLARE, June 19, 1747. S. of John, of Waresley, Hunts. B. at Waresley. School, Bury. Matric. 1747; B.A. 1750-1; M.A. 1754. Fellow, 1752-64. Ord. priest (Peterb., *Litt. dim.* from Lichfield) Dec. 18, 1757. Probably R. of Abington Pigotts, Cambs., 1773. R. of Hawnes, Beds. Buried there Oct. 24, 1780. (*G. Mag.*)

HAGAR, THOMAS. Matric. sizar from ST JOHN'S, Michs. 1566.

HAGGAR, THOMAS. B.A. (? 1609-10); M.A. from QUEENS', 1613. Minister at Oakington, Cambs., c. 1609. V. of Ridgwell, Essex, 1615-33. Perhaps R. of Tilbury-by-Clare, 1633-7. Will (P.C.C.) 1638; of Sudbury, Suffolk, clerk.

HAGAR, ——. Adm. pens. at TRINITY HALL, May 14, 1743; Fell.-Com. 1744. School, Bury. Perhaps John, brother of Robert (1747).

HAGGARD, HINTON. M.A. from CLARE, 1738. Matric. from St John's College, Oxford, May 28, 1712; B.A. (Oxford) 1716. V. of Rodbourne Cheney, Wilts., 1737. (*Al. Oxon.*)

HAGGARD, JOHN. Adm. pens. at CLARE, May 21, 1740. S. of John, of Bromley St Leonards, Middlesex. Matric. 1740; B.A. 1743-4; M.A. 1747. Ord. priest (Lincoln) Dec. 24, 1752. R. of Little Birch, Essex, 1754. R. of Bennington, Herts., 1756-1813. Died Mar. 21, 1813, aged 90. (Burke, *L.G.*)

HAGGARD, MATTHEW. 'B.A. of QUEENS' College' when ord. deacon (York) June, 1626; priest, Sept. 1626.

HAGARDE, ——. Matric. pens. from NICHOLAS HOSTEL, Michs. 1544.

HAGGAS, BENJAMIN, *see* AGAS.

HAGGERSTON, CUTHBERT. B.A. 1532-3; M.A. 1538-9. Fellow of ST CATHARINE'S. Of Northumberland. Perhaps s. of Henry, of Haggerston. R. of Layer Breton, Essex, 1552-4; of Toppesfield, 1553-4. Died 1554. (*Vis. of Durham*, 1666.)

HAGARSTON, H. Matric. Fell.-Com. from QUEENS', Easter, 1561.

HAGGERSTON, ——. B.A. 1476-7; B.D. 1490-1. Probably George 'Hacktyrston,' fellow of CLARE, 1489.

HAGGITT, GEORGE. Adm. sizar (age 18) at SIDNEY, May 24, 1746. S. of William, seaman, of Scarborough, Yorks. B. there. School, Thornton (Mr Ward). Matric. 1747; B.A. 1749-50; M.A. 1753. Ord. deacon (York) June 10, 1750; priest, June 2, 1751. R. of St Peter's and All Saints', Rushton, Northants., 1756.

HAGGET, HUMPHREY. Adm. sizar (age 19) at ST JOHN'S, July 10, 1675. S. of William, husbandman, of Barnard Castle, Durham. Bapt. there, Oct. 23, 1655. School, Strickland.

HAGGET, PAUL. Adm. pens. at TRINITY, Easter, 1645.

HAGGETT, STEPHEN. Adm. sizar at QUEENS', June 17, 1598. Of London. B.A. (? 1602-3); M.A. 1606; B.D. 1615. Fellow, 1605-16. Proctor, 1612-3. Incorp. at Oxford, 1610. V. of St Andrew-the-Great, Cambridge, 1607-16. V. of Wigtoft, Lincs., 1616. R. of Gt Mongeham, Kent, 1617. Will (P.C.C.) 1618.

HAIECCIUS, SIMEON, *see* HAYET.

HAIGH or HAGE, CHRISTOPHER. Matric. pens. from CHRIST'S, Easter, 1584; B.A. from Clare, 1588-9; M.A. 1592. Ord. deacon (Lincoln) Apr. 18; priest, July 27, 1593. V. of Dunton, Beds., 1593-1634.

HAGHE, FRANCIS. Adm. pens. at EMMANUEL, Nov. 10, 1595. Matric. 1595.

HAIGH, FRANCIS. Adm. sizar (age 20) at CHRIST'S, June 8, 1717. S. of John. B. at Thurlstone, Yorks. School, Penistone (Mr Ramsden). Scholar, 1719; B.A. 1720-1. Ord. deacon (York) Mar. 1720-1; priest, Sept. 1722. C. of Cumberworth, Yorks., 1728; also C. of Midhope, where he was a tutor (*see* Samuel). V. of Bolsterstone, 1728-*c.* 1746. (*Peile*, II. 192.)

HAIGH, JAMES. Adm. sizar (age 16) at JESUS, May 23, 1679. Of Lancashire. Matric. 1679; B.A. 1682-3. Ord. priest (Chester) Dec. 19, 1686.

HAIGE or HAGUE, JEREMIAH. Adm. sizar (age 19) at MAGDALENE, June 8, 1671. S. of Thomas, of Horbury, Wakefield. School, Wakefield (private). Matric. 1671; B.A. 1674-5. Ord. deacon (Norwich) May, 1675; priest (York) Sept. 19, 1680.

HAIGH, JOSEPH. Adm. sizar (age 25) at MAGDALENE, June 11, 1738. S. of Henry, of Overden, Halifax. B. there, 1710. School, Halifax. Matric. 1738; B.A. 1741-2. Ord. deacon (*Litt. dim.* from York) Sept. 1742; priest (York) May 20, 1744. C. of Rochdale, 1745. V. of Milnrow, Lancs., 1759-95. Died Aug. 22, 1795. Buried at Rochdale. (H. Fishwick, *Rochdale*, 213.)

HAGUE, JOSEPH. Adm. sizar (age 21) at TRINITY, Mar. 31, 1743. S. of Joshua, of Birstall, Yorks. School, Batley, Yorks. (Mr Dixon). Matric. 1744; LL.B. 1754. Ord. deacon (York) Sept. 23, 1744; priest, Sept. 1747. C. of Birstall. C. of Thornto , Bradford, 1746. P.C. of Holbeck, Leeds, 1754-74. Died 1774.

HAIGH, RICHARD. Adm. sizar (age 18) at ST JOHN'S, June 6, 1722. S. of Henry, husbandman, of Yorkshire. B. at Quarmby, near Huddersfield. Schools, Bradford (Mr Hill) and Sedbergh. Matric. 1722; B.A. 1725-6.

HAIGH, SAMUEL. Adm. sizar (age 19) at CHRIST'S, Apr. 9, 1743. S. of William. B. at Thurlstone, Penistone, Yorks. School, Midhope (Mr Fra. Haigh). Matric. 1743; B.A. 1746-7. Ord. deacon (York) Sept. 20, 1747; priest, Sept. 24, 1749. C. of Dinnington. (*Peile*, II. 243.)

HAGUE, THOMAS. M.A. 1675 (Incorp. from Edinburgh). Only s. of Ralph, of Bilsdale, Yorks. Schools, Eston (Mr Hardwick) and Pickering (Mr Grey). M.A. of Edinburgh, 1670.

HAILSBY, THOMAS. Adm. sizar (age 17) at PEMBROKE, June 26, 1627. S. of Richard, husbandman. B. at West Ashby, Lincs.

HAIME, JOHN. Adm. sizar at EMMANUEL, May 24, 1647. Of Somerset. Matric. 1647; B.A. 1650-1; M.A. 1654. Probably V. of Foxcote, Somerset, 1661-8.

HAYMES, THOMAS. Adm. pens. at EMMANUEL, Lent, 1624-5.

HAIMES, THOMAS. Adm. at KING'S, a scholar from Eton, 1658. B. at Hillingdon, Middlesex, 1641. Matric. 1658; B.A. 1661-2; M.A. 1665. Fellow, 1661-9.

HAISHE, JOHN. Matric. pens. from EMMANUEL, Easter, 1616.

HAKE, ANTHONY. Matric. pens. from EMMANUEL, Michs. 1649.

HAKE, GILES. Adm. sizar (age 19) at PEMBROKE, July 28, 1670. S. of Ralph, of Exeter, farmer. Matric. 1671; B.A. 1674. Admon. of one of these names (Exeter) 1674; of Broadclist, Devon.

HAKE, THOMAS. Adm. pens. at EMMANUEL, Apr. 21, 1647. Of Northamptonshire. B.A. 1650-1; M.A. 1654. Will of one of these names (Exeter) 1675; of Walkhampton, Devon, clerk. Probably brother of William (1647).

HAKE, WILLIAM. Adm. Fell.-Com. at EMMANUEL, Feb. 12, 1618-9. Probably s. of William, of Peterborough; age 17 in 1618. Matric. 1618-9. (*Vis. of Northants.*, 1618.)

HAKE, WILLIAM. Adm. pens. at EMMANUEL, Apr. 21, 1647. Of Northamptonshire. Probably brother of Thomas (1647).

HAKEN, AMOS. Matric. pens. from JESUS, Easter, 1564-5.

HAKEWILL, GEORGE. M.A. 1607 (Incorp. from Oxford). S. of John, of Exeter. Bapt. at St Mary Arches, Exeter, Jan. 25, 1577-8. School, Exeter. Matric. from St Alban's Hall, Oxford, May 15, 1595, age 16; B.A. (Oxford) 1599; M.A. 1602; B.D. 1610; D.D. 1611. Fellow of Exeter College, 1596-1611. Lector, 1642-9. Adm. at Lincoln's Inn, Mar. 22, 1613-4. R. of Heanton Punchardon, Devon, 1611-49. Archdeacon of Surrey, 1617-49. Chaplain to Charles, Prince of Wales. Author. Buried at Heanton, Apr. 5, 1649. (*Al. Oxon.*; *D.N.B.*; *Vis. of Devon*, 1620.)

HAKTOPE, WILLIAM. Matric. pens. from MAGDALENE, Michs. 1642.

HALBOROUGH, ——. Probably M.A. in 1460. (Gr. *Bk*, A, 28.)

HALCOTT, JAMES, *see* HOLCOT.

HALCOTT, JOHN. Adm. pens. (age 17) at CAIUS, Sept. 26, 1666. S. of Matthew, tanner, of Litcham, Norfolk. School, Scarning (Mr Burton). Matric. 1667, as Hellcoate; Scholar, 1667-71; B.A. 1670-1. Adm. at the Middle Temple, Feb. 10, 1670. Buried at Litcham, Apr. 20, 1682. M.I. (*Venn*, I. 428.)

HALCOT or HELCOTT, MATTHEW. Adm. pens. at CAIUS, Feb. 12, 1689-90. S. of Matthew, tanner, of Litcham, Norfolk. B. there. Schools, Gt Dunham (Mr Ransome) and Wymondham (Mr Clarke). Matric. as Fell.-Com. 1691. Of Litcham, Esq. Married Ann, dau. of Thomas Wood, of Bracon Ash, Norfolk. Died Aug. 7, 1707. (*Venn*, I. 487.)

HALDANBY, EDWARD. Matric. pens. from CHRIST'S, July, 1620. S. of Francis, of Haldenby, Yorks. B.A. 1623. Adm. at Gray's Inn, Aug. 7, 1623. Barrister, 1633. (*Peile*, I. 335.)

HALDENBYE or HAWDENBYE, FRANCIS. Matric. sizar from MAGDALENE, Easter, 1588. Probably s. of Gerald.

HALDENBY, JOHN. Scholar at KING'S HALL, 1474-80. One of these names R. of Armthorpe, Yorks., 1486-1523.

HALDENBY, ROBERT. Matric. pens. from CLARE, Michs. 1566. One of these names s. of Francis, of Haldenby, Yorks. Died before his father. (*Vis. of Yorks.*, 1585.)

HALDENBY, ROBERT. Matric. Fell.-Com. from CORPUS CHRISTI, Michs. 1619. Of Yorkshire. Perhaps s. of Francis, of Haldenby, Yorks.; age 12 in 1612. If so, brother of Edward (1620). (*Vis. of Yorks.*)

HALDENBY, THOMAS. B.Can.L. 1519-20.

HALDENBY, WILLIAM DE. Scholar at KING'S HALL, 1360.

HALDYE, WILLIAM. Matric. Fell.-Com. from EMMANUEL, Easter, 1618.

HALDILSAY, ——. D.Can.L. 1479-80.

HALDSWORTH, *see* HOLDSWORTH.

HALE, BERNARD. Adm. pens. at PETERHOUSE, May 2, 1625. 6th s. of William, of King's Walden, Herts. Matric. 1625; B.A. 1628-9; M.A. 1632; B.D. 1639 (*Lit. Reg.*); D.D. 1660 (*Lit. Reg.*). Fellow, 1632-4. Master, 1660-3. Archdeacon of Ely, 1660-3. Preb. of Ely, 1660-1. R. of Fen Ditton, Cambs., 1660. Died Mar. 29, 1663. Buried in Peterhouse Chapel, Mar. 30, 1663. Will, P.C.C. Benefactor to the College. Brother of Rowland (1616) and John (1631-2). (*Vis. of Herts.*, 1634; *Vis. of Essex*, 1612; *T. A. Walker*, 31.)

HALE, BERNARD. Adm. pens. (age 17) at Peterhouse, July 1, 1695. S. of William (1649), of King's Walden. Bapt. Mar. 18, 1677–8. School, Eton. Matric. 1695; Scholar, 1695; B.A. 1698–9; M.A. 1702. Fellow, 1700–15. Adm. at Gray's Inn, Oct. 14, 1696; and at Lincoln's Inn, Feb. 15, 1709–10. Called to the Bar, 1704. Bencher, 1724. Lord Chief Baron of the Irish Exchequer, 1722–5. Baron of the Exchequer in England, 1725–9. Knighted, Feb. 4, 1725–6. Of King's Walden, Herts. Died in London, Nov. 7, 1729. Buried at Abbots Langley. Father of the next, and of William (1734), brother of Rowland (1679). (*T. A. Walker*, 197; *D.N.B.*, where his College career is omitted.)

HALE, BERNARD. Adm. pens. (age 18) at Peterhouse, Jan. 14, 1742–3. S. of Sir Bernard (1695). School, Harrow. Matric. 1743; Scholar, 1743. Colonel of the 20th Regiment, 1769–13. Lieut.-General, 1777. General, 1793. Lieut.-Governor of Chelsea Hospital, 1773–98. Died Mar. 13, 1798. Brother of William (1734). (*T. A. Walker*, 281; *D.N.B.*; A. B. Beaven.)

HALE, CHARLES. Adm. pens. (age 15) at Christ's, Oct. 16, 1684. S. of Thomas. B. in London. School, St Albans (Dr James). Matric. 1684. Resided one year. Adm. at the Middle Temple, July 24, 1688. Of Hertfordshire. Died in Red Lion Square, Sept. 13, 1739. (*Peile*, II. 97; G. *Mag.*)

HALE or HALL, EDMUND. Matric. sizar from Christ's, 1593–4; B.A. 1597–8; M.A. 1601. One of these names V. of Willingdon, Sussex, 1607. (*Peile*, I. 213.)

HALE or HAYLL, GEORGE. Adm. at King's (age 18) a scholar from Eton, Aug. 14, 1504. Of Ruislip, Middlesex. B.A. 1508–9; M.A. 1512–3. Perhaps B.D. 1523–4. Fellow, 1507–19. Ord. priest (Lincoln) May 21, 1513. Perhaps will (P.C.C.) 1550; 'priest; New Windsor, Berks.'

HALE, JOHN. 'Fellow of King's' (not found in *Harwood*). Of London diocese. Ord. sub-deacon (Ely) Dec. 21, 1454; deacon, Mar. 1, 1454–5. R. of Doddington, Cambs., 1454.

HALE or HAYLE, JOHN. Pens. at Gonville Hall, 1514–21. A Benedictine monk from Norwich.

HALE, JOHN. Matric. pens. from Clare, Easter, 1584.

HALE, JOHN. Matric. sizar from Christ's, Mar. 1620–1; B.A. 1623–4; M.A. 1627. Ord. deacon (Peterb.) Feb. 18; priest, Feb. 19, 1626–7. One of these names V. of Tolleshunt D'Arcy, Essex, 1633. Another of Mildenhall, Suffolk, clerk. Will (P.C.C.) 1652. (*Peile*, I. 336.)

HALE, JOHN. Adm. pens. at Emmanuel, Jan. 18, 1629–30. Of Middlesex. Matric. 1631. Perhaps s. of Richard, of Tewin, Herts.; adm. at Lincoln's Inn, Nov. 15, 1632.

HALE, JOHN. Adm. pens. (age 15) at Peterhouse, Feb. 23, 1631–2. 7th s. of William, of King's Walden, Herts. Matric. 1632. Adm. at Gray's Inn, Nov. 21, 1634. Knighted, 1660. High Sheriff of Herts., 1663–4. Died Jan. 27, 1672–3. M.I. at King's Walden. Brother of Bernard (1625) and Rowland (1616). (*Vis. of Herts.*, 1634; *Vis. of Essex*, 1612; *T. A. Walker*, 46.)

HALE, JOHN. Adm. sizar (age 18) at Magdalene, Apr. 6, 1679. S. of John, gent. B. at Ince, Cheshire. School, 'Witton' (Weston) (private). Matric. 1679; and again as pens. 1683; B.A. 1683–4; M.A. 1687. Fellow, 1685. Brother of William (1683).

HALE, JOHN. Adm. sizar at Pembroke, July 7, 1724. S. of John, citizen and weaver, of London. B. at Lambeth, Surrey. Exhibitioner from Christ's Hospital. Matric. 1724; B.A. 1727–8. V. of Albrighton, Salop, 1747–82. Died 1782. Will, P.C.C.

HALE, Sir MATHEW. University Counsel, 1645. S. of Robert. B. at Alderley, Gloucs., Nov. 1, 1609. Matric. from Magdalen College, Oxford, Oct. 20, 1626, age 16. Adm. at Lincoln's Inn, Nov. 8, 1628. Barrister, 1636. Bencher, 1649. Serjeant-at-law, 1654. M.P. for Gloucs., 1654–5 and 1660; for Oxford University, 1659. Justice C.P. 1654–8. Lord Chief Baron of the Exchequer, 1660–71. Knighted, Jan. 30, 1661–2. Lord Chief Justice King's Bench, 1671. Author. Died Dec. 25, 1676. Buried at Alderley. M.I. there. Will (P.C.C.) 1677. (*D.N.B.*; *Al. Oxon.*)

HALE, OLIVER. Matric. pens. from King's, Easter, 1645. One of these names s. of Simon, of Clifton, Beds. Buried at Pulloxhill, Sept. 27, 1694. (*Vis. of Beds.*, 1634.)

HALE or HALES, RICHARD DE. 'King's scholar,' 1331. Incorp. in King's Hall, 1337. Died Aug. 7, 1361.

HALE, RICHARD. Matric. pens. from Trinity, Easter, 1623. One of these names, s. and h. of Richard, of Claberrie, Essex, Esq., adm. at Gray's Inn, Jan. 31, 1625–6.

HALE, RICHARD. Adm. sizar (age 15) at Sidney, Oct. 7, 1631. S. of Gamaliel, farmer. B. at Hoddesden, Herts. School, Deane, Beds. (Joseph Kemp, M.A.). Matric. 1632; B.A. 1635–6. Ord. priest (Lincoln) June 5, 1642. V. of Newnham, Herts., 1642–5. Signs as minister of Roxton, Beds., 1669–84. Buried there Aug. 17, 1684. (W. M. Noble.)

HALE, ROWLAND. Matric. pens. (age 16) from Peterhouse, Easter, 1616. 3rd s. of William, of King's Walden, Herts. Adm. at Gray's Inn, Nov. 5, 1619. Of King's Walden, Esq. High Sheriff of Herts., 1647. Succeeded to the family estate. Died Apr. 7, 1669. Brother of Bernard (1625) and John (1631–2). (*T. A. Walker*, 1; *Vis. of Essex*, 1612; *Vis. of Herts.*, 1634.)

HALE, ROWLAND. Adm. pens. (age 17) at Peterhouse, June 13, 1679. S. of William (1649), of King's Walden, Herts. School, Hertford. Matric. 1679. Adm. at Gray's Inn, Nov. 15, 1681. Brother of Bernard (1695) and probably of William (1680).

HALE, THOMAS. B.D. 1519–20; D.D. 1523–4. Perhaps fellow of St John's, 1520.

HALE or HAYLE, THOMAS. Matric. pens. from St John's, Michs. 1573. B. in London. Migrated to Oxford. B.A. from Exeter College, 1576–7; M.A. (Cambridge) 1580. Incorp. at Oxford, 1585. Fellow of Exeter College, 1579–83. Ord. deacon (London) Dec. 21, 1581, age 27. R. of St Olave, Hart St, 1583–90. R. of Beaumont, Essex, 1591–9. Perhaps V. of Stoke Nayland, Suffolk, 1599–1600. (*Al. Oxon.*)

HALE, THOMAS. Adm. pens. from Queens', Easter, 1609. Of Suffolk.

HALE, THOMAS. Adm. sizar at Queens', June 5, 1626. Of Hertfordshire. S. of Nicholas. Exhibitioner from Tonbridge School. (Hughes, *Tonbridge*.)

HALE, WILLIAM. Matric. pens. from Trinity, Easter, 1582–3; B.A. 1585–6. One of these names, of London, adm. at Gray's Inn, Nov. 14, 1586.

HAYLE, WILLIAM. Matric. sizar from Sidney, Easter, 1631; B.A. 1633–4; M.A. 1637. Ord. deacon (Peterb.) June 4, 1637. Probably R. of Gt Hallingbury, Essex, 1643–89. Died 1689. Will (Cons. C. London) 1689. (J. Ch. Smith.)

HALE, WILLIAM. Adm. Fell.-Com. at Trinity, May 28, 1649. Of Hertfordshire. S. and h. of Rowland (1616), of King's Walden, Herts. Adm. at Gray's Inn, May 3, 1651. Succeeded his father at King's Walden. M.P. for Herts., 1669–79. Died Aug. 25, 1688. M.I. at Walden. Father of Rowland (1679) and Bernard (1695). (*Clutterbuck*, III. 132; A. B. Beaven.)

HALE, WILLIAM. Adm. pens. at Christ's, June 18, 1680. Probably s. of William (above), of King's Walden, Herts. B. there, Feb. 17, 1663–4. Matric. 1682; B.A. 1683–4; M.A. 1687. Probably brother of Rowland (1679) and Bernard (1695). (*Vis. of Essex*; *Peile*, II. 80.)

HALE, WILLIAM. Adm. sizar (age 20) at St John's, May 30, 1683. S. of John, husbandman. B. at Ince, Cheshire. School, Weston (private; Mr Liptrott). Matric. 1683; B.A. 1686–7. Brother of John (1679).

HALE, WILLIAM. Adm. pens. at Christ's, Mar. 19, 1694–5. One of these names adm. at Leyden, Oct. 13, 1699.

HALE, WILLIAM. Adm. pens. (age 17) at Trinity, May 3, 1712. S. of John, of Enfield, Staffs. School, Stourbridge, Worcs. (Mr Wentworth). Matric. 1713–4; Scholar, 1714; B.A. 1715–6; M.A. 1719.

HALE, WILLIAM. Adm. Fell.-Com. (17) at Peterhouse, Dec. 17, 1730. S. of William, of King's Walden, Herts. School, Eton. Of King's Walden, Esq. Died Feb. 16, 1741. (*T. A. Walker*, 262; Ord's *Cleveland*, 232.)

HALE, WILLIAM. Adm. pens. (age 18) at Peterhouse, July 12, 1734. S. of Bernard (1695), Baron of the Irish Exchequer. Bapt. at Lincoln's Inn Chapel, July 7, 1716. School, Eton. Matric. 1734; Scholar, 1734. Adm. at Lincoln's Inn, June 6, 1730. Succeeded to the family estate at King's Walden, Herts. Died at Chelsea, Sept. 14, 1793. M.I. at Walden. Brother of Bernard (1742). (Burke, *L.G.*; *T. A. Walker*, 268.)

HALE, WILLIAM. Adm. pens. at Queens', Feb. 20, 1743–4. Of Worcestershire. Matric. 1744; B.A. 1747–8; M.A. 1751.

HALE or HALL, ——. B.A. 1478–9; M.A. 1482–3.

HALE or HALY, ——. B.A. 1507–8; M.A. 1510.

HALE, ——. B.A. 1508–9.

HALE, ——. Adm. pens. at Trinity Hall, 1745–6; name off, 1749.

HALES, ALEXANDER. Adm. Fell.-Com. at St Catharine's Hall, 1640. Of Kent.

HALES, CHARLES. Matric. Fell.-Com. from Queens', Easter, 1619. S. and h. of Stephen, of Newland, Warws., Esq. Adm. at Gray's Inn, Oct. 22, 1617. Of Snitterfield, Warws., Esq. Perhaps will (P.C.C.) 1639. (Le Neve, *Knights*, 29.)

HALES, CHARLES. Adm. pens. (age 18) at Trinity, June 16, 1686. S. of Thomas. B. at Howlet, Kent. Bapt. at Beaksbourne, Sept. 17, 1667. School, Westminster. Matric. 1686. Adm. at the Inner Temple, Aug. 18, 1686. Of New Windsor, Berks. Married and had issue. Died at Flushing, Holland, Aug. 5, 1747. Buried there. (Burke, *Ext. Bart.*; H. G. Harrison.)

HALES, CHRISTOPHER. B.A. 1538-9 (1st in the *ordo*); M.A. 1541. S. of Thomas, of Hales-place, Kent. Fellow of ST JOHN'S, 1539. An exile at Frankfort under Queen Mary, 1555. (*Cooper*, I. 154.)

HALES, EDWARD. Ord. deacon (Peterb.) Sept. 19, 1641; 'of MAGDALENE College, literate.'

HALES, EDWARD. Adm. Fell.-Com. at TRINITY, Oct. 23, 1646. Of Kent. S. and h. of Samuel (1625), Esq. Matric. 1649; B.A. 1649-50. Adm. at Gray's Inn, Jan. 30, 1651-2. Of Chilston, Kent, Esq. Married Elizabeth, dau. of Sir John Evelyn, of Lee Place, Godstone. Died *c.* 1697. (*Archaeol. Cantiana*, XIV. 66.)

HALES, HUMPHREY. Matric. pens. from PEMBROKE, Easter, 1568. S. of Humphrey (according to the *Visitation*), of the Dungeon, Canterbury. B.A. 1571-2. Bluemantle pursuivant, 1583-7. York herald, 1587-91. Died June 16, 1591. Will (Comm. C. London) 1591. Probably brother of the next. (*Vis. of Kent*, 1619; *Cooper*, II. 103.)

HALES, JAMES. Matric. pens. from TRINITY, Easter, 1560 (*impubes*); Scholar, 1560; B.A. 1563-4. Fellow of Pembroke, *c.* 1565. One of these names adm. at Gray's Inn, 1565. Probably s. of Humphrey. Knighted, 1573. Married Alice, dau. of Sir Thomas Kemp, Knt. Treasurer to the Expedition made to Portugal. Died at sea, 1589. Will (P.C.C.) 1590. Brother of Humphrey, above. (*Hasted*, IV. 440.)

HALES, JAMES. M.A. from EMMANUEL, 1728. S. of John, of Rochester, gent. Matric. from University College, Oxford, Feb. 11, 1716-7, age 18; B.A. (Oxford) 1720-1. V. of Bearsted, Kent, 1723-33. V. of Chart Sutton, 1733-66. Died 1766. (*Al. Oxon.*; H. G. Harrison.)

HALES, JOHN. Matric. pens. from ST JOHN'S, Michs. 1561. One of these names adm. at Gray's Inn, 1563.

HAYLES, JOHN. Matric. sizar from TRINITY, Lent, 1564-5.

HAYLES, JOHN. Matric. Fell.-Com. from TRINITY, Michs. 1576. Perhaps s. and h. of Edward, of Tenterden, Kent, Esq. Married Mary, dau. of Robert Horne, Bishop of Winchester. Died without issue. (*Vis. of Kent*, 1619.)

HALYS, JOHN. Matric. pens. from CHRIST'S, Easter, 1579. One of these names adm. at Gray's Inn, 1578.

HALES, JOHN. Adm. at CORPUS CHRISTI, 1600. B. 1583. B.A. 1603-4; M.A. 1607. Ord. deacon (Norwich) Sept. 20, 1607; priest, May 22, 1608. V. of Farlsthorpe, Lincs., 1611.

HALES, JOHN. Adm. Fell.-Com. at EMMANUEL, June 3, 1619. Doubtless s. and h. of Sir Edward, of Tenterden, Bart.; age 16 in 1619. Matric. 1619. Knighted, May 24, 1625. Married Christiana, dau. of Sir James Cromer, Knt., of Tunstall. Died before his father, *c.* 1652. Buried at Tunstall. Brother of Samuel (1625). (*Vis. of Kent*; *Hasted*, II. 576; *G.E.C.*)

HALES, JOHN. Adm. at CORPUS CHRISTI, 1635. Of Kent.

HALES, JOHN. M.D. 1651 (Incorp. from Padua). Incorp. at Oxford, 1663, as of EMMANUEL. F.R.C.P. 1657. Doubtless John Hale, M.D., of Twickenham. Buried there May 21, 1669. Admon. (P.C.C.) 1669. (*Al. Oxon.*; Munk; J. Ch. Smith.)

HALES, JOHN. Adm. sizar (age 15) at SIDNEY, Apr. 22, 1667. 1st s. of John. B. in St James' parish, London. School, Bishop's Stortford. Matric. 1667; B.A. 1670-1; M.A. 1674.

HALES, JOHN. Adm. pens. at KING'S, *c.* 1677.

HALES, ROBERT. B.A. 1559-60; M.A. 1563. Fellow of TRINITY, 1561. Ord. deacon (Ely) Nov. 24, 1560. One of these names R. of St Clement, Eastcheap, London, 1583-8. R. of St Nicholas Acons, 1580-8. Buried there Dec. 10, 1588. Admon. (Cons. C. London) 1589. (J. Ch. Smith.)

HALES, ROBERT. Matric. pens. from CHRIST'S, Easter, 1563; Scholar, 1564; B.A. 1565-6; M.A. from Pembroke, 1569. Fellow of Pembroke, *c.* 1568.

HALES, ROBERT. Matric. pens. from PEMBROKE, Easter, 1579; B.A. 1581-2 (*fil. nob.*).

HAYLES, ROBERT. Matric. sizar from PETERHOUSE, Michs. 1582; B.A. 1586-7.

HALES, ROBERT. Adm. pens. at CORPUS CHRISTI, 1626. Of Kent. Probably s. and h. of Thomas, of Beakesbourne, Kent. B. *c.* 1610. Matric. Easter, 1627. Adm. at the Inner Temple, 1628. Barrister, 1637. M.P. for Hythe, 1659. Created Bart., July 12, 1660. Married Catherine, dau. of Sir William Ashcomb, of Oxford, Knt. Died *c.* 1695. (*Hasted*, III. 716; *G.E.C.*)

HAYLES, SAMUEL. Matric. pens. from PEMBROKE, Michs. 1562; B.A. 1567-8.

HALES, SAMUEL. Adm. Fell.-Com. at EMMANUEL, Michs. 1606. Matric. 1606.

HALES, SAMUEL. Matric. Fell.-Com. from TRINITY, Easter, 1625. 2nd s. of Sir Edward, of Tenterden, Kent, Knt. and Bart. Adm. at Gray's Inn, June 16, 1626. Age 10 in 1619. Married Martha, dau. of Stephen Heronden, of Staple Inn, Middlesex. Died at Davington, Kent, June 13, 1638. Brother of John (1619), father of Edward (1646). (*Vis. of Kent*; *Archaeol. Cantiana*, XIV. 65.)

HALES, STEPHEN. Adm. (age 19) at CORPUS CHRISTI, 1696. S. of Thomas. Bapt. at Beakesbourne, Kent, Sept. 20, 1677. Matric. Michs. 1697; B.A. 1699-1700; M.A. 1703; B.D. 1711; D.D. (Oxford) 1733. Fellow of Corpus Christi, 1703-19. Ord. priest (London) June 19, 1709. P.C. of Teddington, Middlesex, 1709-61. R. of Porlock, Somerset, 1717-23. F.R.S. 1718. V. of Farringdon, Hants., 1722. Copley medallist, 1739. A member of the French Academy, 1753. Founder and Vice-President of the Society of Arts. Clerk of the closet to the Princess dowager Augusta. Well known as a physiologist and inventor. Died Jan. 4, 1761. (*Masters*, 302; *D.N.B.*)

HALES, WILLIAM. Matric. pens. from CHRIST'S, Michs. 1567. One of these names adm. at Gray's Inn, 1571.

HALES, ——. B.A. 1479-80; M.A. 1482.

HALES, ——. B.D. 1479-80.

HALES, ——. Adm. at CORPUS CHRISTI, 1571.

HALESWORTH, DANIEL. Matric. pens. from ST JOHN'S, Michs. 1572.

HALEY, DROPE. Adm. pens. at CLARE, Nov. 16, 1704. Of 'Ellsware' (? Edgware), Middlesex. S. and h. of John, late of Stanmore, Middlesex, gent. School, Winchester. Age 13 in 1700. Matric. 1705. Adm. at Gray's Inn, Nov. 2, 1708.

HALY or HALEE, JOHN. Matric. pens. from QUEENS', Michs. 1587. Of Suffolk.

HALFHEAD, FRANCIS. Matric. pens. from JESUS, Michs. 1594.

HALFEHEAD or HALFHEIDE, FRANCIS. Matric. sizar from TRINITY, Easter, 1629; Scholar, 1631; B.A. 1632-3; M.A. 1636. V. of Trumpington, Cambs., 1638-42. R. of Bawsey, Norfolk, 1661-79. Will of one of these names proved (V.C.C.) 1642.

HALHEAD or HAWLHED, HENRY. Adm. at KING'S (age 19) a scholar from Eton, Aug. 12, 1513. Of Cambridge. B.A. 1517-8; M.A. 1521. Fellow, 1516-8. Assistant Master at Eton. Afterwards graduated M.A. at Louvain. (*Harwood.*)

HALFHEAD, HENRY. Matric. pens. from TRINITY, Easter, 1575.

HALFEHEAD, JAMES. Adm. pens. at SIDNEY, Feb. 7, 1613-4. Matric. 1614; B.A. 1617-8.

HALFHEAD, ——. Adm. Fell.-Com. at CORPUS CHRISTI, 1579.

HALFHYDE, EDMUND. Adm. pens. at ST CATHARINE'S, Mar. 29, 1701. B. in Cambridgeshire, 1683. Matric. 1701; B.A. 1704-5; M.A. 1708. Fellow, 1707-27. Incorp. at Oxford, 1712. Ord. deacon (Ely) Sept. 20; priest, Dec. 20, 1719. R. of Coton, Cambs., 1719. R. of Girton, 1723.

HALFHYDE, EDWARD. Adm. pens. at ST CATHARINE'S, Jan. 14, 1678-9.

HALFHIDE, JAMES. Matric. pens. from ST JOHN'S, Easter, 1570.

HALFHYDE, THOMAS. Adm. pens. at ST CATHARINE'S, May 21, 1680.

HALFORD, *see also* HAWFORD *and* HOLFORD.

HALFORD, ANDREW. Adm. Fell.-Com. at CHRIST'S, Apr. 1621. 1st s. of Sir Richard, of Wistow, Leics., Knt. (afterwards Bart.). Matric. 1621. Adm. at the Middle Temple, May 21, 1622. Of Kilby, Esq. Died *v.p.* 1657, aged 54. Buried at Wistow. Said to have been condemned to death, by Cromwell, for having hanged a party of rebels against the King; but spared for a bribe of £30,000. Brother of George (1621). (*Peile*, I. 339; *G.E.C.*)

HALFORD, CHARLES. Matric. pens. from ST CATHARINE'S, Michs. 1640. Of Northamptonshire. Probably s. of Richard (1613), of Edith Weston, Rutland. Adm. at Gray's Inn, Nov. 23, 1645. Died Nov. 25, 1696, aged 73. (*Nichols*, II. 876.)

HALFORD, GEORGE. Adm. Fell.-Com. at CHRIST'S, Apr. 1621. S. of Sir Richard, of Wistow, Leics., Knt. Matric. 1621. Adm. at the Middle Temple, May 21, 1622. Of Turlangton, Leics., Esq. Died Aug. 18, 1659, aged 54. Admon. (Leicester) 1663. Brother of Andrew (1621). (*Peile*, I. 339.)

HALFORD, HENRY. Adm. pens. (age 14) at CHRIST'S, July 3, 1658. S. of William (1632). B. at Welham, Leics. School, Uppingham. B.A. 1661-2; M.A. 1665. Adm. at Gray's Inn, Nov. 24, 1662. Barrister-at-law, 1670. Ancient, 1685. Refused the bench, 1699. Brother of William (1658). (*Peile*, I. 582; *Nichols*, II. 864.)

HALFORD or HAWFORD, JOHN. Matric. pens. from CHRIST'S, Dec. 1609. Probably 5th s. of William, of Welham. If so, of Laundy Abbey, Northants. Married Jane, dau. of Sir Matthew Saunders, Knt. Subscribed to the new buildings of Christ's. Probably brother of William (1598-9). (*Peile*, I. 275; J. H. Hill, *Market Harborough*, 330.)

HALFORD or HOLFORD, JOHN. Adm. sizar at EMMANUEL, Easter, 1624. Matric. 1624; B.A. 1628; M.A. 1633. Perhaps proposed for the living of Slimbridge, Gloucs., Sept. 11, 1646.

HALFORD, JOHN. Adm. pens. (age 17) at CHRIST'S, Mar. 3, 1641-2. 3rd s. of William (1598), of Welham, Leics. B. there. School, Oakham. Slain at Oakham, Rutland, 1647. Brother of William (1632) and Thomas (1635). (*Peile*, I. 480; *Nichols*, II. 864.)

HALFORD, JOHN. Adm. sizar (age 18) at SIDNEY, June 17, 1657. S. of Richard, gent. B. at Kibworth Beacham, Leics. Schools, Kibworth Beacham (Mr Ambrose Bent) and Harborough (Mr Jo. Berry). Matric. 1657; B.A. 1660-1.

HALFORD, RICHARD. Matric. pen. from CHRIST'S, Michs. 1613. S. and h. of Richard, of Edith Weston, Rutland, Esq. Adm. at Gray's Inn, May 21, 1617. Sheriff of Ruts., 1631. Died Oct. 28, 1675, aged 81. M.I. at Edith Weston. Brother of Thomas (1618-9), probably father of Charles (1640). One of these names, of Leics., knighted, Jan. 5, 1641-2. (Said to have been born in 1584, in *Lincs. Pedigrees*, 438; age 21 in 1618, by *Vis. of Ruts.*) (*Nichols*, II. 868.)

HALFORD, RICHARD. Adm. pens. (age 16) at CHRIST'S, June 11, 1638. S. of Henry. B. at Little Bowden, Northants. School, Rugby (Mr Green). Matric. 1638; B.A. 1641-2.

HALFORD, RICHARD. Adm. pens. (age 17) at SIDNEY, June 28, 1647. S. of George (1621), Esq. B. at Turlangton, Leics. School, Uppingham (Mr Meeres). Of Lutterworth. Married Frances, dau. of William Halford, of Welham. Living, 1683. (*Nichols*, II. 874.)

HALFORD, RICHARD. Adm. pens. (age 18) at ST JOHN'S, Oct. 27, 1686. S. of Sir Thomas, Bart. B. at Wistow, Leics. School, Kibworth (Mr Daune). Matric. 1686; B.A. 1690-1. In holy orders. Succeeded as 5th Bart., 1695. Died Sept. 5, 1727. M.I. at Wistow. Admon. Leicester. (*Nichols*, II. 873; *G.E.C.*, where he is confused with the next.)

HALFORD, RICHARD. Adm. sizar at QUEENS', June 29, 1697. Of London. B. Jan. 15, 1678-9. School, Merchant Taylors'. Matric. 1697; B.A. 1700-1; M.A. 1704. Incorp. at Oxford, 1704. Ord. deacon (London) May 31, 1702; priest, May 23, 1703. V. of Lyminge, Kent, 1713; R. 1715-26. Died May 24, 1726.

HALFORD, RICHARD. Adm. pens. (age 19) at PEMBROKE, Apr. 30, 1745. S. of Thomas, of Leicester, Esq. Matric. Fell.-Com. Apr. 1748; B.A. 1749. Ord. deacon (Lincoln) May 21, 1749; priest, Mar. 1750-1. V. of Enderby, Leics., 1750-6.

HALFORD, THOMAS. Adm. pens. at SIDNEY, Feb. 6, 1618-9. S. of Richard, of Edith Weston, Rutland. B.A. 1622-3; M.A. 1626. Ord. deacon (Peterb.) June 3; priest, June 4, 1625. R. of Edith Weston. Died 1648. Brother of Richard (1613). (*Lincs. Pedigrees*, 439; *Vis. of Rutland*, 1618.)

HALFORD, THOMAS. Adm. pens. (age 18) at CHRIST'S, Apr. 30, 1635. 2nd s. of William (1598), of Welham. B. at Green's Norton, Northants. (his mother's home). Bapt. there, Mar. 27, 1616. Schools, Oakham and Oundle. Matric. 1635. Adm. at Gray's Inn, Mar. 18, 1639-40. Of Newhall, Thurlaston, Leics. Will dated Feb. 11, 1678: leaves £120 for a scholarship at Christ's. Brother of William (1632) and John (1641). (*Peile*, I. 436; *Nichols*, II. 864.)

HALFORD, WILLIAM. Matric. pens. from CHRIST'S, 1598-9, as Hawford. Doubtless s. of William, of Welham, Leics., Esq. B.A. 1600-1. Adm. at Gray's Inn, Feb. 2, 1604-5. Of Welham, Esq. Sheriff of Leics., 1640. Will proved, Feb. 9, 1646. Probably brother of John (1609), father of Thomas (above), John (1641) and William (1632). (*Peile*, I. 229; J. H. Hill, *Market Harborough*, 330.)

HALFORD or HAWFORD, WILLIAM. Matric. sizar from CHRIST'S, Dec. 1611; B.A. 1614-5; M.A. 1618. Ord. deacon (Peterb.) Sept. 19; priest, Dec. 19, 1619. (*Peile*, I. 284.)

HALFORD, WILLIAM. Adm. Fell.-Com. (age 17) at CHRIST'S, May 28, 1632. S. and h. of William (1598), of Welham, Leics. B. at Green's Norton, Northants. Bapt. there, Apr. 20, 1615. School, Oundle. Matric. 1632. Of Welham, Esq. Married Mary, dau. of Sir Henry Atkyns, of Clapham, Surrey, Knt. Died Apr. 16, 1652. Father of William (1658) and Henry (1658), brother of Thomas (1635) and John (1641). (*Peile*, I. 419; H. I. Longden.)

HALFORD, WILLIAM. Adm. Fell.-Com. (age 15) at CHRIST'S, July 3, 1658. S. of William (1632). B. at Welham, Leics. School, Uppingham (Mr Meares). Of Welham. Knighted, June 24, 1673. Died Dec. 28, 1682. Brother of Henry (1658). (*Peile*, I. 582; Le Neve, 286.)

HALFORD, WILLIAM. Adm. sizar (age 18) at PETERHOUSE, May 21, 1664. Of Leicester. School, Market Harborough. B.A. 1667-8.

HALFORD or HOLFORD, WILLIAM. Adm. sizar at QUEENS', July 7, 1693. Of Leicestershire. Matric. 1695; B.A. 1696-7. Ord. deacon (Lincoln) Sept. 25, 1698; C. of Bayford, Herts.; priest, Sept. 22, 1700.

HALFORD, ——. Adm. Fell.-Com. at TRINITY, June 24, 1647. Of Leicestershire.

HALFPENNY, JOHN. Adm. sizar at TRINITY, June 29, 1674. Matric. 1674-5; Scholar, 1676; B.A. 1677-8.

HALHEAD, *see* **HALFHEAD.**

HALITREHOLME, ——. B.Can.L. 1489-90. Perhaps Robert. Of Beverley. R. of Biddenham, Beds. Will, 1527. (M. H. Peacock.)

HALKE, JOHN. Adm. pens. at CORPUS CHRISTI, 1618. Matric. Lent, 1618-9; B.A. 1621-2; M.A. 1625; B.D. 1631-2 (*Lit. Reg.*). Ord. deacon (Peterb.) Sept. 21; priest Sept. 22, 1623. R. of Upminster, Essex, 1638. Sequestered, 1648; restored, 1660-2. Will (P.C.C.) 1678; as of Kensington, Middlesex. (Davids' *Essex*, 502.)

HALKE, MICHAEL. Adm. at CORPUS CHRISTI, 1602; B.A. 1606-7; M.A. 1613. Ord. deacon (Peterb.) Sept. 26, 1614. R. of Upminster, Essex, 1615; deprived, *c.* 1628. (Davids' *Essex*, 502; H. Smith.)

HALKE, WILLIAM. Matric. Fell.-Com. from CLARE, Easter, 1585. B. at Hastingley, Kent. B.A. 1588-9. Probably M.A. (St Andrews) 1590; Incorp. at Oxford, 1591. B.D. (Oxford) 1613. Ord. deacon (London) Mar. 16, 1605-6, age 40, as 'M.A.' C. of Wye, Kent. R. of Upminster, Essex, 1614-5. Died 1615. Will, P.C.C. (*Al. Oxon.*)

HALL, *see also* **HALLS.**

HALL, ABRAHAM. Adm. pens. (age 17) at TRINITY, Apr. 27, 1717. S. of Abraham, of Boothtown, Yorks. School, Wakefield, Yorks. (Mr Clark). Matric. 1718; Scholar, 1719; M.B. 1725; M.D. 1728 (*Com. Reg.*). F.R.C.P. 1732. Censor, 1734, 1745. Elect, 1749. Physician to St Thomas's Hospital and the Charterhouse. Died at Charterhouse, Feb. 5, 1751. (*Munk*, II. 126.)

HALL, ADAM. B.A. from ST JOHN'S, 1593-4; M.A. 1597. Will (P.C.C.) 1612; clerk, of Preston, Suffolk.

HALL, ANTHONY. Adm. pens. at EMMANUEL, Mar. 1584-5. S. of Anthony, Queen's messenger. Matric. 1585; Scholar. Studied the law at Barnard's Inn. Clerk in the office of the prothonotaries of the Common Pleas. (*Cooper*, II. 174.)

HALL, ARTHUR. Studied in Cambridge. Probably at ST JOHN'S, as he was a ward of Sir William Cecil. S. of Francis, of Grantham (John, according to *Cooper*). M.P. for Grantham, 1571, 1572-81, 1584-6. Expelled, 1581, for an offensive pamphlet. Confined in the Tower, 1581-3. First English translator of Homer. Buried at Grantham, Jan. 7, 1605-6. (*Cooper*, II. 397; *D.N.B.*; *Lincs. Pedigrees*, 441.)

HALL, ARTHUR. Matric. pens. from KING'S, Easter, 1603. Perhaps same as the next.

HALL, ARTHUR. B.A. from CHRIST'S, 1611-2; M.A. 1615. B. at Pidley, Hunts. Ord. deacon (Peterb.) Sept. 25, 1614; priest (London) June, 1623, age 30.

HALL or HOLL, AUGUSTIN. Adm. Fell.-Com. at EMMANUEL, Apr. 15, 1607. Matric. 1607.

HALL, CHARLES. Matric. pens. from TRINITY, Easter, 1619. Probably s. and h. of Thomas, of Barlow Lees, Derbs., gent., deceased; adm. at Lincoln's Inn, Nov. 15, 1619. M.P. for Lincs., 1654. Died Dec. 1, 1669. Buried at Kettlethorpe. Probably father of Charles (1668) and Thomas (1667). (*Lincs. Pedigrees*, 441.)

HALL, CHARLES. Matric. pens. from ST JOHN'S, Easter, 1629; B.A. 1632-3.

HALL, CHARLES. Adm. pens. (age 16) at ST JOHN'S, Nov. 26, 1668; afterwards Fell.-Com. S. of Charles (? 1619), gent., of Kettlethorpe, Lincs. B. there. School, Kettlethorpe (Mr Hall). Matric. 1668. Brother of Thomas (1667). (*Lincs. Pedigrees*, 441, 1342.)

HALL, CHARLES. Adm. sizar (age 16) at CHRIST'S, Apr. 7, 1669. S. of Richard, of Barlow Lees, Derbs. B. there. School, Wirksworth (Mr Crosdale). Matric. 1669; B.A. 1672-3; M.A. 1676. Ord. priest (York) May 29, 1681. Probably V. of Hault Hucknall, Derbs., 1682-90. R. of Kettlethorpe, Lincs., 1690-1728. Preb. of Lincoln, 1700-1. Died *c.* 1728. Father of Thomas (1701), Charles (1702) and Gilbert (1711). (*Peile*, II. 20; *F.M.G.*, 567.)

HALL, CHARLES. Adm. sizar at JESUS, June 24, 1680. S. of Robert, of Kellingley, Pontefract, Esq. Matric. 1680; Scholar, 1682; B.A. 1683-4; M.A. 1689. Ord. deacon (York) Dec. 1684; priest, Sept. 1689.

HALL, CHARLES. Adm. sizar at JESUS, May 26, 1702. Of Derbyshire. S. of Charles (1669), R. of Kettlethorpe, Lincs. Matric. 1702; B.A. 1705-6; M.A. 1726. Ord. deacon (Lincoln) Sept. 25, 1709; priest, Dec. 24, 1710. R. of Harrington, Lincs. V. of Immingham, 1710. C. of Killingholme. Died *c.* 1769, aged 82. Brother of Gilbert (1711). (*F.M.G.*, 568.)

HALL, CHARLES. Adm. sizar at JESUS, Sept. 6, 1729. Of Yorkshire. Matric. 1730; Scholar, 1731; B.A. 1733-4. Ord. deacon (Lincoln) Dec. 23, 1733. One of these names R. of Kirkley, Suffolk, 1748-70.

HALL, CHARLES. M.A. 1734 (Incorp. from Oxford). S. of John, of Stockport, Cheshire, gent. Matric. from Brasenose, Nov. 12, 1716, age 16; B.A. (Oxford) 1720; M.A. 1723. Ord. deacon (Peterb.) Mar. 1, 1723-4, as fellow of Brasenose College. (*Al. Oxon.*; H. I. Longden.)

HALL, CHARLES. M.A. 1743 (Incorp. from Oxford). S. of John, of Basingstoke, Hants., gent. Matric. from Corpus Christi, Oxford, Dec. 17, 1733, age 15; B.A. (Oxford) 1737; M.A. 1741; B.D. 1749; D.D. 1757. V. of Herne Hill, Kent, 1758-60. R. of All Hallows, Bread St, 1760-1. Dean and R. of Bocking, Essex. R. of Southchurch. Died Sept. 6, 1774. (*Al. Oxon.*; J. Ch. Smith.)

HALL, CHRISTOPHER. Matric. sizar from JESUS, Michs. 1549 (*impubes*). One of these names R. of Gestingthorpe, Essex; deprived, 1565.

HALL, CHRISTOPHER. Matric. pens. from ST JOHN'S, Michs. 1572. S. of Rodolph, gent., of York (Lord Mayor, and M.P.). School, Eton. Migrated as Fell.-Com. to Caius, Aug. 14, 1573, age 21. B.A. 1574-5. R. of Escrick, Yorks. 'Learned, able to preach, and of good conversation' (Return of 1592, *Lambeth MS.*). (*Venn*, I. 74.)

HALL or HAULL, CHRISTOPHER. Matric. sizar from TRINITY, Michs. 1578; B.A. 1582-3; M.A. 1586.

HALL, CHRISTOPHER. Matric. sizar from KING'S, Michs. 1602 (entry erased).

HALL, CHRISTOPHER. Matric. sizar from CLARE, Michs. 1622; B.A. 1625-6. Ord. deacon (Peterb.) Dec. 16, 1627. C. at Litlington, Cambs., 1630. Probably minister at Elstow, Beds., 1640. Buried there, as vicar, May 20, 1666.

HALL, CHRISTOPHER. Adm. sizar at CHRIST'S, June 16, 1626. S. of Richard, of Yorkshire. School, Giggleswick (Mr Dockwray). Matric. 1626.

HALL, CLIFFORD. Adm. pens. (age 18) at ST JOHN'S, Aug. 28, 1688. S. of John (1645), clerk. B. at Fordingbridge, Hants. School, Eton. Matric. 1688; B.A. 1692-3; M.A. 1696.

HALL, CORNELIUS. Adm. pens. (age 16) at CHRIST'S, Apr. 18, 1661. S. of Thomas, Esq. B. at Donington, Lincs. School, Uppingham (Mr Freer). Matric. 1661; B.A. 1664-5. Adm. at Gray's Inn, Feb. 9, 1664-5. Captain in the army. Buried at Donington, Nov. 6, 1679. Brother of George (1655). (*Peile*, I. 596; *Lincs. Pedigrees*, 440.)

HALL, DIVE. Matric. pens. from QUEENS', Michs. 1589. Of Bedfordshire.

HALL, EDMUND. B.A. 1487-8.

HALL, EDMUND. Licensed to practise surgery, 1542-3.

HALL, EDMUND. Matric. pens. from CORPUS CHRISTI, Easter, 1569.

HALL, EDMUND. M.A. 1653 (Incorp. from Oxford). S. of Richard, of Worcester. Matric. from Pembroke College, Oxford, July 8, 1636, age 16; M.A. (Oxford) 1649-50. Fellow of Pembroke. Captain in the Parliamentary army. Minister at Chipping Norton, Oxon. R. of St Mary-le-Crypt, Gloucester, 1662-5. R. of Seizencot (sinecure), 1669-79. R. of Abington St Nicholas, Berks., 1676-86. R. of Gt Rissington, Gloucs., 1680-6. Author. Buried Aug. 5, 1686, at Rissington. Will, Gloucester. (*D.N.B.*; *Al. Oxon.*)

HALL, EDMUND. Adm. pens. at CHRIST'S, Apr. 14, 1673; afterwards Fell.-Com. S. of Martin. Educated at Edinburgh University for four years. Probably M.A. 1674, as 'Edward,' *see* below. (*Peile*, II. 47.)

HALL, EDMUND. Adm. pens. (age 18) at TRINITY, June 18, 1701. S. of Edmund, of Bedwin, Wilts. School, Westminster. Matric. 1702; Scholar, 1702. Buried at St Michael's, Cambridge, Oct. 3, 1704.

HALL, EDWARD. Adm. at KING'S, a scholar from Eton, 1514. S. of John, of Northall, Salop. B. in St Mildred's, London. Fellow, 1517-8. No degree recorded. Common serjeant of London, 1532-5. Autumn reader at Gray's Inn, 1534. M.P. for Bridgnorth, 1542. Author, *Chronicle*: continued by Grafton. Died 1547. (*Cooper*, I. 92; *D.N.B.*)

HALL, EDWARD. Adm. sizar (age 15) at ST JOHN'S, Dec. 13, 1660. S. of Richard, blacksmith, of Sigglesthorne, Yorks. B. there. School, Beverley (Mr Sherwood). Matric. 1660; B.A. 1664-5. Ord. priest (Durham) Sept. 19, 1675. R. of Aspley Guise, Beds., 1682-1718. Father of Edward (1696-7) and Martin (1696-7).

HALL, EDWARD. M.A. 1674 (Incorp. from Edinburgh).

HALL, EDWARD. Adm. sizar (age 14) at CHRIST'S, Jan. 20, 1696-7. S. of Edward (1660), R. of Aspley Guise, Beds. B. at Munden, Herts. School, Guilsborough, Northants. Scholar, 1696-7; Matric. 1697; B.A. 1700-1; M.A. 1706. Ord. deacon (Peterb.) Sept. 20, 1702; priest (Lincoln) Sept. 28, 1709. R. of Hockliffe, Beds., 1713-8. R. of Aspley Guise, 1718. Brother of Martin (1696-7).

HALL, FRANCIS. Matric. pens. from ST JOHN'S, Michs. 1550; B.A. 1557-8; M.A. from Queens', 1562. Fellow of Queens', 1559. Perhaps R. of Aston Sandford, Bucks., 1558.

HALL, FRANCIS. Matric. pens. from PEMBROKE, Easter, 1579-80; B.A. 1583-4.

HALL, FRANCIS. Matric. sizar from TRINITY, Easter, 1627; B.A. from St John's, 1630-1; M.A. 1634. Perhaps the man of these names created B.D. at Oxford, Nov. 1642. R. of St Pancras, Soper Lane, 1660-2. Preb. of St Paul's, 1660-82. R. of St Anne and St Agnes, 1660. R. of St Michael Bassishaw, 1662-74. Minister of Knightsbridge Chapel, 1667-9. R. of Market Deeping, Lincs., 1669-73. Preb. of Chichester, 1679-81. Buried at Hillingdon, Middlesex. M.I. Will (P.C.C.) 1681. (*Al. Oxon.*; J. Ch. Smith.)

HALL, FRANCIS. Adm. at KING'S, a scholar from Eton, 1702. B. in London. Matric. Easter, 1702-3; B.A. 1706-7; M.A. 1710. Fellow, 1705; resigned on succeeding to an estate. Comptroller of the Salt duties, 1718-28. Died at Bath, Nov. 18, 1728. (*Harwood.*)

HALL, FRANCIS. Adm. pens. (age 18) at ST JOHN'S, June 16, 1738. S. of Francis, attorney-at-law, of Yorkshire. B. at Swaithe. School, Chesterfield, Derbs. (Mr Burrows). Matric. 1738; B.A. 1741-2; M.A. 1748. Ord. deacon (Rochester) Dec. 18, 1743; priest (York) Feb. 19, 1743-4. R. of Sprotborough, Yorks., 1744-7. R. of Kirksmeaton, 1749-59. R. of Harpole, Northants., 1759-63. R. of Thurnscoe, Yorks., 1763-71. R. of Tankersley, 1771-82. V. of Hartshead, in 1779. Married Mary, dau. of Sir Samuel Armitage, of Kirklees, Bart. Died Feb. 2, 1782. (*Scott-Mayor*, III. 494; M. H. Peacock.)

HALL, GEORGE. Matric. sizar from TRINITY, Michs. 1562.

HALL, GEORGE. 'Two years at CLARE, with his uncle Richard. Of Oakington, Cambs.,' when ord. deacon (Ely) July 7, 1560, age 32. Nephew of Richard (1552). One of these names R. of Hurworth, Durham, 1584-91.

HALL or HAULL, GEORGE. Scholar of CAIUS, 1586-96; B.A. 1588-9; M.A. 1592. Probably ord. priest (Lincoln) Dec. 11, 1593. C. of Cowlinge, Suffolk, in 1604. V. of Wickhambrook; sequestered, 1645. (*Venn*, I. 128 suggests his will proved (Norwich C.C.) 1628.)

HALL, GEORGE. Matric. pens. from CORPUS CHRISTI, *c.* 1594; B.A. 1596-7; M.A. 1601. Fellow, 1599-1606. Ord. deacon and priest (Norwich) July 25, 1602. R. of Searning and Syderstone, Norfolk, 1605. Died Dec. 6, 1628. M.I. at Coxford Priory.

HALL, GEORGE. Adm. sizar at EMMANUEL, Apr. 15, 1611; B.A. 1612-3. One of these names ord. priest (Norwich) Dec. 24, 1615; C. of Saxthorpe, Norfolk, in 1617.

HALL, GEORGE. Matric. Fell.-Com. from MAGDALENE, Easter, 1614.

HALL, GEORGE. Adm. at KING'S (age 16) a scholar from Eton, Aug. 16, 1625. Of Costock, Notts. Matric. 1625; B.A. 1629; M.A. 1633. Fellow, 1628-37. Chaplain to Lord Goring.

HALL, GEORGE. M.A. 1635 (Incorp. from Oxford). S. of Joseph (1589), Bishop of Exeter. Matric. from Exeter College, Oxford, 1628, age 16; B.A. (Oxford) 1631; M.A. 1633-4; D.D. 1660. Fellow of Exeter, 1632-8. V. of Menheniot, Cornwall, 1637-45, sequestered. Preb. of Exeter, 1639-61. Archdeacon of Cornwall, 1641. V. of Willingdon, Sussex, 1647. V. of St Botolph, Aldersgate, 1655. Canon of Windsor, 1660-2. Archdeacon of Canterbury, 1660-8. Bishop of Chester, 1662-8. R. of Wigan, 1662. Died Aug. 23, 1668. Buried at Wigan. Will, P.C.C. (*Al. Oxon.*; *D.N.B.*)

HALL, GEORGE. Adm. Fell.-Com. (age 17) at CHRIST'S, June 26, 1655. S. of Thomas, of Donington, Lincs. B. there. School, Donington (Mr Hurst). Matric. 1656. Adm. at Gray's Inn, Jan. 26, 1655-6. Brother of Cornelius (1661). (*Peile*, I. 568; *Lincs. Pedigrees*, 440.)

HALL, GEORGE. Adm. sizar (age 18) at ST JOHN'S, June 30, 1720. S. of John, clerk, of Durham (P.C. of Darlington). B. at Chester-le-Street. School, Darlington (Mr Richardson). Matric. 1720; B.A. 1723-4. Ord. deacon (Carlisle) May 31, 1724; priest, Aug. 7, 1726. Perhaps C. of St Nicholas, Newcastle. Buried there Nov. 25, 1741. (*Scott-Mayor*, III. 335; H. M. Wood.)

HALL, GEORGE. Adm. sizar (age 18) at ST JOHN'S, July 1, 1727. S. of William, shoemaker, of Middlesex. B. in London. School, Merchant Taylors'.

HALL, GILBERT. Adm. sizar (age 18) at CHRIST'S, Apr. 3, 1711. S. of Charles (1669), R. of Kettlethorpe, Lincs. B. Nov. 7, 1691. School, Gainsborough (Mr Waterworth). Matric. 1712; Scholar, 1713; B.A. 1715-6. Ord. deacon (Lincoln) May, 1716; priest, Sept. 24, 1716. R. of Kettlethorpe, Lincs., 1728-79. Married, at Barnborough, Aug. 12, 1725, Ann Mompesson. Buried at Kettlethorpe, Mar. 14, 1779. Brother of Charles (1702). (*Peile*, II. 177; *F.M.G.*, 567.)

HALL, GODFREY. Matric. sizar from ST JOHN'S, *c.* 1590.

HALL, GUISE. Adm. pens. (age 16) at TRINITY, Apr. 2, 1707. S. of Nicholas, of London. School, Eton. Matric. 1707. Adm. at Lincoln's Inn, Feb. 14, 1705-6, as s. and h. of Nicholas, of Bishop Middleham, Durham, Esq. Died Mar. 10, 1761. Buried at Richmond, Surrey. M.I. (J. Ch. Smith.)

HALL, HENRY. Matric. Fell.-Com. from TRINITY, Easter, 1561. One of these names adm. at Gray's Inn, 1565.

HALL, HENRY. Matric. pens. from CHRIST'S, Dec. 1606. One of these names, s. and h. of Henry, of York, gent., adm. at Gray's Inn, Feb. 2, 1608-9.

HALL, HENRY. Matric. sizar from TRINITY, Michs. 1620; Scholar, 1624; B.A. 1624-5; M.A. 1628; B.D. 1638. Fellow, 1627. V. of Kendal, Cumberland, 1640-4.

HALL, HENRY. Matric. pens. from ST JOHN'S, Easter, 1628. Perhaps s and h. of Henry, of Gretford, Lincs., Esq.; adm. at Lincoln's Inn, Apr. 24, 1630. Of Gretford, and Burton Coggles, Esq. Married, at Grantham, Elizabeth, dau. of Sir Edward Harto , Feb. 23, 1653-4. Will dated, Aug. 22, 1672. Probablpfather of Henry (1674). (*Lincs. Pedigrees*, 442; M. H. Peacock.)

HALL, HENRY. Adm. pens. at TRINITY, June 2, 1635. S. of Henry, of East Lilling, Sheriff Hutton, Yorks. Bapt. at All Saints Pavement, York, Dec. 15, 1618. Adm. at Gray's Inn, Jan. 16, 1638-9. Married Mary, dau. of William Hobson, of 'Siston' (? Easton), Lincs. Died Jan. 8, 1674. Buried at Sheriff Hutton. Will, York. (*Vis. of Yorks.*, 1665; J. Ch. Smith.)

HALL, HENRY. Adm. Fell.-Com. at CAIUS, Feb. 1674. S. of Henry (? 1628), of Gretford, Lincs., Esq. B. at Easton. School, Grantham (Mr Walker and Mr Peters). Matric. 1675. (*Venn*, I. 452; not given in *Lincs. Pedigrees*, 442.)

HALL, HENRY. Adm. sizar (age 17) at CHRIST'S, June 9, 1679. S. of Anthony. B. at Thirsk, Yorks. School, Thirsk (Mr Wildman). Matric. 1682; B.A. 1682-3. (Perhaps signature repeated in 1683-4.) Ord. deacon (Lincoln) Feb. 1683-4. C. of Wexham St Mary, near Slough, Bucks. Perhaps emigrant minister to Maryland, Jan. 11, 1697-8. One of these names consecrated a non-juror bishop, June 11, 1725. Died Nov. 1731. (*Peile*, II. 73 and 90.)

HALL, HENRY. Adm. sizar (age 17) at ST JOHN'S, Jan. 14, 1691-2. S. of Thomas (1657), clerk. B. at Castle Camps, Cambs. School, Bury. Matric. 1692. Brother of Joseph (1696).

HALL, HENRY. Adm. sizar (age 18) at PETERHOUSE, Feb. 20, 1693-4. Of Sussex. School, Horsham. Matric. 1697; B.A. 1697-8. Ord. priest (London) Nov. 11, 1697.

HALL, HENRY. Adm. scholar at CHRIST'S, Feb. 21, 1700-1. Matric. pens. Apr. 1701; B.A. 1703-4; M.A. 1707. Ord. deacon (London) Sept. 1706; priest (Lincoln) Sept. 25, 1709. V. of Elmdon, Essex, 1712-9. R. of Fowlmere, Cambs., 1719-51. Inherited a fortune from his uncle, Rumbold, who kept the Rose Tavern, Cambridge. Died at Fowlmere, Feb. 17, 1756-7, aged 74. Father of Thomas Rumbold (1740). (*Peile*, II. 151.)

HALL, HENRY. Adm. Fell.-Com. at ST JOHN'S, Oct. 30, 1701.

HALL, HENRY. Adm. at KING'S, a scholar from Eton, 1735. S. of Henry. Bapt. Mar. 5, 1716-7, at St Ethelburga, London. Matric. Michs. 1736; B.A. 1740-1; M.A. 1744. Fellow, 1739. Probably adm. at the Inner Temple, May 10, 1737, as s. and h. of Henry, of Hutton Hall, Essex, Esq. Librarian to the Archbishop of Canterbury. Ord. priest (Norwich) Dec. 1749. R. of Harbledown, Kent, 1750-63. V. of Herne, 1752-6. R. of Orpington, 1755-63. V. of East Peckham, 1756-63. Treasurer of Wells, 1762-3. Buried at Harbledown, Nov. 7, 1763. Will, P.C.C. (*Harwood*; H. G. Harrison.)

HALL, HEZEKIAH. Adm. Fell.-Com. at JESUS, July 7, 1707. Of Longnor, Staffs. Matric. 1708.

HALL, HUMPHREY. Matric. pens. from ST JOHN'S, Easter, 1575; B.A. 1578-9; M.A. 1582. Ord. deacon (Peterb.) May 13; priest, July 19, 1582. One of these names R. of Patrington, Yorks., in 1607.

HALL, HUMPHREY. Matric. pens. from ST JOHN'S, Easter, 1621; B.A. 1624-5.

HALL, JAMES. B.A. of NICHOLAS HOSTEL, 1557, when his admon. was granted (V.C.C.). R. of Harlton, Cambs., 1553. Perhaps matric. pens. from Clement Hostel, Easter, 1545.

HALLE, JOHN. Fellow of KING'S HALL. Adm. Nov. 16, 1435; resided till 1456. Ord. deacon (Norwich) Apr. 7, 1436; priest, June 2, 1436.

HALL, JOHN. Adm. at KING'S, a scholar from Eton, 1490.

HALL, JOHN. Incorp. from Oxford, 1500-1. R. of Burwell, Cambs. R. of Leverington, 1519.

HALL, HAYLE or HALE, JOHN. B.Can.L. 1512-3. Fellow or scholar of KING'S HALL, 1532-5. M.A. of Paris. Had studied Canon Law 12 years. (*Gr. Bk*, Γ, 106.) Probably R. of Cranford, Middlesex, 1505-21. V. of All Saints', Isleworth, 1521-35. The first secular priest to suffer martyrdom. Executed at Tyburn, with the Carthusians, May 4, 1535. The Warden of King's Hall writes to Cromwell, Apr. 30, 1535, saying that he has sequestered his goods. (B. Camm, *Eng. Martyrs*, I. 17.)

HALL, JOHN. Matric. pens. from ST JOHN'S, Michs. 1578; B.A. 1582-3; M.A. 1586. Ord. deacon (Peterb.) Aug. 1; priest, Aug. 28, 1586. One of these names, M.A., R. of Marnham, Notts., 1593-4.

HALL, JOHN. Matric. pens. from PETERHOUSE, Easter, 1579-80; B.A. 1583-4; M.A. 1587. Fellow. Ord. deacon and priest (Peterb.) July 9, 1587. One of these names (M.A.), R. of Sandal Parva, Yorks., 1591-7.

HALL, JOHN. B.A. from TRINITY, 1582-3; M.A. 1586. Perhaps adm. June, 1578. Author, Italian verses on death of Dr R. Cosin, 1598. Died Feb. 16, 1617-8, aged 57. M.I. at Bovingdon, Herts. (*Cooper*, II. 270.)

HALL, JOHN. Matric. sizar from PEMBROKE, Easter, 1586; B.A. from St Catharine's, 1588-9, as Hale.

HALL, JOHN. Matric. pens. from QUEENS', Michs. 1589. Of Bedfordshire. B.A. 1593-4; M.A. 1597, as Hale. One of these names, M.A., was R. of Rise, Yorks., in 1601.

HALL, JOHN. Matric. pens. from ST JOHN'S, *c.* 1593.

HALL, JOHN. Adm. sizar (age 18) at CAIUS, July 14, 1618. S. of Richard, husbandman, of Brington, Hunts. School, Oundle, Northants. (Mr Pemberton and Mr Spencer). Matric. 1618-9; B.A. 1621-2; M.A. 1625. Licensed schoolmaster at Eye, Suffolk, 1624. Afterwards at Hoxne. Master of Yarmouth School, 1646. Died 1647. Will (Norwich) 1648. Brother of Thomas (1608). (*Venn*, I. 240.)

HALL, JOHN. Adm. pens. at EMMANUEL, Sept. 30, 1644. Of London. Matric. 1644.

HALL, JOHN. Adm. at KING'S, a scholar from Eton, 1645. B. at Windsor, 1627. Matric. Michs. 1645; B.A. 1649; M.A. 1653. Fellow, 1648-61. R. of Horstead, Norfolk, 1658. V. of Fordingbridge, Hants., 1660-1700. Died 1699-1700. Father of Clifford (1688). (*Harwood*.)

HALL, JOHN. Adm. pens. (age 18) at ST JOHN'S, Feb. 26, 1645-6. S. of Michael, gent. (of Consett, Durham). Bapt. Aug. 20, 1627. School, Durham. Matric. as Fell.-Com. 1646. Adm. at Gray's Inn, 1647. Accompanied Cromwell to Scotland, 1650. A friend of Hobbes and Samuel Hartlib. Poet and pamphleteer. Died Aug. 1, 1656. (*D.N.B.*; Surtees, *Durham*, II. 297.)

HALL, JOHN. Adm. pens. (age 14) at CHRIST'S, June 1, 1648. S. of Robert, of Derbyshire. School, Nottingham (Mr Leake). Matric. 1648.

HALL, JOHN. Adm. sizar at TRINITY, May 29, 1652. Of Salop. Scholar, 1655; B.A. 1655-6; M.A. 1659; B.D. 1666. Fellow, 1658. R. of Hanwell, Middlesex, 1664-6. Preb. of St Paul's, 1664-1707. R. of St Christopher-le-Stocks, London, 1666-1707. R. of Finchley, Middlesex, 1666-1707. President of Sion College, London, 1694. Author of devotional works and poems. Buried at St Christopher's, Dec. 19, 1707. Will, P.C.C. Father of John (1695-6). (*D.N.B.*)

HALL, JOHN. Adm. pens. at JESUS, Feb. 22, 1655-6. Of Staffordshire. Matric. 1657; Scholar, 1658. Perhaps B.A. 1659-60, as Jonathan; M.A. 1663.

HALL, JOHN. Adm. sizar (age 17) at CHRIST'S, Nov. 19, 1658. S. of Henry. B. at York. School, Leeds (Mr Garnet). B.A. 1662-3. Ord. deacon (York) Sept. 1663; C. of Whitkirk, near Leeds. One of these names R. of Guisborough-in-Cleveland, 1694-1722. One R. of Strensall, near York, about 1719. (*Peile*, I. 583.)

HALL, JOHN. Adm. sizar at CHRIST'S, June 26, 1661. He may be the same as the next.

HALL, JOHN. Adm. pens. (age 16) at MAGDALENE, Feb. 23, 1662-3. S. of William, citizen of Lincoln. School, Nottingham. Matric. 1663; B.A. 1666-7; M.A. 1670. Fellow, 1668. Incorp. at Oxford, 1675. Ord. deacon (Peterb.) Sept. 24, 1670.

HALL, JOHN. Adm. pens. (age 17) at ST JOHN'S, Sept. 14, 1675. S. of Samuel (1638), D.D. of Bardfield, Essex. B. there. School, Colchester. Matric. 1675; B.A. 1679-80. Probably R. of Lambourne, Essex, 1700-7. Buried there May 10, 1707.

HALL, JOHN. Adm. sizar (age 20) at PETERHOUSE, Feb. 7, 1679-80. Of Yorkshire. School, Northallerton. Scholar, 1680; B.A. 1683-4. Ord. deacon (Durham) June 2, 1683; priest, Sept. 21, 1684.

HALL, JOHN. Matric. pens. from ST CATHARINE'S, Michs. 1681. One of these names, s. and h. of Thomas, of Chew Magna, Somerset, adm. at Lincoln's Inn, May 14, 1681.

HALL, JOHN. Adm. pens. at CLARE, Sept. 18, 1683. Of Deptford, Kent. School, Lewisham. Matric. 1683; M.B. 1689. Fellow, 1689.

HALL, JOHN. Adm. pens. (age 17) at TRINITY, Jan. 9, 1695-6. S. of John (1652), of St Christopher's, Threadneedle St, London. Bapt. there, Feb. 26, 1677-8. School, North Weald, Essex (Mr Hewet). Matric. 1696; Scholar, 1699; B.A. 1699-1700; M.A. 1703. Ord. deacon (Lincoln) Sept. 21, 1701; priest (London) Dec. 20, 1702. One of these names V. of Erith, Kent, 1705-14.

HALL, JOHN. Matric. sizar from TRINITY HALL, Dec. 1700. Of Yorkshire. Scholar, 1702; B.A. 1703-4. Ord. deacon (York) Oct. 1707; priest, 1708.

HALL, JOHN. Adm. sizar (age 16) at PETERHOUSE, Apr. 23, 1703. Of Yorkshire. School, Richmond, Yorks.

HALL, JOHN. Adm. sizar at JESUS, June 4, 1714. S. of John, clerk, of Fishlake, Yorks. Matric. 1714; Scholar, 1717; B.A. 1717-8; M.A. 1721. Fellow, 1721-2. Ord. deacon (York) May, 1719; priest, 1720-1. C. of Guisborough, Yorks., 1722. Died same year, aged 26. M.I. at Hatfield Chase, Yorks.

HALL, JOHN. Adm. Fell.-Com. (age 17) at JESUS, June 16, 1735. Afterwards (1738) Hall-Stevenson. S. of Joseph, of Durham, Esq. Adm. at the Inner Temple, Nov. 21, 1735. Inherited Skelton Castle, Yorks. Friend of Laurence Sterne. Married Ann, dau. of Ambrose Stevenson, of Lanchester, Durham. Author, *Crazy Tales*, etc. Died at Skelton, Mar. 25, 1785. Buried there. (*D.N.B.*; H. M. Wood.)

HALL, JONATHAN. Adm. sizar at QUEENS', July 9, 1658. Of Wales. Matric. 1661; B.A. 1661-2; M.A. 1665.

HALL, JONATHAN. B.A. from JESUS, 1659-60; M.A. 1663. But *see* John (1655-6). Perhaps ord. deacon (Norwich) July 13, 1662.

HALL, JONATHAN. Adm. pens. (age 15) at ST JOHN'S, Apr. 10, 1696. S. of John, gent. (alderman and draper), of Durham. B. there. School, Durham (private; Mr Ross). Matric. 1696; B.A. 1699-1700; M.A. 1703; B.D. 1710; D.D. 1723. Fellow, 1701-22. Ord. deacon (Ely) May 19, 1706; priest (London) June 8, 1707. R. of Swaffham Bulbeck, Cambs., 1714. R. of Cockfield, Suffolk, 1720-43. Chaplain to Lord Cadogan, ambassador to the States General. Chaplain to the Governor of Berwick. Preb. of Durham, 1723-43. Buried in Durham Cathedral, June 15, 1743. (H. M. Wood.)

HALL, JOSEPH. Adm. pens. at EMMANUEL, Lent, 1588-9. S. of John. B. at Bristow Park, Ashby-de-la-Zouch, July 1, 1574. Matric. 1589; Scholar; B.A. 1592-3; M.A. 1596; B.D. 1603; D.D. 1610. Fellow, 1595. Incorp. at Oxford, 1598. Ord. priest (Colchester) Dec. 14, 1600. R. of Hawstead, Suffolk, 1601-8. Accompanied Sir Edmund Bacon to Spa, 1605. V. of Waltham, Essex, 1608. Archdeacon of Nottingham, 1611-27. Adm. at Gray's Inn, 1615. Dean of Worcester, 1616-27. Bishop of Exeter, and R. of St Breoc, 1627-41. Bishop of Norwich, 1641-56. After his removal as Bishop he retired to Heigham, Norwich, where he continued to ordain until his death. Author, satires and controversial works. Died at Heigham, Sept. 8, 1656, aged 82. M.I. there. Will, P.C.C. Father of George (1635) and Robert (1622), brother of Samuel (1597). (*D.N.B.*)

HALL, JOSEPH. Adm. sizar at EMMANUEL, July 19, 1645. S. of Thomas, of Milborne, Dorset, clerk. B.A. 1646; M.A. 1649. Previously matric. from Wadham College, Oxford, Mar. 11, 1641-2, age 16.

HALL, JOSEPH. Adm. sizar at EMMANUEL, May 22, 1672. Of Cheshire. Matric. 1675; B.A. 1675-6. One of these names R. of Hadleigh, Essex, 1709-12. V. of Blackmore, 1712-7. (J. Ch. Smith.)

HALL, JOSEPH. Adm. sizar (age 17) at SIDNEY, July 9, 1675. 1st s. of John, mercer, deceased. B. at Hull. School, Hull. Matric. 1676; B.A. 1679-80; M.A. 1683. Ord. priest (London) Mar. 12, 1681-2. Incorp. at Oxford, 1683. R. of Croxton, Lincs., 1687. R. of Nettleton, 1690. V. of Grasby, 1697. (*Al. Oxon.*)

HALL, JOSEPH. Adm. sizar (age 16) at ST JOHN'S, Oct. 10, 1696. S. of Thomas (1657), clerk. B. at Castle Camps, Cambs. School, Bury, Suffolk. Matric. 1696. Brother of Henry (1691-2).

HALL, JOSEPH. Adm. sizar at QUEENS', June 30, 1703. Of Essex. Matric. 1703; B.A. 1706-7. Ord. deacon (London) Mar. 9, 1706-7; priest, Sept. 25, 1709. Perhaps Master of Chelmsford Grammar School, till 1731. R. of Bowers Gifford.

HALL, JOSEPH. Adm. sizar (age 18) at SIDNEY, Apr. 2, 1712. Only s. of John (? 1675), deceased, R. of Lambourne, Essex. B. Dec. 1, 1693, at Ightham, Kent. School, Merchant Taylors'. Migrated to St Catharine's, Nov. 10, 1712. Matric. 1712; B.A. from St Catharine's, 1715-6. Adm. at the Inner Temple, Nov. 20, 1714; and at the Middle Temple, Apr. 25, 1721.

HALL, JOSEPH. M.A. from QUEENS', 1734. S. of Richard, of Tiverton, Devon. Matric. from Balliol College, Oxford, Mar. 4, 1723-4, age 17; B.A. (Oxford) 1727. Ord. deacon (Carlisle) Dec. 18, 1726; priest (Exeter) Sept. 21, 1729. V. of Welham, Leics., 1734-67. R. of Gt Wigston. V. of Newbottle, Northants., 1735-8. Died 1767. (*Nichols*, II. 867.)

HALL, JOSIAS. Adm. pens. (age 17) at PEMBROKE, May 24, 1652. S. of Samuel. B. at Hutton Hang, Yorks. Matric. 1653; B.A. 1655-6.

HALL, LANCELOT. Matric. sizar from CHRIST'S, Dec. 1610; B.A. 1614-5; M.A. 1620. Ord. deacon (Durham) Sept. 20, 1618; priest (York) May, 1619. Licensed to preach. (*Peile*, I. 280.)

HALL, LIONEL. Matric. sizar from CLARE, Easter, 1579.

HALL, MARTIN. Adm. sizar (age 13) at CHRIST'S, Mar. 19, 1696-7. S. of Edward (1660), R. of Aspley Guise, Beds. B. there. School, Guilsborough, Northants. (Mr Worling). Matric. 1696-7; Scholar, 1696-7; B.A. 1700-1. Ord. deacon (Peterb.) Mar. 12, 1703-4; priest (Lincoln) Sept. 25, 1709. C. of Linslade, Bucks., 1711. R. of High Laver, Essex, 1727. Died there, 1734. Brother of Edward (1696-7). (*Peile*, II. 138.)

HALLE, MATTHEW. Adm. pens. (age 15) at CAIUS, Aug. 5, 1672. S. of Matthew, chandler, of Yarmouth. Bapt. at St Nicholas, Mar. 21, 1657-8. Schools, Feltwell, Norfolk (Mr Fish) and Melton (Mr Ward). Matric. 1672-3; Scholar, 1673-8; B.A. 1676-7; M.A. 1680. Fellow, 1680. Probably afterwards a Romanist. (*Venn*, I. 447.)

HALL, MICAH. Matric. sizar from KING'S, Easter, 1618; B.A. 1621-2; M.A. 1627. Ord. deacon (Peterb.) Apr. 6, 1624.

HALL, NATHANIEL. Matric. pens. from CHRIST'S, Mar. 1610-1; B.A. 1614-5; M.A. 1618. One of these names, minister, buried at St Antholin's, London, Aug. 14, 1624. Perhaps brother of William (1628). (*Peile*, I. 281.)

HALL, NATHANIEL. Adm. pens. (age 16) at CHRIST'S, Apr. 26, 1659. S. of William. B. in London. (? Bapt. at St Bartholomew-the-Less, Oct. 2, 1643; s. of William, vicar, of 1628.) School, Bury, Suffolk. Matric. 1659. (*Peile*, I. 585.)

HALL, NICHOLAS. Adm. pens. at EMMANUEL, Mar. 26, 1619. Of Newcastle-on-Tyne. S. of Thomas, merchant adventurer. Bapt. at All Saints', Newcastle, Jan. 13, 1604-5. Matric. 1619; Scholar; B.A. 1622-3; M.A. 1626; B.D. 1633. Fellow, 1627. R. of Loughborough, Leics., 1642; ejected, 1642; re-instated, 1662. Master of St Mary's Hospital, Newcastle. Died May 12, 1669. M.I. at Loughborough. Will, P.C.C. (*Nichols*, III. 900; Surtees, *Durham*, I. 126.)

HALL, NICHOLAS. M.A. 1676 (Incorp. from Oxford). S. of Emmanuel, of Bridford, Devon. Matric. from Wadham College, May 5, 1665, age 18; B.A. (Oxford) 1668-9; M.A. 1671; D.D. 1683. R. of St Leonard's, Exeter, 1671. Preb. of Exeter, 1672-1709. Sub-dean, 1675. Treasurer, 1675-1709. R. of Stoke-in-Teignhead, Devon, 1675. R. of Whitstone, 1681. R. of Farringdon, 1704. Died Apr. 25, 1709. Will (Exeter) 1709. (*Al. Oxon.*)

HALL, OLIVER. B.A. from ST CATHARINE'S, 1583-4. Of Cowlinge, Suffolk (perhaps curate); licensed to teach grammar, May, 1586. Probably s. of Richard; bapt. at Cowlinge, Nov. 30, 1567. (V. B. Redstone.)

HALL, OLIVER. Adm. at CORPUS CHRISTI, 1622. Of Norfolk. B.A. 1625-6; M.A. 1629. Ord. deacon (Norwich) Feb. 18, 1626-7; priest, 1630. V. of Hoxne, Suffolk, 1644. R. of Stoke Ash, 1646.

HALL, PETER. Adm. sizar at JESUS, Nov. 22, 1687. Of Yorkshire.

HALL, PHILIP. Adm. pens. (age 17) at CHRIST'S, June 5, 1668. S. of Matthew. B. at Leventhorp, Swillington, Yorks. School, Leeds (Mr Mich. Gilbert). Matric. 1668. Adm. at Lincoln's Inn, June 20, 1668. Buried at Swillington, Oct. 21, 1688. (*Vis. of Yorks.*, 1665; *Peile*, II. 16.)

HALL, PHILIP. Adm. sizar at JESUS, Mar. 9, 1742-3. Of Yorkshire. Scholar, 1743; B.A. 1746-7; M.A. 1750. Fellow, 1751-74. Ord. deacon (York) Mar. 1746-7; priest (Norwich, *Litt. dim.* from York) Dec. 1748. C. of St Mary, Hull, 1747. Died, unmarried, 1774; having been for some time disordered in his mind. Admon. (P.C.C.) 1775; of South Cave, Yorks. (A. Gray.)

HALL, RALPH. Adm. sizar (age 19) at CHRIST'S, Dec. 1, 1670. S. of James. B. at Bulwell, Notts. School, Mansfield (Mr Samson). Matric. 1671; B.A. 1674-5. Ord. deacon (York) May, 1675. V. of Saxelby, Leics., 1685. (*Peile*, II. 32.)

HALL, REGINALD. Matric. pens. from CHRIST'S, Nov. 1559. S. of Simon, of Burton Pedwardine, Lincs. B. 1542. Scholar, 1560–1. Of Ayscoghfee Hall, Lincs. Buried at Pinchbeck, Jan. 4, 1598–9. Father of Robert (1584). (*Peile*, I. 70; *Lincs. Pedigrees*, 444.)

HALL, RICHARD. Matric. pens. from CLARE, Michs. 1552. Migrated to Christ's.

HALL, RICHARD. Licensed to practise medicine and surgery, 1553.

HALL, RICHARD. Matric. pens. from PEMBROKE, Michs. 1553. Of Lincolnshire. B.A. 1555–6; M.A. 1559. Fellow, 1556. D.D. (perhaps from St Omer). Migrated to Caius. Adm. Fell.-Com. there, June 12, 1561, age 25. Ord. deacon (Lincoln) 1565. Afterwards a Romanist. At Douay College, 1575; lecturer there. Canon of Cambray. Canon of St Omer and official of the diocese. Author, theological. Probably died at St Omer. Buried in the Cathedral there, Feb. 26, 1603–4. (*Venn*, I. 46; *D.N.B.*, following *Cooper*, confuses this man with Richard (1552).)

HALL, RICHARD. Matric. sizar from TRINITY, Easter, 1580–1; B.A. 1584–5; M.A. 1588.

HALL, RICHARD. Matric. pens. from TRINITY, Easter, 1613.

HALL, RICHARD. B.D. 1617 (Incorp. from Oxford). Matric. from Balliol College, June 11, 1602, age 16; B.A. (Oxford) 1604; M.A. 1607; B.D. (All Souls) 1617; D.D. 1620. V. of Barking, Essex, 1620. Admon. (P.C.C.) May 25, 1649. (*Al. Oxon.*)

HALL, RICHARD. Matric. sizar from TRINITY, Easter, 1628; B.A. 1631–2; M.A. 1635.

HALL, RICHARD. M.A. 1629 (Incorp. from Oxford). Of Hampshire, gent. Matric. from Hart Hall, Oxford, July 1, 1603, age 14; B.A. (Oxford) 1608–9; M.A. 1612. (*Al. Oxon.*, not quite clear as between this man and the one of 1617.)

HALL, RICHARD. Matric. sizar from KING'S, Michs. 1647; B.A. 1650–1; M.A. 1654.

HALL, RICHARD. Adm. sizar (age 18) at ST JOHN'S, June 7, 1655. S. of Richard, blacksmith, of Catwick-in-Holderness, Yorks. B. there. School, Beverley (Mr Sherwood). Matric. 1655; B.A. 1658–9; M.A. 1662. One of these names M.A., ord. deacon (Lincoln) Aug. 31, 1662.

HALL, RICHARD. Adm. pens. at JESUS, Apr. 5, 1682. Of Nottinghamshire. Matric. 1682; Scholar, 1682; B.A. 1685–6. Died 1686.

HALL, ROBERT. B.Can.L. 1496.

HALL, ROBERT. B.Can.L. 1525–6.

HALL, ROBERT. Adm. at KING'S (age 17) a scholar from Eton, Aug. 13, 1550. Of Horningsea, Cambs. Matric. 1550. Left in 1552.

HALL, ROBERT. Matric. pens. from ST JOHN'S, Easter, 1557–8. S. of Robert, of Keighley, Yorks. School, Skipton. B.A. 1560–1. Migrated to Caius, Feb. 1, 1560–1, age 20. (*Venn*, I. 45.)

HALL, ROBERT. Adm. pens. at CAIUS, Sept. 14, 1560. S. of John, of Norwich, gent., deceased. B. at Scottow, Norfolk. Matric. 1560.

HALL, ROBERT. Matric. pens. from TRINITY, Easter, 1563–4. This, or the next, B.A. 1567–8. One of these names (B.A.), ord. priest (Lincoln) July 17, 1577, was V. of Burton, Lincs.

HALL, ROBERT. Matric. sizar from TRINITY, Easter, 1564–5.

HALL, ROBERT. Matric. sizar from ST JOHN'S, Michs. 1578; B.A. 1582–3.

HALL, ROBERT. Matric. pens. from CHRIST'S, Nov. 1584. S. of Reginald (1559), of Pinchbeck, Lincs. Adm. at Gray's Inn, May 9, 1589. Married at Spalding, to Mary Jackson, Feb. 6, 1607–8. Buried at Boston, Apr. 12, 1627. (*Peile*, I. 180; *Lincs. Pedigrees*, 444.)

HALL, ROBERT. Matric. pens. from EMMANUEL, Easter, 1622. Adm. May 9. S. of Joseph (1589), Bishop of Exeter. B.A. 1625–6. Incorp. at Oxford, 1628; M.A. from Exeter College, Oxford, 1628–9; D.D. 1643. Adm. at Lincoln's Inn, Feb. 26, 1628–9. Preb. of Exeter, 1629–67. Treasurer, 1629–67. R. of Stoke-in-Teignhead, Devon, 1631. Archdeacon of Cornwall, 1633–41. Sequestered, but restored, 1660. R. of Clyst Hydon, 1634. Died May 29, 1667, aged 61. Will (Exeter) 1667. Brother of George (1635). (*Al. Oxon.*)

HALL, ROBERT. Adm. sizar at EMMANUEL, Easter, 1624. Matric. 1624; B.A. 1627–8; M.A. 1631. Possibly R. of Warham, Norfolk; *see* Robert (1667).

HALL, ROBERT. Adm. Fell.-Com. at CLARE, June 30, 1648.

HALL, ROBERT. Matric. sizar from ST CATHARINE'S, Easter, 1650; B.A. 1653–4.

HALL, ROBERT. Adm. sizar at EMMANUEL, July 2, 1667. Of Yorkshire. Matric. 1667; B.A. 1670–1; M.A. 1674. Ord. deacon (York) June, 1671; priest, Sept. 1672. Incorp. at Oxford, 1674.

HALL, ROBERT. Adm. sizar (age 17) at PEMBROKE, July 3, 1667. S. of Robert, clerk, of Warham, Norfolk.

HALL, ROBERT. Adm. at CORPUS CHRISTI, 1704. Of Nottinghamshire. Matric. 1704; B.A. 1707–8; M.A. 1711. Ord. deacon (York) June, 1712; priest (Norwich) June 11, 1713. R. of Lopham, Norfolk, 1713–60. Probably brother of Thomas (1702).

HALL, ROBERT. Adm. pens. at JESUS, June 25, 1708. Of Sussex. Matric. 1709; B.A. 1711–2; M.A. 1715. One of these names V. of Leybourne, Kent, 1720–3. Buried Dec. 9, 1723.

HALL, ROBERT. Adm. at CORPUS CHRISTI, 1736. Of Nottinghamshire. Doubtless s. of Thomas (1702). Matric. Michs. 1736; B.A. 1739–40; M.A. 1743. Ord. deacon (Lincoln) Mar. 14, 1741–2; priest, May 29, 1743. Perhaps R. of Hawton, Notts. Died Mar. 9, 1785. Will (P.C.C.) 1785, of Robert Hall, of Stubton, Lincs., clerk. Probably brother of Thomas (1735). (G. *Mag.*; *Lincs. Pedigrees*, where he is called the 1st son.)

HALL, SAMUEL. Adm. pens. at EMMANUEL, Apr. 6, 1597. S. of John. Matric. 1597; Scholar; B.A. 1600–1; M.A. 1604; B.D. 1611. Fellow, 1606–11. V. of Donington, Lincs., 1611. Died at Lincoln, 1612. Will, Lincoln. Brother of Joseph (1589). (*Lincs. Pedigrees*, 440.)

HALL, SAMUEL. Matric. pens. from CORPUS CHRISTI, Michs. 1638. Of Derbyshire. B.A. 1640–1; M.A. 1645; D.D. 1671. Ord. deacon (Lincoln) Dec. 22, 1644. P.C. of Little Bardfield, Essex, 1650. R. of Gt Bardfield, 1656. R. of Theydon Mount, 1663–94. Died May 15, 1694. Buried at Theydon. Will (Consist. C. London) 1694. Father of John (1675). (H. Smith; J. Ch. Smith.)

HALL, SAMUEL. Adm. sizar (age 18) at PEMBROKE, July 3, 1650. S. of Robert, of Coventry, Warws., shoemaker. Matric. 1650.

HALL, SAMUEL. Adm. sizar at JESUS, May 14, 1652. Of Cheshire. S. of Ralph, of Mear. Matric. 1652; B.A. 1655–6. V. of Barlaston, Staffs., 1656–62; ejected, 1662. (*Calamy*, II. 390.)

HALL, SAMUEL. Adm. pens. at CORPUS CHRISTI, 1681. Of Kent. Matric. 1681; M.B. 1686.

HALL, SAMUEL. Adm. sizar (age 19) at ST JOHN'S, Mar. 27, 1725. S. of Joseph, shoemaker, of Cheshire. B. at Coggleshall (Essex). School, Coggleshall (Mr Malbon). Matric. 1725; B.A. 1728–9. Perhaps V. of Long Houghton, Northumberland, 1730–52. V. of Chatton, 1752–75. C. of Doddington, 1766–75. Buried at Chatton, Mar. 31, 1775. (H. M. Wood.)

HALL, SAMUEL. Adm. pens. (age 17) at TRINITY, Nov. 2, 1731. S. of Joseph, of Lincoln. School, Lincoln (Dr Goodall). Matric. 1732; Scholar, 1732; B.A. 1735–6; M.A. 1739. Ord. deacon (Lincoln) Dec. 24, 1738.

HALL, STEPHEN. Matric. pens. from PEMBROKE, Easter, 1611. B. in All Hallows, Barking, London. B.A. 1614–5; M.A. 1618; B.D. from Jesus, 1625. Fellow of Jesus, 1619–44; ejected; restored, 1660. Incorp. at Oxford, 1619. V. of Guilden Morden, Cambs., 1627. V. of All Saints', Cambridge, 1629–38. V. of Fordham, Cambs., 1639. Imprisoned in the Compter, Southwark, for three years. Preb. of Ely, 1660–1. R. of Harlton, Cambs., 1661. Died Aug. 18, 1661. Buried in Jesus College Chapel. M.I. Will (V.C.C.) 1661. Benefactor to Jesus College. (Le Neve, *Mon.* III. 83; A. Gray.)

HALL, THOMAS. B.D. 1472–3. V. of Barrington, Cambs., 1476.

HALL, THOMAS. B.A. 1498–9; M.A. 1502. Perhaps V. of Earlham, Norfolk, 1504–26.

HALL, THOMAS. M.B. 1503–4; M.D. 1506. Scholar at KING'S HALL, 1505–6. S. and h. of Nicholas, of Colby, Lincs. Of Huntingdon. Received a pardon, May 8, 1510. (*Trin. Coll. Adm.*, I. 128.)

HALL or HAYLL, THOMAS. M.Gram. 1506–7. A priest.

HALL, THOMAS. Matric. sizar from CLARE, Easter, 1544; B.A. 1547–8. Fellow of Peterhouse, 1548–56. One of these names R. of Hitcham, Bucks., 1566–92.

HALL, THOMAS. Matric. sizar from ST JOHN'S, Easter, 1582; B.A. 1584–5; M.A. 1588. One of these names R. of Bradnam, Bucks., 1592–3. One, master of Warwick Grammar School, 1589–94; and V. of St Mary, Warwick, for 46 years. Will (P.C.C.) 1639. (*Vict. Hist. Warws.*, II.)

HALL, THOMAS. Matric. pens. from ST JOHN'S, *c.* 1590.

HALLE (?), THOMAS. Matric. pens. from CHRIST'S, 1592–3.

HALL, THOMAS. Matric. sizar from QUEENS', *c.* 1593. B. at Wigston, Leics., 1578. B.A. 1596–7; M.A. 1600. Fellow, 1599–1608. Incorp. at Oxford, 1600. Taxor, 1607–8. Ord. priest (Colchester) Apr. 5, 1601. R. of Abbots Ripton, Hunts., 1607–18. Died 1618.

HALL, THOMAS. Adm. sizar (age 16) at CAIUS, May 3, 1608. S. of Richard, husbandman. B. at Brington, Hunts. School, Oundle (Mr Spencer). Matric. 1608; Scholar, 1610–2; B.A. 1611–2; M.A. 1615. Ord. priest (Norwich) May 26, 1616. R. of Osmondeston, Norfolk, 1618–42. R. of Frenze, 1618–42. Will proved (Norwich) 1642. Brother of John (1618). (*Venn*, I. 197.)

HALL, THOMAS. Adm. scholar at JESUS, Feb. 28, 1609–10. Of Warwickshire. Migrated to Oxford. Matric. pens. (age 18) from Magdalen Hall, May 24, 1611; B.A. (Oxford) 1613–4. Perhaps adm. at Gray's Inn, Feb. 21, 1615–6, as s. of Thomas, of Priors Marston, Warws.

HALL, THOMAS. Matric. sizar from ST JOHN'S, Easter, 1616; B.A. 1620–1.

HALL, THOMAS. Adm. sizar (age 15) at MAGDALENE, Apr. 2, 1645. S. of Robert, of Wilton, Lincs. School, Mansfield. Matric. 1645; B.A. 1648–9.

HALL, THOMAS. Adm. sizar (age 14) at MAGDALENE, July 6, 1647. S. of John, clerk, of Upton Pyne, Exeter. School, Exeter.

HALL, THOMAS. Adm. at CORPUS CHRISTI, 1657. Of Leicestershire. B.A. 1660–1; M.A. 1664; B.D. 1671. Fellow, 1663–9. Incorp. at Oxford, 1664. Ord. deacon (Lincoln) Sept. 21, 1662; priest (Ely) Mar. 10, 1665–6. C. of St Benet, Cambridge, 1666. R. of Castle Camps, Cambs., 1669–91; ejected as nonjuror. Living at Linton, Cambs., 1695. Father of Henry (1691–2) and Joseph (1696). (*Al. Carthus.*)

HALL, THOMAS. Adm. at CORPUS CHRISTI, 1665. Of Nottinghamshire. Matric. Easter, 1665; B.A. 1668–9; M.A. 1672. Ord. deacon (York) *c.* Feb. 1670–1. V. of Eccles, Lancs., 1678–1721. Fellow of the Collegiate Church of Manchester, 1688–1721. Died 1721. (*Vict. History of Lancs.*, IV. 358.)

HALL, THOMAS. Adm. pens. at EMMANUEL, June 17, 1664. Of Leicestershire. Matric. 1665.

HALL, THOMAS. Adm. pens. (age 17) at ST JOHN'S, June 17, 1667; afterwards Fell.-Com. S. of Charles (? 1619), gent., of Kettlethorpe, Lincs. B. there. School, Kettlethorpe. Matric. 1667–8. Of Kettlethorpe, Esq. Buried there Nov. 15, 1698. Brother of Charles (1668). (*Lincs. Pedigrees*, 441.)

HALL, THOMAS. Adm. pens. (age 18) at TRINITY, Mar. 30, 1687. S. of Thomas, of Hindcourt, Middlesex. School, Enfield (Dr Udall). Matric. 1687.

HALL, THOMAS. Adm. sizar at MAGDALENE, May 23, 1688. B. at Gt Massingham, Norfolk. Matric. 1688.

HALL, THOMAS. Adm. sizar at JESUS, Apr. 23, 1701. Of Lincolnshire. S. of Charles (1669). Matric. 1701; B.A. 1704–5. Ord. deacon (Lincoln) June 8, 1707; priest, June 19, 1709. One of these names Master of Bradford School, Yorks., 1718–28.

HALL, THOMAS. Adm. at CORPUS CHRISTI, 1702. Of Nottinghamshire. Matric. 1702; B.A. 1705–6; M.A. 1709. Ord. deacon (York) Sept. 1709; priest, 1710. R. of Westborough, Lincs. Died May 7, 1754. Probably brother of Robert (1702), father of Robert (1736) and Thomas (1735). (*Lincs. Pedigrees*, 445.)

HALL, THOMAS. Matric Fell.-Com. from KING'S, Easter, 1703.

HALL, THOMAS. Adm. sizar (age 18) at ST JOHN'S, June 13, 1706. S. of Matthew, shoemaker. B. at Shrewsbury. School, Shrewsbury. Matric. 1706.

HALL, THOMAS. Adm. sizar at JESUS, May 3, 1711. Of Spott, Staffs. Matric. 1711; B.A. 1715–6; M.A. 1731. Ord. deacon Lincoln) Sept. 24, 1727.

HALL, THOMAS. Adm. pens. (age 17) at PETERHOUSE, Mar. 4, 1719–20. Of Cheshire. School, Congleton. Matric. 1720; Scholar, 1720. Perhaps s. and h. of Edward, of Cranage, Cheshire. B. June 3, 1702. If so, Sheriff of Cheshire, 1745. Died June 27, 1748. (*Ormerod*, III. 74.)

HALL, THOMAS. Adm. at CORPUS CHRISTI, 1735. Of Nottinghamshire. Doubtless s. of Thomas (1702). Matric. Easter, 1736; B.A. 1738–9; M.A. 1742. Ord. deacon (Lincoln) June 1, 1740. Probably R. of Westborough, Lincs. Died July 19, 1775. Probably brother of Robert (1736). (*Lincs. Pedigrees*, 445, where Robert is called the 1st s.)

HALL, THOMAS. Adm. sizar at EMMANUEL, July 8, 1736. Of Middlesex.

HALL, THOMAS. Adm. pens. at JESUS, June 2, 1741. S. of Joseph, of Durham. Scholar, 1741. General in the army. Lived at Weston Colville, Cambs. Brother of John (1735). (A. Gray.)

HALL, THOMAS. Adm. pens. (age 18) at EMMANUEL, Feb. 10, 1746–7. Of Baxterley, Warws. S. of Thomas, gent. School, Appleby. Matric. 1748. Afterwards Fell.-Com. Perhaps ord. priest (Lincoln) Dec. 18, 1756. R. of Shackerston, Leics., 1756–79. Died 1779. Will (P.C.C.) 1779, of Thomas Hall, of Warwick, clerk.

HALL, THOMAS RUMBOLD. Adm. pens. (age 18) at ST JOHN'S, Sept. 27, 1740. S. of Henry (1701), R. of Fowlmere, Cambs. B. at Fowlmere. School, Scarning, Norfolk (Mr Brett). Matric. 1740; B.A. 1744–5. Of Hildersham, Cambs. High Sheriff of Cambs. and Hunts., 1780–1. (*Scott-Mayor*, III. 509.)

HALL, URBAN. Adm. sizar (age 17) at PETERHOUSE, Nov. 10, 1715. Of Lincolnshire. School, Lincoln. Migrated to St Catharine's, Oct. 12, 1716. Matric. 1715–6; B.A. 1719–20.

HALL, WILLIAM. LL.B. R. of Little Wilbraham, Cambs. Exchanged for Withebrook, Warws., 1456.

HALL, WILLIAM. M.Gram. 1519–20. A priest.

HALL, WILLIAM. Matric. sizar from JESUS, Easter, 1544.

HALL, WILLIAM. Matric. pens. from TRINITY, Easter, 1574; B.A. 1577–8; M.A. 1581. Fellow, 1579. Perhaps R. of Little Stukeley, Hunts., 1581. R. of Orwell, Cambs., 1612–9. Buried at Orwell, Mar. 29, 1619. Will, P.C.C.

HALL, WILLIAM. Matric. pens. from ST JOHN'S, Easter, 1577–8. Of Lincolnshire. B.A. 1580–1; M.A. 1584; B.D. 1591. Fellow, 1587. Incorp. at Oxford, 1584. Perhaps ord. priest (Norwich) 1587. V. of Redgrave and Botesdale, Suffolk, 1597.

HALL, WILLIAM. Adm. pens. at QUEENS', Oct. 23, 1579. Of London.

HALL, WILLIAM. Matric. sizar from TRINITY, Michs. 1617; Scholar, 1620; B.A. 1621–2; M.A. 1625. Ord. deacon (York) Mar. 1625–6; priest (Peterb.) Mar. 2, 1628–9. V. of Kellington, Yorks., 1633. Probably held the living till *c.* 1661.

HALL, WILLIAM. Adm. sizar (age 17) at SIDNEY, Jan. 29, 1619–20. S. of William. B. at Grimsby, Lincs. School, Grimsby. Matric. 1620.

HALL, WILLIAM. Adm. pens. (age about 17) at CAIUS, Feb. 25, 1622–3. S. of William, gent. Of Risby, Suffolk. School, Bury St Edmunds. Matric. 1623; Scholar, 1624–7. (*Venn*, I. 260, where the latter part of the description probably belongs to William of 1628.)

HALL, WILLIAM. Matric. sizar from ST JOHN'S, Easter, 1624; B.A. 1627–8.

HALL, WILLIAM. Adm. pens. (age 16) at CHRIST'S, June 14, 1628. S. of Nathaniel. B. in London. Bapt. at St Bartholomew-the-Less, Oct. 5, 1610. School, Christ's Hospital. Matric. 1628; B.A. 1631–2; M.A. 1635; D.D. 1660 (*Lit. Reg.*). Perhaps V. of St Bartholomew-the-Less, 1636–54. R. of St Michael Bassishaw, 1660–2. Preb. of St Paul's, 1660–2. Died Apr. 13, 1662. Admon. (P.C.C.) 1662. Probably father of Nathaniel (1659). (*Peile*, I. 392.)

HALL, WILLIAM. Matric. sizar from TRINITY, Michs. 1628; B.A. 1631–2; M.A. 1635. One of these names, M.A., ord. priest (Norwich) Dec. 18, 1642. C. of St Saviour, Norwich. Perhaps R. of Hevingham, Norfolk, 1644–59. Buried there May 16, 1659. Will (P.C.C.) 1660.

HALL, WILLIAM. Matric. sizar from QUEENS', Easter, 1633. Of Leicestershire.

HALL, WILLIAM. Adm. sizar (age 15) at ST JOHN'S, May 9, 1635. S. of Charles, tailor, of Middle-Rasen, Lincs. B. there. School, East-Rasen. Matric. 1635; B.A. 1640–1. Ord. deacon (Peterb.) Dec. 18, 1642.

HALL, WILLIAM. Adm. sizar at JESUS, May 22, 1639. Of Nottinghamshire. Matric. 1639; Scholar, 1642; B.A. 1642–3.

HALL, WILLIAM. Adm. sizar (age 18) at SIDNEY, June 30, 1662. S. of William, farmer. B. at Cropton, Pickering, Yorks. School, Edston, York (Mr Hardwick). Matric. 1662; B.A. 1665–6; M.A. 1669. Ord. deacon (Peterb.) Sept. 23, 1666. Signed for priest's orders (London) June 16, 1671; C. of Little Yeldham, Essex. One of these names, M.A., V. of Good Easter, Essex, 1671. Died 1711.

HALL, WILLIAM. Adm. sizar (age 18) at CHRIST'S, May 27, 1664. S. of Thomas. B. at Hornby, Yorks. School, Northallerton (Mr Smelt). Matric. 1664.

HALL, WILLIAM. Adm. pens. at CLARE, Feb. 2, 1671–2. Doubtless s. of Josias, R. of Gt Addington, Northants. Matric. 1672; B.A. 1675–6; M.A. 1679. Ord. deacon (London) Feb. 24, 1677–8. One of these names R. of Acton, Middlesex, 1720–6. (H. I. Longden.)

HALL, WILLIAM. Adm. sizar at JESUS, June 28, 1711. Of Congleton, Cheshire. Matric. 1712; B.A. 1714–5; M.A. 1728. P.C. of Siddington, Cheshire, 1716–24. P.C. of Marton, 1718–24. R. of Gawsworth, 1724. Died at Gawsworth, July 20, 1769, aged 76. M.I. (A. Gray.)

HALL, WILLIAM. Adm. at KING'S, a scholar from Eton, 1724. S. of William. Bapt. at St Botolph's, Aldersgate, July 31, 1705. Matric. Easter, 1724–5; B.A. 1728–9; M.A. 1732. Fellow, 1727. Adm. at the Middle Temple, Feb. 23, 1727–8. Barrister-at-law. Deputy Master of the Exchequer. Solicitor to the Post Office. Secretary to the Pipe Office. Died Feb. 28, 1767. Will, P.C.C. (*Harwood*, 314; *G. Mag.*)

HALL, WILLIAM. Adm. Fell.-Com. at CHRIST'S, Mar. 15, 1724-5. Resided about four years. (*Peile*, II. 210.)

HALL, WILLIAM. Adm. sizar at CHRIST'S, June 23, 1738. B. at Kirkham, Lancs. School, Kirkham (Mr Taylor). Matric. 1738; Scholar, 1739. Died before June, 1741. (*Peile*, II. 237.)

HALLE, ——. Fellow of CORPUS CHRISTI shortly after 1441.

HALL, ——. B.A. 1461-2.

HALL, ——. B.A. 1462-3; M.A. 1466-7.

HALL, ——. B.A. 1468-9.

HALL, ——. B.A. 1475-6.

HALL, ——. B.A. 1476-7. Perhaps M.A. 1478-9.

HALL, ——. Fee for degree; perhaps B.D.; 1484-5. A friar.

HALL, ——. B.A. 1489-90. Perhaps Thomas of KING'S.

HALL, ——. B.Can.L. 1489-90. Perhaps John of KING'S.

HALL, ——. Of ST WILLIAM'S HOSTEL. B.A. 1503.

HALL, ——. B.A. 1519-20.

HALL, ——. B.D. 1520-1; D.D. 1523-4. Preacher, 1519-20.

HALL, ——. Matric. pens. from CHRIST'S, May, 1544. Probably Thomas. B.A. from Clare, 1547-8. Fellow of Peterhouse, 1548 (whom *see*).

HALL, ——. Adm. pens. at SIDNEY, Nov. 1599.

HALL, ——. Adm. Fell.-Com. at EMMANUEL, Easter, 1626.

HALLAM, GEORGE. B.A. from CLARE, 1573-4. R. of St Nicholas Cole Abbey, London, 1581-2. Died 1582.

HALLAM, HENRY. B.A. from ST JOHN'S, 1582-3; M.A. 1586. V. of Mettingham, Suffolk, 1591-1634.

HALLAM, JAMES. Matric. sizar from ST JOHN'S, Easter, 1631; B.A. 1633-4; M.A. 1637. V. of Manuden, Essex, *c.* 1655.

HALLAM, JOHN. Adm. at KING'S, a scholar from Eton, 1747. S. of John. Bapt. at Boston, Lincs., Oct. 17, 1728. Matric. Michs. 1748; B.A. 1753; M.A. 1756; D.D. 1781. Fellow, 1751. Ord. deacon (Lincoln) May 25, 1755. Canon of Windsor, 1775-1811. Dean of Bristol, 1781-1800. Died Aug. 26, 1811. Buried in St George's Chapel, Windsor, Sept. 3.

HALLAM, NICHOLAS. Matric. sizar from CHRIST'S, Oct. 1579. Of Nottinghamshire. B.A. 1584-5. R. of Trowell, Notts., 1588-1626. Died 1626. (A. B. Beaven.)

HALLAM, NICHOLAS. Matric. pens. from CHRIST'S, July, 1620; B.A. 1623-4; M.A. 1627. Incorp. at Oxford, 1624. Ord. deacon (Peterb.) Mar. 2, 1625-6; priest, Mar. 3, 1625-6. (*Peile*, I. 334.)

HALAM, ROBERT. D.Can.L. 1497-8. Principal of ST PAUL'S HOSTEL, 1504. V. of Little Eversden, Cambs., till 1520. (*Cooper*, I. 8.)

HALAM, THOMAS. B.A. 1458-9. Perhaps V. of Babraham, Cambs., 1479.

HALLAY, ——. Fee for M.A. or higher degree, 1468-9.

HALLELEY, CHRISTOPHER. Adm. pens. at TRINITY, Sept. 14, 1667.

HALLILEY, ROBERT (1575), *see* ALLALEY.

HALLELY, ROBERT. B.A. from CHRIST'S, 1607-8; M.A. 1611. V. of Calkwell, Lincs., 1614-5.

HALLEN or HALLEY, FRANCIS. Matric. pens. from JESUS, Michs. 1562.

HALLERD, ——. B.A. 1481.

HALLETT, JOSEPH. Adm. sizar (age 18) at SIDNEY, May 27, 1676. 1st s. of Joseph, nonconformist minister. B. at Bridport, Dorset. Schools, Bridport (Mr Tho. Thompkins) and Tiverton. Ordained in 1683. Appointed his father's assistant at 'James' Meeting,' Exeter, 1687. Pastor of the Meeting, 1713. Conducted a nonconformist Academy at Exeter. Excluded from James' meeting on a charge of unorthodoxy, 1715. Author. Died 1722. One of these names adm. at Leyden, July 13, 1685. (*D.N.B.*)

HALLET, ——. B.A. (?) 1482-3.

HALLEY, GEORGE. Matric. pens. from ST JOHN'S, Michs. 1613; B.A. 1617-8; M.A. 1621. Ord. deacon (York) May, 1619; priest, Dec. 1619. V. of Skipwith, Yorks. One of these names R. of Clowne, Derbs., till 1680. Died Aug. 19, 1680.

HALLEY or HAWLEY, GEORGE. Adm. sizar (age 16) at ST JOHN'S, Feb. 3, 1671-2. B. at York. School, York. Matric. 1672, as Halley; B.A. 1675-6, as Hawley; M.A. 1679; D.D. 1702, as Halley. Ord. deacon (York) May, 1676. V. of Holy Trinity, York, 1679-83; of St Cuthbert, 1683-1708. Preb. of Ripon, 1696-1708. Married Sarah, dau. of Cuthbert Hesketh, R. of Monkton Moor, Yorks. Buried July 21, 1708. (M. H. Peacock.)

HALLEYE, JOHN. Matric. pens. from ST JOHN'S, Lent, 1564-5.

HALLEY, JOHN. Matric. sizar from PEMBROKE, Easter, 1584.

HALLEY, THOMAS. Adm. sizar (age 19) at ST JOHN'S, June 1, 1727. S. of George, husbandman, of Yorkshire. B. at Bubwith. School, Pocklington (Mr Baker). Matric. 1727; B.A. 1730-1; M.A. 1734. One of these names V. of St Peter's, Colchester, 1739-60.

HALLYBREAD, THOMAS. Matric. pens. from TRINITY, Easter, 1557-8; B.A. 1560-1.

HALLYBURTON, ANTHONY. Adm. sizar (age 16) at CAIUS, Apr. 20, 1630. S. of Andrew, minister. B. at Itteringham, Norfolk. Scholar, 1630-6; Matric. 1631; B.A. 1633-4; M.A. 1637. Fellow 1636-46, ejected. C. of Impington, Cambs., 1637. R. of Longford (diocese Lichfield, ? Salop), 1640. Author. Died before 1654. (*Venn*, I. 294.)

HALYDAY, ALAN. Matric. sizar from ST JOHN'S, Easter, 1573.

HALLIDAY, THOMAS. B.A. 1565-6; M.A. from TRINITY, 1569. Ord. deacon (London) June 4, 1566. V. of Thaxted, Essex, 1566-83. Died 1583.

HALLIDAY, ——. B.Can.L. 1477-8.

HALLIDAY, ——. B.A. 1478-9; M.A. 1482.

HALLIDANCE, ——. M.B. 1486-7. *See* HARRIDANCE.

HALLYFAX, CHRISTOPHER. Matric. pens. from CORPUS CHRISTI, Easter, 1574; B.A. 1577-8.

HALLIFAX, JOHN. Matric. sizar from TRINITY, Easter, 1632; B.A. 1635-6; M.A. 1639. Ord. deacon (Peterb.) Sept. 24, 1637; priest, June 9, 1639.

HALLIFAX, SAMUEL. Adm. sizar at JESUS, Oct. 21, 1749. S. of Robert, apothecary, of Mansfield, Notts. School, Mansfield. Matric. 1750; Scholar; B.A. 1754; M.A. 1757; LL.D. from Trinity Hall, 1764; D.D. 1775 (*Lit. Reg.*). Chancellor's medallist, 1754. Fellow of Jesus, 1756-60. Fellow of Trinity Hall, 1760-75. Professor of Arabic, and Lord Almoner's Reader, 1768-70. Regius Professor of Civil Law, 1770-82. Ord. deacon (Ely) Sept. 21, 1755; priest, Mar. 6, 1757. R. of Cheddington, Bucks., 1765. R. of Warsop, Notts., 1778. Chaplain to the King, 1774. Bishop of Gloucester, 1781-9. Bishop of St Asaph, 1789-90. F.S.A. Author, miscellaneous. Died Mar. 5, 1790. (*D.N.B.*)

HALLIMAN, ——. Fee for M.A. or higher degree, 1479-80.

HALLINGDALE, SAMUEL. Matric. sizar from PETERHOUSE, Easter, 1575.

HALLINGS, WILLIAM. M.A. from KING'S, 1726. S. of William, of Hereford. Matric. from Brasenose College, Oxford, Mar. 28, 1705, age 18. B.A. (Oxford) 1708. R. of Evesbatch, Heref., 1714. (*Al. Oxon.*)

HALLIWELL, ABRAHAM. Adm. pens. (age 17) at CHRIST'S, Mar. 6, 1636-7. S. of James. B. at Pike House, near Rochdale, Lancs. Schools, Wakefield and Rochdale (Mr Ormerod). Matric. 1637; B.A. 1640-1; M.A. 1644. Of Pike House, gent., in 1668. Died before Sept. 1688. (*Peile*, I. 447.)

HALLYWELL, CHARLES. Adm. sizar (age 17) at CHRIST'S, May 25, 1689. S. of Henry (1657), clerk, R. of Ifield, Sussex. B. there. Educated at home. Matric. 1689; Scholar, 1690; B.A. 1692-3. Ord. deacon (Chichester) Sept. 1694. V. of Seaford with Sutton, Sussex, 1697. Author. Buried at Seaford, 1707. (*Peile*, II. 113.)

HALLIWELL, EDWARD. Adm. at KING'S (age 18) a scholar from Eton, May 17, 1532. Of Farthingstone, Northants. B.A. 1535-6; M.A. 1539. Fellow, 1535-48. Author of *Dido*, acted before the Queen at King's College, 1564. (*Cooper*, I. 240.)

HALLIWELL or HOLYWELL, GILES. Matric. sizar from QUEENS', Easter, 1633. Of Lincolnshire.

HALLIWELL, HENRY. Matric. pens. from TRINITY, Michs. 1616; B.A. 1620-1; M.A. 1624. Ord. deacon (Chichester) May 20, 1625; priest by the same. R. of Crawley, Sussex, 1626. V. of Ifield, till 1666. Died Feb. 1665-6. Buried at Ifield. M.I. Father of the next. (W. C. Renshaw, *N. and Q.*, 6 S., III. 324.)

HALLIWELL, HENRY. Adm. pens. (age 17) at CHRIST'S, May 11, 1657. S. of Henry (above). B. at Twineham, Sussex. School, Horsham (Mr Nesbitt). B.A. 1660-1; M.A. 1664. Fellow, 1662-7. V. of Ifield, 1667. R. of Slaugham, 1679-92. Chaplain extraordinary to the King. R. of Plumpton, Sussex, 1681. Preb. of Chichester, 1690-1703. V. of Cowfold, 1692-1703. Author, theological. Buried Mar. 9, 1702-3. Father of Charles (1689). (*Peile*, I. 577.)

HALLIWELL, JOHN. Adm. pens. at JESUS, Feb. 15, 1689-90. Of Lancashire. Matric. 1690; Scholar, 1691.

HALLIWELL, NATHANIEL. Adm. sizar at EMMANUEL, June 26, 1669. Of Yorkshire.

HALLIWELL, NICHOLAS. B.A. 1484.

HALYWELL, RICHARD. Matric. sizar from TRINITY, Easter, 1631; Scholar, 1634; B.A. 1634-5; M.A. 1638.

HALLIWELL, THEOPHILUS. Matric. sizar from TRINITY, Easter, 1622; Scholar, 1627; B.A. 1627–8; M.A. 1631. Ord. deacon (Peterb.) June 5; priest, Sept. 25, 1631.

HALLOWELL or HOLWELL, WILLIAM. Matric. sizar from PEMBROKE, Easter, 1608; B.A. 1611–2. Ord. deacon (Peterb.) June 7, 1612.

HALLYWELL, WILLIAM. Adm. sizar at QUEENS', Jan. 8, 1727–8. Of London. Matric. 1728; B.A. 1731–2.

HALLMORYNGE, HENRY. Matric. sizar from TRINITY HALL, Easter, 1557.

HALLOW, ——. B.Can.L. 1483–4.

HALOGH, ——. B.A. 1477–8.

HALLOWS, BRABAZON. Adm. pens. (age 20) at ST JOHN'S, Mar. 18, 1736–7. S. of Thomas, Esq., of Dethick and Glapwell, Derbs. B. at Nottingham. School, Chesterfield (Mr Burrow). Matric. 1737. High Sheriff of Derbs., 1769–70. His mother was Catharine Brabazou, dau. of the Earl of Meath. Married Anne, dau. of John Jackson, of Clapham, Surrey, nephew and heir of Pepys. Brother of the next, and of John (1747–8). (*Scott-Mayor*, III. 482; *F.M.G.*, 469; Burke, *L.G.*)

HALLOWS, CHAWORTH. Adm. pens. (age 20) at ST JOHN'S, June 16, 1738. S. of Thomas, Esq., of Dethick and Glapwell, Derbs. B. at Dublin. School, Chesterfield (Mr Burrows). Matric. 1738; B.A. 1741–2; M.A. 1756. R. of Pleasley, Derbs., 1757–93. Brother of the above, and of John (1747–8). (*F.M.G.*, 469.)

HALLOWS, DANIEL. Adm. Fell.-Com. at ST CATHARINE'S, Dec. 29, 1687. S. of Nathaniel, of Dethick. Matric. 1688; B.A. 1691–2; M.A. 1695. Ord. deacon (Lincoln) Sept. 25, 1692; priest, June 7, 1696. R. of All Saints', Hertford, 1701–41. R. of Gilston, Herts., 1729–41. Died Oct. 6, 1741, aged 71. Father of Nathaniel (1729).

HALLOWES, EPHRAIM. Adm. pens. at EMMANUEL, Apr. 12, 1644. Of Derbyshire.

HALLOWS, JOHN. Adm. pens. (age 18) at ST JOHN'S, Mar. 3, 1747–8. S. of Thomas, Esq., of Glapwell Hall, Derbs. B. at Glapwell. School, Chesterfield. Matric. 1748. Adm. at the Inner Temple, Aug. 16, 1748. Captain in the army. Brother of Brabazon (1736–7) and Chaworth (1738). (*Scott-Mayor*, III. 574; *F.M.G.*, 470.)

HALLOWS, NATHANIEL. Adm. pens. at ST CATHARINE'S, Sept. 26, 1729. Of Hertfordshire. S. of Daniel (1687), of Herts., clerk. B. Mar. 1, 1710–1. School, Winchester. Matric. 1729–30. Migrated to Oxford. Matric. from New College, Aug. 6, 1730, age 19; B.C.L. (Oxford) 1737. (*Al. Oxon.*)

HALLOWES, SAMUEL. Adm. sizar at EMMANUEL, Michs. 1588. Matric. 1588. Will (Gloucester) 1639, of one of these names; of Dursley, Gloucs. (J. Ch. Smith.)

HALLOWS, SAMUEL. Adm. pens. (age 18) at CHRIST'S, Feb. 16, 1652–3. S. of Nathaniel, of Dethick, Derbs. (M.P. for Derby). B. at Derby. School, Westminster. Matric. 1655. Of Norton, Derbs., Esq.; and afterwards of Nottingham. Sheriff of Derbs., 1673–4. Buried at St Mary's, Nottingham. (*Peile*, I. 550; *F.M.G.*, 468; Burke, *L.G.*)

HALLS or HALL, ANTHONY. Matric. Fell.-Com. from PEMBROKE, Easter, 1548; B.A. 1548–9. Fellow, 1549. Will proved (V.C.C.) 1551.

HALLS, CHARLES. Adm. Fell.-Com. at EMMANUEL, Apr. 24, 1707. Of Lincolnshire.

HALLES, EDWARD. Matric. pens. from ST CATHARINE'S, Easter, 1639. 5th s. of Miles (1579), deceased, late R. of Sawtrey, Hunts. B. there. School, Peterborough (Mr Wilbore). Migrated to St John's Jan. 25, 1639–40, age 18. Doubtless ord. deacon (Lincoln) Apr. 26, 1645, as 'B.A.' Usher of Uppingham School, *c.* 1644. R. of Holcott, Northants., 1654: conformed and instituted, 1663. Married Anne, dau. of T. Dalton, D.D. Died Jan. 13, 1715–6. Buried at Holcott. M.I. (*Bridges*, II. 146; H. I. Longden.)

HALLS, HENRY. Matric. pens. from QUEENS', Easter, 1607. Of Huntingdonshire. B.A. 1610–1; M.A. 1614; B.D. 1623. Fellow, 1613–29. Incorp. at Oxford, 1624. Ord. deacon (Peterb.) Mar. 9; priest, Mar. 10, 1622–3.

HALLS or HALLYS, JOHN. Matric. sizar from PEMBROKE, Easter, 1545.

HALLS or HALL, JOHN. Matric. p . from QUEENS', Easter, 1615. Of Huntingdonshire. B.A. 1619–20; M.A. 1623.

HALLS, JOHN. Adm. pens. (age 17) at ST JOHN'S, Nov. 30, 1725. S. of Robert, attorney, of Essex. B. at Colchester. School, Bury, Suffolk. Matric. 1727; LL.B. 1731. R. of East Thorpe, Essex, 1735–95. Will (P.C.C.) 1795.

HALLS, MILES. Matric. sizar from PEMBROKE, Easter, 1579; B.A. 1583–4; M.A. 1587. Ord. deacon and priest (Lincoln) Oct. 25, 1587. R. of Sawtrey All Saints', Hunts., 1587–1630. Buried there Feb. 3, 1629–30. Will, P.C.C., 1630. Father of Edward (1639), Miles and William (1629).

HALLS, MILES. Matric. pens. from QUEENS', Easter, 1622. Of Huntingdonshire. 1st s. of Miles (above). Brother of Edward (1639) and William (1629). (J. Ch. Smith.)

HALLS, MILES. Adm. pens. at QUEENS', May 16, 1670. Of Lincolnshire. Matric. 1670; B.A. 1673–4. Fellow, 1675, till his death, Sept. 1676.

HALLS, PURBECK. Adm. pens. at EMMANUEL, July, 1664. Of Rutland. B.A. 1667–8; M.A. 1671. Ord. deacon (Peterb.) Sept. 19, 1669; priest, May 12, 1670. R. of Marholm, Northants., 1670–5. R. of Collyweston, 1675–1711. Died 1711. (H. I. Longden.)

HALLS or HALL, THOMAS. Matric. sizar from CLARE, Easter, 1620; B.A. 1623–4; M.A. 1627. Ord. deacon (Peterb.) Sept. 19; priest, Sept. 20, 1624.

HALLS, THOMAS. Adm. pens. at ST CATHARINE'S, 1638. Of Northamptonshire.

HALS, THOMAS. Adm. Fell.-Com. (age 16) at TRINITY, Aug. 22, 1716. S. of Thomas, of Clarendon, Jamaica. School, Kensington, London. Matric. 1719.

HALLS or HALL, WILLIAM. Matric. pens. from PEMBROKE, Easter, 1568; B.A. 1571–2; M.A. 1575; B.D. 1582. Fellow, 1574. Ord. deacon (Norwich) Dec. 16, 1577; priest, Sept. 13, 1579. University preacher, 1580. R. of Little Stukeley, Hunts., 1581–1618. R. of Wistow, 1587–1618. Died 1618. Buried at Little Stukeley, Aug. 12.

HALLS or HALL, WILLIAM. Adm. sizar at QUEENS', May 12, 1614. Of Essex. B.A. from Clare, 1617–8; M.A. 1621. Ord. deacon (Peterb.) Aug. 22; priest, Aug. 24, 1618. Perhaps V. of Ellington, Hunts., 1629–36.

HALLS, WILLIAM. Adm. pens. at QUEENS', Apr. 11, 1629. Of Huntingdonshire. Doubtless 3rd s. of Miles (1579). B.A. 1632–3; M.A. 1636. Ord. deacon (Peterb.) Dec. 18, 1636; priest, Mar. 10, 1638–9, as Hall. One of these names R. of Glaston, Rutland, 1639; preb. of Peterborough, 1642. (But *see* a contemporary in *Al. Oxon.*)

HALLES, WILLIAM. Adm. sizar (age 15) at CHRIST'S, July 4, 1682. S. of John. B. at Glaston, Rutland. School, Peterborough (Mr Smith). Matric. 1684; Scholar; B.A. 1685–6; M.A. 1689. Ord. priest (Lincoln) Sept. 1689; C. of Taplow, Bucks. (*Peile*, II. 89.)

HALLES, WILLIAM. Adm. pens. at EMMANUEL, Aug. 2, 1699. Of Northamptonshire. Matric. 1700; B.A. 1703–4.

HALMAN, EDMUND. Matric. pens. from QUEENS', Lent, 1578–9. Of Norfolk. Probably of Swaffham, Norfolk; adm. at Gray's Inn, July 1, 1584.

HALMAN, EDMUND. Matric. sizar (age 18) from PEMBROKE, Easter, 1625. S. of Thomas, of (?) Lakenheath, Suffolk. B.A. 1628–9.

HALMAN, JAMES. Adm. sizar (age 16) at CAIUS, June 27, 1655. S. of Nicholas (1616), clerk, of Thursford, Norfolk. B. there. School, Holt (Mr Wright). Matric. 1655; Scholar, 1655–62; B.A. 1658–9; M.A. 1662. Fellow, 1662–1700. Taxor, 1675. Master of Caius, Aug. 24, 1700. University Registrary, 1683–1701. Buried in the College Chapel, Dec. 23, 1702. Will (V.C.C.) 1703. Benefactor to the College. (*Venn*, I. 391.)

HALMAN, JAMES. Adm. sizar (age 16) at CAIUS, Apr. 6, 1697. S. of Thomas, gent., of Wiveton, Norfolk. B. at Walsingham. School, Holt (Mr Bainbrigge and Mr Reynolds). Matric. 1697; Scholar, 1697–1704; B.A. 1700–1. Ord. deacon (Norwich) Sept. 23, 1705; priest, July 2, 1710. V. of Croxton, Norfolk, 1711–38. R. of Illington, 1712–56. (*Venn*, I. 500.)

HALMAN, JOHN (1507–8), *see* **ALMAN.**

HALLMAN or HALMAN, NICHOLAS. Adm. scholar at CAIUS, July 9, 1616. S. of Thomas, husbandman, of Gt Walsingham, Norfolk. Schools, Walsingham (Mr Bucke) and Norwich. B.A. 1619–20; M.A. 1623. Incorp. at Oxford, 1627. Ord. deacon (Peterb.) June 11, 1620; priest (Norwich) Dec. 17, 1620. V. of Thompson, Norfolk, 1622–33. R. of Thursford, 1626–61. V. of Barney, 1633–61. Registrar there, 1653. Died 1661. Father of James (1655). (*Venn*, I. 234.)

HALMAN, ——. B.A. 1473.

HALME or HOLME, JOHN. M.A. from SIDNEY, 1673. S. of William, of Brodsworth, Yorks. Matric. from Lincoln College, Oxford, May 13, 1664, age 21; B.A. (Oxford) 1667–8. Ord. deacon (York) June 6, 1680. (*Al. Oxon.*)

HALME, JOHN. Adm. sizar (age 16) at ST JOHN'S, Apr. 27, 1693. Probably John Holmes, s. of John. B. at Hatfield, near Doncaster, Yorks. School, Hatfield (Mr Eratt). Matric. 1693; B.A. 1696–7. R. of Sandal parva, 1719–48. Died 1748, aged 72. Buried at Hatfield. (M. H. Peacock.)

HALOCK, WILLIAM. Matric. sizar from Jesus, Easter, 1551. School, Saffron Walden. B.A. 1559-60. Perhaps ord. deacon (Ely) July 17, 1560; 'Haylock, of Christ's'; age 23. V. of Walden St Paul's, Herts., 1560. Admon. (Cons. C. London) 1595.

HALRYSTON, ——. M.A. 1481.

HALSALL, MICHAEL. Adm. at King's (age 18) a scholar from Eton, Aug. 24, 1560. Of Prescot, Lancs. Matric. 1560; B.A. 1564-5. Fellow, during 1563-4. Afterwards Master of the school at Cranbrook, Kent.

HALSALL, THOMAS, *see* **HASSELL.**

HALLSALL, WILLIAM. Adm. sizar at Jesus, Mar. 26, 1722. Of Everton, Lancs. Scholar, 1725; B.A. 1725-6; M.A. 1729. Fellow, 1730-2. Taxor, 1731. Ord. deacon (Lincoln) Nov. 1; priest, Nov. 7, 1731. V. of Helston with Wendron, Cornwall, 1732. Married Mary Huske, of St Sepulchre's parish, Cambridge, Feb. 19, 1732. Died at Helston, 1747.

HALSE, JOHN. Matric. pens. from Clare, *c.* 1596; B.A. 1599-1600; M.A. 1603. Incorp. at Oxford, 1603. Author, Latin verses. (*Cooper*, II. 434.)

HALSETUR, DANIEL. Adm. sizar at Trinity, July 2, 1652. Of Worcestershire. Probably brother of John (1652).

HALLSETER, JOHN. Matric. sizar from Clare, Michs. 1623; B.A. 1627-8; M.A. 1631. R. of Thorley, Herts., 1643. One of these names R. of Little Laver, Essex, 1670. Admon. (Cons. C. London) 1690; to s. John.

HALSETUR, JOHN. Adm. sizar at Trinity, July 2, 1652. Of Worcestershire. Perhaps s. of the above. Scholar, 1655; B.A. 1655-6; M.A. 1659. Probably brother of Daniel (1652).

HALSEY, EDWARD. Matric. sizar from Clare, Easter, 1620; B.A. 1623-4.

HALSEY, JAMES. Adm. pens. at Sidney, May 27, 1606. S. of Robert, of Gt Gaddesden, Herts. Matric. 1606; B.A. 1609-10; M.A. from Clare, 1613; D.D. 1631 (*Lit. Reg.*). Fellow of Clare. Incorp. at Oxford, 1617. R. of Buttermere, Wilts., 1629. Preb. of Winchester, 1631-41. Chaplain to the Lord Treasurer. R. of Watton-at-Stone, Herts., 1636-41. Of Little Burstead, Essex, 1637-8. R. of St Alphage, London, 1638-41. Died 1641. Buried at St Alphage, Mar. 12, 1640-1. Will (P.C.C.) 1641. (Pedigree in Cussan's *Herts.*, III.; the name is printed 'John' in *Hennessy*.)

HALSEY, JOSEPH. Adm. sizar at Trinity, Apr. 23, 1645. Of Leicestershire. Matric. 1645; Scholar, 1647; B.A. 1648-9; M.A. 1652. Fellow, 1649. R. of Penkevil, Cornwall; ejected, 1662. For many years chaplain to Mr Hugh Boscawen. Died Oct. 1, 1711, aged 85. (*Calamy*, I. 285.)

HALSEY, THOMAS. Adm. pens. (age 18) at Peterhouse, Mar. 27, 1740. Of Sussex. School, Amberley. Matric. 1740; Scholar, 1740; B.A. 1743-4. Ord. deacon (Norwich, *Litt. dim.* from Canterbury) Feb. 1745-6.

HALSTEAD, DOMVILLE. Adm. pens. at Trinity Hall, Feb. 23, 1741-2. Matric. 1743-4; LL.B. 1749. Of Lymm, Cheshire, Esq. Adm. at Lincoln's Inn, Mar. 15, 1738-9. Ord. deacon (Norwich) June, 1747. Of Dane Bank, Lymm, Cheshire. His son, Domville, assumed the name Poole.

HALSTEAD, EDMUND. Matric. pens. from Trinity, Michs. 1578.

HALSTEAD, GERARD. Adm. pens. (age 17) at Trinity, Aug. 16, 1715. S. of John, of Jamaica, West Indies. School, Chelsea, London (Mr Hall).

HALSTEAD or HALESTEAD, HENRY. Matric. sizar from Trinity, June, 1575; B.A. 1578-9; M.A. from Christ's, 1582. Ord. priest (London) Dec. 1588; C. of Notley, Essex. V. of St Paul's, Walden, Herts., *c.* 1597, till 1634. Died 1634. Will (Archd. St Albans) 1634. (*Peile*, I. 135.)

HALSTEAD, JOHN. Matric. sizar from St John's, Michs. 1606; B.A. 1610-1; M.A. 1614.

HALSTEAD, JOHN. Adm. pens. (age 16) at Jesus, June 10, 1670. Of Lancashire. School, Manchester. Matric. 1670; M.B. 1675. Practised at Wigan. Will proved (Chester) 1688. (A. A. Mumford.)

HALSTED, LAURENCE. Adm. pens. (age 18) at St John's, Nov. 8, 1656. S. of John, yeoman, of Burnley, Lancs. B. there. Bapt. at Burnley, May 24, 1638. School, Burnley (Mr Aspden). Keeper of the Records in the Tower of London. Married Abee, dau. of John Barcroft, Esq. Will dated, May 1, 1690. (J. Parker; *N. and Q.*, 3 S., IV. 187, 295.)

HALSTED, RICHARD. Matric. sizar from St John's, Michs. 1615; B.A. 1618-9; M.A. 1622. Ord. deacon (Peterb.) Sept. 20, 1618; priest, Feb. 21, 1618-9. Master of Blackburn Grammar School, 1625.

HALSTEAD, RICHARD. Adm. sizar at Jesus, Sept. 27, 1700. Of Yorkshire. S. of Henry. Bapt. at Horbury, Yorks., Apr. 2, 1685. Matric. 1701; B.A. 1704-5. Ord. deacon (York) Oct. 1707; priest, 1710. C. of Horbury, Yorks. V. of Hooton Paguel, 1710-23. Married, at Normanton, Oct. 28, 1710, Elizabeth Wadsworth, of Horbury, Yorks., spinster. Died Apr. 18, 1723, aged 38. Buried at Hooton Pagnel. (A. Gray; J. Parker.)

HALSTED, ROBERT. Adm. sizar (age 17) at Jesus, Apr. 25, 1670. Of Lancashire. Matric. 1670; B.A. 1674-5.

HALSTED, WILLIAM. Matric. pens. from St John's, Michs. 1572; B.A. 1576-7; M.A. 1580. V. of Bracebridge, Lincs., 1614-23.

HALSTEAD, WILLIAM. Adm. pens. (age 17) at Christ's, June 20, 1709. S. of Thomas. B. at Cambridge. School, Eton. Matric. 1710; Scholar, 1710-1; B.A. 1713-4; M.A. 1719. Ord. deacon (London) Dec. 1715. Master of the Free School, Buckingham, 1723-4. Perhaps R. of Farnborough, Hants., 1724. R. of Padbury, Bucks., 1729-63; also R. of Thornborough. Buried at Thornborough, Dec. 29, 1763. Admon. (P.C.C.) 1764. (*Peile*, II. 173; but *see Al. Oxon.* for another of these names.)

HALSTED, ——. A monk. Incorp. from Oxford, 1479-80.

HALSTON, JOHN. B.A. 1458-9.

HALTOFT, T. B.A. 1462.

HALTON, FRANCIS. Adm. pens. at Sidney, Jan. 17, 1617-8. Matric. 1618; B.A. 1621-2; M.A. 1625. One of these names, s. of Sir Roger, of Gt Carlton, Lincs., bapt. at Grimsby, Apr. 11, 1598. Adm. at the Inner Temple, 1624. Called to the Bar Feb. 10, 1633-4. (*Lincs. Pedigrees*, 446.)

HALTON, ROGER. Matric. pens. from St John's, Lent, 1582-3. S. and h. of Robert, serjeant-at-law, deceased. Age 16 in 1582. Adm. at the Inner Temple, 1583. Knighted, July 23, 1603. Of Gt Carlton, Lincs., Knt. Buried at St Leonard's, Shoreditch, Dec. 26, 1616. Father of the next and of William (1609). (*Lincs. Pedigrees*, 446.)

HALTON, ROGER. Adm. pens. at Jesus, Jan. 20, 1620-1. Of Lincolnshire. 2nd s. of Sir Roger (above). Matric. 1621; Scholar, 1622; B.A. 1624-5; M.A. 1628. C. of Theydon Boys, Essex, 1637-40. C. of Castle Camps, Cambs., 1642-3. R. of , Essex, *c.* 1643-4. Died 1664. Brother of William (1609). Rayne

HALTON, THOMAS. Adm. pens. (age 18) at Christ's, Jan. 26, 1628-9. S. of Robert. Bapt. at Wickenby, Lincs., Mar. 23, 1609-10. School, Stortford (Mr Leigh). Matric. 1629. One of these names, of Sawbridgeworth, adm. at the Inner Temple, June 15, 1631. (*Peile*, I. 397; *Lincs. Pedigrees*, 446.)

HALTON, THOMAS, *see* **HORTON** (1664).

HALTON, WILLIAM. Matric. pens. from St John's, Michs. 1584. S. of Robert, serjeant-at-law, deceased, of the Middle Temple. Knighted, June 16, 1618. Died Nov. 20, 1639, aged 70. Buried at Abington, Cambs. Brother of Roger (1582-3). (*Lincs. Pedigrees*, 446.)

HALTON, WILLIAM. Matric. Fell.-Com. from St John's, Easter, 1609. S. and h. of Sir Roger (1582-3), of Castle Carlton, Lincs., Knt. Adm. at the Inner Temple, 1610. Married Hannah, dau. of Sir William Wray, Bart. Died Sept. 16, 1624. Buried at Clerkenwell. Will, P.C.C. Brother of Roger (1620-1). (*Vis. of Lincs.*, 1592.)

HALYOR, EDWARD. M.A. 1480-1.

HAM, JOHN. Adm. pens. (age 19) at Sidney, June 29, 1674. S. of John, gent. B. at Uplowman, Devon. School, Tiverton. Matric. 1674; B.A. 1677-8; M.A. 1681. Brother of the next.

HAM, ROBERT. Adm. pens. (age 18) at Sidney, May 18, 1669. 2nd s. of John, gent. B. at Uplowman, Devon. School, Tiverton. Matric. 1669; B.A. 1672-3; M.A. 1676. Incorp. at Oxford, 1676. R. of Sandford, Devon. Died there Jan. 30, 1731. Will (Exeter) 1731, of Robert Ham, clerk, of Crediton. Father of the next.

HAM, WILLIAM. Adm. pens. (age 17) at Sidney, June 18, 1702. S. of Robert (above), R. of Sandford, Devon. School, Tiverton.

HAMBALL, THOMAS, *see* **HANNIBALL.**

HAMBLETON, HENRY. Matric. pens. from Peterhouse, Easter, 1544; B.A. 1544-5. Perhaps R. of Stansfield, Suffolk, till 1554.

HAMBLETON, ——. M.A. from Sidney, 1623 (in *ordo*).

HAMBLY, WILLIAM. Adm. Fell.-Com. at Pembroke, Feb. 18, 1723-4. S. of William, of St Neot's, Cornwall, gent. Matric. 1723-4; LL.B. 1724. Matric. at Oriel College, Oxford, Oct. 10, 1717, age 18.

HAMBY, ALLEN. B.A. from Christ's, 1593-4; M.A. 1597. S. of John, of Maltby, Lincs., auditor of the Treasury. B. in London, *c.* 1572. R. of Navenby, Lincs., 1599-1607. Died Sept. 1607. Brother of the next. (*Vis. of Lincs.*, 1592; *Peile*, I. 202.)

HAMBYE, RICHARD. Matric. pens. from CHRIST'S, Dec. 1582. 3rd s. of John, of Maltby, Lincs. B.A. 1586-7; M.A. 1590. Incorp. at Oxford, 1593. R. of Raithby, Lincs., 1592. V. of Tathwell, 1613. V. of Hougham, 1613. Admon. (Lincoln) 1616. Brother of the above. (*Lincs. Pedigrees*, 448; *Peile*, I. 171.)

HAMBY or HANSBY, WILLIAM. Scholar of ST JOHN'S, 1561. Of Lincolnshire. Perhaps s. of Edward, of Brocklesby, Lincs. B.A. 1564-5; M.A. 1568. Fellow, 1567. R. of Brocklesby, Lincs. (*Lincs. Pedigrees*.)

HAMCOTTS, ALEXANDER. Matric. pens. from TRINITY, Michs. 1554.

HAMPCOTES, ALEXANDER. Matric. Fell.-Com. from JESUS, c. 1592.

HAMCOOTES, PAUL (1547), see AMCOTTS.

HAMECOTES, RICHARD DE. LL.B. Scholar at KING'S HALL, 1350. Of Lincoln diocese. Promoted to a benefice, 1363. Canon of Westbury-on-Trym, Worcester. R. of Marsham, Norfolk. (*Cal. of Papal Petitions*, I. 404.)

HAMCOTS, RICHARD. Matric. Fell.-Com. from TRINITY, Michs. 1584.

HAMELYN, THOMAS. Adm. at CORPUS CHRISTI, 1441. V. of Grantchester, Cambs., 1441.

HAMMERSHAM, THOMAS. Adm. pens. at KING'S, a scholar from Eton, 1496.

HAMES, WILLIAM. Adm. at MAGDALENE, June 23, 1666.

HAMMERSLY, CHAMBERLAIN. Adm. sizar at CLARE, Apr. 1658. S. of William, of Wedgwood, Staffs. Migrated to Jesus, Apr. 27, 1658. Afterwards at Oxford. Matric. from St Alban's Hall, Mar. 22, 1658-9; B.A. from Oxford; M.A. from Clare, Cambridge, 1681. V. of Burton Dassett, Warws., 1662-89. V. of Avon Dassett, 1681. Non-juror. Buried at Newbottle, Northants., June 6, 1715. He left the bulk of his property to be distributed amongst 'the deprived clergy of our Communion.' (*Al. Oxon.*; *Vis. of Warws.*, 1682; H. I. Longden.)

HAMERSLEY, HUGH. Matric. sizar from KING'S, Easter, 1655; B.A. 1659. Adm. at the Inner Temple, May 5, 1662; of London, gent. Probably father of the next.

HAMMERSLEY, HUGH. Adm. pens. (age 16) at PETERHOUSE, May 31, 1680. Of London. School, Hertford. Scholar, 1680; Matric. 1681; B.A. 1683-4; M.A. 1687. Adm. at the Inner Temple, Apr. 29, 1703; s. and h. of Hugh (? above), late of London, citizen and goldsmith. Barrister-at-law. (*T. A. Walker*, 166.)

HAMERSLEY, STEVEN. Adm. sizar at ST CATHARINE'S, June 16, 1665.

HAMERSLEY, THOMAS. Adm. pens. at PETERHOUSE, Jan. 10, 1628-9. S. of Sir Hugh, alderman, of London. Adm. at Gray's Inn, Aug. 3, 1629. Knighted at Whitehall, Aug. 8, 1641. (*T. A. Walker*, 38.)

HAMERSLEY, THOMAS. Adm. pens. at PEMBROKE, June, 1661.

HAMERTON, GEORGE. Matric. sizar from CHRIST'S, Apr. 1620. Ord. deacon (Peterb.) Aug. 24, 1622. R. of Orton Longueville, Hunts., 1652. 'A constant preaching minister.' Buried there c. 1661. (*Peile*, I. 332.)

HAMERTON, JAMES. Matric. pens. from CHRIST'S, Michs. 1564. B. c. 1546. Ord. priest (Lincoln) May 8, 1569. V. of Wainfleet St Mary, Lincs., 1574-82. V. of Edlington, 1578; 'knows but little Latin.' Admon. (Lincoln) 1588. One of these names s. of Thomas, of Horncastle. (*Lincs. Pedigrees*, 1247.)

HAMEY, WILLIAM. Adm. pens. at EMMANUEL, May 28, 1656. Of Huntingdonshire. Matric. 1656.

HAMILTON, ARCHIBALD. Adm. pens. (age 17) at CAIUS, Mar. 10, 1718-9. S. of Richard, of County Antrim, Ireland. B. in Scotland. School, Westminster. Matric. 1718-9. Adm. at the Middle Temple, 1718. Barrister, 1732. (*Venn*, II. 11.)

HAMILTON, FREDERIC. Adm. pens. at CLARE, May 29, 1746. S. of Lord Archibald. B. in London. School, Westminster. Matric. 1746. Afterwards Fell.-Com. M.A. 1749. Ord. deacon (London) May 24, 1752; priest (Peterb.) Jan. 14, 1753. V. of Wellingborough, Northants., 1753-6. R. of Stanton, Suffolk, 1790-1811. Died 1811.

HAMILTON, GEORGE. M.A. 1624 (Incorp. from St Andrews).

HAMYLDEN, JOHN. Matric. sizar from QUEENS', Michs. 1571; B.A. 1574-5.

HAMILDEN, THOMAS. Adm. Fell.-Com. at QUEENS', June 18, 1608. Of Surrey.

HAMILTON, WILLIAM. (*Dominus*.) M.A. 1635-6 (*Lit. Reg.*).

HAMILTON, WILLIAM. Matric. pens. from KING'S, Easter, 1676.

HAMLE, ——. Perhaps B.Can.L. 1496.

HAMLET, ——. *Cautio* for degree, 1516-7.

HAMLIN, ROBERT. B.A. 1474-5; M.A. 1477.

HAMLIN, THOMAS. Adm. sizar at CLARE, July 11, 1741. B. at Lindfield, Sussex. Matric. 1742; B.A. 1745-6.

HAMMAN, EDWARD. Matric. pens. from ST JOHN'S, Michs. 1570.

HAMON, THOMAS. Matric. pens. from ST JOHN'S, Michs. 1572.

HAMAN, WILLIAM. Matric. pens. from CHRIST'S, Nov. 1551. Perhaps B.A. 1555. Fellow, 1555-6. (*Peile*, I. 48.)

HAMMATT, JOHN. M.A. from CHRIST'S, 1681. S. of John, of Taunton, Somerset. Matric. from St Edmund Hall, Oxford, June 25, 1674, age 16; B.A. (Oxford) 1678. V. of Stantonbury, Bucks., 1679. R. of Emmington, Oxon., 1684. R. of Clyst St George, Devon, 1695. (*Al. Oxon.*; *Peile*, II. 57.)

HAMMENT or HEMANT, HENRY. Adm. sizar (age 20) at ST JOHN'S, Feb. 9, 1708-9. S. of Thomas, husbandman. B. at Whittlesey, Cambs. School, Wisbech (Mr Carter). Matric. 1711; B.A. 1712-3; Hemant.

HAMMOND, ALEXANDER. Matric. pens. from CHRIST'S, Nov. 1566. One of these names, s. of Edward, of New Chipping, Herts., was adm. at the Inner Temple, Nov. 10, 1567. Another adm. at Gray's Inn, 1568. (*Peile*, I. 97.)

HAMMOND, ANTHONY. M.A. 1629 (Incorp. from Montauban).

HAMMOND, ANTHONY. Adm. Fell.-Com. (age 16) at ST JOHN'S, Apr. 2, 1685. S. of Anthony, gent. B. at Somersham, Hunts. School, St Paul's. Matric. 1685; M.A. 1698 (*Lit. Reg.*: nominated for mandate, Oct. 17, 1689). Adm. at Gray's Inn, Dec. 4, 1684. M.P. for Hunts., 1695-8; for the University, 1698-1701; for Huntingdon, 1702-5; for Shoreham, 1708. F.R.S., 1700. Commissioner for the Navy, 1702. Treasurer of the forces in Spain, 1711. Poet and pamphleteer. Died, Mar. 30, 1739, in the Fleet Prison. (*D.N.B.*)

HAMMOND, ANTHONY. Adm. pens. (age 18) at CAIUS, Oct. 7, 1703. S. of Richard, gent., of South Wootton, Norfolk. B. there. Schools, Lynn (Mr Horne) and West Bradenham (Mr Needham). Matric. 1703; Scholar, 1703-7. Lord of the Manor of Congham. Married Susan, sister of Sir Robert Walpole, Earl of Orford. Died Feb. 7, 1743. M.I. at South Wootton. (*Venn*, I. 511.)

HAMOND, ANTHONY. Adm. at CORPUS CHRISTI, 1711. Of Kent. Probably s. of William, of St Alban's Court, Kent. Matric. 1711. Married Catherine Kingsford. Died 1722. Father of William (1737). (Burke, *L.G.*)

HAMOND, CHARLES. Matric. Fell.-Com. from QUEENS', Michs. 1580. Of Yorkshire. Perhaps s. of Bryan, of Scarthingwell, Yorks. Died unmarried, 1588.

HAMMOND, CHARLES. Adm. pens. at JESUS, June 15, 1660. Of Cambridgeshire. Matric. 1660; Scholar, 1662; B.A. 1663; M.A. 1667. Ord. deacon (Ely) Mar. 1663-4; priest (York) 1667. V. of Ledsham, Yorks., 1668-1719. Buried Aug. 13, 1719.

HAMOND, CHARLES. Adm. sizar at JESUS, June 29, 1693. Of Yorkshire. Matric. 1694; B.A. 1696-7. V. of Chatton, Northumberland, 1700-11. P.C. of Doddington Chapel. Buried at Doddington, May 4, 1711. (Contemporary in *Al. Oxon.*)

HAMMOND, EDMUND. Adm. pens. (age 16) at CHRIST'S, Mar. 24, 1658-9. S. of Anthony. B. at Wootton, Norfolk. School, Lynn (Mr Bell). Matric. 1659; B.A. 1662-3; M.A. 1673. Extra-licentiate, R.C.P., June 21, 1697. Died Jan. 30, 1703. M.I. at South Wootton. Will (P.C.C.) 1704. (*Peile*, I. 584.)

HAMMOND, EDWARD. Adm. pens. (age 18) at CAIUS, Oct. 3, 1567. S. of William, of Edgefield, Norfolk. School, Holt. One of these names ord. priest (Norwich) Oct. 21, 1569. R. of Cawston, Norfolk, 1574-1621. Died June 10, 1621. M.I. at Cawston. Will (Norwich) 1621. (*Venn*, I. 60.)

HAMMONT, EDWARD. Adm. pens. (age 17) at CAIUS, Apr. 28, 1596. S. of Edward (? above), R. of Cawston, Norfolk. School, Aylsham. Scholar, 1597-1601; B.A. 1599-1600; M.A. 1603. Ord. deacon (Norwich) Sept. 26, 1603; C. of Skeyton, Norfolk. V. of Aldborough, 1615. Brother of Gilbert (1601).

HAMMOND, EDWARD. Adm. pens. at JESUS, June 2, 1627. Of London. Matric. 1629; Scholar, 1629; B.A. 1630-1; M.A. 1634.

HAMMOND, EDWARD. Adm. pens. at JESUS, Jan. 15, 1648-9. Of Cambridgeshire. Matric. 1648-9; B.A. 1652-3.

HAMMOND, EDWARD. M.A. 1731 (Incorp. from Oxford). S. of E., of London, gent. Matric. from Christ Church, July 19, 1707, age 17; B.A. (Oxford) 1711; M.A. 1713-4. Ord. deacon (Bristol) June 11, 1715. V. of Chippenham, Wilts., 1731. Archdeacon of Dorset, 1733-62. R. of Watton, Herts., 1734-62. Died Apr. 26, 1762, aged 72. M.I. at Watton. (*Al. Oxon.*; F. S. Hockaday.)

HAMMOND, GEORGE. Adm. pens. (age 19) at CAIUS, Feb. 19, 1573-4. S. of George. B. at Westmill, Herts. School, Ely. Matric. 1574; B.A. 1577-8; M.A. 1581. Ord. deacon (London) Mar. 30, 1580; priest (Ely) Apr. 7, 1580. V. of Eltisley, Cambs., 1580. R. of Papworth Everard, 1580. Brother of Maurice (1577-8) and Robert (1575). (*Venn*, I. 77.)

HAMMOND, GEORGE. Matric. sizar from KING'S, Easter, 1577-8. 'B. at Taplow, Bucks.; of Magdalene College, aged 23'; when ord. deacon (London) Dec. 15, 1578. R. of Althorpe, Lincs., 1599-1618.

HAMMOND, GEORGE. Matric. pens. from ST JOHN'S, Michs. 1616; B.A. 1620-1.

HAMMONDE, GERVASE. Matric. pens. from TRINITY, Easter, 1611. One of these names, of Scarthingwell, Saxton, Yorks., Esq., s. of Brian. Died Oct. 4, 1646, aged 52. Buried in Saxton Church. M.I. Admon. (York) 1647. Probably brother of William (1611). (F.*M.G.*, 878; W. Wheater, *Hist. of Sherburn and Cawood*.)

HAMMONDE, GILBERT. Adm. sizar (age 16) at CAIUS, Mar. 26, 1601. S. of Edward (? 1567), R. of Cawston, Norfolk. B. there. School, Cambridge (Mr Edwards). Brother of Edward (1596).

HAMMOND, HENRY. Adm. sizar (age 15) at CAIUS, Sept. 13, 1561. S. of John, of Swaffham. School, Swaffham. Matric. 1561; Scholar, 1564; B.A. 1565-6; M.A. 1569. Fellow and tutor, 1568-72. Ord. deacon (Ely) Dec. 21, 1568; priest (Ely) Sept. 1570. R. of Letchworth, Herts., 1576. V. of Broxbourne, 1582-92. Preb. of St Paul's, 1585-92. Died 1592. Will, P.C.C. (*Venn*, I. 46.)

HAMMOND, HENRY. Matric. sizar from TRINITY, Easter, 1582.

HAMMOND, HENRY. Adm. pens. (age 18) at CAIUS, Jan. 29, 1582-3. S. of Robert, of Wendling, Norfolk. Schools, (?) Necton and Scarning. Scholar, 1586-90; B.A. 1586-7; M.A. 1590. Fellow, 1594-1616. Buried at St Michael's, Cambridge, Oct. 13, 1616. Will proved (V.C.C.) 1616. (*Venn*, I. 116.)

HAMMOND, HENRY. Matric. pens. from TRINITY, *c.* 1596; scholar from Westminster; B.A. 1599-1600; M.A. 1603; B.D. 1610. Probably V. of Rainham, Essex, 1605-8. R. of St John Zachary, London, 1608-23. V. of Mucking, Essex, 1610-5. R. of St Peter-le-Poer, 1615-23.

HAMMOND, HENRY. M.A. 1626 (Incorp. from Oxford). Of Surrey. S. of John (1579), M.D. B. Aug. 18, 1605. Matric. from Magdalen College, Oxford, June 26, 1621, age 15; B.A. 1622; M.A. 1625; B.D. 1633-4; D.D. 1638-9. Fellow of Magdalen College, 1625-34. Public orator at Oxford, 1645-8. Canon of Christ Church. R. of Penshurst, Kent, 1633-46, sequestered. Archdeacon of Chichester, 1643. Chaplain to Charles I, 1645. Deprived and imprisoned, but afterwards placed in the custody of Sir Philip Warwick at Clapham, Beds. Removed, 1649, to the seat of Sir John Pakington. Author, theological. Died Apr. 25, 1660. (*Al. Oxon.*; *D.N.B.*)

HAMOND, HORACE. Adm. at CORPUS CHRISTI, 1735. Of Norfolk. Matric. Michs. 1736; B.A. 1739-40; M.A. 1743; D.D. 1755. Fellow, 1740-6. Ord. priest (Norwich) Dec. 1744. R. of Harpley and Gt Bircham, Norfolk, 1744-86. Preb. of Bristol, 1754-6. Preb. of Norwich, 1756-86. Died at Norwich, Oct. 11, 1786. M.I. at South Wootton. Will, P.C.C. (*G. Mag.*)

HAMOND, HUMPHREY. Matric. pens. from TRINITY, Easter, 1579-80. Of Kent. B.A. 1583-4; M.A. from Queens', 1587. Fellow of St John's, 1589.

HAMOND, HUMPHREY. Matric. pens. from TRINITY, Easter, 1604.

HAMMOND, HUMPHREY. Matric. pens. from QUEENS', Easter, 1635. Of Hertfordshire. B.A. 1637-8; M.A. 1641.

HAMMOND, HUMPHREY. M.A. from CORPUS CHRISTI, 1711. S. of Robert, of Waldron, Sussex. Matric. from All Souls, Oxford, June 18, 1697, age 19; B.A. (Oxford) 1701. R. of East Guildford, Sussex, 1706. Author, *Sermons*. (*Al. Oxon.*)

HAMMOND, JAMES. Adm. pens. (age 18) at PEMBROKE, May 23, 1637. S. of John, of Nonington, Kent. Migrated to Peterhouse, Apr. 7, 1638. Scholar, 1639.

HAMOUND, JOHN. Scholar at KING'S HALL, 1446-57.

HAMMOND, JOHN. Matric. pens. from CORPUS CHRISTI, Easter, 1552; B.A. 1554-5.

HAMMOND, JOHN. LL.B. from TRINITY HALL, 1561. B. at Whalley, Lancs., *c.* 1542. LL.D. 1569. Fellow in 1557, till 1574. Adm. advocate, May 11, 1569. Master in Chancery, 1574. Chancellor of London diocese, 1575. A delegate to the Diet of Smalkald, 1578. M.P. for Rye, 1584-6; for West Looe, 1586-8. Died Dec. 1589. Will (P.C.C.) 1590. Perhaps father of John (1579). (*D.N.B.*; *Cooper*, II. 75; *Suff. Man. Fam.*)

HAMMOND, JOHN. Matric. pens. from TRINITY, Easter, 1570; Scholar, 1573; B.A. 1573-4; M.A. 1577. Fellow, 1576. Incorp. at Oxford, 1578. (*Al. Oxon.*, where he is confused with John (1579).)

HAMMOND, JOHN. Matric. pens. from CLARE, Michs. 1572. B. at Debden, Essex, *c.* 1558. B.A. 1575-6; M.A. 1579. Fellow. Ord. deacon and priest (Peterb.) Sept. 29, 1588. R. of Malden, Beds., 1598. V. of Gt Gransden, Hunts., 1599-1604. Buried at Malden, Feb. 24, 1603-4. Probably the author of a large Plan of Cambridge, dated Feb. 22, 1592, 'from Clare Hall.' (*Cooper*, III. 16; A. Gray.)

HAMMOND, JOHN. Matric. pens. from ST JOHN'S, Easter, 1579. One of these names adm. at Gray's Inn, 1579-80.

HAMMOND, JOHN. Matric. sizar from TRINITY, Easter, 1579. Said (by *Munk*) to be s. of John Hammond, LL.D. (1561). B.A. 1582-3; M.A. 1586; M.D. 1597. Incorp. at Oxford, 1605. Fellow, R.C.P., 1608. Physician to James I and Prince Henry. Died 1617. Will, P.C.C.; of Chertsey, Surrey. Father of Henry (1628). (*Munk*, I. 147; *D.N.B.*, where his College career is confused with that of John, of Trinity (1570).)

HAMMOND, JOHN. Adm. sizar at PETERHOUSE, June 1, 1622. Of Norfolk. One of these names ord. priest (Llandaff); C. or chaplain of Thompson, Norfolk, in 1635.

HAMMOND, JOHN. Matric. pens. from ST JOHN'S, Michs. 1627; B.A. 1631-2; M.A. 1635. Ord. priest (Peterb.) June 4, 1637. R. of Strethall, Essex, 1638-69.

HAMMOND, JOHN. B.A. from TRINITY, 1636-7. One of these names, s. and h. of Robert, late of Chertsey, Surrey, deceased, adm. at Lincoln's Inn, Feb. 10, 1635-6.

HAMMOND, JOHN. Adm. pens. at QUEENS', Sept. 15, 1648. Of Suffolk. One of these names s. of Thomas, of Cresseners-in-Hawkedon, Suffolk. Of East Bergholt, gent., in 1664. Living, 1693. (*Vis. of Suffolk*; *Suffolk Man. Fam.*, I. 261.)

HAMMOND, JOHN. Adm. sizar (age 17) at SIDNEY, Mar. 26, 1663. 2nd s. of Francis, yeoman. B. at Lavenham, Suffolk. Schools, Lavenham and Bury. Matric. 1663; B.A. 1666-7; M.A. 1670. Ord. priest (Ely) Dec. 18, 1669. C. of Raydon, Suffolk. Perhaps R. of Stanway, Essex, 1677. Died 1703. Will (Comm. C. Essex) 1703.

HAMMOND, MAURICE. Adm. pens. (age 16) at CAIUS, Mar. 24, 1577-8. S. of George, yeoman, of Westmill, Herts. Schools, Standon, Herts. (Mr Michswell) and Ely. Matric. 1578; B.A. from Christ's, 1581-2; M.A. 1585. Ord. deacon and priest (Lincoln) July 8, 1586. R. of Barnwell All Saints', Northants., 1592-1617. Buried there Feb. 16, 1616-7. Will (Peterb.) 1617. Brother of George (1573-4) and Robert (1575). (*Venn*, I. 96.)

HAMMOND, MICHAEL. Matric. pens. from CLARE, Michs. 1566.

HAMMOND, MILES. Matric. pens. from PETERHOUSE, Easter, 1585; Scholar, 1587-8. Buried in Little St Mary's, Cambridge, 1588.

HAMMOND, NATHANIEL. Adm. pens. at TRINITY, Jan. 14, 1663-4. Of Cambridge. Matric. 1664. Migrated to Peterhouse, Nov. 14, 1667. Scholar, 1667; B.A. 1667-8; M.A. 1671. Fellow of Peterhouse, 1668-72. Mandate for LL.D. 1689 (*Lit. Reg.*). One of these names V. of Erith, Kent, 1693-1705.

HAMMOND, NATHANIEL. Adm. sizar (age 18) at SIDNEY, Apr. 11, 1683. S. of William, brewer, of Westleton, Suffolk. Schools, Kelshall (Mr Barton) and Layston (Mr Toy). Matric. 1683. Ord. deacon (Norwich) June, 1693; priest, June, 1696. R. of Boulge, Suffolk, 1696. R. of Debach, 1701.

HAMMONDE, NICHOLAS. Adm. pens. (age 15) at CAIUS, Mar. 16, 1619-20. S. of Robert, husbandman, of Norfolk. School, Norwich (Mr Thornton). Matric. 1621; Scholar, 1622-7; B.A. 1623-4; M.A. 1627. Ord. deacon (Norwich) Sept. 20, 1628. C. of Lingwood, Norfolk, in 1635.

HAMMOND, PETER. Adm. sizar (age 17) at SIDNEY, May, 1620. S. of John, husbandman. B. at Sancton, Yorks. School, Newbald. Matric. 1620; B.A. 1623-4; M.A. 1627. Ord. deacon (York) Dec. 1623; priest, Dec. 1624. R. of Everingham, Yorks., 1655-69. Buried there Jan. 8, 1669.

HAMMOND, PHILIP. B.A. from CLARE, 1573-4; M.A. 1577. Perhaps 2nd s. of Richard, of Debden, Essex, whose will (Cons. C. London) 1585. (J. Ch. Smith.)

HAMMOND, PHILIP KNIGHT. Adm. pens. (age 16) at CAIUS, Sept. 26, 1734. S. of Philip, Esq., of Boxted, Suffolk. B. there. Bapt. Oct. 9, 1718. School, Bury. Scholar, 1734-6; Matric. 1735. Died Oct. 4, 1758. Buried at Boxted. (*Venn*, II. 40; G. H. Holley.)

HAMOND, RICHARD. B.Civ.L. 1495-6.

HAMOND, RICHARD. Matric. sizar from CAIUS, Oct. 1567.

HAMMOND, RICHARD. Matric. pens. from ST JOHN'S, Easter, 1570.

HAMMOND, RICHARD. Matric. pens. from ST JOHN'S, Michs. 1579. One of these names, of Norfolk, adm. at Lincoln's Inn, June 26, 1586, from Furnival's Inn.

HAMMOND, RICHARD. Matric. sizar from TRINITY, Lent, 1582-3. B. at Gt Bardfield, Essex. Ord. deacon (London) Feb. 24, 1587-8, age 24; C. of Finchingfield ('B.A.'). Perhaps R. of Tilbury-by-Clare, 1592-1633.

HAMMOND, RICHARD. Adm. Fell.-Com. at EMMANUEL, Feb. 9, 1636-7. Of Norfolk.

HAMMOND, RICHARD. Adm. pens. (age 18) at PEMBROKE, June 3, 1718. S. of Nicholas, of Swaffham, Norfolk, gent. Matric. 1719. Adm. at the Middle Temple, July 16, 1722.

HAMOND, ROBERT. B.A. 1483-4.

HAMMOND, ROBERT. Adm. pens. (age 19) at CAIUS, Feb. 19, 1574-5. S. of George. B. at Westmill, Herts. School, Ely. Matric. 1574-5; B.A. from Christ's, 1578-9; M.A. 1582. Fellow of Christ's, 1582-4. Ord. deacon and priest (Lincoln) Mar. 23, 1581-2. Brother of George (1573-4) and Maurice (1577-8). (*Peile*, I. 135; *Venn*, I. 81.)

HAMMOND, ROBERT. Adm. pens. at JESUS, Jan. 15, 1648-9. Of Cambridgeshire. Matric. 1648-9. One of these names buried at Little St Mary's, Cambridge, July 18, 1663.

HAMOND, ROBERT. Adm. pens. at CORPUS CHRISTI, 1664. Of Norwich. Matric. 1664.

HAMMOND, SAMUEL. Matric. sizar from KING'S, Michs. 1638. B. in York (s. of a butcher). B.A. 1641-2; M.A. 1645. Fellow of Magdalene, 1645. Ord. deacon (Lincoln) June 5, 1642; priest, Dec. 8, 1642. Chaplain to Sir A. Hesilrige, 1648. Intruded minister at Bishop Wearmouth. V. of Newcastle, 1652-60. Minister to the merchants at Hamburg. 'Married Mr Justice Ogle's daughter, of Eglingham.' Died in London, Dec. 10, 1665. (*D.N.B.*; *Calamy*, II. 267; *Surtees Soc.*, L. 142.)

HAMMOND, SAMUEL. Adm. at ST CATHARINE'S, Apr. 17, 1662. Of Suffolk. Matric. 1663; B.A. 1665-6. Perhaps V. of South Benfleet, Essex, 1680. Admon. (Cons. C. London) 1688. (J. Ch. Smith.)

HAMMOND, THOMAS. B.A. 1500-1; M.A. 1503. One Hammond was scholar at KING'S HALL, 1501-5.

HAMMOND, THOMAS. Matric. sizar from CHRIST'S, Michs. 1555; Scholar, 1557-8.

HAMMOND, THOMAS. Scholar of TRINITY HALL, 1561; LL.B. 1561; LL.D. 1569. Fellow, 1566-78. Chancellor of the diocese of Carlisle, 1577-86; and perhaps of diocese of Hereford. Married Anne, dau. of Edward Ward, of Mendham, Suffolk. Died Mar. 11, 1599. Buried at Ash-by-Campsey, Suffolk. Will (P.C.C.) 1599. Brother of John (1561), father of Thomas (1608). (*Suff. Man. Fam.*, I. 254.)

HAMMOND, THOMAS. Matric. pens. from CHRIST'S, Nov. 1566. (*Cooper*, II. 434, confuses him with the last.)

HAMMOND, THOMAS. Matric. pens. from ST JOHN'S, Michs. 1579; B.A. 1583-4; M.A. 1587. Ord. deacon (Peterb.) Dec. 5, 1588; priest, Jan. 24, 1588-9. One of these names (M.A.), R. of Smeaton, Yorks., 1598-1615.

HAMMOND, THOMAS. Adm. Fell.-Com. at CORPUS CHRISTI, 1583. Matric. Easter, 1584.

HAMMOND, THOMAS. M.A. 1597 (Incorp. from Oxford). Of Wiltshire. Matric. from Christ Church, June 12, 1584, age 18; B.A. (Oxford) 1587; M.A. 1590. One of these names V. of Dillwyn, Heref. Will (P.C.C.) 1617.

HAMOND, THOMAS. Matric. pens. from CHRIST'S, Dec. 1608. Doubtless s. of Thomas (1561), of Bury St Edmunds. B. c. 1592. Adm. at Gray's Inn, Oct. 29, 1611; of Ash, Suffolk. Barrister, 1617. Benefactor to Christ's. Mentioned in his grandfather Ward's will, Oct. 17, 1632. (*Peile*, I. 271; *Suffolk Man. Fam.*, I. 254.)

HAMMOND, THOMAS. Matric. pens. from CORPUS CHRISTI, Easter, 1620-1. Of Norfolk. B.A. 1624-5; M.A. 1628. Perhaps s. of Edward (1567). If so, buried at Cawston, Norfolk, May 28, 1630. (G. H. Holley.)

HAMMOND, THOMAS. Adm. sizar at EMMANUEL, Easter, 1623. Matric. 1623; B.A. 1626-7.

HAMMOND, THOMAS. Adm. pens. at EMMANUEL, Feb. 8, 1636-7. Of Norfolk.

HAMMOND, THOMAS. Adm. Fell.-Com. (age 18) at CAIUS, June 4, 1659. S. of John, Esq., of Ellingham, Norfolk. Bapt. there, Dec. 22, 1640. School, Cotton, Suffolk (private; Mr Smith). Matric. 1659. Of Ellingham, Esq. Died unmarried. Will proved (Norwich) 1677. (*Venn*, I. 407; *Vis. of Norfolk*, 1664.)

HAMMOND, THOMAS. Adm. sizar (age 16) at PEMBROKE, Jan. 31, 1677-8. S. of Joseph, farmer. B. at Liston, Essex. Matric. 1678.

HAMMOND, THOMAS. Adm. Fell.-Com. (age 16) at ST JOHN'S, June 24, 1717. S. of Antony, gent., of Middlesex. B. in London. School, Westminster. Matric. 1717.

HAMMOND, THOMAS. M.A. 1717 (*Com. Reg.*). Perhaps the above.

HAMMOND, WILLIAM. Matric. sizar from TRINITY HALL, Michs. 1546.

HAMMOND, WILLIAM. Matric. sizar from KING'S, Easter, 1573.

HAMMOND, WILLIAM. Matric. pens. from CHRIST'S, Mar. 1580-1. Perhaps s. of Ralph, of Kent. B. in London. Scholar. Migrated to St John's. B.A. 1584-5; M.A. 1588. Adm. at Gray's Inn, May 25, 1582. (*Peile*, I. 162.)

HAMMAND, WILLIAM. Matric. pens. from CLARE, c. 1596. One of these names adm. at Gray's Inn, Feb. 22, 1596-7.

HAMMOND, WILLIAM. B.A. from PEMBROKE, 1604-5; M.A. 1608. Probably s. of Henry, of Bury, Suffolk. Ord. priest (Norwich) Sept. 25, 1608, age 23. C. of Trimley, Suffolk. R. of Stratford St Andrew, 1619-30. (*Suff. Man. Fam.*, I. 254.)

HAMMOND, WILLIAM. Adm. pens. at SIDNEY, Apr. 21, 1610. Matric. 1610; B.A. 1613; M.A. from Clare, 1617; B.D. 1623. Ord. deacon (Peterb.) Dec. 20; priest, Dec. 21, 1618, as Hamon. Incorp. at Oxford, 1622.

HAMMOND, WILLIAM. Matric. pens. from TRINITY, Easter, 1611. One of these names, s. of Bryan, of Scarthingwell, Yorks., Esq., adm. at Lincoln's Inn, Oct. 30, 1613. Probably brother of Gervase (1611).

HAMMOND, WILLIAM. Adm. pens. at EMMANUEL, Feb. 15, 1612-3. Matric. 1613.

HAMMOND, WILLIAM. Adm. pens. (afterwards Fell.-Com.) at EMMANUEL, Easter, 1626. S. of John, of Ellingham, Norfolk, gent. Buried at Gt St Andrew's, Cambridge, Oct. 8, 1629. (*Vis. of Norfolk*, 1664.)

HAMMOND, WILLIAM. Matric. sizar from ST JOHN'S, Easter, 1627.

HAMMOND, WILLIAM. Adm. sizar at EMMANUEL, Jan. 15, 1630-1. Of Cambridgeshire. Matric. 1630-1; B.A. 1634-5.

HAMMOND, WILLIAM. Matric. p . (age 17 *sic.*) from PEMBROKE, Easter, 1633. S. of William, of 'Talbourne.' Of Kent. B. Mar. 27, 1620. Schools, Merchant Taylors (and Charterhouse; exhibitioner). B.A. 1636-7; M.A. 1640. Fellow, 1633; ejected, 1644. Died before the Restoration.

HAMMOND, WILLIAM. Adm. sizar (age 17) at ST JOHN'S, July 2, 1677. S. of Christopher, attorney-at-law, of Monk-Frystone, Yorks. B. there. School, Sherburn (Mr Wright). Matric. 1677; B.A. 1683-4.

HAMOND, WILLIAM. Adm. pens. (age 15) at PETERHOUSE, Dec. 7, 1682. S. of Thomas, of Bury St Edmunds, apothecary. Bapt. Sept. 24, 1668. School, Bury. Scholar, 1682-3; Matric. 1683; B.A. 1686-7; M.A. 1690. Usher at Bury School, 1687. Died Aug. 1690. M.I. in Bury churchyard. (*T. A. Walker*, 172.)

HAMMOND, WILLIAM. Adm. pens. (age 18) at ST JOHN'S, June 26, 1736. S. of William, druggist, of Sussex. B. at Battle. Bapt. Jan. 9, 1718-9. School, Charterhouse, London. Exhibitioner. Matric. 1736; B.A. 1739-40. Became a Moravian minister. Author, religious. Buried in their burial ground, Chelsea, 1783. (*Scott-Mayor*, III. 474.)

HAMMOND, WILLIAM. Adm. pens. (age 16) at PEMBROKE, Sept. 17, 1737. S. of Anthony (? 1711), of St Albans Court, Kent, gent. Matric. 1738. Of St Albans Court, Esq. Married Charlotte, dau. of Dr William Egerton, preb. of Canterbury, 1745. (*Hasted*, III. 709; Burke, *L.G.*)

HAMMOND, ——. Fellow of PEMBROKE, 1465. M.A. Probably William, grammar master; rented a tenement belonging to Peterhouse, 1469-72. (*T. A. Walker*.)

HAMOND, ——. B.A. 1520-1.

HAMMOND, ——. Pens. of GONVILLE HALL, 1538.

HAMOND, ——. Matric. pens. from ST JOHN'S, Easter, 1544.

HAMMOND, ——. Adm. Fell.-Com. at KING'S, Michs. 1641.

HAMMONDSON, JOSEPH, *see* EADMONDSON.

HAMOR, RALPH. Adm. at EMMANUEL, July 1, 1607.

HAMORE, WILLIAM. Matric. pens. from QUEENS', Michs. 1572.

HAMMUNDISHAM, *see* AGMONDESHAM.

HAMPDEN, ALEXANDER. Adm. Fell.-Com. at EMMANUEL, May 7, 1633. Of Northamptonshire. S. of Sir Edmund, Knt., of Abington, Northants. School, Oundle. Buried Apr. 2, 1675, at Gt Missenden, Bucks. (*Lipscomb*, II. 376.)

HAMDEN, EDMUND. Adm. at KING'S, a scholar from Eton, 1445; B.A. 1449. Proctor, 1453-4. Afterwards D.D. (*Harwood*). Excused from regency, 1466. Warden of Chapel at Kingston-on-Thames, 1476-85. Nominated by the University as a chantry priest at St George's, Windsor, 1481-2. (*Gr. Bk*, A, 160, 161; *Surrey Arch. Soc.*, VIII. 288.)

HAMPDEN, EDWARD. Adm. pens. at CORPUS CHRISTI, 1611. Of Northamptonshire. Matric. Easter, 1612.

HAMPDEN, HUMPHREY. 'M.A. Cambridge; Incorp. at Oxford, July 10, 1593.' (*Al. Oxon.*, not found in our records.)

HAMPDEN, JOHN. Adm. Fell.-Com. at EMMANUEL, Sept. 18, 1639. Of Buckinghamshire. Perhaps 1st s. of John ('the patriot'). Captain in his father's regiment, 1642. Died c. 1643. (*D.N.B.*)

HAMDEN, WILLIAM. Matric. Fell.-Com. from PEMBROKE, Easter, 1586.

HAMPSHIRE, RICHARD. Adm. at KING'S, a scholar from Eton, 1483. Died as schoolmaster of the Choristers at Windsor. (*Harwood*.)

HAMPSHIRE, RICHARD. Adm. at KING'S (age 17) a scholar from Eton, Aug. 12, 1520. Of Windsor. Died as scholar.

HAMPSHIRE, WILLIAM. Adm. at KING'S, a scholar from Eton, 1479.

HAMSON, JOHN. Matric. sizar from ST CATHARINE'S, Easter, 1635. Of Cambridgeshire. B.A. 1638-9. Ord. deacon (Peterb.) Dec. 22, 1639. Priest (Hereford) June 20, 1641. R. of Yelling, Hunts., -1648-51-; 'a preaching minister.' V. of Chigwell, Essex, 1652-60. V. of Chickney, 1660-90. R. of Broxted, 1663-90. Died 1690.

HAMPSON, JOHN. Adm. sizar (age 14) at CHRIST'S, July 7, 1699. S. of John. B. in Cambridge. School, King's College (Mr Rosewell). Matric. 1699-1700; Scholar, 1702-3; B.A. 1703-4; M.A. 1709. Ord. deacon (Norwich) Sept. 1706; priest (Ely) Sept. 19, 1708, as C. of East Church, Isle of Sheppey. C. of Kegworth, Leics. Died there Aug. 18, 1716. M.I. Will, Leicester. (*Peile*, II. 145.)

HAMPSON, THOMAS. Adm. sizar at QUEENS', Apr. 3, 1577. Of Hertfordshire.

HAMSON, WILLIAM. Matric. sizar from CORPUS CHRISTI, Easter, 1670.

HAMPTON, CHARLES. D.D. from CHRIST'S, 1677. S. of William, R. of Bletchingley, Surrey. Bapt. there, Mar. 15, 1630. Matric. from Exeter College, Oxford, Feb. 13, 1648-9; B.A. (Oxford) 1651-2; M.A. 1654. R. of Worth, Sussex, 1659-1704. R. of Bletchingley, 1677-1704. Chaplain to Lord Paget, of Beaudesert. Died June 2, 1704. Buried at Bletchingley. Will, P.C.C. (*Al. Oxon.*; *Vis. of Surrey*, 1662; *Peile*, II. 67.)

HAMPTON, CHRISTOPHER. Scholar of TRINITY, 1570. S. of John, of Hampshire, clerk. B.A. 1571-2; M.A. 1575; B.D. 1582; D.D. 1598. Fellow, 1574. V. of Chesterton, Cambs., 1585-9. Nominated to the See of Derry, 1611, but not consecrated. Vice-Chancellor of the University of Dublin, 1612. Archbishop of Armagh, 1613-25. Restored Armagh Cathedral. Died, unmarried, at Drogheda, Jan. 3, 1624-5. Buried there in St Peter's Church. (*Coll. Top. et Gen.*, VI. 294; *D.N.B.* is apparently wrong in stating that he was educated at Corpus Christi.)

HAMPTON, CORNWALLIS. Adm. sizar (age 20) at PETERHOUSE, Apr. 14, 1653. Of Essex.

HAMPTON, EDWARD. Matric. sizar from TRINITY, Easter, 1576; Scholar, 1580; B.A. 1580-1; M.A. 1584. Fellow, 1583. Ord. deacon and priest (Peterb.) Nov. 30, 1585.

HAMPTON, EDWARD. Adm. sizar (age 18) at CAIUS, Oct. 15, 1595. S. of Edward. B. at Rainham, Norfolk. School, Rainham. Scholar, 1596-9; B.A. 1598-9; M.A. 1602. Ord. deacon (Norwich) Mar. 25, 1601; priest, Sept. 26, 1603, as C. of East Rudham. R. of Rainham St Martin, Norfolk, c. 1600; and of Stanhow, 1612-34. (*Venn*, I. 157.)

HAMPTON, JOHN. Adm. pens. at QUEENS', June 10, 1594. Of Hertfordshire. B.A. 1597-8; M.A. 1602.

HAMPTON, JOHN. Matric. sizar from CLARE, 1607-8; B.A. 1611-2; M.A. 1615. One of these names V. of Stoke, Kent, 1623-4.

HAMPTON, JOHN. Adm. sizar at TRINITY, July 2, 1660. Matric. 1661; Scholar, 1664; B.A. 1664-5; M.A. 1668. Ord. priest (Peterb.) Sept. 20, 1668. Perhaps R. of Little Ilford, Essex, 1669-80. Died, unmarried, 1680. Admon., Feb. 13, 1679-80.

HAMPTON, ROBERT. Matric. sizar from CLARE, Easter, 1610.

HAMPTON, THOMAS. B.Can.L. (? 1510-1); D.Can.L. 1520-1. A Benedictine monk. Last Prior of Hertford. Licensed to preach by his monastery. (*Gr. Bk*, A, 100.)

HAMPTON, THOMAS. Matric. pens. from QUEENS', Michs. 1618.

HAMPTON, W. Matric. pens. from ST JOHN'S, Easter, 1562.

HAMPTON, WILLIAM. Matric. sizar from TRINITY, Michs. 1568; Scholar, 1571; B.A. 1572-3; M.A. 1576. Perhaps V. of Reigate, Surrey, 1599. Author, *Sermon*, 1601. Buried May 14, 1636. (*Cooper*, III. 16.)

HAMPTON, WILLIAM. Matric. sizar from ST JOHN'S, Easter, 1588.

HAMPTON, WILLIAM. Adm. pens. at CLARE, July 11, 1640. Matric. 1640.

HAMPTON, ——. Scholar at KING'S HALL, 1473-5.

HAMUNDER (? SUMANDER), ——. B.A. 1495-6.

HANADYNE, THOMAS. Matric. sizar from PETERHOUSE, Easter, 1552. Received tonsure (London) May, 1554. C. (?) of Fen Stanton, Cambs.

HANDBY, EDWARD. B.Can.L. 1506-7.

HANBIE or HANSBIE, EDWARD. Matric. pens. from KING'S, Michs. 1573.

HANDBIE, FRANCIS. Matric. pens. from KING'S, Easter, 1606.

HANBYE, JOHN. Matric. pens. from PETERHOUSE, Michs. 1579.

HANBYE, WILLIAM. Matric. pens. (age 9 *sic.*) from JESUS, Michs. 1552. One of these names V. of Dallinghoe, Suffolk, 1569-1613. R. of Little Glemham, 1594-1610. Described as M.A.; ord. priest (Winchester) Mar. 3, 1560-1; Chaplain to Lord Buckland. (A. Gray.)

HANBIE or HANSBIE, WILLIAM. Matric. pens. from KING'S, Michs. 1573.

HANBURY, CHARLES. Adm. pens. (age 17) at ST JOHN'S, Oct. 31, 1670. S. of Edward (below), deceased, of Northamptonshire. B. there. School, Kimbolton (Mr Taylor). Matric. 1671. Brother of Thomas (1673).

HANBURY, EDWARD. Adm. Fell.-Com. (age 15) at SIDNEY, Aug. 17, 1622. S. of John, gent., of Kelmarsh, Northants. B. in London. Schools, Northampton (private) and Naseby (Mr Edward Wright). Matric. 1622. Married (1) Dorothy, dau. of Edward Shukborough, of Naseby, Esq.; (2) Lucy Martin. Died 1656. Father of Thomas (1673) and Charles (above). (*Vis. of Northants.*, 1618; *Bridges*, II. 40.)

HANBURY, NATHANIEL. Adm. pens. (age 18) at TRINITY, June 20, 1677. S. of Philip. B. in London. School, Westminster. Scholar, 1678; Matric. 1680; B.A. 1680-1; M.A. 1684; B.D. 1703. Fellow, 1683. C. of St Michael's, Cambridge. Author. Buried in Trinity College Chapel, Nov. 18, 1715. Will proved (V.C.C.) 1715. (*Al. Westmon.*, 180.)

HANBURY, THOMAS. Adm. pens. (age 15) at JESUS, Sept. 24, 1673, from Pembroke Hall (residence there from July 24, 1673). S. of Edward (1622), of Kelmarsh, Northants, Esq. Matric. 1674; Scholar, 1676; B.A. 1676-7; M.A. from Trinity Hall, 1680. Adm. at the Middle Temple, July 13, 1675. Died 1685. Buried at St Margaret's, Westminster. M.I. Brother of Charles (1670).

HANBURY, THOMAS. Adm. pens. (age 17) at ST JOHN'S, Feb. 24, 1685-6. S. of John, gent. B. at Kelmarsh, Northants. School, Westminster. Matric. 1686. Adm. at the Middle Temple, Feb. 6, 1685-6. Serjeant-at-law, 1715. Died Jan. 30, 1721-2.

HANCE, WILLIAM. Matric. sizar from TRINITY, Michs. 1570. One of these names V. of Steeple, Essex, 1586. Will (P.C.C.) 1614. (J. Ch. Smith.)

HANCH, SAMUEL. Matric. pens. from ST CATHARINE'S, Michs. 1635. Of London. S. and h. of Robert, of All Hallows-in-the-Wall, London. Bapt. there, Aug. 17, 1620. B.A. 1638-9. Adm. at Gray's Inn, Feb. 20, 1640-1. Perhaps buried at All Hallows, Apr. 12, 1643.

HANCHETT, EDWARD. Adm. sizar (age 15) at CHRIST'S, July 8, 1702. S. of Edward. B. at Buntingford, Herts. School, Buntingford (Mr England). Matric. 1704; Scholar, 1704-5; B.A. 1706-7. Fellow, 1708. Died before Jan. 12, 1709-10. (*Peile*, II. 155.)

HANCHETT, JOHN. B.A. from ST JOHN'S, 1619-20. Of Hertfordshire. M.A. 1623. Fellow, 1623-7. Will proved (V.C.C.) 1627.

HANCHETT, JOHN. Adm. pens. at ST CATHARINE'S, Easter, 1646; B.A. 1650-1. Buried at St Benet's, Cambridge, Feb. 12, 1650-1.

HANCHETT, RICHARD. Matric. sizar from QUEENS', Easter, 1624. Of Hertfordshire. B.A. 1626-7; M.A. 1631. One of these names V. of Rainham, Essex, 1662. Will (P.C.C.) 1666.

HANCHETT, THOMAS. Adm. Fell.-Com. (age 15) at CAIUS, Apr. 16, 1575. S. of Thomas. B. at Albury, Herts. School, Walden, Essex. Matric. 1575. Adm. at the Inner Temple, Apr. 15, 1578. J.P. for Herts. Sheriff, 1591, 1600. Of Braughing, gent. (*Venn*, I. 82; *Vis. of Herts.*, 1634.)

HANCKE, GILBERT. Adm. pens. (age 17) at Caius, Apr. 5, 1682. S. of Gilbert, druggist, of Norwich. B. there. School, Norwich. Matric. 1682; Scholar, 1682–5. Died in College. Buried at St Michael's, Cambridge, Nov. 6, 1685. (*Venn*, I. 469.)

HANCOCK, BENJAMIN. Adm. sizar (age 19) at St John's, June 30, 1744. S. of Benjamin, clerk, of Somerset (R. of Breane). B. at Portbury. School, Wells (Mr Bryan). Matric. 1744; B.A. 1747–8. Doubtless V. of Wiveliscombe, Somerset, 1754–67. Will (P.C.C.) of one of these names; of Wiveliscombe, clerk. (But *see* his father in *Al. Oxon.*)

HANCOCKE, 'CHARLES.' Matric. sizar from Emmanuel, Easter, 1686. *See* George.

HANCOCK, EDWARD. Adm. at King's, a scholar from Eton, 1444; D.Civ.L. (*Harwood.*)

HANCOCKE, EDWARD. Matric. pens. from Trinity, Lent, 1577–8. Of Combe Martin, Devon. One of these names s. of William, adm. at the Inner Temple, 1580. Barrister, 1590. Recorder of Exeter. M.P. for Plympton, 1597; and for Barnstaple, 1601.

HANCOCKE, FRANCIS. Adm. pens. (age 16) at Caius, May 14, 1577. S. of Thomas. B. at Fulbourn, Cambs. Bapt. at All Saints', July 6, 1559. Schools, Fulbourn and Walden, Essex (Mr D[13]berow and Mr Wright). Scholar, till 1584; B.A. 1581–2; M.A. 1585. V. of Mattishall, Norfolk, 1585–1603. V. of Reymerstone, 1603. Will (P.C.C.) 1603. (*Venn*, I. 92.)

HANCOCK, FRANCIS. Adm. sizar (age 17) at Caius, Mar. 18, 1701–2. S. of Samuel (? 1664), clerk, of Hethel, Norfolk. B. there. Schools, Stratton, Norfolk (private; Mr Vynne) and Bergh Apton (Mr Conold). Matric. 1702; Scholar, 1702. Died in College. Buried at St Michael's, Cambridge, Nov. 13, 1702. (*Venn*, I. 508.)

HANCOCK, GEORGE. Matric. sizar from St John's, 1598; B.A. 1601–2. Schoolmaster at Shottesham, Norfolk, in 1604. Ord. deacon (Norfolk) Sept. 22; priest, Dec. 22, 1605, age 25. C. of Shottesham.

HANCOCK, GEORGE. Adm. sizar at Emmanuel, May 5, 1686. Probably matric. as 'Charles.' Of Staffordshire. B.A. 1689–90. Ord. priest (London) Dec. 20, 1691. R. of Bramshall, Staffs., 1691. Married, at Bramshall, May 10, 1691, Sarah Horton. Father of the next. (*Wm. Salt Arch. Soc.*, 1915.)

HANCOCK, GEORGE. Adm. pens. (age 19) at Trinity, June 8, 1717. S. of George (above), R. of Bramshall, Staffs. School, Uttoxeter, Staffs. (Mr Phillips). Scholar, 1718; B.A. 1720–1.

HANCOCK, HENRY. Matric. sizar from Jesus, Easter, 1608; B.A. 1611; M.A. 1615. Ord. deacon (Hereford) May 19, 1611; priest (Lincoln) Sept. 22, 1611. C. of Westmill, Herts., 1611. V. of Furneaux Pelham, 1615–43, sequestered. Died 1666. (*Shaw*, I. 315.)

HANCOCK, JAMES. Adm. sizar at Clare, July 1, 1654. B. July 15, 1637. Matric. 1655; B.A. 1657–8. Ord. deacon (Lincoln) May 28; priest, May 30, 1661. R. of Bridgnorth, Salop, 1663–1707. Died Jan. 22, 1706–7. (Le Neve, *Mon.*, II. 117.)

HANCOCKS, JAMES, *see* HANCOX.

HANCOCK, JOHN. Matric. sizar from St John's, *c.* 1596; B.A. 1600–1; M.A. 1604. Ord. deacon (York) May, 1608; priest, Aug. 1608. Perhaps R. of Ashover, Derbs., 1615–20. Died 1620. One of these names, of Sheffield, M.A., licensed to marry Alice Fanshawe, 1609.

HANCOCK, JOHN. Adm. pens. (age 17) at St John's, May 21, 1666. Fell.-Com. 1670. S. of John, deceased, of Belton, near Whitchurch, Salop. B. there. School, Barthomley (Mr Caudrey).

HANCOCKE, JOHN. M.A. from St John's, 1671 (*Lit. Reg.*); D.D. 1691. R. of St Margaret, Lothbury, 1699–1728. Chaplain to the Duke of Bedford. Preb. of Canterbury, 1719–28. Died June 21, 1728. Buried at St James', Clerkenwell. Will, P.C.C. Father of the next, of Pusey (1705–6), Ralph (1702), Thomas (1691) and William (1702).

HANCOCK, JOHN. Adm. pens. (age 17) at St John's, June 2, 1691. S. of John (above). B. at Chester. Matric. 1691. Adm. at the Inner Temple, June 18, 1691. Brother of Pusey and Thomas (1691).

HANCOCK, JOHN. Adm. at Corpus Christi, 1703. Of Norwich. Perhaps s. of Nathaniel, of Norwich, gent. Matric. Easter, 1704. Probably migrated to Brasenose College, Oxford, and matric. there, Mar. 20, 1706–7, age 19; B.A. (Oxford) 1708. (*Al. Oxon.*)

HANCOCK, JOHN. Adm. at King's, a scholar from Eton, 1720. B. at Combe Martin, Devon. Matric. Easter, 1721; B.A. 1724–5; M.A. 1728. Fellow, 1723. Became insane.

HANCOCK, JONATHAN. M.A. 1663 (Incorp. from Oxford). Matric. from Exeter College, July 20, 1654; B.A. (Gloucester Hall) 1660; M.A. not recorded. V. of Beddington, Sussex, 1664. (*Al. Oxon.*)

HANCOCK, PUSEY. Adm. pens. (age 16) at St John's, Mar. 19, 1705–6. S. of John (1671), D.D. B. in London. School, Charterhouse. Exhibitioner. Matric. 1706; B.A. 1709–10; M.A. 1713; B.D. 1722 (from Queens'). Fellow of Queens', 1714–23. Ord. deacon (London) Mar. 22, 1712–3; priest, Sept. 19, 1714. R. of Eversholt, Beds., 1721–31. One of these names R. of Walkington, Yorks.; died before 1777. Brother of John (1691), etc.

HANCOCK, RALPH. Adm. pens. (age 16) at St John's, June 25, 1653. S. of Ralph, deceased, of Whitwell, Derbs. B. there. School, Staveley, Derbs. Matric. 1653; B.A. 1656–7; M.A. 1660; B.D. from Emmanuel, 1667. Fellow of Emmanuel, Dec. 24, 1662 (by mandate). Brother of Thomas (1660).

HANCOCK, RALPH. Adm. sizar (age 16) at St John's, June 30, 1702. S. of John (1671), D.D. B. at Chester. Educated at home. Matric. 1705; B.A. 1705–6; M.A. 1711; D.D. 1717 (*Com. Reg.*). Ord. priest (London) Sept. 25, 1709. V. of Pulloxhill, Beds., 1716. Brother of John (1691), etc.

HANCOCK, RANDAL. Matric. sizar from Christ's, July, 1608. B. at Astbury, Cheshire. B.A. 1611–2; M.A. 1615. Ord. deacon (Rochester); priest (London) Sept. 1619, age 33; C. of Worplesdon, Surrey. (*Peile*, I. 270.)

HANCOCK, RANDAL. Adm. sizar (age 18) at Trinity, June 7, 1735. S. of Randal, of Chesterton, Staffs. School, Nantwich, Cheshire (Mr Adderly). Matric. 1735; LL.B. 1742. Ord. deacon (Lincoln) May 28, 1738.

HANCOCK, RICHARD. Adm. sizar (age 16) at Christ's, Nov. 1, 1642. S. of John (tailor). B. at Newcastle-on-Tyne. Bapt. at All Saints', May 4, 1627. School, Newcastle (Mr Oxley). Matric. 1642.

HANDCOCKE, ROBERT. Matric. pens. from Queens', Michs. 1615. Of Cambridgeshire. B.A. 1618–9; M.A. 1622.

HANCOCK, ROBERT. M.A. 1653 (Incorp. from Oxford). S. of Robert, of St Germain's, Cornwall, gent. Matric. from Exeter College, Oxford, Nov. 27, 1640, age 17. Created M.A. (Oxford) 1648. Fellow of Exeter College, 1648–57. R. of St Martin-by-Looe, Cornwall, 1653. Will of one of these names (Exeter) 1693; of St Martyn. (*Al. Oxon.*)

HANCOCK, ROBERT. Adm. pens. at Clare, Apr. 7, 1659. B. in Bedfordshire. Matric. 1659; B.A. 1662–3; M.A. 1666. Fellow. Signs as minister at Northill, Beds., 1673–83. Author, *Sermons*. Buried at Northill, Sept. 10, 1683.

HANCOCK, SAMUEL. Adm. sizar (age 18) at Caius, May 9, 1631. S. of George (? 1598), late V. of Shottesham, Norfolk. School, Shottesham (Mr Edw. Boone). Matric. 1631; B.A. 1634–5; M.A. 1638. Licensed schoolmaster at Shottesham, 1635. Ord. deacon (Norwich) Sept. 22, 1638; priest, Sept. 22, 1639. R. of Framlingham Earl and Pigot (signs the Bishop's book, May 17, 1645). Died 1661. (*Venn*, I. 299.)

HANCOCK, SAMUEL. Adm. at Corpus Christi, 1664. Of Norfolk. Probably s. of Samuel, above. Matric. 1664; B.A. 1667–8; M.A. 1671. Ord. priest (Norwich) May, 1673. R. of Framlingham Earl and Pigot, Norfolk, 1677–83. Perhaps R. of Hethel; and father of Francis (1701–2).

HANCOCK or HANDCOCK, STEPHEN. Adm. (age 21) at Caius, May 9, 1679. S. of William, of Athlone, Ireland. B. there. School, private. B.A. from Trinity College, Dublin, 1679; Scholar of Caius, 1679–81. Fellow, 1681–3. Dean of Clonmacnois, 1689–97; of Kilmacduagh, 1697–1719. Married Margaret, dau. of A. T. Warner, and widow of Francis Evatt, of Kilgriffe. Will (Dublin) 1719. (*Venn*, I. 461; H. B. Swanzy.)

HANCOCK, THOMAS. Adm. at King's, a scholar from Eton, 1459.

HANCOCK, THOMAS. Matric. sizar from Christ's, Mar. 1582–3 B.A. from Corpus Christi, 1585–6. Perhaps V. of Rede, Suffolk, 1588–90.

HANCOCKE, THOMAS. Matric. sizar from St John's, Michs. 1615; B.A. 1618–9; M.A. 1622. Ord. deacon (Peterb.) July 7, 1622. Perhaps R. of Todwick, Yorks., 1623–47. Died 1647.

HANCOCKE, THOMAS. Adm. pens. (age 17) at St John's, May 5, 1660. S. of Ralph, deceased, of Dronfield, Derbs. B. there. School, Dronfield (Mr Whitaker). Matric. 1660; B.A. 1663–4; M.A. 1671. Brother of Ralph (1663).

HANCOCK, THOMAS. Adm. pens. (age 16) at St John's, June 2, 1691. S. of John (1671), clerk. B. at Asbury, Cheshire. School, Chester. Matric. 1691; M.B. 1696. Brother of John (1691), etc.

HANCOCK, THOMAS. Adm. sizar (age 17) at Pembroke, July 2, 1744. S. of Thomas Saul (next), V. of Hollingbourne, Kent. B. at Harrietsham, Kent. 'Grecian' from Christ's Hospital. Matric. 1744; B.A. 1748–9.

HANCOCK, THOMAS SAUL. Adm. sizar (age 18) at TRINITY, Feb. 18, 1715-6. S. of Thomas, citizen and harness maker, of St Martin-in-the-Fields, London. 'Grecian' from Christ's Hospital. Matric. 1716; Scholar, 1718; B.A. 1719-20; M.A. 1723. Ord. deacon (Lincoln) Mar. 13, 1719-20; priest, Mar. 5, 1720-1. R. of Wormshill, Kent, 1721-41. V. of Hollingbourne, 1727-41. Died Aug. 15, 1741. Father of the above.

HANCOCK, WILLIAM. Matric. pens. from ST JOHN'S, c. 1597; B.A. 1602-3; M.A. from Pembroke, 1606. Fellow of Pembroke, 1605. Incorp. at Oxford, 1607. Ord. priest (Peterb.) Sept. 24, 1609 (*see Cooper*, II. 529). One of these names, minister, buried at St Nicholas, Newcastle-on-Tyne, Mar. 23, 1639-40. S. of Richard, V. of Hartburn. Will proved, 1640. (H. M. Wood.)

HANCOCK, WILLIAM. B.A. 1619 (Incorp. from Oxford). S. of Edward, of Combe Martin, Devon, Esq. Matric. from Corpus Christi College, Oxford, June 7, 1616, age 14; B.A. (Oxford) 1618-9. Adm. at the Middle Temple, June 8, 1618. Died May 2, 1625. (*Al. Oxon.*)

HANCOCK, WILLIAM. Adm. sizar (age 14) at ST JOHN'S, June 30, 1702. S. of John (1671), D.D. B. at Chester. Educated at home. Matric. 1705; B.A. 1705-6. Ord. deacon (London) Mar. 5, 1709-10. Brother of John (1691), etc.

HANCOCK, WILLIAM. Adm. pens. at QUEENS', Mar. 19, 1734-5. Of Somerset. Matric. 1735; M.B. 1741. Probably adm. at Leyden, Sept. 12, 1738. Died June 9, 1798. Will (P.C.C.) 1798; of New Sarum. (*G. Mag.*)

HANCORN, RICHARD. Adm. pens. (age 18) at ST JOHN'S, May 14, 1746. S. of Richard, of Hereford. B. at Whitney. School, Hereford (Mr Willim). Matric. 1746; B.A. 1749-50; M.A. 1753. Ord. deacon (Lincoln) Aug. 24, 1752; priest (Rochester) June 10, 1753. V. of Stoke, Kent, 1753-65. Perhaps his will (P.C.C.) 1789, as 'Rich. Duppa, formerly Rich. Hauccru.' (*Scott-Mayor*, II. 558.)

HANCOX, JAMES. Adm. at EMMANUEL, June 24, 1697. S. of John, mercer, of Kidderminster. B. there. Schools, Kidderminster (Mr Beavans) and Overley (Mr Read). Matric. 1698; B.A. 1701. Migrated to Caius, Oct 18, 1701, age 21. Scholar of Caius, 1702. Died Jan. 22, 1706-7. (*Venn*, I. 508; A. B. Beaven.)

HAND, CHRISTOPHER. Adm. sizar at EMMANUEL, Apr. 22, 1717. Of Oakham, Rutland. School, Oakham. Matric. 1717; Scholar; B.A. 1720-1; M.A. 1724; B.D. 1731. Fellow, 1723. Ord. deacon (Peterb.) Sept. 24, 1721; priest (Lincoln) June 5, 1726. R. of Aller, Somerset, 1743. Perhaps will (P.C.C.) 1778.

HAND, FRANCIS. Matric. sizar from CLARE, Michs. 1572; B.A. 1575-6; M.A. 1579. Author, *Latin Dialogue*, 1585. (*Cooper*, II. 40.)

HAND, JOHN. Matric. sizar from CHRIST'S, Easter, 1579-80.

HAND, TIMOTHY. Matric. pens. from QUEENS', Easter, 1632. Of Ely. B.A. 1635-6. Buried at Gt St Mary's, Cambridge, Apr. 3, 1637.

HAND, WILLIAM. Adm. sizar (age 17) at MAGDALENE, June 23, 1663. S. of William, schoolmaster, of Turnditch, Derbs. School, Duffield. Matric. 1663; B.A. 1666-7.

HANDBY, *see* HANBY.

HANDFORDE, EDWARD. Matric. pens. from CHRIST'S, 1598-9.

HANDFORD, JOHN. Adm. at KING'S (age 15) a scholar from Eton, Aug. 16, 1539. Of Beaconsfield, Bucks. B.A. 1543-4. Fellow, 1542-5.

HANDFORD, THOMAS. Adm. at KING'S (age 17) a scholar from Eton, Aug. 13, 1547. Of Beaconsfield, Bucks. B.A. 1551-2. Fellow, 1550, till 1555.

HANDFORD, WILLIAM. M.A. from KING'S, 1735. S. of Thomas, of Milverton, Somerset, gent. Matric. from Christ Church, Oxford, Mar. 26, 1728, age 18; B.A. (Oxford) 1731. (*Al. Oxon.*)

HANDFORTH, JOHN. Adm. sizar (age 16) at ST JOHN'S, Sept. 15, 1679. S. of Robert, husbandman. B. in Cheshire. School, Stockport (Mr Needham). Matric. 1679.

HANDFORTH, WILLIAM. Adm. sizar (age 19) at ST JOHN'S, June 17, 1679. S. of William. B. at Newton, Cheshire. School, Stockport (Mr Needham). Matric. 1679. Migrated to Christ's, Mar. 2, 1681-2. B.A. 1682-3. V. of Middlewich, Cheshire, 1695. (*Peile*, II. 86.)

HANDIDIE, THOMAS. M.A. 1657 (Incorp. from Oxford). S. of William, cutler. B. in All Hallows, Barking, May 26, 1630. Of St John's College, Oxford, from Merchant Taylors' school. B.A. (Oxford) 1650-1; M.A. 1653. Fellow of St John's, 1650.

HANDLABY, *see* ANLABY.

HANDLEY or HANLEY, HENRY. Adm. at KING'S (age 18) a scholar from Eton, Aug. 1, 1508. Of Sedbergh, Yorks. B.A. 1512-3; M.A. 1516. Fellow, 1511-8. Ord. sub-deacon (Ely) June 6; priest, Dec. 19, 1517.

HANDLEY or HANLEY, JAMES. Adm. at KING'S (age 18) a scholar from Eton, Aug. 16, 1518. Of Nun Monkton, Yorks. B.A. 1522-3; M.A. 1526. Fellow, 1521-4. (Two of these names are recorded as B.A., respectively, 1523-4 and 1524-5. Perhaps the same.) Probably B.D. 1536-7.

HANDLEY or HANLEY, RICHARD. Matric. sizar from PETERHOUSE, Easter, 1635. Of Lincolnshire. B.A. 1638-9. Ord. deacon (Peterb.) June 9, 1639.

HANDLEY, WILLIAM. Adm. sizar (age 16) at CHRIST'S, June 2, 1721. S. of William. B. at Wimbolds Traford, Cheshire. Matric. 1721; LL.B. 1726.

HANDLEY, ——. Pens. at GONVILLE HALL, 1535-8.

HANDS or HANNES, ROBERT. Matric. sizar from TRINITY, Easter, 1574; B.A. 1578-9; M.A. 1583.

HANDS, WILLIAM. Adm. sizar (age 18) at TRINITY, July 6, 1697. S. of William, of Monks Kirby, Warws. B. at Brocks, Warws. School, Rupley (Mr Holiake). Matric. 1697; Scholar, 1699; B.A. 1701-2. Ord. deacon (Lincoln) May 23, 1703.

HANDSOM, *see also* HANSON.

HANDSOM, JOHN. Matric. pens. from CHRIST'S, June, 1565; Scholar, 1566-7.

HANDSON, JOHN. Matric. pens. from TRINITY, *c.* 1596.

HANDSOM, THOMAS. Adm. pens. at SIDNEY, July 6, 1614. Matric. 1614.

HANE, JAMES or JACOB. Adm. pens. at TRINITY, June 29, 1665. School, Westminster. Scholar, 1666; Matric. 1668; B.A. 1668-9. Ord. deacon (Lincoln) Jan. 31; priest, Feb. 1, 1670-1.

HANGAR, JOHN. B.A. from TRINITY, 1598-9. B. in Cambridge, 1579. M.A. from Corpus Christi, 1602; B.D. 1610; D.D. 1620. Incorp. at Oxford, 1608. Ord. priest (Colchester) July 1, 1604. R. of Water Newton, Hunts., 1606-29. R. of Stibbington, 1613-38. R. of Polebrook, Northants., 1629. Died 1638. Will, P.C.C.

HANGER, RICHARD. Adm. sizar at QUEENS', July 20, 1599. Of Cambridgeshire. B.A. from St John's, 1603-4; M.A. 1607. Perhaps M.D. 1615. Incorp. at Oxford, 1608. Ord. deacon (Peterb.) Mar. 20; priest, Mar. 21, 1613-4. R. of Leven, Yorks., 1617-25.

HANKEY, HENRY. Adm. sizar (age 16) at CHRIST'S, June 10, 1674. S. of Henry. B. at Knutsford, Cheshire. School, Tamworth (Mr Antrobus). Matric. 1674; B.A. 1677-8. Ord. deacon (Worcester) Dec. 1679, as C. of Tamworth. Perhaps R. of Wanstead, Essex, Nov. 26, 1689. Died there before July, 1707. (*Peile*, II. 54.)

HANKEY, HENRY. Adm. pens. (age 17) at ST JOHN'S, May 25, 1747. S. of Sir Joseph, Knt., of Middlesex. B. in London. School, Dedham, Essex (Mr Grimwood). Matric. 1747; B.A. 1750-1; M.A. 1755. Ord. deacon (Ely) June 17, 1753; priest (Norwich) Apr. 28, 1754. R. of Brantham and Bergholt, Suffolk, 1754-82. R. of Peldon, Essex, 1761-82. Chaplain to the Earl of Ilchester. Died Apr. 24, 1782. Will, P.C.C. (*Scott-Mayor*, III. 566; *G. Mag.*)

HANKIN, EDMUND. Adm. pens. at CHRIST'S, Sept. 4, 1625. S. of John, of Suffolk. School, Halstead (Mr Whiston). Matric. 1626; B.A. from Magdalene, 1629-30; M.A. 1633. One of these names R. of Creacombe, Devon, 1664. (*Peile*, I. 371.)

HANKIN, JOHN. Adm. pens. (age 17) at CAIUS, Sept. 14, 1581. S. of William, gent. B. at Heywood, Staffs. School, Burton. Ord. deacon (Suffragan Bishop of Colchester) Dec. 29; priest, Dec. 30, 1596. R. of East Donyland, Essex, 1598-1600. V. of Stoke Nayland, Suffolk, 1600-27. (*Venn*, I. 111.)

HANKYN, THOMAS. B.A. 1489; M.A. 1491. Probably of ST BERNARD HOSTEL, 1499. Will proved (V.C.C.) 1509.

HANKINS, FARWELL. M.A. from TRINITY, 1732. S. of John, of Thornford, Dorset, gent. Matric. from Exeter College, Oxford, Mar. 19, 1718-9, age 19; B.A. (Oxford) 1722. (*Al. Oxon.*)

HANKINSON, ROBERT. Adm. sizar (age 16) at CHRIST'S, June 27, 1728. S. of Henry. B. at Kirkham, Lancs. School, Kirkham (Mr Taylor). Matric. 1728; Scholar, 1729; B.A. 1731-2; M.A. 1735. Fellow, 1740-52. Ord. deacon (Lincoln) Dec. 24, 1732; priest, July, 1736. R. of Clipston, Northants., 1751-71. Buried there Sept. 20, 1771. Will (Archd. Northants.) 1771. (*Peile*, II. 217; H. I. Longden.)

HANKYS, ROGER. Matric. pens. from ST JOHN'S, Easter, 1573.

HANMER, EDWARD. Adm. pens. (age 18) at ST JOHN'S, June 1, 1668. S. of James, yeoman, of Maesbrooke-in-Kinnerley, Salop. B. there. School, Oswestry. Matric. 1668; B.A. 1671-2; M.A. 1675.

HANMER, GRIFFIN. Matric. pens. from JESUS, Easter, 1569. Probably 4th s. of William, of Fennes Hall, Co. Flint. Brother of the next. (*Lipscomb*, IV. 341.)

HANMER, HUMPHREY. Matric. pens. from ST JOHN'S, Michs. 1560. 3rd s. of William, of Fennes Hall, Co. Flint. B.A. 1563-4. Doubtless adm. at Gray's Inn, 1561. Probably M.P. for Flint, 1572-83. (*Lipscomb*, IV. 341.)

HANMER, HUMPHREY. Adm. pens. at ST CATHARINE'S, July 30, 1725. Of Fens, Flints. Doubtless s. of William, of Fennes Hall, Co. Flint, deceased. Matric. 1726; B.A. 1729-30; M.A. 1733. Fellow, 1730-40. Incorp. at Oxford, 1733. Married Elizabeth Quartermaine, June, 1766. Died 1773. Brother and heir of Thomas (1720). (*Lipscomb*, IV. 342.)

HANMER, JOHN. Matric. Fell.-Com. from JESUS, Easter, 1571. Perhaps 's. of Sir Thomas, of Hanmer, Flint; adm. at Gray's Inn, 1574, from Staples Inn.'

HANMER, JOHN. Matric. Fell.-Com. from KING'S, Michs. 1637. Perhaps s. of Sir Thomas, 2nd Bart., and Elizabeth Baker. Knighted, 1660. Succeeded as 3rd Bart., 1678. M.P. for Flint, 1659, 1685, 1689; for Evesham, 1669-79; for Co. Flints., 1681. Died 1701. (*G.E.C.*)

HANMER, JOHN. Adm. pens. (age 17) at ST JOHN'S, June 30, 1659. S. of Jonathan (1624), of Bideford, Devon. B. there. School, Barnstaple (Mr Hughes). Matric. 1659. Ordained 1682, by Mr Ant. Palmer. Nonconformist minister at Barnstaple, 1682. Died Jan. 19, 1707, aged 65. (*Calamy*, I. 438; *D.N.B.*)

HANMER, JONATHAN. Adm. pens. at EMMANUEL, Easter, 1624. B. at Barnstaple, Devon, 1606. S. of John Hanmer, *alias* Davies. Matric. 1624, as 'Harmer'; B.A. 1627-8; M.A. 1631. Ordained, Nov. 23, 1632. R. of Instow, Devon, 1632. V. of Bishop's Tawton; and Lecturer at Barnstaple; ejected, 1662. Author. Died at Barnstaple, Dec. 18, 1687. Father of John (1659). (*Calamy*, I. 340; *D.N.B.*)

HANMER, JOSEPH. Adm. sizar at TRINITY, Sept. 10, 1652. Of Cheshire. Matric. 1653; B.A. 1657; M.A. 1661; D.D. 1678. C. of Ellenbrook Chapel, Lancs., 1664-9. Married Martha, dau. of Ralph Eddowes, gent. Father of the next. (*F.M.G.*, 113.)

HANMER, JOSEPH. Adm. sizar (age 17) at TRINITY, Oct. 9, 1677; pens. June 5, 1678. Of Shropshire. S. of Joseph (above). School, Chester (Mr Goldman). Matric. 1678; Scholar, 1681; B.A. 1681-2; M.A. 1685. Fellow, 1684. C. of Biddenham, Beds., 1686-9-; and C. of Clapham, 1686-91-. (F.*M*.G., 113.)

HANMER, ROGER. Matric. Fell.-Com. from QUEENS', Easter, 1620, as 'Anworth.' Of Flintshire.

HANMER, THOMAS. Matric. pens. from ST JOHN'S, Michs. 1560.

HANMER, THOMAS. Matric. pens. from MAGDALENE, Michs. 1602; B.A. 1605-6.

HANMOR, Sir THOMAS, Bart. Matric. Fell.-Com. from KING'S, Easter, 1627. S. and h. of John, of Hanmer, Flints. Succeeded as Bart., 1624. M.P. for Flint, 1640; for Co. Flints., 1669-78. Died 1678. Father of the next and of William (1663). (*G.E.C.*, I. 152; *Vis. of Shrops.*, 1623.)

HANMER, THOMAS. Adm. Fell.-Com. (age 13) at PEMBROKE, July 17, 1663. 3rd s. of Sir Thomas (above), of Hanmer, Flint, Knt. and Bart. Adm. at the Inner Temple, Oct. 27, 1666. Barrister, 1673. Solicitor-General to Queen Catharine, 1676-85. Knighted, Dec. 27, 1676. Died Feb. 7, 1682-3. Buried in the Temple Church, London. M.I. there. Brother of William (1663). (Burke, *Ext. Bart.*)

HANMER, THOMAS. Adm. pens. (age 18) at TRINITY, Apr. 13, 1700. S. of Roger, of Selattyn, Salop. School, Shrewsbury (Mr Lloyd). Matric. 1700; Scholar, 1702; B.A. 1703-4; M.A. 1707. Ord. deacon (Ely) Dec. 21, 1707. R. of Selattyn, 1719-50. Died Feb. 4, 1750.

HANMER, Sir THOMAS, Bart. LL.D. 1705 (*Com. Reg.*). S. of William (1663), of Bettesfield, Flints., gent. B. Sept. 24, 1677. Schools, Bury St Edmunds and Westminster. Matric. from Christ Church, Oxford, Oct. 17, 1693, age 17. Succeeded as 4th Bart., 1701. M.P. for Thetford, 1701-2, 1705-8; for Co. Flint, 1702-5; for Suffolk, 1708-27. Speaker of the House of Commons, 1713. Distinguished literary critic. Died May 5, 1746. Buried at Hanmer. (*Al. Oxon.*; A. B. Beaven.)

HANMER, THOMAS. Adm. Fell.-Com. at ST CATHARINE'S, Apr. 25, 1720. S. of William, of the Fenns, Shropshire. Matric. 1720; B.A. 1723-4; M.A. 1729. Incorp. at Oxford, 1731. M.P. for Castle Rising, 1734-7. Died Apr. 1, 1737. Brother of Humphrey (1725). (*Al. Oxon.*)

HANMER, THOMAS. Adm. sizar (age 19) at ST JOHN'S, May 13, 1751. S. of Henry, farmer, of Salop. B. at Montiord. School, Shrewsbury. Matric. 1751; B.A. 1755; M.A. 1758. Ord. deacon (Lichfield) Sept. 24, 1758; priest, Sept. 23, 1759, as C. of Montford, Salop. V. 1775-96. (*Scott-Mayor*, III. 606.)

HANMER, W. Matric. pens. from TRINITY, Michs. 1564.

HANMER, WILLIAM. Adm. Fell.-Com. (age 15) at PEMBROKE, July 17, 1663. S. of Sir Thomas (1627), of Hanmer, Flint., Knt. and Bart. B. at Angies, France. Married Peregrine, dau. of Sir Henry North, Bart. Father of Thomas (1705), 4th Bart., brother of Thomas (1663). (Burke, *Ext. Bart.*; *Lipscomb*, IV. 342; *G.E.C.*)

HANMER, WILLIAM. Adm. at KING'S, a scholar from Eton, 1736. S. of Henry. Bapt. at Montiord, Salop, Dec. 21, 1717. Matric. Michs. 1737; B.A. 1741-2; M.A. 1745. Fellow, 1740. Vice-provost. Ord. deacon (Lincoln) May 25; priest, Sept. 21, 1755. R. of Horstead, Norfolk, 1761-86. R. of Coltishall, 1761-86. Will (P.C.C.) 1786.

HANN, WILLIAM. M.A. 1650 (Incorp. from Oxford). S. of William, of Haslebury, Dorset. Matric. from Queen's College, Oxford, Feb. 11, 1641-2, age 19. Created M.A. from Pembroke, 1648. Fellow of New College, 1648-60, ejected. Licensed to practise medicine, 1657. (*Al. Oxon.*)

HANNAM, JOHN. B.D. 1662 (*Lit. Reg.*). S. of John, of Calne, Wilts. Matric. from All Souls, Oxford, Nov. 7, 1634, age 20; B.A. (Oxford) 1634; M.A. 1637. R. of Dogmersfield, Hants., 1642-6, sequestered. (*Al. Oxon.*)

HANNAM, PHILIP. Matric. pens. from MAGDALENE, Easter, 1639; B.A. 1642; M.A. 1646.

HANNAM, WILLIAM. Adm. at KING'S (age 18) a scholar from Eton, Aug. 25, 1559. Of Combe, Somerset. Matric. 1559; B.A. 1563-4; M.A. 1567. Fellow, 1562-75. Tenant, under the College, of Toft Monk's Wood, 1574. (*Cooper*, II. 1; *Harwood*, who makes the name 'Harman.')

HANNIBAL or HAMBALL, THOMAS. B.Civ.L. 1496; D.Civ.L. 1502; D.Can.L. 1504. Incorp. at Oxford, 1513. Preb. of York, 1504-9. Chancellor of Worcester, 1514. Entered the service of Wolsey and was engaged by him in negotiations with merchants at Bruges, 1515 and 1520. Ambassador at Rome, 1522-4. Master of the Rolls, 1523-7. Author. Died 1531. (*Cooper*, I. 37; *D.N.B.*)

HANNINGTON, HENRY. Adm. p . (age 18) at CAIUS, May 3, 1637. S. of Henry, V. of Hengham, Kent. Bapt. there, Sept. 28, 1617. School, Canterbury (Mr Ludde). Matric. 1639. C. of St James, Dover; and of Buckland, Kent, 1639. V. of Elham, till 1691. Married, 1671, Barbara, dau. of John Dawson, and widow of Wm Somner, the antiquary. Died 1691. (*Venn*, I. 326; H. G. Harrison.)

HANNY, GEORGE. Adm. Fell.-Com. (age 18) at TRINITY, July 8, 1718. S. of James, of Barbadoes, West Indies. School, Caddington, Herts. Matric. 1719.

HANNY, JOHN. Adm. at KING'S, a scholar from Eton, 1450.

HANSARD, HAMMOND. '4 years at Cambridge.' B.A. (Oxford) 1555-6. S. of Richard, of Biscathorpe, Lincs. Ord. priest (Suffragan Bishop of London) Apr. 28, 1547. R. of Scartho, Lincs., 1560. Of the same names were the V. of Chilham, Kent, 1552; the R. of Routh, Yorks., 1575; and of St Ewe, Cornwall, 1579. Will proved (Lincoln) Mar. 25, 1595. Perhaps father of the next. (*Al. Oxon.*; *Lincs. Pedigrees*, 452.)

HANSARD, RICHARD. Matric. pens. from MAGDALENE, Easter, 1581-2. Perhaps s. of Hammond (above). B.A. 1581-2; M.A. 1585.

HANSBY, EDWARD. Matric. pens. from ST JOHN'S, Lent, 1557-8. S. of Richard, of New Malton, Yorks. B.A. 1560-1; M.A. 1564; B.D. 1569. Fellow, 1561. Ord. deacon (Ely) July 29, 1565; priest, Aug. 24, 1566. University preacher, 1566. Chaplain to the Duke of Norfolk. R. of Greystoke, Cumberland, 1568-85. Preb. of Carlisle, 1584. Married Margaret, dau. of Brian Snawsell. (*Cooper*, I. 283; Hunter, *S. Yorks.*; *Vis. of Yorks.*, 1584.)

HANSBY, RALPH. Matric. pens. from ST JOHN'S, Easter, 1604. Of Cumberland. B.A. 1607-8; M.A. 1611. Fellow, 1609. Taxor, 1616. Incorp. at Oxford, 1611. Ord. priest (Peterb.) May 26, 1616. R. of Barton-in-Fabis, Notts., 1616-35. V. of St Mary's, Nottingham, 1617-35. Died Nov. 20, 1635. Buried at Nottingham. M.I. at St Mary's.

HANSBY, WILLIAM. Matric. pens. from ST JOHN'S, *c.* 1596. Of Cumberland. B.A. 1600-1; M.A. 1604. Fellow, 1602. Incorp. at Oxford, 1612. Ord. deacon (York) June, 1612; priest (Peterb.) May 26, 1616.

HANSCOMBE, JAMES. Adm. sizar (age 16) at PETERHOUSE, Mar. 24, 1700-1. Of Bedfordshire. S. of William. Bapt. at Shillington, Nov. 22, 1684. School, Pertenhall, Beds. Matric. 1701; Scholar, 1701; B.A. 1704-5; M.A. 1708. Ord. deacon (Ely) May 30, 1708; priest, Sept. 25, 1709. R. of Meppershall, Beds., 1712-4. Buried there June 17, 1714. (W. M. Noble.)

HANSCOMBE, JOHN. Adm. pens. at EMMANUEL, Apr. 17, 1628. Of Hertfordshire. Matric. 1628, as 'Lanscombe.'

HANSCOMBE, MATTHEW. Matric. pens. from ST JOHN'S, Easter, 1621. Migrated to Emmanuel, 1623. B.A. 1624-5; M.A. 1628. Ord. deacon (Peterb.) Sept. 19; priest, Sept. 20, 1629.

HANSCOMBE, MATTHEW. Matric. pens. from PETERHOUSE, Michs. 1632. Of Bedfordshire. B.A. 1636-7; M.A. 1640. Fellow, 1639. Ord. deacon (Peterb.) Sept. 19, 1641. Buried at Little St Mary's, Cambridge, Mar. 19, 1643-4.

HANSCOMBE, MATTHEW. Adm. scholar (age 17) at SIDNEY, June 1, 1710. 3rd s. of Robert, gent., of Henlow, Beds. B. there. Bapt. Sept. 4, 1692. School, Wrestlingworth (Mr Bristow). Matric. 1710; B.A. 1713-4. Ord. deacon (Lincoln) Sept. 23, 1716; priest, Sept. 22, 1717. Signs as minister of Langford, Beds., 1726. V. of Old Warden, 1727-38. (W. M. Noble.)

HANSCOMBE, ROBERT. Adm. pens. at ST CATHARINE'S, Easter, 1649; B.A. 1652-3; M.A. 1656.

HANSCOMBE, THOMAS. Matric. pens. from TRINITY, Easter, 1613. B. at Purton, Herts. Migrated to Emmanuel, Dec. 13, 1614. B.A. 1616-7; M.A. 1620. Fellow of Emmanuel, 1620. Ord. priest (London) May 23, 1624. Died at Hildersham, Cambs. Buried there Oct. 13, 1625. Will proved (V.C.C.)

HANSCOME, WILLIAM. Matric. pens. from ST JOHN'S, Easter, 1610.

HANSE, EVERARD. Stated to have been at Cambridge and for some years to have held a living. Of Northamptonshire. Joined the Church of Rome. Adm. at Rheims College, June 11, 1580. Ord. priest, Mar. 25, 1581. Sent to England, and seized soon afterwards. Executed at Tyburn, July 31, 1581. Beatified by Leo XIII, 1886. (Camm's *Martyrs*, II. 249.)

HANSES, CHARLES. Adm. sizar (age 17) at MAGDALENE, May 4, 1677. Migrated to St John's, Oct. 15, 1677. S. of John, gent., of York. B. at Selby, Yorks. School, Archbishop Holgate's, York. Adm. at Gray's Inn, June 17, 1681. Barrister, 1683.

HANSFYLDE, CHARLES. Matric. pens. from QUEENS', Michs. 1545.

HANSLEP, ——. B.Can.L. 1489.

HANSLEY, JOHN. Matric. sizar from PETERHOUSE, Easter, 1546.

HANSLEY, JOHN. Adm. sizar at PETERHOUSE, July 4, 1618. Of Yorkshire. Matric. 1618; B.A. 1621-2; M.A. 1625. Ord. deacon (Peterb.) Sept. 24, 1626; probably priest, Feb. 1626-7. Chaplain to Bishop of London. Preb. of St Paul's, 1639-67. R. of St Christopher-le-Stock, London, 1640-3. R. of Paglesham, Essex, Oct. 2, 1641. Archdeacon of Colchester, 1660-7. R. of Albury, Surrey, 1660. Died 1667. Will, P.C.C. (*T. A. Walker*, 10.)

HANSLEY, LEONARD. Matric. sizar from PEMBROKE, Michs. 1546.

HANSON, *see also* HANDSOM.

HANSON, ANTHONY. Adm. sizar (age 20) at ST JOHN'S, Apr. 29, 1717. S. of Thomas (1675), clerk, of Yorkshire. B. at Thornton, near Skipton. School, Sedbergh. Matric. 1717; B.A. 1720-1; M.A. 1724. Ord. deacon (York) June 4, 1721; priest (Ely) May 19, 1722. (*Scott-Mayor*, III. 309.)

HANSON, EDMUND. B.A. 1463-4; M.A. 1467; B.D. 1471-2. D.D. 1488. Proctor, 1471-2. V. of Orwell, Cambs., 1481-1504. Preb. of Lincoln, 1504-12. Precentor, 1506-12. Probably R. of Hemingford Abbots, Hunts., 1492-1512. Died 1512.

HANSOM, GEORGE. Matric. sizar from MAGDALENE, Michs. 1565. B. 1549. Ord. priest (Lincoln) Apr. 11, 1568; 'married; resides; skilled in Latin.' Perhaps V. of Alford, Lincs., 1574-5. V. of Tathwell, 1575. R. of Withcall, 1592-1600. Will of one of these names (Lincoln) 1607; of Trusthorpe, Lincs., clerk. (*Lib. Cler. Linc.*, 1576.)

HANSOME or HANDSON, JOHN. Matric. pens. from MAGDALENE, Easter, 1560; B.A. 1564-5; M.A. from Trinity, 1568. Fellow of Trinity, 1565. University preacher, 1575. Preacher at St James, Bury St Edmunds. Deprived for nonconformity, 1581. (*Cooper*, I. 452.)

HANSOME or HANDSON, JOHN. Matric. sizar from PETERHOUSE, Easter, 1560; Scholar of Trinity, 1562; B.A. 1562-3; M.A. 1566; B.D. 1573; D.D. 1583. Fellow of Trinity, 1565. Lady Margaret Professor of Divinity, 1573-4. Ord. deacon (Ely) June 2, 1570; priest, Dec. 21, 1572. V. of Chesterton, Cambs., 1574. Preb. of Lincoln, 1576-1618. R. of Irnham, Lincs., 1583. V. of All Saints', Stamford. Buried at Nassington, 1618. Will (P.C.C.) 1618; of Nassington, Northants.

HANSON, JOHN. B.A. from PETERHOUSE, 1603-4. Author, poetical. (*D.N.B.*; *Cooper*, II. 399.)

HANSON, JOHN. Adm. sizar (age 16) at ST JOHN'S, June 24, 1657. S. of William, ironmonger, of Boston. B. there. School, Boston (Mr Ashon). Matric. 1657; B.A. 1660-1; M.A. 1664. Ord. deacon (Lincoln). One of these names V. of Honley, Yorks., till 1681. Buried Dec. 27, 1681.

HANDSON, JONATHAN. Adm. pens. at ST JOHN'S, June 17, 1714. Matric. 1714. S. of John, druggist. B. in Lancashire. School, Sedbergh. Adm. at Trinity College, Dublin, May 27, 1710, age 18; B.A. (Dublin) 1714. Ord. deacon (York) Sept. 1715.

HANDSON, JOSEPH. Adm. sizar (age 18) at TRINITY, June 27, 1698. S. of George, of Staffordshire. School, Uttoxeter (Mr Bouquet). Matric. 1699, as Hanson.

HANSON, SIMON. Matric. sizar from CORPUS CHRISTI, Easter, 1632. Of Derbyshire. Migrated to Jesus, Mar. 17, 1633-4. Scholar of Jesus; B.A. 1635-6; M.A. 1639. Fellow of Jesus, 1638-44, ejected. Died before 1660. (A. Gray.)

HANSON or HAMPSON, THOMAS. B.A. 1524-5.

HANSON, THOMAS. Adm. sizar (age 17) at ST JOHN'S, Apr. 24, 1675. S. of Thomas, clothdresser, of Southowram, Yorks. B. there. School, Sedbergh. Matric. 1675; B.A. 1678-9; M.A. 1682. Ord. deacon (York) June 6, 1680. R. of Thornton-in-Craven, Yorks., 1678-99. Died 1699. Buried Jan. 26. Father of Anthony (1717). (*Vis. of Yorks.*, 1665; H. M. Peacock.)

HANSON, WILLIAM. Matric. sizar from ST JOHN'S, Easter, 1621; B.A. 1624-5; M.A. 1628. Perhaps V. of Twerton, Somerset, 1638-68. One of these names R. of Little Braxted, Essex, *c.* 1650.

HANTON (? HUNTON), HENRY. Matric. sizar from PETERHOUSE, Easter, 1588-9.

HANWAY or HANNEY, JOHN. Adm. pens. (age 19) at TRINITY, June 28, 1690. S. of William. B. at Westminster. School, Westminster. Matric. 1690; Scholar, 1691; B.A. 1693-4.

HANWORTH, NICHOLAS DE. Proctor, 1335-6.

HAPGOOD, THOMAS. Adm. pens. (age 18) at PETERHOUSE, Oct. 14, 1710. Of Middlesex. School, Eton. Matric. 1711; Scholar, 1711.

HARBARD, EDWARD. Matric. Fell.-Com. from PETERHOUSE, Michs. 1561. Probably Edward Herbert, 2nd s. of William, 1st Earl of Pembroke, Knighted 1574. Of Powys Castle. Brother of Henry Herbert. (*T. A. Walker*.)

HARBERT, *see also* HERBERT.

HARBERT, ABIEZER. Matric. sizar from CLARE, Easter, 1613; B.A. 1616-7.

HARBERT or HERBERT, GEORGE. Matric. sizar from CHRIST'S, Easter, 1604. S. of Ralph, of Holmyers, Durham. Bapt. Feb. 24, 1584-5. B.A. 1607-8; M.A. 1611. V. of Renhold, Beds., 1616-35. Brother of Henry (next), Steven (1606) and perhaps Robert (1606). (*Peile*, I. 250; *Surtees*, II. 205.)

HARBART or HERBERT, HENRY. Matric. pens. from CHRIST'S, July, 1610. S. of Ralph, of Holmyers, Chester-le-Street, Durham. Brother of the above. (*Peile*, I. 276; Surtees, *Durham*, II. 205.)

'HARBART,' JOHN. Matric. pens. from EMMANUEL, Easter, 1647; *see* Hobart.

HARBART, RICHARD. Matric. Fell.-Com. from TRINITY, Lent, 1623-4.

HARBART, ROBERT. Matric. sizar from CHRIST'S, July, 1606. Perhaps brother of George (1604).

HARBART, ROWLAND. Matric. pens. from TRINITY, Easter, 1588-9.

HARBART or HERBERT, STEVEN. Matric. pens. from CHRIST'S, Apr. 1606. Kept some terms at Cambridge. Migrated to Oxford. B.A. (Jesus College, Oxford) 1609; M.A. 1612. Probably ord. deacon (Lichfield) Oct. 1614; and C. of Letchworth, Herts. Brother of George (1604). (*Peile*, I. 255.)

HARBATYLL, RALPH. B.D. 1465-6. Studied also at Oxford.

HARBIN, GEORGE. Adm. pens. at EMMANUEL, Mar. 13, 1682-3. Matric. 1683; B.A. 1686-7. Migrated to Jesus, as Fell.-Com. Mar. 30, 1688. Chaplain to Bishop Turner, of Ely, and to Viscount Weymouth. Friend of Bishop Ken. Non-juror. Author. Died Sept. 1744. Will, P.C.C. (*D.N.B.*; *L. Mag.*)

HARBIN, JOSEPH. Adm. pens. (age 16) at ST JOHN'S, Mar. 16, 1701-2. S. of John, schoolmaster. B. at Trent, Somerset. School, Dorchester (Mr Place). Matric. 1702; B.A. 1705-6. Master of Beminster School, Dorset, 1709-11. V. of Poor-Stock, 1711-38. Died 1738. (*Hutchins*, II. 322.)

HARBORNE, WILLIAM. Matric. pens. from TRINITY, Easter, 1623. Of Norfolk; probably Mundham. Migrated to St Catharine's. B.A. 1626-7; M.A. 1630. V. of Kirton, Notts.; ejected, 1662. Retired into Norfolk. Perhaps the same who was presented to Chevening, Kent, 1645. (*Calamy*, II. 289.)

HARBOROUGH, JOHN. Adm. Fell.-Com. at EMMANUEL, July 2, 1679. Of Norfolk. Matric. 1680; M.D. 1683. Will (P.C.C.) 1705; of St Gregory's, London, M.D. (J. Ch. Smith.)

HARBREED, WILLIAM. Matric. Fell.-Com. from St John's, Easter, 1623. Perhaps s. and h. of Richard, of Ledsham, Leeds, Yorks.; age 7 in 1612. Probably of Wistow, Yorks. Married Mary, dau. of Thomas Best, of Wath, 1630. Died before his father. (M. H. Peacock; *Vis. of Yorks.*)

HARBREDE, ——. B.A. 1484–5.

HAREBRON or HARBURNE, HUGH. Adm. at King's (age 16) a scholar from Eton, Aug. 1, 1508. Of Liverpool. B.A. 1512–3. Fellow, 1511–4. Died 1514.

HARBROUNE, THOMAS. Matric. pens. from Jesus, Michs. 1555.

HARBROWNE, THOMAS. Adm. at Corpus Christi, 1560.

HARBYE, ANTHONY. Matric. pens. from Trinity, Easter, 1559.

HARBY, CLEMENT. Matric. pens. from Trinity, Easter, 1622. Probably 3rd s. of Francis, of Adston, Northants., Esq.; adm. at Lincoln's Inn, Feb. 7, 1625–6. Died unmarried in Ireland. Probably brother of Edward (1614). (*Baker*, II. 19.)

HARBY, CLEMENT. Adm. Fell.-Com. at Emmanuel, Easter, 1635. 2nd s. of Sir Thomas, Knt., of Wallington, Surrey. Matric. 1635. Adm. at the Inner Temple, 1638. Knighted, Apr. 21, 1669. (*Le Neve*, 221.)

HARBY, EDWARD. Adm. Fell.-Com. at Sidney, May 28, 1614. Matric. 1614. Probably s. and h. of Francis, of Adston, Northants., Esq., deceased; adm. at Lincoln's Inn, May 11, 1618. Sheriff of Northants., 1643–4. M.P. for Higham Ferrers, 1645–53, 1659, 1660. Married Elizabeth, dau. of Henry Freeman, of Higham Ferrers. Died July 9, 1674. Probably brother of Clement (1622). (*Baker*, II. 19; A. B. Beaven.)

HARBY, EDWARD. Adm. pens. (age 19) at Peterhouse, Mar. 20, 1718–9. Of Huntingdonshire. S. of Francis, of Wapenham, Northants. School, Wollaston, Northants. Matric. 1719; Scholar, 1719; LL.B. 1724. R. of Cowden, Kent, 1732–61. Died May 22, 1761. M.I. at Cowden.

HARBY, FRANCIS. Matric. Fell.-Com. from King's, Easter, 1680–1. Doubtless s. of Edward; age 19 in 1681. Of Adston, Northants. Sold Adston, 1720. Married Parnel, dau. of Samuel Trist, of Culworth and Whitfield, Esq. (*Baker*, II. 19.)

HARBIE, JOHN. Described as 'M.A. from Christ's,' when ord. deacon (London) Mar. 18, 1603–4, age 25. B. in the parish of St Michael, Cornhill. Probably s. of Erasmus, citizen and skinner of that parish. Ord. priest, Mar. 25, 1604. C. of Ockendon, Essex. Will (Consist. C. London) 1612; minister of the word of God. (Not found in Cambridge records.) (*Vis. of Northants.*, 1564; J. Ch. Smith.)

HARBY or HARVEY, JOHN. Matric. pens. from Corpus Christi, Easter, 1618–9; B.A. 1622–3; M.A. 1626. Ord. deacon (Peterb.) May 23, 1624; priest, June 4, 1626. P.C. of Tiltey, Essex, 1628. R. of Little Yeldham, 1635–42. Died 1642. Will (P.C.C.) 1645; Harvey, *alias* Harby.

HAREBY, JOHN. Matric. pens. from Magdalene, Easter, 1620–1; B.A. 1624–5; M.A. 1628.

HARBY, JOHN. Matric. sizar from Magdalene, Easter, 1627; B.A. 1630–1; M.A. 1634. Ord. deacon (Peterb.) Dec. 18, 1631. V. of Hibaldstow, Lincs., 1637. Father of the next.

HARBY, JOHN. Adm. sizar (age 16) at Magdalene, June 5, 1657. S. of John (1627) clerk, of Halston (? Hibaldstow), Lincs. School, Lincoln. Matric. 1657; B.A. 1660–1; M.A. 1665. Ord. deacon (Lincoln) Aug. 31, 1662; priest (Lincoln) Sept. 24, 1671. R. of Snelland, Lincs.

HARBY, THOMAS. Adm. pens. at Queens', Aug. 28, 1622. Of Middlesex. Matric. 1622. Migrated to Emmanuel, Oct. 1622.

HARBY, WILLIAM. B.A. from Magdalene, 1613–4; M.A. 1617. Ord. deacon (York, for Lincoln) Sept. 1616; priest (Peterb.) June 15, 1617. P.C. of Ramsey, Hunts., 1618–29.

HARBY, WILLIAM. Matric. sizar from Christ's, Apr. 1617, as 'Harvey'; B.A. 1620–1; M.A. 1624.

HARBY, WILLIAM. Adm. sizar at Jesus, June 25, 1694. Of Hampshire. Matric. 1696; B.A. 1697–8.

HARBY, ——. Adm. Fell.-Com. at Emmanuel, 1624–5.

HARCOCKE, EDMUND. Adm. pens. (age 17) at Caius, June 14, 1643. S. of Gregory, attorney-at-law, of Norfolk. School, Norwich (Mr Lovering). Matric. 1643; Scholar, 1644–7. Adm. at Gray's Inn, May 28, 1647; of Worstead, Norfolk. Brother of the next. One of these names buried at Worstead, Mar. 8, 1657–8. (*Venn*, I. 350.)

HARCOCKE, HENRY. Adm. pens. (age 17) at Caius, May 23, 1650. S. of Gregory, attorney, of Worstead, Norfolk. B there. Schools, North Walsham (Mr Warnes) and Norwich (Mr Lovering). Matric. 1650; Scholar, 1650–7; B.A. 1653–4; M.A. 1657. Incorp. at Oxford, 1657. Probably V. of East Ruston, Norfolk, 1657–61; appointed June 19, 1657, by the Trustees for the maintenance of ministers (*Lamb MS.*, 968, p. 118). Married Mary, dau. of Arthur Branthwaite, of Hethel, Norfolk. Brother of the above. (*Venn*, I. 380; *Vis. of Norfolk*, 1664.)

HARCOTT, GEORGE. Matric. sizar from Trinity, Michs. 1550.

HARCOURT, BOYS. Adm. sizar at Corpus Christi, 1691. S. of John, of Barton Turf, Norfolk. Matric. 1691; M.B. 1696. Died 1697, aged 22.

HARCOURT, FRANCIS. Adm. pens. at Emmanuel, Easter, 1623. Doubtless s. of Sir Robert, and brother of Vere (1623). Matric. 1623; B.A. 1626–7; M.A. 1630. R. of Plumtree, Notts., 1647.

HARCOURT, HENRY. Adm. pens. (age 19) at Peterhouse, Dec. 27, 1749. Of Middlesex. S. of Henry, of Hertfordshire. School, Luton (private). Matric. 1750; Scholar, 1750; B.A. 1754; M.A. 1757. Fellow, 1756. Ord. priest (Lincoln) Dec. 22, 1754. R. of Warbleton, and of Crowhurst, Sussex. Died Aug. 21, 1800, at Warbleton. Will, P.C.C. Brother of Richard (1742). (*T. A. Walker*; *Lipscomb*, IV. 591.)

HARCOURT, JOHN. Adm. at Corpus Christi, 1701. Of Norfolk. Matric. 1702; B.A. 1705–6.

HARCOURT, RICHARD BARD. Adm. pens. (age 18) at Caius, Nov. 26, 1742. S. of Henry, Esq., of Pendley, Herts. B. in London. School, Eton. Matric. 1743. Adm. at Lincoln's Inn, Feb. 11, 1743. Of Pendley, Herts., Esq. Married Rachel, dau. of Albert Nesbitt, Esq., 1756. Died Jan. 27, 1815. Brother of Henry (1749). (*Venn*, II. 52; *Clutterbuck*, I. 285; *Lipscomb*, IV. 591.)

HARCOURT, VERE. Adm. pens. at Emmanuel, 1623. S. of Sir Robert, Knt. Matric. 1623–4; B.A. 1626–7; M.A. 1630; D.D. 1661 (*Lit. Reg.*). R. of Plumtree, Notts. Lecturer at St Andrew, Holborn, 1642. Archdeacon of Nottingham, 1660–83. Preb. of Lincoln, 1661–83. Died 1683. (Burke, *L.G.*; *Lipscomb*, IV. 591.)

HARCOURT, ——. Adm. Fell.-Com. at Trinity, 1654.

HARDACRE, HENRY. Adm. sizar at Emmanuel, Jan. 27, 1691–2. Of Yorkshire. Matric. 1695; B.A. 1695–6; M.A. 1699. Ord. priest (Lincoln) Feb. 28, 1696–7. R. of Little Brickhill, Bucks., c. 1694–6. C. of Husborne Crawley, Beds., 1695–1707. R. of Millbrook, 1703. C. of Litlington, 1704–25. R. of Drayton Parslow, Bucks., 1708.

HARDANE, GUY. B.Can.L. 1466–7.

HARDCASTLE, CYRIL. Adm. pens. (age 18) at St John's, May 31, 1715. S. of Thomas, clerk, deceased. B. in Ireland. School, Threshfield, Yorks. Matric. 1715; B.A. 1718–9.

HARDCASTLE, JOHN. Adm. sizar (age 18) at Christ's, Apr. 14, 1680. S. of Thomas. B. at Leeds. School, Leeds (Mr Gilbert). Matric. 1680; B.A. 1683–4; M.A. 1693. Ord. deacon (London) Feb. 24, 1683–4; priest, Dec. 20, 1685. (*Peile*, II. 77.)

HARDCASTLE, JOHN. Adm. sizar (age 17) at Peterhouse, Mar. 15, 1715–6. Of Middlesex. Schools, Stockton, Durham, and Richmond, Yorks. Scholar, 1716; LL.B. 1721.

HARDCASTLE, THOMAS. Adm. sizar (age 15) at St John's, June 21, 1652. S. of John, yeoman, of Barwick-in-Elmet, Yorks. B. there. School, Sherburn, Yorks. (Mr Ginnings). Matric. 1652; B.A. 1655–6. V. of Bramham, Yorks.; ejected, 1662. Preacher in Yorks. Suffered frequent imprisonment for Nonconformity. Baptist minister at Broadmead, Bristol. Author, *Sermons*. Died Sept. 29, 1678. (*Calamy*, II. 557; *D.N.B.*)

HARDCASTLE, THOMAS. Adm. sizar (age 15) at St John's, July 3, 1654. S. of William, of Kirkby Malzeard, Yorks. B. there. School, Wakefield (Mr Doughty).

HARDCASTLE, THOMAS. Adm. pens. (age 16) at Christ's, Apr. 21, 1671. S. of William. B. at Laverton, near Kirkby Malzeard, Yorks. School, Ripon (Mr Oxley). Matric. 1671; B.A. 1674–5; M.A. 1678. Ord. priest (London) Sept. 23, 1677. (Burke, *L.G.*)

HARDCASTLE, WILLIAM. Matric. pens. from Clare, Easter, 1584–5; B.A. 1588–9.

HARDCASTLE, WILLIAM. Matric. pens. from Trinity, Michs. 1610.

HARDEN, RICHARD. B.A. in 1533–4, when he was taking duty at Croxton, Cambs. Perhaps of Christ's. (*Peile*, I. 19.)

HARDER, JOHN. Adm. sizar (age 18) at St John's, July 20, 1668. S. of Henry, of Barnstaple, Devon. B. there. School, Barnstaple. Matric. 1668. Will of one of these names (Exeter) 1722; of Bittadon, Devon, clerk.

HARDEST, WILLIAM. B.Civ.L. 1483–4. Of Ely diocese. Ord. deacon (Norwich) Sept. 24; priest, Dec. 17, 1485; title, St Rhadegunde's.

HARDESTEE, CHARLES. Adm. sizar at JESUS, Apr. 20, 1702. Of Derbyshire. Matric. 1702-3; B.A. 1705-6. R. of Fenny Bentley, Derbs., 1707-47.

HARDISTY, JOHN. Adm. sizar at EMMANUEL, Apr. 1, 1678, as Hartistie. Of Yorkshire. Matric. 1678.

HARDESTY or HARDESTRE, WILLIAM. Matric. sizar from TRINITY, Easter, 1575; B.A. 1578-9; B.D. 1608. Incorp. at Oxford, 1608, as M.A. V. of Lanteglos-by-Fowey, Cornwall, 1597; or V. of Otley, Yorks., 1603. (*Al. Oxon.*)

HARDESTY or HARDESTRY, WILLIAM. Adm. sizar at JESUS, June 26, 1668. Of Derbyshire. Matric. 1668; B.A. 1671-2; M.A. 1677. Usher at Repton School, 1672-6. Master of Ashbourne School, 1677-1712. Perhaps R. of Fenny Bentley, Derbs., 1702-7 (*see* Charles, above). Died 1712.

HARDHED, ——. B.A. 1464-5; M.A. 1467-8. Will (P.C.C.) 1483, of John Hardheede, M.A., of TRINITY HALL; of Rattlesden, Suffolk. (J. Ch. Smith.)

HARDHED, ——. Fee for M.A. or higher degree, 1465-6.

HARDINGE, BROWNELL (? BROWNHILL). Adm. pens. (age 17) at TRINITY, Aug. 29, 1678. Of Northamptonshire. S. of Nicholas. B. at Stilton, Hunts. (his mother's home). School, St Paul's.

HARDINGE, CALEB. Adm. pens. at JESUS, June 18, 1717. S. of Gideon (1684), late V. of Kingston-on-Thames. Bapt. Mar. 23, 1700-1. Rustat scholar, 1718; B.A. 1720-1; M.A. 1724. Grace for M.D. 1728 (*Com. Reg.*). Fellow, 1722-33. Physician to George III. Physician to the Tower. F.R.S. 1753. Died at Mansfield, Nov. 1775. Brother of Nicholas (1718). (A. Gray; G. *Mag.*; *Manning and Bray*, I. 383.)

HARDING, CHARLES. Adm. sizar at TRINITY, Apr. 23, 1669. One of these names s. of Nathan, of Agmondesham, Bucks., matric. from Merton College, Oxford, May 11, 1669, age 16. (*Al. Oxon.*)

HARDING, CHARLES. Matric. sizar from KING'S, 1697. B. in London. Doubtless elected colleger at Eton, 1693, age 14. Left Eton, 1696. B.A. 1700-1.

HARDING, DANIEL. Matric. sizar from MAGDALENE, 1633; B.A. 1636-7; M.A. 1640. Of Rolleston, Notts., clerk (*see* Francis (1661)).

HARDING, DANIEL. Adm. sizar (age 19) at ST JOHN'S, June 19, 1714. S. of Hugh, deceased. B. at Farnsfield, near Southwell, Notts. School, Southwell. Matric. 1714; B.A. 1718-9. Ord. deacon (York) Nov. 1718; priest, 1720.

HARDING, FRANCIS. Adm. pens. (age 17) at MAGDALENE, June 10, 1661. S. of Daniel (1633), clerk, of Rolleston, Notts. School, Melton, Leics. Matric. 1661; B.A. 1664-5.

HARDYNG, GEORGE. Matric. sizar from PETERHOUSE, Easter, 1545.

HARDING, GEORGE. Matric. sizar from TRINITY, 1637-8; B.A. 1640-1. P.C. of Whittington, Staffs., 1651-82. Buried Jan. 30, 1681-2. (*Wm. Salt Arch. Soc.*, 1915.)

HARDINGE, GIDEON. Adm. pens. at JESUS, May 31, 1684. Of Derbyshire. S. of Sir Robert, of King's Newton, Melbourne, Derbs., Kut., Recorder of Nottingham. School, Loughborough. Matric. 1684; Scholar, 1684; B.A. 1687-8; M.A. 1691. V. of Kingston, Surrey, 1692-1713. Buried Jan. 28, 1712-3. Father of Caleb (1717) and Nicholas (1718), brother of Robert (1674) and Nicholas (1674), ancestor of the present Viscount Hardinge. (Le Neve, *Knights*, 297.)

HARDING, JOHN. Scholar of QUEENS', 1562; B.A. 1564-5.

HARDINGE, JOHN. Matric. pens. from JESUS, Easter, 1577; B.A. 1580-1; M.A. 1584.

HARDING, JOHN. M.A. 1584 (Incorp. from Oxford). B.A. (Oxford) 1577-8; M.A. 1581; B.D. 1592; D.D. 1597. Proctor, 1589. Fellow of Magdalen College, Oxford; President, 1607-10. Regius Professor of Hebrew, Oxford, 1591-8. R. of Gt Haseley, Oxon., 1597. Preb. of Lincoln, 1604-10. Died 1610. Will (P.C.C.) 1611. (*Cooper*, III. 33; *Al. Oxon.*)

HARDING, JOHN. Matric. sizar from CHRIST'S, July, 1616. Doubtless s. of Richard, of Betley, Staffs. B. June 8, 1600. B.A. 1619-20; M.A. 1623. Incorp. at Oxford, 1623. Fellow of Trinity College, Dublin, by *mandamus* of Lord Deputy, 1636. Vice-Provost, 1637. Tutor to the s. of the Lord Deputy. Chancellor of Christ Church, 1639; deprived, 1643. Died June, 1664. (*Peile*, I. 310; Burke, *L.G.*; *Al. Dub.*)

HARDING, JOHN. Adm. sizar (age 17) at MAGDALENE, May 28, 1666. S. of John, farmer, of Bonsall, Derbs. School, Wirksworth. Matric. 1667; B.A. 1670-1. Ord. priest (Lincoln) Sept. 24, 1671. R. of Maplethorpe, Lincs.

HARDING, JOHN. Adm. pens. (age 16) at PETERHOUSE, May 19, 1670. Of Bedfordshire. School, Bedford. Matric. 1670; Scholar, 1670; B.A. 1673-4. Probably ord. priest (Lincoln) May 29, 1681; C. of Langford, Beds. V. of Riseley, 1690.

HARDING, JOHN. Adm. Fell.-Com. at EMMANUEL, Oct. 21, 1704. Of Derbyshire. Doubtless s. and h. of Robert (1674), of King's Newton, Derbs. Bapt. at Melbourne, Sept. 26, 1685. Matric. 1704; M.A. 1705 (*Com. Reg.*). Deputy Remembrancer in the Exchequer, 1715. Buried at Melbourne, Jan. 27, 1728-9. M.I. (Le Neve, *Knights*, 297; J. J. Briggs, *Melbourne*.)

HARDING, JOHN. M.A. from KING'S, 1732. S. of Egerton, of Whitmore, Staffs., clerk. Matric. from Balliol College, Oxford, May 29, 1717, age 18; B.A. (Oxford) 1720-1. R. of Wolstanton and Keele, Staffs. Died Apr. 24, 1743. Brother of Robert (1732). (*Al. Oxon.*)

HARDING, MICHAEL. M.A. 1676 (Incorp. from Oxford). S. of William, of Holywell parish, Oxford. Matric. from Trinity College, Oxford, Dec. 12, 1665, age 16; B.A. (Oxford) 1669; M.A. 1672; B.D. 1684. Fellow of Trinity College. Will (Oxford) 1697. (*Al. Oxon.*)

HARDING, NICHOLAS. Adm. pens. (age 16) at ST JOHN'S, June 4, 1674. S. of Robert, barrister, of Brancote, Notts. B. there. School, Repton. Probably adm. at Gray's Inn, Nov. 24, 1669. Died before 1679. Brother of Robert (1674) and Gideon (1684). (*Vis. of Derbs.*, 1662.)

HARDINGE, NICHOLAS. Adm. at KING'S, a scholar from Eton, 1718. S. of Gideon (1684), V. of Kingston-on-Thames. B. at Canbury, Kingston, 1699. Matric. Easter, 1718-9; B.A. 1722-3; M.A. 1726. Fellow, 1722. Adm. at the Middle Temple, Oct. 12, 1721. Barrister-at-law. Clerk of the House of Commons, 1731-48. M.P. for Eye, Suffolk, 1748-58. Secretary of the Treasury, 1752-58. Author, poetry. Married Jane, dau. of Sir John Pratt. Died Apr. 9, 1758. Buried at Kingston. Brother of Caleb (1717). (*D.N.B.*; A. B. Beaven.)

HARDINGE, RANDOLPH. Adm. sizar at JESUS, Feb. 26, 1625-6. Of Salop. Matric. 1626.

HARDING, RANDOLPH. Adm. sizar (age 19) at CHRIST'S, June 3, 1671. S. of Randolph. B. at Minshull, Cheshire. Teacher, Mr Coulton. Matric. 1671; B.A. 1674-5. (*Peile*, II. 36.)

HARDING, RICHARD. Adm. sizar at QUEENS', Easter, 1581.

HARDING, RICHARD. Matric. sizar from JESUS, Lent, 1581-2.

HARDING, RICHARD. M.A. 1641-2 (on King's visit).

HARDING, ROBERT. Matric. sizar from KING'S, Easter, 1659; B.A. from Trinity Hall, 1662.

HARDING, ROBERT. Adm. pens. (age 14) at ST JOHN'S, June 4, 1674. S. of Robert, of Newton Regis, Derbs., barrister. B. there. School, Repton. Adm. at Gray's Inn, May 8, 1676. Of King's Newton, Esq. Married Jane, dau. of William Buxton, of Youlgrave, Derbs. Died Oct. 16, 1709. Buried at Melbourne. M.I. Brother of Nicholas (1674) and Gideon (1684), father of John (1704). (J. J. Briggs, *Melbourne*.)

HARDING, ROBERT. M.A. from KING'S, 1732. S. of Egerton, of Whitmore, Staffs., clerk. Matric. from Balliol College, Oxford, Mar. 2, 1724-5, age 18; B.A. (Oxford) 1728. Ord. deacon (London) Dec. 22, 1728; priest (Llandaff) Mar. 14, 1729-30. R. of Potterspury, Northants., 1729-67. R. of Ashton, 1739-67. Buried at Potterspury, Apr. 18, 1767. M.I. Brother of John (1732). (*Al. Oxon.*; *Baker*, II. 127.)

HARDING, SAMUEL. Adm. pens. at EMMANUEL, Nov. 6, 1599. Matric. 1599; B.A. 1603-4; M.A. 1607. Ord. deacon (Colchester) May 21, 1607; priest, Sept. 20, 1607. C. of Pirton, Herts., 1613. Perhaps R. of Gt Ellingham, Norfolk, 1631-9. Died 1639.

HARDING, SAMUEL. Matric. sizar from ST JOHN'S, Easter, 1607. B. in Westminster. B.A. 1610-1; M.A. 1614. Incorp. at Oxford, 1615. Ord. deacon (London) Feb. 25, 1615-6; priest, May 31, 1618. C. of Petworth, Sussex. R. of Christon, Somerset, 1619-39. Died 1639.

HARDING, SAMUEL. Matric. sizar from ST CATHARINE'S, Easter, 1632. Of Suffolk. S. of Robert, of Ipswich. Migrated to Exeter College, Oxford. Matric. there, Apr. 17, 1635, age 19; B.A. (Oxford) 1638. Ord. deacon (Norwich) Sept. 25, 1642. V. of St Stephen, Norwich, 1642-62. R. of Barford, Norfolk, 1662-94; and of Colney, 1670-94. Dramatist. (*Al. Oxon.*; *D.N.B.*)

HARDING, SAMUEL. Adm. sizar at EMMANUEL, May 29, 1651. Of Norfolk. Matric. 1651; B.A. 1654; M.A. 1658. C. of St Saviour, Norwich, 1673.

HARDING, SAMUEL. Adm. sizar (age 18) at MAGDALENE, July 2, 1739. S. of Samuel. B. in London. Matric. 1740.

HARDING, SAMUEL. Adm. sizar (age 20) at TRINITY, Apr. 8, 1740. S. of Samuel, of Fylingdales, Whitby, Yorks. School, Beverley, Yorks. (Mr Clark). Matric. 1740; B.A. 1743-4. Ord. deacon (York) May 20, 1744; priest, Sept. 1747. C. of Terrington, Yorks. V. of Pickering; and V. of Ellerburn, *c.* 1775. (M. H. Peacock.)

HARDING, THOMAS. B.A. from ST JOHN'S, 1604–5; M.A. 1608; B.D. 1629. Incorp. at Oxford, 1611. Second Master of Westminster School, 1610–22. R. of Soulderne, Oxon., 1622–48. An eminent scholar. His history 'of Church and State affairs' was recommended for publication by Parliament, 1641, but never issued. Died Oct. 10, 1648. (*Al. Oxon.*; *D.N.B.*)

HARDING, WALTER. Adm. sizar (age 18) at CHRIST'S, July 4, 1668. S. of George, of Staffordshire. School, Tamworth (Mr Antrobus). B.A. 1671–2.

HARDING, WILLIAM. Adm. at KING'S, a scholar from Eton, 1458.

HARDING, WILLIAM. Adm. sizar at JESUS, Jan. 28, 1726–7. Of Cheshire. Matric. 1727. Doubtless LL.B. from St John's, 1734.

HARDING, WILLIAM ST JOHN. Adm. sizar (age 20) at ST JOHN'S, June 13, 1739. S. of John, druggist, of Huntingdonshire. B. at Kimbolton. School, Oakham (Mr Adcock). Matric. 1740; B.A. 1742–3. Ord. deacon (Lincoln) May 27, 1743; priest, Sept. 22, 1745. C. of Tilbrook, Beds. Perhaps V. of Gt Hale, Lincs., 1758–85. (*Scott-Mayor*, III. 501.)

HARDINGE, WILLIAM. Adm. sizar at JESUS, Oct. 10, 1739. Of Nottinghamshire. Matric. 1740; Scholar; B.A. 1743–4. Ord. deacon (Lincoln) Sept. 23, 1744; priest, May 25, 1746.

HARDYN, ——. Fee for M.A. or higher degree, 1496–7.

HARDING, ——. M.A. (CHRIST'S) 1593, *see* HARDIE, SAMUEL (1589).

HARDINGTON, ROBERT. B.Civ.L. 1516–7.

HARDISWAY, PETER. 'Student of TRINITY HALL' when adm. extra-licentiate R.C.P. Aug. 3, 1719.

HARDMAN, HENRY. B.Civ.L. 1455–6.

HARDMAN, JOHN. Adm. sizar (age 17) at JESUS, Apr. 19, 1667. Of Lancashire. Matric. 1667; B.A. 1670–1.

HARDMETT, THOMAS. Adm. pens. at CLARE, July 6, 1665. Matric. 1667; B.A. 1668–9; M.A. 1672.

HARDNES, HUMPHREY. Matric. sizar from PEMBROKE, c. 1594.

HARDRES, CHARLES. Adm. pens. at QUEENS', May 17, 1656. Of Kent. 1st s. of Thomas (1629), of Gray's Inn. Adm. at Gray's Inn, Oct. 24, 1653. Barrister, 1661. Ancient, 1676. Half-brother of Edmund (1669), James (1668) and Thomas (1667). (*Archaeol. Cantiana*, IV. 56.)

HARDRES, CHARLES. Adm. sizar at QUEENS', Mar. 2, 1682–3. Of Kent. Doubtless s. of Thoresby. B. 1663. Matric. 1683; B.A. 1686–7; M.A. 1691. Fellow, 1690–3. Married, at Canterbury Cathedral, Mar. 27, 1693, Elizabeth Reeves, of Holy Cross, Canterbury. Died 1696. Buried at Upper Hardres. (*Archaeol. Cantiana*, IV. 56.)

HARDRES, EDMUND. Adm. pens. at ST JOHN'S, May 5, 1669. S. of Thomas (1629), recorder of Canterbury. B. there. Matric. 1669. Adm. at Gray's Inn, Jan. 31, 1667–8. Of Canterbury. Died 1723. Buried at Upper Hardres. Brother of the next and Thomas (1667). (*Archaeol. Cantiana*, IV. 56.)

HARDRES, JAMES. Adm. pens. (age 15) at ST JOHN'S, June 3, 1668. S. of Thomas (1629), recorder of Canterbury. B. there. Matric. 1668. Adm. at Gray's Inn, Mar. 7, 1663–4. Barrister, 1673. Died 1688. Buried at Upper Hardres. Brother of Thomas (1667) and the above.

HARDRES, PETER. Matric. pens. from QUEENS', Michs. 1623. Of Kent. S. of Sir Thomas, Knt. B. 1608. B.A. 1626–7; M.A. 1630; B.D. 1637; D.D. 1660 (*Lit. Reg.*). Fellow, 1630–4. R. of Upper Hardres, Kent, 1632–78. Preb. of Canterbury, 1660–78. Buried in the Cathedral, July 15, 1678. Brother of Thomas (1629).

HARDRES, PETER. Adm. Fell.-Com. at QUEENS', Apr. 21, 1651. Of Kent. S. and h. of Sir Richard, of Hardres Court, Kent, Bart. Bapt. at St Giles', Gripplegate, Feb. 15, 1635. Adm. at Gray's Inn, June 28, 1651. Succeeded as Bart., Oct. 1669. Buried at Upper Hardres, Mar. 6, 1673–4. Father of Thomas (1677–8), brother of Thoresby (1659) and Thomas (1657). (Burke, *Ext. Bart.*; *Vis. of Kent*; G.E.C.)

HARDRES or HARDES, THOMAS. Matric. pens. from QUEENS', Easter, 1629. Of Kent. 4th s. of Sir Thomas, late of Hardres Court, Kent, Knt. B. 1610. Adm. at Gray's Inn, June 15, 1629, from Staple Inn. Barrister, 1636. Ancient, 1654. Bencher, 1659. Reader, 1663. Treasurer, 1666. Steward of the Manor of Lambeth, 1649–81. M.P. for Canterbury, 1664–79; and again, 1679–81. Serjeant-at-law, 1669. King's serjeant, 1675. Knighted, May 17, 1676. Recorder of Canterbury. Died Dec. 18, 1681. Buried at Canterbury. Father of Charles (1656), Edmund (1669), James (1668) and Thomas (1667), brother of Peter (1623). (*D.N.B.*)

HARDRES, THOMAS. Matric. pens. from QUEENS', Easter, 1657. Doubtless 3rd s. of Sir Richard, of Hardres Court, Kent. B. 1641. B.A. 1659–60; M.A. 1663. Subscribed for deacon's orders (London) May 20, 1665; for priest's, June 7, 1666. R. of Lower Hardres, Kent, 1669–1711. R. of Upper Hardres, 1678–1711. Died 1711. Brother of Peter (1651) and Thoresby (1659).

HARDRES, THOMAS. Adm. Fell.-Com. (age 15) at ST JOHN'S, June 19, 1667. S. of Thomas (1629), recorder of Canterbury. B. there. Matric. 1667; M.A. 1669 (*Lit. Reg.*). Adm. at Gray's Inn, Mar. 7, 1663–4. Barrister, 1673. Ancient, 1687. Of Canterbury. Married Mary, dau. of John Short. Died 1688. Buried at Upper Hardres. Brother of James (1668) and Edmund (1669).

HARDRES, Sir THOMAS, Bart. Adm. Fell.-Com. (age 18) at MAGDALENE, Mar. 22, 1677–8. S. of Sir Peter (1651), deceased. B. at Upper Hardres, Kent. Bapt. Dec. 21, 1660. School, Canterbury. Succeeded as Bart., 1673. Married Ursula, dau. of Sir William Rooke. Died 1688. Buried at Upper Hardres, Feb. 26, 1688. (*G.E.C.*)

HARDRES, THORESBY. Adm. pens. at QUEENS', Nov. 23, 1659. Of Kent. 4th s. of Sir Richard, of Upper Hardres, Kent, Bart. Matric. 1660; M.A. 1663. Adm. at Gray's Inn, Jan. 23, 1662–3. Barrister, 1670. Ancient, 1686. Died 1686. Buried in Canterbury Cathedral, Mar. 16, 1685–6. Will, P.C.C. Brother of Peter (1651) and Thomas (1657). (*Vis. of Kent*, 1663; *Archaeol. Cantiana*, IV. 56.)

HARDSEDE, ——. Fee for B.A. 1463–4. *See* perhaps —— Hardhede.

HARDWARE, JOHN. Matric. pens. from QUEENS', Michs. 1632. Of Norfolk. B.A. 1635–6; M.A. 1639. Fellow of St John's, 1642. Ord. priest (Peterb.) Sept. 20, 1646. R. of Kirby Cane, Norfolk, 1662–90. Died Feb. 21, 1689–90, aged 75.

HARDWARE, THOMAS. Conduct of KING'S College. Will proved (V.C.C.) 1541.

HARDWICK, EDWARD. Adm. sizar at ST JOHN'S, Feb. 4, 1669–70. B. in Herefordshire. Matric. 1675; B.A. 1675–6; M.A. 1679.

HARDWICKE, JOHN. Adm. pens. at QUEENS', June, 1644. Of Surrey. Matric. Easter, 1645–6; B.A. 1647–8.

HARDWICKE, LAURENCE. Adm. sizar at PETERHOUSE, July 6, 1626. Of Yorkshire. Matric. 1626; B.A. 1629–30; M.A. 1634. V. of Middleton-in-Pickering, Yorks., 1632–52. Perhaps V. of Gt Edstone, 1660–80. Father of Thomas (1653). (*T. A. Walker*, 34.)

HARDWICK, MATTHEW. Adm. sizar at CLARE, Mar. 5, 1668–9. Of Yorkshire. (? S. of Laurence, above.) B.A. 1672–3. Ord. deacon (York) Sept. 1672; priest, Dec. 1674. Probably brother of the next.

HARDWICK, RALPH. Adm. sizar at CLARE, Feb. 24, 1670–1. Of Middleton, Yorks. (? S. of Laurence, above.) Matric. 1671; B.A. 1674–5. Ord. deacon (York) Dec. 1674; priest, Sept. 1675. Probably brother of Matthew, above.

HARDWICKE, RICHARD. Adm. pens. (age 18) at MAGDALENE, Feb. 20, 1712–3. S. of Robert, clerk. B. at Eresby, Lincs. School, Newark. Matric. 1713; B.A. 1716–7; M.A. 1720. Fellow, 1717.

HARDWICK, ROBERT. Adm. sizar (age 17) at SIDNEY, May 8, 1669. S. of William, yeoman, of Dyke, Lincs. B. at Scottesthorpe. Schools, Bourne, Lincs. and Rial, Rutland. Matric. 1669; B.A. 1672–3; M.A. 1676. Ord. deacon (Peterb.) June 14, 1674; priest, Feb. 20, 1675–6. Master of Wigston's Hospital, Leicester, till 1717–8. Died Mar. 1717–8. Admon. (P.C.C.); of Eresby, Spilsby, Lincs. (*Nichols*, IV. 497.)

HARDWICK, SOLOMON. Adm. pens. at QUEENS', July 1, 1695. Of Yorkshire.

HARDWICK, THOMAS. Adm. sizar (age 17) at ST JOHN'S, Oct. 28, 1653 (probably already adm. at Magdalene, July 7, 1653). S. of Laurence (1626), clerk, of Middleton-in-Pickering, Yorks. B. there. Matric. 1653. V. of Kirkby Moorside, Yorks., 1660.

HARDWICK, WILLIAM. Matric. sizar from TRINITY, Easter, 1607; Scholar, 1608; B.A. 1610–1; M.A. 1614; B.D. 1622. Fellow, 1612. Ord. deacon and priest (York) Dec. 1619. Will proved (V.C.C.) 1627.

HARDWICK, WILLIAM. Matric. pens. from TRINITY, Easter, 1612; Scholar, 1614; B.A. 1615–6; M.A. 1619. Ord. deacon (Peterb.) May 31; priest, June 1, 1618. V. of Swineshead, Lincs., 1619–31. V. of Bicker, 1631.

HARDWICKE, WILLIAM. Matric. sizar from PEMBROKE, Easter, 1614.

HARDWICK, WILLIAM. Adm. sizar (age 17) at PEMBROKE, June 25, 1622. S. of Ralph, of London. Matric. 1623. Migrated to Jesus, July 1, 1625. B.A. 1625; M.A. 1629.

HARDWICK, ——. M.Gram. 1520–1.

HARDWYN, THOMAS. B.A. 1511-2.

HARDY, BENJAMIN. M.A. from ST JOHN'S, 1677. S. of Matthew, of Hull, Yorks. Matric. from Lincoln College, Oxford, Apr. 6, 1666, age 15; B.A. (Oxford) 1669. Ord. deacon (York) June, 1671; priest, Sept. 1673. V. of Humbleton, Yorks., in 1676. R. of Sproatley, 1680-1714. V. of Aldborough, 1684-1714. (*Al. Oxon.*)

HARDY, EDWARD. Adm. sizar (age 18) at CHRIST'S, June 16, 1733. S. of William, yeoman, of Park House, Tunstall, Lancs. B. there. Bapt. at Tunstall, July 31, 1714. School, Kirkby Lonsdale (Mr Noble). Matric. 1733; Scholar, 1735; B.A. 1736-7. Ord. deacon, 1736; priest, 1737. R. of Halstead, Kent, 1771-97. Master of Sevenoaks School. R. of Sevenoaks, 1775-7. Married, 1749, Esther, dau. of Thomas Curtis, of Sevenoaks, clerk. Author, theological. Died 1797. Will, P.C.C. Brother of Joseph (1746). (C. F. Hardy.)

HARDYE, EHUD. Adm. sizar (age 18, *sic.*) at CHRIST'S, May 19, 1646. S. of Elisha. B. at Harwood, Lancs. Bapt. at Bolton-le-Moors, Apr. 21, 1622. School, Bolton-le-Moors (Mr Duckworth). Migrated to Queens', 1647. Matric. sizar there, 1647. (*Peile*, I. 506.)

HARDY, ENOCH. Adm. sizar (age 17) at PEMBROKE, May 19, 1663. S. of John. B. in London. Matric. 1664. Signed for deacon's orders (London) Sept. 21, 1672; for priest's, Dec. 19, 1673. C. of Corringham, Essex.

HARDY, JAMES. Adm. sizar (age 17) at ST JOHN'S, Apr. 26, 1666. S. of James, innkeeper, of Mansfield, Notts. B. there. School, Mansfield. Matric. 1667; B.A. 1669-70. Ord. deacon (Peterb.) Sept. 24, 1670.

HARDY, JOHN. B.Civ.L. 1493-4. Perhaps ord. deacon (Lincoln) as 'Geoffrey,' Mar. 31; priest, Apr. 14, 1498; 'of Boston; LL.B.; title, House of St John the Evangelist.' (Bishop's register.)

HARDY, JOHN. Matric. sizar from CLARE, Easter, 1674.

HARDY, JOHN. Adm. at CORPUS CHRISTI, 1678. Of Norfolk. Matric. 1678; B.A. 1681-2. Ord. deacon (Norwich) Oct. 1682; priest, Dec. 1683. R. of Welborne, Norfolk, 1694-7.

HARDY, JOHN. Adm. pens. (age 17) at CHRIST'S, Feb. 4, 1696-7. S. of Richard. B. at Garstang, Lancs. School, Kirkby Lonsdale (Mr Firbank). Matric. 1697, as 'Harvey.' V. of Kinoulton, Notts., 1729-35. V. of Melton Mowbray, 1731-40. Chaplain to the Countess dowager of Lincoln. Died June 28, 1740. M.I. at Melton Mowbray. Will, Leicester. Father of Richard (1731). (*Peile*, II. 138.)

HARDY, JOSEPH. Adm. sizar (age 17) at ST JOHN'S, Apr. 10, 1684. S. of Thomas, shoemaker. B. at Ipswich. School, Ipswich. Matric. 1684; B.A. 1687-8. Ord. priest (Norwich) Sept. 1692. C. of Monk Soham, Suffolk. V. of Bentley, 1697-1722. R. of Wolverston, 1709. Died Jan. 27, 1722. (*E. Anglian*, VII. 22.)

HARDY, JOSEPH. Adm. sizar at CHRIST'S, Mar. 20, 1745-6. S. of William, yeoman, of Barbon, Tunstall, Lancs. Bapt. Feb. 11, 1732-3, at Kirkby Lonsdale, age 10. In deacon's orders. LL.B. 1755. Ord. priest (York) Mar. 1747-8. Head Master of Sutton Valence School, Kent, 1746-86. V. of Headcorn, Kent, 1762. P.C. of Bilsington, 1770-86. V. of Monkton and Birchington, 1772. Died Aug. 5, 1786, aged 63. Buried in Lambe's Chapel, Sutton Valence. M.I. Admon. P.C.C. Brother of Edward (1733). (*Peile*, II. 249; *Hardys of Barbon*.)

HARDY, NATHANIEL. M.A. 1639 (Incorp. from Oxford). S. of Anthony, of St Martin's, Ludgate, London. B. in the Old Bailey, Sept. 14, 1618. Matric. from Magdalen Hall, Oxford, Oct. 11, 1633, age 14; B.A. (Oxford) 1635; M.A. from Hart Hall, 1638; D.D. 1660. Preacher at St Dionis Backchurch, 1643; R. 1660. Dean of Rochester, 1660-70. R. of Henley-on-Thames, 1660-1. V. of St Martin-in-the-Fields, 1661-70. R. of Leybourne, Kent, 1667-70. Archdeacon of Lewes, 1667-70. Author, *Sermons*. Died at Croydon, June 1, 1670. Buried at St Martin-in-the-Fields. M.I. Admon., P.C.C. (*Al. Oxon.*; *D.N.B.*)

HARDY, PETER. Canonicus. B.D. 1505-6.

HARDY, PETER. Adm. sizar (age 16) at MAGDALENE, Apr. 2, 1647. S. of Peter, late of Ipswich. School, Ipswich. Matric. 1647; B.A. 1651-2; M.A. 1655.

HARDY, RICHARD. Adm. pens. (age 16) at PEMBROKE, May 31, 1667. S. of William, mercer. B. at Louth, Lincs. Matric. 1667; B.A. 1670-1; M.A. 1674. Ord. deacon (Lincoln) Sept. 22, 1672; priest (Peterb.) Dec. 22, 1672. C. of Pilling, Lancs., 1686-8. R. of North Meols, 1688-1708. Admon. (Chester) 1708. (R. Stewart-Brown.)

HARDY, RICHARD. Adm. sizar at CHRIST'S, June 5, 1671. Doubtless s. of Richard, of Whittington, yeoman (Will, Richmond, 1702). B. at Widdington, Lancs. School, Kirby (? Kirkby-Ireleth), Lancs. Matric. 1671; B.A. 1677. Ord. deacon (Chester) May 21, 1676; priest, Sept. 21, 1679. (E. Axon; J. Ch. Smith.)

HARDY, RICHARD. Adm. pens. (age 17) at MAGDALENE, Apr. 7, 1727. S. of George, gent., deceased. B. at South Somercotes, Lincs. School, Brigg.

HARDY, RICHARD. Adm. pens. (age 21) at CHRIST'S, June 12, 1731. S. of John (1696). B. at Nottingham. School, Nottingham (Mr Brickhill). Matric. 1731; Scholar, 1731; LL.B. 1737. V. of Kinoulton, Notts., 1735-45. V. of Langar, 1753-75. Master of Melton Mowbray School, Leics., 1757. V. of Eaton, 1768. Died Aug. 6, 1775, at Langar. Buried there. M.I. (*Nichols*, II. 258; *Peile*, II. 224.)

HARDY, RICHARD. Adm. sizar at JESUS, June 10, 1737. S. of Thomas, V. of Bispham, Lancs. Bapt. there, May 18, 1719. Matric. 1737; Rustat scholar, 1737; B.A. 1741-2.

HARDIE, ROBERT. Matric. pens. from ST JOHN'S, Easter, 1588; B.A. 1591-2; M.A. 1595. One of these names, s. of Robert, of Manchester, adm. at Gray's Inn, May 3, 1596. Barrister, 1603.

HARDEY, ROBERT. Matric. sizar from TRINITY, Easter, 1631; B.A. 1634-5; M.A. 1638. One of these names, s. of Nicholas, of King's Newton, Derbs., adm. at Gray's Inn, June 18, 1639. Barrister, 1645. Ancient, 1662.

HARDY, ROBERT. Adm. pens. at CLARE, Feb. 15, 1703-4. B. in London. Matric. 1704; B.A. 1707-8. Perhaps ord. deacon (Lincoln) *c.* 1711.

HARDIE SAMUEL. Resident student at CHRIST'S, 1589. S. of Robert, of Manchester. Perhaps B.A. 1589-90; M.A. 1593 (in the *ordo*, as 'Harding'). Owned property at Manchester and Collyhurst. (*Peile*, I. 198.)

HARDY, SAMUEL. Adm. sizar at EMMANUEL, June 11, 1737. Of Ipswich. School, Oakham. Matric. 1738; B.A. 1741-2. Ord. priest (Exeter) Dec. 1744. R. of Little Blakenham, Suffolk. Schoolmaster and lecturer at Enfield, Middlesex. Author, theological. Died at Tottenham High Cross, Dec. 14, 1793, aged 73. Buried at Tottenham M.I. (G. *Mag.*)

HARDY, THOMAS. Adm. sizar at SIDNEY, June 13, 1616. B. in Yorkshire. Matric. 1616; B.A. 1619-20. Ord. deacon (York) Dec. 1622; probably priest (Durham) Sept. 19, 1630.

HARDY, THOMAS. Adm. sizar (age 18) at MAGDALENE, June 14, 1682. S. of George. B. at Saltfleetby, Lincs. School, Louth. Matric. 1682; B.A. 1686-7.

HARDY, THOMAS. Adm. sizar (age 28) at CHRIST'S, July, 1715. In holy orders. S. of Edward. B. at Barbon, Westmorland (in Tunstall parish, Lancs.). Bapt. at Kirkby Lonsdale, Sept. 23, 1683. School, Kirkby Lonsdale (Mr Firbank). Had been Head Master of Huddersfield School. V. of Mirfield, Yorks., May 15, 1716-39. Buried there, Dec. 19, 1739. Father of William (1738). (*Peile*, II. 188; C. F. Hardy.)

HARDY, THOMAS. Adm. pens. (age 18) at MAGDALENE, June 11, 1733. S. of Thomas (? 1682). B. at Louth, Lincs. School, Lincoln. Matric. 1733; B.A. 1736-7; M.A. 1749.

HARDY, WILLIAM. Adm. sizar (age 17) at PEMBROKE, Apr. 20, 1666. S. of Mark. B. at 'Hyse,' Suffolk. Matric. 1667.

HARDY, WILLIAM. Adm. sizar at CHRIST'S, May 26, 1738. S. of Thomas (1715), V. of Mirfield, Yorks. B. there, July 4, 1719. School, Kirkby Lonsdale. Matric. 1738; B.A. 1741-2; M.A. 1745. Ord. deacon (Lincoln) Mar. 14, 1741-2; priest (Rochester) Sept. 23, 1744. R. of Eastwell, Kent, 1745-7. V. of Burley-on-the-Hill, Rutland, 1747-52. R. of Milton-Keynes, Bucks., 1752. Died Oct. 25, 1752, aged 34. (*Rutland Mag.*, V. 133; *Peile*, II. 236; C. F. Hardy.)

HARDY, WILLIAM. Adm. sizar (age 18) at TRINITY, Mar. 31, 1742. S. of John, C. and schoolmaster of Kirkburton, Yorks. School, Almondbury, Yorks. (Mr Brooke). Matric. 1742; B.A. 1745-6. Ord. deacon (York) Sept. 20, 1747; priest, May, 1749. C. of Kirkburton. (C. F. Hardy.)

HARDYMAN, JOHN. D.D. 1538; probably Incorp. at Oxford same year. Prior of the Augustinian friars in Cambridge. R. of St Martin, Ironmonger Lane, London, 1539-41. Preb. of Lincoln, 1548-53. Preb. of Westminster, 1560-7. V. of Lydd, Kent, 1560-7, where grave charges were made against him. Preb. of Chester, 1567, deprived. R. of Snargate, Kent, 1567-9. (*Cooper*, I. 251.)

HARDYMAN, THOMAS. M.A. 1682 (*Com. Reg.*).

HARE or HARES, ANDREW. Adm. sizar (age 16) at CAIUS, Feb. 12, 1632-3. S. of Robert. B. at Calverley, Yorks. Bapt. Apr. 28, 1616. School, Wakefield (Mr Yonge). Matric. 1633; B.A. 1636-7. V. of Huntington, Yorks., 1642-75. Died 1675.

HARE, CHRISTOPHER. Adm. at CORPUS CHRISTI, 1562.

HARE, EDMUND. Matric. sizar from PETERHOUSE, Easter, 1555. 5th s. of John, of St Mary-le-Bow, London, mercer (brother of Sir Nicholas, the Speaker). Bapt. Apr. 20, 1540. B.A. 1557-8. Adm. at the Inner Temple, 1558. Brother of Nicholas (1545).

HARE, FRANCIS. Adm. at KING'S, a scholar from Eton, 1688. S. of Richard, of Leigh, Essex. B. in London, Nov. 1, 1671. Matric. Easter, 1689; B.A. 1692-3; M.A. 1696; D.D. 1708. Fellow, 1692. Tutor to the Marquis of Blandford. Chaplain-general to the army in Flanders, 1704. Preb. of St Paul's, 1707-40. R. of Barnes, Surrey, 1713-23. Chaplain to George I, 1715-8. Dean of Worcester, 1715-26. Dean of St Paul's, 1726-40. Bishop of St Asaph, 1727-31. Bishop of Chichester, 1731-40. Married (1), 1709, Bethaia Naylor, through whom Hurstmonceaux was inherited. Author, classical. Died Apr. 26, 1740, at the Vatcbe, Chalfont St Giles, Bucks. Buried there. Will, P.C.C. Father of the next. (*D.N.B.*)

HARE, FRANCIS. Adm. Fell.-Com. at CLARE, Sept. 28, 1728. B. in London. Doubtless s. of Francis (above), Bishop of Chichester, and Bethaia Naylor. B. May 14, 1713. Inherited the estate of Hurstmonceaux, Sussex, from his uncle George Naylor, and took the name. Married Carlotta Alston, his stepmother's sister. Lived for a time at Little Thurlow, Suffolk. The Francis Hare who died in Calcutta, 1772 (*G. Mag.*, 198), was his half-brother. (A. J. C. Hare, *Memorials*, I. 84.)

HARE, GEORGE. Adm. pens. (age 15) at CAIUS, Nov. 12, 1707. S. of Sir Thomas (1672), Bart., of Stow Bardolph, Norfolk. B. in London. School, Wisbech (Mr Carter). Matric. 1707. Major of Dragoons. Succeeded his brother Thomas as 5th Baronet, 1760. Of Stow Hall. Died Mar. 18, 1764. M.I. at Stow Bardolph. (*Venn*, I. 517; G. *Mag.*; *G.E.C.* supposes him to have been born *c.* 1701.)

HARE, HUGH. Adm. pens. at EMMANUEL, May 23, 1645. Of Northamptonshire. Matric. 1647.

HARE, HUGH. Adm. nobleman (age 16) at TRINITY, May 12, 1684. Of East Betchworth, Surrey. 1st s. of Henry, Baron Coleraine. B. at Totteridge, Herts. School, Salisbury (Mr Edward Hardwicke). Adm. at the Inner Temple, Feb. 11, 1685-6. M.P. for Bletchingley, Surrey, 1698-1700. Translator, assisted in the translation of the *Works of Lucian*. Married Lydia, dau. of Matthew Carlton, of Edmonton, Middlesex. Died *v.p.* Buried at Tottenham, Mar. 1, 1706-7. (*D.N.B.*; *G.E.C.*)

HARE, HUGH. Adm. Fell.-Com. at CLARE, Oct. 11, 1748. S. and h. of Thomas. B. at Harpham, Norfolk. Matric. 1748.

HARE, HUGH CHARLES. Adm. pens. (age 18) at TRINITY, Mar. 1, 1693-4. S. of Charles, of Docking, Norfolk. B. at Tottenham, Middlesex. School, Eton. Matric. 1694; Scholar, 1697; B.A. 1697-8. Ord. deacon (Norwich) Mar. 1700-1; priest (Lincoln) June 29, 1701. Died Jan. 28, 1743. M.I. at Docking. Will (P.C.C.) 1744.

HARE, JOHN. Matric. pens. from QUEENS', Easter, 1623. Of Oxfordshire.

HAIRE, JOHN. Adm. pens. (age 17) at CAIUS, *c.* May, 1657. S. of Edmund, attorney-at-law. B. at Norwich. Bapt. at St Michael-at-Plea, Oct. 11, 1640. School, Norwich (Mr Lovering). Matric. 1657. Buried at St Michael-at-Plea, July 24, 1666.

HARE, JOHN. Adm. pens. (age 17) at ST JOHN'S, July 2, 1685. S. of John, gent. B. at Syderstone, Norfolk. School, Lynn (Mr Horne). Matric. 1685; B.A. 1688-9. Adm. at the Inner Temple, Nov. 29, 1690, as s. and h. of John, of Branthorpe, Norfolk, deceased. Rouge Dragon Pursuivant, 1701-4. Richmond Herald, 1704-20. Died May 14, 1720. Will, P.C.C.

HARE, JOHN. Adm. pens. (age 19) at ST JOHN'S, May 27, 1717. S. of John, of Middlesex. B. in London. Schools, Eton and Merchant Taylors'. Matric. 1717. Migrated to Emmanuel, Oct. 3, 1718. B.A. 1720-1; M.A. 1724. Ord. deacon (London) Feb. 18, 1721-2.

HARE, JOHN. Adm. at CORPUS CHRISTI, 1723. S. of Ralph (1671-2), of Harpham, Norfolk. Matric. Michs. 1724; LL.B. 1728 (*Com. Reg.*). R. of Wilby, Norfolk, 1730-69. V. of Harpham, 1730. Died Apr. 2, 1769, aged 62. Brother of Ralph (1725). (*Masters*.)

HARE, MICHAEL. Matric. Fell.-Com. from GONVILLE HALL, Michs. 1545. S. of Sir Nicholas (1509), Master of the Rolls. Adm. at the Inner Temple, Dec. 1, 1547. Of Bruisyard Hall, Suffolk. Fined and imprisoned as a recusant. Buried at Bruisyard, Apr. 11, 1611. Will (P.C.C.) 1611; 'now confined for religion.' Brother of Robert (1545) and William (1545). (*Venn*, I. 34; Davy, *Suff. MSS.*)

HARE, NICHOLAS. Probably pens. at GONVILLE HALL, in 1509. 1st s. of John, of Homersfield, Suffolk. M.P. for Downton, Wilts., 1529-36; for Norfolk, 1539-40; for Lancaster, 1545-7; for Taunton, 1547-52. Reader at the Inner Temple, 1532. Recorder of Norwich, 1536. Knighted, 1538. Speaker of the House of Commons, 1539-40. Master of Requests, 1540. Chief Justice of Chester and Flint, 1538-45. Master of the Rolls, 1553-57. Died Oct. 31, 1557. Buried in the Temple Church. Will, P.C.C. Father of Michael (1545), Robert (1545), and William (1545). (*Cooper*, I. 172; *D.N.B.*)

HARE, NICHOLAS. Matric. pens. from TRINITY HALL, Easter, 1545, *impubes*. 1st s. of John, of London, mercer, brother of Sir Nicholas. Adm. at the Inner Temple, 1548. Bencher, 1574. M.P. for Horsham, 1572-83, 1584-7, 1588-9. Recorder of Lynn, 1593-7. Of Stow Bardolph, Norfolk, Esq. Died 1597, aged 67. Will (P.C.C.) 1597. Brother of Edmund (1555). (Carthew, *Launditch*, II. 658; A. B. Beaven.)

HARE, NICHOLAS. Matric. Fell.-Com. from CHRIST'S, 1598-9. Perhaps s. and h. of John, Master of the Bench of the Inner Temple. Adm. at the Inner Temple, June, 1596. Died 1622. Will, P.C.C. (*Peile*, I. 230.)

HARE, NICHOLAS. Adm. pens. at EMMANUEL, Dec. 9, 1647. Of Norfolk. 3rd s. of Sir John, Knt. B. 1632. Matric. 1647. Adm. at the Inner Temple, 1651. Of Harpham Manor, Norfolk. Married Catherine, dau. of William Geary, of Bushmead Abbey, Beds., Esq. Buried Nov. 17, 1689, at Harpham. Father of Ralph (1671-2). (*Blomefield*, I. 414.)

HARE, PHILIP. Matric. pens. from CORPUS CHRISTI, Michs. 1564; B.A. 1566-7; M.A. from Magdalene, 1570. Perhaps Master of Dedham School, Essex, 1573-9.

HARE, RALPH. Matric. Fell.-Com. from TRINITY, Michs. 1584. 2nd s. of John, of Stow Bardolph, Norfolk. Adm. at the Inner Temple, 1584. Barrister, 1596. Bencher, 1605. M.P. for St Mawes, 1601. Died Aug. 1623. Will (P.C.C.) 1625.

HARE, RALPH. Adm. Fell.-Com. (age 14) at PEMBROKE, Jan. 16, 1671-2. S. of Nicholas (1647), Esq., of London. Adm. at the Inner Temple, June 27, 1674; of Stow Hall, Norfolk. Of Harpham, Norfolk. Married Anne, dau. of Sir John Willis, Bart., of Fen Ditton, Cambs. Buried Nov. 18, 1709, at Harpham. Will (P.C.C.) 1710. Father of the next, of John (1723) and perhaps Thomas (1710). (*Blomefield*, I. 414.)

HARE, RALPH. Adm. at CORPUS CHRISTI, 1725. Of Norfolk. S. of Ralph, of Harpham, Norfolk. Matric. Michs. 1724; B.A. 1727-8; M.A. 1731. Fellow, 1729-40. Ord. deacon (Lincoln) June 4, 1732; priest (Ely) July, 1738. R. of Duxford St Peter, Cambs., 1738-61. Died 1761. Will, P.C.C. Brother of John (1723). (*Masters*.)

HARE, RICHARD. Matric. pens. from TRINITY, Easter, 1587.

HARE, ROBERT. Matric. Fell.-Com. from GONVILLE HALL, Nov. 1545. S. of Sir Nicholas (1509). Adm. at the Inner Temple, Dec. 1, 1547. Clerk of the Pells, 1560-70. M.P. for Dunwich, 1563. Of Bocking Hall, and Bruisyard, Suffolk. Well known for his antiquarian collections in the University Registry, and for his donation to the 'Causey Fund' for the improvement of the pathways round Cambridge. Died Nov. 2, 1611. M.I. in Old St Paul's. Will (P.C.C.) 1611. Brother of Michael (1545) and William (1545). (*Venn*, I. 34; *D.N.B.*)

HAYRE, ROBERT. Matric. pens. from ST JOHN'S, Michs. 1546.

HARE, ROBERT. Matric. sizar from QUEENS', Easter, 1579-80. B. at Goldington, Beds. B.A. 1583-4. Ord. deacon and priest (London) Mar. 16, 1599-1600, age 36. R. of Barnesley, Gloucs., 1600-1. Admon., P.C.C. (F. S. Hockaday.)

HARE, ROBERT. Matric. pens. from TRINITY, Easter, 1585.

HARE, ST JOHN. Adm. pens. at JESUS, May 29, 1700. Of Middlesex. Matric. 1700, as 'John'; Scholar, 1700.

HARE, SAMUEL. Adm. pens. (age 20) at CHRIST'S, Apr. 29, 1646. S. of John. B. at Hampton, Middlesex. School, Cobham (Mr Goldwire). Matric. 1646. One of these names, of Leigh, Essex, adm. at the Inner Tempie, 1648. Barrister, 1656. (*Peile*, I. 505.)

HARE, SAMUEL. Adm. pens. at TRINITY HALL, June 29, 1749. Matric. 1750; Scholar, 1750; LL.B. 1755. Ord. deacon (Lincoln) May 24; priest, June 11, 1752. R. of Beachampton, Bucks., 1752-94. R. of Simpson, 1772. V. of Wolverton, 1782. Died Jan. 19, 1794. Buried at Hatfield, Herts. Will, P.C.C. (*Lipscomb*, II.)

HARE, THOMAS. Incorp. LL.D. from Oxford, 1503-4. V. of Twickenham, Middlesex, *c.* 1500-15. Vicar-general of the Bishop of Norwich, 1501-20. Chancellor of diocese of Norwich, 1501-21. R. of Walsoken, Norfolk, 1502-20. V. of Reydon and Southwold, Suffolk, 1503. R. of Gt Massingham, Norfolk, 1506. R. of Grimston, 1508. Will (P.C.C.) 1521; 'of Homerfield, Suffolk. To be buried at St Mary-in-the-Fields, Norwich.' Probably uncle of Sir Nicholas (1509).

HARE, THOMAS. B.A. 1538-9; M.A. 1543; M.D. from PETERHOUSE, 1559. Fellow of Peterhouse, 1543-50. Will (P.C.C.) 1570; of St Michael-in-Bedwardine, Worcester.

HARE or HARES, THOMAS. Adm. sizar at EMMANUEL, Mar. 5, 1621-2. Matric. 1622; B.A. 1625-6.

HARE, THOMAS. Adm. sizar (age 20) at CAIUS, Nov. 10, 1655. S. of Thomas, gent., of Edmonton, Middlesex. B. there. Taught by his father. (*Venn*, I. 396.)

HARE, THOMAS. Matric. sizar from KING'S, Easter, 1657; B.A. 1659-60.

HARE, Sir THOMAS, Bart. Adm. Fell.-Com. (age 14) at CAIUS, Oct. 17, 1672. S. of Sir Ralph, of Stow Bardolph, Norfolk, Bart. B. there. Schools, Denver (Mr Sanderson), Thetford (Mr Keen) and Cambridge (Perse). Matric. 1672; M.A. 1673-4. Succeeded as Bart., Feb. 1671-2. M.P. for Norfolk, 1685-7. Died Jan. 1, 1693-4. Buried at Stow Bardolph. M.I. there. Father of George (1707). (*Venn*, I. 447; *G.E.C.*)

HARE, THOMAS. Adm. Fell.-Com. at CLARE, Oct. 18, 1710. Probably s. and h. of Ralph (1671-2). B. June 13, 1692. Of Harpham, Esq. Buried there 1736. Brother of Ralph (1725) and John (1723). Contemporary at Oxford. (*Blomefield*, I. 414.)

HARE, THOMAS. Adm. pens. (age 19) at TRINITY, June 2, 1743. S. of Thomas, of London. School, Westminster.

HARE, WILLIAM. Matric. pens. from TRINITY HALL, Easter, 1545 (*impubes*). S. of Sir Nicholas (1509). Adm. at the Inner Temple, 1551. Married and had issue. Died Apr. 16, 1597. Brother of Michael (1545) and Robert (1545). (*E. Anglian*, I. 56.)

HARE, WILLIAM. Adm. sizar from QUEENS', Dec. 2, 1582.

HARE, WILLIAM. Adm. sizar (age 18) at CAIUS, June 15, 1622. S. of Andrew, of Calverley, Yorks. School, Calverley (Mr Smith). Matric. 1622; Scholar, 1625; B.A. 1625-6. Died in College, 1629. Will proved (V.C.C.) 1629. (*Venn*, I. 257.)

HAIRE, WILLIAM. Adm. pens. (age 16) at ST JOHN'S, Apr. 24, 1630. S. of Anthony, mayor of Lincoln. B. there. School, Lincoln (Mr Clarke).

HARE, WILLIAM. Matric. pens. from MAGDALENE, Easter, 1631; B.A. 1633-4.

HARE or HAYRE, ——. Scholar of CHRIST'S, 1537; B.A. 1538-9; M.A. 1542. One Robert Hare, B.A., appointed by the College, to Helpstone, Northants., 1540. (*Peile*, I. 25.)

HARE, ——. Matric. Fell.-Com. from CHRIST'S, *c.* 1597.

HARES, THEOPHILUS. Adm. pens. at EMMANUEL, Jan. 21, 1618-9. Matric. 1618-9; B.A. 1622-3; M.A. 1626.

HARES, THOMAS. Matric. pens. from TRINITY, Easter, 1588; Scholar, 1590; B.A. 1592-3; M.A. 1596. Incorp. at Oxford, 1598. R. of Gaywood, Norfolk, 1598-1634. Died Mar. 7, 1634-5, aged 62. M.I. at Gaywood. (Le Neve, *Mon.*, I. 358.)

HAREWELL, HENRY. Matric. pens. from QUEENS', Easter, 1653. Of London. B.A. 1656-7; M.A. 1660.

HAREWELL, ISAAC. Matric. pens. from CHRIST'S, Easter, 1567.

HAREWELL, WILLIAM. M.A. from ST JOHN'S, 1638. S. of Henry, of Coventry, gent. Matric. from Oriel College, Oxford, Oct. 31, 1634, age 18; B.A. (Oxford) 1635-6. Ord. priest (Peterb.) Dec. 18, 1641. R. of Stourbridge, Worcs., 1641. V. of St Peter-le-Grand, Worcester, 1662. (*Al. Oxon.*)

HAREWOOD, *see* HARWOOD.

HARFLET, CHARLES. Matric. pens. from QUEENS', Michs. 1624. Of Kent. Doubtless s. of William, of Sandwich. B.A. 1628-9; M.A. 1632. C. of Stelling, Kent, 1634. V. of St Nicholas, Newington, Kent, till 1671. Died *c.* 1671.

HARFLET, EDWARD. Matric. pens. from ST JOHN'S, Easter, 1563. One of these names s. of Thomas, of Ash, Sandwich.

HARFLEET, HENRY. Matric. pens. from QUEENS', Easter, 1625. Of Kent. Adm. at Gray's Inn, Apr. 28, 1630; s. and h. of Henry, of Ash, author, for whom *see D.N.B.* Married Dorothy, dau. of Anthony Combe, of Greenwich. Will of 'Henry Harfleet, the elder, of Ashe' (P.C.C.) 1651. (*Vis. of Kent*, 1663; J. R. Planché, *A Corner of Kent*, 348.)

HARFLETT, MICHAEL. Matric. pens. from TRINITY, Easter, 1606. Perhaps s. of Sir Thomas, of Ash, Sandwich. Died Nov. 1618. Will proved, Mar. 10, 1618-9. (J. R. Planché, *A Corner of Kent.*)

HARFLET, SAMUEL. Matric. pens. from ST JOHN'S, Easter, 1583. Doubtless s. of Christopher, of Ash, Sandwich, deceased. Bapt. May, 1566. Adm. at the Inner Temple, 1584. Married Winifred, dau. of Sir Robert Peyton, Bart., Sept. 4, 1592.

HARFORD, ANTHONY. Scholar at CHRIST'S, 1577-8; B.A. 1579-80; M.A. 1583, as Hertford.

HARFORD, GEORGE. Matric. sizar from TRINITY, Easter, 1626; B.A. 1629-30; M.A. 1633. Ord. deacon (Peterb.) July 24; priest, July 25, 1630. R. of Stuckbury, Northants., 1635-43. Probably died 1643. (H. I. Longden.)

HARFORD, HERITAGE. Matric. pens. from MAGDALENE, Easter, 1623; B.A. 1626; M.A. 1630. Presented to Cherlton, Hants., Oct. 4, 1647.

HARFORD or HARFORTH, RICHARD. B.A. 1533-4. One of these names preb. of Hereford, 1551. But *see* a contemporary in *Al. Oxon.*

HARFORD, ——. Adm. Fell.-Com. at EMMANUEL, Easter, 1632.

HARGRAVE or HARGREAVES, BENJAMIN. Adm. sizar at JESUS, May 16, 1681. Of Yorkshire. Matric. 1681; Scholar, 1683; B.A. 1684-5. Ord. priest (Norwich) May, 1686.

HARGRAVES, BOLTON. Adm. pens. (age 18) at TRINITY, May 18, 1714. S. of ——, of Gildersome, Batley, Yorks. School, Gildersome. Matric. 1714. Adm. at the Inner Temple, Jan. 20, 1715-6.

HARGREAVES, CHRISTOPHER. Adm. pens. at EMMANUEL, May 15, 1669. Of Lancashire. B.A. 1672. Ord. deacon (York) June, 1674; priest (London) May 21, 1676. V. of Holy Cross, Westgate, Canterbury, 1679, resigned same year. V. of Westwell, Kent, 1680-1706. Died 1706. (H. G. Harrison.)

HARGREAVE, GEORGE. B.C.L. at Oxford 'Incorp. from Cambridge,' 1585 (not found in our records).

HARGREAVES, GEORGE. Adm. pens. at JESUS, June 6, 1666. Of Staffordshire. Matric. 1667.

HARGRAVES, HENRY. Matric. sizar from ST JOHN'S, Michs. 1571. One of these names ord. deacon and priest (Peterb.) Aug. 20, 1574. R. of Pilton, Rutland, 1582. R. of Whitwell, 1584-90. R. of Stretton, 1590. (H. I. Longden.)

HARGREAVES, HENRY. Adm. sizar at EMMANUEL, Dec. 31, 1673. Of Lancashire. Matric. 1674; B.A. 1677-8. Ord. deacon (York) June, 1679; priest (Chester) Sept. 21, 1679. V. of Burton-on-Stather, Lincs.

HARGREAVES, HENRY. Adm. sizar (age 18) at ST JOHN'S, May 6, 1698. S. of James (1655), clerk, deceased. B. at Colne, Lancs. School, Beverley (Mr Lambert). Matric. 1698; B.A. 1701-2. Ord. deacon (York) May, 1702; priest, 1703. V. of Farnworth, Lancs., 1718-32. Will proved at Chester, 1732. Brother of James (1681) and Robert (1707).

HARGRAVES, HUGH. Matric. sizar from ST JOHN'S, Michs. 1567; B.A. 1570-1. R. of Bardwell, Suffolk, 1576-96.

HERGRAVES, JAMES. Matric. sizar from TRINITY, Michs. 1573. One of these names R. of Felsham, Suffolk, 1583-9. Probably brother of John (1575).

HARGRAVE, JAMES. B.A. from TRINITY, 1603-4; M.A. 1607. Ord. deacon (Norwich) Sept. 29, 1604, age 25; priest, Dec. 23, 1604. C. of Arminghall, Norfolk. R. of Blickling, 1605-45. Buried there 1645. M.I.

HARGRAVE, JAMES. Adm. sizar (age 18) at ST JOHN'S, Apr. 17, 1655. S. of John, yeoman, of Greenfield, Colne, Lancs. Bapt. there, Feb. 7, 1637-8. School, Colne (Mr Rakes). Matric. 1655; B.A. 1658-9. P.C. of Colne, 1669-93. Schoolmaster at Colne. Buried there, Jan. 11, 1693-4. Will (Chester) 1694. Father of Henry (1698), James (1681) and Robert (1707). (*Vict. Hist. Lancs.*, IV. 534; J. Parker; E. Axon.)

HARGREAVES, JAMES. Adm. sizar (age 17) at JESUS, May 15, 1677. Of Lancashire. Matric. 1679; B.A. 1680-1; M.A. 1694. Ord. deacon and priest (London) Mar. 4, 1682-3. V. of Elmstead, Essex, 1683-1705. R. of Greenstead by Colchester, 1693-1700. Father of James (1718).

HARGREAVES, JAMES. Adm. sizar (age 16) at ST JOHN'S, Apr. 16, 1681. S. of James (1655), P.C. of Colne, Lancs. School, Wakefield (Mr Baskerville). Matric. 1681; B.A. 1684-5; M.A. 1700. R. of Brandesburton, Yorks., 1693-1723. Married Jane, dau. of John Saunders, of Grosmont Abbey. Buried at Brandesburton, June 1, 1723. Brother of Henry (1698) and Robert (1707), father of James (1723).

HARGRAVES, JAMES. Adm. sizar at CLARE, June 19, 1708. S. of Nathaniel, of Wakefield. B. there. School, Wakefield. Matric. 1709; B.A. 1711-2; M.A. 1715; D.D. 1728 (*Com. Reg.*). Fellow, 1714-24. Ord. deacon (Ely) Feb. 1, 1712-3. R. of East Hoathley, Sussex, 1719-41. Preb. of Chichester, 1723-32. Chaplain to the King, 1724-39. Preb. of Westminster, 1725. R. of St Margaret, Westminster, 1730-4. Dean of Chichester, 1739-41. Died Nov. 15, 1741.

HARGRAVE, JAMES. Adm. pens. (age 17) at CHRIST'S, Sept. 28, 1717. S. of Nathaniel, attorney. Bapt. at St Nicholas, Newcastle-on-Tyne, Jan. 2, 1700-1. Schools, Newcastle and Morpeth (Mr Salkeld). Matric. 1717; Scholar, 1718; Fell.-Com. 1720-5; B.A. 1721-2. One of these names adm. at Lincoln's Inn, Apr. 16, 1725. Of Shawdon, Whittingham, Northumberland. Died Oct. 1777. (H. M. Wood.)

HARGRAVES, JAMES. Adm. sizar at JESUS, Nov. 1, 1718. S. of James (1677), deceased, of Suffolk. Matric. 1719; Scholar; B.A. 1722-3. Ord. deacon (London) June 9, 1723; priest (Norwich) June, 1725. R. of Polstead, Suffolk, 1725-30. Perhaps R. of Little Wigborough, Essex. F.R.S., 1726. Died Feb. 23, 1774. Father of James (1746).

HARGREAVES, JAMES. Adm. sizar (age 17) at ST JOHN'S, May 30, 1723. S. of James (1681), clerk, of Yorkshire. B. at Brandsburton. School, Beverley (Mr Tatham). Matric. 1723; B.A. 1726-7. Ord. deacon (Lincoln) Mar. 17, 1727-8. C. of Skirbeck, Lincs. (*Scott-Mayor*, III. 362.)

HARGRAVES, JAMES. Adm. pens. (age 17) at CAIUS, June 16, 1746. S. of James (1718), late R. of Polstead, Suffolk. B. there. School, Lavenham (Mr Smythies). Matric. 1746; Scholar, 1746-50; B.A. 1749-50. Ord. deacon (London) Sept. 24, 1752; priest (Norwich) Mar. 18, 1753. Patron of Polstead, in 1750. C. of Polstead, 1753-7. R. 1757-63. Will proved (Archd. Sudbury) 1763. (*Venn*, II. 58.)

HERGRAVES, JOHN. Matric. sizar from TRINITY, Easter, 1575. Probably brother of James (1573).

HARGRAVES, JOHN. Adm. sizar (age 17) at ST JOHN'S, Feb. 13, 1644-5. S. of Richard, of Langsthawe, in Craven, Yorks. School, Giggleswick (Mr Lucas). Matric. 1648; B.A. 1648-9. One of these names, 'a minister,' buried in Durham Cathedral, Nov. 21, 1653. Another, P.C. of Halton Gill, in Craven, buried May 6, 1673. (H. M. Wood.)

HARGRAVE, JOHN. Adm. pens. (age 16) at SIDNEY, Apr. 24, 1648. S. of John, clothier. B. at Leeds, Yorks. School, Leeds (Mr Smith and Mr Garnet). Matric. 1648; B.A. 1651-2. Perhaps P.C. of Halton Gill, Yorks., 1673-90. Buried May 6, 1690.

HARGREAVES, JOHN. Adm. sizar (age 21) at MAGDALENE, Apr. 2, 1656. S. of John, of Morton, Keighley, Yorks. Matric. 1656.

HARGREAVES, JOHN. Adm. sizar (age 17) at ST JOHN'S, Feb. 24, 1691-2. S. of Robert (? 1657-8), clerk. B. at Paston, Northants. School, Peterborough (Mr Waring). Matric. 1692; B.A. 1695-6; M.A. 1699. Fellow, 1700-8. Ord. priest (Peterb.) Sept. 20, 1702. C. of Walgrave, Northants.

HARGRAVE, JOHN. Adm. sizar at CORPUS CHRISTI, 1697. Of Kent. Matric. 1697; B.A. 1700-1. Ord. priest (Peterb.) Sept. 20, 1702.

HARGREAVES, JOHN. Adm. sizar at JESUS, Apr. 1, 1703. Matric. 1703; B.A. 1706-7; M.A. 1728. Probably R. of Islip, Northants.; and father of the next. One of these names V. of Barlaston, Staffs., 1754-9. Died 1759.

HARGREAVES, JOHN. Adm. sizar (age 19) at ST JOHN'S, May 15, 1729. S. of John, R. of Islip, Northants. B. at Islip. School, Oakham (Mr Adcock). Matric. 1729; B.A. 1733-4. Ord. deacon (Lincoln) Sept. 22, 1734; priest, Sept. 21, 1735. V. of Guilsborough, Northants., 1741-4. R. of Cranford St Andrew, 1744-61. Admon. (Archd. Northants.) 1761; to widow Rachel. (*Scott-Mayor*, III. 421.)

HARGRAVE, ROBERT. Matric. sizar from CHRIST'S, Dec. 1582; B.A. 1585-6.

HARGRAVES, ROBERT. Adm. sizar (age 19) at ST JOHN'S, Feb. 3, 1657-8. S. of John, deceased, of Higham, High Booth in Whalley, Lancs. B. there. School, Burnley (Mr Aspden). Matric. 1658; B.A. 1661-2; M.A. 1665. Ord. deacon (Lincoln) Oct. 15, 1662; priest (Peterb.) Sept. 20, 1663. Perhaps minister at Paston, Northants., and father of John (1691-2).

HARGREAVES, ROBERT. M.A. from CHRIST'S, 1707. S. of James (1655), clerk, of Colne, Lancs. Matric. from Brasenose, Oxford, July 15, 1693, age 17; B.A. (Oxford) 1697. Incorp. M.A. at Oxford, 1707. Perhaps C. of Warrington, Lancs., in 1705. Brother of Henry (1698) and James (1681).

HARGREAVES, ROBERT. Adm. sizar (age 15) at ST JOHN'S, Sept. 15, 1709. S. of James, shopkeeper. B. at Kildwick, Skipton, Yorks. School, Threshfield (Mr Marshall). Matric. 1710; B.A. 1714-5. Ord. deacon (York) Sept. 1716; priest (Lincoln) Sept. 21, 1718. P.C. of Todmorden, Lancs., 1742; engaged in a severe contest with his parishioners as to the right of appointing churchwardens, 1750. Died 1770. (H. Fishwick, *Rochdale*, 185, who takes him to be a s. of Robert.)

HARGREAVES, ROBERT. Adm. sizar (age 18) at TRINITY, Mar. 31, 1732. S. of Robert, of Pickering, Yorks., clerk. School, Shipton, Yorks. (Mr Clarke). Matric. 1732; Scholar, 1734; B.A. 1735-6; M.A. 1739. Fellow, 1738. Ord. deacon (*Litt. dim.* from York) Sept. 1736; priest (Lincoln) Feb. 27, 1742-3. V. of Thirsk, Yorks., 1745-7. R. of Langton, 1746-54. V. of Harewood, 1747-54. Author, *Sermons*. Died 1754.

HARGREAVES, THOMAS. Adm. sizar at CHRIST'S, May 29, 1680. S. of John. B. at Gisborne, Yorks. School, Earby (Mr Rakes). Matric. 1680; M.B. 1685.

HARGRAVES, THOMAS. Adm. sizar (age 18) at CHRIST'S, Feb. 23, 1711-2. S. of James. B. at Knight Stainforth, Giggleswick, Yorks. School, Giggleswick (Mr Armitstead). Matric. 1712; B.A. 1716-7; M.A. 1722. Ord. deacon (York) Feb. 1715-6; priest, Dec. 1716. One of these names buried at Giggleswick, Apr. 3, 1757. M.I. (*Peile*, II. 178.)

HARGRAVE, WILLIAM. Adm. sizar at JESUS, Apr. 3, 1707. S. of William, of the Isle of Ely. B. 1688. Matric. 1708; B.A. 1710-1. Ord. deacon (Ely) Sept. 23, 1711; priest, Sept. 21, 1712. C. of Manea, Cambs., 1711. R. of Heyford, Northants., 1721-63. Died Dec. 30, 1763. Buried at Heyford. Will (Archd. North.) 1764. (H. I. Longden.)

HARGRAVES, WILLIAM. Adm. sizar at CLARE, Dec. 22, 1742. S. of Joseph, of Wakefield, Yorks., innkeeper. Bapt. there, Sept. 29, 1724. School, Wakefield. Matric. 1743; Scholar, 1744; B.A. 1746-7. Ord. deacon (Peterb.) Dec. 20, 1747. (M. H. Peacock.)

HARGRAVES, ZACHARIAS. Adm. pens. at JESUS, Sept. 11, 1690. Of Lancashire. Matric. 1690; Scholar, 1693; B.A. 1694-5; M.A. 1698. Ord. deacon (London) Mar. 27; priest, Sept. 20, 1696. R. of Polstead, Suffolk, 1696-1700. R. of Greenstead, 1700.

HARGRAVE, ——. Matric. pens. from CHRIST'S, May, 1548.

HAREGROVE, WILLIAM. Scholar at KING'S HALL, 1394-8.

HARKER, JOHN. B.A. 1525-6. Perhaps R. of Boothby Pagnell, Lincs. Died 1575.

HARKYN, JOHN. Matric. pens. from CHRIST'S, May, 1555.

HARKNESS, WILLIAM. Matric. pens. from TRINITY HALL, Dec. 1750; Scholar, 1752. One of these names 'major of the Cambs. Militia,' died July 18, 1775. (G. *Mag.*)

HARLAKENDEN, GEORGE. Matric. sizar from MAGDALENE, Easter, 1580. Probably s. of John, of Warchorn, Kent, Esq. B.A. 1583-4; M.A. 1587. R. of Gt Yeldham, Essex, 1593. (*Top. and Geneal.*, I. 233.)

HARLAKENDEN, HENRY. Matric. pens. from ST JOHN'S, *c.* 1593. S. of Walter, of Tunstall, Kent, Esq. Bapt. there, Mar. 19, 1574-5. 'Slain, Oct. 15, 1601.' Buried at Tunstall, Oct. 18, 1601. (*Top. and Geneal.*, I. 231; *Archaeol. Cantiana*, XIV. 361.)

HARLAKENDEN, RICHARD. Matric. pens. from MAGDALENE, Easter, 1583. 2nd s. but h. of Roger, of Earls Colne, Essex, Esq. B. July 22, 1568. B.A. 1586-7. Migrated to Emmanuel, June, 1588. Adm. at Gray's Inn, Apr. 17, 1592, from Staple Inn. Of Earls Colne, Esq. Married Margaret, dau. of Edward Hubbard. Died Aug. 22, 1631. Buried at Earls Colne. Will (P.C.C.) 1631. Father of Richard (next), brother of Thomas (1585) and Roger (1582-3). (*Vis. of Essex*, 1634; *Top. and Geneal.*, I. 234.)

HARLAKENDEN, RICHARD. Adm. pens. at EMMANUEL, 1623. S. of Richard (above). B. Dec. 21, 1606. Matric. 1623; B.A. 1626-7; M.A. 1630. Adm. at Gray's Inn, May 16, 1623. Of Earls Colne. Sheriff of Essex, 1646. Married Alice, dau. of Sir Henry Mildmay, Knt. Died Sept. 4, 1677. Buried at Earls Colne. Father of the next. (*Vis. of Essex*, 1634.)

HARLACKENDEN, RICHARD. Adm. Fell.-Com. at JESUS, June 20, 1649. Of Essex. S. and h. of Richard (above), of Earls Colne. B. July 19, 1631. School, Earls Colne (Mr Joscelyn). Matric. 1649. Adm. at Gray's Inn, June 6, 1649. Married Mary, dau. of Christopher Meredith, of London, 1652. Died Mar. 25, 1659, at Worcester. Buried at Earls Colne. Admon., P.C.C. (*Vis. of Essex*, 1634; *Josselin's Diary*, 128.)

HARLAKYNDEN, ROGER. Matric. pens. from MAGDALENE, Lent, 1582-3. 1st s. of Roger, of Earls Colne, Essex, Esq. (Will, P.C.C., 1603). Buried at Earls Colne, Dec. 30, 1583. Brother of Richard (1583) and Thomas (1585). (*Vis. of Essex*, 1634; *Top. and Geneal.*, I. 232.)

HARLAKENDEN, THOMAS. Matric. pens. from MAGDALENE, Easter, 1585. S. of Roger, of Earls Colne, Essex. Migrated to Emmanuel, 1588. Adm. at Gray's Inn, Apr. 17, 1592, from Staple's Inn. Of Earls Colne, Esq. Married (1) Dorothy, dau. of John Cheney; (2) Jane, dau. of Edward Hubbard. Buried at Earls Colne, Mar. 27, 1648. Brother of Richard (1583) and Roger (above), father of the next, and of William (1618). (*Vis. of Essex*, 1634; J. B. Peace.)

HARLAKENDEN, THOMAS. Matric. pens. from CHRIST'S, July, 1616. S. of Thomas (above), gent., of Earls Colne, Essex. Bapt. at Earls Colne, Nov. 4, 1599. Lived at Earls Colne. Buried there Sept. 29, 1652. Will (P.C.C.) 1653. Brother of the next. (*Peile*, I. 310; *Vis. of Essex*, 1634.)

HARLAKENDEN, WILLIAM. Matric. pens. from MAGDALENE, Easter, 1618. S. of Thomas (1585), of Earls Colne, Essex. B.A. 1621-2. Of New House, Esq. Married Smithee, dau. of Edward Scroggs, of Hertford. Died Mar. 18, 1674. Buried at Earls Colne. (*Vis. of Essex*, 1634; *Top. and Geneal.*, I. 234.)

HARLAND, JOHN. Adm. pens. (age 17) at ST JOHN'S, Oct. 26, 1658. S. of Richard, gent., of Sutton-in-the-Forest, Yorks. B. there. School, Pocklington (Mr Luellin and Mr Greenwood). Matric. 1658. Married Mary, dau. of Everingham Cressy, of Birkin. Father of Michael (1695).

HARLAND, MICHAEL. Adm. pens. (age 16) at SIDNEY, Mar. 28, 1695. 2nd s. of John (1658), gent. B. at Sutton-on-Forest, Yorks. Schools, Shipton (Mr Hutchkin) and Laughton, Yorks. (Mr Broomhead). Matric. 1695; B.A. 1698-9; M.A. 1702. Ord. deacon (York) May, 1700; priest, 1702. Probably V. of Hockley, Essex, 1703-14. Died 1714.

HARLATON, JOHN DE. Fellow of CLARE, in 1364. B.Can.L. and B.Civ.L. V. of Hinton, Northants. Petitioned the Pope for a canonry at Lichfield, 1363.

HARLEY, ROBERT. Matric. pens. from CAIUS, Easter, 1605. (Not in the College register; probably a blunder for Robert Yardley.)

HARLEY, THOMAS. Adm. pens. from TRINITY, Mar. 10, 1645-6; M.A. 1648 (*fil. nob.*). Incorp. at Oxford, 1649. Fellow of All Souls, 1648, by the Parliamentary visitors. Perhaps 3rd s. of Sir Robert, of Brampton Bryan, Heref., K.B.; adm. at Lincoln's Inn, Feb. 10, 1647-8. One of these names F.R.S., 1667. (*Al. Oxon.*)

HARLEY, WILLIAM. Adm. pens. at EMMANUEL, Sept. 7, 1631. Of Salop. Matric. 1631. Will of one of these names (P.C.C.) 1658; of Eastchurch, Kent, clerk.

HARLEY, WILLIAM. Adm. pens. (age 18) at MAGDALENE, Apr. 28, 1655. S. of Edward, of London, 'rei monetariae custos.' School, Charterhouse; Exhibitioner, Apr. 5, 1655, till Dec. when suspended for some misdemeanour through a 'frantic distemper in his head.' (*Al. Carthus.*) Matric. 1655. One of these names V. of Happisburgh, Norfolk, 1692.

HARLING or LING, RICHARD. LL.D. Of Norfolk. Chancellor of the University, 1337-9, 1351. Benefactor; founder of a 'chest.' Archdeacon of Norwich, 1349-55. 'Of Reedham, Lyng, Elsing, Norfolk, and Wincanton, Somerset.' Will (Lambeth) 1355. Portrait in the Council Room, University Library.

HARLING, WILLIAM. Adm. pens. (age 18) at TRINITY, June 2, 1738. S. of Christopher, of Carlisle. School, Westminster. Matric. 1738; Scholar, 1739; B.A. 1741-2; M.A. 1745. Fellow, 1744.

HARLSTONE, JOHN. Matric. pens. from ST JOHN'S, Easter, 1627. Doubtless s. of John, of South Ockendon, Essex, gent. Adm. at Gray's Inn, Apr. 28, 1629. Brother of Robert (1635-6) and Thomas (1629-30).

HARLESTONE, ROBERT. Adm. pens. (age 16) at PEMBROKE, Jan. 20, 1635-6. S. of John, Esq. B. at South Ockendon, Essex. Matric. 1636; B.A. 1639-40; M.A. 1643. Brother of John (1627) and Thomas (1629-30).

HARLASTON, ROGER DE. 'King's scholar' at Cambridge, 1333. Adm. into KING'S HALL. Left Nov. 21, 1354.

HARLESTONE, SAMUEL. Matric. pens. from CORPUS CHRISTI, Michs. 1565. Migrated to Oxford. B.A. (Oxford) 1569-70; M.A. 1572-3. Incorp. at Cambridge, 1574. R. of Ickham, Kent, 1568-1616. Died 1616. (*Al. Oxon.*; *Archaeol. Cantiana*, XIV. 130.)

HARLSTON, THOMAS. Fellow of GONVILLE HALL in 1421, when ord. deacon (Ely) Mar. 8, 1420-1; and priest, May 17, 1421. V. of Foulden, Norfolk, 1421-8; of Narborough, 1428-31; of Framingham Pigot, 1431-4. (*Venn*, I. 5.)

HARLESTON, THOMAS. Matric. pens. from KING'S, Michs. 1617; B.A. 1619-20.

HARLESTON, THOMAS. Adm. pens. (age 18) at ST JOHN'S, Feb. 8, 1629-30. S. of John, gent., of South Ockendon, Essex. B. there. School, Eton. Migrated to Pembroke. Matric. 1631; B.A. 1633; M.A. 1637. Brother of John (1627) and Robert (1635-6).

HARLSTON or HARLISTON, ——. M.A. 1490-1.

HARLOWE, EZECHIEL. Adm. at KING'S (age 18) a scholar from Eton, Aug. 24, 1560. Of Saffron Walden, Essex. Matric. 1560; B.A. 1564-5, as Harlowe *alias* Taylor. Fellow, 1563-6. Ord. priest (London) Dec. 3, 1567. R. of Thorpe-on-the-Hill, Lincs., 1576. V. of Swinderby, 1581.

HARLOYS or HARLOW, ——. B.Can.L. 1497.

HARLTON, ——. B.A. 1482.

HARMAN, *see also* HERMAN.

HARMAN, GEOFFREY. Scholar of GONVILLE HALL, 1519-23; B.A. 1521-2; M.A. 1525. Incorp. at Oxford, 1525. Supp. for B.D. 1531. Junior Canon of Cardinal College (afterwards Christ Church). One of Wolsey's Cambridge importations. Fellow of Eton, 1532. Died 1533. Buried at Eton. *See also* Richard. (*Harwood*; *Venn*, I. 24.)

HARMAN, HENRY. B.A. 1491-2; M.A. 1503-4.

HARMAN, JOHN. D.D. 1474-5.

HARMAN, JOHN. D.D. 1479-80. A friar. Perhaps the above.

HARMAN, JOHN. Adm. pens. at EMMANUEL, June 26, 1712. Of Middlesex. Matric. 1712. 'Executed in 1724 for a highway robbery.'

HARMAN or HERMAN, MILES (MICHAEL). Adm. sizar (age 16) at CAIUS, 1619. School, Norwich (Mr Briggs). Matric. Easter, 1620; Scholar, 1621-5; B.A. 1623-4. Ord. deacon and priest (Norwich) Dec. 18, 1625. V. of Ringland, Norfolk, 1626-62. (*Venn*, I. 246.)

HARMAN, NICHOLAS. B.A. 1537-8; M.A. 1540. Fellow of GONVILLE HALL, 1541-7. Ord. deacon (Norwich) Feb. 28, 1533-4. C. of Gt St Mary's, Cambridge, 1539. R. of Newtown, Montgom., 1546; of All Saints', Worcester, 1552. C. of All Saints', Northampton, 1556-8. Perhaps R. of Broughton, Northants. R. of Pitsford, 1558-60.

HARMAN, RICHARD. Adm. at KING'S, a scholar from Eton, 1510. Vacated his scholarship, probably for religion, and went to Jesus (*Harwood*). M.A. from Jesus, probably in 1515. Became chaplain to Cranmer. Afterwards junior canon of Cardinal College, Oxford. Imprisoned at Oxford for religion. According to *Cooper* who follows Strype (*Cranmer*, I. 48) he died in 1533, but this seems a confusion with Geoffrey: were there really two Harmans at Cardinal's College? One of these names R. of Crayford, Kent, 1524, to his death, 1570. (A. Gray.)

HARMAN, RICHARD. Adm. pens. (age 17) at SIDNEY, Mar. 28, 1638. S. of Richard, alderman, of Norwich. B. at St Andrew's, Norwich. School, Norwich (Mr Briggs). Matric. 1638. Adm. at Gray's Inn, Mar. 18, 1639-40. Perhaps M.P. for Norwich, 1640-6. Died 1646.

HARMAN, ROGER. B.A. 1513-4; M.A. 1517. Fellow of ST JOHN'S, 1516. Ord. deacon (Ely) Apr. 3, 1518. Probably R. of Deal, Kent, 1544. Will (P.C.C.) 1551.

HARMAN, THOMAS. Matric. pens. from ST JOHN'S, Michs. 1578; B.A. from Magdalene, 1581-2.

HARMAN, WALTER. B.A. 1504-5; M.A. 1508. Probably pens. at GONVILLE HALL, 1510-2.

HARMAN, ——. B.A. 1461-2; probably M.A., as Herman, 1464-5.

HARMAY, JAMES. Matric. pens. from TRINITY, *c.* 1596.

HARME or HAROME, ROBERT. B.A. 1473-4; M.A. (? 1477). Ord. deacon (Lincoln) Mar. 1497; title, the Hospital of ST JOHN, Cambridge.

HARMER, JOHN. M.A. 1584 (Incorp. from Oxford). Of Newbury, Berks. School, Winchester. Matric. from New College, Oxford, Jan. 10, 1574-5; B.A. (Oxford) 1576-7; M.A. 1582; B.D. and D.D. 1605. Fellow of New College, Oxford. Proctor, 1587. Regius Professor of Greek, 1585-9. Warden of St Mary's College, Winchester, 1596-1613. Head Master of Winchester College, 1588-95. Canon of Winchester, 1594-1613. R. of Compton, Hants., 1595; and of Droxford, 1596. One of the translators of the New Testament, 1604. Author. Died Oct. 11, 1613. Buried in the Chapel of New College. M.I. there. Will (P.C.C.) 1614. (*Al. Oxon.*; *D.N.B.*)

HARMER, JOHN. Adm. sizar at CORPUS CHRISTI, 1626. Of Norfolk. Matric. Easter, 1627; B.A. 1630-1; M.A. 1637. Ord. priest (Norwich) Dec. 23, 1632. Licensed as schoolmaster, 1633. Perhaps V. of St Andrew's, Norwich.

HARMER, JOHN. Adm. at CORPUS CHRISTI, 1667. Of Norfolk. Matric. Easter, 1667; B.A. 1670-1. Ord. priest (Norwich) Sept. 1673.

HARMER, RICHARD. Matric. pens. from ST JOHN'S, Michs. 1581.

HARMER (?), ROBERT. Matric. pens. from CLARE, *c.* 1596. One Robert Harmer was V. of Steeple Morden, Cambs., 1620-8. Buried there June 26, 1628. But *see* a contemporary in *Al. Oxon.*

HARMER, ROBERT. Matric. sizar from ST JOHN'S, Easter, 1626; B.A. 1629-30; M.A. 1633. Common preacher or lecturer of Colchester, Essex, 1639-48. (*Morant*, I. 100.)

HARMER, ROBERT. Adm. at CORPUS CHRISTI, 1666. Of Norfolk. Matric. Easter, 1667-8; B.A. 1669-70. Perhaps brother of John (1667).

HARMER, ROBERT. Adm. pens. (age 16) at PETERHOUSE, May 6, 1697. Of Norfolk. School, Bury St Edmunds. Matric. 1697; Scholar, 1697; B.A. 1700-1. Ord. deacon (Norwich) Sept. 1703; priest, June, 1707. V. of Heacham, Norfolk, 1704. V. of Sedgeford, 1708.

HARMER, WILLIAM. Adm. pens. at CLARE, Apr. 4, 1667. Matric. 1669; B.A. 1670-1; M.A. 1674. Ord. deacon (Norwich) June; priest, Sept. 1674. R. of Stiffkey, Norfolk, 1679. Died Oct. 1702, aged 52. M.I. at Stiffkey.

HARMER, WILLIAM. Adm. pens. (age 19) at CAIUS, Feb. 17, 1701-2. S. of William, attorney, of Swafield, Norfolk. B. there. Schools, North Walsham (Mr Harvey) and Bury (Mr Leeds). Matric. 1702; Scholar, 1702-7; M.B. 1707. Died Sept. 12, 1727. M.I. at Swafield. (Venn, I. 508.)

HARMER, WILLIAM. Adm. at CORPUS CHRISTI, 1706. Of Norwich. B. 1691. Matric. 1707; B.A. 1710-1. Ord. deacon (Norwich) Sept. 1714; priest (Ely) Sept. 25, 1715. R. of Hardwick, Norfolk, 1715.

HARMITAGE, *see also* ARMITAGE.

HARMYTAGE, NICHOLAS. Matric. sizar from CLARE, Lent, 1557-8.

HARMYTAGE, THOMAS. Matric. sizar from ST JOHN'S, Lent, 1581-2.

HARMSTON, JOHN. Adm. pens. (age 17) at CHRIST'S, Apr. 17, 1663. S. of Richard. B. at Carlton, Lincs. School, Newark (Mr Leeds). B.A. 1666. Ord. priest (Lincoln) Apr. 1670. R. of East Barkwith, Lincs., 1670; of Wickenby, 1671. (*Peile*, I. 602.)

HARMSTON, SAMUEL. Adm. at MAGDALENE, Apr. 1736. Matric. 1736.

HARNYSS or ARNESSE, EDWARD. Matric. sizar from ST JOHN'S, Michs. 1554. B. at Richmond, Surrey. Migrated to Queens'. B.A. 1558-9; M.A. 1562. Fellow of Queens', 1558-60. Ord. priest (London) Dec. 27, 1559, age 26.

HARNESSE, JOHN. Adm. sizar (age 16) at SIDNEY, Aug. 10, 1650. S. of Thomas, deceased. B. at Laceby, Lincs. School, Riby, Lincs. (Mr Taylour). Matric. 1650-1. Migrated to Magdalene, July 8, 1653. B.A. 1654-5; M.A. 1658. R. of Badsworth, Yorks. R. of Irby, Lincs., 1667-79. Died Jan. 17, 1678-9. Father of Thomas (1680). (*Lincs. Pedigrees*, 459, 1252.)

HARNEIS, RICHARD. Adm. sizar (age 18) at MAGDALENE, Sept. 27, 1723. S. of John. B. at Lincoln. School, Lincoln. Matric. 1723; B.A. 1727-8; M.A. 1731. Fellow, 1728. Ord. deacon (Lincoln) May 20, 1733; priest, Sept. 19, 1736. Died July 7, 1745. Buried at St Peter-at-Arches, Lincoln. (*Lincs. Pedigrees*, 460.)

HARNESS, THOMAS. Adm. pens. (age 16) at MAGDALENE, June 5, 1660. S. of Theophilus, of Laceby, Lincs. School, Louth. Matric. 1660. Married and had issue. Buried at Laceby, Aug. 24, 1719. (*Lincs. Pedigrees*, 459, 1252.)

HARNEIS, THOMAS. Adm. sizar at JESUS, May 31, 1680. S. of John (1650), R. of Irby, Lincs. Matric. 1680; Rustat scholar; B.A. 1683-4; M.A. 1687. C. of Brigsley, Lincs., 1688. R. of Rothwell, Lincs. Buried at Laceby, Feb. 9, 1732-3. (*Lincs. Pedigrees*, 459.)

HARNHAM, JOHN. B.Civ.L. Commissary-general to the Bishop of Ely, 1444. R. of Leverington, Cambs., 1452. Preb. of Salisbury, 1455-73. Died 1473. Will, P.C.C.

HAROLD, Earl of (ANTHONY GREY). Adm. nobleman (age 17) at TRINITY, June 6, 1712. S. of Henry, Duke of Kent. Bapt. at Flitton, Beds., Mar. 2, 1695-6. Matric. 1713-4; LL.D. 1717 (*Com. Reg.*). Summoned to the House of Lords, 1718, as Baron Lucas of Crudwell. Died *s.p.* and *v.p.*, July 21, 1723. (*G.E.C.*)

HARROLD, CORNELIUS. M.A. from ST CATHARINE'S, 1715. S. of C., of Coventry. Matric. from St John's College, Oxford, Oct. 16, 1703, age 15; B.A. (Oxford) 1707. Subscribed as deacon (Peterb.) May 30, 1708. C. of Clay Coton, Northants., 1708. R. of Croft, Leics., 1731. (*Al. Oxon.*)

HAROULD, EDWARD. Matric. sizar from JESUS, Michs. 1571.

HAROLD, WILLIAM. Adm. at CORPUS CHRISTI, 1703. Of Norwich. Matric. Easter, 1703; B.A. 1706-7. Died 1709, aged 23. Buried in St Peter Mancroft, Norwich. (*Masters*.)

HARPAM, RICHARD. B.A. 1497-8. One of these names R. of Springthorpe, Lincs., 1530-9. Died 1539.

HARPENYE, ANTHONY. Matric. pens. from CHRIST'S, June, 1584; B.A. from Magdalene, 1586-7.

HARPENY, JOHN. Adm. at KING'S (age 16) a scholar from Eton, Sept. 7, 1546. Of St Gregory, London. Matric. 1546. Left 1549.

HARPUR, EDWARD. Adm. at CORPUS CHRISTI, 1733. 3rd s. of Sir John, of Calke, Derbs., Bart. Matric. 1733.

HARPUR, FRANCIS. Adm. pens. at TRINITY, June 29, 1670. School, Westminster. Matric. 1671; Scholar, 1671. One of these names Head Master of the Free School, Chester, 1699-1713. Buried in Chester Cathedral, Nov. 26, 1713. Will (Chester) 1716. (E. Axon.)

HARPUR, HENRY. Adm. pens. (age 16) at ST JOHN'S, Mar. 1, 1748-9. S. of Henry, gent., of Middlesex. B. at Islington. School, Maidstone, Kent (Mr Russel). Matric. 1748-9; B.A. 1753. Ord. priest (Rochester) June 29, 1756. V. of Tonbridge, Kent, 1756-90. Buried there Oct. 11, 1790. M.I. Admon., P.C.C.

HARPUR, ISAAC. Adm. sizar (age 16) at ST JOHN'S, Apr. 7, 1660. S. of Fraucis, mercer, of Stockport, Cheshire. B. there. School, Stockport (Mr Tho. Combes). Matric. 1660; B.A. 1663-4. Ord. deacon (Chester) Sept. 25, 1664; priest (Lichfield) Dec. 17, 1665. C. of St Mary's, Oldham, Lancs., 1669-96. Buried at Chester Cathedral, Jan. 17, 1706-7; 'schoolmaster at the abbey Court.' (E. Axon.)

HARPUR, JOHN. Matric. Fell.-Com. from ST JOHN'S, Michs. 1588. 2nd s. of Sir John, of Swarkestone, Derbs. Adm. at the Inner Temple, 1590. Knighted, Apr. 21, 1603. M.P. for Co. Derbs., 1604-11. Married Dorothy, dau. of John Dethick, of Breadsall, Derbs. Will (P.C.C.) 1622. Brother of Richard (1588).

HARPER, JOHN. Adm. pens. at EMMANUEL, Jan. 30, 1614-5. Matric. 1615; B.A. 1618; M.A. 1622. Ord. deacon (Peterb.) May 23, 1619; priest, June 11, 1620. Perhaps V. of Cubbington, Warws., 1627. Marriage licence (Peterb., Oct. 2, 1632) between John Harpur, of Cottesmore, Rutland, clerk, and Anne Wells, of Uppingham, at Normanton, Rutland. (H. I. Longden.)

HARPER, JOHN. Matric. pens. from QUEENS', Easter, 1618-9. Of Suffolk. B.A. 1622-3; M.A. 1626. Perhaps Incorp. at Oxford, 1628. Ord. deacon (Norwich) Dec. 18, 1625; priest, 1626. R. of Withersdale, Suffolk, 1628. One of these names V. of Weybread, 1663.

HARPUR, JOHN. Adm. pens. at EMMANUEL, Oct. 29, 1620. Matric. 1621; B.A. 1624-5; M.A. 1628. One of these names V. of Nazing, Essex, 1645; of Epping, 1650-60, ejected. Minister of St Mary Aldermanbury, 1666-70. Perhaps P.C. of Theydon Bois, 1667. V. of Witham, 1668-70. Died 1670. Will (P.C.C.) 1671; of Epping, clerk.

HARPER, JOHN. Adm. sizar (age 17) at CHRIST'S, Apr. 5, 1630. S. of John. B. at North Mimms, Herts. School, Hertford (Mr Minors). Matric. 1631; B.A. 1633-4; M.A. 1637. Licensed to teach grammar at Northaw, Herts., 1637. V. of Sandridge, 1643-50. One of these names R. of Morley, Derbs., 1647; episcopally instituted, 1662. Died 1690. (*Peile*, I. 404; Cox, *Churches of Derbs.*, IV. 323; see also *Al. Oxon.*)

HARPER, JOHN. Adm. sizar (age 18) at ST JOHN'S, Oct. 9, 1654. S. of Edward, yeoman, of Bishop Wearmouth, Durham. B. there. School, Sedbergh. Matric. 1654; B.A. 1658-9; M.A. 1662. V. of Berwick-on-Tweed, till 1686. V. of Northallerton, Yorks., 1686-94. Buried June 29, 1694. (H. M. Wood.)

HARPER, JOHN. Adm. pens. at EMMANUEL, Feb. 15, 1659-60. Of Hertfordshire. Matric. 1660; B.A. 1663. Signed for deacon's orders (London) Mar. 5, 1663-4, as tutor in the house of Richard Atkins (probably at Clapham, Surrey). One of these names licensed to teach at Dulwich College, May 19, 1664. (J. Ch. Smith.)

HARPUR, JOHN. Adm. sizar at JESUS, July 5, 1708. Of Middlesex. Matric. 1708; B.A. 1711-2; M.A. 1716. Ord. deacon (Norwich) Dec. 1714. C. of Little Over, Derbs. Perhaps R. of Stanton-by-Bridge, 1723-44. P.C. of Calke, 1727-37. Chaplain to Sir John and Sir Henry Harpur. Died July 7, 1744. Buried at Calke. (Cox, *Churches of Derbs.*, III. 350.)

HARPUR, JOHN. M.A. from JESUS, 1709. B. at Oldham, Lancs., *cler. fil.* Matric. from Brasenose College, Oxford, Mar. 18, 1691-2, age 17; B.A. (Oxford) 1695. P.C. of Gorton, Lancs., 1704. (*Al. Oxon.*)

HARPER, JOHN. Adm. pens. (age 17) at TRINITY, June 11, 1718. S. of Miles, of London. School, Westminster. Matric. 1718; Scholar, 1719; B.A. 1721-2.

HARPER, JOHN. M.A. from CLARE, 1721. S. of Edward, of Hartlebury, Worcs. Matric. from University College, Oxford, Apr. 3, 1701, age 17; B.A. (Oxford) 1704-5. V. of Ashleworth, Gloucs., 1716-24. V. of Beckford, 1724-54. Married, 1719, Elizabeth Dee, of Bredon, Worcs. Buried at Beckford, 1754, aged 71. M.I. (*Al. Oxon.*; F. S. Hockaday.)

HARPER, RALPH. Adm. sizar at JESUS, June 22, 1682. Of Salop. S. of Ralph, V. of Audley, Staffs. Matric. 1682; B.A. 1685-6.

HARPUR, RICHARD. Matric. Fell.-Com. from ST JOHN'S, Michs. 1588. S. and h. of Sir John, of Swarkstone, Derbs. Adm. at the Inner Temple, 1590. Knighted, Aug. 6, 1608. Sheriff of Derbs. Will (P.C.C.) 1619. Brother of John (1588), father of the next.

HARPER, RICHARD. Matric. pens. from PEMBROKE, Michs. 1606. Doubtless s. and h. of Sir Richard (above), of Littleover, Derbs., Knt.; adm. at Gray's Inn, Nov. 20, 1610. Perhaps knighted, Apr. 14, 1617.

HARPER, RICHARD. Adm. pens. at PETERHOUSE, Apr. 28, 1634. Of Nottinghamshire. Matric. 1634.

HARPER, ROBERT. Matric. sizar from QUEENS', Michs. 1626. Of Suffolk. B.A. 1629-30.

HARPER, SAMUEL. Adm. pens. (age 17) at TRINITY, Mar. 12, 1749-50. S. of Robert, of London. School, Fulham, London (Mr Croft). Matric. 1750; Scholar, 1750; B.A. 1754; M.A. 1757. Ord. deacon (York) June 13, 1756; priest, Mar. 1757. C. of Gamston, Notts. Perhaps F.R.S., 1766; V. of Rothwell, Leeds, in 1775.

HARPER, THOMAS. Matric. pens. from ST JOHN'S, Michs. 1616. B. in St Olave, Southwark. Doubtless s. of Henry, of Southwark. B.A. 1620–1; M.A. 1624. Incorp. at Oxford, 1626. Ord. deacon (London) Dec. 23, 1621, age 23. R. of Witherley, Leics., 1622. Perhaps R. of Norbury, Derbs., 1627. (*Vis. of Surrey*, 1623; *Al. Oxon.*)

HARPER, THOMAS. Adm. sizar (age 15) at PETERHOUSE, May 10, 1676. Of Leicestershire. School, Market Harborough. Matric. 1676; Scholar, 1679; B.A. 1679–80; M.A. 1683. Fellow, 1682–7. Ord. priest (London) Feb. 28, 1685–6. R. of Grafton Underwood, Northants., 1686–92. R. of St Catherine Coleman, London, 1692–1714. R. of Orsett, Essex, 1700–14. Died 1714. Will, P.C.C.

HARPER, THOMAS. Adm. sizar (age 18) at TRINITY, June 16, 1687. S. of Thomas. B. at Southwark. School, Southwark (Mr Brattle). Matric. 1687–8; Scholar, 1691; B.A. 1691–2. C. of Nettlestead, Kent. R. of Orlestone. Perhaps V. of Teston, 1710–1. Died Mar. 20, 1719, aged 51. Buried at Nettlestead.

HARPER, WALTER. Matric. pens. from ST JOHN'S, Easter, 1565; B.A. 1569–70.

HARPUR or HARPER, WILLIAM. Adm. pens. (age 18) at ST JOHN'S, June 16, 1729. S. of William, gent., of Durham. B. at Gateshead, Newcastle. School, Sedbergh. Matric. 1729; B.A. 1732–3; M.A. 1749. Ord. priest (Durham) Sept. 1733. C. of Gateshead. R. of Barwick-in-Elmet, Yorks., 1740–9. Married, at Gateshead, Feb. 17, 1734–5, Frances Rudstone. Died May 14, 1749. (*Scott-Mayor*, III. 423.)

HARPER, ——. B.A. 1520–1; M.A. 1524.

HARPHAM, MARTIN. Adm. sizar (age 18) at MAGDALENE, June 22, 1680. S. of Philip. B. at North Kelsey, Lincs. School, Caistor, Lincs. Matric. 1680, as 'Harper.'

HARPLE or HAPPLE, HUGH. Scholar at KING'S HALL, 1383–1406.

HARPELE, JOHN DE. M.A. Of Norwich diocese. Fellow of PETERHOUSE in 1331. (*Papal Letters*.)

HARPUM, PETER. Matric. pens. from JESUS, Easter, 1614.

HARRIDANCE or HARRYDANCE, MICHAEL. Matric. pens. from CORPUS CHRISTI, Michs. 1579. B. at Fakenham, Norfolk. B.A. 1582–3. Ord. deacon (London) Nov. 30, 1585, age 24. C. of East Mersey, Essex. R. of Dunton-*cum*-Doughton, Norfolk, 1599–1604.

HARRIDANCE or HALYDANCE, ROBERT. B.A. 1477–8; M.A. 1482; M.B. 1486–7; M.D. 1499–1500, as Harridawnce. Of Norwich. Died 1513. M.I. at St Michael Coslany.

HARRYDANCE, SAMUEL. Matric. pens. from CHRIST'S, Nov. 1570. Ord. deacon and priest (Peterb.) Mar. 16, 1572–3. R. of Frating, Essex, 1576–1607. Died before Nov. 1607. (*Peile*, I. 115.)

HARRYDANCE, WILLIAM. Adm. pens. (age 15) at CAIUS, Oct. 31, 1648. S. of William, gent., of Fakenham. Schools, Fakenham (Mr Wells), Sculthorpe (Mr Turner) and Norwich (Mr Lovering). Of Fakenham, gent. Will proved, 1664. (*Venn*, I. 373.)

HARRIMAN, GAVIN (GAWEN, OWEN). Probably matric. sizar from PEMBROKE, Michs. 1587, as 'Harrimer'; B.A. from Trinity, 1590–1. Ord. deacon and priest (Lincoln) Sept. 27, 1592. R. of Braceborough, Lincs., 1592. Married, at Glinton, Northants., Nov. 6, 1598, Marian, dau. of Robert Wildbore. (*Vis. of Northants.*, 1618; H. I. Longden.)

HARRYMAN, JOHN. Adm. pens. at EMMANUEL, May 21, 1688. Of Huntingdonshire. Matric. 1688; B.A. 1691–2; M.A. 1695. Ord. deacon (Lincoln) Feb. 28, 1696–7; priest, Mar. 5, 1698–9. R. of Peckleton, Leics., 1712. Died June 13, 1743. Will, Leicester. (*Nichols*, IV. 873.)

HARRIMAN, THOMAS. Matric. sizar from ST JOHN'S, Michs. 1554. One of these names V. of Rugeley, Staffs., in 1574. (*Wm. Salt Arch. Soc.*, 1915.)

HARRIMAN, THOMAS. Matric. pens. from ST JOHN'S, Lent, 1620–1.

HARRINGTON, ANDREW. Matric. sizar from KING'S, *c.* 1595; B.A. 1598–9; M.A. from Sidney, 1602. Ord. deacon (Norwich) Mar. 25, 1601; priest (Peterb.) Dec. 23, 1604. V. of Saxby, Lincs., 1610–2. V. of Stainton-by-Langworth, Lincs., 1612–24.

HARRINGTON, EDMUND. Adm. at CORPUS CHRISTI, 1606. Of Essex.

HARRINGTON, EDWARD. Matric. Fell.-Com. from CHRIST'S, *c.* 1598. S. of James (afterwards Bart.). B. at Ridlington, Rutland. Migrated to Sidney, Sept. 1598. B.A. 1599–1600. Knighted, May 11, 1603. Succeeded as Bart., 1614. Sheriff of Rutland, 1621–2, 1636–7. Died 1653. (*G.E.C.*, I. 53; *Vis. of Rutland*, 1618.)

HARRINGTON, EDWARD. Matric. pens. from QUEENS', Easter, 1624. Of Essex. B.A. 1627–8; M.A. 1631. One of these names R. of Aspenden, Herts., 1650.

HARRINGTON, FRANCIS. Adm. Fell.-Com. at SIDNEY, June, 1615. 1st s. of Thomas, of South Witham and Boothby Pagnell, Lincs. B. at Boothby, Lincs. Adm. at the Inner Temple, 1616. (*Lincs. Pedigrees*, 462.)

HARRINGTON, HENRY. Matric. from CORPUS CHRISTI, 1567; B.A. from Christ's, 1570–1. Went to Ireland, where he had a command in the army. Knighted, at Dublin, Apr. 24, 1578. M.P. for Wicklow, 1585–6. One of the Privy Council in Ireland, *c.* 1603. Will (P.C.C.) 1613. (*Peile*, I. 100; A. B. Beaven.)

HARRINGTON, HENRY. Adm. Fell.-Com. at SIDNEY, May, 1600. S. of Sir James. (*Vis. of Rutland*, 1618.)

HARRINGTON, HENRY. Matric. sizar from CORPUS CHRISTI, Michs. 1610. Of Essex. B.A. 1613–4.

HARRINGTON, HENRY. Adm. Fell.-Com. at SIDNEY, June 2, 1613. Matric. 1613. One of these names, of Ridlington, Rutland, adm. at Gray's Inn, Feb. 2, 1620–1.

HARRINGTON, HENRY. Adm. pens. (age 15) at SIDNEY, Sept. 29, 1658. 3rd s. of John, Esq. B. at Hunnington, Warws. Schools, Westminster and Oakham (Mr Frere). Matric. 1658.

HARRINGTON, JAMES. Adm. Fell.-Com. at KING'S, 1570–1.

HARRINGTON, JAMES. Adm. Fell.-Com. at CHRIST'S, Easter, 1594–5. Probably 3rd s. of Sir James, of Exton, Rutland. Knighted, Apr. 18, 1603. Created Bart., June 29, 1611. Died Feb. 2, 1613–4. Buried at Ridlington. M.I. Will (P.C.C.) 1614. (*Peile*, I. 216; *Rutland Mag.*, II. 132.)

HARRINGTON, JAMES. M.A. 1634 (Incorp. from Oxford). S. of Sir James, of Ridlington, Ruts. Matric. from Hart Hall, Oxford, Oct. 11, 1605, age 17; B.A. (Oxford) 1608; M.A. 1610–1. Fellow of Wadham College, 1613–27.

HARINGTON, JAMES. Adm. sizar (age 15) at ST JOHN'S, June 1, 1643. S. of William, gent., of Gt Maplestead, Essex. B. there. School, Felsted (Mr Holbeach). Matric. 1645; B.A. 1646–7.

HARRINGTON, JAMES. Adm. sizar (age 17) at PETERHOUSE, Apr. 3, 1675. Of Yorkshire. School, Melton (? Malton, *see* John, 1662–3), Yorks. Matric. 1675.

HARINGTON, JOHN. Incorp. LL.D. 1492–3. Perhaps R. of Colne Wake, Essex, 1504–47. Died 1547.

HARINGTON, JOHN. Matric. Fell.-Com. from KING'S, Michs. 1576. S. of John, of Stepney, Cheshunt Park, and Kelston, Somerset, Esq. School, Eton. B.A. 1577–8 (1st in the *ordo*); M.A. 1581. Adm. at Lincoln's Inn, Nov. 27, 1581; of Somerset. High Sheriff of Somerset, 1591. Accompanied Lord Essex to Ireland, 1598. Knighted, July 30, 1599. Scholar and poet. Godson of Queen Elizabeth. Buried at Kelston, Somerset, Dec. 1, 1612. Will (P.C.C.) 1614. (*Misc. Gen. et Her.*, IV. 191; *D.N.B.*, where he is wrongly assigned to Christ's College.)

HARRINGTON, JOHN. Adm. Fell.-Com. at CHRIST'S, *c.* 1594. Died before 1606, when he left a legacy of £40 to the College. (*Peile*, I. 216.)

HARRINGTON, JOHN. Matric. from Trinity College, Oxford, Dec. 7, 1604, age 15. S. of Sir John, of Kelston, Somerset. Migrated to Cambridge; Incorp. there, 1607. Adm. at Lincoln's Inn, Apr. 30, 1608. Barrister-at-law, 1615. Treasurer, 1651. M.P. for Somerset, 1645–53; and probably 1654, 1656. (*Al. Oxon.*)

HARINGTON, Sir JOHN. Adm. Fell.-Com. (age 15) at SIDNEY, July 6, 1607. S. of Sir John, Baron Harington, of Exton, Rutland. B. at Combe Abbey, near Coventry. Bapt. at Stepney, May 3, 1592. K.B., 1605. Friend and correspondent of Henry, Prince of Wales. Succeeded as Baron, Aug. 1613. A good linguist, 'well read in logic and philosophy.' Benefactor of his College. Died at Kew, Feb. 27, 1613–4. Buried at Exton. (*G.E.C.*; *D.N.B.*)

HARRINGTON, JOHN. B.A. from CLARE, 1625–6.

HARRINGTON, JOHN. Matric. Fell.-Com. from TRINITY, Michs. 1626. Perhaps s. and h. of Thomas, of Boothby Pagnell, Lincs., Esq.; adm. at Gray's Inn, May 10, 1627. Married and had issue. (*Lincs. Pedigrees*, 462.)

HARRINGTON, JOHN. Adm. sizar (age 17) at PETERHOUSE, Mar. 21, 1662–3. Of Yorkshire. School, Malton. Matric. 1663; B.A. 1666–7; M.A. 1670. Ord. deacon (York) 1667; priest, 1667. One of these names clerk, of Settrington, Yorks., married Anne, dau. of Philip Wreathe, of Langtoft, Jan. 21, 1672–3. (M. H. Peacock.)

HARINGTON, JOHN. Matric. pens. from CHRIST'S, Easter, 1663. One of these names, s. and h. of Benjamin, of Weymouth, Dorset, Esq., adm. at Lincoln's Inn, Nov. 30, 1669.

HARRINGTON, JOSEPH. Matric. pens. from EMMANUEL, Easter, 1637.

HARRINGTON, RALPH. Matric. pens. from PETERHOUSE, Easter, 1608.

HARRINGTON, ROBERT. B.A. 1482-3; M.A. 1486-7.

HARRINGTON, ROBERT. Matric. sizar from CORPUS CHRISTI, Michs. 1567.

HARRINGTON, ROBERT. Matric. pens. from QUEENS', Easter, 1567. Of Essex. B.A. 1570-1; M.A. 1574; B.D. 1582. Fellow, 1572-6. V. of Sible Hedingham, Essex, 1574-94. Died 1594.

HARRINGTON, ROBERT. Adm. pens. (age 17) at SIDNEY, Jan. 23, 1668-9. S. of Sir James, Bart. B. at Swakeley, Middlesex. School, Isleworth (Mr Henry Willis). (*Vis. of Rutland*, 1618.)

HARRINGTON, VILLIERS. Adm. pens. at CLARE, Apr. 10, 1638. Matric. 1638.

HARINGTON, WILLIAM. B.Civ.L. 1492-3. Incorp. (as Heryngton). LL.D. from Bologna, 1499-1500. Doubtless s. of William, of Newbigging, Cumberland. B. at Eastrington, Yorks. Preb. of St Paul's, 1497-1523. R. of St Anne, Aldersgate, London, 1505-10. Caused his tomb to be erected in St John's Chapel, St Paul's Cathedral, shortly before his death. Will (P.C.C.) dated Oct. 12, 1523; proved Jan. 1523-4. (*D.N.B.*; H. G. Harrison.)

HARRINGTON, WILLIAM. Matric. pens. from ST JOHN'S, Michs. 1553. Of Yorkshire. B.A. 1556-7. Fellow, 1557.

HARRINGTON, WILLIAM. Adm. at KING'S (age 18) a scholar from Eton, Aug. 25, 1578. Of London. Matric. 1578. Left in 1581. Probably adm. at Lincoln's Inn, May 9, 1581. 'Travelled beyond the sea.' (*Harwood*.)

HARRINGTON, WILLIAM. Matric. from Magdalen College, Oxford, Mar. 29, 1639, age 16. Migrated to SIDNEY, Nov. 4, 1641. S. of Sir John, Knt. B. at Spalding, Lincs. School, Spalding (Mr Heaton). Matric. 1641; B.A. 1642-3; M.A. from Cams, 1646; LL.D. 1652 (by Visitor's mandate): he had served in the Parliamentary army. Fellow of Caius, 1645-54. Incorp. at Oxford, 1653. R. of Pattesley, Norfolk, 1653. V. of Orwell, Cambs., 1654. Will (P.C.C.) 1697; of London, LL.D. (*Venn*, I. 354.)

HARINGTON, ——. B.Civ.L. 1479-80. Perhaps Richard, V. of Haslingfield, Cambs., 1485.

HARRYNGTON, —— (*maximus*). Matric. pens. from CHRIST'S, May, 1544. (For possible identifications *see Peile*, I. 34.)

HARRYNGTON, —— (*major*). Matrie. pens. from CHRIST'S, May, 1544.

HARRYNGTON, —— (*minor*). Matric. pens. from CHRIST'S, May, 1544.

HARRYNGTON, —— (*minimus*). Matric. pens. from CHRIST'S, May, 1544.

HARRINGTON, ——. Fell.-Com. at PETERHOUSE, Easter, 1559.

HARRINGTON, ——. Matric. pens. from ST JOHN'S, *c.* 1594.

HARRIOTT, JOHN. Matric. pens. from ST JOHN'S, Michs. 1567.

HARRIOTT, RICHARD. Adm. sizar at QUEENS', 1612. B. at Wellingborough, Northants. Matric. Easter, 1613; B.A. 1615-6; M.A. 1619. Ord. deacon (London) Sept. 20, 1618, age 23; priest, Sept. 1619. C. of Hanwell, Middlesex. V. of Eynesford, Kent, 1631-51. V. of Lullingstone, 1631-51. Buried at Eynesford, Apr. 30, 1651. (C. H. Fielding.)

HARRIOTT, ROBERT. Adm. sizar at SIDNEY, Oct. 1599. B. at Wellingborough, Northants. B.A. 1603-4; M.A. 1607. Ord. deacon (London) Sept. 22, 1611, age *c.* 30; priest, Dec. 18, 1613. C. of Gt Greenford, Middlesex. Master of Wellingborough School, Northants. Buried there June 19, 1636. Will (Archd. Northants) 1636. (H. I. Longden.)

HARRIATT, WILLIAM. B.A. from CHRIST'S, 1603-4; M.A. 1607. Ord. deacon (Peterb.) Dec. 20, 1607; priest, May 22, 1608.

HARRIS, ARTHUR. Matric. pens. from ST JOHN'S, Easter, 1589. One of these names adm. at Lincoln's Inn, Apr. 25, 1591; of Salop.

HARRIS, ARTHUR. Adm. Fell.-Com. at SIDNEY, Feb. 1601-2. Of Essex. S. and h. of Sir William, of Cricksey, Essex, Knt. Matric. 1602. Adm. at Gray's Inn, Nov. 20, 1605; and perhaps at Lincoln's Inn, Apr. 28, 1607. Of Cricksey and Woodham Mortimer, Essex, Knt. Knighted, July 15, 1606. M.P. for Malden, 1624-5 and 1628-9 (but elected to serve for Essex County), 1625. Married (1) Anne, dau. of Robert Cranmer, of Kent; (2) Anne, dau. of Sir Nicolas Salter, of Enfield, Middlesex. Died Jan. 9, 1631-2. Father of the next, Cranmer (1623), John (1628), Thomas (1644-5) and Salter (1639). (*Vis. of Essex*, 1612; A. B. Beaven; *Morant*, I. 363.)

HARRIS or HERRIS, ARTHUR. Adm. pens. (age 16) at CHRIST'S, Mar. 18, 1644-5. S. of Sir Arthur (above), Knt. B. at Woodham Mortimer, Essex. School, Chelmsford (Mr Peake). Matric. 1645. Of Stock, Essex, Esq. Brother of Cranmer (1623), John (1628), Salter (1639) and Thomas (1644-5). (*Peile*, I. 492.)

HARRIES, CHARLES. M.A. from KING'S, 1743. Probably s. of John, of Ystrad, Cardigan. Matric. from Jesus College, Oxford, Mar. 30, 1726, age 17; B.A. (Oxford) 1729. R. of Llanllwchaiarn, Montgom.; exchanged this for Cricklade, Wilts. R. of Llangyniew, 1756-61. (*Al. Oxon.*)

HARRIS, CHRISTOPHER. Matric. Fell.-Com. from TRINITY, Michs. 1614. Perhaps s. and h. of Sir William Herris, of Shenfield, Essex, Knt.; adm. at Lincoln's Inn, Jan. 3, 1616-7. Probably M.P. for East Looe, 1620-2; for Ipswich, 1624-5, 1626, 1628. Married Elizabeth, dau. of Sir Harbottle Grimstone, Knt. and Bart. Died 1628. (*Vis. of Essex*, 1634; A. B. Beaven.)

HERRYS, CHRISTOPHER. Adm. at CORPUS CHRISTI, 1647. Of Essex.

HARRIS, CHRISTOPHER. M.A. from TRINITY HALL, 1683. S. of Andrew, of Totnes, Devon, clerk. Matric. from Christ Church, Oxford, Mar. 14, 1662-3, age 15; B.A. (Oxford) 1666-7. P.C. of Wingham, Kent, 1672-1719. R. of Bircholt, 1673. R. of Stourmouth, 1690-1719. Died Nov. 24, 1719, aged 73. Buried at Wingham. M.I. (*Al. Oxon.*; *Hasted*, III. 703.)

HARRIS, CRANMER. Adm. Fell.-Com. at JESUS, Oct. 10, 1623. Of Essex. S. and h. of Sir Arthur (1602), of Saltwood, Kent, and Cricksey, Essex, Knt. Matric. 1624. Knighted, June 21, 1629. Succeeded his father, in 1632. Of Cricksey. High Sheriff of Essex, 1634-5. Brother of Arthur (1644-5), etc. (*Vis. of Essex*, 1612.)

HARRIS, CRANMER. Adm. pens. (age 15) at MAGDALENE, Mar. 24, 1647-8. S. of John (1628), late of Chipstead, Kent, Esq. School, Hertford. Matric. 1648. Adm. at Lincoln's Inn, Nov. 4, 1651.

HARRIS, DANIEL. Adm. sizar (age 19) at MAGDALENE, June 22, 1712. S. of Daniel, grocer. B. at Bewdley, Worcs. School, Bewdley. Matric. 1712; B.A. 1715-6. Perhaps R. of Portland, Dorset, 1730-46. Died 1746.

HARRIS, EDWARD. Adm. at CORPUS CHRISTI, 1579; B.A. 1585-6. One of these names R. of Shelton, Notts., 1595-1625. Died 1625.

HARRYS, EDWARD. Matric. sizar from ST JOHN'S, Easter, 1583.

HARRIS, EDWARD. Matric. pens. from EMMANUEL, Lent, 1588-9. One of these names adm. at Lincoln's Inn, Oct. 8, 1590; of Essex.

HARRYS, EDWARD. Matric. pens. from ST JOHN'S, Easter, 1616; B.A. 1619-20; M.A. 1623. One of these names (M.A.), V. of South Grantham, Lines., 1634' V. of Rushton St Peter, Northants., 1639-52. Buried there Apr. 8, 1652. (T. P. Dorman.)

HARRIS, EDWARD. Adm. pens. (age 16) at PEMBROKE, Sept. 28, 1652. S. of ——, of London, carpenter. Matric. 1653-4. One of these names s. and h. of Richard, of St Paul's, Middlesex, gent.; adm. at Lincoln's Inn, June 12, 1654.

HARRIS, GEORGE. B.A. 1543-4; M.A. 1545; B.D. from TRINITY, 1551 (died before admission). Fellow of Trinity, 1546. Will proved (V.C.C.) 1551.

HARRIS, GEORGE. B.A. from ST JOHN'S, 1620-1; M.A. 1624; B.D. 1631-2 (*Lit. Reg.*). Fellow, 1624. Of Surrey. Ord. deacon (Peterb.) May 15; priest, May 16, 1625. V. of Holy Trinity, Cambridge, 1628. Will (P.C.C.) 1638, of George Harryes, B.D., deceased abroad.

HARRIS, GEORGE. Matric. sizar from PEMBAOKE, Michs. 1627; B.A. 1627-8; M.A. from Corpus Christi, 1647.

HARRIS, GEORGE. Adm. sizar (age 18) at ST JOHN'S, Apr. 8, 1648. S. of William, husbandman, of Wetton, Staffs. B. there. School, Grindon (Mr Peck). Matrio. 1648.

HARRIS, GEORGE. Adm. at KING'S, a scholar from Eton, 1706. B. in Eton. Matric. 1706; B.A. 1710-1; M.A. 1714; D.D. 1734. Fellow, 1709. Fellow of Eton College, 1731. Vice-Provost, 1746-52. Ord. deacon (London) Mar. 16, 1711-2; priest, Sept. 21, 1712. V. of Ringwood, Hants. R. of Worplesdon, Surrey, 1746-52. Died Apr. 4, 1752. Father of John (1747). (*Manning and Bray*, III. 101.)

HARRIS, GEORGE. Incorp. B.A. at KING'S, 1734, from Balliol College, Oxford. Matric. there, Mar. 19, 1715-6. S. of Thomas, of St Ewen's, Bristol. B.A. (Oxford) 1721. (*Al. Oxon.*)

HARRIS, GEORGE. Adm. at CORPUS CHRISTI, 1736. Of London. Matric. 1736; B.A. 1738-9. Probably ord. priest (Peterb.) Dec. 20, 1747.

HARRIS, HENRY. Adm. sizar at CORPUS CHRISTI, 1633. Of London. Matric. Easter, 1634. Perhaps migrated to Oxford and matric. from Magdalen College, Feb. 10, 1636-7, age 17.

HARRIS, HENRY. Adm. pens. at CLARE, Oct. 2, 1662. Matric. 1663; B.A. 1666–7; M.A. 1670. Ord. priest (Gloucester, at the Ely Chapel, Holborn) Feb. 27, 1669–70. R. of Conington, Hunts., 1670–99. Died 1699.

HARRIS, HENRY. Adm. pens. (age 13) at ST JOHN'S, June 26, 1710. S. of Henry, grazier. B. in Surrey. School, Edmonton (Mr Button). Matric. 1710; B.A. 1713–4; M.A. 1717. Adm. at the Inner Temple, Jan. 2, 1717–8, as s. and h. of Henry, of Southwark, Surrey.

HARRIS, ISAIAH. Adm. pens. at TRINITY, Apr. 9, 1646. Of Northamptonshire. LL.B. 1660 (*Lit. Reg.*). Probably of Bucks., clerk, and father of Samuel (1673).

HARRYS, JAMES. Matric. sizar from JESUS, Easter, 1578; B.A. 1581–2. One of these names (B.A.), usher of Boston School, 1586.

HARRIS, JAMES. Adm. at CORPUS CHRISTI, 1699. Of Huntingdonshire. Matric. 1699–1700.

HARRIS, JAMES. Adm. at CORPUS CHRISTI, 1723. Of Cambridgeshire. Matric. Easter, 1724; B.A. 1727–8; M.A. 1734. Perhaps R. of Little Bradley, Suffolk, 1743–5 and R. of Cheveley, Cambs. Will (P.C.C.) 1778.

HARRIS, JAMES. M.A. from KING'S, 1750. S. of Richard, of Newton, Somerset, clerk. Matric. from Hart Hall, Oxford, Mar. 3, 1725–6, age 17; B.A. (Oxford) 1729. Ord. deacon (Bath and Wells) Dec. 20, 1730; priest, Dec. 24, 1732. R. of Abbotsbury, Dorset, 1741–72. Chaplain to Countess Temple. R. of Winterbourne Monkton, 1749–72. Died at Abbotsbury, May 4, 1772, aged 64. (F. S. Hockaday.)

HARRIS, JOHN. Adm. at KING'S, a scholar from Eton, 1480.

HARRIS or HARRYSE, JOHN. Matric. sizar from CHRIST'S, Nov. 1569; B.A. 1574–5.

HARRIS, JOHN. Matric. pens. from ST JOHN'S, Easter, 1617. One of these names, s. and h. of John, of Rickmansworth, Herts., adm. at Gray's Inn, Aug. 11, 1619.

HARRIES, JOHN. Adm. sizar at QUEENS', July 3, 1622. Of Salop. One of these names V. of Little Horwood, Bucks., in 1627.

HARRIS, JOHN. Adm. Fell.-Com. at JESUS, Apr. 30, 1628. Of Kent. 2nd s. of Sir Arthur (1601–2), of Cricksey, Essex, Knt. Matric. 1628. Adm. at Lincoln's Inn, Apr. 14, 1630. Of Chevening, Kent, where he succeeded his father, 1632. Died before 1651. Father of Cranmer (1647–8), brother of Arthur (1644), etc. (*Vis. of Essex*, 1612; A. Gray.)

HARRIS, JOHN. Matric. pens. from TRINITY, Easter, 1631; Scholar from Westminster, 1631; B.A. 1634–5.

HARRIS, JOHN. M.A. 1638 (Incorp. from Oxford). S. of Robert, of Hanwell, Oxon., clerk. Matric. from Magdalen Hall, Oxford, 1626; B.A. (Oxford) 1630; M.A. 1633; B.D. 1641. R. of Passenham, Northants., 1632–60. R. of Overstone, 1633–43. Preb. of Hereford, 1660–78. V. of Merstham, Surrey, 1660. Buried there Oct. 29, 1678. (*Al. Oxon.*; *Manning and Bray*, II. 264; H. I. Longden.)

HARRIS, JOHN. Adm. at PEMBROKE, June 19, 1649. S. o John, of Radford, Devon, Esq. Doubtless of Radford, Esq.; and father of John (1685).

HARRIS, JOHN. Matric. pens. from QUEENS', Michs. 1650. Of Dorset.

HARRIS, JOHN. Adm. pens. (age 16) at CAIUS, June 30, 1658. S. of Thomas, attorney-at-law, of Kirby, Norfolk. School, Norwich (Mr Lovering). Matric. 1658; Scholar, 1658–64; B.A. 1661–2; M.A. 1665. Probably ord. priest (Norwich) Sept. 23, 1665; C. of Poringland. R. of Elsing, 1667–82; of Bawdeswell, 1676–82. Will proved (Norwich) 1682. (*Venn*, I. 403.)

HARRIS, JOHN. Adm. sizar (age 19) at ST JOHN'S, Mar. 4, 1663–4. S. of John, deceased, of Arkholme, Lancs. B. there. School, Kirkby Lonsdale (Mr Garthwaite). Matric. 1664; B.A. 1667–8; M.A. 1671. Signed for deacon's orders (London) Sept. 18, 1668. One of these names R. of Hawstead, Suffolk, 1673.

HARRIS, JOHN. Adm. pens. (age 18) at ST JOHN'S, Mar. 21, 1682–3. S. of Edward, deceased. B. in London. School, Chiltington, Sussex (private; Mr Rushworth). Matric. 1684.

HARRIS, JOHN. Adm. sizar (age 17) at ST JOHN'S, May 28, 1684. S. of John, deceased. B. at Leicester. School, Leicester (Mr Wm. Thomas). B.A. 1687–8; M.A. 1691; B.D. 1699; D.D. (Lambeth) 1706. Fellow, 1691–1702. Ord. deacon (Lincoln) Sept. 20, 1696; priest, Feb. 28, 1696–7. F.R.S. 1696. Secretary, R.S. Preb. of Rochester, 1708–19. R. of St Mildred, Bread Street, with St Margaret Moses, London, 1708–19. R. of East Barming, Kent, 1715–7. P.C. of Strood, 1716–9. Lectured on mathematics in London. Author, scientific, topographical, etc. Died Sept. 7, 1719, in great poverty. Buried at Norton, Kent. Admon., P.C.C. (*D.N.B.*; C. H. Fielding.)

HARRYS, JOHN. Adm. Fell.-Com. (age 16) at TRINITY, Nov. 3, 1685. S. of John (? 1648), of Radford, Devon. School, Plymouth (Mr John Bedford).

HARRIS, JOHN. Adm. at CORPUS CHRISTI, 1688. Of Norfolk. B.A. 1691–2; M.A. 1695. Ord. priest (London) May, 1696.

HARRIS, JOHN. Adm. pens. at CLARE, Dec. 5, 1720. B. at Georgeham, Devon. Matric. 1720. One of these names V. of Furneaux Pelham, Herts., 1723–6.

HARRIS, JOHN. D.D. 1728 (*Com. Reg.*). S. of George, of Melford, Pembs. Matric. from Jesus College, Oxford, June 15, 1697, age 17; B.A. (Oxford) 1701; M.A. 1715. Fellow of Oriel College. Probably R. of Rudbaxton, Pembs., 1700–33. R. of Lampeter Velfrey, 1708–29. Preb. of Canterbury, 1728–38. V. of Ticehurst, Sussex, 1729–38. Dean of Hereford, 1729–36. Bishop of Llandaff, 1729–38. Dean of Wells, 1736–8. Died Aug. 28, 1738. (*Al. Oxon.*)

HARRIS, JOHN. M.A. from KING'S, 1734; of Exeter College, Oxford. (Identification uncertain.) (*Al. Oxon.*)

HARRIS, JOHN. M.A. from TRINITY, 1736. S. of John, of Easton Gray, Wilts., clerk. Matric. from Oriel College, Oxford, Feb. 6, 1720–1, age 17; B.A. (Oxford) 1724. (*Al. Oxon.*)

HARRIS, JOHN. Adm. at KING'S, a scholar from Eton, 1747. S. of George (1706), V. of Ringwood, Hants. B. there. Matric. 1748; B.A. 1752; M.A. 1756. Fellow, 1751. Ord. deacon (Ely) Dec. 25, 1752. R. of Stourminster Marshall, Dorset, 1753–1805. Died June 29, 1805. (F. S. Hockaday.)

HARRIS, JOSEPH. Adm. pens. (age 19) at TRINITY, June 4, 1730. S. of Thomas, of London. School, Westminster. Matric. 1731; Scholar, 1731. One of these names R. of Shadingfield, Suffolk, 1733. R. of Easton Bavent, 1734.

HARRIS, MALACHI. Adm. sizar at EMMANUEL, Easter, 1623. S. of Robert, R. of Hanwell, Oxon. B. at Banbury. B.A. 1626–7; M.A. 1630; B.D. 1637; D.D. 1660 (*Lit. Reg.*). Fellow, 1631. Incorp. at Oxford, 1669. V. of Navestock, Essex, 1656–60, ejected. R. of Farthinghoe, Northants., 1662–84. Accompanied Sir Thomas Rowe on two embassies, as chaplain. Chaplain to Mary, Princess of Orange. Buried at Farthinghoe. Apr. 19, 1684, aged 77. M.I.

HARRIS, MATTHEW. Adm. sizar at JESUS, June 4, 1629. Of Essex. Matric. 1629.

HARRIS, NICHOLAS. Adm. at EMMANUEL, Jan. 17, 1644; B.A. 1644–5. S. of John, of Maidstone, Kent. Previously at Corpus Christi College, Oxford. Matric. there, May 20, 1640.

HARRIS, NICHOLAS. Adm. at CORPUS CHRISTI, 1717. Of London. Adm. at the Inner Temple, Dec. 24, 1718; s. of Richard, merchant, of London. Adm. at Lincoln's Inn, May 27, 1731.

HARRIS, PERCY. Adm. pens. at EMMANUEL, Sept. 11, 1627. Of Cornwall. Probably s. of John, of Lanrest, Cornwall. Matric. 1627. Migrated to Queens', Easter, 1628. (Vivian, *Vis. of Cornwall.*)

HARRIS, PHILIP. Matric. pens. from TRINITY HALL, Easter, 1618–9. Perhaps 5th s. of John, of Hayne, Devon, and Kenegie, Cornwall. B.A. 1621–2; M.A. 1625. Incorp. at Oxford, 1622. Admon. (Exeter) 1661; of Kenwyn, Cornwall, clerk.

HARRYES, RICHARD. Matric. pens. from ST JOHN'S, Michs. 1568. Ord. priest (Norwich) Oct. 17, 1571. Perhaps V. of Stallingborough, Lincs., 1576.

HARRIS, RICHARD. Matric. pens. from ST JOHN'S, Easter, 1576. Of Salop. B.A. 1579–80; M.A. 1583; B.D. 1590; D.D. 1595. Fellow, 1581. Incorp. at Oxford, 1584. R. of Gestingthorpe, Essex, 1599. R. of Bradwell-by-Sea, 1612. Author of *Concordia Anglicana*, in reply to Becane's *De dissidio Anglicano*. Will (P.C.C.) 1621. (*D.N.B.*)

HARRIS, RICHARD. Matric. pens. from QUEENS', c. 1595; B.A. 1598–9. Perhaps M.D. from Pembroke, 1607.

HARRIS, RICHARD. Matric. pens. from QUEENS', Easter, 1631. Of Salop. Age 8 in 1623. S. and h. of Richard, of Stockton, Salop. Adm. at the Inner Temple, 1634. (*Vis. of Shrops.*)

HARRIS, RICHARD. Adm. pens. (age 18) at PEMBROKE, May 14, 1645. S. of Richard, of Leigh, Essex. Matric. 1645; B.A. 1648–9. Perhaps R. of Southchurch, Essex, 1667–80. Died 1680. Will (P.C.C.); of Prittlewell.

HERRYS, ROBERT. B.Can.L. 1498.

HARRYS, ROBERT. Matric. pens. from PEMBROKE, Michs. 1584. One of these names R. of Mellis, Suffolk, c. 1590.

HARRIS, ROBERT. Adm. pens. (age 17) at CAIUS, June 21, 1626. S. of Robert, gent. B. at Kirby Bedon, Norfolk. School, Norwich (Mr Stonham). Matric. 1626; Scholar, 1628–33; B.A. 1629–30; M.A. 1633. Ord. deacon (Norwich) Dec. 22, 1633; priest, Mar. 2, 1633–4. Probably minister of Mellis, Suffolk (where he signed the Solemn League and Covenant, in 1643), 1636–60. One of these names, clerk, buried at Kirby Bedon, Oct. 31, 1668. Another V. of Dunston and Swardeston, Norfolk, 1640. (*Venn*, I. 277.)

HARRIS, ROBERT. Adm. at CORPUS CHRISTI, 1671. Of Essex. Matric. 1671.

HARRIS or HERRIS, SALTER. Adm. Fell.-Com. (age 16) at CHRIST'S, June 28, 1639. S. of Sir Arthur (1601–2), of Woodham-Mortimer, Essex, Knt. B. there. Education, private (Mr Leech). Matric. 1639. Probably died before 1645. Brother of Arthur (1644–5), etc. (*Peile*, I. 462.)

HARRIS, SAMUEL. Matric. pens. from CLARE, Easter, 1622; B.A. 1625–6. Ord. deacon (Llandaff); priest (Norwich) May 20, 1627.

HARRIS, SAMUEL. Adm. pens. (age 17) at CHRIST'S, Apr. 29, 1648. S. of Richard. B. at Truro. School, Truro (Mr White).

HARRIS, SAMUEL. Adm. sizar (age 16) at SIDNEY, July 2, 1673. S. of George. B. at Eaton Socon, Derbs. (*sic*). School, Basford, Nottingham (taught by his father). Matric. 1674; B.A. 1676–7; M.A. 1680. Ord. priest (London) Dec. 23, 1677. V. of Fingringhoe, Essex, 1680–91. R. of St Ethelburga, London, 1691–1704. Preb. of Lincoln, 1695. R. of Walgrave, Northants., 1704–8. Died Jan. 14, 1707–8, aged 54. M.I. at Walgrave. (Blore; *Rutland*, 179; H. I. Longden.)

HARRIS, SAMUEL. Adm. sizar (age 16) at JESUS, Apr. 14, 1673. S. of Isaiah (? 1646), of Buckinghamshire, clerk, deceased. Matric. 1673; Rustat scholar, 1674; B.A. 1676–7; M.A. 1680.

HARRIS, SAMUEL. Adm. pens. (age 17) at PETERHOUSE, May 15, 1700. Of Middlesex. B. Dec. 9, 1682. School, Merchant Taylors'. Scholar, 1700; Matric. 1701; B.A. 1703–4; M.A. 1707. Craven scholar, 1701. Fellow, 1709–15. Regius Professor of Modern History, 1724–33. Ord. deacon (Norwich) May, 1708; priest, June, 1708. R. of Intwood and Keswick, Norfolk, 1708–20. F.R.S., 1722. Author. Died Dec. 21, 1733. (*D.N.B.*)

HARRIS, SAMUEL. D.D. 1728 (*Com. Reg.*). Perhaps the above.

HARRYS, THOMAS. Matric. pens. from TRINITY HALL, Michs. 1546.

HARRYS, THOMAS. Matric. pens. from JESUS, Michs. 1562.

HARRIS, THOMAS. Matric. pens. from CORPUS CHRISTI, Michs. 1573. Of Kent. B.A. 1576–7; M.A. 1580. Fellow, 1579–86.

HARRYSE, THOMAS. Matric. pens. from CLARE, Easter, 1574; B.A. 1577–8.

HARRYS, THOMAS. Matric. pens. from ST JOHN'S, Easter, 1577.

HARRIS, THOMAS. Adm. pens. (age 21) at CAIUS, Oct. 29, 1608. From Exeter College, Oxford; adm. there, in 1606 (not recorded in *Al. Oxon.*). S. of Anthony, gent., of the parish of St Issey, Cornwall. School, Bodmin (Mr Cole). B.A. 1609–10; M.A. 1613. Probably V. of Paul, Cornwall, 1624–61. Will (Exeter) 1661. (*Venn*, I. 200.)

HARRIS, THOMAS. Matric. pens. from MAGDALENE, Easter, 1622; B.A. 1625–6; M.A. 1629. Ord. deacon (Peterb.) July 9; priest, Aug. 3, 1630. Of this name were the R. of Kettering, Northants., 1633–8; the R. of Cranford St Andrew, 1648; and the R. of Hinton, 1653–61. The latter died at Hinton, Dec. 23, 1661. M.I. (J. P. Dorman.)

HARRIS, THOMAS. Matric. sizar (age 17) from TRINITY, Easter, 1636. Perhaps s. of Christopher, of Woodford, Northants., gent. School, Oundle. B.A. 1638–9; M.A. 1642. Ord. deacon (Peterb.) June 5, 1642; priest (Lincoln) Mar. 8, 1644–5.

HARRIS or HERRIS, THOMAS. Adm. pens. (age 18) at CHRIST'S, Mar. 18, 1644–5. S. of Sir Arthur (1601–2), Knt. B. at Woodham Mortimer, Essex. School, Chelmsford (Mr Peake). Adm. at the Inner Temple, Dec. 10, 1644. One of these names an elder for Maldon at Dengie *Classis*, 1648. Brother of Arthur (1644–5), etc. (*Peile*, I. 492.)

HARRIS, THOMAS. Matric. sizar from QUEENS', Michs. 1650. Of Leicestershire. B.A. 1654–5. Ord. deacon (Lincoln) Feb. 22; priest, Feb. 23, 1661–2. One of these names R. of Lawford, Essex, 1693–9. Died Mar. 28, 1699, aged 65. (*Essex Arch. Soc.*, N.S., VIII. 289.)

HARRIS, THOMAS. Adm. sizar at EMMANUEL, May 9, 1660. Of Leicestershire. Matric. 1660.

HARRIS, THOMAS. Adm. sizar (age 17) at MAGDALENE, May 30, 1678. S. of Thomas, clerk, deceased. B. at Sutton-in-the-Field, Lincs. School, Stamford. Matric. 1678; B.A. 1681–2; M.A. 1685. One of these names V. of Duxford St John, Cambs., 1689.

HARRIS, THOMAS. Adm. pens. at EMMANUEL, Apr. 19, 1694. Of Lincolnshire. Matric. 1696; B.A. 1697–8. Ord. deacon (Lincoln) May 26, 1700; priest, May 23, 1703.

HARRIS, THOMAS. Adm. pens. (age 19) at TRINITY, Jan. 30, 1712–3. S. of Thomas, of Newport, Salop. School, Newport (Mr Greenwood). Matric. 1713; Scholar, 1715; B.A. 1716–7. One of these names R. of Flyford Flavel, Worcs., 1717–31. (But *see* a contemporary in *Al. Oxon.*)

HARRIS, THOMAS. Adm. pens. at QUEENS', July 3, 1716. Of Middlesex. Matric. 1716. Adm. at the Inner Temple, Apr. 18, 1716; s. and h. of Robert, citizen of London, and apothecary.

HARRIS, THOMAS. Adm. at CORPUS CHRISTI, 1747. Of Huntingdonshire. Matric. 1748–9. Ord. priest (Lincoln) Sept. 21, 1755, as B.A.

HARRIS, WALTER. M.A. 1631 (Incorp. from Oxford). Of Worcestershire. Matric. from Balliol College, Oxford, July 16, 1621, age 18; B.A. (Oxford) 1623; M.A. 1626. Perhaps R. of Shire Newton, Monmouth, 1633; and R. of Wolves Newton, 1633. (*Al. Oxon.*)

HARRIS, WALTER. M.D. 1679 (Incorp. from Oxford). S. of Walter, of Gloucester. School, Winchester. Matric. from New College, Oxford, Feb. 22, 1666–7, age 19; B.A. 1670. Fellow of New College, 1666–73. M.D. from Bourges, 1675; Incorp. at Oxford. F.R.C.P., 1682. Treasurer, 1714–7. Lumleian lecturer, 1710. Physician to William III. Author, medical. Died in London, Aug. 1, 1732. Admon. (P.C.C.) as of St George-the-Martyr, Middlesex. (*D.N.B.*; *Munk*, I. 423.)

HARRYSE, WILLIAM. Matric. sizar from ST JOHN'S, Easter, 1572. Perhaps matric. again Michs. 1572. S. of Robert, weaver, of St Giles', Cripplegate. B. *c.* 1554. Exhibitioner from Christ's Hospital. B.A. 1575–6; M.A. 1579. (A. W. Lockhart.)

HARRISHE, WILLIAM. Matric. pens. from PEMBROKE, Easter, 1577–8; B.A. 1580–1.

HARRIS, WILLIAM. Matric. pens. from ST JOHN'S, Lent, 1579–80. Of Salop. B.A. 1583–4; M.A. 1587; B.D. 1594. Fellow, 1589. Ord. deacon and priest (Peterb.) Apr. 13, 1589. R. of Titchwell, Norfolk, 1591. Perhaps R. of Wickford, Essex, 1591–1610. Died 1610. Will, P.C.C.

HARRYES, WILLIAM. Matric. sizar from ST JOHN'S, Easter, 1580; B.A. 1583–4.

HARRIS or HERRIS, WILLIAM. Matric. Fell.-Com. from PEMBROKE, Easter, 1608; B.A. 1611–2. Perhaps s. of Sir William, of Cricksea, Essex, Knt.; adm. at Lincoln's Inn, Feb. 25, 1612–3.

HARRIS, WILLIAM. Matric. sizar from CHRIST'S, Apr. 1610; Scholar, 1610–1; B.A. 1612–3; M.A. 1616. Probably ord. priest (Norwich) 1614. Perhaps V. of Hunstanton, Norfolk, 1631. (*Peile*, I. 275.)

HARRIS, WILLIAM. M.A. 1620 (Incorp. from Oxford). Of Buckinghamshire. School, Merchant Taylors'. Matric. from St John's College, Oxford, June 19, 1610, age 18; B.A. 1611; M.A. 1615; B.D. 1621.

HARRIS, WILLIAM. M.A. 1637 (Incorp. from Oxford). Of London. Matric. from St Alban's Hall, Oxford, Nov. 28, 1617, age 18; B.A. (Brasenose College) 1621; M.A. 1624.

HARRIS, WILLIAM. Adm. sizar at CLARE, Feb. 1, 1685–6. Matric. 1686; B.A. 1689–90. Ord. priest (York) June, 1699.

HARRIS, WILLIAM. Adm. at CORPUS CHRISTI, 1702. Of London. Matric. Easter, 1702; B.A. 1705–6. Ord. deacon (London) May 30, 1708; priest, June 19, 1709. One of these names R. of Gt Totham, Essex, 1711.

HARRIS, WILLIAM. Adm. sizar (age 16) at ST JOHN'S, Jan. 8, 1707–8. S. of William, coal-merchant. B. at Cambridge. School, King's, Cambridge (Mr Cole). Matric. 1708; B.A. 1711–2. Ord. deacon (Norwich) May, 1713; priest (Lincoln, *Litt. dim.* from Canterbury) May 27, 1716. C. of Appledore, Kent, 1714. Died at Ebony, Kent. Buried there Nov. 18, 1717. (H. G. Harrison.)

HARRIS, WILLIAM. M.A. from QUEENS', 1719. S. of Joseph, of Gulval, Cornwall, gent. Matric. from Exeter College, Oxford, Apr. 3, 1707, age 18; B.A. (Oxford) 1710. (*Al. Oxon.*)

HARRIS, ——. B.Civ.L. 1473.

HARRIS, ——. B.Can.L. 1493–4 (? 1497).

HARRIS, ——. B.A. 1520–1; M.A. 1523.

HERRIS, ——. Adm. at CORPUS CHRISTI, 1544.

HARRIS, ——. Adm. sizar at KING'S, Lent, 1569–70. Perhaps Thomas Harris, ord. deacon (Lincoln); priest (Ely) Dec. 1569, age 35.

HARRIS, ——. Adm. at CORPUS CHRISTI, 1584.

HARRIS, ——. B.A. from JESUS, 1606–7 (in *ordo*).

HARRIS, ——. Matric. pens. from ST JOHN'S, Michs. 1608.

HARRIS, ——. Adm. Fell.-Com. at ST CATHARINE'S, Oct. 25, 1659. Of Essex.

HARRISON, ABRAHAM. Adm. pens. at EMMANUEL, 1638. Probably 3rd s. of John, Esq., afterwards of Balls, Herts. Migrated to St Catharine's, 1639. Probably brother of John (1633) and William (1637) and half-brother of Richard (1662–3). (*Clutterbuck*, II. 184.)

HARRISON, ALEXANDER. Scholar of QUEENS' (butler) 1542-7. Matric. pens. Easter, 1544; B.A. 1546-7. Will proved (V.C.C.) 1552.

HARRISON, ALEXANDER. Adm. pens. at QUEENS', May 3, 1692. Of Somerset. Matric. 1692; B.A. 1695-6.

HARRISON, ALLINGTON. Adm. pens. (age 17) at CAIUS, Jan. 27, 1673-4. S. of Henry (1628), D.D., of West Wickham, Cambs. B. there. Schools, Saffron Walden, Essex (Mr Burrows) and Bury, Suffolk. Matric. 1674; Scholar, 1674-9; B.A. 1677-8. P.C. of West Wickham, Cambs., 1690-1731. R. of Elmstead, Essex, 1716-8 (resigned). Died May 2, 1731. M.I. at Wickham. Father of the next, and of Henry (1706), brother of William (1674). (*Venn*, I. 450 where his son's ordination is assigned to him.)

HARRISON, ALINGTON. Adm. pens. (age 16) at CAIUS, July 7, 1699. S. of Allington (above), R. of West Wickham, Cambs. B. at Sudbury, Suffolk. School, Bury. Matric. 1699-1700; Scholar, 1699-1703; B.A. from Trinity Hall, 1703-4; M.A. from Caius, 1707. Ord. deacon (Ely) Dec. 21, 1707; priest, Feb. 28, 1707-8. C. of West Wickham, Cambs., 1711. R. of Elmstead, Essex, 1718. P.C. of West Wickham, 1731-3. Died Jan. 8, 1732-3. (*Venn*, I. 503; J. Ch. Smith.)

HARRISON, ANTHONY. Matric. sizar from KING'S, Easter, 1579-80. Perhaps s. of Wyllyam, of Over, Cambs. B. 1563. R. of Catfield, Norfolk, 1609. Secretary to the Bishop of Norwich. Died 1638. One of these names R. of Bisley, Surrey, 1588. (*N. and Q.*, 5th S., X. 212.)

HARRISON, ANTHONY. Matric. sizar from ST JOHN'S, Michs. 1587. Probably ord. deacon and priest (Peterb.) Mar. 15, 1595-6. (*Lambeth MSS.*)

HARRISON, BENJAMIN. Matric. pens. from QUEENS', Michs. 1644. (Already matric. from St John's, Oxford, Apr. 1, 1642, age 18.) S. of George, of London. B.A. (Cambridge) 1645-6. One of these names presented to St Clement's, Sandwich, 1648; there till 1653. V. of South Tawton, Devon, 1653-60. Returned to Sandwich, 1660-6. Afterwards in West of England. (*W. A. Shaw*, I. 363; *Hasted*, IV. 286.)

HARRISON, BERNARD. Matric. pens. from ST JOHN'S, Easter, 1627. Migrated to Oxford, Jan. 1630-1. Incorp. there as B.A. M.A. (Magdalen College, Oxford) 1633. Perhaps adm. at Gray's Inn, Feb. 21, 1633-4, as s. and h. of Gilbert, of London, mercer. (*Al. Oxon.*; *Vis. of London*, 1634.)

HARRISON, CHARLES. Matric. sizar from TRINITY, Easter, 1618; Scholar, 1619; B.A. 1621-2; M.A. 1625. Ord. deacon (Peterb.) Oct. 25; priest, Oct. 26, 1625. V. of Long Stanton All Saints', Cambs., 1625-8. V. of Gt Wymondley, Herts., 1630-46. Sequestered to Bredfield, Suffolk, May 19, 1647, and to Middleton, Essex, 1657. (*Add. MS.*, 15,671, f. 34.)

HARRISON or HERISON, CHRISTOPHER. B.A. 1501-2; M.A. 1504. Perhaps V. of Wickersley, Yorks., 1524.

HARRISON, CHRISTOPHER. Matric. pens. from ST JOHN'S, c. 1592. One of these names, of Durham, gent., adm. at Gray's Inn, Nov. 7, 1595. *See* references in *Gray's Inn Pension Book*.

HARRISON, CHRISTOPHER. M.A. 1658 (Incorp. from Oxford). Matric. from Queen's College, Oxford, June 14, 1649; B.A. (Oxford) 1651; M.A. 1653-4. Fellow of Queen's, 1654. V. of Brough-under-Stainsmore, Westmorland, 1664-94. Died 1694. (*Al. Oxon.*)

HARRISON, CORNELIUS. Adm. pens. (age 17) at PEMBROKE, July 4, 1718. S. of John, of Birmingham, gent. B. at Lichfield, Staffs. Matric. 1719; B.A. 1722-3; M.A. 1726. Fellow, May 29, 1731. Ord. deacon (Norwich) Sept. 1726; priest (Lincoln) Mar. 17, 1727-8. P.C. of Darlington, 1727-8. Died Oct. 4, 1748. Buried at Darlington. Kinsman of Dr Samuel Johnson. (Pedigree in Plantagenet-Harrison's *Yorks.*, 348.)

HARRISON, CUTHBERT. Adm. pens. at CLARE, June 13, 1651. Had kept some terms at Oxford (not in *Al. Oxon.*). B. at Newton, Kirkham, Lancs. Ord. presbyter, Nov. 27, 1651, when he is styled B.A. For a time at Singleton, Lancs. Minister at Shankell-*cum*-Lurgan, Armagh, 1657. At Tullamain and Tubbrid, Tipperary, 1660, till 1662. Afterwards preached in Lancs. Buried at Kirkham, Oct. 16, 1681. (*Calamy*, II. 105; E. Axon.)

HARISON, EDMUND. Adm. pens. at QUEENS', July 28, 1589. Of Essex. Perhaps s. and executor of William (1569).

HARRISON, EDMUND. Matric. pens. from CHRIST'S, 1591-2; B.A. 1592-3; M.A. 1596; B.D. 1603. Probably R. of St Olave's, Jewry, London, 1602-5. (*Peile*, I. 203.)

HARRISON, EDMUND. Adm. pens. at JESUS, May 14, 1652. Of Rutland. Matric. 1652; Scholar, 1653.

HARISON, EDWARD. Matric. pens. from ST JOHN'S, Michs. 1559.

HARRISON, EDWARD. Matric. pens. from CLARE, Easter, 1574.

HARRISON, EDWARD. B.A. from JESUS, 1603-4; M.A. 1607; B.D. 1614. Ord. deacon (Peterb.) Sept. 20; priest, Sept. 27, 1607. One of these names, M.A., R. of Orlestone, Kent, 1613-26.

HARRISON, EDWARD. Matric. sizar from ST JOHN'S, Easter, 1604.

HARRISON, EDWARD. Adm. pens. at EMMANUEL, June 9, 1612.

HARRISON, EDWARD. Adm. sizar at EMMANUEL, Oct. 20, 1613. Matric. 1613; B.A. 1617-8; M.A. 1621. Incorp. at Oxford, 1623. Ord. deacon (York) Sept. 1627; priest, Dec. 1627. R. of Wallasey, Cheshire, c. 1656. Buried there Sept. 5, 1659. (*Ormerod*, II. 478.)

HARRISON, EDWARD. Adm. pens. at JESUS, June 7, 1633. Of Kent. Matric. 1633; Scholar, 1634; B.A. 1636-7; M.A. 1640.

HARRISON, EDWARD. Adm. pens. at JESUS, May 24, 1634. S. of Lancelot (1611), of Orlestone, Kent, clerk. Matric. 1634. Migrated to St John's, Mar. 14, 1635-6, age 17. B.A. 1637-8; M.A. from Hart Hall, Oxford, 1640.

HARRISON, EDWARD. Adm. pens. (age 15) at MAGDALENE, July 3, 1663. S. of Edward, of Passenham, Northants. School, Huntingdon. Matric. 1663. Adm. at the Inner Temple, May 18, 1670.

HARRISON, EDWARD. Adm. pens. at ST CATHARINE'S, May 6, 1671.

HARRISON, EDWARD. Adm. sizar (age 17) at PEMBROKE, Nov. 6, 1703. S. of George, of Lancashire. Matric. 1704; B.A. 1707-8. Ord. deacon (London) Sept. 19, 1708; priest, May 27, 1716. One of these names P.C. of Leeds, Kent, 1725-55.

HARRISON, EURYE. Matric. sizar from ST JOHN'S, Easter, 1609; B.A. 1612-3. Ord. deacon (York) Dec. 1615; priest, Sept. 1616.

HARRISON, FRANCIS. Matric. sizar from ST JOHN'S, c. 1593; B.A. 1596-7; M.A. 1600. Ord. priest (Colchester) Nov. 23, 1600. R. of Aldham, Suffolk, 1602-32. Died 1632.

HARRISON, FRANCIS. Adm. sizar (age 20) at CAIUS, c. May, 1653. S. of John (1606), R. of Mashbury, Essex. B. at Chelmsford. School, Hatfield (Mr Fra. Bridge). Brother of John (1636).

HARRISON, FRANCIS. Adm. at KING'S, a scholar from Eton, 1666. Doubtless 4th s. of Richard, of Hurst, Berks. B. at Hurst, Berks. Matric. 1667. Died as a student, of smallpox. (*Harwood*; *Vis. of Berks.*, 1665.)

HARRISON, GABRIEL. Adm. sizar (age 15) at CAIUS, Jan. 13, 1633-4. S. of Gabriel. B. at Cambridge. Bapt. at Gt St Mary's, Nov. 21, 1616. School, Perse (Mr Lovering). Matric. 1634; Scholar, 1634-41; B.A. 1637-8; M.A. 1641.

HARRISON, GEORGE. Matric. sizar from PETERHOUSE, Michs. 1551. B. at Willesley, Leics. Ord. deacon (London) May 15, 1552; priest, 1554. Perhaps preb. of Wells, 1576-92. One of these names V. of Friston, Suffolk, 1558-62.

HARRISON, GEORGE. Matric. sizar from TRINITY, c. 1596; B.A. 1599-1600; M.A. 1603.

HARRISON, GEORGE. Matric. sizar from ST JOHN'S, c. 1601; B.A. 1604-5; M.A. 1608. Ord. deacon (Peterb.) Feb. 10, 1604-5; priest, Sept. 21, 1606. Perhaps minister at Triplow, Cambs., 1604-6; and R. of South Somercotes, Lincs., 1612-38. Admon. (Lincoln) 1638.

HARRISON, GEORGE. Matric. sizar from TRINITY, Easter, 1612; B.A. 1615-6. Ord. deacon (York) Sept. 1616; priest, Sept. 1618. V. of Scalby, Yorks., 1621.

HARRISON, GEORGE. M.A. 1631 (Incorp. from Oxford). S. of William, of London. Matric. from St John's College, Oxford, Oct. 24, 1623, age 16; B.A. (Oxford) 1626-7; M.A. 1629.

HARRISON, GEORGE. Adm. sizar (age 14) at CHRIST'S, May 20, 1646. S. of Peter. B. at Cottenham, Cambs. School, Cambridge (Mr Hamond). Matric. 1647; B.A. 1649-50; M.A. from King's, 1653. One of these names R. of Fleet-Marston, Bucks., 1668. Died 1696. (*Peile*, I. 507.)

HARRISON, GEORGE. Adm. pens. (age 17) at SIDNEY, May 21, 1697. 1st s. of Edward, yeoman. B. at St Andrew's, Holborn, London. School, Charterhouse, exhibitioner.

HARRISON, GEORGE. Adm. pens. at CHRIST'S, Oct. 20, 1733. B. in the Barbados. Matric. 1733; M.B. 1740. Probably student at Leyden, Oct. 12, 1736.

HARRISON, GERARD. Matric. sizar from ST JOHN'S, Easter, 1611; B.A. 1614-5; M.A. 1620. R. of Harpham, Norfolk, 1651-62.

HARYSON, GUY. Matric. sizar from CAIUS, Michs. 1578. Steward (scholar) of the College, 1581-6. Licensed by the Bishop of Ely to teach grammar at Chesterton, Cambs., Nov. 2, 1587. (*Venn*, I. 99.)

HARRISON, HENRY. Adm. pens. (age 17) at CAIUS, May 25, 1628. S. of Henry, gent., of Kent. B. at Mersham. School, Canterbury (Mr Lud). Matric. 1628; Scholar, 1629–35; B.A. 1631–2; M.A. 1635; D.D. 1664 (*Lit. Reg.*). Fellow, 1636–48. Ord. deacon (Norwich) Dec. 22, 1639; priest, Apr. 25, 1662. Preb. of Ely, 1675–90. V. of Wethersfield, Suffolk; and R. of Snailwell, Cambs., 1679. V. of West Wratting, 1685–90. He had been ejected during the Civil Wars, and travelled widely on the Continent. Buried Sept. 30, 1690. Will, P.C.C. M.I. at West Wickham, Cambs. Father of William (1674) and Allington (1673–4). (*Venn*, I. 284.)

HARRISON, HENRY. Adm. pens. (age 17) at CHRIST' , Apr. 8, 1651. 2nd s. of Sir Thomas, of Copgrove, Yorks.,sKnt. B. at York. Bapt. at Belfrey's, York, Dec. 20, 1633. School, York (Mr Wallis). Matric. 1651. Adm. at Gray's Inn, June 30, 1651. Of Holtby, Yorks., Esq. Buried at Hornby, Yorks., Mar. 9, 1668–9. M.I. (*Peile*, I. 541; *Vis. of Yorks.*; M. H. Peacock.)

HARRISON, HENRY. Adm. pens. (age 17) at MAGDALENE, Apr. 2, 1706. S. of Allington (1673–4), Esq. B. at West Wickham, Cambs. School, Bishop's Stortford. Matric. 1706; B.A. 1711–2; M.A. 1719. Ord. deacon (Ely) Dec. 23, 1711; priest (London) Dec. 19, 1714. Perhaps R. of Mundford, Norfolk, 1720; and R. of West Tofts, 1732.

HARRISON, HUGH. Matric. sizar from JESUS, Easter, 1612. One of these names C. of Smeeth, Kent. Will (Cant.) 1645.

HARRISON, HUGH. Adm. sizar (age 19) at ST JOHN'S, July 2, 1646. S. of Roger, yeoman, deceased, of Monyash, Derbs. B. there. School, Rowsley (Mr Howis). Matric. 1646.

HARRISON, ISAAC. Adm. sizar (age 15) at CAIUS, June, 1631. S. of John (? 1578), R. of Sudbury, Suffolk. B. there. School, Halstead (Mr Whiston). Matric. 1631; B.A. 1634–5; M.A. 1638; D.D. 1657. R. of Hadleigh, Suffolk, 1643. Minister of the *classis*, *c.* 1646. V. of Assington, 1664–75. V. of Dagenham, Essex, 1674–82. Died 1682. Brother of John (1631). (*Venn*, I. 300.)

HARRISON, JACOB. Matric. sizar from CHRIST'S, 1592–3; B.A. 1597–8; M.A. 1601; B.D. 1609. Fellow, 1601. Incorp. at Oxford, 1608. Lady Margaret preacher, 1610. Died in College. Buried at Gt St Andrew's, Apr. 25, 1613. Will proved (V.C.C.) 1613. (*Peile*, I. 210.)

HARRYSON, JACOB. Matric. sizar from ST JOHN'S, Easter, 1602.

HARRISON, JAMES. B.A. 1479–80; M.A. 1483–4. One of these names V. of Aycliffe, Durham, 1508–10. (H. M. Wood.)

HARRISON, JAMES. Matric. pens. from ST JOHN'S, Michs. 1554.

HARRISON, JAMES. Matric. pens. from ST JOHN'S, Michs. 1588; B.A. 1592–3; M.A. 1596. Incorp. at Oxford, 1608. Ord. deacon and priest (Peterb.) Mar. 18, 1596–7. V. of Breesworth, Suffolk, 1601. Perhaps R. of Staumer, Sussex, 1615–39. Buried Mar. 19, 1638–9. (*Essex Archaeol. Soc.*, N.S., VI. 312.)

HARRISON, JAMES. Adm. pens. (age 17) at CHRIST'S, Nov. 27, 1671. S. of Peter (1641). B. at Cheadle, Cheshire. School, Charterhouse. Matric. 1671, as 'John.' No degree recorded, but one of these names, 'B.A. of Corpus,' was ord. deacon (London) May 21, 1676; priest, as 'B.A. of Christ's,' Sept. 23, 1677. One (M.A.) V. of Medmenham, Bucks., 1716. (*Peile*, II. 39.)

HARRISON, JAMES. M.A. from MAGDALENE, 1726. Perhaps s. of James, of Campden, Gloucs., clerk. Matric. from Merton College, Oxford, Mar. 27, 1708, age 17; B.A. (Oxford) 1712. Will (P.C.C.) 1761, of one of these names, R. of Buscot, Berks. (*Al. Oxon.*; J. Ch. Smith.)

HARISON, JEREMY. Adm. sizar (age 19) at ST JOHN'S, Jan. 12, 1636–7. S. of North, gent., of Cambridge. B. there. School, Cambridge (Perse). Matric. 1637. Brother of Ralph (1636–7).

HARRISON, JEREMIAH. Adm. pens. (age 17) at CHRIST'S, Nov. 25, 1645. S. of Peter. B. at Hindley, Lancs. School, Leigh (Mr Greenhalgh). Matric. 1645. Lieut.-Col. in the Parliamentary army. Died July 16, 1683. Will at Chester. Brother of Peter (1641) and Nathaniel (1645). (*Peile*, I. 500; *D.N.B.*)

HARRISON, JERVIS. M.A. 1642–3 (Incorp. from Oxford). Created M.A. at Oxford, 1642.

HARRISON or HERRISON, JOHN. Probably M.A. 1455–6 (*non-incepit*); M.D. 1463–4 (*non-incepit*). Transcriber of the *Historiola* in CAIUS College MSS. (No. 249) in which he claims to be M.D. 1457. Chancellor of the University, 1465–8. (Tanner, *Bibliotheca*.)

HARRISON or HERISON, JOHN. B.A. 1509–10. Perhaps M.A. 1514–5.

HARRISON, JOHN. B.A. 1532–3. One of these names R. of Rushbrook, Suffolk, 1555.

HARYSON, JOHN. Matric. pens. from MAGDALENE, Easter, 1548.

HARRISON, JOHN. Adm. at KING'S, a scholar from Eton, 1570. S. of Rychard, R. of Bradeston and Narford, Norfolk. B. in London, 1552. B.A. 1574–5; M.A. 1578. Fellow, 1573–9. Incorp. at Oxford, 1585. Sur-Master of St Paul's School, 1580. Head Master, 1581–96. 'Died 1596.' (*Cooper*, II. 222.) According to *N. and Q.* (5th S. X. 175) he was afterwards steward to Prince Phillip; resided at Brissingham, Norfolk, and died there 1628.

HARRYSON, JOHN. Matric. pens. from ST JOHN'S, Michs. 1571; B.A. 1575–6; M.A. 1579.

HARRISON, JOHN. Matric. pens. from ST JOHN'S, Michs. 1575. Of Yorkshire. B.A. 1579–80; M.A. 1583; B.D. 1591. Fellow, 1581. Ord. deacon (Peterb.) Jan. 4, 1582–3; priest, Mar. 28, 1583. V. of Histon St Etheldreda, Cambs., 1582–1607, but refused to conform. (*Cooper*, II. 477.)

HARRISON, JOHN. Matric. sizar from TRINITY, Easter, 1576; B.A. from Jesus, 1579–80.

HARRISON, JOHN. Matric. sizar from PETERHOUSE, Easter, 1578; B.A. 1581–2; M.A. 1586. Perhaps ord. priest (Norwich) Mar. 10, 1582–3. Probably C. of St Gregory, Sudbury, 1594. Vicar, 1605. Minister of St Peter's, Sudbury. Died 1641. If so, father of Isaac (1631) and John (1631). (V. B. Redstone.)

HARRISON, JOHN. Matric. sizar from CHRIST'S, Feb. 1579–80; B.A. from Corpus Christi, 1585–6; M.A. 1591. Probably subscribed for deacon and priest (Lincoln) Apr. 12, 1587. One of these names V. of Gt Cornard, Suffolk, 1595. Perhaps R. of Abington Pigotts, Cambs., 1604–33. Buried there Nov. 2, 1633.

HARRISON, JOHN. Matric. sizar from ST JOHN'S, *c.* 1592; B.A. 1595–6; M.A. 1599. Ord. deacon and priest (Peterb.) Dec. 23, 1599. R. of Yelvertoft, Northants., 1600–61 (sequestered, but restored). Buried there May 25, 1661. (H. I. Longden.)

HARRISON, JOHN. Matric. sizar from TRINITY, Michs. 1601; B.A. 1605–6; M.A. 1609. This, or the next, ord. deacon (Norwich) May 22, 1608, age 23; 'B.A.'; C. of Wreningham, Norfolk.

HARRISON, JOHN. Matric. sizar from CHRIST'S, Easter, 1606. B. at Gt Bentley, Essex. B.A. 1609–10; M.A. 1613; B.D. 1620. Ord. deacon (London) Sept. 1611, age 24. R. of Mashbury, Essex, in 1629. Will (Consist. C. London) 1637. Father of Francis (1653) and John (1636). (*Peile*, I. 260; J. Ch. Smith.)

HARRISON, JOHN. B.A. from TRINITY, 1607–8.

HARRISON, JOHN. Matric. sizar from TRINITY, Michs. 1610; B.A. 1613–4; M.A. 1619. One of these names (B.A.), R. of Alderton, Suffolk, 1617–23. R. of Burgh, 1617. R. of Trimley, 1645–6.

HARRISON, JOHN. Adm. pens. (age 18) at CAIUS, Aug. 30, 1612. S. of John, gent., alderman of York (Lord Mayor, 1612). School, York. Matric. 1612; B.A. 1615–6; M.A. 1619. According to the *Genealogist* (XXV. 35) he became M.D. Buried at Belfreys, York, July 30, 1632. Will (York) 1633.

HARRISON, JOHN. Matric. pens. from TRINITY, Easter, 1620; B.A. 1623–4; M.A. 1627. Ord. deacon (Peterb.) May 19; priest, May 20, 1627. One of these names V. of Rowston, Lincs., 1631.

HARRISON, JOHN. Matric. sizar from TRINITY, Easter, 1627; Scholar, 1631; B.A. 1631–2; M.A. 1635; B.D. 1648. Fellow, 1633. Senior proctor, 1646–7. Ord. deacon (Peterb.) Sept. 24, 1637; priest, May 20, 1638.

HARRISON, JOHN. Adm. pens. (age 16) at CAIUS, *c.* June, 1631. S. of John, R. of Sudhury, Suffolk. B. there. School, Halstead (Mr Whiston). Matric. 1631; Scholar, 1633–5; B.A. 1634–5; M.A. 1638. Probably R. of Little Waltham, Essex, 1643–62. Licensed 'teacher' at Pebmarsh, in 1672. Buried at Little Waltham, Jan. 10, 1677–8. Brother of Isaac (1631). (*Venn*, I. 300.)

HARRISON, JOHN. Adm. sizar at EMMANUEL, June 30, 1632. Of Sussex. Matric. 1632; B.A. 1636–7. Perhaps the presbyterian divine, said to have been educated at Cambridge. If so, s. of Peter, of Hindley, near Wigan, Lancs. B. 1613. Minister of Ashton-under-Lyne, Lancs., 1642. R. 1653–62. An active member of the Manchester *Classis*, 1646–60. Imprisoned as a royalist, 1651 and 1659–60. Died Dec. 30, 1670. Perhaps brother of Jeremiah (1645). (*D.N.B.*)

HARRISON, JOHN. Adm. n. (age 15) at SIDNEY, Apr. 25, 1633. S. and h. of John of London, afterwards of Balls, Herts., Knt. B. at St Olave's, Hart Street. Bapt. Feb. 12, 1617–8. Matric. 1633. Adm. at the Inner Temple, 1634. Brother of William (1637). Probably brother of Abraham (1638) and half-brother of Richard (1662–3). (*Clutterbuck*, II. 186.)

HARRISON, JOHN. Adm. pens. at EMMANUEL, Oct. 1634. Of Ireland. B.A. 1634 (Incorp. from Dublin); M.A. (Cambridge) 1636.

HARRISON, JOHN. Matric. pens. (age 16) at PEMBROKE, Easter, 1636. S. of John (1606), R. of Mashbury, Essex. B.A. 1639-40. Brother of Francis (1653).

HARRISON, JOHN. Adm. at CORPUS CHRISTI, 1636. Of Yorkshire.

HARRISON, JOHN. Adm. sizar (age 15) at SIDNEY, Mar. 3, 1648-9. S. of John, farmer. B. at Halles, Bassinthwaite, Cumberland. Schools, Halles (Mr Clerke) and Crosthwaite (Mr Sanderson). Matric. 1649.

HARRISON, JOHN. Adm. sizar at TRINITY, Apr. 11, 1649. Of Cambridgeshire. Matric. 1649; B.A. 1652-3.

HARRISON, JOHN. Adm. pens. (age 19) at ST JOHN'S, Feb. 2, 1655-6. S. of Lancelot, deceased, of Durham. B. there. School, Durham.

HARRISON, JOHN. Adm. pens. at ST CATHARINE'S, Apr. 11, 1662. Of Essex. Matric. 1663; B.A. 1665-6; M.A. 1669. Signed for deacon's orders (London) Sept. 9, 1672. Ord. priest (London) Sept. 23, 1677. C. of Colne Engaine, Essex.

HARRISON, JOHN. Adm. pens. at TRINITY, May 2, 1662. Matric. 1662; Scholar, 1664; B.A. 1665-6; M.A. 1669. Fellow, 1668. Ord. deacon and priest (Peterb.) May 21, 1676.

HARRISON, JOHN. Adm. sizar (age 25) at MAGDALENE, May 29, 1663. S. of Thomas, of Whickham, Durham, deceased. Bapt. there, July 2, 1637. School, Houghton-le-Spring. Matric. 1663; B.A. 1666-7; M.A. 1670. Perhaps ord. priest (Lincoln) Mar. 11, 1667-8. One of these names V. of Felton, Northumberland, 1672-83. Buried there Mar. 29, 1683. (H. M. Wood.)

HARRISON, JOHN. M.D. 1682 (*Lit. Reg.*). Created F.R.C.P. by Charter of James II; adm. Apr. 12, 1687. Perhaps practised at Colchester. *See* Ralph (1710). (*Munk*, I. 460.)

HARRISON, JOHN. Adm. Fell.-Com. (age 17) at PETERHOUSE, Aug. 1, 1687. S. of Richard (1662-3), of Balls, Hertford. School, Hertford. Matric. 1688. Died young, before his father. (*T. A. Walker.*)

HARRISON, JOHN. Adm. pens. (age 22) at TRINITY, Feb. 1, 1689-90, from Trinity College, Dublin. Adm. there, Oct. 2, 1685. S. of James. B. at Loghin Island, County Down, Ireland. School, Lisburn, Lisnagarry, Antrim (Mr Rob. Harvey). Migrated to Corpus Christi, 1690.

HARRISON, JOHN. Adm. pens. at QUEENS', June 12, 1691. Of Essex. Matric. 1691; B.A. 1694-5. Ord. deacon (London) Dec. 19, 1697; priest, Sept. 24, 1699. One of these names V. of Burnham, Essex, 1705-50.

HARRISON, JOHN. Adm. sizar (age 19) at ST JOHN'S, May 9, 1698. S. of Robert, deceased. B. at Appleby, Westmorland. School, Sedbergh. Matric. 1698; B.A. 1701-2. Ord. priest (London) Sept. 19, 1703; 'M.A.' Perhaps R. of Stoke (S. Med.), 1709-24; V. of South Grantham, 1711-36. Died 1736. (Turnor, *Grantham*, 34.)

HARRISON, JOHN. Adm. sizar (age 17) at ST JOHN'S, May 13, 1701. S. of George, husbandman. B. at Cropton-in-Middleton, Pickering, Yorks. School, Thornton (Mr Robinson). Matric. 1701.

HARRISON, JOHN. Adm. pens. (age 16) at ST JOHN'S, Nov. 2, 1717. S. of John, clerk, of Walton, Bucks. B. at Walton. School, Eton; colleger, 1715. B.A. 1721-2; M.A. 1726. Ord. deacon (Lincoln) Dec. 22, 1722. Perhaps priest, Dec. 20, 1724. R. of Stoke (S. Med.), Lincs., 1724-85. V. of Wragby, 1735. R. of Terrington, 1735-85. Died Dec. 22, 1785, aged 86. (*Scott-Mayor*, III. 315; Turnor, *Grantham*, 142.)

HARRISON, JOHN. B.D. 1728 (Incorp. from Oxford). S. of Joseph (1702), V. of Cirencester. Matric. from Corpus Christi College, Oxford, Feb. 22, 1712-3, age 15; B.A. (Oxford) 1716; M.A. 1720; B.D. 1727. Perhaps V. of Over Penne, Staffs., till 1793. Died Jan. 23, 1793. (*Al. Oxon.*)

HARRISON, JOHN. Adm. pens. at QUEENS', May 11, 1731. Of Essex. B. 1712. Matric. 1731; B.A. 1734-5; M.A. 1761. Ord. deacon (Ely) June 1, 1735. V. of Good Easter, Essex, 1745-6. R. of Faulkbourne, 1746-97. Died Dec. 18, 1797, aged 84. Buried at Faulkbourne. M.I. (*Essex Archaeol. Soc.*, N.S., I. 247.)

HARRISON, JOHN. Adm. scholar at TRINITY HALL, Jan. 7, 1739-40. Of Poplar, Middlesex. Perhaps 1st s. of Benjamin, of Mile End, Stepney, Middlesex, apothecary; adm. at Lincoln's Inn, Jan. 23, 1737-8.

HARRISON, JOHN. Adm. sizar (age 17) at PEMBROKE, June 26, 1751. S. of John, of Courbeck (*sic.*), Cumberland. Matric. 1751; B.A. 1755. Perhaps b. Oct. 3, 1733; s. of ——, of Appleby. Died June 19, 1808. (*F.M.G.*, 724.)

HARRISON, JOSEPH. Matric. sizar from KING'S, Easter, 1655; B.A. 1658-9.

HARRISON, JOSEPH. Adm. pens. (age 18) at ST JOHN'S, May 17, 1662. S. of John, cooper, of Hull, Yorks. B. there. School, Hull (Mr Shaw). Matric. 1662. Probably buried at All Saints', Cambridge, July 17, 1663, as 'John.'

HARRISON, JOSEPH. M.A. from EMMANUEL, 1702. S. of Richard, of Brindle, Lancs., clerk. Matric. from Brasenose College, Oxford, Nov. 20, 1685, age 15; B.A. (Oxford) 1689. P.C. of Cirencester, 1690-1753. R. of Daglingworth, Gloucs., 1729-53. Died Nov. 28, 1753. Father of John (1728). (*Al. Oxon.*; *G. Mag.*)

HARRISON, JOSEPH. Adm. pens. (age 17) at TRINITY, May 10, 1703. S. of William, of Orgrave, Rotherham, Yorks. School, Eton. Matric. 1703; Scholar, 1704; B.A. 1706-7.

HARRISON, JOSEPH. Adm. sizar (age 20) at ST JOHN'S, Apr. 18, 1724. S. of William, plumber, of Yorkshire. B. at Glusburn-in-Kildwick. School, Threshfield (Mr Marshall). Matric. 1724. Ord. deacon (York) Aug. 16, 1730. C. of Pateley Bridge.

HARRISON, JOSEPH. Adm. pens. (age 19) at ST JOHN'S, June 24, 1734. S. of William, Esq., of Yorkshire. B. at Orgrave, Rotherham. School, Chesterfield, Derbs. Matric. 1735; B.A. 1737-8; M.A. 1741. Ord. deacon (Lincoln) June 29, 1740; priest (York) May 25, 1746. 'Of Pontefract, clerk.' Died July 12, 1796. (*F.M.G.*, 830.)

HARRISON, JOSEPH. Adm. sizar (age 19) at PEMBROKE, June 17, 1743. S. of Joseph, of Woodbridge, Suffolk. Bapt. there, Mar. 1, 1723-4. School, Woodbridge. Matric. 1743; B.A. 1746-7. Ord. deacon (Norwich) Mar. 1746-7; priest, Feb. 17, 1748-9. C. of Dallinghoe, Suffolk. C. of Letheringham, 1751-99.

HARRISON, JOSHUA. Matric. pens. from TRINITY, Easter, 1616.

HARRISON, KNIGHTLEY. Adm. pens. (age 16) at SIDNEY, May 10, 1634. S. of John (1592), R. of Yelvertoft, Northants. B. there. Schools, Rugby and Coventry (Mr White). Matric. 1634; B.A. 1637-8; M.A. 1641. V. of Stanford-on-Avon, Northants., 1674-84. Head Master of Rugby, 1669-74. Buried at Stanford-on-Avon, Feb. 22, 1683-4. Admon. Archd. Northants.) 1684.

HARRISON, LANCELOT. Matric. sizar from ST JOHN'S, Michs. 1565; B.A. 1568-9.

HARRISON, LANCELOT. Matric. pens. from JESUS, Michs. 1607. B. at Sledborne, Brancepeth, Durham. B.A. 1610-1; M.A. 1614. Ord. deacon (Chichester); priest (London) Mar. 8, 1611-2. P.C. of Kingsbury, Middlesex, 1612. R. of Ickenham, Middlesex, 1626-35. Perhaps R. of Waddingham St Mary, Lincs., 1635.

HARRISON, LANCELOT. Matric. sizar from JESUS, Easter, 1611; B.A. (? 1613-4); M.A. 1617. R. of Bircholt, Kent, 1623-41. R. of Orlestone, 1626-41. Died 1641. Father of Edward (1634) and the next.

HARRISON, LANCELOT. Adm. pens. at JESUS, May 24, 1634. Of Kent. Doubtless s. of Lancelot (above), R. of Orlestone. Matric. 1634; Scholar, 1637; B.A. 1637; M.A. 1641; M.D. 1661 (*Lit. Reg.*). Elected hon. fellow, R.C.P., Dec. 1664. Living at Faversham, in 1670. Father of Lancelot (1670), brother of Edward (1634). (*Munk*, I. 347.)

HARRISON, LANCELOT. Adm. pens. at QUEENS', Mar. 29, 1646. Already matric. from Queen's, Oxford, Dec. 10, 1641, age 15. S. of Thomas, of Smeeth, Kent.

HARRISON, LANCELOT. Adm. pens. (age 19) at ST JOHN'S, May 28, 1670, from Christ Church, Oxford, where he had been adm. Apr. 1, 1668. S. of Lancelot (1634), M.D., of Faversham, Kent. B. there. Exhibitioner from Charterhouse. Matric. 1672; B.A. 1672-3; M.A. 1676; M.D. (St Andrews). Incorp. at Cambridge, 1683. Candidate R.C.P., 1683. F.R.C.P., 1687. (*Munk*, I. 474.)

HARRISON, MARTIN. Matric. sizar from CORPUS CHRISTI, 1601. Of Yorkshire.

HARRISON, MAURICE. Adm. pens. (age 18) at ST JOHN'S, Aug. 2, 1654. S. of John, clerk (presbyterian minister), of Hindley-in-Wigan, Lancs. B. there. School, Manchester (Mr Wickins). Matric. 1654; B.A. 1658-9; M.A. 1664. V. of St Julian's, Shrewsbury. Died 1689. (Mumford, *Manch. Gr. Sch.*)

HARRISON or HERRISON, MICHAEL. B.A. 1503-4.

HARRISON, MICHAEL. Matric. pens. from TRINITY, Easter, 1565; B.A. 1570-1, as 'Nicholas'; M.A. 1574. Incorp. at Oxford, 1580. Ord. priest (Lincoln) Feb. 25, 1573-4. V. of Wirksworth, Derbs., 1577-1608.

HARRISON, MICHAEL. Matric. sizar from TRINITY, Easter, 1573; Scholar, 1575; B.A. 1576-7; M.A. 1580. Fellow, 1579. Ord. deacon and priest (Peterb.) Mar. 19, 1586-7.

HARRISON, NATHANIEL. Adm. pens. (age 16) at CHRIST'S, Nov. 25, 1645. S. of Peter. B. at Hindley, Lancs. School, Leigh (Mr Greenhalgh). Matric. 1645. Probably died young. Brother of Jeremiah (1645), Peter (1641) and perhaps of John (1632). (*Peile*, I. 500.)

HARRISON, NICHOLAS. Matric. sizar from TRINITY, *c.* 1589.

HARRISON, NICHOLAS. Matric. sizar from CHRIST'S, Easter, 1612.

HARRISON, PETER. M.A. 1641 (Incorp. from Dublin). S. of Peter, of Hindley, near Wigan. B.D. 1648; D.D. 1661 (*Lit. Reg.*). Intruded fellow of CHRIST'S, 1644-7. R. of Cheadle, Cheshire, 1652-60 and 1660-74. Died Mar. 17, 1673-4. Will (Chester) 1674. Brother of Jeremiah (1645), Nathaniel (1645) and perhaps of John (1632), father of James (1671). (*Peile*, I. 434; Earwaker, *Cheshire*, I. 222.)

HARRYSON, PHILIP. Matric. pens. from TRINITY, Michs. 1568; Scholar, 1571; B.A. 1572-3; M.A. from Clare, 1576. V. of St John's, Margate, 1601-7. Buried there Aug. 14, 1607.

HARRISON, PHILIP. Adm. sizar (age 18) at ST JOHN'S, Dec. 14, 1733. S. of John, of Middlesex. B. at Kingston. School, Peterborough (Mr Bradfield). Matric. 1733.

HARRISON, RALPH. Adm. pens. at EMMANUEL, Nov. 1632. Of Essex. Matric. 1633; B.A. 1636-7; M.A. 1640; D.D. 1661 (*Lit. Reg.*). Ord. priest (Kilmore) Dec. 11, 1648. R. of St Bartholomew-the-Great, London, 1660-3. R. of St Christopher-le-Stock, 1663-5. Died of the plague. Buried at St Christopher's, Oct. 14, 1665. Will (P.C.C.). (J. Ch. Smith.)

HARRISON, RALPH. Adm. pens. (age 15) at CAIUS, Feb. 8, 1636-7. S. of North, scrivener. B. in Cambridge. School, Perse (Mr Lovering). Scholar, 1636-44; Matric. 1637; B.A. 1640-1. Usher of the Perse School, 1642-4. Brother of Jeremy (1636-7). (*Venn*, I. 323.)

HARRISON, RALPH. Adm. pens. at EMMANUEL, Aug. 30, 1660. Of Essex. Matric. 1661; M.B. 1666; M.D. (New College, Oxford) 1676.

HARRISON, RALPH. Adm. pens. (age 16) at TRINITY, July 4, 1710. S. of John (? 1682), M.D., of Colchester. School, Merchant Taylors', London. B. Feb. 26, 1693-4.

HARRISON, RICHARD. Scholar and fellow of KING'S HALL, 1517-42. B.Can.L. 1501-2. Probably D.Can.L. 1515-6. Official of Ely diocese. R. of Milton, Cambs., 1506-42. Will (V.C.C.) 1542. (*Cooper*, I. 83.)

HARYSON, RICHARD. Matric. sizar from ST JOHN'S, Lent, 1557-8. One of these names V. of Harlow, Essex, 1564-1601. Will (Consist. C. London) 1602.

HARRYSON, RICHARD. Matric. sizar from ST JOHN'S, Easter, 1568.

HARRYSON, RICHARD. Matric. sizar from TRINITY, Michs. 1569; B.A. 1572-3. Ord. deacon and priest (Peterb.) Mar. 16, 1573-4. V. of Quadring, Lincs., 1578. V. of Barnetby, 1578. V. of Horbling, 1583. Admon. (Lincoln) 1593.

HARRISON, RICHARD. Matric. pens. from CHRIST'S, June, 1575; B.A. 1578-9; M.A. 1582. Perhaps R. of Beaumont, Essex; deprived before July, 1586. (*Peile*, I. 131.)

HARRISON, RICHARD. Matric. sizar from TRINITY, Easter, 1577; B.A. from Christ's, 1578-9; M.A. 1582.

HARRISON, RICHARD. Adm. at KING'S (age 18) a scholar from Eton, Aug. 27, 1579. Of Hurst, Berks. S. of Thomas, of Finchampstead, Berks. Matric. 1579. Left in 1581. Married and had issue. Buried at Hurst, Jan. 6, 1585-6. Grandfather of William (1668). (J. Ch. Smith.)

HARRISON, RICHARD. M.A. 1633 (Incorp. from Oxford). S. of Richard, of Minshul Vernon, Cheshire. Matric. from Brasenose College, Oxford, June 10, 1630, age 19; B.A. 1629-30; M.A. 1632. Perhaps minister of Warmingham, Cheshire, 1641. V. of St Mary's, Lichfield, 1645-7 and 1660-76. C. of Tettenhall, 1650; V. 1652-8. R. of Blithfield, 1668-76. Buried at St Mary's, Lichfield, Apr. 3, 1676. (*Al. Oxon.*; *Wm. Salt Arch. Soc.*, 1915.)

HARRISON, RICHARD. Adm. sizar (age 20) at CHRIST'S, June 23, 1655. S. of Robert. B. at Kendal, Westmorland. School, Kendal (Mr Jackson). Matric. 1655.

HARRISON, RICHARD. Adm. Fell.-Com. (age 19) at PETERHOUSE, Jan. 8, 1662-3. S. of Sir John, Knt., of Balls, Herts. B. Oct. 1646. Matric. 1663. Adm. at the Middle Temple, Mar. 20, 1662-3. J.P. for Herts. M.P. for Lancaster, 1669-79. Lieut.-Col. of Militia. Succeeded to the Balls estate in 1705. Buried at All Saints', Hertford, Jan. 17, 1725-6. Probably half-brother of Abraham (1638) and John (1633), father of John (1687). (*T. A. Walker*, 122; *Clutterbuck*, II. 186.)

HARRISON, RICHARD. Adm. sizar at CLARE, Feb. 18, 1731-2. S. of William, of Wakefield, Yorks. Bapt. there, Feb. 12, 1713. School, Wakefield. Matric. 1732; Scholar, 1732; B.A. 1735-6. *Litt. dim.* from York, Feb. 1737-8, for deacon. Usher of Wakefield School, 1735-7. Head Master of Pontefract School, 1737-42. (M. H. Peacock.)

HARRISON, ROBERT. Scholar of JESUS, 1538-9. Possibly the same as the next.

HARRISON, ROBERT. Adm. at KING'S, Easter, 1545 (*see* above); B.A. 1545-6; M.A. 1549. Fellow of Jesus, 1547-9. C. of 'Jesus Church,' Cambridge, 1547. V. of Linton, Cambs., 1554. V. of Gt Stukeley, Hunts., 1561-81. Died 1581. (A. Gray.)

HARRISON, ROBERT. Matric. pens. from ST JOHN'S, Michs. 1564; B.A. from Corpus Christi, 1567-8; M.A. 1572. For a short time Master of Aylsham School, 1573-5. Helped Robert Brown, the Separatist, to form a congregation, and went with him to Middelburg, where he died, *c.* 1585. Author, theological tracts. (*Cooper*, II. 177; *D.N.B.*)

HARRISON, ROBERT. Matric. sizar from MAGDALENE, Easter, 1589. B. *c.* 1566. B.A. 1593-4. Ord. deacon (Durham); priest, Feb. 1594. V. of Laughton, Lincs., 1612. Sequestration of the fruits of the vicarage of St Helen's, York, granted to Rob. Harrison, B.A., 1618; and of St Mary's, Castlegate, 1619. (M. H. Peacock.)

HARRISON, ROBERT. Matric. sizar from TRINITY, Easter, 1597-8; B.A. from King's, 1603-4; M.A. 1607.

HARRISON, ROBERT. Matric. sizar from CLARE, Easter, 1621. S. of Robert, of Manchester. B.A. 1624-5; M.A. 1628. Lecturer at St Andrew-by-the-Wardrobe, London.

HARRISON, ROBERT. Adm. pens. at EMMANUEL, 1623. Matric. 1624; B.A. 1627-8; M.A. 1631.

HARRISON, ROBERT. Adm. pens. at EMMANUEL, May 26, 1636. Of Lincolnshire. Matric. 1636.

HARISON, ROBERT. Matric. sizar from MAGDALENE, Easter, 1637; B.A. 1640-1.

HARRISON, ROBERT. Adm. pens. (age 10) at TRINITY, June 18, 1638. Matric. 1639; B.A. 1641-2; M.A. 1645. Fellow of Peterhouse, 1646. Perhaps s. of Thomas, late of Cayton Grange, Yorks.; adm. at Gray's Inn, Oct. 23, 1646. Afterwards of Cayton. (*T. A. Walker*, 88.)

HARRISON, ROBERT. Adm. pens. (age 16) at CHRIST'S, July 25, 1640. S. of Robert. B. at Belshford, Lincs. School, Caistor (Mr Metcalf and Mr Welfit). Matric. 1640. One of these names minister of Hampton, Middlesex, 1659. (*Peile*, I. 472.)

HARRISON, ROBERT. Adm. sizar at CHRIST'S, July 7, 1674. B. at Hadleigh, Suffolk, 1657. Matric. 1677; B.A. 1677-8; M.A. 1682. Ord. deacon (London) Dec. 1678; priest (Norwich) Dec. 1682. Perhaps R. of Gt Horkesley, Essex, 1683-1733. Died 1733. (*Peile*, II. 55.)

HARRISON, ROBERT. Adm. pens. at QUEENS', June 12, 1691. Of Essex. Matric. 1691; B.A. 1694-5. Perhaps R. of Luddenham, Kent, 1713-55; and P.C. of Oare, till his death, May 1, 1755.

HARRISON, ROBERT. Adm. sizar (age 18) at TRINITY, Mar. 21, 1737-8. S. of Thomas, of Wakefield, Yorks. Bapt. June 20, 1719. School, Wakefield (Mr Wilson). Matric. 1738; B.A. 1741. Ord. deacon (Lincoln) Dec. 20, 1741; priest (York) Sept. 22, 1745. Perhaps P.C. of Hartshead Chapel, Yorks., 1744-62. Died 1762.

HARRISON, SAMUEL. Adm. sizar (age 18) at ST JOHN'S, Apr. 26, 1680. S. of Robert, husbandman. B. at Little Ireton, Derbs. School, Dalbury (private; Mr Ainsworth). Matric. 1680. Drowned in the Cam. Buried at St Sepulchre's, Cambridge, May 26, 1681.

HARRISON, SAMUEL. Adm. pens. (age 19) at TRINITY, May 17, 1729. S. of Thomas, of York. School, York (Dr Jackson). Matric. 1729; Scholar, 1730. Adm. at Lincoln's Inn, Feb. 10, 1729-30.

HARRISON, THOMAS. Adm. pens. at KING'S, Easter, 1562.

HARRISON, THOMAS. Matric. pens. from CHRIST'S, Easter, 1568.

HARRISON, THOMAS. Matric. pens. from ST JOHN'S, Michs. 1572. School, Merchant Taylors'. B.A. 1576-7.

HARRISON, THOMAS. Matric. pens. from TRINITY, Michs. 1573; Scholar, 1575; B.A. 1577-8; M.A. 1581; B.D. 1588. Fellow, 1579-1631. Vice-Master, 1611-31. Incorp. at Oxford, 1585. Perhaps V. of Gt Cornard, Suffolk, 1596-1630. A noted Hebraist. One of the revisers of James I's bible. Died 1631. Buried in the College Chapel. Will pr. (V.C.C.) 1631. (*D.N.B.*, where he is confused with Thomas of 1572.)

HARRISON, THOMAS. Matric. pens. from CLARE, Michs. 1579; B.A. from Magdalene, 1582-3. Subscribed for priest's orders (Lincoln) July 8, 1586, as 'of Lincs. diocese.' C. of Ramsey, Hunts., *c.* 1591.

HARRISON, THOMAS. Matric. sizar from CHRIST'S, Nov. 1584; B.A. from St Catharine's, 1588-9; M.A. 1592. Perhaps licensed, 1592, to teach boys in the province of Canterbury. One of these names (M.A.), R. of Peper-Harow, Surrey, 1598-1600. Died 1600. (*Peile*, I. 181.)

HARRISON, THOMAS. Matric. sizar from St John's, c. 1592.

HARRISON, THOMAS. Matric. sizar from Christ's, 1593-4; B.A. 1597-8. One of these names (B.A.), V. of Donnington, Sussex, 1598-1630. Will (Chichester) 1630. (*Peile*, I. 213.)

HARRISON, THOMAS. Matric. pens. from Trinity, c. 1596. Of Sussex. Migrated to Sidney, June, 1599. B.A. 1599-1600; M.A. 1603. One of these names (M.A.), V. of Burwash, Sussex, 1606-41. Died 1641. Pedigree in Dugdale's *Vis. of Yorks.* (H. G. Harrison.)

HARRISONNE, THOMAS. Matric. pens. from Christ's, c. 1598; B.A. from Magdalene, 1601-2. One of these names V. of Crambe, Yorks., 1620-3.

HARRISON, THOMAS. B.A. from St John's, 1630-1; M.A. 1634.

HARRISON, THOMAS. Adm. pens. (age 18) at Christ's, June 26, 1632. S. of Thomas, of Cayton, Ripley, Yorks. B. there. School, Helmsley (Mr Coniers). Matric. 1632. Adm. at Gray's Inn, June 12, 1635.

HARRISON, THOMAS. Adm. pens. (age 16) at Sidney, Apr. 12, 1634. S. of Robert, merchant. B. at Hull, Yorks. School, Hull (Mr Ja. Burney). Matric. 1634; B.A. 1637-8. Went to Virginia, in 1642, as Chaplain to Sir Wm. Berkeley, the Governor. Pastor of a Puritan Church there. Afterwards at Boston, Mass., for two years. Minister at St Dunstan-in-the-East, London, 1651-3. Accompanied Henry Cromwell to Ireland. Afterwards at Chester; minister at St Oswald's, 1661-2. Had a licence as preacher in Cheshire, 1672. Married (1) in New England, 1648, Dorothy, dau. of the Hon. Samuel Symonds; (2) at St Oswald's, Chester, Feb. 28, 1659-60, Katharine Bradshaw. Generally styled 'Dr.' Author, *Topica Sacra*. Said to have died in Dublin, 1682. (*D.N.B.*; J. G. Bartlett; E. Axon.)

HARRISON, THOMAS. Adm. sizar (age 16) at St John's, June 8, 1646. S. of James, of Hatfield Broad Oak, Essex, clerk. School, Bishop's Stortford. Matric. 1646; B.A. 1649; M.A. 1653. Incorp. at Oxford, 1650-1 and 1653. R. of Wanstead, Essex, 1660-7. Died 1667. (*Al. Oxon.*)

HARRISON, THOMAS. Adm. sizar at Trinity, July 3, 1663.

HARRISON, THOMAS. Adm. sizar at St Catharine's, 1665-6. Matric. 1667; B.A. 1669-70.

HARRISON, THOMAS. Adm. Fell.-Com. (age 16) at Sidney, Mar. 22, 1666-7. S. of Thomas, Esq. B. at Willesden, Middlesex. School, York. Matric. 1668, as 'Matthew.' One of these names (Thomas), s. and h. of Thomas, of Allerthorpe, Burneston, Yorks., Esq., adm. at Gray's Inn, Mar. 29, 1667. Barrister, 1673. Ancient, 1688. Bencher, 1698. Perhaps M.P. for Boroughbridge, Yorks., 1695-8.

HARRISON, THOMAS. Adm. pens. (age 16) at Peterhouse, May 1, 1682. Of Lancashire. School, Hertford. Matric. 1683; Scholar, 1683; B.A. 1685-6; M.A. 1689. Ord. priest (London) June 15, 1690.

HARRISON, THOMAS. Adm. (age 20) at Sidney, June 4, 1685. 1st s. of Thomas, yeoman. B. at Hull, Yorks. School, Hull. Matric. 1685; Scholar, 1687; B.A. 1688-9; M.A. 1692; B.D. 1699. Fellow, c. 1691. Taxor, 1694. Incorp. at Oxford, 1698. Ord. deacon (London) Sept. 30, 1689; priest, Dec. 20, 1691. Perhaps V. of Stowe, Bucks., 1697; and Chaplain in the army. Died abroad.

HARRISON, THOMAS. Adm. sizar (age 16) at St John's, May 25, 1692. S. of William, deceased. B. at St Ives, Hunts. School, Peterborough (Mr Waring). Matric. 1692; B.A. 1695-6.

HARRISON, THOMAS. Adm. pens. (age 16) at Magdalene, Nov. 16, 1694. S. of Thomas, gent. B. at Alford, Lincs. School, Alford. Matric. 1695; B.A. 1698-9; M.A. 1702. Fellow, 1700. Ord. deacon (Lincoln) Mar. 14, 1702-3.

HARRISON, THOMAS. Adm. sizar (age 15) at Sidney, Oct. 10, 1710. 1st s. of Alexander. B. at York. Schools, Hull (Mr Pell) and Oakham. Matric. 1710-1; B.A. 1714-5; M.A. 1718; B.D. 1725. Fellow, 1718. Senior proctor, 1723-4. Ord. deacon (Ely) Mar. 9, 1717-8; priest (Lincoln, *Litt. dim.* from Ely) Mar. 5, 1720-1. Perhaps V. of South Kilvington, Yorks., 1728-45; and R. of St Martin's, Micklegate, York, till 1745.

HARRISON, THOMAS. Adm. sizar (age 16) at St John's, July 9, 1713. S. of William (? 1674), clerk. B. at Snailwell, Cambs. School, Saffron Walden (Mr Kilburne). Matric. 1714; B.A. 1717-8; M.A. 1721; D.D. 1747. Fellow, 1721. Ord. deacon (Ely) Dec. 20, 1719; priest, Sept. 24, 1721. V. of Ryhall, Rutland, 1727-73. R. of Gt Casterton, 1734-82. R. of Market Overton, 1773-82. Died Aug. 10, 1782, at Stamford. Buried at Ryhall. (Blore, *Rutland*, 56; H. I. Longden.)

HARRISON, THOMAS. Adm. pens. (age 17) at Trinity, Oct. 27, 1733. S. of Thomas, of Stoke Edith, Heref. School, Malvern (Mr Hallings). Matric. 1733; Scholar, 1734; B.A. 1737-8; M.A. 1741; B.D. 1751. Fellow, 1740. Regius Professor of Hebrew, 1748-53. Ord. deacon (Lincoln) Dec. 20, 1741; priest, May 29, 1743. V. of Stow-*cum*-Quy, Cambs. Died July 3, 1753. (*G. Mag.*)

HARRISON, THOMAS. Adm. pens. at St Catharine's, Apr. 20, 1734. Of Coggeshall, Essex. Matric. 1734; B.A. 1737-8; M.A. 1745.

HARRISON, W. Matric. sizar from Jesus, Michs. 1567.

HARRISON, W. Matric. sizar from King's, Michs. 1576.

HARRISON, WALTER. Matric. pens. from Trinity, Easter, 1563. Probably V. of Woodnesborough, Kent, 1568-96; described as 'scholar.' Died 1596.

HARRISON or HERYSON, WILLIAM. B.Can.L. 1505-6. Of Burdon Hostel and St Paul's. Will proved (V.C.C.) 1508.

HARRISON, WILLIAM. Matric. sizar from St John's, Michs. 1567. Of Norfolk. B.A. 1571-2; M.A. 1575. Fellow, 1573. Ord. priest (Peterb.) Sept. 15, 1575. One of these names V. of Marton, Lincs., 1599-1633.

HARRISON, WILLIAM. B.D. 1569. Of London. B. Apr. 18, 1534. Schools, St Paul's and Westminster. B.A. from Christ Church, Oxford, 1556; M.A. 1560. Chaplain to Lord Cobham. R. of Radwinter, Essex, 1559-93. R. of St Olave, Silver St, 1567-71. V. of Wimbish, 1571-81. V. of St Thomas the Apostle, 1583-7. Canon of Windsor, 1586-93. Author, historical. Died 1593. Will, P.C.C. (*Cooper*, II. 163; *D.N.B.*; *Al. Oxon.*)

HARRISON, WILLIAM. Matric. sizar from Trinity, Easter, 1576; B.A. 1580-1; M.A. 1584.

HARRISON, WILLIAM. Matric. pens. from Clare, Michs. 1579.

HARRISON, WILLIAM. Adm. at King's, a scholar from Eton, 1582. B. at Fotheringay, c. 1566. Matric. 1582; B.A. 1586-7; M.A. 1590. Fellow, 1585-92. Fellow of Eton, 1593. Vice-provost. Ord. deacon (London) Feb. 26; priest, Feb. 27, 1592-3, age 30. C. of Sutton, Essex. R. of Everdon, Northants., Nov. 11, 1611. Died same year. (*Cooper*, III. 49.)

HARRISON, WILLIAM. Matric. sizar from Queens', Michs. 1582. Of Derbyshire.

HARRISON, WILLIAM. Adm. sizar at Emmanuel, May 28, 1588. Matric. 1588; Scholar; B.A. 1591-2; M.A. 1595. Incorp. at Oxford, 1609. Ord. priest (Peterb.) Sept. 6, 1594. One of these names King's preacher in Lancs., at Huyton, 1601-4. R. of Eccleston, Cheshire, 1619-25. Will (Chester) 1625. (E. Axon.)

HARRISON, WILLIAM. Matric. sizar from Trinity, Michs. 1588.

HARRISON, WILLIAM. Matric. pens. from St John's, Easter, 1589.

HARRISON, WILLIAM. Matric. pens. from Christ's, Dec. 1589.

HARRISON, WILLIAM. Matric. pens. from Magdalene, Easter, 1605; B.A. 1608.

HARRISON, WILLIAM. Matric. pens. from Trinity, Easter, 1606; B.A. from Christ's, 1609-10.

HARRISON, WILLIAM. Matric. sizar from Trinity, Michs. 1610; B.A. 1613-4; M.A. 1619. Ord. deacon (York) Feb. 1615-6; probably priest (Durham) Sept. 20, 1618. V. of Sockburn, Durham, 1620-62. R. of Middleton St George, 1636-77. (H. M. Wood.)

HARRISON, WILLIAM. Matric. sizar from Christ's, July, 1620. B.A. 1629-30; M.A. 1638. Ord. deacon (Peterb.) Apr. 22, 1624; priest, Mar. 13, 1624-5. Probably V. of Canwick All Saints', Lincs., 1626. (*Peile*, I. 336.)

HARRISON, WILLIAM. Matric. pens. from Trinity Hall, Michs. 1629. Of Hampshire. LL.B. 1635. Fellow, 1633-5. Died Mar. 11, 1634-5. Will (V.C.C.) 1635.

HARRISON, WILLIAM. Matric. Fell.-Com. from St Catharine's, Easter, 1637. Of London. Doubtless s. of John, of St Olave's, Hart St, London, Esq. Bapt. there, Sept. 24, 1619. B.A. 1637-8. Adm. at Gray's Inn, Oct. 13, 1637. Said to have died at Oxford of a fall from his horse, 1643, and to have been buried in Exeter College Chapel. Brother of John (1633). (J. Ch. Smith; *Clutterbuck*, II. 186.)

HARRISON, WILLIAM. Adm. sizar at Emmanuel, May 4, 1663. Of Lancashire. Matric. 1663; B.A. 1666-7; M.A. 1670. Perhaps LL.D. 1674 (*Lit. Reg.*).

HARRISON, WILLIAM. M.A. 1668 (Incorp. from Oxford). S. of Sir Richard, of Hurst, Berks. School, Winchester. Matric. from Wadham College, Apr. 11, 1660; B.A. (Oxford) 1664; M.A. 1667; D.D. (Lambeth) 1675. V. of Warlingham, Surrey, 1667. R. of Shalden, Herts., 1669. Preb. of Lincoln, 1669-94. R. of Cheriton, Hants., 1672. Master of St Cross, Winchester, 1676. Preb. of Winchester, 1681-94. Died Aug. 7, 1694. Buried at Hurst. M.I. Will (P.C.C.) as of St Cross. Benefactor to St Cross. (*Al. Oxon.*; J. Ch. Smith.)

HARRISON, WILLIAM. Adm. sizar (age 18) at ST JOHN'S, June 21, 1669. S. of William, of Upton, Salop. B. there. School, Shrewsbury. Matric. 1669; B.A. 1672-3.

HARRISON, WILLIAM. Adm. at CORPUS CHRISTI, 1669. Of Northamptonshire. B.A. 1673-4. Ord. deacon (Peterb.) Sept. 21, 1673; priest, Sept. 20, 1674. One of these names V. of Roade, Northants., 1677; and R. of Grafton Regis, 1681. (*Baker*, II. 235.)

HARRISON, WILLIAM. Adm. pens. (age 17) at ST JOHN'S, Dec. 29, 1674. S. of Henry (1628), D.D. B. at West Wratting, Cambs. School, St Paul's, London. Matric. 1675; B.A. 1678-9; M.A. 1682. Ord. deacon and priest (Norwich) Dec. 1682. Probably R. of Snailwell, Cambs., 1682; and father of Thomas (1713), brother of Allington (1673-4).

HARRISON, WILLIAM. Adm. sizar (age 21) at ST JOHN'S, Jan. 15, 1713-4. S. of Anthony, carpenter. B. at Isell, near Cockermouth, Cumberland. School, Sedbergh. Matric. 1713-4.

HARRISON, WILLIAM. Adm. sizar (age 17) at ST JOHN'S, May 19, 1719. S. of William, husbandman, of Lancashire. B. at Hode, near Kirkham. School, Hode (Mr Taylor). Matric. 1719.

HARRISON, WILLIAM. Adm. sizar (age 18) at TRINITY, Apr. 25, 1734. S. of John, of Malton, Yorks. School, Shipton, Yorks. (Mr Clarke). Matric. 1734; Scholar, 1737; B.A. 1737-8; M.A. 1752. Ord. deacon (Lincoln) May 28, 1738; priest (Lincoln, *Litt. dim.* from York) Dec. 23, 1739. Perhaps R. of Hooton Roberts, Yorks., 1757-94. Also V. of Rotherham. Died Mar. 8, 1794, aged 79. Will, P.C.C.

HARRISON, ——. M.A. or higher degree. Referred to in 1455-6 (*Gr. Bk*, A, 4). Perhaps John.

HARRISON, ——. B.A. 1469-70.

HARRISON, ——. B.A. 1477-8; M.A. 1480.

HARRISON, ——. Of CHRIST'S. Fee for B.A. (? M.A.) 1519-20, or 1520-1.

HARRISON, ——. B.A. 1526-7.

HARRISON, ——. Adm. Fell.-Com. at CORPUS CHRISTI, 1554.

HARISON, ——. Student at PETERHOUSE, Nov. 20, 1563.

HARYSON, —— (*junior*). Adm. pens. at PETERHOUSE, June 10, 1581.

HARRISON, ——. Adm. pens. at PETERHOUSE, 1605. Resided till 1608.

HARRISON, ——. Adm. Fell.-Com. at TRINITY HALL, Mar. 30, 1705. Name off, Dec. 1706.

HARROP, JAMES. Adm. sizar (age 16) at ST JOHN'S, May 30, 1656. S. of James, butcher, of Newcastle-under-Lyne. B. there. School, Newcastle (Mr Richell). Matric. 1656; B.A. 1659-60. P.C. of Lamesley, Durham, 1677-1700. Father of Obadiah (1690).

HARRAP, JOB. Adm. sizar at ST JOHN'S, 1748. S. of John, blacksmith, of Yorkshire. B. at Osset, near Wakefield. School, Rishworth. Matric. 1748; B.A. 1752.

HARROP, JOHN. Adm. sizar at ST CATHARINE'S, Apr. 27, 1739. Of Ashton-under-Lyne, Lancs. Matric. 1739; B.A. 1742-3. Ord. deacon (Ely) Feb. 26, 1742-3; priest (York) June, 1748. P.C. of Holmfirth, Yorks., 1743-95. Died Feb. 6, 1795, aged 75. (Morehouse, *Kirkburton*.)

HARROPE, OBADIAH ('ABDY'). Adm. pens. (age 18) at ST JOHN'S, May 30, 1690. S. of James (1656), P.C. of Lamesley, Durham. B. there. School, Usworth (Mr Stawnik). Matric. 1691; B.A. 1693-4; M.A. 1697. Ord. priest (Durham) May 26, 1700.

HARROPY, REYNOLD. Adm. pens. at QUEENS', July 3, 1578. Of Cheshire.

HARROW, JOHN. Matric. sizar from KING'S, Easter, 1669; B.A. 1672-3.

HARRY, MARK. Adm. pens. at EMMANUEL, Easter, 1621. Matric. sizar, 1621; B.A. 1624-5; M.A. 1628. Ord. deacon (Peterb.) Dec. 24, 1626; priest, June 22, 1628. V. of East Dean, Sussex, 1630-44, sequestered.

HARSFIELD, RICHARD. Matric. pens. from TRINITY, Easter, 1629.

HARSICK, WILLIAM. D.D. of Cambridge. Prior of the Carmelite House there in 1400. A famous teacher. Prior afterwards of Burnham Norton, Norfolk. (*Pits*, 594; B. Zimmerman.)

HARSLET, HENRY. Matric. pens. from ST JOHN'S, Easter, 1571.

HARSLETT, WILLIAM. Matric. sizar from CORPUS CHRISTI, Easter, 1644.

HARSLEY or ARSLEY, ROBERT. Adm. at KING'S, a scholar from Eton, Jan. 16, 1499-1500. Of Scarborough, Yorks. B.A. 1503-4; M.A. 1507. R. of West Wretham, Norfolk, 1509. Died 1551. (*Harwood*.)

HARSNETT, ADAM. Matric. sizar from PEMBROKE, *c.* 1597. S. of Adam, joiner, of Colchester. B. there. B.A. 1600-1; M.A. from St John's, 1604; B.D. from Pembroke, 1612. Ord. priest (London) Dec. 22, 1605, age 25. C. of Shenfield, Essex. V. of Hutton, 1609-39. R. of Cranham, 1612-39. Author, religious. Died 1639. Will proved (P.C.C.) Sept. 16, 1639, by brother Samuel, a grocer. Father of the next. (*D.N.B.*)

HARSNET, EZEKIEL. Adm. at CORPUS CHRISTI, 1647. Of Essex. 3rd s. of Adam (above). B. at Cranham, Essex. School, Colchester. V. of Whitehaven, Cumberland, 1657-62. (*Essex Archaeol. Soc.*, N.S., II. 256.)

HARSNETT or HERSENT, PETER. Adm. at TRINITY, a scholar from Westminster, 1617; B.A. 1620-1; M.A. 1624, as Harsnet. College librarian, 1625-31. Incorp. at Oxford, 1628.

HARSNETT, ROBERT. M.A. 1676 (Incorp. from Oxford). S. of Roger, of Pakington, Staffs., gent. Matric. from Christ Church, June 17, 1664, age 17; B.A. (Oxford) 1668; M.A. 1671; B.D. 1682; D.D. 1685. Preb. of Wells, 1677-94, deprived. *Al. Oxon.* assigns to him preferment probably belonging to the next.

HARSNETT, ROBERT. Adm. sizar (age 18) at PEMBROKE, Feb. 24, 1682-3. S. of Robert, of Somerset, mercer. Migrated to Emmanuel, Mar. 2, 1682-3. Matric. 1683; B.A. 1686-7; M.A. 1695. Ord. deacon (Norwich) May, 1687; priest, June, 1688. Doubtless V. of Griston, Norfolk, 1688-94. R. of Colney, 1694-1701.

HARSNET, SAMUEL. Matric. sizar from KING'S, Easter, 1579. S. of William, baker, of Colchester. B. there. Bapt. June 20, 1561. B.A. from Pembroke, 1580-1; M.A. 1584; D.D. 1606. Fellow of Pembroke, 1583. Proctor, 1592. Master, 1605-16. Vice-Chancellor, 1606-7, 1614-5. Master of Colchester Grammar School, 1587-88. V. of Chigwell, Essex, 1597-1605. Preb. of St Paul's, 1598. R. of St Margaret, Fish St, 1599-1604. Archdeacon of Essex, 1603-9. R. of Shenfield, Essex, 1604. V. of Hutton, 1606-9. Chaplain to Bishop Bancroft. R. of Stisted, 1609-19. Bishop of Chichester, 1609-19; of Norwich, 1619-28. Archbishop of York, 1629-31. Founder of Chigwell School. Author, religious. Died May 25, 1631. Buried at Chigwell. M.I. there. Will, P.C.C. (*Loder*; *D.N.B.*)

HARSNETT, SAMUEL. Matric. Fell.-Com. from CORPUS CHRISTI, Easter, 1656. Of Norfolk.

HARSWELL, HENRY. Matric. pens. from CLARE, *c.* 1592; B.A. 1595-6.

HART, CHARLES. Adm. Fell.-Com. at EMMANUEL, Aug. 26, 1726. Of Derbyshire.

HART, DAVID. Matric. pens. from QUEENS', Michs. 1635. Of Sussex.

HART, EDWARD. Adm. sizar (age 17) at CHRIST'S, Aug. 8, 1689. S. of Edward. B. at Massingham, Norfolk. School, Lynn (Mr Horne). Matric. 1689; Scholar, 1690; B.A. 1693-4. Ord. deacon (Ely) Dec. 1694; priest (Norwich) June, 1696. Probably R. of South Wootton, Norfolk. (*Peile*, II. 114.)

HART, FRANCIS. Matric. pens. from GONVILLE HALL, Easter, 1555. One of these names adm. at Gray's Inn, 1564.

HARTE, HENRY. Adm. Fell.-Com. at KING'S, Easter, 1546.

HART, JAMES. B.D. 1473-4 (*non intravit*).

HART, JAMES. Adm. sizar (age 17) at CAIUS, June 10, 1669. S. of Robert, gent., of Westleigh, Lancs. School, Ringley (Mr Taylor). Matric. 1669; Scholar, 1672-5; B.A. 1672-3; M.A. 1676. Probably R. of Ightham, Kent, 1693-1725. Buried there Dec. 20, 1725. (*Venn*, I. 438.)

HART, JOHN. Matric. pens. from TRINITY HALL, Easter, 1544; LL.B. 1553. Fellow, till 1572. Perhaps V. of Bentley, Suffolk, 1576-80. One of these names R. of South Creake, Norfolk, 1581.

HART, JOHN. Matric. pens. from TRINITY, Michs. 1568. One of these names V. of Bramford, Suffolk, 1578-81. Will of another (P.C.C.) 1625; of St Nicholas Cole Abbey, clerk.

HART, JOHN. Adm. sizar at CLARE, July 28, 1709. B. in Staffordshire. Matric. 1710; B.A. 1713-4.

HART, JOHN. M.A. from KING'S, 1723. S. of J., of Compton, Somerset, clerk. Matric. from St John's, Oxford, Mar. 31, 1712, age 17; B.A. (Oxford) 1715. V. of Stockland, Bristol, 1722. (*Al. Oxon.*)

HART, JOHN. Adm. sizar at QUEENS', Mar. 31, 1736. Of Suffolk.

HART, LEWIS. Adm. sizar (age 17) at ST JOHN'S, June 25, 1632. S. of Simon, R. of Little Torrington, Devon. B. there. School, Exbourne, Devon (Mr Fynny). Matric. 1632; B.A. 1635-6; M.A. 1639. C. of South Weald, Essex, in 1640.

HART, MICHAEL. Adm. sizar (age 17) at CAIUS, May 27, 1684. S. of Philip, gent., of Aylsham, Norfolk. B. there. School, Norwich. Matric. 1684; Scholar, 1685-8; B.A. 1687-8; M.A. 1691. Ord. deacon (Norwich) Dec. 21, 1688; priest (St David's) May 26, 1689. V. of Tunstead, Norfolk, 1689. C. of Landbeach, Cambs., in 1689. R. of Thorpe Market, Norfolk, 1692-1700; of Cantley, 1696-1703. Buried there May 29, 1703. Will (Norwich Archd. C.) 1704. (*Venn*, I. 476.)

HART, NICHOLAS. B.A. 1475-6; M.A. 1479. Received 'letters of conversation,' 1480-1. V. of Foxton, Cambs., till 1498.

HARTE, RICHARD. Matric. sizar from CHRIST'S, June, 1587; B.A. 1590-1; M.A. 1594; B.D. 1608. Ord. priest (Bishop of Colchester, at Norwich) Feb. 1594-5. V. of Swilland, Suffolk, 1597. V. of Ash-Bocking, 1608. Will (P.C.C.) 1630. (*Peile*, I. 190.)

HART, RICHARD. Matric. pens. from ST CATHARINE'S, Easter, 1617; B.A. 1618-9; M.A. 1622. R. of Hargrave, Suffolk, 1634.

HART, RICHARD. B.A. 1620-1 (Incorp. from Oxford). B.A. from Trinity College, Oxford, 1619-20; B.C.L. (Oxford) 1625; D.C.L. (St Alban's Hall) 1628. Adm. advocate, Oct. 14, 1629. A popish recusant, in 1632. Doubtless s. of John, of St Gregory's, London, proctor in the Court of Arches; whose will he proved, 1635. (*Al. Oxon.*; H. G. Harrison.)

HART, RICHARD. M.A. from EMMANUEL, 1738. S. of Thomas, of Furness, Lancs. Matric. from Queen's College, Oxford, June 27, 1716, age 21; B.A. (Oxford) 1720. (*Al. Oxon.*)

HART, ROBERT. Adm. pens. (age 16) at SIDNEY, Mar. 17, 1684-5. Only s. of Joshua, gent. B. at Holbeach, Lincs. Schools, Spalding (Mr Johnson) and Holbeach (Mr West). Matric. 1685; B.A. 1688-9; M.A. 1692. Incorp. at Oxford, 1693.

HART, ROBERT. Adm. pens. (age 17) at ST JOHN'S, May 22, 1717. S. of Rawson, Esq., of Lincolnshire. B. at Grantham. Bapt. there, Oct. 21, 1699. School, Grantham (Mr Ellis). Matric. 1717. Probably adm. at the Inner Temple, Apr. 10, 1717. Of Grantham and Turnley Woodside. An officer in the army. (*Lincs. Pedigrees*, 465.)

HARTE, THOMAS. Adm. at KING'S, a scholar from Eton, 1450. Of Gloucester. B.A. 1454-5; M.A. 1457. Ord. deacon (Ely) Feb. 21, 1455-6. Will of one of these names (P.C.C.) 1509; of Sopworth, Wilts., clerk.

HARTE, THOMAS. Matric. sizar from CHRIST'S, Easter, 1575.

HARTE, THOMAS. Matric. pens. from ST JOHN'S, Michs. 1585.

HARTE, THOMAS. Matric. pens. from CORPUS CHRISTI, Easter, 1589. Of Suffolk. B.A. 1592-3; M.A. 1596. Ord. deacon (Norwich) Oct. 3; priest, Dec. 21, 1596. V. of Brome, Suffolk, 1600.

HART, THOMAS. Adm. sizar at EMMANUEL, Jan. 28, 1594-5. Matric. 1595; Scholar; B.A. 1598-9; M.A. from Sidney, 1602. Fellow of Sidney. Ord. deacon and priest (Peterb.) Sept. 23, 1604. One of these names R. of Chelsworth, Suffolk, 1638.

HARTT, THOMAS. Matric. sizar from TRINITY, Easter, 1613.

HARTE, THOMAS. Matric. pens. from TRINITY, Easter, 1626. One of these names, s. and h. of William, of Uttoxeter, Staffs., gent., adm. at Lincoln's Inn, Jan. 27, 1628-9. Will (P.C.C.) 1647.

HART, THOMAS. Adm. sizar (age 16) at PEMBROKE, Oct. 29, 1636. S. of John. B. at Rickinghall, Suffolk. Matric. 1637; B.A. 1640-1.

HART, W. Matric. sizar from QUEENS', Easter, 1563.

HARTE, W. Matric. pens. from CHRIST'S, Oct. 1583.

HART, WALTER. Matric. sizar from QUEENS', Easter, 1563.

HARTE, WILLIAM. Matric. sizar from TRINITY, Michs. 1561; Scholar, 1563; B.A. 1565-6; M.A. 1570. One of these names R. of Pettaugh, Suffolk, 1566.

HARTE, WILLIAM. Matric. sizar from ST JOHN'S, Easter, 1579: B.A. from Corpus Christi, 1582. Perhaps M.A. 1594, as Heart. Licensed to teach grammar in Norwich diocese, 1584. Perhaps C. of Attleborough.

HART, WILLIAM. Adm. pens. at EMMANUEL, Feb. 24, 1594-5. Matric. 1595. One of these names, of Chilswell, Berks., adm. at the Inner Temple, 1601.

HART, WILLIAM. Adm. pens. at QUEENS', July 2, 1616. Of Lincolnshire.

HART, WILLIAM. Adm. sizar at PETERHOUSE, Oct. 2, 1623. Matric. 1623; Scholar, 1625-6; B.A. 1627-8; M.A. 1631. Ord. deacon (Peterb.) Dec. 20; priest, Dec. 21, 1629. One of these names C. at Abson, Gloucs., in 1642.

HART, WILLIAM. Adm. pens. at CHRIST'S, May 8, 1626. S. of William, of Norfolk, gent. School, Bury. Matric. 1626. One of these names, of Beeston, Norfolk, adm. at Gray's Inn, Feb. 23, 1623-4. (*Peile*, I. 373.)

HART, WILLIAM. Adm. sizar at CHRIST'S, Mar. 22, 1666-7. S. of William. B. at Lynn, 1650. School, Lynn (Mr Bell). Matric. 1667; B.A. 1670-1; M.A. 1674. Ord. deacon (Norwich) May, 1673; priest (London) Dec. 1673. R. of Walpole St Peter, Norfolk, 1675-1726. V. of Walpole St Andrew, 1684-1725. Died May 2, 1726, aged 78. M.I. there. (*Peile*, II. 9.)

HARTE, ——. M.A. 1459. Perhaps Walter Hart, R. of Rochford, Essex, 1454. Preb. of St Paul's, 1467-84. V. of Sporle, Norfolk. R. of St Martin Vintry, London. Will (P.C.C.) 1484. (*Hennessy*.)

HART, ——. B.Can.L. 1473-4.

HARTBORNE, NICHOLAS. Matric. Fell.-Com. from CHRIST'S, Nov. 1546.

HARTBURNE, ROBERT. B.A. from CLARE, 1538-9. Of Durham. M.A. 1541; B.D. 1556. Fellow, 1539. Fellow of St John's, 1555.

HARTCLIFFE, JOHN. M.A. 1658 (Incorp. from Oxford). Matric. from Corpus Christi, Oxford, Feb. 20, 1648-9; (? B.A.); M.A. (Oxford) 1651-2. Of Windsor. Will (P.C.C.) 1676; of St Giles-in-the-Fields; mentions s. John, at King's. Father of the next. (*Al. Oxon.*)

HARTCLIFFE, JOHN. Adm. at KING'S, a scholar from Eton, 1668. S. of John (above), of Windsor, clerk. B. at Henley-on-Thames. Matric. Easter, 1669; B.A. 1672-3; M.A. 1676; B.D. 1689 (*Lit. Reg.*). Fellow, 1671. Received a mandate for Provost, 1689, but the College refused. Previously matric. from Magdalen College, Oxford, Mar. 29, 1667, age 16. Head Master of Merchant Taylors' School, 1681-6. Canon of Windsor, 1691-1712. V. of Twickenham, Middlesex, 1708-12. Author, *Sermons*. Died Aug. 16, 1712. Buried in St George's Chapel, Windsor. (*Harwood*, 258; *Robinson*, I. xiv; *D.N.B.*; *Al. Oxon.*)

HARTENES, HUMPHREY. B.A. from ST JOHN'S, 1598-9; M.A. 1602; B.D. 1610.

HARTFLET, THOMAS. Matric. Fell.-Com. from TRINITY, Michs. 1580.

HARTFORD, Earl of. M.A. from TRINITY, 1703. (*See* Seymour.)

HARTFORD, ——. Adm. sizar at EMMANUEL, Apr. 26, 1645.

HARTGRAVE, GEORGE. Matric. sizar from MAGDALENE, Michs. 1633. S. of Paynell, of Hartgrave, Lincs. R. of Wilksby, Lincs., 1644. Will proved, Nov. 8, 1644; to be buried at Tattersall. (*Lincs. Pedigrees*, 466.)

HARTGRAVE, PAYNELL. Matric. sizar from MAGDALENE, Michs. 1633; B.A. 1636-7. Ord. deacon (Peterb.) Mar. 10, 1638-9; priest, Sept. 19, 1641, as M.A. Perhaps brother of George (above) (not in *Lincs. Pedigrees*).

HARTIS, JOHN. Adm. at SIDNEY, June 28, 1695, as B.A. of Dublin. B. in Dublin. School, Dublin. Migrated to Magdalene. M.A. there, 1695. R. of St Mary-le-Bow, Durham, 1695. V. of Bywell St Peter, Northumberland, 1699-1703. Died 1703.

HARTISTIE, JOHN, *see* HARDISTY.

HARTLEY, ALDERSON. M.A. from MAGDALENE, 1749. S. of Edward, of Hartforth, Yorks. Matric. from Queen's College, Oxford, Mar. 21, 1737-8, age 18; B.A. (Oxford) 1741. (*Al. Oxon.*)

HARTLEY, ANDREW. Adm. sizar at CLARE, Apr. 14, 1662. Of Yorkshire. Matric. 1662; B.A. 1665-6; M.A. 1670.

HARTLEY, CHRISTOPHER. Matric. sizar from ST JOHN'S, Easter, 1614; B.A. 1617-8; M.A. 1621. Incorp. at Oxford, 1623, as 'Hartler.' Ord. deacon (York) May, 1618; priest, Sept. 1618.

HARTLEY, DAVID. Adm. sizar at JESUS, Apr. 21, 1722. S. of David, clerk, deceased, of Ovenden, Halifax, Yorks. B. 1704. School, Bradford. Matric. 1722; B.A. 1725-6; M.A. 1729. Fellow, 1727-30. Master of Newark Grammar School, 1729. Practised physic at Newark, Bury St Edmunds and London. F.R.S., 1736. Author, philosophical. Died at Bath, Aug. 28, 1757. (*D.N.B.*; *F.M.G.*, 615.)

HARTLEY, GEORGE. Adm. pens. (age 17) at CHRIST'S, Apr. 14, 1743. S. of Leonard. B. at Middleton-Tyas, Yorks. School, Kirkheaton (? Kirkleatham), Yorks. (Mr Clarke). Matric. 1743. Migrated to Magdalene, Jan. 19, 1746-7. B.A. 1747-8; M.A. 1751. Fellow of Magdalene, 1747. Adm. at Lincoln's Inn, May 15, 1747, and at the Middle Temple, Jan. 30, 1749. Barrister. Died Apr. 29, 1780. (G. *Mag.*; *Peile*, II. 244.)

HARTLEY, JAMES. 'Of TRINITY HALL,' when ord. priest (York) Sept. 1668.

HARTLIE, JOHN. Matric. sizar from CLARE, Easter, 1587.

HARTLEY, JOHN. Matric. sizar from TRINITY, Easter, 1588.

HARTLEY, JOHN. Matric. sizar from QUEENS', *c.* 1593. Adm. June, 1594. Of Cumberland.

HARTLEY, JOHN. Adm. sizar at EMMANUEL, July 5, 1670. Of Yorkshire. Matric. 1671; B.A. 1674-5.

HARTLEY, JOHN. Adm. sizar (age 20) at TRINITY, June 27, 1689. S. of John, of Gisburn, Yorks. School, Burnsall (Mr Robert Hey). Matric. 1689. One of these names, attorney-at-law, buried at St Mary Castlegate, York, Apr. 12, 1722.

HARTLEY, JOSEPH. Adm. pens. (age 18) at PETERHOUSE, May 29, 1696. Of Buckinghamshire. School, Stony Stratford.

HARTLEY, LANCELOT (? LAURENCE). Matric. sizar from ST JOHN'S, Michs. 1567.

HARTLEY, RICHARD. Adm. sizar (age 17) at TRINITY, July 3, 1734. S. of Richard, of Yorkshire. Matric. 1734; B.A. 1737-8. Usher of Wakefield School, 1738-9. V. of Bingley, Yorks., 1740-89. Died Apr. 20, 1789. M.I. at Bingley. (M. H. Peacock.)

HARTLEY, ROBERT. Adm. sizar at TRINITY, June 2, 1668. Migrated to Christ's, June 29, 1671. B.A. 1671-2. Ord. deacon (York) Sept. 1671; priest, Sept. 1672. P.C. of Farnley, and of Bramley, Yorks., 1673. C. of Burnley, Lancs., 1674-88. Buried there Feb. 9, 1687-8. (*Peile*, II. 38.)

HARTLEY, THOMAS. Adm. at KING'S (age 17) a scholar from Eton, Aug. 14, 1548. Of Guisborough, Yorks. B.A. 1552-3. Fellow, 1551-5.

HARTLEY, THOMAS. Scholar of ST JOHN'S, 1549. B. in Lancashire. School, Sedbergh. B.A. 1552-3; M.A. 1556. Fellow, 1553-7. Will proved (V.C.C.) 1557.

HARTLEY, THOMAS. Adm. sizar (age 16) at ST JOHN'S, May 10, 1725. S. of Robert, bookseller, of Middlesex. B. in London. School, Kendal, Westmorland (Mr Towers). Matric. 1725; B.A. 1728-9; M.A. 1745. Ord. deacon (Gloucester, *Litt. dim.* from Rochester) Mar. 14, 1730-1; priest (London) Sept. 24, 1732. V. of Claydon, Bucks., 1741-6. R. of Winwick, Northants., 1744-84. Expositor and translator of Swedenborg. Died at East Malling, Kent, Dec. 10, 1784. Buried there. Admon., P.C.C. (*D.N.B.*; *Scott-Mayor*, III. 385.)

HARTLEY, W. Matric. sizar from PEMBROKE, Easter, 1585.

HARTELEY, WILLIAM. Matric. pens. from JESUS, Michs. 1555; Scholar of Trinity, 1560; B.A. from Trinity, 1561-2.

HARTNOLL, GEORGE. Adm. Fell.-Com. (age 21) at SIDNEY, July 2, 1646. S. of George, Esq., of Devon. B. at Tiverton. School, Tiverton. Adm. at the Middle Temple, Apr. 24, 1647.

HARTON, AMBROSE. Adm. sizar (age 18) at CHRIST'S, June 6, 1640. S. of John. B. at Wykeham, Yorks. School, Middleton (Mr Hardwick). Matric. 1640.

HARTOPP, EDGAR (? EDWARD) WILLIAM. Adm. Fell.-Com. at EMMANUEL, Nov. 14, 1750. S. of Samuel, Esq. B. at Little Dalby, Leics. School, Broughton Astley. Age 20. Matric. 1750-1. Of Little Dalby, Esq. High Sheriff of Leics. Died 1773. (Burke, *L.G.*; *Nichols*, II. 159.)

HARTOP, EDWARD. Adm. Fell.-Com. at CHRIST'S, Sept. 7, 1624. S. of Sir Edward, Bart. B. at Buckminster, Leics., 1608. Educated at home (Mr Valentine). Matric. 1624. Adm. at Lincoln's Inn, Feb. 15, 1626-7. Knighted, July 26, 1634. Raised a regiment for the service of the Parliament. Succeeded as Bart., 1652. Died 1657. (Burke, *Ext. Bart.*; *Peile*, I. 361; *D.N.B.*; *G.E.C.*)

HARTEP, GEORGE. Matric. pens. from TRINITY, Lent, 1597-8. Perhaps 5th s. of William, of Burton Lazars, Leics., gent.; adm. at Gray's Inn, Apr. 21, 1600. (Burke, *Commoners*, III. 401.)

HARTOPP, JOHN. Adm. Fell.-Com. at EMMANUEL, Oct. 4, 1596; B.A. 1600-1. Probably adm. at Lincoln's Inn, Oct. 11, 1601; of Surrey. Perhaps s. of Thomas, goldsmith, of London. If so, married a dau. of George Evelyn, of Long Ditton, Surrey. Of Kingston-upon-Thames. (*Manning and Bray*, II. 435.)

HARTOPP, MARTIN. Adm. pens. at CLARE, Mar. 30, 1680. Of London. Doubtless 2nd s. of Sir William (1642), of Rotherby, and Agnes, dau. of Sir Martin Lister, of Thorpe-Arnold. Matric. 1680. Migrated to Oxford. B.A. (Merton College) 1683-4; M.A. 1688; M.B. 1689. Practised at Leicester. Died Feb. 24, 1722, aged 60. M.I. at Rotherby. (*Al. Oxon.*; *Nichols*, II. 267; III. 400.)

HARTOP, THOMAS. Matric. pens. from TRINITY, Michs. 1584. One of these names adm. at Gray's Inn, May 10, 1587.

HARTOPP, THOMAS. Matric. Fell.-Com. from QUEENS', Michs. 1616. Of Leicestershire. S. and h. of William (next), of Burton Lazars, Leics., Esq. Adm. at Gray's Inn, Nov. 1, 1619. Of Burton Lazars. Knighted, Aug. 8, 1624. Married Dorothy, dau. of Sir Thomas Bendish, 1661. Will (P.C.C.) Father of William (1642).

HARTOPE, WILLIAM. Matric. pens. from TRINITY, c. 1591. Doubtless s. and h. of Valentine, of Burton Lazars. Probably adm. at Lincoln's Inn, Feb. 2, 1592-3; of Leicestershire. Knighted, Sept. 2, 1617. Will (P.C.C.) 1623; of Burton Lazars. Father of the above.

HARTOPP, WILLIAM. Adm. Fell.-Com. (age 16) at ST JOHN'S, Apr. 20, 1642. S. of Sir Thomas (1616), Knt., of Burton Lazars, Leics. B. there. School, Bumstead, Essex (private; Mr Thornbecke). Adm. at the Middle Temple, Nov. 20, 1646. Of Rotherby. Knighted, June 19, 1660. M.P. for Leicester, 1661-79. Father of Martin (1680). (Le Neve, *Knights*, 78.)

HARTOPP, WILLIAM. Adm. pens. (age 19) at ST JOHN'S, Apr. 19, 1726. S. of Samuel, clerk, V. of Little Dalby, Leics. B. at Dalby. School, Oakham, Rutland (Mr Adcock). Matric. 1726; B.A. 1729-30; M.A. 1741. Ord. deacon (Lincoln) Sept. 20; priest, Dec. 20, 1730. V. of Little Dalby, Leics., 1741-62. R. of Cold Overton, 1749-62. Died July 7, 1762. (*Scott-Mayor*, III. 397.)

HARTRIDGE, DENNIS. Adm. pens. at EMMANUEL, May 22, 1588. Matric. 1588. Afterwards Fell.-Com.

HARTRIDGE, WILLIAM. Adm. pens. (age 16) at ST JOHN'S, July 2, 1647. S. of John, yeoman, of Goudhurst, Kent. B. there. School, Tonbridge (Mr Horne). Matric. 1647.

HARTSHORN, MICHAEL. Adm. sizar (age 19) at PETERHOUSE, Feb. 20, 1718-9. Of Yorkshire. School, Laughton-en-le-Morthen. Matric. 1718-9; B.A. 1722-3. Ord. deacon (Lincoln) May 20, 1722. R. of Langwith, Derbs., 1730-78.

HARTSHORNE, RICHARD. Adm. sizar at QUEENS', June 21, 1653. Of Staffordshire.

HARTSTONGUE, FINCH. Matric. sizar from PEMBROKE, Michs. 1621. 3rd s. of Henry, of Mulberton, Norfolk, and Joyce, dau. of Ralph Finch, of Kingsdown, Kent. (*Vis. of Norfolk.*)

HARTSTONGE, FRANCIS. Adm. Fell.-Com. (age 17) at CAIUS, Oct. 10, 1668. Previously adm. at Trinity College, Dublin, Apr. 10, 1668. S. and h. of Standish, gent., of Limerick, Ireland (afterwards Bart.). B. at Norwich. Schools, Norwich (Mr Lovering), Limerick (Mr Smith) and Cork (Mr Canowell). Adm. at the Middle Temple, Aug. 10, 1668. Brother of John (1676) and Standish (1676) and perhaps Guyn (1700). Died *v.p.* Will proved, 1688. (*Venn*, I. 435.)

HARTSTONGUE, GUYN. Adm. Fell.-Com. (age 15) at CAIUS, Apr. 3, 1700. S. of Standish, gent., of Herefordshire. B. in Dublin. (Perhaps s. of Sir Standish, Bart., by his 3rd wife, Johanna Gwynne.) School, Hereford (Mr Rod). Matric. 1700. Afterwards matric. from Balliol College, Oxford, Oct. 19, 1701. Adm. at the Middle Temple, July 3, 1699. (*Venn*, I. 504.)

HARTSTONGUE, JAMES. Matric. sizar from GONVILLE HALL, Easter, 1544. One of these names, of Norfolk, barrister of Furnival's Inn, adm. at Lincoln's Inn, July 12, 1579. Probably of South Repps, Norfolk. Lay rector of Houghton, in 1597.

HARTSTONGUE, JOHN. Adm. pens. (age 18) at CAIUS, June 19, 1676. 3rd s. of Standish, Esq. (afterwards Bart.). B. at Catton, Norfolk. School, Charleville, Ireland. Adm. at Trinity College, Dublin, May 20, 1673; and at the University of Glasgow. Matric. 1676; B.A. (Dublin) 1677; B.A. (Cambridge) 1677-8; M.A. (Dublin) 1680. Incorp. at Cambridge, 1681. Fellow of Caius, 1681-4. D.D. (Oxford, by diploma) 1693. Ord. priest (Norwich) Mar. 1681-2. Archdeacon of Limerick, 1684-93. Chaplain to the Duke of Ormonde. Bishop of Ossory, 1693; of Derry, 1714-7. Died Jan. 30, 1716-7. Brother of Francis (1668) and the next. (*D.N.B.*; *Venn*, I. 456.)

HARTSTONGUE, STANDISH. Adm. pens. (age 19) at CAIUS, June 19, 1676. 2nd s. of Standish, Esq., of Bruffe, Limerick (afterwards Bart.). B. at Catton, Norfolk. School, Kilkenny (Mr Jones). Adm. at Trinity College, Dublin, Apr. 15, 1673; then at the University of Glasgow. M.A. there. Adm. at the Middle Temple, Oct. 13, 1673. Called to the Irish Bar, 1680. Recorder of Kilkenny. M.P. for Kilkenny, 1695, 1703. Brother of Francis (1668) and John (1676). (*Venn*, I. 405; *Al. Dub.*)

HARTSTONGUE, WILLIAM. Adm. sizar (age 15) at CAIUS, May 4, 1700. S. of Robert, clock-maker, of Norwich. B. there. School, Norwich (Mr Burton and Mr Robinson). Matric. 1700; Scholar, 1700-7; B.A. 1703-4; M.A. 1707. Usher at Norwich Grammar School, 1706. Ord. deacon (Norwich) Mar. 20, 1708-9; priest, July 2, 1710. Perhaps died 1746. (*Venn*, I. 505.)

HARTUS, WILLIAM. Adm. sizar (age 19) at SIDNEY, July 1, 1676. 2nd s. of William, deceased. B. at Coxwold, Yorks. School, Coxwold. Matric. 1676. Migrated to St John's, Mar. 5, 1676-7. B.A. 1679-80; M.A. 1684. Ord. deacon (London) Mar. 16, 1689-90.

HARTWELL, ABRAHAM. Adm. at King's (age 17) a scholar from Eton, Aug. 25, 1559. B. at Burnham (? Dorney), Bucks. Matric. 1559; B.A. 1563–4; M.A. 1567. Fellow, 1562–7. Ord. deacon (London) Oct. 13, 1566, age 25, as fellow of King's. R. of Stanwick, Northants., 1568. R. of Toddington, Beds., 1570. R. of Tingrith, 1572. Established a library at Toddington. His widow, Anne, married, 1585, John Ponde, of St Sepulchre's, London. Author, *Regina Literata* (an account of the Queen's visit to Cambridge in 1564); *A Sight of the Portugal Pearl*, 1565. There were certainly two authors of the name. *See* the next. (*Harwood*; *Cooper*, II. 383.)

HARTWELL, ABRAHAM. Matric. sizar from Trinity, Easter, 1568; Scholar, 1571; B.A. 1571–2; M.A. 1575. Fellow, 1574. There has been much confusion between this and the last. He was almost certainly the secretary to Archbishop Whitgift; and adm. as such, to Gray's Inn, Aug. 10, 1592. Married Elizabeth, dau. of Robert Garnet, of Broxbourne, Herts. Author, *A Report of the Kingdom of Congo*, 1597, translated from the French; *A true Discourse upon the Matter of Martha Brossier* and other works. (All the authorities: *D.N.B.*; *Cooper*, *Harwood*, *Brit. Mus. Cat.*, assume that there was but one author.) Buried at Lambeth, Dec. 17, 1606. Will (P.C.C.) 1607. One of these names M.P. for East Looe, 1586; for Hindon, 1593.

HARTWELL, JOHN. Adm. at King's (age 18) a scholar from Eton, Aug. 15, 1505. Of the city of London. Fellow, during 1508. No degree. Became a Carthusian friar at Shene. (*Harwood*.)

HARTWELL, ROGER. Adm. at King's (age 18) a scholar from Eton, Aug. 9, 1512. Of the City of London. B.A. 1516–7; M.A. 1520. Fellow, 1515–26. Ord. acolyte (Lincoln) Mar. 15, 1521–2.

HARTWELL, THOMAS. Adm. at King's (age 17) a scholar from Eton, May 8, 1503. Of the City of London. B.A. 1507–8; M.A. 1511; B.D. 1519–20; D.D. 1525–6. Fellow, 1506–27. Deputy Vice-Chancellor, 1526–7. Ord. priest (Lincoln) Mar. 12, 1512–3. University preacher, 1515–6. V. of Wootton Wawen, Warws., 1523–45.

HARTWELL, THOMAS. M.Gram. 1520–1. A priest. Schoolmaster at Northampton. Probably V. of Horton, Northants., 1524.

HARTWELL, WILLIAM. Adm. at King's, a scholar from Eton, 1498; B.A. 1503. Fellow, till 1504. Doubtless V. of Dallington, Northants., 1509–11. V. of Spratton, 1511–5. V. of Brayfield, 1515. Will (Archd. Northants.) dated, 1520; speaks of his 'scholars present and past.' (H. I. Longden.)

HARTWELL, WILLIAM. M.A. 1675 (*Lit. Reg.*). Doubtless s. of Richard, of London. Matric. from Lincoln College, Oxford, May 6, 1670, age 16; D.D. from Trinity, Cambridge, 1690 (*Com. Reg.*). Ord. deacon (Durham) Aug. 3, 1680; priest, Aug. 26, 1681. R. of Whickham, Durham, 1681. R. of Stanhope, 1685–1725. Preb. of Durham, 1710–25. Married, at St Nicholas, Newcastle, Aug. 18, 1702, Frances Marley. Buried in Durham Cathedral, June 4, 1725. (*Al. Oxon.*; H. M. Wood; D. S. Boutflower.)

HARTWICK or ARTWICK, EDWARD. Of Hertfordshire. B.A. 1506–7; M.A. 1510; B.D. 1519–20; D.D. 1527–8. Fellow of St Catharine's, c. 1508; and of Jesus, in 1536–7. Principal of St Thomas Hostel, 1512–3. University preacher, 1513–4. Auditor, 1527. V. of St Olave Jewry, 1542–5. R. of St Mary Whitechapel, 1544–52. R. of Little Ilford, Essex, 1548–9. Died 1552. Admon. (Consist. C. London) 1553. (*T. A. Walker*.)

HARVARD, JOHN. Adm. pens. at Emmanuel, Dec. 19, 1627. Of Middlesex. B. 1607. S. of Robert, butcher, of Southwark. Matric. 1631; B.A. 1631–2; M.A. 1635. Went to Charlestown, Mass., New England, Aug. 1637. Settled there, and acted as assistant preacher to the pastor of the First Church in Charlestown. Founder of Harvard College, bequeathing half his estate and his library to the proposed college. Married, Apr. 19, 1636, Ann, dau. of John Sadler, V. of Ringmer, Sussex; sister of the Master of Magdalene. Died Sept. 14, 1638, of consumption. A tablet to his memory was erected by old Harvard students in Emmanuel Chapel, 1904. (*Em. Coll. Hist.*, 72; *D.N.B.*; J. G. Bartlett.)

HARVEL, WILLIAM. Adm. pens. at Queens', Oct. 1564. *See* HARWELL.

HARVEST, GEORGE. Adm. Fell.-Com. (age 18) at Magdalene, July 20, 1734. S. of William, Esq., brewer, of Thames Ditton. B. at Kingston, Surrey. School, Eton. Matric. 1735; B.A. 1738–9; M.A. 1742. Fellow, 1745. Adm. at the Middle Temple, May 17, 1734. Ord. deacon (Lincoln) May 24, 1741. P.C. of Thames Ditton, Surrey, c. 1741–80. Author, *Sermons*. Died Dec. 25, 1780. Buried at Thames Ditton. M.I. (*Mag. Coll. Hist.*, 159; *G. Mag.*; *Manning and Bray*, I. 464.)

HARVEST, TOBIAS. Adm. sizar at Trinity, June 2, 1643. Matric. 1643; B.A. 1646. Adm. at Clare, Nov. 20, 1646.

HARVEY, BENJAMIN. Adm. at Corpus Christi, 1703. Of Norwich. B. 1686. Matric. 1704; B.A. 1707. Ord. deacon (Ely) Dec. 18, 1709; priest, Sept. 23, 1711. V. of Gayton, Norfolk, 1711. V. of Witton, 1711. R. of Stody, 1733.

HARVEY, BRIAN. Matric. sizar from St John's, Easter, 1575.

HARVEY, CAREW (1614), *see* MILDMAY.

HERVEY (*alias* MILDMAY), CAREW. Adm. Fell.-Com. at Emmanuel, Apr. 2, 1677. S. of Francis, of Marks, Essex. B. 1658. Matric. 1677; B.A. 1679–80. Succeeded his father at Marks, 1703. Sheriff of Essex, 1713. Married Anne, dau. of Rich. Barrett Lennard, of Essex. Died May 1, 1743. (*Morant.*, I. 68; J. B. Peace.)

HERVEY, CARR. [illegible] from Clare, Easter, 1710. Eldest s. of John (1683), Baron Hervey, of Ickworth. B. in London, Sept. 17, 1691 (*sic.*, *G.E.C.*). M.A. 1710 (*fil. nob.*). M.P. for Bury St Edmunds, 1713–22. Died at Bath, Nov. 14, 1723. Buried at Ickworth. Brother of the next, of John (1713) and Henry (1744). (Musgrave, *Ob.*; *D.N.B.*; *G.E.C.*)

HERVEY, CHARLES. Adm. Fell.-Com. at Queens', Oct. 28, 1724. S. of John (1683), Earl of Bristol. B. Apr. 1703. School, Bury. Matric. 1724; M.A. 1728; D.D. 1749. Ord. deacon (Lincoln) Aug. 27; priest, Sept. 3, 1732. R. of Kirkby Laythorp, Lincs., 1732. R. of Ickworth, Suffolk. R. of Sproughton and Shotley, 1735. R. of Chedburgh, 1736–48. Preb. of Ely, 1742. Died Mar. 20, 1783. Will, P.C.C. Brother of the above, of John (1713) and Henry (1744).

HERVEY, CHRISTOPHER. Adm. Fell.-Com. at Clare, July 9, 1750. Doubtless s. of John, a Welsh judge. B. at Betchworth, Surrey. Matric. 1750; B.A. 1755; M.A. 1758. Married Hannah Hake. Died Sept. 9, 1786. (*Manning and Bray*, II. 208.)

HARVEY, DANIEL. Adm. Fell.-Com. (age 15) at Caius, Nov. 12, 1646, from Pembroke College, Oxford; adm. there, Mar. 3, 1643. S. of Daniel, gent., of London. Of Combe Nevill, Surrey. School, Croydon, Surrey (Mr Webb). Matric. 1646; B.A. 1647. M.P. for Surrey, 1660. Custodian of New Park, Richmond, 1660. Knighted, May 26, 1667. Ambassador to Turkey, 1669–72. Died at Constantinople, Aug. 1672. Buried at Hempstead, Essex. Will (P.C.C.) 1677. Nephew of the physiologist. (*Venn*, I. 367; *Essex Pedigrees*.)

HARVEY, EDMUND. Matric. pens. from Jesus, Easter, 1566; B.A. 1569–70; M.A. 1573. V. of Harston, Cambs., 1572–3. Will of Edmund Harvey, clerk, C. of All Hallows, Bread St, proved (P.C.C.) 1576; mentions father, William, a grocer.

HARVEY, EDMUND. LL.B. 1570. Resident student at Trinity Hall, Aug. 1564.

HARVEY, EDMUND. Matric. pens. from St John's, Easter, 1611. Perhaps s. of John, of Ickworth. Bapt. there, Oct. 17, 1594. One of these names, of Eye, Suffolk, gent., adm. at Gray's Inn, July 6, 1614, from Barnard's Inn. Colonel in the Parliamentary army. One of the King's judges, but did not sign the death-warrant. Perhaps M.P. for Gt Bedwin, Wilts., 1646; for Middlesex, 1654; for Suffolk, 1656–8. Died June 25, 1673. (A. B. Beaven.)

HARVEY, EDMUND. Adm. pens. (age 18) at Peterhouse, Apr. 1, 1707. Of Suffolk. School, Stoke Ash (private). Matric. 1707; Scholar, 1707; M.B. 1712.

HARVEY, EDMUND. Adm. pens. at Emmanuel, Oct. 3, 1722. Of Bedfordshire. Matric. 1723; B.A. 1726–7. Fellow, 1727. Ord. deacon (Lincoln) Sept. 22, 1728.

HARVEY, EDWARD. Adm. Fell.-Com. (age 17) at Trinity, Aug. 14, 1697. S. of Edward, of Combe, Surrey. School, Eton. Adm. at the Inner Temple, Dec. 24, 1695. Of Tilton-on-the-Hill, Leics. Died Feb. 9, 1707–8, aged 26. M.I. at Hempstead, Essex. (*Misc. Gen. et Her.*, 2nd S., III. 364; *Manning and Bray*, I. 402, where he seems to be confused with his father.)

HARVEY, ELIAB. Adm. pens. (age 19) at Trinity, June 17, 1734. S. of William, of Chigwell, Essex. School, Westminster. Matric. 1734; Scholar, 1735; B.A. 1737–8; M.A. 1741. Fellow, 1740. Adm. at the Inner Temple, May 5, 1733. Of Claybury, Essex. K.C., 1758. M.P. for Dunwich, 1761–8. F.R.S., 1764. Died Oct. 23, 1769. Buried in the Harvey vault, Hempstead, Essex. (*Al. Westmon.*, 310; *Essex Pedigrees*; *G. Mag.*; *Misc. Gen. et Her.*, 2nd S., III. 335.)

HARVEY, FRANCIS. Adm. pens. from Christ's, Mar. 1582–3. Perhaps s. of Stephen, of Hardingston, Northants. (*Peile's* suggestion that he was s. of John, of Ickworth and Pensioner to Queen Elizabeth is apparently wrong.) B.A. from Corpus Christi, 1585–6; M.A. from Emmanuel, 1589. Knighted, July 2, 1626. Justice of Common Pleas. Buried at Hardingston, Aug. 2, 1632. (*Vis. of Essex*, 1612; *Baker*, I. 74; *Peile*, I. 174.)

HARVEY, FRANCIS. Adm. pens. (age 15) at CAIUS, June 9, 1629. S. of Richard, merchant, of Lyme Regis, Dorset (Mayor of Lyme). B. there. School, Ilminster (Mr Conduit). Matric. 1629. Merchant of Lyme, 1644. M.P. for Clomines, 1661. Mayor of Wexford, 1671. Sheriff, 1673. Died Nov. 1692. (*Venn*, I. 290; Burke, *L.G.*)

HARVEY, FRANCIS. Adm. pens. at JESUS, June 23, 1635. Of Cambridgeshire. Matric. 1635.

HARVEY, FRANCIS. Adm. pens. at EMMANUEL, May 5, 1685. Of Middlesex. Matric. 1686.

HARVEY, FRANCIS. Adm. pens. at CLARE, Nov. 16, 1692. Of Cockfield, Suffolk. Matric. 1694; B.A. 1696–7; M.A. 1700. Fellow, 1698. Ord. deacon (Norwich) Mar. 1698–9; priest, June, 1699. V. of Haverhill, Suffolk, 1699. R. of Barham, 1704.

HARVEY, FRANCIS. Adm. pens. at JESUS, Oct. 28, 1702. S. of Francis, citizen of Lincoln. B. there, *c.* 1686. School, Newark, Notts. Matric. 1703; B.A. 1706–7; M.A. from Magdalene, 1710. Fellow of Magdalene, 1708. Ord. deacon (Peterb.) June 19, 1709. Perhaps R. of Lawshall, Suffolk, till 1732. Died Feb. 23, 1732–3. Buried at Lawshall.

HARVEY, FRANCIS. Adm. scholar (age 16) at SIDNEY, May 6, 1707. S. of John, gent. B. at Bridgwater, Somerset. School, Bridgwater (Mr Darby). Matric. 1707.

HERVEY, FREDERICK AUGUSTUS. Adm. at CORPUS CHRISTI, 1747. 3rd s. of John, Lord Hervey, Baron of Ickworth. School, Westminster. M.A. 1754. Created D.D. (Dublin) 1768; and (Oxford) 1770. Adm. at Lincoln's Inn, Feb. 24, 1747–8. Principal clerk of the Privy Seal, 1753. Travelled in Italy and Dalmatia; studied volcanic phenomena. Ord. priest (Ely) Jan. 26, 1755. Bishop of Cloyne, 1767–8. Bishop of Derry, 1768–1803. Succeeded as 4th Earl of Bristol, 1779. F.R.S., 1782. Succeeded to the barony of Howard de Walden, 1799. Died when cruising in the Mediterranean, at Albano, Italy, July 8, 1803. Buried at Ickworth. Brother of William (1751). (*Masters*; *D.N.B.*; H. P. Stokes, *Hist. of Corpus Christi*; *G.E.C.*)

HARVEY, GABRIEL. Matric. pens. from CHRIST'S, Easter, 1566. S. of John, of Saffron Walden, Essex, yeoman and rope-maker. B. there, *c.* 1550. School, Saffron Walden, B.A. 1569–70; M.A. from Pembroke, 1573; LL.B. from Trinity Hall, 1585; D.C.L. (Oxford) 1585. Fellow of Pembroke, 1570. Fellow of Trinity Hall, 1578. Deputy proctor for part of 1583. Elected Master of Trinity Hall, 1585, but the election was set aside by royal Mandate. Friend of the poet Spenser; the 'Hobbinol' of *The Shepheard's Calender*. Author and critic. Retired, after some years, to Saffron Walden, where he practised physic. Buried there Feb. 11, 1630–1. Brother of Richard (1575) and John (1578). (*D.N.B.*; *Peile*, I. 95; G. M. Benton.)

HARVEY, GEORGE. Matric. sizar from TRINITY HALL, Michs. 1544. Nominated an original Fellow of Trinity by King Henry VIII, 1546. B.A. from Trinity, 1551–2. Received tonsure (London) 1553, when he is called a Fellow. R. of Watton-at-Stone, Herts., till 1571. Died 1571.

HARVEY, GEORGE. Matric. pens. from QUEENS', Easter, 1545. One of these names R. of Tollerton, Notts., 1581–1604. Buried Apr. 7, 1604. (Godfrey, *Notts.*)

HARVEY, GEORGE. Adm. pens. (age 19) at ST JOHN'S, July 2, 1715. S. of William, clerk, deceased. B. in Buckinghamshire. School, Wokingham, Berks. Matric. 1715; B.A. 1720–1.

HARVEY, GIDEON. M.D. from ST CATHARINE'S, 1698 (*Lit. Reg.*). S. of Gideon, of Richmond, Surrey (M.D., in his will, P.C.C. 1702). B. *c.* 1669. Matric. from St John's, Oxford, May 20, 1686, age 15. Adm. at Leyden May, 12, 1688. M.D. there, 1690. Candidate R.C.P., 1699. Fellow, 1703. Censor, elect, etc. Physician to the Tower of London. Author, medical. Died Apr. 24, 1755. (*Munk*, II. 10; *Al. Oxon.*; *D.N.B.*)

HARVEY, HENRY. LL.B. from TRINITY HALL, 1538; LL.D. 1542. S. of Robert, of Stradbrooke, Suffolk. Adm. advocate, 1550. Master of Trinity Hall, 1559–85. Vice-Chancellor, 1560. Archdeacon of Middlesex, 1551–4. Vicar-general of London and subsequently of the province of Canterbury. Precentor of St Paul's, 1554. R. of Littlebury, Essex, 1554–82. Commissioner for the detection of heretical books at Cambridge, 1556. Preb. of Salisbury, 1558–72; of Lichfield, 1559–61. Preb. of Ely, 1567–85. Master in Chancery, 1568. Died Feb. 20, 1584–5. Will (V.C.C. and P.C.C.) 1585. Benefactor to Trinity Hall and other colleges. (*Cooper*, I. 505; *D.N.B.*; *Trin. Hall Hist.*)

HARVEY, HENRY. Licensed to practise medicine, 1543–4.

HARVY, HENRY. Matric. pens. from TRINITY, Michs. 1582. Robert (1579–80) had a brother Henry.

HARVEY, HENRY. M.A. from CAIUS, 1744. S. of John (1683), Earl of Bristol. Matric. from Christ Church, Oxford, June 8, 1719, age 17. For some time a cornet in Kerr's dragoons. Ord. priest (Ely) Sept. 1743. R. of Shotley, Suffolk, 1743. Assumed the name Aston, in 1744. Died Nov. 16, 1748. Brother of Carr (1710), Charles (1724) and John (1713). (*Venn*, II. 54.)

HARVEY, HUMPHREY. M.A. from TRINITY HALL, 1685. S. of Humphrey, of Sampford Courtney, Devon, clerk. Matric. from Exeter College, Oxford, Apr. 4, 1679, age 18; (? B.A. Oxford). V. of Dawlish, Devon, 1690. Will (Exeter) 1729. (*Al. Oxon.*)

HARVEY, JAMES. Matric. Fell.-Com. from ST JOHN'S, Easter, 1613. One of these names, s. and h. of James, of Dagenham, Essex, adm. at the Inner Temple, 1615. Brother of John (1619).

HARVEY, JAMES. Matric. pens. from ST JOHN'S, Easter, 1615; B.A. 1618–9.

HARVEY, JAMES. Adm. at PEMBROKE, 1631.

HARVEY, JAMES. Adm. sizar at JESUS, Oct. 12, 1632. Of Hertfordshire. Matric. 1632; B.A. 1636–7; M.A. 1640.

HARVY, JAMES. Adm. pens. at TRINITY, Apr. 12, 1675. Probably s. of Francis, of Cockfield, Suffolk. School, Bury St Edmunds. Adm. at the Middle Temple, Nov. 9, 1674. Recorder of Colchester. Died Apr. 1728, aged 69. (*Bury School*, *S.H.A.H.*; *Vis. of Suffolk*, 1664.)

HARVEY, JAMES. Adm. at CORPUS CHRISTI, 1717. Of Norfolk.

HARVEY, JAMES. Adm. Fell.-Com. at CLARE, Mar. 24, 1720–1. B. at Cockfield, Suffolk. Matric. 1721. Adm. at the Middle Temple, Nov. 6, 1722.

HARVEY, JOHN. Fee for B.A. 1493. One of these names V. of Burnham, 1495–1536.

HARVEY, JOHN. Matric. pens. at QUEENS', Easter, 1578. S. of John, yeoman and rope-maker, of Saffron Walden, Essex. Bapt. there, Feb. 13, 1563–4. School, Saffron Walden. B.A. 1580–1; M.A. 1584. Licensed to practise medicine, 1587. Incorp. at Oxford, 1585. Practised at Lynn. Married Martha, dau. of Mr Justice Meade, of Wendon Lofts, Essex. Author, astronomical, etc. Died July, 1592. Brother of Gabriel and Richard (1575). (*Cooper*, II. 126; *D.N.B.*; G. C. M. Smith.)

HARVEY, JOHN. Matric. pens. from CHRIST'S, Easter, 1586. One of these names adm. at Lincoln's Inn, Aug. 12, 1585; of Hampshire.

HARVEY, JOHN. Adm. pens. at EMMANUEL, Aug. 12, 1587. Matric. 1587.

HARVIE, JOHN. Adm. sizar (age 15) at CAIUS, Apr. 21, 1601. S. of Robert, glover, of Newport, Essex. School, Newport (Mr Morden). Succeeded his father, in 1608, as lord of the manor of Elmes, Essex. (*Venn*, I. 175.)

HARVEY, JOHN. Adm. Fell.-Com. at EMMANUEL, May 4, 1619. Matric. 1619. One of these names, s. of James, of Dagenham, Essex, adm. at the Inner Temple, 1620. Brother of James (1613).

HARVEY, JOHN. Adm. pens. at CAIUS, June 25, 1620. S. of Edmund, merchant, of London. Matric. 1620. Brother of William (1623).

HARVEY, JOHN. Matric. sizar from CAIUS, Easter, 1620 (probably adm. at Corpus Christi, 1619, as 'of Cambs.'). Scholar of Caius, 1620–3; B.A. 1623. Incorp. at Oxford, May 11, 1624. (*Venn*, I. 250, where this and the above are confused.)

HARVEY, JOHN. Adm. pens. at PETERHOUSE, Mar. 31, 1623. Of Essex. Matric. 1623.

HARVEY, JOHN. Adm. pens. at CHRIST'S, June 17, 1626. S. of Oliver, of Thurleigh, Beds. Bapt. there, Feb. 26, 1609–10. School, Brentwood (Mr Plumtree). Matric. 1626; B.A. 1628–9. Adm. at Gray's Inn, Feb. 21, 1627–8. Of Thurleigh, Beds., Esq. Married Elizabeth, dau. of Stephen Hervey, of London, merchant. Will proved, 1664. Father of John (1667). (*Peile*, I. 375; *Vis. of Beds.*, 1634; *Geneal. Bedford*, 441.)

HARVEY, JOHN. Adm. pens. (age 15) at CHRIST'S, Feb. 9, 1630–1. S. of John, of Thurleigh, Beds. Bapt. Oct. 12, 1615. School, Deane, Beds. (private; Mr Harris). Matric. 1631. Adm. at Lincoln's Inn, May 21, 1636. Barrister. Married Lady Dorothy Erskine, dau. of the Earl of Buchan. (*Peile*, I. 406; *Vis. of Beds.*, 1634.)

HARVEY, JOHN. Adm. pens. (age 13) at PEMBROKE, June 24, 1631. S. of Sir Simon, Knt. B. in London. Matric. 1631; B.A. 1633–4.

HARVEY, JOHN. Adm. pens. (age 17) at SIDNEY, July 1, 1633. S. of (John), Esq., of Wantisden, Suffolk. B. at Bedingfield. Schools, Eye (Mr Jo. Hall) and Southolt. Adm. at Gray's Inn, Jan. 29, 1635–6; as S. and h. of John, of Bedingfield, Suffolk.

HARVEY, JOHN. Adm. Fell.-Com. (age 15) at CAIUS, Mar. 11, 1645-6. Eldest s. of Robert, gent., of Quainton, Bucks. B. at Ipswich. Schools, Godmanchester, Hunts. (Mr Sell) and Cambridge (King's Coll. Sch.; Mr Hammond). Matric. 1646. Adm. at the Inner Temple, 1647; called to the bar, 1653. Of Ickwellbury, Beds., Esq. Will proved (P.C.C.) Apr. 20, 1692. Probably brother of Robert (1655) and perhaps father of John (1682). (*Venn*, I. 361; *Vis. of Warws.*, 1682.)

HARVEY, JOHN. Adm. pens. at QUEENS', May 2, 1647. Of Essex. Perhaps s. and h. of Samuel, late of Dagenham, gent.; adm. at Lincoln's Inn, Nov. 20, 1648.

HARVIE, JOHN. Matric. pens from TRINITY HALL, Easter, 1651.

HARVEY, JOHN. Matric. pens. from CHRIST'S, Easter, 1667. Doubtless s. of John (1626). Bapt. at Thurleigh, Jan. 27, 1649-50. Major in the army. Died at Thurleigh, July 14, 1715. He left, by will, a messuage in Bedford for scholarships at Christ's. (*Peile*, II. 18.)

HARVEY, JOHN. Adm. pens. at ST CATHARINE'S, 1668. Matric. Easter, 1669. Adm. at the Inner Temple, Mar. 21, 1668-9.

HARVIE, JOHN. Adm. Fell.-Com. at ST CATHARINE'S, July 29, 1682. Perhaps adm. at the Inner Temple, Feb. 27, 1681-2, as s. and h. of John (? 1645-6), of the Inner Temple. If so, M.P. for Beds.

HERVEY, JOHN. Adm. Fell.-Com. at CLARE, June 28, 1683. S. of Sir Thomas (1641), of Bury St Edmunds, Knt. B. Aug. 27, 1666. School, Bury. Matric. 1684; LL.D. 1705 (*Com. Reg.*). Deputy-lieut. of Suffolk, 1692. M.P. for Bury, 1694-1703. Created Lord Hervey, 1703. Earl of Bristol, 1714. Inherited Ickworth, 1700. Died Jan. 20, 1750-1. Buried at Ickworth. Father of Carr, Charles (1724), John (1713), Henry (1744) and Thomas.

HARVEY, JOHN. Adm. at CORPUS CHRISTI, 1712. Of Norfolk. Matric. 1712.

HERVEY, JOHN. Adm. at CLARE, Nov. 20, 1713. 2nd s. of John (1683), Earl of Bristol. B. Oct. 13, 1696, in Jermyn St, London. School, Westminster. Matric. 1714; M.A. 1715. M.P. for Bury St Edmunds, 1725-33. Vice-Chamberlain and Privy Councillor, 1730. Lord Privy Seal, 1740-2. Called to the House of Lords in his father's life-time, as Baron Hervey of Ickworth. Author, historical. Died Aug. 5, 1743. Buried at Ickworth. Brother of Carr, Charles (1724) and Henry (1744). (*D.N.B.*; *G.E.C.*)

HARVEY, JOHN. Adm. pens. (age 16) at PEMBROKE, Nov. 9, 1727. S. of Robert, of Stockton, Warws., Esq. Matric. 1728.

HARVEY, JOSEPH. Adm. pens. at EMMANUEL, May 30, 1645. Of Middlesex. Matric. 1647. Migrated to Oxford. B.A. from Merton College, 1648; M.A. 1651; D.C.L., 1665. Fellow of Merton College, 1648. Adm. at Gray's Inn, Feb. 9, 1652-3. Advocate, Doctors' Commons, July 1, 1674. (*Al. Oxon.*)

HARVEY, JOSEPH. Adm. sizar at EMMANUEL, June 29, 1682. Of Leicestershire.

HARVEY, JOSEPH. Adm. sizar (age 18) at ST JOHN'S, Jan. 2, 1712-3. S. of Thomas (? 1681), clerk. B. at Laver-Magdalen, Essex. School, Bishop's Stortford (Dr Took). Matric. 1713-4; B.A. 1716-7; M.A. 1724. Ord. deacon (London) Sept. 22, 1717; priest, May 24, 1719. R. of Laver-Magdalen, Essex, 1720-48. Died 1748. Will (Commis. C. Essex) 1748; of Springfield. (J. Ch. Smith.)

HARVEY, JOSIAH. Adm. pens. at QUEENS', June 16, 1693. Of Derbyshire. Matric. 1695; B.A. 1696-7. Ord. deacon (Lincoln) May 30, 1697; priest, June 19, 1698. R. of Laver-Magdalen, Essex, 1700-2. Died 1702.

HARVEY, MARTIN. Adm. pens. (age 16) at CHRIST'S, May 19, 1627. S. of Stephen, merchant (of Weston Favell, Northants.). B. in London. Schools, London (Mr Brinsley) and Mickleham, Surrey (Mr Wall). Matric. 1627; B.A. 1630. Adm. at the Middle Temple, Oct. 10, 1629. Of Weston Favell, Northants. (*Vis. of London*, 1634; *Vis. of Northants.*, 1618; *Peile*, I. 383.)

HARVEY, MATTHEW. Matric. sizar from CLARE, Easter, 1669.

HARVEY, MICHAEL. Adm. Fell.-Com. at EMMANUEL, Mar. 1, 1650-1. Of Middlesex and Clifton Mabanke, Dorset. S. of Michael, late of London, merchant, deceased. Adm. at Gray's Inn, Oct. 21, 1650. J.P. for Dorset. M.P. for Weymouth and Melcombe Regis, Dorset, 1679-81, 1689-1701. Died Feb. 19, 1711-2. M.I. at Bradford Abbas, Dorset. (Le Neve, *Mon.*; *Misc. Gen. et Her.*, 2nd S., III. 362.)

HARVEY, RICHARD. Matric. pens. from PEMBROKE, Easter, 1575. S. of John, yeoman and rope maker, of Saffron Walden. Bapt. there, Apr. 15, 1560. School, Saffron Walden. B.A. 1577-8; M.A. 1581. Fellow. Ord. deacon and priest (Peterb.) Dec. 12, 1585. R. of Chislehurst, Kent, 1586-1631. Author, astrological, theological, etc. Died 1631. Will (Consist. C. Rochester). Left his estate to his brother Gabriel. Brother of Gabriel (1566) and John (1578). (*D.N.B.*; *Cooper*, II. 282; H. G. Harrison.)

HARVEY, RICHARD. Adm. pens. (age 16) at CAIUS, July 4, 1614. S. of John, of Grimstone, Norfolk. School, Lynn (Mr Armitage). Matric. 1615; B.A. 1617-8; M.A. 1622. Ord. priest (Peterb.) June 11, 1620. Probably R. of Wyberton, Lincs., 1626; and V. of Tachbrook, Warws., 1626. Perhaps R. of South Burgh, Norfolk, 1646. (*Venn*, I. 226.)

HARVEY, RICHARD. Adm. pens. (age 16) at CHRIST'S, June 29, 1626. S. of Richard, of Dorset. Schools, Dorchester and Colyton, Devon. Matric. 1626; B.A. 1629-30; M.A. 1633. R. of Broadmayne, Dorset, 1638-55. (*Peile*, I. 377.)

HARVEY, RICHARD. Adm. sizar (age 17) at CAIUS, Apr. 17, 1628. S. of John, gent., of Norfolk. B. at South Creake. School, South Creake (Mr Stimson, Linge and Legge). Matric. 1628; B.A. 1631-2; M.A. 1635. Ord. deacon (Norwich) Dec. 23, 1632; priest, Sept. 1, 1634. Perhaps R. of Ickburgh, Norfolk, 1654-7. Buried there Aug. 7, 1657. One of these names also R. of South Burgh, Norfolk, 1646. (*Venn*, I. 283.)

HARVYE, RICHARD. Adm. sizar (age 16) at CAIUS, Sept. 24, 1632. S. of Stephen, gent. B. at Chipping Barnet, Herts. School, Chipping Barnet (Mr Langley and Geo. Smallwood). Matric. 1632. Scholar, 1635-9; B.A. 1636-7; M.A. 1640. Adm. at Peterhouse, May 9, 1640. V. of Doncaster, Yorks., 1645-9. Buried Dec. 22, 1649. Father of Stephen (1662).

HARVEY, ROBERT. Matric. pens. from ST JOHN'S, Lent, 1563-4.

HARVEY, ROBERT. Matric. pens. from CLARE, Lent, 1564-5; B.A. 1570-1. Minister at Norwich; suspended, 1576; author (*Cooper*, II. 2, who seems to confuse him with the preceding). A Robert Harvey, B.A., was Incorp. at Oxford, 1591.

HARVEY, ROBERT. Adm. scholar at TRINITY HALL, Jan. 31, 1575-6; LL.B. 1583. Fellow, 1583-96. Nephew of Henry (1538); mentioned in his will. 'S. of Lewis, my nephew, late of Rye, Sussex.' He leaves him a small legacy.

HARVEY, ROBERT. Matric. sizar from CHRIST'S, Feb. 1579-80; B.A. 1582-3; M.A. 1586. Probably R. of St Alban, Wood St, 1588-95. R. of St Botolph, Billingsgate, 1595-7. Died 1597. Will (Consist. C. London) 1598. (*Peile*, I. 158, who seems to confuse him with the last.)

HARVEY, ROBERT. Adm. pens. at ST CATHARINE'S, 1655. Of Huntingdonshire. Probably 4th s. of Robert, of Quainton, Bucks. Matric. Easter, 1657; B.A. 1659-60; M.A. 1663. One of these names C. of Wrenbury, Cheshire, 1671-83. Died 1683. Probably brother of John (1645-6).

HARVEY, ROBERT. Adm. sizar at EMMANUEL, June 29, 1667. Of Suffolk. Matric. 1667; B.A. 1670-1; M.A. 1674. Ord. priest (Peterb.) June 14, 1674. Perhaps R. of Antingham, Norfolk, 1690-1701.

HARVY, ROBERT. Adm. sizar at JESUS, Feb. 12, 1689-90. S. of Robert (? 1655), clerk, deceased (of Stockton, Warws.). Of Cheshire. Matric. 1691; B.A. 1694-5. Brother of Thomas (1689-90).

HARVEY, ROBERT. Adm. sizar (age 19) at PETERHOUSE, Feb. 17, 1717-8. Of Lancashire. School, Blackrod, Lancs. Scholar, 1720; B.A. 1721-2. Perhaps minister of Horwich, Lancs., 1724. P.C. of Westhoughton, 1732-55. Master of Codd's Hospital, Norwich, 1744. Will (Chester) 1755. (E. Axon.)

HARVEY, SAMUEL. Matric. pens. from CHRIST'S, 1593-4; B.A. 1597-8; M.A. 1601. One of these names s. of John, of Thurleigh, Beds., Esq. Bapt. there, Mar. 1, 1576-7. Of Shenfield and Brentwood, Essex. Buried Dec. 5, 1638. (*Willey Hundred*, 510.)

HARVEY, SAMUEL. Matric. pens. from ST CATHARINE'S, Easter, 1640. Of Hertfordshire. B.A. 1643; M.A. 1647.

HARVY, SAMUEL. Adm. pens. (age 16) at ST JOHN'S, June 1, 1647. S. of Edmund, merchant, of St Mary Colechurch, Poultry, London. B. there. School, Tonbridge (Mr Horne). Matric. 1647. Adm. at the Inner Temple, 1649; of Fulham, Middlesex.

HARVEY, SAMUEL. Adm. pens. at ST JOHN'S, June 18, 1750. S. of James, gent., of Bedfordshire. B. at Warden. School, Hoddesdon, Herts. (Mr Bennet).

HARVEY, SOLOMON. Adm. pens. (age 17) at ST JOHN'S, June 3, 1707. S. of Solomon, husbandman. B. in the Isle of Thanet, Kent. School, Canterbury (Mr Jones). Matric. 1707; B.A. 1711-2.

HERVEY, STEPHEN. Adm. pens. at TRINITY, May 17, 1641. Probably s. of Stephen, of London. Matric. 1641. (*Vis. of Surrey*, 1662; *Vis. of London*, 1634.)

HARVEY, STEPHEN. Adm. sizar (age 16) at ST JOHN'S, Apr. 26, 1662. S. of Richard (1632), clerk, deceased, of Doncaster, Yorks. B. there. School, Doncaster (Mr Doughty). Matric. 1662; B.A. 1665–6; M.A. 1669. Incorp. at Oxford, 1669. Ord. deacon (Ely) Dec. 22, 1667; priest (Peterb.) Sept. 20, 1668. V. of Arksey, Yorks., 1668–74. Died Mar. 8, 1673–4.

HARVEY, THOMAS. Matric. pens. from JESUS, Easter, 1565; B.A. 1569–70; M.A. 1573.

HARVEY, THOMAS. Matric. pens. from ST JOHN'S, Michs. 1569.

HARVYE, THOMAS. Matric. pens. from PEMBROKE, Lent, 1584–5.

HARVEY, THOMAS. Matric. sizar from CLARE, Easter, 1614.

HARVEY, THOMAS. Adm. pens. (age 15) at PEMBROKE, Apr. 3, 1641. S. of Sir William, Knt. B. at Bury, Suffolk. M.P. for Bury, 1679–81, 1685–7, 1689–90. 'Knighted by Charles II' (not recorded by *Shaw*). Married Isabella, dau. of Sir Humphrey May, 1658. Died May 27, 1694. Brother of William (1636), father of John (1683). (*Vis. of Suff.*, 1664; Gage, *Suffolk*, 286; A. B. Beaven.)

HARVEY, THOMAS. Adm. sizar at QUEENS', July 4, 1681. Of Derbyshire. B.A. 1684–5. Probably will (Consist. C. London) 1708; of Laver-Magdalen, Essex, clerk. Property in Derbyshire. (J. Ch. Smith.)

HARVY, THOMAS. Adm. sizar at JESUS, Feb. 12, 1689–90. S. of Robert, clerk, deceased, of Cheshire. Matric. 1690; B.A. 1693–4. Brother of Robert (1689–90).

HERVEY, THOMAS. 'Sent to a University, probably to Cambridge' (*D.N.B.*). 2nd s. of John (1683), Earl of Bristol. B. Jan. 20, 1698. Probably adm. at Lincoln's Inn. Equerry to Queen Caroline, 1728–37; Vice-Chamberlain, 1733. M.P. for Bury, 1733–47. Eloped with the wife of Sir Thomas Hanmer. An eccentric pamphleteer. Died Jan. 16, 1775. (*D.N.B.*)

HARVEY, TOBIAS. Adm. Fell.-Com. at CLARE, Mar. 30, 1676. Of London. S. of Tobias, of Coleman Street, St Stephen's, London. Matric. 1676. Adm. at the Inner Temple, Jan. 19, 1677–8. Gave £50 to the College building fund.

HARVYE, W. Matric. pens. from CLARE, Lent, 1564–5.

HARVEY, WILLIAM. B.A. 1507–8, 1st in the *ordo*; M.A. 1511; B.D. 1520. Fellow of QUEENS', 1509–30. Lady Margaret preacher, 1525–48. Perhaps preb. of Westminster, 1540. (*Cooper*, I. 38.)

HARVEY, WILLIAM. Matric. sizar from TRINITY, Easter, 1569; B.A. 1572–3.

HARVEY, WILLIAM. B.A. (? 1591–2); M.A. from MAGDALENE, 1595. B. in Colchester. Ord. deacon (London) Nov. 23; priest, Dec. 22, 1595, age 25. C. of Edmonton, Middlesex.

HARVIE, WILLIAM. Adm. scholar (age 16) at CAIUS, May 31, 1593. 1st s. of Thomas, yeoman. B. at Folkestone, Apr. 1, 1578. School, Canterbury. Scholar, 1593–1600; B.A. 1596–7; M.D. (Padua) 1602. Incorp. at Cambridge, 1602. Incorp. at Oxford, 1642. Warden of Merton, 1645. Fellow, R.C.P., 1607. Physician to St Bartholomew's Hospital, 1609. Elected Lumleian lecturer, Aug. 4, 1615. In these lectures he first publicly stated his theory of the circulation of the blood. Physician to James I, 1618. Adm. at Gray's Inn, Mar. 6, 1624–5. Travelled with the Duke of Lenox, visiting France and Spain, 1630. Author, medical. Died June 3, 1657, at Roehampton, Surrey. Buried at Hempstead, Essex. Will (P.C.C.) 1657. (*Venn*, I. 149; *D.N.B.*)

HERVY, WILLIAM. Adm. pens. at SIDNEY, Sept. 10, 1604.

HARVYE, WILLIAM. Adm. pens. (age 16) at CAIUS, Oct. 5, 1623. S. of Edmund, merchant, of the city of London. Matric. 1623–4; Scholar, 1623–4. Brother of John (1620).

HARVEY, WILLIAM. Adm. sizar (age 17) at CAIUS, Mar. 10, 1627–8. S. of William, tanner, of Norfolk. B. at Swaffham. School, Swaffham (Mr Tidd and Mr Melvin). Matric. 1628; Scholar, 1629–33; B.A. 1631–2; M.A. 1635. Ord. priest (Norwich) Sept. 21, 1634. Perhaps V. of Walpole, 1660. C. of Westacre, Norfolk, 1662. One of these names V. of Croydon, Cambs., 1660–74. Died Sept. 27, 1674. (*Venn*, I. 282.)

HARVEY, WILLIAM. Adm. Fell.-Com. (age 17) at PEMBROKE, Apr. 5, 1636. S. of Sir William, Knt. B. at Bury St Edmunds. Matric. 1636; B.A. 1639–40; M.A. 1641–2 (*Lit. Reg.*). Died in College, May 16, 1642. Buried at Ickworth. Brother of Thomas (1641).

HARVEY, WILLIAM. Matric. pens. from PEMBROKE, Easter, 1649. Perhaps a mistake for Herby; whom see.

HERVEY, WILLIAM. Adm. at CORPUS CHRISTI, 1670. Of Northamptonshire. Doubtless s. of Francis, of Weston Favell, Northants. Bapt. Sept. 22, 1653. Matric. 1671; B.A. 1674–5; M.A. 1678. Perhaps patron and R. of Weston, 1677, and Collingtree, Northants., 1679. Died Dec. 3, 1736. Buried at Weston. But *see Al. Oxon.* for a contemporary. (*Baker*, I. 74.)

HARVEY, WILLIAM. Adm. pens. (age 16) at TRINITY, Apr. 15, 1680. S. of Sir Eliab, of Chigwell, Essex. Bapt. at St Peter-le-Poor, Dec. 18, 1663. School, St Paul's. M.P. for Old Sarum, Wilts., 1689–1705, and again, 1708–10; for Appleby, 1705–7; for Weymouth and Melcombe Regis, 1711–3, 1714–5; for Essex, 1715–6, 1722–7. Died Oct. 31, 1731. (*Misc. Gen. et Her.*, 2nd S., III. 334; *Essex Pedigrees*.)

HARVEY, WILLIAM. Adm. sizar (age 18) at PEMBROKE, Feb. 11, 1698–9. S. of William, farmer. B. at Wickhambrook, Suffolk. Matric. 1699; B.A. 1702–3. Ord. deacon (Norwich) Sept. 1703; priest, Sept. 23, 1705. V. of Digby, Lincs., 1703. V. of Metheringham, 1706–18.

HARVEY, WILLIAM. Adm. pens. (age 17) at CHRIST'S, Apr. 25, 1703. S. of Thomas. B. at East Grinstead. Exhibitioner from Charterhouse. Matric. 1704; Scholar, 1704–5; B.A. 1706–7; M.A. 1710. Ord. priest (Chichester) Sept. 1710. V. of Hollington, Sussex, 1711–2. V. of Warnham, 1712–38. Buried there July 31, 1738. Admon. (P.C.C.) 1739. (*Peile*, II. 156.)

HARVEY, WILLIAM. Adm. Fell.-Com. at CLARE, Sept. 26, 1712. B. at Caldecote, Warws. Matric. 1713.

HARVEY, WILLIAM. Adm. sizar (age 18) at CAIUS, Sept. 14, 1713. S. of Robert, of Crimplesham, Norfolk, gent. B. at Beechamwell. School, Norwich (Mr Pate). Matric. 1713–4; Scholar, 1713–8; B.A. 1717–8; M.A. 1726. Ord. deacon (Norwich) July 13, 1718, as C. of Cockley Cley, Norfolk; priest, June 12, 1720. R. of West Winch, 1732–86. V. of Crimplesham, 1735–85. R. of Fincham, 1745–86. Buried at Crimplesham, 1786. (*Venn*, I. 531.)

HARVEY, WILLIAM. Adm. at CORPUS CHRISTI, 1723. Of Norwich. Matric. 1724; B.A. 1726–7. Ord. deacon (Norwich) Sept. 1727; priest, June, 1728. Perhaps R. of Lyng and Marsham, Norfolk, 1729–48. Died Mar. 5, 1747–8, aged 44. (*E. Anglian*, I. 266.)

HERVEY, WILLIAM. Adm. at CORPUS CHRISTI, 1751. 4th s. of John, Baron Hervey, of Ickworth. B. May 13, 1732. Matric. Lent, 1750–1; M.A. 1754. Major in the army, 1782. Lieut.-General, 1793. General, 1798. Died Jan. 15, 1815. Buried at Ickworth. Brother of Frederick Augustus (1747). (Gage, *Suffolk*, 288.)

HARVYE, ——. Matric. Fell.-Com. from CLARE, Easter, 1544.

HARVEY, ——. Adm. Fell.-Com. at EMMANUEL, Easter, 1626.

HARVEY, ——. Adm. at PEMBROKE, 1641.

HARVEY, ——. Adm. Fell.-Com. at ST CATHARINE'S, Easter, 1653. Probably Hugh, 3rd s. of Robert, of Quainton, Bucks. 'Of Cambridge University' (*see Burke*). Of Cole Park, Malmesbury, Wilts. Died 1677. Probably brother of John (1645–6) and Robert (1655). (*Vis. of Warws.*, 1682–3.)

HERVEY, ——. Adm. pens. at MAGDALENE, Aug. 31, 1720.

HARWAR, JOSEPH. Adm. sizar (age 19) at TRINITY, Feb. 27, 1702–3. S. of Thomas, of Bridgemere, Cheshire. School, Madeley, Staffs. (Mr Branker). Matric. 1702–3; B.A. 1706–7; M.A. 1722. R. of Swettenham, Cheshire, 1715–22. V. of Acton, 1722–45. Died 1745.

HARWARD, ANDREW. Adm. at KING'S, a scholar from Eton, 1615. B. at Odiham, Hants., 1598. Matric. Easter, 1615; B.A. 1619–20; M.A. 1623; B.D. 1630. Fellow, 1618–35. V. of Tring, Herts. R. of Grinstead-by-Ongar, Essex, 1641–7. V. of Asholt, Somerset, 1660–2. Chaplain to the Earl of Montgomery. Will (Taunton) 1662.

HARWARD, BENET. Scholar at KING'S HALL, 1539–40.

HARWARD, CHARLES. Adm. pens. at CLARE, Apr. 1, 1743. B. at Plimtree, Devon. Matric. 1742; B.A. 1745–6; M.A. 1755. R. of Whistoo with moiety of Denton, Northants., 1755–62. Preb. of Exeter, 1790. Dean, 1790–1802. Died July 15, 1802, aged 79.

HARWARD, HENRY. Adm. pens. (age 16) at ST JOHN'S, May 26, 1668. S. of John, yeoman, of Pirbright, Surrey. B. there. School, Cobham (Mr Carter). Matric. 1668; B.A. 1671–2; M.A. 1675. Fellow, 1684. Ord. deacon (Ely) Sept. 18, 1675; priest (London) Feb. 24, 1677–8. V. of Gt Thurlow, Cambs., 1687–1715. Died 1715.

HARWARD, JOSEPH. Matric. from QUEENS', Michs. 1727; LL.B. 1728. Of St Mary Hall, Oxford (not found in *Al. Oxon.*).

HARWARD, KEMP. M.D. 1714 (Incorp. from Trinity College, Dublin). S. of Kemp, of Upton Hole, Worcs., gent. Matric. from Merton College, Oxford, Jan. 7, 1696–7, age 15; B.A. (Magdalen Hall, Oxford) 1700; M.B. and M.D. (Dublin) 1708. (*Al. Oxon.*)

HARWARD, PHILIP. Adm. at CORPUS CHRISTI, 1666. Of Suffolk.

HARWARD, RICHARD. Adm. pens. (age 18) at CAIUS, July 25, 1567. 1st s. of Robert, of Yarmouth. School, Yarmouth. Father's will (Norwich) 1577.

HARWARD, SIMON. Matric. pens. from CHRIST'S, Dec. 1572; B.A. 1574-5. Incorp. at Oxford, 1577, where he was chaplain of New College; M.A. (Oxford) 1578. R. of Warrington, Lancs., 1579-81. Perhaps R. of Shipdham, Norfolk, 1587-91. V. of Cromer, 1587-91. 'Preacher' at Crowhurst, Surrey, 1592. Resident at Tandridge, 1596, where he kept a school and practised physic. R. of Banstead, Surrey, 1604. Married Mary, dau. of Richard Langley, at Manchester, Sept. 25, 1582. Author, *Sermons*. (*D.N.B.*; *Peile*, I. 124; *Cooper*, II. 478.)

HARWARD, THOMAS. Adm. sizar (age 17) at CAIUS, June 20, 1633. S. of Edward, minister. B. at Strumpshaw, Norfolk. School, Norwich (Mr Briggs). Matric. 1633; B.A. 1636-7. Ord. deacon (Norwich) Dec. 22, 1639; C. of Ilketshall St John's, 1662; priest (London) Mar. 6, 1663-4. R. of Dickleburgh, Norfolk, 1664. C. of Sampford, Essex. (*Venn*, I. 319.)

HARWARD, WILLIAM. Matric. pens. from ST JOHN'S, Michs. 1546; B.A. 1549-50; M.A. from Queens', 1553. Fellow of Queens', 1550-9, deprived. R. of St Clement Danes, 1559-89. V. of Cowfold, Sussex, 1560. Canon of Windsor, 1562-89. Perhaps R. of Shadoxhurst, Kent. Licensed (Bishop of London) Sept. 25, 1568, to marry Alice Cavell, widow. Died 1589. Will (P.C.C.) 1589. (*Cooper*, II. 51.)

HARWARD, WILLIAM. Matric. sizar from KING'S, Michs. 1625.

HARWELL, THOMAS. Adm. sizar (age 19) at CHRIST'S, Feb. 22, 1714-5. S. of William. B. at Chippenham, Cambs. School, Bury (Mr Randall). Matric. 1715; Scholar, 1715; B.A. 1718-9; M.A. 1722. Fellow, 1723-41. Ord. deacon (Lincoln) June 12, 1720; priest (Norwich) Dec. 1721. V. of Gateley, Norfolk, 1733. V. of Ingoldsby, 1740-69. Died Feb. 9, 1770. Buried in Chippenham Churchyard. Will (P.C.C.) 1770. (*Peile*, II. 186.)

HARWELL, WILLIAM. Adm. pens. at QUEENS', Oct. 1564. Matric. Michs. 1564. Perhaps William Harwell, of 'Fetcham,' Surrey; adm. at the Inner Temple, 1567.

HARWEN, ——. M.A. 1476-7.

HARWICK, THOMAS. Adm. sizar (age 20) at CAIUS, Aug. 26, 1696. S. of Thomas, gent., of (? Wiggenhall) St Mary, Norfolk. B. there. School, Lynn (Mr Horne). Scholar, 1696-1700; Matric. 1697. (*Venn*, I. 499.)

HARWOOD, *see also* HORWOOD.

HARWOOD, ANTHONY. Adm. sizar (age 15) at SIDNEY, Jan. 12, 1630-1. S. of Henry, gent., of Uppingham, Rutland. School, Uppingham. Matric. 1631; B.A. 1634-5; M.A. 1638. Created B.D. (Oxford) 1642. Ord. deacon (Peterb.) Mar. 10, 1638-9. R. of Barnoldby, Lincs., 1642. R. of Harby, Leics., 1660, till 1703. R. of Corby, Northants., 1660. Preb. of Lincoln, 1660-1703. Died May 12, 1703, aged 89. M.I. at Corby. (*Nichols*, II. 422; *Al. Oxon.*)

HARWOOD, AUGUSTINE. Matric. sizar from QUEENS', Michs. 1627. Of London.

HARWOOD, BARTHOLOMEW. Adm. sizar at CORPUS CHRISTI, 1674. Of Norwich. Matric. Easter, 1675; B.A. 1678-9; M.A. 1682. Ord. deacon (Norwich) Nov. 1679; priest Nov. 1681. V. of Easton, Norfolk, 1681-1700. Settled in Boston, New England, in 1697. (*Masters*.)

HARWOOD, CHRISTOPHER. Matric. pens. from PETERHOUSE, Easter, 1575.

HARWOOD, EDWARD. Adm. sizar (age 17) at ST JOHN'S, July 5, 1704. S. of Edward, gent. B. at Shrewsbury. School, Shrewsbury. Matric. 1705; B.A. 1707-8; M.A. 1711. V. of Erith, Kent, 1714-34. Perhaps R. of Thornton-le-Moors, Cheshire, 1733-60. Died 1760. Father of the next.

HARWOOD, EDWARD. Adm. sizar (age 18) at ST JOHN'S, July 2, 1751. S. of Edward (above). B. at Erith, Kent. School, Shrewsbury. Matric. 1751; B.A. 1755; M.A. from Clare, 1758. Fellow of Clare, 1755. Ord. deacon (Chester) June 11, 1755; priest (Llandaff) July 25, 1756. V. of Shenstone, Staffs., 1759-82. R. of Sutton, Shrewsbury, 1775-82. Died at Chester, Apr. 18, 1782. Will (P.C.C.) 1783. (*Scott-Mayor*, III. 609; *G. Mag.*)

HARWOODE, FRANCIS. Matric. sizar from ST JOHN'S, Michs. 1606.

HARWOOD, JAMES. Matric. sizar from ST JOHN'S, Easter, 1618; B.A. 1621-2; M.A. 1626. Ord. deacon (York) June, 1623; priest, Mar. 1624-5. One of these names (James H., *junior*), of Beverley, licensed to marry Elizabeth Dove, in 1622.

HARWOOD, JOHN. B.A. 1460-1.

HARWOOD, JOHN. B.A. from TRINITY, 1569-70.

HARWOOD, JOHN. Matric. pens. from CHRIST'S, Mar. 1586. School, Lincoln. A blind scholar, allowed 40s. a year by the Lincoln town authorities. (*Vict. Co. Hist. Lincs.*; *Peile's* identification (I. 185) must be wrong.)

HARWOOD or HARWARDE, JOHN. Adm. pens. (age 16) at CAIUS, Apr. 12, 1625. S. of John, woolstapler, of Bury St Edmunds. School, Bury (Mr Dickinson). Matric. 1625; B.A. 1628-9; M.A. 1632. Probably ord. priest (Ardfort and Aghadoe) Jan. 5, 1650-1. Probably V. of Mendham, Suffolk, 1653. C. of St Luke's, Norwich, 1662. R. of St Simon and St Jude, *c.* 1662. *See* the next. (*Venn*, I. 270.)

HARWOOD, JOHN. Matric. sizar from CORPUS CHRISTI, Easter, 1644. Of Cambridgeshire. B.A. 1647-8; M.A. 1651. Perhaps V. of Lakenham, Norfolk, 1666. V. of Catton, 1666-92. (*Masters*.)

HARWOOD, JOHN. Adm. pens. at QUEENS', Jan. 6, and Fell.-Com. Jan. 20, 1681-2. S. of John, of Hagbourne, Berks. Matric. 1683; LL.B. 1684; LL.D. 1688. Matric. from Christ Church, Oxford, Mar. 28, 1679, age 18. F.R.S., 1686. F.S.A., 1717. Of Doctors' Commons. Commissary of St Paul's; official of St Mary's, Salop. Died Jan. 1, 1730-1. Will (P.C.C.) 1731. (*Al. Oxon.*)

HARWOOD, JOHN. Adm. pens. (age 19) at PEMBROKE, Mar. 23, 1704-5. S. of John, of Cambridge. Probably colleger at Eton. Matric. 1705; B.A. 1708-9; M.A. 1712; D.D. 1736. Fellow, 1711. Ord. deacon (London) June 15, 1712; priest (Norwich) Sept. 1713. C. of Framlingham, Suffolk, in 1713. V. of Shepreth, Cambs., 1727. R. of Hatley St George, Hunts., 1730. V. of Soham, Cambs., 1731. Died May 24, 1755, aged 67. Perhaps M.I. at Walkern, Herts.

HARWOOD, NATHANIEL. Matric. pens. from QUEENS', Lent, 1623-4. Of London. B.A. 1626-7; M.A. 1631. One of these names of St Giles', Cripplegate, clerk; admon. (P.C.C.) Apr. 8, 1639. (J. Ch. Smith.)

HARWOOD, RICHARD. Matric. sizar from ST JOHN'S, Michs. 1576; B.A. 1580-1; M.A. 1584. One Richard Harward V. of Kempsey, Worcs., 1607. Perhaps preb. of York, 1614-5.

HARWOOD, ROLAND. Adm. pens. (age 18) at ST JOHN'S, Sept. 26, 1716. S. of Thomas, gent., of Salop. B. at Shrewsbury. School, Eton. Matric. 1716; B.A. 1720-1; M.A. from Queens', 1724, as 'Roland Harwood Hill.' Ord. deacon (Lincoln) May 31, 1724; priest (Norwich) June, 1725. R. of Forncett, Norfolk, 1725-30. R. of Hodnet, Salop, 1730-3. R. of Thornton, Cheshire, 1730-3. Died 1733. (*Scott-Mayor*, III. 307.)

HARWOOD, THOMAS. B.A. 1514-5; M.A. 1517; M.D. 1530-1. Perhaps fellow of CLARE, 1515. One of these names fellow of King's Hall, 1530-44. Proctor, 1526-7.

HARWOOD, WALTER. Matric. pens. (age 11) from CLARE, Easter, 1559.

HARWOOD or HARWARDE, WALTER. Adm. scholar (age 15) at CAIUS, June 5, 1580. S. of William, of Windsor, Berks. School, Kelmarsh, Northants. B.A. 1583-4; M.A. 1587.

HARWOOD or HERWOOD, ——. Pens. at PETERHOUSE, July 26, 1578. Resided, till 1580.

HAREWOOD, ——. Pens. at GONVILLE HALL, 1586-8.

HASBERT, JOHN. Matric. sizar from CORPUS CHRISTI, Easter, 1656. Of Norwich. B.A. 1659. Ord. deacon (Lincoln) Mar. 10, 1660-1, as 'Hasbant.'

HASKARD, GREGORY. Adm. sizar at EMMANUEL, Michs. 1657. Matric. 1657; B.A. 1660-1; M.A. 1664; D.D. 1671 (*Lit. Reg.*). Ord. deacon (Lincoln) May 28. R. of St Michael, Queenhithe, 1669-71. R. of Brickhill Bow, Bucks., 1669-71. Canon of Windsor, 1671-1708. Preb. of Sarum, 1671-1708. Chaplain to the King, 1677-1708. R. of St Clement Danes, 1678-1708. Dean of Windsor and Wolverhampton, 1684-1708. Author, *Sermons*. Died Nov. 15, 1708. M.I. at Stoke Poges, Bucks. Will, P.C.C. Father of the next. (*Lipscomb*, IV. 566.)

HASCARD, HENRY. Adm. pens. at EMMANUEL, Feb. 22, 1720-1. Of Buckinghamshire. S. of Gregory (above), D.D. Bapt. at Stoke, Bucks., Mar. 15, 1703-4. Colleger at Eton. Matric. 1721; B.A. 1724-5; M.A. 1728. Ord. deacon (Lincoln) Dec. 22, 1728; priest, Mar. 2, 1728-9.

HASE, *see also* HAYES.

HASE or HAYES, EDMUND. Matric. sizar from MAGDALENE, *c.* 1593; B.A. from St John's, 1596-7; M.A. 1600, 'Hause.' Incorp. at Oxford, 1605.

HASE, EDWARD. Adm. pens. (age 18) at CAIUS, Jan. 12, 1750-1 and Fell.-Com. Nov. 7, 1752. S. of John, Esq., of Gt Melton, Norfolk. B. at Dereham. Schools, Searning and Horsted (private; Mr Parr). Matric. 1750-1. Of Gt Melton and Sall, Norfolk, Esq. Sheriff of Norfolk, 1773-4. J.P. Died May 11, 1804. M.I. at Sall. Brother of John (1748). (*Venn*, II. 65.)

HASE, JOHN. Adm. sizar (age 16) at CAIUS, Apr. 28, 1623. S. of Edmund (? 1593). B. in Norwich. School, Norwich (Mr Stonham). Migrated to Magdalene College. Matric. there, Easter, 1623; Scholar, 1627-9. Readm. at Caius, Apr. 1627. B.A. 1627-8; M.A. 1631. Ord. deacon (Peterb.) Sept. 12; priest, Sept. 13, 1629. C. of Kessingland, Suffolk, in 1636. C. of Herringfleet, 1650. One of these names, minister, buried at Somerleyton, Suffolk, Oct. 7, 1651. (*Venn*, I. 262.)

HASE, JOHN. Adm. Fell.-Com. (age 17) at CAIUS, Apr. 10, 1748. S. of John, clothier, of Dereham, Norfolk (and Mary, dau. of Edward Lombe). B. there. School, Scarning (Mr Brett). Matric. 1748. Adm. at Lincoln's Inn, Oct. 18, 1749. Of Gt Melton, Esq. Assumed his mother's name, Lombe, 1762, on succeeding to the estates of his uncle, Edward Lombe. Sheriff of Norfolk, 1772-3. Created Bart., Jan. 22, 1784. Died unmarried, May 27, 1817, at Gt Melton. Brother of Edward (1750-1). (*Venn*, II. 61; *G.E.C.*)

HASEL, *see* HASSELL.

HASELBECK or HESILBECK, ——. B.Can.L. 1489-90.

HASELDEAN, RICHARD. B.A. 1518-9; M.A. 1522.

HASELDIN, *see* also HESLEDEN.

HASELDIN, ROBERT. Adm. pens. at EMMANUEL, Mar. 21, 1617-8. S. and h. of Robert, of Goldington, Beds., Esq. Matric. 1618. Adm. at Gray's Inn, Oct. 20, 1619. Of Goldington, Beds. Buried there Apr. 21, 1632. (*Vis. of Beds.*, 1634.)

HASELDINE, WILLIAM. M.A. 1737 (Incorp. from Oxford). S. of William, of Close, Lincoln, gent. Matric. from Lincoln College, May 14, 1730, age 16; B.A. from Magdalen, 1733-4; M.A. 1736; B.D. 1747; D.D. 1748. Fellow of Magdalen College, Oxford, 1733-64. V. of Dinton, Wilts., 1762. R. of Wishford and Cobberley, Gloucs., 1764-71. Died Dec. 3, 1773. Buried at Dinton. (*Al. Oxon.*; *G. Mag.*)

HASSELLGRAVE, JOHN. Adm. sizar (age 20) at ST JOHN'S, Mar. 13, 1665-6. S. of John, deceased, of Ashton-under-Lyne, Lancs. B. there. School, Stockport (Mr Combs). B.A. 1669-70. Licensed as schoolmaster at Willingham, Cambs., Feb. 1666-7.

HASELHURST, HENRY. Matric. sizar from JESUS, Easter, 1615.

HAZELHURST, JOSEPH. Adm. sizar (age 21) at ST JOHN'S, Feb. 19, 1722-3. S. of Henry, husbandman, of Cheshire. B. at Synderland, Bowdon. School, Lymm, Cheshire (Mr Spencer). Matric. 1723; B.A. 1726-7. Ord. deacon (Lincoln) Feb. 26, 1726-7; priest, Mar. 14, 1730-1. V. of Middle Drax Rasen, Lincs., 1731-68. V. of North Willingham, 1734-68. Father of the next. (*Scott-Mayor*, III. 358.)

HASLEHURST, JOSEPH. Adm. sizar (age 18) at ST JOHN'S, Apr. 26, 1748. S. of Joseph (1723), clerk. B. at Ireswell. Educated by his father. Matric. 1748-9; B.A. 1752. Ord. deacon (Lincoln) May 24, 1752; priest, June 9, 1754.

HASELHORST, PETER. Matric. sizar from ST JOHN'S, Easter, 1603; B.A. 1606-7.

HASLEHURST, ROBERT. Adm. sizar (age 20) at MAGDALENE, July 2, 1664. S. of William, of Cheshire, deceased. School, Manchester.

HASELRIGGE, *see* HESELRIGGE.

HASELTOPP, EDWARD. Matric. sizar from CHRIST'S, Easter, 1613.

HASELWOOD, ANTHONY. Adm. pens. at CLARE, Apr. 7, 1635. Doubtless of Burbage, Leics., gent. S. of Robert, of Draughton, Northants. Died in London. Will (P.C.C.) 1675. Father of the next. (Fr. *Haslewood*.)

HASLEWOOD, ANTHONY. Adm. pens. at CLARE, June 25, 1673. Of Burbage, Leics. 1st s. of Anthony (above), of Burbage. Matric. 1673; B.A. 1676-7.

HASELWOODE, EDMUND. Matric. pens. from PEMBROKE, Michs. 1555.

HASELWOOD, EDMUND. Matric. pens. from JESUS, Michs. 1568.

HASELWOOD, EDWARD. Matric. pens. from PEMBROKE, Easter, 1561. Perhaps 5th. s of John, of Maidwell, Northants. Died 1589. Will, Northampton.

HASELWOOD, FRANCIS. Matric. sizar from TRINITY, Easter, 1560, *impubes*. One of these names adm. at Gray's Inn, 1567. Perhaps of Belton, Rutland, clerk. S. of Thomas. (*Fr. Haslewood*.)

HASELWOOD, HENRY. Matric. pens. from JESUS, Easter, 1570; B.A. 1573-4. Fellow, 1575-7. Perhaps 5th s. of Thomas; brother of Francis (above).

HASELWOOD, JOHN. Matric. sizar from ST JOHN'S, Easter, 1566.

HASELWOOD, ROBERT. Matric. pens. from PEMBROKE, Michs. 1560.

HASELWOOD, ROBERT. Matric. pens. from ST JOHN'S, Easter, 1612. Of London. Migrated to Oxford after 16 terms. Matric. from Christ Church, Dec. 8, 1615, age 19; B.A. (Oxford) 1615; M.A. 1618. Incorp. at Cambridge, 1623. R. of Fleet, Lincs., 1622-43, sequestered. R. of Kirkby Underwood, Lincs., 1622-51. Buried in Christ Church Cathedral, Oxford, Apr. 20, 1658. (*Al. Oxon.*)

HASELWOOD, ROBERT. Adm. at CORPUS CHRISTI, 1637. Of London. Matric. as 'Harlewood,' 1637; B.A. 1640; B.D. 1662 (*Lit. Reg.*). R. of Fleet, Lincs., 1662-84. Preb. of Lincoln, 1672-84. R. of Kirkby Underwood, 1673-84. Buried at Fleet, Dec. 6, 1684. (C. W. Foster.)

HASLEWOOD, ROBERT. Adm. sizar (age 17) at PEMBROKE, July 6, 1670. S. of Robert (? above), clerk. B. at Fleet, Lincs. B.A. 1673-4.

HASLEWOOD, THOMAS. Adm. at CORPUS CHRISTI, 1682. Of Norwich. Matric. Michs. 1683; B.A. 1686-7; M.A. 1690; B.D. 1698; D.D. 1712. Fellow, 1690-8. Ord. deacon (London) Feb. 24, 1688-9. One of these names R. of Covingham, Essex, 1703-13. Died 1713.

HASFIELD, WILLIAM. B.Can.L. 1467.

HASHMAN, ——. B.D. 1474-5.

HASLAM, ANTHONY. Matric. sizar from QUEENS', Easter, 1607. Of Nottinghamshire. B.A. 1610-1.

HASELEM or HASLEHAM, EDWARD. Adm. sizar (age 19) at ST JOHN'S, Apr. 10, 1746. S. of Edward, husbandman, of Yorkshire. B. at Grassington. School, Threshfield (Mr Knowles). Matric. 1746; B.A. 1749-50. Ord. deacon (York) June 10, 1750; priest (Carlisle) Oct. 22, 1758. P.C. of St Mary's, Honley, Yorks., 1760. Master of the Grammar School, Almondbury, Huddersfield. Buried at Honley, Jan. 14, 1788. (*Scott-Mayor*, III. 558.)

HASLAM, WILLIAM. Adm. sizar (age 19) at ST JOHN'S, Apr. 4, 1720. S. of Edward, druggist, of Lancashire. B. at Rochdale. Bapt. there, Aug. 3, 1700. Schools, Rochdale (Mr Kippax) and Stockport (Mr Dale). Matric. 1720.

HASLERTON, ROBERT, *see* HESLERTON.

HASLINGFIELD, STEPHEN. M.A. Chancellor of the University, 1300-3, 1307.

HASLINGTON, ——. Fee for B.A. 1480-1; M.A. 1482, as Hislington.

HASLOCK, WILLIAM (1645), *see* ASLACK.

HASLOCKE, ——. Sizar or College servant at PETERHOUSE, 1639-45. Possibly above. (*T. A. Walker*.)

HASLOP, *see* also HESLOP.

HASLOP, HENRY. Matric. sizar from KING'S, Easter, 1709; B.A. 1712-3; M.A. 1716. Ord. priest (Norwich) Sept. 1716. R. of Syderstone, Norfolk, 1721-4. R. of Dry Drayton, Cambs., 1725-8.

HASELOP, JOHN. Matric. sizar from KING'S, Michs. 1676; B.A. 1680-1; M.A. 1684. Taxor, 1701. Chaplain of King's College. V. of Gt Wilbraham, Cambs., 1688-1705. V. of Sawston, 1690-1705. Buried at Sawston, Mar. 14, 1705-6.

HASELUPP, THOMAS. Matric. sizar from TRINITY, 1598; Scholar, 1599; B.A. 1601-2; M.A. 1605; B.D. 1612. Incorp. at Oxford, 1607. Ord. deacon and priest (Norwich) Sept. 22, 1605, age 24. V. of Ludham, Norfolk, 1610-1. R. of Eccles-by-the-Sea, 1611. R. of Hempstead, 1611.

HASLOP, WILLIAM. Matric. sizar from KING'S, Lent, 1705-6; B.A. 1709-10.

HASLYHEAD, JOHN. Matric. sizar from ST JOHN'S, Michs. 1618; B.A. 1622-3; M.A. 1626.

HASSALL, ROGER. Matric. pens. from JESUS, Michs. 1606.

HASSALL, THOMAS. Matric. sizar from TRINITY, *c.* 1591; Scholar, 1593; B.A. 1594-5; M.A. 1598, as 'Hassald.' V. of Gt Amwell, Herts., 1599-1657. As chaplain to Lord Hunsdon he had a dispensation, Sept. 15, 1619, to hold St Alphage, London, with Amwell. Died Sept. 24, 1657, aged 84. M.I. at Amwell. Will, P.C.C.

HASSANT, JOHN. Adm. sizar at ST CATHARINE'S, May 24, 1733. Of Earl Soham, Suffolk.

HASSARD, *see also* HAZARD.

HASSARD or HAZARD, JOHN. Matric. pens. from ST CATHARINE'S, Easter, 1633. Of Kent.

HASSARD, ——. Adm. sizar at SIDNEY, Nov. 1600.

HASSELL, AMBROSE. Matric. sizar from TRINITY, Easter, 1578. Ord. priest (Norwich) 1582. R. of Stanfield, Norfolk, 1597.

HASSELL, EDMUND. Matric. sizar from TRINITY, Michs. 1631; Scholar, 1634; B.A. 1635-6; M.A. 1640.

HASELL, EDWARD. Matric. pens. from ST JOHN'S, Easter, 1595; B.A. 1599-1600; M.A. 1603. Ord. deacon and priest (Peterb.) Nov. 20, 1603. V. of Swaiton *with* Spanby, Lincs., 1611.

HASE[illegible] EDWARD. Matric. pens. from CLARE, Easter, 1624. 3rd s. of John, of Bottisham, Cambs. Bapt. Apr. 15, 1604. B.A. 1627-8; M.A. 1631. Fellow. Taxor, 1641. R. of Middleton Cheney, Northants., 1640-2. Buried at Hildersham, Cambs., Aug. 4, 1642. Will, P.C.C. (Burke, *L.G.*)

HASSELL, EDWARD. Adm. at CORPUS CHRISTI, 1676. Of Ely. Matric. Easter, 1677; B.A. 1680-1.

HASYLL, HENRY. Scholar of TRINITY HALL, 1589. B. at Bury, Suffolk. Ord. deacon and priest (London) Feb. 6 and 7, 1597-8, age 24. C. of St Leon., Shoreditch.

HASELL, JEREMY. Matric. pens. from ST JOHN'S, Easter, 1616, as 'Haslepe'; B.A. 1619-20. Probably s. of Thomas, of Conisthorpe, Yorks. Ord. deacon (York) Dec. 1621; priest, June, 1622. (*Vis. of Yorks.*, 1665.)

HASELL, JOHN. Matric. sizar from TRINITY, Easter, 1576.

HASSELL, JOHN. Adm. pens. at QUEENS', May 10, 1717. Of Middlesex. S. of Ralph, of London, gent. Adm. at Lincoln's Inn, May 28, 1720. Barrister. Died Dec. 8, 1749. Brother of Richard (1717). (*G. Mag.*; *L. Mag.*)

HASSEL, LANCELOT. Adm. sizar (age 20) at PETERHOUSE, Apr. 22, 1647. Of Yorkshire. School, Durham.

HASELL, OWEN. Matric. Fell.-Com. from PEMBROKE, Lent, 1607-8.

HASELL, PETER. Adm. pens. (age 16) at CAIUS, Sept. 5, 1676. S. of William, of Sudbury, Suffolk. B. there. School, Burstall. Scholar, 1676-8. Migrated to St Catharine's, 1684. M.A. 1686 (*Lit. Reg.*), 'engaged beyond the seas on urgent occasions.' Ord. deacon (Norwich) May, 1686; priest, May, 1687. R. of Kettlebaston, Suffolk, 1699-1711. Died 1711. (*Venn*, I. 457.)

HASSALL, RALPH. Adm. pens. at EMMANUEL, Apr. 15, 1611. Matric. 1611; B.A. 1614-5; M.A. 1618. One of these names s. of Thomas, of Conisthorpe, Yorks. *See* Jeremy and Samuel (1606). (*Vis. of Yorks.*, 1665.)

HAZELL, RICHARD. Adm. sizar (age 15) at CAIUS, Nov. 3, 1624. S. of Richard, merchant, of London. School, Mercers' (Mr Augar). Matric. 1625; Scholar, 1627-9; B.A. 1628-9. Perhaps V. of Compton, Berks. Admon. (Consist. C. Sarum) 1684. (*Venn*, I. 269.)

HASSELL, RICHARD. Adm. pens. at QUEENS', May 10, 1717. Of Middlesex. 1st s. of Ralph, late of Barnet, gent. Adm. at Lincoln's Inn, Feb. 8, 1719-20. F.R.S., 1726. Of Barnet. Died Mar. 16, 1770. Brother of John (1717).

HASELL, ROBERT. Matric. sizar from TRINITY, Michs. 1565; B.A. 1570-1. One of these names V. of Buckden, Hunts., *c.* 1591. Perhaps preb. of Lincoln, 1591-1605.

HASELL, ROBERT. Adm. sizar (age 18) at SIDNEY, May 30, 1622. S. of John, yeoman. B. at Sutton, Chew Magna, Somerset. School, Wells. Matric. 1622; B.A. 1625-6; M.A. 1629.

HASEL, SAMUEL. Matric. pens. from CHRIST'S, Easter, 1606. One of these names, s. of Thomas, of Conisthorpe, Yorks., gent., adm. at Gray's Inn, Oct. 17, 1608. Of Hutton-on-Darwent, Yorks. Married Mary, dau. of Richard Conyers, of Horden, Durham. Died 1655. (*Peile*, I. 257; *Vis. of Yorks.*, 1665; M. H. Peacock.)

HASSELL, SAMUEL. Adm. pens. (age 17) at PEMBROKE, May 20, 1659. S. of Samuel, of Sudbury, mercer.

HASSELL, SAMUEL. Adm. sizar (age 18) at ST JOHN'S, July 5, 1703. S. of Charles, upholsterer. B. at Brotherton, Ferrybridge, Yorks. School, Pocklington (Mr Ferrour). Matric. 1703; B.A. 1706-7. Ord. priest (Lincoln) July 5, 1713; C. of Digswell, Herts. Perhaps R. of Ayot St Lawrence, till his death, Jan. 23, 1758. (*G. Mag.*)

HASSELL, SAMUEL. Adm. sizar (age 20) at ST JOHN'S, May 31, 1712. S. of Talbott, barrister. B. at Knayton, in Leake parish, Yorks. School, Guisborough (Mr Jaques). Matric. 1712; B.A. 1715-6. Ord. deacon (York) Dec. 1716; priest, 1718.

HASSELL, SAMUEL. Adm. pens. (age 20) at ST JOHN'S, May 10, 1743. S. of Thomas, gent., of Yorkshire. B. at Thorpe. School, Beverley (Mr Clarke). Matric. 1743; LL.B. 1749. Ord. deacon (York) Sept. 21, 1746; priest, June 5, 1748. C. of Carnaby, Yorks., 1746. Died July 4, 1752. (*Scott-Mayor* III. 535; *G. Mag.*)

HASSEL or HASEL, THOMAS. Adm. sizar (age 17) at PETERHOUSE, June 22, 1652. Of Yorkshire. School, Bridlington. Matric. 1652; B.A. 1655-6.

HASOLL, THOMAS. Adm. sizar at QUEENS', 1660. Matric. 1660.

HASSEL, THOMAS. Adm. sizar (age 17) at PETERHOUSE, May 3, 1680. Of Yorkshire. School, Thornton, Yorks. Scholar, 1680; Matric. 1681; B.A. 1683-4; M.A. 1687. One of these names R. of Holwell, Beds., 1690-3.

HASSALL, THOMAS. Adm. sizar at QUEENS', June 22, 1683. Of Worcs. Matric. 1683-4. Perhaps V. of Malvern, 1692-8.

HASSELL, THOMAS. Matric. pens. from TRINITY HALL, 1713.

HASSELL, WILLIAM. Adm. pens. (age 17) at ST JOHN'S, July 5, 1712. S. of John, citizen of London. B. there. School, Haydon, Essex (Mr Goodwyn). Matric. 1712; B.A. 1716-7; M.A. 1720. Fellow of Peterhouse, 1720-5. Ord. deacon (Norwich) Mar. 1722-3; priest (Ely) Mar. 1, 1723-4. R. of Horsemonden, Kent, 1724-85. Buried there Mar. 11, 1785. M.I. Will, P.C.C.

HAZELL, ——. Adm. sizar at ST CATHARINE'S, July 4, 1682.

HASELL, ——. Adm. scholar at TRINITY HALL, Jan. 6, 1714-5.

HASSET, SAMUEL. Matric. pens. from ST JOHN'S, Michs. 1569.

HASSET, THOMAS. Matric. pens. from TRINITY, Michs. 1560.

HASSET, THOMAS. Matric. pens. from ST JOHN'S, Michs. 1571

HASSETT, ——. Pens. at GONVILLE HALL, 1535.

HASTE, THOMAS. Matric. pens. from ST JOHN'S, Easter, 1584. Perhaps adm. scholar at Trinity Hall, June 18, 1585.

HAST, WILLIAM. Adm. sizar (age 17) at ST JOHN'S, June 3, 1670. S. of Richard, of Sherburn, Yorks. B. there. School, Sherburn (Mr Wright). Matric. 1671; B.A. 1674-5; M.A. 1678. Ord. priest (London) Sept. 23, 1677. R. of Mount Bures, Essex, 1679. Died 1721.

HASTE, ——. Scholar at CHRIST'S, 1553-4.

HASTED, EDWARD, *see* HAUSTEAD.

HASTELEYE, JOHN. Of the House of Carmelites, Cambridge. Licensed (Ely) to preach and hear confessions, Feb. 1375-6. (B. Zimmerman.)

HASTINGS, EDWARD. Adm. Fell.-Com. at SIDNEY, July 2, 1605. Doubtless 3rd s. of Francis (1572). M.A. 1610 (*fil. nob.*). Captain R.N. Died unmarried on the voyage to Guiana under Sir Walter Raleigh, 1617. Brother of George (1605). (Burke.)

HASTINGS, EDWARD. Adm. Fell.-Com. at QUEENS', Feb. 24, 1608-9. Of Huntingdonshire. Adm. at the Middle Temple, July 13, 1610. Brother of Henry (1601).

HASTINGS, FERDINANDO. Adm. Fell.-Com. at QUEENS', Lent, 1625-6. S. and h. of Henry, Earl of Huntingdon. B. at Ashby-de-la-Zouch, Jan. 18, 1608. Adm. at Lincoln's Inn, Aug. 4, 1623. M.P. for Co. Leics., 1625 and 1628-9. Summoned to Parliament as Baron Hastings, 1640. Succeeded as 6th Earl, Nov. 14, 1645. Died at Donnington Park, Leicestershire, Feb. 13, 1655. Buried at Ashby. Brother of Henry (1627). (Burke; *G.E.C.*)

HASTINGS, FRANCIS. Matric. Fell.-Com. (age 12) from TRINITY, Easter, 1572. S. of George, of Gopshall, Derbs.; afterwards Earl of Huntingdon. B. *c.* 1560. Resided at the Old Place, near Ashby Castle. Adm. at Gray's Inn, 1574. Died Dec. 17, 1595. Buried at Ashby. Father of the next and of Edward (1605). (*Cooper*, III. 5; *G.E.C.*)

HASTINGS, GEORGE. Adm. Fell.-Com. at SIDNEY, July 2, 1605. Of Ashby-de-la-Zouch, Leics., Esq., brother of Henry, Earl of Huntingdon. 2nd s. of Francis (above) and grandson of George, 4th Earl. Adm. at Gray's Inn, Mar. 22, 1610-1. Knighted, Nov. 1615. M.P. for Co. Leics., 1614, 1620-2; for Leicester, 1625-6. Died June 4, 1641. Buried at Gt St Bartholomew, Smithfield. Brother of Edward (1605). (*Collins*, VI. 658; A. B. Beaven.)

HASTINGS, HARRISON. Adm. pens. (age 18) at MAGDALENE, May 14, 1672. S. of John, gent., of East Keal, Lincs. School, Alford. Matric. 1672; B.A. 1675-6.

HASTINGS, Sir HENRY. Adm. at QUEENS', *c.* 1548. S. of Francis, Earl of Huntingdon. B. *c.* 1536. K.B., 1547. Summoned to Parliament as Baron Hastings, 1559. Succeeded as 3rd Earl, June 20, 1560. Claimed the succession to the throne, through his mother. A supporter of the Puritans. Associated with Shrewsbury in the custody of Mary Queen of Scots. K.G., 1570. Lord Lieutenant of Leics. and Rutland, 1572. President of the North, 1572. Assisted at the trial of Norfolk, 1573. Compiled a history of his family. Died Dec. 14, 1595. Buried at Ashby-de-la-Zouch. Benefactor to Emmanuel College. (*D.N.B.*; *Cooper*, II. 200; *G.E.C.*)

HASTINGS, HENRY. Adm. Fell.-Com. at EMMANUEL, June 17, 1592. Matric. *c.* 1592. Probably s. of Walter, of Kirkby, Leics., Esq. Adm. at Gray's Inn, June 27, 1595. Knighted, Apr. 23, 1603. M.P. for Co. Leics., 1620-2, 1624-5, 1626. Died Sept. 15, 1649. Probably matric. from Lincoln College, Oxford, May 25, 1593. (*Al. Oxon.*)

HASTINGS, HENRY. Adm. Fell.-Com. at QUEENS', Oct. 1601; M.A. 1615, on King's visit. Adm. at Gray's Inn, Mar. 17, 1597-8. Doubtless of Humberstone, Leicester. 4th s. of Sir Edward (and grandson of the Earl of Huntingdon). Died 1629. Brother of Edward (1605). (*G.E.C.*)

HASTINGS, HENRY. Adm. Fell.-Com. at QUEENS', June 30, 1627. Doubtless 2nd s. of Henry, Earl of Huntingdon. A zealous royalist. Sheriff of Leicestershire, 1642. Fought at Edgehill, 1642. Created Baron Loughborough, 1643. Governor of Leicester, 1645. Held Ashby House against the Parliament, till 1646. Called 'Rob-Carrier' from the frequency with which he intercepted communications between London and the North. Escaped to Holland, 1649. Appointed Lord Lieutenant of Leicestershire, 1661, and granted a pension. Died Jan. 1666–7. Buried at Windsor. Brother of Ferdinando. (*D.N.B.*)

HASTINGS, JOHN. Studied at Cambridge. B.A. (Oxford) 1513–4; M.A. 1516; B.D. 1524; D.D. 1536. Chaplain to the King. R. of Baynton, Yorks., 1507–54 (sub-deacon).

HASTINGS, MARTIN. Matric. pens. from TRINITY, Easter, 1618. S. and h. of Thomas, of Hindringham, Norfolk, deceased. Adm. at Gray's Inn, Nov. 7, 1621. (*Vis. of Norfolk.*)

HASTINGS, PHILIP. Adm. at CORPUS CHRISTI, 1626. Of Norfolk. Probably brotber of Martin (above).

HASTINGS, ROBERT. Scholar of MAGDALENE, 1604; B.A. 1608–9; M.A. 1612. R. of East Keale, Lincs., 1612. But *see* a contemporary at Oxford.

HASTINGS, ROGER. Adm. at KING'S (age 17) a scholar from Eton, Aug. 17, 1507. Of the City of London. Name off, 1508. 'Went away scholar, and entered into the order of a friar.' (*Harwood.*)

HASTINGS, THEOPHILUS HENRY. Adm. sizar at ST JOHN'S, May 25, 1748. S. of Henry, shoemaker (*sic.*), of Leicestershire. B. at Lutterworth. School, Leeds. Matric. 1748; B.A. 1752; M.A. 1764. Ord. deacon (Peterb.) Feb. 23, 1752; and probably priest (Lincoln, *Litt. dim.* from York) Mar. 10, 1754. V. of Belton, Leics., 1763–95. R. of Osgathorpe, 1764–95. R. of West Leake, Notts., 1795–1804. Died Apr. 2, 1804. On the death of Francis, Earl of Huntingdon, Oct. 2, 1789, be became hereditary successor. The title was afterwards allowed to his nephew. (*Scott-Mayor*, III. 577.)

HASTINGS, WILLIAM. Matric. pens. from MAGDALENE, Michs. 1619; B.A. 1623–4. One of these names V. of Woodford, Northants., till 1637. Buried there July 14, 1637. (*See Al. Oxon.* for a contemporary.) (*Baker*, I. 538; *Bridges*, I. 131.)

HASTINGS, WILLIAM. Adm. pens. (age 17) at SIDNEY, Oct. 8, 1619. S. of Robert. B. at Bilsby, Lincs. School, Alford. Matric. 1619. Adm. at the Middle Temple, Nov. 24, 1621. Married and had issue. (*Lincs. Pedigrees*, 467.)

HASTINGS, WILLIAM. Adm. pens. at TRINITY, Sept. 13, 1671. Perhaps s. of William, of Hinton, Northants. Matric. 1671–2. Afterwards Fell.-Com. Probably adm. at Lincoln's Inn, Aug. 4, 1673. Married Priscilla, dau. of Lady Dewes, 1693. Buried at Woodford, Northants., Jan. 31, 1701–2. (*Baker*, I. 538.)

HASTLER, EDWARD. B.A. from CHRIST'S, 1616–7; M.A. 1620. B. at Southminster, Essex. Ord. deacon (London) Mar. 1619–20, age 24. Perhaps R. of Bignor, Sussex, 1632. (*Peile*, I. 294.)

HASTLER, JOHN. Adm. sizar at CHRIST'S, June 30, 1623. S. of John. B. at Maldon, Essex. School, Romford (Mr Formin). Matric. 1623; B.A. 1626–7. Ord. deacon (Peterb.) Sept. 20; priest, Sept. 21, 1629. C. of Wendon, Essex, 1631. (*Peile*, I. 353.)

HASTLER or HOSLER, RICHARD. Matric. sizar from ST JOHN'S, Easter, 1629; B.A. 1631–2; M.A. 1635.

HASTLER, THOMAS. Adm. sizar at CORPUS CHRISTI, 1620. Of Essex. S. of Edward, of Maldon, Essex. Matric. Easter, 1621; B.A. 1623–4. Mentioned in his father's will (P.C.C.) 1622. Perhaps V. of Chertsey, Surrey, 1633. ('M.A.')

HASTLING, NICHOLAS. Adm. pens. at CLARE, Mar. 20, 1644 5.

HASTY, JOHN. Matric. sizar from PEMBROKE, *c.* 1593. S. of William. Bapt. at Catterlen, Penrith, Cumberland, Jan. 27, 1575–6. B.A. 1595–6; M.A. 1599. Ord. priest (Carlisle) Mar. 1601. V. of Penrith, 1601–53. Buried there June 6, 1659. (*B. Nightingale.*)

HASWELL, WILLIAM. Adm. sizar (age 20) at ST JOHN'S, Oct. 25, 1701. S. of Robert, husbandman. B. t Cornforth, Durham. Bapt. at Bishop Middleham, Jana 30, 1680–1. School, Durham (Mr Rosse). Matric. 1702.

HATCH, CROPLEY. Adm. at CORPUS CHRISTI, 1740. Of Norfolk. Matric. Michs. 1741; B.A. 1743–4. Ord. deacon (Norwich) May, 1744; priest, Sept. 1745. C. of Hackford, Norfolk. Minor canon of Norwich Cathedral. Minister of Bowthorpe and Bawburgh. (*Masters.*)

HATCH, JOHN. Adm. sizar at QUEENS', Mar. 9, 1587–8. Of Essex.

HATCH, JOHN. Matric. pens. from ST JOHN'S, Easter, 1604; B.A. 1607–8.

HATCH, JOHN. Adm. sizar at PETERHOUSE, Sept. 21, 1625. Of Cambridgeshire. Matric. 1626. Migrated to Pembroke. B.A. 1629–30; M.A. 1633. Will of one of these names (P.C.C.) 1648; of Benenden, Kent, clerk.

HATCHE, JOHN. Adm. sizar (age 17) at CAIUS, June 24, 1738. S. of John, butcher, of Thetford, Norfolk. B. there. School, Thetford (Mr Price and Mr Everson). Matric. 1738; Scholar, 1738–42; B.A. 1741; M.A. from Clare, 1745. Fellow of Clare, 1742. Ord. deacon (Norwich) Mar. 14, 1741–2, as C. of Thornham; priest, Sept. 23, 1744, as C. of Rudham. V. of Sedgeford, 1751–93. R. of Ashwicken, 1771–93. (*Venn*, II. 44.)

HATCH, JOSEPH. Matrie. pens. from ST CATHARINE'S, Easter, 1644; B.A. 1647–8.

HATCH, MORRYSON. Adm. pens. (age 16) at CHRIST'S, Aug. 4, 1668. S. of Joseph. B. at Brent-Pelham, Herts. School, Bishop's Stortford (Mr Leigh and Mr Cudworth). Matric. 1668.

HATCH, RICHARD. Adm. sizar (age 17) at ST JOHN'S, June 1, 1681. S. of Thomas, gent. B. at Simpson, Bucks. School, Newport Pagnell (private; Mr Howard). Matric. 1681; LL.B. 1686. C. of Stony Stratford, 1691–1703.

HATCHE, WILLIAM. Matric. pens. from ST JOHN'S, Michs. 1579; B.A. 1582–3; M.A. 1586. Head Master of Tonbridge School, 1586–1615. Will of one of these names (P.C.C.) 1616; of Frant, Sussex, clerk. (J. Ch. Smith.)

HATCHER, FRANCIS. Adm. pens. (age 16) at SIDNEY, June 12, 1634. S. of William, Esq. B. at St Martin-in-the-Fields, London. Bapt. there, Nov. 13, 1618. Schools, Charterhouse, Eton and Stamford (Mr Dugard). Matric. 1636. Adm. at Gray's Inn, as 's. and h. of William, late of Sutterton, Lincs.,' Feb. 3, 1636–7.

HATCHER, HENRY. Matric. pens. from ST JOHN'S, Lent, 1579–80; B.A. 1583–4; M.A. 1587. S. of Thomas (1555).

HATCHER, JOHN. B.A. 1531–2. Of Surrey. M.A. 1535; M.D. 1543–4. Fellow of ST JOHN'S, 1533. Regius Professor of Physic, *c.* 1554. Vice-Chancellor, 1579–80. Of Careby, Lincs. Married Alice, dau. of Edward Green, of London. In 1545 he acquired the site of the Augustinian Friary at Cambridge. Buried at St Edward's, Cambridge, Mar. 24, 1586–7. Will proved (V.C.C. and P.C.C.) 1587. Father of Thomas (1555). He left money for the clock of Gt St Mary's; and, in default of male issue, the site of the Friars, to found a Hall to be called Hatcher's Hall. (H. P. Stokes; *Lincs. Pedigrees*, 469; *Cooper*, II. 7.)

HATCHER, JOHN. Adm. at KING'S, a scholar from Eton, 1584; left in 1587. S. of Thomas (1555), of Careby, Lincs. (and grandson of John, above). Bapt. Dec. 14, 1566. Adm. at the Inner Temple, 1586. Succeeded to his grandfather's estate in Lincs. Knighted. Sheriff of Lines., 1610–1. Buried at Careby, July 27, 1640. Probably father of Thomas (1603). (*Lincs. Pedigrees*, 469.)

HATCHER, THOMAS. Adm. at KING'S, a scholar from Eton, 1555. S. of John (1531–2), M.D. B. at Cambridge. Matric. Michs. 1555; B.A. 1559–60; M.A. 1563. Fellow, 1558–66. Adm. at Gray's Inn, 1565. Of Careby, near Stamford. Antiquary. A friend of Dr John Caius and J. Stow. Author of miscellaneous works, including a catalogue of the fellows and scholars of King's College up to 1572. Buried at Careby, Lincs., Nov. 14, 1583. Will (P.C.C.) 1583. Father of John (above) and Henry (1579–80). (*Cooper*, I. 483; *Lincs. Pedigrees*, 469; *D.N.B.*)

HATCHER, THOMAS. Adm. Fell.-Com. at EMMANUEL, June 18, 1603. Matric. 1603. Doubtless s. of John (1584), of Careby, Lincs., Knt. Adm. at Lincoln's Inn, May 9, 1607. M.P. for Lincoln, 1624–5; for Grantham, 1628–9; for Stamford, 1640–8; for Lincolnshire, 1654–5, 1656–8, 1659–60; for Boston, 1660. Commissioner to Scotland, 1643. Present at the battle of Marston Moor, 1644, and at the siege of York, 1644. Buried at Careby, July 11, 1677. (*D.N.B.*)

HATCHER, THOMAS. Adm. Fell.-Com. at ST CATHARINE'S, Dec. 15, 1675. Doubtless s. of John, of Careby, Lincs., Sheriff of Lincs., 1676. B. Nov. 3, 1660. Sheriff of Lincs., 1712–3. Of Careby, Esq. Died Sept. 6, 1714. (*Lincs. Pedigrees*, 470.)

HATCHETT, ANDREW. Matric. pens. from CHRIST'S, Nov. 1547; B.A. 1550–1; M.A. 1554. Fellow of Jesus, till 1555. Possibly 'Andrew of Walesby, Lincs.; adm. at the Inner Temple, Apr. 25, 1556.' (*Peile*, I. 43.)

HATCHEMAN, RICHARD. Matric. Fell.-Com. from JESUS, Michs. 1544.

HATCLIFF, DAVID. Matric. pens. from PETERHOUSE, Michs. 1566. S. of Christopher. B.A. from Trinity, 1570–1. Ord. deacon and priest (Lincoln) Nov. 23, 1573. V. of Frodingham, Lincs., 1577. R. of Thoresway, 1579. Will (Lincoln) 1615. (*Lincs. Pedigrees*, 471.)

HATLYFFE, GEORGE. Matric. pens. from JESUS, Easter, 1566. Probably s. of William, of Hatcliffe, Lincs. Married Elizabeth, dau. of Sir Francis Ayscough, of South Kelsey, Lincs. Will proved (P.P.C.) July 2, 1602. Probably brother of Thomas (1564). (*Lincs. Pedigrees*, 473.)

HATCLIFF, R. Resident pens. at JESUS, Aug. 1564.

HATTACLYFF, RICHARD. Matric. pens. from TRINITY, Michs. 1547.

HATLEFF or HATLYFF, ROGER. B.A. 1505–6; B.D. 1513–4 (Incorp. from Turin). Will of one of these names (Consist. C. London) 1519; of St Sepulchre's, London, priest. Bequest to PEMBROKE HALL. (J. Ch. Smith.)

HATLEFE, THOMAS. Matric. pens. from JESUS, Michs. 1564. Probably s. of William, of Hatcliffe. Married Judith, dau. of Sir Francis Ayscough, of South Kelsey, Lincs. Living, 1610. Probably brother of George (1566) and father of William (1582).

HATLIFFE, VINCENT (*alias* **JOHN SPENCER**). Matric. pens. from CORPUS CHRISTI, Easter, 1619. Of Lincolnshire. Doubtless s. of George, of Gt Grimsby. Bapt. there, Aug. 31, 1600. B.A. 1622–3. Converted to the Roman Catholic faith while at Cambridge. Entered the Society of Jesus, 1620. Assumed the name of John Spencer. Professor at Liége, 1642. Missioner at Antwerp, 1655. Returned to England, *c.* 1657. Appointed Superior of the Worcester [illegible], *c.* 1658–67. Author of controversial works. Died [illegible] 17, 1670–1. (*Lincs. Pedigrees*, 473; *D.N.B.*)

HATCLIF, WILLIAM. B.A. at PETERHOUSE, 1436–7; M.A. 1439. Fellow, 1437. Probably same as the next.

HATCLYFFE, WILLIAM. M.D. 1454. One of the original scholars of KING'S College, 1441. Proctor, 1440. Physician and secretary to Edward IV. Master of requests and royal councillor. Employed in negotiations with Scotland, 1471; and with German Hanse, 1472. Ambassador to Denmark, 1476. Died 1480. Will, P.C.C. (*Harwood*; *D.N.B.*)

HATCLEFF, WILLIAM. B.A. 1495–6; M.A. 1499. Of Scottow, Norfolk. Fellow of CLARE, 1497. Ord. deacon (Lincoln) Mar. 30, 1499.

HATCLYFF, WILLIAM. Matric. Fell.-Com. from JESUS, Michs. 1582. Probably 1st s. of Thomas (1564), of Hatcliffe, Lincs. Age 24 in 1592. Adm. at Gray's Inn, Nov. 4, 1586. Of Gt Grimsby, 1610; and of Hatcliffe, Esq., 1614. (*Vis. of Lincs.*, 1592; *Lincs. Pedigrees*, 473.)

HATFELT, ——. Scholar at KING'S HALL, *c.* 1461–5.

HATFIELD, ALEXANDER. Matric. pens. from CHRIST'S, July, 1628. Doubtless s. of Ralph, of Letwell, Yorks. Bapt. Sept. 19, 1611. B.A. 1631–2. Fellow of Trinity College, Dublin, 1635. M.A. (Dublin) 1638. R. of Cloghran, Apr. 1, 1640. Married Alice, dau. of Robert Tinley, D.D. Buried Sept. 3, 1650. (*Peile*, I. 395; Hunter, *S. Yorks.*; *Al. Dub.*; M. H. Peacock.)

HATFIELD, CHARLES. Adm. sizar (age 23) at ST JOHN'S, May 16, 1733. S. of Charles, grazier, of Chapel-en-le-Frith, Derbs. School, Chapel-en-le-Frith (Mr Brooks).

HATFIELD, GEORGE. Adm. pens. (age 19) at ST JOHN'S, May 1, 1736. S. of John, gent., of Hatfield, Yorks. B. at Hatfield. School, Chesterfield (Mr Burrow). Matric. 1736; B.A. 1739–40; M.A. 1763. Ord. deacon (Chester) June 1, 1740; priest, Sept. 19, 1741. V. of Long Parish, Hants., 1746–62. V. of Doncaster, Yorks., 1762–85. V. of Otley, 1782–5. Married Catharine, dau. of Thomas Hallows, and widow of John Cromwell. Died May 25, 1785. Buried at Doncaster. (*Scott-Mayor*, III. 473; M. H. Peacock.)

HATFIELD, GERVASSE. Adm. Fell.-Com. (age 16) at CAIUS, Feb. 2, 1590–1. S. of Henry. B. at Wilford, Notts. Schools, Hickling, Notts. and Milton, Leics. Probably of Hatfield Hall, near Wakefield. Married Grace, dau. of Edward Savile, of Stanley Hall, Wakefield. Buried at Wakefield, June 4, 1654. Will proved, 1654. (*Venn*, I. 142; M. H. Peacock.)

HATFIELD, THOMAS. Scholar at KING'S HALL. Left, Apr. 21, 1381.

HATFIELD, WILLIAM. Adm. sizar (age 17) at ST JOHN'S, Dec. 17, 1712. S. of William, gent. B. at Lynn, Norfolk. School, Wisbech (Mr Carter). Matric. 1713; B.A. 1719; M.A. 1726. Incorp. at Oxford, 1735. Ord. priest (Lincoln) Mar. 5, 1720–1. R. of Lilley, Herts., 1721–67. V. of Caddington, Beds., 1729. Died 1767.

HATFORD or HARTFORD, ANTHONY. Matric. sizar from QUEENS', Michs. 1575.

HATHAWAY, EDWARD. Adm. pens. at CLARE, July 6, 1675. Of Osgathorpe, Leics. S. of Edward, of Osgathorpe, clerk. Matric. at Trinity College, Oxford, June 7, 1671, age 15. Probably R. of Thorpe-in-the-Glebe, Notts., 1679. (*Al. Oxon.*)

HATHWAY, ROBERT. Adm. pens. (age 18) at ST JOHN'S, Jan. 9, 1682–3. Previously matric. from Brasenose, Oxford, Mar. 30, 1680. S. of James, clerk. B. at Marden, Heref. School, Hereford (Mr Harvey). Matric. 1683; B.A. 1683–4; M.A. 1687. R. of Evesbatch, Heref., 1686. R. of Castle Frome, 1693. Father of the next. (*Al. Oxon.*)

HATHAWAY, ROBERT. Adm. pens. (age 20) at ST JOHN'S, Feb. 2, 1712–3. S. of Robert (above). B. at Castle Frome, Heref. School, Hereford (Mr Trehern). Matric. 1713; B.A. 1716–7; M.A. 1721. Ord. deacon (London) Mar. 9, 1717–8.

HATHAWAY, SAMUEL. Adm. pens. at EMMANUEL, Jan. 9, 1710–1. Of Hertfordshire. Matric. 1712; B.A. 1715–6.

HATHEWAY, THOMAS, *see* **HADWAY.**

HATHORNWHAIT, GAWEN. Adm. sizar (age 18) at ST JOHN', June 11, 1632. S. of James, husbandman, of Wardle, Rochdale, Lancs. B. there. School, Blackburn, Lancs. (Mr Halstead). Matric. 1632; B.A. 1635–6.

HATHORNTHWAITE, RICHARD. Matric. pens. from CHRIST'S, Apr. 1707. Adm. scholar, Mar. 11, 1708–9; B.A. 1710–1. C. of Heswall, Cheshire, 1718. C. of Neston, 1722. (*Peile*, II. 166.)

HAWTHORNTHWAITE, ——. B.Can.L. 1490.

HATKYILL, THOMAS. Matric. sizar from TRINITY, Michs. 1572.

HATKILL, THOMAS. Adm. sizar (age 19) at CHRIST'S, June 8, 1671. S. of Richard. B. at Settle, Yorks. School, Giggleswick (Mr Briggs). Matric. 1672.

HATLEY, ANDREW. Adm. at CORPUS CHRISTI, 1671. Of Norwich. S. of Christopher (1619), R. of All Saints', Norwich. Matric. 1671; B.A. 1674–5; M.A. 1678. Ord. deacon (Norwich) May, 1675; priest, Dec. 1677. R. of Morningthorpe, Norfolk, 1679. V. of Watton, 1681–91. R. of Threxton, 1681–98.

HATLEY, ARTHUR. Adm. sizar at TRINITY, June 23, 1641.

HATLEY, CHRISTOPHER. Matric. sizar from TRINITY, Easter, 1619; B.A. 1622–3; M.A. 1626. Ord. deacon (Norwich) Dec. 19, 1624. R. of All Saints', Norwich, 1627–79. R. of Morningthorpe, Norfolk, until 1679. Died July 8, 1679, aged 76. Father of Andrew.

HATLEY, EDMUND. Matric. pens. from TRINITY, Easter, 1587; B.A. 1590–1; M.A. 1594.

HATLEY, EDMUND. Matric. sizar from TRINITY, *c.* 1596. Probably ord. priest (Peterb.) Dec. 19, 1619, as B.A. C. of Little Barford, Beds., 1619–26. Buried there Oct. 5, 1626. (W. M. Noble.)

HATLEY, GRIFFITH. Adm. pens. at EMMANUEL, Lent, 1623–4. S. of Robert, of Goldington, Beds., gent. Bapt. Jan. 8, 1605–6. Matric. 1624; B.A. 1627–8; M.A. 1631. V. of Haslingfield, Cambs., 1639. Perhaps 'Griff. Hatley, of Trinity Hall; Taxor, 1641.' (*Vis. of London*, 1634.)

HATLEY, GRIFFITH. Adm. pens. (age 15) at PEMBROKE, May 14, 1645. S. of John, of London, grocer.

HATLEY, GRIFFITH. Matric. pens. from PEMBROKE, Michs. 1658. S. of Robert, of Goldington, Beds. Exhibitioner from Charterhouse. B.A. 1658–9; M.A. 1662; M.D. 1669. Incorp. at Oxford (M.D.) 1669. Practised as physician at Maidstone 40 years. J.P. Died in London, July 31, 1710, aged 71. Buried at Maidstone. Will (P.C.C.) 1710. (*Cole MS.*, 5871, 188, who makes him s. of John Hatley.)

HATLEY, GRIFFITH. Adm. pens. (age 18) at CAIUS, Apr. 22, 1689. S. of Henry, gent. (of Hunton, Kent), citizen of London. B. there. Schools, Maidstone (Mr Lawes) and St Paul's. Matric. 1689; Scholar, 1689–93. Died Apr. 15, 1693. Buried at Hunton, Kent. (*Venn*, I. 487.)

HATLEY, JOHN. B.A. from CLARE, 1590–1. B. at Haslingfield, Cambs. M.A. 1594. Ord. deacon and priest (perhaps Chichester) Mar. 31, 1597. V. of Wadhurst, Sussex, 1603. Married, at Frant, June 5, 1609, Mary Boots. Will (P.C.C.) 1647. (W. C. Renshaw.)

HATELEY, JOHN. Matric. pens. from ST JOHN'S, Easter, 1604.

HATLEY, JOHN. Matric. sizar at TRINITY, Michs. 1637; Scholar, 1641; B.A. 1642–3.

HATLEY, NATHANIEL. Matric. sizar from QUEENS', Michs. 1624. Of Cambridgeshire. B.A. 1627–8; M.A. 1633. C. of Waltham Cross, Essex, 1635–79. (H. Smith.)

HATLEY, PHILIP. Adm. pens. at PETERHOUSE, 1600–1. S. of William, of Caxton, Cambs. Scholar, 1602–8; B.A. 1604–5; M.A. 1608. Perhaps R. of Lammas *with* Little Hautbois, Norfolk. One of these names, clerk, buried at Over, Cambs., Mar. 1, 1651–2. One of these names proved the will (P.C.C.) of his father, William, of Caxton, Cambs. (*Vis. of Cambs.*, 1619; J. Ch. Smith.)

HATLEY, PHILIP. Matric. sizar from KING'S, Easter, 1617.

HATLEY, RICHARD. Matric. pens. from CLARE, Easter, 1560.

HATLEY, RICHARD. Matric. pens. from TRINITY, Easter, 1587.

HATLEY, RO. Matric. sizar from CLARE, Michs. 1547.

HATLEY, ROBERT. Matric. pens. (age 12) from ST JOHN'S, Easter, 1565. One of these names adm. at Gray's Inn, 1569.

HATLEY, ROBERT. Matric. sizar from CLARE, c. 1592; B.A. 1601-2; M.A. 1605. Will of one of these names (P.C.C.) 1629; of Mountfield, Sussex, clerk.

HATLEY, ROBERT. Adm. pens. at EMMANUEL, Mar. 26, 1604. Matric. 1604. Probably s. of Robert. Bapt. at Goldington, Beds., Aug. 4, 1588. One of these names, of Goldington, adm. at the Inner Temple, 1607.

HATLEY, THOMAS. Matric. sizar from CLEMENT HOSTEL, Easter, 1544.

HATLEY, THOMAS. Matric. sizar from TRINITY, Lent, 1580-1.

HATLEY, —— ('rector'). Fee for M.A. or higher degree, 1461-2. Perhaps Walter, V. of St Mary's, Cambridge.

HATLEY, ——. Incorp. 1514-5.

HATLIFFE, *see* **HATCLIFFE.**

HATSELL, JOHN. Adm. pens. at QUEENS', Oct. 6, 1750. Of London. Matric. 1751; B.A. 1755; M.A. 1760. Adm. at the Middle Temple, Dec. 22, 1750. Called to the Bar, May 20, 1757. Clerk of the House of Commons, 1768-1820. An authority on parliamentary procedure. Died Oct. 15, 1820. Buried in the Temple Church. (*D.N.B.*)

HATSELL, NEEDHAM. Adm. pens. (age 17) at TRINITY, Apr. 4, 1716. S. of William, of London. School, Bishop's Stortford, Herts.

HATSELL, THOMAS. Adm. pens. at QUEENS', Jan. 9, 1743-4. Of Surrey. Possibly s. of William (next). Matric. 1744; B.A. 1747-8; M.A. 1751. Ord. priest (Lincoln) Feb. 23, 1752.

HATSELL, WILLIAM. M.A. from EMMANUEL, 1726. S. of Sir Henry, of St Andrew's, Holborn, Knt. Matric. from Jesus College, Oxford, Oct. 10, 1717, age 16; B.A. (Oxford) 1722. Ord. deacon (Peterb.) Mar. 10, 1722-3; chaplain of the Duke of Marlborough; age 23. Probably V. of Mitcham, Surrey, 1724-34. Died Sept. 21, 1772. Will (P.C.C.) 1773; as of Rivenhall, Essex. (*Al. Oxon.*; H. I. Longden.)

HATT, EDWARD. Matric. sizar from ST JOHN'S, Micha. 1601.

HATT, PIGOTT. Adm. Fell.-Com. (age 17) at CHRIST'S, June 22, 1692. S. of Richard. B. at Orsett, Essex. School, Brentwood (Mr Bernard). Adm. at the Inner Temple, Feb. 20, 1692-3. (*Peile*, II. 125.)

HATTERLEY, WILLIAM. Matric. sizar from QUEENS', Easter, 1634. Of Leicestershire. B.A. 1636-7.

HATTON, ALEXANDER. Adm. sizar (age 18) at ST JOHN'S, June 26, 1710. S. of Thomas, gent. B. at Shrewsbury. School, Shrewsbury. Matric. 1710; B.A. 1713-4; M.A. 1718. 'Accidence Master' at Shrewsbury, 1715-54; 3rd Master, 1754-5. Died Aug. 10, 1755. (G. W. Fisher, *Shrewsbury*.)

HATTON, ARTHUR. Adm. pens. at EMMANUEL, Sept. 25, 1656. Of Nottinghamshire. Perhaps s. of William, of Derby, M.D. Matric. 1656. Adm. at Gray's Inn, Feb. 17, 1654-5; and at the Inner Temple, 1658.

HATTON, BENEDICT. Matric. pens. from TRINITY, Lent, 1580-1.

HATTON, CHRISTOPHER. High Steward of the University, 1588. S. of William, of Holdenby, Northants. B. 1540. Of St Mary Hall, Oxford. Adm. at the Inner Temple, Nov. 1559. Became one of Elizabeth's gentleman-pensioners, 1564. Received grant of estates, court offices and an annuity M.P. for Higham Ferrers, 1571; for Northampton, 1572-83; for Co. Northants., 1584-6. Knighted, 1577. Vice-Chamberlain, 1578. A member of the Commissions for the trials of Babington, 1586; and Mary Queen of Scots., 1586. A friend and patron of Spenser. Lord Chancellor, 1587-91. K.G., 1588. Chancellor of Oxford University, 1588. Died Nov. 20, 1591. Buried in St Paul's Cathedral. (*D.N.B.*; *Vis. of Shrops.*, 1623.)

HATTON, CHRISTOPHER. Adm. Fell.-Com. at JESUS, Jan. 12, 1619-20. S. of Sir Christopher, of Kirby, Northants. Bapt. at Barking, Essex, July 11, 1605. M.A. 1622 (*fil. nob.*); D.C.L. (Oxford) 1642. Adm. at Gray's Inn, Mar. 18, 1619-20. M.P. for Peterborough, 1625; for Clitheroe, 1626; for Higham Ferrers, 1640-2. K.B., 1626. Created Baron Hatton of Kirby, 1643. Comptroller of the King's household, 1643-6. Privy Councillor, 1643. Royal commissioner at Uxbridge, 1645. Retired to France, 1648. Governor of Guernsey, 1662-70. F.R.S., 1663. A lover of antiquities; assisted Dugdale during the Civil War. Author, *The Psalter of David*. Died at Kirby Hall, July 4, 1670. Buried in Westminster Abbey. Benefactor to Jesus College. (*D.N.B.*; *G.E.C.*)

HATTON, CHRISTOPHER. Adm. Fell.-Com. at JESUS, Apr. 16, 1669. 3rd s. of Sir Thomas, of Long Stanton, Cambs., Knt. and Bart. Matric. 1669. Adm. at the Middle Temple, May 7, 1670. Succeeded as 5th Bart., Mar. 15, 1684-5. Died Oct. 1720. Buried at Long Stanton. Brother of John (1660), father of John (1700-1) the next. (*G.E.C.*)

HATTON, CHRISTOPHER. Adm. pens. (age 16) at ST JOHN'S, June 8, 1694. S. of Sir Christopher (above), Bart. B. at Thriplow, Cambs. School, Eton. Died *s.p.* before his father. Brother of John (1700-1). (Burke, *Ext. Bart.*)

HATTON, CHRISTOPHER. Adm. pens. (age 16) at ST JOHN'S, June 10, 1732. S. of William (1704), former fellow. B. in London. School, Bury (Mr Kinsman). Matric. 1732; B.A. 1736-7; M.A. 1740. Ord. deacon (Lincoln) Mar. 2; priest, Mar. 9, 1739-40. R. of Girton, Cambs., 1740-56. R. of Marston-Mortain, Beds., 1746-95. R. of Maulden, 1756-95. Chaplain to the Duchess of Bridgewater. Died at Bath, Feb. 20, 1795. Buried at Maulden. (*Scott-Mayor*, III. 443; *G. Mag.*)

HATTON, EDWARD. Matric. sizar from PEMBROKE, Michs. 1585; B.A. (? 1589-90); M.A. from St Catharine's, 1597. Ord. priest (Norwich) Aug. 14, 1591. R. of Brampton, 1592-1601. V. of Westhall, 1596-1614. Preb. of Norwich, 1604-5. Perhaps preb. of Southwell, 1604-25.

HATTON, FRANCIS. Adm. Fell.-Com. (age 17) at SIDNEY, May 30, 1636. S. of Sir Christopher, Knt. B. at Old Palace, Westminster. Matric. 1636; B.A. 1639; M.A. from Jesus, 1643. Ord. deacon (Lincoln) Dec. 14, 1644. Brother of William (1636).

HATTON, GEORGE. Adm. at KING'S, a scholar from Eton, 1629. S. of Sir Robert, of Oakington, Cambs. B. in Westminster. Bapt. at St Margaret's, Dec. 29, 1612. Matric. Michs. 1628. Died as a student, about 1630.

HATTON, HENRY. Adm. pens. (age 19) at ST JOHN'S, Sept. 1634. Previously matric. from Christ Church, Oxford, Sept. 1, 1634. S. of Christopher, gent., of Sulby Abbey, Welford, Northants. B. there. School, Harborough (Mr Orpin). B.A. 1637-8; M.A. 1641. Fellow, 1643; ejected, 1644. Probably minister of Overchurch, Cheshire, in 1648; and in Co. Wexford, 1658. Preb. of Clone, Ferns and Leighlin diocese, 1662. (Burke, *L.G.*)

HATTON, HUMPHREY. Adm. at KING'S, Easter, 1574.

HATTON, JAMES. Matric. sizar from CHRIST'S, Easter, 1576; B.A. 1579-80. Licensed to teach grammar in Norwich diocese, 1583. Ord. priest (Norwich) 1590. R. of Thwaite, Norfolk, 1590-1632. Died 1632.

HATON, JEREMIAH. Adm. sizar (age 17) at CHRIST'S, May 14, 1661. S. of Edward. B. at Calverley, Yorks. School, Bradford (private; Mr Hensliff). Matric. 1661; B.A. 1664-5. Ord. deacon (York) 1666. (*Peile*, I. 597.)

HATTON, JOHN. Adm. Fell.-Com. at JESUS, Sept. 27, 1625. Of Northampton. Matric. 1626; B.A. 1628-9. One of these names, of London, adm. at the Inner Temple, 1630.

HATTON, JOHN. Adm. Fell.-Com. (age 15) at CHRIST'S, Sept. 28, 1660. 2nd s. of Sir Thomas, of Long Stanton, Cambs., Bart. B. there. Taught by Mr Wisborough. Matric. 1661. Died young, *s.p.* Brother of Christopher (1669).

HATTON, JOHN. Adm. sizar at ST CATHARINE'S, 1677. Matric. Easter, 1677.

HATTON, JOHN. Adm. pens. (age 16) at ST JOHN'S, Jan. 13, 1700-1. S. of Sir Christopher (1669). B. at Thriplow, Cambs. School, Bishop's Stortford (Mr Tooke). Matric. 1701. Succeeded as 7th Bart., June 23, 1733. Died July 1, 1740. Brother of Christopher (1694). Father of Thomas (1745). (G.E.C.)

HATTON, RICHARD. Adm. at KING'S (age 16) a scholar from Eton, 1470. B. at Bath (or St Stephen Walbrook). B.A. (? 1474-5); M.A. 1478. Incorp. LL.D. from abroad, 1483-4. Chaplain to Henry VII. Master in Chancery, employed on an embassy to the Emperor Maximilian, 1486. Ord. (Ely) 1495. V. of East Greenwich, Kent. R. of Hanslope, Bucks., 1496. Ambassador to the Low Countries, and to Scotland, 1499. Preb. of St Stephen's, Westminster, 1499-1509. Provost of King's, 1507-9. Died June, 1509. Will, P.C.C. and King's College. (*Cooper*, I. 13; *Harwood*.)

HATTON, RICHARD. Adm. Fell.-Com. (age 14) at SIDNEY, Feb. 22, 1622-3. S. of Sir Robert, Knt. B. at Tottenham, Middlesex. School, Croydon (Mr Wm. Nicolson). Matric. 1623; B.A. 1625. Adm. at Gray's Inn, Mar. 18, 1619-20; s. and h. of Robert, of Lambeth, Knt. Perhaps knighted, Jan. 27, 1644-5. (*Vis. of Surrey*, 1662.)

HATTON, RICHARD. Adm. sizar at TRINITY, Apr. 18, 1668. S. of George. B. at Chowbent, Lancs. Taught by Mr Tayler. Migrated to Christ's, Feb. 27, 1669-70, age 21. Matric. 1668; B.A. 1671-2; M.A. 1676. Ord. deacon and priest (Chester) Feb. 5, 1671-2. V. of Deane, Lancs., 1673. Buried there Sept. 26, 1712. (*Peile*, II. 27; B. Axon.)

HATTON, RICHARD. Adm. scholar at TRINITY HALL, Jan. 3, 1728–9. Of Market Harborough, Leics. Matric. 1728.

HATTON, ROBERT. Adm. pens. (age 12) at PETERHOUSE, June 28, 1657. Of Northamptonshire. Matric. 1658; M.B. 1661. Fellow, 1663–7. Granted leave of absence, Dec. 20, 1663, to travel to Spain with the ambassadors.

HATTON, ROBERT. Adm. pens. at JESUS, Dec. 15, 1703. Of Kent. School, Sevenoaks. Matric. 1704.

HATTON, Sir THOMAS, Bart. Adm. Fell.-Com. (age 17) at ST JOHN'S, Oct. 8, 1745. S. of Sir John (1700), of Long Stanton, Cambs., Bart. B. at Melbourne. School, Bishop's Stortford, Herts. (Mr Mall). Matric. 1745. Succeeded as 8th Bart., July 1, 1740. Died Nov. 7, 1787. Buried at Long Stanton. (*G.E.C.*)

HATTON, WILLIAM. M.D. 1636–7 (Incorp. from Oxford); M.D. of Padua; Incorp. at Oxford, 1633.

HATTON, WILLIAM. Adm. Fell.-Com. (age 16) at SIDNEY, May 30, 1636. S. of Sir Christopher, Knt. B. at Old Palace, Westminster. Bapt. at St Margaret's, Aug. 21, 1619. M.A. from Jesus, 1641–2, on King's visit. Brother of Francis (1636).

HATTON, WILLIAM. Adm. pens. at TRINITY, Apr. 24, 1649. Of Middlesex. Matric. 1649.

HATTON, WILLIAM. Adm. pens. at ST JOHN'S, Mar. 27, 1704. S. of Sir Christopher, Bart. B. at Cambridge. School, Eton. Matric. 1704; B.A. 1707–8; M.A. 1711. Fellow, 1710–6. Taxor, 1711. Ord. priest (Ely) Dec. 20, 1713. Father of Christopher (1732).

HATWELL, or ATWELL, JOHN. Adm. at KING'S, a scholar from Eton, 1498; B.A. 1502–3; M.A. 1506. Of London. Appears in Vol. I as Atwell.

HAUGHTON, *see also* HOUGHTON.

HAUGHTON, ADAM. Adm. pens. at CHRIST'S, 1712. S. of Adam Houghton (1670), R. of Hockliffe, Beds. Bapt. May 3, 1695. Matric. Michs. 1713; Scholar, 1713; B.A. 1717–8. Ord. deacon (Peterb.) Sept. 21, 1717; priest (Lincoln) May 24, 1719. R. of Hockliffe, Beds., 1719. C. of Battlesden, 1730–2. Buried at Hockliffe, May 10, 1743. M.I. (*Peile*, II. 181.)

HAUGHTON, ANTHONY. Matric. sizar from ST JOHN'S, Easter, 1602; B.A. 1605–6; M.A. 1609.

HAUGHTON, EDWARD. M.A. 1641 (Incorp. from Oxford). Probably s. of Thomas, of Houghton, Lancs., *pleb.* Matric. from Merton College, Oxford, Oct. 10, 1634, age 19; B.A. (Oxford) 1637; M.A. not recorded. (*Al. Oxon.*)

HAUGHTON, GEORGE. Matric. pens. from TRINITY, Easter, 1632. Perhaps Geo. Hoton, V. of Bottisham, Cambs., 1635.

HAUTON or HAWTON, HENRY. Matric. sizar from PETERHOUSE, Lent, 1588–9.

HAUGHTON, HENRY. Matric. pens. from TRINITY, Lent, 1625–6; B.A. 1625–6.

HAUGHTON, HENRY. Adm. pens. (age 16) at CHRIST'S, Mar. 8, 1655–6. S. of Francis. B. at Beckbury, Salop. School, Wolverhampton (Mr Rawlet). Matric. 1656. Ord. deacon and priest (Lichfield) Sept. 25, 1663. V. of Lilleshall, Salop, 1663. (*Peile*, I. 570.)

HAUGHTON, HUMPHREY. Matric. sizar from CHRIST'S, Nov. 1575. B. at Stockport, Cheshire. Migrated to Corpus. B.A. 1578–9; M.A. 1582. Ord. priest (London) 1585–6. R. of Chignal St James, Essex, 1585–1620. Will (Consist. C. London) 1620. (J. Ch. Smith.)

HAUGHTON or HAWTON, JOHN. Matric. sizar from CHRIST'S, Easter, 1587. Probably s. of John, R. and patron of Little Chesterford, Essex. B.A. (? 1591–2); M.A. 1595. Succeeded as R. of Little Chesterford, 1617–52. Died 1652. Brother of William (1605) and perhaps of Thomas (1606). (J. Ch. Smith.)

HAUGHTON, JOHN. Matric. Fell.-Com. from CLARE, Easter, 1610.

HAUGHTON, JOHN. Adm. sizar at JESUS, Feb. 4, 1638–9. Of Leicestershire. Matric. 1639, as 'Houton'; B.A. 1642–3.

HAUGHTON, THOMAS. B.A. from ST JOHN'S, Michs. 1606; Licensed to practise medicine, 1610; M.D. 1624. Perhaps brother of John (1587) and William (1605). The R. of Chesterford in his will (Consist. C. London) 1617, mentions a son Thomas. (J. Ch. Smith.)

HAUGHTON, THOMAS. Adm. sizar at EMMANUEL, June 14, 1656. Of Salop. Matric. 1656; B.A. 1659–60. One of these names (M.A.), V. of Sneinton, Notts., 1663–7.

'HAUGHTON, WILLIAM. Incorp. M.A. from Oxford, 1604.' (*Cooper*, II. 299. This rests upon a blunder in Richardson's *Catalogue*, for Wm. Langton. William Haughton, the dramatist, did not graduate.)

HAUGHTON, WILLIAM. Matric. sizar from ST JOHN'S, Easter, 1605. S. of John, R. of Little Chesterford. B. at Chesterford, Essex. B.A. 1608–9; M.A. 1612. Ord. deacon (London) Mar. 8, 1611–2, age 23; C. of Finchingfield, Essex; priest, Dec. 18, 1614. R. of Little Parndon, Essex, 1621–59. Died Nov. 14, 1659, aged 71. Will (P.C.C.) 1666. M.I. Brother of John (1587) and perhaps of Thomas (1606). (J. Ch. Smith.)

HAULSEY or HALSEY, JOHN. Matric. pens. from CLARE, Easter, 1626; B.A. 1629–30; M.A. 1633.

HAULT, ADAM. Matric. sizar from ST JOHN'S, Michs. 1589.

HAULTAIN, PHILIP DE. Adm. Fell.-Com. at EMMANUEL, July 26, 1600.

HAUNTLER, ROBERT. Matric. sizar from CAIUS, Oct. 1593.

HAUSBYE, RALPH. Matric. pens. from ST JOHN'S, Michs. 1554.

HAUSTEAD or HASTED, EDWARD. Adm. sizar at EMMANUEL, June 11, 1602. Matric. 1602, as Hasted; Scholar; B.A. 1606–7. Buried in Trinity Church, Cambridge, Sept. 27, 1607.

HAWSTED, GEORGE. Matric. sizar from TRINITY HALL, Michs. 1544, *impubes*.

HAUSTED, PETER. Matric. sizar from QUEENS', Easter, 1620. Of Northamptonshire. B. at Oundle. B.A. 1623–4; M.A. 1627; D.D. (Oxford) 1642. R. of Hadham, Herts. V. of Gretton, Northants., 1640. R. of Wold, 1643. Chaplain to the Earl of Northampton. Poet and dramatist. His *Rival Friends* was acted before the King and Queen on their visit to Cambridge, Mar. 22, 1631–2. Died in Banbury Castle, 1645, during the siege. (*D.N.B.*; Cooper, *Annals*; H. G. Harrison.)

HAUSTED, WILLIAM. Matric. sizar from QUEENS', Easter, 1629. Of Northamptonshire. B.A. 1632–3; M.A. 1636. Perhaps V. of Saltby, Leics., 1652–6; and also R. of Muston, 1662–5. Admon. (Leicester) 1665.

HAUSTHORPE, *see* OUSTHORPE.

HAUXLEY, HENRY. Adm. sizar (age 16) at CHRIST'S, Apr. 18, 1667. S. of John, of Milton, Derbs. B. there. School, Repton (Mr Ullock). Matric. 1669; B.A. 1670–1. Ord. deacon (Peterb.) Mar. 3, 1671–2; priest, Sept. 24, 1676. (*Peile*, II. 10.)

HAU(?N)YSTON, WILLIAM. Matric. sizar from ST JOHN'S, Easter, 1605.

HAVARD, DAVID. M.A. from ST JOHN'S, 1719. S. of Thomas, of Llanybyther, Carmarthen. Matric. from Jesus College, Oxford, July 7, 1694, age 18; B.A. (Oxford) 1698. R. of Llanvihangel-by-Usk, Monmouth, 1700. V. of Aberguilly, Carmarthen, 1709. Canon of St David's, 1709. R. of Llanedy, Carmarthen, 1721. (*Al. Oxon.*)

HAVER, THOMAS. Matric. pens. from TRINITY, Michs. 1559.

HAVERCROFT, WILLIAM. Adm. sizar at TRINITY, Easter, 1636. Matric. pens. Michs. 1637.

HAVERS, CLOPTON. Adm. pens. at ST CATHARINE'S, May 6, 1668. S. of Henry (? 1637), clerk. Extra-licentiate R.C.P., 1684. M.D. of Utrecht, 1685. Practised in London. F.R.S., 1686. Author, anatomical; his name is commemorated in the term 'Haversian canals.' Died Apr. 1702. Admon. (P.C.C.) 1702; as of Fenchurch St. (*D.N.B.*)

HAVERS, GILBERT. Adm. at TRINITY, June 20, 1649; a scholar from Westminster, 1650. Of Suffolk. 2nd s. of Gilbert, of Tuddenham St Martin, Suffolk, Esq. B.A. 1652–3; M.A. 1658. Adm. at Gray's Inn, June 6, 1649. Student of physic; assisted in the translation of Dr Sydenham's works. One of these names, of Kew, Surrey, buried at Richmond, Sep. 30, 1697. Admon. (P.C.C.) 1698. (J. Ch. Smith; *Al. Westm.*; *Pedigree in Vis. of Suff.*, 1664.)

HAVERS or HAVER, HENRY. Matric. sizar from ST CATHARINE'S, Michs. 1637. Of Essex. Chaplain to the Earl of Warwick. V. of Chipping Ongar, Essex, *c.* 1643. Minister at Fifield, 1649–50. R. of Stambourne, 1651; ejected, 1662. In presbyterian orders. (*Calamy*, I. 521; *Davids*, 470.)

HAVERS or HAVER, JOHN. Adm. Fell.-Com. (age 16) at CHRIST'S, June 5, 1629. S. of Thomas. B. in London. School, Stockerston, Leics. (Mr Nunne). Matric. 1629. Adm. at Gray's Inn, Aug. 7, 1629. (*Peile*, I. 400.)

HAVERS, JOHN. Matric. sizar from ST CATHARINE'S, Easter, 1633. Of Suffolk. B.A. 1636–7.

HAVERS, PHILIP. 'B.A. of ST CATHARINE'S' when ord. deacon (Norwich) May, 1674. No such graduate found.

HAVERS, THOMAS. Adm. pens. at TRINITY, June 30, 1675. Matric. 1675; B.A. 1678–9; M.A. 1682. Ord. deacon (Norwich) Feb. 1680–1; priest, Aug. 1683. R. of Framlingham Earl, Norfolk, 1683. Licensed by the Bishop to practise medicine, 1692.

HAVERYDGE, JOHN. Matric. sizar from TRINITY, Easter, 1560. V. of Roxton, Beds.; 'ord. priest (Lincoln) Sept. 19, 1563; bred in the schools.' Will (P.C.C.) 1605; Haverigge.

HAVETT, JAMES. Adm. at CORPUS CHRISTI, 1683. Of Norfolk. Matric. 1683; B.A. 1686-7. R. of Sternfield, Suffolk, 1691.

HAVETT, JOHN. Adm. at CORPUS CHRISTI, 1682. Of Norwich. Matric. 1682; B.A. 1685-6; M.A. 1689. R. of Marsham, Norfolk, 1707-14. P.C. of St Giles', Norwich, 1709-14. Buried at St Andrew's, Norwich, May 3, 1714.

HAVILL, GEORGE. Adm. sizar (age 18) at ST JOHN'S, Nov. 8, 1650. S. of George, husbandman, of Dedham, Essex. B. there. School, Dedham (Mr Eaden).

HAVISETT or HETHERSETT, THOMAS. Matric. pens. (age 17) from PEMBROKE, Easter, 1634. S. of Edmund. B. at Thetford, Norfolk. B.A. from Trinity, 1637-8; M.A. 1641. Ord. deacon (Norwich) May 9, 1638-9; priest, Sept. 1661.

HERWARDEN, HENRY DE. LL.D. Chancellor of the University, 1335-7. Imprisoned in Newgate for maintaining the privileges of the University. (Cooper, *Annals*, I. 16.)

HAWARDEN, HUMPHREY. D.Can.L. 1470-1. (Had studied at Oxford.) Dean of the Arches and Dean of the Peculiars, 1503-15. Preb. of Lichfield, 1482. V. of Shoreham, Kent, 1487-1500. R. of Wrotham, Kent, till 1515. Commissary of the Archbishop of Canterbury. R. of St Mary Aldermary, London, 1493. Will (P.C.C.) 1515. (*Hennessy*.)

HAWARDEN, SAVAGE. Adm. at KING'S, a scholar from Eton, 1599. S. of John, of Widnes, Lancs., gent. B. at Prescot, Lancs., Sept. 29, 1582. Fellow, 1602, till 1603. Adm. at Gray's Inn, Feb. 20, 1601-2. Author, Latin poems. (*Vis. of Chesh.*, 1613; *Vis. of Lancs.*, 1613; *Cooper*, II. 385.)

HAWERDEN, ——. B.A. 1477-8.

HAWBOROUGH, ROBERT. D.D. 1475-6. Fellow of CLARE, as 'Hawburn,' May 1, 1448. 'B.A.' Proctor, 1456-7.

HAWCRED, ——. Adm. at EMMANUEL, Lent, 1627-8.

HAWE, GEORGE. Adm. sizar (age 16) at ST JOHN'S, Oct. 7, 1650. S. of George, chandler, deceased. B. at Worcester. School, Biddenden, Kent. Probably matric. 1650, as 'Shawe.'

HAWE, JAMES. Adm. pens. at QUEENS', Oct. 23, 1583. Of London.

HAWE, JOHN. Matric. pens. from TRINITY, Lent, 1577-8.

HAWGH, NICHOLAS. Matric. Fell.-Com. from MAGDALENE, Lent, 1564-5.

HAWGHE, WALTER. Matric. pens. from CORPUS CHRISTI, Michs. 1551; B.A. 1554-5. Fellow of Jesus, 1563-4. (Perhaps at Christ's, in 1555-6.) Probably licensed to practise medicine, 1559. One of these names Head Master of Norwich School, 1562-70. (*Peile*, I. 62.)

HAUGH, ——. Adm. at CORPUS CHRISTI, 1544. Perhaps Robert, Commissary to the Archdeacon of Suffolk, 1573.

HAWDON, FRANCIS. Adm. pens. (age 16) at SIDNEY, Mar. 16, 1671-2. Only s. of Cuthbert, gent. B. at Durham. School, Durham. Adm. at Lincoln's Inn, May 9, 1673.

HAWDEN, GEORGE. Matric. sizar from TRINITY, 1598, as 'Hoyden'; B.A. 1601-2; M.A. 1605. Ord. deacon and priest (Peterb.) Sept. 23, 1604. R. of Swayfield, Lincs., 1608. V. of Bytham, 1614-24.

HAWDEN, GEORGE. Adm. sizar (age 20) at ST JOHN'S, June 28, 1671. B. at Grantham, Lincs. School, Grantham. Matric. 1674; B.A. 1674-5. Ord. deacon (Peterb.) Sept. 19, 1675; priest, May 21, 1676.

HAWDEN, JOHN. B.A. from ST JOHN'S, 1610-1; M.A. 1614. Perhaps eldest s. of the next.

HAWDYN, RALPH. Matric. sizar at CHRIST'S, Dec. 1572; B.A. 1576-7; M.A. 1580. Probably V. of Maldon, Essex, 1600-20. Will (Consist. C. London) 1620; mentions son John. (J. Ch. Smith.)

HAWDEN, RALPH. Adm. sizar (age 17) at SIDNEY, Sept. 17, 1619. S. of Cuthbert. B. at Durham. School, Durham. Matric. 1619; B.A. 1623-4; M.A. 1627. Master at Houghton-le-Spring Grammar School, Durham, 1631-2.

HAWDON or HAUDON, WILLIAM. Adm. sizar (age 19) at PEMBROKE, May 22, 1635. S. of James. B. at Lead Hall, Tadcaster, Yorks. B.A. 1638-9.

HAWES, HAWYS or HAYES, CHARLES. Adm. pens. at TRINITY, May 27, 1674, as Hayes. Matric. 1674; B.A. 1674-5, as Hawys. Perhaps V. of Chebsey, Staffs.

HAWES, CHRISTOPHER. At MAGDALENE for two terms. B. in the parish of St Mary Abchurch, London, c. 1562. Ord. priest (London) June 8, 1591. At Revesby, Lincs. (curate) for nine years. Preacher (London). V. of Rowston, Lincs., 1602. Father of Edward (1606).

HAWYS, EDMUND. Adm. pens. (age 18) at CAIUS, May 18, 1636. S. of Stephen, gent., of Cotes, in North Pickenham, Norfolk. B. at Griston. School, East Dereham (Mr Ives). Matric. 1636. Adm. at Gray's Inn, June 22, 1642. (*Venn*, I. 321.)

HAWES, EDWARD. Matric. sizar from KING'S, c. 1596.

HAWES, EDWARD. Adm. pens. at ST JOHN'S, June 23, 1606. S. of Christopher (above), V. of Rowston, Lincs. School, Westminster. Migrated to Caius, June 9, 1607, age 17. Scholar, 1607. Author of *Trayterous Percyes and Catesbyes Prosopopeia*, while still at school. A copy of this work was sold to Dr Rosenbach, of New York, Mar. 10, 1921, for £200. (*Venn*, I. 195; *D.N.B.*)

HAWES, FRANCIS. B.A. from TRINITY, 1644-5. Ord. priest (Down) Feb. 22, 1648-9. R. of Kessingland, Suffolk, 1661-3.

HAWES, GEORGE. Matric. pens. from ST JOHN'S, Easter, 1607.

HAWES, GREGORY. Matric. pens. from CORPUS CHRISTI, Easter, 1607, as 'George.' Of Suffolk.

HAWES, GUSTAVUS. Adm. sizar at TRINITY, Feb. 11, 1656-7. Matric. 1656-7; B.A. 1661-2; M.A. from King's, 1665. Ord. deacon (Ely) Mar. 14, 1662-3; priest (Lincoln) Mar. 6, 1663-4. Chaplain at King's, 1663. Chaplain to the Duke of Rutland. V. of Croxton Kerrial, Leics., 1669-80. R. of Redmile, 1680-94. R. of Ailestone, 1694-1715-6. Died Feb. 20, 1715-6, aged 76. M.I. at Ailestone. Will, Leicester. (Le Neve, *Mon.*, III. 272.)

HAWES, HENRY. Matric. pens. from TRINITY, Michs. 1551; Scholar, 1552; B.A. 1555-6; M.A. 1559. Fellow, 1555. Will of 'H. Hawes, M.A., Trinity,' proved (V.C.C.) 1559. One of these names (Hausse, House), M.A., ord. priest (Ely) Dec. 21, 1576.

HAWES, HENRY. Adm. sizar at TRINITY, July 7, 1641.

HAWES, HENRY. Adm. pens. (age 18) at TRINITY, May 28, 1695. S. of John, of Stanwell, Middlesex. B. there. School, Westminster. Matric. 1695; Scholar, 1696; B.A. 1698-9; M.A. 1702. Fellow, 1701. Ord. deacon (Lincoln) Apr. 12, 1702; priest (Norwich) Apr. 1702. One of these names preb. of Salisbury, 1750-9. Died Mar. 13, 1759.

HAWES, HENRY. Adm. sizar (age 18) at TRINITY, May 2, 1727. S. of William, of Devon. School, Plymouth (Mr Bedford). Matric. 1727; B.A. 1730-1.

HAWES, JAMES. Adm. pens. at EMMANUEL, Feb. 22, 1630-1. Of Middlesex. Matric. 1631.

HAWES, JOHN. Matric. sizar from EDMUND'S HOSTEL, Easter, 1545. Probably the same who was scholar at Gonville Hall, in 1551. Ord. deacon (London) Oct. 4, 1551; 'had been 7 years at Gonville Hall. B. at Walsham-in-the-Willows, Suffolk; aged 26.' Probably s. of John, of Cranmer, in Walsham. Ord. priest (Norwich) Dec. 1551. Probably re-ordained by Dr Bonner, the Marian Bishop of London, 1554. R. of Rickinghall Inferior, Suffolk, 1554-60. Buried Apr. 1, 1560. (*Venn*, I. 36; *Frere*; V. B. Redstone.)

HAWES, JOHN. Adm. pens. at CORPUS CHRISTI, 1576. Matric. Lent, 1577-8; B.A. 1580-1. Perhaps V. of Brandeston, Suffolk.

HAWES, JOHN. Adm. scholar (age 17) at CAIUS, Feb. 17, 1585-6. S. of John, of Walsham, Suffolk. School, Bury St Edmunds (Mr Wright). Resident, 1589. (*Venn*, I. 127.)

HAWES, JOHN. Adm. pens. at CORPUS CHRISTI, May 17, 1615. B. at Wymondham, Norfolk. Matric. 1615; Scholar, 1618; B.A. 1618-9; M.A. 1622; M.D. 1629. Fellow, 1619-22. Licensed to practise medicine, 1623. Practised physic at Wymondham. Died Dec. 15, 1679. M.I. at Wymondham. Father of the next. (Le Neve, *Mon.*, III. 152; *Masters*.)

HAWES, JOHN. Adm. pens. at CORPUS CHRISTI, Apr. 24, 1650. S. of John (above), of Wymondham, Norfolk. Matric. 1650; B.A. 1653; M.B. 1655; M.D. 1660. Practised at Wymondham. Died there Aug. 19, 1683. M.I. there. (*Masters*.)

HAWES, JOHN. Adm. scholar at CORPUS CHRISTI, 1674. Of Norwich. (? S. of the above.) Matric. 1676; B.A. 1677-8; M.A. 1681; M.D. 1688. Fellow, 1682-5. Practised as physician for many years at Wymondham, Norfolk. F.R.C.P., 1692. Censor. Harveian orator, 1721. Died May 19, 1736. Perhaps brother of William (1680-1). (*Munk*, I. 496; *Masters*.)

HAWES, JOHN. Adm. sizar (age 15) at PEMBROKE, Apr. 24, 1684. S. of Edward, of Sussex, gent. Matric. 1684; B.A. 1687-8; M.A. 1691. Fellow of Peterhouse, 1691-4. Ord. priest (Lincoln) Feb. 12, 1692-3. R. of Berwick, Sussex, 1695. V. of Alciston, 1696-1743. Buried at Berwick, Jan. 7, 1742-3. Father of John (1715-6). (W. C. Renshaw; *T. A. Walker*, 189.)

HAWES, JOHN. Adm. at CORPUS CHRISTI, 1688. Of Suffolk. Matric. 1689; B.A. 1692-3. Probably died 1727, aged 58. M.I. at Wymondham. (*Masters*.)

HAWES, JOHN. Adm. pens. (age 17) at PETERHOUSE, Mar. 2, 1715–6. S. of John (1684), R. of Berwick and Alciston, Sussex. School, Lewes. Matric. 1715–6; Scholar, 1716; B.A. 1719–20; M.A. 1723. Ord. deacon (London) Mar. 5, 1720–1. R. of All Saints', Lewes, 1725–33; or V. of Glynde, 1725–50. R. of Berwick, Sussex, 1743. V. of Alciston, 1743–7. (*T. A. Walker*, 233.)

HAWES, JOHN. Adm. scholar at JESUS, Feb. 21, 1729–30. Of Kent. School, Sevenoaks. Matric. sizar Michs. 1730; B.A. 1733–4. R. of Charlton, Dover, 1742–7. Died 1747.

HAWES, JOHN. Adm. sizar at TRINITY, Oct. 2, 1734. Matric. 1734. One of these names, s. of Henry, of Stoke Damarell, Devon, clerk, matric. at Exeter College, Oxford, May 3, 1737, age 19; B.A. (Oxford) 1738; M.A. 1741. Will of one of these names (P.C.C.) 1788; of Fugglestone, Wilts., clerk. (*Al. Oxon.*)

HAUES, NATHANIEL. Matric. pens. from ST CATHARINE'S, Lent, 1637–8. Of London. S. of Andrew, of London, fishmonger. Age 12 in 1633. Died Jan. 20, 1700–1, aged 79. M.I. in Christ's Hospital Cloisters, London, to Nathaniel Haws, late citizen of London and treasurer of Christ's Hospital, 1683–99. Father of Thomas (1678). (*Vis. of London*, 1633–4.)

HAWES, RICHARD. Adm. pens. at CORPUS CHRISTI, June 10, 1620. Of Suffolk. School, Ipswich. Matric. 1620; B.A. 1623–4; M.A. 1627. R. of Humber, Heref. R. of Ilketshall St John's, Suffolk, 1627. R. of Kentchurch, c. 1640–60. R. of Leintwardine, 1659–62, ejected. Tried by a royalist council for supposed conspiracy; the charge was dismissed, but he was subjected to much persecution from the soldiery. Afterwards lived at Weobley, then at Abergavenny and latterly at Awre, Gloucs. Died Dec. 1668, aged 64. (*Calamy*, II. 31; *Masters*; *D.N.B.*)

HAWES, ROBERT. Matric. pens. from TRINITY, c. 1592; B.A. 1596–7; M.A. from Jesus, 1600. Ord. deacon and priest (Peterb.) Nov. 17, 1598. C. of Gaywood, Norfolk. R. of Gunton, Suffolk, 1623–39. Father of Thomas (1631–2).

HAWYS, ROGER. Adm. sizar at KING'S, c. 1692. S. of William, mercer, of Norwich. B. there. School, Norwich (Mr Burton). Matric. Lent, 1692. Migrated to Caius, May 15, 1694, age 19. Scholar, 1694–9; B.A. 1695–6; M.A. 1699; D.D. 1713. Fellow, 1699–1709. Moderator, 1704. Ord. deacon (London) June, 1699; priest (Norwich) Dec. 23, 1699. R. of Weeting, Norfolk, 1709. Died May 21, 1749. Father of the next. (*Venn*, I. 495.)

HAWYS, ROGER. Adm. pens. (age 17) at CAIUS, July 3, 1729. S. of Roger (1694), R. of Weeting, Norfolk. B. there. Schools, Thetford and Bury. Matric. 1729; Scholar, 1729–31. Died Dec. 18, 1731. M.I. at Weeting St Mary. Will (Norwich C.C.). (*Venn*, II. 31.)

HAWES, SAMUEL. Adm. pens. (age 16) at PETERHOUSE, Sept. 23, 1645. Of London. School, Coventry. B.A. 1649–50; M.A. 1655.

HAWE, SAMUEL. Adm. pens. (age 15) a ST JOHN'S, Oct. 30, 1695. S. of George, clerk. B. at Chatteris, Cambs. School, Burwash, Sussex (private; Mr Goldham). Matric. 1696. Buried at All Saints', Cambridge, Sept. 22, 1699.

HAWISSE, THOMAS. B.D. 1515–6. A friar.

HAWES, THOMAS. Matric. pens. from CHRIST'S, Nov. 1570; B.A. 1574–5; M.A. from Pembroke, 1578. Fellow of Caius, 1578–84. Possibly R. of St Leonard's, Colchester, 1615–40. 'Mr Thomas Hawes, Cantabrigiensis' was adm. at Basel University, Sept. 1584. (*Venn*, I. 96.)

HAWES, THOMAS. Matric. sizar from CLARE, c. 1595. Migrated to Peterhouse. Scholar there, 1596–1602; B.A. 1598–9; M.A. 1602. Perhaps ord. deacon and priest (Peterb.) Nov. 17, 1598. Preacher at Little St Mary's, Cambridge, 1610. V. of Gaywood, Norfolk. Perhaps R. of St Leonard's, Colchester, 1615–40.

HAWES, THOMAS. Adm. pens. (age 16) at SIDNEY, Mar. 4, 1621–2. S. of Thomas, alderman of Bedford. B. there. Bapt. at St Mary's, Dec. 8, 1605. School, Ravensdon (private; Mr Dan. Gyst). Matric. 1622; B.A. 1625. Adm. at Lincoln's Inn, Jan. 21, 1625–6. Probably brother of William (1632).

HAWYS or HAWTIS, THOMAS. Adm. pens. (age 18) at CAIUS, Feb. 11, 1631–2. S. of Robert (1592), minister, of Lowestoft, Suffolk. School, Lowestoft, under his father. Matric. 1632; Scholar, 1633–6; B.A. 1635–6.

HAWES, THOMAS. Adm. sizar (age 16) at MAGDALENE, Apr. 2, 1647. S. of Thomas, of Berkhampstead, Herts. Matric. 1647; Scholar; B.A. 1650–1; M.A. 1654. Doubtless of Berkhampstead St Peter, Herts., clerk. (*Clutterbuck*, I. 303.)

HAWES, THOMAS. Adm. sizar at ST CATHARINE'S, June 19, 1678. Of Coventry. Matric. 1678, as 'Haus'; B.A. 1681–2; M.A. 1685. Incorp. at Oxford, 1684. Ord. deacon (Norwich) Mar. 1681–2; priest, Sept. 1683. V. of Ramsbury, Wilts., 1685–1717. Preb. of Salisbury, 1695–1717. R. of Avingtou, Berks. Died 1717. (*Al. Oxon.*)

HAWES, THOMAS. M.A. 1678 (Incorp. from Oxford). S. of Nathaniel (1637–8), of London, gent. B. May 23, 1655. School, Merchant Taylors'. Matric. from St John's College, Oxford, Nov. 21, 1671, age 15; B.A. (Oxford) 1675; M.A. 1678. Adm. at Gray's Inn, 1682. Will (P.C.C.) 1697. (*Al. Oxon.*; J. Ch. Smith.)

HAWES, THOMAS. Adm. pens. at EMMANUEL, Jan. 19, 1679–80. 'Grecian' from Christ's Hospital. Of Middlesex. Matric. 1681; B.A. 1683–4; M.A. 1687. Ord. deacon (London) May 26, 1689; priest, Mar. 16, 1689–90. Perhaps R. of Ampton, Suffolk, 1690. R. of Croxton, Cambs., 1705.

HAWES, THOMAS. Adm. sizar at EMMANUEL, Jan. 23, 1721–2. Of Middlesex. B.A. 1725–6. Ord. deacon (Ely) Dec. 18, 1726; priest (Lincoln) Mar. 2, 1728–9.

HAWYS, THOMAS. M.B. 1741 (*Lit. Reg.*). One of these names, M.D., physician to the Charterhouse. Buried there Jan. 22, 1763. Admon., P.C.C.

HAWES, WILLIAM. Matric. pens. from TRINITY, Michs. 1560; B.A. 1564–5; M.A. 1568; B.D. from Clare, 1586. Proctor, 1584–5. Ord. deacon (Ely) Sept. 21, 1570. R. of Lawford, Essex, 1585–1615. University preacher, 1586. Died 1615. Will (consist. C. London) 1615.

HAUES (?), WILLIAM. B.A. from TRINITY, 1573–4.

HAWES, WILLIAM. Adm. pens. at EMMANUEL, Oct. 12, 1632. Of Bedfordshire. (Doubtless s. of Thomas; bapt. at St Mary's, Bedford, June 11, 1615.) Matric. 1632; B.A. 1636–7. One of these names, M.D. of Padua, 1644, was incorp. at Oxford, 1663. Hon. fellow R.C.P., 1664. Will (P.C.C.) 1689, of Wm. Hawes, of Islington, Middlesex, M.D. Probably brother of Thomas (1621–2). (J. Ch. Smith; *Munk*, I. 333.)

HAWES, WILLIAM. Adm. scholar at CORPUS CHRISTI, Mar. 8, 1680–1. Of Norwich. Matric. 1681; B.A. 1684–5; M.A. 1693. V. of Wymondham, Norfolk, 1691. V. of Wicklewood, 1697–1701. Died May 16, 1701. M.I. at Wymondham. Perhaps brother of John (1674). (*Masters*.)

HAWES, ——. *Cautio* for degree, 1482–3.

HAWES, —— 'Junior.' Adm. at CORPUS CHRISTI, 1576.

HAWES, ——. Adm. at KING'S, 1592–3.

HAWFEN or HAUGHFEN, JOHN. Adm. Fell.-Com. (age 18) at ST JOHN'S, July 4, 1668. S. of Geoffrey, deceased, of Alderton, near Woodbridge, Suffolk. B. there. School, Woodbridge (Mr Broome). Matric. 1669, as Haufen. Of Little Bealings, Suffolk. Married Elizabeth, dau. of Robert Fynn, of Barham. Died July 24, 1719. Buried at Barham. (Davy, *Suff. MSS.*)

HAWFEENE, WILLIAM. Matric. pens. from TRINITY, Michs. 1615.

HAWFIELD, ROBERT. Matric. sizar from ST JOHN'S, Michs. 1606.

HAWFORD, *see also* HALFORD *and* ALFORD.

HAWFORD, BASIL. Matric. pens. from CHRIST'S, July, 1611; B.A. 1614–5.

HAWFORD, DANIEL. Matric. pens. from CHRIST'S, Nov. 1568. Nephew of the Master. B.A. 1573–4; M.A. 1577. Incorp. at Oxford, 1584. Ord. deacon (Peterb.) May 18, 1580; priest, Aug. 10, 1581. R. of Clipston, Northants., 1580; and of East Farndon, 1588. Died at East Farndon, Nov. 11, 1622. Buried there. M.I. Will (P.C.C.) 1622. Left £5 for books for the library at Christ's College. Brother of Henry (1574). (*Peile*, I. 109; H. I. Longden.)

HAWFORD, EDWARD. B.A. from JESUS, 1542–3. S. of Thomas, of Clipston, Northants. M.A. from Christ's, 1545; B.D. 1554; D.D. 1564. Proctor, 1552–3. Fellow of Christ's, 1543. Master of Christ's, 1559–82. Vice-Chancellor, 1563–4. R. of Glemsford, Suffolk, 1553–74. R. of Clipston, Northants., 1554. R. of Kegworth, Leics., 1560. Preb. of Chester, 1561–82. Chiefly responsible for the University Statutes drawn up in 1570. Died Feb. 14, 1581–2. Benefactor to Christ's. (*Peile*, I. 28; *Cambs. Vis.*, 1619; *D.N.B.*; *Cooper*, I. 448.)

HAWFORD, EDWARD. Matric. pens. from CHRIST'S, Nov. 1570. Perhaps s. of William, brother of the Master. Probably ord. priest (Peterb.) Sept. 18, 1572. One of these names R. of Gilmorton, Leics., 1573–1605. (*Peile*, I. 115.)

HAWFORD, EDWARD. Adm. sizar at CHRIST'S, Mar. 3, 1641–2; previously adm. Apr. 10, 1632, age 17. S. of Edward. B. at Kegworth. School, Repton. Matric. 1632; B.A. 1641–2. (*Peile*, I. 480.)

HAWFORD, HENRY. Matric. sizar from CHRIST'S, May, 1574. Nephew of the Master. Given (under the Master's will) the third choice of the three livings: Clipston, Glemsford and Oxborough. Brother of Daniel (1568). (*Peile*, I. 129.)

HAWFORD, RICHARD. Matric. pens. from Christ's, June, 1584.

HAWFORD, ROBERT. Matric. pens. from Christ's, Dec. 1587. B. at Aslackby, Lincs., *c.* 1570. B.A. (? 1593–4); M.A. 1597. Ord. deacon and priest (Lincoln) Sept. 17, 1597. V. of Butterwick, Lincs., 1599. R. of Haceby, 1599–1604. R. of Brigsley, 1604–42. Father of Robert Alford (1619). (*Peile*, I. 191.)

HAWFORD, THEOPHILUS. Adm. sizar at Emmanuel, Easter, 1617. Matric. 1617; B.A. 1620–1. Ord. deacon (Peterb.) June 8; priest, Sept. 21, 1623. R. of Stanton-by-Bridge, Derbs., 1638.

HAWFORD or HALFORD, WILLIAM. Adm. sizar (age 16) at Christ's, May 3, 1665. S. of John. B. at Kegworth, Leics. School, Repton (Mr Ullock). Matric. 1665; B.A. 1668–9; M.A. 1672. Ord. deacon (Peterb.) June 18, 1671; priest (Lincoln) Feb. 6, 1671–2. R. of Longford, Derbs. R. of Bradley, 1672. (*Peile*, I. 617; H. I. Longden.)

HAWFORD, ZACHARY. Matric. pens. from Christ's, May, 1574. S. of Gyles, of Clipston, Northants., yeoman (brother of Edward, 1542–3). B.A. 1577–8; M.A. 1581. Subscribed for priest's orders (Lincoln) July 18, 1587. R. of Thorpe Arnold, Leics., 1586. The father's will (Archd. Northampton) 1608, suggests that Zachary was an only son. (H. I. Longden; *Peile*, I. 129.)

HAWFORD, ——. Scholar of Christ's, 1541–2.

HAWGHE, *see* **HAWE.**

HAWGOBART, ABRAHAM. Matric. pens. from Peterhouse, Michs. 1581. Afterwards at Queens'. B.A. from St Catharine's, 1584–5.

HAWIN, GEORGE. Matric. pens. from Queens', Easter, 1634; B.A. 1637–8; M.A. 1641. Ord. priest (Lincoln) June 5, 1642. R. of Gretford, Lincs., 1641.

HAWKE, ED. Matric. pens. from Peterhouse, Easter, 1605; B.A. 1608–9; M.A. 1612.

HAWKE, ——. Fee for B.A. 1479–80.

HAWKEBROKE, LEWIS. Adm. at King's, a scholar from Eton, 1488.

HAWKER, EDWARD. Adm. pens. (age 18) at Pembroke, May 20, 1712. S. of Edward, of GagBaddow, Essex, Esq. Matric. 1712. Adm. at Lincoln's Inn, May 6, 1712. Perhaps died Oct. 25, 1756. (L. *Mag.*)

HAWKER, JOHN. M.A. 1631 (Incorp. from Oxford). Of Kent. Matric. from Corpus Christi, Oxford, Jan. 21, 1619–20, age 17; B.A. (Oxford) 1621; M.A. 1624. Perhaps R. of Quendon, Essex, 1632. Probably will (P.C.C.) 1652; of White Notley, Essex, clerk. (*Al. Oxon.*)

HAWKER, RICHARD. Matric. sizar from Magdalene, Easter, 1640.

HAWKES, EDWARD. Adm. sizar (age 16) at Christ's, Apr. 21, 1653. S. of Samuel. B. at Burton-on-Trent. School, Newark (Mr Hill). Matric. 1653; B.A. 1656; M.A. 1660.

HAWKES, JOHN. Adm. at King's (age 18) a scholar from Eton, Aug. 22, 1551. ('Hookes' in *Harwood*.) Of Cambridge. Left in 1554. One of these names V. of Kirby Grindalyth, Yorks., 1561–83.

HAWKES, JOHN. Adm. pens. (age 17) at Peterhouse, July 5, 1670. Of Bedfordshire. School, Winchester. Matric. 1671; Scholar, 1671. Migrated to Corpus Christi, 1672. B.A. 1673–4.

HAWKES, KENELM. Matric. from St John's, *c.* 1592; B.A. 1595–6.

HAWKES, THOMAS. Matric. sizar from St John's, Easter, 1627; B.A. 1630–1. One of these names C. of North Benfleet, Essex, in 1637. R. of Althorne, *c.* 1650–61. Died 1661. Will (Consist. C. London) 1661. (H. Smith.)

HAWKES, THOMAS. Adm. sizar (age 16) at St John's, Nov. 4, 1662. S. of Isaac, sadler, of Kent. B. there. Matric. 1662.

HAWKES, WILLIAM. M.A. 1444. Afterwards D.D. Fellow of Pembroke, 1444. Of Yorkshire. Ord. sub-deacon, Sept. 18, 1445. Perhaps will (P.C.C.) 1512; of All Hallows, Barking, London. One of these names R. of Berwick-in-Elmet, Yorks., 1457–71. Probably the University scribe referred to in *Gr. Bk*, A, 10, 13.

HAWKES, WILLIAM. Matric. sizar from Peterhouse, Michs. 1547.

HAWKES, WILLIAM. Matric. sizar from St Catharine's, Easter, 1631. Of London. B.A. 1634–5; M.A. 1638. One of these names V. of Woolwich, 1646–62, ejected.

HAWKEY, DANIEL. Adm. sizar (age 19) at Pembroke, Apr. 8, 1713. S. of Daniel, of Penzance, Cornwall, mercer. Matric. 1713–4.

HAWKEY, HENRY. Adm. sizar (age 19) at Pembroke, Apr. 30, 1678. S. of John, of Pelynt, Cornwall, gent. Matric. 1678; B.A. 1681–2.

HAWKEY, JAMES. Adm. pens. (age 17) at Pembroke, Feb. 26, 1680–1. S. of Reynold, of St Winnow, Cornwall, gent.

HAWKYN, GEORGE. Matric. pens. from Trinity, Easter, 1560.

HAWKINS, ABEL. Adm. sizar (age 17) at Caius, Dec. 19, 1681. S. of Philip, burgess of Cambridge. B. there. School, Perse (Mr Griffith). Matric. 1682; Scholar, 1682–6; B.A. 1685–6. Licensed schoolmaster at Trumpington, Cambs., June 3, 1691. (*Venn*, I. 469.)

HAWKINS, ABEL. Adm. at Corpus Christi, 1745. Of Norfolk. Matric. 1745.

HAWKINS, ABRAHAM. Matric. pens. from St Catharine's, Michs. 1639. Of Essex.

HAWKINS, ADRIAN. Matric. sizar from King's, Easter, 1625; B.A. 1629–30; M.A. 1633. Incorp. at Oxford, 1633. V. of Aberguilly, Carmarthen, 1634. R. of Merthyr, 1635. (*Al. Oxon.*)

HAWKINS, CHRISTOPHER. Adm. pens. (age 17) at Pembroke, June 16, 1711. S. of Thomas, of Trewinnard, St Erth, Cornwall, gent. Matric. 1712. Adm. at the Middle Temple, Dec. 16, 1710. Clerk of Assizes, Western Circuit, 1729. Succeeded his father at Trewinnard. e haps died Apr. 28, 1767. Father of Thomas (1741). (G.r *Mag.*; *Collectanea Cornubiensia.*)

HAWKINS, EDWARD. Matric. pens. from Queens', Easter, 1631 (adm. 1629). Of Hertfordshire. B.A. 1632–3.

HAWKINS, EDWARD. Adm. pens. (age 17) at Christ's, Jan. 3, 1669–70. S. of Edward. B. at Bishop's Stortford. School, Stortford (Mr Cudworth). Matric. 1670. Adm. at the Inner Temple, Nov. 15, 1671. (*Peile*, II. 27.)

HAWKINS, EDWARD. Adm. at Corpus Christi, 1736. Of Hereford. Matric. 1736; B.A. 1739–40. V. of Roughton, Norfolk, 1746–7. Perhaps also R. of North Runcton. Nov. 16, 1779. Will, P.C.C. (G. *Mag.*)

HAWKINS, FRANCIS. Adm. sizar (age 16) at Peterhouse, Jan. 24, 1659–60. Of Northamptonshire. School, Fotheringhay. Matric. 1661; B.A. 1663–4; Scholar, 1664; M.A. 1667; D.D. 1679. V. of Willesden, Middlesex, 1670–99. R. of Gedney, Lincs., 1677. Preb. of St Paul's, 1688–99. Dean of Chichester, 1688–99. Chaplain of the Tower. Died Feb. 19, 1698–9. Admon., P.C.C. Father of Francis (1689), William (1686) and George (1704). (*T. A. Walker*, 115.)

HAWKINS, FRANCIS. Adm. pens. (age 16) at Peterhouse, May 2, 1666. Of Huntingdonshire. School, Peterborough. Matric. 1667.

HAWKINS, FRANCIS. Adm. pens. at Jesus, July 1, 1689. S. of Francis (1659–60), D.D., Dean of Chichester. Matric. 1690; B.A. 1693–4. Will proved, 1743. Brother of William (1686).

HAWKINS, FRANCIS. Adm. at Corpus Christi, 1731. Of Huntingdonshire. Matric. 1731; B.A. 1734–5; M.A. 1738. Ord. deacon (Lincoln) Sept. 21, 1735; p es , Sept. 25, 1737. R. of Higham Gobion, Beds., 1737. ri Perhaps V. of Hexton, Herts., 1772–5. Died Aug. 1775. Will (P.C.C.) 1775; of Higham Gobion. (G. *Mag.*)

HAWKINS, GEOFFREY. Adm. sizar at Emmanuel, 1636. Matric. Easter, 1637; B.A. 1639–40. Ord. priest (peterb.) Sept. 19, 1641. R. of Chesterton, Hunts., *c.* 1640; deprived 1641. R. of Water Newton, 1660–1700. Died 1700. Buried Mar. 31. Father of Geoffrey (1689).

HAWKINS, GEOFFREY. Adm. sizar at Trinity, Feb. 15, 1661–2; B.A. 1665–6; M.A. from King's, 1669. Chaplain at King's, 1666. Ord. priest (Peterb.) June 2, 1667; of King's College.

HAWKINS, GEOFFREY. Adm. sizar (age 15) at Sidney, Dec. 12, 1689. 1st s. of Geoffrey (1636), R. of Water Newton, Hunts. Schools, Peterborough (Mr Warren) and Oundle. Matric. 1690; B.A. 1693–4; M.A. 1708. Ord. deacon (Peterb.) June 3, 1694; priest, May 30, 1697. R. of Water Newton, 1700–19. R. of Higham Gobion, Beds., 1719–26.

HAWKINS, GEORGE. Adm. pens. (age 18) at St John's, June 5, 1704. S. of Francis (1659–60), D.D. B. in London. School, Eton. Matric. 1707; B.A. 1707–8; M.A. 1711. Ord. priest (London) May 23, 1714. Probably R. of St Mary-at-Hill, London, 1737–49. Buried there Nov. 6, 1749, as D.D.

HAWKINS, HENRY. Matric. pens. from Peterhouse, Easter, 1568. S. of John, of Essex (and Ann Yelverton). B.A. 1571–2; M.A. 1575; LL.D. 1591. Fellow, 1575. Proctor, 1583–4. Incorp. at Oxford, 1577. Adm. at Gray's Inn, Mar. 11, 1583–4. Civilian and diplomatist. Received the Queen's pass, July 2, 1586, to go beyond seas with Lord Zouch. In Prague, 1589. Fellowship resigned, 1599. Will (P.C.C. 1631) of St Andrew's, Holborn. Benefactor to the College. (*T. A. Walker*; *Al. Oxon.*)

HAWKINS, ISAAC. Matric. pens. from TRINITY, Easter, 1723; B.A. 1725–6. One of these names s. of William. of Newport, Salop. Attorney, of Burton-on-Trent. Died Feb. 8, 1800, aged 91. (*Misc. Gen. et Her.*, N.S., III. 44.)

HAWKINS, JAMES. Mus.Bac. 1719. Chorister of ST JOHN'S. B. 1662. Organist of Ely Cathedral, 1682–1729. Composer. Died Oct. 18, 1729. Buried in the Cathedral. Father of William (1705). (*D.N.B.*)

HAWKYNS, JOHN. Matric. sizar from TRINITY HALL, Easter, 1550.

HAWKYNS, JOHN. Matric. pens. from MAGDALENE, Easter, 1581.

HAWKINS, JOHN. M.D. 1616 (Incorp. from Padua). 4th s. of Sir Thomas, of Nash, Kent. A staunch Catholic. Resided in Charterhouse Court, London, 1624. Married Frances, dau. of Francis Power, of Bletchington, Oxon. Grammarian and translator. (*Vis. of Kent*, 1619; *D.N.B.*)

HAWKINS, JOHN. Adm. sizar at SIDNEY, June 28, 1619. B. in Devon. Matric. 1619; B.A. 1622–3; M.A. 1626.

HAWKINS, JOHN. Adm. pens. (age 16) at CHRIST'S, July 4, 1627. S. of George. B. at Bishop's Stortford (Mr Newens, Chadwick and Leigh). Matric. 1627. One of these names sequestered to Springfield, Essex, Aug. 1645; gone in 1647.

HAWKINS, JOHN. Adm. pens. at TRINITY, Mar. 7, 1645–6. Of London. Matric. 1646; Scholar, 1647; B.A. 1649–50; M.A. 1653; B.D. 1661. Fellow, 1650. V. of Enfield, Middlesex, 1662–4, resigned. Brother of William (1662).

HAWKINS, JOHN. Adm. sizar at TRINITY, Nov. 1660. Matric. 1661; B.A. 1664–5; M.A. 1668. Ord. deacon (Peterb.) Sept. 23, 1666; priest, Sept. 20, 1668.

HAWKINS, JOHN. Matric. sizar from TRINITY, Michs. 1663.

HAWKINS, JOHN. Adm. sizar at CLARE, May 15, 1674. S. of Henry, of Wellingborough, Northants. Matric. 1674; B.A. 1677–8. Ord. priest (Peterb.) Sept. 19, 1680. Usher at Wellingborough School, 1677. Master, 1681–7. Probably V. of Milton Ernest, Beds., 1684–1721. Married, at Colmworth, Beds., Dec. 17, 1713, Mary Robinson. Buried at Milton Ernest, June 25, 1721.

HAWKINS, JOHN. M.A. from PEMBROKE, 1677. S. of Henry, of Creed, Cornwall. Matric. from New Inn Hall, Oxford, May 30, 1666, age 19. B.A. (Oxford) 1670. V. of St Erney-by-Lelant, Cornwall, 1676. (*Al. Oxon.*)

HAWKINS, JOHN. Matric. from ST JOHN'S, Easter, 1704. Perhaps a mistake for George, above.

HAWKINS, JOHN. Adm. pe . (age 17) at PEMBROKE, Feb. 25, 1708–9. Afterwards Fell.-Com. S. of Philip, of Pennans, in the parish of Creed, Cornwall, gent. Matric. 1709; B.A. 1712–3; M.A. 1716; D.D. 1728. Master, 1728; resigned, 1733. Died Aug. 2, 1736. Brother of Philip (1715–6). (*Coll. Hist.*)

HAWKINS, JOHN. M.A. 1749 (Incorp. from Oxford). S. of John, of St Andrew's, Holborn, clerk. Matric. from Pembroke College, Oxford, Oct. 30, 1742, age 16; B.A. (Oxford) 1746; M.A. 1749. (*Al. Oxon.*)

HAWKINS, JOHN SANDERSON. Adm. pens. (age 17) at ST JOHN'S, July 5, 1712. S. of Robert, clerk. B. at Goldington, Beds. Bapt. June 13, 1695. School, Haydon, Essex (Mr Goodwyn). Matric. 1713; B.A. 1716–7.

HAWKINS, NICHOLAS. Adm. at KING'S, a scholar from Eton, 1514. B. at Putney, *c.* 1496. Nephew of Bishop West, of Ely. B.A. 1518–9; M.A. (? 1522). Said to have been LL.D. R. of Doddington, Cambs., 1519–27. R. of East Dereham, Norfolk, 1520. R. of Snailwell, Cambs., 1526. Archdeacon of Ely, 1527–34. Advocate, 1528. Attended the Convocation, 1529. Ambassador to the Emperor and to Rome, 1532. Nominated Bishop of Ely, 1533. Died of dysentery at Balbase, Arragon (not at Barcelona, as sometimes stated) on his way home, Jan. 1533–4. Will (P.C.C.) dated Dec. 29, 1533; proved, Oct. 20, 1535. (*Cooper*, I. 48; *D.N.B.*)

HAWKINS, PHILIP. Adm. pens. (age 15) at PEMBROKE, Mar. 7, 1715–6. S. of Philip, of Pennans-in-Creed, Cornwall, gent. Adm. at the Middle Temple, Mar. 2, 1716–7. Doubtless of Trewithan, Cornwall. M.P. for Grampound, 1727–38. Died Sept. 6, 1738. Brother of John (1708–9). One of these names, s. of Philip, of Caerleon, Monmouth, clerk, matric. from Jesus College, Oxford, Mar. 31, 1720. (G. *Mag.*; L. *Mag.*)

HAWKINS, REGINALD. Adm. sizar (age 17) at PEMBROKE, June 21, 1684. S. of John, gent. B. in Cornwall. Matric. 1684; B.A. 1687–8; M.A. 1691; D.D. 1719. Fellow, 1691. Proctor, 1708–9. Ord. priest (Lincoln) Feb. 21, 1691–2. V. of Waresley, Hunts., 1712–8. V. of Soham, Cambs., 1718–31. Died Apr. 18, 1731. Will (P.C.C.) 1731.

HAWKINS, RICHARD. Matric. pens. from CORPUS CHRISTI, Lent, 1577–8. One of these names, of London, adm. at the Inner Temple, 1580.

HAWKINS, THOMAS. Adm. sizar (age 17) at PETERHOUSE, July 5, 1656. Of Northamptonshire. School, Peterborough. Matric. 1657; Scholar, 1660; B.A. 1660–1. Ord. deacon (Peterb.) Sept. 22, 1661. Buried at Little St Mary's, Cambridge, Jan. 3, 1661–2.

HAWKINS, THOMAS. Adm. sizar (age 17) at PETERHOUSE, Feb. 29, 1683–4. Of Cambridge. Schools, Cambridge and St Paul's, London. Matric. 1684; Scholar, 1684; B.A. 1687–8; M.A. 1700. Ord. priest (York) Dec. 1690. Perhaps preb. of Southwell, 1704–18. Buried there Jan. 14, 1717–8. (A. B. Beaven.)

HAWKINS, THOMAS. Adm. sizar (age 19) at PEMBROKE, June 6, 1709. S. of George, V. of Sithney, Cornwall. B. at Mawgan, Cornwall. Matric. 1709; B.A. 1714–5.

HAWKINS, THOMAS. Adm. sizar at JESUS, Mar. 31, 1724. Of Nottingham. S. of ——, clerk, deceased. Matric. 1724; Scholar, 1725; B.A. 1727–8. Ord. deacon (Lincoln) June 1, 1729.

HAWKINS, THOMAS. Adm. Fell.-Com. (age 17) at PEMBROKE, Nov. 10, 1741. S. of Christopher (1711), of Trewinnard, Cornwall, Esq. Matric. 1741. Adm. at the Middle Temple, Feb. 12, 1739–40. Colonel in the Guards. M.P. for Grampound, 1747–54. Died at Trewithan, Dec. 1, 1765. (*Bibliotheca Cornubiensis.*)

HAWKYNS, WILLIAM. Matric. pens. from PEMBROKE, Lent, 1563–4. Resident, as scholar, Aug. 1564. One of these names V. of Postling, Kent, till 1588. V. of Waltham, 1588–95.

HAWKINS, WILLIAM. Matric. sizar at CHRIST'S, July, 1619. B. at Long Stanton or Oakington, Cambs. B.A. 1622–3; M.A. 1626. Ord. deacon (Peterb.) Sept. 25; priest, Sept. 26, 1625. C. of Fen Drayton, Cambs., in 1626. C. of Hadleigh, Suffolk; and Master of Hadleigh School, 1626. Poet. Probably died of the plague. Buried at Hadleigh, June 29, 1637. (*Peile*, I. 330; *D.N.B.*)

HAWKINS, WILLIAM. M.A. 1662 (Incorp. from Oxford). B.A. (Oxford) 1653; M.A. 1656; B.D. 1665; D.D. 1676. Fellow of Magdalen College, Oxford, 1653–69. R. of Droxford, Hants. Preb. of Winchester, 1662–91. Married Anne, dau. of Isaac Walton. Died 1691. Buried in Winchester Cathedral. Will (P.C.C.) 1691. Father of William (1698), brother of John (1645–6). (*Al. Oxon.* has confused him with a namesake; J. Ch. Smith; *N. and Q.*, 9th S., VI. 371.)

HAWKINS, WILLIAM. Adm. pens. (age 18) at PETERHOUSE, Sept. 18, 1672. Of Cambridge. School, Leverington, Isle of Ely. Scholar, 1673.

HAWKINS, WILLIAM. Adm. pens. (age 16) at ST JOHN'S, June 26, 1686. S. of Francis (1659–60), D.D. B. at Barn Elms, Surrey. School, Stamford (Mr Smith). Matric. 1687; B.A. 1689–90; M.A. 1693. Fellow, 1692–1701. Ord. deacon (London) June 11, 1693; priest, May, 1696. V. of Willesden, Middlesex, 1699–1736. V. of St Andrew's, Kingsbury, 1699–1736. R. of St Peter-ad-Vincula, Tower. Preb. of St Paul's, 1707–36. Died June 12, 1736. Will (P.C.C.) 1736; of the Tower. Brother of Francis (1689). (*D.N.B.* has confused him with a barrister.)

HAWKINS, WILLIAM. Adm. pens. (age 19) at TRINITY, Oct. 3, 1698. S. of William (1662), deceased, of Winchester. Bapt. Feb. 24, 1678–9, in Winchester Cathedral. School, Winchester. Matric. 1698. Died at Salisbury, Nov. 29, 1748. M.I. in the Cathedral. (*N. and Q.*, 9th S., VI. 371.)

HAWKINS, WILLIAM. Adm. sizar (age 16) at ST JOHN'S, Feb. 2, 1705–6. S. of James (1719), organist. B. at Ely. School, Ely (Mr Tenant). Matric. 1705–6; B.A. 1709–10.

HAWKRIDGE, ROGER. Adm. sizar at CHRIST'S, Jan. 14, 1625–6. S. of William, of Essex. School, Brentwood (Mr Herne). Matric. 1626.

HAUKSBEE, JOHN. Adm. sizar (age 20) at CAIUS, Oct. 17, 1593. S. of John, baker, of Ely. School, Ely (Mr Spight). B.A. 1596–7; M.A. 1600. V. of Earls Colne, Essex, till 1640. Died 1640. Admon. (Consist. C. London) 1640. (*Venn*, I. 150.)

HAWXEY, WILLIAM. Adm. sizar at CLARE, Apr. 14, 1641. Matric. 1641; B.A. 1644. V. of North Shoebury, Essex, 1650. R. of Bulvan, 1661–81. R. of Little Stambridge, 1664–81. Died 1681. (H. Smith.)

HAWKSHAW, BENJAMIN. Adm. pens. (age 16) at ST JOHN'S, Nov. 4, 1689. S. of Richard, deceased. B. at Dublin. Matric. 1689; B.A. 1691–2. Adm. at Trinity College, Dublin, Apr. 15, 1688. B.A. (Dublin) 1693; M.A. (Dublin) 1695. V. of St Nicholas, Dublin. Author, poetical. Died 1738. (*D.N.B.*)

HAWKSHURST, CHRISTOPHER. Matric. pens. from ST JOHN'S, Michs. 1551, as 'Hawksnest.' Of Nottinghamshire. B.A. 1554–5; M.A. 1558. Fellow, 1555.

HAWKESWORTH, EDWARD. Adm. pens. at ST CATHARINE'S, Apr. 9, 1669. Perhaps s. of Joseph (? 1629), late of Burwash, Sussex, clerk. Matric. 1669. Adm. at Gray's Inn, Sept. 20, 1670. Perhaps brother of Josiah (1662).

HAWKESWORTH, FRANCIS. Adm. pens. at JESUS, Nov. 8, 1704. Matric. 1704.

HAWKESWORTH, GEORGE. Adm. sizar (age 17) at ST JOHN'S, J 21, 1650. S. of Nathaniel, clerk. B. at Melsonby, Richmond. School, Danby-on-Wisk (private; Mr Smelt). Matric. 1650; B.A. 1653-4.

HAUKESWORTH, ISRAEL. Adm. sizar at MAGDALENE, June 22, 1652. S. of Thomas (1628), clerk, of Hunslet, Yorks. School, Leeds. Matric. 1653; B.A. 1655. Brother of Thomas (1655).

HAWKESWORTH, JAMES. Matric. sizar from CORPUS CHRISTI, Easter, 1571. B. at Otley, Yorks. B.A. 1573-4; M.A. 1577. Ord. deacon (London) July 21, 1585, age 34. V. of Middleton Tyas, Yorks., 1585-1628.

HAWKSWORTH, JOHN. Adm. sizar (age 18) at MAGDALENE, June 30, 1681. S. of John. B. at Conisborough, Yorks. School, Doncaster. Matric. 1681, as 'Hawkes'; B.A. 1684-5. Ord. deacon (York) Sept. 1685. C. of Barnburgh.

HAWKSWORTH, JONAS. Adm. sizar (age 16) at SIDNEY, Apr. 27, 1629. S. of John, tanner. B. at Denby, Yorks. School, Denby (Mr Ra. Ward). B.A. 1632-3; M.A. 1636. C. of Sandy, Beds., 1641. Brother of Josiah (1625).

HAWKSWORTH, JOSEPH. Adm. pens. at EMMANUEL, May 18, 1629. Of Yorkshire. Matric. 1629; B.A. 1632-3; M.A. 1636. Perhaps R. of Burwash, Sussex, in 1662. (*See* Josiah (1662) and Edward (1669).)

HAWKSWORTH, JOSIAH. Adm. sizar (age 16) at CAIUS, June 18, 1625. S. of John, currier, of Yorkshire. School, Denby (Mr Ward). Matric. 1625; B.A. 1630-1. Ord. deacon (Peterb.) June 5, 1631; priest, May 27, 1632. Probably R. of Conington, Hunts., in 1650. Married, June 12, 1632, Elizabeth, dau. of John Nodder, of Hansworth, Yorks. Brother of Jonas (1629). (M. H. Peacock.)

HAUKSWORTH, JOSIAH. Adm. pens. (age 17) at SIDNEY, Apr. 25, 1662. S. of Joseph (? 1629), R. of Burwash, Sussex. B. at Preston, Sussex. School, Wadhurst (Mr Wilcox). Perhaps brother of Edward (1669).

HAWKESWORTH, PETER. B.A. from ST JOHN'S, 1595-6.

HAWKESWORTH, PETER. Matric. sizar from TRINITY, *c.* 1601.

HAWKSWORTH, PETER. Adm. pens. at EMMANUEL, May 18, 1629. Of Yorkshire. Perhaps s. of Peter (? above), of High Hoyland, Wakefield. Matric. 1629; B.A. 1632-3.

HAWKSWORTH, THOMAS. Matric. sizar from MAGDALENE, Easter, 1628; B.A. 1631-2; M.A. 1635. Ord. priest (York) Sept. 1632. C. of Hunslet, Yorks., 1636. Ejected, 1662. Died at Alverthorpe, Wakefield, Nov. 23, 1667. Father of Israel (1652) and Thomas (1655). (*Calamy*, II. 564.)

HAWKESWORTH, THOMAS. Adm. sizar (age 17) at ST JOHN'S, Dec. 4, 1647. S. of George, husbandman, deceased, of Edlington, near Doncaster, Yorks. B. there. School, Edlington (Mr Kendall). Matric. 1648; B.A. 1651-2; M.A. 1661. Perhaps Master of Doncaster School, 1659-72.

HAWKSWORTH, THOMAS. Adm. sizar (age 15) at MAGDALENE, Apr. 28, 1655. S. of Thomas (1628), clerk, of Hunslet, West Riding of Yorkshire. Matric. 1655; B.A. 1658-9. Brother of Israel (1652).

HAWKSWORTH, WALTER. Matric. pens. from TRINITY, Easter, 1588. S. of John, officer in the Exchequer. Scholar, 1590; B.A. 1591-2; M.A. 1595. Fellow, 1593-1605. Went to Spain as secretary to Sir Charles Cornwallis, 1605. Dramatist. Died of the plague (said to have been poisoned) at Madrid, Oct. 1606. One of these names adm. at Gray's Inn, Aug. 12, 1592. (*Cooper*, II. 441; *Vis. of Yorks.*, 1666; *D.N.B.*; *F.M.G.*, 972).

HAWKSWORTH, WALTER. Adm. pens. (age 18) at CHRIST'S, Dec. 31, 1667. S. of Sir Richard, of Hawksworth, Northallerton. B. at Ainderby, Yorks. School, Northallerton (Mr Smelt). Matric. 1667-8. Adm. at Lincoln's Inn, May 25, 1668. (*Peile*, II. 13; Burke, *Ext. Bart.*; M. H. Peacock.)

HAWKYARD, MATTHEW. Adm. sizar at QUEENS', Oct. 14, 1611. Of Lancashire.

HAWKYARD, THOMAS. Matric. sizar from QUEENS', Easter, 1606. Of Yorkshire.

HAWLEY, CHRISTOPHER. Matric. sizar from MAGDALENE, Easter, 1632; B.A. 1635-6; M.A. 1639.

HAWLEY, FRANCIS. Matric. pens. from CLARE, Easter, 1578; B.A. 1581-2.

HAWLIE, GABRIEL. Matric. pens. from JESUS, Easter, 1560. One of these names Sheriff of Somerset, 1584. Will (P.C.C.) 1604; of Buckland, Somerset, Esq. (*Vis. of Somerset*, 1573.)

HAWLEY, GEORGE, *see* **HALLEY.**

HAWLEY, HENRY. Adm. Fell.-Com. (age 16) at SIDNEY, Oct. 1, 1621. S. of Sir Henry, Knt. B. at Curry Mallett, Somerset. School, Eton. Matric. 1621.

HAWLEY, HENRY. M.A. 1657 (Incorp. from Oxford). S. of Henry (? Richard), M.D., of Oxford. Matric. from Merton College, Oct. 31, 1646, age 15; B.A. (Oxford) 1649; M.A. (Oriel) 1653. Fellow of Oriel. Proctor, 1661. M.B. (Oxford) 1668. (*Al. Oxon.*)

HAWLEY, HENRY. Adm. pens. at EMMANUEL, Feb. 9, 1675-6. Of Stamford, Notts. S. of William, of Loughborough, Leics. Matric. 1675-6; B.A. 1679-80; M.A. 1683; B.D. 1690. Fellow, 1684-1710. R. of Aller, Somerset, 1709-15. Died Jan. 31, 1715. (H. G. Harrison.)

HAWLEY, JOHN. Adm. pens. at TRINITY, Apr. 20, 1636; Scholar, 1638, as Hewley.

HAWLEY, ROBERT. Adm. pens. (age 16) at SIDNEY, Sept. 15, 1621. S. of Thomas, gent. B. at Alford, Lincs. School, Alford. Matric. 1621.

HAWLEY, ROUSE. Mus.Bac. 1719.

HAWLEY, SETH. Adm. sizar at TRINITY, Dec. 12, 1667. Perhaps of Lynn, Norfolk. S. of Seth. Matric. 1667-8; B.A. 1671-2; M.A. 1675. Ord. deacon (Norwich) May, 1673; priest, Aug. 1674. R. of South Wotton, Norfolk, 1674.

HAWLEY, THOMAS. Matric. sizar from QUEENS', Easter, 1575. Of Leicestershire. B.A. 1578-9; M.A. 1582. Perhaps R. of Little Massingham, Norfolk, 1591-1603.

HAWLY, WILLIAM. Matric. sizar from ST CATHARINE'S, Michs. 1627; B.A. from Magdalene, 1631-2.

HAWLEY, ——. B.A. 1465-6. Perhaps B.D. 1477-8. One Robert Hawley, V. of Gt Wilbraham, Cambs., 1473-80.

HAWLEY, ——. Adm. at SIDNEY, 1642.

HAWLING, BENJAMIN. Matric. from TRINITY HALL, 1677, as 'Holley'; B.A. 1680-1. Doubtless s. of William, of Amwell, Herts., clerk, whose will (Comm. C. Essex) 1683, mentions sons Joseph and Benjamin. (J. Ch. Smith.)

HAWLING, JOSEPH. Adm. pens. (age 19) at PETERHOUSE, May 7, 1667. Of Hertford. School, Hertford. Scholar, 1667; Matric. 1668; B.A. 1670-1. Ord. deacon (Lincoln) Mar. 19, 1670-1; signs for priest's orders (London) May 30, 1672. C. of Amwell, Herts.; to his father William. Brother of Benjamin (above).

HAWLTONE, ——. B.D. 1518-9. A monk.

HAWOOD, *see* **HAYWOOD.**

HAWORTH, *see also* **HOWORTH.**

HAWORTHE, CHARLES. Matric. pens. from CLARE, c. 1593.

HAWORTH, JOHN (1653), *see* **HAYWARD.**

HAWORTH, JOHN. Adm. sizar at ST CATHARINE'S, June 26, 1722. Of Rockcliff, Boroughbridge, Yorks. Matric. 1722; B.A. 1725-6.

HAWORTH or HAYWARD, MICHAEL. B.A. from TRINITY, 1585-6; M.A. from Clare, 1589; B.D. from Trinity, 1595. Ord. deacon and priest (Durham) Apr. 12, 1593. R. of Skinnand, Lincs., 1597. Will (P.C.C.) 1616.

HAWORTH, PETER. Matric. sizar from QUEENS', Lent, 1584-5. Of Yorkshire. Probably ord. deacon and priest (Peterb.) July 9, 1594, as literate. V. of Everton, Notts., 1598-1625. Died 1625.

HAWORTH or HAYWORTH, RANDALL. Matric. sizar from TRINITY, Michs. 1570. One Ralph Hayworth Master of Solihull Grammar School, *c.* 1570.

HAWORTH, RICHARD. Adm. sizar at CLARE, Feb. 26, 1674-5. Of Wellingborough, Northants. B.A. 1679-80. Ord. deacon (Peterb.) Sept. 19, 1680; priest, May 29, 1681. Married, at Wellingborough, Oct. 4, 1688, Mary Markham. (H. I. Longden.)

HAWORTH, SAMUEL. Adm. sizar (age 17) at SIDNEY, Apr. 24, 1677. S. of William (1652), clerk. B. in Hertfordshire. Adm. extra-licentiate of the R.C.P., Oct. 12, 1680, when he claimed to be M.D. of Cambridge and of Paris. Physician to James II. Author, medical. (*Munk*, I. 416; *D.N.B.*)

HAWORTH, THOMAS. Adm. sizar (age 18) at CHRIST'S, June 27, 1728. S. of Richard. B. at Kirkham, Lancs. School, Kirkham (Mr Taylor). Matric. 1728; Scholar, 1729; B.A. 1731-2. R. of Ringstead St Andrew's, Norfolk, 1735-61. (*Peile*, II. 218.)

HAWORTH, WILLIAM. Adm. sizar at ST JOHN'S, Aug. 24, 1652. S. of Laurence, of Preston-in-Amounderness, Lancs. B. there. School, Sedbergh (Mr Jackson). Matric. 1652; B.A. 1656-7. Ejected from St Peter's, St Albans, 1662. Afterwards preacher at Hertford. Died 1703. Father of Samuel (1677). (*Calamy*, II. 40; *Sedbergh Sch. Reg.*)

HAWORTHINGHAM, ADAM DE. 'King's scholar' at Cambridge, 1329-32. Possibly the same as Adam Wormyngworth. (*Trin.* Coll. *Admissions*, I. 89.)

HAWSOPP or **ALSOPP, GEORGE.** Matric. pens. from ST JOHN'S, Michs. 1546; B.A. 1550-1; M.A. 1554. Fellow of Queens', 1551-61. Incorp. at Oxford, 1560. C. of St Giles', Cambridge. Will proved (V.C.C.) 1561.

HAWSTED, *see* **HAUSTEAD.**

HAWSYN, ROBERT. Matric. sizar from KING'S, Lent, 1581-2.

HAWSTWICK, ——. B.Can.L. 1481.

HAWTEYNE, WILLIAM. M.A. from KING'S, 1707. S. of William, R. of Farthinghoe, Northants. Bapt. there, Dec. 29, 1680. School, Rugby. Matric. from Trinity College, Oxford, Oct. 26, 1697, age 17; B.A. (Oxford) 1701. Ord. deacon (Peterb.) Sept. 20, 1702; priest, Dec. 19, 1703. R. of Elstree, Herts., 1706-18. Army chaplain in Flanders and Germany. R. of Datchworth, Herts., 1709-47. V. of Sheephall, 1713-33. V. of Leighton Buzzard, Beds., 1734-48. Author, *Sermons*. Died Jan. 2, 1747-8. M.I. at Datchworth. (*Al. Oxon.*; H. I. Longden.)

HAWTHORNE, GILBERT. B.D. 1622 (Incorp. from Oxford). Of Somerset. S. of Adrian, principal of Magdalen Hall, Oxford, and preb. of Wells. Matric. from Christ Church, Feb. 7, 1588-9, age 16; B.A. (Oxford) 1593; M.A. 1596-7; B.D. 1605. V. of Devynock, Brecon, 1608. V. of Carhampton, Somerset, 1614-8. R. of Caundle Bishop, Dorset, 1618-34. Will (P.C.C.) 1634. (*Al. Oxon.*)

HAWTHORNTHWATE, *see* **HATHORNTHWAITE.**

HAWTINS or **HAWTON, NATHANIEL.** Adm. sizar at JESUS, May 13, 1647. Of London. Eldest s. of John, college receiver in London (of Aldermanbury, citizen and merchant taylor). Matric. 1647; Scholar, 1647; B.A. 1650-1; M.A. 1654. Fellow, 1652-7. Incorp. at Oxford, 1654. R. of Graveley, Cambs., 1656. Buried there June 20, 1696. (A. Gray.)

HAWTOFT, *see* **HOTTOFF.**

HAWTREY, CHARLES. Adm. at KING'S, a scholar from Eton, 1706. S. of John (1664). Bapt. at Maple Durham, Aug. 1687. Matric. Michs. 1707; B.A. 1710-1; M.A. 1714. Fellow, 1710. Ord. deacon (Ely) Mar. 13, 1714-5. R. of Dunton, Essex. R. of Fulmer, Bucks., 1722. Preb. of Exeter, 1725-70. R. of Wootton Courtney, Somerset, 1729. Chaplain to Weston, Bishop of Exeter. R. of Heavitree, Exeter. Sub-dean of Exeter, 1731-70. Married Anne, dau. of Richard Sleech, canon of Windsor. Died May 3, 1770, aged 83. Buried in the Cathedral. M.I. Will, P.C.C. Probably brother of John (1705) and William (1711). (*Harwood*.)

HAWTREY, EDWARD. Adm. at KING'S, a scholar from Eton, 1622. B. at Ruislip, Middlesex, *c.* 1605. S. of John. B.A. 1625-6; M.A. 1629. Fellow, 1625-43. Ord. deacon (Peterb.) Sept. 25, 1631. V. of Burnham, Bucks., 1643; ejected, 1650. R. of Denham; ejected in the Civil War; restored, 1661. Died Oct. 29, 1669, aged 68. Buried at Burnham. M.I. (*Middlesex Pedigrees*; Lipscomb, *Pedigrees*, III. 212.)

HAWTREY, JOHN. Adm. at KING'S, a scholar from Eton, 1646. S. of John, of Ruislip, Middlesex. B.A. 1650-1; M.A. 1654. Fellow, 1650-5. Incorp. at Oxford, 1654. Adm. at Gray's Inn, May 22, 1650. Barrister-at-law, 1654. Perhaps of Pinner Hill. Nephew of Edward (1622). (Lipscomb, *Pedigrees*, III. 213.)

HAWTREY, JOHN. Adm. at KING'S, a scholar from Eton, 1661. S. of Ralph, citizen and merchant taylor, of London. Of Sanderstead, Surrey. Bapt. there, Jan. 10, 1642-3. Matric. Easter, 1662; B.A. 1665-6; M.A. 1669. Fellow. Ord. priest (Ely) Sept. 24, 1670. R. of Sanderstead, 1674-8. Buried there Oct. 11, 1678, aged 35. M.I. (*Manning and Bray*, II. 577; J. Ch. Smith.)

HAWTREY, JOHN. Adm. at KING'S, a scholar from Eton, 1664. S. of Edward (1622). B. at Hitcham, Bucks. Matric. Easter, 1665; B.A. 1668-9; M.A. 1672. Fellow, 1668. Fellow of Eton, 1680-1715. Travelled in France and Italy. V. of Maple Durham, Oxon., 1684-1715. Died Jan. 24, 1715, at Eton. Buried at Maple Durham. Father of Charles (1706) and of William (1711). (J. Ch. Smith; *Harwood* seems in error.)

HAWTREY, JOHN. Adm. Fell.-Com. at KING'S, 1672-3. Colleger at Eton, 1670-2. 1st s. of Ralph, of Ruislip, Middlesex. Died 1673, aged 19. Buried in King's Chapel.

HAWTREY, JOHN. Adm. pens. (age 19) at ST JOHN'S, May 22, 1705. S. of John. B. at Eton, Bucks. School, Eton. Matric. 1705; B.A. 1708-9. Probably brother of Charles (1706) and William (1711).

HAWTREY, ROBERT. Adm. pens. at TRINITY, Apr. 15, 1673. Adm. Fell.-Com. the same day. M.A. 1675 (*Lit. Reg.*).

HAWTREY, WILLIAM. Adm. at KING'S, a scholar from Eton, 1711. S. of John (1664), V. of Maple Durham. Bapt. there, May 30, 1693. Matric. Easter, 1712. Died whilst a student. Brother of Charles (1706) and probably of John (1705).

HAXBY, STEPHEN. B.A. from ST JOHN'S, 1604-5. Of Yorkshire. M.A. 1608; B.D. 1616. Fellow, 1607. R. of Bodney, Norfolk, 1611. Preb. of Lichfield, 1619-22. R. of Coppenhall, Cheshire, 1621-7. (E. Axon.)

HAXBY, THOMAS. Adm. sizar (age 17) at CHRIST'S, Nov. 19, 1658. S. of Thomas. B. at Hartwith, near Pateley Bridge, Yorks. School, Bradford (Mr Cotes). Matric. 1658; B.A. 1662-3; M.A. 1666. Ord. priest (Lincoln) Dec. 1667. V. of Potton, Beds. R. of Wrestlingworth, 1681-9. Married Mary Dowle, Jan. 5, 1683-4. One of these names, V. of Harlington, Beds., died 1693. Buried May 5, 1693, at Potton. (*Peile*, I. 583.)

HAXHAM, ANDREW. Matric. pens. from MAGDALENE, Easter, 1606.

HAXSTEDE, JOHN. Of the Cambridge House of Carmelites. Ord. deacon (Ely) Sept. 18, 1378.

HAXUP, *see* **HACKSUP.**

HAY, *see also* **HEY.**

HAY, GEORGE. Adm. sizar at TRINITY, June 30, 1682. Matric. 1682; Scholar, 1685; B.A. 1685-6; M.A. 1689. Perhaps R. of Horsted Keynes, Sussex. Buried there Nov. 8, 1737. (*Misc. Gen. et Her.*, 2nd S., I. 195.)

HAY, HERRICUS. M.A. 1621 (Incorp. from Edinburgh). M.A. (Edinburgh) 1621.

HAY, ISAAC. Matric. pens. from ST JOHN'S, *c.* 1597; B.A. 1600-1. One of these names, of Battle, Sussex, adm. at the Inner Temple, 1599.

HAY, JAMES. M.A. 1641-2 (on Prince Charles' visit). James Hay, 2nd Earl of Carlisle. K.B., 1626. Colonel of Horse in the Royal army. Died Oct. 30, 1660. Buried at Waltham Abbey. (*G.E.C.*)

HAY, JOHN. M.A. 1633 (Incorp. from Edinburgh). Fellow of ST JOHN'S, 1634, by royal mandate.

HAY, JOHN. Adm. Fell.-Com. at QUEENS', Apr. 26, 1645. Of Sussex. Perhaps s. of Herbert, of Glynde, Sussex; age 8 in 1634. (*Vis. of Sussex*.)

HAY, JOHN. Matric. sizar from QUEENS', Easter, 1656. Of Salop. Migrated to Trinity, Nov. 17, 1656. Scholar of Trinity, 1659; B.A. 1659-60.

HAY or **HAYES, JOHN.** Adm. sizar (age 18) at SIDNEY, June 20, 1666. S. of John, farmer. B. at Aislaby, Pickering, Yorks. Schools, Middleton (Mr Wilson) and Salton (Mr Syth). Matric. 1667; B.A. 1669-70. Signed for deacon's order (London) Sept. 18, 1673. C. of Higham Gobion, Beds.

HAY, JOHN. Adm. sizar (age 19) at TRINITY, June 22, 1714. S. of George, of Tedstone, Heref. School, Hereford (Mr Rodd). Matric. 1714; Scholar, 1717; B.A. 1717-8; M.A. 1721. One of these names C. of St Dionis Backchurch, London, 1729. Buried Nov. 27, 1738. (J. Ch. Smith.)

HEY, LAURANCE. Matric. pens. from ST JOHN'S, Easter, 1544; B.A. 1546-7.

HAYE, RALPH. Adm. sizar (age 19) at ST JOHN'S, Sept. 11, 1647. S. of William, yeoman, of Aislaby, Yorks. B. there. School, Middleton (Mr Hardwick).

HAYE, RICHARD. Matric. sizar from ST JOHN'S, Easter, 1588.

HEY, RICHARD. Adm. pens. at ST CATHARINE'S, June 26, 1751. S. of Richard, of Pudsey, Yorks. Of Hertingfordbury, Herts.

HEYE, ROBERT. Adm. sizar (age 16) at CHRIST'S, Jan. 15, 1674-5. S. of John. B. at Skipton. School, Burnsall. Matric. 1674-5; B.A. 1678-9; M.A. 1684. Master of Burnsall School, 1682-95. Died Jan. 19, 1694-5, aged 36. (*Peile*, II. 57.)

HAYE, ROGER. Matric. sizar from ST JOHN'S, Easter, 1548; B.A. 1553-4. Perhaps fellow, 1554, as 'Houe,' of Lancashire.

HEY, ROGER. Matric. sizar from KING'S, Michs. 1589.

HAY, THOMAS. Matric. sizar from TRINITY, 1636; B.A. 1639-40.

HEY, THOMAS. Adm. at CORPUS CHRISTI, 1746. Of London. Matric. 1746; B.A. 1749-50; M.A. 1753; D.D. Lambeth. Ord. deacon and priest (Canterbury) 1755. Perhaps R. of Wickhambreux, Kent, 1755-1807. V. of Eastchurch, 1755-1807. Preb. of Rochester, 1788-1807. Died at Wingham, 1807, aged 80.

HAY, THOMAS, Viscount DUPPLIN. M.A. 1749. S. and h. of George, Earl of Kinnoull. B. 1710. M.P. for Cambridge, 1741-58. Commissioner of Irish revenue, 1741. A lord of trade, 1746; of the treasury, 1754. Chancellor of the duchy of Lancaster, 1758. Privy councillor, 1758. Succeeded to the Earldom, 1758. Ambassador-extraordinary to Portugal, 1759. Chancellor of St Andrews, 1765. Died Dec. 28, 1787. (*D.N.B.*; *Collins*, VII. 212.)

HAYE, WILLIAM. Matric. Fell.-Com. from PEMBROKE, Michs. 1612.

HAYE, WILLIAM. Matric. Fell.-Com. from CLARE, Michs. 1612.

HAY, WILLIAM. Matric. Fell.-Com. from ST CATHARINE'S, Easter, 1640. One of these names, s. and h. of William, of Horstead, Sussex, adm. at Gray's Inn, July 1, 1644. Perhaps M.P. for Rye, 1641, 1656-8, 1659-60.

HAY, WILLIAM. Adm. sizar at TRINITY, June 2, 1666.

HAY, WILLIAM. Adm. Fell.-Com. at CORPUS CHRISTI, 1689. Of Sussex. Matric. Easter, 1689; M.A. 1690. (*Com. Reg.*)

HAY, WILLIAM. M.A. 1728 (*Com. Reg.*). One of these names V. of Barton Turf, Norfolk, 1727–62 (?).

HAYBAR, THOMAS. Matric. pens. from TRINITY, Michs. 1584.

HEYBARN, *see* HEIBURNE.

HAYCOCKE or HEACOCKE, FRANCIS. Matric. pens. from CHRIST'S, July, 1582. (Possibly matric. from Merton, Oxford, Nov. 24, 1581, age 20. Of Leicestershire.) B.A. 1584–5; M.A. 1588. One of these names of Haconby, Lincs., clerk. Admon. (Lincoln) 1607.

HAYCOCKE, JOHN. Matric. sizar from CHRIST'S, Dec. 1586.

HAYCOCK or HEICOCK, JOHN. Adm. pens. at EMMANUEL, May 15, 1665. Of Middlesex. Matric. 1665; B.A. 1668–9. Expelled, Apr. 28, 1669. Whilst an undergraduate, 'whipped in the butteries for foul misconduct' (contemporary note).

HEACOCK, NATHANIEL. Adm. sizar at EMMANUEL, Aug. 20, 1611. Matric. 1611.

HEYCROFT, *see* **HEICROFT.**

HAYDOCK, JOHN, *see* **HADDOCK.**

HAYDOCK, WILLIAM. Adm. sizar (age 18) at ST JOHN'S, May 27, 1665. S. of Roger, yeoman, of Standish, Lancs. Bapt. there, Feb. 8, 1645–6. School, Sedbergh. Matric. 1667; B.A. 1668–9; M.A. 1672. R. of Standish, 1678. Died Apr. 13, 1713. (*Sedbergh Sch. Reg.*, 120.)

HAYDON, *see also* **HEYDON.**

HAYDON, ALEXANDER. Adm. pens. (age 17) at ST JOHN'S, June 15, 1671. S. of Nathaniel, deceased, of Devon (will, Exeter, 1668; of Alwington, clerk). School, Tiverton. Matric. 1671.

HAYDON, GIDEON. M.A. 1668 (Incorp. from Oxford). S. and h. of Nicholas, of Ottery, Devon, Esq. Matric. from Exeter College, May 20, 1664, age 16; B.A. (Oxford) 1667–8. Adm. at Lincoln's Inn, June 27, 1666. (*Al. Oxon.*)

HAYDON, RICHARD. M.A. from PEMBROKE, 1738. S. of William, of Tiverton, Devon, gent. Matric. from Balliol College, Oxford, Mar. 14, 1725–6, age 19; B.A. (Oxford) 1729. Will (Exeter) 1788; of Okeford, Devon, clerk. (*Al. Oxon.*)

HAYECK, SIMEON, *see* **HAYET.**

HAYES, *see also* **HASE.**

HAYES, ABELL. Matric. sizar from PEMBROKE, Easter, 1610; B.A. from Clare, 1612–3.

HAYES, BENJAMIN. Matric. Fell.-Com. from ST JOHN'S, Easter, 1615. Doubtless s. of Sir Thomas, of London, Knt. and alderman. Bapt. Mar. 12, 1597. Perhaps adm. at the Inner Temple, 1616; of London. Brother of Nathaniel (1617) and Robert (1608). (Phillimore, *London and Middlesex Notebook*, 260.)

HEYES, CHARLES. Matric. pens. from TRINITY, Easter, 1610.

HAYES, CHARLES (1674), *see* **HAWES.**

HAYES, CHERRY. Adm. at KING'S, a scholar from Eton, 1715. B. at Bray, Berks. Matric. 1715–6; B.A. 1719–20; M.A. 1723; M.D. 1728 (*Com. Reg.*). Fellow, 1719. Practised physic at Windsor. Died Oct. 25, 1763. (*L. Mag.*)

HAYES, DANIEL. Adm. sizar at EMMANUEL, Mar. 29, 1644. Matric. 1644; B.A. 1647–8; M.A. 1651. V. of Preston, Kent, 1662. R. of Papworth, Cambs., 1674.

HAIES, EDWARD. Matric. Fell.-Com. from KING'S, Easter, 1571.

HAYES, HENRY. Adm. at KING'S (age 18) a scholar from Eton, Aug. 24, 1560. Of London. Matric. 1560; B.A. 1564–5; M.A. 1568; B.D. 1579. Fellow, 1563–83. Vice-provost, 1581–2. Scrutator, 1581–2. R. of Stower Provost, Dorset, 1583–5. Died 1585. (F. S. Hockaday.)

HAYES, JAMES. Adm. sizar at EMMANUEL, Jan. 26, 1660–1. Of Norfolk. School, Lynn. Matric. 1661; B.A. 1664–5; M.A. 1668.

HAYES, JAMES. Adm. at KING'S, a scholar from Eton, 1733. S. of James. Bapt. at Bray, Oct. 27, 1715. Matric. Easter, 1734; B.A. 1737–8; M.A. 1741. Fellow, 1737. Barrister-at-law, Middle Temple. Recorder of Wokingham, Berks. M.P. for Downton, Wilts., 1753–7, 1761–8, 1771–4. 2nd Judge of Anglesey, Carnarvon and Merioneth, 1761–8. Chief Justice, 1778–93. Died Sept. 9, 1800, aged 85. M.I. at Bray. Brother of Richard (1740). (*Harwood*, 323; J. Ch. Smith; A. B. Beaven.)

HAYES, JOHN. Matric. pens. from QUEENS', Lent, 1687; B.A. 1690–1; M.A. 1694; B.D. 1702; D.D. 1716. Fellow, 1692. Taxor, 1696. Perhaps C. of Higham Gobion, Beds., 1695–1706.

HAYES, JOHN. Adm. at CORPUS CHRISTI, 1723. Of Staffordshire. Matric. Lent, 1724.

HAYES, NATHANIEL. Adm. at EMMANUEL, Feb. 1616–7. Doubtless s. of Sir Thomas, of London, Knt. and alderman. Bapt. Sept. 28, 1600. Matric. 1617. Perhaps adm. at the Inner Temple, 1616. Of London. Living, 1648. Brother of Benjamin (1615) and Robert (1608).

HAYES or HEYES, PETER. Matric. sizar from QUEENS', Michs. 1615. Of Cheshire.

HAYES, PHILEMON. Adm. pens. at CLARE, June 6, 1657. Matric. 1657; B.A. 1660–1.

HAYES, PHILIP. Adm. at KING'S, a scholar from Eton, 1558. Migrated to Oxford, 1561. B.A. from Christ Church, 1562; M.A. 1565–6. R. of Alexton, Leics., 1567. (*Al. Oxon.*)

HAYHES, RICHARD. Matric. sizar from JESUS, Easter, 1611. One of these names ord. priest (Peterb.) June 16, 1622. V. of Bitchfield, Lincs., 1630. (H. I. Longden.)

HAYSE, RICHARD. Adm. pens. at JESUS, June 20, 1640. Of Cheshire. Matric. 1640.

HAYES, RICHARD. Adm. pens. (age 19) at CHRIST'S, June 4, 1740. S. of James, of Holyport, Berks. B. at Clewer. School, Eton. Matric. 1740; Scholar, 1740; B.A. 1743–4; M.A. 1747. Fellow, 1745. Ord. deacon (Norwich) May; priest, Sept. 1746. V. of Caxton, Cambs., 1754. R. of Arborfield, Berks. Will (P.C.C.) 1797. Brother of James (1733). (*Peile*, II. 240.)

HEYES, ROBERT. Matric. sizar from MAGDALENE, Easter, 1605. One of these names schoolmaster at Bolingbroke, Lincs., in 1611.

HAYES, ROBERT. Matric. Fell.-Com. at ST JOHN'S, Michs. 1608. Doubtless 1st s. of Sir Thomas, of London, alderman. Married Katherine Sherwood. Brother of Benjamin (1615) and Nathaniel (1617). (*Vis. of Herts.*, 1634.)

HAYES, THOMAS. Matric. pens. from CORPUS CHRISTI, Michs. 1656. Of Norfolk. One of these names B.A. from Brasenose, Oxford, 1658–9; M.A. 1664; B. and D.Med. 1669. (*Al. Oxon.*)

HAYES, THOMAS. Adm. pens. (age 17) at PEMBROKE, June 22, 1732. S. of Samuel, of Neston-*cum*-Parkgate, Cheshire, gent. Matric. 1732–3; B.A. 1735–6; M.A. 1739; M.D. 1747. Fellow, 1736. Doubtless of Chichester, M.D. Will (P.C.C.) 1767.

HAYES, WILLIAM. Matric. sizar from PEMBROKE, Easter, 1629. Migrated to Emmanuel, May 7, 1631. B.A. 1632–3; M.A. 1636. R. of Papworth St Agnes, Cambs., 1638–73. Buried there Dec. 10, 1673.

HAYES, WILLIAM. Adm. Fell.-Com. at ST CATHARINE'S, 1640. Of Sussex.

HAYES, WILLIAM. Matric. sizar from QUEENS', Easter, 1677. Buried at St Botolph's, Cambridge, Nov. 9, 1677.

HEYES, ——. Adm. Fell.-Com. at KING'S, Michs. 1643.

HAYET, SIMEON. Matric. Fell.-Com. from CORPUS CHRISTI, 1581–2; 'Boemus.' B.A. 1581–2, as Haiecius.

HAYET, WILLIAM, *see* **HAYT.**

HAYFORD or HEYFORD, DENNIS. M.A. from PETERHOUSE, 1682. S. of Christopher, of Pontefract, Yorks. Matric. from Magdalen College, Oxford, Dec. 1, 1671, age 16; B.A. (Oxford) 1675. V. of Rastrick, Yorks., 1676–88. V. of Meltham, 1683–8.

HAYGARTH, CHRISTOPHER. Adm. sizar (age 20) at ST JOHN'S, Apr. 9, 1673. S. of Thomas, yeoman, of Dent, Yorks. B. there. School, Dent. Matric. 1673. Married, at Gt Stainton, June 4, 1702, Jane Baxter. (H. M. Wood.)

HAYGARTH, GEORGE. Matric. sizar from TRINITY, Michs. 1554; Scholar; B.A. 1559–60.

HAYGARTH, JOSIAS. Adm. sizar (age 18) at ST JOHN'S, May 30, 1719. S. of Matthew, husbandman, of Yorkshire. B. at Hollins, near Sedbergh. School, Sedbergh (Mr Saunders). Matric. 1719; B.A. 1722–3; M.A. 1726. Ord. deacon (London) Dec. 20, 1724; priest, Dec. 19, 1725. Perhaps C. of Much Hadham, Herts. Died June 28, 1768. (G. *Mag.*)

HEYHOE, EDWARD. Adm. at CORPUS CHRISTI, 1691. S. of Edward, of Hardingham, Norfolk. Matric. Easter, 1692; B.A. 1695–6; M.A. 1699. Ord. deacon (Norwich) May, 1697; priest, Sept. 1698. C. of Yaxham, Norfolk. R. of Welborne, 1700–20. R. of Rockland St Peter's, 1737. Father of the next.

HEIGHOE, EDWARD. Adm. pens. (age 16) at CAIUS, Nov. 10, 1736. S. of Edward (above), of Hardingham, Norfolk, clerk. B. there. Schools, Wymondham and Scarning (Mr Brett). Scholar, 1736–40; Matric. 1737. Killed at Cambridge. Brother of Grigson (1727). (*Venn*, II. 43.)

HAYHOE or **HAIHOE, GEORGE.** Adm. pens. (age 16) at CAIUS, Mar. 7, 1637–8. S. of Robert, gent., of Saham Toney, Norfolk. B. at Ashill. School, Saham Toney (Mr Gilbert). Matric. 1638; Scholar, 1639–45; B.A. 1641–2; M.A. 1645. Ord. deacon and priest (Lincoln) July 30, 1646. R. of Harpley, Norfolk, 1648–68. Will proved (Norwich) 1668. (*Venn*, I. 330.)

HEYHOE or HEIGHOE, GRIGSON. Adm. pens. (age 18) at CAIUS, May, 1727. S. of Edward (1691), of Hardingham, Norfolk, clerk. B. at Mattishall. School, Wymondham (Mr Sayer and Mr Brett). Scholar, 1727-33; Matric. 1728; B.A. 1730-1. Ord. deacon (Lincoln) Sept. 14, 1732; priest, Dec. 24, 1732. C. of Pertenhall, Beds. R. of Yaxham and Welborne, Norfolk, 1734-63. Died Apr. 7, 1763. M.I. at Hardingham. Will, P.C.C. Brother of Edward (1736). (*Venn*, II. 27.)

HAYHOE, JAMES. Adm. pens. (age 17) at CAIUS, July 3, 1635. S. of William, gent. B. at Watton, Norfolk. Bapt. July 26, 1618. School, Bury St Edmunds (Mr Dickinson). Matric. 1635; Scholar, 1636-40; B.A. 1638-9.

HAYHOW, THOMAS. Matric. sizar from CAIUS, May, 1559. Resident, Aug. 1564.

HAYGHYNTON, ROBERT. Matric. pens. from CHRIST'S, Nov. 1545. Probably secretary to the Earl of Northumberland. Living at Namur, 1577. (*Peile*, I. 38.)

HAYHURST, BRADLEY. Adm. sizar at EMMANUEL, Mar. 31, 1629. Of Lancashire. S. of Richard, of Ribchester, Lancs. Matric. 1629; B.A. 1632-3. Minister at Leigh, Lancs., c. 1646-61. R. of Taxall, Cheshire, c. 1661-2. Minister at Macclesfield, 1671-82. Died 1685. (Earwaker, *Cheshire*, II. 505, 546; E. Axon.)

HAYHURST, RICHARD. Matric. sizar from CHRIST'S, July, 1622.

HAYHURST, ROBERT. Adm. sizar at EMMANUEL, Apr. 27, 1622. Matric. 1622; B.A. 1625-6; M.A. 1629.

HAYHURST, ——. Adm. sizar at CHRIST'S, June 23, 1687.

HAYLET, *see also* HEYLET.

HAYLET, JOHN. Matric. pens. from PEMBROKE, Easter, 1584; B.A. 1587-8; M.A. 1591.

HAYLET or HEYLET, WILLIAM. Adm. sizar at CORPUS CHRISTI, May 23, 1644. Of Norfolk. Scholar, 1647; B.A. 1647-8; M.A. 1651. For a time in presbyterian orders, by Bishop Joseph Hall's advice. R. of Hevingham, Norfolk, 1659-1720. Ord. priest (Norwich) Nov. 10, 1661. R. of Stratton Strawless, 1675. Died Sept. 18, 1720, aged 92. Buried at Stratton. M.I. there. (*Masters*, 309.)

HAYLEY, JOHN. Adm. at KING'S, a scholar from Eton, 1686. B. at Winchester. Matric. Easter, 1687; B.A. 1690-1; M.A. 1694. Fellow, 1690. Junior Proctor, 1719-20. Died in College, 1720.

HAYLEY, THOMAS. D.D. 1717 (*Com. Reg.*). S. of William, of Cleobury, Salop. Matric. from All Souls, Oxford, July 1, 1698, age 17; B.A. (Oxford) 1702; M.A. (Lambeth) 1705. Preb. of Chichester, 1705-35. R. of Dry Drayton, Cambs., 1718-24. V. of Amport, Hants., 1723. Preb. of Winchester, 1728-39. Dean of Chichester, 1735-9. Author, *Sermons*. Died Aug. 12, 1739. Will, P.C.C. (*Al. Oxon.*)

HAYLEZ, ROBERT. M.A. 1456-7. Probably s. of Robert, of Roughton, Norfolk. Fellow of GONVILLE HALL, in 1455. V. of Cromer, 1462-97. (*Venn*, I. 9; Rye, *Cromer*.)

HAYLOCK, JAMES. Adm. sizar at CORPUS CHRISTI, 1667. Of Norfolk. Matric. 1667; B.A. 1670-1. Ord. priest (Norwich) Dec. 1675.

HAYLOCK, JAMES. Adm. sizar at CLARE, Feb. 4, 1723-4. B. at West Wratting, Cambs. Matric. 1724; B.A. 1727-8.

HAYMAN, *see* HEYMAN.

HAYMER, *see* HEYMAR.

HAYMES, THOMAS. Adm. pens. at EMMANUEL, Easter, 1625.

HAIMES, THOMAS. Adm. at KING'S (age 17) a scholar from Eton, July 9, 1658. Of Hillingdon, Middlesex. Matric. 1658; B.A. 1661-2; M.A. 1665. Fellow, 1661-9. Probably V. of Tunstall, Kent, 1670-3 (resigned).

HAYNE or HAYNES, ABRAHAM. Adm. pens. at EMMANUEL, Oct. 16, 1619. Matric. 1619; B.A. 1620-1; M.A. 1625. (Probably matric. from St John's, Oxford, Dec. 4, 1618. S. of William, Head Master of Merchant Taylors' School. Bapt. at St Laurence Pountney, Jan. 24, 1601-2.) Adm. at Lincoln's Inn, Aug. 10, 1626, as of Middlesex, gent. V. of Oadby, Leics., 1632. R. of St Olave's, Hart St, London, 1633-42, ejected. Buried at St Olave's, Mar. 29, 1650. (*Al. Oxon.*)

HAYNE, JAMES. Adm. sizar (age 15) at SIDNEY, July 6, 1630. S. of Francis, retail dealer. B. at Dover. Schools, Christ's Hospital and Charterhouse. Matric. 1631; B.A. 1633-4; M.A. 1637.

HAYNE or HAYNES, JOHN. Adm. pens. at SIDNEY, Aug. 4, 1609. B. in St Laurence parish, Exeter. Matric. 1609; B.A. 1612-3; M.A. 1616. Ord. deacon (London) Sept. 25, 1616, age 23. The R. of Stanway, Essex, 1668-70, was probably J. Haynes (1657).

HAYNE, JOHN. Adm. pens. at EMMANUEL, Mar. 27, 1620. Matric. 1620; B.A. 1623-4.

HAYNE, JOSEPH. Adm. sizar (age 18) at SIDNEY, July 18, 1625. S. of Philip, citizen of Exeter. B. in St Laurence parish, Exeter. Schools, Exeter and Tiverton. Matric. 1625; B.A. 1628-9; M.A. 1632; B.D. 1639. Fellow, 1661-4. V. of Almondsbury, Gloucs., 1661-4. Will of Joseph Hayne (Exeter) 1691; of Pinhoe, clerk. (F. S. Hockaday.)

HAYNE, RICHARD. Adm. pens. at EMMANUEL, Mar. 27, 1620. Matric. 1620; B.A. 1623.

HAYNE, ROBERT. Adm. sizar at EMMANUEL, 1623. Matric. Easter, 1624; B.A. 1627-8; M.A. 1631. Perhaps R. of Weston Colville, Cambs., 1645-63. Buried there June 12, 1663.

HAYNE or HEANE, THOMAS. M.A. 1615 (Incorp. from Oxford). S. of Robert, of Thrussington, Leics. Matric. from Lincoln College, Oxford, Oct. 19, 1599, age 17; B.A. (Oxford) 1604-5; M.A. 1612. Usher of Merchant Taylors' School, 1608; and of Christ's Hospital. Author, theological. Died July 27, 1645. (*Al. Oxon.*; *D.N.B.*)

HAYNE, HAYNES or HEANE, WILLIAM. Matric. sizar from CHRIST'S, Easter, 1579. S. of —— Haynes, of Bristol, yeoman. School, Merchant Taylors'. B.A. 1582-3; M.A. 1588. Head Master of Merchant Taylors' School, 1599-1625. A distinguished grammarian. Author, grammatical. Died c. 1631. (*D.N.B.*)

HAYNES, CHARLES. Adm. pens. (age 17) at PEMBROKE, June 18, 1659. S. of Emmanuel, of Much Hadham, Herts.

HAYNES, CHARLES. Matric. from CLARE, Easter, 1722. 4th s. of Hopton, of the Tower of London, Esq. Adm. at Lincoln's Inn, Dec. 24, 1723. One of these names adm. at Leyden, Aug. 29, 1725. Brother of Hopton (1715), Samuel (1718) and Newton (1722).

HEYNES, EDWARD. Adm. at KING'S (age 18) a scholar from Eton, Aug. 12, 1528. Of Cambridge. Died as scholar, at Grantchester.

HAINES, EDWARD. Adm. pens. at EMMANUEL, June 5, 1671. Of Middlesex.

HAYNES, HENRY. 'M.A. Cambridge; Incorp. at Oxford, July 9, 1622' (*Al. Oxon.*). Not found in our records.

HAINES, HENRY. Adm. pens. at EMMANUEL, May 6, 1720. Of Derbyshire. Matric. 1720; B.A. 1723-4. Ord. priest (Lincoln) June 20, 1736.

HAINES, HEZEKIAH. Adm. pens. (age 17) at SIDNEY, Jan. 26, 1702-3. 1st s. of John, gent. B. at Copford, Essex, May 14, 1685. Schools, Colchester and Merchant Taylors'. Matric. 1703; B.A. 1706-7. Of Copford Hall, Colchester. Died Nov. 16, 1763. (G. *Mag.*; L. *Mag.*)

HAYNES, HOPTON. Adm. pens. at CLARE, June 4, 1715. S. of Hopton, Assay Master of the Mint, of Queen's Square, Westminster (will, P.C.C., 1749). B. in London. Matric. 1715; B.A. 1718-9; M.A. 1722. Fellow, 1721-6. Ord. deacon (Ely) Sept. 23, 1722; priest, Mar. 10, 1722-3. R. of Elmsett, Suffolk, 1726-65. R. of Brettenham, 1727-8. R. of Stansfield, 1728-66. Died June 25, 1766, aged 60. Buried at Elmsett. Admon., P.C.C. Brother of Charles (1722), Samuel (1718) and Newton (1722) and probably father of the next. (J. Ch. Smith.)

HAYNES, HOPTON. Adm. Fell.-Com. at CLARE, June 1, 1749. B. in London. Matric. 1750; B.A. 1753. Probably one of the 'three hopeful sons' of Hopton, above; mentioned in the grandfather's will, 1749. (J. Ch. Smith.)

HAINS, HUMPHREY. Adm. pens. (age 18) at SIDNEY, Apr. 20, 1694. S. of John, farmer. B. at Layton, Staffs. Schools, Norbury (Mr Smith) and Newport (Mr Edwards). Matric. 1695; B.A. 1697-8. Ord. deacon (Lincoln) Dec. 22, 1700. R. of Croft, Leics., 1718-33. R. of Kirby Mallory, 1727-33. Buried Jan. 15, 1733. M.I. at Kirby. Father of Thomas (1739). (*Nichols*, IV. 585.)

HAINES, JAMES. Adm. pens. at CHRIST'S, May 17, 1682. S. of Hezekiah. B. at Copford, Essex. School, Felsted (Mr Glascock). Matric. 1682.

HAYNES, JOHN. Matric. sizar from CHRIST'S, Michs. 1611. B. at Berkhampstead. B.A. 1614-5; M.A. 1618. Ord. deacon (London) Mar. 1619-20, age 24. (For conjectures *see* *Peile*, I. 285.)

HAYNES, JOHN. M.A. 1614-5 (on King's visit).

HAYNES, JOHN. Adm. sizar at QUEENS', May 27, 1642. Of Sussex. Perhaps same as the next.

HAINES, JOHN. Adm. sizar (age 17) at CHRIST'S, May 28, 1642. S. of Thomas, of Hastings, schoolmaster. Exhibitioner from Tonbridge School. Matric. 1642; B.A. 1645-6; M.A. 1652. One of these names licensed to preach at Widford, Herts., 1662. (*Peile*, I. 480.)

HAYNES, JOHN. B.A. 1657 (Incorp. from Cambridge, New England). S. of John, gent. B. at Cambridge, New England. M.A. from Pembroke, 1660. Fellow of Pembroke, 1660–1. Ord. priest (Ely) Mar. 14, 1662–3. One of these names, M.A., R. of Stanway, Essex, 1668–71. Perhaps R. of Hemingston, Suffolk, 1663. V. of Henley, 1664. Will (Comm. C. Essex) 1671.

HAINES, JOHN. Adm. sizar (age 17) at Magdalene, Jan. 9, 1660–1. S. of Richard, of Shrewsbury. School, Shrewsbury. Matric. 1661; B.A. 1664–5; M.A. 1668. Second Master at Shrewsbury, 1668–72. Probably father of the next and of Matthew (1689).

HAYNS or HEYNES, JOHN. Adm. sizar at Jesus, Jan. 14, 1687–8. Of Salop. Matric. 1688. Doubtless s. of John, of Shrewsbury. Matric. from Wadham, Oxford, Mar. 23, 1688–9, age 17; B.A. 1691; M.A. from Lincoln College, 1700. (*Al. Oxon.*)

HAYNES, JOHN. Adm. sizar at Jesus, May 30, 1700. Of Salop. Matric. 1700; Scholar, 1703; B.A. 1703–4; M.A. 1707. R. of Babcary, Somerset, 1729–35 (resigned).

HAYNES, JOSEPH. Matric. pens. from Queens', Easter, 1567 LL.B. 1572–3. Doubtless s. of Simon (1515) and brother of Simon (1568). (*Vis. of Bucks.*, 1634.)

HAYNE, JOSEPH. Adm. sizar at Emmanuel, Apr. 8, 1676. Of Derbyshire. Matric. 1676; B.A. 1679–80.

HAYNES, MATTHEW. Matric. pens. from St John's, Easter, 1616.

HEYNES, MATTHEW. Adm. sizar at Jesus, July 5, 1689. S. of John (? 1660–1), clerk, deceased. Of Salop. Matric. 1690; B.A. 1693–4; M.A. 1697. R. of Preston Bagot, Warws., 1714–31. Perhaps V. of Luton, Beds., 1721. Probably brother of John (1687–8). (A. Gray.)

HAYNES, NEWTON. Adm. pens. at Clare, May 5, 1722. 3rd s. of Hopton, of the Tower of London (Assay Master of the Mint). B. in London. Adm. at Lincoln's Inn, Dec. 24, 1723. One Newton Haynes, 'LL.D.,' died in the Tower, Oct. 17, 1736. Brother of Charles (1722), Hopton (1715) and Samuel (1718). (G. *Mag.*; L. *Mag.*)

HAYNES, RALPH. Matric. sizar from St John's, Michs. 1647 (not found in College register).

HAINES, ROBERT. Adm. sizar at Trinity, July 1, 1674.

HEINES, SAMUEL. Matric. sizar from King's, Easter, 1602.

HAYNES, SAMUEL. M.A. from King's, 1685. S. of John, of Ditcheat, Somerset, clerk. Matric. from Lincoln College, Oxford, Apr. 2, 1677, age 15; B.A. (Oxford) 1680. V. of New Windsor, Berks., 1685–9. (*Al. Oxon.*)

HAYNES, SAMUEL. Adm. at King's, a scholar from Eton, 1718. S. of Hopton, Assay Master of the Mint. B. in London. Matric. Michs. 1719; B.A. 1723–4; M.A. 1727; D.D. 1748. Fellow, 1722. Adm. at Gray's Inn, Sept. 6, 1720. Tutor to James Cecil, Earl of Salisbury. R. of Hatfield, Herts., 1737–52. Canon of Windsor, 1743–52. R. of Clothall, Herts., 1747–52. Edited the Hatfield State Papers. Died June 9, 1752. Brother of Charles (1722), Hopton (1715) and Newton (1722). (G. *Mag.*; *D.N.B.*)

HAYNES or HEYNES, SIMON. B.A. 1515–6; M.A. 1519; B.D. 1528; D.D. 1531. Fellow of Queens', 1516. President, 1528–37. Vice-Chancellor, 1532–3, 1533–4. R. of Barrow, Suffolk, 1528. V. of Stepney, Middlesex, 1534–7. Canon of Windsor, 1535–52. R. of Fulham, 1535–52. Dean of Exeter, 1537–52. R. of Newton Ferrers, Devon, 1538. Preb. of Westminster, 1540–52. Much employed in state affairs. Assisted in the compilation of the first English Liturgy. Died Oct. 1552. Will (P.C.C.) 1552. (*Cooper*, I. 111; *Vis. of Bucks.*, 1634; *D.N.B.*)

HAYNES, SIMON. Matric. pens. from Jesus, Easter, 1568. Probably s. of Simon (above). B.A. from St John's, 1571–2. (*Vis. of Bucks.*, 1634.)

HAYNES or HEYNES, SIMON. Adm. pens. at Queens', June 10, 1596. Of Essex. Matric. 1596.

HAYNES, THOMAS. Of St John's, *c.* 1598–1602. Author, Latin letters. (*Cooper*, II. 344.) Not found in our records.

HAINES, THOMAS. Adm. pens. at Emmanuel, Feb. 18, 1679–80. Previously matric. from St Edmund's Hall, Oxford, Dec. 17, 1678, age 17. Of Somerset. S. of Thomas, of Bristol. Matric. 1680. Adm. at the Middle Temple, Nov. 28, 1681.

HAINS, THOMAS. Adm. sizar at Jesus, July 4, 1739. Of Croft, Leicestershire. S. of Humphrey (1694), clerk, deceased. Matric. 1740; B.A. 1742–3. Ord. deacon (Lincoln) Sept. 23, 1744; priest, May 25, 1746. V. of All Saints', Leicester, 1746–86. V. of St Martin's, 1753–86. Died 1786, aged 65.

HAINES, WALTER. Matric. sizar from Queens', Easter, 1626. Of Bedfordshire. B.A. 1629–30; M.A. 1633. V. of Renhold, Beds. Buried there Apr. 28, 1638.

HEINES, WILLIAM. Matric. pens. from Trinity, *c.* 1595; B.A. 1597–8; M.A. 1601.

HAINSWORTH, GEORGE. Adm. at Corpus Christi, 1750. Of Norwich. B.A. 1755; M.A. 1758. Fellow, 1758–61. Ord. deacon (Ely) Sept. 21, 1756; priest, Mar. 6, 1757. Died 1761.

HAYNTON, JOHN. Carmelite friar. D.D. Cambridge; also at Oxford. Ord. acolyte (Ely) May 25, 1415; whilst student at the Carmelite Priory at Cambridge. Prior at Lincoln. (B. Zimmerman.)

HAYNSWORTH, OLIVER, *see* AINSWORTH.

HAYNTON, MICHAEL DE. M.A. Fellow of Clare, 1355. Chancellor of the University, 1361–2. Licentiate in Theology. V. of Moulton, Lincs. Petitions the Pope, 1363, for canonry of Lincoln. Benefactor to the University and Clare Hall. (*Cal. Pap. Pet.*, I. 435.)

HAYRE, THOMAS. Scholar of Christ's, 1537–8; B.A. 1538–9; M.A. 1543.

HAYSETT, EDWARD. Adm. at Corpus Christi, 1635. Of Norfolk.

HEYT, JOHN. Adm. pens. at Queens', Mar. 6, 1583–4. Of Kent.

HAYTE or HAITE, WALTER. Resident pens. at Queens', Aug. 1564. Probably ord. deacon (Lincoln) 1565; priest (Rochester) 1566. V. of Halling, Kent, 1567–87. V. of Shorne, 1576. Preb. of Rochester, 1586. V. of St Margaret's, Rochester, 1587–9. V. of Goudhurst, 1589. R. of Caxton, 1597–1610. Buried in Rochester Cathedral, 1610. (H. G. Harrison.)

HAYT or HAYET, WILLIAM. B.A. 1565–6; M.A. from St John's, 1569. Ord. deacon (Ely) Apr. 1568, age 23. V. of Osmington, Dorset, 1572. Preb. of Sarum. Will (P.C.C.) 1588.

HAYTER, JOHN. Adm. pens. (age 15) at Magdalene, Nov. 16, 1671. S. of John, of Brentwood, Essex. School, Brentwood.

HAYTER, THOMAS. M.A. from Emmanuel, 1727; D.D. 1744. S. of George, of Chagford, Devon, clerk. School, Tiverton. Matric. from Balliol College, Oxford, May 30, 1720, age 17; B.A. (Oxford) 1723–4. Ord. deacon (York) June 9, 1727; priest, July, 1727. Preb. of York, 1728–49. Preb. of Southwell, 1728–49. R. of Kirkby Overblow, Yorks., 1729–49. Sub-dean of York, 1730–49. Archdeacon of York, 1730–51. R. of Etton, Yorks., 1731. Chaplain to the King, 1734–49. V. of Kirkby-in-Cleveland, 1737–49. Preb. of Westminster, 1739–49. Bishop of Norwich, 1749. F.R.S., 1750. Preceptor to the Prince of Wales, 1751. Bishop of London, 1761. Created a privy councillor, 1761. Author, *Sermons*. Died Jan. 9, 1762. Buried at Fulham. Admon. (P.C.C.) 1762. (*Al. Oxon.*; *D.N.B.*)

HAYTON, JAMES. Adm. sizar (age 17) at St John's, June 3, 1706. S. of Robert, husbandman. B. at Gayles, Yorks. School, Threshfield (Mr Marshall). Matric. 1707; B.A. 1710–1. Ord. priest (York) Dec. 1712. V. of Hornby, Yorks., 1716–70. Buried Jan. 17, 1770.

HAYTON, WILLIAM, *see* HEYDON.

HAYTON, WILLIAM. Adm. sizar at Christ's, May 11, 1680. Of Derbyshire.

HAYWARDE, CHRISTOPHER. Scholar of Trinity, 1562; B.A. 1564–5; M.A. 1568. Fellow, 1565. Ord. deacon (Ely) Dec. 21, 1568. V. of St Martin-in-the-Fields, London, 1577–87. Buried Dec. 27, 1587. Admon. (P.C.C.) 1588.

HEYWARD, EDWARD. Adm. at Corpus Christi, 1600. Of Reepham, Norfolk. S. of Richard. Adm. at the Inner Temple, 1604. Barrister, 1618. Died Sept. 25, 1658, 'aged 64.' M.I. at Reepham.

HEYWARD, EDWARD. Matric. sizar from Magdalene, Easter, 1617; B.A. from Christ's, 1620–1; M.A. 1621. Incorp. at Oxford, 1626. Ord. deacon (Peterb.) May 23; priest, May 24, 1624. V. of Leake, Lincs., 1631. (*Peile*, I. 310.)

HAYWARD, EDWARD. Adm. pens. at Trinity, July 6, 1635. Matric. 1638, as Howard; Scholar, 1638; B.A. 1638–9; M.A. 1642. Fellow, 1640.

HAYWARD, FRANCIS. Matric. Fell.-Com. from Trinity Hall, Easter, 1550.

HEYWARD, FRANCIS. Matric. pens. from Corpus Christi, Easter, 1658. Of Norwich. Adm. at the Inner Temple, 1657.

HAWARD, GEORGE. Matric. Fell.-Com. from Emmanuel, Michs. 1601. One of these names, of London, knighted, Aug. 6, 1604.

HAWARD, HUMPHREY. Matric. Fell.-Com. from Christ's, Dec. 1611. Doubtless s. of John (1586), barrister, of Tandridge Hall, Surrey, J.P.; age 25 in 1623. B.A. 1612–3 (on visit of Prince Charles). Adm. at the Inner Temple, 1613. His father by will (1630) excluded him, as unworthy. Brother of John (1623). (*Vis. of Surrey*, 1623; *Manning and Bray*, II.)

HAYWARD, JOHN. Matric. pens. from Trinity, Michs. 1572. Of Walsingham, Norfolk. B.A. 1578–9. R. of St Mary Woolchurch, London, 1594–1618. R. of Stepney, 1604–18. Buried at St Mary Woolchurch, Oct. 15, 1618, as B.D. (References to the family in Foley's *Records of the S.J.*, I. 175.)

HAYWARD, JOHN. B.A. from PEMBROKE, 1580–1; M.A. 1584; LL.D. 1591. *Supp.* for Incorp. at Oxford, 1616. Adm. advocate, Aug. 5, 1616. Chancellor of Lichfield, 1615. Knighted, Nov. 9, 1619. Adm. at Gray's Inn, Aug. 1, 1619. Master in Chancery. Brought before the Star Chamber for publishing a treatise dealing with the accession of Henry IV and the deposition of Richard II; imprisoned, 1599–1601. Historiographer of Chelsea College, 1610. Practised in the Court of Arches. Master in Chancery, 1616–27. M.P. for Bridgnorth, 1620–2; for Saltash, 1626. Died June 27, 1627. Buried in Gt St Bartholomew's, Smithfield. (*D.N.B.*)

HAYWARD, JOHN. Matric. pens. from CHRIST'S, Mar. 1586. Probably s. of Henry, of Tandridge, Surrey, an alderman of London. Adm. at the Inner Temple, Nov. 1588. Barrister, 1598. Bencher, 1613. Of Tandridge, Surrey. Probably brother of Rowland (1591–2): father of Humphrey (1611) and John (1623). (*Peile*, I. 185; *Manning and Bray*, II. 379.)

HAYWARD, JOHN. Scholar of TRINITY, Easter, 1602; B.A. (? 1602–3); M.A. 1606; B.D. from Pembroke, 1613. Fellow of Pembroke. Ord. deacon and priest (Ely) Sept. 20, 1607. R. of Coton, Cambs., 1607–51. University preacher. R. of Covington, Hunts., 1613. Buried at Coton, May 25, 1643. Will (P.C.C.) 1651; of Coton, clerk.

HAYWARD, JOHN. Adm. Fell.-Com. at EMMANUEL, June 4, 1603. Matric. 1603.

HAYWARD, JOHN. Adm. pens. at EMMANUEL, Feb. 28, 1611–2. Matric. 1612.

HAWARD, JOHN. Adm. pens. (age 16) at CHRIST'S, Nov. 6, 1623. S. of John (1586), barrister, of Tandridge (Tandridge Hall, Surrey). B. there. School, Westerham, Kent (Mr Knight). Matric. 1623. Brother of Humphrey (1611). (*Vis. of Surrey*, 1623, 1662; *Manning and Bray*, II. 305.)

HEYWARD, JOHN. Adm. sizar (age 15) at ST JOHN'S, Apr. 9, 1653. S of Robert, yeoman, of Newtown, Yorks. B. there. School, Melton, Yorks. (Mr Bedford). Matric. 1653, as Haworth.

HAYWARD, JOHN. Adm. pens. (age 16) at PEMBROKE, Feb. 12, 1660–1. S. of John. B. at Brundish, Suffolk.

HAYWARD, JOHN. M.A. from KING'S, 1735. S. of John, of Redmarley, Worcs. Matric. from Pembroke College, Oxford, July 1, 1725, age 20; B.A. (Oxford) 1731–2. V. of Frocester, Gloucs., 1729–76. R. of Nympsfield, 1754–72. Chaplain to Lord Ducie. Died May 14, 1776, aged 71. Buried in Frocester Church. (*Al. Oxon.*; *Misc. Gen. et Her.*, 3rd S., IV. 207; F. S. Hockaday.)

HAYWARD, JOHN. Adm. sizar at CLARE, July 5, 1736. B. at Woolwich, Kent. Matric. 1736; B.A. 1739–40. Fellow, 1742.

HAYWARD, NICHOLAS. Adm. pens. at EMMANUEL, May, 1590. Probably s. of Robert, of Bacton, Suffolk. Bapt. there, May 3, 1573. Matric. 1591; (? B.A. 1594–5). Schoolmaster at Bacton, 1601. (V. B. Redstone.)

HAYWARD, PENGREY. M.A. 1735 (Incorp. from Oxford). S. of Samuel, of Gloucester. Matric. from Brasenose, Mar. 24, 1701–2, age 16; B.A. (Oxford) 1705; M.A. 1708. Treasurer of the Infirmary, Westminster. Died Aug. 27, 1758. Buried in Westminster Abbey. (*Al. Oxon.*)

HAWARD, PHILIP. Adm. at KING'S, a scholar from Eton, 1493. Assistant Master at Eton.

HAYWARD or HAWARD, PHILIP. Adm. pens. (age 18) at CAIUS, Mar. 21, 1637–8. S. of Philip, gent., of Carlton, Suffolk. B. there. School, Loddon, Norfolk (Mr Child). Matric. 1638; Scholar, 1639–42; B.A. 1641–2. Of Carlton Colville, Cambs., gent. Will proved (Archd. Suffolk) 1665. (*Venn*, I. 331; *Vis. of Suffolk*, 1664.)

HEYWARD, RICHARD. Adm. at CORPUS CHRISTI, 1614. Of Canterbury.

HAYWARD, RICHARD. Matric. sizar from QUEENS', Easter, 1622. Of Suffolk. B.A. 1625–6; M.A. 1629.

HAYWARD or HEWARD, RICHARD. Adm. pens. at JESUS, July 4, 1660. Of Suffolk. Matric. sizar, 1660; Scholar, 1662; B.A. 1663–4. Signed for deacon's orders (London) June 4, 1664. C. of Hintlesham, Suffolk. Probably father of the next.

HAYWARD, RICHARD. Adm. sizar at JESUS, July 2, 1687. S. of Richard (? above), clerk, deceased, of Suffolk. Matric. 1688; B.A. 1691–2; Rustat scholar. Ord. priest (Norwich) May, 1695. Perhaps R. of Trimley St Mary, Suffolk; and of St Martin, 1696.

HAYWARD, ROGER. Presumably a member of the University. Expelled for some reason, Oct. 4, 1527; restored, 1528, on good behaviour. (Cooper, *Annals*, I. 326.)

HAYWARD, ROGER. Adm. sizar (age 15) at MAGDALENE, May 6, 1654. S. of John, baker, of Shrewsbury. B. there. School, Shrewsbury. Migrated to St John's, 1656. B.A. 1656–7; M.A. 1661; D.D. 1674 (*Lit. Reg.*). V. of St Chad's, Shrewsbury, 1662. Preb. of Lichfield, 1669–80. Author, *Sermons*. Died 1680. (H. G. Harrison.)

HAWARD, HAUWARD or HEYWOOD, ROWLAND. Matric. pens. from CHRIST'S, 1591–2. Probably s. of Henry, of Tandridge, Surrey. B.A. 1595–6; M.A. 1599. Ord. priest (Salisbury) June, 1606. Probably brother of John (1586). (*Peile*, I. 203; *Vis. of Surrey*, 1623.)

HAYWARD, STEPHEN. Matric. Fell.-Com. from CLARE, Easter, 1623. Doubtless of Faversham, Kent, gent. Adm. at Gray's Inn, May 7, 1624.

HAYWARDE, THEODORE. Matric. sizar from QUEENS', Michs. 1602. Of Essex. B.A. from St Catharine's, 1605–6. R. of Candlesby, Lincs., 1621–9.

HAYWARD, THOMAS. Matric. pens. from ST JOHN'S, Lent, 1584–5.

HAYWARD, THOMAS. Adm. Fell.-Com. (age 15) at TRINITY, Mar. 16, 1692–3. S. of John. B. at Hutton, Essex. School, Eufield (Mr Robert Udall). Matric. 1693.

HAYWOOD, THOMAS. B.D. 1709 (Incorp. from Oxford). S. of Valentine, of London. B. Apr. 1678. School, Merchant Taylors'. Matric. from St John's College, Oxford, July 7, 1694, age 16; B.A. (Oxford) 1698; M.A. 1702; B.D. 1708; D.D. 1714. Ord. priest (Norwich) June, 1701. V. of Harrington, Wilts., 1709–11. V. of Fyfield, Berks., 1709–26. V. of Gt Staughton, Hunts., 1721. R. of Gt Canford, Dorset, during 1722–3. V. of Charlbury, Oxon., 1726–46. Author. Died at Charlbury, Sept. 17, 1746. (*Al. Oxon.*)

HAYWARD, WILLIAM. Matric. pens. from PETERHOUSE, Michs. 1578. Of Walsingham, Norfolk, where he probably resided. B.A. from Jesus, 1582–3. (There are references to the family in *Records of the S. J.*, I. 175.)

HAWARD, ——. D.D. 1470–1. *See* HOWARD.

HAYWARD, ——. Adm. at CORPUS CHRISTI, 1580.

HAYWARD, ——. Adm. pens. at EMMANUEL, Feb. 18, 1633–4. Of Essex.

HAYWOOD, EDMUND. Adm. sizar (age 18) at ST JOHN'S, June 25, 1651. S. of John, husbandman, of Birtle, near Bury, Lancs. B. there. School, Bury, Lancs. Matric. 1651; B.A. 1654–5; M.A. 1658. V. of Wimbish, Essex, 1657–1706. Ord. priest (Ardfert) July 11, 1660. Died 1706. Father of the next.

HEYWOOD, EDMUND. Adm. sizar (age 18) at ST JOHN'S, May 5, 1682. S. of Edmund (above), V. of Wimbish, Essex. B. there. School, Felsted (Mr Glascock). Matric. 1682; B.A. from Queens', 1685–6. Ord. priest (London) May 26, 1700. Probably R. of St Giles', Colchester, 1702. V. of Gt Bentley, Essex, 1708. Died 1728.

HEYWOOD, GILES. Adm. at TRINITY, July 20, 1639; M.A. 1641. S. of Francis, of London. Matric. from Magdalen College, Oxford, May 8, 1635; B.A. (Oxford) 1635–6.

HEYWOOD, HENRY. Matric. sizar from CHRIST'S, Nov. 1581. Of Derbyshire. Ord. deacon (Lichfield) May 19, 1585; priest (London) May 7, 1586. C. of Breedon, Leics., 1599. (*Peile*, I. 167.)

HAYWOOD, JAMES. Matric. sizar from ST JOHN'S, Easter, 1614.

HEYWOOD, JAMES. M.A. 1697 (Incorp. from Oxford). S. of Thomas, of Westminster, gent. Matric. from Christ Church, Dec. 17, 1683, age 19; B.A. (Oxford) 1687; M.A. 1690. V. of Godmanchester, Hunts., 1691. Died Aug. 16, 1729, aged 67. (*Al. Oxon.*)

HEYWOOD, JAMES MODYFORD. Adm. Fell.-Com. (age 17) at TRINITY, June 8, 1747. S. of James, of Maristow, Devon. School, Eton. Matric. 1747. Lord of the Admiralty, 1783–4. (A. B. Beaven.)

HEYWOOD, JOHN. Matric. sizar from QUEENS', Easter, 1571. Of Nottinghamshire. B.A. from Christ's, 1574–5; M.A. 1578. Perhaps V. of Chobham, Surrey, 1575–95.

HEYWOOD, NATHANIEL. Adm. sizar at TRINITY, June 13, 1648. S. of Richard. B. at Little Lever, Lancs. Bapt. at Bolton-le-Moors, Sept. 16, 1633. Matric. 1649; B.A. 1651–2. C. of Illingworth, Yorks., 1652–5. V. of Ormskirk, Lancs., 1656–62, ejected. Afterwards preacher there and elsewhere. Author, *Christ displayed*. Died Dec. 16, 1677. Buried at Ormskirk. Brother of Oliver (1647). (*Calamy*, II. 102.)

HEYWOOD or HEAWOOD, OLIVER. Adm. pens. at TRINITY, June 12, 1647. S. of Richard, of Little Lever. Bapt. at Bolton, Lancs., Mar. 15, 1629–30. Matric. 1646; B.A. 1650. Ord. presbyter at Bury, Lancs. Minister at Coley Chapel, Halifax, Yorks., 1650–62, ejected. Afterwards preacher in Yorks.; imprisoned, etc. Author. Died May 4, 1702. Brother of Nathaniel (1648). (*D.N.B.*; *Calamy*, II. 559; *F.M.G.*, I. 62.)

HEYWOOD, PETER. Matric. pens. from MAGDALENE, Easter, 1620.

HEYWOOD, PETER. Adm. pens. (age 18) at ST JOHN'S, July 5, 1680. S. of Robert, Esq. B. at Heywood, in the parish of Bury, Lancs. Bapt. at Bury, June 19, 1662. School, Chester (Mr Harpur). Matric. 1680, as 'Hewitt.' Attorney-general of the Isle of Man. Married Leonara Connel. Died July 24, 1699. Buried at Kirk Malew. (E. Axon; *Vis. of Lancs.*, 1664; *F.M.G.*, 385.)

HEYWOOD, PETER. Adm. pens. at TRINITY HALL, Dec. 10, 1751; Scholar, 1752.

HAYWOOD or HARWOOD, RALPH. Matric. pens. from CHRIST'S, Lent, 1597-8. Perhaps of East Hagbourne, Berks. (Harwood). B.A. (? 1602-3); M.A. 1606. Died 1623. *Peile's* suggestion that he was brother of John Harwood (1586) must be wrong.

HAYWOOD or HEYWOOD, RALPH. Adm. sizar (age 20) at PETERHOUSE, May 28, 1646. Of Derbyshire. School, Repton. Matric. 1649; Scholar, 1649-50; B.A. 1649-50. Fellow, 1650-3.

HEAWOOD or HAIWOOD, RALPH. Adm. sizar (age 18) at ST JOHN'S, Apr. 18, 1666. S. of John, deceased, of Repton, Derbs. B. there. School, Repton (Mr Ullock). Matric. 1667; B.A. 1669-70.

HAYWOOD, RICHARD. Matric. p s. from CHRIST'S, Nov. 1566. One of these names R. of Lyng, Norfolk, 1574-5.

HEYWOOD, ROBERT. Matric. pens. from MAGDALENE, Easter, 1567. One of these names, 'bred in the schools,' was ord. priest (Chester) 1562; 'age 33; understands Latin; married; preacher' (*Lib. cler. Linc.*, 1576). R. of Rothwell, Lincs. R. of Ashby with Fenby. Will (P.C.C.) 1593.

HAYWOOD, ROBERT. Matric. pens. from MAGDALENE, Easter, 1624; B.A. 1627. Incorp. at Oxford, 1628. M.A. (Brasenose College, Oxford) 1631-2; B.D. 1642-3. Proctor (Oxford) 1639.

HEYWOOD, THOMAS. Fellow of QUEENS', 1448.

HEYWOOD, THOMAS. The dramatist; certainly of Cambridge as he states in his *Apology for Actors*; and probably of PETERHOUSE. Engaged as a member of Henslowe's company, 1598. One of the theatrical retainers of Henry Wriothesley, Earl of Southampton. Afterwards a member of the company belonging to Edward Somerset, Earl of Worcester. Attended the Queen's funeral in 1619 as 'one of her Majesty's players.' His literary labours were not confined to the drama. For an account of his works *see D.N.B.* Probably died *c.* 1650. Possibly identical with the next.

HEYWOOD, THOMAS. Matric. pens. from EMMANUEL, *c.* 1591 (*see* the above).

HAYWOOD, WILLIAM. Matric. pens. from ST JOHN'S, Michs. 1571.

HEYWOOD, WILMOT. Matric. from CHRIST'S, Michs. 1720. Scholar, Jan. 28, 1719-20; B.A. 1722-3; M.A. 1726. Ord. deacon (Lincoln) Sept. 1724; priest, Dec. 18, 1726. R. of Ladbrooke, Warws., 1734. V. of Paxton, Hunts., June, 1745-65. Died 1765. (*Peile*, II. 196.)

HAYWORTH, *see* HEYWORTH.

HAZAND, ——. B.A. 1478.

HAZARD, GABRIEL. Adm. sizar (age 17) at ST JOHN'S, Apr. 19, 1675. S. of Robert. B. at Nottingham. School, Nottingham. Matric. 1675; B.A. 1678-9. Usher at Mansfield Grammar School, *c.* 1682.

HAZARD, MICHAEL. Adm. sizar (age 16) at CHRIST'S, May 13, 1662. S. of Michael. B. at Wakefield. School, Wakefield (Mr Doughty). Matric. 1662; B.A. 1665-6; M.A. 1669. Ord. deacon and priest (Lichfield) Sept. 1665. Master of Burton-on-Trent School, May, 1669-97. Licensed to preach in Lichfield diocese, Sept. 5, 1673. Father of the next. (*Peile*, I. 599.)

HAZARD, MICHAEL. Adm. sizar at CHRIST'S, May 28, 1687. S. of Michael (above), Master of Burton-on-Treut School. B. there. Matric. 1687; B.A. 1690-1. Ord. deacon and priest (Lichfield) Sept. 1692. R. of Thorpe Constantine, Staffs., 1708-19. Buried there Jan. 24, 1719. (*Peile*, II. 105; Shaw, *Staffs.*, I. 437.)

HAZARD or HASSARD, NATHANIEL. Matric. sizar from QUEENS', Michs. 1615. B. at Ashby, Leics. B.A. 1619-20; M.A. 1623. Incorp. at Oxford, 1627. Ord. deacon (London) Sept. 18, 1624; priest, Mar. 13, 1624-5.

HAZARD, ROBERT. Matric. pens. from TRINITY, Michs. 1623; scholar from Westminster, 1624.

HAZARD, THOMAS. Adm. sizar at CHRIST'S, May 31, 1656. Matric. 1656.

HAZELAND, WILLIAM. Adm. sizar (age 15) at ST JOHN'S, May, 1746. S. of William, baker, of Wiltshire. B. at Wilcott. School, Marlborough (Mr Stone). Matric. 1746; B.A. 1749-50 (senior wrangler); M.A. 1753. Fellow, 1751-5. Ord. deacon (Lincoln) June 17, 1753; priest (London) Dec. 23, 1754. V. of Bengeo, Herts., 1761-3. Master of the Grammar School, Hertford. Lecturer at Whitechapel. Author, *Sermons*. Died June 21, 1763. (*Scott-Mayor*, III. 558; *G. Mag.*; *L. Mag.*)

HAZLEWOOD, *see* HASELWOOD.

HAZWELL, JOSEPH. M.A. from EMMANUEL, 1675. S. of Christopher, of London. School, Christ's Hospital. Matric. from Pembroke College, Oxford, Apr. 3, 1669, age 18; B.A. (Oxford) 1672. R. of North Benfleet, Essex, 1685-1733. Died Feb. 9, 1732-3. Will (Comm. C. Essex) 1738. (*Al. Oxon.*)

HEAD, FRANCIS. Adm. at KING'S, a scholar from Eton, 1655. S. and h. of Richard (of Hermitage, Rochester; afterwards Bart.). B. at Rochester, 1639. Matric. 1655; B.A. 1658-9. Fellow, 1658, till 1662. Adm. at the Middle Temple, Nov. 26, 1657. Age 25 in 1664. Died Oct. 16, 1678, *v.p.*, aged 37. Buried at St Margaret's, Rochester. Brother of Meric (1662). (*Vis. of Kent*, 1664; *G.E.C.*)

HEAD, JOHN. Adm. pens. (age 17) at ST JOHN'S, June 26, 1723. S. of William, farmer, of Kent. B. at Tonbridge. School, Tonbridge (Mr Spencer). Matric. 1723; B.A. 1726-7; M.A. 1730. Ord. deacon (El) July 14, 1728; priest, Sept. 21, 1729. V. of Kennington, 1729-30. V. of Woodnesborough, Kent, 1730-6. (*Scott-Mayor*, III. 363.) Sellinge and Burmarsh were held by an Oxford contemporary.

HEAD, MERIC. Adm. at KING'S, a scholar from Eton, 1662. S. of Sir Richard, Bart. B. at Rochester. Matric. Lent, 1663; B.A. 1666-7; M.A. 1670; D.D. 1683. Fellow, 1665. Incorp. at Oxford, 1672. V. of Ulcombe, Kent, 1672-87. R. of Leybourne, 1675-87. Died Mar. 6, 1686-7. Buried at Leybourne. M.I. there. Benefactor to the College Chapel. Brother of Francis (1655). (*Vis. of Kent*, 1664; C. H. Fielding.)

HEADE, RICHARD. Matric. sizar from PETERHOUSE, Michs. 1616.

HEAD, RICHARD. M.A. from KING'S, 1728. S. of Richard, of Whaddon, Wilts. Matric. from Hart Hall, Oxford, Feb. 10, 1710-1, age 17; B.A. (Oxford) 1714. R. of Sherrington, Wilts., 1726. R. of Orcheston St George, 1728. Admon. (P.C.C.) 1772. (*Al. Oxon.*)

HEAD, RICHARD. Adm. sizar (age 19) at ST JOHN'S, June 9, 1742. S. of Henry, clerk, of Wiltshire (Master of Amesbury School). B. at Amesbury. Matric. 1742; B.A. 1745-6; M.A. 1749. Ord. deacon (Salisbury) Sept. 21, 1746. V. of Compton Chamberlayne, Wilts., 1748-1800. R. of Rollestone, 1756-1800. Died 1800. (*Scott-Mayor*, III. 528.)

HEAD, THOMAS. B.A. 1478-9; M.A. 1482; D.D. 1496 (*Loder*). Fellow of PEMBROKE, 1488; Heede. Perhaps Head Master of Ipswich School, *c.* 1488. R. of Orton Waterville, Hunts., 1494-1500. Died 1500.

HEAD, THOMAS. Adm. at CORPUS CHRISTI, 1713. Of Kent. Matric. Lent, 1713-4; B.A. 1716-7; M.A. 1720. Ord. deacon (London) Feb. 22, 1718-9; priest, Dec. 20, 1719. Probably R. of Birdbrook, Essex, 1719-59.

HEDDE, ——. B.D. 1493-4; D.D. 1500. Perhaps Thomas, R. of St Ann, Aldersgate, 1510-5. R. of Laingdon, Essex, 1513-7. Treasurer of St Paul's, 1516-20. Preb. of St Paul's, 1519. Died 1520.

HEDLAM, JOHN. Adm. pens. at PETERHOUSE, Lent, 1588-9. Matric. 1589; Scholar.

HEADLAM, JOHN. Adm. at CORPUS CHRISTI, 1632. Of Yorkshire. Probably s. and h. of Leonard, Town Clerk of York, gent.; adm. at Gray's Inn, June 20, 1632. Of Kexby. Married Margaret dau. of Sir John Lister, of Hull, Knt. Died June 28, 1664. Buried at Catton. Admon. (York) 1664. Probably father of William (1665) and brother of William (1646). (*Vis. of Yorks.*, 1666; J. R. Wallran, *Gainsford.*)

HEADLAM, PHILIP. Matric. pens. from CORPUS CHRISTI, Michs. 1632. Perhaps a mistake for John, above.

HEADLAM, RICHARD. Adm. pens. (age 17) at ST JOHN'S, May 26, 1682. S. of John (1632), Esq., deceased. B. at Kexby, Yorks. School, Pocklington (Mr Elletson). Matric. 1682, as 'Heldam'; B.A. 1685-6; M.A. 1696. Fellow, 1688-97. Ord. deacon (Lincoln) Feb. 28, 1696-7; usher of Pocklington School; priest, May 30, 1697. V. of North Stoke, Oxon., 1698-1730. Said to have been a non-juror. Married, at St Olave's, York, Jan. 17, 1698-9, Susanna Fairfax, widow. Buried Apr. 29, 1730. (*Kettlewell's Life*; M. H. Peacock.)

HEADLAM, WILLIAM. Matric. Fell.-Com. from TRINITY HALL, Michs. 1646. Perhaps s. of Leonard, Town Clerk of York. Bapt. at St Michael-le-Belfry, Nov. 27, 1629. Adm. at Gray's Inn, May 28, 1647. Died unmarried. Brother of John (1632).

HEADLAM, WILLIAM. Adm. pens. (age 16) at ST JOHN'S, June 29, 1665. S. of John (? 1632), Esq., of York. B. there. School, York. Adm. at the Inner Temple, May 17, 1667. Of Kexby, Esq. Buried at Catton, Apr. 16, 1679. (*Vis. of Yorks.*, 1666.)

HEADLAM, ——. B.Can.L. 1482.

HEADLAM, ——. Adm. Fell.-Com. at PETERHOUSE, June 29, 1577.

HEADLAM, ——. Adm. Fell.-Com. at PETERHOUSE, Jan. 22, 1586–7.

HEADLEY, HENRY. Adm. sizar at JESUS, Aug. 7, 1745. Of Cambridgeshire. Matric. 1745; Scholar; B.A. 1749–50; M.A. 1753. Fellow, 1755–63. Ord. deacon (Lincoln) Dec. 23, 1750; priest (London) May 24, 1752. R. of Belaugh and of Instead, Norfolk, 1762. V. of Barton Turf, 1762–85. V. of North Walsham and Antingham, 1768–85. Will (P.C.C.) 1786.

HEADLEY, JOHN. Adm. sizar (age 20) at ST JOHN'S, June 12, 1674. S. of John, deceased, of New England. B. there. School, Westerham, Kent.

HEADLEY, JOHN. Adm. sizar at CLARE, July 26, 1728. B. at Newmarket. Matric. 1729; B.A. 1732–3.

HEADLEY, THOMAS. Matric. sizar from ST CATHARINE'S, Michs. 1571; B.A. from Trinity, 1575–6; M.A. 1579.

HEDLEY, THOMAS. Matric. pens. from QUEENS', Michs. 1582. (Adm. as 'Netley,' of Nottinghamshire, in College register.)

HEADON, MARMADUKE. Adm. pens. at SIDNEY, July 1, 1617. S. of Henry, of Marton. B. in Yorkshire. Age 13 in 1612. Matric. 1617. (*Vis. of Yorks.*, 1612.)

HEADSLEY, JOHN, *see* HADSLEY.

HEALD, PETER. Adm. sizar (age 17) at PETERHOUSE, Feb. 15, 1677–8. Of Yorkshire. School, Pocklington. Matric. 1677–8; B.A. 1681–2; M.A. 1685. Preb. of Chichester. V. of Cowfold, Sussex, 1704–28. Died Aug. 30, 1728, aged 73. (*T. A. Walker*, 161.)

HEALD, THOMAS. Adm. sizar (age 18) at JESUS, June 27, 1679. Of Yorkshire. Matric. 1682; B.A. 1682–3; M.A. 1686. Ord. deacon (York) Feb. 1694–5; priest, 1696. V. of Huddersfield, 1714–34. Master of Hipperholme School. Died 1734. Father of the next, and of Whitley (1709). (A. Gray.)

HEALD, THOMAS. Adm. pens. at JESUS, May 28, 1716. S. of Thomas (above), V. of Huddersfield. Matric. 1716; Scholar, 1716; B.A. 1719–20. Ord. deacon (York) Sept. 1720; priest, June, 1723. Brother of Whitley (1709).

HEALD, THOMAS. Adm. sizar (age 18) at TRINITY, June 19, 1742. S. of Robert, of Norwich. B. at Ashbourne, Derbs. School, Repton. Matric. 1744; M.B. 1749; M.D. 1754. F.R.C.P., 1760. Gulstonian lecturer, 1763. Harveian orator, 1765. Removed to London, 1767. Physician to the London Hospital, 1770. F.R.S., 1770. Croonian lecturer, 1770 and 1784–6. Gresham Professor of Physics, 1771–89. Lumleian lecturer, 1786–9. Author, medical. Died Mar. 26, 1789. Will, P.C.C. (*D.N.B.*; *Munk*, II. 231.)

HEALD, WHITLEY. Adm. pens. (age 15) at ST JOHN'S, Oct. 28, 1709. S. of Thomas (1679), V. of Huddersfield. B. at Wakefield, Yorks. School, Wakefield (Mr Clark). Matric. 1710; B.A. 1713–4; M.A. 1717; B.D. 1724. Fellow, 1717–32. Incorp. at Oxford, 1723. Ord. priest (London) Dec. 20, 1719. V. of North Stoke, Oxon., 1730–6. C. and lecturer at St George, Southwark. Died suddenly, when preaching in St Nicholas Cole Abbey, London, Feb. 22, 1735–6. Brother of Thomas (1716).

HEALD, WILLIAM. Adm. pens. at EMMANUEL, Feb. 13, 1644–5. Of Lancashire. (Previously at Oxford.) One of these names minister of Walton-le-Dale, Lancs., 1651–3–. (E. Axon.)

HEALE, *see* HELE.

HEALEY, GEORGE. Matric. pens. from MAGDALENE, Easter, 1621. Doubtless s. of Thomas, of Burringham, Lincs. Buried at Bottesford, May 8, 1677, aged 73. Brother of Thomas (1627) and father of Thomas (1656–7). (*Lincs. Pedigrees*, 478.)

HEALEY or HEYLEY, JOHN. Adm. sizar at EMMANUEL, Nov. 1586. Matric. 1586; Scholar; B.A. 1590–1; M.A. 1594. Ord. deacon and priest (London) June 24 and 26, 1603. R. of Rushbrook, Suffolk, 1618–33. R. of Gt Whelnetham, 1619–33. Buried at Rushbrook, Apr. 4, 1633. Will (P.C.C.) as Heiley. (V. B. Redstone.)

HELEY, JOHN. Matric. pens. from MAGDALENE, Easter, 1628; B.A. 1631–2; M.A. 1635. Doubtless ord. priest (Norwich) Sept. 25, 1635. Perhaps R. of Snailwell, Cambs., 1641.

HEALY, JOHN. Adm. pens. at EMMANUEL, June 4, 1670. Of Wiltshire. Matric. 1670. One John [illegible]ly, s. and h. of James, of the City of London, gent., adm. at Lincoln's Inn, May 14, 1670.

HEALEY, JOHN. Adm. scholar at TRINITY HALL, Nov. 7, 1735. Of Hull, Yorks. Matric. 1735.

HELY, ORLANDO. Matric. sizar from MAGDALENE, Michs. 1627.

HEALY, SAMUEL. Adm. sizar (age 16) at MAGDALENE, July 1, 1687. S. of Thomas, gent. B. at Batley, Yorks. School, Leeds. Scholar, 1686–9; Matric. 1688; M.A. 1700 (*Lit. Reg.*). Ord. priest (Norwich) May, 1692. V. of Little Massingham, Norfolk. Master of the School at Gt Massingham.

HEALY, SAMUEL HENRY. Adm. sizar (age 17) at SIDNEY, May 7, 1740. S. of Thomas, druggist, of Oakham, Rutland. School, Oakham. Matric. 1740; Scholar; B.A. 1743–4. Ord. deacon (Lincoln) Dec. 22, 1745; priest, June 14, 1747.

HELEY, THOMAS. Matric. pens. from MAGDALENE, Easter, 1627. 3rd s. of Thomas, of Burringham, Lincs. B.A. 1630–1; M.A. 1634. Fellow. V. of Haxey, Lincs., 1641. Brother of George (1621). (*Lincs. Pedigrees*.)

HEALEY, THOMAS. Adm. pens. (age 17) at MAGDALENE, Feb. 5, 1656–7. S. of George (1621), gent., of Messingham, Lincs. Bapt. at Bottesford, Aug. 28, 1639. School, Gainsborough. Matric. 1657. Adm. at Lincoln's Inn, June 23, 1658, as s. and h. of George. Of Burringham, Lincs., Esq. Buried at Bottesford, Jan. 4, 1681–2. (*Lincs. Pedigrees*, 478.)

HELEY or HELLEY, WILLIS. B.A. from MAGDALENE, 1606–7; M.A. from Trinity, 1610.

HEAN, ROBERT (1644), *see* HEARNE.

HEANE, THOMAS (1615), *see* HAYNE.

HEAPE, ABEL. Adm. sizar at EMMANUEL, 1624; B.A. from Peterhouse, 1627–8; M.A. 1631.

HEPE, FRANCIS. Matric. sizar from TRINITY, Easter, 1585; B.A. 1588–9. One of these names, B.A., V. of Binsted, Sussex, 1605–34. Will (Chichester) 1634. (H. G. Harrison.)

HEAPE, GEORGE. Adm. pens. (age 18) at ST JOHN'S, Mar. 8, 1658–9. S. of Francis, gent., of Stoke, Notts. B. there. School, Repton (Mr Ullock). Matric. 1659.

HEAPE, RICHARD. Adm. sizar at JESUS, Apr. 29, 1682. S. of Joseph, of Lancashire. Matric. 1682; Scholar, 1683; B.A. 1685–6. Ord. deacon (Chester) Sept. 25, 1687. Usher of the Free School, Manchester. Admon. (Chester) 1696. (E. Axon.)

HEAPE, THOMAS. Matric. sizar from CHRIST'S, Michs. 1580; B.A. 1583–4. Ord. priest (Chester); licensed preacher (Lincoln). Described as M.A. when presented to V. of Little Marlow, Bucks., 1596.

HEARD, BRYAN. Adm. sizar at CLARE, Nov. 15, 1639. Matric. 1639.

HERD, JOHN. Adm. at KING'S, a scholar from Eton, 1529. B. 1512, at Southwark, Surrey. B.A. 1533–4; M.A. (? 1546); M.D. 1558. Fellow, 1532–6. Ord. priest (Lincoln) 1564. Preb. of Lincoln, 1557. Preb. of York, 1559. R. of Gedney, Lincs. R. of Waddington. Author, historical. Died 1588. (*Cooper*, II. 40; *D.N.B.*)

HEARD, JOHN. Matric. sizar from TRINITY, Easter, 1570; B.A. 1574–5; M.A. 1578; B.D. 1586–7. University preacher, 1586. Incorp. M.A. at Oxford, 1578. R. of St Leonard's, Eastcheap, London, 1583–1610. Died 1610.

HEARD or HERD, JOHN. Matric. sizar from ST JOHN'S, Michs. 1571; B.A. from Trinity, 1576–7. Ord. deacon (Lincoln) July 22, 1578; priest, June 26, 1579. V. of Bishop's Norton, Lincs., 1593.

HERD, THOMAS. B.A. 1488–9.

HEARD, TIMOTHY. Matric. sizar from TRINITY, Easter, 1610. (? S. of John, 1570.) B. in St Leonard's, Eastcheap, London. B.A. 1613–4. Ord. deacon (London) June 15, 1617, age 25; C. of St Mary-le-Bow, London. V. of Takeley, Essex, 1629–43, sequestered.

HEARD, WILLIAM. Adm. pens. at EMMANUEL, Jan. 23, 1640–1.

HEARD, ——. B.A. 1485–6.

HEARDSON or HERDSON, FRANCIS. Matric. sizar from ST JOHN'S, Lent, 1629–30. Doubtless s. of Henry (1588), R. of Stutton. B.A. 1631–2; M.A. 1635. Ord. deacon (Norwich) Sept. 21, 1634; priest, Sept. 25, 1636. C. of Stutton, Suffolk. V. of Eye, 1661. Father of the next.

HEARDSON, FRANCIS. Adm. sizar (age 16) at ST JOHN'S, Apr. 23, 1662. S. of Francis (above), of Wilby (or Westley), Suffolk. B. there. School, Eye (Mr Brown). Matric. 1662; B.A. 1665–6; M.A. 1669. Fellow of Emmanuel, 1668. Buried at St Andrew's, Cambridge, Mar. 6, 1669–70.

HERDSON, HENRY. Matric. pens. from ST JOHN'S, Michs. 1588. Of Nottinghamshire. B.A. 1591–2; M.A. 1596. Fellow, 1594. Probably R. of Stutton, Suffolk. Will (P.C.C.) 1637; proved by s. Francis (? 1629–30). (J. Ch. Smith.)

HERDSON, HENRY. Matric. sizar from ST JOHN'S, Michs. 1626; B.A. 1629–30. He styled himself 'Professor of the art of memory in the University of Cambridge'; afterwards he taught his art in London. Perhaps R. of Harkstead, Suffolk, 1632. Author of *Ars Mnemonica*. (*D.N.B.*)

HEARE, JOHN. Matric. sizar from CORPUS CHRISTI, Michs. 1586. Of Norfolk. B.A. 1590-1; M.A. 1594. Ord. priest (Peterb.)

HEARLE, FRANCIS. Adm. (age 17) at CAIUS, June 25, 1595. S. of James. B. at Tawstock, Devon. Bapt. Aug. 6, 1577. School, Tawstock (Mr Stribling). Scholar, 1598-1603; B.A. 1599-1600; M.A. 1603. Ord. deacon and priest (Peterb.) July 12, 1601. R. of St Erme, Cornwall, 1606. Brother of William (1590). (*Venn*, I. 156.)

HEARLE, FRANCIS. Adm. pens. at TRINITY, June 12, 1675.

HEARLE or HARRELL, WILLIAM. Adm. sizar (age 19) at CAIUS, Oct. 12, 1590. S. of James. B. at Tawstock, Devon. Bapt. Oct. 7, 1571. School, Tawstock. Scholar, 1592-6; B.A. 1593-4; M.A. 1597. Fellow, 1596-1603. Ord. deacon and priest (Peterb.) July 12, 1601. R. of Berrynarbor, Devon. Will (Exeter) 1631. Brother of Francis (1595). (*Venn*, I. 141.)

HEARLE or HEARLES, WILLIAM. Adm. pens. (age 17) at CAIUS, Mar. 29, 1631. S. of John, of Tawstock, Devon. Bapt. Sept. 21, 1613. School, Ilfracombe (Mr Mathews). Matric 1631; Scholar, 1633-6; B.A. 1636-7. Perhaps R. of St Erme, Cornwall.

HEARLEY or HERLEY, STEPHEN. Adm. at TRINITY, Easter, 1641.

HEARLY, WILLIAM. Matric. sizar from MAGDALENE, Michs. 1610.

HEARNE, *see also* **HIERON.**

HEARNE or HERNE, ARTHUR. Matric. pens. from KING'S, *c.* 1595; B.A. from Christ's, 1597-8; M.A. 1601. Incorp. at Oxford, 1601. Ord. deacon (Salisbury) May, 1605; priest, Sept. 1605. Master of Marlborough School, 1602. R. of St Peter's and St Paul's, Marlborough, 1611-30. Buried Sept. 24, 1630. Will (P.C.C.) 1630. (*Peile*, I. 216.)

HEARNE or HERON, ARTHUR. Matric. sizar from ST JOHN'S, Easter, 1622. Of Devon. B.A. 1625-6; M.A. 1629; B.D. 1636. Fellow, 1628. R. of Bardwell, Suffolk, 1631-76. Died 1676. Will of John, of Westminster, gent., proved (P.C.C.) 1649; by s. Arthur, clerk. Father of the next and John (1683).

HERON, ARTHUR. Adm. sizar (age 15) at ST JOHN'S, Aug. 25, 1679. S. of Arthur (above), clerk, deceased, R. of Bardwell, Suffolk. B. there. School, Bury. Matric. 1680; B.A. 1683-4; M.A. 1687. Fellow, 1685-98. V. of Northstoke, Oxon., 1697-8. R. of Moreton, Essex, 1698-1733. R. of Laver Magdalen, 1708-20. Said to have been a non-juror. Married, at Romford, Aug. 6, 1713, Philadelphia, dau. of Carew Henry Mildmay. Buried at Moreton, 1733. Brother of John (1683). (*Scott-Mayor*.)

HERNE, BENJAMIN. Adm. pens. at CLARE, Mar. 18, 1645-6. Matric. 1646; B.A. 1649-50; M.A. 1654.

HERN, CHARLES. Adm. pens. (age 18) at PETERHOUSE, June 30, 1707. Of Middlesex. School, Eton. Matric. 1707; Scholar, 1707. Probably 4th s. of Sir Joseph, of London, Knt., deceased; adm. at the Inner Temple, Nov. 25, 1710.

HERON, CHARNOCK. Adm. pens. at TRINITY, Nov. 3, 1671. S. of John, of Godmanchester, Hunts., Esq. Matric. 1671-2. Adm. at Gray's Inn, Feb. 10, 1672-3.

HIRNE, CHRISTOPHER. Matric. Fell.-Com. from CORPUS CHRISTI, Easter, 1585.

HYRNE, CLEMENT. Adm. Fell.-Com. (age 15) at CAIUS, July 1, 1600. S. of Thomas, alderman, of Norwich (afterwards Knt.). Of Haveringland, Esq. Died Jan. 25, 1655-6. M.I. at Haveringland. Father of John (1623) and Thomas (1620). (*Vis. of Norfolk*; *Venn*, I. 173.)

HERNE or HIRNE, CLEMENT. Adm. Fell.-Com. (age 16) at CAIUS, June 22, 1655. S. of Thomas, gent. (? 1620), of Metton. B. at Mountjoy, Norfolk. Schools, Tharston (Mr Firmary) and Ingworth (Mr Ransom). Matric. 1655. Adm. at Gray's Inn, June 16, 1657. Of Metton and Roughton. Died 1720. Father of Thomas (1684). (*Venn*, I. 391.)

HERON, CUTHBERT. Adm. sizar (age 18) at CHRIST'S, Aug. 19, 1633. S. of Thomas. B. at Crawley, Northumberland. School, Morpeth (Mr Oxley). Matric. 1633. Perhaps father of Matthew (1661). (*Peile*, I. 429.)

HERN, DANIEL. Adm. sizar at PETERHOUSE, Apr. 6, 1593 (possibly matric. from Trinity, 1595). S. of Daniel, serving man. 'Grecian' at Christ's Hospital; sent to Cambridge, *c.* 1592. B.A. from Peterhouse, 1595-6; M.A. 1601; B.D. 1614. V. of Henley, Suffolk, 1607. V. of Bramford, 1623-31.

HEARNE, EDWARD. Matric. pens. from ST JOHN'S, Lent, 1557-8. Perhaps s. of Richard, of Halstead, Essex. Adm. at Lincoln's Inn, Nov. 13, 1564. Barrister, 1575. Recorder of Stamford, 1588. Serjeant-at-law, 1595. Knighted, July 23, 1603. Baron of the Exchequer. Died July 4, 1609. Perhaps father of James (1603). (*Lincs. Pedigrees*, 488.)

HEARNE, EDWARD. Matric. pens. from TRINITY, *c.* 1601. S. of Edmund (? Edward), of Maidstone. B.A. 1605-6; M.A. 1609; B.D. 1616; D.D. 1631-2 (*Lit. Reg.*). Incorp. at Oxford, 1611. Perhaps ord. deacon and priest (Lincoln) Mar. 8, 1611-2. R. of Yelling, Hunts., 1612-9. Preb. of Lincoln, 1616. R. of Coston, Leics., 1620-49. R. of Burton Coggles, Lincs., 1632. Buried at Knipton, Leics., Mar. 12, 1649-50. Will (P.C.C.) 1650; as Heron. (*Al. Oxon.*; *Lincs. Pedigrees*, 486.)

HERON, EDWARD. Adm. pens. at TRINITY, May 22, 1682. Perhaps s. and h. of Thomas, late of London, Esq., deceased; adm. at Lincoln's Inn, May 15, 1682.

HEARNE, FRANCIS. Matric. pens. from TRINITY, Michs. 1572.

HERNE, FRANCIS. Adm. Fell.-Com. (age 18) at CAIUS, Oct. 10, 1720. S. of Francis, of Arminghall, Norfolk. B. in London. School, Harrow. Matric. 1720. Of Harrow-on-the-Hill, Esq. Living, unmarried, in 1748. Sold Arminghall, and had an estate at Tibenham. (*Venn*, II. 15.)

HERNE, GEORGE. Adm. pens. at CLARE, Apr. 20, 1664. Matric. 1664; B.A. 1667-8.

HEARNE, GEORGE. Adm. scholar at TRINITY HALL, Jan. 4, 1742-3. Of Kent. Exhibitioner from King's School, Canterbury. Matric. sizar Dec. 1744. For a short time usher at King's School, Canterbury, in 1743.

HERON, HALY. Matric. sizar from QUEENS', Michs. 1565; B.A. 1569-70. Author, *Discourse of Moral Philosophy*. (*Cooper*, I. 452; *D.N.B.*)

HEARNE, HENRY. Matric. sizar from TRINITY, Easter, 1575.

HERRON, HENRY. Matric. sizar from TRINITY, Easter, 1614.

HEARNE, HENRY. Matric. sizar from MAGDALENE, Michs. 1642; B.A. 1648-9; M.A. 1652.

HEARNE, HENRY. Adm. pens. at EMMANUEL, Mar. 11, 1680-1; Fell.-Com. Sept. 1681. Of Middlesex. Matric. 1686; M.B. 1686.

HERON, JAMES. Adm. at CORPUS CHRISTI, 1603. Of Lincolnshire. Perhaps s. of Sir Edward (? 1557-8), of Stamford and Cressy Hall. Adm. at Lincoln's Inn, Feb. 7, 1604-5. Of Panfield Hall, Essex. Married Anne, dau. of Sir John Hatcher, 1609. (*Lincs. Pedigrees*, 488; *Vis. of Essex*, 1634.)

HEARNE or HERON, JEREMY. Adm. pens. at EMMANUEL, May 1, 1603. Matric. 1603; Scholar; B.A. 1606-7; M.A. 1610. Ord. deacon (Peterb.) June 4; priest, June 5, 1615.

HERON, JOHN. Matric. Fell.-Com. from QUEENS', Michs. 1565.

HERON, JOHN. Matric. Fell.-Com. from CLARE, Lent, 1607-8. Doubtless s. of Richard (alderman and sheriff), of London, gent.; adm. at Lincoln's Inn, Jan. 27, 1610-1. Bencher, 1637. M.P. for Newport, Cornwall, 1628, but unseated. Counsel for Prynne, 1634; and for Laud, 1644, when he delivered 'a learned and eloquent speech.' Will (P.C.C.) 1649, of Hendon, Esq. Probably father of John (1631) and brother of Richard (1607-8). (*D.N.B.*; *Vis. of London*, 1634.)

HERON or HEARNE, JOHN. M.A. 1612 (Incorp. from Oxford). Of Oxfordshire, gent. Matric. from Magdalen College, Oxford, Dec. 15, 1592, age 15; B.A. 1600; M.A. 1604; *Supp.* for B.D. 1611. Fellow of Magdalen, 1599-1612. Perhaps R. of Chale, Isle of Wight, 1612-49. (*Al. Oxon.*; *Vis. of London*, 1634.)

HYRNE, JOHN. Adm. pens. (age about 17) at CAIUS, Apr. 25, 1623. S. of Clement, Esq. (1600), of Hoxne, Suffolk. School, Eye (Mr Dorman). Matric. 1623-4. Brother of Thomas (1620). (*Venn*, I. 262.)

HERON, JOHN. Matric. sizar from PEMBROKE, Easter, 1629; B.A. 1631-2. Ord. deacon (Norwich) May 24, 1635; priest, Sept. 25, 1636. C. of Lound, Suffolk. V. of Kirby-le-Soken, Essex, 1645-79. Died 1679.

HERON, JOHN. Adm. pens. at CLARE, Oct. 19, 1631. Matric. 1632. Probably s. of John (1607-8). Adm. at Lincoln's Inn, Feb. 11, 1635-6. Translator of *The Learned Reading of John Herne, Esq.* (his father), 1659. (*D.N.B.*)

HERNE, JOHN. Adm. pens. (age 16) at PEMBROKE, July 15, 1633. S. of John, of Godmanchester, Hunts., gent. Matric. 1633. Adm. at Lincoln's Inn, Feb. 4, 1636-7.

HEARNE or HERON, JOHN. Adm. sizar (age 16) at CAIUS, Jan. 17, 1639-40. S. of John, cutler, of the parish of Gt St Mary, Cambridge. B. there. Bapt. Feb. 28, 1623-4. School, Perse. Matric. 1640; Scholar, 1640-4; B.A. 1643-4. Fellow, 1644-6.

HEARNE, JOHN. Adm. Fell.-Com. at CLARE, Apr. 20, 1664. B. in London. One of these names, s. and h. of John, of Godmanchester, Hunts., adm. at Lincoln's Inn, May 23, 1666.

HERNE, JOHN. Adm. pens. at CLARE, Feb. 26, 1672–3. Of Tibenham, Norfolk. Matric. 1672–3; B.A. 1676–7; M.A. 1680; D.D. 1690 (*Com. Reg.*). Fellow, 1680. Incorp. at Oxford, 1681. Ord. deacon (London) Apr. 25, 1683. Canon of Windsor, 1690–1707. Chaplain to the King, 1690. Perhaps R. of East Woodhay, Hants., 1691–1707. R. of East Shefford, Berks., 1694–1707. Died Apr. 24, 1707. Will, P.C.C. (*Al. Oxon.*; Le Neve, *Mon.*)

HYRNE, JOHN. Adm. pens. (age 13) at MAGDALENE, Mar. 16, 1674–5. S. of Henry, schoolmaster. B. at Parson's Green, Fulham, Middlesex. School, Parson's Green. Matric. 1675. One of these names, of Kensington, Middlesex, adm. at the Inner Temple, 1676.

HEARN, JOHN. M.A. from CLARE, 1677. S. of Robert, of Sherborne, Dorset. Matric. from Wadham College, Oxford, Mar. 3, 1663–4, age 17; B.A. (Oxford) 1667. R. of Hammoon, Dorset, 1667–88. R. of Blandford Forum, 1680–2. (*Al. Oxon.*)

HERON, JOHN. Adm. sizar (age 16) at ST JOHN'S, July 14, 1683. S. of Arthur, 1622 (of Bardwell, Suffolk), deceased. Bapt. Apr. 3, 1667, at St James', Bury St Edmunds. Exhibitioner from Charterhouse. Matric. 1683–4; B.A. 1687–8. R. of Shipdham, Norfolk, 1696–1706. Buried at Bardwell, Oct. 5, 1706. Brother of Arthur (1679). (*Al. Carthus.*; V. B. Redstone.)

HYRNE, JOHN. Adm. sizar (age 16) at CAIUS, June 27, 1689. S. of William, citizen of Norwich. B. there. School, Norwich (Mr Burton). Matric. 1689. Buried Oct. 21, 1689. Brother of William (1687). (*Venn*, I. 487.)

HERON, JOHN. Adm. sizar (age 17) at ST JOHN'S, July 2, 1725. S. of Robert, husbandman, of Northumberland. B. at Hexham. School, Durham (Mr Thompson). Matric. 1725.

HERON, JOHN. Adm. p[illegible]. (age 17) at TRINITY, June 21, 1735. S. of Robert, of Newark, Notts. School, Westminster. Matric. 1735. Adm. at the Middle Temple, Aug. 4, 1732. Recorder of Newark, 1748–52.

HEARNE, JOSEPH. Adm. Fell.-Com. at CLARE, Aug. 15, 1639. Matric. 1639. Perhaps 2nd s. of John (? 1607–8), bencher of Lincoln's Inn, adm. there, Jan. 19, 1641–2.

HERN, JOSEPH. Matric. Fell.-Com. from KING'S, Lent, 1697. Perhaps 2nd s. of Sir Joseph, of the City of London, Knt.; adm. at Lincoln's Inn, June 24, 1696; and at the Inner Temple, Oct. 23, 1701. If so, brother of Charles (1707). Died Dec. 19, 1723; of the Inner Temple.

HERON, MATHEW. Adm. pens. (age 17) at ST JOHN'S, Sept. 11, 1661. S. of Cuthbert (? 1633), deceased, of Acton, Northumberland. B. there. School, Bilsthorp, Notts. (Mr Bennet). Matric. 1661. Adm. at the Inner Temple, 1662; of Kirkheron, Northumberland.

HEARNE, MICHAEL. Matric. pens. from JESUS, Easter, 1577; B.A. 1580–1; M.A. 1584. V. of St Ives, Hunts., 1595–1602.

HERNE, NICHOLAS. Matric. pens. from ST JOHN'S, Lent, 1577–8. Perhaps adm. at Lincoln's Inn, Feb. 17, 1581–2, from Clement's Inn. Will of one of these names (P.C.C.) 1612; of Arminghall, Norfolk, Esq.

HERNE, PASTON. Matric. pens. from KING'S, Easter, 1722 (adm. as Fell.-Com.). Perhaps captain in the Norfolk militia. Died Mar. 12, 1761. (G. *Mag.*; L. *Mag.*)

HERON, POYNINGS. Matric. Fell.-Com. from QUEENS', Michs. 1565. S. of Sir Nicholas, of Addiscombe House, Surrey. Served in the wars in Ireland and the Netherlands. Married Elizabeth, dau. of Gregory Lovell. Died Jan. 1595–6. Will (P.C.C.) 1596. (*Vis. of Surrey*, 1623.)

HERON, RICHARD. Matric. Fell.-Com. from CLARE, Lent, 1607–8. Doubtless s. of Richard, of London (alderman and sheriff). Bapt. at St Vedast's, May 17, 1597. Brother of John (1607–8). (G. E. Cokayne, *Mayors and Sheriffs of London*.)

HEARNE, RICHARD. Adm. at KING'S (age 16) a scholar from Eton, Jan. 30, 1614–5. Of London. Matric. 1615; B.A. 1617–8; M.A. 1623. Fellow, 1618, till 1623.

HEARNE or HERON, RICHARD. Matric. sizar from KING'S, Easter, 1620; B.A. 1624–5; M.A. 1628. Ord. deacon (Peterb.) Mar. 9; priest, Mar. 10, 1627–8. Signs as C. of Odell, Beds., 1634.

HIRON or HERNE, ROBERT. M.A. 1600 (Incorp. from Oxford). Of Lincolnshire. Matric. from St Alban's Hall, Nov. 4, 1586, age 18; B.A. from Brasenose, 1590; M.A. 1594. Buried at St Mary's, Oxford, May, 1603. Will (Oxford). (*Al. Oxon.*)

HERON, ROBERT. Adm. Fell.-Com. (age 16) at SIDNEY, Jan. 31, 1622–3. S. of Sir Edward, K.B. B. at Surfleet, Lincs. School, Westminster. Matric. 1623. Died *s.p.*, before 1634. (*Lincs. Pedigrees*, 489.)

HERNE, ROBERT. Adm. pens. (age 16) at CAIUS, Mar. 28, 1635. S. of Robert, gent. B. t Tibenham, Norfolk. Schools, Aylsham (Mr Knolles) andaNewport (Mr Lee). Matric. 1635. Adm. at Lincoln's Inn, Oct. 18, 1637. Of Tibenham, Esq. Died Mar. 2, 1685–6. M.I. at Tibenham. (*Venn*, I. 317; *Vis. of Norfolk*, 1664.)

HERON or HERNE, ROBERT. Adm. pens. at CLARE, Oct. 9, 1639. Exhibitioner from Charterhouse. Matric. 1639; B.A. 1643–4; M.A. 1647.

HEARN, ROBERT. Adm. sizar at TRINITY, Apr. 18, 1644, as 'Heane,' as sizar (age 16) at Christ's, May 1, 1645. S. of Nicholas. B. in London. Bapt. at St Vedast's, Sept. 2, 1627. School, St Paul's. Matric. 1645. (*Vis. of London*, 1634.)

HERNE, ROBERT. Adm. pens. at CLARE, Jan. 23, 1670–1. Of Ameringhall, Norfolk. Matric. 1671; B.A. 1674–5; M.A. 1678. Fellow, 1678–1705. Senior proctor, 1694–5., V. of Everton, Hunts., 1691–1705. Died 1705.

HERNE, ROBERT. Adm. pens. at CLARE, Feb. 26, 1672–3. Of Tibenham, Norfolk. S. and h. of Robert (? 1635), of Tibenham, Esq. Matric. 1672–3. Adm. at Lincoln's Inn, July 1, 1674.

HERON, ROBERT. Adm. pens. at CLARE, June 11, 1742. B. at Newark, Notts. Matric. 1743; B.A. 1745–6; M.A. 1749. Ord. deacon (Lincoln) June 14, 1747; priest, Sept. 25, 1748. V. of Basingthorpe, Lincs., 1748. R. of Cotgrave, Notts., 1750–6.

HEARNE or HERON, SAMUEL. Matric. pens. from TRINITY, Easter, 1575, scholar from Westminster. S. of John, of Lincoln. B.A. 1578–9; M.A. 1582; B.D. 1589; D.D. 1595. Fellow. Incorp. at Oxford, 1598. University preacher, 1588. V. of Trumpington, Cambs., 1588–90. V. of Kendal, Westmorland, 1591–2. V. of Kirkby Lonsdale, 1591. V. of Normanton, 1594. V. of Chesterton, Cambs., 1596–9. V. of Enfield, Middlesex, 1598–1601. R. of Cheadle, Staffs., 1602. V. of Fakenham, Norfolk, 1610–6. R. of Tokenham, Wilts., 1610–6. Died 1616. Will (V.C.C. and P.C.C.) 1616. (*Lincs. Pedigrees*, 488; *D.N.B.*)

HERON, SAMUEL. Matric. sizar from TRINITY, Lent, 1634–5. Of Lincolnshire. B.A. 1643–4; M.A. from St John's, 1647. Intruded fellow of St John's, 1644. Junior proctor, 1651–2. Will proved (V.C.C.) 1652.

HERNE, SAMUEL. Adm. pens. at CLARE, June 23, 1663. Of London. Exhibitioner from Charterhouse. Matric. 1663; B.A. 1666–7; M.A. 1670. Fellow, 1671–8. Author, *Domus Carthusiana*. (*Al. Carthus.*)

HEARNE, SIMON. Matric. pens. from TRINITY, Easter, 1572.

HEARNE or HERN, SIMON. Adm. pens. (age 15) at CAIUS, Apr. 19, 1596. S. of Simon, of Tibenham, Norfolk. School, Tibenham. Matric. c. 1596. Migrated to Emmanuel, Apr. 3, 1598. B.A. 1599–1600; M.A. 1604.

HERON, THOMAS. B.Can.L. 1480. One of these names, s. of Sir John, Knt., treasurer of the King's chamber, died Mar. 18, 1517–8.

HERON, THOMAS. Matric. sizar from PETERHOUSE, Michs. 1570; B.A. 1574–5; M.A. 1578. Ord. priest (Peterb.) May 11, 1581. V. of Gt Staughton, Hunts., 1586–93. Probably V. of Gt Marlow, Bucks., 1593. Died Dec. 30, 1599. Buried at Gt Staughton.

HEARNE, THOMAS. Adm. at KING'S, a scholar from Eton, 1598; B.A. 1601–2. Fellow, till 1605. V. of Lyminster, Sussex, 1605–32. Will (P.C.C.) 1632.

HYRNE, THOMAS. Adm. Fell.-Com. (age 16) at CAIUS, July 1, 1620. S. of Clement (1600), of Norwich. School, Aylsham (Mr Knowles). Matric. 1621; B.A. 1623–4. Adm. at Gray's Inn, Feb. 15, 1623–4. Of Haveringland, Esq. Brother of John (1623). (*Venn*, I. 250.)

HERNE or HERON, THOMAS. Matric. sizar from ST JOHN'S, Easter, 1629; B.A. 1632–3. Ord. deacon (Norwich) June 1; priest, Dec. 21, 1634.

HERON, THOMAS. Adm. sizar (age 16) at ST JOHN'S, Sept. 14, 1646. S. of Thomas, R. of Otham, Kent. B. at Wainfleet, Lincs. School, Maidstone (Mr Lamb). Matric. 1646; B.A. 1651–2; M.A. 1655. One of these names V. of Bekesborne, Kent, 1650. Buried there Mar. 1, 1659–60. (H. G. Harrison.)

HERNE, THOMAS. Adm. pens. (age 17) at CAIUS, July 19, 1684. S. of Clement (1655), gent., of Haveringland, Norfolk. B. there. School, Norwich. Matric. 1684; Scholar, 1685. Adm. at Gray's Inn, Feb. 11, 1685–6. Died Oct. 30, 1726. Buried at Haveringland. (*Venn*, I. 477.)

HERON, THOMAS. Adm. sizar at JESUS, July 5, 1703. Matric. 1703; Scholar, 1706; B.A. 1706–7. Ord. deacon (Peterb.) June 8, 1707; priest (London) Mar. 5, 1709–10. C. of Northborough, Northants. (H. I. Longden.)

HERNE, THOMAS. Adm. pens. at CORPUS CHRISTI, Oct. 29, 1711. Of Suffolk. 1st s. of Francis. Matric. 1712; Scholar; B.A. 1715; M.A. (Oxford) 1718. Fellow of Merton College, Oxford, 1716. Domestic tutor to the sons of the Duke of Bedford. Took part in the Bangorian controversy. Author of political and religious pamphlets. Died at Woburn, 1722. (*D.N.*B.; *Masters*.)

HERNE, THOMAS. Adm. scholar at TRINITY HALL, Jan. 6, 1725–6. Of Haveringland, Norfolk. Matric. 1725.

HEARNE, WILLIAM. Matric. pens. from CLARE, Michs. 1570; B.A. 1573–4; M.A. 1577. Perhaps William Hieron, R. of Hemingby, Lincs., 1597.

HERNE or HEARNE, WILLIAM. Adm. pens. at JESUS, June 23, 1635. Of Huntingdonshire. Matric. 1635. One of these names R. of High Hoyland, Yorks., 1660.

HYRNE or HERNE, WILLIAM. Adm. sizar (age 16) at CAIUS, Oct. 15, 1687. S. of William, citizen of Norwich. B. there. School, Norwich. Scholar, 1687–94; Matric. 1688; B.A. 1691–2; M.A. 1695; D.D. 1709. Ord. deacon (London) Sept. 24, 1692; priest (Norwich) Sept. 1696. R. of Harkstead, Suffolk, 1697; of St George Colegate, Norwich, 1715–45. Brother of John (1689), father of William (1717). (*Venn*, I. 484.)

HERON or HIRON, WILLIAM. Adm. sizar (age 20) at TRINITY, June 27, 1688. S. of John. B. at Sutton Agri, Gloucs. School, Combrook, Warws. (Mr John Fancourt). Matric. 1688; B.A. 1691–2. V. of Blyth, Notts., 1695–1731. Buried there Mar. 14, 1731.

HERNE or HYRNE, WILLIAM. Adm. sizar (age 17) at CAIUS, Oct. 15, 1717. S. of William (1687), D.D., R. of St George Colegate, Norwich. B. there. School, Norwich (Mr Pate). Matric. 1717; Scholar, 1717–25; B.A. 1721; M.A. 1725. Ord. deacon (Oxford) Dec. 23, 1722, as C. to his father; priest (Norwich) May, 1724. R. of Horningtoft, Norfolk, 1728. V. of Hemblington, 1729–65; of St James and St Paul, Norwich, 1735–76. R. of Garveston, Norfolk, 1744–76. V. of Alderford, 1762–76. (*Venn*, II. 9.)

HERON, ——. B.A. 1537.

HEATH, ANTHONY. Matric. sizar (age 9) from CAIUS, Easter, 1559.

HEATH, BAILY. Adm. at CORPUS CHRISTI, 1733. S. of Thomas, of Mile-end, Stepney. B. in Middlesex. School, Felsted. Of Stanstead Mountfichet, Essex, Esq. High Sheriff of Essex, 1748. Died July 9, 1760. Perhaps brother of Thomas (1734–5). (*G. Mag.*; *Manning and Bray*, I. 498.)

HEATH, BARTHOLOMEW. Matric. pens. from PETERHOUSE, Michs. 1562. 2nd s. of John, of London, merchant, and warden of the Fleet, who founded a family at Kepier, Durham, to which Bartholomew's brother, John, succeeded. B.A. 1564–5; M.A. 1568; M.D. 1576. Fellow, 1566–79. Brother of Edward (next) and Nicholas (1570). (*T. A. Walker*; Cooper, I. 452.)

HEATH, EDWARD. Matric. pens. from PETERHOUSE, Michs. 1570. 5th s. of John, of London, merchant. Brother of Bartholomew (above) and Nicholas (1570). (*T. A. Walker*.)

HEATH, EDWARD. Matric. Fell.-Com. from CLARE, Easter, 1626. 1st s. of Robert (1587), recorder of London. Age 7 in 1619. Adm. at the Inner Temple, 1625. Barrister, 1634. K.B., Apr. 26, 1661. Brother of George (1633), John (1626) and Robert (1634). (*Vis. of Kent*.)

HEATH, ELLIS. Adm. pens. (age 17) at TRINITY, Apr. 4, 1692. S. of Roger. B. in London. School, Rotherham, Yorks. (Mr Edm. Farrer). Migrated to Oxford. Matric. from St Alban Hall, May 12, 1692.

HEATH, FRANCIS. Matric. pens. from TRINITY, Michs. 1626, a scholar from Westminster; B.A. 1628–9; M.A. 1632; B.D. from Corpus Christi, 1640; LL.D. 1662 (*Lit. Reg.*). Fellow of Trinity Hall, 1662–79 (he had been elected in 1644). Perhaps V. of Sutton-on-the-Forest, Yorks., 1632–5. (*See Al. Oxon.* for a contemporary.)

HEATH, FRANCIS. Adm. at CORPUS CHRISTI, 1633. Of Kent.

HEATH, GEOFFREY. Adm. Fell.-Com. (age 25) at ST JOHN'S, June 4, 1653. S. of Nicholas, gent., of London. B. there. School, London.

HEATH, GEORGE. Matric. Fell.-Com. from CORPUS CHRISTI, Easter, 1633. Of Kent. S. of Robert (1587), recorder of London. B.A. 1636–7; M.A. 1640. Fellow, 1641–2. R. of West Grinstead, Sussex, 1642 (ejected, *c.* 1644) and 1660. Preb. of Chichester, 1660–72. One of these names preb. of Lincoln, 1643. Brother of Edward (1626), John (1626) and Robert (1634). (*Vis. of Kent*, 1619; *Masters*.)

HEATH, HENRY. Matric. sizar from CORPUS CHRISTI, Easter, 1617. Of Northamptonshire. S. of John. Bapt. at Peterborough, Dec. 16, 1599. B.A. 1620–1. No M.A. recorded. Ord. deacon (Peterb.) Oct. 29; priest, Oct. 30, 1622. Afterwards became a Roman Catholic. Adm. at the English College at Douay. Entered the Franciscan Convent, 1623; became a member of the Order. Appointed vicar of his house, 1630; Custos custodum with the office of commissary of his English brethren in Belgium, 1637. Lector of scholastic theology, 1640. Went on the English Mission. Arrested in London; convicted as a returned priest. Executed at Tyburn, Apr. 17, 1643. (*D.N.B.*)

HEATH, JOHN. Matric. Fell.-Com. from CHRIST'S, Dec. 1585. Doubtless s. of John, of Kepier, Durham. Of Kepier, Esq. Married Dorothy, dau. of John Blakiston. Buried at St Giles', Durham, Jan. 6, 1639–40, aged 71. Father of the next. (*Peile*, I. 182; *Surtees*, IV. 70.)

HEATH, JOHN. Matric. sizar from CHRIST'S, July, 1618; B.A. 1621; M.A. 1625. One of these names R. of Little Shelford, Cambs., 1626–41; and of Snailwell, 1641. (*Peile*, I. 325.)

HEATH, JOHN. Adm. pens. (age 16) at PETERHOUSE, May 16, 1620; Fell.-Com. afterwards. S. of Thomas, of East Grange and Kepier, Durham. Bapt. at Pittington, Sept. 20, 1604. Matric. 1620. Adm. at Gray's Inn, Aug. 8, 1620. Of Kepier, Durham, Esq. Married Margaret, dau. of William Smith, of Durham. Subscribed to the building of the College Chapel. Buried Mar. 7, 1664–5, at St Giles', Durham. (*T. A. Walker*, 16; *Surtees*, IV. 70.)

HEATH, JOHN. Matric. pens. (age 16) from PEMBROKE, Easter, 1624. S. of John, pewterer, of London. B.A. 1627–8; M.A. 1631. Fellow, 1634–44 (ejected).

HEATH, JOHN. Matric. Fell.-Com. from CLARE, Easter, 1626. 2nd s. of Robert (1587), recorder of London. Adm. at the Inner Temple, 1625. Barrister, 1634. Bencher, 1660. Attorney-general for the duchy of Lancaster, 1660. M.P. for Clitheroe, 1661–79. Knighted, May 27, 1664. Married Margaret, dau. of Sir John Mennes. Brother of Edward (1626), George (1633) and Robert (1634). (*Vis. of Kent*; *D.N.B.*)

HEATH, JOHN. Adm. pens. at CHRIST'S, Feb. 20, 1642–3. Matric. 1645; B.A. 1646–7; M.A. 1650.

HEATH, JOHN. Matric. pens. from QUEENS', Lent, 1645–6. Of Middlesex. B.A. 1648–9; M.A. from St John's, 1652. Fellow of St John's, 1650 (by order of the visitors).

HEATH, JOHN. Adm. pens. (age 15) at SIDNEY, July 11, 1685. 1st s. of Joseph, yeoman. B. at Cambridge. Schools, Haslingfield (Mr Barber) and Perse (Mr Griffiths). B.A. 1689–90; M.A. 1693; B.D. 1700. Fellow, 1693.

HEATH, JOHN. Adm. at KING'S, a scholar from Eton, 1719. S. of William. B. at Bathwick, Somerset. Matric. 1720; B.A. 1723–4; M.A. 1727. Fellow, 1723. Ord. deacon (London) Feb. 21, 1724–5; priest (Ely) Sept. 24, 1732. R. of Sampford Courtney, Devon, 1738. Will (Exeter) 1772.

HEATH, NEVILL. Matric. sizar from CLARE, Easter, 1631; B.A. 1634–5; M.A. 1638. R. of Calbourne, Isle of Wight. Father of the next.

HEATH, NEVILL. Adm. pens. (age 17) at ST JOHN'S, May 7, 1677. S. of Nevill (above), R. of Calbourne, Isle of Wight. B. at Atherton. School, Newport, Isle of Wight (Mr Chamberlain). Matric. 1677; B.A. 1680–1; M.A. 1684.

HETHE, NICHOLAS. at KING'S HALL, 1384. Clerk. S. of Walter, of Huntingdon. Expelled at the Bishop's visitation, May 19, 1385. (*Trin. Coll. Adm.*, I. 107.)

HEATH, NICHOLAS. B.A. 1519–20. Of the family at Aspley, Tamworth. B. *c.* 1501, in London. M.A. 1522; D.D. 1535. Fellow of CHRIST'S, 1521; of Clare, 1524. Said to have been at Corpus Christi, Oxford, *c.* 1515. University chaplain, 1529–32. Chaplain to Cardinal Wolsey. R. of Hever, Kent, 1531–3. Archdeacon of Stafford, 1534–40. Chaplain to the King. R. of Bishopsbourne, Kent, 1537; and of Cliffe, 1538. Dean of Shoreham, 1538. Bishop of Rochester, 1540–3; of Worcester, 1543–51; deprived; reinstated, 1553–5. Archbishop of York, 1555–9. Lord Chancellor, 1556–8. Deprived of the Archbishopric for refusing the oath of supremacy, 1559. Retired to Chobham, Surrey, where he died and was buried, 1579. Admon. (P.C.C.) 1579. (*Cooper*, I. 403; *Peile*, I. 11; *D.N.B.*)

HEATH, NICHOLAS. Matric. pens. from PETERHOUSE, Michs. 1570. S. of John, of London and Kepler, Durham. Of East Greenwich, Kent. Purchased Little Eden, Durham, 1617. Married Anne, dau. of John Topp. Will proved (Durham) 1627. Brother of Bartholomew (1562) and Edward (1570). (*T. A. Walker*; *Surtees*, I. 38.)

HEATH, RICHARD. Adm. sizar (age 20) at CHRIST'S, June 17, 1631. S. of John. B. at Lilley, Herts. School, Clifton (Mr Bedford). Matric. 1632; B.A. 1634–5. Minister of Hopesay, Salop, 1645. V. of St Alkmund's, Shrewsbury, 1650–62. Retired to Wellington, where he died, May, 1666. One of the correctors of the Press for Walton's Polyglott Bible. (*Peile*, I. 412.)

HEATH, RICHARD. Adm. pens. (age 18) at TRINITY, June 12, 1707. S. of Sir Richard, of Guildford, Surrey, Baron of the Exchequer. School, Westminster. Matric. 1707; Scholar, 1708; B.A. 1710-1; M.A. 1714. R. of East Clandon, Surrey, 1717-29. Died Apr. 18, 1729. (*Al. Westmon.*, 249; G. *Mag.*)

HEATHE, ROBERT. Matric. pens. from TRINITY HALL, Easter, 1553. Of Edenbridge, Kent. Adm. at the Inner Temple, 1564. Of Brasted, Kent. Father of the next.

HEATH, ROBERT. Adm. pens. at ST JOHN'S, June 26, 1587. S. of Robert (above), of Brasted, Kent, barrister. B. at Edenbridge, May 20, 1575. School, Tonbridge. Matric. 1589; D.C.L. (Oxford) 1642-3. Adm. at Clifford's Inn, 1591; and at the Inner Temple, May 23, 1593. Barrister-at-law, 1603. Bencher, 1617. Treasurer, 1625. Recorder of London, 1618-21. M.P. for London, 1620-2; for East Grinstead, 1624-6. Knighted, Jan. 28, 1620-1. Solicitor-general, 1621-5. Attorney-general, 1625. Conducted the principal Star Chamber prosecutions, 1629-30. Chief Justice, C.P., 1631-4. King's serjeant, 1636. Justice K.B., 1641-3. Chief Justice K.B., 1643. Impeached by the Parliament of high treason, 1644; his place declared vacant, 1645. Fled to France, 1646. Died at Calais, Aug. 30, 1649. Buried in Brasted Church. Father of Edward (1626), John (1626), George (1633) and Robert (1634). (*Al. Oxon.*; *D.N.B.*)

HEATH, ROBERT. Matric. pens. from PEMBROKE, Easter, 1611.

HEATH, ROBERT. Adm. Fell.-Com. at CORPUS CHRISTI, 1634. Of London. Doubtless 4th s. of Sir Robert (1587), Knt. Matric. 1634-5. Adm. at the Inner Temple, 1637. Barrister, 1652. Auditor in the Court of Wards. Brother of Edward (1626), George (1633) and John (1626). *D.N.B.* suggests his identity with the poet, author of *Clara Stella*, etc.

HEATH or HEYT, ROBERT. Adm. sizar at CLARE, Nov. 22, 1637. Matric. 1637; B.A. 1641-2.

HEATH, ROBERT. Adm. Fell.-Com. at EMMANUEL, May 19, 1638. Perhaps s. and h. of William, of Lewes, Sussex. Matric. 1639. Adm. at the Inner Temple, 1640. Perhaps barrister, 1654. (*Vis. of Sussex.*)

HEATH, ROBERT. Adm. pens. at CORPUS CHRISTI, 1643. Of London. Exhibitioner from Charterhouse. Matric. Easter, 1644; B.A. 1647-8; M.A. 1651. Ord. deacon (Lincoln) June 3; priest, June 7, 1662.

HEATH, ROBERT. Adm. sizar (age 13) at MAGDALENE, May 15, 1667. S. of Robert, of South Weald, Essex. School, Brentwood. Matric. 1667; B.A. 1670-1; M.A. 1674. Ord. deacon (Ely) Dec. 24, 1671.

HEATH, ROBERT. Adm. pens. at CLARE, June 30, 1673. Of London. Matric. 1674; B.A. 1676-7; M.A. 1680.

HEATH, ROWLAND. Adm. sizar at QUEENS', July 2, 1675. Of Salop. Matric. 1675, from King's.

HEATHE, THOMAS. Matric. Fell.-Com. from CAIUS, Easter, 1559. One of these names R. of Feltwell St Nicholas, Norfolk, 1575-85; V. of Easton, 1594-7; R. of Sutton, 1617-25. (*Venn*, I. 41.)

HEATH, THOMAS. Matric. sizar from TRINITY, Easter, 1607; B.A. 1610-1. Perhaps schoolmaster at Thetford, 1623, but *see* the above.

HEATH, THOMAS. Adm. pens. (age 15) at CHRIST'S, June 8, 1654. S. of Nicholas, of Little Eden, Durham. B. there. Bapt. Apr. 2, 1639. School, Houghton-le-Spring (Mr Caunt). Matric. 1654. Died *c.* 1671. (*Peile*, I. 563; H. M. Wood.)

HEATH, THOMAS. Adm. pens. (age 17) at ST JOHN'S, May 7, 1703. S. of Thomas, deceased. B. at Morton Corbett, Salop. School, Shrewsbury. Matric. 1703; B.A. 1706-7; M.A. 1710. Perhaps adm. at the Inner Temple, May 12, 1704; s. and h. of Thomas, of Hanley Park, Cheshire.

HEATH, THOMAS. M.A. from PEMBROKE, 1728. S. of William, of Carswell, Staffs. Matric. from Hart Hall, Oxford, Feb. 5, 1713-4, age 18; B.A. (Oxford) 1717-8. Perhaps R. of Hathern, Leics., 1733-65; and V. of Sheepshed, 1735-65. Died Oct. 18, 1765. M.I. at Sheepshed. Will, P.C.C. (*Al. Oxon.*; *Nichols*, III. 845)

HEATH, THOMAS. Adm. Fell.-Com. (age 17) at SIDNEY, Mar. 19, 1734-5. S. of Thomas, Esq., of Mile End Green, London. School, Eton. Matric. 1735. Perhaps brother of Bailey (1733).

HEATH, WILLIAM. Adm. sizar at PETERHOUSE, Feb. 11, 1617-8. Of London. S. of Timothy, draper, of St Laurence Pountney. Matric. 1618. Ramsey exhibitioner from Christ's Hospital, 1621. Transferred to Lincoln College, Oxford, but took no degree there. (A. W. Lockhart.)

HEATH, WILLIAM. Matric. pens. from CORPUS CHRISTI, Michs. 1623 (possibly adm. pens. at Peterhouse, June 28, 1622; left Oct. 1623). Of Kent. B.A. 1626-7; M.A. 1630; B.D. 1643. R. of Stoke Newington, 1639-44 and 1662-4. One of these names V. of Bengeo, Herts., during the Interregnum.

HEATH, WILLIAM. Matric. sizar from KING'S, Easter, 1639.

HEATH, WILLIAM. Adm. sizar at ST CATHARINE'S, 1665-6. Matric. 1667; B.A. 1673-4; M.A. 1681. Perhaps R. of Walcot, Somerset, 1707-21. Died 1721.

HEATH, WILLIAM. Adm. pens. (age 18) at CAIUS, June 7, 1683. S. of William, gent., of Blofield, Norfolk. B. at Hemblington, Norfolk. Bapt. July 10, 1665. School, Norwich. Matric. 1683; Scholar, 1683-90; B.A. 1686-7; M.A. 1690. Ord. deacon and priest (London) Sept. 1691. R. of Burlingham St Edmund and St Andrew, Norfolk, 1691-1741. Died Jan. 25, 1740-1. Buried at Burlingham St Edmund. M.I. Will (Norwich, Archd. C.) 1741; 'of Lingwood,' where he gave the communion flagon. (*Venn*, I. 474.)

HEATHCOTE, EDWARD. Adm. sizar (age 18) at ST JOHN'S, June 15, 1746. S. of Ralph (1714), of Leicestershire, R. of Morton. B. at Barrow. School, Chesterfield (Mr Burrow). Matric. 1746; B.A. 1749-50; M.A. 1753. Ord. deacon (Lincoln) Sept. 23, 1750; priest, May 24, 1752. V. of Buckminster and Sewstern, Leics., 1764. Died Apr. 13, 1801. Brother of Ralph (1741). (*Scott-Mayor*, III. 560; *F.M.G.*, 475.)

HEATHCOTE, GEORGE. Adm. Fell.-Com. at CLARE, June 9, 1720. B. in Jamaica. Matric. 1720. One of these names adm. at Lincoln's Inn, June 17, 1721.

HEATHCOTE, GILBERT. Adm. at CORPUS CHRISTI, 1665. S. of Michael. B. at Buxton. School, Bakewell (Mr Beardmore). Migrated as pens. to Christ's, June 11, 1666, age 18. Matric. 1667; B.A. 1669-70; M.A. 1673. *D.N.B.* wrongly identifies him with the Lord Mayor of London, Knt. and Baronet, etc.; who was, however, s. of Gilbert, of Chesterfield; bapt. there, Jan. 8, 1651-2. A more probable identification is by Dr Brady (*Records of Cork*, II. 115), i.e. that he was C. of Youghal, 1683, and Chancellor of Cloyne, 1685-93. But he makes him son of one Gilbert. (*Peile*, II. 5; *G.E.C.*, v. 74.)

HEATHCOTE, GILBERT. Adm. pens. at CHRIST'S, Apr. 22, 1681. One of these names entered at Leyden, 1686 and 1688. (*See Peile*, II. 82.)

HEATHCOTE, GILBERT. Adm. Fell.-Com. at QUEENS', May 12, 1741. Doubtless s. of Sir John, 2nd Bart., of Normanton, Ruts. Succeeded as Bart., 1759. M.P. for Shaftesbury, 1761-8. Sheriff of Rutland, 1771-2. Died at Hampstead, Dec. (? Nov.) 2, 1785. Buried at Normanton. (*G.E.C.*; *G. Mag.*)

HEATHCOTE, JOHN. Adm. Fell.-Com. at QUEENS', May 4, 1744. Probably s. of Sir John, of Normanton, Rutland, Bart. Adm. at Lincoln's Inn, May 4, 1744. If so, brother of Gilbert (above).

HEATHCOTE, RALPH. Matric. sizar from TRINITY, Michs. 1620, as Jethcote; B.A. 1624-5. Ord. deacon (Peterb.) Dec. 18, 1625; priest, Apr. 23, 1626. Will (P.C.C.) 1654; of Tideswell, Derbs., clerk.

HEATHCOTE, RALPH. Adm. pens. (age 18) at MAGDALENE, May 30, 1651. Perhaps s. of Ralph (? Godfrey), of Chesterfield, Derbs. Matric. 1651; B.A. 1654-5; M.A. 1662. Incorp. at Oxford, 1663. R. of Staveley, Derbs., 1661-1716. Married Abigail, dau. of Richard Hall, of Barlow, Jan. 20, 1657-8. Died 1716. Father of Ralph (next). (*F.M.G.*, 474; M. H. Peacock; Jewitt, *Reliq.*, XVI. 144.)

HEATHCOTE, RALPH. Adm. pens. (age 17) at CHRIST'S, July 8, 1681. S. of Ralph (above). B. at Staveley, Derbs. Bapt. there, Nov. 3, 1663. School, Repton (Mr Litherland). Matric. 1682; B.A. 1684-5; M.A. 1688. Fellow (by mandate) 1686-95. Taxor, 1691. Incorp. at Oxford, 1693. Ord. deacon (Lincoln) Feb. 20; priest, Feb. 27, 1686-7. R. of Staveley, Derbs. R. of Morton, Derbs., 1710-39. Married Elizabeth West, of Aston, May 30, 1695. Died 1739. Father of the next. (*F.M.G.*, 474; *Peile*, II. 84.)

HEATHCOK or HEATHCOTE, RALPH. Adm. sizar at JESUS, Apr. 29, 1714. S. of Ralph (above), R. of Staveley, Derbs. Matric. 1714; B.A. 1717-8; M.A. 1722. Ord. deacon (London) Mar. 13, 1719-20; priest (Lincoln) Feb. 18, 1721-2. V. of Sileby, Leics., 1730-65. R. of Morton, Derbs., 1739-65. P.C. of Prestwold, Leics., 1746. Married Mary, dau. of Simon Ockley, Professor of Arabic. Died June 9, 1765, aged 68. Father of Edward (1746) and the next. (*F.M.G.*, 475.)

HEATHCOTE, RALPH. Adm. sizar at JESUS, Apr. 29, 1741. S. of Ralph (above), of Leicestershire. B. at Barrow-on-Soar, Dec. 19, 1721. School, Chesterfield. Matric. 1742; B.A. 1744-5; M.A. 1748; D.D. 1760. Ord. deacon (Lincoln) Sept. 22, 1745; priest, May 25, 1746. C. of St Margaret's, Leicester, 1748. V. of Barkby, Leics., 1749. Took part in the Middletonian Controversy, 1752. Boyle lecturer, 1763-5. V. of Sileby, Leics., 1765. R. of Sawtry All Saints', Hunts., 1767-95. Preb. of Southwell, 1768-95. Author, miscellaneous. Died May 28, 1795. Will, P.C.C. Brother of Edward (1746). (*F.M.G.*, 475; A. Gray; *G. Mag.*; *D.N.B.*)

HEATHCOTE, SAMUEL. Adm. at Corpus Christi, 1740. Of London. S. of Samuel, of Beeralston, Devon. Matric. 1741. Of St George's, Hanover Square; adm. at Lincoln's Inn, July 19, 1740.

HEATHCOTE, THORNHIL. Adm. pens. (age 18) at St John's, Mar. 25, 1746. S. of Samuel, attorney-at-law, of Derbyshire. B. at Derby. School, Derby (Mr Winter). Matric. 1746; B.A. 1749-50. Afterwards Lieut.-Colonel of Marines. Died June 29, 1785. (*Scott-Mayor*, III. 557.)

HEATHER, WILLIAM. Matric. pens. from Queens', Easter, 1658. Of Surrey.

HEATHERFIELD, JOSEPH. Adm. sizar (age 16) at Magdalene, Feb. 28, 1655-6. S. of J., citizen of London. School, St Paul's. Matric. 1656; B.A. 1659-60. Signed for priest's orders (London) Mar. 5, 1663-4. V. of Boxted, Essex, 1667-9. R. of Otterden, Kent, 1668-70.

HEATHERLEY, SEAWELL. Adm. sizar (age 19) at Pembroke, May 13, 1718. S. of William, of London, citizen and carpenter. Matric. 1717; 'Grecian' from Christ's Hospital. B.A. 1721-2; M.A. 1725. Ord. deacon (Norwich) Feb. 1721-2. Under Master at Christ's Hospital, 1725. Head Master, 1738-53. V. of Clavering, Essex, 1753-62. Died Feb. 5, 1762. (*G. Mag.*)

HEATLY or HETLEY, FRANCIS. Matric. Fell.-Com. from St Catharine's, Michs. 1637. Of Huntingdonshire. S. and h. of Thomas, serjeant-at-law, of Brampton, Hunts. Adm. at Gray's Inn, Aug. 7, 1623. Brother of the next. (*Vis. of Hunts.*, 1613.)

HEATLY or HETLEY, WILLIAM. Adm. Fell.-Com. at St Catharine's, 1638. Of Huntingdonshire. S. of Thomas, serjeant-at-law, of Brampton, deceased. Adm. at Gray's Inn, Feb. 2, 1637-8. Married Carina, dau. of Henry Williams, *alias* Cromwell. (*Vis. of Hunts.*, 1613.)

HEATON, *see also* **ETON** *and* **HETON.**

HEATON, EDWARD. Matric. sizar from Magdalene, Easter, 1626; B.A. 1629-30; M.A. 1634. Probably R. of Normanton, Rutland, 1654; conformed in 1662; dead before 1677. (H. I. Longden.)

HETON, FRANCIS. Matric. sizar from Peterhouse, Easter, 1577. 2nd s. of Francis, of London, goldsmith. B.A. 1580-1, as Eaton. Specially adm. at the Inner Temple, Nov. 1582. Brother of the next. (*T. A. Walker.*)

HETON, GEORGE. Matric. pens. from Peterhouse, Easter, 1577. 1st s. of Francis, of London, goldsmith. Adm. at the Inner Temple, Nov. 1579. Brother of Francis (above). (*T. A. Walker.*)

HETON, GEORGE. Matric. pens. from Trinity, Easter, 1612. S. of Thomas, bailiff of the Isle of Ely. Scholar, 1614; B.A. 1616-7; M.A. 1620; B.D. 1632. Fellow, 1618. Will (P.C.C.) 1638. (*Chesters of Chicheley*, 71.)

HEATON, HENRY. Adm. at Corpus Christi, 1730. S. of William. B. at Doncaster, 1710. Colleger at Eton, 1723-7. Matric. 1730; B.A. 1733-4; M.A. 1737; B.D. 1745. Fellow, 1735-54. Taxor, 1738. Ord. deacon (Lincoln) June 5, 1737. Chaplain to Archbishop Herring. V. of Boughton-under-Blean, Kent, 1752-77. V. of Herne Hill, 1752-4. Master of Eastbridge Hospital, 1753. R. of Ivychurch, 1754-77. Preb. of Ely, 1759-77. Died July 8, 1777. Buried at Boughton. Will, P.C.C. (*G. Mag.*)

HEATON, JAMES. Adm. sizar (age 17) at Magdalene, May 23, 1728. S. of James, gent. B. at Gedney, Lincs. School, Boston. Matric. 1728; LL.B. 1733. Ord. deacon (Lincoln) May 20, 1733.

HEATON, JONATHAN. Adm. sizar (age 18) at Trinity, Mar. 15, 1730-1. S. of William, of Oakworth, Yorks. School, Highley, Salop (Mr Blakey). Matric. 1731; B.A. 1735-6. Ord. deacon (Lincoln) June 9, 1734. P.C. of Ashworth, Lancs., 1735-7.

HEATON, HETON or EATON, MARTIN. M.A. 1581 (Incorp. from Oxford). S. of George, of Heton Hall, Lancs. B. there, 1552. School, Westminster. Adm. at Christ Church, 1571; B.A. (Oxford) 1574; M.A. 1578; B.D. 1583; D.D. 1585. Canon of Christ Church, 1582-99. Vice-Chancellor, 1588-9. Dean of Winchester, 1589-99. R. of Houghton, Hants., 1590. R. of Abbots Anne, 1595. Bishop of Ely, 1599-1609. Died July 14, 1609. Buried in Ely Cathedral. Will (P.C.C.) 1610. (*Al. Oxon.*; *D.N.B.*)

HEATON, MARTIN. Adm. sizar at Queens', May 11, 1658. Of Lincolnshire. Doubtless s. of Solomon (1623). Matric. as 'Henton'; B.A. 1661-2. Ord. priest (Peterb.) Feb. 20, 1675-6.

HEATON, PETER. Adm. sizar (age 19) at St John's, Mar. 26, 1717. S. of Henry, linendraper, of Lancashire. B. at Preston. Schools, Preston and Sedbergh (Mr Saunders).

HEATON, RICHARD. Matric. sizar from St John's, Easter, 1620; B.A. 1623-4; M.A. 1627.

HEATON, SOLOMON. Matric. pens. from Magdalene, Easter, 1623; B.A. 1626-7; M.A. 1630. Will of one of these names (P.C.C.) 1658; of Lincs., schoolmaster; mentions s. Martin, 'under age.' (J. Ch. Smith.)

HEATON, WILLIAM. Adm. sizar (age 18) at Peterhouse, Feb. 20, 1721-2. Of Yorkshire. School, Doncaster. Matric. 1723.

HEATON, ——. Adm. student at Peterhouse, Mar. 27, 1574.

HEAVER, JOHN. Adm. sizar at Clare, Aug. 20, 1635. Matric. 1636; B.A. 1639-40; M.A. 1643; D.D. 1661 (*Lit. Reg.*). Fellow, 1642-4 (ejected); restored, 1660. Incorp. at Oxford, 1664. Fellow of Eton College, 1661-70. Canon of Windsor, 1662-70. V. of New Windsor, 1662. Died June 23, 1670. Buried in St George's Chapel, Windsor. M.I. Gave £740 towards rebuilding Clare Hall. (*Harwood.*)

HEAVERS, HENRY. Adm. pens. at Sidney, May 16, 1666. 1st s. of ——, clerk. B. at Stamborne, Essex. School, Felsted.

HEAVYSEAD or HEVISED, THOMAS. Adm. sizar (age 17) at St John's, Oct. 20, 1684. S. of Thomas, shoemaker. B. at Cambridge. School, Cambridge (Mr Brian). Matric. 1684; B.A. 1688-9. Ord. priest (London) Mar. 9, 1706-7.

HEAWOOD, *see* **HAYWOOD.**

HEBB, JOSEPH. Adm. sizar at Emmanuel, 1619. Perhaps s. of Roger Hebbs, of Weybridge, Surrey. Matric. 1619; B.A. 1623-4. *See Vis. of Surrey*, 1623. (J. Ch. Smith.)

HEBBE or HELBE, RICHARD. B.A. 1535-6. Of Leicestershire. M.A. 1539-40. Fellow of Pembroke, 1538. V. of Soham, Cambs., 1552. Admon. (P.C.C.) 1576.

HEBBER, WILLIAM, *see* **HABER.**

HEBBERT, HENRY (1645), *see* **HIBBERT.**

HEBBORN, JOHN. B.Civ.L. 1488. V. of St Vigors, Fulbourn, Cambs., 1514. One of these names R. of Langenhoe, Essex, 1499-1516.

HEBBURNE or HOLBURNE, OTTIWELL. B.Civ.L. 1533. Perhaps scholar at King's Hall, 1516-36.

HEBDEN, WILLIAM. Adm. sizar (age 21) at St John's, May 13, 1701. S. of James, husbandman. B. at Appleton-le-Street, Yorks. School, Sedbergh. Matric. 1701; B.A. 1704-5; M.A. 1708. Ord. deacon (York) June, 1705; priest, 1706. V. of Yeddingham, Yorks., 1717-40. V. of Appleton-le-Street, 1728-40. Buried June 4, 1740.

HEBDEN, WILLIAM. Adm. pens. (age 17) at Trinity, Apr. 16, 1747. S. of George, of Easthorp Park, Yorks. School, Beverley, Yorks. (Mr Clark). Matric. 1747; Scholar, 1748; B.A. 1750-1. Ord. deacon (York) Sept. 22, 1751; priest, June, 1753. C. of Thorpe Bassett.

HEBELTHWAYTE, *see* **HEBLETHWAYTE.**

HEBENER, HENRY. Adm. Fell.-Com. at Trinity, June 6, 1656. Of Middlesex.

HEBER, FRANCIS. Matric. pens. from Jesus, Michs. 1614. Perhaps eldest s. of Thomas, of Marton, Yorks.; if so, died before 1633. (*Vis. of Yorks.*, 1612, 1665.)

HEBER, JOHN. Adm. pens. at St John's, June 2, 1727. Already matric. from University College, Oxford, May 30, 1723, age 17. S. of Reginald (not the next), of Marton, Yorks., Esq. Bapt there, Nov. 23, 1703. R. of Marton, Yorks., 1728-75. V. of Ribchester, Lancs., 1739-75. Married Dorothy Nowell. Died June 27, 1775. Buried at Marton. Brother of Thomas (1715). (*Al. Oxon.*; *G. Mag.*; M. H. Peacock.)

HEBER, REGINALD. Adm. Fell.-Com. (age 14) at Trinity, Aug. 21, 1689. S. of Thomas, of West Marton, Yorks., Esq. B. July 29, 1675. Bapt. at Holy Trinity, Micklegate, York. Migrated to Oxford. Matric. from Queen's College, Oxford, J[illegible] 3, 1690. Of Marton and Stainton, Yorks. J.P. Married Hester, dau. of Sir William Cayley, of Brompton, Yorks. Buried at Marton, Aug. 26, 1715. (Burke, *L.G.*; *Al. Oxon.*; M. H. Peacock.)

HEBER, THOMAS. Adm. sizar (age 18) at St John's, May 7, 1715. S. of Reginald (not the above), R. of Marton, Skipton, Yorks. Bapt. there, Dec. 7, 1695. School, Skipton. Matric. 1715; B.A. 1718-9. Of Gargrave, Yorks. Buried at Gargrave, Feb. 5, 1774. (J. Parker; M. H. Peacock.)

HEBERDEN, WILLIAM. Adm. sizar (age 15) at St John's, Dec. 23, 1724. S. of Richard, gent., of St Saviour's, Southwark, Surrey. B. in Southwark. School, St Saviour's (Mr Symonds). Matric. 1725; B.A. 1728; M.A. 1732; M.D. 1739. Fellow, 1731-52. F.R.C.P., 1746. Practised in London after 1748. Gulstonian lecturer, 1749. Harveian orator and censor, 1750. F.R.S., 1750. Croonian lecturer, 1760. Distinguished physician and scholar. Attended Dr Johnson. Author, medical. Died May 17, 1801. Buried at Windsor. M.I. (*Munk*, II. 159; *D.N.B.*)

HEBLETHWAT, HENRY. Matric. pens. from ST JOHN'S, Michs. 1553. One of these names 3rd s. of John, of Sedbergh, Yorks. B. there. Mercer of the City of London. Died unmarried 1587. Benefactor to St John's. (*Misc. Gen. et Her.*, N.S., I. 418; *Sedbergh Sch. Reg.*, 12.)

HEBBLETHWAITE, HENRY. Adm. sizar (age 17) at CHRIST'S, May 8, 1641. S. of Henry. B. at Killington, Westmorland. School, Kirkby Lonsdale (Mr Tatham). Matric. 1641; B.A. 1644-5; M.A. 1648.

HEBLETHWAITE, JAMES. Matric. Fell.-Com. from ST JOHN'S, Easter, 1626. S. and h. of Thomas (1594), of the Middle Temple. Of Norton, Yorks. Bapt. there, Sept. 14, 1607. Adm. at the Middle Temple, Nov. 17, 1626. Married Ann, dau. of Thomas Hungate, of North Dalton, Yorks. Buried at Norton, Apr. 11, 1653. Will, P.C.C. (*Vis. of Yorks.*, 1665; *Misc. Gen. et Her.*, N.S., I. 418.)

HEBLETHWAYT, JAMES. Adm. sizar (age 19) at ST JOHN'S, Apr. 30, 1647. S. of Christopher, gent., of Sedbergh, Yorks. B. there. School, Sedbergh. Matric. 1647. One of these names V. of Huttons Ambo, Yorks., 1674-6. Brother of John (1659).

HEBLTHWAITE, JAMES. Adm. sizar (age 17) at ST JOHN'S, Apr. 9, 1673. S. of Richard, yeoman, of Dent, Yorks. B. there. School, Sedbergh. Matric. 1673; B.A. 1676-7; M.A. 1680.

HEBLETHWAITE, JAMES. Adm. sizar (age 18) at ST JOHN'S, June 14, 1680. S. of Thomas, husbandman. B. at Sedbergh, Yorks. Bapt. July 8, 1661. School, Sedbergh. Matric. 1680; B.A. 1683-4. Ord. deacon (Carlisle) Dec. 21, 1684; priest (Chester) June 7, 1691. V. of Crosthwaite, Westmorland, 1685-1707. Married Agnes Dickinson, Aug. 7, 1688. Buried at Crosthwaite, May 12, 1707. (B. Nightingale.)

HEBLTHWHAITE, JOHN. Adm. sizar (age 17) at ST JOHN'S, Apr. 29, 1659. S. of Christopher, yeoman, of Sedbergh. B. there. School, Sedbergh. Matric. 1659; B.A. 1662-3. Ord. priest (Peterb.) Dec. 20, 1663. V. of Pytchley, Northants., 1663-73. Married, at Harrington, Northants., Sept. 14, 1675, Mary Hurst, of Denton. Will proved (Archd. Northants.) May 2, 1693. Brother of James (1647). (H. I. Longden.)

HEBBLETHWAITE, JOHN. Adm. sizar at EMMANUEL, June 2, 1737. Of Nottinghamshire. S. of Thomas. Matric. 1738; B.A. 1740-1. Ord. deacon (Lincoln) Sept. 20, 1741; priest, Mar. 18, 1753. R. of Oulton, Suffolk, 1758-74.

HEBLETHWAITE, ROBERT. B.A. 1537-8; M.A. 1541. Fellow of ST JOHN'S, 1538-9. S. of John. Master of the Chantry School, Sedbergh, 1544-52; and first Master of the Grammar School, 1552-85. Perhaps preb. of Chester, 1561. Living, in 1590. Died unmarried. (*Genealogist.*, 2nd S., XIV. 48; *Sedbergh Sch. Register.*)

HEBLETHWAIT, ROBERT. Matric. sizar from ST JOHN'S, Michs. 1583. B. at Sedbergh, *c.* 1567. B.A. 1586-7; M.A. 1590; B.D. 1598. Fellow, 1590. Ord. priest (Peterb.) June 2, 1596. University preacher. V. of Kirkby-le-Thorpe, Lincs., 1601. R. of Beckingham, 1603-26. Died 1626. (*Misc. Gen. et Her.*, 3rd S., II. 17.)

HEBLETHWAITE, ROBERT. Matric. sizar from ST JOHN'S, Easter, 1626; B.A. 1629-30; M.A. 1633. Ord. deacon (Norwich) Sept. 24, 1637. C. of South Lynn, Norfolk. One of these names V. of Melling, Lancs., 1633-48. Buried there Feb. 19, 1647-8. (E. Axon.)

HEBLETHWAITE, ROBERT. Matric. pens. from ST JOHN'S, Easter, 1627; B.A. 1630-1; M.A. 1634.

HEBBLETHWAITE, THOMAS. Adm. at ST JOHN'S, 1553. School, Sedbergh. (*Sedbergh Sch. Reg.*, 80.)

HEBLETHWAITE, THOMAS. Matric. sizar from ST JOHN'S, *c.* 1594. Perhaps s. of John. Of the Middle Temple. Royalist. M.P. for Malton, 1640-5. Buried at Norton, Mar. 27, 1647. Will, York. Father of James (1626). (M. H. Peacock; J. Ch. Smith.)

HEBLETHWAYTE, THOMAS. Adm. pens. (age 16) at ST JOHN'S, July 10, 1646. S. of James (1626), gent., of Norton, Yorks. Bapt. there, June 19, 1628. School, Coxwold (Mr Smelt). Matric. 1646. Adm. at the Middle Temple, Oct. 26, 1647. Of Norton. Knighted, June 9, 1660. M.P. for Malton, 1660-8. Married Barbara, dau. of Sir George Marwood, Bart. Buried at Norton, June 21, 1668. (Le Neve, *Knights*, 69; *Vis. of Yorks.*, 1666.)

HEBLETHWAITE, THOMAS. Adm. sizar (age 19) at ST JOHN'S, June 25, 1713. S. of Edward, husbandman. B. at Ripon, Yorks. School, Ripon (Mr Lloyd). Matric. 1713; B.A. 1716-7. Ord. deacon (York) Sept. 1718; priest, 1719. C. of Tithby, Notts., 1726. R. of Treswell, 1733.

HEBLETHWAIT, THOMAS. Adm. sizar (age 18) at ST JOHN'S, Mar. 15, 1721-2. S. of Joshua, yeoman, of Yorkshire. B. at Dent. School, Sedbergh. Matric. 1722; B.A. 1725-6. Ord. deacon (Ely) Dec. 17, 1725; priest, Dec. 16, 1726. C. of Stuntney, Cambs. Vicar-choral at Ely, 1725. (*Scott-Mayor*, III. 347.)

HEBELTHWAIGHT, WILLIAM. Matric. pens. from TRINITY, Michs. 1547; Scholar, 1548.

HEBBLETHWAITE, WILLIAM. Matric. sizar from ST JOHN'S, Easter, 1602. Migrated to Sidney, Mar. 1603-4. B.A. 1605-6; M.A. 1612. Ord. deacon (Lincoln) Mar. 12, 1608; priest, Sept. 3, 1609. V. of Dunston, Lincs., 1613. V. of Alkborough, 1620.

HECHSTETTER, DANIEL. Matric. pens. from PEMBROKE, Easter, 1607; B.A. 1610-1; M.A. 1614. Perhaps V. of Newburn, Northumberland, 1636. See another of these names at Oxford.

HECHSTETTER, DAVID. Adm. pens. at QUEENS', Mar. 21, 1592-3. Matric. 1593. Of Cumberland; of the Keswick family. Migrated to Oxford. Matric. from Queen's, June 28, 1594, age 20; B.A. (Oxford) 1596-7; M.A. 1600; B.D. 1611. V. of Brough, Westmorland, 1611-23. Died 1623. (*Al. Oxon.*)

HECHSTETER, EMMANUEL. Adm. sizar (age 16) at PEMBROKE, May 6, 1641. S. of Nathaniel. B. at Keswick, Cumberland. Matric. 1641; B.A. 1644-5.

HECHSTETTER or HEXETER, ROGER. Matric. pens. from PEMBROKE, Easter, 1607; B.A. 1610-1; M.A. 1614. Fellow, 1612. Taxor, 1617. Junior proctor, 1630-1. V. of Soham, Cambs., 1631.

HECKER, WILLIAM, *see* **HOOKER.**

HECKFORD, RAYNER. Adm. pens. at JESUS, Jan. 19, 1726-7. Of Essex. B.A. 1730-1; M.A. 1734. Fellow, 1733-58. Lived at Thaxted, Essex.

HECKFORD, THOMAS. Adm. at CORPUS CHRISTI, 1706. Of Suffolk. B.A. 1709-10; M.A. 1713. Ord. deacon (London) July 4, 1710; priest (Norwich) Mar. 1712-3. C. and V. of Gt Cornard, Suffolk, 1713-61. R. of Chilton, 1726-75. V. of Little Waldingfield, 1762-73. Died Nov. 1774. Father of the next.

HECKFORD, THOMAS. Adm. sizar at JESUS, Sept. 21, 1737. B. at Thaxted, Essex. S. of Thomas (above), V. of Gt Cornard, Suffolk. School, Bury. Matric. 1738; B.A. 1742-3. Ord. deacon (Norwich) Mar. 1741-2; priest, June, 1743. R. of Somersham, Suffolk, 1751-1803. V. of Gt Cornard, 1761-1803. Died May, 1803, aged 84.

HECKLE, JEREMIAH. Adm. sizar at TRINITY, Mar. 30, 1658. Matric. 1658, as Hockle; B.A. 1662-3.

HECLETON, RICHARD. Matric. pens. from TRINITY, Michs. 1547; Scholar, 1548.

HECKSTALL, ABRAHAM. Adm. sizar (age 19) at CHRIST'S, Apr. 11, 1677. S. of Abraham. School, Nottingham (Mr Jer. Cudworth). Matric. 1680; B.A. 1680-1. Ord. deacon (York) Sept. 1681; priest, June, 1683. V. of Ruddington, Notts., 1683. Father of the next. (*Peile*, II. 63.)

HECKSTALL, ABRAHAM. Adm. sizar (age 19) at ST JOHN'S, Apr. 29, 1713. S. of Abraham (above), deceased. B. at Ruddington, Notts. School, Nottingham (Mr Johnson). Migrated to Jesus, July 7, 1714. B.A. 1717-8; M.A. 1722. Ord. deacon (London) Mar. 9, 1717-8. C. of Lewisham, Kent, 1725. Lecturer at St Michael Bassishaw, London. Died Mar. 28, 1754. Buried at Lewisham. M.I. Father of the next. (J. Ch. Smith.)

HECKSTALL, BROOKE. Adm. pens. at EMMANUEL, Jan. 21, 1740-1. S. of Abraham (above). B. at Newington Butts, Surrey. Bapt. Apr. 22, 1724. School, Merchant Taylors'. Matric. 1742; LL.B. 1747. R. of St Anne and St Agnes, London, 1764-80. Died Apr. 5, 1780. Buried at Lewisham, Kent. M.I. Will, P.C.C. (J. Ch. Smith; *Robinson*, II. 89; *G. Mag.*)

HECTON, ——. B.Can.L. 1462.

HEDDALL, BRIAN. B.A. 1491-2.

HEDGE, CHRISTOPHER. Elected scholar at TRINITY, from Westminster, 1568. (*List of Queen's Scholars.*)

HEDGE, EDWARD. Fellow of CORPUS CHRISTI, 1509. R. of St Benet, Cambridge, 1512-32. Died 1532. Will (V.C.C.).

HEDGE, JOHN. B.A. 1492-3; M.A. 1496. Will of one of these names (P.C.C.) 1510; of Burnham Thorpe, Norfolk, clerk.

HEDGE, JOHN. Elected to Cambridge, as scholar from Westminster, 1570. (*List of Queen's Scholars.*)

HEDGE, JOHN. Adm. pens. (age 18) at SIDNEY, June 21, 1644. S. of Anthony, Esq. B. at Sall, Norfolk. Schools, Norwich and Epping, Essex (Mr Wm. North). Matric. 1645-6.

HEDGE, THOMAS. B.Can.L. 1492-3.

HEDGE, W. B.A. 1496-7; M.A. from PHYSICK HOSTEL, 1501. Will (P.C.C.) 1537, of William Hedge, of Stoke-by-Nayland, Suffolk, clerk.

HEDGE, WILLIAM. Matric. pens. from TRINITY, Easter, 1571; Scholar, 1571. (Possibly the same as Christopher or John, above, who are not recorded at Trinity.)

HEDGE, ——. M.A. Of ST BERNARD'S HOSTEL. Perhaps Edward, above.

HEDGES, CHARLES. Adm. Fell.-Com. at PETERHOUSE, June 6, 1747. Of Hertfordshire. Perhaps s. of Charles, and grandson of Sir William, Knt., alderman of London. Matric. 1747; B.A. 1750–1; M.A. 1754. Fellow, 1751. Married Anne, sister of Charles, Lord Bayning. Died 1783. (*T. A. Walker.*)

HEDGES, JOHN. Adm. Fell.-Com. (age 17) at PETERHOUSE, May 6, 1706. Of Middlesex. Matric. 1706. Adm. at the Inner Temple, Feb. 11, 1707–8; 3rd s. of Sir William, of London, Knt., deceased. M.P. for St Michael's, 1722–7; for Bossiney, 1727–34; for Fowey, 1734–7. Envoy extraordinary to Sardinia, 1726. Treasurer to the Prince of Wales, 1728–37. Died June 21, 1737. (*T. A. Walker*; A. B. Beaven.)

HEDGES, JOHN. M.A. from KING'S, 1726. S. of Francis, of Reading, Berks., clerk. Matric. from St John's College, Oxford, Feb. 8, 1705–6, age 18; B.A. (Oxford) 1709. R. of Orlestone, Kent, 1721–8. V. of East Peckham, 1723. V. of East Farleigh, 1727–52. M.I. at Thribergh, Yorks. Father of the next. (*Al. Oxon.*)

HEDGES, JOHN. Adm. sizar (age 17) at PEMBROKE, Feb. 10, 1735–6. S. of John (above), V. of Peckham, Kent. Matric. 1736; B.A. 1740–1; M.A. 1744. V. of Tudeley, Kent, 1750–87. Died Aug. 1, 1787, aged 68. M.I. (J. Ch. Smith.)

HEDON, ROBERT. B.A. 1537–8. Of Durham. Fellow of PEMBROKE, 1540. One of these names, a priest, age 32 in 1548, was Master of Cuckfield Grammar School, in 1548. (*Vict. Hist. of Sussex*, II.)

HEDWORTH, JOHN. Matric. pens. from CHRIST'S, May, 1563; Scholar, 1564. Doubtless 2nd s. of Anthony, of Jarrow, Durham. Adm. at the Middle Temple, Nov. 7, 1566. Called to the Bar, 1576. Knighted, Mar. 14, 1603–4. Will dated, 1622. (*Peile*, I. 79.)

HEDWORTH, RALPH. Matric. Fell.-Com. from PETERHOUSE, Easter, 1575. Probably s. and h. of John, of Harraton, Durham; age 14 in 1575. Adm. at the Middle Temple, Oct. 17, 1579. Married Jane (? Joan), dau. of Nicholas Rutland. Buried Aug. 20, 1590. (*Vis. of Durham*; *Surtees*, II. 184; *T. A. Walker.*)

HEESOME, WILLIAM. Adm. sizar at TRINITY, May 13, 1664, as 'Husome.' Matric. 1664; B.A. 1667–8; M.A. 1671. Ord. deacon (Lincoln) Sept. 20, 1668; priest, Sept. 24, 1671.

HEET, RICHARD. Matric. sizar from ST JOHN'S, Michs. 1580.

HEFELD, MICHAEL. B.Civ.L. 1516–7.

HEGARDIN, CHRISTOPHER. Matric. pens. from TRINITY, c. 1597.

HEGARDIN, ROBERT. Matric. sizar from TRINITY, c. 1597.

HEGG, STEPHEN. 'M.A. of ST JOHN'S,' when ord. deacon (York) Mar. 1625–6; priest, June, 1626. P.C. of Whitworth, Durham, 1628–62. Probably s. of Stephen, of Durham. Bapt. at St Mary's, Dec. 30, 1599. Buried at Whitworth, Sept. 28, 1662. Father of the next. (H. M. Wood.)

HEGG, STEPHEN. Adm. pens. (age 15) at ST JOHN'S, June 12, 1660. S. of Stephen (above), P.C. of Whitworth, Durham. B. there. Educated by his father. Matric. 1661. Will (Durham) 1668.

HEGG, THOMAS. Adm. pens. (age 17) at ST JOHN'S, Nov. 7, 1661. S. of Mark, deceased, of Wath, Yorks. B. there. School, Welton, Lincs. (Mr Walker). Matric. 1661.

HEIBURNE, HEBORNE or HEYBORNE, FERDINAND. Adm. Fell.-Com. (age 17) at PEMBROKE, Apr. 27, 1635. S. of Sir Ferdinand, Knt. (groom of the Privy Chamber to Queen Elizabeth). B. at Tottenham High Cross, Middlesex. Matric. 1635. (*Middlesex Pedigrees.*)

HEICROFT, HENRY. Matric. pens. from ST JOHN'S, Easter, 1565. Of Hampshire. B.A. 1566–7; M.A. 1570. Fellow, 1567.

HEIGH, JOHN. Matric. pens. from PEMBROKE, Easter, 1608.

HEIGHAM or HIGHAM, ABRAHAM. Adm. sizar at EMMANUEL, June 25, 1714. Of Somerset. Matric. 1714; B.A. 1717–8.

HEIGHAM, ARTHUR. B.A. from TRINITY, 1621–2; M.A. 1625. S. of Sir Clement (1594–5), Knt., of Barrow, Suffolk. Bapt. Sept. 20, 1602. Ord. deacon (Peterb.) Sept. 23; priest, Sept. 24, 1626. R. of Redgrave, Suffolk, 1638–48. Married Anne, dau. of Thomas Coell, of Depden, Suffolk. Died Jan. 28, 1648–9. Will (Bury) 1650. Father of the next. (Burke, *L.G.*; *Gage*, 9.)

HEIGHAM, ARTHUR. Adm. pens. at QUEENS', June 22, 1660. S. of Arthur (above), R. of Redgrave, Suffolk. Bapt. May 11, 1643. Matric. 1660, as Hyem; B.A. 1663–4; M.A. 1667. Ord. priest (Norwich) Sept. 1677. R. of Hopton, Suffolk, 1677–90. Married Hannah, dau. of John Symonds, of Gislingham. Died June, 1690. Father of John (1698). (Burke, *L.G.*; Davy, *Suff. MSS.*)

HEIGHAM, ARTHUR. Adm. pens. (age 16) at CAIUS, Jan. 23, 1722–3. 2nd s. of John, Esq. (1698), of Rougham, Suffolk. B. at Gislingham, Aug. 23, 1706. Schools, Lavenham (Mr Drift) and Bury (Mr Kinnesman). Matric. 1723; Scholar, 1724–5. Adm. at the Inner Temple, Jan. 27, 1724. Of Hunston Hall, Suffolk. Married, Mar. 28, 1733, Martha, dau. of Roger Cooke. Died June 25, 1787. M.I. at Hunston. Brother of John (1720). (*Venn*, II. 17.)

HYHAM, CLEMENT. Matric. pens. from ST JOHN'S, Michs. 1593.

HEIGHAM or HIGGAM, CLEMENT. Matric. pens. from ST JOHN'S, Easter, 1589. Of Suffolk. Probably s. of Thomas, of Rougham, Suffolk. Bapt. there, 1572. B.A. 1592–3; M.A. 1596. Fellow, 1597. Ord. priest (Lincoln) Sept. 23, 1599. R. of Ampton, Suffolk, 1597–8 (while deacon). V. of Barnham St Gregory, Suffolk, 1598–1610. V. of Barnham St Martin and St Andrew, 1607–10. Perhaps brother of Edmund (c. 1592). (J. J. Howard, *Vis. of Suffolk*, II. 275.)

HEIGHAM, CLEMENT. M.A. 1594–5 (special Congregation). Doubtless of Barrow, Suffolk, Knt. S. of Sir John, of Barrow, Suffolk, Knt. Knighted, 1591. M.P. for Suffolk, 1593. Buried at Barrow, May 26, 1634. Father of Arthur (1621–2). (Burke, *L.G.*; *Gage*, 9.)

HEIGHAM, CLEMENT. Adm. at CORPUS CHRISTI, 1626. Of Suffolk. Doubtless 1st s. of John, of Barrow, Suffolk. Bapt. at Ditchingham (his mother's home), Jan. 10, 1605. One of the knights of the projected order of the Royal Oak. Buried at Barrow, May 6, 1686. Grandson and heir to Clement (above). Father of the next, and of John (1657), William (1664) and brother of John (1627). (J. J. Howard, *Vis. of Suffolk*, II. 294; *Gage*, 9.)

HEIGHAM, CLEMENT. Matric. pens. from ST CATHARINE'S, 1660. S. of Clement (above), of Barrow Hall, Suffolk. B.A. 1662–3. Migrated to Jesus, 1664. M.A. 1666. Signed for deacon's orders (London) Dec. 21, 1666. R. of Sculthorpe, Norfolk, 1667–86. R. of Barrow, Suffolk, 1685–1714. Married (1) Susan, dau. of Luke Skippon, D.D. Buried at Barrow, Apr. 15, 1714. Brother of John (1657) and William (1664). (A. Gray; Le Neve, *Mon.*, III. 174.)

HEIGHAM, CLEMENT. Adm. at CORPUS CHRISTI, 1680. Of London.

HEIGHAM or HIAM, EDMUND. Matric. pens. from ST JOHN'S, c. 1592. Perhaps s. of Thomas. Bapt. at Rougham, Suffolk, 1575. B.A. 1595–6; M.A. 1599.

HIGHAM, FRANCIS. Matric. pens. from TRINITY, c. 1592.

HIGHAM, FRANCIS. Matric. Fell.-Com. from KING'S, Easter, 1640. Probably s. and h. of Sir Richard, late of East Ham, Essex, Knt., deceased. Adm. at Lincoln's Inn, May 4, 1642. Married Susan, dau. of Richard Glover, of East Ham.

HEIGHAM or HYEM, GEORGE. Adm. sizar at EMMANUEL, Mar. 13, 1682–3. Of Suffolk. Matric. 1683–4.

HIGHAM, JAMES. Adm. pens. (age 17) at CAIUS, July 8, 1605. S. of Robert, of Abington, Cambs. School, Newport, Essex. Matric. 1606; Scholar, 1606–8.

HYHAM, JOHN. Matric. pens. from TRINITY HALL, Michs. 1555. Perhaps brother of Thomas (1555).

HYHAM, JOHN. Matric. pens. from CORPUS CHRISTI, Michs. 1561; B.A. from Queens', 1565–6, as Heigham. Ord. deacon (Ely) May 26, 1566; priest, Mar. 23, 1566–7. Of Walden, Essex (? C.) in 1566.

HIGHAM, JOHN. Adm. at CHRIST'S, Apr. 17, 1624. Perhaps s. of William, of Barrow, Suffolk. Bapt. there, Oct. 21, 1606. Matric. pens. 1624. Migrated to Magdalene, 1627. B.A. 1627–8; M.A. 1631. One of these names, of Heigham Hall, buried at Gazeley, Apr. 10, 1658. (*Peile*, I. 357.)

HEIGHAM, JOHN. Matric. pens. from CORPUS CHRISTI, Easter, 1627. Of Suffolk. Doubtless 2nd s. of John, of Barrow, Suffolk. Bapt. there, May 5, 1610. Died *s.p.* Probably brother of Clement (1626). (J. J. Howard, *Vis. of Suffolk*, II. 294.)

HIGHAM, JOHN. Adm. Fell.-Com. (age 16) at CHRIST'S, Oct. 20, 1647. S. of John. B. at Chelmsford. Schools, Chelmsford (Mr Peake) and Springfield (Mr Joyner). Perhaps the only s., 'aged 4 in 1634,' of John and Elizabeth, of Chelmsford. (*Vis. of Essex*, 1634; *Peile*, I. 516.)

HIGHAM, JOHN. Adm. sizar (age 16) at CHRIST'S, Mar. 31, 1657. S. of John. B. at Bury St Edmunds. School, Bury (Mr Stephens). Matric. 1657; B.A. 1660–1; M.A. 1664. Perhaps R. of Beighton, Norfolk, 1680. Died 1680–1. (*Peile*, I. 576.)

HEIGHAM, JOHN. Adm. Fell.-Com. (age 17) at ST JOHN'S, Nov. 6, 1657. S. of Clement (1626), Esq., of Barrow, Suffolk. Bapt. there, Jan. 23, 1640–1. School, Cambridge (Mr Moore). Matric. 1657. Buried at Barrow, Apr. 13, 1676. Brother of Clement (1660) and of William (1664).

HEIGHAM, JOHN. Adm. Fell.-Com. (age 19) at CAIUS, May 26, 1698. S. of Arthur (1660), R. of Hopton, Suffolk. B. there. Bapt. July 20, 1679. Schools, Gislingham, Suffolk (Mr Sparrow) and Bury. Matric. 1698. Of Rougham and Hunston, Suffolk, Esq. Buried at Gislingham, Oct. 10, 1734. Father of Arthur (1722-3) and the next. (*Venn*, I. 500.)

HEIGHAM, JOHN SYMONDS. Adm. Fell.-Com. (age 18) at CAIUS, June 24, 1720. S. of John, Esq. (above), of Rougham, Suffolk. B. at Gislingham. Bapt. at Hunston, June 30, 1702. School, Bury. Matric. 1720. Buried Nov. 22, 1769. Brother of Arthur (1722-3). (*Venn*, II. 14.)

HEIGHAM, ROBERT. Matric. [illegible]. from ST JOHN'S, Easter, 1575; B.A. 1578-9; M.A. 158[illegible]. Ord. deacon (Peterb.) July 10, 1582; priest, Mar. 26, 1582-3. R. of Wotton, Surrey, 1583-1612. Buried June 10, 1612.

HYGHAM, THOMAS. Matric. pens. from TRINITY HALL, Michs. 1555. One Thomas Heigham adm. at Lincoln's Inn, Mar. 7, 1557-8. Perhaps brother of John (1555).

HEIGHAM, THOMAS. Adm. pens. at PETERHOUSE, Easter, 1620. Of Essex. Migrated to Queens', Oct. 5, 1621. B.A. 1623-4. A Thomas Higham 'of London, doctor in phisick,' was living in 1634; 2nd s. of John, of Chelmsford, mercer. His will (P.C.C.) 1672; Dr in Philosophy and Physic. (*T. A. Walker*, 17; J. Ch. Smith.)

HEYHAM, W. M.A. or higher degree, 1474-5.

HIGHAM, WILLIAM. B.A. 1462-3. S. of Thomas, of Higham. M.A. 1466; B.D. 1472-3; D.D. 1479-80. Perhaps ord. deacon (Norwich) Apr. 27, 1467; priest, Sept. 22, 1470. R. of Elsete. R. of Elveden and Gazeley; also of Cheveley, in 1476. Said to have been elected Bishop of Ely. Died 1490. (Davy, *Suff. MSS.*; J. J. Howard, *Vis. of Suffolk*, II. 272.)

HEIGHAM, WILLIAM. M.A. 1612 (on visit of Prince of Wales).

HEIGHAM, WILLIAM. Adm. pens. at JESUS, June 17, 1664. Of Suffolk. S. of Clement (1626), of Barrow, Suffolk, Esq. Bapt. at Horningsheath, Jan. 15, 1647-8. Matric. 1664. Adm. at Lincoln's Inn, Feb. 11, 1667-8. Brother of Clement (1660) and of John (1657). (A. Gray; J. J. Howard, *Vis. of Suffolk*, II. 295.)

HIGHAM, ——. Adm. Fell.-Com. at KING'S, Lent, 1598-9.

HEIGHAM, ——. Adm. pens. at ST CATHARINE'S, Michs. 1658.

HEIGHINGTON, AMBROSE. Adm. pens. (age 18) at ST JOHN'S, Apr. 20, 1672. S. of William, gent. B. at Durham. Bapt. at St Margaret's, Durham, May 30, 1654. School, Durham. Matric. 1672. Buried at Durham, May 5, 1683. (H. M. Wood.)

HEIGHTON, AMBROSE. Matric. sizar from CHRIST'S, Dec. 1586.

HELASDON, ——. A friar. Fee for degree (perhaps D.D.) 1496-7.

HELISDON or ELISDON, ——. M.A. 1503.

HELCOCKE or HELCOTT, PHILIP. Adm. sizar (age 18) at CAIUS, Sept. 10, 1624. S. of Thomas, glover, of Elsing, Norfolk. School, Elsing (Mr Robinson). Matric. 1624; B.A. 1628-9. Ord. deacon and priest (Norwich) Sept. 21, 1628. (*Venn*, I. 269.)

HELDER, *alias* SPICER, RICHARD. Adm. pens. (age 17) at CAIUS, June 21, 1675. S. of William, gent., of Offley, Herts. B. there. Bapt. Feb. 11, 1658-9. School, Hitchin (Mr Draper). Matric. 1675; Scholar, 1675-8. Adm. at Gray's Inn, July 9, 1677. Lord of Little Offley Manor. Died Feb. 25, 1718-9. (*Venn*, I. 454.)

HELE, ARTHUR. Adm. pens. (age 18) at ST JOHN'S, Sept. 28, 1730. Previously matric. from Trinity College, Oxford, June 20, 1728. S. of Richard (1727), Preb. of Salisbury. B. there. School, Salisbury. Matric. 1730; B.A. 1732-3; M.A. 1766. Ord. deacon (Salisbury) July 9, 1734. Usher of the Grammar School, Basingstoke, 1749-58. V. of Corston, Somerset, 1755-78. Master of the Grammar School, Bath, 1758-78. R. of Charlcombe, 1762-78. R. of Porlock, 1763-78. Preb. of Wells, 1764-78. Buried at Corston, Apr. 30, 1778. (*Scott-Mayor*, III. 424; H. G. Harrison.)

HELE, HENRY. M.D. 1728 (*Com. Reg.*). Died at Salisbury, June 24, 1778. Will (P.C.C.) 1778; of Salisbury.

HELE, MUSGRAVE. Adm. pens. (age 19) at PETERHOUSE, Nov. 12, 1715. Previously matric. from Exeter College, Oxford, Feb. 11, 1714-5. Of South Molton, Devon. School, Eton. Matric. 1715, as 'Hill'; Scholar, 1715; B.A. 1718-9. R. of South Perrot, Dorset, 1740-50. Died 1750.

HELE, RENATUS. Adm. sizar (age 17) at PEMBROKE, Apr. 21, 1731. S. of Samson (1677), of Exeter, gent. Matric. 1732; LL.B. 1737. Admon. (Exeter) 1756; of Poltimore, Devon, clerk.

HELE, RICHARD. Adm. pens. (age 19) at PETERHOUSE, June 27, 1705. Of South Molton, Devon. School, Eton. Scholar, 1705; Matric. 1706; B.A. 1708-9; M.A. 1713. Ord. priest (London) Mar. 5, 1709-10. A Richard Hele was V. of Chardstock, Dorset, 1734. Died 1770. (*T. A. Walker*, 213.)

HELE or HEALE, RICHARD. M.A. from KING'S, 1727. S. of Richard, of Salisbury. Matric. from Balliol College, Oxford, Mar. 24, 1696-7, age 15; B.A. (Oxford) 1700. R. of Pampisham, Dorset, 1713-55. Preb. of Salisbury, 1729-55. Died June, 1755. M.I. at Pampisham. Father of Arthur (1730). (*Al. Oxon.*; *Hutchins*, II. 693.)

HELE, SAMSON. Adm. pens. (age 18) at SIDNEY, May 26, 1677. 1st s. of Samuel, gent., of West Prawle, Devon. B. at Portlemouth. School, Kingsbridge (Mr Duncomb). Adm. at Gray's Inn, Feb. 1, 1677-8. Father of Renatus.

HELE, THOMAS. Adm. pens. at EMMANUEL, Oct. 11, 1613. Matric. 1613.

HELE, THOMAS. Adm. at KING'S, a scholar from Eton, 1716. B. at South Molton, Devon. Matric. 1716; B.A. 1720-1; M.A. 1738. Fellow, 1719. Ord. priest (London) June 26, 1720. 'Kept a school, and was preferred in Lincolnshire.' (*Harwood*, 296.)

HELEFIELD or HEALIFIELD, ROGER. Adm. sizar at TRINITY, June 30, 1669. Matric. 1669; B.A. 1672-3. Ord. deacon (York) Sept. 1672; priest, June, 1674.

HELIN, *see* **ELIN.**

HELL or HILL, CHRISTOPHER, *see* **HILL.**

HELL, MAURICE. B.Can.L. 1499-1500.

HELLARD, STEPHEN. B.Can.L. 1474-5. Perhaps D.Can.L. 1492-3. Of Yorkshire. Probably R. of Upminster, Essex, 1470-72. R. of Stevenage, Herts., till 1506. Preb. of St Asaph. Will (P.C.C.) 1506. M.I. at Stevenage.

HELLDER, MARTIN. Matric. sizar from JESUS, Michs. 1610; B.A. 1613-4; M.A. 1617.

HELLIAR or HELIAR, HENRY. Matric. Fell.-Com. from MAGDALENE, Easter, 1609. S. of William, of Exeter. Adm. at Lincoln's Inn, June 26, 1610.

HELLIAR, JOHN. Adm. sizar at QUEENS', Nov. 2, 1694. Of Wiltshire.

HELEY or HELY, *see* **HEALEY.**

HELYAR, WILLIAM. B.A. from MAGDALENE, 1584-5; M.A. 1588. One of these names preb. of Chester, 1624-7.

HELLOT, *see* **ELLIOT.**

HELLYARD, *see* **HILDYARD.**

HELMAN, JOHN, *see* **ELMAN.**

HELME, JAMES. Matric. sizar from QUEENS', Easter, 1612. Of Lancashire. B.A. 1615-6; M.A. 1619. Ord. deacon (Peterb.) Sept. 19; priest, Sept. 20, 1619. Perhaps V. of Manuden, Essex, till 1663.

HELME, ROBERT. Matric. Fell.-Com. from JESUS, Michs. 1567.

HELMES, JOHN. A German (Alemanus). M.A. 1631-2 (*Lit. Reg.*); M.D. 1638.

HELMES, SHADRACKE. Adm. sizar (age 19) at ST JOHN'S, July 3, 1646. S. of Thomas, scrivener, of St Sepulchre's, West Smithfield, Middlesex. B. there. School, Christ's Hospital. Head Master of Christ's Hospital, 1662-78.

HELMES, THOMAS. Adm. pens. at JESUS, Oct. 7, 1633. Of London. Matric. 1634; B.A. 1637-8; M.A. 1641.

HELMES, ——. Adm. pens. at EMMANUEL, Easter, 1623.

HELMESLEY, JOHN. Scholar at KING'S HALL, 1385-91.

HELMESMERE, *see* **ELSMER.**

HELPERBY, THOMAS. Scholar of GONVILLE HALL, 1534-7; B.A. 1535-6; M.A. 1538; B.D. from Trinity, 1546. Fellow of Michaelhouse. One of the original fellows of Trinity, 1546. V. of Long Stanton, Cambs., 1548. Died 1554. Will proved (V.C.C.) 1554.

HELPERBY, WILLIAM DE. Fellow of PETERHOUSE, 1388-93.

HELPERBY, ——. M.A. 1456-7. Perhaps Richard, V. of Langley, Essex, 1460. Mentioned in the will (P.C.C., 1500) of P. Whiting.

HELPERBY, ——. B.A. 1477-8; M.A. 1481-2.

HELSHAM, RICHARD. M.D. 1714 (Incorp. from Dublin). S. of Joshua. B. at Kilkenny. Adm. at Trinity College, Dublin, June 18, 1698; Scholar, 1700; B.A. 1702. Fellow, 1704. Incorp. at Oxford, 1712. Professor of Natural Philosophy at Dublin, 1724-38. Regius Professor of Physic, 1733-8. Died Aug. 1, 1738. Will, Dublin. (*D.N.B.*; *Al. Dub.*)

HELTON, WILLIAM. B.A. from CLARE, 1625-6.

HELWYS, *see also* **ELWES.**

HELWIS, JOHN. B.A. 1483-4.

HELWYS, NICHOLAS. Adm. Fell.-Com. (age 17) at CAIUS, May 20, 1679. S. of William, citizen and alderman of Norwich. B. there. School, Norwich (Mr Burton). Adm. at the Middle Temple, Sept. 4, 1680. Of Morton, Norfolk, Esq. Lord of the manor. Died 1724. M.I. at Ringland. (*Venn*, I. 462.)

HELWYS or ELWYS, RICHARD. B.Can.L. 1501–2.

HELWYS, WILLIAM. Adm. pens. (age 14) at CAIUS, Apr. 6, 1605. S. of Nicholas, gent. B. at Norwich. School, Norwich (Mr Stonham). Scholar, 1605–9; Matric. 1606; B.A. 1609.

HELWYS, WILLIAM. Adm. pens. (age 17) at CAIUS, Sept. 14, 1682. S. of Nicholas, alderman of Norwich. B. there. School, Norwich (Mr Burton). Matric. 1683; Scholar, 1683–6. Adm. at the Middle Temple, Apr. 20, 1686. Called to the Bar, May 26, 1693. Died 1723. M.I. at St Peter Mancroft, Norwich. (*Venn*, I. 471.)

HELY, ——. B.A. 1481–2. For later degrees *see* ELY.

HEMBLING, JOHN. Adm. at CORPUS CHRISTI, 1614. Previously at St Catharine's. Of Norwich. B.A. 1616–7; M.A. 1620. Fellow, 1618–24. Ord. deacon (Peterb.) Dec. 24, 1620; priest (Norwich) Dec. 18, 1625. V. of Hickling and Palling, Norfolk, 1624; sequestered, *c.* 1645. (*Masters.*)

HEMYNGTON, JOHN. Matric. sizar from PETERHOUSE, Michs. 1544.

HEMINGTON, SAMUEL. Adm. sizar (age 18) at TRINITY, July 7, 1730. S. of John, of Needingworth, Hunts. School, Needingworth. Matric. 1731; Scholar, 1732; B.A. 1733–4. Ord. deacon (Lincoln) Mar. 2, 1734–5; priest, Mar. 18, 1738–9. V. of Houghton, 1742–82. V. of Binham, Norfolk, 1750–83.

HEMINGTON, WILLIAM. Adm. pens. at QUEENS', June 21, 1597. Of Bedfordshire. Matric. 1597; B.A. 1600–1. One of these names married, at Elstow, Beds., Dec. 12, 1605, Martha Clerke.

HEMINGWAY, ISAAC. Adm. sizar at EMMANUEL, Sept. 22, 1718. Of Yorkshire. Matric. 1719; B.A. 1722–3. Ord. deacon (York) Sept. 22, 1723; priest, July 21, 1728. V. of Attercliffe, Yorks., 1729–31. Died Mar. 3, 1730–1, aged 29. M.I. at Attercliffe. (M. H. Peacock.)

HEMINGWAY, JOSHUA. Adm. sizar (age 18) at CHRIST'S, May 6, 1671. S. of Henry. B. at Halifax. School, Drighlington (Mr Baskerville). Matric. 1672; B.A. 1674–5; M.A. 1678.

HEMINGWAY, JOSHUA. Adm. sizar at CHRIST'S, Apr. 23, 1684, as 'Joseph.' S. of Samuel, of Yorkshire. School, Halifax (Mr Doughty). Matric. 1685; B.A. 1687–8. Ord. priest (London) Feb. 1688–9. V. of Egmanton, Notts., 1695–1706. V. of Orston, 1706–36. Married, at St Peter's, Nottingham, Mar. 3, 1718–9, Mary Maltby, of Orston. Died 1736. (*Peile*, II. 95; Godfrey, *Churches of Notts.*)

HEMMESBY, SIMON DE. M.A. Of Norwich diocese. Fellow of MICHAELHOUSE, 1331. (*Papal Letters.*)

HEMMING, JOHN. Adm. at KING'S, a scholar from Eton, 1734. S. of William (1706). B. at Ringwood, Hants. Matric. 1735; B.A. 1739–40; M.A. 1743 (adm. to degree, 1750). Fellow, 1738. Ord. deacon (Lincoln) June 17, 1739; priest, Mar. 14, 1741–2. Chaplain to the factory at Aleppo, 1742. R. of Waterden, Norfolk, 1750. V. of Holkham, 1750. R. of Durweston with Knighton, Dorset, 1750–65. Dean of Guernsey for seven years. Died June 5, 1765. Will, P.C.C. (*Hutchins*, I. 267.)

HEMMING, ROBERT. Matric. pens. from TRINITY, Easter, 1597; Scholar, 1582; B.A. 1582–3; M.A. 1586; B.D. 1593. Fellow, 1585. Incorp. at Oxford, 1591. V. of Brabourne and Meopham, Kent, 1593. V. of Alkham and Chislet, 1594. R. of Harbledown, 1597–1601. Died 1601. (*Al. Oxon.*)

HEMMING, WILLIAM. Adm. at KING'S, a scholar from Eton, 1706. B. in Middlesex, 1687. Matric. 1706; B.A. 1710–1; M.A. 1714. Fellow, 1709. Ord. deacon (Ely) Feb. 25, 1710–1. C. of Ringwood, Minstead and Shalborn, Hants. R. of East Soham, Suffolk. Father of John (1734).

HEMING, WILLIAM. Matric. pens. at TRINITY HALL, Dec. 1708. B. in Westminster, 1688.

HEMMINGS, JOSEPH. M.A. 1668 (Incorp. from Oxford). One of these names, s. of John, of Lacock, Wilts., matric. from Magdalen Hall, May 13, 1642, but no degree recorded. R. of Swineshead, Hunts., 1666. (*Al. Oxon.*)

HEMPRYNGAM, ROBERT. Matric. pens. from CHRIST'S, Oct. 1564.

HEMPSON, WILLIAM. Adm. pens. at EMMANUEL, June 27, 1675. Of Kent. Exhibitioner from Charterhouse. Matric. 1678; B.A. 1678–9. Doubtless s. and h. of William, late of the City of London, Esq., deceased; adm. at Lincoln's Inn, May 13, 1679. Registrar of Charterhouse, 1700–39. Died May 4, 1739. (*G. Mag.*)

HEMSLEY, JOHN. Adm. sizar at TRINITY, Apr. 22, 1669. Matric. 1669; Scholar, 1671; B.A. 1672–3; M.A. 1676. Ord. deacon (Peterb.) May 21, 1676.

HEMSLEY, ——. Fee for M.A. or higher degree, 1476–7.

HEMSON, ——. Fee for M.A. or higher degree, 1480. Perhaps B.D. 1489.

HEMSON, ——. Fee for B.A. 1496–7.

HEMSTED, JOHN. Adm. sizar (age 20) at EMMANUEL, May 21, 1724. Of Suffolk. Matric. 1724. Afterwards pensioner. B.A. 1727–8; . . 1733. Ord. deacon (London) Sept. 24, 1727; priest (EM)A June 1, 1729. V. of Haverhill, Suffolk, 1730–69. Died 1769.

HEMSWORTH, GEORGE. M.A. from CHRIST'S, 1700. S. of Francis. B. at Berkhampstead, Herts. Matric. from Christ Church, Oxford, 1691, age 16; B.A. (Oxford) 1694–5. Ord. priest (London) Dec. 19, 1703. (*Peile*, II. 149; *Al. Oxon.*)

HEMUS, DANIEL. M.A. from CLARE, 1747. S. of John, of Stourbridge, Worcs. Matric. from Balliol College, Oxford, Oct. 10, 1737, age 18; B.A. (Oxford) 1741–2. One of these names, of Broseley, Salop, clerk. Will (P.C.C.) 1799. (*Al. Oxon.*)

HEN, Dr. Augustinian friar. Fee for degree, 1500–1.

HENCHBORNE, ——. B.Civ.L. 1504–5.

HENCHMAN, CHARLES. Adm. pens. at CHRIST'S, June 30, 1636. S. of Richard. B. at Rushton, Northants. Schools, Salisbury (Mr Warwick) and Blandford (Mr Eaton). Migrated to Queens'. B.A. 1639–40. (He seems to have matriculated at Oxford, Mar. 3, 1636–7, age 15.) (*Peile*, I. 445.)

HENCHMAN, CHARLES. Adm. pens. (age 18) at ST JOHN'S, May 28, 1726. S. of Charles, clerk (canon of Chester). School, Chester (under his father). Matric. 1726; B.A. 1729–30; M.A. 1744. Incorp. at Oxford, 1744. Ord. deacon (Chester) 1730; priest, Oct. 31, 1731. Minor canon of Chester. R. of Stanton-in-the-Wolds, Chester, 1733–80. P.C. of St Olave, 1748–61. R. of Thurstaston, 1752–61. Precentor of Chester, 1754. V. of St Oswald's, 1761–80. Buried in the Cathedral, July 4, 1780. Brother of Humphrey (1731). (*Scott-Mayor*, III. 398.)

HENCHMAN, HUMPHREY. Matric. pens. from CHRIST'S, Dec. 1609. S. of Thomas, skinner, of London (and Wellingborough, Northants.). B. at Barton Seagrave, Northants. Bapt. there, Dec. 22, 1592. B.A. 1612–3; M.A. 1616; B.D. from Clare, 1623; D.D. 1628. Fellow of Clare, 1617. Incorp. at Oxford, 1617. Preb. and Precentor of Salisbury, 1623–60. R. of Rushton St Peter and All Saints', Northants., 1624. V. of Westbury, Wilts., 1631. R. of Wyke Regis, Kingsteignton and Portland, 1639. Deprived of all his preferments during the Rebellion. Lived in retirement at Salisbury. Maintained a secret correspondence with the Royalist leaders. Assisted Charles II to escape after the battle of Worcester, 1651. Bishop of Salisbury, 1660–3. Member of the Savoy Conference, 1661. Bishop of London, 1663–75. F.R.S., 1665. Died Oct. 7, 1675, aged 83. Buried in Fulham Church. Benefactor to Christ's and Clare. Perhaps brother of Richard (1602). (*Peile*, I. 274; *D.N.B.*; *Hutchins*, II. 831.)

HENCHMAN, HUMPHREY. Adm. pens. (age 19) at ST JOHN'S, Apr. 29, 1731. S. of Charles, clerk, of Cheshire. B. at Chester. Bapt. in the Cathedral, Apr. 22, 1712. School, Chester (under his father). Perhaps preb. of Salisbury, 1775–9. Died 1779. Brother of Charles (1726). (A. B. Beaven.)

HENCHMAN, JOHN. Adm. pens. at QUEENS', Feb. 2, 1670–1. Of London. Matric. 1671. Migrated to Clare, Nov. 22, 1671. B.A. 1674–5; M.A. 1678. Ord. deacon (Peterb.) Feb. 20, 1675–6; priest (London) May 26, 1678. One of these names of Sherborne, Dorset, clerk. Will (Blandford) 1699.

HENCHMAN, JOSEPH. Adm. sizar at JESUS, July 7, 1682. Matric. 1682; Scholar; B.A. 1685–6. Ord. priest (London) Feb. 24, 1688–9 ('M.A.'). R. of Shelfhanger, Norfolk, 1689. R. of Burston, 1706. Father of the next.

HENCHMAN, JOSEPH. Adm. sizar (age 17) at ST JOHN'S, May 26, 1721. S. of Joseph, clerk (above). B. at Chatham. School, Botesdale, Suffolk (Mr Maybourn). Matric. 1721–2; B.A. 1724–5. Ord. deacon (London) May 23, 1725. C. of Wilby, Suffolk. Buried there 1750. (*Scott-Mayor*, III. 339.)

HENCHMAN, RICHARD. Matric. sizar from ST JOHN'S, Easter, 1602. Perhaps s. of Thomas, of London. B.A. 1605–6; M.A. 1609; B.D. 1616; D.D. 1623. Ord. priest (Peterb.) Sept. 25, 1614. R. of Cottesbrooke, Northants., 1614. R. of Rushton All Saints' and St Peter's, 1616–24. Died 1624. Perhaps brother of Humphrey, Bishop of London, if so, father of Thomas (1636). (*N. and Q.*, 3rd S., III. 256; *Hutchins*, II. 831; H. I. Longden.)

HENCHMAN, RICHARD. Matric. sizar from ST CATHARINE'S, Easter, 1634. Of Northamptonshire. B.A. 1637–8; M.A. from Clare, 1641; D.D. 1666. Fellow of Clare, May 8, 1638. Ord. deacon (Peterb.) Sept. 19, 1641; priest (Lincoln) Sept. 24, 1643. Minister of St James, Garlickhythe, London, 1659. V. of Chigwell, Essex, 1661–72. V. of Christ Church, Newgate St, 1662–72. Preb. of St Paul's, 1663–72. Treasurer, 1664–71. Author, sermons. Died at Chigwell, Mar. 11, 1671–2. Buried at Christ Church. Will, Consist. C. London. Nephew of Humphrey, Bishop of London.

HENCHMAN or **HINCHMAN, THOMAS.** Adm. at CLARE, Sept. 7, 1636. Perhaps s. of Richard (1602). Matric. pens. Easter, 1637; B.A. 1640–1; D.D. 1666. Ord. deacon (Peterb.) June 5, 1642. Probably presented to Harrowden, Northants., 1648–51. Preb. of Salisbury, 1660–74. R. of St George, Botolph Lane, London, till 1661. Archdeacon of Wilts., 1663–74. R. of Much Hadham, Herts., 1669–74. Preb. of St Paul's, 1672–4. Died Dec. 1674. Will (P.C.C.) 1675. Nephew of the Bishop of London. Probably brother of William (1637). (*Shaw*, I. 359; *Hennessy*.)

HENCHMAN, THOMAS. Adm. pens. at CLARE, June 10, 1670. Eldest s. of William (1637), R. of Barton Seagrave, Northants. Bapt. there, Aug. 31, 1654. Matric. 1670. Died at Cambridge, July 29, 1671. Buried at Barton. (H. I. Longden.)

HENCHMAN, THOMAS. Adm. pens. at CLARE, Mar. 20, 1681–2. S. of Thomas, of Crutched Friars, London, and of Fulham, Middlesex. Matric. 1682; B.A. 1685–6; M.A. 1690. Fellow, 1688. Incorp. at Oxford, 1693. Ord. deacon and priest (London) June 11, 1693. V. of Norton-by-Daventry, Northants., 1702. Preb. of Salisbury, 1717–46. Died Dec. 1746. (*Hutchins*, II. 831.)

HENCHMAN, WILLIAM. Adm. sizar (age 15) at ST JOHN'S, Nov. 2, 1637. S. of William, baker, of Wellingborough, Northants. B. at Raunds. School, Higham Ferrers (Mr Freear). Matric. 1639; B.A. 1641–2; M.A. 1647. R. of Barton Seagrave, Northants., 1653–86. Conformed, in 1662. Preb. of Peterborough, 1668–86. Married, at Barton, Sept. 21, 1653, Anne, dau. of Thomas Bletso, of Mills Cotton. Died Sept. 14, 1686. Buried at Barton. M.I. (H. I. Longden.)

HENCHMAN or **HENSMAN, WILLIAM.** Matric. pens. from CLARE, Michs. 1637; B.A. 1641–2. Probably s. of Richard (1602); and brother of Thomas (1636).

HENCHMAN, WILLIAM. Adm. pens. at CLARE, Mar. 21, 1673–4. Of Deptford, Kent. Matric. 1674.

HENDEN, EDWARD. Adm. Fell.-Com. (age 17) at ST JOHN'S, Apr. 1, 1646. 1st s. of Sir John, of Biddenden, Kent, Knt. B. there. School, Biddenden (Mr Worrall). Adm. at Gray's Inn, Feb. 2, 1638–9. Brother of the next and of Simon.

HENDEN, JOHN. Adm. Fell.-Com. (age 16) at ST JOHN'S, July 1, 1646. 2nd s. of Sir John, Knt., of Hackney, Middlesex. B. there. School, Biddenden, Kent (Mr Worrall). Adm. at Gray's Inn, May 28, 1647. Of Biddenden, Kent. Brother of Edward and Simon. (*Vis. of Kent*, 1663.)

HENDEN, SIMON. Adm. Fell.-Com. (age 15) at ST JOHN'S, Mar. 7, 1648–9. 3rd s. of Sir John, of Biddenden, Kent, Knt. School, Amersham, Bucks. (Mr Angel). Matric. 1649. Adm. at Gray's Inn, May 28, 1647. Brother of Edward and John.

HENDEN, SOLOMON. Adm. sizar (age 17) at ST JOHN'S, June 24, 1689. S. of William, bailiff. B. at Marksbury, Somerset. School, Haverford (Mr Williams). Matric. 1689; B.A. 1692–3; M.A. 1696. Incorp. at Oxford, 1700.

HENDEN, ——. Adm. pens. at EMMANUEL, Apr. 25, 1638. Of Kent. Perhaps John, s. and h. of Sir Simon, of Benenden, Kent, Knt.; adm. at Gray's Inn, Mar. 24, 1637–8.

HENDERSON, HENRY. Adm. sizar (age 16) at ST JOHN'S, Mar. 14, 1678–9. S. of Thomas, gent. B. at Penrith, Cumberland. School, Kelvedon, Essex (Mr Henderson; ? Samuel, of 1670). Matric. 1679; B.A. 1682–3. V. of White Notley, Essex, 1692. R. of Tendring, 1707. Perhaps brother of Samuel (1670).

HENDERSON or **HINDERSON, JOHN.** M.A. from ST JOHN'S, 1713. S. of John (Hinderson), of London, gent. Matric. from Merton College, Oxford, Feb. 23, 1696–7, age 17; B.A. (Oxford) 1700. One of these names V. of Roydon, Essex, 1707–12. V. of Felsted, 1713–29. Died 1729. (J. Ch. Smith.)

HENDERSON, ROBERT. Adm. sizar at TRINITY, June 24, 1674. Matric. 1674; B.A. 1678–9; M.A. 1685. Ord. deacon (London) Dec. 18, 1681; priest (Durham) June 2, 1683. V. of Felton, Northumberland, 1683–1726, resigned. Married, Aug. 28, 1695, at Bishop Wearmouth, Frances, dau. of George Middleton, of Silksworth, Durham. Rebuilt the vicarage house at Felton. Buried there May 1, 1730, aged 71. Father of William (1719). (H. M. Wood.)

HENDERSON, SAMUEL. Adm. sizar (age 17) at ST JOHN'S, May 28, 1670. S. of Thomas, mercer, of Plumpton, Cumberland. B. there. School, Sedbergh. Matric. 1670; B.A. 1673–4. Fellow, 1675. Ord. priest (London) May 26, 1678. V. of Gt Totham, 1682–90. V. of Messing, Essex, 1690–3. Perhaps schoolmaster at Kelvedon; *see* Henry, above. Died 1693. Buried at Messing, Dec. 5, 1693. Will (p.C.C.). Probably brother of Henry (1678–9).

HENDERSON, THOMAS. Matric. pens. from TRINITY, Michs. 1555.

HENDERSON, WILLIAM. Adm. pens. (age 17) at PETERHOUSE, July 3, 1719. Of Northumberland. S. of Robert (1674). School, Houghton-le-Spring, Durham. Matric. 1719; Scholar, 1719; B.A. 1722–3. Ord. deacon (Durham) Aug. 18, 1723; priest, Aug. 23, 1724. V. of Felton, Northumberland, 1726–72. Died there Sept. 29, 1772. Buried at Felton.

HENDLE, ——. Adm. at CORPUS CHRISTI, 1552. One Peter Hendle R. of Otham, Kent, 1567.

HENDLEY, WILLIAM. Adm. pens. (age 16) at PETERHOUSE, July 5, 1704. 1st s. of Bowyer, of Otham, Kent. School, Eton. Adm. at Gray's Inn, Apr. 15, 1706.

HENDLEY, WILLIAM. Adm. sizar (age 17) at PEMBROKE, May 28, 1708. S. of William, of 'Soham' (? Otham), Kent, gent. B. at Bearstead. Matric. 1708; B.A. 1711–2. Ord. deacon (Ely) Dec. 21, 1712; priest (London) June 12, 1715. Lecturer of St James's, Clerkenwell, 1716; and of St Mary, Islington, 1718. Chaplain to Baron Willoughby. An ardent advocate of Charity Schools. Brought to trial on a charge of procuring unlawful gains under the guise of collecting Charities, 1719. Author, theological. Died 1724. (*D.N.B.*)

HENDRYE or **HENDRIE, JOHN.** Matric. sizar from CLARE, Easter, 1583. Licensed schoolmaster at Gt Bircham, Norfolk, 1586.

HENDRIE, RICHARD. Fellow of CORPUS CHRISTI, 1412. Ord. deacon (Ely) 1412; priest, Sept. 23, 1413. Perhaps V. of West Thurrock, Essex, to 1457. Died 1457.

HENEAGE or **HENNIDGE, EDWARD.** B.A. from CLARE, 1600–1; M.A. 1605. Ord. priest (Norwich) June 11, 1609. C. of Boxford.

HENEAGE, ELIAS. Adm. sizar (age 18) at MAGDALENE, June 4, 1684. S. of James. B. at Donington-on-Bain, Lincs. School, Louth. Matric. 1685; B.A. 1687–8. Ord. priest (Lincoln) Dec. 23, 1688. R. of Bratoft, Lincs., 1689. R. of Mablethorpe St Mary, 1696. Will proved (Lincoln) July 22, 1732. (*Lics. Pedigrees*, 1257.)

HENEAGE, GEORGE. B.Can.L. 1510. S. of John, of Hainton, near Wragby, Lincs. Incorp. at Oxford, 1522. Preb. of Lincoln, 1518–22, 1528–47. Chaplain to Wolsey. Treasurer of Lincoln, 1521–2. Archdeacon of Oxford, 1522–8. R. of Maidswell St Mary, Northants., 1524–33. Dean of Lincoln, 1528–44. Preb. of York, 1533. Archdeacon of Taunton, 1533–42. R. of Sutton Coldfield, 1534. Preb. of Sarum, 1539–46. Archdeacon of Lincoln, 1542–9. Died *c.* Sept. 1549. Buried in Lincoln Cathedral. Will (P.C.C.). Uncle of Thomas (1549). (*Cooper*, I. 95; *D.N.B.*; A. B. Beaven.)

HENEAGE, MICHAEL. Matric. pens. from ST JOHN'S, Easter, 1559. S. of Robert, auditor of the Duchy of Lancaster. B. in Middlesex, Sept. 27, 1540. B.A. 1562–3; M.A. 1566. Fellow, 1563. Adm. at Gray's Inn, 1567. M.P. for Arundel, 1571; for East Grinstead, 1572–83; for Tavistock, 1588; for Wigan, 1592. Keeper of the records in the Tower, 1578. Married Grace, dau. of Robert Honeywood, of Charing, Kent, 1577. Author, antiquarian. Died Dec. 30, 1600. Will (P.C.C.) 1601. Brother of Thomas (1549). (*Cooper*, II. 293; *D.N.B.*; *Lincs. Pedigrees*, 482.)

HENEAGE, MICHAEL. Adm. Fell.-Com. at EMMANUEL, Oct. 4, 1649. Of Surrey. Only s. of Thomas, of Gray's Inn, and Battersea, Surrey. B. Oct. 14, 1632. Matric. 1649. Adm. at Gray's Inn, Nov. 26, 1652. Of Hatton Garden. Knighted, July 30, 1664. Died Dec. 1711. Father of Thomas (1687). (*Lincs. Pedigrees*, 482; Le Neve, *Knights*, 184.)

HENEAGE or **HENNEDGE, THOMAS.** Matric. pens. from QUEENS', Easter, 1549. S. of Robert, of Lincoln. M.A. 1564, on the Queen's visit. Doubtless adm. at Gray's Inn, 1565. M.P. for Stamford, 1553; for Boston, 1562–3; for Co. Lincs., 1563, 1571, 1572–6; for Essex, 1584–7, 1588–9, 1593. Treasurer of the Chamber, 1570. Knighted, Dec. 1, 1577. Keeper of the records, *c.* 1577, with his brother Michael (1559). Vice-Chamberlain to Queen Elizabeth, 1589. Privy Councillor, 1589. Chancellor of the Duchy of Lancaster, 1590–5. Died Oct. 17, 1595. M.I. in old St Paul's. Will (P.C.C.) 1595. (*Cooper*, II. 193; *D.N.B.*; *Lincs. Pedigrees*, 481.)

HENADGE, THOMAS. Matric. pens. (age 10) from ST JOHN'S, Michs. 1564. Probably Sir Thomas, of Hainton, Lincs. S. of William, of Hainton. Knighted, July 23, 1603. Died June 5, 1613, aged 59. (*Lincs. Pedigrees*, 483; Burke, *L.G.*)

HENEAGE, THOMAS. Adm. pens. (age 17) at TRINITY, Sept. 29, 1687. S. of Sir Michael (1649). B. in London. School, Lincoln's Inn Fields (Mr Mordant Webster). Perhaps of Cadeby, Lincs. Died Jan. 2, 1739–40. (*G. Mag.*) Not mentioned in *Lincs. Pedigrees*, 482.

HENEAGE, ——. M.A. 1456–7.

HENGHAM, RICHARD, *see* BURY, Abbot of.

HENKS, ROGER. B.A. from ST JOHN'S, 1576–7.

HENLEY, ANDREW. Adm. Fell.-Com. at CLARE, June 2, 1679. Of London. 2nd s. of Sir Andrew, of Henley, Somerset, Bart. Succeeded his brother Robert, as 3rd Bart., c. 1689. Of Bramshill, Hants. In 1695 'killed a man, and fled for it.' Buried at St James', Westminster, Sept. 14, 1703. (Burke, *Ext. Bart.*; *G.E.C.*)

HENLEY, HENRY. Adm. pens. (age 16) at ST JOHN'S, July 3, 1656. S. of Henry, gent., of Colway-in-Lyme, Dorset. School, Dorchester (Mr Cromlum). Matric. 1657; B.A. 1659–60. Adm. at the Middle Temple, Jan. 26, 1660–1. Married Mary, dau. of John Bulkeley. Buried at Lyme Regis, Dorset, Jan. 17, 1683. (Burke, *L.G. Supp.*)

HENLEY, HENRY CORNISH. Adm. Fell.-Com. at KING'S, 1749–50. S. of Henry Holt, recorder of Lyme Regis, Dorset, and Sarah, dau. of Henry Cornish, of London, Esq. Sheriff of Dorset, 1773. Died at Sandringham, Norfolk, Nov. 17, 1773. (G. *Mag.*; *Hutchins*, III. 742.)

HENLEY, JAMES. Matric. pens. from ST JOHN'S, Easter, 1565.

HENLEY, JOHN. Matric. sizar at TRINITY, Easter, 1573. B. at Offley, Herts. B.A. 1577–8. Ord. deacon (Ely) Apr. 17, 1580; priest (London) Dec. 21, 1580, age 28. R. of Holwell, Beds., 1580–1636. Will proved (Archd. Beds.) 1636; to be buried at Holwell. (H. I. Longden.)

HENLEY, JOHN. M.A. 1664 (Incorp. from Oxford). Matric. from Christ Church, Nov. 26, 1650; B.A. (Oxford) 1654; M.A. 1657. Ord. deacon and priest (Norwich) Sept. 1661. V. of Towcester, Northants., 1662–c. 1676. Father of Simon (1679). (*Al. Oxon.*)

HENLEY, JOHN. Adm. Fell.-Com. (age 17) at TRINITY, June 17, 1695. S. of Sir Robert, of Northington Grange, Alresford, Hants. School, Winchester. Matric. 1695, as 'George.' Elected M.P. for Milborne Port, 1702, but not returned. One of these names s. of Sir Robert, of Abbots Wotton, Dorset. (*Hutchins*, III. 742.)

HENLEY, JOHN. Adm. pens. (age 17) at ST JOHN'S, June 15, 1709. S. of Simon (1679). B. at Melton Mowbray, Aug. 3, 1692. Schools, Melton and Oakham (Mr Wright). Matric. 1709; B.A. 1712–3; M.A. 1716. Generally known as 'Orator Henley.' Ord. deacon (Lincoln) June 12, 1715; priest, Sept. 21, 1718. C. to his father, in 1715; and Master at Melton School, 1716. He applied to the Vice-Chancellor, at one time, to hold an 'oratory' at Stourbridge Fair, but was refused. Came to London, 1721. Reader at the Church of St George the Martyr. R. of Chelmondiston, Suffolk, 1723. Began his 'orations' at Newport, 1726. Established himself in Lincoln's Inn Fields, 1729. Ridiculed by Pope in the *Dunciad*. Caricatured by Hogarth. Author, theology, grammar, etc. Died Oct. 14, 1756. (*D.N.B.*)

HENLEY, PETER. Matric. pens. from CLARE, Easter, 1553. One of these names R. of Swanscomb, Kent, 1569–76.

HENLEY, SIMON. Adm. at CORPUS CHRISTI, 1679. Of Northamptonshire. S. of John (1664), V. of Towcester. B. there, Aug. 12, 1664. Matric. 1680; B.A. 1683–4; M.A. 1694. Ord. priest (Peterb.) Sept. 19, 1686, as of Knipton, Leics. V. of Melton Mowbray, 1690–1731. Died June 15, 1731, aged 66. M.I. at Melton. Will, Leicester. Father of John (1709). (*Nichols*, II. 252; H. I. Longden.)

HENLEY, THOMAS. Adm. at CORPUS CHRISTI, 1698. Previously matric. from Pembroke College, Oxford, Feb. 25, 1696–7. Of Dorset. S. of Henry, of Lyme Regis. M.B. 1703; M.D. 1708. Adm. at Leyden, Oct. 22, 1699. Doubtless practised at Lyme. Admon. (Blandford) 1740; M.D. of Lyme. (J. Ch. Smith.)

HENLEY, ——. Adm. Fell.-Com. at TRINITY HALL, Apr. 12, 1714. (Name off, 1716.)

HENMAN, ALLEN. Matric. pens. from ST JOHN'S, Easter, 1622. Of Kent. Scholar; B.A. 1625–6; M.A. 1629. Fellow, 1629–30; ejected; and 1660–2.

HENMAN, THOMAS. Matric. pens. from ST JOHN'S, Easter, 1618; B.A. 1621–2. Perhaps P.C. of Towersey, Bucks., 1629, as Hennam or Hennant. Succeeded, 1664, at Thame, Oxon. Died there. (*Lipscomb*, I. 460.)

HENMAN, THOMAS. Adm. pens. (age 17) at ST JOHN'S, Oct. 28, 1671. S. of Richard, gent., deceased, of Milton, Kent. B. there. School, Wye (Mr Parris). Matric. 1671; B.A. 1675–6.

HENMER, JOHN. 'King's scholar' at Cambridge, 1328. S. of Richard de Henmer.

HENNANT, HENRY. Adm. sizar at CORPUS CHRISTI, 1643. Of Norfolk. Matric. Michs. 1644; B.A. 1646–7.

HENNANT, THOMAS. Adm. at CORPUS CHRISTI, 1614. Of Norfolk. B.A. 1617–8. Probably R. of Smallburgh, Norfolk, 1629. (For another of these names *see Al. Oxon.*)

HENRISON, RICHARD. B.A. (? 1501); M.A. 1504.

HENRY, the Bedell. University Bedell, c. 1350. (Stokes, *Bedells*, 55.)

HENRY, ——. University 'scriptor,' 1460. (*Gr. Bk*, A, 28.)

HENRY, ——. Of BERNARD HOSTEL. B.A. 1465.

HENRY, ——. D.D. 1466. Prior of St Mary of Overesse. Formerly of QUEENS'.

HENRY, ——. Of TRINITY HALL. B.Can.L. 1466–7.

HENRY, ——. Dominican friar. D.D. 1475–6.

HENRY, ——. Canonicus. B.D. 1480–1.

HENRY, ——. ('Hon. Dominus.') Matric. Fell.-Com. from KING'S, Easter, 1705.

HENSHALL, EDMUND. Matric. sizar from CLARE, Michs. 1602; B.A. 1605–6; M.A. 1609. Perhaps V. of Sutton Valence, Kent, 1614. R. of Crundale. V. of Brenchley. Will (P.C.C.) 1645. But *see* Edward Henshaw in *Al. Oxon.* (H. G. Harrison.)

HENSHAW, BENJAMIN. Adm. at CORPUS CHRISTI, 1717. Of London. Adm. at the Inner Temple, Dec. 5, 1717; s. and h. of Benjamin, of London, merchant. Bapt. Mar. 17, 1700. Married Elizabeth Bethell, of London, 1734. Will proved, Oct. 24, 1767. Brother of Joseph (1720).

HENSHAWE or HYNSHAW, BRIAN. Adm. sizar (age 17) at CAIUS, May 6, 1599. S. of James, of Spofforth, Yorks. B.A. 1602–3; Scholar, 1604–6; M.A. 1606. Licensed as schoolmaster at Morpeth, Northumberland, Oct. 10, 1618. (*Venn*, I. 168; H. M. Wood.)

HENSHAW, EDWARD. Adm. sizar at EMMANUEL, Easter, 1603. Matric. 1603; Scholar; B.A. 1606–7; M.A. 1610. Fellow, 1611–3. Died in College.

HENSHAW, GEORGE. Adm. pens. at JESUS, Mar. 21, 1677–8. S. of Hugh, of Henshaw, Cheshire, Esq. Living, 1681. Died *s.p.* (Earwaker, *E. Cheshire*, II. 400.)

HENSCHAWE, JOHN. B.A. 1473–4; M.A. 1477–8; B.D. 1483–4 (? 1490–1). Fellow of QUEENS', 1484–96. R. of St Botolph, Cambridge, 1495. Died 1499.

HENSHAW, JOHN. Adm. pens. at TRINITY, May 9, 1651, a scholar from Westminster. 2nd s. of John, of Lewes. B. in Sussex. B.A. 1654–5. Adm. at the Middle Temple, Nov. 23, 1654. Called to the bar, Apr. 25, 1662.

HENSHAW or HENSHALL, JOHN. Adm. sizar at JESUS, June 21, 1704. Matric. 1704; B.A. 1707–8.

HENSHAWE, JOSEPH. M.A. from PEMBROKE, 1628. S. of Thomas, of Sussex, solicitor-general of Ireland. School, Charterhouse. Matric. from Magdalen Hall, Oxford, Dec. 7, 1621, age 18; B.A. (Oxford) 1624–5; B.D. 1635; D.D. 1639. Chaplain to George Villiers, Duke of Buckingham. Preb. of Chichester, 1628. V. of St Bartholomew-the-Less, London, 1631–6. Held with this, by dispensation, the livings of East Lavant, Stedham and Hayshot, Sussex. Sequestered and had to compound for his estate. Dean and precentor of Chichester, 1660–3. Bishop of Peterborough, 1663–79. Author. Died Mar. 9, 1678–9. Buried at East Lavant, Sussex. Will, P.C.C. Father of Thomas (1664). (*Al. Oxon.*; *D.N.B.*; H. G. Harrison.)

HENSHAW, JOSEPH. Adm. at CORPUS CHRISTI, 1720. Of London. S. of Benjamin, merchant, of London. Bapt. Nov. 25, 1701. B.A. 1723–4; M.A. 1727. Ord. deacon (London) June 5, 1726. R. of High Ongar, Essex, 1733–88. Will (P.C.C.) 1788. Brother of Benjamin (1717). (Burke, *L.G.*; J. Ch. Smith.)

HENSHAW, MICHAEL. Matric. pens. from ST JOHN'S, Easter, 1614. Of Staffordshire. B.A. 1616–7; M.A. 1620. Fellow, 1618. Ord. deacon (Peterb.) Apr. 21; priest, Apr. 22, 1622. V. of Hanbury, Staffs., 1636–8. Buried July 20, 1638. Will at Lichfield. (*Wm. Salt Arch. Soc.*, 1915.)

HENSHAW, PHILIP. Adm. Fell.-Com. (age 17) at ST JOHN'S, Mar. 18, 1695–6. S. of Thomas (? 1641), gent. B. at Billingshurst, Sussex. Taught privately by Mr Maddison. Matric. 1696. Adm. at Gray's Inn, May 7, 1700. Married Mabel, dau. of Sir Jonathan Raymond, Knt., of Hookland Park, Sussex and of Bussock Court, Berks. Died Aug. 4, 1753.

HENSHAW or HONSHAWE, ROBERT. Matric. pens. from CHRIST'S, Mar. 1580–1. Of Leicestershire. B.A. 1584–5; M.A. 1588.

HENSHAW, THOMAS. Adm. pens. at QUEENS', June 10, 1603. B. in St Mary Magdalene, Milk St, London. B.A. from St John's, 1606; M.A. 1610. Fellow of St John's, 1608. Ord. deacon (London) Mar. 8, 1611–2, age 24.

HENSHAW, THOMAS. Adm. pens. at TRINITY, Apr. 7, 1641. Matric. 1641. One of these names, s. of Thomas, of Billingshurst, Sussex, adm. at the Inner Temple, 1648. Barrister, 1656. Died 1680. But *see Al. Oxon.* for another.

HENSHAW, THOMAS. M.A. 1664 (Incorp. from Oxford). Probably s. of Joseph (1628), Bishop of Peterborough. Matric. from Queen's, Oxford, Nov. 7, 1655; B.A. (Oxford) 1657; M.A. 1661. Fellow of All Souls. Died before Sept. 8, 1675. Buried at East Lavant, Sussex. (*Al. Oxon.*; Burke, *L.G.*)

HENSHAW, TOBIAS. Adm. sizar at CLARE, May 24, 1639. Matric. 1639; B.A. 1642-3; B.D. 1661 (*Lit. Reg.*). Ord. deacon and priest, Nov. 16, 1660. Archdeacon of Lewes, 1670-81. V. of Henfield, Sussex, 1672. V. of Cuckfield, 1672-81. Treasurer of Chichester, 1672-81. Buried at Cuckfield, Nov. 25, 1681. Will, P.C.C. (W. C. Renshaw.)

HENSHAW, WILLIAM. Adm. sizar at EMMANUEL, Dec. 14, 1630. Of Leicester. Matric. 1631. Buried at Gt St Andrew's, Cambridge, Nov. 8, 1634.

HENSHAW, ——. Adm. pens. at TRINITY HALL, July 2, 1723. (Name off, Sept. 1723.)

HENSLEY, FRANCIS. Matric. pens. from ST JOHN'S, Michs. 1585.

HENSLYE, JOHN. Matric. sizar from TRINITY, Michs. 1566.

HENSLEY, ——. M.A. or higher degree, 1484-5.

HENSMAN, HENRY. Matric. pens. from TRINITY, Easter, 1588.

HENSMAN, WILLIAM, *see* **HENCHMAN.**

HENSON, GREGORY. Adm. sizar at QUEENS', Nov. 5, 1706. Of Lincolnshire. Matric. 1706; B.A. 1710-1; M.A. 1718. V. of Somerby, Leics., 1717-59. R. of St John's, Stamford, Llues. Perhaps also V. of Dalby Magna, Leics., 1717-57. Died June 10, 1759. M.I. at Somerby. (*Nichols*, II. 320.)

HENSON, JOHN. Matric. sizar at CORPUS CHRISTI, Easter, 1644. Of Norfolk. B.A. 1647-8; M.A. 1651. Ord. priest (Bishop Jos. Hall) Apr. 1, 1650. V. of Terrington St Clement's, Norfolk, 1651-1711. R. of North Lynn, 1663-1711. Died 1711, aged 86.

HENSON, JOHN. Adm. sizar (age 24) at SIDNEY, June 3, 1731. S. of John. B. at Nottingham. School, Nottingham (Mr Swale). *Litt. dim.* for priest (York) May, 1740. C. of Edwalton, Notts.

HENSON, ROBERT. Adm. sizar at EMMANUEL, June 7, 1611. Matric. 1611. Ord. deacon (Peterb.) Sept. 24, 1615; priest, Dec. 20, 1618. R. of West Lynn, Norfolk, 1620. R. of North Lynn, 1649.

HENSON, SAMUEL. Adm. sizar (age 19) at SIDNEY, May 3, 1669. 1st s. of William, farmer. B. at Hartshorn, Derbs. Schools, Staffordshire (Mr Haslor) and Selby, Yorks. Matric. 1672; B.A. 1672-3. Perhaps died Nov. 23, 1715; 'owner of considerable estates in Yorks. and Derbs.' (M. H. Peacock.)

HENSON, WILLIAM. Adm. pens. at CORPUS CHRISTI, 1558. Matric. Easter, 1559 (*impubes*).

HENSON, WILLIAM. Adm. at KING'S (age 17) a scholar from Eton, Aug. 13, 1564. Of Hemington, Northants. Matric. 1564; B.A. 1568-9; M.A. 1572; B.D. 1579. Fellow, 1567-79. Ord. deacon and priest (Lincoln) Oct. 25, 1576. V. of Fordingbridge, Hants., 1579-1626. Buried May 16, 1626. Will (P.C.C.) 1626.

HENSTON, W. Matric. pens. (age 12) from PEMBROKE, Easter, 1567.

HENSTRIDGE, JAMES. Adm. pens. (age 18) at ST JOHN'S, July 3, 1693. S. of Daniel, organist (for whom *see D.N.B.*). B. at Rochester. School, Eton. Matric. 1696; B.A. 1696-7; M.A. 1703. Ord. deacon (London) Sept. 24, 1699; priest, Sept. 22, 1700. V. of Seasalter, Kent, 1700. R. of St Mildred, Canterbury, 1710-45. R. of Brooke, 1734-45. Minor Canon of Canterbury. Died Dec. 8, 1745. (*G. Mag.*)

HENTON, GEORGE, *see* **HINTON.**

HENTY, THOMAS. Matric. Fell.-Com. from CORPUS CHRISTI, Michs. 1702.

HENVILL, PHILIP. Adm. sizar (age 16) at ST JOHN'S, Jan. 13, 1719-20. S. of William, husbandman, of Dorset. B. at Haydon. School, Sherborne (Mr Gerard). Matric. 1720; B.A. 1724-5.

HENWOOD, JAMES. Adm. sizar (age 20) at PEMBROKE, May 30, 1685. S. of John, farmer. B. in Cornwall. Matric. 1685. Will of one of these names (Exeter) 1721; of Warkley, Devon, clerk.

HEPDEN, JOHN. Adm. pens. at EMMANUEL, May 7, 1600; B.A. 1601-2.

HEPE, FRANCIS, *see* **HEAPE.**

HEPPENSTALL, BRIAN. Matric. pens. from EMMANUEL, July 6, 1608; Scholar; B.A. 1611-2; M.A. 1615. Incorp. at Oxford, 1612. Ord. deacon (York) Sept. 1615; priest, May, 1616. R. of Barlborough, Derbs., 1616. Licensed, Dec. 21, 1619, to Marry Frances Jenkinson, of Kirk Sandal, Yorks. (M. H. Peacock.)

HEPWOOD, THOMAS. Matric. sizar from TRINITY, Michs. 1625; B.A. 1627-8; M.A. 1636. Ord. deacon (Peterb.) Sept. 22; priest, Sept. 23, 1627.

HEPWORTH, JOHN. B.A. from ST JOHN'S, 1612-3; M.A. 1616. Ord. deacon (Peterb.) Dec. 4; priest, Dec. 5, 1614.

HEPWORTH, JOHN. Adm. sizar at CLARE, May 21, 1649. Matric. 1649; B.A. 1652-3. V. of Harewood, Yorks., 1699-1704.

HEPWORTH, RICHARD. Matric. sizar from TRINITY, Easter, 1551; Scholar, 1552. Perhaps V. of Habrough, Lincs., till 1573.

HEPWORTH, STEPHEN. M.A. Chancellor of the University, 1257, 1287, 1299. Benefactor.

HEPWORTH, THOMAS. Adm. sizar (age 17) at CHRIST'S, June 30, 1671. S. of Thomas, of Yorkshire. School, Thornhill, near Dewsbury (Mr Wilson). Matric. 1672; B.A. 1674-5; M.A. 1678. Ord. deacon (York) Sept. 1677; priest, May 29, 1681. V. of Birstall, Yorks., 1681-1701. Buried July 14, 1701. (*Peile*, II. 38.)

HERBERT, *see also* **HARBERT.**

HERBERT, CHARLES. Adm. at KING'S, a scholar from Eton, 1677. B. at Newton, Hereford. Matric. 1678; B.A. 1681-2; M.A. 1686. Fellow, 1681. Chaplain to Lord Herbert, 1683. Schoolmaster at Abergavenny, and lecturer of 'Jones Charity,' Monmouth, 1685. V. of Ringwood, Hants., 1708. Resided at Monmouth, till his death, Mar. 1722-3. (*Harwood*, 264; F. S. Hockaday.)

HERBERT, CHRISTOPHER. Matric. pens. from TRINITY, Michs. 1588. Probably s. of Christopher, merchant, of York. Bapt. at St Crux, July 22, 1571. Scholar, 1590; B.A. 1592-3. Adm. at Gray's Inn, Feb. 6, 1594-5, from Barnard's Inn. Of Lasingcroft, Yorks. Married Elizabeth, dau. of Anthony Wright, of Maltby, Yorks. (*Yorks. Arch. and Top. Journal*, I. 214; M. H. Peacock.)

HERBERT, EDWARD (1561), *see* **HARBARD.**

HERBERT, Sir EDWARD. University Counsel, 1641. S. of Charles, of Aston, Montgomeryshire. Adm. at the Inner Temple, Nov. 1609. Barrister, 1618. Treasurer, 1638. M.P. for Montgomery, 1620; for Downton, 1625-9; for Old Sarum, 1641. A manager of Buckingham's impeachment, 1626; one of Selden's counsel, 1629. Solicitor-general, 1640. Knighted, Jan. 28, 1640-1. Attorney-general, 1641. Impeached and imprisoned for his share in the abortive impeachment of six members, 1642. Joined the Royalists; sequestered as a delinquent, 1646. Went to sea with Prince Rupert, 1648. Accompanied the Duke of York to Paris, 1651. Lord Keeper to Charles II, while abroad, 1653. Died Dec. 1657, at Paris. Buried in the Huguenot cemetery in the Faubourg St Germain. (*D.N.B.*; A. B. Beaven.)

HERBERT, EDWARD. Matric. sizar from QUEENS', Easter, 1642. S. of Nathaniel, gent., of Hargrave, Northants. Migrated to St John's, Jan. 11, 1644-5, age 20. B.A. 1645-6; M.A. from King's, 1654; D.D. 1661 (*Lit. Reg.*). V. of Nantcwnlle, Cardigan. R. of North Ockendon, Essex, 1658-97. R. of Cranham, 1669-97. Died 1697, aged 72.

HERBERT, EDWARD. Adm. Fell.-Com. (age 17) at ST JOHN'S, July 22, 1745. S. of Edward, gent., of Ireland (M.P. for Ludlow). B. at Muckross, Co. Kerry. School, Killarney (Mr Power). Matric. 1746. Adm. at the Middle Temple, Oct. 7, 1745. M.P. for Innistioge, 1749-60; for Tralee, 1761-70. Died Feb. 24, 1770, in the same year as his father. Brother of Thomas (1744) and Nicholas (1749). (*Scott-Mayor*, III. 554; A. B. Beaven.)

HERBERT, GEORGE. Matric. pens. from TRINITY, Michs. 1609. 5th s. of Sir Richard, of Montgomery Castle. B. there, Apr. 3, 1593. A scholar from Westminster, 1608. B.A. 1612-3; M.A. 1616. Fellow, 1616. Public orator, 1619-27. Ord. priest, 1630. R. of Bemerton and Fugglestone, Wilts., 1630-3. As the writer of official letters to the government he proved himself an accomplished courtier. On terms of intimacy with Nicholas Ferrar whose influence doubtless induced him to adopt a religious life. Married Jane, dau. of Charles Danvers, of Baynton, Wilts. A classical scholar and a good musician. The well-known religious poet. Author of *The Temple, Sacred Poems and Private Ejaculations.* Buried at Bemerton, Mar. 3, 1633. (*D.N.B.*)

HERBERT, Sir HENRY. Educated at PETERHOUSE, under Whitgift. S. of William, Earl of Pembroke. Created M.A. (Oxford) 1592. K.B., 1553. Gentleman of the Chamber to King Philip of Spain, 1554. Succeeded as 2nd Earl, 1570. Took a prominent part in the trials of Norfolk (1572), of Arundel (1589) and of Mary, Queen of Scots (1586). K.G., 1574. Lord president of Wales, 1587-1601. A patron of antiquaries. Married Catherine, sister of Lady Jane Grey, 1553. Died at Wilton, Jan. 19, 1600-1. Buried in Salisbury Cathedral. (*Cooper*, II. 294; *D.N.B.*; *G.E.C.*)

HERBERT, HENRY. Adm. Fell.-Com. at MAGDALENE, May 30, 1728. Matric. 1728; LL.D. 1728 (*Com. Reg.*).

HERBERT, JOHN. Adm. pens. (age 17) at MAGDALENE, May 26, 1682. S. of John. B. at North Duffield, near Howden, Yorks. School, Howden. Matric. 1682; B.A. 1685-6.

HERBERT, JOHN. Adm. sizar (age 17) at TRINITY, Aug. 20, 1687. S. of William (1631), D.D., of Bury St Edmunds. School, Bury (Mr Leeds). Matric. 1687; B.A. 1691-2. Brother of William (1679).

HERBERT, JOHN. Adm. pens. (age 18) at TRINITY, June 25, 1688. S. of Nathaniel, of London. School, Westminster. Matric. 1688; Scholar, 1689; B.A. 1691-2; M.A. 1695. Ord. deacon (London) Dec. 18, 1698; priest, Feb. 25, 1699-1700. V. of Ridge, Herts., 1718-20. Died 1720. Admon. (P.C.C.) June 23, 1720. (Not to be confused with his namesake, the D.D. of Oxford: *see Al. Oxon.*)

HERBERT, NICHOLAS. Adm. pens. (age 19) at ST JOHN'S, May 27, 1749. S. of Edward, Esq., of Muckross, Ireland. B. at Muckross, Co. Kerry. School, Killarney. Matric. 1749; LL.B. 1757. Ord. deacon (Ely) Dec. 25, 1752; priest (Hereford) Sept. 9, 1753. R. of Ludlow, Salop, 1753-62. Died 1802. Brother of Edward (1745) and Thomas (1744). (*Scott-Mayor*, III. 589.)

HERBERT, PHILIP. Adm. Fell.-Com. (age 19) at ST JOHN'S. Oct. 29, 1708. S. of James, gent., of Northwood, Kent. B. in London. School, Eton. Matric. 1709. Of Northwood, Kent. Died 1747. (*Hasted*, II. 663.)

HERBERT, RALPH. Adm. Fell.-Com. (age 16) at ST JOHN'S, Aug. 10, 1647. S. of Herbert, mercer, of Biddenden, Kent, gent. School, Biddenden (Mr Worrall). Matric. 1647.

HERBERT, ROWLAND. Matric. pens. from ST JOHN'S, Easter, 1615.

HERBERT, THOMAS. S. of Christopher, of York. Said to have been of Jesus College, Oxford, 1621, and afterwards of TRINITY, Cambridge (no University or College record). Went to Persia with Sir Dodmore Cotton and Sir Robert Shirley, 1628. Commissioner with Fairfax's army, 1644. Groom of the bedchamber to Charles I, 1647-9. Created Baronet, 1660. Wrote an account of his Eastern travels; also reminiscences of the captivity of Charles I. Died at York, Mar. 1, 1681-2. Buried there in the Church of St Crux. M.I. Will, York. (*Al. Oxon.*; *D.N.B.*; M. H. Peacock.)

HERBERT, THOMAS. Matric. sizar from TRINITY, Easter, 1639.

HERBERT, THOMAS. Adm. Fell.-Com. at CHRIST'S, Apr. 28, 1731. S. of Thomas, of Whitefriars, Cardiff. B. in Pembrokeshire. School, Eton. Adm. at the Inner Temple, Feb. 2, 1727-8.

HERBERT, THOMAS. Adm. Fell.-Com. (age 17) at ST JOHN'S, July 12, 1744. S. of Edward, gent., of Ireland (of Muckross, Co. Kerry). B. at Killarney. School, Hackney, Middlesex (Mr Graham). Matric. 1744. Adm. at the Middle Temple, Nov. 1, 1743. Barrister, 1750. M.P. for Ludlow, 1743-54. Died May 16, 1754. Brother of Edward (1745) and Nicholas (1749). (*Scott-Mayor*, III. 546; A. B. Beaven.)

HERBERT, WILLIAM. Matric. pens. from PETERHOUSE, Easter, 1566; B.A. 1568-9.

HERBERT, WILLIAM. Adm. pens. at EMMANUEL, Easter, 1626. Matric. 1627; B.A. 1629-30; M.A. 1633.

HERBERT, WILLIAM. Scholar of TRINITY, Easter, 1631; B.A. 1631-2; M.A. 1635; D.D. 1661 (*Lit. Reg.*). Fellow, 1633. Ord. deacon (Norwich) Sept. 22, 1639; perhaps priest (Lincoln) June 5, 1642. V. of Trumpington, Cambs., 1641-2. R. of Gt Whelnetham, Suffolk, 1646-80. Preacher at St Mary's, Bury St Edmunds, 1662-3. Buried at Gt Whelnetham, Feb. 1680-1. Will (Bury) 1681. Father of William (1679) and John (1687).

HERBERT, WILLIAM. Adm. pens. at TRINITY, Nov. 12, 1649. Of Carmarthen. Matric. 1650. One of these names, of Swansea, Glamorgan, Esq., adm. at Gray's Inn, Dec. 10, 1650.

HERBERT, WILLIAM. Adm. pens. at TRINITY, July 6, 1667. Matric. 1667; B.A. 1671-2. Ord. deacon (Norwich) Sept. 1672. Minor canon of Norwich Cathedral.

HERBERT, WILLIAM. Adm. pens. (age 16) at TRINITY, May 14, 1679. S. of William (1631), D.D. B. at Bury St Edmunds, Suffolk. School, Bury (Mr Leeds). Matric. 1679; Scholar, 1681; B.A. 1682-3; M.A. 1686. Fellow, 1685. Brother of John (1687).

HERBERT, WILLIAM. M.A. from ST JOHN'S, June 25, 1701. S. of Thomas, of Llanvihangel, Cardigan, clerk. Matric. from St John's, Oxford, Mar. 23, 1688-9, age 22; B.A. (Oxford) 1693. V. of Llansantffraid, Cardigan, 1693. (*Al. Oxon.*)

HERBERT, WILLIAM. Adm. Fell.-Com. at CLARE, June 5, 1720. Probably s. of William, 2nd Marquis and titular Duke of Powis. B. in London. Matric. 1720. Died Mar. 8, 1748. (*D.N.B.*)

HERBY, WILLIAM. Adm. pens. (age 17) at PEMBROKE, June 10, 1649. S. of William, of Newport, Isle of Wight, clerk.

HERCY, LOVELACE. Adm. pens. (age 18) at ST JOHN'S, Sep. 17, 1668. 3rd s. of John, of Winkfield, Berks. B. there. School, Eton. Matric. 1669. Of Cruchfield, Berks., and of the Inner Temple. Barrister, 1676. Died 1730. (Burke, *L.G.*; *Vis. of Berks.*, 1665.)

HERD, *see* HEARD.

HERDINGE, BROWNELL, *see* HARDING.

HERDMAN or HARDMAN, BARTIN. B.A. from JESUS, 1609. Ord. deacon (York) June, 1609; priest, Sept. 1610.

HERDMAN, EDMUND. B.A. from JESUS, 1609.

HERDMAN, GABRIEL. Matric. sizar from JESUS, Michs. 1588. One of these names matric. from Lincoln College, Oxford, Apr. 22, 1586. Of Yorkshire.

HERDMAN, LAURENCE. Adm. sizar (age 18) at ST JOHN'S, June 17, 1701. S. of John, husbandman. B. at Quernmore, Lancaster. School, Lancaster (Mr Bordley). Matric. 1701; B.A. 1704-5. Ord. deacon (Ely) June 3, 1705; priest (London) Sept. 19, 1708. V. of Islington, Norfolk.

HERDMAN, THOMAS. Matric. sizar from TRINITY, Easter, 1604.

HEARDSMAN, WILLIAM. Adm. sizar (age 20) at SIDNEY, Oct. 22, 1726. S. of Richard, farmer. B. at Bishop Wilton, Yorks. Schools, Pocklington and Coxwold. Matric. 1726; B.A. 1730-1. Ord. deacon (Lincoln) May 24, 1730; priest (York) July 18, 1731. R. of Sneaton, Yorks., 1734-62.

HEREFORD, ROGER DE. Said to have studied at Cambridge. Flourished *c.* 1178. Mathematician and astrologer. (*D.N.B.*; *Pits.*, 237.)

HEREWARDEN, HENRY DE, *see* HAWARDEN.

HERFORD, JOHN DE. Carmelite friar at Cambridge. Ord. deacon (Ely) Mar. 20, 1343-4. (B. Zimmerman.)

HERFORD, WALTER. Scholar at KING'S HALL, 1364. Died May 2, 1376.

HERGRAVES, *see* HARGRAVES.

HERISHAM, ——. Adm. at CORPUS CHRISTI, 1562.

HERKS, JOHN, *see* GARBRAND.

HERLING, *see* HARLING.

HERMAN, *see also* HARMAN.

HERMAN, REYNARD. Adm. sizar (age 17) at CLARE, Oct. 19, 1633. B. at Nijmwegen, Gelderland, Holland. School, Westminster. Matric. 1633; B.A. from Pembroke, 1637-8; M.A. 1641. Ord. deacon (Peterb.) Dec. 18, 1641; priest, Aug. 17, 1662. Head Master of Stamford School, 1657-62. Confrater of Brown's Hospital, Stamford, 1662-8. R. of Tinwell, Rutland, 1662-8. Buried there Oct. 18, 1668. (*Scott-Mayor*, I. xxxv; *Genealogist*, III. 108.)

HERMAN, WILLIAM. Adm. sizar at TRINITY, May 30, 1648. Matric. 1649.

HERMAN, ——. B.D. 1473-4. Perhaps John, R. of Capel St Mary, Suffolk, 1477-9. Died 1479.

HERMAN, ——. B.Can.L. 1482; probably adm. 1484-5.

HERMITAGE, THOMAS. Matric. sizar from TRINITY, Michs. 1584.

HERNEMAN, BERNARD. Matric. sizar from ST JOHN'S, Easter, 1612; B.A. from Clare, 1615-6; M.A. 1619. Incorp. at Oxford, 1619. R. of Lifton, Devon, 1631.

HERON, *see* HEARN *and* HIERON.

HERRICK, *see also* HEYRICK.

HERRICK or HEYRICK, JOHN. M.A. 1679 (Incorp. from Oxford). S. of Richard (1620), of Manchester, clerk (warden of Manchester College). Matric. from St Edmund Hall, Oxford, July 1, 1670, age 17; B.A. (Christ Church) 1674; M.A. 1676-7. V. of Lockington, Leics., 1680-7. Chaplain to the Earl of Derby. Buried at Lamport, Northants., May 30, 1687. (*Al. Oxon.*; *Vis. of Lancs.*, 1664; E. Axon.)

HERRICK or HEYRICK, RICHARD. B.A. 1620 (Incorp. from Oxford); M.A. 1633. S. of Sir William, goldsmith, of London, and of Beaumanor Park, Leicester. B. in London, May 25, 1600. School, Merchant Taylors'. Matric. (Oxford) May 30, 1617, age 17; B.A. (Oxford) 1619; M.A. 1622. Fellow of All Souls, 1624-5. Ord. deacon (Rochester); priest (Norwich) Sept. 24, 1625. R. of North Repps, Norfolk, 1626-36. Warden of Manchester Collegiate Church, 1635. R. of Ashton-on-Mersey, 1640. Attacked Romanists and episcopalians, 1641. Chief pillar of the Presbyterian party in Lancashire. Arrested and imprisoned for implication in Christopher Love's plot, 1651; pardoned and released. Author, sermons, etc. Died Aug. 6, 1667. Father of John (above). (*Al. Oxon.*; *Vis. of Lancs.*, 1664; *D.N.B.*)

HERRICK, ROBERT. Adm. Fell.-Com. at ST JOHN'S, 1613. 4th s. of Nicholas, goldsmith, of Cheapside, London. B. in London, Aug. 24, 1591. School, Westminster. Migrated to Trinity Hall, 1616. B.A. 1616-7; M.A. 1620. Ord. deacon (Peterb.) Apr. 24; priest, Apr. 25, 1623. V. of Dean Prior, Devon, 1629-47; ejected, lived in Westminster; restored to his living, 1662-74. Though professing a distaste for his Devonshire vicarage he frankly acknowledged that his best poetry was written at Dean Prior. Poet. Buried there, Oct. 15, 1674. M.I. For an account of his work *see D.N.B.*

HERRICK, SAMUEL. Matric. sizar from CORPUS CHRISTI, Easter, 1714.

HERRICK, THOMAS. Adm. pens. (age 15) at MAGDALENE, May 30, 1677. S. of William (next), Esq. B. at Beaumanor, Leics. School, Loughborough. Matric. 1677. Half-brother of William (1676). (Burke, *L.G.*; *Misc. Gen. et Her.*, 2nd S., I. 63.)

HERRICK, WILLIAM. Adm. Fell.-Com. at MAGDALENE, July 4, 1676. S. of William, of Beaumanor, Leics. B. 1624. Of Beaumanor, Leics. Died 1693. Father of the next, with whom he was admitted and of Thomas (above). (Burke, *L.G.*)

HERRICK, WILLIAM. Adm. Fell.-Com. at MAGDALENE, July 4, 1676. S. and h. of William (above), Esq. B. at Beaumanor, Leics., 1650 (so Burke, *L.G.*). Married Dorothy, dau. of James Wootton, of Weston, Derbs. Died 1705. Half-brother of Thomas (1677). (Burke, *L.G.*; *Misc. Gen. et Her.*, 2nd S., I. 63.)

HERRIES, WILLIAM. Adm. pens. (age 16) at CHRIST'S, Mar. 1, 1623-4. S. of Sir William, Knt. B. at Margaretting, Essex. School, Brentwood (Mr Plumtree). Matric. 1624; B.A. 1627-8; M.A. from Pembroke, 1631. Fellow of Pembroke, 1631. An intimate friend of Rich. Crashaw, who has commemorated him in several poems. Died Oct. 15, 1631. (*Peile*, I. 357.)

HERRIES, ——. Scholar of QUEENS', 1534-5.

HERRING, ATHANASIUS. Matric. sizar from KING'S, Easter, 1742; B.A. 1745-6; M.A. 1749. Ord. deacon (Lincoln) May 25, 1746; priest, Sept. 25, 1748. Chaplain of King's. C. of Barton, Cambs., 1750. R. of Hemingby, Lincs. Died Jan. 3, 1791. (*E. Mag.*)

HERRING, FRANCIS. Adm. pens. at CHRIST'S, Apr. 22, 1582. Of Nottinghamshire. Matric. 1582; B.A. 1585-6; M.A. 1589; M.D. 1597 (?). F.R.C.P., 1599. Censor. Author, medical. Died 1628. Will (Archd. London) 1628. (*Peile*, I. 170; *D.N.B.*)

HERRING, HENRY. Adm. at CORPUS CHRISTI, 1736. Of Norwich. Doubtless s. of William (1708). Matric. 1736; B.A. 1740-1; M.A. 1744. Fellow, 1741-6. Incorp. at Oxford, 1746. Ord. deacon (Norwich) June, 1742; priest, May, 1744. V. of Eynesford, Kent, 1748. R. of Toppesfield, Essex. Died before Feb. 1, 1801. Nephew of Thomas, the Archbishop, brother of William (1735).

HERRING, JAMES. Adm. at KING'S, a scholar from Eton, 1649. B. at Coventry, 1634. Matric. 1649; B.A. 1653; M.A. 1657. Fellow, 1652-7. R. of Hitcham, Bucks., 1660-7. Perhaps preb. of Chichester, 1664-73.

HERRING, JAMES. Adm. sizar at JESUS, Mar. 28, 1688. Of Sussex. Matric. 1688; Scholar, 1691; B.A. 1691-2; M.A. 1695.

HERRING, JOHN. Adm. sizar (age 15) at SIDNEY, May 20, 1625. S. of Henry, mercer. B. at Saltash, Cornwall. Schools, Saltash and Maristow, Devon (Mr Wm. Williams). Matric. 1625; B.A. 1628-9; M.A. 1632. V. o Maristow, 1632-62, ejected. Afterwards kept school. Died 1688. Brother of Richard (1633). (*Calamy*, I. 383.)

HERRING, JOHN. Adm. pens. (age 19) at TRINITY, June 3, 1661. Matric. 1661; Scholar, 1664; B.A. 1664-5; M.A. 1668. Ord. deacon and priest (Peterb.) Sept. 22, 1667. One of these names V. of Foxton, Cambs., 1669. R. of Walsoken, Norfolk, 1693-1717. Buried June 2, 1717. M.I. there, by his s. Thomas (1710), Archbishop of Canterbury. Probably father of William (1708). (*Blomefield*, IV. 727.)

HERRING, JOHN. Adm. pens. (age 16) at TRINITY, Aug. 17, 1695. S. of John. B. at Cambridge, Aug. 31, 1679. School, Merchant Taylors'. Matric. 1696.

HERRING, JOHN. Adm. pens. at QUEENS', Oct. 11, 1738. Of Norfolk. Matric. 1739.

HERRING, JOHN. Adm. at CORPUS CHRISTI, 1748. Of London. Matric. 1748; B.A. 1752; M.A. 1755. Fellow, 1754-8. Ord. priest (Peterb.) Sept. 19, 1756. Perhaps R. of Gt Mongeham, Kent, 1757. Died 1802. Nephew of the Archbishop.

HERRING, JULINES. Adm. scholar at SIDNEY, May, 1600. Perhaps s. of Richard, of Coventry. B. at Flambere-Mayre, Montgomeryshire, 1582. School, Coventry. B.A. 1603-4. Ord. by an Irish bishop. V. of Calke, Derbs., *c.* 1610-8. Preacher at Shrewsbury, 1618, suspended for nonconformity. Pastor of the English Church at Amsterdam, 1637-44. Died there Mar. 28, 1644. Will (P.C.C.) 1645-6; as of Shrewsbury. (*D.N.B.*)

HERRING, JULINES. Adm. sizar at JESUS, July 9, 1713. Of Wisbech, Isle of Ely. B. 1692. Matric. pens. 1713; B.A. 1716-7; M.A. 1720. Incorp. at Oxford, 1731. Ord. deacon (Ely) Dec. 20, 1719; priest (London) Mar. 7, 1727-8. R. of Kingsbury, Somerset, 1727.

HERING, JULINES. Adm. pens. at ST CATHARINE'S, Oct. 15, 1725. Of Jamaica. Matric. 1725. Will of one of these names (P.C.C.) 1775; of Heybridge, Essex, clerk.

HERRING, LAURENCE. Adm. pens. (age 18) at CAIUS, Nov. 18, 1614. Of Norwich. S. of George, husbandman. School, Norwich (Mr Thornton). Matric. 1615.

HERRING, NICHOLAS. Matric. sizar from MAGDALENE, Easter, 1606. Probably s. of George, yeoman, of Thorpe, Lincs. B.A. 1609-10. Ord. priest (Peterb.) Sept. 19, 1613. C. of Brinkley, Lincs., in 1614. V. of Gt Steeping, 1618. Will proved, Nov. 26, 1667. (*Lincs. Pedigrees*, I. 258.)

HERRING, RICHARD. Adm. sizar (age 17) at SIDNEY, Mar. 30, 1633. S. of Henry, mercer. B. at Saltash, Cornwall. School, Saltash (Mr Edw. Coffin). Matric. 1633; B.A. 1636-7; M.A. 1640. Sequestered to Drewsteignton, Devon, *c.* 1646; ejected, 1660. Died *c.* 1675. Perhaps will (Exeter) 1674; of Kenn, Devon. Brother of John (1625). (*Calamy*, I. 356.)

HERRING, RICHARD. Adm. sizar (age 16) at CHRIST'S, June 28, 1661. S. of Richard. B. at Newark. School, Newark (Mr Leeds). Matric. 1661; B.A. 1664; M.A. 1668 (*Lit. Reg.*). One of these names (M.A.), V. of Haxey, Lincs., 1672-1712. Buried there Mar. 30, 1712. M.I. (*Peile*, I. 597.)

HERRING, RICHARD. Adm. sizar (age 17) at CHRIST'S, Jan. 4, 1694-5. S. of William. B. at Newark. School, Newark (Mr Jo. Twells). Matric. 1695; Scholar, 1695-6; B.A. 1698-9. (*Peile*, II. 132.)

HERRING, SAMUEL. Adm. pens. at QUEENS', June 25, 1743. Of Norfolk. Matric. 1743; B.A. 1746-7; M.A. 1750. Fellow, 1748. Ord. deacon (Ely) June 4; priest, Oct. 7, 1750. R. of Eastry, Kent, 1753-7.

HERRING, THEODORE. Adm. pens. at EMMANUEL, Mar. 24, 1610-1. B. May, 1596. School, Merchant Taylors'. Scholar; B.A. 1614-5; M.A. 1618. Ord. deacon (Peterb.) Sept. 19; priest, Sept. 20, 1619. Minister of St Anne's, Blackfriars, 1624-8. R. of Doddinghurst, Essex, 1628. Probably sequestered, 1645. Married Elizabeth, dau. of Randolph Carleill, of Sowerby, Yorks. Will (P.C.C.) 1645; of York, property in Doddinghurst. (J. Ch. Smith; M. H. Peacock.)

HERRING, THOMAS. Matric. pens. from CHRIST'S, May, 1571. Perhaps of Heigham, Norfolk, Esq. Died Mar. 21, 1636-7, aged 82. One of these names V. of Burgh-in-the-Marsh, Lincs., 1577-8. (*Peile*, I. 118.)

HERRING, THOMAS. Adm. pens. at PETERHOUSE, July 3, 1621. Of Suffolk. Fell.-Com. 1622.

HERRING, THOMAS. Adm. pens. at ST CATHARINE'S, Apr. 8, 1684. Previously matric. from Lincoln College, Oxford, Mar. 26, 1680, age 18. S. and h. of Robert, f London, gent. Matric. 1684; LL.B. 1685. Adm. at theo Middle Tempie, Jan. 26, 1682-3. (*Al. Oxon.*)

HERRING, THOMAS. Adm. pens. at JESUS, June 21, 1710. S. of John (1661), R. of Walsoken, Norfolk. B. there, 1693. School, Wisbech (Dr Carter). Matric. 1710; B.A. 1713-4. Migrated to Corpus Christi, July 13, 1714. M.A. 1717; D.D. 1728 (*Com. Reg.*). Fellow of Corpus Christi, 1716-23. Ord. deacon (Ely) Sept. 23, 1716; priest, 1719. V. of Shelford, Cambs.; of Stow-*cum*-Quy; and Holy Trinity, Cambridge, 1722. Chaplain to Fleetwood, Bishop of Ely, 1722. R. of Rettendon, Essex, 1722. R. of Barley, Herts., 1722-31. Preacher at Lincoln's Inn, 1727-33. Chaplain to the King, 1727-32. R. of Bletchingley, Surrey, 1731-8. Dean of Rochester, 1732-43. Bishop of Bangor, 1738-43. Archbishop of York, 1743-7. Archbishop of Canterbury, 1747-57. Author, sermons. Died Mar. 13, 1757. Buried at Croydon. Benefactor to Corpus Christi. (*Masters*; *D.N.B.*)

HERRING, THOMAS. Adm. at CORPUS CHRISTI, 1737. Of Cambridgeshire. Matric. 1737; B.A. 1740-1; M.A. 1744. Fellow, 1743-6. Ord. deacon (York) Sept. 25, 1743; priest, May, 1744. R. of St Mary Stoke, Ipswich. Preb. of York, 1747-74. Preb. of Southwell, 1747-74. R. of Harbledown, Kent, 1749-50. R. of Coulsdon, Surrey. R. of St Anne, Soho. R. of Chevening, Kent, 1751-74. Precentor of Chichester, 1761-74. Died Mar. 25, 1774. (*Masters*; *Cole.*)

HERRING, WILLIAM. Scholar of TRINITY HALL, 1708. Probably s. of John (1661). LL.B. 1713; LL.D. 1722. Ord. deacon (Lincoln) Mar. 4; priest, Mar. 5, 1720-1. R. of Intwood and Keswick, Norfolk, 1720-43. V. of Tibbenham, 1721. R. of Edgefield, 1729. R. of Carlton, Notts., 1743. Preb. of York, 1746-62. Chancellor of York diocese, 1748-62. Died Jan. 8, 1762. Will (P.C.C.) 1763. Father of the next. (*D.N.B.* apparently confuses him with the next.) (A. B. Beaven.)

HERRING, WILLIAM. Adm. pens. at CLARE, Oct. 9, 1735. S. of William (above), LL.D., of Norwich. B. there, 1718. School, Norwich. Matric. 1735; B.A. 1739–40; M.A. 1743; D.D. (Lambeth) 1751. Fellow, 1740–3. R. of Alburgh, Norfolk, 1742–7. R. of Edgefield, 1743–7. Preb. of York, 1744–74. Chancellor of York diocese. Preb. of Southwell, Apr. to July, 1747. R. of Bolton Percy, Yorks., 1747–74. Dean of St Asaph, 1751–74. Precentor of Salisbury, 1756–74. Died May 23, 1774. Will, P.C.C. Perhaps brother of Henry (1736). (A. B. Beaven.)

HERRINGDON, CHRISTOPHER. Adm. pens. at CAIUS, c. Sept. 1590.

HERRINGHAM, JOHN. M.A. from SIDNEY, 1730. S. of James, of Aldgate, London, *pleb*. B. Oct. 25, 1701. School, Merchant Taylors'. Matric. from Balliol College, Oxford, Dec. 8, 1719, age 18; B.A. (Oxford) 1723–4. V. of Beckenham, Essex. R. of Chadwell St Mary, 1735–64. Admon. (P.C.C.) 1761; as of St James', Westminster. (*Al. Oxon.*)

HERRINGHOECK, DANIEL. M.D. 1639 (Incorp. from Leyden).

HERINGTON, W. D.Civ.L. 1499–1500 (Incorp. from Bologna).

HERRINGTON, ——. M.A. 1511–2.

HERRIOTT, CHARLES. Adm. at KING'S, a scholar from Eton, 1688. B. in London. Matric. 1689; B.A. 1692–3; M.A. 1696; LL.D. 1701 (*Lit. Reg.*). Fellow, 1692. Studied afterwards at Utrecht. LL.D. there. (*Harwood*, 273.)

HERRIS, *see* **HARRIS.**

HERSENT, PETER, *see* **HARSNETT.**

HERSET, ——. B.A. 1463.

HERSLEY or **HURSLEY, ——.** Canonicus. B.Can.L. 1519–20.

HERSORY, WALTER. Scholar at KING'S HALL, 1363.

HERTE, JOHN. Adm. at KING'S, a scholar from Eton, 1492; B.A. (? 1494–5); M.A. 1498. Archdeacon of Cleveland. One of these names, M.A., Chantry priest of St Mary, at Scarborough, Yorks., in 1525.

HERT, RICHARD. R. of 'Berkelow' (? Bartlow), Ely diocese. License for absence for three years, for study in Cambridge, 1405.

HERTFORD, EDWARD, Earl of, *see* **SEYMOUR.**

HERTFORD, JOHN. Matric. sizar from TRINITY, Michs. 1578.

HERTFORD, ——. Rector of. D.Can.L. 1485–6. Possibly Richard Stephens; B.Can.L. 1478; R. of St Mary's.

HERTWELL, WILLIAM, *see* **HARTWELL.**

HERVEY, *see* **HARVEY.**

HERWARDSTOKE, WILLIAM. B.C.L. R. of Bunwell, Norfolk. Petitions the Pope, 1363, for a canonry. Afterwards clerk of Bishop of Lismore. (*Cal. Pap. Pet.*, I.)

HESCRYCKE, WILLIAM. Matric. sizar from TRINITY, Michs. 1550.

HESILL, THOMAS. Scholar at KING'S HALL, 1423; M.A. in 1430.

HESILRIG, ARTHUR. Matric. Fell.-Com. from MAGDALENE, Easter, 1617. Doubtless s. and h. of Sir Thomas, of Noseley, Leics., Bart. Adm. at Gray's Inn, Jan. 29, 1622–3. Succeeded as 2nd Bart., 1629. M.P. for Leicestershire, 1640; for Newcastle-on-Tyne, 1654, 1656 and 1659. One of the five members impeached by the King, 1642. Fought at Edgehill, 1642; wounded at Lansdowne and Roundway Down, 1643. Took his place in parliament as a leader of the independents. Accompanied Cromwell to Scotland, 1648. A member of every council of State elected during the Commonwealth. Refused nomination as one of the King's judges. Opposed Cromwell's government after the dissolution of the Long Parliament, 1653. Opposed the recognition of Richard Cromwell. Became the recognised leader of parliament. Raised troops against Lambert, 1659. Appointed one of the five Commissioners for the government of the army, 1660. Outwitted by Monck. Arrested at the Restoration; Monck's intervention saved his life. Died in the Tower, Jan. 7, 1661–2. Father of Thomas (1649), Robert (1650) and brother of Donald, etc. (*D.N.B.*; *G.E.C.*)

HAZELRIGG, ARTHUR. Adm. at KING'S, July 23, 1651, by order of the Parliamentary Committee. S. of John, and Elizabeth. B. at Harlaston, Northants. Bapt. Sept. 13, 1633. Of Eton College. B.A. 1654–5. Fellow, 1654 till 1656. 'Went away, being in possession of a large estate.' (*Harwood*.)

HESILRIDGE, ARTHUR. Adm. Fell.-Com. (age 16) at ST JOHN'S, Mar. 28, 1720. S. of Sir Robert (1685), Bart., of Northamptonshire. B. at Northampton. Bapt. at St Peter's, Mar. 28, 1704. School, Carleton, Leics. (Mr Salter). Matric. 1720. Succeeded as 7th Bart., May 18, 1721. Died Apr. 23, 1763. Buried at Noseley. (*G.E.C.*, I. 203; H. I. Longden.)

HASELRIGG, BARTEN. Adm. Fell.-Com. at CHRIST'S, Nov. 1, 1622. S. of Edward, of Leicester. B. in Middlesex. School, Leicester (Mr St John Burrough). Matric. 1622. Captain of the Leics. train-bands. Killed in London in a duel, Mar. 4, 1630–1, aged 23. M.I. in Old St Clement Danes. (*Peile*, I. 347.)

HESILRIG, DONALD. Matric. Fell.-Com. from MAGDALENE, Easter, 1617. Previously matric. from Brasenose, Oxford, June 3, 1608, 'aged 15.' S. of Sir Thomas, of Noseley, Leics. Bapt. at Alderton, Northants., Jan. 24, 1599–1600. Adm. at Gray's Inn, Mar. 14, 1621–2. Of Noseley, Leics., Esq. Died before 1629. Brother of the next, William (1631) and Arthur (1617). (*Nichols*, II. 756.)

HESILRIGG, JOHN. Matric. pens. from MAGDALENE, Easter, 1617. S. of Sir Thomas, of Noseley, Leics., Bart. Bapt. at Alderton, July 10, 1602.

HESILRIDGE, ROBERT. Adm. Fell.-Com. at EMMANUEL, Apr. 17, 1650. Of Northamptonshire. S. of Sir Arthur (1617), of Noseley, Leics., Bart. Adm. at Gray's Inn, Nov. 1, 1658. Succeeded his nephew, as 5th Bart., July 11, 1700. Died May 22, 1713. Brother of Thomas (1649), father of the next. (*G.E.C.*, I. 202.)

HASILRIGGE, ROBERT. Adm. pens. (age 19) at SIDNEY, June 30, 1685. S. of Robert (above), Esq., of St Peter's, Northampton. B. at Noseley, Leics. Schools, Northampton (Mr Archer) and Knotting, Beds. (Mr Scriven). Matric. 1685. Adm. at Gray's Inn, Feb. 11, 1683–4. Succeeded as 6th Bart., 1713. Sheriff of Leics., 1715. Died May 19, 1721. Father of Arthur (1720). (*G.E.C.*, I. 208; *Burke*.)

HASELRIGGE, THOMAS. Adm. Fell.-Com. at EMMANUEL, Oct. 15, 1649. Of Leicestershire. 1st s. of Sir Arthur (1617), of Noseley, Leics., Bart. Adm. at Gray's Inn, Nov. 20, 1652. Succeeded as 3rd Bart., 1661. Died Feb. 24, 1680, aged 55. Brother of Robert (1650), father of the next. (*G.E.C.*; *Burke*.)

HESILRIGE, Sir THOMAS, Bart. Adm. as nobleman, at CLARE, Nov. 4, 1682. Of London. S. and h. of Sir Thomas (above), Bart., of Noseley Hall, Leics. Succeeded as 4th Bart., 1680. Sheriff of Leics., 1686–7. M.P. for Leics., 1690–5. Died unmarried, July 11, 1700, aged 36. (*G.E.C.*, I. 202.)

HESELRICKS, WILLIAM. Adm. pens. at JESUS, Apr. 14, 1631. Of Leicestershire. 6th s. of Sir Thomas, of Noseley. Migrated to Magdalene and matric. pens. there, Easter, 1632, as Heselridge. Brother of Donald (1617), Arthur (1617), etc. (*Nichols*, II. 756.)

HESKETH, CUTHBERT. Matric. pens. from TRINITY, Easter, 1631. Probably s. of Thomas, of Heslington, Yorks. Scholar, 1631; B.A. 1634–5; M.A. 1638. R. of Monkton Moor, Yorks., 1662–5. Died Sept. 14, 1665, aged 52. *See* a contemporary in *Al. Oxon.* (M. H. Peacock; H. G. Harrison.)

HESKETH, HENRY. M.A. 1664 (Incorp. from Oxford). Matric. from Brasenose, May 26, 1653; B.A. (Oxford) 1656; (? M.A. at St Mary Hall). R. of Ashton-on-Mersey, Cheshire, 1662–3. R. of Long Ditton, 1662. R. of Charlwood, Surrey, 1663–1711. R. of St Helen, Bishopsgate, 1678–95. Chaplain to William III. Nominated Bishop of Killala, 1689–90, but not consecrated. Author of religious works. Died Dec. 1710. (*D.N.B.*; *Al. Oxon.*)

HESKETH, HUAN, *alias* **BLACKLEACH.** Educated at Cambridge. S. of Robert, of Rufford, Lancs. Bishop of Sodor and Man, 1487. Died 1525. (*Cooper*, I. 45.)

HESKETH, ROBERT. Adm. sizar (age 20) at CHRIST'S, July 7, 1725. S. of Samuel. B. at Bretherton, Lancs. (Robert, s. of Simon Hesketh, bapt. at Croston, Apr. 2, 1704.) School, Heskin (Mr Johnson). Matric. 1725; Scholar, 1727. Left, 1728. Will (Chester) 1753, of Robert Hesketh, of Bretherton, clerk. (*Peile*, II. 211; E. Axon.)

HESKETH, THOMAS. Educated at Cambridge. 2nd s. of Gabriel, of Aughton, Lancs. B. 1548. Perhaps adm. at Gray's Inn, 1572. Barrister. M.P. for Preston, 1586; for Lancaster, 1597, 1604; for Co. Lancs., 1601. Recorder of Lancaster, 1589. Attorney of the Court of Wards and Liveries, 1589. Counsel for the University, c. 1600. Knighted, June, 1603. Of Heslington, Yorks. Died Oct. 15, 1605. Buried in Westminster Abbey. M.I. erected by his widow Julian. (*Cooper*, II. 412, 554; A. B. Beaven.)

HESKETT, THOMAS. Adm. pens. at TRINITY, Mar. 3, 1653–4. Of Yorkshire. School, Pocklington. Perhaps of Heslington, Yorks., Esq.; adm. at Gray's Inn, Dec. 10, 1655. Deputy-Lieutenant for East Riding, 1687–8. Married Margaret, dau. of John Calverley of Eryholme, Yorks., Apr. 7, 1670. Buried at St Laurence, York, Jan. 8, 1707–8. (M. H. Peacock.)

HESKETH, THOMAS. Adm. Fell.-Com. (age 17) at CHRIST'S, June 9, 1664. S. of Robert, Esq., of Rufford, near Ormskirk, Lancs. B. there. School, Aughton (Mr Stanninough). Matric. 1664. Of Rufford, Esq. Married Anne, dau. of Sir Richard Graham, of Norton Conyers, Yorks., at Wath, June 17, 1697, and had issue. (*Vis. of Lancs.*, 1664; *Peile*, I. 610.)

HESKET, THOMAS. Adm. pens. (age 17) at TRINITY, May 10, 1690. S. of John. B. at Exeter. School, St Paul's. Matric. 1690; Scholar, 1693; B.A. 1693-4; M.A. 1697.

HESKEY, ROBERT. Matric. pens. from CHRIST'S, Michs. 1553.

HESKINS, DOMINIC. B.A. 1542-3, after five terms at Cambridge and seven at Oxford.

HESKINS, THOMAS. M.A. 1540; B.D. 1548; D.D. 1557. Fellow of CLARE, c. 1540. Studied also twelve years at Oxford. R. of Hildersham, Cambs., 1551-6. R. of Duxford St Peter's, 1551. Chancellor of Sarum, 1558. R. of Brixworth, Northants., 1558. Deprived in 1559, for refusing the oath of supremacy. Retired to Flanders; became a Dominican and confessor to the English nuns at Bergen-op-Zoom. Vicar-general of the English Dominicans, c. 1579. Anthor, *Parliament of Chryste*, 1565. (*Cooper*, I. 419; *D.N.B.*; H. G. Harrison.)

HESELDEN, *see also* HASELDIN.

HESLELTEN or HASELDEN, JOHN. Adm. pens. at TRINITY, May 6, 1667. Matric. 1667.

HESLEDEN, JOHN. Adm. sizar (age 19) at PEMBROKE, Apr. 18, 1695. S. of John, of Bracken Bottom, Horton-in-Ribblesdale, Yorks. Matric. 1695; B.A. 1698-9. Ord. deacon (York) June, 1699.

HESLEDEN, JOSIAS. Adm. sizar (age 24) at PEMBROKE, June 30, 1680. S. of Anthony, of Horton-in-Ribblesdale, Yorks., farmer. Perhaps V. of Redmire, Yorks., 1686-7.

HASELDEN, ROBERT. Adm. pens. at TRINITY, Apr. 17, 1667. Matric. 1667.

HESLEDEN, THOMAS. Adm. sizar (age 20) at PEMBROKE, May 7, 1681. S. of Thomas, of Bracken Bottom, Horton, Yorks. Matric. 1681; B.A. 1684-5; M.A. 1688. Ord. deacon (Norwich) May, 1684; priest (Peterb.) Sept. 19, 1686 (when he was of Southwell). R. of Barnoldby, Lincs., 1697-1715. R. of Hatcliffe, 1697-1715.

HESLEDEN, WILLIAM. Adm. sizar (age 24) at ST JOHN'S, June 4, 1740. S. of William, husbandman, of Yorkshire. B. at Horton-in-Ribblesdale. School, Horton (Mr Thornton). Matric. 1740; B.A. 1743-4; M.A. 1749. Ord. deacon (Lincoln) May 20, 1744; priest, Sept. 23, 1744. R. of Grimoldby, Lincs., 1746-73. V. of Gt Grimsby, 1750-73. R. of Irby, 1773-4. (*Scott-Mayor*, III. 505.)

HESLERTON, ROBERT. Adm. sizar (age 16) at ST JOHN'S, June 13, 1656. S. of Joseph, gent., of High Hutton, near New Malton, Yorks. B. there. School, Pocklington (Mr Llewellin). Matric. 1659; B.A. 1659-60; M.A. 1663; B.D. 1683 (*Lit. Reg.*). Ord. priest (Chichester) Jan. 15, 1662-3. V. of Gt Canfield, Essex. V. of Boreham, 1670-83. Died 1683.

HESLETINE, RICHARD. Matric. sizar from TRINITY, Easter, 1607; B.A. 1611-2. Ord. deacon (York) Dec. 1614; priest, Mar. 1614-5. V. of Brayton (? near Selby), Yorks., 1614.

HESLINGTON, JOHN, *see* ISLINGTON.

HESLOCK, ABRAHAM, *see* HOUSELOCK.

HESLOP, *see also* HASLOP.

HESLOP, GEORGE. Adm. pens. (age 17) at CURIST'S, June 28, 1636. S. of William. B. at Hexham. School, Hexham (Mr Fowbery and Mr Forster). Adm. at Gray's Inn, Nov. 6, 1651, as s. and h. of William, of Hermitage, Hexham, deceased.

HESLOPP or HASELOPP, JOHN. Matric. sizar from ST JOHN'S, Easter, 1617. Of Northumberland. Matric. from St Edmund's Hall, Oxford, O t. 3, 1620, age 19, 'after 12 terms at Cambridge'; B.A. (Oxford) 1620. Ord. deacon (Durham) Sept. 23, 1621. V. of Tynemouth, 1623-37. Buried there Aug. 2, 1637. (*Al. Oxon.*; H. M. Wood.)

HESLOP, JOHN. Adm. sizar (age 20) at PETERHOUSE, Jan. 23, 1723-4. Of Yorkshire. School, Appleby. Matric. 1724; Scholar, 1724; B.A. 1728-9.

HESSE, FRANCIS. Scholar of CLARE, 1521.

HESSHAM, THOMAS. Adm. at KING'S, c. 1545. Perhaps V. of Swaffham Prior, Cambs., 1554.

HEST, RICHARD. Adm. sizar at PETERHOUSE, Apr. 4, 1733. Previously matric. from Brasenose, Oxford, May 13, 1727, age 17. S. of Richard, of Warton, Lancs. Scholar, 1733; Matric. 1734; B.A. 1735-6. Ord. deacon (Norwich) Sept. 1734; priest, July, 1736.

HESTERTON, THOMAS. Matric. pens. from ST JOHN'S, Easter, 1611.

HESTON, WALTER. D.D. of Cambridge before 1345. Carmelite friar of Stamford, Lincs. Adm. (Ely) for confessions and preaching, 1337. Distinguished philosopher and theologian. Author. Died c. 1350. (*Pits*; *D.N.B.*)

HETHER, THOMAS. Matric. sizar from ST JOHN'S, Michs. 1555.

HETHERFULL, ——. Adm. Fell.-Com. at CHRIST'S, c. 1590-1.

HETHERINGTON, *see also* ETHERINGTON.

HETHERINGTON, FRANCIS. Adm. sizar (ten year man) at CHRIST'S, June 10, 1751. Already in holy orders. S. of John, of Kirklinton, Cumberland. Matric. 1751; B.D. 1761. R. of Evedon, Lincs. V. of Lavington (Lenton), 1764. Died Oct. 26, 1768, at Lenton. Buried there. M.I. Will, P.C.C. (*Peile*, II. 256.)

HETHERINGTON, GEOFFREY. Adm. pens. (age 17) at PETERHOUSE, Jan. 29, 1708-9. Of Middlesex. S. of Humphrey, of Essex St, Strand. School, Eton. Matric. 1709; Scholar, 1709; B.A. 1712-3. Adm. at the Middle Temple, May 14, 1707. Barrister, 1715. Of North Cray, Kent. Died June 17, 1767. Buried at North Cray. Brother of John (next) and William (1716).

HETHERINGTON, JOHN. Adm. at KING'S, a scholar from Eton, 1712. B. in London. Matric. 1713; B.A. 1716-7; M.A. 1720. Fellow, 1716. Travelled abroad as tutor to Lord J. Russell. Brother of Geoffrey (1708-9) and of William (1716).

HETHERINGTON, RALPH. Matric. pens. from ST JOHN'S, Michs. 1559; B.A. 1561-2; M.A. 1565. Probably fellow of Pembroke, 1562. One of these names adm. at Gray's Inn, 1565.

HETHERINGTON, WILLIAM. Adm. pens. (age 17) at PETERHOUSE, Apr. 10, 1716. S. of Humphrey, of Essex Street, Strand, London. School, Eton. Matric. 1716; Scholar, 1716; B.A. 1719-20; M.A. 1723. Adm. at the Middle Temple, Apr. 18, 1716. Ord. deacon (Ely) Sept. 8; priest, Sept. 22, 1728. R. of Dry Drayton, Cambs., 1728-53. Fellow of Eton, 1749-71, when he resigned. R. of Farnham Royal, Bucks., 1753-78. Inherited the large estate of his brother Geoffrey. Known for his generous philanthropy. Built a chapel at Eton for the use of the inhabitants. Died Dec. 1, 1778. Will (P.C.C.); as of St George-the-Martyr. Brother of Geoffrey (1708) and John (1712). (*Harwood*; *N. and Q.*, June 28, 1917.)

HETHERSET, RICHARD, *see* WETHERSET.

HETHERSETT, THOMAS (1634), *see* HAVISETT.

HETHERSETT, THOMAS DE. LL.D. Warden of KING'S HALL, 1385-91. Chancellor of the University, Nov. 27, 1386. Archdeacon of Sudbury, 1389-98. Official of Ely. Preb. of Sarum, 1398-1406. Canon of Rochester. R. of Hayes, Middlesex, 1398-9. V. of Gillingham, Kent, till his death, c. 1405. Will, P.C.C.

HETHYN, WALTER. Adm. at KING'S, a scholar from Eton, 1454.

HETLEY, *see* HEATLEY.

HETON, *see also* ETON *and* HEATON.

HETON, CHARLES. Adm. sizar (age 18) at TRINITY, July 8, 1724. S. of Thomas (1704), of Buntingford, Herts., clerk. School, Buntingford (Mr Sherson). Matric. 1724; B.A. 1727-8; M.A. 1731. Ord. deacon (Lincoln) June 1, 1729. V. of Layston, Herts., 1748-54. Died 1754. Will, P.C.C.

HETON, JAMES. Adm. sizar (age 18) at ST JOHN'S, May 12, 1740. S. of James, husbandman, of Lancashire. B. at Bolton. School, Bolton (Mr Ashburnell).

HETON, THOMAS. M.A. from CHRIST'S, 1704. S. of James, of Bolton, Lancs. Matric. from Brasenose, Oxford, Jan. 19, 1690-1, age 20; B.A. (Oxford) 1694. Ord. priest (Lincoln) Dec. 22, 1695. R. of Holwell, Beds., 1701. R. of Layston, Herts., 1703-48. R. of Widdial, 1710. Died 1748. Admon. (P.C.C.) 1748. M.I. Layston Church. Father of Charles (1724). (*Al. Oxon.*)

HETON, THURSTON. Fellow of CORPUS CHRISTI, 1445-62-. For an account of his quarrels in College, see *Masters*, 45.

HETTON, RALPH or ROBERT. M.A. 1485. *See* EATON.

HEVENING, THOMAS, *see* KENNINGHAM.

HEVENINGHAM, ANTHONY. Matric. Fell.-Com. from ST JOHN'S, Michs. 1626.

HEVENINGHAM, HENRY. Matric. pens. from QUEENS', Easter, 1605. Of Norfolk. Doubtless s. of Sir Arthur, of Heveningham, Suffolk. Bapt. at Ketteringham, Norfolk, Dec. 13, 1586. Buried there Aug. 18, 1657. Probably brother of John (1592) and Thomas (1601). (*Norfolk Archaeology*, III. 284.)

HEVENINGHAM, HENRY. Adm. pens. (age 16) at PEMBROKE, Apr. 24, 1666. S. of Arthur, of Hockwold, Norfolk, gent. B. there, 1651. Matric. 1667. M.P. for Dunwich, 1695-1700. Died Nov. 21, 1700. Buried at Ketteringham, Norfolk. Brother of John (1663). (Le Neve, *Knights*, 291; *Suckling*, II. 390.)

HEVENINGHAM, JOHN. Matric. pens. from KING'S, Michs. 1572. Fell.-Com. in College.

HEVENINGHAM, JOHN. Adm. Fell.-Com. at QUEENS', July 1, 1592. Of Suffolk. S. of Sir Arthur, of Heveningham, Suffolk. Bapt. there, Mar. 26, 1577. Adm. at the Inner Temple, 1594. Knighted, May 11, 1603. High Sheriff of Norfolk, 1615. M.P. for Norfolk, 1628-9. Died June 17, 1633. Buried at Ketteringham. Father of William (1621). Probably brother of Henry (1605) and Thomas (1601). (*Suckling*, II. 389.)

HEVENINGHAM, JOHN. Adm. pens. (age 16) at PEMBROKE, Apr. 21, 1663. S. of Arthur, Esq. B. at Hockwold, Norfolk. Matric. 1663. Brother of Henry (1666).

HEVENINGHAM, THOMAS. Matric. Fell.-Com. from CORPUS CHRISTI, Easter, 1601. Of Norfolk. Doubtless s. of Sir Arthur, of Heveningham, Suffolk. B. 1584. Adm. at the Inner Temple, 1604. Buried at Ketteringham, Sept. 20, 1651. Probably brother of John (1592) and Henry (1605).

HEVENINGHAM, WILLIAM. Adm. Fell.-Com. at PEMBROKE, Apr. 19, 1621. S. of Sir John (1592), of Ketteringham, Knt. B. at Hockwold, Norfolk. Matric. 1621. Sheriff of Norfolk, 1633. M.P. for Stockbridge, 1640. Member of the High Court, but did not sign the King's death warrant. Member of the Council of State, 1649. Vice-Admiral of Suffolk, 1651. Surrendered at the Restoration. Deprived of his estates and imprisoned in Windsor Castle. His life saved by the exertions of his wife's relations. Married (1) Catherine, dau. of Sir Henry Wallop, of Farley, Wilts.; (2) Lady Mary Casey, dau. of John, Earl of Dover. Died Feb. 21, 1677-8. Buried in Ketteringham Church. Father of the next. (*D.N.B.*)

HEVENINGHAM, WILLIAM. Adm. Fell.-Com. (age 14) at ST JOHN'S, Oct. 5, 1671. S. of William (above), of St Martin-in-the-Fields, London. B. there. School, Windsor. Matric. 1671; M.A. 1673 (*fil. nob.*). (One of these names was adm. at Lincoln's Inn, May 21, 1674, as s. and h. of William, of Heveningham Hall, Suffolk, Esq. Knighted, May 19, 1674. Buried at Heveningham, Oct. 14, 1674.)

HEVER, THOMAS. Matric. pens. from JESUS, Michs. 1561.

HEWARD or HOWARD, ROBERT. M.B. 1539-40.

HEWARD, THOMAS. Adm. at CORPUS CHRISTI, 1628. Of Norfolk.

HEWERDINE, FRANCIS. Adm. sizar (age 17) at SIDNEY, 1691-2. S. of Thomas. B. at Morton (? Morton-on-Swale), Yorks. Schools, Northallerton (Mr Smelt) and Coxwold. Matric. 1692; B.A. 1695-6. Ord. deacon (York) June, 1698; priest, 1698. V. of Squire, 1699. Perhaps brother of Thomas (1677).

HEWARDYNE, ROBERT. Matric. pens. from PETERHOUSE, Michs. 1578.

HEWERDINE, THOMAS. Adm. sizar (age 17) at SIDNEY, June 3, 1677. 1st s. of Thomas, yeoman. B. at Linton, Yorks. School, Coxwold. Matric. 1677; B.A. 1680-1; M.A. 1684. Ord. deacon (Peterb.) June 3, 1683. C. at March, Cambs., 1686-. C. of Abington Pigotts; R. 1724-38. V. of Bassingbourne. Perhaps brother of Francis (1691-2).

HEWARTE, JOHN. Matric. sizar from CHRIST'S, Oct. 1567.

HEWES, *see* **HUGHES.**

HEWITT or HUITTE, ANTHONY. Matric. pens. from MAGDALENE, Easter, 1571. Will of one of these names (Lincoln) 1600; of Horncastle, clerk.

HEWITT, ANTHONY. Matric. pens. from CHRIST'S, July, 1617; B.A. 1620-1; M.A. 1624. Doubtless the man of these names Incorp. M.D. 1637, from Padua.

HUIT, BENJAMIN. Matric. pens. from TRINITY, Michs. 1626; a scholar from Westminster, 1627, as Hewet; B.A. 1630-1.

HUETT, EDMUND. Matric. pens. from TRINITY, Michs. 1550; B.A. 1553-4. Ord. priest (Winchester) June 12, 1557. R. of Maulden, Beds., till 1597. R. of Millbrook. Buried at Maulden, Sept. 17, 1597.

HUITT, EPHRAIM. Matric. sizar from ST JOHN'S, Easter, 1611. C. in Cheshire and at Knowle, Warws. Perhaps the 'Mr Huett, lecturer at Shotwick,' in 1622. When chaplain at Wroxhall, Warws, he was silenced by Archbishop Laud. Went to New England, 1639. Teacher at Windsor, Conn., till his death, Sept. 4, 1644. M.I. there, the oldest in the State. Author, *Anatomy of Conscience*, 1626. *Prophecies of Daniel*, 1644. (*Felt*, 563; J. G. Bartlett.)

HEWET, FRANCIS. Matric. pens. from QUEENS', Easter, 1566. S. of Henry. Probably of Yorkshire. (*Chesters of Chicheley*, 228.)

HEWYTT, GARDINER. Adm. Fell.-Com. (age 16) at ST JOHN'S, June 25, 1656. S. of William, Esq. B. at Beccles, Suffolk. School, Beccles (Mr Cannon). Matric. 1657. Adm. at Gray's Inn, Nov. 17, 1662; s. and h. of Sir William (1633), of Breccles, Norfolk, Knt. Sold his estate at Breccles. Died a pensioner in the Charter house, c. 1720. (Le Neve, *Knights*, 119; *Blomefield*, II. 276.)

HEWET, GEORGE. Adm. sizar (age 18) at MAGDALENE, June 7, 1656. S. of James (1622), R. of Whittington, Derbs. School, Chesterfield. Matric. 1656; B.A. 1659. Ord. deacon (Lincoln) June 8; priest, June 10, 1661. V. of Sutton-on-Lound, Notts. Admon. of one of these names (Consist. C. London) 1706; of Rayleigh, Essex, clerk. (*F.M.G.*, 1009; J. Ch. Smith.)

HEWETT, GILBERT. Adm. pens. at TRINITY, July 5, 1675. School, Westminster. Matric. 1675; Scholar, 1676; B.A. 1678-9; M.A. 1682.

HEWETT, ISRAEL. Matric. sizar from CHRIST'S, Easter, 1602. Of Norfolk. Migrated to Queens', Dec. 1604. B.A. from Christ's, 1605-6; M.A. 1609; B.D. 1616. Fellow of Christ's, 1610-21. V. of Maldon, Essex, 1620-49. Minister of the Dengie *Classis*, 1648. R. of Tendring, 1649. Died there 1663. Brother-in-law of Owen Stockton. (*Peile*, I. 240; *Shaw*, II. 379.)

HUIT or HEWET, JAMES. Matric. sizar from TRINITY, Easter, 1622; B.A. 1626-7. Doubtless s. of Robert, of Whittington, Derbs. Ord. deacon (York) Dec. 1627. R. of Whittington. Father of George (1656). (*F.M.G.*, 1009.)

HEWITT, JAMES. Adm. pens. (age 16) at SIDNEY, May 4, 1664. Only s. of Marmaduke, woollen draper, deceased. B. at Pocklington, Yorks. Schools, Pocklington (Mr Winne) and Beverley (Mr Sherwood). Married Jane, dau. of Thomas Hardy, of Hilston, June 17, 1669. (M. H. Peacock.)

HEWIT, JAMES. Adm. pens. (age 18) at ST JOHN'S, June 7, 1746. S. of William, steward, of Salop. B. near Moreton. Schools, Trentham, Staffs. and Wem, Salop (Mr Appleton). Matric. 1746; B.A. 1749-50. Ord. deacon (Lichfield) June 30, 1751; priest, Dec. 10, 1752. C. of Stoke. (*Scott Mayor*, III. 559.)

HEWITT, JOHN. B.A. 1522-3; M.A. 1526; B.D. 1533-4.

HEWET, JOHN. Matric. Fell.-Com. from CORPUS CHRISTI, Michs. 1565. One of these names R. of 'Gesterton' (? Geldeston), Norfolk, 1567.

HEWETT, JOHN. Adm. sizar (age 16) at ST JOHN'S, Feb. 7, 1631-2. S. of John, of Ingoldsby, Lincs. B. there. School, Grantham (Mr Wilkinson). Matric. 1632. (John, s. of James, of Ingoldsby, seems to have succeeded to the family estate; *v. Lincs. Pedigrees.*)

HEWETT, JOHN. Matric. sizar (age 18) from PEMBROKE, Easter, 1633. S. of Thomas, clothworker, of Eccles, Lancs. B. there, Sept. 1614. Schools, Bolton-le-Moors and Merchant Taylors'. Created D.D. (Oxford) 1643. Chaplain to Charles I; and to the Earl of Lindsey. V. of St Gregory by St Paul's, London, c. 1653-58. R. of St Mary Magdalene, Old Fish St. Executed on Tower Hill for complicity in a royalist plot, June 8, 1658. Author of devotional works. Buried at St Gregory's. (*F.M.G.*, 1030; *D.N.B.*; *Al. Oxon.*)

HEWET or HUETT, JOHN. Adm. Fell.-Com. at CLARE, Oct. 30. 1637. S. of Sir John, of Waresley, Hunts., Bart. Matric. 1637. Succeeded as Bart., 1657. Sheriff of Cambs. and Hunts., 1661-2. Died Sept. 30, 1684. Father of John (1677-8), Thomas (1692) and Tyrrill (1684). (G.E.C.)

HEWYTT, JOHN. Adm. pens. at JESUS, Apr. 3, 1662. Of Norfolk. Matric. 1663.

HEWET, JOHN. Adm. Fell.-Com. at CLARE, Feb. 2, 1677-8. Of Waresley, Hunts. S. and h. of Sir John (1637), Bart. Adm. at the Inner Temple, Feb. 13, 1681-2. Of Waresley, Hunts. Succeeded as 3rd Bart., Sept. 30, 1684. Sheriff of Cambs. and Hunts., 1685-6. Died Fep. 3, 1737. Will (P.C.C.) 1740. Brother of Thomas (1692) and Tyrrill (1684). (*G.E.C.*)

HEWETT, JOHN. Adm. sizar (age 17) at CAIUS, Sept. 16, 1679. S. of Richard, gent., of Eccles, Lancs. B. there. School, Eccles (Mr Atkinson). Brother of Richard (1675). (*Venn*, I. 463.)

HEWITT, JOHN. Adm. pens. (age 18) at ST JOHN'S, Aug. 5, 1682. S. of John, gent (died c. 1668; s. of Dr John Hewitt, of 1633). B. in Surrey. Exhibitioner from Charterhouse. Matric. 1682. Migrated to Oxford. B.A. from Magdalen College, 1686; M.A. (Magdalen Hall) 1693. R. of Harthill, Yorks., 1695-1715. Resided at Leytonstone, Essex, where he kept a school. Father of the next. (*Al. Carthus.*; *F.M.G.*, 1030.)

HEWETT, JOHN. M.A. from CHRIST'S, 1724. S. of John (above), clerk, of Wallingford, Berks. Adm. at Magdalen Hall, Oxford, Oct. 22, 1709, age 19; B.A. (Oxford) 1712-3. Succeeded his father as R. of Harthill, Yorks., 1715-57. Died Apr. 22, 1757, aged 68. Buried at Harthill. M.I. (*Al. Oxon.*; *Peile*, II. 193; *F.M.G.*, 1030; M. H. Peacock.)

HEWYTT, JOHN. Adm. sizar (age 19) at ST JOHN'S, June 19, 1713. S. of Henry, deceased. B. at Paythorne, in Gisburn parish, Yorks. School, Threshfield. Matric. 1713-4; B.A. 1717-8. Ord. priest (York) June 1718. Probably V. of Broughton-in-Craven, 1732-41. (M. H. Peacock.)

HEWITT, MATTHEW. Matric. sizar from MAGDALENE, Easter, 1623; B.A. 1626-7; M.A. 1630. Ord. deacon (Peterb.) May 19; priest, May 20, 1627. V. of Hilton, Dorset, 1633-9; and father of Thomas (1659). (F. S. Hockaday.)

HEWIT, MATTHEW. Adm. at ST JOHN'S, May 14, 1639. S. of Robert, gent. B. at Linton-in-Craven, Yorks. School, Burnsall, Yorks. (Mr Mason). Matric. 1639. Migrated to Christ's, Mar. 24, 1641-2. B.A. 1642-3; M.A. from Sidney, 1652. V. of Gargrave, Yorks., in 1643. R. of one mediety of Linton, Yorks., c. 1651-74. Founder of the Grammar School at Threshfield; and also of Exhibitions at St John's. Died 1674. (*Peile*, I. 480; *Founders and Benefactors*, 56.)

HUIT or HEWITT, MICHAEL. Adm. sizar (age 17) at CAIUS, Apr. 28, 1615. Of Northamptonshire. S. of Robert. School, Higham Ferrers (Mr Burton). Matric. 1615; B.A. 1618-9. Ord. deacon (Peterb.) Sept. 24; priest, Sept. 25, 1620. C. of Hargrave, 1620-34. R. of Newton Bromswold, Northants., 1634-55. Chosen as 'parish register,' 1653. Married, at Hargrave, Apr. 11, 1621, Elizabeth Henchman, widow. Buried at Newton Bromswold, Jan. 9, 1655-6. Father of Robert (1644-5). (*Venn*, I. 228; H. I. Longden.)

HEWET, MORDECAI. Adm. sizar at CORPUS CHRISTI, 1659. Of Nottinghamshire. Matric. Lent, 1660.

HEWITT, NATHANIEL. Adm. pens. (age 20) at CAIUS, May 28, 1718. S. of Nathaniel, gent., of Sproughton, Suffolk. B. there. School, Sproughton (Mr Harwood). Scholar, 1718-20; Matric. 1720. Adm. Fell.-Com. Feb. 3, 1720-1. (*Venn*, II. 10.)

HEWET or HUIT, NICHOLAS. Matric. pens. from ST JOHN'S, Easter, 1554. B. at Blyth, Notts. Migrated to Queens', c. 1555. B.A. 1557-8; M.A. 1561. Fellow of Queens', 1558-68. Ord. deacon (London) Dec. 27, 1559, age 23. R. of Blickling, Norfolk, 1566.

HEWITT, RICHARD. Adm. sizar (age 19) at CAIUS, June 21, 1675. S. of Richard, gent., of Eccles, Lancs. B. there. School, Eccles (Mr Alston). Matric. 1675; Scholar, 1675-80; B.A. 1678-9; M.A. 1682. Ord. deacon (London) Sept. 21, 1679; priest, June 18, 1682. Master of North Weald School, Essex. V. of Norton Mandeville and Roothing Berners, Essex, 1700. R. of Greenstead, to 1724. Died Apr. 26, 1724. Buried at Greenstead. M.I. Brother of John (1679). (*Venn*, I. 454.)

HUET, ROBERT. Matric. pens. from TRINITY, Michs. 1576; B.A. 1580-1, as Hewite.

HEWITT or HUET, ROBERT. Adm. sizar (age 18) at CAIUS, June 29, 1622. S. of Simon, husbandman, of Elsing, Norfolk. School, Elsing (Mr Robinson). Matric. 1623; Scholar, 1625-7; B.A. 1625-6; M.A. 1629. Ord. deacon and priest (Norwich) Feb. 18, 1626-7. C. of Swanton Morley, Norfolk, in 1636. R. of Brandiston, 1642. R. of Bintry, 1642. Will (Norwich Archd. C.) 1665. (*Venn*, I. 258.)

HEWETT or HUITT, ROBERT. Matric. pens. from TRINITY, Easter, 1634. S. of Sir Thomas, Knt., of Shire Oaks, Notts. Bapt. Jan. 24, 1618-9. B.A. 1637-8; M.A. from St John's, 1641. (*F.M.G.*, 1029.)

HEWETT, ROBERT. Adm. sizar (age 16) at ST JOHN'S, Mar. 19, 1644-5. S. of Michael (1615), R. of Newton Bromswold, Northants. Bapt. at Hargrave, Feb. 9, 1628-9. School, Wymington, Beds. (Mr Anderson). Matric. 1645; B.A. 1648-9. Succeeded his father at Newton Bromswold, 1656, probably till 1664. Ord. deacon and priest (Peterb.) Aug. 17, 1662. (H. I. Longden.)

HEWITT, ROBERT. Adm. sizar (age 18) at ST JOHN'S, Apr. 16, 1720. S. of James, yeoman, of Yorkshire. B. at Threshfield, near Skipton. School, Threshfield (Mr Mashall). Matric. 1720; B.A. 1723-4. Ord. priest (York) June 9, 1727; C. of St Mary's, Hull. V. of Caistor, Lincs., 1743-75. V. of Kirmond, 1752-8. R. of Thoresway, 1755-75. R. of Rothwell, 1758-75. (*Scott-Mayor*, III. 333.)

HEWITT, ROBERT. Adm. sizar (age 17) at TRINITY, Apr. 7, 1733. S. of Robert, of Northwich, Cheshire. Matric. 1733. Ord. deacon (Lincoln) June 20, 1736. Probably brother of Thomas (1740).

HEWETT, THOMAS. Adm. at KING'S (age 18) a scholar from Eton, Aug. 14, 1504. Of Newton, or Nowton, Lincoln diocese. Left before 1506.

HUET, THOMAS. Matric. sizar from CORPUS CHRISTI, Michs. 1545. Probably B.A. 1562-3. The Welsh scholar, pensioned Master of the College of the Holy Trinity, Pontefract, at the dissolution. R. of Treffe Egloyse, Pembrokeshire, 1560. Precentor of St David's, 1562-88. Translator of the New Testament into Welsh. Died Aug. 19, 1591. (*Cooper*, II. 108; *D.N.B.*)

HUET, THOMAS. Matric. sizar from MAGDALENE, Michs. 1561.

HEWET, THOMAS. Adm. Fell.-Com. at ST JOHN'S, Feb. 1608. S. of Thomas, gent., of Ketton, Rutland. School, Ketton (Mr Little). Matric. 1609. Migrated to Caius, Oct. 10, 1611. Scholar, 1612-3; B.A. 1612-3. Ord. deacon (Peterb.) Dec. 21; priest, Dec. 28, 1617. Perhaps V. of March, Cambs., 1620. (*Venn*, I. 215.)

HEWYTT, THOMAS. Adm. Fell.-Com. (age 16) at SIDNEY, Apr. 6, 1622. S. of Sir William, Knt., of Pishiobury, Herts. B. at Ilketshall St Laurence, Suffolk. School, Eton. Matric. 1622. Adm. at the Inner Temple, Nov. 1617. M.P. for New Windsor, 1628. Sheriff of Herts., 1638-9 and 1660-1. Knighted, July 10, 1641. Created Bart., July 19, 1660. Buried at Sawbridgeworth, Aug. 19, 1662. (*G.E.C.*)

HEWITT or HUYTE, THOMAS. Adm. sizar (age 22) at ST JOHN'S, Oct. 10, 1659. S. of Matthew (1623), clerk, deceased, V. of Hilton Dorset. B. there. Matric. 1659.

HEWETT, THOMAS. Adm. pens. at CLARE, July 14, 1692. S. of Sir John (1637), of Thornton, Bucks., Bart., and Waresley, Hunts. Matric. 1694; B.A. 1696-7; M.A. 1700; M.D. 1707. Fellow, 1698-1707. One of these names, 'medicus,' of Warwick, died Jan. 31, 1738. Brother of John (1677-8) and Tyrrill (1684). Doubtless father of Thomas (1724-5).

HEWETT, THOMAS. Adm. sizar (age 18) at SIDNEY, Apr. 3, 1721. S. of Richard, chemist. B. at Dunster, Somerset. School, Tiverton. Matric. 1721; B.A. 1724-5.

HEWET, THOMAS. Adm. pens. at CLARE, Feb. 11, 1724-5. S. of Thomas (1692), M.D. B. in London. Matric. 1724-5; B.A. 1728-9; M.A. 1732.

HEWYTT, THOMAS. Adm. sizar (age 19) at PETERHOUSE, Mar. 7, 1734-5. Of Derbyshire. Matric. 1735; Scholar, 1735; B.A. 1738-9. Ord. deacon (Norwich) Mar. 1738-9; priest, Sept. 1741. C. of Walcott, Norfolk.

HEWITT, THOMAS. Adm. sizar (age 19) at TRINITY, Oct. 8, 1740. S. of Robert, of Northwich, Cheshire. School, Beverley, Yorks. (Mr Clark). Matric. 1741; Scholar, 1744; B.A. 1744-5. Ord. deacon (Norwich) Sept. 1745. One of these names, of Whitton, Norfolk, clerk, died Apr. 2, 1791. Probably brother of Robert (1733).

HUIT, TOBIAS. B.A. from CLARE, 1607-8; M.A. 1611. R. of Bulphan, Essex, 1616-61. Licensed (Bishop of London) Jan. 28, 1618-9, to marry Elizabeth, dau. of Richard Wignall, V. of Barking. Died 1661. Will (Consist. C. London) 1661.

HEWYTT, TOBIAS. Adm. sizar at TRINITY, May 19, 1659; B.A. 1662-3.

HEWETT, TYRRILL. Adm. pens. at CLARE, June 10, 1684. S. of Sir John (1637), Bart. B. at Thornton, Bucks. (his mother's home). Of Waresley, Hunts. Matric. 1684; B.A. 1687-8; M.A. 1691. Ord. priest (Lincoln) Sept. 22, 1689. R. of Denton, Hunts., 1689-98. R. of Scotter, Lincs., 1698-1721. Brother of John (1677-8) and Thomas (1692). (Burke, *Ext. Bart.*)

HUET, W. Matric. pens. from QUEENS', Michs. 1564.

HEWITT, WILLIAM. B.A. 1516-7; M.A. 1520.

HUETT, WILLIAM. Matric. pens. from TRINITY, Michs. 1550.

HEWET, WILLIAM. Matric. sizar from ST JOHN'S, Michs. 1580; B.A. 1583-4; M.A. 1588.

HUIT, WILLIAM (1597), *see* CORNWALLIS.

HEWET, WILLIAM. Matric. pens. from TRINITY, Easter, 1612, as Howatt; B.A. 1614-5. Ord. deacon (Peterb.) May 26, 1616; priest, Sept. 21, 1617. V. of Sharnbrook, Beds., 1618-33. Buried there Mar. 26, 1633.

HEWET, WILLIAM. Matric. Fell.-Com. from CHRIST'S, July, 1621. Probably of Dunston, Leics. Adm. at Gray's Inn, May 31, 1622, as s. of William, of Millbrook and Ampthill, Beds. Died 1662, aged 58. (*Peile*, I. 338; Burke, *L.G.*)

HEWETT, WILLIAM. Ord. deacon (Peterb.) June 12, 1625, as 'late of TRINITY College literate'; priest, May 19, 1627. One of these names minister at Cotgrave, Notts., in 1650. Buried there Jan. 22, 1653-4. Will, P.C.C. (Godfrey, *Notts.*)

HEWYT, WILLIAM. Adm. pens. (age 17) at SIDNEY, May, 1633. S. of Sir William, Knt. B. in Suffolk Street, London. Schools, Hadley, Middlesex and Eton. Matric. Fell.-Com. 1633. Adm. at the Inner Temple, 1631. Of Breccles, Norfolk. Knighted, Nov. 20, 1660. Married Ursula, dau. of John Webbe, of Breccles, Norfolk, Esq. Died Apr. 4, 1667, aged 52. Buried in Breccles Church. Father of Gardiner (1656). (*Norfolk Archaeology*, VIII. 316.)

HEWIT, WILLIAM. Adm. sizar (age 17) at CAIUS, Aug. 18, 1740. S. of John, clothier, of Mattishall, Norfolk. B. there. School, Scarning (Mr Brett). Matric. 1740-1; Scholar, 1740-7; B.A. 1744-5; M.A. 1750. Fellow, 1747-67. Ord. deacon (Norwich) Sept. 23, 1744; priest, Dec. 25, 1746. R. of Bodham, Norfolk, 1767-80. R. of Baconsthorpe, 1767-88. Died at Baconsthorpe, Mar. 17, 1788. Will, P.C.C. (*Venn*, II. 47.)

HEWET, ——. B.A. 1492-3.

HEWITT, ——. B.A. 1526-7. One William Hewet V. of All Saints', Cambridge, *c.* 1535.

HEWETSON or **HUITSON, CHRISTOPHER.** Matric. sizar from Jesus, Lent, 1580-1; B.A. 1584-5; M.A. 1588.

HUITSON, NATHANIEL. Matric. sizar from St Catharine's, Easter, 1631. Of Essex. B.A. from King's, 1633-4; M.A. 1637. C. of Cold Norton, Essex, 1637. R. of Woodham Mortimer, 1640-71. V. of Burnham, 1660-71. Died 1671. Will (Consist. C. London) 1671; mentions s. Nathaniel.

HEWITSON or **HUSON, NATHANIEL.** Adm. sizar at Queens', Feb. 25, 1668-9. Of Essex. Doubtless s. of Nathaniel (above). Matric. 1669; B.A. 1672-3. Signed for deacon's orders (London) June 11, 1674; C. of Burnham, Essex.

HEWETSON or **HOWTSON, MILES.** B.Can.L. 1494-5.

HEWETSON, ——. B.Can.L. 1501.

HEWGOE, JOHN. Adm. pens. at Trinity, Jan. 4, 1681-2. Matric. 1685, as Hughoc; Scholar, 1685; B.A. 1685-6.

HEWGOE, JOHN. Adm. sizar at Queens', Mar. 11, 1709-10. Of Cornwall. Matric. 1710; B.A. 1713-4; M.A. 1717.

HEWGOE, STEPHEN. Adm. sizar at Queens', Apr. 7, 1689. Of Cornwall. Matric. 1689; B.A. 1692-3. Probably will (Exeter) 1758; of St Austell, Cornwall, clerk.

HEWGOE, WALTER. Adm. sizar at Queens', May 27, 1685. Of Cornwall. Matric. 1685; B.A. 1688-9. Preb. of Exeter, 1735-41. Will (Exeter) 1741; of Holy Trinity, Exeter, clerk.

HEWIS, *see* **HUGHES.**

HEWKE, WALTER. B.Can.L. 1490. Of Norwich diocese. S. of John Hewke. D.Can.L. 1494-5. Fellow of Trinity Hall. Ord. deacon (Lincoln) Feb. 29, 1490-1; priest, Mar. 19, 1490-1. R. of Holywell, Hunts., 1500-17. Master of Trinity Hall, 1512-7. Died 1517. Buried in the Chapel. M.I. there. Will (P.C.C.). Benefactor to Trinity Hall. (*Cooper*, I. 18; *Coll. Hist.*, 66.)

HEWLER, GEORGE. Matric. sizar from Emmanuel, Easter, 1608.

HEWLEY, THOMAS. Adm. pens. (age 18) at Sidney, Apr. 14, 1648. S. of George, attorney. B. at Wistow, Yorks. Schools, Nun-Monkton (Mr Hen. Constantine) and Selby (Mr Rob. Hulley). Matric. 1648; B.A. 1651-2; M.A. 1655. Incorp. at Oxford, 1657. Of Wistow, Esq.

HEWLING, ——. Scholar of Christ's, 1530-1.

HEWORTH, ——. Scholar at King's Hall, *c.* 1461-5.

HEWSON, BARTHOLOMEW. Matric. sizar from Trinity, Easter, 1626.

HEWSON, MATTHEW. Matric. sizar from Jesus, Easter, 1623; B.A. 1626-7; M.A. 1637. Ord. deacon (Peterb.) Nov. 29; priest, Nov. 30, 1627. V. of Ellington, Hunts., 1636-67. Signs as C. of Yelden, Beds., in 1638. Died 1667.

HEWSON, NATHANIEL. Matric. sizar from Magdalene, Easter, 1622; B.A. 1625-6; M.A. 1629. Ord. deacon (Peterb.) Sept. 23, 1627. V. of Little Addington, Northants., 1646; conformed; instituted, 1663. Buried there Mar. 22, 1692-3. (H. I. Longden.)

HUSON, RICHARD. M.A. from St Catharine's, 1675. S. of Richard, of Hensbridge, Somerset. Matric. from Exeter College, Oxford, July 9, 1668, age 15; B.A. (Oxford) 1672. Ord. priest (London) Dec. 23, 1677. V. of Fifehead Magdalen, Dorset, 1677-1726. (*Al. Oxon.*)

HUSON, SAMUEL. Adm. sizar (age 18) at Peterhouse, July 7, 1720. Of Durham. School, Durham. Matric. 1720; B.A. 1723-4. Ord. deacon (Durham) Aug. 23; priest, Sept. 19, 1724. C. of Grindon, Durham, 1724. V. of Bishopton, 1740-65. Married, at Grindon, July 10, 1739, Ann Tweddell. (H. M. Wood; D. S. Boutflower.)

HEWSON or **HUSON, THOMAS.** B.A. (? 1602-3); M.A. from Trinity, 1623. Probably ord. deacon (Norwich) Sept. 29, 1603, as 'B.A., aged 25.' C. of Holton, Norfolk.

HUGHSON, WILLIAM. Matric. sizar from Queens', Easter, 1641. Of London.

HUSON, ——. B.Civ.L. 1478. Probably John, R. of Reepham and Kerdiston, Norfolk, in 1490.

HEWSON, ——. B.Can.L. 1502-3.

HUSON, ——. B.Civ.L. 1504-5.

HEWTHWAITE, JOHN. Adm. sizar (age 18) at St John's, Jan. 13, 1746-7. S. of Thomas, attorney-at-law, of Yorkshire. B. at Pickering. School, Threshfield (Mr Knowles). Matric. 1747; B.A. 1750-1; M.A. 1757. Ord. deacon (York) June 2, 1751; priest, May 24, 1752. V. of Cottingham, Yorks., 1757-66. V. of Morton and Haconby, Lincs., 1766-8. V. of Messingham and Bottesford, 1768-73. V. of Bicker, 1776-1802. Died Sept. 16, 1802. (*Scott-Mayor*, III. 564.)

HEXAM, JOHN. Matric. sizar from Jesus, Easter, 1570; B.A. 1573-4.

HEXT, FRANCIS. Adm. sizar at Queens', July 9, 1686. S. of Francis, of Trenarren, Cornwall, deceased. B. Jan. 11, 1665-6. Exhibitioner from Charterhouse. Matric. 1686. Succeeded his uncle, Samuel Hext, at Trenarren, 1714. Author, poems. Buried at St Austell, Mar. 31, 1729. (*Al. Carthus.*)

HEXTALL, ABRAHAM, *see* **HECKSTALL.**

HEY, *see also* **HAY.**

HEY, JOHN. Adm. pens. at St Catharine's, 1750-1. S. of Richard, dry salter, of Pudsey, Leeds. B. July, 1734. Matric. 1752-3; B.A. 1755; M.A. from Sidney, 1758; B.D. 1765; D.D. 1780. Fellow of Sidney, 1758-79. Seatonian prizeman, 1763. Norrisian Professor of Divinity, 1780-95. Ord. deacon (Bangor) Feb. 2, 1757; priest (Ely) Mar. 2, 1760. R. of Passenham, Northants., 1779-1814. R. of Calverton, Bucks., 1780-1814. Died Mar. 17, 1815, in London. Buried at St John's Chapel, Marylebone. M.I. at Passenham. Will, P.C.C. (*D.N.B.*; H. I. Longden.)

HEY, THOMAS. Adm. sizar (age 17) at Caius, Mar. 10, 1666-7. S. of Christopher, mercer, of Watton, Norfolk. B. there. Bapt. Dec. 21, 1649. School, Scarning (Mr Burton). Matric. 1667; Scholar, 1667-71; B.A. 1670-1. Ord. priest (York) June 9, 1695. R. of Headon, Notts., 1695-1707. Died 1707. (*Venn*, I. 430.)

HEY, W. Matric. pens. from Corpus Christi, Lent, 1750-1.

HEYDEY, ——. Resident pens. at Jesus, 1561-2.

HEYDON, *see also* **HAYDON.**

HEYDON, CHRISTOPHER. Matric. Fell.-Com. from Peterhouse, Easter, 1576. S. of Sir William, of Baconsthorpe, Norfolk. B.A. 1578-9 (1st in the *ordo*). M.P. for Norfolk, 1588. Travelled abroad. Knighted at the capture of Cadiz, 1596. Suspected of complicity in Essex's rising, 1601, but pardoned. Author, astrological. Died 1623. Buried at Baconsthorpe. Brother of John (1577-8), father of William (1597-8). (*D.N.B.*)

HAIDON, HENRY. Matric. Fell.-Com. from Peterhouse, Michs. 1570. Probably adm. at Lincoln's Inn, Mar. 19, 1572-3; of Norfolk.

HEYDON, HENRY. Matric. pens. from St John's, Easter, 1609.

HAYDON, JAMES. Matric. Fell.-Com. from St John's, Easter, 1605.

HEYDON, JOHN. D.D. Prior of the Carmelites at Cambridge, 1397.

HEYDON, JOHN. Adm. at King's, a scholar from Eton, 1496.

HEYDON, JOHN. Adm. pens. (age 15) at Caius, Mar. 14, 1577-8. S. of William, of Wroxham, Norfolk. Schools, Holt, Norwich and Ryburgh. Served in Ireland. Knighted there, Aug. 5, 1599. In a duel with Sir John Mansfield, in 1599, he lost his left hand (it is preserved in Canterbury Museum). Concerned in the conspiracy of Essex, but pardoned, in 1601. Brother of Christopher (1576). (*Vis. of Norfolk*; *Venn*, I. 96.)

HEIDON, JOSEPH. Matric. pens. from King's, Lent, 1597-8.

HAYDON, MICHAEL. Scholar of Trinity, 1565; B.A. 1567-8; M.A. 1571. One of these names, of Herts., adm. at Lincoln's Inn, Aug. 2, 1572.

HEEDON, NICHOLAS. Probably member of the University before 1279. (Stokes, *Chaplains*, 3.)

HEIDON, NICHOLAS. Matric. pens. from Trinity, Michs. 1559.

HEEDON, ROGER. Probably a member of the University. Founder of chaplaincies. (*See* Stokes, *Chaplains*, 3.)

HAYDON, THOMAS. M.A. 1658 (Incorp. from Oxford). Matric. from Exeter College, Nov. 12, 1650; B.A. (Oxford) 1653; M.A. 1656. Perhaps V. of Stowe, Bucks., 1672-97, resigned.

HEYDON, THOMAS. Adm. at Corpus Christi, 1665. Of Hertfordshire. B.A. 1668-9, as Heden.

HEYDON, W. Matric. Fell.-Com. from Magdalene, Michs. 1567.

HEYDON, WILLIAM. Adm. Fell.-Com. at Peterhouse, Apr. 3, 1580. Perhaps matric. as Haton, 1578. S. of William, of Baconsthorpe. If so, adm. at the Inner Temple, 1578.

HEIDON, W. Matric. pens. from Trinity, Michs. 1576.

HEIDON, WILLIAM. Adm. Fell.-Com. (age 12) at Caius, Feb. 7, 1597-8. S. of Sir Christopher (above). B. at Saxlingham, Norfolk. Educated at home (Mr Blackbourne). Afterwards knighted. Killed, 1627, in the action off the Isle of Rhé. Will, P.C.C. 'A worthy gentleman and valiant soldier: an expert engineer.' There is a volume of MS. letters from his father in the Caius College library. (*Venn*, I. 164; Weever, *Mon.*)

HEYDON, ——. Pens. at Gonville Hall, 1538. Probably Sir Christopher, Knt. (*Blomefield*, VI. 504.)

HEYDON, ——. Adm. Fell.-Com. at TRINITY, 1658.

HEYES, *see* HAYES *and* HASE.

HEYFIELD, NATHANIEL. Matric. sizar from KING'S, Easter, 1631.

HEYFIELD, ——. B.D. 1592 (in the *ordo*).

HEYGAT, REGINALD. Matric. Fell.-Com. from MICHAEL HOUSE, Michs. 1544. Perhaps adm. at Gray's Inn, 1546.

HEIGATE, ROBERT. Adm. Fell.-Com. (age 35) at CAIUS, Jan. 19, 1608–9. Of Ramsholt, Suffolk. S. of Edmund, gent. Perhaps s. of Edmund, of Rendlesham; in *Vis. of Suffolk*, 1612. Will (P.C.C.) 1638. (*Venn*, I. 200.)

HEYHOE, *see* HAYHOE.

HEYLES, JOSEPH, *see* HOYLE.

HEYLET, *see also* HAYLET.

HEYLET, DANIEL. Matric. sizar (probably from CHRIST'S), July, 1606; B.A. from Christ's, 1609–10; M.A. 1613. R. of St Michael-at-Plea, Norwich, 1612–7. Died Sept. 4, 1617, aged 27. (*Peile*, I. 261.)

HAILET or HEYLETT, DANIEL. Adm. sizar at EMMANUEL, June, 1631. Of Norfolk. Perhaps s. of the above. Matric. 1631; B.A. 1634–5.

HEYLIE, CHRISTOPHER. B.A. from ST JOHN'S, 1578–9; M.A. 1582, as Helowe.

HEYLING or HELIN, JOHN. Matric. pens. from QUEENS', Lent, 1618–9. Of London. B. Feb. 7, 1600–1. From Merchant Taylors' School. Migrated to Emmanuel, Oct. 15, 1622. B.A. 1622–3; M.A. 1626. Incorp. at Oxford, 1624. Perhaps adm. at Gray's Inn, 1627, as s. and h. of Peter, of London, gent.

HEYLIN, JOHN. Adm. pens. (age 19) at TRINITY, June 7, 1705. S. of John, citizen and saddler, of London. School, Westminster. Matric. 1706; Scholar, 1706; B.A. 1708–9; M.A. 1714; D.D. 1728 (*Com. Reg.*). Ord. priest (London) Dec. 18, 1709. V. of Haslingfield, Cambs., 1714–9. R. of St Mary-le-Strand, 1724–59. Lecturer at All Hallows, Lombard Street, 1729. Chaplain to George II, 1733–48. Preb. of St Paul's, 1736–59. V. of Sunbury, Middlesex, 1742–7. Preb. of Westminster, 1743–59. Author, theological. Died Aug. 11, 1759. Buried in Westminster Abbey. Will, P.C.C. (*D.N.B.*; *Al. Westmon.*, 246.)

HEYLIN, PETER. M.A. 1621 (Incorp. from Oxford). 2nd s. of Henry, of Burford, Oxon. B. there, Nov. 29, 1599. School, Burford. Matric. from Magdalen College, Oxford, Jan. 19, 1615–6, age 15; B.A. 1617; M.A. 1620; B.D. 1629; D.D. 1633. Fellow of Magdalen, 1618–30. Chaplain to Charles I, 1630. Canon of Westminster, 1631–62; sub-dean, 1660. R. of Hemingford Abbots, Hunts., 1631–2. R. of Houghton-le-Spring, Durham, 1632–3. R. of Alresford, Hants., 1633; of South Warnborough, Hants., 1639. Proposed a conference between Convocation and the Commons, 1640. Obtained a money grant from convocation for Charles I, 1640. V. of Minster Lovell, Oxon.; sequestered from his preferments. Retired to Lacy's Court, Abingdon. A noted controversialist. Author, ecclesiastical. Died May 8, 1662. Buried in Westminster Abbey. (*D.N.B.*)

HEYMAN, HENRY. Matric. pens. from TRINITY, Easter, 1572. Perhaps s. of Ralph, of Somerfield, Sellinge, Kent. Succeeded his father, 1601. Died 1613. (Burke, *Ext. Bart.*)

HEYMAN, HENRY. Adm. pens. (age 16) at PEMBROKE, June 6, 1674. S. of Peter, of Wye, Kent, gent. Matric. 1674. (*Vis. of Kent*, 1663.)

HEYMAN, PETER. Adm. Fell.-Com. at EMMANUEL, June 27, 1597. S. of Henry, of Somerfield, Kent, Esq. M.P. for Hythe, 1620–4, 1624–5, 1626, 1628–9; for Dover, 1640. Died 1641. (*D.N.B.*; *Vis. of Kent*, 1663; A. B. Beaven.)

HEYMAN or HAYMER, ROBERT. Adm. pens. at EMMANUEL, Nov. 18, 1637. Of Kent. Matric. 1637; B.A. 1643–4; M.A. from Pembroke, 1647. Fellow of Pembroke. Died in Cambridge, *c.* 1705; 'hominum miserrimus.' (*Loder.*)

HAYMAN, WILLIAM. Matric. pens. from TRINITY, Lent, 1578–9. Perhaps s. of Ralph, of Somerfield, Kent, Esq. Established scholarships at King's School, Canterbury and at Trinity College. (Burke, *Ext. Bart.*)

HEYMER or HAYMER, ROBERT. Adm. pens. at EMMANUEL, Oct. 11, 1639. Of Suffolk. Matric. 1639, as 'Heymone'; B.A. 1643–4.

HEYNES, *see* HAYNES.

HEYNEY, THOMAS. B.A. from CLARE, 1617–8. Perhaps s. of John, R. of Chailey, Sussex, whose will (P.C.C.) 1603. M.A. 1621. Ord. deacon and priest (Chichester) May 31, 1618. V. of Arundel, Sussex, 1620. R. of Newtimber, 1625. (W. C. Renshaw; J. Ch. Smith.)

HEYRICK, *see also* HERRICK.

HEYRICK, JOHN. Matric. sizar from TRINITY, Easter, 1631. S. of Tobias (1588). Scholar, 1634; B.A. 1635–6; M.A. 1639. Sometime of Gray's Inn (not in the register). Afterwards lived as a private gentleman at Grey Friars, Leicester. Died 1682, aged 71. Brother of William (1627), father of William (1681) and Samuel (1682). (J. H. Hill, *Market Harborough.*)

HEYRICK, NATHANIEL. Adm. sizar (age 17) at TRINITY, May 1, 1716. S. of Samuel (1682), of Loddington, Northants., clerk. Probably b. at Gt Glen, Leics. School, Rugby. Matric. 1716; Scholar, 1718; B.A. 1719–20; M.A. 1723. Fellow, 1722. Senior proctor, 1739–40. Ord. deacon (Lincoln) May 31, 1724; priest (London) Feb. 21, 1724–5. V. of Barrington, Cambs., 1740. R. of Loddington, Northants., 1741. Died May 13, 1767. Buried at Loddington. Will, P.C.C. Brother of Tobias (1729). (*G. Mag.*; J. H. Hill, *Market Harborough*; H. I. Longden.)

HEYRICK, SAMUEL. Adm. sizar at TRINITY, Aug. 30, 1682. S. of John (1631), of Leicester. Matric. 1682; Scholar, 1685; B.A. 1686–7; M.A. 1690. Incorp. at Oxford, 1693. V. of Gt Glen, Leics., 1693–1703. Chaplain of Trinity, 1696–8. R. of Loddington, Northants., 1703–41. Died Jan. 4, 1741–2, aged 76. Buried at Loddington. M.I. there. Will (Archd. Northants.). Father of Tobias (1729) and Nathaniel (1716), brother of William (1681). (J. H. Hill, *Market Harborough*, 118; *Al. Oxon.*)

HEYRICK or HERRICK, THOMAS. Adm. sizar (age 16) at PETERHOUSE, June 27, 1667. S. of Thomas, of Market Harborough, Leics. Bapt. Mar. 4, 1648–9. School, Market Harborough. Matric. 1667; B.A. 1670–1; Scholar, 1671; M.A. 1675. Incorp. at Oxford, 1675. Ord. deacon (Peterb.) Sept. 22, 1672; priest, Dec. 18, 1681. P.C. of Market Harborough, 1685. Author, poetical. Buried Aug. 9, 1694. Admon. (Leicester) 1694. (*D.N.B.*; *Al. Oxon.*)

HEYRICK, TOBIAS. Adm. pens. at EMMANUEL, June, 1588. S. of Robert, of Leicester. Matric. 1588; B.A. 1591–2; M.A. from St John's, 1596. Incorp. at Oxford, 1596. B.D. (Oxford) 1603. *Supp.* for D.D. 1605–6. Fellow of Lincoln College. R. of St Clement's, Oxford, 1604. R. of Houghton-on-the-Hill, Leics., 1605. Died 1627. Father of John (1631) and William (1627). (*Al. Oxon.*)

HEYRICK, TOBIAS. Adm. pens. (age 18) at TRINITY, Mar. 29, 1729. S. of Samuel (1682), R. of Loddington, Northants. Bapt. there, Sept. 6, 1711. School, Rugby. Matric. 1729; Scholar, 1730; B.A. 1732–3; M.A. 1736; B.D. 1750. Fellow, 1735. Ord. deacon (Lincoln) Dec. 22, 1734; priest, June 20, 1736. V. of Barrington, Cambs., 1750. V. of Over, 1750. V. of Gainford, Durham, 1754–82. Died Mar. 30, 1782. M.I. at Gainford. Brother of Nathaniel (1716). (*G. Mag.*)

HEYRICK, WILLIAM. Matric. pens. from TRINITY, Michs. 1627. S. of Tobias (1588). B. 1609. B.A. 1631. Adm. at Gray's Inn, Oct. 19, 1631. Brother of John (1631). (J. H. Hill, *Market Harborough*, 120–4.)

HEYRICK, WILLIAM. Adm. p . at PETERHOUSE, 1657; B.A. 1657–8. From Corpus Christi, Oxford; adm. there, Nov. 7, 1655. Buried at Little St Mary's, Cambridge, Apr. 30, 1660.

HEYRICK or HERRICK, WILLIAM. Adm. pens. (age 17) at ST JOHN'S, June 9, 1681. S. of John (1631), gent. B. at Leicester. School, Melton Mowbray (Mr Daffy). Matric. 1681. Died Jan. 11, 1696–7, aged 32. Brother of Samuel (1682). (J. H. Hill, *Market Harborough.*)

HEYRINGTON, EDMUND. Matric. sizar from ST CATHARINE'S, Michs. 1546.

HEYT, JOHN, *see* HAYT.

HEYTHOON or HEYTTON, THOMAS. B.Civ.L. 1518–9.

HEYWOOD, *see* HAYWOOD.

HEYWORTH, JOHN. Matric. pens. from ST JOHN'S, Easter, 1609.

HEIWORTH, WILLIAM. Matric. sizar from EMMANUEL, Easter, 1606.

HAYWORTH, ——. Grace (? for B.A.) 1483–4.

HIAM, *see* HEIGHAM.

HIBBENS, CHARLES. Adm. pens. at EMMANUEL, May 17, 1617. Matric. 1617. One of these names s. and h. of Thomas, of Weo and Rowton, Salop. B. *c.* 1600. (*Vis. of Salop*, 1623.)

HIBBENS, THOMAS. Matric. sizar from TRINITY, Michs. 1621; B.A. 1624–5. Ord. deacon (Peterb.) Nov. 1, 1624; priest, Sept. 23, 1627. V. of Tallington, Lincs., 1631.

HIBBERT or HEBBERT, HENRY. Adm. sizar (age 18) at ST JOHN'S, Aug. 4, 1645. S. of William, yeoman, of Marple, Cheshire. School, Glossop, Derbs. (Mr Grinley). Possibly the man 'of Hessle *cum* Hull' mentioned by Walker (*Sufferings*, II. 373.)

HIBBERT, HENRY. B.D. 1664 (*Lit. Reg.*); D.D. 1665. Of Cheshire. S. of William, of Marple. Chaplain to the Duke of York. Matric. from Brasenose College, Oxford, Jan. 28, 1619–20, age 18; B.A. (Oxford) 1622; D.D. (Oxford) 1665. V. of Preston in Holderness, Yorks., 1625–43. V. of Mottram in Longdendale, Cheshire, 1649. Minister at Settrington, Yorks., 1652; of Holy Trinity, Hull, 1652. V. of All Hallows the Less, London, 1662. V. of St Olave, Old Jewry, 1662–78. Preb. of St Paul's, 1669–78. Author, theological. Died Sept. 1678. Buried in St Olave's. Will, P.C.C. (*D.N.B.*)

HIBBINS, HENRY. M.A. 1675 (Incorp. from Oxford). S. of Jer., of Rowton, Salop, gent. Matric. from Magdalen Hall, Jan. 31, 1665–6, age 15; B.A. (Oxford) 1669; M.A. (Balliol College) 1672; B.D. 1680. (*Al. Oxon.*)

HIBBINS, JAMES. Adm. pens. (age 20) at MAGDALENE, July 1, 1732. S. of James, gent. B. at Holbeach, Lincs. School, Lincoln. Matric. 1733; B.A. 1735–6; M.A. 1747.

HICKOCK, HENRY. Adm. sizar (age 18) at PETERHOUSE, Mar. 31, 1669. Of Warwickshire. Matric. 1670; B.A. 1672. Ord. deacon (Peterb.) May 25, 1673.

HICCOCK, JOHN. Adm. sizar (age 18) at ST JOHN'S, Aug. 28, 1706. S. of John, husbandman. B. at Wervin, Cheshire. School, Bridge-Trafford, Cheshire (Mr Gibson). Matric. 1707, as 'Hinock'; B.A. 1710–1. Perhaps R. of Shelton, Beds., 1733–4.

HICCOCKS, WILLIAM. Matric. pens. from QUEENS', Easter, 1644. Of Surrey. B.A. 1647–8; M.A. 1652. R. of Little Laver, Essex, 1654. R. of Lee, Kent, 1655; ejected, 1662. (*Calamy*, II. 62.)

HICK, ——. B.A. 1469–70.

HICKE or HIKE, THOMAS. B.A. 1539–40.

HICKES, BAPTIST. Matric. Fell.-Com. from TRINITY, Michs. 1568. 3rd s. of Robert, mercer, of Cheapside. Adm. at the Inner Temple, 1573. Joined his father's business; supplied the court with silk and mercery. Knighted, July 24, 1603. Created Baronet, 1620. M.P. for Tavistock, 1620–2; for Tewkesbury, 1624–5, 1626, 1628. Deputy-Lieutenant for Middlesex, 1625. Created Baron Hickes and Viscount Campden, 1628. Died Oct. 28, 1629. Buried at Campden, Gloucs. Brother of Michael (1559). (*D.N.B.*; *Vis. of Gloucs.*, 1623; A. B. Beaven; *G.E.C.*)

HYX, EDWARD. Matric. pens. from CHRIST'S, Easter, 1563; Scholar in 1564–5. One of these names scholar of Queens', 1563–5.

HICKS, EDWARD. M.A. 1653 (Incorp. from Oxford). S. of John, V. of Gt Barrington, Gloucs. Matric. from Oriel College, Mar. 27, 1640, age 15; B.A. (? 1646); M.A. 1649; D.D. 1660. Royalist captain of horse. R. of Hertingfordbury, Herts.; ejected, 1662. R. of St Margaret Pattens, London, 1661–82. R. of Buckland, Herts., 1667–82. Died 1682. (*Al. Oxon.*; *Clutterbuck*.)

HICKES, GEORGE. Adm. Fell.-Com. (age 18) at PEMBROKE, June 24, 1618. S. of George, of Glemsford, Suffolk. Matric. 1618.

HICKES, GEORGE. M.A. 1668 (Incorp. from Oxford). S. of William, of Newsham Hall, Kirby Wiske, Yorks. B. there, June 20, 1642. School, Northallerton (Mr Thomas Smelt). Matric. from St John's College, Oxford, May 19, 1659; B.A. from Magdalen College, 1662–3; M.A. from Lincoln, 1665; B.D. 1675; D.D. 1679. Fellow of Lincoln College, 1664–80. Ord. deacon, June 10; priest (Oxford) Dec. 23, 1666. R. of St Ebbe's, Oxford, 1675. Chaplain to the Duke of Lauderdale, 1676. V. of Wolverley, Worcs., 1680. Preb. of Worcester, 1680–3. V. of All Hallows, Barking, 1680–6. Chaplain to the King, 1681. Dean of Worcester, 1683–91. R. of Alvechurch, Worcs., 1686. Deprived for refusing the oath of allegiance to William and Mary, 1689. Went to St Germains, 1693. Nominated Suffragan of Bishop Sancroft. On his return to England consecrated non-juror 'Bishop of Thetford,' 1694. Author, miscellaneous. Died Dec. 15, 1715. Buried at St Margaret's, Westminster. Will, P.C.C. Brother of Ralph (1681). (*D.N.B.*; *Al. Oxon.*)

HYCKES, HENRY. Matric. pens. from TRINITY, Easter, 1567; Scholar, 1567, as Hix; B.A. 1570–1.

HICKS, HENRY. Adm. at CORPUS CHRISTI, 1569.

HICKS, JAMES. Adm. sizar (age 18) at CAIUS, June 11, 1742. S. of Francis, grocer, of Watton, Norfolk. B. there. School, Watton (private; Mr Pigge and Mr Edgerly). Scholar, 1742–9; Matric. 1745; B.A. 1745–6; M.A. 1749. Fellow, 1750–69. President, 1767–9. University scrutator, 1767. Ord. deacon (Norwich) June 7, 1747, as C. of Ovington; priest, May 21, 1749, as C. of Shropham. Officiating minister at Little Shelford, Cambs., 1766. R. of Denver, Norfolk, 1769–88. R. of Moulton, 1769–88. Died Apr. 30, 1788. Buried at Denver. M.I. there. (*Venn*, II. 51.)

HICKS, JOHN. B.D. 1608 (Incorp. from Oxford). Of London. Matric. from Christ Church, Jan. 25, 1582–3, age 18; B.A. (Oxford) 1586; M.A. 1589; B.D. 1596. V. of Carlton, Skipton, Yorks., and of Kildwick, 1594. R. of Whitburn, Durham, 1599. Preb. of York, 1615. Married, at Lamesley, Durham, Feb. 20, 1603–4, Alice Blaikston. Buried at Whitburn, Dec. 31, 1630. (*Al. Oxon.*; H. M. Wood.)

HICKS, JOHN. Adm. sizar (age 16) at PETERHOUSE, Sept. 19, 1650. Of Warwickshire. School, Coventry. Scholar, 1652; Matric. 1654; B.A. 1654–5; M.A. 1658.

HICKES, JOHN. Adm. sizar (age 18) at ST JOHN'S, Mar. 19, 1652–3. S. of Richard, R. of Whitburn, Durham. B. there. School, Bishop Wearmouth (Mr Walker). Matric. 1653; B.A. 1656–7. P.C. of Monkwearmouth, Durham, 1662–9. Died 1669. (*Surtees*, II. 54.)

HICKES, MICHAEL. Matric. pens. from TRINITY, Michs. 1559. 1st s. of Robert, mercer, of Cheapside. B. Oct. 21, 1543. Bapt. at St Pancras, London. Adm. at Lincoln's Inn, Mar. 10, 1563–4. Secretary to Lord Burghley and Sir Robert Cecil. M.P. for Truro, 1584–6; for Shaftesbury, 1588, 1592–3; for Gatton, 1597–8; for Horsham, 1601, 1604–11. Knighted, Aug. 6, 1604. Of Beverstone, Gloucs. and Ruckholt, Essex. Died Aug. 15, 1612. Buried at Leyton, Essex. Will (P.C.C.) 1612. Brother of Baptist (1568). (*D.N.B.*; A. B. Beaven.)

HICKES, MICHAEL. Matric. Fell.-Com. from TRINITY, Easter, 1618. Probably s. of the above.

HICKES, MICHAEL. Adm. Fell.-Com. at TRINITY, June 24, 1661.

HICKES, NICHOLAS. M.A. 1662 (Incorp. from Oxford). Matric. from Queen's, Oxford, Apr. 2, 1652. Demy of Magdalen College, Oxford. B.A. (Oxford) 1665; M.A. 1658; B.D. 1665–6. Fellow of Magdalen College, 1658–82. Canon of Chichester, 1682. R. of West Thorney, Sussex, 1684. R. of Charfield, Gloucs., 1701–10. Died Sept. 12, 1710, aged 75. M.I. at Cromhall, Gloucs. (*Al. Oxon.*)

HICKES, RALPH. M.A. from JESUS, 1681. S. of William, of Newsham, Yorks. Matric. from Lincoln College, Oxford, Nov. 13, 1668, age 17; B.A. (Oxford) 1672. Licentiate R.C.P., 1692. Said to have been M.D. Died Apr. 5, 1711. Buried at St Peter's, Cornhill, as Dr of Physic. Will, P.C.C. Brother of George (1668). (*Al. Oxon.*; A. Gray; J. Ch. Smith.)

HICKS or HICKE, RICHARD. Matric. sizar from TRINITY, Michs. 1562; B.A. 1566–7. Ord. deacon (Ely) Apr. 16, 1568, age 24. V. of Hatfield Regis, Essex, 1568–70; patron, Trinity College.

HICKS or HIXE, ROBERT. Matric. sizar from PETERHOUSE, Michs. 1552; B.A. 1556–7; M.A. from Corpus Christi, 1560. Fellow of Corpus Christi, 1558. Received the tonsure (London) 1557. For some time minister at Fotheringay, Northants. R. of Tansor, 1576–1601. Will, P.C.C. (*Bridges*, II. 475; H. I. Longden.)

HICKS, ROBERT. Adm. sizar (age 17) at MAGDALENE, July 2, 1702. S. of Francis, bookseller. B. at Cambridge. School, Histon (private). Matric. 1702–3; B.A. 1705–6; M.A. from King's, 1710. Ord. deacon (Ely) Sept. 21, 1707; priest (Peterb.) Dec. 18, 1709. Chaplain at King's, 1709. V. of Potton, Beds., 1720. R. of Wrestlingworth, 1730.

HICKS, SAMUEL. Adm. sizar at CLARE, Jan. 5, 1738–9. B. in London. Matric. 1739; B.A. 1742–3. Ord. deacon (Lincoln) June 13, 1742; priest, Sept. 23, 1744.

HICKES, STEPHEN. M.A. from MAGDALENE, 1729. S. of William, of Cardinham, Cornwall. Matric. from Exeter College, Oxford, Mar. 26, 1713, age 19; B.A. (Oxford) 1716. R. of Blisland, Cornwall, 1718–80. Died 1780. (*Al. Oxon.*)

HICKES, WILLIAM. Matric. sizar from TRINITY, Michs. 1601; Scholar, 1605; B.A. 1605–6; M.A. 1609. College librarian, 1609–12. One of these names preb. of Lincoln, 1612–46 (but *see Al. Oxon.*). Perhaps R. of Stoke Hammond, Bucks., 1625–45. Died 1646. (*Lipscomb*, IV. 362.)

HICKES, WILLIAM. Said to have been educated at Cambridge. S. and h. of Michael (1559). Created Baronet, July 12, 1619. J.P. and Deputy-Lieutenant of Essex. M.P. for Gt Marlow, 1625 and 1640. Married Mary, dau. of Lord Paget. Died Oct. 15, 1680, aged 84. Probably brother of Michael (1618), father of William (1646). (*D.N.B.*; *Morant*, I. 24.)

HICKS, WILLIAM. Adm. pens. at TRINITY, May 15, 1637. Matric. 1637; Scholar from Westminster, 1638; B.A. 1641–2; M.A. 1645. Perhaps Master of Oundle School, 1646–9. Probably ord. priest (Lincoln) July 14, 1662. V. of Little Baddow, Essex, 1666–9. V. of Hatfield Peverel, 1668–72. R. of South Shoebury, 1672–9. Perhaps R. of Downham, Cambs., 1676–7. Died 1679.

HICKES, WILLIAM. Adm. Fell.-Com. at TRINITY, Mar. 26, 1646. Of Essex. S. of Sir William (above), of Beverstone, Gloucs., Bart. B. Dec. 1629. Succeeded as Bart., 1680. Sheriff of Essex, 1684–5. Died Apr. 22, 1703. Buried at Low Layton. M.I. (*G.E.C.*)

HICKES, WILLIAM. Adm. sizar (age 18) at SIDNEY, June 23, 1671. 2nd s. of John. B. at Middleton, Yorks. School, Pickering, Yorks. (Mr Grey).

HICKFORD, JAMES. Adm. pens. at EMMANUEL, Jan. 16, 1629–30. Of Meddleson, Yorks. Matric. 1629–30; B.A. 1633–4; M.A. 1637. One of these names R. of Ightham, Kent, 1644.

HICKFORTHE, JOHN. Matric. Fell.-Com. from ST JOHN'S, Michs. 1559.

HICKINGTON, PETER. Adm. sizar at ST CATHARINE'S, Nov. 4, 1724. Of Shipton, near York. Matric. 1724–5; B.A. 1728–9. Ord. priest (York) Aug. 16, 1730. C. of Beeford. V. of South Cave, Yorks., *c.* 1730. V. of Elloughton. Perhaps chaplain of H.M. ships *Berwick* and *Culloden*. Died at St George's, Southwark. Will (P.C.C.) 1760. (M. H. Peacock; J. Ch. Smith.)

HICKINGTON, WILLIAM. Adm. pens. (age 17) at TRINITY, June 29, 1748. S. of Peter (? above), of Elloughton, Yorks. School, Beverley (Mr Clark). Matric. 1748; Scholar, 1749; B.A. 1752.

HICKLING, JOHN. Matric. sizar from QUEENS', Michs. 1561; B.A. 1564–5. Perhaps R. of Spixworth, Norfolk, 1567. Presented to Ab-Kettleby, Leics., 1578. V. of Hose, 1582. Will (Leicester) 1614. One of these names ord. priest (Peterb.) Mar. 11, 1574–5.

HICKLIN, THOMAS. Adm. sizar (age 14) at SIDNEY, May 28, 1664. 1st s. of Thomas, yeoman, deceased. B. at Dunston, Staffs. School, Oakham (Mr Jo. Jenner). Matric. 1664.

HICKLING, ——. Adm. pens. at EMMANUEL, Oct. 1629.

HICKMAN, ANTHONY. Matric. pens. from ST JOHN'S, Michs. 1575. 4th s. of Anthony, of Woodford Hall, Essex. Migrated to Peterhouse. B.A. 1579–80; M.A. 1583; LL.D. Fellow of Corpus Christi, 1583–8, where he had a long dispute with the College. Adm. advocate, June 16, 1585. Died Dec. 13, 1597. Will (Comm. C. London) as LL.D. Brother of Henry (1565). (*Masters*, 328; *Lincs. Pedigrees*, 494.)

HICKMAN, CHARLES. Adm. sizar (age 15) at ST JOHN'S, July 8, 1665. S. of John (? 1634), clerk, of Fordham, Norfolk. B. there. School, Lynn (Mr Bell).

HICKMAN, DIXIE. Adm. pens. at EMMANUEL, Apr. 8, 1604. S. of Walter (? William), of Kew, Surrey. Matric. Fell.-Com. 1604; M.A. 1612–3 (on visit of Prince Charles). Adm. at the Inner Temple, 1613; and at Gray's Inn, Aug. 15, 1622. Married and had issue. Buried at Richmond, Surrey, Oct. 10, 1631. (*Lincs. Pedigrees*, 494.)

HICKMAN, HENRY. Matric. pens. from ST JOHN'S, Michs. 1565. Of Middlesborough. S. of Sir Anthony, of Woodford, Essex. B.A. 1568–9; M.A. 1572; LL.D. 1584. Fellow, 1571. Proctor, 1583–4. Incorp. at Oxford, 1572. Adm. advocate, May 14, 1595. Chancellor of diocese of Peterborough. Master in Chancery, 1601. M.P. for Northampton, 1601. Will proved (Peterb.) Sept. 4, 1618. Brother of Anthony (1575). (*Al. Oxon.*; *Lincs. Pedigrees*, 494.)

HICKMAN, HENRY. Matric. pens. from ST CATHARINE'S, Easter, 1647; B.A. 1647–8. Fellow of Magdalen College, Oxford, 1648–60. M.A. (Oxford) 1649–50. Incorp. at Cambridge, 1651. B.D. (Oxford) 1658. Minister of St Aldate's, Oxford. Intruded V. of Brackley, Northants., 1650–9. Retired to Holland. Carried on controversies with Peter Heylin and others. Wrote in defence of nonconformity. Adm. at Leyden, 1663; and again, as English pastor, Apr. 18, 1675. Minister of the English Church there, till his death in 1692. (*D.N.B.*; *Al. Oxon.*; *Baker*, I. 576.)

HICKMAN, JOHN. Adm. pens. at CLARE, May 16, 1634. Matric. 1634; B.A. 1637–8; M.A. 1642. Fellow, 1643; ejected, 1644. University under-librarian, 1640. Ord. deacon (Norwich) May 24, 1644, age 26, C. of Southery, Norfolk; priest, June 16, 1644. R. of Wimbotsham, Norfolk, 1662–71. R. of Bexwell, 1666. Died 1671.

HICKMAN, RICHARD. Matric. sizar from MAGDALENE, Easter, 1607. Of Leicestershire. Migrated to Corpus Christi, 1607. Ord. deacon (Peterb.) Dec. 20, 1612; priest, Feb. 28, 1612–3. C. of Gonerby, Lincs., 1614. Probably will (P.C.C.) 1654; of Kingston, Notts., clerk.

HICKMAN, ROBERT. Matric. sizar from CAIUS, June 26, 1583. S. of Roger, husbandman. B. at Leighton, Beds., *c.* 1572. School, Toddington, Beds. (Mr Proude). Scholar, 1592–5; B.A. 1592–3; M.A. 1596. Ord. deacon and priest (Peterb.) May 14, 1595. Probably buried at Leighton Buzzard, June 3, 1609; described as 'M.A., of Egginton.' (*Venn*, I. 146.)

HICKMAN, THOMAS. Matric. sizar from PETERHOUSE, Easter, 1604; B.A. 1607; M.A. 1611. Incorp. at Oxford, 1611. Ord. deacon (Oxford) Sept. 5; priest, Dec. 18, 1608. C. of Waddesden, Bucks., 1609. R. of Little Kimble, 1615. R. of Upton Lovell, Wilts., 1619–47, sequestered. Buried at Boyton, Wilts., Apr. 22, 1659. (*T. A. Walker*.)

HICKMAN, THOMAS. Matric. pens. from PETERHOUSE, Easter, 1620. Not found in the College register. Perhaps a mistake for Thomas Heigham, whom *see*. (One Thomas Hickman, s. of William, of Gainsborough, Lincs., Knt. Bapt. Feb. 21, 1607–8, adm. at Gray's Inn, Nov. 21, 1627. Died *s.p.*) (*Lincs. Pedigrees*, 495.)

HICKMAN, THOMAS. Adm. Fell.-Com. (age 17) at ST JOHN'S, May 7, 1672. S. of Thomas, gent., of Ireland. B. there. School, Westminster. Matric. 1672.

HYCKMAN, W. Matric. pens. from TRINITY, Easter, 1565.

HICKMAN, WILLIAM. Matric. Fell.-Com. from KING'S, Easter, 1612.

HICKMAN, ——. Adm. Fell.-Com. at KING'S, 1718–9. Perhaps Neville, s. of Sir Willoughby, Bart. Bapt. at Gainsborough, Lincs., May 13, 1701. Succeeded as Bart., 1720. Died June 11, 1733. (Burke, *Ext. Bart.*; *G.E.C.*)

HICKHORNGILL or HICKERINGILL, EDMUND. Adm. pens. (age 16) at ST JOHN'S, June 17, 1647. S. of Edmund, gent., of Aberford, Yorks. B. there. School, Pocklington (Mr Sedgwick). Matric. 1647; B.A. 1650–1. Fellow of Caius, 1651–2. Chaplain in Lilburne's regiment, 1653. Successively baptist, quaker, deist. Governor of Meikleour Castle, Perthshire. A soldier and captain (by sea and land) in the Swedish service. Visited Spain and Portugal and returned to England as Swedish envoy. Afterwards a captain in Fleetwood's regiment. Held a post in Jamaica. Returned to England, 1660. Ord. deacon (Lincoln) May 28; priest, May 31, 1662. V. of Boxted, Essex, 1662–4. R. of All Saints', Colchester, 1662–1708. P.C. of Wickes Priory, Essex. Licensed to preach at St Christopher-le-Stocks, 1662. Engaged in conflicts with the high church party and nonconformists, in the courts and in the press. Publicly recanted, 1684. Excluded from his living, 1685–8. Author, pamphlets, etc. Died Nov. 30, 1708. Buried at Colchester. M.I. in All Saints'. Will, P.C.C. (*Venn*, I. 381; *D.N.B.*)

HICKSON, *see also* **HIGSON.**

HICKSON or HIGSON, JAMES. Adm. sizar (age 17) at ST JOHN'S, June 22, 1667. S. of Robert, clerk, of Malton, Yorks. B. there. Educated at home. Matric. 1667; B.A. 1670–1; M.A. 1677. Incorp. at Oxford, 1677. Ord. deacon (York) June, 1671; priest, Sept. 1672. R. of All Saints', North Street, York, 1674. R. of St Cuthbert, York, 1679. Author, sermon. Brother of Walter (1667).

HICKSON, ROBERT. Matric. pens. from PEMBROKE, Easter, 1567. B. at Elton, Hunts. Ord. deacon (London) Apr. 16, 1579, age 33, as of North Fambridge, Essex (probably curate). V. of Mundon, Essex, till his death, 1604. Admon. (Cons. C. London) to relict, Eastclaramonda. (J. Ch. Smith.)

HICKSON or HIGSON, THOMAS. Adm. sizar (age 17) at ST JOHN'S, July 1, 1650. S. of James, husbandman, of Settle, Yorks. B. there. School, Giggleswick (Mr Walker). Matric. 1650, as Hickson. Migrated to Caius, 1652. Scholar, 1652–3. V. of Willingdon, Sussex, 1662–4; of Selmeston, 1664–81. Buried there Aug. 2, 1681. (*Venn*, I. 386.)

HICKSON or HIGSON, WALTER. Adm. sizar (age 16) at ST JOHN'S, June 22, 1667. S. of Robert, clerk, of Malton, Yorks. B. there. Taught by his father. Matric. 1668; B.A. 1672–3; M.A. 1677. Incorp. at Oxford, 1667. Ord. deacon (York) May, 1673; priest, Sept. 12, 1675. V. of Mappleton, Yorks., 1675–1720. C. of Cottingham, 1678; V. 1699–1722. R. of Swillington, 1706–22. Died 1722. Brother of James (1667).

HICKSON, WILLIAM. Matric. pens. from ST JOHN'S, Michs. 1572.

HICSON or HIGSON, ——. Adm. pens. at EMMANUEL, Easter, 1623. Matric. 1623.

HICKYN, W. Matric. pens. from ST JOHN'S, Easter, 1586.

HIDE, *see* **HYDE.**

HIDER, RICHARD. Matric. pens. from PETERHOUSE, Easter, 1624; Fell.-Com. Apr. 1626.

HIDGEM, RICHARD. Matric. pens. from PETERHOUSE, Easter, 1607. (Probably a mistake for Hodgson, whom *see*.)

HIDGLEY, SAMUEL. Matric. pens. from CLARE, Easter, 1651.

HIERON, *see also* **HEARNE.**

HIERON, JOHN. B.A. 1544–5.

HIERON, JOHN. Adm. sizar at CHRIST'S, May 2, 1625. S. of Walter (V. of Stapenhill), Derbs. School, Repton (Mr Whitehead). Matric. 1625; B.A. 1628–9; M.A. 1632. Ord. deacon and priest (Lichfield) May, 1630. Chaplain to Sir Henry Leigh, at Eggington. Lecturer at Bretby; also at Ashbourne, 1633. R. of Breadsall, 1644–62 (ejected). Author. Died at Losco, July 6, 1682, aged 73. Buried at Heanor. Father of Joseph (1658), brother of Samuel (1637). (*Peile*, I. 367; *Calamy*, I. 306.)

HIERON, JOHN. Adm. pens. (age 18) at CHRIST'S, June 21, 1628. S. of Richard, of Bockenfield, Northumberland. B. there, 1614. School, York (Mr Garthwait). Matric. 1628. Sheriff of Northumberland. Sold Bockenfield, 1672. Died Aug. 18, 1678. Buried in Beverley Minster. (*Vis. of Northumberland*, 1665; H. M. Wood.)

HIERON, JOHN. Adm. sizar (age 18) at TRINITY, May 29, 1719. S. of William, of Blyth, Notts., clerk. School, Glamford Bridge, Lincs. (Mr Waterworth). Matric. 1719. Buried at St Edward's, Cambridge, June 3, 1721.

HIERON, JOSEPH. Adm. pens. (age 16) at CHRIST'S, May 6, 1658. S. of John (1625). B. at Ashbourne, Derbs. School, Repton (Mr Ullock). Matric. 1658. Adm. at Gray's Inn, June 9, 1665; s. and h. of John, of Little Eaton, Derbs. (*Peile*, I. 581.)

HIERON, ROGER. Adm. pens. at EMMANUEL, June 17, 1617. Matric. 1617; B.A. 1620–1; M.A. from Sidney, 1624.

HIERON, SAMPSON. Adm. pens. at EMMANUEL, Easter, 1628. Matric. 1628; B.A. 1631–2. Presented to Harbledown, Kent, Oct. 26, 1647. Probably died *c.* 1655. (*Shaw*, I. 346; H. G. Harrison.)

HIERON or HEARNE, SAMUEL. Adm. at KING'S (age 18) a scholar from Eton, Aug. 24, 1590. Of London. S. of Roger, V. of Epping, Essex. Matric. *c.* 1590; B.A. 1594–5; M.A. 1598. Fellow, 1593–9. Ord. deacon (London) Dec. 21, 1595, age 24. Successful preacher in London. Afterwards R. of Modbury, Devon. Author, sermons, etc. Many of his sermons were published. Died at Modbury, 1617. Will (Exeter) 1617. (*D.N.B.*)

HIERON, SAMUEL. Adm. pens. at JESUS, Mar. 27, 1637. Of Derbyshire. S. of Walter, V. of Stapenhill. Matric. 1635. Perhaps V. of Shirley, Derbs., 1657–62, ejected. Afterwards preacher in Derbyshire. Died Mar. 24, 1687. Brother of John (1625). (*Calamy*, I. 334.)

HIERON, THOMAS. Matric. sizar from QUEENS', Easter, 1616. Of Lincolnshire. B.A. 1619–20; M.A. 1628. Incorp. at Oxford, 1624 (probably adm. there previously in 1614). Ord. priest (Peterb.) Sept. 23, 1621, as B.A. of Trinity College, Oxford. V. of Alderminster, Worcs., 1624–30. V. of Hernhill, Kent, 1630.

HIET, JAMES. Matric. sizar from PETERHOUSE, Easter, 1607. S. of Robert, cordwainer. B. in London. 'Grecian' from Christ's Hospital. B.A. 1610–1; M.A. 1614; B.D. 1621. V. of Childwall, Lancs., 1624–5. R. and V. of Croston, 1625–62, ejected for nonconformity. C. at Wigan, in 1662. Preacher at Liverpool, Oct. 20, 1662. Buried at Croston, Apr. 8, 1663, as V. of Croston. (*Calamy*, II. 89; E. Axon.)

HIGAT, JAMES. M.A. 1598 (Incorp. from Glasgow).

HIGBIE, JOHN. Matric. sizar from QUEENS', Easter, 1620. Of Huntingdonshire. Ord. deacon (Peterb.) Dec. 10; priest, Dec. 19, 1624, as 'B.A.' P.C. of Bury, Hunts., till 1663. Died 1663.

HIGBIE or HIGHBID, WILLIAM. Matric. sizar from PEMBROKE, Easter, 1575; B.A. 1578–9.

HIGHDEN, JOHN. Adm. pens. at SIDNEY, Oct. 9, 1604. S. of John, of Ebberston, Pickering, Yorks. Of Laxton, Esq. Father of the next. (*Vis. of Yorks.*, 1612.)

HIGHDON, JOHN. Adm. pens. (age 14) at SIDNEY, June 30, 1632. S. of John, Esq. (above). B. at Laxton, Howden, Yorks. School, Howden (Mr Wm. Weeks). Matric. 1632.

HIGDEN, JOSEPH. Matric. sizar from CORPUS CHRISTI, Easter, 1624. Of Berkshire.

HIGDEN, MERLIN. Matric. pens. from CORPUS CHRISTI, *c.* 1594. Of Middlesex. B.A. 1596–7; M.A. 1600; B.D. 1608. Fellow, 1601–16. V. of Grantchester, Cambs., 1613–6. Died June 10, 1616. Buried at St Benet's, Cambridge. Will, V.C.C.

HIGDON, LAURENCE. Adm. pens. at TRINITY, May 21, 1636. Matric. 1636; B.A. 1639–40; M.A. from Magdalene, 1643. Perhaps father of William (1682).

HIGDEN, ROBERT. B.A. 1514–5; M.A. 1518–9; B.D. 1535–6. Fellow of QUEENS', 1517–29. Ord. sub-deacon (Ely) Mar. 7, 1516–7. V. of Northall, Middlesex, *c.* 1526–44. Preb. of St Paul's, 1541–4. R. of St Botolph, Bishopsgate, 1541–4. Died *c.* June, 1544.

HIGDEN, WILLIAM. Matric. sizar from KING'S, Easter, 1682. Previously matric. at St Edmund's Hall, Oxford, Feb. 23, 1680–1, age 18. Perhaps s. of Laurence (? 1636), of Corfe Castle, Dorset, clerk. B.A. 1684–5; M.A. 1688; D.D. 1710. R. of St Paul's, Shadwell, 1711–5. Preb. of Canterbury, 1713–5. Claimed as a non-juror, when C. of Camberwell, but afterwards conformed. Author, theological. Died Aug. 28, 1715. Buried in the New Chapel, Westminster, Sept. 5, 1715. (*Al. Oxon.*; *D.N.B.*)

HIGFORD, HENRY. Adm. pens. (age 18) at TRINITY, July 4, 1692. S. of Richard. B. at Boxley, Kent. School, Rochester (Mr Paul Bairstow). Matric. 1693; Scholar, 1695; B.A. 1695–6; M.A. 1699.

HIGFORD, HENRY. M.A. from CORPUS CHRISTI, 1738. S. of William, of Ashton-under-Hill, Gloucs., gent. Matric. from Balliol College, Oxford, Mar. 16, 1726–7, age 17; B.A. (Oxford) 1730. Ord. deacon (Gloucester) Sept. 3, 1732; priest (Winchester). C. of Alderton, Gloucs., 1732; R. 1738–95. Lord of the manor. Lived at Dixton House. Will (P.C.C.) 1795. (F. S. Hockaday; *Al. Oxon.*)

HIGGETT, JOHN. Adm. sizar (age 19) at ST JOHN'S, May 27, 1715. S. of Humphrey, mason. B. in London. School, St Paul's. Matric. 1715; B.A. 1719–20; M.A. 1723. Ord. deacon (London) Oct. 9, 1720. Probably confessor to the Household, 1736–61. Died 1761. One of these names was R. of Slapton, Bucks., 1775–80. Died 1780. Admon. (P.C.C.) 1789; R. of Slapton, formerly of Ealing, Middlesex, but late of Fulham. (J. Ch. Smith.)

HIGGINBOTHAM or HEGYNBOTHAM, JOHN. Adm. sizar at KING'S, Easter, 1564.

HIGGINBOTHAM, THOMAS. Adm. sizar at TRINITY, June 9, 1664. Matric. 1664; B.A. 1668–9, as Hegginbothom. Ord. deacon (Lincoln) June 6, 1669.

HIGGENBOTHAM, ——. Adm. at PEMBROKE, July 6, 1659.

HIGGINS, ANTHONY. Matric. pens. from ST JOHN'S, Michs. 1568. Of Lancashire. Perhaps s. of Thomas, of Manchester. B.A. 1571–2; M.A. 1575; B.D. 1582. Fellow, 1574. Ord. priest (Gloucester) 1572. Preb. of Gloucester, 1578. University preacher, 1581. R. of Kirk Deighton, Yorks., 1583–1624. Master of St Michael's Hospital, Well, 1605. Dean of Ripon, 1608–24. Died Nov. 17, 1624. Will, York. Benefactor to St John's and to Ripon Minster. (*Founders and Benefactors*, 36; M. H. Peacock.)

HIGGONS, BEVILL. Matric. Fell.-Com. from TRINITY HALL, Michs. 1688. Previously matric. from St John's, Oxford, Mar. 5, 1685–6, age 16. S. of Sir Thomas, of Grewell, Hants., Knt. B. at Kezo, 1670. Adm. at the Middle Temple, Nov. 12, 1687. Lived for some years in France, whither he had followed his family into exile. Arrested on a charge of conspiracy against William III, 1696, subsequently released. Historian and p[illegible]. Died at Chiswick, Middlesex, Mar. 1, 1735–6. Buried at St Pancras Churchyard, London, Mar. 6, 1735–6. (*Al. Oxon.*; *D.N.B.*)

HIGGONS, CHRISTOPHER COMYN. Adm. scholar (age 18) at SIDNEY, May 15, 1695. S. of John, gent. B. at Linton, Staffs. Matric. 1695.

HIGGINS, EDWARD. M.A. 1583 (Incorp. from Oxford). B.A. from Queen's College, Oxford, 1575–6; M.A. 1581. Fellow of Brasenose, 1583. Ord. deacon and priest (Lincoln) 1587. Will proved V.C.C. (Oxford) 1588. (*Al. Oxon.*)

HIGGINS, FRANCIS. Adm. sizar (age 16) at ST JOHN'S, Mar. 25, 1704. S. of Richard, clerk. B. at Tonbridge, Kent. School, Tonbridge (Mr Roots). Matric. 1704; B.A. 1708–9. Ord. deacon (London) May 23; priest, Sept. 19, 1714. Probably C. of Farnborough, Kent, 1714.

HIGGINS, GEORGE. Matric. pens. from ST JOHN'S, Michs. 1570. Of Lancashire. B.A. 1574–5; M.A. 1578; B.D. 1585. Fellow, 1577.

HIGGINS, GEORGE. Matric. pens. from ST CATHARINE'S, Easter, 1634. One of these names, of All Saints', Chichester, scholar at Winchester in 1627.

HIGGINS or HYGENS, JOHN. Adm. sizar at PETERHOUSE, Mar. 23, 1641–2. Of London. School, St Paul's. Matric. 1642; B.A. 1645–6. Buried at Little St Mary's, Cambridge, Feb. 1647–8. (*T. A. Walker.*)

HIGGINS, JOHN. Adm. sizar at MAGDALENE, July 1, 1665. S. of Henry, of Wyke, Bradford, Yorks. Ord. deacon (York) *c.* 1666; priest, June, 1667. One of these names V. of Ferry Fryston, Yorks., 1684–90.

HIGGINS, JOHN. Adm. sizar at TRINITY, June 12, 1669. Matric. 1669; B.A. 1672–3; M.A. 1676. Perhaps Master of Aylesbury School, Bucks., during 1680.

HIGGONS, RICHARD. B.A. 1609 (Incorp. from Oxford). Of Salop, gent. Matric. from St John's College, Oxford, Mar. 22, 1604–5, age 15; B.A. (Oxford) 1608; M.A. 1611. Admon. V.C.C. (Oxford) June 2, 1626. (*Al. Oxon.*)

HIGGINS, ROWLAND. Matric. sizar from CHRIST'S, Dec. 1587.

HIGGONS, THOMAS. Matric. pens. from TRINITY, Easter, 1613; B.A. 1615–6; M.A. from Trinity Hall, 1619. Fellow of Trinity Hall, 1619–23. Incorp. at Oxford, 1619. Ord. priest (Norwich) 1623. R. of Drayton, Norfolk, 1623.

HIGGONS, THOMAS. M.A. from KING'S, 1715. S. of Richard, of North Newnton, Wilts. Matric. from Hart Hall, Oxford, July 9, 1701, age 16; B.A. (Merton) 1705–6. V. of Tilshead, Wilts., 1711. V. of Shrewton, 1715. (*Al. Oxon.*)

HIGGINS, ——. Adm. pens. at ST CATHARINE'S, 1695.

HIGGINSON, FRANCIS. Matric. sizar from ST JOHN'S, Michs. 1602. S. of John (1561), V. of Claybrook, Leics. Bapt. there, Aug. 6, 1586. B.A. from Jesus, 1609-10; M.A. 1613. Ord. deacon (York) Sept. 1614; priest, Dec. 1614. C. at Scrayingham, Yorks. R. of Barton-in-Fabis, Notts., 1615. V. of Claybrooke, Leics., 1615. Lecturer at St Nicholas, Leicester, 1617-29. Deprived for nonconformity. Went to New England, 1629, with his wife and eight children. 'Teacher' at Salem; salary £30 a year. Married at St Peter's, Nottingham, Jan. 8, 1615-6, Anna Herbert. Author of *New England's Plantation*. Died at Salem, Aug. 6, 1630, aged 43. (*D.N.B.*; *Felt*, 103; *Annals of Salem*; J. G. Bartlett.)

HIGGINSON, FRANCIS. Adm. sizar (age 18) at ST JOHN'S, July 1, 1678. S. of John, clerk, of Leicestershire (and grandson of Francis above). B. in New England. School, Sedbergh (Mr Wharton). Matric. 1679; B.A. 1681-2.

HIGGINSON, GEORGE. Matric. sizar from JESUS, Easter, 1614; B.A. 1617-8; M.A. 1621.

HIGGINSON, JOHN. Matric. pens. from TRINITY, 1561. B. 1564. B.A. 1564-5; M.A. 1568. V. of Claybrooke, Leics., 1571. Ord. priest (Peterb.) Dec. 22, 1572. Father of Francis (1602).

HIGGINSON, JOHN. Matric. pens. from ST JOHN'S, Easter, 1572.

HIGGINSON, JOHN. Adm. sizar (age 17) at TRINITY, June 30, 1719. S. of Joseph, of Peover, Cheshire. School, Peover (Mr Allen). Matric. 1719.

HIGGINSON, JOSHUA. Adm. sizar (age 17) at TRINITY, June 24, 1709. S. of Peter, of Wem, Salop. School, Wem (Mr Williams). Matric. 1709; B.A. 1714.

HIGGINSON, SAMUEL. Adm. sizar (age 17) at PEMBROKE, July 2, 1623. S. of John, of Anabury, near Coventry, husbandman. One of these names C. of Lower Peover, Cheshire, 1661-4.

HIGGINSON, THOMAS. Adm. pens. (age 18) at CHRIST'S, May 9, 1645. S. of Thomas. B. at Shockerley, Lancs. School, Winwick (Mr Pickering). Matric. 1645. Migrated to Oxford. Scholar of Brasenose, 1648; B.A. (Oxford) 1648. Perhaps V. of Church Minshull, Cheshire; ejected, 1662. (*Peile*, I. 495; *Al. Oxon.*)

HIGGINSON, TIMOTHY. Matric. pens. from CHRIST'S, 1595-6. Of Leicester. B.A. 1598-9; M.A. 1602. Fellow of St John's, 1602. (*Peile*, I. 217.)

HIGGINSON, TOBIAS. Matric. sizar from MAGDALENE, Easter, 1632; B.A. 1635-6; M.A. 1639.

HIGGS, CHRISTOPHER. Adm. sizar (age 17) at SIDNEY, June 23, 1679. 1st s. of Clement, physician, deceased, of Yorkshire. B. at Malton, Yorks. School, Malton (Mr Carteret). (*Vis. of Warws.*, 1682.)

HIGGES, GEORGE. M.A. 1600 (Incorp. from Oxford). Of Staffordshire. Matric. from Balliol College, May 2, 1581, age 17; B.A. (Oxford) 1583; M.A. 1599. Ord. priest (Coventry) Oct. 4, 1584. Perhaps C. of Chearsley, Bucks., in 1585.

HIGGES, GRIFFIN. M.A. 1623 (Incorp. from Oxford). S. of Griffin, of South Stoke, Oxon. B. there, 1589. School, Reading. Matric. from St John's, Oxford, July 4, 1609, age 18; B.A. (Oxford) 1610; M.A. 1615; B.D. 1625. Fellow of Merton, 1611. Proctor, 1622. Adm. at Leyden, Feb. 6, 1629-30. D.D. (Leyden) 1629-30. *Supp.* for incorp. at Oxford, 1629-30. Chaplain at the Hague for twelve years, to the Queen of Bohemia. R. of Gamlingay, Cambs., 1625. V. of Diddington, Hunts., 1626-30. R. of Cliffe-at-Hoo, Kent, 1630-45. Precentor of St David's, 1631-59. Dean of Lichfield, 1638. Author, theological. Died at South Stoke, Henley, Oxon., Dec. 16, 1659. Buried there. M.I. Will (P.C.C.) 1660. (*Al. Oxon.*; *D.N.B.*)

HIGGS, JOHN. Adm. pens. (age 18) at TRINITY, June 17, 1747. S. of John, of London. School, Westminster. Matric. 1747. Scholar, 1748; B.A. 1750-1; M.A. 1754; B.D. 1768. Fellow, 1753-5. Ord. deacon (Ely) Feb. 23; priest, Sept. 21, 1755. V. of Marsworth, Bucks., 1777-80. R. of Grundisburgh, Suffolk, 1780-1816. (*Al. Westmon.*, 341.)

HIGGES, NICHOLAS. B.D. 1600 (Incorp. from Oxford). Matric. from Merton College, Nov. 24, 1581; B.A. (Balliol) 1588; M.A. 1591; B.D. 1600; D.D. 1603. R. of High Ham, Somerset, 1606-31. Preb. of Wells, 1614-31. R. of Spaxton, Somerset, 1622-4. R. of North Cadbury, 1626-7. Died 1631. (*Al. Oxon.*)

HIGHAM, *see* HEIGHAM.

HIGHELORD, JOHN. Matric. pens. from TRINITY, *c.* 1592.

HIGHER or HYAR, GEORGE. Adm. sizar at TRINITY, Jan. 20, 1649-50. S. of George, citizen and grocer, of London. Matric. 1650. 'Grecian' from Christ's Hospital. Migrated to Caius. Scholar, 1650-6; B.A. 1653-4; M.A. 1657. Ord. deacon (Lincoln) June 8; priest, June 10, 1661. V. of Steeple Bumpstead, Essex, 1662-5. C. of Weathersfield, in 1662. Will (Cons. C. London) 1665-6. (*Venn*, I. 379; J. Ch. Smith.)

HIGHGATE, ROBERT. Adm. pens. (age 17) at CHRIST'S, May 14, 1684. S. of Nicholas. B. in London. School, Ware (Mr Burgoine). Matric. 1684. Resided till Michs. 1687. (*Peile*, II. 96.)

HIGHMORE, ROBERT. Adm. sizar at JESUS, Oct. 17, 1698. Of Dorset. S. of William (next), of Barnsley, Dorset, clerk. Matric. from Balliol College, Oxford, Nov. 22, 1699, age 17; B.A. (Magdalen Hall) 1703. R. of Winterbourne Anderstone, Dorset, 1708-10. Died 1710. (*Al. Oxon.*; *Hutchins*, I. 162.)

HIGHMORE, WILLIAM. M.A. from JESUS, 1685. S. of William, of Barnsley, Dorset, clerk. Matric. from Trinity College, Oxford, Apr. 2, 1666, age 16; B.A. (Oxford) 1669-70. R. of Winterbourne Zelston, Dorset, 1674-1707. R. of Winterbourne Anderstone, 1685-1707. Chaplain to the Earl of Shaftesbury. Buried at Winterbourne Zelston, Dec. 16, 1707. Father of Robert (above). (*Hutchins*, I. 337; F S. Hookaday.)

HIGNEY, JAMES. Adm. sizar (age 15) at CAIUS, July 7, 1629. S. of Timothy, burgess of Cambridge. Bapt. at Gt St Mary's, Nov. 20, 1614. School, Cambridge (Mr Shilbourn and Mr Winterton). Matric. 1629; Scholar, 1629-36; B.A. 1632-3; M.A. 1636. Fellow, 1636-7. Probably died 1637. (*Venn*, I. 291.)

HIGNEY, THOMAS. Adm. at KING'S, a scholar from Eton, 1504.

HIGSAW, ——. M.A. 1614 (on King's visit).

HIGSON, *see also* HICKSON.

HIGSON, GEORGE. Adm. sizar (age 17) at ST JOHN'S, Jan. 3, 1645-6. S. of William, minister, of Weston, Notts. B. at Stony Middleton, Derbs. School, Louth, Lincs. Matric. 1645-6.

HIGSON, SAMUEL. Matric. pens. from TRINITY, *c.* 1596; Scholar, 1599; B.A. 1599-1600; M.A. 1603. Fellow, 1602, as Hickson. Senior proctor, 1626-7. Buried in the College Chapel, Oct. 5, 1637. Will (V.C.C.) 1637.

HILARY, JOHN. Adm. pens. (age 18) at TRINITY, June 30, 1707. S. of John, of London. School, St Paul's. Matric. 1707; Scholar, 1708; B.A. 1710-1; M.A. 1741. Ord. deacon (London) May 27, 1711. Will of one of these names (P.C.C.) 1766; of Dulwich, Surrey, clerk.

HILARY, THOMAS. Adm. scholar at TRINITY HALL, Apr. 2, 1737. Of Yorkshire. Matric. 1737.

HILBERT, NICHOLAS. Adm. at KING'S (age 17) a scholar from Eton, Feb. 19, 1525-6. Left *c.* 1529. Of Yarmouth, Norfolk.

HILDERSHAM, ARTHUR. Matric. pens. from CHRIST'S, Michs. 1576. S. of Thomas, of Stetchworth, Cambs. B. there, Oct. 6, 1563. School, Saffron Walden, Essex (Mr Desborough). Scholar; B.A. 1580-1; M.A. 1584. Fellow of Trinity Hall, 1584. Lecturer at Ashby-de-la-Zouch (before ordination) 1587. V. there, 1593-1632. An active manager of the 'millenary' petition, 1604. Silenced by his bishop for nonconformity, 1605; restored, 1609. Imprisoned for three months for refusing the 'ex officio' oath, 1615. Returned to Ashby, 1625. Author, theological. Died Mar. 4, 1632. Will, Leicester. Father of Samuel (1609). (*Peile*, I. 139; *Warren*, 342; *D.N.B.*)

HILDERSHAM, NEHEMIAH. Adm. pens. at EMMANUEL, 1623. Matric. 1623; B.A. 1626-7.

HILDERSHAM, SAMUEL. Adm. pens. at EMMANUEL, May 6, 1609. S. of Arthur (1576), V. of Ashby-de-la-Zouch. Matric. 1609; Scholar; B.A. 1612-3; M.A. 1616; B.D. 1623. Fellow, 1618. Incorp. at Oxford, 1623. R. of West Felton, Salop, 1628-62, ejected. One of the Assembly of Divines. Died at Erdington, near Birmingham, Apr. 1674, aged 80. (*D.N.B.*; *Calamy*, II. 327.)

HILDERSHAM, THOMAS. Matric. pens. from PEMBROKE, Michs. 1575.

HILDESLEY, JOHN. Adm. pens. (age 13) at MAGDALENE, Sept. 27, 1673. S. of Mark, Esq. (next), of Surbiton, Surrey. School, Brentwood. Matric. 1674. Adm. at Lincoln's Inn, Aug. 8, 1676, as s. and h. of Mark, of Lincoln's Inn, Esq. (*Vis. of Surrey*, 1662.)

HILDESLEY, MARK. Adm. pens. at EMMANUEL, Nov. 20, 1645. S. and h. of Mark, of London, gent. Scholar of Corpus Christi, Oxford, by visitors' mandate, 1649; B.A. (Cambridge) 1650. Fellow of New College, Oxford, 1650. Adm. at Lincoln's Inn, Dec. 30, 1648. Barrister-at-law, 1656. Father of the above. (*Al. Oxon.*; *Vis. of Surrey*, 1662.)

HILDESLEY, MARK. Adm. pens. (age 18) at TRINITY, Mar. 29, 1717. S. of Mark, R. of Witton, Hunts. B. at Murston, Kent, Dec. 9, 1698. School, Charterhouse. Matric. 1717; Scholar, 1718; B.A. 1720-1; M.A. 1724. Fellow, 1723. D.D. (Lambeth) 1755. Ord. deacon (Lincoln) Sept. 23, 1722; priest, Mar. 10, 1722-3. Nominated preacher at Whitehall, 1725. V. of Hitchin, Herts., 1731-55. Chaplain to Henry St John, Lord Bolingbroke, 1734. R. of Holwell, Beds., 1735-67. Preb. of Lincoln, 1754-72. Bishop of Sodor and Man, 1755-72. Master of Sherburn Hospital, Durham, 1767-72. Promoted the translation of the Bible and Prayer Book into the Manx language. Died Dec. 7, 1772, at Bishop's Court, Isle of Man. (*D.N.B.*; G. *Mag.*)

HILDESLEY, WILLIAM. Adm. at KING'S, a scholar from Eton, 1676. B. at Stepney, Middlesex. Matric. Easter, 1677. Died, as student, of small-pox, Aug. 1, 1678.

HILDRETH, CHRISTOPHER. Matric. sizar from CHRIST'S, 1613; B.A. 1616-7. Licensed to teach in the parish of Leake, Yorks., Apr. 30, 1619. (M. H. Peacock.)

HILDYARD or HYLLIARD, CHRISTOPHER. Matric. pens. from ST JOHN'S, Michs. 1584. 1st s. of Richard, of Routh, Yorks. Adm. at the Inner Temple, 1586. Of Winestead, Yorks. M.P. for Hedon, 1588-9, 1593, 1597-8, 1601, 1604-11, 1624-5, 1626, 1628-9; for Beverley, 1620-2. High Sheriff of Yorks., 1595, 1613. Knighted, Apr. 17, 1603. Member of the High Commission of York. Married Elizabeth, dau. of Henry Welby, of Goxhill, Lincs. Buried at Winestead, Nov. 23, 1634. Will, York. Father of Christopher (1633) and Henry (1626). (Foster's *Yorks. Pedigrees*; H. M. Wood; A. B. Beaven.)

HELLYARD, CHRISTOPHER. Matric. Fell.-Com. from TRINITY, Easter, 1618. Probably s. and h. of Robert, of Pulford, Durham. Bapt. Sept. 24, 1602. Buried Nov. 29, 1675. (M. H. Peacock.)

HILLIARD, CHRISTOPHER. Matric. Fell.-Com. from TRINITY, Easter, 1633. Doubtless 3rd s. of Sir Christopher (1584), of Winestead, Yorks. B. Sept. 10, 1615. Adm. at the Inner Temple, 1634. Barrister (?1660). Recorder of Hedon, Yorks. Antiquary and friend of Thoresby. Died May, 1694. Buried at St Mary, Castlegate, York. Brother of Henry (1626).

HILDYARD, CHRISTOPHER. Adm. pens. (age 16) at PETERHOUSE, June 10, 1653. Of Yorkshire. Probably s. of Leonard, of Skeffling, Yorks. School, Lund, Yorks. Matric. 1655; Scholar; B.A. 1656-7; M.A. 1661 (*Lit. Reg.*). R. of Routh, Yorks., 1661-1712. Buried there, May 19, 1712. (*Vis. of Yorks*, 1665; Poulson, *Holderness*, II. 498; *T. A. Walker*.)

HILDYARD or HILLIARD, CHRISTOPHER. Adm. pens. (age 17) at PETERHOUSE, July 5, 1686. Of Winestead, Yorks. Doubtless s. of Christopher (above), R. of Routh. B. Nov. 8, 1668. School, Beverley Parks, Yorks. Scholar, 1686; Matric. 1688; B.A. 1689-90. Ord. deacon (York) June 15, 1690; priest (Lincoln) May 22, 1692. C. of West Rasen, Lincs. R. of Claxby, 1693. V. of Usselby. V. of North Willingham. R. of Winestead, Yorks., 1711-22. R. of Rowley, 1715-34. Buried at Rowley, Sept. 24, 1734. Father of the next.

HILDEYARD, CHRISTOPHER. Adm. sizar (age 18) at MAGDALENE, 1714. S. of Christopher (above). B. at Claxby, Lincs. School, Beverley. Matric. 1715; M.A. (Edinburgh) 1722. R. of Winestead, Yorks., 1722-55. V. of Grasby, Lincs., 1722. Married Mary Isabel, dau. of Simon Empringham, of Kettleby Thorpe, Lincs.

HYLIARD, EDWARD. Matric. Fell.-Com. from TRINITY HALL, Easter, 1661. S. of Henry (1626), of Winestead and East Horsley, Surrey. M.A. 1663. Adm. at the Inner Temple, 1663. Barrister-at-law, 1673. Judge in Barbadoes. Married Mary, dau. of David Stokes, D.D., canon of Windsor. Died in Barbadoes, July, 1703. Brother of Philip (1661). (Poulson, *Holderness*, II. 467; M. H. Peacock.)

HILLIARD, EZECHIEL. B.A. from PETERHOUSE, 1573-4; M.A. 1577. Fellow, 1577. Obtained leave for two years' travel, Oct. 1592. Ord. deacon and priest (Peterb.) June 9, 1595. Senior proctor, 1596-7. Fellowship resigned on acceptance of a benefice, 1599. Will (Exeter) 1614; V. of Stoke Climsland. (*T. A. Walker*.)

HILDEYARD, FRANCIS. Adm. pens. (age 15) at PEMBROKE, July 18, 1683. S. of John (1656), of Cawston, Norfolk. Matric. 1684; B.A. 1687-8. Brother of John (1679-80).

HILLIARD, HENRY. Matric. pens. from TRINITY, Michs. 1602. Of Yorkshire. Probably s. of William, bencher of the Inner Temple and recorder of York. Bapt. at Beverley, Jan. 2, 1585-6. Adm. at the Inner Temple, 1603.

HILDYARD, HENRY. Matric. Fell.-Com. from TRINITY, Michs. 1626. Doubtless 1st s. of Christopher (1584), of Winestead, Yorks. Bapt. there, Feb. 1, 1609-10. Of Winestead, Yorks. and East Horsley, Surrey. Royalist sufferer. M.P. for Hedon, 1660. Married Lady Anne Leake, dau. of Francis, Earl of Scarborough. Died Jan. 1674. Will proved, Jan. 15, 1674. Brother of Christopher (1633). (Burke, *L.G.*; Poulson, *Holderness*, II. 467.)

HILDEYARD, HENRY. Adm. Fell.-Com. at TRINITY HALL, Apr. 26, 1701. S. of Philip (1661), of East Horsley, Surrey, Esq. B. at East Horsley, Aug. 29, 1684. Adm. at the Inner Temple, Dec. 5, 1702. Of Goxhill, Lincs., Esq. J.P. Married, at Barton St Mary's, Apr. 23, 1706, Frances, dau. of William Long, of Barton-on-Humber. Died Sept. 16, 1722. Buried at Goxhill. (Burke, *L.G.*; M. H. Peacock.)

HILLIARD, JOHN. Matric. sizar from MAGDALENE, Easter, 1571.

HILDYARD, JOHN. Adm. pens. at TRINITY, May 14, 1656. Of Yorkshire. S. of Christopher, of Ottringham, Yorks. School, Westminster. Scholar, 1656; Matric. 1659. Migrated to Trinity Hall. LL.B. 1663; LL.D. 1669. Ord. deacon and priest (Lincoln) Dec. 23, 1660. R. of Swannington, Norfolk, 1662-1703. R. of Cawston, 1675. Preb. of Norwich, 1683-1703. Chancellor of the diocese of Norwich. Father of the next, and of Francis (1683).

HILDEYARD, JOHN. Adm. pens. (age 17) at PEMBROKE, Mar. 23, 1679-80. S. of John (above), LL.D., R. of Cawston, Norfolk. Matric. 1680. Brother of Francis (1683).

HILLIARDS or HILLYARD, LAURENCE. Adm. sizar (age 18) at ST JOHN'S, Mar. 25, 1714. S. of Joseph, deceased. B. at Heversham, Westmorland. School, Kirby (Mr Gibson). Matric. 1714. Migrated to Christ's, May 5, 1715. B.A. 1717-8. P.C. of Hornby, Lancs., 1718. (*Peile*, II. 187.)

HYLIARD, PHILIP. Matric. pens. from TRINITY HALL, Easter, 1661. Doubtless 4th s. of Henry (1626). M.A. 1663. Of East Horsley, Surrey. Chamberlain of the Exchequer. Married Elizabeth, dau. of Sir Francis Vincent, Bart. Buried at East Horsley, May 1, 1693. Brother of Edward (1661), father of Henry (1701). (Burke, *L.G.*)

HILDYARD, RICHARD. B.D. 1532. Perhaps s. of Peter. D.D. 1534. Fellow of ST JOHN'S, 1524. M.A. of Oxford. Chaplain to Bishop Tunstall. R. of Barmston and Winestead, Yorks., in 1525-6. R. of Norton, Durham, 1538-9. Important actor in the Pilgrimage of Grace. Having advised the religious houses not to surrender, he fled to Scotland, where he was supported by Cardinal Beaton. A pensioner of the Cardinal, at St Andrew's, 1543. (*Cooper*, I. 534.)

HYLLYARD, Sir ROBERT, Bart. Adm. nobleman (age 18) at TRINITY, June 13, 1688. S. of Christopher, of Winestead, in Holderness, Yorks. School, Hull (Mr Pell). Matric. 1689, as Hildyard. Succeeded his grandfather, as 2nd Bart., Mar. 7, 1684-5. M.P. for Hedon, 1701-2. Died Nov. 1729. Buried at Winestead. Brother of William (1695). (Burke, *Ext. Bart.*; *G.E.C.*)

HILDYARD, ROBERT. Adm. Fell.-Com. (age 14) at PETERHOUSE, Apr. 9, 1731. Of Winestead, Yorks. S. of William (1695), R. of Rowley, Yorks. Bapt. at York, July 15, 1716. Matric. 1731. Succeeded as 3rd Bart., 1729. M.P. for Gt Bedwyn, 1754-61. Died at Gilling, Yorks., Feb. 1, 1781. (Burke, *Ext. Bart.*; *T. A. Walker*, 262; *G.E.C.*)

HILLIARD, SAMUEL. M.A. from PEMBROKE, 1700. S. of Samuel, of St Saviour's, Southwark, scrivener. B. June 3, 1676. Matric. from University College, Oxford, Aug. 25, 1693, age 16; B.A. (Trinity, Oxford) 1697. Lecturer at St Mary, Lothbury, 1698. Preb. of Lincoln, 1704. R. of Stifford, Essex, 1709-42. R. of Rainham, 1718-42. Buried at Stifford, Mar. 26, 1742. Will (Consist. C. London) 1742. (*Al. Oxon.*; J. Ch. Smith.)

HYLYARD, WILLIAM. Matric. pens. from ST JOHN'S, Easter, 1557. Probably s. of Martin, of Winestead, Yorks. Recorder of York. M.P. for York, 1586-7. Buried at St Michael Belfry, York, Aug. 20, 1608. (M. H. Peacock.)

HILLYARD, WILLIAM. Matric. pens. from TRINITY, c. 1591. Perhaps s. and h. of William, of Morne, bencher of the Inner Temple; adm. there, 1593. Perhaps s. of the above. B. July 11, 1577. Of Bishop Wilton, Yorks. Knighted, July 9, 1603. Died Oct. 6, 1632. M.I. at Bishop Wilton. (M. H. Peacock.)

HILDYARD, WILLIAM. Adm. pens. (age 16) at SIDNEY, June 26, 1695. S. of Christopher, Esq. B. at Hull, Yorks., 1679. School, Hull (Mr Pell). Matric. 1698; B.A. 1698-9; M.A. 1702. Ord. deacon (York) June, 1704; priest, 1704. R. of Rowley, Yorks., 1704-15. Married Nancy, dau. of Thomas Croft, of Stillington, 1712. His s. Robert (1731), succeeded as Bart., 1729. Buried at Rowley, Nov. 10, 1715. Brother of Robert (1688). (Burke, *Ext. Bart*; *G.E.C.*)

HILDYARD, ——. Adm. Fell.-Com. at TRINITY, 1654.

HILKSTON, ——. D.Civ.L. 1488-9.

HILL, ANTHONY. Matric. sizar from CHRIST'S, Easter, 1576; B.A. 1579–80. Ord. deacon and priest (Lincoln) Oct. 27, 1580. R. of Blyborough, Lincs., 1582–93. V. of Billingborough, 1592–1621. Described, in 1611, as 'M.A., non-resident, living in Ireland.' Admon. (Lincoln) 1621. (*Lib. Cler.*; *Peile*, I. 173.)

HILL, ANTHONY. M.A. from CLARE, 1668. S. of William, of Moreton, Staffs. Matric. from Lincoln College, Oxford, Feb. 21, 1661–2, age 18; B.A. (Oxford) 1665. R. of Little Gidding and Steeple Gidding, Hunts., 1674–91. Died 1691. Father of Josiah (1684). (*Al. Oxon.*)

HILL, ARNOLD. Adm. pens. at EMMANUEL, May 7, 1608. Doubtless 2nd s. of Martin, R. of Asfordby, Leics. Matric. 1608. Of Barrow-upon-Soar. Living, 1647. Brother of Francis (1608), Percival (1613) and John (1626). (*Genealogist*, N.S., XV. 103.)

HILL, AUGUSTINE. Matric. sizar from TRINITY, Lent, 1615–6; B.A. 1618–9; M.A. 1622. Ord. deacon (Peterb.) Sept. 19; priest, Sept. 20, 1619. V. of Horton, Northants., 1623. V. of Bengeo, Herts., 1625–9. R. of Dengie, Essex, 1630–60. Died 1660. Will (Comm. C. Essex) 1660.

HILL, BEVILL. Matric. pens. from TRINITY, Michs. 1629. 1st s. of Thomas, of Lewisham, Kent. Age 7 in 1619. Will (P.C.C.) 1637. (*Vis. of Kent.*)

HILL, CHRISTOPHER. Scholar of CHRIST'S, 1531–2; B.A. 1531–2. Probably R. of Ufford, Suffolk, 1531. One of these names R. f Alphamstone, Essex, 1538–57. V. of Wakering Magna, aso B.D., 1545. R. of Belchamp-Otton, 1548. Deprived, 1565. (J. Ch. Smith.)

HILL, CHRISTOPHER. Adm. sizar (age 17) at SIDNEY, May 26, 1635. S. of Christopher, citizen of London. B. there. Schools, Oakham (Mr Montagu) and Mercers', London. Matric. 1635; B.A. 1638–9; M.A. 1642. Admon. (Exeter) 1677, of one of these names; of Michaelstow, Cornwall, clerk.

HILL, CHRISTOPHER. Adm. pens. at JESUS, July 2, 1680. Of Staffordshire. Matric. 1680; B.A. 1683–4.

HILLS, DANIEL. Matric. pens. from CHRIST'S, Mar. 1610–1.

HILL, DANIEL. M.A. 1702 (Incorp. from Oxford). S. of Daniel, of Salisbury. School, Westminster. Matric. from Christ Church, Oxford, July 13, 1666, age 19; B.A. (Oxford) 1670; M.A. 1673; D.D. (Lambeth) 1720. R. of Southfleet, Kent, 1679–1729. Preb. of Rochester, 1684–1729. R. of St Margaret's, Rochester, 1691–1729. Head Master of Faversham School. Married, at Rochester Cathedral, May 28, 1713, Hester Wilbraham, widow. Died June 25, 1729. Buried in Rochester Cathedral. Father of Thomas (1701). (*Al. Oxon.*; H. G. Harrison.)

HILLS, EDMUND. M.A. 1617 (Incorp. from Oxford). Of Oxfordshire, gent. Matric. from Magdalen Hall, June 16, 1610, g 15; B.A. (Oxford) 1613; M.A. 1616. One of these namesaVe of West Farleigh, Kent, 1640.

HILL or HILLS, EDWARD. Matric. pens. from JESUS, Easter, 1603; B.A. from Trinity, 1607–8; M.A. 1611; B.D. 1618. Fellow, 1610. Incorp. at Oxford, 1611. Ord. deacon (Peterb.) Sept. 9, 1615; perhaps priest (Lincoln) Feb. 25, 1615–6. One Edward Hills, R. of Ludborough, Lincs., 1615–27. Preb. of Lincoln, 1626–7.

HILL, EDWARD. Matric. sizar from CHRIST'S, July, 1607. Probably s. of Richard. B.A. 1610–1; M.A. 1614. Probably V. of Huddersfield, Yorks., 1619–46. R. of Crofton, near Wakefield, c. 1649, till 1662. Died 1669, aged 79. (*Peile*, I. 265; *Duc. Leod.*, 209.)

HILL or HILLES, EDWARD. Adm. sizar at SIDNEY, July, 1624. B. at Sheffield. School, Sheffield. Matric. 1624; B.A. 1627–8, as Hilles.

HILL, EDWARD. Adm. Fell.-Com. at EMMANUEL, July 3, 1658. Of Northamptonshire. Doubtless s. and h. of John (1626), V. of Higham Ferrers. B. at Higham, Mar. 12, 1635. Of Rothwell. Married Susanna, dau. of John Maunsell, of Thorpe Malsor, Northants. Died Aug. 1, 1705, aged 69. Probably father of John (1683), Nathaniel (1690), Robert (1691) and Theophilus (1700). (*Genealogist*, N.S., XV. 235.)

HILL, EDWARD. Adm. at CORPUS CHRISTI, 1663. Of Suffolk. Matric. 1663; B.A. 1666–7; M.A. 1670. One of these names R. of Besselsleigh, Berks. Will (P.C.C.) 1703.

HILL, FRANCIS. Adm. pens. at EMMANUEL, May 7, 1608. 3rd s. of Martin, R. of Asfordby, Leics. Matric. 1608; B.A. 1611–2; M.A. 1615. Ord. deacon (Peterb.) Dec. 22; priest, Dec. 23, 1616. R. of Asfordby, 1621. Perhaps R. of Trowell, Notts., 1626 (but *see Al. Oxon.* for a contemporary). Died May 10, 1666. Brother of Arnold (1608), Percival (1613) and John (1626). (*Nichols*, III. 18; *Genealogist*, N.S., XV. 232.)

HILL, FRANCIS. Adm. sizar (age 17) at ST JOHN'S, June 7, 1677. S. of Francis, husbandman, of Farnsfield, Notts. B. at Hartington, Derbs. School, Southwell (Mr Myres). Migrated to Magdalene, June 3, 1680. B.A. 1680–1. Ord. deacon (York) May, 1681. Brother of Hugh (1667).

HILL, GEORGE. Adm. sizar at QUEENS', Feb. 1, 1577–8. Of Suffolk.

HILL, GEORGE. Matric. sizar from TRINITY, Easter, 1608; B.A. 1611–2. Ord. deacon (York) Mar. 1613–4; priest, Sept. 1614.

HILLS, GEORGE. B.A. from TRINITY, 1626–7.

HILL, GEORGE. Adm. sizar at EMMANUEL, Apr. 10, 1672. Of Staffordshire. Matric. 1672–3; B.A. 1675–6. Ord. deacon (London) Feb. 24, 1677–8. R. of Clippesby, Norfolk, 1719–21. Died Oct. 22, 1721, aged 66.

HILL, GEORGE. Adm. Fell.-Com. at CLARE, June 27, 1733. Doubtless 1st s. of Nathaniel (1690). B. at Waddington, Lincs., c. 1716. Adm. at the Middle Temple, Jan. 5, 1733–4. Barrister, 1741. Of Lincoln's Inn, 1765. Serjeant-at-law and King's serjeant, 1772. Married Anne Barbara, dau. of Thomas Medlycott, of Cottingham, Northants. Died Feb. 21, 1808. Buried at Rothwell, Northants. Brother of John (1734–5). (*D.N.B.*; *Genealogist*, XV. 239.)

HILL, GILBERT. Adm. sizar at CLARE, Dec. 24, 1705. B. in London. Matric. 1706. Exhibitioner from Charterhouse.

HILL, HARRYE. Matric. sizar from TRINITY, Easter, 1603.

HILLS, HEIGHAM. Matric. pens. from QUEENS', Michs. 1628. Of Cambridgeshire. B.A. 1631; M.A. 1635; B.D. 1643. Fellow, 1635–44 (ejected). Ord. deacon (Peterb.) June 4, 1637; priest, Dec. 22, 1639.

HILL, HENRY. Adm. Fell.-Com. at QUEENS', May 29, 1587. Of London. Perhaps adm. at the Inner Temple, 1588.

HILLS, HENRY. Matric. sizar from ST JOHN'S, Easter, 1612; B.A. 1615–6. One of these names (B.A.), R. of Dymchurch, Kent, 1619–25.

HILL, HENRY. Matric. sizar from CORPUS CHRISTI, Easter, 1633; B.A. 1636–7; M.A. 1640. Ord. deacon (Norwich) Sept. 25, 1642, age 26; C. of Thorndon, Norfolk; priest, Dec. 18, 1642. Perhaps R. of Dunton, Bucks., 1662–3.

HILL or HILLS, HENRY. Adm. sizar at QUEENS', June 29, 1670. Of Leicestershire. Matric. 1670; B.A. 1673–4.

HILL, HENRY. Adm. pens. (age 18) at CAIUS, June 4, 1734. 2nd s. of Thomas (1696–7), D.D., R. of Buxhall, Suffolk. B. there. School, Bury (private; Mr Thorp) and public (Mr Kynnesman). Matric. 1734; Scholar, 1734–9; B.A. 1737–8; M.A. 1751; D.D. 1763. Ord. deacon (Norwich) Dec. 24, 1738, as C. of Buxhall, Suffolk; priest, Dec. 21, 1740, as C. of Brettenham. R. of Tostock, Suffolk, 1741; of Buxhall, 1743–75. Died Nov. 8, 1775. Buried at Buxhall. M.I. to him and wife Susan. Will, P.C.C. Brother of Martin (1737). (*Venn*, II. 39.)

HILLS, HERCULES. Adm. sizar (age 16) at SIDNEY, Apr. 2, 1644. S. of Hercules, carpenter. B. at Bolton, Kent. Schools, Faversham (Mr Billingsley) and Ashford (Mr Piggot). Matric. 1644. Migrated to Queens', Aug. 6, 1644.

HILL or HILLS, HUGH. Matric. pens. from ST JOHN'S, Michs. 1552. Of Staffordshire. B.A. 1555–6; M.A. 1559. Fellow, 1556. Perhaps Preb. of Lichfield, 1568–81.

HILL, HUGH. Adm. sizar (age 19) at SIDNEY, May, 1667. S. of Francis, of Hartington, Derbs. School, Sheffield. Matric. 1667; B.A. 1670–1. Ord. priest (York) June, 1671. Brother of Francis (1677).

HILL, HUMPHREY. Matric. sizar from ST JOHN'S, Lent, 1579–80; B.A. 1583–4; M.A. 1587. Ord. deacon and priest (Lincoln) July 25, 1592. R. of Tingrith, Beds., 1606.

HILL, JAMES. Matric. pens. from TRINITY, Michs. 1548.

HILL, JAMES. Matric. pens. from ST JOHN'S, Michs. 1565. Of Lancashire. School, Eton. B.A. 1568–9; M.A. 1572; B.D. 1579. Fellow, 1572. Incorp. at Oxford, 1580. Acted in the tragedy of *Richard III*, by Dr Legge, 1570. V. of Braintree, x, 1585. Will (Cons. C. London) 1608. (*Cooper*, II. [illegible]

HYLL, JAMES. Matric. sizar from TRINITY, Easter, 1586; Scholar, 1588; B.A. 1590–1; M.A. 1594. V. of Over, Cambs., 1594.

HILL, JAMES. Adm. sizar (age 22) at MAGDALENE, Apr. 29, 1659. S. of James, of Sterndale, Derbs. School, Sheffield. Matric. 1659; B.A. 1663–4.

HILL, JAMES. Adm. sizar (age 16) at SIDNEY, Apr. 13, 1667. S. of John, yeoman, of Titchmarsh, Northants. Schools, Oundle and Uppingham. Brother of John (1658).

HILL, JAMES. Adm. pens. (age 18) at PEMBROKE, July 5, 1670. S. of Robert, gent. B. at Stifford, Essex. Exhibitioner from Charterhouse. Matric. 1670.

HILLS, JOEL. Adm. pens. (age 15) at TRINITY, Apr. 26, 1676. S. of Thomas. B. at Newington, Kent. School, Wye (Mr John Paris).

HILL or ATTEHILL, JOHN. Fellow of GONVILLE HALL, till 1455, and perhaps later. Proctor, 1430–1. Ord. deacon (Norwich) Jan. 11, 1431–2; priest, Apr. 1432. Died before Oct. 2, 1461. (*Venn*, I. 7.)

HILL, JOHN. B.Can.L. 1487–8. V. of itham, Essex, 1491. R. of Finchley, Middlesex, 1492. PreWof St Paul's, 1493–6. R. of South Ockendon, Essex, 1493. V. of Leyton, 1494.

HILL, JOHN. B.A. 1490–1; M.A. 1494–5.

HILL, JOHN. Scholar of QUEENS', 1531–4.

HYLLS, JOHN. Matric. sizar from JESUS, Michs. 1549 (*impubes*).

HILL, JOHN. Matric. pens. from TRINITY, Easter, 1577; B.A. 1581–2; M.A. 1585. Preacher at St Mary's, Bury St Edmunds, till 1590. Suspended for nonconformity. (*Cooper*, II. 99.)

HILL, JOHN. Matric. sizar from TRINITY, Easter, 1578.

HILLS, JOHN. Matric. sizar from JESUS, Michs. 1579. B. at Fulbourn, Cambs. B.A. 1582–3; M.A. from St Catharine's, 1586; B.D. from Jesus, 1593; D.D. 1605. Fellow of St Catharine's. Master, 1607–26. Vice-Chancellor, 1616–7. Ord. priest (Peterb.) May 20, 1585. R. of Fulbourn St Vigors, Cambs., 1591. Preb. of Ely, 1601–26. Preb. of Lincoln, 1609–26. Archdeacon of Stow, 1610–2; and of Lincoln, 1612–26. Died Sept. 26, 1626. Buried at Horseheath, Cambs. Will proved (V.C.C.) 1626. (*Hist. of St Catharine's*, 107; A. Gray.)

HILLS, JOHN. Matric. sizar from CORPUS CHRISTI, Michs. 1580; B.A. 1583–4.

HILL, JOHN. Matric. sizar from PEMBROKE, Lent, 1584–5; B.A. from Jesus, 1587–8.

HILL, JOHN. Matric. sizar from KING'S, *c.* 1597.

HILL, JOHN. Matric. sizar from CORPUS CHRISTI, Lent, 1597–8. Of Norfolk. B.A. 1601–2; M.A. 1605. Ord. deacon and priest (Norwich) May 26, 1605, age 24. R. of Braisworth, Suffolk. Perhaps R. of Hemley, Suffolk, 1606–27. One of these names R. of Thorndon, Suffolk, 1615–57, sequestered.

HILLS or HILL, JOHN. Matric. pens. from CHRIST'S, Easter, 1605. S. of Daniel, merchant, of London. B.A. 1608–9; M.A. 1612. Incorp. t Oxford, 1610. Ord. deacon (Peterb.) Sept. 24; priest, Sept. 25, 1615. R. of St Michael Queenhithe, London, 1618–42, sequestered. R. of Eastwick, Herts., 1622–43. As chaplain to the Bishop of Exeter he had dispensation to hold the two, 1622. Will (P.C.C.) 1658; as of Gt Parndon, Essex. (*Peile*, I. 252; *Vis. of London*, 1634; J. Ch. Smith.)

HILL, JOHN. B.A. from TRINITY, 1605–6. Probably ord. deacon (York) Dec. 1612, as 'B.A. of Trinity College.'

HILL, JOHN. Adm. sizar at EMMANUEL, May 20, 1606. Matric. 1606; Scholar; B.A. 1609–10.

HILL or HILLS, JOHN. Adm. pens. at EMMANUEL, Mar. 2, 1608–9. Matric. 1609; Scholar; B.A. 1612–3; M.A. 1616. Licensed to practise medicine, 1621. One of these names ('M.A.'), R. of Coveney, Cambs., 1617–40.

HILL, JOHN. Adm. sizar at EMMANUEL, June, 1614; Scholar; B.A. 1617–8; M.A. 1621. Ord. deacon (Peterb.) Mar. 26; priest, Mar. 27, 1630. Will of one of these names (P.C.C.) 1673; of Edmonton, Middlesex, clerk.

HILL or HILLS, JOHN. Matric. . from CORPUS CHRISTI, Easter, 1616. Of Suffolk. B.A.pe619–20.

HILLS, JOHN. Matric. pens. from ST CATHARINE'S, Michs. 1622; B.A. 1624.

HILL or HILLS, JOHN. Adm. sizar at JESUS, June 3, 1626. S. of Martin, R. of Asfordby, Leics. Matric. 1626; B.A. 1629–30; M.A. 1633. V. of Higham Ferrers, Northants., 1631–5. R. of HoldenPy, 1635–55; ejected, but reinstated, 1660–9: V. of Rothwell, 1639–41, 1660–9. V. of St Sepulchre, Northampton, 1641–2. Married, at Desborough, Northants. July 25, 1626, Susanna, dau. of Edward Lamb, of Rothwell. His wife inherited the manor of Rothwell. Buried at Rothwell, Apr. 24, 1669, as Dr of Physic. Father of Edward (1658), brother of Arnold (1608), Francis (1608) and Percival (1613). (H. I. Longden.)

HILL, JOHN. Matric. pens. from MAGDALENE, Lent, 1626–7.

HILL, JOHN. Adm. sizar at CORPUS CHRISTI, 1627. Of Suffolk. Matric. Easter, 1628; B.A. 1630–1; M.A. 1634. Ord. deacon (Norwich) Sept. 21; priest, Dec. 21, 1634. V. of Thorpe by Ixworth, Suffolk, 1660–84. Died 1684, aged 73. M.I. at Ixworth. (Le Neve, *Mon.*, III. 154.)

HILL or HILLS, JOHN. Matric. sizar from QUEENS', Michs. 1628. Of Nottinghamshire. B.A. 1632–3; M.A. 1636. Ord. deacon (Peterb.) June 11; priest, Sept. 25, 1636. One of these names V. of Dunholme, Lincs., 1642.

HILL, JOHN. Adm. Fell.-Com. from ST CATHARINE'S, 1628. Perhaps s. and h. of Edward, of Cosby, Leics., gent.; adm. at Gray's Inn, Apr. 14, 1632. Age 51 in 1663. (*Staffs. Pedigrees.*)

HILL, JOHN. Adm. pens. (age 16) at CAIUS, May 16, 1634. S. of Joseph (1601), preb. of Lichfield. B. in London. Matric. 1634.

HILL or HILLS, JOHN. Matric. sizar from KING'S, Easter, 1637; B.A. 1640–1.

HILL, JOHN. M.A. from JESUS, 1642. S. of Richard, of Combe Florey, Somerset, clerk. Matric. from Wadham College, Oxford, June 30, 1637, age 18; B.A. (Oxford) 1640. R. of Combe Florey, Somerset, 1645 and 1660–87. Died 1687.

HILL, JOHN. Matric. pens. from ST CATHARINE'S, Easter, 1644; B.A. 1647–8; M.A. (Oxford) 1651; M.B. and M.D. (Oxford) 1659. Fellow of All Souls, 1649. Candidate R.C.P., 1660. Will (P.C.C.) 1661. (*Al. Oxon.*)

HILL or HILLS, JOHN. Adm. sizar (age 19) at SIDNEY, May 18, 1658. S. of John, farmer. B. at Titchmarsh, Northants. School, Oundle. Matric. 1658; B.A. 1661–2; M.A. 1665. One of these names ord. priest (Oxford) Mar. 15, 1662–3; C. of Gt Samford, Essex, in 1664. Brother of James (1667).

HILL, JOHN. Adm. sizar at TRINITY, Nov. 19, 1659. Matric. 1660; B.A. 1663–4; M.A. 1668. Subscribed for deacon's orders (London) May 19, 1665. C. of Wrotham, Kent.

HILL, JOHN. Matric. pens. from ST CATHARINE'S, Easter, 1663; B.A. 1665–6.

HILL, JOHN. Matric. sizar from CAIUS, Michs. 1664. Of Lincolnshire. Scholar, 1665–7; B.A. 1666–7; M.A. 1670. Ord. deacon (Lincoln) Feb. 16, 1667–8, as C. of Broxbourne, Herts.; priest, May 17, 1668. V. of Mutford, Suffolk, 1681–1701. Died *c.* 1701. (*Venn*, I. 419.)

HILL, JOHN. Adm. pens. (age 16) at PEMBROKE, May 2, 1666. S. of Joseph, of Nottingham, druggist. Matric. 1667.

HILL, JOHN. Adm. sizar (age 17) at PETERHOUSE, June 17, 1670. Of Yorkshire. School, Tadcaster. Migrated to Emmanuel. Matric. there, 1673; B.A. 1673–4. Ord. deacon (York) June, 1674.

HILL, JOHN. Adm. scholar (age 17) at SIDNEY, Jan. 2, 1671–2. S. of John, gent. B. at York. Schools, Thornton, Yorks. (Mr Grey) and Pickering (Mr Singleton).

HILL or HILLS, JOHN. Adm. sizar (age 18) at JESUS, May 6, 1674. Of Lancashire. Matric. 1674; Scholar, 1676; B.A. 1677–8; M.A. 1681. Probably Incorp. at Oxford, 1678. One of these names (M.A.), R. of Benacre, Suffolk, 1690.

HILL, JOHN. Adm. pens. ('age 24') at ST JOHN'S, July 6, 1675. S. of Robert, deceased, of St Nicholas Acons, London. B. there. Bapt. Dec. 25, 1645. Matric. 1677–8; B.A. 1678–9. Ord. deacon and priest (Gloucester) May 31, 1678.

HILL, JOHN. Adm. pens. at CHRIST'S, June 22, 1681. B. at Isleworth, Middlesex. Bapt. there, Feb. 8, 1664–5. Adm. at the Inner Temple, Jan. 7, 1683–4, as s. and h. of Roland, of London, merchant, deceased. (*Peile*, II. 83; J. Ch. Smith.)

HILL, JOHN. Adm. Fell.-Com. (age 16) at SIDNEY, Apr. 17, 1683. 1st s. of Edward (? 1658), Esq. B. at Rothwell, Northants. School, Kettering (Mr Fowler). Matric. 1683. Died unmarried and before his father, Nov. 16, 1701. Buried at Rothwell. Brother of Nathaniel (1690), Robert (1691) and Theophilus (1700). (*Genealogist*, N.S., XV. 235.)

HILL, JOHN. M.A. 1698 (Incorp. from Oxford). S. of J., of 'Pottum, Llac' (? Porth din Lleyn), Carnarvonshire, gent. Matric. from Jesus College, Oxford, Mar. 19, 1691–2, age 15; B.A. (Oxford) 1695; M.A. 1698. (*Al. Oxon.*)

HILL, JOHN. Adm. sizar at EMMANUEL, July 8, 1709. Of Rutland. Matric. 1710; B.A. 1713–4; M.A. 1717. Incorp. at Oxford, 1718. Ord. deacon (Ely) May 23, 1714; priest (London) Dec. 2, 1717. R. of Preston, Suffolk.

HILL, JOHN. M.A. from TRINITY, 1724. S. of John, of Aveley, Salop. Matric. from University College, Oxford, Feb. 11, 1707–8, age 18; B.A. (Oxford) 1711. (*Al. Oxon.*)

HILL, JOHN. Adm. pens. at CLARE, Feb. 22, 1734–5. 2nd s. of Nathaniel (1690), clerk, Lord of the Manor of Rothwell, Northants. B. at Waddington, Lincs., *c.* 1718. Matric. 1735; LL.B. 1742; LL.D. 1768. Ord. deacon (Lincoln) Dec. 23, 1739; priest (Bangor) Apr. 4, 1742. R. of Thorpe Malsor, Northants., 1742–93. R. of Kelmarsh, 1759–93. J.P. for Northants. Died Apr. 7, 1793. Buried at Rothwell. M.I. Admon. (Archd. Northants.) 1793. Brother of George (1733). (*Genealogist*, N.S., XV. 236; H. I. Longden.)

HILL, JOHN. Adm. pens. (age 17) at PEMBROKE, July 1, 1742. S. of Thomas, M.A. B. at Bradford, Yorks. Matric. 1742. Migrated to Jesus, July 2, 1746. M.B. 1747.

HILL, JOHN. Adm. scholar at TRINITY HALL, Jan. 5, 1743–4. Of London.

HILL, JOHN. Adm. sizar (age 19) at TRINITY, Apr. 4, 1746. S. of Thomas, of Dunstable, Beds. School, St Paul's. Matric. 1746.

HILL, JOHN SAMUEL. Adm. sizar (age 16) at St John's, June 20, 1732. S. of Richard, clerk. B. in Cambridge. School, Shipton, Yorks. (Mr Clarke). Matric. 1734; B.A. 1737–8; M.A. 1741. Fellow, 1742–5. Ord. deacon (Lincoln) Sept. 24, 1738; priest (Ely) Apr. 12, 1740. R. of Easington, Yorks., 1745–57. R. of Thornton Dale, 1745–57. Preb. of York, 1747–57. R. of Hollingbourne, Kent, 1751–7. Preb. of Ely, 1751–7. Died at Thornton, Sept. 1757. (*Scott-Mayor*, III. 444.)

HILL, JOSEPH. M.A. 1601 (Incorp. from Oxford). B. in Kent, *canonici fil.* Matric. from Corpus Christi, Oxford, Mar. 2, 1592–3, age 17; B.A. 1597; M.A. 1599; B.D. from Hart Hall, 1606. R. of Hinton Waldrist, Berks., 1604. Preb. of Lichfield, 1617–39. R. of Loddington, Northants., 1618–37. Buried there July 24, 1639. Will (Archd. Northants.) 1639; proved by s. John (1634). (*Al. Oxon.*; H. I. Longden.)

HILL, JOSEPH. Adm. pens. (age 20) at St John's, Aug. 20, 1646. S. of Joshua (? 1608), deceased, minister, of Bramley, Leeds, Yorks. B. there. School, Pocklington (Mr Sedgwick). Matric. 1646; B.A. 1649; M.A. from Magdalene, 1651; B.D. 1660. Fellow of Magdalene, 1649–62 (ejected). Proctor, 1658–9. Probably adm. at Gray's Inn, July 7, 1652, as 'Joseph Hill, of Bramley, Yorks.' Adm. at Leyden University, Mar. 29, 1664. Pastor of the Scotch Church at Middleburg, Zeeland, 1667–73, dismissed. Minister at Rotterdam, 1678–1707. Edited a Greek Lexicon. Died Nov. 5, 1707. He left his library to his old school, Pocklington. Probably brother of Joshua (1650), father of —— Hill (1700). (*D.N.B.*)

HILL, JOSEPH. Adm. sizar at St Catharine's, Nov. 14, 1664. Of Northamptonshire. Matric. 1664. Migrated to Jesus, Apr. 26, 1666. B.A. 1668–9. Perhaps s. of John (1626), V. of Rothwell, Northants.; age *c.* 34 in 1681. If so, buried at Rothwell, July 13, 1732. (*Vis. of Northants.*; A. Gray; *Genealogist*, N.S., XV. 234.)

HILL, JOSHUA. Matric. sizar from Trinity, Easter, 1608. Probably s. of Richard. B.A. 1611–2; M.A. 1615. Probably minister of Walmsley Chapel, Lancs. and afterwards of Bramley, Leeds. Died Dec. 13, 1632. Probably brother of Edward (1607) and father of the next and of Joseph (1646). (Thoresby, *Duc. Leod.*, 209.)

HILL, JOSHUA. Adm. pens. (age 16) at Magdalene, July 3, 1650. S. of Joshua (above), clerk, of Leeds, Yorks. School, Leeds. Of Beeston, Yorks., merchant. Died Mar. 20, 1708. Probably brother of Joseph (1646).

HILL, JOSHUA. Adm. sizar (age 17) at Christ's, May 20, 1679. S. of Thomas. B. at Wilsden, near Bradford, Yorks. School, Earby, near Skipton (Mr Rakes). Matric. 1679; B.A. 1682–3. Perhaps ord. deacon (Lichfield) Mar. 1697–8; C. at the Chapel of Brear (Halifax). Ord. priest (York) Sept. 1716. (*Peile*, II. 72.)

HILL, JOSIAH. Adm. pens. (age 14) at Sidney, Sept. 19, 1684. 1st s. of Anthony (1668), R. of Steeple Gidding, Hunts. B. there. School, Oundle. Matric. 1685; M.B. 1690.

HILLS or HILL, MARTIN. Adm. sizar (age 16) at St John's, May 31, 1656 ('Merlin' in College register). S. of William, gent., of London. B. there. School, Westminster. Matric. 1656; B.A. 1659–60; M.A. 1663; B.D. 1682; D.D. 1703. Incorp. at Oxford, 1664. Ord. deacon (Lincoln) May 2; priest, May 4, 1661. V. of Penn, Bucks., 1661–3. V. of Swaffham St Cyriac, Cambs., 1664–1712; of Swaffham St Mary, 1667–1712. Will (P.C.C.) 1713. Father of Thomas (1697–8).

HILL, MARTIN. Adm. pens. (age 18) at Caius, May 31, 1737. S. of Thomas (1696–7), D.D., R. of Buxhall, Suffolk. B. there. Schools, Stowmarket (Mr King) and Bury (Mr Kinnesman). Scholar, 1737–42; Matric. 1738; B.A. 1741–2. Ord. deacon (Norwich) Dec. 20, 1741, as C. of Brettenham. Will (P.C.C.) 1774; of Brettenham, clerk. Brother of Henry (1734). (*Venn*, II. 43.)

HILL, MATTHEW. Adm. sizar (age 16) at Magdalene, May 4, 1649. S. of Matthew, of York. School, York. Matric. 1649; B.A. 1652–3; M.A. 1656. Preacher at Healaugh, Yorks. Ejected from Thirsk, 1662. Went to Maryland, 1669. One Mathias Hill, M.A., was P.C. of Maer, Staffs., 1664–81. (*Calamy*, II. 595.)

HILL, MAURICE. Matric. sizar from Trinity, Easter, 1569.

HILL, MICHAEL. Adm. at King's (age 19) a scholar from Eton, Sept. 1, 1572. Of London. Matric. 1572. Fellow, 1575–7. Expelled without a degree. R. of St Anne, Aldersgate, London, 1587–1604. R. of Brockhall, Northants., 1604–27. Buried there July 21, 1627. (H. I. Longden.)

HILL, MICHAEL. Adm. sizar at Trinity, July 2, 1653. Of Warwickshire. Ord. deacon and priest (Lichfield) July 26, 1663, as 'M.A. of Trinity College.' R. of Thorpe Constantine, Staffs., 1668. (*Wm. Salt Arch. Soc.*, 1915.)

HILL, NATHANIEL. M.A. 1631 (Incorp. from Oxford). S. of Humphrey, of Tingrave, Beds., clerk. Probably matric. from Pembroke College, Oxford, Dec. 16, 1625, age 18; B.A. (Oxford) 1627–8; M.A. 1630. Signs as minister at Husborne Crawley, Beds. R. of Bergh Apton, Norfolk, 1638. V. of Renhold, Beds., 1640–1. Perhaps R. of Fordwich, Kent, till 1663. Probably P.C. of Teddington, Middlesex. Will (P.C.C.) 1664; of Teddington. (*Al. Oxon.*; J. Ch. Smith.)

HILL, NATHANIEL. Adm. sizar at Trinity, July 1, 1665.

HILL, NATHANIEL. Adm. pens. (age 17) at Peterhouse, Mar. 28, 1690. S. of Edward (? 1658), of Rothwell, Northants., Esq. School, Oundle. Matric. 1690; Scholar, 1690; B.A. 1693–4; M.A. 1697. Fellow, 1694–1703. Ord. deacon (Lincoln) May 30, 1697; priest, June 19, 1698. R. of Stanhow, Norfolk, 1700. R. of Waddington, Lincs., 1701. Resided at Rothwell, Northants., where he was Lord of the Manor. Died Apr. 28, 1732. Buried at Rothwell. M.I. Brother of John (1683), Robert (1691) and Theophilus (1700), father of George (1733) and John (1734–5). (*Genealogist*, N.S., XV. 236.)

HILL, OLIVER. Adm. pens. (age 18) at St John's, Oct. 23, 1648. S. of Adam, Esq., of Huntingdonshire. F.R.S., 1676. Author.

HILL, ORMUND. B.A. 1533–4.

HILL, OTWELL. Matric. pens. from St John's, Easter, 1573. Of Lancashire. B.A. 1576–7; M.A. 1580. Fellow, 1579. Taxor, 1588–9. Proctor, 1591. University Commissary, 1605. One of these names, 'LL.D.,' was Chancellor of Lincoln diocese. Died May 19, 1616, aged 56. (Hacketts' *Epitaphs*, 86.)

HILL, PERCIVAL. Matric. sizar from Pembroke, Michs. 1613. Doubtless s. of Martin, R. of Asfordby, Leics. B.A. 1617–8; M.A. 1621. Ord. deacon (Peterb.) Sept. 23; priest, Dec. 23, 1621. V. of Tilton, Leics., 1625. V. of Dagenham, Essex, 1637–40. R. of St Catherine Coleman, London, 1640–1. Brother of Arnold (1608), Francis (1608) and John (1626). (*Genealogist*, N.S., XV.)

HILL, PHILIP. Adm. at Corpus Christi, 1659. Of Norwich. Matric. 1660; B.A. 1663–4; M.A. *c.* 1667. Ord. priest (Norwich) July, 1681. R. of Hardingham, Norfolk, 1681–1702.

HILL, PHILIP. Adm. sizar at Emmanuel, May 9, 1679. Of Devonshire. Matric. 1679; B.A. 1682–3; M.A. 1686. Will of one of these names (Exeter) 1734; of St Columb Minor, Cornwall, clerk.

HILL, PHILIP. Adm. sizar at Emmanuel, May 26, 1709. Of Nottinghamshire. Doubtless s. of Hugh, of Farnsfield, Notts., clerk. Matric. 1709. Matric. from Balliol, Oxford, Dec. 5, 1711, age 20. (*Al. Oxon.*)

HILL, RALPH. Matric. sizar from Peterhouse, Michs. 1556. Perhaps B.A. 1557.

HILL, RALPH. Matric. pens. from Clare, *c.* 1595; B.A. 1599–1600.

HILLS, RALPH. Matric. sizar from Queens', Easter, 1626; B.A. 1629–30; M.A. 1633. Minister at Shalford, Essex, 1645; at Ridgewell, 1648; and at Pattiswick, 1653; ejected, 1662. (*Davids*, 440.)

HILL, RICHARD. B.A. 1526–7; M.A. 1530; B.D. 1541–2. Fellow of Christ's, 1531–9. (*Peile*, I. 15.)

HILL, RICHARD. Matric. pens. from Trinity, Michs. 1559; Scholar, 1560; B.A. 1562–3. Author, *Poems*. (*Cooper*, II. 147.)

HILL, RICHARD. Matric. sizar from Pembroke, Michs. 1578.

HILL, RICHARD. Adm. sizar at Queens', Apr. 21, 1596. Of Lincolnshire. Matric. 1596; B.A. 1599–1600; M.A. 1603. One of these names V. of Hanbury, Staffs., 1602–10. Buried there Feb. 14, 1609–10.

HILL or HILLS, RICHARD. Matric. sizar from Trinity, Easter, 1606. B. *c.* 1586. Scholar, 1606; B.A. (? 1609–10); M.A. 1613. Incorp. at Oxford, 1618, as Hills. Ord. deacon and priest (Oxford) May 3, 1611. Probably R. of Croxby, Lincs., 1613; and father of Vincent (1633).

HILL, RICHARD. Adm. at King's (age 17) a scholar from Eton, Aug. 24, 1611. Of Farnham Royal, Bucks. Matric. 1611. Died whilst a student, 1612. (*Harwood*.)

HILL, RICHARD. Adm. sizar (age 20) at St John's, Mar. 10, 1637–8. S. of William, yeoman, of Burscough, Lancs. B. at Up-Holland, Lancs. School, Ormskirk (Mr Bragg). Matric. 1637–8.

HILL, RICHARD. B.A. 1641 (Incorp. from Oxford). S. of James, of Upton-on-Severn, Worcs., *pleb.* Matric. from Balliol College, July 4, 1634, age 17; B.A. (Oxford) 1638; M.A. 1641.

HILL, RICHARD. Adm. pens. at TRINITY, May 9, 1654. Of Kent. School, Westminster. Scholar, 1654; Matric. 1657; B.A. 1657-8; M.A. 1661. Fellow, 1659. Taxor, 1665. Ord. deacon (Ely) Sept. 20; priest, Dec. 20, 1662. V. of St Michael's, Cambridge, 1663. One of these names preb. of York, 1671-1704.

HILL, RICHARD. Adm. pens. at QUEENS', Feb. 15, 1666-7. Of Somerset. Matric. 1667; B.A. 1670-1; M.A. 1674. One of these names, M.A., R. of Combe Florey, Somerset, 1687-1731. Died 1731.

HILL, RICHARD. Adm. sizar (age 18) at ST JOHN'S, Jan. 19, 1671-2. S. of Richard, yeoman, of Shefford, Beds. B. there. School, Clifton, Beds. Matric. 1672; B.A. 1765-6. One of these names V. of Pulloxhill, Beds., 1685-6.

HILL, RICHARD. Adm. pens. (age 19) at ST JOHN'S, June 18, 1675. S. of Rowland, gent., of Hawkstone, Salop. B. there, Mar. 23, 1655. Schools, Eton and Shrewsbury. Matric. 1675; B.A. 1678-9; M.A. 1682. Fellow, 1679-92. Envoy to Elector of Bavaria, 1696. Ambassador at the Hague, 1699. Lord of the Treasury, 1699-1702. Member of the Admiralty Council, 1702-8. Envoy to Savoy, 1703. D.C.L. (Oxford) 1708. Fellow of Eton, 1714. Died at Richmond, Surrey, June 11, 1727. Buried at Hodnet, Salop. Will, P.C.C. Benefactor to St John's. (*D.N.B.*; *Al. Oxon.*)

HILL, RICHARD. Adm. sizar at EMMANUEL, Dec. 10, 1675. Of Shenstone, Worcs. S. of Humphrey. Schools, Chadgely, Worcs. and Uppingham, Rutland. Matric. 1676; B.A. 1679-80; M.A. 1683; B.D. 1690. Fellow, 1682-1702. Ord. deacon (Lincoln) Sept. 21, 1681; priest, Dec. 23, 1683. R. of Thurcaston, Leics., 1701-33. Died Feb. 7, 1732-3, aged 77. M.I. at Thurcaston. Will, Leicester. (*Nichols*, III. 1060, 1074.)

HILL, RICHARD. Adm. pens. (age 17) at ST JOHN'S, Jan. 11, 1675-6. S. of Francis, clerk, of Essex. B. there. School, Mercers', London. Matric. 1676; B.A. 1679-80; M.A. 1684. Ord. deacon and priest (Norwich) Feb. 27, 1680-1. V. of Owston, Leics., 1683-1723. R. of Withcote, 1706-23. Died Oct. 26, 1723. M.I. at Owston. Will (Leicester) 1724. Brother of William (1676). (*Nichols*, II. 763.)

HILL, RICHARD. Adm. pens. (age 18) at SIDNEY, Mar. 6, 1712-3. S. of John, gent., of Thornton, Yorks. School, Beverley. Matric. 1713; LL.B. 1724. V. of Burton Agnes, Yorks., 1727. One of these names V. of Normanby, Yorks., 1719-24. R. of West Heslerton, 1723-34.

HYLL, ROBERT. Matric. sizar from JESUS, Michs. 1560. One of these names, died, R. of South Pickenham, Norfolk, 1570.

HILL, ROBERT. Matric. sizar from JESUS, Michs. 1597; B.A. from Peterhouse, 1583-4; Scholar, 1584. One of these names, B.A. of Peterhouse, ord. deacon (York) June, 1617.

HILL, ROBERT. Matric. pens. from CHRIST'S, July, 1581. B. at Ashbourne, Derbs. B.A. 1584-5; M.A. 1588; B.D. from St John's, 1595; D.D. 1609. Fellow of St John's, 1588-9. Incorp. at Oxford, 1605. P.C. of St Andrew, Norwich, 1591-1602. Lecturer at St Martin-in-the-Fields, London, 1602. R. of St Matthew, Friday Street, 1607-12. R. of St Bartholomew-on-the-Exchange, 1614-23. R. of St Bartholomew-the-Great, 1614-23. Married Margaret, dau. of Mr Wyts, a Dutchman. Author of devotional works. Buried at St Bartholomew-the-Great, Aug. 1623. Will (P.C.C.) 1623. (*Peile*, I. 164; *D.N.B.*; Cole, *MS.*, 5871, 14.)

HILL, ROBERT. B.A. from EMMANUEL, 1590-1.

HILL, ROBERT. Matric. sizar from MAGDALENE, Easter, 1612; B.A. 1615-6; M.A. 1619. Ord. deacon (Peterb.) May 26, 1616; priest, Sept. 19, 1619. Probably V. of Tugby, Leics., 1622.

HILL, ROBERT. M.A. from ST CATHARINE'S, 1642. S. of Robert, of London, gent. Matric. from Wadham College, Oxford, June 1, 1635, age 16; B.A. (Oxford) 1638-9. R. of Kilvington, Notts., 1637. Preb. of Lichfield, 1660-2. Perhaps R. of Staunton-in-the-Vale, Notts., till 1662. Died 1662.

HILL, ROBERT. Adm. pens. (age 16) at PEMBROKE, Jan. 16, 1663. 2nd s. of Robert, ge1 . B. at Stifford, Essex. Matric. 1664. Adm. at the Middle Temple, Aug. 5, 1670.

HILL, ROBERT. Adm. sizar (age 18) at SIDNEY, June 3, 1676. S. of William, yeoman, deceased. B. at Morton, Staffs. School, Oakham. Matric. 1676; B.A. 1679-80.

HILL, ROBERT. Adm. pens. at CLARE, Apr. 6, 1678. Of Leire, Leics. Matric. 1678; B.A. 1681-2; M.A. 1685. Ord. priest (London) Dec. 20, 1685. Perhaps R. of Sharnford, Leics., 1694-8. Buried there Dec. 9, 1698. Admon. (Leicester) 1701. (*Nichols*, IV. 244, 920.)

HILL, ROBERT. Adm. pens. (age 17) at PETERHOUSE, June 23, 1691. Of Northamptonshire. 5th s. of Edward (? 1658), of Rowell (? Rothwell), Esq. Schools, Norwich and Oundle. Matric. 1691; Scholar, 1691; B.A. 1694-5; M.A. 1698. Ord. deacon (Norwich) May; priest, June, 1701. V. of Gt Barwick, Norfolk, 1701. R. of Stanhow, 1704-31. Author, *Sermon*. Brother of Nathaniel (1690) and Theophilus (1700).

HILL, ROGER. Matric. sizar from ST JOHN'S, Easter, 1622. Doubtless s. of William, of Poundesford, Somerset, Esq. Adm. at the Inner Temple, Mar. 22, 1624. Barrister, 1632. Serjeant-at-law, 1655. M.P. for Taunton, 1640; for Bridport, 1640-53. Baron of the Exchequer, 1657-60. Died Apr. 21, 1667. Father of the next. (Le Neve, 217; *D.N.B.*; A. B. Beaven.)

HILL, ROGER. Adm. Fell.-Com. at JESUS, June 8, 1658. Of London. S. of Roger, of Poundesford, Somerset (above), Baron of the Exchequer. B. 1642. Adm. at the Inner Temple, 1657. Barrister, 1666. Knighted, July 18, 1668. J.P. Sheriff of Bucks., 1673. M.P. for Agmondesham, 1679-81; for Wendover, 1702, 1705-22. Succeeded to the estate of Poundesford, which he sold, and settled at Denham, Bucks. Died Dec. 29, 1729, aged 88. M.I. at Denham. (Le Neve, *Knights*, 217; *Lipscomb*, IV. 458; A. B. Beaven.)

HILL, ROGER. Adm. pens. at CLARE, June 27, 1715. S. of Lockey, of London, gent. B. in London. Matric. 1715; B.A. 1718-9. Probably adm. at Lincoln's Inn, Feb. 10, 1720-1. Of Heath, Derbs.

HILL, ROWLAND. Adm. at KING'S (age 18) a scholar from Eton, Aug. 27, 1579. Of London. Matric. 1579; B.A. 1583-4; M.A. 1587. Fellow, 1582-92. Incorp. at Oxford, 1594. V. of Shalbourn, Berks., 1593. Preb. of Lincoln, 1607-30. Died 1636, aged 74. M.I. at Shalbourn. Will (P.C.C.) 1636. (*Al. Oxon.*; J. Ch. Smith.)

HILL, ROWLAND. Adm. Fell.-Com. (age 18) at ST JOHN'S, 1724. S. and h. of John, gent., of Wem, Salop (apothecary; brother of Sir Richard, Envoy to Brussels, etc.). B. at Hawkstone. Bapt. Sept. 28, 1705. School, Richmond, Surrey. Matric. 1724. Succeeded to the Hawkstone estate. Created Baronet, Jan. 20, 1726-7. High Sheriff of Salop, 1731-2. M.P. for Lichfield, 1734-41. Married (1) Jane, dau. of Sir Brian Broughton, May 27, 1732. Died Aug. 7, 1783. (*Scott-Mayor*, III. 366; *G.E.C.*)

HILL, ROLAND HARWOOD, *see* HARWOOD.

HILL, SAMSON. Adm. pens. (age 17) at PEMBROKE, Dec. 15, 1705. S. of Samson, of Cornwall, Esq. B. in Cornwall. Matric. 1705.

HILL, SAMUEL. Matric. pens. from TRINITY, Easter, 1585. B. at Blunham, Beds. Scholar, 1588; B.A. 1588-9; M.A. 1592; B.D. 1599; D.D. 1608. Fellow, 1591. Ord. deacon and priest (Peterb.) July 11, 1595. V. of Trumpington, Cambs., 1599-1600. R. of Boduey, Norfolk, 1604. Preb. of Chichester, 1606-39. R. of Rotherb , Leics., 1610. R. of Medbourne, 1610-1-39. R. of Church Langton, Leics., 1631-9. Licensed (Peterb. Jan. 22, 1615-6) to marry Anne Brookes, of Uppingham. Died May 8, 1639. M.I. at Church Langton. (*Nichols*, II. 667.)

HILL, SAMUEL. Matric. pens. from EMMANUEL, *c.* 1591.

HILL, SAMUEL. Matric. pens. from ST JOHN'S, Michs. 1615; B.A. 1618-9; M.A. 1622. Incorp. at Oxford, 1623. Ord. deacon (Peterb.) Sept. 21; priest, Sept. 22, 1623.

HILL, SAMUEL. Adm. sizar at EMMANUEL, Aug. 28, 1678. Of Leicestershire. Matric. 1679; B.A. 1682-3.

HILL, *alias* BARBOUR, SAMUEL. Adm. Fell.-Com. (age 16) at ST JOHN'S, Apr. 29, 1707. B. at Hawkstone, Salop (his mother's home), 1690-1. School, Eton. Matric. 1707. Adm. at the Middle Temple, as Hill, *alias* Barbour; s. and h. of Samuel Barbour, of Prees, Salop, July 22, 1708. M.P. for Lichfield, 1715-22. Registrar of the Admiralty, 1715-58. Married Lady Elizabeth Stanhope. Died Feb. 21, 1758, aged 67. Buried at Shenstone, Staffs. Nephew of Richard (1675), who acted as his guardian. (*S. Shaw*, II. 44.)

HILL, SAMUEL. M.A. from EMMANUEL, 1717. S. of Samuel, of Kilmington, Somerset, clerk. Matric. from Queen's College, Oxford, Mar. 22, 1709-10, age 17; B.A. (Oxford) 1713-4. R. of Little Somerford, Wilts., 1730-53. V. of Elsey, 1731-3. R. of Kilmington, Somerset, 1733-53. Preb. of Wells, 1741-51. (*Al. Oxon.*)

HILL, THEOPHILUS. Adm. pens. (age 17) at PETERHOUSE, Apr. 19, 1700. Of Northamptonshire. 7th s. of Edward (? 1658), of Rothwell, Esq. School, Kilworth, Leics. (private). Scholar, 1700-1; Matric. 1701, as 'Thomas'; M.B. 1705. Ord. deacon (Peterb.) Dec. 18, 1709; priest, Sept. 23, 1710. Perhaps R. of Hedgerley, Bucks., 1743-5. Died Oct. 1746. Will (Archd. Bucks.) 1746. Brother of Nathaniel (1690) and Robert (1691). (*Genealogist*, N.S., XV. 103; *Lipscomb*, IV. 506.)

HILL, THEOPHILUS. Adm. sizar at EMMANUEL, July 9, 1725. Doubtless eldest s. of Theophilus (above). Bapt. at Rothwell, Mar. 2, 1705-6. Matric. 1725; B.A. 1729-30. Ord. deacon (Lincoln) June 16, 1728, as B.A.; priest, Sept. 20, 1730. Probably of Leadenham, Lincs., clerk. Will (P.C.C.) 1793. (*Genealogist*, N.S., XV. 229.)

HILL, THOMAS. B.Can.L. 1459-60. Probably R. of St Martin, Iremonger Lane, London, 1481-2. V. of Saffron Walden, Essex, 1447-50. R. of Hadstock.

HILL, THOMAS. B.A. 1518–9. Perhaps V. of Thurston, Suffolk, 1557–62. Will (Bury) 1562.

HYLL, THOMAS. Matric. sizar from CHRIST'S, May, 1551; B.A. 1553–4. R. of Wickmere, Norfolk, 1557. R. of Kedington, Suffolk, 1558–69. Preb. of Ely, 1564; resigned same year. (*Peile*, I. 48.)

HYLLS, THOMAS. Adm. pens. at KING'S, Easter, 1566.

HYLL, THOMAS. Matric. sizar from JESUS, Lent, 1579–80; B.A. 1583–4.

HILLS, THOMAS. Matric. sizar from PEMBROKE, Easter, 1606; B.A. 1609–10. Buried at Little St Mary's, Cambridge, July 13, 1610.

HILLS, THOMAS. Matric. sizar from TRINITY, Michs. 1608.

HILL, THOMAS. Matric. pens. from PETERHOUSE, Easter, 1615; Scholar, 1616–21; B.A. 1618–9; M.A. 1622; D.D. 1634–5. Incorp. at Oxford, 1622. Ord. deacon (Peterb.) Sept. 22; priest, Sept. 23, 1622. R. of Bredfield, Suffolk, 1626–39. V. of Ash Bocking, 1630–9. Will (P.C.C.) 1639. (H. I. Longden.)

HILL, THOMAS. Adm. pens. at EMMANUEL, Oct. 19, 1618. B. at Kington, Worcs. Matric. 1618; Scholar; B.A. 1622–3; M.A. 1626; B.D. 1633; D.D. from Trinity, 1646. Fellow of Emmanuel. Master of Trinity, 1645–53. Vice-Chancellor, 1645–7. Ord. deacon (Peterb.) Jan. 23; priest, Jan. 24, 1628–9. R. of Titchmarsh, Northants., 1633–48. Perhaps R. of Easton Maudit, 1636. One of the original members of the Westminster Assembly. An ardent Calvinist. Author, *Sermons*. Died Dec. 18, 1653. Will proved (V.C.C.) 1653. (*D.N.B.*)

HILL, THOMAS. Matric. pens. from CLARE, Michs. 1621; B.A. 1625–6; M.A. 1629. Ord. deacon (Peterb.) Sept. 23, 1632; priest, Dec. 18, 1636. One of these names (M.A.), V. of Braybrooke, Northants., 1647–57. Buried there Mar. 23, 1656–7.

HILL, THOMAS. Adm. pens. at QUEENS', Mar. 29, 1632. Of Cambridgeshire.

HILL, THOMAS. M.A. 1641–2 (on King's visit).

HILL or HILLS, THOMAS. Adm. pens. (age 19) at EMMANUEL, Jan. 30, 1642–3. Of Hertfordshire. Matric. 1643. Migrated to Peterhouse, Dec. 3, 1644.

HILL, THOMAS. Adm. sizar at CORPUS CHRISTI, 1645. Of Derbyshire. School, Repton. Matric. Easter, 1646; B.A. 1649–50. Chaplain to the Countess of Chesterfield, at Tamworth Castle, Warws. Preacher at Elvaston, Derbs. 'Ordained' at Wirksworth, 1652. Minister at Orton, Leics., 1653–60; and at Shuttington, Warws., 1660–2. Afterwards nonconformist preacher in Warws., etc. Died aged *c.* 50. (*Calamy*, II. 488; *D.N.B.*)

HILL, THOMAS. Adm. pens. at TRINITY, June 18, 1652, a scholar from Westminster. Of Ireland. Matric. 1652; B.A. 1655–6; M.A. 1659; D.D. 1670 (*Lit. Reg.*). Fellow, 1658; ejected, and restored, 1660. Incorp. at Oxford, 1663. Signed for deacon and priest (London) Sept. 24, 1664. Preb. of St Patrick's, Dublin, 1667. Dean of Ossory, 1670. Chaplain to the Duke of Ormond. Died Nov. 1, 1673. Buried in the Cathedral, Kilkenny. Will, Dublin. (E. E. Hill.)

HILL, THOMAS. Matric. sizar from CORPUS CHRISTI, Easter, 1657.

HILL, THOMAS. Adm. sizar (age 16) at PETERHOUSE, May 17, 1664. Of Yorkshire. School, Tadcaster. Matric. 1664; B.A. 1667–8. Ord. deacon (York) June, 1668; priest, Dec. 1668. Perhaps R. of Crawley, Bucks., 1679–86. Died 1686.

HILL, THOMAS. Adm. sizar at QUEENS', Mar. 3, 1668–9. Matric. 1669; B.A. 1672–3; M.A. 1680. Possibly s. of Thomas (1646). If so, a nonconformist tutor; conducted an Academy for training ministers at Derby. Published a selection of Psalms in Latin and in Greek verse. Died Mar. 2, 1720. (*D.N.B.*)

HILL, THOMAS. Adm. sizar at JESUS, Sept. 7, 1687. S. of Thomas (? 1664), clerk, deceased. Exhibitioner from St Paul's School. Matric. 1688; Rustat Scholar, 1688; B.A. 1691–2.

HILL, THOMAS. Adm. pens. at QUEENS', July 6, 1694. Of Wiltshire. Matric. 1695; B.A. 1697–8; M.A. 1701. Ord. deacon (Lincoln) Mar. 16, 1700–1; priest, Mar. 4, 1704–5. One of these names V. of East Malling, Kent, 1705–18. Buried there Sept. 16, 1718. (C. H. Fielding.)

HILL, THOMAS. Adm. pens. (age 18) at ST JOHN'S, Mar. 18, 1696–7. S. of Martin (1656). B. at Swaffham Prior, Cambs. School, Bury St Edmunds. Matric. 1697; B.A. 1700–1; M.A. 1704; D.D. 1719. Ord. deacon (Ely) July 5, 1702; priest, May 30, 1703. R. of Buxhall, Suffolk, 1709–43. Married Sarah, dau. of Henry Copinger, of Buxhall. Died Sept. 4, 1743, aged 65. Buried at Buxhall. Father of Henry (1734) and Martin (1737).

HILL, THOMAS. Adm. pens. (age 18) at TRINITY, June 18, 1701. S. of Daniel (1702), of Southfleet, Kent. School, Westminster. Scholar, 1702; B.A. 1704–5; Matric. 1705; M.A. 1708. Fellow, 1707. F.R.S., 1725. Secretary to the Lords Commissioners of Trade, 1737–58. Poet. Died Sept. 20, 1758. Will, P.C.C.; as of Richmond, Surrey. (*Al. Westmon.*, 239; A. B. Beaven; J. Ch. Smith.)

HILL, THOMAS. Adm. pens. at CHRIST'S, July 8, 1702. S. of James. B. in Cambridge. School, Saffron Walden (Mr Kilborn). Scholar, 1702; Matric. 1702–3; B.A. 1706–7; M.A. 1710. Ord. deacon (Peterb.) Mar. 5, 1709–10; C. of Clapton, Northants., 1710; priest (London) Sept. 21, 1712. One of these names R. of Downham, Essex, 1713–46. Admon. (Comm. C. Essex) 1746. (J. Ch. Smith.)

HILL, THOMAS. Adm. sizar at JESUS, Apr. 19, 1710. S. of ——, clerk, deceased, of Leicestershire. Matric. 1711.

HILL, THOMAS. Adm. sizar (age 17) at ST JOHN'S, June 4, 1710. S. of Abraham. B. at Carlton, near Skipton, Yorks. School, Threshfield (Mr Marshall). Matric. 1710; B.A. 1713–4; M.A. 1718. Fellow, 1717–20. Ord. deacon (London) Mar. 17, 1716–7.

HILL, THOMAS. Adm. pens. (age 19) at SIDNEY, June 30, 1714. S. of Hugh, of Luton, Beds. B. there. School, Houghton Conquest (Mr Clark). Matric. 1714. Migrated to Trinity, Nov. 4, 1715, 'aged 17.' B.A. 1717–8; M.A. 1731. Ord. deacon (Lincoln) Mar. 13, 1719–20; priest (York) Sept. 22, 1723. Probably V. of Litlington, Beds., 1725–8. Perhaps R. of Dunstable; and father of William (1748).

HILL, THOMAS. M.A. from KING'S, 1720. S. of Thomas, of Hereford. Matric. from Magdalen Hall, Oxford, Nov. 23, 1709, age 18; B.A. (Oxford) 1713. Ord. deacon (Worcester) Sept. 20, 1713; priest (Gloucester) Oct. 9, 1715. C. of Newland, 1715. R. of Tintern Parva, Monm., 1719. V. of Llanarth, 1723. Chaplain to Baron Wakefield. R. of Staunton, Gloucs., 1727–64. Buried there July 9, 1764. (*Al. Oxon.*; F. S. Hockaday.)

HILL, THOMAS. Adm. sizar (age 18) at ST JOHN'S, June 26, 1740. S. of John, clerk, of Wiltshire. B. at Stourton. School, Braughton (Mr Goldsborough). Matric. 1740; B.A. 1743–4.

HILL, TIMOTHY. Adm. sizar at TRINITY, June 29, 1667. S. of Robert, of Manchester. Bapt. there, Apr. 11, 1647. M.A. of Glasgow, 1670. Chaplain to Sir Richard Hoghton. Went to the Indies as ship's chaplain, 1675. C. of Stoak, Cheshire. Died at Chester, Aug. 29, 1680. (E. Axon.)

HILLS, VINCENT. Adm. sizar (age 15) at SIDNEY, June 3, 1633. S. of Richard (? 1606), M.A., R. of Croxby, Lincs. B. at Nettleton, Lincs. Matric. 1633; B.A. 1636–7.

HILL, WALTER. Matric. sizar from JESUS, Michs. 1555; B.A. 1563–4.

HILL, WILLIAM. B.Can.L. 1467–8. One of these names R. of Newton, Suffolk, 1470–93. Will (P.C.C.) 1493; B.Can.L.

HILL, WILLIAM. B.A. 1517–8.

HILL or HILLS, WILLIAM. Matric. pens. from PETERHOUSE, Easter, 1568; B.A. 1568–9; M.A. 1572. Ord. deacon (Ely); priest, Apr. 1578. R. of Marham (? Marholm), Northants., 1577–1602. Preb. of Peterborough, 1577–1602. Will (P.C.C.) 1602.

HILL, WILLIAM. Matric. sizar from TRINITY, Easter, 1584; B.A. 1588–9.

HILL, WILLIAM. M.A. 1585 (Incorp. from Oxford). Scholar of Balliol College, Oxford, 1577–8; B.A. (Oxford) 1581; M.A. 1583; B.D. 1591; D.D. 1605. Probably ord. deacon and priest (Lincoln) 1585. R. of Mells, Somerset, 1591–1619. Preb. of Bristol, 1607–19. (F. S. Hockaday; H. G. Harrison.)

HILL or HILLS, WILLIAM. Matric. pens. from JESUS, Easter, 1588. B. at Fulbourn, Cambs. B.A. 1591–2; M.A. 1595; B.D. 1604. Fellow, 1597–1611. Incorp. at Oxford, 1602. Ord. priest (Lincoln) Dec. 21, 1598. V. of Whittlesford, Cambs., 1606–19. V. of Fordham, Cambs., 1611–38. V. of Guilden Morden, 1627. V. of All Saints', Cambridge, 1629. Buried at Fordham, Dec. 25, 1638. Will (P.C.C.) 1639. (A. Gray.)

HILL, WILLIAM. Adm. sizar (age 17) at CAIUS, Nov. 9, 1592. S. of William, gent. B. in the parish of St Michael, Colchester. School, Colchester (Mr Hasnett). Matric. *c.* 1593; B.A. from Clare, 1595–6; M.A. from King's, 1599. One of these names R. of Roudham, Norfolk, 1600–40. Buried there Nov. 22, 1640. (*Venn*, I. 147.)

HILL, WILLIAM. Adm. sizar at EMMANUEL, Aug. 2, 1593.

HILL, WILLIAM. Adm. pens. (age 17) at CAIUS, June 28, 1625. S. of William, gent., of Hales, Norfolk. Matric. 1625; B.A. 1628–9. Adm. at Gray's Inn, Nov. 21, 1627. Of Hales, Esq. J.P. (*Venn*, I. 272; *Vis. of Norfolk*, 1664.)

HILL, WILLIAM. Adm. pens. (age 16) at ST JOHN'S, June 9, 1676. S. of Francis, clerk, of Essex. B. there. School, Colchester. Matric. 1676; M.B. 1681. Ord. deacon (London) Feb. 24, 1683-4; priest, Feb. 24, 1688-9. Doubtless the 'clerk, of St John's,' who became M.A. 1705 (*Lit. Reg.*). Brother of Richard (1675-6).

HILL, WILLIAM. M.A. from KING'S, 1707. Matric. from Christ Church, Oxford, Mar. 28, 1696; B.A. (Balliol) 1699. V. of Dulverton, Somerset, 1704-37. Died 1737. (*Al. Oxon.*)

HILL, WILLIAM. Adm. at KING'S, a scholar from Eton, 1748. S. of Thomas (? 1714), R. of Dunstable, Beds. Matric. 1749; B.A. 1753; M.A. 1757. Fellow, 1752. V. of Dunton, Essex.

HILL, ——. B.Civ.L. 1519-20.

HILL, ——. Adm. Fell.-Com. at KING'S, 1592-3.

HILL, ——. Adm. pens. at KING'S, Lent, 1593-4.

HILL, ——. Adm. sizar at ST CATHARINE'S, Easter, 1652.

HILL, ——. (Doubtless 'Peter.') Adm. Fell.-Com. at MAGDALENE, June 22, 1700. S. of Joseph (1646), former Fellow. B. at Rotterdam. Perhaps P.C. of Cholesbury, Bucks., 1702-54. If so, died 1754, aged 'c. 84.' (Thoresby, *Duc. Leod.*, 209; *Lipscomb*, III. 322.)

HILLEIENSIS, THOMAS. 'D.D. Cambridge'; flourished c. 1290. Of Suffolk. Carmelite friar. (*Pits*, 376.)

HILLENDEN, LAURENCE. B.A. from QUEENS', 1582-3.

HILLERSDON, GUY. Adm. pens. at CLARE, July 6, 1664. S. of John (next), R. of Castle Ashby. B. at Stoke Goldington. B.A. 1666-7; M.A. 1671. Incorp. at Oxford, 1673. Signed for deacon's orders (London) Sept. 22, 1671; for priest's, Sept. 20, 1673. R. of Castle Ashby, Northants., 1680-1719. Buried there Feb. 27, 1718-9, aged 70. (H. I. Longden.)

HILLERSDEN, JOHN. M.A. 1639 (Incorp. from Oxford). S. of John, of Stoke Hamond, Bucks., gent. Matric. from Corpus Christi College, Oxford, Nov. 25, 1631, age 18; B.A. (Oxford) 1631-2; M.A. 1634-5; B.D. 1642. R. of Odstock, Wilts., 1645; and of Castle Ashby, Northants., 1664-80. Archdeacon of Buckingham, 1671-84. Died Nov. 1, 1684. Buried at Stoke Goldington. Will, P.C.C. Father of Guy (1664). (*Al. Oxon.*; *Vis. of Bucks.*, 1634.)

HILLESDEN, JOHN. Matric. pens. from CLARE, Easter, 1667.

HILLERSDEN, JOHN. Adm. Fell.-Com. at CORPUS CHRISTI, 1671. Of Bedfordshire. Probably s. of Thomas, of Elstow, Beds. B. there, Feb. 2, 1655-6. Matric. 1671. Adm. at the Inner Temple, Nov. 2, 1670. Called to the Bar, Nov. 14, 1679. Buried at Elstow, Apr. 20, 1684. M.I.

HILLERSDEN, JOHN. Adm. at CORPUS CHRISTI, 1695. Of Bedfordshire. S. of Thomas, of Elstow, Beds. Bapt. there, Dec. 27, 1678. Adm. at the Inner Temple, May 14, 1696.

HILLERSDON, THOMAS. Matric. Fell.-Com. from KING'S, Michs. 1648. Doubtless s. and h. of Sir Thomas, of Ampthill, Beds., Knt. Bapt. at Kuebworth, Feb. 16, 1630-1. Buried at Elstow, Jan. 17, 1656-7. (*Vis. of Beds.*, 1634; *Vis. of Bucks.*, 1634.)

HILESDEN, ——. Adm. Fell.-Com. at EMMANUEL, Easter, 1626. Possibly Thomas Hillersden, s. and h. of John, of Stoke Hamond, Bucks. If so, brother of John (1639). (*Vis. of Bucks.*, 1634.)

HILLIARD, *see* HILDYARD.

HILLING, THOMAS. B.Can.L. 1477-8.

HILLING, WILLIAM. Adm. sizar at PETERHOUSE, 1600-1; B.A. 1604-5.

HILLMAN, JOHN. M.A. from SIDNEY, 1690. S. of J., of Kinver, Staffs., *pleb.* Matric. from Balliol College, Oxford, Mar. 31, 1682, age 17; B.A. (Oxford) 1685. Preb. of Wolverhampton, 1695-1720. Usher at the Grammar School, 1691-1720. Died Apr. 15, 1720. M.I. at St Peter's, Wolverhampton. Father of John (1709). (*Al. Oxon.* which has probably confused him with the next; *Wm. Salt Arch. Soc.*, 1915.)

HILMAN, JOHN. M.A. from PETERHOUSE, 1707. S. of Francis, of Salisbury. Matric. from Hart Hall, Oxford, Feb. 11, 1692-3, age 16; B.A. (Oxford) 1696-7. Perhaps V. of St Stithian, 1706; and R. of St Michael Penkevel, 1707. R. of Mabyn, Cornwall, 1723. Admon. (Exeter) 1726; of Mabyn. (*Al. Oxon.*)

HILLMAN, JOHN. Adm. sizar at ST CATHARINE'S, July 23, 1709. (Previously matric. from Trinity College, Oxford, Mar. 27, 1708.) S. of John (1690), of Wolverhampton. Bapt. there, Feb. 17, 1692-3. Matric. 1710; B.A. 1711-2; M.A. 1719. (*Al. Oxon.*)

HILLS, *see* HILL.

HILLYARD, *see* HILDYARD.

HILSEY, JOHN. Studied at Cambridge. B.D. (Oxford) 1527. Of Berkshire. Dominican friar; recommended by Cranmer as prior of their house at Cambridge. Prior at Bristol, 1532. Master-general of his order. Bishop of Rochester, 1535-9. Entertained by the University, 1537-8 (*Gr. Bk*, B 2, 217). Compiled a service-book in English, which appeared in 1539 as *The Manual of Prayers*. Died Aug. 4, 1539. (*Cooper*, I. 70; *D.N.B.*; A. B. Beaven; H. G. Harrison.)

HILTAFT, RICHARD. Matric. pens. from CLARE, Michs. 1578.

HILTON, JAMES. Adm. sizar (age 16) at CHRIST'S, June 7, 1670. S. of Joseph. B. at Eye, Suffolk. School, Eye (Mr Browne). Matric. 1670. Buried Dec. 14, 1673, at Gt St Andrew's, Cambridge. (*Peile*, II. 29.)

HILTON, JOHN. Matric. sizar from ST JOHN'S, Michs. 1570; B.A. 1574-5. A priest. Condemned to recant and do penance for heresy and blasphemy, 1584. (*Cooper*, I. 509.)

HILTON, JOHN. Mus.Bac. from TRINITY, 1626. Organist of St Margaret's, Westminster, 1628. Married, at St Margaret's, June 15, 1627, Frances Trapp. Musical composer; madrigals, etc. Buried Mar. 21, 1657, in St Margaret's, Westminster. (*D.N.B.*)

HILTON, JOHN. Adm. pens. (age 16) at ST JOHN'S, Sept. 7, 1635. S. of John, Esq., of Monkwearmouth, Durham. B. at Whitwell House, Durham (his mother's home). School, Houghton-le-Spri (Mr Segg). Matric. 1635. Adm. at Gray's Inn, Mayng, 1638. Captain in the King's service. Succeeded his father at Hilton Castle, Durham. Buried June 21, 1670. (*Vis. of Durham*, 1666; H. M. Wood.)

HILTON, JOHN. Adm. pens. (age 18) at TRINITY, June 18, 1685. S. of John, of Middlesex. School, Westminster. Matric. 1685; Scholar, 1686; B.A. 1688-9; M.A. 1692. Fellow, 1691-1700. Buried in the College Chapel, Sept. 25, 1700.

HILTON, JOHN. Adm. Fell.-Com. (age 19) at ST JOHN'S, Apr. 13, 1687. 1st s. of Henry, Esq. B. at Worsall-on-Tees, Yorks. (his mother's home). School, Durham (Mr Battersby). Married Dorothy, dau. of Sir Richard Musgrave, of Hayton Castle, Cumberland. Buried Apr. 16, 1712. Probably brother of Thomas (1689). (*Surtees*, II. 26.)

HILTON, JOHN. Adm. sizar at ST CATHARINE'S, June 24, 1704. Matric. 1704; B.A. 1707-8. Ord. deacon (York) May, 1708; priest, Sept. 1721. V. of Willerby, Yorks., 1721-3.

HYLTON, MATTHEW. Matric. pens. from TRINITY, Easter, 1573.

HILTON, NATHANIEL. Matric. pens. from JESUS, Michs. 1606. Perhaps s. of Henry, of South Shields, Durham. If so, V. of Billingshurst, Sussex. Buried there July 16, 1655, aged 65. Will (P.C.C.) 1655. (*Surtees*, II. 29.)

HILTON, RALPH. Matric. sizar from TRINITY, Easter, 1570; B.A. 1573-4; M.A. 1577; M.B. 1585; M.D. 1586.

HILTON, SAMUEL. Matric. sizar from CHRIST'S, July, 1608.

HILTON, THOMAS. Adm. p . (age 17) at PETERHOUSE, May 23, 1689. Of Durham. School, Houghton, Durham. Matric. 1689. Probably 2nd s. of Henry. If so, married Margaret Burdett, at Bishopwearmouth, Aug. 11, 1707. Buried Jan. 1, 1717. Probably brother of John (1687). (*T. A. Walker*, 185; H. M. Wood.)

HILTON, WILLIAM. Matric. Fell.-Com. from PETERHOUSE, Easter, 1555. 1st s. of William, of Biddick, and grandson of Sir William, Baron of Hylton. Knighted, Aug. 28, 1570. Married Anne, dau. of Sir John Yorke, of Gowthwaite. Baron of Hylton. Buried at Hylton Chapel, Sept. 9, 1600. (*G.E.C.*; *T. A. Walker*; H. M. Wood.)

HILTON, WILLIAM. Matric. sizar from TRINITY, Michs. 1608.

HILTON, WILLIAM. Adm. sizar at EMMANUEL, July, 1629. Of Lancashire. Matric. 1629; B.A. 1632-3. One of these names was minister at Ringley, Lancs., c. 1635; and at Prestwich, c. 1642. (E. Axon.)

HILTON, WILLIAM. Adm. pens. (age 18) at CAIUS, Sept. 26, 1637. S. of Edward, gent., of Lingwood, Norfolk. B. at Burlingham. School, Westfield (Mr Chapman). Matric. 1637; Scholar, 1640-2; B.A. 1641-2. Ord. deacon (Norwich) Sept. 20, 1640; C. of Lingwood; priest, Mar. 6, 1664. R. of Brooke, Norfolk, 1668-93. Will proved (Norwich C.C.) 1693. (*Venn*, I. 328.)

HILTON, ——. B.A. 1501.

HINBERFIELD, THOMAS. Adm. pens. at JESUS, Mar. 26, 1621. Of London.

HINCHINBROOKE, *see* MONTAGUE.

HINCHLIFFE, JOHN. Adm. pens. (age 18) at Trinity, June 14, 1750. S. of Joseph, of London. School, Westminster. Matric. 1750–1; Scholar, 1751; B.A. 1754; M.A. 1757; D.D. 1764 (*Lit. Reg.*). Fellow, 1755. Master of Trinity, 1768–88. Vice-Chancellor, 1768–9. Ord. deacon (Ely) Dec. 28, 1756; priest, May 19, 1757. Assistant Master at Westminster, 1757–64; Head Master, in 1764, for three months. Tutor to the Duke of Devonshire, 1764–6. V. of Greenwich, 1766–9. Chaplain to George III, 1768–9. Bishop of Peterborough, 1769–94. Dean of Durham, 1788–94. He took a prominent part in the Debates in the House of Lords on the American War. Died at Peterborough, Jan. 11, 1794. Buried in the Cathedral. Will, P.C.C. (*D.N.B.*; *Al. Westmon.*, 353.)

HINCHLIFFE, THEOPHILUS. Adm. sizar (age 17) at St John's, Feb. 3, 1639. S. of Tristram (next), V. of Timberland, Lincs. B. at Baumber or Bamburgh, Lincs. School, Lincoln (Mr Clarke). One of these names buried at Timberland, Aug. 2, 1662.

HINCHLIFFE, TRISTRAM. Matric. sizar from St John's, Easter, 1605; B.A. 1612–3. Ord. deacon (Peterb.) Mar. 20; priest, Mar. 21, 1613–4. C. of Kirkby Underwood, Lincs., 1614. V. of Timberland, 1620–40–; but not in 1662. Buried at Timberland, Sept. 6, 1665. Perhaps his will, proved, Dec. 14, 1665, at Lincoln; described as 'gentleman.' Father of Theophilus (above). (C. E. Foster.)

HINCHMAN, JOSEPH (1682), *see* **HENCHMAN.**

HINCKES, EDWARD. Matric. from Jesus, Easter, 1679; B.A. 1682–3. Probably called 'William' in College register. Ord. deacon (York) June, 1683; priest, Dec. 1684.

HINCKES, SAMUEL. Adm. pens. (age 18) at Caius, Mar. 15, 1609–10. S. of Roger, R. of Taverham, Norfolk. B. there. School, Norwich (Mr Briggs). Matric. 1610; Scholar, 1610–4; B.A. 1613–4; M.A. 1617. Ord. priest (Norwich) 1614. R. of Sporle and Palgrave, Norfolk, 1616. R. of Burlingham St Peter's, 1621–52. R. of Wickmere, 1628. Buried at Burlingham, Oct. 14, 1652. (*Venn*, I. 206.)

HINKS, WILLIAM. Adm. sizar (age 17) at Magdalene, June, 1646. S. of William, of Nun Monkton, Yorks. Matric. 1646. Migrated to Oxford. B.A. from Magdalen Hall, 1650, as 'Hicks.'

HINKES, WILLIAM. Adm. sizar at Jesus, May 5, 1679. S. of ——, clerk. Of Yorkshire. (*See* Edward, above.)

HINCKESMAN, JOHN. Adm. pens. at Queens', June 4, 1739. Of Derbyshire. Matric. 1739; B.A. 1742–3.

HINCKESMAN, THOMAS. Adm. pens. (age 19) at Trinity, Mar. 30, 1742. S. of Thomas, of Chesterfield, Derbs. School, Chesterfield (Mr Burroughs). Matric. 1742; Scholar, 1742; B.A. 1745–6.

HINXMAN, WILLIAM. Adm. scholar at Trinity Hall, Jan. 5, 1729–30. Of Hinton Christchurch, Hants. Matric. 1729–30; LL.B. 1734. V. of Gazeley, Suffolk. Died Nov. 12, 1755. Buried at Gazeley. M.I. (*G. Mag.*)

HINCKLEY, HENRY. Matric. from King's, Easter, 1749. Previously matric. from Pembroke College, Oxford, July 8, 1742, age 18. S. of Henry, of Harbourne, Staffs., gent. M.B. 1749–50; M.D. 1754. F.R.C.P., 1755. Physician to the Middlesex Hospital, 1752; to Guy's, 1756. Censor. Treasurer. 1762–79. Died Nov. 1, 1779. Will, P.C.C. (*Munk*, II. 198.)

HINCKLEY, THOMAS. Matric. sizar from Trinity, Easter, 1633. S. of Samuel, of Tenterden, Kent, yeoman. Bapt. at Hawkhurst, Mar. 19, 1619–20. In 1635, he went with his family to New England. At Scituate, Mass., 1635–40; afterwards at Barnstaple, Plymouth Colony. Deputy-governor, and finally Governor, of the Plymouth Colony, till it was absorbed in Massachusetts, 1692. Retired to legal practise, in which he acquired a great reputation. Married (1) Mary, dau. of Thomas Richards, of Weymouth, Mass., Dec. 4, 1641; (2) Mary, dau. of John Smith, and widow of Nathaniel Glover, Mar. 16, 1659–60. He had a large family by each. Died in Barnstaple, Apr. 16, 1705. His papers were published by the Massachusetts Historical Society, Ser. IV., Vol. 5. (J. G. Bartlett.)

HINCON, JOHN. Adm. pens. at St Catharine's, Jan. 19, 1669–70.

HIND, BENJAMIN. Adm. pens. at Trinity, May 22, 1669. School, Westminster. Matric. 1669.

HIND, BENJAMIN. Adm. sizar at St Catharine's, June 16, 1672. Matric. 1672; B.A. 1675–6.

HINDE, EDMUND. Matric. sizar from Trinity, *c.* 1596; Scholar, 1599.

HYNDE, EDMUND. Adm. at King's (age 17) a scholar from Eton, Sept. 19, 1597. Of Mortlake, Surrey. Doubtless 3rd s. of Edward, of the City of London, gent., whose will (P.C.C.) 1602, leaves property at Mortlake. Matric. *c.* 1597; B.A. 1601–2. Fellow, 1600, till 1603. Left on succeeding to an estate. Brother of Edward (1594). (*History of King's*, 83; J. Ch. Smith.)

HINDE, EDMUND. B.A. from St John's, 1632–3; M.A. 1637; B.D. (Oxford) 1642. Ord. priest (Peterb.) Feb. 18, 1637–8. R. of Pickworth, Rutland, 1636. V. of Weston, Herts., 1662–5. Died 1665.

HYNDE, EDMUND. Adm. sizar (age 18) at Christ's, May 10, 1634. S. of Edmund. B. at Watton, Herts. Schools, Bramfield (Mr Deacon) and Hertford (Mr Minors). Matric. 1634; B.A. from Corpus Christi, 1637–8. One of these names R. of Whepstead, Suffolk, 1642–3; 'went away to the King's army.' (*Peile*, I. 432.)

HINDE, EDWARD. Adm. Fell.-Com. at Corpus Christi, 1571. S. of Sir Francis (1546), of Madingley, Cambs. Matric. 1572. Succeeded to the Madingley estate. Knighted, Oct. 14, 1615. Brother of John (1571) and probably of William (1572).

HYNDE, EDWARD. Adm. at King's (age 17) a scholar from Eton, Aug. 24, 1594. Of London. Doubtless 2nd s. of Edward, of London. Matric. *c.* 1594; B.A. 1598–9; M.A. 1602; B.D. 1615. Fellow, 1597–1622. Vice-Provost, 1621. Chaplain to the Earl of Pembroke. Presented to Broad Chalk, Wilts., 1621. V. of Dunton Waylet, Essex, 1622–5. Died 1625–6. Brother of Edmund (1597). (*Harwood*; J. Ch. Smith.)

HYNDE, FRANCIS. Matric. pens. from St John's, Michs. 1546. S. of Sir John (next), of Madingley, Cambs. Adm. at Gray's Inn, 1549. Succeeded his father. Knighted, 1578. Died Mar. 21, 1595–6. Brother of Thomas (1551), father of Edward (1571), John (1571) and probably of William (1572). (*Cambs. Vis.*)

HYNDE, JOHN. Said to have been educated at Cambridge. Afterwards barrister of Gray's Inn, where he was reader, 1519. J.P. for the Isle of Ely, 1515. Recorder of Cambridge, 1520. Serjeant-at-law, 1531. King's serjeant, 1535. Knighted, Nov. 4, 1545. Justice Common Pleas, 1546. Of Madingley, Cambs. Buried Oct. 18, 1550, at St Dunstan's, Fleet St. Father of the above and Thomas (1551). (*Cooper*, I. 100; *D.N.B.*; Hailstone, *Bottisham*.)

HYNDE, JOHN. Adm. Fell.-Com. at Corpus Christi, 1571. S. of Sir Francis (1546), of Madingley. Matric. 1572, age 10. One of these names adm. at Gray's Inn, 1578, from Barnard's Inn. Brother of Edward (1571) and William (1572). (*Vis. of Cambs.*)

HINDE, JOHN. Matric. pens. from Trinity, Easter, 1577. One of these names R. of St Peter's, Paul's Wharf, 1589. Another (will, P.C.C., 1618) of Milford, Hants., clerk.

HIND, JOHN. Matric. pens. from Trinity, *c.* 1592; Scholar, 1593; B.A. 1595–6; M.A. 1599. Author, *Eliosto Libidinoso*, 1606. Probably grandson of Sir John Hynde, K.B. (*Cooper*, II. 446; *D.N.B.*)

HINDE, JOHN. Matric. sizar from Magdalene, Easter, 1631; B.A. 1633–4; M.A. 1637.

HYNDE, JOHN. Adm. sizar (age 16) at Christ's, May 11, 1639. S. of John. B. at Heversham, Westmorland. School, Heversham (Mr Lucas). Matric. 1639; B.A. 1642–3; M.A. 1646. Ord. deacon and priest (Lincoln) Mar. 6, 1645–6. Perhaps minister at Longton, Lancs., in 1651; and the 'John Hinde, clerk, of Warton' whose will (Richmond) 1669. (*Peile*, I. 460; E. Axon.)

HINDE, JOHN. Adm. sizar (age 18) at Sidney, Feb. 25, 1651–2. S. of John, farmer. B. at Fenlake, Beds. Schools, Fenlake (private; Mr J. Infeli) and Hitchin (Mr Kempe). Matric. 1652, as 'Hides' B.A. 1655; M.A. 1659. Ord. deacon and priest (Norwich) Sept. 1661. Will of one of these names (Archd. Wells) 1689; of Rowde, Wilts., clerk.

HIND, JOSEPH. Adm. pens. (age 13) at Magdalene, Apr. 16, 1650. S. of Edmund, of Leeds, Yorks. School, Leeds. Matric. 1650; B.A. 1653–4.

HIND, LIPTROT. Adm. sizar (age 15) at Christ's, June 2, 1721. S. of William. B. at Ince, Cheshire. School, Ince. Matric. 1721; Scholar, 1722; B.A. 1724–5. (*Peile*, II. 203.)

HINDE, NATHANIEL. Adm. sizar at Emmanuel, June 29, 1622. Matric. 1622; B.A. 1626–7; M.A. 1630. V. of Penkridge, Staffs., 1646–73. Buried there Nov. 5, 1673. (*Wm. Salt Arch. Soc.*, 1915.)

HYNDE, PERCIVAL. Matric. sizar from Clare, Easter, 1577. One of these names, of Kent, matric. from Magdalen College, Oxford, 1571, age 18; Demy, 1571–6. (*Al. Oxon.*)

HINDE, RICHARD. Matric. pens. from St John's, Easter, 1611. Of Essex. B.A. 1614–5; M.A. 1618; B.D. 1626. Fellow, 1616. V. of Higham, Kent, 1627–8.

HIND, RICHARD. B.D. 1749 (Incorp. from Oxford). S. of Thomas, of Lillingstone Lovell, Oxon., clerk. Matric. from Christ Church, May 5, 1730, age 14; B.A. (Oxford) 1732–3; M.A. 1736; B.D. 1745; D.D. 1750. Proctor, 1744. V. of Sheering, Essex, 1754. V. of Bishop's Stortford, 1754–66. V. of St Anne's, Soho, London, 1766–78. Preb. of St Paul's, 1773–90. V. of Rochdale, Lancs., 1778. V. of Skipton, Yorks., 1778–90. Died Feb. 10, 1790. Will, P.C.C. (*Al. Oxon.*)

HIND, ROBERT. B.A. 1514–5; M.A. 1518.

HYNDE, ROBERT. Matric. sizar from CHRIST'S, June, 1583. Perhaps 4th s. of Edward (s. of Sir Francis, above). Adm. at Peterhouse, Oct. 29, 1586; B.A. 1587–8.

HYNDE, ROBERT. Adm. sizar (age 17) at CHRIST'S, May 3, 1636. S. of Nicholas. B. at Casterton, Westmorland. School, Kirkby Lonsdale (Mr Carr). Matric. 1636. (*Peile*, I. 442.)

HYNDE or HINDS, SAMUEL. B.A. from CHRIST'S, 1606–7; M.A. 1610. Ord. deacon and priest (Norwich) Sept. 25, 1608, age 24. R. of Gt Waldingfield, Suffolk (patron John Hynde), 1610–21.

HINDE, SAMUEL. Matric. sizar from KING'S, Easter, 1627; B.A. 1628–9. Perhaps created B.D. from Merton College, Oxford, Aug. 1636. V. of Richmond, Surrey (B.D.), 1653–5. V. of Banstead, 1658–60 (D.D.). One of these names R. of Standish, Lancs., 1640. Chaplain to James, Earl of Derby.

HIND, THOMAS. B.Civ.L. 1501–2. Preb. of St Paul's, 1532–45. R. of Little Eversden, Cambs., 1537. Probably R. of Little Shalford, Cambs., 1539–59. R. of Girton. R. of Cottenham, 1539. Uncle of Sir Francis (1546).

HYNDE, THOMAS. Matric. sizar from CLARE, Michs. 1546.

HYNDE, THOMAS. Matric. pens. from ST JOHN'S, Easter, 1551. S. of Sir John, of Madingley. Adm. at Gray's Inn, 1552. Brother of Francis (1546). (*Vis. of Cambs.*)

HINDE, THOMAS. M.A. 1668 (Incorp. from Oxford). Matric. from Brasenose College, May 19, 1659; B.A. (Oxford) 1662–3; M.A. 1666; B.D. 1678; D.D. 1680. Archdeacon of Aghadoe, 1676. Precentor of Christchurch, Dublin, 1679. Dean of Limerick, 1680–9. Died Nov. 1689. Will, Dublin. (*Al. Oxon.*)

HYNDE, W. Matric. sizar from ST CATHARINE'S, Michs. 1568.

HINDE, WILLIAM. Matric. Fell.-Com. from QUEENS', Michs. 1572. Of Cambridgeshire. Doubtless s. of Sir Francis (1546), of Madingley. Knighted, May 11, 1603. One of these names adm. at Gray's Inn, 1577. Died 1606. Will (P.C.C.) 1606. Probably brother of Edward (1571) and John (1571). (*Vis. of Cambs.*)

HINDE, WILLIAM. Matric. sizar from CHRIST'S, July, 1612; B.A. 1615–6; M.A. 1620. Incorp. at Oxford, 1627. Ord. deacon (Peterb.) May 22; priest, May 23, 1619. R. of Fittleworth, Sussex, 1625. (*Peile*, I. 287.)

HYNDE, ——. Pens. at PETERHOUSE, July, 1547.

HYNDE, ——. Fell.-Com. at PETERHOUSE, July 25, 1579. Resided till 1580.

HINDERSON, JOHN, *see* HENDERSON.

HINDLE, JAMES. Matric. sizar from TRINITY, 1639; B.A. 1640–1. V. of Gt Bookham, Surrey, 1641. Died 1670.

HINDLE, NATHANIEL. Adm. sizar at CHRIST'S, Apr. 23, 1672. S. of Henry. B. at Halifax. School, Halifax (Mr Doughty). B.A. 1676–7. Ord. deacon (Norwich) Mar. 1673–4; priest, Feb. 1674–5. V. of Ludham, Norfolk, 1675. V. of Hickling, 1681–1706. R. of Potter-Heigham, 1699. (*Peile*, II. 42.)

HINDLEY, CHRISTOPHER. Adm. sizar (age 19) at ST JOHN'S, May 20, 1641. S. of Ralph, of Rishton, Lancs., husbandman. School, Blackburn (Mr Ri. Halsted). Matric. 1641; B.A. 1644–5; M.A. 1648. Fellow, 1647. Incorp. at Oxford, 1653. V. of Urchfont, Wilts., 1652. V. of Manningford Bruce, 1661.

HINDLEY, HENRY. B.D. 1609 (Incorp. from Oxford). Of Lancashire. Matric. from St John's, Oxford, June 15, 1588, age 18; B.A. (Corpus Christi, Oxford) 1591; M.A. 1594; B.D. 1603. Licensed to preach, 1607.

HINDLEY, HUGH. Adm. pens. (age 15) at ST JOHN'S, May 7, 1666. S. of Hugh, lawyer, deceased, of London. B. there. School, Sedbergh (Mr Fell). Matric. 1667. Adm. at Gray's Inn, Mar. 10, 1669–70, as s. and h. of Hugh, late of Hindley, Lancs., deceased.

HINDLEY, ROBERT. Adm. pens. at JESUS, June 22, 1695. Previously matric. from Corpus Christi, Oxford, June 1, 1693, age 18. S. of Robert, clerk, of Lancashire. Matric. 1695; Scholar, 1695; B.A. 1696–7; M.A. 1700. Ord. deacon (Peterb.) June 3, 1699; priest (London) Sept. 22, 1700. R. of Aughton, Lancs., 1701–20. Buried there Nov. 12, 1720. (*Al. Oxon.*; H. I. Longden.)

HYNDMAN, JOHN. Adm. pen. at EMMANUEL, May 25, 1627. Of Leicestershire. Scholar from Market Bosworth School. Matric. 1627; B.A. 1630–1; M.A. 1634. Dixie fellow, 1631.

HINDMARSH, HERBERT. Matric. sizar from MAGDALENE, c. 1596. B. at Gt Carlton, Lincs., 1578. B.A. 1599–1600; M.A. 1605. Ord. priest (Lincoln) June 15, 1606. R. of Saltfleetby St Clement, Lincs., 1607.

HYNDMARSH or HYMERS, JOHN. Adm. pens. (age 17) at CHRIST'S, July 15, 1639, as Hymers. S. of Reuben, of Wallsend, Durham. B. at Wallsend. Schools, Morpeth and Newcastle (Mr Oxley). Matric. 1639. Adm. at Gray's Inn, Aug. 14, 1640. Of Wallsend. Married, July 17, 1645, Elizabeth Bainbrigge. Father of the next two. (H. M. Wood.)

HYNDMARSH, JOHN. Adm. pens. (age 16) at CHRIST'S, Apr. 29, 1665. S. of John (above). B. at Wallsend, Durham. School, Newcastle (Mr Oxley). Matric. 1665. Adm. at Gray's Inn, June 5, 1667. Buried at All Saints', Newcastle, July 31, 1694. Brother of the next. (*Peile*, I. 616.)

HINDMARSH or HENMARSH, RICHARD. Adm. pens. (age 17) at CHRIST'S, June 30, 1662. S. of John (1639). B. at Wallsend. School, Berwick (Mr Webbe). Matric. 1662. Married, May 1, 1673, Ann Broomley, of Monk Hesledon. Buried at Wallsend, Apr. 18, 1703. Brother of John (above). (*Peile*, I. 599; H. M. Wood.)

HINDMARSH, THOMAS. Adm. sizar at QUEENS', May 29, 1667. Of Lincolnshire. Migrated to Corpus Christi. Matric. 1667; B.A. 1670–1; M.A. 1676. Ord. deacou (Lincoln) Sept. 22, 1672.

HYNDMER, JOHN. Matric. pens. from CHRIST'S, Nov. 1552; B.A. 1557–8. Fellow, 1558. Nephew of Reginald, parson of Wensley, on whose death he succeeded to the family estate at Aislabie. Died 1589. (*Peile*, I. 51.)

HYNDMER, ROBERT. B.Civ.L. 1520; D.Civ.L. 1526; D.Can.L. 1528. Chancellor of the diocese of Durham. R. of Bluntisham, Hunts., 1527–53. Dean of the Collegiate Church of Lanchester, Durham, 1532. Dean of Auckland, 1541. R. of Stanhope, 1545–58. Commissioner to treat with the Queen of Scots, 1557. Died 1558. Will (Durham); as of Sedgefield. (*Cooper*, I. 180, 551.)

HINDMER, HYNMERS or HYMNERS, W. Matric. pens. from ST JOHN'S, Michs. 1564.

HINGE, THOMAS. Adm. at KING'S (age 17) a scholar from Eton, Aug. 23, 1537. Of Coventry. Name off, *c.* 1540.

HINGESTON, CHARLES. Adm. sizar (age 18) at CHRIST'S, June 29, 1745. 6th s. of Peter (? 1711). B. at Ipswich, July 8, 1727. School, Monk Soham (Mr Ray). Scholar, 1745; Matric. 1745–6; B.A. 1748–9; M.A. 1752. Ord. deacon (Norwich) May, 1750; priest (Ely) Dec. 1752. R. of Trimley St Martin, Suffolk, 1778–87. R. of Rishangles. Died Feb. 4, 1787. Buried at Capel. (*Peile*, II. 248; Davy, *Suff. MSS.*)

HINGESTONE, JAMES. Adm. sizar at EMMANUEL, June 15, 1751. 3rd s. of Robert (1716), Master of Ipswich School. B. Aug. 14, 1733. School, Ipswich. Matric. 1751; B.A. 1755; M.A. 1758. Ord. deacon (Norwich) Oct. 1756; priest, May, 1758. V. of Reydon and Southwold, Suffolk, 1758–77. Died Mar. 30, 1777. Buried at Reydon. Brother of Samuel (1747). (*G. Mag.*)

HINGESTON, PETER. Adm. pens. (age 17) at PEMBROKE, June 16, 1711. S. of Peter, of Ipswich, gent. B. June 6, 1694. Matric. 1712; B.A. 1714–5; M.A. 1718. Ord. deacon (Norwich) Oct. 1719. V. of Wenham Parva, Suffolk, 1726. R. of Capel St Mary, 1726–86. Died July 18, 1786. Brother of the next.

HINGESTON, ROBERT. Adm. sizar (age 17) at PEMBROKE, June 27, 1716. S. of Peter, of Ipswich, organist. B. Mar. 8, 1698–9. Matric. 1716; B.A. 1719–20; M.A. 1723. Ord. deacon (Norwich) May, 1722; 'reader at Ipswich'; priest, May, 1724. R. of West Creeting, Suffolk. R. of Gt Bealings, 1726. R. of Newborne, 1727. R. of St Helen's, Ipswich, 1730. Head Master of Ipswich Grammar School, 1743–66. Died Apr. 9, 1766. Admon., P.C.C. Brother of the above, father of the next and James (1751). (*E. Anglian*, IX. 130.)

HINGESTON, SAMUEL. Adm. sizar (age 17) at CAIUS, July 6, 1747. S. of Robert (above), R. of West Creeting, Suffolk and Head Master of Ipswich. B. at Ipswich, Oct. 27, 1729. School, Ipswich (Mr Bolton and his father). Matric. 1747; B.A. 1750; M.A. 1756. Ord. deacon (Ely, *Litt. dim.* from Norwich) Dec. 25, 1751; priest (London) Dec. 23, 1753. R. of Boyton, 1765–1807; of Holton, 1786–1807. Died Feb. 8, 1807. Buried at Boyton. Brother of James (1751). (*Venn*, II. 60.)

HINGLEY, AUGUSTINE. Adm. sizar at EMMANUEL, Apr. 1, 1661. Of Derbyshire. Matric. 1661.

HINGLY, JOHN. Adm. sizar (age 19) at ST JOHN'S, June 25, 1646. S. of Oliver, farmer, of Newton Solney, Derbs. B. there. School, Repton (Mr Uttock). Matric. 1646; B.A. 1649–50.

HINKS, *see* HINCKES.

HINLEY, ——. Adm. pens. at EMMANUEL, June 17, 1618. Matric. 1618.

HINN, THOMAS. B.Civ.L. 1498–9.

HINNINGHAM, GILBERT. Adm. sizar at EMMANUEL, Sept. 17, 1611; B.A. 1614–5.

HINSON, JOHN. Matric. pens. from ST JOHN'S, Michs. 1583.

HINSON or HENSON, JOHN. Adm. sizar at JESUS, July 20, 1627. Of London. Matric. 1628; Scholar, 1629; B.A. 1630–1; M.A. 1635.

HINSON, JOHN. Adm. pens. (age 17) at CAIUS, May 27, 1630. S. of Thomas (1588), of Fordham, Cambs. B. at Soham. Bapt. Sept. 6, 1612. School, Thurlow (Mr Moore). Matric. 1631; B.A. 1633-4; M.A. 1637. Ord. deacon (Peterb.) June 9; priest (Norwich) Sept. 22, 1639. Probably died young. (*Venn*, I. 295.)

HYNSON, THOMAS. Matric. pens. from CHRIST'S, May, 1567. S. of Thomas, gent. B. at Fordham, Cambs. Scholar; B.A. 1570-1; M.A. from Corpus, 1574. Fellow and tutor of Caius, 1575, till 1576. Incorp. at Oxford, 1577. Appointed agent to his former pupil Lord Bath, in Devon. J.P. for Devon. M.P. for Barnstaple, 1586, 1588, 1597, 1604-11. Died Apr. 17, 1614. M.I. in Tawstock Church. Father of Thomas (1603) and William (1594). (*Vis. of Middlesex*, 1663; *Peile*, I. 99; *Venn*, I. 81.)

HYNSON, THOMAS. Matric. pens. from MAGDALENE, Easter, 1588.

HINSON, THOMAS. Adm. pens. (age 16) at CAIUS, July 6, 1588. S. of William. B. at Fordham, Cambs. School, Bury St Edmunds (Mr Wright). Scholar, 1589-92. Of Fordham, Esq. Married Ann, dau. of Thomas Petchy, of Soham, Cambs. Father of John (1630). (*Venn*, I. 134; *Vis. of Middlesex*, 1663.)

HYNSON, THOMAS. Adm. pens. (age 18) at CAIUS, June 10, 1603. S. of Thomas (1567), of Tawstock, Devon. Bapt. May 8, 1586. School, Barnstaple (Mr Butler). Of Hunts Court, Gloucs., Esq. Married Mary, dau. of William Lawrence, of Sherrington. Brother of William (1594). (*Venn*, I. 182; *Vis. of Gloucs.*, 1623.)

HINSON, WILLIAM. Adm. (age 14) at CAIUS, May 20, 1594. S. of Thomas (1567), gent. B. at Tawstock, Devon. Bapt. June 7, 1580. Schools, Tawstock and Ely (Mr Bande and Mr Spight). B.A. 1598-9. Adm. at Lincoln's Inn, Nov. 6, 1602. Died 1616. Brother of Thomas (above). (*Vis. of Gloucs.*, 1623.)

HINSON, WILLIAM. Matric. pens. from TRINITY HALL, Michs. 1613; LL.B. 1620. Fellow, 1620-9.

HINSON, ——. Fell.-Com. at JESUS, 1589-91.

HINTON, ANTHONY. Adm. (age 30) at MAGDALENE, Mar. 1746-7. Ord. priest (London) Dec. 23, 1754. V. of Hayes, Middlesex, 1757-92. Died Mar. 12, 1792. Will, P.C.C.

HINTON, BENJAMIN. Matric. pens. from TRINITY, *c.* 1593; Scholar, 1593, as Henton; B.A. 1596-7; M.A. 1600; B.D. 1607. Fellow, 1599. V. of Sedbergh, Yorks., 1615-24. R. of Little Stanmore, Middlesex, 1619-32. V. of Hendon, 1626-43, sequestered. Married Joan, sister of Richard Love, D.D., Dean of Ely. Her will (P.C.C.) 1645.

HINTON, GEORGE. Adm. pens. (age 17) at SIDNEY, Oct. 1640. S. of George, Esq. B. at Eversholt, Beds. Bapt. Sept. 28, 1622. Schools, Woburn (Mr Roberts) and Houghton Conquest (Mr Wm. Taylor). Matric. 1641. (*Vis. of Beds.*, 1634.)

HINTON, JOHN. Adm. at CORPUS CHRISTI, 1625. Of Norfolk.

HINTON, JOHN. Adm. pens. at TRINITY, Sept. 10, 1662. Matric. 1663; M.B. 1668. Will (P.C.C.) 1698; of Linton, Kent, M.D.

HINTON, JOHN. Adm. pens. (age 19) at TRINITY, Dec. 18, 1689. From Trinity College, Dublin. Adm. there, Apr. 5, 1686, age 14. S. of Edward, D.D., of Kilkenny. B. at Chipping Norton, Oxford. School, Kilkenny. B.A. 1689-90; B.A. (Dublin) 1690; LL.B. and LL.D. (Dublin) 1704. Dean of Tuam, 1712-43. Died Aug. 1743. Will, Dublin. (A. B. Beaven; *Al. Dub.*)

HINTON, LAURENCE. M.A. 1626 (Incorp. from Oxford). S. of Thomas, of Bourton, Berks. Matric. from Queen's College, Oxford, Apr. 26, 1616, age 17; B.A. (Oxford) 1618; M.A. 1624; D.D. 1642-3. Fellow of Merton College, Oxford, 1619. R. of Chilbolton, Hants., 1633. Preb. of Winchester, 1644-58. Died 1658. Will, P.C.C. (*Al. Oxon.*; J. Ch. Smith.)

HINTON, SAMUEL. Matric. pens. from TRINITY, Michs. 1614. S. of William (1570), Archdeacon of Coventry. B. Jan. 17, 1598-9. Scholar, 1614; B.A. 1616-7; M.A. 1620. Fellow, 1618. LL.D. (Oxford) 1636. Royalist sufferer. Died at Lichfield, Jan. 5, 1668, aged 71. (Blyth's *Hist. of Stoke, Staffs.*; *Gen. et Her.*, N.S., IV. 148.)

HYNTON, THOMAS. Matric. sizar from GONVILLE HALL, Easter, 1552.

HINTON, THOMAS. Matric. pens. from TRINITY, Easter, 1578. Probably s. of Thomas, of Bourton, Berks. Died *c.* 1634. One of these names knighted July 1, 1619. Father of Laurence (1626). (*Vis. of Berks.*, 1665-6.)

HINTON, THOMAS. Adm. sizar at TRINITY, June 3, 1704. S. of Giles, of Biddenden, Kent. School, Cranbrook, Kent (Mr Crowde). Matric. 1704; B.A. 1707-8; M.A. 1712. Ord. deacon (Lincoln) Feb. 25, 1710-1; priest (Ely) Feb. 21, 1713-4. C. of Thornton, Bucks., 1713. R. of Alderton, Northants., 1729-46. Buried there May 20, 1746.

HINTON, WILLIAM. Scholar of TRINITY, 1570, as Henton. S. of Richard. B.A. 1571-2; M.A. 1575; B.D. 1582; D.D. 1587. Fellow, 1574. University preacher, 1581. V. of St Michael, Coventry, 1583-1631. Archdeacon of Coventry, 1584-1631. Precentor of St David's, 1597-1631. Preb. of Lichfield, 1597-1631. Preb. of Hereford, 1605-27. Died June 21, 1631, aged 78. Buried at St Michael's, Coventry. Will (P.C.C.) 1631. Father of Samuel (1614). (*Staffs. Pedigrees*; Blyth's *Stoke*.)

HINTON, WILLIAM. Matric. sizar from CORPUS CHRISTI, Easter, 1634; B.A. 1637-8; M.A. 1641. Ord. deacon (Norwich) Feb. 1; priest, Feb. 25, 1642-3, age 26. R. of Kirkley, Suffolk, 1642.

HINTON, ——. Student at PETERHOUSE, 1563. Probably sizar.

HINTYS, ——. M.A. 1484. Probably Nicholas Hyntes (whom *see*) fellow of CLARE, 1486.

HINXMAN, WILLIAM, *see* HINCKESMAN.

HINXWORTH or INGSWORTH, RICHARD. Adm. at KING'S (age 17) a scholar from Eton, Aug. 15, 1505. Of London. B.A. 1509-10; M.A. 1513. Fellow, 1508-16. Ord. sub-deacon (Lincoln) June 14; deacon, Sept. 20, 1511.

HION, ROWLAND, *see* ION.

HIPPISLEY, JOHN. Adm. sizar at QUEENS', July 1, 1662. Of Somerset. Matric. 1663; B.A. 1665-6; M.A. 1673. Signed for deacon's orders (London) Sept. 24, 1670. Ord. priest (Ely) Mar. 3, 1671-2. R. of Meesden, Herts., 1674-94. Died 1694. Will (Consist. C. London) 1694.

HIPPISLEY, RICHARD. M.A. from KING'S, 1744. S. of John, of Emborough, Somerset, gent. Matric. from Christ Church, Oxford, Oct. 14, 1726, age 16; B.A. (Oxford) 1730. Ord. deacon (Bath and Wells) Dec. 19, 1731; priest, Dec. 23, 1733. R. of Stanton Fitzwarren, Wilts. Chaplain to Lord Borthwick. R. of Stow-on-the-Wold, Gloucs., 1744. Died 1764. Will (P.C.C.) 1765. (*Al. Oxon.*; F. S. Hockaday.)

HIPSLEY, SAMUEL. Adm. scholar at TRINITY HALL, Jan. 7, 1678-9. Previously matric. from St Edmund's Hall, Oxford, Mar. 9, 1675-6. S. of Thomas, of Stanton Drew, Somerset, gent. Matric. 1679; B.A. 1679-80. (*Al. Oxon.*)

HIRD, WILLIAM, *see* HURD.

HIRN, *see* HEARNE *and* HIERON.

HIRST, *see also* HURST.

HIRST or HEARST, CHRISTOPHER. M.A. 1600 (Incorp. from Oxford). Of Wiltshire. Matric. from Magdalen College, Oxford, Nov. 5, 1585, age 16; B.A. (Oxford) 1590-1; M.A. 1594; B.D. 1604. Fellow, 1590-1605. R. of Rimpton, Somerset, 1604-5. V. of Eling, Hants., 1604. R. of Chilbolton, 1609. V. of Hambledon, 1612. R. of Droxford, 1613. Preb. of Winchester, 1614-28. Will (P.C.C.) 1631. (*Al. Oxon.*)

HIRST, EDWARD. B.D. 1609 (Incorp. from Oxford). B.A. from St Mary's Hall, 1587-8; M.A. (Brasenose College) 1592; B.D. 1600. R. of Hackington, Canterbury, 1605-12. V. of Linsted, Kent, 1612-8. V. of Teynham, 1612-8. Died 1618. (*Vis. of Kent*, 1663.)

HIRST, HENRY. Adm. pens. at EMMANUEL, Easter, 1625. Matric 1625; B.A. from St Catharine's, 1629-30; M.A. 1633. Perhaps V. of Huddersfield, Yorks., *c.* 1639-73. Died 1673.

HURST or HYRST, JAMES. M.A. 1609 (Incorp. from Oxford). B.A. from Brasenose College, 1601-2; M.A. 1606-7. V. of West Hythe, Kent, 1610-5. R. of Hackington, Canterbury, 1615-42. Died Sept. 24, 1642. Will (Canterbury) 1642. (H. G. Harrison.)

HIRST, JOHN. Adm. pens. at ST CATHARINE'S, Sept. 30, 1742. Of Halifax, Yorks. Matric. 1742; B.A. 1746-7; M.A. 1750. Fellow, 1748-53. Ord. deacon (Ely) June 5, 1748; priest, June 4, 1750.

HIRST, THOMAS. Matric. pens. from ST CATHARINE'S, Easter, 1621; B.A. 1622-3; M.A. 1626. One of these names, M.A., R. of Long Leadenham, Lincs., 1627. R. of Lurbar, 1627.

HIRST, THOMAS. Adm. pens. (age 17) at PETERHOUSE, Apr. 20, 1748. Of Hertfordshire. Doubtless s. of William (1718). School, Hertford. Matric. 1748; Scholar, 1748; B.A. 1752; M.A. 1755. Fellow, 1754. Perhaps F.R.S., 1755. R. of Little Shelford, Cambs., 1758. R. of Boxworth, 1760-91. Married, May 17, 1761, at Little St Mary's, Bridget Christian. Died Feb. 19, 1791. Will, P.C.C. (G. *Mag.*; *T. A. Walker*.)

HIRST or HURST, WILLIAM. Adm. sizar (age 17) at JESUS, Apr. 17, 1676. Of Yorkshire. Matric. 1676; B.A. 1679-80. Perhaps R. of Broughton Hackett, Worcs., 1692-1702.

HIRST, WILLIAM. Adm. sizar at EMMANUEL, Apr. 26, 1718. Of Yorkshire. Matric. 1718; B.A. 1721-2; M.A. 1734; D.D. 1746. Ord. priest (Lincoln, *Litt. dim.* from Bath and Wells) Mar. 6, 1725-6. V. of Bengeo, Herts., 1729-60. R. of Sacomb, 1739-60. Master of Hertford Grammar School. J.P. for the County. Died Dec. 14, 1760, aged 59. Will, P.C.C. Father of the next and Thomas (1748). (*Cussans*, II.)

HIRST, WILLIAM. Adm. pens. (age 17) at PETERHOUSE, Apr. 2, 1747. S. of William (above), D.D. School, Hertford. Matric. 1747; Scholar, 1747; B.A. 1750-1; M.A. 1754. F.R.S., 1755. Became a Navy chaplain. Present at the sieges of Pondicherry and Vellore. Distinguished as an astronomer. Chaplain to the factory at Calcutta, 1762-4. Returned to England. Started again, in 1769, as chaplain to the Commission of the East India Company to Bengal. The ship was lost at sea, c. Dec. 1769. Brother of Thomas (1748). (*D.N.B.*; H. B. Hyde, *Annals of Bengal*.)

HISLINGTON, *see* HASLINGTON.

HISSON, FRANCIS. Matric. sizar from CLARE, Michs. 1579.

HISSON or HIGSON, WILLIAM. B.A. from ST JOHN'S, 1603-4.

HITCH, HENRY. Adm. pens. at QUEENS', Mar. 26, 1636. Of Cambridgeshire. Matric. 1636. Migrated to Jesus, Feb. 23, 1636-7. Scholar; B.A. 1639-40; M.A. 1643; LL.D. 1661 (*Lit. Reg.*). Incorp. at Oxford, 1680. Chancellor of Ely.

HITCH, HENRY. Adm. pens. (age 18) at TRINITY, Mar. 19, 1722. S. of Robert (1687), of Leathley, Yorks., Esq. School, Westminster. Matric. 1722; Scholar, 1723. Adm. at the Inner Temple, Nov. 27, 1721. Receiver-general for the West Riding. Married Alethoea, dau. of Colonel Robert Brandling, of Leathley. Died Mar. 2, 1765. Brother of Robert (1722). (M. H. Peacock.)

HITCH, JEREMIAH. Adm. pens. at TRINITY, Dec. 19, 1667.

HITCH or HECHE, JOHN. B.D. 1521-2. Dominican friar.

HITCH, JOHN. Adm. sizar at JESUS, Apr. 25, 1650. Of the Isle of Ely. Matric. 1652; Scholar, 1652; B.A. 1653-4; M.A. 1657; LL.D. 1669 (*Lit. Reg.*). Fellow, 1662-84. Incorp. at Oxford, 1662. Died 1684. (A. Gray.)

HITCH, ROBERT. Matric. sizar from TRINITY, Easter, 1611, as Hich; Scholar, 1614; B.A. 1615-6; M.A. 1619; B.D. 1628; D.D. 1661 (*Lit. Reg.*). Fellow, 1617. Ord. deacon (Peterb.) June 11, 1625. R. of Adel, Yorks., 1627. Preb. of York, 1660. Archdeacon of Leicester, 1661-2. Archdeacon of East Riding, 1662. Dean of York, 1665-77. Died Feb. 10, 1676-7.

HITCH, ROBERT. Adm. pens. (age 16) at TRINITY, June 11, 1687. S. of Henry, of Leathley, Yorks. School, Wakefield (Mr Armitage). Adm. at Gray's Inn, May 15, 1690. Of Leathley. M.P. for Knaresborough, 1715-22. Died Nov. 6, 1723. Father of the next and of Henry (1722), brother of Walter (1699).

HITCH, ROBERT. Adm. pens. (age 18) at TRINITY, Dec. 22, 1722. S. of Robert (1687), of Yorkshire. School, Westminster. Matric. 1723; Scholar, 1724; B.A. 1726-7; M.A. 1730. *Litt. dim.* from York, for priest, Nov. 1730. R. of Adel, Yorks., 1733-7. V. of Bramhope, 1740-7. V. of Bassall, 1740-2. Brother of Henry (1722).

HITCH or HYTHE, THOMAS. Matric. sizar from JESUS, Michs. 1571; B.A. 1575-6. Ord. deacon (Ely) Dec. 21, 1576; priest, Nov. 17, 1577. C. and schoolmaster of Stretham, Cambs., 1579. Head Master of Ely Cathedral school for many years.

HITCHE, THOMAS. Matric. sizar from CHRIST'S, Apr. 1582. Of Cambridgeshire, probably of Melbourne. (*Peile*, I. 169.)

HITCH, THOMAS. Adm. sizar (age 15) at PETERHOUSE, June 18, 1637. Of the Isle of Ely. School, Ely. Migrated to Jesus, Nov. 6, 1637. B.A. 1640-1; M.A. 1644. Perhaps ord. deacon (Ely) Sept. 19, 1662; priest, Sept. 19, 1663. Precentor, sacrist and librarian of Ely Cathedral. C. of Trinity Church, Ely, 1676. (A. Gray.)

HITCH, THOMAS. Adm. pens. (age 17) at PETERHOUSE, Apr. 24, 1671. Of Cambridgeshire. Doubtless s. of Robert, of Melbourne. School, Bourn, Cambs. Of Melbourne, Cambs. Married Catherine, dau. of Geoffrey Nightingale, of Kneesworth. (*Genealogist*, III. 300.)

HITCH, WALTER. Adm. pens. (age 19) at TRINITY, June 30, 1699. S. of Henry, of Leathley, Yorks. School, Bradford, Yorks. (Mr Clapham). Matric. 1699; B.A. 1702-3. Brother of Robert (1687).

HITCH, WILLIAM. Matric. sizar from QUEENS', Easter, 1606. Of Cambridgeshire. B.A. 1609-10; M.A. 1614. Probably vicar-choral of Ely, ejected.

HITCH, WILLIAM. Adm. sizar at QUEENS', 1644. Of the Isle of Ely. Migrated to Jesus, Mar. 29, 1645. Matric. 1645; Scholar, 1645; B.A. 1647-8.

HITCHAM, ROBERT. Matric. pens. from PEMBROKE, Michs. 1587. B. at Levington, Suffolk, c. 1572. School, Ipswich. Adm. at Gray's Inn, Nov. 3, 1589, from Barnard's Inn. M.P. for West Looe, 1597-8; for Lynn, 1604-11; for Cambridge, 1614; for Orford, 1624-5, 1626. Attorney-general to the Queen Consort, 1603. Knighted, June 29, 1604. Serjeant-at-law, 1614. King's serjeant, 1616. Died Aug. 15, 1636. Buried at Framlingham. M.I. there. Will (P.C.C.) 1636-7. Benefactor to Pembroke College. (*D.N.B.*; *Loder*, 303.)

HITCHCOCK, GEORGE. Adm. sizar at QUEENS', Dec. 19, 1646. Of Wiltshire. Adm. at Gray's Inn, May 17, 1655, as s. of John, of Preshute, Wilts., Esq. Barrister, 1661. He probably migrated to Oxford. Scholar of New College; B.A. 1649; M.A. 1652. Fellow of Lincoln; ejected, 1662. (*Al. Oxon.*)

HITCHCOCK, GEORGE. Adm. sizar (age 17) at ST JOHN'S, Apr. 22, 1681. S. of Richard, shoemaker. B. at Stafford. School, Stafford (Mr Taylour). Matric. 1681, as 'Hitch'; B.A. 1684-5.

HITCHCOCK, HENRY. Matric. sizar from TRINITY, c. 1591.

HITCHCOX, ISAAC. Adm. pens. (age 16) at JESUS, Apr. 15, 1669. Of Hertfordshire. S. of Robert, M.B., of Ware. Died Jan. 19, 1678-9. M.I. at Hunsdon, Herts.

HITCHCOCK, JAMES CHARLES. Adm. sizar (age 18) at PEMBROKE, June 15, 1747. S. of Thomas, citizen and haberdasher of London. 'Grecian' from Christ's Hospital. Matric. 1748; B.A. 1750-1; M.A. 1754. Ord. deacon (London) June 17, 1753; priest, June 9, 1754. Of Bittiswell, Leics. Died Jan. 24, 1789. (*G. Mag.*)

HITCHCOCKE, JOHN. Adm. pens. at JESUS, July 2, 1675. Previously matric. from St Edmund's Hall, Oxford, July 1, 1672, age 16. S. of Edward, of Islington, Middlesex. Matric. 1675; B.A. 1676-7; M.A. 1680. V. of Pawlett, Somerset, 1685-90. R. of Piddletown, Dorset, 1691-4. Author, *Sermon*. Died 1694.

HITCHCOCK, LAURENCE. Matric. pens. from MAGDALENE, Michs. 1565; B.A. from Christ's, 1569-70. Will proved (V.C.C.) 1573.

HITCHCOCK, MILES. Matric. sizar from ST JOHN'S, Michs. 1564. Will of one of these names (P.C.C.) 1610; of Uxbridge, Middlesex, gent.

HITCHCOCK, WILLIAM. Matric. pens. from CHRIST'S, Oct. 1564; Scholar. Perhaps R. of Strixton, Northants., 1595, till 1622. Died 1622. (*Peile*, I. 86.)

HITCHING, JOHN. Adm. pens. (age 15) at ST JOHN'S, May 9, 1650. S. of Thomas, gent., of Pontefract. B. there. Bapt. at Carleton, Sept. 20, 1631. School, Pontefract (Mr Elliot). Matric. 1650. Adm. at Gray's Inn, July 6, 1650. Of Carleton, Esq. Married Faith, dau. of William Wakefield, of Pontefract. Buried at Pontefract, Feb. 24, 1715-6. (M. H. Peacock.)

HITCHING, JOHN. Adm. sizar (age 18) at ST JOHN'S, June 29, 1717. S. of Nicholas, husbandman, of Yorkshire. B. at Threapland, Skipton. School, Threshfield (Mr Marshall). Matric. 1717; B.A. 1720-1.

HITCHIN, THOMAS. Adm. pens. at PETERHOUSE, Lent, 1603-4. Matric. 1604.

HITCHINSON, ISAAC. Adm. pens. (age 18) at MAGDALENE, Mar. 2, 1662-3. S. of Thomas, of Carsington, Derbs. School, Wirksworth. Matric. 1667. His name appears for ordination as deacon at London, Mar. 5, 1663-4, to the curacy of St Mary Woolnoth, but no signature. Brother of the next.

HITCHINSON, THOMAS. Adm. sizar (age 17) at MAGDALENE, Mar. 28, 1653. S. of Thomas, of Carsington, Derbs. Matric. 1653; B.A. 1656; M.A. 1660; B.D. 1661 (*Lit. Reg.*); D.D. 1673. Ord. deacon (Lincoln) c. 1660. Brother of Isaac (above).

HITE, WILLIAM. M.A. from EMMANUEL, 1722. S. of William, of Goathurst, Somerset, clerk. Matric. from Wadham College, Oxford, Mar. 28, 1705, age 18; B.A. (Oxford) 1708. V. of Knowstone and Molland, Devon, 1719. R. of Lympston, 1733. R. of Babcary, Somerset, 1735. (*Al. Oxon.*)

HOADLY, BENJAMIN. Adm. pens. at ST CATHARINE'S, Feb. 18, 1691-2. S. of Samuel, Head Master of Norwich School (for whom *see D.N.B.*). B. at Westerham, Kent. Bapt. Dec. 22, 1676. Matric. 1692; B.A. 1695-6; M.A. 1699. Fellow, 1697-1701. D.D. (Lambeth) 1715. Ord. deacon (London) 1698; priest, Dec. 22, 1700. Lecturer of St Mildred Poultry, 1701-11. R. of St Peter-le-Poer, 1704-20. R. of Streatham, Surrey, 1710-23. Chaplain to George I, 1715. R. of Llandyssnan, Anglesey. R. of Llandurnog, Vale of Gwyd. Bishop of Bangor, 1716-21; of Hereford, 1721-2; of Salisbury, 1723-34; and of Winchester, 1734-61. An eminent controversialist; leader of the latitudinarian party in Church and State. His sermon on the 'Nature of the Kingdom or Church of Christ' caused the 'Bangorian Controversy,' 1717-20. Author, controversial, etc. Died at his palace at Chelsea, Apr. 17, 1761, aged 85. Buried in Winchester Cathedral. Father of the next, and of John (1730), brother of John (1693). (*D.N.B.*; *Cath. Coll. Hist.*)

HOADLY, BENJAMIN. Adm. at CORPUS CHRISTI, 1722. S. of Benjamin (above), Bishop of Winchester. B. in London, Feb. 10, 1706. School, Hackney. Matric. 1724; M.B. 1727; M.D. 1728 (*Com. Reg.*). Made Registrar of Hereford, by his father whilst bishop. F.R.S., 1727. F.R.C.P., 1736. Gulstonian lecturer, 1737. Harveian orator, 1742. Physician to the Royal household, 1742-5. Author of comedies. Died Aug. 10, 1757. Brother of John (1730). (*Munk*, II. 132; *D.N.B.*; A. B. Beaven.)

HOADLY, JOHN. 'Of St John's, Cambridge,' when ord. priest (Gloucester) Oct. 25, 1678. One of these names R. of Halstead, Kent, 1678–1725. (F. S. Hockaday.)

HOADLY, JOHN. Adm. pens. at St Catharine's, Aug. 11, 1693. S. of Samuel, Head Master of Norwich School. B. at Tottenham, Middlesex, Sept. 27, 1678. Matric. 1694; B.A. 1697–8; M.A. 1703; D.D. 1717 (*Com. Reg.*). Incorp. at Dublin, 1730, and perhaps again, in 1743. Ord. deacon (Norwich) Dec. 1701; priest, Sept. 1703. Assistant Master at Norwich under his father. R. of Spixworth, Norfolk, 1704–6. Preb. of Salisbury, 1706–13. Archdeacon of Salisbury, 1710–27; and Chancellor, 1713–27. Chaplain to the King, 1717–27. R. of Ockham, Surrey, 1717–27. Preb. of Hereford, 1722–7. Bishop of Leighlin and Ferns, 1727–30. Archbishop of Dublin, 1730–42. Archbishop of Armagh, 1742–6. Vice-Chancellor, Trinity College, Dublin, 1742. Died July 19, 1746. Buried at Tallaght. Brother of Benjamin (1691–2). (*D.N.B.*)

HOADLY, JOHN. Adm. at Corpus Christi, 1730. S. of Benjamin (1692), Bishop of Winchester. B. in London, Oct. 8, 1711. School, Hackney. Matric. 1731; LL.B. 1736; LL.D. (Lambeth) 1748. Adm. at the Middle Temple, Nov. 1, 1726. Ord. deacon, Dec. 7; priest, Dec. 21, 1735. Chancellor of the diocese of Winchester, 1735–76. Chaplain to the Prince of Wales. R. of Michelmersh, Hants., 1737. R. of Alresford, 1737. R. of Wroughton, Wilts., 1737–60. Preb. of Winchester, 1737–60. R. of St Mary, Southampton, 1743–76. R. of Overton, Hants., 1746–76. Master of St Cross, Winchester, 1760–76. Poet and dramatist. Died Mar. 16, 1776. Buried in Winchester Cathedral. Will, P.C.C. Brother of Benjamin (1722). (*D.N.B.*; *Cath. Coll. Hist.*, 167.)

HOAKE, ——. Sizar at Peterhouse, 1589–90.

HOALE, *see* HOLLE.

HOARD, SAMUEL. M.A. 1622 (Incorp. from Oxford); B.D. 1632. B. in London, 1599. Matric. from All Souls, Oct. 10, 1617, age 18; B.A. (St Mary Hall, Oxford) 1618; M.A. 1620–1; B.D. 1630. Chaplain to the Earl of Warwick. R. of Moreton, Essex, 1625. Preb. of St Paul's, 1637–58. Author, theological. Died Jan. 15, 1658–9. Buried in Moreton Church. His father, William, buried there, Mar. 6, 1644–5. Father of the next. (*D.N.B.*; *Al. Oxon.*)

HOARD, WILLIAM. Adm. at King's, a scholar from Eton, 1656. S. of Samuel (above), R. of Moreton, Essex. Matric. 1656; B.A. 1659–60; M.A. 1663. Fellow, 1659–69. Ord. deacon (Ely) Sept. 20, 1662. P.C. of St Edward's, Cambridge, 1663. V. of Sturminster Marshall, Dorset, Jan. 8, 1669–70. Died there before Oct. 12, 1670. (F. S. Hockaday.)

HOAR, ARTHUR. Adm. pens. (age 17) at Peterhouse, Aug. 29, 1674. Of Surrey.

HOARE, FRANCIS. Adm. sizar at Clare, June 24, 1697. S. of William, of Green's Norton, Northants. Bapt. there, June 10, 1680. Matric. 1698; B.A. 1702–3. Ord. deacon (Peterb.) May 23, 1703; priest, Sept. 23, 1705. C. of Alderton, Northants., 1703. Master of Towcester Grammar School. Died Oct. 21, 1711. Buried at Towcester. Will (Archd. Northants.) 1712. (*Baker*, II. 336; H. I. Longden.)

HOARE, HENRY. Adm. pens. at St Catharine's, Apr. 1, 1688. Of London. Matric. 1688. Probably s. of James, late of the Middle Temple, deceased; adm. at the Inner Temple, May 26, 1688. (Not found in Edward Hoare's *Pedigree of the Hoare Family.*)

HOARE, JOHN. Adm. at King's, a scholar from Eton, 1445. B. at Winchester. B.A. 1449. Ord. deacon (Ely) Dec. 21, 1454; priest, Apr. 5, 1455. Perhaps canon of Windsor, 1451. Died 1472.

HOARE, JOHN. Adm. sizar at Christ's, Oct. 26, 1640. Previously matric. from Christ Church, Oxford, Dec. 8, 1637, age 19. S. of Richard. B. at Amersham, Bucks. B.A. 1640–1; M.A. from Queens', 1644. Fellow of Queens', 1644–50, ejected. Probably R. of Shere, Surrey, 1656. Buried there Feb. 4, 1658–9. (*Peile*, I. 473; *Manning and Bray*, I. 528.)

HOAR, JOHN. M.A. from Christ's, 1743. S. of John, of West Haddon, Northants. Matric. from Pembroke College, Oxford, Mar. 2, 1727–8, age 18; B.A. (Oxford) 1731. (*Al. Oxon.*; *Peile*, II. 233.)

HOARE, LEONARD. M.A. 1654 (Incorp. from Cambridge, New England). M.D. 1671 (*Lit. Reg.*). 4th s. of Charles and Joanna Hinkesman, of Gloucester. Emigrated to America and graduated at Harvard, 1650. Returned to England, 1653. R. of Wanstead, Essex, 1656–62, ejected. In 1673, he again went to Massachusetts. Pastor of the South Church at Boston, New England. President of Harvard College, 1672–5. Married Bridget, dau. of Lord Lisle. Author of *Index Biblicus* and of *The First Catalogue of Members of Harvard College.* Died Nov. 28, 1675, aged 45. Buried at Braintree, Mass. (*D.N.B.*; *Calamy*, I. 525.)

HOAR, MARTIN. Adm. pens. (age 18) at Trinity, June 26, 1676. S. of James. B. in the Tower of London, July 23, 1658. School, Merchant Taylors'. (*Vis. of London*, 1664.)

HOARE, WILLIAM. Matric. sizar from Trinity, Michs. 1606. One of these names C. of Margaretting, Essex, in 1637; V., in 1664.

HOARE, WILLIAM. Adm. Fell.-Com. at Peterhouse, July 1, 1653. Previously matric. from Brasenose, Oxford, May 6, 1651. Of Middlesex. M.B. 1655; M.D. 1660. Candidate R.C.P., Dec. 24, 1660. One of the original fellows of the Royal Society, 1663. Will (P.C.C.) 1666; of St Martin-in-the-Fields, London, M.D. (*Munk*, I. 298.)

HOARE or HORE, WILLIAM. LL.D. from Trinity Hall, 1683. Matric. from Exeter College, Oxford, July 20, 1654; B.A. (Oxford) 1657; M.A. 1660. Chaplain to the King, 1676–87. Preb. of Worcester, 1676–87. R. of Coulsdon, Surrey, 1678–87. Died 1687. Will (P.C.C.) 1688. (*Al. Oxon.*)

HORE or HARE, WILLIAM. Adm. pens. (age 17) at Trinity, July 26, 1715. S. of William, of Chagford, Devon. School, Exeter (Mr Reynolds). Scholar, 1717; Matric. 1718; B.A. 1719–20; M.A. 1723. Ord. priest (Lincoln) Dec. 23, 1722. R. of Bow Brickhill, Bucks., 1722–42. R. of Tingrith, Beds., 1724–42. Died 1742. Buried at Tingrith. *See* a namesake in *Al. Oxon.*

HOBART, *see also* HUBBARD.

HOBBART, BARTHOLOMEW. Adm. sizar at Emmanuel, Aug. 1, 1675. Of Norfolk. Matric. 1676.

HOBART, BENJAMIN. Adm. pens. at Emmanuel, Apr. 28, 1675. Of Lincolnshire. Afterwards Fell.-Com.

HOBART, DRUE. Adm. pens. (age 16) at Caius, Oct. 7, 1599. S. of Miles, Esq. B. at Plumstead, Norfolk. Bapt. July 7, 1583. School, (private; Mr Dilham). Adm. at Lincoln's Inn, Nov. 17, 1602. (*Vis. of Norfolk.*)

HOBART, EDWARD. Adm. at King's (age 16) a scholar from Eton, Aug. 24, 1583. Of Loddon, Norfolk. Matric. 1583; B.A. 1587–8; M.A. 1591. Fellow, 1586–91. Perhaps adm. at Lincoln's Inn, Feb. 13, 1591–2. One of these names died May 16, 1638, aged '74.' M.I. at Langley, Norfolk. (*Vis. of Suffolk*, 1664; *E. Anglian*, II. 300.)

HOBERT, EDWARD. Matric. Fell.-Com. from St John's, Easter, 1623. 7th s. of Sir Henry (1570), Knt. and Bart., Chief Justice, K.B. Adm. at Lincoln's Inn, Jan. 17, 1624–5. 'Slain in the Low Countries.' Brother of Robert, etc. (*Middlesex Pedigrees.*)

HOBART, FRANCIS. Adm. pens. (age 16) at Pembroke, Sept. 18, 1619. S. of John, of Salhouse, Norfolk. Matric. 1619. Adm. at Lincoln's Inn, Nov. 15, 1621.

HOBART, GEORGE. Adm. pens. at Emmanuel, Apr. 2, 1687. Of Middlesex. Matric. Fell.-Com. 1689; M.A. 1690 (*Com. Reg.*).

HOBART, GREGORY. Adm. sizar at Clare, May 16, 1644. Eldest s. of Gregory. B. at Long Melford, Suffolk, 1625. Matric. 1644; B.A. 1647. Ord. deacon (Lincoln) Apr. 6; priest, Apr. 10, 1661. Perhaps V. of Grayne, Kent, 1661–8. V. of Easton Maudit, Northants., 1662–8. Died Jan. 11, 1667–8. Will (Archd. Northants.) 1668. (H. I. Longden.)

HOBART or HUBBARD, HENRY. Matric. Fell.-Com. from Peterhouse, Michs. 1570. 2nd s. of Thomas, of Plumstead, Norfolk. Adm. at Lincoln's Inn, from Furnival's Inn, July 30, 1575. Called to the Bar, 1584. Bencher, 1596. Reader, 1600–1, 1602–3. Serjeant-at-law, 1602. M.P. for St Ives, 1588, 1589; for Yarmouth, 1597 and 1601; for Norwich, 1604–10. Knighted, July 23, 1603. Attorney-general, 1606–13. Created Baronet, 1611. Lord Chief Justice of C.P., 1613. Built Blickling Hall. Married Dorothy, dau. of Sir Robert Bell, of Beaupré Hall. Author, *Reports in the Reign of James I.* Died Dec. 26, 1625. Buried at Blickling. Father of Miles (1611), Edward (1623), Robert (1623) and perhaps of Thomas (1620). (*T. A. Walker*; *D.N.B.*)

HOBART or HUBBARD, HENRY. Matric. Fell.-Com. from Trinity, Easter, 1573. S. and h. of James, of Hales Hall, Norfolk. B. Apr. 6, 1553. Of Blythford, Suffolk. Married Margaret, dau. of Thomas Rous, of Donnington. Admon. (Norwich) Apr. 19, 1605. (*T. A. Walker.*)

HOBARD, HENRY. Adm. Fell.-Com. at St Catharine's, Lent, 1635–6. Of Norfolk. Perhaps of the Blickling family of Norfolk.

HOBART, HENRY. Adm. pens. at Emmanuel, May 28, 1673. Of Norfolk. Buried at St Andrew's, Cambridge, Oct. 30, 1675, as Hubard.

HOBART, Sir HENRY, Knt. Adm. Fell.-Com. (age 16) at St John's, May 6, 1674. S. of Sir John (1643–4), Bart., of Norfolk. B. there. School, Thetford. M.A. 1675. Knighted, Sept. 29, 1671. M.P. for Lynn, 1681; for Norfolk, 1689–90, 1695–8; for Beeralston, 1694–5. Succeeded as Baronet, Aug. 1683. At the battle of the Boyne with William III. Killed in a duel, at Cawston Heath, with Oliver Le Neve, Aug. 21, 1698. Buried at Blickling. Father of John (1710), brother of John (1682) and Thomas (1682). (G.E.C.)

HOBART, JAMES. Adm. Fell.-Com. (age 17) at CAIUS, May 2, 1668. S. of James, of Mendham, Norfolk, Esq. B. there, Oct. 21, 1652. Schools, Hoxne (Mr Hall), Diss (Mr Barber and Mr Wales) and Thorpe Abbots (Mr Jarmy). Matric. 1668. Buried at Mendham, Mar. 31, 1673. M.I. (*Venn*, I. 434; *Vis. of Suffolk*, 1664.)

HOBARD, JOHN. Matric. pens. from CLARE, Michs. 1568.

HOBART or HUBBARD, JOHN. Matric. pens. from PETERHOUSE, Michs. 1583. Doubtless 3rd s. of John, of Thwaytes, Norfolk. Bapt. July 24, 1568. Perhaps scholar of Trinity Hall, 1584. Married Dorothy, dau. of Arthur Fountaine, of Salle, Norfolk. Died at Salle, Oct. 14, 1630. Father of John (1618). (*T. A. Walker*.)

HOBART or HUBBARD, JOHN. Adm. at CORPUS CHRISTI, 1600. Of Norfolk. B.A. from Trinity, 1604-5, as Hobart.

HOBART, JOHN. Adm. pens. (age 17) at PEMBROKE, July 7, 1618. S. and h. of John (above), of Salle, Norfolk. Bapt. Dec. 14, 1600. Matric. 1618. Adm. at Lincoln's Inn, Oct. 20, 1619.

HOBART, JOHN. Adm. Fell.-Com. at EMMANUEL, Mar 5, 1643-4. Of Norfolk. Perhaps s. and h. of Miles (1611), late of Intwood, Norfolk, deceased. Bapt. at Ditchingham, Mar. 20, 1627-8. Matric. 1644. Adm. at Lincoln's Inn, May 20, 1645. Succeeded his uncle (Sir John) as Baronet, Apr. 20, 1647. M.P. for Norfolk, 1654-5, 1656-8, 1673, 1678-9, 1681. Member of Cromwell's House of Lords, 1657-8. Buried at Blickling, Aug. 30, 1683. Father of Henry (1674), John (1682) and Thomas (1682). (G.E.C.)

HOBART, JOHN. Adm. pens. at EMMANUEL, May 4, 1647. Of Suffolk. Matric. 1647, as Harbart. One of these names, s. and h. of John, of Outwell, Cambs., Esq., adm. at Lincoln's Inn, Nov. 15, 1647.

HOBART, JOHN. Adm. pens. (age 17) at SIDNEY, June 28, 1682. 2nd s. of Sir John (1643-4), of Blickling, Norfolk, Bart. B. in London. School, Wymondham, Norfolk (Mr Ri. Clarke). Matric. 1683. Adm. at Lincoln's Inn, Jan. 5, 1683-4. Brigadier-general in the King's army. Governor of Pendennis Castle, Cornwall. Died Nov. 7, 1734. Buried at Blickling. Brother of Henry (1674) and Thomas (1682). (*Collins*, IV. 367.)

HOBART, JOHN. Adm. at CORPUS CHRISTI, 1699. Of Suffolk. Matric. 1702.

HOBART, JOHN. Adm. Fell.-Com. at CLARE, May 20, 1710. S. of Sir Henry (1674), Bart., deceased. B. at Blickling, Norfolk, Oct. 11, 1693. Matric. 1710. M.P. for St Ives, Cornwall, 1715 and 1722-7; for Norfolk, 1727-8. Vice-Admiral of Norfolk, 1719. A commissioner for trade and plantations, 1721-7. K.B., 1725. Treasurer of the Chamber, 1727-34. Created Baron Hobart of Blickling, 1728. Lord-Lieutenant of Norfolk, 1740-56. Privy Councillor, 1745. Created Earl of Buckinghamshire, 1746. Died in London, Sept. 22, 1756. Father of the next. (*D.N.B.*; *G.E.C.*; A. B. Beaven.)

HOBART, JOHN. Adm. nobleman (age 17) at CHRIST'S, Oct. 30, 1739. S. of John (above), Baron Hobart. B. at Greenwich. School, Westminster. Matric. 1740. Deputy Lieutenant for Norfolk, 1745. M.P. for Norwich, 1747-56. Comptroller of the household, 1755. Succeeded as 2nd Earl of Buckinghamshire, 1756. Privy Councillor, 1756. Lord of the Bed Chamber, 1756. Ambassador to Russia, 1762-5. Lord Lieutenant of Ireland, 1776-80. F.S.A., 1784. F.R.S., 1785. Died Aug. 3, 1793, at Blickling Hall. (*Peile*, II. 238; *D.N.B.*; *G.E.C.*)

HOBART, MILES. Matric. Fell.-Com. from ST JOHN'S, Michs. 1566. Adm. at Lincoln's Inn, Feb. 7, 1569-70. Of Norfolk.

HOBART, MILES. Matric. Fell.-Com. from KING'S, Easter, 1611. 2nd s. of Sir Henry (1570), Knt. and Bart. Adm. at Lincoln's Inn, Mar. 16, 1611-2. Buried at St Paul's, Covent Garden, Dec. 6, 1639, aged 44. Father of John (1643-4). (Apparently wrongly identified in the Peerages and by other authorities with the M.P. for Gt Marlow (another Sir Miles, s. of Miles, of London). For evidence of identification *see Gent. Mag.*, 1851, Pt 2, 383.)

HOBART, MILES. Matric. Fell.-Com. from QUEENS', Easter, 1620, as 'Hubbard.' Of Norfolk.

HOBART or HOBARD, NATHANIEL. Adm. pens. at EMMANUEL, June 13, 1654. Of Suffolk. Perhaps 2nd s. of Nathan, of the City of London, Esq.; adm. at Lincoln's Inn, Nov. 28, 1655. Of Chancery Lane; Master in Chancery; Knighted, May 12, 1661.

HOBART, NICHOLAS. Adm. at KING'S, a scholar from Eton, 1621. S. of William, of Ravenshall. B. at Lindsey, Suffolk, *c.* 1605. Matric. 1620-1; B.A. 1623-4; M.A. 1627. Fellow, 1624-50. Proctor, 1641. Secretary to Sir Thomas Bendish, ambassador to Turkey. Lived at Salisbury. Married Sarah, dau. of Matthew Bust, Master of Eton. Died May 17, 1657. Benefactor to the College, to Eton, and to the University Library. (*Harwood*; Davy, *Suff. MSS.*)

HOBART, ROBART. Matric. Fell.-Com. from ST JOHN'S, Easter, 1623. 6th s. of Sir Henry (1570), Knt. and Bart., Chief Justice K.B. Adm. at Lincoln's Inn, Jan. 17, 1624-5. Died *s.p.* Brother of Edward (1623). (*Middlesex Pedigrees*.)

HOBART, ROBERT. Adm. pens. (age 17) at CAIUS, Nov. 2, 1652. S. of John, Esq., of Norwich. B. at Weybread, Suffolk. School, Norwich (Mr Lovering). Matric. 1653. Readm. Fell.-Com. Oct. 4, 1653-4. Died Mar. 5, 1681-2. Buried at Weybread. (*Venn*, I. 386.)

HOBART, TALBOT. Adm. pens. (age 16) at CHRIST'S, Feb. 11, 1688-9. S. of Thomas. B. in London. Matric. 1689; Scholar, 1690; B.A. 1692-3; M.A. 1696. Ord. deacon (Ely) Mar. 1697-8; priest, Sept. 1698. R. of Upwell, Norfolk, 1698-1701, when he died. (*Peile*, II. 111.)

HOBART, THOMAS. Adm. Fell.-Com. at QUEENS', Oct. 7, 1596. Of Norfolk. Matric. *c.* 1597.

HOBART or HUBBARD, THOMAS. Matric. Fell.-Com. from QUEENS', Easter, 1620. Of Norfolk. Probably 6th s. of Sir Henry (1570), Knt. and Bart., Chief Justice K.B.; adm. at Lincoln's Inn, Dec. 20, 1620 (or, '2nd' s. of Sir Thomas, of Plumpstead, Norfolk, Knt.; adm. at Lincoln's Inn, Nov. 8, 1623).

HOBART, THOMAS. Adm. pens. (age 16) at SIDNEY, June 28, 1682. 3rd s. of Sir John (1643-4), Bart. B. at Blickling, Norfolk. School, Wymcudham (Mr Clarke). Matric. 1683. Adm. at Lincoln's Inn, Jan. 5, 1683-4. Died unmarried. Brother of John (1682) and Henry (1674).

HOBART, THOMAS. Adm. pens. (age 18) at TRINITY, June 5, 1687. S. of Thomas, of London. School, Westminster. Matric. 1687; Scholar, 1688; B.A. 1690-1; M.A. 1694. Fellow, 1693.

HOBART, THOMAS. M.D. from CHRIST'S, 1700. Fellow of Christ's, 1699-1728. His early career is unknown, but he probably entered at Leyden, Aug. 30, 1691, and studied medicine there. He was appointed Fellow on the nomination of the Earl of Nottingham. Held some College offices, but spent most of his time travelling, as a tutor. Died before Apr. 27, 1728. (*Peile*, II. 127.)

HOBART, THOMAS. Adm. at CORPUS CHRISTI, 1703. Of Norfolk. Matric. 1703; B.A. 1706-7.

HOBART or HUBBERT, WILLIAM. Adm. pens. (age 19) at CAIUS, July 6, 1582. S. of John, gent. B. at Thwaite, Norfolk. School, Gt Downham, Norfolk. B.A. 1585-6. Succeeded his father as lord of the manor of Erpingham, Norfolk. Died Nov. 5, 1612. Buried at Erpingham. M.I. Will (P.C.C.) 1612. (*Venn*, I. 115; *Vis. of Norfolk*.)

HOBBS, BENNETT. M.A. 1673 (Incorp. from Oxford). S. of Richard, of Ardington, Berks., gent. School, Winchester. Matric. from New College, Sept. 11, 1661, age 19; B.A. (Oxford) 1665; M.A. 1668-9; B.D. 1679. Fellow of New College. Died Nov. 6, 1680. Buried in the College Chapel. Will, Oxford. (*Al. Oxon.*)

HOBBYS, JOHN. Matric. sizar from KING'S, Easter, 1660; B.A. 1663-4; M.A. 1667. V. of Bacton, Norfolk, 1677-81.

HOBBES or HOBBYS, RICHARD. M.A. from EMMANUEL, 1632. Of Berkshire. Matric. from Magdalen College, Oxford, Nov. 16, 1621, age 17; B.A. (Oxford) 1625. R. of Erpingham, Norfolk, 1642. (*Al. Oxon.*)

HOBBES, ROBERT. M.D. 1461-2. Had studied at Oxford.

HOBBES or HOBYS, ROBERT. Adm. at KING'S, a scholar from Eton, 1495. B. at Peterborough. B.A. 1499-1500; M.A. 1503. Esquire Bedell, *c.* 1504-29. Registrary, 1506. Resided in Gt St Mary's parish, where he held various posts. Enrolled in the *Missa pro Benefactoribus*. Died *c.* 1543. (*Cooper*, I. 83; Stokes, *Bedells*, 71.)

HOBBS, ROBERT. Matric. pens. from TRINITY, 1598, a scholar from Westminster; B.A. 1601-2; M.A. 1605. Ord. deacon and priest (Peterb.) July 25, 1605. R. of Wainfleet All Saints', Lincs., 1605-15. Will of one of these names (Chichester) 1629; of Madehurst, Sussex, clerk.

HOBBES, THOMAS. B.A. 1608 (Incorp. from Oxford). S. of Thomas, clerk, of Westport, Wilts. B. there, 1588. School, Malmesbury. B.A. (Magdalen Hall, Oxford) 1607-8. The well-known philosopher. For many years tutor and secretary to William Cavendish, Earl of Devonshire and his son. Travelled in France, Germany and Italy. Resided in Paris, 1641-52; during this period he wrote his famous book, *Leviathan*; also acted as mathematical tutor to Charles II. Returned to England in 1651, and submitted to the Council of State. Engaged in controversies on philosophical and mathematical questions. Received a pension from Charles II. At 84, he wrote his autobiography in Latin verse. For an account of his numerous works, *see D.N.B.* Died at Hardwick, Derbs., Dec. 4, 1679. Buried in Hault Hucknall Church. (*D.N.B.*)

HOBBES, W. Matric. pens. from PEMBROKE, Easter, 1588. Buried at Little St Mary's, Cambridge, Mar. 14, 1590-1.

HOBBES, WILLIAM. M.A. 1627 (Incorp. from Oxford). Matric. at Oxford, July 1, 1614; B.A. (Trinity College, Oxford) 1617; M.A. (Brasenose) 1621; B.D. from Trinity, 1630; D.D. 1639. R. of Kimpton, Hants., 1653. R. of Sherrington, Wilts., 1657. Preb. of Sarum, 1662-70. Died 1670. Will (Cons. C. Sarum) 1670. (*Al. Oxon.*; J. Ch. Smith.)

HOBBES, WILLIAM. M.A. 1652 (Incorp. from Oxford). Matric. (Oxford) Oct. 10, 1634; B.A. (Magdalen College) 1637; M.A. 1640. Fellow of Magdalen, 1639-54.

HOBBES, WILLIAM. Adm. sizar at EMMANUEL, July 4, 1677. Of Rutland. B.A. 1680-1; M.A. 1684.

HOBBS, WILLIAM. Adm. sizar at QUEENS', Feb. 12, 1682-3. Of Cornwall. Matric. 1683; B.A. 1686-7.

HOBBES, ——. Doctor in some faculty. Incorp. from Oxford, 1505-6.

HOBBYE, RICHARD. Matric. pens. from TRINITY, Easter, 1577, a scholar from Westminster; B.A. 1580-1; M.A. 1584. Incorp. at Oxford, 1584.

HOBBY, ROBERT. Adm. at CORPUS CHRISTI, 1670. Of Norwich. B.A. 1674 (according to *Masters*).

HOBY, THOMAS. Matric. pens. from ST JOHN'S, Easter, 1545. S. of William, of Leominster, Herefordshire. B. 1530. Travelled abroad. Inherited an estate at Bisham, Berks., from his brother Sir Philip. Knighted, 1565-6. Ambassador to France, 1566. Author, translations. Died at Paris, July 13, 1566. Buried at Bisham, Berks. Will (P.C.C.) 1566; 'ambassador resident with the French King.' (*Cooper*, I. 242; *D.N.B.*; Burke, *Ext. Bart.*)

HOBY, WILLIAM. Adm. Fell.-Com. at EMMANUEL, June 13, 1618. Matric. 1618. Perhaps s. and h. of William, of Hailes, Gloucs., Esq., deceased; adm. at Gray's Inn, Apr. 26, 1621. William Hobby, of Hales, was knighted, July 14, 1622.

HOBDAY, STEPHEN. Adm. pens. at EMMANUEL, May 24, 1700. Of Kent. Matric. 1700; B.A. 1703-4; M.A. 1707. Ord. deacon (London) June 8, 1707. V. of Waldershare, Kent, 1708-29. R. of Lower Hardres, 1711-43. V. of St Dunstan's, Canterbury, 1728-43. Died Sept. 29, 1743.

HOBELEN, PETER. Adm. pens. at PETERHOUSE, Mar. 20, 1633-4. Of Lincolnshire. Matric. 1634. (*T. A. Walker*, 33.)

HOBKYN, NICHOLAS. Matric. sizar from TRINITY, Michs. 1566.

HOBLYN, RICHARD. Adm. pens. (age 18) at PEMBROKE, Apr. 10, 1717. S. of Edward, of Egloshayle, Cornwall, gent. LL.B. 1725. Died before Mar. 11, 1744. (Maclean, *Trigg Minor*, I. 474.)

HOBLYN, WILLIAM. Adm. sizar (age 17) at PEMBROKE, Sept. 2, 1729. S. of John, of St Columb, Cornwall, gent. Matric. 1730; B.A. 1733-4. Admon. (Exeter) 1759, of one of these names; of Lydford, Devon, clerk.

HOBMAN, FRANCIS. Adm. pens. (age 16) at CAIUS, Nov. 27, 1609. S. of Thomas, of St Andrew's, Holborn, London. School, Westminster. Matric. 1609; Scholar, 1609-17; B.A. 1613-4; M.A. 1617; B.D. 1628. Fellow, 1619-28. Ord. deacon (Lincoln) Mar. 1, 1617-8; priest (Peterb.) Mar. 12, 1619-20. C. of Barnwell Chapel (? Cambridge), 1619. R. of Greenford Parva, Middlesex, 1621-49. R. of Foulden, Norfolk, 1627. R. of All Saints', Weeting, 1637. R. of St Mary, Weeting, 1651, when he signed Bishop Hall's book, Sept. 17. Author. Buried there, Nov. 23, 1669. M.I. Will (Norwich) 1670. Brother of the next. (*Venn*, I. 205.)

HOBMAN, JOHN. Adm. sizar (age 15) at CAIUS, July 7, 1614. S. of Thomas, retail dealer, of London. School, St Paul's (Mr Gill). Matric. 1614; Scholar, 1615-20; B.A. 1617-8; M.A. 1621. Master at Newport School, Essex, about 1621-3. Licensed Master at Bury St Edmunds Grammar School, 1633; undermaster there, 1641. Perhaps R. of West Barkwith, Lincs., 1641-2. Brother of Francis. (*Venn*, I. 226.)

HOBMAN, WILLIAM. Adm. sizar at EMMANUEL, Oct. 17, 1596; B.A. from Pembroke, 1599-1600. Ord. priest (York) Sept. 18, 1601. V. of Swinderby, Lincs., 1608; previously at Darfield, and Mexborough, Yorks. Admon. (Lincoln) 1617.

HOBSON, CHRISTOPHER. Adm. sizar at QUEENS', June 23, 1598. Of Yorkshire. Will (P.C.C.) 1628, of one of these names; of St Bride's, London, schoolmaster. (J. Ch. Smith.)

HOBSON, CLEMENT. Adm. pens. (age 15) at CHRIST'S, May 20, 1651. S. of William, of Surrey. School, Southwark (Mr Augur). B.A. 1654-5; M.A. 1658. Adm. at Gray's Inn, May 11, 1657. V. of Eltham, Kent, 1658-1725. Died Oct. 31, 1725. Buried at Eltham. M.I. there. (*Peile*, I. 542.)

HOBSON, ED. Matric. pens. from TRINITY, Easter, 1611.

HOBSON, GODFREY. Matric. . from KING'S, Lent, 1591-2. Probably adm. at Lincoln'sInn, May 15, 1594, from Davies' Inn. Of Yorkshire.

HOBSON, JOHN. Scholar of QUEENS', 1487-9; B.A. 1488. Fellow, 1489-93. Ord. acolyte (Ely) Sept. 24, 1491.

HOBSON, JOHN. B.A. 1517-8. Fellow of QUEENS', 1518-20.

HOBSON, JOHN. Matric. sizar from ST CATHARINE'S, Michs. 1564. Of Nottinghamshire. B.A. 1568-9; M.A. 1572. Fellow, as 'Hobbes,' 1569. Probably R. of Hardwick, Cambs., 1572.

HOBSON, JOHN. Matric. sizar from TRINITY HALL, Easter, 1639; B.A. 1642-3. One of these names R. of Kirk Sandall, Yorks., 1642-62. Died 1671. But *see Al. Oxon.* for a contemporary.

HOBSON, JOHN. Adm. Fell.-Com. (age 17) at MAGDALENE, Nov. 12, 1650. S. of William (? 1621), gent., of Syston and Stamford, Lincs. School, Botolph Bridge. Matric. 1651. Adm. at Gray's Inn, Jan. 23, 1652-3. Of Syston, Esq. Married Mary, dau. of Sir Daniel De Ligne, of Harlaxton, Lincs. Buried at Spalding, Dec. 13, 1676. (*Lincs. Pedigrees*, 499.)

HOBSON, JONAS. Adm. sizar (age 21) at ST JOHN'S, May 31, 1631. S. of Edmund, currier, of Wakefield. B. at Sandal Magna, Wakefield, Yorks. School, Chaplethorpe (in Sandal) (private; Mr Oats).

HOBSON, JOSHUA. Adm. sizar at ST JOHN'S, Mar. 11, 1674-5. S. of John, currier, of Dodworth, Yorks. B. there. School, Wakefield. Matric. 1674-5; B.A. 1678-9; M.A. 1682. Fellow, 1681-92. Incorp. at Oxford, 1682. Ord. deacon (York) Sept. 19, 1680. Non-juror.

HOBSON, RICHARD. B.A. 1518-9; M.A. 1520-1; B.D. 1528; D.D. 1530. *Cooper* identifies him with the Gilbertine; prior of their house at Newstead, Lincs. Surrendered, 1538. (*Cooper*, I. 69.)

HOBSON, RICHARD. Adm. pens. at EMMANUEL, May 5, 1618. Probably s. and h. of William, of Spalding, Lincs., Esq. Matric. 1618. Adm. at Lincoln's Inn, Feb. 13, 1619-20. Married and had issue. Will proved, Feb. 12, 1654-5. (*Lincs. Pedigrees*, 498.)

HOBSON, RICHARD. Adm. pens. at JESUS, May 30, 1724. Of Yorkshire. Matric. 1724. Probably of Kirkby Moorside, Esq. Married Mary, dau. of Sir John Statham, of Tidswell. (M. H. Peacock.)

HOBSON, ROBERT. B.A. 1529-30; M.A. 1533. Fellow of ST JOHN'S, 1533. One of these names R. of Rossington, Yorks., 1551-6. V. of Doncaster, 1554-70.

HOBSON, ROBERT. Matric. pens. from TRINITY, Easter, 1633. S. of Lancelot, of St George's, Southwark, glazier. Scholar, 1634; B.A. 1636-7; M.A. 1640; M.D. from Magdalene, 1659. Buried at Southwark, Nov. 9, 1658, aged 42. M.I. Brother of William (1629-30). Father's will (P.C.C.) 1640. (J. Ch. Smith; *Manning and Bray*, III. 640.)

HOBSON, ROBERT. Adm. sizar (age 20) at ST JOHN'S, Sept. 8, 1645. S. of Edmund, of Smallfield, Yorks. School, Wakefield (Mr Doughty). B.A. 1649-50. R. of Flixton, Suffolk, 1669-81. R. of Lound, 1670-81.

HOBSON, ROGER. 'Late student of ST JOHN'S,' when ord. priest (York) May, 1627. No College or University record. V. of Ulrome, in Holderness, Yorks., 1626-62. (M. H. Peacock.)

HOBSON, THOMAS. Matric. pens. from TRINITY, Easter, 1611.

HOBSON, THOMAS. Matric. sizar from QUEENS', Michs. 1612. Of Yorkshire. B.A. 1619-20. Ord. deacon (York) Sept. 1, 1621; priest, June, 1623.

HOBSON, THOMAS. Adm. at CORPUS CHRISTI, 1667. Of Cambridgeshire. B.A. 1671, according to *Masters*.

HOBSON, THOMAS. Adm. sizar at PEMBROKE, June 26, 1690. S. of John, of Barton. B. in Westmorland.

HOBSON, THOMAS. Adm. sizar (age 19) at ST JOHN'S, Feb. 13, 1701-2. S. of Thomas, joiner. B. at Hett, Durham. Bapt. at Kirkmerrington, Oct. 15, 1682. School, Durham (Mr Ross). Matric. 1702; B.A. 1707-8. Ord. deacon (Durham) June 8, 1707; priest, Sept. 24, 1710. C. of Ryton, Durham, 1722. Perhaps V. of Bossall, Yorks., 1729-40. Buried there Oct. 16, 1740.

HOBSON, WILLIAM. Matric. pens. from TRINITY, Michs. 1588.

HOBSON, WILLIAM. Matric. pens. from MAGDALENE, Easter, 1621; B.A. 1624. Probably adm. at Gray's Inn, Nov. 17, 1624, as s. and h. of John, of Boston, Lincs. Age 23 in 1627. Married and had issue. Buried at Spalding, July 6, 1660. Will proved, Aug. 16, 1660. Probably father of John (1650). (*Lincs. Pedigrees*, 499.)

HOBSON, WILLIAM. Matric. pens. from TRINITY, Lent, 1629-30. S. of Lancelot, of St George's, Southwark, glazier. Scholar, 1631; B.A. 1633-4; M.A. 1637; D.D. 1660 (*Lit. Reg.*). R. of St George's, Southwark, 1639. V. of Twickenham, Middlesex, 1661-8. Buried Sept. 9, 1668. M.I. at Southwark. Will (P.C.C.) 'to be buried with his father and brother' (Robert). (*Manning and Bray*, III. 640; J. Ch. Smith.)

HOBSON, WILLIAM. Adm. pens. at EMMANUEL, May 8, 1638. Of Lincolnshire. Probably s. and h. of Richard, of Spalding, Esq. Bapt. at Spalding, Aug. 16, 1621. Matric. 1638. Adm. at Lincoln's Inn, May 10, 1641. Living at Wykeham, 1653. Married and had issue. (*Lincs. Pedigrees*, 498.)

HOBSON, ——. B.A. 1513–4; M.A. 1517; B.D. 1527. Perhaps fellow of CLARE, 1521.

HOCKENHALL, JOHN. Adm. pens. at ST CATHARINE'S, May 11, 1670.

HOCKET, *see* HACKET.

HOCKIN, JOHN. Adm. sizar (age 19) at PEMBROKE, Apr. 19, 1728. S. of Thomas, of Camborne, Cornwall. Matric. 1728; B.A. 1731–2; M.A. 1737. V. of Okehampton, Devon. R. of Lydford. Chaplain to George, Lord Littleton. Had a grant of arms, 1764. Married Elizabeth, dau. of Rev. J. Pearce, of St Earth. Author, *Sermon*. Died at Caduscot, Cornwall. Buried at St Pinnock. Will (P.C.C.) 1778. (*Collect. Cornub.*)

HOCKLEY, NICHOLAS. Adm. pens. (age 19) at ST JOHN'S, June 4, 1631. S. of Nicholas, husbandman, of Godalming, Surrey. B. at Puttenham, Surrey. School, Guildford (Mr Hill). Matric. 1631.

HOCKMORE, PHILIP, *see* HUCKMORE.

HOCKNELL, LANCELOT. Matric. pens. from CHRIST'S, Nov. 1568; Scholar; B.A. 1572–3; M.A. 1576. Ord. deacon and priest (Lincoln) July, 1580. R. of Ringstead St Andrew's, Norfolk, 1587–1626. R. of Bayfield. Died before Apr. 1626. (*Peile*, I. 108.)

HOCKNELL, ROBERT. Adm. sizar at EMMANUEL, Sept. 18, 1621. Matric. 1622; B.A. 1625. Ord. deacon (Peterb.) June 12, 1625; priest, Sept. 23, 1627.

HODDER, GEORGE. Adm. sizar at CHRIST'S, June 5, 1684. S. of George, of Dorset. Matric. 1684; B.A. 1687–8. (*Peile*, II. 97.)

HODDER, JOHN. Adm. pens. at TRINITY, July 7, 1645. Previously matric. from Wadham College, Oxford, Apr. 1, 1642, age 15. S. of John, of Bemister, Dorset. B.A. 1645–6. R. of Hawkchurch, Dorset, probably from 1645; ejected, 1662. Afterwards preacher in Dorset. Buried at Hawkchurch, Mar. 24, 1679–80. (*Al. Oxon.*; F. S. Hockaday.)

HODDER, ROBERT. Adm. sizar at CAIUS, Apr. 21, 1620. Previously matric. from Magdalen Hall, Oxford, Apr. 1618, age 18. Of Dorset. B.A. 1620–1. Perhaps adm. at the Middle Temple, June 30, 1620. R. of Puncknowle, with Bexington, Dorset, 1631–9.

HODDESDON, *see* HODGSON.

HODE or HODD, ——. B.A. 1481–2; M.A. 1485.

HODEBRIDGE, *see* WOODBRIDGE.

HODEROFF, *see* WOODRUFF.

HODETHORPE, *see* WOODTHORPE.

HODGE or HODGES, ABEL. Matric. sizar from PEMBROKE, Easter, 1606. B. at Rawreth, Essex. B.A. 1608–9; M.A. 1612. Ord. deacon (London) Mar. 4, 1609–10; C. of Dengey, Essex; priest, Sept. 22, 1611. V. of Littleport, Cambs., 1612–8. R. of Tydd St Giles', 1618. Married at Elm, Jan. 22, 1638–9, Dorothy Gyles. Father of the next.

HODGES, ABEL. Matric. pens. from PEMBROKE (age 17) Easter, 1631. S. of Abel (above), of the Isle of Ely, clerk. B.A. 1634–5; M.A. 1638. Ord. priest (Peterb.) Mar. 1, 1639–40. R. of Tibenham, Norfolk, 1641. R. of Tharston, 1661–78. Died 1678. Father of the next.

HODGES, ABEL. Adm. pens. at JESUS, July 4, 1664. 1st s. of Abel (above), R. of Tharston, Norfolk. B. at Norwich. School, Ely. Matric. 1664; Scholar, 1665; B.A. 1667–8; M.A. 1671. R. of Tharston, Norfolk, 1678–1720. Father of the next and Robert (1696).

HODGES, ABEL. Adm. sizar (age 18) at PEMBROKE, May 22, 1706. S. of Abel (above), of Tharston, Norfolk, clerk. B. at Tharston. Matric. 1706; B.A. 1709–10. Ord. deacon (Norwich) July, 1712; priest, July, 1714. R. of Tharston, Norfolk, 1721. R. of Little Wacton, 1721–5. R. of Brockdish, 1725–9. Died 1729. Brother of Robert (1696).

HODGE, ALEXANDER. M.A. 1656 (Incorp. from Oxford). Matric. from Wadham College, Jan. 17, 1650–1, 'doctoris fil.'; B.A. (Oxford) 1652; M.A. 1654. Fellow of Wadham, 1654. V. of St Thomas, Exeter; ejected, 1662. Chaplain at Amsterdam, 1669. Died Dec. 1689. (*Al. Oxon.*)

HODGES, FRANCIS. Adm. sizar (age 16) at SIDNEY, July 5, 1641. S. of William, farmer. B. at Oundle, Northants. School, Oundle (Mr Tho. Johnson). Matric. 1642; B.A. 1644–5. Brother of William (1631–2).

HODGE, GEORGE. Adm. sizar at QUEENS', Nov. 28, 1689. Of Cornwall. Matric. 1689.

HODGES, JAMES. Adm. pens. at TRINITY, June 25, 1646. Of London. Scholar, 1647; Matric. 1649; B.A. 1649–50; M.A. 1653. Fellow, 1650. Incorp. at Oxford, 1653.

HODGES, JOHN. M.A. *c.* 1624; B.D. from TRINITY HALL, 1634. One of these names R. of Westerfield, Suffolk, 1629–30. Perhaps R. of Falkenham, 1641.

HODGES, JOHN. M.A. 1631 (Incorp. from Oxford). Of Somerset. Matric. from Brasenose College, Feb. 14, 1588–9, age 18; B.A. 1591–2; M.A. 1595; B.D. and D.D. 1631. Fellow of Lincoln College, 1599–1604. R. of Drayton Parslow, Bucks., 1602. R. of Misterton, Leics., 1608–42. Probably preb. of Lichfield, 1628–42. Will (P.C.C.) 1642; bequests to Drayton Parslow. (*Nichols*, IV. 314; J. Ch. Smith.)

HODGES, JOHN. Adm. sizar at QUEENS', Oct. 21, 1644. From King's College, Edinburgh; adm. there, Oct. 2, 1643. Of Gloucestershire.

HODGES, JOHN. Adm. pens. (age 16) at SIDNEY, May 18, 1654. S. of John, of Hunton, Kent. School, Maidstone (Mr Thomas). Matric. 1654; B.A. 1657–8; M.A. 1661. Fellow. Ord. deacon (Ely) Sept. 20; priest (Lincoln) Oct. 13, 1662. Buried at All Saints', Cambridge, Sept. 18, 1663. Will proved (V.C.C.) 1663.

HODGES or HODGETS, JOHN. Adm. pens. at ST CATHARINE'S, July 2, 1716. Of Worcestershire.

HODGES, JOHN. Adm. at EMMANUEL, May 31, 1727, as 'LL.B. from Oxford.' (Not found in *Al. Oxon.*)

HODGES, JOSEPH. Adm. pens. at CLARE, Nov. 23, 1728. B. in Jamaica. Perhaps adm. at Leyden, Aug. 22, 1731.

HODGE, LAURENCE. Incorp. at Oxford, 1654, as M.A. of Cambridge. Not found in our records.

HODGES, NATHANIEL. Matric. Fell.-Com. from JESUS, Easter, 1615. S. of Richard, of Churchdown, Gloucs. B. July 30, 1600. School, Merchant Taylors'. B.A. 1617. Apprenticed to a merchant taylor, 1617.

HODGES, NATHANIEL. Elected scholar to TRINITY College from Westminster, 1646; afterwards, 1648, adm. at Christ Church, Oxford. S. of Thomas (1620), D.D. B. in Kensington, Sept. 13, 1629. B.A. (Oxford) 1651; M.A. 1654; M.D. 1659. Fellow, R.C.P., 1672. Censor, 1682. Harveian orator, 1683. Attended patients in London throughout the plague, 1665. Published an account of the plague, 1672. Died in debt, in Ludgate prison, June 10, 1688, aged 59. M.I. at St Stephen Walbrook. (*D.N.B.*; *Munk*, I. 361; *Al. Oxon.*)

HODGES, NATHANIEL. Adm. Fell.-Com. at QUEENS', Oct. 16, 1727. Of Middlesex. Matric. 1727. S.P.G. Missionary at Nassau, Bahamas; arrived there, Feb. 1742–3. Died July 3, 1743.

HODGES, RICHARD. Adm. pens. at TRINITY, May 13, 1651. B. in Middlesex. Scholar from Westminster. Matric. 1651; B.A. 1654–5; M.B. 1657.

HODGES, ROBERT. M.A. 1631 (Incorp. from Oxford). Of Somerset. Matric. from Magdalen Hall, Oxford, Apr. 17, 1618, age 17; B.A. (Oxford) 1621; M.A. 1624. R. of Elm, Somerset, 1628. R. of Tellisford, 1644. (*Al. Oxon.*)

HODGES, ROBERT. Adm. sizar (age 16) at PEMBROKE, Sept. 21, 1696. S. of Abel (1664), R. of Tharston, Norfolk. B. at Tharston. Matric. 1697; B.A. 1700–1; M.A. 1704; B.D. 1711. Fellow, 1703. C. at Saxstead, Suffolk and reader at Framlingham, 1704. V. of Darenth, Kent, 1712. R. of St Mary, Hoo, 1719–51. V. of All Hallows, 1724–51. Buried at St Mary, Hoo, May 8, 1751. Brother of Abel (1706). (H. G. Harrison.)

HODGES, THOMAS. Adm. pens. at JESUS, June 17, 1620. Matric. 1620; B.A. 1623–4; M.A. 1627; D.D. 1660 (*Lit. Reg.*). V. of Kensington, 1641–72. Dean of Hereford, 1661–72. R. of St Peter's, Cornhill, 1662–71. Died Aug. 22, 1672, aged 72. Will, P.C.C. Father of Nathaniel (1646). Apparently the man who was created D.D. at Oxford, Dec. 20, 1642; 'preacher before the Long Parliament, and one of the Assembly of Divines.' (Le Neve, *Mon.*, IV. 152; *Al. Oxon.*)

HODGES, THOMAS. Adm. sizar at EMMANUEL, Feb. 27, 1632–3. Of Northamptonshire. S. of Thomas, gent. B. at Cotterstock. School, Oundle; adm. there, Apr. 2, 1627, age 10. Matric. 1633; B.A. 1636–7; M.A. 1640; B.D. from St John's, 1648. Fellow of St John's, 1644. Taxor, 1646.

HODGE, WILLIAM. Matric. sizar from ST JOHN'S, *c.* 1594.

HODGES or HODGE, WILLIAM. Adm. sizar (age 14) at SIDNEY, Jan. 12, 1631–2. S. of William, farmer. B. at Oundle, Northants. School, Oundle. Matric. 1632; B.A. 1635–6; M.A. 1639; B.D. 1646. Fellow. Ord. deacon (Peterb.) Sept. 19, 1641; priest, June 5, 1642. R. of Tichmarsh, Northants. 1648–58. Died 1658. Father of William (1672–3), brother of Francis (1641). (H. I. Longden.)

HODGES, WILLIAM. M.A. 1635–6 (*Lit. Reg.*). One of these names R. of Ripple, Worcs. Archdeacon of Worcester, 1645–76. Will (P.C.C.) 1676. (J. Ch. Smith.)

HODGE, WILLIAM. Adm. scholar (age 16) at SIDNEY, Mar. 12, 1672-3. S. of William (1631-2), R. of Tichmarsh, Northants. B. there. School, Wellingborough. Matric. 1673.

HODGES, WILLIAM. M.A. 1699 (Incorp. from Oxford). S. of William, of London. Matric. from Wadham College, Mar. 23, 1682-3, age 15; B.A. (Oxford) 1686; M.A. 1689. Fellow of Wadham, 1691. R. of St Swithin and St Mary Bothaw, London, 1700-2. Died 1702. Will, P.C.C. One of these names preb. of Wells, 1695-1702. (*Al. Oxon.*)

HODGES, ——. Adm. Fell.-Com. at TRINITY, 1654.

HODGETS, THOMAS. Adm. pens. (age 17) at TRINITY, July 10, 1694. S. of John. B. at Kingswinford, Staffs. School, Stourbridge, Worcs. (Mr John Brown). Matric. 1696-7; Scholar, 1699; B.A. 1699-1700; M.A. 1703.

HODGEKYN, ANTHONY. Matric. sizar from St JOHN'S, Easter, 1584. One of these names of Wilsby, Lincs., clerk. Admon. (Lincoln) 1596.

HODGKINS or HODSKYNS, HENRY. Adm. at KING'S (age 19) a scholar from Eton, Aug. 27, 1576. Of Hailes, Gloucs. Matric. 1576. Left in 1579.

HODGKINS, JOHN. Adm. at KING'S, a scholar from Eton, 1450; M.A. 1457; B.D. 1476-7. Engaged to supervise the rebuilding of Gt St Mary's, Cambridge. V. of Ringwood, Hants. 'A celebrated mathematician whom Henry VII favoured so much as frequently to visit him privately at Ringwood.' (*Harwood.*)

HODGKYN, JOHN. Studied thirteen years in Cambridge and three years in Paris. Dominican friar. B.D. 1520-1; D.D. 1524-5. Provincial of English Dominicans, 1527; deposed; reinstated, 1536. Bishop of Bedford (suffragan to London) 1537-54. V. of Maldon, Essex, 1541-4. R. of Laingdon, 1544-54. Preb. of St Paul's, 1547-54, 1559-60. R. of St Peter, Cornhill, 1555. Deprived of his preferments, as married, 1554. Restored by Elizabeth, 1559. Died 1560. (*Cooper*, I. 206; H. G. Harrison.)

HODGSKIN, RANDOLPH. Adm. sizar (age 15) at CAIUS, Oct. 22, 1618. 4th s. of Francis, V. of Earls Barton, Northants. Bapt. there, Feb. 12, 1603-4. School, Sywell. One of these names ord. deacon, as literate (Peterb.) Sept. 24, 1620; priest, Sept. 22, 1622. Will (Leicester) 1664, of Ralph Hodgkin, of Knipton, Leics., clerk. (H. I. Longden.)

HODGEKYNS, RICHARD. Adm. at KING'S, a scholar from Eton, 1479.

HODGKYNS, ROBERT. Described as 'Fellow of St CATHARINE'S HALL,' when ord. deacon (London) Mar. 1557-8. Perhaps ord. priest (Chester) June 4, 1558. R. of Knebworth, Herts. Will (P.C.C.) 1605.

HODGKINS, WILLIAM. Adm. sizar at EMMANUEL, June 12, 1592. Matric. c. 1592; B.A. 1595-6; M.A. 1599. Ord. deacon (Norwich) July 25; priest, Sept. 29, 1603. C. of Yarmouth, and Master of the Grammar School. R. of Rushmere, Suffolk, 1610.

HODGKIN, WILLIAM. Adm. scholar at TRINITY HALL, Mar. 26, 1606; LL.B. 1612. Fellow, 1611-29. V. of Wood Dalling, and Swannington, Norfolk. Buried at St Edward's, Cambridge, Apr. 27, 1629.

HODGKIN, WILLIAM. B.A. from St CATHARINE'S, 1609; M.A. 1614. Probably the man ord. (as literate), deacon (Peterb.) Sept. 20, 1607; priest (London) May 22, 1608, as 'late of Pembroke Hall, aged 24. B. at Studham, Beds. C. of Stamford Rivers, Essex.'

HODGKINS, ——. B.A. 1482-3.

HODGKINS, ——. Incorp. B.D. 1522-3. A friar.

HODGKINSON, BENJAMIN. Adm. pens. at EMMANUEL, Lent, 1641-2. Of Warwickshire. Matric. 1641, as Hopkinson.

HODGKINSON, JOHN. Adm. pens. at EMMANUEL, Lent, 1641-2. Of Warwickshire. Matric. 1641, as Hopkinson.

HODGKINSON, PAUL. Matric. sizar from CHRIST'S, Michs. 1598. B. at Swinford, Leics. B.A. 1601-2. Ord. deacon (London) Dec. 1605, age 27. C. of Ashdon, Essex. (*Peile*, I. 229.)

HODGKINSON, THOMAS. Adm. pens. at EMMANUEL, June 4, 1692. Of Lancashire. Probably of Preston.

HODGKINSON, TILLEMAN. Adm. at KING'S, a scholar from Eton, 1739. S. of Henry. Bapt. at Woodstock, Oxon., June 30, 1721. Matric. 1739; B.A. 1743-4; M.A. 1747. Fellow, 1742. Ord. deacon (Lincoln) Sept. 25, 1743. For many years schoolmaster at Exeter. Preb. of Llandaff, 1761-86. Died May 28, 1786. Will (P.C.C.) 1786; of Oxford, clerk. (*Harwood*, 328; A. B. Beaven; J. Ch. Smith.)

HODGKINSON, WILLIAM. Matric. pens. from CHRIST'S, July, 1613; B.A. 1616-7; M.A. 1621. R. of Elton, Notts., 1621-34. Buried there May 24, 1634. (*Peile*, I. 292.)

HODGKINSON, ——. Adm. sizar at St CATHARINE'S, 1628.

HODGSON or HODDSON, AARON. Matric. sizar from CHRIST'S, July, 1676; B.A. 1679-80; M.A. 1683. Ord. priest (London) Feb. 1685-6. Probably usher at Stanstead Abbots School. Non-juror. (*Peile*, II. 61; H. G. Harrison.)

HODGESON, ALEXANDER. Matric. pens. from PEMBROKE, Michs. 1571.

HODGSON, ALEXANDER. Adm. sizar (age 19) at St JOHN'S, Apr. 29, 1686. S. of William, husbandman. B. at Dent, Yorks. School, Sedbergh (Mr Wharton). Matric. 1686; B.A. 1689-90.

HODSON, AMOUR. Adm. sizar at KING'S, c. 1669.

HODGSON or HODSON, ANTHONY. Adm. sizar (age 18) at CAIUS, Dec. 2, 1609. Of Newton, Penrith, Cumberland. S. of Thomas, husbandman. School, Blencowe (Mr Jo. Davyes). Matric. 1609.

HODSON, ARTHUR. Matric. pens. from TRINITY HALL, Easter, 1647. 5th s. of Phineas (1590), D.D. Bapt. at St Michael-le-Belfry, York, Mar. 22, 1626-7. Adm. at Gray's Inn, May 28, 1647. Buried in York Minster, May 13, 1656. Brother of Edward (1631), Timothy (1643) and Tobias (1641).

HODSON, BENJAMIN. Adm. sizar (age 17) at MAGDALENE, May 15, 1666. S. of Robert (? 1633), clerk, of Knightsbridge, London. School, Grantham. B.A. 1669-70; M.A. 1673. Ord. deacon (Peterb.) May 29, 1670; priest, June 2, 1672. R. of Broughton, Hunts., 1680-97. Died 1697. Father of Robert (1705).

HODSON, BENJAMIN. Adm. pens. (age 19) at MAGDALENE, May 11, 1693. S. of Joshua (1669), clerk. B. at Barlinge, Lincs. School, Lincoln. Matric. 1695; B.A. 1696-7. Ord deacon (Lincoln) May 30, 1697; priest, Sept. 25, 1698. V. of Bracebridge, Lincs., 1701.

HODSON, CHRISTOPHER. Matric. pens. from St JOHN'S, Michs. 1572; B.A. 1575-6. One of these names, clerk, buried at Hamsterley, Durham, Apr. 5, 1612.

HODGSON, CHRISTOPHER. Matric. sizar from PEMBROKE, Michs. 1581. Perhaps of Beeston, Yorks. Attorney to the Council of the North.

HODGSON, CHRISTOPHER. Adm. at CORPUS CHRISTI, 1623. Probably s. of the above. B. 1606. Of Cottingley Hall, Yorks. Buried at Beeston, Feb. 20, 1642. Brother of John (1618). (M. H. Peacock.)

HODSON, CHRISTOPHER. Adm. pens. (age 18) at St JOHN'S, June 26, 1649. S. of John (1618), gent., of Leeds, Yorks. Probably adm. at Gray's Inn, Dec. 28, 1649, as s. of John, of Newhall, Beeston Park, Leeds, gent. Married Elizabeth, sister of Sir Edmond Jennings. (Thoresby, *Duc. Leod.*)

HODGSON, CHRISTOPHER. Adm. sizar (age 27) at TRINITY, May 15, 1722. S. of Marmaduke, schoolmaster, of Sutton, Yorks. School, Ripley, Yorks. (under his father). Matric. 1723, as 'Charles'; B.A. 1725-6; M.A. 1732. Ord. deacon May 23, 1725; priest, Dec. 19, 1725. Chaplain to the Duke of Buccleuch. V. of Spratton, Northants., 1738-76. R. of Creaton, 1754-73. Buried at Spratton, Jan. 22, 1776. (H. I. Longden.)

HODGSON, CHRISTOPHER. Adm. pens. (age 17) at TRINITY, July 10, 1725. S. of Christopher, of Westerton, near Wakefield, Yorks. Schools, Coventry (Mr Jackson) and Wakefield. Matric. 1726; Scholar, 1727; B.A. 1729-30; M.A. 1733. Fellow, 1732. M.D. Governor of Wakefield School, 1743-68. Married Elizabeth, dau. of Marmaduke Rookes, of Barrowby, Yorks. Buried at Wakefield, Jan. 14, 1768, aged 60. M.I. (M. H. Peacock.)

HODGSON, CLEMENT. B.A. from MAGDALENE, 1592-3. Perhaps s. of John (1566). One of these names R. of Roughton and Bardney, Lincs. Will proved (Lincoln) 1614.

HODSON, EDWARD. Adm. sizar (age 18) at CAIUS, June 28, 1613. Of Felmingham, Norfolk. S. of Edmund. Schoolmaster, Mr Tills.

HODGSON, EDWARD. Adm. Fell.-Com. (age 15) at CHRIST'S, Apr. 22, 1631. S. of Phineas (1590), D.D. B. at York. Educated at home (Mr Tennant). Matric. 1631. Adm. at Gray's Inn, Jan. 11, 1638-9. Probably of Ripon, Esq. Died Mar. 17, 1705-6; 'after 67 years faithful and useful service to the Church and City.' Brother of Arthur (1647), of Timothy (1643) and Tobias (1641). (*Peile*, I. 409; M. H. Peacock.)

HODGSON, EDWARD. Adm. Fell.-Com. at JESUS, Dec. 14, 1691. 1st s. of Sir Thomas, Knt. Of Yorkshire. Matric. 1692.

HODGSON, ELEAZAR. Matric. pens. from St JOHN'S, Easter, 1588. S. of William, of Newcastle. B. in Durham. B.A. 1591-2; M.A. from Jesus, 1595. Incorp. at Oxford, 1608. M.D. (Padua) 1612. Incorp. at Oxford, 1616. Candidate R.C.P., 1616. Fellow, 1618. Censor. Registrar, 1637-9. Elect. Died in St Stephen's, Coleman St, London, Jan. 19, 1638-9. Will, P.C.C. 1639. Brother of Phineas (1590). (*Munk*, I. 172; *Vis. of London*, 1634.)

HODGSON, FARRAND. Adm. sizar (age 17) at ST JOHN'S, June 21, 1692. S. of Thomas, gent. B. in Craven, Yorks. School, Threshfield (Mr Motley). Matric. 1692; B.A. 1695-6. Schoolmaster of Leyland, Lancs. P.C. of Heapey, 1706. (*Vict. Hist. of Lancs.*, VI. 51.)

HODGSON, FRANCIS. Matric. pens. from ST JOHN'S, c. 1596.

HODSON, GAWIN. Scholar of QUEENS', 1535; B.A. 1535-6, 1st in the *ordo*; M.A. 1538. Fellow, 1535-47. R. of Atherington, Devon, 1554-7. Perhaps preb. of Lincoln, 1555-60, deprived.

HODGESON, GEORGE. Adm. pens. at SIDNEY, June 22, 1619. B. in Yorkshire. Matric. 1619; B.A. 1622-3; M.A. 1626. Ord. deacon (York) Dec. 1623; priest, May, 1624.

HODGSHON, GEORGE. Adm. sizar (age 19) at ST JOHN'S, Feb. 20, 1638-9. S. of Lancelot, clerk, of Glassonby-in-Addingham, Cumberland. B. there. School, Blencow (Mr Wm. Wilkinson). Matric. 1639.

HODSON, GEORGE. Adm. sizar (age 16) at ST JOHN'S, Mar. 19, 1717-8. S. of John, clerk, of Cheshire. B. at Christleton. Probably bapt. at Bruera, Cheshire, Oct. 9, 1701; s. of John, C. of Bruera. B.A. 1721-2; M.A. 1737. C. of West Kirby, 1726-58. R. of Overchurch, 1737-57. *See Al. Oxon.* for a contemporary.

HODDESDON, HENRY. Matric. pens. from CORPUS CHRISTI, Easter, 1583. S. of Nicholas. B. at Edgware, Middlesex. B.A. 1586-7; M.A. 1590. Ord. deacon (London) Apr. 12; priest, Apr. 13, 1597. C. of Stanford-le-Hope. R. of 'Iseldon.' R. of Blyborough, Lincs., 1610-8. (*Vis. of London*, 1568.)

HODGSON, HENRY. Matric. pens. from ST JOHN'S, Easter, 1626; B.A. 1629-30; M.A. 1633. Ord. deacon (Peterb.) Dec. 18, 1631. One of these names dean of Harthill, Yorks., in 1648-9.

HODSON, HENRY. Adm. sizar (age 16) at CHRIST'S, Mar. 20, 1699-1700. S. of John (1669). B. at Titchwell, Norfolk. School, Brancaster (under his father). Matric. 1701; Scholar, 1702; B.A. 1703-4. Ord. deacon (Lincoln) June 8, 1707; priest, Feb. 29, 1707-8. R. of Conisholme, Lincs., 1711. V. of Headcorn, Kent, 1716-23. R. of Sandhurst, 1722-53. Died Dec. 24, 1771. Father of John (1741) and Henry (1737), brother of John (1699). (*Peile*, II. 147.)

HODGSON, HENRY. Adm. sizar (age 16) at MAGDALENE, July 9, 1715. S. of Miles (1682), clerk. B. at Louth, Lincs. School, Alford. Matric. 1716; B.A. 1719-20; M.A. 1723. Fellow, 1720. Ord. deacon (Lincoln) Sept. 10, 1721; priest, May 31, 1724.

HODSDEN, HENRY. M.A. from PETERHOUSE, 1720. S. of H., of London. Matric. from St John's College, Oxford, July 10, 1678, age 16; B.A. (Oxford) 1682. R. of Willingdon, Sussex, 1698. V. of Westham, 1719. (*Al. Oxon.*)

HODSON, HENRY. Adm. pens. (age 18) at ST JOHN'S, May 27, 1737. S. of Henry (1699-1700), V. of Headcorn, Kent. B. at Headcorn. School, Tonbridge (Mr Spencer). Matric. 1737; B.A. 1740-1; M.A. 1744. Ord. deacon (Rochester) Apr. 5, 1747; priest, Oct. 7, 1753. R. of Sandhurst, 1753-81. V. of Thornham, 1768-81. Chaplain to the Duke of Bolton. Died Oct. 1781. Will, P.C.C. (*Scott-Mayor*, III. 485.)

HODGSON, JAMES. Matric. pens. from CHRIST'S, 1595.

HODGSON, JAMES. Matric. sizar from CHRIST'S, 1601; B.A. 1605-6; M.A. 1609. Ord. deacon (Norwich) Sept. 21, 1607, age 24; priest, Sept. 1610. C. of Livermere, Suffolk, 1621. Licensed to preach in the diocese. Will (P.C.C.) 1655; of Gt Livermere, clerk.

HODGSON, JAMES. Matric. sizar from CHRIST'S, July, 1614; B.A. 1617-8. Probably ord. deacon (Norwich) Dec. 19, 1619.

HODGSON, JAMES. Matric. pens. from ST JOHN'S, Michs. 1619. One of these names adm. at Gray's Inn, Aug. 11, 1619; 's. of James, of London, gent.' Probably brother of Richard (1606-7). (*Lincs. Pedigrees*, 501.)

HODGSON, JOHN. Scholar of QUEENS', 1509-11.

HODGSON, JOHN. Matric. sizar from ST JOHN'S, Michs. 1566. Probably ord. priest (Lincoln) Dec. 21, 1570. R. of Hemingby, Lincs., 1573; R. of Dalderby, 1575. 'Aged 28; married; well skilled in Latin; preacher.' Will proved, Nov. 17, 1614; mentions s. Clement (? 1592-3). (*Lib. Cler. Linc.*, 1576; *Lincs. Pedigrees*, 501.)

HODSON, JOHN. Matric. sizar from QUEENS', Michs. 1568.

HODGESON, JOHN. Matric. sizar from CHRIST'S, Michs. 1575.

HODGSON, JOHN. B.A. from CHRIST'S, 1592-3. Perhaps M.A. 1596. Ord. priest (Lincoln) Mar. 1596. V. of Stradsett, Norfolk, 1603-51. Died 1651. (*Peile*, I. 198.)

HODSON, JOHN. Matric. sizar from CORPUS CHRISTI, c. 1596; B.A. 1599-1600. Ord. deacon (Norwich) Mar. 25, 1601, age 24. C. of Bramerton. Perhaps R. of Honington, Suffolk, 1610-9; and R. of Coney Weston, 1620-44. Died 1644.

HODGSON, JOHN. B.A. from ST CATHARINE'S, 1599-1600; M.A. 1606. Ord. deacon (Colchester) Oct. 12, 1600.

HODGSON or HOEGSON, JOHN. Adm. pens. at PETERHOUSE, Jan. 25, 1607-8. Matric. 1608. Doubtless s. and h. of John, of London, gent.; adm. at the Middle Temple, Jan. 15, 1611-2. Gave £20 to the Chapel Fund, in 1628. Brother of William (1617). (*T. A. Walker.*)

HODGSON, JOHN. Matric. Fell.-Com. from TRINITY, Easter, 1618. Doubtless s. and h. of Christopher (1581), of Beeston, Yorks.; adm. at Gray's Inn, Aug. 10, 1618. Age 11 in 1612. Of New Hall, Leeds. Alderman and mayor of Leeds. Married Elizabeth, sister of Sir George Radcliffe. Brother of Christopher (1623). Father of Christopher (1649). (*Vis. of Yorks.*, 1612; Thoresby, *Duc. Leod*, 72; M. H. Peacock.)

HODGSON, JOHN. Adm. sizar at JESUS, July 2, 1623. Matric. 1623; B.A. from Clare, 1626-7; M.A. 1630. One of these names R. of Donington, Lincs., 1642.

HODSON, JOHN. Adm. sizar at TRINITY, June 9, 1657. Of Durham. Matric. 1657; Scholar, 1659; B.A. 1660-1.

HODSON, JOHN. Adm. sizar (age 17) at CHRIST'S, June 17, 1669. S. of Thomas (1626). B. at Ringstead, Norfolk. School, Scarning (Mr Burton). Matric. 1669; B.A. 1672-3; M.A. 1676. Ord. priest (Norwich) Dec. 1674. V. of Holme, Norfolk, 1675-1704; of Thornham, 1679-1704; and of Titchwell, 1687. Master of Brancaster School. Father of Henry (1699) and John (1699). (*Peile*, II. 23.)

HODGSON, JOHN. Adm. pens. at KING'S, c. 1675. One of these names adm. at Leyden, Aug. 26, 1676.

HODGSON or HODSON, JOHN. Adm. sizar (age 15) at CHRIST'S, Apr. 11, 1699. S. of John (1669). B. at Ringstead, Norfolk. School, Brancaster (under his father). Matric. 1699; Scholar, 1700; B.A. 1702-3. Ord. deacon (Lincoln, *Litt. dim.* from Norwich) May 23, 1703. Perhaps R. of Thurstaston, Cheshire, 1705-52. Buried there July 8, 1752. Father of the next and perhaps of George (1717), brother of Henry (1699). (*Peile*, II. 145; *Ormerod*, II. 279.)

HODSON, JOHN. Adm. sizar (age 17) at ST JOHN'S, May 30, 1724. S. of John (above), R. of Thurstaston, Cheshire. B. at Thurstaston. Matric. 1724; B.A. 1727-8. Ord. deacon (Chester) June 17, 1728; priest, May 24, 1730. C. of Thurstaston. C. of Woodchurch in 1740. (*Scott-Mayor*, III. 369.)

HODSON, JOHN. Adm. pens. (age 18) at ST JOHN'S, May 16, 1741. S. of Henry (1699-1700), clerk, of Kent. B. at Sandhurst. Schools, Battle, Sussex (Mr Jenkin) and Sutton, Kent (Mr Clendon). Matric. 1743-4; B.A. 1744-5; M.A. 1748. Ord. deacon (Rochester) Dec. 7, 1746.

HODSON, JOSHUA. Adm. pens. (age 18) at MAGDALENE, June 23, 1669. S. of Benjamin, of Scalesby, Lincs., deceased. School, Melton Mowbray, Leics. Matric. 1670; B.A. 1672-3; M.A. 1682. Ord. deacon (Lincoln) May 25, 1673; C. of Fiskerton, Lincs. Father of Benjamin (1693).

HODGSHON, MALACHI. Adm. at KING'S, a scholar from Eton, 1746. S. of Theodore. Bapt. at Wandsworth, Surrey, Sept. 8, 1727. Matric. 1747; B.A. 1750-1; M.A. 1754. Fellow, 1750. Retired to Wales, and died there, Nov. 21, 1769. (*Harwood.*)

HODGSON, MILES. Adm. sizar (age 18) at ST JOHN'S, May 9, 1682. S. of Rowland, husbandman. B. at Dent, Yorks. School, Sedbergh. Matric. 1682; B.A. 1685-6; M.A. 1693. Ord. priest (Lincoln) Feb. 21, 1691-2. V. of Cawkwell, Lincs. R. of Blyborough, 1705. V. of Fairforth, 1708. P.C. of Scamblesby. Master of Louth School. Father of Henry (1715).

HODGSON, NATHANIEL. Adm. pens. (age 16) at SIDNEY, Apr. 18, 1724. S. of Thomas (1670), clerk, of Boynton, Yorks. B. there. Schools, Thornton and Kirkleatham, Yorks. (Mr Clark). Matric. 1724; B.A. 1727-8; M.A. 1754. Ord. deacon (Lincoln) Dec. 25, 1729; priest (York) June 4, 1732. C. of Normanby. C. of Birdsall, Yorks., c. 1747. R. of Scawton and Terrington, 1753-83. R. of Adlingfleet, 1754-93. Married, at Belfreys, York, Aug. 21, 1755, Emma, dau. of the Hon. Thomas Willoughby. Died Jan. 31, 1793. (Foster, *Yorks. Pedigrees.*)

HODGSON, NOAH. Adm. sizar at TRINITY, Aug. 31, 1674; B.A. 1678-9. Ord. deacon (York) Sept. 1682; priest, 1682-3.

HODSON, PHILIP. Matric. sizar from TRINITY, Michs. 1607.

HODGSON, PHILIP. Matric. Fell.-Com. from ST CATHARINE'S, Lent, 1615-6; B.A. 1618-9.

HODGSON, PHILIP. B.A. 1654 (Incorp. from Oxford). Perhaps s. of John, of Croft and Metheringham, Lincs. Age 7 in 1640. Matric. from Queen's College, Oxford, Nov. 10, 1651; B.A. 1654. Adm. at Gray's Inn, Jan. 26, 1656-7. Of Stixwold, Lincs. (*Lincs. Pedigrees*, 500.)

HODGSON, PHINEAS. Matric. pens. from JESUS, *c.* 1590. S. of William, of Newcastle. B.A. 1593–4; M.A. 1597; D.D. 1609. Incorp. Oxford, 1602. R. of Elvington, Yorks., 1600–5. R. of Etton, 1605–11. R. of Sigglesthorne, 1608–24. Chancellor of York Cathedral, 1611–46. Chaplain to the King. Married Jane, dau. of John Hutton, of York. Buried in York Minster, Nov. 28, 1646. Will, York, 1647. Brother of Eleazer (1588), father of Arthur (1647), Edward (1631), Timothy (1643) and Tobias (1641); and 20 others. (*Vis. of London*, 1634; M. H. Peacock.)

HODSON, PHINEAS. Matric. sizar from CLARE, Michs. 1621.

HODSON, RICHARD. Matric. sizar from CLARE, Easter, 1558. One of these names, B.A., V. of Calverley, Yorks., *c.* 1570–3.

HODGSON, HODSHON or HODSON, RICHARD. Matric. pens. from CHRIST'S, June, 1565; Scholar, 1565–6; B.A. 1567–8; M.A. 1571. Ord. deacon (Ely) Dec. 21, 1569, age 24. One of these names R. of Debden, Essex. Will (P.C.C.) 1612. One R. of Camerton, Somerset, 1584–1632. (*Peile*, I. 91.)

HODSON or HODGSON, RICHARD. Matric. pens. from PETERHOUSE, Easter, 1578; B.A. 1581–2.

HODGSON, RICHARD. Matric. sizar from ST JOHN'S, *c.* 1594; B.A. (? 1594–5); M.A. 1599. V. of Ilkley, Yorks., 1607–40. Died Apr. 7, 1640, aged 66. M.I. at Ilkley. Father of Robert (1621).

HODGSON, RICHARD. Probably adm. at PETERHOUSE, as pens., 1606–7. Of London. S. of James, citizen. Matric. Easter, 1607, as 'Hidgem'; B.A. from St John's, 1610–1; M.A. 1614; B.D. 1621. Fellow, 1612. Incorp. at Oxford, 1620. Ord. deacon (Peterb.) June 10; priest, June 11, 1620. R. of Rathby, in Bolingbroke, Lincs., 1623. R. of West Keal, 1643. Probably brother of James (1619). (*Lincs. Pedigrees*, 501.)

HODSON, ROBERT. Matric. pens. from CHRIST'S, 1592–3.

HODGESON, ROBERT. Adm. pens. (age 17) at SIDNEY, Apr. 20, 1621. S. of Richard (1594), M.A., V. of Ilkley. B. at Tadcaster, Yorks. Educated by his father. Matric. 1621; B.A. 1624–5; M.A. 1630. Ord. deacon (York) Mar. 1625–6; priest, Feb. 1626–7. P.C. of Stillington, Yorks. Died Dec. 30, 1639, aged 36. M.I. at Ilkley. (M. H. Peacock.)

HODSON, ROBERT. Matric. pens. from MAGDALENE, Easter, 1633; B.A. 1636–7; M.A. 1643. Ord. deacon (Peterb.) June 9, 1639; priest, Mar. 1, 1639–40. R. of Broughton, Hunts., 1668–80. Died 1680. Perhaps father of Benjamin (1666).

HODSON, ROBERT. Adm. sizar at JESUS, Feb. 8, 1704–5. S. of Benjamin (1666), deceased, R. of Broughton, Hunts. B. 1688. Matric. 1705; Rustat scholar, 1706; B.A. 1708–9. Ord. priest (Ely) Dec. 21, 1712. R. of Broughton, Hunts., 1713–74. Died 1774.

HODGSON, ROBERT. Adm. sizar (age 17) at ST JOHN'S, Mar. 22, 1711–2. S. of James, furrier. B. at Threshfield, Yorks. School, Threshfield (Mr Marshall). Matric. 1712; B.A. 1715–6. Ord. deacon (York) Dec. 1716; priest, June, 1720.

HODSON, ROBERT. Adm. pens. at CLARE, July 5, 1744. B. in London. Matric. 1744; M.A. 1762 (*Lit. Reg.*). Ord. priest (Lincoln) Sept. 22, 1751. R. of Huntingdon St Mary, 1757–1803; and of All Saints', 1762–1803. R. of Offord Cluny, Hunts., 1765–1803. Preb. of Lincoln, 1773–1803. Chaplain to Bishop Newton. Died Jan. 17, 1803, aged 77. Will, P.C.C.

HODGSON, SAMUEL. Matric. pens. from ST JOHN'S, Easter, 1571. Of London. B.A. 1574–5; M.A. 1578. Fellow, 1577. (*Cooper*, II. 23.)

HODGSON, HOGSON or HODSON, SAMUEL. Matric. sizar from CHRIST'S, June, 1602; B.A. 1605–6; M.A. 1609. One of these names, of Carlisle, adm. at Gray's Inn, Feb. 2, 1607–8. Ord. deacon (London) Dec. 1614, age 29; 'b. at Carlisle; now of Mountnessing, Essex.' (*Peile*, I. 240.)

HODGSON, THOMAS. Adm. sizar at QUEENS', Feb. 1, 1591–2. Of Lancashire. Matric. 1592.

HODGSON, THOMAS. Adm. sizar at CHRIST'S, Apr. 15, 1626. S. of Richard, of Norfolk. School, Lynn (Mr Robson). Matric. 1626; B.A. 1629–30; M.A. 1633. Ord. priest (Norwich) 1634. R. of Heacham, Norfolk, 1634–9. R. of Ringstead St Andrew, 1639–61. Died 1661. Father of John (1669). (*Peile*, I. 372.)

HODGSON, THOMAS. Adm. sizar (age 18) at ST JOHN'S, May 6, 1670. S. of Enoch, yeoman, of Richmond, Yorks. B. there. School, Sedbergh (Mr Fell). Matric. 1670; B.A. 1673–4. Ord. deacon (York) June, 1674; priest, Feb. 1674–5. One of these names (B.A.), V. of Kilburn, Yorks., 1677–1716.

HODGSON, THOMAS. Adm. pens. (age 17) at ST JOHN'S, May 13, 1670. S. of Thomas, yeoman, of Ingleton, Yorks. B. there. School, Sedbergh (Mr Fell). Matric. 1675; B.A. 1675–6; M.A. 1679. Ord. deacon (York) Sept. 1677; priest, Dec. 1677. Probably R. of Kirk Deighton, Yorks., 1693–1703. V. of Boynton, 1706–27. V. of Carnaby, 1706–27. V. of Appleton-le-Street, 1706–27. Married Mary, dau. of Robert Ward, of Gray's Inn. Buried Dec. 27, 1727, at Appleton-le-Street. Father of Nathaniel (1724). (*Sedbergh Sch. Reg.*, 120; Foster, *Yorks. Pedigrees*.)

HODGSON, THOMAS. M.A. 1736 (Incorp. from Oxford). S. of Thomas, of Lazonby, Cumberland. Matric. from Queen's College, Oxford, Dec. 1, 1714, age 16; B.A. (Oxford) 1719; M.A. 1722. V. of Brough-under-Stainmore, Westmorland, 1735–68. (*Al. Oxon.*)

HODGSON or HODSON, TIMOTHY. Adm. pens. (age 17) at PETERHOUSE, June 14, 1643. S. of Phineas (1590), D.D., Chancellor of York. Migrated to Trinity Hall. B.A. 1646–7; M.A. 1650. Brother of the next, of Edward (1631) and of Tobias (1641). (*Vis. of London*, 1634.)

HODGSON, TIMOTHY. Adm. sizar (age 18) at ST JOHN'S, Mar. 19, 1684–5. S. of Christopher, gent. B. in Craven, Yorks. School, Threshfield (Mr Hen. Motley). Matric. 1685; B.A. 1688–9. Ord. priest (Peterb.) July 18, 1697. V. of Weston-by-Welland, Northants., 1697–1739. Married, at Weston, Dec. 28, 1698, Anne Ireland. Died 1739. (H. I. Longden.)

HODSON, TOBIAS. Adm. at KING'S (age 17) a scholar from Eton, Sept. 4, 1641. Of York. S. of Phineas (1590), D.D. B.A. and Fellow for a short time. Left in 1647. 'In possession of a good estate, afterwards major of a regiment of horse.' Married Mary, dau. of Sir John Lister, of Hull, Yorks. Brother of Timothy (1643), etc. Father of the next. (*Harwood*; *Vis. of London*, 1634.)

HODSON, TOBIAS. Adm. pens. (age 13) at ST JOHN'S, June 29, 1665. Later Fell.-Com. S. of Tobias (above), Esq., of Bishop Burton, Yorks. B. there. Educated at home. Adm. at the Inner Temple, May 6, 1669. Brother of William (1682).

HODSON, TOBIAS. Adm. pens. at QUEENS', May 18, 1698. Of Yorkshire. Matric. 1698.

HODGESON, WILLIAM. Adm. at KING'S (age 18) a scholar from Eton, Aug. 14, 1534. Of Pontefract, Yorks. B.A. 1538–9; M.A. 1542. Fellow, 1535–46. Probably B.D. 1546; chaplain to the Duke of Norfolk.

HODGESON, WILLIAM. B.A. 1560–1.

HODGSON, WILLIAM. Matric. pens. from ST JOHN'S, Michs. 1564. B. at 'Nows,' Richmondshire, Yorks. Ord. deacon (London) July 25, 1569, age 27; 'student of St John's.'

HODSON, WILLIAM. Matric. pens. from ST JOHN'S, Michs. 1571. One of these names adm. at Gray's Inn, 1578, from Staple Inn. (But *see Al. Oxon.*)

HODSON, WILLIAM. Adm. pens. at PETERHOUSE, May 3, 1617. S. of John, citizen of London. Matric. 1617; B.A. 1620–1; M.A. 1624. Executor of his father, 1628; at that time of Tottenham, Middlesex. Author, poetical and theological. Brother of John (1607–8). (*T. A. Walker*, 5; *D.N.B.*)

HODGSON, WILLIAM. Adm. sizar at CHRIST'S, May 17, 1652. B. at Killinghall, Yorks. Matric. 1652. Ord. priest (York) 1662. V. of Brampton, Yorks., till 1667. V. of Scarborough, 1667–76. Died 1676. (*Peile*, I. 548.)

HODSON, WILLIAM. Adm. pens. (age 18) at ST JOHN'S, Apr. 15, 1682. S. of Tobias (1665). B. at Bishop t, Yorks. School, Beverley (Mr Lambert). Matric. 1682; B.A. 1685–6. Probably ord. deacon (Durham) Sept. 20, 1691; priest, Sept. 25, 1692.

HODSON, WILLIAM. M.A. from ST JOHN'S, 1705. S. of G. (? Gulielmus), of Oxford, clerk. Matric. from St John's, Oxford, Dec. 17, 1689, age 15; B.A. (Oxford) 1693. Perhaps R. of Swanton Novers, Norfolk, 1708–36; and R. of Wood Norton, 1708. Married, at Loddington, Northants., Feb. 20, 1717–8, Frances, dau. of John (?) Allicodde, Esq. (*Al. Oxon.*; H. I. Longden.)

HODGSHON, WILLIAM. Adm. sizar (age 25) at JESUS, May 7, 1714. S. of Hugh, of Whitcham, Cumberland. B. at Milham. School, St Bees. Matric. 1714; B.A. 1717–8. Ord. deacon (Norwich) Mar. 1717–8; priest (Ely) May 24, 1719.

HODGSON, WILLIAM. Adm. sizar at CLARE, Mar. 31, 1716. S. of Timothy (1684–5), V. of Weston-by-Welland, Northants. B. there. School, Oakham. Matric. 1716; B.A. 1719–20; M.A. 1723. Fellow, 1722–30. Ord. deacon (Peterb.) Feb. 18, 1721–2; C. of Weston-by-Welland; priest (Lincoln) Dec. 18, 1726. V. of Standen, Herts., 1728. Died 1747.

HODGSON, ——. B.A. 1475–6; M.A. 1479–80.

HODSON, ——. Matric. sizar from CHRIST'S, Michs. 1553.

HODDESON, ——. Adm. at CORPUS CHRISTI, 1571.

HODILOW, ARTHUR. Matric. pens. from KING'S, *c.* 1595. Doubtless s. and h. of Edmund, of Kelvedon, Essex. Bapt. there, Feb. 24, 1577–8. Of Grafton Underwood, Northants., Esq. Married (1) Jane, sister of Dr Humphrey Henchman, Bishop of London; (2) Lady Susannah Humfrey, widow of Sir Thomas Humfrey, Knt., of Leicestershire. Died May, 1641, aged 63. Father of the next. (*Top. and Gen.*, II. 28.)

HODILOW, ARTHUR. Matric. pens. from CLARE, Easter, 1624. S. of Arthur (above). B.A. 1627-8; M.A. 1631. Settled at Stansty, Wrexham. Married Ermine, dau. of Hugh Meredith, of Wrexham. Will (P.C.C.) 1647; of Stansty, Wrexham, clerk. (*Top. and Gen.*, II. 52.)

HODILOE, BARNABAS. Matric. pens. from CHRIST'S, Nov. 1578. (*See Peile*, I. 147.)

HODILOW, STEPHEN. Matric. sizar from TRINITY, Michs. 1562; Scholar, 1563.

HUDDELOWE, ——. Adm. at CORPUS CHRISTI, 1561.

HODLING, JOHN. B.A. 1535-6.

HODY, EDWARD. Adm. pens. (age 18) at ST JOHN'S, Sept. 26, 1716. S. of John, gent., of Spettisbury, Dorset. B. at Holt Lodge, near Wimbourne. Scholar from Charterhouse. Entered as medical student at Leyden, 1719. M.D. of Rheims, 1723. F.R.S., 1733. L.R.C.P., 1740. Physician to St George's Hospital. Died Nov. 1, 1759, in Hanover Square, London. Admon., P.C.C. (*Scott-Mayor*, III. 307; *G. Mag.*)

HOE, JOHN. Adm. sizar at CHRIST'S, Apr. 28, 1681. S. of John. B. at Nottingham. School, Nottingham (Mr Cudworth). Matric. 1681; B.A. 1684-5. Ord. deacon (London) Feb. 1685-6. (*Peile*, II. 83.)

HOET, JAMES. Adm. Fell.-Com. (age 25) at CAIUS, June 7, 1671. S. of Peter, merchant, of London. B. at St Martin Orgar, Sept. 4, 1645. School, Merchant Taylors'. Perhaps adm. at Leyden, Aug. 11, 1671. Matric. 1672; B.A. 1673-4; M.A. from Sidney, 1677. Ord. deacon (London) Dec. 23, 1677; priest, Dec. 24, 1682. R. of Debden, Essex, 1697-1712. Buried at St Dionis, London, as from St Mary Magdalen, Old Fish St, June 28, 1717. Father of the next. (*Venn*, I. 444; J. Ch. Smith.)

HOET, LAWRENCE. Adm. pens. (age 17) at SIDNEY, Aug. 17, 1700. Only s. of James (above), R. of Debden, Essex. B. in London. School, Felsted. Matric. 1704, as 'Host'; B.A. 1706-7. Ord. priest (London) Feb. 1, 1712-3. R. of Debden, 1713-45. Will (Comm. C. Essex) 1745.

HOFFMAN, BENJAMIN. M.A. 1680 (Incorp. from Oxford). S. of John, R. of Wootton, Oxon. (a German). Matric. from St Edmund Hall, Oxford, Nov. 23, 1666, age 15; B.A. (Oxford) 1670; M.A. (Balliol) 1673. R. of Woodmancote, Sussex, 1682. R. of Albourne, 1689-1711. Author, Sermon at St George's, Botolph Lane, London. (*Al. Oxon.*; H. G. Harrison.)

HOGAN, *see* **HOOGAN.**

HOGDEN, RICHARD. Matric. sizar from ST JOHN'S, Easter, 1588; B.A. (? 1591-2); M.A. 1595, as 'Hogbin.'

HOGGE or HOGGET, ANTHONY. Matric. sizar from CHRIST'S, July, 1604; B.A. 1607-8; M.A. 1612. Perhaps R. of St Thomas-at-Cliffe, Lewes, 1611-42. R. of Glynde, Sussex; sequestered, 1642.

HOGG, RICHARD. B.A. from TRINITY, 1609; M.A. 1612. Ord. deacon (Norwich) Dec. 22, 1611; priest, May 30, 1613. C. of Hardwick, Bucks., 1613.

HOGGE, ROGER. Matric. pens. from ST JOHN'S, Easter, 1570; B.A. 1574-5.

HOGG, STEPHEN. Matric. pens. from ST JOHN'S, Michs. 1616; B.A. 1620-1; M.A. 1624.

HOGGE, THOMAS. Matric. pens. from TRINITY, Easter, 1631; Scholar, 1634; B.A. 1634-5; M.A. 1641. Ord. deacon (Peterb.) Dec. 17, 1641. R. of Farthingstone, Northants., 1650-79. Buried there Jan. 1, 1679-80. (*Bridges*, I. 64; H. I. Longden.)

HOGG, THOMAS. Adm. pens. at ST JOHN'S, Feb. 10, 1662-3. B. at Rochester.

HOGGARD or HOGARD, DANIEL. Adm. at CORPUS CHRISTI, 1679. Of Nottinghamshire. Matric. 1679; B.A. 1682-3. Ord. deacon (York) June, 1683.

HOGARDE, JOHN. Matric. sizar from JESUS, Michs. 1556.

HOGGARD, JOHN. Adm. sizar (age 18) at ST JOHN'S, July 6, 1720. S. of Nathaniel, husbandman, of Nottinghamshire. B. at Tresswell, near Retford. School, Tresswell (Mr Newcombe). Matric. 1721; B.A. 1723-4. Ord. deacon (Lincoln) Sept. 20, 1724; priest, Sept. 25, 1726. Perhaps V. of Skellingthorpe, Lincs., 1750-82. R. of Aisthorpe, 1752-82. R. of Scampton, 1762-82.

HOGGARD, THOMAS. Adm. sizar (age 18) at SIDNEY, June 2, 1702. S. of Philip, deceased. B. at Burton Agnes, Yorks. School, Beverley. Matric. 1704; B.A. 1705-6. Ord. deacon (York) Sept. 1706; priest, 1708. V. of Hutton Cranswick, Yorks., 1711. Perhaps C. of Watton, Hull, c. 1745.

HOGLEY, JAMES. Adm. at Cambridge, c. 1642. S. of James. B. at Dunham, Norfolk. Schools, Saham Toney and Norwich. Afterwards at Furnival's and Lincoln's Inn. Adm. at the English College at Rome, Nov. 25, 1655. Left for England, 1657; drowned near Leghorn. (*Records S.J.*, I. 268.)

HOGLYE, WILLIAM. Matric. sizar from QUEENS', Easter, 1566; B.A. 1569-70. Perhaps V. of Beighton, Norfolk.

HOKE, SAMUEL. Matric. pens. from MAGDALENE, Lent, 1564-5.

HOLBECK or HOLBECH, BARNABAS. Adm. pens. at EMMANUEL, June 17, 1618. S. of William, of Birchley Hall, Fillongley, Warws., gent. Matric. 1618. Adm. at Gray's Inn, Aug. 12, 1622. Perhaps will (P.C.C.) 1635; of Fillongley. Brother of Thomas (1622). (*Vis. of Warws.*, 1682.)

HOLBEACH, GABRIEL. Matric. sizar from QUEENS', Michs. 1619. Of Warwickshire. Probably 3rd s. of George, of Fillongley, Warws. Brother of Martin (1617). (*Vis. of Warws.*, 1619.)

HOLBEACH, HENRY, *see* **RANDS.**

HOLBEACH, MARTIN. Adm. pens. at QUEENS', Sept. 24, 1617. Probably 2nd s. of George, of Fillongley, Warws. B. there. Matric. 1621; B.A. 1621-2; M.A. 1625. Ord. deacon (London) May 23, 1624. Master of Braintree School, 1626-7; of Halstead, c. 1627; and for 21 years the famous puritan Master of Felsted, 1628-49. V. of High Easter, Essex, 1648-62, where he acted as ordaining presbyter, and commissioner for the removal of scandalous ministers. Ejected, 1662, and retired to Dunmow. Buried at Felsted, 1670. Brother of Gabriel (1619). (*Calamy*, I. 304; J. Sargeaunt.)

HOLBECH, MATTHEW. Adm. pens. at TRINITY, July 4, 1663. Perhaps of Meriden Hall, Warws. S. of Matthew, of the Inner Temple, bencher. School, Westminster. Matric. 1663; Scholar, 1664. Adm. at the Inner Temple, July 12, 1660. Called to the Bar, Nov. 27, 1670.

HOLBEACH, RALPH DE. Fellow of PETERHOUSE, 1339. Master, 1344-9. Resigned, and became fellow, 1349-c. 1373. Ord. acolyte (Ely) Sept. 13, 1349. Petitions the Pope for a living in the gift of the Abbot of Bury St Edmunds, July, 1351. He was M.A. and B.C.L. (*Cal. of Pap. Pet.*, I. 212.)

HOLBECH, SIMON DE. Fellow and scholar of PETERHOUSE, 13th or 14th century. (M. R. James, *Catalogue of Peterhouse MSS.*)

HOLBECKE, THOMAS. Matric. pens. from QUEENS', Michs. 1579. One of these names 3rd s. of Martin, of Fillongley, Warws. Of Meriden Hall, Warws. (*Vis. of Warws.*, 1619.)

HOLBECH, THOMAS. Adm. pens. at EMMANUEL, Apr. 30, 1622. Probably 3rd s. of William, of Birchley Hall, Fillongley, Warws. B. at Fillongley, Warws. Age 13 in 1619. Matric. 1622; B.A. 1625-6; M.A. 1629; B.D. 1636; D.D. 1660 (*Lit. Reg.*). Fellow, 1629. Master, 1675-80. Vice-Chancellor, 1677-8. V. of Epping, 1641-43, sequestered, and 1660-80. Preb. of St Paul's, 1660-80. R. of St Augustine, London, 1662-80. Died 1680. Will (P.C.C. and V.C.C.) 1680. Brother of Barnabas (1618). (*Vis. of Warws.*, 1619.)

HOLBECH, THOMAS. Adm. sizar at EMMANUEL, Apr. 1678. Afterwards pens. Dec. 1680. S. of William, grocer, of Westminster (and great nephew of Thomas (1622)). Matric. 1678; B.A. 1681-2; M.A. 1685. R. of Holdenby, Northants., 1685-90. Died 1690. (*Bridges*, I. 529; *Baker*, I. 208.)

HOLBEAM, ROBERT. Adm. at KING'S, a scholar from Eton, Aug. 24, 1560. Matric. 1560; B.A. 1564-5; M.A. 1568. Fellow, 1563-72. R. of Elsworth, Cambs., 1571-87. Died 1587.

HOLBERNE, WILLIAM. Matric. sizar from QUEENS', Lent, 1578-9. Of Suffolk. Probably s. of William, of Southwold.

HOLBEY, ROBERT. Matric. sizar from CORPUS CHRISTI, Easter, 1670. Of Norwich. B.A. 1673-4.

HOLBURNE, ANTHONY. Matric. pens. from CHRIST'S, May, 1562. One of these names, of London, adm. at the Inner Temple, 1565. Perhaps musical composer, and member of the Chapel Royal. (*Peile*, I. 77; *D.N.B.*)

HOLBORNE, OTTIWELL, *see* **HEBBURNE.**

HOLBORNE, SAMUEL. Matric. sizar from ST JOHN'S, c. 1593.

HOLBOURN, WILLIAM. Adm. sizar (age 16) at CHRIST'S, July 4, 1663. S. of Robert. B. at York. School, York (Dr Preston). Matric. 1663; B.A. 1666-7; M.A. 1671. Ord. priest (Ely) June, 1671. R. of Thornton Watlass, Yorks., 1672-9. Died 1679. (*Peile*, I. 606.)

HOLBOROUGH, THOMAS. Adm. pens. at EMMANUEL, Feb. 18, 1617-8. Matric. 1618; Scholar; B.A. 1621-2; M.A. 1625. V. of Battisford, Suffolk, 1628-62, ejected. R. of Akenham, 1661. (*Calamy*, II. 415.)

HOLBOROUGH, THOMAS. Adm. sizar at EMMANUEL, Apr. 10, 1651. Of Suffolk. Matric. 1652; B.A. 1654-5.

HOLBROOK, ANTHONY. Adm. pens. at SIDNEY, July 3, 1694. S. of John (1654), R. of Edgmond, Salop. B. at Ashton. School, Newport, Salop. Matric. 1695; B.A. 1697-8; M.A. 1701. R. of Panfield, Essex, 1705. R. of Little Waltham, 1709. Author, sermons. Will (Comm. C. Essex) 1749. Brother of Thomas (1695) and Theophilus (1700), father of John (1728). (H. G. Harrison.)

HOLBROKE, EDWARD. Adm. at CORPUS CHRISTI, 1713. Of Staffordshire. Matric. 1713-4; B.A. 1716-7; M.A. 1721. Incorp. at Oxford, 1730. Usher at Stafford School. Will (P.C.C.) 1772; of Lichfield, clerk.

HOLBROOK, JOHN. Fellow of PETERHOUSE, 1393, being then B.A. Proctor, 1397-8. D.D. 1418. Master of Peterhouse, 1421-36. Chancellor of the University, 1429-30. Ord. sub-deacon (Ely) 1412; deacon, Dec. 17, 1412; priest, Apr. 22, 1413. R. of South Repps, Norfolk, 1421-37. Chaplain to Henry V and Henry VI. V. of Cherry Hinton, Cambs., 1430. Author, mathematical. Died July 12, 1437. M.I. (Brass) at Little St Mary's, Cambridge. (*D.N.B.*, where the account contains serious inaccuracies; *T. A. Walker*.)

HOLBROOKE, JOHN. Adm. sizar (age 18) at ST JOHN'S, June 8, 1654. S. of Ralph, yeoman, of Over, Cheshire. B. there. School, Northwich, Cheshire (Mr Hulme). Matric. 1654; B.A. 1657-8; M.A. 1661. Ord. deacon (Lincoln) Mar. 10, 1660-1; priest, Feb. 21, 1662-3. Probably V. of Titsey, Surrey, 1662-91; also V. of Edgmond, Salop, 1667. Died Aug. 7, 1691, aged 56. M.I. at Titsey. Father of Anthony (1694), Thomas (1695) and Theophilus (1700). (*Manning and Bray*, II. 407; *Al. Oxon.*, where he is apparently wrongly identified.)

HOLBROOKE, JOHN. Adm. sizar (age 20) at ST JOHN'S, June 28, 1718. S. of Edward, of Stafford (*juristae*). B. at Wolverhampton. School, Wolverhampton (Mr Dawbry). Matric. 1717. Ord. deacon (London) Dec. 18, 1720. Will of one of these names (P.C.C.) 1764; of Hailes, Gloucs., clerk.

HOLBROOK, JOHN. Adm. pens. (age 18) at TRINITY, June 26, 1728. S. of Anthony (1694), R. of Little Waltham, Essex. B. there. School, Westminster. Matric. 1728; Scholar, 1729; B.A. 1731-2; M.A. 1735. Fellow, 1734. Ord. deacon (Lincoln) Mar. 5, 1731-2.

HOLBROOKE, RICHARD. B.A. 1608 (Incorp. from Oxford). Of Kent. S. of John, merchant taylor. School, Merchant Taylors'. Matric. from St John's College, Oxford, Mar. 1, 1604-5, age 18; B.A. (Oxford) 1606; M.A. 1610; B.D. 1617. V. of Evenley, Northants., 1615. V. of St Giles', Northampton, 1620-39. Died 1639. (*Al. Oxon.*)

HOLBROOKE, RICHARD. Adm. pens. at TRINITY, Mar. 26, 1649. S. of Edward, of Manchester. Bapt. there, May 12, 1633. Matric. 1649; Scholar, 1650; B.A. 1652-3; M.A. 1656. Probably chaplain of Manchester College, 1661. Minister of Trinity Chapel, Salford, 1661; ejected, 1662. Afterwards turned to physic. Licensed as presbyterian teacher at Pilkington, Prestwich, 1672. Died July 9, 1676, aged 43. Father of William (1681). (*Calamy*, II. 105; E. Axon.)

HOLBROOKE, SAMUEL. Adm. pens. at KING'S, *c.* 1675. One of these names, s. of Andrew, of Wem, Salop, matric. from St Mary Hall, Oxford, May 4, 1674. (*Al. Oxon.*)

HOLBROOK, THEOPHILUS. Adm. sizar (age 19) at SIDNEY, Oct. 19, 1700. S. of John (1654), R. of Edgmond, Salop. B. at Aston, Salop. School, Newport (Mr Edwards). Matric. 1700; B.A. 1704-5. R. of Lolworth, Cambs., 1717. Brother of the next and of Anthony (1694).

HOLBROOKE, THOMAS. Prior of the Carmelite House at Cambridge, 1456; probably a graduate.

HOLBROOK, THOMAS. Adm. sizar (age 17) at TRINITY, June 22, 1695. S. of John (1654), R. of Aston, Salop. B. there. School, Newport (Mr Samuel Edwards). Matric. 1695; Scholar, 1697; B.A 1698-9. Brother of Anthony (1694).

HOLBROOKE, WILLIAM. M.A. from TRINITY, 1668. S. of Edward, of Bolas, Salop, clerk. Matric. from Oriel College, Oxford, Apr. 10, 1663, age 18; B.A. (Oxford) 1666. R. of Hawton-by-Newark, Notts., 1675. (*Al. Oxon.*)

HOLBROOK, WILLIAM. Adm. pens. (age 17) at MAGDALENE, Apr. 27, 1681. S. of Richard (1649). B. at Manchester. School, Manchester. Matric. 1681; M.B. 1686. Probably died at Salford, 1728. (Mumford, *Manchester Gr. School.*)

HOLBROOKE, WILLIAM. Adm. pens. (age 18) at SIDNEY, Mar. 24, 1731-2. S. of William, of Newport, Salop. B. there. School, Newport (Mr Lea). Matric. 1732. Migrated to Trinity, Jan. 17, 1734. B.A. 1735-6.

HOLCAN, DIONYSIUS. D.D. of Cambridge. Carmelite friar. Of Burnham Norton monastery, Norfolk. Died 1466. (*Pits.*)

HOLCOMBE, GEORGE. Adm. sizar (age 19) at ST JOHN'S, Feb. 13, 1733-4. S. of G., gent., of Pembrokeshire. B. at Brownslett. School, Denbigh (Mr Weston). Matric. 1734; B.A. 1737-8; M.A. 1741. Ord. deacon (Lincoln) Sept. 24, 1738; priest (St David's) Mar. 18, 1738-9. R. of Nash, Pembs., 1739-64. Preb. of St David's, 1742. R. of Pwllcrochan, 1743-89. V. of Llanvihangel Penbryn, Cardigan, 1764-89. Archdeacon of Carmarthen, 1768-89. Died *c.* Feb. 1789. Will, P.C.C. (*Scott-Mayor*, III. 450.)

HOLCOMBE, JOHN. Adm. pens. (age 16) at ST JOHN'S, Oct. 24, 1720. S. of William, gent., of Wales. B. at Mounton, near Pembroke. Schools, Pembroke and Westminster. Matric. 1720; B.A. 1724-5; M.A. 1728. Fellow, 1727-31. Ord. deacon (Lincoln) Sept. 25, 1726; priest, Dec. 24, 1727. R. of Gumfreston, Pembs., 1730-70. R. of Tenby St Mary, 1730-70. Preb. of St David's, 1737-41. Preb. of Brecon, 1741-70. (*Scott-Mayor*, III. 336.)

HOLCOMBE, SAMUEL. Adm. pens. (age 16) at PEMBROKE, May 22, 1682. S. of Humphrey, of London, mercer. Matric. 1684; B.A. 1685-6; M.A. 1689; D.D. 1717 (*Com. Reg.*). Fellow, 1687-93. V. of Cherry Hinton, Cambs. Chaplain to the King, 1716. Preb. of Canterbury, 1721-61. R. of Grafton Flyford, Worcs. V. of Severn Stoke, 1724. P.C. of Christ Church, Old Southgate. R. of St Benet, Gracechurch St, 1728-49. Died Apr. 1, 1761, aged 95. Buried in Canterbury Cathedral. M.I. Will, P.C.C. (J. Ch. Smith; *Misc. Gen. et Her.*, 3rd S., II. 123.)

HOLCOT or HALCOTT, JAMES. Adm. sizar at EMMANUEL, June 15, 1673. Of Yorkshire. Matric. 1673; B.A. 1676-7; M.A. 1682. Ord. deacon (York) Dec. 1677; priest, May, 1684. Probably Master of Mansfield Grammar School, *c.* 1682. V. of Fotheringay, Northants., 1697-1735. Married, Sept. 16, 1734, Elizabeth Loveling. Buried at Fotheringay, Dec. 23, 1735. (H. I. Longden.)

HOLCOT, ROBERT. Dominican friar. Said to have been at Cambridge.

HOLCROFT, FRANCIS. Adm. pens. at CLARE, June 24, 1647. S. of Sir Henry, Knt., of Eastham, Essex. Matric. 1647; B.A. 1650; M.A. 1654. Fellow, 1651-60, ejected. V. of Bassingbourne, Cambs., 1655. A well-known independent preacher. Imprisoned in Cambridge Castle, 1663-72, and in the Fleet, London. Died Jan. 6, 1692-3. Buried at Triplow, Cambs., in the dissenting graveyard. M.I. at Oakington. Brother of Henry (1638) and St John (1636). (*Calamy*, I. 201; *Vis. of Essex*, 1634; *D.N.B.*; H. P. Stokes.)

HOLCROFT, HENRY. Matric. Fell.-Com. from ST JOHN'S, *c.* 1601. Perhaps knighted, May 1, 1622; of London; father of the next, of St John (1636) and Francis (above).

HOLCROFT, HENRY. Adm. pen. (age 16) at CHRIST'S, June 10, 1638. S. of Sir Henry, of Eastham, Essex, Knt. (his mother was dau. of Baron Longford). B. at Dublin. School, Bishop's Stortford (Mr Leigh). Matric. 1638; B.A. 1641-2; M.A. 1645. Fellow of Clare, 1645-50. Incorp. at Oxford, 1671-2. Ord. deacon and priest (Galloway) Jan. 17, 1660-1. R. of Cliffe-at-Hoo, Kent, 1652-62. V. of Patcham, Sussex, 1662-1712; and of Blatchington, 1664. Buried at Patcham, Dec. 12, 1712. Will (P.C.C.). Brother of the next and Francis (1647). (*Peile*, I. 454; *Vis. of Essex*, 1634; W. C. Renshaw.)

HOLCROFT, ST JOHN. Adm. pens. (age 16) at CHRIST'S, July 5, 1636. S. and h. of Sir Henry, of Eastham, Essex, Knt. B. at Dublin. Schools, Battersea (Mr Carroll), Eton and Bishop's Stortford (Mr Leigh). Matric. 1636. Adm. at Lincoln's Inn, June 13, 1638. Succeeded his father. Married Elizabeth, dau. of Sir Ri. Higham, of Eastham. Brother of Henry (above) and Francis (1647). (*Vis. of Essex*, 1634; *Peile*, I. 446.)

HOLECROFT, THOMAS. Adm. sizar (age 18) at ST JOHN'S, June 11, 1645. S. of John, gent., of Balderton, Notts. School, Southwell (Mr Palmer). Matric. 1645; B.A. 1648-9. Minister of Car Colston, Notts., 1658; instituted as rector, 1662-9. R. of Normanton, 1662. Buried May 22, 1669. (Godfrey, *Notts.*)

HOLDEN or HOULDEN, ANTHONY. Adm. pens. at EMMANUEL, Apr. 1, 1636. Of Lincolnshire. Matric. 1636; B.A. 1639-40; M.A. 1643. Fellow of St John's, 1645. Ord. deacon and priest (Norwich) Sept. 22, 1644. C. of Islington, Norfolk. V. of Holme-on-Spalding-Moor, Yorks., 1659-67. Died 1667.

HOLDEN, BENJAMIN. Adm. pens. (age 16) at JESUS, May 24, 1672. S. of Andrew, of Todd Hall, Haslingden, Lancs. Matric. 1672; Scholar, 1675; B.A. 1675-6; M.A. 1679. C. of Middleton, Lancs., 1677-86. V. of Hampsthwaite, Yorks., 1686-1716. R. of Staveley, 1691-1716. Will (York) 1716. (A. Gray.)

HOLDEN, CALEB. Adm. sizar (age 16) at ST JOHN'S, Apr. 14, 1651. S. of George, barber, deceased. B. in Westminster. Exhibitioner from Charterhouse. Matric. 1651.

HOLDEN, CHRISTOPHER. Adm. at KING'S (age 17) a scholar from Eton, Aug. 14, 1548. Of Haslingden, Lancs. Matric. 1548. Left in 1550. Afterwards sur-master at St Paul's School, 1561-78. 'Became a great lawyer.' (*Harwood*.)

HOULDEN, EDWARD. Matric. sizar from ST CATHARINE'S, Michs. 1572; B.A. 1575-6; M.A. 1579; B.D. 1586. Ord. deacon and priest (Lincoln) Feb. 13, 1581-2.

HOULDEN, EDWARD. Matric. pens. from MAGDALENE, Easter, 1605. B. *c.* 1587. B.A. 1608-9; M.A. 1612. Fellow. Ord. deacon (Peterb.) Oct. 4; priest, Dec. 20, 1612. R. of Trusthorpe, Lincs., 1613-.

HOLDEN, EDWARD. Adm. pens. (age 25) at ST JOHN'S, June 24, 1659. B. near Giggleswick, Yorks. School, Giggleswick. One of these names schoolmaster at Whittington, Lancs., c. 1663-77. Buried there Apr. 20, 1677. (E. Axon.)

HOULDEN, EDWARD. Adm. pens. (age 18) at ST JOHN'S, Apr. 5, 1660. S. of Robert, gent., of Aston, Derbs. B. there. School, Repton. Matric. 1660; B.A. 1663-4; M.A. 1667. R. of Ampthill, Beds. Married, at Ampthill, Apr. 3, 1673, Maria (Rebecca), dau. of John Watson, of Little Park, Ampthill. Brother of Samuel (1651), father of Robert (1696). (F. A. Blaydes.)

HOLDEN, GEORGE. Of ST JOHN'S College, when ord. deacon (Peterb.) Mar. 2, 1617-8. Admon. (Lincoln) 1639, of one of these names; of Castle Carlton, Lincs. (H. I. Longden; J. Ch. Smith.)

HOLDEN, GILBERT. Matric. sizar from JESUS, Michs. 1547.

HOLDEN, GILBERT. Matric. sizar from QUEENS', Lent, 1582-3. Of Lancashire. Probably C. of Church, Lancs., 1591-1627. Will (Chester) 1627. (E. Axon.)

HOLDEN, HUGH. M.A. 1634 (Incorp. from Oxford). S. of John, of Dover, gent. B. Mar. 12, 1603-4. School, Merchant Taylors'. Matric. from Magdalen College, Oxford, Nov. 25, 1622, age 18; B.A. (Oxford) 1622; M.A. 1625; B.D. 1633-4. Fellow of Magdalen, 1623-48; ejected; restored, 1660-5. R. of Noke, Oxon., 1636. V. of Sele, or Beeding, Sussex, 1644-7, sequestered. Will (P.C.C.) 1668. (*Al. Oxon.*)

HOLDEN, HUMPHREY. Adm. . (age 14) at PETERHOUSE, July 2, 1652. S. of Simon, of Bedington, Warws. B. May 4, 1638. School, Coventry. Married and had issue. (*Vis. of Warws.*, 1682.)

HOLDON, HUMPHREY. Adm. sizar (age 20) at ST JOHN'S, June 23, 1718. S. of Humfrey, furrier, of Durham. B. there. School, Durham (Mr Wren). Matric. 1718; B.A. 1721-2; M.A. 1727. Ord. deacon (Gloucester, *Litt. dim.* from Durham) Feb. 14, 1721-2; priest (Durham) Sept. 23, 1722. C. of Sadberge. Master of Morpeth Grammar School. Buried at Morpeth, Mar. 23, 1771.

HOLDEN, JEROME. Matric. sizar from CHRIST'S, Easter, 1570; B.A. 1573-4; M.A. 1577. Ord. priest (Peterb.) Nov. 11, 1584. R. of St Mary's, Mablethorpe, Lincs., 1585. Will (Lincoln) 1585, of one of these names; of Mablethorpe.

HOLDEN, JOHN. D.D. 1513-4 (Incorp. from Oxford). A friar. S. of John, of Chaigley, Lancs. B.D. (Oxford) 1508; D.D. 1510. Probably R. of Cricklade St Mary, Wilts., 1510. Succeeded as heir to his brother Thomas. By deed, Nov. 3, 1514, enfeoffed trustees to use of brother Ralph. Died 1514. (*Al. Oxon.*; J. Parker.)

HOULDEN, JOHN. Adm. scholar at TRINITY, Easter, 1565. One of these names B.A. at Oxford, 1569. Perhaps R. of Bildeston, Suffolk, 1570.

HOLDEN, JOHN. Matric. sizar from CHRIST'S, May, 1567; B.A. 1570-1; M.A. from St Catharine's, 1574. Fellow of St Catharine's. Probably R. of St Peter Hungate, Norwich, 1590-8. R. of Bixley, 1601-10. (*Peile*, I. 100.)

HOULDEN, JOHN. Matric. sizar from ST JOHN'S, Michs. 1606.

HOLDEN, JOHN. Matric. sizar from TRINITY, Michs. 1635. Ord. deacon (Peterb.) Dec. 22, 1639, as B.A.; priest (Lincoln) June 5, 1642.

HOLDEN, JOHN. Adm. pens. (age 17) at PEMBROKE, Oct. 19, 1654. S. of Robert. B. at Cranbrook, Kent. Brother of Robert (1654). Robert, the father, died Aug. 27, 1653; and desired his sons John and Robert to be brought up in learning and piety. (H. G. Harrison.)

HOLDEN, JOHN. Adm. sizar (age 17) at ST JOHN'S, Mar. 1, 1659-60. S. of James, yeoman, of Westhoughton, Lancs. Bapt. at Deane, Lancs., Feb. 15, 1642-3. School, Bury St Edmunds (Mr Stephens). Matric. 1660; B.A. 1663-4.

HOLDEN or HOULDEN, JOHN. Adm. sizar (age 17) at ST JOHN'S, July 4, 1701. S. of Thomas, husbandman. B. at Friston, Lincs. School, Boston (Mr Kelsall). Matric. 1702; B.A. 1705-6, as 'Haulden.' Ord. priest (Lincoln) Sept. 25, 1709. V. of Coleby, Lincs., 1709.

HOLDEN, JOHN. Adm. sizar (age 18) at ST JOHN'S, May 3, 1732. S. of Robert (1696), R. of Weston-on-Trent, Derbs. B. at Weston. School, Loughborough (Mr Martin). Matric. 1732; B.A. 1735-6; M.A. 1747. Ord. deacon (Lincoln) Mar. 21, 1735-6; priest, Mar. 6, 1736-7. R. of Weston-on-Trent, 1740-59. R. of Newton Regis, Warwa., 1747-59. Chaplain to the Earl of Ashburnham. Died July 21, 1759. M.I. at Weston. (*Scott-Mayor*, III. 439.)

HOLDYN, JOSEPH. Matric. pens. from QUEENS', Easter, 1659. Of Middlesex.

HOLDEN, MARTIN. Matric. sizar from TRINITY, Easter, 1573. Ord. priest (Lincoln) July 27, 1579, as 'M.A.' R. of Driby, Lincs., 1580. R. of Sutterby, 1583.

HOLDEN, PETER. Matric. pens. from ST JOHN'S, Michs. 1583. One of these names, ord. priest (Lincoln) May 18, 1580, was R. of Goulceby, Lincs., 1589-1637.

HOLDEN, RALPH. Adm. sizar (age 18) at MAGDALENE, Mar. 28, 1673. S. of Ralph, of St Columb, Cornwall. School, Bodmin. Matric. 1673. Probably M.A. 1698 (*Lit. Reg.*). R. of St Ives, Cornwall, 1692-1705. Buried there Jan. 24, 1705.

HOLDEN, RICHARD. B.A. 1534-5. Probably R. of Stanford-le-Hope, Essex, 1548-54. Died 1554.

HOLDEN, RICHARD. Matric. pens. from JESUS, Michs. 1565; B.A. 1570-1.

HOLDEN, RICHARD. Matric. sizar from ST JOHN'S, Michs. 1576; B.A. 1579-80. Perhaps V. of Sellinge, Kent, 1580-90. One of these names R. of Tostock, Suffolk, 1581-1625.

HOLDEN, RICHARD. Matric. sizar from TRINITY, Easter, 1619; Scholar, 1624; B.A. 1624-5; M.A. 1628. V. of Felmersham, Beds., 1635-41 and 1660-74. Buried there Mar. 15, 1681-2. Will (Archd. Bedford) 1682. (W. M. Noble.)

HOULDEN, RICHARD. Adm. pens. at EMMANUEL, 1641-2. S. of William (1605), V. of Whaplode, Lincs. Matric. 1642. Migrated to St John's, Nov. 1, 1645, age 18. B.A. 1645-6; M.A. 1649. Fellow of St John's, 1650. R. of Deptford, Kent, 1672-1702. Perhaps R. of St Dunstan-in-the-East, 1686-98. Buried at Deptford, 1702.

HOLDEN, ROBERT. Matric. sizar from TRINITY, Michs. 1571.

HOLDEN, ROBERT. Adm. pens. (age 15) at PEMBROKE, Oct. 19, 1654. S. of Robert, of Hawkridge, Cranbrook, Kent. B. there. Brother of John (1654).

HOLDEN, ROBERT. Adm. pens. (age 17) at ST JOHN'S, Apr. 17, 1673. S. of Ralph, gent., of Holden, Lancs. B. there. School, Manchester. Matric. 1673. Married Catherine, dau. of Leonard Clayton, V. of Blackburn. Admon. (Chester) 1684, of Robert Holden, of Holden, Esq. (*Vis. of Lancs.*, 1664.)

HOLDEN, ROBERT. Adm. Fell.-Com. at TRINITY, Apr. 15, 1680. Perhaps 1st s. of Samuel (1651). Barrister-at-law. Died June 17, 1746, aged '70.' Perhaps half-brother of Thomas (1696). (Glover, *Derbs.*, II. 60, where the age is apparently wrong, his mother having died in 1668.)

HOLDEN, ROBERT. Adm. pens. at EMMANUEL, July 2, 1696. Of Bedfordshire. S. of Edward (1660), R. of Ampthill. Bapt. at Ampthill, Sept. 18, 1678. Matric. 1699; B.A. 1699-1700; M.A. 1703. Ord. deacon (Lincoln) Dec. 21, 1701; priest, Sept. 20, 1702. R. of Weston-on-Trent, Derbs. Married Ann, dau. of Robert Huntingdon, R. of Whiston, Northants. Died Nov. 9, 1739, aged 61. M.I. at Weston. Father of John (1732). (*Scott-Mayor*, III. 439.)

HOLDEN, ROBERT. Adm. Fell.-Com. at QUEENS', Jan. 7, 1731-2. Of Middlesex. S. and h. of Richard, of Lincoln's Inn, gent. Adm. at Lincoln's Inn, Feb. 8, 1728-9. Died Mar. 24, 1779, aged 64. M.I. at Hinxworth, Herts. Brother of Thomas (1732).

HOLDEN, ROBERT. M.A. 1744 (Incorp. from Oxford). S. of Andrew, of Rochdale, Lancs. Matric. from Brasenose, Mar. 28, 1721, age 16; B.A. (Oxford) 1724-5; M.A. 1728. (*Al. Oxon.*)

HOLDEN, SAMUEL. Ord. deacon and priest (Peterb.) Mar. 2, 1617-8, as 'of St John's College.' No College or University record.

HOLDEN or HOULDEN, SAMUEL. Adm. pens. at EMMANUEL, Sept. 3, 1651. Of Derbyshire. S. of Robert, of Aston-on-Trent, Derbs., gent. B. 1636. Matric. 1651. Adm. at Gray's Inn, Nov. 26, 1651. Of Aston, Derbs., Esq. Married, 1665, Mary, dau. of Edmund Lathwell, of Ruislip, Middlesex. Died Aug. 1692. Buried at Aston. Brother of Edward (1660), father of Thomas (1696) and perhaps of Robert (1680). (*Vis. of Derbs.*, 1662; Glover, *Derbs.*, II. 351.)

HOULDEN, THIMBLEBY. Matric. sizar from CHRIST'S, July, 1606; B.A. 1609-10; M.A. 1613. Ord. deacon (York) Sept. 1610. R. of St Peter-at-Arches, Lincoln, 1615-27. Preb. of Lincoln, 1623-60. R. of Beelsby, Lincs., 1626-32. R. of Little Warley, Essex, May, 1632-53. Buried there Jan. 6, 1652-3. Will (P.C.C.) 1653. (*Peile*, I. 261.)

HOLDEN, THOMAS. M.A. 1572 (Incorp. from Oxford). B.A. (Brasenose College) 1566-7; M.A. 1570. V. of St Peter, St Alban's, 1584-8. V. of Wennington, Essex, 1587-8. R. of Chadwell, 1590-5. Buried there Nov. 9, 1595. Admon. (Cons. C. London) 1595. (*Al. Oxon.*; *Vis. of Lancs.*, 1567.)

HOLDEN, THOMAS. Ord. priest (Peterb.) Feb. 17, 1626-7, as 'of SIDNEY College, literate.' C. of Keysoe, Beds., in 1638.

HOLDEN, THOMAS. Adm. sizar (age 19) at ST JOHN'S, Feb. 28, 1670-1. S. of William, deceased, of Pinchbeck, Lincs. B. there. School, Oakham (Mr Love). Matric. 1671; B.A. 1674-5; M.A. 1678. Ord. deacon (Ely) Sept. 18, 1675.

HOLDEN, THOMAS. Adm. pens. (age 17) at ST JOHN'S, July 6, 1680. S. of Thomas, Esq. B. at Leeds, Yorks., May 3, 1663. School, Chester (Mr Harpur). Matric. 1680. One of these names, s. and h. of Thomas, of Lincoln's Inn, adm. at Lincoln's Inn, June 30, 1680.

HOLDEN, THOMAS. Adm. pens. at CLARE, July 9, 1696. S. of Samuel (1651), of Aston, Derbs. B. 1678. School, Derby. Migrated to Emmanuel, Apr. 22, 1697. Matric. 1697; B.A. 1700-1; M.A. 1704. Ord. deacon (Lincoln) June 29, 1701; C. of Blackfordby, Ashby-de-la-Zouch; priest (Lincoln, *Litt. dim.* from Lichfield) May 31, 1702. R. of Aston, 1702-26. Married Elizabeth, dau. of Gilbert Millington, of Felly Priory, Nottingham. Died June 26, 1726. Perhaps half-brother of Robert (1680). (Burke, *L.G.*)

HOLDEN, THOMAS. Adm. pens. at QUEENS', Dec. 26, 1732. Of Middlesex. S. of Richard. Matric. 1733; B.A. 1736-7; M.A. 1740. Ord. deacon (Lincoln) Mar. 18, 1738-9; priest, Dec. 23, 1739. R. of Hinxworth, Herts., 1739-77. Died Feb. 16, 1777, aged 61. Buried in Hinxworth Church. Will, P.C.C. Brother of Robert (1731-2).

HOLDEN, WILLIAM. Matric. sizar from TRINITY, Easter, 1562; Scholar, 1563; B.A. 1565-6; M.A. 1569. Ord. deacon (Ely) Sept. 21, 1567; priest (London) Apr. 16, 1568. R. of Brisingham, Norfolk, 1569-70. V. of Pakenham, Suffolk, 1571-1621. Buried there Nov. 1, 1621. (V. B. Redstone.)

HOLDEN, WILLIAM. Matric. sizar from ST JOHN'S, Easter, 1563; B.A. 1566-7.

HOULDEN, WILLIAM. Matric. sizar from ST JOHN'S, Easter, 1605; B.A. 1608-9; M.A. 1612. Incorp. at Oxford, 1612. Ord. deacon (Lincoln) June 11; priest, Sept. 3, 1609. V. of Whaplode, Lincs., 1630. R. of Gt Casterton, Rutland, 1646. Will of Wm. Holden, of Brig Casterton (P.C.C.) 1654; property in Whaplode. Father of Richard (1641-2).

HOLDEN, WILLIAM. B.A. 1616 (Incorp. from Oxford). Matric. (Oxford) Dec. 16, 1614; B.A. (Christ Church) 1616; M.A. 1619. *Al. Oxon.* perhaps confuses this man with the above.

HOLDEN, WILLIAM. Adm. pens. at EMMANUEL, June 25, 1635. Of Lincolnshire. Matric. 1635; B.A. 1638-9; M.A. 1642. Probably buried at St Andrew's, Cambridge, Apr. 13, 1642.

HOLDEN, WILLIAM. Adm. sizar (age 19) at MAGDALENE, June 29, 1664. S. of William, of Lincolnshire. School, Pinchbeck. Matric. 1665; Scholar of Trinity Hall, July 8, 1667; B.A. 1667-8. Signed for deacon's orders (London) Mar. 5, 1663-4; for priest's, June 2, 1664. C. of Ashingdon, Essex. Licensed to teach grammar at Stiffkey, Norfolk, 1671.

HOLDEN, WILLIAM. Adm. sizar at ST CATHARINE'S, May 15, 1696. Matric. 1696; B.A. 1699-1700. Ord. deacon (Lincoln) Sept. 22, 1700; priest, Oct. 11, 1702. V. of Sproxton, Leics., 1704-41. V. of Saltby, 1716-41. Died Jan. 27, 1741, 'aged 71.' Will, Leicester. (*Nichols*, II. 330.)

HOLDEN, WILLIAM. Adm. Fell.-Com. at TRINITY HALL, Oct. 22, 1739 (name off, 1741).

HOLDEN, ——. Adm. sizar at KING'S, Easter, 1577.

HOLDENBE, FRANCIS. Matric. sizar from CLARE, Easter, 1571.

HOLDER, CLEMENT. Matric. pens. from MAGDALENE, Easter, 1579. Migrated to Caius. Scholar there, 1580-2; B.A. 1582-3; M.A. 1586. Incorp. at Oxford, 1614. Preb. of Southwell, 1590-1638. R. of Kilvington, Notts., 1609-37. R. of South Wheatley, 1610. Buried at Southwell, Feb. 1, 1637-8. Father of Henry (1635) and William (1633). (*Venn*, I. 110.)

HOLDER, CLEMENT. Adm. sizar (age 17) at PEMBROKE, Mar. 5, 1685. S. of George, citizen of Lichfield. Matric. 1686; B.A. 1689-90; M.A. 1693. Ord. priest (Lincoln) Mar. 4, 1693-4. V. of Hutton, Essex, 1698. Died 1749.

HOLDER or HOWLDRE, EDMUND. Adm. at CORPUS CHRISTI, 1554. Matric. pens. from Christ's, Nov. 1556; B.A. 1560-1.

HOLDER or HOULDER, HENRY. Adm. pens. at PETERHOUSE, Apr. 25, 1635. S. of Clement (1579), priest. B. at Southwell, Notts. Matric. 1635; Scholar, 1635; B.A. 1638-9; M.A. 1642. Fellow, 1642-4; ejected; restored, 1660. Senior proctor, 1675-6. Brother of William (1633). (*T. A. Walker*, 52.)

HOLDER, JOHN. Scholar of QUEENS', 1539-44; B.A. 1541-2. R. of Gamlingay, Cambs., 1539-44. Perhaps will proved (V.C.C.) 1544.

HOLDER, NATHANIEL. Adm. sizar at EMMANUEL, Aug. 5, 1675. Of Kent. Matric. 1675; B.A. 1679-80; M.A. 1683. Ord. priest (Lincoln) Feb. 24, 1683-4. V. of Stoke-by-Ipswich, 1689.

HOLDER, THOMAS. Matric. pens. from TRINITY, Easter, 1616; Scholar, 1619; B.A. 1619-20; M.A. 1623.

HOLDER, WILLIAM. Matric. pens. (age 17) from PEMBROKE, Easter, 1633. S. of Clement (1579), clerk. B. at Southwell, Notts. B.A. 1636-7; M.A. 1640. Fellow, 1640-2. Incorp. at Oxford, Mar. 21, 1643-4. D.D. (Oxford) 1660. Ord. deacon (Lincoln) Dec. 20, 1640. R. of Barnoldby-le-Beck, Lincs., 1641-2. R. of Blechingdon, Oxon., 1642. Preb. of Ely, 1652-98. Preb. of Southwell, 1660-4. Master of Mere Hospital, Lincoln, 1660. R. of Northwold, Norfolk, 1662-7. R. of Tydd St Giles', 1663. F.R.S., 1663. Preb. of St Paul's, 1672-98. Sub-dean of the King's Chapel, 1674-89. Canon residentiary of St Paul's, 1680-98. R. of Therfield, Herts., 1687. Author of *Elements of Speech*, and treatises on harmony. Died at Hertford, Jan. 24, 1697-8, aged 82. Buried in St Paul's Cathedral. Will, P.C.C. Brother of Henry (1635). (*Al. Oxon.*; *D.N.B.*)

HOLDERNESS, Earl of. Adm. as nobleman at TRINITY HALL, Nov. 18, 1732. S. of Robert Darcy (1698). School, Westminster. Succeeded his father as 4th Earl, 1722. Lord-Lieutenant of the North Riding, 1740-77. Ambassador to Venice, 1744-6. Minister at the Hague, 1749-51. Secretary of State, 1751-61. Warden of the Cinque Ports, 1765-78. Died May 16, 1778, aged 59. (*D.N.B.*; *G.E.C.*)

HOLDERNESS, IGNATIUS. Matric. sizar from PEMBROKE, Lent, 1584-5; B.A. 1588-9; M.A. 1593. Ord. priest (Colchester) Nov. 8, 1594. R. of Holton, Suffolk, 1600-1. V. of Wicklewood, Norfolk, 1600-13. V. of Docking, 1612. Father of the next.

HOLDERNES, ROBERT. Adm. sizar (age 18) at PEMBROKE, Oct. 19, 1622. S. of Ignatius (above), of Wicklewood, Norfolk. Schools, Wymondham (Mr Eston) and Frenze (Mr Steers). Migrated to Christ's, Mar. 20, 1622-3. B.A. 1626-7; M.A. 1631. Ord. deacon (Peterb.) Sept. 19; priest, Sept. 20, 1629. (*Peile*, I. 348; H. I. Longden.)

HOLDERNESSE, WILLIAM. M.Gram. 1516.

HOLDGILL or HOLGYLL, WILLIAM. Adm. at KING'S (age 17) a scholar from Eton, Sept. 5, 1527. Of Kendal, Westmorland. Name off, 1530. Perhaps B.A. (Oxford) 1534-5; and R. of Dengie, Essex, 1533-5.

HOLDICH, EDWARD. Adm. pens. (age 17) at SIDNEY, May 30, 1700. 1st s. of Edward, farmer. B. at Wadenhoe, Northants. School, Oundle. Matric. 1700, as 'Hollis'; B.A. 1703-4. Ord. deacon (Peterb.) Sept. 22, 1706; priest, Sept. 25, 1709. C. of Woodford-by-Thrapston. (Burke, *L.G.*; H. I. Longden.)

HOLDITCH, GEOFFREY. Adm. sizar at CLARE, June 3, 1720. S. of Edward. B. at Wadenhoe, Northants. Matric. 1720; B.A. 1723-4. Ord. deacon (Lincoln) Dec. 20, 1724; priest, Dec. 24, 1727. C. of Aldwincle All Saints', Northants., 1724. R. of Stibbington, Hunts., 1744-80. Died 1780. Will, P.C.C.

HOLDYCH or HOLDEGE, HENRY. Adm. Fell.-Com. (age 19) at CAIUS, May 31, 1584. Eldest s. of John, of Ranworth, Norfolk, Esq. B. there. Schools, Ely, and Eye, Suffolk. Matric. 1584. Adm. at Lincoln's Inn, Oct. 26, 1585, and at the Inner Temple, 1585. Succeeded his father at Ranworth. Brother of Richard (1585) and Thomas (1585). (*Vis. of Norfolk*; *Venn*, I. 120.)

HOLDYCHE, JOHN. Matric. pens. from TRINITY HALL, Easter, 1545 (*impubes*).

HOLDYCHE, NICHOLAS. Matric. pens. from ST JOHN'S, Michs. 1567.

HOLDICH, RICHARD. Adm. scholar (age 18) at CAIUS, June 15, 1585. S. of John, Esq., of Ranworth, Norfolk. Schools, Ely (Mr Spight), and Eye, Suffolk (Mr Popson). Matric. 1585. Probably died young. Brother of Thomas (1585) and Henry (1584). (*Vis. of Norfolk*; *Venn*, I. 125.)

HOLDITCH, THEODORE. Matric. pens. from ST JOHN'S, Easter, 1620. S. of Jeffery, of Wadenhoe, Northants. B. there, 1604. B.A. 1623-4; M.A. 1627. Ord. deacon (Peterb.) Dec. 21; priest, Dec. 22, 1628. Chaplain to the East India Co., 1633. Of Lynn, Norfolk. Died 1658. (F. Penny; *Misc. Gen. et Her.*, 3rd S., v. 282.)

HOLDICH, THOMAS. Adm. scholar (age 16) at CAIUS, June 15, 1585. Of Ranworth, Norfolk. S. of John, Esq. Schools, Ely (Mr Spight), and Eye, Suffolk (Mr Popson). Of Ranworth, Esq. Died 1617. Brother of Richard (1585) and Henry (1584). (*Vis. of Norfolk*; *Venn*, I. 125.)

HOLDINGE, CHRISTOPHER. Matric. sizar from TRINITY, Michs. 1553; Scholar, 1555.

HOLDIP, HILLIARD. Adm. pens. at EMMANUEL, Aug. 10, 1671. 3rd s. of Richard, late of the City of London, deceased. B. in Barbadoes. Adm. at Lincoln's Inn, Jan. 31, 1670-1.

HOLDYSWORTH, EDWARD. Matric. pens. from CHRIST'S, Nov. 1545.

HOLDROYD, GEORGE. Adm. pens. at TRINITY, June 3, 1670; B.A. 1674-5; M.A. 1679. Ord. deacon (York) Sept. 1678; priest, Dec. 1684. R. of Skipton, Yorks., 1686-1705. Died Jan. 1713.

HOLDRED or HOLROYD, JONATHAN. Adm. at KING'S, a scholar from Eton, 1646. B. at Brentford, Middlesex, 1628. B.A. 1650-1; M.A. 1654. Fellow, 1649-57. R. of Dunton Waylett, Essex, 1656-8.

HOULDRED, MARK. Matric. sizar from CHRIST'S, Mar. 1588; B.A. (1591-2); M.A. 1595. V. of Little Abington, Cambs., 1607-17.

HOLYROYD, THEOPHILUS. Matric. pens. from CORPUS CHRISTI, Easter, 1649. Of Yorkshire.

HOLDSWORTH, FRANCIS. Adm. sizar (age 16) at ST JOHN'S, May 18, 1654. S. of Robert, husbandman, of Saxton, Yorks. B. there. School, Sherburn (Mr Clark). Matric. 1655; B.A. 1657-8; M.A. 1661. Signs for deacon's orders (York) Aug. 17, 1662. V. of Speeton, Yorks., 1683-91.

HOLDSWORTH, GEORGE. M.A. from EMMANUEL, 1667. Matric. from Magdalen Hall, Oxford, July 25, 1655, *cler. fil.*; B.A. (Oxford) 1658-9. R. of Lawford, Essex, 1674-93. Married, 1672, Amy, dau. of Giles Archer, R. of Farnham, Essex. Died 1693. Buried Aug. 14, 1693. Admon. (Cons. C. London) 1693. (*Al. Oxon.*; J. Ch. Smith.)

HOLDSWORTH, HENRY. Matric. sizar from TRINITY, Michs. 1571; B.A. 1575-6. Ord. deacon (Lincoln) Oct. 31, 1583. R. of Branswell, Lincs., 1585. Admon. (Lincoln) 1614. (But *see also Al. Oxon.*)

HOULDSWORTH, HENRY. Matric. sizar from TRINITY, Easter, 1576.

HOLDSWORTH, JAMES. Adm. sizar (age 21) at ST JOHN'S, June 30, 1709. S. of George, deceased. B. at Bradford, Yorks. School, Threshfield. Matric. 1709; B.A. 1712-3; M.A. 1725. Ord. deacon (York) May, 1713; priest, 1716. C. of Woolley and Royston, Yorks. Afterwards vicar.

HOWLESWORTH, JOHN. Resident student at TRINITY HALL, Aug. 1564.

HOLDSWORTH, JOHN. Adm. sizar (age 18) at CHRIST'S, June 30, 1671. S. of John. B. at Birstall, Yorks. School, Birstall (Mr Noble). Probably adm. at Mr Frankland's Academy at Rathmell, Yorks., 1672. Ord. minister, after twelve years as preacher, Sept. 4, 1689. Nonconformist minister at Cleckheaton, West Riding, Yorkshire. Died there Dec. 15, 1711. Buried at Birstall. (*Peile*, II. 38.)

HOLDSWORTH, JOHN. Adm. at CORPUS CHRISTI, 1674. Of Yorkshire. Matric. 1675; B.A. 1677-8.

HOLDSWORTH, JOHN. Adm. sizar (age 19) at ST JOHN'S, May 26, 1707. S. of John, deceased. B. at Pontefract, Yorks. School, Sedbergh (Mr Wharton). Matric. 1707; B.A. 1710-1; M.A. 1717. Ord. deacon (York) Oct. 1711; priest, 1712. V. of Coley, Yorks., 1733-41. Master of Halifax School, 1733.

HOLDSWORTH, JOHN. Adm. pens. (age 19) at TRINITY, Mar. 28, 1748. S. of Robert, of Loscoe, Yorks. School, Wakefield (Mr Wilson). Matric. 1748; Scholar, 1749; B.A. 1752; M.A. 1755. Fellow, 1753. C. of Burghwallis, Yorks., 1755-64. V. of Normanton, 1765-93. Preb. of Ripon, 1788-1800. Died 1800.

HOULSWORTH, JOSEPH. Matric. pens. from MAGDALENE, Easter, 1625; B.A. 1629-30. R. of Ramsden Crays, Essex, 1630-45.

HOLDSWORTH, JOSIAH. Adm. sizar (age 17) at ST JOHN'S, Apr. 9, 1655. S. of John, clothier, of Wakefield. B. there. School, Wakefield (Mr Doughty). Matric. 1655; B.A. 1658-9. Ejected from Sutton, Lower Poppleton, Yorks., 1662. Preacher at Heaton and Heckmondwike, 1672. Died there 1685. (*Calamy*, II. 595.)

HOLDSWORTH, JUDE. Adm. pens. (age 17) at CHRIST'S, June 27, 1677. S. of John. B. at Middleham, Yorks. School, Bedale (Mr Nicholson). Matric. 1677; B.A. 1680-1; M.A. 1684. Fellow, 1682-94. Minister of Trinity Church, Cambridge, 1691-3. R. of Reed, Herts., 1693-1718. V. of Northamstead Chapel, 1694. V. of Barkway, 1694-1718. Died, probably at Reed, 1718. Admon., P.C.C. Father of the next. (*Peile*, II. 65.)

HOLDSWORTH, JUDE. Adm. pens. at CHRIST'S, 1713. S. of Jude (above), R. of Reed, Herts. Matric. 1713; Scholar, 1713; B.A. 1718-9; M.A. 1723. Ord. deacon (London) June 7, 1719. R. of Hinxhill, Kent, 1722-59. V. of Tonge, 1723-50. R. of Ruckinge, 1750. Chaplain to the Archbishop. Died Nov. 27, 1759. (*Peile*, II. 182.)

HOULDSWORTH, RICHARD. Matric. sizar from ST JOHN'S, Easter, 1607. S. of Richard, V. of Newcastle-on-Tyne. B. there. Bapt. at St Nicholas, Dec. 20, 1590. School, Newcastle. Scholar, 1607; B.A. 1610-1; M.A. 1614; B.D. 1622; D.D. from Emmanuel, 1637. Fellow of St John's, 1613. Master of Emmanuel, 1637-43; sequestered and imprisoned; ejected, 1644. Vice-Chancellor, 1640-3. Lady Margaret Professor, 1643 (elected whilst a prisoner in the Tower). Incorp. at Oxford, 1617. Ord. deacon (Peterb.) Oct. 21; priest, Oct. 22, 1617. R. of St Peter-le-Poer, 1623-43, sequestered. Gresham Professor of Divinity, 1629-41. Preb. of Lincoln, 1633-49. Archdeacon of Huntingdon, 1634-49. Adm. at Lincoln's Inn, Aug. 9, 1635. President of Sion College, 1639. Chaplain to Charles I. Dean of Worcester, 1647. Author, theological. Died Aug. 22, 1649, aged 58. Will (P.C.C.); as of St Peter-le-Poer. Left many books to Emmanuel and the University Library. (*D.N.B.*; *Emmanuel College History*, 87.)

HOLDSWORTH, ROBERT. Adm. at KING'S (age 17) a scholar from Eton, Aug. 25, 1603. Of Halifax, Yorks. and s. of John, of Astey, Halifax, Yorks. B.A. 1607-8; M.A. 1611. Fellow, 1606-9. Master of the School at Sevenoaks, Kent. V. of Modbury, Devon. Probably R. of Wretham, Norfolk, 1613-4. Married Mary Newman, 1610. Admon. (Exeter) 1632; of Modbury. (*Harwood*; Burke, *L.G.*; *Vis. of Yorks.*, 1666.)

HOLDSWORTH, ROBERT. Adm. sizar at QUEENS', June 23, 1688. Of Yorkshire. Matric. 1688; B.A. 1691-2; M.A. 1695. Ord. deacon (York) Mar. 12, 1692-3. R. of Peper Harow, Surrey, 1695. Died 1749. (*Manning and Bray*, II. 37.)

HOLDSWORTH, THOMAS. Adm. sizar (age 15) at PEMBROKE, May, 1641. B. at Middleham, Yorks. Migrated to Emmanuel. (He was probably a nephew of Richard, the Master.) Matric. 1641; B.A. 1644-5; M.A. 1648. Dean of Middleham, Yorks., 1660-80. Went to Paris in 1661, as chaplain to a special Embassy. Preb. of Durham, 1675-80. Wrote a short biography of Richard, the Master, for his *Praelectiones*. Died 1680. (J. B. Peace.)

HOLDSWORTH, THOMAS. Adm. sizar (age 19) at TRINITY, June 27, 1726. S. of Thomas, of Southowram, Yorks. School, Sedbergh. Matric. 1726; B.A. 1729-30. Ord. deacon (York) Aug. 16, 1730. V. of Brearley, Halifax, 1730. (Water, *Halifax*, 380.)

HOLDWORTH, WILLIAM. Matric. sizar from CLARE, Lent, 1588-9; B.A. 1592-3; M.A. 1596. Probably V. of Linton, Cambs., 1597-1602. *See* next.

HOLDSWORTH, WILLIAM. Adm. sizar at EMMANUEL, Sept. 4, 1590; B.A. (? 1594-5); M.A. 1598. Ord. deacon (Lincoln) Sept. 27, 1601; priest, Mar. 12, 1608-9. C. of Shilton Chapel, Leics., 1602. Possibly V. of East Tilbury, Essex, 1603. Author, *Heroologia seu Martyrologia*. Will (Cons. C. London) 1625. (*Cooper*, II. 495, who is wrong as to his degree.)

HOLDSWORTH, WILLIAM. Adm. pens. (age 17) at ST JOHN'S May 18, 1655. S. of William, yeoman, of Kirby Malzeard, Yorks. B. there. School, Burnsall-in-Craven (Mr Clark). Matric. 1655; B.A. 1658-9.

HOLDSWORTH, ——. Adm. sizar at TRINITY HALL, July 5, 1703 (name off, 1706).

HOLE, *see* HOLLE.

HOLESANS, JOHN. 'Fellow of KING'S,' when ord. sub-deacon (Ely) Feb. 22, 1493-4. Not found in *Harwood*, unless he be John Hall.

HOLFORD, *see also* HALFORD.

HOLFORD, ABRAHAM. Adm. pens. (age 17) at CAIUS, Apr. 23, 1633. S. of John, draper. B. at Wivelsfield, Sussex. School, Cuckfield (Mr Sicklemore). B.A. 1636-7; M.A. 1640. Licensed (Bishop of Chichester) to teach writing and grammar, 1637.

HOLFORD, BENJAMIN. Matric. pens. from PETERHOUSE, Michs. 1623. Of London. Probably created M.A. (Oxford) Aug. 31, 1636. Incorp. at Cambridge, 1639.

HOLFORD or HOLDFORT, GEORGE. Adm. pens. at EMMANUEL, Apr. 24, 1604. Matric. 1604.

HOLFORD, HENRY. Adm. Fell.-Com. at PETERHOUSE, Mar. 13, 1615-6. S. of Christopher, of Purfleet. Matric. 1615-6. Adm. at the Middle Temple, Oct. 16, 1612. Called to the Bar, June 30, 1620. Of West Thurrock and Purfleet, Esq. Perhaps his will (P.C.C.) 1624; as of Long Stanton, Cambs. (*Vis. of Essex*, 1612; *T. A. Walker*.)

HOLFORD, PETER. Adm. pens. (age 17) at ST JOHN'S, May 3, 1736. S. of Robert, Master in Chancery, of London. School, Westminster. Matric. 1736. Adm. at Lincoln's Inn, uly 25, 1735. Barrister, 1740. Bencher. Treasurer. Perhaps F.R.S., 1746. Master in Chancery, 1750-1804. Married Anne, dau. of William Nutt, of Buxted, Sussex. Died July 14, 1804. Will, P.C.C. (Burke, *L.G.*)

HOLFORD, PETER. Adm. sizar (age 18) at CHRIST'S, July 6, 1749. S. of Elms. B. at Warrington, Lancs. School, Macclesfield (Mr Atkinson). Scholar, 1749; Matric. 1750; B.A. 1753. (*Peile*, II. 254.)

HOLGATE, BENJAMIN. Matric. sizar from PEMBROKE, Easter, 1579; B.A. 1581-2. R. of one mediety of Burnsall, Yorks., 1582-96. Buried there June 20, 1596. He may be s. of Anthony, R. there, till 1569.

HOLGATE, JOHN. Adm. pens. (age 17) at CAIUS, Feb. 1622-3. S. of William, gent., of Newport, Essex. School, Newport (Mr Hobman). Adm. at the Middle Temple, June 29, 1626. Of Walden, Essex, Esq. Died May 5, 1673. Father of William (1648) and Robert (1658). (*Venn*, I. 261; *Vis. of Essex*, 1634.)

HOLGATE, JOHN. Adm. pens. at QUEENS', Apr. 3, 1673. Of Essex. S. and h. of William (1648), of Walden, Essex. Adm. at Lincoln's Inn, July 4, 1674. Died unmarried.

HOLGATE or HOLDEGATE, ROBERT. D.D. 1537. Gilbertine Canon. S. of Thomas. Probably educated at their house in Cambridge. University preacher, 1524. Prior of St Catharine's. Priory, Lincoln. Afterwards prior of the house at Watton, Yorks.; surrendered, 1539. V. of Codney, Lincs. Chaplain to Henry VIII. Bishop of Llandaff, 1537-45. Archbishop of York, 1545. Lord President of the Council of the North. Deprived of his see, 1554, for being married. Founded hospital and schools at Hemsworth and York. Died Nov. 15, 1556, at his (monastic) house in Cow Lane, Smithfield, London. Will (P.C.C.) 1556. (*Cooper*, I. 164; *D.N.B.*; H. G. Harrison.)

HOLGATE, ROBERT. Matric. pens. from CHRIST'S, Mar. 1557-8. Of Yorkshire. B.A. 1560-1; M.A. from St John's, 1564. Fellow of St John's, 1561. Will of one of these names (P.C.C.) 1592; V. of Wedmore, Somerset. (*Peile*, I. 65.)

HOLGATE, ROBERT. Adm. pens. (age 14) at SIDNEY, Sept. 27, 1658. S. of John (1622-3), Esq. B. at Saffron Walden, Essex. Schools, Saffron Walden, Newport (Mr Woolley) and Thurlow (Mr Billingsley). Matric. 1658. Half-brother of William (1648).

HOLGATE, THOMAS. Matric. pens. from CHRIST'S, Michs. 1560. Probably adm. at the Inner Temple, May 9, 1564; of Pontefract, Yorks. (*Peile*, I. 74.)

HOLGATE, WILLIAM. Adm. pens. at QUEENS', Feb. 1634-5. Of Essex. S. of William, of Gt Bardfield, Essex. Age 16 in 1634. Matric. 1636. (*Vis. of Essex.*)

HOLGATE, WILLIAM. Adm. Fell.-Com. (age 16) at SIDNEY, Oct. 1, 1648. S. of John (1622-3), Esq. B. at Walden, Essex. School, Walden (Mr Mathews). Matric. 1648-9. Adm. at the Inner Temple, 1651. Married Hester, dau. of James Quarles. Died Aug. 31, 1672. Father of John (1673), half-brother of Robert (1658). (*Vis. of Essex*, 1634.)

HOLDGATE, WILLIAM. Adm. sizar (age 17) at ST JOHN'S, Apr. 27, 1693. S. of Edward, husbandman, of Hatfield, near Doncaster, Yorks. School, Hatfield (Mr Eratt). Matric. 1693; B.A. 1696-7. Ord. deacon (Lincoln) Dec. 22, 1700; priest, Sept. 21, 1701. C. of Alkborough, Lincs. R. of Bigby, 1730-46. P.C. of Whitton. Died 1746. Father of the next.

HOLDGATE, WILLIAM. Adm. sizar (age 19) at ST JOHN'S, May 28, 1730. S. of William (above), R. of Bigby, Lincs. B. at Normanby. School, Brigg (Mr Waterworth). Matric. 1730; B.A. 1733-4. Ord. deacon (Lincoln) Mar. 10, 1733-4; priest, Sept. 22, 1734. V. of Roxby and Risby, Lincs., 1743-79. (*Scott-Mayor*, III. 426; *Lincs. Pedigrees*, 1260.)

HOLGYLL, *see* HOLDGILL.

HOLHEAD, JOHN. Adm. pens. at EMMANUEL, May 9, 1633. Of Northamptonshire.

HOLIDAY, ADAM. B.D. 1572. Preb. of Durham, 1560-90. R. of Bishop Wearmouth, 1560-90.

HOLIDAY, GEORGE. Adm. sizar (age 18) at ST JOHN'S, June 1, 1710. S. of George, husbandman. B. at Beverley, Yorks. School, Beverley (Mr Lambert). Matric. 1710; B.A. 1713-4. Ord. deacon (Ely) May 23, 1714; priest (York) Dec. 1715. R. of Saxby, Lincs., 1719.

HOLIDAY, JAMES. Adm. sizar (age 27) at ST JOHN'S, June 11, 1742. S. of Christopher, farmer, of Yorkshire. B. at Goodmanham. School, Coxwold (Mr Midgley). Matric. 1742.

HOLLIDAY, JOHN. Adm. Fell.-Com. at EMMANUEL, July 3, 1599.

HOLLIDAY, NATHANIEL. Matric. sizar from KING'S, Michs. 1624; B.A. 1629-30. Subscribed for deacon's orders (Bristol) Dec. 19, 1630. V. of Climping, Sussex, 1648. (F. S. Hockaday.)

HOLIDAY, THOMAS. Matric. sizar from EMMANUEL, Easter, 1615. Scholar from Lynn School. B.A. 1618-9. Ord. deacon (Peterb.) Dec. 19, 1619.

HOLIDAY, WILLIAM. 'Late of TRINITY HALL.' (Probably matric. pens. from Christ's, 1566.) B. in Cambridge. Ord. deacon (London) Mar. 15, 1591-2, age 38; C. of Laindon, Essex; priest, Dec. 21, 1592.

HOLIDAY, ——. Scholar of TRINITY HALL, Jan. 18, 1636-7.

HOLKAR or HOULKER, JAMES. Matric. sizar from CHRIST'S, July, 1605. Probably of Lancashire. B.A. 1608-9; M.A. 1612. Ord. deacon (Chester) June 11, 1609; priest (York, for Lincoln) May 26, 1616. C. of Navenby. Schoolmaster there, 1614; 'stipend £4, and his diet.'

HOLKER, JOHN. Matric. pens. from CHRIST'S, Easter, 1555. Of Cheshire. Described as 'Chaplain of Christ's' when he received the tonsure (London) Dec. 1554.

HOULKER or HOWKER, JOHN. Matric. sizar from CHRIST'S, July, 1620; B.A. 1623-4; M.A. 1627. Ord. deacon (Lichfield) Sept. 1627. Probably V. of Elvaston, Derbs. (*Peile*, I. 236.)

HOLKER, LAWRENCE. Adm. pens. (age 19) at PEMBROKE, Oct. 17, 1712. S. of Thomas, of Gravesend, Kent, gent. Matric. 1714.

HOLLAND, Earl of, *see* RICH, HENRY.

HOLLAND, ABRAHAM. Scholar of TRINITY, Easter, 1614. S. of Philemon (1566). B.A. 1616-7. Author, poetical. Died Feb. 18, 1625-6. (*D.N.B.*)

HOLLAND, ADAM. Matric. pens. from CHRIST'S, July, 1607.

HOLLAND, ADAM. Adm. sizar at JESUS, June 4, 1683. Of Lancashire. One of these names adm. student at Leyden, Aug. 20, 1686. M.D. 1687. Afterwards a nonconformist minister at Macclesfield. Died Apr. 1716. (E. Axon.)

HOLLANDE, BL[AISE]. Matric. pens. from CHRIST'S, May, 1545. S. of Blaise, of Howell, Lincs. Age 2 in 1530. Of Swineshead, Lincs. Married Alice, dau. of Sir Giles Hussey, of Caythorpe, Lincs., Knt. Died 1552-3. (*Lincs. Pedigrees*, 506; *Peile*, I. 38.)

HOLLAND, BRIAN. Matric. sizar from PETERHOUSE, Michs. 1584.

HOLLAND, CHRISTOPHER. Matric. pens. from PEMBROKE, Michs. 1561. S. of Thomas, of Spalding, Lincs. Bapt. there, Aug. 26, 1546. Migrated to Peterhouse, Jan. 29, 1563-4. B.A. 1564-5. Father of Edward (1597-8), brother of Henry (1556).

HOLLAND, CORNELIUS. Matric. pens. from PEMBROKE, Easter, 1615. Probably s. of Ralph, of St Lawrence Pountney, London. B. Mar. 3, 1599-1600. School, Merchant Taylors'. B.A. 1618-9. Clerk-comptroller to the Prince of Wales, 1635. A commissioner for the Treaty with Scotland, 1643. Said to have drawn up the charges against the King, but did not sign the warrant for execution. A member of the Council of State, 1649-52. Fled to Holland, in 1660. Probably died at Lausanne. (*Robinson*, I. 63; *D.N.B.*)

HOLLAND, EDMUND. Matric. Fell.-Com. from CHRIST'S, Lent, 1620-1. S. of Sir Thomas, of Quiddenham, Norfolk, Knt. Adm. at the Middle Temple, Feb. 7, 1622-3. Brother of John (1620). (*Peile*, I. 337.)

HOLLAND, EDMUND. Adm. sizar at PEMBROKE, Mar. 16, 1708-9. S. of Edmund, of Walsingham, Norfolk, chemist. Matric. 1709; M.B. 1715.

HOLLAND, EDWARD. Matric. pens. from CORPUS CHRISTI, Lent, 1597-8. S. of Christopher (1561). (*Lincs. Pedigrees*, 506.)

HOLLAND, EDWARD. Adm. Fell.-Com. at ST JOHN'S, Sept. 5, 1646. S. of Richard, Esq., of Denton, Lancs. B. there. School, Denton (Mr Greenhalgh). Married Anne, dau. of Edward Warren, of Poynton, Esq. Died before his father, July, 1655. M.I. at Denton. (*Vis. of Lancs.*, 1664.)

HOLLAND, EDWARD. Adm. sizar at EMMANUEL, May 22, 1656. S. of Richard, of Salop. B. in Gloucestershire. Matric. 1658; B.A. 1659-60; M.A. 1663. Incorp. at Oxford, 1664. Ord. deacon (Lincoln) Feb. 22, 1661-2; priest (Peterb.) Sept. 20, 1663. V. of Weekley, Northants., 1663-70. R. of Waltham-on-the-Wold, Leics., 1670-87. Preb. of Lincoln, 1670-87. R. of Stibbington, Hunts., 1678-80. Married, at St Helen's, London, July 14, 1683, Honora Orson, widow. Died 1687. Father of Edward (1683) and Epiphanius (1693). (*Al. Oxon.*; *Nichols*, II. 385, 424; J. Ch. Smith.)

HOLLAND, EDWARD. Adm. Fell.-Com. (age 17) at ST JOHN'S, June 27, 1679. S. of William (1635), clerk. B. at Malpas, Cheshire. School, Chester (Mr Harpur). Matric. 1679. Of Heston and Denton, Lancs., Esq. Buried at Prestwich, Feb. 14, 1683-4. (J. Booker, *Chapel of Denton*; E. Axon.)

HOLLAND, EDWARD. Adm. pens. at EMMANUEL, July 3, 1683. Of Northamptonshire. S. of Edward (1656), R. of Waltham-on-the-Wolds, Leics. Matric. 1685; B.A. 1687-8; M.A. 1692. Ord. priest (London) Dec. 20, 1691. R. of Waltham, Leics., 1692-1722. Died July 23, 1722, aged 56. M.I. at Waltham. Brother of Epiphanius. (*Nichols*, II. 386.)

HOLLAND, EPIPHANIUS. Adm. sizar at JESUS, June 29, 1693. S. of Edward (1656), R. of Waltham-on-the-Wolds, Leics. Exhibitioner from Charterhouse. Rustat scholar, 1693; Matric. 1694; B.A. 1696-7; M.A. 1700. Ord. deacon (Peterb.) Sept. 24, 1699; priest (London) Dec. 22, 1700. Probably C. of St Helen's, London, 1711-3. Brother of Edward (above). (J. Ch. Smith.)

HOLLAND, FRANCIS. Adm. sizar (age 18) at CAIUS, Mar. 12, 1663-4. S. of Matthew (or 'Henry'), of Colkirk, Norfolk. B. at Witchingham, Norfolk (his mother's home). Schools, Witchingham and Searning (Mr Burton). Matric. 1664; Scholar, 1664-8; B.A. 1667-8. Ord. deacon (Gloucester) June 23, 1675. C. of Docking, Norfolk, 1675; of Sedgeford, till his death, in 1709. M.I. at Sedgeford. (*Venn*, I. 420; Carthew, *Launditch*, III. 80.)

HOLLAND, FRANCIS. Adm. pens. (age 17) at TRINITY, Apr. 17, 1707. S. of William, of Wigan, Lancs. School, Wigan (Mr Duckworth). Matric. 1707; Scholar, 1708; B.A. 1710-1; M.A. 1714. Fellow, 1713. Ord. deacon (York) Oct. 1711; priest (Ely) May 23, 1714.

HOLLAND, GARRET. Adm. sizar at EMMANUEL, May 29, 1594. B. at Newton, Lancs., c. 1577. Matric. 1594, as pens.; Scholar; B.A. 1597-9; M.A. 1601. Ord. priest (Lincoln) Nov. 22, 1601. V. of Willoughton, Lincs., 1604-12.

HOLLAND, GEORGE. Adm. sizar (age 18) at TRINITY, June 20, 1699. S. of George, of Alstone, Salop. School, Hadley, Salop (Mr Roe). Matric. 1699; B.A. 1702-3. Ord. deacon (London) May 19, 1706; priest, Dec. 18, 1709.

HOLLAND, GREGORY. B.A. from CHRIST'S, 1604-5; M.A. 1609. R. of West Bergholt, Essex, 1613-c. 1652. R. of Wickham Bishops, 1613. Will (P.C.C.) 1659. (*Peile*, I. 238.)

HOLLAND, GUY. Matric. pens. from ST JOHN'S, Easter, 1602. B. in Lincolnshire, c. 1587. B.A. 1605-6. Converted to Roman Catholicism. Entered the English College at Valladolid. Sent to England, 1615; joined the Jesuits. Arrested in London, 1628. Laboured 45 years on the English mission. Author, theological. Died Nov. 26, 1660. (*D.N.B.*)

HOLLAND, HENRY. B.A. 1519-20; M.A. 1523. One of these names, 'M.A.,' R. of Llangelynin, Carnarvonshire; 'resident and keepeth house.' (Bishop of Bangor's 'Return,' in 1561.)

HOLLAND, HENRY. Matric. Fell.-Com. from GONVILLE HALL, May, 1556. S. of Sir Thomas, of Estovening, Lincs., Knt. B.A. 1559-60; M.A. 1563; B.D. 1570. Fellow and tutor, 1561-72. President, 1568. Ord. deacon (Lincoln) July 11, 1564; priest (Ely) July 29, 1565. V. of Boston, Lincs., 1571-84. Buried at Boston, Apr. 20, 1584. Admon., Lincoln. Brother of Christopher (1561). (*Venn*, I. 39; *Lincs. Pedigrees*, 506.

HOLLAND, HENRY. Matric. sizar from ST JOHN'S, Easter, 1579. Perhaps s. of Hugh, of Conway. B.A. from Magdalene, 1579-80; M.A. 1583. Ord. deacon (St Asaph's); priest (Ely) Dec. 21, 1580, age 24. V. of Orwell, Cambs., 1580-92. V. of St Bride's, London, 1594-1603. Author, *Treatise against Witchcraft*, etc. Died Aug. 1603. Will (Cons. C. London) Oct. 29, 1603. Perhaps brother of Robert (1577). (*Cooper*, III. 8; *D.N.B.*; *Archaeol. Cambrensis*, 3rd S., XII. 183; J. Ch. Smith.)

HOLLAND, HENRY. Adm. sizar at EMMANUEL, May 27, 1656. Of Salop. Matric. 1658; B.A. 1659-60; M.A. 1663. Incorp. at Oxford, 1671. V. or C. of Hicham (? Heacham), Norfolk, 1662. R. of Wheathill, Salop, 1667.

HOLLAND, HUGH. M.Gram. 1511-2. Schoolmaster.

HOLLAND, HUGH. Matric. pens. from JESUS, Easter, 1582.

HOLLAND (*alias* ROBERTS), HUGH. Scholar of TRINITY, 1590, from Westminster. S. of Robert, of Wales. B.A. 1593-4; M.A. 1597, as 'Robert.' Became a Romanist. Travelled to Rome, Jerusalem and Constantinople. Resided for a time at Balliol, Oxford, after his return to England. Patronised by Buckingham. A member of the Mermaid Club. Wrote the Sonnet prefixed to the first Shakespeare folio. Latin and English poet. 'Of Westminster, widower,' at his burial in the abbey, July 23, 1633. (*D.N.B.*; *Al. Westmon.*)

HOLLAND, HUGH. B.A. from CLARE, 1601-2; M.A. 1605. R. of Wistaston, Cheshire, 1606-7; V. of Eastham, 1610-3; R. of Heswall, 1613-24. Buried there Apr. 5, 1624. (E. Axon.)

HOLLANDE, JAMES. Matric. pens. from TRINITY HALL, Easter, 1544.

HOLLAND, JAMES. Matric. from CHRIST'S, 1595-6; B.A. 1596-7; M.A. 1605. One of these names instituted to the 4th mediety of the rectory of Darley, Derbs. Died 1644, aged 69. Buried at Darley. (*Peile*, I. 216.)

HOLLAND, JAMES. Adm. pens. (age 15) at CAIUS, July 3, 1620. S. of Ralph, gent., of London. Bapt. at St Laurence Fountney, Sept. 22, 1604. School, Merchant Taylors'.

HOLLAND, JOHN. Proctor, c. 1436.

HOLLAND, JOHN. D.D. Elected as foundationer at KING'S, 1444. V. of Ringwood, Hants.

HOLLAND (*alias* TEMPLE), JOHN. Adm. at KING'S (age 18) a scholar from Eton, Aug. 13, 1506. Of Barton, Staffs. Left, c. 1509. One of the Knights Templars of St John of Jerusalem. (*Harwood*.)

HOLLAND, JOHN. Matric. sizar from KING'S, 1547.

HOLLAND, JOHN. Matric. pens. from QUEENS', Easter, 1549. Of Bangor diocese. B.A. 1552-3; M.A. 1555. Fellow of Clare when ord. priest (London) 1563. V. of Gt Dunmow, Essex, 1564-78. Died 1578. Will (Cons. C. London) 1578; mentions sons Philemon (1566) and John (? 1572). One of these names, M.A., s. of William, of Hendrefawr, Abergele. (*Archaeol. Cambrensis*, 3rd S., XIII. 170; J. Ch. Smith.)

HOLLAND, JOHN. Matric. pens. from ST JOHN'S, Michs. 1565.

HOLLAND, JOHN. Matric. pens. from TRINITY, Easter, 1572; B.A. 1576-7. Perhaps s. of John (1549); and R. of Chadwell, Essex, 1581-4; V. of Ashford, Kent, 1584-91; and R. of Halden, 1587.

HOLLAND or HOLLONDE, JOHN. Matric. sizar from ST JOHN'S, Michs. 1607; B.A. 1610-1. Probably admon. (Lincoln) 1623; of Barrow, Lincs., B.A.

HOLLAND, JOHN. M.A. 1614 (Incorp. from Oxford). Of Co. Denbigh, gent. Matric. from Hart Hall, June 20, 1606, age 18; B.A. (Oxford) 1609; M.A. 1613. R. of Llansantffraid, Conway, 1613. V. of Llansannan, 1614. R. of Cegidog St George, 1617. Preb. of St Asaph, 1624. R. of Llandulas, Conway, 1629. (*Al. Oxon.*)

HOLLAND, JOHN. Matric. Fell.-Com. from CHRIST'S, Lent, 1620. S. and h. of Sir Thomas, of Quiddenham, Norfolk, Knt. B. Oct. 1603. Created Baronet, June 15, 1629. On the Norfolk Commission in the Civil War. Colonel in the Parliamentary army. M.P. for Norfolk, Apr. to May, 1640; for Castle Rising, 1640-8; for Aldborough, 1661-79. Member of the Council of State, 1660. Died Jan. 19, 1700-1, aged 98. Buried at Langley. Benefactor of Christ's. Brother of Edmund (1620-1). (*Peile*, I. 337; *G.E.C.*; A. B. Beaven.)

HOLLAND, JOHN. Matric. sizar from ST JOHN'S, Michs. 1627; B.A. 1629-30. Ord. deacon (Peterb.) May 23, 1630; priest, May 27, 1632. Perhaps V. of Sausthorpe, Lincs., 1641.

HOLLAND, JOHN. Matric. sizar from TRINITY, Easter, 1631; B.A. 1634-5; M.A. 1638.

HOLLAND, JOHN. Adm. pens. (age 17) at CHRIST'S, May 14, 1639. S. of John. B. in London. School, Norwich (Mr Lovering). Matric. 1639; B.A. 1642-3. (*Peile*, I. 460.)

HOLLAND, JOHN. Matric. pens. from PEMBROKE, Easter, 1640. Probably s. and h. of Anthony, of Swineshead, Lincs.; adm. at Lincoln's Inn, May 28, 1642. Heir of his grandmother Winifred Vaughan. *See* Thomas, 1640. (*Lincs. Pedigrees*, 507.)

HOLLAND, JOHN. Adm. sizar at TRINITY, Apr. 2, 1646. Of Gloucestershire. Matric. 1648-9; Scholar, 1649; B.A. 1649-50; M.A. 1653. Fellow, 1650. Incorp. at Oxford, 1653. R. of St Mary, Guildford, 1650-91. R. of Holy Trinity, Guildford, 1661. R. of Albury, Surrey, 1667. Died July 6, 1691. M.I. at Holy Trinity Church. (*Vis. of Surrey*, 1662; *Manning and Bray*, I. 62.)

HOLLAND, JOHN. Adm. sizar (age 19) at CHRIST'S, June 12, 1647. S. of John. B. at Minshull Vernon, Cheshire. School, Macclesfield (Mr Crosdale). Perhaps the minister at Minshull, 1668-87, mentioned in Shaw's *Manchester Classis Minutes*, III. 433. (*Peile*, I. 515.)

HOLLAND, JOHN. Adm. pens. at EMMANUEL, Lent, 1648-9. Probably s. of William, of Chorlton, Lancs. Bapt. at Manchester, Jan. 22, 1631-2. Matric. 1649; B.A. 1652-3. Ord. to Weaverham, Cheshire, July 9, 1656, by Manchester *Classis*. V. of Weaverham, 1656-62; conformed and reappointed, 1662-8. Probably his will at Chester, 1668; of Weaverham. The C. of Minshull was probably the above. (E. Axon.)

HOLLAND, JOHN. Adm. Fell.-Com. at CHRIST'S, Sept. 1685. S. of Thomas (who was s. of Sir John, of 1620). B. at Quiddenham, Norfolk. School, Bury (Mr Leeds). Matric. 1686. Succeeded his grandfather as 2nd Bart., Jan. 19, 1701. M.P. for Norfolk, 1701-10. Comptroller of the household to Queen Anne, 1709-11. Died 1724. Admon. 1724; as of Bury St Edmunds. (Burke, *Ext. Bart.*; *G.E.C.*)

HOLLAND, JOHN. Adm. sizar at CLARE, July 6, 1692. Of Epworth, Lincs. Matric. 1692; B.A. 1695-6. Ord. priest (Lincoln) Sept. 19, 1703. V. of Appleby, Lincs., 1705.

HOLLAND, JOHN. Adm. sizar (age 17) at TRINITY, Apr. 18, 1717. S. of John, of London. B. in London. School, St Paul's. Matric. 1717. Ord. deacon (Peterb., *Litt. dim.* from Winchester) Mar. 17, 1727-9. C. of Rotherhithe.

HOLLAND, JOHN. Adm. sizar at QUEENS', Mar. 9, 1728-9. Of Lincolnshire. Matric. 1729-30; LL.B. 1737. Ord. deacon (Lincoln) Feb. 18, 1732-3; priest, Mar. 2, 1734-5.

HOLLAND, NICHOLAS. B.A. 1511-2.

HOLLAND, NOEL. Adm. sizar (age 17) at SIDNEY, Apr. 29, 1629. S. of Ralph, Esq. B. at Brooke, Rutland. School, Oakham. Matric. 1629.

HOLLAND, PHILEMON. Matric. pens. from TRINITY, Easter, 1566. S. of John (1549), clerk. B. at Chelmsford. School, Chelmsford. B.A. 1570-1; M.A. 1574; M.D. 1597. Fellow, 1573. Incorp. at Oxford, 1585. Usher at Coventry Grammar School, 1608. Head Master during 1628. Practised physic at Coventry. Author, classical, etc. Died Feb. 9, 1636-7, aged 85. Buried at Coventry. Father of Abraham (1614) and probably brother of John (1572). (*D.N.B.*, where it is wrongly assumed that the M.D. degree is unrecorded.)

HOLLAND, PHILIP. Adm. sizar at SIDNEY, Nov. 1598. Matric. 1598. One of these names C. of Macclesfield, Cheshire, 1616–48. Buried there Oct. 1648. (E. Axon.)

HOLLAND, RALPH. Adm. at KING'S (age 19) a scholar from Eton, Aug. 23, 1537. Of Prescot, Lancs. B.A. 1542–3; M.A. 1545. Fellow, 1540–51. Afterwards Registrar of the College, and public notary. Will of one of these names (P.C.C.) 1586; of the Isle of Ely, gent.

HOLLAND, RALPH. Matric. pens. from CAIUS, Michs. 1559. Probably 1st s. of Thomas, of Estovening, Swineshead, Lincs. Brother of Thomas (1563). (*Lincs. Pedigrees*, 506.)

HOLLAND, RICHARD. M.A. 1612 (Incorp. from Oxford). Of Leicestershire, *cler. fil.* Matric. from Balliol College, June 28, 1604, age 18; B.A. (Oxford) 1607; M.A. 1610. R. of Eastwood, Notts., 1618. (*Al. Oxon.*) The Oxford mathematician, recorded in *D.N.D.*, was another man.

HOLLAND, RICHARD. Adm. pens. (age 18) at ST JOHN'S, May 31, 1636. S. of Robert, blacksmith, of Greenwich. B. in London. School, Greenwich (private; Mr Young). Matric. 1636; B.A. 1639–40; M.A. 1643. R. of Hascombe, Surrey, till 1694. Died there May 23, 1694, aged 76. M.I. (*Manning and Bray*, II. 67.)

HOLLAND, RICHARD. Adm. sizar at CLARE, May 12, 1663; B.A. 1666–7. Ord. deacon (Peterb.) Mar. 3, 1666–7.

HOLLAND, RICHARD. Adm. sizar at EMMANUEL, Mar. 13, 1670–1. Of Leicestershire. B.A. 1674–5; M.A. 1678. Incorp. at Oxford, 1679. Ord. deacon (Ely) Oct. 2, 1675. Chaplain to the Duke of Richmond. Lecturer at All Hallows-the-Great, London. C. of St Magnus. R. of Stamford St George, Lincs., 1681–91. R. of Sculthorpe, Norfolk, 1686–9. R. of East Mersey, Essex, 1703–6. Author, *Sermons*. Died 1706. (*Al. Oxon.*; *D.N.B.*)

HOLLAND, RICHARD. Adm. pens. at ST CATHARINE'S, May 31, 1705. S. of John, merchant, of Brewood, Staffs. Matric. 1708; B.A. 1708–9; M.A. 1712; M.D. 1723. F.R.C.P., 1725. F.R.S., 1726. Censor, 1728. Author, medical. Died Oct. 29, 1730. (*D.N.B.*; *Munk*, II. 92.)

HOLAND, ROBERT DE. Adm. scholar at KING'S HALL, 1360. Clerk. Left Aug. 4, 1381.

HOLLAND, ROBERT. B.A. 1516–7. Perhaps M.A. 1522–3. Probably V. of Gt Shelford, Cambs., 1555–69.

HOLLAND, ROBERT. Matric. sizar from CHRIST'S, May, 1559. Of Yorkshire. B.A. 1562–3; M.A. 1566. Probably fellow of St John's, 1565. Fellow of Christ's, 1566–70. Perhaps V. of Sheffield, 1569–97. R. of Whiston, near Rotherham, 1578–97. Died 1597. Buried at Sheffield, Aug. 24, 1597. (*Peile*, I. 69.)

HOLLAND, ROBERT. Matric. pens. from CLARE, Easter, 1577. 3rd s. of Hugh, of Conway. B. there, 1557. B.A. from Magdalene, 1577–8; M.A. from Jesus, 1581. Ord. deacon (Bangor); priest (Ely) Apr. 1580. C. of Weston Colville, Cambs. Schoolmaster at Dullingham, 1580. R. of Prendergast, Pembrokeshire, 1591; also of Walwyn's Castle, 1607; of Robeston West, 1612; of Llandowror, Carmarth. Author, religious p . Died *c.* 1622. Perhaps brother of Henry (1579). (*Cooper*, II. 174; *D.N.B.*)

HOLLAND, ROBERT. Matric. sizar from CHRIST'S, Dec. 1586. Probably s. of John, of Ely. (*Peile*, I. 188.)

HOLLAND, ROBERT. Matric. pens. from ST JOHN'S, *c.* 1593; B.A. 1596–7; M.A. 1600.

HOLLAND, THOMAS. B.A. 1506–7.

HOLLAND, THOMAS. B.Can.L. 1528–9.

HOLLAND, THOMAS. Adm. (age 14) at CAIUS, Sept. 30, 1563. Of Swineshead, Lincs. 3rd s. of Thomas, of Estovening, Swineshead. School, Boston. Brother of Ralph (1559). (*Lincs. Pedigrees*, 506.)

HOLLAND, THOMAS. Incorp. at Oxford, as B.D., July 17, 1572. Not found in our records.

HOLLAND, THOMAS. Adm. at KING'S (age 16) a scholar from Eton, Aug. 24, 1583. Of Steyning, Sussex. Matric. 1583; B.A. 1587–8. Fellow, 1586–90. V. of Kirdford, Sussex. Will (Chichester) 1647. (*Cooper*, II. 41.)

HOLLAND, THOMAS. Adm. pens. (age 15) at PEMBROKE, May, 1640. S. of Thomas, Esq. B. in Lincolnshire. If he is really a different man from John, matric. at this time, he is probably his younger brother; 2nd s. of Anthony, of Swineshead. (*Lincs. Pedigrees*, 507.)

HOLLAND, THOMAS. Adm. Fell.-Com. at CLARE, May 25, 1664. Of Anglesey, Wales.

HOLLAND, THOMAS. Adm. pens. (age 16) at PETERHOUSE, Feb. 20, 1693–4. Of Flintshire. School, Llanrwst, Denbigh. Scholar, 1694; Matric. 1695. Admon. (Chester) 1704, of one of these names; schoolmaster, of Stenny, Cheshire.

HOLLAND, THOMAS. Adm. Fell.-Com. (age 17) at CHRIST'S, Mar. 24, 1701–2. S. of Thomas. B. in Anglesey. School, Ruthin (Mr Winn). (*Peile*, II. 152.)

HOLLAND, TIMOTHY. Adm. sizar at TRINITY, May 24, 1665. Matric. 1665; Scholar, 1668; B.A. 1668–9; M.A. 1672. Incorp. at Oxford, 1674. R. of Denton, Kent, 1678.

HOLLAND, TOBIAS. Matric. sizar from ST JOHN'S, Michs. 1562. S. of John, of Colchester. School, Colchester. B.A. 1566–7. Migrated to Caius, Jan. 15, 1566–7, age 18. Ord. deacon (Norwich) Sept. 27, 1570; priest, Oct. 17, 1571. C. of Gt Whelnetham, Suffolk. V. of St Stephen's, Norwich, 1575–80. R. of Winterton, Norfolk, 1577–1601. (*Venn*, I. 59.)

HOLLAND, WILLIAM. Licensed to practise surgery, 1559. Will proved (V.C.C.) 1562.

HOLLAND, WILLIAM. Matric. sizar from CLARE, Michs. 1570; B.A. 1574–5; M.A. 1578. One of these names R. of East Farleigh, Kent, 1580–9.

HOLLAND, WILLIAM. Matric. pens. from ST JOHN'S, Michs. 1576. Of Denbighshire. B.A. 1579–80; M.A. 1583; B.D. 1591. Fellow, 1584. Ord. priest (St Asaph) Nov. 3, 1583. R. of Ashby, Norfolk, 1591–1603. R. of North Creake, 1605. Died 1608. Will (P.C.C. and V.C.C.) 1608. (*Cooper*, II. 473.)

HOLLAND, WILLIAM. M.A. 1635 (Incorp. from Oxford). S. of Edward, of Denton and Heaton, Lancs. Adm. at Brasenose College, Oxford, 1627; B.A. (Oxford) 1630–1; M.A. 1633. R. of Malpas, Cheshire, in 1648 and 1662–80. Resigned on succeeding to the family estates. Died Apr. 25, 1682, aged 76. Buried at Prestwich. Will (Chester) 1682. Father of Edward (1679). (*Al. Oxon.*; E. Axon.)

HOLLAND, WILLIAM. Adm. sizar (age 16) at ST JOHN'S, June 14, 1636. S. of John, tailor, of Woodham Ferrers, Essex. B. there. School, Chelmsford (Mr Peake). Matric. 1636; B.A. 1639–40. Perhaps V. of Gt Wakering, Essex, 1663–7, resigned. Will (Cons. C. London) 1677.

HOLLAND, WILLIAM. Adm. pens. at EMMANUEL, Apr. 21, 1638. S. of George, merchant, of Doncaster. B. there. School, Sheffield (Mr Rawson). Matric. 1639. Migrated to St John's, as sizar, Oct. 29, 1640, age 20. B.A. 1641–2. Probably ord. deacou and priest (Lincoln) Sept. 24, 1646. One of these names P.C. of All Hallows Staining, 1663–77. Died Oct. 1677. Will, P.C.C.

HOLLAND, WILLIAM. Adm. sizar (age 17) at ST JOHN'S, July 5, 1659. S. of Robert, yeoman, of Eglwys Fach, Denbighs. B. there. School, Beaumaris (Mr Williams).

HOLLAND, ——. B.A. 1512–3.

HOLLAND, ——. B.A. 1513–4, 1st in the *ordo*; M.A. 1517.

HOLLAND, ——. B.A. 1522–3; M.A. 1525.

HOLLAND, ——. B.A. 1529–30; M.A. 1532.

HOLLAND, ——. Adm. pens. at KING'S, Michs. 1565.

HOLLAND, ——. Matric. from TRINITY, *c.* 1597.

HOLLE, EDWARD. Matric. sizar from TRINITY HALL, Easter, 1549.

HOLL or HOULE, EDWARD. Adm. pens. (age 16) at CAIUS, Apr. 12, 1615. Of Metton, Norfolk. S. of John, gent. School, Roughton (Mr Browne). Matric. 1615–6; B.A. 1618–9. Ord. priest (Norwich) Mar. 17, 1621–2. R. of Langhale and Kirstead, Norfolk, 1626–77. Died 1677. Will (Norwich) 1677. (*Venn*, I. 228; *Vis. of Norfolk*.)

HOLE or HOYLE, HENRY. Adm. sizar at EMMANUEL, Apr. 28, 1615, as Hoole. *See* Hoyle.

HOLE, HENRY. M.A. 1635 (Incorp. from Oxford). S. of Christopher, of Totnes, Devon. Matric. from Exeter College, Oxford, Dec. 13, 1622, age 17; B.A. (Oxford) 1626–7; M.A. 1629. Fellow of Exeter College, 1628–34. V. of Egloshayle, Cornwall, 1633. Buried there Mar. 20, 1659–60. (*Al. Oxon.*)

HOLE or HOOLE, JASPER. Matric. pens. from ST JOHN'S, Michs. 1567. B. at Halifax, Yorks. B.A. 1571–2. Ord. deacon (London) Dec. 20, 1571, age 23; of Ashdon, Essex (probable curate).

HOOLE, HOLLE or HOLE, JOHN. Scholar and fellow of KING'S HALL, 1489–97; B.Can.L. 1497–8. Archdeacon of Cleveland, 1496–7; of East Riding, 1497–1501. Died 1501.

HOALE or HOWELL, JOHN. Adm. sizar at SIDNEY, Nov. 1598. Matric. 1598; B.A. 1601–2; M.A. 1605. Fellow. Incorp. at Oxford, 1606. Ord. priest (Gloucester) Dec. 18, 1608. R. of Cromhall, Gloucs., 1612–44. Will (Gloucester) 1644; as Howell. (F. S. Hockaday.)

HOLE, JOHN. M.A. from KING'S, 1731. Probably s. of Joshua, of South Molton, Devon, clerk. Matric. from Trinity College, Oxford, Mar. 16, 1720–1, age 18; B.A. (Oxford) 1724. Will of one of these names (Exeter) 1782; of Romansleigh, Devon. (*Al. Oxon.*)

HOLE, RICHARD. Adm. pens. (age 18) at SIDNEY, July 1, 1696. S. of Thomas, gent. B. at Zeal Monachorum, Devon. School, Tiverton. Matric. 1697; B.A. 1699–1700; M.A. 1703. Probably will (Exeter) 1747; of North Tawton, Devon, clerk.

HOLE, RICHARD. Matric. sizar from CLARE, Michs. 1747; B.A. 1752; M.A. 1774. (Probably adm. in College as 'Robert.') Will of one of these names (P.C.C.) 1796; of Exeter, clerk.

HOLL, ROBERT. Matric. Fell.-Com. from CLARE, Easter, 1648.

HOLE, ROBERT. Adm. sizar at CLARE, July 17, 1747. B. at Zeal Monachorum, Devon. Perhaps a mistake for Richard (whom *see*).

HOLE, SYDNEY. Matric. sizar from ST JOHN'S, c. 1593.

HOLE or HOLLE, THOMAS. B.A. 1474-5. Of Yorkshire. M.A. 1478-9; B.D. 1483-4. Fellow of PEMBROKE, 1475. Proctor, 1481-2. Ord. deacon (Ely) Sept. 21, 1476. Died 1484.

HOLL, THOMAS (*senior*). Matric. pens. from PETERHOUSE, Easter, 1580. This and the next are probably cousins; sons of Thomas, of Heigham and Edward, of Asham. One of them became Fell.-Com. in 1581. (*T. A. Walker*.)

HOLL, THOMAS (*junior*). Matric. pens. from PETERHOUSE, Easter, 1580.

HOLL, THOMAS. Matric. sizar from CORPUS CHRISTI, Easter, 1607. Of Suffolk.

HOLLE, THOMAS. Adm. pens. (age 17) at CAIUS, May 3, 1671. S. of Robert, gent., deceased, of Heigham, Norfolk. B. at Thursford (his mother's home). School, Aylsham (Mr Ransome). Matric. 1671. Adm. at the Inner Temple, July 2, 1672. Of Heigham, Norwich, gent. (*Venn*, I. 444.)

HOLE, THOMAS. Adm. pens. (age 18) at SIDNEY, Nov. 14, 1719. S. of Thomas. B. at Colebrook, Devon. Schools, Morchard Bishop and Molton (Mr Dean). Matric. 1719. Adm. at the Inner Temple, July 10, 1717; s. and h. of Thomas, of Colebrook, Esq.

HOLE, ——. Scholar at CHRIST'S, in 1547-8.

HOLLED, JEREMIAH. D.D. 1661 (*Lit. Reg.*). S. of John, of Sempringham, Lincs., gent. Matric. from New Inn Hall, Oxford, Apr. 16, 1641, age 15. R. of Walgrave, Northants., 1651; conformed, in 1660, and held the living, till 1681. R. of Thorpe Malzor, 1669-81. Married Dorothy Claypole, a kinswoman of Oliver Cromwell. Died 1681. Brother of the next. (*Al. Oxon.*; H. I. Longden.)

HOLLED, JONATHAN. D.D. 1661 (*Lit. Reg.*). S. of John, of Sempringham, Lincs., gent. Matric. from New Inn Hall, Oxford, Feb. 22, 1638-9, age 16; B.A. (Oxford) 1642. R. of Easton-by-Stamford, Northants., 1647-59. R. of Cottingham and Middleton, 1660-80. Married, at St Mary Aldermanbury, London, Anne, dau. of Sir Seymour Knightley, Nov. 19, 1646. Buried at Cottingham, May 20, 1680. Brother of the above. (*Al. Oxon.*; H. I. Longden.)

HOLLED, KNIGHTLEY. Adm. at CORPUS CHRISTI, 1665. S. of Jonathan (above). Matric. 1667; B.A. 1668-9; M.A. 1672. Ord. deacon (Peterb.) June 2, 1672; priest, Sept. 21, 1673. R. of Barby, Northants., 1677-1700. Buried there Aug. 20, 1700. (*Baker*, I. 264; *Nichols*, IV. 342; H. I. Longden.)

HOLLENDEN, LAURENCE. Matric. sizar from CLARE, Michs. 1566. V. of Teynham, Kent, 1570-95. V. of Preston, 1579-95. Died 1595.

HOLLES, *see* HOLLIS.

HOLLEY, *see also* HOLLY.

HOLLEY, BENJAMIN. Matric. sizar from TRINITY HALL, Easter, 1677. *See* Hawling.

HOLLIBRAND, THOMAS. Matric. sizar from TRINITY, Michs. 1615; B.A. 1618-9.

HOLLIER or HOLLYER, JAMES (? JOHN). Adm. Fell.-Com. at KING'S, 1669-70.

HOLLIER, JOHN. M.A. 1671 (*Lit. Reg.*). If the above is really John, probably the same man.

HOLLIER, ROBERT. Adm. sizar (age 18) at ST JOHN'S, June 4, 1698. S. of John, deceased. B. at Shrewsbury. School, Shrewsbury. Matric. 1698; B.A. 1701-2. C. of Holy Trinity, Chester, till 1709. Buried May 26, 1709.

HOLIER, WILLIAM. M.A. from CAIUS, 1710. S. of William, of Wolverhampton. Adm. at Brasenose College, Oxford, Apr. 6, 1693; B.A. (Oxford) 1696. Ord. deacon (Winchester) Dec. 9, 1697; priest, Nov. 15, 1703. R. of Carshalton, Surrey, 1703-37. Died Mar. 7, 1736-7. (*Venn*, I. 523.)

HOLYNS, ADAM DE. 'KING'S scholar' at Cambridge, 1329.

HOLLIMAN, *see* HOLYMAN.

HOLLIMAN, EDWARD. Matric. sizar from ST JOHN'S, Michs. 1616; B.A. from Trinity Hall, 1620; M.A. from St John's. 1624.

HOLLINS, JOHN. Adm. pens. (age 16) at MAGDALENE, Apr. 5, 1651. S. of John, of Methley, Yorks. School, Leeds. Matric. 1651; B.A. 1654-5; M.A. 1658; M.D. 1665. Fellow. Practised in Shrewsbury. Admon. (P.C.C.) 1712. Father of the next.

HOLLINS, JOHN. Matric. pens. from EMMANUEL, Easter, 1700. S. of John (above), M.D. B. at Shrewsbury. School, Shrewsbury. Migrated to Magdalene, Mar. 27, 1700, age 17; M.B. 1705; M.D. 1710. F.R.C.P. 1726. F.R.S., 1727. Physician to the King, 1727-39. Harveian orator, 1734. Physician-general to the army. Died May 10, 1739. Will, P.C.C. Father of John (1724) and Richard (1724). (*Munk*, II. 94; *D.N.B.*)

HOLLINGS, JOHN. Adm. pens. (age 16) at TRINITY, Feb. 12, 1723-4. S. of John (1700), M.D. B. at Shrewsbury. Matric. 1724; M.A. 1728 (*Com. Reg.*); M.D. 1736 (*Lit. Reg.*). Died Dec. 28, 1739. Will, P.C.C. Brother of Richard (1724). (G. *Mag.*)

HOLLINS, PHILIP. Adm. pens. at EMMANUEL, June 20, 1691. Of Staffordshire. Perhaps s. of Philip, of Moseley. Matric. 1693; B.A. 1694-5. R. of Ackworth, Yorks., 1702. Father of the next. (*Staffs. Pedigrees*.)

HOLLINS, PHILIP. Adm. sizar (age 19) at ST JOHN'S, June 29, 1723. S. of Philip (above), R. of Ackworth, Yorks. B. at Ackworth. School, Eton. Matric. 1723; B.A. 1726-7. Ord. deacon (York) July 21, 1728; priest (Lincoln) Mar. 2, 1734-5. V. of Lavendon and Brayfield, Bucks., 1735-64. Died 1764. (*Scott-Mayor*, III. 363.)

HOLLINGS, RICHARD. Adm. pens. (age 15) at TRINITY, Feb. 12, 1723-4. 2nd s. of John (1700), M.D., of St James', Westminster. B. at Shrewsbury. Matric. 1724. Adm. at the Middle Temple, May 26, 1725. Called to the Bar, June 20, 1729. Solicitor-general to the Prince of Wales, 1736-41. Died Dec. 7, 1741. Brother of John (1724). (G. *Mag.*; A. B. Beaven.)

HOLLINS, SAMUEL. 'Student of TRINITY,' when ord. deacon (York) June, 1626; priest, Dec. 1626. Samuel Hollings, clerk, of St Lawrence, York, was licensed to marry Mary Allen, of York, 1627.

HOLLINGS, THOMAS. Adm. sizar (age 17) at SIDNEY, June 13, 1660. Only s. of Thomas, brewer. B. at Nottingham. School, Nottingham (Mr Hen. Pitts). Matric. 1660; B.A. 1663-4. Ord. deacon (York) c. 1663-4.

HOLLYNS, WILLIAM. B.A. 1550-1.

HOLLYNSHED, EDWARD. Matric. pens. from TRINITY, Easter, 1549. 5th s. of Hugh, of Bosley, Cheshire. Adm. at the Inner Temple, 1559. Succeeded his father. Brother of Ottiwell (1537-8) and probably of Hugh. (*Vis. of Cheshire*, 1613.)

HOLLINGHEDGE, EDWARD. Adm. pens. at EMMANUEL, Apr. 1, 1593. Matric. c. 1596.

HOLLINGHEDGE, ROBERT. Adm. sizar at EMMANUEL, 1586, as Hollingshed. Matric. 1586; B.A. (? 1589-90); M.A. 1593. Ord. deacon and priest (Peterb.) Sept. 5, 1591. V. of Horncastle, Lincs., 1595. Admon. (Lincoln) 1633.

HOLLINGHEDGE, THOMAS. Matric. pens. from CLARE, Michs. 1578; B.A. 1581-2; M.A. 1585. Ord. deacon (Peterb.) Nov. 7, 1585; priest, Mar. 25, 1586.

HOLINGSHEAD, EMANUEL. Adm. pens. (age 19) at ST JOHN'S, June 17, 1667. S. of Edward, clerk, of Brassington, near Wirksworth, Derbs. B. there. School, Ashbourne (Mr Twigg).

HOLLYNSHED, HU. Matric. sizar from TRINITY, Michs. 1547. Probably Hugh Holinshed, of Bosley, Cheshire; adm. at the Inner Temple, 1553. Brother of Ottiwell (1537-8) and Edward (1549). (*Vis. of Cheshire*, 1613.)

HOLINGSHEAD, HUGH. Adm. pens. at JESUS, May 16, 1659. Of Cheshire. S. of Hugh, Esq., of Heywood, Lancs. Bapt. at Alderley, Oct. 2, 1638. C. of Alderley, Cheshire, 1662-4. R. of Gawsworth, 1664-5. Died Jan. 12, 1664-5. Buried at Gawsworth. (*Ormerod*, III. 555; E. Axon.)

HOLLINGSHEAD, OBADIAH. Adm. sizar (age 16) at MAGDALENE, May 27, 1667. S. of Edward, of Ashford, Derbs. School, Derby. Matric. 1668.

HOLINSHED, OTTIWELL. Scholar at CHRIST'S, 1537-8. S. of Hugh, of Sutton Downs, Esq. B.A. 1540-1; M.A. 1544. One of the original fellows of Trinity, 1546. Canon of Windsor, 1550-4, though a layman. Probably will (P.C.C.) 1568; of Ashby-de-la-Zouch, gent. Brother of Edward (1549) and Hu[gh] (1547). (*Cooper*, I. 431; *Vis. of Cheshire*, 1613; *D.N.B.*)

HOLLINSHED, RAPHAEL. Said to have been educated at Cambridge. S. of Ralph, of Cophurst, Cheshire. Cousin of Ottiwell. Steward to Thomas Burdet, of Bromcote, Warws. Author, *The Chronicles*. Died c. 1580. Will (P.C.C.) 1581; of Bromcote. (*Cooper*, I. 430; *D.N.B.*)

HOLLINSHEAD, THOMAS. Matric. pens. from ST CATHARINE'S, Lent, 1623-4; B.A. 1627-8; M.A. (Queen's College, Oxford) 1630. V. of Hartley Wintney, Hants., 1642.

HOLLINGSHEAD, THOMAS. Adm. pens. at ST CATHARINE'S, May 17, 1695. Matric. 1695. Perhaps s. and h. of Francis, of Ashenhurst, Staffs., Esq.; adm. at the Inner Temple, Feb. 12, 1700-1.

HOLINSHED, ——. Matric. pens. from CHRIST'S, May, 1544.

HOLLINGTON, NATHANIEL. Adm. sizar at EMMANUEL, Sept. 7, 1602. Matric. 1602. Perhaps adm. sizar at Sidney, June, 1602.

HOLLINGTON, WILLIAM. LL.D. 1661 (*Lit. Reg.*). S. of John, of Tarbeek, Worcs. Matric. from Oriel College, Oxford, Apr. 1, 1636, age 16. R. of Alvechurch, Worcs.; sequestered, 1646. R. of Long Marston, Gloucs., 1663–86. Chaplain to Charles I and II. Died *c.* 1686. (*Al. Oxon.*; F. S. Hockaday.)

HOLLINGWORTH, ANTHONY. Matric. sizar from TRINITY, Easter, 1618; B.A. 1621–2. Ord. deacon (Peterb.) Mar. 10, 1621–2; priest, Dec. 21, 1623.

HOLLINGWORTH, BENJAMIN. Adm. sizar (age 19) at ST JOHN'S, June 6, 1681. S. of Abraham, husbandman. B. at Allthill-on-the-Lyne, Lancs. School, Manchester (Mr Barrow). Matric. 1681; B.A. 1684–5. Ord. deacon (York) Sept. 1685; priest (Chester) Sept. 25, 1687. C. of Ashworth. C. of Cheadle, 1687–90. Probably C. of Throwley, Kent, till 1696. V. of Sheldwich, 1694–6. V. of Stone, Oxney, 1696. Buried at Cranbrook, May 7, 1716.

HOLLINGWORTH, BENJAMIN. Adm. sizar at JESUS, May 14, 1698. Of Yorkshire. Matric. 1698; Scholar, 1701; B.A. 1701–2; M.A. 1705. Fellow, 1707–12. Ord. deacon (London) Dec. 24, 1704; priest (Ely) Dec. 21, 1707. R. of Nutfield, Surrey, 1711–28. Died Mar. 11, 1727–8. M.I. (J. Ch. Smith.)

HOLLINGWORTH, JAMES. Matric. pens. from TRINITY, Easter, 1588; resided there ten years. S. of Martin, of Lincoln, draper. B. 1570. Scholar, 1590; B.A. (? 1591–2); M.A. 1595; B.D. from St Catharine's, 1603. Fellow of St Catharine's. University preacher. Taxor, 1601. Ord. deacon and priest (Lincoln) Dec. 16, 1599. R. of Trusthorpe, Lincs., 1599–1613. R. of North Claypole, 1605–41. (*Lincs. Pedigrees*, 511.)

HOLLINGWORTH, JAMES. Adm. pens. at TRINITY, Apr. 9, 1658. Of London. Matric. 1658; Scholar, 1659; B.A. 1661–2. Probably s. of Arthur, of St Andrew's, Holborn, London, gent.; adm. at Gray's Inn, May 8, 1661.

HOLLINGWORTH, PHILIP. Adm. sizar at EMMANUEL, Apr. 21, 1666. Of Derbyshire. Matric. 1667; B.A. 1669–70; M.A. 1674.

HOLLINGWORTH, RICHARD. Matric. sizar from MAGDALENE, Easter, 1623. S. of Francis, merchant, of Salford, Lancs. School, Manchester. B.A. 1626–7; M.A. 1630. C. at Middleton, Lancs., 1631–5. Minister at Trinity Chapel, Salford, 1636. Chaplain of the Collegiate Church, Manchester, 1643; Fellow, 1643–56. Assisted Richard Heyrick in establishing Presbyterianism in Manchester. Imprisoned, 1651. Engaged in a literary controversy with the Congregationalists. Wrote the first history of Manchester. Died Nov. 3, 1656. Buried in Manchester Collegiate Church. (Mumford, *Manchester School*, 48; *D.N.B.*)

HOLLINGWORTH, RICHARD. Adm. sizar at EMMANUEL, Feb. 5, 1654–5. B. in Lincolnshire, 1639. Matric. 1655; B.A. 1658–9; M.A. 1662; D.D. 1684. Ord. deacon (Lincoln). V. of West Ham, 1672–82. P.C. of St Botolph, Aldgate, 1682–93, deprived. V. of Chigwell, Essex, 1690–1701. Author, controversial. Died 1701. Admon. (P.C.C.) 1701. (*D.N.B.*)

HOLLINGWORTH, THOMAS. Adm. pens. at TRINITY, July 6, 1668.

HOLLIS or HOLLES, DENZIL. B.A. from CHRIST'S 1612–3 (on Prince Charles' visit); M.A. 1616. 2nd s. of John (1579), Earl of Clare. B. Oct. 31, 1599. Adm. at Gray's Inn, Mar. 9, 1614–5. M.P. for St Michael, Cornwall, 1624–5; for Dorchester, 1628–9; and again, 1640–8, 1660. Took an active part against the King. Fined and imprisoned. Opposed Buckingham's foreign policy. Endeavoured to save his brother-in-law, Strafford. Supported the Grand Remonstrance, 1641. One of the five members impeached, Jan. 3, 1642. A member of the Committee of Safety, 1642. In command of a regiment at Edgehill and Brentford. Opposed the Independents and projected the impeachment of Cromwell, 1644. Parliamentary representative at the Uxbridge Treaty, 1645; and again in 1648, at Newport. Impeached by the Army; escaped to France. Commissioner to Charles II at the Hague. Created Baron Holles of Ifield, Sussex, Apr. 1661. Privy Councillor, 1661. Ambassador at Paris, 1663–7. A negotiator of the Treaty of Breda, 1667. Author, political pamphlets and 'Memoirs.' Died Feb. 17, 1679–80. Buried in St Peter's, Dorchester. Father of the next. (*D.N.B.*; *Peile*, I. 278; *G.E.C.*)

HOLLIS, FRANCIS. Adm. at CLARE, Michs. 1651. S. of Denzil (above) and grandson of John, Earl of Clare. (His name was on the College boards for 20 years.) B. at Dorchester, Aug. 19, 1627. Adm. at the Middle Temple, Feb. 9, 1647–8. Called to the Bar, June 28, 1661. M.P. for Lostwithiel, 1647–8; for Co. Wilts., 1654–5; for Northallerton, 1660; for Dorchester, 1679–80. Created Bart., June, 1660. Succeeded as 2nd Baron Holles, 1680. Died at Aldenham, Herts., Mar. 1, 1689–90. Buried at Ifield, Sussex. Will (P.C.C.) 1695. (J. Ch. Smith; A. B. Beaven.)

HOLLIS, GEORGE. Matric. pens. from CHRIST'S, 1593–4. S. of Denzil, of Irby, Lincs. Bapt. there, Sept. 1, 1577. Knighted, July 2, 1609. Buried in Westminster Abbey, May 23, 1626. Will, P.C.C. Brother of (John) (1579). (*Peile*, I. 214.)

HOLLES, GERVASE. Matric. Fell.-Com. from CHRIST'S, May, 1559. S. of Sir William and Anne Densil. B. at Haughton, Notts., in 1547. Knighted, 1621. Married Frances, dau. of Peter Freschville, of Staveley, Derbs. Buried at Grimsby, Mar. 5, 1627–8. Will (P.C.C.) 1628. (*Peile*, I. 67; *Lincs. Pedigrees*, 508.)

HOLLIS, JAMES. Adm. pens. at CLARE, June 20, 1663. Of London. School, Charterhouse. Matric. 1663; B.A. 1666–7; M.A. 1670. Fellow. Senior Proctor, 1685–6. Ord. deacon (Ely) Dec. 18, 1669; priest (Peterb.) Sept. 25, 1670. V. of Everton, Hunts., 1685–91. Died 1691.

HOLLES, JOHN. Matric. pens. (age 12) from CHRIST'S, Apr. 1579; Fell.-Com. 1580. S. of Denzil. Adm. at Gray's Inn, as of Haughton, Notts., Nov. 8, 1583. Served in Ireland, where he was knighted, 1593. Joined the expedition to the Azores, 1597. Fought against the Turks in Hungary. M.P. for Co. Notts., 1604–11, 1614. Comptroller of the household of Prince Henry, 1610. Created Baron Holles of Haughton, Notts., July 9, 1616; and Earl of Clare, Nov. 2, 1624. Opposed Buckingham. Prosecuted for implication in the proceedings of Sir Robert Dudley; dismissed with a reprimand. Died Oct. 4, 1637, at Clare Palace, Nottingham. Buried at St Mary's, Nottingham. M.I. Brother of George (1593–4), father of Denzil (1612–3). (*Peile*, I. 151; *D.N.B.*; *G.E.C.*)

HOLLIS, JOHN. Adm. sizar (age 17) at ST JOHN'S, June 7, 1684. S. of Richard (1657), deceased. B. at Hutton Buscel, near Scarborough, Yorks. School, Wykeham (Mr Kirby). Matric. 1684; B.A. 1687–8. Probably V. of Brompton, Yorks. A non-juror. Brother of William (1692)

HOLLISS, RICHARD. Adm. sizar at JESUS, May 21, 1657. Of Salop. Matric. 1657; B.A. 1660–1. Ord. deacon (Lincoln) Apr. 20; priest, Apr. 25, 1661. V. of Hutton Buscel, Yorks., 1662–74. V. of Wykeham, 1663–74. Died Aug. 1674. Father of the above and of William (1692).

HOLLIS, ROBERT. Adm. pens. (age 16) at CHRIST', Apr. 13, 1655. S. of Maccabeus, merchant (Chamberlain of Hull). B. at Hull. School, Hull (Mr Shore). Matric. 1655. Adm. at Gray's Inn, June 12, 1656. Recorder of Hull. Died Sept. 4, 1697. M.I. at St Mary's, Hull. (*Peile*, I. 565.)

HOLLYS, THOMAS. Matric. pens. from PEMBROKE, Easter, 1550, *impubes*.

HOLLIS, THOMAS. Adm. sizar at CLARE, Dec. 9, 1714. S. of John, farmer, of Northamptonshire. B. at Kilsby. School, Rugby, Warws. (Mr Holyoake). Matric. 1715. Migrated to St John's, July 23, 1715, age 20. B.A. 1718–9.

HOLLYS, WILLIAM. Matric. pens. from PEMBROKE, Easter, 1550, *impubes*.

HOLLIS or HOLLES, WILLIAM. Adm. pens. (age 15) at PEMBROKE, Oct. 2, 1635. S. of Francis, Esq. B. at Berwick-on-Tweed. Bapt. there, Feb. 27, 1619–20. Matric. 1635; B.A. 1639–40.

HOLLIS, WILLIAM. Adm. sizar (age 17) at ST JOHN'S, May 20, 1692. S. of Richard (1657), deceased. B. at Hutton Buscel, Yorks. School, Wykeham Abbey (Mr Kirby). Matric. 1692. Migrated to Queens', Nov. 3, 1693. B.A. 1695–6. Ord. deacon (York) May, 1697. V. of Ganton, Yorks., 1697–1708. V. of Scalby, 1708–37. V. of Hackness, 1733. Brother of John (1684).

HOLLYS (possibly HOBBYS), ——. B.A. 1498–9. *See* ROBERT HOBBES.

HOLLIS, ——. Adm. Fell.-Com. at CORPUS CHRISTI, 1571.

HOLLIS, ——. Matric. pens. from CHRIST'S, *c.* 1597. Perhaps Thomas; brother of John (1579) and George (1593). (*Peile*, I. 151.)

HOLLOLYE, W. Matric. pens. from QUEENS', Easter, 1577.

HOLLOWE, ——. Adm. at CORPUS CHRISTI, 1589. Perhaps B.A. 1593–4. (*Masters*.)

HOLLOWAY, BENJAMIN. Adm. pens. (age 17) at ST JOHN'S, Feb. 4, 1707–8. S. of Joseph, maltster. B. at Stony Stratford, Bucks. School, Westminster. Matric. 1708; LL.B. 1713. Ord. deacon (Lincoln) July 5, 1713; priest, May 27, 1716. V. of Renhold, Beds., 1713. V. of Willington, 1713. F.R.S., 1723. R. of Waddesdon, Bucks., 1726–36. R. of Middleton-Stoney, Oxford, *c.* 1730–59. R. of Bladon, Bucks., 1736–9. Author, sermons and translations. Died Apr. 10, 1759. Buried at Middleton. (*D.N.B.*)

HOLLOWAY, GAMALIEL. M.A. 1608 (Incorp. from Oxford). 1st s. of Thomas, V. of Cropredy, Oxon. Bapt. there, Dec. 19, 1584. Matric. from Brasenose College, Oxford, May 7, 1601, age 15; B.A. (Oxford) 1604; M.A. 1607. R. of Thorpe Mandeville, Northants., 1610–1. R. of Kislingbury, Oxon., 1611–46, sequestered; and of Wigginton, 1612. Married, Jan. 5, 1608–9, at Cropredy, Philip Swyfte. Buried at Kislingbury, Apr. 26, 1651. (*Al. Oxon.*)

HOLLOWAY, HENRY. Adm. sizar (age 20) at ST JOHN'S, Oct. 20, 1670 (previously adm. at Hart Hall, Oxford, Oct. 14, 1669). S. of Jonadab, of St Clement Danes, London, gun-maker, deceased (whose will, P.C.C., 1669). School, Winchester. Matric. 1670. Returned to Oxford. B.A. (Hart Hall) 1674; M.A. (from Magdalen College) 1677. V. of Portsea, Hants., 1675. R. of Laverstoke, 1691. (*Al. Oxon.*)

HOLLOWAY, THOMAS. M.A. 1608 (Incorp. from Oxford). Of Worcestershire, pleb. Matric. from Balliol College, Oxford, Apr. 4, 1600, age 15; B.A. (Oxford) 1603; M.A. 1606; B.D. 1613; D.D. 1616. V. of St Laurence, Old Jewry, London, till Aug. 1616. Will (P.C.C.) 1616.

HOLLOWAY, THOMAS. Adm. sizar at TRINITY, July 7, 1645. (Previously matric. from University College, Oxford, June 8, 1638, age 15.) Probably s. of Thomas, of Leverton, Berks. Matric. 1645; B.A. 1645-6; M.A. 1649. Chaplain of Trinity College, 1648.

HOLLY, BENJAMIN. Adm. Fell.-Com. (age 17) at CAIUS, Oct. 13, 1657. S. of Benjamin, gent, of Lynn. Bapt. there, Apr. 17, 1640. School, Lynn (Mr Bell). Matric. 1657. Adm. at Gray's Inn, Mar. 24, 1659-60. (*Venn*, I. 399.)

HOLIE, RICHARD. Matric. sizar from ST JOHN'S, Easter, 1589.

HOLLY, WILLIAM. Adm. pens. at EMMANUEL, Dec. 18, 1703. Of Norfolk. S. of William, of Lynn (mayor of Lynn). B. 1686. School, Lynn. Matric. 1704. Made freeman of Lynn, in 1708. Died Apr. 2, 1735. (G. H. Holley.)

HOLMAN, *see also* HALMAN.

HOLMAN, DIGORY. Matric. pens. from PEMBROKE, Easter, 1615. Afterwards matric. from Exeter College, Oxford, Oct. 24, 1617, age 17; B.A. from Trinity Hall, 1619-20. Probably Incorp. at Oxford, 1622, as 'Francis.'

HOLMAN, EDWARD. Adm. pens. at EMMANUEL, Nov. 8, 1658. Of Norfolk. Matric. 1657.

HOLMAN, EVERARD. Matric. pens. from CLARE, Michs. 1626; B.A. 1630-1; M.A. 1634. Admon. (Leicester) 1644; of Kirby Bellars, Leics.; to brother Leonard (1629-30). (J. Ch. Smith.)

HOLMAN, GEOFFREY. Adm. Fell.-Com. (age 19) at SIDNEY, Sept. 13, 1641. S. of George, perfumer, of Pendhill, Bletchingley, Surrey, deceased. B. at Godston, Surrey. School, Cockham, Kent (Mr Knight). Died May 1, 1644. M.I. at Bletchingley. (*Vis. of Surrey*, 1623; *Manning and Bray*, II. 307.)

HOLLMAN, JOHN. Matric. pens. from KING'S, Easter, 1618. One of these names s. of Philip, a scrivener, of London, adm. at the Inner Temple, 1619.

HOLMAN, JOHN. Adm. pens. at EMMANUEL, Sept. 28, 1639. Of Sussex. Matric. 1640; B.A. 1643.

HOLMAN, JOHN. Adm. Fell.-Com. at TRINITY, Nov. 24, 1651. Of Northamptonshire. 2nd s. of Philip, of Warkworth, Northants. Knighted, 1661. M.P. for Banbury, 1661-81. Created Bart., June 1, 1663. Married Jane, dau. of Samuel Fortrey (? Forbes), of Surrey, Esq. Died 1700. Probably brother of —— Holeman (1647). (*G.E.C.*; *Baker*, I. 740.)

HOLMAN, JOHN. Adm. pens. (age 17) at PEMBROKE, July 4, 1718. S. of John, of Tenterden, Kent, gent. Matric. 1719; LL.B. 1724. Ord. deacon (Lincoln) Mar. 17, 1727-8; priest, Mar. 25, 1728. R. of Limpsfield, Surrey, 1728-57. R. of Tatsfield, 1728-57. Died 1757.

HOLMAN, LEONARD. Matric. pens. from CLARE, Lent, 1629-30; B.A. 1633-4; M.A. 1637. R. of Goadby, Leics., 1643-56. Buried there Jan. 1655-6. Admon. (Leicester) 1661. Brother of Everard (1626).

HOLMAN, MICHAEL. Adm. pens. at TRINITY, Mar. 7, 1645-6. Of Middlesex. S. and h. of Michael, of Whitton, Middlesex, Esq. Matric. 1646; Scholar, 1647. Adm. at Lincoln's Inn, Jan. 2, 1649-50; and at the Inner Temple, 1651. Barrister, 1658. (*Vis. of London*, 1634.)

HOLMAN, NICHOLAS, *see* HALMAN.

HOLMAN, RICHARD. Adm. pens. (age 18) at ST JOHN'S, June 13, 1687. S. of Matthew, gent. B. at Hawkhurst, Kent. School, Sutton (Mr Foster). Matric. 1687.

HOLMAN, WILLIAM. Adm. pens. (age 18) at ST JOHN'S, Oct. 23, 1648. S. of Robert, grazier, of Beckley, Sussex. B. there. School, Tonbridge (Mr Horne). Matric. 1648.

HOLEMAN, ——. Adm. Fell.-Com. at TRINITY, Nov. 10, 1647. Of Northamptonshire. Probably George, s. and h. of Philip, of Warkworth, Northants. Married Anostatici, dau. of William (Howard), Viscount Stafford. Died May 19, 1698, aged 67. M.I. at Warkworth. Probably brother of John (1651). (*Baker*, I. 740.)

HOLMDENE, JOHN. Matric. pens. from ST JOHN'S, Michs. 1568.

HOLMDEN, JOHN. Matric. pens. from KING'S, Michs. 1645. Perhaps adm. at the Inner Temple, 1646; s. and h. of Sir Thomas, Knt., of Limpsfield, Surrey. Of Tencheleys, Surrey. Married, 1662, Sarah Middleton. Died 1692. (Burke, *L.G.*)

HOLMDEN, JOHN. Matric. pens. from QUEENS', Michs. 1650. Of Surrey. B.A. 1653-4; M.A. 1657. One of these names s. and h. of Robert, of Brookehouse, Kent, Esq. Adm. at Lincoln's Inn, July 1, 1656.

HOLMEDEN, ROBERT. Adm. Fell.-Com. at PETERHOUSE, Apr. 29, 1623. Probably s. and h. of Henry, of London, Esq., deceased (probably citizen and leather-seller, of Grace Church St; will, P.C.C. 1606). Matric. 1623. Adm. at Lincoln's Inn, Feb. 1, 1625-6.

HOLMDEN, THOMAS. Matric. pens. from KING'S, Easter, 1603 (adm. as 'Handen, of Hackney'). Probably adm. at the Inner Temple, 1605.

HOLMDEN, THOMAS. Matric. Fell.-Com. from KING'S, Michs. 1645.

HOLME, ADAM DE, *see* WICKMERE.

HOLMES, ADAM. Adm. pens. (age 18) at CAIUS, June 20, 1579. S. of William, yeoman. B. at Bishop Wearmouth, Durham. School, Durham. Married Alice, dau. of George Dale, of Dalton-le-Dale. Buried at Bishop Wearmouth, Dec. 13, 1618. Will (Durham) 1619. Twin-brother of Nicholas. (*Vis. of Cambs.*, 1619; *Vis. of Yorks.*, 1564; *Antiquities of Sunderland*, III. 96.)

HOLMES, ANTHONY. B.A. 1530-1; M.A. 1534. Ord. priest (Lincoln) 1536. R. of Normanby, Lincs. R. of Oadby, Leics. Will (Lincoln) 1588.

HOLMES, BARNEHAM. Matric. sizar from TRINITY, 1645. B.A. 1647. Created M.A. from Magdalen Hall, Oxford, 1648. R. of Armthorpe, Yorks., 1648; there in 1662.

HOLME or HULME, BENJAMIN. Adm. sizar (age 12) at JESUS, June 21, 1680. Of Lancashire. S. of James, nonconformist minister, some time of Leigh. Migrated to Oxford. Matric. from Brasenose College, Mar. 10, 1681-2, age 14. Taken by his father to Holland to be trained for the ministry. Entered at Leyden, July 27, 1684. Pastor at Uxbridge, Middlesex. Died Oct. 5, 1691. Buried at Bunhill Fields. M.I. (E. Axon; H. G. Harrison.)

HOLMES or HOLME, CHRISTOPHER. Adm. pens. at SIDNEY, May 28, 1610. Matric. 1611. Perhaps s. of Henry, of Paull Holme, Yorks., age 21 in 1612. Royalist. Lived in the garrison of York. Compounded, and fined £350, 1646. Married Margaret, dau. of Sir John Langton, of Langton, Leics., 1620. Died 1665. (*Vis. of Yorks.*, 1665; Poulson, *Holderness*, II. 488.)

HOLMES, CHRISTOPHER. Adm. pens. at CLARE, Apr. 8, 1656. Matric. 1656; B.A. 1659-60; M.A. 1663; B.D. 1671 (*Lit. Reg.*). Master of Little Thurlow School, Suffolk, 1659. Ord. priest Dec. 17, 1660. R. of Little Bradley, Suffolk, 1660. V. of Gt Thurlow, 1666-87. Died 1687.

HOLME, EDWARD. B.A. 1517-8; M.A. 1520. Of Yorkshire. Scholar and fellow of KING'S HALL. Left, 1528. Ord. priest (Lincoln) Mar. 26, 1524.

HOLMES, EDWARD. Matric. sizar from ST JOHN'S, Easter, 1613. Of Yorkshire. Probably s. of Henry, of Paull Holme, Esq. B.A. 1616-7; M.A. 1620. Fellow, 1620. (M. H. Peacock.)

HOLMES, EDWARD. Adm. sizar (age 16) at CAIUS, May 16, 1637. S. of John, gent. B. at Dickleborough, Norfolk. School, Diss (Mr Lancetter). B.A. 1641-2; M.A. 1645. R. of Morningthorpe, Norfolk, 1645; commended by the Parliamentary Committee. (*Venn*, I. 326.)

HOLMES, EDWARD. Adm. sizar (age 19) at ST JOHN'S, June 6, 1722. S. of John, hosier, of Yorkshire. B. at Sedbergh. School, Sedbergh (Mr Saunders). Matric. 1722; B.A. 1725-6; M.A. 1729. Ord. priest (Lincoln) May 26, 1728; C. of Ayott, Herts.

HOLMES, FRANCIS. Matric. pens. from QUEENS', Michs. 1580. Of Yorkshire. Perhaps s. and h. of John, of Hampole, Yorks. Francis Holmes, of Hampole, married, Apr. 17, 1582, Agnes, dau. of Martin Aune, Esq., of Frickley, Yorks. Brother of William (1580). (*Vis. of Yorks.*)

HOLMES, FRANCIS. Adm. pens. (age 19) at ST JOHN'S, June 27, 1651. S. of John, gent., of Owston, Yorks. B. there. School, Selby (private; Mr Masgill). Matric. 1651.

HOLMES, GEORGE. Matric. sizar from TRINITY, Easter, 1611; B.A. 1613-4; M.A. 1617. Ord. deacon (York) Sept. 1617; priest, Dec. 1617. R. of Armthorpe, Yorks., 1617. R. of Little Sandal, 1626-43. Married, 1617, Elizabeth Postiethwaite, of Armthorpe. (M. H. Peacock.)

HOLMES, GERVASE. Adm. sizar at EMMANUEL, Mar. 24, 1714-5. Of Wigtoft, Lincs. Matric. 1715; B.A. 1718-9; M.A. 1722; B.D. 1729. Fellow, 1721. Ord. deacon (Ely) June 14, 1724; priest, June 11, 1727. R. of Withersdale, Suffolk. V. of Fressingfield, 1738-76. Died Aug. 1776, aged 85. (*Cole MSS.*, 5872, 13.)

HOLMES or HOLME, GILBERT. Matric. pens. from ST JOHN'S, Michs. 1555. Of Yorkshire. B.A. 1559-60; M.A. 1563 (died before admission). Fellow, 1562-3. Ord. deacon (Ely) July 7, 1560.

HOLMES, HENRY. Matric. pens. from ST JOHN'S, Lent, 1584-5.

HOLMES, HENRY. Matric. pens. from ST JOHN'S, Michs. 1610; B.A. 1613-4. Migrated to Peterhouse, July 1, 1615. M.A. 1617.

HOLMES, HENRY. Adm. pens. (age 18) at ST JOHN'S, Apr. 22, 1654. S. of Henry, merchant, of Newcastle-on-Tyne. B. there. Bapt. at All Saints', May 21, 1637. School, Houghton-le-Spring. Matric. 1654. Adm. at Lincoln's Inn, Aug. 25, 1654.

HOLMES or HOLME, HENRY. Adm. pens. at TRINITY, Oct. 26, 1667. S. of Henry, of Paull Holme, Yorks., age 14 in 1665. Matric. 1667-8; B.A. 1671-2; M.A. 1675. Ord. priest (York) Sept. 1675. V. of Cottingham, Yorks., 1673-99. V. of Burstwick, 1678-91. Married Beatrix, dau. of Christopher Stoke, D.D., Chancellor of York. (*Vis. of York*, 1665; M. H. Peacock.)

HOLMES, HENRY. Adm. sizar (age 15) at ST JOHN'S, May 19, 1690. S. of Henry, husbandman. B. at Sedbergh, Yorks. School, Sedbergh (Mr Wharton). Matric. 1690; B.A. 1693-4; M.A. 1697. Perhaps R. of Waberthwaite, Cumberland, 1698-1719. Married Frances, widow of Rev. William Grainger, Apr. 13, 1702. Buried at Waberthwaite, Apr. 7, 1719. (E. Axon.)

HOLME, HENRY. Adm. sizar (age 16) at TRINITY, June 9, 1712. S. of George, of Penrith, Cumberland. School, Newcastle-on-Tyne (Mr Jurin). Matric. 1712; Scholar, 1714; B.A. 1715-6; M.A. 1719; B.D. 1727. Fellow, 1718. Taxor, 1721. Ord. deacon (Lincoln) Sept. 19, 1725; priest, June 5, 1726. V. of Barrington, Cambs., 1734. Died 1737.

HOLMES, HENRY. Adm. sizar at CHRIST'S, July 1, 1721. School, Skipton. Matric. 1721; Scholar, 1722; B.A. 1724-5. Perhaps ord. priest (Lincoln) June 9, 1734. 'V. of Severby and Burnby, Lincs., 1734.'

HOLME, HUGH. Adm. pens. (age 18) at ST JOHN'S, May 4, 1726. S. of Edward, attorney, of Holland House, Upholland, Lancs. B. there. Bapt. Sept. 17, 1707. School, Winwick (Mr Wright). Matric. 1726. Adm. at the Inner Temple, May 9, 1726. Married, Feb. 14, 1731-2, Anne, dau. of Thomas Bankes, of Winstanley Hall.

HOLME, JOHN DE. Scholar at KING'S HALL, 1417. Bachelor (arts or law) in 1420. Left, 1429. Brother of Richard (1406), the Warden.

HOLME, JOHN. Matric. pens. from ST JOHN'S, Michs. 1567. One of these names R. of Wickham Episcopi, Essex, 1569. Will (Cons. C. London) 1600. (J. Ch. Smith.)

HOLME, JOHN. Matric. sizar from CHRIST'S, June, 1584. A north country man. B.A. 1587-8; M.A. 1591. One of these names V. of Ampleforth, Yorks., 1623. Author, *Sermon*, 1592. (*Peile*, I. 179; *Cooper*, II. 146.)

HOLME, JOHN. Matric. sizar from TRINITY, Michs. 1589.

HOLMES, JOHN. Matric. sizar from CLARE, Easter, 1614; B.A. 1617-8; M.A. 1621. Ord. deacon and priest (York) Feb. 1618-9. Licensed to teach at Thirsk, Yorks., Nov. 13, 1618. One of these names, M.A., buried at Hatfield, Yorks., 1680.

HOLMES, JOHN. Adm. pens. (age 17) at CAIUS, Oct. 4, 1643. S. of William, gent., of Shotesham, Norfolk. Schools, Bungay (Mr Creed) and Norwich (Mr Lovering). Matric. 1644; B.A. 1647-8; M.A. 1651. Fellow, 1650-2. Signed for deacon (Norwich) Apr. 25; for priest, May 26, 1670, age 40. R. of Sisland, Norfolk, 1670-3. Will proved (Norwich); of Loddon, May 26, 1673. (*Venn*, I. 351.)

HOLMES, JOHN. Adm. sizar (age 17) at SIDNEY, June 26, 1656. S. of John, Esq. B. at Thornhirst, Doncaster. Schools, Selby (Mr Alex. Mascall) and Doncaster (Mr Marm. Cooke). Matric. 1656; B.A. 1660. One of these names V. of Paull, Yorks., 1680-1701. Perhaps V. of North Clifton, Yorks.; recorded as a non-juror.

HOLME, JOHN. 'Of EMMANUEL' when ord. deacon (York) Sept. 1700; and 'of St John's' when ord. priest, May, 1708. (Not found in our records.)

HOLME, JOHN. Adm. sizar (age 18) at PETERHOUSE, Mar. 11, 1726-7. Of Yorkshire. School, Beverley. Matric. 1727; Scholar, 1727; B.A. 1731-2. *Litt. dim.* from York for deacon, Feb. 1731-2. C. of Doncaster. Perhaps priest (York) Aug. 5, 1733. R. of Kirk or Little Sandal, Yorks., 1748, till 1761. Died 1761.

HOLME, JOHN. Adm. pens. (age 17) at ST JOHN'S, May 23, 1728. S. of John, gent., of Skeffling, Holderness, Yorks. B. at Iklingtou. School, Beverley (Mr Jefferson). Matric. 1728; B.A. 1731-2; M.A. 1735; B.D. 1742. Fellow, 1736-57. Ord. deacon (Lincoln) Sept. 22, 1734; priest, Dec. 21, 1735. V. of Ulrome, Yorks., 1745-75. R. of Huggate, 1752-60. R. of Brandesburton, 1755-75. R. of Barmston, 1760-75. Died Nov. 25, 1775. M.I. at Skeffling. (*Scott-Mayor*, III. 417.)

HOLMES, JOHN. Adm. sizar (age 18) at TRINITY, May 21, 1746. S. of Gervase, of Rampton, Notts. School Rampton (Mr Howlet). Matric. 1747; Scholar, 1748; B.A. 1749-50; M.A. 1753. Ord. priest (Lincoln) Feb. 23, 1752. Senior vicar-choral of Southwell. R. of Beilsby, Lincs. V. of Farnsfield and Kirklington, Notts. Died Sept. 1784. (*G. Mag.*)

HOLMES, JOSEPH. Adm. sizar (age 17) at ST JOHN'S, Mar. 26, 1722. S. of Joseph, maltster, of Yorkshire. B. ataLightcliffe, Halifax. School, Threshfield (Mr Marshall). M tric. 1723. Probably buried at All Saints', Cambridge, Feb. 13, 1724-5, as 'John.'

HOLMES, LEONARD. Incorp. M.A. 1680, from Glasgow.

HOLMES or HOLME, MARMADUKE. Adm. sizar (age 19) at ST JOHN'S, May 9, 1700. S. of John, tailor. B. at Sedbergh, Yorks. School, Sedbergh. Matric. 1700; B.A. 1703-4. Master of Ravenstonedale Grammar School, 1704-7. Perhaps R. of Cliburn, Westmorland, 1739-60. Died 1760.

HOLMES, MATTHEW. Perhaps adm. at PETERHOUSE, Aug. 2, 1561. B.A. when ord. priest (Ely) Apr. 16, 1568. One of these names, 'chaunter of Westminster Abbey,' buried there Aug. 6, 1621. Will, P.C.C. (J. Ch. Smith.)

HOLMES or HOMES, NATHANIEL. D.D. 1658 (Incorp. from Oxford). Of Wiltshire. S. of George, clerk, of Kingswood, Wilts. Matric. from Magdalen Hall, Oxford, Apr. 11, 1617, age 18; B.A. (Exeter College) 1620; M.A. (Magdalen Hall) 1623; B.D. 1633; D.D. 1637. R. of Whipsnade, Beds., 1631-42. R. of St Mary Staining, London, 1643-62, ejected. Became a Millenarian and joined Henry Burton, B.D., in establishing an independent congregation, 1643. Went to reside in the parish of St Giles', Cripplegate, 1662. Author of Millenarian works. Died June, 1678. Buried in St Mary Aldermanbury. (*D.N.*B.)

HOLMES, NICHOLAS. Adm. pens. (age 18) at CAIUS, June 20, 1579. S. of William, yeoman. B. at Bishop Wearmouth, Durham. School, Durham. Buried at Monkwearmouth, Oct. 31, 1603. Twin-brother of Adam (1579). (*Vis. of Cambs.*, 1619; *Vis. of Yorks.*, 1564.)

HOLME, PORTER. Adm. pens. (age 16) at PEMBROKE, June 30, 1680. S. of John, of London, chemist. Matric. 1681; B.A. 1683-4.

HOLMES, RALPH. Adm. sizar (age 16) at PETERHOUSE, May 12, 1638. Of Yorkshire. Matric. 1639. (*T. A. Walker.*)

HOLM, RICHARD DE. 'KING'S scholar' at Cambridge, 1325. Left, Dec. 3, 1328.

HOLME, RICHARD. Scholar at KING'S HALL, 1406; LL.B.; Warden, 1417-24. R. of Wearmouth, Durham. Preb. of York, 1393-1424. Employed in political missions. Will dated at Cambridge, Apr. 18, 1424. Brother of John (1417). (*Test Ebor.*, I. 405 and III. 58; *Lambeth.*)

HOLME, RICHARD. Matric. pens. from ST JOHN'S, Easter, 1560.

HOLME, RICHARD. Adm. sizar (age 16) at ST JOHN'S, June 11, 1672. S. of James, of Sedbergh, Yorks. B. there. School, Sedbergh (Mr Fell). Matric. 1672; B.A. 1675-6; M.A. 1679. Ord. deacon (Carlisle) Mar. 7, 1676-7. V. of Aspatria, Cumberland, 1686-95. R. of Lowther, Westmorland, 1694-1738. V. of Aikton, Cumberland, 1707-38. Preb. of Carlisle, 1727-38. Buried at Lowther, Nov. 10, 1738. Will dated, 1735. Benefactor to Sedbergh School. (B. Nightingale.)

HOLMES, RICHARD. Adm. sizar (age 16) at ST JOHN'S, Apr. 30, 1747. S. of Henry, druggist, of Derbyshire. B. at Derby. School, Mansfield, Notts. (Mr Depleidge). Matric. 1747; B.A. 1750-1. Ord. deacon (Lichfield) June 9, 1754; priest, Sept. 24, 1758. C. of Sawley, Derbs. (*Scott-Mayor*, III. 566.)

HOLME, ROBERT. Matric. Fell.-Com. at CHRIST'S, Nov. 1559. One of these names V. of Leamington; resigned, 1570. One, R. of Greensted, near Colchester, 1586-9; and of St James', Colchester, 1586-91. (*Peile*, I. 69.)

HOLMES, ROBERT. Adm. pens. at SIDNEY, June, 1601. Of Yorkshire. Matric. 1601. Probably adm. at Gray's Inn, Feb. 4, 1602-3; s. of Seth, of Huntingdon, Yorks. Perhaps of Barnby, Yorks., Esq. Married Joan, dau. of Richard Beaumont, of Emley. (M. H. Peacock.)

HOLMES, ROBERT. Adm. sizar (age 16) at ST JOHN'S, July 8, 1681. S. of Christopher (? 1656), clerk. B. at Little Thurlow, Suffolk. School, Peterborough (Mr Ro. Smith). Matric. 1682; B.A. 1685-6; M.A. 1689.

HOLMES, ROGER. B.Civ.L. 1534-5.

HOLME, ROGER. Adm. sizar (age 16) at SIDNEY, June 21, 1628. S. of John, dyer. B. at Ripon, Yorks. School, Ripon (Mr Palmer). B.A. 1631-2; M.A. 1635. Ord. priest (Peterb.) June 9, 1639. Head Master of Ripon School, 1650-61.

HOLMES, SAMUEL. B.A. from MAGDALENE, 1667-8; M.A. 1684. Probably V. of Childerditch, Essex, 1695-1709. Died 1709.

HOMES, THOMAS. B.A. from TRINITY HALL, 1547-8.

HOLMES, THOMAS. Matric. sizar from QUEENS', Michs. 1583. Of Leicestershire. Probably ord. deacon (Lincoln) May 2; priest, May 31, 1591. V, of St Martin, Leicester, 1626-34. Buried there Mar. 3, 1633-4. Will (Leicester) 1634. (J. Ch. Smith.)

HOLME, THOMAS. Matric. pens. from TRINITY, *c.* 1593. Perhaps migrated to Oxford. B.A. from Broadgates Hall, 1596-7; M.A. 1601.

HOLMES or HOLME, THOMAS. Adm. sizar at SIDNEY, May, 1602. Of Yorkshire. Matric. 1602; B.A. 1605-6. Probably ord. deacon (Lincoln) Dec. 20, 1612. C. of Gt Ponton, Lincs., in 1614. One of these names (B.A.), V. of Rocester, Staffs., *c.* 1629.

HOLMES, THOMAS. Matric. pens. from QUEENS', Easter, 1604. Of Essex. B.A. 1606-7; M.A. 1610. Ord. deacon (Peterb.) Sept. 26, 1616. Perhaps ord. priest (Peterb.) Apr. 19, 1617.

HOLMES, THOMAS. Adm. pens. at EMMANUEL, Apr. 29, 1609. Probably became Fell.-Com. Nov. 24, 1611. S. of Christopher, late of London, gent. Matric. 1609. Adm. at Gray's Inn, May 14, 1612. The father seems to have been a citizen and haberdasher, of London. His will (P.C.C., 1597) mentions s. Thomas, a minor. (J. Ch. Smith.)

HOLMES, THOMAS. Adm. sizar (age 17) at CAIUS, Oct. 3, 1701. S. of Thomas, gent., of Mundham, Norfolk. B. there. Schools, Carlton (Mr Pullyn) and Wymondham (Mr Clarke). Matric. 1701; Scholar, 1701-9; B.A. 1705-6; M.A. 1709. Ord. deacon (Norwich) June 8, 1707; priest, June 19, 1709. R. of Fritton, Norfolk, 1715-29; of Flordon, 1719-29. Died Aug. 1729. Buried at Fritton. (*Venn*, I. 508.)

HOLME, THOMAS. Adm. sizar (age 15) at ST JOHN'S, June 7, 1748. S. of Thomas, clerk, of Lancashire, Master of Wellingborough School, and V. of Kirkby Ireleth, in Furness. Bapt. at Kirkby, July 29, 1732. School, Wellingborough, under his father. Matrie. 1749; B.A. 1752. P.C. of St Thomas the Martyr, Upholland, Lancs., 1758-67. Probably R. of Blyborough, Lincs., 1769. R. of Covenham St Mary, 1769-98. Died Aug. 17, 1803. (*Scott-Mayor*, III. 578; E. Axon.)

HOLMES, WALTER. Matric. pens. from TRINITY, Michs. 1612; scholar from Westminster. B. in St Andrew's, Holborn. B.A. 1616-7; M.A. 1622. Ord. priest (London) Dec. 23, 1621, age 25. Schoolmaster at St Olave, Silver St. V. of Frindsbury, Kent, 1620-6. V. of Southchurch, Essex, 1626.

HOLME, WILLIAM. B.A. from CLARE, 1578-9.

HOLMES, WILLIAM. Matric. pens. from QUEENS', Michs. 1580. Of Yorkshire. Probably 2nd s. of John; adm. at Lincoln's Inn, Oct. 26, 1584, from Furnival's Inn. Brother of Francis (1580). ('Holmes of Hampole,' in *Vis. of Yorks.*, 1585.)

HOLMES, WILLIAM. Matric. sizar from QUEENS', Easter, 1607. Of Cambridgeshire. B.A. 1610-1; M.A. 1614; B.D. 1623. Fellow, 1617-23. Ord. deacon (Peterb.) Jan. 3, 1616-7; priest, Sept. 21, 1617. V. of Meldreth, Cambs., 1617. V. of Raunds, Northants., 1623, sequestered. Buried there June 9, 1653. M.I. Will (Archd. Northants.) proved, 1672, by widow Margaret. (*Bridges*, II. 187; H. I. Longden.)

HOLMES or HOLME, WILLIAM. Adm. sizar at EMMANUEL, Dec. 11, 1632. Of Lancashire. Matric. 1632; B.A. 1636-7; M.A. 1640. Ord. deacon (Peterb.) Dec. 22, 1639; priest, Mar. 1, 1639-40. One of these names intruded V. of Guilsborough, Northants., 1645-60. Perhaps V. of Mears Ashby, 1661-70. R. of Rushden, 1670-86. (H. I. Longden.)

HOLMES, WILLIAM. Adm. pens. at TRINITY HALL, July 3, 1679. 1st s. of Jonathan, R. of Cruwys-Morchard, Devon. B. there. Schools, Tiverton and Exburn (private). Migrated to Sidney, Apr. 7, 1680, age 18. Matric. 1680; B.A. 1682-3.

HOLMES, WILLIAM. Adm. sizar (age 24) at TRINITY, Jan. 25, 1742-3. S. of William, of Pontefract, Yorks. School, Burnsall (Mr Allcock). Became a 'ten-year-man,' 1746. Ord. priest (York) May 25, 1746. C. of Ferry Fryston. C. of Pontefract and Knottingley, to 1777. Perhaps V. of Thorner, Yorks., 1770-7. Died July 31, 1777.

HOLME, ——. M.A. or higher degree, 1460-1.

HOME, —— (*senior*). Matric. sizar from CHRIST'S, Nov. 1544.

HOME, —— (*junior*). Matric. sizar from CHRIST'S, Nov. 1544. This, or the above, B.A. from Trinity Hall, 1547-8, as 'Thomas Homes.' *See* shove.

HOLME, HOLMES or HELME, ——. Resident at PETERHOUSE, Aug. 1561.

HOLNEY, JOHN. Matric. sizar from PEMBROKE, Easter, 1611; B.A. 1614-5. Probably V. of Witley, Surrey; and father of John (1640).

HOLNEY, JOHN. Matric. sizar (age 17) from PEMBROKE, Michs. 1635. S. of John, of Boxgrove, Suffolk. B.A. 1638-9; M.A. 1642. Fellow, 1635; ejected, 1644.

HOLNEY, JOHN. Matric. sizar (age 18) from PEMBROKE, Easter, 1640. S. of John (1611), V. of Witley, Surrey. B. there. B.A. 1644-5. Probably C. of West Thorney. R. of Dunsfold, Surrey, 1652-80. Buried there Oct. 6, 1680. (H. G. Harrison.)

HOLNEY, JOHN. Adm. sizar at MAGDALENE, July 6, 1646. Migrated to Clare, Oct. 2, 1647. Matric. 1647-8.

HOLNEY, JOHN. Adm. sizar at JESUS, Apr. 26, 1667. B. at Hurstpierpoint, Sussex. Colleger at Eton, 1664. Matric. 1667; Scholar, 1670; B.A. 1670-1; M.A. 1674. Fellow, 1674-83. Signed for deacon's orders (London) Mar. 13, 1673-4. V. of Whittlesford, Cambs., 1680-2. Buried in the College Chapel, Nov. 6, 1682. Will proved (V.C.C.). (A. Gray.)

HOLOREN, ——. Matric. sizar from ST JOHN'S, Michs. 1609.

HOLROYD, *see* **HOLDRED.**

HOLSTEED, WILLIAM. Matric. sizar from ST JOHN'S, *c.* 1594.

HOLT, ARTHUR. Adm. sizar (ag 20) at CHRIST'S, Dec. 8, 1716. Afterwards pens. and Fell-Com. S. of Joseph (1684). B. in Virginia. School, Sedbergh. Scholar, 1717; LL.B. 1723. Ord. deacon (York) Sept. 1718; priest, Sept. 1719. (*Peile*, II. 190.)

HOLT, CHARLES. Adm. pens. at EMMANUEL, Feb. 13, 1590-1. Matric. *c.* 1591.

HOLT, CHRISTOPHER. Adm. sizar at ST CATHARINE'S, July 10, 1696. Matric. 1696; B.A. 1699-1700. Ord. deacon (York) May, 1700; priest, 1702. V. of Burley-in-Wharfedale, Yorks., 1703-20. V. of Calverley, 1720-41. Died Jan. 9, 1741, aged 69.

HOULT, EDMUND. Adm. sizar at EMMANUEL, May 28, 1588. Matric. 1588. Probably 'of Lancaster,' in 1613. Perhaps father of Ellis (1613).

HOLTE, EDWARD. B.A. 1527-8; M.A. 1530. Will of one of these names (P.C.C.) 1531; of St Mary in the Market-place (? Cambridge) clerk.

HOLT, ELLIS. Adm. sizar (age 18) at CAIUS, July 2, 1613. S. of Edmund (? 1588), of Lancaster. Matric. 1614; B.A. 1616-7; M.A. 1620. Usher at Ipswich Grammar School, 1623-30. Licensed to teach grammar at Ipswich, 1627. (*Venn*, I. 221.)

HOLTE, FRANCIS. Matric. pens. from ST JOHN'S, Michs. 1566. Of Lancashire. Probably 2nd s. of Francis, of Grislehurst. B.A. 1569-70; M.A. 1573; B.D. 1580. Fellow, 1573. Ord. deacon (London); priest (Ely) Apr. 29, 1576. V. of Boxworth, Cambs., 1576. Probably brother of Ralph (1577-8) and John (1577-8). (*Vis. of Lancs.*, 1567.)

HOLT, FRANCIS. LL.B. from TRINITY HALL, 1679. Probably S. of Thomas (1622), of Wells, Somerset, D.D. Matric. from College, Oxford, Dec. 4, 1674, age 18. (*Al. Oxon.*)Trinity

HOLT, GILBERT. Adm. scholar at TRINITY HALL, Apr. 12, 1680. Matric. 1680; B.A. 1683-4; M.A. 1687. Probably chaplain to the Hon. Sackville Tufton, of Newbottle, Northants. (H. I. Longden.)

HOLT, HENRY. Matric. sizar from QUEENS', Michs. 1612. Of Derbyshire.

HOLT, HENRY. Adm. pens. (age 19) at ST JOHN'S, Dec. 7, 1720. 4th s. of Rowland, protonotary of the King's Bench, of Redgrave, Suffolk. B. in London. Schools, Botesdale, Suffolk and Eton. Matric. 1720. Brother of John (1709). (Le Neve, *Knights*, 33.)

HOULT, HENRY. Matrie. Fell.-Com. from CHRIST'S, Easter, 1722.

HOULT, JAMES. Matric. pens. from ST JOHN'S, Michs. 1568; B.A. from Magdalene, 1574-5. One of these names V. of Thriplow, Cambs., 1573.

HOLT, JAMES. M.A. 1634 (Incorp. from Oxford). Of Surrey, gent. Matric. from Corpus Christi, Oxford, Nov. 9, 1621, age 15; B.A. (Oxford) 1624-5; M.A. 1627-8. R. of Cranley, Surrey, 1633-45, sequestered. Died *c.* Sept. 1645. (*Al. Oxon.*; *Surrey Arch. Soc.*, IX. 267.)

HOLTE, JEREMIAH. Matric. sizar from ST JOHN'S, *c.* 1596. Of Suffolk. B.A. 1599-1600; M.A. 1603; B.D. 1610. Fellow, 1603. Incorp. at Oxford, 1608. R. of Horton, Bucks., 1612. R. of Stonham Aspal, Suffolk, 1613-44, ejected. R. of Thurlton, Norfolk (B.D.). Buried there Nov. 27 (year missing). (*Al. Oxon.*; *Blomefield*, X. 182.)

HOLT, JOHN. Matric. sizar from PEMBROKE, Easter, 1566; B.A. 1569-70; M.A. 1573; B.D. 1580. Fellow, 1570. Ord. deacon and priest (Peterb.) Aug. 30, 1573. V. of Trumpington, Cambs., 1573. Chaplain to Archbishop Whitgift. Perhaps R. of Bradfield Combust, Suffolk, 1573; and R. of Stanningfield, 1573. V. of St Stephen, Norwich, 1581. V. of Stokesby and Herringsby, 1584. V. of Thrigby, 1607.

HOULTE, JOHN. Matric. pens. from St John's, Lent, 1577-8. Probably 5th s. of Francis, of Grislehurst, Lancs. Brother of Francis (1566) and Ralph (1577-8). (J. J. Howard, *Vis. of Suffolk*, II. 50.)

HOULTE, JOHN. Matric. pens. from St John's, Michs. 1589; B.A. 1593-4; M.A. 1597. Incorp. at Oxford, 1597. One of these names (M.A.), R. of Welbury, Yorks., 1612-4.

HOULT, JOHN. Matric. Fell.-Com. from St John's, c. 1594. One of these names, of Stubley, Lancs., Esq., adm. at Gray's Inn, May 14, 1595. Perhaps s. of Charles, of Whitwall, Lancs. If so, married Dorothy, dau. of Nicholas Banastre, of Altham, Lancs. Died Aug. 31, 1622. (*Chetham Soc.*, LXXXV. 151; Fishwick, *Rochdale*, 428.)

HOLT, JOHN. Adm. Pens. of Peterhouse, 1598-9. In residence, 1599-1606. Matric. pens. from Pembroke, c. 1596; B.A. 1601-2; M.A. from Peterhouse, 1606. C. of West Wickham, Cambs., 1618.

HOLT, JOHN. Adm. sizar at Jesus, May 9, 1655. Of Cheshire. One of these names 'pastor' of Blackrod, Lancs., in 1658. One of these names V. of Tadcaster, Yorks., 1660. (*See* a contemporary in *Al. Oxon.*)

HOLT, JOHN. Adm. pens. (age 16) at St John's, Sept. 20, 1660. S. of Edward, R. of Alfold, Surrey (whose will, P.C.C., 1679). B. there. School, Westminster. Matric. 1660; B.A. 1664-5. Brother of Richard (1679).

HOLT, JOHN. Adm. pens. at Trinity, June 12, 1668; Scholar, 1669, from Westminster.

HOLT, JOHN. Adm. Fell.-Com. (age 16) at Peterhouse, Apr. 23, 1709. Of Middlesex. Doubtless s. and h. of Rowland, Chief Prothonotary of the King's Bench. School, Eton. Adm. at Gray's Inn, Nov. 1, 1703. Married Lady Jane, sister of Philip, Duke of Wharton, 1723. Buried at Redgrave, Suffolk, Feb. 3, 1728-9. Brother of Henry (1720). (*T. A. Walker*, 222; J. J. Howard, *Vis. of Suffolk*.)

HOULT, JOHN. Adm. scholar at Trinity Hall, Jan. 5, 1719-20. Matric. sizar Dec. 1719; B.A. 1722-3. Ord. deacon (York) Dec. 22, 1723; priest, Sept. 1726. C. of St Peter's, Nottingham, 1726.

HOLT, JOSEPH. Matric. sizar from St John's, Michs. 1626; B.A. 1629-30.

HOLT, JOSEPH. Adm. sizar at Jesus, June 4, 1684. Of Lancashire. B. 1668. Matric. 1684; B.A. 1688-9. Went to Virginia; in holy orders. Father of Arthur (1716). (A. Gray.)

HOULT, LEONARD. Matric. sizar from St John's, Easter, 1602.

HOULTE, RALPH. Matric. pens. from St John's, Lent, 1577-8. Probably 4th s. of Francis, of Grislehurst, Lancs. Adm. at Gray's Inn, from Staple Inn, June 3, 1589. Probably brother of Francis (1566) and John (1577-8). (*Vis. of Lancs.*, 1567.)

HOLT, RICHARD. Matric. sizar from St John's, Michs. 1573; B.A. 1577-8.

HOLTE, RICHARD. Matric. sizar from St John's, Easter, 1577; B.A. 1580-1. Probably V. of Rushall, Staffs., 1604-52.

HOLT, RICHARD. Adm. at King's (age 17) a scholar from Eton, July 18, 1609. Of Staines, Middlesex. Matric. 1609. Died as a student, about 1610. Brother of Thomas (1604).

HOLT, RICHARD. Adm. sizar (age 14) at Trinity, June 27, 1679. S. of Edward, R. of Alfold, Surrey. B. there, July 12, 1663. School, Merchant Taylors'. Matric. 1679; Scholar, 1681; B.A. 1682-3. Brother of John (1660).

HOLTE, ROBERT. Matric. sizar from St John's, Michs. 1561; B.A. 1564-5; M.A. 1568. Ord. deacon (Ely) July 29, 1565.

HOULT, ROGER. Matric. pens. from Magdalene, Easter, 1622.

HOLT, THOMAS. Matric. sizar from Christ's, Lent, 1563-4; B.A. 1566-7; M.A. from Pembroke, 1571. Reader at Welton, Lincs., in 1585. Admon. of one of these names (Lincoln) 1587; of Stainton-by-Langworth, Lincs., M.A.

HOLTE, THOMAS. Matric. sizar from Trinity, Easter, 1574; B.A. 1578-9.

HOLT, THOMAS. Matric. pens. from Pembroke, c. 1596.

HOLTE, THOMAS. Adm. at King's, a scholar from Eton, 1604. Doubtless s. of Richard, of Staines, whose will (P.C.C., 1611) mentions s. Thomas. B. at Staines, Middlesex. B.A. 1608; M.A. 1612. Fellow, 1607-22. Ord. deacon and priest (London) Sept. 19, 1619, age 33. V. of Ringwood, Hants., 1621-52. Died 1652. Brother of Richard (1609). (J. Ch. Smith.)

HOLT, THOMAS. M.A. 1622 (Incorp. from Oxford); D.D. 1665 *Lit. Reg.*). Probably 'of Oxon., gent.' Matric. from Magdalen College, Oxford, June 7, 1611, age 15; B.A. (Oxford) 1614; M.A. 1617; B.D. 1627. Fellow of Magdalen College, 1616-28. R. of Weston Zoyland, Somerset, 1638-42, ejected. R. of Lamyatt, 1641-86. Preb. of Wells, 1641-89; Chancellor, 1660-89. P.C. of Batcombe, Somerset, 1666-89. R. of Wraxall, 1686-9. Died 1689. Will (P.C.C.) 1689. Father of Francis (1679). (*Al. Oxon.*; Walker, *Sufferings*, 74; J. Ch. Smith.)

HOLT, THOMAS. Matric. sizar (age 15) from Pembroke, Easter, 1628. S. of Edward. B. at Peterborough. B.A. 1630-1; M.A. 1634. Ord. priest (Peterb.) Sept. 20, 1635.

HOLT, THOMAS. Matric. pens. from Queens', Easter, 1645. Of Hampshire. Migrated to St John's, Oxford, 1648. B.A. (Oxford) 1648; M.A. 1651. Fellow of St John's, Oxford, 1648. (*Al. Oxon.*)

HOLT, THOMAS. Adm. pens. (age 16) at St John's, Nov. 21, 1649. S. of Thomas, clerk, of Stamford. School, Stamford (Mr Humphries). Matric. 1650.

HOLT, THOMAS. M.A. 1680 (Incorp. from Oxford). S. of Thomas, of Petersfield, Hants., gent. Perhaps matric. from New Inn Hall, May 27, 1671, age 15; B.A. (Magdalen College) 1675; M.A. 1678. Perhaps R. of Streatham, Surrey, 1688-1710. Died Nov. 30, 1710, aged 56. M.I. at Streatham. Will, P.C.C. (*Al. Oxon.*; *Manning and Bray*, III. 395.)

HOLT, WILLIAM. M.A. 1573 (Incorp. from Oxford). B. in Lancashire, c. 1545. B.A. (Oxford) 1566; M.A. 1571-2. Fellow of Oriel, 1568. Went to Douay, 1574, where he was ord. priest. Adm. Jesuit, 1578. Intrigued with Lennox in Scotland, 1581-2; arrested but allowed to escape. R. of the College at Rome, 1586. Spanish agent at Brussels, 1588-98. Sent to Spain. Died at Barcelona, 1599. (*Cooper*, II. 284; *D.N.B.*)

HOLT, WILLIAM. Adm. sizar at Christ's, Apr. 6, 1670. B. at Kinoulton, Notts. School, Ashby-de-la-Zouch. Matric. 1670; B.A. 1673-4. Died in College. Buried Mar. 26, 1675, at Gt St Andrew's, Cambridge. (*Peile*, II. 28.)

HOLTBY, *see* HOULTBIE.

HOLTON, WILLIAM, *see* HOULTON.

HOLWELL, BENJAMIN. Adm. sizar at Emmanuel, Dec. 12, 1720. B. at Melton Mowbray, Leics., c. 1702. Matric. 1721; B.A. 1724-5. Ord. deacon (Peterb.) Feb. 21, 1724-5; priest (Lincoln) June 16, 1728, as 'Hollowell.' C. of Oakham, Rutland, 1725. C. of Nailstone, Leics., 1728-55. R. of Braunston, 1739-55. Died July 20, 1755, aged 54. M.I. at Nailstone. (*Nichols*, II. 108, IV. 809; H. I. Longden.)

HOLWELL, WILLIAM (1608), *see* HALLOWELL.

HOLWELL, WILLIAM. Adm. sizar at Emmanuel, Dec. 31, 1702. Of Leicestershire. Matric. 1702-3, as 'Howell'; B.A. 1706-7. Ord. deacon (Lincoln) June 8, 1707; priest (Peterb.) June 3, 1710; C. of Naseby, Northants. R. of Castle Carlton, Lincs., 1711; of Little Carlton, 1711; of Grimoldby, 1717.

HOLWEY, MOSES. Adm. pens. at St Catharine's, June 13, 1670; M.A. 1677 (*Lit. Reg.*). Incorp. at Oxford, 1677. Subscribed for priest's orders (Bristol) Dec. 17, 1677. R. of Michaelstow, Cornwall, 1678-95. Benefactor to St Catharine's. (*Cath. Coll. Hist.*, 155.)

HOLWEY, THOMAS. Adm. sizar at Queens', May 4, 1587. Of Dorset.

HOLWORTHY, DISBROWE. Adm. Fell.-Com. at Clare, June 6, 1718. S. and h. of Matthew, of Hackney. B. at Hackney, Middlesex. Adm. at the Middle Temple, Oct. 19, 1717. (Le Neve, *Knights*, 193.)

HOLYAR, JOHN. Matric. sizar from Trinity Hall, Michs. 1547.

HOLYER, ROBERT. Matric. pens. from St Catharine's, Michs. 1551.

HOLYMAN, LIONEL. Matric. pens. from Trinity, Michs. 1582. (Previously matric. from Magdalen Hall, Oxford, May 18, 1582.) Probably 2nd s. of Richard, citizen and mercer, of London, whose admon. (P.C.C.) 1572, refers to him as a minor. B. in London. School, St Paul's. B.A. 1585-6; M.A. 1589; B.D. from Corpus Christi, 1597. Said to have been D.D. Fellow of Corpus Christi, 1589-98. Incorp. at Oxford, 1594. University preacher, 1597. R. of Boyton, Wilts., 1600. R. of Sherrington, till 1609. Author, Greek and Latin verses. Died 1609. (*Cooper*, II. 270, III. 94; J. Ch. Smith.)

HOLYOKE or HOLLYOKE, FRANCIS. Adm. sizar at Emmanuel, Apr. 1, 1594. B. at Nether Whitacre, Warws. Migrated to Peterhouse, Lent, 1595-6. B.A. 1595-6; Matric. c. 1596; M.A. from Emmanuel, 1599. Ord. deacon (London) June 28; priest, June 29, 1601, age 28. C. of Thames Ditton, Surrey. R. of Southam, Warws., 1604; sequestered, c. 1642. Author of an Etymological Dictionary. According to *D.N.B.* (which does not mention his Cambridge career) he had been at Queen's College, Oxford, c. 1582; died Nov. 13, 1653, aged 87; and was buried at St Mary's, Warwick: dates which do not agree with his age at ordination.

HOLYWELL, *see* HALLIWELL.

HOME, ALEXANDER, *see* HUME.

HOMER, ATHELBERT Matric. pens. from Pembroke, Lent, 1564-5.

HOMER, ISAAC, *see* HONYWOOD.

HOMOCKE, ARTHUR. Matric. sizar from Clare, Michs. 1568.

HONDEN (? HOMDEN), GEORGE. Matric. Fell.-Com. from CLARE, c. 1596.

HONE, BARTHOLOMEW. Adm. pens. (age 15) at CAIUS, Feb. 16, 1602-3. S. of John (next), LL.D., Master in Chancery. B. in London. Schools, Eton and London (private; Mr Spight). Matric. 1603; B.A. 1605-6. Fellow, 1606-7. Incorp. M.A. at Oxford, 1621. Adm. at the Middle Temple, Aug. 8, 1605. Of Ewelme, Oxon., Esq. Married Jane, sister of Sir Edward Pinchon, of Writtle, Essex, Knt. (*Venn*, I. 181; *Vis. of Essex*, 1634.)

HONE, JOHN. Matric. pens. from CLARE, Michs. 1564. S. of William, of London. LL.B. 1573; LL.D. 1579. Incorp. at Oxford, 1600. Canon of Lincoln, 1564. Admitted advocate, July 8, 1589. Adm. at the Middle Temple, Aug. 8, 1605. Will (P.C.C.) 1616; of St Benet, Paul's Wharf, London. Father of Bartholomew (1602-3). (*Vis. of Essex*, 1634.)

HONE, THOMAS. Adm. pens. (age 16) at CHRIST'S, July 3, 1635. S. of Thomas. B. at Farnham, Essex. School, Bishop's Stortford (Mr Leigh). Matric. 1635; B.A. 1638-9; M.A. 1642; M.D. from Sidney, 1655. Ord. deacon (Lincoln) Dec. 8, 1642. (*Vis. of Essex*, 1634; *Peile*, I. 439.)

HONE, WALTER. Matric. pens. from TRINITY HALL, Michs. 1561.

HONE or HOON, WILLIAM. M.A. 1504-5 (Incorp. from Oxford); B.D. 1514-5. Tutor to the Prince, 1505. Chaplain to the King.

HONELING, BENJAMIN. Ord. deacon (London) June 6, 1680; described as 'B.A. of TRINITY HALL.'

HONY, FREDERICK (Captain). M.A. 1635-6 (*Lit. Reg.*).

HONEY, ——. B.A. 1480.

HONYFOLD, GABRIEL. B.D. 1612 (Incorp. from Oxford). Of Kent, *pleb.* Matric. from Corpus Christi, Oxford, Feb. 4, 1591-2, age 14; B.A. (Oxford) 1597; M.A. 1602; B.D. 1610. R. of North Cove, Suffolk, 1611-2. V. of Willingham St Mary, 1612-3. V. of Ardley, Essex, 1614. Sequestered from Ardley, in 1642, and suffered much. (*Al. Oxon.*; *Newcourt*.)

HONYNGE or HUNNING, HENRY. Matric. pens. from CHRIST'S, May, 1572. 3rd s. of William, of Carlton, Suffolk. Brother of the next. (*Peile*, I. 122; *Vis. of Suffolk*, 1577.)

HONYNGE, WILLIAM. Matric. pens. from CHRIST'S, May, 1572. 2nd s. of William, of Carlton, Suffolk. (*Peile*, I. 122.)

HONYWOOD, ANTHONY. Matric. Fell.-Com. at CHRIST'S, Oct. 1567. Perhaps s. of Robert, of Charing, Kent. Founded a hospital at Lenham. (*Peile*, I. 100; *Vis. of Essex*, 1634.)

HONEYWOOD, EDWARD. Adm. at CORPUS CHRISTI, 1647. S. and h. of Sir John (1604), of Elmsted, Kent, Knt. Adm. at Gray's Inn, May 6, 1647. Created baronet, 1660. Died 1670, aged 42. Buried at Elmsted. Father of John (1693). (*Hasted*, III. 309; G.E.C.)

HONIWOOD, HENRY. Matric. pens. from CHRIST'S, July, 1611. 5th s. of Robert, of Markshall, Essex. B. July 14, 1593. Adm. at Gray's Inn, Jan. 30, 1614-5. Of West Hawkes, Kingsnorth, Kent. Will proved, Nov. 1663, by his brother Sir Peter. Brother of Michael (1611), of Matthew (1606) and Peter (1606). (*Vis. of Essex*, 1634, Pt. II., App. 733; *Peile*, I. 283.)

HONYWOOD, ISAAC. Adm. pens. (age 16) at ST JOHN'S, Apr. 15, 1659. (Apparently matric. sizar Easter, 1659, as 'Homer.') S. of Edward, draper, of London. B. there. School, Guildford (Mr Graine). Matric. 1659. Adm. at the Middle Temple, Jan. 25, 1660-1. Married Rebecca, dau. of William Pycheford, of London, haberdasher. Will proved (P.C.C.) Nov. 3, 1720. (*Top. and Gen.*, II. 191.)

HONYWOOD, JOHN. Matric. pens. from TRINITY, Easter, 1604. Probably s. and h. of Sir Thomas, of Elmsted, Kent, Knt. Adm. at Gray's Inn, Feb. 16, 1607-8. Knighted, June 18, 1619. Sheriff of Kent, 1643-5. Died Nov. 24, 1652, aged 68. Buried at Elmsted. Will (P.C.C.) 1653. Father of Edward (1647). (*Hasted*, III. 309.)

HONYWOOD, JOHN. M.A. from EMMANUEL, 1693. S. of Edward (1647), of Elmsted, Kent, Bart. Matric. from Jesus College, Oxford, Mar. 24, 1682-3, age 17; B.A. (Hart Hall, Oxford) 1686. V. of Petham, Kent, 1691-1737. V. of Waltham, 1691-1737. R. of Burmarsh, 1706-37. Died Sept. 16, 1737. (*Al. Oxon.*; Pedigree in *Vis. of Kent*, 1663.)

HONYWOOD, JOHN LAMOT. Adm. Fell.-Com. (age 15) at CHRIST'S, May 3, 1665. 5th s. of Sir Thomas, of Mark's Hall, Essex, Knt. B. there. School, Felsted. Matric. 1665. Adm. at the Inner Temple, June 6, 1668. Succeeded his brother Thomas, 1672. M.P. for Essex, 1674-81, 1693-4. Sheriff, 1689-90. Died Jan. 1693-4. Brother of Thomas (1656). (*Peile*, I. 616; *D.N.B.*; A. B. Beaven.)

HONYWOOD, MATTHEW. Adm. Fell.-Com. at EMMANUEL, Apr. 26, 1606. Probably 3rd s. of Robert, of Charing, Kent, and Mark's Hall, Essex. B. Dec. 21, 1587. Matric. 1606. Adm. at the Inner Temple, 1605; 'of South Mimms, Middlesex.' Barrister, 1616. Married Elizabeth, dau. of Sir George Rivers, Bart. Died c. 1638. Will (P.C.C.) 1638; of Bishopstone, Sussex. Brother of the next, of Peter (1606) and Henry (1611). (*Vis. of Essex*; *Top. and Gen.*, I. 399.)

HONYWOOD, MICHAEL. Matric. pens. from CHRIST'S, July 8, 1611. 6th s. of Robert, of Charing, Kent, and Mark's Hall, Essex. B. in London, Oct. 1, 1597. B.A. 1614-5; M.A. 1618; B.D. 1636; D.D. 1660 (*Lit. Reg.*). Fellow, 1618-43. Taxor, 1623. Proctor, 1628. Incorp. at Oxford, 1621. Ord. deacon (London) Dec. 1618; priest, Feb. 1618-9. R. of Kegworth, Leics., 1639-45 and 1660. Lived at Utrecht during the protectorate. Canon of Lincoln, 1660. Dean, 1660-81. Died Sept. 7, 1681. Will, P.C.C. Benefactor to Christ's and to Lincoln Cathedral library. Brother of Henry (1611), of Matthew (1606) and the next. (*D.N.B.*; *Peile*, I. 283; *Vis. of Essex*, 1634.)

HONYWOOD, PETER. Adm. Fell.-Com. at EMMANUEL, Apr. 26, 1606. Probably s. of Robert, of Charing, Kent, and Mark's Hall, Essex. Matric. 1606. Adm. at the Inner Temple, 1605; of South Mimms. Barrister, 1618. Died 1685, aged 96. M.I. in Temple Church. Will proved in London, Dec. 15, 1685. (*Musgrave*; *Vis. of Essex*, Pt. II., App. 734.)

HONYWOOD, ROBERT. D.D. 1661 (*Lit. Reg.*).

HONYWOOD, THOMAS. Matric. pens. from PEMBROKE, Easter, 1546. One of these names adm. at Gray's Inn, 1547.

HONYWOOD, THOMAS. Adm. Fell.-Com. at JESUS, Nov. 12, 1656. Of Essex. S. of Sir Thomas, Knt., of Mark's Hall, Essex. Adm. at the Inner Temple, 1658. Succeeded his father, in 1666. Died Nov. 24, 1672. Buried at Mark's Hall. Brother of John Lamot (1665). (For the father *see D.N.B.*)

HONYWOOD, VICESIMUS. Adm. pens. (age 17) at CHRIST'S, Nov. 22, 1639. S. of Sir Robert, of Petts Court, Charing, Kent. B. there. Schools, Hollingbourne (Mr Benham) and Sellinge (Mr Coppinge). Matric. 1639. (*Peile*, I. 464.)

HOO, CLEMENT. Adm. pens. (age 16) at CAIUS, July 25, 1591. S. of John, gent., of Walsingham, Norfolk. B. at Norwich. School, Lynn (Mr Roberts). Perhaps adm. at Gray's Inn, Feb. 11, 1594-5. Of Burnham Thorpe, Norfolk, gent. Father of John (1618). (*Venn*, I. 143; *Vis. of Norfolk*.)

HOO, GERARD DE. First Master of PETERHOUSE, 1284.

HOO, JOHN. Adm. Fell.-Com. at QUEENS', Oct. 9, 1618. Of Norfolk. S. and h. of Clement (above), of North Creake, and Burnham Thorpe, Norfolk, Esq. Adm. at Gray's Inn, Feb. 7, 1620-1. (*Vis. of Norfolk*.)

HOO, THOMAS. Adm. Fell.-Com. (age 15) at SIDNEY, July 14, 1628. S. of William (? below), Esq., of Hoo, Herts. School, Hertford (Mr Minors). Matric. 1628. Married Mary, dau. of Sir Francis Bickley. (*Vis. of Herts.*, 1634; *Clutterbuck*, III. 72.)

HOO, WILLIAM. Matric. Fell.-Com. from CLARE, c. 1596. Perhaps s. of Thomas, of Walden and Kimpton, Herts. Sheriff of Herts., 1629. Died Mar. 14, 1636, aged 56. Buried at St Paul's, Walden, Herts. Perhaps father of Thomas (above). (*Clutterbuck*, III. 72, 143.)

HOO, ——. B.Can.L. 1485-6.

HOODE, ARTHUR. B.Can.L. 1494-5.

HOOD, ARTHUR WILLIAM. Adm. sizar at ST JOHN'S, 1747. S. of Samuel, clerk, of Somerset. B. at Butleigh, near Somerton. School, Ilminster (Mr Davies). Matric. 1747; B.A. 1750-1; M.A. 1754; D.D. 1766. Ord. priest (London) Feb. 28, 1755. R. of Butleigh, 1761-70. Preb. of Wells, 1763-70. (*Scott-Mayor*, III. 568.)

HOODE, JOHN. Matric. sizar from CORPUS CHRISTI, Easter, 1544.

HOOD, JOHN. Matric. pens. from PETERHOUSE, Michs. 1554. R. of Skirbeck, Lincs., 1559-82. 'Ord. priest (Peterb.) Dec. 19, 1561; aged 39. Married; resides; understands Latin competently; B.A. of Cambridge.' (*Lib. Cler. Lincoln*, 1576.)

HOOD, PAUL. M.A. 1614 (Incorp. from Oxford). Of Leicestershire, *pleb.* Matric. from Balliol College, Oxford, Nov. 19, 1602, age 16; B.A. (Oxford) 1606; M.A. 1609; B.D. (Lincoln College) 1617; D.D. 1623. R. of Lincoln College, 1620-68. Vice-Chancellor, 1660-1. R. of Broughton Gifford, Wilts., 1621. R. of Ketesby, Lincs., 1630. Preb. of Lincoln, 1630-3. R. of Eydon, Northants., 1631-49. R. of Ickford, Bucks., 1660. Preb. of Southwell, 1661-2. Died Aug. 2, 1668, aged 84. Buried in All Saints', Oxford. Will, P.C.C. (*Al. Oxon.*)

HOOD, RICHARD. Adm. sizar at EMMANUEL, Apr. 20, 1694. Of Leicestershire. Matric. 1696; B.A. 1697-8; M.A. 1701. Ord. deacon (Lincoln) May 26, 1700; priest, Sept. 22, 1700. R. of Barham, Suffolk, 1704. R. of Heveningham, 1704-35. V. of Wenhaston, 1707. Died Feb. 23, 1735-6, aged 59. (*Suckling*, II. 398.)

HOOD, THOMAS. Matric. pens. from TRINITY, Michs. 1573. S. of Thomas, merchant tailor, of London (of St Leonard's, Eastcheap; will, P.C.C., 1563). School, Merchant Taylors'. B.A. 1577-8; M.A. 1581. Fellow, 1579. Licensed to practise medicine, 1585. First 'Thomas Smith lecturer' in mathematics in London, 1582. Licentiate R.C.P., 1597, being then M.D. of some University. Author, mathematical. Died 1598. (*Cooper*, II. 270; *D.N.B.*)

HOOD or HOODS, THOMAS. Matric. sizar from JESUS, Easter, 1605; B.A. 1608-9.

HOOD, TIMOTHY. Adm. sizar at PETERHOUSE, May 20, 1623. S. of Michael. B. at Richmond, Yorks. Schools, Newcastle (Mr Foley) and Richmond (Mr Bathurst). Migrated to Christ's, June 12, 1623. B.A. 1626-7; M.A. 1635. Licensed to preach at St Clement Danes, 1635-6. Perhaps R. of Bentworth, Hants., 1637. Perhaps V. of Coulsdon, Surrey, 1677. Died there Dec. 6, 1677. Will, P.C.C. (*Peile*, I. 352; *Manning and Bray*, II. 459.)

HOODSON, RICHARD. Matric. sizar from ST JOHN'S, Michs. 1569.

HOOGAN or HOGAN, EDWARD. Adm. pens. (age 16) at CAIUS, Apr. 26, 1692. S. of Thomas (1658), of Dunham, Norfolk. B. there. Schools, Dunham (Mr Ransome), Norwich (Mr Burton) and Fakenham (Mr Oaborn). Matric. 1692; Scholar, 1692-9; B.A. 1695-6; M.A. 1699. Ord. deacon (Norwich) Dec. 18, 1698; priest, Feb. 25, 1699-1700. R. of Beeston, Norfolk, 1709-34; of Shingham, 1709-34. Died 1734. Brother of Thomas (1688). (*Venn*, I. 491.)

HOOGAN, HENRY. Matric. pens. from CHRIST'S, Dec. 1618. Perhaps s. and h. of Thomas (? 1594-5), of Castle Acre and Gt Dunham, Norfolk. Bapt. July 5, 1604. Adm. at Gray's Inn, Jan. 21, 1620-1. Died Oct. 14, 1658. Perhaps brother of Thomas (1628). (*Peile*, I. 325; Carthew, *Launditch*, II. 804.)

HOOGAN, HENRY. Adm. pens. at TRINITY, p . 17, 1655. Of Norfolk. Doubtless s. of Thomas (1628).AMatric. 1656; Scholar, 1657; B.A. 1658-9; M.A. 1662; M.D. 1670. Fellow, 1661. Of Lynn. Married Anne, dau. of Sir Edward Chester, Knt. and widow of Robert Eade, M.D., of Cambridge. (Carthew, *Launditch*, II. 804.)

HOGAN or HUGGONS, JOSEPH. Adm. pens. (age 18) at CAIUS, July 1, 1633. S. of Roland, gent. B. at Roughton, Norfolk. School, Cromer (Mr Colby). Scholar, 1636-40; B.A. 1636-7; M.A. 1640. Ord. priest (Norwich) Dec. 18, 1642' as C. of Buxton, Norfolk. C. of Swanton Abbot, 1642-62. V. of Witton, 1665. V. of North Walsham. Buried at Roughton, Dec. 18, 1692. M.I. (*Venn*, I. 310.)

HOGAN, JOSEPH. Adm. sizar (age 17) at ST JOHN'S, Apr. 10, 1705. S. of Robert, gent. B. at Hanworth, Norfolk. School, Norwich (Mr Hoadley). Matric. 1705; B.A. 1708-9. Ord. deacon (Peterb.) June 3, 1710; priest, June 24, 1712. R. of Twyford, Norfolk, 1715-20. R. of Themelthorpe, 1715-21. V. of Roughton, 1719-46. R. of Foxley, 1747-63. R. of Ingworth, till 1747. R. of Sparham, 1747-63. Died 1763.

HOOGAN, ROBERT. Adm. Fell.-Com. (age 14) at CAIUS, June 12, 1604. S. and h. of Henry, of East Bradenham, Norfolk, Esq. Adm. at Gray's Inn, Feb. 2, 1609-10. Died July 30, 1612. (*Venn*, I. 185; *Carthew*, II. 695.)

HOOGAN, THOMAS. Adm. pens. (age 15) at CAIUS, 1594-5. S. of Anthony, gent. B. at Castle Acre, Norfolk. Schools, Castle Acre and Scarning (Mr Denby). Of Gt Dunham. Knighted, July 23, 1603. Buried at Dunham, Feb. 3, 1656-7. Father of the next and perhaps of Henry (1618).

HOOGAN, THOMAS. Matric. pens. from ST CATHARINE'S, Easter, 1628. Of Norfolk. Doubtless s. of Sir Thomas (above), of Gt Dunham, Norfolk, Knt. Bapt. Dec. 10, 1610. B.A. 1631-2; M.A. 1635. Of Lynn. Father of Henry (1655) and perhaps brother of Henry (1618). (Carthew, *Launditch*, II. 804.)

HOOGAN, THOMAS. Adm. Fell.-Com. (age 16) at CAIUS, July 5, 1658. S. of Henry, of Gt Dunham, Norfolk, Esq. B. there. Schools, Norwich (Mr Lovering) and Lynn (Mr Bell). Matric. 1660, as Hugins. Adm. at Gray's Inn, June 26, 1662. Of Gt Dunham, Esq. Buried there Nov. 9, 1686. Will (Norwich Archd. C.) 1686. Father of Edward (1692) and the next. (*Venn*, I. 403; *Vis. of Norfolk*, 1664.)

HOOGAN, THOMAS. Adm. Fell.-Com. (age 16) at CAIUS, July 3, 1688. S. of Thomas (above), of Gt Dunham, Norfolk. B. there, Apr. 10, 1671. School, Norwich. Matric. 1688. Of Gt Dunham, Esq. Married, June 6, 1700, Helena Halcott, of Litcham. Buried at Gt Dunham, Feb. 5, 1734-5. Brother of Edward (1692), father of the next. (*Venn*, I. 485; *Norf. Arch. Soc.*, I. 359.)

HOOGAN, THOMAS. Adm. pens. (age 16) at CAIUS, Apr. 26, 1720. S. of Thomas (above), of Gt Dunham, Norfolk. B. there. School, Wymondham (Mr Sayer). Matric. 1720; Scholar, 1720-6; M.B. 1726. Adm. at Leyden, Aug. 6, 1726. A lunatic. Died May 3, 1779. Buried at Dunham. M.I. (*Venn*, II. 13.)

HOOKE, AMBROSE. Adm. pens. (age 16) at ST JOHN'S, Feb. 17, 1701-2. S. of James, deceased. B. in Lincolnshire. School, West Bradenham, Norfolk (Mr Needham). Matric. 1702; B.A. 1706-7. Ord. deacon (Lincoln) June 19, 1709; priest, Sept. 23, 1710. C. of Algarkirk, Lincs., 1710.

HOOKE, FRANCIS. Adm. pens. at EMMANUEL, Easter, 1623. Matric. 1623; B.A. 1626-7; M.A. 1630.

HOOK, GILBERT. Adm. pens. at JESUS, May 6, 1683. S. of Richard (1639), D.D., V. of Halifax, Yorks. Matric. 1683; Scholar, 1684; B.A. 1686-7; M.A. 1690; B.D. 1710. Fellow, 1690-1715. V. of Hinxton, Cambs., 1693. V. of Fordham, 1696-1713. R. of Harlton, 1712-5. Died 1715. Will proved (V.C.C.) 1715. Brother of Samuel (1679), William (1674) and Thomas (1674).

HOOKE, HUGH. Matric. sizar from MAGDALENE, Lent, 1564-5. Probably V. of Holy Trinity, York, 1586-1605. R. of Ergham, Yorks., 1587-1605. Died 1605.

HOOKE, HUMPHREY. Adm. pens. (age 15) at PEMBROKE, Mar. 15, 1623-4. Previously matric. from Magdalen College, Oxford, Feb. 28, 1622-3. S. of Henry, of Bramshott, Hants., Esq. Matric. 1623-4. Mentioned in his father's will, 1640. Probably brother of John (1629-30).

HOOKE, JOHN. Chancellor of the University, 1270-5.

HOOKE, JOHN. B.A. from ST JOHN'S, 1587-8; M.A. 1591; B.D. 1598. Fellow, 1589. Of Sussex. Will proved (V.C.C.) 1602.

HOOKE, JOHN. Matric. sizar from EMMANUEL, Easter, 1602.

HOOKE, JOHN. Adm. pens. (age 17) at PEMBAOKE, May 31, 1620. S. of Henry, D.D., Archdeacon of York. (W. W. Capes, *Bramshott*.)

HOOK, JOHN. Adm. Fell.-Com. at QUEENS', Mar. 8, 1629-30. Probably 1st s. of Henry, of Bramshott. If so, matric. from Magdalen College, Oxford, Feb. 28, 1622-3, age 17. M.P. for Haslemere, 1659; unseated same year. M.P. for Winchester, 1660. According to W. W. Capes (*Bramshott*) he was a graduate of Harvard, and R. of Bramshott, 1672-85. Died May 14, 1685, aged 80. M.I. Brother of Humphrey (1623-4).

HOOKE, JOHN. M.A. 1657 (Incorp. from Oxford). Probably s. of Richard (1620). Matric. from Magdalen College, Oxford, Jan. 22, 1648-9; B.A. (Oxford) 1651-2; M.A. 1654. Fellow of Magdalen, 1655-64. Usher of the College School, 1651-5. R. of Blechingdon, Oxon., 1662-73. Buried there Feb. 20, 1673-4. Admon. (Archd. Oxon.) 1674. Probably brother of Theophilus (1653) and Richard (1660). (*Al. Oxon.*; Le Neve, *Mon.*, I. 102.)

HOOKE, JOHN. Matric. pens. from CLARE, Easter, 1660.

HOOKE, JOHN. Adm. pens. (age 15) at TRINITY, Mar. 25, 1719. S. of John. School, Norwich (Mr Reddington). Matric. 1719; Scholar, 1721; B.A. 1723-4; M.A. 1727. Ord. deacon (Lincoln) June 16, 1728. V. of Hatfield Regis, Essex, 1728-53. Died 1753.

HOOK, JOHN. Adm. sizar at CORPUS CHRISTI, 1749. Of Nottinghamshire. Matric. 1750-1; B.A. 1754; M.A. 1757. Fellow, 1758-64. Ord. deacon (Lincoln) June 24, 1755; priest, Mar. 6, 1757. R. of Little Wilbraham, Cambs., 1762-77. V. of Grantchester, 1762. Tutor to the Princess Elizabeth, and Prince Ernest Augustus, 1772. Died Aug. 12, 1777, aged 45. M.I. in Chancel of Little Wilbraham. (H. P. Stokes.)

HOOKE, NATHANIEL. Adm. sizar (age 16) at SIDNEY, July 6, 1681. Previously adm. at Trinity College, Dublin, July 16, 1679; and at Glasgow University, 1680. S. of John, (?) clerk. B. at Corbale, Dublin. Schools, Dublin (Mr Shaw), Dath (Mr Scot) and Kilkenny (Mr Jones). Matric. 1681. Went to Holland. Joined the Duke of Monmouth and landed with him at Lyme Regis, 1685. Sent secretly to London to raise an insurrection. Gave himself up and was pardoned, 1688. Served with the Jacobites in Ireland, and with the French in Flanders. Undertook missions to Scottish Jacobites, 1705 and 1707. Became a Brigadier in the French army, 1708, and a Marechal de camp, 1718. Naturalised, Jan. 1720. Died Oct. 25, 1738. (*D.N.B.*)

HOOKE, PETER. Adm. pens. at CLARE, May 28, 1718. B. at Norwich. Matric. 1717; M.B. 1723; M.D. 1728. Adm. at Leyden, Oct. 21, 1726, age 26. F.R.C.P., 1729. Admon. (P.C.C.) May, 1736; of St Olave, Hart St, London. (*Munk*, II. 113; J. Ch. Smith.)

HOOKE, PETER. Adm. pens. at ST CATHARINE'S, Feb. 27, 1748-9. Of London. Matric. 1749; B.A. 1753; M.A. 1756. Adm. extra-licentiate R.C.P., 1769. Physician to the Norfolk and Norwich Hospital, 1772. Died at Norwich, Sept. 1804. (*Munk*, II. 286.)

HOOKE, RICHARD. Matric. sizar from CLARE, Easter, 1620; B.A. 1623-4; M.A. 1629. Probably R. of Little Baddow, Essex, 1632-76. R. of Gt Stanmore, Middlesex, 1663-76. R. of Cranford, 1664-76. Died 1676. Will (P.C.C.) 1677; to be buried at Cranford. According to *Hennessy* he was D.D. and chaplain to Charles II (but *see* the next).

HOOKE, RICHARD. Adm. sizar (age 16) at PETERHOUSE, June 14, 1639. Of Wigan. Matric. 1639; B.A. 1642-3; M.A. 1651; D.D. 1665 (*Lit. Reg.*). Probably ord. deacon and priest (Lincoln) July 25, 1646. V. of Halifax, 1662-88. R. of Thornton-in-Craven. Preb. of Ripon, 1662-89. Preb. of York, 1670-89. Preb. of Southwell, 1675-89. Died Jan. 1, 1688-9. Father of Gilbert (1683), Samuel (1679), Thomas (1674) and William (1674). (*T. A. Walker*, 68.)

HOOKE, RICHARD. M.A. from CHRIST'S, 1641 (Incorp. from Oxford). S. of Francis, of Northampton. Bapt. at St Peter's, Northampton, Dec. 6, 1612. Matric. from New Inn Hall, Feb. 1, 1632-3, age 19; B.A. (Oxford) 1635; M.A. not recorded. Appointed minister at Boughton, Northants., Aug. 30, 1644. V. of Desborough, 1646. V. of Moulton (on presentation of Oliver Cromwell), 1655-61. V. of Rothersthorpe, 1661. R. of Creaton, 1661; ejected, 1662. Taught school at Creaton and afterwards at Northampton, where he was licensed Presbyterian preacher, 1672-5. Married, at Stoke Albany, Northants., July 19, 1646, Mary Rolston, widow. Buried at St Peter's, Northampton, July 1, 1679. M.I. Will (Archd. Northants.) 1679. (*Peile*, I. 430; H. I. Longden; *Al. Oxon.*)

HOOK, RICHARD. Adm. pens. at CLARE, June 21, 1660. Probably s. of Richard (1620). B.A. 1663-4; M.A. 1667; D.D. 1705. Fellow. Ord. deacon (London) Dec. 24, 1676. R. of St George's, Southwark, 1681-1715. V. of Gt Stanmore, Middlesex, 1687-1715. Died Feb. 8, 1714-5. Buried at Stanmore. Will, P.C.C. Father of Theophilus (1711), brother of John (1657) and Theophilus (1653). (Le Neve, *Mon.*, II. 304.)

HOOKE, ROBERT. Matric. Fell.-Com. from MAGDALENE, Easter, 1568.

HOOK, ROBERT. Adm. pens. (age 19) at CAIUS, Jan. 6, 1623-4. S. of John, shipowner, of Welborne, Norfolk. School, Norfolk. Matric. 1623-4; Scholar, 1625-8; B.A. 1627-8; M.A. 1631. Ord. deacon (Peterb.) Oct. 16; priest, Oct. 17, 1628. C. of Sheringham, Norfolk, in 1636. V. of Hemsby, 1643-65. Will proved, 1665. (*Venn*, I. 264.)

HOOKE, SAMUEL. Matric. sizar from ST JOHN'S, Easter, 1588; B.A. 1591-2; M.A. 1595. Ord. deacon (Norwich) June 24; priest, Sept. 29, 1600. C. of Westacre, Norfolk.

HOOKE, SAMUEL. Matric. sizar from KING'S, Easter, 1605. 1st s. of Ambrose, V. of Blakesley, Northants. Bapt. there, July 29, 1588. Ord. deacon (Peterb.) May 22, 1608; priest, Dec. 20, 1612. C. of Little Billing, Northants. C. of Ecton, 1616. Licensed, Feb. 17, 1609-10, to marry Maude, dau. of James Bracegirdle, R. of Little Billing. (H. I. Longden.)

HOOKE, SAMUEL. Adm. pens. (age 16) at JESUS, June 28, 1679. S. of Richard (1639), V. of Halifax, Yorks. Matric. 1679; Scholar, 1679; B.A. 1682-3; M.A. 1686. Fellow, 1683-7. Died Aug. 12, 1687. Buried at Halifax. Will proved (V.C.C.) 1688. Brother of Gilbert (1683), William (1674) and Thomas (1674). (A. Gray.)

HOOKE, SAMUEL. Adm. sizar at JESUS, June 29, 1700. Of Cambridgeshire. S. of William (1674), R. of Girton. Matric. 1700; B.A. 1703-4; M.A. 1707. Ord. deacon (Peterb.) Sept. 24, 1704; priest, Dec. 30, 1705. V. of Elmstead, Essex, 1706-10. Minor canon of Peterborough, in 1717. Married, June 9, 1717, at the Cathedral, Anne Andrew. Buried in the Cathedral, Dec. 7, 1728, aged 45. M.I. (H. I. Longden.)

HOOKE, THEOPHILUS. Adm. pens. at CLARE, Apr. 14, 1653. Probably s. of Richard (1620). Matric. 1653; B.A. 1656-7; M.A. 1660. Incorp. at Oxford, 1661. Ord. priest (Bishop Brownrigg, of Exeter) Feb. 19, 1658-9. R. of Hollesley, Suffolk. R. of Garboldisham, Norfolk, 1663-89. R. of Sudborne, Suffolk, 1666-1700. Probably brother of Richard (1660) and John (1657).

HOOK, THEOPHILUS. Adm. pens. at CLARE, July 2, 1711. S. of Richard (1660), V. of Staumore. B. at Gt Stanmore, Middlesex. School, Winchester. Migrated to Oxford. Matric. from New College, Oxford, Feb. 29, 1711-2, age 18; B.A. (Oxford) 1715. (*Al. Oxon.*)

HOOKE, THOMAS. Matric. sizar from PEMBROKE, Michs. 1620. S. of Benjamin, of Cirencester, Gloucs. B.A. 1623-4; M.A. 1627. Ord. deacon (Peterb.) Dec. 23; priest, Dec. 24, 1626.

HOOK, THOMAS. Adm. pens. (age 17) at PETERHOUSE, Apr. 7, 1674. Of Nottinghamshire. S. of Richard (1639), of Worcestershire. School, Halifax. Matric. 1675; Scholar, 1675; B.A. 1677-8; M.A. 1681. Brother of William (1674), Gilbert (1683) and Samuel (1679).

HOOKE, THOMAS. Adm. pens. (age 15) at ST JOHN'S, Sept. 10, 1708. S. of Thomas, advocate. B. at Bradford, Yorks. School, York (Mr Tomlinson). LL.B. 1714. Ord. deacon (Ely) May 23, 1714; priest (York) July 21, 1728. P.C. of Carlton-in-Snaith, Yorks., 1715-72. V. of Drax, 1727-30. Married, May 19, 1719, Ellen, dau. of Hugh Taylor, of Coats. Died June 15, 1772. Buried at Carlton. (Robinson, *Snaith*; M. H. Peacock.)

HOOKE, WALTER. B.A. 1515-6; M.A. 1519.

HOOKE, WALTER. Adm. sizar at PEMBROKE, 1654. S. of William, V. of Axmouth, Devon (deprived and emigrated to New England). B. at Axmouth. For two years at Harvard College, Mass. Matric. 1656; B.A. 1656-7. Chaplain to the East India Company, 1668, at Masulipatam. Died there 1670. (F. *Penny*.)

HOOK, WILLIAM. Adm. pens. (age 15) at PETERHOUSE, Oct. 30, 1674. Of Yorkshire. S. of Richard (1639). School, Halifax. Matric. 1675; Scholar, 1675; B.A. 1678-9; M.A. 1682. Ord. deacon (York) Dec. 1680. R. of Girton, Cambs., 1683. Brother of Thomas (1674), Gilbert (1683), Samuel (1679) and father of Samuel (1700).

HOOKE, ——. B.A. 1539-40.

HOOKEL or HUCKLE, PHILIP. One of the original fellows of TRINITY College, Dec. 19, 1546. B.A. (Oxford) 1534-5; M.A. 1539. Fellow of Merton College, 1537.

HOOKER, CORNELIUS. Adm. pens. (age 18) at CHRIST'S, June 27, 1639. S. of Edward, merchant, of St Mary Hill, London. B. Mar. 31, 1621. School, Merchant Taylors'. Matric. 1639. Adm. at Gray's Inn, June 12, 1641. (*Peile*, I. 461.)

HOOKER, EDWARD. Matric. sizar from CORPUS CHRISTI, Easter, 1640. Of Lincolnshire. B.A. 1644; M.A. 1648.

HOOKER, JOHN. Adm. pens. at EMMANUEL, Feb. 4, 1649-50. Of Essex. Matric. 1650.

HOOKER, JOHN. Adm. sizar (age 18) at CAIUS, Apr. 22, 1701. S. of Edward, ironmonger, of Harrow, Middlesex. B. there. School, Harrow. Matric. 1701; Scholar, 1701-8; B.A. 1704-5; M.A. 1708. Ord. deacon (London) Dec. 19, 1708; priest, June 4, 1710. Second Master at Harrow, 1705-22. Died 1722. M.I. at Harrow. (*Venn*, I. 507.)

HOOKER, JONATHAN. Adm. pens. (age 17) at ST JOHN'S, July 9, 1714. S. of Jonathan, R. of Sandy, Beds. Bapt. there, July 5, 1697. School, Stamford (Mr Turner). Matric. 1714. Died at Sandy. Buried Mar. 18, 1715-6. (W. M. Noble.)

HOOKER or OKER, THOMAS. B.Can.L. 1510-1. A monk.

HOOKER, THOMAS. Matric. sizar from QUEENS', Easter, 1604. S. of Thomas, yeoman, of Birstall, Leics. B. there, 1586. School, Market Bosworth. Migrated to Emmanuel. Scholar there, 1604; B.A. 1607-8; M.A. 1611. Dixie fellow, 1609-18. C. of Esher, Surrey, and lecturer at Chelmsford. Silenced by Archbishop Laud, 1626. Kept a private school at Little Baddow, Essex, where John Elliott was his assistant. Went to Rotterdam, 1630, and to New England, 1633. Minister at Cambridge, Mass.; and afterwards at Hartford, Conn., till his death, July 7, 1647. Famous both as preacher and statesman. Married at Amersham, Bucks., Apr. 3, 1621, Susan Garbrand. Author of many theological works. (*D.N.B.*; J. G. Bartlett.)

HOOKER, ——. B.Civ.L. 1487-8.

HOOKER or HOKKAR, ——. B.A. 1511-2; M.A. 1515.

HOOKER, ——. Adm. Fell.-Com. at KING'S, 1707-8.

HOOKES, JOHN. Matric. Fell.-Com. from CHRIST'S, 1595-6.

HOOKES, JOHN. Adm. pens. (age 17) at TRINITY, Apr. 2, 1703. S. of John, of Stockwell, Surrey. School, Wimborne, Dorset (Mr Lloyd). Matric. 1703; Scholar, 1704; B.A. 1706-7. Probably adm. at the Inner Temple, Feb. 8, 1702-3; s. and h. of John, of Clifford's Inn. Clerk of the House of Commons. Died at Gaunts, Dorset, Dec. 16, 1760. (G. *Mag.*; *Hutchins*, III. 245.)

HOOKES, NICHOLAS. Adm. sizar (age 17) at CHRIST'S, Apr. 29, 1634. S. of Nicholas. B. at Conway. Schools, Conway (Mr Roberts) and Westminster. Matric. 1633; B.A. 1637; M.A. 1641. (*Peile*, I. 432, 'Folkes.')

HOOKES, NICHOLAS. Matric. pens. from TRINITY, Easter, 1649, a scholar from Westminster; B.A. 1652-3. Author, *Amanda*, and other poetry. Died Nov. 7, 1712. Buried in Lambeth. (*Al. Westmon.*; *D.N.B.*)

HOOKES, ROBERT. Adm. pens. (age 17) at ST JOHN'S, June 27, 1671. S. of John, gent., of Conway, Carnarv. B. there. Matric. 1671.

HOOKES, THOMAS. Adm. sizar (age 15) at ST JOHN'S, June 15, 1636. S. of William, gent., of Shropham, Norfolk. B. in the Isle of Ely. School, Ely (Mr Hitch). Matric. 1636; B.A. 1639-40.

HOOKES, WILLIAM. B.A. from JESUS, 1582-3; M.A. 1586.

HOOKES, WILLIAM. Matric. pens. from ST JOHN'S, Easter, 1619.

HOOLE, JAMES. Adm. sizar (age 19) at MAGDALENE, Apr. 26, 1671. S. of John, of Crook, Sheffield. School, Sheffield.

HOOLE, JOHN. 'Of TRINITY College, literate,' when ord. priest (York) June, 1667. C. of Coley, Yorks.

HOOLE, JOSEPH. M.A. from SIDNEY, 1727 (*Lit. Reg.*). V. of Haxey, Lincs., 1712-36. R. of St Ann's, Manchester, 1736-45. Died Nov. 27, 1745. Buried at St Ann's.

HOOLE, NATHANIEL. Adm. sizar (age 21) at SIDNEY, May 27, 1721. S. of Thomas. B. at Elswick, Lancs. Schools, Kirkham, Lancs., and Wakefield, Yorks. Ord. deacon (Lincoln) Sept. 23, 1722. Perhaps schoolmaster at Wanstead. Died July 2, 1737. Admon., P.C.C. (G. *Mag.*)

HOOLE, ROBERT. Adm. sizar (age 19) at PEMBROKE, May 25, 1663. S. of Ralph, farmer. B. at Davenham, Cheshire.

HOOLE or HOULE, WILLIAM. Matric. sizar from QUEENS', Easter, 1607. Of Yorkshire.

HOOLE, WILLIAM. Adm. sizar at EMMANUEL, Dec. 20, 1677. Of Yorkshire. Matric. 1678; B.A. 1681-2. Ord. deacon (York) Sept. 1682; priest, Dec. 1684. V. of Lund, Yorks., 1684.

HOOPER, EDWARD GILES. Adm. pens. at QUEENS', Sept. 2, 1741. S. of John (1701), V. of St Mary's, St Neots, Hunts. School, Bury. Matric. 1742; B.A. 1745-6. Ord. deacon (Norwich) May, 1746.

HOOPER, FRANCIS. Adm. pens. (age 18) at TRINITY, Apr. 4, 1713. S. of Joseph, of Manchester. School, Warrington (Mr Shaw). Matric. 1713; Scholar, 1715; B.A. 1716-7; M.A. 1720; D.D. 1728 (*Com. Reg.*). Fellow, 1719. Incorp. at Oxford, 1754. Keeper of the Chetham Library, Manchester, 1719-26. Chaplain to Lady Bland. V. of Didsbury, Lancs., 1721-6. Died 1763. (Mumford, *Manchester Grammar School*; E. Axon.)

HOOPER, HENRY. Adm. sizar (age 19) at PETERHOUSE, July 8, 1730. Of Yorkshire. School, Ripon. Scholar, 1730; Matric. 1731; LL.B. 1737.

HOOPER, ISAAC. Adm. sizar (age 16) at CHRIST'S, Aug. 2, 1695. S. of John. B. at Cambridge. School, King's College, Cambridge (Mr Wm. Donne). Matric. 1695; Scholar, 1696-7; B.A. 1700-1. Ord. deacon (London) June, 1701. (*Peile*, II. 134.)

HOOPER, JOHN. B.A. from KING'S, 1614-5; M.A. 1618. Ord. priest (Peterb.) Dec. 19, 1619. V. of Scothorne, Lincs., 1624.

HOOPER, JOHN. Adm. sizar at CLARE, May 31, 1632. Probably s. of John, parish clerk and notary, of Tonbridge. Exhibitioner from Tonbridge School. Matric. 1632; B.A. 1635-6.

HOOPER, JOHN. Adm. sizar at QUEENS', Sept. 11, 1701. Of London. Matric. 1702; B.A. 1705-6; M.A. 1740. Ord. deacon (Peterb.) Mar. 9, 1706-7; priest, Dec. 18, 1709; C. of Whilton, Northants. V. of St Neots, Hunts., 1713-42. R. of Sawtry St Andrew's, 1739-42. Died 1742. Father of Edward Giles.

HOOPER, NICHOLAS. Adm. pens. (age 17) at CAIUS, Nov. 6, 1671. S. of Nicholas, gent., of Braunton, Devon. School, Barnstaple (Mr Humes and Mr Allanson). Matric. 1671; Scholar, 1672-4. Adm. at the Inner Temple, Dec. 29, 1671. Barrister, 1678. Serjeant-at-law and bencher. M.P. for Barnstaple, 1695-1715. Knighted, 1713. Of Fulbroke, Pilton and Barnstaple. Died May 13, 1731. Will, P.C.C. Father of the next and of Peter. (*Venn*, I. 445; *Vis. of Devon.*)

HOOPER, NICHOLAS. Adm. Fell.-Com. (age 17) at CAIUS, May 30, 1705. S. of Nicholas (1671), of Barnstaple, Devon. B. at Otterton. Schools, Barnstaple (Mr Reyner) and Winchester. Matric. 1705. Adm. at the Inner Temple, Nov. 10, 1700. Married Mary, dau. of Sir John Davy, Bart. Brother of Peter (1689). (*Venn*, I. 513.)

HOOPER, PETER. Adm. pens. (age 17) at CAIUS, Apr. 25, 1689. S. of Nicholas (1671), of Braunton, Devon. B. there. School, Sherwell (Mr Remphry). Matric. 1689; Scholar, 1689-95; B.A. 1692-3. Died without issue. Brother of Nicholas (1705). (*Venn*, I. 487.)

HOOPER, ROBERT. Matric. sizar from KING'S, Michs. 1576. B. at Kymmersley, Salop. B.A. 1580-1; M.A. 1584. Ord. deacon (London) Mar. 30, 1580, age 23.

HOOPER, THOMAS. Matric. Fell.-Com. from KING'S, Lent, 1629-30. Probably s. and h. of John, of Stockbury, Kent, deceased; adm. at the Inner Temple, 1632. Perhaps knighted, June 29, 1644.

HOOPER, WALTER. Adm. pens. (age 16) at SIDNEY, June 8, 1653. S. of Thomas, Esq. (? above), of Stockbury, Kent. B. at Goudhurst. School, Maidstone (Mr Thomas). Matric. 1654. Adm. at the Inner Temple, 1655. Barrister, Nov. 22, 1663. (*Vis. of Kent*, 1663.)

HOORDE, GEORGE. Matric. pens. from ST JOHN'S, Lent, 1579-80. Doubtless brother of Richard and William. (*Vis. of Shropshire*, 1623.)

HOORDE or HORD, RICHARD. Matric. pens. from ST JOHN'S, Michs. 1586. Of Salop. Doubtless s. of John, of Park Bromage. B.A. 1590-1; M.A. 1594; B.D. 1601. Fellow, 1593. Minister at Horningsea, Cambs. R. of Thorington, Essex, 1620-6. Will (P.C.C.) 1626. (*Vis. of Shropshire*, 1623; J. Ch. Smith.)

HOORDE, W. Matric. pens. from ST JOHN'S, Lent, 1579-80. Probably William, brother of George and Richard, above; perhaps of Furnival's Inn, adm. at Lincoln's Inn, 1582. (*Vis. of Shropshire*, 1623.)

HOORE, RICHARD. B.A. 1510-1; Scholar of GONVILLE HALL, 1513-5; M.A. 1514-5. Fellow, 1515-21. University preacher, 1520. R. of All Hallows, Lombard St, 1534-8. V. of North Tuddenham, Norfolk. Died 1538. Will (P.C.C.) 1538; to be buried at Tuddenham. (*Venn*, I. 21.)

HOORE or HORE, ——. B.D. 1462-3. Perhaps V. of Arkesden, Essex, 1496-1517. Will (Cons. C. London) 1517. (J. Ch. Smith.)

HOOTON, JOHN. Adm. sizar (age 17) at ST JOHN'S, Feb. 2, 1710-1. S. of Edward, husbandman. B. at Sherrington, Bucks. School, Northampton (Mr Styles). Matric. 1711; B.A. 1715-6. Ord. deacon (Peterb.) Sept. 21, 1717; priest, Sept. 20, 1718. C. of Easton Maudit. R. of South Luffenham, Rutland, 1725-6. (H. I. Longden.)

HOOTON, ——. B.Can.L. 1480-1.

HOPE, CHARLES. Adm. pens. (age 19) at CHRIST'S, Sept. 1, 1627. S. of Robert, of Grangefield, Sutton-on-the-Hill, Derbs. B. at Trusley, Derbs. School, Repton (Mr Whitehead). Matric. 1627. Of Grangefield. Married and had issue. (*Peile*, I. 387.)

HOPE, CHARLES. Adm. pens. (age 17) at ST JOHN'S, June 25, 1750. S. of William (1719), M.D., of Derbyshire. B. at Derby. School, Derby (Mr Almond). Matric. 1750; B.A. 1754; M.A. 1761. Ord. deacon (Lichfield) Mar. 14, 1756; priest (Lincoln) Mar. 6, 1757. V. of Weston, Lincs., 1757-74. V. of All Saints', Derby, 1774-98. V. of St Michael and St Werburgh, Derby, 1774-98. Married, at Bradfield, Yorks., May 19, 1762, Susanna Stead. Died Dec. 6, 1798. Buried at All Saints', Derby. M.I. (*Scott-Mayor*, III. 600; M. H. Peacock.)

HOPE, JAMES. Adm. sizar (age 17) at ST JOHN'S, June 22, 1677. S. of John, husbandman, of Ormsby, Yorks. B. there. School, Brignall (private; Mr Johnson). Matric. 1677.

HOPE, JOHN. Matric. pens. from KING'S, Easter, 1575.

HOPE, JOHN. Matric. from MAGDALENE, *c.* 1591; B.A. 1595-6; M.A. 1599. Perhaps ord. deacon (Lincoln) May 15, 1602; priest, Mar. 4, 1603-4. R. of Cumberworth, Lincs., 1603.

HOPE, JOHN. M.A. 1622 (Incorp. from Edinburgh). S. of Sir Thomas, of Craighall, Lord advocate to Charles I. Incorp. at Oxford, 1622. Lord of Session, as Lord Craighall, 1632-50. Knighted, and appointed Lord of Session, 1632. One of Cromwell's Committee for the administration of justice, 1652. Representative for Scotland in the English Parliament, 1653. Died at Edinburgh, Apr. 28, 1654. (*Al. Oxon.*; *D.N.B.*)

HOPE, JOHN. Adm. at CORPUS CHRISTI, 1670. Of London. Matric. 1670; B.A. 1673-4. One of these names R. of Swanscombe, Kent, 1686-1705. Buried there Jan. 18, 1705-6.

HOPE, JOHN. Adm. pens. (age 16) at ST JOHN'S, Apr. 24, 1682. S. of Mark (1640), R. of Kedleston, Derbs. B. there. School, Derby (Mr Ogden). Matric. 1683; B.A. 1685-6. Apparently M.D. *see* William, (1719). Fellow, 1689-1700. Said to have been a non-juror. Died July 15, 1710. Buried at St Alkmund's, Derby. M.I. Father of William (1719). (*Kettlewell's Life*; Glover, *Derbs.*, II. 564.)

HOPE, JOHN. Adm. sizar at PETERHOUSE, May 28, 1720. Of Durham. School, Houghton-le-Spring. Matric. 1720; B.A. 1723-4. Ord. priest (Durham) Sept. 16, 1727. C. of Chester-le-Street. Buried at Houghton, Mar. 27, 1728.

HOPE, MARK. Adm. sizar at JESUS, May 6, 1640. Of Derbyshire. 4th s. of Robert, of Grangefield, Sutton-on-the-Hill, Derbs. Bapt. Nov. 5, 1620. School, Repton. Matric. 1640; Scholar, 1643; B.A. 1643-4; M.A. 1650. R. of Kedleston, Derbs., 1654-94. V. of Mackworth, 1663-94. Buried Nov. 15, 1694. Father of John (1682), brother of Charles (1627). (Glover, *Derbs.*, II. 564.)

HOPE, RALPH. Adm. at KING'S (age 19) a scholar from Eton, Aug. 25, 1578. Perhaps of Northall Court, Middlesex. B. at Watford. Matric. 1578; B.A. 1582-3; M.A. 1586. Fellow, 1581-6. Died Oct. 26, 1624. (*Middlesex Pedigrees.*)

HOPE, ROBERT. Adm. sizar at CLARE, Dec. 22, 1634.

HOPE, WILLIAM. Adm. pens. (age 17) at ST JOHN'S, Apr. 1, 1719. S. of John (1682), M.D., of Derbyshire. B. at Derby. School, Derby (Mr Blackwell). Matric. 1719; M.B. 1724; M.D. from Christ's, 1728 (*Com. Reg.*). Died Feb. 1, 1776. Buried at St Alkmund's, Derby. Father of Charles (1750). (*Peile*, II. 217.)

HOPER, DUDLEY. Matric. pens. from CHRIST'S, Easter, 1624. S. of Richard, of St Andrew's parish, Middlesex. B.A. 1627-8; M.A. from Peterhouse, 1631; B.D. 1638; D.D. 1661 (*Lit. Reg.*). Fellow of Peterhouse, 1636. R. of Holme Hale, Norfolk, 1639-61. Brother of John (1628) and Nathaniel (1628). (*Peile*, I. 362; *T. A. Walker*, 42.)

HOPER, GOLDWELL. Adm. pens. (age 17) at CAIUS, May 23, 1662. S. of Richard, Esq., of London. B. there. School, Cheam, Surrey (Mr Aldrich). Matric. 1662; LL.B. 1667. Adm. at Gray's Inn, Jan. 29, 1669-70. (*Venn*, I. 416.)

HOPER, JOHN. Adm. pens. (age 14) at CHRIST'S, Mar. 29, 1628. S. of Richard, gent., of St Andrew's, Holborn. B. in London. School, London (Mr Harnaby). Matric. 1628; B.A. 1631-2; M.A. from Trinity Hall, 1635. (*Peile*, I. 390; *Genealogist*, v. 275.)

HOPER, NATHANIEL. Adm. pens. (age 15) at CHRIST'S, Mar. 29, 1628. S. of Richard, gent., of St Andrew's, Holborn. B. in London. School, London (Mr Harnaby). Matric. 1628. Adm. at Gray's Inn, 1631. Of Sunning, Berks. Living, 1664. Brother of Dudley and John (1628). (*Peile*, I. 390; *Genealogist*, v. 275.)

HOPES or HOPPS, FRANCIS. Adm. sizar (age 18) at ST JOHN'S, June 9, 1660. S. of Joseph, draper, of Richmond, Yorks. B. there. School, Durham. Matric. 1660; B.A. 1663-4; M.A. 1667. R. of Haceby, Lincs. R. of Aswarby, 1682-1705. His dau. Christian, married Sir Stephen Fox, and was the grandmother of Charles James Fox. Died Mar. 13, 1704-5. M.I. at Aswarby. (*Westminster Abbey Register*, 262.)

HOPES, OSBERT. Scholar of TRINITY, 1602; B.A. 1603-4; M.A. 1607. Ord. priest (Ely) 1607. V. of Ash Wicken, Norfolk, 1608-17. R. of Hardwick and Gt Setchey, 1616-52. R. of North Runcton, 1616-50. Died Nov. 20, 1652, aged 70. Buried at North Runcton. Will, P.C.C. Brother of Thomas (1582).

HOPES, SAMPSON. Matric. sizar from TRINITY, Easter, 1588; B.A. 1591-2; M.A. 1595. Ord. priest (Durham) June 27, 1592. V. of East Winch, Norfolk, 1592.

HOPES, THOMAS. Matric. sizar from TRINITY, Easter, 1582; B.A. 1586-7; M.A. 1590. Ord. deacon and priest (Lincoln) Oct. 2, 1587. R. of West Winch, Norfolk, 1588-90. V. of East Walton, 1590. R. of Colveston, 1592-1616. R. of North Runcton and Setchey, 1592-1616. V. of Didlington. Buried July 24, 1616. Brother of Osbert (1602).

HOPKINS, CHARLES. Adm. pens. at QUEENS', May 14, 1687. From Trinity College, Dublin. Adm. there, July 7, 1685, age 14. Of Devon. S. of Ezekiel, Bishop of Derry. B. at Dublin. Matric. 1687; B.A. 1688-9. Friend of Dryden and Congreve. Poet. Died *c.* 1700. Perhaps brother of John (1690). (*D.N.B.*; *Al. Dub.*)

HOPKINS, DANIEL. Adm. sizar (age 17) at TRINITY, June 6, 1676. S. of Thomas, of London. B. there, Nov. 19, 1657. School, St Paul's. Matric. 1676; Scholar, 1679; B.A. 1679-80; M.A. 1683; D.D. 1707. Fellow, 1682. V. of Orwell, Cambs., 1693-1700. R. of Fakenham, Norfolk, 1700-32. R. of Toftrees, till 1732. Died Apr. 16, 1732. M.I. at Fakenham.

HOPKINS, DANIEL. Adm. sizar (age 18) at TRINITY, Apr. 3, 1713. S. of Richard (1683), V. of Whitkirk, Yorks. School, York (Mr Herbert). Matric. 1713; Scholar, 1716; B.A. 1716-7. Ord. deacon (Ely) Sept. 22, 1717; priest (York) Dec. 1717. V. of Kellington, Yorks., 1717-35, resigned. V. of Whitkirk, 1735-43. Married Lydia, dau. of James Favell, of Normanton. Died 1743. Father of Favell (1745). (M. H. Peacock.)

HOPKINS, EDMUND. Adm. sizar at EMMANUEL, Oct. 5, 1591. Matric. *c.* 1592; Scholar; B.A. 1595-6; M.A. 1600. Ord. deacon (London) Jan. 18, 1600-1. R. of Danbury, Essex, 1605.

HOPKINS, EDMUND. Adm. pens. at EMMANUEL, Michs. 1627. Of Essex. Perhaps s. of the above. Matric. 1629-30; B.A. 1630-1; M.A. 1634.

HOPKINS, EDWARD. Matric. sizar from TRINITY, *c.* 1596.

HOPKINS, FAVELL. Adm. sizar (age 19) at TRINITY, Mar. 27, 1745. S. of Daniel (1713), V. of Whitkirk, Yorks. School, Leeds (Mr Barnard). Matric. 1745; Scholar, 1748; B.A. 1748-9; M.A. 1751. Ord. priest (Lincoln) Dec. 24, 1752. P.C. of Bury, Hunts., 1751-88.

HOPKINS, GEORGE. Matric. pens. from CORPUS CHRISTI, Michs. 1598. Of Norwich. Scholar of Trinity Hall, 1600.

HOPKINS, HENRY. Matric. pens. from CLARE, Easter, 1616; B.A. 1619-20; M.A. 1623. Fellow. One of these names, of London, Esq., adm. at Lincoln's Inn, Mar. 7, 1638-9.

HOPKINS, HUGH. Adm. sizar (age 17) at CHRIST'S, Apr. 27, 1702. S. of Marmaduke (1665). B. at Colchester, Oct. 30, 1685. Bapt. at St Vedast, London. School, Cheneys, Bucks. (Mr Burroughs). Matric. 1702; Scholar, 1704; B.A. 1705-6. (*Peile*, II. 152-3.)

HOPKINS, JAMES. Scholar of PETERHOUSE, 1597-1604. Probably s. of William, of Littleport, Cambs. B.A. 1600-1; M.A. 1604. Fellow. Ord. priest (Ely) 1609. V. of Gt Wenham, Suffolk, 1612-3. Author, *Sermon*. Died Dec. 1634. Will (Norwich C.C.) 1635. Brother of Robert (1575). (*Cooper*, III. 16.)

HOPKINS, JAMES. Adm. pens. at EMMANUEL, Mar. 9, 1629-30. Of Suffolk. Perhaps s. of James, above. Matric. 1631; B.A. 1633-4; M.A. 1637. Ord. deacon (Norwich) Sept. 22, 1638; priest, Dec. 22, 1639.

HOPKIN, JOHN. B.A. 1477-8; M.A. 1481. Probably V. of Histon St Etheldreda, Cambs., 1491.

HOPKINS, JOHN. Adm. pens. at QUEENS', Michs. 1599; B.A. 1603-4; M.A. 1607. Author, *Sermon*. (*Cooper*, III. 59.)

HOPKINS, JOHN. Scholar of TRINITY, 1619; B.A. 1620-1.

HOPKINS, JOHN. Adm. sizar at QUEENS', July 4, 1627. Of Dorset.

HOPKINS, JOHN. Matric. sizar from KING'S, Easter, 1632. Perhaps s. of Samuel (? 1606-7), V. of Studham, Beds. Bapt. there, June 18, 1616. B.A. 1636-7; M.A. 1640. Ord. deacon (Peterb.) May 20, 1638. One of these names V. of Flitwick, Beds., 1642.

HOPKINS, JOHN. Adm. sizar (age 18) at SIDNEY, May 19, 1636. S. of Edward, clothier. B. at Tiverton. School, Tiverton (Mr Butler). Matric. 1636; B.A. 1639-40.

HOPKINS, JOHN. Adm. sizar at ST JOHN'S, June 2, 1662. S. of Henry, deceased, of Burton-on-Trent, Staffs. B. there. School, Repton (Mr Ullock). Matric. 1662; B.A. 1665-6; M.A. 1669.

HOPKINS, JOHN. Adm. sizar at JESUS, May 10, 1690. Of Yorkshire. Perhaps s. of Ezekiel, Bishop of Derry. B. Jan. 1, 1675. Matric. 1690; B.A. 1693-4; M.A. 1698. Ord. deacon (Norwich) Mar. 1697-8; priest (York) Sept. 1698. Perhaps the verse-writer. If so, brother of Charles (1687). (*D.N.B.*)

HOPKINS, JONATHAN. Adm. sizar at TRINITY, June 7, 1648. Of Salop. Matric. 1648. Perhaps C. of Lightcliffe, Yorks., *c.* 1655. 'An old friend of mine in Cambridge, but a monstrous drunkard, and had a prodigious end.' (Ol. Heywood, *Diaries*, IV. 324.)

HOPKINS, MARMADUKE. Adm. sizar at CHRIST'S, July 1, 1665. Matric. 1667; B.A. 1668-9; M.A. 1677. Ord. deacon (Lincoln) Dec. 1669; priest, Mar. 29, 1670. R. of Tydd St Mary, Cambs., 1675-84. R. of St Michael-le-Querne, 1684. R. of St Vedast, Foster Lane, 1684-1707. President of Sion College, 1705. Author, *Sermon*. Buried at St Vedast, Oct. 21, 1707. Father of Hugh (1702). (*Peile*, I. 619.)

HOPKINS, NICHOLAS. 'Of TRINITY College,' when ord. deacon (Ely) Mar. 23, 1566-7; priest, Sept. 21, 1567. R. of Harrington, Northants. (age 34 in 1576) till 1599. R. of Dingley, 1599-1608. Died 1608. (H. I. Longden.)

HOPKINS, RICHARD. Matric. pens. from ST JOHN'S, Michs. 1589.

HOPKINS, RICHARD. Adm. sizar at EMMANUEL, Apr. 5, 1619. Matric. 1619. Perhaps R. of Frodsham, Cheshire, in 1657.

HOPKINS, RICHARD. Matric. Fell.-Com. from TRINITY, Easter, 1631. 2nd s. of Sampson, alderman of Coventry, deceased. Adm. at the Inner Temple, 1630. Barrister, 1639. Serjeant-at-law. Bencher. Steward of Coventry, 1647. Doubtless M.P. for Coventry, 1660. Knighted, Sept. 1, 1660. Lord of Foleshill. Died Jan. 1682. Brother of Samuel (1631), father of Richard (1657). (*Lipscomb*, I. 377.)

HOPKINS, RICHARD. Adm. Fell.-Com. at MAGDALENE, June 3, 1647. Of the Wood Houses.

HOPKINS, RICHARD. Adm. pens. at TRINITY, Sept. 28, 1657. S. of Sir Richard (1631). Matric. 1657. Adm. at the Inner Temple, 1658. Barrister, 1665. M.P. for Coventry, 1678-81, 1690-5, 1698-1707. Died Feb. 1, 1707, aged 68. Buried at Coventry. (*Lipscomb*, I. 377; A. B. Beaven.)

HOPKINS, RICHARD. Adm. sizar (age 17) at TRINITY, June 11, 1683. S. of Thomas. School, St Paul's. Matric. 1683; Scholar, 1687; B.A. 1687-8; M.A. 1693. V. of Whitkirk, Yorks., 1688-1701. Died Feb. 15, 1701. Father of Daniel (1713).

HOPKINS, RICHARD. Adm. Fell.-Com. at QUEENS', Feb. 13, 1745-6. Of Coventry. S. and h. of Edward, of Coventry, Esq., deceased. B. 1728. Matric. 1746. M.P. for Dartmouth, 1766-80, 1784-90; for Thetford, 1780-4; for Queenborough, 1790-6; for Harwich, 1796-9. Lord of the Admiralty, 1782-3, 1784-91. Lord of the Treasury, 1791-7. Died Mar. 19, 1799, aged 71. Buried at Coventry. (*Lipscomb*, I. 377; A. B. Beaven.)

HOPKINS, ROBERT. Matric. sizar from JESUS, Michs. 1575. Probably s. of William, of Littleport, Isle of Ely; and brother, by the 1st wife, of James (1597). B.A. 1578-9. Catechist of the House of Bridewell. Will proved (P.C.C.) Apr. 13, 1587. (W. M. Noble.)

HOPKINS, SAMPSON. Adm. pens. (age 17) at PEMBROKE, Dec. 31, 1657. S. of Sampson, gent. B. at Coventry. Matric. 1660; B.A. 1661-2; M.A. 1669. One of these names V. of Gt Wigston, Leics. Will (Leicester) 1693.

HOPKINS, SAMUEL. B.A. from TRINITY, 1606-7; M.A. 1612. (Perhaps matric. from Trinity College, Oxford, May 6, 1603. Of Essex. Age 16.) (Perhaps s. of Edward, V. of Nasing.) B. at Nasing, Essex, c. 1585. Ord. deacon (Lincoln) Dec. 18, 1608; priest, Sept. 24, 1609. V. of Studham, Beds., 1610-21. V. of Pulloxhill, 1621. Married Parnell Whitley. Died at Pulloxhill, 1657. Perhaps father of John (1632).

HOPKINS, SAMUEL. Matric. Fell.-Com. from TRINITY, Easter, 1631. S. and h. of Sampson, alderman of Coventry, deceased. Adm. at the Inner Temple, 1630. Brother of Richard (1631).

HOPKINS, SAMUEL. Adm. pens. (age 17) at ST JOHN'S, May 21, 1657. S. of Richard, clerk, of Frodsham, Cheshire. B. there. School, Shrewsbury (Mr Piggott). Matric. 1660; B.A. 1660-1.

HOPKINS, SAMUEL. Adm. pens. at QUEENS', Jan. 25, 1687-8. Of Devon.

HOPKINS, STEPHEN. Adm. at KING'S (age 17) a scholar from Eton, Aug. 15, 1532; B.A. 1536; M.A. 1539. Fellow, 1535-52. Vice-Provost. R. of West Wretham, Norfolk, 1551; and of East Wretham, 1556-8. Chaplain to Cardinal Pole. Deprived on the accession of Elizabeth, and for a time imprisoned in the Fleet. Admon. (P.C.C.) Feb. 1569-70, of one of these names; of Berks., clerk. (*Cooper*, I. 212.)

HOPKYNS, THOMAS. Matric. pens. (age 13) from JESUS, Michs. 1552. Perhaps LL.B. 1564.

HOPKINS, THOMAS. Matric. sizar (age 12) from ST JOHN'S, Michs. 1562.

HOPKINS, THOMAS. Adm. pens. at TRINITY, Apr. 8, 1675. Matric. 1675; B.A. 1678-9. One of these names V. of Enderby, Leics., 1678; and afterwards of Kirkby Mallory.

HOPKINS, WILLIAM. B.A. from JESUS, 1606-7; M.A. 1610. Ord. deacon (Peterb.) Sept. 20, 1607; priest, Dec. 17, 1609. One of these names R. of Harvington, Worcs., 1625.

HOPKINS, WILLIAM. Matric. pens. from TRINITY, Easter, 1613; B.A. 1616-7; M.A. 1620.

HOPKINS, WILLIAM. Adm. Fell.-Com. at TRINITY, 1656. Matric. 1658. Perhaps adm. at the Inner Temple, 1658.

HOPKINS, WILLIAM. Adm. at PETERHOUSE, Nov. 15, 1675. Matric. 1675; B.A. 1677-8; M.A. 1681. Previously matric. from Balliol College, Oxford, Apr. 3, 1674, age 16, as s. of John, of Martin, Worcs. B. June 7, 1659. R. of Llanfihangel Ystern Llewerne, Mon. Buried Nov. 4, 1708. Will proved, Oct. 4, 1709. (*Misc. Gen. et Her.*, 2nd S., III. 260.)

HOPKINS, WILLIAM. M.A. from CHRIST'S, 1700. S. of Charles, of Sutton-at-Hone, clerk. B. at Sutton. Matric. from Oriel, Oxford, 1693, age 18; B.A. (Oxford) 1696. Ord. priest (Rochester) 1698. V. of Horton Kirby, Kent, 1698-1742. Buried there Nov. 5, 1742. (*Al. Oxon.*; *Peile*, II. 149.)

HOPKIN, WILLIAM. Adm. pens. (age 18) at PEMBROKE, July 6, 1705. S. of Thomas (? 1675), R. of Kirkby Mallory, Leics. B. there.

HOPKINS, WILLIAM. Adm. at CORPUS CHRISTI, 1711. Of Hertfordshire. Matric. 1712; B.A. 1715-6; M.A. 1721. Ord. deacon (London) Dec. 20, 1719; priest, Mar. 13, 1719-20. R. of Strethall, Essex. V. of Elmdon, 1720-80. Will (Archd. Colchester) 1780. (J. Ch. Smith.)

HOPKINS, WILLIAM. Adm. sizar (age 19) at TRINITY, Jan. 14, 1716-7. S. of James, of Axbridge, Somerset. School, Wells (Mr Creighton). Matric. 1718; Scholar, 1720; B.A. 1720-1.

HOPKINS, WILLIAM. Adm. pens. (age 16) at PETERHOUSE, Jan. 2, 1743-4. Of Essex. School, Bishop's Stortford. Matric. 1743-4; Scholar, 1744.

HOPKINSON, EDMUND. Adm. sizar at CLARE, May 30, 1722. B. at Burton Coggles, Lincs. Matric. 1723; B.A. 1725-6; M.A. 1729. Fellow, 1727-54. Ord. deacon (Ely) Dec. 19, 1731; priest, Mar. 5, 1731-2. V. of Everton, Hunts., 1743-54. R. of Hardingham, Norfolk, 1754-9. Died 1759.

HOPKINSON, EDWARD. Matric. pens. from ST JOHN'S, Michs. 1616.

HOPKINSON, HENRY. Matric. pens. from ST JOHN'S, Michs. 1613; B.A. 1617-8. One of these names, s. and h. of Anthony, of Wirksworth, Derbs., gent., adm. at Lincoln's Inn, Oct. 30, 1616. (*Vis. of Derbs.*, 1662.)

HOPKINSON, HENRY. Adm. sizar at CLARE, June 15, 1714. B. at Burton, Lincs., 1697. Matric. 1714; B.A. 1717-8; M.A. 1721. Fellow, 1720-5. Ord. deacon (Ely) Sept. 19; priest, Sept. 25, 1725. R. of Patrington, Yorks., 1725-34. Died 1734.

HOPKINSON, JABEZ. Matric. pens. from ST JOHN'S, Michs. 1602.

HOPKINSON, JEREMY. Matric. sizar from ST JOHN'S, Easter, 1595. B. at Halifax. B.A. 1599-1600; M.A. 1603. Ord. deacon (Peterb.) Aug. 28, 1603; priest (London) June 10, 1609, age 29. C. of St Antholin's, London. V. of Little Wakering, Essex, 1609-11. Died 1611. Admon. (Cons. C. London) 1611.

HOPKINSON, JOHN. Adm. pens. at SIDNEY, Oct. 22, 1614. Of Lincolnshire. Matric. 1614. Migrated to Queens', Jan. 31, 1617-8; B.A. 1618-9.

'**HOPKINSON, JOHN BENJAMIN.**' Mistake in ***Matric. and Degrees for*** **HODGKINSON.**

HOPKINSON, JOHN. Adm. pens. (age 17) at TRINITY, Mar. 21, 1728-9, from St Catharine's Hall, where he had matric. 1729. S. of Robert, of Wakefield, Yorks. School, Sandal, Yorks. (Mr Zouch). Scholar, 1730; B.A. 1732-3; M.A. 1737. Ord. deacon (Lincoln) Dec. 22, 1734; C. of Adel, Yorks. Perhaps R. of Yarm and Kirk Levington, Yorks. Died Oct. 23, 1794, 'aged 87.' (*G. Mag.*)

HOPKINSON, JUDAH. Matric. sizar from ST JOHN'S, c. 1596; B.A. 1600-1; M.A. 1604. Ord. deacon (Peterb.) Sept. 17, 1604; priest, Sept. 22, 1605.

HOPKYNSON, RICHARD. Matric. pens. from ST JOHN'S, Michs. 1569.

HOPKINSON, RICHARD. B.A. from ST JOHN'S, 1593-4; M.A. 1597. Ord. deacon (Peterb.) Mar. 27, 1595; priest, Feb. 14, 1595-6. One of these names buried at Alderton, Northants., May 7, 1604. (H. I. Longden.)

HOPKINSON, RICHARD. Matric. pens. from CLARE, Easter, 1612; B.A. 1615-6.

HOPKINSON, RICHARD. Adm. sizar (age 13) at PETERHOUSE, Apr. 25, 1627. S. of John, of Lincoln's Inn, Counsellor-at-law, sometime of Boston. Bapt. at Alford, Lincs., July 9, 1614. Matric. 1627. Afterwards of Alford. (*T. A. Walker*, 35.)

HOPKINSON, W. B.Civ.L. 1510-1.

HOPKINSON, WILLIAM. Matric. sizar from ST JOHN'S, Lent, 1564-5; B.A. 1567-8; M.A. 1571. Ord. deacon (Ely) May 26, 1566. R. of Holton *with* Beckering, Lincs., till 1571. Author, religious. (*Cooper*, II. 5; *D.N.B.*)

HOPKINSON, ——. Matric. pens. from CHRIST'S, Easter, 1544.

HOPPER, JOHN. B.A. 1532-3. Of Sutton, Lincs. M.A. 1535; B.D. 1548. Fellow of ST JOHN'S, 1554. Ord. deacon (Lincoln) Mar. 13, 1534-5; priest, Mar. 27, 1535 (then fellow of Clare). V. of Barkway, Herts., 1554-63. R. of Reed, 1556-62.

HOPPER, RALPH. Adm. pens. (age 19) at PETERHOUSE, May 28, 1750. S. of John, of Shincliffe, Durham. Bapt. at St Oswald's, Durham, May 25, 1731. School, Durham. Scholar, 1750; Matric. 1751. Adm. at Lincoln's Inn, Jan. 29, 1750-1; and at the Inner Temple, Feb. 3, 1753. Barrister-at-law. Recorder of Hartlepool, 1758-81. Married Philadelphia, dau. of William Cuthbert, recorder of Newcastle. Died Jan. 11, 1786. Buried at Bishop Middleham. M.I. there. (*T. A. Walker*, 298; H. M. Wood.)

HOPPER or HAPPER, RICHARD. Matric. pens. from QUEENS', Michs. 1622. Of London.

HOPPER, RICHARD. Adm. Fell.-Com. (age 18) at PETERHOUSE, June 29, 1658. Of London. Doubtless s. of Richard, of St Andrew's, Holborn. Adm. at the Middle Temple, Feb. 25, 1658-9. (*T. A. Walker*, 114.)

HOPPER, THOMAS. Adm. sizar (age 18) at PETERHOUSE, May 21, 1750. Of Durham. School, Durham. Matric. 1751; Scholar, 1753; B.A. 1754; M.A. 1757. Probably fellow. Chaplain to the Bishop of Chester. V. of Bowdon, Cheshire. Preb. of Ely, 1772-9. R. of Little Gransden and Barley, Herts., 1774. Died 1779. Buried at Barley. Probably brother of Ralph (1750). (*T. A. Walker*, 298.)

HOPPER, ——. B.A. 1537-8. The fellow of CLARE in 1549 was probably John above.

HOPPERTON or HOPPERSON, NICHOLAS. Matric. sizar from CORPUS CHRISTI, Lent, 1580-1; B.A. 1585-6.

HOPPEY, MATTHEW. Matric. pens. from ST JOHN'S, Michs. 1560.

HOPPS, FRANCIS. Adm. pens. at SIDNEY, June 3, 1605. Matric. 1605; B.A. 1608-9; M.A. from St Catharine's, 1612. Ord. deacon (Peterb.) Sept. 26; priest, Sept. 27, 1613.

HOPTON, INGRAM. Adm. Fell.-Com. (age 16) at ST JOHN'S, May 12, 1631. S. of Ralph, Esq., of Armley, Yorks. B. there. Bapt. Feb. 25, 1614-5. School, Wakefield (Mr Doughty). Matric. 1631. Adm. at the Middle Temple, Feb. 1, 1632-3. Lord of the Manor of Armley and Wortley. Knighted, 1642. Colonel in the Royalist army. Married, 1634, Eleanor Lindley, of Leathley. Killed at Winceby, Oct. 11, 1643. Buried at Horncastle. M.I. Will, York. (M. H. Peacock.)

HOPTON, JOHN. S. of William, probabl of Mirfield, Yorks. A Dominican friar. Prior of the orderyat Oxford. Studied also at Cambridge. B.D. Oxford, 1521-2; D.D. Bologna. Incorp. at Oxford, 1529. D.D. Oxford, 1532. R. of St Anne, Aldersgate, London, 1539-48. R. of Fobbing, Essex, 1548. Chaplain to the Princess Mary. Bishop of Norwich, 1554-8. R. of Gt Yeldham, Essex, till 1558. One of the most active persecutors of protestants. Died Dec. 1558. Will (P.C.C.) 1559. (*Cooper*, I. 186; *D.N.B.*)

HOPTON, JOHN. Adm. pens. (age 17) at SIDNEY, May 23, 1682. S. of John, captain, deceased. B. at Northallerton, Yorks. School, York. Matric. 1682. One of these names of Hingerskil, Yorks., Esq. Died Apr. 24, 1703. (*Duc. Leod.*, 188.)

HOPTON, THOMAS. Matric. sizar from TRINITY HALL, *c.* 1593. Probably of Mirfield, Yorks. Licensed, 1596, to marry Bridget, dau. of Thomas Metham, of Metham. (M. H. Peacock.)

HOPTON, ——. B.Can.L. 1468-9. This, or the next (if two), must be William Hopton, of ST CLEMENT'S HOSTEL. Admon. (V.C.C.) 1508, to John Wakefield, of Clement's Hostel.

HOPTON, ——. B.Can.L. 1477-8.

HOPWOOD, ANTHONY. Matric. pens. from ST JOHN'S, Michs. 1589; B.A. 1593-4; M.A. 1597. R. of South Rasen, Lincs., 1618-35.

HOPWOOD, DANIEL. Adm. pens. at EMMANUEL, July 12, 1598.

HOPWOOD, EDMUND. Adm. Fell.-Com. (age 16) at ST JOHN'S, May 24, 1706. S. of John, of Hopwood, near Middleton, Lancs. B. there. Bapt. at Middleton, Oct. 22, 1689. School, Oxford (Mr Badjer). Matric. 1706. Adm. at Gray's Inn, June 18, 1708.

HOPWOOD, JOHN. Adm. at CLARE, June 18, 1641. Matric. sizar from King's, 1641. S. of Edmund, chaplain to the Collegiate Church, Manchester. School, Manchester. In 1647, a child of 'Mr John Hopwood, minister,' was bapt. at Manchester. (E. Axon.)

HOPWOOD, JOHN. Adm. Fell.-Com. at ST CATHARINE'S, Sept. 18, 1678. Probably s. and h. of John, of Hopwood, Lancs., Esq.; adm. at Gray's Inn, May 12, 1680.

HOPWOOD, JOHN. Adm. Fell.-Com. (age 19) at ST JOHN'S, Oct. 25, 1731. S. of John, Esq., of Essex. B. at Stannaway. Educated by his father.

HOPPWOOD, LEONARD. Adm. sizar at EMMANUEL, June 13, 1591.

HOPWOOD, RALPH. Probably fellow of JESUS, *c.* 1530. V. of Fen Ditton, Cambs., 1517-38. Died Oct. 2, 1538. (A. Gray.)

HOPWOOD, RICHARD. Adm. sizar (age 18) at ST JOHN'S, May 9, 1674. S. of James, of Oldham, Lancs. B. there. School, Manchester. Matric. 1674.

HORBERRY, HUGH. Matric. sizar from PEMBROKE, Easter, 1588. Ord. deacon (York) Oct. 26, 1597; priest (Lincoln) Feb. 1, 1600-1. C. of South Hykeham, Lincs., in 1614. Will (Lincoln) 1615.

HORBERY, JAMES. Matric. sizar from CORPUS CHRISTI, Michs. 1625. Of Nottinghamshire. B.A. 1628-9; M.A. 1632.

HORBURY, JOHN. Adm. sizar at JESUS, May 19, 1682. Of Lincolnshire. S. of ——, clerk, deceased. Matric. 1682; Scholar, 1682; B.A. 1685-6. One of these names R. of Gumley, Leics. Admon. (Leicester) 1716.

HORBERY, MARTIN. Matric. sizar from CORPUS CHRISTI, Easter, 1639. Of Nottinghamshire. B.A. 1641-2; M.A. 1660. Preb. of Southwell, 1660-72. Died 1672.

HORBERRY, MARTIN. Adm. sizar at QUEENS', June 11, 1679. Of Nottinghamshire. Matric. 1679. Probably ord. priest (Lincoln) Dec. 19, 1686. R. of Althorpe, Lincs., 1702-21.

HORBERIE, WILLIAM. Adm. pens. (age 16) at ST JOHN'S, May 29, 1632. S. of William, husbandman, of Walkeringham, Notts. B. there. School, Southwell (Mr Sechell). Matric. 1632; B.A. 1635-6; M.A. 1639. Fellow, 1641.

HORDEN, JOHN. Adm. pens. at TRINITY, May 25, 1658. School, Westminster. Scholar, 1659; Matric. 1660; B.A. 1661-2; M.A. 1665; D.D. 1682 (*Lit. Reg.*). Fellow, 1664. Subscribed for deacon's orders (London) May 19, 1665; for priest's, June 2, 1665. V. of St Michael Queenhithe, London, 1671-90. V. of Isleworth, Middlesex, 1681-90. Married Anne, dau. of Thomas Morice, M.P. Died 1690. Will (Consist. C. London) 1690. (*Genealogist*, XXX. 235.)

HORDIS, JOHN. Adm. sizar at CLARE, June 12, 1673.

HORE, *see* **HOARE.**

HORLEE, JOHN DE. 'KING'S scholar' at Cambridge, 1327.

HORLEY, JOHN. B.D. One of those nominated to assist William Bingham in founding his college of God's House, afterwards CHRIST'S.

HORMAN, WILLIAM. At one time of KING'S College. B. at Salisbury. School, Winchester. Fellow of New College, Oxford, 1477-85. Head Master of Eton, 1489-92. Head Master of Winchester, 1495-1502. Fellow of Eton, 1502-35. Vice-Provost. R. of East Wretham, Norfolk, 1494-1503. Author. Died Apr. 12, 1535. Buried in the College Chapel at Eton. (*Cooper*, I. 51; *D.N.B.*; *Harwood*, 55.)

HORNBY, EDMUND. Adm. Fell.-Com. (age 18) at SIDNEY, May 30, 1747. 1st s. of Geoffrey (1703), Esq., of Poulton and Scale Hall, Lancs. Bapt. at Preston, Oct. 8, 1728. School, Preston (Mr Oliver). Matric. 1747. Married Margaret, dau. of John Winckley, Esq., of Preston. Died Sept. 30, 1766. Brother of Geoffrey (1748). (J. Foster, *Lancs. Pedigrees.*)

HORNBY, EDWARD. Adm. pens. at JESUS, Sept. 27, 1696. Eldest s. of Edmund, of Poulton and Scale Hall. Matric. 1697. Scholar. Adm. at the Inner Temple, Nov. 16, 1696. Died *v.p.* Brother of the next, and George (1705-6). (J. Parker.)

HORNBY, GEOFFREY. Adm. pens. (age 18) at ST JOHN'S, Sept. 18, 1703. S. of Edmund, of Poulton, Lancs. Bapt. at Poulton, Apr. 9, 1684. School, Sedbergh. Adm. at the Inner Temple, Nov. 25, 1701. Of Poulton-le-Fylde, Lancs. Married Susanna, dau. and heiress of Edward Sherdley, of Poulton. Died Mar. 27, 1732. Buried in Poulton Church. Brother of George (1705-6). (*Sedbergh School Register*; J. Foster, *Lancs. Pedigrees.*)

HORNBY, GEOFFREY. Adm. pens. (age 18) at SIDNEY, Mar. 28, 1748. 2nd s. of Geoffrey (above), of Preston, Lancs. B. there, Jan. 24, 1730. School, Preston (Mr Oliver). Matric. 1748-9. Died at Preston, Nov. 24, 1801. Brother of Edmund (1747). (J. Foster, *Lancs. Pedigrees.*)

HORNBY, GEORGE. Adm. pens. (age 18) at ST JOHN'S, Jan. 21, 1705-6. 3rd s. of Edmund, of Poulton-le-Fylde, Preston. Bapt. at Preston, Aug. 26, 1685. School, Sedbergh (Mr Wharton). Matric. 1705-6; B.A. 1709-10; M.A. 1713. Ord. deacon (Peterb.) Sept. 20, 1712; C. of Stoke Albany, Northants. R. of Whittington, Lancs., 1706-48. Died Nov. 15, 1747. Brother of Geoffrey (1703). (*Sedbergh School Register.*)

HORNEBY, HENRY. B.D. 1489-90; D.D. 1495. Fellow of CLARE; afterwards of Michaelhouse. Dean of St Chad's, Shrewsbury, 1492-3. R. of Burton Bradstock, Dorset, 1495-1517. Probably R. of Thrapston, Northants., 1495-8. Preb. of Southwell, 1496-1518. Preb. of Lincoln, 1501-18. Dean of Wimborne, Dorset. R. of Over, Cambs. R. of Orwell, 1508-18. Master of Peterhouse, 1509. Master of the College at Tattershall, Lincs., 1513. As secretary to the Lady Margaret he was largely instrumental in the foundation of St John's College. Died Feb. 12, 1517-8. Buried in Little St Mary's, Cambridge. Will, P.C.C. Benefactor of Peterhouse and Clare. Endowed the Mastership of a school at Boston. (*Cooper*, I. 19; *D.N.B.*; *T. A. Walker.*)

HORNBY, JOHN. D.D. of Cambridge. Flourished *c.* 1374. Carmelite friar. B. in Lincolnshire. (*Pits*, 514.)

HORNBY, JOHN. Adm. sizar (age 17) at SIDNEY, Mar. 21, 1677-8. 1st s. of John, shopkeeper, deceased. B. at Snaith, Yorks. School, Yarborough (private; Mr Shaw). Matric. 1678; B.A. 1681-2. Ord. deacon (York) Sept. 1682. Perhaps V. of Mentmore, Bucks.; committed suicide by hanging himself, 1697. (*Lipscomb*, III.)

HORNEBY, NICHOLAS. B.A. 1528-9; M.A. 1532. Fellow of PETERHOUSE, 1531-43.

HORNEBY, ROBERT. Adm. at KING'S, a scholar from Eton, 1484. Will of one of these names (Consist. C. London) 1517; of St John Walbrook, London.

HORNBY, THOMAS. Matric. pens. from MAGDALENE, Michs. 1642; B.A. 1646.

HORNBY, WALTER. Adm. pens. at EMMANUEL, Apr. 20, 1609. S. of Walter. Matric. 1609; Scholar; B.A. 1612-3; M.A. 1616. Ord. deacon (Peterb.) Dec. 19, 1613; priest, Mar. 16, 1616-7. R. of Marston Trussel, Northants., 1622. Married, at Welford, Northants., Dec. 14, 1626, Constance Cowper, of Market Harborough. Buried at Marston, Aug. 6, 1662. M.I. Father of the next. (H. I. Longden.)

HORNBY, WALTER. Matric. pens. from EMMANUEL, Michs. 1647. S. of Walter (above), R. of Marston Trussel, Northants. Bapt. there, Jan. 11, 1628–9. B.A. 1649–50; M.A. 1653. Took holy orders, but refused to conform. His father had bought the advowson of Marston, but he refused presentation. Preached in Northants. Of Lubenham, Leics. Patron of Marston. Died Dec. 20, 1687, at Lubenham. Buried at Marston Trussel. M.I. (*Nichols*, II. 675; H. I. Longden.)

HORNBY, WALTER. Adm. pens. at EMMANUEL, June 22, 1683. Of Middlesex. Became Fell.-Com. 1684.

HORNEBY, WILLIAM. Adm. pens. at EMMANUEL, May 3, 1682. Of Bedfordshire. Matric. 1685; B.A. 1685–6.

HORNCASTLE, WILLIAM. Adm. sizar (age 16) at SIDNEY, Nov. 1, 1636. S. of Richard, yeoman. B. at Wentbridge, Badsworth, Yorks. School, Wakefield (Mr Ro. Doughty). Matric. 1637; B.A. 1640–1. Perhaps married Jane, dau. of Godfrey Copley, Esq., of Shelbrooke, Yorks. (M. H. Peacock.)

HORNCASTLE, ——. M.A. or higher degree, 1473–4. Perhaps 'Thomas,' V. of Cuddington, Surrey, 1490–1500. Died 1500.

HORNE, CHARLES. Matric. pens. from TRINITY, Easter, 1569, a scholar from Westminster; B.A. 1572–3. Migrated to Peterhouse, Mar. 31, 1576. M.A. 1577; B.D. 1585. Fellow of Peterhouse, 1576. Scrutator, 1587. R. of Sturry, Kent, 1597–1618. V. of Chislet, 1601–18. Author, Greek and Latin poems. Died 1618. (*Cooper*, II. 222.)

HORNE, CHRISTOPHER. M.B. from ST CATHARINE'S, 1679. Probably s. of Christopher, of Birmingham, gent. Matric. from Magdalen Hall, Oxford, June 2, 1674, age 17; B.A. (Oxford) 1677–8. (*Al. Oxon.*)

HORN, CORNELIUS. Adm. sizar (age 19) at PETERHOUSE, July 3, 1714. Of Derbyshire. School, Mansfield. Matric. 1714; B.A. 1719–20. Ord. deacon (York) Dec. 1717; priest, Sept. 15, 1726. Head Master of Drighlington School, Yorks., 1719. V. of Hartshead, Yorks., 1726–38. R. of Farnley, 1729–34.

HORNE, COTTON. Matric. sizar from CLARE, Easter, 1620; B.A. 1623–4. Ord. deacon (York) June, 1625; priest, Sept. 1625. O e of these names s. of Cotton, of Hemsworth, was steward ofithe Honour of Pontefract. Died 1656. Possibly brother of William (1631). (*Vis. of Yorks.*, 1666.)

HORNE, GABRIEL. B.A. from ST JOHN'S, 1604–5.

HORN, GEORGE. Adm. sizar (age 19) at PETERHOUSE, Jan. 23, 1723–4. Of Derbyshire. School, Chesterfield. Matric. 1724; Scholar, 1724; B.A. 1729–30. Ord. deacon (Lincoln) Dec. 24, 1732. C. of Sutton-in-Ashfield, Notts.

HORNE, GUSTAVUS. M.A. 1633 (*fil. nob.*). Created M.A. at Oxford, Mar. 21, 1632–3. Adm. at Lincoln's Inn, Mar. 21, 1632–3. Lord of Kankas and Purkala, in Sweden.

HORNE, HEZEKIAH. Adm. at KING'S, a scholar from Eton, 1666. B. at Eton. Matric. 1667; B.A. 1670–1. Fellow, 1670. Died young.

HORNE, ISAAC. Matric. sizar from ST JOHN'S, Easter, 1583; B.A. 1587–8. Perhaps R. of St Martin, Wareham, Dorset, 1602–5. Will of one of these names (P.C.C.) 1634; of Ellisfield, Hants., clerk. (J. Ch. Smith.)

HORNE, JOHN. Adm. at KING'S (age 17) a scholar from Eton, 1453. Of Cambridge.

HORNE, JOHN. M.A. 1629 (Incorp. from Oxford). Of Hertfordshire, gent. Matric. from Oriel College, Oxford, Oct. 27, 1615, age 16; B.A. (Oxford) 1616; M.A. 1620; B.D. 1640. Fellow of Oriel, 1617–48, ejected. V. of Headington, Oxon., 1636.

HORNE, JOHN. Matric. sizar from TRINITY, Michs. 1633. B. at Long Sutton, Lincs., 1614. B.A. 1636–7. Ord. deacon (Peterb.) June 9; priest, Dec. 22, 1639. V. of Sutton St James, Lincs. R. of All Hallows, Lynn, in 1659; ejected, 1662. Author, religious, controversial. Died Dec. 14, 1676, aged 61. Father of the next. (*D.N.B.*; *Calamy*, II. 198.)

HORNE, JOHN. Adm. pens. (age 14) at CAIUS, Feb. 17, 1658–9. S. of John (above), of Lynn. B. at Sutton St James, Lincs. School, Lynn. Matric. 1659; Scholar, 1659–63; B.A. 1662–3; M.A. 1666. Incorp. at Oxford, 1684. Usher of Lynn Grammar School, 1668. Head Master, 1678–1728; not in orders. Married Ann, dau. of Thomas Donne, of Holt Market, Norfolk. Died 1732. Buried at St Nicholas, Lynn. M.I. (*Venn*, I. 404.)

HORNE, JOSIAH. Matric. sizar from TRINITY, c. 1593. B. at Luton, Beds. B.A. 1596–7; M.A. 1600. Ord. deacon and priest (London) Jan. 25 and 26, 1597–8, age 25. V. of Orwell, Cambs., 1599. R. of Winwick, Lancs., 1616–26. Died 1626.

HORNE or LE HORNE, JOSIAS. Adm. pens. at JESUS, June 8, 1619. Of Surrey. Matric. 1620; B.A. 1622–3; M.A. 1626.

HORNE, JOSIAS. Matric. pens. from PETERHOUSE, Lent, 1626–7. Of Berkshire. Migrated to Oxford. B.A. from Pembroke College, 1630, as 'Joshua.' V. of Nocton, Lincs., 1632; and of Aston, Warws., 1647. (*Al. Oxon.*)

HORNE, MOSES. Adm. pens. (age 16) at CAIUS, June 9, 1636. S. of Moses, tailor. B. at Cambridge. Bapt. at Gt St Mary's, Nov. 13, 1619. School, Perse (Mr Lovering). Matric. 1636. Probably a professional copyist in Cambridge. Died June 18, 1656. M.I. at Gt St Mary's. (*Venn*, I. 322.)

HORNE, NICHOLAS. Adm. at KING'S, a scholar from Eton, 1561. B. at Saffron Walden, Essex, 1543. Matric. 1561; B.A. 1565–6; M.A. 1569; B.D. 1577. Fellow, 1564–79. Ord. deacon (London) Sept. 21, 1569; priest (Ely) Dec. 21, 1569. University preacher, 1573.

HORNE, RICHARD. Adm. pens. (age 18) at SIDNEY, Apr. 25, 1649. S. of Francis, Esq. B. at Almondbury, Yorks. School, Almondbury (Mr Geo. Ferrand). Matric. 1649; B.A. 1652–3. P.C. of Stowe-by-Chartley, Staffs., in 1655. Perhaps V. of Cosby, Leics., 1659.

HORNE, ROBERT. B.A. 1536–7. S. of John, of Cleator, Cumberland. M.A. 1540; B.D. 1546; D.D. 1559. Fellow of ST JOHN'S, 1536. Hebrew lecturer, 1545–6. Incorp. at Oxford, 1568. V. of Matching, Essex, 1546–53. R. of Bunwell, Norfolk, 1549. R. of All Hallows, Bread St, 1550–2. Chaplain to Edward VI. Dean of Durham, 1551–3. Preb. of York, 1552. Retired to Zurich and Frankfort, during the reign of Mary. Adm. at Basel University, 1558. Restored to his deanery, 1559–61. Appointed one of the visitors of the University of Cambridge and of Eton College; a fanatical enforcer of conformity. Bishop of Winchester, 1561–80. Assisted in the revision of the authorised version known as the *Bishops' Bible*. Author, sermons, etc. Died at Winchester Place, Southwark, June 1, 1580. Buried at Winchester. (*Cooper*, I. 407; *D.N.B.*)

HORNE, ROBERT. Matric. pens. from QUEENS', Lent, 1653–4. Of Nottinghamshire.

HORNE, SAMUEL. M.A. 1598 (Incorp. from Oxford). Of Hertfordshire, gent. Matric. from Queen's College, Oxford, Oct. 17, 1589, age 15; B.A. 1593; M.A. 1596. Perhaps minister at Impington, Cambs., 1629–31.

HORNE, SAMUEL. Adm. pens. at PETERHOUSE, Dec. 17, 1620. Of Middlesex. Scholar, 1623–9; B.A. 1624; M.A. 1628. Fellow, 1630. Buried at Little St Mary's, Cambridge, Feb. 13, 1634–5, aged 30. Will proved (V.C.C.). (*T. A. Walker.*)

HORNE, THOMAS. Adm. sizar at QUEENS', Oct. 7, 1596.

HORNE, THOMAS. Adm. pens. (age 17) at ST JOHN'S, May 25, 1655. S. of William, gent., of Hemsworth, Yorks. B. there. School, Melton, Yorks. (Mr Bedford). Perhaps 's. of William, of Mexburgh; aged 24 in 1666; married Mary, dau. of —— Eyre, of Sproxton, Lincs.' (*Vis. of Yorks.*)

HORNE, THOMAS. Adm. at KING'S (age 16) a scholar from Eton, July 7, 1659. S. of Thomas, Master of Eton. B. at Tonbridge. B.A. 1662–3; M.A. 1666. Fellow, 1662–83. Senior Proctor, 1682–3. Ord. deacon (Peterb.) Sept. 22, 1667. Chaplain to the Earl of St Alban's. Chaplain to Charles II. Fellow of Eton College, 1682. Vice-Provost, 1697–1708. R. of Piddle Hinton, Dorset, 1685. R. of Bramshot, Hants., 1685–1702. R. of Clewer. Died Nov. 4, 1720. Brother of William (1657). (*Harwood*; *D.N.B.*)

HORNE, THOMAS. Adm. sizar (age 18) at CAIUS, June 16, 1749. S. of Thomas, grazier, of Pulham, Norfolk. B. there. School, St Bees, Cumberland. Matric. 1749; Scholar, 1749–53; B.A. 1753. Ord. deacon (Norwich) June 17, 1753, as C. of Tivetshall; priest, July 13, 1755. (*Venn*, II. 63.)

HORNE, WILLIAM. Matric. sizar from ST JOHN'S, Easter, 1571.

HORNE, WILLIAM. Matric. pens. from QUEENS', Easter, 1575; B.A. 1578–9; M.A. 1582. Probably C. of St Mary's, Stafford, 1587.

HORNE, WILLIAM. Matric. sizar from CLARE, Easter, 1631; B.A. 1634–5. One of these names s. of Cotton, steward of the Honour of Pontefract. Age 50 in 1666. Of Mexborough, Yorks., Esq. Died Mar. 26, 1679. Perhaps brother of Cotton (1620). (*Hunter*, I. 391.)

HORNE, WILLIAM. Adm. at KING'S, a scholar from Eton, 1657. S. of Thomas, Master of Eton. B. at Leicester. Matric. 1657; B.A. 1660–1; M.A. 1664. Fellow, 1660–70. Assistant Master at Eton. Head Master of Harrow, 1669–85. Died 1685. M.I. at Harrow. Will (P.C.C.) 1685. Brother of Thomas (1659). (*Harwood*; *D.N.B.*)

HORNE, ——. B.A. 1473–4; M.A. 1477, as Horner.

HORNECK, ANTHONY. Adm. at CAIUS, c. Apr. 1681, as M.A. (Incorp. from Oxford). S. of Philip Elias. B. at Bacharach on the Rhine, 1641. Naturalized, Oct. 1665. Entered at Queen's College, Oxford, 1663; M.A. (Oxford) (Incorp. from Heidelberg) 1664; D.D. (Cambridge) 1681. V. of All Saints', Oxford. Chaplain of Queen's College. Chaplain to the Duke of Albemarle and tutor to his son. F.R.S., 1668. Preb. of Exeter, 1670–94. R. of Dolton, Devon, 1670–1. Preacher at the Savoy, 1671–96. Chaplain to the King, 1689–97. Preb. of Westminster, 1693–6; of Wells, 1694–7. Licensed, Feb. 19, 1671–2, to marry Jane Boulton, of St Margaret's, Westminster. Author, religious. Died Jan. 31, 1696–7. Buried in Westminster Abbey. Will, P.C.C. Father of the next. (*D.N.B.*; *Venn*, I. 466.)

HORNECK, PHILIP. Adm. pens. (age 16) at ST JOHN'S, Nov. 1, 1690. S. of Anthony (above), preb. of Westminster. B. in London. School, Charterhouse. Matric. 1690. Migrated to Sidney, May 26, 1697. LL.B. 1698. Ord. deacon (London) May 7, 1698. Chaplain to Lord Guildford, solicitor to the Treasury, 1716–28. Author, *The High German Doctor*, a play. Died Oct. 13, 1728.

HORNER, ABRAHAM. Adm. sizar at TRINITY, Apr. 21, 1682. Ord. priest (York) as 'literate,' Sept. 1684. V. of Helperthorpe, Yorks.

HORNER, ANDREW. Matric. sizar from TRINITY, Lent, 1629–30; B.A. 1634–5; M.A. 1638.

HORNER, BENJAMIN. Adm. sizar (age 14) at ST JOHN'S, Feb. 25, 1660–1. S. of William, clerk, of Kent. B. there. School, Biddenden, Kent (Mr Paris). Matric. 1661; B.A. 1664–5. Signed for priest's orders (London) May 25, 1670. V. of Rolvenden, Kent, 1670. R. of Hawkhurst, 1692–7. Brother of Hachaliah.

HORNER, GEORGE. Matric. sizar from TRINITY, Easter, 1587.

HORNER, HACHALIAH. Adm. sizar (age 17) at ST JOHN'S, Apr. 15, 1659. S. of William, clerk, of Essex. B. there. School, Biddenden, Kent (Mr Paris). Doubtless brother of Benjamin (1660).

HORNER, JOHN. Matric. sizar from QUEENS', Michs. 1581. Of Essex. B.A. from St Catharine's, 1584–5. Ord. priest (Norwich) Nov. 7, 1587. V. of Roydon, Norfolk, 1591–1625. Buried there, July 30, 1625. Will (P.C.C.) 1626. Father of Robert (1616). (Le Neve, *Mon.*, I. 98.)

HORNER, JOHN. Adm. sizar (age 15) at ST JOHN'S, Mar. 22, 1668–9. S. of John, deceased, of Hull, Yorks. B. there. School, Hull. Matric. 1669; B.A. 1672–3. Signed for deacon's orders (London) Dec. 19, 1673; C. of Luton, Beds.

HORNER, JOHN. Adm. sizar (age 17) at PEMBROKE, June 19, 1680. S. of John, of 'Sykes,' Yorks. Matric. 1680; B.A. 1683–4. Ord. deacon (York) June, 1694; priest, Feb. 1694–5. C. of Masham, 1696.

HORNER, ROBERT. Adm. sizar (age 16) at CAIUS, June 19, 1616. S. of John (1581), R. of Roydon, Norfolk. Matric. 1616; Scholar, 1619–23; B.A. 1619–20; M.A. 1623. Ord. deacon (Norwich) Dec. 19, 1624; priest, 1625. R. of Roydon, 1625–75. Died July 7, 1675. M.I. at Roydon. Father of the next. (Le Neve, *Mon.*, III. 110; *Venn*, I. 233.)

HORNER, ROBERT. Adm. pens. (age 16) at CAIUS, May, 1664. S. of Robert (1616), of Roydon, Norfolk. B. there. Schools, Diss (Mr Locke and Mr Barber) and Botesdale (Mr Ives). Matric. 1664; Scholar, 1664–71; B.A. 1667–8; M.A. 1671. Fellow, 1671–4. Of Bressingham, gent. Died Dec. 4, 1708. M.I. at Roydon. Will (Norwich C.C.) 1708. (*Venn*, I. 421; Le Neve, *Mon.*, III. 225.)

HORNER, THOMAS. Matric. sizar from TRINITY, Lent, 1581–2.

HORNER, THOMAS. Matric. pens. from PETERHOUSE, Lent, 1582–3. Probably s. of Thomas, of London, salter. School, Merchant Taylors'. Migrated to Oxford. Matric. from St John's, June 7, 1583, age 17; B.A. (Oxford), counting one term at Cambridge, 1586. (*Al. Oxon.*)

HORNER, THOMAS. Adm. Fell.-Com. (age 16) at SIDNEY, Feb. 6, 1620–1. S. and h. of Sir John, of Mells, Somerset, Knt. B. at Pounsford, Somerset. School, Wells. Matric. 1620–1. Adm. at Lincoln's Inn, July 10, 1622. M.P. for Minehead, 1626, 1628. Married and had issue. (Le Neve, *Knights*, 80; A. B. Beaven.)

HORNER, W. Matric. pens. from CHRIST'S, June, 1565. One of these names, of Lincoln diocese, was ord. at the College at Rheims, 1579, and sent to England the same year. (*Peile*, I. 92; *Douay Diary*.)

HORNER, ——. M.A. 1477, *see* HORNE.

HORNESBY, ROBERT. Adm. sizar at EMMANUEL, Aug. 28, 1660. Of Cumberland. Ord. deacon (York) June, 1667.

HORNEWAD, JOHN. Matric. sizar from TRINITY, Easter, 1565.

HORNIGOLD, ANTHONY. Adm. at KING'S, a scholar from Eton, Aug. 15, 1532. Of Orwell, Cambs. B.A. 1535–6. Fellow, 1535. Left soon after.

HORNINGOLD, BENJAMIN. Matric. pens. from CORPUS CHRISTI, Easter, 1631. Of Suffolk. (Probably of Ipswich.) B.A. 1634–5; M.A. 1638.

HORNINGSHEATH, THOMAS DE. B.Civ.L. Rural dean of Thingoe, Suffolk. Petitions the Pope, 1363, for a benefice. (*Cal. Pap. Pet.*, I. 405.)

HORNOLD, DANIEL. Adm. sizar at QUEENS', May 27, 1601. Of Kent. B.A. 1604–5; M.A. 1608.

HORNSEY, HENRY. B.A. 1500–1.

HORNSEY, THOMAS. M.A. 1502. One of these names R. of Little Waltham, Essex, 1519–52. V. of Bradfield, 1526. Will (Comm. C. Essex) 1552. (J. Ch. Smith.)

HORROCKS, ALEXANDER. Matric. sizar from CHRIST'S, June, 1602. Perhaps b. at Turton, Lancs. B.A. 1605–6; M.A. 1609. C. of Deane, near Bolton, 1619. Minister of Westhoughton Chapel (in Deane parish), 1648. One of the Westminster Assembly of Divines. Died at Turton. Buried July 27, 1650. (*Peile*, I. 241; Shaw, *Bury Classis*, II. 234.)

HORROK, JAMES. Matric. sizar from ST JOHN'S, Easter, 1589; B.A. 1592–3; M.A. 1596. Perhaps the 'auncient and eminent servant of God, James Horrocks' who seems to have been at Walmesley Chapel, Lancs.; commended in O. Heywood's *Diaries* (I. 43).

HORROCKS or HORRAX, JAMES. Adm. sizar (age 17) at TRINITY, June 3, 1751. S. of James, of Wakefield, Yorks. School, Wakefield (Mr Wilson). Matric. 1751; Scholar, 1754; B.A. 1755; M.A. 1758. Fellow, 1756. Ord. deacon (Peterb.) Sept. 25, 1757. Usher of Wakefield School, 1757. Minister of Petsworth and Kingston, Virginia, 1762–4. President of the College of William and Mary in Virginia, 1764–71. R. of Williamsbury, 1764–71. Commissary to the Bishop of London. Died at Oporto, Mar. 20, 1772, on his way to England. (M. H. Peacock; H. I. Longden.)

HORROX, JEREMIAH. Adm. sizar at EMMANUEL, May 18, 1632. B. at Toxteth, Lancs., c. 1617. Matric. 1632. Resided three years. C. of Hoole, Lancs., 1639. A distinguished astronomer. Predicted, and observed with Will. Crabtree, the transit of Venus across the sun, Nov. 24, 1639. Resigned his curacy and returned to Toxteth, 1640. Began the first tidal observations. His writings were published by the Royal Society in 1672 and 1678. Died suddenly Jan. 3, 1641. A marble scroll to his memory in Westminster Abbey, faces the monument to Newton. (*D.N.B.*)

HORRACKS, JOHN. Adm. sizar at EMMANUEL, 1588–9. Matric. Michs. 1589; B.A. 1593–4; M.A. 1597. Probably R. of South Fambridge, Essex, 1609–27. Buried at Ashingdon, Jan. 12, 1626–7. Will (Cons. C. London), (J. Ch. Smith.)

HORROCKS, JOHN. Matric. sizar from CHRIST'S, July, 1612; B.A. 1615–6. Ord. deacon (York) Sept. 1616; priest, Dec. 1616. Probably P.C. of Colne, Lancs., 1645–69. Died there Sept. 7, 1669, aged 77. Will, York. (*Peile*, I. 287; *Vict. Hist. Lancs.*, VI. 534; E. Axon.)

HORROCKS, JOHN. Adm. pens. at EMMANUEL, June 8, 1622. Matric. 1622; B.A. 1625–6; M.A. 1629. Perhaps Head Master of Heskin Grammar School, Lancs., 1627.

HORROCKS, JOHN. Adm. pens. at EMMANUEL, Apr. 30, 1671. Of Lancashire. Matric. 1671; B.A. 1674–5. Ord. deacon (York) May, 1676; priest, Mar. 1684–5. V. of Gisburn, Yorks., 1686–1723.

HORROCKS, JOHN. Adm. sizar (age 18) at ST JOHN'S, May 26, 1707. S. of John, clerk. B. at Bolton Abbey, Yorks. School, Threshfield (Mr Marshall). Matric. 1707. Buried at All Saints', Cambridge, Feb. 7, 1708–9.

HORRAX, THOMAS. Matric. sizar from MAGDALENE, c. 1593; B.A. from St Catharine's, 1596–7.

HORROK, THOMAS. Matric. sizar from ST JOHN'S, c. 1593; B.A. 1596–7; M.A. 1600. V. of East Rasen, Lincs., 1603–10. Will (Lincoln) 1610.

HORROCKES, THOMAS. Adm. sizar (age 17) at ST JOHN'S, Apr. 9, 1631. S. of Christopher, fuller, of Bolton-le-Moors, Lancs. B. there. School, Bolton (Mr Duckworth). Matric. 1633; B.A. 1634–5; M.A. 1638. Ord. by the Bishop of Durham. Master of Romford School. P.C. of Roxwell, Essex, 1645. Minister at Stapleford Tawney, 1646–50. V. of Maldon, 1650–62, ejected. Settled at Battersea. Died about 1687. (*Calamy*, I. 511; *Davids*, 423.)

HORREX, THOMAS. Adm. sizar (age 18) at CAIUS, June 25, 1734. S. of Edmund, of Foulden, Norfolk. B. there. Schools, Brandon (Mr Kemball) and Northwold (private; Mr Egerley). Matric. 1734; Scholar, 1734–8; B.A. 1737–8; M.A. 1742. Ord. deacon (Norwich) Dec. 24, 1738; priest, Dec. 21, 1740. R. of Whepstead, Suffolk, 1742–58; of Langford and Ickburgh, Norfolk, till 1758. Died 1758. (*Venn*, II. 39.)

HORRAX or HORROCKS, WILLIAM. Matric. pens. from CLARE, Easter, 1614; B.A. 1617–8. Ord. deacon (York) Sept. 1618; priest, Feb. 1618–9. One of these names C. of Newchurch, Rossendale, Lancs., 1622–c. 1640. (E. Axon.)

HORROBIN, JOHN. Matric. sizar from JESUS, Easter, 1698. Of Lancashire. School, Frankland's Academy, Rathmell, Yorks. Scholar, 1700; B.A. 1702-3. P.C. of Billinge, Lancs., 1704-8. Admon. (Chester) 1708. (E. Axon.)

HORRABIN, MALIN. Adm. sizar (age 18) at ST JOHN'S, June 13, 1663. S. of William, yeoman, of Orgrave, in Stafford Hundred, Yorks. B. there. School, Sedbergh (Mr Fell). Matric. 1663; B.A. 1666-7. Ord. deacon (York) Sept. 1668; priest, June, 1669. V. of Laneham, Notts. R. of Carsington, Derbs., 1679-87. Died Nov. 13, 1687. Buried at Carsington. M.I. (*Peile*, I. 605, wrongly assigns him to Christ's.)

HORROBIN, ROBERT. Adm. sizar at JESUS, June 24, 1698. Of Lancashire. R. of Winfrith, Dorset, 1715-29. Archdeacon of Sodor and Man, 1718; resigned, 1725. Probably R. of Andreas and Chaplain of St Mary's, Castletown, Isle of Man, 1719. Died 1729. (A. Gray; *Manx Soc. Publ.*, 29, 43.) Probably distinct from John, of the same date, though there was only one admission and one matriculation.

HORSEFIELD, ——. Adm. Fell.-Com. at TRINITY HALL, Mar. 1, 1744-5. (Name off, 1746.)

HORSEY, GEORGE. Matric. pens. from TRINITY, Michs. 1619. Scholar from Westminster. B.A. 1623-4; M.A. 1627. Fellow, 1624. Incorp. at Oxford, 1627.

HORSEY, JASPER. Matric. Fell.-Com. from TRINITY, Easter, 1577. 2nd s. of George, of Digwell, Herts., Esq. Adm. at Gray's Inn, Nov. 23, 1584; of Digwell, Herts.; late of Barnard's Inn. Married Helen, dau. of Thomas Docwra, of Putteridge, Herts. Will (P.C.C.) 1637. Brother of the next. (*Vis. of Herts.*; *Clutterbuck*, II. 322.)

HORSEY, RALPH. Matric. Fell.-Com. from TRINITY, Easter, 1577. S. and h. of George, of Digwell, Herts., Esq. M.P. for Dorset, 1586-7, 1597-8. Knighted, 1590-1. Married Edith, dau. of William Mohun, of Melcombe Horsey, Dorset. Died 1612. Buried at Melcombe. Brother of Jasper (above). (*Hutchins*, IV. 427.)

HORSFALL or HORSEFAL, HENRY. Adm. pens. (age 18) at ST JOHN'S, June 25, 1746. S. of John, of Yorkshire. B. at Batley, near Wakefield. School, Chesterfield, Derbs. (Mr Burrow). Matric. 1746. Of Malsis Hall, in Craven, gent. Married Grace Mortimer, of Caxton, Cambs., dau. of Samuel, of Swaffham. Buried May 3, 1760. (*F.M.G.*, 1183; M. H. Peacock.)

HORSFALL, JOHN. Matric. sizar from ST JOHN'S, Michs. 1560. One of these names R. of St Peter's, Paul's Wharf, 1573-87. R. of St Mary Mounthaw, London, 1574-87. Possibly Bishop of Ossory, 1586-1610. 'Of Yorkshire.' Died Feb. 13, 1609-10. (Cotton, *Fast. Hib.*, II. 278.)

HORSFALL, JOHN. Adm. pens. at EMMANUEL, May 20, 1680. Of Yorkshire. Perhaps s. of William, of Stotthes Hall; age 4 in 1666. Matric. 1680. Died July 8, 1722. Buried at Kirkburton. M.I. (*Vis. of Yorks.*, 1666.)

HORSFALL, MIDGELY. Adm. sizar (age 21) at CHRIST'S, Mar. 19, 1745-6. B. at Haworth, Yorks. School, Rishworth (Mr Wadsworth). Matric. 1747. Expelled, Apr. 16, 1747 (College order). (*Peile*, II. 249.)

HORSFALL, WILLIAM. Adm. pens. (age 18) at SIDNEY, June 18, 1653. S. of Richard, Esq., of Stotthes Hall. B. at Kirkburton, Yorks. Bapt. May 4, 1634. Schools, Almondbury (Mr Greene) and Thornhill (Mr Wiglesworth). Matric. 1653. Married Dorothy, dau. of John Ellerker, of York. Buried at Kirkburton, Feb. 8, 1711. (*Vis. of Yorks.*, 1666.)

HORSFALL, WILLIAM. Adm. pens. (age 19) at TRINITY, Feb. 13, 1743-4. S. of Richard, of Strensall, Yorks. School, Ripon, Yorks. (Mr Slide). Matric. 1743-4.

HORSINGTON, THOMAS. M.D. 1663 (*Lit. Reg.*).

HORSLEY or HORSELEY, BENJAMIN. Adm. pens. (age 16) at MAGDALENE, May 10, 1653. S. of John, of Milburn Grange, Northumberland, Esq. School, Berwick. Matric. 1653; B.A. 1656-7.

HORSLEY, ISAAC. Adm. sizar (age 18) at CAIUS, July 3, 1745. S. of Thomas (1720), R. of Melton Constable, Norfolk. B. at Saxthorpe. School, Holt (Mr Holmes). Matric. 1745-6; Scholar, 1745-50. Ord. deacon (Ely) Dec. 8, 1748; priest (Norwich) Sept. 23, 1750. V. of Briston, Norfolk, 1750-1803. R. of Antingham St Mary, 1754-1803. C. of Worstead, 1764-73. Died Apr. 29, 1803. M.I. at Swafield. (*Venn*, II. 57.)

HORSELEY, JOHN. Matric. pens. from ST JOHN'S, Easter, 1567.

HORSELEYE, NICHOLAS DE. Scholar at KING'S HALL, 1337. Died Apr. 21, 1349.

HORSLEY, NICHOLAS. Matric. sizar from CORPUS CHRISTI, Easter, 1544; B.A. 1546-7. Perhaps Nicholas Hornsey, R. of Frostenden, Suffolk, 1561-79. V. of Reydon and Southwold, 1566-82.

HORSLEY, SAMUEL. Adm. pens. at TRINITY HALL, Oct. 24, 1751. S. of John, of St Martin's, Westminster, clerk. Scholar, 1753; LL.B. 1758. Incorp. at Oxford, 1767. D.C.L. (Oxford) 1774. R. of St Mary, Newington, Surrey, 1758-93. F.R.S., 1767. Secretary R.S., 1773. R. of Albury, Surrey, 1774-9. R. of Thorley, Herts., 1777-82. Archdeacon of St Albans, 1781-8. V. of South Weald, Essex, 1782-93. Preb. of St Paul's, 1783-94. Preb. of Gloucester, 1787-93. Bishop of St David's, 1788-93; of Rochester, 1793-1802. Dean of Westminster, 1793-1802. Bishop of St Asaph, 1802-6. Author, scientific and theological. Died at Brighton, Oct. 4, 1806. Buried in Newington, Surrey. (*Al. Oxon.*; *D.N.B.*)

HORSLEY, THOMAS. Scholar and fellow of KING'S HALL, 1521-39; B.Can.L. 1516-7. R. of Wicken Bonant, Essex, and of Stoke College, Suffolk. Preb. of Southwell, 1537-9. Died 1539. Will (P.C.C.) 1540; mentions 'my great chamber at Cambridge.' Left a legacy to the College. (J. Ch. Smith.)

HORSLEY, THOMAS. Matric. sizar from PETERHOUSE, Michs. 1565; B.A. 1565-6. One of these names (B.A.), buried at St Oswald's, Durham, June 16, 1612.

HORSLEY, THOMAS. Adm. sizar (age 17) at CAIUS, July 7, 1720. S. of Thomas, packer, of London. B. there. School, Holt, Norfolk (Mr Duncombe). Matric. 1720; Scholar, 1720-4. Subscribed for deacon's orders (Norwich) Sept. 25, 1726, as C. of Thornage, Norfolk. R. of Melton Constable, 1734-54. C. of Edgefield. Died Aug. 25, 1754. M.I. at Edgefield. Father of Isaac (1745). (*Venn*, II. 15.)

HORSLYNGE, EDWARD. Matric. sizar from ST JOHN'S, Michs. 1585.

HORSMAN, ANDREW. M.A. from EMMANUEL, 1623. Of Devon, *pleb.* Matric. from Broadgates Hall, Oxford, Mar. 8, 1610-1, age 18; B.A. (Oxford) 1616.

HORSEMAN, JOHN. Adm. sizar (age 17) at ST JOHN'S, July 2, 1751. S. of James, clerk, of Durham. B. at Greatham. Educated by his father. Matric. 1751; B.A. 1755; M.A. 1758; B.D. 1766. Fellow, 1757-73. Ord. deacon (Lincoln) Sept. 19, 1756; priest (Durham) Sept. 25, 1757. R. of Soulderne, Oxon., 1772-1806. Died June 25, 1806. M.I. at Soulderne. (*Scott-Mayor*, III. 609.)

HORSMAN, LEONARD. B.A. 1522-3; M.A. 1525. Fellow of CHRIST'S, 1524-33. University preacher, 1532-3. V. of Masham, Yorks., 1534-51. Died 1551.

HORSEMAN, OLIVER. Adm. pens. at EMMANUEL, Oct. 3, 1676. Of Hertfordshire. Probably M.D. of Leyden, Sept. 19, 1680. Licentiate R.C.P., Sept. 30, 1692. Resided in Hatton Gardens. Died there Nov. 24, 1717. Buried in St Andrew's, Holborn. Admon. (P.C.C.) Dec. 10, 1717. (*Munk*, I. 494.)

HORSEMAN, PHILIP. M.A. 1664 (Incorp. from Oxford). Matric. from Magdalen Hall, Oxford, Mar. 28, 1655; B.A. (Oxford) 1658; M.A. 1661. Fellow of Magdalen Hall, 1663-8. Died 1668. (*Al. Oxon.*)

HORSMAN, RALPH. B.A. 1534-5.

HORSEMAN, ROBERT. Adm. Fell.-Com. at KING'S, Michs. 1605; B.A. 1607-8; M.A. 1611. Incorp. at Oxford, 1614.

HORSMAN, ROBERT. Adm. Fell.-Com. (age 15) at SIDNEY, June 30, 1632. S. of Robert, Esq., of Kensington, Middlesex. B. at Titchmarsh, Northants. (home of his mother, Elizabeth Pickering). Bapt. there, Sept. 24, 1615. Schools, Oundle, Oakham and Stretton, Rutland. Matric. 1632. Adm. at Gray's Inn, Nov. 12, 1634, as s. and h. of Robert, of Stretton. (H. I. Longden.)

HORSMAN, SAMUEL. M.D. 1728 (*Com. Reg.*). Of Middlesex. Adm. at Leyden, Sept. 7, 1719, age 21. M.D. there, 1721. F.R.C.P., 1737. Censor. Treasurer, 1746-51. Elect, 1751. Died Nov. 22, 1751. Admon. (P.C.C.); of St Andrew's, Holborn. (*Munk*, II. 135.)

HORSMAN, THOMAS. Matric. pens. from TRINITY HALL, Michs. 1555; LL.B. 1563. Fellow, 1559-72. One of these names, 'of Suffolk, barrister, Furnival's Inn,' adm. at Lincoln's Inn, June 20, 1581. Perhaps knighted, Mar. 14, 1603-4.

HORSMAN, THOMAS. Matric. sizar from TRINITY, Easter, 1607; B.A. 1610-1; M.A. 1614. Fellow of St Catharine's, 1614. Junior proctor, 1618-9. Incorp. at Oxford, 1621. R. of Bergh Apton *with* Holvestone, Norfolk, 1627-58. Died 1658.

HORSEMAN, THOMAS. Matric. sizar from PEMBROKE, Easter, 1627. S. of Henry, vintner, of Norwich. B. at Lynn. Migrated to Caius, May 10, 1628, age 16.

HORSMAN, THOMAS. Matric. pens. from ST CATHARINE'S, Easter, 1650. Buried at St Benet's, Cambridge, Jan. 26, 1652-3.

HORSMAN, ——. B.Can.L. 1476-7.

HORSMONDEN, DANIEL. B.A. from ST JOHN'S, 1603-4. Of Kent. S. of Richard (next), R. of Ulcombe. M.A. 1607; B.D. 1614; D.D. 1627. Fellow, 1605. Taxor, 1604. Incorp. at Oxford, 1617. R. of Whipsnade, Beds., 1622. V. of Goudhurst, Kent, 1625-40. R. of Ulcombe, 1627-39. Sequestered. Married Ursula, dau. of Sir Warham St Leger, Knt., at Ulcombe, 1627. Died 1655. Will (P.C.C.) 1656; of Maidstone. (J. Ch. Smith; H. I. Longden.)

HORSMANDEN, RICHARD. Matric. pens. from CHRIST'S, Nov. 1570. R. of Ulcombe, Kent, till his death, Oct. 27, 1627. Father of the above.

HORSMONDEN, THOMAS. Matric. sizar from ST JOHN'S, c. 1593. Of Kent. Probably s. of Richard, above. B.A. 1594-5; M.A. 1598; B.D. 1606; D.D. 1614. Fellow, 1596-7. Incorp. at Oxford, 1614. Preb. of Lincoln, 1606-33. V. of Goudhurst, Kent, 1613-24. Preb. of Canterbury, 1618-22. R. of Purleigh, Essex, 1624-32. Died 1633. Buried at Throwley, Kent, Jan. 30, 1632-3. M.I. Will, P.C.C. Brother of Daniel (1603-4). (H. I. Longden; J. Ch. Smith.)

HORSNAYLE, ASHABIA. Adm. pens. at TRINITY, Mar. 6, 1667-8. Matric. 1667-8; Scholar, 1671; B.A. 1671-2; M.A. 1675.

HORSNELL, FERDINANDO. Adm. pens. at TRINITY, Mar. 5, 1666-7. Matric. 1667-8.

HORSENELL, JOHN. Adm. at KING'S, a scholar from Eton, 1673. B. in London. Matric. 1674; B.A. 1677-8; M.A. 1681; B.D. 1690 (*Com. Reg.*). Fellow, 1677. Incorp. at Oxford, 1697. Apparently P.C. of Upwood, Hunts., 1684-8. V. of Fordingbridge, Hants., 1700. Died there May, 1724. (*Harwood*).

HORSEPOLE, JOHN. B.A. 1463-4. Perhaps M.A. 1467-8; B.D. 1473-4. Fellow of PETERHOUSE, 1466-83. P.C. of Little St Mary's, Cambridge, 1472-5. (*T. A. Walker*.)

HORSEPOLE, RICHARD. Fee for M.A. or higher degree, 1467-8. Perhaps a mistake for John, above.

HORSEPOOLE, ——. Adm. sizar at SIDNEY, June, 1602.

HORSTON, THOMAS. Scholar at KING'S HALL, 1375; left, Aug. 15, 1384. One of these names, *alias* Vanshapwyck, R. of Gt Hallingbury, Essex, 1393-1410. Preb. of St Paul's, 1404-10. Will (P.C.C., and Court of Hustings) 1410; to be buried at St Nicholas Sherehog, near his father. Leaves his *Pupilla Oculi* and *Legenda Sanctorum* to Hallingbury Church. (J. Ch. Smith; H. G. Harrison.)

HORT, JOSIAH. Adm. sizar at CLARE, Apr. 28, 1704. S. of John, of Marshfield, Gloucs., Esq. B. there, c. 1674. Ord. priest (Ely) Sept. 25, 1705. Chaplain to Earl of Wharton, Lord-Lieutenant of Ireland. Dean of Cloyne, 1718-20; of Ardagh, 1720-2. Bishop of Ferns and Leighlin, 1722-7. Bishop of Kilmore and Ardagh, 1727-41. Archbishop of Tuam, 1742-51. Died Dec. 14, 1751. Will, Dublin. (*D.N.B.*)

HORTON, ALEXANDER. Adm. pens. at JESUS, Apr. 30, 1678. Migrated to St John's, July 26, 1678. S. of Walter, of Catton, Derbs., Esq. School, Ashby-de-la-Zouch (Mr Shaw). Previously matric. from Oriel College, Oxford, May 21, 1674, age 15 (as s. of William); B.A. (Oxford) 1677; M.A. from St John's (Cambridge) 1681. Fellow of St John's, 1684-9. Ord. deacon (London) Sept. 23, 1683. R. of Tydd St Giles', Cambs., 1687-8. R. of Kelshall, Herts., 1688-91, ejected as a non-juror. Brother of Walter (1679). (R. Ussher, *Croxall*, 174.)

HORTON, EDWARD. Matric. sizar from QUEENS', Easter, 1544.

HORTON, JOHN. Matric. pens. from TRINITY, Easter, 1606, as 'Orton'; B.A. 1610-1. Perhaps M.A. from St Catharine's, 1617. One of these names presented to Halford, Warws., Mar. 1, 1647-8. (*Shaw*, I. 352.)

HORTON, JOHN. Adm. sizar at JESUS, Oct. 27, 1653. Of Warwickshire. Matric. 1653; B.A. 1657. Ord. deacon (Lincoln) May, 24; priest, Aug. 5, 1662. Probably V. of Horninghold, Leics. Will (Leicester) 1677.

HORTON, JOHN. M.A. from KING'S, 1740. Perhaps s. of John, of Worcester. Matric. from Hart Hall, Oxford, Nov. 7, 1730, age 18; B.A. (Oxford) 1734. One of these names ord. priest (Lincoln) Dec. 19, 1736. R. of Sharnford, Leics., 1738-93. R. of Little Peatling, 1765-93. Died May 27, 1793, aged 81. M.I. at Sharnford. Will (P.C.C.). (*Al. Oxon.*; *G. Mag.*; *Nichols*, IV. 920.)

HORTON, RICHARD. Adm. pens. (age 17) at PEMBROKE, Feb. 23, 1724-5. 2nd s. of William, of Howroyd, Halifax, Yorks. Bapt. at Ripponden, Nov. 7, 1706. Matric. 1724-5. Adm. at the Inner Temple, Aug. 11, 1725. Died at Howroyd, June 8, 1742. M.I. at Elland. Will, York. (*Vis. of Yorks.*, 1666; M. H. Peacock; J. Ch. Smith.)

HORTON, THOMAS. Adm. at KING'S (age 17) a scholar from Eton, 1537. Perhaps 2nd s. of John, of Catton, Derbs. B. at Catton. B.A. 1541-2; M.A. from Pembroke, 1549. Fellow of King's, 1540-2. Fellow of Pembroke, c. 1548. Ord. deacon (London) Aug. 10, 1550; priest, Mar. 30, 1560. Preb. of Durham, 1560-1. R. of St Magnus, London, 1560-4. Died 1564.

HORTON, THOMAS. Adm. pens. at EMMANUEL, May 13, 1597. B. in St James', Garlickhithe, London. Matric. c. 1597; B.A. 1600-1; M.A. 1604. Incorp. at Oxford, 1607. Ord. deacon (London) Oct. 3; priest, Dec. 21, 1606, age 26. C. of St James', Garlickhithe. Probably R. of Tredington, Worcs., 1607-20. R. of Barcheston, Warws., 1631-9. Will (Worcester) 1639; of Barcheston.

HORTON, THOMAS. Adm. pens. at EMMANUEL, 1623. S. of Laurence, citizen of London. Matric. Easter, 1624; B.A. 1626-7; M.A. 1630; B.D. 1637; D.D. from Queens', 1649. Fellow of Emmanuel, 1631. Professor of Divinity, Gresham College, 1641-61. President of Queens', 1647-60. Vice-Chancellor, 1649-50. Incorp. at Oxford, 1652. Minister of St Mary Colechurch, London, 1638-49, and in 1666. Preacher at Gray's Inn, 1647-51. R. of St Helen's, Bishopsgate, 1666-73. Author, sermons. Buried Mar. 29, 1673, at St Helen's. Will, P.C.C. (*D.N.B.*; *Al. Oxon.*; A. B. Beaven.)

HORTON, THOMAS. Matric. sizar from TRINITY, Lent, 1664-5. Probably adm. as 'Halton' in the College register. One of these names, s. and h. of William, of Barslam, Halifax, Yorks., adm. at Gray's Inn, Feb. 7, 1667-8.

HORTON, THOMAS. Matric. pens. from CHRIST'S, Dec. 1678. Probably s. of Joshua, of Horton, near Bradford, Yorks. B. Nov. 26, 1660. M.B. 1683. Practised physic in London. Married a dau. of —— Watmough, M.D. Died *s.p.*, Mar. 4, 1693-4. Buried at St Thomas, Southwark. Will (P.C.C.). (*Peile*, II. 68.)

HORTON, THOMAS. Adm. Fell.-Com. (age 24) at ST JOHN'S, June 12, 1729. B. in London. School, Highgate. V. of Beenham, Berks., 1731-3. V. of Heston, Middlesex, 1733-50. R. of Hascombe, Surrey, 1750-80. Died Nov. 4, 1791. (*Scott-Mayor*, III. 423.)

HORTON, WALTER. M.A. 1679 (Incorp. from Oxford). S. of Walter, of Catton, Derbs., Esq. Matric. from St Edmund's Hall, Oxford, May 17, 1672, age 16; B.A. from Oriel, 1675-6; M.A. 1678. V. of Walton-on-Trent, Derbs., 1680. V. of All Saints', Derby. Preb. of Lichfield, 1693-1728. Died 1728. Brother of Alexander (1678). (*Al. Oxon.*; Ri. Ussher, *Croxall*, 174.)

HORTON, WALTER. Adm. pens. (age 17) at ST JOHN'S, Apr. 18, 1694. S. of Christopher, gent., of Catton, Derbs. School, Tamworth, Staffs. (Mr Antrobus). Married Elizabeth, dau. of Thomas Kynnersley, of Staffs. Buried July, 1716, at Croxall, aged 38. (Glover, *Derbyshire*, II. 204, 331.)

HORTON, WILLIAM. Adm. pens. at CLARE, July 3, 1690. Of Gumley, Leics. (Grandson of John, of Gumley, yeoman, whose will, Leicester, 1667.) Matric. 1691; B.A. 1694-5; M.A. 1703. Ord. deacon (Norwich) Dec. 1697. V. of Gretton, Northants., 1702-27. Chaplain to Christopher Lord Hatton. R. of Corby, 1703-42. Buried there, Jan. 8, 1741-2. (H. I. Longden; L. G. H. Horton-Smith.)

HORTON, WILLIAM. Adm. Fell.-Com. at CLARE, Aug. 11, 1731. S. of Thomas, of Chaderton, Lancs., Esq. B. there, Dec. 13, 1712. Adm. at Gray's Inn, Apr. 22, 1729. Created Baronet, Jan. 22, 1764. Sheriff of Lancashire, 1764-5. Married Susannah, dau. of Francis Watts, Esq., of Barnes Hall, Yorks. Died Feb. 25, 1774. (Burke, *Ext. Bart*; G.E.C.)

HORTON, ——. Adm. pens. at EMMANUEL, 1604.

HORWOOD; *see also* HARWOOD.

HORWOOD or HARWOOD, JOHN. Adm. at KING'S, a scholar from Eton, 1489; B.A. 1492-3; M.A. 1497. Fellow till his death, 1500. Ord. acolyte (Ely) Sept. 20, 1494; deacon, Mar. 14, 1494-5; priest, Apr. 4, 1495. Admon. granted by King's College.

HORWOOD, JOHN. Matric. sizar from PEMBROKE, Michs. 1580.

HORWODE, RICHARD DE (? ROBERT). 'KING'S scholar' at Cambridge, 1331.

HORWOOD, THOMAS. Adm. sizar (age 17) at SIDNEY, Apr. 9, 1739. S. of George. B. at Marwood, Devon. School, Barnstaple. Matric. 1739; B.A. 1742-3.

HORWODE, WALTER. Scholar at KING'S HALL, 1353. Died Oct. 3, 1367.

HORWOOD or HARWOOD, ——. B.Can.L. 1497-8.

HOSBOSTON, WILLIAM. Matric. pens. from ST JOHN'S, 1547.

HOSIER, GEOFFREY. Adm. pens. (age 17) at CAIUS, Sept. 29, 1584. S. of John, deceased. B. in London. School, Merchant Taylors'. Matric. 1584; Scholar, 1584-7. One of these names C. of Stanford Rivers, Essex, 1598. (*Venn*, I. 121.)

HOSIER, JAMES. Adm. sizar at EMMANUEL, Easter, 1621. Matric. 1621; B.A. 1625-6. C. of Mucking, Essex, in 1637. R. of Chadwell, 1649-53. Will (P.C.C.) 1653; of Chadwell, clerk. (J. Ch. Smith.)

HOSIER, RICHARD. Matric. pens. from KING'S, Easter, 1637.

HOSKEN or HOSKIN, ANTHONY. Adm. sizar (age 18) at PEMBROKE, Feb. 10, 1728-9. S. of George, of St Anthony-in-Meneage, Cornwall, farmer. Matric. 1729; B.A. 1732-3; M.A. 1738. Will (P.C.C.) 1766; of Bodmin, clerk.

HOSKINS, CHARLES. Matric. Fell.-Com. from QUEENS', Lent, 1618-9. Of Oxted, Surrey. Doubtless s. of Sir Thomas, of Oxted, Knt. Married Anne, dau. of William Hale. Died Sept. 10, 1657, aged 54. Buried at Oxted. M.I. (*Vis. of Surrey*; *Manning and Bray*, II. 386.)

HOSKEN, JOHN. Adm. sizar (age 16) at CHRIST'S, Dec. 12, 1663. S. of John. B. at Perran, Cornwall. School, Truro (Mr Jago). Matric. 1663; B.A. 1667-8. Ord. deacon (Exeter) June, 1669; priest, May, 1670. Will (Exeter) 1725; of Perranzabuloe, clerk. (*Peile*, I. 607.)

HOSKINS, NICHOLAS. M.A. from PEMBROKE, 1732. S. of Nicholas, of Whitstone, Cornwall, clerk. Matric. from Queen's College, Oxford, May 25, 1720, age 18; B.A. (Oxford) 1723-4. Probably R. of St Ervan, Cornwall. Admon. (Exeter) 1749. (*Al. Oxon.*)

HOSKYN, THOMAS. Matric. sizar from CHRIST'S, Nov. 1554. Of Shellow Bowels, Essex. Ord. sub-deacon (London) Dec. 1556. Probably R. of Lambourne, Essex, Apr. 15, 1557. R. of Magdalen-Laver, where he died before Dec. 1588. Licensed (Bishop of London) Feb. 10, 1567-8, to marry Margery Wylls, of Magdalen-Laver. Will (Consist. C. London) 1589. (*Peile*, I. 59; J. Ch. Smith.)

HOSKYN, WILLIAM. Adm. sizar (age 20) at PEMBROKE, Oct. 10, 1677. S. of Thomas, farmer. B. at South Wenn, Cornwall.

HOST, JAMES. Adm. Fell.-Com. at TRINITY, June 21, 1680. Matric. 1680.

HOSTE, JAMES. Adm. at CORPUS CHRISTI, 1722. Of Sandringham, Norfolk, Esq.

HOSTENIUS (?), PETER. Matric. pens. from MAGDALENE, Lent, 1564-5.

HOTBLACK, ANTHONY. Adm. sizar at CHRIST'S, Oct. 20, 1738. Of Westmorland. Matric. 1738. Resided one year. Ord. deacon (Lincoln) Dec. 23, 1739; priest, Dec. 21, 1740. C. of Holwell, Beds., and Hitchin, Herts. (*Peile*, II. 237.)

HOTCHKIN, ANTHONY. Matric. sizar from CORPUS CHRISTI, c. 1593. B. at 'Saighton-on-the-Hill,' Cheshire, 1574. B.A. 1596-7. R. of Stonesby, Leics., 1598. V. of Sproxton, 1621.

HOTCHKINS, HENRY. Matric. sizar from MAGDALENE, Easter, 1613; LL.B. from Trinity Hall, 1625. Ord. deacon (Peterb.) May 19, 1623; priest, June 5, 1626. Presented to Swanning-ton, Norfolk (in gift of Trinity Hall), 1628, as 'William Hotchkis, LL.B.' Will of William Hotchkin, LL.B., proved (V.C.C.) 1629.

HOTCHKINS, JOHN. Matric. sizar from TRINITY, Easter, 1648. Of Bedfordshire. B.A. 1651-2.

HOTCHKIN, RALPH. Matric. sizar from CHRIST'S, Dec. 1618; B.A. 1621-2; M.A. 1625. Ord. deacon (London) June, 1626, age 24. R. of Knipton, near Belvoir, Leics., 1627. (*Peile*, I. 326.)

HOTCHKIN or HODGSKIN, WILLIAM. Adm. sizar (age 18) at ST JOHN'S, Mar. 8, 1665-6. S. of John, yeoman, of Bourne, Lincs. B. there. School, Bourne (Mr Eaton). Matric. 1667, as 'Hodgsden.' Ord. deacon (Peterb.) June 18; priest, Sept. 24, 1671, as Hotchking.

HOTCHKIS, JAMES. Adm. pens. (age 18) at ST JOHN'S, July 5, 1720. S. of Joshua, V. of Kingsey, Bucks. B. at Moulsoe, Bucks. School, Charterhouse. Matric. 1720; B.A. 1723-4; M.A. 1727. Ord. deacon (Lincoln) Sept. 20, 1724; priest, Dec. 18, 1726. V. of Kingsey, 1726-49. Usher of Charterhouse, 1731; Head Master, 1732-48. R. of Wolverston, Bucks., 1732. R. of Brettenham, 1739-51. R. of Balsham, Cambs., 1749-51. Died Nov. 11, 1751. Buried in Charterhouse Chapel. (*Scott-Mayor*, III. 336; H. G. Harrison.)

HOTCHKIS, LEONARD. Adm. sizar (age 18) at ST JOHN'S, June 9, 1709. S. of Richard. B. at Chirbury, Salop. School, Shrewsbury. Matric. 1709; B.A. 1712-3; M.A. 1716. Head Master of Shrewsbury, 1735-44. Died Nov. 1771. Will (P.C.C.) 1771; of Shrewsbury, clerk. Brother of the next.

HOTCHKIS, RICHARD. Adm. sizar (age 19) at ST JOHN'S, June 28, 1716. S. of Richard, deceased, of Salop. B. at Chirbury. School, Shrewsbury. Matric. 1716; B.A. 1719-20. Ord. priest (London) Nov. 20, 1720. Brother of the above. Proved his brother Leonard's will in 1771.

HOTCHKIS, THOMAS. Matric. sizar from CORPUS CHRISTI, Easter, 1627; B.A. 1630-1; M.A. 1634. (Entered, in *Masters*, as Henry Hotchins, of Shropshire.)

HOTHAM, *see also* HOWTHAM.

HOTHAM, CHARLES. Adm. pens. (age 16) at PETERHOUSE, Nov. 22, 1631. S. of Sir John, governor of Hull. B. at Scorborough, May 12, 1615. School, Westminster. Matric. 1631. Migrated to Christ's, May 7, 1632. B.A. 1635-6; M.A. 1639. Fellow of Peterhouse, 1644-51, ejected. Proctor, 1646. V. of Withernsea, Yorks., 1640-4. V. of Hollym, 1640-4. R. of Wigan, 1653-62, ejected. Went as minister to Bermuda, 1662. F.R.S., 1667. Translated Boehme's *Consolatory Treatise of the Four Complexions*. Died at Bermuda, 1672. Will (P.C.C.) 1673-4. Father of the next, brother of Durand (1632) and Francis (1651). (*D.N.B.*; *Peile*, I. 419; *T. A. Walker*, 45.)

HOTHAM, CHARLES. Adm. pens. (age 16) at ST JOHN'S, Apr. 9, 1681. S. of Charles (above). B. at Wigan (? Bermuda). Spent his early years in Bermuda. School, Sedbergh. Matric. 1681; B.A. 1684-5; M.A. 1688. Fellow, 1685-92. Ord. deacon, but afterwards entered the army; became brigadier-general, 1710; and colonel of the royal regiment of dragoons. Succeeded his cousin as 4th Baronet, 1691. M.P. for Scarborough, 1695-1702; for Beverley, 1702-23. Died at Bristol. Buried at South Dalton, Jan. 20, 1722-3. Will, York. (*Sedbergh School Register*; *D.N.B.*; A. B. Beaven.)

HOTHAM, DURAND. Adm. pens. (age 15) at CHRIST'S, Nov. 9, 1632. S. of Sir John, Bart. B. at Scorborough. Schools, Scorborough (private; Mr Sugden) and Westminster. Matric. 1632; B.A. 1636-7; M.A. 1640. Adm. at the Middle Temple, Jan. 26, 1640-1. Of Lockington, Yorks. Married, Aug. 23, 1645, Frances, dau. of Richard Remington, of Lund, Yorks. Author. Died in St James', Westminster, 1691. Buried there. Admon. (P.C.C.) 1691. Brother of Charles (1631) and half-brother of Francis (1651). (*Peile*, I. 424; *D.N.B.*; M. H. Peacock.)

HOTHAM, FRANCIS. Adm. Fell.-Com. (age 16) at PETERHOUSE, Apr. 19, 1651. Of Yorkshire. S. of Sir John, by his 4th wife. Buried at St Michael le Belfry, York, July 14, 1653. Will (P.C.C.) 1653. Half-brother of Charles (1631) and Durand (1632). (*T. A. Walker*, 97.)

HOTHAM, JAMES. Matric. Fell.-Com. from ST JOHN'S, Easter, 1605.

HOTHAM, JOHN. Adm. Fell.-Com. (age 16) at PETERHOUSE, May 13, 1648. S. of Sir John, Knt., and grandson of Sir John, 1st Bart. Bapt. at Glentworth, Lincs. (his mother's home), Mar. 21, 1631-2. M.P. for Beverley, 1660-81 and 1689. Succeeded his grandfather as Bart., Sept. 15, 1666. Married, at Burton, Lincs., Aug. 8, 1650, Elizabeth, dau. of Sapcote, Viscount Beaumont of Swords. Buried at South Dalton, Yorks., Sept. 29, 1689. (*T. A. Walker*; M. H. Peacock; *G.E.C.*)

HOTHAM, RALPH. B.A. 1462-3; M.A. 1466. Probably 4th s. of Sir John Hotham, Knt. Fell.-Com. at PETERHOUSE, 1464-5. Perhaps M.P. for Scarborough, 1472. (*T. A. Walker*.)

HOTHAM, ROBERT. Adm. sizar (age 20) at ST JOHN'S, June 1, 1727. S. of John, farmer, of Yorkshire. B. at Storthwood, in Thornton parish. School, Pocklington (Mr Baker). Matric. 1727; B.A. 1730-1. Ord. deacon (Lincoln) Mar. 14, 1730-1.

HOTHAM, THOMAS. B.A. 1507-8.

HOTHAM, WALTER. B.D. 1472-3. A monk. Studied at Cambridge and Oxford.

HOTHERSALL, BURCH. Adm. Fell.-Com. at EMMANUEL, Jan. 29, 1681-2. Of Barbados. M.A. 1682 (*Com. Reg.*). Incorp. at Oxford, 1682.

HOTOFT, JOHN. Scholar at KING'S HALL, 1416. One of the children of the Chapel Royal. Died Aug. 17, 1420.

HOTTOFTE, RICHARD. Matric. sizar from TRINITY, c. 1593; B.A. 1596-7; M.A. 1600. R. of Stourbridge, Worcs., 1602. Perhaps will (Worcester) 1641; of Old Swinford, clerk.

HOTTOF or HAWTOFT, ROBERT. Adm. at KING'S (age 18) a scholar from Eton, Aug. 16, 1546. Of Flintham, Notts. Matric. 1546. Name off, 1549.

HOTTON, HUGH DE. The first known Chancellor of the University, c. 1246.

HOTTON, RICHARD, *see* HUTTON.

HOTTYS, ——. B.A. 1524-5.

HOUBLON, DANIEL. Licensed to practise medicine, 1629.

HOUBLON, JACOB. Adm. Fell.-Com. at PETERHOUSE, July 24, 1654; and incorp. as B.A. S. of James, of London, merchant. Matric. from Pembroke College, Oxford, Nov. 27, 1650; B.A. (Oxford) 1652-3; M.A. (Cambridge) 1655. Fellow of Peterhouse, 1654. Incorp. at Oxford, 1655. R. of Moreton, Essex, 1662-97. Buried there, Dec. 18, 1697, aged 62. Will (Consist. C. London) 1698. Father of the next. (*Essex Pedigrees*; *T. A. Walker*, 106.)

HOUBLON, JACOB. Adm. at CORPUS CHRISTI, 1683. Of Essex. S. of Jacob (above), R. of Moreton. B. there, Feb. 12, 1666-7. Matric. 1683-4; B.A. 1687-8; M.A. 1691. Ord. priest (London) Sept. 20, 1691. R. of Bobbingworth, Essex, 1692-1740. (*Essex Pedigrees*; Burke, *L.G.*)

HOUBLON, JACOB. Adm. at CORPUS CHRISTI, 1725. Of London. S. of Charles, merchant. B. July 31, 1710. Matric. 1725. Migrated to Emmanuel, Feb. 9, 1729-30. M.A. 1730 (*Lit. Reg.*). M.P. for Colchester, 1735-41; for Herts., 1741-7, 1761-8. Married Mary, dau. of Sir John Hinde Cotton, of Madingley, Cambridge, Bart. Died Feb. 15, 1770. (*Essex Pedigrees*; G. *Mag.*)d

HOUGH, EDMUND. Adm. pens. at JESUS, June 25, 1651. Of Cheshire. Matric. 1651; Scholar, 1652; B.A. 1654-5; M.A. 1658. Fellow, 1656-62, ejected. Incorp. at Oxford, 1660. R. of Thornton, Yorks., 1668-89. V. of Halifax, 1689. Married Mary, dau. of John Copley, of Doncaster. Died Apr. 1, 1691, aged 59. Father of Nathaniel (1690). (*Calamy*, I. 205; A. Gray.)

HOUGH, EDMUND. Adm. sizar at JESUS, May 29, 1686. Of Cheshire. Ord. deacon (Chester) Dec. 19, 1686, age 23. V. of Penistone, Yorks., 1690-1717. Licensed to marry Sarah Hill, at Alderley, Cheshire, July 25, 1687; at that time of Goostrey, clerk. Buried at Penistone, Aug. 26, 1717, aged 53. (E. Axon.)

HOUGH or HOFF, GEORGE. Adm. sizar (age 16) at ST JOHN'S, Apr. 27, 1665. S. of George, potter, of Ticknall, Derbs. B. there. School, Repton (Mr Ullock). Matric. 1665; B.A. 1668-9; M.A. 1672.

HOUGH, HENRY. Adm. sizar (age 19) at ST JOHN'S, May 17, 1749. S. of Richard, grazier, of Leicestershire. B. at Bottesford. Schools, Southwell, Notts. and Oakham. Matric. 1749; B.A. 1753. Ord. deacon (Lincoln) June 17, 1753; priest, June 9, 1754. V. of Granby, Notts., 1756-1800. V. of Howes, Leics., 1756-1800. V. of Gretton, Northants., 1768-70. R. of Redmile, Leics., 1770-1800. Died Aug. 25, 1800. (*Scott-Mayor*, III. 589.)

HOUGH or HOGH, JOHN. B.Can.L. 1519-20. A priest.

HOUGH, JOHN. Adm. sizar at PETERHOUSE, June 8, 1629. Of Derbyshire. Matric. 1629; B.A. 1632-3; Scholar, 1633; M.A. 1636.

HOUGH, JOHN. D.D. 1689 (Incorp. from Oxford). S. of John, of London, gent. B. Apr. 12, 1651. Matric. from Magdalen College, Oxford, Nov. 13, 1669, age 16; B.A. (Oxford) 1673; M.A. 1676; B.D. 1687; D.D. 1687. Fellow of Magdalen, 1674-8. President, 1687; deprived, 1687; restored, 1688-1701. R. of North Aston, Oxon., 1678-87. Preb. of Worcester, 1686-90. R. of Tempsford, Beds., 1687. Bishop of Oxford, 1690-9; of Lichfield, 1699-1717; and of Worcester, 1717-43. Died May 8, 1743, aged 93. (*D.N.B.*; *Al. Oxon.*)

HOUGH, NATHANIEL. Adm. pens. at JESUS, July 4, 1690. S. of Edmund (1651), V. of Halifax, Yorks. Matric. 1691; Rustat Scholar; B.A. 1694-5; M.A. 1698; D.D. 1717. Fellow, 1703-9. Incorp. at Oxford, 1707. R. of St George's, Southwark, 1715-37. R. of Newington, Surrey, 1731-7. Died May 3, 1737. M.I. at Newington. (*Al. Oxon.*; A. Gray.)

HOUGH, RICHARD. B.Can.L. 1517-8. Canonicus.

HOUGH, THOMAS. Adm. pens. (age 18) at TRINITY, Apr. 8, 1718. S. of James, of London. Exhibitioner from St Paul's School. Matric. 1719; Scholar, 1719; B.A. 1721-2; M.A. 1725. Fellow, 1724-31. Taxor, 1730. Ord. priest (Lincoln) Dec. 18, 1726. Preached at St Paul's School Feast, 1728. Admon., Dec. 10, 1731.

HOUGH, THOMAS. Adm. sizar (age 18) at ST JOHN'S, Apr. 16, 1725. S. of T., clerk, of Yorkshire. B. at Penistone. School, Penistone (Mr Ramesden). Matric. 1725; B.A. 1728-9. Ord. deacon (Lincoln) Dec. 21, 1729; priest, Sept. 20, 1730. C. of Middleton Keynes, Bucks. R. of Thurnscoe, Yorks., 1734-48. Died Jan. 25, 1748-9. (*Scott-Mayor*, III. 383.)

HOUGHAM, *see* HUFFAM.

HOUGHTON; *see also* HAUGHTON.

HOUGHTON or HAUGHTON, ADAM. Adm. at CORPUS CHRISTI, 1670. Of London. Matric. 1671; B.A. 1673-4; M.A. 1677. Incorp. at Oxford, 1677. V. of Milton Ernest, Beds., 1677-82. V. of Clapham, 1677. V. of Sundon, 1684-7. R. of Hockliffe, 1687-1713. Married Rebecca, dau. of Hezekiah Slingsby, Jan. 3, 1687-8. Buried at Hockliffe, Apr. 20, 1713, aged 59. M.I. Father of Adam Haughton, 1713. (W. M. Noble.)

HOUGHTON, FRANCIS. Adm. sizar (age 17) at TRINITY, May 31, 1699. S. of Thomas, of Nottinghamshire. School, Chesterfield, Derbs. (Mr Browne). Matric. 1699; Scholar, 1702; B.A. 1702-3. Ord. deacon (York) June, 1704; C. of Tankersley.

HOWGHTON, GEORGE. Matric. sizar from PEMBROKE, Easter, 1548.

HOUGHTON, JOCELIN. Adm. sizar at EMMANUEL, Apr. 20, 1640. Of Lancashire. Inventory (Chester) 1668; of Billington, clerk.

HOUGHTON, JOHN. B.Civ.L. 1496-7.

HOUGHTON, JOHN. 'Of Essex; B.A., LL.B. and B.D. of Cambridge' (according to *Cooper*, but the degrees cannot be found recorded). At the age of 28 entered the Carthusian Order in London, of which he became prior, 1531. Supreme visitor of the order in England. Hanged for denying the King's supremacy, May 4, 1535, aged 47. (*Cooper*, I. 52; *D.N.B.*; *Pits*, 724.)

HOUGHTON, JOHN. Matric. pens. from ST JOHN'S, Easter, 1559.

HOUGHTON, JOHN. Matric. sizar from ST JOHN'S, Michs. 1565.

HOUGHTON, JOHN. Matric. sizar from TRINITY, Easter, 1573; B.A. 1577-8; M.A. 1581. Ord. deacon and priest (Lincoln) Nov. 22, 1580. R. of Scrivelsby, Lincs. Perhaps R. of Eaton Bray, Beds., 1604-25.

HOUGHTON, JOHN. Adm. pens. at EMMANUEL, June 4, 1594. Possibly of Cheshire. Matric. from Brasenose, Oxford, Oct. 14, 1597, age 19.

HOUGHTON, JOHN. M.A. 1618 (Incorp. from Oxford). Of Northamptonshire, *pleb.* Matric. from Trinity College, Oxford, May 26, 1609, age 16; B.A. (Oxford) 1613-4; M.A. 1616. Perhaps R. of Little Chesterford, Essex, 1616. One of these names R. of Lutton, Northants. *cum* Washingley, Hunts., 1628-61. Died 1661. (*Al. Oxon.*)

HOUGHTON, JOHN. Matric. pens. from CLARE, Easter, 1624; B.A. 1627-8; M.A. 1631.

HOUGHTON, JOHN. Adm. pens. (age 16) at CAIUS, Sept. 11, 1645. S. of Robert, Esq., of Itteringham, Norfolk. B. there. Schools, Massingham (Mr Woolsey) and Norwich (Mr Lovering). Matric. 1645; Scholar, 1645-9. Adm. at Lincoln's Inn, Oct. 7, 1648. Of Ranworth, Esq. Brother of Richard (1633). (*Venn*, I. 359.)

HOUGHTON, JOHN. Adm. at CORPUS CHRISTI, 1664. Of Norfolk. Perhaps s. and h. of Robert (? 1639), of Ranworth, Norfolk, Esq.; adm. at Lincoln's Inn, May 4, 1665.

HOUGHTON, JOHN. Adm. at CORPUS CHRISTI, 1720. Of Norfolk. Matric. 1720. Perhaps of Bramerton. Died Oct. 1762. (G. *Mag.*)

HOUGHTON, JOHN. Adm. sizar (age 17) at ST JOHN'S, Apr. 30, 1728. S. of Ralph, gent., of Lancashire. B. in Manchester. School, Macclesfield, Cheshire. Probably matric. 1735. Adm. at the Middle Temple, Oct. 31, 1728, as s. and h. of Ralph, of Baguley, Cheshire. John Houghton, of Baghill, Esq., was High Sheriff of Cheshire in 1761, for a few days. (*Scott-Mayor*, III. 416.)

HOUGHTON, JONATHAN. Adm. sizar (age 17) at PETERHOUSE, Feb. 15, 1661-2. S. of John, of Eaton Bray, Beds. School, St Paul's. Matric. 1661-2. Migrated to Oxford. Matric. from Corpus Christi, Oxford, Nov. 26, 1662; B.A. (Oxford) 1665-6. Died Mar. 29, 1667. (*Al. Oxon.*)

HOUGHTON, OLIVER. Matric. sizar from KING'S, Easter, 1545. B. *c.* 1521. Ord. priest (Peterb.) Sept. 20, 1561. V. of Easton Maudit, Northants., 1564-1605. V. of Bozeat, till 1576. V. of Fawsley, 1580-2. Buried at Easton Maudit, Dec. 27, 1605. Will proved (Archd. Northants.) by widow Margaret. (H. I. Longden.)

HOUGHTON, RICHARD. Adm. Fell.-Com. (age about 18) at CAIUS, July 5, 1633. S. and h. of Robert, Esq., of Itteringham, Norfolk. B. there. Schools, Aylsham (Mr Knowles) and Itteringham (Mr Amyraut). Matric. 1633. Adm. at Lincoln's Inn, Oct. 28, 1635. Probably succeeded his father. Will proved (of Norwich, gent.) Feb. 1693. Brother of John (1645). (*Venn*, I. 310.)

HOUGHTON, ROBERT. B.Can. (or Civ.) L. 1489-90.

HOUGHTON, ROBERT. Matric. sizar from TRINITY, Michs. 1581. B. at Burnley, Lancs., c. 1563. Migrated to Emmanuel. One of the original scholars in 1584. B.A. 1585-6; M.A. 1589. Fellow of Emmanuel, 1588. Ord. priest (Lincoln) June 8, 1593. V. of Tickhill, Yorks., 1594-6, resigned. Perhaps V. of Nocton, Lincs., 1596. V. of St Mary's, Lincoln, 1601-10. R. of South Kelsey St Mary's, Lincs., 1610-29. Will (P.C.C.) 1629.

HOUGHTON, ROBERT. Adm. at CORPUS CHRISTI, 1639. Of Norfolk. This, or the next, s. and h. of John, of Ranworth, Norfolk, Esq., adm. at Lincoln's Inn, May 4, 1642.

HOUGHTON, ROBERT. Adm. at CORPUS CHRISTI, 1641. Of Norfolk.

HOUGHTON, ROGER. Adm. Fell.-Com. at EMMANUEL, Apr. 20, 1640. Of Lancashire. Probably s. of Sir Gilbert, of Hoghton Tower, Lancs. Matric. 1640. Killed in the battle at Hessam Moor, 1643. (Foster, *Lancs. Pedigrees*; *Vis. of Lancs.*, 1664.)

HOUGHTON, SAMUEL. Adm. sizar at EMMANUEL, Oct. 12, 1637, as 'Haughton.' Of Lincolnshire. Matric. 1637-8; B.A. 1641-2. Ord. deacon (Lincoln) June 16, 1644. Perhaps R. of Buckenham Ferry, Norfolk, 1669-94.

HOUGHTON, SAMUEL. Adm. sizar at CLARE, Mar. 13, 1666-7. Matric. 1667.

HOGTON, STEPHEN DE. B.Can.L. Priest, of Norwich diocese. R. of Swannington, Norfolk. Petitions the Pope, 1363, for a benefice. Has lectured two years in Canon Law. (*Cal. Pap. Pet.*, I. 405.)

HOUGHTON, THOMAS. Matric. pens. from JESUS, Easter, 1586. One of these names, of London, adm. at Lincoln's Inn, May 5, 1588.

HOUGHTON or HAUGHTON, THOMAS. Adm. sizar at EMMANUEL, Easter, 1624. Matric. 1624. Brother of William (1621).

HOUGHTON, THOMAS. Adm. pens. at TRINITY, Dec. 1, 1646. Of Sussex. Probably s. of Thomas, of Mayfield, Sussex; age 6 in 1634. Matric. 1646. (*Vis. of Sussex.*)

HOUGHTON, THOMAS. Adm. pens. at EMMANUEL, May 23, 1649. Of Salop. Matric. 1649; B.A. 1659-60.

HOUGHTON, THOMAS. Adm. sizar at CLARE, Dec. 22, 1662. Matric. 1663; B.A. 1666-7; M.A. 1670. Fellow. (For a contemporary *see Al. Oxon.*)

HOUGHTON, TOBIAS. Matric. pens. from KING'S, Lent, 1564-5.

HOUGHTON, WILLIAM DE. Adm. at KING'S HALL, 1341; Scholar, 1346. Died Apr. 26, 1347.

HOUGHTON, WILLIAM. B.Civ.L. 1521-2. R. of Sessay, Yorks., 1550-3.

HOUGHTON, WILLIAM. Matric. sizar from EMMANUEL, Easter, 1621; B.A. 1624-5; M.A. 1628. Ord. deacon (Peterb.) Sept. 24; priest, Sept. 25, 1626.

HOUGHTON, WILLIAM. Adm. sizar at TRINITY, Feb. 21, 1652-3. Of Norfolk. B.A. 1656-7; M.A. 1660. One of these names V. of Shernborne, Norfolk, 1660. V. of Dersingham, 1660-1700. V. of Heacham, 1699.

HOUGHTON, WILLIAM. Adm. sizar at EMMANUEL, Aug. 29, 1692. Of Norfolk. Matric. 1696; B.A. 1696-7. Ord. priest (Norwich) June 4, 1699. R. of Anmer, Norfolk, 1709-48.

HOGHTON, ——. B.A. 1481-2.

HOUGHTON, ——. B.A. 1490-1; M.A. 1494.

HOUGHTON, ——. B.Can.L. 1534-5. A priest. Perhaps Thomas, V. of Caldecot, Cambs., 1538-43. One —— Houghton was a scholar at JESUS, 1535-6.

HOUGHTON, ——. Adm. at CORPUS CHRISTI, 1571.

HOULDEN; *see* HOLDEN.

HOULKER, *see* HOLKER.

HOULTBY, GEORGE. Matric. pens. from CHRIST'S, Nov. 1569. Doubtless s. of Lancelot, of Fryton, Yorks. Succeeded his father at Fryton. Probably of Scackleton, Yorks. Married Elizabeth, dau. of Roger Meynill, of Kilvington. Brother of Richard (1571), the Jesuit. (*Vis. of Yorks.*, 1584; M. H. Peacock.)

HOULTBIE, MARMADUKE. Matric. pens. from ST JOHN'S, Michs. 1572.

HOLTBIE or HOULBYE, RICHARD. Matric. pens. (age 18) from CHRIST'S, Nov. 1571. S. of Lancelot. B. at Fryton, Yorks. School, Northallerton. Migrated to Caius, Aug. 19, 1573. Migrated to Hart Hall, Oxford, 1574. B.A. (Oxford) 1575-6. A Jesuit priest. Adm. at Douay, 1578, and sent to England the same year. Most of his labours were in Yorkshire, where, though constantly hunted by spies, he escaped apprehension. Became Superior of the English Jesuits after the execution of Garnet, May 3, 1606. Died in Yorks., May 25, 1640. Brother of George (above). (*Venn*, I. 75; *D.N.B.*; *Vis. of Yorks.*, 1584.)

HOLTBY, ——. B.Civ.L. 1499-1500. One Christopher Holtby, of Bury St Edmunds, Suffolk, and Mavis Enderby, Lincs., priest. Will (P.C.C.) 1522.

HOULTON, JOSEPH. Matric. pens. from CORPUS CHRISTI, Michs. 1615. Of Suffolk. B.A. 1618-9; M.A. 1622. R. of Barton St Mary, Norfolk, 1644.

HOULTON or HOUGHTON, ROBERT. Matric. sizar from CORPUS CHRISTI, Easter, 1571. Probably adm. 1570, as H°w'ter.

HOULTON, ROBERT. M.A. from SIDNEY, 1703. S. of R. of Warminster, Wilts. Matric. from Hart Hall, Oxford, Apr. 21, 1680, age 16; B.A. (Oxford) 1683-4. R. of Winterbourne Monkton, Dorset, 1692-1708; and of Middle Chinnock, Somerset, 1703-8. Died 1708. Father of the next. (*Al. Oxon.*)

HOULTON, ROBERT. M.A. from TRINITY, 1721. S. of Robert (above), of Monkton, Dorset, clerk. Matric. from Wadham College, Oxford, Mar. 22, 1710-1, age 17; B.A. (Oxford) 1714. R. of Penselwood, Somerset, 1719-45. R. of Middle Chinnock, 1732-7. V. of Milton Clevedon, 1737-44. (*Al. Oxon.*)

HOULTON, THOMAS. Matric. sizar from CLARE, Easter, 1612.

HOLTON, WILLIAM. Matric. pens. from ST JOHN'S, Easter, 1552.

HOUNDE, *see* HOWNDE.

HOURDE, THOMAS. Matric. pens. from ST JOHN'S, Easter, 1577.

HOUSDEN, *see* HOWSDEN.

HOUSEGO, ROBERT. Matric. sizar from ST JOHN'S, Michs. 1562. B. at Norwich. B.A. 1565-6; M.A. 1569. Fellow of Corpus Christi, 1569, for a few months. Ord. deacon (London) July 29, 1568. V. of Stanstead Abbots, Herts., 1573-5. (J. Ch. Smith.)

HOUSEHOLD, JOHN. Pens. at GONVILLE HALL, 1510-6; B.D. 1513. Cluniac monk of Castleacre. Signed the surrender, 1537. V. of East Barsham, Norfolk, 1538-51. Will (Norwich) 1551. He leaves gifts, books, vestments, etc., to Gonville Hall. (*Venn*, I. 20.)

HOUSELOCK, ABRAHAM. Adm. sizar (age 16) at PETERHOUSE, Feb. 12, 1641-2. Of Kent. Matric. 1642.

HOWSMAN, JOHN. Carmelite of Cambridge. Ord. deacon (Ely) Dec. 17, 1495.

HOUSEMAN, JOHN. Matric. Fell.-Com. from MAGDALENE, Easter, 1558.

HOUSEMAN, JOHN. Adm. sizar (age 18) at ST JOHN'S, Apr. 28, 1640. S. of William, yeoman, lately deceased, of Slyne, near Lancaster. B. there. Schools, Lancaster (Mr Scholecraft) and Sedbergh (Mr Nelson). Matric. 1640; B.A. 1643-4; M.A. 1647; B.D. 1654. Fellow, 1644; senior fellow, 1652. Ord. priest (Bishop Maxwell, of Kilmore) Oct. 15, 1651. V. of Great Thurlow, Suffolk. Died *c.* 1690.

HOUSEMAN, THOMAS. Adm. pens. at CLARE, May 19, 1660. Of Yorkshire. Matric. 1660; B.A. 1663.

HOUSTWAYTE, *see* HUSTWAITE *and* HUTHWETT.

HOVEDEN, RICHARD. Matric. pens. from TRINITY, Easter, 1577, as 'Owenden'; B.A. 1580-1. One Ri. Hovenden, of Middlesex, adm. at Lincoln's Inn, Dec. 5, 1582.

HOVENDEN, ROBERT. Adm. pens. at PETERHOUSE, Oct. 20, 1564. Doubtless s. of William, of Canterbury. Matric. 1564-5. Migrated to Oxford. B.A. there, 1566; M.A. 1570; B.D. and D.D. 1581. Fellow of All Souls; Warden, 1571-1614. Vice-Chancellor, 1582. Chaplain to Archbishop Parker. Preb. of Lincoln, *c.* 1570-1614. Preb. of Canterbury, 1589-1614. Died Mar. 25, 1614. Buried in the College Chapel. (*Al. Oxon.*; *D.N.B.*)

HOVEDEN, ROBERT. M.A. 1625 (Incorp. from Oxford). Of Kent. S. of George, R. of Harrietsham. Bapt. there, Nov. 21, 1602. Matric. from Brasenose College, Oxford, June 27, 1617, age 14; B.A. (Oxford) 1620-1; M.A. 1623-4. Fellow of All Souls. Died 1640. (*Al. Oxon.*)

HOVENDEN, THOMAS. Matric. pens. from TRINITY, Michs. 1564.

HOVELL, *see also* HOWELL.

HOVILL, EDMUND. Adm. pens. (age 16) at CAIUS, June 20, 1637. S. of Nicholas, gent. B. at North Walsham, Norfolk. Bapt. there, Mar. 15, 1621-2. School, North Walsham (Mr Acres).

HOVELL (*alias* SMITH), GEORGE. B.A. from ST CATHARINE'S, 1600-1; M.A. 1604. Ord. priest (Norwich) Dec. 23, 1604, age 24. V. of Framsden, Suffolk, 1606-12. (Pedigree of 'Hovell, *alias* Smith,' of Ash Bocking, in *Vis. of Suffolk*, 1664.)

HOVELL, GREGORY. Adm. scholar (age 19) at CAIUS, Mar. 27, 1609. S. of Thomas, gent., of Winston, Suffolk. School, Botesdale (Mr Fowle). B.A. 1617-8. Ord. deacon (Norwich) 1619. (*Venn*, I. 201.)

HOVELL, HUGH. Adm. pens. (age 16) at CAIUS, June 9, 1632. S. of William, gent., of Gaywood, Norfolk. B. at Holkham. School, Lynn (Mr Woodmansey). Matric. 1632; Scholar, 1634-9; B.A. 1635-6; M.A. 1639. Of Kenninghall Park, Norfolk, Esq. Died Oct. 25, 1690. Buried at Mildenhall, Suffolk. M.I. (*Venn*, I. 305.)

HOVEL, RICHARD. Adm. Fell.-Com. at EMMANUEL, Jan. 23, 1626-7. Doubtless s. and h. of Richard, of Hillington, Norfolk; adm. at Gray's Inn, Nov. 1, 1624. Knighted, 1641. Royalist. Of Hillington. Buried Aug. 26, 1654. Father of the next. (*Suff. Man. Fam.*, II. 36; *Blomefield*, IV. 566.)

HOVELL, WILLIAM. Adm. Fell.-Com. (age 12) at CAIUS, Oct. 10, 1649. S. of Sir Richard (above), Knt., of Hillington, Norfolk. B. in London. School, Wimpole (Mr Bagge). Matric. 1649; B.A. 1653-4 (1st in the *ordo*). Adm. at Gray's Inn, Jan. 26, 1654-5. Of Hillington. Knighted, June 5, 1660. M.P. for Lynn, 1661-70. Died Mar. 4, 1669-70. Buried at Hillington. Will, P.C.C. (*Venn*, I. 376; *Vis. of Norfolk*, 1664.)

HOVELL, WILLIAM. Adm. pens. (age 17) at ST JOHN'S, Dec. 23, 1732. S. of Oliver, gent. B. at Bury, Suffolk. School, Bury. Matric. 1737; M.B. 1740. Of Badwell Ash, Suffolk. Married, Mar. 30, 1736, Elizabeth, dau. of Alexander Burrell, R. of Adstock, Bucks. Buried at Badwell, July 21, 1769. M.I. Will (Bury) 1769. (*Suff. Man. Fam.*, II. 103; *G. Mag.*; Burke, *L.G.*)

HOVENDEN, *see* HOVEDEN.

HOVENER, ROBERT. Adm. pens. at ST CATHARINE'S, Nov. 8, 1687. Of Surrey. Matric. 1688; B.A. 1691-2.

HOVINGTON, CHRISTOPHER. Matric. sizar from JESUS, Easter, 1614; B.A. 1617-8; M.A. 1621. Ord. deacon (York) May, 1619; priest, Sept. 1621.

HOVY, GEORGE. M.A. 1679 (Incorp. from Edinburgh). V. of Coley, Halifax, Yorks., 1676-81.

HOW, *see* HOWE.

HOWARD, Sir CHARLES. M.A. 1571. 1st s. of William (1564), Baron Howard of Effingham. M.P. for Surrey, 1562-7 and 1572-3. Succeeded as 2nd Baron Howard of Effingham, 1573. Lord Lieutenant of Surrey, 1573-4; of Sussex, 1585-1624; of Devon, 1585-7; and of Cornwall, 1585-1614. K.G., 1575. Lord Chamberlain of the Household, 1583-5. Privy Councillor, 1583. Lord High Admiral, 1585-1618. Chief in command against the Spanish Armada, 1588. Captured Cadiz, 1596. Created 1st Earl of Nottingham, 1596. Commissioner at Essex's trial, 1601. Ambassador extraordinary to Spain, 1605. Died Dec. 13, 1624. Buried at Reigate. M.I. at St Margaret's, Westminster. (*D.N.B.*; A. B. Beaven.)

HOWARD, CHARLES. Matric. pens. at KING'S, a scholar from Eton, Michs. 1640. S. of Sir Charles. B. at Bray, Berks. Fellow, till 1645. Captain of a Troop of Horse in the Royal army. Slain near Newark. (*Harwood*.)

HOWARD, CHARLES. Adm. Fell.-Com. (age 17) at ST JOHN'S, Apr. 26, 1735. 2nd s. of Henry Bowes, 4th Earl of Berks. B. at Elford, Staffs. School, Eton. Matric. 1735. Adm. at Lincoln's Inn, Feb. 12, 1736-7. Died 1773. (*Scott-Mayor*, III. 466.)

HOWARD DE WALDEN, CHARLES WILLIAM. Adm. nobleman (age 18) at MAGDALENE, June 27, 1710. S. of Henry (1685), Earl of Suffolk and Bindon. School, Walden. Matric. 1711. Succeeded his father as 7th Earl of Suffolk, 1718. Recorder of Saffron Walden, 1718. Lord-Lieutenant of Essex, 1718-22. Married Arabella, dau. of Sir Samuel Astry, of Henbury, Gloucs. Died Feb. 9, 1721-2, *s.p.* Buried at Walden. (G.E.C.)

HOWARD, CHARLES. LL.D. 1717. 3rd s. of Henry, 5th Earl of Suffolk. B. 1675. An officer in the army, 1703. Groom of the Bedchamber, 1714-27. Succeeded his brother Edward as 9th Earl of Suffolk, 1731. Married Henrietta, dau. of Sir Henry Hobart, Bart. Died Sept. 28, 1733. Buried at Walden. Brother of Edward (1685) and Henry (1685). (G.E.C.)

HOWARD, EDEN. Adm. sizar (age 21) at TRINITY, Oct. 25, 1726. S. of John, of Market Street, Bedford. Taught by his father. Matric. 1726; B.A. 1730-1. Ord. deacon (Lincoln) June 1; priest, Dec. 21, 1729. Chaplain to the East India Company, 1732-45. Will (P.C.C.) 1781; of Rendlesham, Suffolk. (J. Ch. Smith.)

HOWARD, EDWARD. Adm. Fell.-Com. (age 13) at MAGDALENE, Nov. 2, 1685. S. of Henry (afterwards Earl of Suffolk). B. in St James', Middlesex. School, Panton St (Mr Froholk). Matric. 1685. Succeeded his nephew Charles William (1710) as 8th Earl of Suffolk, 1722. Died unmarried, June 22, 1731. Buried at Walden. Brother of Henry (1685) and Charles (1717). (*Collins*, III. 159; G.E.C.)

HOWARD, EPHRAIM. Adm. sizar (age 16) at ST JOHN'S, Sept. 7, 1681. S. of Thomas, deceased, of Middlesex. B. there. Exhibitioner from Charterhouse. Matric. 1681; B.A. 1685-6; M.A. from Queens', 1690. Fellow of Queens', *c.* 1686. A nonjuror.

HOWARD, FRANCIS. Matric. Fell.-Com. from QUEENS', Easter, 1550 (*impubes*). 3rd s. of Thomas, Viscount Howard of Bindon. Brother of Henry (1550) and Thomas (1550).

HOWARD, HENRY, Earl of Surrey (by courtesy). High Steward of the University with his father, 1539-40. S. of Thomas, 3rd Duke of Norfolk. B. *c.* 1516. K.G., 1541. Distinguished as a scholar and soldier. With the imperial troops at Landrecy, 1543. Appointed Commander of Boulogne, 1545-6. Defeated at St Etienne, 1546. Superseded by his enemy, Lord Hertford, 1546. Married Francis Vere, dau. of the Earl of Oxford. Poet, introduced the Sonnet from Italy into England. Condemned on a frivolous charge of treasonably quartering royal arms. Executed on Tower Hill, Jan. 21, 1547-8. Father of Henry (1564) and Thomas (1564). (*G.E.C.*; *D.N.B.*)

HOWARD, HENRY. Matric. Fell.-Com. from QUEENS', Easter, 1550 (*impubes*). Eldest s. of Thomas, Viscount Bindon. Succeeded as 2nd Viscount, 1582. Married Frances, dau. of Sir Peter Meautys, of Westham, Essex. Admon. granted to his brother, Jan. 16, 1590-1. Brother of Francis (1550) and Thomas (1550). (*G.E.C.*)

HOWARD, HENRY. Matric. Fell.-Com. from KING'S, Michs. 1564. 2nd s. of Henry, Earl of Surrey. B. 1540, at Shottisham, Norfolk. M.A. 1566. Migrated to Trinity Hall. Read Latin lectures on Rhetoric and Civil Law. Chancellor of the University, 1612-4. Incorp. at Oxford, 1568. Went to Court, *c.* 1570. Failed to gain a secure position owing to his relations with Mary Queen of Scots. Retired to Audley End, and directed the education of his brother's children. Re-adm. to court, 1600. Adm. at the Middle Temple, Feb. 2, 1603-4. Commissioner for the trials of Raleigh, 1603; Guy Fawkes, 1605; and Garnet, 1606. Created Earl of Northampton, 1604. Privy Councillor. Warden of the Cinque Ports, 1604-14. K.G., 1605. Lord Privy Seal, 1608-14. First Commissioner of the Treasury, 1612-4. Lived and died a Roman Catholic. Reputed the most learned noble of his day. Built Northumberland House. Endowed three hospitals, including Norfolk College, Greenwich. Died June 15, 1614. Buried in the Chapel of Dover Castle. M.I. at Greenwich. Brother of Thomas (1564). (*D.N.B.*)

HOWARD, HENRY. M.A. 1605. 3rd s. of Thomas (1605), 1st Earl of Suffolk. Married Elizabeth, dau. of William Bassett, of Blore, Staffs. Died young. Brother of Theophilus (1598) and Thomas (1598). (Burke, *Peerage*.)

HOWARD, HENRY. Adm. pens. (age 16) at CAIUS, June 9, 1629. S. of Robert, gent. B. at Tibenham, Norfolk. Schools, Moulton (Mr Matchet) and Eye (Mr Hall). Matric. 1629. Perhaps scholar of Trinity Hall, 1632. Perhaps father of Henry (1667).

HOWARD, HENRY. Adm. Fell.-Com. at ST JOHN'S, July 4, 1640. 2nd s. of Henry Frederic, 3rd Earl of Arundel. B. 1628. D.C.L. (Oxford) 1668. Went abroad; visited John Evelyn at Padua, 1645. High Steward of Guildford, 1663-73. F.R.S., 1666; presented a library to the Royal Society and the Arundel Marbles to Oxford. Created Baron Howard of Castle Rising, 1669. Envoy to Morocco, 1669. Created Earl of Norwich, 1672. Hereditary Earl Marshal, 1672-84. Succeeded his brother Thomas, as 6th Duke of Norfolk, Dec. 1677. Married (1) Lady Anne Somerset, dau. of Edward, Marquis of Worcester; (2) Jane, dau. of Robert Bickerton, gentleman of the wine-cellar to Charles II. Died Jan. 11, 1683-4. Buried at Arundel. Brother of Philip Thomas (1640) and of Thomas (1640). (*D.N.B.*)

HOWARD, HENRY Adm. pens. at CAIUS, Oct. 12, 1667. S. of Henry (? 1629), gent., deceased. B. at Moulton. School, Moulton (Mr Wickham). Matric. 1667; Scholar, 1668-75; B.A. 1671-2; M.A. 1675. Ord. deacon (Norwich) Dec. 1675, as C. of Moulton; priest, Feb. 1675-6. V. of Mutford, Suffolk, 1675-80. Buried there Dec. 8, 1680. (*Venn*, I. 432.)

HOWARD, HENRY. Adm. Fell.-Com. (age 15) at MAGDALENE, Nov. 2, 1685. S. of Henry (afterwards Earl of Suffolk) and grandson of Theophilus (1598). B. in Duke Street, St James. School, Panton St (Mr Froholk). Matric. 1685. M.P. for Arundel, 1695-8; for Essex, 1705-6. Commissary-general of the Musters, 1697-1706. Created Baron Chesterford, Co. Essex, and Earl of Bindon, Co. Dorset, 1706. Privy Councillor, 1707 and 1714. Succeeded his father as 6th Earl of Suffolk, 1709. Lord-Lieutenant of Essex, 1714-8. President of the Board of Trade, 1715-8. Died Sept. 19, 1718. Buried at Walden. Brother of Edward (1685) and Charles (1717), father of Charles William (1710). (G.E.C.)

HOWARD, HENRY. Adm. sizar at CLARE, June 23, 1705. S. of John (1684), R. of Marston Trussel, Northants. Bapt. there, Nov. 11, 1686. Matric. 1705; B.A. 1708-9. Perhaps R. of Saxelby, Leics., 1727. Died 1728. (H. I. Longden.)

HOWARD, HENRY. Said to have been at MAGDALENE. S. and h. of Charles (1717). B. 1706. M.P. for Beeralston, 1728-33. Succeeded his father as 10th Earl of Suffolk, 1733. Married Sarah, dau. of William Hucks, of London, brewer. Died at Audley End, Apr. 22, 1745. Buried at Walden. (G.E.C.)

HOWARD, JAMES, **Earl of Suffolk.** M.A. 1664. S. and h. of Theophilus (1598). Bapt. at Walden, Feb. 10, 1619-20. M.A. (Oxford) 1663. K.B., 1626. Succeeded his father as 3rd Earl of Suffolk, 1640. Lord-Lieutenant of Suffolk, 1642. High Steward of Ipswich, 1653. Lord-Lieutenant of Suffolk and Cambridgeshire, 1660-81. Gentleman of the Bedchamber, 1665. Commissioner for the office of Earl-Marshal, 1673. Hereditary visitor of Magdalene College, Cambridge. Died without male issue, Jan. 7, 1688-9. Buried at Saffron Walden. (*G.E.C.*; *D.N.B.*)

HOWARD, JOHN. Adm. at CAIUS, Apr. 10, 1641. S. of William, goldsmith, of Cambridge. B. 1625. Bapt. at Gt St Mary's, Apr. 19, 1625. School, Perse (Mr Lovering and Mr Watson). Matric. pens. 1641; B.A. 1644-5; M.A. 1648. Perhaps V. of Stantonbury, Bucks., 1675-8; and of Newport Pagnell, 1678-85. (*Venn*, I. 341.)

HOWARD, JOHN. Adm. sizar at TRINITY, May 27, 1667. Matric. 1667; B.A. 1670-1. Ord. deacon (Norwich)uSept. 1672. One of these names (B.A.), V. of Thurston, S ffolk, 1675-85. R. of Westhorpe ('M.A.'), 1685-8. Died 1688.

HOWARD, JOHN. M.A. 1684 (Incorp. from Oxford). S. of Robert, of Guilsborough, Northants. Matric. from Wadham College, Oxford, Dec. 17, 1666, age 19; B.A. (Oxford) 1670; M.A. 1673. Ord. deacon (Peterb.) Sept. 21, 1673; priest, Sept. 20, 1674. R. of Marston Trussel, Northants., 1682-1701. R. of Little Bowden, 1691-6. V. of Kidderminster, 1701. Father of the next and of Henry (1705). (*Al. Oxon.*; *Lipscomb*, IV. 286.)

HOWARD, JOHN. Adm. sizar (age 18) at MAGDALENE, Apr. 18, 1698. S. of John (above), clerk. B. at Marston Trussel, Northants. Educated at Marston Trussel. Brother of Henry (1705).

HOWARD, MATTHEW. Matric. pens. from MAGDALENE, Easter, 1634. Of Essex. Migrated to Queens', Nov. 1, 1639. B.A. 1639-40.

HOWARD, MICHAEL WILLIAM. Adm. pens. at ST CATHARINE'S, July 1, 1739. Of Maryland. Matric. 1739.

HOWARD, PHILIP. M.A. 1576. Educated at ST JOHN'S. Known by the courtesy title of Earl of Surrey. 1st s. of Thomas (1564), 4th Duke of Norfolk. B. 1557. Summoned to the Peers as Earl of Arundel, Jan. 1580-1. Became a Roman Catholic, 1584. In an attempt to leave England he was captured and subsequently, 1589, condemned to death for treason. The sentence was not carried out, but he remained a prisoner. Died in the Tower, Nov. 19, 1595. Brother of William (1577) and Thomas (1605), father of Thomas (1605). (*D.N.B.*; A. B. Beaven.)

HOWARD, PHILIP THOMAS. Adm. Fell.-Com. at ST JOHN'S, July 4, 1640. 3rd s. of Henry Frederic, 3rd Earl of Arundel. B. 1629. Educated at Utrecht and Antwerp. Became a Dominican, 1646. Studied at Naples and Rennes. Ord. priest, 1652. First prior of his own English foundation of Bornhem, Flanders, 1657. Sent on a secret royalist mission to England, 1659. Promoted the marriage of Charles II, 1662; appointed chaplain to Queen Catherine, afterwards grand-almoner. Driven from England by popular feeling, 1674. Created Cardinal, 1675. Arch-priest of S. Maria Maggiore, Rome, 1689. Died June 17, 1694, at Rome. Buried there. Brother of Henry (1640) and Thomas (1640). (*D.N.B.*)

HOWARD, RICHARD. Adm. sizar at TRINITY, Mar. 5, 1659-60. Matric. 1660; B.A. 1663-4. Signed for deacon's orders (London) Feb. 17, 1664-5; for priest's, May 31, 1671. V. of Chislet, Kent, 1672-82. Buried there Nov. 28, 1682. (H. G. Harrison.)

HOWARD, RICHARD. Matric. sizar from CLARE, Easter, 1675.

HOWARD, ROBERT. Of MAGDALENE. 6th s. of Thomas (1598), Earl of Berkshire. Great nephew of Thomas, 1st Earl of Suffolk. Bapt. at St Martin-in-the-Fields, Jan. 19, 1625-6. Knighted at Newbury, 1644. Imprisoned at Windsor under the Commonwealth. M.P. for Stockbridge, 1661-79; and for Castle Rising, 1679-81, 1689-98. Auditor of the Exchequer, 1673-98. Privy Councillor, 1689. Dramatist. Died Sept. 3, 1698. Buried in Westminster Abbey. (*D.N.B.*; *Magdalene College History*.)

HOWARD, SAMUEL. Adm. Fell.-Com. at CLARE, May 29, 1735. B. in London. One of these names, s. of Richard, of Hackney, Esq., adm. at Lincoln's Inn, Oct. 22, 1730.

HOWARD, THEOPHILUS. Matric. Fell.-Com. from MAGDALENE, Michs. 1598. 1st s. of Thomas (1605), 1st Earl of Suffolk. B. 1584. M.A. 1605. Incorp. at Oxford, 1605. Adm. at Gray's Inn, Mar. 18, 1605-6. M.P. for Maldon, 1605-10. Governor of Jersey, 1610-40. Summoned to the Peers as Baron Howard de Walden, 1610. Joint Lord-Lieutenant of the Northern counties, 1614-33. Lord-Lieutenant of Cambridgeshire, Suffolk and Dorset, 1626-40. Privy Councillor, 1626. Succeeded as 2nd Earl of Suffolk and 2nd Baron de Walden, May, 1626. K.G., 1627. Warden of the Cinque Ports, 1628-40. Governor of Berwick, 1635. Died June 3, 1640. Buried at Saffron Walden. Brother of Thomas (1598) and Henry (1605), father of James (1664). (*D.N.B.*; A. B. Beaven.)

HOWARD, THOMAS. High Steward of the University, with his s. Henry, 1530-47, 1553-4. S. of Thomas, Duke of Norfolk. B. 1473. Knighted, 1497. K.G., 1510. Lord Admiral, 1513-25. Fought at Flodden. Earl of Surrey, 1514. Lord-Lieutenant of Ireland, 1520-2. Lord Treasurer, 1522-47. Succeeded as 3rd Duke of Norfolk, 1524. As President of the Privy Council incensed Henry VIII against Wolsey. Earl Marshal, 1533-47 and 1553-4. Acquiesced in the execution of his niece, Anne Boleyn, 1536. Active in the suppression of the Pilgrimage of Grace. Opposed Cromwell. Sent to wage war against Scotland, 1542. Lieutenant-General of the army in France, 1544. Ousted from favour by the Earl of Hertford. Imprisoned in the Tower, 1547, till 1553. Died Aug. 25, 1554. Buried at Framlingham. (*D.N.B.*)

HOWARD, THOMAS. Matric. Fell.-Com. from QUEENS', Easter, 1550, *impubes*. 2nd s. of Thomas, Viscount Howard of Bindon. Succeeded his brother Henry (1550), as 3rd Viscount, 1591. K.G., 1606. Married Grace, dau. of Bernard Duffield. Died *s.p.*, Mar. 1, 1610-1. Brother of Henry (1550) and Francis (1550). (*G.E.C.*)

HOWARD, THOMAS. M.A. 1564 (on the Queen's visit). 1st s. of Henry, Earl of Surrey. B. Mar. 10, 1536. M.A. (Oxford) 1568. K.B., 1553. Succeeded as 4th Duke of Norfolk, Aug. 1554. Earl Marshal, 1554-72. Lord-Lieutenant of Norfolk and Suffolk, 1558. K.G., 1559. Employed in Scotland, 1559-60. Privy Councillor, 1562. Formed a project of marriage with Mary Queen of Scots; imprisoned, 1569-70. Involved in Ridolfi's plot. Executed, June 2, 1572. Benefactor to Magdalene College. Brother of Henry (1564), father of Thomas (1605), of Philip (1576) and William (1577). (*Cooper*, I. 302; *D.N.B.*)

HOWARD, THOMAS. Matric. from MAGDALENE, Michs. 1598. 2nd s. of Thomas, 1st Earl of Suffolk. M.A. 1605. K.B., 1605. M.P. for Lancaster, 1605-11; for Co. Wilts., 1614; for Cricklade, 1620-2. Created Baron Howard of Charlton and Viscount Andover, 1622. K.G., 1625. Earl of Berkshire, 1626. Candidate for Chancellorship of the University, 1626. Privy Councillor, 1639. Governor to the Prince of Wales, 1643-6. Died July 16, 1669, aged about 90. Buried in Westminster Abbey. Brother of Theophilus (1598) and Henry (1605), father of Robert. (*G.E.C.*; A. B. Beaven.)

HOWARD, THOMAS. M.A. 1605. Educated at ST JOHN'S. 2nd s. of Thomas (1564), 4th Duke of Norfolk. B. 1561. Knighted, 1588. Distinguished himself against the Armada, 1588. Commander in the attack off the Azores, 1591. Admiral of the Third Squadron in the Cadiz Expedition, 1596. K.G., 1597. 1st Baron Howard de Walden, 1597. Adm. at Gray's Inn, Feb. 2, 1597-8. Lord-Lieutenant of Cambridgeshire, 1598-1626; Suffolk, 1605-26; and Dorset, 1611-26. Constable of the Tower. High Steward of the University, 1601-14. Created 1st Earl of Suffolk, 1603. Lord Chamberlain, 1603-14. Privy Councillor, 1603. Chancellor of the University, 1614-26. Lord High Treasurer, 1614-8; fined and imprisoned for embezzlement, 1619. High Steward of Exeter, 1621. Died May 28, 1626. Father of Theophilus (1598), Thomas (1598) and Henry (1605), brother of Philip (1576) and William (*c.* 1577). (*D.N.B.*)

HOWARD, THOMAS. M.A. 1605. 1st s. of Philip (1576), 1st Earl of Arundel. B. 1586. School, Westminster. 'Went to TRINITY College' (*D.N.B.*; not recorded in the register). Restored in title and blood, 1604; becoming Earl of Arundel, 1604. Travelled in the Low Countries, France and Italy. Lord-Lieutenant of Sussex, 1608-36; of Norfolk, 1615; of Northumberland and Cumberland, 1633-9. K.G., 1611. Became a protestant, 1615. Privy Councillor, 1616. President of the Committee of Peers on Bacon's case, 1621. Joint Commissioner of the Great Seal, 1621. Earl Marshal, 1621-46. Imprisoned for hostility to Buckingham, 1626. Chief Justice in Eyre, North of Trent, 1634-46. Sent to Vienna to urge the restitution of the Palatinate to Charles I's nephew, 1636. General of the army against Scotland, 1639. Lord Steward, 1640-1. Presided at Strafford's trial, 1641. Left England, 1642, and settled at Padua. Created Earl of Norfolk, June, 1644. Formed the first considerable art collection in England, including statues, pictures, and the famous Arundel marbles presented to Oxford University, 1667. Died at Padua Oct. 4, 1646. Buried at Arundel. (*D.N.B.*; A. B. Beaven.)

HOWARD, THOMAS. Adm. Fell.-Com. at CORPUS CHRISTI, Oct. 12, 1637. 1st s. of Edward, 1st Baron Howard of Escrick. Bapt. at Saffron Walden, Oct. 24, 1625. Succeeded his father as 2nd Baron Howard of Escrick, 1675. Went to the assistance of the King in Lancashire, with 100 horse. Died at Bruges, Aug. 24, 1678. Buried at St Martin-in-the-Fields. Brother of William (1646). (*Masters*; *G.E.C.*)

HOWARD, THOMAS. Adm. Fell.-Com. at ST JOHN'S, Easter, 1640. S. and h. of Henry Frederic, 3rd Earl of Arundel. B. 1627. Suffered from brain fever at Padua, 1645, which impaired his mental faculties. Succeeded his father as Earl of Arundel, 1652. Restored by Act of Parliament to the Dukedom of Norfolk, 1660. Died, unmarried, at Padua, Dec. 13, 1677. Buried at Arundel. Brother of Henry (1640) and Philip Thomas (1640). (*G.E.C.*)

HOWARD, THOMAS. M.A. from KING'S, 1741. S. of Samuel, of Ribbesford, Worcs. Matric. from Trinity College, Oxford, Apr. 24, 1724, age 17. (B.A. not recorded.) (*Al. Oxon.*)

HOWARD, WALTER. Scholar at KING'S HALL, 1397-1404.

HOWARD, WILLIAM. M.A. 1454-5; B.D. 1465-6; D.D. 1469-70. Prior of the Carmelite House at Cambridge, 1468.

HOWARD, Sir WILLIAM. Educated at TRINITY HALL, under Stephen Gardiner. M.A. 1564 (on Queen's visit). S. of Thomas, 2nd Duke of Norfolk. M.A. at Oxford, 1566. Employed in embassies to Scotland, 1531, 1535 and 1536. Ambassador to France, 1537 and 1541. Governor of Calais, 1552-3. Lord High Admiral, 1553-8. Created 1st Lord Howard of Effingham, 1554. K.G., 1554. Privy Councillor, 1554. Lord Chamberlain, 1558-72. Lord-Lieutenant of Surrey, 1559-73. Adm. at the Inner Temple, 1562. Lord Privy Seal, 1572-3. Died Jan. 12, 1572-3. Buried at Reigate. Father of Sir Charles (1571). (*D.N.B.*)

HOWARD, Lord WILLIAM. Probably of ST JOHN'S, *c.* 1577. 3rd s. of Thomas (1564), 4th Duke of Norfolk. B. at Audley End, Dec. 19, 1563. Involved in the fortunes of his brother Philip, imprisoned with him, 1583; joined the Church of Rome, 1584. Restored Naworth Castle, Cumberland; settled there. Improved his estates and encouraged agriculture. Warden of the Western Marches. Scholar and antiquary. An intimate friend of Cotton. Married Elizabeth, sister and co-heir of George, Lord Dacre, of Gillesland, Cumberland. Died Oct. 7, 1640. Benefactor to the College Library. Brother of Philip (1576) and Thomas (1605). (*D.N.B.*)

HOWARD, WILLIAM. Matric. sizar from JESUS, Easter, 1611; B.A. 1614-5; M.A. 1618.

HOWARD, WILLIAM (*dominus*). Matric. Fell.-Com. from ST JOHN'S, Easter, 1624. Doubtless 3rd s. of Thomas (1605), Earl of Arundel. B. Nov. 30, 1614. K.B., 1625-6. Created Baron Stafford, 1640. Retired to Flanders on the outbreak of the Civil War. F.R.S., 1665. Married Mary Stafford, sister and heir to Henry, 5th Baron Stafford. Accused on the testimony of Titus Oates and others of being concerned in the Popish plot. Imprisoned in the Tower of London, 1678. After two years' imprisonment, found guilty and beheaded on Tower Hill, Dec. 29, 1680. Buried in the Chapel of St Peter ad Vincula, in the Tower. (*G.E.C.*; *D.N.B.*)

HOWARD, WILLIAM. Adm. Fell.-Com. (age 15) at CHRIST'S, June 20, 1642. 1st s. of Sir William Howard, of Naworth; great grandson of Lord William (*c.* 1577). M.A. 1642 (on King's visit). Died 1644. (*Peile*, I. 481; *Collins*, III. 503.)

HOWARD, WILLIAM. Adm. Fell.-Com. at CORPUS CHRISTI, July 1, 1646. 2nd s. of Edward, 1st Baron Howard of Escrick. Adm. at Lincoln's Inn, Nov. 2, 1648. M.P. for Winchelsea in the Convention Parliament, 1660. Imprisoned for republican plots, 1657; and again in 1674, for engaging in secret correspondence with Holland. Succeeded his brother Thomas as 3rd Baron, Aug. 1678. Arrested for implication in the Rye House plot. Notorious for his evidence against Russell and Sidney, 1683. Died Apr. 1694. Brother of Thomas (1637). (*D.N.B.*; *Masters*, 316.)

HOWCHIN, JEREMY. Matric. pens. from CORPUS CHRISTI, Easter, 1634. Of Suffolk. Probably s. of Robert, of Rickinghall Superior; bapt. there, Mar. 12, 1616-7. Died in College. Buried at St Benet's, Cambridge, May 3, 1635. (V. B. Redstone.)

HOWCHIN, THOMAS. Matric. pens. from CORPUS CHRISTI, Michs. 1615. Of Suffolk. B.A. 1618-9; M.A. 1622. R. of Palgrave, Suffolk.

HOWDAN (?), WILLIAM. Matric. sizar from PEMBROKE, Easter, 1635.

HOWDELL, JOHN. Matric. sizar from TRINITY, Michs. 1572.

HOWDELL, JOHN. Adm. sizar (age 15) at ST JOHN'S, June 23, 1742. S. of William (1719), clerk, of Kent. B. at Staple, Kent. School, Sedbergh, Yorks. Matric. 1743; B.A. 1746-7. Usher at King's School, Canterbury, 1748. Ord. deacon (Rochester) Sept. 24, 1749; priest (Canterbury) Sept. 23, 1750. R. of Bircholt, Kent, 1750-62. Brother of William (1745). (*Scott-Mayor*, III. 529.)

HOWDELL, WILLIAM. Adm. sizar (age 19) at ST JOHN'S, Mar. 26, 1719. S. of William, husbandman, of Yorkshire. B. at Louth. School, Louth (Mr Williams). Matric. 1719; B.A. 1722-3; M.A. 1726. Ord. deacon (York) Sept. 23, 1722; priest (Canterbury) Sept. 19, 1725. R. of Bircholt, Kent, 1731-43. V. of Leysdown, 1735-56. Father of John (1742) and the next. (*Scott-Mayor*, III. 322.)

HOWDELL, WILLIAM. Adm. sizar (age 17) at ST JOHN'S, June 7, 1745. S. of William (above), clerk, of Kent. B. at Staple, near Sandwich. School, Beverley, Yorks. Matric. 1745; B.A. 1748-9. Ord. deacon (Lichfield) Dec. 23, 1750; priest (Peterb.) Feb. 23, 1752. V. of West Hythe, Kent, 1753-1804. Second Master of King's School, Canterbury, 1777-9. Died Nov. 24, 1804. Brother of John (1742). (*Scott-Mayor*, III. 552; H. G. Harrison.)

HOWDEN, ROBERT. Matric. sizar from JESUS, Easter, 1575; B.A. 1578-9, as 'Howdyll'; M.A. 1582.

HOWE or HOW, GERVASE. Adm. sizar at CHRIST'S, Oct. 21, 1664. Matric. 1667; B.A. 1668-9; M.A. 1672. Ord. deacon (Ely) May, 1670; priest, June, 1671. R. of St Peter, Sandwich, 1673-79. (*Peile*, I. 614.)

HOWE, HENRY. Matric. sizar from JESUS, Easter, 1577; B.A. 1580-1; M.A. 1584. Ord. deacon (Lincoln) Nov. 29, 1582; priest, Dec. 31, 1584. V. of Langford, Beds., 1584. Perhaps R. of St Andrew Hubbard, London, 1593-8, resigned. R. of Calverton, Bucks., 1598-1600. Died 1600.

HOW, JAMES. M.A. 1728 (*Com. Reg.*). Perhaps R. of Milton, Gravesend, 1728-65. R. of St Margaret, Lothbury, 1728-65. Died Aug. 30, 1765, aged 74. M.I. at Milton. Will, P.C.C.

HOWE, JOHN. Matric. pens. from JESUS, Easter, 1557.

HOWE, JOHN. Matric. pens. from ST JOHN'S, Michs. 1588.

HOW, JOHN. Adm. pens. at QUEENS', Oct. 15, 1597. Of Essex.

HOWE, JOHN. Adm. pens. at PETERHOUSE, July 1, 1615. Matric. 1616; B.A. 1618-9; M.A. 1622. Incorp. at Oxford, 1623. Ord. deacon (Peterb.) May 23, 1619. Probably C. at Loughborough, 1628-34. One of these names R. of Ampthill, Beds., 1641; V. of Horbling, Lincs., 1641; of Marston Mortain, Beds., 1643 (but *see* the next).

HOWE, JOHN. Matric. sizar from MAGDALENE, Michs. 1623; B.A. 1626-7. Ord. deacon (Peterb.) Mar. 17, 1624-5.

HOWE, JOHN. Adm. sizar (age 17) at CHRIST'S, May 19, 1647. S. of John (? 1615), clerk. B. at Loughborough. School, Winwick (Mr Gorse). Matric. 1647. Migrated to Oxford. Adm. at Brasenose, 1648; B.A. 1649-50; M.A. 1652. Fellow of Magdalen, 1652-5. 'Ordained' at Winwick, 1652. Minister of Gt Torrington, Devon, 1654-62, ejected. Chaplain to Cromwell. Preached in Devonshire, till 1670. Chaplain to Viscount Massereene in Ireland, till 1676. Joint pastor at Haberdashers' Hall, London, 1676. Began a controversy on predestination, 1677; and with Defoe on occasional conformity, 1700. Author, theological. Died in London, Apr. 2, 1705. Buried in All Hallows Church, Bread Street. (*Peile*, I. 513; *D.N.B.*; *F.M.G.*, 443.)

HOWE, JOHN. Adm. Fell.-Com. (age 17) at SIDNEY, Mar. 11, 1711-2. 1st s. of George, M.D., deceased, of London. B. in Aldermanbury. School, Hackney, Middlesex (Mr Ben. Morland). Matric. 1712. One of these names adm. at Leyden, Sept. 21, 1723. Dead 1729. Perhaps brother of Philip (1712-3). (*F.M.G.*, 443.)

HOW, NATHANIEL. Adm. pens. at EMMANUEL, June 30, 1595.

HOWE, PHILIP. Adm. pens. at QUEENS', Jan. 14, 1712-3. Of Middlesex. Matric. 1713. One of these names 2nd s. of George, M.D. Dead 1729, *s.p.* Perhaps brother of John (1711-2). (*F.M.G.*, 443.)

HOWE, RICHARD. Adm. sizar (age 16) at ST JOHN'S, Dec. 4, 1639. S. of Richard, of Glemsford, Suffolk. B. there. School, Thurlowe (Mr Moore). Matric. 1640; B.A. 1643-4; M.A. 1647.

HOW, RICHARD. Adm. Fell.-Com. (age 17) at CHRIST'S, Feb. 26, 1667-8. S. of Thomas. B. at Stapleford, Essex. School, Felsted (Mr Glascock). Matric. 1667-8. Probably adm. at the Inner Temple, May 13, 1670. (*Peile*, II. 13.)

HOW, RICHARD. Adm. Fell.-Com. (age 17) at PETERHOUSE, Mar. 7, 1693-4. B. in Essex. School, Felsted. Probably s. and h. of Richard, of Broxbourne, Herts.; adm. at Lincoln's Inn, Nov. 6, 1693. Perhaps Sheriff of Essex, 1730. If so, died Sept. 28, 1748. (*T. A. Walker*, 194; *Morant*, I. 188.)

HOWE, RICHARD. Matric. sizar from KING'S, Michs. 1722; B.A. 1725-6; M.A. 1730. Ord. deacon (Lincoln) Sept. 19, 1725; priest, Feb. 22, 1729-30.

HOWE, ROBERT. Matric. pens. from ST CATHARINE'S, Easter, 1639; B.A. 1641-2. (Probably adm. at Emmanuel, 1637.)

HOWE, ROBERT. Adm. sizar at EMMANUEL, June 26, 1672. Of Lincolnshire.

HOW, SAMUEL. Adm. pens. at EMMANUEL, July 8, 1730. Of Middlesex. Matric. 1732; B.A. 1733-4; M.A. 1737.

HOWE, THOMAS. Matric. pens. from ST JOHN'S, Lent, 1557-8.

HOWE, THOMAS. Adm. pens. at EMMANUEL, Mar. 8, 1658-9. Of Yorkshire.

HOW, THOMAS. Adm. pens. (age 16) at ST JOHN'S, June 25, 1673. S. of Alexander, gent., of Battersea, Surrey. B. there. School, St Paul's. Matric. 1673; LL.B. 1678.

HOWE, THOMAS. Adm. pens. (age 23) at CHRIST'S, Oct. 25, 1739. Already M.A. of Aberdeen University. 3rd s. of John, Baron Chedworth. B. at Miserdine, Gloucs. School, Mickleton, Gloucs. (Mr Smith). Matric. 1739; M.A. 1741. Ord. deacon (Gloucester) Jan. 6, 1739-40; priest (Salisbury) June, 1740. R. of Wishford, Wilts. R. of Kingston Deverill, Feb. 24, 1741-2. Married Frances, dau. of Thomas White, of Tattington Place, Suffolk. Died 1776. For his s. Thomas *see D.N.B.* (*Peile*, II. 239; F. S. Hockaday.)

HOW, THOMAS. Adm. pens. (age 17) at TRINITY, Nov. 24, 1739. S. of Thomas, of Tiverton, Devon. School, Tiverton (Mr Westley). Matric. 1740; Scholar, 1740. Probably adm. at the Inner Temple, Apr. 7, 1739; s. and h. of Thomas, late of Gray's Inn.

HOWE, WILLIAM. Matric. pens. from CLARE, Easter, 1577; B.A. 1580-1.

HOWE, WILLIAM. Adm. sizar (age 16) at CAIUS, May 14, 1631. S. of James, gent., of Orsett, Essex. B. there. Educated by Mr Walmesley and Mr Yarver. Matric. 1631; B.A. 1634-5; M.A. 1638. Ord. deacon (Norwich) Mar. 9, 1638-9; priest, Dec. 22, 1639. Licensed to teach grammar at Witnesham, Suffolk, or elsewhere in the diocese, 1639. R. of Dunton Waylett, Essex, 1648. Perhaps R. of Little Braxted, Essex, 1680-91. Died 1691. Perhaps father of the next. (*Venn*, I. 299.)

HOW, WILLIAM. Adm. pens. at JESUS, July 2, 1661. Of Essex. (? S. of the above.) Matric. 1661; Scholar, 1663; B.A. 1664-5; M.A. 1668. Ord. deacon (London) June, 1669; priest (Gloucester, at Holborn) Feb. 27, 1669-70. C. of Witham, Essex, 1669. One of these names R. of Snailwell, Cambs., 1683. Perhaps R. of Woodham Ferrers, Essex, 1691-1700. Will (Cons. C. London) Jan. 1700-1. (J. Ch. Smith.)

HOW, WILLIAM TAYLOR. Adm. pens. (age 18) at PEMBROKE, May 15, 1751. S. of William, of Hadham, Herts., Esq. Matric. 1751; B.A. 1760. Fellow, 1760. Adm. at Lincoln's Inn, Nov. 22, 1752.

HOWE, ——. B.Can.L. 1482-3. Prior of Aldeby, Norfolk.

HOW, ——. Adm. sizar at SIDNEY, Oct. 1599.

HOW, ——. B.A. from TRINITY, 1608-9 (in the *ordo*).

HOWELL, *see also* HOVELL.

HOWELL, DAVY. Matric. pens. from TRINITY, Michs. 1623.

HOWELL, EDWIN. Matric. pens. from QUEENS', Lent, 1563-4. Of Cambridgeshire. B.A. 1567-8; M.A. 1571. Fellow, 1568-72. Ord. deacon (London) July 27; priest (Ely) Dec. 21, 1568. R. of Willingale Spain, Essex, 1571-3. Died 1573.

HOWELL, FRANCIS. Matric. pens. from TRINITY HALL, Easter, 1575.

HOWELL, JOHN. B.A. 1484-5; M.A. 1488-9. Perhaps ord. deacon (Norwich) Apr. 2; priest, Sept. 24, 1485, as 'Aphowell.' One of these names, M.A., R. of St Margaret Pattens, London, 1505-6. Died 1506. Will (P.C.C.) 1506.

HOWELL, JOHN. Matric. pens. from ST JOHN'S, Easter, 1571.

HOWELL, JOHN (1598), *see* HOLL.

HOWELL, JOHN. Matric. sizar from EMMANUEL, Easter, 1616.

HOWEL, JOHN. Adm. sizar at JESUS, Sept. 6, 1645. Of Suffolk. Matric. 1646.

HOWELL, LAURENCE. Adm. sizar at JESUS, July 2, 1681. Of Kent. S. of John, of Deptford. Exhibitioner from Colfe's School, Lewisham. Matric. 1681; B.A. 1684-5; M.A. 1688. Ord. deacon (London) Sept. 22, 1706; priest, by George Hickes, Oct. 2, 1712, in his oratory in St Andrew's, Holborn. A firm non-juror. Master of Epping School; and C. of 'Estwich' (? Eastwick, Herts.). Fined and imprisoned and stripped of his gown for his *Case of Schism*, 1717. Author, theological. Died in Newgate, July 19, 1720. (*D.N.B.*; A. Gray.)

HOWEL, PAUL. Adm. sizar at TRINITY, Apr. 8, 1659. Matric. 1659; B.A. 1662-3; M.A. 1666; M.D. 1671 (*Lit. Reg.*).

HOWELL (? HEWITT), RALPH. B.A. 1526-7.

HOWELL, ROBERT. B.Civ.L. 1520-1.

HOWELL, THOMAS. Matric. pens. from CHRIST'S, May, 1569. Perhaps V. of Gt Stambridge, Essex, 1577-88; and R. of Paglesham, 1578-1600. Will (P.C.C.) 1600. (*Peile*, I. 110.)

HOWELL or HOVELL, THOMAS. M.A. 1609 (Incorp. from Oxford). Of Oxfordshire. Matric. from New College, Oxford, Oct. 24, 1600, age 19; B.A. (Oxford) 1604; M.A. 1607-8. R. of Adwell, Oxon., 1621. (*Al. Oxon.*)

HOWELL, THOMAS. M.A. 1614 (Incorp. from Oxford). S. of Thomas, of Carmarthen, *cler. fil.* Matric. from Jesus College, Oxford, Nov. 20, 1607, age 18; B.A. 1608-9; M.A. 1612; B.D. and D.D. 1630. Chaplain to Charles I. R. of West Horsley, Surrey, 1625-46, sequestered. R. of St Stephen Walbrook, 1635-41. Canon of Windsor, 1636-46. R. of Fulham, Middlesex, 1642-6. Bishop of Bristol, 1644-6. A sufferer at the siege of Bristol, when his palace was pillaged. Died of the effects of maltreatment, 1646. Buried in Bristol Cathedral. (*Al. Oxon.*; *D.N.B.*)

HOWELL or HOVELL, THOMAS. Matric. pens. from ST CATHARINE'S, Michs. 1639. Of Norfolk.

HOWELL or HOVELL, THOMAS. Adm. sizar (age 15) at CAIUS, Dec. 1, 1646. S. of William, of Cambridge, tailor. School, Perse, Cambridge (Mr Crabb). Matric. 1646; B.A. 1650-1; M.A. 1654. Ord. deacon and priest (Norwich) Feb. 25, 1663-4. V. of Clare, Suffolk. R. of Wixoe, 1664-98. Buried at Wixoe, Nov. 18, 1698. (*Venn*, I. 367.)

HOWELL, THOMAS. Adm. sizar (age 16) at JESUS, Apr. 4, 1678. Of Suffolk. Matric. 1678; B.A. 1681-2. Ord. deacou (Norwich) Mar. 1682-3.

HOWELL or HOVELL, WILLIAM. Matric. pens. from TRINITY, *c.* 1594.

HOWELL, WILLIAM. Matric. sizar from QUEENS', Easter, 1646. Of London. B.A. 1649-50. One of these names, s. and h. of John, of Lincoln's Inn, Esq., adm. at Lincoln's Inn, May 23, 1652.

HOULE or HOWELL, WILLIAM. Matric. sizar (age 16) from MAGDALENE, Easter, 1648. S. of Robert, late of Walkeringham, Notts. B.A. 1651-2; M.A. 1655; LL.D. 1665 (*Lit. Reg.*). Fellow, 1651. Incorp. at Oxford, 1676. Advocate at Doctors' Commons, Feb. 4, 1678. Chancellor of Lincoln. Author, historical. Died 1683. Admon. (P.C.C.) 1683. (*Al. Oxon.*; *D.N.B.*)

HOWELL, WILLIAM. (EMMANUEL, 1702), *see* HOLWELL.

HOWEN, JOHN. Adm. sizar (age 20) at ST JOHN'S, June 13, 1713. S. of John, husbandman. B. at Guilsborough, Northants. School, Guilsborough (Mr Wortin). Matric. 1713. Re-adm. as Fell.-Com. in 1737. LL.B. 1739. Ord. deacon (Lincoln) May 27, 1716; priest, Feb. 22, 1718-9. V. of Rothersthorpe, Northants., 1728-56. R. of Bradden, 1739-62. Married, at Ashby St Ledgers, Apr. 28, 1730, Mary Clarke, of Hardingston. Buried at Bradden, Jan. 7, 1762. M.I. (*Scott-Mayor*, III. 487; H. I. Longden.)

HOWES, EDMUND. Adm. pens. at CLARE, July 3, 1723. B. at Morningthorpe, Norfolk. Matric. 1723; B.A. 1726-7; M.A. 1730. Fellow, 1730-40. R. of Haynford, Norfolk, 1730-9. Died *c.* 1739-40. Brother of George (1727).

HOWES, GEORGE. Matric. sizar from TRINITY, Michs. 1567. One of these names V. of Harewood, Yorks., 1570-82.

HOWES, GEORGE. Adm. pens. at CLARE, July 4, 1727. B. at Morningthorpe, Norfolk. Matric. 1727; B.A. 1730-1. V. of Wicklewood, Norfolk, 1734. V. of Honingham, 1738. R. of Mattishall Burgh, 1742-86. Brother of Edmund (1723).

HOWES, GILES. Matric. pens. from QUEENS', Michs. 1551.

HOWIS, ISAAC. Adm. pens. at QUEENS', Jan. 23, 1629-30. Of Suffolk. Matric. 1631, as Hewes.

HOWES (? HUES), JOHN. Matric. sizar from ST JOHN'S, *c.* 1590. One of these names R. of Eastwell, Kent, in 1610.

HOWES, JOHN. Matric. pens. from ST CATHARINE'S, Easter, 1613.

HOWES, JOHN. Adm. pens. (age 15) at EMMANUEL, May 29, 1628. S. of Robert, of London. B. in the parish of St Michael's, Thames St. Matric. 1628. Migrated to Caius, June 6, 1631. Scholar, 1631-4; B.A. 1631-2; M.A. 1635. Fellow of Caius, 1634-9. Licensed preacher in London diocese, 1636. V. of Earls Barton, Northants. (Nominated by the Parliamentary Committee, Sept. 21, 1647, but subscribed the Bishop of London's book the same day.) R. of Abington, Northants., 1652-85. Married, May 26, 1648, Mary Garrett, of Earls Barton. Author. Buried at Abington, June 6, 1685. Will (Archd. Northants.) 1685. (*Venn*, I. 300.)

HOWES, JOHN. Adm. sizar (age 17) at ST JOHN'S, May 13, 1666. S. of John, shoemaker. B. at Nottingham. School, Nottingham. Matric. 1667; B.A. 1669-70; M.A. 1673. Ord. deacon (Ely) Sept. 24, 1670; priest (London) June, 1674; C. of Thorington, Essex. V. of Elmstead, 1675-82.

HOWSE, JOHN. Adm. pens. (age 17) at CAIUS, *c.* May, 1678. S. of Thomas, attorney-at-law, of Carlton, Norfolk. B. there. Schools, Barford and Thetford (Mr Keene). Matric. 1679; Scholar, 1679-84; B.A. 1682-3. Of Morningthorpe, Esq. Sheriff of Norfolk, 1718. Died 1737. Father of the next and perhaps brother of Robert (1679). (Burke, *L.G.*)

HOWES, JOHN. Adm. pens. at CLARE, May 22, 1714. S. of the above. B. at Morningthorpe, Norfolk. Adm. at Gray's Inn, July 1, 1715. Of Morningthorpe, Esq. Died 1773. Father of Thomas (1746–7) and John (1743), Perhaps brother of Thomas (1715).

HOWES or HOWESS, JOHN. Adm. sizar (age 18) at TRINITY, Apr. 6, 1727. S. of John, silversmith, of London. Exhibitioner from St Paul's School. Matric. 1727; B.A. 1730–1. Ord. deacon (Lincoln) June 13, 1731; priest, June 4, 1732.

HOWES, JOHN. Adm. pens. at CLARE, Apr. 18, 1743. Afterwards Fell.-Com. Doubtless s. of John (1714). B. at Fritton ('Freton'), Norfolk. Matric. 1743–4. Probably adm. at Gray's Inn, May 2, 1743; s. and h. of John, of Norwich. Probably brother of Thomas (1746–7).

HOWSE, JOHN. Adm. at CORPUS CHRISTI, 1750. Of Norfolk.

HOWES, LEONARD. Matric. pens. from CHRIST'S, Apr. 1612. S. of Robert, of Besthorpe, Norfolk. School, Moulton (Mr Matchett). Migrated to Caius, 1613. Scholar, 1613–5; B.A. 1614–5; M.A. 1618. Ord. priest (Norwich) 1617. C. of Tottington, Norfolk, in 1617. R. of Hackford, 1619–62. Died 1662. (*Peile*, I. 285; *Venn*, I. 222.)

HOWES, RICHARD. Matric. pens. from CORPUS CHRISTI, Michs. 1614. Of Norfolk. B.A. 1617–8; M.A. 1621. Perhaps R. of Knapton, Norfolk, 1626.

HOWES, RICHARD. Matric. pens. from CORPUS CHRISTI, Lent, 1620–1. Of Nottinghamshire. B.A. 1623–4. Ord. deacon (Peterb.) May 23, 1624.

HOWES, ROBERT. Adm. sizar at EMMANUEL, Apr. 25, 1618, as 'Hewes.' Matric. 1618; B.A. 1621–2. Ord. deacon (Peterb.) Nov. 23, 1622; priest, Apr. 5, 1623. License (Peterborough) Feb. 21, 1625–6, for Robert Howes, of Denton, Hunts., to marry Anne Clarke, of Peterborough. (H. I. Longden.)

HOWES, ROBERT. Adm. pens. (age 27) at CAIUS, Oct. 16, 1657. Re-adm. Fell.-Com. Mar. 18, 1657–8. S. of Thomas, of Norfolk. B. at Erpingham. School, Erpingham (Mr Thornington and Mr Tilny). Matric. 1657. Probably Scholar, 1657–8. B.A. 1660. Perhaps V. of Little Baddow, Essex, 1664–6. V. of Hatfield Peveril, 1664–8. R. of Wickham St Paul, 1666–70. Died 1670. Admon. (P.C.C.) 1670. (*Venn*, I. 401; J. Ch. Smith.)

HOWSE, ROBERT. Adm. pens. (age 15) at CAIUS, Sept. 17, 1679. S. of Robert (? Thomas), attorney, of Carlton, Norfolk. B. there. Schools, Thetford (Mr Keen) and Moulton (Mr Wickham). Scholar, 1679–85; B.A. 1682–3; M.B. 1685. Possibly brother of John (1678). (*Venn*, I. 463.)

HOWES, THOMAS. B.Civ.L. 1518–9.

HOWYS, THOMAS. Matric. sizar from CHRIST'S, Dec. 1560.

HOWSE, THOMAS. Adm. pens. (age 18) at CAIUS, Oct. 11, 1573. Of Baconsthorpe, Norfolk. S. of John. School, Holt. Matric. 1573; B.A. 1576–7; M.A. 1580. Fellow, 1579–87. Probably R. of Clenchwarton, Norfolk. (*Venn*, I. 75.)

HOWYS, THOMAS. Matric. sizar from QUEENS', Easter, 1581. Of Nottinghamshire.

HOWIS, THOMAS. Adm. sizar at QUEENS', June 30, 1596. Of Cambridgeshire.

HOWES, THOMAS. Adm. pens. at CLARE, May 2, 1715. B. at Morningthorpe, Norfolk, 1698. Matric. 1715; B.A. 1718–9; M.A. 1722. Fellow, 1721–5. Ord. priest (Ely) Mar. 10, 1722–3. R. of Morningthorpe, 1723. R. of Thorndon, Suffolk, 1724–74. Died 1774. Father of the next. Perhaps brother of John (1714).

HOWES, THOMAS. Adm. pens. at CLARE, June 28, 1743. S. of Thomas (1715). B. at Thorndon, Suffolk. Matric. 1743; B.A. 1746–7. For a time in the army. Ord. deacon (London) Mar. 10, 1754; priest (Norwich) May, 1756. R. of Illington, Norfolk, 1756–87. R. of Morningthorpe, 1756–71. R. of Thorndon, Suffolk, 1771–1814. Author, *Critical Observations on Books, Ancient and Modern*. Died at Norwich, Sept. 29, 1814, unmarried. (*D.N.B.*)

HOWES, THOMAS. Adm. pens. at CLARE, Feb. 20, 1746–7. Doubtless s. of John (1714). B. at Fritton, Norfolk. Matric. 1748; B.A. 1750–1; M.A. 1754. Fellow, 1752–8. Ord. deacon (Norwich) Dec. 1752; priest, Sept. 1753. R. of Fritton, 1763–75. V. of Thurston, 1775–96. Died 1796, aged 64. Probably brother of John (1743).

HOWSE, WALTER. Matric. pens. from QUEENS', Easter, 1585. B. in London. B.A. 1588–9; M.A. 1592; B.D. 1599. Fellow, 1592–1601. A prominent disputant in the schools. Ord. deacon (Lincoln); priest (Bristol). V. of St Andrew's, Cambridge, 1595. R. of Little Bytham, Lincs., 1601–10. R. of West Deeping, 1606–10. Will (P.C.C.) 1610. (*Cooper*, II. 323.)

HOWSE, WILLIAM. Matric. sizar from QUEENS', Easter, 1602; B.A. 1605–6; M.A. 1609.

HOWES, ——. Fee for M.A. or higher degree, 1485–6.

HOWESS, *see* HOWES.

HOWETT or HOWITT, BENJAMIN. Adm. sizar at TRINITY, Apr. 8, 1674. Matric. 1674; B.A. 1677–8.

HOWETT, JOHN. Ord. deacon (Peterb.) June 20, 1577; priest, Oct. 18, 1577, as 'of TRINITY College.' One of these names V. of Westby-in-Bassingthorpe, Lincs. Admon. (Leicester) 1637.

HOWETT, THOMAS. Matric. sizar from TRINITY, 1639; B.A. 1642–3. Ord. deacon (Lincoln) Mar. 17, 1643–4; priest, same day. V. of East Waight, Notts., 1648. (*Shaw*, I. 363.)

HOWITT, THOMAS. Adm. sizar at TRINITY, Apr. 8, 1674. Matric. 1674; B.A. 1677–8.

HOWGILL, ROBERT. Ord. deacon (Peterb.) June 15, 1617, as 'B.A. of ST JOHN'S' (no adm. or degree recorded). Signs as minister of Meppershall, Beds., in 1620; doubtless curate. Will (P.C.C.) 1645; of Willington, Beds.

HOWGRAVE, HENRY. Adm. at KING'S (age 16) a scholar from Eton, Aug. 24, 1593; B.A. 1597–8; M.A. 1601; B.D. 1607–8. Fellow, 1596, till 1619. Vice-Provost, 1617–9. Ord. priest (London) 1603. R. of Horstead, Norfolk. R. of Coltishall, 1619. Chaplain to the Bishop of Lincoln. Married the widow of Richard Sutton his predecessor. Died Jan. 1645–6. Father of the next. (*Harwood*.)

HOWGRAVE, HENRY. Adm. pens. (age 16) at CAIUS, June 27, 1639. S. of Henry (above), R. of Horstead, Norfolk. School, North Walsham (Mr Agurs). Matric. 1639; Scholar, 1640–4; B.A. 1642–3. R. of Lessingham, Norfolk, 1647, till 1662 (subscribed Bishop Joseph Hall's book). (*Venn*, I. 335.)

HOWGRAVE, JOHN. Matric. pens. from KING'S, Michs. 1625. Migrated to Emmanuel, Oct. 4, 1627. B.A. 1629–30; M.A. 1633. Ord. deacon (Norwich) Mar. 2, 1633–4; priest, June 1, 1634. Probably minor canon of Rochester, 1661–77. V. of All Hallows, Hoo, Kent, 1662–3. V. of Halling, 1663–76.

HOWGRAVE, WILLIAM. Adm. at KING'S (age 18) a scholar from Eton, Aug. 22, 1551. Matric. 1551; B.A. 1555–6; M.A. 1559. Fellow, 1554–63. Incorp. at Oxford, 1563. R. of Aldham, Suffolk, 1566; of Lyminge, Kent, 1570. R. of Long Stanton St Michael, Cambs., 1572–95. R. of Longstow, 1573–95. Died 1595. Probably father of Henry (1593). (*Cooper*, I. 350; *Al. Oxon.*)

HOWKES, HUGH. Matric. pens. from CHRIST'S, Nov. 1561.

HOWKINS, EDWARD. Adm. pens. (age 16) at TRINITY, May 20, 1746. S. of Edward, of Leicester. School, Leicester (Mr Andrews). Matric. 1747; Scholar, 1747; B.A. 1749–50; M.A. 1753; B.D. 1768. Fellow, 1752. Proctor, 1767–8. Ord. deacon (Ely) Dec. 25, 1752. R. of North Runcton, Norfolk, 1778–80. (For personalities *see* *Cole MS.*, 5872, 235.)

HOWKINS, JOHN. Adm. pens. at QUEENS', Oct. 4, 1670. Of Warwickshire. Matric. 1671.

HOWLAND, JAMES. Matric. pens. from PETERHOUSE, Michs. 1572. B. in London. B.A. from Trinity, 1576–7; M.A. from St John's, 1580. Fellow of St John's, 1577. Ord. deacon (Peterb.) Nov. 12, 1587. Preb. of Peterborough, 1586–98. Archdeacon of Northampton, 1587–98. Died Mar. 20, 1597–8. Will, P.C.C. Probably a cousin of Richard (1557), certainly not his s. (*Cooper*, II. 235; *T. A. Walker*.)

HOWLAND, JOHN. Adm. pens. (age 17) at CAIUS, 1594–5. S. of John. B. at Wicken Bonhunt, Essex. School, Newport. Scholar, 1595–9; B.A. 1598–9. Adm. at the Middle Temple, Oct. 21, 1602. Called to the Bar, May 15, 1613. Knighted, Mar. 1, 1616–7. Steward of St Albans, 1619; discharged for his loyalty to Charles I. Perhaps will (P.C.C.) 1652. (*Vis. of Herts.*, 1634; *Venn*, I. 155.)

HOWLAND, JOHN. Adm. pens. (age 16) at CHRIST'S, Mar. 17, 1664–5. S. of Jeffrey. B. in London. School, Brentwood, Essex (Mr Barnard). Matric. 1665; B.A. 1668–9. Adm. at the Inner Temple, June 25, 1666. Of Streatham, Surrey. Died 1686. Brother of Samuel (1664–5). (*Peile*, I. 615; *Vis. of Surrey*, 1662.)

HOWLAND, RICHARD. Matric. pens. from CHRIST'S, Lent, 1557–8. B. at Newport Pond, Essex (s. of John, citizen and salter, of St Margaret Moses, London; will, P.C.C., 1570). B.A. 1560–1; M.A. from Peterhouse, 1564; B.D. 1570; D.D. 1578. Fellow of Peterhouse, 1562. Master of Magdalene, 1576. Master of St John's, 1577. Vice-Chancellor, 1577–8, 1583–4. Incorp. at Oxford, 1567. R. of Stathern, Leics., 1569. R. of Sibson, Hunts., 1573. Chaplain to Lord Burghley. Bishop of Peterborough, 1585–1600. Died June 23, 1600. Buried in Peterborough Cathedral. (*D.N.B.*; *Peile*, I. 65; *Cooper*, II. 287; *Vis. of Surrey*, 1623.)

HOWLAND, SAMUEL. Adm. Pell.-Com. (age 18) at CHRIST'S, Mar. 17, 1664-5. S. of Jeffrey. B. in London. School, Brentwood, Essex (Mr Barnard). Matric. 1665. Adm. at the Inner Temple, as of Streatham, Surrey, June 25, 1666. Called to the Bar, Nov. 1679. Died between 1680-90. Brother of John (1664-5). (*Peile*, I. 615; *Vis. of Surrey*, 1662).

HOWLAND, SAMUEL. Adm. pens. at EMMANUEL, Sept. 1668. Of Middlesex. Matric. 1669.

HOWLAND, WALTER. Adm. Fell.-Com. (age 18) at PEMBROKE, Feb. 22, 1656-7. S. of Robert, Esq. B. in Kent.

HOWLAND, ——. Student at PETERHOUSE, June 10, 1564; probably sizar.

HOWLER, JOHN. B.A. from ST JOHN'S, 1633-4.

HOWLETT, CHARLES. Adm. at CORPUS CHRISTI, 1679. Of Yorkshire. Matric. 1680-1; B.A. 1683-4; M.A. 1687. Ord. deacon (York) May, 1684.

HOWLETT, EDWARD. Adm. at CORPUS CHRISTI, 1677. Of Suffolk. Matric. 1677; B.A. 1680-1. Ord. deacon (Norwich) Feb. 1680-1. V. of Pakenham, Suffolk, 1683-96. R. of Ousden, Cambs., 1696-1712. Died 1712.

HOWLETT, HENRY. Adm. sizar at QUEENS', June 25, 1674. S. of Nicholas (1626), deceased. B. at Scalby, Yorks. School, Scarning, Norfolk. Migrated to Sidney, May 15, 1675, age 19. Matric. 1677; B.A. 1677-8; M.A. 1682. Ord. deacon (York) Sept. 1678; priest, June, 1679. R. of Holtby, Yorks., 1684-1717. Perhaps father of Nicholas (1727).

HOWLETT, JOHN. Matric. sizar from TRINITY, Lent, 1626-7; B.A. 1629-30; M.A. 1633. Ord. priest (Norwich) Dec. 23, 1632. R. of Merkeshale, Norfolk, 1637-9.

HOWLETT, JOHN. Matric. pens. from TRINITY, Easter, 1636.

HOWLETT, JOHN. Adm. at CORPUS CHRISTI, 1665. Of Yorkshire. B.A. 1668-9. Pre-elected fellow, but died before admission. Buried at St Benet's, Cambridge, Feb. 18, 1669-70. Will proved (V.C.C.) 1671.

HOWLETT, JOHN. Adm. pens. (age 18) at TRINITY, June 9, 1697. S. of John, of London. B. there. School, Westminster. Scholar, 1698; Matric. 1700; B.A. 1700-1; M.A. from Trinity Hall, 1704. Adm. at the Inner Temple, May 11, 1698. Perhaps V. of Isleham, Cambs., 1704-7.

HOWLETT, JOSHUA. Adm. sizar (age 17) at ST JOHN'S, Oct. 31, 1710. S. of Robert, surgeon. B. at Lynn, Norfolk. School, Histon (Mr Scaife). Matric. 1710.

HOWLETT, LAURENCE. Adm. sizar at SIDNEY, June 19, 1605. Of Rutland. Matric. 1606. Migrated to Emmanuel. Scholar there, 1607; B.A. 1608-9; M.A. 1612; B.D. 1619. Fellow of Emmanuel, 1613-21. Incorp. at Oxford, 1614. Ord. deacon (Peterb.) Sept. 20; priest, Sept. 21, 1618. Lecturer at St Andrew's, Norwich, 1622-6. R. of Milton Malzor, Northants. 1625. Buried Nov. 26, 1626.

HOWLUTT, LEONARD. Matric. pens. from TRINITY HALL, Easter, 1548; LL.B. 1558. Probably R. of Hoveton, Norfolk, 1561.

HOWLETT, NICHOLAS. Matric. sizar from CAIUS, *c.* 1595. S. of John, of Mattishall, Norfolk. Scholar, 1598-1600; B.A. 1598-9; M.A. 1602; B.D. 1609. Ord. deacon (Norwich) Apr. 25, 1600; priest, Dec. 21, 1601. C. of St Peter Mancroft, Norwich, 1600. V. of Mattishall, Norfolk, 1604-41. R. of Reepham, 1613. Preb. of Norwich, 1618. R. of Winterton, in 1650. Died June 17, 1652. M.I. at Mattishall. (*Venn*, I. 167.)

HOWLETT, NICHOLAS. Adm. sizar (age 17) at CAIUS, July 4, 1626. S. of John, gent., of Witchingham, Norfolk. B. at Taverham. School, Norwich (Mr Mat. Stonham). Matric. 1626-7; Scholar, 1627-30; B.A. 1629-30; M.A. 1633. Ord. priest (Norwich) Sept. 23, 1632. Probably V. of Henley, Suffolk, 1632. V. of Scalby, Yorks., 1634; of Seamer, 1663. R. of Thwing, 1663; and of Dunnington, 1665. Chaplain to Lord Bellasis. Father of Henry (1674). (*Venn*, I. 278.)

HOWLETT, NICHOLAS. Adm. sizar (age 18) at TRINITY, Mar. 17, 1726-7. S. of Henry (? 1674), of Dunnington, Yorks., clerk. School, Kirkleatham, Yorks. (Mr Clark). Matric. 1727; B.A. 1733-4. *Litt. dim.* from York for deacon, Feb. 1729-30; for priest, 1731. C. of Normanton, Yorks. Probably R. of Hinderwell, 1763-80. Died July 17, 1780. (G. *Mag.*)

HOWLET, PETER. Matric. sizar from QUEENS', Easter, 1553. Perhaps a mistake for Philip, below.

HOWLET, PHILIP. B.A. 1554-5; M.A. 1557. Probably fellow of CHRIST'S, 1555-63. (*Peile*, I. 55, supposes the fellow to be Thomas Hulett.)

HOWLETT, RICHARD. Adm. sizar at SIDNEY, Mar. 1603-4. Matric. 1604; B.A. 1607-8; M.A. 1611; B.D. 1617. Fellow. Incorp. at Oxford, 1614. Ord. deacon (Peterb.) Sept. 26; priest, Sept. 27, 1613. R. of Latchingdon and Lawling, Essex, 1642-9. Will (P.C.C.) 1649. Perhaps father of Samuel (1659-60).

HOWLETT, RICHARD. Adm. pens. at EMMANUEL, Sept. 29, 1648. Of Cambridgeshire. Matric. 1648; B.A. 1652; M.A. 1656. Ord. priest (Bishop Brownrigg, of Exeter) Dec. 15, 1658. R. of Harkstead, Suffolk, 1663. R. of Snailwell, Cambs., 1654.

HOWLETT, ROBERT. Adm. sizar at EMMANUEL, May 5, 1609. Matric. 1609; B.A. 1612-3; M.A. 1616. R. of Hinderclay, Suffolk, 1627-62, ejected. Kept school at Colchester.

HOWLETT, ROGER. Adm. sizar at EMMANUEL, Apr. 13, 1631. Of Cambridgeshire. Matric. 1631; B.A. 1633-4; M.A. 1637. Ord. deacon (Peterb.) June 4; priest (Norwich) Sept. 24, 1637.

HOWLET, SAMUEL. Adm. sizar at JESUS, Oct. 29, 1644. Of Suffolk. Matric. 1644. One of these names adm. student at Leyden, Nov. 1, 1647.

HOWLETT, SAMUEL. Adm. pens. (age 16) at ST JOHN'S, Jan. 7, 1659-60. S. of Richard (? 1603-4), clerk, deceased, of Baddow, Essex. B. there. Exhibitioner from Charterhouse. Matric. 1660; Scholar; B.A. 1663-4; M.A. 1667. Fellow, 1664. Benefactor to St John's.

HOWLETT, THOMAS. Scholar of TRINITY, 1602; B.A. 1603-4; M.A. 1607. Ord. deacon and priest (Norwich) May 22, 1608, age 24. C. of Belowe, Norfolk. V. of Heverland, 1608-33. R. of Lyng, 1617-53. Perhaps R. of Gt Livermere, Suffolk, 1633. Will (P.C.C.) 1653; of Lyng. Father of Thomas (1637).

HOWLETT, THOMAS. Matric. pens. from TRINITY, Michs. 1619; B.A. 1624-5; M.A. 1628.

HOWLET, THOMAS. Adm. pens. at TRINITY, Mar. 30, 1637. S. of Thomas (1602). Matric. 1637; B.A. 1640-1. Ord. deacon (Norwich) Sept. 24, 1643, age 25; priest, Mar. 17, 1643-4. C. of Lyng. R. of Gt Livermere, Suffolk, 1645. R. of South Creake.

HOWLETT, WILLIAM. Matric. pens. from PEMBROKE, Easter, 1549.

HOWLETT, WILLIAM. Adm. sizar (age 20) at CAIUS, June 22, 1648. S. of John, goldsmith, of Norwich. Bapt. at St Peter Mancroft, Oct. 19, 1628. School, Norwich (Mr Lovering). Matric. 1648; B.A. from King's, 1650-1.

HOWLETT, —— Matric. sizar from SIDNEY, Lent, 1618-9.

HOWLINGE, BARTHOLOMEW. Adm. sizar (age 20) at CAIUS, Aug. 9, 1580. S. of William, of Shipdham, Norfolk. School, Shipdham. Ord. priest (Norwich) Mar. 10, 1582-3. C. of Pentney, Norfolk, 1584. C. of Castle Acre, 1593-1611. R. of Barton Bendish, 1594-1613. Will proved (Norwich C.C.) 1614. (*Venn*, I. 107.)

HOWLYNG, FRANCIS. Adm. at KING'S (age 17) a scholar from Eton, Aug. 25, 1559. Of London. Matric. 1559; B.A. 1563-4; M.A. 1567. Fellow, 1562-9. Probably Head Master of Westminster, *c.* 1570-2.

HOWLTER, ——. Adm. at CORPUS CHRISTI, 1570. *See* HOULTON, ROBERT.

HOWMAN, EDWARD. Adm. pens. (age 17) at CAIUS, Jan. 29, 1693-4. S. of Roger (1658), M.D., of Norwich. B. at Briston, Norfolk. School, Norwich (private; Mr Norridge, and Cathedral). Scholar, 1694-9; Matric. 1696; M.B. 1699; M.D. 1704. Practised at Norwich. Married, Oct. 12, 1704, at Norwich Cathedral, Margaret, dau. of Thomas Palgrave. Died Feb. 13, 1753. Buried at St Stephens, Norwich. Admon. (P.C.C.) to s. Roger. Brother of Roger (1714), father of Roger (1724). (*Venn*, I. 494.)

HOWMAN, GEORGE. Adm. pens. at QUEENS', June 30, 1659. Of Kent.

HOWMAN, HENRY. Matric. pens. from ST JOHN'S, Easter, 1552. Of Norfolk. B.A. 1554-5; M.A. 1558. Fellow, 1555.

HOWMAN, ROGER. Adm. pens. at CHRIST'S, June 9, 1623. S. of William. B. at Whissonsett, Norfolk. School, Holt (Mr Tallis). Matric. 1623; B.A. 1626-7; M.A. 1630. Ord. deacon (Norwich) June, 1634. R. of Salle, Norfolk, 1637. Presented to St Michael's, Norwich, 1637. Died before Dec. 1670. Father of the next. (*Peile*, I. 351.)

HOWMAN, ROGER. Adm. sizar (age 17) at CAIUS, May 17, 1658. S. of Roger (above), R. of Salle, Norfolk. B. there. Bapt. Apr. 17, 1640. Schools, Saxthorp and Norwich (Mr Lovering). Matric. 1658; Scholar, 1658-65; B.A. 1661-2; M.A. 1665; M.D. 1674. Licensed and practised in Norwich, June 2, 1666. Received a grant of Arms, 1684. Author. Died June 4, 1705. Buried at Salle. M.I. Father of Edward (1693-4) and the next. (*Venn*, I. 402.)

HOWMAN, ROGER. Adm. pens. at PEMBROKE, Apr. 14, 1714. S. of Roger (1658), M.D., of Norwich. Matric. 1714; M.B. 1720. Brother of Edward (1693-4).

HOWMAN, ROGER. Adm. pens. (age 17) at CAIUS, July 1, 1724. S. of Edward (1694), M.D., of Norwich. B. there. School, Bury St Edmunds. Matric. 1724; Scholar, 1724-9; M.B. 1730. Died July 30, 1766. Admon. (Norwich) 1766; of Ditchingham. (*Venn*, II. 22.)

HOWNDE, EDMUND. Matric. sizar from TRINITY, Michs. 1558. S. of John, of Calais. B.A. 1563-4; M.A. 1567; B.D. 1574; D.D. 1582. Fellow of Caius, 1573-6. President, 1573. Master of St Catharine's, 1577-98. Incorp. at Oxford, 1572. Ord. deacon and priest (Lincoln) Jan. 20, 1572-3. R. of West Tilbury, Essex, 1581. R. of Burton Coggles, Lincs., 1583-4. R. of Simondsbury, Dorset, 1583-98. Chaplain to the Queen. Died at Simondshury, Feb. 1597-8; said to have hanged himself. Will (P.C.C.) 1598. Pedigree in *Cambs. Vis.*, 1619. (*Cooper*, II. 234; *Venn*, I. 62.)

HOWNDEN or HUNDEN, ——. B.A. 1513-4.

HOWORTH, *see also* HAWORTH.

HOWORTH, EDMUND. Matric. sizar from MAGDALENE, Michs. 1618; B.A. 1621-2; M.A. 1625. Ord. deacon (Peterb.) Dec. 18; priest, Dec. 19, 1625. R. of East Carlton, Northants., 1633-74. R. of Thorpe Acland, 1639-43. Licensed (Peterborough, Aug. 30, 1636) to marry Lucy, dau. of Robert Knightley, of Cottesbrooke, Northants., gent. Buried at Carlton, Jan. 29, 1673-4, aged 73. M.I. Father of the next and of John (1659), brother of John (1617). (H. I. Longden; *Northants. N. and Q.*, III. 183.)

HOWORTH, EDMUND. Adm. pens. (age 16) at MAGDALENE, May 28, 1667. 2nd s. of Edmund (above), R. of East Carlton, Northants. Bapt. there, May 24, 1650. School, Uppingham. Matric. 1667; B.A. 1670-1; M.A. 1674. Fellow, 1671. Ord. deacon (Peterb.) Sept. 19, 1675. Brother of John (1659). (H. I. Longden.)

HOWORTH, GEORGE. Matric. Fell.-Com. from MAGDALENE, Michs. 1639.

HOWORTH, HENRY. Matric. Fell.-Com. from MAGDALENE, Michs. 1639.

HOWORTH, HENRY. Adm. pens. (age 15) at MAGDALENE, Mar. 31, 1669. S. of Theophilus (1633), M.D., of Manchester. B. Sept. 10, 1653. School, Manchester. Migrated to Jesus, June 28, 1670. Adm. at Lincoln's Inn, Apr. 23, 1670. Captain in the Guards. Buried at Rochdale, July 6, 1717. Perhaps father of the next. (H. Fishwick, *Rochdale*, 420.)

HOWORTH, HENRY PROBERT. M.A. from KING'S, 1749. S. of Henry (? above), of Clyro, Radnor, Esq. Matric. from Jesus College, Oxford, May 20, 1735, age 19; B.A. (Oxford) 1738-9. Perhaps V. of Burbage, Wilts. If so, died 1764. (*Al. Oxon.*; Fishwick, *Rochdale*, 420.)

HOWORTH or HAWORTH, JOHN. Matric. sizar from MAGDALENE, Easter, 1617. Of Manchester. B.A. 1620-1; M.A. 1624; B.D. 1631; D.D. 1664 (*Lit. Reg.*). Fellow, 1645, ejected. Master of Magdalene, 1664-8. Vice-Chancellor, 1666. Ord. deacon (Peterb.) May 12; priest, May 13, 1625. Preb. of Peterborough, 1639; ejected; restored, 1660. Died 1668. Will proved (V.C.C.). Admon. (P.C.C.) to brother Edmund (1618). Relation of Theophilus Haworth. (*Mag. Coll. Hist.*)

HOWORTH or HAWORTH, JOHN. Adm. sizar (age 21) at CHRIST'S, Oct. 21, 1651. S. of John, of Lancashire. School, Manchester (Mr Wiggons). Matric. 1651; B.A. 1655-6; M.A. 1660. Schoolmaster at Elmdon, Essex, before 1659. V. of Elmdon, 1669. Head Master of Hertford School, 1670. Died Nov. 4, 1680. M.I. at All Saints', Hertford. (*Peile*, I. 545.)

HOWARTH, JOHN. Adm. sizar (age 16) at CHRIST'S, June 7, 1659. S. of Edmund (1618), R. of East Carlton, Northants. Bapt. there, June 24, 1643. School, Carlton (Mr Archer). Matric. 1659. Migrated to Trinity, Aug. 29, 1660; Scholar; B.A. 1663-4; M.A. 1667. Fellow of Trinity, 1664. Incorp. at Oxford, 1669. Buried at East Carlton, Sept. 12, 1678. M.I. Brother of Edmund (1667). (*Peile*, I. 586.)

HOWORTH, ROBERT. Matric. pens. from CHRIST'S, July, 1620. Perhaps s. of Edmund, of Howorth; age 13 in 1613; bapt. at Rochdale, Feb. 21, 1601-2; succeeded his father at Howorth, 1625. Buried at Rochdale, Mar. 28, 1639. Perhaps brother of the next. (*Peile*, I. 334; *Vis. of Lancs.*, 1613, 1664; Fishwick, *Rochdale*, 420.)

HOWORTH, THEOPHILUS. Scholar of MAGDALENE, Michs. 1633. S. of Edmund, of Howorth, Lancs. Bapt. at Rochdale, Jan. 2, 1613-4. B.A. 1634-5; M.A. 1638; M.D. 1661. Fellow, ejected. Incorp. at Oxford, 1668. Candidate R.C.P., July 25, 1661. Practised in Manchester. Died Apr. 9, 1671. Father of Henry (1669). (*Munk*, I. 303; *Al. Oxon.*; *Vis. of Lancs.*, 1664.)

HOWSDEN, ARTHUR. Matric. sizar from CLARE, Michs. 1585. B. at Hinxton, Cambs. B.A. from St Catharine's, 1588-9; M.A. 1592. Ord. deacon (London) Dec. 3; priest, Dec. 4 1592, age 26. C. of Little Wendon, Essex.

HOUSDEN, EDWARD. B.A. from CHRIST'S, 1593-4; M.A. 1597. Ord. deacon (London) Mar. 19, 1597-8; priest, Mar. 26, 1598. R. of Little Hormead, Herts., 1604-46. Died 1646. Will, P.C.C. (*Peile*, I. 202.)

HOUSDEN, ENOCK. Matric. sizar from JESUS, Easter, 1603.

HOWSDEN, GEORGE. Matric. pens. from JESUS, Easter, 1569. Probably graduated B.A. Ord. deacon (Norwich) Sept. 29, 1599, age 43; C. of Attleborough, Norfolk; priest, June 24, 1600, as B.A. V. of Rendham, Norfolk.

HOWSDEN, JOHN. Matric. pens. from ST JOHN'S, *c.* 1593.

HOWSDEN, RICHARD. Matric. sizar from TRINITY, Easter, 1618; B.A. from St Catharine's, 1621-2; M.A. 1625. Ord. deacon (Peterb.) June 7; priest, June 8, 1623.

HOWSDEN, THOMAS. Matric. sizar from KING'S, Easter, 1665, as 'Hewsden'; B.A. 1668-9.

HOWSONN, BRIAN. Matric. pens. from ST JOHN'S, Lent, 1584-5; B.A. 1588-9; M.A. 1593.

HOWSON, JAMES. Adm. pens. (age 17) at SIDNEY, Nov. 28, 1622. S. of James. B. in the Strand, London. School, Westminster. Matric. 1622; B.A. 1626-7; M.A. 1631. Incorp. at Oxford, 1633.

HOWSON, JOHN. B.A. 1462-3; M.A. 1466-7. Fellow of PEMBROKE, *c.* 1465. V. of Tilney, Norfolk, 1473.

HOWSON, JOHN. Matric. pens. from PEMBROKE, Michs. 1549. Probably R. of Halton Holgate, Lincs. R. of Toynton St Peter. 'Ord. priest (Lincoln) Nov. 25, 1563, aged 42. Married; resides; skilled in Latin' (*Lib. Cler. Linc.*, 1576); or, R. of Frampton, Lincoln, 1579; ord. priest (Lincoln) 1560.

HOWSON, JOHN. Adm. at KING'S, a scholar from Eton, 1577; B.A. 1581-2. Fellow. Left, 1583.

HOWSON, JOHN. M.A. 1583 (Incorp. from Oxford). B. in St Bride's parish, London, *c.* 1556. Adm. at Christ Church, Oxford, 1577; B.A. (Oxford) 1578; M.A. 1581-2; B.D. and D.D. 1601. Vice-Chancellor, 1602-3. Licensed to preach, 1587. Preb. of Hereford, 1587-1603; and of Exeter, 1592. V. of Bampton, Oxon., 1598. Canon of Christ Church, 1601-19. V. of Gt Milton, 1601. R. of Brightwell, 1608. Original fellow of Chelsea College, 1610. Bishop of Oxford, 1618-28. Bishop of Durham, 1628-32. Died in London, Feb. 6, 1631-2. Buried in St Paul's Cathedral. (*Al. Oxon.*; *D.N.B.*; *Lincs. Pedigrees*.)

HOWSON, ROBERT. Fellow of PEMBROKE, *c.* 1444. V. of Tilney, Norfolk, 1470-3.

HOWSON, SAMUEL. Matric. sizar from ST CATHARINE'S, Easter, 1649.

HOWSON, SAVILE. Adm. sizar (age 18) at TRINITY, Apr. 19, 1718. S. of William, of Marnham, Notts. School, Glamford Bridge, Lincs. (Mr Waterworth). Matric. 1717; B.A. 1721-2. Ord. deacon (York) May, 1722; priest (Lincoln, *Litt. dim.* from York) Mar. 8, 1723-4.

HOWSON, WILLIAM. Adm. scholar at TRINITY HALL, Dec. 20, 1608.

HOWSON, WILLIAM. B.A. from TRINITY, 1618-9; M.A. 1622. Ord. deacon (Peterb.) June 15; priest, June 16, 1622. Preb. of Lincoln, 1629. R. of Somerby, Lincs., 1632.

HOWSON, WILLIAM. Adm. pens. (age 16) at MAGDALENE, June 11, 1673. S. of Brian, of Horton, Yorks. Matric. 1673; B.A. 1676-7. Ord. deacon (York) Sept. 1677.

HOWSON, WILLIAM. Adm. sizar (age 17) at PETERHOUSE, Mar. 17, 1678-9. Of Yorkshire. School, Retford, Notts. Matric. 1679; B.A. 1682-3; Scholar, 1683; M.A. 1686.

HOWSON, ——. B.A. 1473-4. Perhaps scholar of KING'S HALL, 1471-4.

HOWTHAM, *see also* HOTHAM.

HOWTHAM, GEORGE. B.A. from JESUS, 1570-1.

HOWTHEN, ROGER. Matric. pens. from JESUS, Easter, 1566. Ord. deacon (Ely) Dec. 21, 1576, as 'Roger Howtham, B.A.'

HOXLE, PETER. Matric. sizar from MAGDALENE, Michs. 1562.

HOYCE, EDWARD. Adm. at CORPUS CHRISTI, 1650. Of Suffolk.

HOYDEN, GEORGE, *see* HAWDEN.

HOYDESAN, ——. Adm. at CORPUS CHRISTI, 1583.

HOYE, CLEMENT. Matric. pens. from CLARE, Michs. 1578. B. at Peldon, Essex. B.A. 1581-2; M.A. 1585. Ord. deacon (London) May 7, 1586, age 29. R. of Wenden Lofts, Essex, 1586-1620. Died 1620. Admon. (Cons. C. London) 1621.

HOYE, GEORGE. Matric. pens. from ST JOHN'S, Easter, 1560.

HOY, HENRY. Adm. at St CATHARINE'S, 1644. Previously matric. from New Inn Hall, Oxford, July 10, 1640, age 17. S. of John, of Harrow, *pleb.* B.A. 1644–5. Incorp. at Oxford, 1648–9. M.A. from Pembroke College, Oxford, 1648–9. Probably R. of Shalston, Bucks., 1658–73. Died 1673. (*Al. Oxon.*)

HOYES, WILLIAM. Adm. sizar at JESUS, Feb. 16, 1742–3. Of Nottinghamshire. Scholar, 1743; LL.B. 1752. Ord. deacon (Lincoln) Dec. 21, 1746; priest, Sept. 25, 1748.

HOYLAND, EDWARD. Adm. sizar (age 19) at ST JOHN'S, Apr. 22, 1720. S. of John, farmer, of Yorkshire. B. at Brearly, near Wakefield. School, Wakefield (Mr Clarke). Matric. 1720; B.A. 1723–4; M.A. 1727. Ord. deacon (London) Mar. 1, 1723–4; priest (Ely, *Litt. dim.* from York) Dec. 17, 1726. V. of Darfield, Yorks., 1726–66. Lecturer at Worsborough. Died 1766.

HOYLAND, FRANCIS. Adm. pens. (age 17) at MAGDALENE, June 18, 1744. S. of James. B. at Castle Howard, Yorks. School, Halifax. Matric. 1744; B.A. 1748–9. Ord. deacon (York) Sept. 22, 1751; C. of Nunnington; priest (London) Dec. 23, 1753. A friend of William Mason. Received an introduction to Horace Walpole, who printed his *Poems* at the Strawberry Hill press, in 1769. Ill-health prevented him from accepting an offer of a living in South Carolina, in 1769. R. of Little Oakley, Northants., 1769–86. V. of Weekley, 1774–86. Died 1786. (*D.N.B.*; H. I. Longden.)

HOYLAND, ISAAC. Adm. sizar (age 15) at MAGDALENE, Mar. 10, 1661–2. S. of John, clerk, of Kirkby Ashfield, Notts. School, Dronfield. Matric. 1661–2; B.A. 1665–6. V. of Diseworth, Leics., 1671–1712. Head Master of Loughborough School, 1686–96. Buried at Diseworth, Apr. 24, 1712. Will, Leicester. Father of the next. (*Nichols*, III. 756.)

HOYLAND, ISAAC. Adm. sizar at JESUS, July 14, 1692. S. of Isaac (above), V. of Diseworth, Leics. School, Loughborough. Matric. 1693, as Hyland; Scholar, 1694; B.A. 1696–7; M.A. 1700. 'M.A. and physician.' Died at Diseworth, 1705. Buried May 28, 1705, aged 27. M.I. (*Nichols*, III. 756.)

HOYLAND, JOHN. Adm. sizar at EMMANUEL, Apr. 15, 1668. Of Derbyshire. Matric. 1670; B.A. 1671–2; M.A. 1675.

HOYLAND, NATHANIEL. Adm. sizar at EMMANUEL, July 3, 1675. Of Nottinghamshire. Matric. 1676; B.A. 1678–9. Ord. priest (York) Sept. 25, 1681. R. of Claypole (south media) Lincs., 1690–1722.

HOYLE, EDWARD. Adm. pens. at TRINITY, May 3, 1652. Of Yorkshire. Matric. 1652; B.A. 1655; M.A. 1659. R. of Catwick, Yorks., 1665–79.

HOYLE, HENRY. Pens. at PETERHOUSE, Lent, 1595–6. 2nd s. of William, of Stead Hall, Halifax. Bapt. there, Feb. 13, 1576–7. B.A. 1596–7; M.A. 1600. V. of Gisburn, Yorks., 1603–36. R. of Moiety of Linton, 1615–21. R. of Bolton-by-Bolland, 1624–6. Married (1), 1599, Barbara, dau. of Richard Rendall, of Ripon; (2) 1637, Jane Waddington, of Gisburn. Died about 1637. Father of William (1626). (J. Parker; *T. A. Walker.*)

HOYLE or HOLE, HENRY. Adm. sizar at EMMANUEL, Apr. 28, 1615. Matric. 1615; B.A. 1618–9; M.A. 1622. Ord. deacon (Peterb.) July 29; priest, July 30, 1622. R. of Sigglesthorpe, Yorks., 1624–57. Married Grace Waterhouse, of Sprotborough, Yorks., 1624. Died Oct. 18, 1657. Will (P.C.C.) 1658. (H. I. Longden; M. H. Peacock.)

HOYLE, HENRY. Adm. sizar (age 15) at ST JOHN'S, Apr. 20, 1655. S. of William (1626), deceased, of Halton-in-Craven, Yorks. B. there. School, Giggleswick (Mr Walker). Matric. 1655; B.A. 1658–9; M.A. 1662. Ord. deacon (Bishop of Galloway) Nov. 13; priest, Dec. 13, 1661. C. at Otley, 1662; and Guiseley, 1663. V. of Kirkby Lonsdale, Westmorland, 1664–76. Father of the next. (J. Parker.)

HOYLE, HENRY. Adm. sizar (age 14) at TRINITY, June 22, 1689. S. of Henry (above), of Kirkby Lonsdale, Westmorland. School, Bindley or Bingley (Mr William Hustler). Matric. 1689; B.A. 1692–3; M.A. 1696.

HOYLE, JOHN. Adm. pens. at EMMANUEL, May 14, 1658. Of Yorkshire. S. of Thomas, late of York, Esq., deceased. Adm. at Gray's Inn, Feb. 27, 1659–60.

HOYLE, JOHN. Adm. sizar at JESUS, May 7, 1692. B. at Leeds, Yorks. Matric. 1692. Died in College, Aug. 27, 1693. Buried in the Chapel. (A. Gray.)

HOYLE, JOSEPH. Adm. sizar at EMMANUEL, June 1, 1680. Of Yorkshire. Matric. 1680, as 'Hail'; B.A. 1683–4; M.A. 1687. Ord. deacon (London) Mar. 16, 1684–5, as 'Heyles.'

HOYLE, MIHILL. Adm. pens. at PETERHOUSE, Lent, 1603–4. Matric. 1604; Scholar, 1604–5. Michael Hoyle, Esq., of West Riding, Yorks.

HOYLE, THOMAS. Adm. sizar (age 19) at TRINITY, May 23, 1719. S. of Edward, of York. School, Clitheroe, Lancs. (Mr Glasbrooke). Matric. 1719; LL.B. 1725. Minister of Hornby, Lancs., 1725.

HOYLE, WILLIAM. Adm. pens. (age 16) at CAIUS, May 5, 1626. S. of Henry (1596), of Gisburn-in-Craven, Yorks. B. there. School, Giggleswick (Mr Docwray). Matric. 1626; B.A. 1629–30; M.A. 1633. 'Mr William Hoile, prisoner, buried at St Mary Castlegate, York, Nov. 30, 1651.' Father of Henry (1655). (*Venn*, I. 275; M. H. Peacock.)

HOYLEY, GEORGE. Matric. sizar from ST JOHN'S, Lent, 1582–3.

HUBBALD, ALEXANDER. Adm. pens. (age 16) at CAIUS, Sept. 2, 1644. 3rd s. of Gervase (next), R. of Rendlesham, Suffolk. B. there, Oct. 13, 1626. School (Mr Housden and Mr Manning). Matric. 1644; Scholar, 1644–9; B.A. 1648–9. Ord. (by *Classis*) for Marlesford, Suffolk, 1652. Ord. deacon and priest (Norwich) Nov. 10, 1661. V. of Wickham Market, Suffolk, 1657. R. of Monewden, 1663–1703. V. of Hacheston, 1675. Married Susan, dau. of Henry Ewen, gent. Died Sept. 1703. (*Venn*, I. 353; Davy, *Suff. MSS.*)

HUBBALD, GERVASE. Matric. sizar from TRINITY, Easter, 1607; Scholar, 1611; B.A. 1611–2; M.A. 1615. R. of Witnesham, Suffolk, 1620. R. of Rendlesham, 1621–45. Died Apr. 13, 1646. Buried at Rendlesham. Father of Alexander (above).

HUBBARD, *see also* HOBART.

HUBBERT, ABRAHAM. Adm. pens. at TRINITY, Apr. 16, 1651. Of Surrey.

HUBBARD, CHRISTOPHER. Scholar and fellow at KING'S HALL, 1505–26.

HUBBARD, CHRISTOPHER. Matric. pens. from PEMBROKE, Michs. 1573; B.A. 1577–8, as Hobart. Probably adm. at Douay College, May 27, 1580, as 'B.A. of Cambridge.'

HUBBART or HOBART (*alias* THORP), CLEMENT. B.A. 1523–4; M.A. 1534. Prior of the house of Carmelites in Cambridge, 1538; surrendered almost immediately. (*Cooper*, I. 68.)

HUBBERT, EDMUND. Matric. pens. from CORPUS CHRISTI, Easter, 1611. Of Suffolk.

HUBBARD, EDWARD. Adm. sizar (age 17) at ST CATHARINE'S, June 9, 1712. Of Ipswich. Matric. 1712; B.A. 1715–6; M.A. 1719; D.D. 1737. Fellow, 1718. Senior Proctor, 1732–3. Master, 1736–41. Vice-Chancellor, 1739–40. Ord. deacon (Ely) Sept. 21, 1718; priest, Feb. 21, 1724–5. Preb. of Norwich, 1736–41. Died Dec. 22, 1741. Buried in Norwich Cathedral. M.I. Will (P.C.C.) 1742. Brother of Henry (1724). (G. *Mag.*; *Cath. Coll. History.*)

HUBBERT, FRANCIS. Adm. sizar at EMMANUEL, Easter, 1589. Matric. 1589.

HUBBART, FRANCIS. Adm. pens. at PETERHOUSE, July 5, 1617. Matric. 1618; B.A. 1620–1; M.A. 1625.

HUBBART, GEORGE. Adm. pens. at TRINITY, Nov. 14, 1657. Probably s. of William, of Reresby, Leics. B. 1638. Of Reresby, Esq. Married Ann, dau. of William Sacheverell, of Barton, Notts. Died Sept. 30, 1684. Buried at Reresby. (*F.M.G.*, 26.)

HUBBERT, HENRY. Matric. sizar from ST JOHN'S, Easter, 1605. Migrated to Sidney, Oct. 28, 1605. B.A. 1608–9; M.A. 1612. Ord. deacon (York) Sept. 1610; priest, May, 1611. R. of Preston-in-Holderness, Yorks., 1624–40.

HUBBARD, HENRY. Adm. sizar at ST CATHARINE'S, Aug. 12, 1724. Of Ipswich. S. of a cabinet-maker. B. Feb. 5, 1707–8. Matric. 1725; B.A. 1728–9; M.A. 1732; B.D. from Emmanuel, 1739. Fellow of St Catharine's, 1730. Fellow of Emmanuel, 1732. Tutor for many years. Taxor, 1733, 1735. Registrary, 1758–78. Ord. deacon (Lincoln) May 24, 1730; priest (Ely) June 25, 1732. Lady Margaret preacher, 1752–74. Left useful MSS. concerning College matters. Died Jan. 23, 1778, aged 70. Will, P.C.C. M.I. in the cloister of Emmanuel. Portrait by Gainsborough. Benefactor to the College. Brother of Edward (1712). (*Emmanuel Coll. Hist.*; Davy, *Suff. MSS.*)

HUBBARD, HENRY. Adm. sizar at CLARE, Sept. 14, 1738. B. at Wardley, Rutland. Matric. 1740; B.A. 1742–3. Ord. deacon (Lincoln) Sept. 25, 1743.

HUBBARD, JOHN. Matric. sizar from KING'S, Easter, 1581. Perhaps scholar of Trinity Hall, 1584.

HUBERT, JOHN. B.A. from PEMBROKE, 1607–8.

HUBBERT, JOHN. Matric. sizar (age 19) from PEMBROKE, Easter, 1625. S. of John, fuller. B. at Bocking, Essex. B.A. 1628–9; M.A. 1632. Ord. deacon (Peterb.) Sept. 19, 1629. V. of Gt Bentley, Essex, 1641–3. V. of Boxted, 1645–50. V. of Panfield, *c.* 1655. R. of Gt Oakley, 1657–62. Buried there, Mar. 19, 1678–9. (*Davids*, 433; H. Smith.)

HUBBARD, JOHN. Adm. sizar at EMMANUEL, Lent, 1625–6. Matric. 1626; B.A. 1629–30; M.A. 1633. Ord. deacon (Peterb.) Sept. 25, 1631; priest (Norwich) Dec. 23, 1632.

HUBBARD or HOBART, JONAS. Adm. pens. at CAIUS, 1685. Matric. 1685.

HUBBARD or HOBART, PETER. B.A. 1522–3. One of these names R. of Swannington, Norfolk. Perhaps V. of Dennington, Suffolk, *c.* 1542. R. of Monk Soham, 1559–68.

HUBBERD or HOBART, PETER. Adm. at QUEENS', Dec. 1, 1621. S. of Edmund and Margaret (Dewey), of Hingham, Norfolk. Bapt. there, Oct. 14, 1604. Migrated to Magdalene. Matric. 1623; B.A. 1625–6; M.A. 1629. Ord. deacon (Norwich) May 20; priest, Dec. 3, 1627. C. at Haverhill (where he married and had a s. Josiah, 1634) and elsewhere. Went to New England, 1635. First at Charlestown, Mass. One of the founders of Hingham; pastor there till his death, Jan. 20, 1678–9. Married (2) Rebecca, dau. of Richard Brook, at Hingham, Mass., July 3, 1646. His MS. Diary and Church Record are preserved. (*Felt*, 214; J. G. Bartlett.)

HUBBARD, RICHARD. Matric. sizar from ST JOHN'S, Easter, 1578; B.A. 1581–2, as Hubbald. One Richard Hubbald was R. of Todwick, Yorks., 1591–*c.* 1623. Probably Master of Doncaster Grammar School, 1590–6 (?). R. of Hedon, Yorks., 1611.

HUBBARD, THOMAS. Adm. pens. at QUEENS', Mar. 14, 1614–5. Of Kent. B.A. 1615–6. One of these names R. of Cold Norton, Essex, 1658–60, ejected. Buried there Apr. 9, 1664. (*Davids*, 431.)

HUBBARD, THOMAS. Adm. sizar (age 18) at CAIUS, *c.* 1735. S. of Thomas, grazier, of Finningham, Suffolk. B. there. Schools, Gislingham (Mr Plays and Mr Cradock) and Westhorpe (private; Mr Rest). Matric. 1735; Scholar, 1735–42; B.A. 1738–9; M.A. 1742. Fellow, 1743–4. Ord. deacon (Norwich) Dec. 24, 1738; priest, Sept. 21, 1740. R. of Sonning, Berks., 1743–81. Buried Oct. 16, 1781. (*Venn*, II. 41.)

HUBBERT, W. Matric. pens. from ST JOHN'S, Michs. 1566. One William Hubbert, V. of Stoke, Kent, 1584–1623.

HUBBARD, WILLIAM. M.A. 1478–9.

HUBBARD, WILLIAM. Matric. pens. from ST JOHN'S, Michs. 1606.

HUBBARD, WILLIAM. Adm. Fell.-Com. at KING'S, Michs. 1608.

HUBBERT, WILLIAM. Matric. pens. from PEMBROKE, Easter, 1611.

HUBBARD, WILLIAM. Adm. sizar at CORPUS CHRISTI, 1645. Of Norfolk. Matric. 1647.

HUBBERD, WILLIAM. Adm. pens. at CAIUS, Oct. 20, 1679. S. of George, gent., of Southery, Norfolk. B. there. Schools, Wisbech (Mr Frisney), Thetford (Mr Keene) and Ely (Mr Petchy). Matric. 1680. Inherited lands in Southery, 1685, by his father's will. (*Venn*, I. 463.)

HUBBARD, WILLIAM. Adm. sizar at CLARE, July 4, 1715. B. at Melton Mowbray, Leics. Matric. 1715; B.A. 1718–9; M.A. 1722. Ord. deacon (Lincoln, *Litt. dim.* from Peterb.) May 24, 1719; priest (Peterb.) Sept. 25, 1720. C. of Teigh, Rutland, 1719; of Langham, 1720. Usher at Oakham School. Head Master of Uppingham, 1734–47.

HUBBARD, ——. M.A. 1462.

HUBBARD, ——. *Grace* for degree, 1468–9.

HUBBARD, ——. (Rector.) B.D. 1473–4.

HUBBARD, ——. B.Can.L. 1484–5.

HUBBARD, ——. M.A. 1490–1.

HUBBERT, ——. B.A. 1493–4.

HUBBERT, ——. B.Civ.L. 1500.

HUBBERT, ——. B.A. 1612–3 (on visit of Prince Charles).

HUBBERSTIE, EDWARD. Matric. sizar from TRINITY, *c.* 1591; B.A. 1594–5; M.A. 1598.

HUBBOCK, WILLIAM. M.A. 1586 (Incorp. from Oxford). Of Co. Durham. Matric. from Magdalen Hall, Oxford, Apr. 15, 1580, age 19; B.A. (Oxford) 1581; M.A. 1585. Scholar and fellow of Corpus Christi, Oxford. Ord. deacon and priest (Lincoln) 1587. R. of St Peter ad Vincula, Tower of London, 1594–1631. Lecturer at St Botolph's Without, Aldgate, 1597. R. of Nailstone, Leics., 1598. Author, *Sermons.* Will (P.C.C.) 1631. (*Cooper*, II. 528; *D.N.B.*; *Al. Oxon.*)

HUBRIGHT, CORNELIUS. Licensed to practise medicine, 1599.

HUCHON, JOHN (1492–3), *see* **HUTCHIN.**

HUCHON, ——. B.Civ.L. 1493–4.

HUCKLE, FRANCIS. Matric. sizar from TRINITY, Easter, 1619.

HUCKLE, JOHN. B.A. from CHRIST'S, 1573–4. Minister of Aythorp Roothing, Essex; suspended by Bishop Aylmer for refusing to wear the surplice, 1573; and again, 1583, for disputing the Athanasian Creed. Will (P.C.C.) 1625; of Hatfield Broadoak, Essex. (*Peile*, I. 113; *Cooper*, II. 23.)

HUCKLE, PHILIP (1546), *see* **HOOKEL.**

HUCKELL, ROBERT. Adm. pens. (age 15) at CHRIST'S, June 6, 1656. S. of Robert. B. in London. School, Christ's Hospital (Mr Perkins). Matric. 1656; B.A. 1659–60; M.A. 1663. (*Peile*, I. 572.)

HUCKMORE or HOCKMORE, PHILIP. M.A. 1598 (Incorp. from Oxford). S. of Gregory, gent., of Devon. Matric. from Broadgates Hall, Oxford, June 14, 1582, age 14; B.A. (Oxford) 1585–6; M.A. 1590. Died Jan. 1, 1617–8. (*Al. Oxon.*)

HUCKS, ——. Adm. Fell.-Com. at TRINITY HALL, Jan. 6, 1716–7. Name off, 1719. Probably Robert, s. of William, of Wallingford, Berks. Adm. at the Inner Temple, Jan. 11, 1719–20. M.P. for Abingdon, 1722, 1727, 1734. Recorder of Wallingford, 1733. Of Clifton Hampden, Oxon. Buried at Aldenham, Herts., Dec. 30, 1745. M.I. (*Cussans*, III. 246.)

HUCKSTABLE, JOHN. Matric. sizar from CHRIST'S, Mar. 1582–3.

HUDD, THOMAS. Matric. pens. from JESUS, Easter, 1566.

HUD, TIMOTHY. Adm. sizar at PETERHOUSE, Easter, 1623.

HUDDELOWE, *see* **HODILOW.**

HUDDLES, THOMAS. 'Student of TRINITY College,' when ord. deacon (London) Mar. 4, 1568–9, age 30. B. at Branton, Cumberland.

HUDLESTON, DERHAM. Adm. sizar at EMMANUEL, Feb. 16, 1677–8. Of Leicestershire. Matric. 1678; B.A. 1681–2. Ord. priest (Peterb.) Sept. 21, 1684. C. of Stoke Albany, Northants. V. of Barkston, Leics., 1689–95. R. of Braunstone, 1691–1704. R. of Woolsthorpe, Lines., 1704. Will (Leicester) 1738; of Husbands Bosworth, clerk.

HUDLESTON, EDMUND. Matric. sizar from CHRIST'S, Michs. 1559. Perbaps the R. of Kelsey St Mary, Lincs., who was ord. priest (Lincoln) Dec. 21, 1570; 'bred in the schools.' (*Lib. Cler.*, 1585.)

HUDDLESTON, GEORGE. Matric. pens. from MAGDALENE, Easter, 1631. Probably s. of Robert, of St Benedict's, Lincoln. B.A. 1634–5; M.A. 1638. Fellow. Ord. priest (Peterb.) Mar. 10, 1638–9. R. of Wadingham. Preb. of Lincoln, 1675–85. Died 1685. Probably father of the next. (*Lincs. Pedigrees*, 519.)

HUDDLESTON, GEORGE. Adm. sizar (age 15) at MAGDALENE, June 25, 1663. S. of George (? above), clerk, of Beesby, Lincs., deceased. School, Alford. Matric. 1663; B.A. 1666–7; M.A. 1670. Ord. deacon (Lincoln) Aug. 7, 1670; priest, Sept. 24, 1671.

HUDDLESTON, GEOFFREY (? GODFREY). Adm. pens. at JESUS, June 27, 1634. Of Lincolnshire. Matric. 1634–5; B.A. 1637–8.

HUDDLESTON, HENRY. Matric. sizar from MAGDALENE, Easter, 1624; B.A. 1627–8. One of these names, clerk, buried at Addlethorpe, Lincs., Mar. 14, 1656–7. (*Lincs. Pedigrees*, 519.)

HUDLESTON, HUGH. Matric. sizar from TRINITY, Michs. 1572, as 'Hurston'; Scholar, 1575, as 'Hurlston'; B.A. 1576–7; M.A. 1580. Fellow, 1579. Suspended and imprisoned for his contumacy; probably 'a distracted man.' (*Cooper*, II. 241.)

HUDLESTON or HODELSTON, JAMES. Matric. sizar from TRINITY, Easter, 1619; B.A. 1622–3; M.A. 1626. V. of East Tilbury, Essex, 1630. Will (P.C.C.) 1653–4.

HUDDLESTON, JOHN. B.A. 1543–4; M.A. 1546.

HUDLESTON, JOHN. Matric. sizar from CHRIST'S, Michs. 1562. One of these names, ord. priest (Lincoln) Jan. 5, 1580–1, and 'bred in the schools,' was V. of Saxelby, Lincs. Will of one of these names (P.C.C.) 1602; of St Stephen, Coleman St, London.

HUDDILSTON, JOHN. Adm. (age 17) at CAIUS, Nov. 4, 1578. S. of Edmund, of South Weald, Essex. Educated at home under Mr Barnham. Died in College, *c.* 1580. The performance of 'Popish ceremonies' over his body was the cause of complaints against the Master. (*Venn*, I. 98.)

HUDDLESTONE, JOHN. Matric. pens. from TRINITY, Michs. 1579. S. of Robert, of Pinchbeck, Lincs. B. at Lincoln, 1561. B.A. 1583–4; M.A. 1587; B.D. 1597. Ord. deacon and priest (Lincoln) May 28, 1589. Doubtless V. of Sleaford, Lincs., 1591–1627. V. of Felmersham and Pavenham, Beds., 1597–8. Chaplain of Trinity, 1601–4. V. of Hitchin, Herts., 1603–20. (*Lincs. Pedigrees*, 520.)

HUDDLESTON, RICHARD. B.A. 1485–6; M.A. 1489. Proctor, 1492–3. R. of Gt Gransden, Hunts., 1494–1501; patron, CLARE College. Died 1501.

HUDDLESTON, THOMAS. Matric. sizar from CORPUS CHRISTI, Easter, 1624. Of Lincolnshire.

HUDDLESTON, TRISTRAM. Matric. pens. from St JOHN'S, c. 1590. S. of George, R. of Burton, Lincs. B.A. 1593-4; M.A. 1597. R. of Mablethorpe St Peter, Lincs., 1598-1630. (*Lincs. Pedigrees*, 518.)

HUDDLESTON, WILLIAM. Matric. pens. from TRINITY, Easter, 1552. (Perhaps re-entered, 1552.) Probably adm. at Lincoln's Inn, Oct. 31, 1555. Will (P.C.C.) 1564; of Lincoln's Inn, and Sharpenhoe, Beds.

HUDDLESTON, WILLIAM. Adm. at CHRIST'S, Nov. 20, 1619. Doubtless s. of Ferdinand, of Millom, Cumberland. Matric. 1620. A strong royalist. Knighted for bravery at Edgehill (according to *Peile*, I. 332.)

HUDLESTON, WILLIAM. Adm. pens. at EMMANUEL, July 10, 1730. S. of Lawson, R. of Kelston, Somerset. Migrated to Oxford. Matric. from Queen's, Dec. 9, 1735, age 19; B.A. (Oxford) 1739; M.A. (Emmanuel) 1747. Preb. of Wells, 1746-66. V. of St Cuthbert's, Wells. V. of South Brent, Somerset. Married, 1743, Mary, dau. of John Burland, of Wells. Died Mar. 1, 1766. M.I. at Kelston. (*Al. Oxon.*; *Misc. Gen. et Her.*, N.S., II. 408.)

HUDDLESTON, ——. Adm. pens. at PETERHOUSE, Sept. 13, 1566.

HUDSON, BENJAMIN. Adm. pens. at SIDNEY, Oct. 27, 1683. 2nd s. of Edward, gent. (afterward Baronet). B. at Melton Mowbray, Leics. Schools, Barkeby, Leics. (Mr Tho. Rawson) and Grantham, Lincs. (Mr Wm. Walker). Matric. 1683. Succeeded his father as Baronet, June 1, 1702. Brother of Edward (1683), half-brother of Skeffington (1701). (*Nichols*, II. 264; *Kimber*, III. 448; *G.E.C.*)

HUDSON, CHRISTOPHER. Matric. sizar from PETERHOUSE, Easter, 1619. Perhaps s. of Christopher, of Newhall, Yorks. B.A. 1626.

HUDSON, CHRISTOPHER. Adm. pens. at CORPUS CHRISTI, 1619. Of Middlesex. S. and h. of William. Matric. Easter, 1620. Adm. at Gray's Inn, Mar. 15, 1619-20. Brother of William (1619).

HUDSONN, CHRISTOPHER. Matric. sizar from MAGDALENE, Easter, 1622; B.A. 1625-6; M.A. 1629. One of these names C. of Middleton, Lancs., 1624-8; C. of Low Church, Walton-le-Dale, 1630-42; of Cartmel, 1648-9. (E. Axon.)

HUDSON, EDWARD. Matric. sizar from St JOHN'S, Easter, 1651. Perhaps a mistake for William (whom *see*).

HUDSON, EDWARD. Adm. pens. at SIDNEY, Oct. 27, 1683. 1st s. of Edward, gent. (afterwards Baronet). B. at Melton Mowbray, Leics., 1668. Schools, Barkeby, Leics. (Mr Tho. Rawson) and Grantham, Lincs. (Mr Wm. Walker). Died 1694. Brother of Benjamin (1683), half-brother of Skeffington (1701). (*Nichols*, II. 264.)

HUDSON, FRANCIS. Adm. sizar (age 15) at SIDNEY, May 7, 1678. S. of Robert, furrier. B. at Newport, Salop. School, Newport (Mr Edwards). Matric. 1678; B.A. 1681-2.

HUDSON, GEORGE. Matric. pens. from St JOHN'S, c. 1590; B.A. 1593-4; M.A. 1597. One of these names, 'M.A.,' R. of Dimchurch, Kent, 1599-1605. One, V. of New Malton, Yorks., 1615.

HUDSON, GEORGE. Matric. sizar from St CATHARINE'S, Easter, 1623; B.A. 1625.

HUDSON, GEORGE. Adm. sizar at TRINITY, Jan. 29, 1658-9. S. of George, of Lea, Salop. Matric. 1661. Migrated to Magdalene, Mar. 20, 1661-2; age 19. B.A. 1662.

HUDSON, GEORGE. Adm. sizar at CHRIST'S, June 22, 1686. One of these names emigrant minister to Virginia, 1694. (*Peile*, II. 102.)

HUDSON, GERVASE. Matric. sizar from TRINITY, Michs. 1629; B.A. 1632.

HUDSON, HENRY. B.Can.L. 1519-20.

HUDSON, HENRY. Matric. sizar from St JOHN'S, Michs. 1579. Of Cumberland. B.A. 1583-4; M.A. 1587; B.D. 1595. Fellow, 1587. V. of Brampton, Cumberland, 1600-6. R. of Stapleton, 1603. V. of Brigham, 1607-17. Buried there Mar. 2, 1617-8. (*B. Nightingale*.)

HUDSON, HENRY. Adm. pens. (age 15) at SIDNEY, May 23, 1625. S. of Robert, retail-dealer (of St Mary Bothaw, London; will, 1641). B. in Candlewick Street, London. Matric. 1625; B.A. 1628-9; M.A. from Trinity Hall, 1632. Adm. at Gray's Inn, Oct. 10, 1634. Created Baronet, July 3, 1660. Buried at Melton Mowbray, Aug. 27, 1690, aged 81. (*Nichols*, II. 264; *Vis. of London*, 1634; *G.E.C.*)

HUDSON, HENRY. Adm. sizar (age 16) at PEMBROKE, Apr. 22, 1680. S. of George, of Acham (? Acomb), Yorks., gent. Matric. 1680; B.A. 1683-4. Ord. priest (Norwich) May, 1686. C. of Thaxted, Essex.

HUDSON, JAMES. Adm. sizar at PETERHOUSE, May 8, 1622. Matric. 1622; B.A. 1625-6; M.A. 1629. Ord. deacon (York) June, 1626; priest, Sept. 1627. V. of Pocklington, Yorks., 1641-3. Apparently ejected, but probably reinstated, 1660. Buried Aug. 2, 1673. (*Yorks. Archaeol. and Top. Journal*, XIV. 113.)

HUDSON, JOHN. B.A. 1505-6.

HUDSON, JOHN. Matric. pens. from CHRIST'S, Mar. 1580-1. One of these names, of Yorkshire, ordained at Rheims, 1584. (*Peile*, I. 162.)

HUDSON, JOHN. Adm. pens. at QUEENS', Oct. 29, 1582. Of Suffolk. One of these names V. of Ashfield Magna, Suffolk, 1603.

HODSON, JOHN. Adm. sizar at PETERHOUSE, Lent, 1604-5. Matric. 1605; B.A. 1609; M.A. 1612.

HUDSON, JOHN. Adm. pens. at EMMANUEL, July 2, 1614. B. at Stratford, Suffolk. Scholar; B.A. 1617-8. Ord. deacon (London) Dec. 24, 1620, age 23. C. of Gt Horkesley, Essex. R. of Capel St Mary, Suffolk, 1623-31. Will (P.C.C.) 1632.

HUDSON, JOHN. Matric. sizar from QUEENS', Easter, 1629. Of Lincolnshire. B.A. 1632-3. Perhaps R. of Calceby, Lincs., 1637. Admon. (Lincoln) 1648, of one of these names; of Hameringham, Lincs., clerk.

HUDSON, JOHN. Adm. pens. (age 18) at SIDNEY, Nov. 9, 1745. S. of Benjamin, gent., of Bridlington, Yorks. B. there. School, Coxwold. Matric. 1745; M.B. 1753. Probably adm. student at Leyden, Oct. 25, 1751. One of these names, of Bessinby, Bridlington, died Oct. 1772. (G. *Mag.*)

HUDSON, JOSEPH. Adm. sizar (age 19) at St JOHN'S, May 30, 1660. S. of William, deceased, of Stratford, Suffolk. B. there. School, Dedham. Matric. 1660; B.A. 1663-4. Signed for deacon's orders (London) June 4, 1664. R. of Benacre, Suffolk, 1671-7. V. of Lowestoft, 1677-91. Buried in Lowestoft vestry, Oct. 31, 1691. (V. B. Redstone.)

HUDSON, MICHAEL. Matric. pens. from CORPUS CHRISTI, Easter, 1623. Of Kent. B.A. 1626-7; M.A. 1630. Ord. deacon (Peterb.) May 30, 1629. R. of West Deeping, Lincs., 1632. Preb. of Lincoln, 1633-6. Possibly R. of St Nicholas, Newington, 1652-5. R. of Witchling, Kent, 1653-61. Not the royalist divine, for whom *see Al. Oxon.*

HUDSON, NATHANIEL. Adm. sizar at EMMANUEL, Apr. 7, 1657. Of Suffolk. Matric. 1658; B.A. 1660-1; M.A. 1664. Ord. deacon (Norwich) Mar. 15, 1662-3; priest (London) Sept. 25, 1664. Licensed to teach grammar, Norwich diocese, 1662. Master of Dedham School, Essex, 1663-5; and C. of Dedham, in 1664. V. of Gt Bentley, 1664-1708. R. of Holton, Suffolk, 1667.

HUDSON, NATHANIEL. Adm. sizar at EMMANUEL, Feb. 11, 1689-90. Of Suffolk. Matric. 1690; B.A. 1693-4; M.A. 1697. Ord. deacon (Norwich) June, 1694; priest (London) Mar. 20, 1697-8. R. of Holton, Suffolk, 1704-37. Died Nov. 10, 1737. M.I. at Holton.

HUDSON, NICHOLAS. Matric. pens. from QUEENS', Easter, 1576.

HUDSON, PETER. Matric. sizar from St JOHN'S, c. 1591.

HUDSON, PETER. Matric. sizar from QUEENS', Easter, 1612. Of Cumberland. B.A. 1615-6. Ord. deacon (Carlisle) Sept. 20, 1618; priest, May 23, 1619, as 'M.A.' R. of Gosforth, Cumberland, 1628-45. Probably V. of Cockermouth for some years before 1645. Buried at Gosforth, Aug. 2, 1645. (*B. Nightingale*.)

HUDSON, RICHARD. LL.B. 1584, from PETERHOUSE (Incorp. from Oxford). LL.D. 1585. Admitted advocate, Jan. 28, 1594-5. One of these names R. of Swainsthorpe, Norfolk, 1556-71. (*Cooper*, II. 223.)

HUDSON, RICHARD. Adm. sizar (age 18) at St JOHN'S, May 23, 1645. S. of Alexander, 'artificer,' of West Deeping, Lincs. School, Stamford (Mr Umphry). Matric. 1645; B.A. 1647-8.

HUDSON, RICHARD. M.A. from KING'S, 1729. S. of Richard, of Hopton Castle, Salop, clerk. Matric. from Christ Church, Oxford, May 16, 1720, age 20; B.A. (Oxford) 1724. (*Al. Oxon.*)

HUDSON, ROBERT. Matric. pens. from CHRIST'S, May, 1560; B.A. 1562-3; M.A. 1566. One of these names ord. priest (Ely) Dec. 19, 1563. Perhaps V. of Gt Yeldham, Essex, 1568. Died there before Sept. 1593. Will (Cons. C. London) 1594.

HUDSON, ROBERT. Adm. sizar at EMMANUEL, Feb. 7, 1734-5. Of Wherstead or Whepstead, Suffolk. Matric. 1735; B.A. 1738. One of these names, 2nd s. of Sir Roger, adm. at Lincoln's Inn, Jan. 23, 1738-9. Ord. deacon (Norwich) Mar. 1738-9; priest, May, 1741. Perhaps R. of Brockley, Suffolk, 1771-85. Died 1785.

HUDSON, ROBERT. Adm. sizar at QUEENS', Nov. 19, 1737. Of Lincolnshire. Matric. 1738; LL.B. 1744. Ord. priest (Lincoln) Nov. 24, 1746. V. of Nassington, Northants., 1746-71. V. of St Neots, Hunts., 1763-96. Died 1796.

HUDSON, ROBERT. Adm. sizar (age 19) at TRINITY, Apr. 16, 1747. S. of James, of Hutton Cranswick, Yorks. School, Beverley (Mr Clark). Matric. 1747; Scholar, 1750; B.A. 1750-1. Ord. deacon (York) Sept. 22, 1751; priest, Sept. 1752. C. of Bridlington. Brother of Thomas (1742).

HUDSON, ROLAND. Ord. priest (Peterb.) Mar. 24, 1587-8, as 'B.A. of TRINITY College.'

HUDSON, SAMUEL. Matric. pens. from CHRIST'S, Dec. 1620. Migrated to Emmanuel, Easter, 1621. B.A. 1624-5; M.A. 1628. Ord. deacon (Peterb.) Dec. 23, 1626; priest (Norwich) Sept. 1628. R. of Capel St Mary, Suffolk, 1631, where he appears as a member for the 1st division of the Suffolk *Classis*, 1645. Said to have been silenced in 1662. Author, religious. (*Peile*, I. 336; *Calamy*, II. 445.)

HUDSON, SAMUEL. Adm. pens. at EMMANUEL, May 4, 1652. Of Suffolk. Matric. 1655; B.A. 1655-6; M.A. 1659. Probably R. of Earl Stonham, Suffolk, 1662. Living, 1695.

HUDSON, SAMUEL. Matric. pens. from CHRIST'S, July, 1678; M.B. 1683. (*Peile*, II. 68.)

HUDSON, SAMUEL. Adm. sizar at JESUS, Feb. 19, 1701-2. Of Suffolk. Matric. 1702; B.A. 1705-6; M.A. 1709. Ord. deacon (London) Sept. 19, 1708. Perhaps V. of Bishopton, Durham, 1740-62.

HUDSON, SIMON. Matric. pens. from TRINITY, Michs. 1586; Scholar, 1590; B.A. 1590-1. V. of Gosberton, Lincs., 1595-1602. Admon. (Leicester) 1602.

HUDSON, SKEFFINGTON. Adm. pens. (age 18) at PETERHOUSE, Apr. 23, 1701. Of Leicestershire. S. of Sir Edward, Bart. Bapt. at Melton Mowbray, May 11, 1683. School, Melton Mowbray. Matric. 1701; Scholar, 1701. Succeeded his nephew Charles as Baronet, 1752. Died Feb. 26, 1760. Buried at Poplar, Middlesex. Half-brother of Benjamin (1683) and Edward (1683). (*Nichols*, II. 264; *Kimber*, III. 449; *G.E.C.*)

HUDSON, THOMAS. At ST JOHN'S one year, c. 1586. B. at 'Deane,' Cambs., 1569. Ord. priest (Lincoln) June 15, 1606. R. of Somersby, Lincs., 1607-19. Admon. (Lincoln) 1620, of one of these names; of Hameringham, clerk.

HUDSON, THOMAS. Matric. pens. from PEMBROKE, Easter, 1606; B.A. 1608-9; M.A. 1614. Perhaps V. of Cowfold, Sussex, 1622-51. If so, father of Thomas (1639).

HUDSON, THOMAS. Matric. pens. from CHRIST'S, Dec. 1617; B.A. 1620-1; M.A. 1624. One of these names, schoolmaster of Little Chester, Derbs., was ord. deacon (Lichfield) Sept. 1624. Perhaps V. of Elvaston, Derbs., 1625-35. One of these names licensed curate at St Michael, Cornhill, 1636. (*Peile*, I. 321.)

HUDSON, THOMAS. Adm. sizar (age 15) at CHRIST'S, Apr. 27, 1629. S. of John. B. at Kirkby Lonsdale. School, Kirkby Lonsdale (Mr Leake). Matric. 1629; B.A. 1632-3. Fellow, 1635. Will proved (V.C.C.) 1635. (*Peile*, I. 400.)

HUDSON, THOMAS. Adm. sizar at PETERHOUSE, Apr. 3, 1630. Of Yorkshire. One of these names V. of St Lawrence, York, 1638-61. (*T. A. Walker*, 41.)

HUDSON, THOMAS. Matric. pens. from ST CATHARINE'S, Michs. 1639. Of Sussex. S. and h. of Thomas (? 1606), of Cowfold, Sussex, clerk. Adm. at Gray's Inn, May 26, 1642.

HUDSON, THOMAS. Adm. sizar (age 19) at SIDNEY, June 2, 1686. S. of Robert, scrivener, of Newport, Salop. School, Newport (Mr Edwards). Matric. 1686; B.A. 1689-90; M.A. 1693. Fellow, 1693.

HUDSON, THOMAS. Adm. sizar (age 18) at ST JOHN'S, May 21, 1711. S. of Richard, bailiff. B. at Bingley, Yorks. School, Bingley (Mr Ellison). B.A. 1714-5. Ord. deacon (York) Sept. 1716; priest, July 21, 1728. C. of Old Byland and Cold Kirby, Yorks., 1728. Head Master of Otley Grammar School, 1729-33. C. of Scruton, 1731. Head Master of Hipperholme, 1733; and of Bingley, till 1756. Died May 13, 1756.

HUDSON, THOMAS. Adm. sizar (age 19) at TRINITY, June 10, 1742, as 'James.' S. of James, of Hutton-Cranswick, Yorks. School, Beverley, Yorks. (Mr Clark). Matric. 1742; B.A. 1745-6. Perhaps M.A. 1786. Ord. deacon (York) Feb. 23, 1745-6; priest, June, 1751. C. of Swine, Yorks. Perhaps R. of Whitfield, Northumberland, 1764-84; but said to have died Apr. 26, 1784; buried at Blanchland. Brother of Robert (1747).

HUDSON, WILLIAM. B.A. 1498-9. Of Durham diocese. M.A. 1502; B.D. 1511-2. Fellow of PEMBROKE, 1498. Preacher, 1509-10. Ord. deacon (Ely) Apr. 18, 1500; priest (Lincoln) June 13, 1500. Will of one of these names (P.C.C.) 1511; of Clerkenwell Priory, Middlesex, clerk.

HUDSON, WILLIAM. Matric. sizar from TRINITY, Michs. 1550; Scholar, 1554; B.A. 1554-5; M.A. 1558. Fellow, 1555. Perhaps V. of Stradbroke, Suffolk, 1556-9. One of these names R. of Thorpe-Abbots, Norfolk, 1558-60; and also R. of Billingford, 1560. Died 1560. Buried at Billingford.

HUDSON, W. Matric. sizar from QUEENS', Lent, 1557-8; Scholar, 1558-9. Perhaps B.A. 1560-1, as 'Hodgson.' One William Hudson R. of Gt Hormead, Herts., 1562-75. Died 1575. Will (Consist. C. London) 1575; property at Alnwick, Northumberland. (J. Ch. Smith.)

HUDSON, WILLIAM. Adm. at CORPUS CHRISTI, 1591. Of Kent. B.A. 1594-5; M.A. 1598. One of these names V. of Swineshead, Lincs., 1599-1614. Admon. (Lincoln) 1614.

HUDSON, WILLIAM. Adm. pens. at CORPUS CHRISTI, 1619. Of Middlesex. 2nd s. of William. Matric. Easter, 1620. Adm. at Gray's Inn, Mar. 15, 1619-20. Brother of Christopher (1619).

HUDSON, WILLIAM. Adm. sizar (age 16) at ST JOHN'S, June 7, 1651. S. of William, of Otley, Yorks. B. there. School, Burnsall, Yorks. (private). One of these names usher at Bradford School, c. 1657. Probably subscribed as deacon (York) Sept. 1662.

HUDSON, WILLIAM. Adm. sizar (age 18) at ST JOHN'S, Feb. 1, 1654-5. S. of John, clerk, of Dublin. B. there. School, Sleaford, Lincs. (Mr Gibson). Matric. 1655; B.A. 1658.

HUDSON, WILLIAM. Adm. at MAGDALENE, July 3, 1663. S. of ——, Head Master of Guiseley, Yorks. B.A. 1666-7. Ord. deacon (York) June, 1669; priest, May, 1670. Head Master of Otley School, Yorks., 1667-76. V. of Fewston, 1677-1705. Died 1705.

HUDSON, ——. B.A. 1523-4.

HUDSON, ——. Adm. at CORPUS CHRISTI, 1581.

HUDSON, ——. Adm. pens. at ST CATHARINE'S, 1675.

HUEMISTON, ——. Degree (? B.A.) 1492.

HUET, *see* HEWITT.

HUFFAM, EDWARD. Matric. pens. from ST JOHN'S, c. 1593; B.A. 1597-8.

HUFFAM, JOHN. Matric. pens. from ST JOHN'S, Easter, 1582; B.A. 1585-6; M.A. 1589.

HUFFAM, JOHN. Adm. pens. at TRINITY, May 22, 1661. Scholar from Westminster, 1662. Matric. 1661; B.A. 1664-5. (*Graduati* wrong.) Ord. deacon (Ely) Dec. 20, 1668.

HUFFAM, MICHAEL. Matric. pens. from QUEENS', Easter, 1628. Of Kent. B.A. 1631-2; M.A. 1635. Probably C. of Kingston, Kent, 1636-42.

HUFFAM, SOLOMON. Matric. pens. from MAGDALENE, Easter, 1617. Doubtless s. of Richard, of Ash, Sandwich, Kent. Bapt. there, Jan. 1, 1599-1600. Mayor of Sandwich, 1639. Married, at Birchington, Kent, Dec. 6, 1619, Mary Beake, of Northbourne. Died 1659. (*Vis. of Kent*; *Hasted*, IV. 231; H. G. Harrison.)

HUFFAM, STEPHEN. Matric. pens. from ST JOHN'S, c. 1591. Probably s. of Richard, of Eastry, Kent. B.A. 1594-5; M.A. 1598. Ord. deacon (Peterb.) Mar. 16, 1598-9; priest, June 10, 1599. V. of St Mary, Sandwich, Kent, 1600-24. V. of Sarre, 1616-29. Died May 6, 1629. Probably brother of the next. (Planché, *A Corner of Kent*, 394.)

HUFFAM, VINCENT. Matric. pens. from ST JOHN'S, Michs. 1581. Doubtless s. of Richard, of Eastry, Kent. Bapt. at Ash, July 26, 1566. B.A. 1584-5; M.A. 1588. V. of Seasalter, Kent, 1596-1611. V. of Benenden, 1608-11. Probably brother of Stephen (above). (Planché, *A Corner of Kent*, 396.)

HUFFINGTON, ——. Doctor (probably of Theology) 1478-9. Franciscan friar.

HUGESSEN, JOHN. Matric. Fell.-Com. from CORPUS CHRISTI, Michs. 1646. Of Kent. Doubtless s. of Sir William, of Linstead. Married Christian, dau. of Samuel Hales, of Davington, Kent. Died 1670. (*Hasted*, II. 741; *Vis. of Kent*, 1663.)

HUGESTON, JOSIAS. Adm. pens. (age 17) at CHRIST'S, May 13, 1635. S. of Josias. B. at Dover. School, Westminster. Matric. 1635. (*Peile*, I. 436.)

HUGGARD, ROGER. Adm. pens. at EMMANUEL, Michs. 1584. Matric. 1584. Probably B.A. 1589-90. Ord. deacon and priest (Colchester) Jan. 12, 1597-8, as 'B.A.'

HUGGEN, ALEXANDER. Matric. pens. from CORPUS CHRISTI, Easter, 1574. Perhaps adm. as Hugger, in 1576. (*Masters*.)

HUGGEN, ANTHONY. B.A. 1541-2. B. at Framlingham. M.A. 1545. Fellow of ST JOHN'S, 1544.

HUGGEN, JOHN. Matric. pens. from ST JOHN'S, Michs. 1546.

HUGGEN, NATHANIEL. B.A. from ST JOHN'S, 1619-20; M.A. 1623. Ord. deacon (Peterb.) Sept. 23, 1621; priest, June 8, 1623.

HUGGEN, STEVEN. Matric. sizar from CHRIST'S, July, 1605; B.A. 1609-10; M.A. 1614. Perhaps V. of All Hallows, Staining, London. Died 1662. Will (P.C.C.) 1663. (*Peile*, I. 253.)

HUGEN, THOMAS (? HUGGENSON). Matric. Fell.-Com. from QUEENS', Easter, 1561.

HUGGEN, THOMAS. Matric. pens. from PETERHOUSE, Easter, 1572; B.A. 1575–6; Scholar, 1576–9; M.A. 1579. Licensed to teach grammar in Norwich diocese, 1583.

HUGGETT, ANTHONY. Matric sizar from TRINITY, Easter, 1634; B.A. 1637–8; M.A. 1641. Ord. deacon (Peterb.) Dec. 18, 1641. R. of Chaldon, Surrey, 1641. Died 1684. Father of the next. (One Anthony Huggett, of Horne, Surrey, clerk, by will, P.C.C., 1647, leaves his cassock, etc., to nephew Anthony, s. of brother Daniel; probably this man.) (*Manning and Bray*, II. 447.)

HUGGETT, ANTHONY. Adm. sizar at TRINITY, July 6, 1670. S. of Anthony, of Chaldon, Surrey, above. Matric. 1671. Migrated to Oxford. Matric. from Gloucester Hall, Dec. 17, 1673, age 19. (*Al. Oxon.*)

HUGGET, PAUL. Adm. pens. at TRINITY, Mar. 28, 1645.

HUGGINS, JOHN. Adm. sizar (age 15) at SIDNEY, Nov. 30, 1677. S. of Henry, shoemaker, deceased. B. at St Martin-le-Grand, London. School, Aldersgate Street (Mr Tho. Dominel). Matric. 1678.

HUGGENS, ——. Perhaps B.A. 1530–1.

HUGGLE, THOMAS. Adm. at KING'S (age 18) a scholar from Eton, Aug. 9, 1512. Of Salisbury. Died as scholar, 1514. (*Harwood.*)

HUGGLESCOTT, WILLIAM. Matric. sizar from QUEENS', Michs. 1615. Of Leicestershire. B.A. 1618–9.

HUGH, ——. Grace for degree, 1455–6. Augustinian friar.

HUGH, ——. M.A. 1481. Perhaps resident at CORPUS CHRISTI, in 1483.

HUGH, ——. B.A. 1483–4.

HUGH, ——. *Cautio* for B.A. 1520–1.

HUGHES or HEWES, ABRAHAM. Adm. sizar at PETERHOUSE, Apr. 16, 1616. Of Cambridgeshire. (Probably s. of Robert, the College butler.) Matric. 1616; B.A. 1619; M.A. 1623. Ord. deacon (Peterb.) June 11, 1620; priest, June 16, 1622. Probably brother of the next, and of Robert (1608).

HEWES, ANDREW. Adm. sizar at PETERHOUSE, 1601–2. (Probably s. of Robert, the College butler.) B. at Cambridge. Matric. 1602; Scholar; B.A. 1605–6; M.A. 1609. Ord. deacon (London) Apr. 17; priest, June 7, 1612, age 26. C. of Wickford, Essex. Brother of Abraham (above) and Robert (1608).

HUGHS or HEWES, ARTHUR. Matric. pens. from JESUS, Michs. 1565; B.A. 1568–9; M.A. 1572; B.D. 1580. Fellow, 1573–80. R. of Harlton, Cambs., 1579–80. Died *c.* Nov. 16, 1580. Will proved (V.C.C.) 1580. (A. Gray.)

HUGHES, BARTHOLOMEW. M.A. from EMMANUEL, 1721. B.A. from Trinity College, Dublin, 1705. Perhaps R. of Trottiscliffe, Kent, 1723–4. Inc. of Laver Parva and Barnston, Essex, till 1745. Died 1745. (J. Ch. Smith.)

HUGHES, BULKELEY. Adm. sizar at JESUS, May 31, 1701. Of Anglesey. Matric. 1701; Scholar, 1701; B.A. 1704–5; M.A. 1712. Ord. priest (Norwich) Sept. 1706. Doubtless father of Owen (1750).

HUGHES, DAVID. Adm. sizar at QUEENS', July 2, 1722. Of Carnarvon. Matric. 1722; B.A. 1725–6; M.A. 1729; B.D. 1738. Fellow, 1727–77. Vice-President. Ord. deacon (Lincoln) May 28, 1727; priest, Dec. 24, 1727. V. of Little Eversden, Cambs., 1743. Died July 11, 1777. Will, P.C.C. Large benefactor to the College. (G. *Mag.*)

HUGHES, EDWARD. Matric. sizar from JESUS, Easter, 1584. B. at Oswestry, Feb. 1563–4. B.A. 1587–8; M.A. 1591; B.D. 1600; D.D. 1616. Fellow, 1594–1602. Ord. deacon and priest (Lincoln) Aug. 2, 1595. R. of Woughton-on-the-Green, Bucks., 1597–1633. R. of Simpson, 1607–33. Archdeacon of Bangor, 1617–33. Chaplain to Archbishops Bancroft and Abbot. Buried at Woughton, Oct. 9, 1633. Will, P.C.C. (A. Gray; *Lipscomb*, IV. 343.)

HUGHES, EDWARD. Matric. sizar from ST JOHN'S, Easter, 1626; B.A. 1629–30.

HUGHES, EDWARD. Adm. sizar (age 18) at ST JOHN'S, May 3, 1677. S. of Ellis, attorney-at-law. B. at Bala, Merioneth. School, Wrexham (Mr Lewis). Matric. 1677; B.A. 1680–1. Probably brother of Humphrey (1674).

HUGHS, EVAN. M.A. from JESUS, 1665. B.A. from Oriel College, Oxford, 1660–1. Incorp. M.A. at Oxford, 1665. Perhaps V. of Llandyfriog, Cardigan; ejected, 1662. (*Calamy*, III. 496; *Al. Oxon.*)

HUGHES, FRANCIS. Adm. at TRINITY, as Westminster scholar, Easter, 1616; B.A. 1619–20; M.A. 1623. Esquire Bedell, 1629–69. Author, MS. notes on University proceedings. Died Oct. 30, 1669. Buried in St Botolph's. Will proved (V.C.C.) 1670. Father of Owen (1644). (Stokes, *Bedells*, 100.)

HUGHES, GEORGE. M.A. 1627 (Incorp. from Oxford). Of Southwark, Surrey. Matric. from Corpus Christi, Oxford, June 28, 1620, age 16; B.A. (Oxford) 1622–3; M.A. 1625; B.D. 1633. Fellow of Pembroke College, Oxford. Lecturer at All Hallows, Bread Street. Chaplain to Lord Brooke. V. of St Andrew's, Plymouth, 1644–62, ejected. V. of Tavistock, Devon, 1648. Imprisoned for nine months in St Nicholas Island, 1665. A noted Presbyterian. Author, theological. Died at Kingsbridge, July 4, 1667, aged 64. Will, P.C.C. (*Al. Oxon.*; *D.N.B.*; *F.M.G.*, 1053.)

HUGHES, GEORGE. Adm. sizar (age 19) at ST JOHN'S, Feb. 2, 1683–4. S. of Edmund, deceased. B. at Llanfachreth, Merioneth. School, Llanegryn (Mr Owen Jones).

HUGHES, GEORGE. Adm. sizar at QUEENS', Mar. 12, 1685–6. Of Hertfordshire. Matric. 1686. Migrated to Trinity Hall, Jan. 28, 1688–9. B.A. 1689–90. One of these names R. of Colkirk, Norfolk, 1712; probably an Oxford graduate.

HUGHES, HENRY. M.A. 1694 (Incorp. from Oxford). S. of 'Hugh Maurice,' of Llanvihangel Gelindroid, Cardigan. Matric. from Jesus College, Oxford, Mar. 22, 1687–8, age 20; B.A. (St John's College, Oxford) 1691; M.A. 1694. One of these names (M.A.), V. of Bethersden, Kent, 1698–1704. R. of Hurst, till 1704. Died 1704. (*Al. Oxon.*)

HUGHES, HOLLAND. Adm. scholar at TRINITY HALL, Jan. 9, 1694–5. S. of Richard (? 1652), R. of Llanfairynghornwy, Anglesey. Matric. 1695; B.A. 1697–8; M.A. 1702. Ord. priest (Lincoln) Mar. 16, 1700–1. V. of Hemingford Grey, Hunts., 1701–23. V. of Gt Stukeley, 1701–23. Died Nov. 21, 1723, aged 46. M.I. at Hemingford Grey. Father of Newman (1724) and perhaps brother of William (1711).

HEWES, HUGH. Matric. sizar from TRINITY, Michs. 1564; B.A. 1567–8. One of these names, of Anglesey, adm. at Lincoln's Inn, May 3, 1571. His will (P.C.C.) 1609.

HUGHES, HUGH. Adm. pens. (age 17) at ST JOHN'S, July 1, 1640. S. of Roger (? 1608), of Porthamel, Anglesey. B. at Llandegvan, Anglesey (his mother's home). School, Perse, Cambridge (Mr Watson). Matric. 1640. Married Jane, dau. of Owen Wynn, Esq., of Glascoed. (Burke, *L.G.*)

HUGHES, HUGH. Adm. sizar (age 19) at ST JOHN'S, Dec. 8, 1675. (Previously matric. from Christ Church, Oxford, Jan. 14, 1673–4.) S. of Thomas, of Bettws Garnon, Carnarvon. B. there. School, Llanrwst. Matric. 1675; B.A. 1677–8.

HUGHES, HUGH. Adm. pens. (age 18) at TRINITY, Nov. 12, 1734. S. of Thomas, of Llanrwst, Carnarvon. School, Hanmer, Flints. (Mr Hughes). Matric. 1734; Scholar, 1737; B.A. 1738–9. Perhaps preb. of Bangor, 1743–50. Precentor, 1748–9. Dean, 1750–3.

HUGHES, HUMFREY. Adm. sizar (age 24) at ST JOHN'S, May 22, 1674. S. of Ellis, of St Asaph. B. there. School, Oswestry, Salop. Matric. 1674. One of these names, of Pembrey, Merioneth, gent., adm. at the Inner Temple, Apr. 9, 1674. Probably brother of Edward (1677).

HEWES, ISAAC, *see* HOWES.

HEWES, JOHN. Matric. sizar from QUEENS', Easter, 1544.

HEWIS, JOHN. Matric. pens. from TRINITY, Easter, 1575.

HUGHES, JOHN. Matric. sizar from CHRIST'S, June, 1587; B.A. 1590–1; M.A. 1594. One of these names precentor of Llandaff, 1611.

HEWES, JOHN. Matric. pens. from MAGDALENE, Easter, 1611; B.A. 1614–5; M.A. 1619. Ord. deacon (Peterb.) Mar. 16; priest, Mar. 17, 1616–7. One of these names (M.A.), V. of Calkwell, Lincs., 1621.

HUGHES, JOHN. Matric. sizar from ST JOHN'S, Easter, 1611; B.A. 1614–5; M.A. 1618.

HUGHES, JOHN. Matric. sizar from JESUS, Easter, 1612; B.A. 1615–6; M.A. 1619. Ord. deacon (Peterb.) June 15, 1617; priest, Mar. 5, 1619–20. One of these names (M.A.), R. of Lower Gravenhurst, Beds., 1625, was father of Richard (1652).

HUGHES, JOHN. Adm. pens. at JESUS, May 1, 1621. Of Wales. Matric. 1621; B.A. 1624–5. In holy orders.

HEWES, JOHN. Adm. sizar (age 17) at PEMBROKE, July 3, 1621. S. of Richard, of Canterbury. Matric. 1623; B.A. 1624–5; M.A. 1628.

HUGHES, JOHN. Adm. sizar at JESUS, Oct. 10, 1667. Of London. School, Lewisham. Matric. 1667; B.A. 1671–2; M.A. 1675. Ord. deacon (Ely) Sept. 22, 1672; priest (London) June, 1674; C. of St Swithin's, London. Chaplain to the Duke of St Albans. V. of Chalk, Kent, 1680–7. R. of Gravesend, 1687–99. Died Oct. 25, 1699. Buried at Gravesend. M.I. Father of John (1699). (A. Gray.)

HUGHES, JOHN. Adm. sizar (age 19) at ST JOHN'S, Feb. 22, 1683–4. S. of Edmund, deceased. B. at Llanfachreth, Merioneth. School, Llanegryn (Mr Owen Jones). Matric. 1684; B.A. 1687–8.

HUGHES, JOHN. Adm. sizar at JESUS, June 12, 1699. Of Kent. S. of John (1667). B. Sept. 6, 1682. School, Merchant Taylors'. Matric. 1699; Rustat Scholar, 1700; B.A. 1702-3; M.A. 1706. Fellow, 1705-10. Ord. deacon (Ely) Sept. 23, 1705; priest (London) June 8, 1707. Author, theological. Died Nov. 18, 1710, aged 28. Buried at St Nicholas, Deptford. M.I. (Le Neve, III. 240; A. Gray.)

HUGHES, JOHN. M.A. from CORPUS CHRISTI, 1712. S. of J., of Probus, Cornwall. Matric. from Queen's College, Oxford, July 12, 1700, age 17; B.A. (Oxford) 1704. Probably R. of Creed, Cornwall, 1704-49. Died Feb. 17, 1749-50, aged 68. M.I. at Creed. Will (Exeter) 1752. (*Al. Oxon.*)

HUGHES, JOHN. Adm. sizar (age 19) at TRINITY, July 5, 1720. S. of Hugh Jones, of Dolgelly, Merioneth. School, Llanegryn, Merioneth (Mr Edwards). Matric. 1720; B.A. 1723-4.

HUGHES, JOHN. Adm. sizar at QUEENS', May 3, 1733. Of Carnarvon. Matric. 1733.

HUGHES, JOHN. M.A. from KING'S, 1740. S. of Samuel, of Laugharne, Carmarthen. Matric. from Jesus College, Oxford, May 5, 1713, age 18; B.A. (Worcester College) 1718. Adm. at Gray's Inn, May 15, 1713. Barrister, 1720. Ord. deacon (Gloucester) Sept. 25, 1720; priest, June 30, 1723. R. of Binton, Warws. R. of Hawling, Gloucs., 1752-65. Died 1765. (F. S. Hockaday.)

HUGHES, JOHN RUDING. Adm. pens. (age 16) at PEMBROKE, Aug. 4, 1713. S. of John, of Leicester, gent. Matric. 1714.

HUGHES, LEWIS. M.A. from PEMBROKE, 1625. Of Co. Anglesey. Matric. from All Souls (Oxford), Mar. 19, 1618-9, age 17; B.A. (Oxford) 1622. Ord. priest (London) May 20, 1627. R. of Shepperton, Middlesex, 1638-60. Died 1660.

HUGHES, MORRIS. B.A. from ST JOHN'S, 1611-2; M.A. 1616. Ord. deacon (Peterb.) Dec. 19, 1613; priest, Sept. 24, 1615. V. of Leighton Bromswold, Hunts., 1623-(?) 58.

HUGHES, NEWMAN. Adm. sizar at JESUS, Apr. 29, 1724. S. of Holland (1694-5), deceased. Matric. 1724; Rustat Scholar, 1726; LL.B. from Trinity Hall, 1731. (Matric. also from Wadham College, Oxford, Oct. 14, 1726, age 18.) Ord. priest (Lincoln) Sept. 24, 1732. V. of Hemingford Grey, Hunts. (A. Gray; *Al. Oxon.*)

HUGHES or HUES, NICHOLAS. Matric. sizar from CHRIST'S, May, 1576; B.A. from Magdalene, 1579-80. One of these names V. of South Weald, Essex, 1611-26. Died Oct. 12, 1626. A note as to his estate (Cons. C. London) Nov. 1, 1626. (J. Ch. Smith.)

HEWES, OWEN. Matric. sizar from TRINITY, Easter, 1566; B.A. from Jesus, 1570-1, as 'Hughe.' Probably V. of Kingston-on-Thames, Surrey, 1607-13. One of these names V. of Newchurch, Kent, till 1608. Will (P.C.C.) 1613.

HUGHES, OWEN. Adm. pens. (age 16) at CAIUS, Sept. 19, 1644. S. of Francis (1616), Esquire Bedell. Bapt. at Gt St Mary's, Cambridge, Mar. 1, 1628-9. School, Felsted (Mr Holbeach). Scholar, 1644-7; Matric. 1645; LL.B. from Trinity Hall, 1650-1; LL.D. 1662. Fellow of Trinity Hall, 1648-62. Adm. at Gray's Inn, 1649. Commissary in Archdeaconry of Norwich and of Norfolk, 1672-9. Official of the Archdeacon of Norwich. Married Ann, dau. of Edmund Colle, of Snettisham, Norfolk. (*Venn*, I. 354.)

HUGHES, OWEN. Adm. scholar at TRINITY HALL, Jan. 6, 1689-90. Of Wales. Matric. 1689; LL.B. 1695; M.A. 1696 (*Lit. Reg.*). Fellow, 1696-1703. Taxor, 1697. Probably M.P. for Beaumaris, 1698-1700. Ord. deacon (Norwich) July, 1702; priest, July, 1702. R. of Swannington and Wood Dalling, Norfolk, 1702-15. R. of Aberffraw, Anglesey, 1715-40. R. of Trefdraeth, 1715-40. V. of Penmynydd, 1720. Treasurer of Bangor, 1720. Preb. 1720-40. Died Dec. 1740. (*Lond. Mag.*; J. Ch. Smith; A. B. Beaven.)

HUGHES, OWEN. Adm. sizar at JESUS, Oct. 19, 1750. Of Carnarvon. S. of Bulkeley (1701), clerk, deceased. Matric. 1750-1; Rustat Scholar, 1751; B.A. 1755; M.A. from Sidney, 1758; B.D. 1765. Fellow of Sidney, 1758-66. Ord. deacon (Norwich) Sept. 1755; priest (Ely) Sept. 21, 1757, as C. of Chatteris, Isle of Ely. Died Oct. 10, 1766. Admon. (P.C.C.); of St George, Bloomsbury.

HUGHES, RHESUS (REES). Adm. sizar at JESUS, May 21, 1632. Matric. 1633; Scholar; B.A. 1635-6; M.A. 1639. Ord. deacon (Peterb.) June 9, 1639. Probably V. of Troedyraur, Cardigan, 1647. R. of Wem, Salop. (A. Gray.)

HUGHES or HEWES, RICHARD. Matric. pens. from PEMBROKE, Easter, 1606; B.A. 1608-9; M.A. 1612.

HUGHES, RICHARD. Matric. sizar from JESUS, Easter, 1611; B.A. 1614-5; M.A. 1618; B.D. 1625. Fellow, 1617-38. V. of Comberton, Cambs., 1625-38. V. of Elmsted, Essex, 1632-3. Died of the plague. Buried at All Saints', Cambridge, June 13, 1638.

HUGHES, RICHARD. Matric. pens. from JESUS, Michs. 1618; B.A. 1621-2; M.A. 1625; B.D. 1634.

HUGHES, RICHARD. Adm. Fell.-Com. at JESUS, Nov. 16, 1629. Of Wales.

HUGHES, RICHARD. Adm. sizar (age 14) at ST JOHN'S, Oct. 29, 1652. S. of John (? 1612), clerk, of Lower Gravenhurst, Beds. B. there. School, Beaumaris, Anglesey. Matric. 1653; B.A. 1656-7. Perhaps R. of Llanfairynghornwy, Anglesey; and father of Holland (1694-5).

HUES, ROBERT. Matric. sizar from ST JOHN'S, Lent, 1557-8.

HEWES, ROBERT. Adm. sizar at PETERHOUSE, May 8, 1608. S. of Robert, butler of the College. B. in St Botolph's parish, Cambridge. Matric. 1608; Scholar, 1609-15; B.A. 1611-2; M.A. 1616. Ord. deacon (Lincoln) Sept. 1616; priest (London) Sept. 1, 1617, age 26. C. of Roxwell, Essex. Brother of Abraham (1616) and Andrew (1601-2).

HUGHES, ROBERT. Adm. sizar at JESUS, July 15, 1670. Of Merioneth.

HUGHES, ROGER. Matric. Fell.-Com. from KING'S, Easter, 1608. Probably s. of Hugh, late of Porthamell, Anglesey, Esq.; adm. at Lincoln's Inn, Jan. 25, 1611-2. Of Plas Côch, Anglesey. Married Winifred, dau. of David Owen, of Llandegfan. Perhaps father of Hugh (1640). (Burke, *L.G.*)

HEUGHES, ROWLAND. Matric. sizar from ST CATHARINE'S, Easter, 1606; B.A. 1607-8. One of these names R. of Essendon, Herts.; and of Little Berkhampstead, till 1624. Died 1624.

HUGHES, ROLAND. M.A. from MAGDALENE, 1731. S. of Lewis, of the Isle of Anglesey. Matric. from Jesus College, Oxford, Mar. 5, 1707-8, age 18; B.A. (Oxford) 1711. R. of Llanllyfni, Carnarvon, 1724. R. of Eglwysail, Anglesey, 1731. Died 1762. (*Al. Oxon.*)

HUGHES, SIMON. Adm. sizar at CORPUS CHRISTI, 1695. Of Kent. S. of Henry, V. of Bethersden. Bapt. at Canterbury Cathedral, Jan. 23, 1676-7. Matric. 1695; B.A. 1698-9; M.A. 1702. Ord. deacon (Peterb.) Sept. 20, 1702. V. of Bethersden, Kent, 1704-11. R. of Smarden, 1710-28. V. of St Stephen, Hackington, 1719. Preb. of Chichester, 1725-8. Died July 23, 1728. Buried in Hackington Church. (H. G. Harrison.)

HUGHES, SIMON. Adm. pens. at QUEENS', July 2, 1723. Of Kent. Probably s. of Simon (above); bapt. at Canterbury Cathedral, Jan. 3, 1705-6. Matric. 1723; B.A. 1726-7; M.A. 1730. Incorp. at Oxford, 1733. V. of Walton-upon-Thames, Surrey, 1750-77. R. of St Olave's, Southwark, 1750-77. Died Mar. 17, 1777. Will, P.C.C. (*Manning and Bray*, III. 605; H. G. Harrison.)

HUHES, THOMAS. Matric. from QUEENS', Michs. 1545 (*impubes*). Probably B.C.L. (Oxford) 1548.

HEWS, THOMAS. Adm. at CORPUS CHRISTI, 1571.

HUGHES or HEWES, THOMAS. Matric. sizar from QUEENS', Michs. 1571. Of Cheshire. B.A. 1575-6, 1st in the *ordo*; M.A. 1579. Fellow, 1576-82. Adm. at Gray's Inn, 1579. Barrister, 1585. Reader, 1606. Dean of the Chapel, 1618. Author of *The Misfortunes of Arthur*, performed before Queen Elizabeth at Greenwich by members of Gray's Inn, 1588. (*D.N.B.*; *Cooper*, II. 24, 543; Gray's *Inn Pension Book*.)

HEWES, THOMAS. Matric. sizar from TRINITY, Michs. 1585.

HEWES, THOMAS. B.A. from TRINITY, 1598-9. Perhaps the above. One of these names buried at Little Staughton, Beds., Oct. 9, 1612. (W. M. Noble.)

HUGHES, THOMAS. Matric. sizar from TRINITY HALL, Easter, 1658; Scholar, till 1666; B.A. 1661-2; M.A. 1665. Fellow, 1672-8. Perhaps ord. priest (Oxford) June 14, 1663; C. of Little Hallingbury, Essex, in 1664. R. of Fenstanton, Hunts., 1666-8. Perhaps R. of Llanfachreth, Anglesey, 1668-82. C. of St Edward's, Cambridge, 1673. For the circumstances of his election to a fellowship, *see Warren*, 175.

HUGHES, THOMAS. Adm. sizar at JESUS, Apr. 5, 1671. S. of Rees (1632), R. of Wem, Salop, deceased. Matric. 1671; Rustat Scholar, 1673; B.A. 1674-5; M.A. 1684. Incorp. at Oxford, 1684.

HUGHES, THOMAS. Adm. pens. at EMMANUEL, July 26, 1673. Of Dublin. Matric. 1674; B.A. 1677-8.

HUGHES or HEWES, THOMAS. Adm. sizar at EMMANUEL, Sept. 4, 1680. S. of 'Thomas,' of St James', Clerkenwell, citizen and butcher. Bapt. there, July 3, 1664, as s. of Roland. Exhibitioner from Christ's Hospital. Matric. 1681; B.A. 1684-5; M.A. 1688. (A. W. Lockhart; J. Ch. Smith.)

HUGHES, THOMAS. Adm. at TRINITY HALL, Oct. 31, 1736. B. Oct. 8, 1718. School, Merchant Taylors'. Matric. 1740; LL.B. 1740. R. of Llanfwrog, Denbs., 1755-76. V. of Llansilin, 1763-6. Head Master of Ruthin School, 1739-68. (Browne Willis, *St Asaph*.)

HUGHES, VINCENT. Adm. sizar (age 16) at TRINITY, June 18, 1712. S. of Moses, of Wem, Salop, clerk. School, Chester (Mr Hinchman). Matric. 1712.

HUGHES, WILLIAM. Matric. sizar from QUEENS', Michs. 1554. S. of Hugh, of Co. Carnarvon. Scholar, 1554-8; B.A. 1556-7; M.A. from Christ's, 1560; B.D. 1565; D.D. 1575. Fellow of Christ's, 1558-67. Lady Margaret preacher, 1565. Incorp. at Oxford, 1568. B.D. (Oxford) 1568; D.D. 1570. Chaplain to Thomas Howard, Duke of Norfolk. R. of Dennington, Suffolk, 1568. Archdeacon and Bishop of St Asaph, 1573-1600; held sixteen Welsh livings *in commendam*. Assisted William Morgan in the translation of the Bible into Welsh. Died Oct. 1600. Will (P.C.C.) 1600. (*Cooper*, II. 289; *Peile*, I. 52; *D.N.B.*)

HEWES, WILLIAM. Matric. pens. from QUEENS', Michs. 1569. B. in London. B.A. 1573-4; M.A. 1577. Ord. deacon (London) May 15, 1577; priest (Ely) Apr. 17, 1580; 'receives £25 a year for reading in Queens'.' Will proved (V.C.C.) 1584.

HEWES, WILLIAM. Adm. pens. at QUEENS', Apr. 7, 1578. Of Cheshire. Perhaps 'ord. priest (Gloucester) Mar. 3, 1582; bred in the schools'; C. of 'Barford,' Herts., in 1585. (*Lib. Cler. Linc.*)

HEWES, WILLIAM. Matric. sizar from ST CATHARINE'S, Easter, 1612.

HUGHES, WILLIAM. Adm. sizar (age 17) at ST JOHN'S, June 11, 1647. S. of William, of Anglesey. B. there. School, Beaumaris. Matric. 1647; B.A. 1650-1; M.A. 1654; B.D. 1661. Fellow, 1652.

HUGHES, WILLIAM. Matric. sizar from TRINITY HALL, Michs. 1657; B.A. 1660-1; M.A. 1664. Probably ord. deacon (Ely) Mar. 1663-4. One of these names (ord. priest (Oxford) July 14, 1663) was C. of Sawbridgeworth, Herts., in 1664; and V., 1669-73. Died 1673. (*Cussans*, I.)

HUGHES, WILLIAM. Adm. sizar at JESUS, May 19, 1711. S. of (? Richard, 1652), clerk, deceased, of Llanfairynghornwy, Anglesey. Matric. 1710-1; Scholar, 1712; B.A. 1714-5. Ord. deacon (Norwich) May, 1716. Perhaps brother of Holland (1694-5).

HUGHES, WILLIAM. Adm. sizar (age 19) at ST JOHN'S, June 25, 1734. S. of Robert, attorney-at-law, of Denbigh. B. at Wrexham. School, Wrexham (Mr Jones). Matric. 1734. Ord. deacon (Lincoln) June 1, 1740; 'student of law in his 6th year.' Perhaps ord. priest (Norwich) June 26, 1743, age 27. (*Scott-Mayor*, III. 457.)

HUGHES, WILLIAM. M.A. from TRINITY, 1749. S. of William, of Sodbury, Gloucs., clerk. Matric. from Merton College, Oxford, Nov. 15, 1737, age 18; B.A. (Oxford) 1742. One of these names V. of Ware, Herts., 1781-91. Died 1791. Will, P.C.C. (*Al. Oxon.*)

HEWES, ——. Sizar at CHRIST'S, 1564.

HUGHES, ——. Adm. pens. at TRINITY HALL, June 24, 1730 (name off, 1740).

HUGHET, WILLIAM. 'KING'S scholar' at Cambridge, 1332.

HUGHGILL, HENRY. Adm. pens. (age 17) at TRINITY, Nov. 11, 1741. S. of Henry, of Smeaton, Yorks. School, Scorton, Yorks. (Mr Noble). Matric. 1742; Scholar, 1742; B.A. 1745-6; M.A. 1749. R. of Smeaton, Yorks., 1755-1804. V. of Appleton-Wiske, in 1775. Died Jan. 26, 1804, aged 80. M.I. at Smeaton.

HUGILL, THOMAS. Matric. Fell.-Com. from KING'S, Easter, 1724; LL.B. 1724. Probably s. of Charles, of St Peter's, Carmarthen. Matric. from Christ Church, Oxford, Mar. 16, 1718-9, age 17. (*Al. Oxon.*)

HUGOE, JOHN, *see* HEWGOE.

HUICKE, ROBERT. M.D. 1538. B.A. (Oxford) 1528; M.A. 1532-3. Fellow of Merton College, 1530. Principal of St Alban Hall, 1536. Incorp. at Oxford, as M.D., 1566. F.R.C.P., 1536. Censor, five times; and President, 1551-3, 1564-8. Member of the Inner Temple, 1564. Physician to Henry VIII, Edward VI, and Elizabeth. Witness to the will of Katharine Parr. Died at his house at Charing Cross. Will (P.C.C.) proved, Apr. 17, 1581. (*Cooper*, I. 244; *Munk*, I. 32; *D.N.B.*)

HUIT, *see* HEWETT.

HUKE, *see* HEWKE.

HUKE, ——. D.Civ.L. 1514-5. Will of Thomas Huicke, Dr of Laws (P.C.C.) 1575; of St Helen's, Bishopsgate.

HULES or HULCE, GEORGE. Matric. sizar from CORPUS CHRISTI, Michs. 1580. One George Hulkes was V. of Kenton, Suffolk, 1603.

HULES, THOMAS. Matric. sizar from QUEENS', Easter, 1626. Possibly the same as Thomas Hale.

HULETT or HEWLETT, THOMAS. Matric. pens. from CHRIST'S, May, 1554 (not the fellow of Christ's, as supposed by *Peile*, I. 55, who was Philip Howlet). Received the tonsure (London) Sept. 1554; 'of Bath and Wells diocese.' Perhaps V. of Royston, Herts., 1557-63.

HULETT, WILLIAM. Matric. sizar from CLARE, Easter, 1632. Perhaps C. of St Ewen and of St Mary de Grace, Gloucester, 1635. C. of Frocester, Glonos., in 1661.

HULKER, JAMES. Adm. pens. (age 15) at MAGDALENE, May 15, 1672. S. of James (tailor), of Chandos Street, Covent Garden. Matric. 1672. Adm. at the Middle Temple, Sept. 17, 1673. Proved the will of his father, 1694.

HULKES, STEVEN. Matric. pens. from JESUS, Easter, 1605.

HULL, EDWARD. Matric. sizar from CHRIST'S, June, 1578; B.A. 1581-2.

HULL, GEORGE. Matric. pens. from ST JOHN'S, Michs. 1555. B. at Hull, Yorks. B.A. 1558-9. Ord. deacon (London) Jan. 13, 1559-60, age 22.

HULL, HENRY. Matric. pens. from ST JOHN'S, *c.* 1591.

HULL, HUMPHREY. Adm. pens. at KING'S, Easter, 1592. Perhaps s. and h. of Thomas, of Godalming, Surrey. Adm. at Gray's Inn, Oct. 23, 1598; of Windsor, gent. Died before 1646. Donor to the College library. (*Manning and Bray*, I. 607.)

HULL, JAMES. Adm. sizar at JESUS, June 23, 1701. Of Lancashire. Matric. 1701; B.A. 1704-5.

HULLE, JOHN DE. 'KING'S scholar' at Cambridge, 1319. Perhaps preb. of Lincoln, 1333.

HULL, JOHN. Adm. pens. (age 16) at CAIUS, Apr. 8, 1586. S. of William, of Cambridge. Bapt. at Holy Trinity, Mar. 27, 1570. School, Ely (Mr Spight). Matric. 1586; Scholar, 1587-93; B.A. 1589-90; M.A. 1593; B.D. 1600. Fellow, 1595-1602. Incorp. at Oxford, 1594. Afterwards in Ireland. V. of Wallstown, Templeroan, 1615-27. V. of Ballintemple, 1615-25. Precentor of Cloyne, 1616-27. R. of Aglishdrinagh, 1616-27. R. of Shandon, Cork, 1617-27. Author, theological. Died 1627. (*Venn*, I. 127; H. B. Swanzy.)

HULL, JOHN. Adm. pens. at JESUS, Apr. 15, 1646. Of Lancaster.

HULL or HOOLE, JOHN. Adm. sizar at JESUS, May 29, 1680. Of Lancashire. Matric. 1680; B.A. 1683-4. Probably ord. deacon (Chester) May 25, 1684. P.C. of Overton, Lancs., 1684. Perhaps P.C. of Low Church, Walton-le-Dale, 1703-21. Buried there Nov. 4, 1721. Father of Thomas (1721-2). (E. Axon.)

HULL, JOSEPH. Adm. pens. (age 18) at PEMBROKE, Jan. 20, 1668-9. S. of John, gent. B. at Stoke, Suffolk. Adm. at Lincoln's Inn, June 26, 1669.

HULL, LIBEUS. Adm. scholar (age 17) at CAIUS, Apr. 21, 1601. S. of William, gent., of Bury St Edmunds, Suffolk. School, Bury (Mr Marten).

HULL, PETER. Adm. pens. at CHRIST'S, June 27, 1684. Probably did not reside.

HULL, RICHARD. Matric. pens. from TRINITY, Michs. 1620; B.A. 1624-5.

HULL, RICHARD. Adm. sizar (age 17) at SIDNEY, May 7, 1634. S. of John. B. at Uppingham. School, Uppingham (Mr Jo. Clarke). Matric. 1634; B.A. 1637-8; M.A. 1641. Ord. deacon (Peterb.) May 20, 1638.

HULL, RICHARD. Adm. sizar at KING'S, Aug. 1687. B. in London. School, Eton (colleger, 1678-86). Matric. 1688. Migrated to Peterhouse, Apr. 27, 1688. Perhaps schoolmaster at March, Cambs., 1690.

HULL, THOMAS. Adm. pens. at SIDNEY, June 24, 1616. Of Kent. Migrated to Corpus Christi, 1618. B.A. 1619-20; M.A. 1623. Ord. deacon (Peterb.) Oct. 25; priest, Oct. 27, 1623. V. of Godmersham, Kent, 1624-5. R. of Boughton Aluph, in 1642. Married, 1626, Jane Mayler, of Sturry. *See* a contemporary in *Al. Oxon.*

HULL, THOMAS. Adm. sizar at JESUS, Feb. 27, 1721-2. S. of John (1680), clerk, deceased, of Walton-le-Dale, Lancs. Rustat Scholar, 1721; Matric. 1721-2; B.A. 1725-6; M.A. 1729. Ord. priest (Lincoln) May 24, 1730. C. of Elstow, Beds., 1725-6. (W. M. Noble.)

HULL, WILLIAM. Scholar at KING'S HALL, 1411; LL.B. before 1430. R. of Muston, Leics., till 1440. Repaired the church and chancel, in 1425. Died June 3, 1440. M.I. at Muston. (*Nichols*, II. 291.)

HULL, WILLIAM. Matric. sizar from CLARE, Michs. 1579; B.A. 1583-4; B.D. 1602; D.D. 1607. R. of Hawkinge, Kent, 1591-7. V. of Alkham, 1596-1600. R. of Snave, 1597-1600. V. of Teynham, 1600-4. Preb. of Canterbury, 1604-18. V. of Hernhill, till 1605. V. of St Clement's, Sandwich, 1616-8. Died 1618.

HULL, WILLIAM. Matric. sizar from CHRIST'S, Mar. 1582-3; B.A. 1586-7. One of these names King's scholar at Durham, 1580.

HULL, WILLIAM. Matric. sizar from PEMBROKE, Easter, 1614. B. at Witham, Essex. B.A. 1617-8. Ord. priest (London) Dec. 23, 1621, age 26. C. at Aldham, Essex. V. of Ulting, 1637-69. Died 1669.

HULL, WILLIAM. M.A. from CORPUS CHRISTI, 1713. S. of Thomas, of Reading, Berks. Matric. from St Edmund Hall, Oxford, Feb. 17, 1704-5, age 18; B.A. (Oxford) 1708. Perhaps R. of Gt Chart, Kent, 1737-42. Died 1742. (*Al. Oxon.*)

HULL, WILLIAM. Adm. Fell.-Com. at CLARE, Sept. 6, 1718. S. and h. of William, of Exeter. B. there. Adm. at the Middle Temple, Aug. 21, 1717. Called to the Bar, June 28, 1723.

HULL or HULE, ——. D.D. 1487-8. A friar.

HULLER, ROBERT. Matric. sizar from ST JOHN'S, Easter, 1616.

HULLIER, JOHN. Adm. at KING'S, a scholar from Eton, 1538. Conduct of King's. V. of Babraham, Cambs., 1549; and preacher at Lynn. Condemned for heresy, and burnt at Cambridge, Apr. 16, 1555. (*Cooper*, I. 126.)

HULLYER, ROBERT. Matric. pens. from QUEENS', Michs. 1568; B.A. 1572-3; M.A. 1576. *Grace* for M.D. 1583 (did not qualify). Ord. deacon and priest (Norwich) Dec. 18, 1608, as 'M.A., aged 57.'

HULLYER, ——. B.A. 1501. One William Hullyer R. of Warkton, Northants., 1515-54. (T. P. Dorman.)

HULME, GEORGE. Matric. sizar at CHRIST'S, May, 1576. Perhaps P.C. of Weston-on-Trent, Staffs., *c.* 1593; 'Scholaris ruralis.' Ordained by William, Bishop of Chester. (*Wm. Salt Arch. Soc.*, 1915.)

HULME, HUGH. Matric. sizar from ST JOHN'S, Michs. 1566.

HULME or HOLME, MATTHEW. Matric. pens. from ST JOHN'S, Easter, 1562. Of Middlesex. B.A. 1564-5; M.A. 1568. Fellow, 1567. Ord. deacon (Ely) Sept. 21, 1567. V. of Leamington Hastings, Warws. Will (P.C.C.) 1619.

HULME, SAMUEL. Adm. sizar (age 16) at MAGDALENE, June 5, 1674. S. of Robert, of Reddish, Manchester. School, Manchester. Matric. 1674. Not mentioned in the will of his father, of Reddish, yeoman, 1695. (E. Axon.)

HULME, SAMUEL. Adm. sizar at JESUS, May 31, 1680. Of Cheshire. Matric. 1681; B.A. 1683-4; M.A. 1691. Perhaps ord. deacon (Chester) May 29, 1681; priest, June 3, 1683. C. of Knutsford, Cheshire, 1687. Minister of Macclesfield, 1689-1711. R. of Lymm, 1700-11. Died Jan. 27, 1710-1. (E. Axon.)

HULME, THOMAS. Kept ten terms at Cambridge. B.A. from Brasenose College, Oxford, 1596-7; M.A. 1600.

HULSBOS or HULSBESSE, CHRISTIAN. Adm. Fell.-Com. at SIDNEY, June 30, 1616. B. in Belgium. Matric. 1616.

HULSE, EDWARD. Adm. pens. at EMMANUEL, May 30, 1653. Of Stanny, Cheshire. B. 1638. Matric. 1656; B.A. 1656-7; M.A. 1660. Fellow, 1658-1662, ejected. Adm. at Leyden, July 4, 1668; M.D. (Leyden) *c.* 1669. Incorp. at Oxford, 1670. Physician to the court of the Prince of Orange. F.R.C.P., 1677. Treasurer, 1704. Of Baldwin's Park, Kent. Died Dec. 3, 1711. Will (P.C.C.) 1712. Father of the next. (*Munk*, I. 397; *G.E.C.*; *D.N.B.*)

HULSE, EDWARD. Adm. at EMMANUEL, June 16, 1699. S. of Edward (above), M.D. Matric. 1700; M.B. 1704; M.D. 1717. F.R.C.P., 1718. Censor. Elect. Physician-in-ordinary to George II. Created Bart., Feb. 7, 1738-9. Married, at Gray's Inn Chapel, Jan. 15, 1712-3, Elizabeth, dau. of Sir Richard Levett, Knt. Died in Golden Square, London, Apr. 10, 1759, aged 77. Buried at Wilmington, Kent. Father of the next and Richard (1744). (*D.N.B.*; *Munk*, II. 62; *G.E.C.*)

HULSE, EDWARD. Adm. Fell.-Com. at EMMANUEL, July 29, 1732. S. of Sir Edward (above), M.D., Bart. Succeeded as Baronet, 1759. Of Breamore, Hants. High Sheriff of Hants., 1765. Died Dec. 1, 1800. Buried at Wilmington, Kent. Will, P.C.C.

HULCE, GEORGE (1580), *see* HULES.

HULSE, GEORGE. Matric. pens. from CORPUS CHRISTI, Easter, 1611. Of Suffolk. B.A. 1613-4; M.A. 1617.

HULSE, JOHN. Adm. sizar at CAIUS, Sept. 29, 1579. Probably S. of John, husbandman. B. at Cossington, Leics. Schools, Cossington and Seagrave (Mr Both and Sim. Parret). Migrated to Trinity. Matric. 1583; B.A. 1588-9. (*Venn*, I. 104.)

HULSE, JOHN. Adm. pens. (age 16) at ST JOHN'S, Sept. 14, 1724. S. of Thomas, of Elworth Hall, Sandbach, Cheshire, gent. B. at Middlewich. Schools, Congleton and Stockport (Mr Dale). Matric. 1724; B.A. 1728. Ord. priest (Lichfield) Sept 24, 1732. C. at Yoxall, Staffs.; and Witton and Goostry, Cheshire, till 1753, when he succeeded to the family estates at Elworth. Founder of the Hulsean endowments in the University. Died Dec. 14, 1790. (*D.N.B.*; J. W. Clark's *Endowments*; *Scott-Mayor*, III. 374.)

HULSE, RICHARD. Adm. pens. (age 17) at PETERHOUSE, Oct. 31, 1744. Of London. S. of Sir Edward (1699), Bart. School, Charterhouse. Scholar, 1744; Matric. 1745. Adm. at Lincoln's Inn, Oct. 23, 1746. Brother of Edward (1732).

HULTON, EDWARD. M.A. from QUEENS', 1722. S. of James, of Todmorden, Lancs. Matric. from Brasenose College, Oxford, Mar. 19, 1710-1, age 17; B.A. (Oxford) 1714. (*Al. Oxon.*)

HULTON, RALPH. 'M.D. of Cambridge.' Incorp. at Oxford, July 3, 1603. Not found in our records. One of these names preb. of Salisbury, 1600.

HULTON, ROBERT. M.A. from CLARE, 1669. S. of Richard, of Blackburn, Lancs., clerk. Matric. from All Souls, Oxford, May 22, 1663, age 19; B.A. (Oxford) 1666-7. V. of Shorwell, Isle of Wight, 1676. V. of Kingston, 1682. (*Al. Oxon.*)

HULTON, ——. Matric. pens. from ST JOHN'S, Easter, 1544.

HULWOOD or HULLWODE, JOHN. Matric. sizar from PEMBROKE, Easter, 1607; B.A. 1610-1; M.A. 1614.

HULYE, WILLIAM. Matric. pens. from ST JOHN'S, Michs. 1575; B.A. 1579-80.

HUMBERSTONE, CHARLES. Matric. pens. from TRINITY, Easter, 1578; B.A. 1581-2.

HUMBERSTON, EDWARD. Matric. pens. from ST CATHARINE'S, Easter, 1641; B.A. 1644-5; M.A. 1652 (Incorp. from Oxford). Incorp. at Oxford (B.A.) 1648. Fellow of St John's, Oxford, 1648-60, ejected. Afterwards of Pembroke College. (*Al. Oxon.*)

HUMBERSTONE, HENRY. Matric. pens. from CORPUS CHRISTI, Michs. 1582; B.A. 1585-6; M.A. 1589.

HUMBERSTON, HENRY. Matric. p . from TRINITY, Michs. 1618. One of these names, s. and h. of William, of Hempton, Norfolk, Esq., adm. at Lincoln's Inn, June 26, 1626, from Furnival's Inn.

HUMBERSTON, JOHN. Adm. pens. at ST CATHARINE'S, 1640. Of Huntingdonshire.

HUMBERSTONE, MATTHEW. Adm. Fell.-Com. at ST JOHN'S, May 23, 1720. S. of Edward, gent., of Hampshire. B. at Portsmouth. Schools, Bishop's Stortford and Enfield. Matric. 1720. Probably of Humberstone, Lincs.; died Jan. 3, 1735-6, aged 31. (*Lincs. Pedigrees*, 522.)

HUMBERSTON, ROBERT. Adm. scholar (age 16) at CAIUS, Apr. 2, 1581. S. of Edward, yeoman. B. at Earith, Hunts. School, Ely. B.A. 1583-4. One of these names adm. at Douay College, Oct. 15, 1587. Left, Sept. 23, 1588. (*Venn*, I. 110.)

HUMBERSTONE, THOMAS. Matric. pens. from TRINITY, Easter, 1612.

HUMBERSTON, THOMAS. Matric. sizar from MAGDALENE, Easter, 1615.

HUMBERSTONE, WILLIAM. Matric. pens. from TRINITY, Easter, 1578. One of these names adm. at Gray's Inn, 1580. Perhaps s. of William, author of *Humberstone's Survey*, 1570. (*Yorks. Arch. Journal*, XVII. 129.)

HUMBERSTON, WILLIAM. Matric. pens. from PEMBROKE, Michs. 1588. One of these names, of Yardley, Herts., adm. at Gray's Inn, Aug. 12, 1592. Perhaps s. of Edward, of Walkern, Herts. (*Lincs. Pedigrees*, 521.)

HUMBERSTON, WILLIAM. Matric. pens. from TRINITY, Michs. 1618. Perhaps of Ripon, Yorks. Married Bridget, dau. of Giles Parker, of Scotton, and widow of Michael Wandesford, Dean of Limerick. (J. Parker.)

HUMBLE, Sir GEORGE, Bart. Adm. Fell.-Com. (age 17) at TRINITY, Apr. 10, 1695. S. of George (and grandson of Sir William, Bart.). B. at Stratford-juxta-Bow, Essex. School, Twickenham, Middlesex. Matric. 1695. Killed in a quarrel at the Blue Posts Tavern, Mar. 1702-3. (Burke, *Ext. Bart.*; *G.E.C.*)

HUMBLE, SAMUEL. M.A. 1677 (Incorp. from Glasgow).

HUMBLE, TIMOTHY. Matric. sizar from EMMANUEL, Michs. 1601; Scholar; B.A. 1605-6; M.A. 1609. Ord. deacon (York) Sept. 1608. V. of Brafferton, Yorks., 1615-34. Died 1634.

HUMBLE, WILLIAM. Adm. Fell.-Com. at TRINITY, June 17, 1671. Probably 2nd s. of Sir William, of London, Bart. Matric. 1671. Created Baronet, Mar. 17, 1686-7. Married (1) Frances, dau. of Sir Anthony Hasilrigge, Bart.; (2) Mary, dau. of —— Fisher, of Isleworth. Died Aug. 12, 1705, *s.p.* Buried at Twickenham. (Burke, *Ext. Bart.*; *G.E.C.*)

HUME or HOME, ALEXANDER. Adm. Fell.-Com. at ST CATHARINE'S, June 17, 1737. S. of Alexander, Earl of Home, deceased. In holy orders. Succeeded his brother William, as 9th Earl of Home, 1761. Died Oct. 8, 1786. Buried at Home Castle. (*G.E.C.*; *The Scots Peerage*, IV. 481.)

HUME, DANIEL. Adm. sizar (age 18) at MAGDALENE, July 3, 1723. S. of James (1691). B. at Laughton, Lincs. School, Brigg. Matric. 1723; B.A. 1726-7. Ord. deacon (Lincoln) May 28, 1727. Brother of John (1722).

HUME ('HUMIUS'), GASPER. M.A. 1633 (Incorp. from Edinburgh). M.A. there, 1619. According to *Al. Oxon.*, one of these names supplicated for B.A. at Oxford, in 1633, after four years at Edinburgh.

HUME, GEORGE. Adm. pens. (age 16) at SIDNEY, May 1, 1675. 1st s. of George, Master at Tiverton School, Devon. B. at Barnstaple. Schools, Barnstaple and Tiverton. Matric. 1675; B.A. 1678-9; M.A. 1682. Probably ord. deacon (Carlisle) Dec. 21, 1684. R. of Beaumont, Cumberland, 1692-1703. Buried there May 12, 1703. (*B. Nightingale.*)

HUME or HUMES, JAMES. Adm. sizar (age 15) at SIDNEY, June 1, 1691. S. of John (1651), R. of Yelling, Hunts. Educated at home. Matric. 1691; B.A. 1694-5; M.A. 1709. Ord. deacon (Lincoln) May 19, 1695; priest, Sept. 20, 1696. R. of Flixburgh, Lincs., 1698. V. of Prodingham. V. of Laughton, 1711. V. of Bradwell, Bucks., 1729-34. Buried there Feb. 7, 1734. Father of John (1722) and Daniel (1723).

HUMES, JOHN. M.A. 1622 (Incorp. from St Andrews). Graduate from Sedan. B.D. from JESUS, 1629. Fellow, 1624-30, by royal mandate. V. of Guilden Morden, Cambs., 1626-7. One of these names V. of Branxton, Northumberland, 1627-62; died 1662.

HUME, JOHN. M.A. 1634 (Incorp. from Edinburgh and Oxford). M.A. (Edinburgh) 1627. Incorp. at Oxford, 1630. R. of Charlton, Kent, 1636-43, ejected. (*Al. Oxon.*; *Calamy*, III. 75.)

HUME or HUMES, JOHN. Adm. sizar (age 16) at ST JOHN'S, June 12, 1651. S. of Robert, clerk, of Crathorne, Yorks. B. at Acklam, Yorks. School, Danby Wiske, Yorks. (private). Matric. 1651; B.A. 1654-5; M.A. 1660. R. of Yelling, Hunts., 1667-92. R. of Offord Cluny, 1678-92. Died 1692. Father of James (1691) and perhaps of William (1677).

HUME, JOHN. Adm. sizar (age 18) at MAGDALENE, Apr. 25, 1722. S. of James (1691), clerk. B. at Laughton, Lincs. School, Glamford Bridge. Matric. 1723; B.A. 1725-6. Ord. priest (Lincoln) June 1, 1729. Brother of Daniel (1723).

HUMES, PETER. Adm. pens. at TRINITY, May 10, 1659. Of Kent. Scholar from Westminster. Matric. 1659. Perhaps adm. at the Inner Temple, Nov. 3, 1670; of Westminster, gent.

HUME, TIMOTHY. Adm. sizar (age 20) at ST JOHN'S, June 29, 1704. S. of Robert, clerk. B. at Lazonby, Cumberland. School, Sedbergh. Matric. 1704; B.A. 1707-8. Ord. deacon (London) Feb. 1707-8.

HUME, WILLIAM. Adm. pens. (age 17) at PETERHOUSE, Apr. 20, 1668. Of Durham. School, Coniscliffe. Matric. 1668, as 'Hines'; Scholar, 1668; B.A. 1671-2; M.A. 1675. P.C. of Chester-le-Street, Durham, 1673-4. (*T. A. Walker.*)

HUME, WILLIAM. Adm. pens. (age 14) at ST JOHN'S, July 6, 1677. S. of John (? 1651), clerk. B. at Crayke, Yorks. School, York (Mr Langley). Matric. 1677; B.A. 1681-2; M.A. 1685. Perhaps P.C. of Ramsey, Hunts., 1686-7.

HUME, WILLIAM. M.A. from MAGDALENE, 1726. Probably s. of James, of Scotton, Lincs., clerk. Matric. from Exeter College, Oxford, Mar. 11, 1714-5, age 14; B.A. (Oxford) 1718. Perhaps ord. deacon (Lincoln) Dec. 23, 1722; priest, Dec. 20, 1724. (*Al. Oxon.*)

HUMPHREYS, ARTHUR. M.A. 1675 (Incorp. from Oxford). S. of 'Humphrey Thomas,' of Mantry, Montgom. Matric. from Balliol College, June 3, 1663, age 17; B.A. (Oxford) 1666-7; M.A. 1670. R. of Bedford St Peter Martin, 1673. R. of Barton-le-Clay, Beds., 1677. (*Al. Oxon.*)

HUMFREY, CHARLES. Adm. sizar at JESUS, June 23, 1682. S. of John, R. of Ruckland, Lincs. B. at Farforth, Lincs., Apr. 23, 1666. Matric. 1682; B.A. 1685-6. Founded scholarships at Jesus. Died May 25, 1719. M.I. at Ruckland. (A. Gray.)

HUMPHREY or UMPHREY, CHRISTOPHER. Adm. sizar at EMMANUEL, Mar. 1608-9. Matric. 1609; Scholar; B.A. 1612-3; M.A. 1616. Incorp. at Oxford, 1616. Ord. deacon (Peterb.) Apr. 2; priest, Apr. 3, 1618. V. of Pinchbeck, Lincs., 1618.

HUMPHREYS, DAVID. Adm. sizar at EMMANUEL, Sept. 5, 1653. Of Chester. Matric. 1653-4; B.A. 1657-8. Perhaps V. of Bromborough, Cheshire, 1660. (E. Axon.)

HUMPHREYS, DAVID. Adm. sizar (age 18) at TRINITY, Mar. 5, 1708. S. of Thomas, of London, citizen and leather-seller. B. Jan. 1689-90. Schools, Merchant Taylors' and Christ's Hospital. Grecian from Christ's Hospital. Matric. 1708; Scholar, 1709; B.A. 1711-2; M.A. 1715; B.D. 1725; D.D. 1728 (*Lit. Reg.*). Fellow, 1719. Supported Bentley at Trinity. Secretary to the S.P.G., 1716-40. Ord. deacon (London) Apr. 25; priest, Apr. 29, 1722. V. of Ware, Herts., 1730-40. V. of Thundridge, 1732. Author, translations, etc. Died 1740. (*D.N.B.*)

HUMPHREY, EDMUND. B.A. 1532-3. Of Ipswich. M.A. 1536-7. Fellow of QUEENS', 1533-44. Proctor, 1540-1. Ord. priest (Norwich) Mar. 13, 1534-5. V. of Melbourne, Cambs., 1544.

HUMPHRY, EDMUND. Matric. Fell.-Com. from TRINITY, Michs. 1610. Perhaps s. of Richard, of Rettendon, Essex, gent.; adm. at Lincoln's Inn, May 12, 1612. Perhaps will (P.C.C.) 1634; of Rettendon, Esq.

HUMFREY, EDMUND. Adm. pens. at TRINITY, Oct. 2, 1635. Perhaps 2nd s. of Richard, of Rettendon, Essex. (*Vis. of Essex*, 1634.)

HUMFREY, EDMUND. Adm. at CORPUS CHRISTI, 1660. Of Essex.

HUMPHREY, EDMUND. Adm. pens. (age 15) at SIDNEY, June 25, 1668. S. of Edmund, yeoman. B. at Clavering, Essex. School, Walden, Essex. Matric. 1668; B.A. 1671-2. Signed for deacon's orders (London) Sept. 20, 1673. C. of Stoke Pelham, Herts.

HUMPHREYS, EVAN. M.A. from ST JOHN'S, 1681. S. of 'Hum. Davis,' of Llanvihangel, Monm., clerk. Matric. from Balliol College, Oxford, May 27, 1669, age 18; B.A. (Oxford) 1672-3. V. of Llanyblodwell, Salop, 1674. R. of Llanymynech, 1686. (*Al. Oxon.*)

HUMPHREY or UMFREY, FINCH. Adm. pens. (age 16) at PEMBROKE, May 14, 1692. S. of Finch, of Kent. Matric. 1692. Adm. at Gray's Inn, Nov. 9, 1692; s. and h. of Finch, of Fawkham, Kent, deceased. Probably of Darenth, Kent, Esq.; and father of the next. (*Hasted*, II. 592.)

HUMFREY or UMFREY, FINCH. Adm. pens. (age 16) at PEMBROKE, June 4, 1718. S. of Finch (? above), of Grimstead Green (*sic.*), Kent, Esq. Matric. 1717. Probably of Dartford, Kent, Esq.

HUMPHREYS, HENRY. Adm. sizar (age 17) at ST JOHN'S, Apr. 12, 1662. S. of Rowland, deceased, of Llaneilian, Anglesey. School, Beaumaris (Mr Williams). Matric. 1662; B.A. 1665-6. Ord. priest (Ely) Dec. 20, 1668.

HUMFREY, HENRY. M.A. from EMMANUEL, 1724. S. of Tobias, of Askern, Yorks. Bapt. at Campsall, Dec. 3, 1675. Matric. from University College, Oxford, Oct. 26, 1694, age 18; B.A. (Oxford) 1698. V. of Otley, Yorks., 1708-43. Buried there Nov. 8, 1743. (*Al. Oxon.*; M. H. Peacock.)

HUMPHREY or UMPHRA, HUGH. B.A. 1480-1; M.A. 1483-4; B.D. 1493. Probably D.D. 1501-2. Preb. of Lichfield (B.D.) 1502-30.

HUMPHREYS, HUGH. Adm. sizar (age 16) at ST JOHN'S, June 30, 1705. S. of Thomas, gent. B. at North Hope, Flints. School, North Hope (Mr Lloyd). Matric. 1706; B.A. 1709-10. Ord. deacon (Ely) Dec. 23, 1711; C. of Haslingfield, Cambs. One of these names C. or minister of Alderley, Cheshire, 1715-42. Buried there Oct. 29, 1742. (Earwaker, *E. Cheshire*, II. 635.)

HOMFRAY, JOHN. Matric. pens. from CHRIST'S, Nov. 1544. (*Cooper*, II. 80, suggests that John is a mistake for Laurence, whom *see*.)

HUMFREY, JOHN. Matric. sizar from KING'S, Lent, 1577-8.

HUMPHREY, JOHN. Adm. pens. at EMMANUEL, June 14, 1609. Matric. 1609; B.A. 1613-4.

HUMFREY, JOHN. Matric. pens. from TRINITY, Easter, 1613. Probably s. of Michael and Dorothy (Bawler), of Chaldon, Dorset. B. *c.* 1596. Scholar, 1614. One of the 'Dorchester adventurers' for trading to New England. Emigrated, in 1634, to Salem, where he held office in the colony; major-general of the militia, etc. Returned to England, *c.* 1642. Colonel in the Parliamentary army. At the trial of the King he bore the sword of state before the president, John Bradshaw. Died Dec. 1651. (J. G. Bartlett.)

HUMFRY, HUMPHREYS or UMFRAY, JOHN. Adm. pens. (age 16) at CHRIST'S, Mar. 21, 1630-1. S. of John. B. at Bocking, Essex. School, Thurlow, Suffolk (Mr Moore). B.A. 1634; M.A. 1638. One of these names V. of Frome Selwood, Somerset, about 1648-62. (*Peile*, I. 407, 446.)

HUMPHREY, JOHN. Adm. sizar at JESUS, Jan. 15, 1633-4. Of Northamptonshire. Matric. 1634; B.A. 1637-8; M.A. 1641. Ord. deacon (Peterb.) Mar. 10, 1638-9. V. of Rothwell, Northants., 1663. Died Oct. 19, 1679.

HUMFRIE, JOHN. Adm. pens. at EMMANUEL, May 28, 1644. Of Lincolnshire. Matric. 1644. Perhaps s. of Christopher, of Pinchbeck; adm. at Gray's Inn, Mar. 10, 1648-9.

HUMPHREY, JOHN. Adm. pens. at CLARE, June 24, 1648. Matric. 1648; B.A. 1651-2.

HUMFREY, JOHN. Adm. sizar at JESUS, May 1, 1650. Of Suffolk. Matric. 1650; B.A. 1653-4; Scholar, 1654; M.A. 1657. One of these names R. of Spexhall, Suffolk, 1691.

HUMPHREYS, JOHN. Adm. sizar (age 17) at JESUS, June 8 1665. Of Flintshire. Matric. 1665; B.A. 1668-9; M.A. 1672. Ord. deacon (York) Mar. 1668-9; priest (Gloucester) Feb. 27, 1669-70. V. of Guilden Morden, Cambs., till 1677. (A. Gray.)

HUMPHREYS, JOHN. Adm. sizar (age 16) at ST JOHN'S, July 14, 1683. S. of Thomas, deceased. B. at Llanvachreth, Merioneth. School, Wrexham (Mr Lewis). Matric. 1684; B.A. 1687-8.

HUMPHREYS, JOHN. Adm. sizar (age 20) at TRINITY, June 21, 1690. S. of John. B. at Llanrwst, Denbigh. School, Ruthin (Mr Henry Price). Matric. 1690; B.A. 1693-4; M.A. 1697. Brother of Thomas (1689).

HUMPHREYS, JOHN. M.A. from KING'S, 1714. S. of Evan (? 1681), of Llangineth, Salop, clerk. Matric. from Merton College, Oxford, Feb. 26, 1706-7, age 17; B.A. (Oxford) 1710-1. R. of Llanfihangel-yng-Nghwynfa, Montgom., 1717-23. V. of Myfod, 1723. Preb. of St Asaph, 1737-40. (*Al. Oxon.*)

HUMPHREY or UMFREY, LAURENCE. D.D. 1569 (Incorp. from Oxford). B. at Newport Pagnell, Bucks. Scholar of Magdalen College, Oxford, 1546; B.A. (Oxford) 1549; M.A. 1551-2; B.D. 1562; D.D. 1562. Fellow of Magdalen College, 1548-56. Regius Professor of Divinity at Oxford, 1560-89. President of Magdalen College, 1561-89. Vice-Chancellor (Oxford) 1571-6. Dean of Gloucester, 1571-85. Dean of Winchester, 1580-9. R. of Meonstoke, Hants., 1581. Author. Died Feb. 1, 1588-9. (*Al. Oxon.*; *D.N.B.*)

HUMFREY, LAURENCE. Matric. sizar from QUEENS', Lent, 1575-6. Of Nottinghamshire.

HUMPHRY, NATHANIEL. Adm. sizar (age 16) at PEMBROKE, May 30, 1640. S. of Simon (1610), clerk. B. at Melton Mowbray, Leics. Matric. 1640; B.A. 1643-4. Ord. deacon (Lincoln) Mar. 2, 1644-5; priest, Mar. 3, 1644-5. Brother of Simon (1645).

HUMFREY, NATHANIEL. LL.D. 1728 (*Com. Reg.*). S. of Raphael, of the Inner Temple, and of Thorpe Mandeville, Esq. B. in London, *c.* 1679. Barrister-at-law. Ord. deacon (Peterb.) Nov. 20, 1720; priest, Sept. 24, 1721. C. of Thorpe Mandeville, Northants., 1720; R. 1727-44. Married there, Mar. 5, 1716-7, Abigail, dau. of Thomas Pargiter, D.D. Died Mar. 3, 1744, aged 68. Buried at Thorpe. M.I. (*Baker*, I. 722; *Nichols*, III. 1050; H. I. Longden.)

HUMPHRE, NUTTALL. Matric. pens. from ST CATHARINE'S, Michs. 1633; B.A. 1636-7.

HUMPHREYS, OWEN. Adm. sizar (age 21) at TRINITY, Nov. 12, 1723. Previously matric. from Jesus College, Oxford, Feb. 21, 1722-3, as s. of Humphrey, of Abererch, Co. Carnarvon. S. of Owen. School, Bangor (Mr Dolben). Age 21. Matric. 1724; B.A. 1726-7.

HUMPHREY or UMFRIE, RICHARD. Matric. pens. from PETERHOUSE, Michs. 1568.

HUMPHREY or UMPHRIE, RICHARD. B.A. from EMMANUEL, 1605-6. B. at Caster, Northants. M.A. 1609. Ord. deacon (London) Sept. 25, 1609, age 30, as C. of Gt Hadham, Herts. Perhaps ord. priest (Chichester) 1614; and R. of Taverham, Norfolk, 1626.

HUMPHREYS, RICHARD. B.A. from JESUS, 1607-8; M.A. 1611. Ord. priest (Peterb.) Sept. 23, 1610. R. of Edgcote, Northants., 1615-21. Died 1621. (H. I. Longden.)

HUMPHREYS, RICHARD. Adm. Fell.-Com. (age 17) at CHRIST'S, Apr. 2, 1658. S. of Richard, of Rettendon, Essex. B. at Fremell, near Downham, Essex. School, Chelmsford (Mr Peake). Matric. 1658. Died in College, Aug. 7, 1659. M.I. in Gt St Andrew's. (*Peile*, I. 580.)

HUMFREY, RICHARD. Adm. at CORPUS CHRISTI, 1739. Of Norwich. S. of Richard, merchant, of Norwich. B. there, 1721. Matric. 1739; B.A. 1742-3; M.A. 1746. Fellow, 1745-9. Ord. deacon (Ely) Mar. 1746-7; priest (Norwich) June, 1747. R. of Thorpe, near Norwich, 1753-1813. R. of Smallburgh, 1762-1813. Died at Thorpe, Jan. 16, 1813, aged 91. (*Masters-Lamb*, 397.)

HUMPHREYS, RICHARD ROBINS. Adm. sizar (age 17) at PEMBROKE, June 6, 1699. S. of John, of London. B. at Hollowell, Guilsborough, Northants. Bapt. there, Apr. 16, 1682. School, Kibworth, Leics. Matric. 1699. (H. I. Longden.)

HUMFREY, RIS (?). Matric. pens. from JESUS, Michs. 1589.

HUMPHREY or UMPHREY, ROBERT. B.A. from CORPUS CHRISTI, 1604-5; M.A. 1608. Ord. deacon (London) Dec. 20, 1612.

HUMPHREY or UMPHRY, SIMON. Adm. sizar at SIDNEY, June 29, 1610. Matric. 1610; B.A. 1613-4; M.A. 1617. Ord. deacon (Peterb.) Sept. 20; priest, Sept. 21, 1618. Head Master of Melton Mowbray. Head Master of Stamford, 1638-57. Buried at St George's, Stamford, Dec. 8, 1657. Will (P.C.C.) 1657. Father of the next and of Nathaniel (1640).

HUMFREY, SIMON. Adm. sizar at CAIUS, May 23, 1645. S. of Simon (above), Master of Stamford School. B. at Melton Mowbray, Leics. Schools, Melton Mowbray and Stamford. Migrated to St John's, Apr. 1, 1646, age 17. B.A. 1647-8. Brother of Nathaniel (1640). (*Venn*, I. 358.)

HUMPHREY or UMFRIE, THOMAS. Matric. pens. from PETERHOUSE, Michs. 1568.

HUMFREY or UMPHREY, THOMAS. Matric. pens. from CHRIST'S, Easter, 1581; B.A. 1584-5; M.A. 1588. Ord. deacon and priest (Lincoln) Sept. 7, 1591. R. of Grainsby, Lincs., 1591-1635. Author, *Jewel for Gentlewomen*. Will (P.C.C.) 1635. (*Cooper*, II. 41.)

HUMPHRIE, THOMAS. Matric. pens. from QUEENS', Easter, 1612. Of Lincolnshire. Died in College. Buried at St Botolph's, Cambridge, Jan. 1, 1614-5.

HUMPHREYS, THOMAS. Adm. pens. at EMMANUEL, Mar. 2, 1635-6. Of Suffolk. Matric. 1636. Perhaps s. and h. of Charles, of Harleston, Suffolk, gent.; adm. at Gray's Inn, Feb. 18, 1641-2, from Furnival's Inn.

HUMPHREY, THOMAS. Adm. pens. at EMMANUEL, Feb. 3, 1640-1. One of these names, s. of Sir Thomas, Knt. (? of Swepston, Leics.), adm. at Oundle School, Mar. 4, 1636-7, age 13.

HUMPHREYS, THOMAS. Adm. sizar (age 18) at TRINITY, Aug. 5, 1689. S. of John, of Llandovery. School, Ruthin, Denbigh (Mr Henry Price). Matric. 1689; Scholar, 1693; B.A. 1693-4; M.A. 1697. Ord. priest (York) Sept. 1697. Brother of John (1690).

HUMPHREYS, THOMAS. Adm. sizar (age 16) at ST JOHN'S, Feb. 22, 1704-5. S. of Thomas, gent. B. in London, Oct. 8, 1686. School, Merchant Taylors'. Matric. 1705.

HUMFREY, WILLIAM. Matric. sizar from ST JOHN'S, *c.* 1595; B.A. 1599-1600; M.A. 1604.

HUMPHRY or UMFRIE, WILLIAM. Matric. sizar from TRINITY, *c.* 1596. S. of Nicholas, of Dorset and Worcester. Scholar, 1599; B.A. 1599-1600; M.A. 1603; B.D. 1610. Fellow, 1602. R. of Humbleton, Yorks., 1606-7. R. of Sproatley, 1607-26. Perhaps R. of Acklam, 1613. Chaplain to King James. Probably R. of Averham, Notts.; and preb. of Southwell, till 1624. Married Anne, dau. of Charles Hall, of Gretford, Lincs. Died 1626. (*Vis. of Yorks.*, 1665.)

HUMPHREY, WILLIAM. Adm. pens. at EMMANUEL, Easter, 1625. Matric. 1625; B.A. 1628-9.

HUMPHREYS, WILLIAM. Adm. at KING'S, a scholar from Eton, 1718. S. of William. Bapt. in Fleet St, Aug. 15, 1699. Matric. 1718-9; B.A. 1722-3. Fellow, 1721. 'Accidentally burnt to death; buried in the College Chapel.' (*Harwood.*)

HUMPHREES, WILLIAM DOBYNS. Adm. pens. (age 17) at TRINITY, Sept. 3, 1743. S. of Thomas, of London. School, Fulham (Mr Croft). Matric. 1743; B.A. 1747-8; M.A. 1751. Ord. deacon (Ely) Oct. 29, 1749; priest, Sept. 22, 1751. R. of Crownthorpe, Norfolk, 1755-1804.

HUMPHREY, ——. M.A. 1507.

HUMPTON, ANTHONY, *see* HUNTON.

HUMPTON, WILLIAM. Adm. sizar (age 18) at ST JOHN'S, May 14, 1703. S. of Richard, husbandman. B. at Hunmanby, Yorks. School, Beverley (Mr Lambert). Matric. 1703; B.A. 1706-7; M.A. 1717. Ord. deacon (York) May, 1708; priest, 1713. V. of Ecclesall, Yorks., 1720-52. Assistant minister of Sheffield. Died June 28, 1752.

HUNDON, THOMAS. Fellow of PEMBROKE. Ord. deacon (Ely) Mar. 18, 1384-5; priest, Apr. 1, 1385.

HUNDEN, ——. B.A. 1468-9.

HUNGATE, HENRY. Adm. Fell.-Com. (age 15) at CAIUS, Nov. 28, 1613. S. of William, Esq., of East Bradenham, Norfolk. Schools, St Julian's and St Albans, Herts. (Mr Heyward). Matric. 1614. Adm. at Gray's Inn, Feb. 8, 1614-5. Knighted, Apr. 20, 1619. M.P. for Camelford, 1625; for Newport (Cornwall) 1626. Of St Martin-in-the-Fields. Probably sequestered as a royalist. Will (P.C.C.) 1648. (*Venn*, I. 223; Carthew, *Bradenham*.)

HUNGATE, RALPH. Matric. pens. from JESUS, Easter, 1614.

HUNGAT, ROBERT. Matric. pens. from ST JOHN'S, Lent, 1563-4. S. of William, of Saxton, Yorks. Adm. at Lincoln's Inn, Nov. 5, 1567. Barrister, 1579. Founder (by will) of the Grammar School and Hospital of Sherburn, Yorks. Of Sand Hutton, Yorks., Esq. Married Catharine, widow of Sir William Bamburgh. Died July 25, 1619. Buried at St Cuthbert's, York. M.I. Will (York) 1620. (*Vis. of Yorks.*; M. H. Peacock.)

HUNGATE, THOMAS. Matric. pens. from St JOHN'S, Michs. 1571.

HUNGATE, WILLIAM. Matric. pens. from TRINITY, Michs. 1565. One of these names adm. at Gray's Inn, 1571, from Staple Inn. Perhaps s. of William, of Saxton, Yorks.; and father of the next.

HUNGAYTE, WILLIAM. Adm. Fell.-Com. (age 16) at CAIUS, Oct. 16, 1585. S. of William (? above). B. at Saxton, Yorks. School, Sherburn. Probably adm. at Lincoln's Inn, Feb. 19, 1589–90. Of Saxton, Esq. Built Huddleston Hall, Sherburn. Knighted, at York, Apr. 11, 1617. Died Dec. 1634. Admon., York. (*Venn*, I. 126; *Vis. of Yorks.*, 1666.)

HUNGATE, WILLIAM. Matric. pens. from JESUS, Easter, 1614. Perhaps adm. at Gray's Inn, Nov. 8, 1615; s. of William, of North Dalton, Yorks.

HUNGERFORD, JOHN. M.A. 1683 (*Lit. Reg.*). S. and h. of Richard, of Wiltshire. Adm. at Lincoln's Inn, Aug. 7, 1677. Barrister. M.P. for Scarborough, 1692–5, 1702–5, 1707–29. Counsel for the East India Company. Commissioner in the Alienation Office, 1712. Died June 8, 1729. Benefactor to King's College. (*D.N.B.*)

HUNGERFORD, JOHN (D.D. 1701), *see* INETT.

HUNKES, FULK. M.A. 1635–6 (*Lit. Reg.*).

HUNLEY (? *R*), **WILLIAM.** Matric. sizar from St JOHN'S, Michs. 1546.

HUNLOCK, HENRY. Matric. Fell.-Com. from PETERHOUSE, Michs. 1580. Doubtless s. of Henry, of Wingerworth, Derbs., Esq. (who died 1612). B.A. 1583–4. Adm. at the Inner Temple, 1584 (printed volume of admissions probably in error as to parentage). Of Wingerworth, Esq. Sheriff of Derbs., 1624. Married (2) Anne, dau. of Richard Alvey, of Derbs. Died Aug. 17, 1624. Father of the next. (*Kimber*, I. 496; *T. A. Walker*; *Her. and Gen.*, III. 422.)

HUNLOCK, HENRY. Matric. Fell.-Com. from CORPUS CHRISTI, Easter, 1633. Of Derbyshire. S. and h. of Henry (above), of Wingerworth, Derbs., Esq., deceased. Bapt. Oct. 28, 1618. Adm. at Gray's Inn, May 14, 1636. Fought at Edgehill, 1642. Knighted there, Mar. 2, 1642–3. Created a Baronet, Feb. 28, 1642–3. Married Marina, dau. of Dixey Hickman, of Kew, Surrey. Died at Wingerworth, Jan. 14, 1647–8. Will, P.C.C. (*G.E.C.*; *T. A. Walker*.)

HUNLOCK, Sir HENRY, Bart. Adm. Fell.-Com. at TRINITY, 1662. S. of Sir Henry (above), of Wingerworth, Derbs., Bart. Bapt. at St Michael's, Bedwardine, Worcs., Nov. 21, 1645. Adm. at Gray's Inn, Dec. 16, 1654. Succeeded his father, Jan. 1647–8. Married Catherine, dau. of Francis Tyrwhitt, of Kettleby, Lincs. Buried at Wingerworth, Jan. 5, 1714–5. Will, P.C.C. (*Kimber*, I. 498; *G.E.C.*)

HUNNE, EDMUND. Adm. sizar at EMMANUEL, June 19, 1603. Matric. 1603; B.A. 1606–7; M.A. 1610.

HUNNE, ERASMUS. Matric. pens. from CHRIST'S, Mar. 1577–8. Migrated to Trinity Hall. Scholar there, 1581; B.A. 1581–2. One of these names P.C. of Raveley Chapel, Hunts., 1605. C. of Hethersett, Norfolk, 1609–15. (*Peile*, I. 144.)

HUNN, JOHN. Adm. sizar (age 17) at St JOHN'S, Feb. 9, 1677–8. S. of John, deceased. B. at Lutton, in Long Sutton, Lincs. School, Grantham (Mr Walker). Matric. 1677–8; B.A. 1681–2; M.A. 1685. Ord. priest (Norwich) Sept. 1687. R. of Little Fransham, Norfolk, 1687–94.

HUNNE, MILES. Matric. pens. from CHRIST'S, May, 1568. Ord. deacon (Norwich) Apr. 1569; priest, Feb. 1572. R. of Hethersett, Norfolk, 1573; deprived, 1596; restored, 1603–15. Also of Forncett St Mary and St Peter, 1588. Chaplain to the Countess of Essex. Will (P.C.C.) 1615; as R. of Hethersett. (*Peile*, I. 104.)

HUNNE, THOMAS. Adm. pens. at EMMANUEL, Apr. 21, 1597. (? S. of the above.) Matric. *c.* 1597; B.A. 1600–1; M.A. 1604. Ord. deacon and p (Norwich) May 22, 1608. C. of Hethersett, Norfolk[illegible]. of Hethersett, 1609–17. R. of Forncett, 1615.

HUNN, ——. Adm. pens. at St CATHARINE'S, 1675. One Tobias Hunn, s. and h. of Thomas, of St Margaret's, Ilketshall, Suffolk, age 5 in 1664. (*Vis. of Suffolk.*)

HUNNALE, JOHN. Adm. at KING'S (age 16) a scholar from Eton, 1476. Of Cambridge B.A. 1480–1; M.A. 1484. *Cautio* for degree (? B.D.), 1489–90.

HUNNINGS or HONNINGE, EDWARD. Matric. pens. from CHRIST'S, Oct. 1567. Afterwards Fell.-Com. Probably eldest s. of William, of Carleton, Suffolk. One Edward Hunings adm. at Gray's Inn, 1570. Of Darsham, Suffolk. (*Peile*, I. 102; *Vis. of Suffolk*, 1577.)

HUNNINGS, NICHOLAS. Matric. pens. from St JOHN'S, Easter, 1576.

HUNNINGE, ROGER. Adm. pens. (age 17) at CAIUS, Apr. 27, 1579. S. of Peter, citizen of London. School, Merchant Taylors'. Matric. 1579; Scholar, till 1586; B.A. 1582–3. Incorp. at Oxford, 1584. (*Venn*, I. 102.)

HUNNINGE, THOMAS. Matric. pens. from CHRIST'S, Nov. 1550. Probably one of the Honnyngs of Carleton, Suffolk.

HUNNINGHAM, THURSTAN. University Bedell, *c.* 1315. Chaplain of the University. (Stokes, *Bedells*, 59; *Chaplains*, 81.)

HUNNYCHURCH, JOHN. Matric. sizar from KING'S, Easter, 1652.

HUNSBY, RALPH, *see* HANSBY.

HUNSDON, Lord, *see* CAREY.

HUNSELEY, THOMAS. Matric. sizar from PEMBROKE, Michs. 1567; B.A. 1571–2.

HUNSTON, FRANCIS. Matric. pens. from QUEENS', Easter, 1635. Of Norfolk. B.A. 1638–9; M.A. 1642. Ord. deacon (Peterb.) Sept. 25, 1642. V. of Islington, Norfolk, 1647.

HUNSTON, HENRY. Matric. pens. (age 9) from CAIUS, Michs. 1559. Brother of Richard (1559).

HUNSTON, HENRY. Adm. pens. at EMMANUEL, Dec. 3, 1590. Matric. 1591.

HUNSTON, HENRY. Matric. pens. from QUEENS', Easter, 1634. Of Suffolk.

HUNSTON, RICHARD. Matric. pens. (age 13) from CAIUS, Michs. 1559.

HUNSTON, RICHARD. Matric. pens. from TRINITY, Easter, 1563.

HUNSTON, W. Matric. Fell.-Com. from PEMBROKE, Michs. 1559. Perhaps William, s. and h. of William, of Boston, Lincs. Age 26 in 1566. Sheriff of Lincs., 1572. Died Aug. 29, 1582. Will (P.C.C.) 1582. (*Lincs. Pedigrees*, 523.)

HUNSTONE, WILLIAM. Adm. pens. (age 16) at CAIUS, July 24, 1576. S. of Henry, of Langham, Suffolk. Schools, Wisbech and Brandon.

HUNSTWYT, ROBERT, *see* HUSTWAYTE.

HUNT, ABRAHAM. B.A. (? 1602–3). S. of Zachariah (1565), R. of Collyweston, Northants. M.A. from CLARE, 1606. Ord. deacon (Peterb.) Sept. 8; priest, Sept. 25, 1608. R. of Collyweston, 1615–35. Probably R. of Pilton, Rutland, 1617–43. V. of Hemington, Northants., 1629–40. R. of Barnwell All Saints', 1640–58. Buried at Barnwell, Nov. 3, 1658. (H. I. Longden.)

HUNT, ABRAHAM. Adm. sizar at SIDNEY, Oct. 11, 1615, from Christ's. B. in Northamptonshire. Matric. 1615–6; B.A. 1618–9; M.A. 1622. Ord. deacon (Peterb.) Sept. 22; priest, Sept. 23, 1622.

HUNT, ABRAHAM. Adm. sizar at SIDNEY, Apr. 29, 1645. S. of Bartholomew, currier, deceased. B. at Collyweston, Northants. School, Collyweston. Matric. 1645. Migrated to Clare, Oct. 21, 1648. B.A. 1648–9.

HUNT, ADAM. Adm. sizar at EMMANUEL, June 29, 1622. Matric. 1622; B.A. 1625–6.

HUNT, ADAM. Adm. sizar (age 18) at CHRIST'S, Feb. 2, 1626–7. S. of Thomas. B. at Yarwell, Northants. School, Fotheringay (Mr Bridger). B.A. 1630–1; M.A. 1634. Ord. deacon (Chester) 1629. V. of Hucknall Torkard, Notts., 1634. (*Peile*, I. 379.)

HUNT, ANTHONY. Matric. pens. from CHRIST'S, Nov. 1568. Ord. p (Peterb.) June 4, 1568; 'bred in the schools' (*Lib. C*[illegible]1585). Probably R. of Tickencote, Rutland, 1568. R. of West Deeping, Lincs., 1573–1606. Will (Lincoln) 1606.

HUNT, BENJAMIN. Adm. at KING'S, a scholar from Eton, 1717. B. at Eton. S. of John, surgeon. Matric. 1718–9; B.A. 1722–3; M.A. 1726. Fellow, 1721. Ord. deacon (Lincoln) Dec. 24, 1727. R. of Lessingham, Norfolk, 1727. 'Soon after marrying he practised the science of farriery.' (*Harwood*, 297.)

HUNT, BRIAN. Adm. at CORPUS CHRISTI, 1704. Of Kent. Matric. 1705; B.A. 1722. Ord. deacon (London) Mar. 5; priest, Mar. 10, 1709–10, 'literate.' V. of Quadring, Lincs., 1717; 'marine chaplain, non-resident.' S.P.G. missionary at St John's, South Carolina, 1723–6. (*Peile*, II. 196.)

HUNT, CHRISTOPHER. Matric. sizar from CORPUS CHRISTI, Easter, 1623. Adm. pens. at Sidney, Dec. 3, 1623, age 14. S. of Christopher, gent. B. in Norfolk. School, Holt (Mr Tallis). B.A. 1627–8; M.A. 1631. R. of Sharrington, Norfolk, 1641.

HUNT, DANIEL. Adm. pens. at EMMANUEL, July, 1607. Matric. 1607; Scholar. Possibly B.A. from Trinity College, Oxford, Nov. 21, 1611.

HUNT, DANIEL. Adm. sizar (age 17) at CHRIST'S, Aug. 19, 1712. S. of Thomas (? 1671–2), V. of Exton, Rutland. School, Oakham (Mr Wright). Matric. 1712; Scholar, 1712; B.A. 1716–7; M.A. 1720. Fellow, 1719. Ord. deacon (Peterb.) Sept. 20, 1719; priest (Ely) Dec. 20, 1719. Chaplain to the Envoy to Sweden, 1720. Died before Oct. 1723. (*Peile*, II. 181.)

HUNT, EUSEBIUS. Matric. pens. from CHRIST'S, Dec. 1610; B.A. from Jesus, 1613-4; M.A. 1618. Ord. deacon (York) Mar. 1613-4; priest, Dec. 1618. V. of Maltby, Yorks. Minister at Fen Drayton, Cambs., 1614. R. of Orton Longueville, Hunts., 1637-52. Minister of Warboys, 1643. R. of Houghton, 1643. R. of Binfield, Berks., 1647. Father of the next. (*Peile*, I. 279.)

HUNT, EUSEBIUS. Adm. pens. (age 16) at CAIUS, Oct. 10, 1647. S. of Eusebius (above), minister of Warboys, Hunts. B. at Maltby, Yorks. Schools, Orton, Hunts. and Huntingdon (Mr Taylor). Matric. 1648; B.A. 1657-8; M.A. 1664. Perhaps V. of Easton, Hunts., 1659. R. of Chesterton, 1660-96. Died 1696. (*Venn*, I. 370, where he is confused with his father.)

HUNT, FRANCIS. Matric. pens. from ST JOHN'S, Easter, 1585; B.A. 1588-9. Will (P.C.C.) 1597, of one of these names; of Stretton-on-the-Foss, Warws., clerk.

HUNT, FRANCIS. Adm. pens. (age 16) at CAIUS, Oct. 22, 1629. S. of Edmund, woollen-draper (and Elizabeth Jellow). B. at Bury St Edmunds. Bapt. Oct. 3, 1614. School, Thetford (Mr Smyth). Matric. 1629; Scholar, 1630-6; B.A. 1633-4; M.A. 1637. Ord. priest (Norwich) Sept. 25, 1636; C. of St Cuthbert, Thetford, Norfolk. Buried at St Mary's, Cambridge, Apr. 7, 1637. (*Venn*, I. 292.)

HUNT, FRANCIS. Adm. pens. (age 17) at TRINITY, Apr. 30, 1690. S. of Richard, of Bishop's Itchington, Warws. School, Canton Hall, Warws. (Mr Thomas Welsbore). Matric. 1690; Scholar, 1693; B.A. 1693-4; M.A. 1697. Ord. deacon (London) Mar. 8, 1695-6.

HUNT, FRANCIS. Adm. sizar at SIDNEY, July 3, 1721. S. of Francis, farmer, of Houghton Conquest, Beds. School, Houghton Conquest (Mr Clark). Matric. 1721; B.A. 1724-5. Ord. deacon (Lincoln) May 23, 1725; priest, June 16, 1728. C. of Haynes, Beds., 1728-31. R. of St Paul and St Cuthbert, Bedford, 1732-8.

HUNT, GEORGE. Matric. pens. from ST JOHN'S, Michs. 1546. One of these names R. of Claydon, Suffolk, 1573-87.

HUNT, GEORGE. M.A. 1680 (Incorp. from Oxford). S. of Robert, of Compton Pauncefoot, Somerset, gent. Matric. from Magdalen Hall, Oxford, Mar. 27, 1675, age 16; B.A. (Magdalen College, Oxford) 1678; M.A. 1681; D.C.L. 1691. Fellow, 1681-99. Adm. at the Middle Temple, 1677. Died Jan. 29, 1699-1700. M.I. in Magdalen Chapel. (*Al. Oxon.*; Le Neve, *Mon.*, IV. 208.)

HUNT, HENRY. Adm. at KING'S, a scholar from Eton, 1451; M.A. 1460.

HUNTE, HENRY. Matric. pens. from CHRIST'S, Easter, 1554. Perhaps adm. at Gray's Inn, 1556.

HUNT, HOLOFERNES. Matric. pens. from CORPUS CHRISTI, Michs. 1626. Of Suffolk. B.A. 1629-30; M.A. 1633. P.C. of Upwood, Hunts., in 1651.

HUNT, ISAAC. Adm. sizar (age 17) at CAIUS, Jan. 25, 1620-1. S. of Robert, leather worker. B. at Stody, Norfolk. School, Holt (Mr Tallis). Matric. 1620-1; B.A. 1624-5. Ord. deacon (Peterb.) June 12; priest, June 13, 1625. V. of Guist, Norfolk, 1626.

HUNT, ISAAC. Adm. sizar (age 17) at SIDNEY, May 9, 1677. S. of Edward, clerk. B. at Dunchideock, Devon. School, Crediton (Mr Viner). Matric. 1677. One of these names R. of Foots Cray, Kent, 1687-91. Died 1691.

HUNT, JAMES. Matric. pens. from ST JOHN'S, Easter, 1575.

HUNT, JAMES. Adm. pens. (age 18) at CAIUS, May 2, 1705. S. of Edmund, attorney, of Hevingham, Norfolk. B. at Westwick. School, Norwich (Mr Hoadley). Matric. 1705; Scholar, 1705-10; B.A. 1708-9; M.A. 1712. Ord. deacon (Norwich) July 2, 1710, as 'C. of Mundesley'; priest, July 6, 1712. R. of Sparham and Foxley, 1712-42. Died 1742. Will (Norwich Archd. C.) 1742. (*Venn*, I. 513.)

HUNTE, JOHN. Matric. pens. from CHRIST'S, Michs. 1559. One of these names, 'bred in the schools,' was ord. priest (Gloucester) Sept. 22, 1571. R. of Caldecote, Hunts., 1578-1610. (*Peile*, I. 70.)

HUNT, JOHN. Adm. at KING'S (age 16) a scholar from Eton, Aug. 27, 1565. 2nd s. of John, of Lyndon, Rutland. B. at Morcott. Adm. at the Middle Temple, Nov. 25, 1567. M.P. for Sudbury, 1571. Knighted, Nov. 10, 1611. Author, classical. Died 1615. Brother of Thomas (1569). (*D.N.B.*; *Cooper*, II. 59.)

HUNT, JOHN. Matric. sizar from TRINITY, Michs. 1566; Scholar, 1570; B.A. 1570-1; M.A. 1574; LL.D. 1581. Fellow, 1572. Admitted advocate, Jan. 26, 1582-3. Will (P.C.C.) 1630; of Burston, Norfolk.

HUNT, JOHN. Matric. pens. from ST JOHN'S, Easter, 1589.

HUNT, JOHN. Matric. sizar from PEMBROKE, c. 1590.

HUNT, JOHN. Matric. pens. from TRINITY, c. 1592, a scholar from Westminster. B.A. 1595-6; M.A. 1599. Fellow, 1597. One of these names V. of Aylsham, Norfolk, 1610. R. of Burgh, 1613-34.

HUNT, JOHN. Adm. at CORPUS CHRISTI, 1600. Of Leicestershire. Perhaps of Coldnewton, Leics., Esq.; adm. at Gray's Inn, Feb. 23, 1604-5.

HUNT, JOHN. Matric. sizar from EMMANUEL, Easter, 1610. Probably a mistake for Richard, whom *see*.

HUNT or LE HUNT, JOHN. Matric. Fell.-Com. from KING'S, Easter, 1618.

HUNT, JOHN. M.A. 1627 (Incorp. from Oxford). Of Wiltshire. Perhaps matric. from Magdalen College, Oxford, Jan. 26, 1598-9, age 14; B.A. (Oxford) 1606-7; M.A. 1609. R. of Fritwell, Oxon., 1608. Perhaps V. of Sulgrave, Northants., 1633-46. (*Al. Oxon.*)

HUNT, JOHN. Adm. sizar (age 15) at SIDNEY, May 9, 1661. 2nd s. of Joseph, yeoman. B. at Geddington, Northants. Schools, Oundle and Bulwick (Mr Wm. Hicks). Matric. 1661; B.A. 1664-5; M.A. 1668. One of these names (M.A.), R. of Eastbridge, Kent, 1671-3. Died 1673.

HUNT, JOHN. Adm. sizar at TRINITY, May 13, 1667. Matric. 1668. One of these names s. of Nicholas. B. 1650. School, Oundle, whence he is said to have gone to Sidney (*see* next).

HUNT, JOHN. Adm. pens. (age 16) at SIDNEY, Nov. 1667. S. of Samuel, gent., of Rutland. School, Uppingham. Matric. 1668; LL.B. 1673. Ord. deacon (Peterb.) June 14, 1674; priest, Sept. 19, 1680.

HUNT, JOHN. M.A. 1675 (*Lit. Reg.*).

HUNT, JOHN. Adm. sizar at EMMANUEL, Sept. 18, 1687. Of Huntingdonshire. Matric. 1690; B.A. 1691-2.

HUNT, JOHN. Adm. sizar (age 21) at CAIUS, May 20, 1693. S. of John, surgeon, of Rostherne, Cheshire. B. there. Schools, Eccles, Lancs. (Mr Atkinson) and Leigh (Mr Duckworth). Matric. 1693; Scholar, 1693-8; B.A. 1696-7. Elected fellow, 1698, but not admitted. Ord. priest (London) Sept. 25, 1698. Probably V. of Thorpe, Essex, 1700-13. (*Venn*, I. 492.)

HUNT, JOHN. Adm. at CORPUS CHRISTI, 1703. Of Suffolk. Matric. 1704; B.A. 1706-7; M.A. 1710. Ord. deacon (London) May 27; priest, Sept. 23, 1711. V. of Mildenhall, Suffolk, 1714-36. Died 1736.

HUNT, JOHN. Adm. sizar at ST CATHARINE'S, June 30, 1712. Matric. 1712.

HUNT, JOHN. Adm. pens. at EMMANUEL, May 27, 1714. Of Northamptonshire. Matric. 1714; B.A. 1717-8; M.A. 1721. One of these names V. of Hoveton, Norfolk, 1731-3.

HUNT, JOHN. Adm. pens. at ST CATHARINE'S, July 28, 1747. Of Worlington, Suffolk. Matric. 1749; B.A. 1752.

HUNT, JOHN. Adm. pens. (age 18) at TRINITY, July 1, 1751. S. of Thomas, of Narborough, Leics. School, Narborough. Matric. 1752; Scholar, 1752; B.A. 1755. Ord. deacon (Lincoln) June 5, 1757. Will of one of these names (P.C.C.) 1794; of St James', Westminster, clerk.

HUNT, JOSEPH. Adm. sizar (age 18) at ST JOHN'S, June 22, 1674. S. of Thomas, chandler. B. at Nottingham. School, Stamford. Matric. 1674; B.A. 1677-8. Ord. deacon (York) June, 1679; priest, June, 1680.

HUNT, JOSIAS. Matric. sizar from TRINITY, c. 1591; Scholar, 1593; B.A. 1594-5; M.A. 1598; B.D. 1611. Fellow, 1597. R. of Alderton, Suffolk, 1609-17. R. of Burgh, 1613-7.

HUNT, LUKE. Adm. sizar (age 18) at MAGDALENE, Apr. 11, 1665. S. of Antony, of Uttoxeter, Staffs. School, Uttoxeter (private). Matric. 1665; B.A. 1669-70.

HUNT, MATTHEW. Adm. sizar (age 16) at SIDNEY, Sept. 10, 1622. S. of Matthew, chandler. B. at Oundle, Northants. School, Oundle. Matric. 1622; B.A. 1626-7; M.A. 1630. Ord. deacon (Peterb.) July 4, 1629. V. of Winwick, Hunts., 1633-57. Buried June 29, 1657.

HUNT, MATTHEW. Adm. sizar at EMMANUEL, June 26, 1677. S. of Matthew, of Northamptonshire. B. 1660. School, Oundle. Matric. 1677; B.A. 1680-1; M.A. 1684. Ord. priest (Peterb.) Sept. 21, 1684. V. of Southwick, Northants., 1684-91. V. of Weekley, 1691-1704. R. of Barton Seagrave, 1703-23. R. of Barnwell All Saints', 1704-29. Died 1729. (H. I. Longden.)

HUNT, MICHAEL. Adm. sizar at PETERHOUSE, June 30, 1627. Of Kent. S. of John, of Herne. Bapt. Feb. 4, 1609-10. Migrated to King's for a time. B.A. from Peterhouse, 1630-1. R. of Goodnestone, Kent, 1636-41. Died 1641. (J. Ch. Smith.)

HUNT, MICHAEL. M.A. from KING'S, 1721. S. of M., of Wells, gent. Matric. from Christ Church, Oxford, Mar. 26, 1713, age 19; B.A. (Oxford) 1716. Preb. of Wells, 1724-49. R. of Burnett, Somerset, 1733. (*Al. Oxon.*)

HUNT, NATHANIEL. Scholar of EMMANUEL, Michs. 1603; B.A. 1603–4; M.A. 1607. Ord. deacon (York) Mar. 1608–9; priest, June, 1609.

HUNT, NICHOLAS. Matric. sizar from KING'S, Easter, 1620; B.A. 1624–5. Ord. deacon (Peterb.) Aug. 11; priest, Aug. 12, 1625.

HUNT, NICHOLAS. Adm. sizar (age 20) at ST JOHN'S, July 9, 1691. (Previously matric. from Exeter College, Oxford, Apr. 9, 1690.) S. of Lewis. B. at Blackawton, Devon. School, Dartmouth (Mr Winston). Matric. 1692; B.A. 1693–4. V. of Holne, Devon, 1699. Will (Exeter) 1709. (*Al. Oxon.*)

HUNT, RALPH LE. 'King's scholar' at Cambridge, 1327.

HUNT, RICHARD. Matric. pens. from TRINITY, Easter, 1560; Scholar, 1560; B.A. 1564–5; M.A. 1568. Fellow, 1566.

HUNT, RICHARD. Matric. pens. from CHRIST'S, Nov. 1571.

HUNT, RICHARD. Matric. sizar from TRINITY, Michs. 1582; Scholar, 1584; B.A. 1585–6; M.A. 1589; D.D. 1608. R. and V. of Terrington, Norfolk, 1609. Preb. of Canterbury, 1614–33. R. of Foulsham. Dean of Durham, 1620–38. Preb. of Lichfield, 1636. Died Nov. 2, 1638. Buried in Durham Cathedral. M.I. there. (Le Neve, *Mon.*, I. 178.)

HUNT, RICHARD. Adm. at TRINITY, a scholar from Westminster, 1605.

HUNT, RICHARD. Adm. sizar at EMMANUEL, May 7, 1610. S. of William, of Manchester. B. Mar. 2, 1593–4. School, Manchester. Scholar; B.A. 1613–4; M.A. 1617; B.D. 1624. Fellow, 1618. Incorp. at Oxford, 1618. Ord. deacon (Peterb.) Sept. 19; priest, Sept. 20, 1619. V. of Acton, Cheshire, 1626–46. Preb. of Lichfield, 1636–62. V. of Walsall, Staffs., 1639. R. of St Mary-on-the-Hill, Chester, 1642–6 and 1655–62. Probably minister at Warmingham, Cheshire, 1647–8. Died Aug. 1662. Buried at St Mary's. Will, Chester. (R. Stewart-Brown; E. Axon.)

HUNT, RICHARD. B.A. from EMMANUEL, 1624.

HUNT, RICHARD. Adm. at KING'S, a scholar from Eton, 1645. S. of Richard, citizen and mercer, of London. B.A. 1649; M.A. 1653. Fellow, 1648–54. Adm. at Gray's Inn, Nov. 12, 1650. Rhetoric professor, Gresham College, 1654–9. His valuable library was lost in the fire of 1666. Latterly resided at Hutton Hall, Essex. A wide and learned scholar. Married Mary, dau. of William Hampton, R. of Bletchingley, Surrey. Died Oct. 25, 1690. Buried at Hutton. Brother of Thomas (1645). (*Harwood.*)

HUNT, RICHARD. Adm. pens. at EMMANUEL, June 12, 1671. Of Surrey. Matric. 1671; B.A. 1674–5.

HUNT, ROBERT. Matric. pens. from CLARE, Easter, 1587; B.A. 1590–1; M.A. 1594. One of these names R. of Themelthorpe, Norfolk. One ('M.A.'), P.C. of Lanchester, Durham, 1624–35.

HUNT, ROBERT. Scholar of TRINITY HALL, 1603; LL.B. 1606. Perhaps s. of Robert, V. of Reculver. Went as chaplain with the first settlers to Virginia, 1606. Probably died soon after, 1608. (*Cooper*, II. 493; *D.N.B.*)

HUNT, ROBERT. Matric. pens. from CHRIST'S, July, 1611.

HUNT, ROBERT. Matric. sizar from QUEENS', Easter, 1613. Of Norfolk. B.A. 1616–7.

HUNT, ROBERT. Adm. pens. (age 16) at CAIUS, Oct. 5, 1625. S. of John, Esq., of Porstone, Charminster, Dorset. School, Rampisham (Mr Allott). Matric. 1625. Adm. at the Middle Temple, May 18, 1625; s. and h. of John, of Speckington, Dorset. Buried at Charminster, June 22, 1692. (*Venn*, I. 273.)

HUNT, ROBERT. Adm. pens. at TRINITY, Oct. 21, 1651. Of Warwickshire.

HUNT, ROBERT. Adm. pens. (age 16) at CAIUS, Apr. 17, 1661. S. of Robert, barrister, of Hempstead, Norfolk. B. there. School, Holt (Mr Wright, Hicks, and Mazy). Matric. 1661. Adm. at Gray's Inn, June 26, 1663. (*Venn*, I. 412; *Vis. of Norfolk*, 1664.)

HUNT, ROBERT. Adm. sizar at TRINITY HALL, Dec. 24, 1722. Matric. from King's, 1723.

HUNT, ROGER. Scholar of TRINITY, 1605; B.A. 1605–6; M.A. 1609. Incorp. at Oxford, 1612. Ord. deacon and priest, June 3, 1610. C. of Houghton, Hunts., 1613. V. of Stagsden, Beds., till 1623. Buried there, Mar. 2, 1622–3.

HUNT, ROWLAND. Matric. pens. from QUEENS', Easter, 1622. Of Salop. S. of Richard, of Shrewsbury, gent. Migrated to Emmanuel, Oct. 1622. Adm. at Gray's Inn, May 10, 1626. Called to the Bar, June 23, 1637. Doubtless brother of Thomas (1617).

HUNT, ROWLAND. Adm. pens. at JESUS, Apr. 5, 1645. Of Salop. S. and h. of Thomas (1617), of Shrewsbury, Esq. Bapt. May 28, 1629. Matric. 1645. Fellow of All Souls (Oxford) 1648. Created B.C.L. (Oxford) 1649. Adm. at Gray's Inn, June 29, 1646. Barrister, 1656. Sheriff of Salop, 1672. Of Boreatton. Married Frances, dau. of Lord Paget. Buried June 10, 1699. (*Al. Oxon.*)

HUNT, SAMUEL. Matric. sizar from TRINITY, Easter, 1566; B.A. 1570–1. Ord. deacon and priest (Peterb.) Nov. 20, 1574. V. of Graffham, Hunts., 1584.

HUNT, SAMUEL. Adm. sizar at PETERHOUSE, June 5, 1651. Of Warwickshire. School, Coventry. Matric. 1651; B.A. 1654–5.

HUNT, STEPHEN. Adm. at CORPUS CHRISTI, 1693. Of Canterbury. Matric. 1694; M.B. 1699.

HUNT, STEPHEN. M.D. from CAIUS, 1694. S. of Richard, of Stratford-on-Avon. Matric. from Pembroke College, Oxford, Apr. 2, 1669, age 14; B.A. from Trinity, Oxford, 1673; M.A. 1676. Adm. licentiate of the College of Physicians, 1693. Admission as candidate, 1695, deferred, he being then in priest's orders. (*Venn*, I. 494; *Munk*; *Al. Oxon.*)

HUNT, STEPHEN. M.A. from EMMANUEL, 1732. S. of William, Archdeacon of Bath. Matric. from Balliol College, Oxford, Apr. 1, 1721, age 15; B.A. (Oxford) 1725. Ord. deacon (Norwich) June, 1731. (*Al. Oxon.*)

HUNT, THOMAS. B.A. 1484.

HUNT, THOMAS. Adm. at KING'S (age 17) a scholar from Eton, Aug. 24, 1569. Doubtless s. of John, of Lyndon, Rutland. Matric. 1569; B.A. 1573–4. Fellow, 1572–7. Brother of John (1565).

HUNT, THOMAS. Matric. pens. from CLARE, Easter, 1575. Probably same as the next.

HUNT, THOMAS. Matric. sizar from CLARE, Easter, 1575. According to *Cooper* (III. 59), he was s. of James, of Chadderton, Lancs. V. of Oldham, 1580; and first Master of Oldham Grammar School. But there was another of these names, of Lancashire, B.A. from Brasenose, 1586. It is possible that the Clare man was the V. of Whitwick, Leics., who was ord. priest (Lincoln) Sept. 17, 1580.

HUNT, THOMAS. Matric. pens. from TRINITY, *c.* 1594. Perhaps Mus.Bac. from Corpus Christi, 1601.

HUNT, THOMAS. Matric. pens. from JESUS, Easter, 1614. Perhaps s. and h. of William, of Hindolveston, Norfolk, Esq.; adm. at Lincoln's Inn, May 2, 1618.

HUNT, THOMAS. Matric. pens. from QUEENS', Easter, 1617. Of Salop. Probably s. of Richard, of Shrewsbury. Bapt. Dec. 25, 1599. B.A. 1620–1; M.A. 1624. Incorp. at Oxford, 1624. Colonel in the Parliamentary army. M.P. for Shrewsbury, 1645–8. Sheriff of Salop, 1656. Purchased Boreatton. Died 1669. Doubtless brother of Rowland (1622) and father of Rowland (1645). (Burke, *L.G.*; A. B. Beaven.)

HUNT, THOMAS. Adm. pens. at QUEENS', Nov. 2, 1645. S. of Richard, mercer, of London. B. there, *c.* 1627. B.A. 1649–50; M.A. 1653. Fellow of Peterhouse, in 1650. Adm. at Gray's Inn, Nov. 12, 1650. Called to the Bar, 1658. Appointed Clerk of Assize to the Oxford circuit, 1659. Resided at Banbury, 1660–83; acted as steward on the estates of the Duke of Buckingham and the Duke of Norfolk. Counsel for Lord Stafford, 1680. Wrote in support of the municipal rights of the City of London and other municipal cities in England. Fled to Holland to escape arrest, 1683. Settled at Utrecht. Author, legal. Died 1688, aged 61. Brother of Richard (1645). (*T. A. Walker*, 96; *D.N.B.*)

HUNT, THOMAS. Adm. pens. at TRINITY, July 6, 1650. Of Worcestershire.

HUNT, THOMAS. Matric. sizar from TRINITY, Michs. 1653. S. of Michael, draper, of St Sepulchre's, London. B. Aug. 23, 1635. School, Merchant Taylors'. B.A. 1657–8; M.A. 1661. Probably R. of South Collingham, Notts., 1665–7. Father of William (1684–5).

HUNT, THOMAS. Adm. sizar (age 15) at ST JOHN'S, Apr. 13, 1659. B. at Repton, Derbs. School, Repton (Mr Ullock). Matric. 1659; B.A. 1662.

HUNT, THOMAS. Adm. sizar at EMMANUEL, Mar. 20, 1671–2. Of Northamptonshire. Matric. 1672; B.A. 1675–6; M.A. 1679. Ord. deacon (Peterb.) Sept. 22, 1678. Perhaps R. of Tickencote, Rutland, 1687–92. V. of Exton, 1693–1700. Died 1700. (H. I. Longden.)

HUNT, THOMAS. Adm. pens. (age 16) at PETERHOUSE, Nov. 22, 1676. Of London. School, Westminster. Matric. 1677; Scholar, 1677; B.A. 1680–1; M.A. 1684.

HUNT, THOMAS. Matric. sizar from SIDNEY, Easter, 1677.

HUNT, THOMAS. Adm. sizar (age 16) at CAIUS, July 3, 1683. S. of Thomas, gent., of Stower-Provost, Dorset. B. there. School, Blandford. Matric. 1683; Scholar, 1683–90; B.A. 1686–7; M.A. 1690. (*Venn*, I. 474.)

HUNT, WILLIAM. Matric. sizar from TRINITY, Easter, 1580. One of these names ord. deacon and priest (Peterb.) Apr. 18, 1596, as M.A. of Trinity. (H. I. Longden.)

HUNT, WILLIAM. Matric. sizar from TRINITY, Easter, 1616; B.A. 1619–20; M.A. 1623. Perhaps V. of Islington, Middlesex, 1639.

HUNT, WILLIAM. Adm. pens. (age 16) at CAIUS, May 20, 1628. S. of William, Esq. B. at Hindolveston, Norfolk. School, Aylsham (Mr Knolles). Matric. 1628. Adm. at Lincoln's Inn, May 12, 1631. Probably buried at Hindolveston, in 1636. (*Venn*, I. 284.)

HUNT, WILLIAM. Matric. sizar from KING'S, Easter, 1637; B.A. 1640-1; M.A. 1644. Ord. priest (Peterb.) Dec. 18, 1641. According to *Calamy*, I. 249, he was of Hampshire; bred at Eton! V. of Sutton, Cambs., 1643-62, ejected. Died aged abou 70.

HUNT, WILLIAM. M.A. from CHRIST'S, 1641. S. of William. B. at Dowlish-Wake, Somerset. Matric. from Wadham College, Oxford, June 13, 1634, age 18; B.A. (Oxford) 1636-7. Master of Salisbury School, 1641-62. Afterwards kept a school at Ilminster. Minister of a congregation at Salisbury. Said to have died 1684, aged 74. The Head Master of Ilminster, 1677-88, was probably his son. (*Peile*, I. 475; *Calamy*, II. 646; *Al. Oxon.*)

HUNT, WILLIAM. Adm. pens. (age 17) at CAIUS, Feb. 6, 1651-2. S. of Thomas, Esq., of Sharrington, Norfolk. School, Bury St Edmunds. Matric. 1652. Of Sharrington, Esq. Married Ann, dau. of John James, of London. Living in 1686. (*Venn*, I. 384; *Vis. of Norfolk*, 1664.)

HUNT, WILLIAM. Adm. pens. at TRINITY, Oct. 8, 1656. Of Norfolk. Matric. 1656. Adm. at the Inner Temple, 1658.

HUNT, WILLIAM. Adm. pens. (age 17) at ST JOHN'S, Apr. 22, 1664. S. of William, D.D., of Adderbury, Oxon. B. there. School, Winchester. Matric. 1664.

HUNT, WILLIAM. Adm. sizar (age 19) at MAGDALENE, Aug. 7, 1674. S. of William. B. at Sutton, Isle of Ely. School, Sutton (private). Matric. 1674. Probably LL.B. from Trinity Hall, 1679.

HUNT, WILLIAM. Adm. sizar (age 17) at ST JOHN'S, Feb. 16, 1684-5. S. of Thomas (1653), clerk. B. at Collingham, Notts. School, Uppingham (Mr Savage). Matric. 1685; B.A. 1688-9; M.A. 1695. Ord. priest (Lincoln) Sept. 20, 1690. R. of Whitwick, Leics., 1691-1700. R. of Cole Orton, 1700-27. Will of one of these names (Leicester) 1736; of Thringstone, Leics.

HUNT, WILLIAM. Adm. sizar at ST CATHARINE'S, Mar. 9, 1719-20. Of Botesdale, Suffolk. Matric. 1721; B.A. 1723-4. Perhaps V. of Hoveton, Norfolk, 1733; and V. of Neatishead, 1733.

HUNT, ZACHARY Matric. sizar from TRINITY, Michs. 1565. V. of Twywell, Northants., 1573-77. R. of Collyweston, 1577-1615, when he resigned for his son Abraham (1602-3). Will (Peterb.) 1616. (H. I. Longden.)

HUNT, ——. Adm. sizar at TRINITY, Aug. 5, 1645.

HUNT, ——. Adm. pens. at ST CATHARINE'S, 1662.

HUNTBATCH, JOHN. Adm. sizar (age 19) at TRINITY, Oct. 28, 1712. S. of John, of Wem, Salop. School, Wem (Mr Edwards). Matric. 1713; B.A. 1716-7.

HUNTER, BETHEL. Matric. pens. from CHRIST'S, Easter, 1620. S. of Robert, of Thornton-by-Pickering, Yorks. B. c. 1603. Married, at Kirkby Misperton, Yorks., 1630, Magdalen, dau. of Thomas Percehay, of Ryton, Yorks. Will (York) Feb. 1660-1. (*F.M.G.*, I. 355; *Peile*, I. 335; *Vis. of Yorks.*, 1665.)

HUNTER, CHRISTOPHER. Adm. pens. (age 18) at ST JOHN'S, Apr. 11, 1693. S. of Thomas, of Medomsley, near Durham. Bapt. July 8, 1675. School, Houghton-le-Spring (Mr Stobart). Matric. 1693; M.B. 1698. Practised at Stockton-on-Tees, and afterwards at Durham. A keen antiquary. F.S.A., 1725. His cabinets of Roman antiquities were acquired by the dean and chapter of Durham Cathedral. Married, Aug. 1, 1702, Elizabeth, dau. of John Elrington. Died at Unthank, Shotley, July 12, 1757. Left manuscript topographical collections. (*Scott-Mayor*; *D.N.B.*; H. M. Wood.)

HUNTER, CHRISTOPHER. Adm. sizar (age 16) at ST JOHN'S, Apr. 16, 1694. S. of Thomas, clerk, of Dent, Yorks. B. there. School, Sedbergh (Mr Wharton). Matric. 1695; B.A. 1697-8; M.A. 1701. C. of Sedgefield, Durham, 1706-18. Probably V. of Northallerton, Yorks., 1718-25. Married, Apr. 22, 1723, Mary, dau. of Richard Metcalfe, of Thornborough Hall, Yorks. Buried at Northallerton, Dec. 6, 1725. (H.M. Wood; M. H. Peacock.)

HUNTER, CYPRIAN. Adm. sizar (age 17) at ST JOHN'S, Apr. 20, 1676. S. of Josiah, deceased, of Ouseburn, Yorks. B. there. School, York. Matric. 1676; B.A. 1679-80. Ord. deacon (York) May, 1681; priest, Mar. 1682-3.

HUNTER, GEORGE. B.A. 1529-30; M.A. 1533; B.D. 1543. Probably fellow of JESUS, 1534-49. Perhaps fellow of St John's, 1554 (of Yorkshire). Preb. of Lincoln, 1558. R. of Swineshead, Hunts., 1558-69. Buried there Oct. 27, 1569.

HUNTER, HENRY. Adm. pens. at TRINITY, June 3, 1670.

HUNTER, JOHN. Adm. sizar at ST JOHN'S, June 2, 1648. S. of John, butcher, of Northumberland. B. there. School, Newcastle (Mr Augur). Matric. 1649.

HUNTER, JOHN. Adm. pens. at JESUS, Apr. 19, 1678. S. of Robert, clerk, of Cheshire, deceased. Matric. 1679; Scholar, 1681; B.A. 1681-2; M.A. 1685. Perhaps R. of Stapleford, Herts., 1717-24. V. of Wragby, Yorks. Brother of Robert (1678). (A. Gray.)

HUNTER, JOHN. Adm. pens. at CLARE, Feb. 21, 1746-7. B. at Lichfield.

HUNTER, JOSIAH. Matric. pens. from ST CATHARINE'S, Easter, 1645; B.A. 1646-7; M.A. 1650. V. of St Michael's, York, 1662.

HUNTER or HUNT, MATTHEW. B.A. 1513-4.

HUNTER, NATHANIEL. Adm. pens. at PETERHOUSE, June 29, 1594. Resided, till 1597.

HUNTER, RICHARD. B.A. 1529-30; M.A. 1533.

HUNTER, RICHARD. Matric. pens. from ST JOHN'S, Michs. 1587; B.A. (1591-2); M.A. 1595. Ord. deacon and priest (Lincoln) Nov. 6, 1603. R. of Colmworth, Beds., 1605-26. Will proved 1628.

HUNTER, RICHARD. Adm. sizar at JESUS, June 13, 1695. Of Lancashire. Matric 1695; B.A. 1698-9; Scholar, 1699; M.A. 1702.

HUNTER, ROBERT. Matric. pens. from ST JOHN'S, c. 1595.

HUNTER, ROBERT. Adm. pens. at JESUS, Apr. 19, 1678. S. of Robert, clerk, of Cheshire, deceased. Matric. 1679; Scholar, 1681; B.A. 1681-2; M.A. 1685. Brother of John (1678).

HUNTER, ROBERT. Adm. sizar at JESUS, June 7, 1708. S. of John (1678), clerk, of Wragby, Yorks.

HUNTER, ROBERT. Adm. sizar (age 21) at SIDNEY, Apr. 3, 1735. S. of Robert, gent. B. at Thornton-by-Pickering, Yorks. School, Thornton. Matric. 1735; B.A. 1738-9. Ord. deacon (Chester, *Litt. dim.* from York) June 17, 1739. C. of Scalby. (*F.M.G.*, I. 356.)

HUNTER, SAMUEL. Adm. sizar (age 19) at ST. JOHN'S, Apr. 25, 1707. S. of Samuel, of North Frodingham, Yorks. School, Beverley (Mr Lambert). Migrated to Peterhouse, Oct. 2, 1708. B.A. 1710-1; M.A. 1724. Ord. deacon (York) May, 1711; priest, Sept. 1715. Perhaps V. of Wragby, Yorks., 1712-6; and R. of Winceby, Lincs., 1719.

HUNTER, THOMAS. Adm. sizar (age 18) at ST JOHN'S, June 30, 1658. S. of Hugh, husbandman, of Furness Fell, Lancs. B. there. School, Urswick, Lancs. (Mr Inman). Matric. 1658; B.A. 1661-2. One of these names P.C. of Dent, Yorks., 1682-1703. Perhaps V. of Ulverstone, 1663-9. C. of Pilling, 1701-15. Buried at Pilling, May 1, 1715. (E. Axon.)

HUNTER, THOMAS. Adm. sizar (age 18) at PETERHOUSE, July 1, 1717. Of Lincolnshire. School, Horncastle, Lincs. B.A. 1720-1. Ord. deacon (Lincoln) Dec. 23, 1722; priest, Sept. 20, 1724.

HUNTER, ——. B.Can.L. 1501-2.

HUNTER, ——. B.Civ.L. 1542-3.

HUNTING or HUNTON, EDWARD. Adm. pens. at EMMANUEL, 1619. Matric. 1619; B.A. 1622-3.

HUNTINGDON, Sir HENRY (HOLAND). Pens. at KING'S HALL, 1439-42. S. and h. of John (Holand), Earl of Huntingdon. B. 1430. Succeeded his father as Earl of Huntingdon and Duke of Exeter, 1447. A zealous Lancastrian; attainted, Nov. 4, 1461, when all his honours were forfeited. Died *s.p.*, 1473. (*G.E.C.*)

HUNTINGDON, JOHN. Matric. pens. from ST JOHN'S, Easter, 1628; B.A. 1631-2. Ord. deacon (Peterb.) May 20, 1638.

HUNTINGTON, JOHN. Adm. sizar (age 16) at SIDNEY, June 4, 1698. S. of John. B. at Rugby. School, Rugby. Matric. 1698.

HUNTINGTON, JOHN. Adm. at CORPUS CHRISTI, 1719. Of Staffordshire. Matric. 1720; B.A. 1723-4. R. of Beeston, Norfolk, 1724-55. R. of Irstead, till 1755. Died Dec. 6, 1755. (*G. Mag.*)

HUNTINGDON, THOMAS. Matric. sizar from CHRIST'S, June, 1577; B.A. from Magdalene, 1580-1.

HUNTINGTON, THOMAS. Adm. sizar (age 18) at ST JOHN'S, May 18, 1681. S. of Jeremy, barber. B. at Derby. School, Derby (private; Mr Ogden). Matric. 1681; B.A. 1684-5. Ord. priest (Lincoln) Aug. 4, 1700.

HUNTINGDON, WILLIAM. Carmelite of Cambridge. Ord. deacon (at Cambridge, by Abp. of Canterbury) Sept. 19; priest, Dec. 18, 1389.

HUNTINGDON, WILLIAM. M.A. from CLARE, 1727. S. of Dennis, V. of Kempsford, Gloucs. Matric. from Merton College, Oxford, July 11, 1701, age 18; B.A. (Oxford) 1711. R. of Bagendon, Gloucs., 1713-37. C. of Baunton, 1717-37. Died Dec. 30, 1737. M.I. at Bagendon. (*Al. Oxon.*; F. S. Hockaday.)

HUNTINGTON, WILLIAM. Adm. sizar at CLARE, Nov. 10, 1727. B. at Hull, Yorks. Matric. 1728; B.A. 1731-2; M.A. 1744. *Litt. dim.* from York for priest, Feb. 1734-5. V. of North Ferriby, Yorks., 1735-66. V. of Kirk Ella, 1735. V. of Drypool, Hull, 1775. Died 1783.

HUNTINGDON, Prior of. Incorp. 1497-8. Doubtless Thomas Forte. Augustinian canon. Prior of the House at Huntingdon, 1492-1503. Bishop of Achonry, Ireland, 1492-1508. (*Dugdale*; Cotton, *Fast. Hib.*)

HUNTINGFIELD, ROGER DE. Student at Cambridge. M.A., B.Can.L. Reservation of a prebend. (*Papal Letters*, 1329.)

HUNTINGTOWER, LIONEL (TOLLEMACHE), *see* TOLLEMACHE.

HUNTLIE, JOHN. Matric. pens. from CORPUS CHRISTI, Easter, 1586.

HUNTLEY, JOHN. M.A. 1608 (Incorp. from Oxford). Of London, gent. (Perhaps s. of Humphrey, citizen of London; if so, 'of Chipsted, Surrey,' in 1623.) Matric. from Queen's College, Oxford, Nov. 29, 1594, age 16; B.A. (St John's, Oxford) 1598; M.A. 1600-1. (*Vis. of Surrey*; *Surrey Arch. Soc.*, XVI. 26.)

HUNTLEY, JOHN. Adm. pens. at TRINITY, May 26, 1638. Matric. 1638; Scholar from Westminster, 1639; B.A. 1642-3.

HUNTLEY, RICHARD. Matric. sizar from ST JOHN'S, Michs. 1575.

HUNTLEY, RICHARD. M.A. from KING'S, 1726. S. of Matthew, of Boxwell, Gloucs. Bapt. Feb. 4, 1689-90. Matric. from St John's College, Oxford, Mar. 22, 1707-8, age 18; B.A. (Oxford) 1711. Ord. deacon (Coventry and Lichfield) June 28, 1724; priest, Sept. 19, 1725. Chaplain to the Bishop of Coventry and Lichfield. R. of Castle Combe, Wilts., 1726-8. R. of Boxwell, Gloucs., 1727-8. Married, 1716, Anne, dau. of Colonel Henry Lee-Warner, of Dane John, Canterbury, and Walsingham Abbey, Norfolk. Buried Apr. 17, 1728. M.I. at Boxwell. Father of the next. (*Al. Oxon.*; F. S. Hockaday.)

HUNTLEY, RICHARD. M.A. from KING'S, 1748. S. of Richard (above), R. of Boxwell, Gloucs. Bapt. Feb. 23, 1721. Matric. from St John's College, Oxford, Nov. 18, 1737, age 16; B.A. (Oxford) 1741. Ord. deacon (Gloucester) Dec. 23, 1744; priest, Dec. 22, 1745. C. of Boxwell, 1745. R. of Shipton-Moyne, Glouces., 1753-94. Chaplain to the Earl of Shaftesbury. R. of Boxwell, 1753-94. Married, 1754, Anne, dau. of Nicholas Beaker, of Nettleton House, Wilts. Died Mar. 6, 1794. Will, P.C.C. (*Al. Oxon.*; F. S. Hockaday.)

HUNTLEY, TH. Matric. sizar from QUEENS', Easter, 1544.

HUNTLY, WILLIAM. Matric. pens. from ST CATHARINE'S, Easter, 1629. S. of Robert, merchant, of Newcastle-on-Tyne. B. there. Bapt. at St Nicholas, Aug. 22, 1611. School, Bradford. Migrated to St John's, Jan. 22, 1630-1, age 19. B.A. 1632-3.

HUNTMAN, THOMAS. Adm. pens. (age 18) at TRINITY, June 29, 1711. S. of Joseph, of Hatfield, Herts. School, Westminster. Matric. 1711; Scholar, 1713; B.A. 1714-5; M.A. 1718. Esquire Bedell, Jan. 13, 1726-7. Died Dec. 10, 1727. (H. P. Stokes, *Bedells*, 108.)

HUNTON or HUMPTON, ANTHONY. Matric. sizar from CHRIST'S, June, 1575; B.A. 1578-9; M.A. 1582. Licensed to practise medicine, 1589. Author, *Verses*. (*Cooper*, II. 241.)

HUNTON, BENJAMIN. Matric. pens. from CHRIST'S, July, 1622; B.A. 1625; M.A. 1629.

HUNTON, DANIEL. Matric. pens. from CHRIST'S, July, 1617; B.A. 1620-1; M.A. 1624. Ord. deacon (Peterb.) June 7, 1623; priest, June 4, 1626. 'Referred to the Assembly for examination,' Aug. 25, 1646. R. of Kelsey St Mary, Lincs., 1646. (*Peile*, I. 316.)

HUNTON, JOHN. B.A. from TRINITY, 1613-4. Ord. deacon (York) Sept. 1617. R. of St Martin's, York, 1618.

HUNTON, MORDECAI. Adm. pens. at EMMANUEL, Dec. 27, 1690. Of Lincolnshire. M.B. 1696.

HUNWICKE, JOHN. Matric. sizar from MAGDALENE, *c.* 1596; B.A. 1599-1600. Ord. deacon (London) June 24; priest, Aug. 19, 1604. V. of Tolleshunt d'Arcy, Essex, 1604-32. Died 1632. Will (Cons. C. London) 1632; as Hunnix.

HUNWYCKE, WILLIAM. Matric. pens. from JESUS, Easter, 1554. Probably adm. at Lincoln's Inn, Feb. 5, 1558-9. One William Huntwick, living at Temple Newsam, Leeds, 1572-3; owner of lands there. (M. H. Peacock.)

HUNWOOD, AARON. Adm. sizar (age 18) at ST JOHN'S, Mar. 24, 1670-1. S. of William, clerk, of Topcliffe, Yorks. B. there. School, Topcliffe. Matric. 1671.

HURD, JOHN. Adm. pens. (age 18) at TRINITY, May 30, 1694. S. of John. B. at Stidd, Derbs. School, Uttoxeter (Mr John Herbert).

HURD, NATHANIEL. Adm. pens. (age 19) at ST JOHN'S, July 9, 1724. S. of N., gent., of Staffordshire. B. at Mashfield. School, Stockport, Cheshire (Mr Dale). Matric. 1724; LL.B. 1731. V. of Longford, Derbs., 1740-73. R. of Lawton, Cheshire, 1743-4. R. of Thorpe, Derbs., 1766-73. Died 1773. (*Scott-Mayor*, III. 374.)

HURD, RICHARD. Adm. sizar at EMMANUEL, Oct. 3, 1733. S. of John, farmer, of Congreve, Staffs. B. there, Jan. 13, 1719-20. School, Brewood. Matric. 1735; B.A. 1738-9; M.A. 1742; B.D. 1749; D.D. 1768. Fellow, 1742. Ord. deacon (Norwich) June, 1742; priest, May, 1744. C. of St Andrew-the-Less, Cambridge, 1753-6. R. of Thurcaston, Leics., 1756-76. R. of Folkton, Yorks., 1762-74. Preacher at Lincoln's Inn, 1765. R. of Dursley, Gloucs., 1767-74. Archdeacon of Gloucester, 1767-74. Warburtonian lecturer, 1768. Bishop of Lichfield, 1774-81. Preceptor to the Prince of Wales and the Duke of York, 1776. Bishop of Worcester, 1781-1808. Elected a member of the Royal Society of Göttingen, 1781. Scholar and critic. Declined the primacy, 1783. Author, classical, etc. Died May 28, 1808. (*D.N.B.*)

HURD, WILLIAM. Matric. pens. from KING'S, Easter, 1622.

HURDIS, THOMAS. Matric. from TRINITY HALL, Easter, 1705; LL.B. 1705 (*Com. Reg.*). Probably s. of Thomas, of London, gent. Matric. from St Edmund Hall, Oxford, June 14, 1692, age 17. Ord. deacon (Lincoln) Sept. 20, 1702, as 'literate,' C. of Holywell, Hunts.; priest (Lincoln) July 30, 1704, as of St Edmund Hall, Oxford. V. of Ringmer, Sussex, 1727-33. Died 1733. Father of the next. (*Al. Oxon.* makes him a barrister, of the Middle Temple, 1698.)

HURDIS, THOMAS. M.A. from CLARE, 1733; D.D. 1766 (*Lit. Reg.*). S. of Thomas (above), of Holywell, Hunts., clerk. Matric. from Merton College, Oxford, July 18, 1724, age 17; B.A. (Oxford) 1728. Preb. of York, 1750-84. Preb. of Chichester, 1755-84. Canon of Windsor, 1766-84. Died Mar. 29, 1784. Will, P.C.C. (*Al. Oxon.*; *G. Mag.*; J. Ch. Smith.)

HURDLESTON or HURLESTON, GEORGE. Matric. sizar from CHRIST'S, May, 1579. Migrated to Trinity Hall. B.A. 1582-3.

HURDMAN, FRANCIS. M.A. 1675 (Incorp. from Magdalen Hall, Oxford). S. of Edward, of Worcester. Matric. from Magdalen Hall, Oxford, May 23, 1667, age 18; B.A. (Oxford) 1670-1; M.A. 1673. (*Al. Oxon.*)

HURLAND, ROBERT. Matric. pens. from CHRIST'S, Nov. 1559.

HURLAND, THOMAS (1538), *see* FULLER.

HURLESTON, WILLIAM. Matric. pens. from ST JOHN'S, Easter, 1582; B.A. from Trinity, 1584-5. One of these names, of Picton, Cheshire, adm. at the Inner Temple, 1588. Perhaps s. of Roger, of Chester; and brother of Roger Hurlton.

HURLOCK, BROOKE. Adm. sizar at EMMANUEL, Dec. 21, 1747. S. of James, farmer, of Elmstead Hall, Essex. School, Dedham, Essex. Matric. 1748-9, age 18; B.A. 1752. Ord. deacon (London) Sept. 24, 1752; priest, Sept. 22, 1754. R. of Lamarsh, Essex, 1761.

HURLOCKE, HENRY Adm. sizar at PETERHOUSE, Lent, 1601-2. Matric. 1602; Scholar, 1604-9; B.A. 1605-6; M.A. 1609.

HURLTON or HURLETON, RALPH. Adm. at KING'S (age 17) a scholar from Eton, Aug. 12, 1543. Of 'Puton,' Cheshire. Probably Randall, s. of Richard Hurleston, of Picton, Cheshire. Matric. 1544. Fellow, but left without a degree, 1546-7. (*Vis. of Cheshire*, 1613; E. Axon.)

HURLTON, ROGER. Matric. pens. from JESUS, Michs. 1568. Perhaps s. of Roger, of Chester. Died 1609. (*Vis. of Cheshire*, 1613.)

HURNE, FRANCIS. Matric. sizar from TRINITY HALL, Michs. 1561.

HURRELL, JAMES. Adm. sizar at QUEENS', Mar. 10, 1573-4. Of Essex. Probably V. of Gt Saling, Essex, till his death, 1617. Will (Cons. C. London) 1617.

HURRELL, JOHN. Matric. sizar from KING'S, Easter, 1680; B.A. 1683-4; M.A. 1687. Ord. priest (London) May 26, 1689. V. of Boxted, Essex, 1689-1720. Died 1720.

HURRELL, RICHARD. Matric. pens. from PEMBROKE, *c.* 1590; B.A. 1593-4.

HURRIE, STEPHEN. Matric. pens. from ST JOHN'S, Michs. 1612. B. at Horningsea, Cambs. B.A. 1614-5; M.A. from Queens', 1618. Ord. deacon (Peterb.) May 23; priest (London) Dec. 19, 1619, age 24. C. of Merstham, Surrey. R. of Aldeburgh, Norfolk, 1629-44, sequestered. Will (P.C.C.) 1647; of Pulham St Mary, clerk.

HURRYE, THOMAS. Matric. sizar from JESUS, Easter, 1548.

HURRION, JOHN. B.A. from ST CATHARINE'S, 1615-6; M.A. 1619.

HURST, *see also* HIRST.

HURST, JOHN. Matric. pens. from ST JOHN'S, Michs. 1617. One of these names, 1st s. of Godfrey, of London, adm. at the Inner Temple, 1618. Barrister, 1625.

HURST, JOSHUA. Matric. pens. from ST CATHARINE'S, Easter, 1631; LL.B. from Trinity Hall, 1639.

HURST, OWEN. Matric. pens. from CLARE, Michs. 1580.

HURST, OWEN. Matric. sizar from MAGDALENE, Michs. 1623; B.A. 1627-8; M.A. 1631.

HURST, RALPH. Adm. sizar (age 16) at CHRIST'S, May 31, 1653. S. of Ralph. B. in London. School, Danby Wiske, Yorks. (Mr Smelt). Matric. 1653.

HURST, ROBERT. Matric. pens. from CHRIST'S, July, 1621; B.A. 1624; M.A. 1628. Ord. deacon (Peterb.) Aug. 5; priest, Aug. 6, 1626. One of these names V. of Clareborough, Notts., till *c.* 1646. (*Peile*, I. 339.)

HURST, ROBERT (1622), *see* **HAYHURST.**

HURST, SAMUEL. Adm. sizar at TRINITY, Sept. 15, 1704. S. of William, of Holwell, Leics. School, Rugby. Matric. 1705; B.A. 1708-9; M.A. 1730. Ord. deacon (Peterb.) June 3, 1710, C. of Easton-on-the-Hill, Northants.; priest, Sept. 22, 1711.

HURST, THOMAS. Matric. pens. from CHRIST'S, Apr. 1614. S. of Richard, of Leicestershire. B.A. 1616-7; M.A. 1620; D.D. 1631 (*Lit. Reg.*). Incorp. at Oxford, 1623. Ord. deacon (Peterb.) May 4, 1621. Chaplain to King Charles. R. of Long Leadenham, Lincs., 1627-45, sequestered. R. of Ludborough, 1627; of Barrowby, 1629-46 and 1660-80; of Branston, 1638. Author. Died Mar. 17, 1679-80. Buried at Barrowby. (*Peile*, I. 295; *Lincs. Pedigrees*.)

HURST, THOMAS. Adm. pens. (age 17) at ST JOHN'S, May 22, 1731. S. of Thomas, gent., of Nottinghamshire. B. at Newark. School, Nottingham (Mr Hardy). Matric. 1731; B.A. 1734-5; M.A. 1752. Ord. deacon (Lincoln) June 20, 1736; pries (London) Dec. 24, 1738. V. of Exton, Rutland, 1750-80. R. of Ropsley, 1752-80. Chaplain to the Duke of Rutland. (*Scott-Mayor*, III. 436.)

HURST, THOMAS. Adm. pens. (age 18) at TRINITY, June 15, 1739. S. of Samuel, of Clayworth, Notts. School, Hemsworth, Yorks. (Mr Trant). Matric. 1739; Scholar, 1740; B.A. 1742-3. Ord. deacon (Lincoln) Feb. 27, 1742-3; priest (York) June 9, 1745. C. of Ordsall. Perhaps R. of Cole-Orton, Leics., 1761-78.

HURST, TIMOTHY. Adm. sizar at JESUS, June 8, 1734. Of Sandal Magna, Yorks. Matric. 1735. Ord. deacon (Lincoln) June 20, 1736.

HURST, VALENTINE. Matric. pens. from ST JOHN'S, *c.* 1590. S. of Ralph, gent., of West Lilling, Yorks. School, York. Migrated to Caius, Dec. 7, 1591, age 18. Perhaps B.A. 1593-4.

HURST, W. Matric. sizar from CLARE, Easter, 1584.

HURST, WILLIAM. Matric. pens. from MAGDALENE, Easter, 1602.

HURST, WILLIAM. Adm. pens. at QUEENS', Apr. 10, 1690. Of Essex.

HURST, ——. Pens. at PETERHOUSE, 1599-1600.

HURSTON, HUGH. Matric. pens. from TRINITY, Michs. 1567.

HURSTON, HUGH (1572), *see* **HUDDLESTON.**

HURT, CHARLES. Adm. Fell.-Com. (age 18) at ST JOHN'S, Dec. 7, 1696. S. of Nicholas, gent. B. at Castern, in Ilam, Staffs. School, in Surrey (Mr Bonwick). Of Alderwasley, Derbs., Esq. Married Catherine, dau. of Gervase Rosell, Esq., of Ratcliffe-on-Trent, Notts. Died 1763. Grandson of Nicholas (1639-40). (Burke, *L.G.*; *Staffs. Pedigrees*.)

HURT, HENRY. Adm. pens. at ST CATHARINE'S, July 4, 1664. (Previously matric. from St John's, Oxford, Oct. 18, 1662, age 19.). Probably s. of William, of Coventry. B.A. 1665-6. Signed for priest's orders (London) Mar. 10, 1665-6. V. of St Mary, Romney Marsh, 1679-1700. (*Al. Oxon.*)

HURT, JOHN. B.Can.L. 1525-6. R. of Little Billing, Northants., till 1532. V. of St Margaret Moses, London, 1532-42. R. of Gt Billing, Northants., 1533-52. R. of Hanbury, Staffs., 1536-52. V. of Ware, Herts., 1542-52.

HURT, JOHN. Matric. pens. from MAGDALENE, Michs., 1598; B.A. 1601-2; M.A. 1605. Ord. deacon and priest (Peterb.) Sept. 18, 1608. Probably C. of West Tilbury, Essex, 1609. V. of Horndon-on-the-Hill, 1628-48.

HURT, JOHN. Adm. pens. (age 18) at ST JOHN'S, July 4, 164 . S. of William, merchant. B. in London. School, St Paul's. (*Vis. of London*, 1634.)

HURT, JOHN. Adm. pens. at ST CATHARINE'S, July 9, 1664. Matric. 1665; B.A. 1667-8.

HURT, LOWE. Adm. pens. (age 17) at ST JOHN'S, June 13, 1727. S. of Francis, gent., of Derbyshire. B. at Hill-Side, near Wirksworth. School, Chesterfield (Mr Burrow). Matric. 1727; B.A. 1730-1; M.A. 1734. C. of Derwent, Derbs., 1738.

HURT, NICHOLAS. Adm. Fell.-Com. at JESUS, Feb. 8, 1639-40. Of Staffordshire. Doubtless s. of Roger. Matric. 1640. Age 42 in 1663. Of Castern, Derbs. Married Isabella, dau. of Sir Henry Harpur, Bart. uri Feb. 7, 1676-7. Grandfather of Charles (1696) and perhaps of Lowe (1727). (Burke, *L.G.*; *Staffs. Pedigrees*; *Glover*, II. 8.)

HURT, THOMAS. B.Can.L. 1496-7. One of these names parish priest of St Magnus, London, in 1506 (will, P.C.C., of T. Steyd.)

HURTE, THOMAS. Matric. sizar from ST JOHN'S, Michs. 1549.

HURTT, THOMAS. Matric. pens. from TRINITY, Michs. 1615. Of Nottinghamshire. B.A. 1617-8; M.A. from St John's, 1621; B.D. 1629. Fellow of St John's, 1621. V. of Faversham, Kent, 1640-3. Died 1643. Buried there Jan. 22, 1642-3.

HURT, W. B.Can.L. 1498-9. One William Hurt succeeded John Hurt, at Gt Billing, Northants., 1532-50. (T. P. Dorman.)

HURTLE, WILLIAM. Adm. pens. at ST CATHARINE'S, July 2, 1716. Of Worcestershire.

HURTON, PREGION. Adm. pens. (age 18) at ST JOHN'S, June 2, 1740. S. of John, yeoman, of Lincolnshire. B. at Apley. School, Lincoln (Mr Gooddall). Matric. 1740; B.A. 1743-4; M.A. 1747. Ord. deacon (Lincoln) Sept. 22, 1745; priest, Sept. 20, 1747. V. of Crowle, Lincs., 1747-52. V. of Stainton-by-Langworth, 1749-87. Buried at Navenby, 1787. Will (P.C.C.) 1788; as Robert Pregion Hurton. (*Scott-Mayor*, III. 505.)

HURTON, THOMAS. Adm. pens. at CAIUS, July 4, 1637. S. of William, gent. B. at Wells, Norfolk. School, Ely (Mr Hitch).

HURTYLBY, ——. B.A. 1464.

HURWOOD, ROLAND. LL.B. from CHRIST'S, 1654. Previously matric. from St Alban Hall, Oxford, Apr. 1641, age 18. Probably s. of Thomas, R. of Otterington, Yorks. R. of Hawnhy, Yorks., 1660-8. Minister of Thornton-le-Street. Married Catharine, dau. of John Talbot, Esq. (*Peile*, I. 479; M. H. Peacock.)

HUSBAND, CHRISTOPHER. Adm. pens. (age 16) at CAIUS, Sept. 8, 1590. S. of Thomas. B. in Norfolk. Scholar, 1591-6; B.A. 1593; M.A. 1597. Fellow, 1596-1624. Taxor, 1621. Incorp. at Oxford, 1607. Lived at Honing, after 1624, on his family estate. Donor to Caius library. Buried at Honing, Nov. 27, 1634. Father of Valentine (1644). (*Venn*, I. 140.)

HUSBAND, HENRY. M.A. from KING'S, 1725. S. of J., of Eyton, Salop. Matric. from Trinity College, Oxford, June 4, 1714, age 15; B.A. (Oxford) 1718. Brother of Richard (1724). (*Al. Oxon.*)

HUSBAND, JAMES. Adm. pens. (age 17) at CAIUS, Feb. 27, 1710-1. S. of Edward, gent., of Horkesley, Essex. B. there. Schools, Ipswich (Mr Coningsby) and Bury. Matric. 1711; Scholar, 1711-6; LL.B. 1715; LL.D. 1724. Fellow, 1716 and 1722-44. Adm. at Lincoln's Inn, Apr. 27, 1711. Ord. deacon (London) Feb. 18, 1721-2. R. of Ashdon, 1729. R. of Fordham, 1743-9. V. of Little Horkesley, Essex. Died there Feb. 22, 1749-50. M.I. Will, P.C.C. Benefactor to the College. (*Venn*, I. 524.)

HUSBAND, JOHN. Adm. pens. (age 16) at CAIUS, May 15, 1650. S. and h. of Thomas, gent., of Somerton, Norfolk. B. there. School, Norwich (Mr Lovering). Matric. 1650; Scholar, 1650-2. Brother of Thomas (1638). (*Venn*, I. 378; *Vis. of Norfolk*, 1664.)

HUSBANDS, JOHN. Adm. sizar at ST CATHARINE'S, 1675. Matric. 1675; B.A. 1678-9; M.A. 1682.

HUSBAND, JOHN. Adm. sizar (age 17) at CHRIST'S, June 17, 1702. S. of John. B. at Lichfield. School, Liehfield (Mr Shaw). Matric. 1702-3; Scholar, 1702; B.A. 1705-6; M.A. 1709. Ord. deacon (Lichfield) May, 1706; priest (London) Feb. 1707-8. Minor canon of St Paul's, 1706-38. Probahly V. of Mucking, Essex, till 1714. V. of Tottenham, 1714-38. Preb. of Lichfield, 1716-26. Died Feb. 6, 1737-8. (G. *Mag.*; *Peile*, II. 154.)

HUSBAND, RICHARD. M.A. from CHRIST'S, 1724. S. of John, of Eyton, Salop. Matric. from St Mary Hall, Oxford, June 4, 1714, age 17; B.A. (Christ Church) 1718. Ord. deacon (Lichfield) 1719; priest (Canterbury) 1721. R. of Ruddington, Salop, 1722. Minor canon of Rochester, 1736-69. P.C. of Strood, Kent, July 12, 1738-47. V. of St Nicholas, Newington, 1738-9. V. of Stockbury, Kent, 1747-50. V. of Wateringbury, 1750-69. V. of Chart Sutton, till 1769. P.C. of Bilsington, till 1769. Buried in Rochester Cathedral, May 26, 1769. Will, P.C.C. (*Al. Oxon.*; *Peile*, II. 193.)

HUSBANDS, SAMUEL. Adm. Fell.-Com. (age 15) at CAIUS, June, 1663. S. of Richard, linen-weaver, of London. Schools, Hackney (Mr Wooliey), St Mary Axe (Mr Spillwater) and Bishop's Stortford (private; Mr Leigh). Matric. 1664. Adm. at the Middle Temple, Oct. 1, 1665. Of Shalford, Essex. Knighted, Apr. 13, 1684. D.L. and J.P. for Essex. Went to the Barbados. Died there. (*Venn*, I. 419.)

HUSBAND, THOMAS. Adm. pens. (age 16) at CAIUS, Mar. 8, 1637-8. S. of Thomas, gent., of Somerton, Norfolk. B. at Cromer. School, North Walsham (Mr Agurs). Matric. 1638. Adm. at Gray's Inn, Feb. 27, 1639-40. Called to the Bar, 1648. M.I. at Belaugh to Tho. Husband, who died Sept. 17, 1660. Will proved (Norwich) 1660. Brother of John (1650). (*Venn*, I. 331.)

HUSBANDS, THOMAS. Adm. at CORPUS CHRISTI, 1684. Of Norfolk. Perhaps of Somerton. Adm. at Gray's Inn, July 2, 1687.

HUSBAND, THOMAS. Matric. sizar from CHRIST'S, Lent, 1705-6; Scholar, 1706; B.A. 1708-9; M.A. 1712. Fellow, 1709. Scrutator, 1720. Ord. deacon (Lincoln) Sept. 23, 1710; priest, June 15, 1712. R. of Hardwick, Cambs., 1721; of Kegworth, Leics., 1723-5. Died before May, 1725. (*Peile*, II. 162.)

HUSBAND, VALENTINE. Adm. pens. (age 16) at CAIUS, May 9, 1644. S. of Christopher (1590). B. at Catfield, Norfolk. Schools, North Walsham (Mr Acres) and Norwich (Mr Lovering). Matric. 1644; Scholar, 1644-51; B.A. 1647-8; M.A. 1651. Ord. deacon and priest (Bishop Joseph Hall) Aug. 4, 1654. R. of Sloley, Norfolk, 1661-2; of Crostwight, 1672-4; and of Congham St Mary and St Andrew, 1673-84. Will proved (Norwich) 1683-4. Father of the next. (*Venn*, I. 352.)

HUSBAND, VALENTINE. Adm. sizar (age 17) at CAIUS, June 20, 1684. S. of Valentine (above). B. at Honing. School, Lynn. Matric. 1684; Scholar, 1684. Migrated to Sidney, Nov. 19, 1687. (Probably one of the Master's Romanist importations.) (*Venn*, I. 477.)

HUSBAND, WILLIAM. Adm. sizar (age 19) at TRINITY, May 30, 1729. S. of Christopher, of Guisborough, Yorks. School, Kirkleatham, Yorks. (Mr Oakley). Matric. 1729; Scholar, 1732. Ord. deacon (Lincoln) Dec. 24, 1732. One of these names V. of Rudby-in-Cleveland, Yorks., 1745-75. V. of Nunthorpe, 1775. (M. H. Peacock.)

HUSBANDS, —— (*junior*). Adm. sizar at ST CATHARINE'S, 1675.

HUSCROFTE, WILLIAM. Matric. sizar from TRINITY, 1598; B.A. 1601-2; M.A. 1605. Ord. deacon and priest (Peterb.) Sept. 29, 1603. V. of Middleton, Norfolk, 1610.

HUSE, EDMUND. Matric. sizar from CAIUS, Oct. 13, 1582.

HUSK, JOHN. Matric. pens. from CORPUS CHRISTI, 1590. Of Suffolk. B.A. 1593-4; M.A. 1597.

HUSK, JOSEPH. Matric. pens. from CORPUS CHRISTI, Michs. 1720.

HUSON, *see* **HEWSON.**

HUSSE, AMBROSE. Matric. sizar from CAIUS, *c.* 1591. Perhaps s. of George, of Rye, Sussex. (*Vis. of London*, 1634.)

HUSSE, ——. Incorp. from Oxford, 1472-3.

HUSSE or HUSSEY, ——. Incorp. 1497-8. 'Canonist,' 1500.

HUSSEBOURN, RICHARD. Scholar at KING'S HALL, 1361. Died Aug. 28, 1368.

HUSSEBOURN, ROBERT DE. Scholar at KING'S HALL, 1358. S. of William. Died Aug. 22, 1368.

HUSSEY or HUSSYE, ALEXANDER. Matric. pens. from ST JOHN'S, Michs. 1551.

HUSSEY, Sir CHARLES, Bart. Adm. Fell.-Com. at TRINITY, Nov. 10, 1675. 1st s. of Sir Charles, of Caythorpe, Lincs., Bart., deceased. Succeeded his father as 2nd Baronet, 1664. Adm. at the Middle Temple, June 28, 1676. Died unmarried. Buried at Caythorpe, Apr. 21, 1680. Brother of Edward (1675). (*Lincs. Pedigrees*, 531; Burke, *Ext. Bart.*; *G.E.C.*)

HUSSEY, CHRISTOPHER. Adm. sizar (age 19) at TRINITY, Mar. 20, 1703. S. of Robert, of London. School, St Paul's. Matric. 1703; Scholar, 1704; B.A. 1706-7; M.A. 1710; D.D. 1731. Fellow, 1709. Ord. deacon (Ely) May 31, 1713; priest, Dec. 23, 1716. R. of West Wickham, Kent, 1720-61. R. of All Hallows-the-Great and Less, London, 1732-61. Chaplain to the Duke of Dorset. Author, *Sermons*. Died Aug. 16, 1761. Will, P.C.C. (H. G. Harrison; J. Ch. Smith.)

HUSSEY, DEERING. Adm. pens. at EMMANUEL, Easter, 1624. Doubtless 2nd s. of George, of Slynfold, Sussex, and Jane, dau. of John Dering, of Egerton, Kent. Matric. 1624; B.A. 1627-8; M.A. 1631. (*Dallaway and Cartwright*, II. 391.)

HUSSEY, EDWARD. Adm. pens. (16) at CAIUS, Aug. 7, 1645. Of Caythorpe, Lincs. Sagd Sir Edward, Bart., of Honington, Lincs. B. there. School, Somerby (Mr Briggs). Migrated to St John's, Mar. 8, 1646-7. Died without issue. Will proved (P.C.C.) 1659. Perhaps brother of John (1640). (*Venn*, I. 359; *Lincs. Pedigrees*, 529.)

HUSSEY, EDWARD. Adm. Fell.-Com. (age 13) at TRINITY, May 18, 1675. S. of Sir Charles, of Caythorpe, Lincs., Bart. Matric. 1675. Succeeded his brother Charles, as 3rd Baronet, Apr. 1680. M.P. for Lincoln, 1689-95, 1698-1700 and 1701-8. Inherited the Honington baronetcy in 1706, on the death of his cousin Sir Thomas (1654-5). Died Feb. 19, 1724-5. M.I. at Caythorpe. Brother of Charles (1675), father of the next and of Henry (1720). (*Lincs. Pedigrees*, 531.)

HUSSEY, EDWARD. Adm. pens. (age 14) at TRINITY, July 1, 1720. S. of Sir Edward (above), Bart., of Caythorpe and Welbourn, Lincs. School, Grantham, Lincs. (Mr Ellis). Succeeded his brother Henry as 5th Baronet, of Caythorpe, 1730. Died Apr. 1, 1734. Brother of Henry (1720). (*Lincs. Pedigrees*, 531; Burke, *Ext. Bart.*)

HUSSEY, EDWARD. Adm. pens. (age 17) at ST JOHN'S, Oct. 25, 1740. S. of Thomas, Esq., of Burwash, Sussex. B. at Burwash. School, Tonbridge, Kent (Mr Spencer). Adm. at the Middle Temple, Oct. 30, 1739. Buried Apr. 15, 1742. Brother of Thomas (1739). (*Scott-Mayor*, III. 510; Burke, *L.G.*)

HUSEY, GEORGE. Adm. sizar (age 19) at KING'S, Nov. 4, 1717. S. of Robert, farmer, of Dorset. B. at Corfe Mullen. Bapt. there, Feb. 1, 1699-1700. School, Taunton, Somerset. Matric. 1717. Migrated to St John's, Oct. 30, 1718. B.A. 1721-2; M.A. 1725; B.D. 1733. Fellow of St John's, 1723-39. Ord. deacon (Oxford) Dec. 22, 1723; priest (Peterb.) Sept. 20, 1724. Chaplain to the Duke of Somerset. R. of Trowbridge, Wilts., 1730-41. Died there July 14, 1741. M.I. at Seend, Wilts. (*Scott-Mayor*, III. 321.)

HUSSEY, HENRY. Matric. pens. from QUEENS', Easter, 1562. Resident pens. Aug. 1564. One of these names s. of John, of Slynfold, Sussex. Clerk of the Spicery to Queen Elizabeth and King James. Died May 23, 1611, aged 64. (*Dallaway and Cartwright*, II. 390.)

HUSSEY, HENRY. Adm. pens. at EMMANUEL, June 9, 1641. Of Kent. Doubtless s. and h. of George, of Egerton, Kent. Matric. 1641. Adm. at the Inner Temple, 1642. Married the dau. of —— Lamb, of Taywell, Kent. Living, 1666. (*Dallaway and Cartwright*, II. 391.)

HUSSEY, HENRY. Adm. Fell.-Com. (age 17) at TRINITY, July 1, 1720. 1st s. of Sir Edward (1675), Bart., of Caythorpe and Welbourn, Lincs. School, Grantham, Lincs. (Mr Ellis). Succeeded his father as 4th Baronet, 1725. Died Feb. 14, 1729-30, *s.p.* Brother of Edward (1720). (*Lincs. Pedigrees*, 531; *G.E.C.*)

HUSSEY, JEREMIAH. Adm. sizar at TRINITY, Sept. 8, 1682. Matric. 1682; Scholar, 1687; B.A. 1687-8. Will (Exeter) 1711; of Okehampton, Devon, clerk.

HUSSEYE, JOHN. Matric. pens. from PEMBROKE, Easter, 1550. One of these names adm. at Gray's Inn, 1553 (*see* Robert). Perhaps s. of George, of Harswell, Yorks. Of North Duffield, Esq. (*Vis. of Yorks.*, 1584.)

HUSSY, JOHN. Matric. pens. from JESUS, Michs. 1560. One of these names adm. at Gray's Inn, 1563.

HUSSEY, JOHN. Matric. sizar from CLARE, Lent, 1607-8; B.A. 1611-2; M.A. 1615. Ord. deacon (York, for Lincoln) Sept. 1616. R. of High Laver, Essex, till 1637.

HUSSEY, JOHN. Adm. Fell.-Com. at ST CATHARINE'S, 1640. Of Lincolnshire. Perhaps 2nd s. of Sir Edward, of Honington, Lincs., Bart. If so, Captain in the army. Slain at Gainsborough. Buried at Honington, July 28, 1645. Perhaps brother of Edward (1645). (*Lincs. Pedigrees*, 529.)

HUSSEY, JOHN. Adm. sizar (age 19) at ST JOHN'S, July 28, 1646. S. of John, V. of Okehampton, Devon. B. there. School, Exeter (Mr Ball). Matric. 1646; B.A. 1650. Perhaps will (Exeter) 1688; of Okehampton, clerk.

HUSSEY, JOHN. Adm. sizar at TRINITY, July 6, 1670. Matric. 1670; Scholar, 1674; B.A. 1674-5; M.A. 1678. Ord. deacon (Ely) Oct. 2, 1675; priest (London) Dec. 24, 1676.

HUSSEY, JOHN. Adm. pens. at EMMANUEL, May 12, 1676. Of Surrey. Matric. 1679; B.A. 1679-80.

HUSSEY, JOHN. Adm. Fell.-Com. at TRINITY, Mar. 29, 1677. Doubtless s. and h. of Peter (below). B. Nov. 30, 1658. Matric. 1678. Adm. at Lincoln's Inn, May 14, 1677. Of Sutton Place, Surrey. Buried July 9, 1685.

HUSSEY, PETER. Adm. pens. at EMMANUEL, Michs. 1637. Of Middlesex. Matric. 1637. Probably s. of Thomas, of the City of London; adm. (special) to Lincoln's Inn, May 22, 1639. Of Sutton Place, Surrey. Donor to Emmanuel chapel. Buried June 24, 1684. Father of John (above). (*Vis. of London*, 1634; *Manning and Bray*, I. 497.)

HUSSEY, ROBERT. Matric. pens. from PEMBROKE, Easter, 1550. Perhaps s. of George, of Harswell, Yorks. One of these names adm. at Gray's Inn, 1553. (*Vis. of Yorks.*)

HUSSEY, Sir THOMAS, Bart. Adm. Fell.-Com. (age 15) at CHRIST'S, Mar. 1654-5. S. of Thomas. B. at Doddington, Lincs. School, Wormley, Herts. (Mr Lovelace). Matric. 1656; M.A. 1656. Succeeded as Bart. Mar. 22, 1647-8. Of Honington, Lincs. Sheriff of Lincs., 1668-9. D.L. 1680. M.P. for Lincoln, 1681; for Lincs., 1685-7 and 1689-98. Died Dec. 19, 1706. Buried at Honington. Father of William (1690). (*Peile*, I. 565; *Lincs. Pedigrees*, 530; A. B. Beaven.)

HUSSEY, THOMAS. Adm. pens. (age 17) at ST JOHN'S, Oct. 13, 1739. S. of Thomas, Esq., deceased, of Burwash, Sussex. B. at Burwash. Bapt. Sept. 18, 1722. Schools, Maidstone (Mr Walwyn) and Staplehurst (private). Matric. 1739. Of Burwash, and Ashford, Kent. Married, Oct. 8, 1747, Anne, dau. of Maurice Berkeley. Died July 3, 1779. Buried at Ashford. Brother of Edward (1740). (Burke, *L.G.*; *Scott-Mayor*, III. 503.)

HUSSEY, WILLIAM. Adm. sizar at JESUS, May 28, 1680. Of Hampshire. Matric. 1680; Scholar, 1683; B.A. 1683-4; M.A. 1687. Fellow, 1684-1703. Taxor, 1689-90. V. of Comberton, Cambs., 1687. V. of Fordham, 1694-6. R. of Graveley, 1696. R. of Tytherley, Hants., succeeding his father.

HUSSEY, WILLIAM. Adm. Fell.-Com. (age 16) at CHRIST'S, Oct. 10, 1690. S. of Sir Thomas (1654-5), of Doddington, Lincs. B. there. Educated at home (Mr Carleton). Matric. 1690. Resided two years. Buried at Honington, Lincs., July 29, 1698. (*Lincs. Pedigrees*, 530; *Peile*, II. 118.)

HUSSY, ——. Adm. Fell.-Com. at ST CATHARINE'S, 1686. Of Surrey.

HUSTLER, JOHN. Adm. sizar (age 16) at MAGDALENE, June 11, 1652. S. of Arthur, of Cottingham, Yorks. School, Beverley. Matric. 1652; B.A. 1655-6; M.A. 1659.

HUSTLER, WILLIAM. Adm. sizar (age 18) at CAIUS, June 23, 1660. S. of Thomas, husbandman. B. at Silsden, Kildwick, Yorks. School, Silsden, Bingley (Mr Lane). Matric. 1660; Scholar, 1660-3; B.A. 1664-5. Ord. priest (York) Dec. 21, 1662, as C. of Coniston. V. of Ilkley, 1665-1703, where he kept school. Head Master of Otley Grammar School, 1680. Died 1703. (*Venn*, I. 409.)

HUSTWAYTE, *see also* **HUTHWETT.**

HOUSTWAYTE or USTWATE, EDWARD. Matric. pens. from PETERHOUSE, Michs. 1565, as 'Houstvell.' 2nd s. of William Husthwaite. B.A. from Pembroke, 1568-9. Ord. priest (Lincoln) Mar. 28, 1572. R. of Miningsby, Lincs., 1572. Will proved Dec. 12, 1620. Brother of Robert (1564). (*Lincs. Pedigrees*, 532.)

HUSTWATE, GEORGE. Matric. pens. from TRINITY, Easter, 1560.

HUSTWAYTE or HOWSTWAT, JOHN. B.A. 1515-6.

HUSTWAYT or HUSTODE, JOHN. Matric. sizar from ST JOHN'S, c. 1592; B.A. 1595-6.

HUSTEWATE or USTWADE, ROBERT. Scholar at KING'S HALL, 1478-84.

HUNSTWYT or HUSTHWAITE, ROBERT. Matric. sizar from PETERHOUSE, Michs. 1564. S. of William. Burgess of Grimsby, Lincs. Buried there Dec. 25, 1615. Will (Lincoln) 1616. Brother of Edward (1565). (*Lincs. Pedigrees*; *T. A. Walker*.)

HUSTWAITE, ROBERT. Matric. sizar from CLARE, Easter, 1610; B.A. 1613-4; M.A. 1617. Ord. deacon (Peterb.) Dec. 20; priest, Dec. 21, 1618. Perhaps R. of Gonalston, Notts., 1620.

HUSUM, ——. B.Civ.L. 1472-3.

HUTCHINGS, EDMUND. Matric. Fell.-Com. from KING'S, Easter, 1693. One of these names, s. and h. of George, of Gray's Inn, adm. at Gray's Inn, Apr. 10, 1686.

HUTCHYN, JOHN. B.A. 1492-3; M.A. 1496-7; B.D. 1506-7. One of the original fellows of JESUS, 1499. Proctor, 1502-3. University preacher, 1505-6. One John Hochyn, B.D., priest of the Chapel of Our Lady at All Hallows, Barking, London, in 1515. Perhaps V. of Over, Cambs., 1518-21. Died 1521. (A. Gray; J. Ch. Smith.)

HUTCHIN, JOHN. Matric. sizar from QUEENS', Easter, 1571. Ord. deacon and priest (Peterb.) June 22, 1573, as 'B.A.; aged 30; married; bred in the schools' (*Lib. Cler.*, 1576). R. of Wyfordby, Leics., 1574. Buried June 3, 1625.

HUTCHIN, JOHN. Adm. sizar (age 15) at ST JOHN'S, Mar. 5, 1669-70. S. of Hugh, shoemaker, of Grantham, Lincs. B. there. School, Grantham (Mr Sistou). Matric. 1670; B.A. 1673-4; M.A. 1677; B.D. 1684. Fellow, 1677-91. Ord. deacon (Ely) Sept. 23, 1676. Perhaps V. of Coulsdon, Surrey, 1688. Chaplain to the Earl of Danby. Died 1689.

HUTCHINS, JOHN. M.A. from MAGDALENE, 1730. S. of Richard, of Bradford Peverell, Dorset, clerk. B. there, Sept. 21, 1698. School, Dorchester. Matric. from Hart Hall, Oxford, May 30, 1718, age 19; B.A. (Oxford) 1721. C. of Milton Abbas, Dorset, 1723; and usher of the school. R. of Swyre, 1729-73. R. of Melcombe Horsey, 1733-44. R. of Wareham (Holy Trinity, Arne, St Mary and St Martin), 1743-73. Historian of Dorset. Died June 21, 1773. Buried in St Mary's, Wareham. M.I. there. (*D.N.B.*; *Al. Oxon.*; F. S. Hockaday.)

HUTCHINS, LEMAN. Adm. Fell.-Com. at CLARE, Apr. 18, 1718. S. of Sir George, of Gray's Inn, Middlesex, Knt. Bapt. Aug. 1, 1700, at Northaw, Herts. (his mother's home). Died at Chelsea, May 20, 1738. Buried at Northaw. (G. *Mag.*; *Clutterbuck*, II. 415.)

HUTCHIN, ROBERT. Matric. sizar from MAGDALENE, Easter, 1617.

HUTCHINSON, ANDREW. Matric. sizar from TRINITY, Michs. 1632.

HUTCHINSON, BOTELER. Adm. pens. (age 18) at SIDNEY, June 9, 1726. 2nd s. of Julius, Esq. B. at Owthorpe, Notts. School, Winchester. Colonel of marines, 1745. Probably died Feb. 3, 1770. Brother of Charles (1728) and Thomas (1723). (*L. Mag.*; *Clutterbuck*, II. 347.)

HUTCHINSON or HUTCHESON, CHARLES. Matric. sizar from CLARE, Easter, 1585; B.A. 1588-9; M.A. 1592. Perhaps R. of Halstead, Kent, 1593-4. R. of Hartley, 1593-1617. R. of Wrotham, 1593-4.

HUTCHINSON, CHARLES. Matric. sizar from CLARE, Michs. 1611; B.A. 1614-5; M.A. 1618. He was one of the actors in the famous play of *Ignoramus*, performed before James I, in 1614. One of these names V. of Pembury, Kent, 1621-39. R. of Shadoxhurst, 1631-6. Perhaps will (P.C.C.) 1650; of Wrotham, Kent, clerk.

HUTCHINSON, CHARLES. Adm. pens. at TRINITY, May 29, 1667. Matric. 1667.

HUTCHINSON, CHARLES. Adm. Fell.-Com. at TRINITY, July 9, 1669. Perhaps adm. at Gray's Inn, Nov. 16, 1669; s. and h. of John, of Pinner, Middlesex.

HUTCHINSON, CHARLES. Adm. pens. (age 17) at SIDNEY, Oct. 23, 1728. S. of Julius, Esq. B. at Owthorpe, Notts. Educated at home. Matric. 1729; B.A. 1732-3; M.A. 1736; D.D. 1754. Incorp. at Oxford, 1755. Ord. deacon (Lincoln) June 9, 1734; priest (*Litt. dim.* from York) Aug. 1735. C. of St Peter's, Nottingham. Will (P.C.C.) 1769; of Claybrooke, Leics., D.D. Brother of Boteler (1726) and Thomas (1723).

HUTCHINSON, CHRISTOPHER. B.A. 1509-10. Probably R. of Scremby, Lincs., 1526. R. of Leasingham, 1535. Will proved July 8, 1556. (*Lincs. Pedigrees*, 535.)

HUTCHINSON, CHRISTOPHER. Matric. pens. from JESUS, Michs. 1549, *impubes*. Probably s. of Christopher (above), R. of Scremby, Lincs.

HUTCHINSON, EDMUND. Matric. sizar from MAGDALENE, Easter, 1634; B.A. 1636-7; M.A. 1660. Ord. deacon (Peterb.) June 9, 1639; priest, Sept. 19, 1641. V. of Butterwick, Lincs., 1642.

HUTCHINSON, EDMUND. Adm. pens. at EMMANUEL, Jan. 19, 1681-2.

HUTCHYNSON, EDWARD. Matric. pens. from TRINITY, Michs. 1558; Scholar, 1560.

HUTTCHISON, EDWARD. Adm. Fell.-Com. at JESUS, June 19, 1629. Of Yorkshire. S. and h. of Stephen, of Wykeham Abbey, Yorks., Esq. Matric. 1629. Adm. at Gray's Inn, Nov. 1, 1634. Colonel of Horse in the royal service. Disinherited by the will of his father, a Parliamentarian, 1646. Married Frances, dau. of Sir Richard Osbaldiston, of Yorks. Buried at St Mary Woolchurch, London, July 1, 1653. (*Vis. of Yorks.*, 1665; *F.M.G.*, 979; M. H. Peacock.)

HUTCHINSON, EDWARD. Adm. sizar at CHRIST'S, July 7, 1720. (Probably s. of Edward, of Clipston, Northants., who died 1727.) B. at Clipston. Matric. 1720; Scholar, 1721. Buried at Clipston, Aug. 6, 1738. (H. I. Longden.)

HUTCHINSON, ELIAS. Adm. sizar (age 18) at SIDNEY, Feb. 9, 1625-6. S. of Thomas (1582-3), R. of Hapton, Norfolk. B. there. School, Norwich Cathedral. B.A. 1629-30; M.A. 1633. V. of Holy Trinity, York; resigned, 1638. V. of Yedingham, Yorks., 1636-8. R. of South Kilvington, 1638-79. Buried Mar. 25, 1679.

HUTCHINSON, FRANCIS. Matric. pens. from ST JOHN'S, Michs. 1606.

HUTCHINSON or HITCHINSON, FRANCIS. Adm. pens. at ST CATHARINE'S, 1677. S. of Edward. B. at Carsington, Derbs., Jan. 2, 1660-1. Matric. 1678; B.A. 1680-1; M.A. 1684; D.D. 1698. Ord. deacon (London) Sept. 23, 1683; priest, Feb. 24, 1683-4. V. of Hoxne, Suffolk, 1690. V. of St James', Bury St Edmunds. R. of Passenham, Northants., 1706-27. Chaplain to the King, 1715-20. Bishop of Down and Connor, 1720-39. Married, at Bury St Edmunds, Apr. 15, 1707, Perigin North. Author. Died at Portglenone, Antrim, June 23, 1739. Buried there. M.I. Will (Dublin) 1740. (*D.N.B.*; A. B. Beaven.)

HUCHENSON, FRANCIS. Adm. pens. at QUEENS', May 14, 1725. Of Middlesex. Matric. 1725.

HUTCHINSON, GABRIEL. Matric. sizar from CLARE, Easter, 1589.

HUTCHINSON, GERVASE. Matric. pens. from ST CATHARINE'S, Easter, 1650.

HUTCHINSON, JAMES. B.A. from CLARE, 1596-7; M.A. 1600; B.D. 1608-9. Perhaps R. of West Grinstead, Sussex, 1622-37. Preb. of Chichester. Will (Chichester) 1637.

HUTCHINSON, JAMES. Adm. sizar (age 17) at MAGDALENE, May 29, 1668. S. of (? Edward), of Carsington, Derbs. School, Wirksworth. Perhaps brother of Francis (1677).

HUTCHINSON, JAMES. Adm. pens. at QUEENS', June 28, 1731. Of Derbyshire. Matric. 1731; B.A. 1734-5.

HUTCHINSON, JOHN. Matric. pens. from PEMBROKE, Michs. 1568; B.A. 1572-3; M.A. 1576; B.D. 1584. Fellow, 1574. Incorp. at Oxford, 1581. University preacher, 1582. V. of Tilney, Norfolk, 1582-1601. R. of Redenhall, 1584-94. Will (P.C.C.) 1601; of Tilney, mentions brothers William (1568) and Ralph, President of St John's, Oxford. (J. Ch. Smith.)

HUTCHINSON, JOHN. Matric. sizar from PEMBROKE, *c.* 1593; B.A. (? 1594-5); M.A. 1598. Ord. deacon (Lincoln) May 26; priest, Sept. 22, 1605. C. of Spalding, Lincs., 1605. One of these names V. of Askham, Westmorland, 1611-35. Buried there Sept. 8, 1644. (*B. Nightingale.*)

HUTCHINSON, JOHN. Matric. pens. from EMMANUEL, Easter, 1617; B.A. 1620-1.

HUTCHINSON, JOHN. Matric. pens. from ST JOHN'S, Easter, 1627. S. of Thomas, of London, Esq. B.A. 1630-1; M.A. 1634; B.D. 1641. Preb. of Lichfield, 1662-1705. Died Jan. 12, 1704-5 aged 94. Brother of Michael (1627). (*Vis. of London*, 1634; Le Neve, *Mon.*, II. 100.)

HUTCHINSON, JOHN. Adm. Fell.-Com. (age 16) at PETERHOUSE, Feb. 29, 1631-2. S. of Sir Thomas (1606), of Owthorpe, Notts. Schools, Nottingham and Lincoln. Matric. 1632; B.A. 1634. Adm. at Lincoln's Inn, May 16, 1636. Parliamentarian. Sat as one of the King's judges, and signed the death warrant. Governor of Nottingham, 1643. M.P. for Co. Notts., 1646-53; and for Nottingham, April-June, 1660. Member of the first two Councils of State, 1649-51. Joined Monck, in 1659-60. Expelled as a Regicide, 1660. Married Lucy, dau. of Sir Allan Apsley, Knt., Lieut. of the Tower of London. Died in prison at Sandown Castle, Kent, Sept. 11, 1664. Buried at Owthorpe. Probably father of Thomas (1658). (*T. A. Walker*, 46; *D.N.B.*)

HUTCHINSON, JOHN. Adm. sizar (age 15) at SIDNEY, Apr. 4, 1653. S. of Thomas, carpenter. B. at Selby, Yorks. School, Selby (Mr Firth). Matric. 1653; B.A. 1656-7; M.A. 1660. Probably R. of Astbury, Cheshire, 1676-1704. Died 1704.

HUTCHINSON, JOHN. Adm. sizar at TRINITY, Feb. 13, 1654-5. B. in London, Apr. 15, 1638. Schools, Merchant Taylors' and Eton. Matric. 1656; Scholar, 1657; B.A. 1658-9. Fellow, 1659-62, ejected. Travelled. Practised physic at Hitchin and Clapham. Kept a school at Hackney, where he died Feb. 9, 1715-6. (*Calamy*, I. 217.)

HUTCHINSON, JOHN. Adm. pens. (age 16) at ST JOHN'S, Apr. 16, 1670. S. of Thomas, yeoman, of Cornforth, Durham. B. there. Bapt. at Bishop Middleham, July 2, 1653. School, Brignall (Mr Johnson). Matric. 1670; B.A. 1673-4. Ord. deacon (Durham) Sept. 19, 1675.

HUTCHINSON, JOHN. Adm. pens. at TRINITY, Nov. 28, 1675. B. in London. Perhaps colleger at Eton, 1668-74. B.A. 1679-80. One of these names, B.A., was V. of Brampton, Hunts., 1688-92. Died 1692.

HUTCHINSON, JOHN. Adm. sizar (age 20) at SIDNEY, Apr. 21, 1682. S. of William, barhour-master at Hull. B. there. Schools, Hull and Cottingham (Mr Steph. Clarke). Matric. 1682; B.A. 1685-6. One of these names V. of Royston, Yorks., 1719.

HUTCHINSON, JOHN. Adm. sizar (age 18) at TRINITY, Mar. 30, 1737. S. of John, of Oundle, Northants. B. at Frodsham, Cheshire. School, Oundle (Mr Jones). Matric. 1737; Scholar, 1740; B.A. 1740-1; M.A. 1744. Fellow, 1743. Ord. deacon (Peterb.) Feb. 24, 1740-1; priest, May 15, 1744. C. of Clapton, Northants., 1741. C. of Polebrook, 1744. V. of Felmersham, Beds., 1756-92. Buried there July 15, 1792. (Harvey, *Willey Hundred, Beds.*, 290; H. I. Longden.)

HUTCHINSON, JOHN. Adm. pens. (age 18) at ST JOHN'S, July 1, 1751. S. of John, gent., of Framwell Gate, Durham. B. there. Bapt. at St Margaret's, Feb. 23, 1732-3. Schools, Durham (Mr Dongworth) and Houghton-le-Spring (Mr Griffith). Matric. 1751; B.A. 1758. Ord. priest (York) Dec. 1758. C. of Kirkby, Notts. Buried at Appleby, Westmorland, Apr. 24, 1776. M.I. at St Michael's, Appleby. (*Scott-Mayor*, III. 608; H. M. Wood.)

HUTCHINSON, JONATHAN. Adm. sizar at EMMANUEL, Feb. 22, 1620-1. Matric. 1625-6; B.A. 1625-6.

HUTCHINSON, JOSEPH. Matric. sizar from MAGDALENE, Michs. 1639.

HUTCHINSON, JOSHUA. Adm. pens. (age 17) at TRINITY, Apr. 10, 1736. S. of Simon, of Ripon, Yorks. School, Ripon (Mr Stephens). Matric. 1736; Scholar, 1737.

HUTCHINSON, LUKE. Adm. sizar (age 18) at PETERHOUSE, May 11, 1695. Of Derbyshire. School, Derby. Matric. 1696; B.A. 1698-9. Ord. deacon (Lichfield) Mar. 4, 1699-1700; priest, Sept. 21, 1701. V. of Ashbourne, Derbs., 1731-49. V. of Doveridge, till 1749. Died 1749. Buried at Mappleton. Will (Lichfield) 1749. (*T. A. Walker*, 196.)

HUTCHINSON, MATHEW. Adm. sizar (age 18) at ST JOHN'S, May 9, 1662. S. of James, gent., of Richmonds. B. there. School, Sedbergh (Mr Buchanan). Matric. 1662; B.A. 1665-6; M.A. 1669. Ord. deacon (Durham) Sept. 23, 1666; priest (Chester) Aug. 3, 1668. V. of East Cowton, Yorks., 1668-81. V. of Gilling, 1681-1705. Died 1705. Buried at Richmond, Yorks.

HUTCHINSON, MICHAEL. Matric. pens. from ST JOHN'S, Easter, 1627. S. and h. of Thomas, of London. Adm. at the Middle Temple, June 24, 1628. Knighted, Aug. 9, 1641. Married Mary, sister to Lord Brereton. Brother of John (1627). (*Vis. of London*, 1634.)

HUTCHINSON, MICHAEL. Adm. pens. at TRINITY, Nov. 2, 1682. Matric. 1682; Scholar, 1685; B.A. 1686-7; M.A. 1690; B.D. 1701; D.D. 1706. Fellow, 1689. Incorp. at Oxford, 1700. V. of Orwell, Cambs., 1701. Preb. of Lichfield, 1703-7 and 1713-30. V. of Packington, Leics., 1706. R. of Cheadle, Staffs., 1713. Will (P.C.C.) 1730; as of Packington.

HUTCHINSON, MICHAEL. D.D. 1713 (Incorp. from Oxford). S. of John, of Morland, Westmorland. Matric. from Queen's College, Oxford, Dec. 15, 1692, age 15; B.A. (Oxford) 1697; M.A. 1700; B.D. 1708; D.D. 1712. Fellow of Queen's, Oxford, 1701. R. of Lillingstone Dayrell, Bucks., 1712-5. P.C. of St Paul's, Hammersmith, 1717-40. R. of Newnham, Hants., 1719. Died May 10, 1740. Buried at Hammersmith. M.I. (*Al. Oxon.*)

HUTCHINSON, PERCIVAL. Matric. sizar from KING'S, Michs. 1576; B.A. from St Catharine's, 1579-80. V. of St George, Naburn, Yorks., 1582-9. R. of St Dionys, York, 1586-1601. V. of North Fordingham, 1586-96. V. of Withernwick, 1603-39. Died 1639. (M. H. Peacock.)

HUTCHENSON, PHILEMON. Matric. sizar from SIDNEY, Easter, 1619.

HUTCHINSON, RALPH. Matric. pens. (age 17) from PEMBROKE, Michs. 1620. S. of William (1568), D.D., of Castle Camps, Cambs. B.A. from Magdalene, 1623-4; M.A. 1628. Incorp. at Oxford, 1628. V. of Colyton, Devon, 1627-36. Died 1636.

HUTCHINSON, RICHARD. Matric. pens. from ST JOHN'S, *c.* 1594. S. of Richard, of Durham. B.A. (? 1594-5); M.A. 1598. Fellow, 1598. Buried at St Margaret's, Durham, May 29, 1603, four days after his father. (*Surtees*, IV. 155. *Vis. of Durham*, 1666.)

HUTCHINSON, RICHARD. Matric. sizar from MAGDALENE, Easter, 1633.

HUTCHINSON, RICHARD. Adm. pens. (age 18) at ST JOHN'S, May 20, 1692. S. of Edward, deceased (in 1688). B. at Wykcham Abbey, Yorks. School, Wykeham Abbey (Mr Kirby). Matric. 1692.

HUTCHINSON, RICHARD. Adm. scholar at TRINITY HALL, Jan. 4, 1716-7. Probably s. of Edward, of Wykeham Abbey. Bapt. there, Sept. 29, 1698. Matric. 1716. Married Elizabeth, dau. of B. Boynton, Esq., of Rawcliffe, Yorks. Assumed the name of Langley, under the will of his uncle Thomas. Died Dec. 7, 1755. Buried at Wykeham. (M. H. Peacock; *F.M.G.*, 980.)

HUTCHYNSON, ROBERT. Matric. sizar from CHRIST'S, May, 1555. One of these names, ord. priest (Lincoln) Mar. 26, 1558, 'bred in the schools,' was P.C. of Bury, Hunts., 1558-96. R. of Woodwalton, 1559-96. Died 1596.

HUTCHINSON, ROBERT. Matric. sizar from TRINITY, *c.* 1593; B.A. 1596-7. Ord. deacon (Norwich) June 24, 1598, age 24; C. of Clopton, Suffolk; priest, June 29, 1599.

HUTCHINSON, ROGER. Of St John's. S. of William. B.A. 1540-1; M.A. 1544. Fellow, 1543; senior fellow, 1547. Fellow of Eton, 1550 (not mentioned by *Harwood*). Author, *Sermons*, etc. His *Image of God* is dedicated to Thomas Cranmer. Died about May, 1555. Will, 1555, mentions wife and children. (*D.N.B.*; *Cooper*, I. 126.)

HUTCHINSON, ROWLAND. Adm. sizar at Peterhouse, June 12, 1621. S. of Richard, of Berkhouse-in-Skelton, Marske, Richmond, Yorks. Matric. 1621. (*T. A. Walker*, 20; *Vis. of London*, 1634.)

HUTCHINSON, SAMUEL. Adm. pens. (age 14) at St John's, Sept. 14, 1700. S. of Samuel, deceased. B. at Boston, Lincs. School, Boston (Mr Kelsall). Matric. 1702; B.A. 1704-5; M.A. 1705 (*Com. Reg.*). Migrated to Emmanuel, June 12, 1705. Ord. deacon (Lincoln) Feb. 25, 1710-1; priest (London) Apr. 2, 1711. C. of Sutterton, Lincs., 1713. V. of Silk Willoughby, 1718. Preb. of Lincoln, 1718-53. Father of Samuel (1738).

HUTCHINSON, SAMUEL. Adm. pens. at Queens', Oct. 18, 1718. S. of Samuel, of Carsington, Derbs. School, Bury St Edmunds. Matric. 1718-9. Migrated to Trinity College, Dublin. Adm. there, Apr. 20, 1721; B.A. (Dublin) 1723; M.A. 1727. Preb. of Dunsport (Down) 1725. Preb. of Rathsarkan (Connor) 1729. Dean of Dromore, 1729. Archdeacon of Connor, 1736. Bishop of Killala, 1759-80. Died Oct. 27, 1780. Buried at Killala. (T. U. Sadleir.)

HUTCHINSON, SAMUEL. Adm. pens. (age 17) at St John's, July 6, 1738. S. of Samuel (1700), of Lincolnshire. B. at Langton. Bapt. Jan. 3, 1721-2. Exhibitioner from Charterhouse. Matric. 1738; B.A. 1741-2; M.A. 1745. Fellow, 1743-53. Candidate for the Professorship of Anatomy, 1746.

HUTCHINSON, SANDYS. Adm. pens. (age 18) at Trinity, June 23, 1724. S. of Edward, of Boston, Lincs. Schools, Wakefield and Kirkleatham, Yorks. (Mr Clark). Matric. 1724; Scholar, 1725; B.A. 1727-8; M.A. 1731. College librarian, 1729-40. Incorp. at Oxford, 1732. Joint editor of *Thesaurus Linguæ Latinæ*, 1734.

HUTCHINSON, SIMON. Adm. sizar (age 17) at Christ's, June 19, 1669. S. of James (Town Clerk of Richmond, Yorks.). B. at 'Halwith,' Yorks. School, Richmond (Mr Parving). Matric. 1669; B.A. 1672-3; M.A. 1676. Ord. deacon (York) May, 1673; priest, Dec. 1674. R. of West Tanfield, near Ripon, 1704-26. Died Mar. 10, 1725-6. (*Peile*, II. 24.)

HUTCHINSON, SIMON. Adm. pens. (age 17) at St John's, Apr. 9, 1725. S. of Matthew, merchant, of Richmond, Yorks. School, Richmond (Mr Close). Matric. 1725. Of Richmond, gent. Will proved (P.C.C.) 1731. (*Scott-Mayor*, III. 382.)

HUTCHINSON, SOLOMON. Matric. sizar from Christ's, July, 1628. Perhaps s. of Thomas (1582-3). B.A. 1631-2; M.A. 1635. Ord. deacon (Norwich) June, 1633; priest, Dec. 1633. P.C. of Hapton, Norfolk, 1636. (*Peile*, I. 396.)

HUTCHINSON, THEOPHILUS. Adm. pens. at Sidney, Sept. 11, 1606. Matric. 1606; B.A. 1610-1; M.A. 1614. Fellow of Magdalene, 1618. Ord. deacon (Peterb.) May 26; priest, May 27, 1616. Buried at St Giles', Cambridge, Feb. 10, 1634-5. Will proved (V.C.C.) 1635.

HUTCHYNSON, THOMAS. Matric. pens. from Trinity Hall, Michs. 1561.

HUTCHINSON, THOMAS. Matric. sizar from Christ's, Mar. 1582-3; B.A. 1586-7; M.A. 1590. Ord. deacon and priest (Peterb.) Mar. 3, 1594-5. P.C. of Hapton, Norfolk, 1603-36. Father of Elias (1625-6) and probably of Solomon (1628). (*Peile*, I. 174.)

HUTCHINSON, THOMAS. Adm. sizar at Queens', Dec. 5, 1592. Of Yorkshire. Matric. 1593. Perhaps V. of North Frodingham, Yorks., 1597-1649. Buriedp there Dec. 20, 1649. (M. H. Peacock.)

HUTCHINSON, THOMAS. Matric. Fell.-Com. from Pembroke, Easter, 1606. Doubtless s. of Thomas, of Owthorpe, Notts. B. 1588. Adm. at Gray's Inn, Feb. 10, 1608-9. Knighted, Mar. 20, 1616-7. M.P. for Notts., 1640-3. Died Aug. 18, 1643. Father of John (1631-2). (Jewitt, *The Reliquary*, IX. 240; A. B. Beaven.)

HUTCHINSON, THOMAS. Adm. sizar (age 15) at St John's, May 12, 1637. S. of Caverley, yeoman, of Scruton, Yorks. B. there. School, Kirkby Fleetham, near Bedale, Yorks. (private; Mr Smelt). Matric. 1637; B.A. 1640-1. R. of Astbury, Cheshire; sequestered; restored, 1660-75. Buried Dec. 17, 1675. (*Ormerod*, III. 27.)

HUTCHINSON, THOMAS. Adm. Fell.-Com. (age 17) at Peterhouse, May 25, 1658. Of Nottinghamshire. Probably s. of John (1631-2). Matric. 1658. Married Jane, dau. of Sir Alexander Ratcliffe. Died *s.p.* (Jewitt, *The Reliquary*, IX. 240.)

HUTCHINSON, THOMAS. Adm. sizar (age 18) at Peterhouse, Apr. 29, 1676. Of Durham. School, Durham. King's scholar there, 1671. Scholar, 1676; B.A. 1679-80; M.A. from St John's, 1683. Incorp. at Oxford, 1683. Ord. deacon (Durham) June 5, 1680. (*T. A. Walker*, 156.)

HUTCHINSON, THOMAS. Adm. pens. (age 17) at Sidney, Mar. 16, 1688-9. 1st s. of Thomas, deceased. B. at Pickering, Yorks. Schools, Pickering and Thornton (Mr Hen. Hunter). Matric. 1688-9; B.A. 1693-4. Ord. deacon (Peterb.) Dec. 22, 1706; priest, Dec. 19, 1708. Perhaps R. of Lyndon, Rutland, 1731-4. (H. I. Longden.)

HUTCHINSON, THOMAS. Adm. Fell.-Com. (age 17) at Sidney, Apr. 24, 1723. 1st s. of Julius, Esq. B. at Owthorpe, Notts. Educated privately. Matric. 1724. Married Anne, dau. of Sir Walter Wrottesley, of Staffs. Buried at Owthorpe, May 7, 1774. Brother of Boteler (1726) and Charles (1728). (*Clutterbuck*, II. 347.)

HUTCHINSON or HUTCHESSON, THOMAS. Adm. sizar (age 17) at Magdalene, Sept. 29, 1743. S. of John. B. at Wisbech, Cambs. School, Wisbech. Matric. 1743; B.A. 1747-8. Ord. deacon (Norwich) Sept. 1749; priest (Peterb.) Sept. 24, 1752. Perhaps R. of Crostwick, Norfolk, 1756. V. of Gt Finborough, Suffolk, 1764-98. V. of Haughley, 1771-98. Died 1798. Will (P.C.C.) 1799.

HUTCHYNSON, W. Matric. sizar from Christ's, Michs. 1561. One of these names ord. deacon (Ely) Dec. 19, 1563.

HUTCHINSON, W. Adm. pens. at Queens', July 12, 1617. Of London.

HUTCHINSON, WILLIAM. Matric. pens. from Queens', Michs. 1568; B.A. 1572-3; M.A. 1576. Probably B.D. (Oxford) 1590. Chaplain to the Bishop of London, 1581. Archdeacon of St Albans, 1581. V. of Rickmansworth, Herts., 1581-4. R. of St Christopher-le-Stocks, London, 1581-7. R. of St Botolph, Bishopsgate, 1584-90. V. of Hutton, Essex, 1588-9. R. of St Michael Bassishaw, London, 1589-1604. R. of Castle Camps, Cambs., 1590-1604. Preb. of St Paul's, 1591-1604. Father of Ralph (1620), brother of John (1568). According to *Al. Oxon.*, he was also Archdeacon of Cornwall, 1603-16. R. of Cheriton Bishop, Devon, 1604. R. of Kenn, 1604-16. Preb. of Exeter, 1608-16. Buried in Exeter Cathedral, July 22, 1616. (Query, if the same man.)

HUTCHINSON, WILLIAM (*senior*). Scholar of Trinity, 1602; B.A. 1603-4; M.A. 1607. Author, *Verses*. (*Cooper*, II. 479.)

HUTCHINSON, WILLIAM (*junior*). Scholar of Trinity, 1602; B.A. 1603-4; M.A. 1611. Ord. deacon (Peterb.) Sept. 25, 1608; priest, Dec. 28, 1608. V. of Barton, Cambs. R. of Bluntisham, Hunts., 1612. V. of Madingley, Cambs., 1612-16. R. of Stickney, Lincs., 1613-38. Admon. (Lincoln) 1638.

HUTCHINSON, WILLIAM. Matric. pens. from Pembroke, Easter, 1604; B.A. 1606-7; M.A. 1610; B.D. from Clare, 1617; D.D. from Pembroke, 1630. Incorp. at Oxford, 1607, 1612. Probably R. of Cheriton Bishop, Devon, 1616. R. of Kenn, 1616-44. Preb. of Exeter, 1624-44. Will (Exeter) 1644. Perhaps father of William (1641).

HUTCHINSON, WILLIAM. Adm. pens. at Emmanuel, Easter, 1628. Matric. 1628; B.A. 1631-2; M.A. 1635. Ord. priest (Peterb.) May 20, 1638.

HUTCHINSON, WILLIAM. Matric. pens. from Clare, Easter, 1629; B.A. 1632-3.

HUTCHINSON, WILLIAM. Matric. pens. from Queens', Easter, 1641. Of Devon. Possibly s. of William (1604) whom he succeeded at Kenn. Will (Exeter) 1675; of Kenn, Devon, clerk.

HUTCHINSON, WILLIAM. Matric. pens. from St Catharine's, Lent, 1645-6. Of Lincolnshire. B.A. 1647-8; M.A. 1651. Fellow, 1649.

HUTCHINSON, WILLIAM Adm. sizar at Clare, June 16, 1724. B. at Greenwich. School, Lewisham. Matric. 1724; B.A. 1727-8; M.A. 1731. Incorp. at Oxford, 1733. R. of Hazeleigh, Essex, 1732-60. R. of Cricksea. Died 1760.

HUTCHINSON, WILLIAM. Adm. pens. (age 17) at Christ's, May 31, 1748. S. of George. B. at Lisbon. School, Appleby (Mr Yates). Matric. 1748. One of these names, s. of George, late of London, merchant, deceased, adm. at Lincoln's Inn, July 7, 1748. (*Peile*, II. 252.)

HUTCHINSON, ——. Adm. sizar at King's, Easter, 1589.

HUTCHMAN, ——. Student at Jesus, *c.* 1546-7.

HUTHERGILL, THOMAS. Matric. sizar from St John's, Easter, 1614.

HUTHWETT, JOHN. Adm. sizar (age 18) at Caius, Jan. 24, 1620-1. S. of William, gent. B. at Kettering, Northants. School, St Paul's, London. Matric. 1620-1; Scholar, 1623-6; B.A. 1624-5; M.A. 1629. Ord. deacon (Peterb.) Mar. 27; priest, Apr. 1, 1627.

HUTHWAITE, ROBERT. Matric. sizar from Corpus Christi, Easter, 1608. Of Nottinghamshire. B.A. 1611–2. Ord. deacon (York) Sept. 1613; priest, Mar. 1613–4.

HUTLEY, HENRY. Matric. sizar from St John's, Easter, 1623; B.A. 1626–7.

HUTT, GEORGE. Adm. pens. at Emmanuel, Lent, 1641–2. Of Essex. Matric. 1642; B.A. 1645–6; M.A. 1649. Buried at St Andrew's, Cambridge, Mar. 27, 1649.

HUTT, JOHN Adm. sizar (age 18) at Pembroke, Apr. 16, 1636–7. S. of John. B. at Maldon, Essex. Matric. 1636; B.A. 1639–40; M.A. 1643. C. of Maldon, in 1664.

HUTTON, ANTHONY. Adm. pens. at Queens', Oct. 31, 1599. S. of Sir William, of Penrith, Cumberland, Knt. Adm. at Gray's Inn, Oct. 26, 1601. Married Elizabeth, dau. of Robert Burdett, of Bramcote, Warws. (? Notts.). Died July 10, 1637. Buried at Penrith. (Hutchinson, *Cumberland*, I. 339; *Whellan*, 590.)

HUTTON, ANTHONY. Adm. sizar (age 17) at Christ's, June 8, 1659. S. of John, R. of Blankney, Lincs. B. at Blankney. School, Lincoln (Mr Clerk). Matric. 1660; B.A. 1662–3. Ord. priest (Ely) 1667, after being deacon four years. R. of Blankney, 1667–98. Died May 15, 1698. Buried at Blankney. (*Peile*, I. 586.)

HUTTON, ARTHUR. B.A. from St John's, 1607–8. Of Richmondshire. S. of Edward (1573). Probably King's scholar at Durham School, 1599. M.A. 1611. Fellow, 1609. Ord. priest (York, for Lincoln) Mar. 1616–7. V. of East Cowton, Yorks., 1618. R. of Kirkby, Northallerton, 1619. Will (P.C.C.) 1655. (*Vis. of Durham*, 1615.)

HUTTON, CHARLES. M.A. from Pembroke, 1669 (*Lit. Reg.*). 4th s. of Richard, of Poppleton, Yorks. Matric. from Magdalen Hall, Oxford, Oct. 18, 1662, age 18. Married Millicent, dau. of Sir Edward Rhodes, of Gt Haughton, Yorks. Died at Brampton, Yorks., Feb. 1, 1695–6. Buried at Darfield. (*Al. Oxon.*; Foster, *Yorks. Pedigrees*.)

HUTTON, CHRISTOPHER. Adm. Fell.-Com. at Queens', Sept. 8, 1607. Probably s. of Edward (1573). B. in Yorkshire. Bapt. at his mother's home. Age 28 in 1615. Married and had issue. Brother of Arthur (1607–8) and Henry (1613). (*Vis. of Durham*; *Surtees*, III. 19.)

HUTTON, CLEMENT. Adm. sizar (age 18) at St John's, Apr. 9, 1661. 3rd s. of Robert, deceased, of Houghton-le-Spring, Durham. Bapt. there, July 16, 1643. School, Houghton-le-Spring (Mr Cant). Matric. 1661. Of Lynn, Norfolk. (Hutchinson's *Durham*, III; Foster, *Yorks. Pedigrees*.)

HUTTON, EDWARD. Matric. sizar from Trinity, Michs. 1573. S. of John, of Streatlam, Durham. LL.B. 1579. Bailiff of the City of Durham, 1615. Married Anne, dau. of Francis Lascelles, of Allerthorpe, Yorks. Buried Nov. 10, 1629, aged 72. Father of Arthur (1607–8), Christopher (1607) and Henry (1613). (*Vis. of Durham*, 1615; H. M. Wood.)

HUTTON, EDWARD. Matric. sizar from Queens', Easter, 1628. Of Cambridgeshire.

HUTTON, GEORGE. Adm. sizar (age 16) at St John's, May 16, 1636. S. of Robert, currier, of Gainford, Durham. B. there. School, Sedbergh (Mr Nelson). Matric. 1636; B.A. 1639–40; M.A. 1643. Fellow, 1641.

HUTTON, GERARD. Matric. pens. from Jesus, Easter, 1611; B.A. 1614–5; M.A. 1618. Incorp. at Oxford, 1619.

HUTTON, HENRY. Matric. pens. from St John's, Easter, 1613. 5th s. of Edward (1573). B.A. 1619–20. P.C. of Witton Gilbert, Durham, 1635–71. Buried Apr. 24, 1671. (H. M. Wood; *Vis. of Durham*.)

HUTTON, HENRY. Matric. pens. from St John's, Easter, 1625. 4th s. of Sir Richard (1565–6), Justice C.P. B.A. 1628–9; M.A. from Jesus, 1632. Fellow of Jesus, 1629–42. Proctor, 1639–40. Adm. at Gray's Inn, Feb. 2, 1624–5. V. of Long Marton, Westmorland, 1640–55. Preb. of Carlisle, 1643, ejected. Married Elizabeth, dau. of John Cosins, Bishop of Durham. Buried at Marton, Mar. 22, 1654–5. Brother of Richard (1615). (B. *Nightingale*; A. Gray.)

HUTTON, JAMES. B.Civ.L. 1476–7; D.Civ.L. 1481–2. V. of Linton, Cambs., 1487–90. Chancellor of Ely. Died 1490.

HUTTON, JAMES. B.A. 1516–7. Of Westmorland. M.A. 1520–1; B.D. 1528–9. Fellow of Pembroke, 1519. President, 1530. Proctor, 1527–8.

HUTTON, JEREMY. Matric. sizar from Trinity, Easter, 1589; B.A. from Pembroke, 1592–3; M.A. 1596.

HUTTON, JOHN. Matric. sizar from Queens', Michs. 1547.

HUTTON, JOHN. Matric. pens. from Jesus, Michs. 1565; B.A. 1569–70; M.A. 1573. Fellow, 1571–5. One of these names, of Ely diocese, ord. deacon and priest (Durham) June 8, 1584 (M.A.). R. of Gateshead, 1595–1612. Preb. of Southwell, 1601–12. Married, at Gateshead, Nov. 14, 1609, Elizabeth Blithman, widow. Buried there Mar. 10, 1611–2.

HUTTON, JOHN. Matric. sizar from Trinity, Easter, 1577; Scholar, 1580; B.A. 1580–1. (The above ordination may possibly refer to this man, who was of standing for M.A. in 1584.)

HUTTON, JOHN. Matric. sizar from Trinity, Easter, 1584; B.A. from St Catharine's, 1585–6; M.A. 1589. Ord. deacon and priest (Peterb.) Aug. 24, 1590. Perhaps V. of Littlebury, Essex, 1596–1615. Probably R. of Dunsby, Lincs., 1614–28. Will (P.C.C.) 1629.

HUTTON, JOHN. Matric. pens. from St John's, Michs. 1624. School, Sedbergh. B.A. 1627–8; M.A. 1631. Probably ord. deacon and priest (Carlisle) May 27, 1632. R. of St Cuthbert, York, 1636–7. One of these names 5th s. of Sir Timothy, of Marske, Yorks. Buried there Aug. 7, 1638. (*Sedbergh Sch. Reg.*; *Yorks. Archaeol. Journal*, VI. 238.)

HUTTON, JOHN. B.A. 1653 (Incorp. from Oxford). Matric. from New College, Oxford, July 17, 1646, age 18; B.A. (Oxford) 1650. Fellow of New College, 1650–2. Admon. (Oxford) Dec. 23, 1652. (*Al. Oxon.*)

HUTTON, JOHN. Adm. at King's, a scholar from Eton, 1694. B. at Harefield, Middlesex. Matric. Easter, 1695; B.A. 1698–9; M.A. 1702. Fellow, 1697. Incorp. at Oxford, 1711. Ord. priest (Lincoln) May 19, 1706. Kept a boarding house for Westminster scholars. Established an infirmary in Westminster. Died aged 74. Perhaps his will (P.C.C.) as of St Clement Danes, London, M.D. (*Harwood*.)

HUTTON, JOHN. Adm. Fell.-Com. at Jesus, Oct. 10, 1709. S. and h. of John, of Marske, Yorks., Esq. Bapt. Nov. 18, 1691. Matric. 1709. Succeeded his father, 1731. Raised a company of foot for the suppression of the Rebellion in 1745. Buried at Marske, Jan. 16, 1768. Brother of Matthew (1710), father of the next. (Burke, *L.G.*; Foster, *Yorks. Pedigrees*.)

HUTTON, JOHN. Adm. Fell.-Com. (age 18) at Christ's, Nov. 7, 1747. S. of John (above), of Marske, Yorks. Bapt. there, Oct. 14, 1730. School, Westminster. Matric. 1747. Married Anne, dau. of Richard Ling, at Marske, Aug. 31, 1779. Died Sept. 24, 1782. Buried in Marske Church. (*Peile*, II. 250.)

HUTTON, JOSHUA. Adm. pens. at Corpus Christi, 1565. Matric. Michs. 1566. Perhaps R. of Reculver, Kent, 1575–84. V. of Hougham, 1584–90; R. of St Alphege, Canterbury, 1594–6. One of these names R. of Bradwell, Suffolk, 1597–1612.

HUTTON, LANCELOT. B.A. 1620–1 (Incorp. from Oxford). Of Cumberland. S. of a knight. Matric. from Queen's College, Oxford, June 30, 1615, age 17; B.A. (Oxford) 1618; M.A. (Oriel College) 1622. R. of Melmerby, Cumberland, 1621. (*Al. Oxon.*)

HUTTON, LUKE. Matric. sizar from Trinity, Michs. 1582. Probably a son, not of the Archbishop, as sometimes stated, but of Robert, either of 1569 or his namesake, a preb. of Durham (*Yorks. Arch. Journ.*, VI. 241). Author, *The Blacke Dogge of Newgate*, etc. Executed for robbery, at York, 1598. (*Cooper*, II. 540; *D.N.B.*)

HUTTON, MARK. Matric. pens. from Trinity, Michs. 1579.

HUTTON, MATTHEW. Of Trinity, in 1546. S. of Matthew, of Warton, Lancs. B. at Priest Hutton, Warton, 1529. B.A. 1551–2; M.A. 1555; B.D. 1562; D.D. 1565. Fellow, 1553. Vice-Master, 1560–2. Lady Margaret Professor of Divinity, 1561. Master of Pembroke, 1562–7. Regius Professor of Divinity, 1562–7. Ord. deacon (Ely) July 7, 1560. Preb. of Ely, 1560–7. R. of Abbots Ripton, Hunts., 1561–5. Preb. of St Paul's, 1562–90. R. of Boxworth, Cambs., 1563–6. Preb. of Westminster, 1565–8. Preb. of Southwell, 1567–89. Dean of York, 1567–89. R. of West Leake, Notts., 1567–8. R. of Settrington, Yorks., 1568–89. Bishop of Durham, 1589–95. Archbishop of York, 1595–1606. Lord President of the North, 1595–1600. Author, sermons. Died at Bishopsthorpe, Yorks., Jan. 15, 1605–6. Buried in York Minster. M.I. Father of Timothy (1588) and of Thomas (1597). (*Cooper*, II. 421; *D.N.B.*)

HUTTON, MATTHEW. Matric. Fell.-Com. from Trinity, Easter, 1615. S. and h. of Timothy (1588). B. Oct. 20, 1597. A noted Royalist. Married Barbara, dau. of Sir Conyers D'Arcy, 1617. Admon. granted in 1666. Brother of Philip (1618). (John Fisher, *Masham*; *Yorks. Archaeol. Journal*, VI. 238.)

HUTTON, MATTHEW. Adm. pens. at Jesus, June 22, 1710. 2nd s. of John, of Marske, Yorks., Esq. B. there, Jan. 3, 1692–3. Schools, Kirkby Hill, Richmond (Mr Loyd) and Ripon. Matric. 1710; B.A. 1713–4; M.A. 1717; D.D. from Christ's, 1728 (*Com. Reg.*). Fellow of Christ's, 1717–27. Ord. deacon (Ely) Sept. 1718; priest, May, 1719. R. of Trowbridge, Wilts., 1726. R. of Spofforth, Yorks., 1729–47. Preb. of York, 1734–48. Chaplain to George II. Canon of Windsor, 1737–9. Preb. of Westminster, 1739–43. Bishop of Bangor, 1743–7. Archbishop of York, 1747–57. Archbishop of Canterbury, 1757–8. Married, Mar. 1731–2, Mary, dau. of John Lutman, of Petworth, Sussex. Died at Lambeth, Mar. 18, 1758. Buried in Lambeth Church. Brother of John (1709). (*D.N.B.*; *Peile*, II. 176–7.)

HUTTON, MATTHEW. Adm. Fell.-Com. (age 16) at CHRIST'S, Jan. 4, 1732-3. S. of Matthew. B. in London. School, Buntingford. Adm. at Lincoln's Inn, Nov. 25, 1732, as s. of Matthew, late of Newnham, Herts., Esq. (*Peile*, II. 228.)

HUTTON, PHILIP. Matric. pens. from TRINITY, Michs. 1618. 4th s. of Timothy (1588). B.A. 1622-3; M.A. 1626. Ord. deacon (York) Dec. 24, 1626; priest, Feb. 15, 1626-7. R. of Langton-on-Swale, Yorks., 1629-37. Married Elizabeth, dau. of Thomas Bowes, of Streatlam, Durham. Buried at Barnard Castle, Jan. 7, 1637-8. Father of Thomas (1652), brother of Matthew (1615).

HUTTON, PHILIP. Matric. pens. from KING'S, Easter, 1621.

HUTTON, RALPH. Adm. scholar at TRINITY HALL, Aug. 9, 1679. Matric. 1679; M.A. 1682 (*Com. Reg.*). Incorp. at Oxford, 1683.

HUTTON or HOTTON, RICHARD. B.A. 1489-90. Of Yorkshire. M.A. 1493; B.D. 1501. Fellow of QUEENS', 1492-1501. Proctor, 1498-9. Ord. sub-deacon (Ely) Apr. 4; deacon, Apr. 18; priest, June 13, 1495.

HUTTON, RICHARD. B.Civ.L. 1500-1. One of these names (LL.D.), V. of Greenwich; died 1509. Perhaps V. of Stoke d'Abernon, Surrey (LL.B.), 1545. Died 1556.

HUTTON, RICHARD. Adm. at JESUS, *c.* 1565-6. Doubtless s. of Anthony, of Hutton Hall, Cumberland. Adm. at Gray's Inn, 1580. Barrister, 1586. Ancient, 1598. Member of the Council of the North, 1599-1619. Serjeant-at-law, 1603. Recorder of York, 1608. Knighted, Apr. 13, 1617. Puisne Judge, Common Pleas, 1617-39. Gave judgment for Hampden in the Ship Money case. Married Anne (? Agnes), dau. of Thomas Briggs, of Canmire, Westmorland. Died Feb. 26, 1638-9. Buried at St Dunstan-in-the-West, London. M.I. there. Will (P.C.C.) 1639; of Goldsborough, Yorks. Father of the next, and Henry (1625). (*D.N.B.*, where he is assigned to Oxford; M. H. Peacock; J. Ch. Smith.)

HUTTON, RICHARD. Matric. Fell.-Com. from ST JOHN'S, Easter, 1615. Doubtless s. of Richard (above). B.A. 1617. Incorp. at Oxford, 1617. Adm. at Gray's Inn, Feb. 2, 1612-3. M.P. for Knaresborough, 1620-2, 1624-5, 1626, 1628-9. Knighted, July 17, 1625. Sheriff of Yorks., 1644-5. Slain at Sherburn, Oct. 15, 1645. Buried at Goldsborough. Brother of Henry (1625). (*Hunter*, II. 143; A. B. Beaven.)

HUTTON, RICHARD. Matric. sizar from PEMBROKE, Easter, 1631; B.A. 1633-4. C. of Norton Mandeville, Essex, in 1640; and of Greenstead, 1641. Sequestered to Brightlingsea, Essex, *c.* 1643. R. of Workington, Cumberland, 1645. V. of Caldbeck, 1645-62. (Foster, in *Al. Oxon.*, seems to have confused this man with the last.) *See B. Nightingale.*

HUTTON, RICHARD. Adm. sizar (age 15) at PEMBROKE, June 19, 1649. S. of Hemshill (*sic.*), Cumberland. Matric. 1649. Probably R. of Bootle, Cumberland, 1655-1704. Ord. deacon (Chester) Sept. 21, 1662. Died July, 1704, aged 71. M.I. at Bootle, which calls him B.D. (*B. Nightingale*, 864.)

HUTTON, RICHARD. Adm. sizar (age 18) at PEMBROKE, June 5, 1699. S. of Leonard, of Cockermouth, Cumberland. B. at Bodmin, Cornwall. School, St Bees, Cumberland. Matric. 1699.

HUTTON, ROBERT. B.Civ.L. 1476-7. One of these names P.C. of St Mary Colechurch, London. Will (P.C.C.) 1514.

HUTTON, ROBERT. Of PEMBROKE; sizar of William Turner, fellow. An exile under Queen Mary. R. of Little Braxted, Essex; and of Wickham Episcopi, 1560-8. Perhaps V. of Catterick, Yorks. Author, *Summe of Divinitie*. Buried at St Mary-le-Bow, Sept. 5, 1568. (*Cooper*, I. 261; *D.N.B.*; J. Ch. Smith.)

HUTTON, ROBERT. Matric. sizar from TRINITY, Michs. 1569. S. of Edmund, and nephew of Matthew the Archbishop. Scholar, 1573; B.A. 1573-4; M.A. 1577; B.D. 1584. Fellow, 1576. Ord. deacon and priest (Lincoln) Dec. 23, 1578. V. of Lissington, Lincs., 1578. University preacher, 1582. V. of Trumpington, Cambs., 1584-5. V. of Shudy Camps, 1584. Preb. of Durham, 1589-1623. R. of Houghton-le-Spring, Durham, 1590-1623. Married Grace, dau. of Leonard Pilkington, D.D. Died at Houghton-le-Spring, 1623. Buried May 19, in the chancel there. (H. M. Wood.)

HUTTON, ROBERT. Adm. sizar at CLARE, Dec. 23, 1653. Matric. 1654; B.A. 1657-8. Perhaps M.A. 1669. V. of Naseby, Northants., 1661-3. V. of Long Buckby, 1663-7. V. of Watford, 1667-71. Buried at Watford, Jan. 22, 1670-1. (H. I. Longden.)

HUTTON, ROBERT. Adm. pens. (age 17) at PETERHOUSE, Mar. 5, 1700-1. S. of Robert, of Houghton-le-Spring, Durham. Bapt. there, Dec. 4, 1683. School, Houghton-le-Spring. Matric. 1701; Scholar, 1701. Of Houghton-le-Spring. Married Elizabeth, dau. of Sir George Wheler, Knt. and R. of Houghton-le-Spring. Buried Oct. 22, 1725, at Houghton. (Burke, *L.G.*; *T. A. Walker*, 206; Surtees, *Durham*.)

HUTTON, ROGER. Adm. pens. at EMMANUEL, 1584. Matric. 1584-5; B.A. 1588-9. Probably adm. at Gray's Inn, Feb. 2, 1590-1; 'cousin of John, of Dry Drayton, Cambs., Esq.'

HUTTON, SAMUEL. Matric. from TRINITY, *c.* 1593-4; Scholar, 1596; B.A. 1597-8; M.A. 1601. Fellow, 1599. Perhaps preb. of York, 1603-28. If so, s. of Robert, D.D. and nephew of Matthew (1546). Admon. granted Apr. 3, 1629. Perhaps father of Timothy (1626). (*Yorks. Archaeol. Journal*, VI. 241.)

HUTTON, SAMUEL. Matric. sizar from KING'S, Michs. 1628; B.A. 1632-3; M.A. 1636. R. of Southery, Norfolk, 1642-70. Father of the next. Died 1670.

HUTTON, SAMUEL. Matric. sizar from KING'S, 1668. S. of Samuel (above), clerk, of Southery, Norfolk. B. there. School, King's College, Cambridge (Mr Wroth). Migrated to St John's, May 4, 1669, age 17. B.A. 1672-3; M.A. 1676. Ord. deacon (Ely) Oct. 2, 1675; priest (London) Mar. 11, 1676-7. Minor canon of Ely. Died Oct. 3, 1718. M.I. in the Cathedral.

HUTTON, STEPHEN. Matric. sizar from KING'S, Easter, 1669, as 'Hatton'; B.A. 1672-3; M.A. 1676.

HUTTON, THEOPHILUS. Adm. pens. at PETERHOUSE, Aug. 29, 1614. Matric. 1615.

HUTTON, THOMAS. D.Civ.L. 1474-5. Principal of BORDEN HOSTEL (tenant of Peterhouse), 1488-9. Preb. of York, 1485-1506. Preb. of Lincoln, 1488-94. Archdeacon of Bedford, 1489-94. R. of Church Brampton, Northants., 1489-93. Archdeacon of Huntingdon, 1494-6. R. of Dry Drayton, Cambs., till 1494. R. of Graveley, 1494. R. of Warboys, Hunts., 1495-7. R. of Upwell, Cambs. R. of Girton, 1498. Will (P.C.C.) 1505-6.

HUTTON, THOMAS. Matric. Fell.-Com. from JESUS, Easter, 1567.

HUTTON, THOMAS. Adm. Fell.-Com. (age 19) at CAIUS, Nov. 24, 1587. S. of William, gent. B. at Greystoke, Cumberland. School, Cockermouth (Mr Lund).

HUTTON, THOMAS. Matric. pens. from QUEENS', Michs. 1589. Of Cambridgeshire. B.A. 1592-3. One of these names R. of Barningham, Yorks., 1596. Will, Dec. 1639.

HUTTON, THOMAS. Adm. Fell.-Com. at QUEENS', Oct. 13, 1597. Of Yorkshire. 2nd surviving s. of Matthew (1546), Archbishop of York. B. 1581. Matric. 1597. Adm. at Gray's Inn, Nov. 1, 1599. Knighted, Aug. 6, 1617. Of Poppleton, Yorks. Married Ann, dau. of Sir John Bennet, of Dawley, near Uxbridge. Died Jan. 23, 1620-1. Buried at Nether Poppleton. M.I. Will, York. Brother of Timothy (1588). (Hutchinson's *Durham*, III; *Vis. of Yorks.*, 1666.)

HUTTON, THOMAS. Matric. pens. from ST JOHN'S, Michs. 1619; B.A. 1622-3. One of these names, s. and h. of Thomas, of Soham, Cambs., adm. at Gray's Inn, Mar. 18, 1619-20.

HUTTON, THOMAS. Adm. sizar (age 18) at SIDNEY, June 27, 1626. S. of Giles, farmer, of Leicestershire. B. there. School, Southwell (Mr Bayes and Mr Brittan). Matric. 1626-7; B.A. 1629-30. One of these names V. of Bicker, Lincs., 1642.

HUTTON, THOMAS. Adm. pens. (age 17) at ST JOHN'S, Oct. 27, 1652. S. of Philip (1618), clerk, deceased, of Langton-on-Swale, Yorks. B. there. School, Romaldkirk, Richmonds. (Mr Roos). Matric. 1652; B.A. 1657; M.A. 1661. (According to *Al. Oxon.* he matric. from Brasenose, July 25, 1655; and was B.A., Oxford, Jan. 19, 1657-8.) Ord. deacon and priest, July 11, 1661. R. of Marske, Yorks., 1659-94. Buried there June 12, 1694. (H. M. Wood.)

HUTTON, THOMAS. Matric. sizar from KING'S, Easter, 1727; B.A. 1730-1; M.A. 1735. Conduct of King's, 1731. Incorp. at Oxford, 1735. Ord. deacon (Lincoln) Mar. 14, 1730-1; priest, Dec. 24, 1732.

HUTTON, THOMAS. Adm. sizar (age 20) at ST JOHN'S, June 2, 1739. S. of Thomas, deceased, of Westmorland. B. at Kirkby Lonsdale. School, Sedbergh (Dr Saunders). Matric. 1739; B.A. 1742-3. Ord. deacon (Norwich) May 30, 1744. C. of Castleacre, Norfolk.

HUTTON, TIMOTHY. Matric. pens. from TRINITY, Michs. 1588. S. of Matthew (1546), Archbishop of York. B. 1569. Adm. at Gray's Inn, Oct. 14, 1590. J.P., 1598. Knighted, Feb. 16, 1605-6. High Sheriff of York, Feb. to Nov. 1606. Married Elizabeth, dau. of Sir George Bowes, of Streatlam, Durham. Died Apr. 6, 1629. Buried at Richmond. M.I. Brother of Thomas (1597) and father of Matthew (1615) and Philip (1618). (*Vis. of Yorks.*, 1666.)

HUTTON, TIMOTHY. Matric. pens. from ST JOHN'S, Michs. 1614. Of Yorkshire. S. of Thomas (? 1589), R. of Barningham, Richmond. B. there. B.A. 1618-9; M.A. 1622; B.D. 1630. Fellow, 1622. Taxor, 1628-9. Ord. deacon (Peterb.) Apr. 28; priest, Apr. 30, 1627. R. of Chelsworth, Suffolk, 1633-8. Buried there Aug. 14, 1638. Will, V.C.C., and also P.C.C. (proved by his father, Thomas). (*Sedbergh School Reg.* 93; V. B. Redstone.)

HUTTON, TIMOTHY. Matric. pens. from ST JOHN'S, Easter, 1626. Of Durham. S. of Samuel (c. 1593-4). B.A. 1629-30; M.A. 1633. Fellow, 1631. Taxor, 1637-8. C. of St Giles', Cripplegate, London, 1642-72.

HUTTON, WILLIAM. B.A. 1538-9; M.A. 1541; B.D. 1549. Fellow of QUEENS', 1540-3. One of these names R. of Bottesford, Leics.; will (P.C.C.) 1559.

HUTTON, W. Matric. pens. from JESUS, Easter, 1565.

HUTTON, WILLIAM. Matric. sizar from TRINITY, Michs. 1578.

HUTTON, WILLIAM. Matric. sizar from ST JOHN'S, Lent, 1579-80; B.A. 1583-4; M.A. 1587.

HUTTON, WILLIAM. Matric. pens. from PETERHOUSE, Michs. 1580.

HUTTON, WILLIAM. Matric. sizar from TRINITY, Easter, 1626. Perhaps William Hutton, 'B.A. of Trinity,' V. of Sockburn, Yorks., 1662. P.C. of Denton, Durham, 1666.

HUTTON, WILLIAM. LL.B. 1632 (Incorp. from Oxford). S. of Thomas, of St Kew, Cornwall, clerk. Matric. from St John's College, Oxford, Jan. 20, 1625-6, age 18; B.C.L. (Oxford) 1630. R. of North Lew, Devon, 1634. R. of Jacobstowe, Cornwall, 1640-53. R. of Bridestowe, Devon, 1662. Will (Exeter) 1671; of North Lew.

HUTTON, WILLIAM. Adm. sizar (age 18) at CHRIST'S, June 29, 1688. S. of Thomas. B. at St Kew, Cornwall. School, Okehampton (Mr Hussey). Matric. 1688; Scholar, 1689; B.A. 1691-2; M.A. 1705. Ord. deacon (Lincoln) Sept. 25, 1692; priest (Ely) June, 1694. V. of Pampisford, Cambs., 1694-7. Admon. (Exeter) 1720, of one of these names; of Lustleigh, Devon, clerk. (*Peile*, II. 111.)

HUTTON, ——. Scholar at CHRIST'S, 1541-2.

HUXLEY, ANTHONY. Matric. sizar from MAGDALENE, Michs. 1614; B.A. 1618-9; M.A. 1630. Incorp. at Oxford, 1624, as 'M.A.' With the Royal garrison in Lichfield, in 1646. V. of Abbots Bromley, Staffs., 1634-46; sequestered; and 1662-5. Married Margaret, sister of John Chadwick, R. of Standish. (*Wm. Salt Arch. Soc.*, 1915.)

HUXLEY, GEORGE. Adm. Fell.-Com. at CLARE, May 3, 1704. S. and h. of Thomas, of Bow, Middlesex. B. there. Matric. 1704. Adm. at the Middle Temple, May 15, 1704. Probably M.P. for Bedford, 1722-5; for Newport, Isle of Wight, 1726-41. Commissioner for victualling the Navy, 1725-9. Commissary General of Musters, 1729-42. Died July 19, 1744. (A. B. Beaven.)

HUXLEY, JAMES. Adm. Fell.-Com. (age 18) at PETERHOUSE, May 27, 1657. S. of John (next), of Edmonton, Middlesex, Esq. Matric. 1657. Adm. at Gray's Inn, Dec. 13, 1654. Brother of John (1648) and Thomas (1657).

HUXLEY, JOHN. Matric. Fell.-Com. from TRINITY, Michs. 1613. S. and h. of George, of Edmonton, Middlesex, Esq. Adm. at Lincoln's Inn, Oct. 23, 1615. Of Wyre Hall, Edmonton, Esq. Died Sept. 29, 1661, aged 65. Father of James (above), the next, and Thomas (1657). (Le Neve, *Mon.*, III. 50; *Middlesex Pedigrees*.)

HUXLEY, JOHN. Matric. Fell.-Com. from KING'S, Michs. 1648. S. and h. of John (above), of Edmonton, Middlesex, Esq. Adm. at Lincoln's Inn, Nov. 19, 1649. Knighted, Mar. 16, 1662-3. Of Eaton Bray, Beds. Married, at St Mary Woolnoth, July 14, 1655, Sarah Hadley, of St Lawrence Jewry. P.C.C., Jan. 16, 1676-7. Brother of James (1657) and Thomas (1657). Will proved (F. C. Cass, *E. Barnet*.)

HUXLEY, RICHARD. Adm. sizar (age 15) at CAIUS, Feb. 21, 1607-8. S. of William, citizen of London. Of the parish of St Sepulchre, London. School, Westminster. Matric. 1608; Scholar, 1608-13; B.A. 1611-2. Ord. priest (Rochester) June 19, 1614. R. of Ashill, Norfolk, 1621-58. Will proved (Norwich) 1658. (*Venn*, I. 197.)

HUXLEY, THOMAS. Adm. sizar (age 18) at CHRIST'S, July 8, 1635. S. of William. B. at 'Crapston,' Leics. Educated by Mr Sterk. Matric. 1635; Scholar; B.A. 1638-9; M.A. 1642. Fellow, 1642-4; ejected; restored, 1660. Ord. deacon (Lincoln) Sept. 25, 1642; priest, Dec. 18, 1642. V. of Stowmarket, Suffolk, 1660-2. R. of Burwell, Cambs., 1665-81. R. of Toft, 1670-81. Chaplain to Lord Willoughby of Parham. Buried at Burwell, Nov. 10, 1681. (*Peile*, I. 438.)

HUXLEY, THOMAS. Adm. Fell.-Com. (age 20) at PETERHOUSE, May 27, 1657. S. of John (1613), of Edmonton, Middlesex, Esq. Matric. 1657. Adm. at Gray's Inn, Dec. 13, 1654. Brother of James (1657) and John (1648).

HUXLEY, WILLIAM. Ord. deacon (Peterb.) July 10, 1664, as 'B.A. of CHRIST'S.' (Not found in the records.) V. of Moulton, Suffolk, 1677, for a short time. Probably C. of Dullingham, Cambs., 1696-1707. Died at St Margaret's, Westminster, July, 1707. Will (Dean and Chapter of Westminster) 1707. (J. Ch. Smith.)

HUYSHE, ALEXANDER. M.A. 1623 (Incorp. from Oxford). Of St Cuthbert, Wells. Matric. from Magdalen Hall, Oxford, 1613; B.A. (Wadham College) 1613-4; M.A. 1616; B.D. 1627. Fellow of Wadham, 1615-29. Licensed to preach, 1627. Preb. of Wells, 1627-50, 1660-8. R. of Beckington, Somerset, 1628-50, 1660-5. R. of Hornblotton, 1639-50, 1660-8. Doubtless s. of Edward, of Wells, orientalist, notary public, mentioned in his will, P.C.C., 1624. Died Apr. 15, 1668. (*Al. Oxon.*; *D.N.B.*; J. Ch. Smith.)

HUYSH, JAMES. Matric. Fell.-Com. from PEMBROKE, 1593.

HUYSHE, ROWLAND. Matric. pens. from TRINITY, Lent, 1577-8. S. of James, citizen of London. Bapt. Apr. 11, 1560. Scholar, 1580; B.A. 1581-2. Adm. at the Inner Temple, 1583. Of South Brent, Somerset, and Sidbury, Devon. Married Anne, dau. of John Wentworth, of Bocking, Essex. Probably died Jan. 19, 1632-3. (Burke, *L.G.*; *Vis. of Devon*, 1620.)

HUYTIN, JOHN. Prior of the Carmelite House at Cambridge in 1504. B.D. in 1505; D.D. in 1509. Prior of Norwich. Delegate of the English Province of the order at Naples, 1510. (B. Zimmerman.)

HYAGE, HENRY. B.A. 1525-6.

HYAM or HIGHAM, ROGER. Matric. pens. from JESUS, Michs. 1580.

HYDE, BALDWYN. B.Can.L. 1471-2. Perhaps canon of Windsor, 1469-72. Will (P.C.C.) 1472, of Baldwyn Hyde, clerk, Master in Chancery, Carmelite Friars, St Dunstan's, London. One of these names R. of Hawkhurst, Kent, in 1470.

HYDE, BENJAMIN. Matric. pens. from CHRIST'S, July, 1606. S. of John, of London. B.A. 1609-10; M.A. 1613. Adm. at Gray's Inn, Mar. 18, 1621-2. Of London, gent. Twin brother of Nathaniel, father of the next. (*Peile*, I. 259; *Vis. of London*, 1634.)

HIDE, BENJAMIN. Adm. pens. (age 19) at PETERHOUSE, June 24, 1648. S. of Benjamin (above), of London. Exhibitioner from Charterhouse. Migrated to Pembroke. Matric. 1648; B.A. 1651-2. 'Fell distracted: allowed 5s. a week, by Charterhouse, for his maintenance in Bedlam, Nov. 1, 1656.' (*Al. Carthus.*)

HYDE, BERNARD. Matric. Fell.-Com. from CLARE, Easter, 1626. Doubtless s. of Bernard, of London, merchant. Adm. at the Middle Temple, Feb. 9, 1628-9. Of Bore Place, Kent. Married Hester, dau. of John Trott. Died Jan. 5, 1655-6. Father of the next, brother of Humphrey (1626). (*Lincs. Pedigrees*, 537.)

HYDE, BERNARD. Adm. Fell.-Com. at CLARE, Feb. 19, 1651-2. Of Bore Place, Kent. S. of Bernard (above). Knighted, Apr. 30, 1661. Sheriff of Kent, 1673. Married Margaret, dau. of Sir William Morley, Knt., of Halnaker, Sussex. Died 1674. Brother of Humphrey (1653). (*Vis. of London*, 1634.)

HYDE, EDWARD. Matric. pens. from QUEENS', Easter, 1568.

HYDE or HIDE, EDWARD. Matric. pens. from TRINITY, Michs. 1625. S. of Sir Laurence, of Salisbury, Knt. Scholar from Westminster, 1626. B.A. 1629-30; M.A. 1633; B.D. 1640. Fellow, 1632. D.D. (Oxford) 1642-3. R. of Brightwell, Berks.; ejected, 1647. Preacher at Holywell Church, Oxford. Nominated dean of Windsor, 1658, but died, before the Restoration, Aug. 16, 1659, at Salisbury. Author, theological. M.I. in Salisbury Cathedral. Will (P.C.C.) 1660. Brother of James (1640). (Le Neve, *Mon.*, III. 41; *D.N.B.*)

HYDE, EDWARD. Matric. sizar from ST JOHN'S, Easter, 1631.

HYDE, GEORGE. B.A. 1490-1.

HYDE, GEORGE. Adm. Fell.-Com. (age 17) at ST JOHN'S, Apr. 2, 1672. S. of George, Esq., deceased, of Sandon, Herts. B. there. School, Hertford. Matric. 1672. Adm. at the Inner Temple, July 10, 1671. Buried at Sandon, Oct. 5, 1687. (*Cussans*, I. ii. 152.)

HIDE, HENRY. Adm. pens. at CLARE, Jan. 15, 1697-8. Of Sundridge, Kent. B. in London. Matric. 1698; B.A. 1701-2; M.A. 1705. Fellow, 1705. Died of small-pox, Feb. 4, 1705-6. Buried at Sundridge, Kent. M.I. there.

HYDE, HUMPHREY. Matric. Fell.-Com. from CLARE, Easter, 1626. 2nd s. of Bernard, of London, merchant. Adm. at the Middle Temple, Feb. 9, 1628-9. Of Baston and Langtoft, Lincs. Died Oct. 31, 1637. Brother of Bernard (1626), probably father of William (1652). (*Lincs. Pedigrees*, 537.)

HYDE, HUMPHREY. Adm. Fell.-Com. at CLARE, June 27, 1653. Matric. 1654. Doubtless s. of Bernard (1626), of London; and brother of Bernard (1651-2). (J. Ch. Smith.)

HYDE, HUMPHREY. Adm. pens. (age 16) at MAGDALENE, July 7, 1677. S. of William (1652), Esq. B. at Langtoft, Lincs. School, Grantham. Matric. 1678; B.A. 1681-2; M.A. 1685. Fellow, 1684. Ord. priest (Lincoln) Dec. 19, 1686. R. of Sutton St Edmund's, St James', and St Mary, 1687. R. of Hayes, *cum* Norwood, Middlesex, 1689. R. of Dowsby, Lincs., 1690. Buried at Dowsby, Apr. 30, 1727. Father of William (1715). (*Lincs. Pedigrees*, 538.)

HYDE, JAMES. M.A. 1640 (Incorp. from Oxford). 11th s. of Sir Laurence, of Salisbury, Knt.; and Principal of Magdalen Hall, Oxford. Matric. from Hart Hall, Oxford, Apr. 13, 1632, age 14; B.A. (Oxford) 1635; M.A. 1638–9; M.B. 1642; M.D. 1646. Fellow of Corpus Christi, Oxford, 1641–8. Principal of Magdalen Hall, 1662–81. Regius Professor of Physic, 1665–81. Died May 7, 1681, aged 64. Buried at St Peter-in-the-East, Oxford. Brother of Edward (1625). (*Al. Oxon.*)

HYDE, JOHN. B.A. 1533–4.

HYDE, JOHN. Matric. pens. from Sr JOHN'S, Michs. 1560. One of these names R. of Hamstall Ridware, Staffs., 1581.

HYDE, JOHN. Matric. pens. from TRINITY, *c.* 1596.

HYDE, JOHN. M.A. from ST JOHN'S, 1668. Matric. from Exeter College, Oxford, June 15, 1657; B.A. (Oxford) 1661. Ord. deacon (Chester) Sept. 25, 1663; priest (York) Mar. 11, 1665–6. C. of Salford, 1667–94. Chaplain, Collegiate Church, Manchester. V. of Bowdon, Cheshire, 1691–1708. Died 1708. (*Al. Oxon.*; E. Axon.)

HIDE, JOHN. Adm. Fell.-Com. at CLARE, May 11, 1683. Of London. Matric. 1683.

HIDE, JOSHUA. Adm. sizar at JESUS, Oct. 12, 1687. Of Cheshire. Matric. 1687. C. of Chorlton, Lancs., 1689. C. of St James' Chapel, Denton, 1691–5.

HYDE, NATHANIEL. Matric. pens. from CHRIST'S, July, 1606. S. of John, of London. Adm. at Gray's Inn, Feb. 2, 1609–10. Twin brother of Benjamin (1606). (*Peile*, I. 259; *Vis. of London*, 1634.)

HIDE, RALPH. B.Can.L. 1482–3.

HYDE, RALPH. Matric. sizar from ST JOHN'S, Easter, 1614; B.A. 1617–8; M.A. 1621. Incorp. at Oxford, 1622. Ord. deacon (Peterb.) Sept. 19; priest, Sept. 20, 1619. R. of Billingsley, Salop, 1624. R. of Sidbury, 1631. Licensed (Peterborough, Oct. 5, 1624) to marry Anne Jennings, at Barrowden, Rutland. Father of Thomas (1652). (H. I. Longden.)

HYDE, RICHARD. Matric. pens. from ST JOHN'S, Michs. 1546; B.A. 1546–7; M.A. 1549. Fellow, 1547.

HYDE, ROBERT. Adm. at KING'S (age 18) a scholar from Eton, Aug. 19, 1531. Of Lichfield, Staffs. Name off, 1535.

HYDE, ROBERT. Matric. pens. from JESUS, Easter, 1604.

HYDE, ROBERT. Adm. Fell.-Com. at TRINITY, June 6, 1646. Of Wiltshire. S. and h. of Laurence. Adm. at the Middle Temple, Nov. 3, 1647.

HYDE, ROBERT. Adm. pens. (age 18) at CHRIST'S, May 4, 1648. S. of Robert, of Denton, Esq. B. in Lancashire. Bapt. at Manchester, Jan. 12, 1629–30. School, Chester (Mr Greenhalgh). Matric. 1648; B.A. 1651–2. Age 36 in 1664. Married Maria, dau. of John Jackson, of Bubnell, Derbs. Died Oct. 25, 1699. (*Vis. of Lancs.*, 1664; *Peile*, I. 519; E. Axon.)

HYDE, THOMAS. B.Civ.L. 1532–3.

HYDE, THOMAS. Matric. pens. from CHRIST'S, 1596–7. Perhaps 3rd s. of Robert, of Norbury, Cheshire. B.A. 1599–1600; M.A. 1603. Incorp. at Oxford, 1606. Ord. deacon (Salisbury) Sept. 1606; priest, 1606–7. R. of Wanstrow, Somerset, 1610. Died 1624. Will, P.C.C. Brother of William (1597–8).

HYDE, THOMAS. B.A. 1629 (Incorp. from Oxford). S. of Thomas, of Salisbury, D.D. Matric. from Balliol College, Oxford, Nov. 9, 1627, age 17; B.A. (Oxford) 1627; M.A. 1630; D.D. 1643. R. of Abbots Ann, Hants., 1633. R. of Leckford, 1660. V. of Kingsteignton, Devon, 1660. Preb. and precentor of Sarum, 1660–6. Died 1666. Admon., P.C.C. (*Al. Oxon.*)

HYDE, THOMAS. Adm. at KING'S, a scholar from Eton, 1652. S. of Ralph (1614), V. of Billingsley, Salop. B. there, June 29, 1636. Adm. at Queen's College, Oxford, Nov. 10, 1654; M.A. (Oxford) 1659; B.D. and D.D. 1682. Bodley's librarian, 1665–1701. Precentor of Salisbury, 1660–6. Preb. 1660–1703. Archdeacon of Gloucester, and R. of Dursley, Gloucs., 1678–1703. Laudian Professor of Arabic, 1691–1703. Regius Professor of Hebrew, and canon of Christ Church, 1697–1703. Assisted Walton in the publication of the Persian and Syriac versions of the Polyglott Bible. Government interpreter of Oriental languages. Died at Christ Church, Oxford, Feb. 14, 1702–3. (*Harwood*; *D.N.B.*)

HIDE, W. Matric. sizar from ST JOHN'S, Easter, 1563.

HYDE, WILLIAM. Matric. pens. from CHRIST'S, 1597–8. Probably 4th s. of Robert, of Norbury, Cheshire, and brother of Thomas (1596–7).

HYDE, WILLIAM. Matric. pens. from JESUS, Easter, 1614. B. at Wimbledon, Surrey. B.A. 1616–7; M.A. 1620. Ord. deacon (London) Dec. 23, 1621, age 25. One of these names R. of Morley, Norfolk, 1631–74. Died 1674.

HIDE, WILLIAM. Matric. sizar from ST JOHN'S, Michs. 1620; B.A. 1623–4; M.A. 1627. Ord. deacon (York) Sept. 1624; priest, Mar. 1625–6. Will of one of these names (P.C.C.) 1657; of Market Weighton, Yorks.

HYDE, WILLIAM. M.A. 1632 (Incorp. from Oxford). Of Berkshire, gent. Matric. from Balliol College, Oxford, July 16, 1621, age 18; B.A. (Oxford) 1624; M.A. 1627.

HYDES, WILLIAM. Adm. pens. (age 17) at CHRIST'S, May 11, 1642. S. of Richard, grocer. B. at Nottingham. School, Nottingham (Mr Leake). Migrated to Caius, Dec. 9, 1643. (*Peile*, I. 480.)

HYDE, WILLIAM. Adm. Pell.-Com. at QUEENS', Nov. 4, 1652. Of Lincolnshire. Doubtless s. of Humphrey (1626), of Baston, and Langtoft, Lincs. B. 1635. School, Oundle. M.P. for Stamford, 1679–81, 1689–94. Captain of Horse, Lincoln Militia, 1680. Died Nov. 21, 1694, aged 59. Father of Humphrey (1677) and William (1675). (*Lincs. Pedigrees*, 537; *Blore*, 50.)

HYDE, WILLIAM. Adm. sizar at CLARE, May 24, 1653. Matric. 1653; B.A. 1656–7.

HIDE, WILLIAM. Adm. sizar (age 18) at ST JOHN'S, Apr. 22, 1673. S. of William, yeoman, of Market Weighton, Yorks. B. there. School, Pocklington (Mr Ellison). Matric. 1673. Migrated to Sidney as pensioner, Feb. 28, 1676–7. B.A. 1676–7. Ord. deacon (London) Mar. 11, 1676–7; priest (York) Sept. 1678. One of these names R. of Eversholt, Beds., 1698–1719. Admon. (Court of Delegates) 1736; as of Eversholt. (J. Ch. Smith.)

HIDE, WILLIAM. Adm. Fell.-Com. (age 16) at MAGDALENE, Apr. 3, 1675. S. of William (1652), Esq. B. at Langtoft, Lincs. School, Grantham. Matric. 1675; B.A. 1676–7. Adm. at the Middle Temple, Oct. 30, 1677. Of Langtoft, Esq. Died May 6, 1703. Brother of Humphrey (1677). (*Lincs. Pedigrees*, 538.)

HYDE, WILLIAM. Adm. pens. (age 17) at MAGDALENE, July 9, 1715. S. of Humphry (1677), R. of Dowsby, Lincs. B. there. School, Eton. Matric. 1715–6; B.A. 1719–20; M.A. 1723. Ord. deacon (Lincoln) Dec. 18, 1720; priest, Feb. 18, 1721–2. V. of Long Sutton, Lincs., 1720–35. Died July 12, 1735. (*Lincs. Pedigrees*, 538.)

HYED, ——. B.A. 1488–9.

HYDES, ——. B.A. 1496–7.

HYE, THOMAS. Matric. sizar from PETERHOUSE, Easter, 1611.

HYER, *see* HIGHER.

HYETT, *see* HIET.

HYHERT, RICHARD. Principal of ST MARY HOSTEL, 1521. (*Cooper*, I. 26.)

HYLAND, ISAAC, *see* HOYLAND.

HYLD, ——. B.A. 1508–9.

HYLGATE, THOMAS. Matric. sizar from TRINITY, Easter, 1550, *impubes*; Scholar, 1555.

HYMERS, JOHN, *see* HINDMARSH.

HYND, *see* HIND.

HYNGSWORTH, *see* HINXWORTH.

'HYNSLAY,' Rector of. B.Can.L. 1502–3.

HYNTES, NICHOLAS. B.A. 1479–80; M.A. 1484; B.D. 1492–3. Fellow of CLARE, 1486.

HYON, ROWLAND, *see* ION.

HYRBY, ——. B.A. 1492–3.

HYRFORDE, IRFORD or HERTFORTH, PETER. D.D. Nominated as one of the framers of the statutes of QUEENS' College, Mar. 30, 1448, himself a fellow, 1448–9. On Feb. 22, 1412–3, when B.A., he had, before the Chancellor of the University, renounced the opinions of Wycliffe. Confessor to John, Duke of Bedford and witness to his will, Sept. 10, 1435. Benefactor to Queens'. (W. G. Searle, *Hist. of Queens'*, 31.)

HYRNE, *see* HEARNE *and* HIERON.

HYSEM, THOMAS. Matric. sizar from QUEENS', Michs. 1548, *impubes*.

HYSHAM, ——. M.A. 1457–8. *See* ISHAM.

HYX, *see* HICKS.

I

IAN, RICHARD. Matric. sizar from PEMBROKE, Michs. 1551.

IANSON, YANSON or JANSON, LANCELOT. Matric. sizar from TRINITY, Easter, 1570. B. at Richmond, Yorks. Scholar, 1574; B.A. 1574-5; M.A. 1578. Ord. deacon (London) Aug. 18, 1577, age 26. R. of Langford, Essex, 1585. V. of Heybridge, 1587-1624. Married (1) 1587, Margaret, dau. of Wm. Whiting, R. of Toppesfield; (2) Ann, dau. of Thos. Morice, R. of Layer Marney. Buried at Heybridge, Sept. 21, 1624. Will (P.C.C.) 1624; proved by widow Elizabeth. (J. Ch. Smith.)

IBBOTT, BENJAMIN. Adm. sizar at CLARE, July 25, 1695. S. of Thomas (1671), R. of Beechamwell, Norfolk. B. there, 1680. B.A. 1699-1700; Scholar of Corpus Christi, 1700; M.A. there, 1703; D.D. 1717 (*Com. Reg.*). Fellow of Corpus Christi, 1706-7. Librarian and chaplain to Archbishop Tenison, 1707. R. of St Vedast and St Michael-le-Querne, London, 1707-16. Treasurer of Wells Cathedral, 1708-25. Boyle lecturer, 1713-4. P.C. of St Paul's, Shadwell, 1715-25. Chaplain to the King, 1717-25. Preb. of Westminster, 1724-5. Preacher assistant at St James', Piccadilly. Married, at St Martin Outwich, July 28, 1714, Susanna Powell. Author, *Sermons*. Died at Camberwell, Apr. 4, 1725. Buried in Westminster Abbey. Will (P.C.C.) 1725. Brother of John (1706) and Thomas (1702-3). (*D.N.B.*; *Masters*.)

IBBOTT, BOYS. Adm. pens. (age 20) at SIDNEY, June 30, 1690. S. of Edmund (below), minister at Deal, Kent. B. there. Schools, Eynesbury, St Neots, and Westminster. Migrated to Pembroke, July 3, 1690. Matric. 1691; B.A. 1693-4; M.A. 1697. V. of Seasalter, Kent, 1699. Died 1700.

IBBOT, EDMUND. Adm. sizar (age 16) at CHRIST'S, Aug. 18, 1649. S. of John. B. at St Neots. School, Huntingdon (Mr Taylor). D.D. 1662 (*Lit. Reg.*). Chaplain of the ship *Naseby*, which brought over Charles II, in 1660. R. of Deal, 1662-77. Died 1677. Father of Boys. (*Peile*, I. 530.)

IBBOTT, JOHN. Adm. sizar (age 18) at MAGDALENE, July 5, 1706. S. of Thomas (1671), V. of Swaffham, Norfolk. B. there. School, Histon, Cambs. Migrated to Corpus Christi, 1707. Matric. 1708; B.A. 1710-1. Ord. priest (Ely) Sept. 23, 1716. C. of Withington, Gloucs., 1718. Brother of Benjamin (1695) and Thomas (1702-3).

IBBOTT, THOMAS. Adm. sizar at CLARE, Dec. 19, 1671. Of St Ives, Hunts. Matric. 1672, as 'Ibbons'; B.A. 1675-6; M.A. 1679. Ord. deacon (London) May 21, 1676. R. of Beechamwell, Norfolk, 1676. V. of Swaffham, 1696-1720. Father of Benjamin (1695), John (1706) and the next.

IBBOTT, THOMAS. Adm. sizar (age 17) at CAIUS, Jan. 19, 1702-3. S. of Thomas (1671), V. of Swaffham, Norfolk. B. at Beechamwell. Schools, New College, Oxford (Mr Ja. Badger) and Wisbech (Mr Carter). Matric. 1702-3; Scholar, 1703-7; B.A. 1706-7. Ord. deacon (Norwich) May 30, 1708; C. of Beechamwell; priest, June 19, 1709. V. of Kenninghall, Norfolk, 1712-7. R. of St Margaret's and St Peter's, South Elmham, 1717. R. of Beechamwell and Fakenham, 1723-37. Married Susanna, dau. of Clement Heigham, R. of Sculthorpe. Will (Norwich) 1737. Brother of Benjamin (1695) and John (1706). (*Venn*, I. 509.)

IBBOT, THOMAS. Adm. sizar (age 17) at CAIUS, July 6, 1736. S. of Henry, attorney, late of Swaffham, Norfolk. B. there. Schools, Swaffham and Necton (private; Mr Pigge) and colleger at Eton, 1733-5. Scholar, 1736-41; Matric. 1737; B.A. 1739-40; M.A. 1743. Ord. deacon (Norwich) Dec. 21, 1740; priest (Ely) Feb. 26, 1742-3. R. of Beechamwell St Mary, Norfolk, 1764-87. C. of Stoke Ferry, 1768-74. Will (P.C.C.) 1787. (*Venn*, II. 42.)

IBETSON, ANTHONY. Adm. sizar at PETERHOUSE, Oct. 29, 1619. Of Yorkshire. Matric. 1619; B.A. 1623-4. Ord. deacon (York) Sept. 1627; priest, Mar. 1627-8.

IBBOTSON, GEORGE. Adm. sizar (age 19) at MAGDALENE, July 2, 1739. B. at Sheffield. School, Sheffield. Matric. 1739; B.A. 1742-3. Ord. deacon (Lincoln) Sept. 25, 1743; priest, June 2, 1751.

IBBOTSON, JAMES. Adm. pens. (age 17) at TRINITY, June 18, 1691. S. of Timothy (1655), of Hanbury, Staffs. School, Uttoxeter (Mr Thomas Mallet). Matric. 1691-2; Scholar, 1693; B.A. 1694-5; M.A. 1698. Ord. deacon (Lincoln) Sept. 19, 1697.

IBBOTSON, JOHN. Matric. pens. from CHRIST'S, Easter, 1584. Probably s. of Henry, of Wightwisle, Bradfield, Yorks.; bapt. Feb. 25, 1568-9. B.A. from St Catharine's, 1588-9. Ord. priest (London) Oct. 1592, age 25; 'resident at Redbourn, Herts.' R. of Walton, Bucks., 1596-7. R. of Grafton Regis, Northants., 1597-1604. Afterwards of Wightwisle, Bradfield. Married, at St Benet's, Paul's Wharf, London, Mar. 22, 1603-4, Bridget Ellis. Buried at Bradfield, Apr. 29, 1649. (*Peile*, I. 178; *F.M.G.*, 651; H. I. Longden.)

IBBOTSON, TIMOTHY. Matric. sizar from ST CATHARINE'S, Easter, 1655. Of Yorkshire. B.A. 1658-9; M.A. 1662. V. of Hanbury, Staffs. 1677. Preb. of Lichfield, 1677-91. Died 1691. Father of James (1691).

IBBETSON, ——. Adm. Fell. Com. at TRINITY HALL, Oct. 21, 1718. Doubtless Samuel, s. and h. of James, cloth merchant, of Denton Park, Otley, Yorks. Adm. at Lincoln's Inn, Apr. 14, 1720. Married (1) Alice, dau. of Edmund Ogden, of Rochdale; (2) Hephzibah, dau. of John Hatfield, Esq. Died Mar. 1768. Will, York. (M. H. Peacock.)

IBGRAVE, BENJAMIN. Adm. Fell.-Com. at PETERHOUSE, May 16, 1579. S. and h. of Ellis, of Abbots Langley, Herts. (whose will, P.C.C., 1564). Bapt. there, May 4, 1561. Matric. 1579. (*Vis. of Herts.*, 1572; J. Ch. Smith.)

IBGRAVE, JOHN. Adm. Fell.-Com. at PETERHOUSE, *c.* 1590.

IBSON, THOMAS. Matric. pens. from CHRIST'S, Easter, 1619. S. and h. of John, of York, gent. B.A. 1622-3. Adm. at Lincoln's Inn, Apr. 11, 1625. Of York. Gave £15 to the New Buildings at Christ's. (*Peile*, I. 329.)

IDEN, JOHN. Adm. pens. at EMMANUEL, June 3, 1645. Of Sussex. Matric. 1647; B.A. 1648-9. Died in College. Buried at St Andrew's, Cambridge, May 27, 1649.

IDEN, RICHARD. B.Can.L. 1504-5. Perhaps will (P.C.C.) 1523; 'of Clayton, Pyecombe, Sussex, clerk.'

IDEN, RICHARD. B.A. 1538-9, *see* EDEN.

IDEN, RICHARD. Matric. pens. from CORPUS CHRISTI, Easter, 1637. Of Kent.

IDLE, HENRY, *see* CARDELL.

IDLE, JOHN. Adm. sizar at TRINITY, Apr. 27, 1647. Of Yorkshire. Matric. 1646; Scholar, 1649; B.A. 1650-1; M.A. 1654. Ord. priest (Bishop of Ardfert) June 22, 1660. V. of Felsted, Essex, 1662-79. Died 1679.

IDLE, JOHN. Adm. pens. (age 16) at SIDNEY, June 14, 1705. 1st s. of Robert (? 1672), gent. B. at Westow, Yorks. School, Beverley. Adm. at the Middle Temple, Oct. 28, 1709. Barrister, 1715. Adm. at Lincoln's Inn, July 9, 1728.

IDLE, RICHARD. Adm. sizar (age 17) at SIDNEY, June 16, 1682. 1st s. of Richard, yeoman. B. at Bulmer, Yorks. Schools, Stittenham (Mr Ben. Colquit) and Barton (Mr Mat. Boice). Matric. 1682; B.A. 1685-6; M.A. 1690. Ord. priest (York) Dec. 1689. V. of South Dalton, Yorks. V. of Chapel Allerton, 1689. V. of Rothwell, Leeds, 1691-1702. Married Abigail, dau. of John Thoresby, of Leeds, May 20, 1687.

IDLE, ROBERT. Adm. pens. (age 16) at SIDNEY, July 27, 1672. 2nd s. of Jeremiah, yeoman and constable of Yorkshire. B. at Bulmer. Matric. 1672; B.A. 1676-7; M.A. 1680. Incorp. at Oxford, 1680.

IDLOTT, WILLIAM. Adm. sizar (age 16) at CHRIST'S, May 1, 1694. S. of Matthew. B. at Wellingborough, Northants. School, Courteenhall (Mr Ashbridge). Scholar, 1694-5; Matric. 1695. Resided about three years. (*Peile*, II. 130.)

IDON, THOMAS. Adm. pens. (age 16) at CAIUS, May 23, 1576. S. of Robert. B. at Spalding, Lincs. School, Spalding.

IGGLESDEN, STEPHEN. Adm. pens. at JESUS, May 29, 1724. Of Surrey. Perhaps s. of Stephen, surgeon, of Mayfield, Sussex. Matric. 1724; Scholar, 1725. (H. G. Harrison.)

IGLEDEN, JOHN. Matric. pens. from QUEENS', Easter, 1551; Scholar, 1551; B.A. 1554-5; M.A. 1557; B.D. 1564. Fellow, 1553-70. Proctor, 1562-3. University preacher, 1564. Perhaps preb. of Chichester, 1565-78. R. of Monks Horton, Kent, 1568-70. R. of Fordwich, 1572-4. V. of Milton, 1584-5.

IGNES, SAMUEL. Matric. pens. from ST JOHN'S, Easter, 1621; B.A. 1624-5; M.A. 1628.

IGO or YGO, JOHN. B.A. 1526-7.

IKEN, JAMES. Adm. pens. (age 16) at CAIUS, Aug. 6, 1604. S. of Thomas, citizen and skinner, of London. Of the parish of St Mildred Poultry, London. School, Merchant Taylors'. Scholar, 1605–11; B.A. 1607–8; M.A. 1611. Fellow, 1611–20. R. of Stifford, Essex, 1619–45. R. of Swanscombe, Kent, 1620–45. Buried there Mar. 30, 1645. Will, P.C.C. Father of the next. (*Venn*, I. 186.)

IKEN, THOMAS. Adm. pens. (age 14) at CAIUS, Sept. 13, 1648. S. of James (above), R. of Stifford, Essex. B. there. School, Brentwood (Mr Dan. Latham). Matric. 1648; Scholar, 1648–54; B.A. 1652–3.

ILANDE, NICHOLAS. Matric. sizar from QUEENS', Easter, 1551, *impubes*.

ILDEN, ——. Adm. at CORPUS CHRISTI, 1578.

ILDERTON, FRANCIS. Adm. pens. (age 19) at ST JOHN'S, May 25, 1744. S. of Thomas, gent., of Northumberland. B. at Bilton Banks, near Alnwick. School, Wooller (Mr Lithgow). Matric. 1744; B.A. 1747–8; M.A. 1751; B.D. 1759. Fellow, 1752–60. Ord. deacon (London) Dec. 16, 1748; priest, Sept. 22, 1754. C. of Gt Braxted, Essex. Buried at Lesbury, Northumberland, May 24, 1760. (*Scott-Mayor*, III. 542.)

ILES, BRIAN. Matric. pens. from JESUS, Easter, 1612. Perhaps of Leeds. Married Elizabeth Pawson, of York, 1628.

ILES, MICHAEL. Adm. sizar at TRINITY, June 30, 1645. Of Hertfordshire. Matric. 1645; Scholar, 1647; B.A. 1648–9; M.A. 1652.

ILGARDE, MICHAEL. Matric. pens. from TRINITY, Michs. 1554; Scholar, 1554, as Ilgate.

ILIFFE, GEORGE. Adm. sizar at TRINITY, July 2, 1733. S. of John, schoolmaster, of Kensington, London. School, Kensington (under his father). Matric. 1733; B.A. 1737–8; M.A. 1741. Brother of John (1732).

ILIVE, GEORGE. Adm. sizar at QUEENS', Nov. 6, 1623. Of Leicestershire.

ILIFFE, JOHN. Adm. sizar (age 17) at TRINITY, Nov. 23, 1732. S. of John, of Kensington, London, schoolmaster and minister of Heston. School, Kensington (under his father). Matric. 1733; B.A. 1736–7. Brother of George (1733).

ILIFFE, THOMAS. Adm. sizar at EMMANUEL, May 27, 1670. B. at Uppingham, Ruts. Matric. 1671; B.A. 1673–4; M.A. 1677; B.D. 1684; D.D. 1699. Fellow, 1677–90. R. of North Cadbury, Somerset, 1689–1712. Preb. of Wells, 1704–12. Will (P.C.C.) 1712.

ILIFF, WILLIAM. Adm. sizar (age 17) at TRINITY, June 23, 1698. S. of William, deceased, of London, citizen and blacksmith, of St Helen's. 'Grecian' from Christ's Hospital. Matric. 1698; Scholar, 1701; B.A. 1701–2; M.A. 1705. Ord. priest (Lincoln) July 25, 1711. Signs as C. of Sundon, Beds., in 1708. V. of Stotfold, 1711–8. V. of Heston, Middlesex, 1731–2. Died Dec. 3, 1732.

ILKESTON, ROBERT. LL.B., of York diocese, when ord. priest (Lincoln) Apr. 11, 1479, on title of HOUSE OF ST EDMUND, Cambridge.

ILKESTON, WILLIAM. B.A. 1470–1; M.A. Fellow of PETERHOUSE, 1474–93. Probably R. of St Peter, Nottingham, 1499–1510. (*T. A. Walker*.)

ILLENDEN, JOHN. Matric. sizar from KING'S, Easter, 1575. Doubtless ord. deacon (Chichester) Oct. 23, 1578; priest (Rochester) Nov. 30, 1579. V. of Bodiam, Sussex, 1587–1624. Buried Jan. 28, 1623–4. (W. C. Renshaw.)

ILLINGWORTH, HENRY. Adm. sizar at EMMANUEL, Mar. 29, 1659. Of Yorkshire. Matric. 1659; B.A. 1662; M.A. 1666.

ILLINGWORTH, JAMES. Matric. sizar from TRINITY, Lent, 1563–4.

ILLINGWORTH, JAMES. Adm. pens. at EMMANUEL, June 19, 1645. S. of Thomas, draper, of Manchester. Bapt. there, Dec. 18, 1625. No matric.; B.A. 1648–9; M.A. 1652; B.D. 1659. Fellow, 1650–60, ejected. Presented by the University to Eccleston, Lancs., June 13, 1660. Afterwards chaplain in Staffordshire. Died Aug. 28, 1693. Buried at Weston-under-Lyziard. (Mumford, *Manchester Grammar School*; *Calamy*, I. 204; E. Axon.)

ILLINGWORTH, JOHN. Adm. pens. at EMMANUEL, July 1, 1659. Of Yorkshire. Matric. 1659; B.A. 1662–3. Head Master of Otley Grammar School, Yorks., 1663–5.

ILLINGWORTH, TEMPEST. Matric. sizar from TRINITY, Easter, 1631; Scholar, 1634.

IMAGE, JOHN. Adm. sizar (age 17) at ST JOHN'S, Apr. 12, 1747. S. of Charles, wigmaker, of Northamptonshire. B. at Peterborough. School, Peterborough (Mr Marshall). Matric. 1748; B.A. 1750–1; M.A. 1754. Fellow, 1752–63. Ord. deacon (Norwich) Dec. 22, 1751; priest (Peterb.) Dec. 23, 1753. V. of Higham, Kent, 1762–7. Chaplain to the Bishop of Peterborough, 1764–9. V. of St John's, Peterborough, 1766–86. R. of Etton, Northants., 1769–86. Precentor and minor canon of Peterborough, 1769. Licensed, Aug. 28, 1764, to marry Mary Cox, of Peterborough. Died Oct. 12, 1786. Will (P.C.C.) 1787. (*Scott-Mayor*, III. 566; *G. Mag.*; H. I. Longden.)

IMBER, JOHN. Adm. scholar at TRINITY HALL, Jan. 8, 1710–1. Of Winchester. Matric. 1710; LL.B. 1715. In holy orders. Probably of Abbots-Worthy, Hants., clerk, in 1740, when his s. John was adm. at University College, Oxford. Died Nov. 1767. (G. *Mag.*)

IMBER, LUKE. Matric. pens. from TRINITY HALL, Apr. 1715; LL.B. 1719. Ord. priest (Norwich) Feb. 1721–2. C. of Popham, Hants. Died at Christ Church, Hants., Sept. 1773, aged 90. (*G. Mag.*)

IMBER, ——. Adm. pens. at TRINITY HALL, July 4, 1739. Perhaps John, s. of John (1710–1). Matric. from University College, Oxford, May 18, 1740, age 16; B.A. (Oxford) 1744–5.

IMMINS or IMMING, SAMUEL. Adm. sizar at TRINITY, June 24, 1674. Matric. 1674; B.A. 1677–8; M.A. 1681.

IMPEY, GEORGE. Adm. pens. (age 18) at CAIUS, July 2, 1634. S. of Thomas, gent., of Flamstead, Herts. B. at Eggington, Beds. School, Eggington (Mr Plumtree). Matric. 1634; B.A. 1637; M.A. 1641. Licensed to practise medicine, 1646. (*Venn*, I. 315.)

IMPY, RICHARD. Adm. at CORPUS CHRISTI, 1671. Of Bedfordshire. Matric. pens. Easter, 1671.

IMPEY, THOMAS. Matric. pens. from TRINITY, *c.* 1594.

IMWORTH, ROBERT DE. One of the first 'KING'S scholars' at Cambridge, Feb. 6, 1317–8. Left, June 24, 1329.

INCE, THOMAS. Adm. sizar (age 17) at ST JOHN'S, Apr. 26, 1718. S. of Nicholas, gent., of Cheshire. B. at Chester. School, Chester (Mr Henchman). Matric. 1718; B.A. 1721–2; M.A. 1725. Ord. deacon (Chester) July 28, 1723; priest, June 20, 1725. Minor canon of Chester. R. of Handley, Cheshire, 1735–66. Married, at Chester Cathedral, Apr. 10, 1737, Susan Robinson, of Holy Trinity. Died Apr. 5, 1766. Buried in Chester Cathedral. (*Scott-Mayor*, III. 317; J. Ch. Smith.)

INCE, WILLIAM. M.A. 1632 (Incorp. from Dublin). Adm. scholar at Trinity College, Dublin, Nov. 6, 1624; B.A. 1627. Fellow, 1629. Died Dec. 21, 1635. (*Al. Dub.*)

INCE or HENS, ——. Scholar at KING'S HALL, 1498–9. Died same year.

INCENT, JOHN. Studied at Cambridge, afterwards at All Souls, Oxford. S. of Robert. B. at Berkhampstead, Herts. B.C.L. (Oxford) 1506; D.C.L. 1513. An advocate. Preb. of St Paul's, 1519–45. Canon residentiary, 1534. Master of Holy Cross Hospital, Winchester, 1537. Dean of St Paul's, 1540–5. Adm. at Gray's Inn, 1542. Founded a free school at Berkhampstead. Died 1545. (*Cooper*, I. 86; *Al. Oxon.*)

INETT, JOHN. D.D. from ST JOHN'S, 1701. S. of Richard, of Bewdley, Worcs. Matric. from University College, Oxford, July 17, 1663, age 16; B.A. (Oxford) 1666; M.A. 1669. Ord. deacon (Gloucester) Sept. 22, 1667 (as Inett, *alias* Hungerford, his mother's name). R. of St Ebbe, Oxford. V. of Nuneaton, Warws., 1678. Precentor and preb. of Lincoln, 1682–1718. R. of Tansor, Northants., 1685–1706. Chaplain to the King, 1700–2, 1714–8. Chaplain to Queen Anne, 1702–14. R. of Clayworth, Notts., 1706. V. of Wirksworth, Derbs., 1715–8. Author of *Origenes Anglicanae*. Died Mar. 4, 1717–8. M.I. in Lincoln Cathedral. Father of John (next), Richard (1701) and Thomas (1707). (*Al. Oxon.*; *D.N.B.*; A. B. Beaven.)

INETT, JOHN. Adm. pens. (age 17) at ST JOHN'S, Sept. 27, 1701. S. of John (above), D.D. B. at Nuneaton, Warws. School, Rugby (Mr Holyoke). Migrated to Oxford. Matric. from Wadham College, Mar. 17, 1702–3, 'aged 16'; B.A. (St Mary's Hall, Oxford) 1709. Ord. deacon (Peterb.) June 19, 1709; priest, June 3, 1710. C. to his father at Tansor. R. of Grainsby, Lincs., 1710. V. of Gt Carleton, 1717. Brother of the next and of Thomas (1707). (*Al. Oxon.*; H. I. Longden.)

INETT, RICHARD. Adm. pens. (age 18) at ST JOHN'S, Sept. 27, 1701. S. of John (1701), D.D. B. at Nuneaton, Warws. School, Rugby (Mr Holyoke). Matric. 1702; B.A. 1705–6; M.A. 1728 (*Com. Reg.*). Ord. deacon (Peterb.) Sept. 23, 1705; priest, Mar. 16, 1706–7. R. of Tansor, Northants., 1706–45. Preb. of Lincoln, 1731–45. R. of Farthingstone, Northants., 1733–45. Died 1745. Brother of the next and of John (above). (*Baker*, I. 374; *Bridges*, II. 477.)

INETT, THOMAS. Adm. pens. (age 18) at MAGDALENE, June 25, 1707. S. of John (1701), D.D., precentor of Lincoln Cathedral. School, Rugby, Warws. Matric. 1710; B.A. 1710–1; M.A. 1714. Ord. deacon (York) Sept. 1711; priest, 1713. V. of Wirksworth, Derbs., 1718–44. Preb. of Worcester, 1726–49. Preb. of Winchester, 1732–49. Died Jan. 4, 1748–9. Brother of Richard (above) and of John (1701).

INFEELDE, RICHARD. Matric. pens. from TRINITY, Michs. 1614. Adm. at the Inner Temple, 1616, as of West Hoathly, Sussex.

INFIELD, ROBERT. Adm. sizar at TRINITY, Nov. 16, 1660. Matric. 1661; B.A. 1664-5.

INFIELD, THOMAS. Matric. sizar from MAGDALENE, Easter, 1625; B.A. 1628; M.A. 1633. Ord. deacon (Peterb.) Feb. 22; priest, Feb. 23, 1628-9. P.C. of St Peter's, Irthlingborough, Northants., 1638-41. (H. I. Longden.)

INFIELD, WILLIAM. Matric. sizar from MAGDALENE, Michs. 1637.

INGALL, WILLIAM. Matric. sizar from ST JOHN'S, Michs. 1573; B.A. 1577-8; M.A. 1581. C. and schoolmaster at Kendal, Westmorland. Buried there Mar. 21, 1612-3.

INGE, RICHARD. Matric. pens. from TRINITY, Michs. 1583; B.A. 1586-7; M.A. 1590. Master of Nuneaton Grammar School, Warws., c. 1603-10. Will (Leicester) 1615; of Oadby, Leics., clerk.

INGE, RICHARD. Matric. sizar from TRINITY, Michs. 1613; B.A. 1617-8. Migrated to Corpus Christi, 1618. M.A. 1621. Ord. deacon (Peterb.) May 23, 1619. Perhaps V. of Petham, Kent, 1627-41. Died June, 1641. Will, Canterbury.

INGE, RICHARD. Adm. pens. at CLARE, June 8, 1699. S. of William, Esq. Matric. 1700; B.A. 1702-3. Migrated to Emmanuel, Nov. 7, 1704. M.A. 1706. Ord. priest (London) Sept. 15, 1705. R. of Nether Seal, Leics., 1705-48. Married Elizabeth Mugeston. Died May, 1748, aged 67. Will (Leicester) 1749. Father of William (1740). (Burke, *L.G.*; *Nichols*, II. 994.)

INGG, THOMAS. Adm. sizar at PEMBROKE, Jan. 14, 1620-1. Matric. 1620-1; B.A. 1624-5. C. of Anstey, Leics., 1628.

INGE, WILLIAM. Adm. pens. at EMMANUEL, May 11, 1740. Of Nether Seal, Leics. S. of Richard (above), clerk. School, Appleby, Leics. Age 19. Matric. 1740; B.A. 1743-4; M.A. 1747. Fellow, 1746. Ord. deacon (Lincoln) June 9, 1745; priest, Sept. 21, 1746. R. of Brereton, Cheshire. R. of Nether Seal, Leics., 1748-59. Preb. of Lichfield, 1780-1807. Canon residentiary and precentor, 1797-1807. Died Apr. 23, 1807, aged 84. (*G. Mag.*)

INGELO, CHARLES. Adm. pens. at QUEENS', Sept. 2, 1680. Of Buckinghamshire. Doubtless born at Eton; colleger, 1675-80.

INGELO, JOHN. Adm. at KING'S, a scholar from Eton, 1670. 2nd s. of Nathaniel (next). B. at Eton. Matric. 1671; B.A. 1675-6. Fellow, 1674. Adm. at the Middle Temple, Oct. 26, 1675. Died young, of small-pox. Brother of Nathaniel (1665).

INGELO, NATHANIEL. M.A. from QUEENS', 1644 (Incorp. from Edinburgh). D.D. 1658. Fellow of Queens', 1644-6. Fellow of Eton, 1650-83. Accompanied Whitelocke to Sweden, as chaplain, 1653. R. of Piddlehinton, Dorset, 1671-7. Divine and musician. Died Aug. 3, 1683, aged 62. Buried in Eton College Chapel. M.I. Father of the next, and of John (above). (*D.N.B.*; *Harwood.*)

INGELO, NATHANIEL. Adm. pens. at QUEENS', Apr. 28, 1665. S. of Nathaniel (above). B. at Bristol. Migrated to King's, as scholar from Eton, 1665. Matric. 1667; B.A. 1669-70; M.A. 1673. Fellow of King's, 1669. Succeeded his father as R. of Piddlehinton, Dorset, 1677-85. Licensed, May 21, 1678, age 26, to marry Ann, dau. of Dr Evans, canon of Windsor, at Hitcham, Bucks. Died 1685. Father of the next, brother of John (1670). (Hutchins, *Dorset*, II. 805.)

INGELO, NATHANIEL. Adm. pens. at JESUS, Nov. 4, 1699. S. of Nathaniel (above). B. at Piddlehinton, Dorset. Colleger at Eton, 1694-9. Matric. 1699; Rostat Scholar; B.A. 1703-4; M.A. 1707. Incorp. at Oxford, 1707. Subscribed for deacon's orders (Bristol) Mar. 12, 1714-5; for priest's, Sept. 23, 1715. R. of Cottisford, Oxon., 1720. R. of Piddlehinton, Dorset, 1726-51. Died 1751.

INGELOND or INGELEND, THOMAS. Student at Cambridge; probably of CHRIST'S, c. 1520. Dramatist. (*Cooper*, I. 240; *D.N.B.*)

INGHAM, *see also* ENGHAM.

INGHAM, CHRISTOPHER. Adm. pens. (age 17) at CAIUS, May 24, 1584. S. of William, yeoman. B. at Nottingham. School, Sheffield (Mr Heywood). Perhaps admon. (York) 1639; of Laxton, Notts.

INGHAM, JOHN. B.D. Of Lincoln diocese. Fellow of CLARE HALL, when ord. deacon (Ely) Sept. 23, 1402. Fellow of King's Hall, when priest, Mar. 10, 1402-3. R. of Teversham, Cambs., till 1452, when he retired on a pension of ten marks.

INGHAM, ROBERT. Adm. sizar (age 17) at CAIUS, May 16, 1699. S. of Thomas, brewer, of Theberton Hall, Suffolk. B. there. Bapt. July 29, 1682. School, Kelsale (Mr Candler). Matric. 1699; Scholar, 1699-1703; B.A. 1702-3. Fellow, 1703-5. Died in College. Buried at St Michael's, Cambridge, Aug. 22, 1705. (*Venn*, I. 502.)

INGHAM, THOMAS. Adm. sizar at EMMANUEL, July 4, 1674. Of Lancashire. (S. of Robert, of Fulledge, Burnley.) Matric. 1677; B.A. 1677-8. P.C. of Coppull, Lancs., 1705-15. Died c. 1729. For an account of his troubles with the Bishop *see* Nicholson and Axon, *Older Nonconformity*, 538.

INGHAM, WILLIAM. Adm. pens. (age 18) at CHRIST'S, June 5, 1649. S. of William. B. at Wirrall, Cheshire. Schools, Haslingden, Manchester and Lancaster. Matric. 1649. Perhaps minister of Shireshead, Lancs., c. 1652. (*Peile*, I. 527; Shaw, *Lancs. Classis*, II. 235.)

INGLAND, *see* ENGLAND.

INGLE or INGYL, JOHN. Scholar at KING'S HALL, 1383. Perhaps the same as John St Ives, who resided till 1412. Died Apr. 14, 1412. (*Trinity College Admissions*, I. 107.)

INGLE, RICHARD. Adm. pens. (age 15) at CAIUS, Apr. 8, 1697. S. of Benjamin, mercer, of Yarmouth (Mayor, 1702). B. there. School, Yarmouth (Mr Reynolds and Mr Pate). Matric. 1697; Scholar, 1697-8. Buried in Yarmouth Church, Mar. 30, 1721. (*Venn*, I. 500.)

INGLEBY, FRANCIS. Adm. pens. (age 17) at ST JOHN'S, May 13, 1689. S. of William, gent. B. at Palethorpe, Yorks. Bapt. at St Martin's, York, May 29, 1672. School, York (Mr Tomlinson). Matric. 1689. Buried at Clapham, Yorks., Jan. 13, 1717. (*Vis. of Yorks.*, 1665.)

INGILBY, HENRY. Adm. Fell.-Com. at QUEENS', Feb. 17, 1651-2. Of Yorkshire. S. of Sir William, of Ripley, Knt. and Bart. Bapt. at Ripley, July 10, 1634.

INGLEBY, JOHN. B.A. 1455-6.

INGLEBY, JOHN. Fined for non-determination in arts, 1467. One John Yngleby R. of Little Laver, Essex, 1455.

INGILBY, JOHN. Adm. Fell.-Com. at TRINITY, Mar. 18, 1722-3. S. of Sir John, of Ripley, Yorks., Bart. B. 1705. Matric. 1723. Succeeded his father, Jan. 21, 1741-2. Died July 14, 1772. (Burke, *Ext. Bart.*; G.E.C.)

INGLEBY, ROBERT. Matric. sizar from QUEENS', Michs. 1566.

INGLEBY, WILLIAM. Adm. pens. (age 18) at CHRIST'S, Apr. 15, 1653. Afterwards Fell.-Com., Apr. 27. S. of William, of Palethorpe, Yorks. B. there. Bapt. at Bolton Percy, Apr. 16, 1635. School, Giggleswick (Mr Walker). Adm. at Gray's Inn, May 25, 1655. Married Mary Hill, of Knaresborough. Buried at St Martin's, Coney Street, York, Dec. 22, 1679. (*Peile*, I. 551.)

INGLEBY, WILLIAM. Adm. sizar (age 16) at PETERHOUSE, Mar. 12, 1671-2. Of Durham. School, Houghton, Durham. Matric. 1672. One of these names buried at St Margaret's, Durham, June 7, 1704. (H. M. Wood.)

INGLES, JOHN DE, *see* ENGLEIS.

INGLESBY, THOMAS. M.A. 1614-5 (on King's visit).

INGLESBY, WILLIAM. Matric. sizar from CLARE, Michs. 1664.

INGLESTHORPE, SIMON DE. Fellow of CLARE, in 1338.

INGLETHORPE, SAMUEL. Matric. pens. from CORPUS CHRISTI, Easter, 1634. Of Suffolk. B.A. 1637-8. Probably of Bury St Edmunds. (V. B. Redstone.)

INGLETON, JOHN. B.A. 1462-3; M.A. 1466.

INGLETT, WILLIAM. Matric. sizar from ST JOHN'S, Easter, 1622. Of Devon. Probably s. of Giles, of Lamberton, Devon. Bapt. Jan. 4, 1606-7. B.A. 1625-6; M.A. 1629; B.D. 1637. Fellow, 1627. V. of Higham, Kent, 1653-60. Died Jan. 14, 1659-60. M.I. (*Vis. of Devon*, 1620.)

INGLIS, ALEXANDER. Adm. scholar at TRINITY HALL, Jan. 5, 1722-3. Of Salisbury. S. of Alexander, army surgeon. School, Westminster. Matric. 1721; LL.B. 1726. Adm. at Lincoln's Inn, Aug. 8, 1721. 'Marrying a person of Cambridge went into the W. Indies, and lived poorly.' (Cole, *MS.*, 5873, 10; *Al. Westmon.*, 276.)

INGLIS or INGLET, ——. Scholar at CHRIST'S, 1570-1. Probably Christopher England (whom *see*).

INGLISH, *see* ENGLISH.

INGOLDSBY, WILLIAM. Adm. pens. at EMMANUEL, May 3, 1615; B.A. 1618. Obtained royal letters of commendation for a fellowship, 1618, but was not elected. One of these names V. of Brigstock, Northants., 1639-41. R. of Watton-at-Stone, Herts., 1640-5. Died 1645. (*Star Chamber Proceedings James I*, 28.)

INGRAM, ARTHUR. Matric. Fell.-Com. from TRINITY, Easter, 1615. Probably s. and h. of Sir Arthur, of London, Knt. Adm. at Lincoln's Inn, Jan. 18, 1615-6. Knighted, July 16, 1621. High Sheriff for Yorks., 1630. J.P. and D.L. Died July 4, 1655. Buried at Whitkirk, Leeds.

INGRAM, ARTHUR. Matric. pens. from TRINITY, Easter, 1622. Probably s. of Sir William (1582), of York, Knt. LL.B. from Trinity Hall, 1628. Adm. at Gray's Inn, Mar. 18, 1621-2. Of Hull and afterwards of Knottingley, Yorks. Surveyor of the Customs. Age 61 in 1665. Married at Brompton, Nov. 26, 1629, Catharine, dau. of Edward Cayley, of Brompton. (*Vis. of Yorks.*, 1665; M. H. Peacock.)

INGRAM, ARTHUR. Adm. pens. at TRINITY, June 22, 1655. Of Yorkshire. S. and h. of Arthur (above), of Knottingley, Yorks. Matric. 1656. Adm. at Gray's Inn, Apr. 20, 1657. Groom of the Stole to Charles II. Of Thorpe-on-the-Hill, Yorks.; age 28 in 1665. Married Helen, dau. of Henry Gasco , Esq. Died before June 28, 1677. (*Vis. of Yorks.*, 1665.)igne

INGRAM, ARTHUR. Adm. pens. at PEMBROKE, July 6, 1658. Perhaps s. of Arthur (1615). Matric. 1659; B.A. 1661-2. Of Barrowby, Esq. Married Jane, dau. of Sir John Mallory, of Studley, Yorks. Died Sept. 12, 1713. (M. H. Peacock.)

INGRAM, BENJAMIN. Adm. sizar at CORPUS CHRISTI, 1680. Of Norwich. Matric. 1680; B.A. 1683-4. Ord. deacon (Norwich) Dec. 1683; priest, Dec. 1686. V. of Thrigby, Norfolk, 1687-93. V. of Narburgh, 1692-1735. V. of Narford, 1713-35. Died Nov. 23, 1735, aged 75. Buried in Narburgh Church. M.I. (*Blomefield*, VI. 158.)

INGRAM, CHARLES. Adm. at PEMBROKE, July 4, 1654; B.A. 1657.

INGRAME, CHRISTOPHER. Matric. sizar from PEMBROKE, Michs. 1575. Of Worcestershire. B.A. 1578-9. Adm. at Douay, with John Fingley, Jan. 13, 1579-80. Ord. priest, Sept. 20, 1582, at Laon. Sent to England, Oct. 21, 1582, where he died *c.* 1586. (*Douay Diary.*)

INGRAM, EDWARD. Adm. sizar (age 18) at PEMBROKE, Feb. 23, 1630. S. of Edward, husbandman. B. in Essex. Matric. 1631.

INGRAM, EDWARD MACHEL, Viscount IRVINE. Adm. Fell.-Com. (age 16) at CHRIST'S, Sept. 10, 1702. S. of Arthur, Viscount Irvine, and Isabella, dau. of John Machel, of Sussex. B. at Temple Newsam, Yorks. School, Eton. Resided two years. Succeeded to the peerage, June 21, 1702. Adm. student at Leyden, Sept. 11, 1704. Lord-Lieutenant of the East Riding, Yorks. Died of small-pox, May 18, 1714. Brother of Richard (1703). (*Peile*, II. 155; *G.E.C.*)

INGRAM, GOODRICKE. Adm. pens. at ST JOHN'S, May 4, 1718. Of Thorpe-on-the-Hill, Yorks. S. of William (1672), of Methley, Yorks. School, Wakefield (Mr Clark). Migrated to Trinity, May 7, 1718, age 18. Matric. 1718; Scholar, 1720; B.A. 1721-2; M.A. 1725. Fellow, 1724. Ord. deacon (Ely) Mar. 17, 1727-8; priest (Lincoln) Dec. 19, 1731. V. of Kirkby Malzeard, and Masham, 1732. Married Grace, dau. of Anthony Wells, of Bolton, Lancs., Dec. 11, 1733. Buried at Knottingley, Apr. 4, 1755. M.I. Will, York. (M. H. Peacock.)

INGRAM, JAMES. Adm. sizar at JESUS, Mar. 22, 1710. S. of John (1665), R. of Chipstead, Surrey. Bapt. Aug. 4, 1692. School, Merchant Taylors'. Matric. 1710; B.A. 1714-5; M.A. 1725. V. of Oving, Sussex, 1720-46. R. of Sedlescomb, and Westfield. Died Dec. 1756. Will (P.C.C.) 1756. (A. Gray; J. Ch. Smith.)

INGRAM, JOHN. Matric. sizar from JESUS, Michs. 1547. Of Yorkshire. Received tonsure (London) 1553.

INGRAM, JOHN. Matric. pens. from CHRIST'S, Nov. 1586.

INGRAM, JOHN. Adm. at KING'S (age 17) a scholar from Eton, Nov. 30, 1612. Of Bucknall, Lincs. Matric. 1612; B.A. 1616-7; M.A. 1620. Fellow, 1615, till his death, in 1623. Buried in the College Chapel. (*Harwood.*)

INGRAM, JOHN. Adm. at MAGDALENE, June 7, 1665. Migrated to Trinity, May 4, 1666. Matric. 1666-7; B.A. 1669-70; M.A. 1673 Ord. deacon (Ely) June 18; priest, Dec. 24, 1671. R. of Chipstead, Surrey, 1679-1718. Buried there Feb. 5, 1717-8. Father of James (1710).

INGRAM, JOHN. Adm. sizar at CORPUS CHRISTI, 1678. Of Norwich. Matric. 1678; B.A. 1681-2; M.A. 1685. Ord. priest (London) May 18, 1683. Probably of Gt Badow, Essex, clerk. Will (Comm. C. Essex) 1694. (J. Ch. Smith.)

INGRAM, RICHARD. Adm. Fell.-Com. (age 14) at CHRIST'S, July 3, 1703. 2nd s. of Arthur, Viscount Irvine. B. at Temple Newsam, Yorks., Jan. 6, 1686-7. School, Eton. Adm. student at Leyden, Sept. 11, 1704. Succeeded his brother Edward as 5th Viscount Irvine, 1714. Governor of Hull. Colonel of the Body Guards, 1715. Appointed Governor of Barbadoes, 1720, but died before setting out, Apr. 10, 1721. Buried in Westminster Abbey. Brother of Edw. Machell (1702). (*Peile*, II. 157; *Duc. Leod.*, 230; *G.E.C.*)

INGRAM, ROBERT. Adm. pens. (age 16) at ST JOHN'S, Nov. 6, 1686. S. of Arthur, merchant. B. in London. School, Hatton Garden (private; Mr Maydwell). Matric. Fell.-Com. 1686. Perhaps adm. at the Middle Temple, Nov. 25, 1684; and at the Inner Temple, Apr. 21, 1692.

INGRAM, ROBERT. Adm. at CORPUS CHRISTI, 1745. Of Beverley, Yorks. B. there, Mar. 9, 1726-7. School, Beverley (Mr John Clarke). Matric. 1746; B.A. 1749-50; M.A. 1753. Fellow, 1754-60. Ord. priest (Lincoln) June 2, 1751. P.C. of Bredhurst, Kent, 1758. V. of Orston, Notts., 1759-60. V. of Wormingford, Essex, 1760-1803. V. of Boxted, 1768-83. Married Catherine, dau. of Richard Acklom. Author, theological. Died at his son's parsonage, Seagrave, Leics., Aug. 3, 1804. (*D.N.B.*, where he is styled D.D.; *G. Mag.*)

INGRAM, SAMUEL. Adm. sizar (age 18) at CAIUS, Jan. 26, 1680-1. S. of Samuel, mercer, of Yarmouth. B. there. School, Eye (Mr Browne). Matric. 1680-1.

INGRAM, SIMON. Matric. sizar from JESUS, Michs. 1607; B.A. 1611-2. Ord. deacon (Peterb.) Mar. 8, 1611-2. Admon. (Lincoln) 1613; of Holbeach, Lincs., B.A.

INGRAM, WILLIAM. Matric. pens. from TRINITY, Easter, 1582. S. of Hugh, merchant, of London. Scholar, 1585; B.A. 1585-6; M.A. from Magdalene, 1589; LL.D. 1604. Esquire Bedell, 1592-*c.* 1605. Adm. at the Inner Temple, 1583; of Earls Court, Worcs. Afterwards of York. Perhaps knighted, Apr. 11, 1617. Secretary of the King's Council for the North. Married Catharine, dau. of John Edmonds, of Cambridge. Died July 24, 1623. Buried in York Minster. Will, York. (*Vis. of Yorks.*, 1665; Stokes, *Bedells*; M. H. Peacock.)

INGRAM, WILLIAM. Matric. pens. from CHRIST'S, *c.* 1592. Perhaps ord. priest (Lincoln) Nov. 7, 1597. V. of St Martin, Lincoln, 1597. C. of St Margaret's. Admon. (Lincoln) 1635; of Lincoln, clerk.

INGRAM, WILLIAM. Adm. pens. (age 16) at ST JOHN'S, May 10, 1672. S. of Arthur (1622), Esq., of Knottingley, Yorks. B. there. School, Pontefract. Matric. 1673. Adm. at Gray's Inn, June 13, 1673. Married Jane, dau. of Captain Henry Goodricke. Father of Goodricke (1718). (J. Ch. Smith; *Vis. of Yorks.*)

INGREY, GILES. Adm. sizar at CLARE, Sept. 22, 1719. B. at Saffron Walden, Essex. Matric. 1720; B.A. 1723-4.

INGSWORTH, RICHARD, *see* **HINXWORTH.**

INGWORTH, RICHARD. B.D. 1522-3; D.D. 1525-6. Dominican friar. General of the Dominican friars. Perhaps Bishop of Dover who was King's visitor for the suppression of houses of mendicant friars, 1538-9. (Stubbs' *Registrum.*)

INHOULD, ROBERT. Matric. sizar from QUEENS', Lent, 1579-80. Of Suffolk. B.A. 1583-4; M.A. 1587.

INMAN, FRANCIS. Matric. sizar from TRINITY, Michs. 1587; B.A. 1592-3; M.A. 1596. Probably R. of Kingsdown St Edmund, Kent, 1599-1638. Will (P.C.C.) 1638.

INMAN, GEORGE. Adm. sizar (age 19) at ST JOHN'S, May 13, 1647. 1st s. of George, yeoman, of Urswick, Lancs. (whose will, Archdeacon Richmond, 1661). B. there. School, Sedbergh (Mr Garthwait). B.A. 1650-1. Master of Urswick School, *c.* 1655. Minister at Cartmell Fell, 1658-9. V. of Urswick, 1660-81. Died 1681. Will, Archdeacon Richmond. Probably brother of Thomas (1669). (*Vict. Hist. Lancs.*, VIII. 337; E. Axon.)

INMAN, GEORGE. Adm. sizar at CLARE, Apr. 3, 1738. B. at Hull, Yorks. Matric. 1738; B.A. 1741-2. Ord. deacon (Lincoln) Mar. 14, 1741-2. V. of Barrington, Somerset, *c.* 1746; R. of Withycombe; and V. of Rowberrow.

INMAN or INGMAN, GODFREY. Adm. sizar at JESUS, June 17, 1686. Of Yorkshire. Matric. 1686; B.A. 1689-90. Ord. deacon (York) May 22, 1692; priest (Lincoln) Dec. 20, 1719. C. of Northorpe, Lincs., 1719. R. of Blyborough, 1720.

INMAN, JOHN. Adm. sizar (age 18) at ST JOHN'S, May 23, 1684. S. of Robert, husbandman, deceased. B. at Woodhouse, Yorks. School, Threshfield (Mr Motley). Matric. 1685; B.A. 1687-8.

INMAN, ROBERT. Adm. sizar (age 14) at SIDNEY, Apr. 2, 1629. S. of John, gent. B. in Nidderdale, Yorks. School, Burnsall (Mr Wilkinson). B.A. 1632-3; M.A. 1636. R. of High Hoyland, Yorks., 1642-62. Died Mar. 1689.

INMAN, THOMAS. Adm. sizar (age 19) at ST JOHN'S, Apr. 24, 1669. S. of George, deceased, of Furness Fells, Lancs. B. there. School, Sedbergh (Mr Fell). Matric. 1669; B.A. 1672-3. Ord. priest (Chester) July 3, 1674. Master of Urswick School, Lancs., 1681. V. of Urswick, 1681-96. Perhaps brother of George (1647).

INMAN, THOMAS. Adm. sizar (age 18) at St John's, Mar. 5, 1742-3. S. of John, of Yorkshire. B. at Sedbergh. School, Sedbergh (Mr Broxholme). Matric. 1743; B.A. 1746-7.

INMAN, WILLIAM. Adm. sizar (age 17) at Sidney, Feb. 6, 1629-30. S. of Robert, gent. B. at Felbeck, Nidderdale, Yorks. School, Burnsall-in-Craven (Mr Tho. Wilkinson). Matric. 1631.

INNESLEY, INSELL or INSLEY, WILLIAM. Scholar at King's Hall, 1481-5.

INWOOD, JOHN. Adm. pens. (age 18) at St John's, June 19, 1656. S. of John, farmer, of Surrey. B. there. School, Guildford. Matric. 1656, as Fell.-Com.

INWOOD, WILLIAM. Adm. pens. at Trinity, May 15, 1640, as 'Imwod.' Perhaps s. of William, of Walton-upon-Thames, Surrey, gent. Matric. 1640; Scholar, 1641. Of Cobham, Esq. Knighted, Feb. 10, 1683-4. Sheriff of Surrey, 1684. Married Katherine, dau. of James Sutton, of Cobham, Surrey. Died c. 1685. (*Vis. of Surrey*, 1662; *Manning and Bray*, II. 736.)

INYON or INIONE, JAMES. Matric. sizar from Pembroke, Michs. 1613; B.A. 1617-8; M.A. 1621.

INYON, THOMAS. Adm. sizar (age 16) at Caius, Aug. 18, 1691. S. of Thomas, carriage-builder, of Cambridge. B. there. School, under Mr Bryan. Matric. 1691; Scholar, 1691-9; B.A. 1695-6; M.A. 1699. Fellow, 1702-4. Ord. deacon (Lincoln) Mar. 5, 1698-9; priest (Norwich) Sept. 1701. R. of Mattishall, Norfolk, 1703-41; of Westfield, 1703-33. Buried at Elsing, Oct. 1741. Will (Norwich C.C.) 1741. Father of the next. (*Venn*, I. 490.)

INYON, THOMAS. Adm. pens. (age 17) at Caius, Aug. 30, 1723. S. of Thomas (above), V. of Mattishall, Norfolk. B. there. Schools, Scarning (Mr Lane) and Bishop's Stortford (Dr Took and Mr Took). Matric. 1724; Scholar, 1724-9; B.A. 1727-8; M.A. 1731. Fellow, 1729-33. Practised medicine at Pulham St Mary Virgin. Married Margaretta Maria, dau. of Thomas Bransby, of Harleston. Died Mar. 20, 1777. M.I. at Pulham. Will (Norwich C.C.) 1777. (*Venn*, II. 18.)

ION, JOSEPH. 'Of St John's College,' when ord. deacon (York) Sept. 1718; priest, Sept. 1720 (not found in the College register).

ION or HYON, ROWLAND. Matric. sizar from Jesus, Michs. 1608; B.A. 1611-2; M.A. 1615. Ord. deacon (Peterb.) June 17, 1612; priest, Mar. 13, 1613-4. R. of Aswarby, Lincs., 1626. Father of the next. (Pedigree of Ion, of Fillingham, in *Vis. of Lincs.*, 1592.)

ION, THOMAS. Matric. pens. from Jesus, Michs. 1649. Of Lincolnshire. S. of Rowland (above). Bapt. at Aswarby, Lincs., Mar. 18, 1626-7.

IPSWELL, ROBERT. D.Can.L. 1470-1, after study at Oxford (similar *grace*, 1479-80). R. of Billingford, Norfolk, 1461-7. R. of Newton, Isle of Ely, to 1495; and Tydd St Giles', Cambs. Will (P.C.C.) 1496.

IPSWICH, THOMAS. B.Can.L. 1496.

IRBY, ANTHONY. Matric. pens. from Caius, Michs. 1559. S. of Thomas, of Whaplode, Lincs., Esq. Adm. at Lincoln's Inn, May 5, 1569. Bencher. M.P. for Boston, 1588-9, 1592-3, 1597-8, 1601, 1604-11, 1614, 1620-2. Recorder of Boston, 1613. Married Alice, dau. of Thomas Welby, of Moulton. Buried at Whaplode, Oct. 6, 1625. Admon., Lincoln. (*Venn*, I. 41; *Lincs. Pedigrees*; A. B. Beaven.)

IRBY, ANTHONY. Adm. Fell.-Com. at Emmanuel, June 12, 1620. Matric. as Erby. S. and h. of Sir Anthony. Adm. at Lincoln's Inn, May 15, 1620. Knighted, June 2, 1624. M.P. for Boston, 1628-9, 1640-8, 1656-8, 1659, 1660-81. High Sheriff for Lincs., 1638. Died Jan. 2, 1681-2. Buried in St Margaret's, Westminster. Brother of Edward (1620). (A. B. Beaven; P. Thompson, *Boston*.)

IRBY, ANTHONY. Adm. sizar at Trinity, Jan. 23, 1662-3. Matric. 1663; Scholar, 1664; B.A. 1666-7; M.A. 1670.

IRBY, EDWARD. Matric. pens. from Queens', Michs. 1554.

IRBY, EDWARD. Adm. Fell.-Com. at Emmanuel, June 12, 1620. S. of Sir Anthony, Knt. Matric. 1620, as Erby. Adm. at Lincoln's Inn, May 15, 1620. Married Anne, dau. of David Hervey, Esq., of Evedon, Lincs. Brother of Anthony (1620).

IRBY, JOHN. B.Can.L. 1468-9; D.Can.L. 1479-80.

IRBY, WILLIAM. M.A.; B.Can.L. Fellow of Peterhouse, c. 1374. Presented to the Bishop for the Mastership, 1397, and again in 1400.

IRBY or JERBY, ——. Incorp. as D.Can.L. 1502-3.

IRELAND, DAVID. Adm. sizar at Jesus, May 19, 1628. Of Wales. Matric. 1628; B.A. 1631-2.

IRELAND, EDWARD. Matric. sizar from Queens', Michs. 1544.

IRELAND, EDWARD. Matric. pens. from St John's, Michs. 1568. Perhaps adm. at Lincoln's Inn, Feb. 15, 1572-3. Of Salop.

IRELAND, FRANCIS. Matric. sizar from Magdalene, Michs. 1642.

IRELAND, HENRY. Matric. sizar from St John's, Easter, 1575. B. at Denbigh. B.A. 1578-9. Ord. deacon (London) Sept. 28, 1579, age 24.

IRELAND, HENRY. Adm. pens. (age 17) at Peterhouse, July 10, 1724. Of Durham. (Perhaps s. of Henry, V. of Saxham, Durham.) School, Durham. Matric. 1724; Scholar, 1724; B.A. 1727-8; M.A. 1731. Ord. deacon (Lincoln) Dec. 24, 1732. P.C. of Wotton Underwood, Bucks., 1744-56. Died Mar. 1756.

IRELAND, HIERLAND or YIRLAND, JOHN. B.A. 1488-9; M.A. 1491; B.D. 1502-3. Fellow of Queens', 1492-1513. R. of Graveley, Cambs., 1518.

IRELAND, JOSHUA. Adm. pens. (age 17) at St John's, May 23, 1667. S. of Samuel, deceased, of Salop. B. there. School, Shrewsbury (Mr Tayler). Matric. 1667; B.A. 1670-1; M.A. 1674. Fellow, 1674. Ord. deacon (Peterb.) Dec. 22, 1672.

IRELAND, JOSIAS. Matric. pens. from Corpus Christi, Michs. 1579.

IRELAND, RICHARD. Matric. sizar from Clare, Michs. 1627; B.A. 1630-1; M.A. 1634. Ord. priest (Norwich) June 16, 1633. R. of St Edmund's, Norwich, 1638-90. R. of Beeston, Norfolk, 1660. Died Sept. 10, 1690, aged 80. Will (Court of Delegates) 1690; as of Catton. The V. of Wilmington, Sussex, was probably an Oxford contemporary. (J. Ch. Smith.)

IRELANDE, THOMAS. Matric. Fell.-Com. from St Catharine's, Easter, 1544.

IRELAND, THOMAS. Matric. sizar from Trinity, Michs. 1611; B.A. from Clare, 1614-5; M.A. 1618. Perhaps R. of Bradley, Lincs., 1625. Will of one of these names (Chester) 1629; of Crowton, clerk.

IRELAND, THOMAS. Matric. Fell.-Com. from St John's, Michs. 1619. Perhaps s. of Sir Thomas, Vice-Chancellor of Chester. Died Jan. 1638. (Gregson, *Lancs.*, 220.)

IRELAND, THOMAS. M.A. 1658 (Incorp. from Oxford). Probably matric. from Magdalen College, Nov. 19, 1650; B.A. (Oxford) 1652-3. M.A. not recorded.

IRELOND or YERLOND, WILLIAM. B.A. 1525-6.

IRELAND, WILLIAM. Matric. from St John's, Easter, 1544; B.A. 1544-5; M.A. 1548. Fellow, 1547. R. of Chelmsford, Essex, 1561. R. of Barley, Herts., 1564-71. Friend of Ascham. Died 1570-1. (*Cooper*, I. 291.)

IREMONGER, WILLIAM. Adm. pens. (age 19) at Sidney, Dec. 20, 1650. S. of Humphrey, attorney, of Ampthill, Beds. Bapt. at Millbrooke, Beds., Dec. 21, 1631. Schools, Clapwell (Mr Greene) and Houghton Conquest (Mr Sams). Matric. 1652. Adm. at Gray's Inn, May 27, 1652.

IRESON, EDWARD. Adm. sizar at Emmanuel, Oct. 23, 1742. Of Middlesex. Matric. 1744; B.A. 1746-7; M.A. 1750; D.D. 1762. Ord. deacon (Lincoln) Sept. 21, 1746; priest, June 14, 1747. R. of Bringhurst, Leics., 1769-71. Buried at Holt, May 10, 1771. (*Nichols*, II. 514.)

IRETON, CHARLES. Adm. pens. at Trinity, May 25, 1650. Of London. Scholar from Westminster. Matric. 1650.

IRETON, GERMAN. Matric. pens. from St John's, Lent, 1564-5; B.A. 1567-8. One of these names s. of John, Lord of Ireton, Derbs. Lord of Ireton, the first Protestant of the family. (*Stem. Shirleiana*, 326.)

IRETON, JOHN. Matric. sizar from St John's, Lent, 1564-5; B.A. 1568-9; M.A. from Christ's, 1572; B.D. 1579. Fellow of Christ's, 1571. Lady Margaret preacher, 1579-82. Incorp. at Oxford, 1578. Ord. deacon (Lincoln); priest (Chester) Oct. 8, 1570. R. of Kegworth, Leics., 1582-1606. Preb. of Lincoln, 1594-1606. Married Anne, dau. of Christopher Nicholson, of Cambridge, widow of Luke Gilpin. Died June 28, 1606. Buried at Kegworth. M.I. Will, P.C.C. (*Peile*, I. 93; *Cooper*, II. 441; H. I. Longden.)

IRETON, W. Matric. Fell.-Com. from St John's, Easter, 1562.

IRTON, WOLFREED (WILFRID). Matric. Fell.-Com. from Pembroke, Michs. 1614. S. and h. of Christopher, of Cockermouth, Cumberland, Esq. Adm. at Gray's Inn, Nov. 18, 1616.

IRETON, ——. Matric. Fell.-Com. from Christ's, 1597-8. Perhaps s. of John (1564-5), R. of Kegworth, 1582-1606. (*Peile*, I. 227.)

IRISH, WILLIAM. Adm. Fell.-Com. (age 17) at St John's, Feb. 9, 1742-3. S. of Samuel, merchant, of Montserrat, America. Family, of Dorset. School, Hackney (Mr Graham). Matric. 1743. Adm. at the Inner Temple, May 2, 1741. Of Montserrat, Esq.

IRONSIDE, EDWARD. Matric. pens. from QUEENS', Easter, 1620. Of London. S. and h. of Richard, of St Faith's, London, citizen and leather seller, whose will he proved, 1623. Age 20 in 1623. Migrated to Emmanuel, Oct. 16, 1622. B.A. 1623-4; M.A. 1627. Incorp. at Oxford, 1624 and 1628. Adm. at Lincoln's Inn, Nov. 27, 1627, as 'son of Richard, of London, Esq., deceased' (special admission). Perhaps adm. student at Leyden, Aug. 24, 1627. (*Vis. of Herts.*, 1634; J. Ch. Smith.)

IRONSIDE, GILBERT. B.D. 1620 (Incorp. from Oxford). S. of Ralph, of Gloucestershire, B.D. (whose will, P.C.C., 1628). B. at Hawkesbury. Matric. from Trinity College, Oxford, June 22, 1604, age 15; B.A. (Oxford) 1608; M.A. 1612; B.D. 1619; D.D. 1666. Fellow of Trinity (Oxford) 1613. R. of Winterborne Steepleton, Dorset, 1619. R. of Winterborne Abbas, 1625-50 and 1662-7. Preb. of York, 1660-2. Bishop of Bristol, 1661-71. R. of Yeovilton, Somerset, 1662-71. Died Sept. 19, 1671. Buried in Bristol Cathedral. Father of the next, and of Gilbert, Bishop of Bristol, and Hereford. (*Al. Oxon.*)

IRONSIDE, RALPH. B.A. 1655 (Incorp. from Oxford). S. of Gilbert, clerk, of Dorset (above). Matric. from Wadham College, Nov. 14, 1650; B.A. (St Mary's Hall) 1652. Perhaps V. of Netherbury, Dorset, 1662-7. Pedigree in Surtees' *Durham*, I. 150.

IRVINE, Viscount, *see* INGRAM, E. M.

IRVING, WILLIAM. Adm. sizar (age 18) at TRINITY, Dec. 23, 1749. S. of Benjamin, of Bury St Edmunds, innkeeper. School, Bury (Mr Garnbam). Matric. 1750; Scholar, 1753; B.A. 1754. Ord. deacon (Norwich) Feb. 1755; priest, Feb. 1758. Usher of Bury School, 1755-63.

IRWELL, THOMAS. Matric. pens. from ST JOHN'S, *c.* 1595.

ISAAC, BAPTIST (NOEL). Adm. pens. (age 18) at EMMANUEL, Sept. 28, 1742. S. of John, R. of Whitwell, Rutland. School, Oakham. Matric. 1742; B.A. 1746-7. Adm. at Lincoln's Inn, Apr. 9, 1741. R. of Horn, Rutland, 1757-61. V. of Henstridge, Somerset, 1761-72. Preb. of Wells, 1761-72. Died June 20, 1772. Will, P.C.C. (*Collinson*, II. 368; H. I. Longden.)

ISAAC GEORGE. Matric. pens. from KING'S, Lent, 1683.

ISAAC, JOHN. Adm. pens. (age 15) at ST JOHN'S, Mar. 13, 1654-5. S. of John, deceased, of Foxearth, Essex. B. there. School, Bury St Edmunds (Mr Stephens). B.A. from St Catharine's, 1658; D.D. 1671 (*Lit. Reg.*). Ord. priest (Ely) Feb. 23, 1661-2. V. of Gestingthorpe, Essex, 1662-8. R. of Bartlow, Cambs., 1667. One of these names V. of Stapleford, Leics., 1711-5.

ISAAC, PHILIP. Adm. sizar (age 18) at CAIUS, Jan. 31, 1599-1600. S. of Thomas, gent. B. at Braunton, Devon. School, Chulmleigh (Mr Hen. Hatswell). Migrated to Emmanuel. Scholar, 1603; B.A. 1603-4; M.A. 1607. Incorp. at Oxford, 1607. Head Master of Wakefield Grammar School, 1607-23. R. of Bideford, Devon, 1625-43. Married, at Wakefield, 1613, Anna Rhodes. Buried at Bideford, May 25, 1643. Will, Exeter. (*Venn*, I. 171.)

ISAAC, SAMUEL. Matric. sizar from KING'S, Michs. 1706. B. at Windsor. Colleger at Eton, 1698-1706. B.A. 1710-1; M.A. 1715. Ord. deacon (London) July 7, 1710; priest, May 27, 1711. V. of Arlington, Sussex, July 23, 1719-38. V. of Wilmington, 1720-38. Buried at Arlington, May 16, 1738. (W. C. Renshaw.)

ISAAC, THOMAS. B.D. 1515-6. Augustinian friar.

ISAAC, THOMAS. Adm. sizar at EMMANUEL, Apr. 4, 1627. Of Suffolk. Matric. 1627. Migrated to Queens', 1628; B.A. 1630-1; M.A. 1634. R. of Twinstead, Essex, 1654.

ISAAC, ——. B.A. 1454-5. Probably M.A. 1457. Perhaps B.D. 1467-8. Probably John, R. of St Christopher-le-Stock, London, 1483-6. R. of Acton, Middlesex. R. of St Mary, Colchester. V. of Bishop's Stortford, Herts. Preb. of St Paul's, 1472-85.

ISAACSON, ANTHONY. Adm. pens. (age 15) at PEMBROKE, May 2, 1642. 9th s. of Henry (below), of London and Fyfield, Essex. Matric. 1642. Treasurer of Bridewell and Bedlam Hospitals. Married Jane, dau. of John Lawson, of Newcastle, Apr. 27, 1665. Buried at St Nicholas, Newcastle, June 18, 1693. Father of John (1683) and brother of William (1632). (*New County Hist. of Northumberland*, XI. 337; H. M. Wood.)

ISAACSON, HENRY. Said to have been of PEMBROKE HALL. 1st s. of Richard, of St Catherine Coleman, citizen and painter-stainer. B. in London, Sept. 1581. Treasurer of Bridewell and Bedlam, 1643-54. Elected Chamberlain of London, 1651, but declined. Amanuensis and intimate friend of Bishop Lancelot Andrewes. Married Elizabeth, dau. of John Fan, of London. Author, historical and theological. Died Dec. 7, 1654. Will (P.C.C.) 1655. Brother of William (1612-3), father of Anthony (above) and of William (1632). (*D.N.B.*; *Vis. of London*, 1634.)

ISAACSON, JOHN. Adm. pens. (age 17) at CAIUS, Apr. 25, 1683. S. of Anthony (above), of Newcastle. Bapt. there, at St Andrews, Jan. 26, 1666-7. School, North Weald, Essex. Matric. 1683; B.A. 1686-7. Adm. at Lincoln's Inn, Jan. 22, 1683-4. Recorder of Newcastle, 1725-38. Married Jane Lambert, of Newcastle, July 7, 1718, at Long Benton. Buried at St Nicholas, Jan. 5, 1737-8. (*Venn*, I. 473; H. M. Wood.)

ISAACSON or IZASON, PHILIP. Matric. sizar from TRINITY, Easter, 1586; B.A. 1590-1.

ISAACSON, RICHARD. Adm. pens. (age 14) at ST JOHN'S, July 1, 1636. S. of William (1612-3), R. of Woodford, Essex. B. there. School, Culmington, Salop (private; Mr Mease). B.A. 1639-40; M.A. 1643. Probably succeeded his father as R. of Woodford, 1645. Died Nov. 1653. (*Vis. of London*, 1634; H. Smith.)

ISAACSON, STEPHEN. Adm. at QUEENS', July 4, 1715. Adm. pens. at Magdalene, Jan. 12, 1715-6, age 18. S. of Stephen, gent. Bapt. at Burwell, Cambs., June 18, 1697. School, Histon, Cambs. Matric. 1715-6; B.A. 1719-20. Ord. deacon (Ely) Sept. 24, 1721. R. of Freckenham, Suffolk, 1723-59. Married Anne, dau. of Thomas Stuteville, of Newmarket. Buried at Freckenham, Oct. 24, 1759.

ISAACSON, WILLIAM. B.A. from PEMBROKE, 1612-3. 2nd s. of Richard, merchant, of London. School, Merchant Taylors'. M.A. from Jesus, 1616; D.D. 1630. Fellow of Jesus, 1614-20. Incorp. at Oxford, 1617. R. of Woodford, Essex, 1617-45. V. of St Peter's, St Albans, till 1628. R. of St Andrew by-the-Wardrobe, London, 1629-43, sequestered. Died 1645. Brother of Henry, father of Richard (1636). (*Vis. of London*, 1634; A. Gray.)

ISAACSON, WILLIAM. Matric. pens. (age 17) from PEMBROKE, Easter, 1632. S. of Henry (above). B.A. 1634-5; M.A. from King's, 1638. Ord. priest (Peterb.) June 4, 1637. V. of Swaffham Bulbeck, Cambs., 1638-43, sequestered. Chaplain to the East India Company at Suratt and Fort St George, 1644-61. Perhaps R. of St Stephen, Ipswich, 1684. Brother of Anthony. (*Vis. of London*, 1634; F. Penny.)

ISBELL, JOHN. Matric. sizar from CORPUS CHRISTI, Easter, 1588.

ISBURN, THOMAS, *see* EASTBOURNE.

ISLEHAM, ISELHAM or ILAM, JOHN DE. Scholar at KING'S HALL, 1365-9. Clerk.

ISHAM, AUGUSTINE. Matric. pens. from CHRIST'S, Apr. 1610. S. of Richard (1579). Bapt. at Lamport, Northants., Apr. 25, 1593. B.A. 1613-4; M.A. 1617. Ord. deacon (Peterb.) Dec. 18; priest, Dec. 21, 1617. V. of Poslingford, Suffolk, 1622. R. of Elmswell, 1626-37. Married, at Ixworth, Suffolk, Apr. 21, 1636, Anne Denton. Buried at Ixworth, Dec. 12, 1637. Will, Cons. C. Norwich. (*Peile*, I. 275; H. I. Longden.)

ISHAM, EUSEBIUS. Matric. pens. from CHRIST'S, Nov. 1568. S. of Gregory, mercer, of London, and of Braunston, Northants. B. Feb. 26, 1552-3. Adm. at the Middle Temple, Nov. 11, 1570. High Sheriff of Northants., 1584. Knighted, May 11, 1603, by James I. Of Braunston and Pytchley, Northants., Esq. Married Anne, dau. of John Borlase, of Little Marlow, Bucks., Esq. Died June 11, 1626. Buried at Pytchley. Will, P.C.C. (Burke, *L.G.*; *Vis. of London*, 1568; *Peile*, I. 106-7; H. I. Longden.)

ISHAM, EUSEBIUS. Adm. pens. at QUEENS', Oct. 28, 1714. 7th s. of Sir Justinian, of Lamport, Northants., Bart. Bapt. at Lamport, Nov. 28, 1697. Matric. 1715. Migrated to Oxford. Matric. from Balliol College, Oct. 22, 1716, age 18; B.A. (Oxford) 1718; M.A. (Lincoln College) 1721; D.D. 1733. R. of Lincoln College, 1731-55. Vice-Chancellor, 1744-7. Ord. deacon (Oxford) May 18; priest, Sept. 22, 1722. R. of Lamport and Hazelbeach, Northants., 1729-55. Died at Tunbridge Wells, June 17, 1755. Buried at Lamport. Will, P.C.C. (*Al. Oxon.*; *Vis. of Northants.*, 1618.)

ISHAM, GREGORY. Adm. at KING'S (age 18) a scholar from Eton, Aug. 24, 1580. Of London. 1st s. of Henry, of London, mercer. Matric. 1580. Left, in 1582. Adm. at the Middle Temple, Jan. 26, 1582-3. Purchased the manor and advowson of Barby, Northants. Married Elizabeth Catelyne, of Raunds, Northants. Buried at St Margaret's, Westminster, Nov. 25, 1634. Father of the next and of Robert (1611).

ISHAM, GREGORY. Adm. pens. (age 18) at SIDNEY, June 30, 1621. 5th s. of Gregory (above), Esq. B. at Barby, Northants. Bapt. at Bugbrooke, June 10, 1600. School, Rugby. Migrated to Queens', 1625. B.A. 1625-6. Buried at St Botolph's, Cambridge, Sept. 24, 1628. Doubtless brother of Robert (1611).

ISHAM, HENRY. Adm. Fell.-Com. (age 16) at CHRIST'S, Mar. 14, 1684-5. 7th s. of Sir Justinian (1627), Bart. B. at Lamport, Northants. Bapt. Sept. 25, 1668. School, Grantham (Mr Walker). Perhaps matric. 1685, as 'Philip.' M.A. 1689. Buried at Lamport, Jan. 11, 1689-90. Admon. (P.C.C.) 1690. Brother of John (1675). (*Peile*, II. 98.)

ISHAM, JOHN. Adm. pens. at QUEENS', Sept. 30, 1597. Of Northamptonshire. Doubtless s. and h. of Eusebius (1568). Of Pytchley and Braunston, Esq. Buried at Braunston, Dec. 13, 1626. Perhaps brother of Thomas (1620). (*Vict. Co. Hist. Northants. Fam.*)

ISHAM, JOHN. Adm. pens. (age 15) at CHRIST'S, May 29, 1675. 4th s. of Sir Justinian (1627), Bart., of Lamport, Northants. Bapt. there, Aug. 10, 1659. Matric. Pell.-Com. Easter, 1675; M.A. 1679. Fellow, 1681. Adm. at the Inner Temple, Nov. 20, 1685. Under Secretary of State, 1702-4. Married Frances, dau. of Sir Richard Ashfield, of Suffolk, Bart. Buried at Lamport, Oct. 20, 1746. Will, P.C.C. Brother of Henry (1684-5). (*Peile*, II. 58; H. I. Longden.)

ISHAM, JUSTINIAN. Adm. Fell.-Com. (age 16) at CHRIST'S, Apr. 18, 1627. Only s. of Sir John, Bart. B. at Lamport, Northants. Bapt. there, Feb. 3, 1610-1. School, Uppingham (Mr Clark). Matric. 1627. Adm. at the Middle Temple, Oct. 11, 1628. Imprisoned as a delinquent, 1644 and 1649. Succeeded as 2nd Baronet, July 8, 1651. M.P. for Northants., 1661-75. F.R.S., 1663. Died at Oxford, Mar. 2, 1674-5. Buried at Lamport. M.I. Will, P.C.C. Father of Henry (1684-5) and John (1675). (*Peile*, I. 382; *D.N.B.*; *G.E.C.*)

ISHAM, RICHARD. Matric. pens. from CHRIST'S, Oct. 1579. 5th s. of John, of Lamport, Northants., mercer of London. Bapt. at St Antholin's, London, Jan. 1564-5. Scholar. Adm. at the Middle Temple, Jan. 26, 1582-3. Buried at Lamport, May 31, 1618. Father of Augustine (1610). (*Peile*, I. 155; *Victoria Co. Hist. Northants. Fam.*)

ISHAM, ROBERT. Scholar of CHRIST'S, 1537-9. S. of Eusebius, of Ringstead and Pytchley, Northants. B. there. School, Rothwell. B.A. 1539-40; M.A. 1542. R. of Grafton Underwood, 1541-61. R. of Islip, 1542-8. R. of Pytchley, 1548-64. Chaplain to Queen Mary. Preb. of Peterborough, 1554-9. Died May 5, 1564. *I.p.m.*, 1564. Will (P.C.C.) 1568. (*Peile*, I. 22; *Vis. of London*, 1568; *Vis. of Northants.*, 1618.)

ISHAM, ROBERT. Matric. Fell.-Com. from KING'S, Easter, 1611. S. and h. of Gregory (? 1580), of Barby, Northants. Buried there Apr. 10, 1656. Brother of Gregory (1621). (*Victoria Co. Hist. Northants. Fam.*)

ISHAM, ROGER. Adm. sizar (age 16) at ST JOHN'S, May 31, 1638. S. of Roger, gent., of Bradon, Isle Brewers, Somerset. B. there. School, Isle Brewers (private). Migrated to Oxford. Matric. from Christ Church, Nov. 15, 1639. Legatee in the will of his father, P.C.C., 1653. (*Al. Oxon.*; *Vis. of Somerset*, 1623; H. I. Longden.)

ISHAM, THOMAS. Adm. pens. (age 18) at SIDNEY, June 17, 1620. 5th s. of Sir Euseby (1568), of Pytchley, Northants., Knt. Bapt. there, Dec. 20, 1600. School, Sutton, Beds. Of Radclive, Bucks., and Wheatfield, Oxon., Esq. Married, at Pytchley, Aug. 28, 1628, Elizabeth, dau. of Sir Thomas Denton, of Hillesden, Bucks., Knt. Died Feb. 6, 1669-70. Buried at Wheatfield. M.I. Will, P.C.C. (*Vis. of Northants.*, 1618; H. I. Longden.)

ISHAM, ——. M.A. 1457-8. Probably Robert, s. of Robert, of Pytchley, Northants. R. of Drayton Beauchamp, Bucks., 1459-61. R. of Heythorpe, Gloucs., 1461. Preb. of Lincoln, 1467-1501. Probably died 1501.

ISHERWOOD, ADAM. Adm. pens. at EMMANUEL, 1623, as 'Sherwood.' Matric. 1623; B.A. 1626-7.

ISHERWOOD, JOHN. Adm. pens. (age 17) at CHRIST'S, June 2, 1646. S. of Francis. B. at Turton, Lancs. Bapt. at Bolton, Mar. 19, 1629-30. School, Rivington (Mr Rudall). B.A. 1649. Minister at Westhoughton, Lancs., 1651. C. of Turton, 1663. P.C. of Flixton, 1664-1715. Buried May 8, 1715, at Eccles. Brother of Thomas (next). (*Peile*, I. 507; *Vict. Hist. of Lancs.*, V. 44; E. Axon.)

ISHERWOOD, THOMAS. Adm. pens. (age 16) at CHRIST'S, June 11, 1647. S. of Francis. B. at Turton, Lancs. Bapt. at Bolton, Aug. 28, 1631. School, Rivington (Mr Fielding). Matric. 1647. Ord. presbyterian minister of Blackrod, Lancs., Apr. 12, 1654; there, till 1656. Afterwards conformed. C. of Bradshaw, 1662-4. V. of Eccles, 1671-8. Died Feb. 17, 1678. Brother of John (above). (*Peile*, I. 515; E. Axon.)

ISLAYE, JOHN. Matric. Fell.-Com. from MICHAELHOUSE, Michs. 1544.

ISLEY, JOHN. Adm. pens. (age 17) at CHRIST'S, June 10, 1637. S. of Robert. B. at Westerham, Kent. Bapt. there, Feb. 6, 1620-1. School, Westerham (Mr Walter). Matric. 1637; M.B. 1644. Buried at Westerham, 1650.

ISLINGTON or HESLINGTON, JOHN. B.A. 1479-80; B.D. 1489-90; D.D. 1493-4.

ISLIP, JOHN. Probably a member of the University. A monk of Westminster; prior, 1498; abbot, 1500-32. Adm. at Gray's Inn, 1492. Greatly added to the Abbey buildings. Died May 12, 1532. Benefactor to the University. (*Cooper*, I. 45; III. 97; *D.N.B.*)

ISLIP, ROBERT. Adm. sizar (age 18) at ST JOHN'S, June 27, 1713. S. of Robert, husbandman. B. in Westmorland. School, Kirkby Stephen (Mr Leathes). B.A. 1716-7. One of these names (? the father) was usher at Kirkby Stephen, 1710.

ISMAY, JOSEPH. Matric. sizar from CHRIST'S, July, 1729; Scholar, 1729; B.A. 1732-3. V. of Hartshead, Yorks., 1738-40. V. of Mirfield, 1739-78. Antiquary. Died 1778. (*Peile*, II. 221.)

ISONS, HARRINGTON (?). Matric. pens. from ST JOHN'S, c. 1592.

ISSOTT, JOHN. Adm. pens. at CLARE, June 12, 1646. Matric. 1646; B.A. 1649. Probably ejected from Nun-Monkton, Yorks., 1662. (*Calamy*, II. 569.)

ISTEEDE, THOMAS. Matric. pens. from MAGDALENE, Michs. 1581. Probably adm. at Lincoln's Inn, Oct. 23, 1585. Of Sussex.

ITALICUS, ——. B.D. 1514-5. A friar.

ITHELL, FULK. Matric. sizar from JESUS, Easter, 1584.

ITHELL, GEORGE. Matric. sizar from MAGDALENE, Easter, 1548.

ITHELL, HUGH. Matric. pens. from JESUS, Easter, 1575.

ITHELL, JOHN. Matric. pens. from TRINITY HALL, Easter, 1560.

ITHELL, JOHN. Matric. pens. from JESUS, Easter, 1575. Perhaps ord. deacon (Peterb.) May 23, 1619, as 'B.A.; late of Jesus College.'

ITHELL, LEONARD. Matric. pens. from JESUS, Easter, 1578. S. of Geoffrey, of Tugby, Leics. B.A. 1579-80; M.A. 1583. Fellow, 1582-92. R. of Childerley, Cambs., 1588. R. of Coveney, 1588. R. of Bratoft, Lincs., 1590-1634. Will proved (Lincoln) Oct. 1, 1634; 'of Bratoft.' In *Brit. Mus. MS.*, 34,195, f. 8 is an acquittance from him for £15, in consideration of his resigning his fellowship to George Deering. (*N. and Q.*, Sept. 16, 1911; *Lincs. Pedigrees*, 544.)

ITHELL, NICHOLAS AB, *see* ABITHELL.

ITHELL, RALPH. Matric. pens. (age 13) from TRINITY HALL, Easter, 1560; Scholar, 1561. One of these names R. of Aldham, Essex, 1599-1600. R. of Wickham Episcopi, 1600-18. Called M.A. Died 1618.

ITHELL, THOMAS. Matric. sizar from MAGDALENE, Easter, 1549. S. of Pierce, of Billesdon, Leics. B.A. 1553-4 (called 'Anthony' in *Grace* for B.A.); M.A. 1557; LL.D. 1563. Fellow. Master of Jesus, 1563-79. Commissary of the University, 1578-9. Chancellor of Ely. Preb. of St Patrick's, Dublin (a layman). Preb. of Ely; and sinecure R. of Elm and Emneth, 1567-79. R. of Kilken, Flints., 1569-79. Admitted advocate, 1569. Died May 17, 1579. Will proved (V.C.C.). (*Cooper*, I. 406; *Vis. of Cambs.*, 1619; A. Gray.)

IVAT, JOHN. Matric. pens. from QUEENS', Michs. 1569.

IVATT, THOMAS. Adm. pens. at EMMANUEL, Easter, 1623. Matric. 1623. Fell.-Com. in 1624. Perhaps adm. at the Inner Temple, 1628, from Clifford's Inn.

IVE, JOHN. Matric. pens. from CORPUS CHRISTI, Michs. 1561.

IVE, ——. Adm. at CORPUS CHRISTI, 1560. Most probably the above man, though *Cooper* and others identify him with Paul, a writer on fortification, who received money from the Crown for the fortification of Falmouth, 1597; employed in fortifying the Isle of Haulbowline, near Cork, 1601-2. Author of works on fortification. Will (P.C.C.) 1605, as Ivey, of Lambeth Marsh, Surrey; to be buried at Castle Parke, 'soe deepe that the wolves and dogges do not scrape it up againe.' (J. Ch. Smith; *D.N.B.*; *Cooper*, II. 241.)

IVER, ELNATHAN. Adm. sizar (age 18) at CHRIST'S, May 9, 1674. S. of George. B. at Brentford, Middlesex. School, Isleworth (Mr Willis). Matric. 1674; B.A. 1677-8. One 'E. Ivor' ord. priest (Chichester) Sept. 1708. V. of Ditchling, Sussex, 1715-21. V. of Wivelsfield, 1718-21. Died July 30, 1721. M.I. at Ditchling. (*Peile*, II. 51.)

IVERS, PETER. Matric. pens. from CHRIST'S, Michs. 1566.

IVES, ASTY. Matric. pens. from CORPUS CHRISTI, Easter, 1626; B.A. 1628-9; M.A. 1632. Ord. deacon (Norwich) Sept. 25, 1636; priest, Sept. 22, 1638. Schoolmaster at Scarning, Norfolk, 1641. R. of Lower Rickinghall, Suffolk, 1662-73. R. of Shipdham, Norfolk, 1673.

IVES, JAMES. Fined for non-determination in arts, 1431.

IVES, JOHN. Matric. pens. from CLARE, Michs. 1573. S. of John, of Saham Toney, Norfolk. School, Ely. Migrated to Caius, Mar. 28, 1574, age 20; B.A. 1576-7; M.A. 1580. Died at Saham Toney, c. 1632, where he gave a font to the Church. (*Venn*, I. 78.)

IVES, JOHN. Adm. sizar (age 17) at CAIUS, May, 1679. S. of Edward, weaver, of Reepham, Norfolk. B. at Scarning. Schools, Scarning and Norwich (Mr Burton). Matric. 1679; Scholar, 1679. Died in College. Buried at St Michael's, Cambridge, Dec. 28, 1679. (*Venn*, I. 462.)

IVES, JOSEPH. Adm. at TRINITY, June 17, 1693, and Incorp. as B.A. from Oxford. S. of Joseph. B. at Whittlesey, Cambs. School, Huntingdon (Mr Mathews). Matric. from Christ Church, June 28, 1689, age 18; B.A. (Oxford) 1693. Ord. deacon (London) Mar. 8, 1695-6; priest (Lincoln) Feb. 28, 1696-7. R. of Overstone, Northants., 1702-3. Buried there Nov. 30, 1703. (*Al. Oxon.*; H. I. Longden.)

IVES, NICHOLAS. Adm. sizar at EMMANUEL, Jan. 13, 1633-4. Of Essex. Matric. 1635; B.A. 1637-8. Ord. deacon and priest (Norwich) Sept. 22, 1644, age 28; C. of Willisham, Suffolk.

IVES, RICHARD. Matric. pens. from QUEENS', Michs. 1586. Of Hertfordshire. Perhaps B.A. 1589-90. Probably ord. deacon (Peterb.) June 11, 1609; 'B.A. of Queens'.'

IVES or IVE, ROGER. Matric. pens. from QUEENS', Lent, 1618-9. Of London.

IVES, SIMON. Adm. at QUEENS', Aug. 5, 1644. Adm. sizar at St John's, Dec. 17, 1645, age 19. S. of Simon, musician, of Earls Colne, Essex. B. there. School, Islington. Migrated to Trinity Hall. Matric. there, 1647-8; B.A. 1647-8. Minor canon of St Paul's, 1661-2.

IVES, THOMAS. Matric. pens. from CLARE, Michs. 1568.

IVES or EVES, THOMAS. Adm. sizar (age 18) at CAIUS, May 1, 1609. S. of Henry, gent., of Tuttington, Norfolk. School, North Walsham (Mr Tilles). Matric. 1609, as Eves; B.A. 1612-3. Probably C. of Parson Drove, Cambs., in 1620. (*Venn*, I. 201.)

IVES, THOMAS. Matric. Fell.-Com. from CORPUS CHRISTI, Easter, 1620. Of Norfolk.

IVES, WILLIAM. Matric. pens. from MAGDALENE, Easter, 1624. B.A. 1627-8; M.A. 1631. Ord. deacon (Peterb.) Sept. 25, 1631; priest, Feb. 26, 1631-2.

IVES, WILLIAM. Adm. sizar (age 16) at CHRIST'S, Mar. 1646-7. S. of William, of Rushden, Northants. Bapt. there, Jan. 23, 1630-1. School, Wymington, Beds. (Mr Anderson). B.A. 1650-1; M.A. 1654. R. of Green's Norton, Northants., with Whittlebury, 1660-97. R. of Bradden, 1688-97. Died without issue, Jan. 23, 1696-7. Buried at Bradden. Will (P.C.C.) 1697. (*Peile*, I. 512; Burke, *L.G.*)

IVES, WILLIAM. Adm. pens. (age 16) at CHRIST'S, June 28, 1688. 1st s. of Francis. B. at Wellingborough, Northants. Bapt. there, June 13, 1672. School, Cottingham (Mr Ashbridge). Scholar, 1689; Matric. 1691; B.A. 1691-2. Adm. at the Middle Temple, Dec. 23, 1689. Inherited the estate at Bradden, Northants., from his uncle William (above). Buried at Bradden, Apr. 19, 1719. (Burke, *L.G.*; *Peile*, II. 110.)

IVESON, ANTHONY. Matric. sizar from ST JOHN'S, Michs. 1575; B.A. 1579-80. Ord. deacon (Ely) Apr. 1580, age 23. Licensed teacher at Lyng, Norfolk, 1583. V. of Levington, Suffolk, 1586-1619. R. of Haynford, Norfolk, 1592.

IVESON, GREGORY. Matric. sizar from PEMBROKE,' Easter, 1548.

IVESON, HENRY. Adm. pens. (age 19) at TRINITY, May 11, 1733. S. of Edward, of Black Bank, Leeds. School, Shipton, Yorks. (Mr Clarke). Matric. 1734. Of Norwich. M.D. Married Maria Larwood, of Norwich. Died July 30, 1768.

IVESON, JOHN. Adm. pens. (age 18) at ST JOHN'S, May 26, 1718. S. of William (? 1676), clerk, of Yorkshire. B. at Catterick. Exhibitioner from Charterhouse. Matric. 1718. Migrated to Emmanuel, Mar. 27, 1723. B.A. 1724.

IVESON, RICHARD. Matric. sizar from ST JOHN'S, Easter, 1625; B.A. 1629-30.

IVESON, THOMAS. Matric. sizar from PEMBROKE, Easter, 1629; B.A. 1631-2; M.A. 1635. Ord. priest (Norwich) Sept. 25, 1636.

IVESON, TIMOTHY. Adm. sizar (age 16) at CHRIST'S, Apr. 28, 1653. S. of James. B. at Langcliff, Yorks. School, Giggleswick (Mr Walker). Probably ord. deacon (Durham) Mar. 15, 1662-3; priest, Sept. 25, 1664. C. of St John, Stanwick, 1665. C. of Hutton Magna, Richmondshire, 1670. Perhaps father of William (1676).

IVESON, WILLIAM. Adm. sizar (age 19) at CHRIST'S, Mar. 27, 1633-4. S. of James. B. at Langcliff, Yorks. School, Giggleswick (Mr Dockwray). Matric. 1634; B.A. 1637-8; M.A. 1641. Ord. deacon (Lincoln) June 5, 1642. Author. (*Peile*, I. 431.)

IVESON, WILLIAM. Adm. sizar (age 17) at ST JOHN'S, May 19, 1676. S. of Timothy (? 1653), clerk, of Forcett, Richmonds., Yorks. B. there. Matric. 1676; B.A. 1679-80; M.A. 1683. Ord. deacon (Durham) Sept. 21, 1679; priest, June 6, 1680. V. of Catterick, Yorks., 1690.

IVORY, EDMUND. Adm. sizar (age 16) at CAIUS, Aug. 17, 1668. S. of John, painter, of Cambridge. B. there. School, Perse (Mr Griffith). Scholar, 1669-74; Matric. 1671; B.A. 1672-3; M.A. 1676. Fellow, 1674-81. Ord. deacon (Chichester) Nov. 20, 1674; priest (London) May 21, 1676. R. of Bawdeswell, Norfolk, 1692-1721. Will proved (Norwich) 1721. (*Venn*, I. 435.)

IVERY, JOHN. Adm. at KING'S (age 16) a scholar from Eton, Sept. 29, 1561. Of 'Torington' (? Terrington), Norfolk. Matric. 1561; B.A. 1565-6; M.A. 1569. Fellow, 1564-72.

IVORY, ROBERT. 'D.D. Cambridge.' B. in London. Carmelite friar. Provincial of his order. Died 1392. (*Pits*, 557.)

IVORY, ROBERT. Matric. sizar from PEMBROKE, Michs. 1625; B.A. 1629-30. Will proved (V.C.C.) 1630.

IVORY, ROBERT. Adm. sizar at PEMBROKE, Jan. 19, 1634-5. S. of Edmund, of Cambridge. Matric. 1634-5; B.A. 1638-9; M.A. 1642. Ord. deacon (Peterb.) June 5, 1642; priest (Lincoln) Sept. 24, 1643. Chaplain to Sir Thomas Ingram. R. of St Magnus, London, 1662-1711. V. of Heston, Middlesex, 1668-1711. Died 1710-1. Will (P.C.C.) 1711. Father of the next.

IVORY, ROBERT. Adm. pens. (age 16) at JESUS, Oct. 15, 1670. S. of Robert (above), of Middlesex, clerk. Scholar (by Dean and Chapter of St Paul's), 1674.

IVY or IVIE, JOHN. Adm. Fell.-Com. (age 16) at SIDNEY, June 28, 1710. S. of Jonathan, mercer, of Exeter. B. there. School, Uffculme, Devon (Mr Deyman). Matric. 1710. Adm. at the Inner Temple, June 28, 1710.

IVY, OLIVER. Adm. sizar (age 22) at ST JOHN'S, Jan. 25, 1694-5. S. of Thomas, gent. B. at Malmesbury, Wilts. School, Eton. Matric. 1698; B.A. 1698-9. Ord. priest (London) Mar. 16, 1711-2.

IVY, RALPH. Adm. at KING'S, Easter, 1545.

IXEM, JOHN. Adm. pens. (age 16) at CHRIST'S, May 29, 1636. S. of John. B. at Norwich. School, Norwich (Mr Stonham and Mr Cushing). Matric. 1636; B.A. 1639-40; M.A. 1646. Ord. priest (Lincoln) June 28, 1646. Probably V. of Well, near Bedale, Yorks. R. of Todwick, 1660. Perhaps R. of Woodford, near Thrapston, Feb. to Sept. 1661. Buried 1676. Father of the next. (*Peile*, I. 443.)

IXEM, JOHN. Adm. pens. (age 17) at ST JOHN'S, May 25, 1668. S. of John (above), clerk, of Well, Richmondshire. B. there. School, Layton (? Laughton-en-le-Morthen) (Mr Bromehead). Matric. 1668. Migrated to Christ's, May 9, 1670. B.A. 1671-2. Perhaps brother of the next. (*Peile*, II. 29.)

IXEM, THOMAS. Adm. sizar (age 17) at CHRIST'S, Apr. 28, 1674. S. of John. B. at Burton-Lazars, Leics. School, Laughton-en-le-Morthen, Yorks. (Mr Bromehead). Matric. 1674; B.A. 1677-8. Ord. deacon (Lincoln) June, 1679; priest, Dec. 1681. V. of Helpston, Northants., 1682-1702. R. of Folkingham, Lincs., 1702-21. Buried there Mar. 3, 1720-1. Perhaps brother of the above. (*Peile*, II. 51.)

IXWORTH, JOHN DE. Scholar of KING'S HALL. Died Aug. 20, 1349.

IXWORTH, JOHN. LL.D. R. of Lower Rickinghall, Suffolk, 1395. Member of the Pope's household. 'Licensed in respect of prebends at Salisbury and Chichester,' Dec. 2, 1405. Preb. of York, 1405-23; of Lincoln, 1406-8, 1420-2; of Chichester, 1407; of St Paul's, 1419-31, of Salisbury, 1420-31. Proxy from the Bishop of Ely to visit the Roman Curia, Oct. 4, 1406. R. of Pulham, Norfolk, 1407. Archdeacon of Worcester, 1412-31. R. of Sevenoaks, Kent. Preb. of Worcester. (*Cal. of Pat. Rolls*; A. B. Beaven; *Papal Letters*.)

J

JAALE, GALE or GOALE, THOMAS. Adm. at KING'S, a scholar from Eton, 1447. Of Tydowe, Yorks.

JACCHAEUS, PATRICK. Incorp. from Aberdeen, 1664.

JACKLER, ROBERT. Matric. pens. from QUEENS', Easter, 1583. Of Norfolk. B.A. 1585-6; M.A. 1589. Ord. deacon (Norwich) Feb. 1, 1593-4; of Gt Yarmouth. Perhaps V. of Ketteringham, Norfolk, 1591-1602.

JACKLER, THOMAS. Matric. pens. from QUEENS', Easter, 1580. Of Norfolk. B.A. 1583-4; M.A. 1589. Ord. deacon (Norwich) June 24; priest, Dec. 21, 1596; title, his patrimony. R. of Linford, Norfolk, 1598. Perhaps V. of Beetley, Norfolk, 1603. Will (P.C.C.) 1626; of Ashill, Norfolk, clerk; where there is a M.I. to his widow.

JACKLING, EDMUND. Matric. pens. from ST JOHN'S, Michs. 1554. Probably C. of Fowlmere, Cambs., in 1567.

JACKLING, ——. Fellow of CORPUS CHRISTI, in 1554. (*Lamb-Masters*, 319.)

JACKMAN, GOODGION. Adm. pens. at ST JOHN'S, May 12, 1686. S. and h. of John, gent., of Skipton, Yorks. (and Elinor Goodgion). Bapt. there, Feb. 17, 1668-9. School, Threshfield (Mr Motley). Matric. 1686. Adm. at the Middle Temple, June 24, 1687. Called to the Bar, May 18, 1694.

JACKSON, ABRAHAM. M.A. 1629 (Incorp. from Oxford). Of Devon, *cler. fil.* Matric. from Exeter College, Oxford, Dec. 4, 1607, age 18; B.A. (Oxford) 1611; M.A. (Christ Church, Oxford) 1616. V. of North Petherwin, Cornwall, 1618. Preb. of Peterborough, 1640-6. Author, religious. Died *c.* 1646. (*Al. Oxon.*; *D.N.B.*; *Northants. N. and Q.*, IV. 212.)

JACKSON, ALEXANDER. B.D. 1476-7.

JACKSON, ANTHONY. Matric. Fell.-Com. from JESUS, Easter, 1614. Probably s. of Richard, of Killingwold Graves, Beverley, Yorks. Age 14 in 1613. Adm. at the Inner Temple, 1616. Barrister, 1635. Bencher, 1660. Knighted, 1650 (by King Charles, when abroad). (*Vis. of Yorks.*, 1612.)

JACKSON, ARTHUR. Matric. sizar from TRINITY, Easter, 1568.

JACKSON, ARTHUR. B.A. from TRINITY, 1613-4. B. at Little Waldingfield, Suffolk. M.A. 1617. Incorp. at Oxford, 1617. Ord. deacon (Lincoln); priest (London) Dec. 24, 1620, age 27. R. of St Michael, Wood Street, London, 1625-43. Minister of St Faith, London, 1642-62, ejected. President of Sion College, 1646. Presbyterian Commissioner at the Savoy Conference, 1661. Retired to Hadley, Middlesex. Author of Annotations on Job, the Psalms, etc. Died at Edmonton, Aug. 5, 1666. Buried in the ruins of St Michael, Wood St. Will, P.C.C. Father of John (1638). (*Calamy*, I. 104; *D.N.B.*; J. Ch. Smith.)

JACKSON, CHARLES. Adm. sizar (age 21) at ST JOHN'S, Nov. 15, 1645. S. of George, merchant, of Buxton, Derbs. School, Bakewell (Mr Cockeyne).

JACKSON, CHARLES. Adm. pens. at EMMANUEL, Sept. 25, 1731. Of Berkshire. S. of Thomas. Bapt. at Cookham, Oct. 18, 1713. Colleger at Eton, 1728-31. Matric. 1731; B.A. 1735-6; M.A. 1739; B.D. 1746; D.D. 1759. Fellow, 1739. Ord. deacon (Lincoln) Feb. 26, 1737-8; priest, June 13, 1742. R. of St Mary's, Bedford. R. of Thornhaugh, Northants., 1753-61. Chaplain to the Duke of Bedford, Lord-Lieutenant of Ireland. Bishop of Ferns, 1761-5. Bishop of Kildare, 1765-90. Dean of Christ Church, Dublin, 1765-90. Gave £100 towards the College buildings, 1770. Died 1790. (H. B. Swanzy; H. I. Longden.)

JACKSON, CHRISTOPHER. B.A. 1523-4. Of Richmondshire. M.A. 1527. Fellow of ST JOHN'S, 1525. Will (V.C.C.) 1528.

JAXON, CHRISTOPHER. Matric. pens. from CLARE, Michs. 1568.

JACKSON, CHRISTOPHER. Matric. sizar from ST JOHN'S, Easter, 1570; B.A. 1573-4; M.A. 1577. V. of Royston, Herts., 1574-81. V. of Haslingfield, Cambs., 1583-93. Died 1593.

JACKSON, CHRISTOPHER. Adm. pens. (age 20) at MAGDALENE, June 22, 1652. S. of Thomas, of Leeds, Yorks. School, Leeds. Matric. 1653; B.A. 1655. V. of Crosby Garrett, Westmorland, 1657-60. After his ejection he continued to live in the neighbourhood. Buried at Crosby, May 29, 1689. (*Calamy*, II. 495; *B. Nightingale*.)

JACKSON, CHRISTOPHER. Adm. sizar (age 16) at ST JOHN'S, May 19, 1654. S. of John, husbandman, of Kildwick, Yorks. B. there. School, Kildwick (Mr Rakes). Matric. 1654; B.A. 1657-8; M.A. 1662. Perhaps schoolmaster at Austwick, Clapham, Yorks., in 1665. Doubtless R. of St Crux, York, 1671; and of All Saints'-in-the-Pavement, 1676. Preb. of York, 1697-1701. Died May 22, 1701, aged 63. M.I. Benefactor to the City of York. (Le Neve, *Mon.*; *Al. Oxon.* identifies him with another Oxonian.)

JACKSON, CYRIL. Adm. pens. (age 18) at MAGDALENE, Dec. 4, 1736. S. of Robert (1678), clerk. B. at Adel, Yorks. School, Chesterfield. Matric. 1737; M.D. 1769 (*Lit. Reg.*). Practised in Stamford, Lincs. Will (P.C.C.) 1798; of Stamford. Father of the Dean of Christ Church, brother of William (1733). (*N. and Q.*, 6th S., VIII. 139; *F.M.G.*)

JACSON, DANIEL. Matric. pens. from TRINITY, Easter, 1589; B.A. 1593-4; M.A. 1597. Will proved (V.C.C.) 1635.

JACKSON, DOMINICK. Of Cambridge. (College not specified.) Ord. deacon (London) Apr. 24, 1560.

JACKSON, EDMUND. B.Civ.L. 1491-2. Fellow of KING'S HALL. Ord. sub-deacon (Ely) Mar. 17, 1491-2; priest, Apr. 21, 1492. R. of Hilgay, 1503-21. Will (P.C.C.) 1521, 'clerk, of Hilgay, Norfolk and Cambridge.'

JACKSON, EDWARD. Matric. sizar from PEMBROKE, Easter, 1575.

JACKSON, EDWARD. Matric. sizar from TRINITY, Easter, 1620; B.A. 1623-4. Ord. deacon (Peterb.) Sept. 21, 1623. Ord. priest (York) Sept. 1624. Perhaps V. of Headon, Notts., 1623-6. Died 1626.

JACKSON, EDWARD. Adm. sizar (age 18) at JESUS, June 6, 1666. Of Cheshire. Matric. 1667. Migrated as pens. to Trinity, June 15, 1668, then back to Jesus. B.A. 1669-70.

JACKSON, EDWARD. Adm. sizar at CLARE, Oct. 5, 1710. Bapt. at Rochdale, Lancs., Aug. 24, 1692; s. of Daniel, of Church Lane. Matric. 1711; B.A. 1715-6; M.A. 1720; D.D. 1741. Ord. deacon (Ely) Feb. 26, 1715-6; priest (York) Dec. 1716. V. of Penistone, Yorks., 1717-22. Master of Coventry Grammar School, 1718-58. V. of Coleshill, Warw. Preb. of Lichfield, 1733-58. Married Alice, dau. of Thomas Bosvile, R. of Sandal Parva, Yorks. Died May 7, 1758. Will, P.C.C. (M. H. Peacock; A. B. Beaven.)

JACKSON, EDWARD. Adm. at CORPUS CHRISTI, 1742. S. of Edward. Bapt. at Christ Church, Surrey, Mar. 4, 1723-4. Colleger at Eton. Matric. 1743; B.A. 1746-7.

JACKSON, ELEAZER. Adm. sizar (age 15) at CAIUS, Sept. 2, 1608. S. of Laurence, husbandman, of Hartlington, Burnsall, Yorks. School, Burnsall. Matric. 1608; Scholar, 1609-12; B.A. 1612-3. Ord. deacon (Gloucester) Dec. 24, 1615; priest (Peterb.) Dec. 22, 1616. V. of Powick, Worcs., 1622.

JACKSON, FRANCIS. Adm. sizar (age 17) at CHRIST'S, May 31, and pens. Aug. 10, 1649. S. of Richard (1619), R. of Halton, Lancs. Bapt. there, Jan. 29, 1631-2. Schools, Kirkby Lonsdale and Giggleswick. B.A. 1652-3; M.A. 1660. Master of Kirkby Lonsdale School, *c.* 1653-5. V. of Warton, Lancs., 1655-70. Died July, 1670. Will (Archd. Richmond) 1670. Brother of Leonard (1668) and William (1644-5). (W. H. Chippindall; *Peile*, I. 526; E. Axon.)

JACKSON, FRANCIS. Adm. pens. (age 18) at SIDNEY, July 4, 1716. 2nd s. of Francis, gent., of Duddington, Northants. School, Stamford. B.A. 1720-1; M.A. 1724. Ord. deacon (Peterb.) Mar. 5, 1720-1; priest, Sept. 24, 1721. R. of Bulwick, Northants., 1721-70. R. of Seaton, Rutland, 1750-3. Died Apr. 10, 1770. (H. I. Longden.)

JACKSON, FRANCIS. Adm. pens. (age 18) at PEMBROKE, May 15, 1742. S. of Richard, of Arrow, Warws. Colleger at Eton, 1735-41. Matric. 1742; LL.B. 1748. One of these names R. of Orford, Suffolk. Died at Islington, Mar. 19, 1780. (*G. Mag.*)

JACKSON, GEORGE. 'B.A. of Cambridge' when Incorp. at Oxford, 1568. Perhaps ord. priest (Lincoln) Nov. 30, 1565; R. of East Keal, Lincs., 1566; and of West Keal, 1567. Called 'M.A.' in 1586. Will (Lincoln) 1612. (*Lib. Cleri.*)

JACKSON, GEORGE. Matric. Fell.-Com. from CORPUS CHRISTI, 1639. Of Kent.

JACKSON, GEORGE. Adm. sizar (age 16) at CHRIST'S, May 12, 1663. S. of Roger (1615), V. of Langford, Derbs. School, Repton (Mr Ullock). Matric. 1663; B.A. 1666; M.A. 1670; M.D. 1677. Usher at Repton School, 1667-72. Master of Ashbourne, 1672-77. Afterwards practised physic at Derby. Died May 28, 1699. Buried at St Peter's, Derby. Will, P.C.C. Father of George (1699) and Roger (1705), brother of John (1650) and William (1653). (*Peile*, I. 603; Burke, *L.G.*)

JACKSON, GEORGE. Adm. sizar at EMMANUEL, Apr. 18, 1671. School, Manchester. Matric. 1671; B.A. 1674-5. Master of Rochdale Grammar School, 1675-96. Ord. deacon (Chester) Dec. 23, 1677. C. at Rochdale, in 1679. P.C. of Ashworth Chapel, Lancs., 1693-8. Buried at Rochdale, Jan. 19, 1697-8. (Mumford, *Manchester Grammar School*; E. Axon.)

JACKSON, GEORGE. Adm. pens. (age 15) at PEMBROKE, Mar. 22, 1674-5. S. of George, baker. B. at Birmingham. Matric. 1675. Migrated to Queens', Apr. 15, 1676. B.A. 1678-9.

JACKSON, GEORGE. Adm. pens. (age 16) at MAGDALENE, Mar. 29, 1675. S. of George, deceased. B. at Hunslet, Leeds, Yorks. School, Leeds. Matric. 1675; B.A. 1678-9. Ord. deacon (York) Feb. 1680-1; priest, Mar. 1682-3.

JACSON, GEORGE. Adm. pens. at JESUS, June 30, 1699. S. of George (1663), M.D., of Derby. B. 1682. Matric. 1699; Scholar, 1699; B.A. 1702-3; M.A. 1706. Ord. deacon (London) May 19, 1706. Perhaps preb. of St Paul's, 1712-9. V. of Leek, Staffs., 1713-9. Died 1719. Brother of Roger (1705).

JACKSON, GERVASE. Matric. pens. from ST JOHN'S, Lent, 1579-80. Perhaps 3rd s. of William, of Snydale, Yorks. (*Vis. of Yorks.*, 1612.)

JACKSON, HENRY. Adm. pens. (age 18) at CAIUS, Oct. 21, 1580. Of Mowthorpe, Terrington, Yorks. S. of Thomas, gent. Schools, York and Terrington (Mr Pullen and Mr Harding). Matric. 1580.

JACKSON, HENRY. Matric. pens. from JESUS, *c.* 1590.

JACKSON, HENRY. Adm. pens. at EMMANUEL, Apr. 13, 1631. Of Middlesex. Matric. 1631; B.A. 1634-5.

JACKSON, HENRY. Adm. pens. at QUEENS', May 14, 1645. Of Staffordshire. One of these names graduated B.A. at Trinity College, Oxford, Mar. 16, 1649-50. V. of Inkberrow, Worcs., 1663. (*Al. Oxon.*)

JACKSON, HUMFREY. Adm. pens. (age 17) at CAIUS, Apr. 30, 1627. S. of Robert, clothworker. B. in the parish of St Dionis Backchurch, London. Bapt. June 10, 1610. School, Braintree, Essex. Matric. 1627.

JACKSON, HUMPHREY. M.A. from JESUS, 1714. S. of H., of Mevison, Staffs. Matric. from New Inn Hall, Oxford, Dec. 12, 1706, age 16; B.A. (Trinity College, Oxford) 1710. R. of Willesley, Derbs., 1721. V. of Stapenhill, 1736-57. Died Dec. 11, 1757. Will (P.C.C.) 1758. (*Al. Oxon.*)

JACKSON, ISRAEL. Adm. sizar at EMMANUEL, June 23, 1642. Of Lincolnshire. Matric. 1643; B.A. 1645-6; M.A. 1649.

JACKSON, ISRAEL. Adm. at TRINITY, Feb. 10, 1672-3 (under name of Isaac). Of Lincolnshire. School, Boston. Matric. 1673. Migrated to Peterhouse, July 8, 1676. Scholar, 1676; B.A. 1676-7; M.A. 1680. Fellow of Peterhouse, 1679-85. Mayor of Boston, 1668 and 1678. Lecturer of Boston, 1685-1707. (*T. A. Walker*, 157.)

JACKSON, JAMES. Matric. pens. from CLARE, Michs. 1626; B.A. 1629; M.A. 1633; M.D. 1657. Fellow, 1631-86. Senior proctor, 1643. Died in College, 1686. Will proved (V.C.C.) 1686.

JACKSON, JAMES. Adm. sizar (age 18) at ST JOHN'S, Sept. 7, 1649. S. of George, of Hough End, Lancs. School, Manchester. Perhaps B.A. 1665-6 from Emmanuel (*see* the next). One of these names, 'B.A.,' when ord. presbyter by Manchester Classis, 1655. Minister of Chorlton, Lancs., 1655-62. Chaplain of Manchester Coll. Church, 1662-5. Perhaps same as J. J., C. at Prestwich, in 1675. Brother of Richard (1662). (E. Axon.)

JACKSON, JAMES. Adm. pens. at EMMANUEL, Mar. 14, 1665-6. Of Lancashire. B.A. 1665-6. (Doubtless the above.)

JACKSON, JOHN. B.A. 1500.

JAXON, JOHN. Matric. pens. from ST JOHN'S, Michs. 1568.

JACKSON, JOHN. Matric. pens. from ST JOHN'S, Michs. 1570. Probably B.A. from Christ's, 1572-3. Scholar of Christ's. Ord. priest (Lincoln) Oct. 7, 1574. R. of Melsonby, Yorks., 1573-1607. Buried at Richmond, Feb. 20, 1606-7. Doubtless father of Timothy (1607-8), John (1613) and Nathaniel (1616). (*Yorks. Archaeol. Journal*, II. 189.)

JACSON, JOHN. Matric. sizar from CORPUS CHRISTI, Michs. 1573. One of these names, 'bred in the schools,' ord. priest (Lincoln) Apr. 8, 1579, was C. of Folkingham, Lincs., 1585. Perhaps V. of Horncastle, 1593-5.

JACKSON, JOHN. Matric. pens. from ST JOHN'S, Michs. 1576.

JACKSON, JOHN. Matric. sizar from ST JOHN'S, Lent, 1577-8; B.A. 1581-2; M.A. 1585; B.D. 1595. Licensed to teach grammar at Swavesey, Cambs., June 22, 1583. Ord. deacon (London) May 28; priest, Sept. 28, 1591. R. of St Alban, Wood Street, London, 1595-1625. Died 1625. Will, P.C.C., as B.D.

JACKSON, JOHN. Matric. sizar from JESUS, Lent, 1580-1; B.A. 1584-5. One of these names (B.A.), V. of Skendleby, Lincs., 1590-3.

JACKSON, JOHN. Matric. sizar from KING'S, Easter, 1581; Scholar of Trinity, 1584; B.A. from Trinity, 1585-6; M.A. 1589. Probably Incorp. at Oxford, 1594. One of these names, 'M.A.,' ord. deacon and priest (Lincoln) Sept. 1, 1592.

JACKSON, JOHN. Matric. pens. from CHRIST'S, Oct. 1583; B.A. 1587-8; M.A. 1591. One of these names V. of Stainton, Yorks., 1592-1629. (*Peile*, I. 177.)

JACKSON, JOHN. Matric. sizar from TRINITY, Michs. 1588.

JACKSON, JOHN. Matric. pens. from CHRIST'S, 1592-3; B.A. 1596-7; M.A. 1600. Fellow, 1600-5. Married, at St Benet's, Cambridge, 1605, Elizabeth, dau. of Robert Browne, draper. (*Peile*, I. 208, who gives him the preferments of John, of Trinity, 1626.)

JACKSON, JOHN. B.A. (? 1602-3); M.A. from TRINITY, 1608.

JACKSON, JOHN. Adm. pens. at SIDNEY, May 5, 1612; B.A. 1614-5.

JACKSON, JOHN. Matric. sizar from CHRIST'S, July, 1613. S. of John (1570), R. of Melsonby, Yorks. B. 1600. B.A. 1616-7; M.A. 1620. (He seems to have matric. at Lincoln College, Oxford, June 7, 1616.) Master of Richmond Grammar School, 1618-20. Ord. deacon (York) as of Christ's, Dec. 19, 1619; priest, Feb. 22, 1623-4. R. of Marske, 1623. Also R. of Barwick-in-Elmet. Member of the Assembly of Divines. Preacher at Gray's Inn, 1642-4. Puritan, but Royalist. Retired to Barwick on the arraignment of the King. Married Oct. 13, 1629, Joan, dau. of Ralph Bowes, at St Mary-le-Bow, Durham. Buried at Barwick, Jan. 22, 1647-8 (?). Brother of Nathaniel (1616) and Timothy (1607-8). (*Peile*, I. 292; *Yorks. Arch. Journal*, VI. 184; H. M. Peacock.)

JACKSON, JOHN. Adm. Fell.-Com. at EMMANUEL, May 1, 1622. Matric. 1622. One of these names, s. and h. of Joseph, of Edmonton, Middlesex, adm. at Lincoln's Inn, Apr. 8, 1622.

JACKSON, JOHN. Matric. sizar from TRINITY, Easter, 1626; B.A. 1628-9; M.A. 1634.

JACKSON, JOHN. Matric. sizar from TRINITY, Easter, 1626; B.A. 1629-30. One of these names (B.A.), ord. priest (Lichfield) Sept. 19, 1630. V. of Madeley, Staffs., 1635-48. V. of Lapley, 1648-59.

JACKSON, JOHN. Adm. pens. at QUEENS', Mar. 6, 1627-8. Of Suffolk. LL.B. 1633.

JACKSON, JOHN. B.A. from CLARE, 1629-30; M.A. 1633. Probably ord. deacon (Peterb.) Aug. 17, 1662; 'of Clare College; M.A.'

JACSON, JOHN. Matric. pens. from TRINITY, Easter, 1634; Scholar, 1634.

JACKESON, JOHN. Adm. sizar (age 19) at ST JOHN'S, June 11, 1636. S. of Richard, husbandman, of Wyersdale, Lancs. B. there. School, Blackburn (Mr Alstein). B.A. 1639-40; M.A. 1643.

JACKSON, JOHN. Matric. pens. from ST CATHARINE'S, Michs. 1638. Of London. S. of Arthur (1613-4). B.A. 1642-3; M.A. from Queens', 1646. Intruded fellow of Queens', 1644-50, ejected. Incorp. at Oxford, 1653. Ejected from Moulsey, Surrey, 1662. (*Calamy*, II. 451.)

JACKSON, JOHN. Adm. sizar (age 17) at ST JOHN'S, Nov. 2, 1639. S. of Timothy (1607-8), clerk, deceased, of Arksey, Yorks. B. at Hessle, Yorks. School, Pocklington (Mr Sedgwick). B.A. 1645-6. V. of Doncaster, 1648; conformed at the Restoration and reinstituted. R. of Sandal, 1663. R. of Rossington, 1668-90. Buried at Doncaster, July 17, 1690. Father of John (1665) and Nathaniel (1669). Will (York) 1690.

JACKSON, JOHN. Adm. pens. at EMMANUEL, Dec. 9, 1644. Of Yorkshire. Matric. 1645; B.A. 1647-8.

JACKSON, JOHN. Adm. pens. (age 16) at CHRIST'S, May 9, 1650. S. of Roger (1615), V. of Sutton-on-the-Hill, Derbs. B. there. School, Repton (Mr Ullock). Matric. 1650; B.A. 1653-4; M.A. 1658. Master of Etwall Hospital, 1657-91. V. of Etwall, 1662. Buried there 1692. Brother of William (1653) and George (1663). (*Peile*, I. 534.)

JACKSON, JOHN. Adm. Fell.-Com. (age 18) at MAGDALENE, Sept. 16, 1658. S. of Robert, gent., of Ash Parva, Whitchurch, Salop. Matric. 1660.

JACKSON, JOHN. Adm. sizar (age 18) at CHRIST'S, Oct. 19, 1664. S. of Robert. B. at Newton, Lancs. School, Kirkby Lonsdale (Mr Garthwaite). Matric. 1664; B.A. 1668-9; M.A. 1672. Ord. deacon (Ely) Sept. 22, 1672; possibly priest (Lincoln) Dec. 1681. (For conjectures *see Peile*, I. 613.)

JACKSON, JOHN. Adm. pens. (age 15) at ST JOHN'S, May 11, 1665. S. of John (1639), clerk, V. of Doncaster. Bapt. there, Apr. 7, 1651. School, Sedbergh (Mr Fell). Matric. 1667; B.A. 1668-9; M.A. 1672. Ord. deacon (Ely) Sept. 24, 1670; priest, Sept. 1675. R. of Sessay, Thirsk, 1676-90. V. of Doncaster, 1690-1706. R. of Rossington, 1690-1706. Preb. of Southwell, 1704-6. Buried at Doncaster, July 19, 1706. Father of John (1702), brother of Nathaniel (1669). (*F.M.G.*, 1263.)

JACKSON, JOHN. Adm. sizar (age 17) at ST JOHN'S, June 8, 1668. B. at Nottingham. School, Nottingham (Mr Birch). Matric. 1669; B.A. 1671-2. Ord. deacon (Ely) Sept. 22, 1672.

JACKSON, JOHN. Adm. sizar at TRINITY, Oct. 17, 1672. Matric. 1673; B.A. 1676-7.

JACKSON, JOHN. Adm. sizar (age 18) at ST JOHN'S, May 23, 1676. S. of Peter, of Hawthornthwaite, Lancs. B. there. School, Lentworth. Matric. 1676; B.A. 1679-80. Perhaps ord. deacon (Chester) Dec. 18, 1681. Schoolmaster and Reader of Prayers at Burtonwood, Lancs., 1681. One of these names minister of Hindley, 1698-1708. Will (Chester) 1708. But *see* the next. (E. Axon.)

JACKSON, JOHN. Adm. sizar at CHRIST'S, June 14, 1680. S. of Robert. B. at Camfield (? Cantsfield, in Tunstall parish), Lancs. School, Sedbergh (Mr Wharton). Matric. 1680. Resided one year. Perhaps ord. deacon (Chester) Dec. 23, 1683. C. of Burton-in-Thornton, Yorks., 1690.

JACKSON, JOHN. Adm. pens. (age 14) at MAGDALENE, June 28, 1686. S. of John. B. at Brampton, Hunts. School, Huntingdon. Matric. 1687; B.A. 1689-90. Nephew of Sam. Pepys.

JACKSON, JOHN. Adm. sizar at EMMANUEL, Feb. 7, 1693-4. Of Somerset. Matric. 1695; B.A. 1697-8; M.A. 1701. Ord. deacon (Peterb.) May 26, 1700.

JACKSON, JOHN. Adm. sizar (age 17) at PETERHOUSE, Apr. 15, 1700. Of Durham. School, Gisburgh. Matric. 1701; B.A. 1703-4. Ord. deacon (York) Jan. 1705-6.

JACKSON, JOHN. Adm. pens. (age 18) at CHRIST'S, June 27, 1700. S. of George. B. at Bradford. School, Bradford. Matric. 1701; B.A. 1703-4; M.A. 1708. Perhaps minister of Denton Chapel, Lancs., 1709-20. One of these names minister of Stretford, Manchester, Nov. 25, 1726. (*Peile*, II. 148.)

JACKSON, JOHN. Adm. pens. at JESUS, Dec. 15, 1702. S. of John (1665), V. of Doncaster. B. at Sessay, Apr. 4, 1686. School, Doncaster. Matric. 1703; Scholar, 1705; B.A. 1706-7 (did not proceed to M.A. owing to his Arian opinions). Ord. deacon (York) Sept. 1708; priest, 1710. R. of Rossington, Yorks., 1710-63. Master of Wigston's Hospital, Leics., 1729-63. Master of Doncaster Grammar School, 1742-7. Author, theological. Died May 12, 1763. Buried at Rossington. M.I. at Wigston's Hospital. (*D.N.B.*; *F.M.G.*, 1263.)

JACKSON, JOHN. Adm. pens. (age 16) at ST JOHN'S, May 30, 1723. S. of Richard, barrister, of Yorkshire. B. at Clapham, near Settle. School, Sedbergh (Dr Saunders). Matric. 1723; B.A. 1726-7.

JACKSON, JOHN. Adm. sizar at CLARE, July 1, 1723. B. at East Retford, Notts. Matric. 1723.

JACKSON, JOSEPH. Adm. pens. at EMMANUEL, Easter, 1621. Matric. 1621; B.A. from Magdalene, 1626-7; M.A. 1630. Fellow of Magdalene. One of these names s. of Joseph, of Edmonton, Middlesex, adm. at Lincoln's Inn, May 12, 1625.

JACKSON, JOSEPH. Matric. sizar from PEMBROKE, Easter, 1627. S. of Arthur, of London, mercer. Exhibitioner from Charterhouse. B.A. 1630-1; M.A. 1634. Ord. deacon (Norwich) June 1, 1634. One of these names V. of Bromley, Kent, 1647-53; of Aylesford, 1654-61; and of Woodnesborough, 1661-7. Died 1667.

JACKSON, JOSEPH. Adm. sizar at EMMANUEL, Easter, 1659. Of Derbyshire. Matric. 1660; B.A. 1663-4; M.A. 1667. R. of Doynton, Gloucs., 1678-1720. Died Jan. 1719-20.

JACKSON, JOSEPH. Adm. sizar (age 19) at SIDNEY, May, 1677. S. of Joseph, yeoman. B. at Woodseats, Derbs. School, Sheffield. Matric. 1677.

JACKSON, JOSEPH. M.A. 1697 (Incorp. from Oxford). S. of James, of Abbey Holme, Cumberland. Matric. from Queen's College, Oxford, Mar. 29, 1677, age 18; B.A. (Oxford) 1681; M.A. 1685. (*Al. Oxon.*)

JACKSON, JOSHUA. Adm. sizar at TRINITY, Apr. 18, 1662. Matric. 1662; B.A. 1666-7. One of these names R. of Northenden, Cheshire, 1675-c. 1684. Perhaps V. of Dewsbury, Yorks., 1687-1715. Died Feb. 28, 1715.

JACKSON, LAURENCE. Adm. pens. (age 18) at ST JOHN'S, June 29, 1709. S. of Laurence, deceased. B. in London. School, Merchant Taylors' (Mr Parsell). Matric. 1712; B.A. 1712-3; M.A. from Sidney, 1716; B.D. 1723. Fellow of Sidney, 1715. Ord. deacon (York) Dec. 1714; priest (Ely) June 8, 1718. V. of Ardleigh, Colchester, 1723. R. of Gt Wigborough, 1730. Preb. of Lincoln, 1747-72. Author, religious. Died Feb. 17 (? Feb. 26), 1772. Will, P.C.C. (*D.N.B.*)

JACKSON, LEONARD. Adm. sizar (age 17) at CHRIST'S, May 20, 1668. S. of Richard (1619), R. of Whittington, Lancs. Bapt. there, Apr. 21, 1650. Schools, Lancaster (Mr Holden) and Kirkby Lonsdale (Mr Garthwaite). Matric. 1668; B.A. 1671-2; M.A. 1677. Ord. deacon (Chichester) May, 1673; priest (York) May, 1676. R. of Claughton-in-Lonsdale, Lancs., 1678-81. R. of Tatham, 1700-26. Died 1726. Brother of Francis (1649) and William (1644-5). (*Peile*, II. 15; *Vict. Hist. Lancs.*, VIII. 224.)

JACKSON, LEWIS. Adm. sizar (age 18) at TRINITY, Oct. 12, 1698. S. of Richard, of Louth, Lincs. School, Louth (Mr Marshall). Matric. 1699; B.A. 1702-3. Ord. deacon (London) Dec. 19, 1703; priest (Lincoln) Sept. 22, 1706.

JACKSON, LIONEL. Matric. sizar from JESUS, Michs. 1586; B.A. 1593-4, as 'Leonard.'

JACKSON, MICHAEL. Matric. pens. from QUEENS', Michs. 1568.

JACKSON, MICHAEL. Adm. sizar at JESUS, May 10, 1704. Of Nottinghamshire. Matric. 1704; B.A. 1707-8. Ord. deacon (York) Sept. 1708; priest, 1711.

JACKSON, NATHANIEL. Matric. sizar from KING'S, c. 1595. B. at Royston. B.A. from St John's, 1598-9; M.A. 1602. Ord. deacon (London) Sept. 29, 1600; priest, Sept. 27, 1607, age 29. C. of Kingsbury, Middlesex, 1608-9.

JACKSON, NATHANIEL. Matric. sizar from CHRIST'S, July, 1616. 3rd s. of John (1570), R. of Melsonby, Yorks. B.A. 1619-20; M.A. 1623. Ord. deacon (York) June 8, 1623; priest, Feb. 22, 1623-4. V. of Hunsingore, 1623-5. R. of Stonegrave, 1629-44. R. of Barwick-in-Elmet, 1647-60, deprived, and retired to York. Buried at All Saints' Pavement, York, Nov. 1, 1662. Will, York. Brother of John (1613) and Timothy (1607-8), father of Phineas (1648). (*Peile*, I. 311; *Thoresby Soc.*, XVII. 68.)

JACKSON, NATHANIEL. Adm. pens. (age 15) at ST JOHN'S, Mar. 23, 1659-60. S. of Nathaniel, deceased, of Boston, Lincs. B. there. School, St Paul's, London. Matric. 1660; B.A. 1663-4; M.A. 1667.

JACKSON, NATHANIEL. Adm. pens. (age 14) at ST JOHN'S, May 13, 1669. S. of John (1639), clerk, V. of Doncaster. Bapt. there, Dec. 25, 1654. School, Doncaster. Matric. 1669; B.A. 1672-3; M.A. 1676. Ord. deacon (Peterb.) June 14, 1674. Buried at Doncaster, Oct. 26, 1683. (*F.M.G.*, 1263; M. H. Peacock.)

JACKSON, NICHOLAS. Adm. sizar (age 19) at ST JOHN'S, May 20, 1706. S. of Thomas, draper. B. at Burnley, Lancs. School, Burnley (Mr Shaw, ? Robertshaw). Matric. 1706; B.A. 1709-10; M.A. 1713. Ord. priest (York) June, 1712. V. of Sowerby, Yorks., 1711-29. Buried Feb. 11, 1728-9.

JACKSON, PETER. Matric. sizar from TRINITY, Easter, 1581; B.A. 1584-5; M.A. 1588. One of these names R. of Ashdon, Essex, 1584-9. R. of Luddenham, Kent, 1590-1604. V. of Preston, Faversham, 1595-1617. Married, at St George's, Canterbury, Oct. 19, 1598, Thomasine Bix, of Canterbury. Died Jan. 1617.

JACKSON, PETER. Adm. sizar (age 18) at SIDNEY, June 14, 1620. S. of John, husbandman. B. at Over Whitby, Cheshire. School, Northwich. B.A. from Christ's, 1623-4. Curates of these names occur at Over Peover, Cheshire, 1625-27; Heslington, 1630-1; Lower Peover, 1636-8; Gt Budworth, 1640-2; and Woodplumpton, Lancs., 1646-7. (E. Axon.)

JACKSON, PETER. Adm. sizar (age 27) at CHRIST'S, Mar. 26, 1629. S. of Richard. B. at Holm, Westmorland. School, Kirkby Lonsdale. Matric. 1629; B.A. 1632-3. Ord. deacon (York) 1632. One of these names V. of Castle Sowerby, Cumberland, 1656-60.

JACKSON, PETER. Adm. sizar at TRINITY, Mar. 13, 1647-8. Of Cheshire. Matric. 1649. Signed for deacon's and priest's orders (London) Sept. 24, 1663; C. of Eastchurch, Kent. C. of Berkeley, Gloucs., 1665.

JACKSON, PHINEAS. Adm. pens. (age 14) at ST JOHN'S, Apr. 24, 1648. S. of Nathaniel (1616), R. of Barwick-in-Elmet. B. at Stonegrave, near Oswaldkirk, Yorks. School, Leeds. B.A. 1651-2. Of Tadcaster, Yorks. Died before 1662. (*F.M.G.*, 1263.)

JACKSON, PHINEAS. Adm. pens. (age 18) at ST JOHN'S, June 25, 1692. S. of Henry, clerk. B. at Inkberrow, Worcs. School, Winchester (Dr Harris). Matric. 1692; B.A. 1696-7.

JACKSON or JAXON, RALPH. Matric. pens. from CHRIST'S, Michs. 1549. Master of the Savoy, 1553–5. Perhaps preb. of Canterbury, in 1556. One of these names (called B.D.) was R. of St Clement Danes, London, 1557–9. Will (P.C.C.) 1559; to be buried in the Savoy. (J. Ch. Smith.)

JACKSON, RANDOLPH. Adm. pens. at JESUS, Nov. 5, 1709. Of Cheshire. B. at Ayton, Yorks. Scholar, 1711; Matric. 1712; B.A. 1714–5. Ord. deacon (Peterb.) Mar. 1727. V. of Ayton Magna, Yorks., 1727–47.

JACKSON, RICHARD. M.A. 1504–5 (Incorp. from Oxford).

JACKSON, RICHARD. Matric. sizar from PEMBROKE, Easter, 1559; B.A. 1561–2; M.A. 1565; B.D. 1572. Probably fellow, 1562. Ord. deacon (Ely) May 26, 1566; priest, Dec. 21, 1568. University preacher, 1569, 1572. One of these names R. of Beeston St Lawrence, Norfolk, 1586. Perhaps R. of Sternfield, Suffolk, 1603.

JACKSON, RICHARD. Matric. pens. from CLARE, Michs. 1567; B.A. 1570–1. Schoolmaster at Ingleton, Yorks. Author, *The Battle of Flodden*, a ballad. (Cooper, II. 118; *D.N.B.*)

JACKSON, RICHARD. Adm. sizar at CORPUS CHRISTI, Easter, 1571. Matric. 1575; B.A. 1578–9.

JACSON, RICHARD. Matric. pens. from ST JOHN'S, Easter, 1575.

JACKSON, RICHARD. Matric. sizar from ST JOHN'S, Michs. 1579.

JACKSON, RICHARD. Matric. pens. from ST JOHN'S, Easter, 1588.

JACKSON, RICHARD. Matric. pens. from CHRIST'S, July, 1619; B.A. 1622; M.A. 1626. R. of Halton, Lancs., 1630–41. R. of Whittington, 1641–80. A member of the Presbyterian *Classis*, but conformed at the Restoration. Will (Archd. Richmond) 1680. Father of Francis (1649), Leonard (1668) and William (1644–5). (*Vict. Hist. of Lancs.*, VIII. 251; E. Axon.)

JACKSON, RICHARD. Matric. sizar from ST JOHN'S, Easter, 1621; B.A. 1624–5; M.A. 1629. Ord. deacon (York) Sept. 1626; priest, Dec. 1626. Perhaps Head Master of Sedbergh School, 1648–56.

JACKSON, RICHARD. Adm. sizar (age 17) at CAIUS, June 13, 1638. S. of Thomas, R. of Itteringham, Norfolk. School, Aylsham (Mr Clare). Matric. 1639; Scholar, 1639–43; B.A. 1641–2. Ord. deacon (Norwich) June 12, 1642; C. of Calthorpe, Norfolk; priest (Bishop Joseph Hall) Feb. 16, 1648–9. R. of Alby, Norfolk, 1646. R. of Beeston St Lawrence, 1658–71. V. of Barton Turf, to 1671. Buried at Beeston, Feb. 12, 1671. (*Venn*, I. 331.)

JACKSON, RICHARD. Adm. sizar at JESUS, Apr. 29, 1641. Of Norfolk. One of these names adm. at Leyden, July 12, 1641.

JACKSON, *alias* KUERDEN, RICHARD. Adm. at EMMANUEL, Feb. 5, 1644–5. Of Lancashire. S. of Gilbert. B. at Cuerden, near Preston. Previously adm. a commoner of St Mary Hall, Oxford, 1638. Migrated to Emmanuel, on the outbreak of the war. B.A. 1644–5. Incorp. at Oxford. M.A. (St Mary Hall) 1647. Created M.D. (Oxford) 1663, as Kuerden. Vice-Principal of St Mary Hall, 1646. A staunch Royalist. Practised as a physician at Preston, Lancs. Antiquary. Friend of Sir William Dugdale. Probably died *c.* 1693. (*D.N.B.*; *Al. Oxon.*, where his admission at St Mary Hall is not recorded.)

JACKSON, RICHARD. Adm. sizar at TRINITY, Jan. 29, 1658–9.

JACKSON, RICHARD. M.A. from ST JOHN'S, 1662. S. of George, of Hough End, Withington, Lancs. Matric. from Brasenose College, Oxford, Mar. 13, 1639–40, age 18; B.A. (Oxford) 1643. In holy orders. Perhaps C. of Nantwich, Cheshire, 1648–77. Buried there Oct. 13, 1677, aged 56. Brother of James (1649). (*Al. Oxon.*; E. Axon.)

JACKSON, RICHARD. Adm. sizar at EMMANUEL, June 4, 1669. Of Leicestershire. Matric. 1669.

JACKSON, RICHARD. Adm. pens. (age 18) at SIDNEY, June 30, 1690. 1st s. of Thomas, barrister-at-law. B. at Nunnington, Yorks. Schools, Thornton and Coxwold. Matric. 1690.

JACKSON, RICHARD. Adm. sizar (age 16) at TRINITY, Apr. 11, 1700. S. of Richard, of Uttoxeter, Staffs. School, Uttoxeter (Mr Bouquet). Matric. 1700; B.A. 1703–4; M.A. 1707.

JACKSON, RICHARD. Adm. sizar at JESUS, Oct. 20, 1703. Of Nottinghamshire. Matric. 1703; Scholar, 1707; B.A. 1707–8. Ord. deacon (York) June, 1709; priest, 1710. V. of Walesby, Notts., 1720.

JACKSON, RICHARD. Adm. sizar at CLARE, Oct. 25, 1720. B. at Rochdale, Lancs. Matric. 1720; B.A. 1723–4; M.A. 1727. Fellow, 1727–43. R. of Gt Waldingfield, Suffolk, 1743–59. Buried there Oct. 27, 1759.

JACKSON, RICHARD. Adm. pens. (age 18) at TRINITY, Sept. 27, 1723. S. of Richard, of Blurton, Staffs., clerk. School, Trentham, Staffs. (Mr Hargreaves). Matric. 1724; Scholar, 1725; B.A. 1727–8; M.A. 1731. Fellow, 1730. Taxor, 1735. Incorp. at Oxford, 1739. Founder of the Jacksonian Professorship. R. of Witley Magna, Worcs. Married Katherine, dau. of Waldyve Willington, of Hurley, Warws. Died at Hurley Hall, Atherstone, Sept. 24, 1782. Buried at Kingsbu , Warws. Will, P.C.C. (*Endowments*, 206; *D.N.B.*; *G. Mag.*)

JACKSON, RICHARD. Adm. pens. at QUEENS', Apr. 30, 1731. Of Cheshire. Matric. 1731; B.A. 1734–5; M.A. 1738; D.D. 1764. R. of St Oswald, Chester, 1739–61. R. of Duddleston, Cheshire. V. of Trees, Salop. Preb. of Lichfield, 1741–96. Preb. of Chester, 1744–96. Preb. of York, 1750–96. Died 1796. Will (P.C.C.) 1797. (A. B. Beaven; J. Ch. Smith.)

JACKSON, RICHARD. Adm. Fell.-Com. at QUEENS', Apr. 16, 1739. Of Middlesex. S. of Richard, of London, merchant. Adm. at Lincoln's Inn, Mar. 15, 1738–9. Barrister, 1744. Adm. at the Inner Temple, 1751. Reader, 1779. King's Council. M.P. for Weymouth, 1762–8; for Romsey, 1768–84. Counsel to the South Sea Company, 1764–7. Counsel to Cambridge University, 1771–87. Died May 6, 1787. 'Omniscient Jackson.' (*D.N.B.*; A. B. Beaven.) According to *D.N.B.*, he was s. of Richard, of Dublin; adm. at Lincoln's Inn, 1740; whose name does not appear in their register.

JACKSON, RICHARD. Adm. pens. (age 19) at SIDNEY, June 28, 1744. Only s. of Richard, serge maker, deceased, of Exeter. B. in Holy Trinity, Exeter. School, Ottery St Mary (Mr Holmes). Matric. 1745; B.A. 1748–9.

JACKSON, ROBERT. Scholar and fellow of KING'S HALL, 1488–1520.

JACKSON, ROBERT. Matric. sizar from CLARE, Easter, 1559.

JACKSON or JACSOUN, ROBERT. Adm. sizar at EMMANUEL, June 20, 1592. Matric. 1592.

JACKSON, ROBERT. Matric. pe . from TRINITY, Easter, 1620; B.A. 1624; M.A. 1627. Incorp. M.A. at Balliol College, Oxford, 1627.

JACKSON, ROBERT. Matric. sizar from QUEENS', Easter, 1628. Of Lincolnshire. B.A. 1630–1; M.A. 1634. Perhaps ord. priest (Norwich) Sept. 24, 1637; C. of Wiggenhall St Peter.

JACKSON, ROBERT. Adm. pens. at QUEENS', Oct. 1, 1645. Of Yorkshire.

JACKSON, ROBERT. Adm. sizar (age 15) at CHRIST'S, Nov. 20, 1678. S. of Robert. B. at Coates Hall, Derbs. School, Wakefield (Mr Baskerville). Matric. 1678; B.A. 1682–3. Ord. deacon (York) Sept. 1684. Perhaps V. of Beighton, Derbs., 1690. R. of Adel, Yorks., 1702–30. Died there June 28, 1730. Father of Cyril (1736) and William (1733). (*Peile*, II. 70.)

JACKSON, ROBERT. Matric. sizar from CHRIST'S, Easter, 1707; B.A. 1710–1. Ord. deacon (York) Dec. 1712; priest, 1713. One of these names R. of Tatham, Lancs., 1726–33. Died 1733. (*Peile*, II. 166.)

JACKSON, ROBERT. Adm. pens. at CHRIST'S, July 1, 1723. School, Leeds (Mr Barnard).

JACKSON, ROBERT. Adm. sizar at CLARE, Oct. 5, 1723. B. at Coventry. Matric. 1723; B.A. 1727–8. One of these names P.C. of Radstone, Northants., 1766–8. Died 1768.

JACKSON, ROBERT. Adm. sizar (age 18) at ST JOHN'S, June 3, 1743. S. of Thomas, miller, of Yorkshire. B. at Pocklington. School, Sedbergh (Mr Broxholme). Matric. 1743; B.A. 1746–7; M.A. 1750. Ord. deacon (York) June 14, 1747; priest, Sept. 25, 1748; C. of Hayton, Yorks. Usher of Pocklington School, 1745–63. (*Scott-Mayor*, III. 536.)

JACKSON, *alias* OVERTON, ROGER. Adm. at KING'S, a scholar from Eton, 1469. Of Overton, Yorks. Age 17.

JACKSON, ROGER. B.A. 1513–4; M.A. 1517–8. Probably University preacher, 1522–3. V. of Poslingford, Suffolk, *c.* 1535–63.

JACKSON, ROGER. Matric. sizar from TRINITY, Easter, 1577 B.A. 1580–1. One of these names V. of Cretingham, Suffolk, 1603.

JACKSON, ROGER. Matric. sizar from CHRIST'S, June, 1584. Probably of East Bridgeford, Notts. B.A. 1587–8; M.A. 1591. V. of Colston Bassett, Notts., 1597–1650. Will (P.C.C.) 1652. (*Peile*, I. 179.)

JACKSON, ROGER. Matric. sizar from CHRIST'S, Dec. 1615. S. of Michael, of East Bridgeford, Notts. B.A. 1618–9; M.A. 1622. Usher at Repton School, 1623–8. V. of Sutton-on-the-Hill, Derbs., 1627. R. of Dalbury, 1650–2. V. of Langford, 1665. Died May 13, 1667. Father of John (1650), George (1663) and William (1653). (*Peile*, I. 307.)

JACKSON, ROGER. Adm. pens. at JESUS, Apr. 6, 1705. 2nd s. of George (1663), M.D., of Derbyshire. B. 1687 Matric. 1705; M.B. 1710. Of Ashbourne, Derbs. and Stradishall, Suffolk. Married, 1721, Frances, dau. of Colonel John Shallcross, of Derbyshire. Died 1743. Brother of George (1699). (Burke, *L.G.*; Foster, *Lancs. Pedigrees*.)

JACKSON, ROWLAND. Adm. Fell.-Com. (age 16) at CHRIST'S, July 9, 1649. S. of Sir John, of Edderthorpe, Yorks., Knt. B. at Hickleton, Yorks. School, Blackburn (Mr Clayton) Adm. at the Inner Temple, Feb. 10, 1648–9. Died unmarried, before 1665. (*Peile*, I. 530; *Vis. of Yorks.*, 1665.)

JACKSON, SAMUEL. Matric. pens. from PETERHOUSE, Easter, 1579; B.A. 1582–3; M.A. 1586. Ord. deacon (Peterb.) June 10, 1586. One of these names R. of Goxhill, Yorks., 1588–94. R. of Catwick, 1591–1602. Died 1602.

JACKSON, SAMUEL. Matric. pens. from TRINITY, Michs. 1613; B.A. 1616–7; M.A. 1620. Ord. deacon (York) June, 1620; priest, Dec. 1620. V. of Bardney, Lincs., 1624.

JACKSON, SAMUEL. Adm. pens. at EMMANUEL, July 3, 1622. Matric. 1623. One of these names matric. from Magdalen Hall, Oxford, Jan. 28, 1624–5, age 17. Of London. (*Al. Oxon.*)

JACKSON, SAMUEL. Adm. sizar (age 18) at CHRIST'S, July 1, 1674. S. of Charles. B. at Oxton, Notts. School, Oxton (Mr Birch).

JACKSON, SETH. Matric. Fell.-Com. from MAGDALENE, Easter, 1568.

JACKSON, SIMON. Matric. pens. from ST JOHN'S, Easter, 1613. B. in All Saints', Cambridge. B.A. 1616–7; M.A. 1620. Ord. priest (London) Dec. 19, 1619, age 24. V. of Lackford, Suffolk, 1630. Will (P.C.C.) 1649.

JACKSON, SIMON. Adm. sizar (age 20) at ST JOHN'S, June 27, 1684. S. of James (? 1649), clerk. B. at Manchester. School, Crosby (Mr John Waring).

JACKSON, SIMON. Adm. pens. (age 17) at ST JOHN'S, June 30, 1744. S. of Simon, merchant, of Cheshire. B. at Chester. School, Bury, Lancs. (Mr Lister). Matric. 1744; B.A. 1748–9; M.A. 1761. Ord. deacon (Lichfield) Sept. 24, 1752; priest, June 17, 1753. R. of Bebington, Cheshire, 1753–77. R. of Tarporley, 1787–1808. Died Apr. 15, 1808. (*Scott-Mayor*, III. 545; Burke, *L.G.*)

JACKSON, STEPHEN. Adm. pens. at EMMANUEL, July 26, 1598. Matric. 1598. One of these names, of Newcastle-on-Tyne, gent., adm. at Gray's Inn, June 15, 1601.

JACKSON, STEPHEN. Adm. pens. (age 17) at CHRIST'S, June 11, 1627. S. of Thomas, of Cowling, Yorks. Schools, Newcastle (Mr Fowbery, Mr Gray and Mr Wigham) and York (Mr Garthwaite). Matric. 1627. Adm. at Gray's Inn, June 9, 1629. (*Peile*, I. 385.)

JACKSON, THOMAS. B.A. 1539–40. Probably scholar of CHRIST'S, 1535–7.

JACKSON, THOMAS. Matric. sizar from ST JOHN'S, Michs. 1565.

JACKSON, THOMAS. Matric. sizar from PEMBROKE, Michs. 1566; B.A. 1571–2; M.A. 1575. Ord. deacon (Peterb.) July 26, 1575. One of these names (M.A.), V. of Norham, Durham, 1590–1612.

JACKSON, THOMAS. Matric. sizar from EMMANUEL, Michs. 1589. B. in Lancashire. Perhaps M.A. 1600 (*see Grace* for B.D.); B.D. 1608; D.D. 1615. C. of Wye, Kent, in 1596–c. 1614. R. of Boughton Aleph, 1611–4. Preb. of Canterbury, 1614–33. R. of Gt Chart, 1616–29. R. of St George's, Canterbury, 1622. R. of Milton, 1624. V. of Chilham, 1624. R. of Ivychurch, 1629. Author, sermons, etc. Buried in Canterbury Cathedral, Nov. 13, 1646. Will (P.C.C.) 1647. (*D.N.B.*)

JACKSON, THOMAS. Adm. pens. at EMMANUEL, Nov. 4, 1594. Matric. *c.* 1595.

JACKSON, THOMAS. Adm. sizar at QUEENS', Oct. 1610. Of Norfolk. Matric. 1612; B.A. 1614–5; M.A. 1618. Perhaps ord. priest (Norwich) 1616. V. of Calthorpe, Norfolk, 1618–. R. of Itteringham, 1619–74.

JACKSON, THOMAS. Matric. sizar from TRINITY, Easter, 1615; B.A. 1619–20. Ord. priest (Peterb.) Sept. 21, 1623.

JACKSON, THOMAS. Matric. sizar from KING'S, Easter, 1620.

JACKSON, THOMAS. Adm. sizar at QUEENS', Jan. 24, 1620–1. Of Cambridgeshire. Matric. 1621. Migrated to Peterhouse, Nov. 30, 1622. Scholar, 1623; B.A. 1624–5; M.A. 1628. Ord. deacon (York) Dec. 1626; priest, Dec. 1627.

JACKSON, THOMAS. Adm. pens. at EMMANUEL, Lent, 1625–6. Matric. 1626.

JACKSON, THOMAS. Matric. sizar from KING'S, Easter, 1626.

JACKSON, THOMAS. M.A. 1627 (Incorp. from Oxford). Of Kent; father D.D. (? Thomas, 1589). Matric. from St Alban's Hall, Oxford, Jan. 26, 1615–6, age 18; B.A. (Oxford) 1616; M.A. 1618–9. (*Al. Oxon.* assigns to him the Kentish preferment which probably belongs to his father, Thomas, of 1589.)

JACKSON, THOMAS. Matric. sizar from TRINITY, Easter, 1631. Doubtless 's. of William, of Leeds, Yorks.; matric. from Corpus Christi, Oxford, Aug. 28, 1634; aged 19; B.A. 1635; M.A. 1638; sometime of Cambs.' (*Al. Oxon.*)

JACKSON, THOMAS. Adm. pens. at JESUS, Nov. 25, 1644. Of Lincolnshire. Matric. 1645–6.

JACKSON, THOMAS. Adm. sizar at EMMANUEL, Feb. 24, 1652–3. Of Derby. Matric. 1653; B.A. 1656–7; M.A. 1660; B.D. 1667. Fellow, 1658. Junior proctor, 1665–6. R. of Aller, Somerset, 1667–1702. Died 1702.

JACKSON, THOMAS. Adm. sizar (age 16) at PETERHOUSE, July 8, 1654. Of Leicestershire. School, Leicester. Matric. 1655; Scholar, 1655. Perhaps R. of Swithland, Leics., 1662–1700. Died Nov. 6, 1700, aged 63. M.I. at Swithland. (*Nichols*, III. 1053.)

JACKSON, THOMAS. Adm. sizar (age 18) at ST JOHN'S, July 3, 1667. S. of John, deceased. B. at Carlisle. School, Sedbergh (Mr Fell). Matric. 1667; B.A. 1670–1. Perhaps V. of Chaldon, Surrey, 1684. Died 1726.

JACKSON, THOMAS. Adm. pens. (age 16) at CHRIST'S, Mar. 4, 1672–3. S. of Thomas. B. at Leeds. School, Leeds (Mr Gilbert). Matric. 1672–3; B.A. 1676–7. Ord. deacon (London) Feb. 1677–8. One of these names V. of Albury, Herts., 1693–1724. Admon. (P.C.C.) Jan. 15, 1723–4. (*Peile*, II. 46.)

JACKSON, THOMAS. Adm. sizar at CHRIST'S, July 10, 1690. Matric. 1690; B.A. 1693–4.

JACKSON, THOMAS. Adm. sizar (age 16) at PEMBROKE, May 1, 1693. S. of William (1668), R. of Beetham, Westmorland. Bapt. there, Oct. 6, 1675. Matric. 1693; B.A. 1696–7. V. and schoolmaster of Over Kellet, Lancs., in 1698–9 (*parish reg.*). R. of Newbiggin, Westmorland, 1698–1730. Buried there Dec. 1730. (*B. Nightingale*; E. Axon.)

JACKSON, THOMAS. Adm. pens. (age 18) at PETERHOUSE, Apr. 3, 1697. Of Lancashire. School, Warton, Lancs.

JACKSON, THOMAS. Adm. pens. (age 18) at TRINITY, Apr. 25, 1701. S. of Charles, of London. School, St Paul's. Matric. 1701; Scholar, 1702; B.A. 1704–5; M.A. 1708. Ord. deacon (Chichester) Dec. 21, 1707; priest (London) Feb. 29, 1707–8. R. of Rushton All Saints', and St Peter's, Northants., 1725–55. Died Jan. 21, 1755–6, aged 73. Admon. (P.C.C.) 1756. (H. I. Longden; T. P. Dorman.)

JACKSON, THOMAS. Adm. sizar (age 20) at ST JOHN'S, May 19, 1716. S. of Richard, husbandman, of Yorkshire. B. at Austwick. School, Sedbergh (Mr Saunders). Matric. 1716; B.A. 1719–20. Ord. deacon (London) Mar. 13, 1719–20; priest (Norwich) Mar. 1723–4. (Not the R. of Green's Norton, Northants., as suggested in Sedbergh register.)

JACKSON, THOMAS. Adm. sizar (age 18) at ST JOHN'S, May 17, 1717. S. of Thomas, steward, of Lancashire. B. at Burnley. School, Burnley (Mr Ro. Shaw). Matric. 1717; B.A. 1720–1; M.A. 1744. Ord. deacon (York) June 4, 1721; priest, Sept. 15, 1726. V. of Waghen, Holderness, Yorks., 1726–40. R. of Kirkby Underdale, 1740–55. V. of Preston and Hedon, 1744–55. Died 1755. Perhaps father of Thomas (1746–7). (*Scott-Mayor*, III. 311.)

JACKSON, THOMAS. Adm. sizar (age 22) at CHRIST'S, June 12, 1725. S. of Adam. B. at Giggleswick. School, Giggleswick (Mr Carr). Resided, till 1728. Ord. deacon (York) June 9, 1727, as 'literate'; C. of Kirkley; priest, July, 1731. Master of Drax School, near Selby, July 12, 1728. Perhaps V. of Drax, in 1745. *Peile* (II. 210) is probably wrong in assigning Preston to him, which most likely belongs to Thomas, above.

JACKSON, THOMAS. M.A. from KING'S, 1730. Perhaps s. of Lancelot, of Bampton, Westmorland. Matric. (Queen's College, Oxford) Nov. 19, 1722, age 23; B.A. (Oxford) 1726. (*Al. Oxon.*)

JACKSON, THOMAS. Adm. sizar (age 19) at ST JOHN'S, Jan. 26, 1746–7. S. of Thomas (? 1717), clerk, of Yorkshire. B. at Hedon. School, Beverley. Matric. 1747; B.A. 1750–1. Ord. deacon (Hereford) Mar. 4, 1750–1; priest (York) May 24, 1752. Perhaps V. of Skeckling and Burstwick, Yorks., 1758–84. Died at Burstwick, 1784. (*Scott-Mayor*, III. 564.)

JACKSON, TIMOTHY. Adm. sizar at SIDNEY, Mar. 22, 1607–8. Doubtless s. of John (1570), R. of Melsonby, Yorks. Migrated to Christ's. B.A. 1611–2; M.A. 1615. Ord. deacon (York) Feb. 28, 1612–3; C. of Hackness, Yorks.; priest, Dec. 19, 1613. V. of Wragby, Yorks., 1622–5. V. of Holy Trinity, King's Square, York, 1631–5. Buried at Arksey, Yorks., Feb. 2, 1635–6. Father of John (1639), brother of Nathaniel (1616) and John (1613). (*Yorks. Arch. Journal*, VI. 189; M. H. Peacock.)

JACKSON, VALENTINE. Matric. sizar from QUEENS', Easter, 1621. Of Warwickshire. B.A. 1625–6. Ord. deacon (Peterb.) Sept. 19; priest, Sept. 20, 1629. Licensed (Peterborough, May 24, 1636) to marry Joan Fletcher, both of King's Cliffe, Northants. (H. I. Longden.)

JACKSON, VAYN. Matric. pens. from ST JOHN'S, Easter, 1567.

JACSON, WALTER. Matric. sizar from TRINITY, Michs. 1582.

JACKSON, WILLIAM. B.Civ.L. 1509–10.

JACKSON, WILLIAM. B.A. 1530–1; M.A. 1533. Fellow of St John's, 1532. Of Coventry and Lichfield diocese.

JAXON, WILLIAM. Matric. sizar from Pembroke, Easter, 1548.

JACKSON, WILLIAM. Matric. pens. from Trinity, Lent, 1564–5; Scholar, 1567; B.A. 1567–8. One of these names R. of Fordley, Suffolk, 1568–77.

JACKSON, WILLIAM. Matric. pens. from St John's, Easter, 1567; B.A. 1570–1.

JACSON, WILLIAM. Matric. sizar from Trinity, Michs. 1573; Scholar, 1578; B.A. 1578–9; M.A. 1582. One of these names R. of East Keal, Lincs., 1596–1612. Will (Lincoln) 1612.

JACKSON, WILLIAM. Matric. sizar from Trinity, Michs. 1602; B.A. 1606–7; M.A. from Emmanuel, 1610. Ord. deacon (London) c. 1613; priest, June 4, 1615, age 28; 'M.A.; late of Emmanuel, tutor in house of Sir William Twysden, Bart. B. in Lincoln.' Perhaps R. of North Ockendon, Essex, 1619. One of these names V. of Gt Bowden, Leics., 1641.

JACKSON, WILLIAM. Matric. pens. from Pembroke, Michs. 1609. Perhaps the man of these names, ord. deacon (Peterb.) June 19, 1614, as 'literate'; priest, Sept. 25, 1614; 'of Emmanuel College.' Another was ord. deacon (London) June 10, 1609; 'aged 24; b. at Warwick; late of Emmanuel College'; priest, Feb. 17, 1610–1; C. of Bletchingley, Surrey. (Neither of these found in Emmanuel register.)

JACKSON, WILLIAM. Adm. pens. at Christ's, Mar. 14, 1624–5. S. of William, of Kent. School, 'Ouburn.' Matric. 1625; B.A. 1628–9. One of these names R. of North Ockendon, Essex, 1629. (*Peile*, I. 365; but *see* William, 1602.)

JACKSON, WILLIAM. Adm. sizar at Jesus, May 12, 1638. Of Nottinghamshire. S. of William. B. at East Bridgford, Notts. School, Newark. Matric. 1638. Migrated to Christ's, Sept. 21, 1639, age 18. B.A. 1641–2; M.A. 1645. R. of Screveton, Notts., 1652. V. of Oxton, in 1658; burnt out there. Married Dorothy Thoroton, aunt of Robert, the historian. Died Feb. 27, 1661. (A. Gray; Foster, *Lancs. Pedigrees*.)

JACKSON, WILLIAM. Adm. sizar (age 16) at St John's, Feb. 13, 1644–5. S. of Richard (1619), R. of Whittington, Lancs. B. at Kirkby Lonsdale, Westmorland. Schools, Sedbergh (Mr Nelson) and Kirkby Lonsdale (Mr Tatham). B.A. 1648–9. Adm. at Gray's Inn, Nov. 6, 1647. Of Coleraine, Londonderry, Esq. Died July 24, 1688. Buried at Coleraine. For funeral certificate *see Genealogist*, N.S., XXXV. 110. Father of William (1688). Presumably brother of Francis (1649) and Leonard (1668) though these are not mentioned in the certificate.

JACKSON, WILLIAM. Adm. pens. (age 16) at Magdalene, May 27, 1647. S. of John, of Barlings, Lincs. School, Kirton. Matric. 1647; B.A. 1650–1.

JACKSON, WILLIAM. Adm. sizar (age 16) at St John's, Apr. 13, 1653. S. of Roger (1615), V. of Sutton, Derbs. B. there. School, Uppingham (Mr Meres). Matric. 1653; B.A. 1656–7; M.A. 1660; B.D. from Jesus, 1668; D.D. 1673. Fellow of Jesus, 1661–73. Ord. deacon (Ely) June; priest, Sept. 1672. R. of St George, Botolph Lane, Sept. 1, 1666 (church burnt next day in the Great Fire). Chaplain to Archbishop Sterne. V. of Swaffham Bulbeck, Cambs., 1671. Preb. of York, 1671–80. R. of Abington-by-Shingay, Cambs., 1673–80. R. of Bedford parish Church. R. of Chelmsford, 1675–80. Died 1680. Brother of John (1650) and George (1663). (A. Gray.)

JACKSON, WILLIAM. Adm. sizar (age 17) at Sidney, June 20, 1661. S. of John, farmer. B. at Bridgford, Notts. School, Melton Mowbray (Mr Pare). Matric. 1661; B.A. 1664–5; M.A. 1668. Incorp. at Oxford, 1669. Signed for deacon's orders (London) Sept. 19, 1668; priest, June 5, 1669. Chaplain to Sir Roland Lytton, in Herts.

JACKSON, WILLIAM. Adm. sizar (age 20) at Pembroke, Apr. 14, 1668. S. of John, farmer. B. at Bootle, Cumberland. Matric. 1668; B.A. 1671–2. Perhaps ord. deacon (Chester) Sept. 22, 1672; priest, Sept. 21, 1673. Schoolmaster at Beetham, Westmorland, 1673. V. of Beetham, 1683–1709. Buried there Sept. 14, 1709. Will (Archd. Westmorland) 1709. Father of Thomas (1693). (*B. Nightingale*.)

JACKSON, WILLIAM. Adm. pens. (age 18) at Trinity, July 1, 1677. S. of William. B. at Nantwich, Cheshire. School, Westminster. Scholar, 1678; Matric. 1680; B.A. 1680–1. Perhaps of Sandbach, Cheshire. Clerk of the Peace. Buried there June 22, 1713.

JACKSON, WILLIAM. Adm. pens. (age 18) at St John's, May 23, 1688. S. of William, Esq. (1644–5). B. in Ireland. School, Kilkenny. Adm. at Gray's Inn, Nov. 11, 1687; 's. and h. of William, of Coleraine.'

JACKSON, WILLIAM. Adm. sizar (age 18) at Pembroke, July 6, 1715. S. of William, sculptor. B. at St Martin-in-the-Fields, Middlesex. Matric. 1716; B.A. 1719–20. Ord. deacon (Ely) Dec. 22, 1728. One of these names V. of Addington, Surrey, 1730–54. Admon. (P.C.C.) 1754; died at All Hallows, Barking.

JACKSON, WILLIAM. Adm. pens. at Magdalene, June 22, 1733, from University College, Oxford. S. of Robert (1678), clerk. B. at Adel, Yorks. Matric. (Oxford) May 3, 1732, age 18; B.A. (Cambridge) 1735–6. Ord. deacon (Lincoln) Mar. 21, 1735–6. R. of Adel, Yorks., 1737–66. Died at Bath, Feb. 17, 1766, aged 52. Buried at Weston, near Bath. M.I. at Adel. Brother of Cyril (1736).

JACKSON, WILLIAM. Adm. sizar (age 19) at St John's, June 19, 1740. S. of Lancelot, deceased, of Westmorland. B. at Brampton Grange, Westmorland. School, Lowther (Mr Wilkinson). Matric. 1740; B.A. 1743–4; M.A. 1747. Ord. deacon (Peterb.) May 15, 1744. C. of Green's Norton, Northants.

JACKSON, WILLIAM. Adm. pens. at St John's, June 18, 1750. S. of Thomas, merchant, of America. B. at Irish Town. School, Hoddesden, Herts.

JAXON, ——. Matric. Fell.-Com. from Jesus, Michs. 1544; 'M.A. of Oxford.' Perhaps William, B.A. (Oxford) 1530; M.A. 1535.

JACKSON, ——. M.A. 1475–6. Incorporated.

JACKSON, ——. B.Can.L. 1477–8.

JACKSON, ——. D.Civ.L. Incorp. 1500.

JACKSON, ——. D.Can.L. Excused from congregations, etc. as commissary, 1501–2.

JACKSON, ——. B.A. 1507.

JACKSON, ——. Adm. at Corpus Christi, 1550.

JACKSON, ——. Adm. Fell.-Com. at Trinity Hall, Dec. 11, 1696. (Name off, Aug. 1697.)

JACOB, *see also* JACOMB.

JACOB or JACOMBE, ABRAHAM. Adm. Fell.-Com. at Trinity, Aug. 10, 1646. Matric. 1646, as Jacombe. Knighted, June 17, 1683. Governor of Walmer Castle. Father of Herbert (1691).

JACOB, FRANCIS. Matric. sizar from King's, Michs. 1612; B.A. from Jesus, 1615–6; M.A. 1619. R. of Dallinghoe, Suffolk, 1618–47, sequestered. Father of the next.

JACOB, FRANCIS. Adm. sizar (age 16) at St John's, Mar. 30, 1638. S. of Francis (above), R. of Dallinghoe, Suffolk. B. there. School, Ipswich (Mr Holt). B.A. 1641–2; M.A. 1647. Ord. deacon and priest (Lincoln) Sept. 20, 1646. Perhaps preb. of Gloucester, 1662–5.

JACOB, GEORGE. Matric. sizar from Clare, Easter, 1629; B.A. 1632–3; M.A. 1636.

JACOB, GISBRIGHT. Matric. sizar from Trinity, Michs. 1568; Scholar, 1571; B.A. 1571–2; M.A. 1575. Fellow of Clare. Senior proctor, 1591–2. Will proved (V.C.C.) 1597 and (P.C.C.) 1598.

JACOB, HENRY. Adm. Fell.-Com. at Trinity, Aug. 10, 1646.

JACOB, HERBERT. Adm. pens. (age 17) at St John's, May 21, 1691. S. of Sir Abraham (1646), Knt., Governor of Walmer Castle. B. in London. School, Eton. Matric. 1691. Adm. at the Inner Temple, June 3, 1692. (Le Neve, *Knights*, 379.)

JACOB, JAMES. D.D. 1475–6. Of St Catharine's.

JACOB, JOHN. Matric. sizar from Jesus, Easter, 1588; B.A. 1590–1; M.A. 1595; B.D. 1602–3. Doubtless ord. priest (Norwich) Apr. 18, 1594; V. of Wangford, Suffolk, 1593.

JACOB, JOHN. Matric. sizar from Jesus, Easter, 1614.

JACOB, JOHN. Adm. pens. (age 16) at Peterhouse, Dec. 20, 1636. Possibly s. of William, of Mendham, Suffolk. School, Netfield, Suffolk. Matric. 1639. One of these names R. of Greenstead, Colchester, 1650. Perhaps brother of William (1637).

JACOB, JOHN. Adm. pens. at Trinity, Dec. 2, 1651. Of Middlesex. Probably 3rd s. of Sir John, of Bromley, Middlesex. Matric. 1651. Adm. at the Middle Temple, Jan. 20, 1654–5.

JACOB, Sir JOHN, Bart. LL.D. 1705 (*Com. Reg.*). S. of Sir John, 2nd Bart. B. c. 1665. Colonel in the army. Fought at the Boyne, etc. Succeeded as 3rd Bart., 1674. Married Lady Dorothy Barry, dau. of Richard, Earl of Barrymore. Died Mar. 31, 1740. (Burke, *Ext. Bart.*; *G.E.C.*)

JACOB, JOHN. Adm. at King's, a scholar from Eton, 1740. S. of John, V. of Fordington, Dorset. Matric. 1741; B.A. 1744–5; M.A. 1748; M.D. 1758. Fellow, 1744. Practised physic at Salisbury. Died May 2, 1789. Will (P.C.C.) as of New Sarum.

JACOB, NICHOLAS. Adm. sizar at Emmanuel, July 4, 1640. Of Suffolk. Matric. 1640. Nicholas Bradlaw (*alias* Jacob) s. and h. of Nicholas, of Laxfield, Suffolk, gent., deceased; adm. at Gray's Inn, Nov. 7, 1644. Called to the Bar, 1651. Ancient, 1667. Donor to the College Chapel, 1667.

JACOB, PHILIP. Adm. sizar at EMMANUEL, June 5, 1602. Matric. 1602; Scholar; B.A. 1605-6; M.A. 1609; B.D. 1616. Ord. deacon and priest (Norwich) May 22, 1608. V. of Little Fakenham, Suffolk, 1608-10. R. of Caldecote, Hunts., 1610-2. R. of Lower Rickinghall, Suffolk, 1615. Member of the Presbyterian *Classis*, 1645.

JACOBE, ROBERT. Matric. pens. from JESUS, Michs. 1559. One of these names, of London, adm. at the Inner Temple, 1564.

JACOB, ROBERT. Matric. sizar from TRINITY, Michs. 1565. Of London. Scholar, 1568; B.A. 1569-70; M.A. 1573; M.D. 1579. Fellow, 1571. Incorp. from Basel, where he was admitted, 1576. Member of the College of Physicians, 1586. Physician to Queen Elizabeth, who recommended him to the Court in Russia, 1581. Returned to England, 1584. Went out to Russia again, 1586. Died 1588. (*Cooper*, II. 76; *Munk*, I. 88; *D.N.B.*)

JACOB, THOMAS. Adm. pens. at QUEENS', June 24, 1602. Of Suffolk.

JACOB, THOMAS. Adm. at CORPUS CHRISTI, 1678. Of Cambridgeshire. Adm. at Gray's Inn, Nov. 29, 1680; s. and h. of Nicholas, 'of Canterbury' (? Camb.).

JACOB, THOMAS. Adm. at CORPUS CHRISTI, 1699. Of Suffolk. Matric. 1699-1700.

JACOBBE, WILLIAM. Matric. sizar from TRINITY, Michs. 1571; B.A. 1575-6; M.A. from Jesus, 1583.

JACOB, WILLIAM. Adm. pens. (age 15) at PEMBROKE, Mar. 6, 1637-8. S. of William. B. at Mendham, Suffolk. Matric. 1638.

JACOB or JACOME, WILLIAM. Adm. pens. at TRINITY, May 16, 1648, as Jacomb. Of Kent. Matric. 1648, as Jacob; B.A. 1651; M.A. 1655. Perhaps R. of Little Dunham, Norfolk. One of these names V. of Sarre, Kent, *c.* 1653-62, ejected. (For a contemporary *see Al. Oxon.*)

JACOB, ——. B.Can.L. 1485-6.

JACOB or JAKOK, ——. B.A. 1498.

JACOB, ——. Scholar of QUEENS', 1534-9.

JACOBYN, ——. D.D. 1489-90. Dominican friar.

JACOCKS, EDMUND. Adm. pens. at JESUS, Sept. 14, 1637. Of Warwickshire. Matric. as 'Leonard Jaycocke,' 1637.

JACOMB, *see also* JACOB.

JACOMB, GEORGE. M.A. 1728 (*Com. Reg.*). V. of Houghton, Norfolk, 1724-31. R. of Syderstone, 1724-59. R. of Pensthorpe, 1727-31. R. of Stanhow, 1731-59. Died Aug. 8, 1759, aged 75.

JACOMBE, SAMUEL. Matric. sizar from QUEENS', Easter, 1644. Of Leicestershire. B.A. 1647-8; M.A. 1651; B.D. 1658. Fellow, 1649-57. V. of St Mary Woolnoth, London, 1655-9. Died June 12, 1659. Buried at St Mary Woolnoth. Will, P.C.C. Brother of the next. (*D.N.B.*)

JACOMBE, THOMAS. Matric. sizar from ST JOHN'S, Michs. 1642 (already matric. at Magdalen Hall, Oxford, May 20, 1640, age 16). S. of John, of Burton Lazars, Leics., *pleb.* School, Melton Mowbray (Mr Edw. Gamble). B.A. 1643-4; M.A. from Trinity, 1647; D.D. 1661 (*Lit. Reg.*). Fellow of Trinity, 1645. R. of St Martin's, Ludgate, 1647-62, ejected. Chaplain to the Countess of Exeter. Took a leading part on the Presbyterian side in drawing up the exceptions against the Prayer Book. Married a dau. of John Gurdon, of Assington, Suffolk. Author, *Sermons*, etc. Died Mar. 27, 1687. Buried at St Anne's, Aldersgate. Will, P.C.C. Brother of the above. (*Al. Oxon.*; *Calamy*, I. 160; *D.N.B.*)

JACYE or JESSEY, HENRY. Matric. pens. from ST JOHN'S, Easter, 1619. Of Yorkshire. Scholar; B.A. 1622-3; M.A. 1626. *Supp.* for incorporation at Oxford, 1627; 'A preacher's son. B. at West Rowton, Yorks., Sept. 3, 1601.' Minister at Aughton, Yorks., 1633; ejected, 1634. Independent pastor at St George, Southwark, 1645-6. Died Sept. 4, 1663. Buried in Bunhill Fields. (*D.N.B.*; *Calamy*, I. 108.)

JAGGARD, JOHN. Adm. at CORPUS CHRISTI, 1677. Of Essex. Matric. 1679, as 'Jeggard'; B.A. 1681-2; M.A. 1685; B.D. 1693. Fellow, 1684-98. Taxor, 1687-8. R. of St Andrew's, Cambridge, 1689. C. of St Nicholas Chapel, Lynn. Died Nov. 11, 1702. (*Masters*.)

JAGARDE, JOHN. 'Of TRINITY College.' Mentioned in the will of John Jaggard, gent., of Edwardeston, Suffolk, proved Dec. 1699.

JAGARDE, THOMAS. Matric. sizar from CHRIST'S, Nov. 1551, *impubes*. William Masterson, R. of Horseheath, Cambs., leaves him 'such small bookes as be inew for his learnying,' 1556. (C. E. Parsons, *Horseheath*.)

JAGGARD, THOMAS. Adm. pens. at EMMANUEL, Easter, 1625. S. of William, the printer and publisher of the first edition of Shakespeare. Matric. from St Catharine's, 1628; B.A. 1628-9; M.A. 1632. Ord. priest (Lincoln) 1632. R. of Kirkby Overblow, Yorks., 1639-47, 'M.A.' (W. Jaggard.)

JAGGARD, THOMAS. Matric. pens. from QUEENS', Easter, 1656. Of Essex. S. and h. of Humphrey, of Gt Parndon. Articled as pupil to his father. Adm. at the Middle Temple, Nov. 19, 1657. Will proved, Sept. 5, 1697, as of the Middle Temple. (W. Jaggard.)

JAGGARD, THOMAS. Adm. pens. (age 15) at ST JOHN'S, Jan. 17, 1682-3. S. of Abraham, merchant, Warden of the Grocers' Company. B. in London. School (private; Dr Goade). Matric. 1683; B.A. 1686-7. Adm. at the Inner Temple, May 31, 1690. The father was a friend of Samuel Pepys; *see* references in the *Diary*. (W. Jaggard.)

JAGGER, (?) FRANCIS. Matric. pens. from ST CATHARINE'S, *c.* 1597.

JAGLETT, WILLIAM. Matric. pens. from ST JOHN'S, Easter, 1622.

JAGO, ROBERT. Adm. pens. (age 18) at PEMBROKE, May 22, 1677. S. of Robert, V. of Wendron and Helston, Cornwall. B. at Wendron. Matric. 1677; B.A. 1680-1.

JAGOE, STEPHEN. Adm. pens. (age 18) at TRINITY, Oct. 30, 1680. S. of Stephen. B. at Gerrans, Cornwall. School, Plymouth (Mr John Bedford). Matric. 1680.

JAGO, THOMAS. Adm. pens. at EMMANUEL, Oct. 24, 1632. Of Cornwall. Matric. 1632.

JAGOE, WILLIAM. Adm. sizar at QUEENS', June 9, 1692. Of Cornwall. Matric. 1693; B.A. 1695-6.

JAKE, ANTHONY. Matric. sizar from CHRIST'S, June, 1575. Perhaps V. of Warcop, Westmorland, 1597-1625, as Jacques. (*Peile*, I. 132.)

JAKE or JACKE, WILLIAM. Adm. sizar at CLARE, Oct. 21, 1668. Matric. 1669; B.A. 1673.

JAKYS, ——. B.Can.L. 1455-6. Possibly William, Chaplain of Holy Trinity, Ely, 1463; and V. of Sutton, Isle of Ely, 1469-70.

JALLAND or JOLLAND, WILLIAM. Adm. sizar at CORPUS CHRISTI, 1686. Of Nottinghamshire. Matric. 1687; B.A. 1690-1, as Jalland. Ord. deacon (York) Sept. 1693; priest (London) Mar. 4, 1693-4.

JAMES, ABRAHAM. Adm. sizar at EMMANUEL, May 18, 1647. Matric. 1647.

JAMES, ABRAHAM. Adm. sizar at MAGDALENE, June 19, 1656. S. of James, of Suffolk. Matric. 1658; B.A. 1659-60.

JAMES, ALEXANDER. Adm. sizar at CLARE, Nov. 4, 1742. B. at Rochester. Matric. 1742; B.A. 1746-7; M.A. from Christ's, 1750. Fellow of Christ's, 1749-75. V. of Fen Drayton, Cambs., 1763-72. V. of St Margaret-at-Cliffe, Kent, 1773; also P.C. of Buckland. R. of Little Canfield, Essex, 1774. Died 1813. Will, P.C.C. (*Peile*, II. 245.)

JAMES (afterwards KECK), ANTHONY. Adm. pens. (age 19) at ST JOHN'S, Feb. 18, 1730-1. S. of David (next), clerk, of Middlesex, R. of Woughton, Bucks. School, Eton. Matric. 1731. Adm. at Lincoln's Inn, July 6, 1731. Barrister, 1736. Bencher, 1754, as 'Keck.' Serjeant-at-law, 1759. Died at Theobalds, Herts., Mar. 3, 1786, aged 75. Buried at Cheshunt. Brother of Thomas (1733). *Scott-Mayor* (III. 432) identifies him with the M.P. for Woodstock, who died in 1767.

JAMES, DAVID. Adm. pens. at QUEENS', June 23, 1687. Of Wiltshire. Matric. 1688; B.A. 1690-1; M.A. 1694. Doubtless R. of Woughton, Bucks., 1713-45. Died 1745. Will (P.C.C.) 1747. Father of Thomas (1733) and the above.

JEAMES, EDMUND. Adm. sizar at PETERHOUSE, Lent, 1590-1. Matric. 1591; B.A. 1594-5. Ord. deacon (Peterb.) June 4; priest, Sept. 24, 1615. Doubtless Master of Wellingborough School, Northants., 1604-14. V. of Duston, 1617-41, sequestered. Married, at Harpole, Northants., Feb. 2, 1641-2, Elizabeth Langley. (H. I. Longden.)

JAMES, EDMUND. Adm. sizar (age 18) at TRINITY, June 22, 1687. S. of Edmund, of Little Houghton, Northants. School, Northampton (Mr Style). Matric. 1687; B.A. 1691-2. Ord. priest (Ely) 1695. V. of Shudy Camps, Cambs., 1696. (*Trin. Coll. Adm. errata*.)

JAMES, EDWARD. Adm. at KING'S, a scholar from Eton, 1677. B. at Witley, Worcs. Matric. 1679; B.A. 1682-3. Fellow. Died in London, of small-pox.

JAMES, EDWARD. Adm. sizar (age 18) at MAGDALENE, Oct. 10, 1714. S. of Thomas, farmer. B. at Reavsby, Lincs. School, Boston. Matric. 1715; B.A. 1718-9. Ord. deacon (Lincoln) May 24, 1719; priest, June 12, 1720.

JAMES, FRANCIS. LL.B. 1584 (Incorp. from Oxford). S. of John, of Little Ore. Staffs. B. 1559. Matric. (Oxford) Nov. 28, 1581, age 22; B.C.L. 1583; D.C.L. 1588. Fellow of All Souls, 1577. Admitted advocate, Oct. 26, 1590. M.P. for Dorchester, 1593; for Shaftesbury and Corfe Castle, 1597; for Minehead, 1601; for Wareham, 1604–11. Adm. at Gray's Inn, Aug. 10, 1606. Master in Chancery, 1614. Chancellor of Bath and Wells, and of London. Judge of the Court of Audience of Canterbury. Married Blanche, dau. of —— Gunter, and widow of Sir William Billingley, of London, Knt. Died 1616. Will, P.C.C. (*Al. Oxon.*; *Vis. of Durham*, 1615; H. M. Wood.)

JAMES, FRANCIS. Matric. from TRINITY HALL, Dec. 1719. S. of Sir Cane, Bart., of Bury. Scholar, 1720; LL.B. 1724; LL.D. 1729. Fellow, 1728–34. Adm. at Lincoln's Inn, Nov. 26, 1722. Ord. deacon (Norwich) Dec. 23; priest, Dec. 28, 1733. R. of Swannington, Norfolk, 1733–9. V. of Wood Dalling, 1733–9. Died *s.p.* (Burke, *Ext. Bart.*; *G.E.C.*)

JAMES, GEORGE. Adm. pens. at CLARE, Mar. 19, 1634–5. Matric. Fell.-Com. 1635.

JAMES, GILES. Adm. pens. at EMMANUEL, Easter, 1611. B. at Bickley, Sussex. Matric. 1611; Scholar; B.A. 1614–5; M.A. 1618. Ord. deacon (London) Dec. 2; priest, Dec. 22, 1616, age 27. Perhaps of Sherston *with* Pinkney, Wilts.; s. of Simon.

JAMES, HENRY. *Cautio* for degree, 1488.

JAMES, HENRY. Matric. sizar from ST JOHN'S, Michs. 1619.

JAMES or JEAMES, HENRY. Adm. pens. (age 16) at PEMBROKE, Oct. 3, 1620. S. of John, of Ightham, Kent. Matric. 1620. Adm. at the Middle Temple, June 18, 1624. (Pedigree of James, of Ightam in *Sussex Vis.*, 1663.)

JAMES, HENRY. M.A. 1626 (Incorp. from Oxford). Of Bristol, Esq. Matric. from Trinity College, Oxford, Apr. 30, 1619, age 17; B.A. (Oxford) 1622; M.A. (Hart Hall) 1625. R. of Machen, Moum., 1626 (another of the same names, M.A., Oxford, 1620) chaplain to the Bishop of Bristol. V. of Kingston-by-Taunton, Somerset, 1636. V. of Crowcombe, 1662–72. Died 1672. Father of the next. (*Al. Oxon.*)

JAMES, HENRY. Adm. pens. at MAGDALENE, 1660. S. of Henry (above), R. of Kingston, Somerset. School, Eton. Migrated to Queens', Aug. 24, 1661. Matric. 1661; B.A. 1663–4; M.A. 1667; B.D. 1675; D.D. 1679 (*Lit. Reg.*). Fellow of Queens', 1664. Taxor, 1673–4. Elected President of Queens', July 29, 1675. Vice-Chancellor, 1683–4, 1696–9. Regius Professor of Divinity, 1699–1717. Incorp. at Oxford, 1671. Ord. deacon (Peterb.) Sept. 22, 1667; priest, Sept. 20, 1668. R. of St Botolph, Cambridge, 1671. Chaplain to the King. Preb. of York, 1687–1717; and R. of Somersham, Hunts. Preb. of Canterbury, 1705–17. Died Mar. 12, 1716–7.

JAMES, HUGH. Adm. pens. (age 17) at TRINITY, June 26, 1691. S. of Samuel. B. at Carlisle. School, Westminster. Matric. 1691; Scholar, 1692; B.A. 1694–5; M.A. 1698. Fellow of Pembroke, 1699. Ord. deacon (Lincoln) June 19, 1698. Chaplain of Trinity, 1698–1700. R. of Upwell and Outwell Cambs., 1702–40. Died 1740.

JAMES, HUMPHREY. Matric. sizar from TRINITY, Lent, 1594–5. B. at Bramlye, Salop. Ord. deacon (London) Nov. 11, 1597, age 25. C. of Bepton, Sussex. Will (Chichester) 1601; as R. of Bepton.

JAMES, JOHN. Matric. pens. from ST JOHN'S, Michs. 1559.

JAMES, JOHN. Matric. sizar from TRINITY, Michs. 1564. Of Hampshire. Scholar, 1565; B.A. 1567–8; M.A. 1571; M.L. 1575; M.D. 1578. Fellow, 1569. M.D. (Leyden). F.R.C.P. 1584. M.P. for St Ives, Cornwall, 1584–6; and for Newcastle-under-Lyne, 1592–3. Physician to the Queen's household, 1595. Died *c.* Jan. 26, 1600–1. (*Cooper*, II. 178; *Munk*, I. 87.)

JAMES, JOHN. Matric. sizar from TRINITY, Michs. 1570. B. 1554. Scholar, 1575; B.A. 1575–6; M.A. 1579; B.D. 1586. Incorp. at Oxford, 1584. Ord. deacon (London) June 10, 1584; priest (Lichfield) June 15, 1584. University preacher, 1585. R. of Skirbeck, Lincs., 1607–12. Will (Lincoln) 1612. Father of Thomas (1611).

JEAMES, JOHN. Matric. pens. (age 12) from MAGDALENE, Easter, 1585.

JAMES, JOHN. Matric. sizar from TRINITY, *c.* 1591; B.A. 1592–3.

JAMES, JOHN. B.A. from CHRIST'S, 1609–10; M.A. 1615. One of these names R. of Tugford, Salop, Aug. 1617. V. of Cardington, Salop, 1633. (*Peile*, I. 261.)

JAMES, JOHN. Adm. pens. (age 18) at PEMBROKE, Mar. 2, 1624–5. S. of William. B. at Kingham, Oxon. Matric. 1625; B.A. 1628. One of these names, s. and h. of William, of Latham, Suffolk, adm. at Gray's Inn, May 8, 1629.

JAMES, JOHN. M.A. 1654 (Incorp. from Oxford). Perhaps s. of Simon, of Woodstock, Oxon. (Matric. from Exeter College, July 24, 1642, age 15, but no Oxford degree recorded.) Nonconformist V. of Flintham, Notts., till 1662. (*Calamy*, III. 97.)

JAMES, JOHN. Adm. sizar at ST CATHARINE'S, June 25, 1694. Matric. 1695; B.A. 1699–1700; M.A. 1705. Ord. deacon (Norwich) Sept. 1701; priest, Sept. 1702. V. of Ubbeston, Suffolk, 1705.

JAMES, JOHN. D.D. 1698 (Incorp. from Oxford). S. of John, of London. Matric. (Christ Church, Oxford) July 12, 1667, age 17; B.A. 1671; M.A. 1674; B.D. 1684; D.D. 1689. Preb. of Exeter, 1689–1703. Chancellor of Exeter, 1689–1703. R. of Southill, Cornwall, 1689. V. of Harberton, Devon, 1691. Died Jan. 28, 1702–3. Will (Exeter) 1703. (*Al. Oxon.*)

JAMES, JOHN. Adm. pens. at CLARE, May 13, 1721. B. in London, Jan. 12, 1702–3. School, Merchant Taylors'. Matric. 1721; B.A. 1724–5; M.A. 1728. Ord. deacon (Peterb.) Oct. 24, 1727, age 24; C. of Polebrooke, Northants.; priest (Lincoln) Dec. 21, 1729. R. of Prenze, Norfolk, 1734.

JAMES, JOHN. M.A. from CHRIST'S, 1750. S. of John, of Rochester. Matric. from Oriel College, Oxford, Mar. 3, 1734–5, age 17; B.A. (Oxford) 1739. R. of Betteshanger, Kent, 1743–75. R. of Deal, 1755–75. Died Nov. 26, 1775. Will (P.C.C.) 1776; to be buried in Betteshanger. (*Al. Oxon.*; *Peile*, II. 246.)

JAMES, JOSEPH. M.A. 1677. Incorp. from Glasgow.

JAMES, LAN(? U)CELOT. Matric. sizar from TRINITY, Easter, 1572.

JEAMES, LOUIS. Matric. pens. from CHRIST'S, Mar. 1584–5.

JAMES, MARMADUKE. Matric. pens. from TRINITY, Lent, 1634–5; B.A. 1638–9. Probably lecturer at St Peter's, Cornhill, 1642. Perhaps R. of Watton, Herts., 1652.

JAMES, NATHANIEL. Adm. pens. (age 17) at MAGDALENE, June 4, 1647. S. of Nathaniel, of London, gent. School, Albury. Matric. 1647.

JAMES, PETER. B.A. 1520–1; M.A. 1524.

JAMES, REUBEN. Matric. sizar from TRINITY, Easter, 1628; Scholar, 1631; B.A. 1631–2; M.A. 1635.

JAMES, RICHARD. Matric. pens. from TRINITY, Easter, 1617; Scholar, 1619; B.A. 1620–1; M.A. 1624. Ord. deacon (Peterb.) Aug. 11; priest, Aug. 13, 1628. Will of one of these names (Exeter) 1640; R. of Thornbury, Devon.

JAMES, RICHARD. B.D. 1627 (Incorp. from Oxford). Of Hampshire, gent. B. at Newport, Isle of Wight. Matric. from Exeter College, Oxford, May 6, 1608, age 16; B.A. (Corpus Christi, Oxford) 1611; M.A. 1614–5; B.D. 1624. Fellow of Corpus Christi, 1615. Arranged the Cottonian library. Perhaps R. of Little Mongeham, Kent, 1629–35. Buried at St Margaret's, Westminster, Dec. 8, 1638. (*Al. Oxon.*)

JEAMES, ROBERT. Matric. sizar from TRINITY, Easter, 1568; B.A. 1571–2.

JAMES, ROBERT. Adm. pens. at SIDNEY, July 1, 1613; B.A. 1616–7; M.A. 1620.

JAMES, ROBERT. M.D. 1728 (*Com. Reg.*). S. of Edward, of Shenston, Staffs., Major in the army. School, Lichfield. Matric. from St John's, Oxford, Oct. 10, 1722, age 17; B.A. 1726. Extra-licentiate, R.C.P., Jan. 12, 1727–8. Licentiate, 1765. Practised for a time at Sheffield, *c.* 1770. Inventor of the 'fever powders.' Author, medical. Died Mar. 23, 1776. Will, P.C.C. (*D.N.B.*; *Munk*, II. 269; *Al. Oxon.*)

JAMES, ROBERT. Adm. sizar (age 20) at ST JOHN'S, July 1, 1730. S. of John, gent., of Suffolk. B. at Sudbury. School, Blackheath, Kent. Matric. 1730. Adm. at the Middle Temple, Apr. 28, 1726; s. and h. of John, of Sudbury, Suffolk, gent., deceased. Perhaps ord. deacon (Lincoln) May 20, 1733; priest, Sept. 22, 1734, as B.A. One of these names V. of Shephall, Herts., 1734–42. Died 1742.

JAMES, ROGER. Adm. pens. at QUEENS', Apr. 14, 1637. Of Surrey. Probably same as next.

JAMES, ROGER. Adm. Fell.-Com. at CLARE, July 13, 1637. Probably s. of Sir Roger, of Reigate, Surrey, Knt. Matric. 1637. Adm. at the Inner Temple, 1639. M.P. for Reigate, 1661–81, 1689–90. Married a dau. of Sir Anthony Aucher, of Bishopsbourne, Kent. Living, 1697. Probably father of the next. (*Vis. of Surrey*, 1623, 1663; *Manning and* Bray, I. 326.)

JAMES, ROGER. Matric. Fell.-Com. from TRINITY HALL, Easter, 1667. Probably s. and h. of Roger (above), of Reigate, Surrey, Esq. Age 14 in 1663. Died before his father. (*Vis. of Surrey*.)

JAMES, ROGER. Adm. sizar at JESUS, Apr. 27, 1671. Of Essex. Matric. 1671; Scholar, 1672; B.A. 1674–5.

JAMES, SAMUEL. Matric. sizar from MAGDALENE, Michs. 1571.

JAMES, SAMUEL. Adm. scholar at TRINITY HALL, June 2, 1577; LL.B. 1585.

JAMES, SAMUEL. Matric. sizar from QUEENS', Easter, 1619. Of Lincolnshire.

JAMES, SAMUEL. Adm. pens. at EMMANUEL, June 9, 1631. Of Norfolk.

JAMES, THOMAS. M.A. 1600 (Incorp. from Oxford). Of Hampshire (of Newport, Isle of Wight). Matric. from New College, Oxford, Jan. 28, 1591-2, age 19; B.A. 1595; M.A. 1598-9; B.D. and D.D. 1614. Fellow, 1593. Bodley's librarian, 1598-1620. R. of St Aldgate, Oxford, 1602. R. of Midley, Kent, 1609. Sub-dean of Wells, 1614-29. R. of Little Mongeham, 1617-29. Author. Died at Oxford, Aug. 1629, aged 58. Buried in New College Chapel. (*Al. Oxon.*)

JAMES, THOMAS. Adm. pens. at SIDNEY, July, 1602.

JAMES, THOMAS. Matric. pens. from EMMANUEL, Easter, 1611. S. of John (1570), R. of Skirbeck. Bapt. at Boston, Oct. 5, 1595. B.A. 1614-5; M.A. 1618. Ord. deacon (Peterb.) Mar. 16; priest, Mar. 17, 1616-7. For some years ministered in Lincolnshire. Went to New England, arriving June 5, 1632. Pastor at Charlestown, Mass. Removed, 1637, to Newhaven, Conn. Returned to England, c. 1647. Minister at Needham Market, Suffolk, 'hired by the town, 1650'; ejected, c. 1661. Presbyterian preacher at West Creeting, 1680. Nonconformist preacher till his death, Feb. 1682-3, aged c. 90. (*Felt*, I. 159; J. G. Bartlett.)

JAMES, THOMAS. Matric. pens. from TRINITY, Easter, 1632; scholar from Westminster, 1629; B.A. 1632-3.

JAMES, THOMAS. Adm. sizar at QUEENS', Apr. 20, 1677. Of Essex. B.A. 1680-1.

JAMES, THOMAS. Adm. sizar (age 19) at PETERHOUSE, Oct. 25, 1708. B. in Monmouthshire, 1687. School, Usk. Matric. 1709; B.A. 1712-3. Ord. deacon (Ely) June 15, 1712; priest, Mar. 1, 1712-3.

JAMES, THOMAS (1712), *see* JANNS.

JAMES, THOMAS. Adm. pens. (age 19) at TRINITY, June 19, 1717. S. of Thomas, of Cowden, Sussex, gent. Bapt. at Cowden, Apr. 30, 1698. School, Westminster. Matric. 1718; Scholar, 1718; B.A. 1720-1; M.A. 1724. Fellow, 1723. Adm. at the Middle Temple, Nov. 17, 1715. Ord. deacon (Llandaff, at Westminster) Mar. 7, 1730-1; priest (Gloucester) 1731. Perhaps R. of Ashurst, Kent, 1740-6. R. of Waldron, Sussex, 1746. V. of East Grinstead, till 1757. Will (P.C.C.) 1757. (J. Ch. Smith; F. S. Hockaday.)

JAMES, THOMAS. M.A. from TRINITY, 1730. S. of John, of Hereford. Matric. from Balliol College, Oxford, Oct. 21, 1708, age 18; B.A. (Oxford) 1712. (*Al. Oxon.*)

JAMES, THOMAS. Adm. pens. (age 18) at ST JOHN'S, Oct. 25, 1733. S. of David (1687), clerk, of Middlesex, R. of Woughton, Bucks. B. in London. Bapt. at St Dunstan-in-the-West. School, Eton. Matric. 1734. Adm. at Lincoln's Inn, Oct. 6, 1733. Brother of Anthony (1730-1).

JAMES, WILLIAM. B.Civ.L. 1524-5. Perhaps of KING'S HALL, 1524-6.

JAMES, WILLIAM. Matric. pens. from PETERHOUSE, Easter, 1562; B.A. 1564-5; M.A. 1568. Fellow, 1566. University librarian, 1577-81. One of these names Head Master of York School, 1575. (*Cooper*, II. 51; III. 97.)

JAMES, WILLIAM. Matric. pens. from PEMBROKE, Easter, 1583; B.A. 1586-7; M.A. 1590. Fellow, c. 1588. Incorp. at Oxford, 1591. (*Cooper*, II. 99.)

JAMES, WILLIAM. M.A. 1603 (Incorp. from Oxford). S. of William, dean of Christ Church (and Bishop of Durham). B. 1576. Matric. from Christ Church, Feb. 10, 1592-3; B.A. (Oxford) 1595-6; M.A. 1599. Public orator (Oxford) 1601-4. Married Anne, dau. of John Doiley, of Overbury, Suffolk. Died before 1615. (*Al. Oxon.*; H. M. Wood.)

JAMES, WILLIAM. Matric. pens. from PEMBROKE, Easter, 1617; B.A. 1619-20.

JAMES, WILLIAM. Adm. pens. (age 17) at CHRIST'S, Apr. 6, 1661. S. of William. B. at Hackforth, Yorks. School, Northallerton. Matric. 1661. Perhaps ord. priest (York) 1678. (For possible identifications *see Peile*, I. 596.)

JAMES, WILLIAM. Adm. sizar (age 15) at PETERHOUSE, May 23, 1674. Of Nottinghamshire. School, Church Fenton, Yorks. Matric. 1674; B.A. 1677-8; M.A. 1681. Ord. priest (York) June, 1682. V. of Bramham, Yorks., 1687-91. V. of Burstwick, 1691-1723. V. of Paull, 1701-23. Endowed a hospital at Cawood. Died 1723. (H. M. Wood.)

JAMES, WILLIAM. M.A. from KING'S, 1719. Probably s. of James Williams, clerk, of Llansawell, Merioneth. Matric. from St Mary Hall, Oxford, Feb. 21, 1672-3, age 17; B.A. (Jesus College, Oxford) 1677. Perhaps R. of Begelly, Pembroke, 1685; and of Yerbeston, 1692. (*Al. Oxon.*)

JAMES, WILLIAM. Adm. Fell.-Com. (age 19) at SIDNEY, Apr. 26, 1722. S. of William, Esq., deceased, of Ightham, Kent. B. there. School, Ludsdown, Kent (Mr Thornton). Of Ightham, Esq. High Sheriff for Kent, 1732. Usher of the Black Rod in Ireland. Married Elizabeth, dau. of Demetricus James of Reigate, Surrey. (Burke, *L.G.*)

JAMES, ——. Fee for M.A. or higher degree, 1467. A foreigner.

JAMES, ——. Dr of some faculty. Incorp. 1485-6.

JAMESON or JAMSON, RICHARD. Matric. sizar from TRINITY, Easter, 1572.

JAMESON, ROBERT. B.A. 1483-4.

JEAMSON, WILLIAM. M.A. 1663 (Incorp. from Oxford). Matric. from St John's College, Oxford, July 25, 1655; B.A. (Oxford) 1658; M.A. (New College) 1661. Chaplain of Christ Church. V. of Shabbington, Bucks., 1662-72. Died Dec. 13, 1672. Buried in Christ Church Cathedral. Admon. (Oxford) 1672. (*Al. Oxon.*)

JAMINEAU, ISAAC. Adm. pens. (age 17) at TRINITY, June 2, 1727. 3rd s. of Claude, of London. School, Westminster. Matric. 1727; Scholar, 1728. Adm. at the Middle Temple, Oct. 5, 1727. Consul at Naples, 1753-79. Afterwards in the General Post Office. Died Nov. 3, 1789. Will, P.C.C. (*Al. Westmon.*, 296; *G. Mag.*)

JANDRELL or JAUNDRELL, JOHN. Adm. sizar (age 18) at ST JOHN'S, June 13, 1711. S. of Abraham, husbandman. B. at Pitchford, near Shrewsbury. School, Shrewsbury (Mr Lloyd). B.A. 1714-5; M.A. 1720.

JANDRELL, JOHN. Adm. sizar (age 18) at ST JOHN'S, June 30, 1714. S. of John, shoemaker. B. at Shrewsbury. School, Shrewsbury (Mr Lloyd). Matric. 1714; B.A. 1717-8; M.A. 1726.

JANE, JOSEPH. M.A. from ST CATHARINE'S, 1712. S. of Thomas, of St Kew, Cornwall. School, Westminster. Matric. from Christ Church, Oxford, Mar. 18, 1688-9, age 17; B.A. (Oxford) 1692-3. Master of Truro School, 1706-28. V. of Gwinear, 1710-1. R. of St Mary, Truro, 1711-45. Buried at Truro, Nov. 19, 1745. (*Al. Oxon.*)

JANE, THOMAS (1488), *see* LANE.

JANE or JAN, THOMAS. Incorp. at Cambridge, 1495-6. Of Dorset. Educated at Winchester and New College, Oxford. D.Can.L. (Oxford). Vice-Chancellor of Oxford, 1459-60, 1468-70. V. of Little Burstead, Essex, 1471. Preb. of St Paul's, 1471-99. V. of Prittlewell, Essex, 1472. V. of Foulness, 1472-80. R. of Hayes, Middlesex, 1473-99. V. of St Sepulchre's, London, 1479-80. Archdeacon of Essex, 1480-99. V. of Walden, Essex, 1484. V. of St Bride's, Fleet St, 1485-99. Canon of Windsor, 1496-9. Bishop of Norwich, 1499-1500. Died at Folkestone Abbey, Kent, Sept. 1500. Buried at Norwich. Will (P.C.C.). (*Al. Oxon.*; *D.N.B.*; *Cooper*, I. 3; III. 97.)

JANEWAY, ABRAHAM. B.A. from ST CATHARINE'S, 1662. S. of William (1623-4), R. of Kelshall, Herts. B. in St Alphage, Oct. 13, 1640. School, Merchant Taylors'. Matric. from Wadham College, Oxford, Oct. 29, 1657. Nonconformist. Resided at Buntingford, Herts. Died Sept. 1665. Brother of William (1649), John (1650) and Joseph (1666). (*Al. Oxon.*)

JANEWAY, ANDREW. B.A. from JESUS, 1587-8; M.A. 1592. S. of John, V. of Manuden, Essex. B. there. Ord. deacon (London) Dec. 20, 1589, age 24; priest, May 10, 1593; C. of Moreton, Essex. P.C. of Tiltey, 1592-8. R. of All Hallows-the-Wall, London, 1593-1643. Died Feb. 20, 1654-5. Buried at All Hallows. (J. Ch. Smith.)

JANEWAY, JACOB. Adm. sizar (age 19) at ST JOHN'S, Apr. 6, 1743. S. of James (1698), of Kent. B. at Wootton. School, Canterbury. Matric. 1743; B.A. 1746-7. Ord. deacon (Norwich) 1747; priest (Lincoln) Sept. 25, 1748. C. of Compton, Beds.

JANEWAY, JAMES. Adm. pens. at CORPUS CHRISTI, 1698. Of Kent. Probably bapt. at Canterbury Cathedral, Aug. 4, 1682; s. of Mr Jacob Janeway. Matric. 1698; B.A. 1701-2; M.A. 1705. Ord. priest (Lincoln) Sept. 22, 1706. R. of Aldington, Kent, 1708-39. R. of Wootton, 1712-39. Died July, 1739. Father of Jacob (1743).

JANAWAYE, JOHN. Matric. sizar from JESUS, Michs. 1549 (*impubes*).

JENEWAY, JOHN. Adm. at CORPUS CHRISTI, 1556. Perhaps V. of Manuden, Essex, 1564-1619. Will (Cons. C. London) 1619; to be buried at Manuden. If so, father of Andrew (1587-8). (J. Ch. Smith.)

JANEWAY, JOHN. Adm. at KING'S, a scholar from Eton, 1650. 2nd s. of William (1623-4). B. at Lilley, Herts., Oct. 27, 1633. Matric. 1650-1; B.A. 1654-5. Fellow, 1654-7. Died of consumption, June, 1657. Buried at Kelshall. M.I. Brother of William (1649), Abraham (1662) and Joseph (1666). His brother James (of Oxford) wrote a notice of his life in 1673. (*Harwood*; *D.N.B.*)

JANEWAY, JOSEPH. M.A. from ST CATHARINE'S, 1666. S. of William (1623-4), R. of Kelshall, Herts. B. in St Giles', Cripplegate, Sept. 15, 1642. School, Merchant Taylors'. Matric. from All Souls, Oxford, Dec. 8, 1658; B.A. (Wadham College, Oxford) 1662-3. Ord. priest (Lincoln) Dec. 18, 1670. Brother of Abraham (1662), John (1650) and William (1649). (*Al. Oxon.*)

JANEWAY, WILLIAM. Adm. sizar at EMMANUEL, 1623. Matric. 1623–4; B.A. 1626–7; M.A. 1630. Ord. deacon (London) June 8, 1628. R. of Ayott St Lawrence, Herts., 1644–6. R. of Kelshall, till 1654. Will (P.C.C.) 1655. Father of John (1650), William (1649), Joseph (1666) and Abraham (1662). For his son James *see D.N.B.*

JANEWAY, WILLIAM. Adm. sizar at ST JOHN'S, May 21, 1649. Adm. at King's, a scholar from Eton, Oct. 13, 1650, age 17. S. of William (above), R. of Kelshall, Herts. School, Eton. Matric. 1650; B.A. 1654; M.A. 1658. Fellow of King's, 1653–55. R. of Kelshall, Herts., 1654–62, ejected.

JANWAY or JENAWAY, ——. Adm. sizar at PETERHOUSE, 1590–1.

JANIAN or JENIAN, GEORGE. Matric. sizar from TRINITY, Easter, 1573; B.A. 1576–7, as Jeniane; M.A. 1580.

JANION or JANINGE, JOHN. Adm. sizar (age 18) at CAIUS, May 25, 1633. S. of Thomas, gent., of Preston-on-Hill, Cheshire. School, Halton (Mr Percevall). Matric. 1633. Died in College, of the plague. Buried at St Michael's, Cambridge, Nov. 2, 1636. (*Venn*, I. 309.)

JANNA or JANUA, W. Matric. sizar from JESUS, Easter, 1588.

JANNINGS, THOMAS. B.A. from ST CATHARINE'S, 1604–5. Of Shelland, Suffolk. Ord. deacon and priest (Norwich) May 22, 1608, age 25.

JANNS, JAMES. Adm. sizar at ST CATHARINE'S, May 26, 1722. Of Wolverhampton, Staffs. Matric. 1722.

JANNS, THOMAS. Adm. pens. at EMMANUEL, Apr. 15, 1651. Of Staffordshire.

JANNS, THOMAS. Adm. pens. (age 17) at PEMBROKE, May 1, 1712. S. of William (1685), V. of Sedgeley, Staffs. B. at Greenhill (*sic.*), Salop. Matric. 1712; B.A. 1715–6. Ord. deacon (Ely) June 16, 1717. Probably V. of Sedgeley, Staffs., till his death, 1730, as Thomas James. (*S. Shaw*, II. 222.)

JANNS, WILLIAM. Adm. pens. (age 18) at PEMBROKE, May 12, 1685. S. of Thomas, clerk. B. in Staffordshire. Matric. 1686; B.A. 1688–9; M.A. 1692. V. of Sedgeley, Staffs. Father of the above.

JANNY, ROBERT. B.A. from JESUS, 1611–2. Ord. deacon (Peterb.) Jan. 7, 1610–1. Doubtless V. of Bowdon, Cheshire, 1616–37. Buried there Jan. 3, 1636–7. Father of the next. (E. Axon.)

JANNY, ROBERT. Adm. sizar (age 18) at ST JOHN'S, June 27, 1656. S. of Robert (above), clerk. B. at Timperley, Bowdon, Cheshire. School, Dronfield, Derbs. Matric. 1656. Ord. deacon (Lincoln) Mar. 10; priest, Mar. 13, 1660–1. P.C. of Shotwick, Cheshire, 1697–1701. V. of Woodchurch, 1704–5. P.C. of Overchurch, 1705–16. Died Oct. 10, 1719. Buried at Birkenhead, as 'minister of Birkenhead and Overchurch.' (R. Stewart-Brown.)

JANSON, LANCELOT, *see* IANSON.

JANSON, NICHOLAS. Scholar of MAGDALENE, Lent, 1618–9. Ord. deacon (Peterb.) June 3; priest, June 4, 1626, as Ianson, M.A.

JANSSEN, WILLIAM. Adm. pens. at TRINITY HALL, Feb. 16, 1725–6. Probably 4th s. of Sir Theodore, of Wimbledon, Surrey, Bart. Matric. 1726. Adm. at the Inner Temple, May 14, 1724. Died 1768. Will, P.C.C. (G. *Mag.*, 303.)

JAQUES or JACQUES, CHARLES. M.A. from KING'S, 1730. S. of John, of Uxbridge, Middlesex, clerk. Matric. from Queen's College, Oxford, May 7, 1716, age 17; B.A. (Oxford) 1719–20. (*Al. Oxon.*)

JAQUES, EDWARD. Adm. sizar at QUEENS', Jan. 1595–6. Of Lincolnshire. Matric. 1596; B.A. 1599–1600. R. of Kirton, Suffolk, 1625.

JAQUES, GEORGE. Adm. pens. at QUEENS', Oct. 13, 1675. Previously matric. (Christ Church, Oxford) June 19, 1672, age 16. S. of John, of Toton, Notts. Matric. 1675; B.A. 1676–7; M.A. 1680. Ord. deacon (York) May, 1681; priest, Sept. 1681.

JAQUES, GEORGE. Matric. Fell.-Com. from KING'S, Easter, 1729; LL.B. 1729.

JAQUES, JOHN. Adm. sizar (age 24) at ST JOHN'S, July 3, 1646. S. of George, yeoman, of Toton, Notts. B. there. School, Repton, Derbs. (Mr Ullock). Perhaps Chaplain in the Navy, 1653.

JAQUES, JOHN. Adm. sizar (age 16) at ST JOHN'S, May 10, 1680. S. of John, clerk. B. at Scarcliffe, Derbs. School, Sheffield (Mr Balguy). Matric. 1680; B.A. 1683–4. Ord. priest (London) Feb. 28, 1685–6. Probably V. of St Lawrence, Cowley, Middlesex, 1705–18; also V. of Uxbridge. Died 1718. M.I. at Hillingdon. Perhaps father of the next.

JACQUES, JOHN. Adm. sizar at JESUS, June 1, 1708. Of Uxbridge, Middlesex. Matric. 1708; Scholar, 1710.

JACQUES, MARMADUKE. Adm. pens. (age 15) at SIDNEY, May 9, 1650. 6th s. of Sir Roger, Knt. B. at York. Schools, York, Selby (Mr Pennill) and Elvington. Matric. 1650; B.A. 1653–4. Adm. at the Middle Temple, June 6, 1654.

JAQUES, PETER. M.A. from EMMANUEL, 1674. S. of William, of Fleckney, Leics. Matric. from Merton College, Oxford, June 14, 1667, age 18; B.A. (Oxford) 1671. Ord. deacon (Lincoln) Sept. 24, 1671; priest, May 25, 1673. V. of Hinckley, Leics., 1683–1704. Died Oct. 11, 1704. M.I. at Hinckley. Will, Leicester. (*Al. Oxon.*; *Nichols*, IV. 688.)

JAQUES, RICHARD. Matric. pens. from PETERHOUSE, Easter, 1576; B.A. 1579–80; M.A. 1583. Ord. priest (Norwich) May 14, 1581. One of these names R. of Althorpe, Lincs., 1582.

JAQUES, RICHARD. M.A. 1584 (Incorp. from Oxford). M.A. (Queen's College, Oxford) 1583. R. of Ashen, Essex, 1581. (*Al. Oxon.*)

JAQUIS, RICHARD. Adm. pens. at JESUS, Apr. 4, 1660. Of Suffolk. Matric. 1660; Scholar, 1661; B.A. 1663–4; M.A. 1667. Incorp. at Oxford, 1669. Signed for deacon's orders (London) Dec. 17, 1664. R. of Ashwelthorpe, Norfolk, 1672. R. of Wreningham, 1672–6. R. of Wetheringsett, Suffolk, 1679–1715.

JAQUES, RICHARD. Adm. pens. at CORPUS CHRISTI, 1692. Of Norfolk. Matric. 1693; B.A. 1696–7; M.A. 1700. V. of Mendlesham, Suffolk, 1700–14. Perhaps R. of Monewdon, Suffolk, 1703.

JARDEFYLDE or JERDFELD, JONAS. Matric. sizar from CHRIST'S, Easter, 1567, as 'Jervyll'; Scholar; B.A. 1570–1. V. of Bishop's Stortford, 1575–80. R. of St Mary Abchurch, London, 1582–97. Admon. (Cons. C. London) 1597. (*Peile*, I. 100; J. Ch. Smith.)

JARDFIELD, RICHARD. Matric. pens. from QUEENS', Easter, 1583. Of Hertfordshire. B.A. 1591–2; M.A. 1595. V. of Ashby-de-la-Zouch, 1605. Perhaps R. of Icklingham All Saints', Suffolk, 1617–8. Will (P.C.C.) 1618.

JARNOCK, NICHOLAS. Incorp. from Oxford, 1494–5.

JARRARD, Sir THOMAS, *see* GERRARD.

JARRAT or GERRARD, JOHN. Adm. sizar (age 17) at SIDNEY, Dec. 7, 1661. S. of John, farmer. B. at Skerne ('Scarnia'), Yorks. School, Beverley (Mr Sherrard). Matric. 1662; B.A. 1666–7. Ord. deacon (York) June, 1667; priest, June, 1671. V. of Nafferton, *c.* 1667–71. Buried at Skerne, July 15, 1671.

JARRETT, ——. Pens. or Fell.-Com. at JESUS, 1614–5.

JARVIS, *see also* JERVIS.

JARVIS, JOHN. Adm. pens. (age 17) at ST JOHN'S, May 18, 1695. S. of John, gent. B. at Burrough Green, Cambs. School, Bradley, Suffolk (private; Mr Cooper). Matric. 1698–9; B.A. 1698–9; M.A. 1702. Ord. priest (Norwich) Sept. 1702.

JARVIS, RICHARD. Adm. pens. (age 17) at ST JOHN'S, Apr. 19, 1698. S. of William, deceased. B. at Warwick. School, Rugby (Mr Hollyoke).

JASLEY, GABRIEL. Matric. pens. from PEMBROKE, Easter, 1572.

JASPER, ROBERT. Matric. sizar from TRINITY, Michs. 1571. S. of Henry, of Boxford, Suffolk. School, Boxford. Migrated as pens. to Caius, Nov. 1, 1573, age 20. Resident student in Sept. 1575. (*Venn*, I. 75.)

JAUMARD, JOHN. Adm. sizar at CLARE, Dec. 11, 1714. B. at Arundel, Sussex. Matric. 1715; B.A. 1718–9; M.A. 1732. Ord. deacon (London) Dec. 20, 1719; priest, Mar. 13, 1719–20. R. of Frome St Quintin with Evershot, Dorset, 1744–7. Chaplain to the Bishop of Waterford. V. of Ardmore, Co. Waterford, 1747. V. of Ringagonagh, 1747–51. Archdeacon of Lismore, 1749–51. Died 1751. Buried at Youghal, Cork. Will (P.C. Dublin) 1752. (Hutchins, *Dorset*, II. 649; H. B. Swanzy.)

JAUNCEY, JOHN. M.A. from CLARE, 1683. S. of J., of Fenny Stratford, Bucks., gent. Matric. from Lincoln College, Oxford, May 31, 1677, age 17; B.A. (St Mary's Hall, Oxford) 1680–1. Ord. deacon (Peterb.) Dec. 18, 1681. R. of Shenley, Bucks., 1684. (*Al. Oxon.*)

JAXLEY, *see* YAXLEY.

JAY, CHARLES. M.A. from ST CATHARINE'S, 1683. S. of Stephen, R. of Chinnor, Oxon. Matric. from Magdalen Hall, Oxford, May 24, 1676, age 15; B.A. (Merton) 1679–80. R. of Chinnor, 1691. (*Al. Oxon.*)

JEYE, GEORGE. Matric. sizar from CHRIST'S, Mar. 1580–1; B.A. from Peterhouse, 1583–4, as 'Gees.' One of these names V. of Scalby, Yorks., 1631–4. Died 1634.

JAY, HENRY. M.A. 1641–2 (*Lit. Reg.*). One of these names adm. at Lincoln's Inn, July 10, 1622; s. and h. of Henry, of Norwich, Esq.

JEY, JOHN. Matric. Fell.-Com. from PETERHOUSE, Easter, 1581. Probably adm. at Gray's Inn, Jan. 24, 1582-3, from Barnard's Inn. Of Holvestone, Norfolk. Married Lucy Johnson. Died 1619, aged 56. M.I. at Holvestone. Father of Suckling, and grandfather of John (1655). (*Blomefield*, IV. 315.)

JAY or JEY, JOHN. Adm. pens. (age 16) at PETERHOUSE, Sept. 11, 1648. S. and h. of Christopher, of the City of Norwich, gent. Adm. at Gray's Inn, Nov. 6, 1651. (*T. A. Walker*.)

JAY, JOHN. Adm. Fell.-Com. (age 16) at PETERHOUSE, Oct. 18, 1655. S. and h. of Suckling Jay, of Holvestone, Norfolk, Esq. (and grandson of John, 1581). School, Norwich. Adm. at Gray's Inn, May 12, 1658. Student at Leyden, Oct. 31, 1659.

JAY, JOHN. Adm. pens. (age 17) at PEMBROKE, May 8, 1678. S. of John, late of Fleet, Lincs. Matric. 1678.

JAY, ROBERT. Matric. sizar from PETERHOUSE, Michs. 1560; B.A. 1563-4; M.A. 1567; B.D. 1574. Fellow, 1566. Ord. priest (Ely) July 29, 1565. P.C. of Little St Mary's, Cambridge, 1568-9. V. of Melton, Suffolk, 1573-1609. Married there, July 29, 1574, Barbery Hicklingam. Buried at Melton, Dec. 13, 1609. (V. B. Redstone.)

JAY, ROBERT. Adm. sizar at PETERHOUSE, 1597-8.

JAY, ROBERT. Adm. at CORPUS CHRISTI, 1627; B.A. 1631. Ord. deacon (Norwich) Dec. 22, 1633; priest, Mar. 2, 1633-4. V. of Henley, Suffolk, 1634; there, in 1650.

JAY, ROBERT. Adm. pens. at CLARE, Apr. 17, 1711. B. at Holvestone, Norfolk. B.A. 1714-5.

JAY, SUCKLING. Adm. pens. at ST CATHARINE'S, June 2, 1683.

JAYCOCKE, *see* JACOCKS.

JEANES, HENRY. B.A. 1632 (Incorp. from Oxford). S. of Christopher, of Kingston, Somerset, *pleb.* Matric. from New Inn Hall, Oct. 27, 1626, age 15; B.A. (Oxford) 1630; M.A. 1633. R. of Beer Crocombe, Somerset, 1635. R. of Cropland, 1635. V. of Kingston; and R. of Chedzoy, 1646-62. Author, theological. Died at Wells, Aug. 1662. Buried in the Cathedral. (*Al. Oxon.*; *D.N.B.*)

JEANES, THOMAS. Adm. pens. at TRINITY, June 30, 1646. Of London. Matric. 1646; Scholar, 1647; B.A. 1649-50. Incorp. at Oxford, 1652. M.A. (Oxford) 1652; M.B. 1655; M.D. 1659. Fellow of Magdalen College, Oxford, 1652. Practised physic at Peterborough. Killed by a fall from his horse, 1668. (*See* Macray, *Magd. Coll.*, v. 178.)

JEBB, ANTHONY. Matric. sizar from MAGDALENE, Michs. 1545; B.A. 1550-1.

JEBB, JOHN. Adm. pens. at ST JOHN'S, June 19, 1722. S. of Samuel, maltster, of Mansfield, Notts. School, Mansfield (Mr Hucklebridge). Matric. 1725; B.A. 1725-6; M.A. from Christ's, 1729. Fellow of Christ's, 1729-34. Incorp. B.D. and D.D. at Dublin, 1743. Ord. deacon (Ely) July, 1728; priest, Aug. 1730. Chaplain to the Lord-Lieutenant of Ireland. Preb. of Ossory, 1736-40. Treasurer of Christchurch, Dublin, 1740-87. Dean of Cashel, 1769-87. Resided latterly at Egham. Married Anne, dau. of David Gansell, Esq., of Low Layton. Died Feb. 6, 1787, aged 82. Buried at Ashford, Middlesex. M.I. Will, P.C.C. Brother of Samuel (1709). (*Peile*, II. 206.)

JEBB, RICHARD. Adm. pens. at EMMANUEL, June 30, 1683. B. at Wem, Salop. Colleger at Eton, 1678-83. Matric. 1683-4; B.A. 1686-7. Admon. (Chester) 1715, of one of these names; of Astbury, clerk.

JEBB, RICHARD. Adm. sizar (age 22) at TRINITY, Apr. 7, 1724. S. of Richard, of Salop. School, Wem (Mr Edwards).

JEBB, SAMUEL. Adm. sizar (age 15) at PETERHOUSE, June 15, 1709. S. of Samuel, maltster, of Mansfield, Notts. School, Mansfield. Matric. 1709; B.A. 1712-3; non-juror. Ord. deacon (by Mr Jeremy Collier) July 25, 1716; priest, Jan. 25, 1717-8. Librarian to Jeremy Collier in London, till 1726. M.D. of Rheims, 1728. L.R.C.P., 1751. Practised at Stratford-le-Bow. Author, historical and classical. Died Mar. 9, 1772. Will, P.C.C. Brother of John (1722). (*T. A. Walker*, 222; *D.N.B.*; *N. and Q.*, 3rd S., III. 244.)

JEBB, SAMUEL. Adm. pens. (age 18) at TRINITY, Mar. 29, 1739. S. of Joshua, of Chesterfield, Derbs. School, Chesterfield (Mr Burroughs). Matric. 1739; Scholar, 1739. Married and had issue. Died 1787. (Burke, *L.G.*)

JEE, *see* GEE.

JEEVE, JOHN. B.A. from EMMANUEL, 1608-9.

JEPFE, NICHOLAS. Matric. pens. from TRINITY, Easter, 1572; scholar from Westminster, 1572.

JEFFE, ROBERT. Matric. sizar (age 13) from TRINITY, Easter, 1573.

JEFFRESON, CHRISTOPHER. Adm. pens. (age 18) at MAGDALENE, July 18, 1717. School, Histon, Cambs. Matric. 1718. Of Dullingham, Cambs., Esq. M.P. for Cambridge, 1744-7, 1748-9. Married Elizabeth, dau. of Sir John Shuckburgh, Bart. Died Jan. 18, 1748-9. (Burke, *L.G.*)

JEAFFRESON, CHRISTOPHER. Adm. sizar (age 19) at MAGDALENE, June 24, 1748. S. of John. B. at Bawdsey, Suffolk. Bapt. at Walton. School, Woodbridge. Matric. 1749; B.A. 1752. Ord. deacon (Norwich) Mar. 1753; priest, Sept. 1755. C. of Butley, Suffolk. Buried at Tunstall, Feb. 1789.

JEFFERSON, HENRY. Matric. pens. from TRINITY, Easter, 1575.

JEFFERSON, HENRY. Matric. pens. from QUEENS', Easter, 1576.

JEFFERSON, HENRY. Adm. pens. (age 18) at ST JOHN'S, Apr. 8, 1680. S. of Henry, husbandman, of Burstwick-in-Holderness, Yorks. B. there. School, Beverley (Mr Lambert). Matric. 1680; B.A. 1683-4. Ord. priest (Peterb.) Feb. 28, 1685-6. V. of North Ferriby, Yorks., 1686-96. V. of Kirk Ella, 1686-96. Preb. of York, 1712-20. Father of the next.

JEFFERSON, HENRY. Adm. sizar (age 18) at ST JOHN'S, July 11, 1715. S. of Henry (above), clerk, of Yorkshire. B. at Beverley. School, Beverley. Matric. 1716; B.A. 1720-1; M.A. 1727. Ord. deacon (York) June 12, 1720; priest, June 9, 1727. Head Master of Beverley School, 1721-35. Lecturer at St Mary's, Beverley, 1726. R. of South Dalton, Beverley, about 1745. (*Scott-Mayor*, III. 297.)

JEFFERSON, JOHN. Adm. pens. (age 16) at ST JOHN'S, Apr. 26, 1652. S. of John, gent., lately deceased, of Durham. Bapt. there, at St Nicholas, Sept. 1635. School, Guisborough, Yorks. Matric. 1652. Adm. at Gray's Inn, Nov. 26, 1651. Serjeant-at-law. Bencher, 1682. Recorder of Durham, 1686. Appointed one of the justices of Ireland, 1691. Knighted (as 'Jeffreyson'), Nov. 5, 1692. Married Elizabeth, dau. of James Coles, Esq., of Gateshead. Died *c.* 1700. (*Surtees*, IV. 156.)

JEFFERSON, JOHN. Adm. sizar at CORPUS CHRISTI, 1670. Of Yorkshire. Matric. 1670; B.A. 1673-4. Ord. deacon (York) June, 1674; priest, Dec. 1674. V. of Wistow, Yorks., 1677-85. Died 1685.

JEFFERSON, JOHN. Adm. sizar (age 24) at ST JOHN'S, May 8, 1732. S. of J., grocer, of Cumberland. B. at Wigton. School, Wigton (Mr Birbeck).

JEFFERSON, MARK. Adm. sizar (age 16) at PEMBROKE, Jan. 18, 1620-1. S. of George, of London. Matric. 1620-1; B.A. 1624-5; M.A. 1628.

JEFFERSON, ROBERT. Adm. sizar (age 17) at PETERHOUSE, July 1, 1675. Of Northamptonshire. School, Huntingdon. Matric. 1675, as 'Cheverson'; B.A. 1678-9; Scholar, 1680; M.A. 1701.

JEFFERSON, SHUTE. Matric. pens. from ST JOHN'S, *c.* 1594. B. at Stamford, Lincs. B.A. from Trinity, 1596-7; M.A. 1600. Ord. deacon and priest (London) May 22, 1608, age 28. C. of Skellingthorpe, Lincs., 1608. R. of Diddington, Hunts., 1608-9. R. of Doddington Piggott, Lincs., 1608-18. Will (P.C.C.) 1618; of Little Bytham.

JEFFERSON, THOMAS. M.A. 1616 (Incorp. from Oxford). Of Cumberland, *pleb.* Matric. from Queen's College, Oxford, June 27, 1606, age 18; B.A. 1610; M.A. 1613. V. of Holme Cultram, with Newton Arlosh, Cumberland, 1618-32. Died 1632. (*Al. Oxon.*)

JEFFERSON, THOMAS. M.A. from ST CATHARINE'S, 1713. S. of Robert, of Denbigh, clerk. Matric. from Queen's College, Oxford, June 22, 1699, age 17; B.A. (Oxford) 1703-4. V. of Holme Cultram, Cumberland, 1715-30. R. of Lamplugh, 1731-68. (*Al. Oxon.*)

JEFFRAY, DEVEREUX. Adm. sizar (age 19) at CHRIST'S, June 10, 1640. S. of Simon. B. at Kenton, Suffolk. Matric. 1640; B.A. 1643-4; M.A. 1651. Ord. priest (Norwich) Sept. 1644. C. of Sotherton, Suffolk. V. of Blyford and Wenhaston, 1650. (*Peile*, I. 472.)

JEFFERY, EDMUND. Adm. pens. (age 17) at PEMBROKE, Oct. 16, 1657. S. of a grocer, of Southminster, Essex. Matric. 1657; B.A. 1661-2; M.A. from Peterhouse, 1665. Fellow of Peterhouse, 1664. Signed for deacon's orders (London) Dec. 16, 1664; for priest's, Sept. 9, 1668. Probably V. of Tolleshunt Major, Essex, 1668. R. of North Fambridge, 1682. V. of Boreham, 1683. He was deprived of both livings, in 1691. Perhaps V. of North Shoebury, 1707-11.

JEFFREY, EDWARD. Matric. pens. from PETERHOUSE, Easter, 1614; B.A. 1617-8; Scholar, 1618-21; M.A. 1621. Ord. deacon (Peterb.) Dec. 19; priest, Dec. 20, 1619. Perhaps V. of Southminster, Essex, till 1642, ejected.

JEFFREYS, EDWARD. Adm. sizar (age 18) at TRINITY, Apr. 18, 1734. S. of John, of London. School, St Paul's. Matric. 1734; Scholar, 1737; B.A. 1737-8. One of these names R. of Throcking, Herts., 1745-86. Died 1786.

JEFFRIE, FRANCIS. Matric. Fell.-Com. from CLARE, Easter, 1586.

JEFFEREY or GEFFREY, GEORGE. B.A. 1631 (Incorp. from Oxford). S. of Thomas, of Stokenham, Devon, *pleb.* Matric. from Queen's College, Oxford, June 9, 1626, age 20; B.A. 1627; M.A. 1631. R. of Thornbury, Devon, 1641. Admon. (Exeter) 1641. (*Al. Oxon.*)

JEFFRYS, GEORGE. Adm. pens. at TRINITY, 1662. 6th s. of John, of Acton Park, Wrexham. B. there, 1648. School, Shrewsbury, 1652; afterwards at St Paul's and Westminster. Adm. at the Inner Temple, May 19, 1663. Barrister, Nov. 22, 1668. Common Serjeant of the City of London, 1671-8. Introduced at court by Chiffinch. Solicitor-general to the Duke of York, 1677. K.C., 1677. Knighted, Sept. 14, 1677. Recorder of London, 1678-80. Prominent in the Popish plot cases. Chief Justice of Chester, 1680-3; notorious for his brutality. Reprimanded by the House of Commons for obstructing petitions for the assembling of Parliament, 1680. Created a Baronet, 1681. Serjeant-at-law, 1683. Lord Chief Justice, 1683-5. Privy Councillor, 1683-8. Conducted the trials of Algernon Sidney, 1683; and Sir Thomas Armstrong, 1684. Presided at the trial of Titus Oates, 1685. Created Baron Jeffrys of Wem, 1685. Held the 'bloody assize' after Monmouth's rebellion, 1685. Lord Chancellor, 1685-8. Chief ecclesiastical commissioner, 1686. One of the privy councillors who regulated the municipal corporations, 1687. Lord-Lieutenant of Shropshire and Buckinghamshire, 1687-9. Present at the trial of the seven bishops, 1688. Carried out James II's tardy reforms. Arrested in disguise at Wapping, Dec. 12, 1688. Died in the Tower, Apr. 8, 1689. Buried in the Tower Chapel. Brother of William (1661). (*D.N.B.*; *G.E.C.*)

JEFFRYES, GEORGE. Adm. pens. (age 18) at TRINITY, June 14, 1676. S. of George. B. at Chelmsford, Essex. School, Westminster. Scholar, 1677; B.A. 1679-80.

JEFFRYS, GEORGE. Adm. pens. (age 16) at TRINITY, Nov. 12, 1694. S. and h. of Christopher, of Gt Weldon, Northants. Schools, Oundle and Westminster. Matric. 1695; Scholar, 1697; B.A. 1698-9; M.A. 1702. Fellow, 1701-10. Taxor, 1707. Adm. at the Middle Temple, Nov. 3, 1694. Called to the Bar, May 23, 1707. Secretary to Dr Hartstongue, Bishop of Derry, 1714-7. Poet and dramatist. Died Aug. 17, 1755. (*D.N.B.*; *Al. Westmon.*, 228.)

JEFFREYS, GEORGE. Adm. pens. (age 18) at TRINITY, Sept. 3, 1718. S. of John, of Gt Grimsby, Lincs. B. there. School, Gt Grimsby (Mr Mattison). Matric. 1719; Scholar, 1720; B.A. 1722-3. Ord. deacon (Bangor) June 9, 1723; priest (Peterb.) Sept. 19, 1725. Minor canon of Peterborough, 1725. Assistant Master, Peterborough School, 1725. P.C. of Eye, Northants., 1726. R. of Northborough, 1756-69. Precentor of Peterborough, 1757-69. Buried in Peterborough Cathedral, Feb. 28, 1769. (H. I. Longden.)

JEFFERY, GEORGE. M.A. from ST JOHN'S, 1727. S. of Thomas, of Bradford, Devon. Matric. from Balliol College, Oxford, Dec. 12, 1718, age 20; B.A. (Oxford) 1722. V. of Liukiuhorne, Cornwall, 1725-80. Died June 10, 1780, aged 83. M.I. at Linkinhorne. Will, P.C.C. (*Scott-Mayor*, III. 388.)

JEFFREYS, GEORGE. Adm. sizar (age 17) at TRINITY, Mar. 13, 1740-1. S. of George, of St Neots, Hunts. School, St Neots (Mr Bidwell). Matric. 1741; B.A. 1744-5. Ord. deacon (Lincoln) Sept. 21, 1746.

JEFFREY or GEOFFREY, GILBERT. B.A. 1506-7; M.A. 1510-1.

JEFFERAY, HENRY. Matric. sizar from EMMANUEL, Easter, 1602; B.A. from Clare, 1605-6. Ord. deacon (York) Sept. 1607; priest, Sept. 1608. V. of Sowerby, Thirsk, Yorks., 1610-3. V. of Alne, 1614. Married Catharine Spendlove, of Nun-Monkton, Yorks., 1614.

JEFFERY, JAMES. Adm. sizar (age 19) at PEMBROKE, Mar. 18, 1700-1. S. of John. B. at Marazion, Cornwall. Matric. 1701; B.A. 1704-5; M.A. 1708. Fellow, 1708. Senior proctor, 1729-30. Ord. deacon (London) Mar. 20, 1708-9; priest, June 19, 1709. V. of Whittlesford, Cambs., 1721-30.

JEFFERYS, JAMES. Adm. pens. at CLARE, May 20, 1732. B. in London. Matric. 1732. Probably 1st s. of John (? 1705), of Lincoln's Inn, Esq.; adm. at Lincoln's Inn, Apr. 25, 1732.

JEFFREY, JOHN. Adm. at KING'S (age 17) a scholar from Eton, 1454. Of London. Ord. deacon (Ely) Apr. 5, 1466; M.A.

GEOFFREY, JOHN. B.Can.L. 1469; D.Can.L. 1471-2. One of these names Archdeacon of Sudbury, 1483-93.

JEFFERAY, JOHN. Matric. pens. from MICHAELHOUSE, Michs. 1546; Scholar of Trinity, 1550; B.A. 1550-1. Fellow, 1552. One of these names ord. priest (Norwich) Sept. 19, 1561. R. of Berwick, Sussex, 1566-1618. Buried there Feb. 1, 1617-8. Will (Lewes) 1618. (W. C. Renshaw.)

JEFFREY, JOHN. Matric. pens. from TRINITY, Easter, 1569.

JEFFREY, JOHN. Matric. pens. from TRINITY, May, 1579. Migrated to Christ's. B.A. from Christ's, 1582-3. One of these names R. of St Peter, Norwich, 1612-3. (*Peile*, I. 157.)

JEFFERY, JOHN. Matric. sizar from CHRIST'S, Apr. 1606; B.A. 1608-9; M.A. 1612. One of these names V. of Billinghurst, Sussex, 1620. R. of Kingston Bowley, 1626. (*Peile*, I. 256.)

JEFERAYES, JOHN. Adm. at CAIUS, c. 1605-6, from Trinity. S. of William, gent. Age 18. B. at Shereford, Norfolk. School, Lynn (Mr Man). B.A. 1607-8. V. of Harston, Cambs., 1616. R. of Gt Easton, Essex, 1627. V. of Ramsey, 1628-39. Admon. (Consist. C. London) Apr. 1639. (J. Ch. Smith.)

JEFFREY, JOHN. B.A. from ST CATHARINE'S, 1610-1. S. of John, silkweaver. School, Merchant Taylors'. M.A. from Pembroke, 1614; B.D. 1621; D.D. 1627. Fellow of Pembroke, 1613. Chaplain to Archbishop Abbot. R. of Old Romney, Kent, 1627. Preb. of Canterbury, 1629. V. of Ticehurst, Sussex, 1639. V. of Faversham, Kent, 1643. Will (P.C.C.) 1655, as D.D.

GEOFFRAYS, JOHN. Adm. pens. at EMMANUEL, Apr. 2, 1627. S. of Robert, merchant, of London. Matric. 1627; B.A. 1630-1; M.A. 1634. One of these names (Jeffrey) R. of Wavendon, Bucks., 1648-60. Died 1660. (*Vis. of London*, 1634.)

JEFFREYS or JEFFREY, JOHN. Adm. pens. at EMMANUEL, Mar. 2, 1635-6. Of Suffolk. Matric. 1636. Afterwards Fell.-Com. Probably s. and h. of Simon, of Bedfield, Suffolk, gent.; adm. at Gray's Inn, Feb. 22, 1640-1.

JEFFREY or JEFFERYES, JOHN. Adm. sizar (age 15) at CHRIST'S, Feb. 13, 1650-1. S. of Simon, of Suffolk. Matric. 1651; B.A. 1654-5; M.A. 1658. Probably V. of Kenton, Suffolk, 1665. (*Peile*, I. 540.)

JEFFERY, JOHN. Adm. sizar at ST CATHARINE'S, Jan. 24, 1664-5. B. at Ipswich, Dec. 20, 1647. School, Ipswich. Matric. 1665; B.A. 1668-9; M.A. 1672; D.D. 1696. Ord. deacon (Ely) Mar. 19, 1670-1; priest (London) June, 1671. Minister of St Peter Mancroft, Norwich, 1678. V. of Falkenham, Suffolk, 1687. R. of Kirton, 1687. Archdeacon of Norwich, 1694-1720. Author, religious. Died Apr. 1, 1720, aged 72. Buried in the chancel of St Peter Mancroft. (*D.N.B.*)

JEFFREYS, JOHN. Adm. pens. (age 16) at JESUS, Sept. 17, 1683. Of York. Matric. 1683-4; Scholar, 1685; B.A. 1687-8. Married, at York Minster, June 19, 1690, Frances Hutchinson. (M. H. Peacock.)

JEFFERIES, JOHN. Adm. pens. at CORPUS CHRISTI, 1693. Of Norfolk. Matric. 1694.

JEFFERY, JOHN. Adm. sizar (age 17) at TRINITY, Mar. 26, 1696. S. of Edmund. B. at Cambridge. School, St Paul's. Matric. 1696; B.A. 1700-1; M.A. 1714. Ord. deacon (London) Dec. 20, 1702. One of these names (M.A.), R. of Gt Wratting, Suffolk, 1727-60; and of Little Wratting, 1728-60.

JEFFERY, JOHN. Adm. sizar at ST CATHARINE'S, Dec. 14, 1697. Of Ipswich. Matric. 1698; B.A. 1701-2; M.A. 1705. Fellow, 1704. Ord. deacon (Norwich) Sept. 1703; priest, June 8, 1707. R. of Trunch and Gimingham, Norfolk, 1709-48. R. of St Peter Mancroft, Norwich, 1714-23. V. of Earlham, Norwich, 1714-23. Died Aug. 1748. M.I. at Ipswich. (E. *Anglian*, IX. 187.)

JEFFERIES, JOHN. Adm. Fell.-Com. at CLARE, Apr. 11, 1705. B. at Canterbury. Bapt. at the Cathedral, Aug. 22, 1689; s. of James, canon. Matric. 1706. Perhaps adm. at Lincoln's Inn, Jan. 22, 1704-5. Perhaps father of James (1732).

JEFFERY, JOHN. Adm. sizar at ST CATHARINE'S, July 6, 1707. Matric. 1708; B.A. 1711-2; M.A. 1715. Ord. deacon (Norwich) Sept. 20, 1713; priest, Oct. 18, 1714. R. of Drayton, Norfolk, 1714-55. Died Nov. 3, 1755.

JEFFERY or JEFFERIES, JOHN. Adm. at CORPUS CHRISTI, 1747. Of Norfolk. Matric. 1748-9; B.A. 1752. Ord. deacon (Norwich) Sept. 1753; priest, Feb. 1755. V. of Ringland, Norfolk, 1755-79. V. of Potter Heigham, 1779-88. V. of Ludham, 1779-88.

JEFFRYES, JOHN. Adm. pens. at ST CATHARINE'S, Feb. 24, 1750-1. Previously adm. at Jesus College, Oxford, Oct. 14, 1748, age 17. S. of John, of Woozton, in the parish of West Felton, Salop. Matric. 1750-1. Ord. priest (Lincoln, *Lit. dim.* from Lichfield) May 25, 1755; 'student in law, of St Catharine's.' (*Al. Oxon.*)

JEFFREY, NICHOLAS. Matric. pens. from CLARE, Easter, 1575; B.A. 1577-8; M.A. 1581. Incorp. at Oxford, 1588. Ord. deacon (London) May 26, 1605; of Lewes, Sussex (perhaps curate). R. of Poole, Dorset, 1611-24. Buried there Mar. 9, 1624-5. Perhaps father of William (1618). (Hutchins, *Dorset*, I. 54.)

JEFFERY, NICHOLAS. Matric. pens. from PEMBROKE, Easter, 1616; B.A. 1622. One of these names sequestered to Stanwell, Middlesex, in 1646.

JEFFERYES, OWEN. Matric. sizar from ST JOHN'S, Easter, 1607.

JEFFERY, ROBERT. Matric. sizar from KING'S, Easter, 1633.

JEFFRY or JEFFERYES, ROBERT. Adm. pens. (age 15) at CHRIST'S, Sept. 29, 1637. S. of Martin. School, Maidstone (Mr Elmaston). Matric. 1637. Adm. at the Middle Temple, Feb. 11, 1640. (*Peile*, I. 451.)

JEFFERYS, ROBERT. Matric. sizar from KING'S, Easter, 1677; B.A. 1680-1.

JEFFERIES, ROBERT. Adm. at CORPUS CHRISTI, 1703. Of Norfolk. Matric. 1704.

JEFFERY, ROGER. Matric. sizar from CHRIST'S, May, 1572. Ord. deacon and priest (Lincoln) Mar. 1581-2. Perhaps V. of Stanford, Norfolk, 1587-1628. Died 1628. (*Peile*, I. 123.)

JEFFERY, SAMUEL. Adm. pens. at EMMANUEL, Apr. 20, 1690. B. at Sawston, Cambs. Matric. 1690; B.A. 1693-4; M.A. 1697; B.D. 1704. Fellow, 1701-15. C. of Babraham, Cambs., 1697. R. of North Luffenham, Rutland, 1714-22. Buried there May 22, 1722.

JEFFERY, STEVEN. Matric. Fell.-Com. from CLARE, Easter, 1610. One of these names barrister, Gray's Inn, 1617; ancient, 1622.

JEFFREYS, THOMAS. Matric. pens. from CHRIST'S, Michs. 1547. Of Yorkshire. B.A. 1549-50; M.A. from Clare, 1553; B.D. from St John's, 1561. Fellow of Clare, 1559. Fellow of St John's, 1560. Ord. deacon (London) 1559. R. of Ashprington, Devon, 1577. (*Cooper*, I. 383.)

JEFFREY, THOMAS. Matric. pens. from QUEENS', Michs. 1561. One of these names adm. at Gray's Inn, 1564.

JEFFREIS, THOMAS. Adm. pens. (age 20) at CAIUS, Jan. 14, 1568-9. S. of William, of Water Orton, Warws. School, Repton. Matric. 1569. One of these names, of Lincoln diocese, subscribed for deacon's orders at Chester, 1573. Probably R. of Snelland, Lincs., 1576. 'Ord. priest (Peterb.) June 9, 1576, aged 30; skilled in Latin.' (*Lib. Cler. Linc.*, 1576.)

JEFFRAYE, THOMAS. Matric. sizar from CLARE, Michs. 1572; B.A. 1574-5. Probably ord. priest (Norwich) Nov. 30, 1579. V. of Debden, Suffolk, 1589.

JEFFRY, THOMAS. Adm. Fell.-Com. at EMMANUEL, Oct. 24, 1595. Matric. 1595.

JEFFRY, THOMAS. Adm. sizar at SIDNEY, Aug. 1, 1611; B.A. 1614-5. Perhaps ord. deacon (? Chichester) June 15; priest, Sept. 21, 1617. R. of Kingston Bowley, Sussex, 1628. Will (P.C.C.) 1654: of Kingston Bowley. One of these names R. of Yaxley, Hunts., 1624-6. (W. C. Renshaw.)

JEFFREY, THOMAS. Adm. sizar at ST CATHARINE'S, Apr. 23, 1673. Matric. 1673; B.A. 1676-7; M.A. 1680. Ord. deacon (Norwich) May, 1678; priest, Sept. 1679. Perhaps R. of Flordon, Norfolk, 1679; and R. of Gissing, 1690-4. Died 1694.

JEFFREY, W. Matric. sizar from PEMBROKE, Michs. 1568.

JEFFREY, WILLIAM. Resident at QUEENS', 1523-4.

JEFFERAYE, WILLIAM. Matric. pens. from CLARE, Easter, 1576; B.A. 1579-80; M.A. 1583. Ord. deacon and priest (Lincoln) 1587. Will of one of these names (P.C.C.) 1595; of Boston, Lincs., B.D.

JEFFRAIES, WILLIAM. Adm. sizar (age 15) at CAIUS, May 21, 1603. S. of William, gent., of Shereford, Norfolk. School, Lynn (Mr Man). Matric. 1603; Scholar, 1604-7; B.A. 1606-7; M.A. 1610. Ord. deacon and priest (Norwich) 1608; C. of Shereford. Teacher at Fakenham, about 1607-9. One of these names preacher or C. at Sandbach, Cheshire, 1614-5; preacher at Nantwich, 1616-9. (*Venn*, I. 181.)

JEFFREYE, WILLIAM. Adm. sizar (age 13) at PEMBROKE, June 29, 1618. S. of Nicholas (? 1575), of Lewes, Sussex. Matric. 1618; Scholar; B.A. 1621-2; M.A. 1625.

JEFFERY, WILLIAM. Matric. sizar from PEMBROKE, Michs. 1618; B.A. 1621-2; M.A. 1625. Perhaps V. of Sheriff Hales, Staffs., 1622-30. Preb. of Lichfield, 1625-30. Archdeacon of Salop, 1628-42. Chancellor of Lichfield, 1630-42. R. of Hamstall Ridware, 1631-42. Will proved (Lichfield) May 11, 1642. (*Wm. Salt Arch. Soc.*, 1915.)

JEFFREY or JEFFREYS, WILLIAM. Adm. sizar at JESUS, Apr. 16, 1626. Of Hampshire. Matric. 1626; Scholar, 1628; B.A. 1629-30.

JEFFREYS, WILLIAM. Adm. pens. (age 18) at ST JOHN'S, June 21, 1661. S. of John, gent., of Bangor, and of Acton Park, Wrexham. B. at Bangor. Schools, Wrexham (Mr Lewis) and Shrewsbury. Matric. 1661; B.A. 1664-5; M.A. 1669. Brother of George (1662). (G. W. Fisher, *Shrewsbury*.)

JEFFERYS, ——. Adm. Fell.-Com. at MAGDALENE, 1712. (Did not reside.)

JEFFREY or GEFFRA, ——. D.D. 1501.

JEFFORD, ROBERT Matric. sizar from ST JOHN'S, Lent, 1579-80. Doubtless Rob. Gifford, whom *see*.

JEFFREN or JEFFRUN, THOMAS. B.Can.L. 1532-3. Perhaps chantry-priest at Lowick, Northants.; legatee and executor of William Beylight, the other chantry-priest, in 1534. (H. I. Longden.)

JEGON, JOHN. Matric. sizar from QUEENS', Michs. 1567. S. of Robert, of Coggeshall, Essex. B. 1550. B.A. 1571-2; M.A. 1575; B.D. 1583; D.D. (?) 1590. Fellow, 1572-90. Proctor, 1581-2. Scrutator, 1584. Preacher, 1585. Master of Corpus Christi, 1590-1603. Vice-Chancellor, 1596-8, 1600-1. Ord. deacon and priest (Peterb.) July 11, 1573. R. of St Botolph, Cambridge, 1574-8. R. of Redmile, Leics., 1588. R. of Beckingham, Lincs., 1595. Preb. of Southwell, 1600-3. Dean of Norwich, 1601-3. Bishop of Norwich, 1603-18. Married Lilia, dau. of Richard Vaughan, Bishop of London. Died at Aylsham, Mar. 13, 1617-8, aged 67. Will, P.C.C. His arms are on the roof of the Catalogue room (ancient Senate House) to commemorate his Vice-Chancellorship. Brother of Thomas (1580). (*Masters*; *D.N.B.*)

JEGON, JOHN. Matric. sizar from CORPUS CHRISTI, Easter, 1612. B. at Sible Hedingham. S. of Dr Thomas Jegon (1580), Master of Corpus Christi. B.A. 1614; M.A. 1618. Fellow, 1614-20, after much opposition from the other fellows. Ord. deacon (London) May 23, 1619, age 23; priest (Norwich) Oct. 14, 1620. R. of Sible Hedingham, Essex, 1634-72. (*Masters*, 158.)

JEGON, JOHN. Matric. pens. from CORPUS CHRISTI, 1627. S. of John (1567), late Master of Corpus Christi. Adm. at Gray's Inn, Nov. 8, 1630. Died young. Buried at Aylsham, Norfolk, Sept. 1631, aged 19. (*Blomefield*, III. 564.)

JEGON, JOHN. Matric. pens. from CORPUS CHRISTI, Michs. 1639. Of Essex. B.A. 1643-4; M.A. 1647.

JEGON, ROBERT. Matric. Fell.-Com. from CORPUS CHRISTI, Michs. 1624. Of Norfolk. Perhaps s. and h. of John (1567); age *c.* 10 in 1617. If so, of Buxton, Norfolk, Esq. (*Blomefield*, III. 564; VI. 446.)

JEGON, ROBERT. Adm. pens. (age 17) at ST JOHN'S, May 23, 1684. S. of Arthur, Esq. (late of Lincoln's Inn). B. at York. School, Kilham (Mr Kenyon). Matric. 1684. Adm. at Gray's Inn, May 14, 1684.

JEGON, THOMAS. Matric. pens. from QUEENS', Easter, 1580. S. of Robert, of Coggeshall, Essex. B.A. 1583-4; M.A. 1587; D.D. 1602. Fellow of Corpus Christi, 1587. Proctor, 1593-4. Master, 1603-18. Vice-Chancellor, 1608-9. R. of Sible Hedingham, 1594-1618. Preb. of Southwell, 1600-4. Archdeacon of Norwich, 1604-18; Preb., 1604-18. R. of Ashen, Essex, 1605-7. Died Mar. 2, 1617-8. M.I. at Sible Hedingham. Will, P.C.C. Brother of John (1567), father of John (1612). (*Masters*.)

JEGON, WILLIAM. Adm. at CORPUS CHRISTI, 1627. Of Norfolk. Perhaps brother of John (1627).

JEGON, WILLIAM. Adm. sizar at TRINITY, July 9, 1668. B. at Buxton, Norfolk, May 6, 1650. Migrated to King's, as scholar from Eton, 1668. Matric. 1669; B.A. 1672-3; M.A. 1676. Fellow of King's, 1671. Ord. deacon (Peterb.) Sept. 21, 1673. R. of Swanton Morley, Norfolk, 1680-1710. Author, sermons. Died Nov. 18, 1710. Buried at Swanton. M.I.

JEKYLL, RICHARD. Adm. pens. (age 17) at SIDNEY, Aug. 24, 1698. 3rd s. of Thomas (1694), D.D., R. of Cottenham, Cambs. School, Westminster. Migrated to Oxford. Matric. from Christ Church, June 25, 1700, age 20; B.A. (Oxford) 1704; M.A. 1707. R. of Gayton-le-Wold, Lincs., 1725. (*Al. Oxon.*)

JEKYLL, SAMUEL. Adm. sizar (age 15) at SIDNEY, June 25, 1640. S. of John, farmer. B. at Tetney, Lincs. Schools, Castor (Mr Wm. Metcalfe), Alford (Mr Tho. Hooper) and Newton (Mr Petley).

JEKYLL, THOMAS. Adm. pens. at QUEENS', Oct. 22, 1658. Of Kent. Matric. 1660; B.A. 1662-3; M.A. 1666; B.D. 1675. Fellow, 1664-80. Signed for deacon (London) June 7, 1666; for priest, Sept. 22, 1666.

JEKYLL, THOMAS. Matric. pens. from QUEENS', Michs. 1667. Perhaps adm. at the Inner Temple, Feb. 7, 1673-4.

JEKYLL, THOMAS. Incorp. D.D. 1694, at SIDNEY. S. of John, of London. B. in St Stephen Walbrook, London, July 16, 1646. School, Merchant Taylors'. Matric. (Trinity College, Oxford) Dec. 11, 1663, age 16; B.A. (Oxford) 1667; M.A. 1670. Ord. deacon (Lincoln) Dec. 18, 1670. V. of Rowde, Wilts., 1671. Minister of Tothill Fields Chapel in St Margaret's, Westminster. R. of Cottenham, Cambs. Author, sermons. Died June 29, 1700. Buried in the New Church, Westminster. Will, P.C.C. Father of Richard (1698). (*Al. Oxon.*; *D.N.B.*)

JEKYLL, THOMAS. Adm. scholar at TRINITY HALL, Jan. 9, 1703–4. Matric. 1703.

JELLETT, THOMAS. Adm. pens. CHRIST'S, Apr. 5, 1626. S. of Robert, of Devon. School at Ely (Mr Hitch). Matric. 1626.

JELLISON, ROBERT. Adm. sizar (age 18) at ST JOHN'S, Jan. 22, 1666–7. S. of Robert, linendraper, of Hull, Yorks. B. there. School, Hull (Mr Catlyn). Matric. 1667; B.A. 1670–1. Ord. deacon (York) June, 1671; priest, Dec. 1674. V. of Burton Pidsea, Yorks., 1692–1717. V. of Keyingham, 1706–17. Buried Oct. 7, 1717. Father of the next.

JELLISON, ROBERT. Adm. sizar (age 21) at SIDNEY, June 6, 1698. Only s. of Robert (above), of Keyingham, Yorks. School, Beverley (Mr Lambert). Matric. 1698; B.A. 1702–3. Ord. deacon (York) May, 1702; priest, 1703. R. of Holmpton; and V. of Welwick, Yorks., 1710–4. Died Jan. 1713–4.

JELLUS or JELLOWES, JAMES. Adm. sizar (age 16) at CAIUS, June 3, 1637. S. of James, gent. B. at Deeping, Lincs. School, Moulton (Mr Smith). B.A. 1640–1. Ord. deacon (Peterb.) June 5, 1642. R. of Marcham-in-the-Fen, Lincs., 1663; will proved at Lincoln, Sept. 2, 1681. (*Venn*, I. 326.)

JELLYBRANDE, THOMAS. Matric. sizar from PEMBROKE, Michs. 1555.

JELOW or GELOW, HENRY. B.Can.L. 1460.

JELY, *see* JOLLY.

JEMBLEIN, JOHN. Adm. pens. (age 19) at ST JOHN'S, June 30, 1735. S. of James, surgeon, of Cambridgeshire (and Elizabeth Ridley; married at Peterborough, Aug. 22, 1714). B. at Thorney, in the Isle of Ely. School, Lincoln (Mr Goodall). Matric. 1735. Migrated to Trinity Hall, June 8, 1736. B.A. 1738–9. Adm. at the Inner Temple, May 10, 1740, as s. and h. of Jacob Jembelin, of Ramsey, Hunts., Esq. (*Scott-Mayor*, III. 470.)

JEMMET, ROBERT. Adm. pens. at CLARE, July 7, 1676. Of Uxbridge, Middlesex. Matric. 1677.

JEMMATT, SAMUEL. Matric. Fell.-Com. from KING'S, Easter, 1697; M.B. 1697. Doubtless s. of Samuel, V. of St Nicholas, Warwick. Colleger at Eton, 1687–8. Matric. from University College, Oxford, Mar. 3, 1691–2, age 17; B.A. (Oxford) 1695.

JEMMET, WILLIAM. M.A. 1623 (Incorp. from Oxford). B. at Reading. B.A. (Magdalen College, Oxford) 1614; M.A. (Magdalen Hall) 1616–7. Preacher at Lechlade, Gloucs. Lecturer at Isleworth, Middlesex, 1633, for 14 years. R. of Nettlestead, Kent, 1643–5. Chaplain to the Earl of Northumberland. V. of St Giles', Reading, 1649–78. Author, religious. Died Jan. 28, 1677–8. Buried in St Giles' Church. Will (P.C.C.) 1678. (*Al. Oxon.*; *D.N.B.*)

JEMSON, SAMUEL. Adm. pens. (age 17) at CHRIST'S, May 18, 1741. S. of Thomas (of Ratcliff, Stepney, sailmaker, and Elizabeth, dau. of Joshua Sheppard, V. of Harrowden, Northants.). B. in Middlesex. School, Guilsborough, Northants. (Mr Horton). Matric. 1741; Scholar, 1744; B.A. 1745; M.A. 1750. Ord. deacon (Lincoln) May 25, 1746. V. of Weedon Beck, Northants., 1748–80. Married, at Maidford, Northants., June 15, 1758, Sarah Green. Died Sept. 10, 1780. Buried at Brockhall, Northants. Will, P.C.C. (*Peile*, II. 242; H. I. Longden.)

JENDEN, WILLIAM. Adm. sizar at TRINITY, May 12, 1668. Matric. 1668; Scholar, 1671; B.A. 1671–2; M.A. 1675. Signed for deacon's orders (London) Dec. 19, 1673; 'C. of Cowfold, Sussex'; for priest's, June 12, 1674. R. of Chiltington, Sussex. Will (Chichester) 1704.

JENIVER, CHRISTOPHER. Matric. sizar from TRINITY, Easter, 1567. B. *c.* 1549. Scholar, 1571; B.A. 1571–2; M.A. 1575. Ord. priest (Ely) Dec. 21, 1574; C. of St Michael's, Cambridge. V. of Bottisham, Cambs., 1575–1611. Buried Sept. 20, 1611.

JENEVER, HENRY. Matric. sizar from TRINITY, Easter, 1572. Probably B.A. Ord. deacon (Peterb.) June 2, 1577; priest (Lichfield) Aug. 8, 1578. V. of Bottesford, Lincs., 1591 (B.A.).

JENEVER, HENRY. Adm. sizar at JESUS, June 10, 1624. Of Lincolnshire. Matric. 1624; B.A. 1627–8; Scholar, 1628.

JENEWAY, *see* JANEWAY.

JENISON, EDWARD. Matric. pens. from CHRIST'S, Nov. 1586. Probabiy of Newark-on-Trent; adm. at Gray's Inn, Feb. 9, 1591; formerly of Staple's Inn.

JENISON, JAMES. Matric. pens. from TRINITY, Michs. 1584. S. of Robert, gent., deceased, of Burnham Westgate, Norfolk. Bapt. there, Jan. 25, 1568–9. School, Fakenham (Mr Warde). Migrated to Caius, June 22, 1585, age 17. Of Keddington, Lincs., Esq. Married Ellen, dau. of —— Holmes, of Weston, Lincs. (*Vis. of Lincs.*, 1592; *Vis. of Norfolk*; *Venn*, I. 125.)

JENISON, JOHN. Adm. at KING'S (age 17) a scholar from Eton, Aug. 27, 1576. Of Wickmere, Norfolk. Fellow; left, 1580, without a degree. Perhaps V. of East Riston, Norfolk, 1605.

JENISON, JOHN. Adm. pens. at CHRIST'S, May 13, 1672. S. of Matthew. B. at Newark. School, Repton. Matric. 1675; B.A. 1675–6; M.A. 1679. Ord. priest (Lincoln) Aug. 4, 1688. V. of Sedgebrook, Lincs. Died Dec. 29, 1714, aged 59. M.I. at Sedgebrook. Brother of Matthew (1672). (*Peile*, II. 43.)

'JENISON,' JOHN, *see* PENISTON.

JENISON, MATTHEW. Adm. pens. at CHRIST'S, May 13, 1672. S. of Matthew, of Newark, Notts., Esq. School, Repton. Adm. at Lincoln's Inn, Nov. 18, 1674. Knighted, Nov. 19, 1683. M.P. for Newark, 1701–5. Of Newcastle-on-Tyne. Confined in the Fleet prison for refusing to pay the costs of a chancery suit. Died there Nov. 1734, aged 81. Brother of John (1672). (*L. Mag.*; *Peile*, II. 43; Dickinson, *Newark*.)

JENISON, MICHAEL. Matric. pens. from TRINITY, Easter, 1589. Perhaps 5th s. of Thomas, of Walworth, Durham. Of Etwall, Derbs. Married Martha, dau. of Sir Thomas Gerrard, Knt. (*Vis. of Northants.*, 1618; *Vis. of Durham*, 1666.)

JENISON or GENISON, PHILIP. Matric. sizar from TRINITY, Easter, 1627.

JENNISON, RALPH. Adm. Fell.-Com. (age 17) at CHRIST'S, Sept. 26, 1691. S. of Henry. Bapt. at St Nicholas, Newcastle, Oct. 30, 1673. School, London (Mr Meure). Matric. 1691. Adm. at Lincoln's Inn, Dec. 19, 1693. Appointed executor of his father's will, 1703. Of Wolsington, Durham, Esq. Married Barbara, dau. of Robert Jenison, of Walworth. Buried Mar. 25, (?) 1722. (*Peile*, II. 122; *Surtees*, III. 412.)

JENISON, RALPH. Matric. Fell.-Com. from CHRIST'S, Mar. 1718–9. Doubtless s. of Ralph, of Elswick, Newcastle. B. 1696. Bapt. at Heighington, Dec. 23, 1696. M.P. for Northumberland, 1722–41; and for Newport, Isle of Wight, 1749–58. Master of the Buckhounds to George II, 1737–57. Of Elswick and Walworth, Durham. Died May 15, 1758. Buried at Heighington. (*Peile*, II. 196; H. M. Wood; A. B. Beaven.)

JENISON, ROBERT. B.A. from EMMANUEL, 1604–5. S. of Ralph, Mayor of Newcastle. Bapt. at St Nicholas, Jan. 6, 1582–3. M.A. from St John's, 1608; B.D. 1616; D.D. 1629. Incorp. at Oxford, 1608. First Master of St Mary Magdalene's Hospital, 1619. Lecturer at All Saints', Newcastle-on-Tyne, 1622; deprived for nonconformity, 1639. V. of Newcastle, 1645–52. R. of St Pancras, Kentish Town, 1647. Married (1) at St Nicholas, Newcastle, June 22, 1619, Anne, dau. of Wm. Bonner. Author, religious. Buried at St Nicholas, Newcastle, Nov. 8, 1652. Will (P.C.C.) 1653. Father of Thomas (1654). (H. M. Wood; *D.N.B.*)

JENISON, THOMAS. Matric. pens. from ST JOHN'S, Easter, 1578.

JENISON, THOMAS. Adm. at KING'S (age 16) a scholar from Eton, Sept. 13, 1585. Probably of Berwick-on-Tweed. Matric. 1585; B.A. 1589. Left, as fellow, in 1589. Perhaps brother of William (1580).

JENISON, THOMAS. Adm. sizar at EMMANUEL, Easter, 1621. Matric. 1621, as Jenson.

JENNISON, THOMAS. Matric. pens. from ST CATHARINE'S, Michs. 1646.

JENISON, THOMAS. Adm. pens. (age 18) at ST JOHN'S, Apr. 5, 1654. S. of Robert (1604–5), D.D., of Newcastle, Northumberland. Bapt. at St Nicholas, May 10, 1636. School, Newcastle. Matric. 1654. Merchant and alderman of Newcastle. Died Dec. 17, 1676. Buried at St Nicholas, Newcastle. (*Surtees*, III. 322; H. M. Wood.)

JENISON or GENISON, WILLIAM. Matric. pens. from KING'S, Michs. 1575.

JENISON, WILLIAM. Adm. (age 18) at KING'S, Aug. 24, 1580. Of Berwick, Northumberland. Matric. 1580. Left, 1583.

JENISON, WILLIAM. Adm. pens. (age 16) at CHRIST'S, Aug. 6, 1668. 3rd s. of Ralph, of Newcastle-upon-Tyne, and of Elswick, Northumberland. B. at Newcastle. Schools, Newcastle and Berwick (Mr Webb). Matric. 1668. Adm. at Lincoln's Inn, June 11, 1670. Town clerk of Newcastle, 1675–99. Of Benwell, Northumberland. Buried at St Nicholas, Newcastle, Jan. 20, 1711–2. Father of the next. (*Peile*, II. 17; *Surtees*, III. 232.)

JENISON, WILLIAM. Adm. pens. (age 14) at CHRIST'S, July 10, 1692. S. of William (above), town clerk, of Newcastle. B. there. Bapt. at St John's, May 2, 1678. School, Westminster. Scholar, 1693; B.A. 1696–7; M.A. 1700. Ord. deacon (London) Mar. 6, 1700–1; priest, May 23, 1703. (*Peile*, II. 126.)

JENKIN, HENRY. Adm. pens. (age 16) at PEMBROKE, May 9, 1672. S. of Thomas, farmer. B. in the Isle of Thanet, Kent. Matric. 1672; B.A. 1675–6; M.A. 1679. Fellow, 1677. Ord. deacon (London) May 29, 1686. V. of Tilney, Norfolk, 1689–1732. R. of Runcton Holme, 1702–32. Died 1732. Father of Robert (1722) and Thomas (1715–6), brother of Robert (1674).

JENKIN, HENRY. Adm. sizar (age 17) at ST JOHN'S, July 5, 1750. S. of Thomas (? 1715-6), clerk, of Norfolk. B. at Westwick. School, Scarning. Matric. 1750; B.A. 1754; M.A. 1757; B.D. 1765; D.D. 1792. Fellow, 1756-77. Ord. deacon (Gloucester, *Litt. dim.* from York) Dec. 21; priest (Lichfield) Dec. 24, 1758. R. of Angmering, Sussex, 1766-75. R. of Ufford, Northants., 1775-1808. R. of Maidwell St Mary, 1778-1808. Dean and R. of St Buryan, Cornwall, 1799-1817. R. of Wotton, Surrey, 1808-17. R. of Abinger, 1808-17. Preb. of Winchester, 1810-7. Died Dec. 21, 1817. (*Scott-Mayor*, III. 602.)

JENKEN, ROBERT. Matric. pens. from CORPUS CHRISTI, Easter, 1644. S. of Henry, proctor, of Canterbury. B.A. 1647-8. Migrated to Emmanuel, Mar. 1, 1650-1, as first Richards Scholar. M.A. 1651. Probably R. of Ingworth, Essex, 1654; ejected, 1660.

JENKIN, ROBERT. Adm. sizar (age 17) at ST JOHN'S, May 12, 1674. S. of Thomas, of the Isle of Thanet, Kent. B. there. School, Canterbury. Matric. 1674; B.A. 1677-8; M.A. 1681; D.D. 1709. Fellow, 1680-9. Master, 1711-27. Lady Margaret Professor, 1711-27. V. of Waterbeach, Cambs., 1680-9. Chaplain to Bishop Lake, of Chichester, and to the Earl of Exeter. Precentor of Chichester, 1688-90. Author, theological. Died at North Runcton, Norfolk, Apr. 7, 1727. M.I. at Runcton Holme. Will proved (V.C.C.). Brother of Henry (1672). (*D.N.B.*)

JENKIN, ROBERT. Adm. sizar (age 18) at ST JOHN'S, Oct. 17, 1722. S. of Henry (1672), V. of Tilney and Holme, Norfolk. B. at Holme. School, Bexwell (Mr Foster). Matric. 1723; B.A. 1726-7; M.A. 1734. Ord. deacon (Lincoln) Dec. 19, 1731; priest (Rochester) Dec. 23, 1733. R. of Westbere, Kent, 1734-78. V. of Brookland, 1737-43. Minor Canon of Canterbury. Married, at Canterbury Cathedral, May 31, 1738, Catharine Blomer. Died Oct. 8, 1778. Brother of Thomas (1715-6). (*Scott-Mayor*, III. 357; G. *Mag.*)

JENKIN, THOMAS. Adm. pens. (age 16) at PEMBROKE, May 19, 1682. S. of Thomas, of Folkestone, Kent, gent. Matric. 1683-4. Adm. at Gray's Inn, Apr. 28, 1682.

JENKIN, THOMAS. Adm. pens. (age 18) at ST JOHN'S, Feb. 9, 1715-6. S. of Henry (1672), clerk, V. of Tilney, Norfolk (and nephew of Robert, the Master). B. at Tilney. School, Eton. Matric. 1716; B.A. 1719-20; M.A. 1723. Fellow, 1721-6. Ord. deacon (Norwich) Mar. 1, 1723-4. R. of North Lynn, 1729-56. R. of Runcton Holme, Norfolk, 1732-56. Author, theological. Died July 21, 1756. Brother of Robert (1722). (*Scott-Mayor*, III. 298.)

JENKIN, THOMAS. Adm. sizar at ST JOHN'S, Dec. 14, 1722. S. of John, barrister, of Kent. B. at Wye. School, Biddenden (Mr Gaudy). Matric. 1723; B.A. 1726-7; M.A. 1735. Ord. deacon (Lincoln) Dec. 24, 1727; priest, Dec. 19, 1736. V. of Bodiam, Sussex, 1736-62. R. of All Saints', Hastings, 1740-62. Perhaps V. of Salehurst. Will (P.C.C.) 1768. (*Scott-Mayor*, III. 358.)

JENKEN, WILLIAM. Adm. pens. (age 16) at CAIUS, Apr. 12, 1600. S. of Robert, gent., of Folkestone. School, Folkestone. B.A. 1603-4; M.A. from Corpus Christi, 1607; B.D. 1613. Fellow of Corpus Christi, 1607-9. C. of St Benet, Cambridge, Oct. 4, 1611. Preacher of All Saints', Sudbury. Buried Nov. 15, 1616. Father of William (1628). (*Vis. of Kent*, 1619.)

JENKEN, WILLIAM. Matric. pens. from CORPUS CHRISTI, Easter, 1608. Of Kent.

JENKIN, WILLIAM. Matric. pens. from ST JOHN'S, Easter, 1628. S. of William (1600). B. at Sudbury. B.A. 1631-2. Migrated to Emmanuel, Apr. 22, 1634. M.A. 1635. Lecturer and preacher in London and Essex. R. of St Leonard's, Colchester, 1640-3. V. of Christ Church, London, 1642-62. Minister at Blackfriars; ejected, 1662. Imprisoned for participation in the plot of Christopher Love, and later for nonconformity. A strong advocate of the presbyterian discipline. Author, controversial. Died in Newgate, Jan. 19, 1685-6. Buried in Bunhill Fields. M.I. Will (P.C.C.); dated, 1682, from All Hallows, Barking. (*Calamy*, I. 97; *Vis. of Kent*, 1619; *D.N.B.*)

JENKIN, WILLIAM. Matric. sizar from QUEENS', Easter, 1721; B.A. 1724-5; M.A. 1732. Ord. deacon (Lincoln) May 23; priest, Sept. 19, 1725. Will of one of these names (P.C.C.) 1764; of the precincts of Bridewell, London, clerk. (J. Ch. Smith.)

JENKINS, GEORGE. B.A. from PETERHOUSE, 1600-1; M.A. 1604. Probably s. of John, of York, receiver-general for Yorks. C. of Wragby, Yorks., 1607. Ord. priest (York) Feb. 1610-1. V. of Holy Trinity, York, till 1619. Buried there July 1, 1619. Brother of Henry (1584-5) and Thomas (1591). (M. H. Peacock; *T. A. Walker*.)

JENKINS or JENKIN, GODMAN. Adm. pens. (age 16) at ST JOHN'S, July 23, 1673. S. of Robert, gent., of Harding, Herts. B. there. School, Harding. Adm. at Lincoln's Inn, Feb. 18, 1673-4. Of Harpenden, Herts., Esq. Married Sarah, dau. of William Kentish, of Burston, Herts. Died Mar. 22, 1746. (*Clutterbuck*, I. 229.)

JENKINS or GENKYNS, HENRY. Matric. pens. from PETERHOUSE, Easter, 1584-5. Doubtless s. of John, receiver-general for Yorks. Age 16 in 1584. Adm. at Lincoln's Inn, July 1, 1588. Called to the Bar, 1596. M.P. for Boroughbridge, 1604-11. High Sheriff of Yorks., 1623. Of Grimston, Yorks. Married Dorothy, dau. of William Tancred, of Tankard Pannal, Yorks. Died 1646. Admon. Aug. 2, 1646. Brother of George (1600-1) and Thomas (1591). (*Misc. Gen. et Her.*, N.S., I. 122; *T. A. Walker*; M. H. Peacock.)

JENKIN, JOHN. Adm. pens. at CLARE, Apr. 18, 1638. Matric. 1638; B.A. 1641-2.

JENKINS, JOHN. M.A. from SIDNEY, 1682. S. of Henry, of East Buckland, Devon, *pleb.* Matric. (Magdalen Hall, Oxford) Mar. 26, 1675, age 18; B.A. (Oxford) 1678. Probably V. of Hitchenden, Bucks., 1687-1713. Admon. (Archd. Bucks.) 1713. (*Al. Oxon.*)

JENKINS, JOHN. Adm. pens. (age 16) at ST JOHN'S, May 20, 1684. S. of John, Esq. B. at Gateshead, Durham. School, St Paul's, London. Matric. 1684. Adm. at the Middle Temple, May 21, 1683. Called to the Bar, May 22, 1691.

JENKINS, RALPH. Matric. pens. from TRINITY, c. 1593. Probably 4th s. of John, receiver-general for Yorks. Adm. at Lincoln's Inn, Mar. 9, 1595-6, from Furnival's Inn. Brother of George, etc.

JENKINS, THOMAS. Adm. pens. at PETERHOUSE, Nov. 15, 1591. 2nd s. of John, receiver-general of Yorks. Matric. c. 1592; B.A. 1594-5. Probably died before Dec. 2, 1596. Brother of George (1600-1), etc. (*T. A. Walker*.)

JENKYNS, THOMAS. Adm. pens. (age 18) at TRINITY, Aug. 10, 1700. S. of John, of Dublin. School, Dublin (Mr Jones). Matric. 1700.

JENKINS, THOMAS. Adm. sizar at JESUS, May 5, 1743. Of Sussex. S. of ——, clerk, deceased. Matric. 1743; Rustat Scholar, 1743; B.A. 1746-7; M.A. 1750.

JENKINS, WILLIAM. Adm. at CORPUS CHRISTI, 1735. Of Devon. Matric. 1736; B.A. 1739-40; M.A. 1768.

JENKINS, ——. Adm. pens. at PETERHOUSE, 1599-1600. Probably John, youngest s. of John, receiver-general of Yorks. Brother of George, etc. (*T. A. Walker*.)

JENKINSON, CHRISTOPHER. Matric. sizar from ST JOHN'S, Easter, 1611.

JENKINSON, DANIEL. Adm. pens. at EMMANUEL, Apr. 3, 1602. Matric. 1602; B.A. 1605-6; M.A. 1609.

JENKINSON, EDWARD. Matric. sizar from TRINITY, Easter, 1614; B.A. 1617-8; M.A. 1621. Ord. deacon (Peterb.) Dec. 24, 1620. R. of Panfield, Essex, 1628-1643, sequestered. P.C. of Little Holland, 1651. Probably will (P.C.C.) 1652; of St Osyth, clerk. (H. Smith; J. Ch. Smith.)

JENKENSON, GEORGE. Adm. sizar (age 22) at CAIUS, Apr. 27, 1604. S. of Walter, minister, of Halvergate, Norfolk. School, Cambridge (Mr Edwards). Matric. 1604; B.A. 1609. Ord. priest (Norwich) 1609; C. of Tunstall, Norfolk. V. of Halvergate, 1608-18, succeeding his father. (*Venn*, I. 185.)

JENKINSON, GODFREY. Matric. sizar from QUEENS', Easter, 1665; B.A. 1668-9. Ord. deacon (Ely) Sept. 24, 1670. Will (Archd. Wilts.) of one of these names, 1705; of Minety, Wilts.

JENKINSON, GRIFFIN. B.A. from TRINITY, 1588-9; M.A. 1592.

JENKINSON, HENRY. Adm. pens. at EMMANUEL, Mar. 26, 1589. Perhaps s. of Anthony, merchant of London, and of Sywell, Northants. Matric. 1589. Adm. at Gray's Inn, Mar. 9, 1592-3. Died 1611. Buried at Tighe, Rutland. Perhaps father of William (1611-2). (*Misc. Gen. et Her.*, 2nd S., v. 7.)

JENKINSON, HENRY. Adm. pens. (age 18) at MAGDALENE, Sept. 30, 1647. S. of Robert, of East Wykeham, Lincs., gent. School, Louth. Matric. 1647. Adm. at Gray's Inn, Dec. 28, 1649. Of East Wykeham. Will proved, June 15, 1702. Father of Robert (1677). (*Lincs. Pedigrees*, 545.)

JENKINSON, HENRY. Adm. pens. (age 18) at MAGDALENE, Sept. 20, 1707. S. of Robert (1677), Esq., citizen of Lincoln. B. there. School, Enfield, Middlesex. Matric. 1707. One of these names adm. at Lincoln's Inn, Nov. 29, 1709. Of London, gent. Brother of John (1709).

JENKINSON, JOHN. Adm. sizar (age 19) at CHRIST'S, Apr. 26, 1660. S. of Richard. B. at Bradford. School, Bradford (Mr Cotes). Matric. 1660; B.A. 1663-4.

JENKINSON, JOHN. Adm. sizar at ST CATHARINE'S, July 21, 1708. Of Stony Stratford, Bucks. Matric. 1709; B.A. 1712-3. Ord. deacon (Norwich) May 31, 1713; priest, Sept. 19, 1714. R. of Passenham, Northants., 1727-62. Buried there June 25, 1762, aged 71. M.I. (H. I. Longden.)

JENKINSON, JOHN. Adm. pens. (age 17) at MAGDALENE, Aug. 27, 1709. S. of Robert (1677), Esq., citizen of Lincoln. B. there. School, Lincoln. Matric. 1710; B.A. 1713-4. Fellow, 1715. One of these names R. of Sevington, Kent, till 1727. Brother of Henry (1707).

JENKINSON, JOHN. Adm. pens. (age 21) at CHRIST'S, May 24, 1731. S. of William. B. at High House, Lancs. School, Kirkby Lonsdale (Mr Noble). Matric. 1731; Scholar, 1734; B.A. 1734-5; M.A. 1738. Ord. deacon (Lincoln) Mar. 2, 1734-5; priest, Oct. 12, 1735. P.C. of Little Raveley, Hunts., 1745-9. C. of Ingoldsby, Lincs., 1759-72. Buried there Dec. 18, 1798. (*Peile*, II. 224.)

JENKINSON, PAUL. Adm. Fell.-Com. (age 17) at SIDNEY, Apr. 15, 1681. Only s. of Richard, gent., deceased. B. at Chesterfield. Schools, Brampton, Derbs. (Mr Low) and Dronfield (Mr Mason). M.A. 1688 (*Lit. Reg.*). Created Bart., 1685. Of Walton, Derbs. High Sheriff of Derbs., 1686-7. Married Barbara, dau. of John Cotes, of Woodcote, Salop. Died 1714. Father of Richard (1703). (Burke, *Ext. Bart.*; *G.E.C.*)

JENKINSON, PAUL. Adm. pens. (age 18) at TRINITY, June 9, 1697. S. of Paul, of Hodsock, Notts. B. at Chesterfield, Derbs. School, Chesterfield (Mr Browne). Matric. 1697; Scholar, 1699; B.A. 1700-1; M.A. 1704. Ord. deacon (York) Sept. 1702; priest, 1704. R. of Weston, Yorks., 1704.

JENKINSON, RICHARD. Scholar of CLARE, 1562. One of these names V. of Scalby, Yorks., 1566-76.

JENKYNSON, RICHARD. Matric. Fell.-Com. from TRINITY, Michs. 1572.

JENKINSON, RICHARD. Matric. Fell.-Com. from PEMBROKE, Michs. 1614. Perhaps s. and h. of Sir Thomas, of Tunstall, Norfolk, Knt.; adm. at Gray's Inn, May 21, 1617.

JENKINSON, RICHARD. Adm. pens. (age 16) at SIDNEY, Apr. 24, 1703. 2nd s. of Sir Paul (1681), Bart. B. at Walton, Derbs. School, Newport (Mr Edwards). Matric. 1703.

JENKINSON, ROBERT. Matric. pens. from CORPUS CHRISTI, Easter, 1570. Of Cambridgeshire. B.A. 1572-3; M.A. 1576. One of these names ord. deacon (Peterb.) Apr. 10, 1575. Perhaps V. of St John, Margate, 1577-1601. Buried May 13, 1601.

JENKINSON, ROBERT. Matric. pens. from ST JOHN'S, Easter, 1609; B.A. 1612-3. Incorp. at Oxford, 1613. Possibly adm. at the Middle Temple, Jan. 14, 1612-3, as 's. and h. of Robert, of London'; if so, then of Walcot, Oxon.; knighted, Apr. 30, 1618. Died 1645. (*Al. Oxon.*; *Lipscomb*, I. 315.)

JENKINSON, ROBERT. Adm. pens. (age 17) at MAGDALENE, May 16, 1677. S. of Henry (1647), of East Wykeham, Lincs., Esq. School, Grantham. Matric. 1677. Died Oct. 30, 1727. Buried at St Peter-at-Arches, Lincoln. Father of Henry (1707) and John (1709). (*Lincs. Pedigrees*, 546.)

JENKINSON, SIMON. Matric. sizar from MAGDALENE, Lent, 1618-9; B.A. 1622-3; M.A. 1626. Ord. deacon (Peterb.) Sept. 25, 1625.

JENKINSON, SIMON. Adm. sizar (age 20) at TRINITY, June 22, 1689. S. of Thomas, of Bolton Agri, Lancs. Bapt. at Bolton-le-Sands, Sept. 28, 1666. School, Lancaster (Mr Thomas Lodge). Matric. 1689; B.A. 1692-3. Ord. deacon (York) June, 1694; priest, Feb. 1694-5. V. of Flintham, Notts., 1695-1700. Buried there Feb. 25, 1700-1. It is possible that he had matric. from Brasenose College, Oxford, July 6, 1683, age 16.

JENKYNSON, THOMAS. Matric. pens. from CHRIST'S, Nov. 1547; B.A. 1550-1. Perhaps fellow of St Catharine's, c. 1562, as 'Thomas Jenkins, of Westmorland.' One of these names R. of St Mary Woolchurch, London, 1560-93. Buried there Dec. 4, 1693. Will (Cons. C. London) 1594; mentions brother-in-law at Kendal. (J. Ch. Smith.)

JENKINSON, THOMAS. Matric. sizar from CLARE, Michs. 1562; B.A. 1566-7.

JENKYNSON, THOMAS. Adm. sizar (age 18) at CAIUS, Nov. 27, 1646. S. of Thomas, gent. B. in Rutland. Schools, Collyweston (Mr Marshall) and Uppingham (Mr Alson).

JENKINSON, THOMAS. Adm. pens. (age 16) at SIDNEY, Oct. 7, 1668. S. of Miles, gent. B. at Wormingford, Essex. School, Wormingford. Matric. 1668; M.B. 1674.

JENKINSON, THOMAS. Adm. sizar (age 19) at MAGDALENE, May 10, 1679. S. of Thomas. B. at Dunham Massey, Cheshire. School, Lymm. Matric. 1681; B.A. 1682-3.

JENKINSON, THOMAS ROBERT. Adm. pens. (age 18) at EMMANUEL, May 27, 1742. S. of Philip, of Gainsborough, Lincs., gent. School, Oakham. Matric. 1742; B.A. 1745-6. Of Lincoln. Died Oct. 27, 1770.

JENKINSON, WILLIAM. Matric. sizar from TRINITY, Easter, 1579; B.A. 1582-3. Master of Thetford School. R. of Thetford St Peter, 1592-3. V. of Croxton, Norfolk, 1598-1632. Perhaps R. of Santon, 1620. Father of William (1617).

JENKINSON, WILLIAM. Matric. sizar from (? CHRIST'S), Easter, 1606.

JENKINSON, WILLIAM. Adm. pens. at EMMANUEL, Feb. 14, 1611-2. Perhaps s. of Henry (1589), of Sywell, Northants. B. 1596. Matric. 1612. Married and had issue. (*Misc. Gen. et Her.*, 2nd S., v. 7.)

JENKINSON, WILLIAM. Adm. sizar (age 16) at CAIUS, May 1, 1617. S. of William (1579), minister of Thetford, Norfolk. School, Thetford, under his father. Matric. 1617; Scholar, 1618-24; B.A. 1620-1; M.A. 1624. Ord. deacon (Peterb.) June 8; priest (Norwich) Sept. 21, 1623. C. of Croxton, Norfolk, 1627. Succeeded his father as V., 1632-75. Schoolmaster at Thetford, 1632; and C. of St Cuthbert's, Thetford. (*Venn*, I. 236.)

JENKINSON, ——. Adm. at CORPUS CHRISTI, 1544.

JENKINSON, ——. Adm. at CORPUS CHRISTI, 1580.

JENKINSON, ——. Adm. pens. at EMMANUEL, Aug. 5, 1611.

JENKINSON, ——. Adm. pens. at ST CATHARINE'S, 1656-7.

JENKS or JYNKS, BARNARD. Matric. sizar from CHRIST'S, Easter, 1579. Of Northamptonshire. Migrated to Peterhouse, Feb. 6, 1579-80. B.A. 1582-3; M.A. 1586. Ord. deacon (Peterb.) May 30, 1586; priest, Mar. 26, 1587. V. of Southwick, Northants., 1586-96. R. of St Dionis Backchurch, London, 1596-1603. Buried there Sept. 12, 1603. Will, P.C.C. (*T. A. Walker*; H. I. Longden; J. Ch. Smith.)

JENKS, DAVID. Matric. sizar from KING'S, Easter, 1736; B.A. 1739-40; M.A. 1743. Conduct of King's, 1741. Ord. deacon (Lincoln) Feb. 22, 1740-1; priest, Mar. 14, 1741-2. V. of Wingrave, Bucks., 1744. R. of Little Gaddesden, Herts., 1754-93. R. of Aldbury, 1767-79. Died Aug. 25, 1793. Will, P.C.C. (*G. Mag.*; *Musgrave*.)

JENKS, HENRY. Adm. at EMMANUEL, Mar. 21, 1646-7. M.A. of King's College, Aberdeen, 1646 (adm. there, 1642). Fellow of Caius, 1653-97. Proctor, 1686-7. Incorp. at Oxford, 1669. Gresham Professor of Rhetoric, 1670-6. F.R.S., 1674. Author, *The Christian Tutor*. Died in College. Buried at St Michael's, Cambridge, Sept. 1, 1697. (*Venn*, I. 387; *D.N.B.*)

JENKS, THOMAS. Adm. pens. (age 18) at ST JOHN'S, Apr. 12, 1705. S. of Thomas, clerk. B. at Whitchurch, Salop. School, Whitchurch. Matric. 1705.

JENKES, WILLIAM. Matric. from TRINITY, c. 1593. Of Salop. B.A. 1596-7; M.A. from Jesus, 1600; B.D. 1615. Fellow of Jesus, 1603-27. V. of Whittlesford, Cambs., 1612. R. of Graveley, 1615. (A. Gray.)

JENNE, JAMES. Matric. pens. from ST JOHN'S, Lent, 1557-8.

JENNER, *see also* JENOUR.

JENNER, DAVID. Adm. sizar at TRINITY, Dec. 22, 1653. Of Northumberland. Matric. 1657; Scholar, 1657; B.A. 1657-8. Migrated to Sidney. M.A. 1662 (*Lit. Reg.*); B.D. (do.) 1668. Fellow of Sidney. V. of St Sepulchre, Cambridge, 1663. Preb. of Salisbury, 1676-91. R. of Gt Wareley, Essex, 1678-87. Chaplain to the King. Author, *The Prerogative of Primogeniture*. Died Sept. 10, 1691. Will (P.C.C.) 1692-3; as of Compton Bassett, Wilts. (*D.N.B.*)

JENNER, JOHN. Adm. pens. (age 15) at CAIUS, May 11, 1599. S. of Thomas, of Little Walsingham, Norfolk. School, Walsingham (Mr Bankes). Scholar, 1599-1604.

JENNER, JONATHAN. Adm. sizar at TRINITY, June 18, 1655; M.A. 1673 (*Lit. Reg.*). R. of Charlton, Kent, 1676-87.

JENNER or GINNER, THOMAS. Adm. sizar at CHRIST'S, Feb. 1623-4. S. of Thomas, of Fordham, Essex, farmer. B. there. Age 17. School, Fordham (Mr Cone). Matric. 1624. Emigrated to New England, 1635, with his father. Settled at Roxbury, Mass., and then at Weymouth as minister, 1636-40. Minister at Saco, Maine, 1640. Resided at Charlestown, 1646-9. Returned to England, 1650. Minister at Coltishall, Norfolk, 1652-8. His library was bought for Harvard College. Author of *Quakerism Anatomiz'd and Confuted*, 1670. Will (Dublin) May 26, 1676. (J. G. Bartlett; D.N.B.)

JENNER, THOMAS. Matric. pens. from QUEENS', Easter, 1655. S. of Thomas, of Waverton, Sussex. B. 1638, at Mayfield. School, Tonbridge. Adm. at the Inner Temple, 1656. Barrister, Nov. 22, 1663. Bencher, 1682. Recorder of London, 1683-6. Knighted, Oct. 4, 1683. King's serjeant, 1684. M.P. for Rye, 1685-8. Baron of the Exchequer, 1686-8. Justice C.P., 1688-9. Of Petersham, Surrey. One of the royal commissioners to enquire into the appointment of a president of Magdalen College, Oxford. Arrested while attempting to escape with James II, 1688; sent to the Tower; released, 1690. Resumed his practice at the Bar. Died Jan. 1, 1706-7. M.I. at Petersham. Will, P.C.C. (*D.N.B.*; Burke, *L.G.*; *Manning and Bray*, I. 442.)

JENNEY, ARTHUR. Adm. Fell.-Com. (age 18) at CAIUS, June 12, 1611. S. and h. of Francis, Esq., of Rendlesham, Suffolk. Schools, Southwold and Worlingworth (Mr Claydon and Mr Barker). Matric. 1611. Adm. at Lincoln's Inn, 1613. Succeeded his grandfather Arthur, of Knoddishall. Knighted, Mar. 26, 1639. Sheriff for Suffolk, 1645–6; and for Norfolk. 1654–5. Died Mar. 24, 1667–8. Buried at Knoddishall. Will (P.C.C.) 1668. Father of Robert (1635). (*Venn*, I. 212; *Lincs. Pedigrees*, 548; *Vis. of Suffolk*, 1664.)

JENNY or JERMEY, CHRISTOPHER. Adm. at KING'S (age 18) a scholar from Eton, Aug. 13, 1541. Of Cressingham, Norfolk. Left, 1542–3.

GINNY or JINNY, EDMUND. Adm. pens. at ST CATHARINE'S, 1665–6. Perhaps of London, gent. Adm. at the Inner Temple, Dec. 9, 1668. Called to the Bar, Nov. 28, 1675.

JENNEY, EDMUND. Adm. Fell.-Com. at ST CATHARINE'S, May 23, 1733. S. of Robert, of Knoddishall, Suffolk. Bapt. Aug. 20, 1712. Of Bredfield, Suffolk. Died 1745. (Burke, *L.G.*)

JENNEY, EDGAR. Adm. pens. (age 18) at EMMANUEL, Sept. 11, 1742. S. of Arthur, Esq., of Bredfield, Suffolk. School, Chattisham. Matric. 1743. Afterwards Fell.-Com. B.A. 1746–7. Died 1746–7. (Burke, *L.G.*)

JENEY, FRANCIS. Matric. pens. from JESUS, Michs. 1576.

JENNY, FRANCIS. Adm. pens. (age 17) at CAIUS, Feb. 11, 1660–1. S. of William, merchant, of London. B. there. Bapt. at St Laurence Pountney, Apr. 5, 1645. Schools, Bury St Edmunds (Mr Stephens) and Merchant Taylors' (Mr Dugard). Matric. 1661; Scholar, 1661–8; B.A. 1664–5; M.A. 1668. Fellow, 1668–71. Ord. deacon and priest (Lincoln) Dec. 19, 1669. R. of Denver, Norfolk, 1669–1715. Married, at Denver, Sept. 23, 1706, Margaret, dau. of Thomas Barber, of Denver. Died Apr. 10, 1715. Buried at Denver. M.I. Will, P.C.C. Benefactor to the College. Brother of William (1653). (*Venn*, I. 411.)

JENEYE, HENRY. Matric. pens. from JESUS, Easter, 1577; B.A. 1580–1.

JENNY, HENRY. Adm. sizar (age 16) at CAIUS, Dec. 20, 1624. S. of Jerningham (next), R. of Belton, Suffolk. B. at Fritton. Educated by his father. Matric. 1625; B.A. 1629–30. One of these names C. of Stalmine, Lancs., 1646–51. Minister (or V.) of St Michael-on-Wyre, 1651–2 (perhaps 1659). In 1650 is described as M.A. (E. Axon; *Venn*, I. 269.)

JENNEY, JERNINGHAM. Matric. sizar from CHRIST'S, 1595; B.A. 1595–6; M.A. 1599. Ord. deacon (Colchester) Nov. 14; priest, Nov. 15, 1599. R. of Fritton, Suffolk, 1600–24. R. of Belton, 1610–24. Father of the above. (*Venn*, I. 269.)

JENNEY, JOHN. M.A. from MAGDALENE, 1663. Matric. from Pembroke College, Oxford, July 25, 1655; B.A. (Oxford) 1658–9. V. of West Drayton, Middlesex, 1660–4 and 1671–97. R. of Harmondsworth, 1664–97. Died 1697. Buried Dec. 9, 1697. (*Al. Oxon.*)

JENNY, ROBERT. Adm. pens. (age 19) at CAIUS, Oct. 17, 1635. S. of Arthur (1611). B. at Knoddishall, Suffolk. School, Southwold (Mr Claydon). Knighted. Married Elizabeth, dau. of Sir John Offley, Knt., of Madeley, Staffs., 1640. Died 1660. (*Venn*, I. 319; Burke, *L.G.*)

JENNEY, SUCKLIN. Adm. pens. (age 15) at CAIUS, Mar. 26, 1684. S. of George, gent., of Norwich. B. at Morton, Norfolk. School, Norwich. Matric. 1684; Scholar, 1684–7. Died *s.p.* Admon. (P.C.C.) 1698. (*Venn*, I. 475; Burke, *L.G.*)

JENNEY, THOMAS. Adm. pens. (age 15) at CAIUS, Sept. 21, 1611. Eldest s. of Ambrose, gent., of Eltham, Kent. B. at Bexwell, Norfolk. School, Croydon, Surrey (Mr Davyes). Matric. 1611; Scholar, 1611–5. Probably died before 1621, when his father died and was buried at Eltham. (*Venn*, I. 214; *Vis. of Norfolk.*)

JENNY, THOMAS. Matric. pens. from ST CATHARINE'S, Easter, 1663; B.A. 1666–7.

JENNY, WILLIAM. Adm. . (age 17) at CAIUS, July 5, 1653. S. of William, gent. Epeats Bexwell, Norfolk. Bapt. there, Nov. 4, 1637. School, Cambridge (Mr More). Adm. at Lincoln's Inn, 1653. Barrister. Of Gt Cressingham, Esq. Married Dinah, dau. of John Goldsmith, of Stradsett, Norfolk. Buried at Gt Cressingham, Mar. 9, 1669–70. Brother of Francis (1660–1). (*Venn*, I. 389.)

JENNEY, ——. B.A. 1469–70; M.A. 1473–4.

JENNEY, ——. B.Can.L. 1482–3. Rector.

JENY, ——. Adm. Fell.-Com. at CORPUS CHRISTI, 1558.

JENNINGS, ABRAHAM. Matric. sizar from TRINITY, Michs. 1639.

JENYNS, CHRISTOPHER. Adm. pens. (age 18) at PEMBROKE, Jan. 31, 1707–8. S. of John, of Hayes, Middlesex, Esq. B. there. Colleger at Eton, 1703–7. Matric. 1708; B.A. 1711–2.

JENINGS, EDMUND. Matric. pens. from JESUS, Easter, 1614. S. of Peter, of Silsden, Yorks. B.A. 1617–8; M.A. 1621. Buried at Kildwick, July 9, 1623, aged 25. Brother of Jonathan (1614) and Peter (1617). (A. Gray.)

JENNINGS, EDMUND. Adm. Fell.-Com. (age 15) at SIDNEY, May 7, 1641. S. and h. of Jonathan (1614), Esq., of Ripon, Yorks. B. at Scotton. Bapt. at Farnham, Nov. 30, 1626. Schools, Silsden and Ripon. Adm. at Lincoln's Inn, Oct. 6, 1646. Of Ripon. M.P. for Ripon, 1659, 1660, 1673–9, 1685–7, 1690–1. High Sheriff of Yorks., 1675. Married Margaret, dau. of Sir Edward Barkham, of Tottenham High Cross. Died 1691. (*Vis. of Yorks.*; A. B. Beaven; M. H. Peacock.)

JENNINGS, EDMUND. Adm. pens. at TRINITY HALL, July 29, 1749; Scholar, 1750.

JENINGS, 'EDWARD,' *see* **PETER.**

JENNINGS, FRANCIS. Adm. sizar (age 16) at SIDNEY, Apr. 29, 1650. S. of William, farmer. B. at Cambridge. School, Perse (Mr Crabbe). Matric. 1650; B.A. 1653–4.

JENNINGS or JENYNS, GEORGE. B.A. 1520–1.

JENNINGS, GEORGE. Adm. pens. at TRINITY, Apr. 27, 1652. Of Hertfordshire.

JENNINGS, GEORGE. Adm. at CORPUS CHRISTI, 1737. Of London. S. of Admiral Sir John Jennings, of Barkway, Herts. Matric. 1738. Comptroller-General of the army. M.P. for Whitchurch, 1757, 1766; St Germans, 1768; Thetford, 1784. Of Newseles, Herts. Married Mary, dau. of Michael, 10th Earl of Clanricarde, 1741. Died June 5, 1790. (*Cussans*, I. ii. 22.)

JENNINGS, HENRY. Matric. sizar from ST CATHARINE'S, Easter, 1621; B.A. 1623–4; M.A. 1627. Ord. deacon (Norwich) Feb. 18, 1626–7; priest, Dec. 23, 1632. Probably R. of Pinningham, Norfolk, till 1638.

JENNINGS, HENRY. Adm. sizar (age 18) at TRINITY, Jan. 21, 1698–9. S. of Henry, of Cambridge. School, King's College (Mr Roswell). Matric. 1699; B.A. 1702–3. Ord. deacon (London) Dec. 24, 1704.

JENNINGS, HUGH. Ord. deacon (Peterb.) Mar. 5, 1619–20; 'literate of TRINITY College'; priest, June 11, 1620. V. of Ferry Fryston, Yorks., 1620–53. Died Sept. 19, 1653. Contemporary at Oxford.

JENNYNS, JAMES. Adm. pens. (age 17) at ST JOHN'S, Mar. 22, 1700–1. S. of John, Esq. B. at Hayes, Middlesex. School, Eton. Matric. 1701. Adm. at the Inner Temple, Feb. 12, 1701–2. Brother of John (1700–1).

JENYN or JENNING, JOHN. B.A. 1492–3; B.D. 1503–4; D.D. 1519–20. Fellow of QUEENS', 1495. Proctor, 1503–4. President of Queens', 1519–25. V. of Harrow, 1509–38. Died 1538. (*Searle*; *Cooper*, I. 67.)

JENYNGS, JOHN. Matric. pens. from CORPUS CHRISTI, Easter, 1572.

JENNINGS, JOHN. B.A. from ST JOHN'S, 1606–7. Ord. priest (Peterb.) Mar. 20, 1613–4.

JINNINGS, JOHN. Adm. pens. at EMMANUEL, Sept. 12, 1629. Matric. 1629–30.

JENNINGS, JOHN. Matric. pens. from CORPUS CHRISTI, Michs. 1656. Of London. R. of Holdgate, Salop. Preb. of Hereford, 1669–75. (*Masters.*)

JENNINGS, JOHN. Adm. sizar at CLARE, Dec. 20, 1667. Of Cambridge. Matric. 1668; B.A. 1671–2. Ord. deacon (Lincoln) Sept. 24, 1671; priest, June 2, 1672.

JENNINGS, JOHN. Adm. pens. at CLARE, May 25, 1687. Of London. Matric. 1687; B.A. 1690–1; M.A. 1694. Fellow, 1693. Ord. priest (Lincoln) June 3, 1694. V. of Gt Gransden, Hunts., 1708–42. V. of Gamlingay, Cambs., 1710. Chaplain to the Bishop of Ely. Died Feb. 19, 1742–3, aged 72. Buried at Gransden.

JENYNS, JOHN. Adm. pens. (age 18) at ST JOHN'S, Mar. 22, 1700–1. S. of John, Esq. B. at Hayes, Middlesex. School, Eton. Matric. 1701. Adm. at the Inner Temple, Feb. 12, 1701–2. Brother of James (1700–1).

JENNINGS, JOHN. Adm. sizar (age 17) at ST JOHN'S, May 24, 1705. S. of John, gent. B. at Solihull, Warws. School, Shrewsbury (Mr Lloyd). B.A. 1708–9; M.A. 1713. Incorp. at Oxford, 1712. Not (as in *Al. Oxon.*) the V. of Gamlingay. (*See* above.)

JENYNS, JOHN. Adm. sizar (age 17) at CAIUS, Jan. 5, 1737–8. S. of John, grazier, of Meppershall, Beds. B. at Therfield, Herts. School, Southill, Beds. (private; Mr Bedford). Scholar, 1738–43; Matric. 1740–1; B.A. 1741–2; M.A. 1750. Ord. deacon (Salisbury) July 10, 1743; priest, June 23, 1745. V. of Idmiston, Wilts., 1747–68. R. of Boscombe, Wilts., 1750–68. Chaplain to the Bishop of London. Died Aug. 5, 1768. Buried at Boscombe. M.I. (*Venn*, II. 43.)

JENNINGS, JOHN. Adm. sizar (age 19) at PEMBROKE, June 13, 1749. S. of John, of Kentish Town, Middlesex, farmer. Matric. 1749. 'Grecian' from Christ's Hospital. B.A. 1754; M.A. 1771. Ord. priest (Lincoln) Sept. 6, 1757. Head Master of a Grammar School, in 1770. (A. W. Lockhart.)

JENNINGS, JONATHAN. Matric. pens. from JESUS, Easter, 1614. 2nd s. of Peter, of Silsden, Yorks., gent. B.A. 1617-8; M.A. 1621. Adm. at Lincoln's Inn, Feb. 18, 1618-9. Of Ripon, Esq., barrister-at-law. Married, at Farnham, Elizabeth, dau. of Giles Parker, of Newby, Yorks., barrister. Compounded for his estates as a royalist. Died Aug. 24, 1649. Buried at Ripon. Admon., York. Brother of Peter (1614) and Edmund (1614), father of Edmund (1641) and the next. (A. Gray; M. H. Peacock.)

JENNINGS, JONATHAN. Adm. pens. (age 17) at CHRIST'S, June 28, 1650. Fell.-Com. S. of Jonathan (above), of Ripon. B. there. School, Ripon (Mr Palmes). Matric. 1650. Adm. at Gray's Inn, Dec. 28, 1649. M.P. for Ripon, 1659-60, 1688-95. Knighted, Mar. 18, 1677-8. High Sheriff of Yorks., 1690. Fought a memorable duel with Mr George Aislaby, of York. Convicted of manslaughter, but protected by the King's pardon, 1675. Buried at Ripon, Jan. 27, 1706-7. Brother of Edmund (1641). (*Peile*, I. 538; *Ripon Millenary Record*, 65.)

JENNINGS, JONATHAN. Adm. Fell.-Com. (age 16) at CHRIST'S, May 19, 1671. S. of Sir Edmund (1641), of Ripon, Knt. B. there. School, Ripon. Matric. 1671. Adm. at Gray's Inn, June 6, 1671. M.P. for Ripon, 1691-1701. Died 1701. (*Peile*, II. 36.)

JENNINGS, PETER. Probably matric. from JESUS, Easter, 1614, as 'Edward.' S. of Peter, of Silsden, Yorks. B.A. 1617-8; M.A. 1621. Died Mar. 4, 1624, aged 24. Buried at St Crux, York. M.I. Brother of Jonathan (1614). (A. Gray.)

JENNINGS, PHILIP. Adm. pens. (age 18) at ST JOHN'S, Jan. 2, 1697-8. S. of Edward, counsellor. B. in London. School, Eton. Adm. at the Inner Temple, Nov. 27, 1698. M.P. for Queenborough, 1715-22. Died *c.* 1742. His s. Philip Jennings-Clerke was created Bart. in 1774. (*G.E.C.*; *Westminster Abbey Register*, 365.)

JENNINGS, RICHARD. Matric. pens. from ST CATHARINE'S, Michs. 1633. B. at Ipswich. B.A. 1635-6; M.A. 1639. Went to New England, 1636-9. Afterwards minister in Northants., Hunts. and North Glemham, Suffolk; 'ordained' in London, Sept. 18, 1645. R. of Grundisborough, Suffolk, 1645-8. R. of Combe, 1647-62. Died at Clapham, Surrey, Sept. 12, 1709. (*Calamy*, II. 416; *Felt*, 258; *Palmer* (1803), vol. III.)

JENNINGS, RICHARD. Adm. pens. at ST CATHARINE'S, 1659. Matric. 1660; B.A. 1663. Ord. priest (Norwich) Dec. 1677; 'M.A.' V. of Mendham, Norfolk, 1677.

JENNINGS, ROBERT. Matric. sizar from CORPUS CHRISTI, Easter, 1578; B.A. 1582-3; M.A. 1586. Ord. deacon and priest (Peterb.) Mar. 5, 1586-7. V. of West Ham, Essex, 1592-1630. Died 1630. Will, Cons. C. London.

JENNINGS, SAMUEL. Adm. pens. at CLARE, June 30, 1677. Of Irby, Lincs. Matric. 1677; LL.B. 1682. Incorp. at Oxford, 1682.

JENYNS, SOAME. Adm. Fell.-Com. (age 17) at ST JOHN'S, July 2, 1722. S. of Sir Roger, Knt., of Middlesex, and grandson of Sir Peter Soame, Bart. B. in London. Educated at home. Matric. 1724. M.P. for Cambs., 1741-54; for Dunwich, 1754-8; for Cambridge, 1758-80. A Lord of Trade, 1755-80. Of Bottisham Hall, Cambs. Author, poetical and religious. Died Dec. 18, 1787. Will (P.C.C.) 1788. (*D.N.B.*; *Scott-Mayor*, III. 352; A. B. Beaven.)

GENYNGES, THOMAS. Resident student at TRINITY HALL, Aug. 1564.

GENNINGS, THOMAS. Matric. sizar from JESUS, Easter, 1566.

JENNINGS, THOMAS. B.A. from PEMBROKE, 1576-7. B. at Rayleigh, Essex. Ord. priest (London) Dec. 21, 1579, age 25. R. of Willingale Spain, Essex; will proved (Consist. C. London) 1607; leaves his books to Sidney College library, 'newly erected'; gifts to the sizars and scholars of Christ's 'of which house I was sometime an unworthy member'; houses in Danbury and Standon, Essex, after death of wife Avis, to Christ's. Gift to 'High Ongar, where I was brought up by my uncle Dr Tabor.' (J. Ch. Smith.)

JENNINGS, THOMAS. 'Sometime of Cambridge' (probably *c.* 1645). S. of a knight. Demy of Magdalen College, Oxford, 1648; B.A. 1648-9; M.A. 1651. Fellow, 1649. Died Jan. 16, 1657-8. Buried in the College Chapel. (*Al. Oxon.*)

JENYNS, THOMAS. Adm. pens. at CLARE, Oct. 31, 1688. Of Hayes, Middlesex. Doubtless s. of Roger, of Hayes, Middlesex, Esq. Matric. 1688; B.A. 1692-3; M.A. 1696. Adm. at the Inner Temple, Feb. 12, 1686-7. Died May 12, 1696, aged 25. Buried at Hayes. M.I.

GENYNGS, ——. Sizar at PETERHOUSE, Easter, 1545.

JENNINGSON or JENYSON, CHRISTOPHER. B.A. 1502-3. Of ST GREGORY'S HOSTEL. M.A. 1506; B.D. 1515. Fellow of Pembroke, 1505. Preacher, 1511.

JENNINGSON, JOHN. B.A. 1502-3; M.A. 1506. Of ST GREGORY'S HOSTEL.

JENNUAR, ADAM. Matric. pens. from QUEENS', Easter, 1680.

JENOUR, *see also* JENNER.

JENOUR, ANDREW. Matric. pens. from CHRIST'S, *c.* 1592. Doubtless 2nd s. of Andrew, of Gt Dunmow. Of New Inn; adm. at the Middle Temple, Feb. 6, 1594-5. Called to the Bar, Nov. 26, 1602. Married Anne, dau. of John Bentley, of Castle Camps, Cambs. Died Nov. 20, 1632. Brother of Richard (1608) and Kenelm. (*Vis. of Essex*, 1612; *Morant*, II. 110.)

JENOURE, ANDREW. Matric. Fell.-Com. from QUEENS', Easter, 1659. Of Essex. Doubtless s. of Sir Andrew, Bart., of Gt Dunmow. Married Sarah, dau. of Robert Milhorn, Esq., of Markshall, Essex. Died before his father. (*Vis. of Essex*; Burke, *Ext. Bart*; *G.E.C.*)

JENNOR, HENRY. Matric. pens. from TRINITY, Michs. 1628. Perhaps 2nd s. of Sir Kenelm (1608), of Bigods, Dunmow, Essex. If so, adm. at the Middle Temple, 1629. Created M.A. (Oxford) Aug. 31, 1636. Brother of William (1637). (*Al. Oxon.*; *Vis. of Essex*, 1634.)

JENOUR, JOHN. Matric. Fell.-Com. from QUEENS', Easter, 1713. S. of Sir Maynard, Bart., and grandson of Andrew (1659). Succeeded as 4th Bart., *c.* 1710. Married Joan, dau. of Richard Day, of Northweld, Essex. Died Apr. 28, 1739. Father of Richard Day (1735). (*G.E.C.*)

JENOUR, KENELM. M.A. 1608 (*fil. nob.*). Doubtless s. of Andrew, of Dunmow, Essex. Created Bart., July 30, 1628. Married Jane, dau. of Sir Robert Clarke, Baron of the Exchequer. Died Aug. 30, 1629. Will, P.C.C. Brother of Andrew (1592) and Richard (1608). (*G.E.C.*; *Vis. of Essex*, 1612.)

JENOUR, RICHARD. Adm. at KING'S (age 16) a scholar from Eton, Aug. 16, 1608. S. of Andrew, of Dunmow, Essex. Matric. 1608; B.A. 1612-3; M.A. 1616. Fellow, 1611, till his death at Padua about 1618. Doubtless brother of Andrew (1592) and Kenelm (1608). (*Harwood*; *Vis. of Essex*, 1612.)

JENOURE, RICHARD DAY. Adm. pens. (age 17) at PETERHOUSE, June 18, 1735; Fell.-Com. May 25, 1739. S. of Sir John (1713), Bart., of Much Dunmow, Essex. School, Felsted. Succeeded as 5th Bart., Apr. 28, 1739. Adm. at Lincoln's Inn, Jan. 19, 1740-1. Died Mar. 23, 1743-4. (*T. A. Walker*, 270; *G.E.C.*)

JENOUR, WILLIAM. Adm. pens. at TRINITY, June 19, 1637. Matric. 1638; Scholar, 1638. Doubtless 4th s. of Sir Kenelm (1608), of Bigods, Dunmow, Essex. Brother of Henry (1628).

JENSON, ROBERT. Matric. pens. from QUEENS', Easter, 1573.

JENSEN, WALTER. Matric. sizar from CLARE, Lent, 1687.

JENTLEMAN, JAMES. Matric. sizar from TRINITY, Easter, 1618. One James Gentleman appears as minister of Higham Ferrers, Northants. in the register, June 19, 1638. (H. I. Longden.)

JENUN, ABRAHAM. Matric. from ST JOHN'S, *c.* 1598; B.A. 1601-2; M.A. 1605.

JEPHCOTT, HENRY. Adm. sizar at TRINITY, May 20, 1669.

JEPHCOT, JAMES. Adm. sizar (age 19) at CHRIST'S, Sept. 27, 1639. S. of Thomas. B. at Anstey, Warws. School, Coventry (Mr White). Matric. 1639; B.A. 1643-4; M.A. 1647. R. of Oidbury, Salop, 1648 (when he subscribed the Bishop of London's register). Head Master of Bridgnorth Grammar School. (*Peile*, I. 463.)

JEPHCOTT, JOHN. Matric. pens. (age 19) from PEMBROKE, Michs. 1659. S. of Henry, farmer. B. at Anstey, Warws. B.A. 1659-60; M.A. 1663; D.D. 1678. Incorp. at Oxford, 1669 and 1696. R. of All Saints', Evesham, Worcs., 1663-92. Preb. of Worcester, 1683-1706. R. of Harvington, 1684-90; of Tredington, 1689-1701; and of Alvechurch, 1690-1713. Warden of St Martin's Hospital, Worcester, 1700-13. R. of Northfield, 1706-13. Died Mar. 26, 1713. M.I. at Northfield. (*Al. Oxon.*; Nash, *Worcs.*, II. 191.)

JEPHSON or JEPSON, FRANCIS. Matric. sizar from CHRIST'S, Nov. 1570; B.A. 1574-5; M.A. 1579.

JEPSON or JEPHSON, FRANCIS. Matric. pens. from ST JOHN'S, Easter, 1617; B.A. 1620-1; M.A. 1632. V. of Saltby, Leics., *c.* 1639-44; ejected, but reinstated, 1660. Buried at Saltby, Dec. 15, 1670. (*Nichols*, II. 306.)

JEPSON, JOHN. Matric. sizar from CHRIST'S, Lent, 1597-8.

JEPSON, JOHN. Matric. sizar from MAGDALENE, Easter, 1617; B.A. 1620-1.

JEPHSON, NORRIS. Adm. Fell.-Com. at EMMANUEL, June 17, 1634. Of Hampshire. 2nd s. of Sir John, of Froyle, Hants., Knt., and Elizabeth, dau. of Sir Thomas Norreys, of Mallow, Co. Cork. Matric. 1637. Adm. at Lincoln's Inn, Apr. 11, 1638.

JEPSON, RICHARD. Adm. sizar (age 18) at ST JOHN'S, Mar. 28, 1670. S. of Richard, yeoman, of Airton, in Settle, Yorks. B. there. School, Langton. Matric. 1670; B.A. 1673-4. Ord. deacon (York) June, 1674; priest, Sept. 24, 1676. P.C. of Armley, Yorks., 1675-80.

JEPSON, ROGER. Matric. pens. from TRINITY, Easter, 1579.

JEPHSON, SYLVESTER. Adm. sizar (age 16) at MAGDALENE, June 19, 1738. S. of Thomas, clerk. B. at Sixhill, Lincs. School, Lincoln. Matric. 1738. Perhaps M.A. of St Andrews. Ord. deacon (Lincoln) Dec. 19, 1742.

JEPHSON, THOMAS. Adm. sizar (age 17) at SIDNEY, June 27, 1667. S. of William. B. at Oakham, Rutland. School, Oakham. Matric. 1667; B.A. 1670-1. Ord. deacon (Peterb.) Mar. 3, 1671-2; priest, Dec. 22, 1672. R. of Hornfield, Rutland, 1683-97. C. of Welney, Norfolk, 1694. R. of Melton St Mary, 1703. R. of Crownthorpe, 1704-14. Father of William (1711-2).

JEPSON, THOMAS. Adm. sizar at MAGDALENE, May 3, 1698. (Perhaps adm. at Emmanuel same day.) S. of Thomas, clerk. B. at Thorney, Cambs. School, Rayson, Lincs. Matric. 1699. Ord. deacon as of Magdalene, May 26, 1700. Probably father of Sylvester.

JEPSON, WILLIAM. B.A. from CLARE, 1574-5. Ord. deacon (Peterb.) Sept. 23, 1575. V. of Norton Cuckney, Notts., 1579-1621. Married Agnes Joy, widow, of Norton Cuckney. Died 1621.

JHEPSON, WILLIAM. Matric. Fell.-Com. from PETERHOUSE, Michs. 1580.

JEPSON, WILLIAM. Matric. pens. from ST JOHN'S, Easter, 1611. One of these names, s. and h. of Roger, of Oakham, Rutland, gent., adm. at Gray's Inn, from Barnard's Inn, Aug. 6, 1615.

JEPSON, WILLIAM. Matric. pens. from ST JOHN'S, Easter, 1628; B.A. 1631-2; M.A. 1635.

JEPHSON, WILLIAM. Matric. Fell.-Com. from QUEENS', Michs. 1703.

JEPHSON, WILLIAM. Adm. sizar (age 17) at ST JOHN'S, Feb. 8, 1711-2. S. of Thomas (1667), clerk, R. of Melton St Mary. B. at Welney, Norfolk. School, Oundle (Mr Caldwell). Matric. 1712; B.A. 1716-7. Ord. deacon (Peterb.) June 15, 1717; priest (Lincoln) June 12, 1720. C. of St Martin's, Stamford, Northants., 1717. Schoolmaster at Stamford, 1720. V. of Holbeach, Lincs., 1731-41. Died Mar. 6, 1740-1. (H. I. Longden.)

JEPHSON, WILLIAM. Adm. pens. (age 13) at ST JOHN'S, June 15, 1748. S. of William (? above), clerk, Master of Camberwell Grammar School. B. there. Educated under his father. Matric. 1750-1; B.A. 1752; M.A. 1755. Fellow, 1754-73. Adm. at the Middle Temple, Feb. 25, 1750-1. Barrister, 1755. Serjeant-at-law, 1765. Died May 18, 1772. (*Scott-Mayor*, III. 579; *G. Mag.*)

JERMY, ANTHONY. Adm. pens. at JESUS, Feb. 19, 1655-6. Of Norfolk. Probably 3rd s. of Francis, and Alice, dau. of Anthony Irby, of Boston, Knt. School, Bury (Dr Stephens). Matric. 1656; Scholar, 1657; B.A. 1659-60; M.A. 1663. R. of Gunton, Norfolk, 1661. V. of Hanworth, till 1723. Died 1723.

JERMY, CLEMENT. Matric. pens. from CLARE, Michs. 1579. Doubtless of Marlingford, Norfolk, gent. Died 1626. Father of William (1617) and Robert (1631).

JERMY, EDWARD. Adm. (age 18) at CAIUS, Oct. 1, 1612. S. of Sir Thomas (1577), K.B., of Brightwell, Suffolk and of Teversham, Cambs. Educated at home (Mr Matthews). Matric. 1612. Of Teversham, Cambs. Married Mary, dau. of Robert Spencer, of Rendlesham. Buried at Teversham, June 26, 1644. (*Venn*, I. 219; *Vis. of Norfolk*.)

JERMYE, FRANCIS. Matric. Fell.-Com. from TRINITY HALL, Easter, 1551. Perhaps s. and h. of Sir John, of Brightwell, Suffolk, K.B. If so, married Elizabeth, dau. of Sir William Fitz-William, of Ireland, Knt. Doubtless father of Thomas (1577) and perhaps of John (1589). (*Vis. of Norfolk*, 1566.)

JERMY, FRANCIS. Adm. Fell.-Com. (age 18) at CAIUS, Apr. 18, 1608. Of Brightwell, Suffolk. S. of William, Esq. Schools, Boxford (Mr Hogan) and Southwold (Mr Claydon). Matric. 1608. Adm. at Gray's Inn, May 19, 1609, as s. and h. of William, of Worlingworth. Married, May 10, 1613, at Metfield, Suffolk, Elizabeth, dau. of Thomas Bateman, of Flixton. (*Venn*, I. 197.)

JERMY, FRANCIS. Matric. Fell.-Com. from CHRIST'S, Dec. 1615. Probably s. and h. of John, treasurer of the Middle Temple, adm. there, Nov. 2, 1614. One of these names was on the Norfolk Committee of the Eastern Counties Association, 1643. Probably brother of Robert (1621). (*Peile*, I. 303.)

JERMY, FRANCIS. Adm. pens. (age 17) at PEMBROKE, Apr. 2, 1624. S. of Francis, of Walsingham, Norfolk, Esq. Matric. 1625; B.A. 1627-8.

JERMY, FRANCIS. Adm. pens. (age 16) at ST JOHN'S, June 24, 1650. S. of Francis, Esq., lately deceased. B. at Gunton, Norfolk. School, Bury St Edmunds. One of these names, of the Middle Temple, Esq.; buried there 1668. Probably brother of John (1647-8). (Hatton, *New View*.)

JERMY, FRANCIS. Adm. pens. (age 16) at JESUS, June 26, 1671. Of Norfolk. Matric. 1671.

JERMY, GEORGE. Adm. at EMMANUEL, June 28, 1614. Of Suffolk. Migrated as pens. to Queens', Mar. 12, 1617-8. B.A. 1618-9; M.A. 1622. Ord. priest (Norwich) May 27, 1621. R. of Knoddishall, Suffolk, 1622. R. of Buxlow, 1622-79. Buried at Knoddishall, June 27, 1679. (V. B. Redstone; Davy, *Suff. MS.*)

JERMY, ISAAC. Matric. Fell.-Com. from TRINITY, Michs. 1582, as Jermyn. Probably s. of Sir John Jermy, of Stutton, Suffolk, Knt. Adm. at Gray's Inn, Feb. 5, 1583-4. Knighted, Dec. 18, 1604. Married Jane, dau. of John Pagrave (? Palgrave), Norfolk. Buried at Stutton. Father of John (1620). (*Vis. of Suffolk*, 1664.)

JERMY, ISAAC. Adm. pens. (age 17) at ST JOHN'S, Apr. 10, 1663. S. of Robert, gent., of Bayfield-in-Saxlingham, Norfolk. B. there. School, Lynn. Matric. 1663; B.A. 1666-7; M.A. 1670. Perhaps brother of John (1646).

JERMY, JOHN. Adm. pens. (age 15) at CAIUS, Sept. 13, 1589. S. of Francis (? 1551), of Brightwell, Suffolk, Esq. School, Sudbury. Matric. 1589; B.A. 1592-3. Adm. at Gray's Inn, Jan. 28, 1593-4. Steward of Norwich, 1629-31. Perhaps brother of Thomas (1577). (*Venn*, I. 137.)

JERMY, JOHN. Adm. pens. at EMMANUEL, Easter, 1620. Doubtless s. of Sir Isaac (1582), of Stutton, Suffolk. Matric. 1620. Adm. at Gray's Inn, Feb. 2, 1620-1. Buried at Stutton, Dec. 23, 1662, aged 61. Probably father of William (1651-2). (*Vis. of Suffolk*, 1664.)

JERMY, JOHN. Adm. Fell.-Com. (age 16) at ST JOHN'S, May 22, 1646. S. of Robert, of Bayfield, Norfolk. School, Norwich (Mr Lovering). B.A. 1648-9. Incorp. at Oxford, Mar. 14, 1649-50. M.A. (Oxford) 1651. Fellow of All Souls, 1648. Adm. at the Middle Temple, May 7, 1647. Died 1679. Perhaps brother of Isaac (1663). Father of John (1669). (*Al. Oxon.*)

JERMY, JOHN. Adm. Fell.-Com. (age 16) at CHRIST'S, Mar. 9, 1647-8. S. of Francis. B. at Gunton, Norfolk. School, Norwich (Mr Lovering). Matric. 1648. Probably brother of Francis (1650).

JERMY, JOHN. Adm. Fell.-Com. at TRINITY, Mar. 31, 1669. S. of John (1646). B. 1652. Probably M.A. 1671 (*Lit. Reg.*). Doubtless adm. at Lincoln's Inn, June 8, 1671; s. and h. of John, late of Bayfield, Norfolk. Married Jane, dau. of John Chare, of Wandsworth, Surrey. Died Dec. 18, 1735, aged 83. Buried at Aylesham. M.I. Perhaps father of the next. (*Blomefield*, VI. 281.)

JERMY, JOHN. Adm. pens. (age 17) at TRINITY, Jan. 17, 1693-4. S. of John (? above), of Bayfield, Norfolk. B. in London. School, Charterhouse. Matric. 1694. Adm. at the Inner Temple, June 12, 1695. Perhaps father of William (1731).

JERMY, ROBERT. Matric. pens. from CHRIST'S, Dec. 1621. Probably S. of John, Master of the Bench, Middle Temple. Adm. there, June 14, 1621. Called to the Bar, June 19, 1629. One of these names one of the Norfolk Commissioners. (*Peile*, I. 341.)

JERMY, ROBERT. Adm. pens. (age 17) at CAIUS, Mar. 31, 1631. S. of Clement (1579), gent., deceased. Bapt. at Marlingford, Norfolk, Oct. 23, 1614. School, Norwich (Mr Stonham). Matric. 1631; Scholar, 1632-4. Died in College. Buried at St Michael's, Cambridge, Nov. 12, 1634. Brother of William (1617). (*Venn*, I. 297.)

JERMYE, THOMAS. Matric. Fell.-Com. from JESUS, Easter, 1577. Doubtless s. and h. of Francis (1551), of Brightwell, Suffolk. B.A. 1580-1 (1st in the *ordo*). Of Teversham, Cambs., Esq. K.B., July 25, 1603. Sheriff of Cambs., 1606. Married Jane, dau. and sole heir of Edward Styward, of Teversham, Cambs. Father of Edward (1612). (*Vis. of Norfolk*; *Blomefield*, V. 387.)

JERMYE, THOMAS (1607), *see* JERMYN.

JERMY, THOMAS. Adm. sizar at QUEENS', May 25, 1654. Of Suffolk. B.A. 1657; M.A. 1662. R. of Hethersett, Norfolk, 1660-70.

JERME, W. Matric. Fell.-Com. from JESUS, Easter, 1584.

JERMY, WILLIAM. Matric. pens. from CHRIST'S, Easter, 1572.

JERMEY, WILLIAM. Adm. pens. (age 15) at CAIUS, Apr. 28, 1617. S. of Clement (1579), gent., of Marlingford, Norfolk. Bapt. there, Aug. 30, 1601. School, Norwich (Mr Stonham). Matric. 1617; Scholar, 1617–24; B.A. 1620–1; M.A. 1624. Incorp. at Oxford, 1628. Ord. deacon (Norwich) Feb. 18, 1626–7. Buried at Marlingford, Aug. 11, 1628. (*Venn*, I. 236.)

JERMY, WILLIAM. Adm. Fell.-Com. at EMMANUEL, Mar. 23, 1651–2. Of Suffolk. Probably s. of John (1620), of Stutton, Suffolk, Esq.; adm. at Gray's Inn, Feb. 14, 1651–2. Of Stutton, Suffolk. J.P., 1664. Buried there Oct. 6, 1669. (*Vis. of Suffolk*, 1664.)

JERMY, WILLIAM. Adm. at CORPUS CHRISTI, 1731. Of Norfolk. Probably s. and h. of John (1693–4). Matric. 1731. Adm. at the Inner Temple, Nov. 24, 1725. Of Bayfield Hall, Norfolk, Esq. (*Masters*.)

JERMYN or JERMAN, *see also* GERMIN.

JERMAN or JERMYN, ANTHONY. Matric. pens. from JESUS, Michs. 1571. 2nd s. of Ambrose, of Hockham, Norfolk. Killed at the siege of Breda. Brother of Edward (1571). (*Suff. Man. Fam.*, II. 257.)

JERMYN, CHARLES. Signed for priest's orders (Gloucester) Dec. 5, 1677, as B.A. of TRINITY, Cambridge.

JERMYN, EDWARD. Adm. at KING'S (age 16) a scholar from Eton, Oct. 3, 1563. S. of John, of Exeter. B. at Windsor. Matric. 1564; B.A. 1567–8; M.A. 1571; D.D. 1586. Fellow, 1566–76. Chaplain to Bishop Wickham, of Lincoln. R. of Upton, Hunts., 1586–92. R. of Coppingford, 1587–92. Preb. of Lincoln, 1588–1623. V. of Alconbury, Hunts., 1589–1606. R. of Stilton, 1592–1623. J.P. for Hunts. (*Vis. of Hunts.*, 1613; *Harwood*.)

JERMAN or JERMYN, EDWARD. Matric. pens. from JESUS, Michs. 1571. 4th s. of Ambrose, of Hockham, Norfolk. Brother of Anthony (1571). (A. Gray.)

JERMIN, EDWARD. Adm. Fell.-Com. at EMMANUEL, Apr. 26, 1586. Matric. 1586. Probably s. of Sir Robert; and brother of Thomas (1585).

JERMYN, GEORGE. Matric. pens. from CHRIST'S, Michs. 1564. S. of Sir Ambrose, of Rushbrook, Suffolk. Adm. at Queens', 1564. M.A. (as *fil. nob.*) 1570. Fellow of Queens', 1572–7. Died 1577. Brother of Robert (1550).

JERMAN, HENRY. Adm. sizar at EMMANUEL, Sept. 13, 1659. Of Huntingdonshire.

JERMIN or GERMAN, HENRY. Adm. pens. at TRINITY, Mar. 26, 1660. Matric. 1660.

JERMYN, JASPAR. Adm. at KING'S (age 17) a scholar from Eton, Aug. 24, 1575. Of Shrewsbury. Matric. 1575. Left, 1577–8.

JERMYN, JOHN. Matric. pens. from CORPUS CHRISTI, Easter, 1576. of Debden, Suffolk; adm. at Gray's Inn, Apr. 24, 158 Perhaps

JERMYN, JOHN. Adm. Fell.-Com. (age 18) at CAIUS, Mar. 14, 1647–8. S. of Thomas, Esq. B. at West Tofts, Norfolk. Schools, Thetford (Mr Ward) and South Pickenham (Mr Eade). Matric. 1648. Of West Tofts, Esq. Married Elizabeth, dau. of Thomas Townshend, of West Wretham. (*Venn*, I. 371; *Suff. Man. Fam.*)

JERMYN or GERMIN, MICHAEL. M.A. 1617 (Incorp. from Oxford). S. of Alexander, merchant (and Sheriff), of Exeter. Matric. from Exeter College, June 20, 1606, age 15; B.A. (Corpus Christi) 1611; M.A. 1614–5. Fellow of Corpus Christi, Oxford, 1615. Adm. at Leyden, June 30, 1624. D.D. (Leyden) 1624. Incorp. at Oxford, 1624. Chaplain to the Electress palatine and afterwards to Charles I. R. of Edburton, Sussex, 1626–55; ejected, 1655. R. of St Martin's, Ludgate, 1626–43, sequestered. Adm. at Gray's Inn, Mar. 19, 1632–3. President of Sion College, 1640. Died at Kemsing, Kent, Aug. 14, 1659. Will (P.C.C.) 1660. (*Al. Oxon.*; *Vis. of London*, 1634; *D.N.B.*; H. G. Harrison.)

JERMYN, ROBERT. Adm. Fell.-Com. at CORPUS CHRISTI, 1550. 2nd s. of Sir Ambrose, of Rushbrook, Suffolk. Adm. at the Middle Temple, Mar. 2, 1560–1. Knighted, Aug. 1, 1578. Sheriff of Suffolk, 1578–9. M.P. for Suffolk, 1584–7; for East Looe, 1588–9. Married Judith, dau. of Sir George Blagge, Knt. Buried at Rushbrook, Apr. 23, 1614. Will (P.C.C.) 1614. Father of Thomas (1585), Robert (1597) and brother of George (1564). (*Cooper*, II. 324; *Suff. Man. Fam.*, II. 255; Copinger, *Manors of Suffolk*, VI. 333.)

JERMYN, ROBERT. Matric. pens. from TRINITY, Michs. 1553; Scholar, 1555, as Germyn.

JERMIN, ROBERT. Adm. Fell.-Com. at EMMANUEL, Apr. 6, 1597. 2nd s. of Sir Robert (1550), of Rushbrook, Suffolk. Bapt. Apr. 1582. Matric. 1597; B.A. 1599–1600. Adm. at the Middle Temple, Nov. 17, 1601. Married Dorothy, dau. of Sir Henry Warner, of Mildenhall, 1603. Buried at Rushbrook. Brother of Thomas (1585). (*Suff. Man. Fam.*, II. 255.)

JERMIN, ROBERT. Matric. Fell.-Com. from CLARE, Michs. 1617. Doubtless eldest s. of Sir Thomas (1585), Knt., of Rushbrook, Suffolk. Bapt. Sept. 1601. Died 1623. (*Suff. Man. Fam.*, II. 255.)

JERMYN, STEPHEN. Adm. pens. at EMMANUEL, June 14, 1728. Fell.-Com. Apr. 2, 1729.

JERMYN, THOMAS. Matric. . from CORPUS CHRISTI, Easter, 1554. Will of one of these names (Bury) 1581; of Depden, Suffolk.

JERMYN, THOMAS. Matric. pens. from CORPUS CHRISTI, Easter, 1576. Probably nephew of the above.

JERMYN, THOMAS. Adm. Fell.-Com. at EMMANUEL, 1585. 1st s. of Sir Robert (1550), of Rushbrook, Suffolk, Knt. Bapt. Feb. 1572. Matric. 1585. Knighted before Rouen, 1591. K.B., 1603. M.P. for Andover, 1604–11; for Suffolk, 1614; for Bury St Edmunds, 1621–2, 1624–5, 1626, 1628–9 and 1640–4. Comptroller of the Household, 1640–1. Lord-Lieutenant of Suffolk, 1640. Married Catherine, dau. of William Killigrew, of Hanworth. Buried at Rushbrook, Jan. 7, 1644–5. Probably father of Robert (1617) and of Thomas (1622). (*Copinger*, VI. 333; J. B. Peace; A. B. Beaven.)

JERMYN, THOMAS. Adm. at CORPUS CHRISTI, 1607. Of Norfolk. Matric. 1607–8, as Jermye; B.A. 1610–1; M.A. 1614. Ord. priest (Norwich) 1611. V. of Ludham, Norfolk, 1611. V. of Belaugh, 1612. Perhaps V. of Buxton, 1613–21. (*Masters* suggests that he may be the 'Pensioner of the Body' to King James and Charles I. Of West Tofts, Norfolk, Esq.)

JERMYN, THOMAS. Adm. pens. at EMMANUEL, June 13, 1622, as Jermy. Matric. 1622; B.A. 1625–6; M.A. 1629. Doubtless s. of Sir Thomas (1585). If so, M.P. for Leicester, 1625–6; for Lancaster, 1626; for Clitheroe, 1628–9; for Bury St Edmunds, 1640–3. Died Nov. 11, 1659. (A. B. Beaven.)

JERMYN, WILLIAM. Matric. sizar from CLARE, *c.* 1594. Probably s. of Sir Ambrose. B.A. 1600–1. Of Rushbrook, in 1640. (V. B. Redstone.)

JERMYN, WILLIAM. Adm. pens. at PETERHOUSE, 1644–5. Previously matric. from Exeter College, Oxford, June 4, 1641, age 17. Afterwards scholar of Wadham, 1642, as of London; expelled by Parliamentary Visitors, 1648. (*Al. Oxon.*)

JERNEGAN, GEORGE. Matric. sizar from QUEENS', Easter, 1641. Of Essex.

JERNEGAN, HENRY. Matric. sizar from ST CATHARINE'S, Michs. 1565. Of Suffolk. Probably of Ashby. B.A. 1568–9; M.A. 1572. Fellow, *c.* 1569.

JERNYNGHAM or JERNEGAN, HENRY. Matric. Fell.-Com. from TRINITY, Michs. 1566. Doubtless s. of Sir Henry, of Huntingfield Hall, Suffolk, and of Cossey, Norfolk, Knt. Died June 15, 1619. Buried in St Margaret's, Westminster. Father of the next and Thomas (1589). (*Suckling*, II. 46; *Blomefield*, II. 415.)

JERMINGHAM, HENRY. Adm. Fell.-Com. at CAIUS, Nov. 23, 1589. S. of Henry (above), of Cossey ('s. of Robert' in College register, but this must be a mistake). Succeeded his father, in 1619. Created Bart., Aug. 16, 1621. Great sufferer as a Royalist. Died Sept. 1, 1646. Buried at Cossey. Brother of Thomas (1589). (*Venn*, I. 138; *G.E.C.*)

JERMINGHAM, HENRY. Matric. pens. from ST JOHN'S, Michs. 1624.

JERNINHAM or GERNYNGHAM, THOMAS. Matric. pens. from TRINITY, Michs. 1560.

JERMINGHAM, THOMAS. Adm. Fell.-Com. at CAIUS, Nov. 23, 1589. S. of 'Robert' (doubtless Henry; *see* Henry, of same date), Esq., of Cossey, Norfolk. School, Cossey. Died without issue. Brother of Henry (1589). (*Venn*, I. 138.)

JEROME, JOHN. Adm. pens. (age 17) at CHRIST'S, Oct. 1, 1622. S. of John, merchant. B. in London, July 28, 1605. School, Merchant Taylors'. Matric. 1622; B.A. 1626–7.

JEROME, STEPHEN. B.A. from ST JOHN'S, 1603–4; M.A. 1607. Ord. deacon (York) Dec. 1607; priest, Mar. 1608–9. V. of Hutton Buscel, Yorks., 1616–20. Preacher at St Nicholas, Newcastle, 1619. Chaplain to the Earl of Cork. Author, miscellaneous. Died *c.* 1650. (*D.N.B.*)

JEROME, WILLIAM. Educated at Oxford and Cambridge. B.D. (Oxford) 1530. Late monk of the Metropolitan Church of Canterbury. V. of Stepney, Middlesex, 1537–40. An early reformer. Burnt at Smithfield, as a heretic, July 30, 1540. (*Cooper*, I. 76; *Hennessy*.)

JERSEY, PETER. Matric. sizar from King's, Easter, 1641; B.A. 1644. Fellow of Pembroke College, Oxford, 1648. Created M.A. (Oxford) Apr. 14, 1648. Proctor, 1652. Delegate of Parliamentary visitors, 1649. Afterwards conformed. Ord. priest (Lincoln) May 25, 1662. V. of St Peter's, Jersey, 1662; and of St Andrew's, 1663. (*Al. Oxon.*)

JERVIS, *see also* JARVIS.

JERVES, EDMUND. Matric. sizar from St John's, Michs. 1581; B.A. 1584-5. Adm. at Douay College, Apr. 17, 1587. Ord. deacon (R.C.) 1590, and sent to Spain. (*Douay Diary*; *Cooper*, II. 529.)

JARVYS, GEORGE. Matric. pens. from Peterhouse, Michs. 1566.

JARVIS, GEORGE. Adm. pens. at Emmanuel, Oct. 28, 1597. Matric. 1597. Probably of Woodchurch, Kent, gent.; adm. at Gray's Inn, Nov. 14, 1599.

JERVIS, HENRY. M.A. 1578 (Incorp. from Oxford). B.A. (Oxford) 1570; M.A. 1576; B.D. 1582; D.D. 1585. Fellow of Merton, 1572-87. Ord. deacon and priest (Lincoln) June 16, 1580. R. of Broughton Astley, Leics., 1586. Will (Leicester) 1587.

JERVESSE, HUGH. Matric. sizar from Christ's, Michs. 1551. Of Lincoln diocese. Migrated to Clare. B.A. 1557-8; M.A. 1561. Ord. deacon (St Asaph, at London) Mar. 30, 1560. Fellow of Eton, 1562. (*Cooper*, I. 219.)

JERVASE, JOHN. Adm. sizar at Christ's, June 30, 1681. S. of Alexander. B. at Darnall, near Sheffield, Yorks. School, Sheffield (Mr Bayly).

JERVIS, JOHN. Adm. sizar (age 17) at Trinity, Mar. 17, 1709-10. S. of John, of Wybunbury, Cheshire. School, Audlem, Cheshire (Mr Evans). Matric. 1710; B.A. 1713-4.

JARVEIS, JOSEPH. Matric. sizar from Trinity, Easter, 1631; B.A. 1631-2.

JERVIS, PETER. Adm. pens. at St Catharine's, 1666. Matric. 1668; B.A. 1669-70. One of these names, s. of John, of Chatkull, Staffs., matric. from Christ Church, Oxford, Nov. 13, 1663, age 13. (*Al. Oxon.*)

JERVYS, RICHARD. Matric. Fell.-Com. from King's, Easter, 1552.

JERVOISE, RICHARD. Adm. Fell.-Com. at Clare, Dec. 1, 1721. Doubtless s. of Thomas, of Herriard, Hants. B. at Salisbury, 1703-4. High Sheriff of Wilts. Of Britford, Wilts., Esq. Married Anne, dau. of Tristram Huddlestone, of Croydon, Surrey. Died Mar. 1762. (*Nichols*, IV. 602.)

JERVIS or GERVAS, ROBERT. Matric. pens. from Trinity, Easter, 1571; scholar from Westminster, 1570. B.A. 1574-5; M.A. 1578. One of these names V. or C. of Shenstone, Staffs., 1598.

JARVIS, SAMUEL. Adm. Fell.-Com. (age 18) at Pembroke, Dec. 10, 1646. S. of William, Esq. B. at Peatling Magna, Leics. Married Elizabeth, sister to Richard Orton, of Lee Grange. Died Apr. 1674. (*Nichols*, IV. 334.)

JERVYS, STEPHEN. Matric. pens. from Queens', Michs. 1569; B.A. 1573-4; M.A. 1577. R. of Hackford-by-Reepham, Norfolk, 1583-9. R. of Salthouse, 1589-92.

JERVYS, THOMAS. Matric. pens. from St John's, *c.* 1595. One of these names, of Chatkull, Staffs., gent., adm. at Gray's Inn, July 14, 1599.

JARVYSE, WILLIAM. Matric. pens. from Pembroke, Michs. 1567; B.A. 1572-3.

JERVIS, WILLIAM. Matric. pens. from Trinity, Easter, 1609; B.A. 1611-2; M.A. 1615. Incorp. at Oxford, 1618. Ord. deacon (Peterb.) Mar. 16; priest, Mar. 17, 1616-7. V. of Tuxford, Notts., 1617-9. R. of Thoresway, Lincs., 1617. Perhaps the William Gervase, 'M.A.,' who was created D.D. (*Lit. Reg.*) 1661.

GERVAS, WILLIAM. Matric. sizar from Corpus Christi, Michs. 1613. Of Warwickshire.

GERVIS, WILLIAM. Matric. sizar from St John's, Easter, 1614.

JERVIS, WILLIAM. Adm. pens. (age 18) at Trinity, Feb. 24, 1714-5. S. of John, of Darlaston, Staffs. School, Coventry (Mr Greenaway). Scholar, 1716; B.A. 1718-9; M.A. 1722. V. of Stone, Staffs., 1723-78. Perhaps preb. of Lichfield, 1727-9. Died June 5, 1778. (Burke, *L.G.*; A. B. Beaven.)

JESSEY, HENRY (1619), *see* JACYE.

JESSON, ABRAHAM. Adm. p . at Emmanuel, Feb. 26, 1655-6. Of Staffordshire. Matric. 1656-7; B.A. 1659-60.

JESON or IDSON, JOHN. Adm. sizar at Peterhouse, 1600-1; B.A. 1604-5; 'Idson' in *ordo*.

JESSON, THOMAS. Matric. sizar from Peterhouse, Michs. 1571. Probably ord. priest (London) Oct. 13, 1577. P.C. of Prestwold, Leics., 1577-81. V. of St Mary's, Leicester. Perhaps V. of St Nicholas, Leicester, whose will, 1614.

JESSON, WILLIAM. Adm. Fell.-Com. (age 15) at Christ's, June 29, 1663. S. of William. B. in London. School, Woodstock (Dr Gregory). Matric. 1663. Perhaps of Coventry. If so, knighted, Feb. 12, 1668-9. Of Rothley Temple, Leics. High Sheriff of Warws., 1678. Died 1725. (*Peile*, I. 606; *Vis. of London*, 1634; *Lipscomb*, III. 3.)

JESSOP, BARTHOLOMEW. LL.D. 1607 (Incorp. from Oxford). S. of Walter, of Chalcombe, Dorset. B.A. from Magdalen College, Oxford, 1580-1; B.C.L. (Gloucester Hall) 1588; D.C.L. (Magdalen College) 1599. Admitted advocate, Oct. 15, 1601. Chancellor of Sarum diocese. Died July 21, 1620. Buried in Christ Church, Newgate. Will, P.C.C. (*Al. Oxon.*)

JESOPE, CHRISTOPHER. Matric. sizar from Christ's, Michs. 1547; B.A. 1553-4; M.A. 1556. Fellow, 1554-9. Received tonsure (London) 1554. R. of Navenby, Leics., 1559-65. (*Peile*, I. 43.)

JESOP, FRANCIS. Matric. pens. from St John's, Easter, 1586; B.A. 1589-90; M.A. 1593.

JESSOP, FRANCIS. Adm. pens. (age 16) at Caius, May 30, 1699. S. of Samuel, medical practitioner, of East Bradenham, Norfolk. B. there. School, West Bradenham (Mr Needham). Scholar, 1699-1705; Matric. 1700; M.B. 1705. Died Feb. 1, 1749-50. M.I. at Swanton Morley. Brother of Samuel (1691). (*Venn*, I. 502.)

JESOPE, JOHN. Matric. sizar from Christ's, May, 1555; Scholar, 1557-8.

JESUP, JOHN. Adm. pens. (age 16) at Caius, Oct. 23, 1613. S. of John, gent., of Revesby, Lincs. School, Oakham (Mr Wallis). Matric. 1614. Adm. at Gray's Inn, Nov. 18, 1616. Of Coningsby, Lincs., Esq. Married Anne, dau. of Robert Sandford, of Chapell, Essex. Father of Robert (1642). (*Venn*, I. 223.)

JESSUPP, JOHN. Adm. pens. (age 18) at Peterhouse, Feb. 6, 1644-5. Of Suffolk. Matric. 1647; B.A. 1648-9.

JESSUP, JOHN. Adm. sizar at Trinity, Nov. 24, 1669. Matric. 1669; B.A. 1673-4. Ord. deacon (Norwich) Sept. 1675. Perhaps R. of Brettenham, Suffolk, 1698-1708, as M.A. R. of Frostenden, 1708-19.

JESSOP, JONATHAN. Matric. pens. from Corpus Christi, Michs. 1649. Of Suffolk. B.A. 1651-2; M.A. 1659. R. of Colkirk and Oxwich, Norfolk, till 1662.

JESSOP, JOSEPH. Adm. at King's, a scholar from Eton, 1579. B. at Sutton, Kent, *c.* 1562. Matric. 1579-80; B.A. 1583-4; M.A. 1587. Fellow, 1582-91. Secretary to Sir Fra. Walsingham. F.R.C.P., 1597 (being then M.D. of Cambridge). Will (P.C.C.) 1599; of St Bartholomew Exchange. (*Cooper*, II. 241; *Munk*, I. 114.)

JESSOPP, MICHAEL. B.A. from Trinity, 1597-8; M.A. 1601. Ord. deacon and priest (Lincoln) July 17, 1603. V. of Rasen Drax, Lincs., 1603-35. Will (Lincoln) 1635.

JESSOPP, RICHARD. Matric. pens. from St John's, Michs. 1576; B.A. 1580-1.

JESSOP, RICHARD. Matric. sizar from Queens', Easter, 1610. Of Lincolnshire. One of these names P.C. of St Chad's, Stafford, 1637.

JESSOP, ROBERT. Adm. sizar at Peterhouse, May 24, 1612. Matric. 1612; B.A. 1615-6. Ord. deacon (Peterb.) May 26, 1616. Contemporary at Oxford who was R. of Kilve, Somerset.

JESUP, ROBERT. Adm. pens. (age 18) at St John's, May 26, 1642. S. of John (1613), gent., of Coningsby, Lincs. B. at Revesby. School, Westminster. (*Lincs. Pedigrees*, 549.)

JESSOP, SAMUEL. Adm. pens. (age 15) at Caius, July 4, 1691. S. of Samuel, medical practitioner, of Bradenham, Norfolk. B. there. Schools, Dunham (Mr Ransome) and West Bradenham (Mr Needham). Scholar, 1691-5; Matric. 1692. Died in College. Buried at St Michael's, Cambridge, Feb. 26, 1695-6. Brother of Francis (1699). (*Venn*, I. 490.)

JESSOP, THOMAS. M.A. 1565 (Incorp. from Oxford). Probably s. of John, R. of West Chickerel, Dorset. B.A. from Merton College, Oxford, 1560; M.A. 1564; M.B. 1566; M.D. 1569. Fellow of Merton, 1560. F.R.C.P. Junior Linacre lecturer at Oxford. Died at Gillingham, Dorset. Buried Oct. 18, 1615. (*Al. Oxon.*; *Munk*, I. 74.)

JESSOPP, THOMAS. Matric. sizar from Trinity, Michs. 1575. Ord. deacon (Lincoln) July 12, 1583, as B.A. Master of Kirton School, Lincs., in 1585.

JESSOP, THOMAS. Matric. sizar from Corpus Christi, Easter, 1639. Of Bedfordshire. Migrated to Clare, Mar. 31, 1640. B.A. 1643. Ord. deacon (Lincoln) May 28, 1643.

JESSOPP, THOMAS. Adm. pens. (age 14) at EMMANUEL, Mar. 3, 1642-3. Of London. Doubtless s. of Thomas, citizen of London. Migrated to Peterhouse, May 13, 1644. Matric. 1645-6; B.A. 1646-7; Scholar, 1647. R. of Little Gransden, Cambs., 1656. Probably ord. priest (Galloway) June 9, 1661; and V. of Coggeshall, Essex, 1662-79. Buried there Jan. 31, 1679. Father of Thomas (1690-1).

JESSOP, THOMAS. Adm. sizar at EMMANUEL, May 12, 1674. Of Suffolk. Matric. 1674. Died in College. Buried at St Andrew's, Cambridge, June 9, 1677.

JESSOP, THOMAS. Adm. sizar (age 16) at SIDNEY, Feb. 6, 1690-1. S. of Thomas (1642), R. of Little Gransden, Cambs. Bapt. Nov. 11, 1673. School, Huntingdon (Mr Jo. Mathews). Matric. 1691; Scholar, 1691; B.A. 1694-5; M.A. 1698. Ord. deacon (Ely) 1697; priest (London) May 27, 1711. Signs as minister at Tempsford, Beds., 1714-31. Perhaps R. of Goldington, 1716. One of these names R. of Pudding Norton, Norfolk, 1711-37; and of Wells, 1717.

JESSOPE, WILLIAM. Matric. pens. from ST JOHN'S, Michs. 1576. Perhaps s. of Richard, of Brownhall, Sheffield; b. Apr. 1561; buried at Sheffield, Sept. 8, 1630. (M. H. Peacock.)

JESSOP, WILLIAM. M.A. from ST JOHN'S, 1589. Of St Alban Hall, Oxford, 1572. Scholar of Trinity, Oxford, 1573; B.A. 1576. Perhaps R. of Long Crichell, Dorset, 1587-1632; and of Chesilbourne, 1588-1632. (*Al. Oxon.*; F. S. Hockaday.)

JESSOPP, WILLIAM. Matric. pens. from MAGDALENE, Easter, 1627.

JESSOP, WILLIAM. Adm. sizar (age 18) at ST JOHN'S, May 23, 1637. S. of Thomas, husbandman, of Wentworth, Yorks. B. there. School, Worsborough (Mr Shaw). B.A. 1640-1.

JESOP, WILLIAM. Adm. sizar (age 18) at MAGDALENE, Jan. 31, 1725-6. S. of William. B. at South Kyme, Lincs. School, Haynton. Matric. 1726; B.A. 1729-30. Ord. deacon (Lincoln) Feb. 22, 1729-30; priest, Sept. 19, 1731.

JESSOPP or JESAPP, WILLIAM SHIERCLIFFE. Adm. pens. (age 18) at ST JOHN'S, June 29, 1733. S. of William, Esq., of Broom Hall, Sheffield, Yorks. B. at Thurnscoe. School, Wakefield. Matric. 1733; B.A. 1736-7. Ord. deacon (Lincoln) June 5, 1737; C. of Lea, Lincs. Of Thurnscoe Manor, Yorks. Buried there July 4, 1751. (M. H. Peacock.)

JESSOP, ——. Adm. Fell.-Com. at TRINITY, 1654.

'JETHCOTE.' RALPH; mistake for HEATHCOTE, whom *see*.

JETHERELL, JOHN. Matric. pens. from TRINITY, Easter, 1627. Perhaps s. of William Jawdrell, of Stoughton, Hunts. (*Vis. of Cambs.*, 1619.)

JETTERELL, ROBERT. Matric. pens. from PEMBROKE, Michs. 1569. Doubtless s. of Thomas, of Sutton, Cambs. Knighted. Buried at Sutton, July 19, 1606. Will (P.C.C.) Jhetherell. (*Vis. of Cambs.*, 1619.)

JETTER, JAMES. Matric. sizar from ST JOHN'S, Lent, 1563-4.

JETTER or GETTER, ROBERT. Matric. pens. from QUEENS', Michs. 1565; Scholar.

JETTER, WILLIAM. Matric. pens. from CLARE, Easter, 1586.

JEVE, JOHN. Matric. pens. from TRINITY, Michs. 1566. One of these names adm. at Gray's Inn, from Staple's Inn, 1573.

JEVE, RICHARD. Matric. sizar from CLARE, Easter, 1577. B. at Steeple Morden, Cambs. B.A. 1580-1; M.A. 1584. Ord. deacon (London) Dec. 21, 1581. V. of Winston, Suffolk, 1589-1636. Buried there Sept. 15, 1636.

JEVEN, DANIEL. Scholar of TRINITY, 1608; B.A. 1608-9; M.A. 1612. Pedigree of Jeven, of Sedgley Hall, Staffs., in S. Shaw, *Staffs.*, II. App. 19.

JEVEN, DANIEL. Matric. sizar from TRINITY, 1637; Scholar, 1641; B.A. 1641-2.

JEW, GEORGE. Adm. sizar (age 18) at SIDNEY, Jan. 7, 1636-7. S. of Thomas. B. at Shelvie, Himbleton, Worcs. Schools, King's School, Worcester, and Warwick (Mr Tho. Dugard). Matric. 1637; B.A. 1640-1. Ord. deacon (Lincoln) Sept. 25, 1642; priest, Sept. 22, 1644.

JEWYLL, GEORGE. Adm. pens. at CAIUS, May 19, 1565. S. of John, of Scoulton, Norfolk. School, Wymondham, Norfolk.

JEWELL, GEORGE. Adm. pens. (age 20) at TRINITY, June 16, 1715. S. of John, of Battersea, Surrey. School, Westminster. Scholar, 1716; Matric. 1718; B.A. 1718-9; M.A. 1722. Fellow, 1721. Usher of Westminster School. Died June 6, 1725. Buried at the Abbey. (*Al. Westmon.*, 266; *Westminster Abbey Register*.)

JEWELL, JOHN. Adm. pens. (age 18) at CAIUS, Sept. 12, 1586. S. of Robert. B. at Carleton Rode, Norfolk. School, Palgrave, Suffolk (Mr More). Scholar, 1587-90; B.A. 1596-7; M.A. 1600. Ord. priest (Norwich) 1593. C. of St Mary's, Bury St Edmunds, 1603, till after 1627. Married, at Rushbrook, Suffolk, Apr. 24, 1623, Mary White. Died *c.* 1650. Will (P.C.C.) 1651; as of Carleton Rode, clerk. (*Venn*, I. 128.)

JEWELL, RICHARD. Adm. sizar (age 16) at PETERHOUSE, 1636. Of London. School, Durham. Matric. 1636; B.A. 1639-40.

JEWELL, SAMUEL. Adm. sizar at JESUS, July 2, 1650 Of Hertfordshire. Doubtless s. of Samuel, —— of St Albans, tailor. B. at St Albans. Matric. 1650; B.A. 1653-4; Scholar, 1654; M.A. 1657. Fellow, 1655-62. Incorp. at Oxford, 1660. V. of Whittlesford, Cambs., 1660-2. Will (V.C.C.) 1662. (A. Gray.)

JEWELL, THOMAS. Adm. sizar (age 18) at PEMBROKE, June 16, 1648. S. of James, grocer, of London. Migrated to Caius, Feb. 26, 1649-50. Matric. 1649-50. One of these names V. of Ilam, Staffs., 1661-8. Died 1668.

JEWETT, JOHN. M.D. 1658 (Incorp. from Dublin). Adm. candidate R.C.P., June 25, 1659.

JEWETT, JOSEPH. Adm. pens. (age 18) at CAIUS, June 29, 1695. S. of Joseph, medical practitioner, of Norwich. B. there. School, Norwich (Mr Burton). Matric. 1695; Scholar, 1695-1700. (*Venn*, I. 497.)

JEWKES, JOHN. Adm. pens. (age 18) at PETERHOUSE, May 25, 1702. Of Sussex. School, Eton. Adm. at the Inner Temple, May 15, 1702; as s. and h. of Humphrey, of Petworth. Adm. at Lincoln's Inn, Apr. 21, 1713. M.P. for Bridport, 1730-4; for Aldborough, 1735-43. Died Sept. 25, 1743, aged 61. (*T. A. Walker*, 209; A. B. Beaven.)

JEWRY, *see also* JURY.

JEWRY, JOHN. Matric. sizar from TRINITY, Michs. 1616; Scholar, 1619; B.A. 1619-20; M.A. 1623. Ord. deacon (Peterb.) Dec. 13; priest, Dec. 14, 1623, as Ivory. R. of Ayott St Peter, Herts., 1630.

JEWRY, JOHN. Matric. pens. from CORPUS CHRISTI, Easter, 1626. Of Cambridgeshire. B.A. 1630-1.

JEX, EDWARD. Adm. sizar (age 16) at ST JOHN'S, May 17, 1656. S. of John, yeoman of Trunch, Norfolk. B. at Edgefield. School, North Walsham. Matric. 1656; B.A. 1659-60. Perhaps adm. at the Inner Temple, May 14, 1667. Called to the Bar, July, 1671.

JOACHIM, BRYTYNNER. M.A. 1504-5; B.D. 1506-7. Incorp. as D.D. 1511-2.

JOBSON, ANDREW. Matric. pens. from TRINITY, Michs. 1564.

JOBSON, JOHN. Recorded as fellow of CLARE, in 1527.

JOBSONNE, JOHN. Matric. pens. from QUEENS', Michs. 1558, *impubes*.

JOBSON, MICHAEL. Matric. pens. from PEMBROKE, Michs. 1571. Probably adm. at Gray's Inn, 1573.

JOBSONNE, RICHARD. Adm. sizar (age 16) at CAIUS, May 15, 1623. S. of Richard, gent., of South Cave, Yorks. School, South Cave (Mr Brabbs). Matric. 1623. Perhaps s. of the traveller in Guinea, 1620-1, for whom *see D.N.B.* One Richard Jobson by will (York, 1643) left lands in Ellerker, adjoining South Cave. (*Venn*, I. 262.)

JOBSON, T. B.A. 1490-1; M.A. 1493.

JOBSON or JOPSON, THOMAS. Matric. sizar from TRINITY, Easter, 1568; Scholar, 1571, as Jopson; B.A. 1571-2; M.A. (Oxford) 1575. R. of Barnbrough, Yorks., 1578-1615. Perhaps V. of Rotherham, 1587-93. V. of Waddington, 1615-9.

JOBSON, WILLIAM. Matric. pens. from ST JOHN'S, Michs. 1572. One of these names V. of Aldborough, Holderness, Yorks., 1578-1613.

JOCELYN, *see* JOSELIN.

JODRELL, EDMUND. Adm. Fell.-Com. (age 17) at ST JOHN'S, June 10, 1653. S. of Edmund, Esq., of Taxall, Cheshire. B. there. Taught at home. Matric. 1653-4. High Sheriff of Cheshire, 1670. Married Elizabeth, dau. of Sir Francys Burdett, of Foremark, Derbs., Bart. (*Ormerod*, III. 382.)

JODRELL, WALTER. Adm. scholar at TRINITY HALL, Jan. 12, 1738-9. Of Westminster. Bapt. at St Paul's, Covent Garden, Dec. 27, 1719. Matric. 1738. Adm. at Lincoln's Inn, Dec. 16, 1738, as s. of William, of Covent Garden, mercer. Solicitor-general of the island of Grenada. Died Aug. 7, 1771. (G. *Mag.*, 378.)

JOET, HENRY. B.A. 1505.

JOHNSON, ABEL. Adm. pens. at TRINITY HALL, June 29, 1749. S. of Rowland (1716), V. of Hemel Hempstead, Herts. B. there. Colleger at Eton, 1743-4. (Name off, 1750.) Perhaps died Apr. 20, 1761. (L. *Mag.*)

JOHNSON, ABRAHAM. Adm. pens. at EMMANUEL, Oct. 20, 1591. S. of Robert (1557-8). B. at North Luffenham, July 5, 1577. Matric. 1591. Created M.A. 1612-3 (on the King's visit). Adm. at Lincoln's Inn, May 11, 1594. Of Rutland. Barrister, 1602. Bought property at South Luffenham, and lived there. High Sheriff of Rutland, 1618. Married (1) Anne Meadows; (2) Elizabeth, dau. of Laurence Chaderton, Master of Emmanuel. Died 1649. Father of Isaac (1614), Ezechiel (1622), Samuel (1620) and Francis (1633). (*Vis. of Rutland*, 1618; J. B. Peace.)

JOHNSON, ALEXANDER. B.A. 1516–7. Licensed to practise surgery, 1540–1. V. of Chatteris, Cambs., 1546–8.

JOHNSON, ALEXANDER. Adm. pens. at KING'S, 1673–4. S. of William (1649), of Rishton Grange, in Bolland, Yorks. B. at Slaidburn, Yorks. Colleger at Eton, 1670–3. Sheriff of Lancs., 1688. Died Aug. 20, 1741. (M. H. Peacock; J. Parker; *Vis. of Lancs.*, 1664.)

JOHNSON, ANDREW. Matric. sizar from QUEENS', Easter, 1613.

JOHNSON, ANDREW. Adm. sizar (age 16) at CHRIST'S, Nov. 11, 1635. S. of Thomas. B. at Offord, Hunts. School, Potton (Mr Shiers). Migrated to Trinity. Matric. 1636; B.A. 1638–9. Perhaps brother of Philip (1630).

JOHNSON, ANTHONY. Pens. at PETERHOUSE, 1554. V. of Trumpington, Cambs. Died 1557. His inventory (V.C.C.) is summarized in *Camb. Ant. Soc.*, LVIII. 186.

JOHNSON, ANTHONY. B.A. from JESUS, 1579–80; M.A. 1583. Schoolmaster at Fen Ditton, Cambs., 1582. V. of Moulton, Lincs., 1584. Probably R. of Richmond, Yorks., 1585–1620. V. of Hauxwell, 1588–1620.

JOHNSON, ARTHUR. Matric. sizar from MICHAELHOUSE, Michs. 1548.

JOHNSON, ARTHUR. Matric. pens. from ST JOHN'S, Easter, 1573. B. at Kendal, Westmorland. B.A. 1576–7; M.A. 1580; B.D. 1586. Fellow, 1581. Ord. deacon (London) Mar. 30, 1580, age 26. Minister of St Benet, Cambridge, 1604–11. Will proved (V.C.C.) 1611.

JOHNSON, ARTHUR. Matric. sizar from KING'S, Michs. 1588.

JOHNSON, ARTHUR. Adm. scholar (age 19) at KING'S, Aug. 29, 1597. Of Widford, Oxon. B.A. 1601–2; M.A. 1605; B.D. 1615. Fellow, 1600–21. Senior proctor, 1613–4. Vice-Provost, 1619. Ord. priest (Peterb.) July 27, 1614. Chaplain to Lord Purbeck. Died Apr. 2, 1621. Buried in the College Chapel. (*Harwood.*)

JOHNSON, BALDWYN. Adm. at KING'S (age 18) a scholar from Eton, Oct. 3, 1563. Of Leighton Buzzard, Beds. Matric. 1563–4; B.A. 1567–8; M.A. 1571. Fellow, 1566–72. Died at Down Hatherley, Gloucs., Aug. 30, 1613. Buried there. M.I. Brother of William (1551). (*Harwood.*)

JONSON, BENJAMIN. The dramatist. Has been assigned to Cambridge (to TRINITY, by Aubrey; and to St John's, by Fuller), but no proof has been found. He states, himself, that he 'was Master of Arts of both Universities, by their favour, not his study.' He was M.A. from Christ Church, Oxford, July 19, 1619, but no Cambridge degree is recorded. He was born in Westminster, educated there under Camden. Died Aug. 16, 1637, aged 63. Buried in Westminster Abbey.

JOHNSON, BENJAMIN. Adm. pens. (age 16) at SIDNEY, May 9, 1660. 2nd s. of Thomas (1627–8), R. of Tinwell, Ruts. B. at Oundle. Bapt there, Aug. 26, 1642. Schools, Stamford (Mr Humphreys), Oundle (under his father) and Charterhouse (exhibitioner, 1660). Matric. 1660; B.A. 1663–4; M.A. 1667; B.D. 1674. Fellow, 1664. Junior proctor, 1672–3. R. of Dunsby, Lincs., 1676. Perhaps preb. of Salisbury, 1685. Died same year, at Boreham, Essex. Admon. (P.C.C.) Mar. 11, 1685–6. (*Al. Carthus.*)

JOHNSON, BENJAMIN. Adm. sizar (age 17) at CHRIST'S, Jan. 25, 1697–8. S. of Oliver (1670). B. at Capel, Suffolk. Educated by Mr Coleman. Matric. 1698; Scholar, 1698–9; B.A. 1701–2. (*Peile*, II. 140.)

JOHNSON, CARINUS. Adm. as sizar of Dr Thimbleby, 1519–20.

JOHNSON, CATLIN. Matric. pens. from CLARE, Michs. 1572; B.A. 1575–6.

JONSON, CHARLES. Matric. sizar from JESUS, Easter, 1566.

JOHNSTON, CHARLES. Adm. pens. at ST JOHN'S, Oct. 20, 1676. 2nd s. of Nathaniel (1654), M.D., of Pontefract, Yorks. B. there. School, Sedbergh. Matric. 1676; M.B. 1682; M.D. 1687. Physician at Pontefract. Married Sarah, dau. of Thomas Burley, of Greenhill, Yorks. Died at Chesterfield. Brother of Cudworth (1671), father of Henry (1712). (*F.M.G.* 927; *Vis. of Yorks.*, 1665.)

JOHNSON, CHARLES. Adm. pens. (age 17) at TRINITY, Sept. 3, 1677. S. of William. B. at Cambridge. School, York (Mr Thomas Cockroft). Died Feb. 3, 1728.

JOHNSON, CHRISTOPHER. Adm. sizar (age 17) at ST JOHN'S, May 31, 1670. S. of Christopher, yeoman, of Clapham, Yorks. B. there. School, Sedbergh (Mr Fell). Matric. 1670; B.A. 1673–4. Ord. deacon (York) June, 1674; priest, Sept. 1677.

JOHNSON, CHRISTOPHER. M.A. from KING'S, 1691; D.D. 1701 (*Lit. Reg.*). S. of John, of Churcham, Gloucs., clerk. Matric. from New Inn Hall, Oxford, July 8, 1676, age 18; B.A. (Queen's College, Oxford) 1680. Incorp. M.A. at Oxford, 1692. Of Richmond, Surrey, schoolmaster. Married, at Charterhouse Chapel, London, Jan. 27, 1706–7, Mary Dyer, of St Giles', Cripplegate. Buried at Richmond, Jan. 6, 1710–1. Will, P.C.C. (*Al. Oxon.*; J. Ch. Smith.)

JOHNSTON, CUDWORTH. Adm. pens. (age 15) at ST JOHN'S, Mar. 30, 1671. S. of Nathaniel (1654), M.D. of Pontefract, Yorks., and Ann Cudworth, of Eastfield, Yorks. B. there, Sept. 21, 1654. Schools, Pocklington and Pontefract. Matric. 1671; M.B. 1676; M.D. 1682 (*Lit. Reg.*). Physician at York. Married Margaret, dau. of John Pelham, of Hull, June 21, 1680. Buried Apr. 17, 1692. Brother of Charles (1676), father of Pelham (1700). (*F.M.G.*, 927.)

JOHNSON, CUTHBERT. Matric. pens. from CHRIST'S, Nov. 1575. Possibly ord. at Rheims, 1583 ('of Durham diocese') and came to England, 1584. 'Cuthbert Johnson, *alias* William Darrel, a Jesuit, publickly disputed with Rob. Cooke, V. of Leeds, before the King's Council.' (*Peile*, I. 134; *Douay Diary*; Whitaker, *Loidis*, 26.)

JOHNSON, CUTHBERT. Matric. sizar from PETERHOUSE, Michs. 1582.

JOHNSON, DANIEL. Matric. pens. from CLARE, Michs. 1572.

JOHNSON, DANIEL. Adm. pens. at EMMANUEL, Apr. 17, 1599. (Possibly a mistake for Samuel.)

JOHNSON, DANIEL. Matric. sizar from CORPUS CHRISTI, Easter, 1631. Of Norfolk. B.A. 1634–5; M.A. 1638; B.D. 1646. Fellow, 1644–50, ejected (*Coll. Hist.*, 105). Ord. priest (Bishop Hall, of Norwich) Oct. 19, 1653. Perhaps R. of Barking and Darmsden, Suffolk, 1649. R. of Postwick, Norfolk, 1661.

JOHNSON, DANIEL. Matric. sizar from CORPUS CHRISTI, Easter, 1649.

JOHNSON, DANIEL. Adm. sizar at EMMANUEL, Feb. 27, 1665–6. Of Leicestershire. Matric. 1667.

JOHNSON, EDMUND. B.A. 1516–7. One of these names canon of Windsor, June–Nov., 1560. Will, P.C.C.; schoolmaster of St Anthony's, London. (Cole, *MS.*, 5873, 64.)

JOHNSON, EDWARD. Matric. sizar from TRINITY, Lent, 1582–3. (Perhaps same as the next.)

JOHNSON, EDWARD ('EDMUND'). Matric. pens. from TRINITY, Michs. 1583; Scholar, 1588; B.A. 1588–9; M.A. 1592. One Edmund Johnson V. of Lilford, Northants., till 1630. Admon. (Peterb.) to widow Alice. Perhaps father of Thomas (1627). (H. I. Longden.)

JOHNSON, EDWARD. Matric. sizar from ST CATHARINE'S, Easter, 1586; B.A. 1588–9; M.A. 1593. One of these names R. of Kirklinton, Cumberland, 1604–11. V. of Beaumont, 1611. (*B. Nightingale.*)

JOHNSON, EDWARD. Mus.Bac. from CAIUS, 1594. Composer, madrigals and psalm tunes. (*Venn*, I. 151; *D.N.B.*; *Cooper*, II. 304.)

JOHNSON, EDWARD. B.A. from TRINITY, 1610–1; M.A. 1614.

JOHNSON, EDWARD. Adm. sizar at QUEENS', July, 1620. Of Cambridgeshire. Matric. 1622; B.A. 1623–4; M.A. 1627. Ord. deacon (Peterb.) Sept. 23, 1627; priest (London) June 8, 1628. V. of Milton, Cambs., 1632. Perhaps R. of Stanstead, Suffolk, 1638.

JOHNSON, EDWARD. Matric. pens. from MAGDALENE, Easter, 1639. One of these names, 'B.A.,' ord. deacon (Lincoln) June 16, 1644; priest, Apr. 9, 1645.

JOHNSON, EDWARD. Adm. pens. at EMMANUEL, May 15, 1667. Of Rutland. Matric. 1668.

JOHNSON, EDWARD. Adm. sizar at QUEENS', June 19, 1669. Of Yorkshire. Matric. 1669. Ord. deacon (York) Dec. 1672; priest, Sept. 21, 1673.

JOHNSON, EZECHIEL. Matric. pens. from CHRIST'S, July, 1608; B.A. 1611–2; M.A. 1615. Ord. deacon (Peterb.) Mar. 19; priest, Mar. 20, 1613–4. R. of Bucknall, Lincs., 1615.

JOHNSON, EZECHIEL. Adm. sizar at EMMANUEL, May 28, 1622. S. of Abraham (1591), of South Luffenham, Rutland. B. 1607. B.A. 1625–6; M.A. 1629. Master of Uppingham School. V. of Paulerspury, Northants., 1631–7. R. of Cranford St John, 1640–c. 1656. Lord of the manor of Clipsham, Ruts. Died Feb. 25, 1687, aged 81. Buried at Olney, Bucks. M.I. Brother of Isaac (1614) Samuel (1620), etc. (*Vis. of Rutland*, 1618; *Vis. of London*, 1634; J. B. Peace; H. I. Longden.)

JOHNSON, FRANCIS. Matric. pens. from CHRIST'S, Apr. 1579. 1st s. of John, Mayor of Richmond, Yorks. Bapt. there, Mar. 27, 1562. B.A. 1581–2; M.A. 1585. Fellow, 1584–9. Ord. deacon (London) Apr. 16; priest, Apr. 28, 1584. Imprisoned and expelled from the University for a sermon preached at St Mary's, Cambridge, in which he maintained presbyterianism to be of divine right, 1589. Withdrew to Holland; chaplain to the English merchants at Middleburg, 1589–92. Returned to England and together with John Greenwood formed a separatist church in London, 1592. Several times imprisoned. Returned to Holland, becoming pastor of the exiled separatists at Amsterdam, 1597. Author of Brownist treatises. Died at Amsterdam, Jan. 10, 1618. Brother of George (1580). (*D.N.B.*)

JOHNSON, FRANCIS. Adm. at EMMANUEL, July 9, 1633. Of Rutland. S. of Abraham (1591), of South Luffenham. Matric. 1633; B.A. 1637; M.A. 1644 (Incorp. from Edinburgh). Brother of Isaac (1614), etc. (J. B. Peace.)

JOHNSON, FRANCIS. Adm. pens. at CHRIST'S, May 30, 1646, as 's. of Thomas; of Lancs.; M.A.; previously admitted at Emmanuel.' Probably s. of Thomas, preacher (R. of Stockport); bapt. at Eccles, Jan. 9, 1619-20. Admitted R. of Stockport, Sept. 17, 1656, but appointment void. (E. Axon; *see Peile*, I. 507 and the above.)

JOHNSON, FRANCIS. Adm. at KING'S, a scholar from Eton, 1680. Probably 7th s. of Robert, of the Park House. B. at Brompton, Middlesex. Bapt. at Kensington, Oct. 3, 1664. Matric. 1681; B.A. 1684-5; M.A. 1688. Fellow, 1684. Died in London, 1690. (*Harwood*; J. Ch. Smith.)

JOHNSON, FRANCIS. Adm. sizar (age 18) at ST JOHN'S, May 20, 1684. S. of Ralph (1648), clerk. B. at Brignall, Yorks. Matric. 1684; B.A. 1687-8. Buried at Brignall, Oct. 19, 1689.

JOHNSON, FRANCIS. Adm. at CORPUS CHRISTI, 1718. Of Norwich. Matric. 1721; B.A. 1722-3. Ord. deacon (London) Sept. 22, 1723; priest (Norwich) Sept. 1727. V. of Brooke, Norfolk, 1728. R. of Thwaite, 1733-60. Died Nov. 1760. (*G. Mag.*, 542.)

JOHNSON, FRANCIS. Adm. pens. (age 17) at CHRIST'S, May 2, 1728. S. of Francis. B. at Newcastle. Bapt. at St Nicholas, Mar. 11, 1710-1. School, Newcastle. Matric. 1728; Scholar, 1728; M.B. 1733. Married Mary, dau. of Jean Huet, of Whickham, Durham, Sept. 17, 1741. Buried at St Nicholas, Aug. 19, 1771. (*Peile*, II. 216; H. M. Wood.)

JOHNSON, FREDERIC. Adm. pens. at EMMANUEL, Jan. 25, 1595-6. Matric. *c.* 1596. Perhaps adm. at Lincoln's Inn, Jan. 27, 1598-9. Of London.

JOHNSON, GEOFFREY. Matric. pens. from CHRIST'S, Mar. 1557-8. Of Lincolnshire. S. of Maurice, alderman, of Stamford, Lincs. B. *c.* 1541. Migrated to St John's. B.A. 1559-60; M.A. 1563. Fellow of St John's, 1560. Chaplain of Wigston's Hospital, Leicester. V. of St Martin's, Leicester, 1570. Preb. of Norwich (B.D.), 1570-8. R. of Stony Stanton, Leics., till 1573. Died Sept. 1585, aged '60.' Brother of Robert (1557-8). (*Peile*, I. 66; *Misc. Gen. et Her.*, N.S., I. 450, where the date of his birth and his age are apparently wrong.)

JOHNSON, GEORGE. Matric. sizar from PEMBROKE, Easter, 1560. One of these names 'ord. priest (Peterb.) Sept. 20, 1561, V. of Kirton, Lincs., aged 40; married; resides; understands Latin.' (*Lib. Cler. Linc.*, 1576.)

JOHNSON, GEORGE. Matric. pens. from JESUS, Michs. 1562. One of these names, of Leighton Buzzard, Beds., adm. at the Inner Temple, 1564.

JOHNSON, GEORGE. Matric. pens. from CHRIST'S, Dec. 1580. S. of John, of Richmond, Yorks. Scholar; B.A. 1584-5; M.A. 1588. Taught in school in St Nicholas Lane, London. Committed as a Brownist to the Fleet, 1593. Sentence changed to one of banishment. Sailed for America, 1597, but the ship meeting with disaster, he returned to England. Escaped to Amsterdam, 1597; settled there with the colony of banished Englishmen. Quarrelled with his brother Francis about his wife's fondness for dress and fine clothing, and was excommunicated, 1604. Returned to England and wrote an account of the dissensions in the church at Amsterdam. Died in Durham gaol, 1605. Brother of Francis (1579). (*Peile*, I. 160; *D.N.B.*; *Cooper*, II. 435; III. 97.)

JOHNSON, GEORGE. Adm. sizar (age 16) at PEMBROKE, Feb. 4, 1624-5. S. of William. Matric. 1625; B.A. 1628-9.

JOHNSON, GUIDO. Adm. at KING'S (age 17) a scholar from Eton, Aug. 1, 1508. Of Fotheringay, Northants. Left, *c.* 1511. Clerk to Sir Robert Brudenell, Lord Chief Justice. (*Harwood*.)

JOHNSON, HENRY. B.A. 1530-1. One of these names V. of Halling, Kent, 1534-45.

JONSON, HENRY. Matric. sizar from PEMBROKE, Easter, 1565; B.A. 1572-3.

JOHNSON, HENRY. Matric. sizar from CORPUS CHRISTI, Easter, 1572.

JOHNSON, HENRY. Matric. pens. from ST JOHN'S, Michs. 1588.

JOHNSON, HENRY. Matric. sizar from TRINITY, 1598. Perhaps B.A. from St John's, 1604-5. Licensed to preach (York) 1607. One of these names (B.A.), V. of Wighill, Yorks., 1608-10.

JOHNSON, HENRY. Adm. pens. at PETERHOUSE, Feb. 1, 1611-2. Matric. 1612; B.A. from Trinity, 1614-5; M.A. 1618. Ord. deacon and priest (York) Feb. 1618-9. One of these names V. of Burton, Westmorland, 1622-46.

JOHNSON, HENRY. Matric. sizar from ST JOHN'S, Easter, 1616; B.A. from Christ's, 1619.

JOHNSON, HENRY. Adm. pens. at PETERHOUSE, June 22, 1622. Of Middlesex. Matric. 1622; Scholar, 1623; B.A. 1625-6; M.A. 1629.

JOHNSON, HENRY. Of TRINITY. Licensed to practise medicine, 1632.

JOHNSON, HENRY. Adm. sizar (age 16) at CHRIST'S, Oct. 16, 1640. S. of Henry. B. at Bothal, Northumberland. School, Newcastle (Mr Oxley). Matric. 1640.

JOHNSON, HENRY. Adm. sizar (age 18) at ST JOHN'S, June 30, 1645. (Previously matric. from Magdalen Hall, Oxford, Apr. 1, 1642, and resided there one year.) S. of Henry, attorney, of Bingley, Yorks. Matric. 1645; B.A. 1645-6; M.A. 1649. Fellow, 1647. Perhaps R. of Elm and Emneth, Cambs., 1651; V. 1661.

JOHNSON, HENRY. Adm. pens. (age 17) at ST JOHN'S, Oct. 28, 1645. S. of Henry, gent., of Breamore, Hants. School, Downton, Wilts. B.A. 1649-50; M.A. 1653. Fellow, 1650. One of these names of Devizes, Wilts., clerk. Admon. (Cons. C. Sarum) 1681.

JOHNSON, HENRY. Adm. sizar (age 15) at ST JOHN'S, Sept. 10, 1649. S. of John, of Wadsworth, Yorks., gent. School, Bingley (Mr Watkins). Matric. 1650; B.A. 1653-4; M.A. 1657. Incorp. at Oxford, 1657. One of these names (M.A.), R. of Washington, Durham, 1662-83. Buried there June 22, 1683. (H. M. Wood.)

JOHNSON, HENRY. Adm. pens. (age 17) at ST JOHN'S, May 31, 1682. S. of Henry, dyer. B. at Shrewsbury. School, Shrewsbury (Mr Taylour). Matric. 1682; B.A. 1685-6. Appointed 3rd Master at Shrewsbury, 1688. Died Sept. 14, 1690. (G. W. Fisher, *Shrewsbury*, 204.)

JOHNSON, HENRY. Adm. pens. at TRINITY, May 30, 1682.

JOHNSON, HENRY. Adm. Scholar (age 17) at SIDNEY, Apr. 22, 1684. 1st s. of Henry, gent. B. at Barnby-on-the-Moor, Yorks. School, Pocklington (Mr Tho. Ellison). Matric. 1684; M.B. 1689.

JOHNSTON, HENRY. Adm. sizar at JESUS, May 2, 1712. S. of Charles (1676), M.D., of Pontefract, Yorks. Bapt. there, Feb. 3, 1694-5. Matric. 1712; B.A. 1715-6; M.A. 1719; LL.D. 1728. Incorp. at Oxford, 1720. Ord. deacon (Lincoln) July 14, 1717; priest (London) Dec. 20, 1719. R. of Whilton, Northants., 1720-2. Preb. of Lincoln, 1727-55. R. of Stowmarket, Suffolk, 1727. R. of Stoke and Monk Soham, 1729-55. Precentor of Llandaff, 1733-50. Chancellor of Llandaff diocese, 1738-55. Married Hannah, sister of Dr John Harris, Bishop of Llandaff. Died Oct. 3, 1755. (*F.M.G.*, 927; Baker, *Northants.*, I. 235; A. B. Beaven.)

JOHNSON, HENRY. Adm. pens. at EMMANUEL, Sept. 21, 1720. Of Middlesex. Matric. 1720.

JOHNSON, HODSON. Adm. pens. (age 17) at ST JOHN'S, June 28, 1651. S. of William, husbandman, of Cherry Burton, near Beverley, Yorks. B. there. School, Leconfield, Yorks. (private). B.A. 1654-5; M.A. 1658.

JOHNSON, HUGH. Matric. sizar from QUEENS', Michs. 1585. Of Cheshire.

JOHNSON, HUGH. Matric. pens. from CORPUS CHRISTI, 1597. Of Suffolk.

JOHNSON, HUGH. Adm. sizar at JESUS, June 26, 1671. Of Carnarvon. Matric. 1671.

JOHNSON, HUMFREY. Adm. sizar (age 15) at ST JOHN'S, June 29, 1724. S. of Joshna (1702), M.A., of Salop. B. at Shrewsbury. School, Shrewsbury. Matric. 1724; B.A. 1727-8; M.A. 1731. 3rd Master at Shrewsbury, 1728-35.

JOHNSON, ISAAC. Adm. pens. at EMMANUEL, June 6, 1600. One of these names s. of Richard, of Claxby, Lincs., Esq. Of the Middle Temple. Councillor-at-law. Living, 1634. (*Lincs. Pedigrees*, 550.)

JOHNSON, ISAAC. Adm. sizar at EMMANUEL, Oct. 1614; afterwards pens. S. of Abraham (1591), of South Luffenham, Rutland, and grandson of Archdeacon Robert (1557-8), founder of Oakham School. Matric. 1614; B.A. 1617-8; M.A. 1621. Adm. at Gray's Inn, Jan. 31, 1620-1. Ord. deacon (Peterb.) Mar. 12, 1619-20; priest, May 27, 1621. Married, 1623, Lady Arbella Fiennes, dau. of Thomas, Lord Clinton, Earl of Lincoln (which caused a family quarrel, the father objecting, and the grandfather supporting him; eventually the archdeacon disinherited Abraham). One of the original members of the Massachusetts Company. Accompanied Winthrop to New England, 1630; his wife died from the effects of the journey, and he died Sept. 30, 1630. Brother of Ezechiel (1622) and Samuel (1620). (J. G. Bartlett; *Vis. of Rutland*, 1618; *D.N.B.*; Waters, *Genealogical Gleanings*, 1033.)

JOHNSON, ISAAC. Adm. sizar at Jesus, Dec. 28, 1733. Of Hertfordshire. S. of William (1692), clerk, deceased. B. Feb. 17, 1714–5. School, Christ's Hospital. Scholar, 1734; Matric. 1735; B.A. 1737–8; M.A. 1741. Ord. deacon (Lincoln) Feb. 26, 1737–8. R. of Wormshill, Kent, 1741–67. V. of St Dunstan, Canterbury, 1743–67. Died Mar. 13, 1767, aged 52. Buried in Canterbury Cathedral. (*G. Mag.*; H. G. Harrison.)

JOHNSON, JAMES. B.A. from Trinity, 1601–2; M.A. 1605. Ord. deacon (Peterb.) Sept. 21; priest, Dec. 21, 1606. Perhaps V. of Car Colston, Notts., 1614–(?) 31. 'The most famous country schoolmaster of his time.' (*Thoroton*.)

JOHNSON, JAMES. Matric. sizar from Corpus Christi, Easter, 1620. Of Suffolk.

JOHNSON, JAMES. Matric. sizar from Corpus Christi, Easter, 1624. Of Norwich. Probably died in College; buried at St Benet's, Cambridge, Sept. 8, 1625.

JOHNSON, JAMES. Matric. sizar from St John's, Easter, 1624; B.A. 1627–8; M.A. 1631. Ord. deacon (Peterb.) Dec. 18, 1631.

JOHNSON, JAMES. Adm. pens. at Emmanuel, Mar. 2, 1635–6. Of Suffolk. Matric. 1636. Migrated to Queens', May, 1639; B.A. 1639; M.A. 1643. Ord. deacon (Norwich) Sept. 25, 1642, age 23; C. of Ellingham, Norfolk; priest, May 28, 1643. One of these names (M.A.), V. of Westleton, Suffolk, 1667.

JOHNSON, JAMES. Adm. pens. (age 15) at Sidney, June 29, 1655. S. of Robert (1620), R. of Bainton, Yorks. B. at Rise. Bapt. there, July 7, 1636. School, Pocklington (Mr Llwelline). Matric. 1656; B.A. 1658–9; M.A. 1662; B.D. 1669; D.D. 1689. Fellow, 1662. Master, 1688–1704. Vice-Chancellor, 1689–90. Incorp. at Oxford, 1663. Adm. at Gray's Inn, June 8, 1657. Died Jan. 1703–4. Will (V.C.C.) 1704. Benefactor to the College.

JOHNSON, JAMES. Adm. pens. (age 16) at St John's, May 5, 1657. S. of John (1631–2), D.D., R. of St Mary, Whitechapel, Middlesex. B. there. School, Felsted (Mr Glascock). Matric. 1657; B.A. 1660–1. Adm. at Sidney, Sept. 29, 1663.

JOHNSON, JAMES. Adm. pens. (age 14) at Caius, July 3, 1664. S. of James, merchant, of Yarmouth (afterwards Knt. and M.P. for Yarmouth). School, Norwich (Mr Lovering). Matric. 1664. Brother of Thomas (1671). (*Venn*, I. 422; *Vis. of Norfolk*, 1664.)

JOHNSON, JAMES. Adm. scholar at Trinity Hall, Jan. 1, 1690–1. Matric. 1691; LL.B. 1696; LL.D. 1702. Fellow, 1697–1727. Chancellor of Ely, c. 1707–28. Master of the Faculties, 1714–28. Died Feb. 3, 1727–8, aged 55. (*Trin. Hall Coll. Hist.*, 180; A. B. Beaven.)

JOHNSTON, JAMES. Adm. Fell.-Com. (age 17) at Magdalene, May 19, 1739. S. of James, Esq. (Secretary of State for Scotland; *see D.N.B.*). B. at Twickenham, Middlesex. School, Westminster. Matric. 1740. Brother of John (1739).

JOHNSON, JAMES. Incorp. D.D. 1749. S. of James, of Melford, Suffolk, clerk. Matric. from Christ Church, Oxford, June 5, 1724, age 18; B.A. (Oxford) 1728; M.A. 1731; D.D. 1742. Second Master of Westminster School, 1733–48. R. of Mixbury, Oxon., 1743–59. V. of Watford, Herts., 1743–59. R. of Berkhampstead, 1743–59. Chaplain to the King, 1744–52. Preb. and canon residentiary of St Paul's, 1748–53. Bishop of Gloucester, 1752–9. Bishop of Worcester, 1759–74. Died at Bath, Nov. 28, 1774. Buried at Laycock, Wilts. Will, P.C.C. (*Al. Oxon.*; A. B. Beaven; *D.N.B.*)

JOHNSON, JEREMIAH. Matric. pens. from Corpus Christi, Easter, 1571.

JOHNSON, JEREMY. Adm. pens. (age 18) at St John's, June 29, 1708. S. of James, plumber. B. at Colchester. School, Colchester (Mr Allen). Matric. 1708; B.A. 1711–2. Ord. deacon (London) Dec. 21, 1712; priest, May 23, 1714.

JOHNSON, JOHN. B.Can.L. 1455–6. R. of Sutton, Isle of Ely, 1470.

JOHNSON, JOHN. B.Civ.L. 1504–5.

JOHNSON, JOHN. B.Can.L. 1510–1; D.Can.L. 1513–4.

JOHNSON, JOHN. Adm. at King's (age 18) a scholar from Eton, Aug. 11, 1523. B. at Eton. B.A. 1527–8; M.A. 1531. Fellow, 1526–41. Travelled beyond the sea and became a physician. Fellow of Eton, 1553; deprived, 1554, as a married priest. (*Harwood*.)

JOHNSON, JOHN. B.Civ.L. 1528–9. R. of Huffington.

JOHNSON, JOHN. Matric. pens. from Queens', Easter, 1544; B.A. 1546–7; M.A. 1549; B.D. 1555. Fellow of Clare, 1553. Fellow of Jesus, 1554–85. Received the tonsure (London) 1553; perhaps ord. priest (Lincoln) 1556. The Jesus fellow was a civilian, and often acted for the University. He died Feb. 9, 1585–6, aged 56. M.I. at Downham Church, Cambs. Will proved (V.C.C. and P.C.C.) 1586. (*Cooper*, II. 241, seems to make but one man of this and the next; A. Gray.)

JOHNSON, JOHN. B.A. 1552–3; M.A. 1556. Perhaps B.D. 1562; and University preacher, 1560. According to *Peile* (I. 41) he may have been fellow of Christ's, 1553–4. Perhaps R. of Westley, Suffolk, 1556–8. (*See* last entry.)

JOHNSON, JOHN. Matric. pens. from Christ's, Michs. 1555; B.A. 1559–60. Probably V. of Calceby, Lincs., 1566; 'ord. priest (Lincoln) 1558; bred in the schools'; or V. of Yarborough, Lincs.; 'ord. priest (Lincoln) Sept. 19, 1563; bred in the schools.' (*Lib. Cler.*, 1585.)

JOHNSON, JOHN. Matric. pens. from St John's, Michs. 1569; B.A. 1573–4; M.A. 1577. Incorp. at Oxford, 1580. One of these names (B.A.), V. of Goldington, Beds., 1574.

JOHNSON, JOHN. Matric. sizar from Peterhouse, Easter, 1572; B.A. 1575–6. Ord. deacon (London) Oct. 6, 1577, age 25; priest (Lincoln) Feb. 5, 1577–8; 'B.A.'

JOHNSON, JOHN. Matric. sizar from St Catharine's, Michs. 1572.

JOHNSON, JOHN. Matric. pens. from St John's, Easter, 1576; B.A. 1579–80; M.A. 1583; D.D. 1594. Incorp. at Oxford, 1620. *Al. Oxon.* considers he may be the R. of Stepney, 1628–68, but the age makes this unlikely. *See* John of 1631–2.

JOHNSON, JOHN. Matric. sizar from Clare, Easter, 1580. B. at Aston, Yorks. School, Leicester. B.A. 1583–4; M.A. 1587. Ord. deacon and priest (Peterb.) July 12, 1601. Tutor to the sons of Sir Thomas Cecil, 1596. Tutor in the family of Lord Exeter at Burleigh House. Head Master of Fotheringhay School, 1596–1601. R. of Tansor, Northants., 1601–20. Died Oct. 28, 1620. Buried at Tansor. M.I. Will, P.C.C. Will of widow, Elizabeth, proved 1621 by son Jonathan (1615–6). (*Bridges*, II. 477; H. I. Longden.)

JOHNSON, JOHN. Matric. pens. from St John's, Michs. 1588. One of these names adm. at Gray's Inn, Nov. 16, 1586, from Staple Inn.

JOHNSON, JOHN. Matric. sizar from Christ's, Michs. 1589; B.A. from Clare, 1592–3. Ord. priest (Lincoln) Mar. 22, 1600. V. of Ravenstone, Bucks., 1603–23.

JOHNSON, JOHN. Matric. Fell.-Com. from St John's, Easter, 1589.

JOHNSON, JOHN. Adm. at Corpus Christi, 1601. Of Kent. B.A. 1604–5; M.A. 1608. Probably R. of Westbere, Kent, 1608; and father of John (1647).

JOHNSON, JOHN. Adm. sizar at Peterhouse, Lent, 1602–3; B.A. 1606–7; M.A. 1610.

JOHNSON, JOHN. Adm. sizar at Sidney, June, 1603. Matric. 1604; B.A. 1607–8; M.A. 1611.

JOHNSON, JOHN. Matric. sizar from Pembroke, Lent, 1607–8; B.A. 1611–2; M.A. 1615. Fellow, 1613. Ord. deacon and priest (Lincoln) Feb. 21, 1618–9.

JOHNSON, JOHN. Matric. sizar from Christ's, July, 1612.

JOHNSON, JOHN. Adm. pens. at Emmanuel, Easter, 1612. Matric. 1612; B.A. 1615–6; M.A. 1619. Incorp. at Oxford, 1619. Ord. deacon (Peterb.) Sept. 19; priest, Sept. 20, 1619.

JOHNSON, JOHN. Matric. sizar from Pembroke, Michs. 1615; B.A. 1618–9; M.A. 1622. Licensed to practise medicine, 1637. One of these names (B.A.), R. of Thoresway, Lincs., 1621–9.

JOHNSON, JOHN. Matric. pens. from Trinity, Easter, 1616.

JOHNSON, JOHN. Adm. at Corpus Christi, 1618. Of Kent. Perhaps s. of John, of Nethercourt, Isle of Thanet. B. 1599. (*Vis. of Kent*, 1619; *Hasted*, IV. 371.)

JOHNSON, JOHN. Matric. pens. from St John's, Easter, 1619. Of Yorkshire. B.A. 1622–3; M.A. 1626; B.D. 1634. Fellow, 1623. Taxor, 1632. Ord. deacon (York) June; priest, Sept. 1623. Will proved (V.C.C.) 1636.

JOHNSON, JOHN. Adm. pens. at Peterhouse, July 4, 1620. Of Yorkshire. Matric. 1620; B.A. 1623–4; M.A. 1627. One John Johnston, R. of Sutton-on-Derwent, Yorks., died 1657, aged 57. (*F.M.G.*, 927.)

JOHNSON, JOHN. 'Late student of Emmanuel'; ord. deacon (York) Mar. 1627–8. Possibly John Juxton, whom *see*.

JOHNSON, JOHN. Matric. sizar from Peterhouse, Easter, 1628. Of Yorkshire. B.A. 1631–2; M.A. 1635. Ord. priest (Peterb.) Sept. 25, 1636.

JOHNSON, JOHN. Adm. sizar at Queens', Easter, 1629. Of Cambridgeshire.

JOHNSON, JOHN. Adm. sizar at Emmanuel, Apr. 14, 1631. Of Northamptonshire. Matric. 1631. Probably ord. deacon (Peterb.) Feb. 18, 1637–8; 'B.A., of Emmanuel College.'

JOHNSON, JOHN. D.D. 1631–2 (*Lit. Reg.*). Probably s. of Henry, of Stratford-le-Bow, Middlesex (admon., 1640, P.C.C.). The will of John, D.D., R. of St Mary Matfallon, Whitechapel, and of Stepney, 1628–69, was proved (P.C.C.) 1669. Father of James (1657). (J. Ch. Smith.)

JOHNSTON, JOHN. M.D. 1634 (Incorp. from Leyden). S. of Simon, of Craigieburn, Nithsdale. B. at Sambter, Poland, Sept. 3, 1603. Matric. (at St Andrews), Jan. 29, 1623–4. Travelled abroad, 1625–9. Took courses of botany and medicine at Cambridge, 1629. M.D. (Leyden) 1632. Practised medicine there and obtained a great reputation. Retired to his estate near Liegnitz in Silesia, 1655. A distinguished naturalist. Author, scientific. Died June 8, 1675. Buried at Lessno, Poland. (*D.N.B.*)

JOHNSON, JOHN. Adm. pens. (age 18) at CHRIST'S, Apr. 28, 1635. S. of John. B. at Anmer, Norfolk. School, West Newton (Mr Ringwood and Mr Webster). Matric. 1635. One of these names, of Anmer, but said to be son of Bartholomew, adm. at Gray's Inn, Nov. 1, 1634.

JOHNSON, JOHN. Matric. pens. from CORPUS CHRISTI, Michs. 1635. Of Lincolnshire. B.A. 1638–9; M.A. 1642. Ord. deacon (Lincoln) May 20, 1646.

JOHNSON, JOHN. Matric. sizar from ST CATHARINE'S, Easter, 1644; B.A. 1646–7; M.A. 1650.

JOHNSON, JOHN. Adm. pens. at EMMANUEL, June 20, 1644. Of Leicestershire. Matric. 1644; B.A. 1647–8. Migrated to Oxford. Fellow of St John's, Oxford, 1649; and of New College, 1650. M.A. 1650. Incorp. at Cambridge, 1651. Student of Egyptian antiquities. R. of Hornchurch, Essex, 1655. V. of Tin ewick, Bucks., 1656–62. Afterwards preacher in London andelsewhere. (*Al. Oxon.*; Davids' *Essex*.)

JOHNSON, JOHN. Adm. sizar (age 18) at MAGDALENE, May 20, 1645. S. of Marmaduke, of Hull, Yorks. School, Hull. B.A. 1649–50.

JOHNSON, JOHN. Adm. pens. (age 16) at SIDNEY, June 4, 1646. S. of Robert (1620), clerk, of the London Convocation (and of Bainton, Yorks.). B. at Rise, Yorks. School, Charterhouse. Matric. 1647; B.A. 1649–50; M.A. 1653. Incorp. at Oxford, 1653. Adm. at Gray's Inn, Nov. 12, 1650.

JOHNSON, JOHN. Adm. at CORPUS CHRISTI, Mar. 11, 1647–8. Of Kent. S. of John (? 1601), clerk, deceased, of Westbere, Kent. B. there. School, Canterbury. Matric. 1649. Migrated to St John's, Apr. 4, 1651, age 20.

JOHNSON, JOHN. Adm. pens. at TRINITY, Mar. 14, 1653–4. Of Lancashire. Matric. 1653–4.

JOHNSON, JOHN. Adm. pens. (age 17) at ST JOHN'S, May 23, 1662. S. of John, deceased, of South Cave, Yorks. B. there. School, Beverley (Mr Sherewood). Matric. 1662.

JOHNSON, JOHN. Adm. pens. at CORPUS CHRISTI, 1663. Of Norwich. Matric. 1664.

JOHNSON, JOHN. Adm. pens. (age 18) at ST JOHN'S, June 1, 1672. S. of Ambrose, yeoman, of Whorlton, Durham. Bapt. there, June 24, 1653. School, Gt Strickland, Westmorland. Matric. 1672; B.A. 1675–6.

JOHNSON, JOHN. Adm. sizar (age 19) at SIDNEY, Apr. 2, 1674. 1st s. of John, clerk. B. at Bishop Burton, Yorks. Educated at home. Matric. 1674; B.A. 1677–8. Ord. deacon (York) Sept. 22, 1678; priest, Dec. 1679. Probably C. of Harfleet, in Holderness, 1680.

JOHNSON, JOHN. Adm. sizar (age 16) at MAGDALENE, Mar. 4, 1677–8. S. of Thomas (1652), deceased. B. at Frindsbury, Kent, Dec. 30, 1662. School, King's, Canterbury. Matric. 1678; B.A. 1681–2; M.A. from Corpus Christi, 1685. Pre-elected to a fellowship, 1685, but not admitted. Ord. priest (Rochester) Dec. 19, 1686. V. of Baughton-under-Blean, Kent, 1687–97. V. of Hernhill, 1687–97. V. of Margate, 1697–1703. V. of Appledore, 1697–1725. V. of Cranbrook, 1707–25. Married, Oct. 24, 1689, Margaret, dau. of Thomas Jenkin. Author, sermons, etc. Died Dec. 15, 1725. Buried at Cranbrook. M.I. there. Father of John (1704). (*D.N.B.*)

JOHNSON, JOHN. Adm. pens. (age 17) at ST JOHN'S, Feb. 4, 1686–7. S. of John, deceased. B. in Lincolnshire. School, Lincoln (Mr Garmston). Matric. 1687.

JOHNSTON, JOHN. Adm. pens. (age 17) at ST JOHN'S, May 5, 1690. S. of Samuel, gent. (physician, of Beverley). B. at Beverley. School, Beverley (Mr Lambert). Matric. 1690; M.B. 1695. Brother of Samuel (1701).

JOHNSON, JOHN. Adm. sizar at CLARE, Apr. 20, 1691. Of Chesterton, Cambs. Matric. 1691; B.A. 1694–5. One of these names 'M.A.,' ord. deacon (Durham) Sept. 25, 1698; priest, Sept. 24, 1699. Perhaps C. of Grindleton, in Craven, 1706–16.

JOHNSON, JOHN. Adm. sizar at JES , May 25, 1698. Of Nottinghamshire. Matric. 1698; B.A. 1701–2. Scholar, 1702; M.A. 1705. Perhaps ord. priest (Peterb.) Mar. 4, 1704–5. V. of Cameringham, Lincs., 1705. C. of Ingham. R. of Willingham-by-Stowe, 1706.

JOHNSON, JOHN. Adm. at CORPUS CHRISTI, 1704. S. of John (1677–8). B. in Kent. Matric. 1705; B.A. 1708–9; M.A. 1712; B.D. from St John's, 1719. Fellow of St John's, 1715–24. Ord. deacon (Peterb.) May 30, 1713; C. of Barrowden, Rutland; priest (London) May 27, 1716. V. of St Clement's, Cambridge, 1721. R. of Standish, Lancs., 1723. Died Jan. 9, 1723–4, aged 33. (*Masters*, 320.)

JOHNSON, JOHN. Adm. pens. at JESUS, June 22, 1715. Of Yorkshire. S. of Henry. Matric. 1715; M.B. 1720.

JOHNSON, JOHN. LL.B. 1724 (Incorp. from Oxford). B.C.L. (Brasenose) 1721; D.C.L. (Oxford) 1726. R. of Hurworth, Durham, 1714–61. Preb. of Durham, 1727–61. Died Oct. 14, 1761, aged 83. M.I. at Hurworth. (*Al. Oxon.*)

JOHNSON, JOHN. M.A. 1728 (*Com. Reg.*).

JOHNSTON, JOHN. Adm. Fell.-Com. (age 17) at MAGDALENE, May 19, 1739. S. of James, Esq. (Secretary of State for Scotland; *see D.N.B.*). B. at Twickenham, Middlesex. School, Westminster. Brother of James (1739).

JOHNSON, JOHN. Adm. sizar (age 19) at ST JOHN'S, Oct. 20, 1740. S. of Maurice, Esq., barrister, of Lincolnshire. Bapt. at Spalding, Apr. 5, 1722. School, Spalding (Mr Whiteing). Matric. 1740; B.A. 1744–5; M.A. 1748. Ord. deacon (Ely) Sept. 23, 1744; priest (Lincoln) Dec. 21, 1746. Minister of Spalding. F.S.A. President of the Spalding Society, 1757. V. of Moulton, Lincs., 1757–8. Died 1758. (*Scott-Mayor*, III, 510; *Genealogist*, I. 112.)

JOHNSON, JONATHAN. Matric. sizar from TRINITY, Lent, 1615–6. S. of John (1580), R. of Tansor, Northants. Bapt. at Fotheringhay, June 4, 1598. Scholar, 1619; B.A. 1619–20; M.A. 1623. Ord. deacon (Peterb.) May 27, 1621; priest, May 4, 1623. V. of Bracebridge, Lincs., 1623. Probably preb. of Lincoln, 1660–3. Licensed (Peterborough, June 25, 1622), as of Tansor, clerk, to marry Elizabeth Awsten, of Oundle. (H. I. Longden.)

JOHNSON, JONATHAN. Adm. sizar (age 20) at ST JOHN'S, May 17, 1744. S. of William, glover, of Cheshire. B. at Chester. School, King's, Chester (Mr Henchman). Matric. 1744; LL.B. 1751. P.C. of Hargreave, Cheshire, 1758–1806. Died 1806.

JOHNSTON, JOSEPH. Adm. sizar (age 18) at ST JOHN'S, Apr. 27, 1661. S. of John (? 1620), deceased, of Beverley, Yorks. B. there. Schools, Sheffield and Pocklington. B.A. 1664–5; M.A. 1668; B.D. 1675. Fellow, 1669–86. Ord. deacon (York) Nov. 1664; priest, *c.* 1667. V. of St John, Peterborough, 1680–5. R. of Polebrook, Northants., 1685–1720. Preb. of Southwell, 1687–1720. Married Mary, dau. of Edward Croft, merchant, of Bristol. Buried at Polebrook, Jan. 26, 1719–20. (*Bridges*, II. 417, 545; H. I. Longden.)

JOHNSON, JOSEPH. Adm. sizar (age 19) at ST JOHN'S, June 29, 1668. S. of Thomas, tailor, of Stamford, Lincs. B. there. School, Stamford (Mr Geery). Matric. 1668; B.A. 1671–2.

JOHNSON, JOSHUA. Adm. sizar (age 18) at ST JOHN'S, June 6, 1702. S. of Richard, deceased. B. at Shrewsbury. School, Shrewsbury (Mr Lloyd). Matric. 1702; B.A. 1706–7; M.A. 1710. 4th Master at Shrewsbury School, 1706–13. Father of Humphrey (1724).

JOHNSON, LANCELOT. Adm. pens. (age 17) at PEMBROKE, Mar. 31, 1651. S. of Lancelot, barrister; grandson of Lancelot Andrews, Bishop of Winchester. Adm. at the Inner Temple, 1649. Barrister, 1658. Bencher, 1674.

JOHNSON, LAURENCE. Matric. sizar from CHRIST'S, May, 1570. Of Kettering, Northants. B.A. 1573–4; M.A. 1577. (*Peile*, I. 114.)

JOHNSON, MALCOLM. Matric. sizar from CORPUS CHRISTI, Easter, 1624. Of Peterborough. B.A. 1627. Ord. deacon (Peterb.) July 22; priest, July 23, 1627. Minister at Parson Drove, Cambs., 1661.

JOHNSON, MARMADUKE. Adm. sizar at JESUS, Feb. 14, 1639–40. Of Yorkshire. Matric. 1640.

JOHNSON, MARMADUKE. Adm. sizar (age 17) at TRINITY, June 6, 1679. S. of Marmaduke. B. at Worksop, Notts. School, Tickhill, Yorks. Matric. 1679; Scholar, 1681; B.A. 1682–3; M.A. 1686.

JOHNSON, MARTIN. Adm. sizar at EMMANUEL, Jan. 11, 1635–6. Of Lincolnshire. (S. of Martin, of Spalding. Bapt. there, Feb. 2, 1620–1.) Matric. 1636; B.A. 1639–40; M.A. 1643; B.D. from Magdalene, 1661. Minister of Spalding. Master of Spalding School. Married Katharine Draper. Buried at Spalding, Feb. 28, 1678. Father of Walter (1677). (*T. A. Walker*; *Genealogist*, I. 105.)

JOHNSON, MARTIN. Adm. sizar at EMMANUEL, June 5, 1716. Of Nottinghamshire. B.A. 1719–20; M.A. 1723. Fellow, 1722. Ord. deacon (Ely) June 9, 1723; priest, Dec. 18, 1726. R. of Henstead, Suffolk, 1727–58. R. of Gisleham, 1730.

JOHNSON, MATTHEW. Matric. sizar from CORPUS CHRISTI, Easter, 1611. Of Kent. B.A. 1614–5.

JOHNSON, MILES. Matric. sizar from TRINITY, Easter, 1611; B.A. 1614–5. Ord. deacon (York) Sept. 1615; priest, Dec. 1617. V. of Muston, Yorks., 1618–43. Will (York) 1630.

JOHNSON or JOHNSTON, NATHANIEL. M.A. 1654 (Incorp. from St Andrews). M.D. from KING'S, 1656. S. of John (? 1620), R. of Sutton-on-Derwent, Yorks. Bapt. at Whitgift, Yorks., Jan. 8, 1628-9. F.R.C.P., 1687. Practised at Pontefract. Antiquarian. Friend of Thoresby. Removed to London, 1687; became a high Tory pamphleteer. After the Revolution lived privately with the Earl of Peterborough, who maintained him. Married, 1653, Anne, dau. of Richard Cudworth, of Eastfield, Yorks. Author, political; also left manuscript collections on Yorkshire Antiquities. Died 1705. Will, P.C.C. Father of Cudworth (1671) and Charles (1676). (*Vis. of Yorks.*, 1665; *F.M.G.*; *D.N.B.*)

JOHNSTON, NATHANIEL. Adm. sizar at QUEENS', Jan. 29, 1685-6. Of Lancashire. Matric. 1686; B.A. 1689-90; M.A. 1693. Ord. priest (London) Dec. 24, 1693.

JOHNSON, NICHOLAS. B.A. from MAGDALENE, 1604-5. B. at South Thoresby, Lincs., 1583. M.A. 1612. Incorp. at Oxford, 1612. Ord. deacon (Lincoln) July 15, 1606; priest (Peterb.) May 22, 1608. V. of South Elkington, Lincs., 1608. Will proved (Lincoln) 1649.

JOHNSON, NICHOLAS. Matric. pens. from MAGDALENE, Easter, 1618; B.A. 1621; M.A. 1625. (*Misc. Gen. et Her.*, N.S., II. 122.)

JOHNSTON, NICHOLAS. M.A. from TRINITY, 1750. S. of William. B. in Armagh. Adm. at Trinity College, Dublin, June 10, 1743, age 19; B.A. (Dublin) 1747. (*Al. Dublin.*)

JOHNSON, OLIVER. Adm. pens. at CORPUS CHRISTI, 1670. S. of Oliver, of Gipping, Suffolk. Matric. 1671; B.A. 1673-4; M.A. 1677. Ord. deacon (Norwich) Mar. 1673-4; priest, Dec. 7, 1674. C. at Gipping, Suffolk. R. of Little Wenham, 1674. R. of Capel St Mary, 1683-1726. Father of Benjamin (1697-8).

JOHNSTON, PELHAM. Adm. sizar (age 19) at ST JOHN'S, May 2, 1700. S. of Cudworth (1671), M.D., deceased. B. at York. School, Sedbergh (Mr Wharton). Matric. 1700; M.B. 1711; M.D. 1728 (*Com. Reg.*). F.R.C.P., Sept. 30, 1732. Married Anne, dau. of Maximilian Western, of Abington, Cambs. Died at Westminster, Aug. 10, 1765. Admon. (P.C.C.) 1765. (*Munk*, II. 126; *F.M.G.*, 927; *D.N.B.*)

JOHNSON, PETER. Matric. sizar from CLARE, Easter, 1581; B.A. 1585-6.

JOHNSON, PETER. Matric. Fell.-Com. from CORPUS CHRISTI, Easter, 1646. Of Kent. B. 1629. Migrated to Oxford. Matric. from Magdalen Hall, Oxford, Feb. 6, 1648-9; B.A. (Oxford) 1648-9; M.A. 1651. Adm. at Gray's Inn, Nov. 29, 1648, as s. of Henry, of Nether Court, Isle of Thanet, gent. Took presbyterian orders, Oct. 26, 1654, in the church of St Olave Jewry. V. of St Laurence, Thanet, 1654-62, ejected. R. of Maresfield, Sussex; ejected, 1660. Inherited the manor of Nether Court. Buried in the Church of St Laurence, 1704. (*Al. Oxon.*; *Hasted*, IV. 380; H. G. Harrison.)

JOHNSON, PHILIP. Adm. pens. (age 17) at ST JOHN'S, Nov. 7, 1630. S. of Thomas, R. of Offord Cluny, Hunts. B. in Hertfordshire. School, private. Matric. 1631; B.A. 1634-5; M.A. 1639. Ord. priest (Peterb.) June 9, 1639. Perhaps brother of Andrew (1635).

JOHNSON, R. M.D. 1488-9.

JOHNSON, RALPH. Adm. sizar (age 18) at ST JOHN'S, May 11, 1648. S. of William, husbandman, of Newsham, in Kirkby Ravensworth (or in Kirkby Wiske), Richmondshire. B. there. School, Sedbergh. Ord. deacon and priest (Whitherne) Aug. 8, 1661. V. of Brignall, Yorks., 1662-95. Master of Brignall School. Father of Francis (1684).

JOHNSON, RALPH. Adm. Fell.-Com. at TRINITY HALL, Feb. 25, 1737-8. Matric. 25, 1738; LL.B. 1738. Perhaps ord. deacon (Lincoln) Apr. 8, 1733.

JOHNSON, RICHARD. Matric. sizar from PEMBROKE, Michs. 1550.

JOHNSON, RICHARD. M.A. 1555. Fellow of TRINITY, 1560. One of these names R. of Ashley, Cambs., 1574-91; and V. of Silverley, 1575.

JOHNSON, RICHARD. Matric. sizar from TRINITY, Easter, 1570.

JOHNSON, RICHARD. Matric. sizar from ST JOHN'S, Michs. 1578; B.A. 1582-3. Ord. deacon (Peterb.) Sept. 29; priest, Mar. 25, 1586. One of these names R. of Holy Trinity, Dorchester, 1585. But *see Al. Oxon.* for a contemporary.

JOHNSON, RICHARD. Matric. sizar from JESUS, Michs. 1579.

JOHNSON, RICHARD. Matric. pens. from TRINITY, c. 1591; Scholar, 1591; B.A. 1594-5; M.A. 1598; B.D. 1608. Fellow, 1597. Incorp. at Oxford, 1600. Head Master of Derby School, till 1610. Probably R. of Barrowden, Rutland, 1603. V. of St Werburgh, Derby, 1606-27. Preb. of Southwell, 1616-24. Married, 1604, Katharine, dau. of Richard Smith, B.D., R. of Bulwick, Northants. (H. I. Longden.)

JOHNSON, RICHARD. Matric. pens. from TRINITY, 1598; B.A. 1601-2.

JOHNSON, RICHARD. Matric. sizar from QUEENS', Easter, 1602. Of Norfolk. B.A. 1605-6; M.A. 1609. Ord. deacon (Norwich) Sept. 21, 1607, age 23; C. of East Dereham, Norfolk; priest, Sept. 25, 1608. Probably V. of Ketteringham, 1611. One of these names, M.A., R. of Partney, Lincs., 1632.

JOHNSON, RICHARD. Matric. sizar from ST JOHN'S, Easter, 1603; B.A. 1606-7. One of these names R. of Bracon-Ash, Norfolk, 1649-59.

JOHNSON, RICHARD. Matric. pens. from JESUS, Easter, 1614. Perhaps V. of St Mary, Bishophill, York, 1632-8. (A. Gray.)

JOHNSON, RICHARD. Adm. at KING'S (age 16) a scholar from Eton, Oct. 3, 1621. Of Chorley, Lancs. 2nd s. of William, of Welch Whittle, Lancs. B.A. 1625; M.A. 1629. Fellow, 1624, till his death, Nov. 19, 1650. College bursar. Taxor, 1638-9. Buried in the Chapel. The fellow of Manchester College was an Oxford contemporary. (*Harwood*; *Vis. of Lancs.*, 1663.)

JOHNSON, RICHARD. Adm. sizar (age 18) at ST JOHN'S, Sept. 15, 1675. S. of Robert, of Harborough, Leics. B. there. School, Harborough. Matric. 1675; B.A. 1679-80. 2nd Master at King's School, Canterbury, 1681-4. Head Master, 1684-9. P.C. of Nackington, Kent, 1684-5. Kept a school in Kensington. Head Master of Nottingham, 1707-19. Author of *Grammatical Commentaries* and other works. Drowned himself. Buried at St Nicholas, Nottingham, Oct. 26, 1721. (*Vict. Hist. of Notts.*, II; *D.N.B.*; A. B. Beaven.)

JOHNSTONE, RICHARD VANDEN-BEMPDÉ. Adm. pens. (age 18) at PEMBROKE, July 2, 1750. S. of Lieut.-Col. John Johnstone (died 1741). B. in London, Sept. 21, 1732. Matric. 1750. Served in the 3rd Foot Guards. Succeeded to the Hackness estate in right of his mother, 1762. Created Baronet, July 6, 1795. Died near Scarborough, Yorks., July 14, 1807. (*G.E.C.*)

JOHNSON, ROBERT. B.A. 1466. Ord. sub-deacon (Ely) Apr. 1; deacon, May 27, 1469.

JOHNSON, ROBERT. B.Civ.L. 1521-2. Of ST NICHOLAS HOSTEL. Proctor in the Court of Arches. Registrar of London diocese. Died Nov. 20, 1558. Buried in St Faith's under St Paul's, London. M.I. to him and his wife Alice. (*Cooper*, I. 185.)

JOHNSON, ROBERT. B.Can.L. 1531. Incorp. at Oxford, 1551. Preb. of Rochester, 1541; of Worcester, 1544-58. Chancellor of diocese of Worcester, 1544-58. Preb. of Tamworth, Staffs., 1547-58. Preb. of Hereford, 1551-9. R. of Clun, Salop, 1553. Preb. of York, 1556-8. Master of York School, c. 1557. R. of Bolton Percy, 1558. Preb. of Southwell, 1558-9. Died 1559. (*Cooper*, I. 203; *D.N.B.*; A. B. Beaven.)

JOHNSON, ROBERT. Matric. sizar from CLARE, Lent, 1557-8. S. of Robert (? Maurice), alderman of Stamford, Lincs. B. c. 1540. School, Peterborough. Migrated to Trinity. B.A. 1560-1; M.A. (from Trinity) 1564; B.D. 1571. Fellow of Trinity, 1563. Incorp. at Oxford, 1565. Ord. priest (London) Dec. 23, 1568, age 27. Chaplain to Lord Keeper Nicholas Bacon. Preacher, 1568. Suspended by Archbishop Parker, but conformed. Preb. of Peterborough, 1569-73; of Rochester, 1569-87; of Norwich, 1570-6; and of Windsor, 1572-1625. R. of North Luffenham, Rutland, 1574-1625. Archdeacon of Leicester, 1591-1625. Best known by the foundation of Oakham and Uppingham Schools, and by his College benefactions. Buried at North Luffenham, July 25, 1625, aged 85. Will, P.C.C. Father of Abraham (1591), brother of Geoffrey (1557-8). (*Cooper*, I. 323, erroneous; *D.N.B.*; *Vis. of Rutland*; *Misc. Gen. et Her.*, N.S., I. 450.)

JOHNSON, ROBERT. Matric. pens. from CORPUS CHRISTI, Michs. 1562. One of these names adm. at Lincoln's Inn, Feb. 16, 1566-7. Of Norfolk.

JOHNSON, ROBERT. Adm. at KING'S (age 17) a scholar from Eton, Aug. 23, 1566. Of London. Matric. 1566; B.A. 1570-1; M.A. 1574. Fellow, 1569-76.

JOHNSON, ROBERT. Adm. pens. at EMMANUEL, Apr. 25, 1593. Matric. c. 1596.

JONSON (?), ROBERT. Matric. pens. from ST JOHN'S, c. 1594.

JOHNSON, ROBERT. Adm. at CORPUS CHRISTI, 1594. Tutor to the Berties, sons of Lord Willoughby. Of Scotland. Doubtless M.A. 1597; Incorp. from Edinburgh. One of these names (M.A.), P.C. of Trinity Minories, London, for a short time, in 1619.

JOHNSON, ROBERT. Matric. sizar from ST JOHN'S, Easter, 1614; B.A. 1617-8; M.A. 1621. Ord. deacon (Peterb.) May 23, 1619. One of these names R. of Covenham St Mary, Lincs., 1627-9.

JOHNSON, ROBERT. Matric. sizar from TRINITY, Easter, 1620; B.A. 1622-3; M.A. 1626; B.D. 1656. Ord. deacon (York) June, 1623; priest, June, 1625. R. of Rise, Yorks., 1628-62. R. of Bainton, 1647-60. One of the Westminster Assembly of Divines. V. of Welton, 1660-70. Died 1670. Father of James (1655) and John (1646). (M. H. Peacock.)

JOHNSON, ROBERT. Adm. sizar (age 16) at CAIUS, Apr. 15, 1630. S. of Henry, preb. of Ely Cathedral. B. at Ely. School, Ely (Mr Hitch). Matric. 1631.

JOHNSON, ROBERT. M.A. 1653 (Incorp. from Oxford). B.A. from New College, 1649; M.A. 1652. Scholar and fellow of New College. (*Al. Oxon.*)

JOHNSON, ROBERT. Adm. sizar (age 18) at PETERHOUSE, May 15, 1683. Afterwards pens. Of Durham. School, Durham. Matric. 1683; Scholar, 1683; B.A. 1686–7. Perhaps V. of Leatherhead, Surrey, 1689–1752. Died Apr. 9, 1752. Will, P.C.C.

JOHNSON, ROBERT. Adm. sizar (age 18) at TRINITY, Oct. 9, 1702. S. of John, of Worcester. School, Worcester. Matric. 1702; B.A. 1706–7; M.A. 1710; B.D. 1725. Fellow, 1709. Taxor, 1712–3. Ord. deacon (Lincoln) June 4, 1710; priest, Mar. 17, 1716–7.

JOHNSON, ROGER. Matric. pens. from CHRIST'S, Easter, 1622. S. and h. of Bartholomew, of Anmer, Norfolk, clerk. Adm. at Gray's Inn, Nov. 1, 1623. Probably brother of John (1635). (*Peile*, I. 343.)

JOHNSON, ROOK. Adm. pens. at QUEENS', May 10, 1602. Of Essex. B.A. 1603–4; M.A. 1607.

JOHNSON, ROWLAND. Matric. sizar from ST CATHARINE'S, Easter, 1559. S. of John, gent., of Hertfordshire. School, Hertford. Migrated to Caius, as 'Jhonsey,' Feb. 14, 1562–3, age 18. (*Venn*, I. 50.)

JOHNSON, ROWLAND. Adm. pens. (age 19) at ST JOHN'S, June 18, 1667. S. of Thomas, deceased, of Whittington, Lancs. B. there. School, Sedbergh (Mr Fell). Perhaps ord. deacon (Chester) as literate, Sept. 24, 1671. Parish clerk of Cartmell, Lancs., 1670; schoolmaster, 1671; and C. 1671. Living, 1696. (E. Axon.)

JOHNSON, ROWLAND. Adm. sizar (age 18) at ST JOHN'S, June 19, 1716. S. of Richard, clerk. B. at Dolgelly, Merioneth. School, Ruthin, Denbigh (Mr Lloyd). Matric. 1716. Migrated to Trinity, Nov. 16, 1717. B.A. 1719; M.A. 1729. Ord. deacon (London) Apr. 19, 1720. Doubtless V. of Hemel Hempstead, Herts., 1729–73. Preb. of Lincoln, 1737–73. Died Feb. 4, 1773. Will (P.C.C.) 1773. Father of Abel (1749). One of these names R. of Fetcham, Surrey, 1737–48. (*Scott-Mayor*, III. 305.)

JOHNSON, SAMUEL. Adm. at KING'S, a scholar from Eton, 1583. Of Highgate, Middlesex. B. *c.* 1566. Matric. 1583; B.A. 1587–8; M.A. 1591. Fellow, 1586–90. Incorp. at Oxford, 1593. (*Cooper*, II. 120.)

JOHNSON, SAMUEL. Matric. pens. from EMMANUEL, Easter, 1599. (Perhaps adm. Apr. 17, 1599, as 'Daniel.') B.A. 1602–3; M.A. 1606.

JOHNSON, SAMUEL. Adm. pens. at EMMANUEL, Easter, 1618. Matric. 1618.

JOHNSON, SAMUEL. Adm. pens. at EMMANUEL, June 15, 1620. 2nd s. of Abraham (1591), of South Luffenham. B. at Stamford, Lincs., Jan. 1604–5. B.A. 1623–4; M.A. 1628; D.D. 1641 (*Lit. Reg.*). Incorp. at Oxford, 1628. R. of Ashdown, Essex, 1640–58. Died July 19, 1658. Will, P.C.C. Brother of Ezechiel (1622), Isaac (1614), etc. (J. B. Peace.)

JOHNSON, SAMUEL. Adm. pens. (age 16) at PEMBROKE, Apr. 30, 1621. S. of Susan, of London, widow. Matric. 1621; B.A. 1623–4; M.A. 1627; M.D. 1641.

JOHNSON, SAMUEL. Matric. sizar from QUEENS', Easter, 1652. Of Huntingdonshire. B.A. 1656–7; M.A. 1660. Probably ord. deacon (Norwich) Sept. 1661; priest, Sept. 21, 1662. C. of Cotton, Suffolk. Perhaps brother of Solomon (1652).

JOHNSON, SAMUEL. Matric. sizar from MAGDALENE, Michs. 1658.

JOHNSON, SAMUEL. Adm. sizar at TRINITY, June 6, 1666. School, St Paul's. Matric. 1666–7; B.A. 1669–70. Ord. priest (Gloucester, at Holborn) Feb. 27, 1669–70. R. of Corringham, Essex, 1670–86 and 1689–1702. Chaplain to William, Lord Russell. Degraded, fined, and whipped for seditious writings, 1686. Restored at the Revolution. Died at Kensington, Middlesex, 1702. Admon. (P.C.C.) Jan. 4, 1702–3. (*D.N.B.*; J. Ch. Smith.)

JOHNSON, SAMUEL. Adm. pens. (age 17) at ST JOHN'S, Sept. 29, 1668. S. of John, deceased, of Gateshead, Durham. Bapt. there, Apr. 17, 1651. School, Newcastle (Mr Oxley). Matric. 1668. Adm. at Gray's Inn, Aug. 12, 1670.

JOHNSON, SAMUEL. Adm. sizar at EMMANUEL, July 5, 1686. Afterwards pens. Of Northamptonshire. Matric. 1686; B.A. 1689–90; M.A. 1693. Ord. priest (Peterb.) Sept. 25, 1692. V. of Alconbury, Hunts., 1701–41. Died 1741.

JOHNSTON, SAMUEL. Adm. pens. (age 16) at ST JOHN'S, Apr. 4, 1701. S. of Samuel, M.D. B. at Beverley, Yorks. School, Beverley (Mr Lambert). Matric. 1701; B.A. 1704–5; M.A. 1708; B.D. 1716. Fellow, 1708–18. Ord. deacon (London) Dec. 24, 1710; priest (York) Dec. 1711. V. of St Mary, Beverley, 1716–67. Married Sarah, dau. of Christopher Tadman, Esq. Died Feb. 2, 1767, aged 82. M.I. Father of Samuel (1738) and brother of John (1690). (*Scott-Mayor*, III. 492.)

JOHNSON, SAMUEL. Adm. sizar at EMMANUEL, Mar. 30, 1722. Of Huntingdonshire.

JOHNSON, SAMUEL. Adm. pens. (age 19) at TRINITY, July 1, 1722. S. of Samuel. School, Norwich (Mr Reddington). Matric. 1723. Adm. at the Middle Temple, Jan. 2, 1723–4. Called to the Bar, Jan. 28, 1732. Died Aug. 18, 1766, aged 63. M.I. at St George, Tombland, Norwich.

JOHNSON, SAMUEL. M.A. 1723 (Incorp. from Oxford). S. of Samuel, of Reading, Berks. Probably matric. from Christ Church, Oxford, 1703; B.A. (Oxford) 1706; M.A. 1710. V. of Gt Torrington, Devon, 1713. R. of Little Torrington, 1719–46. Died Mar. 10, 1745–6. (*Al. Oxon.*)

JOHNSON, SAMUEL. Adm. pens. (age 17) at ST JOHN'S, July 3, 1727. S. of Samuel, gent., of Kent. B. at Canterbury. School, Canterbury (Mr Lehunt). Matric. 1727; B.A. 1730–1; M.A. 1738. Adm. extra-licentiate R.C.P., 1738. Practised at Canterbury. Died there June 20, 1763. (*Munk*, II. 139).

JOHNSON, SAMUEL. Adm. sizar (age 16) at PEMBROKE, Feb. 22, 1736–7. S. of William, of Holt, Norfolk. Matric. 1738; LL.B. 1743. Ord. deacon (Norwich) June, 1743; priest, Dec. 1748. R. of Overstrand, Norfolk, 1748–79.

JOHNSTON, SAMUEL. Adm. sizar (age 20) at ST JOHN'S, Apr. 14, 1738. S. of Samuel (1701), clerk, of Yorkshire. B. at Beverley. School, Beverley (Mr Clarke). Matric. 1738; B.A. 1741–2; M.A. 1745; B.D. 1753; D.D. 1776. Fellow, 1744–77. Ord. deacon (*Litt. dim.* from York) Sept. 1742; priest (Lincoln) Sept. 25, 1743. C. of St Mary, Beverley. R. of Winestead, Yorks., 1759–75. R. of Freshwater, Isle of Wight, 1775. J.P. for East Riding, Yorks. Died at Beverley, July 10, 1791, aged '52' according to G. *Mag.* (*Scott-Mayor*, III. 492; G. *Mag.*, 684.)

JOHNSON, SILAS. Matric. pens. from CORPUS CHRISTI, Easter, 1584. Probably 7th s. of Paul, of the Isle of Thanet. Of Canterbury. Perhaps V. of Stonesby, Leics., 1589; 'Shirus Johnson.' Buried at St Mary Bredin, Canterbury, 1633. (*Vis. of Kent*, 1619; *Hasted*, IV. 311.)

JOHNSON, SOLOMON. Matric. sizar from QUEENS', Easter, 1652. Of Huntingdonshire. B.A. 1656–7; M.A. 1660. Perhaps brother of Samuel (1652).

JOHNSON, TALBOT. Matric. pens. from ST JOHN'S, Michs. 1614. B. at Richmond, Yorks. B.A. 1618–9; M.A. 1622. Ord. deacon (London) Mar. 12, 1619–20, age 25. C. of Upminster, Essex.

JOHNSON, THOMAS. *Grace* for B.A. 1457–8.

JOHNSON, THOMAS. B.A. 1530–1. One of these names R. of Weston Colville, Cambs., 1554, and V. of West Wratting, 1567.

JOHNSON, THOMAS. Matric. pens. from CHRIST'S, Nov. 1549. Fellow (M.A.), 1556–8. Perhaps R. of North Barham, Norfolk, 1555–7.

JOHNSON, THOMAS. Matric. sizar from ST JOHN'S, Michs. 1565.

JOHNSON, THOMAS. Matric. pens. from ST JOHN'S, Michs. 1570. S. of Geoffrey, citizen of London. School, St Paul's. Migrated to Caius, Mar. 25, 1573, age 19. B.A. 1573–4. Ord. priest (London) Oct. 6, 1577. Possibly R. of St Andrew Undershaft, Mar.–June, 1597. One of these names V. of Dorney, Bucks., 1583–96; of Thornborough, 1590–8. Perhaps father of Thomas (*c.* 1601). (*Venn*, I. 72.)

JOHNSON, THOMAS. Matric. pens. from TRINITY, Easter, 1587. One of these names, of Norfolk, adm. at Lincoln's Inn, May 23, 1593, from Furnival's Inn.

JOHNSON, THOMAS. Matric. pens. from ST JOHN'S, *c.* 1593. Probably ord. deacon (Peterb.) Sept. 25, 1614; 'of St John's; literate.'

JOHNSON, THOMAS. Matric. sizar from JESUS, *c.* 1597.

JOHNSON, THOMAS. Matric. sizar from ST JOHN'S, *c.* 1601. Perhaps s. of Thomas (1570). B. at Dorney, Bucks. B.A. 1605–6; M.A. 1609. Ord. deacon and priest (London) Mar. 31, 1610, age 24. V. of Carlton-le-Moorland, Lincs., 1610–4. R. of North Scarle, 1612–4.

JOHNSON, THOMAS. M.A. 1604 (Incorp. from Oxford). Of Bedfordshire, gent. Matric. from St Alban Hall, May 3, 1594, age 16; B.A. (Oriel) 1596; M.A. 1601; M.B. and M.D. 1609. Buried at St Mary's, Oxford, Nov. 16, 1621. Will (P.C.C.) 1622. (*Al. Oxon.*)

JOHNSON, THOMAS. Adm. at KING'S (age 16) a scholar from Eton, Aug. 16, 1608. Of London. B.A. 1612–3. Fellow, 1611–4. 'Married and settled in Windsor.' (*Harwood.*)

JOHNSON, THOMAS. Adm. sizar at EMMANUEL, Aug. 1, 1611. Matric. 1611.

JOHNSON, THOMAS. Matric. pens. from CHRIST'S, July, 1613; B.A. from St Catharine's, 1616-7.

JOHNSON, THOMAS. Adm. pens. at EMMANUEL, Dec. 22, 1617.

JOHNSON, THOMAS. Adm. at EMMANUEL, Feb. 8, 1627-8. Matric. 1629. S. of Edmund (? 1583), V. of Lilford, Northants. School, Oundle. Adm. at Sidney, Feb. 10, 1630-1; B.A. 1631-2; M.A. 1635. Master of Oundle School, 1636-46. R. of Tinwell, Rutland, 1646-62. Married, July 20, 1637, at Oundle, Martha Nethercotts. Buried at Tinwell, May 29, 1662. Father of Benjamin (1660). (H. I. Longden.)

JOHNSON, THOMAS. Adm. pens. (age 18) at SIDNEY, Jan. 23, 1635-6. S. of Thomas, clothier. B. at Hull, Yorks. School, Newark (Mr Poynton). B.A. 1639-40.

JOHNSON, THOMAS. Matric. sizar from TRINITY, Easter, 1636; B.A. 1639-40; M.A. 1643. One of these names V. of Hitchin, Herts. (Trinity living), till 1665. Perhaps R. of Little Saxham, Suffolk, 1665-91.

JOHNSON, THOMAS. Adm. pens. (age 19) at ST JOHN'S, June 8, 1649. S. of Edward, yeoman, of Painthorpe, Yorks. B. there. School, Crigglestone, near Wakefield (Mr Dan. Birt). B.A. 1652-3; M.A. 1656.

JOHNSON, THOMAS. Adm. pens. (age 15) at CHRIST'S, June 29, 1650. S. of William, of Northampton, gent. Bapt. at All Saints', Northampton, Oct. 4, 1633. School, Strixton (Mr Farrow). Matric. 1650. Probably adm. at Gray's Inn, Nov. 20, 1652. Barrister-at-law. If so, of Olney, Bucks. Married Anne, dau. of Rev. Ezechiel Johnson, R. of Paulerspury, Northants. Buried at Olney, Aug. 10, 1696. Brother of William (1650). (*Peile*, I. 538; *Misc. Gen. et Her.*, N.S., II. 122.)

JOHNSON, THOMAS. Adm. sizar at TRINITY, Mar. 3, 1650-1. Of London. Matric. 1651; Scholar, 1652; B.A. 1654-5; M.A. 1661.

JOHNSON, THOMAS. Matric. sizar from CORPUS CHRISTI, Easter, 1652. Of Kent. B.A. 1655-6; M.A. 1659. Ord deacon and priest, 1660. V. of Frindsbury, Kent, 1660 Father of John (1677-8). (H. P. Stokes.)

JOHNSON, THOMAS. M.A. 1660 (Incorp. from Oxford). Matric from Hart Hall, Mar. 17, 1653-4; B.A. (Oxford) 1656; M.A. 1658-9. One of these names V. of Debenham, Suffolk, perhaps father of Thomas (1690). (*Al. Oxon.*)

JOHNSON, THOMAS. Adm. pens. at CORPUS CHRISTI, 1668. Of Kent. Matric. 1668; B.A. 1671-2; M.A. 1676. Signed for deacon's orders (London) Dec. 19, 1672; for priest's, Dec. 20, 1673; C. of Cheriton, Kent. V. of Brookland, 1677-1727. R. of St Mary, Canterbury, 1713-27. Minor canon of Canterbury. Married, 1679, Ann Terry, of St Alphage, Canterbury. Died Nov. 6, 1727, aged 78. Buried in Canterbury Cathedral. (H. G. Harrison.)

JOHNSON, THOMAS. Adm. sizar (age 15) at MAGDALENE, June 10, 1669. S. of Thomas, of Wisbech, Ely. School, Wisbech. Matric. 1669; B.A. 1672-3; M.A. 1676. Ord. deacon (Peterb.) Sept. 23, 1677.

JOHNSON, THOMAS. Adm. pens. (age 15) at CAIUS, Mar. 25, 1671. S. of James, merchant, of Yarmouth. B. there. School, Scarning (Mr Burton). Matric. 1671. Probably buried at Yarmouth, 1684. Brother of James (1664). (*Venn*, I. 444.)

JOHNSON, THOMAS RICHARD. Adm. sizar at QUEENS', May 10, 1672. Of Buckinghamshire. Matric. 1672; B.A. 1675-6; M.A. 1681. Ord. deacon (London) Dec. 21, 1679; priest, May 29, 1681.

JOHNSON, THOMAS. Adm. sizar (age 15) at ST JOHN'S, Aug. 4, 1673. S. of Thomas, of London. B. there. Taught by Dr Moore. Matric. 1673; B.A. 1677-8; M.A. 1681. Fellow, 1679-92. Ord. deacon (London) Apr. 18, 1683; priest, Feb. 24, 1683-4.

JOHNSON, THOMAS. Adm. sizar (age 18) at MAGDALENE, June 28, 1679. S. of Thomas, baker. B. at Glentham-in-Lindsey, Lincs. School, Bawtry, Yorks. Matric. 1679; B.A. 1682-3.

JOHNSON, THOMAS. Adm. at KING'S, a scholar from Eton, 1683. B. at Stodham, Oxon. Matric. 1684; B.A. 1688-9; M.A. 1692. Fellow, 1687. Usher at Ipswich School, 1688-91. Afterwards assistant master at Eton. Lived at Brentford. Head Master of Chigwell, 1715-8. Edited Sophocles. (*Harwood*, 269; *D.N.B.*)

JOHNSON, THOMAS. Adm. sizar at EMMANUEL, July 2, 1684. Of Breton, Lincs. Matric. 1685; B.A. 1688-9; M.A. 1692; B.D. 1699. Fellow, 1690-1709. Taxor, 1695. R. of Spofforth, Yorks.

JOHNSON, THOMAS. Adm. sizar (age 15) at TRINITY, June 20, 1690. S. of Thomas, V. of Debenham, Suffolk. Matric. 1691-2; Scholar, 1693; B.A. 1693-4; M.A. 1697. Ord. deacon (Norwich) Dec. 1697; priest, June, 1699. V. of Debenham, 1699. Father of Thomas (1721).

JOHNSON, THOMAS. Adm. sizar (age 17) at CHRIST'S, Feb. 19, 1714-5. S. of Thomas. B. at Burton-upon-Ure, Masham, Yorks. School, Bedale (Mr Marshall). Matric. 1715; Scholar, 1716; B.A. 1718-9. Ord. deacon (York) Sept. 1720; priest, May, 1722. One of these names Master of Heskin School between 1716 and 1726. Perhaps his admon. (Chester) 1745; as of Heskin. (*Peile*, II. 186.)

JOHNSON, THOMAS. Adm. pens. at QUEENS', Mar. 27, 1717. Of Middlesex.

JOHNSON, THOMAS. Adm. sizar (age 18) at MAGDALENE, June 3, 1721. S. of Thomas (1690), clerk. B. at Debenham, Suffolk. School, Monk Soham. Matric. 1721; B.A. 1724-5; M.A. 1728. Fellow, 1725. Taxor, 1732. Ord. deacon (Ely) Dec. 19, 1725; priest, June 11, 1727. Chaplain at Whitehall. One of the four editors of Stephens's *Latin Thesaurus*. Author, miscellaneous. Died July, 1737. (*D.N.B.*)

JOHNSON, THOMAS. Adm. pens. (age 18) at TRINITY, July 10, 1725. S. of Thomas, of London. Bapt. at St James', Westminster, 1706-7. School, Eton. Matric. 1726; Scholar, 1727; B.A. 1729-30; M.A. 1737. Incorp. at Oxford, 1741.

JOHNSON, THOMAS. Adm. sizar (age 17) at ST JOHN'S, June 11, 1748. S. of Thomas (? James), draper, of Kelsale and Bury, Suffolk. B. at Bury. School, Bury (Mr Garnham). Matric. 1748; B.A. 1752; M.A. 1755. Fellow, 1753-64. Ord. deacon (Ely) Dec. 25, 1753; priest (Norwich) Apr. 13, 1755. R. of Wickham Market, Suffolk, 1755-1803. Died July 9, 1803. (*Scott-Mayor*, III. 579; Growse, *Bildeston*, 13.)

JONSON, TIMOTHY. Matric. pens. from ST JOHN'S, Easter, 1566.

JOHNSON, TIMOTHY. Adm. sizar (age 17) at SIDNEY, June 19, 1686. S. of Matthew, gent., of Hull. B. there. School, Hull. Migrated to Clare, July 3, 1686. Matric. 1686; B.A. 1689-90; M.A. 1693. Ord. deacon (York) Sept.; priest, Dec. 1690. Perhaps R. of Bubwith, Yorks.

JOHNSON, WALTER. Adm. pens. (age 15) at PETERHOUSE, June 2, 1677. Of Lincolnshire. S. of Martin (1635-6). School, Spalding (under his father). Matric. 1677; Scholar, 1677; B.A. 1680-1; M.A. 1685. Master of Spalding Grammar School, 1682. Died 1695. (*Genealogist*, I. 107; *T. A. Walker*.)

JOHNSON, WALTER. Adm. sizar at CLARE, Feb. 19, 1686-7. Of Lincoln. B.A. 1690-1. Ord. deacon (Lincoln) Sept. 23, 1694.

JOHNSON, WALTER. Adm. pens. (age 16) at ST JOHN'S, Mar. 30, 1703. Readmitted as Fell.-Com. Nov. 10, 1722. S. of Martin, gent., of Spalding, Lincs. B. at Southwick, Northants. Bapt. there, June 13, 1686. School, Spalding. Matric. 1703; LL.B. 1723. Ord. deacon (Peterb.) Sept. 22, 1723; C. of Tansor, Northants.; priest (Lincoln) Sept. 19, 1725. Head Master of Spalding Grammar School. Chaplain to the Duke of Buccleuch. V. of Leeke, Staffs., 1735-7. R. of Redmarshall, Durham, 1737-60. Buried there Apr. 18, 1760. 1st cousin of Walter (1677). (*Scott-Mayor*, III. 358; *T. A. Walker*.)

JOHNSON, WILLIAM. B.A. 1485-6. One of these names R. of Slaidburn, Yorks., 1507-9.

JOHNSON, WILLIAM. Educated at Cambridge. Of Worcester. Went to Ireland, and became Master of a Grammar School at Kilkenny, in or before 1552. Dean of Kilkenny, 1559. Died there Oct. 7, 1581. (*Cooper*, I. 445.)

JOHNSON, WILLIAM. Adm. at KING'S (age 17) a scholar from Eton, Aug. 22, 1551. Of Leighton Buzzard, Beds. Matric. 1551; B.A. 1555-6. Fellow, 1554-5. Student at Gray's Inn. 'Married an heiress of large estate at Down Hatherley, Glones.' Died Sept. 12, 1614. Buried at Down Hatherley. M.I. there. Brother of Baldwyn (1563). (*Harwood*.)

JOHNSON, WILLIAM. Matric. sizar from ST JOHN'S, Michs. 1555; B.A. 1558-9. Perhaps will proved (V.C.C.) 1559.

JOHNSON, WILLIAM. Matric. pens. from CORPUS CHRISTI, Michs. 1555.

JOHNSON, WILLIAM. Matric. sizar from PEMBROKE, Michs. 1561; Scholar, 1564.

JOHNSON, WILLIAM. Matric. pens. from ST JOHN'S, Michs. 1565; B.A. 1569-70.

JOHNSON, WILLIAM. Matric. sizar from QUEENS', Easter, 1570. Of Cambridgeshire. B.A. 1572-3. Probably ord. deacon (Peterb.) Sept. 19, 1574, on recommendation of the Mayor of Cambridge and his brethren. Perhaps V. of Poslingford, Suffolk, 1601-27. (H. I. Longden.)

JOHNSON, WILLIAM. Matric. sizar from JESUS, Easter, 1585; B.A. 1588-9; M.A. 1592. Incorp. at Oxford, 1594. One of these names V. of Billinghay, Lincs., 1596.

JOHNSON, WILLIAM. Adm. pens. at EMMANUEL, May 20, 1590. Matric. *c.* 1591.

JOHNSON, WILLIAM. Matric. sizar from PEMBROKE, c. 1593. Exhibitioner from Ipswich School. B.A. 1597-8; M.A. 1601. Ord. deacon and priest (Colchester) Mar. 14, 1601-2.

JOHNSON, WILLIAM. Matric. pens. from CORPUS CHRISTI, Easter, 1608. Of Kent. B.A. 1611-2; M.A. 1615.

JOHNSON, WILLIAM. Matric. pens. from TRINITY, Easter, 1612; B.A. 1615.

JOHNSON, WILLIAM. Matric. pens. from QUEENS', Easter, 1627. Of London. S. of William (and Priscilla, dau. of Wm. Leman), of Beccles, Suffolk. B.A. 1630-1; M.A. 1634; D.D. 1661 (*Lit. Reg.*). Ord. priest (Peterb.) Mar. 1, 1639-40. Sub-almoner of Westminster Abbey. R. of Warboys, Hunts., 1647-67. Archdeacon of Huntingdon, 1666-7. Preb. of St Paul's, 1666-7. Died Mar. 4, 1666-7, aged 56. Buried in Westminster Abbey. Will, P.C.C. (*Westminster Abbey Reg.*)

JOHNSON, WILLIAM. Adm. sizar at JESUS, Apr. 24, 1628. Of Yorkshire. Matric. 1629; Scholar, 1629; B.A. 1631-2; M.A. 1635. Probably ord. deacon (Norwich) Sept. 24, 1637; priest, Sept. 20, 1640 (M.A., personal title). R. of Bessingham, Norfolk, 1645. V. of Hinxton, Cambs., 1657. (A. Gray.)

JOHNSON, WILLIAM. Adm. sizar (age 18) at CAIUS, May 10, 1631. S. of Peter, shoemaker, of Cambridge. Bapt. at Holy Trinity, Nov. 13, 1614. School, Perse (Mr Lovering). Matric. 1631; Scholar, 1633-6; B.A. 1634-5; M.A. 1638. Fellow, 1636-44. Ord. deacon (Peterb.) June 4, 1637; priest, May 20, 1638.

JOHNSON, WILLIAM. Adm. Fell.-Com. (age 16) at CAIUS, Apr. 21, 1632. S. and h. of William, of Monk's Frith, Barnet. B. at East Barnet, Herts. Bapt. Jan. 3, 1615-6. Educated at home (Mr Langley). Matric. 1632. Adm. at Lincoln's Inn, Aug. 11, 1634. Living at Barnet, 1644. (*Venn*, I. 305.)

JOHNSON, WILLIAM. Adm. pens. (age 17) at CHRIST'S, June 1, 1649. S. and h. of Alexander, of Rushton Grange, Craven, Yorks. Schools, Bolton and Giggleswick. Matric. 1649. Adm. at Gray's Inn, Dec. 31, 1650. J.P. for Lancs., and West Riding. High Sheriff of Lancs., 1679-80. Married Mary, dau. of Dr Thomas Comber, Master of Trinity. Died 1681. Father of Alexander (1673-4). (*Peile*, I. 526; *Vis. of Lancs.*, 1664; J. Parker.)

JOHNSON, WILLIAM. Adm. pens. (age 14) at CHRIST'S, June 29, 1650. S. of William. B. at Northampton. Bapt. at All Saints', Mar. 29, 1635. School, Strixton (Mr Farrow). Matric. 1650; B.A. 1653-4; M.A. 1657. Fellow of Clare, May 1, 1654-63. Incorp. at Oxford, 1657. Perhaps adm. at the Inner Temple, 1655, as 's. of William, of Olney.' Buried at St Edward's, Cambridge, Feb. 16, 1662-3. Brother of Thomas (1650). (*Peile*, I. 538; H. I. Longden.)

JOHNSON, WILLIAM. Adm. sizar at EMMANUEL, July 2, 1663. Of Yorkshire. Matric. 1663.

JOHNSTON, WILLIAM. Adm. sizar (age 15) at ST JOHN'S, Mar. 30, 1671. S. of John, druggist, of Pontefract, Yorks. B. there, Feb. 5, 1654-5. School, Pontefract. Matric. 1671; B.A. 1674-5; M.A. 1679. Incorp. at Oxford, 1675.

JOHNSON, WILLIAM. Adm. sizar (age 17) at ST JOHN'S, July 1, 1678. S. of Robert, husbandman. B. at Firbank, Kirkby Lonsdale, Westmorland. School, Sedbergh (Mr Wharton). Matric. 1678. Probably ord. deacon (Chester) Sept. 18, 1681. C. of Garsdale-in-Sedbergh, Mar. 23, 1686-7.

JOHNSTONE, WILLIAM. M.D. 1682 (Incorp. from Anjou). Of Warwickshire. Perhaps student at Leyden, Mar. 25, 1678. F.R.C.P., 1685. Censor, 1688. Practised in London and Warwick. Died Nov. 22, 1725, aged 82. Buried at Warwick. (*Munk*, I. 435.)

JOHNSON, WILLIAM. Adm. pens. (age 17) at PETERHOUSE, Apr. 19, 1692. Of Hertfordshire. School, Hertford. Scholar, 1693; Matric. 1696; B.A. 1696-7; M.A. 1715. Ord. deacon (Lincoln) June 4, 1699; priest, Apr. 12, 1702. R. of St Andrew, Hertford, 1707-23. R. of Hertingfordbury, Herts., 1715-23. Died 1723. Father of Isaac (1733).

JOHNSON, WILLIAM. Adm. pens. at CLARE, July 2, 1711. Doubtless s. of William, of Olney, Bucks. Bapt. there, Apr. 13, 1694. Matric. 1711. Buried at Olney, Mar. 9, 1720-1. Brother of Woolsey (1714).

JOHNSON, WILLIAM. Adm. sizar (age 18) at ST JOHN'S, July 25, 1716. S. of Thomas, currier, of Northumberland. B. at Hexham. Bapt. there, Feb. 14, 1699-1700. School, Hexham (Mr Bewick). Matric. 1717. Ord. deacon (Carlisle) Sept. 17, 1721. Probably Master of Hexham Grammar School. Married, at Hexham, Feb. 22, 1720-1, Frances Heron. One of these names buried at Morpeth, Northumberland, Apr. 24, 1742; 'a clergyman, out of the gaol.' (H. M. Wood.)

JOHNSON, WILLIAM. Adm. sizar (age 20) at TRINITY, June 29, 1723. S. of Richard, of Merioneth., clerk. School, Ruthin, Denbigh (Dr Lloyd).

JOHNSON, WILLIAM. M.A. from TRINITY, 1728 (*Com. Reg.*).

JOHNSON, WILLIAM. Adm. sizar (age 18) at MAGDALENE, Mar. 6, 1729-30. S. of James. B. at Ellingham, Norfolk. School, Loddon. Matric. 1731; B.A. 1733-4. Perhaps ord. deacon (Lincoln) May 19; priest, June 9, 1734. V. of Whalley, Lancs., 1738. Retired to Prescot. Died there 1792. (*Vict. Hist. Lancs.*, VI. 358.)

JOHNSON, WILLIAM. Adm. pens. (age 20) at MAGDALENE, Apr. 2, 1730. S. of William. B. at Lincoln. School, Brigg. Matric. 1731; B.A. 1733-4; M.A. 1737. Fellow. Ord. deacon (Lincoln) June 9, 1734, as fellow.

JOHNSON, WILLIAM. Adm. sizar at CLARE, Jan. 9, 1738-9. Afterwards Fell.-Com. S. of Harry, of Milton Bryant, Beds. Bapt. at Olney, Bucks., Nov. 29, 1721. Matric. 1739. Died Dec. 13, 1745. Buried at Olney. (*Misc. Gen. et Her.*, N.S., II. 124.)

JOHNSON, WOOLSEY. Adm. pens. at CLARE, May 19, 1714. S. of William, Esq., and grandson of Thomas Woolsey, D.D. Bapt. at Olney, Bucks., June 19, 1696. Matric. 1715; B.A. 1717-8; M.A. 1721. Ord. deacon (Peterb.) Sept. 25, 1720 (title, his estate at Sharrington, Norfolk). R. of Wilby, Northants., 1729-56. V. of Olney, 1735-53. V. of Wytham-on-the-Hill, Lincs. In 1752 he built the Manor House and enclosed the Park at Wytham. Died there Apr. 21, 1756, aged 59. M.I. at Wytham. Brother of William (1711). (*Misc. Gen. et Her.*, N.S., II. 123; G. *Mag.*)

JOHNSON, ——. B.D. 1492. A friar. Prior of the Carmelites.

JOHNSON, ——. B.A. 1498-9; M.A. 1502-3.

JOHNSON, ——. B.A. 1500-1.

JOHNSON, ——. B.A. 1526-7.

JOHNSON, ——. Matric. sizar from CHRIST'S, 1544.

JOHNSON, ——. Adm. at CORPUS CHRISTI, 1550.

JOHNSON, ——. Adm. at CORPUS CHRISTI, 1575.

JOHNSON, ——. Adm. at CORPUS CHRISTI, 1580.

JOHNSON, ——. Adm. sizar at PETERHOUSE, 1599-1600.

JOHNSON, ——. Adm. sizar at KING'S, Michs. 1602.

JOHNSON, ——. Adm. sizar at PETERHOUSE, Apr. 30, 1615.

JOHNSON, ——. Adm. at TRINITY, 1645.

JOISE, *see* JOYCE.

JOLLAND, GEORGE. Adm. at CORPUS CHRISTI, 1716. Of Norwich. B.A. 1719-20; M.A. 1723. Ord. deacon (Lincoln) Sept. 10, 1721; priest, Sept. 23, 1722.

JOLLAND, GEORGE. Adm. pens. (age 16) at ST JOHN'S, July 7, 1726. S. of George, gent., of Lincolnshire. B. at Glemsford Bridge. Schools, Bury St Edmunds and Colchester. Matric. 1727. Will (P.C.C.) 1780, of one of these names, of Stafford, clerk.

JOLLAND, GEORGE. Adm. pens. (age 18) at ST JOHN'S, Mar. 9, 1748-9. S. of George, gent., of Derbyshire. B. at Wirksworth. School, Manchester (Mr Brooke). Matric. 1748-9; B.A. 1753; M.A. 1756. Fellow, 1754-9. Ord. deacon (Lincoln) Sept. 22, 1754. Perhaps V. of Newton Bishop, Lincs., 1758. Said to have died 1760. (*Scott-Mayor*, III. 585.)

JOLLAND or JELLAND, JOHN. Adm. at CORPUS CHRISTI, 1676. Of London. Matric. 1676; B.A. 1679-80; M.A. 1683. Fellow, 1682-90. Ord. priest (Lincoln) June 3, 1683. Preb. of Salisbury, 1697-1727. R. of Denton, Lincs., 1698. Died 1727. Perhaps father of the next.

JOLLAND, WILLIAM (1686), *see* JALLAND.

JOLLAND or JOLLANDS, WILLIAM. Adm. pens. (age 19) at MAGDALENE, Apr. 24, 1717. (? S. of John, above.) B. at Tillingham, Lincs. School, Brigg. Matric. 1717; B.A. 1720-1. Ord. deacon (Lincoln) Feb. 18, 1721-2. Perhaps V. of 'Geringham,' Lincs. Died Mar. 13, 1732-3. (G. *Mag.*)

JOLLIFFE or JOYLIFFE, GEORGE. M.A. from CLARE, 1650 (Incorp. from Oxford); M.D. 1652. S. of John, of East Stower, Dorset, gent. Matric. from Wadham College, Oxford, Mar. 31, 1637, age 16; B.A. (Pembroke College, Oxford) 1640; M.A. 1643. Lieutenant in the King's forces, under Lord Hopton. His discovery of the lymph ducts was published by Francis Glisson, in 1654. F.R.C.P., 1658. Settled latterly in London. Died Nov. 11, 1658. Buried at St James', Garlickhithe, London. Will, dated Nov. 16, 1658; proved (P.C.C.) 1658. (*Al. Oxon.*; *Munk*, I. 280; *D.N.B.*; *Vis. of Dorset*, 1623.)

JOLIFFE, HENRY. B.A. 1522-3; M.A. 1526; B.D. 1537-8. Fellow of CLARE, and of Michaelhouse. Proctor, 1536-7. R. of Bishop's Hampton, Worcs., 1538. Preb. of Worcester, 1542-59. Probably R. of Houghton, Hunts., 1548-60, deprived. Dean of Bristol, 1554-9. Resisted Bishop Hooper and wrote against Ridley. Deprived under Elizabeth, and retired to Louvain. Author, theological. Admon. Jan. 28, 1573-4. (*Cooper*, I. 320; *D.N.B.*)

JOLLIFFE, JAMES. Adm. sizar at CLARE, June 20, 1646. Matric. 1646; B.A. 1649-50; M.A. 1653. Ord. deacon and priest (Peterb.) Sept. 22, 1661. R. of Irthlingborough All Saints', Northants., 1661-4. R. of Gedling, Notts., 1682-1703. Buried Apr. 21, 1703. (H. I. Longden.)

JOLLIFFE, RICHARD. B.A. 1616 (Incorp. from Oxford). Of Dorset, *pleb.* Matric. from Merton College, Nov. 6, 1607, age 18; B.A. 1616; M.A. 1621.

JOLLIS, ROBERT, *see* JULLYS.

JOLLY, BARTHOLOMEW. B.Can.L. 1483-4.

JOLLEY, EDWARD. Adm. pens. at TRINITY, May 22, 1661. School, Westminster. Matric. 1661; Scholar, 1662. Perhaps of Emberton, Bucks. Died 1695. Admon. (Archd. Bucks.) 1695.

JOLLEY, EDWARD. M.A. 1684 (Incorp. from St Andrews). One of these names V. of Gt Wigston, Leics., 1706-29. Buried there Oct. 16, 1729. Will (Leicester) 1729. (*Nichols*, IV. 383.)

JOLLY, GEORGE. Adm. pens. (age 14) at CAIUS, Sept. 17, 1589. S. of Sigismund, of Ilketshall St Andrew's, Suffolk.

JOLLY, HENRY. Matric. sizar from QUEENS', Easter, 1623. Of London. B.A. 1626; M.A. 1630.

JOLLEY, JAMES. Adm. sizar at TRINITY, Apr. 22, 1645. Of Lancashire. S. of James (of Droyslden, Lancs., clothier), Major in the Parliamentary army. Bapt. at Gorton Chapel, Manchester, June 17, 1627. School, Manchester. Matric. 1645; Scholar, 1646; B.A. 1648-9; M.A. 1652. Fellow, 1649. Living, in 1666 (father's will); probably died before 1692. Brother of Thomas (1645). (*F.M.G.*, 1050; E. Axon.)

JOLLY, JOHN. Adm. pens. (age 15) at ST JOHN'S, Apr. 18, 1646. S. of Philip, counsellor, of Spalding, Lincs. B. there. School, Spalding (Mr Trew). Adm. at Gray's Inn, May 21, 1650.

JOLLY, JOHN. Adm. sizar at QUEENS', Apr. 13, 1709. Of Warwickshire. B. Sept. 17, 1689. School, Merchant Taylors'. Matric. 1709; B.A. 1712-3.

JOLLY, JOHN. Adm. sizar at ST CATHARINE'S, May 30, 1722. Of Derbyshire. Matric. 1722; B.A. 1725-6. Ord. deacon (Lincoln) June 5, 1726.

JOYLIE, THOMAS. Matric. pens. from CHRIST'S, Apr. 1584; Scholar, 1586; B.A. 1587-8; M.A. 1591. Ord. deacon and priest (Peterb.) July 14, 1591. Probably P.C. of Ashford, Middlesex, 1592-3. V. of Gt Wakering, Essex, 1594. R. of Thundersley, 1600-19. Buried there Apr. 17, 1619. (*Peile*, I. 178; H. I. Longden.)

JOLLEY, THOMAS. Adm. sizar at TRINITY, Jan. 28, 1645-6. S. of James, of Manchester. B. at Droylsden. Bapt. at Gorton Chapel, Manchester, Sept. 29, 1629. Matric. 1646. Minister at Altham, Lancs., 1649-62, ejected. Afterwards a preacher in Lancs.; frequently imprisoned. Author of *The Surrey Demoniack*. Died Mar. 14, 1702-3, aged 72. Buried at Altham. Brother of James (1645). His notebook printed by the Chetham Society. (*Calamy*, II. 79; *F.M.G.*, 1050; *D.N.B.*; E. Axon.)

JOLLY, THOMAS. Adm. sizar at QUEENS', Aug. 25, 1679. Of Suffolk. Matric. 1680; B.A. 1683-4. Fellow, Oct. 5, 1686-Apr. 28, 1687.

JOLLY, WILLIAM. Adm. pens. at QUEENS', June 23, 1674. B. at Chute, Wilts. Colleger at Eton, 1670-3. Matric. 1674; B.A. 1677-8.

JOLLY or JELY, ——. M.A. 1501; M.D. 1510-1. Perhaps fellow of KING'S HALL. Buried at St Mary's, 1519.

JOLLYBRAND, THOMAS. Matric. pens. from TRINITY, Lent, 1584-5.

JON, JOSEPH. Adm. sizar (age 16) at ST JOHN'S, May 15, 1711. S. of Thomas, deceased. B. at Eamont Bridge, Westmorland. School, Appleby (Mr Banks).

JONES, ABRAHAM. Matric. Fell.-Com. from PEMBROKE, Michs. 1611. Doubtless s. and h. of Sir Francis, Sheriff of London, and of Welford, Berks. B. *c.* 1595. Of the Middle Temple, and of Welford. Married and had issue. Buried at Welford, Jan. 14, 1628-9. (*Vis. of Berks.*; *N. and Q.*, 9th S., VIII. 309, 316.)

JONES, ALEXANDER. Matric. pens. from ST CATHARINE'S, Michs. 1622.

JONES, ALEXANDER. Adm. sizar at JESUS, Apr. 2, 1653. S. of John, V. of Eccles, Lancs. Bapt. there, Feb. 9, 1633-4. School, Manchester. Matric. 1653; B.A. 1656-7; Scholar, 1657; M.A. 1660. Fellow, 1657-63. Incorp. at Oxford, 1660. V. of Ashby-de-la-Zouch, 1662-71. V. of Piddletown, Dorset, 1671. Died there 1672. Brother of Edmund (1645). (*Al. Oxon.*; Mumford, *Manchester Grammar School*.)

JONES, BENJAMIN. Adm. scholar at TRINITY HALL, Jan. 9, 1694-5. Matric. 1695.

JONES, BERNARD. B.A. from ST JOHN'S, 1593-4; M.A. 1597. Ord. deacon and priest (Peterb.) Dec. 10, 1599. C. of Little Wymondley, Herts., 1607. R. of Hoggeston, Bucks., 1618-*c.* 46. Will dated 1646; to be buried in Hoggeston.

JONES, CADWALLADER. Matric. pens. from MAGDALENE, Lent, 1618-9.

JONES, CADWALADER. Adm. sizar (age 17) at ST JOHN'S, Mar. 17, 1634-5. S. of John Williams, yeoman, of Abererch, Carnarvon. B. there. School, Bangor (Mr Tho. Meridith). Matric. 1634-5; B.A. 1638-9; M.A. 1642. Ord. priest (Peterb.) Sept. 19, 1641. R. of Reresby, Leics., 1660-76. R. of Broughton, 1661-76.

JONES, CADWALADER. Adm. sizar (age 18) at ST JOHN'S, Dec. 1, 1726. S. of John, husbandman, of Carnarvon. B. at Llangyby. School, Pwllheli (Mr Jones). Matric. 1726; B.A. 1730-1. One of these names was R. of Bodfean, Carnarvon, 1747-52. (*Scott-Mayor*, III. 402.)

JONES, CHARLES. Matric. pens. from ST JOHN'S, Easter, 1611. One of these names adm. at Lincoln's Inn, Jan. 1612-3; s. of William, of Beaumaris, Anglesey.

JONES, CHARLES. Matric. pens. from TRINITY, Easter, 1620; B.A. 1624-5; M.A. 1628. Fellow, 1627. V. of Kirkby Lonsdale, Westmorland, 1637-40. One of these names preb. of Chester, Feb.-May, 1635.

JONES, CHARLES. Adm. sizar at TRINITY, June 8, 1664. Matric. 1664; B.A. 1667-8; M.A. 1671.

JONES, CHARLES. Adm. pens. at TRINITY, June 25, 1672.

JONES, DAVID. Matric. sizar from JESUS, Easter, 1615; B.A. 1618-9; M.A. 1624. Ord. priest (York) Sept. 1620. V. of Orston, Notts., 1638. (Godfrey, *Notts.*)

JONES, DAVID. Adm. sizar (age 16) at ST JOHN'S, Jan. 21, 1650-1. S. of Thomas Jones, yeoman, of Llanrwst, Denbigh. B. there. School, Llanrwst (Mr Roger Wyn).

JONES, DAVID. Adm. pens. (age 20) at ST JOHN'S, Aug. 21, 1682. S. of John, gent. B. in Carmarthen. School, Shrewsbury (Mr Tayler). Matric. 1682; B.A. 1686-7. Said to have been refused the M.A. as a non-juror.

JONES, DAVID. Adm. pens. at ST CATHARINE'S, June 30, 1742. Of Llandovery, Carmarthen.

JONES, DEARING. Adm. pens. (age 17) at CHRIST'S, 1737. B. at Ely. Taught by his father. Matric. 1737; Scholar, 1738; B.A. 1740-1; M.A. 1744. Fellow, 1743-53. Ord. deacon (Ely) Sept. 1743; priest, Sept. 23, 1744. V. of Impington, Cambs., 1750. R. of Navenby, Lincs., 1753-1803. V. of St Andrew, Cambridge. Died Nov. 12, 1803. Buried in Navenby Church. (*Peile*, II. 234; *G. Mag.*, 1098.)

JOHNES, ED. Matric. sizar from CHRIST'S, May, 1562.

JONES, EDMUND. Adm. sizar (age 21) at ST JOHN'S, Oct. 17, 1645. 7th s. of John, V. of Eccles, Lancs. B. there. Bapt. Sept. 12, 1624. School, Eccles (Mr Jones). B.A. 1649-50; M.A. from Jesus, 1660. Ord. by the Manchester *Classis*, Jan. 25, 1649-50. Assisted his father at Eccles. V. of Eccles, 1653-62. Licensed as presbyterian teacher in 1672. An active member of the Manchester *Classis*. Died May 2, 1674. Buried at Eccles. Will (Chester) 1674. Brother of Alexander (1653). (A. Gray; *Lancs. and Chesh. Ant. Soc.*, XXXVI.)

JONES, EDWARD. Matric. pens. from QUEENS', Lent, 1577-8. Of Wales. B.A. 1580-1; M.A. 1584; D.D. 1597. R. of Barton, Norfolk, 1585-1603. Preb. of Lincoln, 1586-98. R. of Stretham, Cambs., 1592-98. Probably R. of Hickham, Lincs., 1592-5.

JONES, EDWARD. Matric. pens. from ST JOHN'S, Easter, 1588. 3rd s. of William, of Shrewsbury. Adm. at Lincoln's Inn, Feb. 21, 1588-9. Of Sandford, Salop. Married Mary, dau. of Robert Powell, Esq., of Salop. Father of Thomas (1629) and William (1629).

JONES, EDWARD. Matric. sizar from JESUS, Easter, 1606; B.A. 1609-10; M.A. 1613. Ord. deacon (York) Sept. 1613. One of these names (M.A.), P.C. of Kinver, Staffs., *c.* 1620-30.

JONES, EDWARD. LL.B. from MAGDALENE, 1622. Incorp. at Oxford, 1630. One of these names adm. at Lincoln's Inn, Feb. 23, 1626-7; s. of John, of Penmark, Glamorgan.

JONES, EDWARD. Adm. pens. at TRINITY, May 22, 1661. S. of Richard. B. at Llwyn-rhirid, Fordon, Montgom., July, 1641. School, Westminster. Matric. 1661; Scholar, 1662; B.A. 1664-5; M.A. 1668. Fellow, 1667. Master of Kilkenny School, where he had Swift as a pupil. Signed for deacon and priest (London) May 30, 1667. Chaplain to the Duke of Ormonde. Preb. of Ossory, 1677-83. Dean of Lismore, 1678-83. Bishop of Cloyne, 1683-92. R. of Aber-Hafesp, 1690. Bishop of St Asaph, 1692. R. of Halkin, 1694. R. of Caerwys, 1695. R. of Llansaintffraid, 1696. Suspended for simony and maladministration, 1701-2. Died in Westminster, May 10, 1703. Buried at St Margaret's. Father of Thomas (1693) and Richard (1692-3). (*D.N.B.*)

JONES, EDWARD. Adm. scholar at TRINITY HALL, Oct. 29, 1662. Of Denbigh. Matric. 1662.

JONES, EDWARD. Adm. pens. at EMMANUEL, Jan. 22, 1670–1. Of Salop. S. of Sir Thomas (1629), Chief Justice C.P., of Sandford, Salop. Matric. 1674; B.A. 1674–5; M.A. 1678; D.D. 1720. Fellow, 1677–82. Incorp. at Oxford, 1682. Ord. deacon and priest (London) May 29, 1681. V. of St Mary's, Brithdir, Llanfyllin, 1682–1705. Chaplain to the Lord Keeper. Canon of Windsor, 1684–1728. Chancellor of St Paul's, 1720–33. R. of Hodnet, Salop. Died 1738. Brother of Thomas (1655) and William (1655).

JONES, EDWARD. Adm. sizar at CHRIST'S, May 23, 1682. S. of Benjamin. B. at Hertford. School, Hertford. Matric. 1682; B.A. 1685–6.

JONES, EDWARD. M.A. from KING'S, 1716. S. of Thomas, of Usk, Moum., Esq. Matric. from Oriel College, Oxford, Oct. 22, 1708, age 19; B.A. (Oxford) 1712. Probably ord. priest (Winchester) Jan. 19, 1713–4. V. of Burton Pedwardine, Lincs., 1717. (*Al. Oxon.*)

JONES, EDWARD. M.A. from KING'S, 1719. Matric. from Christ Church, Oxford, 1710. Probably B.A. (Oxford). This, or the last, ord. priest (London) June 29, 1721. (*Al. Oxon.*)

JONES, EDWARD. Adm. sizar (age 17) at ST JOHN'S, May 18, 1724. S. of Randle, attorney, of Wales. School, Wrexham (Mr Appleton). Matric. 1724; B.A. 1727–8. One of these names V. of Huyton, Lancs., 1737–65. Died 1765.

JONES, ELLIS. Adm. sizar at TRINITY, July 2, 1652. Of Flintshire. Matric. 1653.

JONES, FRANCIS. Adm. at CORPUS CHRISTI, 1746. Of Hampshire. S. of Edward, and Catherine. Bapt. at Mottisfont, Nov. 9, 1727. Exhibitioner from Charterhouse. Matric. 1746; B.A. 1749–50; M.A. 1753. Ord. priest (Norwich) Dec. 1752. R. of Cratfield, Suffolk, 1753–8. Will of one of these names (P.C.C.) 1764; of Huntingfield, clerk.

JONES, GAWEN (appears also as GAWEN). B.D. 1531–2. A friar.

JONES or JOHNS, GEOFFREY. B.Civ.L. 1536–7. V. of White Notley, Essex. R. of St Mary Woolchurch, London, 1539–54. R. of St Swithin, 1554. Buried in St Mary Woolchurch, Jan. 23, 1559–60.

JONES, GEOFFREY. Matric. pens. from MAGDALENE, Easter, 1545. R. of Ashley, Cambs., till 1563, and V. of Silverley, 1554–63.

JONES, GEOFFREY. Matric. sizar from QUEENS', Michs. 1572. Of Wales. B.A. 1575–6, as 'Griffin.'

JONES, GEORGE. Matric. pens. from MAGDALENE, Easter, 1625; B.A. 1628–9; M.A. 1632. One of these names (M.A.), R. of Heveningham, Suffolk, 1666. R. of Cockley, 1670.

JONES, GEORGE. B.A. from TRINITY HALL, 1658. Perhaps the 'Grecian' from Christ's Hospital, 1652. Probably V. of Sittingbourne, Kent, 1662–c. 1705. R. of Blackmanstone, 1667. R. of Burmash, 1673–1705. Died 1705.

JONES, GEORGE. Adm. sizar at CAIUS, Mar. 11, 1677–8. S. of John, clothier, of Sudbury, Suffolk. B. there. At school under Mr Fairclough and Mr Chapman. Matric. 1678; Scholar, 1678–82; B.A. 1681–2. Ord. deacon (Norwich) Dec. 1682; priest (London) Sept. 21, 1684. Will proved (P.C.C.) 1702. (*Venn*, I. 458.)

JONES, GEORGE. M.A. from KING'S, 1712. S. of Griff., of Daylsford, Worcs., clerk. Matric. from Trinity College, Oxford, Apr. 8, 1701, age 18; B.A. (Oxford) 1704–5. Ord. deacon (Peterb.) June 3, 1705; priest, Sept. 22, 1711. C. of Helmdon, Northants., 1705. R. of Upper Swell, Gloucs., 1712–8. R. of Helmdon, Northants., 1717–23. Buried there Nov. 6, 1723. (*Al. Oxon.*; *Baker*, I. 631; H. I. Longden.)

JONES, GEORGE LEWIS. Adm. at KING'S, a scholar from Eton, 1741. S. of Theophilus. Bapt. at St Giles', Cripplegate, London, Sept. 12, 1725. Matric. 1742; B.A. 1746–7; M.A. 1750; D.D. 1772. Fellow, 1745. Ord. deacon (Peterb.) Nov. 29; priest, Dec. 20, 1747. R. of Winkfield, Wilts. R. of Limpsfield, Surrey, 1757–75. R. of Tatsfield, 1757–66. V. of Renninghall, Norfolk, 1770. Chaplain to Lord Harcourt, Lord-Lieutenant of Ireland. Bishop of Kilmore, 1774–90. Bishop of Kildare, 1790–1804. Dean of Christ Church, Dublin, 1790–1804. Privy Councillor, Ireland, 1793. Died in London, Mar. 9, 1804.

JONES, GIBBON. Adm. pens. (age 18) at TRINITY, May 19, 1733. S. of Thomas, of London. Bapt. at St Margaret's, Westminster, Aug. 24, 1714. Exhibitioner from Charterhouse. Matric. 1733; Scholar, 1735; B.A. 1736–7. Ord. deacon (Lincoln) Sept. 19, 1736; priest (Norwich, *Litt. dim.* from Canterbury) Aug. 1738. R. of Monewdon, Suffolk, 1738.

JONES, GODFREY. Adm. sizar (age 18) at ST JOHN'S, Apr. 29, 1709. S. of John. B. at Ruthin, Denbigh. School, Ruthin (Mr Williams). Matric. 1709. Ord. priest (London) Dec. 21, 1712, as 'B.A.' R. of Chipping Ongar, Essex, 1720–33. Died 1733.

JONES, GRIFFITH, alias GWIN. Cambridge scholar; age 25 in 1576. Ord. by Bishop Scamler, Mar. 25, 1574. R. of Barton Seagrave, Northants., 1575–1610.

JONES, GRIFFITH. M.A. from MAGDALENE, 1719. S. of Rowland, of Llangany, Merioneth. Matric. from Jesus College, Oxford, Jan. 20, 1702–3, age 19; B.A. (Oxford) 1707–8. Probably schoolmaster of Llanrwst, 1702. R. of Bodvary, 1715. Died at Denbigh, 1726. (*Al. Oxon.*)

JONES, HENRY. Matric. sizar from CHRIST'S, c. 1591.

JONES, HENRY. Adm. Fell.-Com. at QUEENS', Sept. 7, 1596. Of Carmarthen. Probably adm. at Lincoln's Inn, Oct. 28, 1599. Of Co. Carmarthen. Doubtless s. and h. of Sir Henry, of Abermarles, Carmarthen, Knt. If so, Sheriff of Carmarthen, 1638–9. Knighted, Sept. 7, 1642. Created Bart., July 25, 1643. Died c. May, 1644. Probably brother of Thomas (1596). (*G.E.C.*)

JONES, HENRY. Matric. sizar from CLARE, Easter, 1625; B.A. 1628–9; M.A. 1632. Ord. deacon (Peterb.) Feb. 18, 1637–8.

JONES, HENRY. Matric. sizar from ST JOHN'S, Easter, 1628; B.A. 1631–2.

JONES, HENRY. Adm. pens. (age 18) at PETERHOUSE, May 4, 1669. Of Suffolk. School, Gipping. Scholar, 1669; Matric. 1670; B.A. 1672–3; M.A. 1676. Probably R. of Naughton, Suffolk, 1681–1723.

JONES, HENRY. Adm. sizar at QUEENS', July 7, 1681. Of Carmarthen.

JONES, HENRY. Adm. sizar (age 20) at ST JOHN'S, May 26, 1683. S. of Roger. B. at Llandilo Vawr, Carnarvon (? Carmarthen). School, Carnarvon (Mr Maddock). Matric. 1683.

JONES, HENRY. Adm. sizar (age 18) at PETERHOUSE, Oct. 9, 1711. Of Monmouth. School, Usk. Matric. 1712; LL.B. 1718. Ord. deacon (Hereford) Sept. 25, 1715; priest, Nov. 10, 1717. R. of Woolston, Gloucs., 1720–9. V. of Tewkesbury, 1728–9. Died 1729. (F. S. Hockaday.)

JONES, HENRY. Adm. at KING'S, a scholar from Eton, 1712. S. of Charles, clerk. B. at Langton, Dorset. Matric. 1713; B.A. 1716–7; M.A. 1720. Fellow, 1716. F.R.S., 1724. Abridged the *Philosophical Transactions*, 1700–20. Died at Kensington, Jan. 1726–7. Admon. (P.C.C.) granted to his father. (*Harwood*; *D.N.B.*)

JONES, HENRY. Adm. sizar (age 18) at PETERHOUSE, Oct. 4, 1722. Of Suffolk. School, Lavenham. Matric. 1724.

JONES, HOWELL. Adm. sizar (age 20) at ST JOHN'S, Feb. 7, 1683–4. S. of John Morrice, victualler, deceased. B. at Dolgelly, Merioneth. School, Llanbrynmair, Montgomery (private; Mr Thomas). Matric. 1683–4. Buried at All Saints', Cambridge, May 3, 1686, as 'Hugh.'

JONES, HUGH. Matric. sizar from MAGDALENE, Michs. 1551. One of these names R. of Glatton, Hunts., 1558–(?) 63.

JONES, HUGH. Matric. pens. from CHRIST'S, Nov. 1565; B.A. from Corpus Christi, 1566–7. One of these names R. of Elstree, Herts., 1576–89. Died 1589. Another R. of Chalfont St Peter, Bucks., 1587–1604. (*Peile*, I. 93.)

JONES, HUGH. Matric. sizar from JESUS, Easter, 1585; B.A. 1588–9; M.A. 1592. Ord. priest (Lincoln); a preacher. R. of Bolnhurst, Beds., 1596–1641. Father of John (1623).

JONES, HUGH. M.A. from TRINITY HALL, 1740. S. of William, of Llanverres, Denbigh, clerk. Matric. from Jesus College, Oxford, Mar. 21, 1715–6; B.A. (Oxford) 1719. Probably R. of Llanverres, Denbigh, 1725–43. Preb. of St Asaph, 1741–64. V. of Gresford, Flint, 1743. Chaplain to Bishop Maddox, of St Asaph. (*Al. Oxon.*)

JONES, HUMPHREY. Matric. sizar from CHRIST'S, Easter, 1579.

JONES, HUMPHREY. Adm. Fell.-Com. at QUEENS', May 24, 1668. Of Wales. Matric. 1668; M.A. 1669 (*Lit. Reg.*).

JONES, JAMES (JACOB). Matric. sizar from KING'S, Easter, 1606; B.A. 1609–10; M.A. 1613. Incorp. at Oxford, 1615. Probably R. of Clewer, Berks., 1625. (*Al. Oxon.*)

JONES, JAMES. Adm. sizar (age 16) at PEMBROKE, Mar. 29, 1681. S. of Humphrey, of London, draper. Matric. 1681.

JONES, JOHN. Licensed to practise medicine, 1564. Of Wales. Studied at Oxford. No record of any degree. Practised in Notts. and Derbs., also at Bath and Buxton. Patronised by Henry Herbert, Earl of Pembroke, and George Talbot, Earl of Shrewsbury. Author, medical. (*Cooper*, I. 419; *D.N.B.*)

JONES, JOHN. Matric. sizar from CORPUS CHRISTI, Michs. 1567. One of these names R. of Walton, Bucks., 1572–96. Died 1596.

JONES, JOHN. Matric. pens. from PEMBROKE, c. 1593; B.A. 1596–7; M.A. 1600; B.D. 1607. Fellow, 1598.

JONES, JOHN. Matric. sizar from ST JOHN'S, c. 1595; B.A. 1598–9; M.A. 1602. Probably fellow of Pembroke, 1601–5; buried at Little St Mary's, Apr. 26, 1605.

JONES, JOHN. Matric. from CHRIST'S, Easter, 1596. Perhaps B.A. 1603-4; M.A. from Pembroke, 1607.

JOHNES, JOHN. Matric. sizar from QUEENS', Michs. 1608. Of Northamptonshire. B. about 1593. B.A. 1612-3; M.A. 1616. Ord. deacon (Peterb.) Dec. 19, 1613. Probably R. of Abbots Ripton, Hunts., 1619-30, deprived. Arrived at Boston, New England, Oct. 3, 1635. Joined in founding the town of Concord, Mass. Pastor there, 1637-44; and afterwards at Fairfield, Conn. Died there Jan. 1664-5. (J. G. Bartlett.)

JONES, JOHN. Matric. pens. from ST JOHN'S, Michs. 1611; B.A. 1615-6.

JOANES, JOHN. Adm. sizar (age 17) at CAIUS, July 4, 1615. S. of William, printer, of the parish of St Giles, Cripplegate, London. School, Harlington, Middlesex (Mr Durant). B.A. 1618-9; M.A. 1622. Ord. deacon (Peterb.) Sept. 24, 1620; priest, Sept. 23, 1621. One of these names V. of Chapel-at-Hanney, Berks., 1650. (*Venn*, I. 230.)

JONES, JOHN. Adm. sizar at EMMANUEL, Apr. 28, 1623. S. of Hugh (1585). B. at Bolnhurst, Beds. Bapt. there, May 16, 1608. School, Ravensden, Beds. (? Mr Gubet). Matric. 1623. Migrated to Christ's, July 3, 1623. B.A. 1626-7; M.A. 1630. Ord. deacon (Lichfield) Dec. 19, 1629. *Peile* (I. 353) identifies him with the ejected minister of Marple, Lancs., but this seems very doubtful.

JONES, JOHN. Matric. sizar from ST CATHARINE'S, Easter, 1626; B.A. 1628-9.

JONES, JOHN. Adm. at KING'S (age 16) a scholar from Eton, Aug. 23, 1627. Of Barnet, Herts. Matric. 1627; B.A. 1630-1; M.A. 1634. Fellow, 1630-7. Conduct of Eton College. R. of St Mary Magdalene, Milk St, London, 1637-42, sequestered.

JONES, JOHN. Matric. sizar from QUEENS', Easter, 1632. Of Denbigh. B.A. 1635-6; M.A. 1639. One of these names V. of Winslow, Bucks., 1681. Died Oct. 27, 1681.

JONES, JOHN. Adm. pens. at QUEENS', July 1, 1645. Of Devon. Migrated to Oxford. B.A. (New Inn Hall) 1648; M.A. (New College) 1651. Admon. (Exeter) 1698, of one of these names; of Nether Exe, Devon, clerk.

JONES, JOHN. Adm. sizar (age 17) at ST JOHN'S, June 30, 1660. S. of Thomas, yeoman, of Denbigh. B. there. School, Newport (Mr Chaloner). Matric. 1660; B.A. 1663-4; M.A. 1669. Subscribed for deacon's orders (London) June 3, 1664; for priest's orders, May 19, 1665. C. of Barkway, Herts. Perhaps R. of Beachampton, Bucks., 1687-1714. Died 1714.

JONES, JOHN. Adm. sizar at TRINITY, May 12, 1664. B. at Pentraeth, Anglesey, June 2, 1650. Matric. 1664; Scholar, 1668; B.A. 1668-9; M.A. 1672; M.D. 1679 (*Lit. Reg.*); D.D. 1689. R. of Abergarthcelyn and Llanllechyd, Carnarvon. Dean of Bangor, 1689-1727. Preb. of St Asaph, 1696-1727. Died at Bangor, May 6, 1727. (Br. Willis, *St Asaph*; A. B. Beaven.)

JONES, JOHN. Adm. sizar at QUEENS', June 7, 1682. Of Worcestershire. Matric. 1683; B.A. 1685-6. 'Ord. deacon at Worcester by Bishop Thomas; and priest by Bishop Lloyd. C. of Sutton-under-Brails, Gloucs., for 18 years, in 1717.' (*Letter to Bishop of Gloucs.*) (F. S. Hockaday.)

JONES, JOHN DAVIES, *see* DAVIES, JOHN (1684).

JONES, JOHN. Adm. sizar (age 20) at TRINITY, Jan. 18, 1693-4. S. of Charles. B. at Penmorfa, Carnarvon. School, Ruthin, Denbigh (Mr Robert Morgans). Matric. 1693-4.

JONES, JOHN. Matric. sizar from KING'S, Michs. 1704; B.A. 1707-8; M.A. 1712.

JONES, JOHN. Adm. sizar (age 18) at MAGDALENE, Apr. 17, 1704. S. of William. B. at Llanymawddwy, Merioneth. School, Ruthin. Matric. 1704; B.A. 1707-8.

JONES, JOHN. Adm. sizar (age 19) at MAGDALENE, Feb. 3, 1721-2. S. of John. B. at Dolley, Salop (? Dolace, Radnor). School, Knighton, Radnor. Matric. 1722; B.A. 1726-7.

JONES, JOHN. M.A. from SIDNEY, 1727. S. of Matthew, of Brindle, Lancs., *pleb.* Matric. from Brasenose College, Oxford, Apr. 3, 1718, age 18; B.A. (Oxford) 1721. One of these names (M.A.), P.C. of Flixton, Lancs., 1723. Buried there Sept. 8, 1751, aged 52. M.I. (E. Axon.)

JONES, JOHN. M.A. from TRINITY HALL, 1728. B.A. from Jesus College, Oxford. (For alternatives *see Al. Oxon.*)

JONES, JOHN. Matric. Fell.-Com. from MAGDALENE, Lent, 1729; M.B. 1729.

JONES, JOHN. Adm. pens. at TRINITY, June 6, 1735. School, Westminster. Matric. 1735; Scholar, 1736.

JONES, JOHN. Adm. pens. at EMMANUEL, June 1, 1742. Previously matric. from Lincoln College, Oxford, Feb. 7, 1740-1. S. of John, of Oundle, Northants., clerk. Matric. 1744; LL.B. 1748. Ord. deacon (Lincoln) June 9, 1745; priest, May 25, 1746. Perhaps R. of Caterham, Surrey, 1769-75. Died 1775. Will (P.C.C.) Dec. 1775.

JONES, JOHN NOYES. Adm. at CORPUS CHRISTI, 1733. Of Bristol. Matric. 1735; B.A. 1736-7; M.A. 1740. Fellow, 1738-47. Incorp. at Oxford, 1748. Ord. deacon (Winchester) Dec. 18, 1737; priest (Bath and Wells) Sept. 19, 1742. R. of St Peter's, Bristol, 1746-57. Chaplain to Lord Halkerton. R. of Kilve, Somerset, 1751-7. Died Mar. 3, 1757. (F. S. Hockaday.)

JONES, JONATHAN. Adm. sizar (age 17) at TRINITY, May 2, 1721. S. of Robert, of London. School, St Paul's. Matric. 1721.

JONES, JOSHUA. Adm. at KING'S, a scholar from Eton, 1651. B. at Mellis, Somerset (? Wells, Wools, Hants.). B.A. 1654-5; M.A. 1659. Fellow, 1654-67. Ord. deacon (Lincoln) Dec. 23, 1661; priest same day. Chaplain in Norfolk to John Coke, Esq. R. of Huntingfield, Suffolk, 1666. R. of Cockley, 1670-5. Preb. of Norwich, 1670-5. (*Harwood.*)

JONES, LEWIS. Adm. sizar at JESUS, June 29, 1742. Of the Isle of Ely. B. 1725. Matric. 1744; B.A. 1745-6; M.A. 1749. Ord. deacon (Ely) Dec. 6, 1747; priest (Norwich) Dec. 1749. Doubtless V. of Lakenheath, Suffolk, 1750; of Kenninghall, Norfolk, 1770-1807. V. of Witchford, Isle of Ely, 1772. Died in the College at Ely, Jan. 6, 1807, aged 82. (A. Gray.)

JONES, MATTHEW. Adm. sizar at CLARE, Sept. 10, 1686; B.A. 1690-1. Ord. priest (Lincoln) Sept. 24, 1693. C. of Yelden, Beds. Signs as minister of Renhold, Beds., 1696-1711. V. of Willington, 1698-1713. Buried there Mar. 20, 1712-3.

JONES, MAURICE. Adm. Fell.-Com. at EMMANUEL, July 10, 1649. Of Carnarvon.

JONES, MAURICE. Adm. Fell.-Com. (age 16) at MAGDALENE, Aug. 27, 1690. S. of Humphrey, Esq., deceased. B. at Corwen or Dole, Merioneth. School, Ruthin, Denbigh. Matric. 1690. Adm. at Gray's Inn, Sept. 8, 1693.

JONES, MEREDITH. Adm. sizar at MAGDALENE, Oct. 8, 1712. S. of John, carpenter. B. at Llansannan, Denbigh. Matric. 1712. Probably ord. priest (London) Sept. 22, 1717, as 'Marmaduke Jones, of Magdalene College.'

JONES, MORGAN. Adm. sizar (age 18) at ST JOHN'S, Dec. 13, 1710. S. of William, gent. B. at Llanvair, Montgomery. School, Oswestry (Mr Poole). Matric. 1710; B.A. 1714-5.

JONES, NATHANIEL. Adm. sizar at EMMANUEL, Mar. 2, 1597-8. Matric. *c.* 1597.

JONES, NICHOLAS. Matric. pens. from QUEENS', Easter, 1566. One of these names V. of Windrush, Gloucs., 1567-72. R. of Farmington, 1571-9. 'Understandeth Latin well.' Died before Aug. 1579. Will (Gloucester) 1579. (F. S. Hockaday.)

JONES, NIMROD. Adm. sizar (age 18) at TRINITY, June 23, 1724. S. of Richard, of Denbigh. School, Beaumaris, Anglesey (Mr Morgan). Matric. 1723; B.A. 1726-7. Ord. priest (Lincoln) May 20, 1733. R. of Radwell, Herts., 1733. Died Oct. 19, 1749.

JONES, OWEN. Matric. sizar from CHRIST'S, *c.* 1596. B. at Clinocke, Carmarthen (? Clynnog, Carnarvon). B.A. from Trinity, 1599-1600. Ord. deacon (London) Sept. 25 1608; priest (York) May, 1613. R. of Rumpington (? Ruddington, Notts.), 1612.

JONES, OWEN. Adm. sizar (age 16) at ST JOHN'S, June 10, 1676. S. of Thomas, of Bangor. B. there. School, Beaumaris. Matric. 1676; B.A. 1679-80.

JONES, OWEN. Adm. sizar (age 20) at ST JOHN'S, June 19, 1676. S. of John, of Merioneth. B. there. School, Llanasaph or Llanasa. Matric. 1676; B.A. 1679-80. Probably M.A. 1683.

JONES, OWEN. M.A. 1678 (Incorp. from Oxford). S. of Thomas, of Manafon, Montgomery. Matric. from Pembroke, Oxford, Mar. 10, 1644-5, age 17; B.A. (Oxford) 1668; M.A. 1671. (*Al. Oxon.*)

JONES, OWEN. Adm. sizar (age 17) at ST JOHN'S, May 10, 1742. S. of Rowland. B. at Drwsdeugoed, Llanarmon, Carnarvon. School, Pwllheli. Matric. 1742; B.A. 1745-6; M.A. 1763. Ord. deacon (London) Sept. 21, 1746; priest (Canterbury) Nov. 5, 1748. V. of Mountnessing, Essex, 1758-65. R. of West Thorndon, 1764-65. Died Sept. 24, 1765. (*Scott-Mayor*, III. 525.)

JONES, OWEN. M.A. from KING'S, 1746. B.A. from Jesus College, Oxford. (For possible identifications *see Al. Oxon.*)

JONES, PERRY. Matric. sizar from KING'S, Easter, 1718.

JONES, PETER. Matric. sizar from JESUS, Easter, 1562.

JONES or JOHNES, PETER. Adm. pens. (age 16) at PETERHOUSE, Apr. 18, 1639. Of Chester. Matric. 1639; Scholar, 1639; B.A. 1642-3.

JONES, PETER. Adm. sizar (age 19) at PETERHOUSE, Apr. 20, 1748. Of the Isle of Ely. School, Ely. Matric. 1748.

JONES, PHILIP. Adm. sizar (age 19) at CHRIST'S, May 13, 1668. S. of Philip. B. in Southwark. Schools, Southwark (Mr Augur) and Merchant Taylors' (Mr Goad). B.A. 1671-2. Ord. deacon (Ely) June 18; priest, Dec. 24, 1671. Perhaps V. of Downe, Kent, 1672-87. V. of Addington, Surrey, 1680-1706. R. of Farley, 1685. Admon. (Comm. C. Surrey) Nov. 1706; as of St Olave, Southwark. (*Peile*, II. 15; J. Ch. Smith.)

JONES, RALPH. Matric. sizar from QUEENS', Lent, 1563-4; B.A. 1565-6; M.A. 1569; B.D. 1576; D.D. 1581. Fellow, 1566-82. University preacher, 1574. V. of St Paul's, Bedford, 1579. R. of Melford, Suffolk, 1583-90.

JONES, RALPH. B.A. from ST JOHN'S, 1593-4; M.A. 1597.

JONES, RALPH. B.A. from ST JOHN'S, 1607-8. Ord. deacon (Norwich) Sept. 24, 1609, age 23. C. of Shimplingthorne, Suffolk.

JONES, RANDOLPH. Adm. sizar (age 18) at ST JOHN'S, May 12, 1673. S. of Edward. B. at Bangor. School, Bangor. Matric. 1673.

JONES, RICE. Matric. sizar from QUEENS', Michs. 1602; B.A. 1605-6. Will of one of these names (Cons. C. Sarum) 1622; of Luckington, Wilts., clerk.

JONES, RICE. Adm. sizar at CLARE, June 25, 1666. Matric. 1667; B.A. 1669-70; M.A. 1674.

JHONES, RICHARD. Matric. Fell.-Com. from CHRIST'S, Nov. 1544; M.A. 1545. Possibly s. of Richard Jonas, who translated Eucherius' *Book of Midwifery*. (*Peile*, I. 36.)

JONES, RICHARD. Matric. sizar from MAGDALENE, Michs. 1545.

JHONES, RICHARD. Matric. sizar from ST CATHARINE'S, Easter, 1550.

JONES, RICHARD. Matric. sizar from JESUS, Michs. 1566. Of Bala, Merioneth. B.A. from Christ's, 1568-9; M.A. 1572, as 'Robert'; B.D. from Magdalene, 1579; D.D. 1584. Fellow of Magdalene. Ord. deacon (Ely) Dec. 21, 1569, age 22. R. of Mistley, Essex, 1580-5. Died 1585. Admon. (Cons. C. London) Dec. 4, 1585; as of Mistley, D.D. (J. Ch. Smith.)

JONES, RICHARD. Matric. sizar from JESUS, c. 1596; B.A. 1598-9; M.A. 1603.

JONES, RICHARD. Matric. sizar from JESUS, Easter, 1603; B.A. 1605-6; M.A. 1609; B.D. 1619. One of these names (B.D.), V. of Tremeirchion, Flintshire.

JONES, RICHARD. B.A. from JESUS, 1606-7; M.A. 1610. Ord. deacon (Peterb.) Sept. 25; priest, Dec. 28, 1608.

JONES, RICHARD. Matric. sizar from MAGDALENE, Easter, 1631.

JONES, RICHARD. M.A. from KING'S, 1665. Matric. from All Souls, Oxford, Oct. 29, 1657; B.A. (Oxford) 1661. Incorp. as M.A. at Oxford, 1665. One of these names (M.A.), V. of Oswestry, Salop, 1680-90. R. of Darowen, Montgomery, 1684. V. of Llangollen, Denbigh, 1702-6.

JONES, RICHARD. Adm. pens. at QUEENS', May 28, 1667. Of Wales. Matric. 1667. One of these names, s. and h. of Morgan, of Carmarthen, Esq., adm. at Gray's Inn, Nov. 16, 1669.

JONES, RICHARD. Adm. Fell.-Com. (age 14) at TRINITY, June 26, 1683. S. of Sir William. B. in London. M.A. 1685. Probably ord. deacon (London) June 7, 1691.

JONES, RICHARD. Adm. sizar at CLARE, Dec. 18, 1691. Of Bangor, Wales. Matric. 1692; B.A. 1695-6; M.A. 1701. Ord. deacon (London) Feb. 28, 1696-7; priest (Bangor) Dec. 19, 1697. Master of Oundle School, 1698-1761. R. of Glendon, Northants., 1719-61. V. of Weekley, 1722-44. R. of Hemington, 1744-61. Died 1761. Father of Richard (1736). (H. I. Longden.)

JONES, RICHARD. Adm. pens. (age 16) at TRINITY, Mar. 9, 1692-3. S. of Edward (1661), D.D., Bishop of St Asaph. B. at Kilkenny, Ireland. School, Westminster. Matric. 1693. Brother of Thomas (1693).

JONES, RICHARD. Matric. sizar from EMMANUEL, Easter, 1731. S. of Thomas, of Llandewi, Cardigan. Matric. (Jesus College, Oxford) Mar. 28, 1729, age 20. Migrated to Emmanuel, Mar. 8, 1730-1.

JONES, RICHARD. Adm. sizar at JESUS, May 14, 1736. S. of Richard (1691), Master of Oundle School. B. at Kettering, Northants. Matric. 1736; B.A. 1739-40; Scholar, 1740; M.A. 1743. Ord. deacon (Lincoln) Dec. 20, 1741; priest (Peterb.) May 15, 1744. C. of Weekley, Northants., 1744. V., 1745-73. R. of Luddington, 1755-73. Chaplain to Mary, dowager Lady Griffin. Died 1773. Admon. (P.C.C.) 1774. (H. I. Longden.)

JONES, RICHARD. Adm. pens. at TRINITY HALL, Nov. 8, 1748. (Name off, 1751.)

JONES, ROBERT. Scholar of JESUS, 1538-9.

JONES, ROBERT. Matric. sizar from TRINITY, Lent, 1564-5.

JONES, ROBERT. Matric. Fell.-Com. from TRINITY HALL, Easter, 1565.

JONES, ROBERT. Matric. sizar from TRINITY, Easter, 1566.

JONES, 'ROBERT.' M.A. from CHRIST'S, 1572 (doubtless a mistake for Richard, 1566).

JONES, ROBERT. B.A. from MAGDALENE, 1573-4. B. c. 1550. Ord. deacon (Ely) Dec. 21, 1574; priest, Apr. 17, 1575. C. of Toft, Cambs. C. of Cottenham.

JONES, ROBERT. Matric. sizar from JESUS, c. 1595; B.A. 1598-9.

JONES, ROBERT. Adm. pens. at QUEENS', Jan. 21, 1610-1. Of Denbigh. Died in College. Buried at St Botolph, Cambridge, Mar. 10, 1610-1.

JONES, ROBERT. Matric. sizar from TRINITY, Easter, 1617; B.A. 1620-1; M.A. 1626. Ord. deacon and priest (Norwich) Sept. 23, 1627.

JONES, ROBERT. Adm. pens. (age 19) at CHRIST'S, June 5, 1641. S. of Edward. B. at Ysgwennant, Denbigh. School, Shrewsbury (Mr Chaloner). Matric. 1641. One of these names B.A. from Brasenose, Oxford, 1645; M.A. 1648. Yate fellow, 1646.

JONES, ROBERT. LL.B. 1653 (Incorp. from Oxford). Matric. from New College, Nov. 16, 1650; B.C.L. 1650. Fellow of New College, 1649-60, ejected.

JONES, ROBERT. Adm. sizar at EMMANUEL, Apr. 9, 1664. Of Cheshire. Matric. 1664.

JONES, ROBERT. Adm. pens. (age 16) at ST JOHN'S, May 21, 1681. S. of Thomas, attorney-at-law. B. at Wellington, Salop. School, Wellington (Mr Binnell). Matric. 1681. Probably adm. at Gray's Inn, June 17, 1682, as s. and h. of Thomas, of Longden-super-Terne, Salop, gent.

JONES, ROBERT. Adm. sizar (age 19) at ST JOHN'S, June 18, 1707. S. of Randal, husbandman. B. at Ashton-upon-Mersey, Cheshire. School, Manchester (Mr Barrow).

JONES, ROBERT. Adm. sizar (age 16) at PETERHOUSE, May 24, 1711. Of Bedfordshire. School, Roxton, Beds. Matric. 1714; B.A. 1714-5. Ord. deacon (Peterb.) May 26, 1716; priest (Lincoln) June 12, 1720. C. of Twywell, Northants., 1716. One of these names V. of Claxton, Leics., 1725-9; R. of Knipton, 1730-50. Died Nov. 7, 1750. (H. I. Longden.)

JONES, ROBERT. Adm. sizar at QUEENS', May 15, 1739. Of Lincolnshire. Matric. 1739; B.A. 1742-3. Ord. deacon (Lincoln) Sept. 25, 1743; priest, Sept. 25, 1748.

JONES, ROBERT. Adm. sizar (age 16) at ST JOHN'S, June 27, 1750. S. of Thomas, clerk, of Denbigh. B. at Llangniven. School, Ruthin (Mr Hughes). Matric. 1750; B.A. 1754; M.A. 1757. Fellow, 1755-63. Ord. deacon (Lincoln) June 5; priest, Sept. 25, 1757. V. of Henllan, Denbigh, 1759-66. V. of Llangwm, 1760-81. (*Scott-Mayor*, III. 600; Br. Willis, *St Asaph*.)

JONES, ROGER. Adm. pens. (age 19) at ST JOHN'S, June 2, 1635. S. of William, R. of Llangadvan, Montgomery. B. at Drayton, Salop. School, Coventry (Mr White). B.A. 1638-9; M.A. 1642. Fellow, 1641-4, ejected. One of these names presented to Llanerfyl, Montgomery, June 10, 1647. One of these names (M.A.), preb. of Lincoln, 1690-1700.

JONES, ROLAND. Adm. pens. (age 16) at CAIUS, May 11, 1641. S. of William, gent., of Pentraeth, Isle of Anglesey. B. there. School, Beaumaris (Mr Vaughan). Matric. 1641. One of these names V. of Llanrhaiadr, Denbigh, 1651. One, V. of Wendover, Bucks., 1663-5; and V. of Dorney, 1667-85.

JONES, ROWLAND. Adm. pens. (age 16) at SIDNEY, Apr. 17, 1706. 2nd s. of William, gent. B. at Pentraeth. School, Bangor (Mr Rice Morgan). Matric. 1706. Brother of William (1706).

JONES, SAMUEL. B.A. from CORPUS CHRISTI, 1609. Perhaps ord. deacon (Peterb.) June 11, 1609; 'of Trinity College.'

JONES, SAMUEL. Matric. sizar from QUEENS', Easter, 1613. B. at Lewes, Sussex. B.A. 1616-7; M.A. 1620. Ord. deacon (Chichester); priest (London) Dec. 19, 1619, age 23.

JONES, SAMUEL. Matric. sizar from CORPUS CHRISTI, Easter, 1622; B.A. 1625-6; M.A. 1629. Ord. deacon (Peterb.) July 13, 1626; priest (Norwich) Sept. 23, 1627. Perhaps R. of Fordley, Suffolk, 1633-9.

JONES, SAMUEL. Adm. sizar at EMMANUEL, Mar. 23, 1639-40. Of Sussex. Matric. 1640. Died in College. Buried at St Andrew's, Cambridge, Dec. 18, 1640.

JONES, SAMUEL. Matric. sizar from CORPUS CHRISTI, Easter, 1650. Of Norfolk. B.A. 1653-4; M.A. 1657. Probably ord. priest (Bishop of Galloway) Nov. 3, 1660. R. of Halesworth, Suffolk, 1662-90.

JONES, SAMUEL. Adm. pens. at CORPUS CHRISTI, 1694. Of Suffolk. Matric. 1695; B.A. 1697-8; M.A. 1701. Ord. deacon (Norwich) June, 1699; priest, July, 1702. R. of Spixworth, Norfolk, 1706.

JONES, SAMUEL. Adm. sizar (age 17) at St John's, June 25, 1719. S. of Samuel, of Salop. B. at Shrewsbury. School, Shrewsbury (Mr Lloyd). Matric. 1719; B.A. 1722-3. Probably ord. deacon (Hereford) Aug. 9, 1724; priest, Sept. 11, 1726. R. of Frodesley, Salop, 1741-60. V. of St Alkmund's, Shrewsbury, 1758-63. Died Feb. 2, 1763. Will, P.C.C. (*Scott-Mayor*, III. 327.)

JONES, SIMON. Adm. pens. at Christ's, May 7, 1709, from King's. Perhaps migrated to Oxford, as s. of John, of Llangollen, Denbigh, and matric. there, from Jesus College, Mar. 27, 1710, age 19. One of these names R. of Llandegla, Denbigh, 1737. (*Al. Oxon.*)

JONES, STEPHEN. Matric. sizar from St John's, Michs. 1628; B.A. 1632-3; M.A. 1636. One of these names R. of Shenley, Herts. Probably C. of Poddington, Beds., in 1632.

JONES, THOMAS. Matric. sizar from Trinity Hall, Easter, 1544.

JOHNS, THOMAS. Matric. pens. from Christ's, May, 1561.

JONES, THOMAS. Matric. sizar from Christ's, Nov. 1565. S. of Henry, of Middleton, Lancs. B.A. 1569-70; M.A. 1573; D.D. (Dublin) 1614. Chancellor of St Patrick's, 1577-1611; Dean, 1581-4. Bishop of Meath, 1584-1605. Preb. of St Patrick's, 1601-12. Archbishop of Dublin, and Lord Chancellor of Ireland, 1605-19. Died Apr. 10, 1619. Buried in St Patrick's Cathedral. Ancestor of the Viscounts Ranelagh. (*Vis. of Beds.*, 1634; *Peile*, I. 93; *D.N.B.*; A. B. Beaven.)

JOANES, THOMAS. B.A. (? 1595-6); M.A. from Clare, 1599. Ord. priest (Peterb.) Feb. 24, 1599-1600. One of these names, 'M.A.; late usher of the Free School, Middleton, Lancs.; and now Master of the Free School at Dyvelin, Ireland, buried at Middleton, 1610.' (E. Axon.)

JONES, THOMAS. Adm. Fell.-Com. at Queens', Sept. 7, 1596. Of Carmarthen. Matric. 1596. Probably adm. at Lincoln's Inn, Oct. 28, 1599. Of Co. Carmarthen. Probably brother of Henry (1596).

JONES, THOMAS. B.A. (? 1602-3); M.A. from St John's, 1606.

JONES, THOMAS. Matric. sizar from Jesus, Easter, 1606. B. at Meyllteyrn, Carnarvon. B.A. 1609-10; M.A. 1619. Ord. deacon (London) Dec. 22, 1611, age 24; priest, Sept. 23, 1615. One of these names V. of Barnes, Surrey, 1614-34. Died 1634.

JOHNES, THOMAS. Matric. sizar from St John's, Easter, 1614; B.A. 1617-8; M.A. 1621.

JONES, THOMAS. Adm. pens. (age 16) at Caius, Mar. 23, 1618-9. S. of Edmund (? Edward, of 1577-8), of Barton, Norfolk. School, Lynn (Mr Armitage). Matric. 1619; Scholar, 1620-1; B.A. 1622-3; M.A. 1626.

JONES, THOMAS. Adm. pens. at Corpus Christi, 1623. Of London. Matric. Easter, 1624; B.A. 1626-7; M.A. 1630. Ord. deacon (Peterb.) July 11; priest, July 15, 1629.

JONES, THOMAS. Adm. pens. at Sidney, Sept. 1624. B. in London.

JONES, THOMAS. Adm. pens. at Emmanuel, May 9, 1629. 2nd s. of Edward (1588), of Shrewsbury, Esq. School, Shrewsbury. B.A. 1632-3. Adm. at Lincoln's Inn, May 6. 1629. Barrister, 1634. M.P. for Shrewsbury, 1660-76. Justice North Wales, 1662-70. Serjeant-at-law, 1669. Chief Justice, 1670-6. King's serjeant, 1671. Knighted, 1671. Justice K.B., 1676-83. Chief Justice C.P., 1683-6. Committed to custody by the House of Commons, 1689, for judgment against the Serjeant-at-Arms, in 1682. Buried in St Alkmund's Church, Shrewsbury, June 3, 1692. Brother of William (1629), father of Edward (1670-1), Thomas (1655) and William (1655). (*D.N.B.*; A. B. Beaven.)

JONES, THOMAS. Matric. sizar from Trinity, Easter, 1631.

JONES, THOMAS. Adm. at King's, a scholar from Eton, 1640. B. at Windsor, 1623. Matric. 1639; B.A. 1644; M.A. 1648. Fellow, 1643-50.

JONES, THOMAS. Adm. pens. at Emmanuel, June 5, 1655. Of Salop. S. of Thomas (1629). Adm. at Gray's Inn, June 14, 1656, as s. and h. of Thomas, of Dole Cothye, Carmarthen. Barrister-at-law. Adm. at Lincoln's Inn, Nov. 25, 1669. K.C., 1683. Married Jane Wilkinson. Died 1711. Brother of Edward (1670-1) and William (1655).

JONES, THOMAS. Adm. Fell.-Com. at Emmanuel, Mar. 14, 1684-5. Of Denbigh. Probably s. and h. of Thomas (above). Died July 31, 1715, aged 48. Buried at Shrewsbury. M.I. (*Archaeol. Cambrensis*, 4th S., IX. 47; *Powy's Land Club*, XIV. 266.)

JONES, THOMAS. Adm. pens. (age 16) at Trinity, Dec. 2, 1693. S. of Edward (1661), D.D., Bishop of St Asaph. School, Westminster. Matric. 1694; Scholar, 1697; B.A. 1697-8; M.A. 1701. Ord. priest (Lincoln) Sept. 21, 1701. Perhaps B.D. and D.D. from Jesus College, Oxford, 1721. Preb. of St Asaph, 1702-20. V. of Bettws-yn-Rhos, 1702-17. V. of Llanrhiadr-yn-Mochnant, 1702-20. V. of Llanfair-Caereinion, Montgomery, 1705-11. V. of Abergele, 1716-42. Buried there, 1742. Brother of Richard (1692-3). *Al. Oxon.* assigns him to Trinity, Oxford.

JONES, THOMAS. Adm. at King's, a scholar from Eton, 1697. B. at Llangasty, Brecon, 1676. Matric. 1697; B.A. 1701-2; M.A. 1705; B.D. 1713. Fellow, 1700. Ord. deacon (Ely) June 19, 1709; priest, Mar. 5, 1709-10. Chaplain to Fleetwood, Bishop of Ely. R. of Downham, Cambs., 1715-50. Preb. of Ely, 1722-59. Died Dec. 18, 1759. Father of Thomas (1738).

JOHNES, THOMAS. Adm. Fell.-Com. (age 16) at St John's, Mar. 3, 1701-2. S. of Thomas, gent. B. at Llanginning, near Carmarthen.

JONES, THOMAS. M.A. from Peterhouse, 1736; B.A. from Jesus College, Oxford. (For possible identifications *see Al. Oxon.*)

JONES, THOMAS. Adm. at Corpus Christi, 1737. Of Cardiganshire.

JONES, THOMAS. Adm. sizar at Clare, Nov. 15, 1738. S. of Thomas (1697), preb. of Ely. Matric. 1738; B.A. 1742-3; M.A. 1746. Fellow, 1746-51. Ord. deacon (Norwich) Sept. 1745; priest, Dec. 1746. R. of Downham, Cambs., 1750. R. of Conington, 1762. Chaplain to the Archbishop of Canterbury. Lecturer at St Magnus Martyr, and St Margaret, New Fish St, London. Went to South Carolina, 1787. R. of St George, Winyaw. Declined an Irish bishopric, offered him by his College contemporary the Marquis of Townshend. Died at Winyaw, Oct. 10, 1788. Admon. (P.C.C.) 1790. (Dalcho, *S. Carolina*; E. A. Jones.)

JOHNES, THOMAS. Matric. Fell.-Com. from Corpus Christi, Easter, 1738. Perhaps Thomas of 1737.

JONES, THOMAS. Matric. sizar from King's, Lent, 1745-6; B.A. 1750-1; M.A. 1754. Chaplain of St Saviour's, Southwark, 1753-62. Died June 6, 1762, aged 33. M.I. at Southwark. Will, P.C.C. (*Manning and Bray*, III. 576.)

JONES, WALTER. Matric. sizar from Trinity, Michs. 1572; Scholar, 1575; B.A. 1576-7; M.A. 1580. Fellow, 1579. One of these names V. of Easington, Yorks., 1583-96. Another, V. of Benenden, Kent, 1586-1606, deprived, 'M.A.'

JONES, WALTER. Adm. sizar at Queens', Apr. 14, 1669. Of Huntingdonshire. Matric. 1669.

JONES, WALTER. D.D. 1728 (*Com. Reg.*). S. of Richard, of 'Thatcham,' Berks., gent. Matric. from Christ Church, Oxford, July 3, 1708, age 15; B.A. (Oxford) 1712; M.A. 1715. Ord. deacon (Worcester) Sept. 19, 1714; priest (Oxford) Aug. 5, 1716. R. of Halford, Warws., 1716. R. of Upton-on-Severn, Worcs., 1717-39. V. of Powick, 1717-29. Chaplain to George I and II, 1724-39. R. of Woolston, Gloucs., 1729-39. Died 1739. Admon. (P.C.C.) 1739, of one of these names; of Overbury, Worcs., clerk. (*Al. Oxon.*; F. S. Hockaday; J. Ch. Smith.)

JONES, WATTS. Adm. pens. at Emmanuel, Apr. 22, 1611. Matric. 1611; Scholar; B.A. 1614-5. Ord. deacon (York) Dec. 1619.

JONES, WILLIAM. Matric. sizar from King's, Easter, 1545. Conduct of King's. One of these names R. of Hayes, Middlesex, 1565-1602.

JONES, WILLIAM. Matric. pens. from Jesus, Easter, 1573; B.A. from Magdalene, 1576-7; M.A. 1580. Ord. deacon (Ely) Dec. 21, 1578, age 23; priest, July 5, 1579. V. of Frostenden, Suffolk, 1596.

JONES, WILLIAM. Matric. sizar from Jesus, Easter, 1575; B.A. 1579-80; M.A. 1583. One of these names R. of Cranfield, Beds., 1587 and 1603.

JONES, WILLIAM. Matric. sizar from Trinity, Easter, 1576. B. 1561. B.A. from Clare, 1579-80; M.A. 1583; B.D. from Emmanuel, 1590; D.D. 1597. One of the original fellows of Emmanuel, 1584. Ord. deacon and priest (Lincoln) Sept. 23, 1585. R. of East Bergholt, Suffolk, 1591-1636. Author of biblical commentaries. Died Dec. 12, 1636. Buried at East Bergholt. M.I. Will (Norwich) 1637. Father of William (1615). (*D.N.B.*)

JOHNS, WILLIAM. Matric. pens. from St John's, *c.* 1591; B.A. 1594-5; M.A. 1598.

JONES, WILLIAM. Adm. at King's (age 17) a scholar from Eton, Aug. 25, 1599. Of Chacombe, Northants. B.A. 1603-4; M.A. 1607; B.D. 1613. Fellow, 1602-16. Ord. priest (Lincoln) May 31, 1607. Chaplain to the Countess of Southampton. 'Afterwards a lecturer in the Isle of Wight, and beneficed there.' Author, religious. (*Harwood*; *D.N.B.*)

JONES, WILLIAM. Matric. pens. from Peterhouse, Easter, 1602; Scholar, 1604-9; B.A. 1605-6; M.A. 1609. Ord. priest (Norwich) Sept. 24, 1609, age 24.

JONES, WILLIAM. Matric. pens. from St John's, Michs. 1602; B.A. from Jesus, 1605-6; M.A. 1609. Ord. deacon (Peterb.) May 26, 1611; priest, Apr. 8, 1616.

JOANES, WILLIAM. Adm. pe . (age 16) at CAIUS, Oct. 12, 1615. S. of William, D.Dns(1576), of Bergholt, Suffolk. School, Bergholt (Mr Owles). Matric. 1615; Scholar, 1615-21; B.A. 1618-9; M.A. 1622. Ord. priest (Llandaff) 1624. R. of Bergholt and Brantham, 1636-44, sequestered. V. of Ashen, Suffolk; and of Bardfield, Essex. 'Hath three cures; hath been absent from Ashen 6 or 7 years; and hath employed malignant curates.' Will (P.C.C.) 1661. (*Venn*, I. 231.)

JONES, WILLIAM. Matric. sizar from ST JOHN'S, Michs. 1621; B.A. 1625-6; M.A. 1629. Ord. deacon (Norwich) Sept. 23, 1627; priest (Peterb.) Mar. 3, 1627-8.

JONES, WILLIAM. Adm. pens. at EMMANUEL, May 9, 1629. Of Salop. S. and h. of Edward (1588), of Shrewsbury, Esq. Adm. at Lincoln's Inn, Apr. 6, 1629. Of Sandford Hall, Esq. Married Mary, dau. of Sir Richard Greaves, Knt., of Moseley, Worcs. Brother of Thomas (1629). (Burke, *L.G.*)

JONES, WILLIAM. M.A. 1639 (Incorp. from Oxford). B.A. (Balliol College) 1631. M.A. 1634.

JONES, WILLIAM. Adm. pens. at EMMANUEL, June 5, 1655; Fell.-Com. 1657. Of Salop. S. and h. of Thomas (1629). Adm. at Lincoln's Inn, May 26, 1655. Of Sandford, Salop, and of Carreghova, Denb., Esq. Married Grace, dau. of Sir Peter Pyndar, of Chester. Brother of Edward (1670-1) and Thomas (1655). (Le Neve, *Knights*, 269.)

JONES, WILLIAM (1670), *see* JOYNES.

JONES, WILLIAM. Adm. sizar (age 18) at MAGDALENE, Aug. 25, 1671. S. of Aaron, of Wantage, Berks. School, Wantage. Migrated to Oxford. Matric. from New Inn Hall, Mar. 22, 1671-2. One of these names P.C. of Mortlake, Surrey, 1681-1720. Died Aug. 5, 1720.

JONES, WILLIAM. Adm. sizar at ST CATHARINE'S, Feb. 11, 1691-2. Of London. Matric. 1692; B.A. 1695-6. Ord. deacon (London) Mar. 8, 1695-6; priest, May, 1696. One of these names Minister of Chesham Bois, Bucks., 1704-40. Will (Archd. Bucks.) 1741. Another of St Alban, Wood St, London, clerk. Admon. (P.C.C.) 1705. (J. Ch. Smith.)

JONES, WILLIAM. Adm. sizar (age 18) at TRINITY, Mar. 26, 1702. S. of Thomas, of Beaumaris, Anglesey. School, Beaumaris (Mr Wynne). Matric. 1702; B.A. 1705-6.

JONES, WILLIAM. Adm. pens. (age 17) at SIDNEY, Apr. 17, 1706. 1st s. of William, gent. B. at Pentraeth. School, Bangor (Mr Rice Morgan). Matric. 1706.

JONES, WILLIAM. M.A. from KING'S, 1718. Probably s. of Philip, of St Peter's, Cardigan. Matric. from Jesus College, Oxford, July 3, 1708, age 18; B.A. (Oxford) 1712. (*Al. Oxon.*)

JONES, WILLIAM. Adm. pens. (age 17) at ST JOHN'S, Oct. 28, 1725. S. of Samuel, gent., of Cheshire. B. at Frodsham. School, Tarvin (Mr Thomason). Matric. 1725. Migrated to Oxford. Matric. (Wadham) June 3, 1727, age 18; B.A. (Oxford) 1729; M.A. 1732. (*Al. Oxon.*)

JONES, WILLIAM. Matric. Fell.-Com. from KING'S, Easter, 1726; M.B. 1726; M.D. 1731.

JONES, ZACHARY. B.A. from CHRIST'S, 1577-8. Of Devon, gent. Matric. from Christ Church, Oxford, *c.* 1574. Adm. at Lincoln's Inn, Feb. 17, 1579-80. Barrister at Lincoln's Inn, 1596. (*Al. Oxon.*)

JHONES, ——. Matric. pens. from ST JOHN'S, *c.* 1594.

JOPE, WILLIAM. M.A. from MAGDALENE, 1731. S. of Joseph, of St Stephen's, Cornwall, gent. Matric. from Exeter College, Oxford, May 6, 1717, age 17; B.A. (Oxford) 1720-1. One of these names, of Tamerton Foliot, Devon, clerk. Admon. (P.C.C.) 1774. (*Al. Oxon.*)

JOPS or JOPES, JOHN. Matric. sizar from ST JOHN'S, Michs. 1565; Scholar of Trinity, 1567. One of these names ord. priest (Lincoln) 1571. Schoolmaster at Moulton, Lincs., 1581. R. of North Thoresby, Lincs., 1590-1.

JOPSON, THOMAS (1568), *see* JOBSON.

JOPSON, THOMAS. Adm. Fell.-Com. at TRINITY, June 19, 1646. Of Yorkshire. S. and h. of Thomas, of Cudworth, Yorks., Esq. Adm. at Gray's Inn, Mar. 1, 1646-7. (*Vis. of Yorks.*)

JORDAN, ABRAHAM. Adm. pens. (age 17) at TRINITY, June 26, 1679. S. of Abraham. B. in London. School, Westminster. Matric. 1680; Scholar, 1680; B.A. 1682-3; M.A. 1686. Fellow, 1685. V. of Bottisham, Cambs., 1696.

JORDEN, BENJAMIN. Adm. sizar (age 17) at SIDNEY, June 16, 1671. 4th s. of Richard, yeoman, deceased. B. at Dawly, Salop. School, Ariston (private). Matric. 1672.

JOURDAYNE, CYPRIAN. Matric. sizar from TRINITY, Lent, 1564-5.

JORDEN, EDWARD. Adm. Fell.-Com. at PETERHOUSE, Jan. 23, 1579-80. S. of Edward, of Cranbrook, Kent. B.A. 1582-3, as 'Forden'; M.A. 1586; M.D. (Padua) *c.* 1591. L.R.C.P., 1595. F.R.C.P., 1597. Practised as physician at Bath. Author, medical. Died at Bath, Jan. 7, 1632-3, aged 63. Buried in the Abbey Church. (*Munk*, I. 113; *T. A. Walker*; *Genealogist*, N.S., VI. 93; *D.N.B.*, which makes him probably of Hart Hall, Oxford; born, *c.* 1569.)

JORDEN, EDWARD. Adm. pens. at EMMANUEL, Nov. 16, 1607. S. of Richard, of Cranbrook, Kent. Bapt. there, Nov. 21, 1591. Matric. 1607. Probably B.A. from Jesus, 1617-8. His father's will (1595) directed that he should go to Cambridge. (*Misc. Gen. et Her.*, N.S., IV. 227.)

JORDAN, FRANCIS. Adm. pens. (age 17) at CAIUS, June 15, 1660. S. of Edmund, jurisconsultus. B. at Parham, Suffolk. School, Brooke, near Norwich (Mr Clerke). Matric. 1660; B.A. 1663. Of Parham, Suffolk, gent. Buried there May 20, 1712. (*Venn*, I. 409.)

JORDAN, GEORGE. M.A. from JESUS, 1717. S. of Thomas, of Charlewood, Surrey, gent. Matric. from Pembroke College, Oxford, Mar. 16, 1705-6, age 20; B.A. (Oxford) 1709. V. of Heathfield, Sussex, 1713-31. V. of Burwash, 1717-55. Preb. of Chichester, 1723-45. Chancellor of diocese of Chichester, 1725-50. R. of Ivychurch, Kent, 1731-54. Died Oct. 26, 1754. Will, P.C.C. (*Al. Oxon.*; A. B. Beaven.)

JORDAN, GEORGE. Adm. pens. at JESUS, May 13, 1718. Previously matric. from Trinity College, Oxford, Apr. 7, 1715, age 17. S. of William, of Buckland, Surrey. Matric. 1718-9; B.A. 1719. Probably ord. priest (Norwich) Dec. 1721. C. of Newdigate, Surrey.

JORDAN, HEARTOAKE. Adm. pens. (age 17) at MAGDALENE, Oct. 12, 1683. 2nd s. of Sir Joseph, Knt., and Vice-Admiral (for whom *see* *D.N.B.*). B. at Woodside House, Hatfield. School, Hertford. Matric. 1688; LL.B. 1689. Fellow, 1689.

JURDEN, HENRY. Matric. sizar from KING'S, Easter, 1626. One of these names B.A. from Magdalen College, Oxford, 1633. Probably V. of Sunbury, Middlesex, 1648-62. V. of Walberton, Sussex, 1652-62, ejected. (*Al. Oxon.*)

JORDAN, HUMPHREY. B.A. 1530-1. Of CHRIST'S. Perhaps will (P.C.C.) 1558; 'of Grimston, Norfolk, gent.'

JORDAN, JAMES. Adm. pens. (age 17) at CHRIST'S, Apr. 2, 1628. S. and h. of John, gent., of Charlwood, Surrey. B. at Worth, Sussex. School, Charlwood (Mr Mulcaster). Matric. 1628. Resided four terms. Adm. at the Middle Temple, Oct. 24, 1629. (*Peile*, I. 390; *Vis. of Surrey*, 1623.)

JOURDEN, JOHN. Matric. pens. from ST JOHN'S, Easter, 1565.

JORDAN, JOHN (BELGA). M.A. 1624. Signs amongst the incorporations.

JORDAN, JOHN. Adm. pens. at EMMANUEL, Mar. 23, 1645-6. B. in St Petrock's, Exeter. B.A. 1649. V. of Stoke Canon, Devon, 1655-62, ejected. Died aged 80.

JORDAN, JOHN. Adm. sizar at EMMANUEL, Apr. 28, 1704. Of Suffolk. Matric. 1704.

JORDAN, JOHN. Adm. sizar at ST CATHARINE'S, May 28, 1705. S. of Thomas, of Aldridge, Staffs., Esq. Matric. 1706; B.A. 1708-9; M.A. 1713. Fellow, 1713. Taxor, 1717-8. V. of Inglesham, Wilts., *c.* 1735-63. Died Aug. 28, 1763, aged 76. Buried at Inglesham. M.I. Will, P.C.C. (*Shaw*, II. 100.)

JORDEN, MARIOTT. Adm. sizar (age 19) at TRINITY, Oct. 17, 1716. S. of William, of Kettering, Northants. School, Kettering (Mr Jones). Matric. 1716; Scholar, 1720; B.A. 1720-1; M.A. 1724. College Chaplain, 1724-5. Ord. deacon (Peterb.) Sept. 25, 1720; priest (Lincoln) Sept. 23, 1722. C. of Loddington, Northants., 1720.

JORDAYN, RICHARD. B.Can.L. 1502-3.

JORDAN, RICHARD. Matric. Fell.-Com. from JESUS, Michs. 1617.

JORDAN, ROBERT. Matric. pens. from CORPUS CHRISTI, Michs. 1635. Of Chichester. B.A. 1638; M.A. 1642.

JORDAN, ROGER. Adm. at KING'S, a scholar from Eton, 1450; M.A. 1459. Perhaps B.Can.L. 1465-6. Fellow. Ord. (Ely) Apr. 5, 1466. V. of Wootton Wawen, Warws. (*Harwood.*)

JORDAN, SAMUEL. Adm. sizar (age 18) at ST JOHN'S, Mar. 8, 1631-2. S. of Robert, deceased, of Oakham, Rutland. B. there. School, Oakham (Mr Stackhouse). B.A. 1635-6.

JORDAN, SAMUEL. Adm. sizar at ST CATHARINE'S, July 3, 1728. Of Kent.

JORDAN, THOMAS MARSHALL. Adm. sizar at ST CATHARINE'S, May 27, 1733. Of Maidstone, Kent. Matric. 1734; B.A. 1737-8; M.A. 1759. R. of Barming, Kent, 1758-86. R. of Iden, Sussex. Died Feb. 26, 1786, aged 72. Admon. (P.C.C.) 1792. (*G. Mag.*)

JOURDAYNE, W. Matric. pens. from CLARE, Michs. 1567.

JURDEN, WILLIAM. Matric. sizar from KING'S, Easter, 1611; B.A. 1617-8; M.A. 1621. Ord. priest (Peterb.) Mar. 12, 1619-20. V. of St Paul's, Canterbury, until 1637, and 1661-80. R. of Orgarswick, Kent, till 1680. Died 1680. Probably buried in Canterbury Cathedral, Aug. 21, 1680; minor canon of Canterbury.

JORDAN, WILLIAM. Adm. sizar at QUEENS', July 5, 1670. Of Kent. Matric. 1670; B.A. 1673-4.

JORDAYN, ——. B.A. 1500.

JORDAN, ——. B.A. 1524-5; M.A. 1527.

JORDEN, ——. Matric. Fell.-Com. from CLARE, Easter, 1611.

JORTIN, JOHN. Adm. pens. at JESUS, May 16, 1715. S. of Renatus Jordain, a Huguenot refugee (for whom *see D.N.B.*). B. in St Giles-in-the-Fields, London, 1693. School, Charterhouse. Matric. 1715; Scholar; B.A. 1718-9; M.A. 1722; D.D. (Lambeth) 1755. Fellow, 1721-8. Taxor, 1723-4. Boyle lecturer, 1749. Ord. deacon (Peterb.) Sept. 22, 1723; priest (Ely) June 14, 1724. V. of Swavesey, Cambs., 1727-31. Reader at New Street Chapel, Bloomsbury, 1731. R. of Eastwell, Kent, *c.* 1737-42. R. of St Dunstan-in-the-East, 1751. V. of Kensington, 1762-70. Preb. of St Paul's, 1762-70. Archdeacon of London, 1764-70. Author, theological. Died Sept. 5, 1770. Buried in Kensington. Will, P.C.C. (*D.N.B.*)

JOCELYN, EDWARD. Adm. pens. at QUEENS', May 30, 1676. 3rd s. of Sir Robert (1640), Bart., of Hyde Hall, Hertford. School, Felsted. Matric. 1677; B.A. 1679-80; M.A. 1683; B.D. 1690 (*Com. Reg.*). Fellow, 1681-95. Adm. at the Middle Temple, May 16, 1678. R. of High Roothing, Essex, 1694. Died Sept. 9, 1732. Brother of Strange (1670) and Robert (1669).

JOSSELIN, FRANCIS. Matric. pens. from JESUS, *c.* 1592. 2nd s. of Henry, of Essex. Adm. at the Middle Temple, June 28, 1595. Brother of Henry (*c.* 1592). (*Vis. of Essex, 1612.*)

JOSLYN, GEOFFREY. Matric. pens. from JESUS, Easter, 1571; B.A. 1574-5; M.A. 1578. Ord. deacon (Peterb.) July 7, 1581; priest, July 5, 1582. R. of Shellow Bowels, Essex, 1581-5. V. of Good Easter, until 1635.

JOSSELIN, HENRY. Matric. pens. from JESUS, *c.* 1592. S. of Henry, of Essex. B.A. 1595-6; M.A. 1599. Fellow, 1597-1606. Brother of Francis (*c.* 1592). (A. Gray; *Vis. of Essex, 1612.*)

JOSSELYN, HENRY. Adm. at CORPUS CHRISTI, 1623. Of Kent. S. of Sir Thomas, of Torrells Hall, Essex, and Theodora, dau. of Edmund Cooke, of Bexley, Kent, widow of Clement Bere, of Dartford. B. 1606. In 1634 he went to Portsmouth, New Hampshire, as agent to the patentee. Thence to Black Point, Maine, where he was a large landowner. Chief Justice of Maine, 1668. Justice at Pemaquid, till his death in 1683. Married *c.* 1644, Margaret, widow of Capt. Thomas Cammock. (J. G. Bartlett; *D.N.B.*)

JOCELIN, HEZEKIAH. Adm. pens. (age 17) at CAIUS, Mar. 30, 1630. S. of Hezekiah, gent. B. at Farnham, Essex. School, Newport (Mr Leigh). Scholar, 1630-7; Matric. 1631; B.A. 1633-4; M.A. 1637. Schoolmaster at Harlow, Essex, in 1640. R. of Copford, Essex, 1662-71. Will (P.C.C.) 1671. (*Venn*, I. 293.)

JOSCELYN, JOHN. Matric. pens. from QUEENS', Michs. 1545. 3rd s. of Sir Thomas, of Hyde Hall, Herts., K.B. B. in Essex, 1529. B.A. 1548-9; M.A. 1552. Fellow, 1549-7. Preb. of Hereford, 1560-77. R. of Hollingbourne, Kent, 1577. Latin secretary to Archbishop Parker. Founded a Hebrew lectureship at Queens'. Anglo-Saxon scholar. Author of *Historiola Collegii Corporis Christi*, etc. Died Dec. 28, 1603. Buried at High Roding, Essex. M.I. Will (Comm. C. Essex) 1604. (*Cooper*, II. 366; *D.N.B.*; *Masters*, 97.)

JOSLINGE, JOHN. Adm. pens. at EMMANUEL, 1588-9. Probably s. of Richard, of Sawbridgeworth, Herts. Bapt. there, Aug. 18, 1573. Matric. 1589. Adm. at Gray's Inn, Oct. 11, 1591. Married Elizabeth, dau. of William Wiseman, Esq., of Mayland, Essex. Buried at Sawbridgeworth, Dec. 11, 1613. Probably father of the next. (*Clutterbuck*, III. 204.)

JOCELYN, JOHN. Adm. pens. at EMMANUEL, Apr. 18, 1616. Probably s. of John (above). Bapt. at Sawbridgeworth, Herts., Oct. 15, 1600. Matric. 1616. Adm. at Gray's Inn, as 's. and h. of John, late of the Inn,' Nov. 15, 1619.

JOSLIN, NATHANIEL. Matric. pens. from MAGDALENE, Easter, 1622; B.A. 1625-6; M.A. 1629. Ord. deacon (Peterb.) July 4; priest, July 5, 1628. R. of Wram lingham, Norfolk, 1638-60. R. of Hardingham, 1656; ejected 1662.

JOSELYN, NATHANIEL. Adm. pens. at EMMANUEL, June 16, 1663. Of Essex. Probably s. of John, of Feering, Essex; age 18 in 1664. Matric. 1663. Adm. at Gray's Inn, Nov. 14, 1662. (*Vis. of Essex*, 1664.)

JOSSELIN, RALPH. Adm. pens. at JESUS, Mar. 5, 1632-3. S. of John, of Roxwell, and Bishop's Stortford, Herts. B. Jan. 26, 1616-7. School, Bishop's Stortford. Matric. 1633; B.A. 1636-7; M.A. 1640. Usher at Deane, Northants., and Cranham, Essex. Ord. deacon (Peterb.) Dec. 22, 1639; priest, Mar. 1, 1639-40. V. of Earls Colne, Essex, 1640-83; and for a short time Master of the school there. Chaplain in the Parliamentary army. Died 1683. His *Diary* was published by the Camden Society, 1908. (A. Gray.)

JOSSELYN, ROBERT. Matric. Fell.-Com. from ST JOHN'S, Easter, 1616. Doubtless s. of Richard, of Sawbridgeworth, Herts. Knighted, May 18, 1621. Of Hyde Hall, Herts., Knt. Sheriff of Herts., 1645-6. Married Bridget, dau. of Sir William Smith, of Hill Hall, Essex. Buried at Sawbridgeworth, May 3, 1664, aged 64. Father of the next. (*Vis. of Herts.*, 1634; *Clutterbuck*, III. 204; *G.E.C.*)

JOCELYN, ROBERT. Adm. Fell.-Com. at QUEENS', June 2, 1640. Of Hertfordshire. Doubtless s. of Sir Robert (above), of Hyde Hall, Knt. Bapt. at Sawbridgeworth, Jan. 14, 1622-3. Created Baronet, June 8, 1665. Sheriff of Herts., 1677. Married Jane, dau. of Robert Strange, of Somerford, Wilts. Buried at Sawbridgeworth, June 12, 1712. Father of the next, of Strange (1670) and Edward (1676). (*Vis. of Herts.*, 1634; *G.E.C.*)

JOCELIN, ROBERT. Adm. Fell.-Com. at QUEENS', Apr. 29, 1669. Of Hertfordshire. S. of Robert (above). Bapt. at Sawbridgeworth, May 6, 1652. Buried Apr. 19, 1675. Brother of Strange (1670) and Edward (1676).

JOSELIN, SIMON. Matric. pens. from QUEENS', Easter, 1629. Of Essex. B.A. 1632-3. Probably s. of Ralph, of Roxwell; and executor of his will (P.C.C.) 1632. Buried at St Benet's, Cambridge, Sept. 12, 1634.

JOCELYN, STRANGE. Adm. pens. at QUEENS', Apr. 29, 1670. Of Hertfordshire. S. of Sir Robert (1640). B. 1651. Matric. 1670; B.A. 1673-4. Succeeded his father as 2nd Baronet, 1712. Married Mary, dau. of Tristram Conyers, of Walthamstow, Essex. Died at Hyde Hall, Sept. 3, 1734. Buried at Sawbridgeworth. (*Clutterbuck*, III. 205; *G.E.C.*)

JOSCELYN, THOMAS. Matric. pens. from QUEENS', Michs. 1545.

JOSTLING, THOMAS. Matric. pens. from QUEENS', Easter, 1604. Of Essex. B.A. 1607-8.

JOSCELIN, THOMAS. Adm. pens. at EMMANUEL, Apr. 13, 1619. Probably s. of John (1588-9). Bapt. Oct. 10, 1602. Matric. 1619; B.A. 1622-3; M.A. 1626. Ord. deacon (Peterb.) Aug. 4; priest, Aug. 5, 1626. One of these names V. of Mayland, Essex, *c.* 1628-39. Doubtless brother of John (1616). (*Vis. of Herts.*, 1634.)

JOCELYN, THOMAS. Adm. pens. (age 18) at ST JOHN'S, June 2, 1647. S. of Thomas, of Chelmsford, grocer. School, Chelmsford. Matric. 1647; B.A. 1650-1.

JOCELYN, THOMAS. Matric. pens. from QUEENS', Michs. 1647. Of Hertfordshire. Probably 4th s. of Sir Robert (1616), of Hyde Hall. Bapt. at Sawbridgeworth, Oct. 26, 1630. B.A. 1650-1. Buried Sept. 14, 1652. Brother of Robert (1640).

JOSELIN, TORRELL. Matric. Fell.-Com. from JESUS, Easter, 1606. S. and h. of Sir Thomas, Knt., of Willingale, Essex, and Anne, dau. of Humphrey Torrell. Adm. at Lincoln's Inn, Apr. 28, 1608. Signed at Cambridge, as one of the Eastern Counties Association. Of Holywell, Hunts., 1633. Buried at Oakington, Cambs., 1656. (*Vis. of Essex*, 1558; A. Gray.)

JOSSELYN or JASLEN, ——. Adm. Fell.-Com. at PETERHOUSE, Jan. 19, 1583-4. Probably Richard, s. and h. of Richard, of Hyde Hall. Of Hyde Hall, Esq. Father of Sir Robert (1616). (*T. A. Walker.*)

JOSSE, JOHN. Matric. sizar from TRINITY, Michs. 1575; B.A. 1579-80. Probably the John Joyce, 'late of Clare; born at Maidstone, aged 26' who was ord. deacon (London) Dec. 21, 1579; priest same day.

JOSS, THOMAS. Adm. pens. at JESUS, Oct. 15, 1649. Of Lincolnshire.

JOVIAN (? JOINAN), JOHN. Matric. sizar from ST JOHN'S, Easter, 1585.

JOWER, JOHN. Adm. pens. (age 18) at ST JOHN'S, Sept. 28, 1654. S. of Luke, turner, of St Clement's, Ipswich. B. in Suffolk. School, Ipswich. Matric. 1654, as 'Gower.' Adm. at Gray's Inn, May 6, 1656.

JOWLE, JOHN. Adm. pens. at SIDNEY, May 22, 1615; B.A. 1618-9.

JOYE, CHARLES. Adm. pens. at EMMANUEL, Mar. 31, 1735. Of Middlesex. Matric. 1735.

JOYE, EDWARD. Matric. pens. from ST JOHN'S, Easter, 1604; B.A. 1607-8; M.A. 1611. Incorp. at Oxford, 1609 and 1611.

JOYE, GEE or JAYE, GEORGE. Also called CLARKE. B.A. 1513-4. Of Bedfordshire. M.A. 1517; B.D. 1524-5. Fellow of PETERHOUSE, 1517-28. An early reformer. Denounced for heresy, in 1527, he fled to Strasburg, Antwerp and elsewhere, where he published various translations of the Scriptures. Died 1553. Father of the next. (For list of his works *see Cooper*, II. 114; *D.N.B.*)

JOY, GEORGE. B.A. from ST JOHN'S, 1563-4. S. of George (above). M.A. 1567; B.D. 1575. Fellow, 1565. Of Canterbury. Ord. deacon (Ely) Dec. 21, 1569, age 26. R. of St Peter's, Sandwich, Kent, 1570-7. V. of Higham, 1573-5. V. of St Clement's, Sandwich, 1574-1600. P.C. of St Mary, Dover, 1574. R. of Elmstone, 1580-1600. Died 1600. Buried at Elmstone. (*D.N.B.*; H. G. Harrison.)

JOYE, PETER. Adm. pens. at EMMANUEL, July 4, 1735. Of Middlesex. Matric. 1735.

JOY, ROBERT. Matric. pens. from ST JOHN'S, Michs. 1564. Of Kent. B.A. 1567-8; M.A. 1571. Fellow, 1568. V. of Hartlip, Kent, 1578-95. P.C. of St Mary, Dover, in 1582. V. of Sittingbourne, 1587-93. V. of Rainham, 1593-5.

JOYE, WILLIAM. Matric. sizar from TRINITY, Easter, 1607; B.A. 1610-1; M.A. 1614. Ord. deacon (Peterb.) Mar. 5; priest, Mar. 6, 1614-5. V. of Warden, Northumberland, 1616-28. Perhaps V. of Merstham, Surrey, 1645.

JOYCE, MARTIN. Adm. pens. at TRINITY, June 27, 1670. School, Westminster. Matric. 1671; Scholar, 1671.

JOISE, JOHN. Matric. Fell.-Com. from CLARE, Michs. 1581.

JOICE, RICHARD. Resident pens. at CORPUS CHRISTI, in Aug. 1564.

JOYNER, ANDREW. Matric. pens. from CHRIST'S, Michs. 1554.

JOYNER, DANIEL. Adm. sizar at EMMANUEL, Easter, 1624; B.A. 1627-8; M.A. 1631. R. of Chipping Ongar, Essex, 1635. R. of Stapleford Tawney, 1643-5. Died 1645. Will (P.C.C.) 1646. Father of the next. (H. Smith.)

JOYNER, DANIEL. Adm. pens. (age 18) at PEMBROKE, Mar. 20, 1654-5. S. of Daniel (above), R. of High Ongar, Essex. Bapt. there, Jan. 19, 1636-7. Ord. priest (Galloway). R. of Hawkwell, Essex, 1662-95. Died May 19, 1695, 'aged 54.' M.I. at High Ongar.

JOYNER, EDMUND. Matric. sizar from ST JOHN'S, Michs. 1559.

JOYNER, FRANCIS. Matric. pens. from TRINITY, Easter, 1579.

JOYNER, ISAAC. Matric. pens. from CHRIST'S, Mar. 1577-8; B.A. from Peterhouse, 1581-2; M.A. 1585. R. of Norton Mandeville, Essex, 1598. V. of White Notley, 1598. Will, 1638, mentions sons Daniel (? 1624) and Isaac (next).

JOYNER, ISAAC. Adm. pens. at EMMANUEL, Mar. 1607-8. S. of Isaac (above), of Inworth, Essex. Matric. 1608; Scholar; B.A. 1611-2; M.A. 1616. Ord. deacon (London) Dec. 18, 1614, age 24; C. of Fifield; priest, Sept. 23, 1615. V. of Clare, Suffolk, 1617-23. R. of Springfield Boswell, Essex, 1629.

JOYNER, ISAAC. Adm. sizar at QUEENS', July 3, 1650. Of Essex. B.A. 1654; M.A. 1658. Probably usher at Felsted School, 1658. R. of South Fambridge, Essex, 1661-6. Died 1666.

JOYNER, RALPH. Matric. pens. from CORPUS CHRISTI, Michs. 1579; B.A. 1582-3.

JOYNER, RICHARD. M.D. 1580. Of Corpus Christi, Oxford, 1559; B.A. (Oxford) 1564; M.A. 1568. Fellow, 1564.

JOYNER, VALENTINE. Adm. pens. at TRINITY, July 1, 1674. S. of Christopher, of London, gent. Migrated to Oxford. Matric. from Magdalen Hall, July 14, 1676, age 18; B.A. (Oxford) 1677-8. Adm. at the Inner Temple, 1677. Buried in the Temple Church, Mar. 2, 1681-2. (*Al. Oxon.*)

JOYNER, WILLIAM. Adm. sizar (age 17) at CAIUS, Nov. 17, 1674. S. of Robert, druggist, of Hingham, Norfolk. B. there. Schools, Wymondham (Mr Morphew) and Scarning (Mr Burton). Matric. 1674-5; Scholar, 1675-81; M.B. 1682. (*Venn*, I. 451.)

JOYNES, HENRY. Matric. sizar from EMMANUEL, Easter, 1625.

JOYNES, JOHN. Adm. pens. (age 17) at CHRIST'S, Apr. 9, 1630. S. of John. B. at Ingleby, Derbs. School, Repton (Mr Whitehead). Matric. 1631; B.A. 1633-4; M.A. 1637. Probably R. of St Peter-at-Arches, Lincoln, 1661. Preb. of Lincoln, 1664-72. R. of Hickham, 1667. An excellent preacher. Died 1672. (*Peile*, I. 404.)

JOYNES, WILLIAM. Adm. sizar at EMMANUEL, Apr. 23, 1670. Of Leicestershire. Matric. 1670, as Jones; B.A. 1673-4. C. of Haslemere, and Godalming, Surrey. Died Aug. 28, 1700; accidentally drowned. M.I. at Haslemere. (*Manning and Bray*, I. 660.)

JOZUE or JOSUA, RICHARD. Matric. pens. from TRINITY, June, 1572; B.A. from Christ's, 1576-7.

JUBBE, FRANCIS. Matric. sizar from ST JOHN'S, Easter, 1584.

JUBB, GEORGE. Adm. pens. at JESUS, Oct. 17, 1702. Of Yorkshire. B. 1684. Matric. 1703; Scholar, 1704; B.A. 1706-7; M.A. 1717. Ord. deacon (Ely) Feb. 29, 1707-8; priest (York) June 9, 1709. V. of Lissington, Lincs., 1709. Perhaps R. of St Mary Stoke, Ipswich, 1749-51.

JUBBES, MARTIN. Adm. pens. (age 16) at CAIUS, Jul 1678 S. of John, gent., of Wymondham, Norfolk. B. there Bapt Jan. 25, 1663-4. School, Wymondham (Mr Clarke). Matric 1679; Scholar, 1679-82. Adm. at Lincoln's Inn, Dec. 2, 1681, as s. and h. of John, of Carlton Road. Barrister-at-law Succeeded his father as lord of the manor at Wicklewood Died June 9, 1732. (*Venn*, I. 460; G. *Mag.*)

JUBBS, RALPH. Adm. sizar (age 17) at CAIUS, Apr. 26, 1720 S. of John, weaver, of Wymondham. B. there. School, Wymondham (Mr Sayer). Scholar, 1720-5; Matric. 1721; B.A. 1723-4. (*Venn*, II. 14.)

JUBES, WILLIAM. Adm. pens. (age 17) at ST JOHN'S, July 6, 1695. S. of William, gent. B. at Wymondham, Norfolk. School, Wymondham (Mr Clarke). Matric. 1696. Migrated to Emmanuel, Apr. 16, 1698.

JUBY, THOMAS. Matric. sizar from CORPUS CHRISTI, Easter, 1588. Of Norfolk. B.A. 1594-5; M.A. 1598. Ord. deacon and priest (Peterb.) Mar. 18, 1596-7. R. of Theydon Mount, Essex, 1602. Licensed (Bishop of London, May 3, 1603) to marry Bridget, dau. of John Deane, of Woodstone, Hunts. Buried at Theydon Mount, Nov. 21, 1637. Will (Cons. C. London) 1638. (H. Smith.)

JUCE, RICHARD. Matric. sizar from ST JOHN'S, *c.* 1594.

JUCE, THOMAS. Matric. pens. from CHRIST'S, July, 1608. One of these names R. of King's Langley, Herts., 1635; died 1670. (*Peile*, I. 268.)

JUCKES, GEORGE. Adm. pens. at QUEENS', Apr. 22, 1650. Of Salop.

JUCKES, THOMAS. Matric. Fell.-Com. from KING'S, Michs. 1612; B.A. 1615. One of these names, 's. and h. of George, of Buttington, Montgomery, Esq.' adm. at Lincoln's Inn, Nov. 21, 1616.

JUDD, DEANE. Adm. sizar at JESUS, May 3, 1732. Of Leicestershire. Matric. 1735; B.A. 1735-6; Scholar, 1736. Ord. deacon (Lincoln) Sept. 19, 1736; priest, May 28, 1738. R. of Gilmorton, Leics., 1738-84. Died Apr. 25, 1784, aged 73. M.I. at Gilmorton. (A. Gray.)

JUDD or JUDE, EDWARD. Adm. pens. at EMMANUEL, Apr. 27, 1596. B. at Bumpstead, Essex, 1580. Matric. 1596; B.A. from St John's, 1599-1600. Ord. deacon (Lincoln) Feb. 23, 1604-5. R. of South Somercotes, Lincs., 1605. V. of Nasing, Essex, 1608-40. R. of Hunsdon, Herts., till 1644. Died 1644. Father of John (1629-30).

JUD, HERBERT. Adm. sizar (age 15) at PEMBROKE, May 10, 1633. Of Wymondham, Norfolk. Matric. 1633, as 'Jurd.'

JUDD, JOHN. Matric. sizar from CLARE, Michs. 1572. One of these names V. of Gt Doddington, Northants., 1588-9. Died 1589. (H. I. Longden.)

JUDE, JOHN. Matric. sizar from ST JOHN'S, *c.* 1595; B.A. 1598-9; M.A. 1603.

JUDE, JOHN. Adm. pens. (age 16) at ST JOHN'S, Mar. 8, 1629-30. S. of Edward (1596), R. of Hunsdon, Herts. B. in Essex. School, (private; Mr Gooderick). Matric. 1631; B.A. 1633-4; M.A. 1637. Fellow, 1635. Junior proctor, 1643-4. Died 1644.

JUDD, NICHOLAS. Adm. pens. at PETERHOUSE, June 27, 1627. Of Lincolnshire. Matric. 1627; Scholar, 1627; B.A. 1630-1; M.A. 1639. Ord. priest (Norwich) Mar. 9, 1638-9. V. of Holy Trinity, Bungay, Suffolk, 1638-40.

JUDD, ROBERT. Adm. pens. (age 18) at PEMBROKE, Feb. 21, 1705-6. S. of Robert, gent. B. at Brandon, Suffolk. Matric. 1705-6.

JUDD, THEOPHILUS. Adm. sizar (age 18) at ST JOHN'S, Mar. 23, 1680-1. S. of William, husbandman. B. at Burton Overy, Leics. School, Kibworth Beauchamp (Mr Dand). Matric. 1681; B.A. 1684-5; M.A. 1692. R. of Milton Bryant, Beds., 1702-10. Buried there Nov. 4, 1710.

JUDD, W. Matric. sizar from JESUS, Easter, 1570.

JUDKIN, EDWARD. Adm. pens. (age 17) at PEMBROKE, July 4, 1694. S. of Edward, of Draycot, gent. B. in Derbyshire. Matric. 1695; M.B. 1699. Student at Leyden, Nov. 16, 1700.

JUDKIN, THOMAS. Adm. sizar at EMMANUEL, Easter, 1612. Matric. 1612; B.A. 1615-6; M.A. 1619. Ord. deacon (Peterb.) Sept. 21; priest, Sept. 22, 1617. Signs as V. of Stagsden, Beds., 1626-41.

JUDKIN, ——. Adm. sizar at TRINITY, Apr. 24, 1645.

JUDSON, RICHARD. Matric. sizar from TRINITY, Michs. 1566; Scholar, 1568; B.A. 1570-1. M.A. (Oxford) 1574. R. of St John, Watling St, London, 1580-6. Perhaps R. of Green's Norton, Northants., 1581-4. R. of St Peter-le-Poer, London, 1583-1615. R. of St Peter Cheap, 1585-1615. Died Aug. 1615.

JUDSON, RICHARD. Adm. sizar at CLARE, July 5, 1634. Matric. 1635; B.A. 1639-40. Ord. deacon (Lincoln) May 28; priest, May 29, 1643. Perhaps V. of Middleton-in-Pickering, Yorks., 1653-61.

JUGGE, JUDGE or GUGGE, RICHARD. Adm. at KING'S, a scholar from Eton, 1531. B. in Cambridgeshire (s. of Richard, of Waterbeach, according to W. K. Clay), *c.* 1514. Afterwards a printer in London. Quecu's printer, 1560. One of the original members of the Stationers' Company, of which he was repeatedly master and warden. Buried at St Faith under St Paul's, Aug. 18, 1577; 'Richard Ingge, prynter to the Queen's Majesty.' Benefactor to King's College. (*Cooper*, I. 383; *D.N.B.*; J. Ch. Smith.)

JUGG, THOMAS. M.A. 1612-3 (on visit of Prince of Wales).

JUKES, *see* JEWKES.

JULIAN, HENRY. Matric. sizar from QUEENS', Michs. 1623. Of Norfolk. B.A. 1627-8; M.A. 1634. Ord. deacon (Peterb.) May 5; priest, May 6, 1629. R. of Rollesby, Norfolk, 1663.

JULIAN, JOHN. Ord. priest (Peterb.) Nov. 10, 1575; 'late of ST JOHN'S College.' S. of John, of Swafield, Lincs. V. of Elsham, Lincs., 1583, as B.A. (*Lincs. Pedigrees*, 553.)

JULIAN, WILLIAM. Adm. pens. at ST CATHARINE'S, July 4, 1682. Adm. at Gray's Inn, Nov. 26, 1683, as s. and h. of James, late of Melton Mowbray, Leics., gent.

JULIAN, WILLIAM. Adm. pens. at CLARE, Apr. 9, 1717. B. at Market Overton, Ruts. One of these names Councellor-at-law to the Church of Market Overton. Buried there 1736. (*Rutland Mag.*, IV. 100.)

JULLYS or JOLLIS, ROBERT. B.D. 1505-6; D.D. 1509-10. Prior of the Dominican friars in Cambridge. Afterwards at Norwich, where he was a witness against the martyr Bilney, in 1531. (*Cooper*, I. 46.)

JUNCATIUS, JOHN. M.A. June 1632 (Incorp. from Bourges).

JURIN, JAMES. Adm. sizar (age 17) at TRINITY, June 30, 1702. S. of John, of London, citizen and dyer. Bapt. Dec. 15, 1684. 'Grecian' from Christ's Hospital. Matric. 1702; Scholar, 1703; B.A. 1705-6; M.A. 1709; M.D. 1716. Fellow, 1708. Adm. student at Leyden, Nov. 2, 1709. Master of the Grammar School, Newcastle, 1709-15. F.R.S., 1717. F.R.C.P., 1719. Censor; Elect, 1744; President, 1750. An ardent Newtonian. Mathematician and physiologist. Author medical and mathematical. Died Mar. 22, 1749-50, at his house in Lincoln's Inn Fields. Buried at St James', Garlickhithe. Will, P.C.C. Father of the next. (*D.N.B.*; *Munk*, II. 65; H. M. Wood.)

JURIN, JAMES. Adm. pens. (age 17) at TRINITY, June 16, 1748. S. of James (above), of London, M.D. School, Hackney, London (Mr Newcombe). Matric. 1748; Scholar, 1749; B.A. 1752; M.A. 1755. Adm. at Lincoln's Inn, May 17, 1749. Of the Hermitage, Hexham, Northumberland. F.R.S., 1756. Married Mary, dau. of John Simpson, of Newcastle, at All Saints', Newcastle, Sept. 26, 1757. Died July 3, 1762, at Hackney, Middlesex.

JURY, *see also* JEWRY.

JURY, NATHANIEL. Adm. at EMMANUEL, June 14, 1626. S. of Thomas, draper. B. at Cambridge. School, Perse. Matric. 1626; Scholar, 1628-33. Migrated as sizar to Caius, Oct. 8, 1628, age 18. B.A. 1629-30; M.A. 1633. V. of Gt Gransden, Hunts., 1650; of Olney, Bucks., 1658-62. (*Venn*, I. 285.)

JURY, NATHANIEL. Adm. pens. at CLARE, Apr. 6, 1659. Matric. 1659; B.A. 1662-3. Fellow.

JUSON, THOMAS. M.A. 1721 (Incorp. from Oxford). S. of T., of Shrewsbury. Matric. from Trinity College, Oxford, Feb. 28, 1710-11, age 18; B.A. (Christ Church) 1714; M.A. 1717. Ord. priest (Lincoln) Jan. 1, 1724-5. R. of Wanstead, Essex, 1725. (*Al. Oxon.*)

JUSTICE, HENRY. Adm. pens. (age 19) at TRINITY, Apr. 27, 1716. S. of William, of York, attorney. School, Wakefield (Mr Clark). Adm. at the Middle Temple, Nov. 12, 1716. Called to the Bar, Feb. 10, 1727. Lord of the manor of Rufforth. Tried at the Old Bailey, May 8, 1736, for stealing books from the College and University Libraries. His sentence of transportation was changed to exile for life. Retired to Italy. Author, *Virgilii Opera*, 1757. Died at the Hague, 1763. (Davy, *MSS.*, 19137; *N. and Q.*, 2nd S., II. 514; Cooper, *Annals*, IV. 233.)

JUSTICE, HUGH. Matric. sizar from ST JOHN'S, Michs. 1576.

JUSTICE, JASPER. Adm. sizar (age 17) at ST JOHN'S, June 14, 1639. S. of Gasper, blacksmith, of Doncaster, Yorks. B. there. School, Doncaster. B.A. 1642-3. Perhaps M.A. 1680. One Mr Justice kept a school at Arksey, near Doncaster, 1646-7.

JUSTICE, JOHN. Adm. sizar (age 18) at SIDNEY, Apr. 27, 1711. 1st s. of John, of Knighton, Staffs. School, Whitchurch, Salop (Mr Tho. Hughes). Matric. 1710-1; B.A. 1714-5. Ord. priest (York) May, 1719. Probably R. of Ightfield. Died July, 1771, aged 79. Brother of William (1716). (G. *Mag.*)

JUSTICE, LUKE. Adm. sizar (age 18) at SIDNEY, Mar. 27, 1702. S. of Roger, gent. B. at Knighton, Staffs. School, Whitchurch, Salop (Mr Fra. Hudson). Brother of the next.

JUSTICE, WILLIAM. Adm. sizar (age 19) at SIDNEY, May 31, 1705. S. of Roger, gent., of Knighton, Staffs. School, Whitchurch, Salop (Mr Fra. Hudson). Matric. 1705. Brother of the above.

JUSTICE, WILLIAM. Adm. pens. (age 18) at SIDNEY, Apr. 27, 1716. 2nd s. of John, of Knighton, Staffs. Matric. 1716; B.A. 1719-20; M.A. 1730. Ord. deacon (York) Sept. 1720; priest, Sept. 1721. C. of Ordsall, Notts., 1726. Brother of John (1711).

JUXON, ELIAS. Adm. at KING'S (age 18) a scholar from Eton, June 29, 1650. Of London. Doubtless s. of Elias, of London, merchant taylor. Matric. 1650; B.A. 1653-4; M.A. 1657. Fellow, 1653, till 1660. R. of Aldington, Kent, 1661. Nephew of Richard (1628). (*Vis. of London*, 1634.)

JUXON, JOSEPH. Adm. pens. at EMMANUEL, Lent, 1639-40. Of London. Perhaps s. of John, of St Laurence Pountney, London. Adm. at the Middle Temple, Nov. 28, 1640. (H. B. Wilson, *St Laurence Pountney*, 136.)

JUXON, JOSEPH. Adm. sizar at CLARE, Feb. 27, 1711-2. B. at Appleby, Derbs. Matric. 1712; B.A. 1715-6; M.A. 1740. Ord. deacon (Lincoln, *Litt. dim.* from Coventry and Lichfield) Nov. 13, 1720; priest (Lincoln) June 4, 1721. R. of Hungerton, Leics., 1723-57. V. of Twyford, 1732-57. R. of Eastwell, 1746. Author of a sermon on Witchcraft. Died Oct. 15, 1757. (*Nichols*, III. 284.)

JUXON, RICHARD. Adm. at KING'S (age 17) a scholar from Eton, Sept. 1628. Of London. Doubtless s. of Thomas, merchant taylor. Matric. 1628; B.A. 1632-3. 'Died suddenly, at a cock-fight at the Blue Boar, Cambridge, 1635, when he laughed extremely.' (*N. and Q.*, 3rd S., III. 257; *Harwood*.)

JUXON, THOMAS. Matric. pens. from QUEENS', Easter, 1619. S. of Thomas, of St Laurence Pountney, London. B. Dec. 1599. School, Merchant Taylors'. B.A. 1622-3. Incorp. at Oxford, Mar. 17, 1622-3.

JUXTON, JOHN. Adm. pens. at EMMANUEL, Easter, 1626. Matric. 1626.

JUYTE (? INYTE), ANTHONY. Matric. sizar from CHRIST'S, May, 1561.

JYRLYNGTON, JOHN, *see* GIRLINGTON.

END OF VOLUME TWO

CAMBRIDGE: PRINTED BY J. B. PEACE, M.A., AT THE UNIVERSITY PRESS

9781333065119

SD - #0014 - 140922 - C0 - 229/152/27 - PB - 9781333065119 - Gloss Lamination